American Casebook Series
Hornbook Series and Basic Legal Texts
Nutshell Series

of

WEST PUBLISHING COMPANY
P.O. Box 43526
St. Paul, Minnesota 55164
January, 1984

ACCOUNTING

Faris' Law and Accounting in a Nutshell, approximately 392 pages, 1984 (Text)

Fiflis, Kripke and Foster's Teaching Materials on Accounting for Business Lawyers, 3rd Ed., approximately 784 pages, 1984 (Casebook)

Siegel and Siegel's Accounting and Financial Disclosure: A Guide to Basic Concepts, 259 pages, 1983 (Text)

ADMINISTRATIVE LAW

Davis' Cases, Text and Problems on Administrative Law, 6th Ed., 683 pages, 1977 (Casebook)

Davis' Basic Text on Administrative Law, 3rd Ed., 617 pages, 1972 (Text)

Davis' Police Discretion, 176 pages, 1975 (Text)

Gellhorn and Boyer's Administrative Law and Process in a Nutshell, 2nd Ed., 445 pages, 1981 (Text)

Mashaw and Merrill's Introduction to the American Public Law System, 1095 pages, 1975, with 1980 Supplement (Casebook)

Robinson, Gellhorn and Bruff's The Administrative Process, 2nd Ed., 959 pages, 1980, with 1983 Supplement (Casebook)

ADMIRALTY

Healy and Sharpe's Cases and Materials on Admiralty, 875 pages, 1974 (Casebook)

Maraist's Admiralty in a Nutshell, 400 pages, 1983 (Text)

Sohn and Gustafson's Law of the Sea in a Nutshell, approximately 250 pages, 1984 (Text)

AGENCY PARTNERSHIP

Fessler's Alternatives to Incorporation for Persons in Quest of Profit, 258 pages, 1980 (Casebook)

Henn's Cases and Materials on Agency, Partnership and Other Unincorporated Business Enterprises, 396 pages, 1972 (Casebook)

Reuschlein and Gregory's Hornbook on the Law of Agency and Partnership, 625 pages, 1979, with 1981 pocket part (Text)

Seavey's Hornbook on Agency, 329 pages, 1964 (Text)

Seavey and Hall's Cases on Agency, 431 pages, 1956 (Casebook)

Seavey, Reuschlein and Hall's Cases on Agency and Partnership, 599 pages, 1962 (Casebook)

Selected Corporation and Partnership Statutes and Forms, 556 pages, 1982

Steffen and Kerr's Cases and Materials on Agency-Partnership, 4th Ed., 859 pages, 1980 (Casebook)

Steffen's Agency-Partnership in a Nutshell, 364 pages, 1977 (Text)

AMERICAN INDIAN LAW

Canby's American Indian Law in a Nutshell, 288 pages, 1981 (Text)

Getches, Rosenfelt and Wilkinson's Cases on Federal Indian Law, 660 pages, 1979, with 1983 Supplement (Casebook)

ANTITRUST LAW

Gellhorn's Antitrust Law and Economics in a Nutshell, 2nd Ed., 425 pages, 1981 (Text)

Gifford and Raskind's Cases and Materials on Antitrust, 694 pages, 1983 (Casebook)

LAW SCHOOL PUBLICATIONS—Continued

ANTITRUST LAW—Continued

Oppenheim, Weston and McCarthy's Cases and Comments on Federal Antitrust Laws, 4th Ed., 1168 pages, 1981 (Casebook)

Posner and Easterbrook's Cases and Economic Notes on Antitrust, 2nd Ed., 1077 pages, 1981, with 1982–83 Supplement (Casebook)

Sullivan's Hornbook of the Law of Antitrust, 886 pages, 1977 (Text)

See also Regulated Industries, Trade Regulation

ART LAW

DuBoff's Art Law in a Nutshell, approximately 290 pages, 1984 (Text)

BANKING LAW

Lovett's Banking and Financial Institutions in a Nutshell, 409 pages, 1984 (Text)

White's Teaching Materials on Banking Law, 1058 pages, 1976, with Case and Statutory Supplement (Casebook)

BUSINESS PLANNING

Epstein and Scheinfeld's Teaching Materials on Business Reorganization Under the Bankruptcy Code, 216 pages, 1980 (Casebook)

Painter's Problems and Materials in Business Planning, 2nd Ed., approximately 1035 pages, 1984 (Casebook)

Selected Securities and Business Planning Statutes, Rules and Forms, 485 pages, 1982

CIVIL PROCEDURE

Casad's Res Judicata in a Nutshell, 310 pages, 1976 (text)

Cound, Friedenthal and Miller's Cases and Materials on Civil Procedure, 3rd Ed., 1147 pages, 1980 with 1984 Supplement (Casebook)

Ehrenzweig, Louisell and Hazard's Jurisdiction in a Nutshell, 4th Ed., 232 pages, 1980 (Text)

Federal Rules of Civil-Appellate-Criminal Procedure—West Law School Edition, 343 pages, 1983

Hodges, Jones and Elliott's Cases and Materials on Texas Trial and Appellate Procedure, 2nd Ed., 745 pages, 1974 (Casebook)

Hodges, Jones and Elliott's Cases and Materials on the Judicial Process Prior to Trial in Texas, 2nd Ed., 871 pages, 1977 (Casebook)

Kane's Civil Procedure in a Nutshell, 271 pages, 1979 (Text)

Karlen's Procedure Before Trial in a Nutshell, 258 pages, 1972 (Text)

Karlen, Meisenholder, Stevens and Vestal's Cases on Civil Procedure, 923 pages, 1975 (Casebook)

CIVIL PROCEDURE—Continued

Koffler and Reppy's Hornbook on Common Law Pleading, 663 pages, 1969 (Text)

McBaine's Cases on Introduction to Civil Procedure, 399 pages, 1950 (Casebook)

Park's Computer-Aided Exercises on Civil Procedure, 2nd Ed., 167 pages, 1983 (Coursebook)

Shipman's Hornbook on Common-Law Pleading, 3rd Ed., 644 pages, 1923 (Text)

Siegel's Hornbook on New York Practice, 1011 pages, 1978 with 1981–82 Pocket Part (Text)

See also Federal Jurisdiction and Procedure

CIVIL RIGHTS

Abernathy's Cases and Materials on Civil Rights, 660 pages, 1980 (Casebook)

Cohen's Cases on the Law of Deprivation of Liberty: A Study in Social Control, 755 pages, 1980 (Casebook)

Lockhart, Kamisar and Choper's Cases on Constitutional Rights and Liberties, 5th Ed., 1298 pages plus Appendix, 1981, with 1983 Supplement (Casebook)—reprint from Lockhart, et al. Cases on Constitutional Law, 5th Ed., 1980

Vieira's Civil Rights in a Nutshell, 279 pages, 1978 (Text)

COMMERCIAL LAW

Bailey's Secured Transactions in a Nutshell, 2nd Ed., 391 pages, 1981 (Text)

Epstein and Martin's Basic Uniform Commercial Code Teaching Materials, 2nd Ed., 667 pages, 1983 (Casebook)

Henson's Hornbook on Secured Transactions Under the U.C.C., 2nd Ed., 504 pages, 1979 with 1979 P.P. (Text)

Murray's Commercial Law, Problems and Materials, 366 pages, 1975 (Coursebook)

Nordstrom and Clovis' Problems and Materials on Commercial Paper, 458 pages, 1972 (Casebook)

Nordstrom and Lattin's Problems and Materials on Sales and Secured Transactions, 809 pages, 1968 (Casebook)

Nordstrom, Murray and Clovis' Problems and Materials on Sales, 515 pages, 1982 (Casebook)

Nordstrom's Hornbook on Sales, 600 pages, 1970 (Text)

Selected Commercial Statutes, 1379 pages, 1983

Speidel, Summers and White's Teaching Materials on Commercial and Consumer Law, 3rd Ed., 1490 pages, 1981 (Casebook)

Stockton's Sales in a Nutshell, 2nd Ed., 370 pages, 1981 (Text)

Stone's Uniform Commercial Code in a Nutshell, 507 pages, 1975 (Text)

Uniform Commercial Code, Official Text with Comments, 994 pages, 1978

LAW SCHOOL PUBLICATIONS—Continued

CORPORATIONS

Hamilton's Cases on Corporations—Including Partnerships and Limited Partnerships, 2nd Ed., 1108 pages, 1981, with 1981 Statutory Supplement and 1984 Supplement (Casebook)

Hamilton's Law of Corporations in a Nutshell, 379 pages, 1980 (Text)

Henn's Cases on Corporations, 1279 pages, 1974, with 1980 Supplement (Casebook)

Henn and Alexander's Hornbook on Corporations, 3rd Ed., Student Ed., 1371 pages, 1983 (Text)

Jennings and Buxbaum's Cases and Materials on Corporations, 5th Ed., 1180 pages, 1979 (Casebook)

Selected Corporation and Partnership Statutes, Regulations and Forms, 556 pages, 1982

Solomon, Stevenson and Schwartz' Materials and Problems on the Law and Policies on Corporations, 1172 pages, 1982 with 1983 Supplement (Casebook)

CORPORATE FINANCE

Hamilton's Cases and Materials on Corporate Finance, approximately 882 pages, 1984 (Casebook)

CORRECTIONS

Krantz's Cases and Materials on the Law of Corrections and Prisoners' Rights, 2nd Ed., 735 pages, 1981, with 1982 Supplement (Casebook)

Krantz's Law of Corrections and Prisoners' Rights in a Nutshell, 2nd Ed., 384 pages, 1983 (Text)

Popper's Post-Conviction Remedies in a Nutshell, 360 pages, 1978 (Text)

Robbins' Cases and Materials on Post Conviction Remedies, 506 pages, 1982 (Casebook)

Rubin's Law of Criminal Corrections, 2nd Ed., 873 pages, 1973, with 1978 Supplement (Text)

CREDITOR'S RIGHTS

Bankruptcy Code and Rules, Law School Ed., 438 pages, 1984

Epstein's Debtor-Creditor Law in a Nutshell, 2nd Ed., 324 pages, 1980 (Text)

Epstein and Landers' Debtors and Creditors: Cases and Materials, 2nd Ed., 689 pages, 1982 (Casebook)

Epstein and Sheinfeld's Teaching Materials on Business Reorganization Under the Bankruptcy Code, 216 pages, 1980 (Casebook)

Riesenfeld's Cases and Materials on Creditors' Remedies and Debtors' Protection, 3rd Ed., 810 pages, 1979 with 1979 Statutory Supplement and 1981 Case Supplement (Casebook)

CRIMINAL LAW AND CRIMINAL PROCEDURE

Cohen and Gobert's Problems in Criminal Law, 297 pages, 1976 (Problem book)

Davis' Police Discretion, 176 pages, 1975 (Text)

Dix and Sharlot's Cases and Materials on Criminal Law, 2nd Ed., 771 pages, 1979 (Casebook)

Federal Rules of Civil-Appellate-Criminal Procedure—West Law School Edition, 343 pages, 1983

Grano's Problems in Criminal Procedure, 2nd Ed., 176 pages, 1981 (Problem book)

Israel and LaFave's Criminal Procedure in a Nutshell, 3rd Ed., 438 pages, 1980 (Text)

Johnson's Cases, Materials and Text on Substantive Criminal Law in its Procedural Context, 2nd Ed., 956 pages, 1980 (Casebook)

Kamisar, LaFave and Israel's Cases, Comments and Questions on Modern Criminal Procedure, 5th ed., 1635 pages plus Appendix, 1980 with 1983 Supplement (Casebook)

Kamisar, LaFave and Israel's Cases, Comments and Questions on Basic Criminal Procedure, 5th Ed., 869 pages, 1980 with 1983 Supplement (Casebook)—reprint from Kamisar, et al. Modern Criminal Procedure, 5th ed., 1980

LaFave's Modern Criminal Law: Cases, Comments and Questions, 789 pages, 1978 (Casebook)

LaFave and Scott's Hornbook on Criminal Law, 763 pages, 1972 (Text)

Langbein's Comparative Criminal Procedure: Germany, 172 pages, 1977 (Casebook)

Loewy's Criminal Law in a Nutshell, 302 pages, 1975 (Text)

Saltzburg's American Criminal Procedure, Cases and Commentary, 2nd Ed., 1193 pages, 1984 (Casebook)

Uviller's The Processes of Criminal Justice: Investigation and Adjudication, 2nd Ed., 1384 pages, 1979 with 1979 Statutory Supplement and 1983 Update (Casebook)

Uviller's The Processes of Criminal Justice: Adjudication, 2nd Ed., 730 pages, 1979. Soft-cover reprint from Uviller's The Processes of Criminal Justice: Investigation and Adjudication, 2nd Ed. (Casebook)

Uviller's The Processes of Criminal Justice: Investigation, 2nd Ed., 655 pages, 1979. Soft-cover reprint from Uviller's The Processes of Criminal Justice: Investigation and Adjudication, 2nd Ed. (Casebook)

Vorenberg's Cases on Criminal Law and Procedure, 2nd Ed., 1088 pages, 1981 (Casebook)

LAW SCHOOL PUBLICATIONS—Continued

CRIMINAL LAW AND CRIMINAL PRO-
CEDURE—Continued

See also Corrections, Juvenile Justice

DECEDENTS ESTATES

See Trusts and Estates

DOMESTIC RELATIONS

Clark's Cases and Problems on Domestic Relations, 3rd Ed., 1153 pages, 1980 (Casebook)

Clark's Hornbook on Domestic Relations, 754 pages, 1968 (Text)

Krause's Cases and Materials on Family Law, 2nd Ed., 1221 pages, 1983 (Casebook)

Krause's Family Law in a Nutshell, 400 pages, 1977 (Text)

Krauskopf's Cases on Property Division at Marriage Dissolution, 250 pages, 1984 (Casebook)

EDUCATION LAW

Alexander and Alexander's The Law of Schools, Students and Teachers in a Nutshell, approximately 395 pages, 1984 (Text)

Morris' The Constitution and American Education, 2nd Ed., 992 pages, 1980 (Casebook)

EMPLOYMENT DISCRIMINATION

Player's Cases and Materials on Employment Discrimination Law, 2nd Ed., approximately 675 pages, 1984 (Casebook)

Player's Federal Law of Employment Discrimination in a Nutshell, 2nd Ed., 402 pages, 1981 (Text)

See also Women and the Law

ENERGY AND NATURAL RESOURCES LAW

Rodgers' Cases and Materials on Energy and Natural Resources Law, 2nd Ed., 877 pages, 1983 (Casebook)

Selected Environmental Law Statutes, 768 pages, 1983

Tomain's Energy Law in a Nutshell, 338 pages, 1981 (Text)

See also Environmental Law, Oil and Gas, Water Law

ENVIRONMENTAL LAW

Bonine and McGarity's Cases and Materials on the Law of Environment and Pollution, approximately 892 pages, 1984 (Casebook)

Findley and Farber's Cases and Materials on Environmental Law, 738 pages, 1981, with 1983 Supplement (Casebook)

Findley and Farber's Environmental Law in a Nutshell, 343 pages, 1983 (Text)

ENVIROMENTAL LAW—Continued

Hanks, Tarlock and Hanks' Cases on Environmental Law and Policy, 1242 pages, 1974, with 1976 Supplement (Casebook)

Rodgers' Hornbook on Environmental Law, 956 pages, 1977 (Text)

Selected Environmental Law Statutes, 768 pages, 1983

See also Energy and Natural Resources Law, Water Law

EQUITY

See Remedies

ESTATES

See Trusts and Estates

ESTATE PLANNING

Kurtz' Cases, Materials and Problems on Family Estate Planning, 853 pages, 1983 (Casebook)

Lynn's Introduction to Estate Planning, in a Nutshell, 3rd Ed., 370 pages, 1983 (Text)

See also Taxation

EVIDENCE

Broun and Meisenholder's Problems in Evidence, 2nd Ed., 304 pages, 1981 (Problem book)

Cleary and Strong's Cases, Materials and Problems on Evidence, 3rd Ed., 1143 pages, 1981 (Casebook)

Federal Rules of Evidence for United States Courts and Magistrates, 327 pages, 1983

Graham's Federal Rules of Evidence in a Nutshell, 429 pages, 1981 (Text)

Kimball's Programmed Materials on Problems in Evidence, 380 pages, 1978 (Problem book)

Lempert and Saltzburg's A Modern Approach to Evidence: Text, Problems, Transcripts and Cases, 2nd Ed., 1296 pages, 1983 (Casebook)

Lilly's Introduction to the Law of Evidence, 486 pages, 1978 (Text)

McCormick, Elliott and Sutton's Cases and Materials on Evidence, 5th Ed., 1212 pages, 1981 (Casebook)

McCormick's Hornbook on Evidence, 3rd Ed., Student Ed., approximately 1006 pages, 1984 (Text)

Rothstein's Evidence, State and Federal Rules in a Nutshell, 2nd Ed., 514 pages, 1981 (Text)

Saltzburg's Evidence Supplement: Rules, Statutes, Commentary, 245 pages, 1980 (Casebook Supplement)

FEDERAL JURISDICTION AND PROCEDURE

Currie's Cases and Materials on Federal Courts, 3rd Ed., 1042 pages, 1982 (Casebook)

LAW SCHOOL PUBLICATIONS—Continued

FEDERAL JURISDICTION AND PROCEDURE—Continued

Currie's Federal Jurisdiction in a Nutshell, 2nd Ed., 258 pages, 1981 (Text)

Federal Rules of Civil-Appellate-Criminal Procedure—West Law School Edition, 343 pages, 1983

Forrester and Moye's Cases and Materials on Federal Jurisdiction and Procedure, 3rd Ed., 917 pages, 1977 with 1981 Supplement (Casebook)

Redish's Cases, Comments and Questions on Federal Courts, 878 pages, 1983 (Casebook)

Vetri and Merrill's Federal Courts, Problems and Materials, 2nd Ed., approximately 250 pages, 1984

Wright's Hornbook on Federal Courts, 4th Ed., Student Ed., 870 pages, 1983 (Text)

FUTURE INTERESTS

See Trusts and Estates

HOUSING AND URBAN DEVELOPMENT

Berger's Cases and Materials on Housing, 2nd Ed., 254 pages, 1973 (Casebook)—reprint from Cooper et al. Cases on Law and Poverty, 2nd Ed., 1973
See also Land Use

IMMIGRATION LAW

Weissbrodt's Immigration Law and Procedure in a Nutshell, approximately 337 pages, 1984 (Text)

INDIAN LAW

See American Indian Law

INSURANCE

Dobbyn's Insurance Law in a Nutshell, 281 pages, 1981 (Text)

Keeton's Cases on Basic Insurance Law, 2nd Ed., 1086 pages, 1977

Keeton's Basic Text on Insurance Law, 712 pages, 1971 (Text)

Keeton's Case Supplement to Keeton's Basic Text on Insurance Law, 334 pages, 1978 (Casebook)

Keeton's Programmed Problems in Insurance Law, 243 pages, 1972 (Text Supplement)

York and Whelan's Cases, Materials and Problems on Insurance Law, 715 pages, 1982 (Casebook)

INTERNATIONAL LAW

Henkin, Pugh, Schachter and Smit's Cases and Materials on International Law, 2nd Ed., 1152 pages, 1980, with Documents Supplement (Casebook)

INTERNATIONAL LAW—Continued

Jackson's Legal Problems of International Economic Relations, 1097 pages, 1977, with Documents Supplement (Casebook)

Kirgis' International Organizations in Their Legal Setting, 1016 pages, 1977, with 1981 Supplement (Casebook)

Weston, Falk and D'Amato's International Law and World Order—A Problem Oriented Coursebook, 1195 pages, 1980, with Documents Supplement (Casebook)

Wilson's International Business Transactions in a Nutshell, 2nd Ed., 476 pages, 1984 (Text)

INTERVIEWING AND COUNSELING

Binder and Price's Interviewing and Counseling, 232 pages, 1977 (Text)

Shaffer's Interviewing and Counseling in a Nutshell, 353 pages, 1976 (Text)

INTRODUCTION TO LAW

Dobbyn's So You Want to go to Law School, Revised First Edition, 206 pages, 1976 (Text)

Hegland's Introduction to the Study and Practice of Law in a Nutshell, 418 pages, 1983 (Text)

Kelso and Kelso's Studying Law: An Introduction, approximately 585 pages, 1984 (Coursebook)

Kinyon's Introduction to Law Study and Law Examinations in a Nutshell, 389 pages, 1971 (Text)

See also Legal Method and Legal System

JUDICIAL ADMINISTRATION

Carrington, Meador and Rosenberg's Justice on Appeal, 263 pages, 1976 (Casebook)

Nelson's Cases and Materials on Judicial Administration and the Administration of Justice, 1032 pages, 1974 (Casebook)

JURISPRUDENCE

Christie's Text and Readings on Jurisprudence—The Philosophy of Law, 1056 pages, 1973 (Casebook)

JUVENILE JUSTICE

Fox's Cases and Materials on Modern Juvenile Justice, 2nd Ed., 960 pages, 1981 (Casebook)

Fox's Juvenile Courts in a Nutshell, 3rd Ed., approximately 290 pages, 1984 (Text)

LABOR LAW

Gorman's Basic Text on Labor Law—Unionization and Collective Bargaining, 914 pages, 1976 (Text)

Leslie's Labor Law in a Nutshell, 403 pages, 1979 (Text)

Nolan's Labor Arbitration Law and Practice in a Nutshell, 358 pages, 1979 (Text)

LAW SCHOOL PUBLICATIONS—Continued

LABOR LAW—Continued

Oberer, Hanslowe and Andersen's Cases and Materials on Labor Law—Collective Bargaining in a Free Society, 2nd Ed., 1168 pages, 1979, with 1979 Statutory Supplement and 1982 Case Supplement (Casebook)

See also Employment Discrimination, Social Legislation

LAND FINANCE

See Real Estate Transactions

LAND USE

Hagman's Cases on Public Planning and Control of Urban and Land Development, 2nd Ed., 1301 pages, 1980 (Casebook)

Hagman's Hornbook on Urban Planning and Land Development Control Law, 706 pages, 1971 (Text)

Wright and Gitelman's Cases and Materials on Land Use, 3rd Ed., 1300 pages, 1982 (Casebook)

Wright and Webber's Land Use in a Nutshell, 316 pages, 1978 (Text)

See also Housing and Urban Development

LAW AND ECONOMICS

Goetz' Cases and Materials on Law and Economics, 547 pages, 1984 (Casebook)

Manne's The Economics of Legal Relationships—Readings in the Theory of Property Rights, 660 pages, 1975 (Text)

See also Antitrust, Regulated Industries

LAW AND MEDICINE—PSYCHIATRY

Cohen's Cases and Materials on the Law of Deprivation of Liberty: A Study in Social Control, 755 pages, 1980 (Casebook)

King's The Law of Medical Malpractice in a Nutshell, 340 pages, 1977 (Text)

Shapiro and Spece's Problems, Cases and Materials on Bioethics and Law, 892 pages, 1981 (Casebook)

Sharpe, Fiscina and Head's Cases on Law and Medicine, 882 pages, 1978 (Casebook)

LEGAL HISTORY

Presser and Zainaldin's Cases on Law and American History, 855 pages, 1980 (Casebook)

See also Legal Method and Legal System

LEGAL METHOD AND LEGAL SYSTEM

Aldisert's Readings, Materials and Cases in the Judicial Process, 948 pages, 1976 (Casebook)

LEGAL METHOD AND LEGAL SYSTEM—Continued

Bodenheimer, Oakley and Love's Readings and Cases on an Introduction to the Anglo-American Legal System, 161 pages, 1980 (Casebook)

Davies and Lawry's Institutions and Methods of the Law—Introductory Teaching Materials, 547 pages, 1982 (Casebook)

Dvorkin, Himmelstein and Lesnick's Becoming a Lawyer: A Humanistic Perspective on Legal Education and Professionalism, 211 pages, 1981 (Text)

Fryer and Orentlicher's Cases and Materials on Legal Method and Legal System, 1043 pages, 1967 (Casebook)

Greenberg's Judicial Process and Social Change, 666 pages, 1977 (Coursebook)

Kempin's Historical Introduction to Anglo-American Law in a Nutshell, 2nd Ed., 280 pages, 1973 (Text)

Kimball's Historical Introduction to the Legal System, 610 pages, 1966 (Casebook)

Mashaw and Merrill's Introduction to the American Public Law System, 1095 pages, 1975, with 1980 Supplement (Casebook)

Murphy's Cases and Materials on Introduction to Law—Legal Process and Procedure, 772 pages, 1977 (Casebook)

Reynolds' Judicial Process in a Nutshell, 292 pages, 1980 (Text)

See also Legal Research and Writing

LEGAL NEGOTIATION

Edwards and White's Problems, Readings and Materials on the Lawyer as a Negotiator, 484 pages, 1977 (Casebook)

Williams' Legal Negotiation and Settlement, 207 pages, 1983 (Coursebook)

LEGAL PROFESSION

Aronson's Problems in Professional Responsibility, 280 pages, 1978 (Problem book)

Aronson and Weckstein's Professional Responsibility in a Nutshell, 399 pages, 1980 (Text)

Mellinkoff's The Conscience of a Lawyer, 304 pages, 1973 (Text)

Mellinkoff's Lawyers and the System of Justice, 983 pages, 1976 (Casebook)

Pirsig and Kirwin's Cases and Materials on Professional Responsibility, 4th Ed., approximately 650 pages, 1984 (Casebook)

Schwartz and Wydick's Problems in Legal Ethics, 285 pages, 1983 (Casebook)

Selected Statutes, Rules and Standards on the Legal Profession, 249 pages, 1984

Smith's Preventing Legal Malpractice, 142 pages, 1981 (Text)

LEGAL RESEARCH AND WRITING

Cohen's Legal Research in a Nutshell, 3rd Ed., 415 pages, 1978 (Text)

LAW SCHOOL PUBLICATIONS—Continued

LEGAL RESEARCH AND WRITING—Continued

Cohen and Berring's How to Find the Law, 8th Ed., 790 pages, 1983. Problem book by Foster and Kelly available (Casebook)

Cohen and Berring's Finding the Law, 8th Ed., Abridged Ed., 556 pages, 1984 (Casebook)

Dickerson's Materials on Legal Drafting, 425 pages, 1981 (Casebook)

Felsenfeld and Siegel's Writing Contracts in Plain English, 290 pages, 1981 (Text)

Gopen's Writing From a Legal Perspective, 225 pages, 1981 (Text)

Mellinkoff's Legal Writing—Sense and Nonsense, 242 pages, 1982 (Text)

Rombauer's Legal Problem Solving—Analysis, Research and Writing, 4th Ed., 424 pages, 1983 (Coursebook)

Squires and Rombauer's Legal Writing in a Nutshell, 294 pages, 1982 (Text)

Statsky's Legal Research, Writing and Analysis, 2nd Ed., 167 pages, 1982 (Coursebook)

Statsky's Legislative Analysis: How to Use Statutes and Regulations, 2nd Ed., 217 pages, 1984 (Text)

Statsky and Wernet's Case Analysis and Fundamentals of Legal Writing, 2nd Ed., 441 pages, 1984 (Text)

Teply's Programmed Materials on Legal Research and Citation, 334 pages, 1982. Student Library Exercises available (Coursebook)

Weihofen's Legal Writing Style, 2nd Ed., 332 pages, 1980 (Text)

LEGISLATION

Davies' Legislative Law and Process in a Nutshell, 279 pages, 1975 (Text)

Nutting and Dickerson's Cases and Materials on Legislation, 5th Ed., 744 pages, 1978 (Casebook)

Statsky's Legislative Analysis: How to Use Statutes and Regulations, 2nd Ed., 217 pages, 1984 (Text)

LOCAL GOVERNMENT

McCarthy's Local Government Law in a Nutshell, 2nd Ed., 404 pages, 1983 (Text)

Michelman and Sandalow's Cases-Comments-Questions on Government in Urban Areas, 1216 pages, 1970, with 1972 Supplement (Casebook)

Reynolds' Hornbook on Local Government Law, 860 pages, 1982 (Text)

Stason and Kauper's Cases and Materials on Municipal Corporations, 3rd Ed., 692 pages, 1959 (Casebook)

Valente's Cases and Materials on Local Government Law, 2nd Ed., 980 pages, 1980 with 1982 Supplement (Casebook)

MASS COMMUNICATION LAW

Gillmor and Barron's Cases and Comment on Mass Communication Law, 4th Ed., approximately 1100 pages, 1984 (Casebook)

Ginsburg's Regulation of Broadcasting: Law and Policy Towards Radio, Television and Cable Communications, 741 pages, 1979, with 1983 Supplement (Casebook)

Zuckman and Gayne's Mass Communications Law in a Nutshell, 2nd Ed., 473 pages, 1983 (Text)

MILITARY LAW

Shanor and Terrell's Military Law in a Nutshell, 378 pages, 1980 (Text)

MORTGAGES

See Real Estate Transactions

NATURAL RESOURCES LAW

See Energy and Natural Resources Law, Environmental Law, Oil and Gas, Water Law

OFFICE PRACTICE

Hegland's Trial and Practice Skills in a Nutshell, 346 pages, 1978 (Text)

Strong and Clark's Law Office Management, 424 pages, 1974 (Casebook)

See also Legal Interviewing and Counseling, Legal Negotiation

OIL AND GAS

Hemingway's Hornbook on Oil and Gas, 2nd Ed., Student Ed., 543 pages, 1983 (Text)

Huie, Woodward and Smith's Cases and Materials on Oil and Gas, 2nd Ed., 955 pages, 1972 (Casebook)

Lowe's Oil and Gas Law in a Nutshell, 443 pages, 1983 (Text)

See also Energy and Natural Resources Law

PARTNERSHIP

See Agency—Partnership

PATENT AND COPYRIGHT LAW

Choate and Francis' Cases and Materials on Patent Law, 2nd Ed., 1110 pages, 1981 (Casebook)

Miller and Davis' Intellectual Property—Patents, Trademarks and Copyright in a Nutshell, 428 pages, 1983 (Text)

Nimmer's Cases on Copyright and Other Aspects of Law Pertaining to Literary, Musical and Artistic Works, 2nd Ed., 1023 pages, 1979 (Casebook)

POVERTY LAW

Brudno's Poverty, Inequality, and the Law: Cases-Commentary-Analysis, 934 pages, 1976 (Casebook)

POVERTY LAW—Continued

LaFrance, Schroeder, Bennett and Boyd's Hornbook on Law of the Poor, 558 pages, 1973 (Text)

See also Social Legislation

PRODUCTS LIABILITY

Noel and Phillips' Cases on Products Liability, 2nd Ed., 821 pages, 1982 (Casebook)

Noel and Phillips' Products Liability in a Nutshell, 2nd Ed., 341 pages, 1981 (Text)

PROPERTY

Aigler, Smith and Tefft's Cases on Property, 2 volumes, 1339 pages, 1960 (Casebook)

Bernhardt's Real Property in a Nutshell, 2nd Ed., 448 pages, 1981 (Text)

Boyer's Survey of the Law of Property, 766 pages, 1981 (Text)

Browder, Cunningham and Smith's Cases on Basic Property Law, 4th Ed., approximately 1368 pages, 1984 (Casebook)

Bruce, Ely and Bostick's Cases and Materials on Modern Property Law, approximately 1000 pages, 1984 (Casebook)

Burby's Hornbook on Real Property, 3rd Ed., 490 pages, 1965 (Text)

Burke's Personal Property in a Nutshell, 322 pages, 1983 (Text)

Chused's A Modern Approach to Property: Cases-Notes-Materials, 1069 pages, 1978 with 1980 Supplement (Casebook)

Cohen's Materials for a Basic Course in Property, 526 pages, 1978 (Casebook)

Cunningham, Whitman and Stoebuck's Hornbook on the Law of Property, Student Ed., approximately 928 pages, 1984 (Text)

Donahue, Kauper and Martin's Cases on Property, 2nd Ed., 1362 pages, 1983 (Casebook)

Hill's Landlord and Tenant Law in a Nutshell, 319 pages, 1979 (Text)

Moynihan's Introduction to Real Property, 254 pages, 1962 (Text)

Phipps' Titles in a Nutshell, 277 pages, 1968 (Text)

Uniform Land Transactions Act, Uniform Simplification of Land Transfers Act, Uniform Condominium Act, 1977 Official Text with Comments, 462 pages, 1978

See also Housing and Urban Development, Real Estate Transactions, Land Use

REAL ESTATE TRANSACTIONS

Bruce's Real Estate Finance in a Nutshell, 292 pages, 1979 (Text)

Maxwell, Riesenfeld, Hetland and Warren's Cases on California Security Transactions in Land, 3rd Ed., approximately 710 pages, 1984 (Casebook)

REAL ESTATE TRANSACTIONS—Continued

Nelson and Whitman's Cases on Real Estate Transfer, Finance and Development, 2nd Ed., 1114 pages, 1981, with 1983 Supplement (Casebook)

Osborne's Cases and Materials on Secured Transactions, 559 pages, 1967 (Casebook)

Osborne, Nelson and Whitman's Hornbook on Real Estate Finance Law, 3rd Ed., 885 pages, 1979 (Text)

REGULATED INDUSTRIES

Gellhorn and Pierce's Regulated Industries in a Nutshell, 394 pages, 1982 (Text)

Morgan's Cases and Materials on Economic Regulation of Business, 830 pages, 1976, with 1978 Supplement (Casebook)

Pozen's Financial Institutions: Cases, Materials and Problems on Investment Management, 844 pages, 1978 (Casebook)

See also Mass Communication Law, Banking Law

REMEDIES

Dobbs' Hornbook on Remedies, 1067 pages, 1973 (Text)

Dobbs' Problems in Remedies, 137 pages, 1974 (Problem book)

Dobbyn's Injunctions in a Nutshell, 264 pages, 1974 (Text)

Friedman's Contract Remedies in a Nutshell, 323 pages, 1981 (Text)

Leavell, Love and Nelson's Cases and Materials on Equitable Remedies and Restitution, 3rd Ed., 704 pages, 1980 (Casebook)

McCormick's Hornbook on Damages, 811 pages, 1935 (Text)

O'Connell's Remedies in a Nutshell, 364 pages, 1977 (Text)

York and Bauman's Cases and Materials on Remedies, 3rd Ed., 1250 pages, 1979 (Casebook)

REVIEW MATERIALS

Ballantine's Problems

Black Letter Series

Smith's Review Series

West's Review Covering Multistate Subjects

SECURITIES REGULATION

Hazen's Hornbook on The Law of Securities Regulation, approximately 520 pages, 1984 (Text)

Ratner's Securities Regulation: Materials for a Basic Course, 2nd Ed., 1050 pages, 1980 with 1982 Supplement (Casebook)

Ratner's Securities Regulation in a Nutshell, 2nd Ed., 322 pages, 1982 (Text)

Selected Securities and Business Planning Statutes, Rules and Forms, 485 pages, 1982

LAW SCHOOL PUBLICATIONS—Continued

SOCIAL LEGISLATION

Brudno's Income Redistribution Theories and Programs: Cases-Commentary-Analyses, 480 pages, 1977 (Casebook)—reprint from Brudno's Poverty, Inequality and the Law, 1976

Hood and Hardy's Workers' Compensation and Employee Protection Laws in a Nutshell, 274 pages, 1984 (Text)

LaFrance's Welfare Law: Structure and Entitlement in a Nutshell, 455 pages, 1979 (Text)

Malone, Plant and Little's Cases on Workers' Compensation and Employment Rights, 2nd Ed., 951 pages, 1980 (Casebook)

See also Poverty Law

TAXATION

Dodge's Federal Taxation of Estates, Trusts and Gifts: Principles and Planning, 771 pages, 1981 with 1982 Supplement (Casebook)

Garbis and Struntz' Cases and Materials on Tax Procedure and Tax Fraud, 829 pages, 1982 with 1984 Supplement (Casebook)

Gunn's Cases and Materials on Federal Income Taxation of Individuals, 785 pages, 1981 with 1983 Supplement (Casebook)

Hellerstein and Hellerstein's Cases on State and Local Taxation, 4th Ed., 1041 pages, 1978 with 1982 Supplement (Casebook)

Kahn's Handbook on Basic Corporate Taxation, 3rd Ed., Student Ed., 614 pages, 1981 with 1983 Supplement (Text)

Kahn and Gann's Corporate Taxation and Taxation of Partnerships and Partners, 2nd Ed., approximately 1300 pages, 1984 (Casebook)

Kragen and McNulty's Cases and Materials on Federal Income Taxation, Vol. I: Taxation of Individuals, 3rd Ed., 1283 pages, 1979 with 1983 Supplement (Casebook)

Kragen and McNulty's Cases and Materials on Federal Income Taxation, Vol. II: Taxation of Corporations, Shareholders, Partnerships and Partners, 3rd Ed., 989 pages, 1981 with 1983 Supplement (Casebook)

McNulty's Federal Estate and Gift Taxation in a Nutshell, 3rd Ed., 509 pages, 1983 (Text)

McNulty's Federal Income Taxation of Individuals in a Nutshell, 3rd Ed., 487 pages, 1983 (Text)

Posin's Hornbook on Federal Income Taxation of Individuals, Student Ed., 491 pages, 1983 (Text)

Rice's Problems and Materials in Federal Estate and Gift Taxation, 3rd Ed., 474 pages, 1978 (Casebook)

Rice and Solomon's Problems and Materials in Federal Income Taxation, 3rd Ed., 670 pages, 1979 (Casebook)

TAXATION—Continued

Rose and Raskind's Advanced Federal Income Taxation: Corporate Transactions—Cases, Materials and Problems, 955 pages, 1978 (Casebook)

Selected Federal Taxation Statutes and Regulations, 1255 pages, 1983

Sobeloff and Weidenbruch's Federal Income Taxation of Corporations and Stockholders in a Nutshell, 362 pages, 1981 (Text)

TORTS

Christie's Cases and Materials on the Law of Torts, 1264 pages, 1983 (Casebook)

Green, Pedrick, Rahl, Thode, Hawkins, Smith and Treece's Cases and Materials on Torts, 2nd Ed., 1360 pages, 1977 (Casebook)

Green, Pedrick, Rahl, Thode, Hawkins, Smith, and Treece's Advanced Torts: Injuries to Business, Political and Family Interests, 2nd Ed., 544 pages, 1977 (Casebook)—reprint from Green, et al. Cases and Materials on Torts, 2nd Ed., 1977

Keeton, Keeton, Sargentich and Steiner's Cases and Materials on Torts, and Accident Law, 1360 pages, 1983 (Casebook)

Kionka's Torts in a Nutshell: Injuries to Persons and Property, 434 pages, 1977 (Text)

Malone's Torts in a Nutshell: Injuries to Family, Social and Trade Relations, 358 pages, 1979 (Text)

Prosser and Keeton's Hornbook on Torts, 5th Ed., Student Ed., approximately 1052 pages, 1984 (Text)

Shapo's Cases on Tort and Compensation Law, 1244 pages, 1976 (Casebook)

See also Products Liability

TRADE REGULATION

McManis' Unfair Trade Practices in a Nutshell, 444 pages, 1982 (Text)

Oppenheim, Weston, Maggs and Schechter's Cases and Materials on Unfair Trade Practices and Consumer Protection, 4th Ed., 1038 pages, 1983 (Casebook)

See also Antitrust, Regulated Industries

TRIAL AND APPELLATE ADVOCACY

Appellate Advocacy, Handbook of, 249 pages, 1980 (Text)

Bergman's Trial Advocacy in a Nutshell, 402 pages, 1979 (Text)

Binder and Bergman's Fact Investigation: From Hypothesis to Proof, approximately 350 pages, 1984 (Coursebook)

Goldberg's The First Trial (Where Do I Sit?) (What Do I Say?) in a Nutshell, 396 pages, 1982 (Text)

Hegland's Trial and Practice Skills in a Nutshell, 346 pages, 1978 (Text)

TRIAL AND APPELLATE ADVOCACY—Continued

Hornstein's Appellate Advocacy in a Nutshell, approximately 270 pages, 1984 (Text)

Jeans' Handbook on Trial Advocacy, Student Ed., 473 pages, 1975 (Text)

McElhaney's Effective Litigation, 457 pages, 1974 (Casebook)

Nolan's Cases and Materials on Trial Practice, 518 pages, 1981 (Casebook)

Parnell and Shellhaas' Cases, Exercises and Problems for Trial Advocacy, 171 pages, 1982 (Coursebook)

Sonsteng, Haydock and Boyd's The Trialbook: A Total System for Preparation and Presentation of a Case, Student Ed., approximately 400 pages, 1984 (Coursebook)

TRUSTS AND ESTATES

Atkinson's Hornbook on Wills, 2nd Ed., 975 pages, 1953 (Text)

Averill's Uniform Probate Code in a Nutshell, 425 pages, 1978 (Text)

Bogert's Hornbook on Trusts, 5th Ed., 726 pages, 1973 (Text)

Clark, Lusky and Murphy's Cases and Materials on Gratuitous Transfers, 2nd Ed., 1102 pages, 1977 (Casebook)

Gulliver's Cases and Materials on Future Interests, 624 pages, 1959 (Casebook)

Gulliver's Introduction to the Law of Future Interests, 87 pages, 1959 (Casebook)—reprint from Gulliver's Cases and Materials on Future Interests, 1959

McGovern's Cases and Materials on Wills, Trusts and Future Interests: An Introduction to Estate Planning, 750 pages, 1983 (Casebook)

TRUSTS AND ESTATES—Continued

Mennell's Cases and Materials on California Decedent's Estates, 566 pages, 1973 (Casebook)

Mennell's Wills and Trusts in a Nutshell, 392 pages, 1979 (Text)

Powell's The Law of Future Interests in California, 91 pages, 1980 (Text)

Simes' Hornbook on Future Interests, 2nd Ed., 355 pages, 1966 (Text)

Turrentine's Cases and Text on Wills and Administration, 2nd Ed., 483 pages, 1962 (Casebook)

Uniform Probate Code, 5th Ed., Official Text With Comments, 384 pages, 1977

Waggoner's Future Interests in a Nutshell, 361 pages, 1981 (Text)

WATER LAW

Getches' Water Law in a Nutshell, approximately 400 pages, 1984 (Text)

Trelease's Cases and Materials on Water Law, 3rd Ed., 833 pages, 1979, with 1984 Supplement (Casebook)

See also Energy and Natural Resources Law, Environmental Law

WILLS

See Trusts and Estates

WOMEN AND THE LAW

Kay's Text, Cases and Materials on Sex-Based Discrimination, 2nd Ed., 1045 pages, 1981, with 1983 Supplement (Casebook)

Thomas' Sex Discrimination in a Nutshell, 399 pages, 1982 (Text)

See also Employment Discrimination

WORKERS' COMPENSATION

See Social Legislation

CONSTITUTIONAL LAW

By

JOHN E. NOWAK

Professor of Law, University of Illinois

RONALD D. ROTUNDA

Professor of Law, University of Illinois

J. NELSON YOUNG

Professor of Law, University of North Carolina at Chapel Hill
Professor of Law Emeritus, University of Illinois

SECOND EDITION

HORNBOOK SERIES

STUDENT EDITION

ST. PAUL, MINN.
WEST PUBLISHING CO.
1983

Library of Congress Cataloging in Publication Data

Nowak, John E.
Handbook on constitutional law.

(Hornbook series)
Includes bibliographical references and index.
1. United States—Constitutional law. I. Rotunda,
Ronald D. II. Young, J. Nelson (Jesse Nelson),
1916– . III. Title. IV. Series.
KF4550.N6   1983a   342.73   83–12334
347.302

ISBN 0-314-73466-X

N., R. & Y. Const.Law 2nd Ed. HB

1st Reprint—1984

To Judy, Marcia, and Zerla

*

PREFACE TO SECOND EDITION

A decade has passed since we first signed an agreement with West Publishing to prepare a one-volume treatise on constitutional law. We are pleased by the acceptance which the first edition, published over five years ago, has received from lawyers, judges, scholars, and students. We hope that the second edition of the treatise will prove to be as valued a research work as was its predecessor.

The scope of judicial activity has expanded in recent decades to the point where our national news magazines have run cover stories on the explosion of legal principles and judicial control of our governance system. Although the popular media no doubt have overstated the magnitude of this development, during the past decade the Supreme Court has decided constitutional issues at a record-breaking pace. The problem of keeping the treatise "within manageable size", to which we referred in the preface to the first edition, has been exacerbated by the passage of time and new Supreme Court decisions. Although we have not deleted coverage of any subjects that appeared in the first edition, we have had to limit our coverage of some issues in order to provide an analytic overview of the constitutional issues which are most studied or litigated today. As in our first edition, we have omitted many issues relating to court jurisdiction, conflict of laws, and criminal procedure; at appropriate points in the treatise we refer the readers to some of the many excellent texts on these subjects. We have attempted to keep the section and subsection divisions in this edition as close as possible to those used in the first edition because we have received many favorable comments from readers who found the subject matter divisions helpful.

As we did for our first edition, we will publish periodic supplements to this treatise, which may include new topic areas as well as an update of developments in areas examined in the text. The cut-off date for cases covered in this volume is May 15, 1983.

The number of persons to whom we are indebted has grown so large as to make it uneconomical for West to print a complete listing of those who have played a role in the publication of both editions of this treatise. Such a list would include not only all those persons mentioned in the first preface but also professors from across the country who have given us their reactions to the first edition and suggestions for this edition, particularly those professors who published reviews of our first edition. We are also grateful to the members of the judiciary who have written to us, commented upon, and cited our work. We also thank our students and staff who have contributed their efforts to this edition, particularly our secretaries, Karen McGuire and Barbara Milazzo, and our student research assistants, Steven Cook, Ellyn Dorf, Mary Lynn Eubanks, Elizabeth Gamsky, Robin Greenwald, Heidi Ladd, Ronald Kneezel, Sherri Knuth, Mary Kay Scott, and Jane Templeton.

PREFACE TO SECOND EDITION

Because of space limitations we have had to limit our references to secondary authorities and to court decisions other than those of the United States Supreme Court. We hope that no scholar or judge will feel slighted by our failure to refer to his or her work. Also to conserve space, we have cited Supreme Court cases only to the official United States Reports; we have omitted parallel citations to the Supreme Court Reporter and Lawyers' Edition, unless a citation to the United States Reports was not yet available for a recent Supreme Court opinion.

J.E.N.
R.D.R.
J.N.Y.

Champaign, Illinois
Chapel Hill, North Carolina
June, 1983

PREFACE TO FIRST EDITION

As has been often noted, it may be impossible to prepare a single volume treatise on Constitutional Law. To keep this volume within manageable size, we have had to exclude a variety of constitutional issues from consideration, and focus instead on selected areas of constitutional adjudication and decision making. We have omitted most issues relating to jurisdiction, conflicts of laws, and criminal procedure; there are many fine texts which examine these specialized subject areas. In general, we have emphasized those areas of Constitutional Law which are most often studied and litigated today as well as those emerging issues that we believe will be of most importance in the years ahead. In the annual supplements to this edition we will include references to all constitutional opinions of the Supreme Court; these later developments, indeed, may alter the scope of our coverage in future editions. But for the present we have had to make subjective judgments concerning the areas that will be of most significance to students and scholars in the next several years.

Within each Chapter the reader will find subsections that differ in length and depth of treatment of particular issues—varying from summations of the Supreme Court's work to lengthy, analytical evaluations of the judicial process. We hope that each major section, when viewed as a unit, will give an accurate picture of what the Court has done and an evaluation of that work in terms of accepted scholarly critiques and our own analyses. We have endeavored to identify those portions of the text that emphasize our interpretive views of issues, as opposed to factual accounts of the work of the Court. In attempting to incorporate the political, historic and economic background of some of the more significant Court decisions, we have of necessity engaged in subjective evaluations and judgments.

It is far too late in the history of constitutional scholarship for the authors of a text such as this to claim full credit for the ideas presented in their work. In a very real sense we are indebted to all of those scholars whose works have gone before us and aided us in our own studies—from the late Professors Corwin and Thayer to the many outstanding scholars of today. In particular, we have been aided by the many excellent casebooks that are currently published for law school use; these texts have served all professors of Constitutional Law as important research resources as well as stimulating teaching tools. We have cited casebooks, texts and articles where we thought that those works would be of particular aid to the reader who refers to this book for study or research guidance; unfortunately, space requirements have limited our citations to secondary authorities.

PREFACE

We also gratefully acknowledge the invaluable suggestions of those professors who have commented upon drafts of our manuscript: Derrick A. Bell, Jr. of Harvard, Jesse H. Choper of the University of California at Berkeley, Martin H. Redish of Northwestern University, William W. Van Alstyne of Duke University, and our colleagues at the University of Illinois, Wayne R. LaFave and Peter H. Hay. Our indebtedness to all these scholars cannot be overstated. Their work is responsible for improvements to the text; responsibility for its failures remains with us alone (though each of us believes that the other two are at fault).

We also wish to express our thanks to the various students at the College who have aided us throughout the last three years with work ranging from research assignments to the drudgery of citation checking. Kimball Anderson, Karen Butler, Nancy J. Clawson, David Crumbaugh, David Finch, Judy Gross, Marianne Guerrini, Mary Hester-Tone, Robert Markowski, Gary Nelson, Judith Perlman, Frances E. Prell, Charles Salowitz, Patricia Smart, James Vroman and Ruth Wilcox. We express our appreciation to our secretaries, Kay Tresslar and Cynthia Utley, and to those who assisted them—Beth Cobb, Patricia Estergard, Linda Graham, Patricia Love, and Judy Nowak.

A note on citation forms: To conserve space we have cited each Supreme Court case only to the official reporter; parallel citations to the Supreme Court Reporter and the Lawyers Edition may be found in the tables in the introductory pages of each bound volume of those reporters. We have cited recent cases to the Supreme Court reporter system when citations to the U.S. Reports were not available. The cut off date for this volume is July 1, 1977. After initial citations and references to Bator, Mishkin, Shapiro and Wechsler, *Hart and Wechsler's The Federal Courts and the Federal System* (2d ed. 1973), we subsequently cite this excellent text only by its title. To make our cross references within sections easier to follow, we have generally used a separate numbering system for the footnotes in each subsection. Footnote cross references refer to the numbers within the same section; there are no cross references solely by footnote number to other portions of the text. We trust that these few peculiarities of our citation pattern will cause no inconvenience to the reader.

J.E.N.
R.D.R.
J.N.Y.

Champaign, Illinois
December, 1977

SUMMARY OF CONTENTS

SUMMARY OF CONTENTS

APPENDICES

TABLE OF CONTENTS

TABLE OF CONTENTS

TABLE OF CONTENTS

PART II. THE FEDERAL SYSTEM AND FEDERAL POWER

CHAPTER THREE. SOURCES OF NATIONAL AUTHORITY

CHAPTER FOUR. THE FEDERAL COMMERCE POWER

CHAPTER FIVE. FEDERAL FISCAL POWERS

TABLE OF CONTENTS

CHAPTER SIX.   INTERNATIONAL AFFAIRS

CHAPTER SEVEN.   PRESIDENTIAL DOMESTIC POWER

CHAPTER EIGHT.   CONGRESSIONAL POWERS AND PRIVILEGES

TABLE OF CONTENTS

CHAPTER NINE. THE COMMERCE CLAUSE AND RESTRICTIONS ON STATE REGULATORY POWERS

CHAPTER TEN. FEDERAL REGULATION AND STATE AUTHORITY

TABLE OF CONTENTS

CHAPTER ELEVEN. STATE TAXATION

TABLE OF CONTENTS

TABLE OF CONTENTS

TABLE OF CONTENTS

PART III. LIMITATIONS ON GOVERNMENT POWER: INDIVIDUAL RIGHTS AND LIBERTIES

CHAPTER TWELVE. INDIVIDUAL LIBERTIES: AN OVERVIEW

CHAPTER THIRTEEN. SUBSTANTIVE DUE PROCESS

TABLE OF CONTENTS

CHAPTER FOURTEEN.   STATE ACTION

CHAPTER FIFTEEN.   PROCEDURAL DUE PROCESS—THE REQUIREMENT OF FAIR ADJUDICATIVE PROCEDURES

TABLE OF CONTENTS

CHAPTER SIXTEEN. EQUAL PROTECTION

TABLE OF CONTENTS

TABLE OF CONTENTS

TABLE OF CONTENTS

TABLE OF CONTENTS

TABLE OF CONTENTS

TABLE OF CONTENTS

CHAPTER NINETEEN. FREEDOM OF RELIGION

TABLE OF CONTENTS

XL

TABLE OF CONTENTS

APPENDICES

*

CONSTITUTIONAL LAW

*

PART I

JUDICIAL REVIEW

CHAPTER ONE

THE ORIGINS OF JUDICIAL REVIEW

I. INTRODUCTION

The power of the Supreme Court to determine the constitutionality and, therefore, the validity of the acts of the other branches of government has been firmly established as a basic component of the American system of Government. But it was not always so and a major part of the Court's history may be described as a continuing effort to establish and maintain this judicial power. In a very real sense this entire text deals with the subject of judicial review. We will return to discuss the establishment and proper scope of the judicial power in connection with a wide variety of subjects ranging from the commerce clause to due process and the first amendment freedoms. Therefore this chapter will not attempt wide-ranging examination of the legitimate scope of judicial review. Instead, it will only set out the primary decisions concerning the power of judicial review coupled with some basic historical and academic commentary upon them. This discussion should provide the reader with a framework for later inquiry into the use of judicial power as it is examined throughout other portions of the text. The remainder of this chapter is divided into two major sections. The first will examine the Supreme Court's decision in *Marbury v.*

Madison [1] and the claim to a judicial power to review the acts of other branches of the federal government. The second major section will examine the primary cases by which the Court established its power to review the actions of state and local governments.

II. MARBURY v. MADISON—THE POWER TO DECLARE ACTS OF THE FEDERAL GOVERNMENT TO BE IN VIOLATION OF THE CONSTITUTION

A. The Setting of the Case

During the last years of the eighteenth century the Federalist Party controlled the national government. The time was one of intense political rivalry. The Federalists had used the powers of the national government for partisan purposes, exemplified by the use of the Sedition Act to punish those who spoke out against President Adams or the Federalist Congress. The political opposition reacted with animosity towards the Federalists and the Federalist judges who enforced the Sedition Act against other political parties.

In 1800 the Federalists lost power for a variety of reasons, including popular reaction against their use of the Sedition Act and the growing tensions with Great Britain. [2] Jefferson won the popular vote for the presidency but there was a tie vote between Jefferson and Burr in the electoral college. Jefferson would have to be chosen president by the House of Representatives. Although the Federalists were facing the end of their era of power, Adams remained as president until the end of his term on March 4, 1801. In December 1800, Oliver Ellsworth, third Chief Justice of the United States, resigned his position on the Supreme Court. President Adams first sought to reappoint former Chief Justice John Jay to the Court, but Jay refused the appointment.

Following the Jay refusal, Adams nominated John Marshall, Adams' secretary of state and a leading figure in the Federalist Party, to be the fourth Chief Justice of the United States. On January 27, 1801, Marshall's nomination was confirmed by the Senate; Marshall took office on February 4, 1801. Only a month remained until Jefferson would take office and, at President Adams' request, Marshall continued to serve as Adams' secretary of state for the remainder of Adams' term.

In the last few weeks before Jefferson and the Republicans (sometimes also referred to as Democratic-Republicans, or Anti-Federalists) took office, the Federalists sought to maintain their power through continued control of an expanded federal judiciary. They passed the Circuit Court Act which reduced the number of Supreme Court Justices and eliminated the practice of having the justices individually hold court in the circuits. [3] The Act also established sixteen new circuit courts and federal judgeships. These were quickly filled with federalist appointees who received confirmation only two days before Jefferson was to take office, and who thus came to be known as the "midnight judges." But it was even later appointments that gave rise to the *Marbury* litigation.

On February 27, 1801, the holdover Federalist Congress authorized the appointment of 42 justices of the peace to serve five-year terms in the District of Columbia and Alexandria. [4] President Adams appointed Federalists to these positions and they were confirmed by the Senate on March 3, the day before the Republicans were to take office. The formal appointments were made by delivery of sealed commissions by the Secretary of State. John Marshall, as Secretary of State, executed and sought to deliver these commissions but, even though he had

1. 5 U.S. (1 Cranch) 137 (1803).

2. R. McCloskey, The American Supreme Court at 37–8 (1960); The Sedition Act is examined in the first section of Chapter 18 on the Freedom of Speech.

3. Act of February 13, 1801, Ch. 4; 2 Stat. 89.

4. Act of February 27, 1801, Ch. 15; 2 Stat. 103.

some assistance, there remained a few unde-livered commissions that night.

Of course, the Republicans were not pleased by the prospect of these new Feder-alist judges and they took several steps to alter the situation. First, Jefferson, through his Secretary of State, James Madison, refused to deliver the remaining commissions for the justices of the peace. Second, the Republican Congress, after a de-bate on the wisdom and constitutionality of altering the judicial structure, repealed the Circuit Court Act in 1802.[5]

William Marbury was one of those justices of the peace appointed by Adams who had failed to receive his commission. He brought suit against the new secretary of state, James Madison, for delivery of his commission by filing an original action in the Supreme Court seeking an order of manda-mus to Madison to compel the delivery. He asserted jurisdiction for this original action under § 13 of the Judiciary Act of 1789, one of the first acts of the Congress.

Jefferson was of the belief that he could not be ordered to take such an action by a court and Madison refused to appear before the Supreme Court. The Court then issued a rule to show cause as to why the manda-mus should not issue and set the case for ar-gument in the 1802 term. However, the Congress was in the process of repealing the Circuit Court Act and it rescheduled the terms of the Supreme Court so as to elimi-nate part of the 1802 term of the Court. Thus, when the Court began its 1803 term it faced the issue of defining the judicial power in relation to the other branches of govern-ment. The Court avoided overruling the re-peal of the Circuit Court Act a week after it ruled it had no jurisdiction to entertain Mar-bury's action.[6] But in the *Marbury* decision

the Supreme Court asserted its power to re-view the constitutionality of the actions of both the executive and legislative branches of the federal government. Although the Republicans disputed this claim to power, political opposition did not mount for a seri-ous attack on the Court for neither ruling actually went against the immediate inter-ests of the Republicans. Had the Court reached other results in the case, the Repub-lican Congress might well have considered impeaching the federalist judges on the Su-preme Court.[7] However, Marshall was able to establish the claim to judicial authority without taking actions which would provoke political reprisals against the Supreme Court.

B. The Opinion of the Court

On February 24, 1803, Chief Justice Mar-shall delivered the opinion of the Supreme Court in *Marbury v. Madison*.[1] In the opin-ion the Court held that Marbury had a right to his judicial commission. In so doing the Court found that the executive was subject to certain legal and constitutional restraints which could be enforced by the judiciary. Yet the Court found that it could not grant the remedy in an original action as it was not within the jurisdiction fixed for the Court by Article III. The opinion inter-preted a section of the Judiciary Act of 1789 as placing this action within its jurisdiction but found that the law conflicted with the Constitution. Marshall concluded by finding that the Supreme Court had the power to de-clare such a law to be invalid as a violation of the Constitution.

Marshall began the opinion by framing the case in terms of three issues. First, wheth-er Marbury had a right to the commission. Second, whether the laws of the country es-

---

5. Act of March 8, 1802, Ch. 8; 2 Stat. 132. For a history of the debate see 1 C. Warren, The Supreme Court in United States History 204–222 (1932).

6. Stuart v. Laird, 5 U.S. (1 Cranch) 298 (1803). In this case the Court upheld part of the act but did not confront the most difficult issues. However, the case is often cited as upholding the repeal act by implica-tion.

7. Indeed the House of Representatives later did impeach Justice Chase, a leading and hated partisan Federalist, but the trial failed in the Senate. See, 1 C. Warren supra note 5 at 289–95.

1. 5 U.S. (1 Cranch) 137 (1803).

tablished a remedy for the deprivation of the right. Third, whether a mandamus could be issued in an original action before the Supreme Court. Marshall found that Marbury had a right to the commission once it was signed by the President and sealed by the Secretary of State. Based on the act of Congress authorizing the appointment of Justices of the Peace for the District of Columbia, the opinion found this to be a "vested legal right".[2] The Court might have held that the right did not vest until delivery of the commission, but the justices stated that an irrevocable right accrued to the individual after the execution of the commission.

On the second issue, the opinion found that the "essence of civil liberty" required a legal remedy for a legal wrong. Since the government of the United States is one "of laws and not of men" it must grant a remedy for violation of vested legal rights.[3] Marshall did note that there would not be a judicial remedy for a wrong where the subject matter was political in nature or otherwise committed to the discretion of the executive.[4] In such instances the individual's remedy would have to be left to the political process. But where individual rights depended on a duty established by law there was a remedy that might be judicially enforced to protect the injured individual. This argument laid the basis for his conclusions in the next section concerning the scope of judicial review.

The crucial issue in the case thus became whether Marbury was entitled to the remedy for which he had applied to the Supreme Court. The opinion by Marshall subdivided this issue into two further questions concerning the nature of the writ of mandamus and the power of the Court.

In examining the nature of the writ, the opinion asserted a judicial power to review the acts of the executive branch. As the writ of mandamus is one to order an officer to take a specific action, Marshall inquired as to whether it could be used against officers of the executive branch. He recognized that the importance of the relationship between the president and the high executive officers, such as cabinet members, was one that should not be examined absent specific legal justification. Indeed, Marshall found two classes of executive acts which could not be made the subject of judicial review. Where the action by the president or executive officers was in its nature "political" the matter was not one for judicial intervention. Similarly where the Constitution or federal law placed a subject matter within the sole discretion of the executive it could not be reviewed by the Court. However, Marshall found that it was not the nature of the executive branch that limited judicial review but only that the judiciary should not seek to review solely political or discretionary acts.[5] Where the Constitution or federal law established some duty for the executive branch, the judiciary could enforce that duty. In such a case there was no intrusion into the power granted the President, but only an inquiry into the charge of a specific illegality.[6] Thus Marshall established the basis for finding that the actions of the executive branch were subject to review under both the Constitution and laws of the United States and that the federal judiciary could order the executive to comply with those principles.

This analysis left only the question of whether the mandamus against the executive should issue in this particular case. Here Marshall found a conflict between the Court's statutory jurisdiction and that fixed by Article III of the Constitution. Although it could have been interpreted in a different manner, he found that Section 13 of the Judiciary Act of 1789[7] authorized original ac-

---

2. Id. at 162.

3. Id. at 163.

4. Id. at 166.

5. 5 U.S. (1 Cranch) at 170.

6. Id.

7. Act of September 24, 1789; Sec. 13; I Stat. 73, 80–81. The provision read:

"And be it further enacted, That the Supreme Court shall have exclusive jurisdiction of all controversies of a civil nature, where a state is a party, except between a state and its citizens; and except also

tions in the Supreme Court for writs of mandamus to officers of the United States such as the action involved in this case. He interpreted Article III as fixing the original jurisdiction of the Supreme Court to exclude such actions.[8] The opinion found that Congress might have the power to alter the appellate jurisdiction of the Court but that the original jurisdiction was intended to be fixed by this provision. As construed, there was a clear conflict between the jurisdictional statute and the Constitution, leading Marshall to consider whether a law which was in conflict with the Constitution could be valid and whether the Supreme Court had the power to invalidate or, at least, disregard such a law.

Marshall found that the question of whether a federal statute contrary to constitutional provisions could be the law of the land was "not of an intricacy proportioned to its interest."[9] The basis for this ruling was the concept that the people of the nation had the right to establish binding principles for the governing of society which had the effect of enforceable law. While the people might have established a government of general powers, they chose instead to create one of defined and limited powers. Marshall found no middle ground between these types of government. This left, in his opinion, the choices of either declaring the Constitution to be the superior and binding law, or allowing the legislature to be an entity of unlimited powers. He found a basis for the superiority of the Constitution in the fact that the nation had sought to establish a written Constitution with fundamental principles to bind it in the future. Therefore the Constitution was the superior law and an act repugnant to it was invalid.

There remained the question of whether the Courts were obliged to follow the act of the legislature despite their view as to its incompatibility with the Constitution. Here Marshall asserted the basis for the judicial review of acts of the federal legislative branch under the Constitution. Marshall's argument is deceptively simple. The essence of the argument is his first point, that "it is emphatically the province and duty of the judicial department to say what the law is."[10] Having previously recognized the Constitution as being the superior "law" in the nation, with this statement Marshall lays claim to final authority on matters of constitutional interpretation for the judicial department. It is this concept of the Constitution as law, and the judiciary as the institution with responsibility to interpret the law, which remains the cornerstone of judicial review today.

Marshall put forth several other points in support of his conclusion concerning the judicial power to find laws to be in violation of the Constitution. Since the Court would be required to follow either the statute or the Constitution in a given case, he found that an inability to reject the law in favor of the

---

between a state and citizens of other states, or aliens, in which latter case it shall have original but not exclusive jurisdiction. And shall have exclusively all such jurisdiction of suits or proceedings against ambassadors, or other public ministers, or their domestics, or domestic servants, as a court of law can have or exercise consistently with the law of nations; and original, but not exclusive jurisdiction of all suits brought by ambassadors, or other public ministers, or in which a consul, or vice consul, shall be a party. And the trial of issues of fact in the Supreme Court, in all actions at law against citizens of the United States, shall be by jury. The Supreme Court shall also have appellate jurisdiction from the circuit courts and courts of the several states, in the cases herein after specially provided for; and shall have power to issue writs of prohibition to the district courts, when proceeding as courts of admiralty and maritime jurisdiction, and writs of mandamus, in cases warranted by the principles and usages of law, to any courts appointed, or persons holding office, under the authority of the United States."

8. U.S.Const. art. III reads in part:

"In all Cases affecting Ambassadors, other public Ministers and Consuls, and those in which a State shall be a Party, the supreme Court shall have original Jurisdiction. In all the other Cases before mentioned, the supreme Court shall have appellate Jurisdiction, both as to Law and Fact, with such Exceptions, and under such Regulations as the Congress shall make."

9. 5 U.S. (1 Cranch) at 176. Indeed the entire discussion of this point took less than two pages. Id. at 176–77.

10. 5 U.S. (1 Cranch) at 177.

Constitution would subvert "the very foundation" of a written Constitution.[11] Within the document he found further support in the extension of the judicial power to "all cases arising under the Constitution."[12] He finds that this jurisdictional power inevitably leads to the conclusion that the framers of that provision must have been willing to allow the judiciary to use and interpret the Constitution in the cases arising under it. The opinion also concluded that the provisions of the Constitution which specifically restricted federal powers support the conclusion that the judiciary would have to choose between enforcing the Constitution or following the legislature in certain cases. Marshall cited several provisions which imposed specific limitations on the acts of government such as the export tax clause,[13] the Bill of Attainder and *ex post facto* prohibitions,[14] and the establishment of requirements for proof of treason.[15] In cases which involve these provisions it was clear to Marshall that the framers of the Constitution must have contemplated that the courts would follow its terms rather than any contrary act of the legislature. He drew further support for this conclusion from the oath for the judges, which required them to support the Constitution.[16] To Marshall this required that the judges follow the Constitution rather than any subordinate law.

Marshall's argument closes as it began with the concept of the Constitution as the superior law. He noted that in the Supremacy Clause of Article VI the Constitution is first mentioned and that the acts of the United States which are granted recognition are "those only which shall be made in *pursuance* of the Constitution."[17] Thus he found that the supreme law of the land must be the Constitution and that the justices are required to follow it rather than any inconsistent provisions of federal legislation.

Thus Marbury was denied his commission as the Supreme Court found that it could not entertain an original action for mandamus consistent with its jurisdiction under Article III. To the extent that Section 13 of the Judiciary Act included a contrary provision it was unconstitutional and "void".[18]

C. Some Notes on the Marbury Decision

1. Criticisms of the Marbury Opinion

For obvious reasons the decision in *Marbury v. Madison* has been the subject of continuing analysis and historical inquiry. Although the doctrine of judicial review is firmly established, a recapitulation of some of the commentary concerning *Marbury* and its historical antecedents remains of importance beyond mere historical interest. Theories concerning the proper scope of judicial actions under the Constitution often focus upon the legitimate claim to authority of the Court and find that the judicial power should be exercised most sparingly if the claim to this authority is weak. This section will summarize some of the past criticisms of

---

11. Id. at 178.

12. U.S.Const. art. III, § 2:

"The judicial Power shall extend to all Cases, in Law and Equity, arising under this Constitution, the Laws of the United States, and Treaties made, or which shall be made, under their Authority;—to all Cases affecting Ambassadors, other public Ministers and Consuls;—to all Cases of admiralty and maritime Jurisdiction;—to Controversies to which the United States shall be a Party;—to Controversies between two or more States;—between a State and Citizens of another State;—between Citizens of different States;—between Citizens of the same State claiming Lands under the Grants of different States, and between a State, or the Citizens thereof, and foreign States, Citizens or Subjects."

13. U.S.Const. art. I, § 9, cl. 5:

"No Tax or Duty shall be laid on Articles exported from any State."

14. U.S.Const. art. I, Sec. 9, cl. 3:

"No Bill of Attainder or ex post facto Law shall be passed."

15. U.S.Const. art. III, § 3:

"Treason against the United States, shall consist only in levying War against, them or, in adhering to their Enemies, giving them Aid and Comfort. No Person shall be convicted of Treason unless on the Testimony of two Witnesses to the same overt Act, or on Confession in open Court."

16. 5 U.S. (1 Cranch) at 180.

17. Id. (emphasis in original).

18. Id.

Marshall's opinion, the sources of an historical inquiry, and commentary on the relationship between the *Marbury* rationale and the proper scope of judicial review. In reviewing this material, one should remember the words of Justice Frankfurter that:

> The courage of *Marbury v. Madison* is not minimized by suggesting that its reasoning is not impeccable and that its conclusion, however wise, not inevitable. I venture to say this but fully aware that, since Marshall's time and largely, I suspect, through the momentum of the experience which he initiated, his conclusion in *Marbury v. Madison* has been deemed by great English speaking Courts an indispensable, implied characteristic of a written Constitution.[1]

Criticisms of John Marshall's opinion in *Marbury v. Madison* are of two general types.[2] First, there is criticism of the way in which Marshall strove to reach the decisions concerning the constitutional authority of the Court over the other branches of government. Second, Marshall's arguments concerning the authority of the Court are sometimes said to be assertions of authority rather than substantial reasons supporting his conclusion.

It is certainly true that Chief Justice Marshall was striving to use this decision to establish a claim to the power of judicial review. Initially, it should be noted that Marshall's merely hearing the case shows his view of its importance and his eagerness to use the decision on behalf of the judicial branch. Marshall did withdraw from a decision concerning the Court's power over the acts of state courts when he had a direct financial interest in the decision,[3] but here his personal stake in the outcome was not so clear. The likelihood that this case might establish the foundation for future relationships between the authority of the three branches of government was such that Marshall was willing to disregard charges of partisanship and author the opinion himself.

Within the opinion Marshall clearly had opportunities to avoid the constitutional questions concerning both the executive and legislative acts. A ruling either that Marbury lacked a right to the commission until delivery or that the political process was to govern the remedy for refusals to honor appointments would have avoided these issues.[4] Similarly a construction of the Judiciary Act as authorizing mandamus only when jurisdiction was otherwise properly invoked would have avoided the ruling on the constitutionality of the statute. Marshall's effort to reach the constitutional question thus is open to criticism under today's generally accepted principle that the Court should avoid ruling on a constitutional issue when a case can be decided on a narrower ground. However this principle is only a general guide for Court action and in no sense is it an ironclad rule which has bound the Court at all times in its history. When justices feel that a constitutional decision is important for the protection of certain values they are always free to decide the issue rather than to avoid it provided the Court has jurisdiction.[5] The extent to which one agrees with the conclusion that the Court should have the power to review the constitutionality of the acts of

---

1. Frankfurter, John Marshall and the Judicial Function, 69 Harv.L.Rev. 217, 219 (1955).

2. The historical criticisms of Marbury are analyzed and supplemented in Van Alstyne, A Critical Guide to Marbury v. Madison, 1969 Duke L.J. 1. We commend this excellent article, which contains a further bibliography, to those interested in more detailed and documented analytical treatment of the opinion. For one of the finest early pieces on the relation between the opinion and the legitimate claim to the power of judicial review see Corwin, Marbury v. Madison and the Doctrine of Judicial Review, 12 Mich.L.Rev. 538 (1914).

3. See the discussion of Martin v. Hunter's Lessee, 14 U.S. (1 Wheat.) 304 (1816) in Section II of this Chapter. In *Marbury* Marshall was the secretary of state who originally was to have delivered the judicial appointment; therefore he might have been called as a witness.

4. The Court has since endorsed a wider power for the executive relating to appointments and discharges. See Myers v. United States, 272 U.S. 52 (1926); Humphrey's Ex'r v. United States, 295 U.S. 602 (1935); Wiener v. United States, 357 U.S. 349 (1958); see also United States v. Smith, 286 U.S. 6, 47–48 (1932); United States v. Le Baron, 60 U.S. (19 How.) 73 (1856). Van Alstyne, supra note 2, at 10.

5. See the Note on the discretionary principles relating to avoidance of constitutional decisions in our chapter on Federal Jurisdiction, Chapter 2, section IV, B,7.

the federal government to a large measure determines one's criticism of Marshall's reaching the constitutional issues in this case. He was clearly correct in perceiving that this case offered the perfect vehicle for laying claim to the power of judicial review while avoiding a direct confrontation with the other branches of government. Had Marshall avoided the constitutional issues in this case, he might not have received a similar opportunity to establish the basis of the judicial power. Whether he would have succeeded without deciding the case in this manner is a matter for conjecture, but the gamble was one which Marshall was unwilling to take.

It is also true that Marshall's arguments concerning the relationship between the actions of the other branches of the federal government and the Constitution can be subdivided into a series of assertions, none of which inexorably leads to the conclusion which Marshall draws from them.[6] His discussion of judicial control of the powers of the executive is especially troublesome for its vagueness as to standards for the exercise of judicial power. While Marshall makes it clear that the president is subject to specific legal restraints established either by statute or the Constitution, he does not further define the nature of the duties that are, or can be made, subject to judicial review. Instead Marshall asserts an open-ended power to review executive actions based upon the principle that the executive can have no right to disregard a specific duty assigned to him by law. Indeed it was this general assertion of authority to review executive acts which gave rise to the greatest dispute at the time of the *Marbury* decision and several presidents have disputed

the claim to some extent.[7] However, it was also this general principle which would provide the Supreme Court with a basis for finding that the President of the United States could not disregard judicial subpoenas for evidence in ongoing criminal cases over one hundred and seventy years later.[8]

Marshall's discussion of the constitutionality of legislative acts falls into two parts. First, Marshall found that a law which was not in conformity with constitutional principles could not be the law of the land. This proposition established the Constitution as a binding law superior to any other federal action. The individual reasons on which Marshall established this conclusion are subject to some question. The fact that the people established a government of limited powers does not of necessity mean that they established a single document to control the actions of their own democratic process. It is at least possible that the legislature was to be guided by these principles, while it was free to interpret them for itself and to have its acts respected by the other branches of government. Marshall, however, sought to shore up the argument by finding that the essence of a written Constitution is that it is to be a fundamental and binding document. Once again, this conclusion is not necessarily true; other nations have employed written Constitutions as general principles for government which are not enforced by the judicial departments against acts of other branches of the government.[9] But despite these individual criticisms of the components of Marshall's opinion, the argument must stand or fall on his ultimate conclusion that the Constitution was intended to be law in its truest sense.

---

6. Thus James Bradley Thayer in his biography of Marshall found himself forced to state that the reasoning did not go beyond that earlier put forth by Hamilton and did not meet the most difficult questions concerning the nature of judicial power. J. Thayer, John Marshall, at 77–78 (1901) as reprinted in Thayer, Holmes & Frankfurter, John Marshall (1967, P. Kurland ed.).

7. Presidents Jefferson, Jackson, Lincoln, and Roosevelt disputed some aspects of the power when ju-

dicial rulings interfered with their implementation of federal policy. For citations to Presidential writings disputing the authoritativeness of Supreme Court decisions, see G. Gunther, Cases and Materials on Constitutional Law at 26–30 (10th ed. 1980).

8. United States v. Nixon, 418 U.S. 683 (1974).

9. See Cappelletti, Judicial Review in Comparative Perspective, 58 Calif.L.Rev. 1017 (1970).

Having found that the Constitution was to be a form of law superior to legislation, Marshall went on to consider whether the judiciary must follow a law which was in conflict with the Constitution. Here Marshall follows his concept of the Constitution as "law." He argued that it is the institutional responsibility of the judiciary to interpret law and apply the law which is superior in any conflict between the Constitution and legislation. However, this principle does not establish that the judiciary is the proper body to make the initial determination of whether the statute is in fact so inconsistent with the provisions of the superior document that it is invalid. He drew support for this position from a number of specific examples of cases that might involve a choice between following legislative acts or a very specific provision of the Constitution. If, for example, Congress passes a statute providing for the conviction of persons for treason on the testimony of less than two witnesses, the judges would be confronted with the question of whether to follow the Constitution or the statute in a trial for treason. But this choice involves no question of interpretation, for there is a clear conflict; it does not even support the conclusion that the judiciary can void the act of Congress. The court might only be able to refuse to apply the statute in the given case.

Marshall found further support for the duties of the judiciary in that the judges take an oath to support the Constitution. But while this oath might give judges some support in choosing not to apply a specific act of Congress in a decision, it furnishes no claim to superior powers regarding constitutional interpretation because the legislators and executive take similar oaths. Nor does the supremacy clause of Article VI solve the problem, for it states only that federal laws were meant to be superior to state laws and state constitutions; it says nothing concerning the relationship between federal actions and the Constitution. Marshall's argument that only laws made in pursuance of the Constitution are the supreme law of the land does not solve the problem: we are left with the question of whether the judiciary or Congress has the final determination of when a law is made in pursuance of the Constitution.

Although Marshall's decision can be divided and attacked, it stands as an impressive argument when taken as a whole. The Chief Justice, in this case, is asserting only that the Constitution is a superior form of law established by the direct will of society and which judges must follow in the course of deciding issues before them. Marshall's claim to a unique judicial power is, as yet, an essentially limited one and, therefore, more easily supported ·by these types of assertions. Professor Corwin noted the concept of judicial review really rests upon three separate bases: (1) that the Constitution binds all parts of the federal government, (2) that it is enforceable by the Court in actions before it, and (3) that the judiciary is charged with interpreting the Constitution in a unique manner so that its rulings are binding on all other departments of the government.[10] The *Marbury* opinion seeks to establish the first two of these principles and only implies the existence of the third. The first two principles are, in fact, both historically and logically easier to prove than the third.[11] But if a strong case can be made that the Constitution is truly a binding law which is capable of being understood and interpreted as are other laws, then the claim to judicial superiority becomes extremely strong. In *Marbury* Chief Justice Marshall admitted of virtually no arguments that would cast doubt on the first two propositions concerning the Constitution as law. His opinion may be faulted for a failure to explore the concept of judicial authority to control the other branches and thereby to reflect upon doubts concerning the binding nature of the Constitution. However, Marshall would explore this concept in later opinions.

10.   Corwin, supra note 2, at 552.

11.   Id.

In *McCulloch v. Maryland,* [12] Chief Justice Marshall laid claim to the judicial authority to bind all branches of government by constitutional interpretation. In that opinion he found the Constitution to be both a law capable of definition by the normal legal process and a document of enduring principles which required an independent judiciary to interpret and apply it throughout changing historical periods. It was the reasoning and effect of this decision on both the claim to judicial supremacy and the establishment of federal authority over the states that led both Professor Thayer and Justice Frankfurter to regard it as Marshall's greatest opinion. [13] But Marshall also explored and explained the concept of judical supremacy and matters of constitutional interpretation in other decisions. In his decisions concerning the reviewability of actions of state government under the contract clause and the commerce clause, Marshall established the Constitution as a law which had to be interpreted and enforced by the judiciary in order to maintain its supremacy. Throughout his thirty-four year tenure as Chief Justice of the United States, John Marshall established the theoretical basis of judicial review with arguments both on and off the Court. [14] That Marshall did not accomplish this goal with a single opinion is hardly an indictment of his ability or contribution to the shaping of our legal history. Indeed, Marshall recognized at the end of his career that the Court had not yet totally secured its role in government. As stated by the late Robert McCloskey:

In his last years, Marshall was beset with misgivings about America's future, full of gloomy convictions that he had failed in his campaign to establish judicial sovereignty and to cement the bonds of national union . . . Not even he, the architect-in-chief, realized how securely the cornerstones of American Constitutionalism had been laid . . . But if we can tolerate, as Marshall could not, a world of half certainty (and if we enjoyed, as he did not, the perspective of the future), we can see that his forebodings were excessive and his accomplishments greater than he knew. The doctrine of judicial sovereignty was still subject to occasional challenge in moments of stress . . . but surely the judicial monopoly, though imperfect, was very impressive. The nation in general thought of the Court as the principal authority and conceded its right to supervise the states in most matters . . . America's devotion to the idea of fundamental law and the Court's ability to capitalize on opponents' errors had made sure of that. [15]

2. *A Note on the Historical Antecedents of the MARBURY Opinion*

A detailed examination of the possible historical basis for the claims to both judicial review and the supremacy of judicial interpretations under the Constitution is beyond the scope of this treatise. The subject is of such intricacy and importance that it has been the subject of entire volumes as well as numerous articles. [1] There is no clear conclusion as to whether the framers or ratifiers of the Constitution clearly intended to establish the Supreme Court as the final body to interpret the Constitution and control the acts of other branches of government. Professor Julius Goebel, in his excel-

---

12. 17 U.S. (4 Wheat.) 316 (1819).

13. Thayer, supra note 6, at 68; Frankfurter, supra note 1, at 214. The opinion is analyzed in the text in Chapter 3 on the National Powers.

14. Marshall defended the *McCulloch* decision and its reasoning in a series of newspaper articles published under the title "A Friend of the Constitution." See G. Gunther, ed., John Marshall's Defense of McCulloch v. Maryland (1969).

15. R. McCloskey, The American Supreme Court at 77–79 (1960).

1. See e.g., C. Beard, The Supreme Court and the Constitution (1912); R. Berger, Congress vs. The Su-

preme Court (1969); J. Goebel, 1 The Oliver Wendell Holmes Devise History of the Supreme Court of the United States—Antecedents and Beginnings to 1801 (1971); 1 A.A.L.S. Selected Essay on Constitutional Law, Chapter 1 (D. Maggs, Ed., 1938); Grey, Origins of the Unwritten Constitution: Fundamental Law in American Revolutionary Thought, 30 Stan.L.Rev. 843 (1978); Meigs, The American Doctrine of Judicial Power and Its Early Origin, 47 Am.L.Rev. 683 (1913); Nelson, Changing Conceptions of Judicial Review: The Evolution of Constitutional Theory in the States, 1790–1860, 120 U.Pa.L.Rev. 1166 (1972); Thayer, The Origin and Scope of the American Doctrine of Constitutional Law, 7 Harv.L.Rev. 1 (1893).

lent volume, concluded that there was indeed an historical basis for Chief Justice Marshall's claim to a judicial power to review the constitutionality of the acts of other branches of government.[2] However, this conclusion has been disputed by others and at a minimum the claim can be made that the precedents for this principle prior to 1803 are not clear.[3]

One can surmise from the historical data that some form of judicial review seems to have been accepted by a number of the drafters of the Constitution and that the concept, at least in part, had been endorsed by some of the states prior to the date of the *Marbury* decision. However, it must be remembered that this power was a truly unique American invention and at its earliest stages was so undefined that debate over the original understanding of the concept can be virtually endless. The late Professor Corwin noted that the concept of judicial review really included three separate assertions: (1) that the Constitution was meant to be the paramount law of the land; (2) that the judiciary had some ability to interpret and apply the Constitution in cases before it; (3) that the judicial interpretation was to be final and controlling over the views of the other branches of government.[4] As Professor Corwin noted, there is strong evidence for the first proposition, somewhat less strong but still substantial historical data supporting the second proposition, and historical data which is subject to totally conflicting interpretations as to the third asserted principle.[5] Herein lies the essence of the debate over the historical basis for Chief Justice Marshall's ruling in *Marbury*. Today we understand "judicial review" as including not only the ability of the Supreme Court to interpret the Constitution but also its power to void the acts of other branches of government on this basis. The evidence supporting judicial review as we know it today was not clear in 1803, but this form of judicial authority was rapidly accepted following the *Marbury* decision.

Professor Nelson, who has challenged Professor Goebel's conclusion that the concept of judicial review was publicly accepted by 1800, has also demonstrated that some form of judicial review seems to have been widely accepted throughout the states by 1820 [6] and that the concept of the judiciary as the ultimate interpreter of the Constitution was generally accepted by the time of the Civil War.[7] This continually expanding acceptance of the principle of judicial review may lead one to believe that there must have been some generally accepted core concept of judicial power at the time of *Marbury*. But the historical data remains subject to continual reexamination and debate. We will list the four main sources of this data so that the student may reflect upon them independently.

The first source of historical inquiry has been the English precedents for judicial review and the colonial experience. There is the widely quoted statement of Lord Chief Justice Edward Coke in *Dr. Bonham's Case:* "When an Act of Parliament is against common right and reason, the common law will control it and adjudge such Act to be void." [8] But there is also no solid historical basis for finding any form of judicial review in British judicial practice. The claim has also been made that the colonists may have understood the system to include some form of judicial review as the English government, pri-

---

2. J. Goebel, 1 The Oliver Wendell Holmes Devise History of the Supreme Court of the United States—Antecedents and Beginnings to 1801 (1971).

3. See 2 W. Crosskey, Politics and the Constitution (1953) (attack on the concept of judicial review). Contra, R. Berger, Congress vs. The Supreme Court (1969); Hart, Book Review, 67 Harv.L.Rev. 1456 (1954).

4. Corwin, Marbury v. Madison and the Doctrine of Judicial Review, 12 Mich.L.Rev. 538, 552 (1914).

5. Id.

6. Nelson, Changing Conception of Judicial Review: The Evolution of Constitutional Theory in the States, 1790–1860, 120 U.Pa.L.Rev. 1166 (1972).

7. Id. See also, E. Corwin, Liberty Against Government (1948).

8. Dr. Bonham's Case, 8 Coke Rep. 107, 116–121 (C.P.1610). See generally, Plucknett, Bonham's Case and Judicial Review, 40 Harv.L.Rev. 30 (1926); Thorne, Dr. Bonham's Case, 54 L.Q.Rev. 543 (1938).

marily through the Privy Council, had the power to review and void acts of the colonial legislatures which were found to be in violation of their charters or other English law.[9] However, this practice was a most limited one and not readily accepted by many colonies. While there is no clear support for judicial review in the English-colonial experience that is not the relevant issue. What is important to a search for the antecedents of *Marbury* is the understanding of the colonists concerning the English experience rather than the currently "correct" view of that history.

The second source of historical data concerning judicial review is the federal constitutional convention and the ratification process. This source offers the most fruitful support for the concept of judicial review. At the Convention almost every statement of a delegate which might be implied as reflecting on the subject of judicial review of the constitutionality of federal laws indicates an acceptance of that concept in some general form.[10] This evidence has led many scholars across the past 50 years to conclude that the framers must have intended to create a new form of judicial review under the Constitution.[11] However, the undefined nature of the judicial power referred to at the Convention leaves the historical support for the current concept of judicial supremacy unclear. In the ratification process The Federalist Papers endorsed a concept of judicial review upon arguments very close to those

which Marshall used in *Marbury* but there was some dispute as to the extent of this power by anti-federalists.[12]

The third area for historical inquiry is the experience in the state courts after the revolution. Between the time of the revolution and 1803, judicial review had been adopted by judicial decisions or provisions in state constitutions in most of the states that had given any specific attention to the issue.[13] However, as Professor Nelson has pointed out, there was still opposition to this concept in a number of states prior to 1800.[14] If we do not limit our examination of the state courts to the period prior to 1803, however, the case for judicial review becomes much stronger. Between 1800 and 1820 the concept of judicial review in terms of whether to apply a statute in a given case had received widespread acceptance. One of the most important courts of the period was the Supreme Court of Pennsylvania. While that Court accepted the concept of judicial review, Justice Gibson of Pennsylvania (later Chief Justice of that court) attacked the historical and philosophical basis for judicial review and the decision in *Marbury*.[15] The growth of the concept was demonstrated by Gibson's eventual conversion to believing that the concept should be adopted out of necessity, if not historical accuracy.[16] The rapid acceptance of the doctrine in the states indicates that there may well have been a commonly shared belief concerning the basic principle of judicial review which had taken

---

9.   J. Goebel, supra note 2, at 50–83; But cf. Nelson, supra, note 6, at 1166–67.

10.   See J. Goebel, supra note 2 at 196–251. For a collection of citations and excerpts from the debates see, P. Bator, D. Shapiro, P. Miskin and H. Wechsler, Hart and Wechsler's The Federal Courts and The Federal System 1–32 (2 ed. 1973) (hereinafter cited as H. Hart & H. Wechsler's, The Federal Courts and The Federal System (2d ed. 1973).

11.   See Corwin, The Establishment of Judicial Review, 9 Mich.L.Rev. 102–25, 284–316 (1910–11); Beard, supra note 1; R. Berger, supra note 3; H. Hart & H. Wechsler, supra note 10 at 9.

12.   The Federalist Nos. 78 and 81 (Hamilton) (Modern Lib. ed. 1937). For an analysis of the ratification debates see, J. Goebel, supra note 2, at 251–412. Marshall defended the concept of the Virginia convention, 3 J. Elliot, Debates in the Several States Conventions in

the Adoption of the Federal Constitution at 553–4 (1836).

13.   See J. Goebel, supra note 2 at 125–42; Corwin, Marbury v. Madison and the Doctrine of Judicial Review (notes follow text) reprinted in, 1 A.A.L.S., Selected Essays in Constitutional Law at 171–2 (D. Maggs ed., 1938).

14.   Nelson, Changing Conception of Judicial Review: The Evolution of Constitutional Theory in the States, 1790–1860, 120 U.Pa.L.Rev. 1166 (1972). See generally, Nelson, The Eighteenth Century Background of John Marshall's Constitutional Jurisprudence, 76 Mich.L.Rev. 893 (1978).

15.   Eakin v. Raub, 51 Pa.Rep. (12 Sargent & Rawle) 330, 343 (1825).

16.   Norris v. Clymer, 2 Pa. 277, 281 (1845).

shape prior to 1800 and which went through its initial growth period following the express adoption of the principle by the Supreme Court of the United States.

The final source of inquiry concerning the legitimate basis of judicial review is the acts of the federal government following the establishment of the Constitution. Here we have a very limited amount of data, but what exists indicates that there was an acceptance of the judicial review of legislation in some form. Individual justices, when in the circuits, refused to assume some duties that they believed were beyond their constitutional authority [17]; there was even correspondence between the Court and President Washington concerning the constitutionality of having the justices conduct trials in the circuits.[18] The Supreme Court upheld or applied actions of the federal and state legislatures in a way which indicated a belief that the justices were free to disregard the acts should they find them to be in violation of the Constitution.[19] However, there was no express adoption of the concept of judicial review in the opinions of the Court prior to *Marbury*. The concept also finds some implied acceptance by the actions of the Congress during this period. The first Congress wrote the Judiciary Act of 1789 which in part implies a power to review the constitutionality of state and federal laws by granting jurisdiction to the Supreme Court to review the actions of state courts which might concern such issues.[20] Additionally when the Republican Congress debated whether to repeal the Circuit Court Act of 1801 which established the "Midnight Judges", there was concern expressed over the constitutionality of the action although there was dispute as to the Court's powers in these debates.[21] While neither source confirms the claim to judicial review set out in *Marbury*,

they do indicate that the concept of judicial review was recognized as at least a plausible interpretation of the Constitution during this period.

3. A Note on the Relationship Between MARBURY and the Standards for Judicial Review

Throughout this text we will indicate at relevant points the ways in which the concepts of judicial authority have been defended or attacked in terms of the role of the Court in enforcing certain principles of the Constitution. Most of the debate on these issues will center on political philosophy concerning the role of this nonelected entity in a democracy. However we should note here that one's view of the judicial function in some measurement may relate to his or her view of the historical basis for Marshall's claim to judicial supremacy.

If one does not believe that there is a solid basis for judicial review in the text or history of the Constitution then one should accept the principle that the power of the Court to void the acts of other branches of government should be exercised rarely and then only out of absolute necessity. Thus, Judge Learned Hand felt that the power should be exercised only when absolutely necessary to prevent the democracy from overturning a clear and paramount constitutional principle.[1] But if one is convinced that the concept of judicial review has a solid historical basis there is somewhat greater room to exercise this judicial power. Professor Wechsler answered Judge Hand that he thought that there was no doubt but that the framers of the Constitution intended to create the power of judicial review and, therefore, he found a somewhat greater constitutional

---

17. See Hayburn's Case, 2 U.S. (2 Dall.) 409 (1792); J. Goebel, supra note 2, chapters 9–17 and Appendix.

18. There was a letter by several Justices to Washington and individual correspondence between Chief Justice Jay and the President. See, H. Hart & H. Wechsler, supra note 10, at 68. The practice was later upheld in Stuart v. Laird, 5 U.S. (1 Cranch) 299 (1803).

19. Hylton v. United States, 3 U.S. (3 Dall.) 171 (1796); Calder v. Bull, 3 U.S. (3 Dall.) 386 (1798).

20. Act of Sept. 24, 1789; 1 Stat. 73; See J. Goebel, supra note 2, chapter 11.

21. 1 C. Warren, The Supreme Court in United States History at 214–15 (1926).

1. L. Hand, The Bill of Rights 11–18 (1958).

role for the judiciary.[2] However, this historical evidence does not lead to a conclusion that the judiciary should overturn the acts of the government whenever judges disagree with the policy adopted by those acts. Professor Wechsler argued that the Court should only intervene against the will of democracy when the justices could identify a clear and "neutral" principle which was not dependent upon their view of the equities of the given case or the practical policies behind governmental actions.[3] This concept of limited, but legitimate, review over the acts of government forms the basis of the philosophy of "judicial restraint" whose most well-known proponents include Justice Frankfurter [4] and Professors Thayer,[5] Wechsler,[6] Bickel,[7] and Kurland.[8]

Acceptance of the position that there is a clear historical and textual basis for judicial supremacy in matters of constitutional interpretation may lead one to the further conclusion that the justices should not be extremely hesitant to strike down acts of other branches of government. Such a view rests upon the belief that there is a unique judicial function guaranteeing that constitutionally recognized rights, as identified by the Court, will be fully protected for future generations even if that means that the current decisions of democracy must be overturned. This view went through an era of disrepute as the justices used their power to strike down a variety of economic and social welfare reform measures between 1887 and 1937.[9] However, as the government has increasingly defined the scope of individual liberty in society, the position has made a new appearance with brilliant defenders. Three of the most notable proponents of this philosophy are Professor Charles Black,[10] Judge J. Skelly Wright [11] and Justice William O. Douglas.[12]

There are an almost limitless number of views of the proper role of the judiciary and the American Constitutional system and we will not attempt to list them in any single place within this text.[13] However, we would

2. Wechsler, Toward Neutral Principles of Constitutional Law, 73 Harv.L.Rev. 1, 3–5 (1959).

3. Id. See Greenawalt, The Enduring Significance of Neutral Principles, 78 Colum.L.Rev. 982 (1978). See generally, Rotunda, Judicial Biography and the Nature of Judicial Review, in R.Rotunda (ed.), Six Justices on Civil Rights (1983).

4. See Frankfurter, John Marshall and the Judicial Function 69 Harv.L.Rev. 217 (1955).

5. See Thayer, The Origin and Scope of the American Doctrine of Constitutional Law, 7 Harv.L.Rev. 129 (1893).

6. See Wechsler supra note 2, and H. Wechsler, Principles' Politics and Fundamental Law (1961).

7. See A. Bickel, The Supreme Court and the Idea of Progress (1969).

8. See Kurland, Toward a Political Supreme Court, 37 U.Chi.L.Rev. 19 (1969).

9. For an examination of these decisions see Chapter 4 on the Commerce Clause and Chapter 13 on Substantive Due Process.

10. See C. Black, The People and the Court (1960).

11. See Wright, Professor Bickel, The Scholarly Tradition and the Supreme Court, 84 Harv.L.Rev. 769 (1971).

12. See W. O. Douglas, The Right of the People (1958); see also, W. O. Douglas, Go East, Young Man (1974).

13. At appropriate points in the text, we will refer the reader to scholarly writings examining the proper scope of judicial review in terms of specific legal issues or court decisions. Today, much of the debate concerning the scope of judicial review focuses on a three-way dispute between scholars who may be classified as part of an "interpretivist," "process-oriented," or "value-oriented" school of constitutional jurisprudence. These labels only very inexactly describe three general approaches to the subject of judicial review. The interpretivists believe that the Supreme Court should only test legislation in terms of the words of the Constitution as they were understood by the persons who wrote or ratified the constitutional provisions at issue in a particular case. Professors Berger and (now Judge) Bork are two of the most read exponents of interpretivist philosophy today. See R. Berger, Government by Judiciary (1977); Bork, Neutral Principles and Some First Amendment Problems, 47 Ind.L.J. 1 (1971). Modern process-oriented scholars have followed in the steps of neutral principle theorists such as Bickel and Wechsler as they have argued that justices should state clearly the reasons which justify their definition of a particular constitutional principle and limit the judicial role to independent examination of only those legislative acts which appear to violate the specific wording of a constitutional provision, restrict the openness of the political process, or discriminate against discrete and insular minorities. Professor Jesse Choper, while not arguing against a wider scope of judicial review than a process-oriented approach would justify, has provided much of the theoretical groundwork for the process-oriented school. See J. Choper, Judicial Review and the National Political Process: A Functional Reconsideration of the Role of the Supreme

strongly suggest that at every point in the text one reflect upon the institutional capabilities of the Court and its proper role in a democracy.[14]

III. REVIEW OF STATE LAWS

A. The Cases

There are three decisions of particular importance in establishing the federal judicial power over state laws. The first of these cases, *Fletcher v. Peck*,[1] is important because it was the first exercise of the Court's authority after a period of intense attack on the Supreme Court between 1803 and 1810.[2] The Court had survived these attacks and now invalidated a state law under the Constitution for the first time.[3] This case involved a Georgia statute which sought to annul earlier conveyances of land to private persons. Those conveyances had been au-

thorized by an earlier, corrupt state legislature and the state now wished to cancel what seemed to be fraudulent acts. However the land had since passed to a private good faith purchaser who sought the enforcement of his contract and ownership rights. Construing the term "contract" to include an executed state contract or grant, the Supreme Court found the annullment to be an impairment of the obligation of contract within the meaning of Article I. The repealing statute was, therefore, unconstitutional. It was immaterial that the state was the grantor, for no distinction was found between the obligation of contracts where the contract was between two individuals and between the state and an individual. Marshall remarked in conclusion:

> The estate having passed into the hands of a purchaser for a valuable consideration, without notice, the state of Georgia was restrained either by general principles which are common to

Court (1980). Commentary on Professor Choper's work includes: Monaghan, Book Review, 94 Harv.L. Rev. 296 (1980); Nowak, Book Review, 68 Calif.L.Rev. 1223 (1980). During the past decade the most widely read and influential advocate of a process-oriented approach to the subject of judicial review has been Professor (now Dean) John Hart Ely. See J. Ely, Democracy and Distrust (1980). Commentary on Professor Ely's work includes: Grano, Ely's Theory of Judicial Review: Preserving the Significance of the Political Process, 42 Ohio St.L.J. 167 (1981); Nowak, Foreword: Evaluating the Work of the New Libertarian Supreme Court, 7 Hastings Constitutional Law Quarterly 263 (1980); Tushnet, Darkness on the Edge of the Town: The Contributions of John Hart Ely to Constitutional Theory, 89 Yale L.J. 1037 (1980). The value-oriented scholars would have the Supreme Court promote the social good by requiring all branches of the government, including the judiciary, to comply with principles of moral and political philosophy which these scholars believe are evidenced by the history and provisions of the Constitution and societal concensus on fundamental values. Although there are differences in their methodology, Professors Perry and Tribe and Dean Wellington provide examples of how a value-oriented approach may be used to define the proper scope of judicial review. See M. Perry, The Constitution, the Courts and Human Rights: An Inquiry into the Legitimacy of Constitutional Policymaking by the Judiciary (1982); L. Tribe, American Constitutional Law (1978); Tribe, The Puzzling Persistence of Process-Based Constitutional Theories, 89 Yale L.J. 1063 (1980); Wellington, Common Law Rules and Constitutional Double Standards: Some Notes on Adjudication, 83 Yale L.J. 221 (1973). Professor Henry Monaghan has forged a most interesting theory of judicial review which combines elements of the interpretivist and process-oriented approaches as

he has attacked those scholars who have advanced value-oriented theories. See Monaghan, Our Perfect Constitution, 56 N.Y.U.L.Rev. 353 (1981). An excellent overview of the problem of choosing between these approaches to judicial review and analysis of the basis for a value-oriented approach to constitutional theory is contained in two articles by Professor Thomas Grey. See Grey, Do We Have an Unwritten Constitution? 27 Stan.L.Rev. 703 (1975); Grey, Origins of the Unwritten Constitution: Fundamental Law in American Revolutionary Thought, 39 Stan.L.Rev. 843 (1978).

14. For a most insightful analysis of how a judge of the United States Court of Appeals can influence the development of constitutional doctrine, see Glennon, The Role Of A Circuit Judge In Shaping Constitutional Law: Jerome Frank's Influence On The Supreme Court, 1978 Ariz.St.L.J. 523.

1. 10 U.S. (6 Cranch) 87 (1810).

2. This included an attempt to impeach Justice Chase, a noted Federalist, that was successful in the House but failed in the Senate. During this period Marshall greatly feared that the Court would lose its power and independence. See, R. McCloskey, The American Supreme Court 44–47 (1960).

3. The Court had earlier overriden state laws on the enforceability of state debts in federal courts in Chisholm v. Georgia, 2 U.S. (2 Dall.) 419 (1793) but this was "reversed" by the eleventh amendment. The Court had previously considered the constitutionality of state acts, thus indicating an early belief in the power, but it upheld the challenged act. See Calder v. Bull, 3 U.S. (3 Dall.) 386 (1798); And the Court had enforced federal treaties; Clerke v. Harwood, 3 U.S. (3 Dall.) 342 (1797).

our free institutions, or by the particular provisions of the Constitution of the United States, from passing a law whereby the estate of the plaintiff in the premises so purchased could be constitutionally and legally impaired and rendered null and void.[4]

The second major decision concerning the federal judicial power in this area is *Martin v. Hunter's Lessee.*[5] This case involved conflicting claims to land in the northern portion of Virginia.[6] Lord Fairfax was a former British national who had become a citizen of Virginia prior to his death. In 1781 he willed the land he held in Virginia, which was quite extensive, to his nephew in England, Denny Martin. Virginia later passed acts to confiscate the lands of those who were British citizens or loyalists during the Revolutionary War. Virginia then granted a portion of Lord Fairfax's land to David Hunter. The stage was set for the litigation between the representatives of Martin and Hunter. The litigation spanned two decades and was complicated by a series of related actions.

Acting on behalf of the British representatives John Marshall had negotiated a compromise and personally purchased a large share of the land. His personal involvement led him to recuse himself from these decisions due to his financial interests. In connection with this agreement, the Virginia legislature had adopted the 1796 Act of Compromise, but the Supreme Court did not mention this act in its original decision on the ownership of the land. The existence of that compromise, and the complicated transactions, make it unclear whether the "right" persons ever did receive the benefits of the property pursuant to the Supreme Court's

mandate.[7] What is important today is that the Court enforced its decision on the constitutionality of state acts over the contrary opinions of the state officials and judges.

Martin's representatives based their claim to the land on the anti-confiscation clauses of treaties between the United States and Great Britain. Hunter, and the State of Virginia, claimed that title had vested in Virginia prior to these treaties so that they were not applicable to his title. The highest court of Virginia, the Court of Appeals, had ruled for Hunter and the state, but in 1813 the Supreme Court of the United States found that the treaties secured title in Martin.[8] Since state law is subordinate to federal treaties under the supremacy clause,[9] the case was returned to the Virginia courts for the entry of a judgment for Martin's representatives and successors. The Virginia Court of Appeals refused to follow this order because it found that the case should have been decided differently on the basis of the compromise under state law, and because the Supreme Court could not constitutionally exercise jurisdiction over a state supreme court. The state decision, if allowed to stand, would have voided section 25 of the Judiciary Act; it constituted a direct challenge to the authority of the national government in general and the Supreme Court in particular. Indeed, the Virginia Court was led by Judge Spencer Roane, who opposed the growth of power of the national government and who was a long-time political foe of John Marshall in Virginia.[10] Marshall was unable to respond for the Supreme Court because of his personal interests in the case; the opinion of the Supreme Court was written by Justice Story.

---

4. 10 U.S. (6 Cranch) at 139.

5. 14 U.S. (1 Wheat.) 304 (1816).

6. For a history of the events which led to this suit and the course of the litigation see 4 Beveridge, The Life of John Marshall (1919); 1 C. Warren, The Supreme Court in United States History 442–53 (1922). Summaries of these events may be found in most casebooks, particularly, G. Gunther, Cases and Materials on Constitutional Law 36–40 (10th ed. 1980); H. Hart & H. Wechsler's, The Federal Courts and the Federal System 442–46 (2d ed. 1973).

7. See W. Lockhart, Y. Kamisar & J. Choper, Constitutional Law: Cases—Comments—Questions 33 (5th ed. 1980); 1 C. Warren, supra note 6 at 450; 2 W. Crosskey, Politics and the Constitution 786 (1953).

8. Fairfax's Devisee v. Hunter's Lessee, 11 U.S. (7 Cranch) 603 (1813).

9. U.S. Const. art. VI, cl. 2.

10. Note, Judge Spencer Roane of Virginia: Champion of States' Rights—Foe of John Marshall 66 Harv. L.Rev. 1242 (1953).

In *Martin v. Hunter's Lessee*[11] the Supreme Court ruled that it had the jurisdiction and authority to review all state acts under the Constitution, laws and treaties of the United States. Writing for the Court, Story found that the Judiciary Act properly recognized the existence of appellate jurisdiction in the Supreme Court over actions in state courts.[12] The supremacy clause of Article VI plainly indicates that the framers realized that federal issues might arise in state cases, and the grant of jurisdiction to the Supreme Court in Article III over all cases within the judicial power of the United States had to include such decisions. Yet Virginia had argued that it was a sovereign and could not be restricted by the rulings of the Supreme Court. Story countered this claim by noting that the people of the nation had chosen to limit state sovereignty when they established a Constitution specifically restricting state acts in a variety of ways such as those included in Article I.[13] There was no reason to exempt actions of the state judiciary from these restrictions which did not unduly impair the functions of the state judiciary since the supremacy clause required those judges to follow federal law.

Story concluded by asserting the Supreme Court's right and duty to be the single, final interpreter of federal law and the Constitution. A national government, whose parts are subject to a single Constitution, must include an entity to give a final interpretation to its laws. Moreover, state courts had to be subject to the rulings of the Supreme Court in federal issues so that the meaning and application of the laws, treaties and Constitution of the United States would have a uniform interpretation and application throughout the country. Finally, the Court did not consider the propriety of issuing a mandamus order against state judges; it merely held that the judgment of the Virginia Court of Appeals had to be reversed.[14]

Marshall had an opportunity to speak for the Court in asserting jurisdiction over state acts in the third primary case, *Cohens v. Virginia*.[15] In this decision the Supreme Court upheld the state prosecution of interstate sellers of lottery tickets but in so doing established its authority to review state criminal proceedings. The decision came at a time when there were severe challenges to the Court as southern states feared the growing national power.[16] In this case Virginia had prosecuted persons who sold lottery tickets in the state in violation of state law. The appellants claimed that the sales were permitted by a federal statute authorizing a lottery in the District of Columbia. Marshall held that the federal act did not protect these persons, and in so deciding he asserted federal authority to review these state acts and criminal proceedings. He found a clear jurisdictional basis in the Constitution and federal statutes to review federal issues that were adjudicated in state courts, as had Story. Further, the opinion stated that the eleventh amendment did not withdraw federal jurisdiction where the suit was not one brought against the state by a non-citizen but was instituted by the state itself. Most importantly, he expounded upon the nature of the Constitution's control of state acts. Marshall found the Constitution to be an original act of the people which was apart from, and superior to, any concept of state sovereignty. To the extent that the people created a national power, the federal judiciary shared in it with the other branches of the federal government. As the Con-

---

11. 14 U.S. (1 Wheat.) 304 (1816). See also Chapter 2, section IV, C for a discussion of the federal issues in this case and the principle of an adequate and independent state ground.

12. Id. at 327–37.

13. Id. at 324–5, 343–4.

14. Id. at 362. Justice Johnson joined the opinion only because it had not taken a position on the mandamus issue. Id.

15. 19 U.S. (6 Wheat.) 264 (1821).

16. This had largely been a reaction to Marshall's opinion for the Court upholding federal law and limiting state power in McCulloch v. Maryland, 17 U.S. (4 Wheat.) 316 (1819), which is discussed in Chapter 3 on National Powers.

stitution was created to be a paramount and enduring law, it would often require enforcement against outside challenges. In Marshall's opinion the federal courts were a proper institution for this purpose.

B. Notes on the Review of State Laws

1. *Theory and Standards of Judicial Review*

The theory of the federal judicial power to review the acts of state governments to determine their constitutionality is easily justified once the basic concept of judicial review of federal statutes is granted. The supremacy clause of Article VI makes state law subordinate to the federal treaties and laws, as well as the Constitution.[1] That provision charges state court judges with the duty of following the Constitution of the United States as opposed to state law whenever the two conflict. As Professor Black has noted, the framers would have taken an incomprehensible, inconsistent position if they intended to have state judges review the constitutionality of state acts under the U.S. Constitution while denying a similar power to the Supreme Court in the appellate jurisdiction granted to it.[2] If nothing else, the supremacy clause strengthens the Court's claim to review state laws as a necessary way of declaring uniform principles of constitutional law. If each of the states was free to go its own way in matters of constitutional interpretation, the Constitution would have little impact as a national law.

These arguments, as well as those made in the three early cases concerning the review of state laws, have found almost universal acceptance among the justices and scholars. Thus, even Justice Holmes, who was opposed to active review of federal laws, found that the review of state acts was a necessary part of the federal judicial function.[3] Professor Thayer in his classic article on the nature of the judicial power in matters of constitutional law found no theoretical difficulty with the independent federal judicial review of state acts.[4]

In addition to the establishment of the power of judicial review over the states, the Court also had to determine what standards to apply when reviewing such acts. A strong argument can be made for allowing the states greater freedom than the federal government when applying the provisions of the Bill of Rights to them, for those were originally drafted to restrict only the federal government.[5] On the other hand, to the extent that the concept of judicial restraint is based on democratic theory, there is less reason for the federal judiciary to defer to state governments. In such a situation the judiciary is confronted with the acts of a subsidiary unit of the federal system rather than those of a coordinate, elected branch of the national government. Much of the modern theory of judicial restraint is based upon the work of Professor James Thayer, but he did not advocate the use of great restraint

---

1. U.S. Const. art. VI, cl. 2:

"This Constitution, and the Laws of the United States which shall be made in Pursuance thereof; and all Treaties made, or which shall be made, under the Authority of the United States, shall be the supreme Law of the Land; and the Judges in every State shall be bound thereby, any Thing in the Constitution or Laws of any State to the Contrary notwithstanding."

2. This point can serve as a strong argument for a grant of judicial power to review federal as well as state acts. C. Black, The People and The Court, 23–25 (1960).

3. Holmes once wrote: "I do not think the United States would come to an end if we lost our power to

declare an Act of Congress void. I do think the Union would be imperiled if we could not make that declaration as to the laws of the several States." O. W. Holmes, Collected Legal Papers at 295–96 (1920).

4. Thayer, The Origin and Scope of The American Doctrine of Constitutional Law, 7 Harv.L.Rev. 129, 154 (1893).

5. This position was advanced by the younger Justice Harlan. See e.g. Williams v. Florida, 399 U.S. 78, 117 (1970) (Harlan, J., concurring) and Chapter 3 section V on Due Process and the application of the Bill of Rights to the States.

when federal courts reviewed state laws. In the words of the Professor:

> But when the question is whether State action be or not be conformable to the paramount constitution, the supreme law of the land, we have a different matter in hand. Fundamentally, it involves the allotment of power between the two governments,—where the line is to be drawn. True, the judiciary is still debating whether a legislature has transgressed its limit; but the departments are not co-ordinate and the limit is at a different point. The judiciary now speaks as representing a paramount constitution and government, whose duty it is, in all its departments, to allow that constitution nothing less than its just and true interpretation; and having fixed this, to guard it against any inroads from without.[6]

The Supreme Court now holds the state and federal governments to identical standards when reviewing their acts under any constitutional guarantee applicable to both. This position is based on two principles. First, the provisions of the Constitution have a single meaning which the judiciary is bound to respect and enforce. Second, the federal judiciary is a similarly non-democratic institution when reviewing the acts of the democratic process in either situation. This principle of a single standard applies whether the constitutional provision involved is one of the provisions of the Bill of Rights that applies to the states [7] or a general guarantee such as due process or equal protection.[8] Indeed, this position has been accepted for so long that few remember Thayer's complete thesis, and his article has been cited as authority for exercising restraint when reviewing state laws.[9]

2. *State Challenges*

It should be noted that, while the Court's authority over state acts has long been accepted, the most serious political challenges to it have come in this area.[10] Prior to the Civil War there were recurring arguments that the individual states had the right to act free of federal constitutional restraints. These arguments resulted in political attempts to limit the Supreme Court's authority ranging from alteration of its statutory jurisdiction to claims of a right to disregard its constitutional interpretation if the state chose to "interpose" its sovereignty between the Court and the people of the state.[11] This interposition theory led to the argument that individual states had the power of "nullification"—the ability to disregard federal laws because the states were independent sovereigns. While this theory had strong support in individual southern states, it was never widespread and the Supreme Court exercised its authority in a manner that solidified its position over the states.[12]

After the Civil War, the power of the nation was firmly established and the arguments for "states' rights" disappeared from the halls of Congress and most of the nation.[13] However, as the Court in recent years began to cause individual states some discomfiture by enforcing the Constitution, new challenges to the Court's authority

6. Thayer, supra note 4, at 154–5.

7. Malloy v. Hogan, 378 U.S. 1 (1964).

8. United States v. Kras, 409 U.S. 434 (1973). However, there may be an exception to this principle in cases involving laws which define or restrict the rights of resident aliens. There is dicta indicating that the Court will subject federal laws which burden aliens as a class to a more lenient standard of review than state laws which burden resident aliens because of unique federal interests in this area. See Nyquist v. Mauclet, 432 U.S. 1, 7 n. 8 (1977). The case is discussed in Chapter 16, Equal Protection, section III, Aliens.

9. San Antonio Independent School District v. Rodriguez, 411 U.S. 1, 60 (1973) (Stewart, J., concurring).

10. This quite interesting point concerning judicial review and attacks on it was noted by Professor Charles Black. C. Black, Structure and Relationship in Constitutional Law 74–6 (1969).

11. See Warren, Legislative and Judicial Attacks on the Supreme Court of the United States—A History of the Twenty-Fifth Section of the Judiciary Act, 47 Am. L.Rev. 1, 161 (1913).

12. R. McCloskey, The American Supreme Court, Chapters 3 & 4 (1960).

13. See Nowak, The Scope of Congressional Power to Create Causes of Action Against State Governments and the History of the Eleventh and Fourteenth Amendments, 75 Colum.L.Rev. 1413, 1460–64 (1975).

arose.[14] But these are nothing more than political attempts to fight a firmly established concept; the states have no power or right to disregard the Constitution or its enforcement by the federal judiciary. The Supreme Court reaffirmed this principle when it held that states could not deter the federal enforcement of desegregation orders regardless of their individual positions on the issue.[15]

As these challenges involve no legitimate principle of constitutional law, they will receive no further treatment in this treatise except to note individual challenges when relevant to an historical explanation of an area of constitutional interpretation. To the extent that state officers choose to disregard federal rulings, they are subject to penalty under the contempt power and individual federal statutes, and the executive branch may be called upon to enforce federal law in these instances.[16]

3. *State Court Review of State Laws*

State courts may be called upon to review the constitutionality of either state or federal laws in the course of deciding issues in cases before them. When reviewing federal laws these courts must follow the rulings of the Supreme Court and enforce federal laws over inconsistent state acts. However, more difficult problems arise when state courts review state laws.

State courts are the final interpreters of state law even though their actions are reviewable under the federal constitution, treaties, or laws. The supreme court of a state is truly the highest court in terms of this body of law and it is not a "lower court" even in relation to the Supreme Court of the United States. It must follow the Supreme Court's rulings on the meaning of the Constitution of the United States or federal law, but it is free to interpret state laws or the state constitution in any way that does not violate principles of federal law.[17]

This power is an extremely important one for it means that the state courts are always free to grant individuals more rights than those guaranteed by the Constitution, provided it does so on the basis of state law.[18] The federal Constitution establishes minimum guarantees of rights and the granting of additional liberties does not violate its provisions. Thus, if a state court found the death penalty to be absolutely barred by the eighth amendment, its ruling could be overturned by the Supreme Court as contrary to its interpretation of federal law,[19] but if the

14. See Note, Interposition vs. Judicial Power—A Study of Ultimate Authority in Constitutional Questions, 1 Race Rel.L.Rep. 465 (1956); see also, Beatty, State Court Evasion of United States Supreme Court Mandates During the Last Decade of the Warren Court, 6 Val.L.Rev. 260 (1972).

15. Cooper v. Aaron, 358 U.S. 1 (1958); Bush v. Orleans Parish School Bd., 364 U.S. 500 (1960), affirming 188 F.Supp. 916.

16. See Note, Enforcement of Court Orders—Federal Contempt Proceeding and Prevention of Obstruction, 2 Race Rel.L.Rep. 1051 (1957); Pollitt, Presidential Use of Troops to Execute the Laws: A Brief History, 36 N.C.L.Rev. 117 (1958).

17. See, e.g., Members of the Jamestown School Committee v. Schmidt, ___ R.I. ___, 405 A.2d 16, 18–19 (1979) (Bevilacqua, C. J.) citing an earlier edition of this work.

18. See e.g., PruneYard Shopping Center v. Robins, 447 U.S. 74 (1980), in which the Supreme Court upheld a state court decision interpreting the state constitution to protect the distribution of pamphlets and petitions at a private shopping center. Although the Supreme Court held that the first and fourteenth amendments did not prevent a private shopping center owner from prohibiting such activities on his property, the expansion of the rights of speech and association could be accomplished by interpretation of the state constitution. For an excellent analysis of the current use of the power, see Howard, State Courts and Constitutional Rights in the Day of the Burger Court, 62 Va. L.Rev. 873 (1976). See generally Developments in The Law—The Interpretation of State Constitutional Rights, 95 Harv.L.Rev. 1324 (1982). For arguments justifying wider use of this power, see Brennan, State Constitutions and the Protection of Individual Rights, 90 Harv.L.Rev. 489 (1977).

19. The Supreme Court has overturned state judicial grants of rights where they were based on the state court's erroneous interpretation of the meaning of federal law. See, e.g., Lehnhausen v. Lake Shore Auto Parts, 410 U.S. 356 (1973); see also Oregon v. Haas, 420 U.S. 714 (1975).

When the Supreme Court reverses a state court decision which invalidated state law on the basis of an erroneous ruling or the meaning of the federal constitution, it normally notes that the state court remains free to review and invalidate the law at issue under the terms

state court based its decision on the state constitution, it could not be overturned, for the eighth amendment only allows the states to execute people under certain circumstances—it does not require it. Thus individual state courts have taken actions which are not required by the Supreme Court such as declaring sex classifications to be "suspect",[20] requiring equal financing of state schools,[21] or actively reviewing economic classifications under their own constitution.[22]

In closing it should be noted that all of the principles discussed in this treatise apply with full force to the ruling of state courts because they are required to follow the Supreme Court's interpretation of the Constitution of the United States. Nevertheless, one must always remember that the state courts may exceed the federal courts in the granting of rights under the state's laws or constitution as long as they do not violate a restriction of federal law. As the state courts are not "lower courts," they are not required to follow the interpretation of lower federal courts, such as the Court of Appeals

with jurisdiction over their state territory, even on matters relating to the Constitution of the United States.[23] The federal court orders are res judicata and binding in individual cases, but when a similar issue appears in a new state case, the state supreme court need only follow the rulings and interpretations of the Supreme Court of the United States. State court rulings contrary to the lower federal court may be a futile action, for the federal court may be able to issue a series of rulings, use habeas corpus, or even impose a state-wide injunction against state officials to enforce its interpretation of federal law. However, if the state supreme court believes that the lower federal court is in error as to the meaning of the Constitution, it may continue to hold an opposite interpretation so long as it does not interfere with a ruling of the federal court in a specific case. When such inconsistent rulings arise, it is common for the Supreme Court of the United States to exercise its appellate jurisdiction over a case involving the issue so that the matter can be finally resolved.[24]

of the state constitution. See, e.g., Minnesota v. Clover Leaf Creamery Co., 449 U.S. 456, 461, n. 6 (1981) (overruling state court invalidation of commercial regulation under equal protection clause of the fourteenth amendment while allowing for independent review of the state law by the state courts under the state constitution). See also County Bd. v. Richards, 434 U.S. 5 (1977) (per curiam); Idaho Dept. of Employment v. Smith, 434 U.S. 100 (1977) (per curiam).

20. Sail'er Inn, Inc. v. Kirby, 5 Cal.3d 1, 95 Cal. Rptr. 329, 485 P.2d 529 (1971); People v. Ellis, 57 Ill.2d 127, 311 N.E.2d 98 (1974).

21. Serrano v. Priest, 5 Cal.3d 584, 96 Cal.Rptr. 601, 487 P.2d 1241 (1971); Robinson v. Cahill, 62 N.J. 473, 303 A.2d 273 (1973).

22. Grace v. Howlett, 51 Ill.2d 478, 283 N.E.2d 474 (1972) (classification within no-fault insurance legisla-

tion); Hetherington, State Economic Regulation and Substantive Due Process of Law, 53 Nw.U.L.Rev. 13, 226 (1958).

23. Similarly a federal district court is only bound to follow the interpretation of the Court of Appeals for its Circuit and one Court of Appeals is not bound to follow the reasoning or results of decision in other circuits. This may result in a "split in the circuits" on a point of federal law which can only be resolved by the Supreme Court.

24. One example was the continuing dispute between the Supreme Court of Maine and the Court of Appeals for the First Circuit and the District Court over the allocation of the burden of proof in manslaughter cases that was finally resolved in Mullaney v. Wilbur, 421 U.S. 684 (1975).

CHAPTER TWO

FEDERAL JURISDICTION

I. A BRIEF INTRODUCTION TO THE DEVELOPMENT OF FEDERAL JURISDICTION: CONSTITUTIONAL AND STATUTORY

A. Overview of the Present Jurisdictional Framework of the Supreme Court

The Supreme Court is the only federal court created directly by the Constitution. Article III mandates that the judicial power be vested in "one Supreme Court." As to the inferior courts, the judicial power is vested only as the Congress "may from time to time ordain and establish" such lower courts.[1]

Under Article III of the Constitution, the jurisdiction of all federal courts is limited in nature and cannot be expanded beyond the contours set out in Article III. Federal courts constitutionally can hear only cases "arising under" the Constitution, laws, and treaties of the United States (including admiralty cases), and certain other cases by virtue of the status of the parties, i.e., cases affecting ambassadors, other public ministers, and consuls, controversies to which the United States is a party, controversies between two or more states, between a state and citizens of another state, between citizens of different states, between citizens of the same state claiming lands under grants of different states, and between a state or its citizens and foreign states, citizens, or subjects.[2]

Congress need not create lower federal courts and, if it does, need not grant them the full Article III jurisdiction. In fact, it has never conferred the full Article III jurisdictional power. For example, while lower federal courts have had jurisdictional power since their creation to hear controversies between citizens of different states, that power has always been subject to a requirement that the amount in controversy be in excess of a certain amount.[3]

In addition to these Article III courts—which are also called constitutional courts, and which may adjudicate only Article III business and are within that Article's guarantee of lifetime tenure and salary protection—Congress also has the power, within

---

1. U.S. Const. art. III, § 1.

2. U.S. Const. art. III, § 2, cl. 1.

3. See, e.g., Judiciary Act of 1789, 1 Stat. 73, section 11 of which provided that in diversity actions the amount in controversy "exceeds, exclusive of costs, the sum or value of five hundred dollars . . . ."

certain limits, to create what are called legislative courts or Article I tribunals, that is, "[t]ribunals inferior to the Supreme Court"[4] which are neither limited by, nor protected by, Article III. These Article I tribunals are really akin to administrative agencies; that is, the "judges" do not have any constitutionally guaranteed lifetime tenure and protection from salary diminution;[5] they are not governed by the case or controversy limitation of Article III[6] and thus may render advisory opinions;[7] however, to some extent these courts (e.g., territorial courts[8]) may receive business which Congress could have sent to an Article III court. But Congress may not simply give any and all Article III business to an Article I court, or otherwise the very concept of a court protected and

limited by Article III would have no meaning.[9] At the present time, Article I courts include territorial courts,[10] certain courts in the District of Columbia,[11] courts martial,[12] and legislative courts and administrative agencies which adjudicate "public rights."[13]

The Supreme Court has original jurisdiction, under Article III,[14] of all cases affecting ambassadors, other public ministers and consuls, and cases in which a state is a party. This original jurisdiction cannot constitutionally be expanded.[15] Also under Article III the Court has appellate jurisdiction of all the other cases within the limited jurisdiction of Article III, but this appellate jurisdiction is given "with such Exceptions, and un-

---

4. U.S. Const. art. I, § 8, cl. 9. See, e.g., Marshall, C. J., in American Insurance Co. v. Canter, 26 U.S. (1 Pet.) 516, 546 (1828): "These courts [the superior courts of the territory of Florida, created by Congress], then, are not constitutional Court, in which the judicial power conferred by the Constitution on the general government, can be deposited. They are incapable of receiving it. They are legislative Court, created in virtue of the general right of sovereignty which exists in the government, or in virtue of that clause which enables Congress to make all needful rules and regulations, respecting the territory belonging to the United States." See generally, Katz, Federal Legislative Courts, 43 Harv.L.Rev. 894 (1930); Currie, The Federal Courts and the American Law Institute, 36 U.Chi.L. Rev. 1 (1968); M. Redish, Federal Jurisdiction: Tensions in the Allocation of Power 35–51 (1980).

5. E.g., Glidden Co. v. Zdanok, 370 U.S. 530, 533–34 (1962) (plurality opinion of Harlan, J., joined by Brennan & Stewart, JJ.); United States v. Fisher, 109 U.S. 143 (1883). See generally, C. Wright, Law of Federal Courts § 11 (4th ed. 1983).

6. Glidden Co. v. Zdanok, 370 U.S. 530, 583 (1962) (plurality opinion of Harlan, J.).

7. 370 U.S. at 579–83 (plurality opinion of Harlan, J.). See also, Jacoby, Recent Legislation Affecting the Court of Claims, 55 Georgetown L.J. 397 (1966).

8. E.g., In re Ross, 140 U.S. 453 (1891) (consular court); American Insurance Co. v. Canter, 26 U.S. (1 Pet.) 516 (1828) (superior court of the territory of Florida).

9. Northern Pipeline Constr. Co. v. Marathon Pipe Line Co., 102 S.Ct. 2858 (1982) (Opinion of Brennan, J., joined by Marshall, Blackmun, & Stevens, JJ.) (violation of Art. III for non-Art. III judges to have the jurisdiction granted by § 241(a) of the Bankruptcy Act of 1978). See generally, Note, Article III Limits on Article I Courts: The Constitutionality of the Bankruptcy Court and the 1979 Magistrate Act, 80 Colum.L.Rev. 560 (1980); Krattenmaker, Article II and Judicial Independence: Why the New Bankruptcy Courts are Un-

constitutional, 70 Georgetown L.J. 297 (1981); Note, Article III Constraints and the Expanding Civil Jurisdiction of Federal Magistrates: A Dissenting View, 88 Yale L.J. 1023 (1979). Cf. Silberman, Masters and Magistrates, 50 N.Y.U.L.Rev. 1070, 1297 (1975).

Contrast, United States v. Raddatz, 447 U.S. 667 (1980), upholding the constitutionality of 28 U.S.C.A. § 636(b)(1)(B), a provision of the Federal Magistrates Act which permits a district court to refer to a magistrate a motion to suppress evidence and authorizes the district court to determine and decide such motion based on the record developed before the magistrate, including the magistrate's proposed findings of fact and recommendations. However, the district court gives the magistrate's proposed findings and recommendations only such weight as the district court decides, and that court makes the ultimate decision. 447 U.S. at 683. Also the district court appoints and may remove the magistrates, and the district court also may decline to defer any matter to the magistrate. 447 U.S. at 685 (Blackmun, J., concurring).

10. See n. 8, supra.

11. Palmore v. United States, 411 U.S. 389 (1973); Kendall v. United States, 37 U.S. (12 Pet.) 524 (1838).

12. Dynes v. Hoover, 61 U.S. (20 How.) 65, 79 (1858).

13. Murray's Lessee v. Hoboken Land & Improvement Co., 59 U.S. (18 How.) 272, 284 (1855); Atlas Roofing Co. v. Occupational Safety Comm'n, 430 U.S. 442, 450 (1972). In Atlas the Court defined "public rights" as, "e.g., cases in which the Government sues in its sovereign capacity to enforce public rights created by statutes within the power of Congress." 430 U.S. at 450. The United States Claims Court is declared to be "established under Article I . . . ." 28 U.S.C.A. § 171(a).

14. U.S. Const. art. III, § 2, cl. 2.

15. Marbury v. Madison, 5 U.S. (1 Cranch) 137 (1803).

der such Regulations as the Congress shall make." [16]

At the present time Congress has created thirteen judicial circuits, numbered one through eleven, plus the District of Columbia Circuit, plus the Court of Appeals for the Federal Circuit.[17] The Federal Circuit Court hears appeals from a final decision of the United States Claims Court, similar appeals from the federal district courts, the Court of International Trade, the Board of Patent Interferences, patent appeals from the federal district courts, and similar miscellaneous matters.[18] Cases heard in the federal court system normally are heard in district courts in one of these circuits. From them the parties may appeal to the court of appeals for that circuit, which normally sits in panels of three, and from there the parties may seek review in the Supreme Court either by way of certiorari (discretionary review); by way of appeal (obligatory review, at least in theory); or by certified questions.[19]

In addition to this basic federal court system, Congress has at times also established more specialized courts pursuant to its powers under Article III, such as a special railroad court, composed of already sitting federal judges designated for part-time sitting on this court.[20]

In the past, challenges to many statutes in federal court had to be heard by a three-judge court. Now, only when a particular statute requires, or when an action is filed challenging the constitutionality of the apportionment of congressional districts or the apportionment of any statewide legislative body, is a federal district court of three judges convened.[21] There is a direct appeal from decisions by these three-judge courts to the Supreme Court.[22] There is also direct appeal from decisions of federal courts invalidating Acts of Congress in which the United States or its officers, employees, or agencies are a party.[23]

The jurisdictional statutes also provide for original jurisdiction in the Supreme Court of certain cases; in some instances this jurisdiction is exclusive, in others it is not.[24]

Decisions from state courts are reviewable by the Supreme Court under the statutes if they involve final judgments or decrees by the highest court of the state from which the decision could be had and (1) where the validity of a treaty or statute of the United States is drawn in question on constitutional grounds, or (2) where a state statute is drawn in question on grounds of its being repugnant to the Constitution, treaties, or laws of the United States, or (3) where any title, right, privilege, or immunity is specially set up or claimed under the Constitution, treaties, or statutes of the United States or a commission is held or authority is exercised under the laws of the United States.[25]

---

16. U.S. Const. art. III, § 2, cl. 2.

17. See, Federal Court Improvement Act of 1982, Pub.L. 97–164. See also, 28 U.S.C.A. §§ 41–48.

18. See 28 U.S.C.A. § 1295, "Jurisdiction of the United States Court of Appeals for the Federal Circuit."

19. See generally, Section II, C, of this Chapter; Boskey & Gressman, the Supreme Court's New Rules for the Eighties, 85 F.R.D. 487 (1980); Bice, The Limited Grant of Certiorari and the Justification of Judicial Review, 1975 Wis.L.Rev. 343; Tushnet, The Mandatory Jurisdiction of the Supreme Court—Some Recent Developments, 46 U.Cinn.L.Rev. 347 (1977). Cf. Gressman, Requiem for the Supreme Court's Obligatory Jurisdiction, 65 A.B.A.J. 1325 (1979); Letter Signed by all Supreme Court Justices on Mandatory Jurisdiction of the Supreme Court, 65 A.B.A.J. 1328–29 (1979) (addressed to Senator De Concini and reprinted in the A.B. A.J.).

20. See 45 U.S.C.A. § 719; see Regional Rail Reorganization Act Cases, 419 U.S. 102 (1974). In recent times, a Temporary Emergency Court of Appeals, also composed of part-time judges, was created to hear cases arising out of wage-price controls imposed for a time by President Nixon. Act of Dec. 22, 1971, Pub.L. 92–210, § 211(b), 85 Stat. 743. See also 12 U.S.C.A. § 1904 note.

21. 28 U.S.C.A. § 2284.

22. 28 U.S.C.A. § 1253.

23. 28 U.S.C.A. § 1252.

24. 28 U.S.C.A. § 1251. See generally, this Chapter, section II, A, for further discussion of original jurisdiction.

25. 28 U.S.C.A. § 1257.

Federal jurisdiction often raises not only statutory questions—when is a state decision "final"; is the review by appeal or certiorari; and so on—but also constitutional questions. These constitutional questions are frequently involved because Article III allows Congress to grant federal courts only limited jurisdiction. For example, is the claim brought before the federal court a "case or controversy" within the meaning of Article III? If the case is brought on diversity grounds, are the parties really citizens of diverse states? In a diversity case, is the amount in controversy requirement of the diversity statute met by the plaintiff?

In addition to these and other such statutory and constitutional questions that must be resolved prior to the court hearing the case on the merits, the Supreme Court has developed many rules of self restraint to avoid exercising its power to strike laws violative of the Constitution. In the remainder of this Chapter we shall consider some of these questions of constitutional jurisdiction, statutory jurisdiction, and self-imposed rules of restraint, and we shall see how they are often used as tools to avoid reaching the merits. But first, we shall look at the long historical development which has led to the present jurisdictional framework of the Supreme Court.

B. The Historical Development of the Jurisdictional Framework of the Supreme Court

While the framers of the Constitution "readily accepted" the notion that there should be a federal judiciary system,[1] the nature of that system was a subject of more than a little dispute. Article III of the Constitution by its own terms declares that there shall be "one Supreme Court," [2] yet there was much less agreement on the nature of lower courts, or even if they should be created. Some of the framers wanted no lower federal courts; others would provide only for lower federal courts of admiralty; some insisted that the Constitution require the establishment of lower federal courts; and others still would have granted Congress the power to create them with jurisdiction over all matters of general concern.[3]

The resolution of the controversy is reflected in the language of the first sentence of Article III, Section 1:

> The judicial Power of the United States, shall be vested in one Supreme Court, and in such inferior courts as the Congress *may* from time to time ordain and establish.[4]

Congress, it would appear, was given discretion as to whether or not to establish lower federal courts,[5] though the language is not without ambiguity. And even assuming Congress need not have created the lower federal courts, some commentators have argued that once having created the lower federal courts, Congress must vest in them, or in some of them, the full scope of the federal judicial power.[6] This view has never been accepted by Congress, which has not given the lower federal courts full Article III jurisdiction. Nor has it been accepted by the Supreme Court, which has in dictum spoken broadly of Congress' power to grant or take

---

1. Farrand, The Framing of the Constitution 79 (1913). See P. Hay & R. Rotunda, The United States Federal System: Legal Integration in the American Experience 12–26 (Giuffrè, Milan 1982).

2. U.S. Const. art. III, § 1.

3. See generally H. Hart & H. Wechsler's The Federal Courts and the Federal System 11–12 (2d ed. 1973). See also, e.g., M. Redish, Federal Courts: Cases, Comments and Questions 140–48 (1983).

4. U.S.Const. art. III, § 1 (emphasis added).

5. See, e.g., 1 Farrand, The Records of the Federal Convention 124–125 (1911) (remarks of Wilson and Madison on June 5, 1787: there is "a distinction between establishing such tribunals absolutely, and giv-

ing a discretion to the Legislature to establish or not establish them.") Professor Julius Goebel is one recent commentator arguing that some lower courts must be created. J. Goebel, I Oliver Wendell Holmes Devise History of the Supreme Court of the United States: Antecedents and Beginnings to 1801, at 246–247 (1971).

6. Justice Story, though admitting that the question whether Congress must establish inferior courts poses a question of some difficulty, still concluded in Martin v. Hunter's Lessee, 14 U.S. (1 Wheat.) 304, 330–331 (1816), "that Congress are bound to create some inferior courts in which to vest all that jurisdiction which, under the Constitution, is exclusively vested in the United States, and of which the Supreme Court cannot

away jurisdiction of the lower federal courts. Thus in *Sheldon v. Sill*,[7] the Supreme Court stated:

> The Constitution has defined the limits of the judicial power of the United States, but has not prescribed how much of it shall be exercised by the Circuit Court; consequently, the statute which does prescribe the limits of their jurisdiction, cannot be in conflict with the Constitution, unless it confers powers not enumerated therein.[8]

While the question of to what extent Article III itself or the due process clause of the Fifth Amendment restricts the congressional power over federal court jurisdiction, is considered in more detail later in this Chapter,[9] it is important to keep this issue in mind as one studies the development of federal jurisdiction.

In order to broaden our perspective, it is useful to very briefly review the continual expansion of federal jurisdiction from its very narrow beginnings with the first Judiciary Act of 1789 [10] until modern times. While it has been charged that the first Act "has

been so smothered in praise that its real significance has become obscured," [11] it has also been recognized that it was of extreme importance for several reasons: (1) it created a court organization which "served the country substantially unchanged for nearly a century;" (2) it created, under section 25 of the Act, a significant "nationalizing" influence by establishing Supreme Court review of state court decisions on federal questions; and (3) it established a system of lower federal courts, which was its "transcendent achievement." [12]

The First Judiciary Act is also significant for what it did not do. Thus, it did not establish any general review in the Supreme Court of federal criminal cases.[13] In fact, it was not until 1889 that there was generally established direct appeals in federal criminal cases,[14] though the collateral attack of a writ of habeas corpus was previously available.[15] Similarly, although the first Act created diversity jurisdiction in the lower federal courts (with a jurisdictional amount of $500) [16] the Act did not provide for any gen-

---

take original cognizance." Yet, the same Justice Story recognized some limitations on jurisdiction when he dismissed a diversity suit under a statute limiting diversity jurisdiction. White v. Fenner, 29 Fed.Cas. 1015 (No. 17,547) (C.C.D.R.I.1818).

More recently, Judge Prettyman held that if a case "arises under the Constitution, laws or treaties of the United States, . . . jurisdiction to entertain it is in some district court by compulsion of the Constitution itself." Eisentrager v. Forrestal, 174 F.2d 961, 966 (D.C.Cir.1949), rev'd on other grounds sub nom. Johnson v. Eisentrager, 339 U.S. 763 (1950).

See generally J. Goebel, 1 Oliver Wendell Holmes Devise History of the Supreme Court of the United States: Antecedents and Beginnings to 1801, at pp. 246–47 (1971); Eisenberg, Congressional Authority to Restrict Lower Federal Court Jurisdiction, 83 Yale L.J. 498 (1974); Redish & Woods, Congressional Power to Control the Jurisdiction of Lower Federal Courts: A Critical Review and a New Synthesis, 124 U.Pa.L.Rev. 45, 52–75 (1975); Rotunda, Congressional Power to Restrict the Jurisdiction of the Lower Federal Courts and the Problem of School Busing, 64 Georgetown L.J. 839 (1976); Sager, Foreword: Constitutional Limitations on Congress' Authority to Regulate the Jurisdiction of the Federal Courts, 95 Harv.L.Rev. 17 (1981).

7. Sheldon v. Sill, 49 U.S. 8 (How.) 441 (1850). The Court specifically upheld the power of Congress to exclude from the diversity jurisdiction cases in which a promissory note or other chose in action was assigned to create diversity jurisdiction.

8. 49 U.S. (8 How.) at 448.

9. See section III, infra.

10. 1 Stat. 73 (Sept. 24, 1789).

11. F. Frankfurter & J. Landis, The Business of the Supreme Court: A Study in the Federal Judicial System 4 (1927).

12. Id. See also id. at 4–5: "No other English-speaking union (not to deal with nations nurtured in legal institutions radically different from our own) has a scheme of federal courts." (footnote omitted).

13. Judiciary Act of 1789, §§ 9, 11, 1 Stat. 73, 76–78. The district courts had jurisdiction of minor offenses; the circuit courts had jurisdiction of more serious crimes. There was provision for appeal from the district courts to the circuit courts. The Judiciary Act of 1802, § 6, 2 Stat. 159 (Apr. 29, 1802) provided for review in the Supreme Court of federal criminal cases if there was a division of opinion of law in the circuit court. See also Judiciary Act of 1872, § 1, 17 Stat. 196 (June 1, 1872).

14. In 1889 Congress granted the Supreme Court direct review of capital cases. Judiciary Act of 1889, § 6, 25 Stat. 656 (Feb. 6, 1889). The Evarts Act, § 5, 26 Stat. 827 (Mar. 3, 1891) expanded this review to all infamous crimes.

15. Ex parte Siebold, 100 U.S. 37 (1880). Cf. Salinger v. Loisel, 265 U.S. 224, 231 (1924).

16. Act of 1789, § 11, 1 Stat. 73, 78.

eral federal question jurisdiction in the lower federal courts. It was not until the Act of March 3, 1875 [17] that Congress finally gave the lower courts basic jurisdiction, of cases arising under the Constitution, laws, or treaties of the United States,[18] though this phrase has been interpreted to be narrower in meaning than its analogous language in the Constitution.[19] It was not until 1914 that the Supreme Court was allowed to review state court decisions in which the state court had upheld the federal claim and held its own statute invalid.[20]

In the Judiciary Act of 1789 Congress divided the country into thirteen districts, each state comprising one district except for Massachusetts and Virginia which were each divided into two districts.[21] Rhode Island and North Carolina had not yet joined the union so they were not included in the Act.[22] Though there have been rare exceptions, in general district lines do not cross state lines.[23] The original district courts created by the Act of 1789 were granted jurisdiction over minor criminal and civil matters, and over admiralty cases; it was as admiralty courts that they exercised their most important jurisdiction.[24]

The original judiciary act also created circuit courts, but unlike the modern courts of appeal, these circuit courts had original jurisdiction as well as some appellate jurisdiction over the district courts.[25] Their own original jurisdiction in some matters was at times concurrent with, or exclusive of, the district courts.[26] The law established three judicial circuits, and each circuit court originally consisted of one of the district judges within the circuit and two Supreme Court justices.[27] The justices objected to the rigors of riding circuit and, in correspondence to then President Washington, some even contended the requirement was unconstitutional.[28] When the issue was actually litigated some years later, the constitutionality of the practice was upheld.[29] In 1793 Congress did reduce somewhat the circuit riding burden of the justices by altering the composition of the circuit courts to include only one justice per-court.[30]

In 1801 the Federalist Congress eliminated circuit riding, created sixteen new circuit judgeships, and authorized a greatly expanded jurisdictional authority;[31] but a year later the Jeffersonians repealed this so-called "Midnight Judges" statute,[32] amid a very lively debate as to the constitutionality of

---

17. 18 Stat. 470 (March 3, 1875).

18. Excluding the short-lived Midnight Judges Statute of 1801, (also called the Circuit Courts Act), discussed below, which greatly expanded federal jurisdiction but which was repealed one year later. Act of 1801, § 11, 2 Stat. 92 (Feb. 12, 1801), repealed by Act of 1802, § 1, 2 Stat. 132 (Mar. 8, 1802). A portion of this Repeal Act which was challenged on constitutional grounds was upheld in Stuart v. Laird, 5 U.S. (1 Cranch) 299 (1803).

19. Compare Article III, § 2, cl. 1 and Osborn v. Bank of the United States, 22 U.S. (9 Wheat.) 738 (1824) (Marshall, C.J.) with, Romero v. International Terminal Operating Co., 358 U.S. 354, 379 n. 51 (1959).

20. Act of 1914, 38 Stat. 790 (Dec. 23, 1914).

21. Act of 1789, §§ 2-3, 1 Stat. 73.

22. F. Frankfurter & J. Landis, The Business of the Supreme Court: A Study in the Federal Judicial System 11 (1927).

23. The Judiciary Act of 1801, § 21, 2 Stat. 89, 96 (Feb. 13, 1801), created a district out of the District of Columbia and parts of Virginia and Maryland. At the present time, the District of Wyoming includes "those portions of Yellowstone National Park situated in Montana and Idaho . . ." 28 U.S.C.A. § 131.

24. The Judiciary Act of 1789, §§ 3, 9, 1 Stat. 73, 76; see also, F. Frankfurter & J. Landis, The Business of the Supreme Court: A Study in the Federal Judicial System 12 (1927).

25. Judiciary Act of 1789, §§ 21, 22, 1 Stat. 83-84.

26. Id. at §§ 9, 11, 12, 1 Stat. 73, 76, 78, 79. These circuit courts had "exclusive cognizance" of federal crimes except that they shared jurisdiction with the federal district courts over minor criminal matters.

27. Id. at § 4, 1 Stat. 73-74.

28. H. Hart & H. Wechsler, The Federal Courts and Federal System 68 (2d ed. 1973). See also F. Frankfurter & J. Landis, The Business of the Supreme Court 14-15, 21-23 (1927).

29. Stuart v. Laird, 5 U.S. (1 Cranch) 299, 309 (1803).

30. Judiciary Act of 1793, 1 Stat. 333 (March 2, 1793).

31. Judiciary Act of 1801, §§ 1-3, 7, 11, 2 Stat. 89-90, 92 (Feb. 13, 1801). See, F. Frankfurter & J. Landis, The Business of the Supreme Court 25 (1927).

32. Judiciary Act of 1802, § 1, 2 Stat. 132 (March 8, 1802).

eliminating courts manned by life-tenured judges.[33] In 1869 Congress further reduced circuit riding by the justices.[34]

In 1875 Congress finally conferred general federal question jurisdiction on the lower federal courts as well as expanding their diversity jurisdiction.[35] This large expansion of jurisdictional authority in 1875, while apparently not appreciated at the time, finally meant that the federal courts "ceased to be restricted tribunals of fair dealing between citizens of different states and became the primary and powerful reliances for vindicating every right given by the Constitution, the laws, and treaties of the United States." [36]

The next fairly significant change in federal jurisdiction came in 1891 with the Evarts Act,[37] named after Senator Evarts, a member of the Judiciary Committee.[38] This act created the circuit courts of appeal and eliminated the limited appellate power of the old circuit courts. The new appellate courts could hear most of the appeals from the original cases brought in the old circuit or district courts. The act also added additional circuit judgeships, and for the first time created a discretionary review system of certiorari in the Supreme Court.[39] Within a few months the number of new cases docketed in the Supreme Court were greatly reduced; in 1890, 623 new cases had been docketed on the appeal docket; in 1892 the number had dropped to 275.[40] The old circuit courts, the existence of which were long difficult to justify, were finally eliminated in

1911 and their remaining original jurisdiction assumed by the district courts.[41]

In 1925 came another important revision of the federal court system with the enactment of the Judges Bill.[42] This law was originally written by a committee of Supreme Court justices and it "drastically" redistributed federal judicial power.[43] The device of discretionary review created by the Evarts Act was significantly enlarged and direct review by the Supreme Court of the district courts was greatly reduced. The Supreme Court achieved its goal of limiting appellate jurisdiction as of right and expanding discretionary jurisdiction for a large class of cases.[44]

In 1948, with the codification and revision of the Judicial Code, the Circuit Courts of Appeal were renamed "United States Court of Appeal for the _____ Circuit" and the name "District Court of the United States" was changed to "United States District Court for the _____ District".[45] The Act also established the District of Columbia Circuit in addition to the ten other circuits, numbered one to ten, throughout the entire United States.[46] Within each of these circuits there is at least one district court and several district judges. Each state has at least one district court.

By 1982 the number of circuits had increased to thirteen, numbered one through eleven, plus the District of Columbia Circuit, and the Federal Circuit. The new Eleventh Circuit was created by dividing the Fifth Circuit, and the Federal Circuit was created to

---

33. See F. Frankfurter & J. Landis, The Business of the Supreme Court 26–28 & n. 75 (1927). A portion of this Repeal Act was upheld in Stuart v. Laird, 5 U.S. (1 Cranch) 299 (1803). See also, Van Alstyne, A Critical Guide to Marbury v. Madison, 1969 Duke L.J. 1, 5.

34. Judiciary Act of 1869, § 2, 16 Stat. 44 (April 10, 1869).

35. Judiciary Act of 1875, 18 Stat. 470 (March 3 1875).

36. F. Frankfurter & J. Landis, The Business of the Supreme Court 65 (1927).

37. Judiciary Act of 1891, 26 Stat. 826 (March 3, 1891).

38. F. Frankfurter & J. Landis, The Business of the Supreme Court 98 (1927).

39. Judiciary Act of 1891, §§ 1, 6, 26 Stat. 826, 828 (March 3, 1891).

40. F. Frankfurter & J. Landis, The Business of the Supreme Court 102 (1927).

41. Judiciary Act of 1911, 36 Stat. 1087 (March 3, 1911).

42. Judiciary Act of 1925, 43 Stat. 936 (Feb. 13, 1925).

43. F. Frankfurter & J. Landis, The Business of the Supreme Court 1 (1927).

44. American Constr. Co. v. Jacksonville, T. & K. Ry. Co., 148 U.S. 372, 382 (1893).

45. 28 U.S.C.A. §§ 43(a); 451.

46. 28 U.S.C.A. § 41.

handle appeals from the United States Claims Court, similar appeals from the federal district courts, patent appeals from federal district courts and from the Board of Patent Interferences, appeals from the Board of Patent Interferences, and similar miscellaneous matters.[47]

The Chief Justice now assigns to each circuit at least one Supreme Court justice,[48] but the justices no longer ride circuit. Their circuit duties include ruling on applications for stays of other court rulings and similar motions. By Supreme Court rule, applications should be "addressed to the Justice allotted to the Circuit within which the case arises." [49] If the application is denied, that fact will not prevent the matter from being renewed before another justice, though such forum-shopping is officially "not favored" unless the earlier denial has been without prejudice.[50]

Along with this general historical background a more specific development should be noted. In 1908, in the decision of *Ex parte Young* [51] the Supreme Court held that an injunction prohibiting the Attorney General of Minnesota from enforcing an unconstitutional act was proper and not barred by the Eleventh Amendment. In 1910 Congress reacted to the pressure from states to withdraw the jurisdiction of federal courts to hear such suits by expanding earlier requirements for a three-judge court to include cases in which plaintiffs desired an interlocutory injunction against the enforcement of state statutes by state officials. At least one of these judges was an appellate judge; appeal was directly to the Supreme Court. This statutory requirement led to a great deal of complicated litigation.[52] In 1976 Congress repealed this statute and now a three-judge court is required only when a statute specifically requires it or when an action is brought challenging the constitutionality of the apportionment of a congressional district or the apportionment of any statewide legislative body.[53] From the decisions of three-judge courts there is still a direct appeal to the Supreme Court.[54]

---

47. See 28 U.S.C.A. § 1295, "Jurisdiction of the United States Court of Appeals for the Federal Circuit." See also 28 U.S.C.A. § 41. The Eleventh Circuit was effective October 1, 1981.

48. 28 U.S.C.A. § 42.

49. Supreme Court Rule 43(4).

To determine whether a Supreme Court circuit justice will stay a final order the following test has been used:

> "In deciding whether to grant a stay pending disposition of a petition for certiorari, the Members of this Court use two principal criteria. First, 'a Circuit Justice should "balance the equities" . . . and determine on which side the risk of irreparable injury weighs most heavily.' [citation omitted]. Second, assuming a balance of equities in favor of the applicant, the Circuit Justice must also determine whether 'it is likely that four Members of this Court would vote to grant a writ of certiorari. [citation omitted]. The burden of persuasion as to both of these issues rests on the applicant, and his burden is particularly heavy when, as here, a stay has been denied by the District Court and by a unanimous panel of the Court of Appeals. [citations omitted]."

Beame v. Friends of the Earth, 434 U.S. 1310, 1312 (1977) (Marshall, Circuit Justice) (stay denied). Cf. New Motor Vehicle Bd. v. Orrin W. Fox Co., 434 U.S. 1345 (1977) (Rehnquist, Circuit Justice) (district court injunction stayed pending appeal because case came within Court's obligatory jurisdiction, four members of

the Court would likely note probable jurisdiction, and the lower court likely in error).

The test as to interlocutory court orders appears even more strict. If a circuit justice believes that the Court would not grant certiorari to review a lower court interlocutory order (even though the Court might grant certiorari to consider the claim if it were presented as a final order or decision), then the petitioner's application for a stay of that order will also be denied "without attempting to inquire further as to what irreparable injury would be suffered by the applicants in the event of such denial." Pacific Union Conference of Seventh-Day Adventists v. Marshall, 434 U.S. 1305, 1306 (1977) (Rehnquist, Circuit Justice) (stay of enforcement of discovery orders denied).

50. Supreme Court Rule 43(5). See, Winters v. United States, 89 S.Ct. 57 (1968) (Douglas J., Circuit Justice). See generally, R. Stern & E. Gressman, Supreme Court Practice §§ 17.17–17.18 (5th ed. 1978). The justice may refer the application for stay or bail to the full court. Supreme Court Rule 50(6).

51. 209 U.S. 123 (1908). See section IV, A of this Chapter.

52. E.g., Sardino v. Federal Reserve Bank of New York, 361 F.2d 106, 114 (2d Cir.), cert. denied 385 U.S. 898 (1966).

53. See 28 U.S.C.A. § 2284.

54. 28 U.S.C.A. § 1253.

By this trial and error method of creating a national judiciary system, Congress over the last two hundred years has in general tended (a) to constantly broaden the jurisdiction of the lower federal courts, (b) to create a nationwide system of Courts of Appeal, which mainly operate to filter cases between the Supreme Court and the federal trial courts, and (c) to give the Supreme Court greater control over its own docket.[55]

II. STATUTORY JURISDICTION OF THE SUPREME COURT

A. Original Jurisdiction

The basic statutes governing Supreme Court jurisdiction are found in title 28 of the U.S. Code. Section 1251 governs original jurisdiction[1] and provides in general that the high court has original *and* exclusive jurisdiction of controversies between two or more states.[2] These cases must be heard by the Supreme Court. The Supreme Court also has original, but not exclusive jurisdiction of cases in which ambassadors or other public ministers or counsels or vice counsels of foreign states are parties; cases between the United States and a state; and cases brought by a state against citizens of another state or aliens. Since these cases may be heard by the district courts as well, the Supreme Court rarely accepts original jurisdiction.

This original jurisdiction in practice accounts for but a small percentage of the Supreme Court caseload. For the 1980 term, for example, of the 4280 cases disposed of, only seven were on the original docket. Of the 864 cases remaining on the docket only seventeen were on the original docket.[3] Typically cases within the original jurisdiction are referred to a special master, to receive evidence and prepare a record.[4]

Although Congress by statute has always provided for the original jurisdiction of the Supreme Court, the Court has often stated in dictum that "the original jurisdiction of the Supreme Court is conferred not by Congress but by the Constitution itself. This jurisdiction is self-executing and needs no legislative implementation."[5] In *California v. Arizona*,[6] the Court raised but avoided the question of Congressional power to limit its original jurisdiction. California sought to invoke the Supreme Court's original jurisdiction in a suit to quiet title. California sued Arizona and the United States. Federal statutes provided that controversies between the United States and a state may be heard originally by the Supreme Court, and controversies between two or more states must be heard originally by the Supreme Court.[7]

---

55. See generally, H. Friendly, Federal Jurisdiction: A General View (1973).

1. § 1251. Original jurisdiction

"(a) The Supreme Court shall have original and exclusive jurisdiction of all controversies between two or more States.

"(b) The Supreme Court shall have original but not exclusive jurisdiction of:

"(1) All actions or proceedings to which ambassadors, other public ministers, consuls, or vice consuls of foreign states are parties;

"(2) All controversies between the United States and a State;

"(3) All actions or proceedings by a State against the citizens of another State or against aliens."

2. The Supreme Court interprets section 1251(a) narrowly. Thus, political subdivisions of states are not states for purposes of this subsection. Illinois v. Milwaukee, 406 U.S. 91 (1972). And cases within section 1251(b)(3) may be dismissed in the Court's judgment if there is another suitable forum when original jurisdiction to protect "the essential quality of the right asserted" is not "necessary for the State's protection." Massachusetts v. Missouri, 308 U.S. 1, 18 (1939).

See also California v. Texas, 102 S.Ct. 2335 (1982) (per curiam) (Court, after acknowledging that it has imposed prudential and equitable restraints on the exercise of its original jurisdiction, concluded that California's motion for leave to file a complaint against Texas under the Court's original jurisdiction should be granted; the issue involved the question of whether Howard Hughes was domiciled in California or Texas at the time of his death).

3. The Supreme Court, 1980, Term, 95 Harv.L.Rev. 91, 342 (1981).

4. E.g., Mississippi v. Arkansas, 402 U.S. 926 (1971); 402 U.S. 939 (1971); 403 U.S. 951 (1971); 411 U.S. 913 (1973); 415 U.S. 289 (1974); 415 U.S. 302 (1974).

5. California v. Arizona, 440 U.S. 59, 65 (1979).

6. 440 U.S. 59 (1979).

7. 28 U.S.C.A. § 1251.

The United States by statute waived its sovereign immunity from suit in actions brought against it to quiet title to land, but a statute also provided that the federal district courts should have exclusive jurisdiction of such suits.[8]

While the Supreme Court agreed that Congress could refuse to waive some or all of its sovereign immunity from suit in any court or all courts, it stated "once Congress has waived the Nation's sovereign immunity, it is far from clear that it can withdraw the constitutional jurisdiction of this Court over such suits."[9] The Supreme Court then avoided the constitutional question by construing the federal statute as excluding only state court jurisdiction over such cases and confining jurisdiction in those cases to the federal courts. Thus it allowed the suit to be brought originally in the Supreme Court.

B. Appellate and Certiorari Jurisdiction

Under "direct appeal" the appellant can bypass the courts of appeal and have the case directly heard by the Supreme Court. If review is by "appeal" the appellant will receive Supreme Court review, in theory, as of right. Under "certiorari", review for the petitioner is discretionary.

Section 1252 of title 28[1] provides in general for a direct appeal to the Supreme Court from any decision of a federal district court holding an act of Congress unconstitutional in a civil case, if the United States, or one of its agencies or officers or employees, in their official capacities, is a party. Previously, there were some provisions for direct appeals in federal criminal cases but now all appeals go to the Courts of Appeal.[2] There is also a direct appeal from decisions of three judge courts,[3] but with the recent revision of the three-judge court requirement severely limiting its application,[4] the number of direct appeals should be correspondingly reduced. Two far more important jurisdictional statutes are 28 U.S.C.A. §§ 1254[5] and

---

8. 28 U.S.C.A. §§ 1346(f), 2409a.

9. 440 U.S. at 67.

1. § 1252. Direct appeals from decisions invalidating Acts of Congress

"Any party may appeal to the Supreme Court from an interlocutory or final judgment, decree or order of any court of the United States, the United States District Court for the District of the Canal Zone, the District Court of Guam and the District Court of the Virgin Islands and any court of record of Puerto Rico, holding an Act of Congress unconstitutional in any civil action, suit, or proceeding to which the United States or any of its agencies, or any officer or employee thereof, as such officer or employee, is a party.

"A party who has received notice of appeal under this section shall take any subsequent appeal or cross appeal to the Supreme Court. All appeals or cross appeals taken to other courts prior to such notice shall be treated as taken directly to the Supreme Court."

Under this section, the Supreme Court may decide all questions of the case. McLucas v. DeChamplain, 421 U.S. 21 (1975).

2. 18 U.S.C.A. § 3731, as amended by Act of Jan. 2, 1971, Pub.L. 91–644, § 14(a), 84 Stat. 1890. The Court of Appeals appeal may be also skipped under the general statute concerning certification of questions directly to Supreme Court. 28 U.S.C.A. § 1254(3).

3. § 1253. Direct appeals from decisions of three-judge courts

"Except as otherwise provided by law, any party may appeal to the Supreme Court from an order granting or denying, after notice and hearing, an interlocutory or permanent injunction in any civil action, suit or proceeding required by any Act of Congress to be heard and determined by a district court of three judges."

4. See 28 U.S.C.A. § 2281 (Injunction against enforcement of state statute; three-judge court required), and 28 U.S.C.A. § 2282 (Injunction against enforcement of federal statute; three judge court required), both repealed by Act of Aug. 12, 1976, Pub. L. 94–381, §§ 1 & 2, 90 Stat. 1119.

U.S.C.A. § 2284 was amended to require a three-judge district court "when otherwise required by Act of Congress, or when an action is filed challenging the constitutionality of the apportionment of congressional districts or the apportionment of any statewide legislative body." 28 U.S.C.A. § 2284(a), as amended by Act of Aug. 12, 1976, P.L. 94–381, § 3, 90 Stat. 1119. See generally, C. Wright, Law of Federal Courts § 50 (4th ed. 1983).

5. § 1254. Courts of appeals; certiorari; appeal; certified questions

"Cases in the courts of appeals may be reviewed by the Supreme Court by the following methods:

(1) By writ of certiorari granted upon the petition of any party to any civil or criminal case, before or after rendition of judgment or decree;

1257.[6] The former governs appeals and writs of certiorari from the courts of appeals of the federal circuits. The latter governs "[f]inal judgments or decrees rendered by the highest court of a State in which a decision could be had. . . ."[7]

If a state court holds a state statute unconstitutional, Supreme Court review is by certiorari—that is, the Supreme Court may, in its discretion, review the case. Since the natural inclination of a state court might be expected to uphold the validity of its state's laws, a decision striking down such a law is contrary to that inclination and thus less protection for the petitioner by way of obligatory review is necessary. Moreover, a state court invalidation of a state statute on federal grounds does not threaten the uniformity of federal statutory law.[8]

If, on the other hand, the state court upholds the validity of a state statute or holds invalid a treaty or statute of the United States, review is by way of appeal—that is, Supreme Court review is obligatory. In

(2) By appeal by a party relying on a State statute held by a court of appeals to be invalid as repugnant to the Constitution, treaties or laws of the United States, but such appeal shall preclude review by writ of certiorari at the instance of such appellant, and the review on appeal shall be restricted to the Federal questions presented;

(3) By certification at any time by a court of appeals of any question of law in any civil or criminal case as to which instructions are desired, and upon such certification the Supreme Court may give binding instructions or require the entire record to be sent up for decision of the entire matter in controversy."

6. § 1257. State courts; appeal; certiorari

"Final judgments or decrees rendered by the highest court of a State in which a decision could be had, may be reviewed by the Supreme Court as follows:

(1) By appeal, where is drawn in question the validity of a treaty or statute of the United States and the decision is against its validity.

(2) By appeal, where is drawn in question the validity of a statute of any state on the ground of its being repugnant to the Constitution, treaties or laws of the United States, and the decision is in favor of its validity.

(3) By writ of certiorari, where the validity of a treaty or statute of the United States is drawn in question or where the validity of a State statute is drawn in question on the ground of its being repugnant to the Constitution, treaties or laws of the United States, or where any title, right, privilege or immunity is specially set up or claimed under the Constitution, treaties or statutes of, or commission held or authority exercised under, the United States.

"For the purposes of this section, the term 'highest court of a State' includes the District of Columbia Court of Appeals."

The leading case interpreting this section is Dahnke-Walker Milling Co. v. Bondurant, 257 U.S. 282 (1921). Cf. also, 28 U.S.C.A. § 1258:

§ 1258. Supreme Court of Puerto Rico; appeal; certiorari

"Final judgments or decrees rendered by the Supreme Court of the Commonwealth of Puerto Rico may be reviewed by the Supreme Court as follows:

(1) By appeal, where is drawn in question the validity of a treaty or statute of the United States and the decision is against its validity.

(2) By appeal, where is drawn in question the validity of a statute of the Commonwealth of Puerto Rico on the ground of its being repugnant to the Constitution, treaties, or laws of the United States, and the decision is in favor of its validity.

(3) By writ of certiorari, where the validity of a treaty or statute of the United States is drawn in question or where the validity of a statute of the Commonwealth of Puerto Rico is drawn in question on the ground of its being repugnant to the Constitution, treaties, or laws of the United States, or where any title, right, privilege, or immunity is specially set up or claimed under the Constitution, treaties, or statutes of, or commission held or authority exercised under, the United States."

7. A great deal of litigation has involved the statutory requirement that the judgment be "final." The leading modern case setting forth the various tests to determine finality is Cox Broadcasting Corp. v. Cohn, 420 U.S. 469 (1975). See also, e.g., San Diego Gas & Elec. Co. v. City of San Diego, 450 U.S. 621 (1981) (no "final judgment" for purposes of 28 U.S.C.A. § 1257 in case where litigant claims uncompensated taking of property but where state court has not yet decided whether any taking has in fact occurred because of disputed factual issues); Moses H. Cone Memorial Hosp. v. Mercury Const. Corp., 103 S.Ct. 927 (1983), holding that case "final" within meaning of 28 U.S.C.A. § 1291—stay of federal suit pending resolution of state suit meant that there would be no further litigation in the federal forum—or was within the exception to the finality rule under Cohen v. Beneficial Loan Corp., 337 U.S. 541 (1949).

8. As the Court explained in Key v. Doyle, 434 U.S. 59, 67 (1977), the mandatory appeal jurisdiction as to state law cases under section 1257 "is reserved for cases threatening the supremacy of federal law." Thus if a state court invalidates a state statute on federal grounds, "uniformity of national [statutory] law is not threatened and there is no automatic right of appeal . . . ."

such cases, the obligatory review tends to work against what might be considered the more natural inclination to guard state interests more than federal interests. There is also the possibility of the discretionary review by certiorari of such cases.

The statute governing the courts of appeals for the various circuits in general follows this same theory: because a federal court's natural inclination might be expected to favor federal interests, if the court of appeals holds a state statute unconstitutional, review is by appeal; review by appeal precludes review by writ of certiorari at the instance of the appellant, and the review on appeal is restricted to the Federal questions presented. In addition, review may also lie by way of a writ of certiorari granted upon the petition of any party in any civil or criminal case, before or after rendition of judgment or decree.[9] A court of appeals may also certify a question of law in a civil or criminal case to the Supreme Court, which may either decide the question or require the entire record to be sent up for decision.[10]

C. Theoretical and Practical Differences Between Certiorari and Appeal

In some situations a case may fall on both sides of the line between certiorari and appeal.[11] But, in theory there is an important distinction between the discretionary review of certiorari and the obligatory review of appeal. Under the Supreme Court's rules, a "review on writ of certiorari is not a matter of right, but of judicial discretion, and will be granted only where there are special and important reasons therefor."[12] Consequently, the Court need not explain its refusal to accept certiorari and one cannot deduce any decision on the merits or other precedential value from such denials.[13]

The members of the Supreme Court have, in recent years, more frequently written lengthy dissents to denials of certiorari. Because denial of certiorari "simply means that fewer than four members of the Court deemed it desirable to review a decision of the lower court as a matter of sound judicial discretion,"[14] some justices have objected to the frequent filing of written dissents to denials of certiorari as "totally unnecessary", "the purest form of dicta", and "potentially misleading."[15] Others have replied: "Be-

---

9. 28 U.S.C.A. § 1254(1).

10. 28 U.S.C.A. § 1254(3).

11. Not only do the relevant statutes allow some cases to be brought under either certiorari or appeal, but even under the section dealing with appellate review from the state courts, 28 U.S.C.A. § 1257(2), a careful lawyer can make his case appear to be included as an appeal by drafting his pleadings to allege that the statute in question was invalid as applied to him. See Dahnke-Walker Milling Co. v. Bondurant, 257 U.S. 282 (1921).

12. Supreme Court Rules, Rule 17(1). The "character of reasons which will be considered," while not "controlling nor fully measuring the court's discretion" are listed in Rule 17(a), (b), (c):

"(a) When a federal court of appeals has rendered a decision in conflict with the decision of another federal court of appeals on the same matter; or has decided a federal question in a way in conflict with a state court of last resort; or has so far departed from the accepted and usual course of judicial proceedings, or so far sanctioned such a departure by a lower court, as to call for an exercise of this Court's power of supervision.

"(b) When a state court of last resort has decided a federal question in a way in conflict with the deci-

sion of another state court of last resort or of a federal court of appeals.

"(c) When a state court or a federal court of appeals has decided an important question of federal law which has not been, but should be, settled by this Court, or has decided a federal question in a way in conflict with applicable decisions of this Court."

13. Maryland v. Baltimore Radio Show, 338 U.S. 912 (1950) (Frankfurter, J.). See Linzer, The Meaning of Certiorari Denials, 79 Colum.L.Rev. 1227 (1979).

14. Opinion of Frankfurter, J., respecting the denial of the petition for writ of certiorari in Maryland v. Baltimore Radio Show, 338 U.S. 912, 917 quoted in Opinion of Stevens, J., respecting the denial of the petition for writ of certiorari in Singleton v. Commissioner, 439 U.S. 940, 943 (1978).

15. Opinion of Stevens, J., in Singleton v. Commissioner, 439 U.S. at 944. Justice Stevens was "puzzled" by the dissent's suggestion that certiorari may have been denied because the tax case was "devoid of glamour and emotion." 439 U.S. at 946. Cf. Reproductive Services, Inc. v. Walker, 439 U.S. 1133 (1979) (statement of Stevens, J.); County of Sonoma v. Isbell, 439 U.S. 996 (1978) (statement of Stevens, J., joined by Brennan and Stewart, JJ., objecting to the Court not-

cause no one knows all that a denial means, does it mean that it means nothing? . . . It is just one of the facts of life that today every lower court does attach importance to denials and to presence or absence of dissents from denials, as judicial opinions and lawyers' arguments show." [16] Individual justices have thus used their dissents to denial of certiorari to express their concern about the facts of the particular case, to re-emphasize their earlier dissents, to urge reconsideration of a settled point, or to comment on the Court's workload.[17]

For appeals, the appellant invokes review as of right.[18] The Supreme Court rules require the appellant to file a jurisdictional statement,[19] which is similar to the petition for certiorari.[20] The appellee may, on the basis of these papers, file a motion to dismiss or affirm.[21] If there is a technical defi-

ciency the Court may dismiss the appeal summarily on this procedural issue.[22] It may also dismiss an appeal on the merits for want of a substantial federal question.[23] "Substantiality" is considered jurisdictional:

> [A]lthough the validity of a law was formally drawn in question, it is our duty to decline jurisdiction whenever it appears that the constitutional question presented is not, and was not at the time of granting the writ, substantial in character.[24]

Thus, unlike certiorari, decisions "to affirm summarily, and to dismiss for want of a substantial federal question . . . are votes on the merits of a case . . . "[25] binding as precedent on the lower courts.[26] But interestingly enough, this precedent is not as binding on the Supreme Court as would be one of its own more considered opinions.[27] This distinction of precedential value accords with reality because, notwith-

---

ing that certiorari denied because of failure to file petition within time limits set by 28 U.S.C.A. § 2101).

16. Brown v. Allen, 344 U.S. 443, 542–43 (1953) (Jackson, J., concurring in the result).

17. See Linzer, The Meaning of Certiorari Denials, 79 Colum.L.Rev. 1227 (1979).

18. E.g., Hart, Foreword: The Time Chart of the Justices, 73 Harv.L.Rev. 84, 88 (1959).

19. Supreme Court Rules, Rule 15.

20. See, Supreme Court Rules, Rule 21(1).

21. Supreme Court Rules, Rule 16.

22. Hart, Foreword: The Time Chart of the Justices, 73 Harv.L.Rev. 84, 89 (1959).

Cf., e.g., Doe v. Delaware, 450 U.S. 382 (1981), where Brennan, J., joined by White J., dissented to the per curiam dismissal of appeal for want of a properly presented federal question and argued that the Court should instead vacate and remand in order to allow the appellants to pursue further court proceedings.

23. Supreme Court Rules, Rule 16(1)(b):

"The Court will receive a motion to dismiss an appeal from a state court on the ground that it *does not present a substantial federal question;* or that the federal question sought to be reviewed was not timely or properly raised and was not expressly passed on; or that the judgment rests on an adequate nonfederal basis." (emphasis added).

And subsection (c) provides, as to federal courts:

"The Court will receive a motion to affirm the judgment sought to be reviewed on appeal from a federal court on the ground that it is manifest that the questions on which the decision of the cause depends *are so unsubstantial* as not to need further argument." (emphasis added).

24. Zucht v. King, 260 U.S. 174, 176 (1922) (Brandeis, J.).

25. Ohio ex rel. Eaton v. Price, 360 U.S. 246, 247 (1959) (Memorandum of Brennan, J.); R. Stern & E. Gressman, Supreme Court Practice 323 (5th ed. 1978).

26. Hicks v. Miranda, 422 U.S. 332, 344 (1975). It is important to note that the summary affirmance by the Supreme Court affirms the judgment of the lower court only and not necessarily the reasoning by which it was reached. Mandel v. Bradley, 432 U.S. 173 (1977) (per curiam).

The late Justice Tom Clark, when he was sitting by designation on a Fourth Circuit case, objected to the Supreme Court's statement in *Hicks,* that a dismissal for want of a substantial federal question is a decision on the merits. That view, he said, seems "to me to fly in the face of the long-established practice of the Court during the eighteen Terms in which I sat. During that time, appeals from state court decisions received treatment similar to that accorded petitions for certiorari and were given about the sme precedential weight." Hogge v. Johnson, 526 F.2d 833, 836 (4th Cir. 1975) (Clark, Justice concurring).

See also, Washington v. Confederated Bands & Tribes of the Yakima Indian Nation, 439 U.S. 463, 476 n. 20 (1979) (while summary dismissals are rulings on the merits, they do not "have the same precedential value here as does an opinion of this Court after briefing and oral argument on the merits."); Illinois State Bd. of Elections v. Socialist Workers Party, 440 U.S. 173, 183–85 (1979).

27. Edelman v. Jordan, 415 U.S. 651, 671 (1974); Caban v. Mohammed, 441 U.S. 380, 390 n. 9 (1979).

standing the important distinction in theory between certiorari and appeal, in fact the Supreme Court in recent years has failed to treat the two modes of review differently. Professor Henry Hart has concluded:

> [I]t has long since become impossible to defend the thesis that all the appeals which the Court dismisses on this ground [of lack of substantiality] are without substance. And any pretense that jurisdictional statements are concerned only with jurisdiction vanished when the Court began to affirm and even reverse judgments on the basis of them. Thus, the Court seems to have proceeded upon the view that a "right" of appeal not only does not include a right to be heard orally but does not include even a right to have the case considered upon plenary briefs. This view is hard enough to accept when it is the appellant who loses. But when the practice works to the prejudice of the appellee through a reversal on the jurisdictional papers, it seems impossible to reconcile with conventional conceptions of due process of law. In such cases the appellee, having had no adequate notice of the possibility, finds himself finally foreclosed without any real opportunity for argument at all.[28]

A former Supreme Court clerk has reported that "jurisdictional statements and petitions for certiorari now stand on practically the same footing and upon the case made in the former, just as in the latter may depend the grant [or denial] of further hearing." [29]

And Professor Charles Wright has concluded that, although technically true, it is "seriously misleading" to think that appeal is a matter of right.[30] Several justices in various dissents have also complained that the Court is insufficiently distinguishing the statutory differences between certiorari and appeal, by accepting certiorari in cases where the circumstances and importance of the issues do not warrant, while not granting a full appeal and issuing summary decisions when it should.[31]

Some commentators, notably Professor Alexander Bickel, have defended the Supreme Court's discretionary treatment of its certiorari review as a technique which should be used to avoid difficult constitutional decisions which, if decided, might legitimate unfortunate doctrine.[32] The desire to avoid difficult constitutional questions also helps justify and explain the pressures on the Supreme Court to treat lightly summary affirmances, reversals, and—in particular—dismissals for want of a substantial federal question. Perhaps Congress should recognize what in fact is being done and provide by statute that dismissals for want of a substantial federal question should be treated only as denials of certiorari rather than as precedent.

28. Hart, Foreword: The Time Chart of the Justices, 73 Harv.L.Rev. 84, 89 n. 13 (1959), citing United States v. Haley, 358 U.S. 644, motion to vacate judgment denied 359 U.S. 977, petition for rehearing denied 359 U.S. 981 (1959). See also, Smith v. Arkansas State Highway Employees, Local 1315, 441 U.S. 463, 465 (1979) (Marshall, J., dissenting, to per curiam, summary reversal of first amendment issues without even a plenary hearing).

29. Willey, Jurisdictional Statements on Appeals to the U.S. Supreme Court, 31 A.B.A.J. 239 (1945).

30. C. Wright, Law of Federal Courts, § 108 (4th ed. 1983).

31. See, e.g., Southern & Northern Overlying Carrier Chapters of the California Dump Truck Owners Ass'n v. Commission, 434 U.S. 9 (1977) (Rehnquist, J., dissenting to per curiam dismissal of an appeal, without prejudice, from a state court, arguing that case should have been decided on the merits); Idaho Dept. of Employment v. Smith, 434 U.S. 100, 102 (1977) (Brennan, J., joined by Marshall, J., dissenting in part to per curiam summary reversal, arguing that certiorari should have been denied), id., 434 U.S. at 103–105

(1977) (Stevens, J., dissenting in part to per curiam summary reversal arguing that certiorari should have been denied); Pennsylvania v. Mimms, 434 U.S. 106, 115 (1977) (Stevens, J., joined by Brennan and Marshall, JJ., dissenting to per curiam reversal, arguing that certiorari should have been denied). Brown Transport Corp. v. Atcon, Inc., 439 U.S. 1014, 1014–25 (1979) (White, J., joined by Blackmun, dissenting to denial of certiorari); Burger, C.J., agreed and cited letters by some of the justices to the Commission that studied proposals for a national court of appeals. 439 U.S. at 1026, 1031 n. 7. Brennan, J., in a separate statement, reaffirmed his opposition to a new national court of appeals. 439 U.S. at 1032. See also, Brennan, The National Court of Appeals: Another Dissent, 40 U.Chi.L.Rev. 473 (1973).

32. A. Bickel, The Least Dangerous Branch: The Supreme Court at the Bar of Politics 133–143, and passim (1962); Bickel, The Passive Virtues, 75 Harv.L. Rev. 40 (1961). Contra, e.g., Gunther, The Subtle Vices of the "Passive Virtues"—A Comment on Principle and Expediency in Judicial Review, 64 Colum.L.Rev. 1 (1964).

To be distinguished from the other types of review is an affirmance by an equally divided Court, which is not entitled to precedential weight;[33] the decision only records the fact that the Supreme Court was equally divided and that the lower court decision stands. A reversal is not possible for no order has been made.[34]

D. Proposals for Reform

Probably the most important of the various proposals for changes in the jurisdiction of the Supreme Court is the Report of the Study Group on the Caseload of the Supreme Court.[35] The Study Group was appointed by the Chief Justice to study the Court's caseload and to make appropriate recommendations. The Group was chaired by Professor Paul Freund and consequently its report is often referred to as the Freund Report.

Its study of the statistics of the Court's current workload, both in absolute terms and in the mounting trend, concluded that there was "impressive evidence that the conditions essential for the performance of the Court's mission do not exist . . . [T]he pressures of the [Supreme Court's] docket are incompatible with the appropriate fulfillment of its historic and essential functions."[36] In 35 years, the number of cases filed in the Court has increased 400% but the oral arguments have remained fairly constant.[37] The Report concluded that issues "that would have been decided on the merits a generation ago are passed over by the Court today; and second, the consideration given to the cases actually decided on the

merits is compromised by the pressures of 'processing' the inflated docket of petitions and appeals."[38]

After considering and rejecting other remedies, such as limiting the Supreme Court's jurisdiction solely to constitutional issues, creating specialized courts of administrative appeals, creating a national court of criminal appeals, and other proposals,[39] the Report recommended the creation of a National Court of Appeals and some procedural changes. It summarized its conclusions as follows:

1. The establishment by statute of a National Court of Appeals, with a membership of seven judges drawn on a rotating basis from the federal courts of appeals and serving staggered three-year terms. This Court would have the twofold function of (1) screening all petitions for certiorari and appeals that would at present be filed in the Supreme Court, referring the most review-worthy (perhaps 400 or 450 per Term) to the Supreme Court (except as provided in clause (2)), and denying the rest; and (2) retaining for decision on the merits cases of genuine conflict between circuits (except those of special moment, which would be certified to the Supreme Court). The Supreme Court would determine which of the cases thus referred to it should be granted review and decided on the merits in the Supreme Court. The residue would be denied, or in some instances remanded for decision by the National Court of Appeals.

2. The elimination by statute of three-judge district courts and direct review of their decisions in the Supreme Court; the elimination also of direct appeals in ICC and antitrust cases; and the substitution of certiorari for appeal in all cases where appeal is now the prescribed procedure for review in the Supreme Court.

---

33. Neil v. Biggers, 409 U.S. 188, 192 (1972); Etting v. Bank of the United States, 24 U.S. (11 Wheat.) 59, 78 (1826); The Antelope, 23 U.S. (10 Wheat.) 66 (1825).

Cf. Ohio ex rel. Eaton v. Price, 360 U.S. 246 (1959) per curiam 4–4 decision noting probable jurisdiction of appeal, which was believed by the four members voting against such action to turn on the same question as that decided eleven months previously in Frank v. Maryland, 359 U.S. 360 (1959), and Ohio ex rel. Eaton v. Price, 364 U.S. 263 (1960) (per curiam affirmance by an equally divided Court).

34. Durant v. Essex Co., 74 U.S. (7 Wall.) 107, 112 (1869). See generally, Note, The Precedential Value of

Supreme Court Plurality Decisions, 80 Colum.L.Rev. 756 (1980).

35. Federal Judicial Center Report of the Study Group on the Case Load of the Supreme Court (Dec. 1972). Hereinafter cited as Freund Report. It is reprinted in 57 F.R.D. 573.

36. Freund Report at 5.

37. Freund Report at 5–6.

38. Freund Report at 6.

39. Freund Report at 10–18.

This recommendation is not dependent on the adoption of the preceding recommendation. If a National Court of Appeals is established, these recommended changes in appellate procedure would become applicable to it.

3. The establishment by statute of a non-judicial body whose members would investigate and report on complaints of prisoners, both collateral attacks on convictions and complaints of mistreatment in prison. Recourse to this procedure would be available to prisoners before filing a petition in a federal court, and to the federal judges with whom petitions were filed.

4. Increased staff support for the Supreme Court in the clerk's office and the Library, and improved secretarial facilities for the Justices and their law clerks.[40]

Of these proposals, the first has created the most controversy. Critics have focused on the screening by the National Court of Appeals of petitions for certiorari. If the Supreme Court has a lessened control of its docket, it would have less of a chance to indicate a shift in constitutional doctrine, for it might not have the opportunity to take a case framed to present the right questions. Because of this screening, it is possible that new areas of constitutional importance, such as the criminal procedure decisions, might never have developed if this screening process had existed a few years before. In addition, critics argue that the Supreme Court is not really overworked, that screening certiorari petitions can be done very quickly and efficiently by the justices themselves, and that the poor and minorities might have less access to the Court.[41] Some of the jus-

tices or former justices of the Supreme Court have joined these attacks on the proposal.[42]

Other commentators have supported the Freund Report, arguing that only by limiting the caseload can we keep the justices from being overworked, to give them the time to think, to develop the law, to reflect, and not merely dispose of thousands of cases a year as quickly as possible. Professor Freund, in defending his report, has answered some of the critics by arguing:

There has been speculation whether cases like *Gideon* and *Miranda* would have reached the Supreme Court under the proposed plan. The fears are really groundless, since, although the individuals may have been inconspicuous, the issues had been considered by the Supreme Court time after time . . . .

Some litigants denied review by the Supreme Court might fare better if their cases were flagged by a National Court of Appeals. Some element of unpredictability concerning particular litigants inheres in the present system itself. Indeed, nothing in the new proposal could approach in magnitude this element in the *Miranda* case itself, in which, it will be recalled, five of some one hundred similar petitions were granted on an undisclosed basis of choice, these petitioners were held entitled to new trials, and the rest were told that, except for the five chosen instruments, the decision would apply prospectively only. . . . [It has been argued that] a court which has jurisdiction to decide a case must also have authority to decide whether to decide. Whence comes this asserted principle? Not, surely, from the

---

40. Freund Report at 47–48.

41. See, e.g., Prof. Charles Black, The National Court of Appeals: An Unwise Proposal, 83 Yale L.J. 883 (1974); Gressman, The Constitution v. The Freund Report, 41 George Wash.L.Rev. 951 (1974). See generally, A. Bickel, The Caseload of The Supreme Court and What, If Anything, To Do About It (1973). For a thorough analysis of the Court's caseload in recent years see, Hellman, The Business of the Supreme Court Under the Judiciary Act of 1925: The Plenary Docket in the 1970's, 91 Harv.L.Rev. 1709 (1978).

The observations that the Court is overworked is hardly a new one. See, "Correspondence," 1 Harv.L. Rev. 43, 44 (1887). See also, Letter Signed by all Supreme Court Justices on Mandatory Jurisdiction of the

Supreme Court, 65 A.B.A.J. 1328–29 (1979) (addressed to Senator De Concini and reprinted in the A.B.A.J.); cf. Gressman, Requiem for the Supreme Court's Obligatory Jurisdiction, 65 A.B.A.J. 1325 (1979). Contra, e.g., Arnold, Professor Hart's Theology, 73 Harv.L.Rev. 1298, 1314 (1960).

42. E.g., Tidewater Co. v. United States, 409 U.S. 151, 174 (1972) (Douglas J., dissenting); Brennan, The National Court of Appeals: Another Dissent, 40 U.Chi. L.Rev. 473 (1973); Warren, Let's Not Weaken the Supreme Court, 60 A.B.A.J. 677 (1974); Brennan, Chief Justice Warren, 88 Harv.L.Rev. 1, 4 (1974); Goldberg, One Supreme Court, The New Republic, Feb. 10, 1973, at 15.

Constitution, as the history of criminal appeals demonstrates. . . .[43]

Some justices have also supported, in varying degrees, the Freund Report.[44]

In addition to the Freund Report, other proposals include increasing the number of cases the Supreme Court accepts for review and having it then assign these cases to a newly created court for decision.[45] Others suggest that the Congress grant power to the Supreme Court to promulgate rules to confer jurisdiction on the newly created national court of appeals—within Congressional guidelines—to decide individual cases or classes of cases referred to it by the Supreme Court. This new court could recommend to the Supreme Court that it hear or deny review of such cases but the Supreme Court would retain final power to accept or reject any case for hearing.[46]

E. "Court Packing" and the Number of Justices on the Supreme Court

It has been argued that judicial review exists with the consent of the people since the high Court's "membership, size, funds, staff, rules of procedure, and enforcement agencies are subject to the control of the 'political' branches."[1] These elements of the judicial structure are certainly not guaranteed or even mentioned in the sparse and incomplete language of Article III. Particularly illustrative of this situation is the number of justices on the Supreme Court. The first Judiciary Act provided for a chief justice and five associate justices.[2] A few years later, the Act of 1801 provided that "after the next vacancy . . . . [the Supreme Court] shall consist of five justices only; that is to say, of one chief justice, and four associate justices," but this entire act was repealed in 1802.[3] The Act of 1807 then increased the number of associate justices to six;[4] in 1837 the number of associate justices was increased once again to eight,[5] and in 1864 to nine.[6] Perhaps the total number on the Court might have remained at nine associate justices and one chief, but Chief Justice Chase joined by other justices thought the Court too large and so informed Congress. Also about this time a vacancy occurred with the death of Justice Catron, and the Senate, rather than act on President Andrew Johnson's nomination, passed a bill reducing the number of associate justices to six, prohibiting any new appointments until two new associate justice vacancies would

---

43. Freund, Why We Need the National Court of Appeals, 59 A.B.A.J. 247, 251 (1973). See also, Griswold, Rationing Justice—the Supreme Court's Caseload and What the Court Does Not Do, 60 Corn.L. Rev. 335 (1975); A. Bickel, The Caseload of the Supreme Court, and What, If Anything, To Do About It (1973).

44. Burger, Defends Freund Study Group's Composition and Proposal, 59 A.B.A.J. 721 (1973); Rehnquist, The Supreme Court: Past and Present, 59 A.B.A.J. 361 (1973).

See also, Brown Transport Corp. v. Atcon, Inc., 439 U.S. 1014 (1978) (White, J., joined by Blackmun, J., dissenting to denial of certiorari): "[W]e are performing at our full capacity. . . . There is no doubt that those concerned with the coherence of the federal law must carefully consider the various alternatives available to assure that the appellate system has the capacity to function in the manner contemplated by the Constitution. . . . [T]here is grave doubt that this function is being adequately performed."

Justice White also referred to cases that seemed deserving of full consideration but which he believed could not be considered because of other demands.

45. Griswold, Rationing Justice—The Supreme Court's Caseload and What The Court Does Not Do, 60 Corn.L.Rev. 335 (1975).

46. Hufstedler, Courtship and Other Legal Arts, 60 A.B.A.J. 545 (1974). See also, Levin & Fickles, A New Proposal for a National Court of Appeals, 59 Judicature 164 (1975).

1. Levy, Judicial Review, History, and Democracy: An Introduction in, Judicial Review and the Supreme Court 1, 12 (1967).

2. Judiciary Act of 1789, § 1, 1 Stat. 73 (Sept. 24, 1789).

3. Judiciary Act of 1801, § 3, 2 Stat. 89 (Feb. 13, 1801), repealed, Judiciary Act of 1802, § 1, 2 Stat. 132 (Mar. 8, 1802).

4. Judiciary Act of 1807, § 5, 2 Stat. 420 (Feb. 24, 1807).

5. Judiciary Act of 1837, § 1, 5 Stat. 176 (Mar. 3, 1837).

6. Judiciary Act of 1864, § 2, 13 Stat. 4 (Feb. 19, 1864).

occur. Johnson signed the act.[7] But the new act did not last for long. In 1869, after the little-liked Johnson left and U.S. Grant became President, Congress passed a new statute setting the number of associate justices at eight with one Chief Justice.[8] President Grant now had two new appointments, one created by the new statute and one by the resignation of an associate justice. He announced these a few hours after the Supreme Court held (5–3) that it was unconstitutional to apply the Legal Tender Acts—which were enacted during the Civil War and made United States notes legal tender for most debts, public and private—to antecedent debts.[9] The justice who had offered his resignation had joined the majority in this legal tender case. After Grant's appointments were confirmed by the Senate the newly enlarged court of nine justices overruled the earlier legal tender decision, with the four members of the old majority in dissent.[10] Charges have been made and countered that Grant "packed" the Court.[11]

While the total number of justices has remained at nine (including the chief justice), President Franklin D. Roosevelt in 1937 proposed to increase that number, also amid charges of a court-packing plan. Under his proposal the President could appoint an additional justice for each justice on the Court who had served at least ten years and had failed to retire within six months of reaching his 70th birthday. The maximum number of justices on the Supreme Court would be set at 15. The proposal included new retirement privileges for Supreme Court justices.[12] Roosevelt argued that new blood was needed on the Court and that the older justices were less efficient. In reality, Roosevelt's legislative programs dealing with the economic depression were being struck down by the bare majority of unsympathetic justices.[13] The great majority of the Congress, led by members of Roosevelt's own party, defeated the plan, which might have set an unfortunate precedent. The Congress did provide retirement benefits for Supreme Court justices in a Judiciary Act passed in 1937,[14] which caused conservative Justice Van Devanter to resign in May of 1937. Also during the fight over the proposal, the Supreme Court appeared to change its position and upheld the validity of several important items of New Deal and state economic legislation.[15] This change was also caused in part by Justice Roberts who appeared to leave the conservative bloc and join the liberal bloc.[16] In any event,

---

7. Judiciary Act of 1866, § 1, 14 Stat. 209 (July 23, 1866). The President could fill no vacancy "until the number of associate justices shall be reduced to six."

8. Judiciary Act of 1869, § 1, 16 Stat. 44 (April 10, 1869). During the period others urged that the Court be increased to 10, 18 and even 24. See F. Frankfurter & J. Landis, The Business of the Supreme Court: A Study of the Federal Judicial System 49 n. 160 & 74–75 (1927).

9. Hepburn v. Griswold, 75 U.S. (8 Wall.) 603 (1869). See A. Kelly & W. Harbison, The American Constitution: Its Origins and Development 485 (4th ed. 1970).

10. Legal Tender Cases, 79 U.S. (12 Wall.) 457 (1871).

11. See, e.g., Ratner, Was the Supreme Court Packed by President Grant, 50 Pol.Sci.Q. 343 (1935); Fairman, Mr. Justice Bradley's Appointment to the Supreme Court and the Legal Tender Cases, 54 Harv.L. Rev. 977 (1941); Choper, The Supreme Court and the Political Branches: Democratic Theory and Practice, 122 U.Pa.L.Rev. 810, 851 (1974).

12. See H.R.Doc. No. 142, 75th Cong., 1st Sess. (1937).

13. For cases striking down New Deal legislation, see, e.g., Railroad Retirement Bd. v. Alton R. R., 295 U.S. 330 (1935); Schechter Poultry Corp. v. United States, 295 U.S. 495 (1935); United States v. Butler, 297 U.S. 1 (1936); Carter v. Carter Coal Co., 298 U.S. 238 (1936).

14. Judiciary Act of 1937, 50 Stat. 24 (Mar. 1, 1937).

15. E.g., West Coast Hotel Co. v. Parrish, 300 U.S. 379 (1937) (state minimum wage law upheld), distinguishing Morehead v. New York ex rel. Tipaldo, 298 U.S. 587 (1936) and overruling Adkins v. Children's Hosp., 261 U.S. 525 (1923). Steward Machine Co. v. Davis, 301 U.S. 548 (1937) (Social Security tax upheld); Helvering v. Davis, 301 U.S. 619 (1937) (Social Security payment of old age benefits upheld); NLRB v. Jones & Laughlin Steel Corp., 301 U.S. 1 (1937) (National Labor Relations Act of 1935 upheld); see also United States v. Darby, 312 U.S. 100 (1941) (Fair Labor Standards Act upheld), overruling Hammer v. Dagenhart, 247 U.S. 251 (1918).

16. See A. Kelly & W. Harbison, The American Constitution: Its Origins and Development 764 (4th ed. 1970), which argues that Justice Roberts' switch vote in West Coast Hotel v. Parrish, 300 U.S. 379 (1937) was

Roosevelt may have lost the battle but appeared to have won the war.

F. The "Rule of Four"

Justice Brennan has explained the Supreme Court's internal procedure to decide if it will accept a case for decision by writ of certiorari or appeal:

> The Court's practice, when considering a jurisdictional statement whereby a litigant attempts to invoke the Court's jurisdiction on appeal is quite similar to its well-known one on applications for writs of certiorari. That is, if four Justices or more are of opinion that the questions presented by the appeal should be fully briefed and argued orally, an order noting probable jurisdiction or postponing further consideration of the jurisdictional questions to a hearing on the merits is entered.[1]

This "Rule of Four" has a long tradition, and there is "ample indication that Congress had the rule of four in mind when it approved the . . . ."[2] Judiciary Act[3]—often called the Judges Bill—in 1925. Even if only eight justices consider a petition, four votes are still required to accept jurisdiction, but "[o]n rare occasions, as when only six or seven Justices are eligible or available, the rule is sometimes but not invariably relaxed so as to permit the granting of certiorari on

the vote of only three Justices—although Mr. Justice Douglas once stated flatly in an in-chambers opinion that 'three out of seven are not enough to grant a petition for certiorari.' "[4]

Justice Frankfurter opposed the rule of four as applied in Federal Employers' Liability Act cases. He objected to accepting a large number of these cases where the sole issue was the sufficiency of the evidence for submission to the jury. Thus, in *Rogers v. Missouri Pacific Ry. Co.*,[5] Frankfurter refused to vote on the merits of the case in which certiorari had been accepted, notwithstanding the "integrity of the certiorari process" or the "rule of four."

> The "rule of four" is not a command of Congress. It is a working rule devised by the Court as a practical mode of determining that a case is deserving of review . . . . The reason for deference to a minority view no longer holds when a class of litigation is given a special and privileged position.[6]

Notwithstanding the strong tradition of the "rule of four," Justice Frankfurter's rejection of it finds some support in other cases where the Court, in several 5 to 4 opinions, has dismissed certiorari as improvidently granted, without adequate discussion.[7]

announced to his fellow justices in December, 1936, after the *Parrish* case had been argued but before the court-packing plan had been announced. Justice Stone's illness at the time delayed publication of the decision. Roberts' switch thus represented an actual change in conviction and not merely a shift with the political winds caused by announcement of the court-packing plan.

See generally, Mason, Harlan Fiske Stone and FDR's Court Plan, 61 Yale L.J. 791 (1952); R. Jackson, The Struggle for Judicial Supremacy (1941); Leuchtenberg, The Origins of Franklin D. Roosevelt's "Court-Packing" Plan, 1966 Sup.Ct.Rev. 347; Frankfurter & Fisher, The Business of the Supreme Court at the October Terms, 1935 and 1936, 51 Harv.L.Rev. 577 (1938).

1. Ohio ex rel. Eaton v. Price, 360 U.S. 246, 246–247 (1959) (separate memorandum by Brennan, J.) In this case the Court, by a vote of 4–4 noted probable jurisdiction of an appeal. Frankfurter, Clark, Harlan, and Whittaker, JJ., voted against probable jurisdiction because they believed the case turned on the same question as that decided by a 5–4 vote a short time earlier. Stewart, J., did not participate.

2. Leiman, The Rule of Four, 57 Colum.L.Rev. 975, 985 (1957). See also 81 Cong.Rec. 2814 (1937).

3. Act of 1925, 43 Stat. 936 (Feb. 13, 1925). Certiorari, or discretionary review, was created for the Supreme Court by the Evarts Act, 26 Stat. 826 (Mar. 3, 1891).

4. R. Stern and E. Gressman, Supreme Court Practice § 5.4 at 346 (5th ed. 1978), citing Pryor v. United States, 404 U.S. 1242, 1243 (1971) (Douglas, Circuit Justice). See also id. at 347 n. 11.

5. 352 U.S. 500, 524 (1957) (dissenting opinion).

6. 352 U.S. at 524, 529 (1957) (Frankfurter, J. dissenting). Frankfurter, however, would vote in an FELA case in order to prevent a 4–4 tie. Inman v. Baltimore & Ohio R. R., 361 U.S. 138, 141 (1959) (separate opinion of Frankfurter, J.). Frankfurter's position on FELA cases has been both defended and attacked. Compare, Hart, Foreword: The Time Chart of the Justices, 73 Harv.L.Rev. 84, 98 (1959), with Arnold, Professor Hart's Theology, 73 Harv.L.Rev. 1298, 1302–1304 (1960).

7. E.g., NAACP v. Overstreet, 384 U.S. 118 (1966), a per curiam, 5–4 dismissal of the writ of certiorari as improvidently granted. There was no opinion for the majority, with a long dissent by Douglas, J., joined by Warren, C.J., Brennan and Fortas, JJ.; Triangle In-

Justice Brennan, joined by Justice Marshall, has argued in one case that dismissals of the writ of certiorari as improvidently granted, after briefs and oral arguments, are "proper only when the more intensive consideration of the issues and the record in the case that attends full briefing and oral argument reveals that conditions originally thought to justify granting the writ of certiorari are not in fact present."[8] But Justice Stevens, concurring in the dismissal of the writ, found no problem: "[I]t is my understanding that at least one Member of the Court who voted to grant certiorari has now voted to dismiss the writ; accordingly, the action of the Court does not impair the integrity of the Rule of Four."[9] It ought not to matter that the change in vote reflects only the factors that motivated the original vote to deny.

G.　Tenure and Salary Protections

All of the federal judges appointed pursuant to Article III have lifetime tenure, and a constitutional guarantee that their salary "shall not be diminished during their Continuance in Office."[1] The concept of separation of powers provides a basis for protecting the financial independence of the members of the judicial branch. Thus, Article III of the Constitution prohibits the diminution of a judge's compensation during his or her term in office. This clause is a specific means of ensuring the independence of the judiciary.[2]

Congress is not required to keep judicial salaries growing with inflation rates;[3] Congress may in its discretion increase the salaries of federal judges or refuse to increase them, so long as it does not reduce the compensation of the judges. Congress can also nullify previously authorized increases in judicial salaries if the Congressional nullification becomes law before the beginning of the fiscal year in which the previously authorized increase was to take effect.[4] However, Congress cannot repeal an increase in judicial salaries which took effect under a formula previously set forth by statute, if the repealing act becomes law after the be-

---

volvement Council v. Ritchie, 402 U.S. 497 (1971) was another 5–4 per curiam dismissal of the writ as improvidently granted. In this case Justice Douglas' dissent, joined by Black, Brennan, and Marshall, JJ., prompted a concurrence from Justice Harlan. Douglas argued:

> "The four who now dissent were the only ones to vote to grant the petition. The rule [of four] should not be changed to a 'rule of five' by actions of the five Justices who originally opposed certiorari. It is improper for them to dismiss the case after oral argument unless one of the four who voted to grant moves so to do, which has not occurred here."

402 U.S., at 508.

Harlan's concurrence argued that the "changed posture of the case" indicated that its adjudication would not be "a provident expenditure of the energies of the Court." 402 U.S. at 502.

Cf. also, some of the War Crimes Cases, Milch v. United States, 332 U.S. 789 (1947) (motion for leave to file petition for writ of habeas corpus denied, 4–4); Everett v. Truman, 334 U.S. 824 (1948) (per curiam) (same; 4–4). See generally, Fairman, Some New Problems of the Constitution Following the Flag, 1 Stan.L. Rev. 589 (1949).

8. Burrell v. McCray, 426 U.S. 471, 473–74 (1976) (Brennan, J., dissenting), relying on The Monrosa v. Carbon Black Export, Inc., 359 U.S. 180 (1959).

9. Burrell v. McCray, 426 U.S. at 472. Justice White also dissented to the per curiam dismissal of the writ; he would affirm the judgment of the 4th Circuit, as would Stevens, Brennan, and Marshall, JJ., if the case had been accepted.

1. U.S.Const. art. III, § 1. See United States v. Will, 449 U.S. 200 (1980) (federal statute unconstitutional to the extent that it purported to repeal judicial salary increase already in effect). See generally The Federalist Papers, No. 79 (Hamilton).

2. For an excellent examination of the clause and the problem of applying it to modern judicial compensation questions, see Rosenn, The Constitutional Guaranty Against Diminution of Judicial Compensation, 24 U.C.L.A.L.Rev. 308 (1976).

3. A number of federal judges filed suit in the Court of Claims to have their salaries raised on the claim that inflation reduced the real value of their salaries and, therefore, that the failure to raise their salaries violated both the compensation clause and the principle of separation of powers. The Court of Claims found no constitutional violation and the Supreme Court refused to review the decision. Atkins v. United States, 556 F.2d 1028 (Ct.Cl.1977), cert. denied 434 U.S. 1009 (1978).

4. United States v. Will, 449 U.S. 200 (1980).

ginning of the fiscal year in which the increase took place.[5]

In addition, Article III judges are protected by lifetime tenure; they can be removed only by impeachment.[6] The purpose of this guarantee is to insulate "the individual judge from improper influences not only by other branches but by colleagues as well, and thus [to promote] judicial individualism."[7]

III. THE CONGRESSIONAL POWER TO LIMIT JURISDICTION

A. Ex Parte McCardle—The Opinion, Its Historical Setting, and the Limitations of Its Holding

The Supreme Court's post Civil War decision of *Ex Parte McCardle*[1] is often relied on by commentators and some courts as supporting a broad power of Congress to limit the jurisdiction of the lower federal courts and the Supreme Court. In that case, under the authority of the Reconstruction Acts, the military government had imprisoned McCardle, who then brought a habeas corpus action alleging that the Reconstruction legisla-

tion was unconstitutional. The lower court upheld the Act, and McCardle appealed under authority of the then recently passed Act of February 5, 1867,[2] providing appeal to the Supreme Court from the circuit courts.[3] After the Court had acknowledged jurisdiction but before a decision on the merits, Congress withdrew the statutory right of appeal,[4] seeking to avoid a Supreme Court determination that the Reconstruction legislation was unconstitutional.[5] The Court complied with the withdrawal and dismissed the case for want of jurisdiction.[6] As the Court noted, while the appellate jurisdiction of the Supreme Court "is, strictly speaking, conferred by the Constitution . . . it is conferred 'with such exceptions and under such regulations as Congress shall make' "[7] according to Article III, section 2, clause 2.

The *McCardle* precedent has been read broadly by some.[8] This case has been used from time to time to support unsuccessful efforts in Congress to assert legislative power over the jurisdiction of the courts in order to control substantive results of court decisions over, for example, reapportionment,[9]

---

5. Id. Federal judges, including justices of the Supreme Court, are not disqualified from deciding cases under this compensation clause, since the disqualification of all federal judges would leave this issue undecided, and the public interest and the independent judiciary unprotected. United States v. Will, 449 U.S. 200 (1980) (common law "rule of necessity" justifies federal judges hearing cases under the compensation clause even though they have some interest in the outcome of the litigation; neither judicial canons of ethics or related statutory provisions operate to disqualify all United States judges in such cases). See T. Morgan & R. Rotunda, Professional Responsibility: Problems and Materials 430–33 (2d ed. 1981).

6. United States ex rel. Toth v. Quarles, 350 U.S. 11, 16 (1955). See also, The Federalist, No. 78 (Alexander Hamilton).

7. Northern Pipeline Constr. Co. v. Marathon Pipe Line Co., 102 S.Ct. 2858, 2865 n. 10 (1982) (Opinion of Brennan, J., joined by Marshall, Blackmun, & Stevens, JJ.). See generally, the article by second circuit judge Irving Kaufman, Chilling Judicial Independence, 88 Yale L.J. 681 (1979).

1. 74 U.S. (7 Wall.) 506 (1869). See generally, Van Alstyne, A Critical Guide to Ex Parte McCardle, 15 Ariz.L.Rev. 229 (1973).

2. Act of February 5, 1867, ch. 26, § 1, 14 Stat. 385.

3. See 74 U.S. (7 Wall.) at 508.

4. Id.

5. See generally C. Fairman, 6 The Oliver Wendell Holmes Devise History of the Supreme Court of the United States: Reconstruction and Reunion 1864–88, pt. 1, at 433–514 (P. Freund ed. 1971); Van Alstyne, A Critical Guide to Ex Parte McCardle, 15 Ariz.L.Rev. 229 (1973).

6. 74 U.S. (7 Wall.) at 515.

7. 74 U.S. (7 Wall.) at 512–13.

8. E.g., National Mutual Insurance Co. v. Tidewater Transfer Co., 337 U.S. 582, 655 (1948) (Frankfurter, J., dissenting); Wechsler, The Courts and the Constitution, 65 Colum.L.Rev. 1001, 1005 (1965). See generally, Elliott, Court-Curbing Proposals in Congress, 33 Notre Dame Lawyer 597 (1958).

Some recent authority limiting congressional power includes, e.g., Sager, Foreword: Constitutional Limitations on Congress' Authority to Regulate the Jurisdiction of the Federal Courts, 95 Harv.L.Rev. 17 (1981); Auerbach, The Unconstitutionality of Congressional Proposals to Limit the Jurisdiction of Federal Courts, 47 Mo.L.Rev. 47 (1982); see also, M. Redish, Federal Jurisdiction: Tensions in the Allocation of Judicial Power 7–34 (1980).

9. E.g., H.R. 11926, 88th Cong., 2d Sess. (1964).

subversive activities,[10] and school busing.[11] But this broad interpretation of *McCardle* is not necessarily required.

The Court there recognized the limited nature of the statutory withdrawal:

> Counsel seems to have supposed, if effect be given to the repealing act in question, that the whole appellate power of the court, in cases of habeas corpus, is denied. But this is an error. The act of 1868 does not except from the jurisdiction any cases but appeals from Circuit Courts under the act of 1867. It does not affect the jurisdiction which was previously exercised.[12]

The Court clarified the meaning of this statement only months later in *Ex parte Yerger*[13] where it held the same statute that was at issue in *McCardle* did not affect its certiorari jurisdiction. The Court concluded that writs of habeas corpus and certiorari could revise the decision of the circuit court and free the prisoner from unlawful restraint.[14] The limitation of the appellate jurisdiction thus had little practical effect.

In the *McCardle* situation Congress was not withdrawing all jurisdiction from the lower federal courts and the Supreme Court. It was only withdrawing one avenue of appeal to the Supreme Court. Even if Congress were to remove all appellate avenues to the Supreme Court, that would only make the lower federal courts the final decision-makers; it would not oust the federal courts from their essential role in the constitutional plan of exercising judicial review.[15] In other words, even a wholesale removal of appellate jurisdiction—a fact situation much broader than that presented in *McCardle*—does not imply a congressional power to prevent all of the federal courts from exercising judicial review; it only implies a power to make lower federal courts the last decision-makers. This latter power is not completely unusual. The original Judiciary Act of 1789, for example, did not provide for any direct review of federal criminal cases in the Supreme Court.[16]

It should also be noticed that the jurisdictional limitation in *McCardle* was neutral. The denial of appeal to the Supreme Court applied to both the Government and a private party. If the Government had lost the habeas action below, as it might lose in a future case, the Government would similarly have been denied an appellate remedy. The neutrality of a jurisdictional limitation helps to assure that Congressional withdrawal will not be an attempt to alter the results of specific cases.

To emphasize the narrowness of its holding, the Court in *McCardle* distinguished the case before it from two other decisions of the state courts that it cited with approval, *State v. Fleming*[17] and *DeChastellux v.*

---

10. E.g., S. 2646, 85th Cong., 1st Sess. (1957).

11. See generally, Rotunda, Congressional Power to Restrict the Jurisdiction of the Lower Federal Courts and the Problem of School Busing, 64 Georgetown L.J. 839 (1976).

12. 74 U.S. (7 Wall.) at 515.

13. 75 U.S. (8 Wall.) 85 (1869).

14. Id. at 103.

Under section 14 of the Judiciary Act of 1789, the Supreme Court and other courts could issue writs of habeas corpus and all other writs necessary in the aid of their respective jurisdictions. The writ of habeas corpus could not extend to prisoners unless they were in custody under color of the authority of the United States. See id. at 96. Marbury v. Madison clarified that the power to issue writs of mandamus under section 13 of the Judiciary Act constitutes an exercise of appellate jurisdiction when exercised by the Supreme Court. See 5 U.S. (1 Cranch) 137, 147 (1803). Four years after *Marbury*, the Court similarly construed the provisions of section 14 relating to writs of habeas

corpus and mandamus. See Ex parte Bollman, 8 U.S. (4 Cranch) 75, 99–101 (1807).

15. See Hart, The Power of Congress to Limit the Jurisdiction of Federal Courts: An Exercise in Dialectic, 66 Harv.L.Rev. 1362, 1365 (1953); see also, Ratner, Congressional Power Over the Appellate Jurisdiction of the Supreme Court, 109 U.Pa.L.Rev. 157, 172 (1960); Ratner, Majoritarian Constraints on Judicial Review: Congressional Control of Supreme Court Jurisdiction, 27 Villanova L.Rev. 929 (1982).

16. C. Wright, Federal Courts § 1 (4th ed. 1983). The Supreme Court continued to exercise habeas jurisdiction, but that review is much narrower, limited to a lack of jurisdiction in the lower courts. This limitation forced the Court to expand the definition of lack of jurisdiction to include the situation where the criminal statute for violation of which the defendant was indicted was unconstitutional. Ex parte Siebold, 100 U.S. 371 (1879).

17. 26 Tenn. 152 (1846).

Fairchild.[18] The *McCardle* court took care to distinguish its facts from these cases where the courts had struck down "the exercise of judicial power by the legislature, or of legislative interference with courts in the exercising of continuing jurisdiction."[19] In the *Fleming* case, the defendant had been indicted under an 1838 statute regulating the sale of liquor, but in 1846, while his prosecution was pending, the Tennessee legislature legalized such sales and provided that no one could be punished for violation of the earlier statute.[20] The Tennessee Supreme Court held the 1846 statute violative of the Tennessee constitution because the legislature had no power to interfere with the judicial function.[21] In *Fairchild* the Pennsylvania Supreme Court held invalid an act that granted a new trial to Fairchild, the unsuccessful defendant in a trespass suit. The court reasoned that the statute was an impermissible attempt by the legislature to exercise judicial power.[22]

In *McCardle*, the Court found that in *Fleming* and *Fairchild* the legislature had exercised judicial power by interfering with the courts' continuing jurisdiction, distinguishing the case before it where Congress had exercised its constitutional power tó make exceptions to the Court's appellate jurisdiction.[23]

It has been argued that the historical evidence surrounding the exceptions clause of Article III, granting Congress power to regulate the Supreme Court's appellate jurisdiction, supports the view that the clause be read in light of the contemporary state practice to confine regulation basically to housekeeping matters and to certain proceedings where neither error nor certiorari tradition-

ally had been available.[24] The framers did not intend that the exceptions clause give Congress the power to control the results of particular cases. Analogously then, Congress may not use the power to restrict the federal courts' jurisdiction in order to control the results of particular cases and achieve the result forbidden by a proper interpretation of the exceptions clause.

A principle implied from Article III and not refuted by the *McCardle* precedent is that the guarantee of an independent federal judiciary limits the legislature in the exercise of its power to regulate federal court jurisdiction. This principle is perhaps most directly supported by a post-*McCardle* decision, *United States v. Klein*,[25] which holds that Congress may not enact legislation to eliminate an area of jurisdiction in order to control the results in a particular case.

Klein sued in the Court of Claims under an 1863 statute which allowed the recovery of land captured or abandoned during the Civil War if the claimant could prove that he had not aided the rebellion.[26] Relying on an earlier Supreme Court decision that a presidential pardon proved conclusively that he had not assisted the rebellion,[27] Klein won his case in the Court of Claims.[28] While the government's appeal to the Supreme Court was pending, Congress passed a statute providing that a presidential pardon would not support a claim for captured property, that acceptance without disclaimer of a pardon for participation in the rebellion was conclusive evidence that the claimant had aided the enemy, and that when the Court of Claims based its judgment in favor of the claimant

---

18. 15 Pa. 18 (1850).

19. 74 U.S. (7 Wall.) at 514 (footnote omitted).

20. 26 Tenn. at 152–53.

21. Id. at 154.

22. 15 Pa. at 20.

23. 74 U.S. (7 Wall.) at 514.

24. See J. Goebel, 1 The Oliver Wendell Holmes Devise History of the Supreme Court of the United States: Antecedents and Beginnings to 1801, at 240 (P. Freund ed. 1971). See also Merry, Scope of the Su-

preme Court's Appellate Jurisdiction: Historical Basis, 47 Minn.L.Rev. 53 (1962).

25. 80 U.S. (13 Wall.) 128 (1871).

See generally, Young, Congressional Regulation of Federal Courts' Jurisdiction and Processes: United States v. Klein Revisited, 1981 Wis.L.Rev. 1189.

26. Id. at 138–39.

27. Id. at 143; see United States v. Padelford, 76 U.S. (9 Wall.) 531, 543 (1869).

28. 80 U.S. (13 Wall.) at 143.

of such a pardon the Supreme Court lacked jurisdiction on appeal.[29]

The Supreme Court declared this restriction of jurisdiction unconstitutional, holding that Congress had the power under Article III to confer or withhold the right of appeal from Court of Claims decisions but that those parts of Article III requiring that the judicial branch be independent of the legislative and executive branches restrict that power.[30] The Court found that the withdrawal of jurisdiction was only a means to deny to presidential pardons the effect that the Court previously had held them to have.[31] Reasoning that such a denial of jurisdiction prescribes for the Court a rule for the decision of its cases, the Court concluded that Congress had exceeded its power to regulate appellate jurisdiction and had passed the limit separating the legislative from the judicial branch.[32]

The decision in *Klein* strongly supports the contention that Congress must exercise its power to limit jurisdiction in a manner consistent with constitutional limitations and the independence of the judiciary. Any jurisdictional limitation must be neutral; that

is, Congress may not decide the merits of a case under the guise of limiting jurisdiction. And, Congress' power under the exceptions clause is subject, like other congressional powers, to the limitations expressed in the Constitution. Thus Congress could not exercise its exceptions power so as to violate the fifth amendment due process clause or other Constitutional limits.[33]

B. Due Process Limitations on Congress's Jurisdictional Powers and a Survey of the Major Statutory Restrictions on Jurisdiction

Although Article III does give Congress power to affect the jurisdiction of the lower federal courts, other provisions of the Constitution limit the reach of that power.[1] Specifically, it should be held that under the due process clause of the fifth amendment Congress may not exercise its Article III power over the jurisdiction of the courts in order to deprive a party of a right created by the Constitution.[2] For example, since the equal protection guarantee of the due process clause of the fifth amendment forbids racial

---

29. Id. at 143–44. The statute also required the Court of Claims to dismiss actions of claimants with presidential pardons who had not previously disclaimed their participation in the rebellion. Id. at 143.

30. 80 U.S. (13 Wall.) at 145–47. However, it is no violation of the separation of powers for Congress, by statute, to require the Government simply to waive one of its affirmative defenses. United States v. Sioux Nation, 448 U.S. 371 (1980) (Congress by statute could waive res judicata effect of prior decision entered against Government).

31. 80 U.S. (13 Wall.) at 145.

32. Id. at 146–47.

33. United States v. Bitty, 208 U.S. 393, 399–400 (1908) (Harlan, J.): "What such exceptions and regulations should be it is for Congress, in its wisdom, to establish, having of course due regard to *all* the provisions of the Constitution." (emphasis added).

1. See generally Van Alstyne, A Critical Guide to Ex parte McCardle, 15 Ariz.L.Rev. 229, 263–69 (1973).

See the interesting discussion in Redish & Woods, Congressional Power to Control the Jurisdiction of Lower Federal Courts: A Critical Review and a New Synthesis, 124 U.Penn.L.Rev. 45 (1975) analyzing the implications of Tarble's Case, 80 U.S. (13 Wall.) 397 (1872). See also, Sager, Foreword: Constitutional Lim-

itations on Congress' Authority to Regulate the Jurisdiction of Federal Courts, 95 Harv.L.Rev. 17 (1981). Redish, Constitutional Limitations on Congressional Power to Control Federal Jurisdiction: A Reaction to Professor Sager, 77 Nw.U.L.Rev. 143 (1982).

For example, although the Constitution gives Congress the power to punish piracies and felonies committed on the high seas, it limits that power by prohibiting ex post facto laws or bills of attainder. See U.S. Const. art. I, §§ 8, 9.

2. United States v. Bitty, 208 U.S. 393, 399–400 (1908). Of course, Congress may eliminate statutorily-created rights simply by repealing the statute. See Battaglia v. General Motors Corp., 169 F.2d 254, 257 (2d Cir.), cert. denied 335 U.S. 887 (1948).

It should also be remembered that the state courts exist with their general jurisdiction to hear constitutional claims. These courts, under the Supremacy Clause, must implement the requirements of the Constitution. Yet the safety valve of the state courts' jurisdiction (assuming that Congress—if it could—does not purport to limit their jurisdiction) should not justify restrictions by the Congress on federal courts when those restrictions violate the due process clause or other such right. The possible exercise of checks on the abuse of power should not be used to justify the exercise of such abuses of power.

discrimination,[3] Congress could not enact a statute totally denying original or appellate jurisdiction over actions brought by members of a particular racial group, for that result would amount to a violation of due process. Indeed, a survey of congressional limitations on the jurisdiction of the lower federal courts suggests that the Supreme Court will not uphold a statutory infringement of constitutional rights under the guise of a jurisdictional statute, nor should such statutes be so construed.

The Norris-LaGuardia Act,[4] perhaps the most famous example of congressional removal of jurisdiction, limits federal courts' power to issue an injunction or restraining order in a labor dispute.[5] This withdrawal of equitable jurisdiction violates neither the Article III principles established in *United States v. Klein*[6] nor any constitutional rights. Although the restriction limits the relief that labor unions and employers may seek during a labor dispute, Congress may properly limit the courts' equitable jurisdiction if the limitation has some rational basis, since neither a union nor an employer is a suspect class.[7] In upholding the Act's limitation, the Supreme Court implicitly acknowledged this conclusion by recognizing that a business does not have a constitutionally vested right to have a federal court issue an injunction in a case involving a labor dispute.[8] Section 7(e) of the Act, which requires a federal court to determine whether the public officer charged with protecting a complainant's property is unable or unwilling to furnish adequate protection before granting the claim for injunctive relief, provides additional support for the conclusion that the Act does not infringe on constitutional rights.[9] This section sufficiently protects any arguable rights of an employer to due process of law before the "taking" of property.[10] The Court did state, in the case upholding the constitutionality of the Act, that "[t]here can be no question of the power of Congress thus to define and limit the jurisdiction of the inferior courts of the United States."[11] And it was on a jurisdiction theory that the Act was passed.[12] But in light of the later development of the law we should not view the Norris-LaGuardia Act of depriving employers of rights that are constitutionally guaranteed. Thus, it is constitutional to prevent the federal courts from enforcing, by the granting of legal or equitable relief, "yellow dog" contracts, i.e., contracts by which employees agree, as a condition of employment, not to become or remain a member of a labor union.[13] Since as a substantive matter such contracts can be forbidden, unless one adopts the discarded theory of substantive due process,[14] to limit federal

---

3. Bolling v. Sharpe, 347 U.S. 497 (1954); Cf. Boddie v. Connecticut, 401 U.S. 371, 380–82 (1971) (due process prohibits states from denying individuals seeking divorce access to the courts solely on the basis of inability to pay); Battaglia v. General Motors Corp., 169 F.2d 254, 257 (2d Cir.), cert. denied 335 U.S. 887 (1948); cf. Youngstown Sheet & Tube Co. v. Sawyer (The Steel Seizure Case), 343 U.S. 579, 646 (1952) (Jackson, J., concurring) (Fifth Amendment gives a private right that limits governmental authority under Article II to execute the laws.)

4. 29 U.S.C.A. §§ 101–15 (1970).

5. Id. § 107.

6. See 80 U.S. (13 Wall.) 128, 146–47 (1871). The Norris-LaGuardia Act requires a court to make findings similar to those of an equity court before enjoining a labor dispute. The court must find that substantial and irreparable injury will occur without an injunction, that the balance of hardships favors the complainant, and that the complainant has no adequate remedy at law. Norris-LaGuardia Act §§ 7(b)–(d), 29 U.S.C.A. §§ 107(b)–(d).

7. See Lauf v. E.G. Shinner & Co., 303 U.S. 323, 330 (1938).

8. See id.

9. See Norris-LaGuardia Act § 7(e), 29 U.S.C.A. § 107(e).

10. In fact, the statute serves to implement the first amendment right to peaceful, noncoercive picketing. Cf. Thornhill v. Alabama, 310 U.S. 88, 102–03 (1940) (labor dispute is within area of free discussion protected by the Constitution).

11. Lauf v. E.G. Shinner & Co., 303 U.S. 323, 330 (1938) (footnote omitted).

12. See S.Rep. No. 163, H.R.Rep. No. 669, 72d Cong., 1st Sess. 10 (1932).

13. 29 U.S.C.A. § 103.

14. Earlier the Supreme Court had held that the employer's right to insist on "Yellow Dog" contracts was protected from interference by the due process clause of the Fourteenth Amendment, Coppage v. Kansas, 236 U.S. 1 (1915), and the Fifth Amendment, Adair v. United States, 208 U.S. 161 (1908). See also, Truax

jurisdiction to enforce such contracts restricts no constitutional right.

Another congressional limitation on the courts' power is found in the anti-injunction provisions of the Internal Revenue Code.[15] The courts have upheld the Act's restriction on suits to restrain the assessment or collection of taxes, but only after finding that Congress has provided the injured taxpayer with other adequate remedies.[16] As Justice Brandeis pointed out in *Phillips v. Commissioner*,[17] "where only property rights are involved, mere postponement of the judicial enquiry is not a denial of due process, if the opportunity given for the ultimate judicial determination of the liability is adequate." [18] Justice Brandeis' reasoning implies that a jurisdictional limitation in tax cases that deprived a person of property without due process of law would be improper. Consistent with this reading of the statute, federal courts have recognized that there may be an exception to the Act where a plaintiff has no other remedy.[19]

The portal-to-portal cases [20] provide another example of constitutional limitations on congressional power over the jurisdiction of the lower federal courts. In the mid-1940s,

the Supreme Court ruled that time spent by workers in previously noncompensable work, such as underground travel in iron ore mines and similar incidental activities, was part of the work week compensable under the Fair Labor Standards Act.[21] This unexpected decision created immense retroactive liability for many businesses.[22] In an effort to eliminate this liability, Congress amended the statute to make such work noncompensable [23] and withdrew the jurisdiction of the courts to hear cases that were presently pending or were to be brought under the old statute.[24] The constitutional problems presented by Congress' removal of jurisdiction were carefully considered by the Second Circuit in *Battaglia v. General Motors Corp.*[25] Finding that an amendment of the Fair Labor Standards Act destroyed the plaintiffs' claim to overtime pay under the Act, the court held that, because no rights had vested in the plaintiffs, the amendment did not constitute a taking of property and the jurisdictional limitation therefore was valid: Congress' jurisdictional power was not exercised to deprive any person of life, liberty, or property without just compensation.[26] By considering and rejecting this constitutional

v. Corrigan, 257 U.S. 312 (1921). Such cases are no longer good law and reflect discarded theories of substantive due process. See Chapter 13 on Substantive Due Process.

15. Int.Rev.Code of 1954, § 7421(a).

16. Bob Jones University v. Simon, 416 U.S. 725, 746 (1974) (where judicial review available, injunction denied university suing to prevent revocation of its tax exempt status); Phillips v. Commissioner, 283 U.S. 589, 597–98 (1931) (summary procedure for collection of unpaid income and property taxes from transfer of property of taxpayer valid since transferee has two alternate methods of judicial review). See generally Note, Nontaxpayer Challenges to Internal Revenue Service Rulemaking: Constitutional and Statutory Barriers to Judicial Review, 63 Georgetown L.J. 1263, 1283–97 (1975).

17. 283 U.S. 589 (1931).

18. Id. at 596–97.

19. See Note, Nontaxpayer Challenges to Internal Revenue Service Rulemaking: Constitutional and Statutory Barriers to Judicial Review, 63 Georgetown L.J. 1263, at 1286, 1288–89 (1975).

20. See Anderson v. Mt. Clemens Pottery Co., 328 U.S. 680 (1946); Jewell Ridge Coal Corp. v. Local No. 6167, 325 U.S. 161 (1945); Tennessee Coal, Iron & R.

Co. v. Muscoda Local No. 123, 321 U.S. 590 (1944). See generally Morgan, The Portal-to-Portal Pay Case, in The Third Branch of Government: 8 Cases in Constitutional Politics 50–83 (C. Prichett & A. Westin eds. 1963).

21. See Anderson v. Mt. Clemens Pottery Co., 328 U.S. 680, 690–93 (1946); Tennessee Coal, Iron & R. Co. v. Muscoda Local No. 123, 321 U.S. 590, 598–99 (1944).

22. See D. Currie, Federal Courts: Cases and Materials 145–46 (1975).

23. Portal-to-Portal Act, ch. 52, 61 Stat. 84 (1947), as amended, 29 U.S.C.A. §§ 216, 251–62.

24. Id. § 2(d), 29 U.S.C.A. § 252(d).

25. 169 F.2d 254 (2d Cir.), cert. denied 335 U.S. 887 (1948).

26. Id. at 257. In *Battaglia* the court held that the Portal-to-Portal Act did not encroach on the independent power of the judiciary, attempt to change previous Supreme Court decision, or impose a rule of decision that violated Article III or contradicted *Klein*. The Court found that while the Portal-to-Portal Act changed the Fair Labor Standards Act, it left private contractual rights enforceable in the courts except to the extent that they referred to the prior statutory law. See id. at 261–62.

claim, this court of appeals explicitly recognized that congressional power over the jurisdiction of the courts is limited by the due process clause.

The Supreme Court has acknowledged constitutional issues concerning the congressional power to restrain federal court review of Selective Service cases, a subject over which courts traditionally have exercised deferential review.[27] In *Oestereich v. Selective Service Board* [28] Justice Harlan noted in a concurring opinion that it would raise serious constitutional problems to interpret section 10(b)(3) of the Selective Service Act,[29] which limits the courts' jurisdiction to review Selective Service decisions, as denying a registrant the opportunity to raise a constitutional issue in some competent forum.[30] To prevent the legislature from using the federal courts to accomplish unconstitutional ends, Congress's Article III power must be subject to the due process guarantees of the fifth amendment.[31]

Cases upholding the federal anti-injunction statute [32]—which in general forbids federal injunctions of state court proceedings—also do not support a broad view of Congressional power over lower Federal Court jurisdiction.[33] The statute by its own terms exempts injunctions which are "expressly authorized by Act of Congress," and the Supreme Court has held that in section 1983 of title 42, which enforces the guarantees of the fourteenth amendment, Congress expressly authorized suits in equity as a means of redress or an exemption to the anti-injunction statute.[34]

> The very purpose of § 1983 was to interpose the federal courts between the States and the people, as guardians of the people's federal rights—to protect the people from unconstitutional action under color of state law, "whether that action be executive, legislative, or judicial." [35]

While the important civil rights guaranteed by section 1983 allow the injunctive remedy where appropriate in spite of the anti-injunction statute, it is also true that principles of equity, comity, and federalism must also be decided before an injunction may issue.[36] Such comity cases, however, do not allow Congress to use a jurisdictional limitation to limit constitutional rights.

Younger v. Harris,[37] one of the leading cases construing the comity requirements, explains that generally no constitutional right is infringed by a statute forbidding injunctions of state proceedings because "the moving party has an adequate remedy at law and will not suffer irreparable injury if

---

27. Compare Falbo v. United States, 320 U.S. 549, 554 (1944) (no judicial review of Selective Service Classification), with Estep v. United States, 327 U.S. 114, 119–20, 123–25 (1946) (judicial review of Selective Service Classification after acceptance for induction permissible despite silence of Act.) See generally H. Hart & H. Wechsler's, The Federal Courts and the Federal System, 365–72 (2d ed. 1973).

28. 393 U.S. 233 (1968).

29. Military Selective Service Act of 1967, § 10(b)(3), 50 U.S.C.A.App. § 460(b)(3).

30. 393 U.S. at 243 n. 6 (Harlan, J., concurring).

31. See also 114 Cong.Rec. 10888 (1968). Senator Tydings submitted opinions of legal scholars that a proposed bill eliminating federal review of the admission of confessions into evidence by state courts and federal habeas jurisdiction over state prisoners was arbitrary and would violate the equal protection guarantees included in the right to due process. Id. at 10888–97.

32. 28 U.S.C.A. § 2283 provides:

> "A court of the United States may not grant an injunction to stay proceedings in a State court except as expressly authorized by Act of Congress, or where necessary in aid of its jurisdiction, or to protect or effectuate its judgments."

33. See generally Mitchum v. Foster, 407 U.S. 225 (1972); Amalgamated Clothing Workers v. Richmond Bros. Co., 348 U.S. 511 (1955); see also, Lynch v. Household Finance Corp., 405 U.S. 538 (1972).

34. Mitchum v. Foster, 407 U.S. 225 (1972).

35. 407 U.S. at 242.

36. 407 U.S. at 243. See generally section IV, D, 5, infra ("Abstention, Comity, and Federal Court Injunctions of State Court Proceedings"). See also, M. Redish, Federal Jurisdiction: Tensions in the Allocation of Judicial Power 259–90 (1980).

37. 401 U.S. 37 (1971) (Black, J.). See, also, the companion cases of Samuels v. Mackell, 401 U.S. 66 (1971); Boyle v. Landry, 401 U.S. 77 (1971); Perez v. Ledesma, 401 U.S. 82 (1971); Dyson v. Stein, 401 U.S. 200 (1971); Byrne v. Karalexis, 401 U.S. 216 (1971).

denied equitable relief." [38] However, the Court made clear that comity considerations could not be applied to prevent the issuance of an injunction where it is necessary to prevent irreparable constitutional injury. It noted, quoting *Fenner v. Boykin:* [39]

> *Ex parte Young*, 209 U.S. 123, and the following cases have established the doctrine that *when absolutely necessary for protection of constitutional rights* courts of the United States have power to enjoin state officers from instituting criminal actions. But this may not be done except under extraordinary circumstances where the danger of irreparable loss is both great and immediate. [40]

The Court has allowed injunctions to issue when necessary to protect constitutional rights. For example: if a state law is " 'flagrantly and patently violative of express constitutional prohibitions,' " [41] or there is "bad faith, harassment, or any other unusual circumstance that would call for equitable relief." [42] *Younger*, though limiting the overly broad dictum in an earlier case,[43] approved the issuance of an injunction if the facts would indicate that equitable relief

was necessary to prevent irreparable injury to constitutional rights.[44]

Another issue concerning Congressional power to control jurisdiction involves the power of Congress to restrict challenges to regulatory action to certain courts and subject to certain procedures. Although two World War II cases could be read to recognize a broad power to restrict jurisdiction in this way, that interpretation is hardly compelled.

In *Lockerty v. Phillips* [45] the Supreme Court upheld a special statutory scheme set up during World War II to control inflation. Under the Emergency Price Control Act of 1942 an Emergency Court of Appeals was created and vested with exclusive jurisdiction to determine the validity of any regulation, order, or price schedule issued under that Act; the litigants had to follow a specified procedure. Judgments of that court could be reviewed by the Supreme Court.[46] In *Yakus v. United States*,[47] the Court upheld the constitutionality of the provisions of the Emergency Price Control Act, which was construed to deprive litigants of the opportu-

---

38. 401 U.S. at 43–44.

39. 271 U.S. 240 (1926).

40. 401 U.S. at 45 (emphasis added).

41. 401 U.S. at 53. See also, Mitchum v. Foster, 407 U.S. 225, 230 (1972).

42. 401 U.S. at 54. See also, Mitchum v. Foster, 407 U.S. 225, 230 (1972). In Perez v. Ledesma, 401 U.S. 82, 85 (1971) the Court stated:

"Only in cases of proven harassment or prosecutions undertaken by state officials in bad faith without hope of obtaining a valid conviction and perhaps in other extraordinary circumstances where irreparable injury can be shown is federal injunctive relief against pending state prosecutions appropriate."

43. Dombrowski v. Pfister, 380 U.S. 479 (1965).

44. 401 U.S. at 47–49. See section IV, D, 5, infra ("Abstention, Comity, and Federal Court Injunctions of State Court Proceedings"), for further discussion of these issues.

See also, Califano v. Sanders, 430 U.S. 99, 109 (1977), interpreting a statute to allow a very limited review of Social Security cases if there is no constitutional question raised. The Court noted that "when constitutional questions are in issue, the availability of judicial review is presumed, and we will not read a statutory scheme to take the 'extraordinary' step of foreclosing jurisdiction unless Congress' intent to do so is manifested by 'clear and convincing' evidence." The Court cited

Weinberger v. Salfi, 422 U.S. 749, 762 (1975) and Johnson v. Robison, 415 U.S. 361, 366–67 (1974). The *Sanders* Court also held that section 10 of the Administrative Procedure Act does not afford to the federal district courts an implied grant of subject matter jurisdiction.

Cf. Oklahoma Natural Gas Co. v. Russell, 261 U.S. 290, 293 (1923) (Holmes, J.) ("[T]he District Court had jurisdiction and a duty to try the question whether preliminary injunctions should issue."); Pacific Telephone & Telegraph Co. v. Kuykendall, 265 U.S. 196, 204–05 (1924) (Taft, C.J.) ("Under such circumstances [where the utility alleges confiscatory rates with no stay available under state law] comity yields to constitutional right, and the fact that the legislative fixing of rates has not been concluded will not prevent a federal court of equity from suspending the daily confiscation, if it finds the case to justify it.").

45. 319 U.S. 182 (1943). See also, M. Redish, Federal Jurisdiction: Tensions in the Allocation of Judicial Power 7–35 (1980).

46. 319 U.S. at 187–89.

47. 321 U.S. 414 (1944). The Court did not reach the issue of whether the Act, to the extent it prohibited all interlocutory relief by the Emergency Court, was unconstitutional. See generally, Price Control in a Cold War—A Symposium, 19 Law & Contemp.Prob. 475 (1954).

nity to attack the validity of a price regulation in a criminal prosecution violating the Act. The Court said:

> Congress, through its power to define the jurisdiction of inferior courts and to create such courts for the exercise of the judicial power, could, subject to other constitutional limitations, create the Emergency Court of Appeals, give to it *exclusive* equity jurisdiction to determine the validity of price regulations prescribed by the Administrator, and *foreclose* any further or other consideration of the validity of a regulation as a defense to a prosecution for its violation.[48]

The extent of Congress' power to prescribe certain procedures which, if not followed, would preclude one from attacking administrative regulations and orders was not entirely clear after *Yakus*. The Court suggested a narrow holding in other parts of its opinion. Thus, it emphasized the special circumstances of wartime inflation.[49] The Court also noted that it was not deciding whether one charged with criminal violation of a duly promulgated regulation could assert a defense that the regulation was unconstitutional on its face, or whether one charged and convicted of a regulation could be deprived of the defense that the regulation was invalid if that person had been diligently seeking a determination of its validity pursuant to the statutory procedure.[50]

Despite the *Yakus* decision, the Court will not readily interpret a Congressional statutory scheme to limit claims to specific courts, as illustrated by *Adamo Wrecking Co. v. United States.*[51] Petitioner was indicted for violating a section of the Clean Air Act of 1970, which makes it a criminal offense to knowingly violate an "emission standard" promulgated by the Administrator of the EPA. Section 307(b) of the Clean Air Act provided a 30-day limitation period following promulgation for challenges to "any emission standard promulgated under section 112" and required all such petitions

to be filed in the District of Columbia Circuit. Further, any action of the Administration that could have been so reviewed could not later be reviewed in a civil or criminal proceeding for enforcement.

The District Court granted petitioner's motion to dismiss the indictment on the ground that the regulation it violated was not really an "emission standard" within the meaning of section 112(c) of the Act. The Sixth Circuit reversed, holding that Congress intended by section 307(b)(2) to preclude petitioner from questioning whether a regulation ostensibly promulgated under section 112(c) was in fact an emission standard. The Sixth Circuit relied heavily on *Yakus*.

The Supreme Court reversed the Sixth Circuit and held in *Adamo Wrecking* that a defendant may assert that a regulation is not really an "emission standard" and thus not within section 112(c) as a defense in an enforcement proceeding: the 30 day limitations period would not bar this claim.

The Court found that the statutory scheme of *Yakus*, which showed clear congressional intent to require all actions of the Price Administrator to be reviewed only in the Emergency Court of Appeals, differed substantially from the scheme of the Clean Air Act, which precludes review of only certain, limited, types of regulations of the EPA Administrator.[52] The Court noted that the complexity of the Clean Air Act statutory scheme, which does not preclude review of most types of regulations, showed Congressional intent to impose the more stringent penalties on violators of "emissions standards" only. Because Congress did not intend to empower the Administrator to make a regulation an "emission standards" by his mere designation, the Government was required to prove, in a prosecution, that the regulation violated was really an emission standard.[53] Underlying the Court's rea-

---

48. 321 U.S. at 443 (emphasis added).

49. 321 U.S. at 439.

50. 321 U.S. at 446–47.

51. 434 U.S. 275 (1978).
Cf. n. 44, supra.

52. 434 U.S. at 279.

53. 434 U.S. at 284.

soning seems to have been a fear that precluding review would create potentially widespread liability of many small businesses.[54]

In a concurring opinion Justice Powell reached the question of whether *Yakus* foreclosed a due process challenge to the Government's interpretation of the Clean Air Act. He noted that *Yakus* might be viewed as an exercise of the war powers. Present day environmental concerns "are not comparable—in terms of an emergency justifying the short-cutting of normal due process rights—to the need for national mobilization in wartime of economic as well as military activity." [55] Powell also emphasized that the 30-day limitation on judicial review imposed by the Clean Air Act would usually not afford adequate time for challenge to the regulations being promulgated. It would be "totally unrealistic" to believe that the many small businesses around the country, or more than a fraction of all persons and entities affected by these regulations, would have access to and knowledge of the Federal Registers and its daily publication of regulations. Thus, even if a lower court were to conclude that a regulation is an emission standard and that the preclusion provisions of section 307(b) would apply, Powell understood the majority opinion to imply no view "as to the constitutional validity of section 307(b) in the context of a criminal prosecution." [56]

IV. OTHER LIMITATIONS ON JUDICIAL REVIEW

A. The Eleventh Amendment

1. Introduction and Historical Note

The eleventh amendment states that:

> The Judicial power of the United States shall not be construed to extend to any suit in law or equity, commenced or prosecuted against one of the United States by Citizens of another State, or by Citizens or Subjects of any Foreign State.

This provision acts as a jurisdictional bar to suits brought against state governments in the federal courts.[1] It does not grant the states true immunity, for it does not exempt them from the restrictions of federal law; it only means that some types of suits against them must be brought in state rather than federal court. This distinction raises extremely important and complex issues. Supreme Court interpretations of the amendment have involved both expansions and restrictions of the literal application of its wording. An in-depth consideration of this jurisdictional point is beyond the scope of this text, but the history of the amendment [2] and rulings under it [3] have been the subject of a number of books and articles to which one can turn for a more thorough treatment. Here we will present only a brief sketch of the import of the amendment so that the reader may consider it as a part of the overview of jurisdiction.

The eleventh amendment was proposed and ratified as a reaction to the Supreme

---

54. 434 U.S. at 282, n. 2.

55. 434 U.S. at 290 (Powell, J., concurring).

56. 434 U.S. at 291 (Powell, J., concurring).

1. See San Diego Unified Port District v. Gianturco, 457 F.Supp. 283, 288 (S.D.Cal.1978) (Schwartz, C.J., quoting an earlier edition of this treatise).

2. C. Jacobs, The Eleventh Amendment and Sovereign Immunity (1972); Nowak, The Scope of Congressional Power to Create Causes of Action Against State Governments and the History of the Eleventh and Fourteenth Amendments, 75 Colum.L.Rev. 1413 (1975). For an analysis of the history and application of the eleventh amendment in connection with an argument

that the amendment granted no constitutional right of sovereign immunity to the states but only allowed for the continuation of a common law doctrine of sovereign immunity, see Field, The Eleventh Amendment and Other Sovereign Immunity Doctrines: Part One, 126 U.Pa.L.Rev. 515 (1978). Field, The Eleventh Amendment and Other Sovereign Immunity Doctrines: Congressional Imposition of Suit Upon the States, 126 U.Pa.L.Rev. 1203 (1978).

3. 13 Wright, Miller & Cooper, Federal Practice and Procedure: Jurisdiction § 3524 (1975); Note, A Practical View of the Eleventh Amendment—Lower Court Interpretations and the Supreme Court's Reaction, 61 Georgetown L.J. 1473 (1973).

Court's decision in *Chisholm v. Georgia*,[4] which was an original action instituted against Georgia in the Supreme Court by Alexander Chisholm as the executor of the estate of a South Carolina decedent, Robert Farquar. During the revolutionary period, Farquar had delivered supplies to Georgia under a contract which remained unpaid at his death. Georgia never contested the debt but, instead, refused to appear on the grounds that the federal court had no jurisdiction over such a suit. After delaying the case for a term so that Georgia might have fair notice of the Court's intention to proceed, the Supreme Court heard the plaintiff's counsel and reached a decision. By a vote of 4 to 1 the Court decided that it had jurisdiction in the case and entered a judgment by default against Georgia.[5] The use of a majority opinion for the Court had not yet been developed and the justices delivered their individual opinions *seriatim*. None of the justices relied on a congressional grant of jurisdiction. The four voting together rested their decisions on a general power under Article III and the concept of states having only limited sovereignty in a national democracy.[6] The one dissenting justice refused to find any federal court jurisdiction over state governments absent congressional authorization.[7] The decision is difficult to evaluate since the history of Article III simply does not resolve the issue of federal jurisdiction over debt actions against states.[8]

The feeling of the populace, if not the historical or legal precedents, soon become clear. The eleventh amendment was proposed immediately after the *Chisholm* decision and it was ratified in less than five years. The reasons for this reaction may have included some popular opinion about the meaning of Article III, theoretical problems concerning the available judicial procedures against a sovereign, if subordinate, unit in the federal system, and fear of suits by Tory creditors.[9] While the individual state debts to British citizens and loyalists were not great, increasing tensions with Great Britain created fear of debts arising from a new conflict and an animosity towards paying any such claims.[10] Thus the proposed amendment was quickly approved by all political factions.

Unfortunately, knowing this historical background does not prove of great help in resolving particular problems under the amendment. The provision passed with such little debate that its history is silent on a great many issues. All that can be said with certainty is that the amendment was to bar federal jurisdiction in suits by non-citizens against a state for the payment of debts and damages for past actions absent specific congressional authorization of the federal cause of action. That is all that was necessary to reverse the *Chisholm* ruling. The application of the provision to suits by citizens of the defendant state, its nonapplication to actions to force prospective compliance with federal law, and the status of Congressional grants of jurisdiction, are all problems of judicial interpretation of the role of such a provision in our federal system.[11]

The earliest interpretation of the amendment, by Chief Justice Marshall, applied it as a narrow reversal of the *Chisholm* form of federal suit. In *Cohens v. Virginia*,[12] the opinion by Marshall indicated that the amendment had no part in suits other than

4. 2 U.S. (2 Dall.) 419 (1793).

5. Id. at 479.

6. The opinions are analyzed in Nowak, supra note 2, at 1431–33.

7. 2 U.S. (2 Dall.) 419, 432–35 (opinion of Iredell, J.). It should be noted that Justice Iredell was the only contrary vote but that the opinion was not labeled as a "dissent."

8. Nowak, supra note 2, at 1422–30.

9. C. Jacobs, supra note 2, at 67–72, I. C. Warren, The Supreme Court in United States History 91–99 (1922).

10. Nowak, supra note 2, at 1433–41.

11. Nowak, supra note 2; Tribe, Intergovernmental Immunities in Litigation, Taxation and Regulation: Separation of Powers Issues in Controversies About Federalism, 89 Harv.L.Rev. 682 (1976); Baker, Federalism and the Eleventh Amendment, 48 Colo.L.Rev. 139 (1977).

12. 19 U.S. (6 Wheat.) 264 (1821).

debt actions and held it inapplicable to suits brought by the state against a private individual such as criminal proceedings. Marshall also wrote for the Court in *Osborn v. Bank of the United States* [13] stating that the amendment was inapplicable whenever the state was not a party of record. The interpretations were to be narrowed in future years, but there was no significant exploration of these issues until the 1880's and thus Marshall's opinions are the only judicial exposition of the meaning of the amendment at a time close to its adoption.

2. *An Outline of the Current Rules*

The eleventh amendment prohibits federal courts from exercising jurisdiction over state governments in certain circumstances. It does not bar state courts from asserting jurisdiction over their own state government or the government of another state. In *Nevada v. Hall*,[14] the Court held that a suit brought in the courts of one state against another state did not violate constitutional principles of federalism or state comity. *Hall* involved California residents who were injured in an automobile accident in California when an employee of the University of Nevada, while on official business and driving an official Nevada vehicle, collided with their car. The California plaintiffs brought suit in the California state court and named the state of Nevada as a party defendant. The California courts ruled that, as a matter of California law, such a suit was proper; the Supreme Court upheld the state judgment on the ground that the suit did not violate the Federal Constitution. Justice Stevens, writing for six members of the Court in *Hall*, first reviewed the history of the doctrine of sovereign immunity and its impact

on the framing of the Constitution.[15] Justice Stevens concluded that traditional notions of sovereign immunity do not extend beyond a bar to suits against the sovereign in the sovereign's own courts. The majority found that the framers of the Federal Constitution were concerned only with the aspect of sovereign immunity involving suits brought in federal courts against the states. Justice Stevens proceeded to find that nothing in the full faith and credit clause of the Constitution required California to give effect to Nevada's statutory provisions concerning its sovereign immunity because those provisions were in conflict with California's public policy to compensate resident motorists injured by accidents on California highways.[16] Respect for the sovereign immunity of Nevada in California courts, the Justice found, was merely a matter of comity and in no sense constitutionally required. Justice Stevens, however, did indicate in a footnote that some constitutional constraints might be placed on the exercise of jurisdiction over a sister state if the court action posed a "substantial threat to our constitutional system of cooperative federalism." [17]

The eleventh amendment acts as a bar to federal jurisdiction over state governments, as such, when they are sued by anyone other than the federal government or another state. The bar applies to all types of suits for damages or retroactive relief for past wrongs, but it is not an effective barrier to forcing the state to prospectively comply with federal law. If the amendment applies, the suit may be heard in federal court with the consent of the state and, in limited circumstances, the state may be held to an implied waiver of its immunity. Congress may create federal causes of action against

13. 22 U.S. (Wheat.) 738 (1824).

14. 440 U.S. 410 (1979).

15. 440 U.S. at 415–21.

16. 440 U.S. at 424.

17. 440 U.S. at 424 n. 24. Justice Blackmun authored a dissenting opinion in which he expressed concern over the effect that the Court's ruling would have on interstate relations and argued that the Constitution implicitly forbade suits against one state in the courts

of another state. 440 U.S. at 427–32 (Blackmun, J., dissenting). Justice Rehnquist and Chief Justice Burger joined Justice Blackmun's opinion; Justice Rehnquist also authored a separate dissent, in which the Chief Justice joined, that attempted to demonstrate that the Court's ruling was in conflict both with prior rulings of the Court and with "the logic of the constitutional plan itself." 440 U.S. at 433 (Rehnquist, J., dissenting).

states without their consent when it acts pursuant to its power to enforce the fourteenth amendment. The extent to which the eleventh amendment restricts other Congressional powers has not yet been determined.

In resolving issues under the eleventh amendment one should ask five basic questions: (1) is the plaintiff one to whom the amendment applies? (2) is the suit truly against the state? (3) is the suit seeking relief in a manner that is barred by the amendment? (4) has the state waived its immunity? (5) is there a congressional statute which can override the immunity in this area?

First, one must determine if the plaintiff is subject to the jurisdictional bar. By its own terms the amendment bars suits by citizens of other states or foreign nationals.[18] Additionally the Court held in *Hans v. Louisiana*[19] that the amendment by implication also bars suits by citizens of the defendant state. Thus all private plaintiffs are subject to the amendment. However, if the state

brings an action against the private person, that suit does not come under the restrictions.[20] Similarly, a state may be sued by another state[21] or the United States.[22] The amendment does not bar jurisdiction by federal courts when a suit is brought by the federal government even where it is suing the state to protect private individuals. Thus the Secretary of Labor of the United States may bring a federal suit against a state government to establish the rights of individual employees whose personal suit would be barred.[23]

The second issue concerns whether a "state" is being sued. Suit is barred only when the state government is the defendant. Agencies of the state come under this heading, but its political subdivisions do not. Thus municipal corporations,[24] counties[25] and school boards[26] may be sued in federal court without raising an eleventh amendment issue. If an entity is found to be merely the instrumentality of state government it shares the immunity, but it has none if it is a politically independent unit.[27] Similarly, state officers may be sued in their per-

18. See, e.g., Principality of Monaco v. State of Mississippi, 292 U.S. 313 (1934); Ex parte State of New York, 256 U.S. 490 (1921); Fitts v. McGee, 172 U.S. 516 (1899).

19. 134 U.S. 1 (1890). For an examination of the historical background of the Supreme Court's nineteenth century decisions interpreting the eleventh amendment, see Orth, The Eleventh Amendment and The End of Reconstruction: The Fair Fame and Name of Louisiana, 2 Tulane Lawyer 2 (1980); Orth, The Eleventh Amendment and the North Carolina State Debt, 59 N.C.L.Rev. 747 (1981).

20. Cohens v. Virginia, 19 U.S. (6 Wheat.) 264 (1821).

21. South Dakota v. North Carolina, 192 U.S. 286, 315–21 (1904).

22. United States v. Mississippi, 380 U.S. 128, 140–41 (1965).

23. Employees of the Dept. of Public Health & Welfare v. Missouri Dept. of Public Health & Welfare, 411 U.S. 279, 285–6 (1973). Cf. EEOC v. Wyoming, 103 S.Ct. 1054 (1983). However, the Court has held that a suit is barred if a plaintiff state is merely acting as an agent to collect and distribute an amount owed to its citizens by the defendant state. New Hampshire v. Louisiana, 108 U.S. 76 (1883).

24. Maybanks v. Ingraham, 378 F.Supp. 913 (E.D.Pa.1974); cf. Port of Seattle v. Oregon & Washington RR. Co., 255 U.S. 56 (1921).

The Supreme Court has held that a municipal corporation is a person, as that term is used by 42 U.S.C.A. § 1983 so that it can be sued in either state or federal court for violating the federal rights of an individual. Monell v. Department of Social Services, 436 U.S. 658 (1978) overruling part of Monroe v. Pape, 365 U.S. 167 (1961).

25. Lincoln County v. Luning, 133 U.S. 529 (1890).

26. Mt. Healthy City School District Bd. of Education v. Doyle, 429 U.S. 274 (1977). The status of a state college or university remains unclear, see generally, Calgue, Suing the University "Black Box" Under the Civil Rights Act of 1871, 62 Iowa L.Rev. 337 (1976); Note, Immunity of Teachers, School Administrators, School Board Members, and School Districts from Suit Under Section 1983 of Civil Rights Act, 1976 U.Ill.L. Forum 1129 (1976).

27. In Lake Country Estates, Inc. v. Tahoe Regional Planning Agency, 440 U.S. 391 (1979) the Court by a 6 to 3 vote held that a defendant created by interstate compact agency was not immune from suit in federal court under the eleventh amendment. 440 U.S. at 402–03. The majority opinion by Justice Stevens did not conclude that all agencies created by interstate compact would be subject to suit in federal court; the opinion merely found that the defendant agency, due to its composition, structure, and function, was a "political subdivision" of the states and not an "arm" of the states. 440 U.S. at 401–03. As such, the agency enjoyed no immunity from suit under the eleventh

sonal capacity for damages in a federal action, because the amendment grants them no immunity from federal action even where they are acting in their official capacity.[28] However, if the suit actually requests that the officer be ordered to pay funds from the state treasury for wrongful acts of the state, or return property in the state's possession, the suit will be barred because the state is the real party in interest.[29] There is no longer any requirement that the state be a named party of record. Thus, if a suit requests that the head of a state department of welfare be ordered to personally pay damages the suit is permissible, but if it requests an order requiring him to pay past due amounts from the state treasury it is barred.[30] The one exception to the real party in interest rule arises in connection with the next issue.

The third issue concerns the nature of relief sought in the federal action. Where the action is one for damages, past debts or retroactive relief of any type, it is barred whether it is brought in law, equity, or admiralty.[31] Thus federal suits at law for return of improperly collected state taxes are barred.[32] Similarly, when the Court of Appeals for the Seventh Circuit attempted to order the payment of illegally withheld welfare payments under an "equitable-restitution" theory it was reversed by the Supreme Court.[33]

The one exception to the amendment based on the form of action is that a private person may bring an equitable action to force state officers to comply with federal law in the future even though they will be required to spend state funds to so comply. The distinction had its genesis in *Ex parte Young*,[34] wherein the Court held that a state officer could be forbidden in a federal suit from enforcing state law. This holding was based on the fiction that the officer could not be given authority to violate federal law so that the suit was not against the state authority itself. Today the fiction is maintained to the extent that a state officer must be the named defendant in such a suit. The use of prospective relief by a federal court will be upheld even if it involves the ordering of the official to use state funds. Although the state is the real party in interest, the eleventh amendment was never intended, nor held, to grant the states the ability to subvert the supremacy clause by granting immunity to the states or their officials from judicial orders to comply with federal law.[35] Thus, in the same suit in which the Court struck the lower federal court's order to the state officer to pay past due welfare checks, it upheld the order which forced him to disburse state payments in conformity with federal laws in the future.[36] The Supreme Court unanimously held that state officers could be subject to a federal cause of action, and ordered by a federal court, to force

amendment. The Court also held that members of the defendant agency were absolutely immune from suit for actions taken in their legislative capacity. 440 U.S. 402–06. Justices Brennan, Marshall, and Blackmun authored separate opinions dissenting in part from the Court's holding. These justices were in accord with the Court's eleventh amendment ruling as it applied to the facts of the case, but did not believe that the immunity issue had properly been resolved by the Court. 440 U.S. at 406–09 (dissenting opinions of Brennan, Marshall, & Blackmun, JJ.).

28. Scheuer v. Rhodes, 416 U.S. 232 (1974).

29. Edelman v. Jordan, 415 U.S. 651 (1974); In re Ayres, 123 U.S. 443 (1887).

30. Edelman v. Jordan, 415 U.S. 651 (1974).

31. Concerning admiralty suits, see, Ex parte Madrazzo, 32 U.S. (7 Pet.) 627 (1833); Platoro Ltd. v. Unidentified Remains of a Vessel, 508 F.2d 1113 (5th Cir. 1975).

32. Ford Motor Co. v. Department of Treasury of the State of Indiana, 323 U.S. 459 (1945).

33. Edelman v. Jordan, 415 U.S. 651 (1974).

34. 209 U.S. 123 (1908).

35. Nowak, The Scope of Congressional Power to Create Causes of Action Against State Governments and the History of the Eleventh and Fourteenth Amendments, 75 Colum.L.Rev. 1413, 1445–56, 1455–58 (1975). The Supreme Court recently reaffirmed the principle that the eleventh amendment does not bar suits in federal courts against state officials for the purpose of obtaining injunctive relief against the enforcement of unconstitutional state laws. Ray v. Atlantic Richfield Co., 435 U.S. 151, 156–57 n. 6 (1978).

36. Edelman v. Jordan, 415 U.S. 651 (1974). The doctrine was so well accepted by this time that the state did not contest the propriety of the injunction.

them to disburse state funds to institute educational programs in connection with a suit to desegregate public schools.[37] If state officials do not comply in good faith with the federal court order of prospective relief, the federal courts may impose monetary penalties upon either the particular state officers or the state itself.[38]

If a plaintiff seeks a federal court order to state government officials to transfer to the plaintiff specifically identified pieces of property there will be an issue in the case regarding the applicability of the eleventh amendment. If the action is brought against the state government itself or if the plaintiff is merely seeking compensation for the state treasury based on a claim that the state has improperly taken funds from him or refused to pay money to him, the suit will be barred by the amendment. However, if the plaintiff brings suit against the state officials and claims that the officials are acting unconstitutionally and beyond the scope of their authority by having in their possession specific pieces of property owned by the plaintiff, a federal court may be able to attach the property and adjudicate all parties' rights to the property in an *in rem* proceeding.[39]

This exception to the amendment's bar to federal court jurisdiction over state governments, allowing federal courts to order state

officers to comply with federal law, does not open the federal courts to all those who seek judgments against state governments that might be described as something other than "retroactive" relief. Federal courts are not allowed to adjudicate claims against state governments unless the cause of action falls into a specific category of actions that the Supreme Court has held not to be barred by the amendment. Thus, the executor of an estate could not use the Federal Interpleader Act, 28 U.S.C. § 1335, as a jurisdictional basis for forcing officials of two state governments to litigate in federal court the states' inconsistent claims of jurisdiction to tax the estate represented by the executor.[40]

The fourth issue is whether the state has waived its eleventh amendment immunity for purposes of the particular suit. The jurisdictional bar is not absolute and the state may consent to the suit in federal court. However, to constitute an express waiver the state must do more than merely allow suits to be brought in courts already having jurisdiction. The Supreme Court has read a state statutory provision permitting taxpayers to sue the state for tax refunds to allow suits only in state courts.[41] But if the state clearly indicates that such suits are generally permissible, or that an agency or corporation otherwise exempt may be sued in its own name, the waiver will stand.

---

37. Milliken v. Bradley (Milliken II), 433 U.S. 267 (1977).

38. See Hutto v. Finney, 437 U.S. 678 (1978), holding that a federal district court was empowered to impose financial penalties, including attorneys fees, on state agencies when officials in those agencies have in bad faith failed to comply with orders of prospective or injunctive relief. As such awards serve only the purpose of a remedial fine similar to a civil contempt penalty, they are allowed as ancillary to the granting of the prospective relief.

39. Florida Dept. of State v. Treasure Salvors, Inc., 102 S.Ct. 3304 (1982). Except for the fact that suits requesting return of specific items of property do not involve an extension of federal court jurisdiction over a state treasury, it is difficult to distinguish this type of case from cases wherein the Supreme Court has held that plaintiffs could not use a restitution theory to justify federal court jurisdiction over a cause of action wherein the plaintiff sought the return of money which the state allegedly had taken or withheld from him on

an unconstitutional basis. *Treasure Salvors* was decided by a 5–4 vote and without a majority opinion. It is possible that the Supreme Court in future years will find that the *Treasure Salvors* decision is used by lower federal courts to justify federal court jurisdiction over cases in which plaintiffs seek compensation from a state treasury for state interference with their property rights. If so, the Court may have to clarify, restrict, or reverse the *Treasure Salvors* ruling. See Florida Dept. of State v. Treasure Salvors, Inc., 102 S.Ct. 3304, 3323 (1982) (White, J., concurring in part and dissenting in part, joined by Powell, Rehnquist and O'Connor, JJ.)

40. Cory v. White, 102 S.Ct. 2325 (1982).

41. Ford Motor Co. v. Department of Treasury of the State of Indiana, 323 U.S. 459 (1945). See also Florida Dept. of Health & Rehabilitation Service v. Florida Nursing Home Ass'n, 450 U.S. 147, 149–50 (1981) (per curiam) (waiver of sovereign immunity for state agency does not constitute waiver of eleventh amendment immunity).

Even if a state does not wish to waive its immunity, under some circumstances the state's actions may imply a waiver. Mere appearance in federal court by the state does not waive its immunity.[42] The state's failure to plead immunity at the trial level does not constitute a waiver; the eleventh amendment is a jurisdictional bar that can be raised on appeal.[43] The Supreme Court can only be said to have implied a waiver of state immunity in two cases, and the first of these may be read as only upholding the principle that interpretation of state waivers is a federal issue. In *Petty v. Tennessee-Missouri Bridge Commission* [44] the Court found that a state waived its immunity from suit for actions relating to an agency created by an interstate compact. The Court found that a rather vague provision in the compact constituted a waiver of immunity. While the majority opinion is not clear on this point, it would appear only to hold that the terms of federally approved compacts are to be interpreted under federal law.[45] Yet this case does offer some basis for finding that states may waive their immunity by willfully engaging in federally regulated activities; the extent to which such activities constitute a waiver should also be determined by federal standards.

The Supreme Court did find an implied waiver in *Parden v. Terminal R.R. Co.*[46] In *Parden,* a state took over the operation of a railroad after the existence of extensive federal regulation of railroad liability. The Court held that the state owned railroad was subject to federal employees' compensation laws and could be sued in a federal court by individuals claiming benefits under such laws. Operation of the railroad constituted the waiver of immunity. Operating a federally regulated enterprise does not automatically waive a states' immunity and, since the *Parden* decision, the Supreme Court has been reluctant to infer a waiver. Today it is unlikely that an implied waiver will be found unless the state has taken actions that are admittedly subject to federal regulations and which are not essential state functions.[47] Congress may require a state to waive immunity in order to be eligible for federal funds, but a state's receipt of the funds will constitute a waiver only if Congress explicitly required such a waiver [48] or explicitly granted a right of action to individuals.[49] Neither the state's participation in a federal program in itself nor a concomitant agreement to obey federal law constitutes a waiver of eleventh amendment immunity.[50]

The final issue is whether Congressional grants of specific jurisdiction to federal courts are subject to the eleventh amendment. The Court has held that federal statutes based upon the Congressional power to enforce the fourteenth amendment are not subject to these jurisdictional rules,[51] a posi-

---

42. Clark v. Barnard, 108 U.S. 436 (1883).

43. Edelman v. Jordan, 415 U.S. 651 (1974). The state may waive its immunity by appearing in federal court and stating through its counsel that it will consent to court orders awarding damages or other forms of retroactive relief to the plaintiff if its position on the merits of the litigation is rejected by the court. See Toll v. Moreno, 102 S.Ct. 2977 (1982).

44. 359 U.S. 275 (1959).

45. Agencies created by interstate compacts would seem to be sufficiently independent from the state governments which form and fund them so that they may be considered a political subdivision of the state governments and not entitled to protection by the eleventh amendment. The determination of whether the eleventh amendment restricts federal court jurisdiction over such an agency will be left for individual, case-by-case determinations. See Lake Country Estates, Inc. v. Tahoe Regional Planning Agency, 440 U.S. 391 (1979), note 27 supra.

46. 377 U.S. 184 (1964).

47. The Court has held that waiver of this right by states should not be implied more readily than the waiver of any personal constitutional right, Edelman v. Jordan, 415 U.S. 651 (1974). For analysis regarding the proper tests for the implication of a waiver, see Nowak, supra note 30, at 1446–50; Comment, Implied Waiver of a State's Eleventh Amendment Immunity, 1974 Duke L.J. 925.

48. Employees of the Dept. of Public Health & Welfare v. Missouri Dept. of Public Health & Welfare, 411 U.S. 279 (1973).

49. Edelman v. Jordan, 415 U.S. 651 (1974).

50. Florida Dept. of Health & Rehabilitation Service v. Florida Nursing Home Ass'n, 450 U.S. 147, 150 (1981) (per curiam), rehearing denied 451 U.S. 933, on remand 648 F.2d 241.

51. Fitzpatrick v. Bitzer, 427 U.S. 445 (1976).

tion clearly supported by history.[52] Some authors have argued that Congress should be free to create federal causes of action against state governments under any of its enumerated powers.[53] Such arguments are based on the premise that Congress is the most institutionally capable entity to balance the competing interests in the federal system.[54] Others see no reason not to trust the justices to set proper standards for the exercise of both state and federal authority [55] even though the Court's last experiment in restricting Congressional power to protect the states literally ended in disaster.[56] The current justices have ruled that they will overturn federal acts under the tenth amendment insofar as they are applied in a manner that unnecessarily restricts the freedom of state governments,[57] which indicates that there may not be a general exception from the eleventh amendment for all Congressional grants of federal jurisdiction.

In *Hutto v. Finney,*[58] the Supreme Court found that the Civil Rights Attorney's Fees Awards Act of 1976 [59] applies to state governments. Congress enacted this statute pursuant to its power to enforce the fourteenth amendment and so neither the tenth nor the eleventh amendment stands as a barrier to awarding attorney's fees against state governments if they are otherwise suable on the basis of a federal civil rights cause of action.[60] Indeed, a federal court may be able to award attorney's fees to a party that prevails on a statutory claim against the state which is pendant to a substantial constitutional claim against state officials.[61]

While the Court has been liberal in its construction of the Civil Rights Attorney's Fees Awards Act when states are otherwise suable in a federal court, it refused to create a general cause of action against state governments for the violation of federal rights as it found that state governments were not "persons" who were suable under 42 U.S.C.A. § 1983. That section creates a cause of action against "persons" who deprive others of federally guaranteed rights.

In *Quern v. Jordan* [62] the Court reaffirmed the holding of *Edelman v. Jordan* [63] that suits against states are permissible in federal court pursuant to § 1983 only to the extent that prospective, and not retrospective, relief is sought by naming a state official as the nominal defendant. Because the eleventh amendment does not bar suits seeking only prospective relief, such suits are

---

52. See, Nowak, The Scope of Congressional Power to Create Causes of Action Against State Governments and the History of the Eleventh and Fourteenth Amendments, 75 Colum.L.Rev. 1413 (1975).

53. Nowak, supra note 52; Tribe, Intergovernmental Immunities in Litigation, Taxation, and Regulation: Separation of Powers Issues in Controversies About Federalism, 89 Harv.L.Rev. 682 (1976).

54. This position relies on the principles previously examined and established by Professor Wechsler. See, Wechsler, The Political Safeguards of Federalism: The Role of the States in the Composition and Selection of the National Government, 54 Colum.L.Rev. 543 (1954).

55. Baker, Federalism and the Eleventh Amendment, 48 Colo.L.Rev. 139 (1977).

56. See Chapter 4, Section III concerning the Court's attempt to take such a position by restricting the federal commerce power from 1887 to 1937.

57. Compare National League of Cities v. Usery, 426 U.S. 833 (1976) with EEOC v. Wyoming, 103 S.Ct. 1054 (1983). These cases are examined in Chapter 4, Section IV, C, 4 of this treatise.

58. 437 U.S. 678 (1978).

59. 42 U.S.C.A. § 1988.

60. In Maine v. Thiboutot, 448 U.S. 1 (1980) the Court allowed an award of attorney's fees against a state government to a party prevailing on a federal, statutory, nonconstitutional claim under Section 1983 of the Civil Rights Act. The Court found that 42 U.S. C.A. § 1983 created a cause of action against persons who deprive others of any rights created by federal constitutional or statutory law. There was no eleventh amendment issue because the case had been brought in a state court. The Court was not required to determine in this case whether Section 1983 applied to state governments because the state did not appeal from the judgment against it.

61. Maher v. Gagne, 448 U.S. 122 (1980). See also New York Gaslight Club, Inc. v. Carey, 447 U.S. 54 (1980) (federal court action may be brought to recover an award of attorney's fees to the prevailing party in state administrative or judicial proceedings concerning federal civil rights. Congressional power under the fourteenth amendment overrides any possible state interest in denying attorney's fees awards in such cases).

62. 440 U.S. 332 (1979).

63. 415 U.S. 651 (1974), discussed at note 30, supra, and accompanying text.

proper under § 1983 when brought against state officials even though the state itself may be the real party in interest. The *Quern* Court held, however, that § 1983 did not manifest congressional intent to abrogate the states' eleventh amendment immunity from suit in federal court. Although the Court did not question congressional power to abrogate eleventh amendment immunity when legislating to implement the terms of the fourteenth amendment, the Court found that no intent to abrogate the immunity could be gleaned from the history of § 1983.[64]

The controversy in *Quern* resulted from the lower court ruling following the remand in *Edelman*. The district court ruled that members of the *Edelman* plaintiff class were entitled to receive notice that they had been deprived of welfare benefits in violation of applicable law, and ordered the state to mail such notices together with notices of the availability of state process by which the injured welfare recipients could seek a remedy. The Seventh Circuit Court of Appeals reversed the lower court because it found that the form of the notice purported to decide that the welfare recipients were in fact entitled to the lost benefits. However, the

Seventh Circuit found that a notice that merely advised the class members that they might have a claim and that state process was available to them would constitute permissible prospective relief.[65] Thus the precise issue presented to the Supreme Court was only whether a Federal court order mandating such notice violated the eleventh amendment bar to retrospective relief declared in *Edelman*.[66]

Justice Rehnquist's opinion for seven members of the Court in *Quern* first noted that cases decided subsequent to *Edelman* had been thought by some to cast doubt on the validity of the *Edelman* precedent.[67] The Justice repudiated any such implications, finding that nothing in cases subsequent to *Edelman* compelled alteration of the *Edelman* ruling. *Monell v. Department of Social Services*,[68] which had held that local governmental units were "persons" within the meaning of § 1983 and thus enjoyed no eleventh amendment immunity, was only a ruling on the applicability of the statute to local governmental units. In support of the majority reaffirmance of the *Edelman* rule,[69] the Justice pointed to the *per curiam* opinion in *Alabama v. Pugh*,[70] holding that the state itself was not a proper

---

64. Because the Court upheld the lower court's grant of prospective relief it was unnecessary to reach this issue but the majority did reach and decide the issue. Justices Brennan and Marshall refused to endorse the § 1983 ruling and Justice Brennan labeled it dicta. 440 U.S. at 349, 350 (Brennan, J., concurring); 440 U.S. at 366 (Marshall, J., concurring).

65. 440 U.S. at 336.

66. 440 U.S. at 334.

67. 440 U.S. at 338.

68. 436 U.S. 658 (1978). The Supreme Court has held that municipalities are "persons" as that term is used by 42 U.S.C.A. § 1983. Monell v. Department of Social Services, 436 U.S. 658 (1978) overruling on this point Monroe v. Pape, 365 U.S. 167 (1961). In *Monell* the Court held that a municipal corporation would be liable for damages if it creates or implements an unconstitutional government policy. However, the opinion states that municipal corporations would not be liable for damages under § 1983 solely on the basis of respondeat superior for the acts of their employees. In so ruling the Court noted that it was not holding that a State could be considered a "person" subject to § 1983. 436 U.S. at 690 n. 54, n. 55. In Newport v. Fact Concerts, Inc., 453 U.S. 247 (1981), the Court limit-

ed the type of damages recoverable in a § 1983 action against a municipality to compensatory damages. The majority opinion in Fact Concerts found that the legislative history of § 1983, when viewed against the common law immunity from punitive damages for municipalities, showed no congressional intention to subject municipalities to awards of punitive damages. Additionally, the majority believed that awards of punitive damages against municipalities would not significantly advance the societal interest in deterring official misconduct.

69. 440 U.S. at 338.

70. 438 U.S. 781 (1978). *Pugh* involved a suit by prisoners alleging that the Alabama state prison system, as administered, constituted cruel and unusual punishment. Plaintiff prisoner named the state of Alabama as a defendant in the action. The Supreme Court held that the federal suit directly against Alabama as a named party violated the eleventh amendment. Justices Brennan and Marshall dissented without opinion. Justice Stevens dissented on the ground that the error in allowing the state to be named as a party was entirely harmless. He noted: "Surely the Court does not intend to resolve summarily the issue [of whether the state is a person within § 1983]." 438 U.S. at 783n.*

party in an action brought pursuant to § 1983 in federal court. Justice Rehnquist found that the legislative history of § 1983 was not sufficiently clear to warrant an inference that state immunity, an important attribute of state sovereignty, had been withdrawn for purposes of § 1983 suits. The majority opinion distinguished *Hutto v. Finney* [71] on the ground that the Civil Rights Attorney's Fees Awards Act had clearly been intended by Congress to override the states' eleventh amendment immunity with respect to attorney's fees in civil rights actions. Finally, Justice Rehnquist's opinion resolved the precise issue of *Quern* by finding that the method of notice proposed by the Seventh Circuit did not violate the ban on retrospective relief declared in *Edelman*. [72]

B. Case or Controversy and Related Doctrines

1. Introduction

Article III, section 2 of the Constitution confines federal court jurisdiction to "cases" and "controversies." [1] Interpreting this jurisdictional requirement is an important example of the self-imposed limitations on judicial review. In addition to its constitutional meaning, this requirement has prompted

nonconstitutional doctrines of judicial self-restraint.

2. Advisory Opinions

Although the framers never accepted a proposal that the President and the House and Senate obtain advisory opinions from the Supreme Court, [2] the justices, very early in the history of the Supreme Court, rendered legal opinions in the form of letters, to the executive. In 1790 Chief Justice John Jay and a minority of the other justices wrote President Washington, in response to his letter to them, that they thought the requirement of their riding circuit was unconstitutional. [3] Washington was apparently unmoved, the circuit riding continued, and when the practice was challenged in litigation over a decade later, the Court upheld circuit riding as justified by historical precedent, without referring to this earlier correspondence. [4] Probably one of the most famous instances of letters to the President concerning the constitutionality of a practice was *Hayburn's Case*. [5] In a footnote to the opinion the court reporter cited letters to the President from two circuit courts objecting on constitutional grounds to the provisions of a particular statute. [6] The Court avoided any constitutional confrontation because Congress amended the statute prior to the

---

Justice Brennan, in his opinion in *Quern*, criticized the majority reliance on *Pugh* because the issue of the inclusion of the state itself within the term "person" in § 1983 was not briefed or argued by the parties in *Pugh*, was not put in issue by the parties in *Pugh*, and was not, as Justice Stevens noted in *Pugh* itself, an issue properly to be decided in a manner so offhand as to be virtually unconscious. Quern v. Jordan, 440 U.S. 332, 351 (1979) (Brennan, J., concurring in the judgment).

71. 437 U.S. 678 (1978).

72. 440 U.S. at 346–49.

1. There is really no difference between "case" or "controversy" except that the latter may be narrower in meaning, including only civil cases. Aetna Life Insurance Co. v. Haworth, 300 U.S. 227, 239 (1937).

See generally, Brilmayer, The Jurisprudence of Article III: Perspectives on the "Case or Controversy" Requirement, 93 Harv.L.Rev. 297 (1979); Tushnet, The Sociology of Article III: A Response to Professor Brilmayer, 93 Harv.L.Rev. 1698 (1980); Brilmayer, A Reply, 93 Harv.L.Rev. 1727 (1980).

2. I.M. Farrand, The Records of the Federal Convention at 1787, at 340–341 (1937).

3. H. Hart & H. Wechsler's The Federal Courts and the Federal System 68 (2d ed. 1973), citing 4 Am.Jurist 294 (1830); 2 J. Story, Commentaries on the Constitution § 1579 n. 1 (5th ed. Bigelow 1891). See also 1 C. Warren, The Supreme Court in United States History 108–111 (1926).

4. Stuart v. Laird, 5 U.S. (1 Cranch) 299, 309 (1803). For other examples of such unofficial letters, see generally, Westin, Out-of-Court Commentary by United States Supreme Court Justices, 1790–1962: Of Free Speech and Judicial Lockjaw, 62 Colum.L.Rev. 633 (1962).

5. 2 U.S. (2 Dall.) 408 (1792). Cf. Tutun v. United States, 270 U.S. 568 (1926). See generally, Rotunda, Congressional Power to Restrict the Jurisdiction of the Lower Federal Courts and the Problem of School Busing, 64 Georgetown L.J. 839, 844–847 (1976).

6. 2 U.S. (2 Dall.) at 410–413 n. (a).

decision, so the case was dismissed.[7] None-theless the case is significant for it reflected the view of several justices who were refusing, on constitutional grounds, to execute a statute on Congress' terms over a decade before the Court decided *Marbury v. Madison*.[8]

One year after *Hayburn's Case*, Chief Justice Jay and the associate justices concluded in an exchange of correspondence involving President Washington and his Secretary of State, Thomas Jefferson, that the federal courts may not constitutionally give advisory opinions:

> [T]he lines of separation [are] drawn by the Constitution between the three departments of the government. These being in certain respects checks upon each other, and our being judges in a court in the last resort, are considerations which afford strong arguments against the propriety of our extra-judicially deciding the questions [previously asked], especially as the power given by the Constitution to the President, of calling on the heads of departments for opinions [Art. II, § 2], seems to have been *purposely* as well as expressly united to the *executive* departments.[9]

The problem of advisory opinions and the case or controversy requirement formed the theoretical framework for the leading case of *Muskrat v. United States*.[10] In 1902 Congress by statute provided for a transfer of Cherokee property from tribal ownership to individual ownership by citizens of the Cherokee Nation as of a certain date. This private ownership was accompanied by certain restrictions on alienation. Two later acts increased the number of Cherokees permitted to enroll as well as increasing the restrictions on alienation. Plaintiffs sued to have these subsequent statutes declared unconstitutional because they increased the number of Indians entitled to share in the final dis-

tribution of property. Other plaintiffs also sued to have the restraints on alienation removed.

A special act of Congress had empowered the plaintiffs to institute suit in the Court of Claims to determine the validity of these acts "in so far as said acts . . . attempt to increase or extend the restrictions upon alienation, encumbrance, or the right to lease the allotments of lands . . . or to increase the number of persons entitled to share in the final distribution of lands and funds. . . ."[11] Jurisdiction was conferred in the Court of Claims with a right of appeal in the Supreme Court. The United States, under the statutory scheme, was the party defendant, and if the plaintiffs were successful the government would pay their attorneys fees.

The Supreme Court reversed the Court of Claims and directed it to dismiss for want of jurisdiction. The government purported to be the defendant, but it had no interest in the outcome of this litigation. Plaintiffs do not "assert a property right as against the Government, or . . . demand compensation for alleged wrongs because of action upon its part."[12] The Court concluded that the jurisdictional act was merely an attempt to provide for a test in the Supreme Court of the validity of an act of Congress, without regard to the requirement of a case or controversy. That attempt was unconstitutional. The power to declare a law unconstitutional exists because the Court finds the law that one of the parties has relied on in conflict with "the fundamental law." The Court rules the act unconstitutional because, in the course of deciding the actual controversy, it must choose the fundamental law over the statute. There is otherwise no gen-

---

7. 2 U.S. (2 Dall.) at 410 & n. (a).

8. 5 U.S. (1 Cranch) 137 (1803). Subsequent cases have approved and relied on the footnote in *Hayburn's Case* as a correct interpretation of the Constitution. See Muskrat v. United States, 219 U.S. 346, 352–353 (1911); United States v. Ferreira, 54 U.S. (13 How.) 40, 49–51 (1851).

9. See 3 H. Johnston, Correspondence and Public Papers of John Jay 486–489 (1891), relied on in Muskrat v. United States, 219 U.S. 346, 354 (1911).

10. 219 U.S. 346 (1911).

11. 219 U.S. at 350.

12. 219 U.S. at 361.

eral power of revision over the actions of Congress.[13]

Part of the law in question, the restriction on alienation, was self-executing. If an Indian were to sell his land to a private party in violation of the alienation provisions, the case of the Indian vs. the private person would create an appropriate case testing the constitutionality of the alienation provisions; the court might have to decide, for example, the claim of the Indian that the land should be returned since the sale was not valid. The private party could also seek a declaratory judgment that his title was valid, if a declaratory judgment procedure existed.

The section of the statute relating to the increasing of the Indian enrollments was not self-executing. The Indians, in another case specifically referred to in *Muskrat*,[14] had brought suit in a lower federal court to enjoin the Secretaries of Interior and Treasury from increasing the enrollments. The Supreme Court, when that case came up the next year, affirmed the lower court decision upholding the acts.[15] Jurisdiction should lie in that case because there was a controversy: parties injured by the actions of a government official sought to enjoin those officials from carrying out statutorily mandated duties on the ground that the statute was unconstitutional. While the Court might reach a constitutional issue in an appropriate case, *Muskrat* shows that Congress cannot grant jurisdiction to give what is really an advisory opinion.

The jurisdictional act in *Muskrat* was poorly drafted, justifying the Supreme Court's decision. The statute struck down in *Muskrat* only gave the Court jurisdiction to decide the constitutional issue. In a real case or controversy the Court might never reach that issue: it might decide, for example, that the plaintiffs were not really Cherokee Indians, or go off on another, narrower ground. It is likely that a more careful statute could have created the appropriate test case.[16]

We now know that coercive relief is not an essential element of the case or controversy requirement. That is, if there is an actual case or controversy, the court may issue only declaratory relief.[17] Thus the constitutionality of a declaratory judgment statute is now accepted.[18] A federal court may even issue prospective relief, but, if it does, the relief must at least apply to the parties before it in order that the opinion not be merely advisory.[19]

The Court of Claims, at the time of the *Muskrat* decision, was an Article I Court, not a Court created pursuant to Article III.[20] Article I Courts, since they are not bound by the case or controversy requirements of Article III may give advisory opinions. In fact, until the Court of Claims was held to be an Article III Court, it routinely fulfilled a congressional reference jurisdiction by rendering advisory opinions to Congress.[21] The Supreme Court did not explain why it did not uphold the part of the *Muskrat* jurisdictional

---

13. 219 U.S. at 361.

14. "Nor can it make any difference that the petitioners had brought suits in the Supreme Court of the District of Columbia to enjoin the Secretary of Interior from carrying into effect the legislation subsequent to the act of July 1, 1902, which suits were pending when the jurisdictional act here involved was passed." 219 U.S. at 362.

15. Gritts v. Fisher, 244 U.S. 640 (1912).

16. Cf. South Carolina v. Katzenbach, 383 U.S. 301, 335 (1966) (test case procedure for testing the validity of the Voting Rights Act of 1965 upheld.)

17. See 28 U.S.C.A. §§ 2201–02 (Federal Declaratory Judgment Act) upheld in Aetna Life Insurance Co. of Hartford, Conn. v. Haworth, 300 U.S. 227 (1937). See generally, Borchard, Declaratory Judgments (2d ed. 1941).

18. Aetna Life Insurance Co. v. Haworth, 300 U.S. 227, 239–240 (1937).

19. Desist v. United States, 394 U.S. 244, 254–55 n. 24 (1964); Stovall v. Denno, 388 U.S. 293, 301 (1967); Firestone Tire & Rubber Co. v. Risjord, 449 U.S. 368, 379 & n. 15 (1981); Kirchberg v. Feenstra, 450 U.S. 455, 463 (1981).

20. Glidden Co. v. Zdanok, 370 U.S. 530 (1962); Katz, Federal Legislative Courts, 43 Harv.L.Rev. 894 (1930). See Section I, A, of this Chapter supra, on Article I courts.

21. Glidden Co. v. Zdanok, 370 U.S. 530, 579–583 (1962). See generally, Jacoby, Recent Legislation Affecting the Court of Claims, 55 Georgetown L.J. 397 (1966).

statute giving, in effect, the Court of Claims the power to render an advisory opinion. The Supreme Court must have thought that the jurisdictional statute was not severable, that is, Congress did not want only the Court of Claims opinion as to the constitutionality of the statute; it wanted the Supreme Court's final judgment.

While the *Muskrat* Court reaffirmed the requirement of an actual case or controversy, it did not articulate some of the reasons justifying this limitation on the jurisdictional powers of Article III Courts. Four reasons are apparent.[22] First, advisory opinions may not be binding on the parties, in that advice given need not be accepted. The power of the Court is then eroded. We have seen that when Chief Justice Jay and several associate justices wrote President Washington contending that the requirement of riding circuit was unconstitutional, he was unpersuaded and the circuit riding continued.[23] Second, advisory opinions also undermine the basic theory behind the adversary system. Suits for advisory opinions may more likely be collusive or the parties, anxious to obtain a certain advisory opinion, may be less likely to fully brief all of the relevant issues. Once again to refer to Jay's letter to Washington on riding circuit, when the issue came in actual litigation before the Court, when it was faced with a concrete situation, it decided contrary to the earlier informal opinion.[24] Third, with a real controversy before it, the Court might be able to avoid the constitutional issue entirely and decide the case on narrower grounds. Advisory opin-

ions unnecessarily force the Court to reach and decide complex, if not impossible, constitutional issues. The jurisdictional statute in *Muskrat* prohibited this narrower alternative. Chief Justice Marshall in *Marbury v. Madison*[25] emphasized that judicial review is a reluctant power, only used because it must be exercised in the litigation at hand. Fourth, the power to render such an advisory opinion is really a greater power than the reluctant judicial review justified by Marshall, because it increases the situations where the Court can exercise this significant power of judicial review. Such a large increase in this power to freeze into Constitutional law the views of unelected judges is inappropriate for a democracy and was specifically rejected by the framers.[26]

3. *Mootness and Collusiveness*

Article III Courts may not decide moot questions, only actual cases or controversies.

> A justiciable controversy is thus distinguished from a difference or dispute of a hypothetical or abstract character; from one that is academic or moot. The controversy must be definite and concrete, touching the legal relations of parties having adverse legal interests. It must be a real and substantial controversy admitting of specific relief through a decree of a conclusive character, as distinguished from an opinion advising what the law would be upon a hypothetical state of facts.[1]

If the case is moot "there is no subject matter on which the judgment of the court's order can operate."[2]

---

22. For an examination of the reasons for rejecting this power see, Frankfurter, Advisory Opinions, 37 Harv.L.Rev. 1002 (1924). These reasons have not precluded some states from adopting the practice for their state courts, though they have sought to limit the power to avoid these objections. Comment, The State Advisory Opinion in Perspective, 44 Ford L.Rev. 81 (1975). Cf. Rotunda, The Public Interest Appellant: Limitations on the Right of Competent Parties to Settle Litigation Out of Court, 66 Nw.U.L.Rev. 199, 214–20 (1971).

23. See text of this section at notes 2–4, supra.

24. Stuart v. Laird, 5 U.S. (1 Cranch) 299, 309 (1803).

25. 5 U.S. (1 Cranch) 137 (1803).

26. The framers did not accept a proposal to give the Supreme Court power to issue advisory opinions. 1 M. Farrand, The Records of the Federal Convention of 1787, at 340–41 (1937).

1. Aetna Life Insurance Co. v. Haworth, 300 U.S. 227, 240–241 (1937). See generally, Brilmayer, The Jurisprudence of Article III: Perspectives on the "Case or Controversy" Requirement, 93 Harv.L.Rev. 297 (1979); Tushnet, The Sociology of Article III: A Response to Professor Brilmayer, 93 Harv.L.Rev. 1698 (1980); Brilmayer, A Reply, 93 Harv.L.Rev. 1727 (1980).

2. Ex parte Baez, 117 U.S. 378, 390 (1900).

While the Supreme Court has sometimes stated that mootness is a constitutional limitation,[3] it has at other times been willing to relax the mootness rule so that the requirement will not be so "rigid" as to prevent the review of important constitutional issues.[4] Mootness should therefore properly be regarded as rooted in part in the constitutional limitation of the judicial power to cases and controversies, although its application is rooted as well in a rule of self-restraint which may be relaxed at times by the Court.

A case may become moot for several reasons. The controversy must normally exist at every stage of the proceeding, including the appellate stages.[5] Thus, a case may become moot because the law has changed;[6] because defendant has paid moneys owed and no longer wishes to appeal, notwithstanding plaintiff's desire to obtain a higher court ruling;[7] because allegedly wrongful behavior has passed, been mooted, and could not reasonably be expected to recur;[8] because a party could no longer be affected by a challenged statute; for example, a law regulating rights of minors when the party, through lapse of time, is no longer within the age brackets governed by the statute;[9] or because a party has died.[10]

3. E.g., St. Pierre v. United States, 319 U.S. 41, 42 (1943); Liner v. Jafco, Inc., 375 U.S. 301, 306 n. 3 (1964); Sibron v. New York, 392 U.S. 40, 57 (1968); California v. San Pablo & Tulare R.R. Co., 149 U.S. 308, 314 (1893).

4. Roe v. Wade, 410 U.S. 113, 125 (1973). See Wirtz v. Glass Bottle Blowers Ass'n, Local 153, 389 U.S. 463, 474 (1968) (public interest in deciding issue helps prevent case from being moot); see also Wirtz v. Hotel, Motel, & Club Employee Union, Local 6, 391 U.S. 492 (1968).

5. E.g., Roe v. Wade, 410 U.S. 113, 125 (1973); Golden v. Zwickler, 394 U.S. 103, 108 (1969); United States v. Munsingwear, 340 U.S. 36, 39 (1950): "The established practice of the Court in dealing with a civil case from a court in the federal system which has become moot while on its way here or pending our decision on the merits is to reverse or vacate the judgment below and remand with a direction to dismiss." (footnote omitted, citing cases, and noting that as to federal civil cases "there are but few exceptions to this practice in recent years.")

Great Western Sugar Co. v. Nelson, 442 U.S. 92 (1979) (per curiam) (where court of appeals dismissed appeal as moot, the district court judgment must be vacated).

6. E.g., United States v. Alaska S.S. Co., 253 U.S. 113 (1920) (pending appeal, Congress passed new law which makes the original case moot because it necessitates changes in the forms of bills of lading required by I.C.C.; the form of these bills of lading was the subject matter of the original case). Accord, Princeton University v. Schmid, 102 S.Ct. 867 (1982).

See also Environmental Protection Agency v. Brown, 431 U.S. 99, 103, (1977) (per curiam): "We decline the [Government's] invitation to pass upon the EPA regulations, when the only ones before us are admitted to be in need of certain essential modifications. Such action on our part would amount to the rendering of an advisory opinion."

Contrast Zablocki v. Redhail, 434 U.S. 374, 382, n. 9 (1978) (revision of state law under constitutional attack does not moot controversy because by its terms the new statute is to be enforced only if enforcement of the old statute is enjoined by court order).

7. E.g., California v. San Pablo & Tulare R.R., 149 U.S. 308, 313–314 (1893) (any obligation of the railroad to pay to the State the sums sued for in the case together with interest, penalties, and costs, has been extinguished by the offer to pay and the deposit of the money in a bank; thus the case is moot).

8. SEC v. Medical Committee for Human Rights, 404 U.S. 403, 406 (1972) (Dow Chemical Co. acquiesces in a request to include a shareholder's proposal for a corporate charter amendment in Dow's proxy material, and the proposal receives less than 3% of the voting shareholder's support; Dow may thus exclude the proposal for a three-year period, and it is extremely doubtful that at the end of that period the shareholders will resubmit the proposal and Dow will refuse it; thus, the decision of the Court of Appeals (overruling the arguments of the SEC) that it had jurisdiction to review the SEC's determination not to oppose Dow's initial refusal of the shareholders' proxy request is now moot).

9. Atherton Mills v. Johnston, 259 U.S. 13 (1922) (father and minor son sued on April 15, 1919, to enjoin corporation from firing son in order that the corporation could comply with the Child Labor Tax Act governing child labor between 14 and 16 years of age; the case was argued before the Supreme Court on December 10, 1919, and restored to the docket for reargument on June 6, 1921, reargued on March 7, 1922, and decided on May 15, 1922. "The lapse of time since the case was heard and decided in the District Court has brought the minor, whose employment was the subject-matter of the suit, to an age which is not within the ages affected by the act. The act, even if valid, can not affect him further." 259 U.S. at 15).

See also, Murphy v. Hunt, 455 U.S. 478, 481 (1982) (per curiam) (constitutional claim to *pretrial* bail is moot once claimant is convicted; he made no claim to a constitutional right to bail pending appeal).

10. Durham v. United States, 401 U.S. 481 (1971) (per curiam):

"Our cases where a petitioner dies while a review is pending are not free of ambiguity. In a recent

To prevent either party from creating a technical mootness as a sham to deprive the court of jurisdiction, the Court has created various exceptions to the doctrine. Thus, if a party voluntarily stops allegedly illegal conduct, that change does not make the case moot, for the defendant would then be free to return to his old ways.[11] Defendant must show that "there is no reasonable expectation that the wrong will be repeated."[12]

Another exception to the general mootness rule concerns those cases which are "capable of repetition, yet evading review." A mere "physical or theoretical possibility"

is not enough to meet the test of "capable of repetition, yet evading review," otherwise "virtually any matter of short duration would be reviewable." There must be a "reasonable expectation" or a "demonstrable probability" that "the same controversy will recur involving the *same* complaining party."[13]

Such cases may be divided into two main categories. In one, the challenged order is so short that it will normally expire before review may be had. Such cases include short sentences in criminal cases,[14] short term orders of agencies that usually contin-

---

mandamus action the petitioner died and we granted certiorari, vacated the judgment below, and ordered the complaint dismissed. . . . In a state habeas corpus case we granted certiorari and vacated the judgment so that the state court could take whatever action it deemed proper. . . . Our practice in cases on direct review from state convictions has been to dismiss the proceedings. . . . In an earlier case the Court announced that the *appeal* had abated . . . while in another the Court stated that the *cause* had abated. . . .

"In federal criminal cases we have developed the practice of dismissing the writ of certiorari and remanding the cause to the court below. . . . [B]eyond [suggesting such disposition on remand as law and justice require] we have basically allowed the scope of the abatement to be determined by the lower federal courts." 401 U.S. at 482 (emphasis in original).

The Court then adopted the rule of the eighth circuit in Crooker v. United States, 325 F.2d 318, 320 (8th Cir. 1963): "death pending direct review of a criminal conviction abates not only the appeal but also all proceedings had in the prosecution from its inception." (401 U.S. at 483, footnote omitted). But cf. Robinson v. California, 370 U.S. 660 and 371 U.S. 905 (1962).

Marshall, Burger and Stewart would have dismissed the petition as moot. Blackmun, in a dissent, said he "would merely dismiss the decedent's petition for certiorari, rather than direct the dismissal of the *indictment*." (461 U.S. at 484, emphasis in original).

11. E.g., United States v. W.T. Grant Co., 345 U.S. 629, 632 (1953); County of Los Angeles v. Davis, 440 U.S. 625 (1979).

12. 345 U.S. at 633, quoting United States v. Aluminum Co. of America, 148 F.2d 416, 448 (2d Cir. 1945). See also, United States v. Oregon State Medical Society, 343 U.S. 326, 333 (1952):

"When defendants are shown to have settled into a continuing practice or entered into a conspiracy violative of antitrust laws, courts will not assume that it has been abandoned without clear proof. . . . It is the duty of the courts to beware of efforts to de-

feat injunctive relief by protestations of repentance and reform, especially when abandonment seems timed to anticipate suit and there is probability of resumption."

St. Paul Fire & Marine Insurance Co. v. Barry, 438 U.S. 531, 537–538 (1978) (case not moot because the conditions complained of have not been shown to have abated even though subsequent events have reduced the practical importance of the case).

A statement of the party that it would not be economical for them to engage in challenged activity, is not, standing alone, sufficient "to satisfy the heavy burden of persuasion which we have held rests upon those in appellees' shoes." United States v. Concentrated Phosphate Export Ass'n, Inc., 393 U.S. 199, 203 (1968). But a court being asked for an injunction in cases of voluntary cessation of allegedly wrongful conduct may on grounds of equitable discretion refuse to issue the requested injunction even if the case is not moot. See SEC v. Harwyn Indus. Corp., 326 F.Supp. 943 (S.D.N.Y.1971).

13. Murphy v. Hunt, 455 U.S. 478, 482 (1982) (per curiam) (emphasis added). See also, Southern Pac. Terminal Co. v. Interstate Commerce Comm'n, 219 U.S. 498, 515 (1911); City of Los Angeles v. Lyons, 103 S.Ct. 1660 (1983).

14. E.g., Sibron v. New York, 392 U.S. 40, 52–53 (1968) (short sentence for "low visibility" minor offense).

See also Gannett Co., Inc. v. DePasquale, 443 U.S. 368, 377 (1979) (a case is capable of repetition yet evading review if the challenged action—exclusion of reporters from pretrial hearing—is too short in its duration to be fully litigated prior to its cessation and there is reasonable expectation that the same complaining party would be subjected to the same action again); Richmond Newspapers, Inc. v. Virginia, 448 U.S. 555, 567–69 (1980) (plurality opinion) (objection of newspaper to closure of trial to public is not mooted by the end of the criminal trial since criminal trials are often of such short duration and the closure order is thus capable of repetition yet evading plenary review by the Court).

ue or will come up again,[15] short term injunctions that may be repeated,[16] and similar circumstances. In the second category, the challenged order is not short term, but the factual circumstances appear to make the order moot by the time of appeal. Election cases illustrate this problem. As Justice Douglas noted: "We are plagued with election cases coming here on the eve of elections, with the remaining time so short we do not have the days needed for oral argument and for reflection on the serious problems that are usually presented." [17] To beat the election clock, the Court may issue its decision as soon as possible prior to the elec-

tion, with the opinion coming later.[18] Or, the Court may decide the issue after the election, if the issue is otherwise capable of repetition yet evading review.[19]

Collateral consequences may also prevent a case from being moot, even though some of the original relief requested may be moot. Thus, a case is not moot as to the party defendant if another party paid the joint judgment rendered against them and served on the other party a demand for contribution. Then, the party "is still subject to a suit because of the original judgment as to its liability." [20] In *Powell v. McCormack*,[21] Congressman Powell's claim of improper

---

15. E.g., Southern Pac. Terminal Co. v. Interstate Commerce Comm'n, 219 U.S. 498, 515 (1911) (ICC rate order); SEC v. Sloan, 436 U.S. 103, 108 (1978).

16. Carroll v. President and Comm'rs of Princess Anne, 393 U.S. 175 (1968). After a white supremacist organization held a public rally, officials of Princess Anne and of Somerset County obtained an ex parte restraining order from local court to prevent the next planned rally, which therefore did not occur. A trial was held and a 10 month injunction was then issued. The state court of appeals reversed as to the 10 month order but affirmed the 10 day restraining order. The case is not moot as to that 10 day order because the petitioners "have sought to continue their activities . . . and it appears that the decision of the Maryland Court of Appeals continues to play a substantial role in the response of officials to their activities." 393 U.S. at 178 (footnote omitted).

17. Ely v. Klahr, 403 U.S. 108, 120–121 (1971) (Douglas, J., concurring).

18. Ray v. Blair, 343 U.S. 154 (1952) (per curiam). (argued March 31, 1952; decided April 3, 1952; primary election to be held May 6, 1952. Mandate issued forthwith.) See also Ray v. Blair, 343 U.S. 214, 216 (1952) (Opinion filed April 15, 1952).

19. E.g., Moore v. Ogilvie, 394 U.S. 814 (1969). Plaintiffs, independent candidates for office of presidential and vice-presidential electors, objected to a state statute requiring nominating petitions to have at least 200 qualified signatures from each of the 50 counties, including the very sparsely settled counties. The election had passed by the time of Supreme Court review and it was urged that there was no possibility of granting relief to the plaintiffs. But the Court found that the burden placed on the nomination of "statewide offices remains and controls future elections, as long as Illinois maintains her present system as she has done since 1935." 394 U.S. at 816. Cf. Hall v. Beals, 396 U.S. 45 (1969) (per curiam): objection to six month residency requirement in presidential election; by the time the case came to the Supreme Court plaintiffs had met the residency requirement, the election had been held, and the state legislature amended the statute to reduce the residency requirements to two months;

held, case moot and Moore v. Ogilvie, 394 U.S. 814 (1969) distinguished because there the same restrictions that affected Moore's candidacy in 1968 could do so again in 1972, and because there the state had not amended the offending statute to solve the problem; Brennan and Marshall, JJ., dissented, relying on Moore v. Ogilvie.

See also First Nat. Bank v. Bellotti, 435 U.S. 765 (1978). A declaratory judgment suit by banks and business corporations challenging state criminal statute forbidding corporations from spending money to influence referendum questions not material to their business interests was held not moot although referendum at issue had taken place already, because short period between proposal and submission to voters would otherwise preclude review, similar referendums were reasonably expected in future, and appellants would again be subject to a threat of prosecution, and the effect on arguably protected speech would persist. The Court thus noted:

"Present here are both elements identified in Weinstein v. Bradford, 423 U.S. 147, 149 (1975), as precluding a finding of mootness in the absence of a class action: '(1) the challenged action was in its duration too short to be fully litigated prior to its cessation or expiration, and (2) there [is] a reasonable expectation that the same complaining party [will] be subjected to the same action again.'"

435 U.S. at 774.

Democratic Party v. LaFollette, 450 U.S. 107, 115 n. 13 (1981).

20. Bank of Marin v. England, 385 U.S. 99, 101 (1966). There was also remaining the issue of costs and that respondents "sole financial interest" is protection against imposition of costs. The Court did not decide what would be the ruling as to mootness if costs alone were involved. 385 U.S. at 101.

See also Deposit Guaranty Nat. Bank v. Roper, 445 U.S. 326 (1980) (neither defendants' tender to individual plaintiffs of the maximum amount they could have recovered, nor the district court's entry of judgment in

---

21. See note 21 on page 68.

exclusion from the House of Representatives was not mooted by his later seating by the time of Supreme Court review, for the issue of his back pay remained.[22]

In criminal cases, the collateral consequences of a conviction also serve to prevent mootness. Serving the sentence does not necessarily mean the case is moot. "[A] criminal case is moot only if it is shown that there is no possibility that any collateral consequences will be imposed on the basis of the challenged conviction."[23] As a corollary to this principle, the state may seek Supreme Court review of a lower court reversal of a criminal defendant's conviction, even if the defendant had already served his sentence. The reversal of the conviction, if allowed to stand, would preclude the state from imposing collateral legal consequences on the defendant.[24]

The application of the general rules are illustrated by a discussion of several of the cases in this area. First, *Roe v. Wade*.[25]

Roe was a case challenging the constitutionality of the Texas abortion legislation. Jane Roe, using a pseudonym, instituted the case in March of 1970, at a time when she was unmarried, pregnant, and desired an abortion. She amended her complaint purporting to sue "on behalf of herself and all other women" similarly situated.[26] At the time of Roe's hearing in the district court several months later, on May 22, 1970, there was no evidence that she was then pregnant. By the time the case was decided by the Supreme Court it was January 22, 1973; thus the appellee suggested "that Roe's case must now be moot because she and all other members of her class are no longer subject to any 1970 pregnancy."[27] The Court made use of the "repetition" exception to the mootness rule:

> [W]hen . . . pregnancy is a significant fact in the litigation, the normal 266-day human gestation period is so short that the pregnancy will come to term before the usual appellate process is complete. If that termination makes a case moot, pregnancy litigation seldom will

favor of plaintiffs—both of which plaintiffs refused to accept—mooted their class action because plaintiffs retained a continuing individual interest in the resolution of the class certification question because they wished to shift part of the costs of the litigation to those who would share in its benefits if the class would be certified and would prevail).

21. 395 U.S. 486 (1969).

22. 395 U.S. at 495–500. Accord, Memphis Light, Gas, and Water Div. v. Craft, 436 U.S. 1, 8–9 (1978) (plaintiffs claim for actual and punitive damages arising out of a power company's termination of services prevents the case from being mooted, even though plaintiffs no longer desire a hearing to resolve the dispute over their bills and there is no allegation of a present threat of termination of services).

In University of Texas v. Camenisch, 451 U.S. 390 (1981), a student sued claiming that the University had, in violation of federal law, discriminatorily refused to pay for a sign language interpreter. The district court issued a preliminary injunction and ordered that the University pay for the interpreter and that the student post a security bond of $3,000 pending outcome of the appeal. By the time the case reached the court of appeals the University had obeyed the preliminary injunction and the student had been graduated. The Supreme Court ruled that while the correctness of the decision to grant a preliminary injunction is moot, the question of whether the University must pay for the interpreter is not moot and remains for trial on the merits. "Thus when the injunctive aspects of a case become moot on appeal of a preliminary injunction, any issue preserved by an injunction bond can generally

not be resolved on appeal, but must be resolved in a trial on the merits. Where, by contrast, a federal district court has granted a permanent injunction, the parties will already have had their trial on the merits, and, even if the case would otherwise be moot, a determination can be had on appeal of the correctness of the trial court's decision on the merits, since the case has been saved from mootness by the injunction bond." 451 U.S. at 396.

23. Sibron v. New York, 392 U.S. 40, 57 (1968). The Court narrowed the earlier broad dictum in St. Pierre v. United States, 319 U.S. 41 (1943). Contrast Lane v. Williams, 455 U.S. 624 (1982) (during their plea acceptances, respondents were never informed that the negotiated sentence included mandatory prison terms; had respondents sought to set aside the guilty pleas the case would not have been moot because of the collateral consequences flowing from the convictions; but respondents only seek to remove the consequence that gave rise to the challenged harm; since the respondents are no longer subject to any direct restraint as a result of the parole term—which has expired of its own accord—that consequence no longer exists; nor can complainants show that they would be subject to any civil liabilities now because they had earlier violated a parole term which has now expired and may have been invalid).

24. Pennsylvania v. Mimms, 434 U.S. 106, 108 n. 3 (1977).

25. 410 U.S. 113 (1973).

26. 410 U.S. at 120 & n. 4.

27. 410 U.S. at 124.

survive much beyond the trial stage, and appellate review will be effectively denied. Our law should not be that rigid. Pregnancy often comes more than once to the same women, and in the general population, if man is to survive, it will always be with us. Pregnancy provides a classic justification for a conclusion of nonmootness. It truly could be "capable of repetition yet evading review." [28]

The case was thus not considered mooted by subsequent events.

A similar conclusion was reached, by a 5–4 vote, in *Super Tire Engineering Co. v. McCorkle.*[29] In New Jersey, where this case arose, employees were eligible for state welfare assistance even though they were engaged in an economic strike. After such a strike occurred, the employers sued for injunctive and declaratory relief against distribution of such welfare payments to the strikers. Before the case was tried, the strike ended. The trial court rejected the union's contention that the case was moot and went on to decide the merits, holding the New Jersey practice not prohibited by federal law. The Supreme Court granted certiorari on the mootness issue after the Court of Appeals had held the case to be moot. The high court found that as to the request for declaratory relief the case was not moot. "If we were to condition our review on the existence of an economic strike, this case most certainly would be the type presenting an issue 'capable of repetition, yet evading review.'" [30]

Seven days later the Court issued its per curiam opinion in *DeFunis v. Odegaard.*[31] DeFunis had claimed that his denial of admission to a state law school constituted discrimination against him on account of his race. DeFunis was not a member of the va-rious minority groups who were given preferential admissions.[32] DeFunis did not bring the case as a class action, and at the trial level, where he won his claim, the court ordered him admitted to the law school. When the case reached the state Supreme Court, where he lost, he was in his second year of law school. Then Justice Douglas, as Circuit Justice, stayed that judgment pending a final judgment by the Supreme Court. DeFunis was in his third year when the Court first considered his certiorari petition; following the submission of briefs and oral arguments the Supreme Court then held the case moot.

During oral argument the respondents indicated that DeFunis was now in his last quarter of his third year and that his registration would not be cancelled "regardless of the outcome of this litigation." [33] Thus, a "determination by this Court of the legal issues tendered by the parties is no longer necessary to compel that result [of DeFunis' finishing school], and could not serve to prevent it." [34]

Perhaps if *DeFunis* had brought a class action, the case would not have been held moot. In *Sosna v. Iowa,*[35] decided the year after *DeFunis*, the Court explicitly held that while there must be a live controversy at the time of Supreme Court review, the "controversy may exist, however, between a named defendant and a member of the class represented by the named plaintiff, even though the claim of the named plaintiff has become moot." [36] Similarly, if the lower court erroneously denies class action certification, the mootness of the named plaintiff's personal claim does not moot the controversy because class certification, if granted by the appellate court, may be treated as related back to

---

28. 410 U.S. at 125 (citations omitted).

29. 416 U.S. 115 (1974).

30. 416 U.S. at 125 (citations omitted).

31. 416 U.S. 312 (1974) (per curiam).

32. The groups were Blacks, Chicanos, American Indians, and Filipinos, 416 U.S. at 320 (Douglas, J., dissenting).

33. 416 U.S. at 316 n. 3. Compare 416 U.S. at 315 with id. at 315 n. 2.

34. 416 U.S. at 317.

35. 419 U.S. 393 (1975). See also, Zablocki v. Redhail, 434 U.S. 374, 382, n. 9 (1978) ("regardless of the current status of appellee's individual claim, the dispute over the statute's constitutionality remains alive with respect to the class appellee represents, and the [alleged mooting event] took place well after the class was certified.")

36. 419 U.S. at 402.

the original erroneous denial. Thus, in a class action the mootness of the named plaintiff's personal claim does not render the controversy moot if the class is certified either before or after the individual's personal claim is mooted.[37]

The majority in *DeFunis* argued that it was not relevant that mootness appeared to be created in part by the university. The argument that "voluntary cessation of allegedly illegal conduct does not . . . make the case moot"[38] was not applicable, the Court argued, because the question of mootness was not a function of a unilateral change in admission procedure. Those procedures were attacked and if they were unilaterally changed, the defendant could always go back to its old ways, unless there were no reasonable expectation that the alleged wrong would be repeated. The case was moot simply because DeFunis' law school status would not be affected by the litigation.[39] Nor was this case one capable of repetition, yet evading review. "[T]here is no reason to suppose that a subsequent case attacking those procedures will not come with relative speed to this Court, now that the Supreme Court of Washington has spoken."[40]

Four justices dissented on the mootness determination. "Any number of unexpected events—illness, economic necessity, even academic failure—might prevent [DeFunis'] graduation at the end of the term."[41] In addition the dissent argued that the public interest should require the Court to decide the case and end the issue. "[W]e should not transform principles of avoidance of consti-

tutional decisions into devices for side-stepping resolution of difficult cases."[42]

These decisions do not easily fit into a pattern. While the majority opinion in *DeFunis* cited *Roe*, none of the opinions in *DeFunis* even cited *Super Tire*, issued one week earlier, which would appear to have supported a conclusion that *DeFunis* was not moot. *Roe* itself would appear to suggest that the Court in *DeFunis* could have applied the "repetition" exception. Of the nine justices participating in *DeFunis* and *Super Tire*, only Powell thought that both cases were moot.[43]

However, the three cases are consistent because in *Roe* and in *Super Tire* the events that had ended could have repeated themselves to the *same* plaintiffs: Jane Roe could have gotten pregnant again and wanted another abortion; the strikers could have gone on strike again and applied for more welfare payments. But DeFunis had graduated from law school; the event—preferential admissions—could not be (or at least would be unlikely to be) repeated to him again.

Closely related to the doctrine of mootness is the doctrine of feigned or collusive cases. In *United States v. Johnson*[44] one party sued another alleging that the rent he paid was in excess of the maximum allowed by federal regulation. The defendant moved to dismiss on the grounds that the Emergency Price Control Act, pursuant to which the rent regulation had been issued, was unconstitutional. The United States intervened and the trial court ruled on the merits that

---

37. United States Parole Comm'n v. Geraghty, 445 U.S. 388 (1980) (plaintiff who filed class action challenging the validity of parole guidelines could continue his appeal of lower court ruling denying certification even though he had been released from prison while appeal was pending).

38. 416 U.S. at 318 (quoting United States v. W.T. Grant Co., 345 U.S. 629, 632 (1953) and other cases).

39. The state law school could moot all future attacks on its preferential admissions program by simply admitting every student like DeFunis who objected to his exclusion. But there is an inner check that operates to prevent this method from being abused: disgruntled applicants will quickly learn that the easiest law school admission ticket is the filing of a law suit.

40. 416 U.S. at 319.

41. 416 U.S. at 348 (Brennan, J., dissenting, joined by Douglas, White, and Marshall, JJ.). Mr. DeFunis did in fact graduate from law school.

42. 416 U.S. at 350 (Brennan, J., dissenting).

43. While Justice Rehnquist dissented in *Roe* based on several arguments, none of them appear to have related to mootness. The closest Justice Rehnquist came to the mootness issue is an argument phrased more in terms of third party standing. 410 U.S. at 171–172 (Rehnquist, J., dissenting).

44. 319 U.S. 302 (1943) (per curiam).

the Act was unconstitutional. The Government then moved to reopen the case on the grounds that the suit was collusive, but the trial court refused. The Supreme Court reversed.

The record showed that plaintiff brought the suit under a fictitious name at the defendant's request. Moreover, plaintiff's counsel, who never met plaintifff, was selected and paid for by the defendant. Plaintiff never read the complaint, defendant assured him that he would incur no expense in connection with the suit, and he had no knowledge of the judgment he asked for, outside of reading about it in a local paper. Plaintiff had not filed a brief on his behalf at the trial court. There was no claim, however, that the original parties submitted any false or fictitious facts to the court. On this record, the case was held to be collusive and was dismissed:

> Here an important public interest is at stake— the validity of an Act of Congress having far-reaching effects on the public welfare in one of the most critical periods in the history of the country. That interest has been adjudicated in a proceeding in which the plaintiff has had no active participation, over which he has exercised no control, and the expense of which he has not borne. He has been only nominally represented by counsel. . . . Whenever in the course of litigation such a defect in the proceedings is brought to the court's attention, it may set aside any adjudication thus procured and dismiss the cause without entering judgment on the merits. It is the court's duty to do so where, as here, the public interest has been placed at hazard by the amenities of parties to

a suit conducted under the domination of only one of them.[45]

Thus, parties may not submit cases on a stipulated statement of facts not in accordance with the actual facts.[46] Neither will the Court accept a case where a contract is made for the purposes of instituting a suit so that the parties may "procure the opinion of this court upon a question of law, in the decision of which they have a common interest opposed to that of other persons, who are not parties to this suit. . . . "[47] Thus the Court would not accept a case where both sides argued and agreed that an anti-busing law was constitutional.[48]

The problem of a collusive suit appeared to be raised in *United States v. Nixon*,[49] where President Nixon's counsel argued that the Court lacked jurisdiction to order the president to respond to a subpoena issued by the Special Prosecutor for presidential tapes and papers relating to a criminal prosecution, because the matter was an intra-branch dispute between subordinate and superior offices within the Executive Branch. Quoting *United States v. I.C.C.*[50] the Court said that "courts must look behind names that symbolize the parties to determine whether a justiciable case or controversy is presented."[51] The *Nixon* case was a criminal case brought in the name of the United States; the Attorney General has the statutory responsibility to conduct such litigation and to appoint subordinate officers to aid him. Pursuant to these statutory powers he issued regulations delegating authority to a Special Prosecutor "with unique authority and tenure."[52] Though the Attorney

---

45. 319 U.S. at 304–305.

46. Swift & Co. v. Hocking Valley R.R., 243 U.S. 281 (1917).

Nor will the court accept a case when an attorney, because of possible conflicts of interest, contrived a test case that might not have existed in legal representation untainted by a conflict. See Wood v. Georgia, 450 U.S. 261 (1981) (employees, unable to pay substantial fines, claimed a violation of the equal protection clause on the basis of wealth; but since the record showed that the employees may have become subjected to such fines because of the divided loyalties of their counsel—who was also the agent of the employer, who may have instructed the lawyer to contrive a test

case—the Court concluded that it would not reach the difficult equal protection issue but instead it remanded for further hearings not tainted by a conflict of interest.)

47. Lord v. Veazie, 49 U.S. (8 How.) 251, 254 (1850).

48. Moore v. Charlotte-Mecklenburg Bd. of Education, 402 U.S. 47 (1971) (per curiam).

49. 418 U.S. 683 (1974).

50. 337 U.S. 426, 430 (1949).

51. 418 U.S. at 693.

52. 418 U.S. at 694 (footnote omitted).

General could amend or revoke these regulations, he had not and, until he did, the United States was bound to respect these regulations. "Moreover, the delegation of authority to the Special Prosecutor in this case is not an ordinary delegation by the Attorney General to a subordinate officer: with the authorization of the President, the Acting Attorney General provided in the regulation that the Special Prosecutor was not to be removed without the 'consensus' of eight designated leaders of Congress."[53] Thus, there was a proper case or controversy for the Court to decide.

To be distinguished from collusive suits are such cases as where there is a default judgment,[54] or where the Solicitor General confesses error,[55] or a state's attorney confesses error,[56] or a party seeks naturalization and no one opposes the petition,[57] because in all of these cases there is a real, not a feigned, case, with real and direct consequences operating on the litigants.

In spite of the general rule as to feigned cases, the Court at times has accepted cases where there was strong evidence the suit was collusive.[58] For example, the Court has accepted cases brought by stockholders seeking to prevent their corporation from complying with allegedly unconstitutional statutes. Thus in *Carter v. Carter Coal Co.*[59] the Court upheld the right of stockholders to sue their corporation to prevent it from paying an allegedly unconstitutional

tax.[60] Since neither the shareholders nor the corporation normally would want the Corporation to pay the tax, it would seem to be the better rule for the Court to have dismissed that, and similar cases.

4. Ripeness, Prematurity, and Abstractness

Just as a case can be brought too late, and thereby be moot, it can be brought too early, and not yet be ripe for adjudication. While this general ripeness principle is not disputed, its application by the Supreme Court has resulted in a line of cases with seemingly inconsistent rulings. At least the grounds distinguishing them are too subtle for the commentators to appreciate.

A leading decision on the ripeness doctrine is *United Public Workers v. Mitchell.*[1] The plaintiffs in this case sought declaratory relief and an injunction against the members of the United States Civil Service Commission to prevent enforcement of a sentence of the Hatch Act which provided that "no officer or employee in the executive branch of the Federal Government . . . shall take any active part in political management or in political campaigns."[2] The provision was challenged as unconstitutional for a variety of reasons, but only one plaintiff had actually violated the provision and the rules promulgated under it. As to the plaintiffs who had not been charged with violations,

---

53. 418 U.S. at 696.

54. Re Metropolitan Ry. Receivership, 208 U.S. 90, 108 (1908): "Jurisdiction does not depend on the fact that the defendant denies the existence of the claim made, or its amount or validity. If it were otherwise, then the Circuit Court would have no jurisdiction if the defendant simply admitted his liability and the amount thereof as claimed, although not paying or satisfying the debt."

55. Compare Young v. United States, 315 U.S. 257, 258–259 (1942), with Casey v. United States, 343 U.S. 808 (1952); and compare, Cheng Fan Kwok v. Immigration and Naturalization Service, 392 U.S. 206, 210 (1968), with Watts v. United States, 422 U.S. 1032 (1975). Cf. Thompson v. United States, 444 U.S. 248 (1980) (per curiam). See also, United States v. Lovett, 328 U.S. 303 (1946). See generally, Note, Government Litigation in the Supreme Court: The Roles of the Solicitor General, 78 Yale L.J. 1442 (1969).

56. Sibron v. New York, 392 U.S. 40, 58–59 (1968).

57. Tutun v. United States, 270 U.S. 568, 576–580 (1926) (Brandeis, J.).

58. E.g., Fletcher v. Peck, 10 U.S. (6 Cranch) 87 (1810). See A. Kelly & W. Harbison, The American Constitution: Its Origins and Development 276 (4th ed. 1970).

59. 298 U.S. 238 (1936).

60. 298 U.S. at 286.

1. 330 U.S. 75 (1947). Justice Reed delivered the opinion of the Court. Murphy and Jackson, JJ., did not participate. Rutledge dissented in part, Frankfurter concurred; Black dissented; Douglas dissented in part.

2. 330 U.S. at 82.

the Supreme Court found the issues not ripe for adjudication:

> [T]he facts of [plaintiffs'] personal interest in their civil rights, of the general threat of possible interference with those rights by the Civil Service Commission under its rules, if specified things are done by appellants, does not make a justiciable case or controversy. Appellants want to engage in "political management and political campaigns" to persuade others to follow appellants' views by discussion, speeches, articles and other acts reasonably designed to secure the selection of appellants' political choices. . . .

> A hypothetical threat is not enough. We can only speculate as to the kinds of political activity the appellants desire to engage in or as to the contents of their proposed public statements or the circumstances of their publication. . . . Should the courts seek to expand their power so as to bring under their jurisdiction ill-defined controversies over constitutional issues, they would become the organ of political theories.[3]

As to the plaintiff who had been charged with political activity, the Court did consider the constitutional issue "as defined" by the Commission's charges and proposed findings and plaintiff's admissions. The Court held that the plaintiff's particular activities could constitutionally be made the basis for disciplinary action.

There are various policy considerations supporting the ripeness theory. Until the controversy has become concrete and focused, it is difficult for the Court to evaluate the practical merits of the position of each party. As one commentator has argued, when the constitutional issues seem to be "extremely close" the Court is more likely to demand a more concrete record, because it needs to know much more about the actual practices of enforcement and other relevant facts, which the bare text of an unenforced statute does not allow.[4] More pragmatic

reasons may also explain the application of the doctrine. If a record is concrete rather than abstract in nature, the Court may find a way of interpreting the statute to avoid or minimize the constitutional issue. The statute may be interpreted to raise constitutional problems as applied to some issues and not to others. Or, the application of customs behind the statute may justify a narrow interpretation of its scope. Not to be excluded is the possibility that if the Court waits for an actual controversy, the whole constitutional problem may just be eliminated by later developments.

A brief look at some of the other important cases applying the ripeness doctrine illustrate some of the themes, policies, problems, and inconsistencies in this area.

In *Adler v. Board of Education*[5] the majority upheld the constitutionality of a state law requiring the dismissal of any teacher who advocated or belonged to any organization advocating the overthrow of the government by force or violence. Black and Douglas dissented on the merits and would have invalidated the law. Only Frankfurter dissented on the ripeness issue, arguing that the facts in this case: "fall short of those found insufficient in the *Mitchell* case. These teachers do not allege that they have engaged in proscribed conduct or that they have any intention to do so. They do not suggest that they have been, or are, deterred from supporting causes or from joining organizations . . . except to say generally that the system complained of will have this effect on teachers as a group."[6]

In *International Longshoremen's & Warehousemen's Union, Local 37 v. Boyd,*[7] the Court, through Justice Frankfurter, ruled that an action was not ripe when a union and some of its alien members sued to enjoin the District Director of the Immigration and Naturalization Service from treat-

---

3. 330 U.S. at 89–91.

4. Scharph, Judicial Review and the Political Question: A Functional Analysis, 75 Yale L.J. 517, 531–532 (1966) (this point illustrated by discussion of United Public Workers v. Mitchell, 330 U.S. 75 (1947) and Adler v. Board of Education, 342 U.S. 485 (1952)).

5. 342 U.S. 485 (1952). On the merits, *Adler* was later substantially rejected. See Keyisihian v. Board of Regents, 385 U.S. 589, 593–595 (1967).

6. 342 U.S. at 504.

7. 347 U.S. 222 (1954).

ing aliens domiciled in the continental United States, but returning from temporary work in Alaska, as if they were aliens entering the United States for the first time. The distinction in treatment is important because newly entering aliens can be excluded for reasons which could not justify deporting aliens lawfully residing here.[8] Plaintiffs also asked for declaratory relief. "Appellants in effect asked the District Court to rule that a statute the sanctions of which had not been set in motion against individuals on whose behalf relief was sought, because an occasion for doing so had not arisen, would not be applied to them if in the future such a contingency should arise."[9]

Only Justices Black and Douglas dissented, pointing out that the immigration officials intended to construe and enforce the law as the union feared; that after the case had begun, they in fact had done so; that 1953 resident aliens were, on their return, processed as if they had never lived here; and that some of the union members "are evidently about to be denied the right ever to return. . . ."[10]

Cramp v. Board of Public Instruction,[11] involved a Florida statute which required every employee to take an oath that, inter alia, he had never lent "aid, support, advice or influence to the Communist party."[12] The plaintiff refused to take the oath but believed that he could truthfully do so as he understood its language. The Court found standing, and implicitly found ripeness, because:

> [T]he very vice of which he complains is that the language of the oath is so vague and indefinite that others could with reason interpret it differently. He argues, in other words, that he could unconstitutionally be subjected to all the risks of a criminal prosecution *despite* the sworn allegations as to his past conduct. . . .[13]

Citing *Mitchell* and *Adler,* the Court found "direct and serious" injury to the plaintiff.[14]

More recent cases have reaffirmed the basic principle of *Mitchell,* though the various fact situations involved show that no mechanical tests can be applied here.[15]

---

8. 347 U.S. at 225 (Black, J., dissenting).

9. 347 U.S. at 223–224.

10. 347 U.S. at 226 (Black, J., dissenting).

11. 368 U.S. 278 (1961).

12. 368 U.S. at 279.

13. 368 U.S. at 284 (emphasis in original).

14. 368 U.S. at 283.

15. An exhaustive list of cases is beyond the scope of this book. Some interesting cases include Poe v. Ullman, 367 U.S. 497 (1961) (statute complained of never enforced; Court does not reach merits); Epperson v. Arkansas, 393 U.S. 97, 109 (1965) (Black, J., concurring) (Court informed that there has "never been even a single attempt" to enforce statute; Court reaches the merits).

With *Mitchell* compare United States Civil Service Commission v. National Ass'n of Letter Carriers, 413 U.S. 548 (1973) (ripeness issue not discussed; Hatch Act issue decided on the merits, slight factual differences from Mitchell case, see 413 U.S. at 551–553 n. 3).

With International Longshoremen's & Warehousemen's Union, Local 37 v. Boyd, 347 U.S. 222 (1954), discussed in the text at nn. 7–10, supra—where the majority appeared unimpressed by the fact that since the case had begun the 1953 resident aliens had been processed as if they had never lived here—should be compared Regional Rail Reorganization Act Cases, 419 U.S. 102, 140 (1974): "[S]ince ripeness is peculiarly a

question of timing, it is the situation now rather than the situation at the time of the District Court's decision that must govern." (footnote omitted). See also, Buckley v. Valeo, 424 U.S. 1, 113–118 (1976) (per curiam).

An important case illustrating the problem of ripeness and decided in terms of the abstract record is Socialist Labor Party v. Gilligan, 406 U.S. 583, 588 (1972): "[W]e know very little more about the operation of the [challenged] Ohio affidavit procedure as a result of this lawsuit than we would if a prospective plaintiff who had never set foot in Ohio had simply picked this section of the Ohio election laws out of the statute books and filed a complaint. . . ."

See also, Duke Power Co. v. Carolina Environmental Study Group, Inc., 438 U.S. 59, 81–82 (1978) (finding ripeness in constitutional challenge to statute limiting liability of nuclear accidents caused by private nuclear power plants because case or controversy requirements were met and prudential considerations argued for prompt resolution of their important public issue; "appellees will sustain immediate injury from the operation of the disputed power plants and that such injury would be redressed by the relief requested" satisfies ripeness requirement).

New Jersey v. Portash, 440 U.S. 450, 456 (1979) (when defendant, who had been granted use immunity before the grand jury, was later informed by trial court during his subsequent prosecution that his grand jury testimony could be used to impeach him if he took

5. Hayburn's Case and the Requirement of Finality

The federal judiciary will not have its decision in case frustrated by having it subjected to revision, suspension, modification, or other review by the executive or legislative branches. Because of the principle of the separation of powers and the independence of the federal judiciary, the federal courts will not act as administrative agencies nor in any other way act as an agent of the executive or legislative branches.

The Supreme Court first spoke directly on the proper relationship between the legislature and the judiciary in *Hayburn's Case* [1] in 1792, only several years after adoption of the Constitution and enactment of the Judiciary Act of 1789. [2] *Hayburn's Case* concerned a statute empowering federal and state courts to determine the propriety and amount of pensions for disabled veterans of the Revolutionary War. [3] The statute provided for the Secretary of War to review the court decision and transmit his opinion to Congress; if Congress agreed with the allowance and amount of the pension, it would appropriate the necessary funds. [4] The Circuit Court for the District of Pennsylvania refused to consider William Hayburn's application for a pension under the statute, and the Attorney General sought a writ of mandamus in the Supreme Court. [5] Prior to the decision, Congress amended the legislation to provide other relief for the pensioners, and the Supreme Court dismissed on grounds of mootness. [6] In a footnote to the dismissal, however, the reporter of decisions noted some of the views of the justices on the constitutional division between the legislative and judicial functions. [7] He quoted Chief Justice Jay and Justice Cushing as Circuit Court Justices, holding that because the duties under the original pension act were not judicial, they could not perform them in their capacity as judges. They agreed, however, to perform the duties as commissioners while court was adjourned. [8] The footnote in *Hayburn's Case* also cited letters to the President from two circuit courts concerning the same statute. In 1792 the Circuit Court for the District of Pennsylvania, consisting of Supreme Court Justices Wilson and Blair and a district judge, protested to the President that the statute was radically inconsistent with the independence of the judicial power that the Constitution vested in the courts. [9] The Circuit Court for the District of North Carolina, including Associate Justice Iredell, also had written the President that no decision of any court of the United States could be liable to revision or suspension by the legislature because the Congress had no judicial power but impeachment. [10]

---

the stand, the fact that the defendant did not take the stand did not render abstract or hypothetical the constitutional question whether the ruling violated his privilege against self-incrimination).

See also, Babbitt v. United Farm Workers Nat. Union, 442 U.S. 289, 295–307 (1979) (provisions of state farm labor act regulating election procedures, consumer publicity, and criminal sanctions are justiciable and presented in a sufficiently concrete case, but challenges to the act's access and compulsory arbitration provisions are premature and their application is not shown to be presently real and concrete).

Hodel v. Virginia Surface Mining and Reclamation Ass'n, Inc., 452 U.S. 264, 294–97 (1981) (challenge against operation of the civil penalties of Surface Mining Act premature because appellees did not allege that they had any civil penalties assessed against them and district court did not find that they had been affected by any of the statutory procedures for the assessment and collection of fines). Accord, Hodel v. Indiana, 452 U.S. 314, 335–36 (1981).

1. 2 U.S. (2 Dall.) 408 (1792).

2. See generally Hart & Wechsler, The Federal Courts and the Federal System (2d ed. 1973), at 1–23, 32–36.

3. See Act of March 23, 1792, ch. 11, 1 Stat. 243.

4. See id.

5. 2 U.S. (2 Dall.) at 408.

6. Id. at 410 & n. (a).

7. Id. at 410 n. (a) (quoting opinion of federal Circuit Court for the District of New York and letters of Circuit Court Justices to the President). Subsequent cases approved and relied on the decisions reported in the margin of *Hayburn's Case* as a correct interpretation of the Constitution. See Muskrat v. United States, 219 U.S. 346, 352–53 (1911); United States v. Ferreira, 54 U.S. (13 How.) 40, 49–51 (1851).

8. See 2 U.S. (2 Dall.) at 410–13n. (a).

9. Id.

10. Id. It was not until a year after *Hayburn's Case* that the Supreme Court concluded, in an exchange of correspondence with President Washington,

The five justices were not speaking lightly; they were refusing, on constitutional grounds, to execute a statute according to Congress' terms over a decade before the Court decided *Marbury v. Madison*.[11]

Cases following *Hayburn's Case* further delineated the boundaries between the legislative and judicial functions. In *Gordon v. United States*[12] the Court held that it had no jurisdiction to hear an appeal from a Court of Claims decision regarding damage done to petitioner by United States troops during the War of 1812.[13] Although the Court did not provide the reasons for its holding, in a draft opinion Chief Justice Taney argued that the Court of Claims was not exercising a judicial function because it did not have the power to enforce its decisions; it was dependent on the Secretary of the Treasury and Congress to estimate and appropriate funds to pay its judgments.[14] The Chief Justice reasoned that the award of a remedy is an essential part of the exercise of judicial power and that rendering a judgment and yet having the remedy subject to Congressional approval is not an exercise of article III jurisdiction.[15] Lending support to this reasoning is *Schneiderman v. United States*,[16] in which a naturalized citizen contested a federal district court's de novo determination under section 15 of the Naturali-

zation Act of 1906 that his grant of citizenship from a naturalization court was invalid.[17] Although the full Court did not reach the issue, Justice Rutledge commented in a concurring opinion that Congress does not have authority both to confer jurisdiction and to nullify the effects of its exercise by other jurisdictional provisions in the same statute.[18] The principle raised by Justice Rutledge reflects the constitutional independence of the judiciary and fosters the separation of powers concept implicit in Article III. The full Court adopted this principle in *Chicago & Southern Airlines Inc. v. Waterman Steamship Corp.*,[19] in which it denied judicial review of a presidentially reviewable order of the Civil Aeronautics Board on the grounds that such dual review would violate article III.[20]

The principle underlying *Hayburn's Case* and its progeny is that the Article III guarantee of an independent federal judiciary prevents the legislature and the executive from reviewing a judicial decision. As the Court stated in *Chicago & Southern Airlines:*

> It has . . . been the firm and unvarying practice of Constitutional Courts to render no judgments not binding and conclusive on the parties and none that are subject to later review or alteration by administrative action.[21]

that the federal courts may not constitutionally give advisory opinions. See H. Johnston, Correspondence and Public Papers of John Jay 486–89 (1891).

11. 5 U.S. (1 Cranch) 137 (1803).

12. 69 U.S. (2 Wall.) 561 (1865); see Gordon v. United States, Appendix I, 117 U.S. 697 (decided 1865, Opinion printed in Oct. Term, 1885).

13. 69 U.S. (2 Wall.) at 561.

14. Gordon v. United States, Appendix I, 117 U.S. 697, 698–99 (decided 1865, Opinion printed in Oct. Term, 1885) (draft opinion of Taney, C.J., published posthumously).

15. Id. at 702. Chief Justice Taney's last judicial writing stated:

"Without such an award the judgment would be inoperative and nugatory, leaving the aggrieved party without a remedy . . . unless Congress should at some future time sanction it, and pass a law authorizing the court to carry its opinion into effect. Such is not the judicial power confided to this Court, in the

exercise of its appellate jurisdiction: yet it is the whole power that the Court is allowed to exercise under this act of Congress."

Id., see Muskrat v. United States, 219 U.S. 346, 354 (1911) (citing Chief Justice Taney's draft opinion as one of "great learning").

16. 320 U.S. 118 (1943).

17. Id. at 120–22.

18. Id. at 168–69 (Rutledge, J., concurring).

19. 333 U.S. 103 (1948).

20. Id. at 113–14. In strong language, Justice Jackson observed that "[j]udgments within the powers vested in the courts by the Judiciary Article of the Constitution may not lawfully be revised, overturned or refused faith and credit by another Department of Government." Id. at 113.

21. Chicago & Southern Airlines, Inc. v. Waterman S.S. Corp., 333 U.S. 103, 113–114 (1948). See also 333 U.S. at 113.

6. *Standing*

a. *Taxpayer and Citizen Standing*

Justice Douglas has warned us that "Generalizations about standing to sue are largely worthless as such,"[1] and Professor Paul Freund has described the problem of standing as "among the most amorphous in the entire domain of public law."[2] While it may not be possible to explain all of the contours of this doctrine, an historical discussion of its development should prove useful.

The first important link in the standing chain is *Frothingham v. Mellon*.[3] Mrs. Frothingham challenged the constitutionality of a federal Maternity Act which provided appropriations to the states if they would comply with its provisions. The intent of the Act was to reduce maternal and infant mortality. Plaintiff alleged that she was a taxpayer and in that capacity she was therefore injured because "the effect of the appropriations complained of will be to increase the burden of future taxation and thereby take her property without due process of law."[4]

The Court found this alleged injury unpersuasive. The Court distinguished the cases where a municipal taxpayer has been held to have standing to sue to object to alleged misuse of municipal moneys because in those situations the injury is "direct and immediate"[5] and the case "is not without some resemblance to that subsisting between stockholder and private corporation."[6] But a federal taxpayer's interest "is comparatively minute and indeterminable; and the effect upon future taxation . . . so remote . . . ."[7] The Court also found that granting standing to a federal taxpayer *qua* taxpayer would allow virtually anyone to challenge any federal act where its administration requires the outlay of money.[8] For the requisite standing the Court required that the following test be met:

> The party who invokes the power [of judicial review] must be able to show not only that the statute is invalid but that he has sustained or is immediately in danger of sustaining some direct injury as the result of its enforcement, and not merely that he suffers in some indefinite way in common with people generally.[9]

There are several important effects and distinctions of *Frothingham* that should be noted. The opinion purported to distinguish federal review of claims of municipal taxpayers,[10] though after the *Flast* case this distinction should not be valid. In addition so-called taxpayer suits such as *Frothingham* are challenges to the spending power, not to the taxing power. Such taxpayers do

---

1. Association of Data Processing Service Organizations, Inc. v. Camp, 397 U.S. 150, 151 (1970).

2. Hearings on S. 2097, before the Subcommittee on Constitutional Rights of the Senate Committee on the Judiciary, 89th Cong., 2d Sess., pt. 2 at 498 (1966).

3. Consolidated with Massachusetts v. Mellon, 262 U.S. 447 (1923). In Massachusetts v. Mellon the Court denied the standing of Massachusetts to attack the constitutionality of the Maternity Act. The state did not have standing on its own behalf because the statute did not coerce the state to do anything. 262 U.S. at 480, 482. Nothing could be done under the statute without the state's consent. The statute "simply extends an option which the State is free to accept or reject." 262 U.S. at 480. Neither can the state sue the federal government as representative of citizens of the state, for only the United States and not a state may be *parens patriae* as against the federal government. 262 U.S. at 485–486. Cf. Texas v. I.C.C., 258 U.S. 158, 162 (1922).

4. 262 U.S. at 486.

5. Id.

6. 262 U.S. at 487.

7. Id.

8. Id.

9. 262 U.S. at 488.

10. 262 U.S. at 486–87. Cf. Everson v. Board of Education, 330 U.S. 1, 3 (1947) ("The appellant, in his capacity as a district taxpayer, filed suit in a state court challenging the right of the Board [of Education] to reimburse parents of parochial school students."). Cf. Doremus v. Board of Education, 342 U.S. 429 (1952). There, an appeal was dismissed because there is no standing for municipal taxpayers objecting to bible reading in public schools where there is no allegation that the challenged activity adds any sum whatsoever to the cost of conducting school or is supported by a separate tax or any particular appropriation. *Everson* was distinguished as a case where there was a "measurable appropriation or disbursement of school district funds occasioned solely by the activities complained of." 342 U.S. at 434. There was also no standing to object to the bible reading by the plaintiffs as parents because, before the appeal was taken to the Supreme Court, the student had graduated and thus that aspect of the case was moot. 342 U.S. at 432.

not really object to the taxes levied but to the uses to which they apply. As Justice Harlan correctly explained in a dissent in another case, such a suit by a taxpayer challenging an expenditure:

> cannot result in an adjudication either of the plaintiff's tax liability or of the propriety of any particular level of taxation. The relief available consists entirely of the vindication of rights held in common by all citizens.[11]

Nor can it be said that such a taxpayer, if successful on the merits in declaring an expenditure unconstitutional, would have his taxation burden reduced, even minutely. Mrs. Frothingham really attacked only the expenditure, not the taxing power. Prohibiting an expenditure does not prohibit the taxation, for the two are not normally tied together:

> Taxes are ordinarily levied by the United States without limitations of purpose; absent such a limitation, payments received by the Treasury in satisfaction of tax obligations lawfully created become part of the Government's general funds.[12]

Taxes which are *earmarked* for a certain purpose may, even under the *Frothingham* ruling, be challenged in a variety of ways. Thus the taxpayer may contest paying the earmarked tax because the purposes for which it is earmarked are alleged to be unconstitutional.[13] Taxpayers, as taxpayers, may also contest the assessment of their tax liability (as opposed to the expenditure of the money received by the Government)—by a suit for refund, in defense of civil suit brought by the Government, or in defense of a prosecution—on the grounds that, for example, the money taxed cannot constitutionally be taxed under the income tax amendment to the Constitution,[14] or that reporting the income to be taxed violates the self-incrimination clause of the fifth amendment,[15] or that the tax is really a penalty in the guise of a tax,[16] or simply that the tax liability was incorrectly assessed under the statutory provisions.

In spite of these distinctions, *Frothingham* has been attacked as going too far in restricting taxpayer suits by not even allowing standing to taxpayers to object to federal monies being used to construct a church of a particular religious denomination in blatant disregard of the establishment clause of the first amendment.[17] Thus, proposals have been made for a statutory modification of the *Frothingham* rule, with most commentators arguing that the decision rested primarily on policy grounds favoring judicial self-restraint and not on the constitutional requirements of an Article III case or controversy.[18] With this background the Supreme Court undertook "a fresh examination of the limitations upon standing to sue in a federal court and the application of those limitations to taxpayer suits," in the case of *Flast v. Cohen*.[19]

In *Flast*, federal taxpayers challenged under the establishment clause the expenditure of federal funds under the Elementary and Secondary Education Act of 1965 to finance teaching of reading, arithmetic, and other subjects in, and purchase of textbooks for use in, religious schools. The *Flast* majority first held that the rule of *Frothingham* was one of judicial self-restraint and not required by the Constitution, for "we find no absolute bar in Article III to suits by federal taxpayers challenging allegedly unconstitutional

---

11. Flast v. Cohen, 392 U.S. 83, 118 (1968) (Harlan, J., dissenting).

12. 392 U.S. at 118 (Harlan, J., dissenting).

13. Bailey v. Drexel Furniture Co., 259 U.S. 20 (1922) (challenge to payment of Child Labor Tax, challenge upheld as a penalty). See also, Flast v. Cohen, 392 U.S. 83, 117 (1968) (Harlan, J., dissenting) (and cases cited therein).

14. E.g., Eisner v. Macomber, 252 U.S. 189 (1920).

15. E.g., Marchetti v. United States, 390 U.S. 39, 48–61 (1968).

16. E.g., Bailey v. Drexel Furniture Co., 259 U.S. 20 (1922).

17. Flast v. Cohen, 392 U.S. 83, 98 n. 17 (1968).

18. See generally, Hearings on S. 2097, before the Subcommittee on Constitutional Rights of the Senate Judiciary Committee, 89th Cong., 2d Sess. (1966); Jaffe, Standing to Secure Judicial Review: Private Actions, 75 Harv.L.Review 255 (1961).

19. 392 U.S. 83, 94 (1968).

federal taxing and spending programs."[20] The Court, however, did not overrule *Frothingham;* rather it established an important exception to its application:

[I]n ruling on standing, it is both appropriate and necessary to look to the substantive issues . . . to determine whether there is a logical nexus between the status asserted and the claim sought to be adjudicated. . . .

The nexus demanded of federal taxpayers has two aspects to it. *First* the taxpayer must establish a logical link between that status and the type of legislative enactment attacked. Thus, a taxpayer will be a proper party to allege the unconstitutionality only of exercises of congressional power under the taxing and spending clause of Art. I, § 8, of the Constitution. It will not be sufficient to allege an incidental expenditure of tax funds in the administration of an essentially regulatory statute. . . . *Secondly*, the taxpayer must establish a nexus between that status and the precise nature of the constitutional infringement alleged. Under this requirement, the taxpayer must show that the challenged enactment exceeds specific constitutional limitations imposed upon the exercise of the congressional taxing and spending power and not simply that the enactment is generally beyond the powers delegated to Congress by Art. I, § 8. When both nexuses are established, the litigant will have shown a taxpayer's stake in the outcome of the controversy and will be a proper and appropriate party to invoke a federal court's jurisdiction.[21]

The Court went on to explain that the *Flast* plaintiffs established both nexuses but Mrs. Frothingham had only met the first nexus. First, both the plaintiffs in *Flast* and in *Frothingham* complained of the exercise of the spending power under Article I, section 8. And, in both cases, the challenged program involved a substantial expenditure of funds, *not an incidental expenditure* of tax funds in the administration of an essentially regulatory statute.[22]

However, only the *Flast* taxpayer fulfilled the second requirement, that there be a nexus between the status as a taxpayer and the precise nature of the constitutional infringement alleged. The Court reached this conclusion after it examined the history behind the establishment clause of the first amendment and concluded that one of the "specific evils feared" was that the taxing and spending power would be used to favor one religion over another.[23] Thus, the challenged statute allegedly exceeded a specific constitutional limitation imposed on the taxing and spending power. The basis of the challenge, unlike the *Frothingham* case, was not simply that the taxing and spending was generally beyond Congress' powers.[24] The tenth amendment, relied on by plaintiffs in *Frothingham*, was not, under the *Flast* analysis, a specific limit on the taxing and spending powers.

Justice Harlan in dissent agreed that plaintiffs suing as representatives of the public interest, bereft of any personal or proprietary interest, are not constitutionally excluded from the federal courts,[25] but he advised that the Court should wait until Congress authorized such public actions, as it has done in the past.[26] The Court's willingness to hear such public actions, he feared "might well alter the allocation of authority among the three branches of the Federal Government."[27] The majority's limits to the public action plaintiff were not satisfactory

20. 392 U.S. at 101.

21. 392 U.S. at 102–103 (emphasis added).

22. The *Flast* Court emphasized that the expenditure of funds must not be an incidental expenditure in the administration of an essentially regulatory statute. "This requirement," the Court said, "is consistent with the limitation imposed upon state—taxpayer standing in federal courts in Doremus v. Board of Education, 342 U.S. 429 (1952)." 392 U.S. at 102. *Doremus* is discussed at note 10, supra. *Doremus* is apparently still law after *Flast.*

23. 392 U.S. at 103.

24. 392 U.S. at 103–105.

25. 392 U.S. at 119–120 (Harlan, J., dissenting).

26. 392 U.S. at 131–132 (Harlan, J., dissenting). See, e.g., Oklahoma v. Civil Service Comm'n, 330 U.S. 127, 137–39 (1947), where the Court found standing by a state because Congress had created such standing by statute. For more recent affirmations of this principle by the Court, see O'Shea v. Littleton, 414 U.S. 488, 493 n. 2 (1974); S. v. D., 410 U.S. 614, 617 n. 3 (1973).

27. 392 U.S. at 130 (Harlan, J., dissenting).

because the criteria "are not in any sense a measurement of any plaintiff's interest in the outcome of any suit." [28] Justice Harlan also was not persuaded that, even accepting the nexus tests, it could be shown historically that the establishment clause met the requirement of the second nexus.[29]

Other than an attack based on the establishment clause, the *Flast* majority offered no examples of what other types of constitutional provisions were specific limitations to grant standing to any taxpayer under the second nexus of the *Flast* test. Neither have later cases. Thus, in *United States v. Richardson*[30] the Court (5–4), held that taxpayers did not meet the *Flast* test and had no standing to challenge a statute for allegedly violating Article I, section 9, clause 7, of the Constitution, which requires that "a regular statement and Account of the Receipts and Expenditures of all public Money shall be published from time to time." Plaintiffs alleged that the challenged statute unconstitutionally allowed the Director of the CIA to avoid the requirement of public reporting of its public funds. Justice Powell, concurring in *Richardson* found that Harlan's critique of the *Flast* nexus test "unanswerable" and predicted that the test's "lack of real meaning and of principled content . . . renders it likely that it will in time collapse of its own weight . . . ." [31]

Similarly in *Simon v. Eastern Kentucky Welfare Rights Organization*[32] the Court denied standing to plaintiffs to sue the Secretary of the Treasury on the theory that a recent Revenue Ruling was inconsistent with the Internal Revenue Code. Plaintiffs claimed that this Ruling, which granted favorable tax treatment to hospitals despite their refusal to give full service to indigents, injured them. They sought a requirement that all hospitals serve indigents as a condition of favorable tax treatment in order to discourage hospitals from denying their services to plaintiffs. The Court found the allegations too speculative in the absence of any federal statute creating standing for such a class of plaintiffs. Justice Stewart's separate concurrence noted that "I cannot now imagine a case, at least outside the First Amendment area, where a person whose own tax liability was not affected ever could have standing to litigate the federal tax liability of someone else." [33]

The same day as *Richardson* was decided, the Court held by a vote of 6–3, in *Schlesinger v. Reservists Committee to Stop the War*,[34] that plaintiffs had no standing, either as taxpayers or as citizens generally, to challenge the membership of Members of Congress in the military reserve as being in violation of Article 1, section 6, clause 2. This incompatibility clause provides that "no person holding any office under the United States, shall be a member of either house during his continuance in office." As to citizen standing, the Court found only "injury in the abstract." [35] And as to taxpayer standing, the Court found that it did not exist because the plaintiffs below "did not challenge an enactment under art. I, § 8, but rather the action of the Executive Branch in permitting Members of Congress to maintain their reserve status." [36]

The narrowness with which the Court has interpreted the *Flast* holding is well illustrated by *Valley Forge Christian College v. Americans United for Separation of Church and State, Inc.*[37] The Secretary of Health, Education, and Welfare (now called the Secretary of Education) disposed of surplus federal property—in this instance, a 77 acre tract of real property—by giving it to

---

28. 392 U.S. at 121 (Harlan, J., dissenting).

29. 392 U.S. at 125.

30. 418 U.S. 166 (1974).

31. 418 U.S. at 183, 184 (Powell, J., concurring).

32. 426 U.S. 26 (1976).

33. 426 U.S. 26, 46 (Stewart, J., concurring).

34. 418 U.S. 208 (1974).

35. 418 U.S. 208, 217.

36. 418 U.S. 208, 228. See also Richardson v. Kennedy, 401 U.S. 901 (1971), affirming 313 F.Supp. 1281 (D.Pa.1970) (taxpayer has no standing, under the second nexus of the *Flast* test, to challenge Congressional salary increases under art. I, § 8).

37. 154 U.S. 464 (1982).

the Valley Forge Christian College, which would use it to train "men and women for Christian service as either ministers or laymen." The Secretary acted pursuant to a federal regulation, which implemented and helped effectuate a federal statute, which in turn was authorized by Article IV, section 3, clause 2 of the Constitution, which vests in Congress the power to "dispose of" and make "all needful Rules" regarding federal property.

Justice Rehnquist for the Court held, surprisingly, that the plaintiffs had failed the first prong of the *Flast* test. First, they "do not challenge the constitutionality of the Federal Property Administrative Services Act itself, but rather a particular Executive branch action arguably authorized by the Act;" thus the "source of their complaint is not a congressional action, but a decision by HEW to transfer a parcel of federal property." Second, "and perhaps redundantly," the property transfer was not pursuant to the taxing and spending clause but rather the property clause of Article IV, section 3.[38] *Flast* would appear to be a case which is limited precisely to its facts.

b. Personal Standing, Nontaxpayer Suits and the Requirement of Injury in Fact

Whether a party has "alleged such a personal stake in the outcome of the controversy as to assure that concrete adverseness which sharpens the presentation of issues" is we are told, "the gist of the question of federal standing. It is, of course, a question of federal law."[39] In the taxpayer suits we have discussed, the Court has attempted to formulate tests to determine when a taxpayer *qua* taxpayer has alleged such a personal

stake in the outcome of a suit. In nontaxpayer actions, the determination of whether plaintiff has suffered something deemed to be an "injury" for purposes of the standing requirement has been the subject of much litigation and changing trends in the Supreme Court.

The nexus requirement of taxpayer suits is not part of the constitutional requirements of standing outside the taxpayer context.[40] For personal standing, the plaintiff must establish at a minimum a "personal stake" in the outcome. This stake requires a two-fold showing: first, a "distinct and palpable injury" to the plaintiff, and second, a "'fairly traceable' causal connection between the claimed injury and the challenged conduct."[41] Plaintiff can meet the second prong of this requirement by showing that there is a "substantial likelihood" that the relief requested of the court will redress the claimed injury.[42]

In general it may be said that if plaintiff is protesting a claimed invasion of a generalized constitutional injury, the Court appears to be more reluctant to find standing—and thus create the need to dispose of a constitutional claim—than in cases where the plaintiff is arguably within the zone of interests protected by a federal statute, or a statute appears to grant standing in the case. In other words, if Congress speaks, either explicitly or implicitly, the Court will accept Congress' decision to confer standing to litigate constitutional or statutory claims. "When Congress has so acted, the requirements of Article III remain: 'the plaintiff still must allege a distinct and palpable injury to himself, even if it is an injury shared by a large class of other possible litigants.'"[43] If Congress has not so spoken,

38. 454 U.S. at 479–480 & n. 15 (footnotes omitted). Brennan, J., joined by Marshall & Blackmun, JJ., filed a lengthy dissent; Stevens, J., also wrote a separate dissent.

39. Baker v. Carr, 369 U.S. 186, 204 (1962). In the Matter of the Application of Northern States Power Co. For a Proposed Increase in Rates for Electric Service, 328 N.W.2d 852, 855 (S.D.1983) (Henderson, J. citing treatise).

40. Duke Power Co. v. Carolina Environmental Study Group, Inc., 438 U.S. 59, 78–79 (1978).

41. 438 U.S. at 72.

42. 438 U.S. at 75 & n. 20. See, Young v. Klutznick, 652 F.2d 617, 629 (6th Cir. 1981) (Keith, J., dissenting), citing an earlier edition of this treatise.

43. Simon v. Eastern Kentucky Welfare Rights Organization, 426 U.S. 26, 41 n. 22 (1976), quoting Warth v. Seldin, 422 U.S. 490, 501 (1975); California Medical

the plaintiff alleging a constitutional injury must not only overcome the Article III standing requirements but also the use of standing as a tool of judicial self-restraint.[44]

Association of Data Processing Service Organizations v. Camp, and *Barlow v. Collins*[45] decided the same day, illustrate the modern approach for nonconstitutional claims.

In *Association of Data Processing* the Court, through Justice Douglas, held that the petitioners, who sold data processing services to businesses generally, had standing to challenge a ruling, by the Comptroller of the Currency, which allowed national banks to make data processing services available to other banks and bank customers. The petitioners claimed that this ruling was contrary to statutory prohibitions restricting the activities of national banks. Justice Douglas noted that unlike *Flast*, the petitioners sued not as taxpayers but as competitors. To determine if these petitioners have standing, Justice Douglas fashioned a two-part test.

First, the plaintiff must allege "that the challenged action has caused him injury in fact, economic or otherwise."[46] Petitioners met this first test because, as competitors with banks, the ruling by the Comptroller threatened them with loss of future profits.

Secondly, the "question is whether the interest sought to be protected by the complainant is arguably within the zone of interests to be protected or regulated by the statute or constitutional guarantee in question."[47] The Court explicitly rejected a more limited test promulgated earlier.[48] This zone of "interests" is also not limited to economic interests any more than the "injury in fact" requirement included only economic injury. To illustrate this latter point Justice Douglas cited other cases showing that the requisite injury may be aesthetic, conservational and recreational, economic, or reflect a spiritual stake in first amendment values of free exercise and establishment.[49] One who is financially injured "may be a reliable private attorney general to litigate the issues of the public interest in the present case."[50] Presumably one suffering a

Ass'n v. Federal Election Comm'n, 453 U.S. 182, 187 n. 6 (1981).

The question of who has standing to assert federal constitutional rights is a federal question which a state court cannot preclude the Supreme Court from deciding when the matter is in federal court. United States v. Raines, 362 U.S. 17, 23 n. 3 (1960); Cramp v. Board of Public Instruction, 368 U.S. 278, 282 (1961); Princeton University v. Schmid, 455 U.S. 100, 102 n.* (1982) (per curiam).

44. Cf. Schlesinger v. Reservists Committee to Stop the War, 418 U.S. 208 (1974):

"It is one thing for a court to hear an individual's complaint that certain specific government action will cause that person private competitive injury, Association of Data Processing Service Organizations, Inc. v. Camp, 397 U.S. 150 (1970), or a complaint that individual enjoyment of certain natural resources has been impaired by such action, United States v. SCRAP, 412 U.S. 669, 687 (1973), but it is another matter to allow a citizen to call on the courts to resolve abstract questions." (418 U.S. at 223; footnote omitted).

See also, Warth v. Seldin, 422 U.S. 490, 500 (1975).

Gladstone, Realtors v. Village of Bellwood, 441 U.S. 91, 99 (1979) affirmed the distinction formulated in this paragraph between standing based solely on Article III

(where plaintiff must satisfy both case or controversy requirements and prudential principles) and standing based on a statute (where Congress may expand standing to the full extent permitted by Article III without regard to prudential standing rules). See generally Varat, Variable Justiciability and the Duke Power Case, 58 Tex.L.Rev. 273 (1980).

45. Association of Data Processing Service Organizations v. Camp, 397 U.S. 150 (1970); Barlow v. Collins, 397 U.S. 159 (1970).

See Young v. Klutznick, 652 F.2d 617, 629 (6th Cir. 1981) (Keith, J., dissenting), citing this section of an earlier edition of this treatise.

46. 397 U.S. 150, 152 (1970).

47. 397 U.S. at 153.

48. 397 U.S. at 153. The earlier, rejected test was issued in Tennessee Elec. Power Co. v. Tennessee Valley Authority, 306 U.S. 118 (1939). In that case the Court denied competitors' standing to object to the T.V.A. operating allegedly in violation of the statutory plan. The Court then held injury in fact was not the test; rather, the right invaded must be a "legal right". See 306 U.S. at 137–139.

49. 397 U.S. at 154, and cases cited therein. See also, Sierra Club v. Morton, 405 U.S. 727, 734 (1972).

50. 397 U.S. at 154.

noneconomic loss will also be a reliable private attorney general.[51]

In *Barlow v. Collins*,[52] the Court, again through Justice Douglas, held that tenant farmers eligible for payments under a federal program had standing to contest the validity of a certain administrative regulation. Applying the *Data Processing* test the Court found that the farmers had standing. Also, after finding standing, the Court found, as it had earlier in the *Data Processing* case, that judicial review of the action of the Secretary of Agriculture was not precluded, either expressly or impliedly, by statute.[53]

Justice Brennan, joined by Justice White, concurred in the result and dissented in both *Data Processing* and *Barlow*. Brennan rejected the two step test and argued that the "first step is the only one that need be made to determine standing." [54] That is, if plaintiff alleges that a challenged action has caused him injury in fact, economic or otherwise, Brennan would find standing.[55]

The fact that the injury alleged need not be limited to economic injury is fortified by the Supreme Court's later decision in *Sierra Club v. Morton*,[56] where the Court stated:

Aesthetic and environmental well-being, like economic well-being, are important ingredients of the quality of life in our society, and the fact that particular environmental interests are shared by the many rather than by the few does not make them less deserving of legal protection through the judicial process.[57]

The 4–3 majority in *Sierra Club* held that the plaintiffs did not have standing to contest a proposed development in the Mineral King Valley because the Sierra Club did not allege that it was among the injured.

The alleged injury [to the environment of the Mineral King Valley] will be felt directly only by those who use Mineral King and Sequoia National Park, and for whom the aesthetic and recreational values of the area will be lessened by the highway and ski resort. The Sierra Club failed to allege that it or its members would be effected in any of their activities or pastimes by the Disney development. Nowhere in the pleadings or affidavits did the Club state that its members use Mineral King for any purpose. . . .[58]

In a footnote the Court explained that its decision does not bar the Sierra Club from amending its complaint to make the proper allegations to secure standing.[59] Once it secures standing, the plaintiff may assert the general public interest in its role as a private attorney general.[60]

Justice Douglas in dissent, argued that the "critical question of 'standing' would be simplified and also put neatly into focus if we fashioned a federal rule that allowed environmental issues to be litigated before federal agencies or federal courts in the name of the inanimate object about to be despoiled, defaced, or invaded by roads and bulldozers and where injury is the subject of public outrage."[61]

A case that Professor Davis has called probably "an all-time high in Supreme Court liberality on the subject of standing,"[62] is *United States v. Students Challenging Regulatory Agency Procedures* (SCRAP).[63]

51. See also, Sierra Club v. Morton, 405 U.S. 727, 737 & 740 n. 15 (1972).

52. 397 U.S. 159 (1970). See also Douglas Oil Co. v. Petrol Stops Northwest, 441 U.S. 211, 218 n. 8 (1979) (defendants in a private antitrust action have standing under Article III to object to a court order releasing grand jury transcripts to the plaintiffs, although the defendants had pled *nolo contendere*).

53. 397 U.S. at 165.

54. 397 U.S. at 168 (Brennan J., concurring in the result and dissenting).

55. 397 U.S. at 172 (Brennan J., concurring in the result and dissenting).

56. 405 U.S. 727 (1972).

57. 405 U.S. at 734.

58. 405 U.S. at 735.

59. 405 U.S. at 735 n. 8.

60. 405 U.S. at 740 n. 15.

61. 405 U.S. at 741 (Douglas, J., dissenting). See generally, Stone, Should Trees Have Standing—Toward Legal Rights for Natural Objects, 45 So.Calif.L. Rev. 450 (1972); C. Stone, Should Trees Have Standing (1974).

62. K. Davis, Administrative Law of the Seventies § 22.02–2 at 489 (1976).

63. 412 U.S. 669 (1973).

SCRAP was an unincorporated association representing five law students with the purpose of enhancing the quality of the environment. SCRAP protested the failure of the Interstate Commerce Commission to suspend a $2^1/2\%$ surcharge on nearly all freight rates. SCRAP claimed standing in that each of its members suffered economic, recreational, and aesthetic harm because of the adverse environmental impact of the freight structure. Each of SCRAP's members, it was alleged, had to pay more for finished products because of this freight structure. The SCRAP members use of the forests, rivers, streams, and so on had been adversely affected by the increased freight rates. Moreover, it was alleged, the air the SCRAP members breathed was being increased in pollution because of this modified rate structure. And, SCRAP alleged, each of its members has been forced to pay increased taxes because of the sums which must be expended to dispose of otherwise reusable waste materials. The surcharge, SCRAP argued, was unlawful because the I.C.C. had failed to file a detailed environmental impact statement, for the 2.5% surcharge allegedly had an adverse impact on recycling and thus was a major federal action significantly affecting the environment.

In part II of the opinion of the Court (written by Justice Stewart and joined by Justices Brennan, Blackmun, Douglas, and Marshall), the Court admitted that "all persons who utilize the scenic resources of the country, and indeed all who breath its air, could claim harm similar to that alleged by the environmental groups here. But we have already made it clear that standing is not to be denied simply because many people suffer the same injury."[64] The majority thus found standing: "We cannot say on these pleadings that the appellees could not prove their allegations which, if proved, would place them squarely among those persons injured

in fact by the Commission's action, and entitled under the clear impact of *Sierra Club* to seek review."[65] The Court specifically refused to limit standing to those "significantly" affected by agency action. An "identifiable trifle" is enough.[66]

To such cases as *Sierra Club* and SCRAP must be compared cases involving constitutional issues. While SCRAP shows that the Article III threshold of case or controversy is very low indeed, it does not follow that the Court will always allow standing to plaintiffs who satisfy this threshold and who seek to litigate constitutional claims. The policies of judicial restraint dictate a higher standard in some constitutional cases. A comparison of two such constitutional cases, *Trafficante v. Metropolitan Life Insurance Co.*[67] and *Warth v. Seldin*[68] will illustrate this distinction.

In *Trafficante* two tenants (one black and one white) of an apartment complex housing about 8,200 residents filed separate complaints with the Secretary of Housing and Urban Development under the Civil Rights Act of 1968. Each alleged that the owner of the complex had discriminated against non-whites in the rental of housing. These two tenants alleged injury in that they had lost the social benefits of living in an integrated community; they had lost the business and professional advantages which would have accrued if they had lived with members of minority groups; and they had suffered embarassment and economic damage in social, business, and professional activities from being stigmatized by being residents in a white ghetto.

While the unanimous Court found the legislative history of the 1968 Civil Rights Act "not too helpful,"[69] the Court found an Article III case or controversy and held that it could give vitality to the particular statutory section "only by a generous construction which gives standing to sue to all in the

---

64. 412 U.S. at 687.

65. 412 U.S. at 689–90.

66. 412 U.S. at 689 n. 14, quoting Davis, Standing: Taxpayers and Others, 35 U.Chi.L.Rev. 601, 613 (1968).

67. 409 U.S. 205 (1972).

68. 422 U.S. 490 (1975).

69. 409 U.S. at 210.

same housing unit who are injured by racial discrimination in the management of those facilities within the coverage of the statute."[70]

In *Warth v. Seldin*,[71] various organizations and individual residents in the Rochester, New York, metropolitan area brought an action against the town of Penfield, adjacent to Rochester, and against members of Penfield's Zoning, Planning and Town Boards. Plaintiffs claimed that Penfield's Zoning Ordinance unconstitutionally excluded persons of low and moderate income from living in the town because of requirements such as lot size, setback, and floor area.

The Court found no standing in the claims of plaintiffs who asserted injury as persons of low or moderate income and as members of racial or ethnic groups. These plaintiffs were not able to allege other than in conclusory terms that they had been personally injured: none of these plaintiffs had any present interest in any Penfield property; none was subject to the ordinance's strictures; none had ever been denied a variance or permit by the defendants; there was no evidence that proposed efforts of third parties to build low and moderate housing would have satisfied the plaintiffs' needs at prices they could afford. In fact, their allegations suggested that "their inability to reside in Penfield is the consequence of the economics of the area housing market, rather than respondents' assertedly illegal acts."[72] Plaintiffs had not sufficiently alleged specific concrete facts that the challenged practices harmed them and that if the Court were to intervene they would personally benefit in a tangible way.

Some of the plaintiffs alleged standing as taxpayers of Rochester who claimed economic injury because Penfield's refusal to allow or facilitate such construction of such low or moderate housing required Rochester to assume a greater burden in this area. The majority also rejected this notion of standing and in so doing relied specifically on the lack of a Congressional statute deemed to create such standing. The only basis, the majority found, of the Rochester taxpayers' claim is that the Penfield ordinance violated the rights of third parties, persons of low and moderate income said to be excluded from Penfield. The prudential standing rule normally bars litigants from asserting the rights or legal interests of others. This "rule of judicial self-governance is subject to exceptions, the most prominent of which is that Congress may remove it by statute. Here, however, no statute expressly or by clear implication grants a right of action, and thus standing to seek relief, to persons in petitioners' position."[73]

One of the organizations claimed standing in part because 9% of its membership is composed of permanent residents of Penfield and these residents were denied the benefits of living in a racially and ethnically integrated community. The majority rejected this claim for standing and distinguished *Trafficante* because in that case the plaintiffs relied on the Civil Rights Act of 1968. Plaintiffs in *Warth* relied on the more general sections 1981, 1982, and 1983 of title 42.[74] The majority emphasized:

As we have observed above, Congress may create a statutory right or entitlement the alleged deprivation of which can confer standing to sue even where the plaintiff would have suf-

---

70. 409 U.S. at 212.

71. 422 U.S. 490 (1975).

72. 422 U.S. at 506 (footnote omitted).

73. 422 U.S. at 509–10.

74. 422 U.S. at 493, 512–13.

When area residents and a village charged real estate brokers with "steering" prospective home buyers to different residential areas according to race in violation of section 812 of the Fair Housing Act, the Supreme Court, in Gladstone, Realtors v. Village of Bellwood, 441 U.S. 91 (1979), found that the standing

granted by Congress under that section was intended to reach as broadly as is permitted by Article III, just as the Court similarly had interpreted section 810 of that Act in *Trafficante*. The Village of Bellwood had standing because it alleged that the racial steering manipulated the housing market in the Village and reduced its tax base. The individuals appeared before the district court in two capacities. First, they acted as "testers" of defendants' practices, i.e., without intending to actually buy homes they pretended to be seeking homes to test the defendants. Before the Supreme Court the plaintiffs did not press the claim of

fered no judicially cognizable injury in the absence of statute. . . . No such statute is applicable here.[75]

Other plaintiffs were also found not to have standing on different grounds or not to have alleged the continued existence of a ripe controversy with the result that no plaintiff was able to bring the law suit.

In *Moose Lodge v. Irvis*,[76] the Court held that a Lodge member's black guest refused service in the Code's dining room because of the Lodge's policy barring blacks from membership and from being guests had no standing to challenge the membership policies because he had never sought to be a member. In *Laird v. Tatum*[77] the majority found that plaintiffs who claimed to be chilled in violation of the first amendment by allegedly illegal surveillance by the U.S. Army lacked sufficient standing to maintain the action. Professor Davis in criticizing this case noted that "[p]robably the five Justices of the majority would not deny that the plaintiffs were injured more than the students were in the SCRAP case. But courts are more comfortable in protecting the environment than they are in restricting an espionage system."[78] Plaintiffs were apparently insufficiently chilled. A statute could have conferred standing on such plaintiffs in this case.[79] In *S. v. D.*[80] where the Court held

that a private citizen lacks a judicially cognizable interest in the prosecution or nonprosecution of another, the majority specifically noted that this lack of standing could be cured by statute.[81]

In *Singleton v. Wulff*[82] the Court found that doctors have standing to raise their rights and the rights of their patients not to have abortions interfered with by a state law forbidding Medicaid payments to be used for certain abortions. The Court appeared to emphasize the concrete commercial injury alleged: if the physicians prevail in their efforts to remove the Medicaid limitation of reimbursable abortions, they will benefit, for they will then receive payments for the abortions; the state and the federal government will be out of pocket by the amount of the payments. "The relationship between the parties is classically adverse, and there clearly exists between them a case or controversy in the constitutional sense."[83]

Related to these cases are those instances where plaintiffs allege that threatened governmental action will injure them in the near future. The Court is not entirely consistent when it finds that a threat is sufficient to confer standing and when it finds the threat insufficient.

In *O'Shea v. Littleton*[84] the majority of the Court found no Article III standing by

standing as testers, and the Supreme Court did not decide that question. Second, plaintiffs sought standing as homeowners in the community at which the racial steering was directed. In that capacity the Court held that they had standing, but that two plaintiffs who did not reside in the target area lacked standing. 441 U.S. at 112 & n. 25. See also, Havens Realty Corp. v. Coleman, 455 U.S. 363 (1982) ("testers," i.e., persons who pose as renters or purchasers for the purpose of gathering information of illegal racial steering, also have standing under this Act).

75. 422 U.S. at 513–14, citing S. v. D., 410 U.S. 614, 617, n. 3 (1973), and Trafficante v. Metropolitan Life Insurance Co., 409 U.S. 205, 212 (1972). For an article analyzing Congressional power to establish standing and suggesting some reforms, see Sedler, Standing and the Burger Court: An Analysis and Some Proposals for Legislative Reform, 30 Rutgers L.Rev. 863 (1977).

76. 407 U.S. 163 (1972).

77. 408 U.S. 1 (1972).

78. K. Davis, Administrative Law of the Seventies § 22.02–8, at 504 (1976).

79. Rotunda, Comment, 27 Harv.L.Bulletin 4 (Spring 1976).

80. 410 U.S. 614 (1973). Leeke v. Timmerman, 454 U.S. 83 (1981) (per curiam) (actions of state officials, which influenced decision of state solicitor to oppose issuance of arrest warrants of prison guards, did not confer standing on prison inmates).

81. Id. at 617 n. 3. In Duke Power Co. v. Carolina Environmental Study Group, Inc., 438 U.S. 59, 79 n.24 (1978), the Court said that in S. v. D., 410 U.S. 614 (1972), the Court denied standing "not because of the absence of a subject matter nexus between the injury asserted and the constitutional claim but instead because of the unlikelihood that the relief requested would redress appellant's claimed injury."

82. 428 U.S. 106 (1976).

83. 428 U.S. at 113.

84. 414 U.S. 488 (1974). See also, City of Los Angeles v. Lyons, 103 S.Ct. 1660 (1983) (lack of case or controversy to justify equitable relief); Ashcroft v. Mattis, 431 U.S. 171 (1977) (per curiam).

plaintiffs, residents of Cairo, Illinois, who brought a civil rights action against the State's Attorney, his investigator, the Police Commissioner, the county magistrate and an associate judge, who allegedly engaged, under color of law, in a continuing violation of Constitutional rights in the administration of the criminal justice system by setting illegal bonds, imposing higher sentences on non-whites, and requiring members of plaintiffs' class to pay for trial by jury. The majority found insufficient allegations of actual continuing injury. Also in *Laird v. Tatum* [85] discussed above, the Court found the alleged chill of first amendment rights insufficient to support the necessary real and immediate threat of injury. Yet in *Doe v. Bolton* [86] the Court found that physicians, who were consulted by pregnant women, had standing to contest the constitutionality of the state's abortion law—

> despite the fact that the record does not disclose that any one of them has been prosecuted, or threatened with prosecution, for violation of the State's abortion statutes. The physician is one against whom these criminal statutes directly operate in the event he procures an abortion that does not meet the statutory exceptions and conditions. The physician-appellants, therefore, assert a sufficiently direct threat of personal detriment. They should not be required to await and undergo a criminal prosecution as the sole means of seeking relief.[87]

Apparently what may have distinguished *Doe* from *Tatum*, *O'Shea* and other such cases is not so much the reality of the threat—which was not dissimilar in all these cases—but in the concreteness of the factual allegations which were more precise in *Doe*, and in the nature of the relief sought, which required less judicial supervision and exertion of continual judicial power in *Doe* than in *Tatum* and *O'Shea*.

This analysis of *Doe*, as well as the reluctance of the Court to find standing in some cases as opposed to others, supports the view that the law of standing, as a practical matter, is used as a decisional tool by the Court to avoid disposing of certain cases on the merits. As the merits of the constitutional issue are more difficult, the Court may be more likely to require plaintiff to demonstrate more standing than in other cases. If Congress steps in and by statute creates standing, the Court is much more ready to decide the case on the merits. Congress then has in effect asked the Court to decide the issue, thus serving to justify the Court's exercise of judicial review. The only limit on Congress' power is that Congress cannot exceed the case or controversy requirements of Article III. But as we have seen in *United States v. SCRAP* [88] the Article III threshold of case on controversy is very low indeed.

This view of the Court has been subjected to much criticism. Professor Davis, for example, has argued:

> Protecting against an excessive judicial role by using the law of standing is likely to mean for some cases not only providing that protection but also preventing judicial review that is needed in the interests of justice. Therefore, the law of standing is the wrong tool to use for confining courts to a role that is appropriate for courts.[89]

Yet, the Court often acts as if it is using standing as another tool for confining courts to a role that is appropriate for courts.

c. Third Party Standing

It is said to be the rule that "one to whom application of a statute is constitutional will not be heard to attack the statute on the ground that impliedly it might also be taken as applying to other persons or other situations in which its application might be unconstitutional."[1] The basis for this rule of self restraint lies in prudential concerns: the desire to avoid constitutional questions and to

---

85. 408 U.S. 1 (1972). See text at nn. 77–79, supra.

86. 410 U.S. 179 (1973).

87. 410 U.S. at 188.

88. 412 U.S. 669 (1973).

89. K. Davis, Administrative Law of the Seventies § 22.21 at 523 (1976).

1. United States v. Raines, 362 U.S. 17, 21 (1960).
See also, H. L. v. Matheson, 450 U.S. 398, 405 (1981) (minor attacking state statute requiring physician's pa-

assure that the most effective and concerned advocate is before the Court.[2]

However, in order to protect civil rights, to this basic rule there are several exceptions allowing third-party standing, that is, standing to assert the rights of others not before the Court. In general the Court will allow litigants standing to assert the rights of third parties after weighing the importance of the relationship between the litigant and the third party, the ability of the third party to vindicate his own rights and the risk that the rights of third parties will be diluted if third party standing is not allowed.[3]

Before considering specific case applications of these exceptions, third party standing should be distinguished from the right sometimes granted to a litigant to challenge a statute as overbroad. Such challenges normally are allowed in the first amendment area. In overbreadth cases, the litigant challenges a statute on its face because, it is argued, that while a narrowly drawn statute could constitutionally prohibit his activity, the challenged statute is overbroad and appears to include activity which is constitutionally protected. The actual litigant before the Court in such cases is injured because the Court finds he has a right to be

prosecuted only under a statute that is narrowly drawn. In third party standing cases, the litigant claims that the law as applied injures not only him but a third party. Such cases are not necessarily in the first amendment area. First amendment overbreadth is discussed in Chapter 18 on free speech.[4]

The leading case illustrating one of the exceptions to the basic third-party standing rule is *Barrows v. Jackson.*[5] Prior to *Barrows,* in *Shelley v. Kraemer,*[6] the Court had held it was a violation of the equal protection clause of the Fourteenth Amendment for the Courts to enforce by injunction racially restrictive covenants in real property. In *Barrows,* a co-covenantor sued at law for damages against another co-covenantor who allegedly broke the agreement. The Court held that the damage action could not be maintained under the Fourteenth Amendment, and in reaching that result it discussed third-party standing and ruled that the white seller could assert the rights of the black purchaser.

The Court noted that unlike *Shelley,* "no non-Caucasian is before the Court claiming to have been denied his constitutional rights. May respondent, whom petitioners seek to coerce by an action to pay damages for her failure to honor her restrictive covenant, re-

---

rental notification prior to performing abortion on a dependent, unmarried, minor girl does not have standing to attack statute as applied to unmarried minors who are mature and emancipated because "she did not allege or proffer any evidence that either she or any member of her class is mature or emancipated.").

2. Duke Power Co. v. Carolina Environmental Study Group, Inc., 438 U.S. 59, 80 (1978) (noting such prudential limits on third party standing).

3. Note, Standing to Assert Constitutional Jus Tertii, 88 Harv.L.Rev. 423, 441 (1972). See generally Sedler, Standing to Assert Constitutional Jur Tertii in the Supreme Court, 71 Yale L.J. 599 (1962). See also, Sedler, The Assertion of Constitutional Jus Tertii: A Substantive Approach, 70 Calif.L.Rev. 1308 (1982) (arguing that a party should be able to prevail in constitutional litigation only if he can show a violation of his own rights). In a recent case Justice Blackmun has emphasized two factors:

"[T]he Court has looked primarily to two factual elements to determine whether the rule [as to third party standing] should apply in a particular case. The first is the relationship of the litigants to the

person whose rights he seeks to assert. If the enjoyment of the right is inextricably bound up with the activity the litigant wishes to pursue, the court can at least be sure its construction of the right is not unnecessary in the sense that the right's enjoyment will be unaffected by the outcome of the suit. Furthermore, the relationship between the litigant and the third party may be such that the former is fully, or very nearly, as effective a proponent of the right as the latter. . . .

"The other factual element to which the Court has looked is the ability of the third party to assert his own right . . . . If there is some genuine obstacle to such assertion . . . the third party's absence from court loses its tendency to suggest that his right is not truly at stake. . . ." Singleton v. Wulff, 428 U.S. 106, 114–16 (1976). (Opinion of Blackmun, J., joined by Brennan, White, & Marshall, JJ.)

4. See Chapter 18, Section III, B.

5. 346 U.S. 249 (1953).

6. 334 U.S. 1 (1948).

ly on the invasion of the rights of others in her defense to this action?"[7] The Court held that she could. She was in fact subject to possible injury, for she was sued for damages of nearly $12,000.[8] And, under the special circumstances of this case, if respondent could not raise the black person's rights, "it would be difficult if not impossible for the persons whose rights are asserted to present their grievance before any court."[9] Thus the Court created an exception to what it termed "only a rule of practice . . . outweighed by the need to protect the fundamental rights which would be denied by permitting the damages action to be maintained."[10]

One wonders if *Barrows* was really an illustration of third party standing. Defendant was injured in fact, being subject to the damage action. Moreover, if a black purchaser has an equal protection right to buy property, without state interference, from a willing white seller, should not a white seller have the same equal protection right to sell that property to a willing black purchaser? Nearly a quarter of a century after *Barrows*, in *Peters v. Kiff*,[11] the Supreme Court held that a white criminal defendant had standing to attack the verdict on the grounds that blacks were excluded from the grand jury and trial jury. But only three of the six justices comprising the majority reasoned that the defendant was injured in fact by the exclusion, and therefore had direct standing.[12]

Whatever might have been the rationale of *Barrows*, its rule as to third party standing has continued. Thus, a medical doctor does not have third party standing to attack

a state anti-contraceptive statute on the grounds that it prevents him giving his professional advice concerning the use of contraceptives to three patients whose condition of health might be endangered by child bearing.[13] But if the person is convicted of prescribing, selling, or giving away contraceptives, in the defense to that action he may then raise the third-party rights of the recipients.[14] Professor Davis argues that while the results in these two cases are completely different, the facts are indistinguishable. "The restriction on medical practice was of the same sort in both cases, although the one involved contraception and the other abortion."[15] This "rule" in contraceptive cases has not been applied in obscenity cases. Thus, although the mere private possession of obscene matter cannot constitutionally be made a crime,[16] there is no constitutional right to distribute or sell obscene materials or to protect the right to sell by raising the rights of the recipients to privately possess obscene materials at home.[17]

In *Warth v. Seldin*[18] the Court refused third party standing to certain litigants attacking a town's zoning regulations. These litigant-taxpayers in Rochester, New York, claimed that the refusal of the town of Penfield to allow construction of low and moderate income housing raised the litigants' taxes because their town provided more such housing than it otherwise would. The Court noted that these taxpayers were not themselves subject to the Penfield's ordinances. Nor did Penfield's laws preclude or adversely affect a relationship existing between them and the persons whose rights were allegedly violated. No other relation-

---

7. 346 U.S. at 254–255.

8. 346 U.S. at 256.

9. 346 U.S. at 257.

10. 346 U.S. at 257.

11. 407 U.S. 493 (1972).

12. 407 U.S. at 500: "[T]he exclusion of a discernible class from jury service injures [all defendants] in that it destroys the possibility that the jury will reflect a representative cross section of the community." (Opinion by Marshall J., joined by Douglas and Stewart, JJ.).

13. Tileston v. Ullman, 318 U.S. 44 (1943) (per curiam). Cf. Doe v. Bolton, 410 U.S. 179, 188–189 (1973).

14. Eisenstadt v. Baird, 405 U.S. 438, 443–46 (1972); see also Griswold v. Connecticut, 381 U.S. 479 (1965).

15. K. Davis, Administrative Law in the Seventies § 22.06 at 516 (1976). See generally, K. Davis, Administrative Law Treatise § 22.06 (1958).

16. Stanley v. Georgia, 394 U.S. 557 (1969).

17. United States v. Reidel, 402 U.S. 351 (1971).

18. 422 U.S. 490, 508–10 (1975).

ship other than an incidental congruity of interests existed between them and the excluded persons. Nor did the taxpayers show that the persons actually excluded from Penfield were disabled from claiming their own rights in a proper case. And, whatever "may occur in Penfield, the injury complained of—increases in taxation—results only from decisions made by the appropriate Rochester authorities, who are not parties to this case."[19] Thus, no third party standing was allowed.[20]

Using the *Barrows* justification, as discussed more thoroughly below, organizations, if injured, have been allowed at times to raise the rights of their members.[21] States may assert the rights of their citizens, as *parens patriae*,[22] but when the defendant is the Federal Government the state may not, at least ordinarily, be *parens patriae* "in respect of their relations with the Federal Government. In that field it is the United States and not the State, which represents them [the citizens] as *parens patriae* . . . "[23] And, as discussed in the beginning of this section, in the first amendment area, a party may challenge a statute as overbroad or vague, where the strict application of third party standing rules would have an inhibitory effect on free speech.[24]

In spite of the Court's attempts to set up tests to determine when the *Barrows* justification will allow third party standing and when it will not, no consistent rationale explains the case law. As Professor Davis has concluded:

> One who tries to find a rational explanation for the contrariety of holdings is driven to the question whether the motivation for the holdings on standing lies in the Court's inclination or disinclination to decide particular substantive issues. If the Court knows of a way to reconcile its recent holdings on the question, it has not disclosed that way in its opinions.[25]

The Court's confused pronouncements of the third party standing issue has resulted in unnecessary litigation preliminary to ever reaching the merits and, to the extent that the Court has created pitfalls for those seeking third party standing, its conclusions in this area conflict with the general loosening of procedural burdens in cases involving personal standing. Assuming that the litigant has suffered injury in fact from the challenged conduct; that the case is sufficiently concrete and ripe; and that prudential concerns do not dictate judicial self restraint, the Court should only forbid third party standing if it is persuaded that the party seeking standing will not be an adequate

---

19. 422 U.S. at 509.

20. Cf. Schweiker v. Gray Panthers, 453 U.S. 34, 40 n. 8 (1981) (respondent, an organization dedicated to assisting the elderly, has standing to sue Secretary of Health and Human Services because respondent alleged and proved that some of its members are persons adversely affected by Secretary's Social Security regulations).

21. NAACP v. Alabama ex rel. Patterson, 357 U.S. 449, 458–459 (1958): "[P]etitioner argues more appropriately the rights of its members, and that its nexus with them is sufficient to permit that it act as their representative before this Court . . . "; NAACP v. Button, 371 U.S. 415, 428 (1963): "[P]etitioner may assert this right on its own behalf, because, though a corporation, it is directly engaged in those activities, claimed to be constitutionally protected, which the statute would curtail."; Pierce v. Society of Sisters, 268 U.S. 510, 535 (1925): "[Appellees] have business and property for which they claim protection. These are threatened with destruction through the unwarranted compulsion which appellants are exercising over present and prospective patrons of their schools."

But cf. McGowan v. Maryland, 366 U.S. 420, 429 (1961):

"[A]ppellants contend here that the statutes . . . [governing closing of certain stores on Sunday] prohibit the free exercise of religion . . . But appellants allege only economic injury to themselves: they do not allege any infringement of their own religious freedoms due to Sunday closing. In fact, the record is silent as to what appellants' religious beliefs are."

The Court did allow appellants, however, to challenge the statutes on grounds of establishment of religion. Id. at 430.

22. Missouri v. Illinois, 180 U.S. 208, 241 (1901).

23. Massachusetts v. Mellon, 262 U.S. 447, 486 (1923).

24. E.g., Thornhill v. Alabama, 310 U.S. 88, 97–98 (1940). For a discussion generally of third party standing, its rationales, and its exceptions, see United States v. Raines, 362 U.S. 17, 21–23 (1960). See also, Chapter 18, section III, B, infra.

25. K. Davis, Administrative Law in the Seventies § 22.06 at 518–19 (1976).

representative of the third parties whose interests he champions.[26]

d. Standing by State Governments, Associations, and Congressmen

A State may sue on behalf of its citizens as *parens patriae*, "to protect the general comfort, health, or property rights of its inhabitants threatened by the proposed or continued action of another State, by prayer for injunction . . . ." but when it joined the Union it "lost power as a sovereign to present and enforce individual claims of its citizens as their trustee against a sister State."[1] The state may also sue as *parens patriae* to protect its citizens from environmental damages,[2] because in general a state "may act as the representative of its citizens in original actions where the injury affects the general population of a state in a substantial way."[3] As Justice Holmes said in *Georgia v. Tennessee Copper Co.:*[4]

> The State owns very little of the territory alleged to be affected, and the damage to it capable of estimate in money, possibly, at least, is small. This is a suit by a State for an injury to it in its capacity of *quasi*-sovereign. In that capacity the State has an interest independent of and behind the titles of its citizens, in all the earth and air within its domain. It has the last word as to whether its mountains shall be stripped of their forests and its inhabitants shall breathe pure air. . . . The alleged damage to the State as a private owner is merely a makeweight . . . .[5]

But a state cannot sue the federal government as representative of its citizens, for only the United States and not a state may be *parens patriae* as against the federal government.[6]

Associations of individuals have standing to invoke judicial protection of the association *qua* association; such associations may also assert the rights of its members "at

---

26. Rohr, Fighting for the Rights of Others: The Troubled Law of Third Party Standing and Mootness in the Federal Courts, 35 U. Miami L.Rev. 393 (1981).

1. North Dakota v. Minnesota, 263 U.S. 365, 375–76 (1923); see New Hampshire v. Louisiana, 108 U.S. 76 (1883); Louisiana v. Texas, 176 U.S. 1, 16 (1900). Maryland v. Louisiana, 451 U.S. 725, 736–39 (1981). (In an original action challenging the constitutionality of a Louisiana use tax on natural gas, the jurisdiction of plaintiff states is supported not only by their alleged substantial injury to their proprietary interests as consumers of natural gas but also by the states' interest in protecting its citizens from substantial economic injury from imposition of the tax.); Alfred L. Snapp & Sons, Inc. v. Puerto Rico ex rel. Barez, 102 S.Ct. 3260 (1982) (Puerto Rico has standing as *parens patriae* to sue members of apple industry in Virginia, claiming that in violation of federal law petitioners had discriminated against Puerto Rican migrant farmworkers; a state has quasi-sovereign interest in the economic well-being of its residents and in not being discriminatorily denied its rightful status in the federal system).

See generally, Malina & Blechman, Parens Patriae Suits for Treble Damages Under the Antitrust Laws, 65 Nw.U.L.Rev. 193 (1970).

2. E.g., Missouri v. Illinois, 180 U.S. 208 (1901); Kansas v. Colorado, 206 U.S. 46 (1907); Georgia v. Tennessee Copper Co., 206 U.S. 230 (1907); New York v. New Jersey, 256 U.S. 296 (1921); Pennsylvania v. West Virginia, 262 U.S. 553 (1923); North Dakota v. Minnesota, 263 U.S. 365 (1923); Illinois v. City of Milwaukee, 406 U.S. 91 (1972); Washington v. General Motors Corp., 406 U.S. 109 (1972).

3. Maryland v. Louisiana, 451 U.S. 725, 737 (1981).

4. 206 U.S. 230 (1907). See generally, Note, The Original Jurisdiction of the United States Supreme Court, 11 Stan.L.Rev. 665 (1959).

5. 206 U.S. at 237. As to the power of states to sue as *parens patriae* to enjoin violations of the federal antitrust laws, see Georgia v. Pennsylvania R. R. Co., 324 U.S. 439 (1945), upholding this power. In 1972 the Supreme Court rejected such a power when the remedy sought is damages rather than injunction. Hawaii v. Standard Oil Co., 405 U.S. 251 (1972). Congress recently created a new procedural device of a *parens patriae* action by states on behalf of their citizens to enforce existing rights of recovery under section 4 of the Clayton Act. See Hart-Scott-Rodino Antitrust Improvements Act of 1976, Pub.L. No. 94–435, 90 Stat. 1383, 1394–96 (1976). However, a majority of the Court has since held that this Act does not change the substantive law that a pass-on theory may not be used either defensively by an antitrust violator or offensively by an indirect purchaser. Illinois Brick Co. v. Illinois, 431 U.S. 720 (1977). See also Hanover Shoe, Inc. v. United Shoe Machinery Corp., 392 U.S. 481 (1968). Malina & Blechman, Parens Patriae Suits for Treble Damages Under the Antitrust Laws, 65 Nw.U.L.Rev. 193 (1970).

6. Massachusetts v. Mellon, 262 U.S. 447, 485–86 (1923). See also, South Carolina v. Katzenbach, 383 U.S. 301, 324 (1966). Cf. Texas v. I.C.C., 258 U.S. 158, 162 (1922).

least so long as the challenged infractions adversely affect its members' associational ties."[7] Such associations may also establish standing (even if they have no injury to themselves) as representative of the injury to their members, but the association must still allege the kind of injury that would satisfy the standing requirement had the individual members themselves brought suit.[8] Then, "so long as the nature of the claim and of the relief sought does not make the individual participation of each injured party indispensable to proper resolution of the cause, the association may be an appropriate representative of its members, entitled to invoke the court's jurisdiction."[9]

Finally, the standing of an association to sue on behalf of its members and assert their rights depends on the nature of the relief sought. It is easier for such an association to secure injunctive, declaratory, or some other form of prospective [10] relief because then "it can reasonably be supposed that the remedy, if granted, will inure to the benefit of those members of the association actually injured."[11] No such assurance exists if the remedy sought is money damages and if the association has not suffered damages *qua* association. Thus, if the damage claims are not common to the entire membership nor shared by all in equal degree, such association does not have standing to sue for such damage claims. In these cases, any alleged injury will have been suffered by the individuals, and both the fact of injury and its degree will require individualized proof.[12]

While the Supreme Court has not yet definitely ruled on the matter,[13] some lower federal courts have found standing in members of Congress *qua* member, while others have rejected this theory.[14]

Government officials do have standing to object to the constitutionality of laws that they are required to enforce if their refusal to enforce could cause their removal from office, but their enforcement of the law might violate their oath to support the Constitution; when they have such a Hobson's choice they have alleged the requisite personal stake in the outcome of the litigation.[15]

e. Standing and Equal Protection

Every challenge to a law claiming that the law violates equal protection by being under-inclusive raises a special standing issue. If

---

7. Warth v. Seldin, 422 U.S. 490, 511 (1975); see also, NAACP v. Alabama, 357 U.S. 449, 458–60 (1958); Pierce v. Society of Sisters, 268 U.S. 510, 534–36 (1925); Sullivan v. Little Hunting Park, Inc., 396 U.S. 229, 237 (1969); Joint Anti-Fascist Refugee Committee v. McGrath, 341 U.S. 123, 183–87 (1951) (Jackson, J., concurring). Thus, in Hunt v. Washington State Apple Advertising Comm'n, 432 U.S. 333 (1977), the Court upheld the standing of what was technically a state agency but actually a trade association to sue on behalf of its member apple growers to challenge the constitutionality of another state's law affecting apple growers.

8. Warth v. Seldin, 422 U.S. 490, 511 (1975); Sierra Club v. Morton, 405 U.S. 727, 734–41 (1972); National Motor Freight Ass'n v. United States, 372 U.S. 246 (1963).

9. Warth v. Seldin, 422 U.S. 490, 511 (1975).

10. E.g., National Motor Freight Ass'n v. United States, 372 U.S. 246 (1963).

11. Warth v. Seldin, 422 U.S. 490, 515 (1975).

12. Id. at 510–11.

13. The issue was raised in the lower federal court but not decided by the Supreme Court in Mink v. EPA, 410 U.S. 73, 75 n. 2 (1973).

14. E.g., Kennedy v. Sampson, 511 F.2d 430, 435–36 (D.C.Cir.1974) (standing upheld for Senator Kennedy seeking declaratory judgment that presidential pocket veto of a bill was ineffective); Holtzman v. Schlesinger, 484 F.2d 1307, 1315 (2d Cir. 1973) (Congresswoman Holtzman does not have standing *qua* Congresswoman, to attack constitutionality of Indo-China war). Other lower court cases include, Nader v. Bork, 366 F.Supp. 104 (D.D.C.1973); Brown v. Ruckelshaus, 364 F.Supp. 258 (D.C.D.Calif.1973). See generally, K. Davis, Administrative Law of the Seventies § 22.02–9 (1976); Note, Congressional Access to the Federal Courts, 90 Harv.L.Rev. 1632 (1977).

15. Board of Education v. Allen, 392 U.S. 236, 241 n. 5 (1968). Some lower courts, however, have concluded that this portion of *Allen* has been overruled sub silentio by the Court's decisions in Schlesinger v. Reservists Committee to Stop the War, 418 U.S. 208 (1974), and United States v. Richardson, 418 U.S. 166 (1974), discussed in this Chapter, supra at Section IV, B, 6, a. Other lower courts believe this *Allen* standing rule to remain good law. In City of South Lake Tahoe v. California Tahoe Regional Planning Agency, 449 U.S. 1039 (1981) the Court refused to decide the issue and denied certiorari. Justice White, joined by Justice Marshall, dissented and wrote a cogent opinion explaining why the *Allen* standing rule is still good law.

a court invalidates the law, the state can respond either by extending the benefits equally to everyone, or denying the benefits equally to everyone. If the person denied benefits sues, the state can argue that he has no standing since, if the state denies benefits to everyone, that person denied benefits will be no better off. If the person granted benefits sues, then the state can argue that he is not injured by the present law. In such circumstances the Supreme Court allows either party standing, otherwise underinclusive statutes could never be challenged. The point is illustrated in *Orr v. Orr*.[1]

In that case a divorced wife instituted contempt proceedings against her former husband for nonpayment of alimony. He challenged as unconstitutional the statutory scheme under which husbands but not wives could be required to pay alimony. The husband had failed to ask for alimony. If the state would respond to a holding of unconstitutionality by neutrally extending alimony to needy husbands as well as needy wives, Mr. Orr would still be obligated to pay the alimony to his former wife. While the state argued that Mr. Orr therefore had no standing, and that only a needy husband denied alimony could sue, the Court noted that if the state would respond to a holding of unconstitutionality by neutrally denying alimony to everyone, then, under the state's theory, the needy husband would lack standing and Mr. Orr would have it. "Because we have no way of knowing how the State will in fact respond, unless we are to hold that underinclusive statutes can never be chal-

lenged because *any* plaintiff's success can theoretically be thwarted, Mr. Orr must be held to have standing here."[2]

7. A Note on the Duty to Avoid Constitutional Decisions

The doctrines related to advisory opinions, mootness, collusiveness, ripeness, prematurity and abstractness, standing, and other such rules of self-restraint are all functions of the general and basic judicial duty to avoid decisions of constitutional questions. This duty, in turn, draws support from Chief Justice Marshall's rationale of judicial review as a reluctant power exercised only because the Court must decide cases brought before it in conformity with the Constitution.[1] There are also more pragmatic considerations for this policy of self-restraint. Judicial review is inconsistent with pure majority rule, and, because of the conflict between the judiciary and the democratic system, may result in popular disapproval of court action. The policy of a strict necessity in disposing of constitutional issues is a useful device that helps assure that judicial review does not take place gratuitously.[2] As Justice Rutledge also frankly acknowledged for the Court in *Rescue Army v. Municipal Court*[3] there are pragmatic justifications for this view:

> It is not without significance for the policy's validity that the periods when the power [to avoid a constitutional decision] has been exercised most readily and broadly have been the ones in which this Court and the institution of judicial review have had their stormiest experiences.[4]

---

1. 440 U.S. 268 (1979).

2. 440 U.S. 273 (emphasis in original). As the Court also noted by way of analogy, "There is no doubt that a state law imposing alimony obligations on blacks but not whites could be challenged by a black who was required to pay."

1. Marbury v. Madison, 5 U.S. (1 Cranch) 137 (1803).

2. Notwithstanding the Supreme Court's policy of strict necessity in deciding constitutional cases, the Court has the power to limit the grant of review to certain questions presented, and its power to decide is not limited to the precise terms of the question presented. E.g., Procunier v. Navarette, 434 U.S. 555, 559–560 n. 6 (1978), citing blonder—Tongue Laboratories, Inc. v.

University of Illinois Foundation, 402 U.S. 313, 320 n. 6 (1971). See also, Hart & Wechsler's The Federal Courts and the Federal System 1599 (2d ed. 1973), and id. at 640 ("Are these practices consistent with the jurisdictional statute's provision for review of 'judgments or decrees', rather than issues?").

3. 331 U.S. 549 (1947). In Re Contest of the Election for the Office of Governor and Lieutenant Governor Held at the General Election on November 2, 1982, 93 Ill.2d 463, 496, 67 Ill.Dec. 131, 44 N.E.2d 170 (1983) (Ward, Goldenhersh, and Clark, JJ. dissenting, citing treatise).

4. 331 U.S. at 572 n. 38, citing Brant, Storm Over the Constitution (1936). See generally, R. McCloskey,

In the *Rescue Army* case Justice Rutledge offered some of the important rationales for this policy, relying in part on Justice Brandeis' concurrence in *Ashwander v. Tennessee Valley Authority*.[5] The Rutledge opinion merits quotation at length:

> From *Hayburn's Case*, 2 Dall. 408 [1792] to [the present] this Court has followed a policy of strict necessity in disposing of constitutional issues. The earliest exemplifications, too well known for repeating the history here, arose in the Court's refusal to render advisory opinions and in applications of the related jurisdictional policy drawn from the case and controversy limitation . . . The same policy has been reflected continuously not only in decisions but also in rules of court and in statutes made applicable to jurisdictional matters, including the necessity for reasonable clarity and definiteness, as well as for timeliness, in raising and presenting constitutional questions. Indeed perhaps the most effective implement for making the policy effective has been the certiorari jurisdiction . . .
>
> The policy, however has not been limited to jurisdictional determinations. For, in addition, "the Court [has] developed, for its own governance in the cases confessedly within its jurisdiction, a series of rules under which it has avoided passing upon a large part of all the constitutional questions pressed upon it for decision." Thus, as those rules were listed in support of the statement quoted, constitutional issues affecting legislation will not be determined in friendly, nonadversary proceedings; in advance of the necessity of deciding them; in broader terms than are required by the precise facts to which the ruling is to be applied; if the record presents some other ground upon which the case may be disposed of; at the instance of one who fails to show that he is injured by the statute's operation, or who has availed himself of its benefits; or if a construction of the statute is fairly possible by which the question may be avoided. . . .
>
> Indeed in origin and in practical effects, though not in technical function, it is a corolla-

ry offshoot of the case and controversy rule. . . .

> The policy's ultimate foundations . . . are found in the delicacy of that function, particularly in view of possible consequences for others stemming also from constitutional roots; the comparative finality of those consequences; the consideration due to the judgment of other repositories of constitutional power concerning the scope of their authority; the necessity, if government is to function constitutionally, for each to keep within its power, including the courts; the inherent limitations of the judicial process, arising especially from its largely negative character and limited resources of enforcement; withal in the paramount importance of constitutional adjudication in our system. . . . Its execution has involved a continuous choice between the obvious advantages it produces for the functioning of government in all its coordinate parts and the very real disadvantages, for the assurance of rights, which deferring decision very often entails . . . .
>
> One aspect of the policy's application, it has been noted, has been by virtue of the presence of other grounds for decision. . . . To the more usual considerations of timeliness and maturity, of concreteness, definiteness, certainty, and of adversity of interests affected, are to be added in cases coming from state courts involving state legislation those arising when questions of construction, essentially matters of state law, remain unresolved or highly ambiguous. They include, of course, questions of incorporation by reference and servability, such as this case involves. Necessarily whether decision of the constitutional issue will be made must depend upon the degree to which uncertainty exists in these respects. And this inevitably will vary with particular causes and their varying presentations. . . .[6]

Statutes thus are normally presumed constitutional, and judges, it is thought, should exercise considerable self-restraint whenever such statutes are under constitutional attack. Illustrating this policy is the fact that

---

The American Supreme Court 220–231 (1960); A. Bickel, The Least Dangerous Branch: The Supreme Court at the Bar of Politics (1962); J. Ely, Democracy and Distrust (1980); J. Choper, Judicial Review and the National Political Process: A Functional Reconsideration of the National Political Process (1980).

5.   297 U.S. 288, 341–356 (1936).

6.   331 U.S. at 568–574 (footnotes and case citations omitted).

some legislators may vote against a measure on the grounds of its unconstitutionality and later, when they become judges and are on the bench, should hold the same challenged law to be constitutional. Though they have not changed their personal viewpoint, they have exercised the self-restraint of the judiciary.[7]

C. Adequate State Grounds and Federal Questions

1. The General Rule

As a general rule it may be stated that the Supreme Court, when it reviews a decision of a state court, only reviews the federal questions and not the state law questions:

> The State courts are the appropriate tribunals, as this court has repeatedly held, for the decision of questions arising under this local law, whether statutory or otherwise. And it is not lightly to be presumed that Congress acted upon a principle which implies a distrust of their integrity or of their ability to construe those laws correctly.[1]

Justice Jackson later offered a much quoted rationale for this rule:

> This Court from the time of its foundation has adhered to the principle that it will not review judgments of state courts *that rest on adequate and independent state grounds.* [Citations omitted] The reason is so obvious that it has rarely been thought to warrant statement. It is found in the partitioning of power between the state and federal judicial systems and in the limitations of our own jurisdiction. Our only power over state judgments is to correct them to the extent that they incorrectly adjudge federal rights. And our power is to correct wrong judgments, not to revise opinions. We are not permitted to render an advisory opinion, and if the same judgment would be rendered by the state court after we corrected its views of federal laws, our review could amount to nothing more than an advisory opinion.[2]

This rationale is not entirely correct. If the Supreme Court were to decide a federal issue when the state decision rested on an alternative adequate and independent state ground, the federal decision is more like a moot decision rather than an advisory one, for the case is a concrete controversy.[3] While the Court has called mootness a constitutional requirement,[4] it has also been more willing to relax the requirement in the public interest, so that the law not be "that rigid." [5] More importantly, there is historical evidence that Congress did intend review of the whole case [6] and on occasions the Supreme Court itself has said that it is unnecessary to determine if the rule is constitutionally based, for there is adequate statutory warrant for the requirement.[7]

---

7. Thayer, The Origin and Scope of the American Doctrine of Constitutional Law, 7 Harv.L.Rev. 129, 144 (1893). See Chapter I, Section II, C, 3.

1. Murdock v. City of Memphis, 87 U.S. (20 Wall.) 590, 626 (1875). An important issue in *Murdock* was whether the Judiciary Act of 1867, § 2, 14 Stat. 385, 386 (Feb. 5, 1867), which amended section 25 of the Judiciary Act of 1789, 1 Stat. 73 (Sept. 24, 1789), conferred upon the Supreme Court the power to decide all of the questions presented by the state case which are necessary to its final judgment or decree; and not just the federal questions. The 1867 amendment eliminated the clause of the 1789 Act which limited Supreme Court review to the federal questions. The Court decided that although the restrictive clause was not enacted Congress did not mean to confer such power. See generally, Note, The Untenable Nonfederal Ground in the Supreme Court, 74 Harv.L.Rev. 1375 (1961).

2. Herb v. Pitcairn, 324 U.S. 117, 125–126 (1945) (emphasis added). See generally, M. Redish, Federal Jurisdiction: Tensions in the Allocation of Judicial Power 216–31 (1980); P. Hay & R. Rotunda, The United States Federal System: Legal Integration in the American Experience 203–18 (Giuffrè, Milan 1982).

3. Compare H. Johnston, Correspondence and Public Papers of John Jay 486–489 (1891) (advisory opinions), with Defunis v. Odegaard, 416 U.S. 312 (1974) (mootness).

4. E.g., Liner v. Jafco, Inc., 375 U.S. 301 (1964).

5. Roe v. Wade, 410 U.S. 113, 125 (1973).

6. C. Wright, Law of Federal Courts § 107 at 543 (3d ed. 1976): "Such a course seems wholly consistent with the temper of the times." See also 2 W. Crosskey, Politics and the Constitution in the History of the United States, 711–817 (1953).

7. Fay v. Noia, 372 U.S. 391, 430 n. 40 (1963) (specifically referring to, but not accepting, Jackson, J.'s constitutional justification in Herb v. Pitcairn, 324 U.S. 117, 125–126 (1945).

2. *Applications of the Rule*

The intricacies of this rule of review of state court opinions are more normally considered in texts on federal jurisdiction,[8] but its basic elements are useful to appreciate some of the restrictions on Supreme Court review of state court decisions.

A state court may rule that a state law is repugnant to both the federal and state constitutions. In general, then, there is no Supreme Court jurisdiction to review this decision, for if the Supreme Court agrees with the state court interpretation of the federal constitution, then the decision would be affirmed. And if the Supreme Court disagrees with the state court interpretation of the federal constitution, the decision would still be affirmed, for the U. S. Supreme Court cannot reverse the state court as to a decision resting on an interpretation of its own constitution.[9]

Similarly, there would be no jurisdiction if the state court, though presented with a federal ground of decision, only chose to base its decision on the nonfederal ground which in itself did not violate federal law.[10] If the state court held the state law valid under both state and federal constitutional provisions, then the Supreme Court could exercise review, for if it disagreed with the state

court's review of the federal constitution (or federal statute or treaty), the state decision would have to be reversed regardless of the interpretation of the state law.

However, if the state court invalidates a statute as prohibited by both a state and federal constitutional provision, but did not intend that its decision rest independently on the state ground, which it automatically interpreted to be as broad as the federal constitutional provision, then there may be Supreme Court review of the federal issue. Since the state court felt compelled in construing its own law by what it understood to be federal constitutional considerations, the Supreme Court may review because the state court may have misapprehended federal law.[11] The state ground is not independent.

If the state court in fact decided the case on a federal ground, there can be Supreme Court review even though the state court ruling might have been decided on an adequate nonfederal ground.[12]

Sometimes the state ground of decision may be viewed as neither adequate nor independent.[13] For example, the state court may strike a statute but the state court opinion may be ambiguous as to its basis.[14] The decision may cite federal cases, reflect federal

---

8. See generally C. Wright, Law of Federal Courts § 107 at 542–548 (3d ed. 1976).

9. E.g., Serrano v. Priest, 5 Cal.3d 584, 96 Cal.Rptr. 601, 487 P.2d 1241 (1971); Cf. Fox Film Corp. v. Muller, 296 U.S. 207 (1935).

10. E.g., Wood v. Chesborough, 228 U.S. 672 (1913).

11. Delaware v. Prouse, 440 U.S. 648, 652–55 (1979); South Dakota v. Neville, 103 S.Ct. 916, 919 n.5 (1983).

12. St. Louis, I. M. & Southern Ry. v. McWhirter, 229 U.S. 265, 275–276 (1913). Orr v. Orr, 440 U.S. 268, 274–75 (1979). Cf. Kentucky v. Whorton, 441 U.S. 786 (1979) (per curiam) (overturning state judicial granting of rights where they were based on state court's erroneous interpretation of the meaning of federal constitutional requirements).

13. It is unclear in the case law if these criteria of "adequate" and "independent" are the same, alternative, or conjunctive. Note, The Untenable Nonfederal Ground in the Supreme Court, 74 Harv.L.Rev. 1374, 1381–1382 (1961).

14. See Herb v. Pitcairn, 324 U.S. 117, 127 (1945) ("it is not necessary to [the state court's] functions to make a sharp separation of the [state and federal questions on which] their discussion is often interlaced.)

When it is unclear whether the state court has relied only on state grounds, the U. S. Supreme Court has developed the following rule:

> "[W]hen, as in this case, a state court decision fairly appears to rest primarily on federal law, or to be interwoven with the federal law, and when the adequacy and independence of any possible state law ground is not clear from the face of the opinion, we will accept as the most reasonable explanation that the state court decided the case the way it did because it believed that federal law required it to do so. If a state court chooses merely to rely on federal precedents as it would on the precedents of all other jurisdictions, then it need only make clear by a plain statement in its judgment or opinion that the federal cases are being used only for the purpose of guidance, and do not themselves compel the result that the court has reached. . . . If the state court decision indicates clearly and expressly that it is alternatively based on bona fide separate, adequate, and independent grounds, we, of course, will not undertake to review the decision."

Michigan v. Long, 103 S.Ct. ___ (1983).

By way of footnote the Court said that there may be circumstances in which clarification is necessary, "and

reasoning, or otherwise indicate its reliance on federal law:

> If the [state] court were only incidentally referring to decisions of this Court in determining the meaning of the state law . . . . [then] this Court would have no jurisdiction to review that question. But, if the state court did in fact intend alternatively to base its decision upon the state statute and upon an immunity it thought granted by the Constitution as interpreted by this Court, these two grounds are so interwoven that we are unable to conclude that the judgment rests upon an independent interpretation of the state law.[15]

Sometimes a state law will incorporate by reference a federal law. A state court decision in such circumstances may be reviewable by the Supreme Court for the state court will be relying on a proper interpretation of federal law to adjudicate rights; usually the federal law is itself operative in the facts of the case. The Supreme Court may decide that federal question and remand to the state courts.[16]

A state court may bar federal court review if a decision on a state procedural ground prevents the state court from reaching the federal substantive issue. For example, the state court may have a consistent practice of declining to answer questions not

reserved.[17] Or the state court may decide not to reach the substantive issue because of res judicata[18] or other requirements of state law.[19] Such procedural hurdles can be overcome:

> Even though the claimed constitutional protection be denied on nonfederal grounds, it is the province of this Court to inquire whether the decision of the state court rests on a *fair or substantial* basis. If unsubstantial, constitutional obligations may not be thus avoided.[20]

For example, a novel procedural requirement that appears to be newly created by the state court in the very decision barring the litigant,[21] or a state court decision overruling its prior case law to bar the litigant's assertion of the federal right[22] will not prevent Supreme Court review. As Justice Holmes has explained, "Whatever springes the State may set for those who are endeavoring to assert rights that the State confers, the assertion of federal rights, when plainly and reasonably made, is not to be defeated under the name of local practice."[23]

Henry v. Mississippi[24] is an unusual case concerning the procedural rules that relate to foreclosing Supreme Court review. Aaron Henry, a civil rights worker[25] was convicted of disturbing the peace by indecent

---

we will not be foreclosed from taking the appropriate action." 103 S.Ct. at ___ n.6.

15. State Tax Comm'n v. Van Cott, 306 U.S. 511, 514 (1939) (footnotes omitted). See also, Minnesota v. National Tea Co., 309 U.S. 551, 556 (1940). In these cases the judgment was vacated and the cases remanded so that the federal and state questions could be clearly presented or that the federal question be "dissected out." 309 U.S. at 556. Orr v. Orr, 440 U.S. 268, 276 (1979) (where ambiguity as to basis of state law exists, the Supreme Court can remand for clarification); Zant v. Stephens, 456 U.S. 410 (1982) (per curiam) (same). See also Herb v. Pitcairn, 324 U.S. 117, 126–128 (1945), discussing other alternatives, including remand of the case for further consideration (as when there are supervening events), or grant of a continuance, so that application may be made to the state court for clarification. See generally, Note, Supreme Court Treatment of State Court Cases Exhibiting Ambiguous Grounds of Decision, 62 Colum.L.Rev. 822 (1962).

16. E.g., Moore v. Chesapeake & Ohio Ry., 291 U.S. 205, 214 (1914); Standard Oil Co. of California v. Johnson, 316 U.S. 481 (1942); St. Martin Evangelical Lutheran Church v. South Dakota, 451 U.S. 772, 780 n. 9 (1981). See generally, Greene, Hybrid State Law in the Federal Courts, 83 Harv.L.Rev. 289 (1969).

17. See Tileston v. Ullman, 318 U.S. 44 (1943). Cf. Webb v. Webb, 451 U.S. 493 (1981) (where petitioner failed to raise her federal claim in the state courts, which failed to rule on the federal issue, the writ of certiorari dismissed for want of jurisdiction).

18. See Postal Telegraph Cable Co. v. City of Newport, 247 U.S. 464, 474–476 (1918).

19. See, Edelman v. California, 344 U.S. 357, 358–359, 361 (1953) (denial of petitioner's motion rested on adequate state ground, his choice of the wrong remedy under local law.).

20. Lawrence v. State Tax Comm'n, 286 U.S. 276, 282 (1932) (emphasis added).

21. E.g., NAACP v. Alabama ex rel. Patterson, 357 U.S. 449, 457–58 (1958).

22. Brinkerhoff-Faris Trust & Savings Co. v. Hill, 281 U.S. 673, 678 & 682 n. 9 (1929).

23. Davis v. Wechsler, 263 U.S. 22, 24 (1923).

24. 379 U.S. 443 (1965).

25. Sandalow, Henry v. Mississippi and the Adequate State Ground: Proposals for a Revised Doctrine, 1965 Sup.Ct.Rev. 187, 190.

proposals to, and offensive contact with, an 18 year-old hitchhiker. Under the state law corroborative evidence was needed for conviction, and the only such evidence was the fruit of a search, which the state Supreme Court found to be illegal. The conviction was reversed, though Henry's counsel had not made an objection to the introduction of the evidence at the time it was introduced. The state court excused Henry's counsel's failure to comply with Mississippi's contemporaneous objection rule because of out-of-state counsel's unfamiliarity with local procedure. After this opinion the state filed a suggestion of error, explaining that Henry had also been represented by competent local counsel as well as out of state counsel. The state court then withdrew its opinion and filed a new one affirming the conviction. The U. S. Supreme Court did not find Henry's federal claims necessarily foreclosed by failure to comply with local procedure.

After purporting to draw some distinctions between state substantive law and state procedural law grounds of decision, Justice Brennan for the majority argued that "a litigant's procedural defaults in state proceedings do not prevent vindication of his federal rights unless the State's insistence on compliance with its procedural rule serves a legitimate state interest." [26] The Court found that the contemporaneous objection rule to the introduction of illegal evidence does serve a legitimate state interest but this purpose "may have been substantially served by petitioner's motion at the close of the State's evidence asking for a directed verdict because of the erroneous admission . . . ." of evidence.[27] Then the

Court remanded to determine if petitioner's counsel deliberately bypassed the contemporaneous objection rule as part of trial strategy, in which case waiver of constitutional rights would be found and the State could insist on its procedural requirements.[28]

What the Supreme Court was apparently doing in this case was to adopt a habeas corpus theory of waiver of constitutional rights in criminal cases and incorporate the habeas theory into a case under the direct review of the Supreme Court. It perhaps was no accident that Justice Brennan, author of *Henry*, was also the author of the leading habeas case developing the waiver theory for collateral review.[29] *Henry* has not had any significant growth in the law; its future development remains unclear and it may simply stand as a sport.[30]

Procedural requirements which are really federal in nature cannot be used to defeat Supreme Court review by a more restrictive state interpretation. Thus, a state court refusal to consider a federal claim on the grounds of mootness does not prevent Supreme Court review, for the question of mootness in such circumstances is itself a question of federal law which the Supreme Court must decide.[31]

Finally, in some cases the Supreme Court may review a state court decision because the state substantive law is connected with important federal interests. For example, normally what is a "contract" is a matter of state law, but the Constitution provides no state shall impair "the Obligation of Contracts . . . ." [32] Thus, "in order that the constitutional mandate may not become a

---

26. 379 U.S. 443, 447.

27. 379 U.S. 443, 448.

28. 379 U.S. 447, 450.

29. Fay v. Noia, 372 U.S. 391, 439 (1963). *Fay* was relied on in *Henry*, e.g., 379 U.S. 443 at 450, 452, 453.

On remand, the state court found waiver and reaffirmed his conviction. Henry v. State, 198 So.2d 213, 202 So.2d 40 (Miss.1967), cert. denied 392 U.S. 931 (1968). See also 388 U.S. 901 (1967). Mr. Henry subsequently won his case when a federal district court, in a habeas corpus proceeding, found no waiver. Henry v. Williams, 299 F.Supp. 36 (D.Miss.1969).

30. Cf. Parker v. North Carolina, 397 U.S. 790 (1970) (failure to follow state procedural rule that required objection to composition of grand jury before guilty plea is adequate state procedural ground of decision; *Henry* not cited). But see Camp v. Arkansas, 404 U.S. 69 (1971) (*Henry* cited and case reversed); Monger v. Florida, 405 U.S. 958, 962 (1972) (*Henry* cited by dissenters urging reversal).

31. Liner v. Jafco, Inc., 375 U.S. 301, 304 (1964).

32. U.S.Const. art. I, § 10.

dead letter, we are bound to decide for ourselves whether a contract was made, what are its terms and conditions, and whether the State has, by later legislation, impaired its obligation. This involves an appraisal of the statutes of the State and the decisions of its courts." [33] Were the rule otherwise, a state court could preclude Supreme Court review of a criminal case allegedly based on a forced confession by accepting the federal rule as to voluntariness but finding that as a factual matter the confession was not coerced. Related to this doctrine is the rule that the Supreme Court is not prevented from review because the state court opinion "put[s] forward the untenable construction [of a corporate charter] more than the unconstitutional statutes in its judgment. To hold otherwise would open an easy method of avoiding the jurisdiction of this court." [34]

It is sometimes unclear whether the federal court merely looks to the state law to assure itself that the state interpretation rests on a fair or substantial basis or whether there is a federal common law of, for example, "contract." [35]

D. The Abstention Doctrine

1. The Pullman Case and the Origins of the Abstention Doctrine

The view that federal courts are under a duty to exercise their jurisdiction in every case where it was properly invoked was one which was followed for many years. As Chief Justice Marshall explained:

> It is most true, that this Court will not take jurisdiction if it should not: but it is equally true, that it must take jurisdiction if it should . . . . We have no more right to decline the exercise of jurisdiction which is given, than to usurp that which is not given.[1]

In many older cases, the Court in fact did reject requests for stays of its jurisdiction pending decision by the state courts.[2] Perhaps the position favoring the exercise of jurisdiction persisted until recently because the conflict between state and federal jurisdiction was not as apparent as it later became.[3]

Such a broad exercise of federal jurisdiction can raise unnecessary constitutional problems when a plaintiff sues in federal court protesting state action and a decision as to the applicable interpretation of state law is relevant to the federal constitutional issue. Where state law is unclear, the federal court is faced with an unpleasant choice of alternatives. The court can proceed and decide the state law question in such a way as to avoid the constitutional issue. Or, it can apply the state law in such a way as to require a decision on constitutional grounds, an alternative not favored if there are any other grounds for decision.[4] Under either alternative, the rule as to the constitutionali-

---

33. Indiana ex rel. Anderson v. Brand, 303 U.S. 95, 100 (1938) (footnote omitted).

34. Terre Haute & R. R. v. Indiana ex rel. Ketcham, 194 U.S. 579, 589 (1904).

Perhaps also justified by this general principle is Martin v. Hunter's Lessee, 14 U.S. (1 Wheat.) 304 (1816), where the Supreme Court reversed the state court judgment that property had been seized prior to a treaty with Great Britain forbidding such seizures in the future. The Court in that case possibly was deciding that when property is forfeit was a matter of federal law in light of the treaty. Or perhaps it was deciding that the state decision was not supported by adequate state grounds or represented an evasion of federal rights.

35. Compare Demorest v. City Bank Co., 321 U.S. 36, 42–43 (1944) (Jackson, J.) (to determine what is a property right under state law the Supreme Court inquires whether the decision of the state court rests on a fair or substantial basis), with D'Oench, Duhme &

Co. v. Federal Deposit Insurance Co., 315 U.S. 447, 470 (1942) (Jackson, J., concurring) (the contract clause is "an example of the part the common law must play in our system").

1. Cohens v. Virginia, 19 U.S. (6 Wheat.) 264, 404 (1821).

2. See McClellan v. Carland, 217 U.S. 268 (1910); Chicot County v. Sherwood, 148 U.S. 529 (1893); Hyde v. Stone, 61 U.S. (20 How.) 170 (1857).

3. Note, The Abstention Doctrine, 40 Denver Law Center Journal 45, 46 (1963). Compare Swift v. Tyson, 41 U.S. (16 Pet.) 1 (1842), with Erie R. R. v. Tompkins, 304 U.S. 64 (1933), overruling Swift and recognizing the supremacy of state courts interpreting their state law even in diversity cases.

4. See, e.g., Ashwander v. Tennessee Valley Authority, 297 U.S. 288, 347 (1936) (Brandeis, J., concurring).

ty of the state law is binding on state courts, but the state courts are still free to apply a different interpretation of the state law in a later case (except in the atypical case where the Supreme Court rules that no interpretation of the state law can save its unconstitutionality). This situation has led to the creation of the "abstention doctrine". Under some circumstances, a federal court may decline to exercise jurisdiction where a constitutional issue rests on an unsettled interpretation of state law. In such cases the Court should abstain from exercising jurisdiction otherwise conferred. An elaboration of this principle follows.

The leading abstention case developing this doctrine is *Railroad Commission v. Pullman Co.*,[5] where Justice Frankfurter first identified and discussed the rule of abstention.[6] The Pullman company sought to enjoin enforcement of an order of the Railroad Commission of Texas requiring that any sleeping car operated in Texas be continuously in charge of a Pullman conductor. If the light traffic justified only one Pullman sleeper the railroads had, prior to this order, put in charge only a porter, who in turn was responsible to the train conductor. If a train carried two or more sleepers, only then was a Pullman conductor to be in charge. The porters on the Pullman were, in those days, black, and the conductors were white. The effect of the order then would be to increase job opportunities for the whites. An issue was whether the order was authorized under Texas law. If it were, the plaintiffs (including the black porters) charged violations of the equal protection, due process, and commerce clauses of the Constitution. The company and others had attacked the order by bringing an action in federal district court, which accepted jurisdiction and

decided the necessary state law issues by holding that the Texas statutes did not allow the commission's order. The Supreme Court, in an opinion by Justice Frankfurter, reversed and remanded to the district court with directions to retain jurisdiction of the case pending determination of the state law question by the Texas courts after plaintiffs brought proceedings there with reasonable promptness. The district court, the high court said, should have exercised abstention of its jurisdiction.

The Court found the authority for its action in the wide discretion generally accorded a court of equity. A unanimous Court noted that a ruling on the constitutional question would involve a sensitive issue of state policy that should be avoided so long as there is another basis for adjudication. A decision by the federal court on the state law issue would be merely a prediction of the law because the Supreme Court of Texas, the final authority on the matter, had not interpreted the scope of the statute. Such a forecast should be avoided, according to the Court, because "[t]he reign of law is hardly promoted if an unnecessary ruling of a federal court is thus supplanted by a controlling decision of a state court. The resources of equity are equal to an adjustment that will avoid the waste of a tentative decision as well as the friction of a premature constitutional adjudication."[7] The abstention doctrine was the result of the Court's attempt to further smooth relations between state and federal authority.

Later cases utilizing the abstention doctrine did not focus as heavily on the sensitivity of the state issue as did the *Pullman* court. The primary focus of the doctrine became the avoidance of unnecessary adjudication of a constitutional issue.[8] Justice

5. 312 U.S. 496 (1941).

6. In earlier cases the Court had in fact abstained but without any broad justification of doctrine. See Thompson v. Magnolia Petroleum Co., 309 U.S. 478 (1940) (federal court should defer to state court to determine state property law issue in bankruptcy proceeding); Pennsylvania v. Williams, 294 U.S. 176 (1935) (federal court, in a diversity case, should defer to state court to state administration of corporate assets by

state officer; petition of Commonwealth of Pennsylvania granted); Langnes v. Green, 282 U.S. 531 (1931) (federal district court, in exercise of its discretion, should permit state court to proceed but retain a petition in its jurisdiction).

7. 312 U.S. at 500.

8. See, e.g., City of Meridian v. Southern Bell Telephone & Telegraph Co., 358 U.S. 639 (1959); Shipman

Frankfurter classified use of the abstention doctrine in this area as an aspect of the basic constitutional principle that federal courts will determine a constitutional question only if there is no alternative basis on which the controversy can be decided.[9] By submitting at least the state issues to the state courts, it is possible that the resulting state construction will avoid the constitutional issue in whole or in part.

The abstention doctrine, particularly as applied outside of a *Pullman* factual situation, raises many complicated issues which are usually considered in more detail in texts on federal jurisdiction.[10] Here we refer specifically to the development of the *Pullman* doctrine mainly to illustrate the significance of the abstention doctrine on the avoidance of constitutional issues, *viz.*, when should a federal court abstain from deciding a federal constitutional issue in cases which it has the jurisdiction to decide.[11]

Given the reasons for *Pullman* abstention, its application would be inappropriate if any possible interpretation of the relevant state law would be unconstitutional[12] or where the state law is settled,[13] or where a state court ruling would not be helpful in a determination of the constitutional issue.[14] Even if there is no prior state court adjudication, abstention is also not appropriate where the meaning of the challenged statute is "pointedly clear."[15]

Abstention also may be raised in a case where jurisdiction is grounded only on diversity and not on a federal question. "[T]he presence of a federal basis for jurisdiction may raise the level of justification needed for abstention."[16]

v. DuPre, 339 U.S. 321 (1950). Cf. Moore v. Sims, 442 U.S. 415, 423–431 (1979) (the fact that the challenge to a complex state statute is very broad-based is a factor militating in favor of abstention, not against it, because of the opportunity in the state courts of a narrowing construction).

9. Burford v. Sun Oil Co., 319 U.S. 315, 338 (1943) (dissenting opinion).

10. E.g., C. Wright, Law of Federal Courts § 52 (4th ed. 1983).

11. One Supreme Court opinion has purported to "confine the circumstances appropriate for abstention to three general categories." Colorado River Water Conservation District v. United States, 424 U.S. 800, 814 (1976). Thus, federal courts may dismiss an action when there is adequate state court review of a complex state regulatory scheme based primarily on local factors; federal courts ought not fashion the domestic policy of a state towards its administrative agencies. Burford v. Sun Oil Co., 319 U.S. 315 (1943); Alabama Public Service Comm'n v. Southern R. Co., 341 U.S. 341 (1951). Similarly, "[a]bstention is also appropriate where there has been presented difficult questions of state law bearing on policy problems of substantial public import whose importance transcends the result in the case then at bar." Colorado River Water Conservation District v. United States, 424 U.S. 800, 814 (1976), citing Louisiana Power & Light Co. v. City of Thibodaux, 360 U.S. 25 (1959). Generally, abstention is appropriate where plaintiff asks the federal court to enjoin a state criminal proceeding, unless plaintiff can show bad faith, harassment by the prosecutors, or a patently invalid state statute. Younger v. Harris, 401 U.S. 37 (1971). But in diversity litigation not involving federal constitutional or statutory issues federal courts ought not "exclude cases from [their] jurisdiction merely because they involve state law or because the law is uncertain or difficult to determine." Meredith v. Winter Haven, 320 U.S. 228, 236 (1943). And there are circumstances which permit the dismissal of a federal suit due to the presence of a concurrent state proceeding "for reasons of wise judicial administration . . . ." These circumstances are "more limited than the circumstances appropriate for abstention," but they do exist, though they are "exceptional." Colorado River Water Conservation District v. United States, 424 U.S. 800, 818 (1976).

12. Harman v. Forssenius, 380 U.S. 528, 534–535 (1965). Compare, Colautti v. Franklin, 439 U.S. 379, 392, n. 9 (1979) (abstention not argued by appellants nor is it appropriate given the extent of the vagueness of the challenged abortion statute for the court to abstain *sua sponte*), with, Anders v. Floyd, 440 U.S. 445 (1979) (per curiam) (possibility of abstention regarding abortion prosecution "suggested" by Supreme Court when state definition of viability is not clear [alternative constructions may obviate the constitutional difficulty] and criminal proceedings are pending in state court).

13. Lindsey v. Normet, 405 U.S. 56 (1972); Toomer v. Witsell, 334 U.S. 385, 392 n. 15 (1948); New Motor Vehicle Bd. v. Orrin W. Fox Co., 439 U.S. 96, 100 n. 3 (1978).

14. Public Utilities Comm'n of Ohio v. United Fuel Gas Co., 137 U.S. 456 (1943).

15. Babbitt v. United Farm Workers Nat. Union, 442 U.S. 289, 297–312 (1979) (no abstention as to challenged election procedures since the statute is clear, but lower court should have abstained as to criminal penalty and consumer publicity provisions because statute is ambiguous and is reasonably susceptible of constructions which would obviate the constitutional problems).

16. Colorado River Water Conservation District v. United States, 424 U.S. 800, 815 n. 21 (1976).

While the abstention doctrine was founded on the discretion vested in a court of equity,[17] it has since been applied to actions at law as well.[18] As the Court pointed out in *Louisiana Power & Light Co. v. City of Thibodaux,*[19] the first decision authorizing abstention in a case at law, "[t]hese prior cases have been cases in equity, but they did not apply a technical rule of equity procedure. They reflect a deeper policy derived from our federalism."[20]

The abstention doctrine may be applied in any type of case regarding state laws and is not limited solely to issues regarding property rights. In *Harrison v. NAACP*[21] the Court by a vote of 6 to 3 indicated that abstention is applicable to cases involving civil rights. That case involved the interpretation of a state's statutes which allegedly infringed upon the plaintiff's civil rights. The Court ordered abstention by the federal district court, indicating that the same criteria used for any other case involving a constitutional question of state statutory validity should be considered where the case involved civil rights. Justice Douglas, joined by Chief Justice Warren and Justice Brennan argued in dissent:

> We need not—we should not—give deference to a state policy that seeks to undermine paramount federal law. We fail to perform the du-

ty expressly enjoined by Congress on the federal judiciary in the Civil Rights Acts when we do so.[22]

The majority did not specifically answer this argument. The Proposed Federal Court Jurisdiction Act of 1973,[23] based on a proposal by the American Law Institute and not yet enacted by Congress, would reverse the majority opinion in *Harrison.*[24]

2. Some Problems and Procedures of Abstention

A major problem with the use of the abstention doctrine is the burden of expense and delay which is placed on the parties when they are forced to return to the state courts. The Supreme Court has not felt that such delay and inconvenience weigh too heavily when balanced against "the much larger issue as to the appropriate relationship between federal and state authorities functioning as a harmonius whole."[1] In the realities of an actual controversy, however, costs cannot be dismissed lightly. Not only may the monetary expenditures of juggling between courts be high, but delay and inconvenience to individual litigants must be considered. In some abstention cases the parties move from court to court arguing procedural issues for years before ever reaching the merits.[2] In some recent cases

---

17. Meredith v. Winter Haven, 320 U.S. 228 (1943); R.R. Comm'n of Texas v. Pullman Co., 312 U.S. 496 (1941).

18. United Gas Pipe Line Co. v. Ideal Cement Co., 369 U.S. 134 (1962); Clay v. Sun Insurance Office, 363 U.S. 207 (1960); Louisiana Power & Light Co. v. City of Thibodaux, 360 U.S. 25 (1959).

19. 360 U.S. 25 (1959).

20. 360 U.S. at 28. See also Clay v. Sun Insurance Office Ltd., 363 U.S. 207 (1960).

21. 360 U.S. 167 (1959).

22. 360 U.S. 167, 184 (dissenting opinion).

23. S. 1876, 93d Cong., 1st Sess. (May 23, 1973) (based on American Law Institute Study of the Division of Jurisdiction Between State and Federal Courts (1969), reprinted in H. Hart & H. Wechsler, The Judicial Code and Rules of Procedure in the Federal Courts 711–42 (1976). For a description of the congressional revisions of the A.L.I. proposal, see statement of Senator Burdick in 93d Cong., 1st Sess., vol. 119, No. 78, at 9637–40.

24. Section 1371(g) of the Proposed Federal Court Jurisdiction Act of 1973 (see note 23 supra) provides:

> "This section ['abstention and stays in certain cases'] is inapplicable, and the district court shall proceed to judgment, in actions to redress the denial, under color of any State law, statute, ordinance, regulation, custom, or usage, of the right to vote or of the equal protection of the laws, if such denial is alleged to be on the basis of race, creed, color, sex, or national origin. This section is also inapplicable, and the district court shall proceed to judgment, in actions brought by the United States or an officer or agency thereof."

1. Chicago v. Fieldcrest Dairies, Inc., 316 U.S. 168, 172–73 (1942).

2. While the Court has argued that abstention does not "involve the abdication of federal jurisdiction, but only the postponement of its exercise . . . ." Harrison v. NAACP, 360 U.S. 167, 177 (1959), that postponement can drag on for years. Wright, The Abstention Doctrine Reconsidered, 37 Tex.L.Rev. 815, 818 (1959). See also, Spector Motor Service, Inc. v. McLaughlin, 323 U.S. 101 (1944) and Spector Motor Service, Inc. v.

some Justices have expressed strong concern over these delaying costs of abstention.[3]

The problems of abstention are magnified by the procedural complexities surrounding its use. The federal court should abstain deciding the federal constitutional issue until the state court has had a chance to rule definitively on the interpretation of the state law in question, by a declaratory judgment action or otherwise. But the state court may decide that it cannot constitutionally give what to it is an advisory opinion.[4] Some states have developed certification procedures, whereby such state law questions may be certified to the state supreme court,[5] but the great majority have not done so.[6] In some cases the state court will refuse to decide a certified question that is not considered ripe.[7] The state courts have no obligation to consider issues brought in this way, for they may refuse to adjudicate until a case comes to them in the normal manner. Even when the state court does take the case, its procedural posture is intriguing. Since the state courts have a duty to enforce and abide by the U.S. Constitution,[8] it would be improper for the state courts to construe the statute without considering it in light of the requirements of the federal Constitution.[9] After obtaining the authoritative state court judgment, the parties may return to the federal district court for the constitutional decision. Or the parties may seek

U.S. Supreme Court review of the final state court decision. "Where, however, the party remitted to the state courts elects to seek a complete and final adjudication of his rights in the state courts, the District Court's reservation of jurisdiction is purely formal, and does not impair [Supreme Court] jurisdiction to review directly an otherwise final state court judgment."[10] If the parties opt for Supreme Court review at this stage of the litigation, then they cannot later return to the district court after Supreme Court review or denial of a writ of certiorari. The Supreme Court has explicitly admitted that this discretionary review or even appellate review is an "inadequate substitute for the initial District Court determination" that plaintiff sought before the court invoked abstention.[11] This inadequate substitute applies not only to issues of law, "it is especially true as to issues of fact."[12]

The Supreme Court attempted to clarify the complexities of the abstention doctrine in *England v. Louisiana State Board of Medical Examiners*,[13] where it outlined the procedural position litigants should take in an abstention case:

> [I]f a party freely and without reservation submits his federal claims for decision by the state courts, litigates them there, and has them decided there, then—whether or not he seeks direct review of the state decision in this Court—he has elected to forgo his right to return to the District Court . . .

O'Connor, 340 U.S. 602 (1951) (nearly seven years delay between decision requiring abstention and decision on merits); United States v. Leiter Minerals, Inc., 381 U.S. 413 (1965) (case dismissed as moot eight years after abstention required).

3. England v. Louisiana State Bd. of Medical Examiners, 375 U.S. 411, 423 (1964) (Douglas, J., concurring); Clay v. Sun Insurance Office, 363 U.S. 207, 228 (Douglas, J., dissenting); and 363 U.S. 207, 224 (Black, J., dissenting, joined by Warren, C.J., and Douglas, J.) (1960).

4. Compare United Service Life Insurance Co. v. Delaney, 328 F.2d 483 (5th Cir.1964) (ordering abstention), with, United Service Life Insurance Co. v. Delaney, 396 S.W.2d 855 (Tex.1965) (decision on state law in this abstention case denied because it would only be advisory opinion).

5. Florida first provided such a certification procedure, Fla.Stat.Ann., § 25.031, in 1945, and the Supreme Court approved of the practice. Lehman Brothers v.

Schein, 416 U.S. 386 (1974); Zant v. Stephens, 102 S.Ct. 1856, 1859 & n. 4 (1982).

6. Only a handful of states have a certification statute or rule of court. See generally Lillich & Mundy, Federal Court Certification of Doubtful State Law Questions, 18 U.C.L.A.L.Rev. 888 (1971).

7. In re Richards, 223 A.2d 827 (Me.1966).

8. Cf. Testa v. Katt, 330 U.S. 386 (1947).

9. Government & Civic Employees Organizing Committee, C.I.O. v. Windsor, 353 U.S. 364, 366 (1957).

10. NAACP v. Button, 371 U.S. 415, 427 (1963).

11. England v. Louisiana State Bd. of Medical Examiners, 375 U.S. 411, 416 (1964). Accord, Colautti v. Franklin, 439 U.S. 379, 392, n. 9 (1979).

12. 375 U.S. at 416.

13. 375 U.S. 411 (1964).

We recognize that in the heat of litigation a party . . . denying the statute's applicability may be led not merely to state his federal constitutional claim but to argue it, for if he can persuade the state court that application of the statute to him would offend the Federal Constitution, he will ordinarily have persuaded it that the statute should not be construed as applicable to him. In addition, the parties cannot prevent the state court from rendering a decision on the federal question if it chooses to do so . . . . [A] party may readily forestall any conclusion that he has elected not to return to the District Court . . . by making on the state record the "reservation to the disposition of the entire case by the state courts" that we referred to [earlier]. That is, he may inform the state courts that he is exposing his federal claims there only for the purposes of complying with [the case law], and that he intends, should the state courts hold against him on the question of state law, to return to the District Court for disposition of his federal contentions.[14]

The Court emphasized that an explicit reservation is not indispensable to preserve the return to the state court: it must "clearly" appear that the litigant litigated his federal claims in the state courts.[15] *Either* party to the litigation may make this reservation.[16] One party's insistence on litigating the federal claim in state court waives his rights to return to federal court but not his opponent's rights.[17]

14. 375 U.S. at 419–421.

15. 375 U.S. at 421.

16. 375 U.S. at 422 n. 13. See also, Zablocki v. Redhail, 434 U.S. 374, 379–380 n. 5 (1978); Will v. Calvert Fire Insurance Co., 437 U.S. 655 (1978) (opinion of Rehnquist, J., joined by Stewart, White, and Stevens, JJ. stating that if there is duplicative litigation in state and federal courts, the decision to defer to state courts is largely in the discretion of the federal district court even if matters of substantive federal law are involved). See also 437 U.S. at 668 (Brennan, J., dissenting, joined by Burger, C.J., and Marshall & Powell, JJ.).

17. 375 U.S. at 422 n. 13.

1. Note, Federal-Question Abstention: Justice Frankfurter's Doctrine in an Activist Era, 80 Harv.Law Rev. 604 (1967).

3. *The Modern Abstention Doctrine*

The abstention doctrine received its greatest use during Justice Frankfurter's years on the Court. It has been said that his retirement in 1962 left the doctrine "a judicial orphan."[1] The Court during the 1960's was far less amenable to use of abstention, as is evidenced by the fact that in the first seven cases on abstention to reach the Court after Justice Frankfurter's retirement, all were found to be improper for the exercise of abstention.[2] In four of these seven decisions the Court overruled lower court decisions to abstain.[3]

This steady decline of the abstention doctrine has been somewhat halted. While the doctrine has not been revived to the peaks reached at earlier times, recent decisions indicate abstention is not a dead doctrine.

After having required abstention in one case in 1970 and after having remanded to consider that issue in a 1971 case, on the grounds that claims might be successfully upheld under the relevant state constitutional provisions,[4] the Court split 6–3 against the propriety of abstention in *Wisconsin v. Constantineau*.[5] The majority, speaking through Justice Douglas, found no unresolved question of state law with respect to the federal constitutional issue and noted that "[w]here there is no ambiguity in the state statute, the federal court should not abstain but should proceed to decide the federal constitutional claim."[6] The majority

2. See id. at 604 n. 3. Harman v. Forssenius, 380 U.S. 528 (1965); Dombrowski v. Pfister, 380 U.S. 479 (1965); Davis v. Mann, 377 U.S. 678 (1064); Baggett v. Bullitt, 377 U.S. 360 (1964); Hostetter v. Idlewild Bon Voyage Liquor Corp., 377 U.S. 324 (1964); Griffin v. County School Bd., 377 U.S. 218 (1964); McNeese v. Board of Education, 373 U.S. 668 (1963).

3. Dombrowski v. Pfister, 380 U.S. 479 (1965); Baggett v. Bullitt, 377 U.S. 360 (1964); Griffin v. County School Bd., 377 U.S. 218 (1964); McNeese v. Board of Education, 373 U.S. 668 (1963).

4. Reetz v. Bozanich, 397 U.S. 82 (1970) (abstention required); Askew v. Hargrave, 401 U.S. 476 (1971) (remand to consider abstention issue).

5. 400 U.S. 433 (1971).

6. 400 U.S. at 439.

struck, as a violation of procedural due process, a state statute which allowed the police chief and certain other officials to post a notice in all retail liquor outlets in a town forbidding sales or gifts of liquor to a named individual for a period of one year on the grounds of excessive drinking. Chief Justice Burger dissenting, disagreed, contending that although "there is no absolute duty to abstain" in cases "involving no urgency or question of large import" a three judge district court would do well to abstain.[7] "For all we know," he said, "the state courts would find this [state] statute invalid under the State Constitution . . ."[8]

In *Harris County Comm'rs Court v. Moore*[9] an 8–1 decision with Justice Douglas dissenting, the Court reversed a three-judge district court and required abstention where the character of the federal right asserted and the availability of the relief sought turned in large part on unsettled state law.[10] The Court explained that "where the applicability of the statute is uncertain, abstention is often proper, while in the case where the vagueness claim goes to the obligations imposed by the statute, it is not, since a single state construction often would not bring the challenged statute 'within the bounds of permissible constitutional certainty.'"[11]

The *Harris* Court distinguished the *Constantineau* case and offered a test of when to apply the abstention doctrine in cases where the allegedly uncertain state law is not a statute but the state constitution:

> [W]e declined to order abstention [in *Constantineau*] where the federal due process claim was not complicated by an unresolved state-law question, even though plaintiffs might have sought relief under a similar provision of

the state constitution. But where the challenged statute is part of an integrated scheme of related constitutional provisions, statutes, and regulations, and where the scheme as a whole calls for clarifying interpretation by the state courts, we have regularly required the district courts to abstain.[12]

The refusal to expand, in a wholesale manner, the abstention doctrine to cases where a claim might also be brought under the state *constitution* is very important, for a contrary ruling could have turned abstention into a requirement of judicial exhaustion. As the Court most explicitly recognized in *Examining Board of Engineers v. Flores de Otero:*[13]

> Indeed, to hold that abstention is required because [a state statute] might conflict with [certain] broad and sweeping [state] constitutional provisions, would convert abstention from an exception into a general rule.[14]

Recently, the Court has reemphasized that "[a]bstention from the exercise of federal jurisdiction is the exception, not the rule",[15] and that the exceptional nature of abstention has confined its use to three general categories of circumstances: (1) "cases presenting a federal constitutional issue which might be mooted or presented in a different posture by a state court determination of pertinent state law", (2) "where there have been presented difficult questions of state law bearing on policy problems of substantial public import whose importance transcends the result in the case then at bar", and (3) "where, absent bad faith, harassment, or a patently invalid state statute, federal jurisdiction has been invoked for the purpose of restraining state criminal proceedings [citations omitted], state nuisance

---

7. 400 U.S. at 443. Mr. Justice Black wrote the second dissent in the case and Mr. Justice Blackmun joined in the opinions of both dissents. See also Lake Carriers Ass'n v. Mac Mullan, 406 U.S. 498 (1972), also rejecting abstention; Powell and Burger dissented.

8. 400 U.S. at 440. (footnote omitted).

9. 420 U.S. 77 (1975). In this case plaintiffs, who were justices of the peace and constables, challenged the constitutionality of a state law relating to their removal from office prior to the end of their terms.

10. 420 U.S. at 88.

11. 420 U.S. at 86 n. 9, quoting Baggett v. Bullitt, 377 U.S. 360, 377–78 (1964).

12. 420 U.S. at 84–85 n. 8, citing Reetz v. Bozanich, 397 U.S. 82 (1970), and City of Meridian v. Southern Bell Telephone & Telegraph Co., 358 U.S. 639 (1959).

13. 426 U.S. 572 (1976).

14. 426 U.S. at 598 (footnote omitted).

15. Colorado River Water Conservation District v. United States, 424 U.S. 800, 813 (1976).

proceedings antecedent to a criminal prosecution, which are directed at obtaining the
closure of places exhibiting obscene films
[citation omitted], or collection of state taxes
[citation omitted]." [16]

4. The ALI Proposal

Confusion as to the scope and wisdom of
the doctrine has led the American Law Institute to attempt to codify the doctrine in its
proposed jurisdiction act.[1] Some of the
more troubling conceptual and procedural
aspects of the abstention doctrine are clarified in proposed section 1371. Subsection (c)
requires:

> (c) A district court may stay an action, other-
> wise properly commenced in or removed to a
> district court under this title, on the ground
> that the action presents issues of State law
> that ought to be determined in a State proceed-
> ing, if the court finds (1) that the issues of
> State law cannot be satisfactorily determined
> in the light of the State authorities, (2) that ab-
> stention from the exercise of Federal jurisdic-
> tion is warranted either by the likelihood that
> the necessity for deciding a substantial ques-
> tion of Federal constitutional law may thereby
> be avoided, or by serious danger of embarrass-
> ing the effectuation of State policies by a deci-
> sion of State law at variance with the view that
> may be ultimately taken by the State court, or
> by other circumstances of like character, (3)
> that a plain, speedy, and efficient remedy may
> be made in the courts of such State, and (4)
> that the parties' claims of Federal right, if any,
> including any issues of fact material thereto,
> can be adequately protected by review of the
> State court decision by the Supreme Court of
> the United States.

Applicability of the doctrine would be
deemed inappropriate to civil rights cases or
to actions brought by the United States.[2] If
the federal court abstains and stays its action (and does not vacate the stay), the case
would then move to the State Court and
from there review will be in the U.S. Supreme Court, not back to the district court.[3]

5. Abstention, Comity, and Federal Court Injunctions of State Court Proceedings

Related to the *Pullman* abstention doctrine and yet representing a distinct line of
cases is the question of when a federal court
may grant a declaratory injunction or declaratory relief which relates to a threatened or
pending state criminal prosecution. Such
federal court intrusion into state proceedings is not favored because of what has been
termed "Our Federalism," that is, a "sensitivity to the legitimate interests of both
State and National Governments . . . "[1]
Several important distinctions between *Pullman* abstention and "Our Federalism" abstention are worth noting.

> In a conventional Pullman-type case, the issue
> is whether the federal plaintiff should himself
> be forced to commence a state proceeding, one
> which might not occur at all except by virtue of
> the abstention order. In the normal ["Our
> Federalism"] case, on the other hand, the
> whole point is that a state proceeding either
> has been or is about to be commenced in any
> event by the state authorities, and the holding
> is that the whole case should be litigated in
> that proceeding.[2]

In addition, in a *Pullman* case, the federal
court stays its own proceedings to allow the
state court to rule on the state law issues;
federal jurisdiction is postponed. In "Our
Federalism" cases, the federal plaintiff
seeks a stay of the state court proceeding
(or threatened proceeding) so that the feder-

---

16. 424 U.S. 814–816 (1976).

1. The proposal, as revised, was introduced in Congress on May 23, 1973, S. 1876, 93d Cong., 1st Sess.,
reprinted in H. Hart & H. Wechsler, The Judicial Code
and Rules of Procedure in the Federal Courts 711–42
(1976). Most of it has not yet been enacted.

2. Proposed § 1371(g). Cf. Harrison v. NAACP,
360 U.S. 167 (1959).

3. Proposed § 1371(d). Cf. England v. Louisiana
State Bd. of Medical Examiners, 375 U.S. 411 (1964).

1. Younger v. Harris, 401 U.S. 37, 44 (1971). See
generally, e.g., Redish, The Doctrine of Younger v.
Harris: Deference in Search of Rationale, 63 Cornell
L.Rev. 463 (1978); Soifer & Macgill, The Younger Doctrine: Reconstructing Reconstruction, 55 Tex.L.Rev.
1141 (1977); Sedler, Younger and Its Progeny: A Variation on the Theme of Equity, Comity and Federalism,
9 U. Toledo L.Rev. 681 (1978).

2. H. Hart & H. Wechsler, The Federal Courts and
the Federal System 1043 (2d ed. 1973).

al court can adjudicate the federal issue. If the federal court refuses to intervene, there is no federal court jurisdiction at all at this stage. If plaintiff is ultimately convicted he only has the chance of Supreme Court review or perhaps a habeas corpus claim in the lower federal courts.[3]

The "Our Federalism" line of cases should also be distinguished from those cases where a civil action or criminal prosecution is commenced in state court and the state defendant seeks removal of the entire case to federal court (where it is still prosecuted by state officials but heard by a federal judge). This removal may be allowed on the statutory grounds that the state defendant is a federal officer, or member of the armed forces, or any person who is denied or cannot enforce in the state courts a right under any law providing for equal civil rights, or any person who is sued for doing any act under color of authority for any law providing for equal rights, or for refusing to do any act on the grounds that it would be inconsistent with such law.[4]

The case law and literature on "Our Federalism" is rapidly expanding[5] and we will not consider this subject in any detail here except to outline a few of the major considerations.

First, any federal injunction of a state court proceeding must pass the hurdle of the federal anti-injunction or comity statute.[6] This hurdle is not a high one because all constitutional claims against state action can be based in part on the constitutional cause of action created by the broadly worded section 1983 of title 42. The Supreme Court has held that section 1983 is an exception to the anti-injunction statute.[7] Thus, for all practical purposes the bar to such injunctions lies not in statutory restrictions but in notions of judicial self-restraint, in comity, in "Our Federalism."

In very brief outline, the comity rules of "Our Federalism" as to federal court injunctions of state criminal proceedings distinguish between "pending" and "not pending but threatened" proceedings. If the state proceedings are pending it is very difficult to obtain a federal court injunction. The federal plaintiff must show that the federal injunction is necessary to prevent "irreparable injury" which is both " 'great and immediate.' "[8] Retreating from an earlier case,[9] the Court now holds that a claim that the state prosecution chills first amendment rights or is based on a statute unconstitutional on its face is insufficient to make the necessary showing of irreparable injury.[10] Plaintiff must show "bad faith, harassment,

---

3. Id. See also Id. at 1044–45.

4. 28 U.S.C.A. §§ 1442, 1442a, 1443.

5. See, e.g., C. Wright, Law of Federal Courts § 52A at 229 n. 1 (3d ed. 1976).

6. 28 U.S.C.A. § 2283:

"A court of the United States may not grant an injunction to stay proceedings in a State court except as expressly authorized by Act of Congress, or where necessary in aid of its jurisdiction, or to protect or effectuate its judgments."

See generally, Redish, The Anti-Injunction Statute Reconsidered, 44 U.Chi.L.Rev. 717 (1977); Mayton, Ersatz Federalism Under the Anti-Injunction Statute, 78 Colum.L.Rev. 330 (1978), which presents a careful study of the anti-injunction statute, 28 U.S.C.A. § 2283.

To be distinguished from federal court injunctions of state court proceedings are state court injunctions of federal court proceedings. It is not within the power of state courts, under the Supremacy Clause, to bar litigants from filing and prosecuting *in personam* actions in federal court. General Atomic Co. v. Felter, 434 U.S. 12 (1977) (per curiam).

7. Mitchum v. Foster, 407 U.S. 225 (1972). As one commentator has noted, "it is difficult to imagine an instance in which such [injunctive] relief could *not* be sought under § 1983 and in which § 2283 might therefore be a bar." H. Hart & H. Wechsler, The Federal Courts and the Federal System 1249 (2d ed. 1973) (emphasis in original; footnote omitted). See Chapter II, § III, B, supra.

The breadth of section 1983 is illustrated, e.g., by Lynch v. Household Finance Corp., 405 U.S. 538 (1972).

A recent case in which a fragmented Court, with no majority opinion, applied 28 U.S.C.A. § 2283 to bar a federal court injunction (though not in a constitutional context) is Vendo Co. v. Lektro-Vend Corp., 433 U.S. 623 (1977).

8. Younger v. Harris, 401 U.S. 37, 46 (1971), quoting Fenner v. Boykin, 271 U.S. 240, 243 (1926); see also Samuels v. Mackell, 401 U.S. 66, 69 (1971).

9. Dombrowski v. Pfister, 380 U.S. 479 (1965).

10. Younger v. Harris, 401 U.S. 37, 50–54.

or any other unusual circumstance that would call for equitable relief." [11]

In pending state prosecutions, the same equitable principles relevant to the propriety of an injunction must be taken into account in determining whether to issue declaratory relief.[12] If injunctive relief would be inappropriate, declaratory relief should "ordinarily" be denied as well.

Next we consider the situation where the state prosecution is not pending but is merely threatened. Plaintiff of course must show a sufficiently immediate threat so as to confer standing.[13] If no state prosecution is pending a federal plaintiff can secure declaratory relief if such a prosecution is threatened even though a showing of bad-faith enforcement or other special circumstances has not been made.[14]

Whether a federal injunction in such circumstances would be allowed appeared to be a much more difficult issue given the distinctions the Supreme Court has drawn between the cases involving the less intrusive declaratory judgments versus the injunctive remedy,[15] but the Supreme Court has allowed injunctions when the state criminal prosecution is not pending.[16]

If state criminal proceedings are begun against the federal plaintiffs "after the federal complaint is filed but before any proceedings of substance on the merits have taken place in the federal court, the principles of *Younger v. Harris* [and Our Federalism] should apply in full force." [17] The phrase "proceedings of substance on the merits" is undefined, but the significance of this rule is substantially lessened since the Court has also held that if no state action is pending and the federal plaintiff is seeking declaratory relief, the federal court could grant a preliminary injunction restraining the defendants from enforcing the disputed law until the end of the trial on the merits, at which time a declaratory judgment could be issued if the facts and law warrant. Such a preliminary injunction should prevent a state proceeding on the merits from starting. In determining whether to issue such a preliminary injunction the trial court, as in other equitable actions, must find a sufficient showing of harm and likelihood of ultimate success on the merits.[18]

These principles of "Our Federalism" apply to state civil proceedings when "the State is a party to the . . . proceeding, and the proceeding is both in aid of and closely related to criminal statutes," [19] as in a state civil action to abate the showing of an allegedly obscene movie as a nuisance, or a state contempt process.[20] These principles are also apparently applied in federal suits seeking to enjoin executive branches of "an agency of state or local governments . . . " [21]; but no such deference based on "Our Federalism" is owed a state administrative board if it is incompetent by reason of bias to adjudicate the issues before it.[22] However, a federal court should invoke "Our Federalism" and abstain from considering a challenge to the constitutionality of a

11. Id. at 54.

12. Samuels v. Mackell, 401 U.S. 66 (1971); Cf. Great Lakes Dredge & Dock Co. v. Huffman, 319 U.S. 293 (1943).

13. Younger v. Harris, 401 U.S. at 42.

14. Steffel v. Thompson, 415 U.S. 452 (1974). Cf. Patsy v. Board of Regents, 102 S.Ct. 2557 (1982) (no exhaustion of state administrative remedies is required before bringing a suit under 42 U.S.C.A. § 1983).

15. E.g., Steffel v. Thompson, 415 U.S. 452 (1974).

16. Wooley v. Maynard, 430 U.S. 705, 707–711 (1977) (threat of repeated prosecutions).

17. Hicks v. Miranda, 422 U.S. 332, 349 (1975).

18. Doran v. Salem Inn, Inc., 422 U.S. 922 (1975).

19. Huffman v. Pursue, Ltd., 420 U.S. 592, 604 (1975).

20. Id.; Juidice v. Vail, 430 U.S. 327 (1977); See also Trainor v. Hernandez, 431 U.S. 434 (1977) (principle of "Our Federalism" applies to civil attachment action brought by the state in its sovereign capacity); Moore v. Sims, 442 U.S. 415 (1979) (principle of "Our Federalism" applies to child abuse civil proceeding in which the state is a party).

21. Rizzo v. Goode, 423 U.S. 362, 380 (1976) (43 U.S. C.A. § 1983 action against mayor of Philadelphia and other city officials). For a narrow interpretation of *Rizzo*, see Lewis v. Hyland, 434 U.S. 931, 933 (1977) (Marshall, J., joined by Brennan, J., dissenting to denial of certiorari).

22. Gibson v. Berryhill, 411 U.S. 564, 575–77 (1973).

state's attorney ethical and disciplinary rules when they are the subject of a pending state disciplinary proceeding.[23] The failure to appeal a state criminal conviction does not bar prospective declaratory and injunctive relief to preclude further prosecution under a statute alleged to violate constitutional rights if a genuine threat of future prosecutions exists.[24]

One of the important unsettled issues of the "Our Federalism" line of cases is the res judicata and collateral estopped effects of federal lower court decisions offering declaratory relief to particular federal plaintiffs.[25] For example, may a lower federal court issue an injunction against a pending state prosecution initiated against a federal plaintiff who had successfully secured declaratory relief? To what extent may other parties rely on the collateral estoppel effects of a lower federal court's declaratory judgment? Answers to such questions remain in the future.

E. Political Questions

1. Introduction

The political question doctrine—which holds that certain matters are really political in nature and best resolved by the body politic rather than suitable for judicial review—is a misnomer. It should more properly be called the doctrine of nonjusticiability, that is, a holding that the subject matter is inappropriate for judicial consideration. The *White Primary Cases*,[1] the reapportionment decisions,[2] the steel seizure case,[3] and *United States v. Nixon*[4] are all cases involving "political" issues in which the Court rendered a decision. As Justice Jackson has noted, "all constitutional interpretations have political consequences."[5]

An important consequence of the political question doctrine is that a holding of its applicability to a theory of a cause of action renders the government conduct immune from judicial review.[6] Unlike other restrictions on judicial review—doctrines such as case or controversy requirements, standing, ripeness and prematurity, abstractness, mootness, and abstention—all of which may be cured by different factual circumstances, a holding of nonjusticiability is more absolute in its foreclosure of judicial scrutiny.

2. The Leading Cases

An early and leading case developing the political question doctrine was *Luther v. Borden*,[7] an 1849 opinion by Chief Justice Taney. The case in theory was a simple action of trespass brought by the plaintiff, Martin Luther, against Luther M. Borden and others, for breaking and entering plaintiff's house. The defendants claimed that

---

23. Middlesex County Ethics Committee v. Garden State Bar Ass'n, 102 S.Ct. 2515 (1982). The Court noted that state bar disciplinary hearings within the constitutionally prescribed jurisdiction of the state supreme court are "ongoing state judicial proceedings;" they implicate important state interests; and there is adequate opportunity in the state proceedings to raise the federal constitutional challenges. 102 S.Ct. at 2522.

24. Wooley v. Maynard, 430 U.S. 705, 710–712 (1977).

25. See, e.g., Steffel v. Thompson, 415 U.S. 452, 470–71 (1974); id. at 477 (White, J., concurring); id. at 482 n. 3 (Rehnquist, J., concurring). See also, Restatement of Judgments, Second, tent. draft No. 1, §§ 68, 68.1 (1973).

1. In these cases the Court opened up black participation in party primaries. E.g., Terry v. Adams, 345 U.S. 461 (1953); Smith v. Allwright, 321 U.S. 649 (1944); United States v. Classic, 313 U.S. 299 (1941); Nixon v. Condon, 286 U.S. 73 (1932); Nixon v.

Herndon, 273 U.S. 536 (1927); Baskin v. Brown, 174 F.2d 391 (4th Cir. 1949); Rice v. Elmore, 165 F.2d 387 (4th Cir. 1947).

2. E.g., Baker v. Carr, 369 U.S. 186 (1962); Reynolds v. Sims, 377 U.S. 533 (1967); Whitcomb v. Chavis, 403 U.S. 124 (1971); Burns v. Richardson, 384 U.S. 73 (1966); Fortson v. Dorsey, 379 U.S. 433 (1965); Gray v. Sanders, 372 U.S. 368 (1963); Davis v. Mann, 377 U.S. 678 (1964); Mahan v. Howell, 410 U.S. 315 (1973).

3. Youngstown Sheet & Tube Co. v. Sawyer, 343 U.S. 579 (1952).

4. 418 U.S. 683 (1974).

5. R. Jackson, The Supreme Court in the American System 56 (1955).

6. As Baker v. Carr, 369 U.S. 186, 209 (1962) illustrated, a reapportionment case is nonjusticiable if brought under the guaranty clause but justiciable if brought under the equal protection clause.

7. 48 U.S. (7 How.) 1 (1849).

their actions were justified because they were agents of the state of Rhode Island and pursuant to military orders broke into the house to search for and arrest plaintiff, who was engaging in insurrection against that state. The plaintiff in turn argued that this justification was invalid because "before the acts complained of were committed, that government had been displaced and annulled by the people of Rhode Island, and that the plaintiff was engaged in supporting the lawful authority of the State, and the defendants themselves were in arms against it." [8] Thus, out of a simple trespass action the Supreme Court was called upon to determine which was the legitimate government of Rhode Island. [9]

Taney turned to Article IV, section 4 of the United States Constitution, the guaranty clause:

The United States shall guarantee to every State in this union a Republican Form of Government, and shall protect each of them against Invasion; and on Application of the Legislature, or of the Executive (when the Legislature cannot be convened) against domestic Violence.

He argued that the Constitution "has treated the subject [of interference in the domestic concerns of a state] as political in nature, and placed the power in the hands of [the general government]." [10] He added:

[I]t rests with congress to decide what government is the established one in a State . . . . And its decision is binding on every other department of the government, and could not be questioned in a judicial tribunal . . . .

After the President has acted and called out the militia [pursuant to authority granted by Act of Congress], is a Circuit Court of the United States authorized to inquire whether his decision was right? . . . . [I]t would [then] become the duty of the court (provided it came to the conclusion that the President had decided incorrectly) to discharge those who were arrested or detained by the troops in the service of the United States, or the government which the President was endeavoring to maintain. [11]

After *Luther* the most significant development of the political question doctrine occurred in *Baker v. Carr*, [12] which upheld the justiciability of legislative reapportionment. The case is considered in more detail below in connection with other reapportionment decisions, [13] but here it is important to outline the general theories and tests of political questions developed in *Baker*.

Baker reviewed in considerable detail the political question cases and argued that in the guaranty clause cases and in other types of political question cases as well, "it is the relationship between the judiciary and the coordinate branches of the Federal Government, and not the federal judiciary's relationship to the states, which gives rise to the 'political question.'" [14] To determine if, given that coordinate relationship, the doctrine should be invoked, the Court fashioned the following test:

Prominent on the surface of any case held to involve a political question is found a textually demonstrable constitutional commitment of the issue to a coordinate political department; or a lack of judicially discoverable and manageable standards for resolving it; or the impossibility of deciding without an initial policy determination of a kind clearly for nonjudicial discretion; or the impossibility of a court's undertaking independent resolution without expressing lack of the respect due coordinate branches of gov-

---

8. 48 U.S. (7 How.) at 35.

9. On the Dorr Rebellion, what the Court called "the unfortunate political differences which agitated the people of Rhode Island in 1841 and 1842", 48 U.S. (7 How.) at 34, see, id. at 35–40, and 2 C. Warren, The Supreme Court in United States History 185–195 (rev.ed. 1926). See also Ex parte Dorr, 44 U.S. (3 How.) 103 (1847).

10. 48 U.S. (7 How.) at 42.

11. 48 U.S. (7 How.) at 42–43. Curiously, in dictum, the Court said that Congress "might, if they had deemed it most advisable to do so, have placed it in the power of a court to decide when the contigency had happened which required the federal government to interfere." Id. at 43. But this dictum has been largely forgotten.

12. 369 U.S. 186 (1962).

13. See Chapter 16, section IX below.

14. 369 U.S. at 210.

ernment; or an unusual need for unquestioning adherence to a political decision already made; or the potentiality of embarrassment from multifarious pronouncements by various departments on one question.[15]

The Court found that the guaranty clause cases involve the elements of a political question and thus are nonjusticiable. But since those reasons for nonjusticiability have "nothing to do with their touching on matters of state governmental organization," [16] a reapportionment case is not foreclosed from judicial review when it is based on a claim of denial of equal protection.[17]

Another leading case articulating a political question standard is *Powell v. McCormack*.[18] After Congressman Adam Clayton Powell was selected to Congress in November of 1966, the 90th Congress refused to seat him. Powell sued to be seated, to receive back pay, and for a declaratory judgment that his exclusion was unconstitutional.

Before reaching the issue of justiciability, the majority opinion by Chief Justice Warren found the case not to be moot [19] nor precluded by the legislative immunity granted by the speech or debate clause.[20] Then the Court found that Powell was "excluded" from the 90th Congress rather than "expelled". Article I, section 5, clause 2 governs expulsions and provides that each House "with the Concurrence of two-thirds" may expel a member. The respondents argued that the House could expel a member for any reason whatsoever.[21] The Court did not have to decide this argument for it ruled that Powell would only be subject to expulsion if he had been allowed to take his seat and *then* required to surrender it.[22]

Powell, the Court ruled, was "excluded"; that is, he was not permitted to take his seat and his oath of office. Only a majority is required for exclusion.[23] Although two-thirds voted against Powell,[24] the Court did not find that it should judge the legality of his exclusion by the expulsion standard. The difference between calling the vote an exclusion rather than an expulsion was one of substance and not form for several reasons: (1) the House treated the vote as one of exclusion and not expulsion;[25] (2) while the law is unclear the historical evidence and the belief of the House members was that expulsion cannot be applied for actions taken during a prior Congress,[26] which was Powell's case; and (3) some Congressmen expressed the view that they would have not voted to "expel" Powell though they did vote to "exclude" him.[27]

---

15. 369 U.S. at 217.

16. 369 U.S. at 218.

17. 369 U.S. at 237.

18. 395 U.S. 486 (1969).

19. Powell was reelected and was seated in the 91st Congress in January, 1969, long before the Supreme Court decision was issued on June 16, 1969. The respondents argued that the case was now moot. The majority held that Powell's claim for back salary prevented mootness. 395 U.S. at 496.

20. The Court held that the Speech or Debate Clause, art. I, § 6, was not a bar to the action:

"The purpose of th[is] protection afforded legislators is not to forestall judicial review of legislative action but to insure that legislators are not distracted from or hindered in the performance of their legislative tasks by being called into court to defend their actions. A legislator is no more or no less hindered or distracted by litigation against a legislative *employee* calling into question the employee's affirmative action than he would be by a lawsuit questioning the employee's failure to act. Nor is the distraction or hindrance increased because the claim is for salary rather than damages, or because the litigation questions action taken by the employee within rather than without the House." (395 U.S. at 505) (emphasis added).

The Court concluded that legislative employees who participate in unconstitutional activity are responsible for their acts even if the action against a Congressman would be barred by the Speech or Debate clause. But the Court also said that it was not deciding that the Speech or Debate clause would in fact bar an action solely against members of Congress where no agents participated and no other remedy was available. 395 U.S. at 506 n. 26.

21. 395 U.S. at 507.

22. 395 U.S. at 507 n. 27.

23. 395 U.S. at 492, 508.

24. 395 U.S. at 493.

25. 395 U.S. at 492, 508.

26. 395 U.S. at 508–510.

27. 395 U.S. at 511.

Then, applying the tests of *Baker v. Carr*,[28] the Court decided that while the vote to expel Powell might not have been justiciable, the vote to exclude Powell was otherwise generally justiciable and was not a political question. Exclusion is governed by Art. I, § 5, cl. 1, which provides that each House is "the Judge of the Elections, Returns and Qualifications of its own Members . . . ." To determine if the Constitution provided a textual commitment to a coordinate branch of the federal government the Court said it had to interpret this clause. After examining the relevant historical materials the Court concluded that "the Constitution leaves the House without authority to *exclude* any person, duly elected by his constituents, who meets all the requirements for membership expressly prescribed in the Constitution.[29] The power to exclude, governed by a majority vote, is narrower than the power to expel, governed by a two-thirds requirement. The Court finally concluded that the House was without power to exclude Powell since it was clear that he met all the requirements of age, residence, and citizenship.

Since the petitions only sought declaratory relief it was unnecessary to express an opinion as to the appropriateness of coercive relief.[30] Notwithstanding the contrary decision of the House of Representatives the Court thought it "an 'inadmissible suggestion' that action might be taken in disregard of a judicial determination." [31] Though the Court did not cite *Glidden Co. v. Zdanok* [32] at this point, it might well have done so. In that case the Court ruled that the Court of Claims exercised Article III judicial power even though the Court of Claims or any federal court is impotent to enforce a money claim against the United States, which the Court of Claims may award.[33] After all, the Supreme Court may render a decision involving a money judgment between States,[34] though the Court cannot enforce that award. And even in private litigation, the Court may award money damages or injunctive relief even though that judgment cannot be enforced because the private litigant is judgment proof or subsequently escapes the jurisdiction of the Court.

The most recent and significant political question case is *United States v. Nixon* [35] where the Supreme Court affirmed the order of the District Court ordering *in camera* examination of certain material including certain taped conversations, subpoenaed by the Watergate Special Prosecutor from President Nixon. In the course of the unanimous opinion Chief Justice Burger rejected the argument that a claim of executive privilege is a political question. The controversy in this case was one the courts traditionally resolve: the production or nonproduction of certain specified evidence deemed by the prosecutor to be relevant to and admissible in a pending criminal case.[36] Such issues, said the Court, are traditionally justiciable and within the Article III power.[37] Enforcements of a subpoena duces tecum "must necessarily be committed" to the trial court's sound discretion.[38] Thus while the Court should defer to each branch, it cannot share this Article III judicial power with the Executive anymore than it could share in the Executive's veto power.[39] The issue of the applicability of executive privilege in these circumstances then is not committed to another branch of government but to the Court.

28.　369 U.S. 186, 217 (1962).

29.　395 U.S. at 522 (emphasis in original; footnote omitted). It was all agreed that Powell met the requirements of age, residence, and citizenship required in Art. I, § 2, cl. 2. Nor were other standing qualifications in dispute. See also, 395 U.S. at 520 n. 41.

30.　395 U.S. at 517, 550.

31.　395 U.S. at 549 n. 86, citing McPherson v. Blacker, 146 U.S. 1, 24 (1892).

32.　370 U.S. 530 (1962).

33.　370 U.S. 530, 568–572 (Opinion of Harlan, J.). See also La Abra Silver Mining Co. v. United States, 175 U.S. 423, 461–462 (1899).

34.　South Dakota v. North Carolina, 192 U.S. 286, 318–321 (1904).

35.　418 U.S. 683 (1974).

36.　418 U.S. at 696–697.

37.　418 U.S. at 697.

38.　418 U.S. at 702.

39.　418 U.S. at 704.

Given the broad exercise of judicial review expressed in *Baker, Powell,* and *Nixon* the present scope of the Political Question Doctrine is not easily summarized. By examining the precedents of a few decided areas which do not appear to have been challenged by the leading cases we may develop some perspective of the problem.

3.   A Few Decided Areas

The lengthy opinion in *Baker v. Carr* [40] discussed several of the areas which have been held to be political questions. It may be useful to consider some of the cases discussed there as well as other cases in order to better illustrate the doctrine.

a.   Foreign Affairs and the War Making Power

The *Baker* Court explicitly rejected the dictum, found in some earlier cases, that anything touching foreign affairs is immune from judicial review.[41] Yet the fact that a matter relates to foreign policy or international affairs is certainly relevant, because of the need to avoid conflicting public postures or because of the nonjudicial discretion that lies with the executive or legislative branches. Thus a court will not usually "inquire whether a treaty has been terminated, since on that question 'governmental action

. . . must be regarded as of controlling importance,' [but] if there has been no conclusive 'governmental action' then a court can construe a treaty and may find it provides the answer." [42]

In connection with the Vietnam War the lower courts have generally ruled that the issue of its legality was nonjusticiable, but the Supreme Court has either denied certiorari or summarily affirmed, over the objection of several justices who wanted full oral argument.[43] Given the sensitive problems of holding a war to be illegal, most issues relating to the constitutionality of a war may well be nonjusticiable. The effect of such a holding would be that, while only Congress can declare war, the President can make war, and Congress can authorize an undeclared war. That is, the decision whether or not war should formally be declared is a political question. Yet, the issue may be different if the President were to seek to make war over clear congressional opposition, while Congress was not in session, so that even an argument of implicit congressional authorization could not be made. It is also unclear if any soldier or other party could even have standing to raise the issue of an illegal war based on the alleged violation of the War Powers Resolution,[44] which was enacted over Presidential veto and concerns

---

40. 369 U.S. 186 (1962). See generally, e.g., Henkin, Is There a "Political Question" Doctrine?, 85 Yale L.J. 597 (1976).

41. 369 U.S. at 211.

42. 369 U.S. at 212, comparing Terlinden v. Ames, 184 U.S. 270, 285 (1902), with Society for the Propagation of the Gospel in Foreign Parts v. New Haven, 21 U.S. (8 Wheat.) 464, 492–495 (1823), and Clark v. Allen, 331 U.S. 503 (1947). See generally 369 U.S. at 212–214. See, Eain v. Wilkes, 641 F.2d 504, 514 (7th Cir. 1981) (Wood, C.J.).

See also Goldwater v. Carter, 444 U.S. 996, 1003 (1979) (Opinion of Rehnquist, J., joined by Burger, C. J., and Stevens & Stewart, JJ.) (decision by President Carter to terminate treaty of defense with Government of Taiwan is political).

43. E.g., Atlee v. Laird, 347 F.Supp. 689 (E.D.Pa. 1972) (3-judge court) (legality of Vietnam War nonjusticiable), affirmed summarily, sub nom. Atlee v. Richardson, 411 U.S. 911 (1973) (Douglas, Brennan & Stewart, JJ. would note probable jurisdiction and set the case for oral argument); see also Holtzman v. Schlesinger,

484 F.2d 1307 (2d Cir. 1973) (Cambodian bombing nonjusticiable; stay granted by District Court order enjoining the bombing); On the stay, see 414 U.S. 1304 (1973) (Marshall, Circuit Justice, in chambers, denying application to vacate stay of Court of Appeals order staying district court injunction of Cambodian bombing), and 414 U.S. 1316 (Douglas, Circuit Justice, in chambers, granting stay of Court of Appeals stay), and 414 U.S. 321 (Marshall, Circuit Justice in chambers; stay of district court order granted; Burger, C. J., Brennan, Stewart, White, Blackmun, Powell & Rehnquist, JJ., agree).

See also, Mora v. McNamara, 389 U.S. 934 (1967); Velvel v. Nixon, 396 U.S. 1042 (1970); McArthur v. Clifford, 393 U.S. 1002 (1968); Massachusetts v. Laird, 400 U.S. 886 (1970); Mitchell v. Laird, 488 F.2d 611 (D.C.Cir. 1973); Orlando v. Laird, 443 F.2d 1039 (2d Cir. 1971). Cf. Gilligan v. Morgan, 413 U.S. 1, 6–12 (1973) (U.S.Const. art. I, § 8, cl. 16).

44. Pub.L. 93–148, 87 Stat. 555 (Nov. 7, 1973), 50 U.S.C.A. §§ 1541–48. See Chapter 6, section III, D, infra.

the war powers of the Congress and the President.

b. Amendments to the Constitution

The leading case in this area is *Coleman v. Miller*,[45] where plaintiffs included members of the Kansas Senate, whose votes against ratification of a constitutional amendment had been overridden. They sued in state court to compel the Secretary of State to erase an endorsement on a resolution ratifying the proposed Child Labor Amendment, and indicate instead that it "was not passed." The court was also asked to restrain the officers of the Senate and House from signing the resolution and the Kansas Secretary of State from authenticating it and delivering it to the Governor. The petitioners had three claims: (1) that the Lieutenant Governor could not cast the deciding vote in the Senate because he was not part of the "Legislature" within the meaning of Article V of the U. S. Constitution; (2) that Kansas could not ratify the amendment because it had previously rejected it; and (3) that the amendment could not be ratified because it was no longer viable, not having been ratified within a reasonable time.

Chief Justice Hughes' opinion for the Court held that the complaining senators had standing,[46] with Justices Frankfurter, Roberts, Black, and Douglas dissenting on this point.[47] The Court was equally divided on the issue of whether the Lieutenant Governor could cast the deciding vote on ratification, with the same four justices arguing that this issue was nonjusticiable.[48]

Petitioners also argued that either a ratification or rejection of a proposed amendment cannot later be changed. The Court held that the "question of the efficacy of ratifications by state legislatures, in the light of previous rejection or attempted withdrawal, should be regarded as a political question pertaining to the political departments, with the ultimate authority in the Congress in the exercise of its control over the promulgation of the adoption of the amendment."[49] Congress, the Court said, could have enacted a statute relating to ratification after rejections (and rejections after ratification) but had not done so then. To this day, in fact, it has left this area barren of clear statutory guidance.

Finally the petitioners argued that the proposed amendment has been spent, lost its force, and could not be ratified because of the length of time—thirteen years—between its proposal and the Kansas ratification. Previously the Supreme Court had held that Congress may fix a reasonable time for ratification.[50] But Congress had not—and still has not—enacted any general statutory provisions governing the length of time. In the past, seven years was used, in various proposed amendments, as a reasonable time.[51] At the time of *Coleman*, the average time to ratify an amendment, excluding the first ten, had been three years, six months, and 25 days.[52] To the extent that economic, political, and social conditions relate to a proposed amendment, make it nonviable, those factors change. Weighing those factors to determine viability, the Court recognized, was inappropriate for the judiciary. Thus it concluded that the issue of a reasonable time "lies within congressional province." And that question should be "regarded as an open one for the consideration of the Congress when, in the presence of certified ratifications by three-fourths of the States, the time arrives for the promulgation of the adoption of the amendment. Th[at] decision by the Congress . . . of the question whether the amendment had been adopted

---

45. 307 U.S. 433 (1939).

46. 307 U.S. at 438.

47. 307 U.S. at 460 (Opinion of Frankfurter, J.).

48. 307 U.S. at 456 (Black, J., concurring).

49. 307 U.S. at 450.

50. Dillon v. Gloss, 256 U.S. 368 (1921).

51. See, e.g., U.S.Const., 18th amend., § 3; 20th amend., § 6; 21st amend., § 3; 22d amend., § 2.

52. 307 U.S. at 453.

within a reasonable time would not be subject to review by the courts."[53]

Justice Butler dissented and would have held that more than a reasonable time had elapsed.[54] The separate opinion of Justice Black joined by Frankfurter, Roberts, and Douglas stated: "Congress, possessing exclusive power over the amending process, cannot be bound by and is under no duty to accept the pronouncements upon that exclusive power by this Court or by the Kansas courts. Neither state nor federal courts can review that power."[55]

The problem of reconciling judicial review with majority rule adds another important reason why decisions on amending the Constitution, particularly decisions preventing amendments, should not be made by the courts. The Child Labor Amendment had been proposed because of earlier Court decisions preventing adequate legislation in this area.

> It is one thing for the Court to strike down the Child Labor Law as incompatible with its choice of constitutional values . . . but it would seem to be quite a different matter if the Court could, by a narrow interpretation of the amendment procedures, prevent the ratifi-

cation of the amendment which was intended to overrule [its earlier decisions] . . . . [I]t is by no means inconceivable that an amendment might be unconstitutional. But this seems to be one instance in which the Court cannot assume responsibility for saying "what the law is" without, at the same time, undermining the legitimacy of its power to say so.[56]

Such a view need not completely exclude the Courts from the amendment process. Thus, the Court has upheld the power of Congress to fix a reasonable time for ratification and it has determined, where statutes required, when an amendment has gone into effect.[57] But if statutes do not provide for a judicial role[58] and if the power of Congress to enact such statutes is not the matter in dispute, it may be the rule that all amendment questions relating to the constitutionality of the amendment procedure should be regarded as political.[59]

c. The Guaranty Clause

From *Luther v. Borden*[60] to the present time the Guaranty clause of Article IV, section 7 has been held not to be "a repository of judicially manageable standards which a court could utilize independently in order to

---

53. 307 U.S. at 454.

54. 307 U.S. at 470 (Butler, J., dissenting).

55. 307 U.S. at 459 (Black, J., concurring).

56. Scharpf, Judicial Review and the Political Question: A Functional Analysis, 75 Yale L.J. 517, 589 (1966). Cf. Leser v. Garnett, 258 U.S. 130 (1922) (upholding the constitutionality of the 19th Amendment, in the course of which the Court said: "official notice to the Secretary [of State], duly authenticated, that [a state legislature] had [ratified a proposed amendment] was conclusive upon him, and, being certified to by his proclamation, is conclusive upon the courts.") 258 U.S. at 137.

57. Dillon v. Gloss, 256 U.S. 368 (1921) (18th Amendment). See also National Prohibition Cases, 253 U.S. 350, 386–388 (1920) (18th Amendment case, holding, inter alia, that the two-thirds vote in each House of Congress required in proposing an amendment is a vote of two-thirds of the members present, assuming a quorum, and not a two-thirds vote of the entire membership, present and absent); Hawke v. Smith, No. 1, 253 U.S. 221 (1920) (18th Amendment case, holding that provision of state constitution requiring submission of ratification to referendum is unconstitutional under Article V of the Constitution); Hawke v. Smith, No. 2, 253 U.S. 231 (1920) (19th Amendment case, hold-

ing same as in Hawke v. Smith, No. 1); United States v. Sprague, 282 U.S. 716 (1931) (18th Amendment; Tenth Amendment does not limit power of Congress to choose ratification by legislature instead of convention); Hollingsworth v. Virginia, 3 U.S. (3 Dall.) 378, 381 (1798) (11th Amendment; President has nothing to do with the proposing or adoption of Amendment to the Constitution).

58. It should be noted that under the present law it is the Administrator of the General Services Administration who is given statutory responsibility to publish his certificate that an amendment "has been adopted, according to the provisions of the Constitution . . . ." 1 U.S.C.A. § 106b.

The judicial role under this statute, and the extent to which the Administrator of the General Services Administration has any discretion to declare the ratification of a state (or a state's rescission of its earlier ratification) valid or invalid are unclear.

59. Compare Rotunda, Running Out of Time: Can the E.R.A. Be Saved, 64 A.B.A.J. 1507 (1978) (arguing in favor of the application of the political question doctrine), with Almond, id., 64 A.B.A.J. 1504 (1978) (arguing for opposing viewpoint).

60. 48 U.S. (7 How.) 1 (1849).

identify a State's lawful government."[61] Thus, a claim that a state initiative and referendum violates the guaranty clause is nonjusticiable.[62] Similarly, a claim that the state of Kentucky's procedure for determining the results of a contested election of Governor and Lieutenant Governor is not justiciable if brought under the guaranty clause.[63]

Occasionally in dissents, some justices have apparently suggested that the guaranty clause ought not always to be regarded as a nonjusticiable right,[64] but the majority has never agreed with that position. The reapportionment cases themselves illustrate that a claim of reapportionment is nonjusticiable if brought under the guaranty clause but justiciable if brought under the equal protection clause of the Fourteenth Amendment.

d. *Political Party Conventions*

Some legal commentators suggest that manageable standards for dealing with the impacts of judicial review of political parties have not yet developed,[65] and that some of the factors which result in nonjusticiability occur in most litigation challenging party activity. Thus it is argued that in political party cases, the Court is faced with the impossibility of deciding without rendering an initial policy determination better left to other branches of government.[66] This argument fails to perceive that the questions subject to judicial review which arise in the context of political parties may be no more political

than the questions decided by the Supreme Court in many cases involving the right to vote.[67]

Exercising judicial review of party regulations does not have to require an initial nonjudicial policy determination. In *Nixon v. Herndon*[68] the State of Texas by statute forbade blacks from voting in the Democratic primary. The Supreme Court ruled the statute unconstitutional. Texas repealed its unconstitutional statute and authorized the state executive committee of the party to pass qualifying party rules. When the party committee immediately barred blacks from voting in the primaries, the Supreme Court in *Nixon v. Condon*[69] reached the same result: the party's rule was unconstitutional. The Court exercised judicial review of a party rule without making "an initial policy determination of a kind clearly for nonjudicial discretion."[70]

In *Ray v. Blair*,[71] the Supreme Court determined the constitutional validity of a party-enacted loyalty pledge. The issue was not rendered nonjusticiable because a political party had promulgated the challenged rule. In *Seergy v. Kings County Republican County Committee*[72] the Second Circuit struck down a New York statute that allowed the county committee for each party to choose an alternative election procedure for determining membership in the committee. The court found a violation of the one man, one vote standard to the extent to

---

61. Baker v. Carr, 369 U.S. 186, 223 (1962).

62. Pacific States Telephone & Telegraph Co. v. Oregon, 223 U.S. 118 (1912).

63. Taylor v. Beckman, No. 1, 178 U.S. 548 (1900). See id. at 581 (Brewer & Brown, JJ., dissenting on 19th Amendment grounds), id. at 585 (Harlan, J., dissenting on 14th Amendment grounds). See generally Baker v. Carr, 369 U.S. 186, 223–226 (1962), and cases cited therein. As *Baker* notes, challenges to congressional action as violative of the guaranty clause are also nonjusticiable. Id. at 224.

64. See Fortson v. Morris, 385 U.S. 231, 249 (1966) (Fortas, J., dissenting, joined by Douglas, J., and Warren, C.J.); Baker v. Carr, 369 U.S. 186, 242 n. 2 (1962) (Douglas, J. concurring).

65. E.g., Comment, One Man, One Vote and Selection of Delegates to National Nominating Conventions,

37 U.Chi.L.Rev. 536 (1970). Contra, Rotunda, Constitutional and Statutory Restrictions on Political Parties in the Wake of Cousins v. Wigoda, 53 Tex.L.Rev. 935 (1975). See generally, Chambers & Rotunda, Reform of Presidential Nominating Conventions, 56 Va.L.Rev. 179 (1970).

66. Kester, Constitutional Restrictions on Political Parties, 60 Va.L.Rev. 735, 782 (1974).

67. See, e.g., Terry v. Adams, 345 U.S. 461 (1953) (White Primary Case).

68. 273 U.S. 536 (1927).

69. 286 U.S. 73 (1932).

70. Baker v. Carr, 369 U.S. 186, 217 (1962).

71. 343 U.S. 214 (1952).

72. 459 F.2d 308 (2d Cir. 1972).

which the party committee performed a governmental function:

> In those rare instances where committeemen perform public electoral functions . . . the county committee . . . is unquestionably playing an integral part in the state scheme of public elections.[73]

It is doubtful that the apportionment scheme forbidden in *Seergy* would become nonjusticiable simply if reenacted as a party rule. This conclusion is true even if the correct substantive decision is that political party representatives should not be subject to the one man, one vote rule. The change in authorship should not suddenly create an initial policy judgment of a kind clearly for nonjudicial discretion. If authorship of the rules were substantively determinative, courts would not be able to exercise any review of even state laws regulating parties, for such laws as a practical matter are authored by the political parties within the state.

The fact that a question relate to politics does not for that reason necessarily make it nonjusticiable. In *Cousins v. Wigoda*,[74] while purporting not to decide the extent to which the political question doctrine counsels against judicial intervention, the Court in fact opened the way to increased judicial involvement in political conventions by restricting contrary language in the earlier case of *O'Brien v. Brown*.[75] *O'Brien* was a per curiam 6–3 opinion which had stayed a judgment of the D.C. Circuit that had granted relief to California delegates (pledged to candidate George McGovern) contesting their unseating at the 1972 Democratic National Convention, but that had denied like relief to the Illinois delegates (Mayor Richard J. Daley et al.). The high court in *O'Brien* said that "these cases involve claims of the power of the federal judiciary to review actions heretofore thought to be in the control of political parties. Highly important questions are presented concerning justiciability. . . . [W]e entertain grave doubts as to the action taken by the Court of Appeals."[76]

Cousins reversed, as an unconstitutional abridgment of the first and fourteenth amendments' guarantee of the right to associate with the political party of one's choice, a state court's contempt citation purportedly based on implementing Illinois statutes that regulated delegation selection to the national convention.[77] Yet, the majority opinion indicated that regulation of national parties and conventions by Congress or of state parties by the states would present different issues.[78] Justice Powell, concurring in part and dissenting in part, also acknowledged that such regulations would require a wholly different balance.[79] If the Court had felt committed to the *O'Brien* dictum that there might be significant problems of justiciability,[80] its decision in *Cousins* would have been much broader. Rather than reversing the state court's order for violating the freedom of association where there was no claim that the party's selection procedure was unconstitutional, where the laws relied on by the state court were state rather than federal, and where the state had no special interest overriding the freedom of association, the Court would simply have held that laws governing political parties are nonjusticiable. The narrower holding suggests that the

---

73. 459 F.2d at 314.

74. 419 U.S. 477 (1975).

75. 409 U.S. 1 (1972) (per curiam).

76. 409 U.S. 1, 4–5 (1972).

77. 419 U.S. 477, 489–490 (1975).

Accord, Democratic Party v. LaFollette, 450 U.S. 107 (1981) which relied on *Cousins* and invalidated—as a violation of the first amendment right to association—a Wisconsin statute conflicting with a rule of the National Democratic Party providing that only those who are willing to affiliate publicly with the Democratic Party may participate in the process of selecting delegates to the Party's National Convention. The Wisconsin statute required that the results of the state's open primary—open to anyone without any requirement of publicly stating one's affiliation with the Democratic Party—bound the delegates' votes at the Convention, even though the delegates were selected as party caucuses open only to those who publicly stated their affiliation with the Party.

78. 419 U.S. 477, 483–484 n. 4.

79. 419 U.S. at 497 n.*.

80. 409 U.S. at 4–5.

Court does not intend to employ the political question doctrine to sidestep future questions concerning delegate selection for a national political convention.

To the extent that party action is not merely an exercise in legitimate political discretion but rather is racially discriminatory or implements other delegate section procedures which, as *Cousins* explained, "are not exercised within the confines of the Constitution,"[81] it is likely that the Court will exercise judicial review. But failing such violations, the Court may not exercise review. Lower courts, for example, have refused to reapportion political party conventions;[82] though the Supreme Court has not yet ruled on the issue,[83] it is extremely unlikely that any inflexible, wooden interpretation of the one man, one vote standard would be implemented which would prohibit the conventions from recognizing legitimate party concerns.

e. Impeachment

Commentators have usually thought that any impeachment proceeding, particularly a presidential impeachment, by the House and then by the Senate is a political question.[84] Certainly the language of the Constitution supports such a view. Article I, section 2 states that the House "shall have the sole power of Impeachment," and section 3 provides that the "Senate shall have the sole Power to try all Impeachments." Since no statute sets out or otherwise defines impeachable offenses, the nature of the proceeding makes it difficult if not impossible for the Court to apply any judicial criteria

for review. In fact any such statute might be unconstitutional for it might interfere with the House's *sole* power of Impeachment.

The Chief Justice would be disqualified from setting on any hypothetical Supreme Court review of the impeachment of the President since the Constitution commands that he preside at the Senate trial.[85] Moreover, the potential for national confusion would be great if the Senate were to declare the presidential office vacant and the impeached president would refuse to leave, apply for Supreme Court or lower court review, and claim, for example, that some of the Senators who voted against him were prejudiced and should have disqualified themselves. Since the framers placed the sole power of impeachment in two *political* bodies—the House and Senate—it would certainly appear that such an issue remains a political question. Yet some commentators have suggested that at least some aspects of impeachment are judicially reviewable.[86]

4. A Functional Test for Political Questions

In addition to the *Baker* test of political question, and some recent cases finding or not finding political questions in limited areas[87] several commentators have proposed various tests for the application of the doctrine.

Professor Bickel has argued:

Such is the foundation, in both intellect and instinct, of the political-question doctrine: the Court's sense of lack of capacity, compounded in unequal parts of (a) the strangeness of the

---

81.　419 U.S. 477, 491 (1975).

82.　E. g., Bode v. National Democratic Party, 452 F.2d 1302, 1307–09 (D.C.Cir.1971), cert. denied 404 U.S. 1019 (1972); Georgia v. National Democratic Party, 447 F.2d 1271, 1278–79 (D.C.Cir.1971) (per curiam), cert. denied 404 U.S. 858 (1971). See generally, Rotunda, Constitutional and Statutory Restrictions on Political Parties in the Wake of Cousins v. Wigoda, 53 Tex.L.Rev. 935, 938–943 (1975).

83.　Cousins v. Wigoda, 419 U.S. 477, 483–484 n. 4 (1975); Gray v. Sanders, 372 U.S. 368, 378 n. 10 (1963).

84.　E. g., Wechsler, Toward Neutral Principles of Constitutional Law, 73 Harv.L.Rev. 1, 8 (1959).

85.　U.S.Const. art. 1, § 3, cl. 6.

86.　R. Berger, Impeachment: The Constitutional Problems (1973).

87.　E.g., Gilligan v. Morgan, 413 U.S. 1 (1973) (art. I, § 8, cl. 16) (political question); but cf. Scheuer v. Rhodes, 416 U.S. 232, 249 (1974) (not political question); Roudebush v. Hartke, 405 U.S. 15, 18–19 (1972) (Article I, § 5) (political question); Elrod v. Burns, 427 U.S. 347, 352 (1976) (Brennan, J., with White & Marshall, JJ.) (not political question).

issue and its intractability to principled resolution; (b) the sheer momentousness of it, which tends to unbalance judicial judgment; (c) the anxiety, not so much that the judicial judgment will be ignored, as that perhaps it should but will not be; (d) finally ("in a mature democracy"), the inner vulnerability, the self-doubt of an institution which is electorally irresponsible and has no earth to draw strength from.[88]

Professor Henkin has proposed another analysis:

The "political question" doctrine, I conclude, is an unnecessary, deceptive packaging of several established doctrines . . . . I see its proper content as consisting of the following propositions:

1. The courts are bound to accept decisions by the political branches within their constitutional authority.

2. The courts will not find limitations or prohibitions on the powers of the political branches where the Constitution does not prescribe any.

3. Not all constitutional limitations or prohibitions imply rights and standing to object in favor of private parties.

4. The courts may refuse some (or all) remedies for want of equity.

5. In principle, finally, there might be constitutional provisions which can properly be interpreted as wholly or in part "self-monitoring" and not the subject of judicial review. (But the only one the courts have found is the "guarantee clause" as applied to challenges to state action, and even that interpretation was not inevitable.)[89]

And finally, among the many articles in this field it is important to consider the formula-

tion of Professor Scharpf.[90] He considers the doctrine best explained in functional terms rather than an unprincipled retreat from difficult cases or the absence of applicable legal standards. Sometimes, he argues, the doctrine is justified when the Court cannot be assured of full clarification of the relevant questions because of difficulties of access to information. This function "is most obvious in the cases touching upon foreign relations where the Court has generally been hesitant to trust its own understanding of the broader situation."[91] In the case of purely domestic issues, this rationale appears weaker but even here its justification is understandable "for the decisions concerning the ratification of constitutional amendments, legislative enactments and the duration of the Civil War."[92] Secondly, the political question doctrine is explained in part as "the Court's deference to the prior decisions of another department within the latter's sphere of specific responsibility."[93] This justification supports the practical need for a uniformity of decision on those matters where the political departments have already committed the United States. Thirdly the Court will defer to the wider responsibilities of the political departments.[94] Thus, the Court has accepted, in *United States v. Pink* [95] the policy of recognition "implied in the Litvinov Assignment as controlling for the question of the validity of Soviet Expropriations in order to avoid any interference with the President's attempt to deal with the problem of Russian debts as a political pre-

---

88. A. Bickel, The Least Dangerous Branch 184 (1962).

89. Henkin, Is There a "Political Question" Doctrine? 85 Yale L.J. 597, 622–623 (1976) (footnote omitted).

90. Scharpf, Judicial Review and the Political Question: A Functional Analysis, 75 Yale L.J. 517 (1966). See also, Finkelstein, Judicial Self-Limitation, 37 Harv. L.Rev. 338 (1924); Finkelstein, Further Notes on Judicial Self-Limitation, 39 Harv.L.Rev. 221 (1925); Weston, Political Questions, 38 Harv.L.Rev. 296 (1925);

Dodd, Judicially Non-Enforceable Provisions of Constitutions, 80 U.Pa.L.Rev. 54 (1931).

91. Scharpf, Judicial Review and the Political Question: A Functional Analysis, 75 Yale L.J. 517, 567 (1966).

92. Scharpf, supra note 91, at 568–569.

93. Scharpf, supra note 91, at 573.

94. Scharpf, supra note 91, at 578.

95. 315 U.S. 203 (1942).

requisite for recognition."[96] But in all these areas the Court limits "the thrust of the functional rationales for the political question by a normative qualification: where im-portant individual rights are at stake, the doctrine will not be applied."[97] Thus it is unusual to apply the doctrine to the Bill of Rights.[98]

96. Scharpf, supra note 91, at 583 (footnote omitted).

97. Scharpf, supra note 91, at 584.

98. Id.

PART II

THE FEDERAL SYSTEM AND FEDERAL POWER

CHAPTER THREE

SOURCES OF NATIONAL AUTHORITY

I. INTRODUCTION

In order to determine whether any action of the federal government complies with the Constitution of the United States, the federal action must be reviewed on two bases. First, it must be determined whether the enactment is made pursuant to one of the powers granted the federal government under the Constitution, for the federal government is one of enumerated rather than inherent powers. It can only act to effectuate the powers specifically granted to it, rather than acting for the general welfare of the populace. Second, it must be determined whether the regulation or legislation violates some specific check on federal power such as those contained in the Bill of Rights. Even if the federal government is acting pursuant to one of its enumerated powers, it may not disregard these constitutional limitations. This two test form of review should be con-

trasted with the way that state laws are reviewed by federal courts. For the purposes of federal law, state governments (or their subsidiaries) are not creatures of limited powers: they are recognized as having a general "police power"—the inherent power to protect the health, safety, welfare or morals of persons within their jurisdiction. It is not for federal courts to determine whether state acts are authorized by state law. Federal courts test only whether a state act violates some specific check on state power contained in the federal constitution. The different basis for review of federal laws relates to the formation of the federal government, and the description of its powers in the Constitution.

It should be remembered that the federal government existed prior to the writing of the Constitution. With the Declaration of Independence and the war against Great

Britain, the country became loosely aligned under the Articles of Confederation.[1] Under these Articles a national government of very limited powers was established. It was clear that this form of national government could not control the activities of the states which were causing commercial problems. During the Revolutionary period and its aftermath, the States enacted conflicting commercial regulations which established trade barriers to the movement of goods and services. These regulations so hampered both national and international commerce that there was a call for a convention to amend the Articles of Confederation to deal with this problem. It became apparent to the delegates attending the convention that a new form of government would be necessary to deal with these national commercial problems. Following this first meeting there was a convention—which we now know as the constitutional convention—to amend the powers of the national government so as to enable it to deal with certain multistate problems.[2] It was this convention, which began in May of 1787, that produced our constitution and the new federal government.

When the convention was called, the Virginia delegation made several specific recommendations concerning the powers that should be granted the new federal government. Edmund Randolph submitted the Virginia proposals which included a provision that empowered the national legislature "to legislate in all cases to which the separate States are incompetent, or in which the harmony of the United States may be interrupted by exercise of individual legislation." This was adopted while other resolutions which indicated more limited powers for the national legislature were rejected by the convention.[3] This proposal was sent to the Committee on Detail which was to draft specific constitutional provisions based on the proposals sent to it by the general convention. The committee's draft of the constitution contained an enumeration of powers for Congress which was very close to that contained in the final draft in Article I, section 8 of the Constitution. Yet at no time did any delegate challenge the committee's deviation from the language of the Randolph plan and the listing of specific powers for the federal government. There was no significant debate on the concept of enumerated powers or on the seemingly sweeping powers granted by the commerce clause or the necessary and proper clause. The history and records of the convention yield little evidence as to whether these proposals were accepted because the delegates thought that the national government should be strictly limited to a specific set of powers or because they assumed that this listing included the sweeping powers which had been implied by the Randolph proposal. During the ratification debates there was concern expressed over the scope of powers given to the national government, but while the debates were vigorous and the ratification process a difficult one, no clear picture emerges as to the general understanding of the powers of the national government.

During the ratification process there did arise a popular concern about the powers of the government and the absence of a bill of rights for individual citizens.[4] Following ratification of the Constitution and establishment of the federal government, the first Congress drafted a series of amendments

---

1. The Articles were ratified on July 9, 1778. The text of the Articles may be found in the Lawyer's Edition of J. Nowak, R. Rotunda, & J. Young, Constitutional Law, Chapter 21 (Hornbook series, 2d ed. 1983).

2. The resolution for a new convention to deal with commercial problems is reprinted in 1 H. Commanger, ed., Documents of American History 132 (5th ed. 1949). It has become conventional wisdom to assert that the decade of the 1780's was a period of intense regional conflict which was reflected in the Articles of Confederation and the weakness of the federal government under those Articles. A student author has challenged this thesis and presented data supporting the thesis that this period was one of increasing federal power which culminated naturally in the formation of a stronger federal government under the Constitution. Note, The United States and the Articles of Confederation: Drifting Toward Anarchy or Inching Toward Commonwealth?, 88 Yale L.J. 142 (1978).

3. I, Farrand, Records of Federal Convention of 1787, (1911) at 47, 53; Vol. II, id. at 25–7, 181–2.

4. See generally B. Schwartz, The Bill of Rights: A Documentary History (1971).

which were submitted to the states in September 1789.[5] Ten of these amendments were accepted and ratified by December 15, 1791 and they are now known as the Bill of Rights.[6] The first eight of these amendments establish certain rights of individuals against infringement by the federal government. The ninth amendment recognizes that certain individual rights were retained by the people even though those rights were not listed in the Constitution.[7] The tenth amendment indicates that the states and individual citizens retained powers which were not specifically granted to the new federal government.[8] The ninth and tenth amendments seem to imply that the actions of the federal government were subject to limitations in the specification of its powers and to recognition of certain individual rights.

Following the establishment of the federal government the debate over its powers continued to rage on for many years. Federalists such as Hamilton advocated control of national problems through federal legislation. The Republicans, also referred to as the Anti-federalists, led by Jefferson, opposed the increasing activity of the federal government because they thought it a usurpation of powers reserved to the states. Prior to 1800 the Federalists enjoyed a period of virtually unchecked success. They passed legislation ranging from the establishment of the national judiciary to creation of a national bank to regulate monetary problems. Indeed, they went so far in their activities as to pass sedition laws which were used to punish those whose political activities might in some way be harmful to the national government.[9] Throughout this period Jefferson and the Republicans continued to advance the theory that the federal government had only those powers which were specifically listed in the Constitution and that those powers must be interpreted narrowly in order to avoid a violation of the rights of states and individual citizens.[10]

Virtually all of the issues concerning the scope of national power during the first century of the country's existence were settled by the political branches of government rather than the judiciary.[11] But the Supreme Court was to play an important part in these debates and the framing of national power by its decision in *McCulloch v. Maryland*.[12] It is to that decision that we now turn.

---

5. Approximately 124 amendments had been offered by the states. The first congress, led by Madison, drafted the specific proposals. The House of Representatives passed seventeen amendments. The Senate rejected two of these and combined the remaining into twelve proposed amendments. Congressional Research Service, the Constitution of the United States of America—Analysis and Interpretation at 898–900 (92d Congress, 2d sess., Senate Doc. No. 92–82, (1972); see also Schwartz, supra note 4, vol. II at 627–980, H. Ames, The Proposed Amendments to the Constitution at 14, 184–5 (1896).

6. The two amendments which were not ratified as a part of this Bill of Rights dealt with the apportionment of representatives to population and the compensation of members of Congress. See sources cited in note 5 supra.

7. "The enumeration in the Constitution, of certain rights, shall not be construed to deny or disparage others retained by the people." U.S.Const. amend. IX.

8. "The powers not delegated to the United States by the Constitution, nor prohibited by it to the States, are reserved to the States respectively, or to the people." U.S.Const. amend. X.

9. These laws are examined in connection with the first amendment's guarantee of free speech in Chapter 18.

10. One of the most famous remarks of Jefferson on the attempts of the Federalists to expand national power concerned their attempt to grant a federal charter to a mining business. Jefferson wrote:

"I do not know whether it is understood that the Legislature of Jersey was incompetent to [do] this, or merely that we have concurrent legislation under the sweeping clause. Congress are authorized to defend the nation. Ships are necessary for defense; copper is necessary for ships; mines, necessary for copper; a company necessary to work the mines; and who can doubt this reasoning who has ever played at 'This is the House that Jack Built'? Under such a process of filiation of the necessities the sweeping clause makes clean work."

1 C. Warren, The Supreme Court in United States History 501 (Rev. ed. 1926) (footnote omitted).

11. In only two cases prior to the Civil War did the Court strike down federal legislation, Marbury v. Madison, 5 U.S. (1 Cranch) 137 (1803); Dred Scott v. Sanford, 60 U.S. (19 How.) 393 (1857).

12. 17 U.S. (4 Wheat.) 316 (1819).

II. McCULLOCH v. MARYLAND AND THE BASIS OF FEDERAL POWER

In the landmark case of *McCulloch v. Maryland*[13] the Supreme Court interpreted the necessary and proper clause [14] so as to establish the legitimate role of federal government in dealing with national problems. Prior to this decision the history of that clause had left the scope of federal authority unclear. The clause had been added to the Constitution by the Committee on Detail when it revised the general proposals into a list of enumerated powers for the new federal government. While this clause did not create any significant debate at the constitutional convention, it was the cause of great debate during the ratification process. Opponents of the Constitution feared that this sweeping power would eliminate all functions of the states. Proponents of the Constitution had attempted to allay these fears but they did so in somewhat less than clear terms. Thus, in the words of one historian, "there still remained a grave anxiety over the indeterminate language contained" in the necessary and proper clause.[15] This anxiety continued through the first federalist administrations as the new federal government embarked upon legislation touching a variety of state and local interests.

The Supreme Court had considered the meaning of that clause only once prior to the *McCulloch* decision. In *United States v. Fisher* [16] the Court upheld federal legislation which gave the payment of debts to the United States priority in settling the estates of insolvent debtors. The opinion, written by Chief Justice Marshall, asserted the principle that "Congress must possess the choice of means, and must be empowered to use any means which are in fact conducive to the exercise of a power granted by the constitution." [17] A majority of the Court in this case found the law to be clearly related to the financial powers of Congress and no detailed analysis of those powers was used to justify the act.[18] Thus, when the Chief Justice examined the problem presented in *McCulloch*, he was writing on an essentially clean slate even though the necessary and proper clause and the Bank of the United States had been the subject of widespread debate throughout the country.

In *McCulloch* the Court considered the ability of the federal government to charter the second Bank of the United States. This was an issue of national concern, for the establishment of a national bank had been a great public controversy since the creation of the republic. Soon after the establishment of the federal government, a national bank was proposed by Alexander Hamilton to regulate currency and national economic problems. This caused the most serious dispute of a constitutional issue during President Washington's administration, since Jefferson and the Republicans protested what they saw to be the usurpation of state powers by the establishment of the Bank.[19] But the Federalists were enjoying a period of widespread political support and they were

---

13. Id.

14. "Congress shall have the Power . . . To make all Laws which shall be necessary and proper for carrying into Execution the foregoing Powers, and all other Powers vested by this Constitution in the Government of the United States, or in any Department or Officer thereof." U.S.Const. art. I, § 8.

15. 1 C. Warren, The Supreme Court in United States History at 500 (Rev. ed. 1926).

16. 6 U.S. (2 Cranch) 358 (1805).

17. Id. at 396.

18. The only specific power of Congress referred to was the power "to pay the debt of the Union." Id. at 396. Art. I, § 8 provides for powers relating to currency and bankruptcy which might have been used to sustain this law.

The Constitutional Convention had rejected a motion to empower the Congress to "grant charters of incorporation" and one may question the *McCulloch* holding in terms of this historical fact. See, 1 P. Freund, A. Sutherland, M. Howe, & E. Brown, Constitutional Law—Cases and Other Problems 142 (3d ed. 1967). Of course, this historical evidence does not mean that Congress was barred from granting charters to effectuate other enumerated powers. See also text at note 28 infra.

19. A good summary of the history of this dispute may be found in G. Gunther, Constitutional Law at 92–106 (10th ed. 1980). For a discussion of the political history and consequences of the bank and the Court's decision see Warren, supra note 15, at 499–540.

Even after *McCulloch*, attacks on the Bank continued. For example, in Osborn v. Bank of the United

able to establish the Bank. The Bank, however, was a somewhat limited success and its charter was allowed to expire in 1811 without being renewed. By this time the Federalists had lost power and there was little interest in establishing a national bank. Only one year later this situation was dramatically changed, for the war against Great Britain brought new economic problems.

Following the war of 1812 the states seemed incapable of dealing with the monetary problems of a disrupted economy. Despite his Anti-federalist heritage, President Madison approved the establishment of a second Bank of the United States in 1816. Unfortunately the Bank did not provide an answer to many of the economic ills of the times. After a few years a very serious economic depression took place and the Bank was blamed for aggravating the situation through its monetary practices. Additionally it appeared that many of the branches were engaged in corrupt practices designed to help specific interests and, indeed, to profit those who controlled the Bank. Accordingly many of the states made attempts to limit the powers of the branches of the bank which were located within their boundaries. It was a state action of this type which gave rise to the *McCulloch* case.

Maryland enacted a tax on the issuance of bank notes which was in effect a discriminatory tax on the national bank. The law required any bank not chartered by the state to pay a $15,000 per year tax or use certain "stamped" paper for its notes which would impose a 2% tax on those notes. Branches of the Bank of the United States continued to operate and issue bank notes in Maryland even though they refused to comply with the statute. The state then brought an action against the cashier of the bank, McCulloch, for the tax and penalties. The Maryland Court of Appeals affirmed a judgment for the state and the case was taken to the Supreme Court of the United States. The Supreme Court reversed the state decision and held the tax invalid in an opinion by Chief Justice Marshall.

In order to determine the validity of the Maryland tax, the Court was required to determine the constitutionality of the national bank legislation. If the Congress could not establish such a bank, then the Maryland statute did not interfere with any legitimate federal authority. Maryland argued that the states did not have to surrender their ability to regulate banks to the national government. This position was based on the theory that the federal government had been given only a limited amount of power from the "sovereignty" of the states. Marshall and the Court rejected this "states' rights" argument and, in so doing, established the basis for federal supremacy.

States, 22 U.S. (9 Wheat.) 738 (1824), the Supreme Court, again speaking through Chief Justice Marshall, affirmed a lower court decision directing defendants to restore to the Bank the sum of $100,000. (The lower court decision as to the awarding of interest was reversed.) Osborn was the auditor of the state of Ohio and had proceeded against the Bank pursuant to an act of the state legislature entitled "an act to levy and collect a tax from all banks and individuals, and companies and associations of individuals, that may transact business in this state without being allowed to do so by the laws thereof." The Bank, under this act, pursued its operations contrary to the laws of the state. In *Osborn* Marshall also proposed a very broad view of federal jurisdiction. He argued that constitutionally Congress may (and did, in the *Osborn* situation) extend federal jurisdiction to all cases where a title or right set up by a party may be defeated or sustained by a construction of the Constitution. The Bank was a creature of federal law; the Bank could make no contract,

bring no suit, nor acquire any right unless authorized to do so by federal law. Thus, he argued, all issues involving the Bank arise under the laws and Constitution of the United States. Marshall readily admitted that the right of the Bank to sue may be settled law, and actually any lawsuit may revolve around a construction of a simple contract construed under state law, but to Marshall that made no difference. The original federal "question forms an original ingredient in every cause. Whether it be, in fact, relied on or not, in the defense, it is still a part of the cause, and may be relied on." 22 U.S. (9 Wheat.) at 824. See also, the companion case of United States v. Planter's Bank of Georgia, 22 U.S. (9 Wheat.) 904 (1824).

Marshall's defense of *McCulloch* and of his broad view of federal jurisdiction took place not only in the case law but in the newspapers, under a pseudonym. See generally, G. Gunther, ed., John Marshall's Defense of McCulloch v. Maryland (1969).

The Chief Justice's opinion in *McCulloch v. Maryland* [20] deals with three distinct aspects of federal power. First, he establishes the principle that the federal government draws its authority directly from the people. Second, he interprets the necessary and proper clause so as to allow Congress a wide scope of authority to implement the enumerated powers. Third, he concludes that state legislation (especially state taxation) which might interfere with the exercise of these federal powers is invalid.

The Chief Justice begins by examining the general basis of authority for the federal government and the Constitution. This designation of the people as the source of authority for the new nation was the theoretical basis for federal supremacy over "states' rights". The states had claimed that the Constitution emanated from their independent sovereignties and that the exercise of the federal power could not predominate over the states' claims to power. Marshall rejects this theory by stating that the federal government emanates from the people and not from the states. [21] Because the power is not derived from the states, they cannot limit grants of power to the Congress. The concept that national sovereignty came from a direct popular base would later be reasserted by Webster and Lincoln and would become one of the "main tenets of American Nationalism." [22]

Following this definition of the source of the federal powers it was incumbent upon the Chief Justice to set guidelines under which the Constitution, as the embodiment of those powers, would be interpreted. Marshall here stressed the differences between a constitution and ordinary legislation: "Its nature, therefore, requires that only its great outlines should be marked, its important objects designated, and the minor ingredients which comprise those objects be deduced from the nature of the objects themselves." [23] This statement justified broad judicial construction of the Constitution far beyond *Marbury v. Madison*, [24] the landmark case providing for federal judicial review of Congressional legislation. [25] In *Marbury* the Court had invalidated a law which was in direct conflict with a constitutional provision. Here Marshall went further and established the Constitution as a statement of binding principles that had the force of law but which could adapt to a changing society without continual alteration. Additionally, this established the authority of the Court to engage in a more general interpretative function when determining the constitutionality of legislation. Thus, Marshall implied the existence of wide ranging powers for the federal government in general, and the judiciary in particular, when he stated that "we must never forget that it is a *constitution* we are expounding." [26]

---

20. 17 U.S. (4 Wheat.) 316 (1819).

21. Id. at 403–7.

22. A. Kelly & W. Harbison, The American Constitution 289 (4th ed. 1970).

In an opinion that can only be described as a judicial aberration, Justice Rehnquist has stated that the states were the vehicle by which the people delegated their commerce power to the federal government. His attempt to justify a judicial role in restricting the federal commerce power on this premise not only cuts against the Court's decisions since 1937, it also runs counter to the theory of the nature of federal power employed by Chief Justice Marshall in McCulloch v. Maryland, 17 U.S. (4 Wheat.) 316 (1819) and Gibbons v. Ogden, 22 U.S. (9 Wheat.) 1 (1824). See Hodel v. Virginia Surface Mining and Reclamation Ass'n, 452 U.S. 264 (1981) (Rehnquist, J. concurring in the judgment). Justice Rehnquist's concurring opinion also is applicable to Hodel v. Indiana, 452 U.S. 314 (1981).

23. 17 U.S. (4 Wheat.) at 407.

24. 5 U.S. (1 Cranch) 137 (1803).

25. For a discussion of the basis of judicial review see Chapter 1. For a scholarly analysis of the principle that Supreme Court rulings constitute "law" which binds government officials not party to a Supreme Court case, see Farber, The Supreme Court and the Rule of Law: Cooper v. Aaron Revisited, 1982 U.Ill.L.Rev. 387.

26. McCulloch v. Maryland, 17 U.S. (4 Wheat.) 316, 407 (1819) (emphasis added). Because of the scope of power implied by this assertion, Justice Frankfurter thought it was the most important of the Court's statements of constitutional principle. Frankfurter, John Marshall and the Judicial Function, 69 Harv.L.Rev. 217, 219 (1955).

The second major part of the opinion deals with the breadth of the powers which can be exercised by the federal government. Flexibility being essential, Marshall defined the broad standards within which federal laws must fall. Here he interpreted the grant of powers to Congress as allowing for the full effectuation of national goals. The necessary and proper clause, when combined with the specific grants of powers, evidenced the granting of generalized powers to Congress. He gave what has become the classic test for the existence of federal power:

> Let the end be legitimate, let it be within the scope of the constitution, and all means which are appropriate, which are plainly adapted to that end, which are not prohibited, but consist with the letter and spirit of the constitution, are constitutional.[27]

Under this test federal acts were valid so long as they bore a reasonable relationship to an enumerated power of the government. Hence, the second Bank of the United States was allowed because a connection could be found between it and the powers granted to "lay and collect taxes; to borrow money; to regulate commerce; to declare and conduct a war; and to raise and support armies and navies." [28]

Using the same doctrine Hamilton had used in support of the first Bank of the United States in 1791, Marshall traced implied federal powers from two sources: (1) the principle that every legislature must have the appropriate means to carry out its powers, and, (2) the necessary and proper clause following the enumerated powers, which indicated an express recognition of the need to provide law-making powers for their execution. As the nation was intended to endure, the federal government had to have been granted the normal discretionary powers of a sovereign to choose how to best effectuate national goals. The enumeration

of powers in the Constitution limited the number of ends which the government could pursue and the Court would not have added "great substantive and independent" powers to this list.[29] But where the government was pursuing a legitimate goal which related to one of its enumerated powers, it had incidental, implied powers to accomplish its ends, which would include powers of sufficient magnitude to deal with national problems.[30] The existence of such powers also could be derived from the necessary and proper clause. According to Marshall, this clause did not require the Congress to use only means which were absolutely necessary to pursue an enumerated federal power. He found that the framers did not use the word "necessary" in this restrictive way and that it would be illogical to establish a nation with only very restricted powers.[31] Instead, this clause authorized the federal government to select any reasonable means to achieve its ends. All such forms of legislation would be reasonably necessary and proper to the exercise of the enumerated powers. Whether a law met this test was a question of degree which the Congress was better suited to answer. Thus the Court would not void the law unless it were clear that it was designed for "the accomplishment of objects not intrusted to the government." [32]

In the third major portion of the opinion, Marshall held that the Maryland tax had to be stricken as it interfered with the exercise of a valid federal action. In all cases of conflict between federal and state laws, the supremacy of federal law was established by the Constitution.[33] From this principle it was found that the states could not possess incompatible powers which might be hostile to the federal actions. Here the Chief Justice found that the power to tax would be

---

27. 17 U.S. (4 Wheat.) at 421.

28. Id. at 407. See note 18, supra.

29. Id. at 411.

30. While these were only "incidental" powers, Marshall was careful to note that they might include

very important powers and that they were not implied merely because they were "inferior." Id. at 407–8.

31. 17 U.S. (4 Wheat.) at 413–16.

32. Id. at 423.

33. Id. at 426.

the power to destroy.[34] Thus, the state had no power to tax the valid federal instrumentality, as this would subject the operations of the federal government to state control. It should be noted that later years would see a revision of the concept of federal immunity from state taxation. However, the principles of federal supremacy and the federal government's freedom from state regulation or taxation which would defeat its powers remain valid today.[35]

III. JUDICIAL REVIEW AND FEDERAL POWERS AFTER McCULLOCH

It must never be forgotten that the federal government is one of enumerated powers and that it does not possess a general police power. In theory, at least, all federal actions must relate to a grant of power in the Constitution or the amendments thereto. In practice, the Supreme Court will accord the more democratic branches of the federal government great deference in their interpretation and implementation of those powers. The justices, in accordance with Marshall's position, will review federal legislation only to see if it can be said to reasonably relate to an express grant of power. So long as it would be reasonable for the Congress to view a problem as connected to one of the Constitution's grants of power, the law will be upheld.

The Court was not always so lenient in how it reviewed the exercise of federal powers by Congress. During the period from the Civil War until 1937 the justices were of the opinion that they should guard against the expansion of federal power. This position was reflective of the majority's opinion that the Constitution protected individual lib-

erty in the market place against government interference.[36] These justices saw their function as protecting such liberties from encroachment by legislative acts. State legislation during this period was subjected to strict review under the due process and equal protection clauses of the fourteenth amendment.[37] Federal legislation was subject to similarly strict scrutiny, but the Court focused on the scope of Congressional power when reviewing these acts, and construed the grants of power very narrowly during this period. It was the view of the majority that the tenth amendment put some forms of local activity beyond federal regulation. Accordingly, they would not approve federal legislation which regulated intrastate activities unless they were convinced that the activity was not relegated to local control by the tenth amendment. This conflict was centered on Congressional attempts to regulate business activities pursuant to its commerce power. In a separate Chapter we shall examine how the Court used the tenth amendment to define the commerce power.[38] But this approach was not limited to commerce problems and the Court used the tenth amendment to define the scope of many federal powers. Such varying pieces of legislation as arid land reclamation statutes [39] or penalties for racial discrimination in public accommodations [40] were stricken as beyond any grant of powers during this period in the Court's history. The Court approved federal legislation only when a majority agreed that it was clearly related to a grant of power and that no legitimate state interest was impaired by the federal act. Thus, laws relating to the moneta-

---

34. Id. at 427.

35. On the subject of intergovernmental immunities, see Chapter 11, section III, C.

36. See the sections on "substantive due process" from 1865–1900 and 1900–1937, Chapter 13, sections II and III, infra.

37. Id.

38. Chapter 4, infra.

39. Kansas v. Colorado, 206 U.S. 46 (1907).

40. Civil Rights Cases, 109 U.S. 3 (1883). It should be noted that in this case Justice Bradley, a chief exponent of judicial control over legislation, specifically used tenth amendment principles to define and restrict congressional power under the fourteenth amendment 109 U.S. at 14–15. For an examination of the "state action" requirement of the fourteenth amendment which was established by this case see Chapter 14, infra.

ry system [41] or the dispensation of electricity from federal dams [42] were upheld.

This restrictive view of federal powers brought the Court into serious conflict with the administration of President Franklin Roosevelt. Following a series of cases in which the Court struck down "New Deal" legislation, the President proposed his now famous (infamous?) Court Packing Plan.[43] During the time when this court packing proposal was under consideration, at least one justice became more lenient in how he reviewed the exercise of federal power and this enabled a new majority to approve federal legislation. Shortly after this, several vacancies occurred on the Court and President Roosevelt appointed new justices who would accord great deference to the acts of the coordinate branches of government, a deference which signaled a return to the original position of the Court in *McCulloch*.

Today the test for validity of a federal act is whether the Congress might reasonably find that the act relates to one of the federal powers. So long as the act bears some reasonable relationship to a grant of power to the federal government, the law must be upheld. If the act arguably relates to such an end, then it is valid so long as it does not violate a specific check on governmental action such as those contained in the Bill of Rights. No longer will the justices substitute their judgment for that of Congress as to the national scope of a problem or the relation of federal legislation to a grant of federal power. We will see this position developed in terms of the federal commerce power in the next chapter, but the principle of *McCulloch* now applies to all federal powers.[44] Thus, deference is granted to Congress in determining whether the reclamation of arid lands statutes relates to federal powers [45] or whether civil rights statutes are related to the civil war amendments.[46]

In assessing the degree of power granted the federal government by granting deference to the other branches of government under the *McCulloch* test, it must be remembered that federal authority is derived from several sources. Article I, section 8, contains the basic grants of federal power in its listing of the powers of Congress.[47] Article II creates federal powers in its definition of the powers and duties of the president.[48] Article III gives Congress the power to

---

41. Legal Tender Cases, 110 U.S. 421 (1884).

42. Ashwander v. Tennessee Valley Authority, 297 U.S. 288 (1936).

43. In February, 1937, the President proposed legislation that would allow him to appoint a new Justice for each one on the Court who was over seventy years old. This would have allowed him to appoint six additional justices and change the majority view in the Court. For excerpts from the plan and the debate which lead to its defeat see, G. Gunther, Constitutional Law at 167–71 (9th ed. 1975); see also, Jackson, The Struggle for Judicial Supremacy (1941); Leuchtenburg, The Origins of Franklin D. Roosevelt's "Court Packing" Plan, 1966 Sup.Ct.Rev. 347. There is no clear evidence that the Court was influenced by this proposal, although Justice Roberts did switch to a position of deference towards legislative acts at this time. There is evidence that he came to this position prior to the court packing plan. Frankfurter, Mr. Justice Roberts, 104 U.Pa.L.Rev. 311 (1955).

44. Several specific powers of the federal government which have been the source of some litigation are mentioned in section IV of this chapter, even though they are not usually covered in constitutional law courses.

As a part of a scholarly examination of the role of the Supreme Court, Professor Jesse Choper has presented the argument that the Supreme Court should not rule on the division of power between the federal and state governments. J. Choper, Judicial Review and the National Political Process (1980). See also Nowak, Book Review, 68 California L.Rev. (1980) (reviewing Choper).

45. United States v. Gerlach Live Stock Co., 339 U.S. 725 (1950); see also, Arizona v. California, 283 U.S. 423 (1931).

46. Jones v. Alfred H. Mayer Co., 392 U.S. 409 (1968) (open housing statutes relate to thirteenth amendment); Katzenbach v. Morgan, 384 U.S. 641 (1966) (voting rights statute relates to fourteenth amendment). Congressional enforcement of the civil war amendments is examined in Chapter 17. It should be noted that the deference accorded congressional judgments in this area does not differ from the modern Court's review of other types of federal legislation.

47. For the complete text see Appendix; as to the history of the enumerated powers, see section 1 of this chapter.

48. The powers of the President are discussed in chapter 7. The complete text of Article II may be found in the Appendix at the end of this volume.

make regulations concerning the jurisdiction of the Supreme Court and power to declare the punishment for treason,[49] and the admiralty jurisdiction within Article III grants Congress powers relating to the judicial process beyond mere control of jurisdiction.[50] Article IV, section 1, gives Congress power to prescribe procedure for proving full faith and credit to the laws and court judgments of states.[51] Section 3 of Article IV grants Congress the power to admit new states to the Union.[52] Additionally that section grants the Federal government a general power over the territories and property of the United States.[53] This power is important because it allows the federal government to act as a state or local government in relation to such property.[54] Several of the Amendments also specifically provide Congress with powers to enact legislation to effectuate their substantive provisions.[55]

There are also unwritten sources of Congressional authority. The most important implication of federal power relates to the conduct of foreign relations.[56] It has been said that power with respect to external affairs is not derived from the Constitution—that power lies outside its words. This unwritten authority is the result of judicial recognition that the country must speak as a single entity in foreign affairs. Because the United States cannot isolate itself from the rest of the world, the national government must be allowed to act in external affairs as does any other nation. As we will study in later Chapters, there are limits placed on these powers by the separation of powers concept and the guarantees of individual liberties,[57] but in terms of the authorization of federal action, the foreign affairs powers are exempted from the traditional enumerated powers theory. Since the states have no individualized interest in external relations, the federal government has by implication an exclusive and general grant of power in this area.

49. For the complete text of Article III see appendix D. Section 1 grants congress power over the lower federal courts. Section 2 grants congress power to alter the jurisdiction of the Supreme Court. Section 3 defines Treason.

50. See, e.g., Panama R. R. v. Johnson, 264 U.S. 375 (1924) (Congress can create causes of action for injured seamen, and other maritime laws, based on article III grant of admiralty and maritime jurisdiction).

51. "Full Faith and Credit shall be given in each State to the public Acts, Records, and judicial Proceedings of every other State. And the Congress may by general Laws prescribe the Manner in which such Acts, Records and Proceedings shall be proved, and the Effect thereof." U.S.Const. art. IV, § 1.

52. "New States may be admitted by the Congress into this Union; but no new State shall be formed or erected within the Jurisdiction of any other State; nor any State be formed by the Junction of two or more States, or Parts of States, without the Consent of the Legislatures of the States concerned as well as of the Congress." U.S.Const. art. IV, § 3, par. 1.

53. "The Congress shall have Power to dispose of and make all needful Rules and Regulations respecting the Territory of other Property belonging to the United States; and nothing in this Constitution shall be so construed as to Prejudice any Claims of the United States, or of any particular State." U.S.Const. art. IV, § 3, par. 2.

54. Berman v. Parker, 348 U.S. 26, 32 (1954) (U.S. has "police power" as to the District of Columbia so that it may exercise powers of eminent domain not connected to another enumerated power.)

55. U.S.Const. amend. 13, § 2 (abolition of slavery); amend. 14, § 5 (citizenship and several forms of civil rights); amend. 15, § 2 (prohibition of discrimination by race for voting); amend. 16 (power to levy an income tax); amend. 19, § 2 (prohibition of discrimination by sex for voting); amend. 23, § 2 (representation for the District of Columbia); amend. 24, § 2 (abolition of poll tax in federal elections); amend. 26, § 2 (grant of franchise to citizens 18 yrs. of age or older). It should also be noted that amendments 20 and 25 grant Congress a role in the selection, retention or replacement of the president or vice-president under certain circumstances.

56. Federal power in this area is examined more closely in Chapter 6, infra. See United States v. Curtiss-Wright-Export Corp., 299 U.S. 304 (1936); L. Henkin, Foreign Affairs and the Constitution 24 (1972); Lofgren, United States v. Curtiss-Wright Export Corporation: An Historical Reassessment, 83 Yale L.J. 1 (1973).

57. See Nowak & Rotunda, A Comment on the Creation and Resolution of a "Nonproblem": Dames & Moore v. Regan, the Foreign Affairs Power, and the Role of the Court, 29 U.C.L.A.L.Rev. 1129 (1982). Special attention is directed to the limits on expatriation, see Chapter 20, infra and the equal protection guarantees for resident aliens, see Chapter 16, section III, infra.

IV. OTHER SOURCES OF FEDERAL POWER

The great bulk of the constitutional cases dealing with Congress' power to enact laws focus on only a few clauses in the Constitution, particularly the interstate commerce clause,[1] the necessary and proper clause,[2] and, more recently, section 5 of the fourteenth amendment. The student of the subject however should bear in mind that there are other sources of federal power in the Constitution which merit at least a brief reference here.

One important source of federal power, for example, is found not in Article I at all but in Article III, the judiciary article. Section 2, clause I of Article III extends the federal judicial power to, inter alia, "all Cases of admiralty and maritime jurisdiction . . . ." The admiralty jurisdiction now "extends to all waters, salt or fresh, with or without tides, natural or artificial, which are in fact navigable in interstate or foreign water commerce, whether or not the particular body of water is wholly within a state and whether or not the occurrence or transaction that is the subject matter of the suit is confined to one state." [3] Yet nowhere does the Constitution establish the source of the law the federal courts should apply in exercising their jurisdiction. The Supreme Court has interpreted this jurisdictional grant to create also a federal common law, substantive law-making power.[4]

The Supreme Court in the era of *Swift v. Tyson* [5] had implied from the diversity jurisdiction of Article III a right to fashion substantive law governing diverse parties in matters of "general commercial law," but the *Swift* rule applied only when the diverse parties brought the case in federal court. The admiralty substantive common law however, applies as true federal substantive law: valid throughout the United States and in all courts. Thus, "no State has power to abolish the well recognized maritime rule concerning measure of recovery and substitute therefore the full indemnity rule of the common law." [6] Moreover, "the substantial rights of an injured person are not to be determined differently whether his case is labelled 'law side' or 'admiralty side.' " [7]

The Supreme Court fairly early recognized Congress' legislative power to change the substantive admiralty rules created by the federal courts, but the language in the opinions derived this congressional power from Congress' power over interstate commerce rather than the Article III jurisdictional grant.[8] But in 1891 Justice Bradley found that it was the admiralty jurisdictional grant itself that was the source of this power in combination with the language of the "necessary and proper clause, which provides, inter alia, that Congress has the power to make all Laws which shall be necessary and proper for carrying into Execution the foregoing Powers [of Article I] and *all other Powers* vested by this Constitution in the

---

1. U.S.Const. art. I, § 8, cl. 3.

2. U.S.Const. art. I, § 8, cl. 18.

3. G. Gilmore & C. Black, The Law of Admiralty § 1–11 at 31–32 (2d ed. 1975). For a brief study of the expansion of admiralty jurisdiction see id. at 31–32 n. 99.

4. See generally Note, From Judicial Grant to Legislative Power: The Admiralty Clause in the Nineteenth Century, 67 Harv.L.Rev. 1214 (1954). See also, e.g., Moragne v. State Marine Lines, 398 U.S. 375 (1970); Romero v. International Terminal Operating Co., 358 U.S. 354, 360–61 (1959). On admiralty problems in general, see, e.g., G. Gilmore & C. Black, The Law of Admiralty (2d ed. 1975).

5. 41 U.S. (16 Pet.) 1 (1842) (Story, J.).

6. Chelentis v. Luckenbach S. S. Co., 247 U.S. 372, 382 (1918). See also, Southern Pacific Co. v. Jensen, 244 U.S. 205 (1917).

7. Pope & Talbot, Inc. v. Hawn, 346 U.S. 406, 411 (1953); Garrett v. Moore-McCormack Co., 317 U.S. 239 (1942).

8. See The Lottawanna, 88 U.S. (21 Wall.) 558, 577 (1875): "Congress undoubtedly has authority under the commercial power, if no other, to introduce such changes as are likely to be needed." See also, The Daniel Ball, 77 U.S. (10 Wall.) 557, 564 (1871); Morre v. American Transp. Co., 65 U.S. (24 How.) 1, 39 (1861).

Government . . . "[9] Thus, Bradley stated:

It is unnecessary to invoke the power given to Congress to regulate commerce . . . in order to find authority to pass the law in question. The act . . . was passed in amendment of the maritime law of the country, and the power to make such amendments is coextensive with that law. It is not confined to the boundaries or class of subjects which limit and characterize the power to regulate commerce; but, in maritime matters, it extends to all matters and places to which the maritime law extends.[10]

Congress' power to modify the substantive admiralty rules should not really create any conceptual problems, for in such cases Congress is not reversing any Supreme Court decision of constitutional dimension but is really only enacting legislation and revising the Court's decision based on federal common law.[11]

Another example of judicial common law making power derived from a jurisdictional grant is the power to create the law governing litigation between states, a power "implied from the jurisdictional grant over interstate controversies and justified by the inappropriateness of using any one state's law."[12] By analogy to the admiralty cases, Congress may also legislate the substantive rules governing this area of disputes between the states.[13]

It also should be remembered that the federal courts have the power to create federal common law when activities arise from and bear heavily upon a federal program, even though there is no federal statute specifically applicable.[14] The Constitution and acts of Congress may require that state law not govern such activities of its own force. In such cases the federal interests are sufficiently implicated to warrant the protection of federal common law, which Congress may

---

9. Art. I, § 8, cl. 18 (emphasis added.).

10. In re Garnett, 141 U.S. 1, 12 (1891). See also, e.g., Crowell v. Benson, 285 U.S. 22, 55 (1932); H. Hart & H. Wechsler's, The Federal Courts and the Federal System 786 (2d ed. 1973). But cf. G. Gilmore & C. Black, The Law of Admiralty §§ 1–16, at 47 (2d ed. 1975).

11. The Supreme Court has invalidated federal statutes in the admiralty area on the theory that Congress had unconstitutionally attempted to delegate to the states its legislative power over admiralty. E.g., Knickerbocker Ice Co. v. Stewart, 253 U.S. 149 (1920); Washington v. W. C. Dawson & Co., 264 U.S. 219 (1924). This theory does not reject the main point, however; as *Knickerbocker* itself stated, the "Constitution itself adopted and established, as part of the laws of the United States, approved rules of the general maritime law and *empowered Congress to legislate* in respect of them and other matters within the admiralty and maritime jurisdiction." 253 U.S. at 160 (emphasis added). In any event, the *Knickerbocker* rule is analytically unsound and makes little sense. By incorporating by reference state laws, Congress has not abdicated the responsibility, rather it is fulfilling it. The *Knickerbocker* theory has not been applied in other areas. See e.g., United States v. Sharpnack, 355 U.S. 286 (1958). And given the direction of the Court in the admiralty area, it is unlikely that this rule will be followed today. Cf. Wiburn Boat Co. v. Fireman's Fund Insurance Co., 348 U.S. 310 (1955) (in the absence of a federal admiralty rule, the Court finds maritime insurance policy governed by state law). Cf. R. Rotunda, Modern Constitutional Law 129–30 (1981).

12. H. Hart & H. Wechsler, The Federal Courts and the Federal System 786 (2d ed. 1973). See, e.g., City of

Milwaukee v. Illinois and Michigan, 451 U.S. 304, 313–14 (1981).

13. Arizona v. California, 373 U.S. 546, 565 (1963): "It is true that the Court has used the doctrine of equitable apportionment to decide river controversies between States. But in those cases Congress had not made any statutory apportionment . . . Where Congress has so exercised its constitutional power over waters, courts have no power to substitute their own notions of an 'equitable apportionment' . . . ." (footnote omitted).

14. When Erie R. R. Co. v. Tompkins, 304 U.S. 64 (1933) overruled Swift v. Tyson, 41 U.S. (16 Pet.) 1 (1842), the Supreme Court did not really eliminate "federal common law." Rather, when federal courts now create a federal common law rule, it applies to all the parties without regard to diversity and whether or not the case is heard in state or federal court. See generally, P. Hay & R. Rotunda, The United States Federal System: Legal Integration in the American Experience 290–310 (Giuffrè, Milan, 1982). By eliminating the false uniformity of *Swift* "and by leaving to the states what ought to be left to them, *Erie* led to the emergence of a federal decisional law in areas of national concern that is truly uniform because, under the supremacy clause, it is binding in every forum, and therefore is predictable and useful . . . . The clarion yet careful pronouncement of Erie, 'There is no federal general common law,' opened the way to what, for want of a better term, we may call specialized federal common law." Friendly, In Praise of Erie—And of the New Federal Common Law, 39 N.Y.U.L.Rev. 383, 405 (1964). See, e.g., Clearfield Trust Co. v. United States, 318 U.S. 363 (1943).

change by statute.[15] Thus in *Cannon v. University of Chicago*,[16] the Court held that title IX of the Educations Amendments of 1972 [17]—which provides that educational programs receiving financial assistance from the federal government shall not discriminate against persons on the basis of sex—impliedly authorizes a private cause of action by persons who claim to have been the victim of such discrimination at the hands of federally funded educational programs.

Federal courts may also imply private rights of actions which arise directly under the Constitution. For example, in *Davis v. Passman*,[18] the Court held that a cause of action and a damages remedy can be applied directly under the Constitution when plaintiff demonstrates that the due process clause of the fifth amendment is violated.[19]

In addition, it should be noted that Congress is given power to dispose of and make "all needful Rules and Regulations respecting the Territory or other Property belonging to the United States . . . " in Article IV.[20] How the Congress disposes of its property, whether by lease or otherwise, is left to its discretion.[21] For example, this property clause was used as a basis to uphold the constitutionality of the government's production and sale of electricity by the Tennessee Valley Authority.[22] The Court explained that water power and the electric energy generated by the government-owned dam was susceptible of disposition as property belonging to the United States. Since the power of disposition is expressly conferred, the ninth and tenth amendments are inapplicable; the Court then rejected the argument that the Congress has authority to dispose of this energy

---

15. United States v. Kimbell Foods, Inc., 440 U.S. 715, 726–27 (1979), relying on Clearfield Trust Co. v. United States, 318 U.S. 363, 366–67 (1943). The criteria to determine when to imply such a cause of action are outlined in the leading case of Cort v. Ash, 422 U.S. 66 (1975).

However it is important to realize that the existence of congressional authority under Article I or under another portion of the Constitution does not mean that federal courts are completely free to develop a common law rule to govern those areas until Congress acts. "Rather, absent some congressional authorization to formulate substantive rules of decision, federal common law exists only in such narrow areas as those concerned with the rights and obligations of the United States, interstate and international disputes implicating the conflicting rights of States or our relations with foreign nations, and admiralty cases. In these instances, our federal system does not permit the controversy to be resolved under state law, either because the authority and duties of the United States as sovereign are intimately involved or because the interstate or international nature of the controversy makes it inappropriate for state law to control." Texas Industries, Inc. v. Radcliff Materials, Inc., 451 U.S. 630, 641 (1981) (footnotes omitted). See also, e.g., City of Milwaukee v. Illinois and Michigan, 451 U.S. 304 (1981).

16. 441 U.S. 677 (1979). Justice Stevens' opinion for the majority focused on four factors for implication of private causes of action, as earlier announced in the leading case of Cort v. Ash, 422 U.S. 66 (1975). On implying private causes of action from federal statutes see generally, Hacker & Rotunda, SEC Registration of Private Investment Partnerships after Abrahamson v. Fleschner, 78 Colum.L.Rev. 1471, 1484–88 (1979) (discussing implied rights of action in the context of the securities laws).

17. 20 U.S.C.A. § 1861 et seq.

18. 442 U.S. 228 (1979). See also Bivens v. Six Unknown Named Agents, 403 U.S. 388 (1971) (damage remedy implied from violation of fourth amendment); Butz v. Economou, 438 U.S. 478 (1978).

19. In that case plaintiff alleged that a U.S. Congressman, in firing her, had discriminated against her on the basis of her sex, in violation of the fifth amendment. The criteria to determine when to imply such a right are different than those used to imply a cause of action based on a statutory right. A private right of action for damages may be implied directly from the Constitution if the remedy is appropriate because, for example, injunctive relief is unavailable, if there is no governmental immunity, and if there is no explicit congressional declaration that money damages are unavailable. 442 U.S. at 241–48. In *Davis* the suit was brought against a former Congressman, who was a Congressman when he fired plaintiff allegedly because of her sex. The Court noted but intimated no view whether the speech or debate clause would shield defendant from liability. 442 U.S. at 233–35, n. 11.

20. U.S.Const. art. IV, § 3, cl. 2.

21. United States v. Gratiot, 39 U.S. (14 Pet.) 526, 533, 538 (1840). For example, the United States, not individual states, has property rights to submerged lands off the national coastline. Congress may yield these rights to the coastal states but the state property rights are dependent on the terms of the federal legislation. United States v. Louisiana, 446 U.S. 253 (1980); Alabama v. Texas, 347 U.S. 272 (1954); United States v. California, 332 U.S. 19 (1947). See also, United States v. California, 447 U.S. 1 (1980).

22. Ashwander v. Tennessee Valley Authority, 297 U.S. 288, 330–38 (1936).

only to the extent that it is a surplus necessarily created in the course of making munitions of war or operating the works for navigation purposes (which were the government's justification for the construction of the dam and the power plant connected with it). The Court found that there is no constitutional prohibition denying the government the right to seek a wider market for its electricity.[23]

As to the territories of the United States, "Congress has the entire dominion and sovereignty, national and local, Federal and state, and has full legislative power over all subjects upon which the legislature of a State might legislate within the State; and may, at its discretion, intrust that power to the legislative assembly of a Territory."[24] Pursuant to this broad power Congress may establish legislative courts with powers *not* derived from Article III but from this property clause section and Congress' Article I powers;[25] thus, Congress may authorize such legislative courts to exercise admiralty jurisdiction even though such courts have not been created pursuant to Article III.[26] Since these territorial courts are not created under Article III the judges do not have that Article's guarantees of lifetime tenure with no reduction of salary.[27]

Section 4 of Article IV empowers the United States to guarantee to every State "a Republican Form of Government . . ." A long line of Supreme Court cases have constantly reaffirmed the position that this clause is nonjusticiable because "it rests with Congress to decide what government is the established one in a State . . . as well as its republican character."[28] The nonjusticiability of this clause is considered elsewhere in this treatise;[29] for purposes of this section it is important to realize that while an issue arising under this clause may be nonreviewable by the Court, nonetheless it may furnish an appropriate basis to justify the exercise of Congressional power.

In 1861 for example, President Lincoln, not wanting to recognize the Southern States as a conventional belligerent, relied on this clause for authorization to put down the rebellion.[30] Later the congressional Republicans justified their Reconstruction legislation and policies in part on this clause.[31] One theory reasoned that when a State was in a state of rebellion in violation of the Constitution it deprived its citizens of a republican form of government, even though it could never leave the Union; thus Congress was justified in using all the means at its disposal, including military

23. 297 U.S. at 330, 333–39. The Court added that "the Government rightly conceded at the bar, in substance, that it was without constitutional authority to acquire or dispose of such energy except as it comes into being in the operation of works constructed in the exercise of some power delegated to the United States." 297 U.S. at 340.

Other cases illustrating Congress' powers over its property include United States v. Fitzgerald, 40 U.S. 407 (1841); Gibson v. Chouteau, 80 U.S. (13 Wall.) 92, 99 (1872); Tameling v. United States Freehold & Immigration Co., 93 U.S. 644, 663 (1877); United States v. McGowan, 302 U.S. 535 (1938); United States v. San Francisco, 310 U.S. 16 (1940).

24. Simms v. Simms, 175 U.S. 162, 168 (1899). This jurisdiction also applies to all things or animals that come on to the territory. Kleppe v. New Mexico, 426 U.S. 529 (1976).

Congress may pass separate legislation for territories and may treat a territory, such as Puerto Rico, differently than the states in terms of federal assistance. This disparate treatment will be upheld "so long as there is a rational basis for its [the Congress'] actions." Harris v. Rosario, 446 U.S. 651 (1980) (per curiam) (up-

holding lower level of federal reimbursement to Aid to Families with Dependent Children program in Puerto Rico).

25. American Insurance Co. v. Canter, 26 U.S. (1 Pet.) 511, 546 (1828) (Marshall, C.J.). On legislative courts, see generally, Glidden Co. v. Zdanok, 370 U.S. 530 (1962). See also H. Hart & H. Wechsler, The Federal Courts and the Federal System 396–400 (2d ed. 1973). Cf. Palmore v. United States, 411 U.S. 389 (1973).

26. Id.

27. Id.

28. Luther v. Borden, 48 U.S. (7 How.) 1, 42 (1849). See also e.g., Georgia v. Stanton, 73 U.S. (6 Wall.) 50 (1868); Texas v. White, 74 U.S. (7 Wall.) 700, 729 (1869); Baker v. Carr, 369 U.S. 186, 218–32 (1962).

29. See Chapter 2, section IV, E.

30. W. Wiecek, The Guarantee Clause of the Constitution 171 (1972).

31. Id. at 167. See generally H. Belz, Reconstructing the Union: Theory and Policy During the Civil War (1969).

might (and presumably, later reconstruction legislation) to fulfill the federal guarantee.[32] In *Texas v. White* [33] the Court appeared to affirm this theory though stating that it was not necessary to determine whether all the actions taken to restore Texas to her proper constitutional relations were, in all respects, warranted by the Constitution.[34]

In addition to the powers discussed and the "necessary and proper clause" discussed above—as well as the congressional power to enforce specific amendments to the Constitution [35]—one should also bear in mind the other enumerated powers of Article I, section 8. Such powers include the powers and restrictions on taxing and spending; [36] the power to borrow; [37] the power over interstate commerce; [38] the powers to establish uniform rules on naturalization and bankruptcies; [39] the power to coin money and punish counterfeiting; [40] the power to establish post offices and post roads; [41] the power to establish copyright and patent protec-

tion; [42] the power to constitute tribunals inferior to the Supreme Court; [43] the power to define and punish piracies and felonies on the high seas and offenses against the law of nations; [44] the war power and related powers; [45] the power to govern the District of Columbia and to govern places where the government has purchased and erected forts, arsenals, and other needful buildings; [46] and the power (albeit not generally exercised) to apply federal choice of law rules in state and federal courts, based on the full faith and credit clause.[47]

V. THE SEPARATION OF POWERS PRINCIPLE

The modern concept of "separation of powers" has its origin in Western European struggles between legislative bodies and monarchs.[1] It was particularly the English experience which formed the basis for the political beliefs most common in the American colonies. From the time of the English

---

32. W. Wiecek, The Guarantee Clause of the Constitution 174–76 (1972), citing an 1861 speech of Maryland Unionist Henry Winter Davis, in J.A.L. Creswell, ed., Speeches and Addresses of Henry Winter Davis 265 et seq. (1867), and an 1862 speech of Charles Sumner, in 37 Cong. 2d sess. 736–37 (Feb. 12, 1862).

33. 74 U.S. (7 Wall.) 700 (1869).

34. 74 U.S. (7 Wall.) at 729–30. See also, White v. Hart, 80 U.S. (13 Wall.) 646 (1871).

35. See Chapter 17.

36. Art. I, § 8, cl. 1; see Chapter 5, sections I and II.

37. Art. I, § 8, cl. 2; see Chapter 5, section III; Knox v. Lee (Legal Tender Cases), 79 U.S. (12 Wall.) 457 (1871), overruling Hepburn v. Griswold, 75 U.S. 603 (1870); Lynch v. United States, 292 U.S. 571 (1934); Perry v. United States, 294 U.S. 330, 351 (1935).

38. Art. I, § 8, cl. 3; see Chapter 4.

39. Art. I, § 8, cl. 4. On naturalization see Chapter 20, sections I and II. On bankruptcy, see generally, e.g., J. MacLachlan, Bankruptcy (1956); see also, Railway Labor Executives Ass'n v. Gibbons, 455 U.S. 457 (1982) (uniformity provision of the bankruptcy clause prohibits Congress from enacting a bankruptcy law that applies only to one regional debtor; nor could Congress escape this limitation by seeking to enact the bankruptcy law under the commerce clause, even though uniformity in the applicability of legislation is not required by the commerce clause).

40. Art. I, § 8, cls. 5 & 6; see Hart, The Gold Clause in United States Bonds, 48 Harv.L.Rev. 1057 (1935). See also Chapter 5, section III.

41. Art. I, § 8, cl. 7; see e.g. Cushman, National Police Powers Under the Postal Clause of the Constitution, 4 Minn.L.Rev. 402 (1920).

42. Art. I, § 8, cl. 8; see generally, M. Nimmer, Nimmer on Copyright (1976); R. Nordhaus, Patent, Trademark and Copyright Infringement (1971); R. Choate, Cases and Materials on Patent Law (1973).

43. Art. I, § 8, cl. 9. See also Article III of the Constitution.

44. Art. I, § 8, cl. 10. See e.g., Ex parte Quirin, 317 U.S. 1, 27–28 (1942); United States v. Flores, 289 U.S. 137 (1933); United States v. Arizona, 120 U.S. 479 (1887); United States v. Furlong, 18 U.S. (5 Wheat.) 184, 200 (1820).

45. Art. I, cls. 11–16. See generally Chapter 6, section III.

46. Art. I, § 8, cl. 17; see generally, W. Tindall, The Origin and Government of the District of Columbia (1903); Palmore v. United States, 411 U.S. 389 (1973); James v. Dravo Contracting Co., 302 U.S. 134, 145 (1937); Mason Co. v. Tax Comm'n, 302 U.S. 186 (1937).

47. See E. Scoles & P. Hay, Conflict of Laws 112–13 (1982).

1. For a comprehensive development of the theory of separation of powers see, W. B. Gwyn, The Meaning of the Separation of Powers (Tulane Univ. 1965); M.J.C. Vile, Constitutionalism and the Separation of Powers (Clarendon Press 1967); Sharp, The Classical American Doctrine of "the Separation of Powers," 2 U.Chi.L.Rev. 385 (1935).

Civil War there was a continual shifting of power between the monarch and parliament. This history led to the practical delineation of functions between the branches of English government which was the basis for John Locke's view of the proper division of powers.[2] But the concept of separation of powers was explained most convincingly by Montesquieu, whose writings were well known throughout Western Europe and the American colonies in the eighteenth century. Montesquieu argued that any combination of the judicial, legislative or executive powers would create a system with an inherent tendency towards tyrannical actions.[3]

At the time of the American Revolution the concept of separation of powers was accepted with virtual unanimity by political leaders in the new states. Indeed, the constitutions of the early state governments sometimes referred to the principle specifically.[4] When the new federal Constitution was drafted the power of the federal government was divided between three branches of government in a manner similar to that recommended by Montesquieu. But while the Constitution created separate executive, legislative, and judicial departments, there was no clear delineation between their functions. Instead, the drafters of the Constitution sought to establish a system of checks and balances between the branches of government to ensure the political independence of each branch and to prevent the accumulation of power in a single department.

Today we may not recognize that the system of "checks and balances" run counter to a separation of functions concept, but that was clearly realized at the time of the

Revolution. One of the most serious charges made against the new Constitution was that it did not sufficiently distinguish between the functions of each branch of government, and thereby failed to follow the separation of powers concept. James Madison answered this argument in *Federalist No. 47* wherein he admitted that this objection was a serious and honest one.[5] However, Madison went on to demonstrate how the separation of powers doctrine, as explained by Montesquieu, did not require a strict division of functions between the three branches of government. Madison defended the Constitution as having a sufficient division of functions between the three branches of government to avoid the consolidation of power in any one branch.

The concept of separation of powers is not one that is capable of precise legal definition and it does not yield clear solutions to intragovernmental disputes. As Professors Frankfurter and Landis noted:

> As a principle of statesmanship the practical demands of government preclude its doctrinaire application . . . In a word, we are dealing with what Sir Henry Maine, following Madison, calls a "political doctrine" and not a technical rule of law. Nor has it been treated by the Supreme Court as a technical legal doctrine. From the beginning that Court has refused to draw abstract, analytical lines of separation and has recognized the necessary area of interaction.[6]

The concept of the separation of powers as a political doctrine, rather than a technical rule of law, is as true today as it was in 1924 when Frankfurter and Landis first expressed their opinion. The Supreme Court has rejected the argument that would have

2. See, Vile, supra note 1, at 64–7 discussing Locke and his role in the development of this theory. For the original theory see, J. Locke, Second Treatise of Government [An Essay Concerning the True Origin, Extent and End of Civil Government].

3. Montesquieu, The Spirit of the Laws, 151–2 (Nugent trans. 1949).

4. See, e.g., Constitution of Massachusetts—1780, Part the First, Art. XXX as reprinted in 5 W. Swindler, Sources and Documents of U.S. Constitutions 96 (Oceana Publ. 1975).

5. J. Madison, The Federalist, No. 47, The Meaning of the Maxim, Which Requires A Separation Of The Departments Of Power, Examined And Ascertained, in the Federalist Papers at 302–3 (new American Library Ed.1961). See also, B. Bailyn, The Ideological Origins of the American Revolution 55–93 (1967); A. Vanderbilt, The Doctrine of the Separation of Powers and Its Present-Day Significance 97–144 (1953).

6. Frankfurter & Landis, Power of Congress over Procedure in Criminal Contempts in "Inferior" Federal Courts—A Study in Separation of Powers, 37 Harv.L. Rev. 1010, 1012–14 (1924).

it limit the activities of each branch of the federal government so that there would be no overlap or blending of functions,[7] but the Court has been cognisant of the principle when confronted with cases involving disputes between branches of the federal government.[8]

Because there is no fruitful rule or test which governs decisions relating to separation of powers, this treatise will not analyze "separation of powers cases" as a unit. Instead we have placed the cases that might arguably fall into such a category in the sections concerning the central issue in each of those cases. Thus, the sections dealing with

such issues as political questions, congressional vetoes, presidential powers, and executive privilege all refer to the separation of powers principle. To find the Court's treatment of the principle in a specific case the reader need only identify the issue or case name in the index or case table to this text. Those interested in an examination of the various areas in which the principle is particularly relevant should consult the topic index under "separation of powers"; in that part of the index we cross reference to all portions of the text which touch upon the principle.

---

7. In Nixon v. Administrator of General Services, 433 U.S. 425, 443 (1977) the majority opinion stated:

"the Court [in U. S. v. Nixon] squarely rejected the argument that the Constitution contemplates a complete division of authority between the three branches . . . Like the District Court, we therefore find that appellant's argument rests upon an 'archaic view of the separation of powers as requiring three outright departments of government.'"

See also, Powell v. McCormack, 395 U.S. 486 (1969) (Court's decision on House refusal to seat Congressman does not violate separation of powers principle).

But see Industrial Union Dept., AFL–CIO v. American Petroleum Institute, 448 U.S. 607, 669 (1980) (Rehnquist, J, concurring in the judgment). In this opinion Justice Rehnquist explicitly relied on the theories of John Locke to advocate a return to the pre-1937 view of the separation of powers principle that would have the Court invalidate delegations of legislative authority to executive agencies whenever a majority of the justices felt that the legislature had not sufficiently limited the power of the executive agency. In this case

the Supreme Court, by a five to four vote, invalidated a health standard promulgated by the Occupational Safety and Health Administration limiting occupational exposure to benzene. The plurality opinion, in contrast, relied on the statutory basis that OSHA had failed to support its proposed standards with appropriate findings of fact. Later, Justice Rehnquist convinced Chief Justice Burger that there should be active judicial review of congressional delegation to lawmaking power to regulatory agencies. See American Textile Mfrs. Institute Inc. v. Donovan, 452 U.S. 490, 543 (1981) (Rehnquist, J., dissenting, joined by Burger, C. J.).

8. Professor Jesse Choper argued that the Supreme Court should rule separation of powers issues to be nonjusticiable. This proposal is a part of a scholarly examination of the role of the Supreme Court. J. Choper, Judicial Review and the National Political Process (1980). See also, Nowak, Book Review, 68 California L.Rev. 1223 (1980) (reviewing Choper).

See generally Quint, The Separation of Powers Under Nixon: Reflections on Constitutional Liberties and the Rule of Law, 1981 Duke L.J. 1.

CHAPTER FOUR

THE FEDERAL COMMERCE POWER

I. INTRODUCTION

A. The Commerce Clause: Its Problems and Development

Article I, Section 8 of the Constitution provides in part that Congress shall have the power "To regulate Commerce with foreign Nations, and among the several States, and with the Indian Tribes." The brevity of this clause belies the fact that its interpretation has played a significant role in shaping the concepts of federalism and the permissible uses of national power throughout our history. It must be remembered from the last chapter that the federal government, at least in form, was not granted a general police power or the inherent right to act on any subject matter in order to promote the health, safety or welfare of the people throughout the nation. But the framers did grant Congress a power to regulate commerce which might, depending on the definition of that seemingly non-technical word, include the power to promote the economic welfare of the citizens throughout the country. The grant of power also may be viewed as committing this subject matter to Congress and thereby removing some of the powers of states to deal with local matters that may be considered a part of the "commerce" described by this clause. Thus it can be seen that, absent some further restriction upon the power, it might indeed be the functional equivalent of a generalized "police power" because much of the activity which takes place within the country, and even within a single state, might be said to relate to economic issues and problems. A broad reading of the clause would not only grant a sweeping power to the federal government but it would also restrict the ability of individual states to adopt laws which burden the forms of commerce which were committed to the control of the federal government.

The history of the commerce clause adjudication is, in a very real sense, the history of the concepts of federalism as well as the development of doctrines supporting a specific federal power. It becomes quite important therefore to look at the treatment which the Supreme Court has given this clause throughout each stage in its history, even though we will summarize the Court's current position in a single section. Therefore, this chapter follows the Court's interpretations of the commerce power on a chronological basis. After some introductory notes we shall turn to the first cases defining the power which demonstrate both historical and theoretical uncertainty on the part of the justices in defining the scope of powers for the new national government. In the next section we will examine the Court's attempt to restrict the power, more out of a desire to protect the role of the states in the federal system than to hold the federal government to an original limited grant of power. Finally, we shall see that modern economic problems made the justices aware that they were not institutionally capable of restricting this power on a principled basis; the other branches of government appear to be the more capable entities for defining the true nature of national commercial problems and the means that are needed to promote the economic well-being of the country. Today, the Court will uphold the decisions of Congress so long as there is some rational argument for finding that the items that they regulate fall within the commerce power. But in order to understand the meaning of the current rules concerning the nature of Congress' power and the slight restrictions placed upon it, one must read the current decisions in light of the past experience of the Court. While we examine the scope of state powers that may be exercised in conformity with the com-

merce clause in a separate chapter, we will note many state regulation cases in our development of the theory of a national commerce power. These decisions evidence the justices' desire to interpret the commerce power in order to define the roles of both the nation and the states in the federal system.

Before going on to an examination of the development of specific commerce clause tests and the modern rules, we briefly discuss two related points. First, we will comment on why the Court has not had significant difficulties in upholding a plenary federal power over all forms of commercial regulations of foreign commerce and dealings with American Indians. This section should sufficiently indicate why the issues under the commerce clause have centered on the ability of Congress to regulate commerce among the states. Second, we will note some of the pre-constitutional commercial problems and the nature of the forces that gave rise to the grant of a national commerce power to Congress. This history will, of course, not be definitive, but it should indicate the range of options which the Court had before it early in its history and the problems of attempting to base any modern decision upon the intention of the framers of this provision. After that, we shall move to a chronological examination of interstate commerce issues and analyze the principles which moved the justices to define the power in particular ways during each era.

B. The Power to Regulate Commerce with Foreign Nations and Indian Tribes

Today it may be said that the congressional power to regulate commerce among the states stands on an equal footing with its powers to regulate commerce relating to foreign nations or Indian tribes. But this state of affairs exists only because the Court has finally committed itself to deferring to congressional power to regulate interstate commerce in the same way that it has always recognized plenary powers to regulate the other two subjects. Even during periods when the justices were debating whether to significantly restrict the congressional power to regulate intrastate activities under the commerce power, there was no serious advocacy of restrictions on the federal powers in these other areas.[1] The reason is quite simple: the justices have never recognized any important or legitimate state interest in foreign affairs or dealings with American Indians. Thus, when the Court was seeking to reserve powers for the states under the tenth amendment, it had no cause to use that concept to restrict the federal powers in these areas.[2]

The Court has always recognized a plenary power in Congress to deal with matters touching upon foreign relations or foreign trade. Indeed, as we note in Chapter 6, the federal powers in this area may constitute an exception to the normal requirement that the federal government justify its acts in terms of specific enumerated powers. The history of the commerce clause and the shaping of the Constitution itself also endorse the finding of an unrestricted power in this area. As noted in the next section, one of the prime areas of commercial problems meant to be solved by the Constitution was

the imposition of restrictions on imports and exports by the states. The Constitution specifically prohibits state government from imposing such duties without the consent of the national government.[3] The Article I section 10 listing of activities that are prohibited to the states primarily focuses upon matters touching upon their foreign trade or relations with foreign countries.[4] Thus it can be safely asserted that there was no constitutional recognition of any "reserved powers" of the states to act in these areas.

The Constitution as originally framed seems also to recognize a virtually unlimited power of Congress over commerce with foreign nations. The primary concern over congressional power in the international area came from the Southern states who feared that a broad power might be used to restrict the importation of slaves following the ratification of the Constitution. This possible use of the power was eliminated by expressly prohibiting Congress from banning the importation of slaves until 1808.[5] There were similar fears that so broad a power in Congress might result in certain states being favored in matters of foreign trade. Thus Section 9 of Article I insures the Congress will not tax exports or give preference

---

1. Although the Constitution grants Congress the power to regulate foreign commerce and commerce among the states in parallel language, "there is evidence that the Founders intended the scope of the foreign commerce power to be the greater." Japan Line Ltd. v. County of Los Angeles, 441 U.S. 434, 447, 99 S.Ct. 1813, 1821 (1979) (footnote omitted). See, e.g., Brolan v. United States, 236 U.S. 216, 222 (1915). An excellent example of the lack of debate is the Lottery Case (Champion v. Ames), 188 U.S. 321 (1903) in which the Court upheld the Congressional Act prohibiting the sending of lottery tickets into states which prohibited lotteries, over the dissents of four justices. Yet these justices indicated that they would not place restrictions on the power of Congress over international trade. Id. at 373–4 (Fuller, C. J., dissenting, joined by Brewer, Shiras, and Peckham, JJ.). See also, United States v. Marigold, 50 U.S. (9 How.) 560 (1850).

2. See, e. g., Board of Trustees v. United States, 289 U.S. 48 (1933) (protective tariffs); Weber v. Freed, 239 U.S. 325 (1915) (prohibition of importation of prize fight films); The Abbey Dodge, 223 U.S. 166 (1912) (prohibition of sponges from Gulf of Mexico or waters off Florida construed as not applicable within the States); Buttfield v. Stranahan, 192 U.S. 470 (1904) (prohibition of importation of certain types of tea).

3. U.S.Const. art. I, § 10, cl. 2.

4. "No State shall enter into any Treaty, Alliance, or Confederation; grant Letters of Marque and Reprisal; coin Money; emit Bills of Credit; make any Thing but gold and silver Coin a Tender in Payment of Debts; pass any Bill of Attainder, ex post facto Law, or Law impairing the Obligation of Contracts, or grant any Title of Nobility.

"No State shall, without the Consent of Congress, lay any Imports or Duties on Imports or Exports, except what may be absolutely necessary for executing it's inspection Laws: and the net Produce of all Duties and Imposts, laid by any State on Imports or Exports, shall be for the Use of the Treasury of the United States; and all such Laws shall be subject to the Revision and Controul of the Congress.

"No State shall, without the Consent of Congress, lay any Duty of Tonnage, keep Troops, or Ships of War in time of Peace, enter into any Agreement of Compact with another State, or with a foreign Power, or engage in War, unless actually invaded, or in such imminent Danger as will not admit of delay."

U.S.Const. art. I, § 10.

5. U.S.Const. art. I, § 9, cl. 1; U.S.Const. art. V.

to certain ports in matters of foreign trade.[6] It would seem clear from the document itself that the power to deal with foreign commerce was very precisely defined and is a plenary one within only the specific restrictions set by that document.

The congressional power to regulate commerce with American Indian tribes was upheld on an even more basic rationale. The Court has continually recognized Indian tribes as constituting separate, though dependent, "sovereigns" within the nation. Part of the reason for the original designation of the Indians as such was the desire to remove the states' ability to control or exploit the Indian tribes.[7] Thus the Court found that they were subject only to federal regulation because of their quasi-sovereign status. The quasi-sovereign status of federally recognized Indian tribes meant that the national government had an inherent right to regulate Indian affairs.[8] The commerce clause provision regarding Indian tribes provided a textual basis for recognition of this power, but the Supreme Court almost certainly would have declared Indian affairs to be a subject for national, rather than local, regulation even if there were no reference to Indian tribes in the commerce clause.[9]

There is an important distinction between governmental acts that classify persons for special treatment because of their Indian ancestry and the regulation of federally recognized Indian tribes. Laws which favor or disfavor persons because of their Indian ancestry should be considered suspect and subject to the most rigorous judicial scrutiny under the equal protection guarantee. However, congressional legislation or federal agency regulations regarding federally recognized Indian tribes and their members does not constitute a violation of the implied equal protection guarantee of the fifth amendment due process clause so long as the classification is "tied rationally to the fulfillment of Congress' unique obligation toward the Indians."[10] The Supreme Court employs a mere rationality test when scruti-

6. U.S.Const. art. I, § 9, cl. 6.

7. Cherokee Nation v. Georgia, 30 U.S. (5 Pet.) 1 (1831); Worcester v. Georgia, 31 U.S. (6 Pet.) 515 (1836). See Washburn, The Historical Context of American Indian Legal Problems, 40 Law & Contemporary Problems, 12 (1976).

8. A detailed examination of the legal status of American Indian tribes and their members is beyond the scope of this treatise. In addition to the cases and authorities referred to in this section, those interested in doing further research into this subject should refer to: F. Cohen, Handbook of Federal Indian Law (Govt. Printing Office 1942); W. Canby, American Indian Law in a Nutshell (1981); L. Gasaway, J. Hoover & D. Warden, American Indian Legal Materials: A Union List (1980); D. Getches, D. Rosenfelt & C. Wilkinson, Federal Indian Law: Cases and Materials (1979); L. Rosen, American Indians and the Law (1976) (reprint of 40 Law & Contemporary Problems 1–223); M. Price, Law and the American Indian: Readings, Notes and Cases (1973); Constitutional Rights of the American Indian, Hearings Before the Subcommittee on Constitutional Rights of the Committee on the Judiciary, United States Senate, Eighty-Seventh Congress, First Session, Part 1 (1961).

9. United States v. Kagama, 118 U.S. 375, 384 (1886). Laurence, The Indian Commerce Clause, 23 Ariz.L.Rev. 204 (1981). Federal authority over Indian tribes has in the past been based on the treaty making power of the President and Senate. See McClanahan v. Arizona State Tax Comm'n, 411 U.S. 164, 172 n. 7 (1973).

Even during the period in the Supreme Court's history in which the justices restricted the federal power over interstate commerce on the basis of the tenth amendment, a majority of the justices recognized a broad federal power to regulate the activities of members of American Indian tribes and non-Indians who had commercial dealings with tribal members. For example, United States v. Nice, 241 U.S. 591 (1916) overruling Matter of Heff, 197 U.S. 488 (1905), the Court held that federal legislation could restrict the sales of intoxicating beverages to Indians even when the transaction otherwise did not involve interstate commerce. Today a law which restricts the access of tribe members to such commodities should be held to violate the implicit equal protection guarantee of the fifth amendment due process clause. See, Johnson & Crystal, Indians and Equal Protection, 54 Wash.L.Rev. 587 (1979).

10. Morton v. Mancari, 417 U.S. 535, 555 (1974) (upholding employment preference for members of Indian tribes in Bureau of Indian Affairs); Washington v. Washington State Commercial Passenger Fishing Vessel Ass'n, 443 U.S. 658, 673 n. 20 (1979) (interpreting federal treaties with certain Indian tribes to guarantee them a share of each run of anadromous fish in areas in the State of Washington and holding both that state laws limiting those rights were invalid and that the granting of these preferential fishing rights to Indians did not violate the principles of equal protection). See Johnson & Crystal, supra note 9.

nizing tribal classifications because such classifications are viewed as political rather than racial. Laws which give preferential employment or economic benefits to members of American Indian tribes may be upheld on this basis without consideration of whether they constitute a form of benign racial classification which might not otherwise survive scrutiny under the equal protection guarantee.[11] This rationality standard should not be used to justify legislation which imposes burdens upon persons because of their American Indian ancestry.[12]

Commentators have questioned whether the unique constitutional status of members of American Indian tribes has benefited tribal members.[13] The status of the tribes as quasi-sovereign entities has resulted in the

Supreme Court refusal to apply the guarantees of the Bill of Rights to tribal regulations of individual tribe members in the same manner as it has applied those provisions to the actions of local governments.[14] The extension of civil liberties protection to members of federally recognized tribes residing on tribal property has come about primarily by congressional action.[15] The congressional power to pass laws limiting the use of tribal property or regulating the action of tribal members is subject to some constitutional restrictions. Although the Supreme Court has not made clear exactly which provisions of the Bill of Rights restrict congressional power in this area, it has held that the just compensation clause ap-

---

11.   Morton v. Mancari, 417 U.S. 535 (1974) (employment preference in Bureau of Indian Affairs upheld). See also, United States v. Antelope, 430 U.S. 641 (1977); Fisher v. District Court, 424 U.S. 382, 390 (1976). See generally, Johnson & Crystal, supra note 9.

12.   In Washington v. Confederated Bands & Tribes of the Yakima Indian Nation, 439 U.S. 463 (1979), the Supreme Court held that a 1953 Act of Congress allows some states by legislative act to modify their jurisdiction so as to assume either full or partial jurisdiction over criminal offenses and civil causes of action regarding tribal Indians and Indian territories. The State of Washington had extended its criminal and civil jurisdiction over Indians and Indian territories except for eight subject matter areas which it would allow to remain within the jurisdiction of the Indian tribe unless the State was requested to assume full jurisdiction by the particular tribe. The Supreme Court found that this partial extension of jurisdiction and "checker board" jurisdictional pattern over Indian lands violated neither the federal statute nor the equal protection clause. So long as the state was acting in response to a federal enabling act allowing for the regulation or reduction of sovereignty of Indian tribes, the law was to be tested under the traditional rational basis standard of review for determining whether the classification violated the equal protection guarantee. Although this was a state law, the separate treatment of jurisdiction over tribal Indians would not be deemed a "suspect" classification, as would a law which classified persons by their Indian heritage rather than their continued status as a member of a tribe officially recognized by federal law. Because of the "unique status" of Indian tribes under federal law, the federal government may enact, as it did here, legislation signaling out tribal Indians. So long as the statute was not designed to discriminate against a tribe, the classification would be upheld if it were not totally irrational or arbitrary.

13.   See, Clinton, Isolated In Their Own Country: A Defense of Federal Protection of Indian Autonomy and

Self-Government, 33 Stan.L.Rev. 979 (1981); Note, The Indian: The Forgotten American, 81 Harv.L.Rev. 1818 (1968).

14.   Proceedings in Indian tribal courts are not subjected to the Bill of Rights. Talton v. Mayes, 163 U.S. 376 (1896). Proceedings in the Indian courts are subjected to the terms of the Indian Civil Rights Act, 25 U.S.C.A. §§ 1301–1303. Thus, federal courts, on the basis of that Act, may review proceedings in tribal courts and grant habeas corpus to persons whose rights under the Act have been violated. However, the Supreme Court in Santa Clara Pueblo v. Martinez, 436 U.S. 49 (1978) found that the Indian Civil Rights Act only applied to proceedings in tribal courts. The Act by its own terms establishes a remedy of habeas corpus, so that federal courts can grant that relief in reviewing tribal court proceedings under the Act. However, the lower federal courts had found that the Act, when coupled with other general jurisdictional statutes, allowed them to review tribal laws and practices. But the Supreme Court found that the Act did not remove tribal immunity from suit, and that it did not create a cause of action against tribal officers. Allowing the federal courts to use the Act as a general grant of jurisdiction would almost necessarily result in the total abrogation of tribal sovereignty, and put an end to the ability of individual tribes to follow their own lifestyles. The Supreme Court would not authorize such an intrusion into the internal workings of Indian tribes, even by lower federal courts, absent clear action by Congress or a conflict with the overriding sovereignty of the United States. Thus, it is for Congress to determine whether it wishes to expand federal court jurisdiction over Indian tribes for violations of the Indian Civil Rights Act. The Court specifically noted that Congress had the power to create such federal jurisdiction and to limit tribal immunity. 436 U.S. at 54–55.

15.   See, e.g., Indian Civil Rights Act, 25 U.S.C.A. § 1301 et seq.

plies to the federal appropriation of tribal property.[16]

The authority of Indian tribes to govern their lands, and the people thereon, is subject to intrinsic limitations arising from the relationship of Indian tribes to the federal government. The primary limitations on tribal sovereignty relate to the transfer of land, external attributes of political sovereignty, and jurisdiction over non-Indians who are on Indian property. Although Congress has wide latitude in dealing with American Indians, the Supreme Court has held that tribal sovereignty is to be honored by federal courts to the extent that it does not conflict with federal statutes, federal treaties, or the overriding sovereignty of the United States.[17]

State and local governments have no jurisdiction over Indian tribes unless they specifically have been granted such jurisdiction by Congress. The rights of tribal Indians under the statutes, treaties, or Constitution of the United States are federal questions; federal law, as interpreted by the federal courts will supersede any conflicting state laws, regulations or court rulings.[18] The nature of the federal interest in Indian affairs, and the extent of federal regulation of American Indian tribes, has resulted in federal preemption of state regulations. State or local attempts to regulate the use of tribal property or the activities of individuals on tribal property ordinarily will be held invalid because of federal preemption.[19] State jurisdiction over activity on Indian reservation lands located in the state is permitted only to the extent that it has been granted to the state by Congress.[20] Members of Indian tribes may be subject to state or local regulation of their off-reservation activities if those local regulations do not conflict with

16. United States v. Sioux Nation of Indians, 448 U.S. 371 (1980) (although the taking of original title is not compensable, the government's acquisition of land held by an Indian tribe with recognized title to the land constitutes a compensable taking under the fifth amendment).

17. See note 14, supra.

Indian courts have only limited jurisdiction because the overriding sovereignty of the United States, as well as specific congressional enactments, limits the scope of tribal court powers. In Oliphant v. Suquamish Indian Tribe, 435 U.S. 191 (1978), the Supreme Court held that Indian tribal courts do not have inherent jurisdiction over non-Indian residents of Indian reservations. The overriding sovereignty of the United States bars tribal authority over non-Indians in criminal matters, absent a congressional statute or treaty provision that would grant the tribe that jurisdiction. However, Indian tribes retain their sovereignty to punish criminal acts committed by tribal Indians, although Congress might restrict or eliminate tribal jurisdiction over such matters. In United States v. Wheeler, 435 U.S. 313 (1978), the Court found that Indian tribes have power to enforce their criminal laws against tribal members because this was not an aspect of tribal sovereignty that was restricted by the relationship to the federal government. The Court stated that: "Indian tribes still possess those aspects of sovereignty not withdrawn by treaty or statute, or by implication as a necessary result of their dependent status." 435 U.S. at 322–23.

18. Washington v. Washington State Commercial Passenger Fishing Vessel Ass'n, 443 U.S. 658 (1979) (state law as written or construed could not interfere with preferential fishing rights given Indian tribes by federal treaties). See also United States v. Clarke, 445

U.S. 253 (1980) (federal statutes do not permit state or local governments to condemn land "allotted in severalty to Indians" by physical intrusion or occupation, nor do they authorize an inverse condemnation action by the Indian landowner. Rather, these statutes require the condemning authority to exercise its eminent domain power and to compensate the Indian owner for the taking of allotted land).

19. See, e.g., United States v. John, 437 U.S. 634 (1978).

20. United States v. John, 437 U.S. 634 (1978); United States v. McBratney, 104 U.S. 621 (1881). See also Rice v. Rehner, 103 S.Ct. 3291 (1983); note 12 supra.

A federal statute, unchanged since 1834, requires a "white person" involved in a trial with an Indian concerning rights to property to bear the burden of proof in the trial whenever the Indian can show prior possession of the property. 25 U.S.C.A. § 194. In Wilson v. Omaha Indian Tribe, 442 U.S. 653 (1979), the Supreme Court found that this statute applies to suits between individual or corporate landowners and Indian tribes, although state governments are not to be burdened by this presumption. The statute, and federal common law, were to control the determination of property rights where the United States and the Indian tribe had never formally relinquished title to lands retained by the Indian tribe in the Territory, and later State, of Nebraska, pursuant to an 1854 federal treaty. However, the Supreme Court found that federal common law, used to interpret the treaty, should incorporate state law to determine if some of the once tribal land which, due to a river course change, was on the Iowa side of the Iowa-Nebraska border and which had been used for years by Iowa residents, belonged to the Indian tribe or to those Iowa residents.

federal regulations, legislation, treaties or constitutional provisions.[21]

In the remaining portions of this chapter we will examine the one federal commerce power which has been subject to differing types of restrictions during its history—the power to regulate commerce "among the states."

C. A Note on the History of the Commerce Clause

As we noted in the previous chapter, there was no debate in the Constitutional Convention over the enumeration of specific powers for the federal government following an initial, unsuccessful proposal to grant it a general "police" power.[1] One of the enumerated powers that was not specifically examined was the grant of power to Congress to regulate commerce "among the several States." Thus we have no direct history as to the meaning of the clause that could even arguably be called determinative of specific legal issues. Not only must we content ourselves with looking at the circumstances surrounding the calling of the Constitutional Convention and the ratification process, but we must note that this clause employs a concept, that of "commerce," that seems by its nature subject to differing definitions with the passing of time. Let us note some of the forces which gave rise to the calling of the convention and drafting of the clause before moving on to the judicial interpretations of both the history and meaning of that provision.

There had been no significant commercial problems prior to the Declaration of Independence, for Britain had controlled the trade between the colonies themselves as well as that with foreign nations. The acts of the colonial governments were subject to the review of the Privy Council, and the British Board of Trade supervised the general commercial transactions through the colonies.[2] Additionally all of the actions of the colonial governments and the forms of trade which they engaged in were at least formally subjected to the authority of the Secretary of State for the Southern Department. It was primarily the Board of Trade supervision over the trade of and the access to goods and services in each colony that eliminated economic conflict during the colonial period.

After the signing of the Declaration of Independence there was no central control over commercial transactions in the new states. The individual states were fearful of having their trade subjected to discriminatory restrictions either by states with conflicting commercial interests or a national government that might be controlled by such interests. Therefore when they formed a national government under the Articles of Confederation they granted the Continental Congress some powers over national affairs but none over commerce between the new states. Not only did they fail to give Congress such a power but they restricted the Continental Congress' powers in foreign affairs by providing that no federal treaties might limit the individual states' powers over commerce and the taxation of imports and exports.[3]

The lack of a centralized authority over commerce and the conflicting economic interests of the new states led to what may best be described as economic chaos under the Articles of Confederation: the loss of a trade relationship with Great Britain; serious diminishing of international trade with a resulting shortage of currency; and the coalition of local economic forces to protect their position in the now limited market place. Individual states then began to set up trade barriers by imposing economic

---

21. Mescalero Apache Tribe v. Jones, 411 U.S. 145 (1973) (upholding nondiscriminating state gross receipts tax as applied to business operated by Indian tribes on off-reservation land).

1. See Chapter 3, section I, supra.

2. A. Kelly & W. Harbison, The American Constitution, Its Origins and Development, 50–54 (4th ed. 1970).

3. Articles of Confederation, art. IX, par. 1 (1777). The Articles are reprinted in the Lawyer's Edition of J. Nowak, R. Rotunda, & J. Young, Constitutional Law, Chapter 21 (hornbook series, 2d ed. 1983).

sanctions against competing products from other states as well as taxing trade passing through their state in order to gain a more solid economic position, further limiting the market place for goods and services.[4] States such as New York which controlled major foreign ports imposed taxes on incoming foreign commerce destined for the other states. In retaliation these states would tax goods brought in from other states at a rate so high as to foreclose access to their markets. The situation became such that many political leaders in the nation feared that the economic warfare would lead to a dissolution of the union and that "at a minimum" the powers of the Continental Congress to deal with commercial problems between the states had to be enhanced.[5] Thus there was a call for a convention to amend the powers of the national government under the Articles of Confederation so as to make it effective to deal with multistate problems.

When the delegates met to amend the Articles of Confederation, they quickly realized that the country needed an entirely new form of government to deal with national problems. Thus there was a call for a new convention, which we now know as the Constitutional Convention, to totally revise the powers of the national government.[6] This convention began in May of 1787 and produced the new federal government with its enumerated (but not debated) power to regulate commerce "among the states." At the constitutional convention, several states expressed concern over the congressional power to regulate foreign commerce. The southern states feared control over this matter might lead to the prohibition of the importation of slaves to such an extent that they proposed limiting the national commer-

cial powers. In the ensuing compromise the powers were not defined narrowly but the southern states received assurance in the Constitution that Congress would not bar the importation of slaves until 1808.[7] Several of the southern states also feared that the Northeast might control the Congress and thereby favor their trade centers and products at the expense of southern agricultural interests. These fears were overcome by the provisions of Section 9 of Article I which guaranteed that no preference would be given to the ports of any state and that Congress could not impose any export taxes.[8]

The congressional power over international commerce was thus specifically defined by the convention, and there is no record of the power over commerce with the Indian tribes as a source of concern. But the power over internal commerce was both undefined and of great importance. Undoubtedly the Federalists intended Congress to have significant powers in this area but there are indications that some of the framers and ratifiers were opposed to granting Congress such a wide power over commercial matters that it would remove all state autonomy in these areas.[9] Thus the question of state power to enact regulations affecting interstate commerce, a question which was to be of the most frequent concern to the Court, did not have a legislative history which would be helpful to the Court. However, the Court could rely upon history to demonstrate two general concerns for the drafting of the Constitution in general and the commerce clause in particular: (1) the power must have been meant to put an end, either in itself or through federal legislation, to the trade barriers and tariffs which had led to the economic problems during the preceding period;

---

4. See, Kelly & Harbison, supra note 2 at 109; F. Broderick, The Origins of the Constitution 1776–1789, at 18 (1964); C. Heathcock, The United States Constitution in Perspective at 20 (1972); P. Hay & R. Rotunda, The United States Federal System: Legal Integration in the American Experience 5–7 (Milan, Giuffrè 1982).

5. Id.

6. The resolution for a new convention to deal with commercial problems is reprinted in 1 H. Commanger, Documents of American History 132 (5th ed. 1949).

7. U.S.Const. art. I, § 9, cl. 1; U.S.Const. art. V.

8. U.S.Const. art. I, § 9.

9. Thus the Federalists felt called upon to answer charges that the scope of federal powers was so great as to endanger the autonomy of the states. See, e.g., The Federalist No. 45 (Madison), see also No. 11 (Hamilton), reprinted in, The Federalist Papers (New American Library Ed. 1961). For an examination of the conflicting economic forces that affected the framing of the Constitution, see generally, C. Beard, An Economic Interpretation of the Constitution of the United States (Rev. ed. 1960).

(2) the national power must have been intended to be broad enough to deal with the type of economic problems of the nation as a unit. The experience under the Articles of Confederation showed that the individual states had literally no success in trying to deal with multistate economic problems. As can be readily seen, this background has given the Court some themes to follow in its interpretation of the commerce clause but left for the justices the task of analyzing the purpose and meaning of the commerce power in the federal system. It is to the Court's work in this area that we now turn.

II. JUDICIAL INTERPRETATIONS OF THE POWER PRIOR TO 1888

In examining the interpretation of the commerce clause during this period, then Professor Felix Frankfurter commented: "Relatively little emerges up to the death of [Chief Justice] Waite in 1888, regarding the Court's attitude towards the commerce clause as an affirmative instrument for promoting 'commerce among the states.' The preoccupation [of earlier periods] is with the restrictive use of the clause." [1] And so it was, because Congress passed little commercial legislation during this period and the Supreme Court reviewed even less. No piece of federal commercial legislation was invalidated by the Court prior to the Civil War. [2] Indeed, the major review of Article I powers prior to the war was *McCulloch v. Maryland*. [3] But the justices did reflect upon the scope of the national commerce power during this period in deciding cases concerning

the validity of state laws under the "dormant" commerce clause. [4]

In *Gibbons v. Ogden* [5] Chief Justice Marshall examined the scope of both federal and state powers under the commerce clause. The opinion today ranks as one of the most important in history. In it Marshall laid the basis for later justices to uphold a federal power to deal with national economic and social problems. But before that time would come, the Court would go through periods disregarding the basis of Marshall's ruling. *Gibbons* concerned the granting of a steamboat monopoly to a private company. New York had granted the exclusive right to engage in steamboat navigation in the waters of New York to a partnership which had transferred the monopoly to Ogden. Gibbons began a competing service between New York and New Jersey. When Ogden sued Gibbons for encroachment on the monopoly, he defended by asserting that the state granted monopoly violated the commerce clause. Instead of giving a definitive ruling on the scope of state powers under that clause, the Court found the monopoly invalid because it conflicted with a valid federal statute. Marshall's opinion held that the federal statute governing the licensing of ships granted those ships the right to engage in coastal trade and that the federal statute governed the issue because it was the supreme law of the land. [6] In the course of the opinion, Marshall gave a broad reading to the powers of Congress under the commerce clause. Marshall defined commerce as "intercourse" and recognized that it extended into each state. Congress had the power to regulate "that commerce which

1. F. Frankfurter, The Commerce Clause Under Marshall, Taney and Waite, at 7 (1964—first published 1937).

   Scott v. Moore, 680 F.2d 979, 1019–20 n. 66 (5th Cir. 1982) (Rubin & Williams, JJ.), quoting an earlier edition of this treatise.

2. Only two federal acts were held unconstitutional during this period: see Marbury v. Madison, 5 U.S. (1 Cranch) 137 (1803) (part of Judiciary Act held unconstitutional grant of original jurisdiction); Dred Scott v. Sandford, 60 U.S. (19 How.) 393 (1857) (Missouri Compromise granting freedom to slaves in certain territories).

3. 17 U.S. (4 Wheat.) 316 (1819).

4. The development of standards to review these issues is examined in Chapter 9.

5. 22 U.S. (9 Wheat.) 1 (1824). See also, P. Hay & R. Rotunda, The United States Federal System: Legal Integration in the American Experience 71–80 (Milan, Giuffrè 1982). For a further discussion of *Gibbons* as it relates to state power over commerce, see Chapter 9, section I, B.

6. 22 U.S. at 210.

concerns more states than one." [7] The federal power extended to commerce wherever it was present, and thus, "the power of Congress may be exercised within a state." [8]

The commerce power, in Marshall's opinion, was not to be restricted by the judiciary. His opinion for the majority of the Court found that the commerce power, "like all others vested in Congress, is complete in itself, may be exercised to its utmost extent, and acknowledges no limitations other than are prescribed in the Constitution." [9] Marshall did state that some "internal" commerce of a state would be beyond the power of Congress to regulate.[10] But this statement was Marshall's expression of his initial view of the scope of the words "commerce among the states." He did not mean to limit the power of Congress in order to protect the powers of individual states. As Felix Frankfurter viewed the opinion:

> Marshall not merely rejected the Tenth Amendment as an active principle of limitation; he countered with his famous characterization of the powers of Congress, and of the commerce power in particular, as the possession of the unqualified authority of a unitary sovereign. He threw the full weight of his authority against the idea that, apart from specific restrictions in the Constitution, the very existence of the states operates as such a limitation . . .[11]

Chief Justice Marshall had only two more opportunities to examine the meaning of the commerce clause prior to his death. Both of these cases focused on particular powers of the states. In *Brown v. Maryland* [12] the Court, in an opinion by Marshall, invalidated a state statute which imposed a license fee or tax on wholesale importers. The tax was invalid for two reasons. First, it constituted a tax on international imports while they were still in their original package and before they became part of the "common mass" of property within the state. Therefore, it violated the constitutional prohibition against state duties on imports or exports.[13] Second, the tax conflicted with the commerce clause and the power of Congress to regulate and permit the sale of imports. Here Marshall described the power of Congress as the power to regulate commercial intercourse which reached into a state.[14] Once again Marshall was only describing a specific aspect of the power; he did not imply that the Court should limit the commerce power to protect state sovereignty.[15]

In *Willson v. Black Bird Creek Marsh Co.*,[16] the Court upheld a Delaware statute which authorized the building of a dam across a navigable creek. Although this dam obstructed the passage of ships, including those with federal licenses, the Supreme Court in an opinion by Chief Justice Marshall found the act consistent with the federal commerce power. He believed the act to be within the police power of the state to protect the public, which the state retained even after the ratification of the federal commerce clause. Also he found that Congress did not intend to grant rights of passage over such creeks and, therefore, the state act did not conflict with an exercise of

---

7. 22 U.S. at 189, 194.

8. 22 U.S. at 195.

9. 22 U.S. at 196.

10. 22 U.S. at 194.

11. F. Frankfurter, supra note 1, at 40; Marshall made the point thus, 22 U.S. at 34:
> "If, as has always been understood, the sovereignty of congress, though limited to specified objects, is plenary as to those objects, the power over commerce with foreign nations, and among the several States, is vested in congress as absolutely as it would be in a single government, having in its constitution the same restrictions on the exercise of the power as are found in the constitution of the United States."

12. 25 U.S. (12 Wheat.) 419 (1827).

13. U.S. Const. art. I, § 10; The "original package" test for imports was abandoned in Michelin Tire Co. v. Wages, 422 U.S. 1040 (1975); see Chapter 11. The original package doctrine was not applied to state taxes on interstate commerce. Woodruff v. Parham, 75 U.S. (8 Wall.) 123 (1869).

14. 25 U.S. (12 Wheat.) at 446.

15. Marshall cited *Gibbons* and reiterated the concept that the power had "no limitations other than are prescribed by the constitution." 25 U.S. (12 Wheat.) at 446.

16. 27 U.S. (2 Pet.) 245 (1829).

the federal power. However, Marshall's opinion did not indicate that he would have placed any restriction on the congressional power to deal with this matter even though it involved a local "police power" issue. Felix Frankfurter noted,[17] that the concepts of commerce formulated in the Marshall opinions could lead to "obscuring formulas" for the proper exercise of both state and national powers. This confusion in fact took place over a long period of time and it was only after 1937 that the Court returned to Marshall's position. But from Marshall's death in 1835 until 1888, few restrictions were placed on the national commerce power.

Between 1837 and 1851, the Supreme Court reviewed several state acts under the commerce clause without formulating clear principles to govern the exercise of either state or national power. But there were statements in the decisions, even by supporters of Marshall's position, that indicated a sharp distinction between the types of commerce that could be regulated by Congress or the states.[18] In 1851 the Court decided *Cooley v. Board of Wardens* [19] and established the basic analysis of state power under the dormant commerce clause. The *Cooley* opinion established the concept of "selective exclusiveness" whereby commercial subjects requiring uniform national regulation could be regulated only by Congress, while subjects of local concern might be regulated to some extent by the states.[20] The opinion did not attempt to define the scope of federal power, but its division between "national" and "local" subjects would one day be used by justices who sought to restrict federal power.

The Court under the leadership of Chief Justice Taney was more lenient in reviewing state legislation than the Marshall Court,[21] but the Court made no attempt to restrain federal commercial powers.[22] Indeed, there were indications during this period that the Court would have been willing to recognize sweeping federal powers under the commerce clause had Congress attempted extensive regulation. Taney seemed ready to defer to federal as well as state legislative judgments.[23] The justices had little difficulty in upholding federal acts to prohibit trade in counterfeit money.[24] The Court also deferred to Congressional judgment over commerce in the *Wheeling Bridge Cases.* In 1852, the Court invalidated Virginia statutes authorizing a bridge over the Ohio River that might interfere with commerce.[25] Congress then passed a federal law declaring the bridge to be lawful.[26] This statute was held by the Court to fall within the federal commerce power.[27]

Following the Civil War, the Supreme Court began to assert its authority to control the actions of the other branches of the federal government. During the chief justiceship of Salmon Chase from 1864 to 1873, eight federal statutes were held to be unconstitutional.[28] The Court did not consider significant commercial issues until 1869. In that year, the justices seemed ready to rec-

---

17.　F. Frankfurter, supra note 1, at 31–2, 61–2.

18.　Id.; see, e.g., the Passenger Cases, 48 U.S. (7 How.) 283, 400 (1849) (opinion of McClean, J.).

19.　53 U.S. (12 How.) 299 (1851).

20.　This is examined in the section of state powers and the commerce clause in Chapter 9.

21.　See, e.g., New York v. Miln, 36 U.S. (11 Pet.) 102 (1837); In fact, Chief Justice Taney never voted to strike down state legislation under the commerce clause; see F. Frankfurter, supra note 1 at 55.

22.　While Taney did not seek to control the commerce power generally, he did write the opinion invalidating the congressional act freeing slaves in certain territories, Dred Scott v. Sandford, 60 U.S. (19 How.) 393 (1857), and it appears that he would have also restricted the commerce power as to slavery issues, see

Groves v. Slaughter, 40 U.S. (15 Pet.) 449 (1841); F. Frankfurter, supra note 1, at 66–8.

23.　F. Frankfurter, supra note 1 at 65–73.

24.　United States v. Marigold, 50 U.S. (9 How.) 560 (1850).

25.　Pennsylvania v. Wheeling & Belmont Bridge Co., 54 U.S. (13 How.) 518 (1852).

26.　Act of August 31, 1852 & 6, c. 111; 10 Stat. 110, 112.

27.　Pennsylvania v. Wheeling & Belmont Bridge Co., 59 U.S. (18 How.) 421 (1856).

28.　C. Fairman, VI Oliver Wendell Holmes Devise History of the Supreme Court of the United States— Reconstruction and Reunion 1864–88, part one, at 1426 (1971).

ognize wide federal powers when they held that Congress could pass a tax on state bank notes that would destroy their marketability.[29] But in the same year the Court upheld the state regulation of interstate insurance business because insurance contracts were not "articles of commerce." [30]

The year 1870 saw the Court temporarily staffed by justices who were ready to restrict the federal power. In the first "legal tender case" the Court held that the Legal Tender Acts were unconstitutional as applied to preexisting debts.[31] In the same month the Court issued the first decision which held a federal commercial statute invalid because it exceeded the congressional power to regulate commerce. In *United States v. Dewitt* [32] the Supreme Court invalidated a federal statute which prohibited the sale of an illuminating petroleum product made of naphtha and oil which was inflammable below certain fire test levels. The opinion by Chief Justice Chase found this statute beyond any federal power because the commerce clause was "a virtual denial of any power to interfere with the internal trade and business of the separate states." [33] Although the Court held that the federal government could only regulate such matters when it was necessary and proper to the effectuation of an enumerated power, the opinion gave no basis for judicial review of these acts.

Two new justices were appointed to the Supreme Court at this time and 1871 saw a shift back to deference toward the other branches of government. The Court quickly reversed the decision on the legality and application of the Legal Tender Acts.[34] The Court also gave a somewhat broader reading to the commerce clause. In *The Daniel Ball* [35] the Court upheld the application of a federal safety regulation to a ship which operated solely on a river in Michigan. Since the ship was used for part of the transportation of goods moving from one state to another, it was an "instrumentality" of that commerce. The Court sustained the regulation without returning to the problem of purely "internal" trade. But the justices in 1871 were still ready to protect the states to some degree from the power of the federal government; the Court held that certain federal taxes could not be applied to state payments to certain state officers.[36]

The last sixteen years in this period witnessed no real changes in the position of the Supreme Court. The justices continued to strike down state legislation which would place significant burdens on interstate commercial transactions,[37] and the Court upheld what seemed already to be traditional exercises of the congressional power regarding the building of bridges,[38] legal tender,[39] or trade with Indians.[40] The Court also upheld the Congressional power to license interstate communications agencies by striking down Florida's attempt to grant exclusive telegraph privileges within its borders.[41] However, the Supreme Court did strike down one more piece of federal commercial legislation during this period. In *The Trade Mark*

29. Veazie Bank v. Fenno, 75 U.S. (8 Wall.) 533 (1869).

30. Paul v. Virginia, 75 U.S. (8 Wall.) 168 (1869). This decision was later overturned, United States v. South Eastern Underwriters Ass'n, 322 U.S. 533 (1944).

31. Hepburn v. Griswold, 75 U.S. (8 Wall.) 603 (1870).

32. 76 U.S. (9 Wall.) 41 (1870).

33. 76 U.S. (9 Wall.) at 44.

34. Knox v. Lee (The Legal Tender Cases), 79 U.S. (12 Wall.) 457 (1871); see also Julliard v. Greenman, 110 U.S. 421 (1884).

35. 77 U.S. (10 Wall.) 557 (1871).

36. Collector v. Day, 78 U.S. (11 Wall.) 113 (1871); see also, United States v. Railroad Co., 84 U.S. (17

Wall.) 322 (1873) (payment on certain municipal bonds exempted). For a discussion of the status of intergovernmental tax immunities today, see Chapter 11.

37. See, e.g., Welton v. Missouri, 91 U.S. 275 (1876) (discriminatory tax invalid); Wabash, St. Louis & Pacific Ry. v. Illinois, 118 U.S. 557 (1886) (state regulation of interstate rates invalid).

38. Newport & Cincinnati Bridge Co. v. United States, 105 U.S. 470 (1882). See F. Frankfurter, supra note 1, at 92–95.

39. Julliard v. Greenman, 110 U.S. 421 (1884).

40. United States v. Forty-Three Gallons of Whiskey, 108 U.S. 491 (1883).

41. Pensacola Telegraph Co. v. Western Union Telegraph Co., 96 U.S. 1 (1878).

Cases [42] the Court held that Congress exceeded its power under the commerce clause when it attempted to establish a trademark registration and regulation system that did not exempt commercial transactions occurring with a single state.[43]

As we turn to the next period in the history of the commerce clause, we can see that the Court in 1887 was relatively free to define the power of Congress. Marshall's original position had been one of great deference to the Congress and of active promotion of national power. Under Taney the Court had given greater leeway to the states in the regulation of commerce and this line of cases helped to create the basis for an interstate/internal commerce dichotomy. Following the war, the Chase Court had asserted a new, independent control over the scope of federal powers and for the first time had stricken down federal commercial legislation. Under Chief Justice Waite the Supreme Court allowed a fair range of congressional actions but again the justices had invalidated some federal commercial legislation that regulated the internal commerce of the states. Although Waite believed in giving deference to other branches of both state and federal governments,[44] the Court

in the 1880's was moving toward more active control over the social and political policies of the other branches.[45] And the language finding "internal" commerce beyond the federal power would give these justices a tool for restricting federal regulation of national, social, and economic conditions.[46]

III. 1888–1936

A. Summary

While this period began with a linguistic distinction between interstate commerce and the internal activities within a state, there were few restraints on federal power. In the first cases during this period, the distinction became stronger as the Court edged toward a concept of "dual federalism." [1] This concept involved the use of the tenth amendment to initially define the powers of Congress; under this theory the tenth amendment reserved the regulation of some activities for the states and federal power could only apply to other activities. This theory was the principle behind the Supreme Court's ruling that the antitrust acts did not apply to manufacturing combinations.[2] The production process was seen as an activity reserved for state regulation and the Court

---

42. The Trade Mark Cases (United States v. Steffens), 100 U.S. 82 (1878).

43. The Court also held that this act was beyond the "patent and copyright" power of art. I, § 8, cl. 8. The effect of the decision was diminished in 1903, when the Court, per Justice Holmes, held that lithograph advertisements could be constitutionally copyrighted; Bleistein v. Donaldson Lithographing, 188 U.S. 239 (1903). Later decisions concerning the nature of advertising materials or labels under the copyright power have eliminated the import of this decision. It is thought that a modern Court might overturn this decision, but it is unlikely that it will have occasion to do so since virtually all business trademarks today are found to have a sufficient relationship to interstate commerce to be regulated under the theory of this decision. See 1 M. Nimmer, Nimmer on Copyright §§ 8.4, 9.1, 24 (1976).

44. F. Frankfurter, supra note 1, at 81–2.

45. It was during this period that the Court invalidated the Congressional act in The Civil Rights Cases, 109 U.S. 3 (1883). The concept of substantive due process was being debated at this time. See Munn v. Illinois, 94 U.S. 113 (1877). Justice Field was the leading exponent of using the judicial power against new activities of government entities in the area of economics

and social welfare. As Felix Frankfurter has stated (supra note 1 at 110):

> "when it comes to fundamental issues—the scope of national powers as against the reserved rights of the states, the unrestricted prerogatives of private property as against its social obligations enforced through law—the period of Waite's Chief Justiceship is in large measure the history of a duel between him and Field."

46. This linguistic distinction had become stronger over the years. In Coe v. Town of Errol, 116 U.S. 517 (1886), the Court held that logs cut and stored in New Hampshire for transport and sale in other states could be taxed by New Hampshire. The rationale of the decision was that the logs had not yet been put into commerce on the tax assessment day. The opinion seemed to use a sharp distinction between interstate commerce and local production or storage. For an analysis of state powers to tax items allegedly in interstate commerce, see generally Chapter 11, section II, A, 3, c.

1. For an analysis the concept and its demise, see Corwin, The Passing of Dual Federalism, 36 Va.L.Rev. 1 (1950).

2. United States v. E. C. Knight Co., 156 U.S. 1 (1895).

required a "direct" connection to interstate commerce to place it under the federal power.

The Court tempered this use of the tenth amendment with the "stream" or "current" of commerce theory. Under this concept, Congress could regulate what seemed to be an intrastate activity if that activity were connected to the interstate movement of goods or services. Thus, stockyards could be subject to regulation because they were part of interstate commerce.[3] But this concept again was based on a finding of a "direct" connection to interstate commercial transactions.

In a very limited area, the justices recognized that the economic impact of some activities might create a sufficient link with interstate commerce to subject them to federal regulation. The Supreme Court upheld the federal regulation of railroad rates and restricted state authority in this area because a majority of the justices recognized that the local rate structures had a real effect on interstate transportation.[4] The Court agreed that the railroads were in need of national regulation, so federal railroad safety laws were also upheld.[5] But the Court did not extend the congressional power based on economic effects of intrastate activities beyond railroad regulation.

When persons or items traveled between two states, there could be no question that they constituted interstate commerce. Congress sometimes sought to set terms for the transportation of goods that in effect regulated activities within the states. These statutes were generally "police" regulations, including the prohibition against transporting women across state lines for certain immoral purposes or the interstate transportation of unwholesome food or drugs. The

Court at first upheld those regulations as a part of the federal commerce power, but the justices restricted the power when Congress tried to regulate the employment conditions of children through such a statute.[6] The Supreme Court restricted congressional power over the interstate transport of goods to the regulation of activities that had a direct, harmful effect on interstate commerce.

These cases set the stage for the Supreme Court's battle against the New Deal legislation of the early 1930's. In a series of cases, the Court struck down major regulations of retirement systems, business practices, labor organizations, and agricultural production. A majority of the justices viewed the tenth amendment as committing the regulation of such activities to the states. They interpreted the commerce clause in terms of what the tenth amendment left for federal regulation. Because these laws were not regulations of interstate transportation or the "stream" of commerce there would have to be a demonstrably "direct" connection between regulated activity and interstate commerce. The justices independently reviewed the basis for the laws, and they refused to accept economic theories that might show the effect of the activities on the national economy and commerce. Indeed, the justices went so far as to strike down some regulations as improper delegations of national authority to regulatory agencies—a concept that has had no place in the cases before or after this short period.[7]

The Court placed similar restrictions on the taxing and spending powers of Congress. After having allowed Congress in the past to place prohibitory taxes on some items, the Court refused to allow a tax that would circumvent its commerce clause rulings by regulating the conditions of labor.[8]

---

3. Swift & Co. v. United States, 196 U.S. 375 (1905).

4. The Shreveport Rate Case (Houston & Texas Ry. v. United States), 234 U.S. 342 (1914).

5. Southern Ry. Co. v. United States, 222 U.S. 20 (1911).

6. Hammer v. Dagenhart (The Child Labor Case), 247 U.S. 251 (1918) overruled by United States v. Darby, 312 U.S. 100 (1941).

7. Panama Refining Co. v. Ryan, 293 U.S. 388 (1935); Schechter Poultry Corp. v. United States, 295 U.S. 495 (1935); cf. Sunshine Anthracite Coal Co. v. Adkins, 310 U.S. 381 (1940).

8. The Child Labor Tax Case (Bailey v. Drexel Furniture Co.), 259 U.S. 20 (1922).

Similarly, the Court used the tenth amendment to restrict the congressional power to spend federal revenues. The justices sought to stop Congress from buying compliance with federal regulation of single-state activities.[9] The taxing and spending powers are discussed in separate sections.[10]

It is interesting to note that during this period the Court gave a wide reading to powers of the federal government when the justices did not think that federal regulation affected a subject reserved to the states by the tenth amendment. Thus, the Court upheld the taxing of firearms,[11] the federal nullification of gold clauses in contracts,[12] and the sale of electricity from federal dams.[13] These decisions emphasize how a combination of tenth amendment interpretation and the justices' personal views of national economic policy shaped the decisions during this period. It must not be forgotten that this period coincides with the period when the same justices controlled both state and federal economic and social welfare legislation with the doctrines of substantive due process and equal protection.

This period ends with President Roosevelt's court-packing plan. The President proposed to alter the path of the Court by appointing a new justice for each current justice over 70 years of age. Although the President was not granted this authority by Congress, the Supreme Court did shift its position on these issues in 1937. Natural vacancies and the appointment process quickly solidified the new position.

B. 1888 to 1933

Two early cases from Iowa concerning the manufacture and sale of alcoholic beverages strengthened the distinction between intrastate activities and interstate commerce, although neither decision concerned the scope of federal power. In *Kidd v. Pearson*[14] the Supreme Court upheld an Iowa statute prohibiting the manufacture of intoxicating beverages within the state. The basis for this ruling was the Court's view that this activity could be regulated by the state because it was "manufacturing" and not "commerce."[15] Thus, in *Leisy v. Hardin*[16] the Supreme Court held that an Iowa ban on the importation of intoxicating beverages violated the commerce clause because it regulated an item of commerce before it became part of the general property within the state.[17]

These cases might still have led to a recognition of wide federal powers. Congress disagreed with the effect of the *Leisy* decision. A federal statute was enacted the same year which subjected liquors transported in interstate commerce to the laws of the state into which they were shipped. The Supreme Court upheld this statute against the claim that it delegated federal powers to the states.[18] The opinion recognized that Congress had simply enacted a national commerce law with a rule of localized control. The statute did not allow any state to control another state's laws. Years later, Congress passed a statute prohibiting the transportation of such beverages into states that had laws against them. This act was also upheld by the Court.[19]

9. United States v. Butler, 297 U.S. 1 (1936).

10. See Chapter 5.

11. Sonzinsky v. United States, 300 U.S. 506 (1937).

12. Norman v. Baltimore & O. R. R. Co., 294 U.S. 240 (1935).

13. Tennessee Electric Power Co. v. Tennessee Valley Authority, 306 U.S. 118 (1939).

14. 128 U.S. 1 (1888).

15. "No distinction is more popular to the common mind, or more clearly expressed in economic and political literature, than that between manufacture and commerce." 128 U.S. at 20.

16. 135 U.S. 100 (1890); see also Bowman v. Chicago & Northwestern Ry., 125 U.S. 465 (1888).

17. The case seemed to resurrect the interstate-original package concept expressed by Marshall in Brown v. Maryland, 25 U.S. (12 Wheat.) 419 (1827). However, the Court had held the concept inapplicable to interstate transactions in Woodruff v. Parham, 75 U.S. (8 Wall.) 123 (1869).

18. Wilson Act, 26 Stat. 313 (1890), sustained in In re Rahrer, 140 U.S. 545 (1891).

19. Webb-Kenyon Act, 37 Stat. 699 (1913), sustained in Clark Distilling Co. v. Western Maryland Ry. Co., 242 U.S. 311 (1917).

A related recognition of the congressional ability to share its power was *Field v. Clark.*[20] Here the Court upheld a tariff statute which allowed the president to suspend the free importation of some items if he found the tariffs of the origin countries "reciprocally unequal and unjust." The majority recognized that the statute did not give true legislative power to the president because it set sufficient standards to guide him. Of course, there was no tenth amendment concept of state interests for the majority to protect.[21]

As the Supreme Court neared the turn of the century, the justices evidenced a growing distaste for federal restrictions on business activities. Although the Court did not invalidate federal legislation, it restricted the scope of economic regulations. Thus the Court held that the new Interstate Commerce Commission lacked statutory authority to issue subpoenas[22] or fix railroad rates.[23] These rulings could be cured by new legislation. That was not true of the way the Court restricted the antitrust laws in *United States v. E. C. Knight Co.*[24] In this case the majority held that the Sherman Antitrust Act could not be applied to a monopoly acquisition of sugar refineries. The majority found that regulation of "manufacture" was reserved to the states by the tenth amendment and, hence, beyond the commerce power. Nor could use of the statute be justified in this case under the theory that the monopoly might adversely affect interstate commerce because this market effect was only "indirect." The act was not stricken but it was interpreted to exclude ap-

plication to such manufacturing enterprises in order to avoid constitutional infirmities.[25]

The Supreme Court quickly eased its most restrictive interpretations of the antitrust acts. The Court held that the acts could be applied to agreements to fix prices by iron pipe manufacturing companies[26] and that joint control of competing parallel railways could be broken up.[27] The majority agreed that these practices had a sufficient connection to commerce. It should be noted that Mr. Justice Holmes dissented in the later case because he did not see how the Court could stop short of allowing Congress to regulate every individual activity under these theories.[28]

In 1905 Holmes created the "current" (or "stream" or "flow") of commerce theory. He wrote the opinion for a unanimous Court in *Swift & Co. v. United States*[29] upholding the application of the Sherman Act to an agreement of meat dealers concerning their bidding practices at the stockyards which would fix the price of meat. Although the stockyard activity took place within a single state, it was but a temporary stop in the interstate sale of cattle. It was, in Holmes' words, only an interruption in "a current of commerce among the States, and the purchase of the cattle is a part and incident of such commerce."[30] Thus, the physical relationship to interstate sales established that the activity was not one that should be reserved to a single state. It had a direct effect on commerce. However, the opinion could be interpreted in a restrictive manner because the test required tangible connections and direct relationships to commerce.

20. 143 U.S. 649 (1892).

21. U.S. Const. art. I, § 8 (Congress has power to regulate commerce with foreign nations). In a similar manner, the Court had no problem upholding the federal acts relating to the exclusion or deportation of Chinese nationals in Fong Yue Ting v. United States, 149 U.S. 698 (1893).

22. Counselman v. Hitchcock, 142 U.S. 547 (1892).

23. Cincinnati, N. O. & T. P. R. Co. v. Interstate Commerce Comm'n, 162 U.S. 184 (1896).

24. (Sugar Trust Case), 156 U.S. 1 (1895).

25. See Hopkins v. United States, 171 U.S. 578 (1898); Anderson v. United States, 171 U.S. 604 (1898).

26. Addyston Pipe & Steel Co. v. United States, 175 U.S. 211 (1899).

27. Northern Securities Co. v. United States, 193 U.S. 197 (1904).

28. 193 U.S. 197, 400 (1904) (Holmes, J., dissenting). President Theodore Roosevelt had appointed Holmes in 1902 believing him to have an opposite opinion. Roosevelt was so angered by Holmes' vote, he stated that he could carve out of a banana a justice with more backbone. C. Bowen, Yankee from Olympus 370 (1944).

29. 196 U.S. 375 (1905).

30. 196 U.S. at 398–99.

In the first few years of this century, the Court sustained the exercise of federal regulation or prohibition of items under the commerce and taxing powers. Taxes designed to prohibit sale of colored oleomargarine [31] and premiums given with tobacco [32] were upheld. The justices did not hold that Congress could exercise its regulatory power with a totally free hand. In *"The Lottery Case" (Champion v. Ames)*,[33] the Court upheld the Federal Lottery Act which prohibited the interstate shipment of lottery tickets. The majority opinion by the elder Justice Harlan held that Congress had the power to prohibit as well as regulate interstate movement or transportation. But it was clear that the majority agreed that lottery tickets were an "evil." [34]

The year 1905 marks the point at which a majority of the justices had enough of what they considered to be unjustified tampering with the economic and social order.[35] In the next half dozen years these justices struck down a wide variety of state and federal laws. The Supreme Court held invalid as beyond the commerce power the regulation of sales of intoxicants to Indians,[36] the quarantine of diseased animals,[37] imposition of liability on employers for employee injuries,[38] and the prohibition of harboring alien women.[39] But the justices' special wrath was reserved for laws that interfered with employer-employee relationships. In 1905, the Court had stricken state maximum hour legislation under the due process clause in *Lochner v. New York*.[40] A similar fate awaited any employment regulation that the justices felt was an unreasonable interference with the free market system.[41] In 1908, the Supreme Court for the first time invalidated a federal statute solely on the basis of substantive due process. The justices struck down a statute prohibiting railroads from firing employees for union membership.[42] When combined with a similar ruling concerning state regulations of employment contracts,[43] "yellow dog" (non-union) contracts were constitutionally insulated from reform movements.

In 1908, the Court also began to apply the antitrust acts to labor unions,[44] starting a series of cases in which the courts moved to stop union activities [45] and which resulted in the Norris-LaGuardia Act restriction of federal court jurisdiction in relation to such matters.[46] At the same time the Supreme

31. In re Kollock, 165 U.S. 526 (1897).

32. Felsenheld v. United States, 186 U.S. 126 (1902).

33. 188 U.S. 321 (1903).

34. 188 U.S. at 354.

35. There had already been evidence of this with the extensive use of the due process and equal protection clauses; see Chapter 13 on substantive due process. In addition to the cases we have already examined, the Court had invalidated a federal income tax in Pollock v. Farmer's Loan & Trust Co., 157 U.S. 429 (1895), and on rehearing, 158 U.S. 601 (1895). This decision resulted in the passage of the Sixteenth Amendment.

36. Matter of Heff, 197 U.S. 488 (1905), overruled in United States v. Nice, 241 U.S. 591 (1916).

37. Illinois Central Ry. v. McKendree, 203 U.S. 514 (1906).

38. The Employer's Liability Cases, 207 U.S. 463 (1908).

39. Keller v. United States, 213 U.S. 138 (1909).

40. 198 U.S. 45 (1905).

41. See, e.g., Hammer v. Dagenhart, 247 U.S. 251 (1918) (child labor); Bailey v. Drexel Furniture Co., 259 U.S. 20 (1922) (child labor); Adkins v. Children's Hosp., 261 U.S. 525 (1923) (minimum wage for women invalidated); Railroad Retirement Bd. v. Alton R. Co., 295 U.S. 330 (1935) (pension for retired railroad workers); Southern Pac. Co. v. Jensen, 244 U.S. 205 (1917) (workman's compensation).

42. Adair v. United States, 208 U.S. 161 (1908).

43. Coppage v. Kansas, 236 U.S. 1 (1915).

44. Loewe v. Lawlor (The Danbury Hatters Case), 208 U.S. 274 (1908).

45. Duplex Printing Press Co. v. Deering, 254 U.S. 443 (1921) (printing); Coronada Co. v. United Mine Workers, 268 U.S. 295 (1925) (mining); United States v. Brims, 272 U.S. 549 (1926) (carpenters); Bedford Co. v. Stone Cutters Ass'n, 274 U.S. 37 (1927) (stone cutters); Local 167 v. United States, 291 U.S. 293 (1934) (poultry handlers); Allen Bradley Co. v. Union, 325 U.S. 797 (1945) (electricians); United States v. Employing Plasterers Ass'n, 347 U.S. 186 (1954) (plasterers); United States v. Green, 350 U.S. 415 (1956) (swampers); Callanan v. United States, 364 U.S. 587 (1961) (extortion obstructing interstate commerce).

46. 29 U.S.C.A. §§ 101–115, limiting judicial power to issue injunctions; upheld in Lauf v. E. G. Shinner & Co., 303 U.S. 323 (1938).

Court restricted the impact of the antitrust laws on business when it held that only "unreasonable" restraints on trade were illegal.[47]

Beginning in 1911 the Supreme Court did evidence a greater tolerance for federal commercial regulation that the majority did not regard as unjustified regulations of labor. In the next several years the Court upheld the establishment of safety standards and regulation of hours for employees of railroads.[48] The Court also approved a restricted form of an employer's liability statute.[49]

After 1911 the Court sustained congressional actions that regulated the nature of items which could be shipped in interstate commerce in order to achieve "police power" ends. The Court upheld prohibition of impure or adulterated food and drugs [50] as well as retail labeling requirements for items which traveled through interstate commerce.[51] The Court reversed an earlier decision and held that Congress could restrict the sale of intoxicating beverages to Indians.[52] Additionally, the Court upheld the Mann Act, which prohibited the transportation of women across state lines for immoral purposes.[53] In 1918, however, the Court would once again step in to restrict labor regulation with which the justices disagreed.

In *Hammer v. Dagenhart*[54] ("The Child Labor Case"), the Court by a 5–4 vote invalidated a federal statute which prohibited the interstate shipment of goods coming from a mining or manufacturing establishment that employed children under certain ages.[55] The majority found the act to exceed the commerce power because it regulated the conditions of production. This subject matter was reserved for state regulation by the tenth amendment. The government justified the law as necessary to eliminate unfair competition against products from states that prohibited child labor. The majority of the Supreme Court found that Congress had no power to equalize market conditions that were not a part of interstate commerce. The majority attempted to distinguish the earlier cases that allowed Congress to prohibit or set the terms of interstate transportation of products. The opinion stated that the earlier prohibitions had all related to the elimination of a harmful item or commercial evil, but in the majority's view, there was nothing harmful about products made by children.

Writing for the dissenters, Holmes expounded an "embargo theory" of congressional power over the interstate transportation of people or products.[56] Holmes stated that the child labor regulation was clearly the regulation of commerce among the states and that the Court was wrong to invalidate it because of its effect or economic basis. He would not interpret the power of Congress in terms of its effect on the states. Thus, Congress could set any terms for the transport of items between the states. In evaluating Holmes' theory, one must remember that he was not addressing a situation where the congressional prohibition of transport infringed a more specific guarantee of the Bill of Rights, such as the first amendment. There is no indication that Holmes would have exempted the commerce power from more specific constitutional restraints. Rather, Holmes did not recognize the tenth

47. United States v. E. C. Knight Co. (The Sugar Trust Case), 156 U.S. 1 (1895).

48. Baltimore & Ohio Ry. v. Interstate Commerce Comm'n, 221 U.S. 612 (1911).

49. The Second Employers Liability Cases, 223 U.S. 1 (1912).

50. Hipolite Egg Co. v. United States, 220 U.S. 45 (1911).

51. McDermott v. Wisconsin, 228 U.S. 115 (1913); United States v. Sullivan, 332 U.S. 689 (1948).

52. United States v. Nice, 241 U.S. 591 (1916), overruling Matter of Heff, 197 U.S. 488 (1905).

53. Hoke v. United States, 227 U.S. 308 (1913); also applied to noncommercial vice, Caminetti v. United States, 242 U.S. 470 (1917).

54. 247 U.S. 251 (1918).

55. The statute required that for thirty days prior to the production, no child under sixteen be employed in a mine and no child under fourteen be employed in a manufacturing establishment. Additionally, it set maximum hours and days of work for children between fourteen and sixteen who were employed in factories.

56. 27 U.S. 251, 278 (dissent).

amendment as a general limitation on the exercise of congressional control of commerce.

Congress sought to circumvent this decision by levying an excise tax on anyone who employed child labor under the terms proscribed in the earlier regulation. The only difference between the two statutes was that this tax applied to businesses whether or not they shipped the goods in interstate commerce. In *The Child Labor Tax Case,*[57] the Court held that this tax was not a true tax but only a "penalty" for violation of a commercial regulation. As such, it was invalid under the prior decision because it exceeded the power of Congress and invaded the areas reserved for control by the states. The Court distinguished earlier cases that had allowed prohibitory taxes. "Incidental" regulatory motives could be tolerated, but there was some point "in the extension of the penalizing features of the so-called tax when it loses its character as such and becomes a mere penalty, with the characteristics of legislation and punishment." [58]

The Child Labor Tax cannot be distinguished in terms of its penalty or regulatory features from other prohibitory taxes that the Court upheld. The Court had upheld such taxes on tobacco premiums [59] and colored oleomargarine.[60] Only three years before the child labor decision, the Court upheld the Narcotic Drug Act tax.[61] That act required those who dispensed certain drugs to pay a $1 tax and to comply with very detailed regulations concerning the dispensation of drugs. The Court held that, as long as there was any relation to revenue, the tax could be upheld. The real distinction between these cases was simply Congress' obvious attempt to circumvent the child labor ruling. Once the Court had stricken the

child labor regulations, it could not uphold this subversion of its ruling on the proper scope of federal and state authority. Even Holmes joined in the invalidation of this "tax." [62]

In a companion decision, the Court invalidated a tax on grain "futures" contracts.[63] The act levied a tax on grain, but it exempted contracts made through a board of trade whose practices had been approved by the Secretary of Agriculture. The Court quickly dispensed with this tax, holding that it was a penalty and a regulation which could not fit under the taxing power. However, this subject matter was not totally beyond the federal power; the next year the Supreme Court upheld the Grain Futures Act which directly regulated these subjects.[64] The tax-penalty distinction ended after these cases.[65]

The Court also upheld a series of new federal commercial regulations. In *Stafford v. Wallace* [66] the Court found that Congress could subject meat stockyard dealers and commission men to regulation by the Secretary of Agriculture. The opinion by Chief Justice Taft was notable because it not only resurrected Holmes' current of commerce theory but also implied that activities that had an economic effect on commerce could be regulated.[67] But the Court did not follow up on this concept until 1937. Between 1922 and 1933, the Supreme Court did uphold several more federal commercial regulations. The period ended on a hopeful note as the Court upheld the regulation of railroad labor relations and railway workers unions because disruption in this field could affect interstate commerce.[68]

As we turn to the period of the New Deal, we can see several distinct lines of decisions

57. (Bailey v. Drexel Furniture Co.), 259 U.S. 20 (1922).

58. 259 U.S. at 38.

59. Felsenheld v. United States, 186 U.S. 126 (1902).

60. In re Kollock, 165 U.S. 526 (1897).

61. United States v. Doremus, 249 U.S. 86 (1919).

62. 259 U.S. 20 (1922).

63. Hill v. Wallace, 259 U.S. 44 (1922).

64. Chicago Bd. of Trade v. Olsen, 262 U.S. 1 (1923).

65. See United States v. Sanchez, 340 U.S. 42 (1950).

66. 258 U.S. 495 (1922).

67. 258 U.S. at 515–16.

68. Texas & New Orleans R. Co. v. Brotherhood of Ry. & S. S. Clerks, 281 U.S. 548 (1930).

regarding the commerce power. Under the *Shreveport Rate Case,*[69] Congress could regulate activities that had an economic effect on commerce among the states. The Court, however, did not apply this theory beyond the railroad regulation cases. The Court had also allowed the regulation of single-state activities which were a part of the stream or current of commerce, but this theory required a tangible connection of the activity to interstate commerce. The Court would allow other regulation of commerce only if the subject matter had a "direct" effect on interstate commercial transactions. At the root of all these distinctions was the Court's use of the tenth amendment to reserve some subjects for state authority and its view that the federal power excepted those subjects. Even when Congress regulated the passage of goods or persons between states, the Court might block the regulation of these subjects under the tenth amendment.

C. 1933–36: The New Deal "Crisis"

The election of 1932 created a public mandate for a new approach to ending the economic depression which beset the country. Franklin D. Roosevelt had been elected president on the promise of a "new deal" and of immediate action. Congress cooperated by passing a wide variety of administrative proposals to alter economic conditions. However, the decisions of the Supreme Court over the previous fifty years indicated that the third branch of government might not acquiesce in the new federal approaches to economic problems.[1] From 1933 to 1937 the Court vacillated in the degree to which it controlled state economic regulations.[2] A majority of the justices, however, exercised

strict control over the scope of federal legislation.

In the first decision on New Deal legislation, the Court for the first time in history struck down a statute as an excessive delegation of legislative power to the executive branch. The National Industrial Recovery Act of 1933 [3] [NIRA] had been designed to regulate competitive practices in hopes of increasing prices and improving the conditions of labor. The president was authorized by the Act to establish and enforce "codes of fair competition" for trades or industries. These codes were to be approved by industrial organizations or trade association in each industry before the president adopted them. The Act also contained a specific provision allowing the president to prohibit the transportation of petroleum products produced in violation of state statutes, so-called "hot" oil. In *Panama Refining Co. v. Ryan,*[4] the Supreme Court held that the Act was an excessive delegation of the legislative power to the executive because it did not set any standards for when the president should exercise his discretionary power to prohibit shipment of these products. The Court did not reach the validity of the basic portion of the Act, the trade codes, at this time. But while the particular defect in this statute was easily remedied by legislative prohibition of all interstate shipments of "hot" oil,[5] the majority's use of the new delegation concept indicated that much New Deal legislation might meet with constitutional disapproval.

In *Railroad Retirement Board v. Alton R. R. Co.,*[6] the Court by a 5–4 vote held that the Railroad Retirement Act of 1934 exceeded the commerce power. The Act required and regulated pension systems for railroad employees. The majority opinion distin-

---

69. 234 U.S. 342 (1914).

1. See Stern, The Commerce Clause and the National Economy, 1933–1946, 59 Harv.L.Rev. 645 (1946).

2. See., e.g., Nebbia v. New York, 291 U.S. 502 (1934) (upholding price control on milk); Baldwin v. G. A. F. Seelig, Inc., 294 U.S. 511 (1935) (invalidating certain provisions of law upheld in *Nebbia* because they touched interstate commerce).

3. 48 Stat. 195 (1933).

4. 293 U.S. 388 (1935).

5. Hot Oil Act, 49 Stat. 30 (1935).

6. 295 U.S. 330 (1935).

guished earlier cases upholding the regulations of railroad employment conditions because those regulations related to safety or efficiency aspects of interstate commerce. Here the majority found the Act to be designed only to help "the social welfare of the worker, and therefore remote from any regulation of commerce." [7] The dissenting justices would have accepted the congressional decision that there was a relationship between the financial well-being and morale of railroad employees and commerce,[8] but this relationship was not a sufficiently direct one in the view of the majority.

The NIRA was next declared to be invalid, this time by a unanimous vote. Pursuant to the code provisions already mentioned, a code of competition set for poultry dealers in and near New York City regulated the conditions and price of labor. In the "sick chicken cases," *Schechter Poultry Corp. v. United States*,[9] the Court invalidated the Act for two reasons: first, allowing the president to approve and adopt the trade codes constituted an excessive and unconstitutional delegation of power; and second, the act exceeded the scope of the federal commerce power. The opinion was troublesome more for what it said than for what it did. The NIRA had proved to be an administrative disaster and the executive branch was allowing the Act to expire without seeking its renewal.[10] The striking of the statute on a delegation theory also proved to be little problem because promulgating some standards could easily be done in legislation. Indeed the delegation concept died out after these cases and the Court has never again invalidated congressional actions on this ground. The majority's discussion of the commerce power, however, showed the Court ready to strike down federal attempts to deal with the national problems of the 1930's. The majority opin-

ion by Chief Justice Hughes found that the employment practices of a poultry business did not have a sufficiently "direct" connection to interstate commerce. The wages that employees engaged in "internal commerce" were paid or the hours they were required to work were subjects reserved for regulation by the States. The majority opinion flatly refused to find a basis in the national economic crisis for a federal power to deal with "internal" matters of the states which only "indirectly" affected commerce.[11] Justices Cardozo and Stone, who usually dissented in such cases, concurred in the judgment, although they rejected the formal "directness" test.[12]

Any continuing hope that the Court would recognize a federal power to counteract the Depression came to an end in 1936.[13] In two decisions the majority made it clear that they would interpret federal powers in terms of the tenth amendment and reserve certain types of regulations as the exclusive province of the states.

In *United States v. Butler*[14] the Court invalidated the Agricultural Adjustment Act of 1933. The Act attempted to end depressed farm prices by authorizing the Secretary of Agriculture to make payments to farmers who agreed to reduce their acreage or production. The fund for the payments came from taxes on the processors of the commodities that were subject to these regulatory agreements. The government sought to defend the Act both as a tax and as a part of its power to spend for the "general welfare" of the country. The majority opinion found it unnecessary to decide the precise scope of the taxing or spending powers because it found the Act to be in violation of the tenth amendment, regardless of the enumerated power on which it was arguably

7. 295 U.S. at 368.

8. 295 U.S. at 379 (dissent).

9. 295 U.S. 495 (1935). For a discussion of the *Schechter* opinion's weaknesses, see Stern, supra note 1 at 662.

10. Stern, supra note 1.

11. 295 U.S. 495, 548 (1935).

12. 295 U.S. 495, 554 (Cardozo, J., concurring).

13. United States v. Butler, 297 U.S. 1 (1936); Carter v. Carter Coal, 298 U.S. 238 (1936). The Court also struck down as a penalty a federal tax on liquor dealers operating in states where selling liquor was illegal; United States v. Constantine, 296 U.S. 287 (1935).

14. 297 U.S. 1 (1936).

based. The Court found that the setting of the quantity and quality of agricultural production was a matter reserved to the state governments and, therefore, outside any of the enumerated powers of Article I. Nor could the government offer payments in return for compliance with these restrictions because that would constitute the purchasing of submission to federal regulation of a subject reserved to the states.[15]

The most important decision of this period came in *Carter v. Carter Coal Co.*[16] when the Court struck down the Bituminous Coal Conservation Act of 1935. Under the Act, all coal producers were required to follow the maximum hour labor terms negotiated between miners and the producers of more than two-thirds of the annual national tonnage production for the preceding calendar year.[17] The minimum wages of employees were fixed in a similar manner, and there was a tax on the coal producers who did not comply with these restrictions. The Act also regulated coal prices, but the majority found it unnecessary to discuss this provision because it found the provision inseparable from the wage and hour requirements which it held invalid. The majority held that the setting of requirements by private producers was an unconstitutional delegation of legislative power to private persons. This Act went beyond the earlier acts which had been stricken as improper delegations because this Act allowed competitors to set the regulations for other members of the industry. However, the delegation point was treated summarily by the opinion which concentrated on the national commerce power. The majority opinion found that federal regulation of the wages and hours of employees involved in mining and production was outside the commerce power. The majority

followed now typical tenth amendment analysis by holding that the relationships between employers and employees in all production occupations "is a purely local activity."[18] As such, the subject matter was reserved for the exclusive jurisdiction of the states unless it had a "direct" effect on interstate commerce. The majority found that employment relationships had only indirect effects on interstate commerce. The majority was simply unconvinced that labor relations had such a close relationship to interstate commerce that they should be removed from those subject matters reserved for the exercise of state power. The *Carter* opinion showed that the Court was going to actively enforce its view of the tenth amendment against the national attempts to deal with the economic depression. The federal government would be precluded from controlling employer-employee relationships unless the Court changed its position.

It should be noted that the Court did not seek to restrict federal power when there was no legitimate state interest at stake. Thus, the Court upheld federal legislation abrogating the gold clauses in contracts as a reasonable measure to regulate the national currency.[19] The states had no tenth amendment interest in the regulation of the monetary system, so the Court had little problem in upholding this legislation. Similarly the Court upheld the establishment of a federal dam and the sale of hydroelectric power from that facility.[20] The Court was not going to protect private businesses from competition by the federal government; there was no tenth amendment principle which was violated in the majority's view by the establishment of such a federal facility. Furthermore, the Court upheld a tax on firearms which was clearly designed to be a

---

15. 297 U.S. at 73.

16. 298 U.S. 238 (1936).

17. 298 U.S. at 283–84; quoting 49 Stat. 991, Sec. 4, Part III, Subdiv. (g).

18. 298 U.S. at 304.

19. Norman v. Baltimore & O. Ry. Co., 294 U.S. 240 (1935). Although the Supreme Court held that Congress could abrogate gold clauses in private contracts,

it held that the Congress could not constitutionally enact legislation that would terminate the express contractual obligation of the federal government to repay with gold rather than currency the holders of previously issued bonds. Perry v. United States, 294 U.S. 330 (1935).

20. Tennessee Electric Power Co. v. Tennessee Valley Authority, 306 U.S. 118 (1939).

regulation of transactions in such items.[21] But the majority here found no constitutionally significant interest of either state governments or private persons in the absence of federal taxes or regulations concerning firearms and, therefore, the majority had no problem upholding this "tax." And in January 1937 the Court upheld a congressional statute prohibiting the transportation of articles made by convict labor into states that had prohibited the sale of such goods.[22] In so doing, the Court recognized a broad power of Congress to set the terms of interstate transactions if it did not transgress any reserved powers of the states. The Court, however, was not headed on a course of deference to legislative judgments concerning economic and social relationships. The country received a vivid reminder of this shortly after the *Carter* decision when the Court held that state laws establishing minimum wages for women violated the due process clause of the fourteenth amendment.[23] Despite the Court's favorable rulings on legislation whose purpose it thought was within the proper sphere of federal objectives, the majority had no intention of permitting legislation to alter what it considered to be the constitutionally protected provinces of either state government or private business.

President Roosevelt was not one to accept the destruction of his economic and social programs for the country without a fight. He did not make the Supreme Court rulings an issue during the 1936 campaign, but his overwhelming victory in that election constituted a mandate to pursue with even greater vigor his previous course of reform. In February of 1937 President Roosevelt unveiled his now famous "Court Packing" plan. The President asked for legislative authority to appoint an additional federal judge for each judge who was 70 years of age and had served on a court for at least ten years. There would be a maximum of 50 judges

who might be appointed under the proposed legislation, with a total maximum of fifteen members on the Supreme Court of the United States. Had this plan been approved, there would actually have been fifteen justices on the Court because six justices were over 70 years of age in 1937. The plan produced one of the greatest political controversies of the century.[24] The president and the staunch supporters of the New Deal legislation fought for the bill as a necessary way to allow social reforms and end the Depression. But the Court was ably defended by many persons, not the least of whom was Chief Justice Charles Evans Hughes. Indeed, the fight over the Court Packing plan first brought into being the alliance between Republican members of Congress and conservative Democratic representatives from Southern states. The plan was eventually defeated, in large measure because the justices "reformed" themselves. Beginning in the spring of 1937 the Court began to defer to the other branches of government in matters of economics and social welfare.[25] No longer would substantive due process and equal protection be used to overturn laws which interfered with traditional views of economic freedom. The Court was willing to follow Chief Justice Marshall's advice and interpret the commerce clause as a plenary power without first considering what subject matters the justices would wish reserved for state authority under the tenth amendment. While the full impact of the majority's change of position could not be appreciated for several years, it was immediately apparent that the Court would no longer threaten economic reforms. Did the Court switch under pressure from President Roosevelt or because of realization of its proper role in reviewing economic and social legislation? It is easy to assume that the switch was a product of the Court Packing plan, but it must be remembered that the same period of

21. Sonzinsky v. United States, 300 U.S. 506 (1937).

22. Kentucky Whip & Collar Co. v. Illinois Central R. R. Co., 299 U.S. 334 (1937).

23. Morehead v. New York ex rel. Tipaldo, 298 U.S. 587 (1936).

24. See Chapter 2, section II, E for further discussion of the Court Packing plan.

25. West Coast Hotel Co. v. Parrish, 300 U.S. 379 (1937); NLRB v. Jones and Laughlin Steel Corp., 301 U.S. 1 (1937).

time saw worsening of national economic conditions, including the outbreak of violent labor disputes. For whatever reasons, Justice Roberts began to vote more consistently to uphold both state and federal legislation. This switch was enough to form a new majority on the Court. In the next four years, President Roosevelt was able to appoint seven new justices, all of whom were committed to the deferential approach towards federal commercial legislation.

IV. 1937 TO PRESENT

A. Summary

The Supreme Court today interprets the commerce cause as a complete grant of power. The tenth amendment is no longer viewed as a reservation of certain subjects for state regulation. Once the justices began to define the commerce power as an independent grant of power rather than in terms of the tenth amendment, the production-commerce and direct-indirect distinctions soon passed away. The Court now will defer to the legislature's choice of economic rationale; the possible economic impact of an activity on commerce among the states will bring it within this power. Thus the old concepts of physical connection to commerce and the "current of commerce" theories have been discarded as inappropriate judicial restrictions on the commerce power. The Court has finally returned to Marshall's definition of commerce among the states as that which concerns more states than one. The justices will defer to the legislative choices in this area and uphold laws if there is a rational basis upon which Congress could find a relation between its regulation and commerce.

There are three ways that an item, person, or activity may come under the federal commerce power. First, Congress can set the regulations, conditions, or prohibitions regarding the permissibility of interstate travel or shipments if the law does not contravene a specific constitutional guarantee. Second, the federal government may also **regulate any activity**, including "single

state" activities, if the activity has a close and substantial relationship to, or effect on, commerce. This relationship or effect may be based on theoretical economic relationships or impact. The activity may be subject to congressional power where it is one of a generic type of activities that have a cumulative effect on commerce. Third, Congress may regulate single-state activities which otherwise have no effect on commerce if the regulation is "necessary and proper" to regulating commerce or effectuating regulations relating to commerce.

These powers, like all federal powers, are subject to specific constitutional constraints, such as the Bill of Rights. From 1937 to 1976, the tenth amendment was not regarded as embodying a specific principle which would serve as the proper basis for a judicially enforced restraint on the federal powers. Then, in 1976 the Court revived the tenth amendment as a check on the ability of the federal government to control the activities of state governments. The amendment is not to be used to restrict the federal regulation of private entities or to reserve subjects for the exercise of state authority. The commerce power is still defined without regard to any reserved power concepts of the tenth amendment, but that amendment will void federal regulation of state governments if the regulations imposed severe burdens on the ability of the state government to engage in an activity essential to its independent existence and sovereignty. The Supreme Court will void a federal commercial statute under this principle only if the Court finds that the federal statute (1) governs the "states as states," (2) regulates "attributes of state sovereignty," and (3) directly impairs the state's ability to structure traditional state functions. This tenth amendment principle should give immunity to state and local governments from the application of some federal commercial regulations to them without interfering with the federal government's ability to regulate the private sector.

Just as the older concepts of the tenth amendment have not been revived, there is no significant "anti-delegation" principle which restricts the exercise of the commerce power. Congress may pass laws that allow states to independently regulate some activity; such laws involve a federal adoption of varying structures for commerce rather than any delegation to the states. The Congress may delegate both rulemaking and administrative functions to the executive branch or agencies it establishes. The political process in modern times has resulted in federal control of wide variety of intrastate and multistate commercial matters; it has become impossible for the Congress to define with precision the scope and meaning of its commercial statutes. The past half century has witnessed increased congressional use of federal executive agencies to administer federal statutes and to promulgate regulations which effectuate legislative policies. Today the Supreme Court will allow Congress to share its legislative power with the executive branch by delegating aspects of

that power to executive agencies. Such legislative delegations will be upheld unless Congress abdicates one of its powers to the executive agency or fails to give legislative definition of the scope of the agency's power.[1] Finally, if Congress were to grant a private group the power to control its competitors, there might be a problem regarding whether the persons regulated were deprived of due process by being subject to the will of entities with interests contrary to theirs. However, this issue does not constitute an excessive delegation problem.[2]

Finally, it must be noted that if Congress is regulating an activity that may be deemed to come under the three-part test for the commerce power, the motive of Congress in passing the regulation is irrelevant. Thus Congress may exercise its commerce power for clearly noncommercial reasons. The Court has upheld a wide variety of legislation under the commerce power including health regulations, criminal laws, and civil

1. Since 1936 no federal statute has been held unconstitutional by the Supreme Court because of an excessive delegation of legislative power to an executive agency. The Court has focused on the need for statutory definition of agency power as both needed to avoid excessive delegation and a reason for upholding the delegation of power to agencies. See, e.g., Lichter v. United States, 334 U.S. 742 (1948); Yakus v. United States, 321 U.S. 414 (1944). The Supreme Court has sometimes invalidated particular agency regulations on the basis that the agency did not have legislative authorization to promulgate the regulation at issue. Hampton v. Mow Sun Wong, 426 U.S. 88 (1976); Industrial Union Dept. v. American Petroleum Institute, 448 U.S. 607 (1980). The Court also at times has claimed that it is narrowly interpreting the scope of an agency's legislative grant of power in order to avoid constitutional delegation of power issues. See, National Cable Television Ass'n, Inc. v. United States, 415 U.S. 336 (1974); Federal Power Comm'n v. New England Power Co., 415 U.S. 345 (1974).

Judges who oppose the growth of federal power may seek to resurrect the anti-delegation principle in vogue in the early 1930's as a means of curtailing federal power. For example, Justice Rehnquist would use the tenth amendment to restrict the growth of federal power, see Hodel v. Virginia Surface Mining & Reclamation Ass'n, 452 U.S. 264, 307 (1981) (Rehnquist, J., concurring). The Justice would also use separation of powers, anti-delegation principle to achieve such a result. Justice Rehnquist's invocation of a separation of powers rationale for this anti-delegation argument seems to be only a means to curtail the growth of federal power that occurs when federal agencies imple-

ment their legislative authority by promulgating regulations governing a variety of economic matters. See Industrial Union Dept. v. American Petroleum Institute, 448 U.S. 607, 671 (1980) (Rehnquist, J., concurring); American Textile Mfrs. Institute v. Donovan, 452 U.S. 490, 543 (1981) (Rehnquist, J., dissenting, joined by Burger, C.J.).

When executive agencies engage in adjudication of individual cases their actions may be restrained by the principles of due process. See Chapter 15, Procedural Due Process, infra. Additionally, some judges and scholars have advocated the development of an anti-delegation principle which would deny an executive agency the ability to promulgate regulations or make administrative decisions that affect the civil liberties of individual persons absent clear legislative circumscription of the agency's powers. See, Kent v. Dulles, 357 U.S. 116 (1958) (construing narrowly a delegation of power to control passports so as to avoid first amendment problems); K. Davis, Administrative Law Treatise § 3:15 (2 ed. 1978); Leventhal, Principled Fairness and Regulatory Urgency, 25 Case Western Reserve L.Rev. 66 (1970); Wright, Beyond Discretionary Justice, 81 Yale L.J. 575 (1972).

2. Compare Eubank v. Richmond, 226 U.S. 137 (1912) (holding invalid a law which gave property owners power to set zoning regulations for neighboring property) with Eastlake v. Forest City Enterprises, Inc., 426 U.S. 668 (1976) (upholding system whereby zoning changes must be approved by voter referendum). See generally Chapter 15, Procedural Due Process, infra.

rights acts. If there is a rational basis for finding a sufficient relationship between the regulation and commerce under one of the three tests discussed above, the act is within the commerce power. If it does not violate a constitutional restriction or fundamental constitutional right the law must be upheld.

B. Development of New Standards

In April of 1937, the Supreme Court by a 5 to 4 vote adopted an approach to defining the commerce power which was quite different from that of the previous period. The Court upheld the National Labor Relations Act and the labor board's orders against an employer's unfair interference with union activities in *NLRB v. Jones & Laughlin Steel Corp.*[3] The majority opinion found no fault in the Act, which by its terms regulated labor practices "affecting commerce." The Act defined commerce in terms of transactions among states and "affecting commerce" as those practices or labor disputes that might burden or obstruct commerce. The case involved orders against practices in steel and iron works, but the Court rejected the production vs. commerce distinction. This was most important for it meant that the Court would no longer define the commerce power in terms of tenth amendment reserved power concepts. The steel company was a vertically integrated enterprise which operated in many states. Labor disruptions in its manufacturing component could affect commerce in several states. The majority, however, did not rest on a stream of commerce theory; it dismissed this phrase as only a metaphor to describe some valid exercises of the commerce power.[4] The discussion of the power showed an institutional awareness of the economic needs of the nation; the decision stated that intrastate activities could be regulated if they had "a close and substantial relation to interstate commerce."[5] The opinion did not completely disregard the direct-indirect distinction; the case involved a large multistate corporation.

In a companion case the Court upheld the application of the National Labor Relations Act to a minor clothes manufacturer.[6] The opinion merely cited the facts that the enterprise shipped goods in interstate commerce and that a general strike in the industry in New York had severe effects on trade. This summary reliance on the *Jones & Laughlin* decision further confirmed a trend toward recognizing economic impact as a sufficient relationship to interstate commerce.

On May 24, 1937 the Supreme Court issued opinions on the tax and spending powers which showed the majority was committed to the economic effects approach.[7] In *Steward Machine Co. v. Davis*[8] the Court upheld the unemployment compensation tax and payment provisions of the Social Security Act. Under this system, employers received a credit for payments to state unemployment systems. A five-member majority held that this law was neither the regulation of activities beyond the federal powers nor an unconstitutional coercion of state government to enact such systems. The opinion found that the national tax and spending powers were properly used to prevent the national economic consequences of unemployment and to eliminate the obstructions to state systems caused by the advantage of businesses in states without unemployment compensation taxes. The opinion rejected the tenth amendment as a general limit upon the subjects of federal power. In *Helvering v. Davis*[9] the Court upheld the old age benefits provision of the Social Security Act by a vote of 7–2. The Court was committed to recognizing at least federal taxing and spending powers of sufficient scope to deal with national economic problems.

---

3. 301 U.S. 1 (1937); Austin Road Co. v. Occupational Safety & Health Review Comm'n, 683 F.2d 905, 907 (5th Cir. 1982) (Politz, J.), citing this section of an earlier edition of this treatise.

4. 301 U.S. at 36.

5. 301 U.S. at 37.

6. NLRB v. Friedman-Harry Marks Clothing Co., 301 U.S. 58 (1937).

7. See the next section of this chapter.

8. 301 U.S. 548 (1937).

9. 301 U.S. 619 (1937).

In the next two years the Supreme Court more clearly evidenced its rejection of the tenth amendment as a definitional limitation on federal powers. The justices upheld laws that regulated employment relationships and single-state production activities. Among the acts upheld were regulation of tobacco warehouses to enforce production quotas,[10] product price-setting provisions,[11] and the application of the National Labor Relations Act to small production enterprises.[12]

In 1941 the justices gave a more definite sign that economic impact was a basis for exercise of the commerce power, as they granted renewed deference to the congressional power to set the conditions for production of items that were the subject of multistate transactions. The Fair Labor Standards Act of 1936 prescribed the minimum wage and maximum hours for employees "engaged in [interstate] commerce or the production of goods for [interstate] commerce." The Act prohibited the interstate shipment of goods made in violation of these regulations and also imposed direct penalties on employers who violated the requirements.[13] The Supreme Court in *United States v. Darby* [14] unanimously upheld both the terms of prohibition and direct regulation of wages and hours. The opinion by Justice Stone first recognized Congress' plenary power to set the terms for interstate transportation. It made no difference that Congress was attempting to regulate production in this way because the "motive and purpose of a regulation of interstate commerce are matters for the legislative judgment upon the exercise of which the Constitution places no restriction and over which the Courts are given no control." [15] So long as Congress did not violate a specific check

on its power such as the provisions of the Bill of Rights, it could set any terms for interstate transportation; that was clearly "commerce among the states." The Court would no longer use a reserved power view of the tenth amendment to place other restrictions on Congress. The only impediment to this interpretation was *Hammer v. Dagenhart* [16] which the Court now overruled.[17]

The *Darby* opinion also upheld the direct regulation of the hours and wages of employees engaged in the production of goods for interstate shipment. The opinion found that Congress could regulate intrastate activities that "so affect interstate commerce or the exercise of the power of Congress over it." [18] The Court discarded the production-commerce distinction as well as the directness test and overruled *Carter Coal*.[19] Congress was free to set the terms of intrastate activities to protect or regulate interstate commerce. Congress could choose to protect commerce from competition by goods made under substandard labor conditions. Because competition was a sufficient economic tie to interstate commerce, it made no difference how small the individual producer's share of shipments in commerce might be.[20] The Court recognized that the tenth amendment did not serve as a basis for restricting the commerce power:

> Our conclusion in unaffected by the tenth amendment . . . . The amendment states but a truism that all is retained which has not been surrendered. There is nothing in the history of its adoption to suggest that it was more than declaratory of the relationship between the national and state governments as it had been established by the Constitution before the amendment or that its purpose was other than to allay fears that the new national govern-

10. Mulford v. Smith, 307 U.S. 38 (1939); Currin v. Wallace, 306 U.S. 1 (1939).

11. United States v. Rock Royal Co-Operative, Inc., 307 U.S. 533 (1939) (milk); Sunshine Coal Co. v. Adkins, 310 U.S. 381 (1940) (coal).

12. NLRB v. Friedman-Harry Marks Clothing Co., 301 U.S. 58 (1937); NLRB v. Fruehauf Trailer Co., 301 U.S. 49 (1937); NLRB v. Fainblatt, 306 U.S. 601 (1939).

13. 52 Stat. 1060, 29 U.S.C.A. § 200 et seq. (1975).

14. 312 U.S. 100 (1941).

15. 312 U.S. at 115.

16. 247 U.S. 251 (1918).

17. 312 U.S. at 116–17.

18. 312 U.S. at 118.

19. Carter v. Carter Coal Co., 298 U.S. 238 (1936).

20. 312 U.S. 100, 117 (1941).

ment might seek to exercise powers not granted, and that the states might not be able to exercise fully their reserved powers.[21]

In *Darby*, the Court also upheld the requirement that employers who sold items for interstate commerce keep records of the hours and wages of all employees. Even if some employees worked solely on an intrastate product not directly affecting commerce, these regulations were necessary to full enforcement of the provision relating to employees who worked in production for interstate commerce.

The Supreme Court followed the theory that intrastate action could be regulated if the regulation was necessary to effectuate federal control of commerce among the states. In *United States v. Wrightwood Dairy*[22] the Court upheld the application of federal milk regulations to milk that was produced and sold in a single state. The opinion found that solely intrastate activities could be regulated because the failure to regulate them would interfere with congressional regulation of interstate commerce. Here, the competition of unregulated intrastate milk might affect the marketing of milk sold in interstate commerce which was federally regulated. The Court applied a necessary and proper clause analysis to find a Congressional power to regulate these intrastate activities.

In 1942, the Court completed the move to recognizing a plenary commerce power based on economic theory. It held that particular intrastate activities of very small scale could be federally regulated if they might affect commerce when combined with similar small-scale activities. In *Wickard v. Filburn*[23] the Supreme Court held that a marketing quota legitimately could be applied to a farmer who grew a small amount of wheat, although the wheat was primarily to be consumed on his own farm with some to be sold locally. The Court had no difficulty in upholding regulation of this farmer even though it would be difficult for him to affect interstate transactions. Total supply of wheat clearly affects market price, just as does the current demand for the product. The marketing quotas were designed to control the price of wheat. If many farmers raised wheat for home consumption, they would affect both the supply for interstate commerce and the demand for the product. The possibility of such an effect justified regulation of the individual farmer. The Court deferred to the legislative judgment concerning economic effects and the relationships between local activities and interstate commerce. It was not for the judiciary to restrict congressional power either by limiting the subject matter of the power or independently reviewing the "directness" of connections to commerce. The opinion explicitly returned to Chief Justice Marshall's broad definition of commerce in *Gibbons v. Ogden*.[24] The Court had come full circle and returned to the broad view of the commerce power that had existed for most of our history. Commerce was once again considered to be intercourse that affected more states than one.

After *Wickard*, the tests for proper exercise of the commerce power were settled. First, Congress could set the terms for the interstate transportation of persons, products, or services, even if this constituted prohibition or indirect regulation of single state activities. Second, Congress could regulate intrastate activities that had a close and substantial relationship to interstate commerce; this relationship could be established by congressional views of the economic effect of this type of activity. Third, Congress could regulate, under a combined commerce clause-necessary and proper clause analysis, intrastate activities in order to effectuate its regulation of interstate commerce. The Court would not independently review the Congressional decision on economic relationships or policy. The only significant checks on the power were specific guarantees of the Constitution such as the Bill of Rights or

---

21. 312 U.S. at 123–24.

22. 315 U.S. 110 (1942).

23. 317 U.S. 111 (1942).

24. 317 U.S. at 120.

similarly fundamental constitutional rights or guarantees. The Court did not see any such guarantee inherent in the tenth amendment although the idea of such a guarantee would be renewed on a very limited basis in 1976.[25] Because the Court has not significantly altered these approaches to reviewing commerce decisions, we will only outline the major decisions that complete the modern view.[26] We will highlight some special problems in the next subsections.

Following these decisions the Court had no trouble in upholding federal legislation regulating interstate commerce in "intangibles" such as insurance contracts or securities issues. In *United States v. South-Eastern Underwriters*[27] the Court reversed decisions from the preceding periods and held that Congress could regulate interstate transactions in insurance.[28] The opinion stated that a business which concerned more than one state "is not deprived of its interstate character merely because it is built up-

on sales contracts which are local in nature."[29] Similarly, the Court upheld regulations of securities by the Securities Exchange Commission, including strict regulation of the entities that could control public utility shares.[30]

The Supreme Court has also continued to recognize a federal power to control the methods of production and the sale of goods in interstate commerce. The Court has not deviated in later years from the ruling on the National Labor Relations Acts. It has upheld federal jurisdiction over employment relationships in single state enterprises that might arguably affect commerce.[31] And the Court has upheld the use of the antitrust laws against a wide variety of business practices that might affect commerce.[32] Activities which might at one time have seemed local in nature, such as the practice of law or real estate brokerage agreements, can be subjected to federal antitrust legislation today.[33] In related cases, the Court has found

---

25. See National League of Cities v. Usery, 426 U.S. 833 (1976). The Supreme Court today uses the tenth amendment to protect state governments from federal regulation of their activities; it no longer restricts the federal power over private sector commerce on this basis. See section IV, C, 4 below.

26. The modern approach to the judicial review of commerce clause legislation outlined in this paragraph was reaffirmed by the Supreme Court in Hodel v. Virginia Surface Mining & Reclamation Ass'n, Inc., 452 U.S. 264 (1981) and Hodel v. Indiana, 452 U.S. 314 (1981). In these cases the Court upheld federal legislation controlling strip mining on land formerly used for farming. Although farmland was not an item of interstate commerce, Congress could regulate its use because it would not be irrational for Congress to conclude that the use of such land for strip mining rather than farming could affect commerce in agricultural products or that the mines could create environmental hazards that might affect more than one state. "A court may invalidate legislation enacted under the Commerce Clause only if it is clear that there is no rational basis for a congressional finding that the regulated activity affects interstate commerce, or that there is no reasonable connection between the regulatory means selected and the asserted ends." Hodel v. Indiana, 452 U.S. 314, 325 (1981). These cases are discussed further in Section IV C 4 of this chapter, infra.

27. 322 U.S. 533 (1944).

28. Id., see Paul v. Virginia, 75 U.S. (8 Wall.) 168 (1869); New York Life Insurance Co. v. Deer Lodge County, 231 U.S. 495 (1913).

29. 322 U.S. at 547.

30. Electric Bond Co. v. SEC, 303 U.S. 419 (1938); North American Co. v. SEC, 327 U.S. 686 (1946); American Power Co. v. SEC, 329 U.S. 90 (1946).

31. Howell Chevrolet Co. v. NLRB, 346 U.S. 482 (1953) (retail auto dealer part of manufacturer's distribution system); Plumbers, Steamfitters, Refrigeration, Petroleum Fitters, and Apprentices of Local 298 v. County of Door, 359 U.S. 354 (1959) (half of construction materials from outside state); NLRB v. Reliance Fuel Co., 371 U.S. 224 (1963) (retail distributor of fuel oil obtained oil from wholesaler who imported it from outside state).

32. See Goldfarb v. Virginia State Bar, 421 U.S. 773 (1975) (attorney pricing agreements violate the Sherman Act); McLain v. Real Estate Bd., 444 U.S. 232 (1980) (Sherman Act suit may be maintained against real estate brokers so long as jurisdictional requirement of connection to commerce is alleged and proved in the particular suit). See also California Retail Liquor Dealers Ass'n v. Midcal Aluminum, Inc., 444 U.S. 988 (mem.) (1980) (Sherman Act applies to resale agreements between grape growers and wine merchants even though authorized by California state law; twenty-first amendment, granting control of local sale or use of alcoholic beverages to states does not preclude federal regulation).

33. Mandeville Island Farms v. American Crystal Sugar Co., 334 U.S. 219 (1948) (refining within single state but interstate distribution); Moore v. Mead's Fine Bread Co., 348 U.S. 115 (1954) (baker allied with bakers in other states subject to antitrust laws for actions within state).

that Congress can restrict the use of items following their transportation in interstate commerce. Thus, the Court has upheld the provision of the Food, Drug, and Cosmetic Act that requires precise labeling for the retail sale of items that have been a part of interstate commerce.[34] The Court rejected any possible "original package" limit on the commerce power and held that Congress could set the labeling requirements after shipment to assure that later sale did not undermine Congressional policies.[35] This concept of regulating items in commerce has also justified congressional police statutes, including one making it a crime for a convicted felon to possess a firearm which had ever been the subject of interstate commerce.[36]

Throughout our history the Court had recognized a broad power to regulate navigable waterways under the commerce clause. This power now includes the regulation of both navigable interstate waterways and streams that might be made navigable. When combined with the power to spend for the public welfare, the federal government has a complete power to regulate all waterways, build dams and establish projects to reclaim arid lands.[37] Although Congress has plenary authority over navigable waters, if federal legislation or regulation deprives the owners of private waterways of significant property rights, the federal government must compensate those owners for the taking of their property.[38]

C. Refinement and Application of the New Standards

1. Introduction

There are decisions in three subject areas—civil rights legislation, federal criminal laws concerning traditionally local crimes, and the regulation of activities of state governmental entities—that further refine general commerce clause principles. One must be aware of the approaches that the Court has taken in the review of the federal legislation in these areas in order to have a complete picture of current commerce clause analysis.

2. Civil Rights Legislation

In 1964, the Supreme Court upheld the constitutionality of Title II of the Civil Rights Act.[1] This provision imposed penalties on anyone who deprived another person of equal enjoyment of places of public accommodation on the basis of the individual's race, color, religion, or national origin. The Act covered all but the smallest rooming houses or hotels, restaurants, entertainment centers, or other retail establishments that made use of products that had moved in interstate commerce or that had otherwise affected commerce. The Court upheld the application of the restrictions to hotels in *Heart of Atlanta Motel Inc. v. United States.*[2] There were no congressional findings connected to the bill regarding the rela-

---

34. United States v. Sullivan, 332 U.S. 689 (1948).

The Supreme Court since 1936 has not restricted the congressional power to subject intrastate activities to federal regulation. However, the Court has required plaintiffs alleging that a defendant's intrastate activity violates federal statutes to prove that the defendant's activity has the relationship to interstate commerce set forth in the federal act as a condition of regulation. See Gulf Oil Corp. v. Copp Paving Co., Inc., 419 U.S. 186 (1974) (suit alleging anti-trust violations of Robinson-Patman Act and Clayton Act by producers of asphalt for highways dismissed due to plaintiff's failure to demonstrate requisite relationship between intrastate asphalt producer's activities and commerce as required by those statutes).

35. U. S. v. Sullivan, 332 U.S. at 698. The original package limitation is found in Lyng v. Mich., 135 U.S. 161 (1890) (if in original packaging, part of interstate

commerce and exempt from state tax); Schollenberger v. Penn., 171 U.S. 1 (1898) (state can't prohibit importation of oleomargarine if still in original package).

36. Barrett v. United States, 423 U.S. 212 (1976); cf. United States v. Bass, 404 U.S. 336 (1971). See also Perez v. United States, 402 U.S. 146 (1971).

37. Pennsylvania v. Wheeling & Belmont Bridge Co., 59 U.S. (18 How.) 421 (1856); Gilman v. Philadelphia, 70 U.S. (3 Wall.) 713 (1866); Monongahela Navigation Co. v. United States, 148 U.S. 312 (1893); United States v. Chandler-Dunbar Co., 229 U.S. 53 (1913); Arizona v. California, 283 U.S. 423 (1931); United States v. Appalachian Power Co., 311 U.S. 377 (1940).

38. Kaiser Aetna v. United States, 444 U.S. 164 (1979); Vaughn v. Vermilion Corp., 444 U.S. 206 (1979).

1. 78 Stat. 241, 42 U.S.C.A. § 2000 et seq.

2. 379 U.S. 241 (1964).

tionship between discriminatory practices in hotels and interstate commerce. However, the opinion found that there was no need for formalized congressional findings to support commerce power legislation because the Supreme Court was not the proper entity to review economic decisions of the legislature. The Court found that commerce power legislation would be upheld if there were any arguable connection between the regulation and commerce which touched more states than one. Congress' motive did not have to be commercial because the interstate commerce power was plenary. The opinion dictated the deference due Congress under the commerce power. It stated the proper questions for judicial review:

> The only questions are: (1) whether Congress had a rational basis for finding that racial discrimination by motels affected commerce, and (2) if it had such a basis, whether the means it selected to eliminate that evil are reasonable and appropriate.[3]

Because the records of the congressional consideration of these bills was "replete with evidence" of the ways in which racial discrimination affected interstate travel by black persons, there was no problem in upholding the statute.[4] The Court recognized, as it had done in the time of Chief Justice Marshall, that interstate transactions and transportation fell under the commerce power regardless of whether they were commercial in character.

In *Katzenbach v. McClung*[5] the Court upheld the application of Title II of the Civil Rights Act to the now famous "Ollie's Barbeque," a family-owned restaurant in Birmingham, Alabama, located over a mile away from an interstate highway or major method of transportation. The Act by its terms applied to any restaurant that either served interstate travellers or that served to intrastate patrons products of which a substantial portion had moved in interstate commerce. No interstate travellers were served

at the restaurant. Ollie's, however, had purchased almost $70,000 worth of meat the previous year from a supplier who received it from out-of-state sources. The opinion found that this purchase both brought the restaurant under the terms of the Act and sustained a constitutional exercise of the commerce power over it. The Court noted that no direct congressional testimony clearly established a relationship between discrimination in such establishments and interstate commerce. However, a search for such detailed evidence would have been based on an erroneous view of the role of the Court in reviewing commerce power legislation. There could be no argument with the rationality of the theory that restricting the availability of food and public accommodations services to members of minority races had a restrictive effect upon their interstate travel. It made no difference that Ollie's Barbeque was quite small; the Court recommitted itself to the *Wickard* principle that Congress could regulate what seemed to be trivial activities if they were of a generic category that had an effect on commerce.[6] There were additional bases for regulating the practices of Ollie's Barbeque based upon the effect of the discrimination on commerce and the regulations of goods that had passed through commerce. The Court's opinion specifically stated that it was not abdicating all responsibilities of judicial review but only affording Congress the deference it deserved on economic matters.[7] Once again, the question was simply whether Congress had a rational basis for finding a chosen regulatory scheme necessary for the protection of commerce.

3. Federal Criminal Laws

Another area in which the Supreme Court has given increased deference to the legislature was its use of the commerce power to establish jurisdiction for federal criminal laws. Congress has the inherent power to

---

3. 379 U.S. at 258–59.

4. 379 U.S. at 252–53.

5. 379 U.S. 294 (1964).

6. 379 U.S. at 301, citing Wickard v. Filburn, 317 U.S. 111 (1942).

7. 379 U.S. at 303–04.

establish criminal penalties for actions that interfere with any federal interest. Thus, Congress may establish crimes related to any action taken on federal lands under its property power,[8] activities relating to interstate communications under the postal power,[9] the evasion of tax statutes under the taxation power,[10] or the violation of federal civil rights under the powers granted by certain amendments to the Constitution.[11]

The commerce power also offers an independent basis for the enactment of federal criminal laws. The tests here are identical to those used to analyze the validity of any federal regulation under the commerce power. To be a proper subject for a commerce-based criminal statute, an activity must either relate to interstate transactions, have an effect on interstate commerce, or be an activity which is necessary and proper to regulate in order to effectuate the commerce power. Perhaps the most far-reaching federal criminal statutes have related to the prohibition of interstate transportation incident to some other crime. These include such well known statutes as the Mann Act which outlaws the transportation of women for immoral purposes,[12] the Dyer Act which punishes the interstate transportation of stolen vehicles,[13] and the Lindbergh Law which punishes kidnappings that are related to interstate transportation or commerce.[14] Congress, when establishing criminal statutes, may also make use of its power to regulate items that have passed in interstate commerce. Thus, Congress has made it a crime for a person who is convicted of a felony to receive or possess a firearm that was transported at any time in interstate commerce.[15] The Supreme Court has not only upheld this statute but has applied it to a person who was not convicted of a felony until after he had received the firearm and long after it had been the subject of interstate commerce.[16]

The Supreme Court has evidenced no greater inclination to review criminal statutes enacted under the commerce power than civil regulations. The extent of the Court's deference to Congress was best demonstrated in *Perez v. United States.*[17] In this case the Court upheld Title II of the Consumer Credit Protection Act which makes a federal crime of extortionate credit transactions, an activity otherwise known as "loan sharking." The statute made it a crime to charge excessive rates of interest, or to use violence or the threat of violence to collect debts. The Act did not require any specific connection between the transaction and interstate commerce to subject it to criminal penalties. However, the opening section of the Act included findings by Congress that organized crime was interstate in character and that a substantial part of the income of organized crime came from extortionate credit transactions. These findings also stated that extortionate credit transactions were carried out to a substantial extent in interstate commerce and that even

---

8. U.S. Const. art. IV, § 3, cl. 2. See, e.g., 18 U.S.C.A. §§ 3, 9a, 10a.

9. Ex parte Jackson, 96 U.S. 727 (1878) (crime to circulate materials relating to lotteries). Public Clearing House v. Coyne, 194 U.S. 497 (1904) (fraudulent orders); Roth v. United States, 354 U.S. 476 (1957) (mailing obscene matter).

10. 18 U.S.C.A. § 3045; 26 U.S.C.A. § 7201 et seq.

11. See, e.g., 18 U.S.C.A. §§ 241–245. The Congressional power to enforce civil rights is examined in Chapter 17.

12. 18 U.S.C.A. § 2421.

13. 18 U.S.C.A. § 2312.

14. 18 U.S.C.A. § 1201.

15. Gun Control Act of 1968, 18 U.S.C.A. §§ 921–928.

16. Barrett v. United States, 423 U.S. 212 (1976). In United States v. Culbert, 435 U.S. 371 (1978) the Supreme Court held that the Hobbs Act, 18 U.S.C.A. § 1951, applied to any person who violated its terms by obstructing, delaying or effecting commerce through robbery, extortion or similar activities; the Act was not to be limited by interpreting it to require that such persons also be involved with any specific category of "racketeering." While the case did not involve a specific commerce power issue, it demonstrates the broad scope of congressional power. The Court did not seriously question the ability or wisdom of Congress in passing the law even though it might "disturb the federal-state balance." 435 U.S. at 379.

17. 402 U.S. 146 (1971), upholding, Title II, 82 Stat. 159 (1968), 18 U.S.C.A. § 891 et seq.

where they were "purely intrastate in character, they nevertheless directly affect interstate and foreign commerce." The defendant Perez had been found guilty of engaging in an extortionate credit transaction in his loans to a person in New York. All of the activities took place in the State of New York and there was no evidence that Perez was connected to organized crime or that he had ever used the instrumentalities of commerce in connection with his loan sharking business. The Court upheld his conviction under the traditional commerce power tests. The majority opinion by Justice Douglas found that it was rational for Congress to conclude that even intrastate loan sharking activities affected interstate commerce by altering property ownership on a massive scale and by financing criminal organizations which might operate in several states. The opinion did note that although the Court gave deference to the Congressional findings, Congress did not need to make particular findings in order to support the statute.[18] The Court would have upheld the act as long as there was a rational argument for finding a connection between the regulated activity and commerce. It made no difference that the regulated activity was one of the traditional subject matters of local police power legislation. The Supreme Court would no longer interpret the congressional power in terms of subject areas reserved to the states by the tenth amendment.

Only Justice Stewart dissented in the *Perez* decision.[19] He stated that there were simply no facts upon which he could make a rational distinction between loan sharking and other local crimes. Because he could find no clear connection between intrastate loan sharking activities and interstate commercial problems, he would have held that the regulation of this local, intrastate crime was "reserved to the states under the Ninth and Tenth Amendments."[20] But no other justice in 1971 was of the opinion that the Constitution required that the states be given primary jurisdiction over any subject matter—even traditional forms of local crime.

4. Regulation of State and Local Governmental Entities

The one significant restriction on the commerce clause today comes in the area of federal regulation of the activities of state and local governmental entities. Of course, the commerce power, like all other federal powers, is subject to the restrictions of the Bill of Rights and other fundamental constitutional guarantees. However, from 1936 until 1976, the tenth amendment was considered a truism and found not to contain a specific or enforceable guarantee that might check the commerce power. The theoretical basis for the judicial refusal to enforce that amendment seemed invincible by the end of this forty-year period. Professor Herbert Wechsler in his classic work on judicial review had noted how the Court had failed to find any neutral principle capable of supporting judicial power to circumscribe the commerce clause in the tenth amendment.[21] In a separate analysis of the federal system, he detailed the ways in which Congress was best suited to balance the national interests and determine the freedom of local governments and the legislation which they might enact in the federal system.[22] Congress was the governmental unit capable of resolving disputes between various parts of the nation and creating the proper balance of national and local interests. Because the states have independent political bases and great influence upon the workings of Congress, they had political safeguards against arbitrary or unreasonable acts by the federal government. For the Supreme Court to actively review commerce decisions, they would have

---

18. 402 U.S. at 155–56.

19. 402 U.S. 146, 157 (Stewart, J., dissenting).

20. 402 U.S. 146, 158 (Stewart, J., dissenting).

21. Wechsler, Toward Neutral Principles of Constitutional Law, 73 Harv.L.Rev. 1, 23–24 (1959).

22. Wechsler, The Political Safeguards of Federalism: The Role of the States in the Composition and Selection of the National Government, 54 Colum.L.Rev. 543 (1954).

to sit as a national policy-making body, overriding the balanced political process by the justices' individual views of the federal system. Recent commentators exhibited virtually uniform agreement with Professor Wechsler that "the Court is on weakest ground when it opposes its interpretation of the Constitution to that of Congress in the interest of the states." [23] However, in 1976 the Supreme Court breathed new life into the tenth amendment and declared it to be a specific check upon the power of Congress to regulate the activities of state and local governments.

Since 1936 the Court had several opportunities to review federal regulations of state activities. Each time it found them to be within the scope of the federal commerce power. Prior to 1968, the Court had upheld the application of statutes setting railroad safety, labor relations, and employer liability requirements for railroad companies owned by state governments.[24] Although at least one majority opinion had held that the states could not block the exercises of federal commercial power to a greater degree than private individuals,[25] the Court had not yet considered the application of federal regulations to employees in the purely governmental enterprises of the state. In 1968, the Supreme Court considered the application of the federal minimum wage requirements to employees of state and local government institu-

tions such as hospitals and schools. In *Maryland v. Wirtz*,[26] the Court upheld such an application of the statute with only two justices dissenting. There was no question that the regulation of the hours, conditions, and wages of laborers in enterprises affecting interstate commerce fell within the power of Congress. The sole issue was whether the Constitution carved out an exemption for the employment practices of state and local governments. The Court found that there was no exemption; the federal government could act to achieve the proper goals of its enumerated powers in a manner that might override important state interests. The majority opinion indicated that Congress could not engage in "the utter destruction of the state as a sovereign political entity" [27] but did not set any specific limits on the commerce power. Only Justices Douglas and Stewart, in dissent, would have held that the tenth amendment prohibited federal regulations that constituted an undue interference with the performance of sovereign or governmental functions of the state.[28]

In the 1970's, following the appointment of several new justices, there were indications that the Supreme Court would establish a tenth amendment principle to protect state governmental entities from certain federal regulations.[29] The Court had not decided in *Wirtz* whether suits could be brought in federal court for individual recoveries for

---

23. Id. at 559. Professor Jesse Choper has published a scholarly study demonstrating the ways in which state voters and their governmental representatives have an impact on the framing and implementation of federal legislation. On this basis, Professor Choper goes beyond the Wechsler argument for judicial deference to the federal legislature in this area; Choper proposes that the Supreme Court rule such federalism issues to be nonjusticiable questions which must be left to the political branches of government. J. Choper, Judicial Review and the National Political Process: A Functional Reconsideration of the Role of the Supreme Court (1980). See also Nowak, Book Review, 68 Calif.L.Rev. 1223 (1980) (reviewing Choper); Nowak, The Scope of Congressional Power to Create Causes of Action Against State Governments and the History of the Eleventh and Fourteenth Amendments, 75 Colum.L.Rev. 1413 (1975); Tribe, Intergovernmental Immunities in Litigation, Taxation, and Regulation: Separation of Powers Issues in Controversies About Federalism, 89 Harv.L.Rev. 682 (1976).

24. United States v. California, 297 U.S. 175 (1936); California v. Taylor, 353 U.S. 553 (1957).

25. United States v. California, 297 U.S. 175, 184–85 (1936).

26. 392 U.S. 183 (1968).

27. 392 U.S. at 196.

28. 392 U.S. 183, 201 (Douglas & Stewart, JJ., dissenting).

29. There is little or no explanation for the shift in the Court's position regarding the judicially enforceable nature of the tenth amendment other than the political background and philosophy of the newly appointed justices. The decisions of the 1970's, attacking the established principle of judicial deference to congressional decisions regarding federalism issues were joined only by Republican justices. Those justices were Blackmun, Powell, Rehnquist, Stewart (who was replaced by the even more states' rights oriented Justice O'Connor) and Chief Justice Burger. Unless one believes that either the Warren Court or the Burger

violations of the Fair Labor Standards Act by state-owned enterprises.[30] When this issue was considered by the Court in 1973, it held that the statute did not grant individuals a right to bring federal court actions to collect damages from the state.[31] The majority opinion by Justice Douglas was hesitant to find that Congress would by implication so severely damage the interests of state governments. And in 1975, when the Court upheld the application of wage "freeze" legislation to state employees, the opinion indicated that it relied in part upon the emergency economic conditions in the nation to sustain the act.[32] The decision indicated that there might be some tenth amendment limitation upon the powers of the federal government to regulate state entities absent emergency conditions.[33] Then in 1976, the Court defined a new tenth amendment principle.

In *National League of Cities v. Usery* [34] the Supreme Court, by a 5–4 vote, held that the minimum wage and overtime pay provisions of the Fair Labor Standards Act could not be applied to the employees of the state governments. In so doing, the majority opinion overruled *Wirtz* and dismissed as "wrong" statements in earlier opinions that the states were not entitled to special exemptions from the exercise of the federal commerce power.[35] But the Court did not otherwise disturb basic commerce clause analysis in any respect.

The opinion reached this result by finding that the regulation of all wages and hours of employees of enterprises such as these fell within the commerce power of the federal government. The tenth amendment, however, invalidated the application of the statute to employees of state and local governments.

It is important to note that the Court did not hold that the wages and hours of state employees were not commerce or that they did not affect commerce. The opinion made it clear that the justices had no intention of disturbing the modern tests for finding relationships between intrastate activities and the commerce power. The Court also disdained any use of the tenth amendment to reserve subject areas of commerce for state regulation. The Court explicitly noted that tenth amendment principles would not limit the ability of the federal government to regulate the activities of nongovernmental entities or employees.[36] When the federal government regulated intrastate activities that affected commerce, it acted within its powers. It could regulate activities of the greatest local importance because all such activities were still subject to sovereignty of the federal as well as the state government. However, the opinion noted that the commerce power, like all federal powers, was limited by the specific guarantees and limitations of the Bill of Rights. The majority found no reason to distinguish the tenth amendment from the other amendments and held that it should serve as a specific limitation upon the exercise of the commerce power just as might the first or fifth amendments.[37]

From past decisions on state and federal relationships, the majority perceived a principle which guaranteed the independent exis-

---

Court was more adept than the other at divining the "true" meaning of federalism, one cannot explain the Court's position on these issues except in terms of the political philosophy of the justices. See Nowak, Foreword: Evaluating the Work of the New Libertarian Supreme Court, 7 Hastings Constitutional Law Quarterly 263 (1980).

Justice Stevens has urged the other justices to avoid ad hoc decisionmaking on federalism issues so as to avoid the charge that constitutional law is nothing more than the exercise of the will of the individuals on the Court. See Florida Dept. of Health and Rehabilitative Services v. Florida Nursing Home Ass'n, 450 U.S.

147 (1981) (Stevens, J., concurring, citing an earlier edition of this treatise).

30.   392 U.S. at 200.

31.   Employees of Dept. of Public Health and Welfare v. Missouri, 411 U.S. 279 (1973).

32.   Fry v. United States, 421 U.S. 542 (1975).

33.   421 U.S. at 548.

34.   426 U.S. 833 (1976).

35.   426 U.S. at 855.

36.   426 U.S. 833, 841 (1976).

37.   426 U.S. at 841–42.

tence and attributes of sovereignty of state and local governments. The tenth amendment guaranteed that Congress would not abrogate a state's plenary authority over matters essential to the state's separate and independent existence.[38]

The tenth amendment principle enforced by the majority was clarified somewhat by its application in the *National League of Cities* decision. First, the Court held that the state's ability to determine its employees' wages and conditions of labor was an "undoubted attribute of state sovereignty."[39] Unfortunately, the majority failed to specify exactly what aspects of the employer-employee relationship made discretionary authority in this area an attribute of sovereignty. However, the discussion of the limitation over the local government's freedom to determine the ways in which it would deliver services to its citizens indicates that the Court will only be concerned with protecting activities of state governments which relate to truly "governmental" activities.[40] The opinion thus appears to leave undisturbed federal regulations of state-owned businesses in the private sector. Thus federal railroad regulations may still be applied to state-owned railway systems. This distinction apparently revives what had been believed to be a thoroughly discredited dichotomy between governmental and proprietary activities of state and local governments.[41] Although the Court has not defined the attributes of sovereignty with great precision, it did make it clear that state subdivisions and local governments had an equal right to these attributes of sovereignty and that interference with integral services provided by such subordinate arms of a state government was therefore beyond the reach of congressional power.[42]

The finding that the activity regulated by the federal government related to the sovereign existence of the state did not alone mean that the regulation violated the tenth amendment. This finding required a further inquiry into whether the particular regulation impaired the essential activities of the state. The majority opinion by Mr. Justice Rehnquist, in making this determination, focused on the financial impact of the regulation on the state governmental entities. The impact of the wage regulation upon them would be twofold. First, it restricted their freedom of choice as to setting the conditions under which their employees worked.[43] Second, it limited their choices as to the delivery of governmental services because it forced them to make a minimum allocation of resources for the employment of certain individuals.[44] Thus, it appears that the degree to which the federal regulation eliminates discretionary judgments by the state over matters directly related to its sovereign functions and the amount of the burden on its financial resources are both factors to be considered in the determination of whether a federal regulation of state activity violates the tenth amendment.

Clearly there must be some federal regulations that touch upon even important state functions which will remain valid following creation of this test. As Mr. Justice Stevens pointed out in dissent, any federal regulation costs money and limits economic choices.[45] It is hard to believe that the federal government requirements that states withhold income tax payments from their employees' wages or that states purchase automobiles

---

38. 426 U.S. at 845.

39. 426 U.S. at 845.

40. 426 U.S. at 852.

41. For a time the Supreme Court held that state governments and their agencies were immune from federal taxation of transactions which were "governmental" in their nature. However, if the state activity was in the nature of a private or "proprietary" business venture, it was not immune from federal taxation. See, e.g., Burnet v. Coronado Oil & Gas Co., 285 U.S. 393 (1932); Ohio v. Helvering, 292 U.S. 360 (1934);

Helvering v. Powers, 293 U.S. 214 (1934). This distinction provided little basis for principled adjudication and was discarded as a sole test for determining tax immunities under either federal or state law. See Helvering v. Gerhardt, 304 U.S. 405 (1938); Graves v. New York ex rel. O'Keefe, 306 U.S. 466 (1939).

42. 426 U.S. 833, 852 (1976).

43. 426 U.S. at 848.

44. 426 U.S. at 848.

45. 426 U.S. 833, 881 (dissent).

with pollution control equipment violate the tenth amendment. But these regulations may increase the cost of employing individuals or operating cars to carry out important governmental functions, just as did the minimum wage regulations. Unfortunately, the majority opinion does not furnish a clear basis for distinguishing these regulations. Some help in understanding the *National League of Cities* decision was furnished by the concurring opinion of Mr. Justice Blackmun who provided the fifth vote for the majority. He understood the opinion to adopt a balancing approach to determine violations of the tenth amendment.[46] Thus, in his opinion, the tenth amendment would not be violated if the federal regulation of state activities fit the normal tests for the commerce clause and if the federal interest in the regulation was "demonstrably greater" than the state's claim for an exemption.[47]

In *Hodel v. Virginia Surface Mining and Reclamation Association*,[48] the Supreme Court upheld a federal statute controlling surface mining and replacing state control over the amount and conditions of such mining. In so doing the Court clarified the standard for the protection of state sovereignty previously established in *National League of Cities v. Usery*.[49] The federal act at issue in *Virginia Surface Mining* empowered the Department of Interior to set standards for surface coal mining on "steep slopes" and the preservation of land or topsoil affected by such mining within each state. While a state could participate in the establishment of standards for mining within its jurisdiction, states were not required to act as enforcement agents for the federal government. However, once permanent

standards were established, states could assume control over mining operations only if they adopted regulations approved by the Secretary of Interior. This federal action removed an element of state sovereignty by taking over the regulation of an activity within these states' jurisdiction, but the Supreme Court found that such federal infringement of state sovereignty was not prohibited by the tenth amendment.

To determine if the act was valid the judiciary was only to test it under the previously established standards for compatibility with the commerce clause; "when Congress has determined that an activity affects interstate commerce, the courts need inquire only whether the finding is rational."[50] The majority opinion in *Virginia Surface Mining* then reviewed the tenth amendment principle relied upon in the *National League of Cities* decision and found that three requirements must be satisfied for judicial invalidation of congressional commerce power legislation.[51] First, the federal statute must regulate "States as States." Second, the federal legislation must regulate "matters that are indisputably attributes of state sovereignty." Finally, the impact of compliance with the federal regulation must directly impair the state's ability "to structure integral operations in areas of traditional functions."

In *Virginia Surface Mining*, the majority opinion distinguished the regulation of "States as States", which required judicial scrutiny under the tenth amendment, from the congressional regulation of private individuals and businesses, which are subject to the dual sovereignty of the United States and their home state. Legislation merely

---

46. 426 U.S. 833, 856 (1976) (Blackmun, J., concurring).

47. Id. Mr. Justice Blackmun's concurrence suggested that federal power is not outlawed in such areas as environmental protection where the federal interest is greater than the state interest and where state compliance is essential.

48. 452 U.S. 264 (1981).

49. 426 U.S. 833 (1976).

50. Hodel v. Virginia Surface Mining and Reclamation Ass'n, 452 U.S. 264, 277 (1981). Only Justice

Rehnquist appeared to want to return to the approach used by the Supreme Court between 1890 and 1937. He advocated a return to a strict judicial review of the perimeters of Congress's commerce clause powers. Id. at 307 (Rehnquist, J., concurring in the judgment). Rehnquist's concurring opinion is also applicable to Hodel v. Indiana, 452 U.S. 314, 336 (1981), a companion case in which the Supreme Court upheld the constitutionality of the Surface Mining and Reclamation Control Act provisions regulating mining on "prime farmland."

51. 451 U.S. at 287–88.

regulating nongovernmental enterprises was not to undergo independent judicial review but only to be tested under the rational basis test employed in previous commerce clause decisions. The tenth amendment, the Court held, does not limit "congressional power to pre-empt or displace state regulation of private activities affecting interstate Commerce." [52]

When the Supreme Court, following *Virginia Surface Mining*, examined a direct clash between federal and local governments over the regulation of public utilities, it again refused to cut back the scope of federal commerce power in the name of the tenth amendment. But in so doing, the Court left open questions concerning the extent to which Congress may force state or local governmental entities to aid in the enforcement of federal statutes. In *Federal Energy Regulatory Commission v. Mississippi*,[53] the justices, by a 5–4 vote, upheld the constitutionality of Titles I and III and Section 210 of Title II of the Public Utility Regulatory Policies Act of 1978, referred to by the Court as PURPA or the Act.[54]

The Act had three features to which state governments objected.[55] First, the Act required each state agency with authority over public utilities to consider specific approaches for structuring utility rates and specific standards relating to the terms and conditions of public utility operations. State regulatory agencies and legislatures were free to adopt different standards than those suggested by the federal legislation so long as the federally suggested standards were considered at state regulatory agency proceedings initiated after November 9, 1980. Consideration of the federal standards was a condition for state regulation of public utilities; failure to consider the federal standard would require state abandonment of regulation in this field and result in federal standards in the state for the regulation of public utilities. Second, the Act prescribed specific procedures to be followed by the state regulatory authorities or nonregulated utilities when considering the proposed standards. This portion of the Act required public notice and hearings for consideration of the federal standards, and also allowed "any person" to bring an action in state court to force the state agency to consider the federal standards. Third, the statute required the Federal Energy Regulatory Commission, FERC, after consultation with state regulatory authorities, to prescribe rules exempting certain cogeneration and small power facilities from state laws governing electric utilities and to issue such rules as necessary to "encourage cogeneration and small power production" and to require each state regulatory authority to implement the FERC rules regarding cogeneration and small power production facilities.

The Court in *FERC v. Mississippi* had no problem in finding that the regulation of public utilities, even those which operated in a single state, was within the scope of congressional power under the commerce clause. All the justices agreed on this point, even those dissenting justices who believed that Congress had exceeded tenth amendment restrictions.

The issue in *FERC v. Mississippi* which created the division among the justices related to the meaning and enforceability of the tenth amendment. Five justices found that there was no violation of that amendment in this case because Congress in this instance was only setting the conditions for the sharing of federal power with the states rather than interfering with the sovereignty of the states or traditional local government functions. Justice Blackmun's majority opinion was quite straightforward in explaining the rationale for upholding the federal legislation. He began with the assertion that Con-

---

52. 452 U.S. at 289–90. See also Hodel v. Indiana, 452 U.S. 314 (1981) (upholding "prime farmland" provisions of Surface Mining and Reclamation Control Act which limited mining on certain farmland and required the preservation of topsoil for farm usage in such areas).

53. 102 S.Ct. 2126 (1982).

54. 16 U.S.C.A. §§ 2601–2645; 15 U.S.C.A. §§ 3201–3211; 16 U.S.C.A. § 324a–3.

55. 102 S.Ct. at 2130.

gress could have entirely pre-empted the field of public utility regulation, a point seemingly agreed to by the dissenters. Since 1936 there has been no serious claim that federal legislation should be judicially invalidated because it supplants or replaces state or local regulation of commercial matters; such a claim would be nothing more than the invocation of the pre-1937 rationale for rejecting the political process which has resulted in the growth of federal power. Because the entire subject of public utilities regulation was within the federal commerce power, Congress could condition the ceding of this power to the states upon state agency consideration of federal interests. Thus, the provisions of the federal statute requiring state regulatory agencies to consider certain standards or rate structures were permissible. It might be true that states would feel required to consider the federal standards rather than abandon the regulation of public utilities, but realistically, "the most that can be said is that [PURPA] establishes a program of cooperative federalism that allows the States, within the limits established by federal minimum standards, to enact and administer their own regulatory programs, structured to meet their own particular needs." [56]

The second feature of the Act to which the states objected, the setting of particular procedures by which the federally suggested standards were to be considered, was also held to be nonobjectionable in terms of the tenth amendment. The setting of procedures to be followed by state agencies only insured that the federal interest would be considered and did not require the state to exercise its sovereign authority in a particular manner by legislating on a subject in conformity with federal dictates, nor did it otherwise interfere with attributes of state sovereignty. The states were free to forego consideration of federal standards if they were willing to allow the federal govern-

ment to exercise its admittedly constitutional commerce power to regulate directly all utilities within the state.

The third provision of the Act to which the states objected, requiring state regulatory authorities to implement FERC rules regarding cogeneration and small electric facilities, also did not violate the tenth amendment. The FERC had found that state commissions could implement this provision by "an undertaking to resolve disputes between qualifying facilities and electric utilities arising under [the act]." [57] The Supreme Court found that the statute-implementing regulations only require state authorities to adjudicate disputes arising under the statute. This type of dispute resolution was upheld by the Court on the basis of *Testa v. Katt*.[58] In that case the Court had upheld a federal statute requiring state courts to adjudicate claims under a federal statute. The supremacy clause of the Constitution expressly recognized state courts as a means by which federal law would be enforced. The majority opinion in *FERC v. Mississippi* did no greater damage to the scope of state and local authority by requiring agencies in states which had decided to regulate public utilities to adjudicate disputes within their jurisdiction than the Supreme Court in earlier years had done by requiring state courts to uphold and implement federal law.

The dissents in *FERC v. Mississippi* highlight the relationship between the political philosophy of the justices currently on the Supreme Court and the outcome of federalism cases in the 1970's. Justice Powell submitted a rather brief dissent limited to the majority's upholding the provision of the Act which prescribed exact procedures that state agencies must follow in considering the proposed standards.[59] Justice Powell felt compelled to agree that the precedents of the Supreme Court prevented a return to older views of federalism such as would justify in-

---

56. 102 S.Ct. at 2141, quoting Hodel v. Virginia Surface Mining and Reclamation Ass'n, 452 U.S. 264, 289 (1981).

57. 102 S.Ct. at 2137.

58. 330 U.S. 386 (1947).

59. 102 S.Ct. at 2143.

validation of the substantive provisions of the federal act, though he found "appeal—and indeed wisdom" in Justice O'Connor's opinion. However, he found no basis on which Congress could be permitted to dictate the procedures by which state agencies determine whether to adopt federal standards as their own regulations.

Justice O'Connor, joined by Chief Justice Burger and Justice Rehnquist, issued a dissent that can only be described as an attempt to invoke the principles of federalism in vogue on the Court before 1937 in order to cut back the scope of federal commercial power and protect a commercial regulatory role for state governments that might otherwise be eliminated by the political process.[60] Justice O'Connor found Titles I and III of the act to be unconstitutional [61] because she determined that they interfered with attributes of state sovereignty and the ability of states to structure integral operations in areas of traditional government functions. In her view, the structure of the federal system, which she found implicit in the text of the Constitution and the tenth amendment, allows for complete preemption of commercial areas by the federal government but does not allow Congress to set conditions for the sharing of federal commercial power with the states when those conditions require state governmental entities to consider or implement federal standards in a manner dictated by federal law.

The Supreme Court, by a 5–4 vote, upheld the application of the Age Discrimination in Employment Act to state and local governments in *Equal Employment Opportunity Commission (EEOC) v. Wyoming.*[62] Justice Brennan wrote the majority opinion and found that this ruling was technically consistent with the *National League of Cities, Hodel,* and *FERC* decisions. Wyoming objected to being prohibited from discharging

state park and game commission employees at age 55; the Act prohibits discrimination based on age against employees or potential employees between the ages of 40 and 70. In denying Wyoming's tenth amendment challenge, Brennan found that the state's claim of immunity must be subjected to the three-part test set forth in *Hodel* and that the conflicting state and federal interests would only have to be balanced if the federal regulation met all three tests.

Justice Brennan readily conceded that the federal law prohibiting discrimination in employment based on age did regulate the "States as States," the first part of the three-part *Hodel* test. Whether the statute met the second part of that test by regulating an "undoubted attribute of state sovereignty"—the majority found presented "significantly more difficulties" because "[p]recisely what is meant" by this phase is "somewhat unclear" and "our subsequent cases applying the *National League of Cities* test have had little occasion to amplify on our understanding of the concept."[63] However, the majority did not have to explore the meaning of this amorphous concept because the Age Discrimination Act did not meet the third prong of the *Hodel* test: it did not " 'directly impair' the State's ability to 'structure integral operations in areas of traditional governmental functions.' "[64]

Justice Brennan's majority opinion rejected the state's claim that its mandatory retirement age of 55 was necessary to assure the physical preparedness of its game wardens. Under the federal law, Wyoming could meet this goal by proceeding in a more individualized manner and dismissing only those wardens who are not physically fit. Alternatively, under the federal act the state could keep its present policy if it could demonstrate that age is a bona fide occupa-

---

60. 102 S.Ct. at 2145. See note 29 supra.

61. 102 S.Ct. at 2145 n. 1 (declining to determine the constitutionality of section 210).

62. 103 S.Ct. 1054 (1983). The decision ruled that the extension of The Age Discrimination in Employ-

ment Act of 1967, 81 Stat. 602, as amended, 29 U.S.C.A. § 621 et seq., was a valid exercise of the federal commerce power.

63. 103 S.Ct. at 1061 n. 11.

64. 103 S.Ct. at 1062.

tional qualification for the job.[65] According to the majority, there was no reason to conclude that the federal law at issue would have any "wide-ranging threat to the structure of state governance." In *National League of Cities*, the Court had concluded that imposing the federal minimum wage on state workers would significantly affect state decisions as to how to spend money for other vital programs. In *EEOC v. Wyoming* the Court refused to find that the Age Discrimination Act would have a similar result; the majority opinion indicated that not all federal commerce regulations which affected state resource allocation decisions would run afoul of the tenth amendment.[66]

Justice Stevens, in a concurring opinion, noted that eight of the nine justices believed that the *National League of Cities* and *EEOC* decisions were inconsistent; he advocated a direct overruling of *National League of Cities*.[67] The *EEOC* majority was composed of the four justices who had dissented in the *National League of Cities* and Justice Blackmun.

Chief Justice Burger and Justices Powell, Rehnquist, and O'Connor dissented in EEOC v. Wyoming. These justices appear ready to return to a pre-1937 model of judicial review and close scrutiny of the basis of federal laws which restrict state sovereignty. The

Chief Justice demonstrates this position when he states: "I have reexamined [the Constitution] and I fail to see where it grants to the national government the power to impose such strictures on the states either expressly or by implication."[68] Justice Powell reads the history of the formation of the Union and the tenth amendment to restrict federal powers in this area almost exactly as did justices of the pre-1937 era. One assumes that Powell's ability to dispense with the views of Chief Justice Marshall in a footnote[69] and his rejection of the argument that the commerce power was a central concern to the drafters of the Constitution[70] is a testament to his unshakable faith in his view of federalism rather than a total inability on his part to assess primary and secondary historical materials.[71] The dissenters did not believe the Act could not be justified as an exercise of congressional power under section 5 of the fourteenth amendment.[72] The majority, having found the law to be a valid commerce power regulation, did not address the fourteenth amendment issue but strongly implied that the Age Discrimination Act could also be upheld on that basis.[73]

The *National League of Cities* decision opened the door to judicial scrutiny of the reach of federal power over state and local

---

65. The Court noted that the limited intrusion on state sovereignty might be upheld even if the federal law were deemed to impair the state's ability to structure integral government operations. The overriding nature of the federal interest in preventing age discrimination in private sector and state employment was not negated by the fact that the Act did not apply to some federal government workers. EEOC v. Wyoming, 103 S.Ct. 1054, 1064 n. 17 (1983).

66. 103 S.Ct. at 1062 n. 14. The majority stated that the examination of impact on state resource allocation decisions was to be "a more generalized inquiry, essentially legal rather than factual. . . ." 103 S.Ct. at 1063.

67. EEOC v. Wyoming, 103 S.Ct. 1054, 1066 (1983) (Stevens, J., concurring).

68. EEOC v. Wyoming, 103 S.Ct. 1054, 1068 (1983) (Burger, C.J., joined by Powell, Rehnquist, & O'Connor, JJ., dissenting).

69. EEOC v. Wyoming, 103 S.Ct. 1054, 1077 n. 5 (1983) (Powell, J., dissenting, joined by O'Connor, J.). Powell stated that Marshall's opinion in Gibbons v.

Ogden, 22 U.S. (9 Wheat.) 1 (1829) concerning the scope of the commerce power was irrelevant to the decision of this case because Marshall's opinion was not concerned with issues of state sovereignty.

70. 103 S.Ct. at 1076–77 nn. 2 & 3 (Powell, J., dissenting).

71. Justice Stevens, in the concurring opinion referred to in note 67 supra, examined the history of the drafting of the Constitution in general, and the commerce clause in particular, and the opinions of Chief Justice Marshall on the scope of federal power as a basis for rejecting strict judicial control of the allocation of power in the federal system. Justice Stevens' analysis mirrors that contained in Chapter 3, Sections 1–3, and Chapter 4, Sections 1 & 2, of this treatise. Justice Powell stated that he wrote separately "to dissent from Justice Stevens' novel view of our Nation's history." 103 S.Ct. at 1075 (Powell, J., dissenting).

72. EEOC v. Wyoming, 103 S.Ct. 1054, 1072–75 (1983) (Burger, C.J., dissenting).

73. EEOC v. Wyoming, 103 S.Ct. 1054, 1064 n. 18 (1983).

governments. That decision, and the renewed interest of some justices in protection
of federalism principles they see embodied in
the tenth amendment, may leave in doubt a
wide variety of federal legislation that regulates or taxes the activities of state and local
governments.[74] Because the cases employing this principle are few in number, there is
little basis at this time for projecting the extent of this new judicial limitation on federal
power. Nevertheless, we should note several points that appear to be settled by these
cases and some of the major issues that are
yet to be resolved by the Court.

First, until such time as the *National
League Cities* decision is overruled (if ever),
there is a tenth amendment principle that restricts congressional power to regulate state
and local governments but does not restrict
congressional power to regulate private sector activities. This principle will only be
used to prohibit the application of some federal statutes or regulations to state and local government activities. Where the federal statute or regulation is found to violate
this tenth amendment principle, state and local governments will be given a constitution-

al exemption from the application of the federal regulation to their activities. Even in
this instance, however, the federal commercial statute or regulation will be upheld in so
far as it regulates the activities of persons
or entities in the private sector.[75]

Second, state and local governments will
only be given an exemption from the application of a federal commercial regulation if the
federal regulation fails a three-part test.
The federal statute will be restricted or invalidated under the tenth amendment only if
it is judicially determined that the federal
statute: (1) regulates "the states as states";
(2) addresses matters that are "indisputably
attributes of state sovereignty"; (3) requires
state compliance with the federal law which
would directly impair a state's ability to
"structure integral government operations
in areas of traditional functions." The federal statute will be invalid if all three tests
are met. Thus, when a state engages in a
function that is not "governmental" but only
a type of business activity traditionally performed in the private sector, there will be no
immunity for the state from the federal statutes regulating or taxing that activity.[76]

---

74. The decision in *National League of Cities* has
not been applied so as to impose tenth amendment limitations upon the taxing power of the federal government. In Massachusetts v. United States, 435 U.S. 444
(1978), the Court held that there was no constitutional
barrier to the federal government imposing an aviation
"user tax" on state governments. This involved a flat
fee registration tax on aircraft including those used by
states solely for police activities. That portion of the
majority opinion which indicated that the most recent
tenth amendment rulings would not affect state tax immunity in any way was joined only by four members of
the court. Indeed these were the same four justices
who had dissented in *National League of Cities*. Two
other justices (Justices Powell and Stewart) joined in
the opinion to the extent that it established a particular
test for determining when "user taxes" on state activities would be permissible. Rehnquist, J., and Burger,
C.J., dissented on the point of whether the tax involved
was a user tax; they would have required further proceedings to determine the nature, impact, and constitutionality of the tax. Justice Blackmun did not participate in the decision. Thus, it remains unclear to what
extent the Supreme Court may apply the resurrected
tenth amendment principle to taxation of state activities or the attempted regulation of state activities
through use of the federal taxing power.

The tenth amendment poses no barrier to the prosecution of state legislators who have violated federal

statutes. See United States v. Gillock, 445 U.S. 360
(1980) (refusing to grant state privilege in federal criminal prosecutions for violations of federal statutes
prohibiting bribe-taking and racketeering activity by
officials).

See generally, Note, the Constitutionality of Federal
Regulation of Municipal Securities Issuers Applying
the Test of National League of Cities v. Usery, 51 N.Y.
U.L.Rev. 982 (1976); cf. Municipal Bankruptcy, the
Tenth Amendment and the New Federalism, 89 Harv.
L.Rev. 1871, 1901–05 (1976).

75. For example, in National League of Cities v.
Usery, 426 U.S. 833 (1976), the Court overruled Maryland v. Wirtz, 392 U.S. 183 (1968) only to the extent
that the earlier case had approved the application of
federal minimum wage requirements to employees of
state and local government. The *National League of
Cities* decision did not invalidate the application of this
federal regulation to private sector (nongovernmental)
business.

76. United Transportation Union v. Long Island R.
R. Co., 102 S.Ct. 1349 (1982) (state-owned railroad must
comply with Railway Labor Act mediation and cooling
off procedures because application of federal law to
state-owned business does not impair state ability "to
structure integral operations in areas of traditional
functions.") See also California v. Taylor, 353 U.S. 553
(1957); United States v. California, 297 U.S. 175 (1936).

Even when all three tests are met, the federal law might not be invalidated. The Court has held open the possibility that it might find some federal interests to be sufficiently important to justify impairment of state autonomy.[77] Perhaps the three part test only masks a judicial balancing of state and federal interests.

Third, Congress possesses some power to modify the immunity of states from federal regulations under the fourteenth amendment. Although the parameters of this power are not clear, the Supreme Court has held that states have neither tenth amendment immunity from civil rights statutes nor eleventh amendment jurisdictional immunity from federal court actions under such statutes.[78] Assuming that the Court will not allow Congress to validate all commercial legislation which the justices would find to violate the tenth amendment merely by labeling such commercial regulations "fourteenth amendment" legislation, we must

await future cases to see if the justices will attempt to circumscribe congressional power under the fourteenth amendment so as to eliminate a congressional ability to avoid the effect of the *National League of Usery* decision in this manner.

The federal government may have some power to secure state waiver of tenth amendment immunity from federal regulation or eleventh amendment immunity from federal court suits by requiring such waiver as a condition of receiving federal funds. Again, we must await further cases to find if the court will employ tenth amendment principles to restrict the federal spending power and ability to demand such waivers of constitutional protection for state sovereignty in exchange for federal dollars.[79]

Finally, in addition to the unresolved questions suggested by the above discussion, it is difficult to determine the extent to which the justices will allow the Congress to make use of the state authorities or agencies

---

77. See Hodel v. Virginia Surface Mining & Reclamation Ass'n, 452 U.S. 264, 288 n. 29 (1981): "Demonstrating that these three requirements are met does not, however, guarantee that a Tenth Amendment challenge to congressional commerce power action will succeed. There are situations in which the nature of the federal interest advanced may be such that it justifies state submission."

The fifth amendment limits the ability of the federal government to take property belonging to state or local governments without just compensation, even though the tenth amendment does not prohibit such federal acts. However, no person or entity may sue the United States without its permission. Legislation imposing a twelve year statute of limitations on suits challenging the taking of property by the federal government could be applied to bar state government suits against the United States. Block v. North Dakota ex rel. Board of University and School Lands, 103 S.Ct. 1811 (1983).

The position taken in this footnote was reaffirmed in later decisions. See United Transportation Union v. Long Island R. R. Co., 455 U.S. 678, 684 n. 9 (1982); Federal Energy Regulatory Comm'n v. Mississippi, 102 S.Ct. 2126, 2139–40 n. 28 (1982).

78. Milliken v. Bradley (Milliken II), 433 U.S. 267, 288–91 (1977) (state may be subjected to federal court orders requiring expenditure of state funds to correct *de jure* school segregation). "The Tenth Amendment's reservation of nondelegated powers to the States is not implicated by a federal court judgment enforcing the express prohibitions of unlawful state conduct enacted by the Fourteenth Amendment." 433 U.S. at 291.

See Fitzpatrick v. Bitzer, 427 U.S. 445 (1976) (fourteenth amendment enforcement power overrides eleventh amendment immunity); Rome v. United States, 446 U.S. 156 (1980) (fifteenth amendment enforcement powers override state sovereignty). Hutto v. Finney, 437 U.S. 678 (1978), (Civil Rights Attorney's Fees Award Act of 1976 is applicable to state governments).

79. In Pennhurst State School and Hosp. v. Halderman, 451 U.S. 1 (1981), the Court held that Congress had not required states to provide minimally restrictive treatment of mentally retarded persons as a condition of receiving federal grants which aid states in providing for such care. However, in dicta in a footnote, Justice Rehnquist's majority opinion stated: "There are limits on the power of Congress to impose conditions on the States pursuant to its spending power . . . Even the Halderman respondents, like the court below, recognize the "constitutional difficulties" with imposing affirmative obligations on the states pursuant to the spending power . . . That issue, however, is not now before us." 451 U.S. at 17 n. 13. In this case the Court also found it unnecessary to consider whether Congress could impose such conditions on the states through the exercise of Congress' fourteenth amendment power. 451 U.S. at 16 n. 12. See notes 73, 78 supra, see also Bell v. New Jersey, 103 S.Ct. 2187 (1983) (state sovereignty is not impaired by enforcement of condition of federal educational grants to states when state admits condition is valid exercise of spending power).

in implementing federal legislative policies. The closeness of the decision in *FERC v. Mississippi* makes it difficult if not impossible to tell how the Court would rule on a federal statute which required state agencies to act as enforcement mechanisms for federal statutes beyond requiring the state to aid in the resolution of disputes which occur between private parties and governmental entities under the federal statute.

The entire scope of federal control of state or local governments remains uncertain, since the difference between the outcome of *National League of Cities v. Usery* and *FERC v. Mississippi* or *EEOC v. Wyoming* is solely the way in which Justice Blackmun strikes a balance between competing federal and state concerns. While Justice Blackmun's balancing of such interests is not the "law" of these cases in a technical sense, it is his vote which at the moment is determinative because the other eight justices are now evenly split between a position advocating judicial deference to the congressional definition of commerce power over state and local governments and active judicial scrutiny of the permissible scope of such power.[80]

---

80. Brennan, Marshall, White and Stevens, JJ., would defer to Congress. Burger, C.J., and O'Connor, Powell and Rehnquist, JJ., would limit congressional power. In National League of Cities v. Usery, 426 U.S. 833 (1976), Rehnquist, J., wrote a majority opinion joined by Stewart, Blackmun, Powell, JJ., and Burger, C.J., Brennan, Marshall, Stevens, and White, JJ., were in dissent. In FERC v. Mississippi, 102 S.Ct. 2126 (1982), Burger, C.J., and Powell, Rehnquist and O'Connor, JJ. (who replaced Stewart) were in dissent. Brennan, Marshall, Stevens and White, JJ., had moved to the majority side by acquiring the vote of Justice Blackmun. In EEOC v. Wyoming, 103 S.Ct. 1054 (1983), the majority was composed of Justices Blackmun, Brennan, Marshall, Stevens and White; Chief Justice Burger and Justices O'Connor, Powell, and Rehnquist were in dissent.

CHAPTER FIVE

FEDERAL FISCAL POWERS

I. INTRODUCTION

Federal fiscal powers are comprehensive and exert a controlling impact upon the nation's economy. It is appropriate to observe not only that these powers are among the most important of the powers granted to the federal government, but also that the constitutional issues with respect to these powers have been firmly established. These powers include the power to tax, the power to coin money and to borrow on the credit of the United States, and the power to spend. Each of these is briefly discussed in the following sections.

1. The following Constitutional provisions directly relate to the substantive taxing powers granted to the federal government:

(a) *Article I, Section 2, clause 3:*

"Representatives and direct Taxes shall be apportioned among the several States which may be included within this Union, according to their respective Numbers . . . ."

(b) *Article I, Section 8, clause 1:*

"The Congress shall have Power To lay and collect Taxes, Duties, Imposts and Excises, to pay the Debts and provide for the common Defence and general Welfare of the United States; but all Duties, Im-

II. POWER TO TAX

A. General Scope of the Taxing Power

Broad powers of taxation are granted to Congress by express provisions of the Constitution.[1] Except for two specific limitations upon the exercise of the power and one prohibition, the power to tax is plenary. The specific limitations upon the exercise of the power to tax are these: (1) direct taxes and capitation taxes must be allocated among the states in proportion to population; and (2) all custom duties and excise taxes must be uniform throughout the United States.

posts and Excises shall be uniform throughout the United States."

(c) *Article I, Section 9, clauses 4 and 5:*

"No Capitation, or other direct, Tax shall be laid, unless in Proportion to the Census or Enumeration herein before directed to be taken.

"No Tax or Duty shall be laid on Articles exported from any State."

(d) *Sixteenth Amendment:*

"The Congress shall have power to lay and collect taxes on incomes, from whatever source derived, without apportionment among the several States, and without regard to any census or enumeration."

The single prohibition is that no duty shall be levied upon exports from any state. The due process clause of the fifth amendment operates, of course, as a general limitation upon the exercise of the power to tax.

The Sixteenth Amendment which permits imposition of a federal income tax without apportionment among the states was necessitated by the five to four decision in *Pollock v. Farmer's Loan & Trust Co.* [2] Forty-two years later, with its decision in *New York ex rel. Cohn v. Graves,* [3] the Court in effect overruled *Pollock* and in so doing rendered the Sixteenth Amendment redundant.

B. Direct vs. Indirect Taxes

1. *Historical Background*

Although the Constitutional grant of taxing power to the federal government is very broad, the dichotomy between direct and indirect taxes ultimately proved to be a stumbling block in the development of our present federal tax structure. Prior to the decision in *Pollock* in 1895, it had been the general consensus that the term "direct" tax employed in the Constitution embraced only taxes on land (real property) and poll or capitation taxes. This consensus was firmly founded. The Court had expressed this view in at least three significant cases. The first was *Hylton v. United States* [4] in which the Court in the early years of the new Constitution sustained a federal tax on carriages as a duty or excise which was not subject to ap-

portionment. The second case was *Veazie Bank v. Fenno* [5] in which the Court sustained as an indirect tax a prohibitory tax (duty) upon the issuance and circulation of state bank notes. The third and most important was the decision in *Springer v. United States* [6] in which the Court sustained the Civil War Income Tax Act as an excise or duty which was not subject to apportionment. In light of existing precedent, the decision in *Pollock* came as a notable surprise. In *Pollock*, the Court held that the Income Tax Act of 1894 was a direct tax and unconstitutional and void because it imposed a tax on income from real estate and personal property without apportionment.[7] It is important to note, however, that in its decision on rehearing, the majority of the Court made the following observation with respect to taxes on the income of business and occupations:

> We have considered the act only in respect of the tax on income derived from real estate, and from invested personal property, and have not commented on so much of it as bears on gains or profits from business, privileges, or employments, in view of the instances in which taxation on business, privileges, or employments has assumed the guise of an excise tax and been sustained as such.[8]

This exception to the basic decision was significant in that the Court made it clear that a tax on income from business and occupations was not a direct tax and could be subjected to taxation without the necessity of apportionment on the basis of population.

2. 157 U.S. 429 (initial decision), 158 U.S. 601 (decision on rehearing) (1895) (tax upon income from real and personal property held invalid in the absence of apportionment).

3. 300 U.S. 308 (1937) (sustaining New York income tax on income derived by New York resident from New Jersey real estate).

4. 3 U.S. (3 Dall.) 171 (1796) Mr. Justice Patterson who had participated in the Constitutional Convention made the following statement in his separate opinion: "I never entertained a doubt that the principal, I will not say the only objects, that the framers of the constitution contemplated as falling within the rule of apportionment [as a direct tax], were a capitation tax and a tax on land." Id. at 3 Dallas 177.

5. 75 U.S. (8 Wall.) 533 (1869). In its decision the Court made the following observation: "It may be

rightly affirmed, therefore, that in the practical construction of the Constitution by Congress, direct taxes have been limited to taxes on land and appurtenances, and taxes on polls, or capitation taxes." Id. at 544.

6. 102 U.S. 586 (1880). The Court summarized its position as to the nature of a direct tax in the following extract: "Our conclusions are, that *direct taxes*, within the meaning of the Constitution, are only capitation taxes, as expressed in that instrument, and taxes on real estate; and that the tax of which the plaintiff . . . complains is within the category of an excise or duty." Id. at 602.

7. The Court also held that under the doctrine of intergovernmental immunity the tax was invalid insofar as it applied to interest on state and municipal obligations.

8. 158 U.S. at 635.

The "undoing" of the *Pollock* decision by the adoption of the sixteenth amendment provides a fascinating chapter in American history.[9] The Populist movement which had produced the Income Tax Act of 1894 continued to gain momentum. In the campaign of 1908, the Democratic platform contained a plank supporting a constitutional amendment to authorize an income tax. William Howard Taft, the Republican candidate, in the course of the campaign expressed the view that the country could have an income tax without a constitutional amendment. In 1909, the pressure for an income tax culminated in a compromise with the addition of the Corporate Excise Tax of 1909 as an amendment to the Payne-Aldrich Tariff Bill and the adoption of a joint resolution by the Senate and House of Representatives submitting the sixteenth amendment to the states for ratification. On February 25, 1913, the Secretary of State issued a proclamation declaring that the amendment had been duly ratified.

In the meantime, the Corporate Excise Tax Act of 1909 had been challenged and sustained in *Flint v. Stone Tracy Co.*[10] The statute provided that every corporation "engaged in business in any state or territory" was required "to pay annually a special excise tax with respect to the carrying on or doing business" at the rate of one percent upon all net income in excess of five thousand dollars. The constitutional challenge was based upon *Pollock* and was premised on the contention that the tax was invalid as an unapportioned direct tax inasmuch as it applied to corporate income derived from real and personal property. In *Pollock*, the majority of the Court had concluded that a tax upon income from property was the equivalent of a direct tax upon the income-producing property itself.

In sustaining the validity of the Corporation Excise Tax Act of 1909, the Court first noted that the statute was structured "as a tax upon the doing of business in a corporate capacity" and that "the measure of the tax [was] . . . income."[11] Having defined the structure of the tax, the Court considered the issue as to whether a tax cast in such form, and computed upon all income including income derived from property, constituted a direct tax upon real and personal property within the proscription of the *Pollock* case.

In reliance upon several decisions, including *Pollock*, the Court concluded that the rationale of the latter was not controlling. First, the Court noted its statement in *Pollock* that the decision therein did not bear "on gains or profits from business, privileges, or employments, in view of the instances in which taxation on business, privileges, or employments has assumed the guise of an excise tax and been sustained as such."[12] Additional reliance was placed by the Court upon *Knowlton v. Moore*,[13] sustaining a federal legacy tax as an excise upon the transmission of property by inheritance, and *Spreckels Sugar Refining Co. v. McClain*,[14] sustaining a special tax measured by gross receipts upon the businesses of refining oil or sugar as an excise with respect to carrying on such businesses. After reviewing several cases relating to state franchise taxes, the Court finally summarized its position with respect to the difference between the subject and the measure of a tax with the following comment:

It is . . . well settled by the decisions of this court that when the sovereign authority has exercised the right to tax a legitimate subject of taxation as an exercise of a franchise or privilege, it is no objection that the measure of taxation is found in the income produced in part from property which of itself considered is non-taxable. Applying that doctrine to this case, the measure of taxation being the income of the corporation from all sources, as that is but the measure of a privilege tax within the

---

9. See R. Paul, Taxation in the United States, Chs. I–III (1954).

10. 220 U.S. 107 (1911).

11. Id. at 146.

12. Id. at 148.

13. 178 U.S. 41 (1900).

14. 192 U.S. 397 (1904).

lawful authority of Congress to impose, it is no valid objection that this measure includes, in part at least, property which as such could not be directly taxed.[15]

Thus, the Court reasserted its adherence to the doctrine that, if the subject of a tax is within the taxing power, the measure of the tax is not a matter of judicial concern.

2. Current Status of Direct vs. Indirect Taxes

As indicated by the citations in *Flint v. Stone Tracy* of intervening decisions subsequent to *Pollock*, and as confirmed by later Court decisions, the dichotomy between direct and indirect taxes is no longer a problem. The Court has held that the following taxes are indirect (excise) taxes and not direct taxes subject to the requirement of apportionment: federal legacy tax of 1898;[16] special federal tobacco tax of 1898;[17] special excise tax of 1898 imposed on the business of refining sugar and computed upon gross annual receipts;[18] federal estate tax enacted in 1916;[19] and the federal gift tax of 1924.[20]

C. Federal Taxing Power and Due Process

On rare occasions and seldom with success,[21] due process objections have been raised with respect to federal tax provisions. In *Brushaber v. Union Pacific R.R. Co.*,[22] the first income tax (enacted in October, 1913, following ratification of the sixteenth amendment) was challenged on several due process grounds, including the fact that it was retroactive to March 1, 1913, and the fact that it provided for graduated rates.

These contentions were brushed aside by the Court with the following observation:

> So far as the due process clause of the Fifth Amendment is relied upon, it suffices to say that there is no basis for such reliance since it is equally well settled that such clause is not a limitation upon the taxing power conferred upon Congress by the Constitution; in other words, that the Constitution does not conflict with itself by conferring upon the one hand a taxing power and taking the same power away on the other by the limitations of the due process clause.[23]

In two subsequent income tax cases, the Court again refused to recognize the taxpayer's due process objections. The first was *Corliss v. Bowers*[24] in which the taxpayer challenged the provisions which taxed the income of revocable trusts to the settlor. The second was *Burnet v. Wells*[25] in which the taxpayer challenged the provisions for taxing the income of irrevocable life insurance trusts to the insured-settlor. In *Corliss v. Bowers*, the Court concluded that it was reasonable to tax one on income which was subject to his unfettered control and which he was free to enjoy at any time he saw fit. In *Burnet v. Wells*, the Court concluded that it was reasonable to tax the settlor on the income applied to maintain insurance policies on his own life for the benefit of family members since, in effect, he had reserved the income for his own peace of mind. The following statement summarizes the rationale of the Court's decision:

> Income permanently applied by the act of the taxpayer to the maintenance of contracts of insurance made in his name for the support of his dependents is income used for his benefit in such a sense and to such a degree that there is

---

15. 220 U.S. at 165.

16. Knowlton v. Moore, 178 U.S. 41 (1900).

17. Patton v. Brady, 184 U.S. 608 (1902).

18. Spreckels Sugar Refining Co. v. McClain, 192 U.S. 397 (1904).

19. New York Trust Co. v. Eisner, 256 U.S. 345 (1921).

20. Bromley v. McCaughn, 280 U.S. 124 (1929).

21. In Nichols v. Coolidge, 274 U.S. 531 (1927), the Court held that there was a violation of due process in

taxing, as part of the decedent's gross estate, a transfer of property which had been completed prior to the enactment of the federal estate tax in 1916.

22. 240 U.S. 1 (1916).

23. Id. at 24. The Court also noted that retroactive provisions of the Civil War Income Tax had been sustained in Stockdale v. Atlantic Insurance Co., 87 U.S. (20 Wall.) 323 (1873).

24. 281 U.S. 376 (1930).

25. 289 U.S. 670 (1933).

nothing arbitrary or tyrannical in taxing it as his.[26]

D.   Federal Taxes as Regulatory Measures

A tax, whatever the type, has an inherent economic impact on business and commerce. This is unavoidable, however desirable the ideal of a neutral tax system. Custom duties which until the turn of the century provided the major portion of federal revenues were also regulatory in that certain tariffs protected American manufacturers against competition from foreign goods. But it was not until 1928 that the Court in *J. W. Hampton Co. v. United States*[1] sustained the validity of protective tariffs which tended to produce little or no revenue. In sustaining the power of Congress to impose protective tariffs, the Court noted the historical background of our tariff policy going back to the first session of Congress and concluded with the following observation:

Whatever we may think of the wisdom of a protection policy, we can not hold it unconstitutional.

So long as the motive of Congress and the effect of its legislative action are to secure revenue for the benefit of the general government, the existence of other motives in the selection of the subjects of taxes can not invalidate Congressional action.[2]

In an earlier decision, *McCray v. United States*,[3] the Court had sustained a federal excise tax of ten cents per pound imposed upon the sale of colored oleomargarine. Taxpayer alleged that the tax was prohibitory and therefore a violation of the due process provisions of the fifth amendment. In its opinion the Court stated:

Since . . . the taxing power conferred by the Constitution knows no limits except those

expressly stated in that instrument, it must follow, if a tax be within the lawful power, the exertion of that power may not be judicially restrained because of the results to arise from its exercise.[4]

The Court continued by noting that it would be improper for the judicial branch to inquire into the underlying motives of the Congress irrespective of the purpose of the Act.

On the point of regulatory taxes, it should be observed that a federal tax *qua* tax may be a valid exercise of the taxing power but subject to specific constitutional limitations such as the prohibition against self-incrimination.[5] It was held in the *Child Labor Tax Case*, that the federal government had violated the tenth amendment by infringing upon the powers reserved to the state.[6] Today the Court does not apply the tenth amendment in this manner although it does consider the tenth amendment to be a check upon the power of the federal government under the commerce clause to control the activities of state and local governments.[7]

E.   Power to Spend

The Constitutional power to spend is a condition imposed on the power to tax. Under the constitutional provision, the power to spend is coupled with the power to tax and is cast in terms of power to tax "and provide for the common Defense and general Welfare."[1] There have been no Court decisions directly involving the issue of the power to spend to provide for the common defense. However, the Court has considered the question as to the nature and extent of the power to spend for the general welfare.[2]

---

26. Id. at 680–81.

1. 276 U.S. 394 (1928).

2. Id. at 412.

3. 195 U.S. 27 (1904).

4. Id. at 59.

5. E.g., Marchetti v. United States, 390 U.S. 39 (1968).

6. 259 U.S. 20 (1922).

7. To date the Court has resurrected the tenth amendment only as a check on the federal regulatory power under the Commerce Clause. See Chapter 4, The Federal Commerce Power, Section IV, C, 4.

1. U.S. Const. art. I, § 8, cl. 1.

2. The dearth of decisions directly bearing on the power to spend is related to the general lack of taxpayer standing to sue to enjoin expenditure of federal funds. Massachusetts v. Mellon, 262 U.S. 447 (1923). Contrary to the state rule applicable at the state and

In *United States v. Butler*,[3] decided in 1936, the Court for the first time provided a definitive guide with respect to the power to spend for the general welfare:

> The Congress is expressly empowered to lay taxes to provide for the general welfare. Funds in the Treasury as a result of taxation may be expended only through appropriation. (Article I, § 9, cl. 7.) They can never accomplish the objects for which they were collected unless the power to appropriate is as broad as the power to tax. The necessary implication from the terms of the grant is that the public funds may be appropriated "to provide for the general welfare of the United States." These words cannot be meaningless, else they would not have been used. The conclusion must be that they were intended to limit and define the granted power to raise and to expend money. How shall they be construed to effectuate the intent of the instrument?
>
> Since the foundation of the Nation sharp differences of opinion have persisted as to the true interpretation of the phrase. Madison asserted it amounted to no more than a reference to the other powers enumerated in the subsequent clauses of the same section; that, as the United States is a government of limited and enumerated powers, the grant of power to tax and spend for the general national welfare must be confined to the enumerated legislative fields committed to the Congress. In this view the phrase is merely tautology, for taxation and appropriation are or may be necessary incidents of the exercise of any of the enumerated legislative powers. Hamilton, on the other hand, maintained the clause confers a power separate and distinct from those later enumerated, is not restricted in meaning by the grant of them, and Congress consequently has a substantive power to tax and to appropriate, limited only by the requirement that it shall be exercised to provide for the general welfare of the United States. Each contention has had the support of those whose views are entitled to weight. This court has noticed the question, but has never found it necessary to decide which is the true construction. Mr. Justice Story, in his Commentaries, espouses the Hamiltonian position. We shall not review the writings of public men and commentators or discuss the legislative practice. Study of all these leads us to conclude that the reading advocated by Mr. Justice Story is the correct one. While therefore, the power to tax is not unlimited, its confines are set in the clause which confers it, and not in those of section 8 which bestow and define the legislative powers of the Congress. It results that the power of Congress to authorize expenditure of public moneys for public purposes is not limited by the direct grants of legislative power found in the Constitution.[4]

Although the Court provided a broad construction of the power to spend for the general welfare, it proceeded to hold the Agricultural Adjustment Act of 1933 to be an unconstitutional invasion of state powers reserved under the tenth amendment. This result was rectified the following year with the decisions in *Steward Machine Co. v. Davis*[5] and *Helvering v. Davis*.[6] In these cases, the Court sustained the Social Security Act of 1935 as a proper exercise of federal authority which did not invade the province of the states under the tenth amendment.

Today the Supreme Court will not attempt to reserve areas of activity for the sole control of state governments. Thus federal spending programs will not be invalidated because they invade the "police power" of the states and influence local activities.[7] The spending program will be upheld so long as its substantive provisions do not violate a

---

local level, taxpayer standing to sue is narrowly circumscribed except for alleged violation of the Establishment Clause of the First Amendment.

3.   297 U.S. 1 (1936).

4.   Id. at 65–66 (footnote omitted).

5.   301 U.S. 548 (1937).

6.   301 U.S. 619 (1937).

7.   See, e.g., Oklahoma v. United States Civil Service Comm'n, 330 U.S. 127 (1947), upholding Congressional power to withhold from a state those highway funds supplied by the federal government unless the state removed a state official who had engaged in certain political activities prohibited by federal law; although Congress had no direct power to place local officials under the Hatch Act, it would require, *as a condition of receiving federal funds*, that the state accept the restrictions of the federal Hatch Act. Cf. United Public Workers v. Mitchell, 330 U.S. 75 (1947). See generally, P. Hay and R. Rotunda, The United States Federal System: Legal Integration in the American Experience 169–84 (Giuffrè, Milan, 1982).

specific check on the federal power. The most recent example of this is *Buckley v. Valeo*[8] wherein the Court upheld the establishment of the Presidental Election Campaign Fund. Since the grant of public funds for presidential candidates did not violate any specific check upon the federal power or limit any fundamental rights the provision was sustained under the rule stated in the *Butler* decision as an expenditure to promote the general welfare.

III. POWER TO BORROW AND TO CONTROL THE CURRENCY

The grant of power to Congress to borrow is general and unlimited.[1] Exercise of the power to borrow is within the exclusive discretion of Congress and is considered in conjunction with the correlative power to coin money and regulate the value thereof.[2] The most significant aspect of the power to borrow and to coin money is the exercise of that power in the establishment of the national banking system,[3] the establishment of the federal reserve system with its control over the currency and money supply,[4] and the establishment of other federal credit facilities such as the federal land bank system.[5] The power to create a national banking system to implement the fiscal operations of the federal government includes the power to limit or to prohibit state taxation of such banks as instrumentalities of the federal government.[6]

Federal power with respect to the national banking system and control of the currency and coin includes the power of devaluation of the monetary unit. In 1933, in the emergency of the Great Depression, Congress abolished the gold standard for our currency and by Joint Resolution invalidated the gold clauses in both private and public obligations. The resolution invalidating the gold clauses provided that every obligation which was by its terms payable in gold "shall be discharged upon payment, dollar for dollar, in any coin or currency which at the time of payment is legal tender for public and private debts." This action was sustained with respect to private obligations in *Norman v. Baltimore & O. R. R. Co.*[7] as within the authority of Congress to regulate the currency and establish the monetary system of the country. Because Congress in the exercise of its sovereign power over the currency may alter or impair the rights of parties under private contracts, there is no deprivation of property without due process of law.

By contrast, in *Perry v. United States*,[8] a case initiated in the Court of Claims upon a gold bond issued by the Government, the Court held that the United States has no constitutional power to abrogate its obligations incurred in the exercise of its power to borrow upon the credit of the Government and that it is liable for damages in the event of breach. The bondholder held a bond in the face amount of $10,000 and contended that he was entitled to recover an amount in dollars equal to the current value of the former gold content of the United States dollar. If he had prevailed, he would have received $16,931. The Court acknowledged that the Government's repudiation of the gold clause

---

For a discussion of the Supreme Court's use of tenth amendment principles to grant local governments immunity from federal regulations see Chapter 4.

8. 424 U.S. 1 (1976) (per curiam).

1. U.S. Const. art. I, § 8, cl. 2 states: The Congress shall have power . . . to borrow Money on the credit of the United States . . . ."

2. Id., cl. 5 reads: The Congress shall have Power . . . to coin Money, regulate the Value thereof, and of foreign Coin . . . ."

3. McCulloch v. Maryland, 17 U.S. (4 Wheat.) 316 (1819) (state tax on national bank notes held invalid as a tax upon an instrumentality of the federal government).

4. First Nat. Bank v. Fellows, 244 U.S. 416 (1917) (sustaining the Federal Reserve Act).

5. Smith v. Kansas City Title & Trust Co., 255 U.S. 180 (1921) (sustaining the Federal Farm Loan Act).

6. Owensboro Nat. Bank v. Owensboro, 173 U.S. 664 (1899) (sustaining the power to limit taxation of national banks to taxes authorized by Congress). See First Agricultural Nat. Bank of Berkshire County v. State Tax Comm'n, 392 U.S. 339 (1968) (holding invalid as unauthorized by Congress a state sales and use tax on purchases by a national bank of tangible personal property for its own use).

7. 294 U.S. 240 (1935).

8. 294 U.S. 330 (1935).

in its bonds was unconstitutional; but it denied recovery on the ground that the bondholder had established no loss since he had received in legal tender the full face amount of the government obligation. A contrary decision would have resulted in an enrichment of the bondholder in the amount of $6,931.

An early historical illustration of the power of the federal government to control the value of the currency is found in *Veazie Bank v. Fenno.*[9] In this decision, the Court sustained a prohibitory ten percent tax on the issuance and circulation of state bank notes to assure a stable national currency. Although the Court discussed at length the issue as to the difference between a direct and indirect tax, the decision was founded on the power of Congress to control the value of the currency.[10] As a corollary to *Veazie Bank,* the Court in the *Legal Tender Cases*[11] later recognized the constitutional authority of the Congress to provide that United States treasury notes shall constitute legal tender in the satisfaction of all obligations whether incurred before or after the enactment of the legislation. Finally, it should be noted that Treasury Regulations governing the ownership of Government obligations are controlling for federal estate tax purposes irrespective of the nature of the interests in the property as determined by local law.[12]

---

9. 75 U.S. (8 Wall.) 533 (1869).

10. Id. at 548–549.

11. 79 U.S. (12 Wall.) 457 (1871), overruling Hepburn v. Griswold, 75 U.S. (8 Wall.) 603 (1870). For interesting background on this reversal by the Court, see Choper, The Supreme Court and the Political Branches: Democratic Theory and Practice, 122 U.Pa. L.Rev. 810, 851 (1974).

12. United States v. Chandler, 410 U.S. 257 (1973) (registration of Government savings bonds in joint tenancy controls in determining decedent's gross estate even though decedent had delivered the bonds to the donee joint tenants as complete, irrevocable, inter vivos gifts).

CHAPTER SIX

INTERNATIONAL AFFAIRS

I. INTRODUCTION—THE ROLE OF THE THREE BRANCHES OF GOVERNMENT

The United States in its capacity as a sovereign nation must interact with other countries in the international realm, for the ability of a nation to conduct foreign relations is inherent in the concept of sovereignty.[1] Because specific constitutional references to foreign relations are, however, sparse, much of the foreign affairs power evolved from constitutionally implied powers and extraconstitutional sources. Our effort in this section to understand the constitutional sources of our foreign relations will be first to study the roles of the president, Congress and the courts in foreign affairs as set forth in the text of the constitution, and then to look closer at specific areas of foreign affairs, the treaty power and the war power.

A. The Executive

Traditionally the president has been considered responsible for conducting the United States' foreign affairs.[2] Justice Sutherland in the leading case of *United States v.*

---

1. L. Henkin, Foreign Affairs and the Constitution 16 (1972); United States v. Curtiss-Wright Export Corp., 299 U.S. 304, 318 (1936).

2. Henkin, supra note 1, at 37.

Curtiss-Wright Export Corp.[3] stated in a unanimous opinion:

> [T]he President alone has the power to speak or listen as a representative of the nation. . . . As Marshall said in his great argument of March 7, 1800, in the House of Representatives, "The President is the sole organ of the nation in its external relations, and its sole representative with foreign nations."[4]

Blackstone acknowledged the historical concept of executive predominance in foreign relations indicating in his *Commentaries*, "What is done by the royal authority, with regard to foreign powers is the act of the whole nation."[5] Such plenary executive power is not, however, found anywhere in the text of the Constitution. Nor will any examination of the affirmative grants of foreign affairs power in the Constitution reveal that the president is the "sole organ" of foreign relations.

Specific enumerations of the executive's foreign affairs powers appear in Article II of the Constitution. The president is empowered to make treaties, with a concurrence of two-thirds of the Senate, and to appoint ambassadors, public ministers and consuls with the Senate's advice and consent.[6] Additionally, the chief executive is authorized, as the representative of the United States, to receive ambassadors and public ministers.[7] The Commander-in-Chief power, constitutionally delegated to the president, profoundly affects United States' international relations.[8] Although these provisions attest to the fact the president has an active role in foreign affairs, the executive, in actuality, has gone far beyond these express grants in conducting international relations.

What sources, in addition to express Constitutional provisions, does the president receive his foreign affairs powers from? Alexander Hamilton, in support of the theory of presidential supremacy in foreign affairs, wrote under the pseudonym "Pacificus" a series of articles published in *The Gazette of the United States* supporting George Washington's "Proclamation of Neutrality," issued in 1793 after the outbreak of war between Great Britian and France. In these articles Hamilton argued the first clause of Article II, "the executive power shall be vested in a President of the United States. . . ." was a general grant of power to the executive and that the following specific grants in Article II, except when expressly limited, serve to interpret the general grant. Hamilton concluded that any foreign affairs power not explicitly granted to the Congress devolves by implication upon the president through the executive power clause.[9] As examples, Hamilton cited the president's power to recognize governments and terminate relations with foreign nations under the auspices of the constitutional provision authorizing the executive to receive foreign ambassadors and consuls.[10] Although treaties are subject to the advice and consent of the Senate, the president, by implication, is empowered to continue or suspend the treaty on his own initiative Hamilton believed. Hamilton warned in *The Federalist* of the danger of restricting the executive's powers too severely.[11]

These implied Constitutional powers were recognized as early as George Washington's administration. Washington, by receiving "Citizen" Genet in accord with the Constitutional provisions allowing the president to receive foreign ambassadors and ministers, recognized the revolutionary government of France, and later, by demanding Genet's recall, ended diplomatic relations with France

---

3. 299 U.S. 304 (1936).

4. 299 U.S. at 319.

5. I, W. Blackstone, Commentaries 252 (Cooley ed. 1871).

6. U.S. Const. art. II, § 2.

7. Id. § 3.

8. Id. § 2.

9. E. Corwin, The President: Office and Powers 179–81 (4th Rev.Ed.1957), citing from A. Hamilton, Works 76 (Hamilton, ed.)

10. U.S. Const. art. II, § 3.

11. See The Federalist Nos. 67, 70; Corwin, The President, supra note 9, at 16–17.

without consulting Congress.[12] Washington also established historical precedent for limiting Congress's role in the area of treaty making when he refused to comply with the House of Representatives' request to give to Congress papers relevant to the negotiations involving the Jay treaty in 1796. The executive's treaty negotiation powers were, Washington believed, exclusive.[13] The president alone was empowered to designate individuals to conduct foreign affairs negotiations abroad and to determine what should be included in international agreements.[14] The Supreme Court indirectly legitimized these extensions of the constitutional foreign affairs power in *Marbury v. Madison*.[15] In *Marbury* the Court stated that judicial review of conflicts between the executive and congress over the foreign affairs power would be inappropriate, terming disputes of this nature as inherently political questions.[16]

Implied foreign affairs powers have also been extrapolated from the Commander-in-Chief clause and the Constitutional provision that the executive shall "take care" that "the laws be faithfully executed."[17] The extension of executive foreign affairs power on the basis of these two grants has not been as successful as the presidential claim to the foreign affairs power premised on the "executive power clause" discussed above.[18] This power attributed to the Commander-in-Chief will be treated later in section III dealing with the War Power. The clause empowering the executive to "take care" that laws are "faithfully executed" has been employed to justify executive action to insure treaty provisions are faithfully adhered to.[19] Presidents have even authorized forceful in-

tervention in foreign conflicts under the auspices of this clause contending that the duty to see all laws are faithfully executed also encompasses international law. These assertions are, however, unpersuasive since it is generally understood that this clause applies only to United States law and international law only to the extent the latter has been incorporated into the law of the United States in situations occurring either within the United States or affecting American citizens or the government.[20]

The Supreme Court acknowledged the unique role of the executive in *United States v. Curtiss-Wright Export Co.*[21] This case involved a controversy surrounding a presidential Embargo Proclamation issued May 28, 1934,[22] prohibiting the sale of arms to countries involved in the Chaco conflict in South America. Authorization for this declaration was granted in a joint congressional resolution passed earlier on the same day empowering the president to issue a proclamation limiting arms and ammunition sales to those involved in the conflict.[23] Revocation of the proclamation occurred in November of 1935.[24] The defendants, indicted in 1936 for conspiring to sell arms to Bolivia, challenged the joint resolution claiming it was an unconstitutional delegation of authority. The Supreme Court upheld the resolution, finding the proclamation valid. Justice Sutherland, writing for the majority, addressed the role of the president in international relations:

> [T]he federal power over external affairs in origin and essential character [is] different from that over internal affairs [and] . . . participation in the exercise of the power is significantly limited. In this vast external realm

---

12. U.S. Const. art. II, § 3; E. Corwin and L. Koenig, The Presidency Today 30 (1956); Corwin, The President, supra note 9, at 181–82.

13. Corwin, The President, supra note 9, at 181–83.

14. Corwin & Koenig, supra note 12, at 31.

15. 5 U.S. (1 Cranch) 137 (1803).

16. 5 U.S. (1 Cranch) at 166.

17. U.S. Const. art. II, § 3.

18. Henkin, supra note 1, at 42.

19. Id. at 54–55.

20. Id. at 55. For example, troops have been sent under presidential authority to Panama (1882), Cuba (1903), Haiti (1916), Korea (1950), Vietnam (1960's); Matthews, The Constitutional Power of the President to Conclude International Agreements, 64 Yale L.J. 345, 360 n. 88, 367 & n. 115–120 (1955).

21. 299 U.S. 304 (1936).

22. 48 Stat. 1744 (1934).

23. 48 Stat. 811 (1934).

24. 49 Stat. 3480 (1935).

. . . the President alone has the power to speak or listen as a representative of the nation. He makes treaties with the advice and consent of the senate; but he alone negotiates.[25]

Sutherland also quoted with approval a statement issued on February 15, 1816 by the Senate Committee on Foreign Relations:

The President is the Constitutional representative of the United States with regard to foreign nations. He manages our concerns with foreign nations . . . The nature of transactions with foreign nations, moreover, requires caution and unity of design, and their success frequently depends on secrecy and dispatch.[26]

Sutherland concluded that it was important to realize that presidential authority to issue the proclamation came not only from the joint resolution of Congress but also from the "very delicate, plenary and exclusive power of the President as the sole organ of the federal government in the field of international relations . . . "[27] This power did not need to be based on an act of Congress, the Court recognized, although it was "of course" to be exercised in subordination to express provisions of the Constitution. A pragmatic look at the international scene supported this view of the Constitutional framework. The President:

not Congress, has the better opportunity of knowing the conditions which prevail in foreign countries. . . . He has his confidential sources of information. He has his agents in the form of diplomatic, consular and other officials. Secrecy in respect of information gathered by them may be highly necessary and the premature disclosure of it productive of harmful results.[28]

Although Sutherland depicts presidential predominance in foreign affairs, it should not be forgotten that in that case the president was acting in accord with congressional policy. Justice Jackson in his concurrence in *The Steel Seizure Case*[29] interpreted the

Curtiss-Wright decision as dealing with situations arising when the presidential actions are in harmony with an act of Congress, not when the President acts contrary to Congress.[30] The Jackson interpretation would place a significant limitation on the theory of the executive plenary foreign affairs powers.

The Supreme Court reaffirmed much of the reasoning of *Curtiss-Wright* as to the unique nature of the president's foreign affairs power when it refused to review an executive order concerning the involvement of United States citizens with foreign air transportation in *Chicago and Southern Air Lines, Inc. v. Waterman Steamship Corp.*[31] In that case the Civil Aeronautics Board, with the express approval of the president, granted an overseas air route to Chicago and Southern Air Lines and denied it to its rival, the Waterman Steamship Corporation. The proceedings were not challenged as to their regularity, but Waterman nonetheless sought review of the CAB decision as approved by the president. The Court recognized that Congress could delegate "very large grants of its power over foreign commerce to the President."[32] And the President possesses his own foreign affairs power. In the *Waterman* case the Court found the President drew his powers from both sources. The Court in that case, where the president was not acting in defiance of Congressional direction, reasoned:

The President, both as Commander-in-Chief and as the Nation's organ for foreign affairs, has available intelligence services whose reports are not and ought not to be published to the world. It would be intolerable that courts, without the relevant information, should review and perhaps nullify actions of the Executive taken on information properly held secret . . . [T]he very nature of executive deci-

---

25. 299 U.S. at 319.

26. Id. at 319 quoting U.S. Senate Reports, Committee on Foreign Relations vol. 8 at 24 (1816).

27. 299 U.S. 304, 320.

28. Id. at 320.

29. Youngstown Sheet & Tube Co. v. Sawyer, 343 U.S. 579 (1952).

30. Id. at 635–636 n. 2 (Jackson, J., concurring).

31. 333 U.S. 103 (1948) (Jackson, J., for the Court).

32. 333 U.S. at 109.

sions as to foreign policy is political, not judicial.[33]

In *Waterman* the Court therefore concluded, in a 5 to 4 opinion, that whatever portion of the CAB order which emanated from the president was not subject to judicial review. The CAB orders, before presidential approval, are premature and not subject to review. After such presidential approval, they "embody Presidential discretion as to political matters beyond the competence of the courts to adjudicate." [34] Thus by constitutional exegesis, practical experience, and Congressional acquiescence, the executive has usually predominated the foreign affairs sphere, but this expansive international relations power is not plenary.[35]

B. The Congress

The continual controversy existing between Congress and the executive as to the extent of each branch's foreign affairs power centers on whether Congress and the president act as constitutional equals in this sphere or whether the executive initiates foreign policy while the Congress acts merely to implement the president's policy.[1] The importance of Congressional participation in international affairs was recognized during the early stages of United States' foreign policy.

In response to Alexander Hamilton's "Pacificus" articles supporting presidential supremacy in foreign affairs James Madison wrote a series of letters under the name of "Helvidius." Madison stated in these writings that Congress, not the president, was empowered to determine United States foreign policy. Hamilton, Madison argued, was attributing quasi-monarchical powers to the Executive branch reminiscent of the role of royalty in British foreign affairs.[2] However one would decide the Hamilton-Madison debate, the fact remains that Congress plays a vital role in the foreign affairs scenario. Success or failure of executive foreign policy depends, to a great extent, on the support of Congress. Congress received foreign affairs powers from express and implied constitutional grants. The specific Constitutional provisions granting Congress authority in foreign affairs matters delegate legislative power, and Article I, § 8 defines these powers broadly: "Congress shall have Power to provide for the common Defence, . . . " [3] to regulate foreign commerce,[4] and to define and punish Piracies and Felonies committed on the high Seas, and Offences against the law of Nations." [5] Additionally, Congress is empowered to declare war, to make rules of war, grant letters of marque and reprisal,[6] and to raise, support and regulate an army and a navy.[7] Two-thirds of the senate must consent to treaties before they are ratified. The Senate also is authorized to advise the president on the contents of the treaty.[8]

These express grants have been used extensively to validate congressionally created foreign policy. The commerce clause [9] legitimizes congressional legislation regulating United States foreign trade. With the increased importance of international business

---

33. 333 U.S. at 111.

34. 333 U.S. at 114. *Waterman* has been read not to preclude judicial review if the CAB's actions are beyond its powers, so that legally it could not place anything before the president. E.g., Pan American World Airways, Inc. v. CAB, 380 F.2d 770 (2d Cir. 1967), aff'd by an equally divided Court, 391 U.S. 461 (1968).

35. See generally, Paust, Is the President Bound by the Supreme Law of the Land?—Foreign Affairs and National Security Reexamined, 9 Hastings Const. L.Q. 719 (1982).

1. E. Corwin, The President: Office and Powers (4th Rev.Ed.1957) at 184–85.

2. Id. at 180–82, citing 6 J. Madison, Writings 138 (Hunt, Ed.)

3. U.S. Const. art. I, § 8, cl. 1.

4. Id. § 8, cl. 3.

5. Id. § 8, cl. 10.

6. Id. § 8, cl. 11.

7. Id. § 8, cls. 12, 13.

8. Id. art. II, § 2.

9. Id. art. I, § 8, cl. 3. For a discussion of the exclusive nature of Congress's power to regulate foreign commerce see United States v. Guy W. Capps, Inc., 204 F.2d 655, 658 (4th Cir. 1953) aff'd 348 U.S. 296 (1955), discussed below in section II, E.

transactions in relation to the world and national economies, foreign commerce has devoloped into a vital area of foreign affairs. Consequently, Congressional control of foreign commerce has a tremendous impact on the structure of United States foreign policy.[10] Congress's power to declare and wage war [11] directly checks the executive's foreign affairs power. These war powers will be discussed in more detail in section III of this Chapter. Specific constitutional grants enabling Congress to define and punish offenses against international law [12] empower Congress to create legislation regulating areas such as international air piracy, counterfeit foreign currency and foreign expropriations of the property of the United States or its citizens.[13] Through these provisions Congress creates binding foreign policy law.

Congress has expanded its foreign affairs powers by reading implied grants to influence foreign policy into express Constitutional provisions. Article I, section 8 authorizes Congress:

> to make all Laws which shall be necessary and proper for carrying into the execution the . . . Powers vested by this Constitution in the Government of the United States or in any Department or Officer thereof.[14]

The "necessary and proper" clause has been used effectively to check presidential foreign affairs power as the president relies on congressional legislation to enact his foreign af-

fairs policy. Congress can also stymie implementation of executive international policy by refusing to appropriate necessary funds.[15] Foreign aid programs depend on Congressional authorization as provided for in the "spending power" clause.[16] Congress, under the auspices of the "postal power" clause, has authorized international postal agreements.[17] These constitutionally implied foreign affairs powers provide a basis for many of the congressional actions which influence foreign policy.

The Supreme Court acknowledges the existence of a constitutionally implied power authorizing Congress to regulate foreign affairs. In *Perez v. Brownell* [18] the Court held that Congress was acting within its foreign affairs power by stating in the Nationality Act of 1940 [19] that any United States citizen voting in a foreign political election would lose his citizenship.[20] Justice Frankfurter, writing for the Court, asked:

> [W]hat is the source of power on which Congress must be assumed to have drawn? Although there is in the Constitution no specific grant to Congress of power to enact legislation for the effective regulation of foreign affairs, there can be no doubt of the existence of this power in the law-making organ of the nation . . . [A] federal Government to conduct the affairs of that nation must be held to have granted that Government the powers indispensible to its functioning effectively in the company of sovereign nations. The Government

---

10. Japan Line, Ltd. v. County of Los Angeles, 441 U.S. 434 (1979) (state tax on instrumentalities unconstitutional because such tax may subject foreign commerce to risk of multiple burdens and may impair federal uniformity in an area where federal uniformity is essential). Cf. Independent Warehouses v. Scheele, 134 N.J.L. 133, 137, 45 A.2d 703, 705 (1946), aff'd 331 U.S. 70 (1947); Gibbons v. Ogden, 22 U.S. (9 Wheat.) 1, 189–90 (1824); Henkin, The Treaty Makers and the Law Makers: The Law of the Land and Foreign Relations 107 U.Penn.L.Rev. 903, 925 (1959).

11. U.S. Const. art. I, § 8, cl. 11.

12. Id. § 8, cl. 10.

13. E.g., 18 U.S.C.A. § 1651, 49 U.S.C.A. § 1472(i) (air piracy); United States v. Arjona, 120 U.S. 479, 484–88 (1887) (Congress has the power to define and punish the offenses which disrupt harmonious foreign relations); The Hickenlooper Amendment, Foreign Assistance Act of 1961, § 620(e) as amended, 22 U.S.C.A. § 2370(e) (Congress authorizes the president to sus-

pend foreign aid to any nation that has seized U.S. property or repudiated or nullified existing contracts with U.S. citizens or businesses when the foreign government fails to give full compensation for such acts within a reasonable time).

14. U.S. Const. art. I, § 8, cl. 18.

15. L. Henkin, Foreign Affairs and the Constitution 76–79 (1972).

16. U.S. Const. art. I, § 8, cl. 1.

17. Id. § 8, cl. 7, see e.g. 39 U.S.C.A. §§ 505, 506; L. Henkin, Foreign Affairs and the Constitution 77 (1972).

18. 356 U.S. 44 (1958).

19. 54 Stat. 1137 § 401 as amended Act of Sept. 27, 1944, 58 Stat. 746.

20. 356 U.S. 44, 62 (1958), overruled in Afroyim v. Rusk, 387 U.S. 253 (1967).

must be able not only to deal affirmatively with foreign nations . . . [i]t must also be able to reduce to a minimum the frictions that are unavoidable in a world of sovereigns sensitive in matters touching their dignity and interests.[21]

Though the precise holding of this case was later overruled there was no doubt cast on the reasoning and principle that Congress was constitutionally empowered to legislate on such matters.[22]

A constitutional doctrine used to legitimize Congressional involvement in foreign affairs was also enunciated in *Fong Yue Ting v. United States.*[23]

> The United States are a sovereign and independent nation and are vested by the Constitution with the entire control of international relations and with all the powers of government necessary to maintain that control . . . The Constitution . . . speaks with no uncertain sound upon this subject. . . . The power . . . being a power affecting international relations, is vested in the political departments of the government, and is to be regulated by treaty or by act of Congress.[24]

The United States, as a sovereign nation, possesses a "foreign affairs power" which is an inherent attribute of sovereignty.[25] Justice Sutherland in the *Curtiss-Wright*[26] case acknowledged that the "foreign affairs power" arising from the sovereign status of the United States expanded Congress' legislative authority in international relations matters.

This broad "foreign affairs power" has been used as a basis for a wide variety of congressional legislation. Alien immigration and registration laws were promulgated on the strength of the "foreign affairs power."[27] Congress, on the basis of sovereignty, may be able to compel United States citizens residing abroad to return to the United States for legal proceedings and to answer for conduct engaged in abroad.[28] Presumably under this power Congress has authorized the Court to modify the act of state doctrine as recognized by the executive so that some acts of foreign governments affecting United States citizens may be challenged.[29] The extent of this congressional "foreign affairs power" at present is uncertain. Congress has yet to exercise this power as fully as the Supreme Court implies that it is empowered to.[30]

One area where the extent of Congressional power—and, in particular, the constitutional limitations on that power—are uncertain concerns the power over the territories. While certainly Congress has the power to govern its territories, it is not always clear to what extent the Constitution follows the Flag, that is, to what extent the Constitution applies to territories which are acquired but not incorporated into the United States.[31] In the beginning of the twentieth century the Court held that the requirement of uniformity of taxes imposed by Congress did not apply to Puerto Rico.[32] The Court at that time saw the need to

---

21. Id. at 57.

22. Perez v. Brownell, 356 U.S. 44 (1958), overruled in Afroyim v. Rusk, 387 U.S. 253 (1967); L. Henkin, Foreign Affairs and the Constitution 326 n. 39 (1972).

23. 149 U.S. 698 (1893).

24. 149 U.S. at 711, 713.

25. E.g., Burnet v. Brooks, 288 U.S. 378, 396 (1933).

26. United States v. Curtiss-Wright Exporting Corp., 299 U.S. 304, 318–19 (1936).

27. The Chinese Exclusion Case, 130 U.S. 581 (1889); Fong Yue Ting v. United States, 149 U.S. 698 (1893).

28. Cf. Vance v. Bradley, 440 U.S. 93, 103–109 (1979); Kinsella v. U. S. ex rel. Singleton, 361 U.S. 234, 245–46 (1960); L. Henkin, Foreign Affairs and the Constitution 75–76 (1972).

29. Blackmar v. United States, 284 U.S. 421 (1932); Banco Nacional de Cuba v. Farr, 383 F.2d 166, 182 (2d Cir. 1967), cert. denied 390 U.S. 956 (1968), rehearing denied 390 U.S. 1037 (1968).

30. L. Henkin, Foreign Affairs and the Constitution 74–76 (1972); Henkin, The Treaty Makers and the Law Makers: The Law of the Land and Foreign Relations, 107 U.Pa.L.R. 903, 922–23 (1959).

31. See generally, Sutherland, The Flag, The Constitution and International Agreements, 68 Harv.L. Rev. 1374 (1955); Green, Applicability of American Laws to Overseas Areas Controlled by the United States, 68 Harv.L.Rev. 781 (1955); Fairman, Some New Problems of the Constitution Following the Flag, 1 Stan.L.Rev. 587 (1949).

32. Downes v. Bidwell, 182 U.S. 244 (1901) (Art. I, § 8, cl. 1 not apply to Puerto Rico).

grant flexibility to Congress in administering its territories not previously subject to common law traditions.[33] However, the Court later held or otherwise indicated that other clauses of the Constitution do apply to Puerto Rico.[34] Moreover, because Congress may make constitutional provisions applicable to territories by statute even though they would not otherwise be controlling, the Court will attach great weight to a legislative determination that a particular constitutional provision may practically and beneficially be applied in a territory.

Thus the Court concluded in *Torres v. Puerto Rico* [35] that Congress' implicit determinations and long experience establish that the fourth amendment restrictions on search and seizure apply to Puerto Rico. The Court did not decide whether the fourth amendment applied directly or by operation of the fourteenth amendment. Justice Brennan, joined by Justices Stewart, Marshall, and Blackmun concurred. They argued that the older cases restricting the applicability of constitutional guarantees in Puerto Rico and cited by the majority should not be given any expansion assuming their validity in modern times.[36]

Clearly, the Constitution grants extensive foreign affairs powers to the Congress as well as to the executive. A third party, the Court, also is authorized constitutionally to participate in the formation of foreign affairs policy. It is to the role of the Court that we now turn.

C. The Court

Although the executive and legislative branches of the federal government dominate United States foreign affairs, the Supreme Court also influences foreign policy. Specific constitutional provisions in Article III, § 2 indicate that the Court is in a position to wield substantial power in international affairs. Historically, however, the Court frequently defers to the judgment of Congress and the executive when a conflict which may have impact on foreign relations arises. The Article III grant of judicial power to the federal courts extends to foreign affairs by use of the following language:

> All Cases, in Law and Equity, arising under this Constitution, the Laws of the United States and Treaties made—or which shall be made under their authority;—to all cases affecting Ambassadors, other public Ministers and Consuls; . . . to Controversies to which the United States shall be a Party, . . . to Controversies . . . between a State or Citizen thereof, and foreign States, Citizens or Subjects . . . . In all Cases affecting Ambassadors, other public Ministers and Consuls . . . the Supreme Court shall have original jurisdiction.[1]

On the basis of these provisions the Court exercises jurisdiction in cases involving foreign nations,[2] suits by United States citizens

---

33. See, e.g., Dorr v. United States, 195 U.S. 138 (1904) (no constitutional requirement that territorial government of the Philippines provide jury trial in criminal cases); Balzac v. Puerto Rico, 258 U.S. 298 (1922) (no constitutional requirement of jury criminal cases in Puerto Rico, which was not an incorporated territory of the United States even though its residents had been granted United States citizenships).

34. E.g., Balzac v. Puerto Rico, 258 U.S. 298, 314 (1922) (Court applies, without discussion, first amendment in Puerto Rico); Calero-Toledo v. Pearson Yacht Leasing Co., 416 U.S. 663, 668–69 n. 5 (1974) (Court applies due process clause in Puerto Rico because " 'there cannot exist under the American flag any governmental authority untrammeled by the requirements of due process of law as guaranteed by the Constitution of the United States.' ") (quoting Magruder, C.J., in Mora v. Mejias, 206 F.2d 377, 382 (1st Cir. 1953); Examining Bd. v. Flores De Otero, 426 U.S. 572, 599–601 (1976) (equal protection guarantee applies to Puerto Rico);

Califano v. Torres, 435 U.S. 1, 4 n. 6 (1978) (per curiam) (Court assumes without deciding that constitutional right to travel extends to Puerto Rico).

35. 442 U.S. 465, 470 (1979). Cf., e.g., Best v. United States, 184 F.2d 131, 138 (1st Cir. 1950), cert. denied 340 U.S. 939 (1957) (court assumes, "and we think it probably so," that fourth amendment extends to protect U. S. citizens in foreign countries under occupation by our armed forces).

36. 442 U.S. at 475 (1979) (Brennan, J., concurring). See also section II, B, infra, of this Chapter, text at nn. 13–14. But see Chief Justice Burger's dictum in Haig v. Agee, 453 U.S. 280, 308 (1981) ("Assuming, arguendo, that First Amendment protections reach beyond our national boundaries, ...).

1. U.S.Const. art. III, § 2.

2. E.g., Banco Nacional De Cuba v. Sabbatino, 376 U.S. 398 (1964).

against aliens or foreign diplomats,[3] and suits to interpret and enforce treaty terms.[4] The Court also hears cases arising under the "Laws of the United States"[5] which include all laws made in pursuance of the Constitution.[6] Since the Congress is constitutionally authorized to define and punish international law violations, thereby incorporating international law into United States law, the Constitution thus grants the Court jurisdiction over cases involving international law.[7] Consequently the Court will occasionally address issues involving international law and will make pronouncements that affect both the structure of United States foreign policy and international law.

The Court hesitates to exercise any authority in the area of foreign affairs that would exceed the scope of these express constitutional grants. Although the Supreme Court is empowered to review acts of the legislature and executive to insure conformance with constitutional provisions, the political question doctrine is an important exception to this judicial review power,[8] and demonstrates the Court's reluctance to take an active role in formulating foreign policy. Justice Brennan, in *Baker v. Carr*,[9] characterized a case involving a political question stating:

> Prominent on the surface of any case held to involve a political question is found a textually demonstrable constitutional commitment of the issue to a coordinate political department; . . . or the potentiality of embarrassment from multifarious pronouncements by various departments on one question.[10]

The area of foreign affairs often fits squarely within the Court's definition of political questions:

> There are sweeping statements to the effect that all questions touching foreign relations are political questions. Not only does resolution of such issues frequently turn on standards that defy judicial application, or involve the exercise of a discretion demonstrably committed to the executive or legislature; but many such questions uniquely demand single-voiced statement of the Government's views.[11]

Justice Brennan continued, citing a passage from *Oetjen v. Central Leather Co.*[12]

> The conduct of the foreign relations of our Government is committed by the Constitution to the Executive and Legislative—"the political"—Departments of the Government, and the propriety of what may be done in the exercise of this political power is not subject to judicial inquiry or decision.[13]

The *Baker* Court indicated there are some instances when the political question doctrine will not exempt foreign affairs issues from judicial review, but these exceptions are primarily limited to situations where the judiciary is acting in the absence of any conclusive action by the executive or Congress.[14]

In practice the Court employs the political question rationale to abstain from foreign affairs cases only infrequently. Primarily, in order to maintain judicial independence and integrity the Court refrains from reviewing executive and legislative action relating to foreign affairs by deciding that the

---

3. 28 U.S.C.A. § 1251 (1970).

4. E.g., Terlinden v. Ames, 184 U.S. 270 (1902); Martin v. Hunter's Lessee, 14 U.S. (1 Wheat.) 304 (1816).

5. U.S.Const. art. III, § 2.

6. Id. at art. VI.

7. U.S.Const. art. I, § 8. See The Paquete Habana, 175 U.S. 677, 700 (1900).

8. Marbury v. Madison, 5 U.S. (1 Cranch) 137, 165–66 (1803) (discussion of judicial review). On political questions see generally Chapter II, section IV, E.

9. 369 U.S. 186 (1962).

10. 369 U.S. 186, 217.

11. Id. at 211 (footnotes omitted).

12. 246 U.S. 297, 302 (1918).

13. 369 U.S. at 211 & n. 31.

14. 369 U.S. 186, 212–13, citing Terlinden v. Ames, 184 U.S. 270, 285 (1902) (Court can construe a treaty to decide if it has been terminated in the absence of conclusive governmental action involving the treaty); The Three Friends, 166 U.S. 1, 63, 66 (1897) (Court can construe executive declarations to determine if American neutrality standards have become operative); Ex parte Peru, 318 U.S. 578 (1943) (Judicial action regarding immunity of foreign ship is permissible in absence of executive declaration).

political branches are acting within the scope of their constitutional authority.[15]

The Supreme Court exercises considerable influence over foreign affairs legislation. The federal judiciary, acting in a quasi-legislative capacity, interprets laws, international law, executive agreements and treaties.[16] The Court's authority to construe international law was discussed in *The Paquete Habana* where the Court stated: "International law is a part of our law and must be ascertained and administered by the courts of justice. . . . "[17] Recently the Court has extended the scope of this "judicial legislation" in the foreign affairs area. In the leading case of *Banco Nacional De Cuba v. Sabbatino* [18] the Supreme Court established a doctrine which had a profound impact on United States foreign relations: the principle theory asserted was "Federal common law" which was binding on the nation.[19]

The complex fact situation in *Sabbatino* involved basically a controversy between a United States commodity broker and the Cuban government over the title to Cuban sugar sold in New York. Banco Nacional, on behalf of the Cuban government, sued the commodity broker, Farr, Whitlock and Company, for conversion of bills of lading and the proceeds from the sale of the sugar. In defense, Farr, Whitlock argued that the proceeds belonged not to the Cuban government but to the Cuban sugar company owned primarily by residents of the United States. The Castro regime, Farr, Whitlock asserted, had illegally expropriated the prop-

erty of this American owned business in violation of international law. The Cuban government's title to the sugar was therefore invalid under international law.[20]

The District Court and the Second Circuit agreed and, holding that Cuba had violated international law, ruled against Banco Nacional.[21] The Supreme Court reversed, relying on the "act of state" doctrine to bar judicial condemnation of Cuba's expropriation actions even though the expropriation violated customary international law.[22] The act of state doctrine "in its traditional formulation precludes the courts of this country from inquiring into the validity of the public acts a recognized foreign sovereign power committed within its own territory."[23] Writing for the majority, Justice Harlan stated that failure to adhere to the act of state doctrine and give effect to the expropriation might interfere with or embarrass the executive branch's foreign affairs policy. The United States, arguing *amicus curiae*, urged that the Court reverse the lower courts on these same grounds.[24] In deciding to uphold the act of state doctrine, however, the Court was not arguing that it was bound to follow the directions of the executive branch. Harlan, protecting the judicial integrity of the Court, held that although the act of state doctrine is not within the text of the Constitution, the doctrine does have " 'constitutional' underpinnings"[25]; "[T]he scope of the act of state doctrine must be determined according to federal law."[26] The Court established the act of state doctrine as federal common law and held that the feder-

15. L. Henkin, Foreign Affairs and the Constitution 213–14, 449–50, n. 26 (1972). See, e.g., Williams v. Suffolk Insurance Co., 38 U.S. (13 Pet.) 415, 420 (1839). (It is not within the Court's province to review actions of the executive done in accordance with its constitutional functions); see also, United States v. Palmer, 16 U.S. (3 Wheat.) 610, 634–35 (1818); Gelston v. Hoyt, 16 U.S. (3 Wheat.) 246, 322 (1818).

16. L. Henkin, Foreign Affairs and the Constitution 216 (1972).

17. 175 U.S. 677, 700 (1900).

18. 376 U.S. 398 (1964).

19. L. Henkin, The Foreign Affairs Power of the Federal Courts: Sabbatino, 64 Colum.L.Rev. 805, 806 (1964).

20. 376 U.S. 398, 401–08.

21. 193 F.Supp. 375 (S.D.N.Y.1961), aff'd 307 F.2d 845 (2d Cir.1962).

22. Banco Nacional de Cuba v. Sabbatino, 376 U.S. 398, 427–37 (1964).

23. 376 U.S. 398, 401 (1964).

24. 376 U.S. 398, 432–33; see also Argument of Deputy Attorney General Katzenbach, 32 U.S.L.W. 3158 (U.S. Oct. 29, 1963).

25. 376 U.S. 398, 423.

26. Id. at 427 (footnote omitted).

al judiciary will not examine expropriation acts of a recognized sovereign within its own territory in the absence of a treaty even if the taking violates customary international law.[27]

The Court's decision was made independently of congressional or executive directives. To that extent, its decision to uphold the act of state doctrine was based upon the Court's belief that it can create foreign relations law. This exercise of judicial power does have important limits, even though the reference to "'constitutional' underpinnings" was somewhat less than crystal clear. While it may hint that the Court's definition was constitutional in origin and therefore Congress cannot change it, the language of the majority opinion suggests otherwise. Thus, immediately after the reference to "'constitutional' underpinnings" the Court states: "It [the act of state doctrine] arises out of the basic relationships between branches of government in a system of separations of powers." [28] Later the Court states:

> [We] decide only that the Judicial Branch will not examine the validity of a taking of property within its own territory by a foreign sovereign government, extant and recognized by this country at the time of suit, *in the absence of* a treaty or other unambiguous agreement regarding controlling legal principles, even if the complaint alleges that the taking violates customary international law.[29]

The better view of *Sabbatino* is that it exemplifies the creation of federal common law,[30] not federal constitutional law. The constitutional underpinnings of the act of state doctrine relate more to the separation of powers than to the constitutional origins of the doctrine. Thus, Congress can change the act of state doctrine and, perhaps, by statute, require the courts to look to "customary international law."

This view of *Sabbatino* is somewhat supported by subsequent events. Congress became concerned over the theories advocated in *Sabbatino*. Shortly after the decision was handed down Congress effectively overruled the *Sabbatino* interpretation of the act of state doctrine by revising the Hickenlooper amendment provisions regarding acts of states.[31] The Supreme Court subsequently denied certiorari in a case involving this legislation, *Banco Nacional de Cuba v. Farr*,[32] which was a suit arising out of the *Sabbatino* sugar transactions where the lower courts applied the new statute and not the *Sabbatino* decision.

In a later decision involving Cuban expropriation of United States citizen's property by the Cuban government, *First National City Bank v. Banco Nacional de Cuba*,[33] the divided Court deferred to the opinion of the executive branch in areas touching foreign affairs. Justice Rehnquist, writing for himself, Chief Justice Burger, and Justice White, acknowledged that the executive had advised the Court that the act of state doctrine should not be applied in the situation under consideration. His plurality opinion recognized, "the primacy of the Executive in . . . foreign relations," concluding:

> where the Executive Branch, . . . expressly represents to the Court that application of

---

27. Id. at 428.

28. Id. at 423.

29. Id. at 428 (emphasis added).

30. See, e.g., Hay, Unification of Law in the United States: Uniform State Laws, Treaties and Judicially Declared Federal Common Law, in Legal Thought in the United States of America Under Contemporary Pressures: Reports from the United States of America on Topics of Major Concern as Established for the VIII Congress of the International Academy of Comparative Law 261, 280–81, 289 (J. Hazard & W. Wagner, eds. 1970).

31. 22 U.S.C.A. § 2370(e)(2); see also the divided Court opinion in First Nat. City Bank v. Banco Nacion-

al de Cuba, 406 U.S. 759, 761–62 (1972) (plurality opinion of Rehnquist, J.).

Provisions of title 28 of the United States Code have been enacted (in October 21, 1976 to be effective 90 days after that) which also relate to the *Sabbatino* issue. See 28 U.S.C.A. § 1330 (Actions against foreign states); 28 U.S.C.A. Chapter 97 (Jurisdictional Immunities of Foreign States). See particularly 28 U.S.C.A. § 1605 of Chapter 97 (General exceptions to the jurisdictional immunity of a foreign state).

32. 243 F.Supp. 957 (S.D.N.Y.), aff'd 383 F.2d 166 (2d Cir.1967), cert. denied 390 U.S. 956 (1968).

33. 406 U.S. 759 (1972).

the act of state doctrine would not advance the interests of American foreign policy, that doctrine should not be applied by the courts.[34]

Not all of the Court was in accord with the theory of judicial acquiescence to the executive and Congress in foreign affairs. In the concurring opinion of Justice Powell and the dissent of Justice Brennan, the justices emphasized the importance of maintaining the integrity and independence of the judiciary.[35] Brennan was particularly adamant in his dissent stressing that any decision should be made on the basis of constitutional authority and not upon recommendations of the executive.[36]

Relying on *Banco Nacional de Cuba v. Sabbatino*,[37] the Court has deferred to the political branch and held that "it is within the exclusive power of the Executive Branch to determine which nations are entitled to sue." [38] Ruling that foreign nations were allowed to sue as "persons" within the meaning of the antitrust laws, allowing private antitrust treble damage actions, the Court specifically referred to a letter from the Legal Adviser of the State Department indicating that it anticipated no foreign policy problems from its holding allowing foreign nations to sue as "persons" under the antitrust laws.[39] Congress responded to this decision by amending the Clayton Act in order to eliminate, in general, the right of foreign governments to recover treble damages.[40]

II. THE TREATY MAKING POWER

A. Introduction

Constitutional provisions confer the treaty making power to the federal government, specifically to the president and the Senate. The Constitution empowers the president ". . . by and with the Advice and Consent of the Senate, to make treaties provided two thirds of the Senators present concur." [1] Other language expressly prohibits states from entering, in their own right, into treaties or alliances.[2] Treaties are proclaimed in the text of the Constitution to be the supreme law of the land and binding upon states.[3] Federal judicial power, in addition, is constitutionally extended to encompass cases involving treaties made under the authority of the federal government.[4] Another constitutional directive relevant to the treaty power is the necessary and proper clause,[5] which enables Congress to enact all law needed to implement and enforce treaties.

From these provisions a specific treaty making process has developed. Generally the executive appoints and supervises a team of individuals who negotiate the agreement. After a satisfactory agreement is concluded the executive submits the proposed treaty to the Senate. If the treaty is approved by two-thirds of the Senate, the president then ratifies it and the treaty becomes an agreement binding as an international obligation.[6] Its effectiveness as domestic law depends on its being either self-executory or, if it is executory, there being the required implementing legislation.[7]

---

34. Id. at 767–68.

35. Id. at 773–76, 776–796.

36. Id. at 776–796.

37. 376 U.S. 398, 408–12 (1964).

38. Pfizer, Inc. v. Government of India, 434 U.S. 308, 320 (1978). The Court also cited Jones v. United States, 137 U.S. 202 (1890) for this proposition.

39. 434 U.S. 308, 319 n. 20. The dissent objected to the reliance on this letter and argued that the decision as to whether foreign nations could sue should be left to Congress. 434 U.S. 308 at 329 n. 3 (Burger, C.J., joined by Powell & Rehnquist, JJ., dissenting); 434 U.S. 308, 331 n. 2 (Powell J., dissenting).

40. See 15 U.S.C.A. § 15(b).

1. U.S.Const. art. II, § 2, cl. 1.

2. U.S.Const. art. I, § 10, cl. 3; art. I, § 10, cl. 1. See Chapter 10, section II, A.

3. U.S.Const. art. VI, cl. 2.

4. U.S.Const. art. III, § 2, cl. 1.

5. U.S.Const. art. I, § 8, cl. 18. See, Missouri v. Holland, 252 U.S. 416 (1920).

6. L. Henkin, Foreign Affairs and the Constitution 130 (1972).

7. See section II, D of this Chapter.

B. Limitations on the Treaty Power

Although there are no express limitations on treaty making in the text of the Constitution the Supreme Court has endeavored to define the scope of the treaty power. The basic Constitutional provision is:

> This Constitution, and the Laws of the United States which shall be made in Pursuance thereof; and all Treaties made, or which shall be made, under the Authority of the United States, shall be the supreme Law of the Land . . .[8]

This clause at one time had been interpreted by legal authorities to suggest that treaties were equal to the Constitution.[9] As a consequence the theory that treaties were not subject to any constitutional limitations developed. The Supreme Court addressed this problem in *Geofroy v. Riggs* [10] where Justice Field in often quoted dicta discussed the constitutionally implied limitations on the treaty power.

> That the treaty power of the United States extends to all proper subjects of negotiation between our government and the governments of other nations, is clear . . . . The treaty power, as expressed in the Constitution, is in terms unlimited except by those restraints which are found in that instrument against the action of the government or of its departments . . . . It would not be contended that it extends so far as to authorize what the Constitution forbids, or a change in the character of the government or in that of one of the States, or a cession of any portion of the territory of the latter, without its consent . . . . But with these exceptions, it is not perceived that there is any limit to the questions which can be adjusted touching any matter which is properly the subject of negotiation with a foreign country.[11]

Thus, while the tenth amendment does not place any reserved restrictions on the treaty power, the specific restraints of the Bill of Rights and other similar constitutional restraints do exist. Also, it is argued that since the treaty power extends to all proper subjects of negotiation, it does not include any matters "which do not essentially affect the actions of nations in relation to international affairs, but are purely internal." [12]

The definitive pronouncement on this constitutional question was made by Justice Black's opinion in *Reid v. Covert.*[13]

> [N]o agreement with a foreign nation can confer power on the Congress, or on any other

---

8. U.S.Const. art. VI, § 2.

9. Nowak & Rotunda, A Comment on the Creation and Resolution of a "Non-Problem": Dames & Moore v. Regan, the Foreign Affairs Power, and the Role of the Courts, 29 U.C.L.A.L.Rev. 1129, 1134–55 (1982); L. Henkin, Foreign Affairs and the Constitution 137 (1972). See Missouri v. Holland, 252 U.S. 416, 433 (1920) where Justice Holmes wrote: "Acts of Congress are the supreme law of the land only when made in pursuance of the Constitution, while treaties are declared to be so when made under the authority of the United States. It is open to question whether the authority of the United States means more than the formal acts prescribed to make the convention."

10. 133 U.S. 258 (1890).

11. Id. at 266–67; see also Ware v. Hylton, 3 U.S. (3 Dall.) 199 (1796); Asakura v. Seattle, 265 U.S. 332, 341 (1924).

12. Hearings on S.J.Res. 1, Before a Subcommittee of the Senate Committee on the Judiciary, 84th Cong., 1st Sess. 183 (1955) (testimony of Secretary of State Dulles). Treaties dealing with and promoting human rights are considered within the treaty power. Restatement of the Law, 2d Foreign Relations Law of the United States, Reporter's Note following § 118 (1965).

13. 354 U.S. 1 (1957). Justice Black announced the judgment for the Court; his opinion was joined in by only three other Justices (Warren, C.J., and Douglas and Brennan, JJ.), but none of the other justices, either concurring or dissenting, questioned his analysis of Missouri v. Holland, 252 U.S. 416 (1920). There was no opinion for the Court. Justice Whittaker took no part in the case; Justice Frankfurter concurred in a separate opinion; Justice Harlan also concurred in another separate opinion; and Justice Clark, joined by Justice Burton, dissented.

Following Justice Black's opinion in Reid v. Covert, 354 U.S. 1 (1957), a special U.S. court, sitting in allied occupied West Berlin, ruled that two East German citizens who were charged with hijacking a Polish airliner and landing it in the U.S. military zone, were entitled to the full protection of the U.S. Constitution, including a trial by a jury of their peers. The special court system was established by the 1945 rules of occupation, and sitting by designation was a U.S. District Judge from New Jersey. The special court was never forced to convene before, and under the rules of procedure applicable to it, the judge's ruling is not appealable. Nat'l Law Jrl., Mar. 26, 1979, at 9, col. 1; N.Y. Times, Mar. 15, 1979, at A3, col. 1–3. Thus, the Constitution may follow the flag not only as to U.S. citizens but also as

branch of Government, which is free from the restraints of the Constitution.[14]

Black concluded that Constitutional provisions limit the acts of the president, the joint actions of the president and the Senate, and consequently they limit the treaty power. Given these limitations on the scope of the treaty making power, the Supreme Court has found treaties to be equal in status to congressional legislation, and, as expressly provided in the text of the Constitution, the supreme law of the land.[15]

The states have sometimes argued that the tenth amendment imposes additional limitations upon the treaty power. Asserting that under the Constitution they retain control over certain matters, the states contended that the federal government cannot alter these reserved powers through treaties. The Supreme Court confronted this issue in *Hauenstein v. Lynham.*[16] *Hauenstein* was a suit by the heirs of a Swiss citizen who died intestate owning property in Virginia; the plaintiffs sought to recover the proceeds from the sale of the property by the local escheator. The heirs, invoking provisions of a treaty between the United States and Switzerland, prevailed over the local law preventing such aliens from taking property by descent or inheritance. The Court stated that treaties are the supreme law of the land and superior to the laws and constitutions of the individual states.[17] "It must always be borne in mind that the Constitution, laws, and treaties of the United States are as

much a part of the law of every State as its own local laws and Constitution."[18]

Any tenth amendment limitation on the federal treaty power was flatly rejected in the landmark case of *Missouri v. Holland.*[19] Initially Congress had enacted a statute to protect migratory birds in danger of extinction.[20] This Act was subsequently held invalid by the lower federal courts for lack of a specific constitutional provision empowering Congress to regulate matters of this nature.[21] Later a treaty was concluded with Great Britain involving the same issues as the statute had covered. New statutes were passed to implement the treaty.[22] In *Missouri v. Holland* the state brought a bill in equity to prevent the Migratory Bird Treaty and the regulations made pursuant to this agreement from being enforced by the federal game warden. Missouri claimed that the treaty and new statutes interfered with her tenth amendment reserved rights and were as a consequence void. Justice Holmes, writing for the Court, concluded that the treaty and statutes did not interfere with rights reserved by states.

> To answer this question it is not enough to refer to the Tenth Amendment . . . because by Article II, § 2, the power to make treaties is delegated expressly, and by Article VI treaties made under the authority of the United States, along with the Constitution and laws of the United States made in pursuance thereof, are declared the supreme law of the land. If the treaty is valid there can be no dispute about

to aliens, at least when they are not enemy aliens. See also section I, B of this Chapter, supra, text at nn. 31–36.

14. 354 U.S. at 16. See also, Geofroy v. Riggs, 133 U.S. 258, 267 (1890); Holden v. Joy, 84 U.S. (17 Wall.) 211, 242–43 (1872); The Cherokee Tobacco, 78 U.S. (11 Wall.) 616, 620–21 (1870); Doe v. Braden, 57 U.S. (16 How.) 635, 657 (1853); New Orleans v. United States, 35 U.S. (10 Pet.) 662, 736 (1836).

15. U.S.Const. art. II, § 2; Martin v. Hunter's Lessee, 14 U.S. (1 Wheat.) 304, 360 (1816); Foster & Elam v. Neilson, 27 U.S. (2 Pet.) 253, 314–315 (1829); Missouri v. Holland, 252 U.S. 416, 433 (1920).

Cf. Stotzky & Swan, Due Process Methodology and Prisoner Exchange Treaties, 62 Minn.L.Rev. 733 (1978); Robbins, A Constitutional Analysis of the Prohibition against Collateral Attack in the Mexican-American Prisoner Exchange Treaty, 26 U.C.L.A.L.Rev. 1 (1978).

See Paust, The Unconstitutional Detention of Prisoners by the United States Under the Exchange of Prisoner Treaties, in R. Lillich, ed., International Aspects of Criminal Law: Enforcing United States Law in the World Community 204–27 (1981).

16. 100 U.S. 483 (1880).

17. Id. at 483–89.

18. Id. at 490.

19. 252 U.S. 416 (1920).

20. Act of March 4, 1913, C. 145, 37 Stat. 847.

21. United States v. Shauver, 214 F. 154 (E.D.Ark. 1914); United States v. McCullagh, 221 F. 288 (D.Kan. 1915).

22. Migratory Bird Treaty Act of July 3, 1918, 16 U.S.C.A. §§ 703–711.

the validity of the statute under Article I, § 8 as a necessary and proper means to execute the powers of the Government . . . . It is said that a treaty cannot be valid if it infringes the Constitution, that there are limits . . . to the treaty making power. . . .[23]

Holmes then rejected the state's argument that the same constitutional limitations applying to acts of Congress should also apply to treaties. He reasoned:

An earlier act of Congress that attempted by itself and not in pursuance of a treaty to regulate the killing of migratory birds within the States had been held bad in the District Court. . . . Acts of Congress are the supreme law of the land only when made in pursuance of the Constitution, while treaties are declared to be so when made under the authority of the United States. It is open to question whether the authority of the United States means more than the formal acts prescribed to make the convention. We do not mean to imply that there are no qualifications to the treaty-making power; but they must be ascertained in a different way. It is obvious that there may be matters of the sharpest exigency for the national well being that an act of Congress could not deal with but that a treaty followed by such an act could . . . .[24]

What Holmes perhaps meant is that before the Treaty the migratory bird act (assuming the correctness of the earlier decisions) did not implement any federal power; after the Treaty, which itself was consistent with federal powers and not violative of any federal limitations, the migratory bird act did implement a federal power, the treaty power. Observing that the provisions of the agreement did not contravene any constitutional provisions, Holmes concluded that any limi-

tation upon the treaty would have to be based upon the general terms of the tenth amendment. Matters of national interest are best protected by national action Holmes reasoned. Because the problem of protecting migratory birds was national in scope no one state could provide as complete a solution as the treaty and resulting statutes.[25] Although Missouri could have regulated the birds in the absence of a treaty, treaties and accompanying statutes are binding both throughout the nation and within the territory of a state. States exercise control over most of their internal activities but a treaty may override such power.[26] It is also argued that the treaty must be a proper subject for negotiation, for the treaty power does not extend to matters "which do not essentially affect the actions of nations in relation to international affairs, but are purely internal." [27]

Attempts to limit federal treaty making power by constitutional amendment have been unsuccessful.[28] During the 1950's proponents of the Bricker Amendment campaigned for a legislative overruling of the *Missouri v. Holland* [29] decision. These individuals were concerned that portions of Justice Holmes' dicta in *Missouri v. Holland* would be interpreted to mean that treaties were not subject to constitutional limitations as were acts of Congress.[30] Ultimately Congress rejected the Bricker Amendment. Constitutional provisions and Supreme Court decisions were found to provide adequate restraints on federal power making the amendment unnecessary.[31]

23. 252 U.S. 416, 432 (1920).

24. Id. at 432–33. See also Hay, Supranational Organizations and United States Constitutional Law, 6 Va.J. of Internat'l Law 195, 198 n. 10 (1966).

25. Id. at 434–35.

26. Id. at 434.

27. Hearings on S.J.Res. 1, Before a Subcommittee of the Senate Committee on the Judiciary, 84th Cong., 1st Sess. 183 (1955) (testimony of Secretary of State Dulles). See also, Restatement of the Law, 2d, Foreign Relations Law of the United States § 117(1) (1965).

28. S.J.Res. 1, 83d Cong., 1st Sess., 99 Cong.Rec. 6777 (1953).

29. 252 U.S. 416 (1920).

30. Id. at 433. Proponents of the Bricker Amendment were specifically concerned with Mr. Justice Holmes' statement, that "Acts of Congress are the supreme law of the land only when made in pursuance of the Constitution, while treaties are declared to be so when made under the authority of the United States," in Missouri v. Holland, 252 U.S. 416, 433 (1920).

31. See generally L. Henkin, Foreign Affairs and the Constitution 146–47 (1972). For a discussion of constitutional and Supreme Court case law limitations

For a time, efforts to limit the treaty power focused on the President's authority to terminate treaties. If the Constitution requires a two-thirds vote of the Senate in order to ratify a treaty, the Constitution, it was argued, must also require a two-thirds vote before the President can abrogate a treaty. A fragmented Court rejected this claim in *Goldwater v. Carter*.[32] Several Senators and others sued for declaratory and injunctive relief against President Carter after he announced that he planned to terminate the mutual defense treaty with Taiwan, the Republic of China. The President gave the one year notice which the termination clause of the treaty required. He also recognized the Peoples Republic of China (the Peking Government) rather than the Nationalist Government of Taiwan as the Government of China.

The Court, without opinion, granted certiorari and ordered the district court to dismiss the complaint. Justice Rehnquist, joined by Chief Justice Burger and Justices Stevens and Stewart, concurred in the judgment and filed a statement concluding that the "basic question presented by the petitioners in this case is political and therefore nonjusticiable because it involves the authority of the President in the conduct of our country's foreign relations and the extent to which the Senate or the Congress is authorized to negate the action of the President." [33] Justice Brennan dissented and rejected the majority's view of the political question doctrine. However, he

nonetheless would not question the presidential decision because it rested on the President's exclusive power to recognize foreign governments. The President abrogated the treaty with Taiwan because he recognized the Peking Government.[34]

Only Justice Powell's concurrence firmly rejected the political question doctrine, either as broadly held by Justice Rehnquist or as more narrowly held by Justice Brennan. Powell argued that there were judicially discoverable and manageable standards because decision in this case "only" required the Court to interpret the Constitution.[35] Nonetheless he concurred in the dismissal of the case on the grounds that the issue was not ripe and would not be until Congress chose to "confront the President," and reached a "constitutional impasse." [36] He hinted that if the Senate would pass a resolution declaring that its approval was necessary for the termination of any mutual defense treaty and further declared that it intended the resolution to have retroactive effect, that might then make the case ripe.

C. Executory and Self–Executing Treaties

Although no provisions in the Constitution discuss the nature of a treaty, the Supreme Court has recognized that two types of treaties exist. Treaties may be either executory, that is a ratified treaty which requires implementing legislation before it takes effect, or self-executory treaties, which take effect im-

on treaty-making see, Association of the Bar of the City of New York—Committee on Federal Legislation, The Risks of the 1956 Bricker Amendment 4–7 (1956); Nowak & Rotunda, A Comment on the Creation and Resolution of a "Nonproblem": Dames & Moore v. Regan, the Foreign Affairs Power, and the Role of the Courts, 29 U.C.L.A.L.Rev. 1101 (1982). Reid v. Covert, 354 U.S. 1, 16–17 (1957).

32. 444 U.S. 996 (1979). See generally, e.g., Note, Resolving Treaty Termination Disputes, 129 U.Pa.L. Rev. 1189 (1981).

33. 444 U.S. at 1001.

34. 444 U.S. at 1007.

35. 444 U.S. at 999. Cf. Roberts, J., in United States v. Butler, 297 U.S. 1, 62 (1936):

"When an act of Congress is appropriately challenged in the courts as not conforming to the consti-

tutional mandate the judicial branch of the Government has only one duty,—to lay the article of the Constitution which is invoked beside the statute which is challenged and to decide whether the latter squares with the former."

Powell also rejected the other tests, outlined in Baker v. Carr, 369 U.S. 186 (1962), to determine whether there was a political question. See Chapter 2, section IV, E, supra.

36. 444 U.S. at 998.

Justice Marshall concurred in the dismissal but without any opinion. Justice Blackmun, joined by Justice White, did not reach the merits and would have set the case for oral argument and plenary consideration.

mediately upon ratification. This distinction was made in the case of *Foster v. Neilson* [37] where the Court indicated that treaties are:

to be regarded in Courts of justice as equivalent to an act of the legislature, whenever it operates of itself without the aid of any legislative provision. But when the terms of the stipulation import a contract, when either of the parties engages to perform a particular act, the treaty addresses itself to the political, not the judicial department; and the legislature must execute the contract before it can become a rule for the Court. [38]

In *Whitney v. Robertson* [39] the Court again acknowledged that executory treaties have no effect until the necessary legislation is enacted.

D. Conflicts Between Treaties and Acts of Congress

While treaties as well as federal statutes are the supreme law of the land, the Constitution provides no solution for the dilemma arising when provisions of a self-executing treaty conflict with acts of Congress. [40] In *Whitney v. Robertson* [41] the Supreme Court addressed the issue of modifying a treaty by subsequent acts of Congress. The case involved a dispute arising between the United States and the Dominican Republic over the terms of a sugar trade treaty to which the two nations were parties. The Court stated that constitutionally treaties and legislative acts are equal, both being the supreme law of the land. When the treaty and statute:

relate to the same subject, the courts will always endeavor to construe them so as to give effect to both, if that can be done without violating the language of either; but if the two are inconsistent, the one last in date will control the other . . . [42]

Acts of Congress passed after the date of the treaty, the Court held, control over the treaty terms.

In the *Chinese Exclusion Case* [43] the Supreme Court affirmed the lower court's decision that an act excluding Chinese laborers from the United States was a constitutional exercise of legislative power even though it conflicted with an existing treaty. The Court rationalized that treaties being equivalent to acts of the legislature, they can, like statutes, be repealed or amended. When a conflict between treaty and statutory provisions develops, the Court stated, ". . . the last expression of the sovereign will must control." [44]

E. Executive Agreements

Although the Constitution expressly confers only a treaty making power upon the president, a power to be exercised with the advice and consent of the Senate, it does not provide that such treaties be the exclusive means by which the United States assumes an international commitment. Thus, through the use of executive agreements, presidents have concluded a variety of international agreements on their own authority without this required approval. [45] These executive agreements, while they cannot be termed treaties as they lack the constitutional requirement of consent by the Senate, frequently cover the same subject matter as treaties. [46]

---

37. 27 U.S. (2 Pet.) 253 (1829). Compare United States v. Percheman, 32 U.S. (7 Pet.) 51 (1833), where the Supreme Court held that the same treaty was self-executing, after the Court examined the Spanish text and Spanish grammatical usage. See generally, Restatement of the Law, 2d, Foreign Relations Law of the United States § 154 (1965).

38. 27 U.S. (2 Pet.) at 314.

39. 124 U.S. 190, 194 (1888).

40. U.S.Const. art. VI, cl. 2.

41. 124 U.S. 190 (1888).

42. Id. at 194.

43. Chae Chan Ping v. United States, 130 U.S. 581 (1889).

44. Id. at 600.

45. See, e.g., Proclamation No. 2761A, 12 Fed.Reg. 8863 (1947) (U.S. participation in GATT, The General Agreement on Tariffs and Trade). Weinberger v. Rossi, 456 U.S. 25, 30 n. 6 (1982). For a discussion regarding the number of executive agreements concluded by the president on behalf of the United States, see L. Henkin, Foreign Affairs and the Constitution 173, n. 1 (1972).

46. The history and nature of executive agreements is discussed extensively in: McDougal and Lans, Trea-

There are basically four types of executive agreements.[47] First, the president may conclude an executive agreement based on his exclusive presidential powers, such as the power as commander-in-chief of the armed forces pursuant to which he conducts military operations with our allies, or his power to receive foreign ambassadors and recognize foreign governments.[48] Second, the president may conclude an executive agreement in pursuance of an authorization contained in a prior treaty.[49] Third, the president may derive his power to conclude an executive agreement from prior Congressional authorization. That is, the House and Senate together delegate certain powers to the president which he exercises together with his independent powers in the areas of foreign affairs.[50] Fourth, the president may obtain Congressional confirmation by both Houses of an agreement negotiated by the Executive.[51]

The Supreme Court discussed the status of the executive agreement in the leading case of the *United States v. Pink*.[52] *Pink* involved a dispute over the title to the New York assets of a Russian insurance company. Russia had nationalized all her insurance companies in 1918 and 1919 by decrees intended to include the foreign assets of all Russian insurance businesses.[53] In 1933, President Roosevelt and the Soviet government concluded the Litvinov Assignment, an executive agreement whereby the Soviet Union assigned its vested rights in the assets of the Russian insurance company located in New York to the United States government. This agreement was the first type of executive agreement discussed above: it was entered into pursuant to the president's constitutional authority. Under the terms of the agreement the United States became entitled to the property; the rights of the United States were to be superior to the claims of the corporation and foreign creditors.[54] The Supreme Court found that the New York state court's policy not to recognize the Soviet government and the state's refusal to enforce the Litvinov Assignment ran counter to the executive agreement

ties and Congressional-Executive or Presidential Agreements: Interchangeable Instruments of National Policy: Parts I and II, 54 Yale L.J. 181, 534 (1945), and Borchard, Treaties and Executive Agreements, A Reply, 54 Yale L.J. 616 (1945). See also, Kefauver, The House of Representatives Should Participate in Treaty Making, 19 Tenn.L.Rev. 44, 48 (1945).

47. Restatement of the Law, 2d, Foreign Relations of the United States §§ 119–121 (1965); Hay, Supranational Organizations and United States Constitutional Law, 6 Va.J. of Internat'l Law 195, 204–09 (1966).

48. Restatement of the Law, 2d, Foreign Relations of the United States, § 121 (1965). See id. at comment *b*. A typical illustration:

"The President makes an agreement with state A whereby the United States will transfer to A a number of destroyers in exchange for the lease of areas for naval and air bases in certain territory of A. The agreement is valid under the President's powers as chief executive and commander-in-chief. Cf. Arrangement with Great Britain Respecting Naval and Air Bases, 54 Stat. 2405, E.A.S. No. 181, 3 Dept. State Bull. 199 (1940). Cf. 39 Ops.Atty.Gen. 484 (1940)."

Id. at Comment *b*, Illustration 2. It has been argued that the president's power to "faithfully execute" the laws, U.S.Const. art. II, § 3, furnishes the president additional and independent power as a basis for executive agreements. But this view is a minority one and is too open-ended to be acceptable.

49. See, e.g., Restatement of the Law, 2d, Foreign Relations Law of the United States, § 119, comment *b*, Illustration 1:

"The United States and state A make a security treaty providing, among other things, that the two states may make administrative agreements governing the disposition of United States forces in A. Pursuant to that provision, the President of the United States makes an executive agreement defining jurisdiction over United States forces in A. The executive agreement is constitutional. Cf. Wilson v. Girard, 354 U.S. 524 (1957)."

50. See, e.g., id. at § 120, Comment *a*, Illustration 1:

"An act of Congress provides that when the President finds that existing duties or import restrictions of the United States or any foreign country are unduly burdening or restricting the foreign trade of the United States, he may enter into trade agreements with foreign governments and proclaim such modifications of existing duties and other import restrictions as may be necessary to carry out any such foreign trade agreement, provided that reductions or increases in any duty rate shall not exceed 50 per cent of any existing rate . . . . This agreement [of the president] is constitutional . . . ."

51. See id. at § 120, Comment *b*.

52. 315 U.S. 203 (1942).

53. Id. at 210.

54. Id. at 234.

made by President Roosevelt in connection with his recognition of the Government of the U.S.S.R.[55]

Justice Douglas, writing for the Court, noted that the Litvinov Assignment was an international compact, an executive agreement, that did not require Senate approval.[56] Citing language from *United States v. Curtiss-Wright Export Corp.*,[57] Douglas stated that the president is the "sole organ of the federal government" in foreign affairs.[58] Failure to find the Litvinov Assignment binding upon the United States and conclusive on the courts would usurp the function of the executive.

> A treaty is a "Law of the Land" under the supremacy clause . . . of the Constitution. Such international compacts and agreements as the Litvinov Assignment have a similar dignity.[59]

Just as state law yields to treaties, Douglas indicated, so must provisions of the executive agreement prevail over state policy.[60] The Court found that the provisions of the Litvinov Assignment passing the vested Soviet right in the property to the United States must be recognized as valid by New York.[61]

The broad presidential power to settle foreign claims by use of executive agreements is well illustrated by *Dames & Moore v. Regan.*[62] After Iranians seized the American Embassy in Tehran on November 4, 1980, and held the occupants hostage, President Carter, acting pursuant to his powers under the International Emergency Economic Powers Act, issued a blocking order that froze all the Iranian Government assets subject to the jurisdiction of the United States. There followed lengthy negotiations and, with the mediation of Algeria, Iran released the American hostages on January 20, 1981 after the United States and Iran signed an Agreement concerning the settlement of claims.

The Agreement required the United States to terminate all suits brought in the U.S. courts against Iran and to "nullify all attachments and judgments obtained therein, to prohibit all further litigation based on such claims, and to bring about the termination of such claims through binding arbitration" before an Iran-United States Claims Tribunal.[63] President Carter, and later President Reagan, signed a series of executive orders to implement this agreement. These orders purported to nullify all attachments, liens, or other non-Iranian interests in Iranian assets subject to President Carter's November 14, 1979 freeze of Iranian assets.

Petitioner sued for declaratory and injunctive relief against the enforcement of the Executive Orders and the Treasury Department's implementing regulations claiming that they were unconstitutional to the extent that they "adversely affect petitioner's final judgment [on a contract claim] against the Government of Iran and the Atomic Energy Organization [of Iran], its execution of that judgment in the state of Washington, its judgment attachments, and its ability to continue to litigate against the Iranian banks."[64]

The Court, per Rehnquist, J., upheld the constitutionality of the Executive Orders re-

---

55. Id. at 231–32. See also Moscow Fire Insurance Co. v. Bank of New York & Trust Co., 280 N.Y. 286, 20 N.E.2d 758 (1939), aff'd by an equally divided Court, sub nom., United States v. Moscow Fire Insurance Co., 309 U.S. 624 (1940) (New York Court of Appeals refused to recognize the superiority of the United States' claims on the basis of the Litvinov Assignment over the claims of others).

56. 315 U.S. 203, 229 (1942). United States v. Belmont, 301 U.S. 324, 330 (1937).

57. 299 U.S. 304, 320 (1936).

58. 315 U.S. at 229.

59. 315 U.S. at 230.

60. Id. at 230–31.

61. Id. at 234.

62. 453 U.S. 654 (1981). See generally, Symposium: Dames & Moore v. Regan, 29 U.C.L.A. L.Rev. 977–1159 (1982)—Brownstein, The Takings Clause and the Iranian Claims Settlement, id. at 984; Carter, The Iran-United States Claims Tribunal: Observations of the First Year, id. at 1076; Miller, Dames & Moore v. Regan: A Political Decision by a Political Court, id. at 1104; Nowak & Rotunda, A Comment on the Creation and Resolution of a "Non-Problem": Dames & Moore v. Regan, the Foreign Affairs Power, and the Role of the Court, id. at 1129.

63. 453 U.S. at 665.

64. 453 U.S. at 667.

lying in large part on Justice Jackson's analysis in *Youngstown Sheet & Tube Co. v. Sawyer*.[65] The Court's opinion was narrowly drafted and attentive to the civil liberties implications when it held that if the President's freeze amounted to a taking of property, the Government must provide just compensation. This opinion provides no support for the proposition that the President has inherent authority to sign an Executive Agreement which is inconsistent with any of the other provisions of the Bill of Rights. On the contrary, the decision reaffirms the supremacy of the Bill of Rights and is a model of realistic jurisprudence.[66]

The Court first concluded that Congress, by statute, had explicitly authorized the President to nullify the post-freeze attachments and to direct that the blocked Iranian assets be transferred to the New York Federal Reserve Bank and later to Iran.[67] The purpose of this statute is to "permit the President to maintain the foreign assets at his disposal for use" as a "bargaining chip" when negotiating with a hostile nation.[68]

Independent of the attachments of the Iranian assets were the underlying claims against Iran. The Court was not able to find any explicit authority to suspend the claims pending in the U.S. Courts. However, while there was no evidence of contrary congressional intent, there was evidence of legislative intent to invite broad presidential action, and there was a long history of congressional acquiescence of similar presidential conduct. "Crucial to our decision today is the conclusion that Congress has implicitly approved the practice of claim settlement by executive agreement." [69]

The exercise of presidential power in this case did not unconstitutionally divest the federal courts of jurisdiction, any more than a finding of sovereign immunity divests the courts of jurisdiction. Rather the President has directed the federal courts to apply a different rule of substantive law.[70]

Petitioner also charged that the suspension of its claims constituted a taking of their property without just compensation, but the Court found this question not ripe for review. However the majority did find ripe the question whether petitioner would have a remedy at law in the Court of Claims if in fact there was a taking. And the Court held that if there were a taking the Court of Claims would have jurisdiction to provide compensation.[71]

Although cases such as *United States v. Belmont*,[72] *United States v. Pink*,[73] and *Dames & Moore v. Regan* [74] indicate that ex-

---

65. 343 U.S. 579, 634 (1952), cited, e.g., at 453 U.S. at 661–62, 674. For a discussion of Jackson, J.'s concurring opinion see this Chapter, section III, C, infra.

66. See 453 U.S. at 660–61, 688. See generally, Nowak & Rotunda, A Comment on the Creation and Resolution of a Nonproblem": Dames & Moore v. Regan, the Foreign Affairs Power, and the Role of the Court, 29 U.C.L.A.L.Rev. 1129 (1982).

67. The Court relied on the "plain language" of the International Emergency Economic Powers Act, 50 U.S.C.A. § 1702, its legislative history, and the legislative history and cases interpreting the Trading with the Enemy Act, 50 U.S.C.A.App. § 5(b), from which was drawn the pertinent language of § 1702.

68. 453 U.S. at 673. See also, Propper v. Clark, 337 U.S. 472, 493 (1949).

69. 453 U.S. at 680. See also 453 U.S. at 679, n. 8: "At least since the case of the 'Wilmington Packet' in 1799, Presidents have exercised the power to settle claims of United States Nationals by executive agreement."

70. 453 U.S. at 684–85. Cf. Chapter 1, section III, supra.

71. 453 U.S. at 688–90. Stevens, J., concurred and would have held that the question as to the jurisdiction of the Court of Claims was not ripe. Powell, J., concurred and dissented in part. He would not have decided whether the president's nullification of the attachments represented a taking. The majority, in a footnote, had rejected petitioner's argument that although the president, when he froze assets, could have forbidden attachments, "once he allowed them the President permitted claimants to acquire property interests in their attachments." The Court, rather, concluded that "because of the President's authority to prevent or condition attachments, and because of the orders he issued to this effect, petitioner did not acquire any 'property' interest in its attachments of the sort that would support a constitutional claim for compensation." 453 U.S. at 674 n. 6.

72. 301 U.S. 324 (1937).

73. 315 U.S. 203 (1942).

74. 453 U.S. 654 (1981).

ecutive agreements are as binding upon the nation as ratified treaties, questions still remain as to what extent an executive agreement is equivalent to a treaty. *United States v. Guy W. Capps, Inc.*[75] for example, involved an executive agreement between Canada and the United States regulating potato exports by Canada. This agreement was the third type of executive agreement discussed above. The Fourth Circuit stated:

> [T]he executive agreement was void because it was not authorized by Congress and contravened provisions of a statute dealing with the very matter to which it related and that the contract relied on, which was based on the executive agreement, was unenforceable in the courts of the United States for like reason.[76]

The court found this executive agreement invalid because the Executive branch had not properly exercised those powers delegated to it by earlier federal statutes:

> There was no pretense of complying with the requirements of [the Agricultural Adjustment Act of 1948]. . . . Since the purpose of the agreement as well as its effect was to bar imports which would interfere with the Agricultural Adjustment program, it was necessary that the provisions of this statute be complied with and an executive agreement excluding such exports which failed to comply with it was void.[77]

Although the Supreme Court has not ruled on this issue directly and affirmed on other grounds,[78] the *Capps* decision suggests that the executive agreements might not be com-

pletely equal to treaties in all respects. The Restatement of the Law, 2d, Foreign Relations Law of the United States, has summarized the effect on domestic law of an executive agreement entered into pursuant to the president's constitutional authority, the first type of executive agreement described above:

> (1) An executive agreement, is made by the United States without reference to a treaty or act of Congress, conforming to the [appropriate] constitutional limitations . . . and manifesting an intention that it shall become effective as domestic law of the United States at the time it becomes binding on the United States.
>
> (a) supersedes inconsistent provisions of the law of the several states, but
>
> (b) does not supersede inconsistent provisions of earlier acts of Congress.[79]

The position of the Restatement, 2d—that an executive agreement entered into by the president pursuant to his constitutional authority, the first type of agreement described above, does not supersede earlier acts of Congress[80]—may not be entirely correct when the president is in fact entering into an agreement pursuant to his *inherent* presidential authority in the field of foreign relations.[81] The Reporter's Notes to the First Tentative Draft of the Restatement of the Law, Foreign Relations Law of the United States (Revised) rejects the position of the Restatement, 2d,[82] and the black letter of

---

75. 204 F.2d 655 (4th Cir. 1953), aff'd on other grounds 348 U.S. 296 (1955).

76. 204 F.2d at 658. The court also stated that no cause of action had been created by Congress for this type of injury. Id.

On the president's powers to regulate international economic affairs, see generally J. Jackson, Legal Problems of International Economic Relations, Chapter 4 (1977).

77. 204 F.2d at 658–59. The Circuit Court also said that the executive agreement is invalid because it affects foreign commerce and the president does not have the power to regulate interstate and foreign commerce since that power is vested in the Congress by the Constitution. This dictum is unpersuasive. "If the President cannot make agreements on any matter on which Congress could legislate, there could be no executive agreements with domestic legal consequences, since, we have seen, the legislative powers of Congress

has few and far limits." L. Henkin, Foreign Affairs and the Constitution 181 (1972).

78. 204 F.2d 655, 658 (4th Cir. 1953), aff'd on other grounds 348 U.S. 296 (1955). See also, Seery v. United States, 127 F.Supp. 601, 606 (Ct.Cl.1955); American Bitumals & Asphalt Co. v. United States, 146 F.Supp. 703, 708 (Cust.Ct.1956), rev'd on other grounds 246 F.2d 270 (C.C.P.A.1957), cert. denied 355 U.S. 883 (1957); Consumer's Union v. Rogers, 352 F.Supp. 1319 (D.D.C.1973).

79. Restatement of the Law, 2d, Foreign Relations Law of the United States, § 144(1) (1965).

80. See text at nn. 47–48, supra.

81. P. Hay & R. Rotunda, The United States Federal System: Legal Integration in the American Experience 59–60 (Giuffrè, Milan 1982).

82. Tent.Draft No. 1, at 70 (Reporter's Notes to § 135) (April 1, 1980).

the Restatement (Revised) also does not adopt the view of the Restatement, 2d.[83]

In short, if the president has authority under the Constitution or otherwise to promulgate an executive order, and if that order is consistent with previously enacted federal law, then that executive agreement is also the supreme law of the land and must prevail over contrary state law and probably also over earlier Congressional enactments if the president is, in fact, entering into an agreement pursuant to his inherent presidential authority in the field of foreign relations.

III. THE WAR POWER

A. Introduction

Constitutional language suggests that the president and Congress share the war power, the dominant authority being vested in the legislature. Congress declares war and is delegated power to tax and finance expenditures necessary for defense. Additionally, Congress determines the rules of warfare, is empowered to raise and support an army and navy and makes all laws necessary and proper for exercising the war power.[1] The president, the Constitution provides, is the Commander-in-Chief of the armed forces.[2] It has been argued that the Commander-in-Chief clause, read in concert with provisions vesting executive power in the president to see that the laws are faithfully executed and peace preserved, authorizes the president to use military force where required to protect national interests unless Congress prohibits such action.[3]

B. Historical Development of the War Power

The nature of the executive and congressional war powers has been the subject of a debate which was initiated when the Constitution was written and continues to the present day. The framers, believing the power to enter into war should be granted to the body most broadly representative of the people, vested the power to declare war in Congress.[4] Alexander Hamilton writing on the executive's role in the *Federalist Papers* endorsed a limited Commander-in-Chief power.[5]

> The President will have only the occasional command of such part of the militia of the nation as by legislative provision may be called into the actual service of the Union. . . . [The Commander-in-Chief power] would amount to nothing more than the command and direction of the military and naval forces, as first general and admiral of the Confederacy.

Hamilton believed the president was powerless to declare war and to raise armies.[6] He expressed fear that the war power would be construed to prohibit raising armies in peace time thereby preventing the nation from preparing to defend itself against future invasions.[7] James Madison, sharing Hamilton's apprehension, asserted that interest in self preservation would prevail over any constitutional barriers that limited military preparations and precautions unless there was a war.[8] Although the framers intended to place a constitutional check upon the president's power to involve the nation in war, they also wanted to be certain that the president had authority to mobilize military forces to repel sudden attacks.[9]

Historically presidents have justified their authorization of military intervention abroad

---

83. Id. at 64, § 135(1). See also, id. at 66, Comment (a).

1. U.S. Const. art. 1, § 8.

2. U.S. Const. art. 2.

3. See E. Corwin, The President: Office and Powers 134 (4th rev. ed. 1957).

4. C. Berdahl, War Powers of the Executive in the United States 79 (1921).

5. A. Hamilton, The Federalist Papers, No. 69 at 417–18 (Rossiter ed. 1961).

6. Id. at 18.

7. A. Hamilton, The Federalist Papers, No. 25 at 162–67 (Rossiter ed. 1961).

8. J. Madison, The Federalist Papers, No. 41 at 256–64 (Rossiter ed. 1961).

9. 2 M. Farrand, The Records of the Federal Convention of 1787 at 313, 318–19 (rev. ed. 1937).

without congressional approval on three theories: Self defense, neutrality and collective security.[10] First, presidents have asserted they have power to order defensive military action in response to aggression without consulting Congress. The second theory, the neutrality theory, developed as a justification for military intervention in foreign countries to protect United States nationals and property. The executive could send troops abroad for a limited security purpose but the troops were to be neutral to any conflict in the foreign country. Third, presidential authorization of military intervention without prior congressional approval has been justified as within the executive's power under collective security agreements such as the Organization of American States (O.A.S.), The North Atlantic Treaty Organization (N.A.T.O.) and the South East Asian Treaty Organization (S.E.A.T.O.).[11]

Self defense was the first theory used to justify expansion of executive war power. President Jefferson's hesitation to take aggressive action against Tripoli without the consent of Congress after the Beys declared war against the United States was criticized by Hamilton. Hamilton wrote that no congressional approval was necessary for any defensive military action taken by the president as long as the United States was not the aggressor.[12] Subsequent presidents have relied on the self defense theory many times since Hamilton made this argument. During the Mexican American War Con-

gress, after heated debate, upheld President Polk's orders authorizing the United States troops to attack first in self defense if the enemy crossed the Rio Grande into disputed territory.[13] In the *Prize Cases*,[14] during the Civil War, the Supreme Court found President Lincoln had the right to blockade southern states without a congressional declaration of war. Writing for a five to four majority, Justice Grier stated that the president has the power to determine if hostilities are sufficiently serious to compel him to act to suppress the belligerency or take defensive measures.

> He [the president] has no power to initiate or declare a war either against a foreign nation or a domestic State. But by the Acts of Congress of February 28, 1795, and 3d of March, 1807, he is authorized to call out the military and naval forces of the United States in case of invasion by foreign nations, and to suppress insurrection against the government of a State or of the United States.
>
> If a war be made by invasion of a foreign nation, the President is not only authorized but bound to resist force by force. He does not initiate the war, but is bound to accept the challenge without waiting for any special legislative authority. And whether the hostile party be a foreign invader, or States organized in rebellion, it is none the less a war, although the declaration of it be "unilateral."[15]

The executive, the Court indicated, was also empowered to determine what degree of force should be used to respond to the conflict.[16]

---

10. The "Pacificus" and "Helvidius" letters on the foreign affairs power also reflect the sentiments of Madison and Hamilton on the division of the war power between the president and Congress. Madison argued the foreign affairs power could be used to commit the nation to a course of action leading to war. He concluded that, by virtue of the constitutional provision expressly granting Congress the power to declare war, the foreign affairs power must also be vested in Congress. The opposing argument was adopted by Hamilton who perceived the determination of the direction of foreign policy to be an inherently executive power although the implementation of such power depended upon subsequent acts of Congress. E. Corwin The President: Office and Powers 177–81 (4th rev. ed. 1957).

11. The "Yale Paper"—Indochina: The Constitutional Crisis 116 Cong.Rec. S 7117–S 7123 (May 13, 1970). See generally, Note, Congress, the President,

and the Power to Commit Forces to Combat, 81 Harv. L.Rev. 1771, 1778–85. (1968).

12. A. Hamilton, Works of Alexander Hamilton 746–47 (J. Hamilton ed. 1851); Note, Congress, the President, and the Power to Commit Forces to Combat, 81 Harv.L.Rev. 1771, 1779 (1968).

13. Act of May 13, 1846, ch. 16, 9 Stat. 9. Later, however, the House of Representatives amended a resolution of thanks to General Taylor to include language charging that Polk had unconstitutionally and unnecessarily involved the United States in a war. Note, Congress, the President, and the Power to Commit Forces to Combat, 81 Harv.L.Rev. 1771, 1780 n. 50 (1968).

14. 67 U.S. (2 Black) 635 (1863).

15. Id. at 668.

16. Id. at 670.

Actions of presidents in this century have led to a steady erosion of the congressional war making power. Under the guise of the neutrality theory Theodore Roosevelt sent troops to Panama in 1903. The troops in reality were being used to fight the Colombian Army.[17] President Truman ordered troops to South Korea to repel the invasion by North Korea without seeking authorization from Congress. Although Truman described involvement in Korea as a police action, not a war, public opposition to the president's action developed as the nation became deeply involved in a major military conflict.[18] During the subsequent administration President Eisenhower was careful to seek congressional approval prior to authorizing military involvement in Formosa and the Suez crisis.[19]

A recent trend has been for the president to secure general Congressional authorization to fall back upon in case the executive's power to authorize military intervention in foreign conflicts is later attacked. President Kennedy justified the adoption of the quarantine during the Cuban missile crisis on the basis of a joint Congressional resolution and the United States' O.A.S. collective security arrangement.[20] The marines sent to the Dominican Republic by President Johnson were initially justified under the neutrality theory as necessary to protect United States' nationals. Later the neutrality rationale was dropped and the explanation was then made

that the president was authorized to order the troops to Santa Domingo under the provisions of the Rio Treaty adopted pursuant to the O.A.S. charter.[21] President Johnson relied upon the Commander-in-Chief clause and the Gulf of Tonkin resolution to justify his authorization of escalated military involvement in Viet Nam.[22]

C. Economic Regulations and the War Power

The power of the president and Congress to impose economic regulations in times of war provides insight into the nature and scope of the war power. In *Woods v. Cloyd W. Miller Co.*[23] the Supreme Court reversed the District Court. The lower court had held that Congress' authority to regulate rent by virtue of the war power ended with the Presidential Proclamation terminating World War II hostilities.[24] The Court found that the war power sustained Title II of the Housing and Rent Act of 1947 citing a passage from *Hamilton v. Kentucky Distillers Co.*[25] that included in the war power the power "to remedy the evils which have arisen from [the war's] rise and progress" and continues until the emergency has ended. Thus, cessation of hostilities is not necessarily the end of a war.[26] Since the power to wage war is the power to wage it successfully,[27] the context of a war or preparations for

---

17. S. Bemis, A Diplomatic History of the United States 515–19 (4th ed. 1955).

18. R. Leckie, The Wars of America 850–58 (1968).

19. T. Bailey, A Diplomatic History of the American People 834–44 (6th ed. 1958). See generally Note, Congress, the President, and the Power to Commit Forces to Combat, 81 Harv.L.Rev. 1771, 1791–93 (1968).

20. See Presidential Proclamation No. 3504, 27 Fed. Reg. 10,401 (1962) where Kennedy justified the quarantine and accompanying measures taken against Cuba and the Soviet Union on the basis of the joint resolution and a resolution passed by the Organization of American States authorizing the quarantine.

See also 2 A. Chayes, T. Ehrlich and A. Lowenfeld, International Legal Process 1107–09 (1969).

21. 2 A. Chayes, T. Ehrlich and A. Lowenfeld, International Legal Process 1179–82 (1969). Excellent accounts of the Dominican Republic Crisis are given in,

N.Y. Times, Apr. 29, 1965, at 1, col. 8 and N.Y. Times, May 3, 1965, at 10, col. 1.

22. Note, Congress, the President, and the Power to Commit Forces to Combat, 81 Harv.L.Rev. 1771, 1793 (1968) citing U.S. Dept. of State, The Legality of the United States Participation in the Defense of Viet Nam, 54 Dept. State Bull. 474, 484–85 (1966).

23. 333 U.S. 138 (1948).

24. Id. at 140.

25. 251 U.S. 146 (1919).

26. 333 U.S. 138, 141 (1948).

27. E.g., United States v. Macintosh, 283 U.S. 605, 622 (1931); Home Building & Loan Ass'n v. Blaisdell, 290 U.S. 398, 426 (1934); Hirabayashi v. United States, 320 U.S. 81, 93 (1943). Thus the war power has been used to justify internment of Japanese-American citizens in World War II. See, e.g., Korematsu v. United

a war or its winding down may justify extensive legislative and executive power.[28]

In *Youngstown Sheet & Tube Co. v. Sawyer* [29] the Supreme Court discussed the president's power to impose economic regulations under the Commander-in-Chief clause and other constitutional provisions. Apprehensive that an impending steel worker's strike would endanger national security, President Truman issued an executive order instructing Secretary of Commerce Sawyer to seize and operate many of the nation's steel mills,[30] Truman justified the executive order as valid under the constitutional and statutory power vested in him as President and Commander-in-Chief. Pursuant to the president's order the Secretary of Commerce seized the steel mills. Sawyer directed the presidents of the mills to operate their facilities in compliance with regulations the Department of Commerce issued. Truman immediately informed Congress of these events, but the legislature failed to take any action.[31] Congress had previously enacted legislation providing methods for handling situations of this nature and in the case of a labor dispute, had expressly refused to condone governmental seizure of property.[32]

The steel companies filed suit against Secretary of Commerce Sawyer in the district court praying for declaratory judgment and injunctive relief. The district court granted the plaintiffs a preliminary injunction which the appellate court stayed. The Supreme Court, in an expedited proceeding, affirmed the district court's order in a six to three decision finding the executive's seizure order invalid.[33]

Justice Black wrote the opinion for the Court in which Justices Frankfurter, Douglas, Jackson and Burton concurred. Justice Clark concurred in the judgment of the Court. Although the appeal was made from the lower court's decision to issue a preliminary injunction, Black stated that the issue of the Constitutional validity of President Truman's order was ripe for determination. The Court found that no express or implied statutory provision authorized the president's seizure order [34] and rejected the argument that the order should be upheld as a valid exercise of the president's Commander-in-Chief power. In response to the government's contention that numerous cases have found military commanders entitled to broad powers, Black stated:

> Such cases need not concern us here. Even though "theater of war" be an expanding concept, we cannot with faithfulness to our constitutional system hold that the Commander in Chief of the Armed Forces has the ultimate power as such to take possession of private property in order to keep labor disputes from stopping production. This is a job for the Nation's law-makers, not for its military authorities.[35]

Black also concluded that the executive power vested in the president by the Constitution, particularly his duty to see that the laws are faithfully executed, refutes the idea that the chief executive can make laws.[36] Congress has "exclusive constitutional authority to make laws necessary and proper to carry out the powers vested by the Constitution" in the federal government.[37] The "necessary and proper" clause applies to Congress, not to the executive branch.

States, 323 U.S. 214 (1944). It is unclear the extent to which *Korematsu* is still good law as to its result.

28. E.g., L. Henkin, Foreign Affairs and the Constitution, 321 n. 15 (1973).

29. 343 U.S. 579 (1952).

30. Id. at 583, Executive Order 10340 April 8, 1952, 17 Fed.Reg. 3139 (1952).

31. 343 U.S. at 583.

32. Corwin, The Steel Seizure Case, 53 Colum.L.R. 53, 55–56 (1953). Corwin indicates Congress provided alternative solutions for similar problems in the De-

fense Production Act of 1950, 50 U.S.C.A.App. § 2071 (1952); The Labor Management Relations (Taft-Hartley) Act of 1947, 29 U.S.C.A. §§ 141–197 (1952); and the Selective Service Act of 1948, 50 U.S.C.A.App. §§ 451–462 (1952).

33. 343 U.S. at 584–86.

34. Id. at 584–86.

35. Id. at 587.

36. Id. at 587.

37. Id. at 588–89.

In his concurring opinion Justice Frankfurter indicated he was not drawing conclusions as to what powers the president would have had in the absence of legislation applicable to the seizure.[38] What was at issue was the president's authorization of the steel seizure after Congress had expressly refused to support this course of action.

> In formulating legislation for dealing with industrial conflicts, Congress could not more clearly and emphatically have withheld authority . . .[39]

Frankfurter warned, however:

> It is an inadmissibly narrow conception of American constitutional law to confine it to the words of the Constitution and disregard the gloss which life has written upon them. In short, a systematic, unbroken, executive practice, long pursued to the knowledge of the Congress and never before questioned . . . may be treated as a gloss on "executive Power" vested in the President by § 1 of Art. II.[40]

Prior incidents of industrial seizures Frankfurter concluded did not indicate a past history of Congressional acquiescence of executive authority in this area.[41]

Justice Douglas stated in his concurring opinion that the branch of government with "the power to pay compensation for a seizure is the only one able to authorize a seizure or make lawful one that the President has effected. That seems to me to be the necessary result of the condemnation provision in the Fifth Amendment."[42]

Justice Jackson, in his separate concurrence, argued that the president's powers "are not fixed but fluctuate, depending upon their disjunction or conjunction with those of Congress."[43] The scope of the president's war powers, Jackson believed, depended upon the conditions existing at the time the executive asserted his authority. He developed a three part analysis. First, when the "President acts pursuant to an express authorization of Congress, his authority is at its maximum."[44] If the president had seized the steel mills pursuant to Congressional grant of authority the constitutional validity of his action would probably have been upheld. Secondly, if the president acted:

> in the absence of either a congressional grant or denial of authority, he can only rely upon his own independent powers, but there is a zone of twilight in which he and Congress may have concurrent authority, or in which its distribution is uncertain. Therefore, congressional inertia . . . may sometimes . . . enable, if not invite, measures on independent presidential responsibility.[45]

When, however, the president acts contrary to the express or implied will of Congress then the executive power falls to the third part of the analysis, an extremely low level, his "lowest ebb" of authority. The president can then:

> rely only upon his own constitutional powers minus any constitutional powers of Congress over the matter. Courts can sustain exclusive presidential control in such a case only by disabling the Congress from acting upon the subject. Presidential claim to a power at once so conclusive and preclusive must be scrutinized with caution.[46]

Jackson concluded that the steel seizure order was contrary to the will of Congress and, as a consequence, could only be upheld if such seizures were found to be within the power of the executive and beyond the scope of congressional authority.[47] And the president's actions were not of that type.

---

38. Id. at 597.

39. Id. at 602.

40. Id. at 610–11.

41. Id. at 613.

42. Id. at 631–32.

43. Id. at 635.

44. Id.

45. Id. at 637.

46. Id. at 637–38.

47. Id. at 640.

The Court endorsed and applied Jackson's analysis in Dames & Moore v. Regan, 453 U.S. 657, 669 (1981), discussed in section II, E, supra, but noted that "it is doubtless the case that executive action in any particular instance falls, not neatly in one of three pigeonholes, but rather at some point along a spectrum running from explicit congressional authorization to explicit congressional prohibition."

Justice Burton stated in his concurrence that the seizure order was repugnant to the separation of powers theory.[48] In a concurring opinion, Justice Clark indicated that although the president has extensive authority to act in times of national emergency this power is subject to limitations prescribed by Congress.[49] In the dissent Justice Vinson joined by Justices Reed and Minton, rationalized that the president was within the scope of his constitutional authority when he ordered the steel mills seized as an emergency situation existed.[50]

48. Id. at 655–60.

49. Id. at 660–67.

50. Id. at 667–710.

51.

PURPOSE AND POLICY

Sec. 2. (a) It is the purpose of this joint resolution to fulfill the intent of the framers of the Constitution of the United States and insure that the collective judgment of both the Congress and the President will apply to the introduction of United States Armed Forces into hostilities, or into situations where imminent involvement in hostilities is clearly indicated by the circumstances, and to the continued use of such forces in hostilities or in such situations.

(b) Under article I, section 8, of the Constitution, it is specifically provided that the Congress shall have the power to make all laws necessary and proper for carrying into execution, not only its own powers but also all other powers vested by the Constitution in the Government of the United States, or in any department or officer thereof.

(c) The constitutional powers of the President as Commander-in-Chief to introduce United States Armed Forces into hostilities, or into situations where imminent involvement in hostilities is clearly indicated by the circumstances, are exercised only pursuant to (1) a declaration of war, (2) specific statutory authorization, or (3) a national emergency created by attack upon the United States, its territories or possessions, or its armed forces.

CONSULTATION

Sec. 3. The President in every possible instance shall consult with Congress before introducing United States Armed Forces into hostilities or into situations where imminent involvement in hostilities is clearly indicated by the circumstances, and after every such introduction shall consult regularly with the Congress until United States Armed Forces are no longer engaged in hostilities or have been removed from such situations.

D. Present Status of the War Power

The ability of the executive to deploy the military to foreign nations to fight in informal wars created a growing discontent with what many have regarded as the president's assumption of congressional war power during the Viet Nam conflict. To restore what has been argued to be the balance intended by the framers, Congress passed the War Powers Resolution over a presidential veto on November 7, 1973; it is reprinted in part in the margin.[51] The War Powers Resolution restricts the executive's authority to involve the United States in foreign controversies without Congressional approval.

REPORTING

Sec. 4. (a) In the absence of a declaration of war, in any case in which United States Armed Forces are introduced—

(1) into hostilities or into situations where imminent involvement in hostilities is clearly indicated by the circumstances;

(2) into the territory, airspace or waters of a foreign nation, while equipped for combat, except for deployments which relate solely to supply, replacement, repair, or training of such forces; or

(3) in numbers which substantially enlarge United States Armed Forces equipped for combat already located in a foreign nation;

the President shall submit within 48 hours to the Speaker of the House of Representatives and to the President pro tempore of the Senate a report, in writing [setting forth "the circumstances necessitating the introduction of armed forces," "the constitutional and legislative authority" under which it occurred, "the estimated scope and duration of the hostilities," and "such other information as the Congress may request."]

CONGRESSIONAL ACTION * * *

Sec. 5. * * * (b) Within sixty calendar days after a report is submitted or is required to be submitted pursuant to section 4(a)(1), whichever is earlier, the President shall terminate any use of United States Armed Forces with respect to which such report was submitted (or required to be submitted), unless the Congress (1) has declared war or has enacted a specific authorization for such use of United States Armed Forces, (2) has extended by law such sixty-day period, or (3) is physically unable to meet as a result of an armed attack upon the United States. . . .

(c) Notwithstanding subsection (b), at any time that United States Armed Forces are engaged in hostilities outside the territory of the United States, its possessions and territories without a declaration of war or specific statutory authorization, such forces shall be removed by the President if the Congress so directs by concurrent resolution. * * *

Specific provisions of the Resolution, however, ensure that the president has authority to send the military into combat without requesting authorization from Congress if the United States or one of her territories is attacked.[52]

The War Powers Resolution raises many interesting and unresolved questions. Is the Resolution binding? If it is, who has standing to sue claiming a violation of the provisions? No specific language in the Resolution resolves the standing issue. Perhaps Justice Brennan's theory, expressed in the different context of other cases, that the only requirement for standing is injury in fact [53] could provide a basis for military personnel sent abroad in violation of the resolution to sue the president. But even if standing is found to exist, it may well be the case that judicial review of cases under this law are foreclosed by the doctrine of political questions.[54] The impact of a resolution may suggest that questions regarding provisions of the War Powers Resolution should be considered justiciable and not immune from judicial review as political questions. Even if this resolution were reviewable and subject to litigation, its constitutionality is subject to a presidential claim that the resolution improperly seeks to subtract from his inherent powers. Under Justice Jackson's analysis in the Steel Seizure case, the president's war powers should be at their lowest ebb: if he would act contrary to the War Powers Resolution, he would then have only his own powers minus any Constitutional powers of Congress to reduce his powers. The final answers to all of these issues are unsettled.

E. Military Courts

1. Overview

Military courts were established by Congress pursuant to its Article I power to make rules for the government and regulation of the land and naval forces and its power to make laws which are necessary and proper for implementing that power.[1] During war or insurrection, military courts dispense justice to both civilian and military transgressors. Martial law can be declared if, by reason of civil disturbance or invasion, the civil courts cannot function; during the period of martial law, all crimes are tried by courts-martial. In wartime, even when civil

INTERPRETATION OF JOINT RESOLUTION

Sec. 8. (a) Authority to introduce United States Armed Forces into hostilities or into situations wherein involvement in hostilities is clearly indicated by the circumstances shall not be inferred—

(1) from any provision of law . . . .

(2) from any treaty . . . . or . . .

(b) Nothing in this joint resolution shall be construed to require any further specific statutory authorization to permit members of United States Armed Forces to participate jointly with members of the armed forces of one or more foreign countries in the headquarters operations of high-level military commands which were established prior to the date of enactment of this joint resolution and pursuant to the United Nations Charter or any treaty ratified by the United States prior to such date.

(c) For purposes of this joint resolution, the term "introduction of United States Armed Forces" includes the assignment of members of such armed forces to command, coordinate, participate in the movement of, or accompany the regular or irregular military forces of any foreign country or government when such military forces are engaged, or there exists an imminent threat that such forces will become engaged, in hostilities.

(d) Nothing in this joint resolution—

(1) is intended to alter the constitutional authority of the Congress or of the President, or the provisions of existing treaties; or

(2) shall be construed as granting any authority to the President with respect to the introduction of United States Armed Forces into hostilities or into situations wherein involvement in hostilities is clearly indicated by the circumstances which authority he would not have had in the absence of this joint resolution. * * *

52. War Powers Resolution, 50 U.S.C.A. §§ 1541–48, § 2 C(3).

See generally, Franck, After the Fall: The New Procedural Framework for Congressional Control Over the War Power, 71 Am.J. of Internat'l L. 605 (1977).

53. See Association of Data Processing Service Organizations v. Camp, 397 U.S. 150 (1970) (Brennan, J. concurring); Barlow v. Collins, 397 U.S. 159 (1970) (Brennan, J. concurring).

54. See Chapter 2, section IV, E, 2, a.

1. U.S. Const. art. I, § 8.

courts continue to function and try nonmilitary crimes, enemy combatants may be tried by courts-martial under the law of war [2] whether the crimes were committed in a war zone or through entrance by stealth into a non-combatant zone. Martial law must end when civil courts can again function; court-martial under the law of war can occur at least until peace has been declared.

During peacetime, military courts play the limited role of governing members of the armed forces. Although courts-martial may try members of the armed forces whether they are stationed within the United States or on foreign soil, these courts do not have jurisdiction to try those family members who accompany the servicemen, nor do they have jurisdiction to try civilian employees. Courts-martial can only try servicemen while they are actively in the military and only then if the crime is service-connected. The United States Supreme Court has severely limited the jurisdiction of courts-martial because, courts-martial, as courts established under Article I, do not need to provide most constitutional safeguards for defendants. Courts-martial do not have an independent judiciary with life tenure,[3] do not provide a jury of the accused's peers,[4] do not provide legal counsel for the accused in all non petty offenses,[5] and do not require indictment by grand jury.[6] Moreover, Article III courts, including the United States Supreme Court, do not have the power to directly review decisions of courts-martial. Military prisoners may petition Article III courts to grant a writ of habeas corpus, but review in even collateral proceedings is limited to ascertaining that the military court had jurisdiction and that it considered the defendant's claims. Civil courts cannot correct errors in the military court's procedure or conclusions. A civil court, furthermore, generally must abstain until the conclusion of the military trial before granting the writ of habeas corpus.

2. Martial Law and the Law of War

Martial law, when applicable, supercedes the law of jurisdiction by granting control of persons and property to military rule and court martial. It is not a true body of law but the principle upon which the military is given control of the law. As Blackstone stated:

[M]artial law, which is built upon no settled principles, but is entirely arbitrary in its decisions, is . . . in truth and reality no law, but something indulged rather than allowed as a law. The necessity of order and discipline in an army is the only thing which can give it countenance, and therefore it ought not to be permitted in time of peace, when the king's courts are open for all persons to receive justice according to the laws of the land.[7]

Ex parte Milligan[8] gave the United States Supreme Court the opportunity to discuss the parameters of the declaration of martial law. Milligan was arrested in Indiana on the orders of the commander of the Indiana military district and tried by court-martial. He was convicted and sentenced to be hanged. He applied for a writ of habeas corpus to the Supreme Court, contending that he, as a civilian and citizen of a non-rebelling state, was not under the jurisdiction of a court-martial. The Supreme Court sustained Milligan's contention, holding that martial law "can never be applied to citizens in states which have upheld the authority of the government, and where the courts are open and their process unobstructed . . . . Martial law cannot arise from a *threatened* invasion. The necessity must be

---

2. The law of war is a branch of international law that prescribes the rights and obligations of belligerents and other persons resident in a theatre of war. For an explication of the law of war, see 2 Winthrop, Military Law and Precedents, The Law of War (2d ed.; 1920 reprint).

3. See, e.g., 10 U.S.C.A. § 826. The requirement of an independent judiciary is found in Article III of the Constitution and applies only to Article III courts.

4. See, e.g., 10 U.S.C.A. § 825.

5. Middendorf v. Henry, 425 U.S. 25 (1976).

6. U.S. Const. amend. V; Ex parte Milligan, 71 U.S. (4 Wall.) 2 (1866).

7. 1 Blackstone, Commentaries 413.

8. 71 U.S. (4 Wall.) 2 (1866).

actual and present; the invasion real, such as effectually closes the courts and deposes the civil administration." [9] If the invasion has ended, there is no basis for martial law. Even if the right of habeas corpus is lawfully suspended, as it may be during time of War or insurrection, a prisoner thus denied habeas corpus is, nevertheless, entitled to a civilian trial with full Constitutional protections.[10]

In 1946, the Supreme Court in *Duncan v. Kahanamoku* [11] confronted a congressional act authorizing the declaration of martial law in case Hawaii were to be threatened with invasion. The Court avoided a constitutional decision on Congress' power to establish martial law by construing "martial law" in the act to authorize merely vigorous action for the maintenance of an orderly civil government and not to authorize the supplanting of civil courts by courts martial.

Rules protecting civilians from courts martial while civil courts can function, however, do not insulate combatants in a war from military jurisdiction. Thus, the Supreme Court in *Ex parte Quirin* [12] permitted trial by court-martial of eight saboteurs who entered the United States secretly and without uniforms. Their status as combatants removed them, including one claiming American citizenship, from the purview of *Milligan's* holding that citizens of states with open civilian courts could not be tried by court martial. *In re Yamashita* [13] extended the jurisdiction of military tribunals to guard against the immediate renewal of the conflict and to remedy the evils which the

military operations have produced. The Court concluded that at least until peace has been officially recognized by treaty or proclamation, military commissions can try violations of the law of war committed before the cessation of hostilities. The Fifth Amendment due process provision does not apply in these circumstances. The Court held that such trials were not subject to the Articles of War standards for military trials because the Articles of War applied only to trials for members of the American army and for prisoners of War who committed crimes while prisoners.

3. Military Law

Military law refers to the legal system, including the courts, by which the military forces are governed.[14] Military courts have limited jurisdiction; they can try only military personnel for service-related crimes. In *United States ex rel. Toth v. Quarles*,[15] the United States Supreme Court held that only present military personnel were subject to court martial. Toth received an honorable discharge after serving in Korea; five months later, he was arrested and tried by court-martial for a murder committed in Korea while he was in the army. The Supreme Court noted that millions of citizens were veterans and that allowing military courts to take jurisdiction on the basis of past association with the military would remove from many citizens the protections of civil trial. After an initial ruling to the contrary, the Court extended the *Toth* ruling in *Reid v. Covert* [16] to remove from military jurisdic-

---

9. 71 U.S. at 121, 127 (emphasis in original).

10. 71 U.S. at 126. But see Korematsu v. United States, 323 U.S. 214 (1944), holding that Japanese-American citizens could be subjected to military authority under Congress's war power, even though civilian courts were functioning. See Chapter 16, on Equal Protection, section II, D, 4, a, Classifications Based on Race or National Origin, for a further discussion of *Korematsu.*

The Constitution permits the writ of habeas corpus to be suspended in time of war or insurrection. U.S. Const. art. I, § 9. The suspension would prevent civil courts from hearing habeas petitions from either civilian or military prisoners. However, Congress must declare the suspension. See, Ex parte Bollman, 8 U.S. (4

Cranch) 75; 1 Winthrop, Military Law and Precedents (Military Law) 830 (2d ed., 1920 reprint).

11. 327 U.S. 304 (1946).

12. 317 U.S. 1 (1942).

13. 327 U.S. 1 (1946).

14. For a discussion of the history of military law, see 1 Winthrop, Military Law and Precedents (Military Law) (2d ed., 1920 reprint). Present military law is codified in the Uniform Code of Military Justice, 10 U.S.C.A., ch. 47.

15. 350 U.S. 11 (1955).

16. 354 U.S. 1 (1957), on rehearing, reversing 351 U.S. 470 (1956).

tion family members who accompanied army personnel to foreign bases. In *Covert*, the civilian wife of an air force sergeant residing on base with him in England was convicted by court-martial of killing her husband. The trial was held pursuant to an executive agreement with England that crimes committed on American army bases could be tried by American courts-martial rather than by English courts. The United States Supreme Court held that, at least in capital offense cases, the military could not try a civilian. Justice Black, in a plurality opinion indicated that the agreement with England which permitted the American court-martial was required to conform to the Constitutional constraints on trials. Because civilian spouses are not members of the land and naval forces, Congress had no power to provide for their trial by other than in an Article III court in conformity with Constitutional restraint. At this time, however, there was no ruling on courts-martial jurisdiction in general because Justices Frankfurter and Harlan found that only capital cases should be excluded from military jurisdiction in these circumstances.

Three years later, the Court clarified and expanded *Reid* in *Kinsella v. United States ex rel. Singleton*[17] when it excluded from court-martial jurisdiction civilian family members being tried for noncapital offenses. Other Supreme Court cases held that civilian employees of the armed forces, like civilian

family members, were not within the purview of military court jurisdiction in either capital cases[18] or noncapital cases.[19] Although through this series of decisions, the Court intended to augment the Constitutional protection available to civilians accompanying the military forces, such civilians constitutionally may be tried by the host country.[20]

Military court jurisdiction is limited to particular types of crimes as well as to particular persons. In *O'Callahan v. Parker*,[21] the Supreme Court invalidated the court martial conviction of a serviceman in Hawaii who had attempted to rape a girl while he was on leave and dressed in civilian clothes. The Court held that only service-connected crimes could be tried by court martial. The Court decision noted that the Fifth Amendment excepts from indictment by grand jury only those cases arising in the land or naval forces when in actual service in time of war or public danger. The Court decided that a soldier on leave was not "in actual service", at least when the crime was unconnected to the soldier's military duties. Therefore, the soldier must be indicted and have a civilian trial.

Two years later in *Relford v. Commandant*,[22] the Court upheld the court martial conviction of a serviceman accused of raping several civilian women. The Court found that *O'Callahan* did not apply because these crimes were committed by a serviceman on

Note that *Reid* applied constitutional protections to the family members who accompanied the American soldiers to foreign bases. The mere fact that the bases were abroad did not serve to negate the application of the U.S. Constitution. See also, e.g., Best v. United States, 184 F.2d 131, 138 (1st Cir. 1950), cert. denied 340 U.S. 939 (1951) ("For present purposes we assume and we think probably so, that the protection of the Fourth Amendment extends to United States citizens in foreign countries under occupation by our armed forces."); Cf. Biddle v. United States, 156 F. 759, 761 (9th Cir. 1907). See generally, Fairman, Some New Problems of the Constitution Following the Flag, 1 Stan.L.Rev. 587 (1949); Sutherland, The Flag, the Constitution, and International Agreements, 68 Harv.L. Rev. 1374 (1955). But cf. Haig v. Agee, 453 U.S. 280, 308 (1981) (Court assumes, arguendo, "that the First Amendment protections reach beyond our national boundaries . . . "). See section I, B, supra, text at nn. 31–36.

17.   361 U.S. 234 (1960).

18.   Grishan v. Hagan, 361 U.S. 278 (1960).

19.   McElroy v. United States ex rel. Gugliando, 361 U.S. 281 (1960).

20.   See Wilson v. Girard, 354 U.S. 524 (1957), holding that the American forces could allow Japan to try an American soldier for the murder of a Japanese woman. For discussions of military court jurisdiction over civilians and civilian-military hybrids, see Bishop, Court-Martial Jurisdiction over Military-Civilian Hybrids: Retired Regulars, Reservists, and Discharged Prisoners, 112 U.Penn.L.Rev. 317 (1964); Everett, Military Jurisdiction over Civilians, 1960 Duke L.J. 366; Girard, The Constitution and Court-Martial of Civilians Accompanying the Armed Forces—A Preliminary Analysis, 13 Stan.L.Rev. 461 (1961).

21.   395 U.S. 258 (1969).

22.   401 U.S. 355 (1971).

the military base against women properly on the base; the crimes were service-connected.[23]

4. The Relation Between Military Courts and Civil Courts

Military courts form a separate judicial system from the Article III judicial system of civil courts. As noted previously, many constitutional protections for criminal defendants do not apply to court martial of servicemen.[24] Congress, after creating the military court system for the governing of the armed forces, provided that court-martial decisions could be reviewed by an appeals panel within the military and by the Secretary of Defense or the President if the offense is capital. By statute, Congress declared that military criminal proceeding shall be final and conclusive and binding upon all departments, courts, agencies, and officers of the United States.[25] The Supreme Court held in *Smith v. Whitney*[26] that this provision prevented direct review of courts martial by civil courts. Collateral attack by application for the writ of habeas corpus, however, is permitted. The Court distinguished direct from collateral review in *Dynes v. Hoover*.[27] A final court martial sentence:

> is altogether beyond the jurisdiction or inquiry of any civil tribunal whatever, unless it shall be in a case in which the court had not jurisdiction over the *subject-matter or charge*, or one in which, having jurisdiction over the subject-matter, it has failed to observe the rules prescribed by the statute for its exercise. . . . Persons . . . belonging to the army and the

navy are not subject to illegal or irresponsible courts martial . . . . In such cases, everything which may be done is void—not voidable, but void; and civil courts have never failed, upon a proper suit, to give a party redress . . . .[28]

Civilian courts can review military court decisions for constitutional defects in jurisdiction; it was on this basis that the Supreme Court limited court martial jurisdiction over service-related crimes perpetrated by military personnel.[29] Apparently, civil courts have jurisdiction also to review nonconstitutional jurisdiction issues; military courts have no common law powers and must obey statutory limits on their jurisdiction.[30]

In *Hiatt v. Brown*,[31] the Supreme Court stated that a federal court should not review such matters as propositions of law, sufficiency of evidence, or competency of counsel in a court-martial proceeding. The federal court could review the military's exercise of discretion conferred by statute to refuse counsel to a defendant only if a gross abuse of that discretion had given rise to a defect in the court-martial's jurisdiction. The Court reaffirmed this position in *Burns v. Wilson*.[32] In *Burns*, petitioners asserted that their confessions had been coerced. A plurality of four justices suggested that some review beyond merely establishing court-martial jurisdiction was proper. A civil court should not reevaluate evidence but should determine if the military court had given fair consideration to every significant defense. However, even if the court found an error in the military court's procedure or evaluation of the evidence, it should not

---

23. In Gosa v. Mayden, 413 U.S. 665 (1973), a plurality of the Court held that *O'Callahan* should have only prospective application. A majority of the Court adhered to the service-connected crime requirement for military court jurisdiction.

24. See notes 3 through 6, supra. See also Everett New Look in Military Justice, 1973 Duke L.J. 649.

25. 10 U.S.C.A. § 876. See Gusik v. Schilder, 340 U.S. 128 (1950) (holding that the finality of court-martial determination does not prevent collateral attack in civil courts). For a summary of intramilitary review procedures, see Wacker, The "Unreviewable" Court-Martial Conviction: Supervisory Relief Under the All Writs Act from the United States Court of Military Ap-

peals, 10 Harv.Civ.Rights—Civ.Liberties L.Rev. 33 (1975).

26. 116 U.S. 167 (1885).

27. 61 U.S. (20 How.) 65 (1857).

28. 61 U.S. at 81 (emphasis in original).

29. See text accompanying notes 14 through 20.

30. See McClaughry v. Deming, 186 U.S. 49 (1902); 1 Winthrop, Military Law and Precedents, (Military Law) (2d ed., 1920 reprint).

31. 339 U.S. 103 (1950).

32. 346 U.S. 137 (1953).

overturn the decision; the military court need only consider the defense.[33]

Recently, in *Middendorf v. Henry*,[34] the Court heard a habeas petition in which several soldiers complained that they had been denied counsel in a summary court-martial. The Court denied the petition on the merits, holding that a summary court-martial, which by statute cannot sentence a defendant to more than forty-five days incarceration, is not a criminal proceeding and no counsel is required, at least when the defendants had the opportunity to choose a type of court-martial which could give longer sentences but at which counsel would have been provided.[35] The defendants had waived their right to counsel in writing, and the military court had not determined the constitutionality of the waiver. Although the Court did not discuss the level of review appropriate, *Henry* fits the *Burns* mold: a federal court may hear a claim that the court-martial has not considered.

A civil court can also hear a challenge to the constitutionality of the particular statute or regulation which a defendant has violated, but the Supreme Court has limited the grounds for challenge. In *Parker v. Levy*,[36] an officer had exhorted enlisted personnel to refuse to fight in Viet Nam. The officer was court-martialed for his refusal to obey the command of a superior officer to estab-

lish a training program and for "conduct unbecoming an officer" for his exhortations. The officer challenged his convictions, claiming that the regulations were overbroad and too vague to satisfy the due process requirement of notice. The Court upheld the statutes on two grounds: first, that they had been interpreted sufficiently to give notice of what type of conduct was proscribed, and second, that the defendant could have no reasonable doubt that his conduct was unlawful. Justice Rehnquist, writing for a majority of the Court, noted that because of the need to maintain military discipline, Congress could legislate with greater breadth and flexibility when prescribing rules for the military than it could when legislating for civilian society.[37]

Because the Supreme Court has emphasized the necessity for comity between the civil and military courts,[38] civil courts should wait to review the basis of a court martial until the issues are clear. Nevertheless, a federal court does not have to abstain from hearing a habeas petition during a court-martial proceeding. In *Parisi v. Davidson*,[39] the defendant claimed conscientious objector status while he was in the armed forces. His claim was denied, and he was ordered to board a plane to Viet Nam. He refused and was court-martialed. The Supreme Court held that under these circum-

---

33. Before *Burns*, a majority of the Court had expressed a similar view of the limited review available on habeas petition. In Humphrey v. Smith, 336 U.S. 695 (1949), the Court refused to consider the defendant's guilt or innocence in a habeas action. In Hiatt v. Brown, 339 U.S. 103 (1950), the Court refused to consider a due process challenge based on insufficiency of evidence and incompetence of counsel. Whelchel v. McDonald, 340 U.S. 122 (1950) foreshadowed *Burns*, with the Court holding that the defendant must have the opportunity to present an insanity defense for a military court to retain jurisdiction. Later the Court heard a case, Jackson v. Taylor, 353 U.S. 569 (1957), in which the Court decided on the merits a military review board's jurisdiction to reduce sentence imposed by court martial. The Court, however, refused to review the sentences. One commentator suggests that habeas review for military prisoners is narrower than habeas review for civilians only because a court reviewing a court martial conviction will not find that the court martial lost jurisdiction by having deprived the accused of constitutional rights; Weiner, Courts Martial and

the Bill of Rights: The Original Practice, 72 Harv.L. Rev. 1, 296–97 (1958). Another commentator, however, suggests that habeas review of court martial should be broader than review of civilian courts. See Development in the Law—Federal Habeas Corpus, 83 Harv.L. Rev. 1038, 1216–25 (1970) (also suggesting that lower courts actually do provide fuller review).

34. 425 U.S. 25 (1976).

35. The Court relied on Gagnon v. Scarpelli, 411 U.S. 778 (1972) (holding that probation revocation was not a criminal proceeding for which counsel must be provided). Other types of courts-martial provide counsel as a statutory requirement; the Court did not discuss the constitutional necessity behind the statute.

36. 417 U.S. 733 (1974).

37. 417 U.S. at 756–57.

38. Parisi v. Davidson, 405 U.S. 34 (1972); Gusik v. Schilder, 340 U.S. 128 (1950).

39. 405 U.S. 34 (1972).

stances, a federal court did not need to abstain from hearing an appeal of the denial of conscientious objector status during the military trial for disobeying orders. The Court noted that the defendant had exhausted his military administrative remedies and he had no other course by which to challenge the decision. He could raise his conscientious objector claim at the court martial as a defense to the charge, but even if the court-martial accepted his claim, the court-martial would not release him from the armed forces. The Court concluded that the two hearings were independent; the civil court did not need to abstain.

In 1975 in *Schlesinger v. Councilman*,[40] the Court limited *Parisi*, holding that although the district court had subject matter jurisdiction over the court martial habeas petition, the balance of factors governing exercise of federal equitable jurisdiction suggested that the court abstain until the completion of court martial proceedings. Normally, a federal court should not interfere with a court-martial if the defendant's only injury would be standing trial at the court martial and if the court martial could resolve the defendant's claim.

40. 420 U.S. 738 (1975).

CHAPTER SEVEN

PRESIDENTIAL DOMESTIC POWER

I. EXECUTIVE PRIVILEGE

The amenability of the President of the United States to service of process is not clearly spelled out in the executive powers and privileges enumerated in the Constitution. As early as 1866 Attorney General Stanberry relied on presidential immunity in arguing that the President is beyond legal process,[1] analogizing that the President was the ultimate sovereign of the country and should enjoy the same type of privilege as other potentates.[2] The Supreme Court dismissed the complaint on different grounds and carefully disclaimed a decision upon the assertion of total presidential immunity from process.[3] Distinguishing the power of the courts to require the president to perform a single ministerial act from power to control the exercise of the executive's broad constitutional discretion in carrying out his duties, the Court held that it had "no jurisdiction of a bill to enjoin the President in the performance of his official duties." [4] Despite the fact that the issue was never clearly reached, some commentators interpreted the *Johnson* holding to mean that the president is immune from legal process when performing what he deems to be his constitutional duties.[5]

1. Mississippi v. Johnson, 71 U.S. (4 Wall.) 475 (1866). On the history of presidents as witnesses, see Rotunda, Presidents and Ex-Presidents as Witnesses: A Brief Historical Footnote, 1975 U. of Ill.L.Forum 1.

Prior to the subpoena of a president upheld in United States v. Nixon, 418 U.S. 683 (1974), the courts have only twice before issued a subpoena to a sitting president. The first was the subpoena issued to President Jefferson in United States v. Burr, 25 Fed.Cas. 30 (No. 14,692) (C.C.Va.1807); the presiding judge was Chief Justice Marshall sitting on circuit during the treason trial of Aaron Burr. See generally, Rhodes, What Really Happened to the Jefferson Subpoenas, 60 A.B.A.J. 52 (1974); Berger, The President, Congress, and the Courts, 83 Yale L.J. 1111 (1974).

On January 3, 1818, President Monroe became the second President to be served with a subpoena while in office. Monroe was summoned as a witness in behalf of the defendant in the court-martial case of one Dr. William C. Barton. Monroe submitted answers to interrogatories forwarded by the court after his Attorney General informed him in a handwritten unpublished opinion, that a subpoena *ad testificandum* could properly be issued to the president. See Opinion of Attorney General Wirt, dated January 13, 1818, in the Records of the Judge Advocate General (Navy), Record Group 125, National Archives Building. A large part of the opinion is reprinted in Rotunda, Presidents and Ex-Presidents as Witnesses: A Brief Historical Footnote, 1975 U.Ill.L.Forum 1, 5–6.

2. 71 U.S. (4 Wall.) at 484.

3. 71 U.S. (4 Wall.) at 498.

4. 71 U.S. (4 Wall.) at 501.

5. See, e.g., C. Burdick, The Law of the American Constitution (1922) § 50, at 125–27; 3 W. Willoughby,

Beginning with *Marbury v. Madison*, [6] the courts had always asserted power to determine and enforce constitutional and other legal obligations of executive officials under the president, even when the alleged wrongs were done under the auspices of presidential command.[7] As the Supreme Court stated in *Marbury*, "[i]t is, emphatically, the province and duty of the judicial department, to say what the law is." [8] The power of the courts to review the boundaries of executive action was further acknowledged in such cases as *Youngstown Sheet & Tube Co. v. Sawyer*,[9] where the judicial branch forced Secretary of Commerce Sawyer to return to their private owners the steel mills which had been seized by the Secretary upon President Truman's order to terminate a wartime labor dispute.

Though the power of the courts to review actions of executive officials was early established, in none of these cases had process issued directly against the president. One of the significant aftermaths of the famous Watergate break-in put this issue squarely before the courts in *United States v. Nixon*.[10] On March 1, 1974, a grand jury sitting in the District of Columbia indicted seven of President Nixon's presidential aides and campaign staff for conspiracy to defraud the United States and to obstruct justice. The President had been named as an unindicted co-conspirator by the same grand jury. The Watergate Special Prosecutor moved the District of Columbia District Court to issue a subpoena *duces tecum*, requiring the president to produce certain memoranda, papers,

and tapes which related to specific meetings between the president and others. Nixon publicly released edited transcripts of 43 conversations, including edited portions of 20 conversations subject to the subpoena; in the courts the president's attorneys moved to quash the subpoena for the actual tapes on the ground of executive privilege.[11]

The district court rejected presidential contentions that the dispute was non-justiciable because the courts lacked authority to review an assertion of executive privilege by the president and ordered the tapes and documents to be delivered to the court on or before May 31. On May 24 the president asked the court of appeals for a writ of mandamus, seeking review of the lower court's action. The same day, the Special Prosecutor filed a petition in the Supreme Court for writ of certiorari before judgment. The petition was granted on May 31, 1974, the effect of which was to bypass the Court of Appeals and to bring the case immediately from the district court to the Supreme Court for review. The Supreme Court ordered production "forthwith" of the subpoenaed materials, affirming the district court's denial of the president's motion to quash. In an unanimous opinion written by Chief Justice Burger,[12] the Court first disposed of the procedural issues by determining that the district court's order was "appealable" notwithstanding the finality requirement of the federal statute governing petitions for certiorari,[13] and that the specific procedural requirements for a subpoena *duces tecum* under the Federal Rules of Criminal

The Constitutional Law of the United States (2d ed. 1929) §§ 979–80, at 1497–1500.

6. 5 U.S. (1 Cranch) 137 (1803).

7. See also, Kendall v. United States ex rel. Stokes, 37 U.S. (12 Pet.) 524 (1838); Land v. Dollar, 190 F.2d 623 (D.C.Cir. 1951), vacated as moot 344 U.S. 806 (1952).

8. 5 U.S. (1 Cranch) at 177.

9. 343 U.S. 579 (1952).

10. 418 U.S. 683 (1974). See generally, Freund, Foreward: On Presidential Privilege, 88 Harv.L.Rev. 13 (1974).

11. Subsequently, Nixon also moved to expunge the grand jury's action naming him as an unindicted coconspirator.

12. Justice Rehnquist took no part in the consideration or decision of the case.

13. Court of appeals jurisdiction under 28 U.S.C.A. § 1291 encompasses only "final decisions of the district courts", but the Supreme Court noted that "[t]o require a President of the United States to place himself in the posture of disobeying an order of a court merely to trigger the procedural mechanism for review of the ruling would be unseemly, and would present an unnecessary occasion for constitutional confrontation between two branches of the Government." 418 U.S. at 691–92.

Procedure, Rule 17(c), had been met. Citing the Attorney General's regulations delegating unique authority and tenure to the Special Prosecutor, the Court concluded that sufficient adverseness existed to make the case "justiciable" notwithstanding the "intra-branch" character of the dispute.[14]

The Court then addressed the key issue of executive privilege. The President's first line of reasoning, that the separation of powers doctrine precludes judicial review of a Presidential claim of privilege, was summarily rejected by the Court. Relying on the principle of *Marbury v. Madison*[15] that it is the ultimate province and duty of the judiciary to decide what the law is, the Court noted that, "[a]ny other conclusion would be contrary to the basic concept of separation of powers and the checks and balances that flow from the scheme of tripartite government."[16]

The President's second argument was that, as a matter of constitutional law, executive privilege prevails over the subpoena *duces tecum*. For the first time, presidential executive privilege was given a stamp of approval by the Supreme Court, though it was a much narrower approval than President Nixon wished. The Court agreed that the President has a prima facie privilege to maintain the confidentiality of internal executive communications, because possible public dissemination of such communications could tend to inhibit frank discussion and advice in the decision-making process. The absence of an express constitutional provision was seen as no bar to the assertion of such a privilege, for "[c]ertain powers and privileges flow from the nature of enumerated powers; the protection of the confidentiality of presidential communications has similar constitutional underpinnings."[17] To the extent the presidential interest in confidentiality "relates to the effective discharge of a President's powers, it is constitutionally based."[18]

While recognizing the need for an executive privilege, the Court made it clear that such a privilege was not absolute and unqualified. The prima facie privilege must yield to the higher claims of judicial process in any criminal case where either the prosecution or defense has demonstrated a need for the evidence subpoenaed, and the evidence would otherwise be admissible upon trial of the indictment.[19] The Court accorded "great deference" to the felt need of the president for complete objectivity and candor from his advisers. However, the Court reasoned:

> [W]hen the privilege depends solely on the broad, undifferentiated claim of public interest in the confidentiality of such conversations, a confrontation of other values arises. Absent a claim of need to protect military, diplomatic, or sensitive national security secrets, we find it difficult to accept the argument that even the very important interest in confidentiality of Presidential communications is significantly diminished by production of such material for *in camera* inspection with all the protection that a district court will be obliged to provide.[20]

In the next paragraph the Court stated that it would upset the constitutional balance to accept a generalized claim of confidentiality by the president in "nonmilitary and nondiplomatic discussions . . . ." No explanation was given as to why there was no reference to "sensitive national security secrets" as there was earlier. Several pages later the Supreme Court also referred to "military or diplomatic secrets,"[21] but not to the more open-ended category of national security. Finally, the Court made it clear that it is for the judicial branch to determine the extent of the duty of the President and other executive officials to produce evidence, i.e., to what extent executive privilege will reach, though the Court would accord "high re-

---

14. 418 U.S. at 692–97.

15. 5 U.S. (1 Cranch) 137, 177 (1803).

16. 418 U.S. at 704.

17. 418 U.S. at 705–06.

18. 418 U.S. at 711.

19. "The generalized assertion of privilege must yield to the demonstrated, specific need for evidence in a pending criminal trial." 418 U.S. at 713.

20. 418 U.S. at 706.

21. 418 U.S. at 710.

spect to the representations made on behalf of the President." [22]

The Court, along with both parties to the litigation, accepted the notion that presidential communications are "presumptively privileged." [23] But the interest in confidentiality in this case was only generalized, and therefore there should be no high deference to the president,[24] and compulsory process to obtain evidence needed "either by the prosecution *or* the defense" is imperative to the function of the courts.[25] The Court concluded that the president's generalized claim could not prevail over the "demonstrated, specific need for evidence in a pending criminal trial." [26] The district court, in conducting its *in camera* examination, was ordered to excise all material not relevant and admissible.[27]

The Court explicitly did not consider its weighing of the balance of interests in a case involving the president's generalized interest in confidentiality and the need for relevant evidence in civil litigation or a congressional demand for information, nor the president's interest in preserving state secrets.[28] It may well be the case that the Court will view itself as the arbiter of all inter-branch disputes over this issue and balance the federal interest in confidentiality against the need of the other branch of government to receive the evidence to effectuate its functions. However, the criminal process is unique in that the president, as chief executive officer, controls it. There is the added measure of unfairness in allowing the executive branch to simultaneously pros-

ecute someone and then deny that party and the court relevant information, particularly when the secrecy of the information is not essential to legitimate executive interests. Thus it is very difficult to predict the course of litigation over the scope of this privilege in future years.

In *Nixon v. Administrator of General Services Administration*,[29] the Court was called upon to decide a unique case focusing on the question of executive privilege. After President Nixon's resignation, Congress enacted the Presidential Recordings and Materials Preservation Act.[30] Title I of this Act directed the Administrator of the General Services Administration to take custody of former President Nixon's presidential papers and tape records; provide for their orderly processing and screening; return to the former president those items that were personal in nature; and establish the terms upon which public access might eventually be had for the remainder of the materials.

The former president brought suit attacking the constitutionality of the Act on a number of grounds, two of which are particularly relevant to this section. The Supreme Court upheld the Act and in so doing decided some important questions of separation of powers and executive privilege.

First the Court rejected the argument that the law violated principles of separation of powers. The executive branch, the Court argued, became a party to the Act's regulation when President Ford signed the bill into law; the new administration of President Carter supports the law; and the materials remain

---

22. 418 U.S. at 707, citing United States v. Burr, 25 Fed.Cas. 187, 190, 191–192 (No. 14,694) (C.C.Va.1807). On the Burr subpoena issued to President Jefferson by Chief Justice Marshall sitting on circuit during the treason trial of Aaron Burr, see Rotunda, Presidents and Ex-Presidents as Witnesses: A Brief Historical Footnote, 1975 U. of Ill.L.Forum 1, 4–5.

23. 418 U.S. at 708.

24. 418 U.S. at 711. The Court contrasted other cases where the Court did grant high deference. C. & S. Air Lines v. Waterman S. S. Corp., 333 U.S. 103, 111 (1948) (foreign policy considerations; no claim of executive privilege); United States v. Reynolds, 345 U.S. 1, 10 (1953) (military matters; claimant's demand for evidence in a Tort Claims Act case rejected).

25. 418 U.S. at 709 (emphasis added).

26. 418 U.S. at 713.

27. 418 U.S. at 714.

28. 418 U.S. at 712 n. 19. One circuit court has, without much reasoning, concluded that a congressional subpoena for information would not be enforced by the Courts because the Court, in engaging in an ad hoc balancing, determined the material was not needed that badly. Senate Select Committee on Presidential Campaign Activities v. Nixon, 498 F.2d 725 (D.C.Cir. 1974).

29. 433 U.S. 425 (1977).

30. Pub.L. No. 93–526, 44 U.S.C.A. § 2107.

in the executive branch in the custody of a presidential appointee, the Administrator of the General Services Administration. To determine whether a breach of the separation of powers exists, all of these facts are relevant because the "proper inquiry focuses on the extent to which [the Act] prevents the Executive Branch from accomplishing its constitutionally assigned functions." [31] On its face the Act does not create undue disruption of the executive branch.

Next the Court turned to the issue of executive privilege. First the Court held that a former president could assert executive privilege. One need not be an incumbent to claim the benefit of the privilege, but, in weighing this qualified privilege, the fact that neither of the incumbent presidents after President Nixon supported his claim detracted from his claim that the Act intrudes into the executive function. Then the Court explained that the presidential privilege would exist only to those materials whose contents would fall within the scope of the privilege recognized in *United States v. Nixon*,[32] where the subpoenaed information was sought by the Special Prosecutor in a criminal case.

Finally the Court concluded that given the screening of materials there is no reason to believe that there will not be adequate safeguards to protect executive privilege. It is true that someone will be doing the screening and thus will be seeing the materials, but the intrusion is limited to personnel already in the executive branch and sensitive to executive concerns. And, this limited intrusion has adequate justification. "[T]he American people's ability to reconstruct and come to terms with their history [should not] be truncated by an analysis of Presidential

privilege that focuses only on the needs of the present." [33]

We may expect future litigation under this Act to raise questions about the screening process and the decision to allow public access to certain materials.

The Nixon Presidency spawned further litigation and elaboration of the immunity attached to the president and his aides in two cases decided the same day, *Nixon v. Fitzgerald*,[34] and *Harlow v. Fitzgerald*.[35] Fitzgerald was a management analyst for the Department of the Air Force; he was dismissed from his job after having "blown the whistle" in certain congressional hearings regarding cost overruns of the C–5A transport plane. The Air Force claimed that he was terminated as part of a reduction in force and not in retaliation for his embarrassing testimony.

After various congressional and Civil Service hearings [36] Fitzgerald sued Butterfield, Harlow, Nixon and others; he relied on various statutes and the first amendment to support his claim. In *Nixon* the Court, speaking through Justice Powell, reasoned that the president "occupies a unique position in the constitutional scheme," [37] that diversion of his energies by concern with private lawsuits would raise unique risks to the effective functioning of government," [38] and the fragmentary historical evidence supports the notion of presidential immunity,[39] but the "most compelling arguments" favoring presidential immunity arise from "the Constitution's separation of powers and the judiciary's historical understanding of that doctrine." [40]

The Court then held that "a former President of the United States is entitled to absolute immunity from damages liability predi-

---

31. 433 U.S. at 443.

32. 418 U.S. 683 (1974).

33. 433 U.S. at 452–53 (footnote omitted).

34. 102 S.Ct. 2690 (1982). As for immunity of federal legislators, see Chapter 8, section II, supra.

35. 102 S.Ct. 2727 (1982).

36. The Civil Service Hearings Examiner concluded that Fitzgerald had been improperly terminated for

"reasons purely personal" to him, but that the evidence did not support a finding of retaliation. 102 S.Ct. at 2696.

37. 102 S.Ct. at 2702.

38. 102 S.Ct. at 2703.

39. 102 S.Ct. at 2702 n. 31.

40. 102 S.Ct. at 2703 n. 31.

cated on his official acts. We consider this immunity a functionally mandated incident of the President's unique office, rooted in the constitutional tradition of the separation of powers and supported by our history." [41] Such absolute immunity exists at least in those cases where Congress has taken no "express legislative action to subject the President to civil liability for his official acts." [42]

The Court in the past has recognized an absolute immunity—e.g., the prosecutor when he files his indictment, a congressman when he makes a speech in Congress—but has limited that immunity to performance of particular functions of his office. [43] Absolute presidential immunity is not so limited: "we think it appropriate to recognize absolute Presidential immunity from damages liability for acts within the 'outer perimeter' of his official responsibility." [44]

Justice White, joined by Justices Brennan, Marshall, and Blackmun, dissented and concluded that "the Court clothes the office of the President with sovereign immunity, placing it above the law." [45] But the majority's response was that alternative remedies protect the nation and place the president under law:

There remains the constitutional remedy of impeachment. In addition, there are formal and informal checks on Presidential action that do not apply with equal force to other executive officials. The President is subjected to constant scrutiny by the press. Vigilant oversight by Congress also may serve to deter Presidential abuses of office, as well as to make credible the threat of impeachment. Other incentives to avoid misconduct may include a desire to earn re-election, the need to maintain prestige as an element of Presidential influence, and a President's traditional concern for his historical stature.

The existence of alternative remedies and deterrents establishes that absolute immunity will not place the President "above the law". For the President, as for judges and prosecutors, absolute immunity merely precludes a particular private remedy for alleged misconduct in order to advance compelling public ends. [46]

Earlier the majority had also noted that the injunctive remedy is still possible, and, in appropriate criminal cases, the President is subject to subpoena. [47] One might add that Congress perhaps could authorize private damage actions against the President—a point that the majority explicitly left open [48]—but even if that alternative is not possible, perhaps Congress could authorize a damage action against the public purse. That is, so that future Fitzgeralds would not be remediless, Congress perhaps could authorize them to sue the public treasury for out of pocket losses in an action brought in the Claims Court or similar tribunal.

In the companion case, *Harlow v. Fitzgerald*, [49] the Court ruled that the scope of immunity for senior presidential aides and advisers was only qualified, not absolute. "For executive officials in general," said the Court, "qualified immunity represents the norm." [50] Executive officials do not derive any absolute immunity from the President, unless the function that they are performing demands such immunity. The official claiming absolute immunity has the burden to demonstrate that the responsibilities of his office embrace such a sensitive function that he requires a total shield from liability and that he was performing such a function for which liability is asserted. Some Presiden-

41. 102 S.Ct. at 2701.

42. 102 S.Ct. at 2701 (footnote omitted).

43. 102 S.Ct. at 2705, 2706 n. 41.

44. 102 S.Ct. at 2705.

45. 102 S.Ct. at 2711 (footnote omitted) (dissenting opinion). See also, 102 S.Ct. at 2726 (Blackmun, J., joined by Brennan & Marshall, JJ.).

46. 102 S.Ct. at 2706 (footnotes omitted).

47. 102 S.Ct. at 2704, citing Youngstown Sheet & Tube Co. v. Sawyer, 343 U.S. 579 (1952), and United States v. Nixon, 418 U.S. 683 (1974).

48. 102 S.Ct. at 2701 & n. 27. Chief Justice Burger, in his concurring opinion, contended that under the Constitution Congress could not create any damage action against the President. 102 S.Ct. at 2709 n. 7 (Burger, C.J., concurring).

49. 102 S.Ct. at 2727 (1982).

50. 102 S.Ct. at 2733.

tial "alter egos" could make such a showing. For example, "a derivative claim to Presidential immunity would be strongest in such 'central' Presidential domains as foreign policy and national security, in which the President could not discharge his singularly vital mandate without delegating functions nearly as sensitive as his own." [51]

The earlier case law had stated that qualified immunity would not be available if the official *"knew or reasonably should have known"* that his actions would violate the plaintiff's constitutional rights *"or if he took the action with malicious intention* to cause a deprivation of constitutional rights or other injury . . . ." [52] However this subjective element made it difficult for the trial courts to weed out insubstantial claims. Therefore the Court fashioned a new rule:

> Reliance on the objective reasonableness of an official's conduct, as measured by reference to clearly established law, should avoid excessive disruption of government and permit the resolution of many insubstantial claims on summary judgment. On summary judgment, the judge appropriately may determine, not only the currently applicable law, but whether that law was clearly established at the time an action occurred. If the law at that time was not clearly established, an official could not reasonably be expected to anticipate subsequent legal developments, nor could he fairly be said to 'know' that the law forbade conduct not previously identified as unlawful. Until this threshold immunity question is resolved, discovery should not be allowed. If the law was clearly established, the immunity defense ordinarily should fail, since a reasonably competent public official should know the law governing his conduct. Nevertheless, if the offi-

cial pleading the defense claims extraordinary circumstances and can prove that he neither knew nor should have known of the relevant legal standard, the defense should be sustained. But again, the defense would turn primarily on objective factors. [W]e conclude today that bare allegations of malice should not suffice to subject government officials either to the costs of trial or to the burdens of broad-reaching discovery. We therefore hold that government officials performing discretionary functions generally are shielded from liability for civil damages insofar as their conduct does not violate clearly established statutory or constitutional rights of which a reasonable person would have known.[53]

II. IMPOUNDMENT OF FUNDS

The power of Congress to provide funds for the programs it has established is a necesssary concomitant to the legislative power granted Congress by the Constitution.[1] In some instances, however, such funds have been authorized and appropriated by Congress for a particular program but are impounded by the President. The issue becomes to what extent Congress has the power to limit the traditional discretionary role of the executive branch in the appropriations process. The spending power of Congress is inherently subject to a limited, overrideable presidential veto.[2] This qualified veto is far less restrictive than would be an absolute power to impound, for such impoundment power would give the executive an unassailable item veto over the area of congressional spending—perhaps the legislative branch's single greatest responsibility.

Proponents of an executive power of impoundment have relied on both language in

---

51.   102 S.Ct. at 2736 n. 19.

The Court also rejected any generalized absolute immunity derived from the President, although the Court had earlier recognized such derivative immunity for congressional aides derived from the Senators' and Representatives' speech and debate immunity. 102 S.Ct. at 2735. See Gravel v. United States, 408 U.S. 606 (1972). See also Chapter 8, section II, infra.

Chief Justice Burger's dissent would have given absolute immunity for the President's "alter ego" or "elbow aides" because these personal aides work more closely with the President on a daily basis than Cabinet officials or other executive officials do. 102 S.Ct. at

2741.   Brennan, J., joined by Marshall & Blackmun, JJ., filed an opinion concurring in the opinion of the Court. Rehnquist, J., also filed a short concurring opinion.

52.   102 S.Ct. at 2737 (emphasis by the Court).

53.   102 S.Ct. at 2739, 2738 (footnotes omitted).

1.   U.S. Const. art. I, § 8, cl. 18 gives the Congress authority to "make all Laws which shall be necessary and proper for carrying into Execution . . . all . . . Powers vested by this Constitution in the Government of the United States . . . ."

2.   U.S. Const. art. I, § 7, cl. 2.

the Constitution and various federal statutes. Article II, § 3, of the Constitution states that the President "shall take care that the laws be faithfully executed . . . ." This broad language, it has been contended, gives rise to an "inherent" executive power over appropriations, as where the expenditure of funds might violate a constitutional provision.[3] Statutory authority to impound has usually been claimed to derive from four general statutes: (1) the Anti-deficiency Act of 1950 [4], (2) the Employment Act of 1946 [5]; (3) the Economic Stabilization Act of 1970 [6]; and (4) the public debt ceiling.[7] The assertion is that where increased federal spending could threaten the goals of these statutes designed to restrict expenditures the President, who is bound by the Constitution to faithfully execute *all* of the laws of the United States, must have the ability to withhold funds to resolve these conflicting statutory duties.

Until recently, courts had no well defined guidelines in resolving the impoundment controversy. This is partly due to the fact that traditionally courts have been reluctant to enter into the impoundment arena. The majority of impoundment controversies have been settled through political and not judicial processes [8]. Courts entered the picture only when other methods failed. When taken to court, impoundment raises difficult questions of judicial review and judicial restraint, for the courts must then define the relative scope of executive and congressional power in an area void of explicit constitutional provisions. Additionally, judicial resolution of impoundment disputes is hampered

by complex problems of proof. Where statutory grounds are asserted as the basis for upholding impoundment, the argument of the Executive is that (1) the withholding of funds is authorized by one of the general laws permitting a restriction on spending,[9] or (2) the specific appropriations bill involved confers upon the president such extensive discretion over the rate of spending that he is entitled to impound for general political and economic motives. Those challenging the executive action are faced with the difficult burden of showing that the executive has exceeded its discretion.[10] Resort to the courts to challenge an impoundment has also been hampered by recognition of the natural judicial deference to administrative judgments in complex areas. Courts are likely to defer to executive expertise and uphold impoundments for which a plausible argument can be made rather than trying to independently evaluate and reassess administrative judgments. A court may also decline to decide cases involving impoundment if the issue is deemed a "political question" and therefore nonjusticiable.[11]

These factors have kept all but a few impoundment controversies out of the courts. In 1838 the Supreme Court considered for the first time the issue of whether the executive has an inherent power under the Constitution to impound even in the face of congressional mandate. The case, *Kendall v. United States ex rel. Stokes* [12], established that when Congress has expressly directed that sums be spent, the president has no constitutional power not to spend them. Congress had passed a private act ordering

---

3. See, Kranz, A Twentieth Century Emancipation Proclamation: Presidential Power Permits Withholding of Funds from Segregated Institutions, 11 Am.U.L. Rev. 48, 67–74 (1962).

4. 31 U.S.C.A. § 665. Later amended to conform with the Impoundment Control Act of 1974, 31 U.S.C.A. § 1401.

5. 15 U.S.C.A. §§ 1021–25.

6. See 12 U.S.C.A. § 1904 note. This act expired on midnight, April 30, 1974.

7. 31 U.S.C.A. § 7576.

8. For a discussion of unimpounding methods which did not rely on judicial intervention, see J. Mills and W.

Munselle, Unimpoundment: Politics and the Courts in the Release of Impounded Funds, 24 Emory Law Journal 313, 315–22 (1975).

9. See footnotes 3–7, and accompanying text, supra.

10. Where the issue is simply whether the President has inherent constitutional power to impound despite congressional mandates, the issue of abuse of discretion does not arise. See Kendall v. United States ex rel. Stokes, 37 U.S. (12 Pet.) 524 (1838), infra.

11. See generally Baker v. Carr, 369 U.S. 186, 208–17 (1962); H. Hart and H. Wechsler's, The Federal Courts and The Federal System 233–41 (2d ed. 1973).

12. 37 U.S. (12 Pet.) 524 (1838).

the Postmaster General to pay petitioner Kendall for services rendered. The Court considered and rejected the executive's argument that the petitioner could not sue in mandamus because the Postmaster General was subject only to the directives of the president, not of Congress.[13] The Court found the constitutional duty of the executive to faithfully execute the law[14] made it necessary that the congressional mandate be carried out.[15] The holding in *Kendall*, however, was limited to those cases where there is an outright refusal by the executive to spend funds which he has been specifically ordered to spend by the Congress.

The courts did not really begin to hear cases involving impoundment of arguably discretionary spending until the era of the Nixon Administration. Unlike previous exercises of impoundment, which had usually occurred in wartime, the Nixon Administration used impoundment as a policy tool on an extensive scale in the domestic area. These impoundments were often permanent and, rather than merely reducing a program's scope, terminated or severely restricted entire projects.[16] The first major cases on impoundment were filed in 1971, before the impoundment policies of the Nixon Administration had reached the scale of a national controversy. In *San Francisco Redevelopment Agency v. Nixon*[17], mandamus was sought to compel the President to allot money appropriated by Congress to various executive agencies. The case was dismissed on the basis of sovereign immunity and the impoundment issues were never reached. The following year, the San Francisco Housing Authority brought action against HUD to compel the executive to spend designated funds.[18] The case was dismissed on grounds of sovereign immunity and that lack of standards for the exercise of executive discretion in the Housing Act made the issue a political question over which the court lacked jurisdiction.

While the San Francisco cases failed, a Missouri suit in 1973 was to become both the first appellate court decision on impoundment and the first to overrule a withholding of funds where executive discretion was an issue. The Eighth Circuit in *State Highway Commission v. Volpe*[19] rejected the federal government's argument that the controversy involved a political question not appropriate for judicial resolution and pointed out that the issue was not of the executive's power to control the rate of expenditure of funds, but rather a matter of statutory construction that was properly within the competence of the court.[20] The statute involved did not give the Executive total discretionary power over spending and courts have the power to review agency actions which exceed or abuse statutory discretion.[21]

The determination of the existence of statutory discretion will generally be dispositive of the political question issue, for statutes found to vest total discretion in the executive have no ascertainable standards for review.[22] Appropriations with no discretion will not be political questions because there are explicit standards for review.[23] As the district court noted in *National Council of Community Health Centers, Inc. v. Weinberger*,[24] "[w]hen Congress directs that mon-

---

13.　37 U.S. at 612–613.

14.　U.S. Const. art. II, § 3.

15.　37 U.S. at 613.

16.　See, OMB Report Under Federal Impoundment and Information Act. 37 Fed.Reg. 7707 (1974).

17.　329 F.Supp. 672 (N.D.Calif.1971).

18.　San Francisco Housing Authority v. HUD, 340 F.Supp. 654 (N.D.Cal.1972).

19.　479 F.2d 1099 (8th Cir. 1973).

20.　479 F.2d at 1106.

21.　See Citizens to Preserve Overton Park, Inc. v. Volpe, 401 U.S. 402, 413. Such review falls under Section 706 of the Administrative Procedure Act, which provides specific standards of review and gives the courts the right to set aside agency actions which are arbitrary, capricious, or otherwise not in accordance with the law or if the action fails to meet statutory, procedural or constitutional requirements. 5 U.S.C.A. §§ 706(2)(A), (B), (C), (D).

22.　San Francisco Housing Authority v. HUD, 340 F.Supp. 654 (N.D.Cal.1972); San Francisco Redevelopment Authority v. Nixon, 329 F.Supp. 672 (N.D.Cal. 1971).

23.　Train v. New York, 420 U.S. 35 (1975).

24.　361 F.Supp. 897, 900 (D.D.C.1973).

ey be spent and the President, as Chief Executive, declines to permit the spending, the resulting conflict is not political." Enactments which permit some discretion present the greatest problem for the courts for they must establish through statutory interpretation first, whether they have the ability to establish limits on the exercise of discretion and then, whether such standards have been exceeded. This problem was illustrated in *Campaign Clean Water, Inc. v. Ruckelshaus*,[25] where the district court found that agency discretion had been exceeded by impounding 55% of the available funds. The lower court found that commitment of only 45% of funds was unacceptable and therefore an abuse of discretion, but did not define adequate standards for compliance. A determination that judicial standards existed for measuring the discretion of the executive was inherent in the finding of abuse; the Supreme Court reversed and remanded on other grounds, not deciding this issue.[26]

Lower courts, as well as the Supreme Court, have studiously avoided consideration of constitutional issues and have instead based most of the holdings on principles of statutory interpretation.[27] *Train v. New York*,[28] the first modern impoundment case to reach the Supreme Court, is a prime example of a decision based on standard methods of statutory interpretation rather than broader constitutional issues.[29] In *Train* the Supreme Court dealt with the refusal of the Administrator of the Environmental Protection Agency to allot six billion dollars during fiscal years 1973 and 1974 under the

Water Pollution Control Act. The Court in *Train* exhaustively considered the legislative history of the Water Pollution Control Act and weighed conflicting interpretations of that history. The allotment provisions in the Act were determined to be mandatory, the Court rejecting the executive's argument that total discretion has been conferred on the Administration:

> We cannot believe that Congress at the last minute scuttled the entire effort by providing the Executive with the seemingly limitless power to withhold funds from allotment and obligation. Yet such was the Government's position in the lower courts—combined with the argument that the discretion conferred is unreviewable.[30]

In emphasizing legislative history and statutory interpretation as the basis for its holding, the *Train* Court continued the lower court trend of steering clear of broader constitutional issues on impoundment. By rejecting the authority of the administration to impound, however, the Court impliedly rejected a constitutional authority to impound in the face of a Congressional mandate to the contrary and in the context of a program where the President could not reasonably claim special powers as the Commander-in-Chief or an inherent power limited to foreign affairs.[31]

Aside from a normal desire to avoid a constitutional decision where other grounds are available, it is clear that the courts are reluctant to freeze into the Constitution a stringent definition of constitutional authority which might impair the system of checks

---

25. 361 F.Supp. 689 (E.D.Va.), modified 489 F.2d 492 (4th Cir. 1973), rev'd sub nom. Train v. Campaign Clean Water, Inc., 420 U.S. 136 (1975) (per curiam), vacating judgment and remanding for proceedings consistent with Train v. New York, 420 U.S. 35 (1975).

26. Id.

27. See, e.g., Train v. New York, 420 U.S. 35 (1975); State Highway Comm'n v. Volpe, 479 F.2d 1099 (8th Cir. 1973).

28. 420 U.S. 35 (1975).

29. Cf. Statement of Deputy Attorney General Joseph Sneed, Before the Ad Hoc Subcommittee on Impoundment of Funds of the Senate Committee on Government Operations and the Senate Subcommittee on Separation of Powers of the Senate Committee on the

Judiciary, 93d Cong., 1st Sess. 364 (1973) (arguing, inter alia, that Congressional mandates to spend may intrude impermissibly into matters reserved to the president over foreign affairs and his role as Commander-in-Chief). See generally, Abascal & Kramer, Presidential Impoundments, Part II: Judicial and Legislative Responses, 63 Georgetown L.J. 149 (1974); Mikva & Hertz, Impoundment of Funds—The Courts, The Congress and the President: A Constitutional Triangle, 69 Nw.U.L.Rev. 335 (1974).

30. 420 U.S. at 45–46.

31. Broad claims of constitutional authority have been asserted by the executive. See generally, Note, Impoundment of Funds, 86 Harv.L.Rev. 1505, 1513–16 (1973).

and balances between Congress and the president. Little precedent exists with regard to the doctrine of inherent authority, although this doctrine has been discussed briefly in *Youngstown Sheet & Tube Co. v. Sawyer*,[32] and *United States v. Curtiss-Wright Exporting Corp.*[33] The Court in *Youngstown* expressly rejected a theory that the president had broad inherent authority to issue an order seizing control of the steel mills, stating "[t]he President's power, if any, to issue the order must stem either from an act of Congress or from the Constitution itself,"[34] and that no such power could be inferred from the "aggregate of his powers under the Constitution."[35]

Increasing friction between the executive and legislative branches over the impoundment issue led to the passing of the Congressional Budget and Impoundment Control Act of 1974.[36] The approach taken by Congress is to require consultation with Congress and its ratification of any executive action which has the effect of impounding funds absent prior congressional authorization. If Congress refuses to ratify the Executive's action, the action must be reversed and ended. In this manner the President cannot curtail programs by refusing to spend funds unless he receives permission

from Congress. The result of this Act is increased congressional control over impoundment, an institutionalization of the role of the courts in the process, and a reduction in the number of the more difficult constitutional problems. Whether the Impoundment Control Act itself, in some circumstances, violates an inherent or reserved presidential power remains an open question.[37]

III. APPOINTMENT AND REMOVAL POWERS

A. The Appointment Powers

The power of the president to appoint and remove officers of the United States stems in part from express provisions of the Constitution and in part from the implications of express grants of power. Article II, section 2, clause 2, establishes in the president the power to appoint officers of the United States; it also provides that Congress may vest the appointment of inferior officers in either the president alone, in the courts, or in the heads of departments. At no time, however, may the legislative branch exercise executive authority by retaining the power to appoint those who will execute its laws. Thus, it was held in *Springer v. Philippine Islands*[1] that the legislature of the Philip-

---

32. 343 U.S. 579 (1952) (seizure of the steel mills by President Truman).

33. 299 U.S. 304 (1936) (presidential powers in foreign trade).

34. 343 U.S. at 585.

35. 343 U.S. at 587.

36. Pub.L. 93–344, 88 Stat. 297, 31 U.S.C.A. § 1001 et seq.

37. A separate, though related, question is the extent to which the President can interfere with agency rule making in order to promote efficiency or for more political purposes. See generally, Sierra Club v. Costle, 657 F.2d 298 (D.C.Cir. 1981); Symposium, 56 Tulane L.Rev. 811–902 (1982); Rosenberg, Beyond the Limits of Executive Power: Presidential Control of Agency Rulemaking Under Executive Order 12,1291, 80 Mich.L.Rev. 193 (1981).

Another area of dispute between the president and Congress concerns the president's use of what is called the "pocket veto." See U.S. Const. art. I, § 7, cl. 2, which provides that if "any Bill shall not be returned by the President within ten Days (Sundays excepted) after it shall have been presented to him, the Same shall be a Law, in like Manner as if he had signed it,

unless the Congress by their Adjournment prevent its Return in which Case it shall not be a Law."

The question of the proper use of the pocket veto—which allows the president to veto legislation without giving the Congress the opportunity to override the veto—has been subject to some controversy. See, e.g., Constitutionality of the President's Pocket Veto Power, Hearings Before the Senate Judiciary Subcommittee on Separation of Powers, 92d Cong., 1st Sess. (1971); A.S. Miller, Presidential Power in a Nutshell 97–103 (1977). It has also been the subject of litigation in the lower courts. Kennedy v. Sampson, 511 F.2d 430 (D.C.Cir. 1974). However there has been no recent Supreme Court decision in this area. The older cases are Wright v. United States, 302 U.S. 583 (1937) and Okanogon Indian Tribe v. United States (The Pocket Veto Case), 279 U.S. 655 (1929). See also 40 Opinions of the Attorney General 274 (July 16, 1943).

1. 277 U.S. 189 (1928). The classic articles in this area include, Corwin, Tenure of Office and the Removal Power Under the Constitution, 27 Colum.L.Rev. 353 (1927); Donovan & Irvine, The President's Power to Remove Members of Administrative Agencies, 21 Cornell L.Q. 215 (1936).

pine Islands could not constitutionally provide for legislative appointment to executive agencies.

This basic principle was recently affirmed in *Buckley v. Valeo*,[2] where the Supreme Court held that Congress had violated Article II in providing that the President pro tem. of the Senate and the Speaker of the House were to appoint a majority of the voting members of the Federal Election Commission. *Buckley* involved a suit seeking a declaratory judgment that the Federal Election Campaign Act as amended in 1974 was unconstitutional and asking for an injunction against its enforcement. The Act provided for certification of constitutional questions concerning its validity to the Court of Appeals. A series of such questions were certified concerning the validity of exercise by the Commission of the various powers granted to it in light of the fact that Congress, and not the President, had appointed most of its members.

Although the Court of Appeals dismissed on the ground that most of the questions were not ripe for adjudication, the Supreme Court found sufficient ripeness to reach the merits. The Court held that Congress had violated the appointments clause because neither of the legislative officers purportedly given the appointment power were deemed to come within the terms "courts of law" or "heads of departments" as required by Article II. Since they had not been appointed in accordance with the power granted the President under Article II to appoint "Officers of the United States," members of the Commission could not exercise the purely executive functions of administering the law.

2. 424 U.S. 1 (1976).

3. 100 U.S. 371 (1879).

4. 100 U.S. at 398. On this no "incongruity" requirement see Hobson v. Hansen, 265 F.Supp. 902, 913–14 (D.D.C.1967); United States v. Solomon, 216 F.Supp. 835 (S.D.N.Y.1963); In re Farrow, 3 F. 112 (1880); Russell v. Thomas, 2 Fed.Cas. No. 12,162 (1874); Birch v. Steele, 165 F. 577 (5th Cir. 1908).

Although the question of the propriety of the courts of law exercising appointment powers has been much discussed recently in connection with proposals for a permanent Special Prosecutor to prosecute, in appropriate cases, governmental officials, there are only a few Supreme Court cases on the subject. In 1879, in *Ex parte Siebold*[3] the Supreme Court held that Congress could authorize the Circuit Courts to appoint election supervisors. *Siebold* read this Article II section 2, clause 2 broadly. That clause provides that "the Congress may by Law vest the Appointment of such inferior Officers, as they think proper, in the President alone, in the Courts of Law, or in the Heads of Departments." *Siebold* held:

> [T]he duty [of the court] to appoint inferior officers, when required thereto by law, is a constitutional duty of the courts; and in the present case there is no such incongruity in the duty required as to excuse the courts from its performance, or to render their acts void.[4]

Other Supreme Court cases offer little more guidance other than this no "incongruity" requirement.[5]

While Congress may not appoint those who execute the laws, it may lay down qualifications of age, experience, and so on. Sometimes these qualifications significantly narrow the field of choice.[6]

B.   The Removal Power

There is no express Constitutional grant of a removal power (other than Congress' removal power in connection with impeachments), although at least one framer of the Constitution, James Madison, felt it "absolutely necessary that the President should have the power of removing from office"[7]

5. Rice v. Ames, 180 U.S. 371 (1901) (court appointment of commissioners to handle extradition matters upheld).

6. See generally, Note, Power of Appointment to Public Office Under the Federal Constitution, 42 Harv. L.Rev. 426 (1929). See also, E. Corwin, The President: Office and Powers 1787–1957, at 363–365 (4th ed. 1957).

7. Annals of Congress 387 (1789) [1789–1791].

appointees to office. It would seem that a presidential removal power was not even formally discussed at the Constitutional Convention.[8] Absent an express presidential grant of removal power, such a power has long been assumed to arise from the grant of executive power under Article II, section 1 of the Constitution and the duty under Article II, section 3 to "take care that the Laws be faithfully executed."[9] Presidential control over purely executive functions would be seriously undermined by any efforts to limit this removal power.

An early judicial statement on the removal power can be found in the seminal case of *Marbury v. Madison*.[10] Marbury had been appointed a Justice of the Peace for the District of Columbia shortly before the end of the administration of President John Adams. Due to the lack of time before the next administration would take over, his commission was never delivered. Jefferson's incoming cabinet was resentful of Marbury and other federalist judges who had been appointed in the "midnight hour" of the prior administration; the new Secretary of State, James Madison, refused to deliver the commission. Marbury went to the Supreme Court seeking mandamus to compel delivery. The Court denied the writ, holding that the Act of Congress which purported to grant the Supreme Court original jurisdiction to issue mandamus was invalid because in conflict with Article III of the Constitution. Writing the opinion for the Court, Chief Justice Marshall stated a narrow view of the executive's power of removal:

> [W]hen the officer is not removable at the will of the executive, the appointment is not revocable, and cannot be annulled: it has conferred legal rights which cannot be resumed. . . .

[A]s the law creating the office, gave the officer a right to hold for five years, independent of the executive, the appointment was not revocable, but vested in the officers legal rights, which are protected by the laws of his country.[11]

The holding of the case that the Supreme Court lacked original jurisdiction in mandamus was not dependent on the removal power; thus, Marshall's assertion that the President had no power to remove Marbury within the five year term of appointment was mere dictum. Indeed, as discussed more fully below, subsequent decisions of the Court did not follow Marshall's statement.[12] On its facts, *Marbury* can also be distinguished from the majority of cases involving presidential removal because it was not an executive office that was involved but a judicial office in the local courts of Washington, D.C.

The next significant Supreme Court addressing the removal question was *Ex parte Hennen*,[13] a case involving a dismissed Clerk of the United States District Court for the Eastern District of Louisiana. Pursuant to an act of Congress granting both the Supreme Court and the federal district courts power to appoint their own clerks, Duncan Hennen had been named to such an appointment. Hennen was later dismissed by a district judge, who also appointed a new clerk. Hennen promptly sought a writ of mandamus to compel his reinstatement by the district court. Mandamus was denied on the ground that the power to appoint clerks for a district court was vested exclusively in that court and the Supreme Court could not control its exercise.[14]

Although no issue of presidential removal was involved in the *Hennen* decision, language in the opinion supports such a power.

---

8. See generally, M. Farrand, The Records of the Federal Convention (1911).

9. See, Myers v. United States, 272 U.S. 52, 164 (1926).

10. 5 U.S. (1 Cranch) 137 (1803). See Chapter 1, section II, supra.

11. 5 U.S. (1 Cranch) at 162.

12. See, e.g. United States v. Smith, 286 U.S. 6, 47 (1932) (completeness of appointment on signing of the commission); United States v. Le Baron, 60 U.S. (19 How.) 73 (1856); Parsons v. United States, 167 U.S. 324 (1897) (term of office). See also the cases on removal of officers discussed below.

13. 38 U.S. (13 Pet.) 230 (1839).

14. 38 U.S. (13 Pet.) at 261.

Noting that "[t]he Constitution is silent with respect to the power of removal from office, where the tenure is not fixed," [15] the Court went on to state that "[i]n the absence of all constitutional provision, or statutory regulation, it would seem to be a sound and necessary rule, to consider the power of removal as incident to the power of appointment." [16]

United States v. Perkins, [17] another examination of the removal powers, established that where Congress vests the power of appointment in some official other than the president, [18] it has the ability to regulate and restrict the manner of removing that appointee. *Perkins* involved a suit in the Court of Claims for lost wages by a naval cadet-engineer whom the Secretary of the Navy had discharged because his services were "not required." Congress had provided that no officer could be dismissed from the armed services except by court-martial. Invalidating Perkins' dismissal, the Court made it clear that "when Congress, by law, vests the appointment of inferior officers in the heads of Departments it may limit and restrict the power of removal as it deems best for the public interest." [19] Since the *Perkins* holding was limited to removal by heads of Departments it did not reach the issue of whether Congress could place restrictions upon the removal power of the president once it had vested him with a power of appointment over inferior officers.

In two decisions following *Perkins*, the Court further avoided deciding whether Congress could constitutionally restrict the president's power to remove officers appointed by him by basing the decisions on constructions of the statutory grants of appointment power. [20] In the second of these cases, *Shurtleff v. United States*, [21] the Court did note that the ability to remove from office was inherent in the power of appointment unless taken away by "plain and unambiguous language" in the enabling statute. [22]

The key issue of Congressional restriction of the president's removal power was finally reached in the leading case of *Myers v. United States*. [23] A postmaster at Portland, Oregon, Myers was discharged in an order issued by the Postmaster General and sanctioned by the president. Congress had provided that postmasters could be removed by the president "with the advice and consent of the Senate" but that until so removed they would hold office for four years. [24] Myers was removed by President Wilson without any attempt on the president's part to secure concurrence by the Senate. The Court of Claims dismissed Myers' suit for lost pay because he had waited too long to sue; the Supreme Court affirmed on different grounds.

Former President William Howard Taft, as Chief Justice, wrote the opinion for the Court, holding that "[t]he power to remove . . . is an incident of the power to appoint" [25] and the Tenure of Office Act was unconstitutional insofar as it restricted the power of the president to remove officers he had appointed. [26] Contrasting the general grant of executive power contained in Article II of the Constitution with the specific grants of enumerated legislative powers found in Article I, the Court deemed the fact that no express limitation was placed on the power of removal a "convincing indication

---

15. 38 U.S. (13 Pet.) at 258.

16. 38 U.S. (13 Pet.) at 259.

17. 116 U.S. 483 (1886).

18. Pursuant to Article II, § 2 of the Constitution, Congress may by law vest the appointment of inferior officers in the heads of Departments.

19. 116 U.S. at 485.

20. Parsons v. United States, 167 U.S. 324 (1897); Shurtleff v. United States, 189 U.S. 311 (1903).

21. 189 U.S. 311 (1903).

22. 189 U.S. at 318.

23. 272 U.S. 52 (1926). See generally, Van Alstyne, The Role of Congress in Determining Incidental Powers of the President and of the Federal Courts: A Comment on the Horizontal Effect of "the Sweeping Clause," 36 Ohio St.L.J. 788, 800–809 (1975).

24. 19 Stat. 80 (1876) provided that: "[P]ostmasters of the first, second, and third classes may be removed by the President by and with the advice and consent of the Senate, and shall hold their offices for four years unless sooner removed according to law . . . ."

25. 272 U.S. at 161.

26. 272 U.S. at 176.

that none was intended." [27] The Court relied heavily on its view of history as well as on the practical necessity of an unfettered removal power for the President to carry out the mandate of Article I to see that "the Laws be faithfully executed." The need for removal as a "disciplinary influence" was recognized by the Court,[28] for "as his [the President's] selection of administrative officers is essential to the execution of the laws by him, so must be his power of removing those for whom he cannot continue to be responsible." [29]

Three justices dissented from the holding of an absolute power of the President to remove in *Myers*. Justice McReynolds felt that an unlimited power of removal could only stem from clear language in the Constitution and should not be implied absent such language. Justice Brandeis noted that Senatorial approval in the removal of officials was a well established legislative practice and, lacking a judicial decision to the contrary, such a practice should be equivalent to judicial construction of the statute granting the appointment power to the president. The remaining dissenter, Mr. Justice Holmes, argued that where Congress creates a position, and has the power to transfer the appointment power to an official other than the President, Congress clearly has the power to restrict the mode of removing the appointee.

Myers was severely criticized for the suggestion by the Chief Justice that the president could remove quasi-judicial officers as, for example, members of independent regulatory agencies.[30] Read broadly, *Myers* would stand for the proposition that under the Constitution the president has unrestricted power to remove any official he had appointed, with the exception of federal judges. Nine years later, the broad language and reach of the *Myers* decision were somewhat limited in the case of *Humphrey's Executor v. United States*,[31] which held that the president cannot remove a member of an independent regulatory agency in violation of restrictions in the statutory framework. Under the Federal Trade Commission Act any commissioner could be removed from office by the president for "inefficiency, neglect of duty, or malfeasance in office." [32] Humphrey was removed from his position as a member of the Commission by President Roosevelt, who candidly admitted that the removal was for policy reasons rather than for one of the causes enumerated in the statute. Suit to cover his lost wages was brought by his executor.

The *Humphrey* Court looked to the nature and function of the Federal Trade Commission and concluded that "its duties are neither political nor executive, but predominantly quasi-judicial and quasi-legislative." [33] Recognizing that the independence of the regulatory agencies could be severely curtailed by a presidential power to remove members at will, the Court held that while *Myers* applied to all purely executive officers, the Constitution does not grant the president unlimited removal power as to quasi-legislative or quasi-judicial officers, even where such hold office through presidential appointment.[34]

Wiener v. United States [35] further clarified the distinction made in the *Humphrey* case between purely executive officers and those whose duties extend to non-executive functions. In *Wiener*, President Eisenhower's dismissal of a Truman appointee to the War Claims Commission was held invalid *even in the absence* of an express congressional restriction on the president's power of

27. 272 U.S. at 128.

28. 272 U.S. at 132.

29. 272 U.S. at 117.

30. See the opinion of the Court, 272 U.S. at 135. This implication led one commentator to call the decision a "menacing challenge to an administrative organization which represents years of planning and experimentation in meeting modern conditions." E. Corwin,

The President's Removal Power under the Constitution, 68 (Nat'l Municipal League 1927).

31. 295 U.S. 602 (1935).

32. 295 U.S. at 623.

33. 295 U.S. at 624.

34. 295 U.S. at 629.

35. 357 U.S. 349 (1958).

removal. Following the unanimous holding in *Humphrey's Executor* that the validity of statutory limitations on presidential removal powers turns on the question of whether the involved agencies included functions either partially legislative or judicial, *Wiener* elaborated on "[t]his sharp differentiation" setting apart "those who are part of the Executive establishment and those whose tasks require absolute freedom from Executive interference." [36]

While the president's power to remove quasi-judicial and quasi-legislative officers has been limited by these holdings, it is clear that he still retains the unlimited power to remove those purely executive officers he has appointed.[37] However, as the *Perkins* case indicated, it must be remembered that different rules apply where the government officer has been appointed by someone other than the president. As a general rule, the government has the power of summary dismissal over its employees. Two exceptions to this rule exist. The first occurs in a *Perkins* situation where Congress has restricted or regulated the manner of removal. Secondly, where an executive department promulgates administrative regulations having the force and effect of law which establish procedures governing dismissal of employees, such regulations are binding on the official who prescribed them for so long as the regulation remains operative.[38] Following these principles, the Supreme Court has twice ruled that an executive department must follow its own administrative regulations governing employee discharge or the discharge will be deemed illegal.[39] The regulations of course may always be changed.

C. Conclusion

The cases on the appointment power establish several general principles. The president has the power to appoint officers of the United States. The Congress may not exercise the power to appoint those who execute the laws; but, as to "inferior officers," the federal courts share with the president the power of appointment. When the court appoints, the office may be unrelated to judicial administration but it should not be "incongruous."

The removal power cases establish four general principles. First, purely executive officers appointed by the President are subject to a presidential removal power that may not constitutionally be limited by Congress. Second, Congress may, however, limit and regulate removal where it has vested the appointment power in some official other than the president. Third, quasi-legislative and quasi-judicial officers may be removed by the president only for cause, regardless of who did the appointing and even if Congress has not expressly limited removal. Finally, where an executive department has established administrative regulations having the force and effect of law to govern employee dismissal, it may not remove any employee in a manner inconsistent with those regulations.

IV. THE PARDONING POWER

By the time of Henry VII's reign in England, common law had developed the principle that the monarch was vested, absolutely and exclusively, with the power to pardon those accused or convicted of crime.[1] The idea of executive pardoning power was so firmly established in the common law that delegates to the Constitutional Convention adopted with little debate a clause perpetuating the power of executive pardon for the

---

36. 357 U.S. at 353.

37. See, e.g., Martin v. Tobin, 451 F.2d 1335 (9th Cir. 1971).

38. The doctrine that the official prescribing such a regulation is bound by it stems from United States ex rel. Accardi v. Shaughnessy, 347 U.S. 260 (1954).

39. Service v. Dulles, 354 U.S. 363 (1957); Vitarelli v. Seaton, 359 U.S. 535 (1959).

1. See Grupp, Some Historical Aspects of the Pardon in England, 7 Am.J.Legal History, 51, 55 (1963). See generally, A.S. Miller, Presidential Power in a Nutshell 307–13 (1977).

President.[2] Based on recognized English principles of pardon, Article II § 2 of the Constitution grants the President ". . . Power to grant Reprieves and Pardons for Offences against the United States, except in Cases of Impeachment." Case law has now developed the extent of the power to pardon far beyond that recognized at common law.

According to Lord Chief Justice Coke, the English King was given great discretion and leeway in the exercise of his power; his pardon could be "either absolute, or under condition, exception, or qualification . . . ."[3] Broad discretion in the use of the presidential pardon was accepted early by American courts. Writing for the Supreme Court in *United States v. Wilson*[4], Chief Justice Marshall recognized that a pardon was an act of mercy, "an act of grace, proceeding from the power entrusted with the execution of the laws. . . ."[5] For almost a full century after *Wilson* most courts adhered to this view of the granting of a pardon as the executive's personal act of mercy toward an individual.[6] Common law remained the basis for resolving questions concerning the reach of this "merciful" power.

The Supreme Court ultimately abandoned the historical "act of grace" approach in *Biddle v. Perovich*.[7] *Biddle* enunciated for the first time a theory of presidential pardon that went beyond simple adherence to common law precepts. The Court upheld a commutation of sentence by the President from death to life imprisonment even though the change in sentence was imposed without the prisoner's consent. An earlier case, *Burdick v. United States*,[8] had held that acceptance of the pardon was essential and that a witness in a grand jury proceeding could refuse to accept a pardon and instead assert his privilege against self-incrimination. The decision in *Burdick* recognized that in some instances the stigma of a pardon would not be wanted and that the "merciful" act could be rejected. In *Biddle*, however, Mr. Justice Holmes' opinion for the Court made it clear that a pardon is an act for the public welfare, "not a private act of grace from an individual happening to possess power."[9] The Court recognized presidential power to impose "less severe" punishments for the public welfare and deemed that consent was not necessary in such a situation, for the prisoner "on no sound principle ought to have any voice in what the law should do for the welfare of the whole."[10]

In addition to changing the theoretical focus of the pardon power from a private act to one for the general welfare, the *Biddle* Court for the first time refused to sanction a technical distinction between the power to pardon and the power to commute sentence, which had previously been viewed as completely different forms of clemency.[11] The Court recognized that the president's power extends to imposition of "less severe" punishments; where the substituted sentence is one generally recognized as being less hard the president need not grant full pardon. Although expanding the scope of the pardoning power to include commutation without the prisoner's consent, the Court did not go so far as to hold that the president has unlimited freedom in substituting punishment.

The effect and operation of a pardon have been further defined by the Supreme Court in other cases. In *Ex parte Garland*,[12] the Court was faced with the effect of a pardon granted by President Andrew Johnson to one Garland for all offenses committed by him arising from his participation in the Civil

2. 2 M. Farrand, The Records of the Federal Convention of 1787 at 626 (1911).

3. E. Coke, The Third Part of the Institutes of the Laws of England 233 (1817).

4. 32 U.S. (7 Pet.) 150 (1833).

5. 32 U.S. at 160.

6. See, e.g., Ex parte Garland, 71 U.S. (4 Wall.) 333, 380 (1866).

7. 274 U.S. 480 (1927).

8. 236 U.S. 79 (1915).

9. 274 U.S. at 486.

10. 274 U.S. at 487.

11. See, e.g., Ex parte Wells, 59 U.S. (18 How.) 307 (1855).

12. 71 U.S. (4 Wall.) 333 (1867).

War. Prior to the pardon, Congress had enacted a law providing that any individual who wished to practice law in the federal courts first had to take an oath stating that he had never voluntarily borne arms against the United States or given aid to its enemies. Finding the Act to be unconstitutional as a bill of attainder, the Court held that the presidential pardon had relieved Garland from all penalties and disabilities, including the oath, for the named acts. In speaking of the scope of the president's power under Article II, section 2, the Court noted that "[i]t extends to every offence known to the law, and may be exercised at any time after its commission, either before legal proceedings are taken, or during their pendency, or after conviction and judgment." [13] A full pardon erases the act and its legal consequences so that "in the eye of the law the offender is as innocent as if he had never committed the offense" and restores the offender to "all his civil rights." [14]

This wide scope of the pardoning power was again emphasized in *Ex parte Grossman*,[15] where the Court held that the power extended not only to indictable crimes but also to contempt of court. Other early decisions have made it clear that the pardoning power encompasses the capacity to remit fines and forfeitures;[16] to commute sentences;[17] to grant amnesty to specified classes or groups;[18] and to pardon conditionally as well as absolutely.[19]

Certain limitations on Article II, § 2 power have also been recognized, however. The Court noted in *Knote v. United States*[20] that pardon could not compensate the offender for personal injuries suffered by imprisonment, nor can a pardon affect any rights which have vested in others due to the judgment against the offender. The opinion of the Court went on to point out that:

However large . . . may be the power of pardon possessed by the President, and however extended may be its application, there is this limit to it, as there is to all his powers—it cannot touch moneys in the Treasury of the United States, except expressly authorized by act of Congress. The Constitution places this restriction upon the pardoning power.[21]

The power of the President to attach conditions to grants of clemency was affirmed by the Court in *Schick v. Reed.*[22] A divided Court[23] upheld the presidential commutation of a death sentence to life imprisonment conditioned on permanent ineligibility for parole, even where the commuted sentence was not one which had been specifically provided for by statute. The majority opinion in *Schick* emphasized that the only limits which can be imposed on the presidential pardon power are those in the Constitution itself, and to require the executive to substitute a punishment already permitted by law would place unauthorized congressional restrictions on the pardoning power.[24]

---

13. 71 U.S. (4 Wall.) at 380. Note that while Congress cannot limit the presidential pardoning power, see also, United States v. Klein, 80 U.S. (13 Wall.) 128 (1872), but cf. note 15, infra, Congress can enact amnesty statutes. The Laura, 114 U.S. 411, 414–17 (1885).

14. 71 U.S. (4 Wall.) at 380. It should be noted, however that acceptance of a pardon will take away one civil right of the offender—the privilege against self-incrimination. See Brown v. Walker, 161 U.S. 591, 598–99 (1896).

15. 267 U.S. 87 (1925). The Court did appear to distinguish criminal contempts, which a presidential pardon would reach, from civil contempts, which the pardon would not reach. Id. at 121–22. It has also been argued that a presidential pardon might not reach a contempt of Congress. E. Corwin, The President: Office and Powers 414 (4th rev. ed. 1957).

16. Illinois Central R.R. v. Bosworth, 133 U.S. 92 (1890).

17. Armstrong v. United States, 80 U.S. 154 (1871).

18. United States v. Klein, 80 U.S. 128 (1869).

19. Ex parte William Wells, 59 U.S. (18 How.) 307 (1865).

20. 95 U.S. 149 (1877).

21. 95 U.S. at 154.

22. 419 U.S. 256 (1974).

23. Chief Justice Burger wrote the majority opinion, Justices Marshall, Douglas and Brennan dissented in an opinion written by Marshall.

24. 419 U.S. at 266–67.

Schick continued the historical trend of the Supreme Court of extending the pardoning power of the President beyond prior judicially recognized boundaries and far beyond the scope of its English common-law counterpart. It may be that one of the few major limitations on the president's power to pardon under Article II, § 2 is that recognized by the majority in *Schick* that the "President may not aggravate punishment."[25]

25. 419 U.S. at 267.

CHAPTER EIGHT

CONGRESSIONAL POWERS AND PRIVILEGES

I. THE CONGRESSIONAL POWER TO INVESTIGATE

A. Introduction

The investigatory power of Congress, buttressed by the sanction of contempt, is a very broad one and raises issues of constitutional history, the role of Congress as a check on the Executive Branch, and the applicability of the first amendment as a check on abusive Congressional investigations. These topics will be considered in this Chapter.

Although nowhere in the Constitution is there expressly granted to either House of Congress a general power to investigate in aid of legislation, or in aid of its function of overseeing the Executive Branch, the Supreme Court has long recognized that such a power is to be implied as an essential concomitant to Congress' legislative authority. Access to outside sources of information is deemed essential to the legislative process, and the Courts have recognized that compulsory procedures are therefore required. *McGrain v. Daugherty,*[1] is a leading case which gives explicit judicial recognition of the right of either House of Congress to

1. 273 U.S. 135 (1927).

commit for contempt a witness who ignores its summons or refuses to answer its inquiries. In *McGrain* the high court upheld a Senate investigation as to whether the Department of Justice was performing or neglecting its duties. Such an investigation was one on which legislation could be based and thus the Senate had the power to compel the attendance of witnesses to give information on the subject, although the Resolution did not expressly state that the investigation was in aid of legislation.[2] Congress' investigative role in exercising its oversight function and exposing corruption has been similarly recognized. As Professor, and later President, Woodrow Wilson explained:

> The informing function of Congress should be preferred even to its legislative function. The argument is not only that discussed and interrogated administration is the only pure and efficient administration, but more than that, that *the only really self-governing people is that people which discusses and interrogates its administration* . . .[3]

Congress also has a right to compulsory process when it exercises its function of judging an election,[4] or determining if a member should be expelled.[5]

Congress' contempt powers in aid of its Article I functions has deep historical roots. The first trial by the Congress for contempt (in this case the trial was by the House of Representatives) was in late 1795 and early 1796, and involved two defendants. One defendant, Randall, was "convicted" of an attempt to corrupt two members of the House of Representatives. The House itself tried and imprisoned Randall; thus the aid of the Courts was not needed. He remained as a prisoner of the House until January 13, 1796. The other, Whitney, was discharged

on January 5, 1796 because the evidence against him was found to be insufficient. There was no appeal of the imprisonment to the Courts by either Randall or Whitney.[6]

In such cases the House used its *common law* power of contempt; there now exists also a *statutory* contempt procedure using the process of the courts to try and sentence offenders.[7] In this section we will first consider the constitutional basis for the common law contempt remedy; then we will briefly analyze the statutory procedure, which is in addition to—and does not preempt—Congress' common law contempt power. Finally we will turn to the various defenses to congressional contempt, concentrating on those based on the Constitution.

B. The Development of Nonstatutory, Common Law Contempt

The first judicial recognition of a common law power of either House of Congress to punish for contempt was in *Anderson v. Dunn,*[8] where the Supreme Court upheld in broad terms the right of either House to attach and punish a person other than a Member of Congress for contempt of its authority, without using the judicial process. The prisoner, however, could still test the validity of his imprisonment by applying for a Writ of Habeas Corpus or suing the Sergeant at Arms.[9]

In *Marshall v. Gordon,*[10] the Court held that Congress has an implied power of contempt but may not arrest a person who only published matter slanderous of the House of Representatives and which presented no immediate obstruction to the legislative process.[11] Appellant in that case applied for habeas corpus after his arrest by the Ser-

---

2. 273 U.S. 135, 177–78. See also Watkins v. United States, 354 U.S. 178, 187 (1957).

3. W. Wilson, Congressional Government 303–04 (1885) (emphasis added).

4. E.g., Barry v. United States ex rel. Cunningham, 279 U.S. 597 (1929) (investigation of senatorial election).

5. In re Chapman, 166 U.S. 661 (1897).

6. Moreland, Congressional Investigations and Private Persons, 40 S.Calif.L.Rev. 189, 190 (1967).

7. 2 U.S.C.A. § 192.

8. 19 U.S. (6 Wheat.) 204 (1821).

9. In Anderson v. Dunn, 19 U.S. (6 Wheat.) 204 (1821), the plaintiff sued the Sergeant at Arms of the House of Representatives for assault and battery and false imprisonment.

10. 243 U.S. 521 (1917).

11. But Congress has the power to order the arrest of a witness to compel his attendance, without first serving a subpoena, if it has reason to believe that the witness will not appear if summoned. Barry v. United States ex rel. Cunningham, 279 U.S. 597, 616–19 (1929).

geant at Arms. The Court ruled that Congress has the implied power of contempt because it has:

> the right to prevent acts which in and of themselves inherently obstruct or prevent the discharge of legislative duty or the refusal to do that which there is inherent legislative power to compel in order that legislative functions may be performed.[12]

Thus the Senate may hold in contempt a witness who had been commanded to produce papers and who instead destroyed them after service of the subpoena. The punishment for a past contempt is appropriate to vindicate the "established and essential privilege of requiring the production of evidence." [13]

This inherent common law power of contempt has been reaffirmed in dicta in several more recent cases. In *Groppi v. Leslie*,[14] for example, the Court reaffirmed that: "Legislatures are not constituted to conduct full-scale trials or quasi-judicial proceedings and we should not demand that they do so although *they possess inherent power* to protect their own processes and existence by way of contempt proceedings." [15]

Nonstatutory contempt has some procedural advantages over statutory contempt,[16] discussed below. Although a United States Attorney has a supposed nondiscretionary duty under the statutory contempt statute to

refer a possible violation to the Grand Jury,[17] it is unclear what procedures are followed if the United States Attorney fails to perform his duty or engages in a less than energetic prosecution. In addition, while the President has pardoned statutory contempt of Congress—pursuant to his constitutional right of pardon—his power to pardon for nonstatutory contempts of Congress is unclear. Professor Corwin, for example, suggested that the president may *not* pardon for nonstatutory contempts of Congress.[18] Perhaps the very broad pardoning power of the president,[19] may not, because of the separation of powers, cover "convictions" by the legislature for contempt of its process. However, no separation of powers theory limits a presidential pardon for contempt of court.[20]

It appears that the power of either House to maintain an individual in custody for nonstatutory contempt is limited to the duration of the current session of that House.[21] Though the Senate is in theory a continuing body,[22] it is nonetheless thought that a confinement by the Senate also only exists until the end of its session.[23] And, in any trial before either House, procedural due process guarantees will require that the contemnor be given notice and an opportunity to be heard prior to conviction and sentencing.[24]

---

12. Marshall v. Gordon, 243 U.S. 521, 542 (1917).

13. Jurney v. MacCracken, 294 U.S. 125, 149–150 (1935).

14. 404 U.S. 496 (1972). The *Groppi* case involved a state legislative body but there is no reason to believe that the case would have been decided differently had it involved Congress or one of its committees.

15. 404 U.S. 496, 500 (1972) (emphasis added). See also Russel v. United States, 369 U.S. 749, 756 & n. 8 (1962).

16. 2 U.S.C.A. § 192.

17. Ex parte Frankfeld, 32 F.Supp. 915 (D.D.C. 1940). However, before the United States Attorney may act on an apparent section 192 violation, there must be a certification to him by either the House involved or the President of the Senate or the Speaker of the House when Congress is not in session. There is no automatic certification to the United States Attorney, for the Committee report of the apparent section 192 violation is then subject to further consideration on

the merits. Wilson v. United States, 369 F.2d 198 (D.C. Cir. 1966) (case construing section 194).

18. E. Corwin, The President: Office and Powers (4th rev. ed. 1957) 414 n. 132. But see, Ex parte Grossman, 267 U.S. 87, 118–120 (1925) (rejecting separation of powers argument that the president may not pardon violations of federal court orders).

19. Schick v. Reed, 419 U.S. 256 (1974); Ex parte Garland, 71 U.S. (4 Wall.) 333 (1867). See Chapter 7, section IV.

20. Ex parte Grossman, 267 U.S. 87 (1925).

21. Anderson v. Dunn, 19 U.S. (6 Wheat.) 204, 231 (1821).

22. McGrain v. Daugherty, 273 U.S. 135, 181–182 (1927).

23. Moreland, Congressional Investigations and Private Persons, 40 S.Calif.L.Rev. 189, 199 n. 31 (1967).

24. Groppi v. Leslie, 404 U.S. 496 (1972).

C. Nonstatutory, Common Law Contempt Procedure

In the case of citations for nonstatutory contempt, normally a subpoena, issued by the committee which desires to question a witness, is personally served on the witness. If he fails to appear, or appears and refuses to answer, the committee reports the matter to the full House or Senate which then adopts a resolution that the Speaker of the House or president pro tempore of the Senate command the Sergeant at Arms or his deputy to arrest the offending party and bring him before the bar of the House in question to answer pertinent questions and to be kept in custody to await further order.[25] The arrest warrant is valid anywhere within the territory of the United States.[26]

The witness is then brought before the House or Senate and again asked the question sought or confronted with the charges against him. He may be given time to prepare a defense or the right to counsel, and allowed to speak in his own behalf. If he refuses to comply with the demand of the relevant House of Congress he is cited for contempt by majority vote of that House and remanded to the custody of the Sergeant at Arms to be held in the common jail of the District of Columbia or in the guardroom of the Capitol Police. He will be held until he has purged himself of the contempt, or until released at the end of the session or by vote of the appropriate House.

The exercise of the inherent contempt power of Congress may of course be tested by a writ of habeas corpus.[27] Congress can exercise its contempt power only within the scope of its constitutional power, and when Congress engages in a "proceeding in a matter beyond their legitimate cognizance . . . " the judiciary will intervene.[28] The

scope of review is, however, limited, for courts have been reluctant to interfere with the exercise by another branch of government of one of its inherent powers. The court will review only the character of the offense to the extent of determining that the House has jurisdiction over the prisoner. As Justice Brandeis explained in *Jurney v. MacCracken* [29] the issue of actual guilt of the charge is left to the judgment of Congress:

> This contention [of MacCracken] goes to the question of guilt, not to that of the jurisdiction of the Senate. . . . Whether he is guilty, and whether he has so far purged himself of contempt that he does not now deserve punishment, are the questions which the Senate proposes to try. The respondent to the petition did not, by demurring, transfer to the court the decision of those questions. The sole function of the writ of habeas corpus is to have the court decide whether the Senate has jurisdiction to make the determination which it proposes.[30]

The scope of a federal court's review in a normal habeas proceeding has expanded considerably since *Jurney*, but the fact still remains that habeas review is considerably more narrow than the review a court would exercise on direct appeal.[31] Thus the scope of a court's inquiry over a House of Congress' common law contempt action should be much narrower than the scope of a court's inquiry over a statutory contempt conviction. For example, in a common law contempt action, the nature of the punishment required as remedial action would be within the discretion of the legislature and should not be judged by the court unless there is "an absolute disregard of discretion and a mere exertion of arbitrary power . . . . ".[32]

Since Congress has in recent years relied exclusively on statutory contempt, there are

25. McGrain v. Daugherty, 273 U.S. 135, 152–154 (1927).

26. Anderson v. Dunn, 19 U.S. (6 Wheat.) 204, 234 (1821).

27. E.g., Ex parte, Nugent, 18 Fed.Cas. (No. 10,375) 471, 481–483 (C.C.D.C.1848); cf. Jurney v. MacCracken, 294 U.S. 125 (1935).

28. Kilbourn v. Thompson, 103 U.S. 168, 197 (1881).

29. 294 U.S. 125 (1935).

30. 294 U.S. 125, 152.

31. See generally, Developments in the Law—Federal Habeas Corpus, 83 Harv.L.Rev. 1038, 1113 et seq. (1970).

32. Marshall v. Gordon, 243 U.S. 521, 545 (1917).

only a few modern cases in which the courts have ruled on the exercise of the inherent contempt power. In two cases involving common law contempt, *Kilbourn v. Thompson*,[33] an 1881 case, and *Marshall v. Gordon*,[34] a 1917 case, the Court refused to uphold the Congressional action. It is therefore not entirely clear as to the limits of Congressional power in this area of common law contempt.[35] At the least, all investigations must be made pursuant to a valid legislative purpose, and lacking that purpose, a witness cannot be punished for refusing to cooperate.[36] But since Congress' investigative power is exceedingly broad, that limitation should not prove to be a significant one, assuming that the committee resolution can reasonably be interpreted to authorize the investigation undertaken.[37] No one can be compelled to disclose information on matters which fall outside the authorized scope of inquiry of a committee, for while the investigative power is inherent in either House of Congress as a whole, a committee is restricted to the mission delegated to it by the Congress.[38] Thus, a question must meet a pertinency standard[39] in order for a contempt to be upheld when judicially tested; if the question fails to pass constitutional muster, "a witness rightfully may refuse to answer where the bounds of the power are exceeded or the questions are not pertinent to the matter under inquiry."[40] Where the witness is called before the entire House and

the questions asked again, perhaps pertinency would be measured by the full scope of the investigatory power of Congress and not that of only the committee before which the testimony originally took place.[41]

Since Congress has the power to judge guilt or innocence of the contempts it charges, a finding of willfulness would be a matter to be determined by the appropriate House of Congress, subject only to the limited review in common law contempt cases. To what extent the requirements read into statutory contempt proceedings, discussed below, may be found to actually be a part of due process, is difficult to determine. To date, due process has been applied to legislative contempt proceedings only to the extent of requiring notice and an opportunity to be heard. It may well be the case that the due process requirements will be extended; thus far, procedural due process guarantees do not require a quasi-judicial proceeding by a legislature in order to have a valid contempt.[42]

D. The Development of Statutory Contempt

1. The Statute

Because of the unclear limitations on non-statutory contempt and because contempt trials are time consuming, in 1857 Congress enacted a statute providing for criminal process in the federal courts with prescribed

---

33. 103 U.S. 168 (1881).

34. 243 U.S. 521 (1917).

35. In modern cases involving *statutory* contempt, Congressional power has been upheld. E.g., Sinclair v. United States, 279 U.S. 263 (1929); Barenblatt v. United States, 360 U.S. 109 (1959).

36. Kilbourn v. Thompson, 103 U.S. 168, 194–196 (1881). In *Kilbourn* the Court released Kilbourn from the District of Columbia common jail. He refused to answer questions concerning some of his financial dealings and some papers related to those dealings, which concerned a real estate pool between him and Jay Cooke, whose banks had failed. Justice Miller for the Court held that the committee's investigation was really judicial in nature and related only to Kilbourn's personal affairs. This part of *Kilbourn* has been interpreted very narrowly. See Sinclair v. United States, 279 U.S. 263 (1929); McGrain v. Daugherty, 273 U.S. 135 (1927). It is likely now that a claim based on an argument that a committee's investigation vested ex-

clusively in the judiciary would fail. See, Hutcheson v. United States, 369 U.S. 599 (1962).

See generally, Hacker & Rotunda, Restrictions on Agency and Congressional Subpoenas Issued for an Improper Purpose, 4 Corp.L.Rev. 74 (1981). See also section II of this Chapter, infra.

37. See Barenblatt v. United States, 360 U.S. 109 (1959); United States v. Rumely, 345 U.S. 41 (1953).

38. Watkins v. United States, 354 U.S. 178, 206 (1957); United States v. Rumely, 345 U.S. 41 (1953).

39. The pertinency standard is discussed in section I, D, 4 dealing with statutory contempt.

40. McGrain v. Daugherty, 273 U.S. 135, 176 (1929).

41. See Sweezy v. New Hampshire, 354 U.S. 234, 256 (1957) (Frankfurter, J. concurring): "The case must be judged as though the whole body of the [state] legislature had demanded the information of the petitioner."

42. Groppi v. Leslie, 404 U.S. 496, 500 (1972).

penalties for contempt of Congress.[43] The present day version of that statute is section 192 of title two of the U.S. Code. This statute is merely supplementary to the nonstatutory power of Congress; it does not preempt the field.[44] However, since Congress by the use of that statute seeks the aid of the federal courts, the courts require that every defendant prosecuted for a statutory violation be accorded all of the guarantees and safeguards which the law gives to every defendant in a federal criminal case—even though the defendant would not constitutionally have the right to all of those guarantees had Congress used its own common law power of contempt and not resorted to the courts.[45]

2 U.S.C.A. section 192 provides as follows:

Every person who having been summoned as a witness by the authority of either House of Congress to give testimony or to produce papers upon any matter under inquiry before either House, or any joint committee established by a joint or concurrent resolution of the two Houses of Congress, or any committee of either House of Congress, willfully makes default, or who, having appeared, refuses to answer any question pertinent to the question under inquiry, shall be deemed guilty of a misdemeanor, punishable by a fine of not more than $1,000 nor less than $100 and imprison-

ment in a common jail for not less than one month nor more than twelve months.[46]

This section has been used extensively in recent years, especially since World War II, and the provision has been considered at length by the courts. Four major elements of the crime have been identified: (a) the investigation during which the contempt occurred must be in aid of a valid legislative purpose; (b) the committee conducting the investigation must be authorized to conduct the particular inquiry in question; (c) the question that was refused an answer or the papers the production of which was required must be pertinent to the authorized inquiry; (d) the default must be willful.

2. Legislative Purpose

The nature of the investigative power requires that each inquiry be based on a constitutional grant of legislative authority. That power is, however, very broad:

It encompasses inquiries concerning the administration of existing laws as well as proposed or possibly needed statutes. It includes surveys of defects in our social, economic or political system for the purpose of enabling the Congress to remedy them. It comprehends probes into departments of the Federal Government to expose corruption, inefficiency or waste.[47]

---

43. 11 Stat. 155 (1857).

44. In re Chapman, 166 U.S. 661, 671–72 (1897).

45. E.g., Watkins v. United States, 354 U.S. 178, 206–208 (1957); Russell v. United States, 369 U.S. 749, 755 (1962); Gojack v. United States, 384 U.S. 702, 707 & n. 6 (1966).

46. See also:

"§ 193. Privilege of witnesses

"No witness is privileged to refuse to testify to any fact, or to produce any paper, respecting which he shall be examined by either House of Congress, or by any joint committee established by a joint or concurrent resolution of the two Houses of Congress, or by any committee of either House, upon the ground that his testimony to such fact or his production of such paper may tend to disgrace him or otherwise render him infamous."

"§ 194. Certification of failure to testify; grand jury action failing to testify or produce records

"Whenever a witness summoned as mentioned in section 192 fails to appear to testify or fails to pro-

duce any books, papers, records, or documents, as required, or whenever any witness so summoned refuses to answer any question pertinent to the subject under inquiry before either House, or any joint committee established by a joint or concurrent resolution of the two Houses of Congress, or any committee or subcommittee of either House of Congress, and the fact of such failure or failures is reported to either House while Congress is in session, or when Congress is not in session, a statement of fact constituting such failure is reported to and filed with the President of the Senate or the Speaker of the House, it shall be the duty of the said President of the Senate or Speaker of the House, as the case may be, to certify, and he shall so certify, the statement of facts aforesaid under the seal of the Senate or House, as the case may be, to the appropriate United States attorney, whose duty it shall be to bring the matter before the grand jury for its action."

47. Watkins v. United States, 354 U.S. 178, 187 (1957). See also Barenblatt v. United States, 360 U.S. 109 (1959).

Still, there is no power to expose the activities of individuals merely for the sake of exposure without justification in terms of functions of Congress; it is not the function of Congress to conduct legislative trials.[48] Private affairs may be inquired into and their exposure compelled, however, in pursuit of an independent legislative purpose.[49] Congress and its Committees do have the power "to inquire into and *publicize* corruption, maladministration or inefficiency in agencies of the Government."[50]

The existence of a valid legislative purpose is to be judged simply by whether the legislative body has jurisdiction over the subject matter of the investigation. The enabling resolution contains the grant and limitations of the committee's power.[51] The fact that a committee has reported no legislation at all as the result of an extended series of hearings does not negate a conclusion that the committee has a legislative purpose.[52]

The Supreme Court declared in *McGrain v. Daugherty*,[53] that a legislative purpose was to be presumed when the subject matter of the investigation was within the jurisdiction of Congress, as the "only legitimate object the Senate could have in ordering the [particular] investigation [before it] was to aid it in legislating." The presumption cannot be rebutted by impugning the motives of individual Congressmen, for motive is irrelevant as long as the assembly's legislative purpose is in fact being served.[54] The Court will simply refuse to hear allegations that the ulterior motive of the investigators is not to aid legislation but to harass individuals for their political beliefs.[55] Once a legislative purpose is established, the permissible scope of the investigation may be as far reaching as the potential legislative function to which it is related.[56] It can encompass all matters necessary to the fulfillment of the legislative purpose.

3. Authority of the Committee

A witness can be punished for refusal to testify before a Congressional committee only if that committee and in turn its subcommittee were authorized by its parent House or committee to conduct the investigation to which the testimony pertained. This requirement is an element of the pertinency requirement and therefore is jurisdictional.[57] Such authority can be conferred by statute or by special resolution. It is an element of the offense which must be pleaded and proved by the government. Thus in *Gojack v. United States*,[58] a contempt citation was reversed because no showing was made that the parent committee had delegated to its subcommittee before whom the witness had appeared the authority to make the inquiry; the full committee also had not specified the area of inquiry as required by its own rules. The authorization defines the subject of the inquiry and thus puts some limits on its scope. As the *Gojack* Court explained: "The jurisdiction of the courts cannot be invoked to impose criminal sanctions in aid of a roving commission. The subject of the inquiry of the specific body before which the alleged contempt occurred must be clear and certain."[59] The requirement of committee authorization is composed of two elements. First, the committee or subcommittee must be empowered to conduct the specific investigation undertaken. Second, it must be

---

48. Watkins v. United States, 354 U.S. 178, 200.

49. 354 U.S. at 200, 206.

50. 354 U.S. at 200 n. 33, citing, inter alia, Landis, Constitutional Limitations on the Congressional Power of Investigation, 40 Harv.L.Rev. 153, 168–194 (1926).

51. United States v. Rumely, 345 U.S. 41, 44 (1953).

52. Townsend v. United States, 95 F.2d 352, 355 (D.C.Cir. 1938).

53. 273 U.S. 135, 178 (1927). But cf. Watkins v. United States, 354 U.S. 178, 200 n. 33 (1959) (upholding right to expose governmental corruption).

54. Barenblatt v. United States, 360 U.S. 109, 132–133 (1959); Watkins v. United States, 354 U.S. 178, 200 (1957).

55. Tenney v. Brandhove, 341 U.S. 367, 377–378 (1951).

56. Townsend v. United States, 95 F.2d 352, 361 (D.C.Cir. 1938).

57. Watkins v. United States, 354 U.S. 178, 201, 206 (1957); Gojack v. United States, 384 U.S. 702, 708 (1966).

58. 384 U.S. 702, 705, 713–714 (1966).

59. 384 U.S. 702, 715 (1966).

shown that the inquiry with respect to which the contempt occurred was within the scope of the delegated authority.[60]

In the case of the House Un-American Activities Committee (HUAC), the Supreme Court has been willing to read the committee's authorizing resolution very broadly. Although the Court has criticized the vagueness of the HUAC resolution and the ambiguity of its operative terms in *Watkins v. United States*,[61] it read *Watkins* narrowly and the authorizing resolution broadly in *Barenblatt v. United States*.[62] *Barenblatt* involved inquiry by a committee investigating alleged Communist infiltration into the field of education, including whether a former teaching fellow at the University of Michigan was then or had ever been a member of the Communist Party. Petitioner Barenblatt refused to answer the committee's questions on Party membership, objecting not on fifth amendment grounds, but rather disclaiming in general the right of the Sub-committee to inquire into his "political" and "religious" beliefs or "other personal or private affairs" or "associational activities." The Court affirmed his contempt conviction and in rejecting the petitioner's contention that the Sub-committee had no such powers of inquiry stated: "Just as legislation is often given meaning by the gloss of legislative reports, administrative interpretation, and long usage, so the proper meaning of an authorization to a congressional committee is not to be derived alone from its abstract terms unrelated to the definite content furnished them by the course of congressional actions." [63] The committee's history forced the Court to conclude that its legislative authority to conduct the instant inquiry was "unassailable." [64]

In other areas, however, the courts have read authorizing resolutions narrowly, particularly where required to avoid the necessity of facing a constitutional question. Thus the Supreme Court has refused to find that the Senate Select Committee on Lobbying Activities was authorized to inquire into attempts to influence general public opinion through the publication and distribution of political books and pamphlets. The Court found that the subject was too remote from the authorized investigation to sustain abridgement of the freedoms of speech and of the press which might be involved.[65]

4. *Pertinency*

Closely related to the problem of the authority of the committee is the requirement that the questions asked be pertinent to the subject under inquiry. Pertinency is an explicit statutory requirement of 2 U.S.C.A. section 193, which refers to a refusal to answer "any question pertinent to the question under inquiry . . . ." Because of the pertinency requirement, authorizations must be clear and specific. Pertinency is an element of the offense, and since in a criminal proceeding the presumption of regularity of Congressional activity is outweighed by the presumption of innocence of the accused, it must be pleaded and proved by the government.[66] It is the particular subject under inquiry at any given time, and not the full investigative authority of the committee, to which the question must be pertinent; the indictment must specify the question under congressional committee inquiry at the time of the defendant's alleged default.[67]

Pertinency is a broader concept than that of relevance in the field of evidence, extending in its broadest reach to the entire field of inquiry permitted by the legislative purpose.[68] It is a question of law to be decided by the court rather than by the jury, and good faith mistake as to the law is not a

---

60. United States v. Lamont, 236 F.2d 312, 314 (2d Cir. 1956). *Lamont* was relied on and approved of in Gojack v. United States, 384 U.S. 702, 714–715 (1966).

61. 354 U.S. 178, 202 et seq. (1957).

62. 360 U.S. 109.

63. 360 U.S. 109, 117.

64. 360 U.S. 109, 122.

65. United States v. Rumley, 345 U.S. 41 (1953) (Frankfurter, J.).

66. Sinclair v. United States, 279 U.S. 263, 296–297 (1929).

67. Russell v. United States, 369 U.S. 749, 771 (1962).

68. United States v. Orman, 207 F.2d 148, 153 (3d Cir. 1953).

defense for the defendant.[69] It is the question and the possible answer which must be pertinent; the pertinence of the actual answer is immaterial.[70] Since pertinency is an element of the offense, lower courts have held that the defense is not waived by a failure to object to a question on pertinency grounds,[71] but the Supreme Court has suggested to the contrary in dictum.[72]

When a question is not clearly pertinent on its face, the government will be allowed to introduce extraneous evidence to establish pertinency.[73] There are generally five methods by which pertinency can be shown: (1) from the definition of the inquiry found in the authorizing resolution or statute; (2) from the opening remarks of the committee chairman; (3) from the nature of the proceeding; (4) from the question itself; and (5) from the response of the committee to a pertinency objection.[74]

Because statutory contempt is a criminal offense subject to the same due process safeguards as any other offense, avoidance of the infirmity of vagueness requires that a witness be able to know when he is violating the law. The pertinency of the question must therefore be made clear to the witness before he is compelled to answer, at least so long as he makes an objection based on pertinency. Since the witness acts at his peril if he refuses to answer, he should be entitled to know in advance the subject of the inquiry to which the committee deems the question pertinent. *Watkins v. United States*,[75] explained that a witness is entitled to be informed of the relation of the question to the subject of the investigation with the same precision as the due process clause requires of statutes defining crimes.[76] Judge, now Chief Justice Burger, while sitting on the District of Columbia Court of Appeals, interpreted *Watkins* as creating a reasonable man standard: it requires not that the witness in fact subjectively appreciate the pertinency of the question, but only that it be demonstrated with sufficient clarity that a reasonable man would have understood it.[77]

5. *Willfulness*

Willful default is the fourth requirement of the statute, and must of course be proved beyond a reasonable doubt.[78] Willfulness does not, however, require action with an evil motive or purpose; all that is required is an intentional and deliberate act not the product of inadvertence or accident. Good faith on the part of the witness is not a defense.[79] The statute encompasses all forms of intentional failure to testify: failing to appear, refusal to be sworn or to answer questions, and leaving the hearing before being excused.[80] The witness is, however, entitled to a clear ruling by the committee on his objections to their demands.[81] He must not be made to guess as to his legal position; it must be made clear to him that the committee demands an answer notwithstanding his objection, and at what point the committee considers him to be in default.[82]

Any withholding of subpoenaed documents is a violation of the statute if it in fact results in obstruction of the inquiry, regard-

69. Sinclair v. United States, 279 U.S. 263, 298–299 (1929); Braden v. United States, 365 U.S. 431, 436 (1961).

70. United States v. Orman, 207 F.2d 148, 154 (3d Cir. 1953).

71. United States v. Orman, 207 F.2d 148, 154 (3d Cir. 1953); Bowers v. United States, 202 F.2d 447, 452 (D.C.Cir. 1953).

72. Barenblatt v. United States, 360 U.S. 109, 123–25 (1959); Deutch v. United States, 367 U.S. 456, 472–73, 475 (1961) (dissenting opinions).

73. Bowers v. United States, 202 F.2d 447, 450, 453 (D.C.Cir. 1953).

74. Watkins v. United States, 354 U.S. 178, 209–214 (1957).

75. 354 U.S. 178 (1957).

76. 354 U.S. 178, 208–209, 214–215.

77. Sacher v. United States, 252 F.2d 828, 835 (D.C. Cir.), rev'd on other grounds 356 U.S. 576 (1958) (per curiam).

78. Quinn v. United States, 349 U.S. 155, 165 (1955).

79. Sinclair v. United States, 279 U.S. 263, 298–299 (1929).

80. Townsend v. United States, 95 F.2d 352, 358 (D.C.Cir. 1938).

81. See, United States v. Kamp, 102 F.Supp. 757, 759 (D.D.C.1952).

82. Quinn v. United States, 349 U.S. 155, 165–166 (1955); Flaxer v. United States, 358 U.S. 147 (1958).

less of the form in which it is manifested, although the default does not mature until the return date of the subpoena. If the witness is in fact unable to comply with the request, the burden is on him to come forward to explain that inability.[83]

E. First, Fourth, and Fifth Amendment Rights of Witnesses

1. Fifth Amendment

The fifth amendment right to refuse to incriminate oneself is available to a witness testifying before a Congressional committee.[84] The privilege is a personal one, however, and cannot be claimed on behalf of a corporation or in relation to documents kept in a representative capacity.[85] No particular form of words is necessary to invoke the fifth amendment privilege. All that is required is that the committee be able to understand the claim; "If an objection to a question is made in any language that a committee may reasonably be expected to understand as an attempt to invoke the privilege, it must be respected both by the committee and by a court . . . ."[86] The burden is then placed on the committee to inquire into objections which are unclear.[87] The privilege is waived unless it is invoked and the witness cannot select the place to stop in his testimony. Once answers to incriminating questions have been given, the privilege is waived as to other questions on the same subject, which can be refused only if they present a real danger of further incrimination. In fact, this waiver may occur

even though the witness was not aware until it was too late that the right had been waived.[88]

The witness is not the sole judge of his claim.[89] The privilege cannot be used by the witness as a subterfuge to avoid answering innocent questions. It can be claimed only when there is a reasonable apprehension on the part of the witness that his answer would furnish evidence or reveal sources of evidence which could lead to his conviction for a criminal offense.[90] He may therefore be asked to explain his claim of such a reasonable apprehension, although he may not be forced actually to disclose the information.[91] He need not disclose the incriminating facts in order to sustain his claim; it need only be evident that an answer or explanation of refusal to answer might result in injurious disclosures.[92]

If a congressional witness is granted immunity from prosecution by a congressional committee, no fifth amendment privilege is applicable.[93] The immunity power of Congress, under the present statutory authority, is limited to offering only "use" immunity, not "transactional" immunity.[94] Under transactional immunity, a witness is immunized from prosecution for the crime about which he is testifying. The narrower, "use," immunity only prohibits the use in a criminal prosecution derived directly or indirectly, from the testimony.[95]

A court has no discretion to deny an immunity request of the legislative branch where procedural prerequisites have been

---

83. United States v. Bryan, 339 U.S. 323, 329–333 (1950).

84. Quinn v. United States, 349 U.S. 155, 162 (1955).

85. McPhaul v. United States, 364 U.S. 372, 380 (1960); Hale v. Henkel, 201 U.S. 43 (1906).

86. Quinn v. United States, 349 U.S. 155, 162–163 (1955).

87. 349 U.S. 155, 162–164.

88. Rogers v. United States, 340 U.S. 367, 370–374 (1951). See generally, Tigar, Foreward: Waiver of Constitutional Rights: Disquiet in the Citadel, 84 Harv. L.Rev. 1, 9–10 (1970).

89. Hoffman v. United States, 341 U.S. 479 (1951).

90. See Quinn v. United States, 349 U.S. 155, 162 (1955).

91. E.g., United States v. Jaffe, 98 F.Supp. 191, 193–194 (D.D.C.1951).

92. Emspak v. United States, 349 U.S. 190, 198–199 (1955).

93. See Kastigar v. United States, 406 U.S. 441, 453 (1972).

94. 18 U.S.C.A. §§ 6001, 6002, 6005.

95. Kastigar v. United States, 406 U.S. 441, 453 (1972).

met.[96] In such a case, the duties of the court are purely ministerial, and "any attempted exercise of discretion on its part, either to deny the requests or to grant immunity with conditions, would be an assumption of power not possessed by the [court]." [97] The function of the court in such a statutory immunity request is to determine first, whether the established procedures have been complied with, and then, to insure that Congress has constitutional jurisdiction over the inquiry area, that the particular agent of Congress has appropriate jurisdiction over the inquiry, and that the information sought is relevant to the matter under investigation.[98] The courts may not go beyond this to question the wisdom of the immunity sought. Nor may the court seek to condition, limit, or deny the immunity order on the grounds of prejudicial pretrial publicity. "[T]he court could not go beyond administering its own affairs and attempt to regulate proceedings before a coordinate branch of government." [99]

2. First Amendment

a. Presence of Communications Media

A witness does not ordinarily have a right to object to the presence of the communications media at a hearing.[100] In one case, however, a lower court held that the presence of TV cameras and reporters made it impossible for the witness to testify in a calm, considered and truthful manner, and thus that condition justified his refusal to testify.[101] But this case has not been extended or followed by other lower courts. In *United States v. Orman*,[102] for example, the court held that the question of whether a witness before a congressional committee should have a right to demand that information given by him which cannot aid the committee in its legislative purpose be withheld from the public is for legislative, not for judicial control.[103]

And in *United States v. Hintz*,[104] the court stated:

> This court has no power to impose upon Congress, a coordinate branch of our government, either a proscription against or a prescription for radio, television, movies or photographs. This court is of the opinion that the mere presence of such mechanisms at an investigative hearing does not infect the hearing with impropriety.[105]

The *Hintz* court specifically rejected any reading of the case law which would *per se* prevent a conviction of any witness who commits a contempt of Congress "while in the presence of spectators and the sensory apparatus which permits the nation to see and to hear." [106] Still, at a trial it would allow the defendant to prove that the conditions of testimony were not reasonably conducive to that clarity and accuracy to which defendant was normally capable. Such a question would be for the factfinder.[107] More recent cases have followed this right of a Committee to open the hearings to the public, for "[i]t is apparent as well that a committee's legislative purpose may legitimately include the publication of information." [108]

Of course if the publicity invoked by the congressional hearing interferes with a subsequent criminal trial on related matters, the court may grant a continuance until the publicity abates or implement other techniques to safeguard the defendant's right to a fair

---

96. Application of Senate Select Committee on Presidential Campaign Activities, 361 F.Supp. 1270 (D.D.C. 1973) (Sirica, J.).

97. 361 F.Supp. at 1272.

98. 361 F.Supp. at 1278.

99. 361 F.Supp. at 1280. See also Delaney v. United States, 199 F.2d 107, 114 (1st Cir. 1952).

100. United States v. Hintz, 193 F.Supp. 325 (N.D. Ill.1961).

101. United States v. Kleinman, 107 F.Supp. 407, 408 (D.D.C.1952).

102. 207 F.2d 148 (3d Cir. 1953).

103. 207 F.2d at 159.

104. 193 F.Supp. 325 (N.D.Ill.1961).

105. 193 F.Supp. at 331–32.

106. 193 F.Supp. at 329.

107. 193 F.Supp. at 332.

108. Application of Senate Select Committee on Presidential Campaign Activities, 361 F.Supp. 1270, 1281 (D.D.C.1973). See also Watkins v. United States, 354 U.S. 178, 200 (1957).

trial. But the court may not interfere with the congressional hearing. It is "for the committee to decide whether considerations of public interest demanded at that time a full-dress public investigation. . . ." [109]

b. Limitations on the Congressional Power to Compel Reporter's Sources

Increasing use has been made of the subpoena power to compel testimony and appearances by journalists. The press has responded by challenging the subpoenas with the argument that the first amendment guarantee of freedom of the press should protect reporters from being compelled to disclose confidential sources of information.

In *Branzburg v. Hayes*,[110] the Supreme Court held in a 5–4 decision that the first amendment affords newsmen no privilege, absolute or qualified, against appearing and testifying before a *grand jury*. The opinion of the Court was delivered by Justice White, joined by Chief Justice Burger and Justices Blackmun, Powell and Rehnquist. Justice Powell filed a brief concurring opinion suggesting that on other facts a first amendment reporter's privilege might be appropriate: "[T]he courts will be available to newsmen under circumstances where legitimate First Amendment interests require protection." [111] Thus the holding in *Branzburg*, as well as Justice Powell's concurrence, while compelling a reporter to comply with a grand jury subpoena issued for a proper purpose, leaves open the issue of the reporter's privilege before a congressional hearing, as well as before an administrative hearing or civil case.

c. Free Speech and Association Limitations on Congressional Inquiry

In more recent times the Court has begun to focus limits on Congressional investigative powers based on the guarantees of the First Amendment, rather than on separation of power principles. A leading case illustrating this trend is *Watkins v. United States*.[112] The House of Representatives had authorized an investigation of alleged Communist activity by the Un-American Activities Committee and its subcommittees.[113] Watkins, a trade-union official, was subpoenaed to appear before one of the subcommittees after two witnesses linked him with the Communist Party during the Second World War. Watkins denied that he had ever been a Communist and testified freely about his personal activities and associations.[114] However, he refused to answer questions as to whether he knew certain persons to have been past members of the Communist Party. Watkins told the Committee: "I will answer any questions which this committee puts to me about myself. I will also answer questions about those persons whom I knew to be members of the Communist Party and whom I believe still are. I will not, however, answer any questions with respect to others with whom I associated in the past. I do not believe that any law in this country requires me to testify about persons who may in the past have been Communist Party members or otherwise engaged in Communist Party activity but who to my best knowledge and belief have long since removed themselves from the Communist movement." [115] He did not invoke his fifth amendment privilege against self-incrimination, but challenged both the power of the committee to ask such questions and the rel-

---

109. Delaney v. United States, 199 F.2d 107, 114 (1st Cir. 1952).

110. 408 U.S. 665 (1972).

111. 408 U.S. at 710.

112. 354 U.S. 178 (1957). Previously, several lower court cases had held that HUAC, the House Committee on Un-American Activities, was not violating the First Amendment in asking witnesses about Communist Party associations. Barsky v. United States, 167 F.2d 241 (D.C.Cir. 1948) cert. denied 334 U.S. 843 (1948); United

States v. Josephson, 165 F.2d 82 (2d Cir. 1974), cert. denied 333 U.S. 838 (1948).

113. H.R. Res. No. 5, 83d Congress, 1st Session, 99 Cong.Rec. 15 (1953).

114. The Government, in its brief, admitted that: "A more complete and candid statement of his past political associations and activities . . . can hardly be imagined." Brief for Respondent, pp. 59–60.

115. 354 U.S. 178, 185.

evance of the questions to the duties of the committee. Watkins was reported to the full House, and subsequently indicted for and convicted of statutory contempt of Congress.[116] A three-judge panel of the Court of Appeals for the District of Columbia reversed,[117] but on rehearing en banc, the conviction was affirmed.[118] The Supreme Court reversed with only one dissent.

The Court, while admitting that the "power of the Congress to conduct investigations is inherent in the legislative process [and] is broad," [119] based its holding on the fact that neither the vague resolution of the House establishing the Committee nor the comments of the subcommittee chairman on the day of questioning gave Watkins a sufficient indication of pertinence so that the defendant could know the conduct required of him by the statute. However, the Chief Justice went beyond this narrow holding and in broad dicta announced principles which placed limits on the congressional power to investigate. Although a broad power to investigate is inherent in the legislative process, each inquiry must be related to, and in furtherance of, a legitimate task of Congress. "[T]he First Amendment freedoms of speech, press, religion, or political belief and association" are thus protected in congressional investigations.[120] The Court had: "no doubt that there is no congressional power to expose for the sale of exposure. The public is, of course, entitled to be informed concerning the workings of its government. That cannot be inflated into a general power to expose where the predominant result can only be an invasion of the private rights of individuals. But a solution

to our problem is not to be found in testing the motives of committee members. . . ." [121] In a footnote the Court distinguished "the power of Congress to inquire into and publicize corruption, maladministration or inefficiency in agencies of the Government." [122] Thus power to question in these protected areas of individual privacy unrelated to governmental inefficiency may not be delegated to committees by resolutions so broad that they provide no standards for the questioners and no yardstick by which the courts can measure the need for information against the competing demands of individual freedom.

The dictum about First Amendment rights in *Watkins* was expanded by a plurality of the Court that same day in *Sweezy v. New Hampshire*.[123] *Sweezy* held invalid, under the 14th Amendment, the contempt conviction of a guest lecturer at a state university who declined to testify to state authorities concerning his lecture and his associates.[124] Chief Justice Warren announced the judgment of the Court and delivered an opinion joined in by Justices Black, Douglas, and Brennan. Warren argued that to question an unwilling witness about his prior expressions of political belief is to chill his exercise of the right of free speech and to inhibit the expression of unorthodox opinion in the community. Such sanctions can be justified only if a countervailing state interest is served by the questioning. In *Sweezy*, the delegation of authority to the attorney general, a one-man legislative committee, had been in such broad terms that the legislature could not have determined a specific need for the information sought. Therefore, the question

116. See 2 U.S.C.A. § 192, which proscribes refusal by a witness "to answer any question pertinent to the question under inquiry" by a congressional committee.

117. Watkins v. United States, 233 F.2d 681, 688 n. * (D.C.Cir. 1956) (dissenting opinion).

118. Watkins v. United States, 233 F.2d 681 (D.C. Cir. 1956).

119. 354 U.S. at 187.

120. 354 U.S. at 188.

121. 354 U.S. at 200 (footnote omitted).

122. 354 U.S. at 200 n. 33. See also Application of Senate Select Committee on Presidential Campaign Activities, 361 F.Supp. 1270, 1281 (D.D.C.1973).

123. 354 U.S. 234 (1957).

124. State law imposed various disabilities on "subversive persons" and "subversive organizations." N.H.Rev.Stat.Ann. §§ 588:1–16 (1955). The legislature, by resolution, appointed the attorney general as a one-man legislative committee to investigate violations of this law. Sweezy was summoned to appear; he answered some questions but was adjudged in contempt by a county court for refusal to answer questions about his speech or associates during the 1948 campaign. The state supreme court affirmed. Wyman v. Sweezy, 100 N.H. 103, 121 A.2d 783 (1956).

of the state interest was not reached. "The lack of any indications that the [state] legislature wanted the information the Attorney General attempted to elicit from petitioner must be treated as the absence of authority." [125] The use of the contempt power violated the due-process requirements of the Fourteenth Amendment by invading protected areas of speech in the absence of a legislation determination of public interest.

Warren's views in *Watkins* and *Sweezy* did not bear fruit in *Barenblatt v. United States*,[126] decided two years later; Justice Harlan delivered the opinion of the Court. Chief Justice Warren with Black and Douglas dissented. In *Barenblatt* the majority actually found subcommittee authority to compel testimony about the witness' membership or part in the Communist Party and Communist infiltration into the field of education.[127] In fact, to determine authorization the Court was willing to consider "the gloss of legislative reports, administrative interpretation, and long usage. . . ." [128] Unlike the facts in *Watkins*, the questions in this case were found to be pertinent to the authorized inquiry.[129] In considering the first amendment defense (the witness explicitly refused to rely on the fifth amendment) [130], the Court argued that where "First Amendment rights are asserted to bar governmental interrogation resolution of the issue always involves a balancing by the courts of the competing private and public interests at stake. . . ." [131] In balancing, the Court noted that the investigation was for a valid legislative purpose, that the Communist Party is not "an ordinary political party", and that thus "investigatory power in this domain is not to be denied Congress solely because the field of education is involved." [132] The conviction was affirmed.

That same day, in *Uphaus v. Wyman* [133] the Court upheld, in spite of a first amendment attack, a one-man legislative investigation by the New Hampshire Attorney General. *Sweezy* was distinguished because the academic and political freedoms discussed there were not present in *Uphaus*. In *Uphaus* the State Attorney General was investigating the allegedly subversive activities of World Fellowship Inc., which had a summer camp in New Hampshire. The Court also accepted the state court decision that the legislature did desire an answer to the inquiries,[134] which sought the lists of names of all the people who had attended the camp during 1954 and 1955. The Attorney General had a "valid reason to believe that the speakers and guests . . . might be subversive persons. . . . " [135] Warren, Black, and Douglas again dissented.[136]

Barenblatt and *Uphaus* do not spell the end of the First Amendment role in legislative investigations. A significant, more recent, case is *Gibson v. Florida Legislative Investigation Committee*.[137] The state legislative committee ordered the president of the Miami branch of the NAACP to bring with him records of the association as to the identity of its members and contributors. The state wanted to investigate the infiltration of Communists into various organizations. The president of the local NAACP told the committee that he would answer questions based on his own personal knowledge but not produce the requested papers. The Supreme Court reversed his contempt conviction.

The Court distinguished *Barenblatt* and other cases where the witness refused to answer questions about his own past or pre-

---

125. 354 U.S. 234, 354 (1957).

126. 360 U.S. 109 (1959).

127. 360 U.S. 109, 114–15 (1959).

128. 360 U.S. 109, 117 (1959).

129. 360 U.S. 109, 123–125 (1959).

130. 360 U.S. 109, 114 (1959).

131. 360 U.S. 109, 126 (1959).

132. 360 U.S. 109, 127–29 (1959).

133. 360 U.S. 72 (1959).

134. 360 U.S. 72, 77 (1959).

135. 360 U.S. 72, 79 (1959).

136. 360 U.S. 72, 82 (1959). Brennan, J. also dissented and in fact wrote this dissent.

137. 372 U.S. 539 (1963).

sent membership in the Communist party. In *Gibson:*

> it is not alleged Communists who are the witnesses before the Committee and it is not discovery of their membership in that party which is the object of the challenged inquiries. Rather it is the N.A.A.C.P. itself which is the subject of the investigation . . .[138]

The Court also distinguished *Uphaus* because in *Gibson* "no semblance of such a nexus between the NAACP and subversive *activities* has been shown here."[139] The Court then summarized the evidence and concluded that it disclosed no existence of "any substantial relationship between the NAACP and subversive or Communist activities."[140] The conviction was reversed.

Several years later the New Hampshire Attorney General was again before the Supreme Court. In *DeGregory v. Attorney General,*[141] the Court reversed a contempt conviction of a witness who refused to answer questions about Communist activities prior to 1957. The Court concluded:

> [W]hatever justification may have supported such exposure in *Uphaus* is absent here; the staleness of both the basis for the investigation and its subject matter makes indefensible such exposure of one's associational and political past—exposure which is objectionable and damaging in the extreme to one whose associations and political views do not command majority approval.[142]

The nature of the organization thus may be important in striking the apparently ad hoc balance between the first amendment's associational interests and the legislature's investigative interests.[143]

3. The Fourth Amendment

The Fourth Amendment's protections against unreasonable search and seizure applies to Congressional investigations[144] but the legislative subpoenas may be very broad in their inquiry and yet be upheld.[145] Improperly seized evidence may not be used in criminal cases.[146]

II. THE SPEECH AND DEBATE CLAUSE

Article 1, section 6 of the Constitution,[1] known as the speech or debate clause, recognizes the need for protection of legislative independence in a governmental system of separation of powers, a theme long found in English law. The language of this clause finds direct kinship in the English Bill of Rights of 1689. As the Court has explained:

> This formulation of 1689 was the culmination of a long struggle for parliamentary supremacy. Behind these simple phrases lies a history of conflict between the Commons and the Tudor and Stuart monarchs during which successive monarchs utilized the criminal and civil law to suppress and intimidate critical legislators. Since the Glorious Revolution in Britain, and throughout United States history, the privilege has been recognized as an important protection of the independence and integrity of the legislature. . . . In the American governmental structure the clause serves the additional function of reinforcing the separation of powers so deliberately established by the Founders.[2]

The clause provides protection of speech in Congress by making conduct of U.S. Sena-

---

138. 372 U.S. 539, 547 (1963). The Court emphasized that the NAACP is "a concededly legitimate and nonsubversive organization." 372 U.S. at 548 (footnote omitted).

139. 372 U.S. 539, 550 (1963) (emphasis in original).

140. 372 U.S. 539, 554–555 (1963).

141. 383 U.S. 825 (1966).

142. 383 U.S. 825, 828–829 (1966). Cf. Doe v. McMillan, 412 U.S. 306 (1973).

143. Cf. Shelton v. United States, 404 F.2d 1292 (D.C.Cir. 1968), cert. denied 393 U.S. 1024 (1969) (Ku Klux Klan investigation upheld).

144. Watkins v. United States, 354 U.S. 178, 188 (1957).

145. E.g., McPhaul v. United States, 364 U.S. 372 (1960).

146. Nelson v. United States, 208 F.2d 505 (D.C.Cir. 1953), cert. denied 346 U.S. 827 (1962).

1. "[F]or any Speech or Debate in either House, they shall not be questioned in any other Place." U.S. Const. art. 1, § 6.

2. United States v. Johnson, 383 U.S. 169, 178 (1966) (footnote omitted). See generally 383 U.S. at 177–83.

The English Bill of Rights of 1689 provided ". . . That the freedom of speech and debates or proceedings in Parliament, ought not to be impeached or questioned in any court or place out of Parliament." 1 W. & M., Sess. 2, c. 2. For a review of the history of this con-

tors or Representatives [3] engaged in legislative functions privileged against civil or criminal suit. That is not to say that there are no restraints on the conduct of federal legislators, for application of the privileges of the clause has been limited through narrow judicial interpretation. In addition, Congress itself has the power to regulate conduct of its members under Article 1, § 5, although in practice such regulation has been neither common nor consistent.

At the present time, the Supreme Court has written only a handful of decisions involving the construction, scope and interpretation of the speech or debate clause. The two earliest cases, *Kilbourn v. Thompson* [4] and *Tenney v. Brandhove*,[5] expressly adhered to a broad, liberal interpretation of the speech or debate clause. In *Kilbourn*, the Supreme Court noted that the privilege should extend "to things generally done in a session of the House by one of its members in relation to the business before it." [6]

Kilbourn dealt with the issues of whether the House possessed general contempt power and the scope of Congressional power to investigate. The scope of the speech or debate clause was a secondary issue. The House was attempting to investigate the history and character of what was termed "the real estate pool" of the District of Columbia. The Jay Cooke Co. held a large portion of the pool when it went bankrupt, with the United States as one of its creditors. In the course of the House investigation Hallett Kilbourn, a member of the Cooke Firm, was summoned by a subpoena duces tecum to appear before the committee of the House investigating the scandal. Kilbourn appeared, answered some questions of the committee, but refused to answer others or to produce subpoenaed books or papers. As a result, he was cited for contempt by resolution and vote of the entire House. While later expansion of Congress' legitimate investigative role have for the most part made the Court's response to the investigative issues questionable, the opinion is still cited with approval by justices on both sides of the speech or debate controversy. The *Kilbourn* Court held that although the investigation was outside the legitimate powers of Congress, the speech or debate clause protected the Congressmen who voted for the contempt from a civil suit for false imprisonment. However, the Sergeant-at-arms who had taken Kilbourn into custody pursuant to the congressional order was held not to be within the ambit of the clause and was therefore liable for damages.[7]

The Court's rationale in denying the privilege to the employees of Congress but upholding it for those giving them orders was unclear in *Kilbourn*, and might have been based on the fact that the arrest was not a usual act in a legislative session. The *Kilbourn* Court did not reach the issue of whether "there may . . . be things done,

---

cept in English law see, C. Wittke, The History of English Parliamentary Privilege (1921).

3. The speech or debate clause applies, by its own terms, only to federal legislators. Neither that clause nor federal common law provides any comparable protection to state legislators in federal prosecutions for bribery or other federal criminal prosecutions. United States v. Gillock, 445 U.S. 360 (1980). As for immunity of the president and executive officers, see Chapter 7, section I, infra.

4. 103 U.S. 168 (1881).

5. 341 U.S. 367 (1951).

6. 103 U.S. at 204.

7. After the Supreme Court decided in favor of Kilbourn, the case went back to the District of Columbia court where Kilbourn eventually recovered a judgment of $20,000, which was paid by order of Congress with interest and the costs of suit. See In re Application of the Pacific Ry. Comm'n, 32 F. 241, 253 (N.D.Cal.1887).

Pacific Railway applied *Kilbourn* and approved of it as a case which "will stand for all time as a bulwark against the invasion of the rights of the citizen to protection in his private affairs against the unlimited scrutiny of investigation by a congressional committee." Id. The opinion was written by Justice Field sitting as circuit judge. This case was later cited with approval in Sinclair v. United States, 279 U.S. 263, 292–93 (1929).

See generally, Hacker & Rotunda, Restrictions on Agency and Congressional Subpoenas Issued for an Improper Purpose, 4 Corp.L.Rev. 74 (1981), demonstrating that the gist of *Kilbourn* should still be good law: "Congress may not issue subpoenas nor use its investigatory powers for an improper purpose (i.e., for the ulterior purpose of aiding a private litigant), though it is not ousted of jurisdiction simply because its investigation incidentally may aid a private litigant." Id. at 78. See also, Landis, Constitutional Limitations on the Congressional Power of Investigation, 40 Harv.L.Rev. 153 (1926).

in the one House or the other, of an extraordinary character, for which the members who take part in the act may be held legally responsible."[8] A second possible rationale for the distinction between Congressmen and their aides can be found in *Tenney v. Brandhove*.[9] *Tenney* was a case brought under the Civil Rights Act in which a former witness attempted to sue a state legislative committee. Though the decision was based on the interpretation of a federal statute in light of common law immunity, the Court surveyed and frequently referred to the speech or debate clause. The majority of the Court held the committee immune from suit, noting that the case would be different where "an official acting on behalf of the legislature" is sued,[10] and thus indicating that the clause's literal protection was only available to members of Congress.

Other significant constructions of the clause, usually in the form of dicta, were also to be found in the three cases which dealt with the speech and debate clause in the 1960's—*United States v. Johnson*,[11] *Dombrowski v. Eastland*,[12] and *Powell v. McCormack*.[13]

The major theme linking these three more recent cases with the two earlier ones is that all, while espousing general principles of liberal interpretation of the clause, were far more narrow and restrictive in its actual application, particularly with regard to the liability of legislative aides for legislatively authorized activities. *Dombrowski* and *Powell*, like *Kilbourn*, declined to extend the immunity of the clause to the activities of legislative employees acting under the authority and direction of Congress or one of its committees. In *Dombrowski* plaintiffs alleged that the Chairman of a Senate sub-

committee and that subcommittee's counsel conspired with Louisiana officials to violate the plaintiffs' Fourth Amendment rights. The Court found sufficient evidence against the counsel of the subcommittee to allow plaintiffs to go to trial. But the complaint against Senator Eastland was dismissed on grounds of the speech and debate clause:

> The record does not contain evidence of his involvement in any activity that could result in liability. It is the purpose and office of the doctrine of legislative immunity, having its roots as it does in the Speech or Debate Clause . . . that legislators engaged "in the sphere of legitimate legislative activity," . . . should be protected not only from the consequences of litigation's results but also from the burden of defending themselves.[14]

In *Powell* the Court decided on the merits a charge by Congressman Powell that he was unlawfully excluded from taking his seat in the House of Representatives. While the Court allowed dismissal of the action against the Congressmen, the Court held the speech or debate clause was not a bar to the action against the House employees who were acting under House orders.[15]

Tenney upheld the privilege as a bar against suit for members of a legislative committee but noted that the issue might have been different had the defendants been officials acting on behalf of the legislature rather than members of it.[16] In *Johnson* the Court determined that a speech delivered by a Senator on the floor of Congress and the Senator's motivation for delivering it, were covered by the clause and could not form the basis of a criminal charge of conspiracy to defraud the government. However, the Court went on to hold that the prosecution could still proceed with the conspiracy charge on the condition the speech itself

---

8. 103 U.S. at 204.

9. 341 U.S. 367 (1951).

10. 341 U.S. at 378.

11. 383 U.S. 169 (1966).

12. 387 U.S. 82 (1967) (per curiam).

13. 395 U.S. 486 (1969).

14. Dombrowski v. Eastland, 387 U.S. 82, 84–85 (1967) (per curiam) quoting Tenney v. Brandhove, 341 U.S. 367, 376 (1951).

15. Powell v. McCormack, 395 U.S. 486, 505–506 (1969). In 395 U.S. at 506 n. 26 the Court said it "need not decide whether under the Speech or Debate Clause petitioners would be entitled to maintain this action solely against members of Congress where no agents participated in the challenged action and no other remedy was available. Cf. Kilbourn v. Thompson, 103 U.S. 168, 204–205 (1881)."

16. 341 U.S. at 377–378.

could not constitute an overt act. This limitation, the *Johnson* Court assumed, would purge the prosecution of all elements offensive to the speech or debate clause.[17]

Liberal rationales combined with narrow, restrictive holdings in these five cases to make the precise scope of legislative privilege under the speech or debate clause unclear. None of these opinions, alone or in tandem, defined with any particularity the nature of legislative activity that would be protected by the clause.

In a trilogy of decisions the Court in recent years has bypassed the broad dicta of these earlier cases to take a narrow view of those activities of Congress protected by Article I, section 6. In *United States v. Brewster*,[18] the Court held that Senator Daniel Brewster could be tried on a criminal charge of general application so long as the Government's case did not rest upon legislative acts or the motives of the Senator in performing those acts. The Court distinguished between legislative acts which are "clearly a part of the legislative process—the *due* functioning of the process"[19] and activities which though legitimate, are unprotected because they are essentially "political in nature."[20] The Court held that the speech or debate clause "does not prohibit inquiry into activities that are casually or incidentally related to legislative affairs but not a part of the legislative process itself."[21]

In the same session, the Court in *Gravel v. United States*[22] further developed the legislative—political distinction of *Brewster* by pointing out that acts do not become "legislative in nature" simply because members of Congress "generally perform [them] in their official capacity"[23] and that:

Legislative acts are not all-encompassing. The heart of the Clause is speech or debate in either House. Insofar as the Clause is construed to reach other matters, they must be an integral part of the deliberative and communicative processes by which Members participate in committee and House proceedings with respect to the consideration and passage or rejection of proposed legislation or with respect to other matters which the Constitution places within the jurisdiction of either House.[24]

Gravel also expressly held that, for purposes of construing the speech or debate clause, a member of Congress and his assistant are to be treated as one in the performance of their legislative functions.[25] Any act which would be protected by the clause if performed personally by a member of Congress is thus equally protected if performed by a legislative aide or assistant. "[I]t is literally impossible, in view of the complexities of the modern legislative process . . . for Members of Congress to perform their legislative tasks without the help of aides and assistants. . . ."[26] Applying these principles, the *Gravel* Court held a senator and his aide immune from questioning by a grand jury concerning their investigatory acts in preparation for a subcommittee hearing, except insofar as those acts were criminal or related to third-party crime. This position did not reject the distinctions between employees and Congressmen found in the earlier cases, for the *Gravel* Court carefully distinguished the previous holdings. *Kilbourn* was interpreted as a case where the House resolution authorizing legislative arrest was immune from judicial review. "But the resolution was subject to judicial review insofar as its execution impinged on a citizen's rights as it did there. That the House could with impunity order an unconstitutional arrest afforded no protection for those who made the arrest."[27] Presumably if a congressman actually made the arrest in *Kilbourn* he would not be protected for that action, though he would be protected for

17.   383 U.S. at 184–185.

18.   408 U.S. 501 (1972).

19.   408 U.S. at 516 (emphasis in original).

20.   408 U.S. at 512.

21.   408 U.S. at 528.

22.   408 U.S. 606 (1972).

23.   408 U.S. at 625.

24.   408 U.S. at 625.

25.   The Court noted that congressional assistants must be treated as the Congressman's "alter ego." 408 U.S. 616–617.

26.   408 U.S. at 616.

27.   408 U.S. at 618.

voting for the arrest. *Dombrowski* was distinguished as a case where the "record contained no evidence of the Senator's involvement in any activity that could result in liability . . . whereas the committee counsel was charged with conspiring with state officials to carry out an illegal seizure of records. . . ."[28] *Powell* was interpreted as a case where the Court could afford relief against House aides seeking to implement invalid resolutions. As in *Kilbourn*, the *Powell* Court had noted that it did not reach the issue of the Congressmen's liability if they themselves would implement the resolution and no other remedy was available.[29]

The clause was also held in *Gravel* not to protect any private republication of materials which had been introduced and made public at a committee hearing. This ruling was a significant narrowing of application of the clause because it excluded from protection the informative function of Congress in publishing information for the benefit of constituents. *Gravel* articulated the principle that before the privilege extends to matters beyond pure speech or debate in either House, "they must be an integral part of the deliberative and communicative processes by which Members participate in committee and House proceedings with respect to the consideration . . . of proposed legislation or with respect to other matters which the Constitution places within the jurisdiction of either House."[30] The extension of the privilege to matters that are not pure speech or debate will occur only when the protection afforded by the privilege is necessary to prevent indirect impairment of the deliberations of the House or Committee functions.

Several years later, in *United States v. Helstoski*,[31] the Court clarified the legislative act—political act distinction. In that case the government had charged that a former congressman had, while a Member of Congress, accepted money in return for promising to introduce and in fact introducing private bills to suspend the application of the immigration laws. The former Member was indicted for violating 18 U.S.C.A. § 201, making it a crime for a public official to corruptly ask for or accept anything of value in return for being influenced in the performance of his official duties.

The government argued that the speech or debate clause did not prohibit it from introducing references to past legislative acts because such references are essential to show the motive for taking money. Also, the government argued that exclusion of references to past acts is not logical since jurors, if they are told of promises to perform legislative acts, will infer that the acts themselves were performed, thereby calling the acts into question.

The majority rejected this reasoning and, relying on the prior law, held that the speech or debate clause precludes any inquiry into acts that occur in the regular course of the legislative process and into the motivation for those acts. While such exclusion will make concededly prosecution more difficult, "references to past legislative acts of a member cannot be admitted without undermining the values protected by the Clause."[32] However, "[p]romises by a Member to perform an act *in the future* are not legislative acts."[33] Thus, the government may demonstrate such corrupt agreements. Even a promise to "deliver a speech, to vote, or to solicit other votes at some future date is not 'speech or debate.' Likewise, a *promise* to introduce a bill is not a legislative act."[34]

As to the question of waiver, the majority went on to hold that, assuming that it is pos-

---

28. 408 U.S. at 619.

29. 408 U.S. at 620.

30. 408 U.S. at 625. But cf. Watkins v. United States, 354 U.S. 178, 200 n. 3 (1957): The power of "Congress to inquire into and publicize corruption, maladministration or inefficiency in agencies of the Government . . . was the only kind of activity described by Woodrow Wilson . . . when he wrote:

'The informing function of Congress should be preferred even to its legislative function.' "

31. 442 U.S. 477 (1979).

32. 442 U.S. at 491.

33. 442 U.S. at 489 (emphasis added).

34. 442 U.S. at 489 (emphasis in original).

sible for a congressman to waive the speech or debate privilege, such a waiver can only be found after explicit and unequivocal renunciation of the privilege, not found in this case. Also, assuming that Congress could institutionally waive the privilege for its Members, 18 U.S.C.A. § 201 is not such a waiver.[35]

The cases discussed above all dealt with the scope of legislative immunity as applied to criminal cases; in *Doe v. McMillan*[36] the Court applied the speech or debate clause to civil litigation, and continued to apply the distinction drawn in the earlier criminal cases between legislative and political acts.

In *McMillan*, parents of District of Columbia school children brought action against members of the House Committee on the District of Columbia, federal legislative employees of the Government Printing Office, and district school officials and employees seeking damages, declaratory and injunctive relief for alleged invasion of privacy resulting from public dissemination of a Committee report on the District of Columbia school system, which report identified, by name, students in highly derogatory contexts.[37]

The Supreme Court found that the scope of the speech or debate clause clearly immunized members of Congress from liability for all of the acts upon which the civil suit was based; the "alter ego" test of *Gravel* was applied to grant similar immunity to the committee staff, the consultant and investigator introducing material at the committee hearings.

The Court then addressed the sole remaining issue in the case: whether the speech or debate clause affords absolute immunity from private suit to persons who, with authorization from Congress, distributed materials which allegedly infringed upon the rights of individuals. The Court acknowledged the importance of informing the public of congressional activities, but felt that the act of informing the public need not always be regarded as an essential part of legitimate legislative activity merely because authorized by Congress. The test to be applied in determining whether an act is immune was the standard of *Gravel:* whether the act of informing the public was " 'an integral part of the deliberative and communicative processes by which Members participate in committee and House proceedings.' "[38] The Court went on to hold that, in private suits such as this, the speech or debate clause affords no immunity to those who, at the direction of Congress, distribute actionable material to the general public. To the extent that the public printer and superintendent of documents had printed excess copies of the report for use other than internally by Congress, a cause of action arose against them.[39]

In *Eastland v. United States Servicemen's Fund*,[40] a later case interpreting the scope of Article 1, § 6, the Supreme Court held that the federal courts may not enjoin the issuance of a subpoena by a Committee of Congress directing a bank to produce the bank records of an anti-war group, the USSF, under investigation by the Committee. The USSF was not in a position to assert its alleged constitutional claim by refusing to comply with the subpoena and then defending itself in a statutory contempt action, since the subpoena was directed to the bank and not the USSF. The Court applied the immunity privilege despite allegations

---

35. 442 U.S. at 491–94. In a companion case the Court also held that if a defendant wished to challenge the validity of an indictment on the grounds that it violates the speech or debate clause, mandamus is not the appropriate remedy. The defendant must use the remedy of appeal. Helstoski v. Meanor, 442 U.S. 500 (1979).

36. 412 U.S. 306 (1973).

37. Among other things, the report listed names of children as being frequent "class cutters", having failed examinations and for disciplinary problems. 412 U.S. at 308–09 and nn. 1–2.

38. 412 U.S. at 314, quoting Gravel v. United States, 408 U.S. at 625.

39. In Davis v. Passman, 442 U.S. 228, 235, n. 11 (1979) the Court noted the issue but intimated no view whether the speech or debate clause would shield a former Congressman from an implied civil damage brought by a former employee fired because of her sex. See, e.g., Comment, Speech or Debate Clause Immunity for Congressional Hiring Practices: Its Necessity and Its Implications, 28 U.C.L.A.L.Rev. 217 (1980).

40. 421 U.S. 491 (1975).

that the contribution lists subpoenaed were the equivalent of membership lists of the anti-war group and that first and fifth amendment rights were therefore in danger of irreparable harm. Chief Justice Burger's majority opinion accepted the Government's argument of absolute congressional immunity and found that the Court had no power to review the subpoena.[41]

Hutchinson v. Proxmire [42] further elaborated on the legislative/political distinction, offered useful, illustrative examples, and held that the speech or debate clause provides no absolute privilege from liability to civil plaintiffs for defamatory statements made outside the legislative chamber, though it would be "wholly immune" if made on the Senate floor,[43] or in a committee hearing, even if held outside the chambers; committee reports are also protected, but their republication in a newsletter is not.[44] While the privilege applies when Congress informs itself by committee hearings and speeches on the floor, a congressman's individual transmittal of such information in order to inform the public and also other Members "is not a part of the legislative function or the deliberations that make up the legislative process." [45] Thus newsletters and press releases are not within the speech or debate privilege. Also, a congressman's "libelous remarks in . . . followup telephone calls to executive agencies and in radio and television interviews are not protected." [46]

In short, the traditional view of the speech or debate clause has come to mean that Con-gressional privilege is limited essentially to purely legislative tasks such as voting, preparation of internal reports, and debate. Despite criticisms from commentators,[47] the Supreme Court has refused to extend the protection of the clause to "political" activities of Congress, although these informative, mediating, and educational functions are now accepted as legitimate roles for legislators. Under the present test for the speech or debate clause, Congressmen and their aides are protected from suit only insofar as their actions are directly, essentially related to the legislative process.

III. THE PRIVILEGE FROM ARREST

Article I, section 6 of the Constitution provides, in addition to the speech and debate clause, the privilege from arrest clause:

> The Senators and Representatives . . . shall in all Cases, except Treason, Felony and Breach of the Peace, be privileged from Arrest during their Attendance at the Session of their respective Houses and in going to and returning from the same. . . .

This clause has been interpreted almost out of existence, and the history behind it justifies this exceedingly narrow interpretation. At the time of the Framers of the Constitution, arrest in civil cases was common.[1] The privilege is limited to protection from this now obsolete practice. Arrest is not the same as service of process, thus the privilege does not protect a congressman from service of process in a civil case,[2] or in a

---

41. Joining Chief Justice Burger were Justices Blackmun, Rehnquist, White & Powell.

In a concurring opinion, Justices Marshall, Brennan, and Stewart agreed that the facts of the instant case made no relief possible, but they suggested that a different procedure and/or different defendants would provide a forum for asserting such constitutional claims. 421 U.S. at 513.

Justice Douglas dissented, and would have ruled in favor of the Servicemen's Fund on the first amendment issue. See, e.g., 421 U.S. at 518 (Douglas, J., dissenting): "[N]o regime of law that can rightfully claim that name may make trustees of . . . vast powers immune from actions brought by people who have been wronged by official action."

42. 443 U.S. 111 (1979).

43. 443 U.S. at 130.

44. 443 U.S. at 130–33.

45. 443 U.S. at 133 (footnote omitted.)

46. 443 U.S. at 121 n. 10 (1979). Justice Stewart joined in all of the opinion except this footnote 10. 443 U.S. at 134.

47. See, e.g., Cella, The Doctrine of Legislative Privilege of Speech or Debate: The New Interpretation as a Threat to Legislative Coequality, 8 Suffolk L.Rev. 1019 (1974); Reinstein and Silverglate, Legislative Privilege and The Separation of Powers, 86 Harvard L.Rev. 1113 (1973).

1. Long v. Ansell, 293 U.S. 76, 83 (1934) (Brandeis, J.).

2. 293 U.S. at 82.

criminal case.[3] Since the privilege is limited by interpretation to civil suits, it affords no protection from arrest in any criminal case.[4] A more expansive reading of this narrowly interpreted [5] privilege clause is neither likely nor consistent with the intent of the Framers.

IV. THE CONGRESSIONAL VETO

Congress in recent years has increasingly employed a device termed the "legislative veto." Congress passes legislation on a subject that gives the president, or an executive agency, the power to enact regulations with the force of law if one or both Houses of Congress do not take certain action. Pursuant to this method of legislative enactment, Congress provides in a statute that the president or other executive official must submit the proposed regulation to Congress. Under one alternative, this proposal then will become law unless one House of Congress (or both Houses, according to some statutes) by resolution affirmatively disapproves of the proposal. Under another form, the proposal only will become law if one House of Congress (or alternatively, both Houses) affirmatively approves of the proposal.[1]

The typical objections to use of the legislative veto are that the legislative veto, to the extent it allows a one House veto, conflicts with section 1 of the Constitution, which vests the legislative power in Congress, consisting of both Houses, not in either House acting alone; that the legislative veto conflicts with the president's veto power; and that the legislative veto generally violates the principle of separation of powers.[2]

Various types of this legislative veto have been constitutionally challenged in the lower courts [3] and discussed by the commentators,[4] but the Supreme Court had generally avoided the issue in the past [5] or denied certiorari.[6] Then, on June 23, 1983, the Supreme Court wrote a broad opinion invalidating the congressional veto. The decision was *Immigration and Naturalization Service v. Chadha*[7] which the Court had held over from the previous term.[8] Chadha was an East Indian, lawfully in the United States on a nonimmigrant student visa which had expired in 1972. Therefore, in 1974 a deportation hearing was held, and Chadha filed a petition to suspend his deportation. Under section 244(a)(1) of the Immigration and Nationality Act, the immigration judge found that the deportation should be suspended

3. United States v. Cooper, 4 U.S. (4 Dall.) 341 (C.C. Pa.1800).

4. Williamson v. United States, 207 U.S. 425, 435–446 (1908) (extensive discussion of historical understanding).

5. Long v. Ansell, 293 U.S. 76, 82 (1934): "Clause 1 defines the extent of the immunity. Its language is exact and leaves no room for a construction which would extend the privilege beyond the terms of the grant."

1. E.g., Javits & Klein, § IV Congressional Oversight and the Legislative Veto: A Constitutional Analysis, 52 N.Y.U.L.Rev. 455, 456 (1977). A list of statutes utilizing various forms of congressional vetoes may be found in Congressional Research Service: Library of Congress, Congressional Review, Deferral and Disapproval of Executive Action: A Summary and an Inventory of Statutory Authority (1976).

2. See, United States v. Atkins, 556 F.2d 1028, 1058 (Ct.Cl.1977) (per curiam), cert. denied 434 U.S. 1009 (1978).

3. Clark v. Valeo, 559 F.2d 642, 649–50 (D.C.Cir. 1977) (not reaching issue), aff'd on appeal sub nom., Clark v. Kimmitt, 431 U.S. 950 (1977); United States v. Atkins, 556 F.2d 1028, 1058–71 (Ct.Cl.1977) (per curiam), cert. denied 434 U.S. 1009 (1978) (upholding veto).

4. E.g., Watson, Congress Steps Out: A Look at Congressional Control of the Executive, 63 Calif.L.Rev. 983 (1975) (attacking constitutionality of the legislative veto); Bruff & Gelhorn, Congressional Control of Administrative Regulation: A Study of Legislative Vetoes, 90 Harv.L.Rev. 1369 (1977) (same); Javits & Klein, Congressional Oversight and the Legislative Veto: A Constitutional Analysis, 52 N.Y.U.L.Rev. 52 (1977) (supporting its constitutionality); Dixon, The Congressional Veto and Separation of Powers: The Executive on a Leash?, 56 N.C.L.Rev. 423 (1978); Nathanson, Separation of Powers and Administrative Law: Delegation, the Legislative Veto, and the "Independent" Agencies, 75 Nw.U.L.Rev. 1064 (1981); Martin, The Legislative Veto and the Responsible Exercise of Congressional Power, 68 Va.L.Rev. 253 (1982).

5. See Buckley v. Valeo, 424 U.S. 1, 140 n. 176 (1976) (per curiam). Justice White's concurrence accepted the legislative veto in that case. 424 U.S. at 285–86.

6. E.g., United States v. Atkins, 556 F.2d 1028 (Ct. Cl.1977) (per curiam), cert. denied 434 U.S. 1009 (1978) (Federal Salary Act of 1967, 2 U.S.C.A. § 359).

7. 103 S.Ct. ___ (1983).

8. See 51 U.S.L.W. 3453 (U.S.1982).

and the Attorney General conveyed this information to Congress.[9]

Under section 244(c)(2) the House of Representatives passed a resolution which was a veto of the Attorney General's decision. This resolution was not treated as "legislation" and therefore was not sent to the Senate nor signed by the President. Chief Justice Burger, for the Court, held that the Constitution requires that legislation be presented to the President for approval or veto, this resolution was really legislation, and hence it violated the Presentment Clause.[10] Moreover, the congressional veto violated the bicameral requirement and the principle of separation of powers.[11]

Whether a resolution is legislation depends not on its form, said the Court, but whether it contained matters regarded as legislative in its character and effect. This resolution met that test:

> Section 244(c)(2) purports to authorize one-House of Congress to require the Attorney General to deport an individual alien whose deportation otherwise would be canceled under § 244. The one-house veto operated in this case to overrule the Attorney General and mandate Chadha's deportation; absent the House action, Chadha would remain in the United States. Congress has *acted* and its action has altered Chadha's status.
>
> The legislative character of the one-house veto in this case is confirmed by the character of the Congressional action it supplants . . . Without the challenged provision in § 244(c)(2), this could have been achieved, if at all, only by legislation requiring deportation. Similarly, a veto by one House of Congress under § 244(c)(2) cannot be justified as an attempt at amending the standards set out in § 244(a)(1), or as a repeal of § 244 as applied to Chadha. Amendment and repeal of statutes, no less than enactment, must conform with Art. I.[12]

The congressional veto violated the structural framework in the Constitution, which was intended to place "enduring checks" on each branch and protect the people "from the improvident exercise of power by mandating certain prescribed steps." The Court also found that section 244(c)(2) was severable from the remainder of the Act.[13]

---

9. The judge found that Chadha met the requirements of section 244(a)(1), in that he had lived in the United States over seven years, was of good moral character, and would suffer extreme hardship if deported.

10. U.S.Const., art. I, § 7, cl. 2, 3.

11. See U.S.Const., art. I, §§ 1, 7, cl. 2.

12. 103 S.Ct. at ___ (emphasis in original) (footnotes omitted).

13. Justice Rehnquist objected to this severability conclusion. Justice White's broad dissent (he was the only justice who dissented on the merits) characterized the majority's opinion as too broad: "The Court's Article I analysis appears to invalidate all legislative vetoes irrespective of form or subject." 103 S.Ct. at ___. Justice Powell said: "The breadth of this holding gives one pause." 103 S.Ct. at ___.

CHAPTER NINE

THE COMMERCE CLAUSE AND RESTRICTIONS
ON STATE REGULATORY POWERS

I. STATE REGULATION AFFECTING INTERSTATE COMMERCE FROM GIBBONS TO DiSANTO

A. Introduction

The Constitution specifically grants to Congress the power to regulate commerce.[1] Thus, when a state regulation conflicts with federal legislation enacted under the commerce clause, the federal statute controls pursuant to the supremacy clause.[2] Similarly, the Court historically has recognized the power of Congress to adopt or approve specific state regulation of commerce.[3] The Constitution itself, however, does not articulate the boundaries of this commerce power vested in Congress, particularly when Congress has not spoken. Whether or not the commerce power is exclusive or to what extent concurrent state regulation may coexist in the absence of an articulated Congressional judgment is not textually demonstrable. Moreover, the text of the commerce clause provides no overt restraint of state impingement of interstate commerce in the absence of Congressional legislation. It has been left to the Court to interpret, as inherent in that affirmative grant of power, self-executing limitations on the scope of permissible

---

1. U.S. Const. art. 1, & 8, cl. 3. The definition of "commerce" in the commerce clause is the same whether used to justify federal control or strike down or restrict state legislation. Philadelphia v. New Jersey, 437 U.S. 617, 623–24. As to federal control over interstate commerce, see generally Chapter 4.

2. See Preemption, Chapter 10, section I.

3. "Although Congress cannot enable a state to legislate, Congress may adopt the provisions of a state on any subject." Gibbons v. Ogden, 22 U.S. (9 Wheat.) 1, 207 (1824). White v. Massachusetts Council of Construction Employers, 103 S.Ct. 1042, 1047 (1983): "The Commerce Clause is a grant of authority to Congress, and not a restriction on the authority of that body." See section I, D, below (discussion of Cooley v. Board of Wardens, 53 U.S. (12 How.) 299 (1851)).

state regulation. When the Court seeks to decide the extent of permissible state regulation in light of a "dormant" commerce clause power, it is in effect attempting to interpret the meaning of Congressional silence when it intervenes in an area where the primary power is that of Congress. As we shall see, a necessary corollary to the implied check of the dormant commerce clause is the acknowledgement that Congress can respond to the Court's decision with subsequent legislation reversing the effect of the Court's prior determination. Thus, Congress may later express its consent to state regulation which would otherwise be barred by the dormant commerce clause and, in effect, reverse a decision of the Supreme Court. Yet there is no true reversal for Congress is only adopting a new, valid federal regulation.

The scope of permissible state regulation in the absence of Congressional action constituted a particularly inexplicable enigma for the early Court. The determination of the proper role for the judicial branch in light of Congressional silence in the exercise of its commerce power has divided members of the Court up until the present century. When a state regulation is challenged as a violation of the commerce clause and Congress has abstained from exercising its plenary power, the Court has reluctantly accepted the role of arbiter of the competing state and national interests. Confronted with no expression of Congressional objectives, the Court has been relegated to the difficult task of finding a national economic policy decision in the silence of Congress.[4]

Initially the Court could have adopted any one of several theories to resolve its dilemma. The Congressional commerce power could have been interpreted as an exclusive power, like the war power. Even in light of Congressional abstention, the existence of this constitutional grant of power to Congress could symbolize a dormant prohibition of any and all state regulation affecting interstate commerce. Designated as the negative implication theory, this line of reasoning inferred that Congressional silence was indicative of a purposeful design to leave the area of interstate commerce unregulated.[5] Conversely, another theory, adopted for example by Chief Justice Kent of the New York Courts, argued that Congressional silence always represented an intent to defer to state regulation in that area.[6]

In its threshold inquiry the Court rejected the notion of an exclusive role for Congress, barring any and all state regulation affecting interstate commerce, as an untenable doctrine. The Court also declined to adopt a state-directed posture validating all state regulation in the absence of specific Congressional prohibition. It has selected a middle ground, sometimes deciding that the area is appropriately regulated by the several states and at other times deciding that the area may not be regulated at all. In formulating its analytical framework, the judicial branch has generally been cognizant of the concerns expressed by the framers of the Constitution.[7] That is, the rationale of the commerce clause was to create and foster the development of a common market among the states, eradicating internal trade barriers, and prohibiting the economic Balkanization of the Union. Approval of discriminatory regulation enacted by one state would merely serve to invite retaliatory legislation by the burdened jurisdictions. Recognition of the predominant goal of estab-

---

4. Powell, The Still Small Voice of the Commerce Clause, Proceedings, National Tax Association 337, 338–39 (1937), in 3 A.A.L.S., Selected Essays on Constitutional Law 931, 932 (D. Maggs ed. 1938): "Now Congress has a wonderful power that only judges and lawyers know about. Congress has a power to keep silent. Congress can regulate interstate commerce just by not doing anything about it. Of course when Congress keeps silent, it takes an expert to know what it means. But the judges are experts. . . ."

5. Sholley, The Negative Implications of the Commerce Clause, 3 U.Chi.L.Rev. 556 (1936).

6. E.g., Livingston v. Van Ingen, 9 Johns, 507 (N.Y.1812) (opinion of Kent. C.J.). See also Taney, C.J., dissenting in Pennsylvania v. Wheeling & Belmont Bridge Co., 54 U.S. (13 How.) 518, 587 (1852).

7. See Alexander Hamilton, The Federalist, No. 32.

lishing a unified, national economy has permeated judicial interpretations of state power to regulate commerce. When local legislation thwarts the operation of the common market entity, it has then exceeded the permissible limits within the federal structure. Congress, of course, may legislatively approve what amounts to discriminatory commercial regulation by the states.[8] Such approval, however, does not violate the intent of the commerce clause; the dangers of a part discriminating against the whole are greater than the whole discriminating against a part, for an inner political check that is not operative in the former is operative in the latter case.

B. The Gibbons Case

The Supreme Court initially struggled with the concept of interpreting the meaning of Congressional silence in the leading case of *Gibbons v. Ogden*.[9] Under the forceful direction of Chief Justice Marshall, not only was a broad definition of commerce enunciated, but the supremacy of the common market concept acknowledging a category of concurrent regulation supposedly emanating from the state's police powers was embraced as the most viable doctrine for the emerging nation.

In *Gibbons* New York had granted an exclusive steamboat operator's license to Livingston and Fulton, who had in turn assigned it to Ogden. The highest court of New York had sustained an order enjoining Gibbons from operating a federally licensed steamboat in New York waters on the grounds of the state-granted monopoly to Ogden. Gibbons argued that the state monopoly violated federal commerce power. In assessing the scope of state power to regulate interstate commerce, Marshall spoke in broad terms. "Commerce" he said, is more than traffic. "[I]t is intercourse. It describes the commercial intercourse between nations and parts of nations . . . ."[10] It includes navigation. "No sort of trade can be carried on between this country and any other to which this power does not extend."[11] The phrase "among the several States" means "intermingled with," for commerce among the states "cannot stop at the external boundary-line of each State, but may be introduced into the interior." These words, however, do not "comprehend commerce which is completely internal . . . and which does not extend to or affect other States."[12] Thus the vessel operated by Gibbons was in interstate commerce.

Then Marshall flirted with—but did not adopt—the idea that the power to regulate commerce among the states is exclusive. That is, Marshall did not adopt the argument that since Congress has power over interstate commerce, a state may not enact legislation, pursuant to its commerce power, that affects also interstate commerce. Those that believed that the states have an interstate commerce power, even though the federal government has it, argued from analogy that the federal government has a taxing power and yet the grant of that power to the federal government did not exclude the

---

8. E.g., Prudential Insurance Co. v. Benjamin, 328 U.S. 408 (1946). Cf. also, U.S. Const. art. I, § 10, cl. 2.

As Western & Southern Life Insurance Co. v. State Bd. of Equalization, 451 U.S. 648, 652–53 (1981), recognized under its plenary commerce clause power, "Congress may 'confe[r] upon the States an ability to restrict the flow of interstate commerce that they would not otherwise enjoy.' If Congress ordains that the States may freely regulate an aspect of interstate commerce, any action taken by a State within the scope of the congressional authorization is rendered invulnerable to Commerce Clause challenge." (internal citations omitted). Cf. Lewis v. BT Investment Managers, Inc., 447 U.S. 27, 45–50 (1980) (federal statute as interpreted does not authorize state statute's discrimination against interstate commerce).

9. 22 U.S. (9 Wheat.) 1 (1824).

10. Id. at 189.

11. Id. at 193.

12. Id. at 194. What is "completely internal" has long been narrowly defined, for the commerce power extends to all matters which *affect* interstate commerce. Such is now the modern view and the early view. See, e.g., The Daniel Ball, 77 U.S. (10 Wall.) 557 (1871) (a vessel operating solely on a river within Michigan's borders is within the stream of interstate commerce). For a short period of time the Supreme Court rejected this broad view. See Chapter 4.

states from also exercising it. Marshall answered this argument by distinguishing the state power to tax from the state power to regulate commerce. State power to tax represented a necessary element for the state's very existence. Conversely, when a state regulates interstate commerce "it is exercising the very power that is granted to Congress, and is doing the very thing which Congress is authorized to do. There is no analogy, then, between the power of taxation and the power of regulating commerce." [13] Then, it was argued that the States have enacted inspection laws; such state laws are specifically recognized by the Constitution,[14] and such laws are indeed regulations of commerce. Marshall answered that the inspection laws may have "a remote and considerable influence on commerce" but their origin is not derived from any commerce power but from what today we would call the state's "police power:"

> [T]hat immense mass of legislation which embraces everything within the territory of a state not surrendered to a general government; all of which can be most advantageously exercised by the states themselves. Inspection laws, quarantine laws, health laws of every description, as well as laws for regulating the internal commerce of a State, and those which respect turnpike roads, ferries, etc., are component parts of this mass.[15]

Since New York's inspection laws and other such concededly valid laws derived—in Marshall's view—from the police powers, the enactment of such laws did not prove that New York had any power to enact legislation deriving from a commerce power.[16]

The "police power" is nowhere mentioned in the Constitution but the term has been a frequently cited concept in Constitutional cases, particularly in the commerce area.

Marshall's inquiring into the derivation or source of the exercise of a power—whether it be the police power, the commerce power or some other power—has not been fruitful because of the difficulty of ascertaining the metaphysical origin of any given power. But, as then Professor Frankfurter has noted, Marshall did not have the opportunity to develop the doctrine; and all we can be certain of is that the test did not prove to be a useful tool when turned over to others.[17] This "origin-of power" question was not laid to rest however until *Cooley v. Board of Wardens* [18] discussed later in this section.

As we shall see in the development of the later case law, a state law may regulate health and safety and yet also regulate or affect commerce among the states. In general, if the regulation is more of a benefit to health and safety than it is a burden to interstate commerce, the Court will not strike down the state legislation. If it is more of a burden than a benefit, the Court will invalidate the state law. Later in this Chapter we shall examine more carefully some of the tests the Court has fashioned to determine when the burdens to interstate commerce exceed the health and safety benefits that the state claims are promoted by its law.

After engaging in this metaphysical discussion of the origin of the exercise of health and safety rules affecting interstate commerce, Marshall turned to the argument that the commerce clause by its own terms exclusively gave to Congress the power to regulate commerce among the states. "There is great force in this argument" he said, "and the court is not satisfied that has been refuted." [19] But Marshall did not decide this issue because in this instance Congress had acted, or rather Marshall inter-

---

13. 22 U.S. (9 Wheat.) at 199–200.

14. U.S. Const. art. I, § 10, cl. 2.

15. 22 U.S. (9 Wheat.) at 203.

16. Historically Congress has acquiesced in State enforcement of Quarantine Laws. Morgan v. Louisiana, 118 U.S. 455 (1886); Louisiana v. Texas, 176 U.S. 1, 21 (1900). Other cases sustaining the validity of state quarantine measures include Mintz v. Baldwin, 289 U.S. 346 (1933); Pacific States Co. v. White, 296

U.S. 176 (1935); and Bourjois, Inc. v. Chapman, 301 U.S. 183 (1937).

17. See, F. Frankfurter, The Commerce Power Under Marshall, Taney and Waite 31–32, 61–62 (1964—first published 1937).

18. 53 U.S. (12 How.) 299 (1851), discussed in section I, D, below.

19. 22 U.S. (9 Wheat.) at 209.

preted the federal act allowing a licensee to engage in coastal trade to conflict with the New York monopoly and hence the state monopoly must fall. New York could not limit the scope of the federal license by creating a state monopoly over an interstate waterway which would render the federally-conferred license useless. Right after this decision, competition in New York and the other states increased which caused the steamboat fare from New York to New Haven to be reduced from five to three dollars.[20]

C. Between GIBBONS v. OGDEN and COOLEY v. BOARD OF WARDENS

An early manifestation of the origin-of-power dichotomy was expounded by the Court in *Willson v. Black-Bird Creek Marsh Co.*[21] There, state law had authorized the company's erection of a dam which, under the *Gibbons* rationale, obstructed an interstate commerce waterway. The dam was broken by Willson's federally licensed ship. The company had successfully sued for damages in state court, and the Supreme Court, per Chief Justice Marshall, affirmed, rejecting appellee's argument that the state law violated the commerce clause. Marshall implied that the Delaware statute was not within the purview of the dormant commerce clause because it was plainly an example of the state's permissible regulation of a local health and property matter. It is also noteworthy that the Delaware legislation resulted in a nondiscriminatory prohibition of all shipping, local as well as foreign, as contrasted with the New York statute invalidated in *Gibbons* which favored local shippers to the disadvantage of non-resident carriers. Nonetheless, the *Willson* decision was construed as a retreat from the absolutist position discussed in *Gibbons*. Marshall appeared to tacitly abandon the idea that a federal license conveyed to the holder an unrestricted right to travel in all commerce.

In the era between *Gibbons* and *Cooley v. Board of Wardens*[22] the Court grappled with Marshall's origin-of-power doctrine. Subsequent decisions failed to formulate a satisfactory criteria for the test, and the members of the Court were unable to elicit majority support for any one position.

Marshall's concept of "police regulation" formed the basis of the decision in *New York v. Miln*[23] upholding a New York statute requiring a report of passenger identification information from every shipmaster arriving in New York from any foreign country or other state of the union. Purportedly, the state measure functioned as a safety regulation protecting the local citizenry from the arrival of undesirables. Adhering to Marshall's description of state police power, Justice Barbour's opinion for the majority hastily dismissed any need to consider state power to regulate commerce. Once the New York statute was defined as within that great mass of legislation emanating from the police power, the Court summarily sustained the law as a proper regulation of the state's internal affairs. The Court's ease in arriving at a conclusion was not necessarily an accurate reflection of the viability of the test.[24] Justice Thompson had writ-

---

20. 1 C. Warren, The Supreme Court in United States History 615 (Rev. ed. 1926).

21. 27 U.S. (2 Pet.) 245 (1829). See generally, F. Frankfurter, The Commerce Power Under Marshall, Taney and Waite 27–34 (1964—first published 1937).

22. 53 U.S. (12 How.) 299 (1851).

23. 36 U.S. (11 Pet.) 102 (1837).

24. A statute requiring masters or owners of every vessel landing passengers from a foreign port to pay to the state $1.50 or provide a $300 bond for each passenger landed to indemnify the locality for expenses for relief or support was struck down in Henderson v. New York, 92 U.S. 259 (1876). *Miln* was narrowly construed. The Court said:

"Nothing is gained in the argument by calling it the police power. Very many statutes, when the authority on which their enactments rest is examined, may be referred to different sources of power, and supported equally well under any of them. A statute may at the same time be an exercise of the taxing power and of the power of eminent domain. . . . It must occur very often that the shading which marks the line between one class of legislation and the other is very nice, and not easily distinguishable.

"But, however difficult this may be, it is clear, from the nature of our complex form of government,

ten the first opinion for the Court, but his approval of concurrent state power to regulate commerce was unacceptable to his colleagues. Justice Story dissented not on the basis that the Court had applied the wrong standard, but because in his opinion the state statute constituted a regulation of commerce, and was, therefore, invalid. Interestingly, the same case had been argued at an earlier date [25] and Marshall, the author of the standard, (who died between the first and second argument) then concurred with Story.

The Court remained impossibly divided over the issue of exclusive Congressional power in the decade between *Miln* and *Cooley*. In *The License Cases* [26] six justices delivering separate opinions sustaining a state license requirement for the sale of imported liquor. The lack of consensus was also illustrated in *The Passenger Cases* [27] where eight justices wrote separate opinions annulling state legislation imposing a tax on alien passengers arriving from foreign ports. Finally, the Court resolved Marshall's dilemma with the concept of exclusive Congressional power in *Cooley v. Board of Wardens* [28] instructing that under certain circumstances a recognition of exclusive Congressional power is appropriate while at other times concurrent state regulation is acceptable.

D. The COOLEY Rule of Selective Exclusiveness

Cooley v. Board of Wardens [29] represents the culmination of the formulative period of a search for an adequate standard for judicial review of state regulation of commerce in the absence of Congressional legislation. This decision set the direction for commerce clause adjudication for almost the next 100 years. In *Cooley* the Court, speaking

through Justice Benjamin Curtis, who resigned after the *Dred Scott* decision and later was counsel to President Andrew Johnson in his impeachment proceedings, affirmed a Pennsylvania law requiring ships entering or leaving the Philadelphia port to engage a local pilot. Cooley had been subjected to the state penalty for his failure to engage such a pilot, and he challenged the law as an impermissible state regulation of interstate commerce. The Court sustained the act on the basis of a distinction between those subjects of commerce which demand a uniform rule throughout the country and those subjects which permit diversity of treatment in order to fulfill local needs. The Court specifically rejected both extreme interpretations of the commerce clause; i.e., either that congressional power was exclusive or that state regulation in the absence of congressional action could go unbridled.

The *Cooley* doctrine delineates the nature of the subject of the challenged regulation as the determinative factor in reviewing its validity. The doctrine of selective exclusiveness expounded in *Cooley* stipulates that if the item is such that national uniformity is necessitated, then Congressional power is exclusive. If, on the other hand, the item is representative of a peculiarly local concern (even though within the reach of the Congressional commerce clause power such as the Pennsylvania pilotage laws) warranting a diversity of treatment, then concurrent state regulation is authorized in the absence of Congressional preemption.

Unfortunately, there were pitfalls in the *Cooley* doctrine as well. First, there is no adequate indicia for the determination of national subjects as opposed to local subjects. It is also doubtful that the Court's inquiry could satisfactorily be limited to the subject

---

that, whenever the statute of a State invades the domain of legislation which belongs exclusively to the Congress of the United States, it is void, no matter under what class of powers it may fall, or how closely allied to powers conceded to belong to the States." 92 U.S. at 271–72.

25. See C. Swisher, American Constitutional Development 196, 197 (2d ed. 1954).

26. 46 U.S. (5 How.) 504 (1847).

27. 48 U.S. (7 How.) 28 (1849).

28. 53 U.S. (12 How.) 299 (1851).

29. 53 U.S. (12 How.) 299 (1851).

matter only, but rather consideration of the state action had to encompass the purpose and effect of the regulation also. Additionally, although a state might be regulating a local subject matter, the legislation could still be discriminatory in purpose or effect, thereby affording residents favorable treatment in relation to non-residents. An important element of the *Cooley* decision was that the Pennsylvania laws were in fact nondiscriminatory, falling with equal weight on Pennsylvania residents. The Court has consistently evinced a greater willingness to sustain state regulations which equally burden local residents. When there is no discrimination against out-of-state citizens or residents, an inner political check operating within the state assures that the effects of the law will not be too harsh, for it will operate equally on the state citizens who enacted it.

E. Federal Incorporation by Reference of State Laws

In considering the application of *Cooley*, it is noteworthy that the Congressional Act of 1789 specifically endorsed the continuation of state regulation until further provisions were established by Congress. Interestingly, the Court in *Cooley* did not appear to hold this statute as binding, and decided the case as if there were no Congressional statute on the scene authorizing the nondiscriminatory state pilotage laws. Justice Curtis did raise the question of whether or not Congress could enact legislation adopting *future* state laws by incorporation. He seemed to indicate that such action was constitutionally an impossibility. Justice Curtis we now know was in error equating the adoption of future laws by incorporation as indistinguishable from the delegation of the power to legislate. For example, Congress

cannot delegate to Illinois the power to legislate federal pollution standards for the whole country. Then Congress would be abdicating interstate commerce control to one state to legislate for the nation. However, Congress can enact legislation prescribing that the federal pollution standard in each state shall be the same as the state standard. Then, it is not abdicating its authority but merely incorporating by reference future legislation. This type of "delegation" is appropriate because those having input into the political process evolving the requisite standard are also bound by it, assuring an inner political check.[30] Congress is incorporating state laws as they are now or are in the future, for:

> [r]ather than being a delegation by Congress of its legislative authority to the States, it is a deliberate continuing adoption by Congress [of laws] as shall have been already put in effect by the respective States for their own government.[31]

Subsequent cases support the view that the validity of judicial interpretation of the need for uniformity applies only in the absence of Congressional action, for Congress has demonstrated its retained power to reverse the Court's opinion by authorizing the annulled state legislation. In *Leisy v. Hardin*[32] the Court invoked the original package doctrine to invalidate state regulation of interstate liquor traffic vis-a-vis an Iowa Statute prohibiting the sale of intoxicating liquor. In a broad application of the *Cooley* national uniformity standard, the Court held that as "transportation, purchase, sale and exchange of commodities is national in its character and must be governed by a uniform system, so long as Congress does not pass any law to regulate it, or allowing the states so to do, it thereby indicates its will that such commerce shall be free and untrammelled."[33] Under this rubric the Iowa

---

30. E.g., United States v. Sharpnack, 355 U.S. 286 (1958) (and examples cited therein); Prudential Insurance Co. v. Benjamin, 328 U.S. 408 (1946); Clark Distilling Co. v. Western Maryland Ry., 242 U.S. 311 (1917). In admiralty some old, poorly reasoned cases do not recognize this type of adoption. E.g., Knickerbocker Ice Co. v. Stewart, 253 U.S. 149 (1924). Cf. Morrison,

Worker's Compensation and the Maritime Law, 38 Yale L.J. 472 (1929).

31. United States v. Sharpnack, 355 U.S. 286, 294 (1958).

32. 135 U.S. 100 (1890).

33. 135 U.S. at 109–110.

statute was struck down. Congress hastily responded by enacting the Wilson Act [34] subjecting interstate liquor traffic to the laws of importation without exception. The Wilson Act was sustained by a unanimous Court in the decision of *In re Rahrer*.[35] The Court explained that the subsequent legislation did not represent Congressional delegation of its power to regulate commerce, but rather a legitimate manifestation of Congressional power under the Commerce Clause to authorize an acceptable form of state regulation. Other cases equally support this principle.[36]

F. The DiSANTO Case and Dowling's Formulation

In formulating a more adequate standard for the evolving nation, the post-*Cooley* Court unanimously embraced a recognition of the states' concurrent power to regulate commerce. The issue of Congressional exclusivity had been resolved, but judicial inquiry as to the extent of permissible, concurrent state power remained. Various verbal touchstones were invoked by successive Courts in an attempt to formulate a predictable dichotomy between permitted and invalid state exercise of regulatory power, but the absence of an adequate standard is evidenced by the plethora of cases that cannot by reconciled merely by an application of the *Cooley* doctrine.[37]

In these decisions one factor becomes imperative to the judicial tribunal—a legitimate state regulation must not burden interstate commerce in either purpose or effect unless the extent of that burden is outweighed by a legitimate state objective that cannot be achieved in a less burdensome manner. In

other words, the Court was more willing to defer to the judgment of the state political process if those burdened by the regulation were represented in that process. Thus, state regulatory measures which fall equally on local residents are more likely to be sanctioned than those parochial schemes which favor local citizens and burden non-residents, for in the former situation an inner political check is operative which helps assure the validity of the law and thus lessen the need for an active judicial review. While discrimination against interstate commerce was acknowledged as one emerging test, this factor alone did not suffice to resolve the Court's continuing difficulty with the practical application of the *Cooley* doctrine.

Di Santo v. Pennsylvania [38] was a typical case in which the Court was called upon to review the validity of a state law in light of the dormant Commerce Clause. A Pennsylvania regulation required sellers of steamboat tickets to apply for and be granted a license. In addition, the licensees were charged an annual fee and subject to license revocation. The putative local benefit to be derived from the state regulation was the protection of local citizens from fraudulent acts.

The Court struck down the regulation as an unnecessary, burdensome interference with foreign commerce. Admonishing the state that such legislation could not be justified by characterizing it as an exertion of the police power to prevent possible fraud, the majority, in a broad application of the *Cooley* doctrine, held that Congress has exclusive authority to regulate foreign commerce because the subject demands uniform treatment, and therefore, state legislation of

---

34. 26 Stat. 313 (1890).

35. 140 U.S. 545 (1891).

36. E.g., Compare Pennsylvania v. Wheeling & Belmont Bridge Co., 54 U.S. (13 How.) 518 (1852) (the Wheeling Bridge seriously obstructs navigation), with Pennsylvania v. Wheeling & Belmont Bridge Co., 59 U.S. (18 How.) 421 (1856) (an Act of Congress declaring the Wheeling Bridge to be a lawful structure and a post road is valid). See also, Western & Southern Life Insurance Co. v. State Bd. of Equalization, 451 U.S.

648, 652–53 (1981). See generally Note, Change in Constitutional Doctrine Through Legislation: Some Recent Developments, 63 Harv.L.Rev. 861 (1950).

37. See Brandeis J., joined by Holmes, J., dissenting, in Di Santo v. Pennsylvania, 273 U.S. 34, 43 & n. 4 (1927). See also Stern, The Problems of Yesteryear—Commerce and Due Process, 4 Vand.L.Rev. 446, 451–52 (1951).

38. 273 U.S. 34 (1927).

this nature is necessarily repugnant to the Congressional power.

In his now famous dissent Justice Stone departed from the majority's position and implored the Court to adopt a more appropriate standard for adjusting the conflicting claims of the federal government and the states to regulate commerce. He reminded the majority that since *Cooley* the Court's decisions had repeatedly acknowledged that the purpose of the Commerce Clause "was not to preclude all state regulation of commerce crossing state lines, but to prevent discrimination and the erection of barriers or obstacles to the free flow of commerce, interstate or foreign." [39] To achieve this objective, Stone advocated the utilization of a more realistic method, abandoning reliance on rigid verbal formulae:

> [T]he traditional test of the limit of state action by inquiring whether the interference with commerce is direct or indirect seems to me too mechanical, too uncertain in its application, and too remote from actualities, to be of value. In this making use of the expressions, "direct" and "indirect interference" with commerce, we are doing little more than using labels to describe a result rather than any trustworthy formula by which it is reached.

> [I]t seems clear that those interferences not deemed forbidden are to be sustained, not because the effect on commerce is nominally indirect, but because a consideration of all the facts and circumstances, such as the nature of the regulation, its function, the character of the business involved and the actual effect on the flow of commerce, lead to the conclusion that the regulation concerns interests peculiarly local and does not infringe the national interest in maintaining the freedom of commerce across state lines. [40]

Stone's dissent received significant support from Professor Noel T. Dowling, who expanded the Justice's ideas into a very influential article. Published in 1940, [41] Dowling's article used the Stone dissent as a foundation for providing the Court with a practical resolution of its century long dilemma with the *Cooley* doctrine. Dowling stressed that the new theory merely involved acknowledgment by the Court of what it had been attempting to do all along; i.e., "deliberately balancing national and local interest and making a choice as to which of the two *should* prevail." [42] Dowling envisioned the new structure as one in which:

> in the absence of affirmative consent a Congressional negative will be presumed in the courts against state action which in its effect upon interstate commerce constitutes an unreasonable interference with national interests, the presumption being rebuttable at the pleasure of Congress. . . . State action falling short of such interference would prevail unless and until superseded or otherwise nullified by Congressional action. [43]

The cornerstone of Dowling's formulation, as he conceded, is that Congressional will controls. The Court's role is to attempt to review existing state legislation in light of the dormant commerce clause weighing the putative local benefits against its interpretation of the competing national interests. If the Court sustains the state action as not constituting an unreasonable burden on interstate commerce, and Congress concurs, no subsequent Congressional action is required. If Congress concludes that the state action is undesirable, it retains the power to terminate its dormant state, and assert its will pursuant to its commerce clause power. Similarly, if the Court invalidates the state regulation, Congress can consequently resurrect the state law by expressing its consent to such state action. Unequivocally Congress has the power to grant such consent pursuant to the commerce clause provision.

Professor Dowling's article had substantial impact on state regulation of commerce decisions. The modern cases discussed immediately below reflect both the Court's willingness to openly engage in a balancing

---

39. 273 U.S. at 43–44.

40. 273 U.S. at 44.

41. Dowling, Interstate Commerce and State Power, 27 Va.L.Rev. 1 (1940).

42. 27 Va.L.Rev. at 21.

43. 27 Va.L.Rev. at 20.

approach and the extent of Dowling's contribution to the development of a more workable formula for dealing with problems in a modern era. The end of formalistic tests and metaphysical attempts to interpret congressional silence has led to an era of more understandable rules. The Court now accepts its judicial role of balancing conflicting economic policies until such time as Congress chooses to act.

II. STATE POWERS OVER TRANSPORTATION

The Court manifested initial acceptance of Dowling's expansion of Stone's *Di Santo* dissent discussed in the preceding section in the early landmark case of *Southern Pacific Co. v. Arizona*.[1] Arizona had charged Southern Pacific with violating a state Train Limit Law prohibiting trains with more than 14 passenger cars or 70 freight cars from operating within the state. Ostensibly, the state regulation was a safety measure. Nonetheless, its practical effect was to impose a much heavier burden on interstate as opposed to intrastate lines.

Chief Justice Stone, writing for the majority, noted the trial court's findings that the operation of long trains is standard practice through the United States; that approximately 93% of the freight traffic in Arizona and 95% of the passenger traffic is interstate; that the train limit law required the Southern Pacific to haul over 30% more trains in Arizona. To comply with such train limit laws, trains must either be broken up as they enter the border of a state or conform to the lowest train limit restriction of all the states they travel through, thus allowing such a state to have a substantial extraterritorial effect for its regulations. Given the interstate nature of the train lines, "the Arizona law often controls the length of passenger lines all the way from Los Angeles to El Paso."[2]

In addition, the safety data presented at the trial debilitated the rationale underlying the local enactment, i.e., the increased safety resulting from shorter trains was more than overcome by the added risks inherent in increasing the number of trains operating within the state. "The decisive question," said the majority, "is whether in the circumstances the total effect of the law as a safety measure in reducing accidents and casualties is so slight or problematical as not to outweigh the national interest in keeping interstate commerce free from interferences which seriously impede it and subject it to local regulation which does not have a uniform effect on the interstate train journey which it interrupts."[3]

The majority, agreeing with the trial court that the Arizona law had no reasonable relation to safety, found that the burdens on interstate commerce outweighed the state's equivocal evidence of safety. The majority clearly weighed and reevaluated the evidence; it did not accept the state's factual assertions of safety because the interests in interstate commerce are "not to be avoided by 'simply invoking the convenient apologetics of the police power.'"[4] The Court thus indicated by its language and actions that the test of "reasonableness" under the interstate commerce clause cases is much stricter than the modern test of "reasonableness" of economic activities under the due process and equal protection cases.

Justices Douglas and Black dissented separately, accusing the majority of adopting for the Court the role of a "super-legislature" and contending that this case presented an issue to be resolved in the political arena not the judicial branch. Thus, in their opinions, it was not that the Court had balanced the competing interests and attained the wrong result, but that the Court should not have engaged in a balancing inquiry at all.

1. 325 U.S. 761 (1945).

2. 325 U.S. at 774–75 (footnote omitted).

3. 325 U.S. at 775–76.

4. 325 U.S. at 780, quoting Kansas City Southern Ry. Co. v. Kaw Valley District, 233 U.S. 75, 79 (1914).

Southern Pacific was decided in the wake of *South Carolina Highway Department v. Barnwell Brothers Inc.*,[5] where a unanimous Court, (Justice Cardozo and Justice Reed not participating), sustained a South Carolina weight and width limitation for trucks operated within the state. Again Stone, then a Justice, and not yet the Chief Justice, wrote the opinion.

In *Barnwell* the Court had upheld a South Carolina statute which prohibited on its highways trucks over 90 inches in width and whose loaded weight exceed 20,000 pounds. All other states permitted the standard width of 96 inches and only four other states prescribed a gross weight as low as 20,000 pounds. The majority emphasized that a state "may not, under the guise of regulation, discriminate against interstate commerce."[6] "[S]o long as the state action does not discriminate, the burden is one which the Constitution permits . . ."[7] The commerce clause prohibits "state legislation nominally of local concern [which] is in point of fact aimed at interstate commerce, or by its necessary operation is a means of gaining a local benefit by throwing the attendant burdens on those without the state."[8] But other language seems quite inconsistent with the later *Southern Pacific* decision written by the same Justice Stone. *Barnwell* argued that it is for Congress and not the Court to decide to what extent "local interests should be required to yield to the national authority and interest."[9] "[C]ourts do not sit as legislatures . . ."[10] "Since the adoption of one weight or width regulation, rather than another, is a legislative not a judicial choice, its constitutionality is not to be determined by weighing in the judicial scales the merits of the legislative choice and rejecting it if the weight of evidence presented in court appears to favor a differ-

ent standard."[11] "[C]ourts are not any the more entitled, because interstate commerce is affected, to substitute their own for the legislative judgment."[12]

These two cases, while difficult to reconcile, are not entirely inconsistent. In *Barnwell* the evidence of the relationship between the state law and safety requirements was much stronger than the *Southern Pacific* case. In spite of the *Barnwell* language quoted above, the Court did in fact summarize and analyze the evidence of safety.[13] For example, 100 miles of South Carolina roads at the time were only 16 feet wide, too narrow for two 96 inch wide trucks. Secondly, the Court emphasized the local nature of the state highway system. While this "localness" is not correct nor applicable in the 1970's, it was very relevant when *Barnwell* was decided in 1938. The Court there said that "[f]ew subjects of state regulation are so peculiarly of local concern as in the use of state highways."[14] *Southern Pacific*, in distinguishing *Barnwell*, thought that the state's powers over "its" highways is "far more extensive" than its control over railroads.[15]

Finally, it is probably true that the political check operated more effectively in *Barnwell* than in *Southern Pacific*. While neither decision carefully articulates this rationale, the references to a *discriminatory* burden on interstate commerce supports the theory. The *Southern Pacific* prohibition of longer trains probably burdens the long haul shipper more than the short haul shipper. The long haul shipper is more likely to be interstate and the short haul shipper is more likely to be intrastate. These intrastate shippers—feeling less of a burden of the state regulation—are less likely to use the political processes to urge the law's repeal. In fact, to the extent the state regulation

---

5. 303 U.S. 177 (1938).

6. 303 U.S. at 189.

7. 303 U.S. at 189.

8. 303 U.S. at 185–86.

9. 303 U.S. at 190.

10. Id.

11. 303 U.S. at 191.

12. Id.

13. 303 U.S. at 191–196.

14. 303 U.S. at 187.

15. 325 U.S. at 783.

places a discriminatory burden on interstate commerce it works to the advantage of the competing, Arizona railroads. In *Barnwell*, the prohibition of larger trucks is more likely to burden equally the intrastate, South Carolina truck shipper. It is relatively easy for the short haul intrastate train to add freight or passenger cars as it crosses the state line. It can then compete effectively with its interstate rivals. But it is harder for these interstate shippers to split a train and add an engine upon crossing the state line. On the other hand, just as it is difficult for an interstate truck shipper to shift to a small truck when entering South Carolina, it is equally difficult for the South Carolina trucker to shift to a larger truck when leaving his state; and if he does not shift, he suffers a competitive disadvantage because he does not have equivalent economies of scale. Because the burden of the South Carolina statute is not discriminatory against the interstate shipper, the South Carolina truckers have an incentive to change the law if it is not really warranted. Evidence that the inner political check worked is supported by the fact that in South Carolina, within three months after the *Barnwell* decision, the state legislature changed its law to expand its weight and width laws.[16]

Thus, an important factor in analyzing all such cases attacking state regulation affecting interstate commerce is not only whether as an absolute matter the burden on interstate commerce is substantial but in addition whether the burden imposed on such commerce is discriminatory in favor of local concerns. To the extent it is not, there is room for operation of an inner political check which lessens the need for an active judicial review. When such a political check is working, the Court is more likely to respect the state's own balancing of legitimate safety concerns with the national necessity for an efficient, uniform transportation system.

Within this rubric the decision in *Bibb v. Navajo Freight Lines, Inc.*[17] invalidated an Illinois safety measure specifying contour mud flaps for trucks operated within its jurisdiction. The state's peculiar variation on mud flap design resulted in disallowing interstate commerce operators from using a mud flap in Illinois that was legal in 45 other states; additionally, the Illinois design was itself illegal in Arkansas, which required straight mud flaps. This permutation in standards retarded the free flow of interstate trucking unnecessarily. The Court noted the trial court's finding that the contour mud flap posed no safety advantage over the conventional or straight mud flap and there was evidence that it created new hazards by accumulating heat in the brake drum. And the special mud flap design—because of the different and conflicting requirements of other jurisdictions—significantly interfered with interstate commerce. In language suggestive of the *Cooley* rule the Court struck down the Illinois requirement:

> This is one of those cases—few in number—where local safety measures that are nondiscriminatory place an unconstitutional burden on interstate commerce. This conclusion is especially underlined by the deleterious effect which the Illinois law will have on the "interline" operation of interstate motor carriers. The conflict between the Arkansas regulation and the Illinois regulation also suggests that this regulation of mudguards is not one of those matters "admitting of diversity of treatment, according to the special requirements of local conditions" . . .[18]

In *Bibb* the Court also noted that if the only issue were the cost of adjustment to these new safety regulations for an interstate commerce carrier, the measure would have to be sustained.[19] Apparently, the enhanced cost factor alone would not have motivated the Court to strike down the train length regulation in *Southern Pacific*. Rather it is the minimal evidence supportive of the safe-

16. South Carolina Acts, No. 845 (1938).

17. 359 U.S. 520 (1959).

18. 359 U.S. at 529, quoting Hughes, C. J., in Sproles v. Binford, 286 U.S. 374, 390 (1932). See also, Ray v. Atlantic Richfield Co., 435 U.S. 151, 179 (1978).

19. 359 U.S. at 526.

ty rationale as contrasted with the onerous impediment to the movement of interstate commerce that is decisive: the burdens on interstate commerce exceeded the benefits of local safety.

The wealth of cases in this area are not all entirely consistent but a brief review of some of them will hopefully illustrate the main techniques employed by the Court. In a long line of cases the Supreme Court has upheld statutes requiring "full-crews" on railroad trains. This requirement, when nondiscriminatorily applied to intra- as well as interstate trains, is sufficiently related to safety that the Court will not second-guess the legislature. Moreover, the added burden of adding crew members when the train crossed a border is not significant compared with the possible safety advantages.[20]

The Supreme Court also held, nearly a decade before *Brown v. Board of Education*[21] integrated the schools, that the state of Virginia could not require the segregation of white and black passengers on interstate motor traffic because "seating arrange-

ments for the different races in interstate motor traffic require a single, uniform rule to promote and protect national travel."[22]

The Court has upheld a city's anti-pollution ordinance that applied nondiscriminatorily to ships in both intra- and interstate commerce. There was no evidence that other communities had actually imposed different or conflicting standards, though in the future they might. Under the law, ships had to make structural changes in their boilers.[23]

The Court reversed state denials of certificates of convenience which were denied to interstate motor carriers on the grounds that the territory was already "adequately" served.[24] In effect, the state was merely using the law to limit competition and burden the interstate shipper. But the state may deny such certificates for bonafide safety reasons: that a new carrier on a particular route that is already congested would cause safety problems.[25]

Commentators on the various problems and court tests in this area abound,[26] but

---

20. Brotherhood of Locomotive Firemen & Enginemen v. Chicago, Rock Island & Pacific R. R. Co., 393 U.S. 129 (1968). See also, Brotherhood of Locomotive Firemen & Enginemen v. Chicago, R. I. & P. R. R. Co., 382 U.S. 423, 438 (1966), where Justice Douglas dissented on the grounds that the Federal Government had preempted such regulation. 382 U.S. at 438. Other cases upholding full crew legislation include: Missouri Pacific Co. v. Norwood, 283 U.S. 249 (1931); St. Louis, Iron Mt. & S. R. R. Co. v. Arkansas, 240 U.S. 518 (1916); Chicago, R. I. & P. R. R. Co. v. Arkansas, 219 U.S. 453 (1911).

21. 347 U.S. 483 (1954).

22. Morgan v. Virginia, 328 U.S. 373, 386 (1946).

23. Huron Cement Co. v. Detroit, 362 U.S. 440 (1960). The Court also found no federal preemption of the area.

24. Buck v. Kuykendell, 267 U.S. 307 (1925); Railroad Transfer Service v. City of Chicago, 386 U.S. 351 (1967).

See also, e.g., Raymond Motor Transport, Inc. v. Rice, 434 U.S. 429 (1978), where the Court struck down a number of Wisconsin regulations implementing statutes that barred trucks longer than 55 feet from operating on state highways. In reversing the district court, Justice Powell noted that Wisconsin had "failed to make even a colorable showing that its regulations contribute to highway safety." The trucking companies had presented a "massive array" of evidence that their 65 foot double trailers were as safe, if not safer,

than the 55 foot trailers permitted by the regulations; Wisconsin's sole witness had admitted that the regulations were not based on considerations of safety, but rather reflected a prejudice against large trucks. 434 U.S. at 438 & n. 11, 437–38. The Court also stressed that the regulations provided for a large number of exceptions that openly discriminated in favor of Wisconsin industries, and that the Wisconsin regulations greatly added to the cost of interstate trucking. The Court cautioned that similar restrictions would be upheld "if the evidence produced on the safety issue were not so overwhelmingly one-sided as in this case." 434 U.S. at 446–47 & n. 24.

Iowa also tried to ban the use of 65 foot double trailers on its highways, but the Court held that the law violated the commerce clause. Kassell v. Consolidated Freightways Corp. of Delaware, 450 U.S. 662 (1981) was similar to *Raymond* except that "Iowa made a more serious effort to support the safety rationale of its law than did Wisconsin in *Raymond*, but its effort was no more persuasive." 450 U.S. at 671–72 (plurality opinion of Powell, J.). In fact, in the lower courts Iowa actually argued that the state law promoted safety and reduced road wear by diverting much truck traffic to other states. 450 U.S. at 667, 677 nn. 23 & 24 (Powell, J.).

25. Bradley v. Public Utilities Comm'n, 289 U.S. 92 (1933).

26. The classic books in this area include, F. Frankfurter, The Commerce Clause Under Marshall, Taney

perhaps the best recent summary of the law in this area is by the Supreme Court itself in *Pike v. Bruce Church, Inc.*[27]

Although the criteria for determining the validity of state statutes affecting interstate commerce have been variously stated, the general rule that emerges can be phrased as follows: Where the statute regulates even-handedly to effectuate a legitimate local public interest, and its effects on interstate commerce are only incidental, it will be upheld unless the burden imposed on such commerce is clearly excessive in relation to the putative local benefits. If a legitimate local purpose is found, then the question becomes one of degree. And the extent of the burden that will be tolerated will of course depend on the nature of the local interest involved, and on whether it could be promoted as well with a lesser impact on interstate activities. Occasionally the Court has candidly undertaken a balancing approach in resolving these issues, but more frequently it has spoken in terms of "direct" and "indirect" benefits and burdens.[28]

III. INCOMING COMMERCE

In the modern era the Court has abandoned the so-called "original package" doctrine[1] as the definitive test for assessing state regulatory power over products of extrastate origin. State legislation permeated with indicia of economic protectionism is now subjected to a more critical judicial analysis. The basic rule is that if the statu-

tory purpose or effect is to isolate state producers from competitive interstate commerce commodities, thereby augmenting the economic security of the local market, the parochial legislation is invalid. State restraint of the national market, even under the guise of local health and safety pursuits, is also untenable if a less burdensome, non-discriminatory alternative is available.

The seminal case invoking these theories to invalidate a state regulatory scheme is *Baldwin v. G. A. F. Seelig, Inc.*[2] Justice Cardozo, writing for a unanimous court, rejected the concept that the original package doctrine or any allusion to a direct/indirect burden distinction could be relied upon by the State of New York to restrict the sale of Vermont milk within its borders.

New York, in the *Baldwin* case, had established minimum milk prices to be paid to producers by dealers. For products originating within the state, the Supreme Court had no problem with New York's minimum price laws.[3] But New York milk dealers, in order to avoid paying the artificially high milk prices—made high as a result of the law—would naturally be encouraged to buy their milk out-of-state. Therefore, to keep the system unimpaired by competition from afar, the Act had a provision whereby the protective prices were extended to that part of the supply (about 30%) which came from other states.[4] In other words, a New

---

and Waite (1937); W. D. G. Ribble, State and National Power over Commerce (1937); B. Gavit, The Commerce Clause of the United States Constitution (1932). See also, Dowling, Interstate Commerce and State Power, 27 Va.L.Rev. 1 (1940); Dowling, Interstate Commerce and State Power—Revised Version, 47 Colum.L.Rev. 597 (1947). More modern pieces include Eule, Laying the Dormant Commerce Clause to Rest, 91 Yale L.J. 425 (1982); Maltz, How Much Regulation is Too Much—An Examination of Commerce Clause Jurisprudence, 50 George Wash.L.Rev. 47 (1981).

27.　397 U.S. 137 (1970).

28.　397 U.S. at 142 (case citations within quotation omitted without any special indications).

1.　The doctrine was delineated by Chief Justice Marshall in Brown v. Maryland, 25 U.S. (12 Wheat.) 419 (1827). The doctrine was rejected as to one state's exports to a sister state. Woodruff v. Parham, 75 U.S. (8 Wall.) 123 (1869). In Leisey v. Hardin, 135 U.S. 100 (1890) the Court held that a state could not prevent the

sale within the state of liquor in the original package from another state. Congress enacted legislation rejecting Leisy v. Hardin. See In re Rahrer, 140 U.S. 545 (1891). *Brown* has now been interpreted—in the context of a case dealing with the state's power to tax goods imported from foreign countries—to allow the state to levy nondiscriminatory and neutral taxes on foreign goods; i.e., a tax may be imposed without regard to the origin of the goods, and even if the goods taxed are in their original package. Michelin Tire Corp. v. Wages, 423 U.S. 276 (1976), overruling Low v. Austin, 80 U.S. (13 Wall.) 29 (1872). See generally Chapter 11, section II, A, 3, b.

2.　294 U.S. 511 (1935).

3.　See Nebbia v. New York, 291 U.S. 502 (1934); Hegeman Farm Corp. v. Baldwin, 293 U.S. 163 (1934); cf. Borden's Farm Products Co. v. Baldwin, 293 U.S. 194 (1934), all cited in Baldwin v. G. A. F. Seelig, Inc., 294 U.S. 511, 519 (1935).

4.　294 U.S. 519.

York milk dealer could not sell his milk in that state unless he has paid the milk producer (wherever the latter is located) whatever the dealer, under the state law, would have to pay the New York producer. Seelig bought its milk from a Vermont creamery at less than the New York set price and so the New York Commission refused to license it to do business in New York. The New York procedure in effect constituted a tariff on the out of state milk. Even though the state collected no money, it artificially raised the price of out of state milk so that it could not underprice the local product.

Legitimate state power to regulate commerce for health and safety reasons could not be invoked to exculpate exclusionary state minimum price regulations. Justice Cardozo argued:

New York has no power to project its legislation into Vermont by regulating the price to be paid in that state for milk acquired there. So much is not disputed. New York is equally without power to prohibit the introduction within her territory of milk of wholesome quality acquired in Vermont, whether at high prices or at low ones. This again is not disputed. Accepting those postulates, New York asserts her power to outlaw milk so introduced by prohibiting its sale thereafter if the price that has been paid for it to the farmers of Vermont is less than would be owing in like circumstances to farmers in New York. The importer in that view may keep his milk or drink it, but sell it he may not.

Such a power, if exerted, will set a barrier to traffic between one state and another as effective as if customs duties, equal to the price differential, had been laid upon the thing transported. . . . Nice distinctions have been made at times between direct and indirect burdens. They are irrelevant when the avowed purpose of the obstruction, as well as its necessary tendency, is to suppress or mitigate the consequences of competition between the states. Such an obstruction is direct by the very terms of the hypothesis. We are reminded in the opinion below that a chief occasion of

the commerce clauses was "the mutual jealousies and aggressions of the States, taking form in customs barriers and other economic retaliation." . . . If New York, in order to promote the economic welfare of her farmers, may guard them against competition with the cheaper prices of Vermont, the door has been opened to rivalries and reprisals that were meant to be averted by subjecting commerce between the states to the power of the nation.[5]

The Court also rejected the argument that the purpose of the New York law was to maintain an adequate supply of pure milk, the supply being put in jeopardy when the farmers of the state are unable to earn a living income. The Court correctly realized that such an argument, if accepted, proves too much for it would allow virtually all state trade barriers against other states. "The Constitution was framed under the dominion of a political philosophy less parochial in range. It was framed on the theory that the people of the several states must sink or swim together, and that in the long run prosperity and salvation are in union and not division."[6]

The New York milk regulatory scheme struck down in *Baldwin* was an attempt to aid local milk producers by making more expensive the importation of milk from a sister state. In effect, it was a wealth transfer to local producers directly financed by the out-of-state producers. There was no inner political check working within New York state to assure that the people of New York directly paid for this wealth transfer. Presumably the Court would have upheld the transfer of direct cash payments or tax subsidies to New York milk producers financed by the New York general taxpayer. An inner political check would then be working to assure that the people within the state, who directly paid for the subsidy, can weigh the costs and benefits. But when there is an attempt to shift the direct costs to out-of-state persons this inner political check is not

5. 294 U.S. at 521–22. See also Polar Ice Cream & Creamery Co. v. Andrews, 375 U.S. 361 (1964).

6. 294 U.S. at 523.

working as well and there is a broader role for judicial review.[7]

Baldwin also does not forbid a state from using its tax laws to subject interstate goods sold in its state to the same tax levied on intrastate goods sold in its state, i.e., a "compensatory use" tax. The tax laws in such a case are nondiscriminatorily applied and are not used to compensate for *natural* competitive advantages of another state; rather, unlike the *Baldwin* situation, such a "compensating use" tax does not smother competition but removes an *artificial* competitive disadvantage otherwise imposed by local tax laws on the local product.[8] Thus, the Supreme Court has approved a 2% sales tax on all retail sales within the state and a 2% compensating use tax for the privilege of using in the state an item purchased at retail out-of-state on which a sales or use tax has not previously been paid. Credit for the out-of-state tax was given.[9]

The *Baldwin* Court has fully supported the policy of invalidating "special interest" legislation designed to enhance the economic prosperity of local citizens by hindering the free flow of products in commerce, for, as Justice Frankfurter has stated: "The very purpose of the Commerce Clause was to create an area of free trade among the several States."[10]

To avoid the *Baldwin* problem, some states have sought to draft more complex schemes which have more than a perfunctory reference to local health and safety interests. To deal with these situations the Court has developed a strict, active judicial review to assure that the legitimate safety measures can be accomplished by the means imposing the least restrictive effects on interstate commerce. This principle is well illustrated by the case of *Dean Milk Co. v. City of Madison*.[11] A Madison ordinance made it illegal to sell milk as pasteurized unless it had been processed and bottled at an approved pasteurization plant within a radius of five miles from the central square of Madison. The state court approved the five mile radius on the grounds that it promoted convenient, economical, and efficient plant inspection. The Court was unimpressed that Madison's law also excluded Wisconsin milk from outside the Madison area as well as interstate milk.[12] Similarly the Court did not accept the health rationale for the restrictive measure, for there were "reasonable nondiscriminatory alternatives, adequate to conserve legitimate local interests" that were available.[13] For example, if the city insisted that its own officials inspect distant milk sources, it could do so and charge the actual

---

7. Cf. Rotunda, The Commercial Speech Doctrine in the Supreme Court, 1976 U.Ill.L.Forum 1080, 1098, 1101. See also id. at 1083:

"A broader scope for judicial review should exist in these instances of legislative judgment based on hidden costs than exists when the costs of the legislative decision are obvious. A court decision that requires a legislative body to reveal the true expense of a legislative decision does not infringe on the majority's substantive right to give aid to [milk producers]. Such a mandate only encourages an open decision-making process: a process that facilitates more rational legislative decisions."

It is certainly true, as the economists tell us, that ultimately it will be the New York milk consumer who pays for the aid given to the New York milk producer. This consumer will pay, either in the form of higher milk prices (under the *Baldwin* quasi-tariff scheme) or in the form of higher taxes (to finance the direct cash, or indirect tax subsidies to the local milk producers).

But when the consumer's cost is more directly borne and the actual costs are less hidden, the inner political check is working more effectively.

8. See Brown, The Open Economy: Justice Frankfurter and the Position of the Judiciary, 67 Yale L.J. 219, 234–36 (1957).

9. Henneford v. Silas Mason Co., 300 U.S. 577 (1937). See also generally Barrett, State Taxation of Indirect Commerce—"Direct Burdens," "Multiple Burdens," or What Have You, 4 Vand.L.Rev. 496 (1951); see Chapter 11, section II, E, 2, c, for an analysis of the *Henneford* case.

10. McLeod v. J. E. Dilworth Co., 322 U.S. 327, 330 (1944).

11. 340 U.S. 349 (1951).

12. 340 U.S. at 354 n. 4, citing Brimmer v. Rebman, 138 U.S. 78, 82–83 (1891).

13. 340 U.S. at 354.

and reasonable cost of such inspection to the importing producers and processors.[14]

To permit Madison to adopt a regulation not essential for the protection of local health interests and placing a discriminatory burden on interstate commerce would invite a multiplication of preferential trade areas destructive of the very purpose of the Commerce Clause.[15]

The Court has also looked with suspicion on state reciprocity agreements. For example, in *Great Atlantic & Pacific Tea Co. v. Cottrell*,[16] the challenged Mississippi law admitted interstate milk for sale only if the producing state had agreed to a reciprocal inspection standards agreement. Reaffirming the vitality of the *Baldwin* and *Dean Milk* standard, the Court refused to limit its inquiry because of the state's assertion of its power to regulate for legitimate health and safety reasons. The Mississippi law permitted Louisiana milk to be admitted to Mississippi if Louisiana entered into a reciprocity agreement with Mississippi, even if Louisiana's standards were lower than Mississippi's. "The reciprocity clause thus disserves rather than promotes any higher Mississippi milk quality standards."[17] And if Mississippi is allowed "to insist that a sister State either sign a reciprocal agreement acceptable to Mississippi or else be absolutely foreclosed from exporting its products to Mississippi," such a rule "would plainly 'invite a multiplication of preferential trade areas destructive of the very purpose of the Commerce Clause.'"[18] Although ostensibly Mississippi sought to guarantee safe milk standards, the Court concluded that the substance of the regulatory scheme was contrived to protect the status of Mississippi milk producers in foreign jurisdictions.[19]

Nonetheless, states are not totally barred from restraining incoming interstate commerce when the alleged local benefit outweighs the degree of the state-imposed burden. In *Breard v. Alexandria*[20] the Court, per Justice Reed, upheld, against all constitutional objections, a municipal ordinance forbidding unrequested door-to-door solicitation. The Court stated that the local homeowners right to privacy outweighed the economic burden even though "interstate commerce itself knocks on the local door."[21] Legislation designed to protect the social welfare interests of the community was, thereby, afforded greater deference than local regulatory schemes manifesting an attempt to preserve local prosperity at the expense of nonresidents.[22] Thus, our federalist system recognizes state power to reasonably regulate incoming commerce pursuant to legitimate local health and safety objectives, *but only* to the extent that the nondiscriminatory burden[23] imposed on the national market place does not exceed the putative local benefits.

---

14. 340 U.S. at 354–55, citing Sprout v. City of South Bend, 277 U.S. 163, 169 (1928), and Miller v. Williams, 12 F.Supp. 236, 242, 244 (D.Md.1935).

15. 340 U.S. at 356.

16. 424 U.S. 366 (1976).

17. 424 U.S. at 375.

18. 424 U.S. at 380.

19. Accord, Sporhase v. Nebraska, 102 S.Ct. 3456 (1982) (reciprocity provision of state statute regulating exportation of water is "explicit barrier to commerce"). Cf. Polar Ice Cream & Creamery Co. v. Andrews, 375 U.S. 361 (1964), invalidating a complex Florida scheme favoring local milk distributors; Minnesota v. Barber, 136 U.S. 313 (1890) disallowing a Minnesota law which required that all fresh meat sold in the state must be inspected by a local Minnesota inspector within 24 hours before slaughter.

20. 341 U.S. 622 (1951).

21. 341 U.S. at 636.

22. The Seventh Circuit invoked a similar preferential balancing test in upholding the validity of a local phosphate ban. Procter & Gamble Co. v. City of Chicago, 509 F.2d 69 (7th Cir.), cert. denied 421 U.S. 978 (1975).

23. See, e.g., Exxon Corp. v. Governor of Maryland, 437 U.S. 117 (1978). A Maryland statute provided that a producer or refiner of petroleum products may not operate any retail service station within the state and must extend all "voluntary allowances" uniformly to all service stations it supplies. The Court upheld the constitutionality of the statute and found that it did not discriminate against interstate commerce. The petroleum refiners were all from out of state, since Maryland has no local producers or refiners. These refiners "will no longer enjoy their same status in the Maryland market, in-state independent dealers will have no competitive advantage over out-of-state dealers. The fact that the burden of a state regulation falls on some interstate companies does not, by itself, establish a claim of discrimination against interstate commerce." 437

The emphasis on nondiscrimination is important, because even products which are concededly harmful are still "commerce" and therefore subjected to standard commerce clause analysis. For example, if an article's worth in interstate commerce is "far outweighed" ·by the dangers in its movement—such as those items which spread pestilence—then the state could prohibit its transportation across state lines.[24] In contrast, a state cannot prohibit the out of state importation of solid or liquid wastes in order to extend the life of landfill within the state and protect its environment. Such wastes are in commerce and protected by the commerce clause. And the state could hardly argue that the movement of wastes cannot be said to endanger health and the environment since state law allowed *nonimported* wastes to be transported within the state. Nor can a state distinguish between in state and out of state wastes by allowing the former but not the latter to be disposed of in landfill sites within the state, for a state cannot slow down or prohibit the flow of commerce (in this case, waste products) in order to conserve for those within its borders a scare resource (land fill).[25]

The present state of this area of the law is probably best summarized by former Solicitor General Robert L. Stern:

> In the absence of discrimination, the Court tends to sustain the state action when interference with commerce is clear and the local interest is not very substantial; where there is discrimination, the *Dean* case holds, it must appear that there is no other reasonable method of safeguarding a legitimate local interest. Where a state law has no other purpose than to favor local industry, this balancing of interest approach probably will not be used, inasmuch as the purpose of the state regulation would be illegitimate.[26]

To be distinguished from state power to regulate commerce in general is the state power to regulate commerce over *liquor*, in light of the twenty-first amendment, section two, which provides: "The transportation or importation into any State, Territory, or possession of the United States for delivery or use therein of intoxicating liquors, in violation of the laws thereof, is hereby prohibited." The twenty-first amendment does not repeal the commerce clause as to state regulation of the importation or transportation of liquor, but it certainly affects it, and serves to give the state "wide latitude." [27]

Thus a state may exact a license fee for the privilege of importing into that state li-

---

U.S. at 126 (footnote omitted). Cf. Lewis v. BT Investment Managers, Inc., 447 U.S. 27, 41–43 (1980) (distinguishing *Exxon*, the Court invalidated a state law which discriminated among affected business entities according to the extent of their contacts with the local economy).

24. Philadelphia v. New Jersey, 437 U.S. 617, 622 (1978).

25. Philadelphia v. New Jersey, 437 U.S. 617 (1978). A different case would be presented if a state regulated all waste deposit in land fill areas, even if interstate waste would thereby be affected, since then there is no *discrimination* against the interstate waste. See, e.g., Minnesota v. Clover Leaf Creamery Co., 449 U.S. 457 (1981), on remand 304 N.W.2d 915 (to conserve energy and resources Minnesota may ban retail sale of milk in plastic, nonrefillable containers; the statute does not discriminate against interstate commerce and the incidental burden on interstate commerce is not excessive in relation to the putative local benefits).

26. Stern, The Problems of Yesteryear—Commerce and Due Process, 4 Vand.L.Rev. 446, 458 (1951) (foot-

note omitted), in R. G. McCloskey, ed., Essays in Constitutional Law 166 (1957). See also, Hunt v. Washington State Apple Advertising Comm'n, 432 U.S. 333 (1977) (North Carolina statute held violative of commerce clause by burdening interstate sale of Washington State apples; the state statute required that all apples sold or shipped into the state in closed containers could be marked only with the relevant federal grade or marked "not graded"; this restriction prohibited the display of the more stringent Washington State grade and hence was invalid); Edgar v. MITE Corp., 102 S.Ct. 2629 (1982) (Illinois Business Takeover Law invalid because the substantial burden on interstate commerce outweighs alleged local benefits, and Illinois has no interest in regulating internal affairs of foreign corporations); Warner Bros., Inc. v. Wilkinson, 533 F.Supp. 105, 107 (D. Utah 1981), citing this section of an earlier edition of this treatise.

27. Seagram & Sons, Inc. v. Hostetter, 384 U.S. 35, 42 (1966). See also, Chapter 18, Section XVII, F, 5 ("Obscenity and the Twenty-First Amendment").

quor from another state,[28] although in the absence of the twenty-first amendment the dormant commerce clause would have forbade such an import fee. However a state cannot tax liquor imported into that state from a foreign country, in violation of the export import clause.[29] Nor does the state power over liquor insulate state regulations in this area from the limitations of the fourteenth amendment.[30] Also, notwithstanding the state's power to control whether to permit the importation and sale of liquor and how to set up the structure of the system to distribute liquor, under the commerce clause Congress has the power to prohibit resale price maintenance in violation of the Sherman Act.[31] The Court in each case challenged under the commerce clause must carefully scrutinize the competing state and federal interests.[32]

IV. OUTGOING COMMERCE

Consistent with the rationale prohibiting discriminatory state regulation of incoming commodities, states are not allowed to facilitate local economic advantage by restraining the entry of home products into the national market. State statutes burdening the exportation of local products are treated as the equivalent of embargoes. Although embargoes *per se* are repugnant to the national common market philosophy, the Court has engaged in a balancing approach recognizing that certain forms of embargoes are legitimate when they represent the least burdensome alternative for achieving a necessitated goal. When laws to protect local economic interests operate equally on domestic and foreign consumers alike, they are not considered "embargoes" but only economic assistance of a nondiscriminatory nature.

In *Parker v. Brown* [1] Justice Stone, delivering the opinion of the Court, cited his *DiSanto* dissent in support of the balancing approach as the appropriate means of resolving the competing state and national interests in the regulation of commerce. In *Parker* the Court sustained a California marketing scheme challenged as a violation of both the commerce clause and the Sherman Antitrust Act and held that a State may fix prices without violating either the dormant commerce clause or the federal antitrust laws.[2] California, pursuant to the state's Agricultural Prorate Act, required each raisin producer to deliver over ⅔ of his crop to a marketing control committee which, in effect, engaged in price fixing in order to attempt to eradicate "injurious" price competition, and, thereby, bolster the stability of the raisin market. The effect on

---

28. State Bd. v. Young's Market Co., 299 U.S. 59 (1936). See also, e.g., Mahoney v. Joseph Triner Corp., 304 U.S. 401 (1938) (state law restricting importation of certain types of liquor upheld); Finch & Co. v. McKittrick, 305 U.S. 395 (1939) (Missouri statute prohibiting the importation into that state any liquor manufactured in another state which has laws which discriminate against the importation of liquor manufactured in Missouri upheld).

29. Department of Revenue v. James Beam Co., 377 U.S. 341 (1964).

30. See, e.g., Craig v. Boren, 429 U.S. 190, 204–09 (1976) (equal protection); Wisconsin v. Constantineau, 400 U.S. 433, 436 (1970) (due process). But cf. New York State Liquor Authority v. Bellanca, 472 U.S. 714 (1981) (per curiam). See also, California v. LaRue, 409 U.S. 109 (1972).

31. California Retail Liquor Dealers Ass'n. v. Midal Aluminum, Inc., 445 U.S. 97 (1980).

32. See generally, Note, The Effect of the Twenty-first Amendment on State Authority to Control Intoxicating Liquors, 75 Colum.L.Rev. 1578 (1975).

1. 317 U.S. 341 (1943).

2. The Court also held that there was no anti-trust violation in this instance as obeying state law cannot be construed as a conspiracy. The meaning of this case in the anti-trust field has been limited however. See, e.g., Goldfarb v. Virginia State Bar, 421 U.S. 773 (1975); Cantor v. Detroit Edison Co., 428 U.S. 579 (1976). The holding does not mean that states can grant immunity from the anti-trust laws, but that one obeying a state law cannot be prosecuted under the Sherman Act. Some commentators state that *Parker* should be limited to the situation where the federal government has spoken and the state measure is consistent with federal law. See generally, Verkuil, State Action, Due Process and Antitrust: Reflections on Parker v. Brown, 75 Colum.L.Rev. 328 (1975); Posner, The Proper Relationship Between State Regulation and the Federal Antitrust Laws, 49 N.Y.U.L.Rev. 693 (1974); Slater, Antitrust and Government Action: A Formula for Narrowing Parker v. Brown, 69 Va.L.Rev. 71 (1974).

interstate commerce was undeniable as between 90 and 95 percent of the raisins
grown in California ultimately entered interstate or foreign commerce, but there was
deemed to be no discrimination against interstate commerce so the local interest could be
advanced.

Justice Stone first examined the question
by applying the mechanical test of whether
or not the state regulation was imposed *before* or *after* the articles entered interstate
commerce. Although he began the discussion by asserting that under this approach
the measure was within state power, since
the regulation did in fact occur *before* interstate commerce operation, he concluded that
courts should not be bound by such mechanical formulations. Citing *DiSanto*, Stone advocated that the more adequate test was
whether or not the local interests to be
served outweighed the competing national
interests. Noting the significance of the raisin industry in the California economy, and
the fact that almost all of this nation's raisins are produced within that one state, the
Court concluded that, on balance, the regulation should be sustained as a legitimate attempt by a state to deal with a peculiarly local problem which Congress might never
specifically address. Therefore, the state
could legitimately fix the prices of goods
within the state even though those commodities would eventually become interstate commerce commodities.[3] Moreover, the Court
found that Congress had recognized the distressed conditions of the agricultural production of the United States and the California program did not interfere with this
Congressional policy.[4]

State regulation restricting outgoing commerce was also validated when the Supreme
Court approved a Pennsylvania minimum
price law affecting milk shipped in interstate
commerce in *Milk Control Board v. Eisenberg Farm Products.*[5] The state law requir-

ing the licensing of milk dealers and their
payment of a minimum price to producers in
the state was challenged as an unconstitutional obstruction of interstate commerce to
the extent it was applied to a New York purchaser procuring the milk for resale outside
of Pennsylvania. *Eisenberg* was the converse of *Baldwin v. G. A. F. Seelig Inc.*[6]
where the State had tried to affect the price
to be paid for milk in a sister state. The
Court had struck down the *Baldwin* statute
but it upheld the *Eisenberg* regulatory
scheme.

The Court noted several important factors
distinguishing this regulation from an embargo. First, the vast majority of the milk
produced by local farmers was consumed
within the state. Thus local consumers
were equally burdened by the state law and
there was therefore some operation of an inner political check. Secondly, the sale itself
took place in Pennsylvania, and for the
Court to allow dealers to ignore the law if
any of their milk was subject to interstate
commerce operation would have nullified the
efficacy of the state's entire price support
program. These two reasons are less than
persuasive: that the sale took place within
the State does not prevent regulation of the
sale from affecting interstate commerce;
moreover, to say that upholding the entire
regulatory scheme, including the effect on
interstate commerce, is essential to the effectiveness of the state scheme is a boot-
strap argument: if the State does not have
the power to deal with a problem, the fact
that it would like the power to deal with the
problem does not grant the power.

More likely *Eisenberg* is justified, if at all,
on the theory that since approximately 90%
of the milk was only shipped within the
state,[7] the problem was essentially local and
the Court was interpreting Congressional silence under the dormant commerce clause to
allow the local solution to what was per-

3. Cf. Lemke v. Farmers Grain Co., 258 U.S. 50
(1922) and Shafer v. Farmers Grain Co., 268 U.S. 189
(1925), both distinguished in Parker v. Brown, 317 U.S.
at 361.

4. 317 U.S. at 367–68.

5. 306 U.S. 346 (1939).

6. 294 U.S. 511 (1935), discussed above in Section
III.

7. 306 U.S. at 350.

ceived as a local problem. Any local police power regulation which increases the cost of goods or services that might go into commerce may be said to burden commerce. However, where there is no discrimination and the effect on interstate commerce does not impair national interests, there is no basis to strike the law. The state in this case had adopted a nondiscriminatory least burdensome alternative for dealing with an essentially local concern.

The significance of discriminatory impact and therefore the lack of an inner political safeguard was underscored by the Court's subsequent decision in *H. P. Hood and Sons v. DuMond*.[8] There, New York refused to grant a Massachusetts milk distributor a license to operate a third milk receiving station in the state on the grounds that the additional diversion of local milk to Massachusetts would impair the supply for the New York market. In a 5–4 decision the narrowly divided court, per Justice Jackson, rejected the existence of state power to develop such a discriminatory plan:

> May Michigan provide that automobiles cannot be taken out of that State until local dealers' demands are fully met? Would she not have every argument in the favor of such a statute that can be offered in support of New York's limiting sales of milk for out-of-state shipment to protect the economic interests of her competing dealers and local consumers?[9]

Justice Black, dissenting, advocated that the majority had abandoned the *Cooley* approach and that the decision, therefore, would ultimately result in the circumscription of a wide range of state regulation. Contemporaneous commentators also criticized the decision as an unwarranted departure from the Court's earlier decisions in *Parker* and *Eisenberg*.

A more accurate evaluation of the opinion reveals that *Hood* is not a departure from the precedent enunciated in those decisions. Unlike those earlier regulatory measures sustained by the Court, in *Hood* the New York ad hoc licensing scheme discriminated against interstate commerce because only a non-resident was burdened by the state's action. In *Eisenberg* the state statute fixing a minimum price applied equally to in-state and out-of-state milk purchasers. But here there was a classic trade barrier to the flow of goods to out of state buyers. Moreover, the nature of that discrimination meant that the persons burdened by such state action were individuals who had no representation in the state political process effecting them; it was this type of trade barrier which the commerce clause was drafted to eliminate. Under these circumstances, the Court correctly and consistently invoked the national market rule prohibiting such a home embargo.

In spite of the continued usage of verbal touchstones such as "incidental" and "indirect", the Court seems to have adopted Stone's balancing formulation. Each case turns upon a weighing of all the relevant circumstances rather than the application of a mechanical test such as does the state regulation effect the product before or after interstate commere operation occurs. The weight afforded the ostensible local interests varies according to their nature; i.e., genuine health and safety concerns are granted greater difference than regulations aimed at preserving a favored position for local industry. While it is not easy to make all of these cases consistent, several illustrations may prove helpful.

The states have not been allowed to unreasonably burden the exportation of local products whether their purpose is to enhance the reputation of local products,[10] retain domes-

---

8. 336 U.S. 525 (1949).

9. 336 U.S. at 539. Cf. Commonwealth Edison Co. v. Montana, 453 U.S. 609, 618 (1981) where the Court upheld a nondiscriminatory severance tax on coal mined in Montana; although 90% of Montana coal is shipped to other states, "the Montana tax is computed at the same rate regardless of the final destination of the coal, and there is no suggestion here that the tax is administered in a manner that departs from this even-handed formula.").

10. The most recent example of the viability of Stone's balancing doctrine as applied to outgoing com-

tic resources for local consumption,[11] insure local employment,[12] or open a particular market only to their own residents.[13]

In very early decisions, the Court had upheld regulation of the consumption of a state's natural resources, such as water,[14] game,[15] but not natural gas.[16] Under the modern view of the dormant commerce clause these water and game decisions allowing embargoes no longer represent good law.

The 1979 overruling of *Geer v. Connecticut*,[17] an 1896 case, illustrates the change in the law. In *Geer*, the Supreme Court had found no violation of the commerce clause in a state statute which had forbidden the transportation outside of the state of game

birds that had been lawfully killed within the state.

In 1979 the Supreme Court, in *Hughes v. Oklahoma*,[18] explicitly overruled *Geer* and rejected its legal fiction that interstate commerce is not involved because the state "owns" all the wild animals within the state. *Hughes* invalidated an Oklahoma statute which prohibited the transporting or shipping outside of the state for sale natural minnows seined or procured within the state. The statute on its face discriminated against interstate commerce of natural minnows by overtly blocking such transportation. In another case the Court concluded that water is an article of commerce.[19] While the state can conserve natural resources it must do so in a nondiscriminatory fashion that recog-

merce is Pike v. Bruce Church, Inc., 397 U.S. 137 (1970). In a unanimous opinion the Court invalidated an Arizona law requiring that cantaloupes be packed within the state; this law was designed to prevent deceptive packaging, and, it was argued, to ensure that the products would enter the national market bearing an Arizona label. The state stipulated that its primary purpose was to enhance its reputation for the production of superior produce by prohibiting deceptive packaging. "[T]he State's tenuous interest in having the company's cantaloupes identified as originating in Arizona cannot constitutionally justify the requirement that the company build and operate an unneeded $200,000 packing plant in the State." 397 U.S. at 145. Cf. Sligh v. Kirkwood, 237 U.S. 52 (1915) (Court upholds Florida statute which prohibits the delivery for shipment of citrus fruits immature or otherwise unfit for consumption as not unconstitutional under the dormant commerce clause).

11. H. P. Hood & Sons v. Du Mond, 336 U.S. 525 (1949).

12. Foster-Fountain Packing Co. v. Haydel, 278 U.S. 1 (1928) (restrictions on shipping shrimp out of state struck down); Pike v. Bruce Church, Inc., 397 U.S. 137 (1970).

13. Toomer v. Witsell, 334 U.S. 385 (1948) (discriminatory license fee on nonresident shrimp travelers struck down as violation of Article IV privileges and immunities clause). See Chapter 10, section II, C.

14. Hudson County Water Co. v. McCarter, 209 U.S. 349 (1908) (prohibition of transportation of water out of state upheld).

15. Geer v. Connecticut, 161 U.S. 519 (1896) (prohibition against shipping game birds out of state upheld).

16. Oklahoma v. Kansas Gas Co., 221 U.S. 229 (1911) and Pennsylvania v. West Virginia, 262 U.S. 553 (1923). Cf., Cities Services Gas Co. v. Peerless Oil & Gas Co., 340 U.S. 179 (1950).

17. 161 U.S. 519 (1896).

18. 441 U.S. 322 (1979). Cf. Baldwin v. Montana Fish and Game Comm'n, 436 U.S. 371, 385–86 (1978) ("States may not compel the confinement of the benefits of their resources, even their wildlife, to their own people whenever such hoarding and confinement impedes interstate commerce."). *Baldwin* was brought not under the commerce clause but under the privileges and immunities clause of Article IV, § 2 and the equal protection clause of the fourteenth amendment; that case rejected challenges to the differences in the cost (as between state residents and nonresidents) of the state hunting license fees; the licenses were needed to hunt Elk, a recreational sport.

19. Sporhase v. Nebraska, 102 S.Ct. 3456 (1982). Nebraska law provided that if anyone intends to withdraw ground water from a well or pit within that state and transport it for use in an adjoining state he must secure a permit, which will only be issued if (1) the withdrawal of the ground water is reasonable; (2) not contrary to conservation; (3) is not otherwise detrimental to the public welfare; and (4) "if the state in which the water is to be used grants reciprocal rights to withdraw ground water from that state for use in the State of Nebraska."

The Court found that the first three conditions did not "indicate that they impermissibly burden interstate commerce" because the state regulates water in time of shortage to protect the health of its citizens, not just the health of the economy; the legal expectation that in some cases a State may restrict water within its borders has been fostered by the Supreme Court's equitable apportionment decrees and interstate compacts; and the state's claim of public ownership of ground water (the surface owner in Nebraska has no unlimited rights in ground water) "may support a limited preference for its own citizens in the utilization of the resource." But the reciprocity requirement of the statute is "an explicit barrier to commerce" among the states and Nebraska did not meet the initial burden of showing a "close fit" between this reciprocity provision and the asserted local purpose of the statute. The reci-

nizes that the relevant economic unit is the nation.[20] Thus a state cannot prohibit the exportation out of state of hydroelectric power produced by private facilities within the state, nor can it reserve for its own citizens the "economic benefit" of that hydroelectric energy.[21]

Finally it should be noted that when the state itself enters the market as a purchaser or seller of interstate commerce, nothing in the dormant commerce clause forbids it from restricting its own purchases or limiting its sales to its own citizens.[22] For example, a state may follow a policy of confining the sale of cement produced at a *state owned* cement plant solely to state residents.[23] But a state may not compel privately owned cement plants within the state to sell their products solely to state residents.[24] When a state actually owns resources and

favors its own citizens it is not violating the commerce clause; it is simply engaging in a form of welfare.[25]

In summary, if the local measure, even under the guise of a more legitimate goal, attempts to afford residents an economic advantage at the expense of a free-flowing national market, the countervailing national interest will override. But even local economic measures are more likely to be upheld if there is no discriminatory purpose or effect. The modern standard incorporating Stone's *DiSanto* dissent,[26] Dowling's theory,[27] and the Court's subsequent decisions was summarized by Justice Stewart in *Pike v. Bruce Church, Inc.*[28]

Where the state regulates even handedly to effectuate a legitimate local public interest, and its effects on interstate commerce are only incidental, it will be upheld unless

---

procity portion of the statute "does not survive the 'strictest scrutiny' reserved for facially discriminatory legislation" and hence violates the Commerce Clause.

See also, City of Altus v. Carr, 255 F.Supp. 828 (W.D. Tex.), aff'd mem. 385 U.S. 35 (1966).

20. See Hicklin v. Orbeck, 437 U.S. 518, 533 (1978), stating that "the Commerce Clause circumscribes a State's ability to prefer its own citizens in the utilization of natural resources found within its borders, but destined for interstate commerce." *Hicklin* voided Alaska's hiring preferences related to its oil and gas resources.

Contrast, White v. Massachusetts Council of Construction Employers Inc., 103 S.Ct. 1042 (1983), holding that there is no commerce clause violation for the mayor of Boston to require that all construction projects funded in whole or in part by city funds, or funds which the city had the authority to administer, should be performed by a work force consisting of at least half bona fide Boston residents, because the city is a market participant. There are limits on a state or local government's ability to reach beyond the immediate parties with which the government transacts business, but these limits have not been breached here. "[T]he Commerce Clause does not require the city to stop at the boundary of formal privity of contract. In this case, the mayor's executive order covers a discrete, identifiable class of economic activity in which the city is a major participant. Everyone affected by the order is, in a substantial if informal sense, 'working for the city.' . . ." 103 S.Ct. at 1046 n. 7.

21. New England Power Co. v. New Hampshire, 455 U.S. 331 (1982).

22. Hughes v. Alexandria Scrap Corp., 426 U.S. 794, 810 (1976) (5 to 4 decision holding that state bounty for scrap automobiles can favor scrap processors with an in-state plant).

See McCready v. Virginia, 94 U.S. (4 Otto) 391, 395–96 (1877):

"If Virginia had by law provided for the sale of its once vast public domain, and division of the proceeds among its own people, no one, we venture to say, would contend that the citizens of other States had a constitutional right to the enjoyment of this privilege of Virginia citizenship. Neither if, instead of selling, the State had appropriated the same property to be used as a common by its people for the purposes of agriculture, could the citizens of other States avail themselves of such a privilege."

23. Reeves v. Stake, 447 U.S. 429 (1980). See generally Anson & Schenkkan, Federalism, the Dormant Commerce Clause, and State-Owned Resources, 59 Tex. L.Rev. 71 (1980).

24. See New England Power Co. v. New Hampshire, 455 U.S. 331 (1982), holding that a state cannot prohibit a private power company from exporting out of state locally generated hydroelectric power. The Court found unpersuasive the argument that the state "owned" the Connecticut River which was used to generate the power. "This product is manufactured by a private corporation using privately-owned facilities." 455 U.S. at 339 n. 6.

25. Cf. McCarthy v. Philadelphia Civil Service Comm'n, 424 U.S. 645 (1976) (residence within a specific area can be a requirement of *public* employment); White v. Massachusetts Council of Construction Employers, Inc., 103 S.Ct. 1042 (1983), n. 20, supra.

26. Di Santo v. Pennsylvania, 273 U.S. 34, 44 (1927).

27. Dowling, Interstate Commerce and State Power, 27 Va.L.Rev. 1 (1940).

28. 397 U.S. 137 (1970).

the burden imposed on such commerce is clearly excessive in relation to the putative local benefits. If a legitimate local purpose is found, then the question becomes one of degree. And the extent of the burden that will be tolerated will of course depend on the nature of the local interest involved, and on whether it could be promoted as well with a lesser impact with interstate activities.[29]

V. PERSONAL MOBILITY

By enlarging the scope of the judicial definition of commerce to include the movement of persons, the commerce clause has been one of several constitutional provisions invoked to challenge state regulations impairing the free mobility of citizens. In the early case of *Crandall v. Nevada*[1] the Court struck down a state law imposing a capitation tax of one dollar upon "every person leaving the state by any railroad, stage coach, or other vehicle engaged or employed in the business of transporting passengers for hire."[2] Justice Miller discussed the applicability of the commerce clause to the resolution of the question, but then held that it was unnecessary to resolve the issue on that ground as the right of the citizenry to enjoy unrestricted travel is inherent in the very fiber of a federal form of government. The federal government, stated Miller, depends upon its ability to call its citizens to any government outpost or office to aid or serve in its multitudinous functions.[3] Concurrently, a citizen also possesses a correlative right to come to the seat of government to assert any claim or to transact any business, "and this right is in its nature independent of the will of any State over whose soil he must pass in the exercise of it."[4]

Justice Clifford agreed with the result, but dissented on the grounds that the Nevada Act should have been negated as inconsistent with Congressional power under the commerce clause. His reasoning was adopted by a later Court in annulling a California law making it a misdemeanor for any person knowingly to bring a non-resident indigent into the state. In *Edwards v. California*[5] the Court held that the state's attempt to bar the entry of indigent citizens was analogous to the economic barrier burdening the importation of milk products struck down in *Baldwin v. G. A. F. Seelig.*[6] Justice Byrnes' opinion quoted the national common market theory advanced by Cardozo in *Baldwin* as support for the assertion that just as a state cannot shut its gates to the influx of competitive commodities, it also is prohibited from thwarting the influx of indigents. In order to maintain the existence of a national entity, the guarantee of unrestricted personal mobility must be equivalent, if not superior to, the guarantee afforded commercial products. The majority rejected the contention that such state legislation could be justified as a valid exercise of the police power noting that the statute's sole purpose was to burden interstate commerce by impeding the movement of people across state lines. The absence of an inner political check was noted as an additional weakness inherent in the California statute; i.e., those persons burdened by the state regulation, non-resident indigents, had no voice in the political process responsible for the enactment of the legislation.

Concurring separately, Justice Douglas urged that ultimately the right of personal mobility could be diluted by relying on the

---

29. 397 U.S. at 142 (case citation within quotation omitted without indication).

1. 73 U.S. (6 Wall.) 35 (1867). In Shapiro v. Thompson, 394 U.S. 618, 630 and n. 8 (1969), the Court noted it had "no occasion to ascribe the source of this right to travel interstate to a particular constitutional provision" but that it has been grounded on the commerce clause; the privileges and immunities clause of Art. IV; § 2, cl. 1, the privileges or immunities clause of the fourteenth amendment; and the due process clause of the fifth amendment.

2. 73 U.S. (6 Wall.) at 36.

3. Justice Miller noted, for example, that if such a tax had existed in Tennessee during the Civil War, the federal Treasury would have been depleted by the prohibitive cost of transporting the army through the state.

4. 73 U.S. (6 Wall.) at 44.

5. 314 U.S. 160 (1941).

6. 294 U.S. 511 (1935).

commerce clause for its efficacy. Douglas, joined by Murphy and Black, reiterated Miller's statement in the *Crandall* decision recognizing that the right of persons to move from state to state is a fundamental right implicit in national citizenship. As such it is incorporated in the privileges or immunities clause of the fourteenth amendment.[7] Moreover, akin to the right to privacy, the right to travel is one of those penumbral rights emanating from the body of the Constitution itself and inuring to the benefit of all citizens prior to and independent of the existence of the fourteenth amendment.

Subsequent personal mobility decisions have incorporated both the majority's reluctance to enlarge the scope of the privileges and immunities doctrine and the concern expressed by Justice Douglas of relegating the protection of the right to travel to the commerce clause provision. Consequently equal protection has increasingly been invoked as a preferential ground for challenging state legislation which impinges the right to travel.[8]

In *Evansville-Vandenburgh Airport Authority District v. Delta Airlines*[9] the Court sustained, inter alia, an Indiana law imposing a tax of one dollar on all commercial airline passengers. Although Justice Douglas argued in dissent that to sustain these laws required overruling *Crandall*, the majority specifically distinguished these contemporary charges as constituting permissible reimbursement to the state for the cost of providing a public facility which in fact aids and advances transportation. Justice Brennan's opinion explained that the Nevada tax was imposed on persons traveling via privately owned facilities, such as the railroads, and therefore, was not analogous to a state-imposed charge limited to travelers benefiting from facilities provided for their use at state expense. Comparing the airport tax to highway tolls, the Court held that "a charge designed only to make the user of state-provided facilities pay a reasonable charge to help defray the costs of their construction and maintenance may constitutionally be imposed on interstate and domestic users alike."[10]

Thus, the Court appears to be saying that a tax imposed on those benefiting from public transportation facilities will not be interpreted as an impermissible burden on interstate commerce although an exit tax unrelated to a state-incurred expense is invalid. it should also be noted that the one dollar tax in the *Delta Airlines* case is fairly nominal. If the tax were more substantial in amount it should be struck because, unlike highway tolls and other actual costs of travelling, such a head tax is no way proportionate to the resources used in travel but really is a tax on exiting, of the kind struck down in *Crandall*.

The privileges and immunities clause of Article IV, section 2, referring to the privileges of state citizenship, would also appear to provide an appropriate basis for voiding restrictive state regulations. Historically, however, the Court has resisted acknowledging the provision as a broad source of individual rights.[11] It has been interpreted narrowly as a prohibition of local legislation which discriminates against non-residents. Although rarely invoked by contemporary Courts, the clause was relied upon to invali-

---

7. Justice Jackson, also concurring separately, preferred basing the decision on the privileges or immunities clause of the fourteenth amendment. He reminded the majority that the right to travel is not absolute; states may legitimately restrict the movement of fugitives from justice or carriers of contagious disease for example. The California statute, however, erred, in his opinion, by enlisting property status as the criterion for determining the right to travel.

8. See Equal Protection, Chapter 16, section X, discussing Shapiro v. Thompson, 394 U.S. 618 (1969) and related cases.

9. 405 U.S. 707 (1972).

10. 405 U.S. at 714. Subsequent to the *Evansville-Vanderburgh* decision, Congress enacted legislation to prohibit states and political subdivisions from imposing airport head taxes. 49 U.S.C.A. § 1513.

11. However, in Corfield v. Coryell, 6 Fed.Cas. 546 No. 3,230 (C.C.D.Pa., 1823), the right to travel under Art. IV privileges and immunities clause was acknowledged in dictum. See Chapter 10, section II, C.

date a discriminatory licensing fee in *Toomer v. Witsell.*[12]

South Carolina in that case had imposed a $2500 licensing fee on out-of-state shrimpers as contrasted with a $25 charge for residents. Ostensibly, the prohibitive charge was necessary to discourage excessive trawling, and thereby enhance the preservation of the state's shrimp supply. Although the Court recognized the goal as a legitimate state purpose, it rejected the means as an unreasonable remedy in violation of the privileges and immunities clause. The South Carolina restriction was directed only at non-residents. Because trawlers follow migrating shrimp, and marginal sea fishing occurs off the coast of several Southern states, the statute inevitably invited retaliatory measures by neighboring jurisdictions. This was the exact situation which the framers of the Constitution intended the privileges and immunities clause to prevent. *Toomer* and the Article IV privileges and immunities clause are discussed more thoroughly below.[13]

12. 334 U.S. 385 (1948).

13. See Chapter 10, section II, C; and Chapter 11, section III, B, 2.

CHAPTER TEN

FEDERAL REGULATION AND STATE AUTHORITY

I. FEDERAL PREEMPTION

A. Introduction

When Congress exercises a granted power, concurrent conflicting state legislation may be challenged via the Preemption Doctrine. The supremacy clause [1] mandates that federal law overrides, i.e., preempts, any state regulation where there is an actual conflict between the two sets of legislation such that both cannot stand, for example, if federal law forbids an act which state legislation requires. Moreover, where Congress acts pursuant to a plenary power, it may specifically prohibit parallel state legislation, [2] i.e., occupy or preempt, the field. Unfortunately, preemption questions seldom arise under such clear cut circumstances.

In recent years Congress has enacted legislation touching more and more areas traditionally subjected to state regulation. Often, state statutory schemes predated Congressional action. In initiating a new regulatory scheme, Congress seldom articulates a specific intent to preempt an entire field of regulation. Indeed, it is common for Congress to include a typical "savings clause" explicitly legitimizing concomitant state regulation. [3] Nonetheless, the judicial branch has shouldered the responsibility for discovering congressional intent and, if necessary, invalidating state laws which are superseded because they "impair federal superintendence of the field" and impermissi-

---

1. U.S. Const. art. VI, cl. 2.

2. Section 408 of Title IV of the Wholesome Meat Act, 21 U.S.C.A. § 678 provides "Marking, labeling, packaging, or ingredient requirements in addition to, or different than, those made under this chapter may not be imposed by any state . . . ."

3. Securities Exchange Act of 1934, 15 U.S.C.A. § 78bb(a) instructs:

" . . . Nothing in this chapter shall affect the jurisdiction of the securities commissioner (or any agency or officer performing like functions) of any State over any security or any person insofar as it does not conflict with the provisions of this chapter or the rules and regulations thereunder."

bly interfere with the effectuation of Congressional objectives.[4] Congress of course can always reverse such decisions by making clear its intent not to preempt the field.

The Court formulated analytical standards for preemption decisions in the early leading cases of *Hines v. Davidowitz*,[5] *Rice v. Santa Fe Elevator Corp.*,[6] and *Pennsylvania v. Nelson*,[7] discussed below. While the touchstones invoked by the Court can be delineated succinctly, there is no simplistic constitutional standard for defining preemption parameters.[8] The difficulty of uniform or generalized analysis of this doctrine arises because of the diversity and complexity of preemption problems.

Preemption decisions pervade the entire range of federal regulation. Before a judicial determination occurs, therefore, the Court must consider the federal law and its operation compared with the state statute and its operation. Then, the decision is based upon the specifics of the relationship between the relevant statutory provisions within the preemption framework. Of necessity the nature of the problem of discovering congressional intent has resulted in judicial ad hoc balancing. Therefore, while the significant criteria may be articulated, here, even more than in other areas, it is difficult to apply the rationale underlying a decision in one field to the problem in another context.[9] Despite the diversity of preemption problems, the underlying constitutional principles are designed with a common end in view: to avoid conflicting regulation of conduct by various official bodies which might have some authority over the subject

matter.[10] Where there are no indicia of congressional intent the Court may have to balance the state and federal interests, to achieve this end.

B. The Traditional Tests

In *Hines v. Davidowitz*.[11] the Court held that the Federal Alien Registration Act of 1940 precluded enforcement of Pennsylvania's Alien Registration Act of 1939. Noting the supremacy of national power in the general field of foreign policy, and the sensitivity of the relationship between the regulation of aliens and the conduct of foreign affairs, the Court concluded that Congressional enactment of uniform national immigration laws "occupied" the field so as to preempt state regulation. Justice Black, speaking for the majority, acknowledged that no rigid verbal formulae are a fortiori determinative of displacement of concurrent state regulation. The test is whether under the circumstances of a particular case the state law "stands as an obstacle to the accomplishment and execution of the full purposes and objectives of Congress."[12]

In the following decade the Court elaborated upon the *Hines* rationale in *Pennsylvania v. Nelson*.[13] Chief Justice Warren enunciated a three-pronged inquiry to ascertain preemption parameters: 1. pervasiveness of the federal regulatory scheme; 2. federal occupation of the field as necessitated by the need for national uniformity; 3. danger of conflict between state laws and the administration of the federal program.[14]

Within this framework the Supreme Court affirmed the Pennsylvania Supreme Court's

---

4. Hines v. Davidowitz, 312 U.S. 52 (1941). Partee v. San Diego Chargers Football Co., 128 Cal.App.3d 501, 180 Cal.Rptr. 416, 419 n.3 (4th Dist. Ct.App.1982) (Cologne, J.), citing an earlier edition of this treatise.

5. 312 U.S. 52 (1941).

6. 331 U.S. 218 (1947).

7. 350 U.S. 497 (1956).

8. Justice Black cautioned in *Hines*: "But none of these expressions provides an infallible constitutional test or an exclusive constitutional yardstick. In the final analysis, there can be no one crystal clear distinctly marked formula." 312 U.S. at 67.

9. Hirsh, Toward a New View of Federal Preemption, 1972 U.Ill.L.F. 515. See, also, Note, Preemption as a Preferential Ground: A New Canon of Construction, 12 Stan.L.Rev. 208 (1959).

10. Amalgamated Association of Street, Electric Ry. & Motor Coach Employees v. Lockridge, 403 U.S. 274 (1971).

11. 312 U.S. 52 (1941). Cf. DeCanas v. Bica, 424 U.S. 351 (1976).

12. 312 U.S. at 67.

13. 350 U.S. 497 (1956).

14. 350 U.S. at 502–505.

decision that federal anti-communist legislation superseded the state's Sedition Act. The Court stressed that the need for national predominance mandated the conclusion that Congress intended to occupy the field. Under this rubric, the state statute proscribing seditious acts against the federal government must succumb to federal regulation of seditious conduct.

Thus, the Supreme Court embarked upon a case-by-case approach, examining state regulatory schemes under established principles of federal preemption. The progeny of *Hines* and *Nelson* have continually narrowed the scope of judicial inquiry to a determination of whether, under the particular facts of the case, the existence of the state regulatory scheme is facilitative or detrimental to the purposes and objectives of the federal statute.

In making this judicial assessment, the balancing of interests is similar to the Court's approach in ascertaining unconstitutional burdens on interstate commerce. Greater deference has been afforded regulation which is traditionally parochial, i.e. health and safety measures. Again, it must be emphasized that each case turns on its own facts. Thus, while local government may not regulate aviation converse to the national scheme to comport with local preferences,[15] federally licensed seagoing vessels may, nonetheless, be compelled to meet local pollution standards.[16] Similarly, Georgia law superseding federal labeling of tobacco was invalidated,[17] while California's imposition of higher maturity standards for federally approved interstate commerce avocados was upheld.[18] States may not enact food labeling requirements which do not permit "reasonable variations" when the federal law allows such reasonable variations in accuracy due to moisture loss during distribution because the state law conflicts with the goal of the federal law to facilitate value comparisons.[19] The National Labor Relations Act does not preempt a state tort action for intentional infliction of emotional distress brought by a union member against the union and union official if the state tort is either unrelated to employment discrimination or a function of the particularly abusive manner in which the employment discrimination is accomplished; the tort may not be a function of the actual or threatened employment discrimination itself.[20]

C. Comparison of Commerce Power Cases

The limited nature of preemption decisions to the specifics of the relevant statutory provisions occurs even within the same statutory scheme so as to produce different results. In *Maurer v. Hamilton*[21] a Pennsylvania statute prohibiting the carrying of cars over truck cabs was challenged as conflicting with the Interstate Commerce Commission's national regulation of the field under the Motor Carrier Act of 1935. The Court, per Justice Stone, sustained the Pennsylvania statute as a weight and height regulation not barred because of the Interstate Commerce Commission's authority to issue safety regulations. The Court acknowledged deference to state legislation where public safety and health are involved.

Without overruling *Maurer*, Justice Black's opinion for the Court in *Castle v. Hayes Freight Lines*[22] in the following decade struck down an Illinois law suspending

---

15. Burbank v. Lockheed Air Terminal, Inc., 411 U.S. 624 (1973).

16. Huron Portland Cement Co. v. Detroit, 362 U.S. 440 (1960).

17. Campbell v. Hussey, 368 U.S. 297 (1961).

18. Florida Lime & Avocado Growers Inc. v. Paul, 373 U.S. 132 (1963).

19. Jones v. Rath Packing Co., 430 U.S. 519 (1977).

20. Farmer v. United Brotherhood of Carpenters & Joiners of America, Local 25, 430 U.S. 290 (1977) (Court

notes that inflexible application of rule of preemption in NLRA cases when state purports to regulate activities protected by section 7 of NLRA or unfair labor practices under section 8 of NLRA is to be avoided, especially where the state has a substantial interest at stake and that interest does not threaten undue interference with the federal regulatory scheme).

21. 309 U.S. 598 (1940).

22. 348 U.S. 61 (1954).

an interstate carrier's right to use Illinois highways for repeated violations of Illinois truck weight limits. The Court purportedly distinguished *Maurer* on the basis that the ICC had exclusive power to regulate *which* motor carriers could operate in interstate commerce. Deferring to the Savings Clause provision in the federal act, the Court concluded that this form of state regulation, unlike the situation in *Maurer*, was not within the powers reserved to the states in the Congressional Act.

D. Modern Developments

In recent decisions the Supreme Court has refused either to presume or infer intent.[23] The Court requires that Congress "manifest its intention clearly. . . . "[24] However, Congress need not manifest its intention by explicitly providing that the federal statute preempts the state law. Rather the Court seeks to find the intent of Congress. If this intent is not clear from the language of the statute—that is, if Congress did not explicitly provide that federal law does, or does not, preempt state law—, then Congress' intention may be clear from the pervasiveness of the federal scheme,[25] the need for uniformity,[26] or the danger of conflict between the enforcement of state laws and the administration of federal programs.[27] But absent persuasive reasons evidencing Congressional intent favoring preemption, the Court will not presume the invalidity of state regulations.[28]

An illustrative case is *New York State Dept. of Social Services v. Dublino*.[29] There the Court sustained New York Work Rules which conditioned receipt of federal A.F.D.C. assistance upon an individual's fulfillment of an additional state requirement. In order to be eligible for federal assistance, the New York statute stipulated that individuals must accept employment. Rejecting

---

23. Goldstein v. California, 412 U.S. 546 (1973); New York State Dept. of Social Services v. Dublino, 413 U.S. 405 (1973). See also, Bryant Radio Supply, Inc. v. Slane, 507 F.Supp. 1325, 1327 n.2 (W.D.Va.1981) (Turk, D.J.), citing an earlier edition of this treatise.

24. New York State Dept. of Social Services v. Dublino, 413 U.S. 405, 413 (1973), quoting Schwartz v. Texas, 344 U.S. 199, 202–203 (1952). See also Exxon Corp. v. Governor of Maryland, 437 U.S. 117, 132 (1978) ("This Court is generally reluctant to infer preemption . . . ."); Hisquierdo v. Hisquierdo, 439 U.S. 572, 581 (1979) (the Court will not find that a state law dealing with family and family property law is preempted unless the state law does "major damage" to "clear and substantial" federal interests; "mere conflict" in the words of the two statutes does not imply federal preemption).

25. E.g., White Mountain Apache Tribe v. Bracker, 448 U.S. 136 (1980) (state taxes as applied to commerce by non-Indians on an Indian reservation preempted by pervasive federal regulation); Local 926, Internat'l Union of Operating Engineers, AFL–CIO v. Jones, 103 S.Ct. 1453 (1983) (state tort action preempted by N.L.R.B.).

26. E.g., Jones v. Rath Packing Co., 430 U.S. 519 (1977) (state may not enact food labeling requirements which do not permit "reasonable weight variations" when the federal law allows such reasonable variations in accuracy due to moisture loss during distribution because the state law conflicts with the goal of the federal law to facilitate value comparisons).

27. E.g., Pennsylvania v. Nelson, 350 U.S. 497, 505–510 (1956) (enforcement of state sedition acts presents serious danger of conflict with administration of the federal program because sporadic local prosecutions—or even prosecutions by private individuals, as allowed by the Pennsylvania law—may obstruct federal undercover operations and enforcement plans).

28. E.g. Malone v. White Motor Corp., 435 U.S. 497 (1978) (state statute relating to pensions not preempted by older federal law even though a new federal statute expressly provided for preemption); Sears, Roebuck & Co. v. San Diego County District Council, 436 U.S. 180 (1978) (no preemption by National Labor Relations Act of state court power to enjoin—as violation of state trespass laws—labor picketing which is arguably but not definitely prohibited or protected by federal law); Philadelphia v. New Jersey, 437 U.S. at 621 n.4 (1978) (no "clear and manifest purpose of Congress" to preempt entire field of interstate waste management on transportation); White Mountain Apache Tribe v. Bracker, 448 U.S. 136 (1980) (state taxes as applied to commerce by non-Indians on an Indian reservation preempted by pervasive federal regulation); Chicago & North Western Transp. Co. v. Kalo Brick & Tile Co., 450 U.S. 311, 317 (1981) (Interstate Commerce Act preempts state law purporting to provide damages to shipper injured as a result of common carrier's failure to provide adequate rail service when I.C.C. had approved the rail carrier's abandonment of the rail line); Pacific Gas & Electric Co. v. State Energy Resources Conservation and Development Commission, 103 S.Ct. 1713, 1722–32 (1983) (California moratorium on new nuclear plants not preempted by Atomic Energy Act). See generally, Note, The Preemption Doctrine: Shifting Perspectives on Federalism and the Burger Court, 75 Colum.L.Rev. 623 (1975).

29. 413 U.S. 405 (1973).

the contention that the New York legislation was preempted due to federal pervasiveness in the field, the Court adopted a state-directed posture. Justice Powell reiterated the presumption favoring the legitimacy of state legislation:

> If Congress is authorized to act in a field it should manifest its intention clearly . . . The exercise of federal supremacy is not lightly to be presumed.[30]

II. INTERGOVERNMENTAL COOPERATION

A. Interstate Compacts

1. The Basic Definitions

Article I, section 10, clause 1, provides, inter alia, that:

> No State shall enter into any Treaty, Alliance, or confederation . . .

But clause 3 of that same section adds that:

> No State shall, without the Consent of Congress, . . . enter into any Agreement or Compact with another State or with a Foreign Power . . .

In *Holmes v. Jennison*,[1] Chief Justice Taney tried to distinguish these two clauses in a plurality opinion

> In the first paragraph, the limitations are absolute and unconditional; in the second, the for-

bidden powers may be exercised with the consent of Congress . . .

> [T]he words "agreement," and "compact," cannot be construed as synonymous with one another; and still less can either of them be held to mean the same thing with the word "treaty" in the preceding clause, into which the states are positively and unconditionally forbidden to enter; and which even the consent of Congress could not authorize.[2]

Taney went on to define "treaty" as "an instrument written and executed with the formalities customary among nations . . . "[3] "Agreement" or "compact" are the more comprehensive terms.[4] An agreement need not even be in writing; it is merely "a verbal understanding to which both parties have assented, and upon which both are acting . . . "[5] Because the framers "anxiously desired to cut off all connections or communication between a State and a foreign power" Taney defined "agreement" to "prohibit every agreement, written or verbal, formal or informal, positive or implied, by the mutual understanding of the parties."[6]

In 1893, in *Virginia v. Tennessee*[7] the Court, speaking through Justice Field, adopted a much narrower definition of "compact" or "agreement," but the two cases are not necessarily in conflict, for Taney's plurality opinion in *Holmes* was written in the

---

30. 413 U.S. at 413, quoting Schwartz v. Texas, 344 U.S. 199, 202–203 (1952). But cf. Douglas v. Seacoast Products, Inc., 431 U.S. 265 (1977).

In contrast, in the European Community, preemption of local law by Community law is considered the norm; that is, when Community law substantially regulates a subject matter, it is generally taken to preempt national legislation except in the cases in which Community law provides for the contrary. For example, in case 41/76 (15.12.76) Suzanne Criel, née Donckerwolke and Henri Schou v Procureur de la République au Tribunal de Grande Instance, Lille and Director General of Customs [1972] E.C.R. 1921 at p. 1937, the Court said that as "full responsibility in the matter of commercial policy was transferred to the Community by means of Article 113(1), measures of commercial policy of a national character are only permissible after the end of the transitional period by virtue of specific authorization by the Community." See generally, A. Tizzano, Lo sviluppo delle competenze materiali delle Comunità europee, 21 Revista di diritto europeo 139, 207–09 (1981); J.-V. Louis, Quelques réflexions sur la répartition des compétences entre la Communauté européene

et ses Etats membres, 2 Revue d'Intégration Européenne 355, 364–70 (1979).

1. 39 U.S. (14 Pet.) 540 (1840). On interstate compacts, see generally P. Hay & R. Rotunda, The United States Federal System: Legal Integration in the American Experience 185–95 (Giuffrè, Milan, 1982); Frankfurter and Landis, The Compact Clause of the Constitution—A Study in Interstate Adjustments, 34 Yale L.J. 685 (1925); F. Zimmerman and M. Wendell, Interstate Compacts Since 1925 (1951); F. Zimmerman and M. Wendell, The Law and Use of Interstate Compacts (1961).

2. 39 U.S. (14 Pet.) at 570, 571.

3. Id. at 571.

4. In a later opinion the Court stated that a "compact" is merely more formal than an "agreement." Virginia v. Tennessee, 148 U.S. 503, 520 (1893).

5. 39 U.S. (14 Pet.) at 572.

6. Id.

7. 148 U.S. 503 (1893).

context of a state and a foreign power while Field's Court opinion in *Virginia v. Tennessee* was written in the context of an agreement between two states. Congressional consent was not required, Field said, as to those "many matters upon which different States may agree that can in no respect concern the United States".[8] Congressional consent, however, is required of any agreement tending to increase the political power of the States, which may encroach upon or interfere with the supremacy of the United States.

He offered several examples. Thus, if Virginia should come into possession and ownership of a small parcel of land in New York, and New York wished to purchase it as a site for a public building, no consent of Congress is necessary. Similarly, if Massachusetts wished to transport its exhibits to the World's Fair at Chicago by using the Erie Canal, the contract between the states could be made without the consent of Congress. But if two states would agree to change their boundary lines with the result that the States, or one of them, may increase political power or influence, consent of Congress is probably required.[9]

8. 148 U.S. at 518.

9. 148 U.S. at 518, 520. Thus in United States Steel Corp. v. Multistate Tax Comm'n, 434 U.S. 452 (1978) the Court applied Virginia v. Tennessee, 148 U.S. 503, 519 (1893) and held that it would not "circumscribe modes of interstate cooperation that do not enhance state power to the detriment of federal supremacy." 434 U.S. at 460. See also id. at 473: "But the test is whether the Compact enhances state power *quoad* the National Government."

See also, New Hampshire v. Maine, 426 U.S. 363 (1976); Stearns v. Minnesota, 179 U.S. 223, 244–48 (1900); Landes v. Landes, 1 N.Y.2d 358, 153 N.Y.S.2d 14, 135 N.E.2d 562 (1956); Duncan v. Smith, 262 S.W.2d 373, 42 A.L.R.2d 754 (Ky.1953).

10. Green v. Biddle, 21 U.S. (8 Wheat.) 1, 85–86 (1823).

11. 21 U.S. (8 Wheat.) at 86–87.

12. Virginia v. West Virginia, 78 U.S. (11 Wall.) 39, 59–60 (1871) (Act of Congress admitting West Virginia into the Union at the request of Virginia is a "clear and satisfactory" inference that Congress intended to consent to the admission of West Virginia with the contingent boundaries provided for in the statute of Virginia which prayed for West Virginia's admission, and in so

2. *The Consent of Congress*

The Constitution does not explain either how Congress' consent to a compact is to be made, nor when it is to be given. The Supreme Court early recognized that the mode or form of consent is to be left to the wisdom of Congress.[10] Thus when Congress consented to the separation of Kentucky from Virginia and the creation of Kentucky as a separate state, it must be taken to have consented to the compact by which the separation was made.[11] Sometimes the consent may be implied from congressional legislation on the subject.[12] Congress may also place conditions on giving its consent.[13]

Congressional consent will usually precede the compact, for example, if "it is to lay a duty of tonnage, to keep troops or ships of war in time of peace, or to engage in war."[14] In fact, sometimes Congress has given its consent years before the proposed compact will have come into existence.[15] But if the compact "relates to a matter which could not well be considered until its nature is fully developed, it is not well perceived why the consent may not be subsequently given."[16]

doing it necessarily consented to the agreement of those States on the subject).

13. See, e.g., Arizona v. California, 292 U.S. 341, 345 (1934) (Congressional approval of Colorado River Compact subject to certain limitations and conditions, the approval to be effective upon the ratification of the compact, as so modified, by the legislature of California and at least five of the other six states).

14. Virginia v. Tennessee, 148 U.S. 503, 521 (1893). Cf. De Veau v. Braisted, 363 U.S. 144, 154 (1960) (Opinion of Frankfurter, J., joined by Clark, Whittaker, & Stewart, JJ.) (Congress expressly gave its consent to implementing legislation not formally part of the compact; "This provision in the consent by Congress to a compact is so extraordinary as to be unique in the history of compacts."). See also, Act of June 6, 1934, 48 Stat. at Large 909 (1934) (Congress consents in advance to agreements for the control of crime).

15. E.g., Cuyler v. Adams, 449 U.S. 433, 441 & n. 9 (1981) (Congress, by enacting the Crime Control Consent Act of 1934, gave consent in advance to the Interstate Agreement on Detainers, initially drafted by the Council of State Governments in 1956).

16. Virginia v. Tennessee, 148 U.S. 503, 521 (1893).

3. Supreme Court Interpretation of Interstate Compacts

The leading case on the power of the Supreme Court to interpret interstate compacts is *West Virginia ex rel. Dyer v. Sims.*[17] In 1940 Congress gave its consent to an eight State Compact entered into for purposes of controlling pollution in the Ohio River system. One of those states was West Virginia and a controversy arose within that State between its officials as to West Virginia's responsibilities under the Compact. The state auditor, Sims, refused to allow payment from the state treasury of a sum of money the state legislature appropriated as its contribution to the expenses of the commission set up under the Compact.

The West Virginia Supreme Court upheld Sims and found the state act approving West Virginia's adherence to the Compact unconstitutional under that *state's* Constitution because it delegated the state's police power to the federal government and other states and because it bound future state legislatures to make appropriations. Justice Frankfurter for the Court stated that just as the Supreme Court has the power to settle disputes between states where there is no compact, "it must have the final power to pass upon the meaning and validity of compacts."[18] Having said all that, Frankfurter appeared to go on in his opinion to construe *not* the Compact but the state constitution. Frankfurter quickly conceded that the state supreme court is, for state purposes, the ultimate tribunal for construing its state constitution. But, "we are free to examine determinations of law by State courts in the limited field where a compact brings in issue the rights of other States and the United

States."[19] Frankfurter states that it "is one of the axioms of modern government" that a state may delegate to an administrative body the power to make rules and decide cases;[20] and he concluded: "the obligation of the State under the Compact is not in conflict with Art. X, § 4 of the State Constitution."[21]

Justice Reed separately concurred and argued that the "interpretation of the meaning of the compact controls over a state's application of its own law through the Supremacy Clause and not by any implied federal power to construe state law."[22] Justice Jackson, also separately concurring, also rejected the Frankfurter analysis, and relied on a federal estoppel theory:

> West Virginia, for internal affairs, is free to interpret her own Constitution as she will. But if the compact system is to have vitality and integrity, she may not raise an issue of *ultra vires*, decide it, and release herself from an interstate obligation. The legal consequences which flow from the formal participation in a compact consented to by Congress is a federal question for this Court.[23]

Both the Reed and the Jackson analysis find more traditional and solid support for federal review of the interstate Compact rather than review of the state constitution. The preferred analysis is that an interstate Compact is sufficiently federal so that all questions interpreting the Compact may be decided ultimately by the Supreme Court as a matter of federal common law.

Subsequently the Court in *Cuyler v. Adams*[24] held explicitly that "the construction of an interstate agreement sanctioned by Congress under the Compact Clause presents a federal question" because "congressional consent transforms an interstate

---

17. 341 U.S. 22 (1951).

18. 341 U.S. at 28.

19. Id. See also, Murdock v. Memphis, 87 U.S. (20 Wall.) 590 (1875). Note that *Murdock* was not decided on constitutional grounds. "It seems entirely plausible that Congress intended by eliminating [a restrictive proviso in 1867] to open the whole case for review by the Supreme Court, if there is a federal question in the case sufficient to take the case to the Supreme Court." C. Wright, Law of Federal Courts 543 (3d ed. 1976).

But, with very few exceptions, it is now considered that state courts speak with final authority on questions of state law. Id.

20. 341 U.S. at 30.

21. 341 U.S. at 32.

22. 341 U.S. at 33 (Reed, J., concurring).

23. 341 U.S. at 35 (Jackson, J., concurring). Justice Black concurred without opinion. 341 U.S. at 32.

24. 449 U.S. 433 (1981).

compact within this Clause into a law of the United States. . . . "[25] In that case the Court held that the construction of an agreement sanctioned by Congress presented a federal question even though the agreement, under the compact clause, did not *require* congressional consent, where the agreement would have been an appropriate subject for congressional legislation. The congressional consent thus *federalized* the interpretation of the Detainers Agreement. "[W]here Congress has authorized the States to enter into a cooperative agreement, and where the subject matter of that agreement is an appropriate subject for congressional legislation, the consent of Congress transforms the States' agreement into federal law under the Compact Clause."[26]

B. Other Forms of State and Federal Cooperation

In addition to the interstate compact clause, the Constitution and tradition have provided other forms of federal/state cooperation to solve particular problems. The federal government, by use of its spending power, often cooperates with, encourages, and aids the states in financing various programs that Congress finds to promote the general welfare. This principle is illustrated by *Steward Machine Co. v. Davis.*[1]

Davis upheld the constitutionality of certain sections of the Social Security Tax Act dealing with unemployment compensation. Under title IX of the Act, an excise tax was levied against employers with eight or more employees. The proceeds then entered the Treasury and were not earmarked, but there were credits allowable of up to 90% of the federal tax for contributions made under

state law to a state unemployment fund, provided that the state law had been certified to the Secretary of the Treasury as satisfying certain minimum criteria. "Some of the conditions thus attached to the allowance of a credit are designed to give assurance that the state unemployment compensation law shall be one in substance as well as name. Others are designed to give assurance that the contributions shall be protected against loss after payment to the state."[2] Thus, the contributions to the state fund had to be paid immediately over to the Secretary of the Treasury who would credit it and invest appropriate amounts of it in government securities.

This social security plan was upheld as constitutional and not violative of the reserved power of the states. For present purposes we refer to it as an illustration of federal state cooperation. Justice Cardozo for the majority emphasized this theme:

> Supporters of the statute say that its operation is not constraint, but the creation of a larger freedom, the states and the nations joining together in a cooperative endeavor to avert a common evil.[3]

He explained that while some states had enacted unemployment compensation programs, others had been deterred for fear that the taxes necessary to support the program would drive industry out of the state.[4] Also the existence of such a system in one state would encourage the needy to migrate there, further burdening that state's resources.[5] "[I]n so far as there was failure by the states to contribute relief according to the measure of their capacity, a disproportionate burden, and a mountainous one, was laid upon the resources of the Government of their nation."[6] The nationwide federal

---

25. 449 U.S. at 438.

26. 449 U.S. at 441 (footnote omitted). In *Cuyler* the Interstate Agreement on Detainers did not demand congressional consent but it was an appropriate subject for congressional legislation under the commerce clause (Art. I, § 8, cl. 3) and the extradition clause (Art. IV, § 2, cl. 2). 449 U.S. at 442 & n. 10. Accord, Texas v. New Mexico, 103 S.Ct. ___ (1983).

1. 301 U.S. 548 (1937). Accord, Carmichael v. Southern Coal & Coke Co., 301 U.S. 495 (1937).

2. 301 U.S. at 575.

3. 301 U.S. at 587.

4. 301 U.S. at 588.

5. Helvering v. Davis, 301 U.S. 619, 644 (1937) (a companion case to Steward Machine Co. v. Davis, 301 U.S. 548 (1937)).

6. Steward Machine Co. v. Davis, 301 U.S. at 588.

program, operating with state cooperation, removed these disadvantages.

In addition to the use of federal grants to induce the states to comply with federal programs, Congress sometimes exercises its powers under the commerce clause to promote state interests by validating state restrictions on interstate commerce that would be invalid without such congressional authorization. Thus, Congress may allow the states to place discriminatory taxes on out-of-state corporations in interstate commerce.[7] And Congress may allow states to prohibit the transportation in their states of certain goods, even though such goods are in interstate commerce.[8]

Cooperation is a two-way street. Thus States, in turn, may not, under the Supremacy Clause, refuse to enforce valid federal laws even though such enforcement is in state court,[9] unless Congress either expressly or impliedly excuses the state from an enforcement role.[10]

C. Interstate Comity

Various sections of the Constitution, particularly sections 1 and 2 of Article IV, serve to insure comity and courtesy among the states "to help fuse into one Nation a collection of independent, sovereign states." [1] The Articles of Confederation specifically referred to this idea of courtesy:

> The better to secure and perpetuate mutual friendship and intercourse among the people of the different States of this Union, the free inhabitants of each of these States, paupers, vagabonds and fugitives from justice excepted, shall be entitled to all privileges and immunities of free citizens in the several States; and the people of each State shall have free ingress and regress to and from any other State . . . .[2]

Section 1 of Article IV provides for "full faith and credit" in each state of the public acts, records, and judicial proceedings of every other state. Congress is also given authority to legislate under this clause.[3] This clause is normally considered in texts on Conflicts of Law or Choice of Law and is not considered here.[4]

Clause 2 of Section 2 is called the interstate rendition clause or fugitive from justice clause and places a duty on states to surrender to their sister states fugitives from justice.[5] The leading case in this area is *Kentucky v. Dennison*.[6] *Dennison* was an original suit brought by Kentucky against Dennison, the Governor of Ohio.

---

7. E.g., Prudential Insurance Co. v. Benjamin, 328 U.S. 408 (1946) (and cases cited therein) (upholding discriminating tax on foreign insurance companies.)

8. E.g., Clark Distilling Co. v. Western Maryland Ry., 242 U.S. 311 (1917) (upholding the Webb-Kenyon Act which divested intoxicating liquor of their interstate character in certain cases).

9. Testa v. Katt, 330 U.S. 386 (1947).

10. See, e.g., Douglas v. New York, N.H. & H.R.R., 279 U.S. 377, 387–88 (1929).

1. Toomer v. Witsell, 334 U.S. 385, 395 (1948).

2. Articles of Confederation, art. IV, cl. 1, reprinted in U.S.C.A., Constitution of the United States, Annotated; and in the Lawyer's Edition to J. Nowak, R. Rotunda & J. Young, Principles of Constitutional Law, Chapter 21 (West Hornbook Series, 2d ed. 1983). Clause 2 of the Article dealt with the rendition of fugitives from justice and Clause 3 is the ancestor of the modern full faith and credit clause.

3. There has not been a great amount of federal statutory law in area. The present federal legislation may be found in 28 U.S.C.A. §§ 1738–1742.

4. See generally, E. Scoles & P. Hay, Conflict of Laws (1982); R. Leflar, American Conflicts Law (1968);

R. Weintraub, Commentary on the Conflicts of Laws (1971); Hay, International Versus Interstate Conflicts Law in the United States, 35 Rabels Zeitschrift 429 (1971); Kirgis, The Roles of Due Process and Full Faith and Credit in Choice of Law, 62 Cornell L.Rev. 94 (1976).

5. Clause 3 of the Section governs fugitives from labor, i.e., runaway slaves. The Civil War Amendments abolishing slavery have made this section obsolete. The main Supreme Court cases in this area include: Prigg v. Pennsylvania, 41 U.S. (16 Pet.) 539 (1842); Jones v. Van Zandt, 46 U.S. (5 How.) 215 (1847); Moore v. Illinois, 55 U.S. (14 How.) 13 (1853); Ableman v. Booth, 62 U.S. (21 How.) 506 (1859); Osborn v. Nicholson, 80 U.S. (13 Wall.) 654 (1872). Justice Story explained that this clause "contemplates the existence of a positive, unqualified right on the part of the owner of the slave, which no state law or regulation can in any way qualify, regulate, control or restrain. The slave is not to be discharged from service or labor, in consequence of any state law or regulation." Prigg v. Pennsylvania, 41 U.S. (16 Pet.) 539, 612 (1842).

6. 65 U.S. (24 How.) 66 (1861).

Kentucky sought a writ of mandamus to require Dennison to turn over a criminal fugitive who had violated Kentucky's laws by assisting a slave to escape. Chief Justice Taney for the Court held the Court had jurisdiction, and also decided, inter alia, that the words "treason, felony, or other crime" "embrace every act forbidden and made punishable by a law of the State." [7] But said Taney, in interpreting the congressional statute implementing this clause as well as the clause itself, the duty of the state to turn over fugitives from justice is only a moral duty:

> [L]ooking to the subject-matter of this law [enacted to implement the fugitive from justice clause], and the relations which the United States and the several States bear to each other, the court is of the opinion, the words "it shall be the duty" were not used as mandatory and compulsory, but as declaratory of the moral duty which this compact created. . . . The act does not provide any means to compel the execution of this duty . . . nor is there any clause or provision in the Constitution which arms the Government of the United States with this power. Indeed, such a power would place every State under the control and dominion of the General Government, even in the administration of its internal concerns and reserved rights. . . .

It is true that Congress may authorize a particular State officer to perform a particular duty; but if he declines to do so, it does not follow that he may be coerced, or punished for his refusal.[8]

Thus, the Court unanimously overruled Kentucky's motion for mandamus.[9] Once the governor of the asylum state exercises his "moral duty" or discretion and grants extradition based on the demanding state's judicial determination that probable cause exists, the judiciary of the asylum state may make no further judicial inquiry on that issue.[10]

In addition to the full faith and credit clause and the interstate rendition clause, the major clause of Article IV dealing with comity is section 2, clause 1, also known as the comity clause or the privileges and immunities clause of Article IV: "The Citizens of each State shall be entitled to all Privileges and Immunities of Citizens in the several States." The terms "citizen" and "resident" are "essentially interchangeable" for "most cases" under this clause.[11]

Some commentators and justices have had great hopes for this clause, seeing it as guaranteeing equal protection to the citizens of each of the several states,[12] or as guaranteeing certain substantive natural rights.[13] But like its kin in section 1 of the fourteenth amendment, the Article IV privileges and immunities clause has not become so important, and when the Court strikes a classifica-

---

7. 65 U.S. (24 How.) at 99.

8. 65 U.S. (24 How.) at 107–108. See 18 U.S.C.A. § 1073 (when illegal to flee state to avoid prosecution) and 18 U.S.C.A. § 3182 (duty of Governor to deliver interstate fugitives from justice).

9. 65 U.S. (24 How.) at 110. Other important cases interpreting this clause include: Roberts v. Reilly, 116 U.S. 80 (1885); Innes v. Tobin, 240 U.S. 127 (1916); Taylor v. Taintor, 83 U.S. (16 Wall.) 366 (1873); Strassheim v. Daily, 221 U.S. 280 (1911); Applegard v. Massachusetts, 203 U.S. 222 (1906); Drew v. Thaw, 235 U.S. 432 (1914); Pettibone v. Nichols, 203 U.S. 192 (1906); South Carolina v. Bailey, 289 U.S. 412 (1933); Ker v. Illinois, 119 U.S. 436 (1886); Nelson v. George, 399 U.S. 224 (1970); United States v. Rauscher, 119 U.S. 407 (1886); Lascelles v. Georgia, 148 U.S. 537 (1893).

10. Michigan v. Doran, 439 U.S. 282 (1978); Pacileo v. Walker, 449 U.S. 86 (1980) (per curiam).

11. Hicklin v. Orbeck, 437 U.S. 518, 524 n. 8 (1978).

12. E.g., Catron, J., concurring in Dred Scott v. Sandford, 60 U.S. (19 How.) 393, 527 (1857): "[T]he right to enjoy the territory as equals was reserved to the States, and to the citizens of the States, respectively. The cited clause [Art. IV, Section 2, cl. 1] is not that citizens of the United States shall have equal privileges in the Territories, but the citizens of each State shall come there in right of his State, and enjoy the common property. He secures his equality through the equality of his State, by virtue of that great fundamental condition of the Union—the equality of the States."

13. E.g., Washington, J. riding circuit in Corfield v. Coryell, 6 Fed.Cas. 546, 551–52 (C.C.E.D.Pa.1823) (No. 3,230): "[W]hat are the privileges and immunities of citizens of the several states? We feel no hestitation in confining these expressions to those privileges and immunities which are, in their nature, fundamental; which belong, of right, to the citizens of all free governments; and which have, at all times, been enjoyed by the citizens of the several States which compose this Union. . . . "

tion based on state citizenship, it is likely to rely on the equal protection aspects of the due process clause of the fifth amendment or the equal protection clause of the fourteenth amendment. Similarly, a decision in name or in fact creating substantive natural law rights is more likely to be based on the due process clauses of the fifth or fourteenth amendments or some other clause.

The narrow scope of this comity clause is illustrated by the fact that corporations are excluded from its protection [14] though of course corporations are protected by the interstate commerce clause and the due process clauses of the fifth and fourteen amendments. Also, the *Dred Scott* [15] case excluded blacks from its coverage, a result reversed by the Civil War Amendments.

The modern cases interpreting the privileges and immunity clause of Article IV fall into several main groups. The first group deals with commercial rights and is well illustrated by the leading case of *Toomer v. Witsell*. [16] Several South Carolina statutes regulated commercial shrimp fishing within three miles of the coast of that state. No federal regulations governed any of the shrimp fishing extending from North Carolina to Florida. The regulations of the various states involved often aimed against non-resident fishing "have now irritated retaliation to the point that the fishery is effectively partitioned at the state lines . . . ." [17] One of the challenged South Carolina laws required payment of a license fee of $25 for each shrimp boat owned by a resident and $2500 for each boat owned by a non-resident. It is that law which was successfully challenged under the privileges and immunities clause of Article IV.

Chief Justice Vinson spoke for the majority in *Toomer* and explained that the test to determine a violation of the Article IV privileges and immunities clause is whether there are valid reasons for a state to make distinctions based on one's state citizenship and whether the degree of discrimination bears a "close relation" to these reasons. [18] This clause outlaws "classifications based on the fact of non-citizenship unless there is something to indicate that non-citizens constitute a peculiar source of the evil at which the statute is aimed." [19]

Vinson then noted that the South Carolina statute frankly and plainly discriminates against non-residents, that it serves to virtually exclude non-residents from South Carolina fishing waters, and that even though the South Carolina statute is written in terms of residence rather than citizenship, it is still within the privileges and immunities clause.

Next, Vinson rejected the state's arguments based on need to conserve natural resources by carefully and actively scrutinizing the means used to achieve such an objective:

[The State's brief mentions], without further elucidation, the fishing methods used by non-residents, the size of their boats, and the allegedly greater cost of enforcing the laws against them. One statement in the [State's] brief might also be construed to mean that the State's conservation program for shrimp requires expenditures of funds beyond those collected in license fees—funds to which residents and non-residents contribute. Nothing in the record indicates that non-residents use larger boats or different fishing methods against residents, that the cost of enforcing the laws against them is appreciably greater, or that any substantial amount of the State's general revenue funds is devoted to shrimp conservation. But assuming that such were the facts, they would not necessarily support a remedy so drastic as to be a near equivalent of total exclusion. The State is not without power, for example, to restrict the type of equipment used in its fisheries, to graduate license fees according to the size of the boats, or even to charge

---

14. E.g., Bank of Augusta v. Earle, 38 U.S. (13 Pet.) 519, 586 (1839); Paul v. Virginia, 75 U.S. (8 Wall.) 168, 181 (1869).

15. Dred Scott v. Sandford, 60 U.S. (19 How.) 393, 403–411 (1857).

16. 334 U.S. 385 (1948).

17. 334 U.S. at 388.

18. 334 U.S. at 396.

19. 334 U.S. at 398.

non-residents a differential which would merely compensate the State for any added enforcement burden they may impose or for any conservation expenditures from taxes which only residents pay. We would be closing our eyes to reality, we believe, if we concluded that there was a reasonable relationship between the danger represented by non-citizens, as a class, and the severe discrimination practiced upon them.[20]

The State finally argued that an unexpressed exception to the privileges and immunities clause of Article IV are *ferae naturae;* in other words, the State argued, that it was the trustee for its citizens who owned in common all of the fish and game within the State.

The Court acknowledged that there were several older cases which supported this theory in dictum,[21] but only one actually upheld a State discriminating against citizens of other States in the area of commercial fishing or hunting where no persuasive independent justification for the discrimination was advanced.[22] That case was *McCready v. Virginia,*[23] an 1876 case. *McCready* had upheld a state law which prohibited all non-Virginia citizens from planting oysters in the tidal waters of a Virginia river. That decision had reasoned that the right of Virginians in Virginia waters is a property right similar to the planting of corn on state-owned land.

Toomer noted two important differences between it and *McCready*. First, the fish in *McCready* would remain in that state until removed from the state by man. The fish in *Toomer* migrated from the water of other states and were in South Carolina only temporarily. The *Toomer* fish were, so to speak, in the stream of interstate commerce. Secondly, the *McCready* decision involved regulation of fishing in the inland waters but the *Toomer* case dealt with fishing in the marginal sea.

The Court thus refused to extend *McCready* and it struck the *Toomer* statute under the privileges and immunity clause. Perhaps equally as significant, the Court's opinion casted significant doubts on the reasoning and conclusions of *McCready*. The majority noted that the ownership theory is "now generally regarded as a fiction expressive in legal shorthand of the importance to its people that a State have power to preserve and regulate the exploitation of an important natural resource."[24] It cited with approval a case decided "only fifteen years after the *McCready* decision"[25] and pointedly noted that in that case the conservation statute upheld did not discriminate in favor of any state's citizens.[26] In a footnote it explained that the origin of the legal fiction laid in a confusion between the Roman concept of *imperium*, or governmental power to regulate, and *dominium* or ownership,

20. 334 U.S. at 398–99 (footnotes omitted).

21. 334 U.S. at 400 n. 33, citing Geer v. Connecticut, 161 U.S. 519 (1896). *Geer* was later overruled in Hughes v. Oklahoma, 441 U.S. 322 (1979). See generally, Chapter 9, section IV.

22. The *Toomer* Court distinguished Patsone v. Pennsylvania, 232 U.S. 138 (1914) on the grounds that the state statute forbidding non-resident aliens from killing game or possessing firearms useful for that purpose found sufficient support in the record before the Court that it could not say that the Pennsylvania legislature was not warranted in assuming that resident aliens were the peculiar source of the evil the state sought to prevent. The state statute was found not to violate the fourteenth amendment. *Patsone* is an old case and, in spite of *Toomer's* effort to distinguish it, it may not be good law under *Toomer's* analysis of the Article IV privileges and immunities clause.

The second case to be distinguished was Haavik v. Alaska Packers Ass'n, 263 U.S. 510 (1924). In that

case the issue was the validity, under a Congressional statute, of a $5 fishing licensing fee imposed on non-residents but not on residents by an Alaskan statute. *Toomer* correctly noted that the issue was not the state's tax powers but Congress'. And, Congress' power to authorize the tax was reasonably exercised in light of the fact that the fee was a reasonable contribution toward the protection which the local government gave nonresidents. In Mullaney v. Anderson, 342 U.S. 415 (1952), the Court did strike an Alaskan licensing differential of $50 on non-resident fishermen and $5 on resident fishermen in territorial waters.

23. 94 U.S. 391 (1876).

24. 334 U.S. at 402 (footnote omitted).

25. 334 U.S. at 402.

26. 334 U.S. at 402 n. 35, citing Manchester v. Massachusetts, 139 U.S. 240, 265 (1891).

and that the state power over fish and game was in origin only *imperium*.[27]

Thus the concept of governmental power to regulate simply restates the issue rather than answers it: does the state's power to regulate fish and game wholly within the state ever allow it under the privileges and immunities clause of Article IV to discriminate in favor of local commercial interests? The *Toomer* majority never completely answered this question for it did not reverse *McCready*, only narrowed its holding; but one would think that under the modern view of the privileges and immunities clause, the modern view of the interstate commerce clause, and simple economic analysis the Court should hold that while a state may—in the absence of preemptive federal authority—conserve its natural resources or exploit them, it may fashion neither policy with a view of discriminating against out-of-state residents or citizens.

The decision in *Douglas v. Seacoast Products, Inc.*[28] supports this conclusion, although it was actually decided on federal preemption grounds: the majority held that Virginia statutes denying federally licensed ships owned by nonresidents of Virginia from fishing in the Virginia portion of Chesapeake Bay and prohibiting such ships owned by non-United States citizens from catching fish anywhere in Virginia denied licensees their federally granted rights to engage in fishing activities on the same terms as state residents. In the course of the majority opinion, the Court significantly rejected the theory of state ownership of fish and wildlife:

A State does not stand in the same position as the owner of a private game preserve and it is

pure fantasy to talk of "owning" wild fish, birds or animals. Neither the States nor the Federal Government, any more than a hopeful fisherman or hunter, have title to these creatures until they are reduced to possession by skillful capture. . . . The "ownership" language of [the older] cases . . . must be understood as no more than a 19th-century legal fiction. . . . Under modern analysis, the question is simply whether the State has exercised its police power in conformity with the federal laws and Constitution.[29]

A year after *Douglas*, in *Hicklin v. Orbeck*,[30] a unanimous Supreme Court invalidated, under the privileges and immunities clause, the Alaska Hire Act. That state law gave employment preference to Alaska residents over nonresidents for all oil and gas leases and other such agreements to which the state was a party. Alaska noted that the oil and gas that was the subject of the Alaska Hire Act was owned by the state.

The Court stated, first, that prior cases have held that such state discrimination against nonresidents seeking to pursue a trade, occupation, or common calling within the state violates this clause. Second, even if a state could seek to alleviate its unemployment problem by requiring such hiring preferences, the state's law could not withstand scrutiny under this clause because it was not sufficiently tailored to aid its intended beneficiaries. Finally, and most importantly, while Alaska's actual ownership of the oil and gas resources are a factor to be considered in judging the law, that ownership was insufficient to justify the pervasive discrimination.[31]

27. 334 U.S. at 402 n. 37. Frankfurter, J., concurring, and joined by Jackson, J., would have read the privileges and immunities clause more narrowly and would have based the *Toomer* result discussed here on the commerce clause. 334 U.S. at 407.

28. 431 U.S. 265 (1977).

29. 431 U.S. 265 at 284–85.

30. 437 U.S. 518 (1978).

31. "Alaska Hire extends to employers who have no connection whatsoever with the State's oil and gas, per-

form no work on state land, have no contractual relationship with the State, and receive no payment from the State. The Act goes so far as to reach suppliers who provide goods or services to subcontractors who, in turn, perform work for contractors despite the fact that none of these employers may themselves have direct dealings with the State's oil and gas or ever set foot on state land." 437 U.S. at 530 (footnote omitted).

However, the mayor of Boston may require that all construction projects funded in whole or in part by city funds or funds which the city had the authority to ad-

Later, in *Hughes v. Oklahoma*,[32] the Court held that the "ownership" of wild game was a fiction and should not be recognized as justifying discrimination against out of state residents whether the challenge is brought either under the privileges and immunities clause or the commerce clause.[33] *Hughes* invalidated a state law forbidding the transporting of natural minnows out of state for sale.

To be contrasted with the protections which the privileges and immunities clause offers nonresidents of a state as to wild animals (or fish) involved in interstate commerce or *commercial* activities is the virtual inapplicability of that clause to protect nonresidents hunting wild animals as *recreational* sport. Thus, in *Baldwin v. Fish and Game Comm'n of Montana*[34] a 6 to 3 majority of the Supreme Court upheld a Montana hunting license system—under which nonresidents were charged 7½ times more than residents for a hunting license entitling one to hunt Elk and other game—[35] against challenges that the system violated the privileges and immunities clause of Article IV and the equal protection clause of the fourteenth amendment. Justice Blackmun for

the majority stated that, while the "contours" of the privileges and immunities clause of Article IV "are not well developed",[36] it was nevertheless the law that States must treat its citizens and nonresidents equally only "with respect to those 'privileges' and 'immunities' bearing upon the vitality of the Nation as a single entity."[37] He concluded that it would be improper to link the right to hunt for sport with such things as the right to travel, the right to vote, and the right to pursue a calling. *Toomer v. Witsell*[38] and other such cases were distinguished as involving "commercial" licensing, but Elk hunting "in Montana is a recreation and a sport."[39]

In addition to the area of fish, game, and natural resources, the Article IV privileges and immunity clause is also invoked in connection with Constitutional challenges to state and local taxation. This topic is considered in detail elsewhere in this treatise.[40] Also because of the privileges and immunities clause the state must guarantee non-citizens reasonable access to its courts, although the access "may not be technically and precisely the same in extent as accorded

---

minister should be performed by a work force consisting of at least half bona fide Boston residents because the city was acting as a market participant and not a market regulator. White v. Massachusetts Council of Construction Employers, Inc., 103 S.Ct. 1042 (1983). *Hicklin* was distinguished because even though the mayor's order affects contracts between public employers and their employees, "the mayor's executive order covers a discrete, identifiable class of economic activity in which the city is a major participant. Everyone affected by the order is, in a substantial if informal sense, 'working for the city.'" 103 S.Ct. at 1046, n. 7.

32. 441 U.S. 322 (1979).

33. 441 U.S. at 333. See generally, e.g., Note, Hughes v. Oklahoma and Baldwin v. Fish and Game Comm'n: The Commerce Clause and State Control of Natural Resources, 66 Va.L.Rev. 1145 (1980).

34. 436 U.S. 371 (1978).

35. If a Montana resident bought the same type of license it would cost him $30 vs. $225 for the nonresident. If the resident wanted to hunt only Elk, his license was $9, but the nonresident still had to purchase a combination license for $225. 436 U.S. at 373.

36. 436 U.S. at 380 (footnote omitted).

37. 436 U.S. at 383. See also 436 U.S. at 387:

"With respect to such basic and essential activities, interference with which would frustrate the purposes of the formation of the Union, the States must treat residents and nonresidents without unnecessary distinctions."

38. 334 U.S. 385 (1948).

39. 436 U.S. at 388. The majority also dismissed the fourteenth amendment equal protection challenge by observing that the Montana licensing scheme is not irrational.

In dissent, Justice Brennan, joined by Justices Marshall and White, argued that the Article IV privileges and immunities clause prohibits a state from unjustifiably discriminating against nonresidents, and that it is irrelevant whether a given right is deemed "fundamental." The out-of-state discrimination, according to the dissent, would only be allowed if "(1) the presence or activity of nonresidents is the source or cause of the problem or affect with which the State seeks to deal, and (2) the discrimination practiced against nonresidents bears a substantial relation to the problem they present." 436 U.S. at 402. The Montana Elk license scheme would fail under this two part test.

40. See Chapter 11, section III, B.

to resident citizens." [41] Thus the Court has upheld a Minnesota statute which applied the statute of limitations of the state where the cause of action arose unless the plaintiff is a Minnesota citizen and owned the cause of action ever since it accrued. The Court emphasized that plaintiff had delayed in asserting the claim and would have been barred in his home state.[42]

In addition, a state may prescribe reasonable conditions upon which a foreign corporation may enter the territory to do business,[43]—for example, by prescribing the condition of consenting, either expressly or impliedly, to appoint an agent to receive service of process within the state [44]—but it may not grant a preference to the in-state creditors ahead of the out-of-state creditors in the administration of the property of an insolvent foreign corporation.[45] A lawyer has no right, under the privileges and immunity clause or elsewhere in the Constitution, to be allowed to practice in one State just because he or she has been admitted to another State's bar.[46]

41. Canadian Northern Ry. Co. v. Eggen, 252 U.S. 553, 562 (1920).

42. Canadian Northern Ry. Co. v. Eggen, 252 U.S. 553 (1920). See also, Chemung Canal Bank v. Lowery, 93 U.S. 72 (1876); Chambers v. Baltimore & Ohio R. R., 207 U.S. 142 (1907); Douglas v. New York, N.H., & H.R. Co., 279 U.S. 377 (1929); New York v. O'Neill, 359 U.S. 1 (1959).

43. Blake v. McClung, 172 U.S. 239, 254 (1898).

44. Doherty & Co. v. Goodman, 294 U.S. 623 (1935).

45. Blake v. McClung, 172 U.S. 239 (1898).

46. Leis v. Flynt, 439 U.S. 438, 442–43 & n. 4 (1979) (per curiam). On "privileges and immunities" analysis generally, see the thorough study in Varat, State "Citizenship" and Interstate Equality, 48 U.Chi.L.Rev. 487 (1981).

CHAPTER ELEVEN

STATE TAXATION

I.   INTRODUCTION

As a matter of convenience, this Chapter embraces all federal constitutional aspects of state and local taxation: due process, commerce clause, equal protection, privileges and immunities, intergovernmental immunity, and state taxation of American Indians. In many state tax cases considered by the Court, the overriding issues involve the concurrent consideration of both due process and the commerce clause. These issues are treated as problems of jurisdiction to tax. Initially, there must be jurisdiction to tax in a substantive due process sense before there can be a question as to whether the particular tax imposes an improper burden on interstate commerce. Since the due process and commerce clause issues are commonly interrelated, the emphasis is upon these aspects of state taxation. Other constitutional issues relating to state taxation, such as equal protection, privileges and immunities, inter-

governmental immunity, and taxation of American Indians are separately treated because the issues more frequently arise as independent problems.

Substantially all types of state and local taxes are treated in this discussion. A comparison of these taxes leads to the conclusion that there has evolved a trend toward some degree of consistency in the application of constitutional doctrine in the arena of state taxation.

II.   JURISDICTION TO TAX

A.   General Ad Valorem Property Taxes

1.   Introduction and Summary

There are three categories of property to which ad valorem property taxes may be applied—real property, tangible personal property, and intangible personal property.

With respect to substantive due process, the Court has established the following general rules as to the jurisdiction of the states to impose ad valorem property taxes. Real property and permanently situated tangible personal property can be taxed only by the state in which the property is located. These items are deemed to have acquired an exclusive tax situs in the state where located since that state is the only state which has provided benefits and protection under its laws. In the case of interstate railroads and other instrumentalities of interstate commerce, the value of these connected properties and rolling stock may be determined as a unit and properly allocated among the several states in which the business operates. Intangible personal property, on the other hand, as distinguished from real property and tangible personal property, may be taxed not only by the state of domicile of the owner under the maxim *mobilia sequuntur personam* (movables follow the person), but also by any other state in which the property interest is deemed to have received benefits and protection. Thus, from the standpoint of due process, real property and permanently situated tangible personal property have a single tax situs; by contrast, intangible personal property may have a multiple tax situs.

2. Real Property

It may be stating the obvious to note that real property, irrespective of the owner's domicile, has an exclusive situs for ad valorem taxation in the state in which it is located. This point was stated in dictum in *Union Refrigerator Transit Co. v. Kentucky* [1] where the Court made the following observation:

> It is . . . essential to the validity of . . . [an ad valorem property] tax that the

property shall be within the territorial jurisdiction of the taxing power. Not only is the operation of state laws limited to persons and property within the boundaries of the state, but property which is wholly and exclusively within the jurisdiction of another state, receives none of the protection for which the tax is supposed to be the compensation. This rule receives its most familiar illustration in the cases of land which, to be taxable, must be within the limits of the state. [2]

The Court proceeded to note that it knew of "no case where a legislature has assumed to impose a tax upon land within the jurisdiction of another state." [3]

The rule that due process requires the taxing state to provide a benefit with respect to the property interest subjected to taxation was applied under interesting circumstances in *Louisville & Jeffersonville Ferry Co. v. Kentucky.* [4] In that case, the taxpayer, a Kentucky corporation, operated a ferry between Louisville and Jeffersonville, Indiana. It had obtained a special grant from the Indiana legislature to operate a ferry from any portion of the public grounds or commons in Jeffersonville bordering upon the Ohio river across from Louisville. To complement the Indiana franchise, the corporation leased ferry privileges from the city of Louisville. In assessing the intangible property of the corporation, the Kentucky authorities included the value of the Indiana franchise. Taxpayer's due process objection to the inclusion of the Indiana franchise as part of the Kentucky property tax assessment was sustained by the Court on the ground that the privilege granted to use the public facilities in Jeffersonville was a property interest in the nature of real property located in Indiana. [5]

---

1. 199 U.S. 194 (1905).

2. 199 U.S. at 204.

3. Id.

4. 188 U.S. 385 (1903).

5. The rationale of the decision was stated as follows:

> "We . . . recognize the general rule that the power of the state to tax is limited to subjects within its jurisdiction or over which it can exercise dominion. No difficulty can exist in applying the general rule in this case; for, beyond all question, the ferry

Senior v. Braden,[6] decided in 1935, is the only case to have directly presented the issue as to the jurisdiction of the state of the owner's residence to impose a property tax upon an interest in out-of-state real property. In this case, an Ohio resident held beneficial interests in certain real estate trusts which owned Illinois, Massachusetts, and Nebraska real property. Each trustee held title to the buildings located in the respective states and managed the properties free of control by the beneficiaries. Beneficial interests in the trusts were represented by transferable trust certificates. Ohio attempted to tax the interests of beneficiaries under the Ohio intangible property tax which provided that income-producing intangibles be taxed at a rate of five percent upon the income therefrom. These provisions were a part of the Ohio general property tax system. The tax was challenged on the ground that this was an attempt to tax an interest in out-of-state real estate in violation of due process. In resolving the issue against the tax authorities, the majority of the Court emphasized the principle of trust law that a beneficial interest under a trust constitutes an interest in the corpus of the trust—in this case, the real property itself.[7] Thus, the Court concluded that the tax was not a tax upon intangible personal property, but rather an invalid tax upon the out-of-state real estate held in trust.[8]

In 1940, in *Wisconsin v. J. C. Penney Co.*[9] the Court through Justice Frankfurter, expressed the due process concept of jurisdiction to tax in terms of "nexus"—a tie or link. The question presented in that case was whether Wisconsin, a non-domiciliary state, could impose a tax of two and one-half percent upon the "privilege of declaring and receiving dividends, out of income derived from property located and business transacted in" Wisconsin. Taxpayer, a Delaware corporation, voted and paid dividends from its principal office in New York with checks drawn upon New York bank accounts. In sustaining the tax in the face of the taxpayer's challenge that there was a violation of due process concepts of jurisdiction, the Court stated the applicable test in the following terms:

> [The due process] . . . test is whether property was taken without due process of law, or, if paraphrase we must, whether the taxing power exerted by the state bears fiscal relation to protection, opportunities and benefits given by the state. The simple but controlling question is whether the state has given anything for which it can ask return. The substantial privilege of carrying on business in Wisconsin, which has here been given, clearly supports the tax . . . . The fact that a tax is contingent upon events brought to pass without a state does not destroy the nexus between such a tax and transactions within a state for which the tax is an exaction.[10]

Although the decision in *J. C. Penney Co.* related to an excise tax rather than a property tax, the substantive due process issue is the same: Has the taxing jurisdiction provided a benefit to the taxpayer with respect to his person, his property, or his business? If

---

franchise derived from Indiana is an incorporeal hereditament derived from and having its legal situs in that state. It is not within the jurisdiction of Kentucky. The taxation of that franchise or incorporeal hereditament by Kentucky is, in our opinion, a deprivation by that state of the property of the ferry company without due process of law in violation of the 14th Amendment of the Constitution of the United States; as much so as if the state taxed the real estate owned by that company in Indiana." (Id. at 397–98).

6. 295 U.S. 422 (1935).

7. For this point the Court relied upon its erlier decision in Brown v. Fletcher, 235 U.S. 589 (1915). In *Brown* the Court held that a provision of the Judicial Code which limited the jurisdiction of the United States District Court to suits brought "to recover upon any promissory note or other chose in action" did not confer jurisdiction to enforce the interest of an assignee of a beneficial interest under a testamentary trust. Emphasis was placed upon the following statement in the *Brown* decision: "If the trust estate consisted of land, it would not be claimed that a deed conveying seventenths interest therein was a chose in action . . . ." 235 U.S. at 597.

8. Justice Stone, joined by Justices Brandeis and Cardozo filed a vigorous dissent on the ground that transferable certificates of beneficial interests in trusts of land are comparable to shares of stock in a corporation and should be considered intangibles for purposes of taxation.

9. 311 U.S. 435 (1940).

10. 311 U.S. at 444–45.

an affirmative answer is forthcoming, the requirements of substantive due process have been met.

3. Personal Property

a. Distinction Between Tangible and Intangible Personal Property

In the decision in *Union Refrigerator Co. v. Kentucky*,[11] the Court noted that there is a fundamental difference in the criteria for imposition of an ad valorem general property tax as between tangible and intangible personal property. With respect to tangible personal property, physical location of the property in the taxing state was held prerequisite as a matter of due process to the quid pro quo requirement of protection for which an ad valorem property tax is imposed as compensation. Consequently, tangible personal property having a permanent location has an exclusive tax situs in the state in which it is located irrespective of the state of domicile of the owner.

By contrast, the Court observed that as a matter of administrative convenience, the Courts apply the maxim *mobilia sequuntur personam* and hold that intangible personal property may be taxed by the state of residence or domicile of the owner even though this rule may result in multiple taxation. The Court expressed the rationale for this distinction in the following manner.

[T]here is an obvious distinction between tangible and intangible property, in the fact that the latter is held secretly; that there is no method by which its existence or ownership can be ascertained in the State of its situs, except perhaps in the case of mortgages or shares of stock. So if the owner be discovered, there is no way by which he can be reached by process in a State other than that of his domicil, or the collection of the tax otherwise enforced. In this class of cases the tendency of modern authorities is to apply the maxim *mobilia sequuntur personam*, and to hold that the property may be taxed at the domicil of the owner as the real situs of the debt, and also, more

particularly in the case of mortgages, in the State where the property is retained. . . .

If this occasionally results in double taxation, it much oftener happens that this class of property escapes altogether. In the case of intangible property, the law does not look for absolute equality, but to the much more practical consideration of collecting the tax upon such property, either in the State of the domicil or the situs. Of course, we do not enter into a consideration of the question, so much discussed by political economists, of the double taxation involved in taxing the property from which these securities arise, and also the burdens upon such property, such as mortgages, shares of stock and the like—the securities themselves.[12]

The potential for multiple taxation of intangible personal property is more fully developed later in this Chapter.

b. Imported Goods and the Demise of the "Original Package" Doctrine

(1) Imports From Abroad

For a century and a half, goods imported from foreign countries were insulated from all forms of state and local taxation so long as such goods remained in the "original package." The decision in *Brown v. Maryland*[13] was the genesis of this "original package" doctrine. Under the Maryland statute that was challenged in *Brown*, "all importers of foreign articles or commodities . . . before they [could] sell" such goods were required to "take out a license" at a cost of fifty dollars. The statute was patently discriminatory since it did not apply to vendors of domestic goods. The Court concluded that the tax violated both Article I, Section 8, Clause 3 which confers upon Congress the power "to regulate Commerce with foreign Nations" and Article I, Section 9 which specifies that "no State shall, without the Consent of the Congress, lay any Imposts or Duties on Imports or Exports."

The issue presented in *Brown* could have been resolved by emphasizing the discrimi-

---

11. 199 U.S. 194 (1905).

12. 199 U.S. at 205–206.

13. 25 U.S. (12 Wheat.) 419 (1827).

natory nature of the license tax. But the
Attorney General of Maryland, Roger Taney
(later Chief Justice Taney), contended that
invalidation of the tax by strict construction
of the literal language of the Constitution
would result in rendering imported goods
permanently free from state and local taxation, thereby depriving the states of a valuable source of revenue. Chief Justice Marshall responded to this argument with the
following observation:

> It is sufficient for the present to say, general-
> ly, that when the importer has so acted upon
> the thing imported, that it has become incorpo-
> rated and mixed up with the mass of property
> in the country, it has, perhaps, lost its distinc-
> tive character as an import, and has become
> subject to the taxing power of the State; but
> while remaining the property of the importer,
> in his warehouse, in the original form or pack-
> age in which it was imported, a tax upon it is
> too plainly a duty on imports to escape the pro-
> hibition in the constitution.[14]

Forty-five years later, the "original package" dictum in *Brown* was adopted by the
Court in *Low v. Austin*[15] as constitutional
doctrine to bar the imposition of a nondiscriminatory ad valorem property tax upon
imported goods which had left the stream of
commerce but which had not been removed
from their original packages. Thus the
"original package" doctrine, although unsupported by sound rationale and inconsistent with the underlying purposes of the
constitutional provision, became firmly wo-
ven into our constitutional fabric. By the
mid-1940's, critical scholarly analysis had established the weakness of the rule[16] and the
Court began to waiver in its adherence.

In *Hooven & Allison Co. v. Evatt*[17] and
Youngstown Sheet & Tube Co. v. Bowers,[18]
the Court adopted the view that imported
raw materials essential to the maintenance
of normal manufacturing inventories had be-

come so committed to the regular on-going
manufacturing process as to warrant imposition of state and local ad valorem property
taxes. However, these decisions left open
the obvious question as to whether manufactured goods which were imported for resale
and which were essential to the maintenance
of normal inventories of a wholesale or retail
merchant should also be deemed to have
passed beyond the veil of protection under
the "original package" doctrine.

With the decision in *Michelin Tire Corp.
v. Wages*,[19] the Court finally discarded the
original package doctrine in its entirety as a
bar to nondiscriminatory state taxation and
overruled *Low v. Austin*:

> Our independent study persuades us that a
> nondiscriminatory ad valorem property tax is
> not the type of state exaction which the Fram-
> ers of the Constitution or the Court in *Brown*
> had in mind as being an "impost" or "duty"
> and that *Low v. Austin's* reliance upon the
> *Brown* dictum to reach the contrary conclusion
> was misplaced.[20]

At a later point, the Court again emphasized
the validity of a nondiscriminatory ad
valorem property tax on imported goods
which are no longer in transit:

> Nothing in the history of the Import-Export
> Clause even remotely suggests that a nondis-
> criminatory ad valorem property tax which is
> also imposed on *imported goods that are no
> longer in import transit* was the type of exac-
> tion that was regarded as objectionable by the
> Framers of the Constitution. By definition,
> such a tax does not fall on imports as such be-
> cause of their place of origin.[21]

(2) Imports From Sister States

In concluding his opinion in *Brown v. Maryland*, Chief Justice Marshall observed as
dictum that "we suppose the principles laid
down in this case to apply equally to impor-
tations from a sister State."[22] During the

---

14. Id. at 441–42.

15. 80 U.S. (13 Wall.) 29 (1872).

16. E.g., Powell, State Taxation of Imports—When
Does an Import Cease to Be an Import?, 59 Harv.L.
Rev. 858 (1945).

17. 324 U.S. 652 (1945).

18. 358 U.S. 534 (1959).

19. 423 U.S. 276 (1976).

20. Id. at 283.

21. Id. at 286 (emphasis added).

22. 25 U.S. (12 Wheat.) at 449.

balance of the nineteenth century, the Court refused to apply this dictum with respect to goods originating in another state.

Woodruff v. Parham,[23] was the first and most notable case to consider the issue as to whether the original package doctrine should be extended to goods imported from a sister state. The City of Mobile imposed a nondiscriminatory tax upon sales at auction. Taxpayer conducted auction sales in Mobile. Included among the goods sold at auction were goods produced in other states which had been consigned to the taxpayer for sale in the original packages. In declining to apply the original package doctrine to bar the tax, the Court explored the history of the export-import clause and concluded that it was inapplicable to interstate goods. With this background, the Court proceeded to emphasize the discriminatory effect which would follow if the doctrine were applied with respect to goods which originated in another state:

Whether we look, then, to the terms of the clause of the Constitution in question, or to its relation to the other parts of that instrument, or to the history of its formation and adoption, or to the comments of the eminent men who took part in those transactions, we are forced to the conclusion that no intention existed to prohibit, by *this clause*, the right of one State to tax articles brought into it from another. If we examine for a moment the results of an opposite doctrine, we shall be well satisfied with the wisdom of the Constitution as thus construed.

The merchant of Chicago who buys his goods in New York and sells at wholesale in the origi-

nal packages, may have his millions employed in trade for a half a lifetime and escape all State, county, and city taxes; for all that he is worth is invested in goods which he claims to be protected as imports from New York. Neither the State nor the city which protects his life and property can make him contribute a dollar to support its government, improve its thoroughfares or educate its children. The merchant in a town in Massachusetts, who deals only in wholesale, if he purchase his goods in New York, is exempt from taxation. If his neighbor purchase in Boston, he must pay all the taxes which Massachusetts levies with equal justice on the property of all its citizens.[24]

The rule of *Woodruff* was applied by the Court in *Brown v. Houston*,[25] where the taxpayer challenged the validity of a nondiscriminatory general ad valorem property tax. Taxpayer, a Pittsburgh firm, shipped coal to its agent in New Orleans for sale by the boatload. The coal was assessed after reaching the dock in New Orleans. Thereafter, more than half was sold to foreign steamships and consumed in foreign commerce; the balance was sold for local consumption. In sustaining the tax, the Court relied upon *Woodruff* for the proposition that goods brought from another state are not imports and emphasized the fact that the coal had become a part of the common mass of goods held for sale within the state.[26]

There were a few cases in the first quarter of this century in which the Court appeared to lend its support to the extension of the "original package" doctrine to goods

23. 75 U.S. 123 (1868).

24. Id. at 136–37.

25. 114 U.S. 622 (1885).

26. The Court's assessment of the underlying factual situation is important to an understanding of its decision:

"The complainants were not exporters; they did not hold the coal at New Orleans for exportation, but for sale there. Being in New Orleans, and held there on sale, without reference to the destination or use which the purchasers might wish to make of it, it was taxed in the hands of the owners (or their agents) like all other property in the city . . . . If after this, and after being sold, the purchaser

thought proper to put it on board of a steamer bound to foreign parts, that did not alter the character of the taxation so as to convert it from a general tax to a duty on exports. . . . [W]here a general tax is laid on all property alike, it cannot be construed as a duty on exports when falling upon goods not then intended for exportation, though they should happen to be exported afterwards. This is the most that can be said of the goods in question, and we are therefore of opinion that the tax was not a duty on exports any more than it was a duty on imports, within the meaning of those terms in the clause under consideration."

(114 U.S. at 629–630).

having their source in another state.[27] These cases may be distinguished on their facts, however, either as involving the constitutional prohibitions on the imposition of excessive state inspection fees or improper sales or license fees upon sales in interstate commerce.

In any event, the question as to extension of the "original package" doctrine to goods imported from a sister state was laid to rest in *Sonneborn v. Cureton*.[28] Texas imposed an occupation tax upon the gross sales of wholesale dealers in refined oil. Taxpayer obtained oil refined by out-of-state producers part of which was sold from its place of business in Texas "in unbroken original packages." It was contended that the tax as applied to these sales was invalid. The Court sustained the tax, stating and summarizing its disposition of the issue in the following terms:

> Our conclusion must depend on the answer to the question: Is this a regulation of, or a burden upon, interstate commerce? We think it is neither. The oil had come to a state of rest in the warehouse of the appellants and had become a part of their stock, with which they proposed to do business as wholesale dealers in the state. The interstate transportation was at an end, and, whether in the original packages or not, a state tax upon the oil as property or upon its sale in the state, if the state law levied the same tax on all oil or all sales of it, without regard to origin, would be neither a regulation nor a burden of the interstate commerce of which this oil had been the subject.[29]

As indicated by the decision in *Sonneborn*, the crucial test with respect to goods imported from a sister state is whether the interstate transportation of the property has been terminated. If it has, the goods have become a part of the common mass of goods within the state and are subject to nondiscriminatory taxation. In *Michelin*, the Court adopted the same test with respect to foreign imports. Thus, whether the goods are imported in interstate or foreign commerce, taxability in the state of destination turns on whether the goods have left the stream of commerce.

In conclusion, it should be emphasized that even though the goods are no longer in transit, a state or local tax cannot be imposed on a discriminatory basis determined by the initial source of the goods. Violation of this basic principle is illustrated by the underlying facts in *I. M. Darnell & Son Co. v. Memphis*.[30] The Tennessee Constitution provided that the legislature should exempt from the general property tax "the direct product of the soil in the hands of the producer and his immediate vendee." To implement this provision, the legislature provided for the exemption of "all growing crops . . . , the direct product of the soil of this state in the hands of the producer and his immediate vendee, and manufactured articles from the produce of the state in the hands of the manufacturer." Taxpayer operated a lumber mill and on tax day held an inventory of logs, and lumber manufactured from logs which had been produced in other states. Taxpayer objected to the taxation of his inventories on the ground that there was a violation of the commerce clause. His position was sustained on the basis of the discrimination against property which had been imported from another state:

> As there can be no doubt within the principles so clearly settled by the decided cases, to which we have referred, that the disputed tax, which the court below sustained, was a direct burden upon interstate commerce since the law

---

27. Bowman v. Continental Oil Co., 256 U.S. 642 (1921) and Askren v. Continental Oil Co., 252 U.S. 444 (1920). (*Bowman* is a continuation of litigation initiated in *Askren*. It is unclear whether the Court found excessive inspection fees, improper license fee upon solicitation of sales of goods to be shipped in interstate commerce, or relied solely on original package doctrine as to a portion of taxes held invalid); Standard Oil Co. v. Graves, 249 U.S. 389 (1919) (excessive inspection fee); Rearick v. Pennsylvania, 203 U.S. 507 (1906) (im-

proper fixed-sum license fee imposed upon solicitation of sales of goods to be shipped in interstate commerce); Norfolk & Western Ry. v. Sims, 191 U.S. 441 (1903) (improper sales tax imposed upon catalogue purchase from out-of-state vendor).

28. 262 U.S. 506 (1923).

29. Id. at 508–509.

30. 208 U.S. 113 (1908).

of Tennessee in terms discriminated against property the product of the soil of other states brought into the state of Tennessee by exempting like property when produced from the soil of Tennessee, it follows that the court below erred in deciding the tax to be valid . . . ."[31]

As stated by the Court in *Michelin*, a parallel rule applies with respect to goods imported from a foreign country. "The Import-Export clause clearly prohibits state taxation based on the foreign origin of the imported goods, [i.e., a discriminatory tax based on foreign source] but it cannot be read to accord imported goods preferential treatment that permits escape from uniform taxes imposed without regard to foreign origin for services which the State supplies."[32]

The only case that is patently inconsistent with the foregoing rule is *Madden v. Kentucky*.[33] In *Madden*, Kentucky imposed an annual ad valorem property tax upon bank deposits held by its citizens. Deposits in Kentucky banks were taxed at 10 cents per one hundred dollars, but deposits in out-of-state banks were taxed at 50 cents per one hundred dollars. The Court sustained the tax on out-of-state bank deposits in the face of a challenge under the due process, equal protection and privileges and immunities clauses of the fourteenth amendment.[34] No question was raised by the taxpayer as to infringement of the commerce clause.

Inasmuch as a bank deposit creates a debt, an item of intangible personal property,[35] and since interstate banking transactions constitute commerce under the commerce clause,[36] it is submitted that the tax

sustained in *Madden* violated the commerce clause. The result in *Madden* was to impose a discriminatory tax upon intangible personal property which had its origin in interstate commerce.

c. *Goods Shipped in Interstate and Foreign Commerce*

(1) *When Commerce Begins*

Under both the Commerce Clause and the Import-Export clause, goods that have entered the stream of commerce, whether interstate or foreign, and whether as imports or exports, are immune from state and local taxation so long as the goods remain in the stream of commerce. This effectuates the constitutional objective of protecting interstate and foreign commerce from both cumulative and discriminatory burdens of taxation which might otherwise result as a consequence of the movement of goods through more than one jurisdiction in the course of commerce itself.[37]

The initial question is whether the goods have entered the stream of commerce—i.e., has the "commerce" which gives rise to constitutional protection actually begun? If the owner is to transport the goods, he must have begun the actual transit of the goods in interstate or foreign commerce. If a common carrier is to transport the goods, possession of the goods must have been surrendered to the carrier for purposes of transit. Neither the intention to ship goods in interstate or foreign commerce, the assembling of goods, the packaging of goods, nor their

---

31. Id. at 125. A recent example of the application of the rule of the *Darnell* decision to invalidate a state excise tax is provided by Boston Stock Exchange v. State Tax Comm'n, 429 U.S. 318 (1977). New York imposed a transfer tax on securities transferred or delivered in New York at a greater rate on those which had been sold on out-of-state stock exchanges than on those which had been sold on the New York stock exchange. Citing *Darnell* among other decisions, the Court noted that a tax which favors local enterprises at the expense of out-of-state businesses violates the prohibition against discriminatory treatment of interstate commerce. 429 U.S. at 329.

32. 423 U.S. at 287.

33. 309 U.S. 83 (1940).

34. The decision in *Madden* was premised upon the broad power of the states to classify for purposes of taxation and the conclusion that the right to deposit money in a bank is not a privilege of national citizenship within the privileges and immunities clause.

35. Fidelity & Columbia Trust Co. v. Louisville, 245 U.S. 54 (1917) (sustaining a Kentucky ad valorem property tax on a resident's bank deposits in St. Louis banks).

36. See California Bankers Ass'n v. Shultz, 416 U.S. 21 (1974).

37. For a helpful discussion, see Page, Jurisdiction To Tax Tangible Movables, 1945 Wis.L.Rev. 125.

warehousing is sufficient to place the goods in the stream of commerce.

Coe v. Town of Errol [38] is the seminal case on this point. Logs had been cut from forests in New Hampshire and held on the banks of the Androscoggin river in that state to be floated down river at some later date to lumber mills in Maine. While held ready for shipment, the property was assessed for general property tax purposes as of the regular assessment date in the same manner as other property in the state. The owners challenged the tax as violating both the Commerce Clause and the Import-Export clause on the ground that the goods were "in transit to market from one state to another."

In sustaining the tax, the Court reviewed a number of earlier cases and stated the following test for determining whether goods have entered the stream of commerce:

> [N]o definite rule has been adopted with regard to the point of time at which the taxing power of the state ceases as to goods exported to a foreign country or to another state. What we have already said, however, in relation to the products of a state intended for exportation to another state will indicate the view which seems to us the sound one on that subject, namely, that such goods do not cease to be part of the general mass of property in the state, subject, as such, to its jurisdiction, and to taxation in the usual way, until they have been shipped, or entered with a common carrier for transportation to another state, or have been started upon such transportation in a continuous route or journey. We think that this must be the true rule on the subject. [39]

The Court has applied the rule of *Coe v. Errol* in a number of cases in determining

whether the goods in question had entered the stream of commerce. [40]

In the most recent case, *Kosydar v. National Cash Register Co.*, [41] the taxpayer had manufactured cash registers and other business machines to meet the specifications of foreign customers. Pending actual shipment, the goods were warehoused at the company's main plant in Dayton, Ohio and were included on the local property tax rolls. Taxpayer contended that the goods were exempt under the Import-Export Clause because of their unique construction and special adaptation to foreign currency transactions which rendered the goods domestically nonsaleable and assured the practical certainty of their exportation. In reliance upon *Coe v. Errol*, and intervening decisions, the Court concluded: "Our prior cases have determined that the protections of the Import-Export Clause are not available until the article at issue begins its physical entry into the stream of exportation. We find no reason to depart from that settled doctrine." [42]

(2) Interruption of Commerce

Assuming that shipment of the goods has once begun, what is the effect of an interruption of the shipment of the goods prior to delivery at the ultimate market destination? If the interruption is for a purpose associated with, or is incidental to, the safe transportation of the property, the goods are deemed to remain in the stream of commerce and to

---

38. 116 U.S. 517 (1886).

39. Id. at 527.

40. In each of the following cases the Court sustained the particular tax on the ground that the goods had not entered the stream of commerce: (1) Empresa Siderurgica, S.A. v. Merced County, 337 U.S. 154 (1949) (ad valorem property tax on portions of cement plant which had been dismantled and crated but not yet delivered to common carrier for export); (2) Federal Compress & Warehouse Co. v. McLean, 291 U.S. 17 (1934) (nondiscriminatory tax upon privilege of operating a cotton compress; cotton compressed, baled and held in

warehouse pending subsequent shipment in interstate commerce); (3) Oliver Iron Mining Co. v. Lord, 262 U.S. 172 (1923) (occupation tax upon business of mining iron ore at 6 percent of value of ore mined; ore shipped to out-of-state customers); (4) Heisler v. Thomas Colliery Co., 260 U.S. 245 (1922) (ad valorem tax upon anthracite coal mined in the state: coal was destined for shipment out-of-state and value was determined after coal had been mined, washed, screened, or otherwise prepared for market).

41. 417 U.S. 62 (1974).

42. Id. at 71.

enjoy constitutional tax immunity.[43]   On the other hand, if the interruption in the shipment of the goods is for a separate business purpose unrelated to safe transportation of the goods, as for example, for processing or for holding the goods pending receipt of orders, the goods will be deemed to have been withdrawn from the stream of commerce. In that case, the property will be considered to have become a part of the taxable mass of goods in the jurisdiction in which movement of the goods has ceased.[44]

There are a few cases which warrant special emphasis on the issue of interruption in interstate or foreign shipment. In *Bacon v. Illinois*[45] the taxpayer purchased grain which was in transit from southern and western states. Through his agents he had contracted for resale of the grain in eastern markets. The southern and western sellers had shipped the grain under contracts with the railroads for shipment to the east coast with reservation of the right to remove the grain from the cars at Chicago for the "purposes of inspecting, weighing, cleaning, clipping, drying, sacking, grading, or mixing, or changing the ownership, consignee or destination" thereof. Upon arrival of the grain in Chicago, taxpayer removed the grain from the railroad cars to his private elevator for the sole purpose of inspecting, weighing, grading, and mixing. As soon as these operations were completed, the grain was reloaded in railroad cars and shipped to customers in eastern cities. No part of the grain was sold or consumed in Illinois. Illinois imposed a general property tax upon the inventory of the grain in the taxpayer's elevator on tax day. In sustaining the tax, the Court premised its decision upon the purpose of the interruption in the shipment:

> But neither the fact that the grain had come from outside the state, nor the intention of the owner to send it to another state, and there to dispose of it, can be deemed controlling when the taxing power of the state of Illinois is concerned. The property was held by the plaintiff in error in Chicago for his own purposes and with full power of disposition. It was not being actually transported, and it was not held by carriers for transportation. The plaintiff in error had withdrawn it from the carriers. . . . He had the privilege of continuing the transportation under the shipping contracts, but of this he might avail himself or not, as he chose. He might sell the grain in Illinois or forward it, as he saw fit . . . . He had established a local facility in Chicago for his own benefit, and while, through its employment, the grain was there at rest, there was no reason why it

---

43. Champlain Realty Co. v. Brattleboro, 260 U.S. 366 (1922) is the leading case on this point. Taxpayer cut logs in Vermont and placed them in an adjoining river to be floated to its mill in New Hampshire. Flood conditions necessitated holding the logs downstream in a boom near Brattleboro until the flood subsided. While held in the boom, the logs were assessed for general property taxes. The Court concluded that the logs in the boom were still in transit in interstate commerce and therefore immune from local property taxes since the interruption of the journey was necessary to the safe delivery of the property at the owner's mill in New Hampshire. It was emphasized that the interruption in transportation was not for the owner's benefit but solely for the purpose of saving the property from loss or destruction.

44. The following cases illustrate the application of the rule stated in the text: (1) In American Steel & Wire Co. v. Speed, 192 U.S. 500 (1904), taxpayer shipped wire and nails from its Illinois manufacturing plant to its warehouse in Tennessee. The goods were sorted and stored in the Memphis warehouse prior to filling orders received from its customers in southern states. The Court sustained a general property tax upon the warehouse inventory on the ground that termination of shipment in Tennessee served a business pur-

pose separate from the safe and convenient transportation of the goods. (2) A similar result was reached in Susquehanna Coal Co. v. South Amboy, 228 U.S. 665 (1913). Taxpayer was a dealer in coal which it purchased or mined in Pennsylvania. The coal was sold to customers in New York and other eastern states. Shipment was made by rail from Pennsylvania mines to the company's coal yards maintained at the harbor in South Amboy, New Jersey. Taxpayer held in storage at dock side quantities of coal which varied from 10,000 tons to 150,000 tons to meet future orders from its customers. A general property tax upon these inventories was sustained on the ground that the coal had been removed from interstate commerce and was stored for a separate business purpose. (3) In Diamond Match Co. v. Ontonagon, 188 U.S. 82 (1903), taxpayer cut logs in Michigan which were floated downstream and held in a boom in Michigan until needed at its mill in Wisconsin. As needed, logs were taken from the boom and delivered to a railroad carrier for transportation to its Wisconsin mill. Held: Logs gathered in the boom awaiting shipment when needed had not entered interstate commerce and were therefore subject to local property taxes.

45.   227 U.S. 504 (1913).

should not be included with his other property within the state in an assessment for taxation which was made in the usual way, without discrimination.[46]

Two additional cases relate to goods destined for foreign export. In *Richfield Oil Corp. v. State Board of Equalization*,[47] the taxpayer sold oil to the New Zealand government at a price f. o. b. Los Angeles harbor. The oil was transported by pipeline from the taxpayer's refinery in California to storage tanks at the Los Angeles harbor where it was pumped into the purchaser's tanker. California assessed a sales tax upon the sale which was held invalid as an export duty in violation of the import-export clause.[48]

Joy Oil Co., Ltd. v. State Tax Commission,[49] presented a more difficult problem. Joy Oil, a Canadian corporation, purchased gasoline from a Michigan refinery for shipment to Canada. The oil was transported to Dearborn, Michigan by rail and placed in storage tanks pending shipment by truck into Canada. The purchase was made in December, 1945 and shipment to Dearborn was completed in February, 1946. By this time, however, federal regulations had been adopted which prohibited shipment of inflammables over an international motor bridge. Taxpayer held the gasoline in storage in Dearborn until July, 1947 when it began shipment by tanker across the Detroit river. Shipment to Canada was completed in August, 1947. On April, 1947, the gasoline in storage was assessed for general property tax purposes by the Dearborn tax authorities. The issue was whether the tax violated the export-import clause. In sustaining the tax, the majority of the Court, relying upon *Richfield Oil* and *Coe v. Errol*, concluded that the extended delay in continuation of the shipment to Canada had removed the property from the stream of foreign commerce:

> But here the period of storage at Dearborn was so long as to preclude holding that the first step toward exportation would inevitably be followed by others. . . . While in storage, the gasoline might have been diverted to domestic markets without disruption of any existing arrangement for its transshipment and without even breach of any contractual commitment to a foreign purchaser. Neither the character of the property nor any event equivalent to its redelivery to a common carrier made export certain for all practical purposes.
>
> . . .
>
> The export-import Clause was meant to confer immunity from local taxation upon property being exported, not relieve property eventually to be exported from its share of the cost of local services.[50]

Maryland v. Louisiana[51] is a recent case to involve the validity of a tax on goods moving in interstate commerce where the taxing state asserted that there was an interruption which validated the tax. Louisiana imposed a "first-use tax" on certain gas imported into Louisiana which was not previously subjected to taxation by another state or the United States. As structured, the tax applied only to gas produced out-of-state on federal Outer Continental Shelf (OCS) lands. OCS gas was piped from wells in the Gulf of Mexico to processing plants located on the

---

46. 227 U.S. at 516.

47. 329 U.S. 69 (1946).

48. The decision in *Richfield Oil* would not stand today in light of *Michelin*. In Department of Revenue v. Association of Washington Stevedoring Co., 435 U.S. 734 (1978), the Court sustained a general business tax upon the business of stevedoring which had been challenged as contravening the Import-Export Clause. In its decision, the Court referred to *Richfield Oil* which had been cited to support the proposition that the Import-Export Clause imposes an absolute ban on all taxation of imports and exports. This argument was dismissed by the Court with the observation that the *Richfield Oil* decision failed to recognize the distinction established by *Michelin* between a "tax" and an

"Impost or Duty." The clear implication is that even though the property was destined for export, the nondiscriminatory tax upon the local sale in *Richfield Oil* would be valid under the rationale of the *Michelin* decision. See text at Section II, E, 1, d, infra.

49. 337 U.S. 286 (1949).

50. 337 U.S. at 288.

51. 451 U.S. 725 (1981). The following year the Court applied the supremacy clause to bar imposition of local property taxes on goods manufactured in Mexico, shipped to the United States, and held in a customs bonded warehouse pending transshipment to Latin America. Xerox Corp. v. Harris County, Texas, 103 S.Ct. 523 (1982).

Louisiana coast where liquifiable hydrocarbons were removed. The gas flowed continuously from the well head to and through the processing plants into interstate pipelines with 98% of the OCS gas distributed to out-of-state consumers in over 30 states. Under the Louisiana statute, exemptions from and credits for the tax with respect to local use or consumption were so designed that in operation the tax applied only to gas that was distributed to out-of-state customers. Several states, joined by the United States and a number of pipeline companies, brought an original action in the Supreme Court to challenge the validity of the tax under both the supremacy clause and the commerce clause. Plaintiffs were successful on both counts.

On the commerce clause issue, Louisiana argued that the local "uses" for which the tax was imposed constituted an interruption in the flow of commerce so that there was a sufficient nexus to validate the tax. In response, the Court observed that although there may have been a sufficient nexus for a valid Louisiana tax, there was no interruption of the movement of the gas in interstate commerce. Relying on the tests laid down in *Complete Auto Transit*,[52] the Court noted that a state tax on interstate commerce can be sustained *provided* there is a substantial nexus with the taxing state, the tax is fairly apportioned, and it does not discriminate against interstate commerce. If a tax fails to meet any one of these tests, it cannot

stand. In view of the patent discriminatory operation of the "first-use tax," the Court concluded that there was a clear violation of the commerce clause.

(3) Termination of Commerce

The final issue for consideration is when the shipment of goods in interstate or foreign commerce has been concluded. Generally, delivery of the goods by the carrier to the consignee purchaser or owner terminates the movement in interstate or foreign commerce and removes them from the protection of the commerce clause or the Import-Export clause. The best example of this principle is the decision in *Michelin*,[53] which emphasized the termination of transit.

d. Taxation of Intangible Personal Property

As indicated previously, multiple ad valorem property taxation of intangible personal property was recognized by the Court at an early date as consistent with principles of substantive due process.[1] The owner's state of domicile can tax intangible personal property by application of the maxim, mobilia sequuntur personam.[2] Under this maxim, a domiciliary corporation is also taxable upon intangibles which have no connection with the state of incorporation and which are directly related to another state, or which are utilized by the corporation in carrying on business in another state.[3] On

---

52. 430 U.S. 274 (1977). See text at Section II, D, 6, infra.

53. 423 U.S. 276 (1976). See text at Section II, A, 3, b, (1), supra.

1. Supra, Section II, A, 3, a.

2. Fidelity & Columbia Trust Co. v. Louisville, 245 U.S. 54 (1917) (bank deposits in out-of-state bank).

3. Cream of Wheat Co. v. Grand Forks County, 253 U.S. 325 (1920) is the leading case on this point. The corporation was organized under the laws of North Dakota but all of its business, manufacturing, commercial and financial, was conducted outside the state. A tax upon the intangible property of the corporation was sustained on the ground that the taxing state was the domiciliary state: "The fact that its property and business was entirely in another state did not make it any the less subject to taxation in the state of its domicile."

253 U.S. at 328. Accord, Newark Fire Insurance Co. v. State Bd. of Tax Appeals, 307 U.S. 313 (1939).

The *Cream of Wheat* decision was followed in sustaining a tax on intangibles of a domestic corporation in Commonwealth v. Universal Trades, Inc., 392 Pa. 323, 141 A.2d 204, appeal dismissed 358 U.S. 129 (1958). In *Universal*, a corporation engaged in the construction business was organized as a Pennsylvania corporation. Its principal office was located in Florida and its construction business was carried on in the British West Indies and Puerto Rico for the United States government. No business activity was conducted in Pennsylvania and the corporation had no property in Pennsylvania. Business of the corporation was directed and conducted entirely through its principal office in Florida. The tax sustained was imposed by Pennsylvania upon the corporation's bank accounts and accounts receivable due from out-of-state debtors.

the other hand, a nondomicilliary state can impose a valid tax upon intangibles under the quid pro quo principle of benefits conferred by its laws in the creation, control, protection, or enforcement of the particular intangible property interest.

Accepting the basic principle that the state of domicile can always tax the owner's intangible personal property, numerous examples of actual or potential multiple taxation can be cited. The state of the debtor's residence can tax a non-resident creditor upon the debt owed to him whether or not such debt is secured by a lien upon local real or personal property.[4] The rationale of these cases may be stated in the alternative: either, (a) upon the ground that the debt is enforcible under the laws of the taxing state, or (b) upon the fact that the debt was acquired by the taxpayer in the conduct of an established business in the taxing state. In the latter case, the debt is deemed to have a commercial or business situs. Similarly, the state of incorporation can impose a property tax upon the shares of stock of a corporation organized under its laws and owned by nonresident shareholders. The underlying principle has been stated by the Court in the following terms:

> [T]he shares represent a property interest, an aliquot proportion of the whole corporate assets. The shareholders, whether domestic or foreign, depend for the preservation and protection of this property upon the law of the state of the corporation's domicile. The property right so represented is of value, arises

where the corporation has its home, and is therefore within the taxing jurisdiction of that state; and this, notwithstanding the ownership of the stock may also be a taxable subject in another state.[5]

Two cases bearing upon the issue of multiple taxation of intangibles warrant special consideration. In *Wheeling Steel Corp. v. Fox*,[6] the taxpayer, a Delaware corporation, maintained its principal office in Wheeling, West Virginia. From this office, the corporate officers conducted the business of the corporation. Although its major manufacturing facilities were in Ohio, all sales orders were accepted, billings were rendered, collections were made and deposits with New York banks were processed through the Wheeling office. Checks drawn upon New York banks were issued from the principal office in Wheeling to pay the operating expenses of the corporation. West Virginia imposed a property tax upon the taxpayer's out-of-state bank accounts and accounts receivable due from out-of-state customers. The issue was whether the West Virginia tax violated principles of due process. In sustaining the tax, the Court held that the out-of-state bank accounts and accounts receivable due from out-of-state customers were localized in West Virginia and properly attributable to that state as the "commercial domicile" of the corporation. As the Court observed: "The corporation has made . . . [Wheeling, West Virginia] the actual seat of its corporate government."[7]

---

4. (1) Liverpool & L. & G. Insurance Co. v. Board of Assessors, 221 U.S. 346 (1911) (premiums due to out-of-state insurance company from policy holders to whom credit had been extended); (2) Metropolitan Life Insurance Co. v. New Orleans, 205 U.S. 395 (1907) (loans made by New York corporation upon insurance policies through local office in New Orleans); (3) New Orleans v. Stempel, 175 U.S. 309 (1899) (mortgage loans made by New York resident through local agent); (4) Savings & Loan Society v. Multnomah County, 169 U.S. 421 (1898) (California resident taxable under Oregon property tax for mortgage loan secured by Oregon real estate).

5. Schuylkill Trust Co. v. Pennsylvania, 302 U.S. 506, 516 (1938) (footnotes omitted). In an earlier case, the Court had reached the same conclusion. Corry v. Baltimore, 196 U.S. 466 (1905). The practical problem of collection of the tax with respect to nonresident

shareholders is avoided by placing the burden of payment upon the corporation with a right of reimbursement against the shareholders.

6. 298 U.S. 193 (1936).

7. Id. at 212.

There is language in the decision which suggests that the "commercial situs" in West Virginia might preclude taxation of the intangibles by Delaware, the domiciliary state:

> "To attribute to Delaware, merely as the chartering state, the credits arising in the course of the business established in another state, and to deny to the latter the power to tax such credits upon the ground that it violates due process to treat the credits as within its jurisdiction, is to make a legal fiction dominate realities in a fashion quite as extreme as that which would attribute to the chartering state all

In the following year, the Court rendered a more sweeping decision in *First Bank Stock Corp. v. Minnesota.*[8] Taxpayer, also a Delaware corporation, owned controlling interests in the shares of a number of financial institutions located in the Ninth Federal Reserve District. Included in this group were shares in Montana and North Dakota banks. Corporate business and fiscal operations were centralized and controlled from its principal office in Minnesota where the stock certificates of its subsidiaries were kept. Taxpayer's shares in the Montana and North Dakota banks had been lawfully taxed under the general property tax laws in those states. Minnesota also imposed a general property tax upon these shares and taxpayer objected on due process grounds. Taxpayer's objection was denied and the Court sustained the Minnesota property tax, concluding its decision with the following statement:

> The economic advantages realized through the protection, at the place of domicil, of the ownership of rights in intangibles, the value of which is made the measure of the tax, bear a direct relationship to the distribution of burdens which the tax effects. These considerations support the taxation of intangibles at the place of domicil, at least where they are not shown to have acquired a business situs elsewhere, as a proper exercise of the power of government. Like considerations support their taxation at their business situs, for it is there that the owner in every practical sense invokes and enjoys the protection of the laws, and in consequence realizes the economic advantages of his ownership. We cannot say that there is any want of due process in the taxation of the corporate shares in Minnesota, irrespective of the extent of the control over them which the due process clause may save to the states of incorporation.[9]

the tangible possessions of the Corporation without regard to their actual location.

"The constitutional authority of West Virginia to tax the accounts receivable and bank deposits in question cannot be denied upon the ground that they are taxable solely in Delaware. The question is whether they should be deemed to be localized in West Virginia." (298 U.S. at 211).

Assuming that each state imposes a general property tax to the full extent of its constitutional power under the federal constitution, implications of the *First Bank* decision for extensive multiple taxation of intangible personal property become readily apparent. This is particularly so when the decision in *First Bank* is read in connection with the long line of existing authority recognizing double taxation of intangibles as impervious to due process objections.[10]

4. *Taxation of Interstate Transportation and Communiction Systems*

a. *Unitary Method of Valuation*

With respect to the valuation of an interstate transportation or communication system, it is readily apparent that a valuation of that portion of the system located solely within a taxing district of a state as physical property wholly separate and apart from the entire system would not accurately reflect its real value. Accurate valuation of a part of an interstate system can be ascertained only by consideration of the value of the entire system as an integrated going concern. To remedy the undervaluation which would result from the separation of out-of-state properties of an interstate system for ad valorem taxation, the states during the last half of the nineteenth century enacted statutes which provided for valuation of interstate railroad systems in their entirety by combining out-of-state portions with in-state portions to arrive at a total unitary value. The value of the entire system then was apportioned to the taxing state on the basis of main track mileage within the state to total track mileage of the entire system. This valuation of the in-state portion in turn was allocated to the various taxing districts on a track mileage basis.[1]

8. 301 U.S. 234 (1937).

9. 301 U.S. at 241.

10. See Section II, A, 3, c, (3), supra.

1. For a comprehensive treatment of the unit rule method of valuation and the history of its development, see 2 J. Bonbright, Valuation of Property, chs. XIX and X (1937).

The unitary method of valuation was first endorsed by the Court in *State Railroad Tax Cases.*[2] This case involved the constitutionality of an Illinois statute which provided that the state board of equalization should value as a unit the railroad track, right of way, rolling stock and intangibles of railroad corporations operating within the state. This unit value was allocated by the board among the various counties on a track mileage basis and reallocated within the respective counties in a similar manner among the several taxing districts through which the railroad operated. Property of all other corporations and individuals was subject to assessment by the local assessor. Although there were some clear overtones of federal constitutional issues, the Court specifically negated any serious challenge under the United States Constitution.[3] The crux of the case was whether the centralization of assessment of railroad operating property (tangible and intangible) in a state board which was required by statute to utilize the unit rule of valuation violated the state constitutional requirement of uniformity. The Court found no support for the position of the railroad companies. In denying relief, the Court endorsed the unit rule of valuation in the following terms:

> [A]s we have already said, a railroad must be regarded for many, indeed for most purposes, as a unit. The track of the road is but one track from one end of it to the other, and, except in its use as one track, is of little value. In this track as a whole each county through which it passes has an interest much more important than it has in the limited part of it lying within its boundary. Destroy by any means a few miles of this track within an interior county, so as to cut off the connection between the two parts thus separated, and, if it could not be repaired or replaced, its effect upon the value of the remainder of the road is out of all proportion to the mere local value of the part of it destroyed. A similar effect on the value of the interior of the road would follow the destruction of that end of the road lying in Chicago, or some other place where its largest traffic centres. It may well be doubted whether any better mode of determining the value of that portion of the track within any one county has been devised than to ascertain the value of the whole road, and apportion the value within the county by its relative length to the whole.[4]

Not until 1894, eighteen years later, was the Court confronted with federal constitutional objections to the unit rule of valuation. In the companion cases of *Pittsburgh, C., C. & St. L. Ry. Co. v. Backus*[5] and *Cleveland, C., C. & St. L. Ry. Co. v. Backus,*[6] the unit rule of valuation was unsuccessfully challenged as violating principles of due process and as imposing an undue burden on interstate commerce. The challenge was premised on the ground that by taking out-of-state portions of the railroad into consideration the unit value reflected the value of out-of-state property and values arising from the conduct of interstate commerce. Relying on the explanation in its earlier decision in *State Railroad Tax Cases,* the Court reaffirmed its acceptance of the unit rule as a reasonable method of arriving at a fair valuation of the in-state portions of an interstate railroad system. With the *Backus* decisions, the unit rule of valuation was firmly established.

In applying the unit rule of valuation, two questions arise: (1) Has the taxing state improperly included in the tax base values representing out-of-state properties which are unrelated to the unitary character of the property comprising the system being valued? (2) Does the formula for allocation of values result in an unreasonable allocation to the taxing state? If either of these circumstances exists, the assessment is invalid

---

2. 92 U.S. 575 (1876). The unit rule had been previously applied, but without specific recognition, in sustaining a state franchise tax upon domestic railroad corporations measured by net earnings and capital stock apportioned to the taxing state on the basis of track mileage. The Delaware R.R. Tax, 85 U.S. 206 (1874).

3. "The validity of the statute is not seriously questioned here on the ground of any conflict with the Constitution of the United States." 92 U.S. at 617.

4. Id. at 608.

5. 154 U.S. 421 (1894).

6. 154 U.S. 439 (1894).

as a violation of both due process and the commerce clause.[7]

Two cases may be cited to illustrate the erroneous inclusion of out-of-state property which was deemed unrelated to the unitary character of the particular interstate enterprise. In *Fargo v. Hart*[8] the Indiana tax authorities, in determining the unit value of the American Express Co., included certain securities held by the express company's New York office as a part of its investment trust operations. Taxpayer's challenge of the inclusion of these securities under both due process and the commerce clause was sustained by the Court on the ground that these assets had no organic relation to the conduct of the express business.

Similarly in *Wallace v. Hines*,[9] the Court held that it was improper to include mortgage loans on out-of-state property held as investments, and out-of-state land grants which were not used for railroad purposes in determining the unit value of an interstate railroad. Justice Holmes, writing for the Court, articulated the underlying purpose of the unit rule of valuation in the following manner:

> The only reason for allowing a State to look beyond its borders when it taxes the property of foreign corporations is that it may get the true value of the things within it, when they are part of an organic system of wide extent, that gives them a value above what they otherwise would possess. The purpose is not . . . to open to taxation what is not within the State. Therefore no property of such an interstate road situated elsewhere can be taken into account unless it can be seen in some plain and fairly intelligible way that it adds to the value of the road and the rights exercised in the State.[10]

Union Tank Line v. Wright[11] is the leading case to illustrate an unreasonable formula for allocation of unit value to the taxing state. Union Tank, a New Jersey corporation, owned 12,000 railroad tank cars which it rented to shippers for shipment of goods over interstate railroads. The company did not carry on business in Georgia, but those companies which leased their equipment transported goods into or through Georgia on interstate rail lines on a regular basis throughout the year. By using a mileage basis formula, the tax authorities allocated $291,195 as that part of the unit value attributable to Georgia. Evidence submitted by the taxpayer established that on the average 57 tank cars were in Georgia at all times during the tax year. At a value of $830 per car, the aggregate value of the 57 tank cars in the state totalled $47,310.

The Court recognized that movables which are regularly and habitually used and employed within a state may be taxed according to their fair values although such property is devoted to interstate commerce. It also recognized the propriety of allocating unit value to the taxing state but added that "if the plan pursued is arbitrary and the consequent valuation grossly excessive it must be condemned because of conflict with the commerce clause or . . . [due process] or both."[12] On the facts, the Court concluded that the taxpayer's "property was appraised according to an arbitrary method which produced results wholly unreasonable and that to permit enforcement of the proposed tax would deprive it of property without due process of law and also unduly burden interstate commerce."[13]

7. For helpful discussions of the unit rule, see Isaacs, The Unit Rule, 35 Yale L.J. 838 (1926); Note, The Unit Rule—What Is Unitary Organization, 41 Harv.L.Rev. 227 (1927).

8. 193 U.S. 490 (1904).

9. 253 U.S. 66 (1920).

10. Id. at 69.

11. 249 U.S. 275 (1919).

12. Id. at 282.

13. Id. at 283. See Norfolk & W. R. Co. v. Missouri State Tax Comm'n, 390 U.S. 317 (1968) wherein the Court held that the rigid application of a mileage formula resulted in an excessive allocation of the value of rolling stock to the taxing state.

b. Allocation of Values of Instrumentalities of Interstate Commerce

(1) Railroad Cars

Allocation among the taxing states of the unitary value of an interstate railroad presents little difficulty with respect to the continuous line of track which extends through or into two or more states. But the allocation of the value of a fleet of railroad cars poses a different problem inasmuch as this type of property has no permanent location and continuously moves from state to state in the transportation of goods and persons. However, the fact that the railroad cars have no permanent location within the taxing state does not bar a property tax thereon even though such property is employed in the conduct of interstate commerce.

Pullman's Palace Car Co. v. Pennsylvania [1] is the leading case which established the propriety of tax apportionment of instrumentalities of interstate commerce to a nondomiciliary state with respect to railroad cars operated within the state during the year. Pullman, an Illinois corporation, in cooperation with the various railroads, operated its sleeping coaches, parlor cars, and dining cars throughout the country receiving separate charges from the passengers for the use of these facilities. Pullman operated its equipment continuously into, through, and out of the state of Pennsylvania and had about 100 cars within the state at any time throughout the year. Pennsylvania assessed a tax upon the taxpayer's property by allocating the value of its capital stock (representing the value of its equipment) on a mileage basis. As indicated by the decision in *Union Tank*, this method of allocation may not have been the most accurate, but in the particular case the result was not significantly different from a valuation based on the average number of cars employed in the state during the year. [2]

Taxpayer objected to the tax on the ground that as a matter of due process the cars had an exclusive situs in Illinois, the state of domicile. In its decision the Court stated that the only issue before it was whether the tax violated the commerce clause. It proceeded to hold that Pennsylvania could tax and that the mileage method of allocation was a just and equitable method of assessment. In its opinion, the Court disposed of both the due process and commerce clause issues with the following observation:

> The cars of this company within the state of Pennsylvania are employed in interstate commerce; but their being so employed does not exempt them from taxation by the state; and the state has not taxed them because of their being so employed, but because of their being within its territory and jurisdiction. The cars were continuously and permanently employed in going to and fro upon certain routes of travel. If they had never passed beyond the limits of Pennsylvania, it could not be doubted that the state could tax them, like other property within its borders, notwithstanding they were employed in interstate commerce. The fact that, instead of stopping at the state boundary, they cross that boundary in going out and coming back, cannot affect the power of the state to levy a tax upon them. The state, having the right, for the purposes of taxation, to tax any personal property found within its jurisdiction, without regard to the place of the owner's domicile, could tax the specific cars which at a given moment were within its borders. The route over which the cars travel extending beyond the limits of the state, particular cars may not remain within the state; but the company has at all times substantially the same number of cars within the state, and continuously and constantly uses there a portion of its property; and it is distinctly found, as matter of fact, that the company continuously, throughout the periods for which these taxes were levied, carried on business in Pennsylvania, and had about 100 cars within the state. [3]

The position of the taxpayer in *Pullman* that the state of domicile has exclusive juris-

---

1. 141 U.S. 18 (1891).

2. 2 J. Bonbright, Valuation of Property 671 (1937).

3. 141 U.S. at 25–26.

diction to tax a fleet of railroad cars is of special significance where the domiciliary state asserts its full power to tax. In these circumstances, the Court has consistently recognized the preferential status of the domiciliary state by imposing upon the taxpayer the burden of proving that the property has a separate tax situs in whole or in part in another jurisdiction.[4] In *Central Railroad Co. of Pennsylvania v. Pennsylvania*,[5] for example, the railroad's rolling stock was used throughout the United States. The railroad, however, could show habitual employment only in New Jersey. Consequently, it was held that Pennsylvania as the domiciliary state could tax all of the rolling stock except for the portion allocable to New Jersey.

(2) Boats and Barges

The rules governing taxation of vessels engaged in interstate commerce are determined by whether the vessels are used on inland waterways or on the ocean. Vessels used upon inland waterways are taxed in the same manner as railroad rolling stock and the state of domicile may tax the entire value of the vessels unless it is established that the vessels have acquired a tax situs elsewhere.[6] In *Ott v. Mississippi Valley Barge Line Co.*,[7] the Court sustained a property tax by a nondomiciliary state determined by an allocation of values on a mileage basis. In its decision, the Court stated: "We see no practical difference so far as either the Due Process Clause or the Com-

merce Clause is concerned whether it is vessels or railroad cars that are moving in interstate commerce."[8] In *Standard Oil Co. v. Peck*,[9] decided three years later, the Court held that Ohio, the domiciliary state, could not impose a general property tax on any portion of the taxpayer's barge line in view of the fact that the barges were used almost continuously outside the state during the year. The barges transported oil on the Mississippi and Ohio Rivers, but the vessels neither loaded nor unloaded oil in Ohio ports.

Ocean going vessels, by contrast, are generally taxed under the "home port" doctrine which recognizes that the domiciliary state has exclusive authority to tax.[10] The rationale for this rule is that nondomiciliary states in which the coastal vessels dock do not provide sufficient protection and benefits to justify recognition of jurisdiction to tax. Merely docking in the port of a nondomiciliary state does not constitute habitual use within the state. In *Southern Pacific Co. v. Kentucky*,[11] the Court endorsed the following quotation from an earlier New York case as the appropriate rationale for establishing the taxable situs of ocean-going vessels: "'To determine their situs, for purposes of taxation, by their longer or shorter stay in a particular port, or by their more or less frequent resort to it, would introduce perpetual uncertainty; it would, practically, subject them to taxation in every port, or exempt them in all.'" There is an exception to this rule, however, if the vessel is used solely within the limits of a nondomiciliary state.

---

4. New York Central & H.R.R. Co. v. Miller, 202 U.S. 584 (1906). *New York Central* is the leading case on the issue of burden of proof. In that case, it was acknowledged that a considerable portion of the company's rolling stock was constantly in use out of state. However, New York, the state of incorporation denied the railroad's claim for exclusion of a portion of its rolling stock in determining the value of the corporate capital employed in the state. The Court sustained the New York tax with the following observation: "In the present case . . . it does not appear that any specific cars or any average of cars was so continuously in any other state as to be taxable there." Id. at 597.

5. 370 U.S. 607 (1962).

6. Upper Missouri River Corp. v. Board of Review, 210 N.W.2d 828 (Iowa 1973), appeal dismissed 419 U.S.

809 (1974). Taxpayer, an Iowa corporation, owned a towboat which was leased and used by the lessee outside Iowa throughout the entire year. Held: Iowa as the state of domicile had jurisdiction to tax in the absence of proof that the property had acquired a taxable situs in another jurisdiction.

7. 336 U.S. 169 (1949).

8. Id. at 174.

9. 342 U.S. 382 (1952).

10. Southern Pac. Co. v. Kentucky, 222 U.S. 63 (1911).

11. Id. at 75–76. The Court was quoting from People ex rel. Pac. Mail S. S. Co. v. Commissioners of Taxes, 58 N.Y. 242, 246 (1874).

In that case, the state in which the vessel is in continuous use is deemed to have exclusive jurisdiction to tax.[12]

(3) Airlines

In establishing the jurisdictional rules for the taxation of fleets of airplanes used by airline companies in interstate commerce, the Court at first adopted the rule that the domiciliary state had exclusive jurisdiction to tax. In *Northwest Airlines v. Minnesota*, the Court in sustaining a Minnesota property tax upon the entire fleet emphasized the unique role of Minnesota as the domiciliary state.[13] Ten years later, however, the Court reconsidered its position and in *Braniff Airways, Inc. v. Nebraska State Board of Equalization & Assessment*[14] embraced the rule of allocation of unit valuation of an airline fleet among the states in which the aircraft are habitually employed. Thus, the rules for the taxation of airplanes operated by an interstate airline are the same as those applicable to the rolling stock of interstate railroads.

c. In Lieu Taxes Measured by Gross Receipts

About the turn of the century, some jurisdictions adopted "in lieu" taxes as a basis for taxing railroads, carline companies, and express companies. These taxes were measured by gross receipts derived from business conducted in the taxing state including gross receipts from the in-state portion of interstate commerce. They were described as "in lieu" taxes because they were a substitute for the regular ad valorem property tax. Since these taxes were measured by gross receipts they were challenged as violating the commerce clause.

Maine v. Grand Trunk Ry. Co.[1] was probably the first case to present the issue. In that case, Maine assessed a tax upon the corporate franchise computed on the average gross receipts per mile of railroad operations in the state. The Court sustained the tax on the ground that the corporate franchise was a valuable property interest which was properly subject to taxation by the state and that the gross receipts were merely utilized as a fair measurement of the value of that property interest. Similar results were reached in other cases including *United States Express Co. v. Minnesota*[2] and *Cudahy Packing Co. v. Minnesota.*[3] The most recent application of this rule is found in the decision in *Railway Express Agency, Inc. v. Virginia.*[4] In *Railway Express*, the in lieu tax was measured by gross receipts from operations in Virginia and was a substitute for all property taxes on intangibles and rolling stock of express companies.

d. Compensatory Charges for Use of Highways and Airports

Although property taxes are not involved, it is appropriate at this point to consider the question as to the validity of highway and

---

12. Old Dominion S. S. Co. v. Virginia, 198 U.S. 299 (1905). The Court stated:

"Our conclusion is that where vessels, though engaged in interstate commerce, are employed in such commerce wholly within the limits of a state, they are subject to taxation in that state, although they may have been registered or enrolled at a port outside its limits."

Id. at 309–10.

13. 322 U.S. 292 (1944). Emphasis upon the domiciliary status of the taxing state was cast in the following terms:

"No other State is the State which gave Northwest the power to be as well as the power to function as Northwest functions in Minnesota; no other State could impose a tax that derives from the significant legal relation of creator and creature and the practi-

cal consequences of that relation in this case. On the basis of rights which Minnesota alone originated and Minnesota continues to safeguard, she alone can tax the personalty which is permanently attributable to Minnesota and to no other State."

Id. at 294–95.

14. 347 U.S. 590 (1954). The Court, citing *Ott*, made the following observation: "We perceive no logical basis for distinguishing the constitutional power to impose a tax on such aircraft from the power to impose taxes on river boats." Id. at 600.

1. 142 U.S. 217 (1891).

2. 223 U.S. 335 (1912).

3. 246 U.S. 450 (1918).

4. 358 U.S. 434 (1959).

airport user chargers in relation to the taxation of interstate systems of transportation. It is firmly established that interstate motor carriers although directly engaged in the conduct of interstate commerce can be subjected to nondiscriminatory state license fees for the privilege of using the highways of the taxing state. These exactions are imposed as a condition precedent to operation upon the highways in the state and have been sustained over constitutional objections on the ground that such exactions are merely compensation to the state for wear and tear upon the state's highway system. This rule prevails even though the tax may be paid into the general revenue fund of the taxing state. Judicial doctrine on this point places upon the taxpayer the burden of proving that the exaction constitutes unreasonable compensation for the service or privilege granted.

Highway taxes sustained by the Court have assumed various forms.[1] In *Capitol Greyhound Lines v. Brice*,[2] the most recent of a long line of definitive cases dealing with this particular issue, the Court considered the validity of a Maryland statute which imposed a tax of two percent upon the fair market value of motor vehicles used in interstate or intrastate commerce as a condition precedent to the issuance of certificates of title which in turn were a further condition to the registration and operation of such vehicles in the state of Maryland. Other taxes including a mileage tax were also applicable to both interstate and intrastate carriers. It was the taxpayer's objection that the tax premised upon vehicle value was invalid under the commerce clause as it applied to an interstate carrier, because it varied for each carrier without relation to road use. In

overruling this objection, the Court observed first that considering other taxes the total charges by Maryland varied with mileage traveled, and added that under the general rule "taxes like that of Maryland . . . are valid unless the amount is shown to be in excess of fair compensation for the privileges of using state roads."[3] On the record, the taxpayer failed to sustain its burden of proof.[4]

More recently, in *Evansville-Vanderburgh Airport Authority v. Delta Airlines, Inc.*,[5] the Court considered the question as to the validity of Indiana and New Hampshire airport user fees. The Indiana fee was one dollar and the New Hampshire fee varied from 50 cents to one dollar for each passenger emplaning on any commercial aircraft. The Indiana fee was imposed by a local airport authority with respect to the use of a particular airport; the New Hampshire fee applied to the use of all publicly owned and operated airports in the state. In each case, the fee was payable whether the passenger was travelling to an intrastate or interstate destination.

In reliance upon the highway user fee cases, the Court sustained the charges on the principle that it is "settled that a charge designed only to make the user of state-provided facilities pay a reasonable fee to help defray the costs of their construction and maintenance may constitutionally be imposed on interstate and domestic users alike."[6] The Court had no difficulty in accepting the fact that the charges were an approximation of the value of the use and that there was a reasonable classification of passengers in the application of the fees. Some passengers, such as those using private planes, members of the military, temporary

---

1. Dixie Ohio Express Co. v. State Revenue Comm'n, 306 U.S. 72 (1939) (manufacturer's rated capacity and weight of trailers); Hicklin v. Coney, 290 U.S. 169 (1933) (carrying capacity); Continental Baking Co. v. Woodring, 286 U.S. 352 (1932) (gross-ton mileage); Interstate Busses Corp. v. Blodgett, 276 U.S. 245 (1928) (mileage within the state); Clark v. Poor, 274 U.S. 554 (1927) (number and capacity of vehicles); Kane v. New Jersey, 242 U.S. 160 (1916); and Hendrick v. Maryland, 235 U.S. 610 (1915) (horsepower).

2. 339 U.S. 542 (1950). The Appendix to Justice Frankfurter's dissenting opinion contains a tabulation and summary of all cases decided by the Court prior to 1950 which considered the question of highway user taxes. Id. at 561.

3. Id. at 547.

4. Id. at 548.

5. 405 U.S. 707 (1972).

6. Id. at 714.

layovers, and deplaning passengers were not subject to the charges. Finally, the Court observed that the airlines had failed to establish that the fees were excessive in relation to costs incurred by the taxing authorities.[7]

5. Taxation of Instrumentalities of Foreign Commerce

Prior to its decision in *Japan Line, Ltd. v. County of Los Angeles*,[1] the Court had not ruled on the question whether a state may impose a nondiscriminatory ad valorem property tax on foreign-owned instrumentalities of international commerce. More than a century ago, the Court applied the "home port" doctrine in determining jurisdiction to tax ocean-going vessels owned by a United States company that transported goods and passengers in interstate commerce between New York and California via way of the Isthmus of Panama.[2] In 1961, the Court denied certiorari in a case where a state court had held invalid under the commerce clause an ad valorem property tax on foreign-owned aircraft, based and registered abroad and used exclusively in international commerce.[3]

In *Japan Line*, the state tax authorities imposed an ad valorem personal property tax on cargo containers owned by Japanese shipping companies that were used in transporting goods by ocean-going vessels in international commerce. The value of the containers was apportioned on the basis of their "average presence" in the taxing district which was three weeks of each year. In this manner, approximately $3/52$ of the total value of the cargo containers was apportioned to the respective California taxing districts. The facts were stipulated on appeal and it was stated that the cargo containers owned by the Japanese companies were subject to property taxes in Japan and were taxed on their total value in that country. Similar American-owned cargo containers temporarily located in Japan were not subjected to Japanese property taxes.

California tax authorities contended that a nondiscriminatory property tax imposed on instrumentalities of foreign commerce on an apportioned basis was comparable to an ad valorem tax on instrumentalities of interstate commerce and valid by application of the same constitutional standards.[4] In refusing to accept the view that commerce clause analysis was controlling, the Court emphasized that two additional inquiries must be made: first, whether the state tax creates a substantial risk of international multiple taxation; and second, whether the state tax prevents the federal government from speaking with one voice in regulating commercial relations with foreign governments.

On the first point, the stipulation of facts clearly established that there was international multiple taxation. On the second, the Court referred to the Customs Convention on Containers entered into by Japan and the United States. Under the Convention, temporarily imported cargo containers are admitted free of "all duties and taxes whatsoever chargeable by reason of importation." This convention, the Court observed, reflects a national policy to remove impediments to the use of containers as instrumentalities of international commerce. Thus, to permit the

---

7. See Chapter 9, section V for a discussion of *Evansville-Vanderburgh* with respect to interference with the freedom of mobility of individuals under the commerce clause. Subsequent to the *Evansville-Vanderburgh* decision, Congress enacted legislation to prohibit states and political subdivisions from imposing airport head taxes. 49 U.S.C.A. § 1513.

1. 441 U.S. 434 (1979).

2. Hays v. Pacific Mail S.S. Co., 58 U.S. (17 How.) 596 (1854).

3. Scandinavian Airlines System Inc. v. County of Los Angeles, 56 Cal.2d 11, 14 Cal.Rptr. 25, 363 P.2d 25, cert. denied 368 U.S. 899 (1961).

4. The factors that California relied upon to sustain the tax were the following: (1) a substantial nexus existed by reason of habitual presence of some of the containers throughout the year; (2) the tax was fairly apportioned on the basis of average presence; (3) the tax did not discriminate: and (4) the tax was fairly related to services provided by the California governmental units. 441 U.S. at 444–46. The Court rejected these arguments as applied to foreign commerce.

California tax to stand would frustrate the attainment of federal uniformity in the negotiation of international trade agreements and set the stage for retaliatory taxes by foreign governments.

6. *Property Interests Held In Trust*

Jurisdiction of a state to impose a general property tax upon property held by a trustee is governed by the same rules as apply to the taxation of property owned by any other person. Real property and tangible personal property located in the taxing state, title to which is held by a trustee, is subject to tax under the quid pro quo doctrine set forth in *Union Refrigerator Transit Co. v. Kentucky.*[1] Similarly, intangible personal property owned by the trustee is subject to property taxation in the same manner as intangibles owned by any other person and subject to the same risks of multiple taxation.[2] The state of the trustee's domicile has jurisdiction to tax by application of the maxim mobilia sequuntur personam or by reason of the commercial or business situs of the trust. Other states may also have jurisdiction to tax for various reasons based on benefits and protection conferred with respect to such property.

There are two aspects of trust ownership which may give rise to additional multiple taxation. If there are co-trustees, each of whom is domiciled in a different state, each state may assert jurisdiction to tax. However, if the trust corpus consists of real property or tangible personal property, only the state in which the property is located has jurisdiction to tax. But if the corpus includes intangibles, the property may have a dual tax situs. This principle is illustrated by the decision in *Greenough v. Tax Assessors*[3] where the Rhode Island statutes provided that intangibles held in trust by more than one trustee should be taxed proportionately in the towns where the co-trustees resided.

In *Greenough,* a decedent who died a resident of New York created a testamentary trust of certain corporate stocks and designated a resident of New York and a resident of Rhode Island as co-trustees. The securities were held at all times in New York and the business of the trust was transacted solely in New York. Pursuant to the Rhode Island statute, the tax authorities assessed one-half the trust corpus as property taxable to the co-trustee residing in that state. The assessment was challenged on due process grounds. In rejecting this contention, the Court emphasized that the courts of Rhode Island were available to other parties for the enforcement of any claims arising with respect to the co-trustee's performance of his duties under the trust. On this basis, the Court concluded that sufficient benefit and protection was afforded to support imposition of the tax.

The second aspect of trust ownership which increases the possibility of additional multiple taxation relates to the interest of the beneficiary. Assume, for example, that the trustee is domiciled in State *A.* All the trust corpus is located in State *A.* The life income beneficiary is domiciled in State *B,* and the designated remainderman is domiciled in State *C.* As a matter of due process, are the several property interests taxable in each of the three states? There is no doubt that State *A* has jurisdiction to tax the entire trust corpus since that is the domicile of the trustee as holder of the legal title. Furthermore, inasmuch as all the property is located in State *A* and all trust business is transacted in that state the trust also has a business situs in State *A.*

The next question is whether State *B* has jurisdiction to tax the value of the interest of the life beneficiary. In *Safe Deposit & Trust Co. of Baltimore v. Virginia,*[4] the settlor, a resident of Virginia, transferred certain securities in trust to a Baltimore

---

1. 199 U.S. 194 (1905). See text discussion at Section II, A, 2, supra.

2. See text discussion beginning at Section II, A, 3, d, supra.

3. 331 U.S. 486 (1947).

4. 280 U.S. 83 (1929).

trust company for the benefit of each of his two minor sons. The trustee was to accumulate income and distribute one-half of the corpus and accumulated income to each of the sons as they attained age 25. Virginia assessed a property tax upon the entire corpus of the trust. Taxpayer contended and the majority of the Court adopted the view that the assessment was upon property wholly beyond the jurisdiction of Virginia. The decision was premised on the conclusion that the maxim mobilia sequuntur personam should not apply "where the possessor of the legal title holds the securities in Maryland, thus giving them a permanent situs for lawful taxation there, and no person in Virginia has present right to their enjoyment or power to remove them." [5] Justice Stone in a concurring opinion agreed with the result but chose to leave open the question as to whether Virginia, the state of domicile of the beneficiaries, could by an appropriate statute tax the beneficiaries upon the value of their equitable interests.[6]

In 1941, the Court was presented with the issue which Justice Stone had raised in *Safe Deposit & Trust Co.* In *Commonwealth v. Stewart*,[7] Pennsylvania provided by statute for valuing and taxing beneficial interests in trusts as personal property. Taxpayer, a resident of Pennsylvania, was life beneficiary under a New York trust. The trustees were domiciled in New York and all trust business was transacted in New York. In sustaining the tax, the Pennsylvania Supreme Court, in reliance upon *Senior v. Braden* [8] among other decisions, recognized the modern trend of equity jurisprudence and the doctrine that the beneficiary has rights in rem with respect to the trust corpus. On this basis, the Pennsylvania court concluded that the tax was upon the taxpayer's interest in the intangible personal property held on trust and within due process concepts of

state jurisdiction to tax. On appeal, the Pennsylvania decision was affirmed in a per curiam opinion by the United States Supreme Court.[9]

As a final observation, it should be added that under the rule of *Senior v. Braden*,[10] a beneficial interest under a trust which holds title to out-of-state real estate would not be within the tax jurisdiction of the state of the beneficiary's domicile. This holding squares with the rule that neither a fee interest nor a legal life estate in out-of-state real property is subject to tax by the state of residence of the owner.

B. Death Taxes

1. Introduction

Jurisdictional concepts with respect to state death taxes parallel those which govern jurisdiction to impose general ad valorem property taxes. Real property and permanently situated tangible personal property have an exclusive tax situs in the state in which the property is located. Intangibles, on the other hand, have a potential multiple tax situs in the same manner and for the same reasons that intangibles are subject to multiple taxation under the general property tax. The potential for multiple death taxation of intangibles has been reduced, however, by the general adoption of reciprocal exemption statutes.

There are two complicating factors which relate to multiple death taxation of intangibles. The first is the fact that states apply different concepts in classifying certain property interests as tangible or intangible property. Second, inasmuch as domicile provides a secure foundation for imposition of death taxes upon intangibles, there may be circumstances in which more than one state claims to be the state of domi-

---

5. Id. at 92.

6. Id. at 95–96.

7. 338 Pa. 9, 12 A.2d 444 (1940).

8. 295 U.S. 422 (1935). See text discussion at Section II, A, 2, supra.

9. 312 U.S. 649 (1941).

10. 295 U.S. 422 (1935).

cile of the decedent. These issues are discussed in sections 4 and 5 which follow.

2. Real Property and Tangible Personal Property

It was generally recognized at an early date that the state of decedent's domicile did not have jurisdiction to impose a death tax upon real property located in another state,[1] but it was not until 1925 that the Court firmly established the same limitation with respect to tangible personal property located in another state. In *Frick v. Pennsylvania,*[2] the decedent, a resident of Pennsylvania owned the Frick Art Collection valued in excess of $13,000,000 which was located in New York in a building especially constructed to house the collection. His estate also included tangible personal property having a value of $325,000 which was permanently located at his country estate in Massachusetts. Under the Pennsylvania statute, an inheritance tax was imposed on the transfer of all the property of a resident decedent wherever located. In *Frick*, the Court relied on its decision in *Union Refrigerator Transit Co. v. Kentucky*[3] in holding that these items had an exclusive tax situs in New York and Massachusetts and that a tax by Pennsylvania would contravene principles of due process.

In *City Bank Farmers' Trust Co. v. Schnader,*[4] the Court was presented with the converse situation. Three years prior to his death, the decedent, a New York resident, lent his art collection to a Philadelphia museum. The loan was made on the condition that the collection would be sold at a stipulated price, provided that the purchaser would make a gift of the collection to the museum. The decedent also reserved the right to remove the collection at any time prior to sale. In this case the Court sustained a Pennsylvania inheritance tax on the transfer of the property on the ground that the property had acquired an actual situs in Pennsylvania.

Treichler v. Wisconsin[5] is the Court's most recent pronouncement of the rule that out-of-state real property and tangible personal property are beyond the death tax reach of the domiciliary state. In *Treichler*, the Court held invalid a Wisconsin statute that assessed a special estate tax computed at 30% of the maximum credit allowed under the federal estate tax after reduction for death taxes paid to other states. The result was to impose the Wisconsin tax upon all the resident decedent's property wherever located which included real property and tangible personal property located in Illinois and Florida. The Court followed the *Frick* decision and held the statute invalid.

3. Intangible Personal Property

a. Development of Constitutional Doctrine

At the turn of the century, Justice Holmes, writing for the Court in *Blackstone v. Miller,*[6] unequivocally endorsed multiple death taxation of intangible personal property. In *Blackstone*, the testator who died domiciled in Illinois held a debt due from a New York resident and a bank deposit in a New York bank. As the domiciliary state,

---

1. Appeal of Commonwealth, 129 Pa. 338, 18 A. 132 (1889). In holding that Pennsylvania lacked jurisdiction to impose an inheritance tax on the transfer of a fee interest in Maryland real estate by a resident-decedent, the court stated:

> "[R]eal estate is not drawn to the person or domicile of the owner, for taxation or any other purpose, and hence cannot be taxed outside of the jurisdiction where it is situate. The taxation of property involves the reciprocal duty of protection on the part of the state levying such tax. . . . [T]he state itself cannot exercise extra-territorial taxing power as to real estate, and carry into another state, and enforce there, its remedies for the collection of taxes."

129 Pa. at 345, 18 A. at 133.

2. 268 U.S. 473 (1925).

3. 199 U.S. 194 (1905).

4. 293 U.S. 112 (1934).

5. 338 U.S. 251 (1949). *Treichler* was applied in determining the appropriate "pick-up" tax under the California death tax provisions. Estate of Fasken, 19 Cal. 3d 412, 138 Cal.Rptr. 276, 563 P.2d 832, cert. denied 434 U.S. 877 (1977).

6. 188 U.S. 189 (1903).

Illinois imposed an inheritance tax on the transfer of this property. The issue was whether New York, a nondomiciliary state, also could tax. In sustaining the New York tax, the Court stated the due process principles for recognizing jurisdiction to tax by both Illinois and New York:

> Power over the person of the debtor confers jurisdiction, we repeat. And this being so, we perceive no better reason for denying the right of New York to impose a succession tax on debts owed by its citizens than upon tangible chattels found within the state at the time of the death. . . .
>
> . . . The fact that two states, dealing each with its own law of succession, both of which the plaintiff in error has to invoke for her rights, have taxed the right which they respectively confer, gives no cause for complaint on constitutional grounds. . . . The universal succession is taxed in one state, the singular succession is taxed in another. The plaintiff has to make out her right under both in order to get the money.[7]

In 1928, in its decision in *Blodgett v. Silberman*,[8] the Court confirmed the corollary aspect of the *Blackstone* doctrine in a case involving the jurisdiction of the state of domicile to impose death taxes. Decedent died a resident of Connecticut. His estate consisted of the following items: (1) an interest as a general partner in a New York limited partnership doing business in New York, the assets of which included New York and Connecticut real estate, merchandise, bank deposits, trade receivables, and other intangible personal property; (2) shares in New York, New Jersey and Canadian corporations; (3) United States bearer bonds held in a New York safe deposit box; (4) a savings account in a New York bank; (5) a life insurance policy issued by a New York life insurance company payable to the estate; and (6) coin and currency in a safe deposit box in New York. Except for the bearer bonds, currency, and coin, the Con-

necticut Court held that the decedent's interest in the various items, including his interest as a general partner in the New York partnership, constituted interests in intangible property which were taxable by Connecticut as the domiciliary state. The bearer bonds, currency and coin were excluded as tangible personal property having an exclusive tax situs in New York, the state in which they were located.

In its decision on appeal, the Supreme Court made several significant points. First, the Court endorsed the principle that the state of domicile has jurisdiction to impose a death tax on the transfer of intangible personal property irrespective of whether the transfer is also taxable in another jurisdiction. Second, the Court affirmed the view that an interest in a partnershp constitutes a chose in action, intangible personal property, rather than a proportionate interest in the underlying assets of the partnership business. Third, the Court reversed the Connecticut Court and held that Government bearer bonds regardless of their form represented debts or choses in action and were taxable by the state of domicile as intangible personal property. Finally, the Court agreed that currency and coin constitute tangible property and have an exclusive tax situs in the state where located.

With the decisions in *Blackstone* and *Blodgett*, multiple death taxation of the transfer of intangible personal property appeared to be firmly established.[9] For a brief period, however, the Court reversed its position. In a series of four cases decided in a brief span of two years, the Court invalidated death taxes imposed by nondomiciliary states and held that as a matter of due process the state of domicile had exclusive jurisdiction to impose a death tax on the transfer of intangible property.[10] This position was short-lived, however, and in 1939 the Court

---

7. Id. at 206–07.

8. 277 U.S. 1 (1928).

9. In 1928, the year in which *Blodgett* was decided, the National Conference of Commissioners on Uniform State Laws and the American Bar Association ap-

proved the Uniform Reciprocal Transfer Tax Act. See the text discussion at Section II, B, 3, b, *infra*.

10. Each of the four decisions are identified chronologically as follows: Farmers' Loan & Trust Co. v. Minnesota, 280 U.S. 204 (1930) (New York decedent held

began its return to the doctrine of the *Blackstone* decision.[11] In *Curry v. McCanless*,[12] decedent died domiciled in Tennessee. During her lifetime she transferred certain securities to an Alabama trust company on trust retaining an income interest for life and reserving a testamentary power of appointment. By her will, decedent appointed the trust corpus to family members; both Tennessee and Alabama assessed death taxes on the transfer of the property. In a proceeding brought under the Tennessee Declaratory Judgments Act, the Supreme Court of Tennessee held that Tennessee, as the state of domicile, had exclusive jurisdiction to impose a death tax. On appeal, the Supreme Court reversed, holding that both Tennessee and Alabama had conferred sufficient benefits under due process concepts with respect to the transfer of the property to warrant death taxes by both states. The rationale of the decision was summarized by the Court in the following statement:

> If it be thought that it is identity of the intangibles with the person of the owner at the place of his domicile which gives power over them and hence 'jurisdiction to tax', and this is the reason underlying the maxim mobilia sequuntur personam, it is certain here that the intangibles for some purposes are identified with the trustee, their legal owner, at the place of its domicile and that in another and different relationship and for a different purpose—the exercise of the power of disposition at death, which is the equivalent of ownership—they are identified with the place of domicile of the testatrix, Tennessee. In effecting her purposes, the testatrix brought some of the legal interests which she created within the control of one state by selecting a trustee there and others within the control of the other state by making her domicile there. She necessarily in-

voked the aid of the law of both states, and her legatees, before they can secure and enjoy the benefits of succession, must invoke the law of both.[13]

On the same day that *Curry v. McCanless* was decided, the Court rendered its decision in *Graves v. Elliott*.[14] Decedent died a resident of New York. Seven years prior to her death, and while residing in Colorado, she transferred certain securities on trust to a Colorado trust company for the benefit of family members, reserving the power to alter the beneficial interests and the power to revoke. She died without having exercised either power and Colorado imposed a tax on the transfer of the trust property. The New York Court of Appeals held that New York lacked jurisdiction to tax inasmuch as the situs of the trust property was in Colorado where the trust had been administered. After acknowledging that the administration of the trust was localized in Colorado so that Colorado had jurisdiction to tax, the Court in reliance on *McCanless* reversed and held that New York also could tax. In its opinion, the Court stated:

> [W]e cannot say that the legal interest of decedent in the intangibles held in trust in Colorado was so dissociated from her person as to be beyond the taxing jurisdiction of the state of her domicile more than her other rights in intangibles. Her right to revoke the trust and to demand the transmission to her of the intangibles by the trustee and the delivery to her of their physical evidences was a potential source of wealth, having the attributes of property. As in the case of any other intangibles which she possessed, control over her person and estate at the place of her domicile and her duty to contribute to the support of government there afford adequate constitutional basis for imposition of a tax measured by the value

---

Minnesota state and municipal bonds); Baldwin v. Missouri, 281 U.S. 586 (1930) (Illinois decedent held Missouri bank accounts and promissory notes of Missouri residents); Beidler v. Tax Comm'n, 282 U.S. 1 (1930) (Illinois decedent held debts due from a South Carolina corporation); First Nat. Bank v. Maine, 284 U.S. 312 (1932) (Massachusetts decedent held stock of a Maine corporation).

11. This change of position by the Court was foreshadowed by its decision in Burnet v. Brooks, 288 U.S. 378 (1933). In *Brooks*, the Court held that the federal

estate tax applied to securities (domestic and foreign) owned by a citizen of Great Britain and resident of Cuba who had placed the securities in the hands of agents in the United States. The decision was premised upon the sovereign power of the United States with respect to securities physically located within its territorial limits.

12. 307 U.S. 357 (1939).

13. Id. at 372.

14. 307 U.S. 383 (1939).

of the intangibles transmitted or relinquished by her at death.[15]

Three years following *McCanless* and *Elliott*, the Court, in *State Tax Commission v. Aldrich*,[16] sustained the jurisdiction of a nondomiciliary state to impose a death tax on the transfer of shares of stock in a corporation organized under the laws of the taxing state. In *Aldrich*, the decedent died holding shares of stock in Union Pacific Railroad Co., a Utah corporation. The Court sustained the jurisdiction of Utah to tax the transfer of the shares on the ground that the corporation owed its existence to the laws of Utah which governed the transfer by the corporation of its shares of stock. But where neither the decedent nor the corporation is domiciled in a state in which the corporation owns property, the Court has refused to expand due process concepts to sanction imposition of a death tax by such state.[17]

During this period of return to the doctrine of *Blackstone v. Miller*, the Court in two additional cases recognized the jurisdiction of the state of domicile to impose death taxes upon the transfer of intangibles administered by out-of-state trusts in which the decedent held either a beneficial interest or a donated power of appointment, or both.

In *Graves v. Schmidlapp*,[18] the decedent's father created a Massachusetts trust consisting of securities giving the decedent a life interest therein coupled with a general testamentary power of appointment. Decedent was domiciled in New York and exercised the general power by appointing the trust corpus to his surviving spouse. In *Central Hanover Bank & Trust Co. v. Kelly*,[19] the decedent, a resident of New Jersey, transferred securities on irrevocable trust to a New York trust company retaining a life interest with a gift over of the remainder at his death. In each of these cases, the Court emphasized domicile of the decedent as the controlling factor in sustaining the death tax imposed on the transfer by the state of residence.[20] By 1943, the Court had returned full circle to its original position with respect to multiple death taxation of intangible personal property.[21]

b. Statutory Modification of Multiple Death Taxation of Intangibles

As a practical matter, double death taxation of intangible property has been substantially alleviated by statute in all states and the District of Columbia.[22] In general, these statutes either grant an exemption on a reciprocal basis or provide a flat exemption

15. Id. at 386–87.

16. 316 U.S. 174 (1942).

17. Rhode Island Hosp. Trust Co. v. Doughton, 270 U.S. 69 (1926). Decedent who died domiciled in Rhode Island held stock in R. J. Reynolds Tobacco Co., a New Jersey corporation, with substantial property holdings in North Carolina. The court held invalid a North Carolina statute which imposed a death tax on the transfer of corporate shares by allocating to North Carolina that portion of the value of the shares equal to the ratio of the corporate assets in North Carolina to total corporate assets.

18. 315 U.S. 657 (1942).

19. 319 U.S. 94 (1943).

20. In Graves v. Schmidlapp, 315 U.S. 657 (1942), the Court explained the basis for its decision in the following terms:

"Intangibles, which are legal relationships between persons and which in fact have no geographical location, are so associated with the owner that they and their transfer at death are taxable at the place of his domicile, where his person and the exercise of his property rights are subject to the control

of the sovereign power. His transfer of interests in intangibles, by virtue of the exercise of a donated power instead of that derived from ownership, stands on the same footing. In both cases the sovereign's control over his person and estate at the place of his domicile, and his duty to contribute to the financial support of government there, afford adequate constitutional basis for the imposition of a tax."

315 U.S. at 660.

In Central Hanover Bank & Trust Co. v. Kelly, 319 U.S. 94 (1943), the Court stated the basis for its decision more succinctly: "Domicile is the single controlling consideration in this situation, as it is in the case of the taxation of income derived from activities outside the state." 319 U.S. at 97.

21. For an excellent comprehensive discussion of problems of multiple death taxation, see H. Marsh, Jr., Multiple Death Taxation in the United States, 8 U.C. L.A.L.Rev. 69 (1961).

22. 4 State Inh. Est. & Gift Tax Rep. (CCH) ¶ 12,080. Nevada by constitutional provision prohibits an inheritance or estate tax. Nev.Const. art. X, § 1.

with respect to intangibles of a nonresident decedent. The impetus for these statutes was the approval in 1928 of the Uniform Reciprocal Transfer Tax Act by the National Conference of Commissioners on Uniform State Laws and the American Bar Association.[23]

4.   What Is Intangible Property?

a.   Currency and Coin

As indicated in the discussion of *Blodgett v. Silberman*,[24] the Court in 1928 held that currency and coin constituted tangible personal property and were taxable only in the state where located. In that case, the currency and coin owned by a Connecticut resident were located in a safe deposit box in New York. In *Thomas v. Virginia*,[25] decided in 1960, the Court reaffirmed that position. In *Thomas*, the decedent was domiciled in Virginia. At his death he held $263,100 in currency in a safe deposit box in the District of Columbia. The Virginia courts sustained a death tax on the transfer of this property as intangible personal property with a tax situs in the domiciliary state. On appeal the Court reversed in a per curiam decision citing the *Blodgett* decision.

b.   Partnership Interests

A partnership interest, as discussed in *Blodgett v. Silberman*,[26] is generally classified as intangible personal property irrespective of the fact that the underlying assets may consist of real property and tangible personal property located in another state. Under the provisions of the Uniform Part-

nership Act, a partner does not hold a proportionate interest in each item of partnership property. Instead, "a partner's interest in the partnership is his share of the profits and surplus, and the same is personal property."[27] This rule is generally recognized for purposes of death taxes upon the transfer of partnership interests.[28]

If a state in which the tangible partnership assets are located has enacted a reciprocal exemption provision with respect to intangible property of a nonresident, it would follow that a partnership interest of a nonresident decedent would escape double death taxes. But this result is not always the case since the state in which partnership assets are located may take the position that the decedent's interest for death tax purposes is an interest in the real estate and chattels owned by the partnership.[29] This alternative involves a construction of the particular state's statutes and is a matter for determination by the state courts. Thus, both the state of domicile and the nonresident state may impose a tax on the same interest.[30]

c.   Real Property and the Doctrine of Equitable Conversion

As a general rule, real property transferred at death is taxable only in the state in which the property is located. Where the decedent resides in one state and the real property is located in another, however, the doctrine of equitable conversion may apply in certain circumstances to convert the decedent's interest into intangible personal property. If both states apply the doctrine in the same manner and if both states have recip-

---

23.   9C Uniform Laws Ann. 72 (1957).

24.   277 U.S. 1 (1928). See text at Section II, B, 3, a, supra.

25.   364 U.S. 443 (1960).

26.   277 U.S. 1 (1928). See text at Section II, B, 3, a, supra.

27.   Uniform Partnership Act § 26.

28.   Lynch v. Kentucky Tax Comm'n, 333 S.W.2d 257 (Ky.1960); Wooten v. Oklahoma Tax Comm'n, 185 Okl. 259, 91 P.2d 73 (1939).

29.   In re Perry's Estate, 121 Mont. 280, 192 P.2d 532 (1948), 34 Iowa L.Rev. 129 (1948). Decedent, a res-

ident of California was a partner in a Montana mining enterprise. Montana had adopted the Uniform Reciprocal Transfer Tax Act. The Montana Supreme Court held that decedent owned an interest in the Montana lands and the mining equipment which did not qualify under the exemption statute.

30.   In re Estate of Havemeyer, 17 N.Y.2d 216, 217 N.E.2d 26 (1966). Decedent, resident of New York, held a partnership interest in a partnership owning Connecticut real estate. Connecticut taxed the decedent's interest in the real estate and New York taxed the decedent's interest in the partnership.

rocal exemption provisions relating to intangibles, there will be a single death tax; but if the two states are inconsistent in their application of the doctrine of equitable conversion, the property interest may be subject to double death taxation,[31] or the property may escape death taxation altogether. This problem is one of the law of conflicts, however, and does not present an issue of federal constitutional law.

Application of the doctrine of equitable conversion may arise either (1) where the decedent has contracted prior to death to sell the out-of-state property or (2) where the decedent directs his executor by testamentary provision to sell the real estate and distribute the proceeds. The prevailing view is to apply the doctrine of equitable conversion in the first situation,[32] but not in the second.[33]

d. Out-of-State Real Estate Held In Trust

In *Senior v. Braden* [34] discussed in section II, A, 6 of this Chapter [35] it was held that the resident owner of a certificate of beneficial interest in an out-of-state land trust could

not be subjected to a general property tax as a matter of due process since such interest is deemed an interest in out-of-state real property.[36] With respect to the jurisdiction of the domiciliary state to impose a death tax upon the transfer of an interest in an out-of-state land trust, there is a conflict of authority in the state court decisions. Michigan, adhering to the rule of *Senior v. Braden*, has held a death tax on the transfer of such interest invalid as an attempt to tax the transfer of out-of-state real property.[37] Kentucky, on the other hand, has refused to follow *Senior v. Braden* and has concluded that an interest in an out-of-state land trust is intangible personal property which is subject to death tax by the domiciliary state.[38]

In *Senior v. Braden*, Justice Stone wrote a vigorous dissenting opinion joined by Justices Brandeis and Cardozo.[39] In his dissent, Justice Stone expressed the view that a transferrable certificate of beneficial interest in an out-of-state land trust is comparable to a share of stock in a corporation. For this reason, he would have sustained the property tax in that case as a tax on intangi-

---

31. An example of double taxation is provided by the decisions in Pennsylvania v. Presbyterian Hospital, 287 Pa. 49, 134 A. 427 (1926) and Land Title & Trust Co. v. Tax Comm'n, 131 S.C. 192, 126 S.E. 189 (1925). Decedent was domiciled in South Carolina and the real property was located in Pennsylvania. By her will, decedent directed her executors to sell the Pennsylvania real estate and distribute the proceeds to certain beneficiaries. Pennsylvania held the transfer of the property taxable as real estate located therein. South Carolina applied the doctrine of equitable conversion to hold the transfer subject to the South Carolina inheritance tax.

32. Doctrine of equitable conversion applied where the decedent had contracted prior to death to sell real property:

(a) By domiciliary state: State ex rel. Hilton v. Probate Court, 145 Minn. 155, 176 N.W. 493 (1920); In re Plasterer's Estate, 49 Wash.2d 339, 301 P.2d 539 (1956), 32 Wash.L.Rev. 127 (1957). Contra: Paul's Estate, 303 Pa. 330, 154 A. 503 (1931), 31 Colum.L.Rev. 1373 (1931), 79 U.Pa.L.Rev. 773 (1931); 41 Yale L.J. 140 (1931).

(b) By non-domiciliary state: In re Briebach's Estate, 132 Mont. 437, 318 P.2d 223 (1957); In re Ryan's Estate, 102 N.W.2d 9 (N.D.1960), 36 N.Dak.L. Rev. 185 (1960); In re Eilermann's Estate, 179 Wash. 15, 35 P.2d 763 (1934). Contra, De Stuer's Estate, 199 Misc. 777, 99 N.Y.S.2d 739 (1950).

33. Doctrine of equitable conversion *not* applied where executor was directed by will to sell real property in non-domiciliary state:

(a) Domiciliary state: Connell v. Crosby, 210 Ill. 380, 71 N.E. 350 (1904); Wegman v. Jungers, 226 Iowa 1260, 286 N.W. 422 (1939); In re Swift's Estate, 137 N.Y. 77, 32 N.E. 1096 (1893). Contra, Land Title & Trust Co. v. Tax Comm'n, 131 S.C. 192, 126 S.E. 189 (1925).

(b) Non-Domiciliary state: Commonwealth v. Presbyterian Hosp., 287 Pa. 49, 134 A. 427 (1926).

34. 295 U.S. 422 (1935).

35. See text at Section II, A, 6, n.10, supra.

36. It is a firmly established principle of trust law that "if the trust property is real property, the interest of the beneficiary is real property unless the interest of the beneficiary is so limited in duration that if it were a legal interest it would be personal property." Restatement (Second) of Trusts § 130.

37. In re Stahl's Estate, 334 Mich. 380, 54 N.W.2d 691 (1952).

38. Security Trust Co. v. Department of Revenue, 263 S.W.2d 130 (Ky.1953).

39. 295 U.S. at 433–41.

ble personal property. Justice Stone stated that there is a fundamental distinction between the ownership of an interest in a land trust represented by transferrable certificates of beneficial interest and the ownership of an interest in a trust of real property not represented by transferrable certificates of beneficial interest.[40] This distinction is persuasive particularly where the land trust certificates are traded on a securities market. In this situation, the majority decision in *Senior v. Braden* may not prevail today.

In the case of the ordinary trust of out-of-state real estate, however, established due process concepts should apply to limit jurisdiction to impose a death tax on the transfer of the beneficial interest to the state in which the real estate is located. Whether the interest in the out-of-state land is a legal interest or an equitable interest should not determine jurisdiction to tax the transfer of immovables.

5. *Multiple Domicile*

a. *The Decisions*

Although the exemption statutes relating to intangible property of a nonresident decedent have substantially alleviated the problem of multiple taxation, it is possible that more than one state will find that the decedent was domiciled within its borders. In *Worcester County Trust Co. v. Riley*,[41] an interpleader suit brought by the executor to resolve conflicting claims of domicile by Massachusetts and California, the Court concluded that neither "the Fourteenth Amendment nor the full faith and credit clause re-

quires uniformity in the decisions of the courts of different states as to the place of domicil, where the exertion of state power is dependent upon domicil within its boundaries."[42] After noting that the suit was in substance one against the states, the Court held that it was barred by the eleventh amendment which provides that: "The judicial power . . . shall not be construed to extend to any suit in law or equity commenced or prosecuted against one of the United States by Citizens of another State."[43] This holding, of course, compounds the problem of multiple taxation and all of the decedent's intangible property may be the basis for more than one death tax since the exemption statutes do not protect the estate if the decedent is held to be domiciled in more than one state.

A notable example of multiple domicile resulting in double taxation involved the Campbell Soup fortune. Dr. John T. Dorrance died owning all of the stock of the corporation which had a value in excess of $100,000,000. Both Pennsylvania and New Jersey held that Dr. Dorrance was domiciled within their borders and each state included the stock in the decedent's taxable estate. Pennsylvania inheritance taxes exceeded fourteen million dollars[44] and New Jersey collected more than twelve million dollars.[45]

A few years later, in *Texas v. Florida*,[46] the Court held that judicial relief is available as between the states only in the rare situation where the taxes assessed by the several claimant states exceed the assets of the estate, a situation not existing in the Campbell Soup case. In the absence of such circum-

---

40. Id. at 439–40.

41. 302 U.S. 292 (1937).

42. Id. at 299.

43. See the discussion of the eleventh amendment in Chapter 2 , section IV, A, supra.

44. In Re Dorrance's Estate, 309 Pa. 151, 163 A. 303 (1932), cert. denied 287 U.S. 660 (1932), on rehearing 172 A. 900 (1933), cert. denied 288 U.S. 617 (1933).

45. In Re Dorrance's Estate, 115 N.J.Eq. 268, 170 A. 601 (1934).

46. 306 U.S. 398 (1939). This case involved the estate of Colonel Green who died owning property having

a net value of approximately $36,137,000 after payment of debts and administration expenses other than death taxes. The bulk of his estate consisted of stocks and bonds; and the balance included real estate and tangible personal property valued at $6,500,000 which were located in Texas, Florida, New York and Massachusetts. All four states contended that Colonel Green was domiciled therein and all four assessed death taxes accordingly. Aggregate death taxes, federal and state, exceeded the net estate by $1,590,000. The Court confirmed the report of a Special Master who concluded that the decedent's domicile was in Massachusetts.

stances, there is no case or controversy between the states and the Court lacks jurisdiction to resolve the issue.[47]

More recently, in *California v. Texas*,[48] four justices indicated that relief may be available to the estate of a decedent in multiple domicile cases by utilizing the federal interpleader statute. In this case, California filed a motion for leave to file a bill of complaint for the purpose of invoking the Court's original and exclusive jurisdiction to settle a dispute with Texas as to the domicile of the late Howard R. Hughes. California alleged that if the estate were subject to death taxes by both California and Texas, the aggregate federal and state death taxes would exceed the total estate. The majority of the Court denied the motion per curiam without explanation. Four justices,[49] however, filed concurring opinions and three [50] of the four joined in an opinion stating that *Texas v. Florida* had been wrongly decided and should be overruled.

The basis for overruling *Texas v. Florida* as urged by the three justices was premised on the ground that there was no justiciable case or controversy within the original and exclusive jurisdiction of the Court since none of the states claiming the right to tax the decedent's estate had reduced its claim to judgment. Moreover, it was asserted that the Court, by analogyzing the suit in *Texas v. Florida* to a bill in the nature of interpleader, "focused erroneously on the plight of the estate" and the " 'substantial likelihood' of multiple and inconsistent tax claims" which did not constitute "a case or controversy" among the claiming states. At another point, the three justices stated their position more fully as follows:

> It must be recognized . . . that what is involved is unfairness to the *estate*, not to the taxing States. The remedy of interpleader exists, if at all, to require litigation of the inconsistent tax claims in a single forum in order to avert the risk of loss *to the estate* that would result from separate adjudications. But the only live controversy in such a suit is between each State and the decedent's estate as to the legal obligation to pay death taxes. There is, in fact, no present dispute *between the claiming States.*[51]

Finally, it should be noted that all four concurring judges were of the view that the subsequent decision in *Edelman v. Jordan* [52] had effectively overruled *Worcester County Trust Co.*, and that the eleventh amendment is no longer a bar to the use of federal interpleader to resolve the issue of a decedent's domicile.

With this prompting by four members of the court, the administrator of the Hughes estate filed a statutory interpleader action for determination of the issue of domicile. This suit was dismissed by the District Court; the Court of Appeals for the Fifth Circuit reversed, and certiorari was granted.[53] Thus the question as to whether an interpleader action could lie was again squarely before the Court. But in *Cory v. White*,[54] the Court reaffirmed the rule of *Worcester County Trust Co.*, and held that the eleventh amendment bars an interpleader action. Concurrently, however, the Court granted California leave to file an original complaint on the ground that a controversy exists between two states within the Court's original jurisdiction.[55]

47. For an interesting discussion of the problem of multiple domicile, see H. Tweed, Death and Taxes are Certain—But What of Domicile, 53 Harv.L.Rev. 68 (1939).

48. 437 U.S. 601 (1978) (per curiam).

49. Justices Brennan, Stewart, Powell, and Stevens.

50. Justices Stewart, Powell, and Stevens.

51. 437 U.S. at 611.

52. 415 U.S. 651 (1974). See the discussion of this decision in Chapter 2, Section IV, A, 2, supra.

53. Lummis v. White, 491 F.Supp. 5 (W.D.Tex. 1979), reversed 629 F.2d 397 (1980), cert. granted sub nom., 452 U.S. 904 (1981).

54. 102 S.Ct. 2325 (1982).

55. California v. Texas, 102 S.Ct. 2335 (1982). Four justices (Powell, Marshall, Rehnquist, and Stevens) vigorously dissented on the ground that there was no ripe controversy. It was their position that there could be no justiciable controversy until both states obtained money judgments against the estate and the estate proved insufficient to satisfy both claims.

b. Statutory Relief

As in the case of multiple taxation of intangibles, a number of states have adopted legislation to cope with the question of multiple domicile. These statutes provide either for arbitration or compromise of conflicting claims of domicile.

In 1943, the National Conference of Commissioners on Uniform State Laws and the American Bar Association approved two statutes to deal with the problem: (1) the Uniform Act on Interstate Arbitration of Death Taxes, and (2) the Uniform Act on Interstate Compromise of Death Taxes.[56] As of July 1, 1977, thirty-two states had adopted some form of statute for compromise or arbitration of domiciliary disputes with respect to the imposition of death taxes.[57]

6. Aggregation of Property by the Non-Domiciliary State in Determining Amount of Death Tax

For the purpose of determining the death tax payable in the estate of a nonresident, a few states aggregate the nontaxable out-of-state property with the taxable property in the state.[58] An amount is then computed upon the aggregate estate, but the tax payable in the estate of the nonresident is that portion of the amount so computed which the taxable property in the state bears to the aggregate estate. Thus, if the taxable property in the non-domiciliary state were valued at $100,000 and there were property having a value of $400,000 located in other states, an amount of tax first would be computed

upon the aggregate sum of $500,000, but the tax payable to the nonresident state would be one-fifth of the amount determined on the aggregate estate.

The New Jersey statute which provided for this method of determining the amount of death taxes in the estate of a nonresident was challenged as violating the privileges and immunities clause, due process, and equal protection. In *Maxwell v. Bugbee*,[59] the Court in a five to four decision sustained the statute. On the privileges and immunities argument, the Court noted that since *Blackstone v. Miller*,[60] it had been established that an estate of a nonresident could be subjected to a death tax with respect to property passing under the laws of the nonresident state even though the entire estate was taxed by the state of residence. With respect to due process, the Court emphasized the fact that the tax was not on the transfer of out-of-state property, but that out-of-state property was merely taken into account in measuring the transfer tax applicable to property within the jurisdiction of the nonresident state.

Finally, stressing the fact that "absolute equality is impractical in taxation," the Court held that the tax did not violate the equal protection clause. The Court stated that the tax, though applied differently to residents and nonresidents, was not so "wholly arbitrary and unreasonable as to be beyond the legitimate authority of the State" and thus did not violate taxpayer's right to equal protection.[61]

---

56. For the texts of the Uniform Acts and record of adoptions, see 8 Uniform Laws Ann. 255 (Arbitration) and 271 (Compromise) (Master ed. 1972) (1977 Supp. at 72 and 74). There may be state constitutional issues as to the validity of these statutes in jurisdictions whose state constitutions provide, as in Illinois, that the "power of taxation shall not be surrendered, suspended, or contracted away." Ill.Const. art. IX, § 1.

57. 4 State Inh. Est. & Gift Tax Rep. (CCH) ¶ 12,035. See H. Marsh, Multiple Death Taxation in the United States, 8 U.C.L.A.L.Rev. 69 (1961). The author concludes that two remaining steps should be taken to resolve the problem of multiple death taxation: (1) each state should adopt a reciprocal exemption stat-

ute with a uniform definition of intangibles; and (2) each state should enact a statute providing for compulsory arbitration of disputes relating to domicile.

58. The following statutes provide this method of determining death taxes in the estate of a nonresident: N.J.Stat.Ann. § 54:34–3 (West 1960); N.C.Gen.Stat. § 105–21 (Michie 1972).

59. 250 U.S. 525 (1919).

60. 188 U.S. 189 (1903). See text at Section II, B, 3, a, supra.

61. See C. Lowndes, Rate and Measure in Jurisdiction to Tax—Aftermath of Maxwell v. Bugbee, 49 Harv.L.Rev. 756 (1936).

C. Income Taxes

1. General Requisites of State Jurisdiction to Tax

a. Income Taxes Upon Individuals

Due process principles governing jurisdiction to impose State income taxes upon individuals, residents and nonresidents, were established initially by two leading cases both of which were decided in 1920. In *Maguire v. Trefry*,[1] a Massachusetts statute imposed a tax upon the income received by a resident-beneficiary of a testamentary trust administered by a Philadelphia trust company. The trust income consisted of interest and dividends upon securities comprising the trust corpus. Taxpayer contended that the tax violated the due process requirements prescribed by *Union Refrigerator Transit Co. v. Kentucky*[2] in that the effect was to tax property outside the jurisdiction of the state. In response, the Court noted that "we are not dealing with the right to tax securities which have acquired a local situs [in another state], but are concerned with the right of the State to tax the [income of the] beneficiary of a trust at her residence, although the trust itself may be created and administered under the laws of another state."[3]

In sustaining the tax, emphasis was placed upon the fact that the taxpayer was domiciled in the taxing state: "The beneficiary is domiciled in Massachusetts, has the protection of her laws, and there receives and holds the income from the trust property. We find nothing in the Fourteenth Amendment which prevents the taxation in Massachusetts of an interest of this character, thus owned and enjoyed by a resident of the state."[4] In concluding its opinion, the Court drew an analogy to the property tax by observing that, in principle, imposition of an income tax upon a taxpayer's out-of-state income does not differ from the imposition of an ad valorem property tax upon a debt owed to the same taxpayer by an out-of-state debtor.

The second case, *Shaffer v. Carter*,[5] resolved the question as to whether a state could constitutionally impose an income tax upon a nonresident citizen of another state. An Oklahoma statute imposed a general income tax upon both residents and nonresidents and provided that the tax applied to "net income from all property owned, and of every business . . . carried on in this State by persons residing elsewhere." Taxpayer, a resident of Illinois, owned oil-producing land and operated oil and gas mining leases in Oklahoma. Taxpayer contended that the tax violated due process, equal protection, and the privileges and immunities clause. Due process was the primary basis for objection, however, and the argument was premised on the proposition that the state lacked jurisdiction to tax the income of nonresidents. The Court disposed of this contention by emphasizing the benefits derived by the taxpayer under the laws of the taxing state:

That the State, from whose laws property and business and industry derive the protection and security without which production and gainful occupation would be impossible, is debarred from exacting a share of those gains in the form of income taxes for the support of the government, is a proposition so wholly inconsistent with fundamental principles as to be refuted by its mere statement. That it may tax the land but not the crop, the tree but not the fruit, the mine or well but not the product, the business but not the profit derived from it, is wholly inadmissible.

Income taxes are a recognized method of distributing the burdens of government, favored because requiring contributions from those who realize current pecuniary benefits under the protection of the government, and because the tax may be readily proportioned to their ability to pay.[6]

---

1. 253 U.S. 12 (1920).
2. 199 U.S. 194 (1905).
3. 253 U.S. at 16.

4. Id. at 17.
5. 252 U.S. 37 (1920).
6. Id. at 50–51.

Although it may have appeared that the decisions in *Maguire* and *Shaffer* had fully resolved the issue as to state power to impose income taxes upon individuals, another decision was required to confirm the power of a state to impose an income tax upon out-of-state income of an individual residing and domiciled in the taxing state. In 1937, the Court was again presented with the issue as to jurisdiction of a domiciliary state to tax out-of-state income.

In *New York ex rel. Cohn v. Graves*,[7] the taxpayer resided in New York. During the tax years in question, the taxpayer as beneficiary of a life estate under her husband's will received rental income from real property located in New Jersey and interest income upon bonds secured by mortgages upon New Jersey real estate. Two of the executors resided in New Jersey and both the bond and mortgages were held for safekeeping in a New Jersey bank. The issue was whether New York had jurisdiction to tax the rentals and interest income derived from the New Jersey properties.

In reliance upon *Pollock v. Farmers' Loan & Trust Co.*,[8] the taxpayer objected primarily on the ground that the tax was in substance and effect a tax on real estate and tangible property located without the state and therefore in violation of due process. In sustaining the tax, the Court distinguished between property taxes and income taxes[9] and emphasized the benefits enjoyed by the taxpayer by reason of her status as a resident of the taxing state:

> That the receipt of income by a resident of the territory of a taxing sovereignty is a taxable event is universally recognized. Domicil itself affords a basis for such taxation. Enjoyment

of the privileges of residence in the state and the attendant right to invoke the protection of its laws are inseparable from responsibility for sharing the costs of government. . . . A tax measured by the net income of residents is an equitable method of distributing the burdens of government among those who are privileged to enjoy its benefits. The tax, which is apportioned to the ability of the taxpayer to pay it, is founded upon the protection afforded by the state to the recipient of the income in his person, in his right to receive the income and in his enjoyment of it when received. These are rights and privileges which attach to domicil within the state. To them and to the equitable distribution of the tax burden, the economic advantage realized by the receipt of income and represented by the power to control it, bears a direct relationship.[10]

The decision in *Cohn* effectively removed any lingering doubts which may have been created by the decision in *Pollock* and the Court reaffirmed the authority of a domiciliary state to tax all income of a resident individual irrespective of its source.

In summary, *Maguire, Shaffer,* and *Cohn* established as a matter of due process the constitutional power of a state to impose taxes upon individuals whether or not domiciled therein. In the case of individuals domiciled in the taxing state, domicile alone is sufficient to sustain the tax because of the personal benefits enjoyed by the individual under the laws of the state. In the case of an individual who is neither domiciled in nor resident of the taxing state, an income tax is justified by the benefits provided by the taxing state in the protection of the taxpayer's income-producing occupation, business, and property located within the state.

---

7. 300 U.S. 308 (1937).

8. 157 U.S. 429 (1895); 158 U.S. 601 (1895). In *Pollock*, the Court held that an income tax upon income produced by real and personal property was in effect a direct tax upon the property itself. On this basis, the *Pollock* decision invalidated the Income Tax Act of 1894 as violating the requirements of Article I, Section 2, Clause 3 and Article I, Section 9, Clause 4, both of which require that all direct taxes shall be apportioned among the states according to population. The decision in *Pollock* led ultimately to the adoption of the

Sixteenth Amendment. See Chapter 5, section B, 1, supra.

9. The Court acknowledged that New York could not impose a property tax upon the New Jersey real estate but noted that "[T]he incidence of a tax on income differs from that on property. . . . The tax on each is predicated upon different governmental benefits; the protection offered to the property in one state does not extend to the receipt and enjoyment of income from it in another." 300 U.S. at 314.

10. 300 U.S. at 312–13.

b. Individual Income Taxes and the Privileges and Immunities Clause

Although a state has broad powers to tax the income of both residents and nonresidents, a state income tax cannot discriminate against nonresidents without violating the Privileges and Immunities Clause.[11] This rule was established by the Court in *Travis v. Yale & Towne Mfg. Co.*[12] New York enacted an income tax which applied to both residents and nonresidents who earned income in the state. Under the statute, personal exemptions were granted to each resident taxpayer and each of his dependents, but no similar provision was made for nonresidents.

In its opinion in *Yale & Towne Mfg. Co.*, the Court referred to the early decision in *Ward v. Maryland*[13] which had invalidated a discriminatory tax upon nonresident traders doing business in the state. In *Ward*, the Court stated that the Privileges and Immunities Clause "secures and protects the right of a citizen of one state to pass into any other state . . . for the purpose of engaging in lawful commerce . . . and to be exempt from any higher taxes or excises than are imposed . . . upon its own citizens."[14] With this earlier case as precedent, the Court concluded that the New York tax constituted "an unwarranted denial to the citizens of Connecticut and New Jersey [who earned income in New York] of the privileges and immunities enjoyed by citizens of New York."[15]

In a more recent case, *Austin v. New Hampshire*,[16] the Court considered the validity of the New Hampshire Commuters Income Tax which imposed an income tax only upon the earnings of nonresidents and wholly exempted New Hampshire residents. The net effect of the statutory provisions was to tax nonresidents on their earnings in New Hampshire at a rate not to exceed that imposed by their respective states of residence. Thus, since the neighboring states in which the taxpayers resided allowed a credit under their respective income taxes for income taxes paid to other states, there was no increase in the aggregate tax burden imposed upon nonresidents.[17]

In considering the New Hampshire statute, the Court first noted that although the states have great freedom of classification for tax purposes based on forms of business organization or types of trade or business, concern for maintenance of the integrity of the Privileges and Immunities Clause requires a more rigorous test of review.[18] To permit discrimination on the basis of noncitizenship or nonresidence would impair the structural balance essential to the concept of federalism. As interpreted by prior cases, this clause guarantees that citizens of State *A* may do business in State *B* on terms of substantial equality with the citizens of State *B*.[19] With this foundation, the Court concluded that the New Hampshire tax could not be sustained.

c. Income Taxes Upon Corporations

The same principles of due process which have developed with respect to jurisdiction to impose income taxes upon individuals appear equally applicable to corporations. If a corporation is organized under the laws of the taxing state, it is taxable as a domicilia-

---

11. The privileges and immunities clause is discussed at this point since, as a practical matter, it operates as a limitation upon the taxing power of the state.

12. 252 U.S. 60 (1920).

13. 79 U.S. (12 Wall.) 418 (1870).

14. Id. at 430.

15. 252 U.S. at 80.

16. 420 U.S. 656 (1975).

17. It was on this basis that the New Hampshire authorities argued that the burden imposed upon non-residents was "not more onerous in effect" if the tax credit they received from their states of residence were taken into account. Another point suggested by the New Hampshire authorities was that the neighboring states could repeal their credit provisions for the New Hampshire income tax and thus remove the diversion of tax revenues from their treasuries. The court answered the latter argument by pointing out that this required retaliatory legislation by the neighboring states which the Privileges and Immunities Clause was intended to eliminate. 420 U.S. at 666–67.

18. 420 U.S. at 661–63.

19. Toomer v. Witsell, 334 U.S. 385 at 396 (1948).

ry corporation upon all of its income whether derived from within or without the state of domicile. Although there appears to be no direct Supreme Court decision on point, it does not seem to be a seriously debatable issue in light of the decisions relating to individuals. Under principles of due process, jurisdiction to tax all the income of a domestic corporation is particularly apropos in view of the fact that the taxpayer-corporation derives its very existence from the taxing state.[20] Similarly, a foreign corporation conducting business or owning income-producing property in the taxing state is taxable upon the income derived from its business operations or property owned therein by virtue of the benefits and protection provided by the state.[21]

2. Net Income From Interstate Business

a. Development of Constitutional Doctrine

(1) Domestic Corporations

The basic constitutional framework for state taxation of the income of interstate manufacturing, mercantile and financial businesses was erected by the Court during the period 1918 to 1931. The first case considered by the Court, *United States Glue Co. v. Town of Oak Creek*,[22] presented the question as to whether the state of corporate domicile could validly tax that portion of the net income of a manufacturing business derived from goods manufactured within the state but sold to out-of-state customers. Sales giving rise to the income in question were of two types: sales made upon orders received from out-of-state customers, the goods being delivered from the company's Wisconsin factory, and sales made upon orders received from out-of-state customers at out-of-state branches with the goods, which had been manufactured in Wisconsin, being delivered from such branches. The specific issue was whether taxation of net income derived from these interstate transactions constituted the imposition of an unconstitutional burden upon interstate commerce. In sustaining the validity of the tax imposed by the *domiciliary* state, the court stressed the point that a tax on net income is not a direct and immediate burden upon interstate commerce since the tax is occasioned not by reason of the commerce itself but by reason of the fact that the transactions in interstate commerce proved to be profitable. Thus the tax was held not to be inherently discriminatory with respect to such commerce. With this decision the Court established the validity of a tax upon the net income of a domiciliary corporation irrespective of whether the income was de-

---

20. See Lawrence v. State Tax Comm'n, 286 U.S. 276 (1932). In *Lawrence* the court sustained a Mississippi income tax which taxed individuals upon their out-of-state income but excluded out-of-state income in taxing domestic corporations. Taxpayer objected on the ground that there was a violation of equal protection. Although the Court sustained the classification, there is a clear implication that such classification was not constitutionally required and that the state could have taxed domestic corporations in the same manner as resident individuals. See also State Tax Comm'n v. Aldrich, 316 U.S. 174 (1942) in which the Court sustained the imposition of an estate tax on the transfer of shares of stock by Utah, the domiciliary state. Decedent died a resident of New York and the shares were bequeathed to beneficiaries who were non-residents of Utah.

This issue should not be dismissed, however, without a caveat. In Northwestern States Portland Cement Co. v. Minnesota, 358 U.S. 450 (1959), reference was made to the possibility that a domiciliary state might tax all the income of a corporation engaged in interstate commerce and that a tax imposed by a non-domiciliary state upon apportioned income would result in double taxation of a portion of the same income. In a footnote on this point, the Court cited the fact that in Standard Oil Co. v. Peck, 342 U.S. 382 (1952), it had struck down an ad valorem property tax imposed by the domiciliary state upon a fleet of barges plying in interstate commerce because it was not apportioned. 358 U.S. at 463, n. 5.

21. This basic principle is supported by Shaffer v. Carter, 252 U.S. 37 (1920) insofar as due process is concerned. The commerce clause issue was finally resolved in Northwestern States Portland Cement Co. v. Minnesota, 358 U.S. 450 (1959), discussed in the text at section II, C, 2, c, infra. See M. V. Marine Co. v. State Tax Comm'n, 606 S.W.2d 644, 652 (Mo.1980) (Morgan, J.), quoting this paragraph of the treatise.

22. 247 U.S. 321 (1918).

rived from intrastate or from interstate commerce.[23]

(2) Foreign Corporations

Two years later, in *Underwood Typewriter Co. v. Chamberlain*,[24] the Court for the first time considered the validity of an apportioned state income tax imposed on a *foreign* corporation engaged in interstate commerce. The Underwood Typewriter Company was a Delaware corporation with its principal office in New York and all of its manufacturing facilities in Connecticut. Under the applicable statutory provisions, net income of the corporation was allocated to Connecticut on the basis of a single-factor property formula, namely, the ratio of the fair cash value of corporate real estate and tangible personal property located in Connecticut to the total fair cash value of all corporate real and tangible personal property wherever located. This formula resulted in an allocation of 47% of Underwood's income to Connecticut. The taxpayer contended, apparently based on the volume of sales consummated within the state, that only 3.3% of its net income was derived from business in Connecticut. The Underwood Typewriter Company challenged the statute as imposing an undue burden upon interstate commerce and as an attempt to tax income arising from business conducted outside the taxing state contrary to principles of due process. The Court gave the commerce clause argument only brief attention, brushing it aside on the basis of *United States Glue Co.*

With respect to the due process argument in *Underwood Typewriter Co.*, the Court found that the taxpayer had failed to sustain the burden of proving "that the method of apportionment . . . was inherently arbitrary, or that its application . . . produced an unreasonable result." [25] On this issue, the Court alluded to the unit rule of valuation relating to the imposition of property taxes on property employed as an integral part of an interstate transportation system and the Court made the following observation:

> The profits of the corporation were largely earned by a series of transactions beginning with manufacture in Connecticut and ending with sale in other States. In this it was typical of a large part of the manufacturing business conducted in the State. The legislature in attempting to put upon this business its fair share of the burden of taxation was faced with the impossibility of allocating specifically the profits earned by the processes conducted within its borders. It, therefore, adopted a method of apportionment which, for all that appears in this record, reached, and was meant to reach, only the profits earned within the State. "The plaintiff's argument on this branch of the case," as stated by the Supreme Court of Errors, "carries the burden of showing that 47 percent of its net income is not reasonably attributable, for purposes of taxation, to the manufacture of products from the sale of which 80 percent of its gross earnings was derived after paying manufacturing costs." The corporation has not even attempted to show this; and for aught that appears the percentage of net profits earned in Connecticut may have been much larger than 47 percent. There is, consequently, nothing in this record to show that the method of apportionment adopted by

---

23. This decision was foreshadowed by Peck & Co. v. Lowe, 247 U.S. 165 (1918) which held that the imposition of the federal income tax upon net income derived from foreign exports did not violate the constitutional proscription of a duty upon exports. Two years later, the Court sustained an income tax upon an individual domiciled within the taxing state with respect to income received by him as a beneficiary of an out-of-state trust. Maguire v. Trefry, 253 U.S. 12 (1920).

Domiciliary corporations, of course, may seek to establish that they are "doing business" outside of the domiciliary state in order to be allowed to apportion their income. See E. F. Johnson Co. v. Commissioner of Taxation, 302 Minn. 236, 224 N.W.2d 150 (1975), ap-

peal dismissed 421 U.S. 982 (1975) (taxpayer's only office and place of manufacture was within the domiciliary state, but it sold products throughout the United States and Canada, and thus contended that it was carrying on business outside of the state and should be allowed to apportion its income). Cf. Blackmon v. Habersham Mills, Inc., 233 Ga. 501, 212 S.E.2d 337 (1975) (whether the taxpayer is "doing business" in other states so as to be subject to their taxing jurisdiction is immaterial).

24. 254 U.S. 113 (1920).

25. Id. at 121.

the State was inherently arbitrary, or that its application to this corporation produced an unreasonable result.[26]

This decision not only asured apportionment among nondomiciliary states of net income derived from interstate commerce, but also bestowed the court's blessing on a statutory formula method of apportionment.

During the next decade, the Court decided two additional cases which involved the validity of a tax upon apportioned net income of a foreign manufacturing corporation where the apportionment was made on the basis of a single-factor property formula. In *Bass, Ratcliff & Gretton v. State Tax Commission*[27] decided in 1924, the Court sustained a formula for allocating net income which included not only real and tangible personal property but also certain intangibles, namely, accounts and bills receivable and investments in the capital stock of other corporations. The taxpayer, a British corporation, was engaged in manufacturing ale in England which was sold both in England and the United States. Sales in the United States were made through branches located in New York and Chicago. The Court sustained the validity of the apportionment relying principally on its decision in *Underwood Typewriter Co.* In its opinion the Court observed that the "company carried on the unitary business of manufacturing and selling ale, in which . . . profits were earned by a series of transactions beginning with the manufacture in England and ending in sales in New York and other places . . . [and] the State was justified in attributing to New York a just proportion of the profits earned by the Company from such unitary business."[28] Based on the record, the Court concluded that the method of apportionment was not "inherently arbitrary or a mere effort to reach profits earned elsewhere."

Two aspects of the decision in *Bass, Ratcliff & Gretton* are of special significance with respect to the matter of taxation of the net income of interstate businesses. The first aspect of importance is the inclusion of intangible property in the allocation formula. The second aspect of importance is the fact that the Court specifically endorsed the "unit rule" concept relating to the allocation of property values of interstate transportation systems for general property tax purposes as a rational basis for determining the taxable income of a unitary business of interstate manufacture and sale. Thus, the stage was set for subsequent articulation of the unitary concept with respect to the apportionment of net income from interstate business.

The last case during this period of development of constitutional doctrine was decided in 1931. In *Hans Rees' Sons v. North Carolina*,[29] a New York corporation was engaged in the business of tanning, manufacturing and selling belting and other heavy leathers. Its manufacturing operations were conducted exclusively in North Carolina. The company maintained its sales office and a warehouse in New York and sold its products both at wholesale and retail. Sales of the company products were made throughout the United States, Canada and Western Europe. Approximately 40% of the output of its manufacturing plant in North Carolina was shipped to the New York warehouse and the balance was shipped direct to customers upon order from the New York sales office. Under the statutory property formula, approximately 80% of the corporate income was allocated to North Carolina. In the trial court, the taxpayer offered evidence to show that its net income was comprised of buying profit, manufacturing profit, and selling profit and that income having its source in the manufacturing and tanning operations within North Carolina was 17 per-

---

26. Id. at 120–21 (footnote omitted).

27. 266 U.S. 271 (1924).

28. Id. at 282. It is of interest to note that the corporation reported no net income for the year from its operations in the United States for purposes of the fed-

eral income tax. Thus, the income apportioned to New York was based upon the worldwide income of the corporation.

29. 283 U.S. 123 (1931).

cent. This evidence was stricken by the trial court. The state supreme court sustained the ruling of the trial court but held that even if the evidence were deemed competent, it would not change the result. On the basis of this record, the United States Supreme Court reviewed the case as if the evidence had been received by the state court as true and accurate but as having no bearing on the validity of the statute in the particular circumstances.

In *Hans Rees' Sons*, the taxpayer's objection was premised upon both due process and the commerce clause. In reaching its decision, the Court observed that with respect to an interstate business where different states have jurisdiction to impose an income tax on the basis of what is done within its own borders, the question becomes one of apportionment. In these circumstances, "evidence may always be received which tends to show that a state has applied a method, which, albeit fair on its face, operates so as to reach profits which are in no just sense attributable to transactions within its jurisdiction." [30] In reliance on the assumption made by the state court with respect to the facts shown, the Court concluded that the taxpayer had sustained the burden of proving that the statutory method as applied to it "operated unreasonably and arbitrarily, in attributing to North Carolina a percentage of income out of all appropriate proportion to the business transacted by the appellant in that state."[31]

With the triumvirate of *Underwood Typewriter Co.*, *Bass, Ratcliff & Gretton*, and *Hans Rees' Sons*, the Court firmly established the rule that a non-domiciliary state could tax, on an apportioned basis, the net income of a corporation engaged in manufacturing and selling in interstate commerce. These cases in general validated the single-factor property formula but the taxpayer's success in *Hans Rees' Sons*, though attributable to a procedural aspect of the case, clearly indicated that such a formula was highly vulnerable. At this point, the Court not only had established the validity of the formula method of apportioning net income from interstate business, but also had provided an impetus for the development of a multiple-factor formula for such apportionment.[32]

b. *Formulas for Apportionment of Income—Requirement of Reasonable Relationship to In-State Activities*

Two major due process limitations have been imposed by the Court on apportionment formulas: (1) the method used must display a "modicum of reasonable relation to corporate activities within the state" [33] and (2) the formula must not operate in an arbitrary manner or produce an unreasonable result.[34] The Court, however, has expressly refrained from endorsing any single apportionment method as being the only method which satisfies due process.[35]

Although the Court upheld the use of a single-factor property formula in *Underwood Typewriter Co.*, the vulnerability of single-factor formulas was established by the decision in *Hans Rees' Sons*. In *General Motors v. District of Columbia*, the Court, without reaching the substantive due

---

30. Id. at 134.

31. Id. at 135.

32. It should be noted that in 1919, Massachusetts, under its corporate franchise tax, initiated the three-factor formula for allocation of income based upon property, payroll and sales. Mass.Gen.Acts, 1919, ch. 355, § 19. This tax was held invalid as applied to a corporation deemed to be engaged exclusively in interstate commerce. Alpha Portland Cement Co. v. Massachusetts, 268 U.S. 203 (1925). The decision in *Alpha Portland Cement Co.* was premised on the ground that the tax was imposed for the privilege of conducting an interstate business where the only in-state

activity consisted of a sales office with orders being forwarded to the taxpayer's principal office in Pennsylvania.

33. General Motors v. District of Columbia, 380 U.S. 553, 561 (1965) (decision based on statutory interpretation of scope of taxing power granted by Congress to the District of Columbia).

34. Underwood Typewriter Co. v. Chamberlain, 254 U.S. 113, 121 (1920); Hans Rees' Sons v. North Carolina, 283 U.S. 123, 134 (1931).

35. General Motors v. District of Columbia, 380 U.S. 553, 561 (1965).

process and commerce clause issues, overturned a single-factor sales formula established by regulation on the ground that the regulation exceeded the congressional grant of taxing power to the District of Columbia.[36] Although the Court's opinion was expressly based on statutory interpretation, the opinion analyzed the reasonableness of the single-factor sales formula and found it lacking, noting that prior decisions "lend little support to the use of an exclusively sales-oriented approach."[37] Subsequently, however, in *Moorman Manufacturing Co. v. Bair*,[38] the Court sustained the application of an Iowa single-factor sales formula in the apportionment of income of an interstate business.

Two-factor formulas, although more likely to withstand a due process attack than single-factor formulas, are still subject to attack as being arbitrary and unreasonable. The supreme courts of both South Carolina[39] and Colorado[40] recently have upheld two-factor formulas which apportion income on the basis of property and sales.

Three-factor formulas are the most prevalent among the various states.[41] Typically the factors included are property, sales, and payroll with some states analogizing loans and interest for financial institutions to property and sales for non-financial corporations.[42] Because the three-factor formula encompasses the three major aspects of business activities within a taxing state, i.e. amount of property owned in the state, amount of salaries paid to personnel within the state, and volume of sales within the state, it is the method of apportionment most likely to withstand attack as being arbitrary or unreasonable. At least one state has upheld as constitutional a taxing scheme which is based upon a three-factor formula, but which allows. (1) manufacturing concerns to elect to use a two-factor formula based on property and payroll; and (2) selling concerns to elect to use a two-factor formula based on property and sales.[43] Such a scheme tends to assure reasonableness by allowing corporations to elect an alternative to the three-factor formula, based on the type of business.

The second due process limitation is that the formula not be applied so as to produce an arbitrary or unreasonable result. Apportionment formulas which are valid on their face are subject to constitutional attack as being improperly applied. The inclusion of each item of income[44] must be based on a

---

36. Id. at 562.

37. Id. at 561. It should be noted that an issue frequently litigated before state supreme courts in relation to the reasonableness of an allocation of income is whether certain sales were effected within the taxing state. See Commonwealth v. Blumenthal Bros. Chocolate Co., 457 Pa. 61, 321 A.2d 369 (1974); Commonwealth v. Safe Harbor Water Power Corp., 458 Pa. 134, 328 A.2d 833 (1974); Commonwealth v. Pincus Bros., Inc., 453 Pa. 525, 309 A.2d 381 (1973); Commonwealth v. Eli Lilly & Co., 439 Pa. 268, 266 A.2d 636 (1970); Commonwealth v. Hellertown Mfg. Co., 438 Pa. 134, 264 A.2d 382 (1970); Grain Belt Breweries, Inc. v. Commissioner of Taxation, 309 Minn. 190, 243 N.W.2d 322 (1976); Ralston Purina Co. v. Commissioner of Revenue, 306 Minn. 321, 236 N.W.2d 779 (1975).

38. 437 U.S. 267 (1978). See the critical evaluation of this decision beginning at section II, C, 2, e, infra.

39. In United States Steel Corp. v. South Carolina Tax Comm'n, 259 S.C. 153, 191 S.E.2d 9 (1972), the taxpayer, a nationwide manufacturing concern, was deemed to be a selling concern within South Carolina. Thus, the taxpayer was restricted to using the three-factor formula or the alternative available to selling concerns, of a two-factor formula based on property

and sales. The taxpayer was barred from electing the manufacturer's alternative of a two-factor property and payroll formula.

40. In General Motors Corp. v. Colorado, 181 Colo. 360, 509 P.2d 1260 (1973), the Colorado Supreme Court held that a two-factor formula based on property and sales meets due process requirements. See also Union Pacific R.R. Co. v. Heckers, 181 Colo. 374, 509 P.2d 1255 (1973), appeal dismissed 414 U.S. 806 (1973).

41. General Motors v. District of Columbia, 380 U.S. 553, 559 n. 9 (1965).

42. Household Finance Corp. v. Franchise Tax Bd., 230 Cal.App.2d 926, 41 Cal.Rptr. 565 (1964).

43. United States Steel Corp. v. South Carolina Tax Comm'n, 259 S.C. 153, 191 S.E.2d 9 (1972).

44. The granting of deductions, although not related to the validity of the method of apportionment, must also pass the constitutional tests of complying with the commerce clause and of satisfying due process. See Alabama v. Western Grain Co., 55 Ala.App. 690, 318 So.2d 719 (1975); cert. denied 294 Ala. 770, 318 So.2d 722, appeal dismissed 424 U.S. 960 (1976); Union Pacific R.R. Co. v. Heckers, 181 Colo. 374, 509 P.2d 1255 (1973), appeal dismissed 414 U.S. 806 (1973); F. W.

determination that the item in issue comes within the scope of the applicable formula. Little litigation has arisen concerning the inclusion of either property or payroll. However, the inclusion of sales has resulted in numerous cases evaluating the factual pattern in issue to determine where a sale was performed.[45] Apportionment, of course, need not be exact, but need only achieve a reasonable approximation to the corporate activities within the taxing state.[46] To establish the invalidity of a formula, *as applied*, the taxpayer must establish that a gross disproportion exists between the income allocated by the statutory formula and the income factually proven to have arisen from activity within the state.[47]

c. In-State Business Activity and the NORTHWESTERN STATES Decision

By 1931 the Court, in its decisions relating to apportionment of income from interstate commerce, had dealt only with cases where the taxpayer-corporation could be considered as having a significant presence in the non-domiciliary state through the ownership of property in the state coupled with the activities of full-time employees. Fifteen years passed before the Court considered the question as to whether a lesser degree of business activity within the taxing state, consisting only of the solicitation of sales, was sufficient to support an apportionment of net income. In 1946, in a per curiam decision in *West Publishing Co. v. McColgan*,[48] the Court sustained the allocation of net income where the principal and only significant activity or presence within the taxing

state consisted of the solicitation of orders for law books published out-of-state and shipped to customers from out-of-state locations. The taxpayer, a Minnesota corporation, employed four full-time salesmen to sell law books in California. These salesmen solicited orders, received payments thereon, collected delinquent accounts, and handled customer complaints. The taxpayer did not rent offices in California, but its salesmen obtained space in the offices of certain attorneys by making available the use of the publisher's sample books which were kept on hand in connection with their sales activities. In legal newspapers and periodicals circulated in California, the taxpayer advertised as its local offices these offices which had been obtained by its employees.

The California statute involved in *West Publishing Co.* imposed a tax on the net income "of every corporation derived from sources within [the] State." Income from sources within the state was defined to include "income from tangible and intangible property located or having a situs in this State and income from any activities carried on in this State, regardless of whether carried on in intrastate, interstate or foreign commerce." The taxpayer challenged imposition of the tax on any of its income, principally on the ground that California could not impose a tax on any part of the net income of a foreign corporation which was engaged exclusively in interstate commerce. The taxpayer also contended that the tax violated the due process clause of the fourteenth amendment, asserting that the state was without jurisdiction to tax.

Woolworth Co. v. Commissioner of Taxes, 130 Vt. 544, 298 A.2d 839 (1972); F. W. Woolworth Co. v. Commissioners of Taxes, 133 Vt. 93, 328 A.2d 402 (1974).

45. See cases cited at note 37, supra. See also Texas Eastern Transmission Corp. v. Kingsley, N.J.State Tax Cas.Rep. (CCH) ¶ 200–709 (1975), petition for certification denied 71 N.J. 533, 366 A.2d 688 (1976), appeal dismissed 430 U.S. 925 (1977).

46. Covington Fabrics Corp. v. South Carolina Tax Comm'n, 264 S.C. 59, 212 S.E.2d 574 (1975), appeal dismissed 423 U.S. 805 (1975); Union Pac. R.R. Co. v. Heckers, 181 Colo. 374, 509 P.2d 1255 (1973), appeal

dismissed 414 U.S. 806 (1973) (Commissioner allocated 3.65% of taxpayer's apportionable income while taxpayer argued for 3.56%; 0.09% difference is "simply too small to constitute an unlawful burden upon interstate commerce, a violation of due process, or a violation of equal protection"); United States Steel Corp. v. South Carolina Tax Comm'n, 259 S.C. 153, 191 S.E.2d 9 (1972).

47. General Motors Corp. v. Colorado, 181 Colo. 360, 509 P.2d 1260 (1973).

48. 328 U.S. 823 (1946), affirming per curiam 27 Cal.2d 705, 166 P.2d 861 (1946).

In a comprehensive opinion the Supreme Court of California sustained the tax, relying principally on *United States Glue Co.* and emphasizing the well established principle that the commerce clause does not bar a tax on net income derived from interstate commerce. In refuting the taxpayer's due process argument, the California court made the following observation:

> The record shows without conflict that plaintiff engages in substantial income-producing activities in California. It has local offices here as well as employees who devote their entire time to soliciting orders, receiving payments, adjusting complaints, collecting delinquent accounts, and performing other services for plaintiff. This state provides a market in which plaintiff operates in competition with local lawbook publishers. Plaintiff's agents receive the same protection and other benefits from the state as agents carrying on business activities for a principal engaged in intrastate business. The state protects plaintiff's business transactions within its borders and maintains courts in which plaintiff enforces payment for the sale of its publications. In West Publishing Co. v. Superior Court, 20 Cal.2d 720, 128 P.2d 777 (1942), certiorari denied 317 U.S. 700 (1943), it was held that by virtue of these activities plaintiff is present in this state and subject to the jurisdiction of its courts.[49]

With its per curiam affirmance of *West Publishing Co.*, the United States Supreme Court endorsed the view that the mere solicitation of sales within the taxing state was a sufficient activity on which to premise an allocation of net income from interstate business. However, a fully definitive decision on this issue was not forthcoming until 1959.

In 1959, the Court, consolidated two cases, now referred to jointly as *Northwestern States Portland Cement Co. v. Minnesota.*[50] The case presented by Northwestern States Portland Cement Company involved the application of the Minnesota income tax.

Minnesota imposed a general income tax on the "taxable net income" of residents and nonresidents including domestic and foreign corporations "whose business within the state during the taxable year consists exclusively of foreign commerce, interstate commerce, or both." The statute incorporated a three-factor formula which provided for allocation of income based on sales, tangible property, and payroll.[51] Northwestern States Portland Cement Company, an Iowa corporation, operated a cement manufacturing plant in Mason City, Iowa, maintained a sales office in Minneapolis, and solicited orders in Minnesota through its salesmen. All orders were forwarded to Mason City for acceptance, all sales were made on a delivered price basis, and all billings and collections were made from the Iowa office. The corporation owned some office equipment but no real estate in Minnesota, and did not warehouse any of its products in that state. Forty-eight percent of the company's sales were made to Minnesota customers.

The second case consolidated under the title of *Northwestern States Portland Cement Co.*, related to Stockham Valves and Fittings, Inc. This case involved application of the Georgia income tax which provided that "every domestic and every foreign corporation shall pay annually an income tax equivalent to five and one-half percent of the net income from property owned or from business done in Georgia," such income to be allocated to the state by a three-factor formula based on inventory, wages and gross receipts. Taxpayer, a Delaware corporation, with its principal office and plant in Birmingham, Alabama, manufactured valves and pipe fittings which were sold to wholesalers and jobbers. Taxpayer maintained a sales-service office in Atlanta, Georgia, which served five states. Except for

49. 27 Cal.2d at 713, 166 P.2d at 866.

50. 358 U.S. 450 (1959).

51. The statute in issue provided for apportionment based on the average of: (1) the percentage which sales within the state is of total sales wherever made; (2) the percentage which total tangible property owned or used in the state is of total tangible property wher-

ever located, owned, or used by taxpayer in connection with his business; and (3) the percentage which taxpayer's total payroll paid or incurred in the state is of the taxpayer's total payrolls paid or incurred in connection with his business. Minn.Stat. § 290.19 (1945). The current version is essentially the same as the 1945 version. See Minn.Stat. § 290.19 (1974).

some office equipment, the company owned no property in Georgia. All sales were processed and filled by the main office in Birmingham, shipment being made direct to the customer on an f.o.b. warehouse basis.

In each case the taxpayer *conceded* that the particular method of allocation of income was fair and reasonable. The challenge to the validity of the tax in each case paralleled the position taken by the taxpayer in *West Publishing Co.*, namely, that the statutes violated both the due process clause and the commerce clause. In its opinion, the Court focused most of its attention upon the commerce clause issue. After reviewing its earlier decisions, the Court concluded with the observation that "these cases stand for the doctrine that the entire net income of a corporation, generated by interstate as well as intrastate activities, may be fairly apportioned among the states for tax purposes by formulas utilizing in-state aspects of interstate affairs." [52] The Court laid particular stress upon *West Publishing Co.* as having dispelled any doubt as to the propriety of an income tax upon net income derived from interstate commerce.

Two aspects of the portion of the Court's opinion in *Northwestern States* which discussed *West Publishing Co.* are of particular importance. The first is the Court's observation that "it is significant . . . that West had not qualified to do business in California." [53] The second is the statement that "the [state court's] opinion was not grounded on the triviality that office space

was given West's solicitors by attorneys." [54] Thus, the Court underscored its position that mere solicitation of sales constituted adequate "in-state aspects of interstate affairs" to support a formula allocation of net income. Proceeding to the due process argument, the Court observed that "the taxes imposed are levied only on that portion of the taxpayer's net income which arises from its activities within the taxing state. These activities form a sufficient 'nexus between such a tax and transactions within a state for which the tax is an exaction'." [55] On the basis of *Northwestern States*, it is reasonably clear that mere solicitation of business by a foreign corporation in a state other than that in which the principal office is located provides a sufficient nexus to warrant apportionment of net income to the market state.[56]

d. Congressional Response to NORTH-WESTERN STATES

The decision in *Northwestern States* was met with an immediate legislative response. Congress promptly enacted Public Law 86–272 which circumscribed the broad rule of *nexus* articulated by the Court. Under this statute, a state is prohibited from taxing income from interstate business where: (1) the only activity within the taxing state is solicitation of sales orders for tangible personal property; (2) the orders are forwarded out-of-state for acceptance; and (3) the goods are shipped from an out-of-state location.[57] In *Heublein, Inc. v. South Carolina*

---

52. 358 U.S. 450, 460 (1959).

53. Id. at 461. With this comment, the Court emphasized the wholly interstate character of the taxpayer's operations.

54. Id. at 461. With this second comment, the Court was apparently emphasizing that a "place of business" within the taxing state was not a prerequisite to the apportionment of net income from interstate commerce.

55. Id. at 464.

56. Concurrent dispositions of other pending interstate income tax cases, all of which sustained imposition of the tax, confirm the conclusion stated in the text. Brown-Forman Distillers Corp. v. Collector of Revenue, 234 La. 651, 101 So.2d 70 (1958), appeal dismissed and cert. denied 359 U.S. 28 (1959) (only in-state

activity was solicitation of orders and goodwill services of "missionary men"); ET & WNC Transp. Co. v. Currie, 248 N.C. 560, 104 S.E.2d 403 (1958), affirmed per curiam, 359 U.S. 28 (1959) (trucking company engaged solely in interstate business maintained local terminals); International Shoe Co. v. Fontenot, 236 La. 279, 107 So.2d 640, cert. denied 359 U.S. 984 (1959) (only in-state activity was solicitation of orders).

57. State courts have been diligent in restricting P.L. 86–272 to its terms. In Heublein, Inc. v. South Carolina Tax Comm'n, 257 S.C. 17, 183 S.E.2d 710 (1971), aff'd 409 U.S. 275 (1972), the South Carolina Supreme Court held that a state may require a corporation, as a condition to selling alcoholic beverages within the state, to establish more than the minimal nexus protected by P.L. 86–272. In Heftel Broadcasting Honolulu, Inc. v. Wong, 57 Haw. 175, 554 P.2d 242 (1976),

Tax Commission the Court held that the major purpose of Congress in enacting Public Law 86–272 was to define the phrase "sufficient nexus" as used by the Court in *Northwestern States*, and thereby provide certainty in the administration of state taxation.[58] By establishing a minimal nexus requirement before a state may tax a foreign corporation, Congress effectively determined that the state's interest in taxing business with less contact was weaker than the nation's interest in an open economy.[59]

The South Carolina Alcoholic Beverage Control Act, which was challenged in *Heublein*, required foreign corporations desiring to sell alcoholic beverages within the state to establish more than the minimal contacts with the state which are protected by Public Law No. 86–272.[60] The taxpayer challenged the validity of imposing an income tax on a foreign corporation which was required, as a condition of doing business within the state, to forfeit the protection of Public Law 86–272 when the corporation would not otherwise have forfeited that protection. The Court found that the requirement was not an attempt by the state to evade Public Law 86–272, but that the requirement had been enacted pursuant to a regulatory scheme that served "legitimate state purposes other than assuring that the State may tax the

firm's income."[61] Because Heublein had done more than the acts protected from state income taxation by Public Law 86–272, Heublein was subject to the state income tax. Although the dicta in *Heublein* deals broadly in terms of legitimate regulatory schemes, the holding may be limited to regulation of alcoholic beverages because the Court, in finding no commerce clause violation, relied heavily on precedent establishing that "a State is totally unconfined by traditional Commerce Clause limitations when it restricts the importation of intoxicants destined for use, distribution, or consumption within its borders."[62]

e. The Single-Factor Sales Formula and the MOORMAN MANUFACTURING CO. Decision—A Backward Step

In its recent decisions relating to state taxes affecting interstate and foreign commerce, the Court appeared to have abandoned a strict doctrinaire approach in determining whether a particular tax conflicted with principles of due process, the commerce clause, or the import-export clause. In lieu of a doctrinaire test, the Court applied a pragmatic test by looking to "economic realities"[63] to determine whether there was a sufficient nexus, or whether there was dis-

---

cert. denied 429 U.S. 1073 (1977), the Hawaii Supreme Court found that a lease of films which was neither negotiated nor executed in Hawaii was effectively an acquisition of intangible telecast rights. P.L. 86–272, of course, does not apply to *intangible* property. Finally, in Texas Eastern Transmission Corp. v. Kingsley, N.J. State Tax Cas. Rep. (CCH) ¶ 200–709 (1975), petition for certification denied 71 N.J. 533, 366 A.2d 688 (1976), appeal dismissed 430 U.S. 925, 97 S.Ct. 1540 (1977), the New Jersey Tax Court found that the *transfer* by the taxpayer of natural gas within New Jersey to a company which delivers the gas out-of-state, even though the sale was negotiated outside of the state and the gas flowed through the state uninterrupted, constituted a sufficient nexus with the state to invoke taxation.

P.L. 86–272 also has been used by the states in a correlative manner to provide the standard for whether a domestic corporation is taxable on income. Such use was endorsed by the Colorado Supreme Court when, in Coors Porcelain Co. v. Colorado, 183 Colo. 325, 517 P.2d 838 (1973), cert. denied 419 U.S. 874 (1974), the court upheld a regulation of the state Department of Revenue which required that all income of a domestic corporation which is not allocable to a foreign state, be-

cause protected by P.L. 86–272, will be allocated to Colorado.

58.   409 U.S. 275, 280 (1972), aff'g 257 S.C. 17, 183 S.E.2d 710 (1971).

59.   409 U.S. at 280. The Court also noted that by the twenty-first amendment, commerce clause limitations do not apply to state regulation of intoxicants. Id. at 283.

60.   Id. at 277–78.

61.   Id. at 282–83.

62.   Id. at 283, citing Hostetter v. Idlewild Bon Voyage Liquor Corp., 377 U.S. 324, 330 (1964).

63.   Complete Auto Transit v. Brady, 430 U.S. 274 (1977) (sustaining Mississippi tax on gross receipts from in-state transportation of property in interstate commerce). In this decision, the Court stated: "There is no *economic consequence* that follows necessarily from the use of the particular words, 'privilege of doing business,' and a focus on that formalism merely obscures the question whether the tax produces a forbidden effect." Id. at 288 (emphasis added).

crimination or risk of multiple burden on interstate or foreign commerce. This shift in the Court's position provided an emerging rationality that previously was lacking in the resolution of these issues.[64]

A series of five cases decided in a period of four years illustrate this development. In *Standard Pressed Steel Co. v. Washington*,[65] the Court sustained the Washington state business and occupation tax on gross receipts from the sale of aerospace fasteners manufactured out-of-state and delivered to the Boeing Company located in Washington. The taxpayer conducted business with Boeing through an engineer residing in the state. The employee's office was in his home and his duties consisted primarily of consulting with Boeing with respect to the use of the taxpayer's products. In a unanimous decision, the Court sustained the tax under both the due process clause and commerce clause. There was sufficient nexus by the presence in Washington of the full-time employee, and there was no demonstrable risk of multiple taxation of the sales to Boeing.

This was followed by the decision in *Colonial Pipeline Co. v. Traigle*,[66] wherein the Court, without overruling *Spector Motor Service, Inc. v. O'Connor*,[67] sustained a nondiscriminatory, fairly apportioned Louisiana franchise tax imposed on a company engaged exclusively in interstate commerce. The tax was sustained on the ground that it was not imposed on the privilege of engaging in interstate commerce but rather on the subject of doing business in Louisiana in the corporate form. This case led the Court in its subsequent decision in *Complete Auto Transit, Inc. v. Brady*[68] to overrule *Spector*

Motor. In *Complete Auto* the Court sustained a Mississippi tax on the "privilege of engaging in business" measured by gross receipts derived from in-state transportation of goods shipped in interstate commerce. In its decision the Court emphasized the fact that the tax was fairly apportioned and nondiscriminatory—i.e., there was no risk of multiple burden on the gross income derived from the rendition of local services in the conduct of interstate commerce.

During this period, the Court also decided *Michelin Tire Co. v. Wages*[69] wherein it repudiated the long-standing "original package" doctrine and sustained a nondiscriminatory property tax on imported goods that were no longer in transit. The most recent decision in this "pragmatic series" is *Dep't of Revenue v. Ass'n of Washington Stevedoring Co.*[70] wherein the Court sustained the Washington state general business tax on gross receipts derived from the business of stevedoring. In this case the Court relied upon *Complete-Auto* and noted that since the business activity was exclusively localized the tax was nondiscriminatory and fairly apportioned. Again, although the local services involved the transportation of goods in interstate or foreign commerce, there was no risk of multiple state taxation of the taxpayer's business activities.

This encouraging development suffered a significant setback, however, with the decision in *Moorman Manufacturing Co. v. Bair*[71] in which the majority of the Court reverted to a strict doctrinaire approach in sustaining the Iowa single-factor destination sales formula for the apportionment of net income of an interstate business engaged in the manufacture and sale of tangible person-

---

64. See W. Hellerstein, State Taxation and the Supreme Court: Toward a More Unified Approach to Constitutional Adjudication?, 75 Mich.L.Rev. 1426 (1977).

65. 419 U.S. 560 (1975). See text at Section II, E, 1, e, at n.67, infra.

66. 421 U.S. 100 (1975). See text at Section II, D, 6, at nn.43–47, infra.

67. 340 U.S. 602 (1951). In *Spector Motor* the Court held that a state could not impose a franchise tax on the privilege of engaging in interstate com-

merce "no matter how fairly it is apportioned to business done within the [taxing] state." See text at Section II, D, 6, infra.

68. 430 U.S. 274 (1977). See text at Section II, D, 6, n.48, infra.

69. 423 U.S. 276 (1976). See text at Section II, A, 3, b, (1), supra.

70. 435 U.S. 734 (1978). See text at Section II, E, 1, d, infra.

71. 437 U.S. 267 (1978).

al property. The issue presented in *Moorman* had previously been considered by the Court in the context of the validity of a District of Columbia administrative regulation. In *General Motors Corp. v. District of Columbia*,[72] a single-factor sales formula had been promulgated by administrative regulation under the District of Columbia Income and Franchise Tax Act. The statute under which the regulation was issued provided that "if the trade or business of any corporation . . . is carried on . . . both within and without the District, the net income derived therefrom shall . . . be deemed to be income from sources within and without the District." The Court noted that if a manufacturing business were located in Maryland and sold its entire output in the District the single-factor sales formula would result in apportioning 100% of the net income of the enterprise to the District. On this basis, the Court concluded that the sales formula for apportionment of net income was contrary to the express requirements of the statute. Although the Court disclaimed taking "any position on the constitutionality of a state income tax based on the sales factor alone," the decision included an incisive appraisal of the single-factor sales formula as contrasted with the typical three-factor formula consisting of property, payroll and sales:

> While the Court has refrained from attempting to define any single appropriate method of apportionment, it has sought to ensure that the methods used display a modicum of reasonable relation to corporate activities within the State. The Court has approved formulae based on the geographical distribution of corporate property and those based on the standard three-factor formula. See, e.g., Underwood Typewriter Co. v. Chamberlain, supra; Butler Bros. v. McColgan, 315 U.S. 501, 62 S.Ct. 701, 86 L.Ed. 991. *The standard three-factor formula can be justified as a rough, practical approximation of the distribution of either a corporation's sources of income or the social costs which it generates. By contrast, the geographical dis-*

tribution of a corporation's sales is, by itself, of dubious significance in indicating the locus of either factor. We of course do not mean to take any position on the constitutionality of a state income tax based on the sales factor alone. For the present purpose, *it is sufficient to note that the factors alluded to by this Court in justifying apportionment measures constitutionally challenged in the past lend little support to the use of an exclusively sales-oriented approach.* In construing the District Code to prohibit the use of a sales-factor formula, we sacrifice none of the values which our scrutiny of state apportionment measures has sought to protect.

> In sum, we find that the language of the authorizing statute does not permit the application of an apportionment formula which makes use of the sales factor alone. *The conclusion which we draw from examination of the statutory language finds support in the conflict with other taxing jurisdictions which would result from a contrary view. It finds further support in the continuing concern for fair apportionment which this Court has displayed over the years in scrutinizing state taxing statutes.*[73]

Although these statements in *General Motors Corp.* were dicta, it appeared likely that the Court, if presented with the issue, would strike a state statute which incorporated a single-factor sales formula as the basis for apportioning the income of an interstate business.

In *Moorman*, the taxpayer was engaged in the manufacture and sale of feed for livestock and poultry. None of its manufacturing plants were located in Iowa, but it maintained six warehouses in Iowa that were supplied with its products manufactured in Illinois. The company also employed 500 persons who were engaged in sales and related activities in Iowa. Under the Iowa statute, the taxpayer was required to apportion its net income solely on the basis of a destination-sales formula. This resulted in an allocation of approximately 50% more income to Iowa than would have been the case

---

72. 380 U.S. 553. See text at Section II, C, 2, b, supra.

73. 380 U.S. at 561–62 (emphasis added).

if the customary three-factor (property, payroll and sales) formula were applied.[74] The taxpayer challenged the Iowa statute as violating both due process and the commerce clause.

The decision in *Moorman* sustaining the Iowa statutory sales formula was by a divided Court with Justice Stevens writing for the six-judge majority. Taxpayer's due process objection was denied on the ground that a single-factor formula is presumptively valid and that the taxpayer failed to prove by "clear and cogent" evidence that the income attributed to Iowa was disproportionate to the business transacted therein. On the commerce clause issue, the majority decision was premised on three propositions: (1) the taxpayer did not prove duplication (multiplicity) of taxation since it failed to establish the source of its net income between Illinois operations and Iowa sales; (2) the commerce clause does not require that the Court accept the three-factor formula as the only constitutionally valid formula since this, in effect, would involve the Court in activity of a legislative nature by requiring the prescription of national uniform rules in the application of such formula—a usurpation of the legislative power of Congress; and (3) the Court need not be concerned with the speculative issue of multiple taxation in view of the fact that Iowa unquestionably could have imposed a gross receipts tax which would be more burdensome than a net icome tax inasmuch as a gross receipts tax is payable irrespective of whether the taxpayer's operations are profitable.

Justice Powell, who wrote the principal dissenting opinion, concluded that the Iowa single-factor sales formula discriminated against interstate commerce by providing a direct commercial advantage to local business. It was his view that the single-factor sales formula operated as a tariff on goods manufactured in other states and as a subsidy to Iowa manufacturers selling their goods outside Iowa. He aptly demonstrated this point by a simple illustration included in a footnote to his dissent.[75] Justice Powell accepted the majority view that, in the absence of clear proof by the taxpayer of an arbitrary allocation of income, there was no violation of due process in the sense that arithmetical perfection is not expected. This point was stated as follows: "Because there is no ideal means of 'locating' any State's rightful share [of net income], such uniformity cannot be dictated by this Court." On the commerce clause issue, however, he proceeded to take judicial notice of the discriminatory effect of the Iowa single-factor-sales apportionment formula with respect to out-of-state businesses in light of the general use of the three-factor formula by other states. In this connection, he cogently distinguished the early income tax cases that sustained single-factor property formulae [76] by pointing out that such statutes discriminate against in-state businesses and consequently do not operate to raise a commerce clause issue. He acknowledged that the Court could not apply the commerce clause with precision; but he noted that the Court has consistently evaluated the validity of state regulatory and taxation statutes by weighing the effect of such measures against the background of practice of other states.[77] This led Justice Powell to conclude that, where a state's departure from general practice results in discrimination against interstate commerce, the Court should not abrogate its constitutional duty to invalidate the statute. In his view, this would not lead to the Court's adoption of fixed or precise rules of apportionment since the "impact on

74. 437 U.S. 271 n. 4.

75. 437 U.S. at 284–285 n. 2.

76. Underwood Typewriter Co. v. Chamberlain, 254 U.S. 113 (1920), see text at Section II, C, 2, a, (2), n.24, supra; and Bass, Ratcliff & Gretton Ltd. v. State Tax Comm'n, 266 U.S. 271 (1924), see text at Section II, C, 2, a, (2), n. 27, supra.

77. On this point, Justice Powell discussed the following cases: Southern Pac. Co. v. Arizona, 325 U.S. 761 (1945) (state statute limiting length of interstate trains); Bibb v. Navajo Freight Lines, Inc., 359 U.S. 520 (1959) (Illinois statute banning type of mudguard permitted in 46 other states); and General Motors Corp. v. District of Columbia, 380 U.S. 553 (1965) (analysis equally applicable to a commerce clause inquiry).

commerce must be weighed in the circumstances of each case."

Justice Blackmun who joined with Justice Powell in the principal dissent, wrote a separate dissent in which he stated that Iowa's "anachronistic single-factor sales formula runs headlong into overriding commerce clause considerations and demands." He concluded his brief dissenting opinion with the following observation:

> Today's decision is bound to be regressive. Single-factor formulas are relics of the early days of state income taxation. The three-factor formulas were inevitable improvements and, while not perfect, reflect more accurately the realities of the business and tax world. With their almost universal adoption by the States, the Iowa system's adverse and parochial impact on commerce comes vividly into focus. But with its single-factor formula now upheld by the Court, there is little reason why other States, perceiving or imagining a similar advantage to local interests, may not go back to the old ways. The end result, in any event, is to exacerbate what the Commerce Clause, absent governing congressional action, was devised to avoid.[78]

Justice Brennan, in a brief separate dissent, expressed the view that Iowa's single-factor sales apportionment formula fails to meet "the Commerce Clause requirement that a State's taxation of interstate business must be 'fairly apportioned to the commerce carried on within the taxing state.' "[79]

As suggested by Justice Blackmun in his dissent, there is little doubt that the decision in *Moorman* will adversely affect the trend toward uniformity in state formulae for apportionment of income from interstate business. Moreover, the majority opinion reflects a reversion to a doctrinaire approach reminiscent of the early income tax apportionment decisions—an about-face from the pragmatic approach which has been followed in the more recent state tax cases.

The majority opinion is premised on the taxpayer's failure to prove "by clear and cogent evidence"[80]—i.e., by "a separate accounting analysis"[81]—that the single-factor sales formula resulted in a grossly disproportionate attribution of income to business transacted in Iowa. This position is fundamentally contrary to the unitary concept of taxation of the income of an interstate enterprise. Under the unitary concept of taxing the income of interstate business, due consideration must be given to the relative contribution of the business activities of the taxpayer in each of the various states to the production of the total unitary income. Thus, the majority was in error in suggesting that "a separate accounting analysis might have revealed that losses in Illinois operations prevented appellant from earning more income from exploitation of a highly favorable Iowa market."[82] This statement implies that, with a separate accounting determination, it would have been appropriate to recognize that the taxpayer's entire net income vis-a-vis its Illinois-Iowa operations may have been derived solely from its business activities in Iowa. As early as the decision in *Butler Bros. v. McColgan*,[83] the Court refused to accept an interstate taxpayer's concededly accurate separate accounting for in-state business activities which established a loss from California operations where the entire interstate enterprise had enjoyed a net profit for the taxable year. The Court adhered to the view that, under the unitary concept, net income of the entire interstate business must be attributed to the activities conducted in each of the several states.[84] Consequently, it would be inappropriate either to recognize a loss from operations in one state, or to allocate the entire net income to another state, however accurate such accounting determination might be.[85]

---

78. 437 U.S. at 282–283.

79. 437 U.S. at 281.

80. 437 U.S. at 274.

81. 437 U.S. at 273.

82. Id.

83. 315 U.S. 501 (1942). This case was litigated solely on the due process issue.

84. 315 U.S. at 509.

85. See Hans Rees' Sons v. North Carolina, 283 U.S. 123, 133 (1931).

The fundamental invalidity of the single-factor sales formula lies in the fact that it reflects only business activity which results in sales in the taxing state. It fails to recognize other business activities that contribute to the production of net income of the enterprise. This point was aptly made in the decision in *General Motors Corp. v. District of Columbia* [86] wherein the Court struck the District of Columbia single-factor sales formula. Justice Stewart who prepared the Court's opinion in that case noted that, if a Maryland manufacturer sold all of its product in the District, the single-factor sales formula would result in allocating the taxpayer's entire net income to the District.

In the concluding portion of the majority opinion, the Court purports to dispose of the multiple burden issue by suggesting that instead of an income tax Iowa could have imposed a gross receipts tax. The latter, according to the Court, would have been more burdensome since it would apply irrespective of profitable operations. But this response is irrelevant to the multiple burden issue raised by the taxpayer with respect to the operation of the single-factor sales formula in the apportionment of net income. If it chose, Iowa could constitutionally impose a sales tax or gross receipts tax *in addition* to its income tax since Moorman's Iowa sales and Iowa gross receipts have an exclusive tax situs within the state. [87] In sum, it is regrettable that the majority ignored the more rational "economic realities" test in resolving the issue presented in *Moorman*. [88]

3. State Statutes Governing Division of Income of Interstate Business

a. Specific Allocation

The various state income tax statutes which provide for the division of net income from interstate commerce generally include provisions for specific allocation of certain types of income realized by multistate corporations. [1] These provisions for specific allocation apply to non-operating items of income such as interest, dividends, and capital gains which are incidental to the principal business income of a corporation. Under these statutes interest and dividends are usually allocated to the legal or commercial domicile of the corporation. [2] Capital gains from real and tangible personal property are generally allocated to the state where the property is located; [3] and capital gains from intangibles are allocated in the same manner

---

86. 380 U.S. 553 (1965).

87. Standard Pressed Steel Co. v. Washington, 419 U.S. 560 (1975).

88. For a more comprehensive treatment of the issue in *Moorman*, see, Young, The Single Factor Sales Formula and the *Moorman Manufacturing Co.* Decision—A Backward Step in the Apportionment of Income of Interstate Business, 56 Taxes 659 (1978).

1. The Willis Committee report includes a comprehensive discussion of this matter based on the statutes in effect at that time. House Judiciary Comm., Special Subcommittee, State Taxation of Interstate Commerce, House Report No. 1480, 88th Cong., 2d Sess., Vol. I, pp. 197–217 (1964). For a chart summarizing the current statutory provisions relating to specific allocation of items of income, see State and Local Tax Service—All States Unit (P-H) ¶ 1046.

2. Proceeds received by the parent corporation from the dissolution of a foreign subsidiary corporation also have been held to be taxable by the domiciliary state. Gross Income Tax Division v. P. F. Goodrich Corp., 260 Ind. 41, 292 N.E.2d 247 (1973) (P. F. Goodrich, an Indiana corporation, was taxed on the receipt of proceeds from the dissolution of a Delaware corporation).

Interest and dividends, however, may be allocated to states in which the corporation receiving the interest or dividends is doing business. In re Goodyear Tire & Rubber Co., 133 Vt. 132, 335 A.2d 310 (1975). In *Goodyear Tire & Rubber Co.* the statute taxed all items of income properly included in the taxpayers federal income tax, thus including dividends received from Goodyear's foreign subsidiaries on the theory that the tax was imposed on the money received by Goodyear, not on the profits of the subsidiaries.

3. At least two states have adopted a test of whether the property, on which the gain was realized, was "employed in the business." See Target Stores, Inc. v. Commissioner of Revenue, 309 Minn. 267, 244 N.W.2d 143 (1976) (taxpayer realized gain on sale of real property in foreign state which it was compelled to purchase incident to the acquisition of other real property required for business expansion; held gain not includible as unitary income for apportionment to taxing state); Johns-Manville Products Corp. v. Commissioners of Revenue Administration, 115 N.H. 428, 343 A.2d 221 (1975), appeal dismissed 423 U.S. 1069 (1976) (taxpayer realized gain on real property located in a foreign state which had been acquired for manufacturing process which was later phased out; held that property was an asset of a unitary business and thus the gain

as interest and dividends. This scheme for treatment of non-business income has been adopted by the Uniform Division of Income for Tax Purposes Act.[4]

The existing pattern for specific allocation of items which usually constitute "non-operating" income is inapplicable to financial institutions. By contrast with manufacturing, mercantile and most service enterprises, interest, dividends and capital gains constitute a major portion of the operating income of financial enterprises. Consequently, the statutory provisions applicable to the division of income of multi-state financial institutions parallel those applicable to the operating income of other multi-state businesses.[5]

As a matter of due process, the debtor's state of commercial domicile has jurisdiction to impose an income tax on interest earned by an out-of-state financial institution on loans utilized by the debtor in the taxing state.[6] Taxation of the net income derived from these transactions presents no commerce clause issue,[7] but the determination of net income in these circumstances does present practical difficulties in ascertaining the proper division of costs and expenses. This leads to a consideration of formula apportionment of net income derived from the operation of interstate business.

b. Formula Method v. Separate Accounting

The decision in *Northwestern States* illustrated the application of the Minnesota three-factor formula, consisting of property, payroll, and sales in the apportionment to a non-domiciliary state of net income from an interstate business. The obvious alternative to the application of a formula method of apportionment of net income is a separate accounting for items of income and expense relating to the business activities conducted within the taxing state. This leads to the question whether the formula method can be required by the taxing state where the taxpayer can demonstrate a reasonably accurate determination of in-state income by its method of separate accounting.

The Court discussed the issue of requiring separate accounting in *Butler Bros. v. McColgan*.[8] Butler Bros. was an Illinois corporation engaged in the wholesale dry goods and general merchandising business, purchasing from manufacturers and others and selling to retailers only. Butler Bros. operated wholesale houses in seven states including California. Each of the seven locations served a separate territory with its own sales force, handled its own collections and credit arrangements, and kept its own books and accounts. All of its sales in California were handled by its San Francisco office. All purchases were handled by the company's home office in Chicago with

---

was subject to apportionment). Another state has adopted a test relying on the relationship between activities within the state and activities outside of the state. Commonwealth v. ACF Industries, Inc., 441 Pa. 129, 271 A.2d 273 (1970) (foreign corporation's operations outside of taxing state were independent of, and did not contribute to, operations within the state; thus gain on sale of stock held by foreign corporation not taxable).

4. Uniform Division of Income for Tax Purposes Act §§ 4–8.

5. If the taxpayer corporation is a parent of foreign subsidiaries, the profits of the subsidiaries may be excluded by finding that the subsidiaries are not taxable entities. See Sun Finance & Loan Co. v. Kosydar, 45 Ohio St.2d 283, 344 N.E.2d 330 (1976), cert. denied 429 U.S. 857 (1976) (business done by foreign subsidiaries

is not includible in apportionment formula used to determine amount of net worth to be allocated to taxing state). If a foreign corporation is engaged in the credit business in the taxing state, dividend income earned by wholly owned subsidiaries outside of the state also may be excluded by finding that the income is nonapportionable. See Transamerica Financial Corp. v. Wisconsin Dept. of Revenue, 56 Wis.2d 57, 201 N.W.2d 552 (1972) (all nonapportionable dividends and interest are deducted from taxable income to the extent of interest and dividends in excess of total interest (whether or not apportionable) paid and allowed as a deduction).

6. Shaffer v. Carter, 252 U.S. 37 (1920).

7. U.S. Glue Co. v. Town of Oak Creek, 247 U.S. 321 (1918).

8. 315 U.S. 501 (1942).

goods being shipped to the various warehouses and charged to each location at cost plus transportation expenses. Costs of operating the central buying division, costs of central advertising, and home office general overhead expenses were allocated to the respective area operations.

At the time that *Butler Bros.* arose, the California statute provided that income from interstate businesses should "be determined by an allocation upon the basis of sales, purchase, expenses of manufacture, payroll, value and situs of tangible property, or by reference to these or other factors, or by such other method of allocation as is fairly calculated to assign to the state the portion of net income reasonably attributable to the business done within this state and to avoid subjecting the taxpayer to double taxation." In the tax year in question, the taxpayer enjoyed net income of approximately $1,150,000 from its entire multistate operations. In applying the three-factor formula based on property, payroll, and sales, the tax commissioner allocated 8.1372% of the total corporate income (approximately $93,500) to California. By contrast, the taxpayer by its method of separate accounting for its California operations, reported a net loss therefrom in the amount of $82,850. The tax commissioner did not challenge the accuracy of the taxpayer's method of separate accounting for costs and expenses allocable to its California operations. The taxpayer contended that the statutory formula which converted a loss of $82,850 into a profit of $93,500 resulted in an allocation of out-of-state income to the taxing state in violation of the due process requirements of the fourteenth amendment.

In resolving this issue the Court relied on the "unit rule" which the Court had developed much earlier in the property tax cases involving the valuation of property employed by businesses engaged in interstate transportation and communication. In its opinion, the Court articulated the analogy to which it had alluded in *Underwood Typewriter Co.* and endorsed in *Bass, Ratcliff & Gretton.* Under the property tax unitary rule, property located within the taxing state which is part of an interstate system may be valued with reference to its connection with such system. Thus, out-of-state property is necessarily taken into account in arriving at the value of the property which is physically located within the taxing state.[9] The unitary rule of property valuation had been aptly described in one of the Court's earlier decisions in the following manner:

> [W]hen . . . property is part of . . . [an interstate] system and has its actual uses only in connection with other parts of . . . [such] system, that fact may be considered by the State in taxing, even though the other parts of the system are outside of the State. The sleepers and rails of a railroad, or the posts and wires of a telegraph company, are worth more than the prepared wood and the bars of steel or coils of wire, from their organic connection with other rails or wires and the rest of the apparatus of a working whole. This being clear, it is held reasonable and constitutional to get at the worth of such a line in the absence of anything more special, by a mileage proportion. The tax is a tax on property . . . [and] is intended to reach the intangible value due to what we have called the organic relation of the property in the State to the whole system. . . . And this principle . . . has been extended . . . to the lines of express companies, although those lines are not material lines upon the face of the earth. There is the same organic connection as in the other cases.[10]

The Court made three preliminary observations in the *Butler Bros.* opinion: (1) the statutory formula, by its terms, was fairly calculated to assign to California that portion of the net income which was reasonably attributable to the business conducted in that state; (2) the burden was upon the tax-

---

9. When a corporation is found to be a unitary operation, all of the corporation's business income is assumed to be reasonably related to the business activity within the taxing state. Johns-Manville Product Corp. v. Commissioner of Revenue Administration, 115 N.H. 428, 343 A.2d 221 (1975), appeal dismissed 423 U.S. 1069 (1976).

10. Fargo v. Hart, 193 U.S. 490, 499 (1904).

payer to show by clear and cogent evidence that the application of the formula resulted in taxation of extraterritorial income and (3) the Court did not need to impeach the integrity of the taxpayer's separate accounting system to establish that the taxpayer's contention was erroneous.

In sustaining application of the unitary concept in the taxation of the net income of an interstate business, the Court pointed to the unity of ownership and management which characterized the taxpayer's interstate business operations. Particular stress was placed on centralized purchasing which admittedly resulted in obtaining more favorable prices for the benefit of the entire enterprise. In answer to the taxpayer's contention that its method of separate accounting for its California operations demonstrated that none of the net income of the multistate enterprise was attributable to California, the court responded with the following observation:

> If factors which are responsible for that net income are present in other States but not present in California, they have not been revealed. At least in [the] absence of that proof, California was justified in assuming that the San Francisco branch contributed its aliquot share

to the advantages of centralized management of this unitary enterprise and to the net income earned.[11]

4. Determining the Unitary Character of Income of an Interstate Business

Butler Bros. was the first case in which the United States Supreme Court specifically determined the issue as to whether the entire income of an interstate enterprise was sufficiently unitary in character to warrant apportionment by formula to the taxing state. Subsequent applications of the unitary rule have been made principally by the state courts and the developments with respect to this aspect of the taxation of income of interstate business are to be found in the state court decisions.[12]

A brief summary of selected state court decisions indicates the factual patterns in which the issue as to the unitary character of an enterprise has arisen and illustrates that some diversity exists in the positions of the state courts. With respect to integrated wholesale and retail merchandising, the courts have been consistent in following the rule of the decision in *Butler Bros.*[13] This consistency also applies to manufacturing concerns.[14] With respect to companies en-

11. Butler Bros. v. McColgan, 315 U.S. 501, 509 (1942).

12. For comprehensive discussions of the problems of apportionment of income of unitary businesses, see J. Hellerstein, Recent Developments in State Tax Apportionment and the Circumscription of a Unitary Business, 21 Nat'l Tax J. 487 (1968); F. Keesling and J. Warren, California's Uniform Division of Income for Tax Purposes Act, 15 U.C.L.A.L.Rev. 156 (1967); F. Keesling and J. Warren, The Unitary Concept in the Allocation of Income, 12 Hastings L.J. 42 (1960); E. Rudolph, State Taxation of Interstate Business: The Unitary Business Concept and Affiliated Corporate Groups, 25 Tax L.Rev. 171 (1970).

13. Western Auto Supply Co. v. Commissioner of Taxation, 245 Minn. 346, 71 N.W.2d 797 (1955) (combination wholesale and retail operations held unitary in view of centralized purchasing and centralized management); Walgreen Co. v. Commissioner of Taxation, 258 Minn. 522, 104 N.W.2d 714 (1960), appeal dismissed 365 U.S. 767 (1961); Rothschild & Co. v. Commissioner of Taxation, 270 Minn. 245, 133 N.W.2d 524 (1965); Zale-Salem, Inc. v. State Tax Comm'n, 237 Or. 261, 391 P.2d 601 (1965) (parent and subsidiary corporations engaged in retail jewelry business taxed as a unitary business on an apportionment basis).

In determining the unitary character of a business, the test is whether the operation of the business within the state is dependent on, or contributory to the operation of the business outside of the state. Associated Dry Goods v. Commissioner, Minn. State Tax Cas. Rep. (CCH) ¶ 200–675 (1974), aff'd per curiam, 306 Minn. 532, 235 N.W.2d 821 (1975), cert. denied 425 U.S. 999 (1976) (Wherein many factors indicated that each of 15 divisions of the foreign corporation engaged in retail sales were independent, while many factors also indicated that the corporation was a unitary operation). Department of Taxation v. Lucky Stores Inc., 217 Va. 121, 225 S.E.2d 870 (1976) (Lucky Stores, a foreign corporation engaged in retail sales, found to be a nationwide unitary business).

14. The test of *Butler Bros.* has been applied by the courts in Coca Cola Co. v. Department of Revenue, 271 Or. 517, 533 P.2d 788 (1975) (parent and subsidiary found to constitute a unitary business by ignoring separate corporate shells), and Commonwealth of Pennsylvania v. Advance-Wilson Industries, Inc., 456 Pa. 200, 317 A.2d 642 (1974) (in determining whether corporation may use separate accounting, court must look to the relationship between the activity within the state and the activity outside of the state).

gaged in production of oil and gas, the cases have been inconsistent. California has denied separate accounting with respect to instate operations and has required determination by formula apportionment on a unitary basis.[15] A contrary position has been taken by the Kansas and Minnesota courts which have recognized separate accounting for oil and gas operations conducted within their states.[16] A similar conflict exists with respect to construction companies. Utah has adopted the unitary rule and has applied the statutory apportionment formula to an Iowa corporation engaged in the general construction business.[17] In the year in question, the corporation was engaged in a number of projects in several states but its operations were centralized in and directed from the home office in Sioux City, Iowa. On the facts of the case, the result was advantageous to the taxpayer inasmuch as its Utah project was more profitable than its operations in other states. In a more recent decision, Oregon applied the separate accounting rule with respect to a foreign corporation which was engaged in the construction of a dam within the state. On the evidence presented, the court concluded that the taxpayer had sustained the requisite burden of proof in establishing that the separate accounting method was the only method which would "fairly and accurately" reflect the net income from the business done within the state.[18] The court thus concluded that apportionment is not mandatory for all unitary businesses. This decision also operated to the taxpayer's advantage inasmuch as its construction projects within Oregon had resulted in a loss whereas its out-of-state projects had produced a net gain. The Oregon Supreme Court subsequently rejected an attempt by the Department of Revenue to require a construction corporation to use the separate accounting method when the taxpayer had established that it was a unitary business entitled to use the apportionment method.[19]

Each state court must apply its own statutory provisions. A majority of state income tax statutes provide that if the business income of a corporation is derived from business activities conducted both within and without the state, such income shall be apportioned, usually by a three-factor formula consisting of property, payroll and sales.[20] Certain items in the nature of investment in-

---

15. Superior Oil Co. v. Franchise Tax Bd., 60 Cal.2d 406, 34 Cal.Rptr. 545, 386 P.2d 33 (1963); Honolulu Oil Corp. v. Franchise Tax Bd., 60 Cal.2d 417, 34 Cal.Rptr. 552, 386 P.2d 40 (1963).

16. Webb Resources, Inc. v. McCoy, 194 Kan. 758, 401 P.2d 879 (1965) (Kansas statutes at this time made separate accounting the preferred method); Skelly Oil Co. v. Commissioner of Taxation, 269 Minn. 351, 131 N.W.2d 632 (1964) (out-of-state production of oil and gas deemed separate from business of refining and marketing where only activity within taxing state was that of marketing). In a recent Mississippi decision, it was held that exploration for and production of gas in Louisiana and Texas was a separate business and not an integral part of an interstate gas transmission pipeline system which originated in the gas producing areas of Louisiana and Texas. Tenneco, Inc. v. Barr, 224 So.2d 208 (Miss.1969).

17. Western Contracting Corp. v. State Tax Comm'n, 18 Utah 2d 23, 414 P.2d 579 (1966).

18. Utah Construction & Mining Co. v. State Tax Comm'n, 255 Or. 228, 465 P.2d 712 (1970).

19. Donald M. Drake Co. v. Department of Revenue, 263 Or. 26, 500 P.2d 1041 (1972).

20. State and Local Tax Service—All States Unit (P-H) ¶ 1046. Separate accounting is generally authorized as an alternative where formula apportionment produces a distorted or inequitable result. At least one state has adopted a scheme involving a three-factor formula, which allows manufacturing corporations to elect to use only the property and payroll factors and which allows selling corporations to elect to use only the property and sales factors. See United States Steel Corp. v. South Carolina Tax Comm'n, 259 S.C. 153, 191 S.E.2d 9 (1972) (although taxpayer may be a manufacturing business in other states, it is a sales organization within South Carolina and thus may not elect to use only the property and sales factors).

The single-factor formula adopted by the District of Columbia was held to be in violation of the statutory grant of authority in General Motors v. District of Columbia, 380 U.S. 553 (1964) (apportionment based solely on percentage of sales made within the District). Although the decision was expressly based on statutory interpretation, the Court's opinion contains extensive dicta which points up both the inconsistency of using a single-factor formula in light of the extensive use of the three-factor formula by other states, and the fact that a single-factor formula does not achieve fair apportionment.

come may be classified as non-business income with an exclusive tax situs. Under the Uniform Division of Income for Tax Purposes Act, for example, items of non-business income include capital gains, rents, royalties, interest and dividends.[21]

"Business income" is defined in the Uniform Act to mean "income arising from transactions and activity in the regular course of the taxpayer's trade or business," [22] but there is no clear cut delineation of business income and nonbusiness income. This is illustrated by the decision in *Montgomery Ward & Co v. Commissioner* [23] where the Minnesota Supreme Court was presented with the issue as to whether income derived from temporary investments of excess working capital constituted income from intangibles employed in the nationwide operations of the company. If such income reflected the unitary characteristics of the company's merchandising operations it was subject to apportionment under the three-factor statutory formula. In the tax year in which this issue arose, the taxpayer had accumulated approximately $300,000,000 in temporary investments with the expectation of ultimately employing these funds in the expansion of its business operations. The case was remanded to the Board of Tax Appeals to enable the taxpayer to present proof that its income from temporary investments was unrelated to the income derived from its general merchandising business. However, prior to reaching its decision to remand, the court made the following observation:

> The record indicates that the intangibles were carried on the corporate balance sheet as current assets and the income derived from the investments was commingled with other corporate business income in accounts used to pay ordinary business obligations. On the present record, the taxpayer has failed to sustain its burden of proving that the intangibles involved were not employed in its principal business. . . . It is possible that the taxpayer could show that for all practical purposes some part of the amounts up to $300,000,000 held during the period in question and invested in liquid securities was not actually used or usable in its merchandising operation in any significant sense. We recognize the possibility that at some point funds accumulated, held, and invested in anticipation of expansion of a business at a future, but indefinite, date have but a minimal relationship to the successful day-to-day operation of a general merchandising business. Presumably, corporate action segregating this fund was possible. But where the fund so held is not set aside as a reserve for future expansion and made unavailable for current operating expenses; where the management of the investment of corporate funds in the intangibles is entrusted to the corporate officers who manage the principal business; where the income from the intangibles is commingled with ordinary business income; and where the operating expenses of the business enterprise are paid generally from such commingled funds, the taxpayer's burden of establishing that the intangibles were not employed in the principal business would seem to be an extremely difficult one.[24]

The foregoing decision, although applicable to a unitary mercantile business, suggests that in the context of the financial industry, it would be unlikely that any significant part of a financial institution's business operations could be isolated as lacking unitary character and thus reduce the base of operating income subject to apportionment by appropriate statutory formula.[25]

---

21. Uniform Division of Income for Tax Purposes Act §§ 4–8.

22. Id., § 1(a). The complete definition is as follows: " 'Business income' means income arising from transactions and activity in the regular course of the taxpayer's trade or business and includes income from tangible and intangible property if the acquisition, management, and disposition of the property constitute integral parts of the taxpayer's regular trade or business operations."

23. 276 Minn. 479, 151 N.W.2d 294 (1967).

24. 276 Minn. at 483–84, 151 N.W.2d at 296–97.

25. As indicated by the quotation from the decision in *Montgomery Ward & Co.*, there is a serious question as to whether any portion of the income of a business corporation can be considered non-business income inasmuch as all economic activity of the corporation is "business." It is also illogical to suggest that capital gains, interest, dividends, and rents are not an integral part of the whole economic fabric of the corporate enterprise. It is likely that the "business" and "non-business" dichotomy has evolved from

A decision markedly relevant to the question of the unitary character of an interstate financial business is *Household Finance Corp. v. Franchise Tax Board.*[26] The issue in this case was whether the separate accounting method of determining income earned with respect to the California operations of the corporation should prevail over an apportionment by statutory formula of the corporation's entire net income. It was the taxpayer's contention that its California operations were clearly separable from its business conducted in other states and that there was no basis for resorting to a formula determination. The court, following the rationale of the *Butler Bros.* decision, noted that if income is derived from or attributable to sources both within and without the state, the statutory requirement of apportionment by formula is valid even though a separate accounting method is reasonably feasible.

In the tax years in question, the taxpayer operated approximately 425 branches, of which 33 offices were located in California. Strong central management was exercised through the Chicago home office. Funds were borrowed by the home office and allocated to the various branches. Excess funds collected by the branches were remitted to the central office. Real estate leases, purchasing, public relations, advertising and personnel were handled or controlled by the home office. In all, the entire organization operated as an integrated unit.

The apportionment formula which was sustained by the California court was based upon three factors—the monthly average of loans outstanding, interest collected, and payroll. In rejecting the taxpayer's objections to the application of this formula, the court drew an analogy to the typical property, sales and payroll formula:

> Plaintiff asserts that basing the formula on outstanding loans, interest collected, and pay-

roll, is erroneous. But for a business dealing in large part in tangible goods, a formula based upon the factors of property, payroll, and sales has been upheld *(John Deere Plow Co. v. Franchise Tax Bd.,* 38 Cal.2d 214, 238 P.2d 569). The "property" of Household Finance Corporation is its outstanding loans represented by notes receivable. Its collections of interest appear entirely analogous to the sales of John Deere Plow Company. The payroll factor is the same in both cases. The formula used for the finance company is based upon factors reasonably and fairly adapting to this different type of business the factors found proper in Deere. We find nothing arbitrary in using them to compare the national and California business of plaintiff, and to determine the proportion of total business attributable to California.[27]

This decision may indicate the pattern for future statutory or administrative formulas which may be adopted for the purpose of apportioning income derived from interstate banking and financial operations. Other formulas would be appropriate but, in view of the nature of financial business operations, the rationale of this decision commends a combination of loans, interest and payrolls as particularly relevant factors in devising a fair formula for apportioning the income of financial institutions.

Another decision which tends to confirm the foregoing pattern as a sound basis for apportionment of income from interstate financial operations is *Equitable Savings & Loan Association v. State Tax Commission.*[28] The taxpayer, an Oregon corporation, was engaged in the business of making loans upon improved real estate with its principal office in Portland. It operated twenty-two branch offices in Oregon, four in Washington, and one in Idaho. All the business activities of the association were centralized in and controlled through the home office in Portland. During the years in question, the corporation made or participat-

---

the accounting concept of stating "operating income" as an item separate from gains and losses from "extraordinary items." For an interesting observation on this point, see J. Dane, Taxation of Interstate Business—Three Alternate Solutions of the Jurisdictional Problem, 22 Tax Executive 248, 260 (1970).

26. 230 Cal.App.2d 926, 41 Cal.Rptr. 565 (1964).
27. 230 Cal.App.2d at 930, 41 Cal.Rptr. at 568.
28. 251 Or. 70, 444 P.2d 916 (1968).

ed in out-of-state loans not only in the states of Washington and Idaho where it maintained branches, but also in California and Hawaii where it had no branch offices. In addition, the association consummated a large volume of Capehart military housing loans which were closed in Washington, D. C. These loans related to construction near military bases in a number of states.

At this time, the Oregon statute provided that "if the gross income of a corporation . . . is derived from business done both within and without the state, the determination of net income shall be based upon the business done within the state, and the commission shall have power to permit or require either the segregated method of reporting or the apportionment method of reporting, under rules and regulations adopted by the commission, so as fairly and accurately to reflect the net income of the business done within the state." The statute further provided that the foregoing rule of apportionment "was designed to allocate to the State of Oregon on a fair and equitable basis a portion of such income earned from sources both within and without the state." Under long-standing regulations, financial institutions had been taxed upon their unitary income by applying a three-factor apportionment formula based upon wages, loans and interest.

The Tax Commission took the position that the association's entire income was taxable in Oregon. The Commission offered the following alternative bases in support of its position. First, the taxpayer's operations in other states did not provide a sufficient nexus to warrant allocation of any of its income to such other states. Second, since the taxpayer was a domestic corporation and was dealing in intangibles, its entire income from such property was taxable by Oregon, the state of domicile, under the rule of mobilia sequuntur personam. The taxpayer countered with the contention that its income was unitary in character and that it was en-

titled by statute and the regulations to apportionment. Both issues were resolved for the taxpayer. On the nexus issue, the court stated its position by quoting from an earlier opinion.

[N]exus exists whenever the corporation takes advantage of the economic milieu within the state to realize a profit. The state is entitled to tax if the benefits it provides are a substantial economic factor in the production of the taxpayer's income. . . .

. . . It is now firmly established that a state may tax the net income of a corporation engaged exclusively in interstate commerce. We would expect the United States Supreme Court to hold, as we do, that due process nexus is established even though the taxpayer has no offices or agents within the taxing state if it could be shown that Oregon's economy was a substantial economic factor in the production of the taxpayer's income subject to tax.[28a]

On the facts the court concluded that "there can be doubt that the 'economic milieu' of the other states in which plaintiff engaged in business was a substantial factor in producing plaintiff's income in those states."

On the issue as to whether Oregon could tax the entire net income of the association on the basis of its domicile within the state, the court pointed to the contrary rule specifically provided by statute and regulations:

The regulations have provided since at least 1938 that as to financial institutions, their unitary income shall be apportioned by the three-factor formula of wages, loans and interest. There is no dispute in this case about the wage factor. It would be pure sophistry to now suggest that by gross loans the commission did not mean loans made in other states to residents thereof and secured by property in those states. The factor of "gross interest collected" obviously was intended to mean the interest paid on out-of-state loans.

We think the tax court properly apportioned plaintiff's unitary income in accordance with the statute and the plain meaning of the commission's own regulations. If there is to be special taxation of the income from intangibles of a domestic corporation, it should be provided

28a. 444 P.2d at 919. The court was quoting from American Refrigerator Transit Co. v. State Tax

Comm'n, 238 Or. 340, 346, 350–351, 395 P.2d 127, 130, 132 (1964).

by the legislature and not initiated either by the commission or by this court.[29]

The *Equitable Savings & Loan Association* decision, rendered by the court of the domiciliary state, is significant in its recognition that loans consummated in other states in which the corporation had no branch offices established a sufficient nexus for apportionment of net income to such other states.[30] These out-of-state loans were secured, of course, by real property located in those states. In the context of commercial banking, however, nexus would not be tied to the geographical location of tangible security for loans made but would be related to in-state activities of solicitation and negotiation and the fact that eventual resort might be had to the courts of the taxing state for the collection of the indebtedness.

5. Affiliated Corporations and the Unitary Rule—Interstate and Foreign Commerce

One of the more difficult problems which has arisen in the allocation of income from multistate business relates to the income of affiliated corporations all of which are concurrently engaged in interstate operations. To what extent does the unitary rule apply to require combination of the income of each of the several affiliated corporations? There are two types of affiliated groups to consider: (1) an affiliated group of corporations which are engaged in the same line of business in different geographical locations through separate corporations and integrated either on a horizontal or vertical basis; and (2) an affiliated group which is comprised of several corporations engaged in different and unrelated lines of business but operating interstate either in the same or different jurisdictions.

Edison California Stores v. McColgan [31] probably ranks as the leading case involving the application of the unit rule to affiliated

corporations which are engaged in the same line of business in different states. In that case, a multistate retail shoe business was operated through a Delaware parent corporation with its headquarters in St. Louis. There were fifteen wholly-owned subsidiary corporations each of which operated in the state in which it was incorporated. All operations were centralized in the home office of the parent corporation which provided centralized management, centralized purchasing, centralized advertising and various other centralized administrative functions. The home office determined operating policies for the entire affiliated group and maintained the principal accounting records for all of the subsidiary corporations. Goods purchased by the central purchasing division were shipped to the various stores operated by the subsidiary corporations which were charged with the cost thereof plus a specified percentage and an allocable portion of general overhead expenses. Each subsidiary operated solely within the geographical confines of its particular state. The manner of operation in Edison California Stores paralleled that of Butler Bros. except that the branches within each state were incorporated under the laws of the state in which they operated.

In *Edison California Stores*, the tax commissioner took the position that the three factor formula should be applied to allocate on a unitary basis the income of the entire business enterprise comprising the parent and all of its subsidiaries. The taxpayer's basic objection to application of the unit rule was premised upon the existence of a separate corporate entity for the California operations coupled with a separate accounting for its operations. In reliance upon the *Butler Bros.* decision, the court brushed aside this argument, in effect stating that the corporate veil of each separate corporation

---

29.   444 P.2d 916, at 920.

30.   See also Sun Finance & Loan Co. v. Kosydar, 45 Ohio St.2d 283, 344 N.E.2d 330 (1976), cert. denied 429 U.S. 857 (1976) (subsidiary financing corporations

neither incorporated nor doing business in taxing state do not qualify as "dealers in intangibles" under Ohio law, and thus are not subject to apportionment).

31.   30 Cal.2d 472, 183 P.2d 16 (1947).

could not be used to cloak the existence of an integrated multistate unitary enterprise:

> In the present case all of the elements of a unitary business are present—unity of ownership, unity of operation by centralized purchasing, management, advertising and accounting, and unity of use in the centralized executive force and general system of operation. The business of the parent and all of its subsidiaries is owned and managed under one centralized system, to the same extent as in the Butler Brothers case and other cases considered therein. Thus the business is unitary regardless of the fact that in the Butler Brothers case there was but one corporation involved, owning as parts of the unitary system seven different branches in as many states, and that in the present case there is a parent corporation owning and controlling as units of one system fifteen different branches organized as corporations in as many states. No difference in principle is discernible. If the crux of the matter is to ascertain that portion of the business which is done within this state, then the same considerations justify the use of the formula allocation method in the one case as in the other.[32]

In a later case involving the Kennecott family of affiliated corporations—a parent and five wholly-owned subsidiaries—the California court has defined, with apparent acceptance by the United States Supreme Court, the extent to which the unitary rule is applicable to the combined income of a legally integrated group of corporations. The tax authorities contended that the unit rule should be applied to require apportionment of the total income of the whole intercorporate group. The California court in its decision in *Chase Brass & Copper Co., Inc. v. Franchise Tax Board*[33] refused to apply the unitary rule in this pervasive manner. The problem presented can best be appraised by analyzing the intercorporate structure of the Kennecott group and their respective business activities.

Kennecott Copper Corporation, a New York corporation and parent of the group, did no business in California. Its business was that of mining copper, gold, silver and molybdenite in a number of other states. Approximately 20% of its total production of copper was sold to Chase Brass & Copper Co., one of its five wholly-owned subsidiaries.

Braden Copper Company, a Maine corporation, mined copper in Chile which it regularly sold to the Chilean government and on the world market. In the years in question, due to a general shortage of copper, Braden sold some of its production in the United States. Chase Brass & Copper Co. was one of its buyers.

Bear Creek Mining Company, a Delaware corporation, was engaged in exploration for new ore deposits. In the years in question, the corporation explored for metals in California, but it made no significant discoveries.

Kennecott Sales Corporation, a New York corporation, handled all the sales of copper for the parent and all United States sales for Braden and was compensated on a commission basis. It made no sales in California; any sales of copper by this corporation which entered California were completed outside the state.

Kennecott Wire and Cable Co., a Rhode Island corporation, purchased copper from the parent and from Braden copper which it manufactured into copper rod, wire and cable for transmission of electricity. None of its manufacturing operations were conducted in California, but its products were warehoused and sold in California by Chase Brass and Copper Co.

The taxpayer, Chase Brass and Copper Co., a Connecticut corporation, manufactured brass, bronze and copper rod, sheet,

---

32. 30 Cal.2d at 479–80, 183 P.2d at 21. In Coca Cola Co. v. Department of Revenue, 271 Or. 517, 533 P.2d 788 (1975), the court ignored separate corporate shells to find that the parent corporation and a wholly-owned subsidiary constituted one unitary business, noting that the existence of separate corporate entities does not bar combination of income for tax apportionment purposes.

33. 10 Cal.App.3d 496, 95 Cal.Rptr. 805, cert. denied 400 U.S. 961 (1970), appeal dismissed for want of Jurisdiction, 400 U.S. 961 (1970). See decision on remand 70 Cal.App.3d 457, 138 Cal.Rptr. 901 (1977), appeal dismissed for want of substantial federal question, 434 U.S. 1029 (1978).

wire and tube outside California. Its business activities in California consisted of warehousing and selling its products and the products of Kennecott Wire and Cable Co.

The operations of Chase Brass and Copper Co. were concededly unitary in character and its income was properly subject to apportionment pursuant to the statutory three-factor formula. There were two facets to the extension of the unitary rule to the other corporations in the affiliated group. The first concerned the treatment of Kennecott copper, Kennecott Sales, and Chase Brass as a single unit in that their operations constituted a vertical integration of mining, manufacturing and marketing of finished products. As to these companies, the court concluded that the unitary rule was properly applicable. This conclusion was premised upon the court's determination that the test of unity of ownership, operation, and use was met in this case. Unity of ownership was obvious. Unity of operation was based upon the following findings: centralized purchasing as to some items; centralized advertising through use of the same agency and reference in the advertising materials to membership in the Kennecott group; utilization of the same firm of public accountants; consolidation of tax accounts; representation of Chase Brass by the staff of Kennecott Copper in the particular tax proceedings; loans by Kennecott Copper to Chase Brass to finance rehabilitation of its Connecticut plant; and administration by Kennecott Copper of a common retirement plan for salaried employees. Unity of use was found in the integration of top level management which was centralized in the president and board of directors of Kennecott Copper. The parties had stipulated that the board of directors of the parent was concerned with the development and maintenance of its fabricating subsidiaries and their basic problems and policies. Futhermore, the parent corporation reviewed and controlled the executive salary scale of all subsidiary employees earning more than $15,000. Conse-

quently, executive control at the highest level was in Kennecott Copper. Finally, the court emphasized the fact that Chase Brass through the years had been a regular and substantial customer of Kennecott Copper, taking about 20% of its total copper production. Relying on these factors, the court concluded that Kennecott Copper, Kennecott Sales, and Chase Brass constituted a unitary enterprise with respect to copper production, manufacture and sale. The operations of Kennecott Copper relating to gold, silver, and molybdenite metals were not included as a part of the unitary business.

A similar issue existed as to whether Braden Copper should be included within the vertical integrated group since it had supplied Chase Brass with raw materials during the years in question. Inasmuch as the relationship with Braden Copper arose only by reason of the shortage of raw material which happened to exist in the years in question and since Braden was not a regular part of the integrated domestic operations of the Kennecott family, the court excluded Braden Copper. The Court also excluded Bear Creek Mining since its operations were unrelated to the production and manufacturing operations of Chase Brass.

The second aspect of extending the unitary rule in *Chase Brass & Copper Co.* was the question of horizontal integration with Kennecott Wire and Cable Co., a sibling corporation, which was also engaged in the manufacture and sale of copper products and subject to common control by the parent, Kennecott Copper. The element of common control and the fact that Chase Brass since 1944 had handled the sale of a major part of the production of Kennecott Wire and Cable through the Chase Brass sales organization led the court to conclude that these two corporations were engaged in a unitary business. The appeal of *Chase Brass & Copper Co.* to the United States Supreme Court was dismissed for want of jurisdiction on December 21, 1970.[34]

---

34. 400 U.S. 961 (1970). See decision on remand, 70 Cal.App.3d 457, 138 Cal.Rptr. 901 (1977), appeal dismissed for want of substantial federal question, 434 U.S. 1029 (1978).

Implications of this decision with respect to the financial industry are readily apparent. The question is the extent to which the unitary rule is applicable to financial holding companies. This turns, of course, on the nature of the businesses conducted by the affiliated corporations. If the lines of business conducted by the non-financial corporations are wholly unrelated to finance, the unitary rule will not embrace the group or any portion of the income of members of the group.[35] On the other hand, to the extent that other corporations in the affiliated group are engaged in finance or related lines of business and to the extent that management and operations are integrated, such corporations within the group will be exposed to the broader unitary concept.[36]

In any case, common ownership of a group of corporations engaged in unrelated businesses does not establish a unitary enterprise for purposes of apportioning net income. As indicated by the decision in *Chase Brass & Copper Co.*, the operations of an affiliated group are unitary only to the extent that the business conducted by any one of the corporations within the taxing state is dependent upon or contributes to the out-of-state business operations of one or more other corporations within such group. Furthermore, as in *Chase Brass & Copper Co.*, the unitary character of the group may be determined to exist only with respect to a part of the business operations of members of the group.

An interesting variation, if not inconsistency, in the application of the unitary rule is found in the decision in *Interstate Finance Corp. v. Wisconsin Department of Taxation.*[37] In that case the taxpayer oper-
ated within the state through its own branch offices and also through offices operated by its wholly-owned subsidiaries. Interstate Finance, an Iowa corporation with its home office in Dubuque, operated five branch offices in Iowa and two in Wisconsin. It also owned all the stock of seventeen subsidiaries located in five different states, including three which operated in Wisconsin. The parent and its subsidiaries were engaged principally in automobile financing at both the wholesale and retail levels. The former involved the financing of inventories of automobile dealers; the latter involved the purchase of dealers' interests in customer sales contracts. Operations of the entire enterprise were centralized at the home office which determined all matters of general company policy and exercised supervisory control over all of its branches and subsidiary operations. All the funds required in the operation of the enterprise were obtained by the home office through lines of credit established with major banks. Branch managers were selected, trained, transferred, and supervised by the home office. The home office participated in loan decisions in connection with its wholesale financing and in all loans over $5,000, maintained a central accounting system, took possession of most security documents, withdrew funds from the local branches, and processed payrolls for all employees.

Two questions were involved. The first was whether Interstate Finance's own branch office operations in Wisconsin were part of a multistate unitary business which would require apportionment of income by the formula method. If the answer to this question were affirmative, the second ques-

---

35. Corporations affiliated through non-bank-originated one-bank holding companies would ordinarily lack unitary character. For a study and description of these groups, see: Hearings on S. 1052 (et al.) and H.R. 6778 Before the Senate Comm. on Banking and Currency, 91st Cong.2d Sess, pt. 2 at 1289–1301 (1970).

36. Corporations affiliated under the umbrella of a bank-originated one-bank holding company would usually constitute a unitary enterprise. As is true generally, the determining factor in the area of bank holding companies is the nature of the business conducted by
each of the affiliated corporations. On this point, P.L. 91–607, the Bank Holding Company Act amendments of 1970, is of interest. This act restricts the investments of a bank holding company to shares of companies "the activities of which * * * [are] so closely related to banking or managing or controlling banks as to be a proper incident thereto." Thus, corporations subsequently acquired by bank holding companies will necessarily possess a unitary character.

37. 28 Wis.2d 262, 137 N.W.2d 38 (1965).

tion would be whether the income of the taxpayer's wholly-owned subsidiaries also should be included in the base subject to apportionment.

On the first issue, the court rejected the taxpayer's contention that its separate accounting method should control. On this point, the case was substantially on all fours with the factual situation described in *Butler Bros.* The taxpayer attempted to establish by its separate accounting procedures that its Wisconsin branches were operated either at a loss or at a lesser profit than that determined by applying the statutory formula of apportionment on a unitary basis.

The second issue relating to the inclusion of the wholly-owned subsidiary corporations as a part of a unitary business was resolved by the court by a strict construction of the Wisconsin statute. The taxpayer argued that if its branches were an integral part of a unitary business, it followed that its wholly-owned subsidiaries were also an integral part thereof. This argument was premised upon the fact that the relationship of the parent and its home office to its subsidiary operations was precisely of the same character as its relationship to its branch offices. In rejecting the argument for inclusion of the subsidiaries, the court relied upon the fact that the Wisconsin statute did not specifically authorize the combination of separate corporate entities in applying the unitary rule. There is a question as to whether the court was correct in recognizing statutory restraints upon application of the unitary rule in the circumstances of this case.[38]

In two cases decided in 1980, *Mobil Oil Corp. v. Commissioner of Taxes of Vermont*[39] and *Exxon Corp. v. Wisconsin Dept. of Revenue,*[40] the Court for the first time since *Butler Bros.* was decided in 1942, considered the question as to whether the *entire income* of a nondomiciliary *interstate and multinational* corporation was

sufficiently unitary in character to warrant apportionment by formula to the taxing state. With these decisions, the Court endorsed a broad application of the unitary concept to the income of interstate and multinational corporations.

In *Mobil* the issue was the propriety of including in the income base subject to apportionment dividends received from foreign subsidiaries and affiliates doing business abroad. Mobil, a New York corporation, conducted an integrated international petroleum business consisting of the production, refining and marketing of petroleum products. Much of its business abroad was conducted through wholly and partly owned subsidiaries and affiliates, none of which operated in Vermont. Mobil's business in Vermont was limited to the wholesale and retail marketing of its products. Management of Mobil's investments in shares of subsidiary and other corporations and the collection of dividends therefrom was directed through its New York headquarters.

Mobil argued that inclusion of dividend income in the apportionable base constituted a violation of both due process and the commerce clause. Its due process argument was premised on alleged lack of nexus—i.e., that Vermont had no connection with either the management of its investments or the business conducted by its foreign subsidiaries and other corporations. In resolving the due process (nexus) issue, the Court emphasized the fact that the dividend income received by Mobil reflected profits derived from a functionally integrated enterprise whether its foreign operations were conducted directly by Mobil or through subsidiary and affiliated corporations. In the absence of proof by Mobil that the dividend income was unrelated to its business conducted in Vermont, the Court concluded that the "underlying economic realities" warranted the application of the unitary business principle to

38. E. Rudolph, State Taxation of Interstate Business: The Unitary Business Concept and Affiliated Corporate Groups, 25 Tax L.Rev. 171, 199–200 (1970).

39. 445 U.S. 425 (1980).

40. 447 U.S. 207 (1980).

the inclusion of the dividends in the apportionable income tax base.[41]

Mobil's commerce clause argument was premised on the risk of multiple taxation of the dividend income. Mobil contended that since New York, as the state of commercial situs, had jurisdiction to tax the dividend income without apportionment, the Vermont tax imposed an unconstitutional burden on both interstate and foreign commerce. The Court rejected this contention, noting that New York's power to tax did not deprive a sister state of its power to tax the income of a unitary business on an apportioned basis.[42] With respect to the alleged burden on foreign commerce as a result of the imposition of the Vermont tax in addition to foreign taxes, the Court noted the illogic of the taxpayer's position in light of its contention that New York, the state of commercial situs should be deemed to have exclusive jurisdiction to tax the dividend income.[43]

In *Exxon*, the taxpayer's challenge was directed at a more fundamental aspect of the unitary concept. As a vertically integrated producer of petroleum products, Exxon organized its management and accounting on a strict functional basis into three categories: (1) exploration and production, (2) refining, and (3) marketing. Its Wisconsin business was limited solely to the marketing of its products. All of its production and refining operations were located in other states. Internally, the corporation accounted for its income and profits separately for each of the three functions of production, refining and marketing. Crude oil was transferred from production to refining at prevailing whole-sale prices. Similarly, refined products were transferred from refining to marketing at wholesale prices. In its Wisconsin income tax returns for the years in question, Exxon reported losses based on separate state accounting that reflected only its Wisconsin marketing operations. The Wisconsin Department of Revenue took the position that as a unitary enterprise, Exxon's marketing activities in the state were an integral part of a unitary business and that its *entire* income—not merely its marketing income—was properly subject to apportionment by formula. Exxon argued that under both due process and commerce clause concepts, the income derived from its production and refining operations constituted income derived from out-of-state activities that were unrelated to its marketing operations in Wisconsin. With this argument, Exxon contended that income attributable to production and refining should be excluded from its unitary base as having no nexus with Wisconsin. In sustaining Wisconsin's apportionment of Exxon's *entire* income, the Court emphasized that the marketing of Exxon products in Wisconsin was an integral part of a unitary business. As explained by the Court, production in the oil fields provides the raw material (crude oil) for the refineries; the refineries provide the products for marketing; and marketing of the refined products assures the cost-efficient operation of the unitary enterprise. With this demonstrated interdependence between the various operating functions, the Court concluded that there was sufficient nexus to support apportionment of Exxon's entire *income* to the taxing state.

---

41. In a dissenting opinion, Justice Stevens questioned the fairness of the allocation in view of the fact that although the dividends were included in the unitary base, the property, payroll and sales of the affiliated corporations were excluded from the denominator of the apportionment formula. On this matter, the majority noted that Mobil had disclaimed any challenge as to the accuracy or fairness of Vermont's apportionment formula. The majority suggested, however, that due process considerations might preclude inclusion of dividends in the apportionable base "where the business activities of the dividend payor have nothing to do with the activities of the recipient in the taxing state." 445 U.S. at 440–43.

42. New York did not tax the dividend income, but the Court assumed without deciding that there was sufficient nexus to permit New York to do so. 445 U.S. at 445–47.

43. Mobil argued that its position on this point was supported by the decision in *Japan Line* wherein the Court held invalid a California property tax imposed on cargo containers used in foreign commerce that were owned by Japanese shipping companies. In that case, the tax resulted in multiple international taxation and was found to be in conflict with the power of the federal government to regulate foreign commerce. See text at Section II, A, 5, supra.

With respect to the commerce clause issue, Exxon argued that income derived from its exploration and production function should be allocated exclusively to the situs state to avoid multiple taxation. This argument was dismissed by the Court on the ground that jurisdiction of the situs state to impose a tax on income derived from production in that state does not deprive the market state of jurisdiction to tax the entire income of a unitary business by fair apportionment.

Although the Court in these two decisions endorsed a broad application of the unitary concept, its endorsement was not without qualification. In *Exxon*, the Court reiterated a suggestion made in *Mobil Oil* that there may be circumstances which would justify excluding certain income from the apportionable base of a unitary business. According to the Court, such exclusion would be warranted if in the light of the "underlying economic realities" the taxpayer proved that the income was derived from " 'unrelated business activity' which constitutes a 'discrete business enterprise.' "[44] One might speculate as to whether this is a significant and meaningful qualification. For example, a conglomerate interstate enterprise may include several distinct and wholly unrelated product lines each of which is produced and marketed in a different group of states. An enterprise of this type differs markedly from the highly integrated product lines of the petroleum industry. Nevertheless, an evaluation of such an enterprise in the light of "underlying economic realities" would likely lead to the conclusion that the several lines of business are economically interdependent and that each constitutes an integral part of a unitary enterprise. To draw upon the basic tests of *Butler Bros.* and the thrust of *Mobil Oil* and *Exxon*, the unitary character of the income of a conglomerate can be established through unity of ownership, centralization of management, and the economic reality that the income and profits

flowing from any one product line necessarily sustain and promote the operation of all other product lines and maintain the financial stability of the whole enterprise. On this rationale the entire income may be deemed unitary in character and subject to formula apportionment among the various states in which the company operates irrespective of the geographical situs of its separate product lines.

As stated in *Mobil* and *Exxon*, the "discrete business" exception to the unitary principle is premised on "underlying economic realities." This would lead one reasonably to conclude that the unitary principle can be applied to require apportionment of income derived by a parent from subsidiaries with respect to which it holds a significant economic (financial) interest and consequent realistic control.

Two recent decisions, however, dispel this notion and clearly indicate that the sine qua non in the application of the unitary principle is the centralization of managerial control over the business operations of subsidiary companies; dominant economic (financial) control through investment is not enough. In both *ASARCO Inc. v. Idaho State Tax Commission*[45] and *F. W. Woolworth Co. v. Taxation and Revenue Department*,[46] the majority of the Court, over vigorous dissent, concluded on due process grounds that dividends, interest, and capital gains derived by a nondomiciliary parent from its subsidiary companies engaged in the same lines of business could not be apportioned to the taxing state in the absence of direct centralized managerial control of their operations.

In *ASARCO*, the taxpayer held major interests in five corporations which varied from 34 percent to 53 percent. Like ASARCO, each of the five was engaged in some aspect of the nonferrous metals business; but ASARCO did not exercise direct centralized managerial control in the opera-

44.   447 U.S. at 223–24.

45.   102 S.Ct. 3103 (1982).

46.   102 S.Ct. 3128 (1982).

tion of the five companies.[47] Pursuant to the Idaho statute, "business" income as contrasted with "nonbusiness" income is subject to apportionment.[48] "Business" income is defined to include income from intangible property when "acquisition, management, or disposition" of such property "constitute[s] integral or necessary parts of the taxpayers' trade or business operations." On this basis, Idaho contended that there was integration between the business use of these intangible assets (shares of the five subsidiary companies) and ASARCO's mining, smelting, and refining operations which made the dividend, interest and capital gain income derived from the subsidiaries a part of its unitary enterprise. In response, the majority (quoting from *Mobil*) concluded that it could not permit a nondomiciliary state to apportion and tax dividend income "[w]here the business activities of the dividend payor have nothing to do with the activities of the recipient in the taxing state." [49]

In its assessment of the underlying facts, the minority emphasized ASARCO's dominant economic position with respect to its investment in each of the five companies and concluded that each company was a part of ASARCO's unitary nonferrous metals business. Justice O'Connor, writing for the minority, concluded: "Both common sense and business reality dictate a different result." [50] Pragmatic considerations in the assessment

of actual economic realities firmly support the position of the minority.

In *F. W. Woolworth Co.*, New Mexico applied similar statutory provisions to apportion dividend income received by Woolworth, a New Jersey corporation, from its ownership of stock in four foreign country subsidiaries. Woolworth held a 100 percent interest in its German, Canadian and Mexican subsidiaries, and a 52.7 percent interest in its English subsidiary. All four subsidiaries were engaged in chain store retailing, and all four operated autonomously in the purchase and marketing of goods. There was no integration and centralization of the business and managerial functions of the several companies. There was, however, frequent mail, telephone and teletype communications between upper echelons of management of the parent and its subsidiaries. Moreover, major financial decisions including the amount of dividends and the creation of substantial debt had to be approved by the parent. Again, the Court divided in the same manner and for the same reasons as in *ASARCO* with the majority holding that apportionment of dividend income received from the subsidiaries was barred by due process considerations.

Constitutional challenges relating to state taxation of income from foreign commerce have extended thus far only to dividends, interest and capital gains income actually received by a multinational corporation from

---

47. The five corporations from which ASARCO derived income and the circumstances relating to its substantial interests therein are detailed as follows: (1) M.I.M. Holdings, Ltd.—ASARCO owned 53% of the stock of this publicly held corporation which is engaged in mining, milling, smelting, and refining of nonferrous metals in Australia and England. M.I.M. sold about 1% of its output to ASARCO on the open market. Although ASARCO held potential control, it elected none of the members of the board and took no part in the selection of M.I.M.'s officers. M.I.M. operated autonomously and independently of ASARCO. (2) Southern Peru Copper Corp.—ASARCO held 51.5% of the stock with the balance owned by three other major metals companies: Phelps Dodge (16%); Newmont Mining (10.25%); and Cerro Copper (22.25%). Southern Peru produces copper in Peru and sells about 35% of its output to ASARCO. Under a management contract with the other shareholders, ASARCO was bound *not* to exercise control of Southern Peru. (3) ASARCO Mexi-

cana, S.A.—ASARCO owned 49% of the stock with the balance owned by Mexican nationals. Mexicana operated autonomously and engages in Mexico in the same general line of business as does ASARCO in the United States. (4) General Cable Corp. and (5) Revere Copper and Brass, Inc.—These are domestic public held companies that respectively fabricate cables and manufacture copper wares. ASARCO owned about 34% of the stock of each. Both are ASARCO customers. Under a 1967 antitrust consent decree, ASARCO was under specific prohibitions as to these two companies with respect to several matters including maintaining common officers, voting their stock, and selling copper to them at advantageous prices.

48. Intangible "nonbusiness" income is allocated entirely to the state of the corporation's commercial domicile. 102 S.Ct. at 3106.

49. 102 S.Ct. at 3115.

50. 102 S.Ct. at 3119.

its foreign subsidiaries. Two pending cases,[51] however, involve the question as to whether a state can constitutionally apply the unitary principle to require apportionment of the combined worldwide income of a group of related corporations. In each case, the parent company is a United States corporation with extensive international operations conducted through a number of foreign subsidiary corporations. Inasmuch as the foreign subsidiaries may be subject to tax on income earned in their respective countries of operation, there is a risk of double taxation. It is contended that unitary apportionment of worldwide income violates both the foreign commerce and due process clauses of the constitution. Support for this position is premised principally on the decision in *Japan Line.*[52] In that case there was in fact both international multiple taxation and a direct conflict with existing treaty provisions. In the pending cases, the Court is called upon to define the scope of the unitary principle and to determine the reach of federal power to regulate foreign commerce vis a vis state power to tax the income of United States corporations derived from multinational operations.

6. Legislative Limitations Upon Taxation of Income Derived From Interstate Commerce

a. Federal Limitations

As a review of the cases has indicated, the states have broad constitutional power, within the limits of the due process and the commerce clauses, to tax income derived from all interstate business operations. What, if any, are the existing general statutory limitations—either federal or state—upon the exercise of this power? Federal limitations can be imposed by Congress in the exercise of its power to regulate interstate commerce. At the state level, the only limita-

tions are those imposed by state constitutional provisions or by self-restraint in the exercise of the taxing power.

As previously observed, there was an immediate response by Congress to the decision in *Northwestern States.* In that case, the Court held that mere solicitation of orders for the sale of goods within the taxing jurisdiction provided a sufficient nexus to warrant allocation of net income from interstate business. Prior to the end of 1959, Congress in the exercise of its power to regulate interstate commerce enacted Public Law 86–272.[1] Although Congress accepted the result reached in the specific cases which had been decided by the Court (each corporation maintained a sales office within the taxing state), it proceeded to blunt the full thrust of *Northwestern States* by prohibiting an allocation of net income solely on the basis of solicitation of sales orders. Specifically, P.L. 86–272 prohibits the imposition of an income tax if the only business activity in the taxing state consists of "the solicitation of orders . . . in such State for sales of tangible personal property . . . which orders are sent outside the State for approval or rejection, and, if approved, are filled by shipment or delivery from a point outside the state." Exemption is also extended to income derived from sales made within a state through independent contractors. This legislation, since it applies only to the sale of tangible personal property in interstate commerce, imposes no restrictions with respect to the allocation of income from interstate financial or banking operations.

As previously noted, the Court has held that Public Law 86–272 is limited by the twenty-first amendment of the Constitution because state regulatory action under that amendment is not restricted by the commerce cause and thus is not subject to legis-

51. Caterpillar Tractor Co. v. Lenckos, 84 Ill.2d 102, 49 Ill.Dec. 329, 417 N.E.2d 1343 (1981), prob. juris. noted 454 U.S. 1029 (1981); Container Corp. of America v. Franchise Tax Bd., 117 Cal.App.3d 988, 173 Cal.Rptr. 121 (1981), prob. juris. noted 454 U.S. 1078 (1982).

52. See the text discussion of *Japan Lines* at Section II, A, 5, supra.

1. 15 U.S.C.A. § 381.

lation enacted under the commerce clause.[2] The states, therefore, are free to impose regulations under the twenty-first amendment which otherwise would be barred by Public Law 86–272.

Concurrently with the enactment of Public Law 86–272, Congress authorized an extensive study of state taxation of interstate commerce. This study was conducted by a subcommittee of the House Judiciary Committee and was completed in 1965.[3] The Willis Committee report recommended enactment of legislation which (1) would limit apportionment of income from interstate commerce to those states in which the taxpayer has a "business location" and (2) would require that the apportionment be made solely on the basis of a two factor—payroll and property—formula.[4] Thus far, no legislation has been enacted to implement these recommendations.

Under the Willis Committee proposals, a taxpayer would be deemed to have a business location within a state if the company owned or leased real property within the State or if the company had one or more employees located in the State. This definition of business location would broaden the nexus compared to the restrictions imposed by P.L. 86–272, inasmuch as the presence of a single employee to solicit orders in the tax-

ing state would provide a basis for apportionment of net income to such state. Although the proposed elimination of the sales factor from the apportionment formula would simplify administration by removing the necessity of determining the state of sale, it would effect a substantial reapportionment of income from the market states to the manufacturing states.

b. State Limitations

Although there have been no developments at the federal level since the enactment of Public Law 86–272, there have been two significant developments at the state level during the past two decades which have had an important effect upon the taxation of net income from interstate business. These developments are (1) the promulgation of the Uniform Division of Income for Tax Purposes Act,[5] and (2) the consummation of the Multistate Tax Compact.[6] The former has been adopted, with some modifications, in twelve states,[7] and the Multistate Tax Compact currently includes nineteen member states and fourteen associate member states.[8] One of the principal objectives of both the Uniform Act and the Multistate Tax Compact which incorporates the Uniform Act is to promote equitable and uniform allocation of the income tax base of in-

2. Heublein, Inc. v. South Carolina Tax Comm'n, 409 U.S. 275 (1972), aff'g 257 S.C. 17, 183 S.E.2d 710 (1971).

3. House Judiciary Comm., Special Subcommittee, State Taxation of Interstate Commerce, H.R. Rep. No. 1480, 88th Cong. 2nd Sess., Vols. 1 and 2 (1964); H.R. Rep. No. 565, 89th Cong. 1st Sess., Vol. 3 (1965); H.R. Rep. No. 952, 89th Cong. 1st Sess., Vol. 4 (1965). The report of this subcommittee is generally referred to as the report of the Willis Committee or Willis Subcommittee.

4. H.R. Rep. No. 952, 89th Cong., 1st Sess., Vol. 4, at 1135 (1965).

5. The Uniform Division of Income for Tax Purposes Act was approved by the National Conference of Commissioners on Uniform State Laws and the American Bar Association in 1957. 7 Uniform Laws Ann. 365 (Master ed. 1970). For background and evaluations of the Uniform Act, see: A. Lynn, Formula Apportionment of Corporate Income for State Tax Purposes: Natura Non Facit Saltum, 18 Ohio St.L.J. 84 (1957); A. Lynn, The Uniform Division of Income for

Tax Purposes Act Re-examined, 46 Va.L.Rev. 1257 (1960); W. Pierce, The Uniform Division of Income for State Tax Purposes, 35 Taxes 747 (1957); J. Wilkie, Uniform Division of Income for Tax Purposes, 37 Taxes 65 (1959).

6. The Multistate Tax Compact was initiated as an alternative to the recommendations of the Willis Committee that Congress enact Federal rules to govern the apportionment of income from interstate business. The Compact, which was drafted in final form in December 1966, was prepared under the auspices of the Council of State governments. It was the joint product of representatives of the National Association of Tax Administrators, the National Association of Attorneys General and the National Legislative Conference. 27 Council of State Governments—Suggested State Legislation C–3 (1968).

7. 7 Uniform Laws Annot. (Master ed. 1970) (Supp. 1971–76, at 271).

8. State & Loc. Taxes—All States Unit (PH) ¶ 5150 and ¶ 5151.

terstate businesses. The Uniform Act utilizes a three-factor apportionment formula which includes property, payroll, and sales, but the Act does not apply to financial organizations and public utilities.[9]

The validity of the Multistate Tax Compact was challenged principally on the ground that it lacked Congressional approval as required by Article I, § 10, clause 3 of the Constitution. In *United States Steel Corp. v. Multistate Tax Commission*,[10] the Court adhered to the doctrine of *Virginia v. Tennessee*[11] in the construction of the compact clause and sustained the compact. In assessing the operating effect of the compact, which provides for joint audits by the states of interstate businesses, the Court concluded that there was no threat to federal supremacy. Thus, the compact met the test prescribed in *Virginia v. Tennessee* that Congressional approval of an interstate agreement is required only where the agreement tends to increase the political power of the states relative to the federal government. Additional objections based on the commerce clause and the fourteenth amendment were deemed to lack merit.

D. Corporate Franchise Taxes

1. Introduction

Creation of a corporation and the continuation of its existence, typically require the payment of two franchise taxes, an initial franchise tax as consideration for issuance of the corporate charter and an annual franchise tax as consideration for continuation of the corporate existence. Similar franchise taxes are imposed by a foreign jurisdiction if the corporation seeks to enter another state to carry on business. In that case, there is an initial franchise tax for the privilege of entering the state to exercise its corporate authority to carry on an intrastate business, and an annual franchise tax for the privilege of continuing its qualified status.[1]

Although the value of the corporate franchise may be determined, for purposes of taxation, by the amount of property owned, the amount of earnings, or the amount of capital, a franchise tax is not a tax on property, earnings, or capital. It is simply a tax on the privilege of carrying on a business in the corporate form.[2] Determining the constitutionality of state franchise taxes and other taxes imposed on corporations engaged in interstate business has been a perennial problem for the Supreme Court.[3] The Court itself has described its many opinions in this area as a "quagmire"[4] and has recognized that efforts to reconcile the opinions would be pointless and futile.[5] Nevertheless, the constitutional principles governing state franchise taxes are discernible and the Court has clarified the issue relating to corporations engaged exclusively in interstate commerce.

---

9. For the complete text of the Uniform Division of Income for Tax Purposes Act, see 7 Uniform Laws Annot. 367–380 (Master ed. 1970). Section 2 excludes financial organizations and public utilities from its provisions. Section 1(d) defines financial organization to mean "any bank, trust company, savings bank, [industrial bank, land bank, safe deposit company] private banker, savings and loan association, credit union, [cooperative bank], investment company, or any type of insurance company."

10. 434 U.S. 452 (1978).

11. 148 U.S. 503 (1893). For a full discussion of the interstate compact provisions, see Chapter 10, section II, A, supra.

1. For examples of the described franchise tax provisions, see: Model Business Corporation Act §§ 132–133 (1974).

2. Home Insurance Co. v. New York, 134 U.S. 594, 599 (1890).

3. Colonial Pipeline Co. v. Traigle, 421 U.S. 100, 101 (1975): "We have once again a case that presents 'the perennial problem of the validity of a state tax for the privilege of carrying on, within a state, certain activities' related to a corporation's operation of an interstate business. Memphis Natural Gas Co. v. Stone, 335 U.S. 80, 85 (1948)."

4. Northwestern States Portland Cement Co. v. Minnesota, 358 U.S. 450, 457–58 (1959).

5. In Freeman v. Hewit, 329 U.S. 249, 252 (1946), the Court stated: "The history of this problem is spread over hundreds of volumes of our Reports. To attempt to harmonize all that has been said in the past would neither clarify what has gone before nor guide the future."

2. Franchise Taxes by Domiciliary State

The authority of a state to impose a franchise tax for the privilege of being incoporated within the state is well established.[6] A state may impose an initial charge for creating the corporation and a recurring charge for permitting its continued existence. The tax is not rendered invalid merely because the corporation is engaged in interstate commerce.[7] Moreover, the tax may be measured by total capital stock which in part may represent property employed in other states,[8] or it may be measured by gross receipts derived from interstate and foreign commerce.[9] The tax is constitutional because interstate commerce is not the subject of the tax.[10] The fee exacted from a domestic corporation merely represents the quid pro quo for the privilege of corporate existence conferred upon the business.

3. Franchise Taxes by Foreign State

A nondomiciliary state may not tax foreign corporations for the privilege of entering the state to engage in interstate commerce.[11] The right to engage in interstate commerce is conferred by the Constitution and is not a privilege granted by the states.[12] The Constitution, however, does not confer the right to engage in intrastate commerce.[13] Therefore, states generally impose an "entrance fee" on foreign corporations for the privilege of entering to engage in intrastate commerce. The amount and reasonableness of the fee is immaterial.[14] Furthermore, the fee may be measured by the total, unapportioned capital of the corporation.[15] The validity of these fees is based on the notion that a corporation is not a "citizen" and is not entitled, therefore, to the benefits of the privileges and immunities clause.[16] In addition to imposing an entrance fee for the privilege of engaging in intrastate commerce, the state may restrict the intrastate business of foreign corporations to particular localities and may impose whatever conditions it deems necessary.[17] A state may even entirely prohibit foreign corporations from engaging in intrastate commerce.[18] In *Railway Express Agency, Inc. v. Virginia*,[19] for example, the Supreme Court upheld a Virginia requirement that all public service corporations obtain a corporate charter from

6. Kansas City, Fort Scott & Memphis Ry. Co. v. Botkin, 240 U.S. 227, 232 (1916).

7. Id.

8. Kansas City, Memphis, & Birmingham R.R. Co. v. Stiles, 242 U.S. 111, 118–19 (1916).

9. In Canton R.R. v. Rogan, 340 U.S. 511 (1951), the Court sustained a domestic franchise tax measured by gross receipts against a carrier operating a marine terminal and rail line in the Baltimore port area moving goods to and from the port in serving connecting interstate railroads. The Court emphasized the fact that the gross receipts in these circumstances were fairly apportioned to the taxing state.

10. Because the Constitution gives authority over interstate commerce to Congress, the states are prohibited from making interstate commerce the subject of a tax. As stated in Crutcher v. Kentucky, 141 U.S. 47, 57 (1891):

"To carry on interstate commerce is not a franchise or a privilege granted by the State, it is a right which every citizen of the United States is entitled to exercise under the Constitution and the laws of the United States . . . ."

11. Western Union Telegraph Co. v. Kansas, 216 U.S. 1, 21 (1909).

12. Crutcher v. Kentucky, 141 U.S. 47, 57 (1891).

13. Atlantic Refining Co. v. Virginia, 302 U.S. 22, 26–27 (1937).

14. Atlantic Refining Co. v. Virginia, 302 U.S. 22, 26–27 (1937).

15. Id. at 28.

16. The 14th Amendment provides in part that "No State shall make or enforce any law which shall abridge the privileges and immunities of citizens of the United States." These privileges and immunities include the right of every citizen to travel freely from state to state. Twining v. New Jersey, 211 U.S. 78 (1908).

17. Horn Silver Mining Co. v. New York, 143 U.S. 305, 314 (1892): "Having no absolute right of recognition in other states, but depending on such recognition and the enforcement of its contracts upon their assent, it follows, as a matter of course, that such assent may be granted upon such terms and conditions as those states may think proper to impose. They may exclude the foreign corporation entirely; they may restrict its business to particular localities, or they may exact such security for the performance of its contracts with their citizens as in their judgment will best promote the public interest. The whole matter rests in their discretion."

18. Id.

19. 282 U.S. 440 (1931).

the state before engaging in intrastate business.

4. Entrance Fees vs. Annual Franchise Tax

Courts distinguish between an entrance fee imposed for the privilege of entering the state to carry on an intrastate business, and a tax imposed after that privilege has been granted.[20] As noted above, the discriminatory nature of entrance fees does not raise constitutional problems. Subsequent taxation, however, cannot discriminate between foreign and domestic corporations. Once admitted to the state for purposes of engaging in intrastate commerce, the foreign corporation becomes entitled to equal protection as a "person" under the fourteenth amendment.[21] In *Hanover Fire Insurance Co. v. Harding*,[22] for example, the Court invalidated an Illinois statute requiring foreign insurance companies which previously had been admitted to the state to pay an annual tax based upon a percentage of net receipts. Domestic insurance companies were not subject to this tax.[23] However, in *Lincoln National Life Insurance Co. v. Read*,[24] the Court sustained the imposition of discriminatory taxes following entry where the foreign corporation had agreed, as a condition to its admission, to pay all future taxes that might be imposed by the taxing state.

With its decision in *Western & Southern Life Insurance Co. v. State Board of Equalization*,[25] the Court abandoned the rule of *Lincoln National Life Insurance Co. v. Read*[26] that permitted a state, in its discretion, to impose a discriminatory tax on foreign corporations seeking to enter the state to carry on intrastate business. In *Lincoln National*, the Court had held that a foreign corporation was not a "person" within a state's jurisdiction for purposes of equal protection unless it had complied with the conditions placed on its entry. In overruling *Lincoln National*, the Court applied the doctrine that a state cannot impose an unconstitutional condition on the grant of a privilege.

Western & Southern Life Insurance Co., an Ohio corporation, challenged the California retaliatory tax on foreign insurance companies that resulted in the imposition of a greater tax than was applicable to other insurance companies doing business in California. Its challenge was premised on both the commerce clause and equal protection. The commerce clause issue was resolved on the ground that the McCarran-Ferguson Act had removed any commerce clause restriction on a state's power to tax the insurance business.[27] Although the Court, in overruling *Lincoln National*, recognized the application of equal protection, it proceeded to sustain the California reciprocal tax by holding that there was a reasonable classification which served a legitimate legislative purpose to promote the interstate business of domestic insurers by deterring other states from

---

20. Hanover Fire Insurance Co. v. Harding, 272 U.S. 494, 510–511 (1926): "In subjecting a law of the State which imposes a charge upon foreign corporations to the test whether such a charge violates the equal protection clause of the Fourteenth Amendment, a line has to be drawn between the burden imposed by the State for the license or privilege to do business in the State, and the tax burden which, having secured the right to do business, the foreign corporation must share with all other corporations and taxpayers of the State. With respect to the admission fee, so to speak, which the foreign corporation must pay, to become a quasi citizen of the State and entitled to equal privileges with citizens of the State, and any inequality as between the foreign corporation and the domestic corporation in that regard does not come within the inhibition of the Fourteenth Amendment, but, after its admission, the foreign corporation stands equal, and is to be classified with domestic corporations."

21. Id.

22. Id.

23. The Court also has invalidated a state law revoking the license of a foreign corporation for exercising its constitutional right to remove suits brought against them from the state courts to the federal courts. Terral v. Burke Constr. Co., 257 U.S. 529 (1921). See also Southern Ry. Co. v. Greene, 216 U.S. 400 (1909) and Air-Way Elec. Appliance Corp. v. Day, 266 U.S. 71 (1924) wherein the Court invalidated discriminatory taxes imposed on foreign corporations after admittance to the state for purposes of intrastate commerce.

24. 325 U.S. 673 (1945).

25. 451 U.S. 648 (1981).

26. 325 U.S. 673 (1945).

27. 451 U.S. at 652–55.

enacting discriminatory or excessive taxes on California corporations.

5. Apportionment of Tax Base

After imposition of the initial entrance fee on a foreign corporation, the subsequent levy of taxes for the privilege of continuing to conduct intrastate business also raises due process and commerce clause considerations. The due process clause requires that a state confer sufficient benefits or protection before the power to tax is established.[28] In addition, the value of the business subject to taxation must be fairly apportioned to the taxing jurisdiction in order to avoid burdening interstate commerce. Consequently, when a business is engaged in both interstate and intrastate commerce, the taxing state must limit application of its annual franchise tax to that portion of the value of the business conducted within the state.[29] However, in determining the amount allocable to the taxing state, the taxing authorities may include interstate commerce activities conducted within the state.[30]

6. Subject of the Tax—Demise of SPECTOR MOTOR

The most difficult constitutional problems arise when a state attempts to tax a business engaged in purely interstate commerce on activities conducted within its borders.[31] Early Court decisions held that a state may not prevent a foreign corporation engaged solely in interstate commerce from entering the State.[32] This proposition led to the notion that a state could not impose a franchise tax for the privilege of doing business within the state when the corporation was engaged exclusively in interstate commerce.[33] Interstate commerce could not be the subject of taxation even though the tax was nondiscriminatory and fairly apportioned.[34]

During the past half century, the Court by its decisions has gradually eroded the strict rule that the conduct of interstate business is insulated from state and local taxation.[35] In the late 1930's, the Court developed the practical "multiple burdens" approach [36] and began to hold that "local incidents" of inter-

---

28. The basic "question is whether the state has given anything for which it can ask return." Wisconsin v. J. C. Penney Co., 311 U.S. 435, 444 (1940).

29. For example, a state may confer sufficient benefits and protection so that it is entitled to levy a tax. The state, however, could not levy a tax on the total capital of a foreign corporation unless the total capital was employed within the State. Therefore, the total capital of the corporation must be apportioned among the taxing jurisdictions. Cudahy Packing Co. v. Hinkle, 278 U.S. 460 (1929).

30. Spector Motor Service v. O'Connor, 340 U.S. 602, 609 (1950): "Our conclusion is not in conflict with the principle that, where a taxpayer is engaged both in intrastate and interstate commerce, a state may tax the privilege of carrying on intrastate business and, within reasonable limits, may compute the amount of the charge by applying the tax rate to a fair proportion of the taxpayer's business done within the State, including both interstate and intrastate."

See also, Interstate Oil Pipe Line Co. v. Stone, 337 U.S. 662 (1948); International Harvester Co. v. Evatt, 329 U.S. 416 (1946); Atlantic Lumber Co. v. Commissioner of Corp. and Taxation, 298 U.S. 553 (1936).

31. For an excellent discussion, see J. Hellerstein, State Franchise Taxation of Interstate Businesses, 4 Tax L.Rev. 95 (1948).

32. Crutcher v. Kentucky, 141 U.S. 47 (1891); International Text-Book Co. v. Pigg, 217 U.S. 91 (1910).

33. Cheney Bros. v. Massachusetts, 246 U.S. 147, 153–54 (1918); Alpha Portland Cement Co. v. Massachusetts, 268 U.S. 203, 217 (1925); Cudahy Packing Co. v. Hinkle, 278 U.S. 460 (1929); Looney v. Crane Co., 245 U.S. 178 (1917).

34. Ozark Pipe Line Corp. v. Monier, 266 U.S. 555 (1925) (corporate capital apportioned on basis of the ratio of property within the state to total property of the corporation).

35. W. Hellerstein, State Taxation of Interstate Business and the Supreme Court, 1974 Term: Standard Pressed Steel and Colonial Pipeline, 62 Va.L.Rev. 149, 177 (1976).

36. In Western Live Stock v. Bureau of Revenue, 303 U.S. 250, 258, 260 (1938) which involved a New Mexico gross receipts tax on a magazine publisher, Justice Stone stated:

"[W]e think the tax assailed here finds support in reason, and in the practical needs of a taxing system which, under constitutional limitations, must accommodate itself to the double demand that interstate business shall pay its way, and that at the same time it shall not be burdened with cumulative exactions which are not similarly laid on local business. . . .

"The tax is not one which in form or substance can be repeated by other states in such a manner as to lay an added burden on the interstate distribution of the magazine. . . ."

state commerce were taxable.[37] In *Spector Motor Service v. O'Connor*,[38] however, the Court firmly adhered to its earlier position that a tax upon the privilege of engaging in interstate business within the state was unconstitutional. In *Spector*, a franchise tax "for the privilege of carrying on . . . business" measured by fairly apportioned net income was assessed against an interstate carrier. "The constitutional infirmity of such a tax persists no matter how fairly it is apportioned to business done within the state." [39] *Spector Motor* was subsequently reaffirmed in *Northwestern States Portland Cement Co. v. Minnesota*,[40] wherein the Court *upheld* a fairly apportioned, nondiscriminatory net income tax imposed upon a foreign corporation engaged exclusively in interstate commerce. The Court distinguished the two cases by noting that the subject of the tax in *Northwestern* was the corporation's net income, whereas in *Spector* it was the privilege of doing business in the state.[41] The measure of the tax in both cases was net income. Thus, in each case, constitutionality was determined by the legal incident or subject of the tax.[42]

In *Colonial Pipeline v. Traigle*,[43] decided in 1975, the Court again upheld the imposition of a nondiscriminatory, fairly apportioned franchise tax based upon local incidents of interstate commerce. The taxpayer in *Colonial* did not engage in intrastate commerce in Louisiana but it did own an interstate pipeline that ran through the state.

The state first attempted to levy a franchise tax for the "privilege of carrying on or doing business" in the state. The Louisiana courts invalidated this tax. The Louisiana legislature then amended the tax to provide that it was payable for "the qualification to carry on or doing business within this state or the actual doing of business within this state in a corporate form". The Supreme Court upheld this tax on the ground that the amendment made the tax constitutional by "limiting its application to operating incidences of activities within Louisiana for which the State affords privileges and protections . . . ." [44] The subject of the tax was not interstate commerce. Instead, the subject was the doing of business in Louisiana in the corporate form.[45] Therefore, the tax was constitutional.

The concurring opinion in *Colonial* by Justices Blackmun and Rehnquist stated that the majority's legal distinctions were "too finespun and far too gossamer".[46] Undeniably, the approach by the majority in reaffirming the rule of *Spector* reflected adherence to a rule of strict precision in the use of statutory language and reliance upon the legal incidents or subject of the tax. It is clear that the Connecticut tax in *Spector* was imposed "upon [the corporation's] franchise for the privilege of carrying on or doing [exclusively interstate] business within the state . . . ." [47] It is difficult, however, to find a comparable degree of precision in the language of the Louisiana statute

---

37. See W. Hellerstein, supra note 35 at page 177–78, citing: Memphis Natural Gas Co. v. Stone, 335 U.S. 80 (1948); Coverdale v. Arkansas-Louisiana Pipe Line Co., 303 U.S. 604 (1938).

38. 340 U.S. 602 (1951).

39. Id. at 609.

40. 358 U.S. 450 (1959). See text at Section II, C, 2, c, supra.

41. W. Hellerstein, supra note 35 at 178–79.

42. Determination of the validity of a tax by reference to the "subject" thereof, irrespective of its measure, has a solid foundation in the Court's prior decisions. E.g., Flint v. Stone Tracy Co., 220 U.S. 107 (1911) discussed in Chapter 5, Section II, B, 1, supra.

43. 421 U.S. 100 (1975).

44. Id. at 113.

45. Id. at 114.

46. Id. at 115. Justices Blackmun and Rehnquist concluded their concurring opinion with the following observation:

"It makes little constitutional sense—and certainly no practical sense—to say that a state may not impose a fairly apportioned, nondiscriminatory franchise tax with an adequate nexus upon the conduct of business in interstate commerce, but that it may impose that same tax on the conduct of business in interstate commerce 'in a corporate form' or, for that matter, in a partnership or individual form . . . . Certainly to the lay mind, or to any other than the purely legal mind, these are distinctions with little substantive difference and this is taxation by semantics."

47. Id. at 112.

which the majority willingly sustained. In any event, the pragmatic approach suggested by Justices Blackmun and Rehnquist provided the catalyst for overruling *Spector* at the next term of Court.

In *Complete Auto Transit, Inc. v. Brady,*[48] the taxpayer, a Michigan corporation, was engaged in the business of transporting motor vehicles by motor carrier for General Motors. General Motors assembled the vehicles at its assembly plants located outside Mississippi and shipped the vehicles by rail to Jackson, Mississippi. The vehicles were unloaded in the railroad yards in Jackson and reloaded on the taxpayer's trucks for transportation to dealers at various points in Mississippi. Each vehicle was shipped under a bill of lading which stated the name and address of the consignee. The tax imposed upon the taxpayer was assessed under a Mississippi sales tax statute which provided that "there is hereby levied and assessed . . . privilege taxes for the privilege of engaging or continuing in business or doing business within this state" at specified rates upon the gross income from designated business activities. The statute required taxpayers to add the tax to the gross sales price of its goods or services.

In reliance on *Spector,* taxpayer contended that the tax was invalid in that it was imposed on the privilege of engaging in the conduct of interstate commerce. The Court acknowledged that the taxpayer was engaged in transporting goods in interstate commerce but noted that those engaged in interstate commerce are not relieved from their just share of the state tax burden even though it increases the cost of doing business. After reviewing numerous cases, the court summarized the underlying factual circumstances of the case before it:

> We note again that no claim is made that the activity is not sufficiently connected to the State to justify a tax, or that the tax is not fairly related to benefits provided the taxpayer, or that the tax discriminates against interstate

commerce, or that the tax is not fairly apportioned.[49]

With this summary as a datum point, the Court observed that the philosophy underlying the rule of *Spector* had been rejected by subsequent decisions and that "the rule itself has been stripped of any practical significance." Turning to the economic consequences, the Court concluded its opinion with the following statement:

> There is no economic consequence that follows necessarily from the use of the particular words, 'privilege of doing business,' and a focus on that formalism merely obscures the question whether the tax produces a forbidden effect. Simply put, the *Spector* rule does not address the problems with which the Commerce Clause is concerned. Accordingly, we now reject the rule of *Spector Motor Service, Inc. v. O'Connor, supra,* that a state tax on the 'privilege of doing business' is *per se* unconstitutional when it is applied to interstate commerce, and that case is overruled.[50]

With its decision in *Complete Auto Transit,* the Court has validated nondiscriminatory taxes on the privilege of engaging in local activities incident to the conduct of interstate commerce provided the tax is fairly apportioned and there is sufficient nexus to establish that benefits and protection have been provided by the taxing state.

E. License, Gross Receipts, Sales and Use Taxes

1. License Taxes

a. Introduction

Most states require that persons engaged in specified activities or occupations obtain a license and pay a fee. The fee may be a fixed sum, or it may be based on volume of production, or on gross receipts from sales. Constitutionality of privilege, occupation, and license taxes depends on whether the taxing state has a sufficient nexus with the taxable activity for purposes of the due process clause and on whether the tax unduly

---

48. 430 U.S. 274 (1977).

49. 430 U.S. at 287.

50. 430 U.S. at 288–89.

burdens interstate commerce. An endless variety of privilege, occupation, and license taxes has resulted in many irreconcilable Court decisions. Nevertheless, an examination of the decisions in this area reveals several emerging themes. To facilitate analysis, the decisions first are grouped on the basis of the measure of the tax, and then consideration is given to whether the taxing jurisdiction is the state in which the goods are produced or the state in which they are marketed.

b. Fixed-Fee License Taxes

The seminal decision in the fixed-fee license cases is *Robbins v. Taxing District of Shelby County*.[1] Robbins, who was a salesman (drummer) for an Ohio firm, displayed sample goods and solicited sales in Memphis, Tennessee. The State of Tennessee required a fixed-fee license from all salesmen who did not maintain a regular place of business within the taxing district and who solicited orders for the sale of merchandise by sample. Orders taken by Robbins were filled by shipment to the customers from the Ohio offices of his principal. Robbins refused to pay the license fee and challenged the constitutionality of the Tennessee statute under the commerce clause. In its decision, the Court held that the imposition of a tax upon the solicitation of the sale of goods to be shipped into the state in interstate commerce constituted "a tax on interstate commerce itself."[2] This decision in *Robbins* continues to be controlling in modern-day

cases.[3] For example, in *Memphis Steam Laundry Cleaner, Inc. v. Stone*,[4] the Supreme Court invalidated a fixed-fee license required by the State of Mississippi of all persons doing business as a transient vendor in the state. Mississippi imposed the fee upon a Tennessee laundry firm that occasionally sent trucks into Mississippi to collect and deliver laundry. The drivers of the truck also solicited new business. Citing the *Robbins* decision, the Court reiterated that solicitation of interstate business was integral to interstate commerce and could not be the subject of state taxation.[5]

It has been aptly concluded that the criterion established by the *Robbins* decision with respect to the constitutionality of fixed-fee license taxes is whether the licensed activity is integral to taxable intrastate commerce or nontaxable interstate commerce.[6] The principle of the *Robbins* decision is easily stated but its application has led to a number of decisions that are difficult to reconcile. In a comprehensive study in 1962, several illustrations were assembled for comparison.[7] For example, it has been held that the taking of photographs to be developed in another state [8] and the assembly of pictures and frames that have been shipped separately into the state [9] are nontaxable incidents of interstate commerce. By contrast, the courts have sustained fixed-fee license taxes imposed upon the repairing and provisioning of ships used exclusively in interstate and foreign commerce [10] and upon

---

1. 120 U.S. 489 (1887).

2. Id. at 497.

3. Developments in the Law—Federal Limitations on State Taxation of Interstate Business, 75 Harv.L. Rev. 953, 1027 (1962). [hereinafter referred to as Developments]. See, e.g., Memphis Steam Laundry Cleaner, Inc. v. Stone, 342 U.S. 389 (1952); Nippert v. City of Richmond, 327 U.S. 416 (1946); Best & Co. v. Maxwell, 311 U.S. 454 (1940).

4. 342 U.S. 389 (1952).

5. The Court stated:

"In the long line of 'drummer' cases, beginning with Robbins v. Taxing District of Shelby County, 120 U.S. 489 (1887), the Court has held that a tax imposed on the solicitation of interstate business is a

tax imposed on interstate commerce itself. Whether or not solicitation of interstate business may be regarded as a local incident of interstate commerce, the Court has not permitted state taxation to carve out this incident from the integral economic process of interstate commerce."

Id. at 392–93.

6. Developments, supra note 3 at 1027.

7. Id. at 1027–28.

8. Commonwealth v. Olan Mills, Inc., 196 Va. 898, 86 S.E.2d 27 (1955).

9. Caldwell v. North Carolina, 187 U.S. 622 (1903).

10. Martin Ship Service Co. v. City of Los Angeles, 34 Cal.2d 793, 215 P.2d 24 (1950).

the installation of lightning rods [11] or railway signal equipment.[12] Furthermore, although the solicitation of orders to be shipped across state lines is a nontaxable incident of interstate commerce,[13] the peddling of food [14] or drink [15] brought into the state before sale is not exempt from state or local taxation.

It was suggested that the differences in the results of these cases could be reconciled by consideration of the degree of the state's interest under the police power.[16] A more pragmatic appraisal, however, leads one to the observation that the magnitude of local incidents or local activity involved in providing the goods or services was significantly greater in those transactions deemed taxable than in those held nontaxable. On this basis, one may conclude that the test is whether the business subjected to the license tax is essentially local in nature.

There is no question as to the validity of a fixed-sum license fee where the state is clearly acting within the scope of its police power. The license fees in these cases are not revenue measures since the charges must be limited to the cost of regulation.[17] The Court's recognition of the valid exercise of the police power by a state is well illustrated in *California v. Thompson* [18] wherein the State of California required that "transportation agents" pay one dollar for a license and post $1,000 bond. "Transportation agents" were defined as those who solicit or sell transportation over public highways in the state. Although highway transportation is an integral part of interstate commerce, the Court upheld the statute. The Court declared that the Statute was "not a revenue measure . . . ." [19] Instead, the statute was a legitimate police

power "measure to safeguard members of the public desiring to secure transportation by motor vehicle." [20]

Fixed license fees, of course, are not apportioned on the basis of volume of business done and may represent a significant financial hurdle for prospective businesses. Consequently, fixed-fee license taxes are suspect if applied to a business engaged in both intrastate and interstate commerce. Many states, therefore, measure the amount of the fee by production or by gross receipts derived from a taxable incident of intrastate activity.

c. License Taxes Based on Production

The cases involving license fees measured by production or use must be distinguished from use tax cases. The use tax is complementary to the sales tax and is imposed on the purchaser of tangible personal property. By contrast, license or privilege taxes measured by production or use are imposed on an individual or business engaging in a licensed activity. For example, in *Oliver Iron Mining Co. v. Lord*,[21] Minnesota imposed an "occupation tax" equal to six percent of the entire value of ore mined or produced during the taxable year. The tax was imposed upon a firm that mined ore in Minnesota and shipped most of its output to other states pursuant to pre-existing contracts. The Court upheld the tax, declaring that "the ore does not enter interstate commerce until after the mining is done, and the tax is imposed only in respect of mining." [22] The activity of mining, according to the Court, was not interstate commerce in itself. Therefore, Minnesota's "occupation tax" did not unduly burden interstate commerce.

11. Browning v. Waycross, 233 U.S. 16 (1914).

12. General Ry. Signal Co. v. Virginia, 246 U.S. 500 (1918).

13. Real Silk Hosiery Mills v. City of Portland, 268 U.S. 325 (1925).

14. Caskey Baking Co. v. Virginia, 313 U.S. 117 (1941).

15. Wagner v. City of Covington, 251 U.S. 95 (1919).

16. Developments, supra note 3 at 1028.

17. E.g., Opinion of the Justices, 112 N.H. 166, 290 A.2d 869 (1972).

18. 313 U.S. 109 (1941).

19. Id. at 112–13.

20. Id.

21. 262 U.S. 172 (1923).

22. Id. at 179.

Similarly, a license tax on the generation of electricity measured by the number of kilowatt hours produced is valid even though the electricity subsequently is distributed throughout several states.[23] Moreover, a tax on the use of electricity, according to the Court in *Coverdale v. Arkansas-Louisiana Pipe Line Co.*,[24] is valid even though the electricity is used to compress natural gas that is then shipped via an interstate pipeline. Like the generation of electricity, the use of electricity is a taxable incident of intrastate activity that is separable from interstate commerce.

The foregoing rule stated in *Oliver Mining Co.* that a tax on mining is valid per se as a tax on local (intrastate rather than interstate) commerce had been fully articulated in *Heisler v. Thomas Colliery Co.*,[25] decided earlier the same Term. But this longstanding rule was discarded in Commonwealth Edison Co. v. Montana.[26] Wherein the Court observed that "a state severance tax is not immunized from Commerce Clause scrutiny by a claim that the tax is imposed on goods prior to their entry into the stream of interstate commerce.[27] In *Commonwealth Edison Co.*, the Court did not question the result of Heisler and the earlier cases; instead the Court concluded that the broader four-part test prescribed by *Complete Auto Transit* should govern.[28] Under *Complete Auto Transit*, a state tax is deemed compatible with the Commerce Clause if it is applied to an activity that has a substantial local nexus, is fairly apportioned, does not discriminate against interstate commerce, and is fairly related to ser-

vices provided by the state. In sustaining the Montana severance tax on coal mining under this four-part test, the Court emphasized the *local* nature of coal mining operations.[29] Thus, the abandonment of the *Heisler* test is essentially a change of form and not of substance.[30]

License fees measured by the volume of production or use generally are valid if imposed by the state that is the source of the production or use since the production or use generally is separable from interstate activity. Considerable difficulty may exist, however, in attempting to separate intrastate (local) from interstate activity in the state that is the market place of the production. For example, in *Cooney v. Mountain States Telephone & Telegraph Co.*,[31] a Colorado firm operated a telephone and telegraph business throughout the United States. The State of Montana imposed a privilege tax whereby every firm engaged in the business of operating telephone lines in the state had to pay a license tax on every phone instrument used. The Court invalidated the tax because it did not distinguish between intrastate and interstate usage of the phones.[32] The Court admitted that a state could require payment of an occupation tax from a business engaged in both intrastate and interstate commerce. The state, however, must restrict its tax to the intrastate portion of the business. The mere fact that a portion of the firm's business is intrastate in character and therefore taxable does not justify a tax upon the interstate portion or an unapportioned tax upon the whole business.[33] It must appear that the tax is im-

---

23. Utah Power & Light Co. v. Pfost, 286 U.S. 165 (1932).

24. 303 U.S. 604 (1938).

25. 260 U.S. 245 (1922).

26. 453 U.S. 609 (1981).

27. Id. at 617.

28. Complete Auto Transit, Inc. v. Brady, 430 U.S. 274 (1977). See text discussion of *Complete Auto Transit* at Section II, D, 6, at n.48, supra.

29. 453 U.S. at 626.

30. The decision in *Commonwealth Edison* should be placed in historical perspective by noting that the

Court in applying *Complete Auto Transit* was merely recognizing that the former dichotomy which had classified mining as intrastate business no longer holds. See text discussion in Chapter 4, section II, A, supra.

31. 294 U.S. 384 (1935); see also, State Tax Comm'n v. Interstate Natural Gas Co., 284 U.S. 41 (1931).

32. 294 U.S. at 390.

33. The Court stated,

"There is no question that the State may require payment of an occupation tax from one engaged in both intrastate and interstate commerce. But a State cannot tax interstate commerce; it cannot lay a tax upon the business which constitutes such com-

posed solely because of the intrastate business and that the amount is not increased because of interstate activity.[34] Under this doctrine, the license fee must be limited by the terms of the statute or ordinance solely to the intrastate portion of a dual business.[35]

Imposition of state taxes on production may be subject, however, to constraint under the supremacy clause. In *Arizona Public Service Co. v. Snead*,[36] the Court, on the basis of a federal statute, struck down a New Mexico Electric Energy Tax on the generation within the state of electricity that was transmitted for sale in other states and the Republic of Mexico. The Court concluded that under the supremacy clause the tax was invalid as in conflict with the following provisions of 15 U.S.C.A. § 391:

> No State, or political subdivision thereof, may impose or assess a tax on or with respect to the generation or transmission of electricity which discriminates against out-of-State manufacturers, producers, wholesalers, retailers, or consumers of that electricity. For purposes of this section, a tax is discriminatory if it results, either directly or indirectly, in a greater tax burden on electricity which is generated and transmitted in interstate commerce than on electricity which is generated and transmitted in intrastate commerce.

Under the New Mexico statute, a tax equivalent of 2% of the retail value of electricity was imposed on all companies generating electricity within the state whether the electricity was sold within or without the state. New Mexico also imposed a 4% gross receipts tax on the retail sale of electricity, a tax borne by the consumer. To avoid pyramiding the tax burden on New Mexico consumers, a credit for the 2% Electric Energy Tax was allowed against the gross receipts tax. The effect of the New Mexico

credit provision was to impose the 2% Electric Energy Tax on the generation of electricity for sale out-of-state, and no tax on the generation of electricity for sale within the state.

The Court recognized that there was some ambiguity in the statutory language of 15 U.S.C.A. § 391 as finally enacted, but concluded from the Congressional debates and Committee Reports that the statute was "aimed directly" at the New Mexico Electric Energy Tax. Moreover, the Court rejected the contention that there was a constitutional issue under the commerce clause and held that enactment of 15 U.S.C.A. § 391, was within the scope of the broad power of Congress to regulate interstate commerce.

d. *License Taxes Measured by Gross Receipts*

Perhaps the most controversial facet of due process and commerce clause protection against state taxation of interstate commerce arises in the license or privilege taxes measured by the gross receipts of a business engaged in multi-state operations. Gross receipts taxes imposed by the marketplace state may contravene the due process clause if the seller conducts little business activity within the State. Furthermore, the unapportioned nature of gross receipts taxes may impose multiple or cumulative burdens upon interstate commerce. At this point, however, the Court has not required apportionment of gross receipts taxes relating to the sale of goods originating in interstate commerce.[37] Moreover, the Court has consistently sustained taxes on manufacturing and production measured by gross receipts as valid taxes on local business activity.[38] If the activity or subject is taxable, the formu-

---

merce or the privilege of engaging in it. And the fact that a portion of a business is intrastate and therefore taxable does not justify a tax either upon the interstate business or upon the whole business without discrimination."

Id. at 392–93.

34. Sprout v. City of South Bend, 277 U.S. 163, 171 (1928). See also, Leloup v. Port of Mobile, 127 U.S. 640 (1888).

35. Developments, supra note 3 at 1030.

36. 441 U.S. 141 (1979).

37. Hellerstein, State Taxation of Interstate Business and the Supreme Court, 1974 Term: Standard Pressed Steel and Colonial Pipeline, 62 Va.L.Rev. 149, 174 (1976) [hereinafter cited as Hellerstein].

38. Id., citing: American Manufacturing Co. v. St. Louis, 250 U.S. 459 (1919); Heisler v. Thomas Colliery

la used to measure the amount of the tax apparently is irrelevant. Accordingly, in *American Manufacturing Co. v. St. Louis*,[39] the Court sustained a gross receipts tax imposed upon every manufacturer doing business within the City of St. Louis. The City required each manufacturer to obtain a license and pay a fee of one dollar for every $1,000 of sales. The tax was valid, according to the Court, even though imposed upon St. Louis manufacturers who engaged in interstate sales. The Court observed that "payment of the tax is not made a condition of selling goods in interstate commerce or in other commerce, but only of continuing the manufacture of goods in the City of St. Louis." [40] Gross receipts merely provided a convenient measure of a legitimate tax on the local activity of manufacturing.[41]

In addition to having sustained taxes on manufacturing, producing, and extracting activities, the Court has held that the publication of a nationally-distributed magazine is local activity subject to a tax on gross receipts.[42] By contrast, until 1978, the Court firmly held to the view that the activity of stevedoring is an integral part of interstate or foreign commerce and could not be the subject of a gross receipts tax.[43] The result of these stevedoring cases was highly ques-

tionable since the activity of loading and unloading cargo from ships at port can be considered local activity separable from actual interstate or foreign transportation of the cargo.[44] Moreover, the activity of stevedoring can not be subjected to multiple taxation by several states.

In *Department of Revenue v. Association of Washington Stevedoring Co.*,[45] the Court reconsidered its position and overruled its prior decisions by sustaining the imposition of state taxes on the business of stevedoring under both the commerce clause and the import-export clause. The Court noted that the commerce clause issue was resolved by its decision in *Complete Auto*.[46] In *Complete Auto*, the Court sustained a tax on the privilege of engaging in interstate business measured by gross receipts derived from the in-state portion of shipment of goods in interstate commerce. Stevedoring activity occurs completely within the taxing state even though it occurs while the goods are in transit. Inasmuch as stevedoring has an exclusively local nexus, it follows that the tax is fairly apportioned, it is nondiscriminatory, and it is clearly related to the services provided by the State.[47] On the import-export clause issue, the Court turned to its decision

---

Co., 260 U.S. 245 (1922); Hope Natural Gas Co. v. Hall, 274 U.S. 284 (1927).

39. 250 U.S. 459 (1919).

40. Id. at 463.

41. The Court stated that,

"In the outcome the tax is the same amount as if it were measured by the sale value of the goods but imposed upon the completion of their manufacture. The difference is that, for reasons of practical benefit to the taxpayer, the city has postponed payment until convenient means have been furnished through the marketing of the goods."

Id. at 464.

42. In Western Live Stock v. Bureau of Revenue, 303 U.S. 250 (1938), the State of New Mexico imposed a tax of 2% of gross advertising revenues upon a New Mexico publisher whose journal circulated throughout several States. In upholding the tax, the Court stated:

"In the present cases the tax is, in form and substance, an excise conditioned on the carrying on of a local business, that of providing and selling advertising space in a published journal, which is sold to and paid for by subscribers, some of whom receive it in

interstate commerce. The price at which the advertising is sold is made the measure of the tax. This Court has sustained a similar tax said to be on the privilege of manufacturing, measured by the total gross receipts from sales of the manufactured goods both intrastate and interstate. American Manufacturing Co. v. St. Louis . . . ."

Id. at 257.

43. Joseph v. Carter & Weeks Stevedoring Co., 330 U.S. 422 (1947); Puget Sound Stevedoring Co. v. State Tax Comm'n, 302 U.S. 90 (1937).

44. In Canton R.R. v. Rogan, 340 U.S. 511 (1951), the Court sustained a domestic franchise tax measured by gross receipts which was assessed against a carrier operating a marine terminal and rail line in the Baltimore port area moving goods to and from the port in serving connecting interstate railroads. The Court emphasized the fact that the gross receipts in these circumstances were fairly apportioned to local activity in the taxing state.

45. 435 U.S. 734 (1978).

46. 430 U.S. 274 (1977).

47. 435 U.S. at 750.

in *Michelin* [48] as a basis for holding that the tax on stevedoring did not constitute a prohibited "Import or Duty" and noted that the following tests laid down in *Michelin* were met: (1) There was no usurpation of the authority of the Federal Government in the regulation of foreign commerce; and (2) the tax did not disturb harmony among the states since it merely exacted compensation for services and protection extended to imports and exports. [49] The Court emphasized the distinction between prohibited "Imports and Duties" that are imposed upon the *value of the goods,* and taxes that are imposed upon the privilege of conducting a local business, namely, the business of transporting cargo within the State.

Thus for purposes of the import–export clause, the distinction made by the Court is premised primarily upon the legal incidence or subject of the tax. This is to be contrasted with the Court's concern under the commerce clause as to whether the tax in question imposes a discriminatory economic burden. In his concurring opinion, Justice Powell lamented the resurrection of the "direct-indirect" test and recommended reliance solely on the test as to whether the particular tax constitutes a discriminatory transit fee. [50]

As indicated by *American Manufacturing Co. v. St. Louis* [51] and its progeny, gross receipts taxes must specify a taxable incident or taxable subject of local activity such as manufacturing. A tax imposed on "gross receipts from all trades, businesses, or commerce" has been held invalid as applied to gross receipts derived from interstate sales. [52] Thus, in *Gwin, White & Prince, Inc. v. Henneford,* [53] the Court invalidated a Washington State gross receipts tax on the privilege of engaging in business activities within the state. The state imposed the tax on a Washington firm that marketed fruit throughout several States. The Court was concerned that "[i]f Washington is free to exact such a tax, other states to which commerce extends may, with equal right, lay a tax similarly measured . . . ." [54] Thus, the failure to specify a taxable incident of local activity raises the possibility of burdening a multistate business with multiple taxation of the same transaction.

e. *Unapportioned Gross Receipts and the Market State*

Another controversial line of cases involves the application of a state's unapportioned gross receipts tax to an out-of-state vendor making sales to in-state customers. These decisions raise familiar due process and commerce clause issues. First, there must be "some definite link, some minimum connection, between a state and the person, property or transaction it seeks to tax." [55] Second, the unapportioned nature of the gross receipts tax must not unduly burden interstate commerce by subjecting the taxpayer to multiple state taxation of the same transaction. [56]

48. 423 U.S. 276 (1976).

49. 435 U.S. at 751–61.

50. 435 U.S. at 762–64.

51. 250 U.S. 459 (1919).

52. See, e.g, Adams Manufacturing v. Storen, 304 U.S. 307 (1938), wherein the State of Indiana imposed a tax on the gross receipts derived from trades, businesses, or commerce. The Court invalidated the tax as applied to an Indiana manufacturing firm that sold 80% of its products to customers in other states. The Court stated:

"So far as the sale price of the goods sold in interstate commerce includes compensation for a purely intrastate activity, the manufacture of the goods sold, it may be reached for local taxation by a tax on the privilege of manufacturing, measured by the value of goods manufactured, or by other permissible forms of levy upon the intrastate transaction. It is because the tax, forbidden as to interstate commerce, reaches indiscriminately and without apportionment, the compensation for both interstate commerce and intrastate activities that it must fail in its entirety so far as applied to receipts from sales interstate."

Id. at 313–14.

53. 305 U.S. 434 (1939).

54. Id. at 439.

55. Miller Bros. Co. v. Maryland, 347 U.S. 340, 344–45 (1954) (question whether out-of-state vendor was liable for use tax).

56. Note the overlap of the commerce and due process clause issues.

Norton Co. v. Department of Revenue,[57] which is a leading sales tax case, has been described as supporting an apportioned gross receipts tax with respect to an out-of-state vendor making sales to in-state customers.[58] The taxpayer in *Norton* was a Massachusetts manufacturer of abrasive machines and supplies with a branch office in Chicago. Illinois imposed a sales tax on all of the manufacturer's sales to Illinois customers. The sales resulted from three categories of transactions. First, the Chicago office made over-the-counter sales from inventory on hand. Second, the Chicago office forwarded to the Massachusetts home office orders for merchandise not on hand. Third, Illinois customers often mailed orders directly to the Massachusetts office without utilizing the services of the Illinois branch. These mail orders were filled by direct shipment to the customers. The Court set forth the rule that a firm that enters a state to do local business can avoid taxation on some sales to in-state customers "only by showing that particular transactions are dissociated from the local business and [are] interstate in nature."[59] Accordingly the Court held that sales arising from the first two categories were not dissociated from the local business because the services rendered by the Chicago office were "decisive factors in establishing and holding this market."[60] Sales arising from the third category of transactions, however, were nontaxable because they were "so clearly interstate in character that the State could not reasonably attribute their proceeds to the local business. . . ."[61]

It is not clear, however, that the *Norton* decision can properly be cited to support an apportioned gross receipts tax with respect to the sale of goods. The Illinois tax was a sales tax—a transactions tax—not a general gross receipts tax. Furthermore, at the time the *Norton* issue arose, Illinois did not have a complementary use tax. Had there been an Illinois use tax in effect, Illinois could have required Norton to collect and remit the tax on mail order sales inasmuch as Norton maintained a local retail outlet in Illinois.[62]

In any event, the Court has not endorsed an apportioned gross receipts tax with respect to the sale of goods. On the contrary, in three significant cases involving the application of the Washington State "business activities" tax, the Court has found "some local incident . . . sufficient to bring the transaction" within the taxing power of the state.[63] In *Field Enterprises, Inc. v. Washington,*[64] a Delaware corporation, with its principal office in Chicago, was engaged in the business of publishing and selling encyclopedias throughout the United States. It maintained a division office in Seattle with a division manager and four employees. This office was used as a headquarters to train salesmen and there were 175 salesmen within the state. Orders for books, which were obtained through personal calls by salesmen, were submitted with the down payments thereon to the division office in Seattle and forwarded by that office to Chicago. Shipments pursuant to these orders were made directly from Chicago to the customer and billings and collections of the unpaid balance of the purchase price were made by the Chicago office. On these facts it was held that the tax upon the gross receipts from sales in Washington did not impose an unconstitutional levy upon interstate commerce. The Court's per curiam affirmance was premised upon its decision in *Norton.*

57. 340 U.S. 534 (1951).

58. Hellerstein, supra note 37 at 161–67.

59. Norton Co. v. Department of Revenue, 340 U.S. 534, 537 (1951). The Court also asserted that "a taxpayer claiming immunity from a tax has the burden of establishing his exemption." Id.

60. Id. at 538.

61. Id. at 539.

62. See Nelson v. Sears, Roebuck & Co., 312 U.S. 359 (1941) and text discussion at Section II, E, 2, d, infra.

63. 340 U.S. 534, 537 (1951).

64. 352 U.S. 806 (1956), affirming per curiam 47 Wash.2d 852, 289 P.2d 1010 (1955).

Field Enterprises was followed by *General Motors Corp. v. Washington* [65] in which the Court dealt with the issue as to whether it was constitutional to apply the Washington business activities tax to the taxpayer's gross receipts from wholesale sales of motor vehicles, parts and accessories delivered to independent retail dealers in the state of Washington. Under the GM organizational structure, distributions of its products were supervised through geographical offices. Chevrolet, Pontiac and Oldsmobile divisions maintained a zone office in Portland, Oregon which served GM operations in Oregon, Washington, Idaho, Alaska and portions of Montana and Wyoming. GM offices and employees located in the State of Washington consisted of the following: (1) The Chevrolet division maintained a branch office in Seattle to service a major part of the state of Washington by expediting deliveries and performing some promotional work. This office was under the jurisdiction of the Portland zone office. (2) GM Parts Division maintained a warehouse in Seattle, employed 20 to 28 employees, and supplied all of the Chevrolet, Pontiac and Oldsmobile dealers in Washington with parts and accessories most often called for. (3) Each district manager of the Chevrolet, Pontiac and Oldsmobile divisions resided in Washington and each regularly visited the dealers under his supervision for the purpose of establishing and maintaining sales of GM automobiles. Each district manager's home served as his office for the transaction of GM business.

With the exception of automobile parts sold from the Seattle office and warehouse of the GM Parts Division, all sales within Washington were consummated on the basis of orders mailed by dealers to out-of-state offices of GM and filled by shipment of goods into the state. The challenge to the tax related to gross receipts from out-of-state shipments to Washington dealers. After carefully summarizing all the facts relating to GM business activity in the state of Washington, the Court concluded that GM had so mingled its taxable business with that which it claimed to be not taxable that, in light of all the evidence, attribution of all its Washington sales to its local activity was justified. Again the Court relied upon *Norton* in which it had stated that a taxpayer "cannot channel business through a local outlet to gain the advantage of a local business and also hold the immunities of an interstate business." [66]

The final chapter in the series of three cases was the Court's decision in *Standard Pressed Steel Co. v. Washington.* [67] Standard Pressed Steel's home office and manufacturing plant were in Pennsylvania. Washington imposed its business and occupation tax upon Standard's gross receipts from the sale of aerospace fasteners to Boeing Company, which is located in the State of Washington. Standard's only Washington-based employee was an engineer whose office was in his home and who primarily consulted with Boeing concerning its use of fasteners. Standard's out-of-state offices handled all sales orders, shipments, negotiations, and payments. Constitutional challenge of the tax was premised on both due process and the commerce clause. The Court brushed aside the due process contention as frivolous with the observation that the presence of the taxpayer's engineer-salesman "made possible the realization and continuance of valuable contractual relations between appellant and Boeing." [68] Thus, the Court found the necessary nexus to meet due process requirements.

---

65. 377 U.S. 436 (1964).

66. 340 U.S. 534, 539 (1951). In *General Motors* the Court stated:

"Thus, in the bundle of corporate activity, which is the test here, we see General Motors' activity so enmeshed in local connections that it voluntarily paid taxes on various of its operations but insists that it was not liable on others. Since General Motors elected to enter the State in this fashion, we cannot say that the Supreme Court of Washington erred in holding that these local incidents were sufficient to form the basis for the levy of a tax that would not run contrary to the Constitution. Norton Co. v. Department of Revenue, supra."

377 U.S. 436, 447–48 (1964).

67. 419 U.S. 560 (1975).

68. Id. at 562.

In disposing of the commerce clause argument, the Court relied on its decision in *General Motors* as "almost precisely in point" and observed that the issue was whether there was a risk of multiple taxation. On this point, the Court noted that the burden was on the taxpayer and no such showing had been made.[69] In effect, the Court concluded that the taxpayer's manner of doing business in the taxing state through the continual presence of an engineer-salesman was sufficient to convert the transactions into intrastate sales.[70]

By contrast with interstate transactions involving the sale of goods, the Court has sustained apportioned gross receipts taxes upon businesses engaged in interstate transportation.[71] In each case, the taxes were imposed on or measured by gross receipts derived from that portion of the transportation conducted within the taxing state. In these cases, there was no risk of multiple taxation and there was no question as to significant localized activity.

2. Sales and Use Taxes

a. Introduction

General sales and complementary use taxes have been adopted by most states[1] and are a very important source of state and local government revenue.[2] The sales tax is usually imposed at the retail level on local sales of tangible personal property. Some statutes, however, also include the sale of services as well as the sale of goods within the scope of the tax. The sales tax is generally added to the selling price and is borne by the consumer, but the vendor is made an agent of the state for purposes of collection.

The complementary use tax is designed to reach out-of-state purchases by residents of the state. It is imposed upon all tangible personal property used, stored or consumed within the state on which a sales tax has not been paid. The use tax serves a dual function.[3] First, it protects the revenue by taxing out-of-state purchases of goods made by residents of the state for use or consumption within the state. Second, it protects local merchants against competition from out-of-state merchants who are not subject to a sales tax or who are taxed at lower rates. In appropriate circumstances, the out-of-state vendor can be required to collect and remit the use tax in the same manner as if the sale had been consummated within the state.

b. Sales Taxes and Interstate Transactions

The fact that goods have been obtained by the vendor from out-of-state does not bar imposition of a sales tax on the subsequent sale thereof.[4] This rule squares with that applicable under the general property tax. If the shipment in interstate commerce has terminated, and the goods have become a

---

69. As a practical matter there is no risk of multiple taxation of these transactions under a sales tax because the requisite incidents of a local sale would not exist in any other jurisdiction.

70. 419 U.S. 560, 564.

71. Canton R.R. v. Rogan, 340 U.S. 511 (1951) (Maryland franchise tax measured by gross receipts of railroad company apportioned on a mileage basis; taxpayer engaged in interstate commerce but operated solely in taxing state); Interstate Oil Pipe Line Co. v. Stone, 337 U.S. 662 (1949) (Mississippi privilege tax on operation of pipelines measured by gross receipts; taxpayer, a foreign corporation, was engaged exclusively in interstate commerce and operated only in Mississippi); Central Greyhound Lines, Inc. v. Mealey, 334 U.S. 653 (1948) (New York tax on gross receipts of public carrier valid to extent applied to receipts apportioned on a mileage basis).

1. Forty-five states and the District of Columbia impose general sales and use tax. Alaska imposes a business license tax measured by gross receipts and authorizes cities and school districts to impose gross receipts taxes. Non-users are Delaware, New Hampshire, Montana and Oregon. 1 All State Sales Tax Rep. (CCH) ¶ 301.

2. The report of the Bureau of the Census for fiscal year 1976 indicates that general sales taxes provided 30.6% of total state revenues. State Tax Collections in 1976, U.S. Dept. of Commerce, Bureau of the Census, GF 76 No. 1, Table A, page 1 (January, 1977).

3. Miller Bros. Co. v. Maryland, 347 U.S. 340, 343 (1954).

4. Sonneborn Bros. v. Cureton, 262 U.S. 506 (1923). The vendor in *Sonneborn Bros.* purchased oil out-of-state which was shipped to its storerooms in Texas. The oil thereafter was sold to local customers in the

part of the common mass of goods in the state of destination, they may be subjected to nondiscriminatory taxation. This is the case whether the tax is an ad valorem property tax based on general ownership or a sales tax based upon the exercise of one of the incidents of ownership. This conclusion is easily reached under circumstances in which the shipment of the goods in interstate commerce precedes the contract to sell. The more difficult question, which was presented in *McGoldrick v. Berwind-White Coal Mining Co.*,[5] is whether the commerce clause bars imposition of a sales tax where the performance of a contract previously entered into by the vendor necessarily requires subsequent shipment of the goods in interstate commerce for delivery to the buyer.

In *Berwind-White*, the taxpayer was engaged in mining coal in Pennsylvania. It maintained a permanent sales office in New York and through that office contracted to sell large quantities of its coal to utility companies and steamship lines. In most instances the coal was shipped by rail to docks in New Jersey and loaded on barges for shipment to the point of delivery in New York alongside purchasers' plants or steamships. The city of New York assessed a two percent sales tax upon these sales and the Court sustained the tax, holding that the sales occurred after the goods had left the stream of commerce. The Court described the tax in the following manner:

> It does not aim at or discriminate against interstate commerce. It is laid upon every purchaser, within the state, of goods for consumption, regardless of whether they have been transported in interstate commerce. Its only relation to the commerce arises from the fact that immediately preceding transfer of possession

to the purchaser within the state, which is the taxable event regardless of the time and place of passing title, the merchandise has been transported in interstate commerce and brought to its journey's end. Such a tax has no different effect upon interstate commerce than a tax on the "use" of property which has just been moved in interstate commerce . . . or the tax on storage or withdrawal for use by the consignee of gasoline, . . . or the familiar property tax on goods by the state of destination at the conclusion of their interstate journey.[6]

On the facts, it is clear that the taxpayer was regularly engaged in maintaining a sales office in New York but was dealing in a commodity in quantities not regularly held in stock prior to sale. Later in its opinion, the Court noted that the economic effect or burden of the tax was no greater "whether the purchase order or contract precedes or follows the interstate shipment." [7] In either case, the vendor's performance of his contractual obligation is deemed to occur after the shipment of the goods in interstate commerce has been terminated. Conversely, a sales tax upon the local sale of goods is valid even though the purchaser plans to ship the goods out-of-state immediately following the purchase.[8]

The scope of the *Berwind-White* decision was more clearly defined in *McLeod v. J. E. Dilworth Co.*,[9] decided in 1944. Taxpayer, a Tennessee corporation with its home office and place of business in Memphis, was engaged in the business of selling mill supplies and machinery. Sales were made to Arkansas customers whose orders were obtained by traveling salesmen and submitted to the home office for approval. Title and possession were transferred to the purchaser upon delivery to the carrier in Memphis and collec-

original packages. The Court, upholding the imposition of a sales tax by Texas, stated:

> "The interstate transportation was at an end, and whether in the original packages or not, a state tax upon the oil as property or upon its sale in the state, if the state law levied the same tax on all oil or all sales of it, without regard to origin, would be neither a regulation nor a burden of the interstate commerce of which this oil had been subject."

Id. at 508–09.

5. 309 U.S. 33 (1940).

6. Id. at 49.

7. Id. at 54.

8. International Harvester Co. v. Department of Treasury, 322 U.S. 340 (1944) (sustaining Indiana gross receipts tax upon sales to out-of-state buyers who took delivery in Indiana and immediately transported the goods to another state).

9. 322 U.S. 327 (1944).

tions were made through the Memphis office. Arkansas imposed its sales tax upon these transactions.

The question presented was whether the Arkansas sales tax violated the commerce clause. In holding the sales tax invalid, the Court adopted the position taken by the state court, namely, that no sale had been made in Arkansas inasmuch as delivery of possession and transfer of title to the purchaser had occurred in Tennessee. The Court, employing commonly used due process concepts to dispose of the commerce clause issue, stated that to permit "Arkansas to impose a tax on such transactions would be to project its powers beyond its boundaries and to tax an interstate transaction." [10]

It should be noted that the Court refused to accept the contention that since a use tax would have been valid in the circumstances, a sales tax should be accepted as permissible in view of the fact that the economic effect would be the same. The Court emphasized that the legislature had chosen not to impose a use tax and stated:

[W]e are not dealing with matters of nomenclature even though they be matters of nicety. . . . Though sales and use taxes may secure the same revenue and serve complementary purposes, they are, as we have indicated, taxes on different transactions and for different opportunities afforded by a State. [11]

Thus, the Court recognized that the *stated subject* of the tax was controlling.

c. Application of the Use Tax

Although a state can not tax a sale consummated out-of-state, it may tax the subsequent use of the goods by the purchaser within the state. In *Henneford v. Silas Mason Co.,* [12] the taxpayer was engaged as a contractor in the construction of the Grand Coulee Dam on the Columbia River in Washington State. In the performance of that work, it brought into the state certain heavy equipment and construction materials purchased out-of-state. Washington imposed a use tax upon the cost of these articles, which the taxpayer challenged as a violation of the commerce clause.

In sustaining the tax, the Court relied upon the principles developed in connection with the general property tax. The rationale of the decision was stated as follows:

The tax is not upon the operations of interstate commerce, but upon the privilege of use after commerce is at an end.

Things acquired or transported in interstate commerce may be subjected to a property tax, non-discriminatory in its operation, when they have become part of the common mass of property within the state of destination. . . . This is so, indeed, though they are still in the original packages. . . . For like reasons they may be subjected, when once they are at rest, to a non-discriminatory tax upon use or enjoyment. . . . The privilege of use is only one attribute, among many, of the bundle of privileges that make up property or ownership. [13]

The principle stated in *Silas Mason Co.* has been applied with respect to goods brought into the state and placed in storage for subsequent use in interstate commerce. In *Southern Pacific Co. v. Gallagher,* [14] for example, an interstate railroad purchased materials and supplies out-of-state and shipped them into California where they were stored until needed in the operation and repair of the railroad system and its equipment. The California use tax by its terms applied to storage or use. The Court sustained the tax, stating that "there was a taxable moment when the . . . [sup-

---

10. Id. at 330. This is illustrative of the fact that the same principle may be applicable to both due process and commerce clause issues. The Court found that there was no sale within the state that could be subjected to a sales tax. To permit a state to tax a sale consummated outside the state would violate both due process and the commerce clause.

11. 322 U.S. at 331.

12. 300 U.S. 577 (1937). See, Allemed, Inc. v. Department of Revenue, 101 Ill.App.3d 746, 748, 57 Ill.Dec. 164, 166, 428 N.E.2d 714 (1981), citing earlier edition of this treatise.

13. 300 U.S. at 582.

14. 306 U.S. 167 (1939).

plies] had reached the end of their interstate transportation and had not begun to be consumed in interstate operation." [15] Prior to *Southern Pacific Co.*, the Court in *Edelman v. Boeing Air Transport* [16] had upheld the imposition of a use tax upon gasoline withdrawn from storage and placed in airplanes that were operated in interstate commerce. The Court observed that the tax was not imposed on gasoline consumed in the operation of the planes, and stated: "It is at the time of withdrawal alone that 'use' is measured for the purposes of the tax." [17] As indicated by the decision in *Boeing*, a use tax imposed on and measured by the amount of gasoline consumed in interstate commerce would clearly violate the commerce clause.[18]

d. Collection of the Use Tax Through Out-of-State Vendors

Although the legal incidence of the use tax is upon the consumer, the states have sought to simplify the administration of the tax by imposing the burden of collection upon the seller. This has led to a major issue concerning the circumstances in which a state can require an out-of-state vendor to collect the use tax from resident consumers without violating due process.

It was established at an early date that it is appropriate to impose the duty of collecting a use tax on an in-state vendor who imports goods from another state for local sale or distribution.[19] With little discussion and solely on the basis of these early cases, the Court in *Felt & Tarrant Manufacturing Co. v. Gallagher* [20] sustained imposition of the burden of collecting the use tax on an

out-of-state vendor whose only activity within the state was the solicitation of sales through local agents. Two years later, the Court, again with little elaboration, sustained imposition of the burden of collecting the use tax with respect to catalogue sales of national mail-order houses that also operated retail outlets in the taxing state.[21] In these decisions the Court held that the catalogue sales, although separable, nevertheless were related to the taxpayers' local retail operations, and it concluded that the burden of collection of the use tax violated neither due process nor the commerce clause.

The next case to present the issue of imposing the burden of collecting the use tax upon the vendor was *General Trading Co. v. State Tax Commission*,[22] decided the same day as *J. E. Dilworth Co.* General Trading, a Minnesota corporation, employed traveling salesmen to solicit orders in Iowa which were subject to acceptance at its Minnesota headquarters. Goods to fill the orders were shipped from Minnesota by common carrier to the Iowa purchasers and the company maintained no office, branch, or warehouse in Iowa. Again, relying on its prior decisions and without elaborating, the Court sustained the imposition of the burden of collection upon the vendor even though the only activity in the taxing state was solicitation of orders.

Not until its decision in *Miller Bros. v. Maryland* [23] did the Court hold the imposition of the burden of collection on an out-of-state vendor to be invalid. Miller Bros. operated a store in Wilmington, Delaware

---

15. Id. at 177.

16. 289 U.S. 249 (1933).

17. I*f*. at 252. A similar result was reached in Nashville, C. & St. L. Ry. v. Wallace, 288 U.S. 249 (1933), wherein the railroad imported gasoline into Tennessee for use as fuel in its interstate railway operations. The Supreme Court upheld Tennessee's use tax imposed upon the storage or usage of gasoline in the state. Local storage of the gasoline provided a sufficient taxable incident separate from interstate commerce.

18. Helson v. Kentucky, 279 U.S. 245 (1928) (held invalid a gasoline tax imposed on gasoline *used* in operating an interstate ferry).

19. Monamotor Oil Co. v. Johnson, 292 U.S. 86 (1934); Bowman v. Continental Oil Co., 256 U.S. 642 (1921).

20. 306 U.S. 62 (1939).

21. Nelson v. Sears, Roebuck & Co., 312 U.S. 359 (1941); Nelson v. Montgomery Ward & Co., 312 U.S. 373 (1941).

22. 322 U.S. 335 (1944).

23. 347 U.S. 340 (1954).

which was patronized by residents of nearby Maryland. Its contacts with Maryland customers included newspaper and radio advertising, occasional mailing of sales circulars, and some deliveries to Maryland customers by common carrier or by its own delivery trucks. On the basis of these activities, Maryland asserted the right to impose upon Miller Bros. the duty of collecting the Maryland use tax. In a five-four decision, the Court held that the imposition of the burden of collection violated due process. The test was stated in the majority opinion as follows: "[D]ue process requires some definite link, some minimum connection, between a state and the person, property or transaction it seeks to tax." [24] In responding to the contention that the decision in *General Trading* was controlling, the Court stated:

> [T]here is a wide gulf between this type of active and aggressive operation within a taxing state [solicitation in *General Trading*] and the occasional delivery of goods sold at an out-of-state store with no solicitation other than the incidental effects of general advertising. *Here was no invasion or exploitation of the consumer market in Maryland.* On the contrary, these sales resulted from purchasers traveling from Maryland to Delaware to exploit its less tax-burdened selling market. That these inhabitants incurred a liability for the use tax when they used, stored or consumed the goods in Maryland, no one doubts. But the burden of collecting or paying their tax cannot be shifted to a foreign merchant in the absence of some jurisdictional basis not present here.[25]

There was a brief but vigorous dissent in *Miller Bros.* written by Justice Douglas. The dissenting justices were of the view that Miller Bros. had enjoyed more than minimal contact with the Maryland market. The dissent stated:

> This is not a case of minimal contact between a vendor and the collecting State. Appellant did not sell cash-and-carry without knowledge of the destination of the goods; and its delivery truck was not in Maryland upon a casual, nonrecurring visit. Rather there has been a course of conduct in which the appellant has regularly injected advertising into media reaching Maryland consumers and regularly effected deliveries within Maryland by its own delivery trucks and by common carriers.[26]

Since *Miller Bros.*, which was decided in 1954, there have been three decisions involving the propriety of imposing the burden of collection of a use tax on an out-of-state vendor. In *Scripto, Inc. v. Carson,*[27] the Court sustained imposition of the burden of collection where the out-of-state vendor solicited sales in the taxing state through "independent contractors" instead of its own salesmen. The Court concluded that the distinction between independent contractors and employee-salesmen was "without constitutional significance." [28]

The next case considered by the Court involved an out-of-state vendor who sold goods in the taxing state only by catalogue on a mail order basis. In *National Bellas Hess, Inc. v. Department of Revenue,*[29] the Court, with three dissenting justices, held that imposition of the burden of collection of the use tax on the out-of-state vendor would violate the commerce clause. The only activity in the taxing state was communication with customers by mail or common carrier as part of a general interstate business. The majority observed that it had "never held that a State may impose the duty of use tax collection and payment upon a seller whose only connection with customers in the state is by common carrier or the United States mail." [30] It was the conclusion of the majority that "it is difficult to conceive of commercial transactions more exclusively interstate in character than the mail order transactions here involved." [31]

As indicated in the dissenting opinion, however, National Bellas Hess, with headquarters in Missouri, had sold $2,174,744 in merchandise to Illinois customers over the

24. Id. at 344–345.

25. Id. at 347 (emphasis added).

26. Id. at 358.

27. 362 U.S. 207 (1960).

28. Id. at 211.

29. 386 U.S. 753 (1967).

30. 386 U.S. at 758.

31. 386 U.S. at 759.

15-month period in issue. These sales were obtained by twice-a-year catalogue mailings, supplemented by additional mailings of special sales books and flyers. A substantial part of the vendor's sales were on credit. The minority concluded that to require the vendor to collect the Illinois use tax in these circumstances would not violate either due process or the commerce clause. The dissenting opinion stated:

> There should be no doubt that this large-scale, systematic, continuous solicitation and exploitation of the Illinois consumer market is a sufficient "nexus" to require Bellas Hess to collect from Illinois customers and to remit the use tax, especially when coupled with the use of the credit resources of residents of Illinois, dependent as that mechanism is upon the State's banking and credit institutions. Bellas Hess is not simply using the facilities of interstate commerce to serve customers in Illinois. It is regularly and continuously engaged in "exploitation of the consumer market" of Illinois (Miller Bros. Co. v. State of Maryland, 347 U.S. 340, 347, 74 S.Ct. 535, 540, 98 L.Ed. 744 (1954)) by soliciting residents of Illinois who live and work there and have homes and banking connections there, and who, absent the solicitation of Bellas Hess, might buy locally and pay the sales tax to support their State. Bellas Hess could not carry on its business in Illinois, and particularly its substantial credit business, without utilizing Illinois banking and credit facilities.[32]

In *National Geographic Society v. California Bd. of Equalization*,[33] the most recent case, the Court again considered the question as to whether the vendor could be required to collect use taxes upon mail order sales. In this case, however, the vendor operated two offices within the taxing state, but the business conducted through these offices consisted solely of soliciting advertis-

ing for its monthly magazine. As such, the California offices were wholly unrelated to its mail order business which was located in Washington, D.C. From the Washington office, the taxpayer sold maps, atlases, and other materials to California residents only on the basis of mail orders. None of these items was sold through its California offices and its California offices provided no customer services with respect to these activities. Taxpayer's opposition to collection of the use tax was premised on both *Bellas Hess* and *Miller Bros.* The Court concluded that the taxpayer's "continuous presence in California in offices that solicit advertising for its magazine provides a sufficient nexus to justify that State's imposition . . . of the duty to act as collector of the use tax."[34]

Although the result in *National Geographic* was predictable,[35] special note should be accorded Justice Blackmun's concurring opinion. He stated first that he is "not at all convinced that the Court's facile distinction of *Miller Bros.* . . . [in the principal opinion] is a proper and acceptable distinction."[36] In this statement, he referred to the alleged lack of knowledge by the seller in *Miller Bros.* that the goods were to be used in another state and he directs attention to the fact that the record disclosed that Miller Bros. Co. delivered merchandise of a value of $9,500 to out-of-state customers either by its own delivery trucks or by common carrier. He also chided the Court for its apparent intention "to rest a distinction on the fact that the sales [in Miller Bros.] were made out of state," and observed that "a use tax is imposed only on sales made out-of-state."[37] He concluded by citing *Complete Auto Transit*[38] and *Coloni-*

---

32. 386 U.S. at 761–762.

33. 430 U.S. 551, 97 S.Ct. 1386 (1977), affirming 128 Cal.Rptr. 682, 547 P.2d 458 (1976).

34. 430 U.S. at 562.

35. In Reader's Digest Ass'n v. Mahin, 44 Ill.2d 354, 255 N.E.2d 458 (1970), appeal dismissed 399 U.S. 919 (1970), the taxpayer maintained offices in Illinois to solicit advertising for its magazine. The Association also advertised its books and phonograph records in local

newspapers and over local radio and television stations. Sales of books and records were made only by mail order from the Association's New York headquarters. Held: Association liable for collection of use tax on mail order sales. Appeal to Supreme Court dismissed for want of jurisdiction.

36. 430 U.S. at 562.

37. 430 U.S. at 563.

38. 430 U.S. 274 (1977).

al Pipeline Co.,[39] with the statement that "we have another instance where this Court's past decisions in the tax area are not fully consistent." [40]

At the risk of reading too much into Justice Blackmun's concurring opinion, there is an implication that he may be prepared to reconsider the rationale of both *Miller Bros.* and *Bellas Hess.* His statement can reasonably be interpreted as indicating that he holds the view that exploitation of the market state by mail order sales and delivery by common carrier are sufficient to create a nexus which would justify imposition on the out-of-state vendor of the duty to collect the use tax. The last chapter in this area remains to be written.

III. OTHER PROBLEMS OF STATE TAXATION

A. State Taxation and Equal Protection

1. *Principles of Equal Protection*

A review of the cases involving the issue of equal protection of state tax statutes indicates that the Court generally defers to the judgment of the state legislative bodies. In *Allied Stores of Ohio v. Bowers,*[1] Ohio had adopted a statute apparently to encourage nonresidents to establish distribution warehousing facilities in the state. The Ohio property tax provided generally for taxing all personal property used in business but added a special exemption by providing that "merchandise or agricultural products belonging to a nonresident . . . is not used in business in this state if held in a storage warehouse for storage only." [2] Plaintiff, a resident taxpayer that maintained a warehouse incident to its merchandising operations, challenged the statute as an unreasonable classification in violation of equal protection inasmuch as the exemption dis-

criminated against in-state businesses. The Court sustained the exemption on the ground that the statute was premised on a reasonable legislative purpose, namely, the promotion of the economy of the state. In its decision, the Court stated the applicable principles governing equal protection with respect to state taxation:

> The States have a very wide discretion in the laying of their taxes. When dealing with their proper domestic concerns, and not trenching upon the prerogatives of the National Government or violating the guaranties of the Federal Constitution, the States have the attribute of sovereign powers in devising their fiscal systems to ensure revenue and foster their local interests. Of course, the States, in the exercise of their taxing power, are subject to the requirements of the Equal Protection Clause of the Fourteenth Amendment. But that clause imposes no iron rule of equality, prohibiting the flexibility and variety that are appropriate to reasonable schemes of state taxation. The State may impose different specific taxes upon different trades and professions and may vary the rate of excise upon various products. It is not required to resort to close distinctions or to maintain a precise, scientific uniformity with reference to composition, use or value. . . . "To hold otherwise would be to subject the essential taxing power of the State to an intolerable supervision, hostile to the basic principles of our government and wholly beyond the protection which the general clause of the Fourteenth Amendment was intended to assure."
>
> . . .
>
> But there is a point beyond which the State cannot go without violating the Equal Protection Clause. The State must proceed upon a rational basis and may not resort to a classification that is palpably arbitrary. The rule often has been stated to be that the classification "must rest upon some ground of difference having a fair and substantial relation to the object of the legislation." "If the selection or classification is neither capricious nor arbitrary, and rests upon some reasonable considera-

---

39.   421 U.S. 100 (1975).

40.   430 U.S. at 563.

1.   358 U.S. 522 (1959). See, Sea-Pac Co., Inc. v. State Department of Fisheries, 30 Wn.App. 659, 661, 638 P.2d 92, 94 (1981), citing an earlier edition of this treatise.

2. This statutory provision was subsequently amended to apply only to merchandise shipped from outside the state to be held in storage for shipment to destinations outside the state. 358 U.S. at 523 n. 1.

tion of difference or policy, there is no denial of the equal protection of the law." . . . That a statute may discriminate in favor of a certain class does not render it arbitrary if the discrimination is founded upon a reasonable distinction, or difference in state policy.[3]

2. Some Examples of Application of Equal Protection

The issue of alleged unreasonable classification has been presented in numerous cases, a few of which have been selected for illustration. In *Fox v. Standard Oil Co. of New Jersey*,[4] the Court considered the validity of the West Virginia annual chain store tax which was graduated by brackets according to the number of retail units in the state. The rate began at $2 for a single unit and increased to $250 for each unit in excess of seventy-five. The Court stated that the issue was whether the consequences of the graduation of rates was "so extreme, so disproportionate to benefits, as to be an arbitrary discrimination" between larger chains and smaller chains, or between chains for the sale of gasoline and chains for the sale of other products.

In sustaining the tax, the Court emphasized three factors: (1) the scope of legislative power; (2) the difference in economic power as between large chains and small chains; and (3) the fact that all taxpayers of the same class (or size) were taxed in the same manner. The following extract summarizes the thrust of the decision:

> When the power to tax exists, the extent of the burden is a matter for the discretion of the lawmakers. The subject was fully considered in *Magnano Co. v. Hamilton*, 292 U.S. 40 (1934) decided at the last term. "Even if the tax should destroy a business it would not be made invalid or require compensation upon that ground alone. Those who enter upon a business take that risk." . . . A chain, as we have seen, is a distinctive business species,

with its own capacities and functions. Broadly speaking its opportunities and powers become greater with the number of the component links; and, the greater they become, the more far-reaching are the consequences, both social and economic. For that reason the state may tax the large chains more heavily than the small ones, and upon a graduated basis, as indeed we have already held. . . . Not only may it do this, but it may make the tax so heavy as to discourage multiplication of the units to an extent believed to be inordinate, and by the incidence of the burden develop other forms of industry. . . . In principle there is no distinction between such an exercise of power and the statute upheld in *Magnano Co. v. Hamilton*, . . . whereby sales of butter were fostered and sales of oleomargarine repressed. A motive to build up through legislation the quality of men may be as creditable in the thought of some as a motive to magnify the quantity of trade. Courts do not choose between such values in adjudging legislative powers. They put the choice aside as beyond their lawful competence. "Collateral purposes or motives of a Legislature in levying a tax of a kind within the reach of its lawful power are matters beyond the scope of judicial inquiry." . . . The tax now assailed may have its roots in an erroneous conception of the ills of the body politic or of the efficacy of such a measure to bring about a cure. We have no thought in anything we have written to declare it expedient or even just, or for that matter to declare the contrary. We deal with power only.[5]

Less than two months later, the Court rendered its decision in *Stewart Dry Goods Co. v. Lewis*.[6] The issue in that case was the validity of a Kentucky annual gross sales tax that was imposed on the graduated basis varying from 1/20th of one percent on the first $400,000 of gross sales to one percent on gross sales in excess of $1,000,000. By contrast with its decision in *Standard Oil*, the majority of the Court concluded that the tax was arbitrary and violated principles of

---

3.   Id. at 526–28.

4.   294 U.S. 87 (1935). Examples of other Court decisions sustaining chain store taxes include the following in chronological order: State Board of Tax Commissioners v. Jackson, 283 U.S. 527 (1931) (tax graduated by brackets); Great Atlantic & Pacific Tea

Co. v. Grosjean, 301 U.S. 412 (1937) (applicable rate determined by total number of units including out-of-state stores).

5.   294 U.S. at 99–101.

6.   294 U.S. 550 (1935).

equal protection. The majority conclusion was premised on the following factors: (1) the use of gross sales as the measure of the tax bore no necessary relationship to net profits and ability to pay; and (2) the tax, in effect, operated as a discriminatory sales tax in that a sale of an article by a store in the lowest bracket was taxed at $^1/_{20}$th of one percent while a sale of the same goods in a store in the highest bracket was taxed at one percent. Contrary to the Court's frequent assertions, the majority appeared to step into the arena of legislative policy by suggesting that an income tax or a flat rate sales tax would accomplish the underlying legislative purpose of alleviating the disproportionate burden of the ad valorem property tax borne by the small merchant.[7]

There was a vigorous dissenting opinion by Justice Cardozo who was joined by Justices Brandeis and Stone.[8] The minority expressed the view that the dollar volume of sales of a business was as much a measure of economic power and ability to pay as the number of business units in the case of a chain store tax. In addition, the graduated rate schedule resulted in a fair and equitable allocation of tax burden and was supported by ample precedent.[9] An objective appraisal of *Stewart Dry Goods* leads one to doubt whether the majority view would prevail today.

In *New York Rapid Transit Corp. v. City of New York*,[10] the Court sustained a gross receipts tax on utilities that was earmarked for unemployment relief. Taxpayer objected on several grounds: (1) it was improper to select utility companies for a special tax; (2) business in general should bear this burden which could be shifted to consumers; and (3) the taxpayer could not effectively shift the tax since its fares were fixed by city charter provision and could only be changed by referendum. In response, the Court emphasized that utility companies are a distinct class of business with distinctive advantages and that the method of adjustment of fares of the taxpayer constituted an incidental hardship in a situation where the tax operated uniformly as to all members of the particular class.

In the following circumstances, the Court has sustained the tax in question on the ground that there was a reasonable classification for purposes of equal protection: a higher rate of tax on motor carriers who hauled for hire than that imposed on those who hauled only their own property;[11] a municipal license tax applicable only to commercial warehouses and not to private warehouses;[12] a personal property tax exemption for individuals but not for corporations;[13] and a property tax exemption for widows but not for widowers.[14]

In *Wheeling Steel Corp. v. Glander*,[15] Ohio pursuant to specific statutory provisions imposed an ad valorem property tax on certain intangibles owned by nonresidents and foreign corporations consisting of accounts receivable derived from sales of goods manufactured in Ohio. The sales were made to out-of-state customers and were billed from and collected at out-of-state offices of the vendor. Residents and domes-

7. Id. at 563.

8. Id. at 566–80.

9. The minority opinion concluded with the following statement: "In fine, there may be classification for the purpose of taxation according to the nature of the business. There may be classification according to size and the power and opportunity of which size is an exponent. Such has been the teaching of the law books, at least until today." Id. at 580. Among the cases cited by the minority as precedent were the following: Pacific American Fisheries v. Territory of Alaska, 269 U.S. 269 (1925); Metropolis Theatre Co. v. Chicago, 228 U.S. 61 (1913); Clark v. Titusville, 184 U.S. 329 (1902); Maine v. Grand Trunk Ry. Co., 142 U.S. 217 (1891).

10. 303 U.S. 573 (1938).

11. Dixie Ohio Express Co. v. State Revenue Comm'n, 306 U.S. 72 (1939).

12. Independent Warehouses v. Scheele, 331 U.S. 70 (1947).

13. Lehnhausen v. Lake Shore Auto Parts Co., 410 U.S. 356 (1973), overruling Quaker City Cab Co. v. Pennsylvania, 277 U.S. 389 (1928).

14. Kahn v. Shevin, 416 U.S. 351 (1974) (classification justified by disproportionately heavy economic burden suffered by a widow as compared to a widower; widow may find it necessary to enter the labor market, whereas the widower usually continues in his business or occupation).

15. 337 U.S. 562 (1949).

tic corporations were not taxed upon similar intangibles. Discriminatory treatment of nonresidents and foreign corporations was conceded. Taxpayers affected by the Ohio statute challenged the tax in the state courts as a violation of due process and the commerce clause. On appeal, the Court disposed of the issue as a violation of equal protection in view of the obvious disparity in treatment based solely on the taxpayer's nonresidence.

In 1968, a significant equal protection case relating to charitable organizations was decided by the Court in *WHYY, Inc. v. Borough of Glassboro.*[16] Taxpayer, a noncommercial public television station was organized as a not-for-profit corporation under the laws of Pennsylvania. The corporation registered and qualified to do business in New Jersey where it constructed a transmittal station and tower. Thereafter, the taxpayer applied for property tax exemption for the year 1964. The New Jersey authorities acknowledged that the taxpayer met all the requirements for exemption except that it had not been organized as a New Jersey corporation as required by statute. The New Jersey statute was sustained by the state courts. On appeal, the Supreme Court first noted that inasmuch as the taxpayer-corporation had been admitted to enter New Jersey to carry on its business, it was entitled to equal protection. In reliance on *Wheeling,* the Court proceeded to hold that the New Jersey statute violated equal protection since tax exemption was denied solely on the basis of the taxpayer's state of domicile.

B. State Taxation and the Privileges and Immunities Clause

1. The Privileges and Immunities Test

In the prior discussion of jurisdiction to impose individual income taxes[1] attention was directed to the limitations imposed on the states by the privileges and immunities clause with respect to the equality of treatment of citizens of other states who seek to carry on business activity in the taxing state.[2] The applicable rule is well stated in the early case of *Ward v. Maryland.*[3] Maryland adopted two taxes applicable to vendors of goods. One was applicable to residents of the state and provided a scale of license fees which varied from $15 to $150 depending on the amount of the vendor's stock in trade. The other applied to nonresidents who sold by catalogue or by sample goods that were not produced or manufactured in Maryland. The annual license fee for these vendors was $300. Failure of an out-of-state vendor to obtain a license subjected the offender to a fine of not less than $400 nor more than $600. Ward, a citizen of New Jersey, who sold harness by sample, failed to obtain the required license and was fined $400 under the provisions of the statute. He challenged the statute on the ground that it violated both the commerce clause and the privileges and immunities clause. Although the Court suggested that the Maryland statute violated the commerce clause, it preferred to base its decision solely on the privileges and immunities clause and held the statute invalid as a clear violation of the constitutional proscription. The Court stated its position on the application

---

16.   393 U.S. 117 (1968).

1.   See text at Section II, C, 1, b, supra, discussing Austin v. New Hampshire, 420 U.S. 656 (1975) and Travis v. Yale & Towne Manufacturing Co., 252 U.S. 60 (1920).

2.   U.S.Const. art. IV, § 2: "The citizens of each state shall be entitled to all Privileges and Immunities of Citizens in the several states." The term "citizen"

as used in this clause means a natural person. Consequently, corporations which are artificial persons are not protected by this clause and a state can constitutionally prohibit the admission of a foreign corporation to carry on intrastate business. Paul v. Virginia, 75 U.S. (8 Wall.) 168 (1869).

3.   79 U.S. (12 Wall.) 418 (1870).

of the privileges and immunities clause in the following terms:

> Attempt will not be made to define the words "privileges and immunities," or to specify the rights which they are intended to secure and protect, beyond what may be necessary to the decision of the case before the court. Beyond doubt those words are words of very comprehensive meaning, but it will be sufficient to say that the clause plainly and unmistakably secures and protects the right of a citizen of one State to pass into any other State of the Union for the purpose of engaging in lawful commerce, trade, or business without molestation; to acquire personal property; to take and hold real estate; to maintain actions in the courts of the State; and to be exempt from any higher taxes or excises than are imposed by the State upon its own citizens.
>
> Comprehensive as the power of the States is to lay and collect taxes and excises, it is nevertheless clear, in the judgment of the court, that the power cannot be exercised to any extent in a manner forbidden by the Constitution; and inasmuch as the Constitution provides that the citizens of each State shall be entitled to all privileges and immunities of citizens in the several States, it follows that the defendant might lawfully sell . . . any goods which the permanent residents of the State might sell . . . without being subjected to any higher tax or excise than that exacted by law of such permanent residents.[4]

It is reasonably clear that the *Ward* case could have been decided under the commerce clause in view of the discrimination against the sale of out-of-state goods. That step was not taken until a later date as noted in connection with the fixed-fee license cases.[5]

2. *Illustrative Applications*

The rule of the *Ward* decision has been applied in a series of cases to invalidate discriminatory license fees imposed on nonresidents. These include, chronologically, the following: (1) a Tennessee annual privilege tax of $100 on foreign construction companies having their chief office outside the state as compared to a license fee of $25 on each domestic and foreign construction company with its chief office in Tennessee;[6] (2) a South Carolina licensing fee for the use of shrimp boats in its coastal waters of $2500 for each boat owned by a nonresident as compared with a fee of $25 for each boat owned by a resident;[7] and (3) an Alaska license fee for commercial fisherman of $50 for nonresidents and $5 for residents.[8] In *Toomer v. Witsell*, holding the South Carolina license invalid, the Court made the following perceptive observation on the objective of the privilege and immunities clause:

> The primary purpose of this clause . . . was to help fuse into one Nation a collection of independent, sovereign States. It was designed to insure to a citizen of State A who ventures into State B the same privileges which the citizens of State B enjoy . . . .
>
> In line with this underlying purpose, it was long ago decided that one of the privileges which the clause guarantees to citizens of State A is that of doing business in State B on terms of substantial equality with the citizens of that State.[9]

In *Travelers' Insurance Co. v. Connecticut*,[10] the Court approved a Connecticut statute which on its face appeared to discriminate against nonresident shareholders of Connecticut corporations. Under the statutory provisions, nonresident shareholders were assessed a state tax of 15 mills per dollar on the market value of their shares, but they paid no local property taxes. Resident shareholders, on the other hand, paid no state tax, but were locally assessed on the fair market value of their shares reduced by the proportionate value of all real estate held by the corporation upon which the corporation had paid Connecticut property taxes. Resident shareholders paid their taxes

---

4. Id. at 430.

5. See text at Section II, E, 1, b, supra.

6. Chalker v. Birmingham & N.W. Ry. Co., 249 U.S. 522 (1919) (nonresident was an Alabama citizen engaged in the business of constructing a railroad in Tennessee).

7. Toomer v. Witsell, 334 U.S. 385 (1948).

8. Mullaney v. Anderson, 342 U.S. 415 (1952).

9. 334 U.S. at 395–396 (footnote omitted).

10. 185 U.S. 364 (1902).

to the respective municipalities in which they resided and the tax rates varied among the different communities. On the basis of this analysis of the factual circumstances, the Court concluded that the statute did not operate in such a manner as to indicate an intention to create unjust discrimination against nonresidents.

C. State Taxes and Intergovernmental Immunity

1. Introduction

The genesis of the doctrine of intergovernmental immunity is found in the decision in *McCulloch v. Maryland*.[1] In that case, which held a discriminatory state tax on the Bank of the United States to be invalid, chief Justice Marshall made his notable observation that "the power to tax involves the power to destroy."[2] From this beginning, the doctrine of intergovernmental immunity expanded during the following century not only to insulate direct government functions from taxation but also to insulate from taxation secondary or derivative transactions relating to the performance of governmental functions.[3] The doctrine reached its zenith when it was extended to exempt the employ-

ees of the state and federal governments from income taxes imposed by the other.[4] This was followed by the extension of the exemption to those leasing government lands.[5]

Although some limits upon the expansion of the doctrine had been established in the early 1930's,[6] reversal of the doctrine did not occur until the later years of that decade. In a brief span of sixteen months, the Court decided a series of four cases, each involving an income tax, which abruptly turned the tide.

2. Income Taxes

James v. Dravo Contracting Co.,[7] the first of the income tax cases, involved the application of a West Virginia gross sales and income tax to the receipts derived by a contractor under a construction contract with the federal government. In sustaining the tax, the Court relied on its prior decision in *Metcalf & Eddy v. Mitchell*,[8] decided in 1926, in which it had upheld the application of the federal income tax to the income of an independent contractor who had performed contractual services for the State of Massachusetts. In *Metcalf & Eddy*, the Court had

---

1. 17 U.S. (4 Wheat.) 316 (1819).

2. Id. at 431. The doctrine of intergovernmental immunity has been stated by the Court in the following terms:

> "The very nature of our constitutional system of dual sovereign governments is such as impliedly to prohibit the federal government from taxing the instrumentalities of a state government, and in a similar manner to limit the power of the states to tax the instrumentalities of the federal government."

Metcalf & Eddy v. Mitchell, 269 U.S. 514, at 521 (1926).

In Memphis Bank & Trust Co. v. Garner, 103 S.Ct. 692 (1983) the Court invoked the *McCulloch* rule to invalidate a discriminatory Tennessee bank tax that applied to interest on federal obligations but exempted interest on Tennessee obligations.

3. It is significant to note that subsequent limitations on the doctrine of intergovernmental immunity were recognized by the Court during the Great Depression. At that time both the states and federal government were seeking additional revenues to meet the added burdens imposed by adverse economic conditions.

4. Dobbins v. Commissioner of Erie County, 41 U.S. (16 Pet.) 435 (1842) (state income tax on federal em-

ployee held unconstitutional); Collector v. Day, 78 U.S. (11 Wall.) 113 (1871) (federal income tax on state judge held unconstitutional). These decisions were premised on the rationale that an income tax on the salaries of the employees constituted a tax on the means by which each government exercised its powers.

5. Gillespie v. Oklahoma, 257 U.S. 501 (1922) (lessees of restricted Indian lands immune to state income taxes); Burnet v. Coronado Oil & Gas Co., 285 U.S. 393 (1935) (lessee of state school lands exempt from federal income taxes).

6. See Educational Films Corp. of America v. Ward, 282 U.S. 379 (1931) (upholding a state franchise tax measured by income including royalties on federally granted copyrights); Alward v. Johnson, 282 U.S. 509 (1931) (sustaining a state tax on gross revenues derived from a federal contract to transport the mail); Pacific Co. v. Johnson, 285 U.S. 480 (1932) (holding valid a corporate franchise tax measured in part by interest on exempt Government bonds); Fox Film Corp. v. Doyal, 286 U.S. 123 (1932) (allowing a gross receipts tax measured entirely by the amount of royalties received under federal copyrights).

7. 302 U.S. 134 (1937).

8. 269 U.S. 514 (1926).

distinguished the position of a private contractor from that of a government employee in determining the applicability of the doctrine of governmental immunity. With respect to the argument that the state tax increased the cost to the federal government, the Court in *Dravo* noted that the gross sales and income tax paid by the contractor were comparable to the property taxes which were paid on the property used in performing the contract, and constituted part of the cost of doing the work.[9]

Two additional income tax cases involved the exemption of state and federal employees from income taxes imposed by the non-employer government. In *Helvering v. Gerhardt,*[10] the Court sustained the imposition of the federal income tax on the salaries of employees of the Port of New York Authority; and in *Graves v. New York ex rel. O'Keefe,*[11] the Court completed the reversal of prior doctrine by sustaining application of the New York income tax on the salary of an employee of the federal government. *Helvering v. Mountain Producers Corp.*[12] completed the chain of reversal of the immunity doctrine in the income tax field by overruling the prior decisions which had extended income tax immunity to lessees of state and federal lands.[13]

3. Sales and Use Taxes

Paralleling the income tax cases, the same process of extension, and then limitation of the immunity doctrine occurred with respect to sales and use taxes.[14] In reversing the extension of the doctrine, and in the absence of specific Congressional legislation, the Court concluded that a state sales tax affecting federal procurement contracts is permissible if the *illegal incidence* of the tax falls on one other than the federal government, notwithstanding the fact that the economic burden may actually be borne by the federal fisc. This rule evolved from the decision in *Alabama v. King & Boozer,*[15] wherein the Court sustained a state sales tax on lumber purchased by a contractor in the performance of a cost-plus contract with the United States. Under the applicable state statute the supplier was required to add the tax to his sale price and collect the tax from the contractor-purchaser. In turn, the contractor-purchaser was reimbursed by the federal government as provided by the terms of the procurement contract. In reaching its decision, the Court emphasized that the contractor was not an agent of and could not pledge the credit of the federal government, and that the contractor, not the government, was legally liable for the purchase price of the materials, including the state sales tax. Reimbursement of these costs was deemed no more an infringement of the immunity of the federal government from state taxation than the tax laid on the contractor's gross receipts in *Dravo.*[16]

The same principle is applicable with respect to federal excise taxes on goods sold to a state. If the legal incidence of the federal excise is on the vendor, the tax is valid.

9. 302 U.S. at 160.

10. 304 U.S. 405 (1938).

11. 306 U.S. 466 (1939).

12. 303 U.S. 376 (1938) (overruling *Gillespie* and *Coronado* cited in note 5).

13. Congress has also acted to end the exemption in any remaining cases in which the question might arise. The Buck Act, 4 U.S.C.A. §§ 105–110, provides that no person shall be relieved from liability for any income tax levied by a state solely because he resides in a federal area or receives income from services performed in such an area. See Howard v. Commissioners of Sinking Fund of Louisville, 344 U.S. 624 (1953) (sustaining occupational license tax imposed by municipality on gross receipts of taxpayers employed at naval ordinance plant).

14. The following are examples of early cases that broadly extended tax immunity with respect to sales taxes: Panhandle Oil Co. v. Mississippi, 277 U.S. 218 (1928) (state sales tax was held inapplicable to sales of gasoline made to the United States for use in its motor vehicles); Graves v. Texas Co., 298 U.S. 393 (1936) (holding invalid a state excise tax on gasoline withdrawn from storage and sold to the United States); Indian Motorcycle Co. v. United States, 283 U.S. 570 (1931) (federal manufacturer's excise tax was invalidated in its application to a sale of motorcycles for use by a municipal police force).

15. 314 U.S. 1 (1941). Accord, Curry v. United States, 314 U.S. 14 (1941). These cases effectively overruled *Panhandle Oil Co.* and *Texas Co.* cited in the preceding footnote.

16. 314 U.S. at 14.

Thus, federal taxes on liquor sold to state-operated liquor stores,[17] and the federal tax on gasoline sold to a state are both valid.[18]

Thirteen years after *King & Boozer*, a majority of the Court, in *Kern-Limerick, Inc. v. Scurlock*,[19] revived the immunity doctrine to bar a state sales tax on the sale of machinery to a cost-plus contractor engaged in the construction of a naval ammunition depot. In *Kern-Limerick*, the Navy had provided in its contract that the "Contractor shall act as the purchasing agent of the government" in the purchase of materials, and further that the "Government shall be directly liable to the vendors for the purchase price."[20] In light of these provisions, the majority concluded that "the purchaser under this contract was the United States," and that by reason of established principles of sovereign immunity "this Court cannot subject the Government or its official agencies to state taxation without a clear congressional mandate."[21]

In a vigorous dissent, the minority asserted that the majority, in effect, had overruled *King & Boozer*. This view was premised on the ground that government agencies and their employees cannot delegate "to private persons power to buy goods for the Government and pledge its credit to pay for them." For this reason, the minority concluded that the provisions of the Navy contract were ineffective to shift the legal incidence of the sales tax from the contractor to the government.

Recently, in *United States v. New Mexico*,[22] the Court in a unanimous decision returned to the basic premise of *Dravo* and *King & Boozer* by sustaining a New Mexico gross receipts and compensating use tax that had been imposed on materials sold to cost and cost-plus contractors engaged in performing management, maintenance, repair and construction work at various atomic energy facilities of the federal government. Each contract provided that the contractor "acts as an agent" of the Government in the purchase of property and in the disbursement of Government funds advanced to finance such purchases. Title to materials purchased vested directly in the Government and the Government held complete control over the disposition of the property.

After noting "the confusing nature of our precedents,"[23] the Court stated that "a narrow approach to governmental tax immunity" is necessary to give "full range to each sovereign's taxing authority," and observed that traditional agency concepts can have no application in resolving this issue.[24] For a state tax to fail, the tax must be *directly* upon the United States.[25] Government contractors, the court concluded, are not instrumentalities of the federal government; therefore, the acquisition and use of property by a contractor in the performance of a Government contract is the conduct of a commercial enterprise that constitutes a separate and distinct taxable activity.

As previously indicated, the federal government can provide immunity from state taxation by statute expressly forbidding the states to levy sales or any other taxes.[26] Moreover, the court has also held that such power does not depend on the nature of the activity Congress seeks to exempt.[27]

---

17. Ohio v. Helvering, 292 U.S. 360 (1934); South Carolina v. United States, 199 U.S. 437 (1905).

18. See notes 15 and 16.

19. 347 U.S. 110 (1954).

20. 347 U.S. at 112, fn. 2.

21. 347 U.S. at 122.

22. 455 U.S. 720 (1982).

23. 455 U.S. at 733.

24. 455 U.S. at 735–36.

25. E.g., United States v. Mississippi Tax Comm'n, 421 U.S. 599 (1975) (invalidating a state tax on liquor sold to military installations, the Court holding that the legal incidence of the tax was on the United States); Federal Land Bank of St. Paul v. Bismarck Lumber Co., 314 U.S. 95 (1941) (state law required the sales tax to be passed on to the purchaser, in this case an instrumentality of the federal government).

26. Carson v. Roan-Anderson Co., 342 U.S. 232 (1952).

27. Federal Land Bank of St. Paul v. Bismarck Lumber Co., 314 U.S. 95 (1941).

An interesting governmental immunity question was presented in *Montana v. United States*[28] relating to the application of a Montana tax of one percent on the gross receipts of "public contractors." Public contractors were defined to include all persons who perform contracts for the State of Montana, its subdivisions and the federal government. The tax did not apply to private construction work. Moreover, public contractors were allowed to credit the gross receipts tax against Montana personal property taxes and the Montana income tax. The substantive issue was whether the gross receipts tax on public contractors—state, local, and federal—but not on private contractors resulted in discrimination against the federal government contrary to the rule established by *Phillips Chemical Co.*[29] as applied in *County of Fresno.*[30] Contention that the tax on public contractors was discriminatory against the federal government was premised on the fact that when a *state* contractor increased his price to the state by the amount of the gross receipts tax, the state in effect received reimbursement for this increased price in the form of the gross receipts tax on the contract price. Although the gross receipts tax was credited against personal property and income taxes, the state was not out-of-pocket. By contrast, the federal government was required to reimburse its contractors for the gross receipts tax through an increased contract price with no way of recovering any portion of the additional out-of-pocket amount. Governmental subdivisions of Montana were in the same position as the federal government with respect to out-of-pocket costs.

In *Montana*, the federal government directed one of its contractors to initiate a suit in the state courts to challenge the validity of the tax. Shortly thereafter, the government instituted this suit in United States District Court to challenge the tax. By stipulation, the parties continued the District Court proceedings pending the decision of the state court. The Montana Supreme Court unanimously sustained the tax.[31] Thereafter, a three-judge District Court considered the instant case on the merits and the majority struck down the tax as violative of the immunity granted the federal government under the supremacy clause. The majority based its decision on the ground that, since private contractors were not subject to the tax, the credit provisions resulted in singling out federal contractors for taxation. The dissenting judge took two alternative positions: First, that inasmuch as the federal government was directly involved in litigating the identical issue in the state court, collateral estoppel applied to bar the federal government from again challenging the tax in this proceeding; and second, that since municipal and state contractors as well as federal contractors were subject to the tax, there was no discrimination under the rule of *Phillips Chemical Co.* On appeal, the Court did not reach the substantive issue; instead, it held that there were no circumstances to bar application of the rule of collateral estoppel enunciated by the dissenting judge below. Thus, the state court decision sustaining the tax was allowed to prevail on this procedural ground.[32]

---

28. 440 U.S. 147 (1979).

29. Phillips Chemical Co. v. Dumas Independent School District, 361 U.S. 376 (1960). (See text at Section III, C, 4, infra).

30. United States v. County of Fresno, 429 U.S. 452 (1977). In *County of Fresno*, the Court emphasized that there is no risk of abuse of the state's taxing power with respect to the federal government if other constituents of the state are subject to the same tax, since they can be expected to impose a political check on the state legislature against oppressive taxation.

31. Peter Kiewit Sons' Co. v. State Bd. of Equalization, 161 Mont. 140, 505 P.2d 102 (1973) (*Kiewit I*) (sus-

taining distinction between public and private contractors as consistent with Supremacy and Equal Protection Clauses); Peter Kiewit Sons' Co. v. Department of Revenue, 166 Mont. 260, 531 P.2d 1327 (1975) (*Kiewit II*) (dismissed a second suit as barred by principles of collateral estoppel and res judicata).

32. 437 F.Supp. 354 (D.Mont.1977) (three judge court), reversed 440 U.S. 147 (1979).

Contrast Washington v. United States, 103 S.Ct. 1344 (1983), a 5 to 4 decision. In this case the Court considered the validity of a Washington sales tax that distinguished between federal and nonfederal construction projects. In the case of nonfederal projects, the sales

4. *Property Taxes*

Since *McCulloch v. Maryland,* it has been the established rule under the supremacy clause that property owned by the federal government is exempt from state and local property taxes.[33] This is the rule unless Congress expressly permits such taxation or authorizes payments in lieu thereof.[34]

Where the government leases its property to private persons for business or personal use, a question arises as to whether the immunity doctrine should bar local taxes on such use. In a series of cases decided in 1958 which involved application of the Michigan statutes, the Court held that lessees of government-owned manufacturing facilities were validly subject to nondiscriminatory property-use taxes on the value of the government facilities used for business purposes.[35] In reaching this conclusion, the Court emphasized the fact that the property-user tax imposed on lessees of tax-exempt property merely served to equalize the tax burden relative to those who leased similar facilities from non-exempt owners.

The Court applied the rule of the Michigan cases in *United States v. County of Fresno*[36] to sustain a nondiscriminatory Califor-

nia annual use or property tax on possessory interests in improvements located on tax-exempt land. In this case, the tax was applied to the rental value of government-owned homes located in National Forests and furnished to employees of the Forest Service as part of their compensation.

5. *Franchise Taxes*

Inherent in the doctrine of governmental immunity and the supremacy clause is the exemption of government obligations from state taxation.[37] For many years, the Congress has expressly prohibited state property taxes on Government obligations and state income taxes on the interest thereon.[38]

There is an important exception, however, with respect to "nondiscriminatory franchise or other nonproperty taxes in lieu thereof imposed on corporations." Thus, the issue in the application of state statutes relating to corporations is whether the tax is a franchise tax or a property tax. If the subject of the tax is the corporate franchise, government obligations or the interest thereon may be included in the measure of the tax.[39] But if the subject of the tax is the capital or the property of the corporation, the tax will be

---

tax was imposed on the landowner and based on the full contract price. In the case of nonfederal projects, however, the tax was imposed on the contractor and based solely on the cost of materials purchased for the project. The Court sustained the tax as applied to federal government projects on the ground that the tax did not impose a discriminatory economic burden on the federal government.

33. E.g., Van Brocklin v. Tennessee, 117 U.S. 151 (1886).

34. Id. at 175.

35. United States v. City of Detroit, 355 U.S. 466 (1958); United States v. Township of Muskegon, 355 U.S. 484 (1958). The Court reached the same conclusion with respect to inventories of raw materials, work-in-process, and finished goods held by a private manufacturer under a government procurement contract which provided that title to the property was vested in the federal government. City of Detroit v. Murray Corp., 355 U.S. 489 (1958).

But the state tax must not discriminate against lessees of government property. In Phillips Chemical Co. v. Dumas Independent School District, 361 U.S. 376

(1960), the Court held invalid a Texas statute which imposed greater tax burdens on lessees of government-owned property than those imposed on lessees of state-owned property.

36. 429 U.S. 452 (1977).

37. Weston v. Charleston, 27 U.S. (2 Pet.) 449 (1829).

38. 31 U.S.C.A. § 742:

"Except as otherwise provided by law, all stocks, bonds, Treasury notes, and other obligations of the United States, shall be exempt from taxation by or under State or municipal or local authority. This exemption extends to every form of taxation that would require that either the obligations or the interest thereon, or both, be considered, directly or indirectly, in the computation of the tax, except nondiscriminatory franchise or other nonproperty taxes in lieu thereof imposed on corporations and except estate taxes or inheritance taxes."

39. Werner Machine Co. v. Director of Division of Taxation, 350 U.S. 492 (1956).

deemed an invalid tax on the government obligations.[40]

6. Death Taxes

The doctrine of intergovernmental immunity has not affected the power of either federal or state government to impose death taxes upon the transfer of governmental obligations.[41] Thus, a state can impose a death tax upon a bequest of federal obligations,[42] and the federal government can impose a death tax upon a bequest of a state obligation.[43] The rationale of these decisions is that a death tax is a tax on the privilege of transferring property at death or a tax on the privilege of inheriting property and is not a direct tax on the government obligations. Similarly, a state may impose a death tax on a bequest to the federal government[44] and the federal government may impose a death tax on a bequest to a state or local governmental unit.[45]

7. Governmental vs. Proprietary Functions

Taxation of essential state or federal governmental functions by the other would, of course, violate the doctrine of intergovernmental immunity and disrupt our federal system. There are certain functions, however, which are not essentially governmental, but rather proprietary (business) in nature, and these may be the proper subject of taxation. For example, the following state activities have been held properly subject to federal taxation: state sales of mineral waters;[46] sales of liquor in state-owned liquor stores;[47] state operations of a railroad;[48] and municipally operated parks and bathing beaches.[49]

A significant question of intergovernmental immunity was considered in *Massachusetts v. United States*,[50] wherein the Court sustained an annual federal registration tax imposed on all civil aircraft that fly in the navigable airspace of the United States as applied to aircraft owned by a State and used exclusively for police functions. The Court relied on its decision in *Evansville-Vanderburgh Airport Authority v. Delta Airlines, Inc.*[51] and emphasized the following aspects of the tax: (1) as a user fee, the tax was nondiscriminatory; (2) it was based on fair approximation of use; and (3) it was not shown to be excessive in relation to the cost of benefits conferred. On these grounds, the Court concluded that there was no violation of the rule of implied immunity of a state government from federal taxation.

By contrast with the supremacy of the federal government, the states do not have as broad a latitude in the taxation of federal activities. For example, governmental immunity has been applied to invalidate a state tax on liquor sold to Government military installations.[52] As previously indicated, Congress has the power to designate those functions of the federal government which may or may not be subjected to state taxation.[53]

---

40. Society for Savings v. Bowers, 349 U.S. 143 (1955); New Jersey Realty Title Insurance Co. v. Division of Tax Appeals, 338 U.S. 665 (1950).

41. See note 38 for express Congressional authorization of estate and inheritance taxes upon United States obligations. 31 U.S.C.A. § 742.

42. Plummer v. Coler, 178 U.S. 115 (1900).

43. Greiner v. Lewellyn, 258 U.S. 384 (1922).

44. United States v. Perkins, 163 U.S. 625 (1896). Inasmuch as the devolution of property at death is within the exclusive control of the states, a state can prohibit testamentary gifts to the federal government. United States v. Burnison, 339 U.S. 87 (1950).

45. Snyder v. Bettman, 190 U.S. 249 (1903).

46. New York v. United States, 326 U.S. 572 (1946).

47. Ohio v. Helvering, 292 U.S. 360 (1934); South Carolina v. United States, 199 U.S. 437 (1905).

48. California v. Anglim, 37 F.Supp. 663 (1941), 129 F.2d 455, cert. denied 317 U.S. 669 (1942).

49. Wilmette Park District v. Campbell, 338 U.S. 411 (1949) (federal admissions tax).

50. 435 U.S. 444 (1978).

51. 405 U.S. 707 (1972) (sustaining state and local government airport-user fees). See text at Section II, A, 3, d, supra.

52. United States v. Mississippi Tax Comm'n, 421 U.S. 599 (1975).

53. Federal Land Bank of St. Paul v. Bismarck Lumber Co., 314 U.S. 95 (1941). In this connection, see 12 U.S.C.A. § 548 (as amended by P.L. 91–156) that lifts the tax immunity previously available to national banks by providing that for tax purposes "a national bank shall be treated as a bank organized and existing

With respect to federal savings and loan associations, Congress has granted state and local governments broad authority to impose any taxes provided such taxes are not "greater than that imposed . . . on other *similar* local mutual or cooperative thrift and home financing institutions." [54] In *First Federal Savings & Loan Association of Boston v. State Tax Comm'n*,[55] it was contended that the Massachusetts income tax violated the federal statutory provisions by discriminating against federally chartered savings and loan associations. The challenge to the Massachusetts tax was premised on two bases: (1) that state savings and loan associations were allowed greater deductions for additions to their reserves than federal associations; and (2) that credit unions, which allegedly compete with savings and loan associations, were wholly exempt from the tax. On the basis of this second point, it was contended that federal savings and loan associations should also be exempt.

The Court denied both objections and sustained the Massachusetts tax. As to the first point, the Court noted that the difference in the allowed deduction for additions to reserves turned on a variation in federal and state regulatory practices and not on the provisions of the Massachusetts income tax which included a neutral standard for the deduction. Moreover, the record did not indicate that in "practical operation" federal associations had suffered either a significant handicap or a competitive disadvantage. As to the second argument, the Court noted that credit unions are not "similar" to federal savings and loan associations since the former are required by law to give prefer-

ence to small personal loans. By contrast, the primary lending role of federal savings and loan associations is "to provide for the financing of homes."

D. Prohibitory State Taxes

1. Due Process Considerations Under Fourteenth Amendment

Imposition of a state tax which operates to prohibit the activity taxed presents a due process issue. If a prohibitory state tax clears the hurdle of the enacting state constitution, it is unlikely to fall under the due process clause of the fourteenth amendment. In *A. Magnano Co. v. Hamilton*,[1] a prohibitory tax of 15 cents per pound imposed by the State of Washington upon all butter substitutes was sustained over the objection that it constituted a taking of taxpayer's property contrary to due process.

In *Magnano*, the Court made it amply clear that if a state statute by its terms is a revenue measure, the language of the statute is controlling and it is inappropriate for the Court to consider underlying legislative motives. This point was forcefully stated in the decision:

The statute here under review is in form plainly a taxing act, with nothing in its terms to suggest that it was intended to be anything else. It must be construed, and the intent and meaning of the Legislature ascertained, from the language of the act, and the words used therein are to be given their ordinary meaning unless the context shows that they are differently used. . . . If the tax imposed had been 5 cents instead of 15 cents per pound, no one, probably, would have thought of challenging its constitutionality or of suggesting that under the guise of imposing a tax another and

under the laws of the State or other jurisdiction within which its principal office is located."

In Chase Manhattan Bank v. City of New York, 440 U.S. 447, 99 S.Ct. 1201 (1979), the Court held invalid a commercial rent and occupancy tax imposed on national banks during the period June 1, 1970 through May 31, 1972. Public Law 91–156 enabled states to impose certain pre-existing taxes on national banks provided the state legislature authorized imposition of the taxes by subsequent "affirmative action". In this case, the Court concluded that subsequent legislation merely in-

creasing the rate of the tax did not constitute *the affirmative legislative action* required by P.L. 91–156, namely, consideration by the state legislature of "the impact of such taxes on the existing balance of taxation between national and state banks." 440 U.S. at 449, 99 S.Ct. at 1202.

54. 12 U.S.C.A. § 1464(h) (emphasis added).

55. 437 U.S. 255 (1978).

1. 292 U.S. 40 (1934).

different power had in fact been exercised. If a contrary conclusion were reached in the present case, it could rest upon nothing more than the single premise that the amount of the tax is so excessive that it will bring about the destruction of appellant's business, a premise which, standing alone, this court heretofore has uniformly rejected as furnishing no juridical ground for striking down a taxing act. . . .

From the beginning of our government, the courts have sustained taxes although imposed with the collateral intent of effecting ulterior ends which, considered apart, were beyond the constitutional power of the lawmakers to realize by legislation directly addressed to their accomplishment. Those decisions, as the foregoing discussion discloses, rule the present case.[2]

2. Conflict in State Court Decisions

State court decisions are in conflict in the application of state due process considerations to prohibitory taxes upon otherwise lawful or harmless businesses. Some courts adhere to the "federal" rule as expressed in *Magnano* and will not consider the underlying legislative motives if the tax is in form a revenue measure.[3]

Other state courts, however, have adopted the rule that the legislature may not prohibit indirectly, by exercise of the taxing power,

2. Id. at 46–47.

3. E.g., Ludwig v. Harston, 65 Wyo. 134, 197 P.2d 252 (1948) (sustaining a prohibitory tax on oleomargarine).

4. E.g. Flynn v. Horst, 356 Pa. 20, 51 A.2d 54 (1947) (holding a prohibitory tax on oleomargarine to be invalid).

1. See Chapter 16, section II, G, infra. For a comprehensive and historical treatment of the taxation of Indians for the period through 1956, see U.S. Dept. of Interior, Federal Indian Law, ch. X (1958).

2. McClanahan v. State Tax Comm'n, 411 U.S. 164, 165 (1973).

3. Historically, this doctrine which combines the principles of federal preemption and tribal sovereignty is traceable to two early cases. The New York Indians, 72 U.S. (5 Wall.) 761 (1866) and the Kansas Indians, 72 U.S. (5 Wall.) 737 (1866). In both of these cases, the Court barred the states of New York and Kansas from imposing property taxes upon Indian-held lands which were protected by treaty from state taxation.

an activity which cannot be prohibited directly by the exercise of the police power. In these jurisdictions, the validity of the statute or ordinance is determined by the nature of the business or activity that is subject to the prohibitory tax.[4]

E. State Taxation of American Reservation Indians

1. Introduction

The unique status of American Indians under the Constitution is discussed in Chapter 16.[1] Article I, Section 8, clause 3 provides that "Congress shall have Power to regulate Commerce . . . with the Indian Tribes;" and Article II, Section 2 provides for exercise of the treaty power by the President with the advice and consent of the Senate. Under these constitutional provisions, the Court has concluded that, with respect to the taxation of reservation Indians, a state cannot interfere with matters "which the relevant treaty and statutes leave to the exclusive province of the Federal Government and the Indians themselves."[2] Thus, the doctrines of federal pre-emption and Indian sovereignty are deemed controlling in resolving the issue of state jurisdiction to tax.[3]

It should be added that for a time the basis of tax exemption of reservation Indians was premised upon the doctrine of immunity of federal instrumentalities. E.g., United States v. Rickert, 188 U.S. 432 (1903). The high-water mark in the application of the federal instrumentality doctrine was reached in Gillespie v. Oklahoma, 257 U.S. 501 (1922) where the Court extended the concept to exempt a non-Indian lessee of restricted and allotted lands from an Oklahoma income tax upon income derived by the lessee from the sale of his share of the oil produced under the lease. With the waning of the doctrine of intergovernmental immunity, the *Gillespie* decision was overruled in a subsequent decision involving imposition of the federal income tax upon income earned by a lessee of oil and gas interests owned by the State of Wyoming. Helvering v. Mountain Producers Corp., 303 U.S. 376 (1938). Following the decision in *Mountain Producers*, the Court in Oklahoma Tax Comm'n v. Texas Co., 336 U.S. 342 (1949), sustained a state gross production tax and a state excise tax imposed on a non-Indian lessee of Indian lands held in trust by the United States for certain Indian Tribes.

The Court has recognized [4] the following quotation from a recent case as an accurate summation of the principles defining the power of the states to tax reservation Indians, their property and business activities on federally established reservations:

> [I]n the special area of state taxation, absent cession of jurisdiction or other federal statutes permitting it, there has been no satisfactory authority for taxing Indian reservation lands or Indian income from activities carried on within the boundaries of the reservation, and *McClanahan* . . . lays to rest any doubt in this respect by holding that such taxation is not permissible absent congressional consent.[5]

This statement of principle as to the power of the states to impose taxes with respect to reservation Indians may be illustrated by summarizing the results of the Court's decisions as to various types of taxes.[6]

2. Property Taxes

With respect to property taxes, states are barred from taxing tribal land, lands individually held within a reservation, improvements upon such lands, and the personal property of Indians located thereon. Two recent cases are illustrative. In *Bryan v. Itasca County*,[7] the Court held that Minnesota could not tax a mobile home owned by a reservation Indian and located on reservation land held in trust by the United States for the Chippewa tribe. In this decision, the Court overturned the Minnesota Supreme Court's conclusion that the federal statutes by implication granted the states power to tax.[8] Similarly, in *Moe v. Confederated Salish & Kootenai Tribes*,[9] the Court held invalid a Montana personal property tax on motor vehicles owned by Indians residing on a reservation.[10]

3. Business License, Gross Receipts and Sales Taxes

In *Warren Trading Post Co. v. Arizona State Tax Commission*,[11] the Court held invalid an Arizona tax of 2% on the "gross proceeds of sales, or gross income" of the taxpayer which had been licensed by the federal government to operate a retail business on the Navajo Indian Reservation. The decision was premised on the principle of federal pre-emption, and specifically on the ground that to permit the tax would "frustrate the evident congressional purpose of ensuring that no burden shall be imposed upon Indian traders for trading with Indians on reservations except as authorized by Acts of Congress or by valid regulations promulgated under those Acts."[12] Relying on *Warren Trading Post*, the Court also invalidated the imposition of Arizona motor carrier license and use fuel taxes on a non-Indian logging company that operated solely on reservation lands harvesting timber for the White Mountain Apache Tribe.[13]

---

4. Bryan v. Itasca County, 426 U.S. 373, 376 (1976).

5. Mescalero Apache Tribe v. Jones, 411 U.S. 145, 148 (1973). The Court was referring to McClanahan v. Arizona State Tax Comm'n, 411 U.S. 164 (1973).

6. Indian Tribes, as sovereign units, have the power to impose taxes on property or business activities on Indian reservations. See discussion at Section III, E, 6, infra. Congress by reason of its paramount authority, has the power to impose federal taxes on reservation Indians. See Choteau v. Burnet, 283 U.S. 691 (1931) (Osage Indian holding certificate of competency held subject to federal income tax on share of income received from tribal mineral leases held in trust by the United States). Finally, property off the reservation which is independently owned by an American Indian, and income earned off the reservation are generally subject to state taxation.

7. 426 U.S. 373 (1976).

8. The statute under consideration was 28 U.S.C.A. § 1360.

9. 425 U.S. 463 (1976).

10. See also Washington v. Confederated Tribes of the Colville Indian Reservation, 447 U.S. 134, rehearing denied 448 U.S. 911 (1980) where the Court held that the State of Washington could not impose a property tax in the guise of an excise tax on mobile homes, campers and trailers owned by tribes and their members and used both on and off reservations.

11. 380 U.S. 685 (1965).

12. Id. at 691. The pre-emption doctrine was also applied by the Court in Central Machinery Co. v. Arizona State Tax Comm'n, 448 U.S. 160, 100 S.Ct. 2592 (1980) to invalidate imposition of a state sales tax with respect to an on-reservation sale of farm machinery to reservation Indians by a non-Indian vendor.

13. White Mountain Apache Tribe v. Bracker, 448 U.S. 136 (1980). In a subsequent case, the Court followed *White Mountain* to bar imposition of a New Mexico tax on the gross receipts of a non-Indian construction company received from a tribal school board

Similarly, in *Moe v. Confederated Salish & Kootenai Tribes*,[14] the Court held invalid a Montana cigarette retailer's license tax, and a cigarette sales tax imposed on tribal members who sold cigarettes on the reservation to reservation Indians. But the Court also held that there was no conflict with congressional policy in requiring the reservation vendor to collect and remit the cigarette sales tax on sales made to non-Indians.[15]

A more difficult issue was presented in *Mescalero Apache Tribe v. Jones*.[16] In that case, the Tribe operated a ski resort on tax exempt non-reservation land leased from the United States Forest Service which bordered their reservation. A few ski trails extended into the reservation, but all the buildings and equipment were located on Forest Service lands. In constructing the facilities, the Indians made out-of-state purchases of certain materials which were used to construct ski lifts at the resort. New Mexico imposed its sales tax on the gross receipts derived from the operation of the ski resort and its compensating use tax on the purchase price of materials used to construct the ski lifts. The Tribe challenged both taxes on three principal grounds: (1) the federal government had exclusive jurisdiction over the Tribe for all purposes; (2) the resort was exempt from taxation as a federal instrumentality; (3) the Indian Reorganization Act under which the venture was undertaken specifically provided for tax exemption. The Court sustained a sales tax on gross receipts, noting that the income-producing activity was off the reservation and that there was no bar to state taxation under either the federal statutes or the Act by which New Mexico was admitted as a State. However, the Court held the use tax invalid since the materials had been permanently attached to the realty. Under the provisions of the Indian Reorganization Act, it was provided that any lands or rights acquired thereunder "shall be taken in the name of the United States in trust for the Indian tribe . . . for which the land is acquired, and such lands or rights shall be exempt from State and local taxation." [17] The Court recognized that a use tax is not a property tax, but concluded that "use of permanent improvements . . . is so intimately connected with use of the land itself that an explicit provision relieving the latter of state tax burdens must be construed to encompass an exemption for the former." [18]

4. Income Taxes

In 1973, the Court for the first time considered the issue as to whether a state could validly impose a personal income tax on a reservation Indian whose entire income was derived from reservation sources. In *McClanahan v. State Tax Commission*,[19] the Court formulated the currently prevailing principle stated above with respect to state jurisdiction to tax reservation Indians, and held that under the relevant treaty and statutory provisions Arizona had no jurisdiction to impose its income tax upon Navaho Indians whose income was derived from reservation sources.

5. Death Taxes

In *Oklahoma Tax Commission v. United States* [20] the Court considered the question of jurisdiction of a state to impose death taxes with respect to the estates of three deceased members of the Five Civilized Tribes who were not reservation Indians. The properties of the estates of the decedents included the following items: (1) land exempt from direct taxation; (2) land not exempt

---

for construction of a school for Indian children. Ramah Navajo School Bd., Inc. v. Bureau of Revenue of New Mexico, 102 S.Ct. 3394 (1982).

14. 425 U.S. 463 (1976).

15. This principle was similarly applied in Washington v. Confederated Tribes of the Colville Indian Reservation, 447 U.S. 134, rehearing denied 448 U.S. 911 (1980).

16. 411 U.S. 145 (1973).

17. 25 U.S.C.A. § 465.

18. 411 U.S. at 158.

19. 411 U.S. 164 (1973).

20. 319 U.S. 598 (1943).

from direct taxation; (3) restricted cash and securities held for the Indians in trust by the Secretary of the Interior; and (4) miscellaneous personal properties and insurance. The aggregate value of the three estates was $1,245,000 of which approximately 90% consisted of cash and securities. Apparently, the cash and securities were derived from oil and gas production upon the Indian lands and by specific Congressional act these minerals were subject "to all State and Federal taxes." [21] With this background, the Court found no general Congressional intent to exempt the entire estate of these Indians from state death taxes, and held that only the lands exempt from direct taxation were excluded from the tax. This decision was followed in *West v. Oklahoma Tax Commission*,[22] in which the Court similarly held that a state inheritance tax was validly imposed on the mineral headrights of a restricted Osage Indian even though the interest and proceeds thereof were held in trust by the United States for the decedent.

6. *Tribal Power to Tax*

At an early date, it was recognized that, in the absence of Congressional action, Indian tribes retain the power to tax transactions occurring on Indian reservation lands as an incident of their power to control access to such lands.[23] This power to tax was succinctly confirmed as a "sovereign" power in *Washington v. Confederated Tribes of Col-*

ville [24] wherein the Court sustained tribal cigarette taxes as applied to sales to non-tribal purchasers. At this point, however, the source of tribal power to tax had not been precisely articulated. An opportunity, if not necessity, for this determination was presented in *Merrion v. Jicarilla Apache Tribe*.[25] Beginning in 1953, the tribe had executed oil and gas leases authorizing the lessees to enter the reservation to drill for and extract oil and gas from reservation lands on a royalty basis. Thereafter, in 1976, the tribe imposed a severance tax on oil and gas production on reservation lands. The lessees challenged the tax on the ground that the tribe's power to tax was derived from the power to control access to their lands; and since the leases granted the lessees this access on the terms and conditions therein provided, the severance tax violated the provisions of the lease. In sustaining the tax, the Court concluded that the tribal power to tax is not derived solely from the power to exclude non-Indians from tribal lands, but rather, from the tribe's general sovereign authority to control economic activity within its jurisdiction and to exact a tax upon such activity to defray the cost of government services. Although the tribe, by executing the leases, had granted to the lessees lawful access to reservation lands, it did not thereby waive or contract away its sovereign power to tax the lessees on the privilege of conducting business on the reservation.[26]

---

21. 319 U.S. at 604 n. 6.

22. 334 U.S. 717 (1948). The *West* decision was followed in United States v. Mason, 412 U.S. 391 (1973) which presented a question as to whether the Government had breached its fiduciary obligation by failing to challenge an Oklahoma inheritance tax assessed in similar circumstances.

23. E.g., Morris v. Hitchcock, 194 U.S. 384 (1904) (sustaining Chickasaw Nation annual privilege tax on

non-Indians for use of reservation lands to graze cattle).

24. 447 U.S. 134, rehearing denied 448 U.S. 911 (1980).

25. 455 U.S. 130 (1982).

26. As emphasized by the Court in its opinion, the power to impose tribal taxes is subject to Congressional control.

PART III

LIMITATIONS ON GOVERNMENT POWER: INDIVIDUAL RIGHTS AND LIBERTIES

CHAPTER TWELVE

INDIVIDUAL LIBERTIES: AN OVERVIEW

I. APPLICATION OF THE TEXTUAL PROVISIONS TO FEDERAL OR STATE GOVERNMENTS

A. Guarantees in the Original Text (Body) of the Constitution

The text of the Constitution contains three specific guarantees of individual rights which are rarely the subject of intensive constitutional study or litigation. Although they are examined elsewhere, the student should note at the outset not only that these guarantees exist but also how they affect the different governmental entities.

Article I section 10 of the Constitution specifically prohibits a state legislature from impairing the obligation of contracts.[1] The terms of this provision only apply to the actions of a state legislature. The due process clause of the fifth amendment, however, would bar any federal legislation that retroactively impaired the obligations of contract in a similar manner.[2]

The ex post facto clauses effectively eliminate the ability of either the federal or state governments to punish persons for actions

---

1. "No State shall . . . pass any . . . Law impairing the Obligation of Contracts . . . ." U.S. Const. art. I, § 10.

2. "No person shall be . . . deprived of life, liberty, or property, without due process of law . . . ." U.S. Const. amend. V. See Chapter 13, section VI, A.

which were not illegal when performed.[3] The federal government cannot enact any ex post facto criminal law because of the specific prohibitions against such provisions in Article I, section 9, paragraph 3. A similar prohibition is applied to the states under Article I, section 10, paragraph 1.

Another prohibited form of retroactive legislation is a law that imposes punishment on specific individuals. Such a law is known as a bill of attainder. Whether or not a legislature enacts a bill of attainder on the basis of a person's prior acts or on the basis of his political beliefs, the measure still is a legislative punishment that denies that person recourse to the courts. Consequently, the Constitution abolished bills of attainder.[4] The federal government is prohibited from enacting such bills by Article I, section 9, paragraph 3. A similar prohibition applicable to state governments is contained in Article I, section 10, paragraph 1.

B. The Bill of Rights and Their Incorporation in the Fourteenth Amendment

The first ten amendments to the Constitution constitute the Bill of Rights. These amendments were submitted to the States by the first Congress in response to expressions of concern for guarantees of individual liberty that had been raised during the debates on the ratification of the Constitution. The ninth and tenth amendments, however, usually are not considered as specific guarantees of individual liberties.[5] Thus the first eight amendments are sometimes referred to as the Bill of Rights. In an early decision the Supreme Court held that the amendments to the Constitution were not applicable to the states.[6] This holding was correct historically because the drafters of the Bill of Rights designed the amendments as a check on the new national government. This judicially perceived intent of the drafters, however, limited the ability of the courts to control the substance of state law under the federal constitution.

After the passage of the fourteenth amendment the argument was made that this amendment, through both its privileges and immunities clause and its due process clause, made the guarantees of the first ten amendments applicable to the states. The Supreme Court, however, continually rejected this theory of total incorporation of the Bill of Rights into the fourteenth amendment. The Court, instead, adopted a theory of selective incorporation. Under this concept only those provisions of the Bill of Rights that the Court considers fundamental to the American system of law are applied to the states through the due process clause of the fourteenth amendment.[7] Therefore, the states cannot violate the first ten amendments directly. They are only capable of violating those amendments insofar as those provisions are incorporated into the fourteenth amendment and applied to the states. Thus, if a state were to abridge the freedom of speech, it would be abridging the first amendment as applied to it through the four-

3. "No Bill of Attainder or ex post facto Law shall be passed." U.S. Const. art. I, § 9.

"No State shall . . . pass any Bill of Attainder, ex post facto Law . . . ." U.S. Const. art. I, § 10. See Chapter 13, section VI, B.

4. See note 3 supra.

5. "The enumeration in the Constitution, of certain rights, shall not be construed to deny or disparage others retained by the people." U.S. Const. amend. IX.

"Powers not delegated to the United States by the Constitution, nor prohibited by it to the States, are reserved to the States respectively, or to the People." U.S. Const. amend. X.

For an expression of the view that at least the ninth amendment recognizes the existence of additional indi-

vidual rights see, Griswold v. Connecticut, 381 U.S. 479, 486–99 (1965) (Goldberg, J. concurring joined by Warren, C. J. & Brennan, J.); Note, The Uncertain Renaissance of the Ninth Amendment, 33 U.Chi.L.Rev. 814 (1966); Paust, Human Rights and the Ninth Amendment: A New Form of Guarantee, 60 Corn.L. Rev. 231 (1975).

6. Barron v. The Mayor and City Council of Baltimore, 32 U.S. (7 Pet.) 243 (1833).

7. The most recent standard for incorporation of a provision into the fourteenth amendment is developed in Duncan v. Louisiana, 391 U.S. 145 (1968). For a further examination of this issue see Chapter 13, section V.

teenth amendment. It would be incorrect to refer to the state as violating the first amendment without noting its application to the state through the fourteenth amendment.

Knowing which of the Bill of Rights the Supreme Court has applied to the state governments is important when determining what specific constitutional limitations may be placed on a state. Under their own terms the ninth and tenth amendments seem inapplicable to the states. Of the first eight amendments the Supreme Court has held explicitly that only three of the individual guarantees are inapplicable to the states. The three unincorporated guarantees are: (1) the second amendment guarantee of the right to bear arms,[8] (2) the fifth amendment clause guaranteeing criminal prosecution only on a grand jury indictment;[9] and (3) the seventh amendment guarantee of a jury trial in a civil case.[10] Two provisions of the Bill of Rights have not been the subject of litigation which would establish their application to the states. The third amendment,[11] which prohibits the quartering of soldiers in private houses, has not been interpreted or applied by the Supreme Court. The Court has not determined whether the "excessive fine" provision of the eighth amendment is applicable to the states. However, as the provision seems logically intertwined with the

other provisions of that Amendment, it may already have been impliedly made applicable to the states.[12]

The eighth amendment's prohibition of the imposition of excessive bail presents a different problem. No specific case exists in which the Court has ruled that this provision is applicable to the states. In a number of state cases, however, the Court has assumed that the clause is applicable.[13] Consequently, the provision for all practical purposes should be treated as incorporated into the fourteenth amendment.

Another specialized problem relates to the just compensation clause of the fifth amendment. The wording of the amendment specifically requires the government to give just compensation for property taken for public use.[14] The due process clause of the fourteenth amendment, however, fails to contain this specific language, though it does prohibit the state governments from taking property without due process of law.[15] The fifth amendment guarantee of just compensation technically has not been incorporated into the fourteenth amendment. Nevertheless, the Court has held that the fourteenth amendment due process guarantee provides the same safeguard against a state's taking of property without just com-

---

8. "A well regulated Militia, being necessary to the security of a free State, the right of the people to keep and bear arms, shall not be infringed." U.S. Const. amend II. United States v. Cruikshank, 92 U.S. 542, 553 (1876).

9. "No person shall be held to answer for a capital, or otherwise infamous crime, unless on a presentment or indictment of a Grand Jury . . . ." U.S. Const. amend. V. Hurtado v. California, 110 U.S. 516 (1884).

10. "In a Suit at common law . . . the right of trial by jury shall be preserved . . . ." U.S. Const. amend. VII. Minneapolis & St. Louis R.R. Co. v. Bombolis, 241 U.S. 211 (1916); Melancon v. McKeithen, 345 F.Supp. 1025, (E.D.La.1972), aff'd 409 U.S. 943, 1098 (1973); Bringe v. Collins, 274 Md. 338, 335 A.2d 670 (1975). Continental Title Co. v. District Court, 645 P.2d 1310, 1316 n. 7 (Colo.1982), citing earlier edition of this treatise.

11. "No soldier shall, in time of peace be quartered in any house, without the consent of the Owner, nor in a time of war, but in a manner to be prescribed by law." U.S. Const. amend. III.

12. "Excessive bail shall not be required, nor excessive fines imposed, nor cruel and unusual punishments inflicted." U.S. Const. amend. VIII.

The technical application of the provision may never be known since the primary problem in this area relates to the imprisoning of indigents for the failure to pay fines, and the Court has analyzed this under the equal protection clause, see, Tate v. Short, 401 U.S. 395 (1971). The cruel and unusual punishment provision is applicable to the states, see Louisiana ex rel. Francis v. Resweber, 329 U.S. 459 (1947); Robinson v. California, 370 U.S. 660 (1962). For the applicability of the excessive bail provision see note 13 and accompanying text.

13. See, e.g., Schilb v. Kuebel, 404 U.S. 357, 365 (1971).

14. "[N]or shall private property be taken for public use, without just compensation." U.S. Const. amend. V.

15. "[N]or shall any State deprive any person of life, liberty, or property, without due process of law . . . ." U.S. Const. amend. XIV, § 1.

pensation.[16] Thus, the rules that govern when a government may take property for public use and when it must pay just compensation to private individuals when exercising its regulatory or eminent domain powers are identical under the two clauses.

C. The Privileges and/or Immunities Clauses

Two clauses of the Constitution guarantee certain privileges to citizens against infringement by the state government. Article IV section 2 requires that the citizens of each state receive all the "privileges and immunities" of citizens of other states.[17] Section 1 of the fourteenth amendment prohibits the states from making laws which would abridge "the privileges or immunities of citizens of the United States."[18] Despite the essentially similar wording of the two provisions they have widely differing applications. The Article IV provision often is referred to as the comity clause. It prohibits any distinctions in law between citizens of a state and citizens of other states if those distinctions are unreasonable. The clause is a specialized type of equal protection provision which guarantees that all classifications which burden persons because they are not citizens of the state must reasonably relate to legitimate state or local purposes.

The privileges or immunities clause of the fourteenth amendment protects very few rights. The Supreme Court held that this clause neither incorporated any of the Bill of Rights nor protected all rights of individual citizens.[19] The Court, instead, decided that the provision only protected those rights peculiar to being a citizen of the federal government; it does not protect those rights which related only to state citizenship. Therefore, the clause only refers to uniquely federal rights such as the right to petition Congress, the right to vote in federal elections, the right to interstate travel or commerce, the right to enter federal lands, or the rights of a citizen while in the custody of federal officers.[20] These rights receive absolute protection in the sense that the states never could have a legitimate interest in terminating completely any of those rights. A state, however, may limit individual liberties without violating the provision as long as it does not eliminate the federal rights. Thus, in the history of the Court only one case has found that a state has violated this provision and that decision was overruled within a few years.[21] Nevertheless, the fourteenth amendment's privilege or immunities clause is still important because it may justify congressional legislation that would prevent a private individual from infringing or impairing federal rights.[22]

II. APPLICATION OF SPECIFIC GUARANTEES FOR AND AGAINST PRIVATE INDIVIDUALS

A. Constitutional Constraints on Individual Actions

Almost all of the constitutional protections of individual rights and liberties restrict only the actions of governmental entities. For example, the Bill of Rights acts as a check only on the actions of the federal government. Moreover, the provisions of the body of the Constitution that protect individual

---

16. Chicago B. & Q. R.R. Co. v. Chicago, 166 U.S. 226 (1897). Today the Supreme Court itself cites the *Chicago B & Q* decision as incorporating the takings clause into the fourteenth amendment, even though that decision does not refer to an incorporation issue. See Webb's Fabulous Pharmacies v. Beckwith, 449 U.S. 155, 159 (1980). The Amendment also bars the state's taking of property for private rather than public uses. Missouri Pacific Ry. v. Nebraska, 164 U.S. 403 (1896).

17. "The Citizen of each State shall be entitled to all Privileges and Immunities of Citizens in the several States." U.S. Const. art. IV, § 2.

18. U.S. Const. amend. XIV § 1.

19. Slaughter-House Cases, 83 U.S. (16 Wall.) 36 (1873).

20. Id. at 79–81.

21. Colgate v. Harvey, 296 U.S. 404 (1935) overruled in Madden v. Kentucky, 309 U.S. 83 (1940).

22. United States v. Classic, 313 U.S. 299 (1941). Congressional power to protect civil rights is examined in Chapter 17.

rights are limited expressly in their application to actions of either the federal or state governments.[1] Finally, the amendments to the Constitution which protect individual liberties only have been applied to the actions of the state or federal governments. The Civil War amendments—thirteen, fourteen, and fifteen—contain the most important applications and the only significant exception to this principle.

The thirteenth amendment prohibits slavery and involuntary servitude within the United States.[2] No governmental action is required to violate the thirteenth amendment's proscription of slavery. The prohibition applies whether a private person or a government entity is seeking to enslave an individual. Nevertheless, the judiciary has hesitated in finding any given practice to violate this amendment absent some congressional guidance.

The terms of the fourteenth amendment only restrict the freedom of states to make certain types of laws or take certain actions.[3] Thus, traditional doctrine suggests that private individuals cannot violate the amendment. When dealing with problems about application of the fourteenth amendment, a checklist approach will facilitate the determination of whether a state has transgressed the strictures of the amendment. Any official act of the state such as legislation, executive orders, or court decrees will always comprise state action. However, when a plaintiff complains about the actions of a seemingly private individual, an issue will arise as to the presence of "state action" related to the specific harm. First, courts will look for some formal connection between the individual and the government.

Government employees generally will be held to be acting for the government unless their actions are clearly outside of both their formal authority and the de facto authority that their official position grants them.[4] Although more complex questions will be analyzed in the chapter discussing state action, as a general rule courts usually will find a connection between a state and an individual if the state has provided significant aid to the individual or if it is fair to treat the individual as a partner or joint venturer with the state.[5] Additionally, a person will be subject to constitutional restraints if he has been allowed to perform an essential "state function."[6] Of course, all lesser governmental units such as county, city, or other local governments are considered to be a part of the state.

When analyzing problems involving the federal government under the Bill of Rights or the fifteenth amendment, the analysis is identical to that used to determine whether a state government has acted under the fourteenth amendment.[7] Thus, all official acts of the Congress, the executive (including agency regulations), and the federal judiciary constitute government action for the purpose of the Bill of Rights or the fifteenth amendment. Similarly, the courts may find that individuals are so involved with the federal government, either through administrative or financial contacts, that these constitutional provisions also will limit their actions.

B. What Individuals Are Protected by the Constitutional Guarantees?

It is important to know that the wording and interpretation of several constitutional

---

1. See U.S. Const. art. I, §§ 9, 10.

2. "Neither slavery nor involuntary servitude, except as a punishment for crime whereof the party shall have been duly convicted, shall exist in the United States . . . ." U.S. Const. amend. XIII, § 1.

3. "*No State* shall make or enforce any law which shall abridge the privileges or immunities of citizens of the United States; *nor shall any State* deprive any person of life, liberty, or property without due process of law . . . ." U.S. Const. amend. XIV, § 1 (emphasis added). See Chapter 14 on State Action.

4. Griffin v. Maryland, 378 U.S. 130 (1964); see also, Lombard v. Louisiana, 373 U.S. 267 (1963).

5. See, e.g., Evans v. Newton, 382 U.S. 296 (1966); Burton v. Wilmington Parking Authority, 365 U.S. 715 (1961).

6. See, e.g., Marsh v. Alabama, 326 U.S. 501 (1946); Terry v. Adams, 345 U.S. 461 (1953).

7. See Columbia Broadcasting System, Inc. v. Democratic National Committee, 412 U.S. 94 (1973).

provisions limit the application of their specific guarantees to certain types of persons or entities. For example, the term "citizen" in Article III, which established the federal judiciary, includes corporations.[8] Therefore, suits involving corporations involve "citizens" for federal jurisdictional purposes. The term "citizen", however, does not include either corporations or aliens under other provisions of the Constitution such as the definition of "citizen" in the fourteenth amendment.[9] Neither corporations nor aliens receive the protection of the privileges or immunities clause of the fourteenth amendment or the comity clause of Article IV, since those clauses protect only citizens.[10]

The term "person" also has been interpreted to give varying protection to corporations. Under the fifth amendment's prohibition of compulsory self-incrimination, "person" fails to include corporations or other business entities.[11] Aliens within the United States, however, receive protection from self-incrimination under this provision. Both aliens and corporations are considered to be "persons" for the purposes of the due process clauses of the fifth and fourteenth amendments and the equal protection clause of the fourteenth amendment.[12] Similarly, aliens and corporations are included within the protection of the fourth amendment which guarantees the right of the people to

be free from unwarranted searches and seizures.[13]

The equal protection clause of the fourteenth amendment only requires that a state not practice unjustified discrimination in law against persons "within the jurisdiction" of the state. Nevertheless, even persons not physically present in the state are protected by the clause because the Supreme Court has interpreted the provision to guarantee equal treatment under the law to all people who are subject to the law of a state.[14] Thus, anyone who is directly affected by a state law may challenge the law on the basis of the equal protection guarantee of the fourteenth amendment even though he is not physically present in the state at the time of the suit.

III.   PROCEDURAL DUE PROCESS vs. SUBSTANTIVE REVIEW

A.   The Due Process Clauses

When the Court reviews a law to determine its procedural fairness, it reviews the system of decision-making to determine whether or not a government entity has taken an individual's life, liberty, or property without the fair procedure or "due process" required by the fifth and fourteenth amendment.[1] This type of review is easily justified because it involves no more than a judicial

---

8.   "The judicial Power of the United States shall extend to all Cases, in Law and Equity, arising under the Constitution, the Laws of the United States, and Treaties made, or which shall be made, under their authority; . . . —between Citizens of different States . . . ." U.S. Const. art. III, § 2. Louisville, Cincinnati & Charleston R.R. Co. v. Letson, 43 U.S. (2 How.) 497 (1844).

9.   "All persons born or naturalized in the United States and subject to the jurisdiction thereof are citizens of the United States and of the State wherein they reside." U.S. Const. amend. XIV, § 1.

10.   As to the fourteenth amendment see its definition of citizen in note 9, supra. As to the protection of the comity clause—the interstate privileges and immunities clause of Article IV—see Blake v. McClung, 172 U.S. 239 (1898). Note also that corporations and aliens will not receive the protection of other amendments which protect the right of citizens, such as the fifteenth amendment. Asbury Hosp. v. Cass Co., 326 U.S. 207 (1945).

11.   Bellis v. United States, 409 U.S. 322 (1973).

12.   Santa Clara County v. Southern Pacific R.R., 118 U.S. 394 (1886), (corporations); Truax v. Raich, 239 U.S. 33 (1915) (aliens); Plyler v. Doe, 102 S.Ct. 2382 (1982) (illegally resident aliens).

13.   "The right of the people to be secure in their persons, houses, papers, and effects, against unreasonable searches and seizures, shall not be violated . . . ." U.S. Const. amend. IV. Silverthorne Lumber Co. v. United States, 251 U.S. 385 (1920) (corporations); United States v. Wong Quong Wong, 94 F. 832 (D.C.Vermont 1899) (aliens); United States v. Toscanino, 500 F.2d 267 (2d Cir. 1974) (aliens).

14.   See Kentucky Finance Corp. v. Paramount Auto Exchange, 262 U.S. 544 (1923).

1.   "No person shall be . . . deprived of life, liberty, or property, without due process of law . . . ." U.S. Const. amend. V.

assessment of a decision-making process that has determined that a specific individual should suffer some burden. It may involve the review of the general fairness of a procedure authorized by legislation or merely the review of the fairness of a decision in an individual case. In either instance, little theoretical complaint exists about a court's active role in reviewing the fairness of a governmental decision-making process as the judiciary seems uniquely suited for such a task.

It is important to realize that procedural review is limited in scope. Procedural due process guarantees only that there is a fair decision-making process before the government takes some action directly impairing a person's life, liberty or property. This aspect of the due process clauses does not protect against the use of arbitrary rules of law which are the basis of those proceedings. It is only necessary that a fair decision-making process be used; the ultimate rule to be enforced need not be a fair or just one. For example, if a state legislature enacted a law which imposed the death penalty upon any person who had been found guilty of double parking an automobile after a determination of guilt through trial by jury and appellate review, the law would clearly comport with the *procedural* restrictions of the due process clauses. The law might violate the eighth amendment, as applied to the states by the fourteenth, in that it constituted cruel and unusual punishment. Indeed the law might also violate the substantive guarantee of the due process clause of the fourteenth amendment insofar as it was an irrational and arbitrary abuse of the government's power to protect against traffic hazards. However, so long as the decision-making process by which the burden of the death penalty was handed out was a fair one the

law could not be stricken on the basis of "procedural" due process.

This brings us to the ability of the judiciary to review the substance of legislation. By "substantive review" we mean the judicial determination of the compatibility of the substance of a law or governmental action with the Constitution. The Court is concerned with the constitutionality of the underlying rule rather than with the fairness of the process by which the government applies the rule to an individual. Therefore, every form of review other than that involving procedural due process is a form of substantive review. For example, if the Court were to strike a law restricting the freedom of the press because it violated the first amendment, the case would involve a form of substantive review by the Court. The Court would have determined that the substance or rule of the legislation was incompatible with the language of the amendment. Substantive review under specific amendments or provisions of the Constitution has not met with intense intellectual criticism. Because the Constitution gives an indication through specific language that certain types of legislation or executive action are beyond the power of government, the ability of the judiciary to overrule state or federal law on the basis of specific textual provisions has not been challenged widely since *Marbury v. Madison.*[2] The Court's ability to determine the constitutionality of state or federal laws or executive actions under the due process and equal protection clauses, however, is subject to much greater criticism.

The next chapter will examine the development of judicial control over state and federal legislation under the due process and equal protection clauses. The student, however, should appreciate how the Court can overrule a piece of legislation because the Court disagrees with its substance under a

---

"[N]or shall any State deprive any person of life, liberty, or property, without due process of Law . . . .." U.S. Const. amend. XIV, § 1.

State v. Manocchio, 448 A.2d 761, 764 (R.I.1982) (Weisberger, J.), citing earlier edition of this section of the treatise.

2. 5 U.S. (1 Cranch) 137 (1803). Continuing disputes which concern the proper role for a Court in a democratic society are discussed in Chapter 1.

portion of the Constitution that speaks only of a process (or procedure) being due an individual. The concept the Court employs to control the substance of legislation under the due process clause is that certain types of lawmaking go beyond any proper sphere of government activity. In short, the Court views the act as incompatible with our democratic system of government and individual liberty. The judicial premise for this position is that any life, liberty or property limited by such a law is taken without due process because the Constitution never granted the government the ability to pass such a law. For example, if the Court assumes that the government does not possess the power to pass legislation establishing the maximum number of hours which workers can be employed in a given week, then the Court can hold that any law which would limit those hours must have been passed by an unconstitutional process. The measure would be void under the due process clause because no piece of legislation could limit the ability of employers or employees to set the terms of employment in a manner compatible with the Constitution. The importance of such a ruling is that it eliminates entirely the ability of the state or federal government to deal with a given type of problem. Because the other branches of government theoretically are responsive to the people, this particular form of substantive review constitutes a judicial rejection of a democratic society's attempt to deal with its social problems. But if the effect of a substantive due process decision is readily apparent, the basis on which a court justifiably can reach such a decision has been a source of continuing controversy.

The Supreme Court used the substantive due process test to control a wide variety of legislation during the period from 1885 to 1937. During this period a majority of the justices concluded that interference with certain types of economic liberty was not a permissible end of government and that the Court was free to determine what types of legislation rationally promoted legitimate economic goals. This role gave the Court the power of a "super legislature." If the justices disagreed with any law, they could declare the measure unconstitutional because it failed to comport with their sense of the legitimate economic role of American government. After 1937, however, a dramatic shift took place in the Court's manner of reviewing legislation under the due process clauses. The Court realized that nothing either in the language of the Constitution or in the basic judicial function gave federal judges a claim to superiority in determining the rationality of economic legislation. The Court, therefore, abandoned the role of an independent reviewer of "economic and social welfare" legislation under the due process clause. The Court no longer would overturn legislation under the due process guarantees unless the law had no rational argument supporting it. If the law can arguably be said to rationally relate to a legitimate goal of government, the Court will uphold the law even though the justices might disagree with the wisdom of its provisions.

The Supreme Court continues to make an independent determination of the legitimacy of laws which affect the "fundamental rights" of individuals under the Constitution. If legislation limits a fundamental right—a specific type of civil liberty as defined by the Court [3] —the Court will more carefully scrutinize the underlying factual basis for the legislation. Thus the standard for reviewing such legislation is called a "strict scrutiny" standard. The Court raises the standard that legislation must meet under the due process guarantees if the law regulates or limits a fundamental civil liberty. Under the strict scrutiny standard the Court requires that the law be necessary to

---

3. These rights include the following: (1) first amendment rights; (2) the right to engage in interstate travel; (3) the right to vote; (4) the right to fair proceedings before a deprivation of personal liberty (although this is somewhat unclear); (5) the right to privacy which includes some rights to freedom of choice in sexual matters; (6) the right to freedom of choice in marriage. This list may not be exclusive; for a discussion of the problems in this area, see Chapter 13, section V.

promote a compelling or overriding interest of government if it is to limit the fundamental rights of individual citizens. If the justices are not satisfied that the law is necessary to promote an end of government which is clearly more important than the limitation of the fundamental liberty, they will find the law violative of the due process clause.

It is important to distinguish the concepts of substantive and procedural due process, even though they may seem to be intermingled in challenges to a specific piece of legislation. The difference between analyzing procedural defects and legislative decisions on substantive issues was well demonstrated in the case of *New Motor Vehicle Bd. of California v. Orrin W. Fox Co.*[4] This case involved a challenge to the California Automobile Franchise Act, under the terms of which an automobile manufacturer could not establish a new dealership franchise nor relocate an existing franchise within a certain radius (approximately ten miles) of an existing franchisee dealing in the same automobile line of that manufacturer if the existing franchisee in the area protested the creation of a competing dealership to the New Motor Vehicle Board. If there was no protest, the new franchise could be established immediately; if there was a protest, the Board informed the manufacturer that, under penalty of law, the manufacturer could not establish or relocate the new dealership until the Board had held a hearing on whether there was good cause for permitting such dealership competition. Under the Act, the Board was required to convene a hearing within 60 days and to render a decision 30 days following the hearing; it was admitted that the vast majority of new dealerships or relocated franchises were allowed because the Act established a presumption in favor of greater competition. In this particular case, the General Motors Corporation attempted to establish a new Buick franchise dealership within ten miles of an existing Buick franchisee and to relocate a Chevrolet dealership within 10 miles of an existing Chevrolet dealer. The Board ordered G.M. not to establish such dealerships pending the hearing; General Motors challenged the ability of the Board to delay the establishment of the dealerships without a prior hearing.

The majority opinion, by Justice Brennan, correctly found that this challenge did not involve a true procedural problem; it was the legislation, not the action of the Board, that limited General Motor's ability to create the new dealerships. There was no ruling that freedom of business activity could not be a liberty or property interest protected by the due process clause. The majority noted that there was no procedural problem here because there was no challenge to the Board's notice and hearing procedures, which were admittedly fair in terms of making the final determination as to whether to allow the new franchise to be established. The "stop notice" that delayed the creation of the dealership was not like an administrative order or a temporary injunction because it was not based on a determination that there was anything specifically wrong with the creation of the proposed new dealership. In operation, the Act merely created a 90-day waiting period to establish a dealership whenever an existing dealer believed that the competitive pressure would cause him some economic problem. Thus, the majority reasoned, this case involved only problems of substantive due process and equal protection; the issue was whether a legislature could delay the creation of dealerships in areas where competitors already existed. The majority opinion cited many of the substantive due process and equal protection decisions of the past 40 years rejecting the older use of strict review of economic regulations. The Court required only that there be some conceivable argument that the Act is rationally related to a legitimate end of government. As this delay might conceivably help to eliminate some harmful economic effects of unrestrained competition, regardless of whether there really were demonstrable

4. 439 U.S. 96 (1978).

harmful effects from free competition, the Court had to uphold the law. Justice Brennan, for the majority, briefly noted that the delegation of powers argument made by General Motors had no merit; the fact that the delay occurred only when an existing competitor complained of the creation of the new dealership did not establish a delegation of any basic power of government to the existing dealer. "An otherwise valid regulation is not rendered invalid simply because those whom the regulation is designed to safeguard may waive its protection." [5]

The Supreme Court also focused on the difference between procedural and substantive due process when it upheld a variety of regulations pertaining to the confinement of pretrial detainees and convicted inmates of a federal correctional facility in New York City. In *Bell v. Wolfish* [6] the Court found that procedural due process would require fair procedures for determining guilt before someone could be punished but that there was no general substantive due process right to have the government create the best possible conditions for the holding of persons awaiting trial.

The conditions at the facility in *Bell* were challenged by persons who were being de-

tained solely because they could not post bail and there were no less drastic means for insuring their presence at trial. The lower federal courts had overturned several practices of the federal facility including the assignment of two persons to rooms originally intended for single occupancy, the prohibition against receiving packages of food and personal items from outside the institution, the use of body cavity searches following contact visits, and the requirement that the pretrial detainees remain outside their rooms during routine searches or "shakedowns." The lower federal courts believed that they had a power to inquire into generalized jail conditions because of a procedural due process right to fair treatment; the Supreme Court recognized that this case actually involved a substantive due process challenge to the government regulations.

The majority opinion, by Justice Rehnquist, determined that the correct standard was a determination of whether or not the specific condition could be considered "punishment of the detainee." [7] The Court thus found a distinction between measures which constituted punishment of the detainee and which therefore could not be imposed prior to a proper determination of guilt and rea-

---

5. 439 U.S. at 109. Two concurring opinions, joined by three justices, indicated varying views of the substantive and procedural due process distinction. Justice Marshall, concurring in a separate opinion, joined the opinion of the Court but stated that he believed that the Act was in fact reasonable because the legislature had to choose whether to place an economic burden on existing franchises or those who sought to establish a new competitive franchise. 439 U.S. at 112 (Marshall, J., concurring).

Justice Blackmun, joined in a concurring opinion by Justice Powell, noted that there was no liberty or property interest at stake as the statute set the terms for the initial right to create a dealership and those terms were rational in allowing for a delay in some situations. Thus, there was no procedural question because there was no challenge to the procedures used to determine whether the Board should allow the creation of a new franchise. 439 U.S. at 113–14 (Blackmun, J., concurring).

Only Justice Stevens dissented; he believed that the law violated the principles of procedural due process because it allowed a competitor, the existing franchisee, to delay the creation of the competitive dealership. His dissent noted that over 99% of the contested new dealerships or relocations were allowed by the

board so that "properly analyzed, the statute merely confers a special benefit on a limited group of private persons who are likely to oppose the establishment or relocation of a new car dealership." 439 U.S. at 120 (Stevens, J., dissenting).

However, Justice Stevens failed to appreciate that this was not a procedural problem; there was no claim that any further procedures would have cured this defect. Justice Stevens' real complaint with the Act was disclosed by his argument that the Act constituted an impermissible delegation of power to invoke a procedure that delayed competition and the right to establish a competing economic unit. Id. at 126. This Act, however, did not delegate a basic governmental power to some private persons to govern or license others; instead, it was merely the legislature creating a preference for some economic units over others. Justice Stevens came close to admitting that the issue was one of substantive due process, id. at 125–26 n. 28 (Stevens, J., dissenting), and his dissent was aimed more at the inadvisability of placing legislative constraints on competition than the need of new procedures to safeguard liberty or property interests.

6. 441 U.S. 520 (1979).

7. 441 U.S. at 535.

sonable regulatory restraints which could be imposed. Justice Rehnquist also stated that great deference should be paid to the decisions of prison officials because of their greater expertise in the assessment of interests in security and prison discipline. Federal courts were not entitled to inquire generally into whether or not government prison regulations are the least burdensome, or best, alternative for regulating the freedom of the detainees or prisoners.[8]

When an inmate at a penal facility claims that he has been subjected to a special type of punishment, or unfavorable conditions to which other inmates have not been subjected, he raises a procedural due process issue in terms of the fairness of the administrative procedures by which he was selected for such punishment.[9] When the prisoner claims that the general conditions in the prison fall below constitutionally acceptable standards of decency, he is raising a substantive issue that can best be analyzed in terms of whether the prison conditions violate the principles of the cruel and unusual punishment clause. The Supreme Court has found that there can be no single test for determining when prison conditions fall below societal standards of decency from which the cruel and unusual punishment clause draws its meaning.[10]

8. The Supreme Court, in *Wolfish*, also upheld a restriction on prisoners, including detainees, that prohibited the receipt of hardbound books by detainees unless they came from a publisher or bookstore. The majority opinion noted that convicted prisoners do not forfeit all of their constitutional rights and that they retain some right to speech, religion, equal protection, and due process. However, the interest in prison discipline allowed for reasonable limitations on those rights, so long as the limitations were related to preserving internal order and discipline at the facility. The fact that prison officials could make a reasonable argument that items could be hidden in the hardbound book, and the difficulty of detecting those items justified the rule. Thus, the Court also approved the use of body cavity searches and shakedowns of inmate living areas outside of the presence of the detainee as reasonable under the circumstances; the majority opinion explicitly employed a balancing test to measure the privacy interest of the detainees against the interests in prison discipline. The majority in *Wolfish* noted that the conditions in some prisons, both state and federal, were deplorable and that federal courts have rightly condemned "these sordid aspects of our prison system" but that this did not give a generalized right to judges to become "enmeshed in the minutiae of prison operations." 441 U.S. at 562.

Thus it would appear that federal judges are restricted in their examination of prison conditions under the cruel and unusual punishment clause and under the due process clauses; both principles will require a high degree of deference to the prison authorities but should allow for the judicial invalidation of punitive measures against pretrial detainees or totally unreasonable restrictions or punishments of convicted inmates.

Justice Powell, agreed with the method of analysis used by the majority but would have restricted the use of body cavity searches because he placed greater weight on the privacy interest of the pretrial detainees; he would have allowed the lower courts to strictly review and revise these prison regulations. Bell v. Wolfish, 441 U.S. 520, 562 (1979) (Powell, J., concurring and dissenting). Justice Marshall, in dissent, would have weighed the detainee's interest against the countervailing interests of the government, 441 U.S. at 562 (Marshall, J., dissenting). Justice Stevens believed that the majority opinion had placed too little value in the principle of substantive due process and that the majority virtually eliminated meaningful protection for the pretrial detainees. He found that the Court should not accept the generalized interest in prison discipline when examining restrictions placed on pretrial detainees because all restrictions of their rights constituted punishment prior to trial. Justice Stevens would have made the prison authorities demonstrate that they could not regulate the pretrial detainees with less burdensome means. However, he did agree with the majority that there should be objective criteria for the determination of punishment. Justice Stevens considered the fact that the Court recognized that the pretrial detainee had a liberty interest in the condition of confinement that should be protected by the due process clause to be a significant step in fashioning a due process principle to review prison conditions. 441 U.S. at 579 (Stevens, J., dissenting, joined by Brennan, J.).

9. See, e.g. Vitek v. Jones, 445 U.S. 480 (1980) (requiring a hearing before the transfer of an inmate from a prison facility to a mental hospital); compare Hewitt v. Helms, 103 S.Ct. 864 (1983) (prisoners are not generally entitled to hearing prior to administrative segregation or transfer; statutory entitlement satisfied by informal hearing).

10. Compare Rhodes v. Chapman, 452 U.S. 337 (1981) (finding that the housing of two inmates in a cell designed for a single inmate does not violate the cruel and unusual punishment clause) with Estelle v. Gamble, 429 U.S. 97 (1976) (failure of prison authorities to provide for prison inmate's medical needs constitutes cruel and unusual punishment). See also Revere v. Massachusetts General Hospital, 103 S.Ct. ___ (1983) (due process requires government official to obtain medical help for a person who was injured when he was arrested but does not require government to reimburse the hospital; eighth amendment principles are not applicable before adjudication of guilt).

In *Rhodes v. Chapman* [11] the Court held that the celling of two inmates in cells originally designed to house only one did not constitute cruel and unusual punishment because there was no evidence that the double celling of inmates in the particular prison examined by the Court inflicted "unnecessary or wanton pain or is grossly disproportionate to the severity of crimes warranting imprisonment." [12]   However the Court indicated that federal judges were to "scrutinize claims of cruel and unusual confinement" in order to determine if conditions of confinement in other prisons amounted to cruel and unusual punishment although the majority opinion indicated that "courts cannot assume that state legislatures and prison officials are insensitive to the requirements of the Constitution or to the perplexing sociological problems of how best to achieve the goals of the penal function in the criminal justice system." [13]

When analyzing a constitutional decision concerning the imposition of punishment for criminal activity, one must be cognizant of the distinction between substantive due process and procedural due process issues. The Court will actively examine whether or not an individual has received fair treatment in terms of the process of adjudication.[14] However, the Court will not use substantive due process principles to invalidate legislatively prescribed penalties for criminal activity.[15] For example, in *Rummel v. Estelle,*[16] the Supreme Court upheld a recidivist statute against claims that it had violated the due process clause of the fourteenth amendment and the cruel and unusual punishment clause of the eighth amendment, applicable to the states through the due process clause.

In *Rummel,* the state required the imposition of a life sentence upon a defendant for his third felony conviction, even though the defendant in the particular case was guilty of what would appear to be rather minor theft offenses: fradulent use of a credit card to obtain $80 worth of goods, the passing of a forged check for $28.36, and the obtaining of $120.75 by false pretenses. The justices in the majority indicated an unwillingness to second guess legislative judgment under either the due process or cruel and unusual punishment clauses. Because the defendant did not claim that his trial or the sentencing hearing was unfair, but only that the sentence was disproportionate to the crime, there was no procedural issue in this case.

B.   The Equal Protection Clause

Analysis under the equal protection clause of the fourteenth amendment is identical to that used under the due process clauses. The only equal protection clause appears in the fourteenth amendment and it only applies to the states.[17] The Court, however, has interpreted the due process clause of the fifth amendment to test federal classifica-

---

11.   452 U.S. 337 (1981).

12.   452 U.S. at 348.

13.   452 U.S. at 352. Justices who concurred in the judgment indicated even more willingness than the majority to examine the details of prison conditions to determine whether they violated our society's standards of human dignity. See Rhodes v. Chapman, 452 U.S. 337, 352 (1981) (Brennan, J., joined by Blackmun and Stevens, J.J., concurring in the judgment); Id. at 368 (Blackmun, J., concurring in the judgment). Justice Marshall challenged the findings of both the majority and concurring justices that the double-celling of inmates in the Ohio prison examined in the *Rhodes* litigation did not adversely affect the prisoners in a way which violated basic concepts of human dignity in our society. Rhodes v. Chapman, 452 U.S. 337, 369 (1981) (Marshall, J., dissenting).

14.   See Chapter 15, Procedural Due Process, for an examination of such issues.

15.   For an excellent analysis of substantive due process and cruel and unusual punishment principles in determining the constitutionality of legislatively prescribed penalties and the relationship of questions of substantive justice to procedural due process issues, see Jeffries and Stephan, Defenses, Presumptions, and Burden of Proof in the Criminal Law, 88 Yale L.J. 1325 (1979).

16.   445 U.S. 263 (1980).

17.   This is because the language of the clause refers only to the states.

"[N]or shall any State . . . deny to any person within its jurisdiction the equal protection of the laws." U.S. Const. amend. XIV, § 1.

tions under the same standards of review.[18] Thus, the Constitution may be said to contain an equal protection guarantee applicable to the federal government even though the fourteenth amendment cannot be applied to federal actions.

Review under both equal protection guarantees is always substantive in nature. The equal protection guarantees require the government to treat similarly situated individuals in a similar manner. They do not govern the process to be employed in decision-making but they do regulate the ability of the government to finally classify individuals as different in type, either for the purposes of dispensing government benefits or punishments. Under the due process clause the Court asks whether the legislation rationally relates to a legitimate end of government. The identical test exists under the equal protection clauses except that legislation reviewed under these guarantees always involves a classification. If a law burdens all persons equally when they exercise a specific right, then the courts will test the law under the due process clause. If, however, the law distinguishes between who may and who may not exercise a right, then judicial review of the law falls under the equal protection guarantee because the issue now becomes whether the distinction between these persons is legitimate. The classification employed is the "means" used to achieve some end. Thus, the Court reviews the issue of whether the classification rationally relates to a legitimate end under the equal protection guarantees.

In the period from 1885 to 1937, the Supreme Court examined many economic legislative classifications to determine if the justices agreed that those classifications were related to legitimate functions of an American government. This examination resulted in the striking of economic and general so-cial legislation, although it was used less often than substantive review under the due process clauses.[19] After 1937, however, the Court abandoned this use of active review of legislation under the equal protection guarantees. Consequently, the justices no longer will scrutinize or determine for themselves the legitimacy of classifications employed in general social welfare or economic legislation. If the classifications arguably relate to a legitimate function of government, the Court will sustain them under the equal protection guarantees.

As with the use of the due process clauses to protect fundamental civil rights, the Supreme Court distinguishes cases involving certain individual rights and liberties from those cases merely involving general police power or social welfare legislation. In cases where fundamental rights or liberties are at issue, the Court will employ "strict scrutiny" in reviewing classifications under the equal protection guarantee. This review means that the justices will independently determine whether or not the classification is constitutionally permissible. As with the due process civil liberties cases, a "strict scrutiny" review involves a determination of whether the legislature's classification is necessary to promote a compelling or overriding governmental interest.

Because equal protection problems involve classification, another situation arises in which an increased level of scrutiny and a compelling interest test should be employed beyond the fundamental rights cases. When certain groups of persons are classified or separated out for specific government benefits or burdens, the Court will employ strict scrutiny of the classifications. The Court, however, will not strictly scrutinize all legislative classifications of people. The Court recognizes that to some degree all legislation classifies people, and to function proper-

---

18. Bolling v. Sharpe, 347 U.S. 497 (1954); United States v. Kras, 409 U.S. 434 (1973). There is dicta indicating that the Court will subject federal laws which burden aliens as a class to a more lenient standard of review because of unique federal interests in this area. See, Nyquist v. Mauclet, 432 U.S. 1, 7 n. 8 (1977). The case is discussed in Chapter 16, Equal Protection, section III, Aliens.

19. R. McCloskey, The American Supreme Court 151 (1960).

ly legislatures must have some freedom to use classification schemes when enacting legislation. Therefore, the Court will employ the strict scrutiny standard to review the legitimacy of classifications (unrelated to fundamental rights) only when a so-called "suspect" classification has been employed by the legislature. Because of the justices' views of the history and purposes behind the fourteenth amendment, laws that classify individuals on the basis of either their status as a member of a racial minority, their national origin, or their lack of United States citizenship are viewed as suspect.[20] The Court will not approve legislation involving such a classification unless a majority of the justices are independently satisfied that the classification is necessary to promote a compelling governmental interest.

The Court clearly has identified classifications based on race or nationality as suspect.

Moreover, the Court has applied some form of strict scrutiny when reviewing legislative classifications based on alienage, gender or legitimacy. The Court at times has referred to alienage classifications as being "suspect", although the Court has not invalidated all uses of such classifications. The Court has refrained from holding that either sex or illegitimacy constitutes a suspect classification, but the justices recently have taken an active role in preventing the government from arbitrarily dispensing benefits or burdens based on these forms of personal status. Therefore, even though legitimacy or sex are not traditional suspect classifications, legislation employing these traits as classifications receives a more intense review from the Court than does general economic or social welfare legislation.[21]

---

20. For further discussion of suspect classifications see Chapter 16, sections I–IV.

21. See Chapter 16, sections III, IV, V for a discussion of the cases dealing with alienage, gender, and legitimacy classifications.

CHAPTER THIRTEEN

SUBSTANTIVE DUE PROCESS

I. JUDICIAL CONTROL OF LEGISLATION PRIOR TO THE CIVIL WAR

Almost since the beginning of the nation the justices of the Supreme Court had suggested that they had an inherent right to review the substance of legislation that either the Congress or state legislatures had enacted. Seventeenth and eighteenth century political theory had built on an earlier philo-sophical base in espousing the position that certain natural rights prevailed for all men and that a governmental body could not limit or impair these rights. In short, these rights existed in every society whether they arose from a social compact or from devine right. From this seventeenth and eighteenth century political thought grew the concept that a higher or natural law limited the restrictions on liberty that a temporal government could impose on an individual. In the case of *Calder v. Bull*[1] the justices for the first time engaged in a debate concerning their ability to overrule legislation on the basis of natural law.

In *Calder* the Court held that the Connecticut legislature had not violated the Constitution when it set aside a probate decree.[2] The case, however, is important for the opposing opinions of Justices Iredell and Chase, rather than for the precise issue or result of the litigation. Justice Chase believed that the drafters of the constitutions of the federal and state governments intended to create governments of limited powers and that natural law, as well as the specific provisions of written constitutions, restricted and regulated governmental power.[3] He felt that the province of the judiciary was to ensure that the government did not violate the rights of the people under the natural law. Therefore, Justice Chase decided that the proper role of the Supreme Court was to invalidate legislation if the justices believed that it interfered with rights that the natural law had vested in the people. Justice Iredell, on the other hand, made a plea for what is now known as judicial restraint.[4] He contended that, even if natural law ought to prevail, no valid legal theory existed that indicated that a court should have the power to enforce the natural law over the will of the people as that will was reflected by the other branches of government. He noted that the people had limited the acts of Congress or the states with specific constitutional checks; if those specific checks were violated, the Court only would be enforcing democratic principles by declaring the legislation void. If the Court relied upon natural law to overturn legislative acts, the justices not only would assume powers not granted them under the Constitution but also would disparage the democratic process. Thus, Justice Iredell believed that the justices had no role in enforcing natural law principles because enforcement of such principles would result in the subservience of the people to the individual views of the justices.

In form, the Supreme Court has adopted the views of Justice Iredell and ruled that it only may invalidate acts of the legislative and executive branches of the federal and state governments on the basis of specific provisions of the Constitution. In substance, however, the beliefs of Justice Chase have prevailed as the Court continually has expanded its basis for reviewing the acts of other branches of government.

During the early years of the republic the Court refrained from overturning acts of the federal government. Indeed, the Court only held two acts of the federal government unconstitutional during the period from the Court's formation to the Civil War.[5] Two reasons account for the Court's seeming acceptance of the actions of the other branches of the federal government during this period. First, the central mission of the Court during its early years—particularly under Chief Justice Marshall—was to build the federal system into a viable government. The rulings of the Court on the commerce power and necessary and proper clause helped to establish the federal power. Second, and more importantly, the new federal government made few attempts to limit the "natural" rights of liberty or property of individual citizens. The restrictions on the freedom to use property came from state rather than federal legislation.

In developing controls and checks over the state governments the federal judiciary moved slowly. The text of the Constitution and the Bill of Rights contain only a limited number of restraints on the actions of state

1. 3 U.S. (3 Dall.) 386 (1798).

2. Id. at 401.

3. Id. at 386–88.

4. Id. at 398–400.

5. The first was the section of the Judiciary Act overturned in Marbury v. Madison, 5 U.S. (1 Cranch) 137 (1803). The second was the Missouri Compromise which was held unconstitutional in Dred Scott v. Sandford, 60 U.S. (19 How.) 393 (1857). Actually the defendant's name in this case was misspelled; it should be "Sanford." C. Wright, Law of Federal Courts 249 n. 5 (3d ed. 1976), citing Latham, The Dred Scott Decision 26 (1968).

governments. No matter how much individual justices may have wanted to limit the authority of state governments on the basis of natural law, they realized that using natural law would be a difficult task. Strong arguments against the ability of any branch of the federal government to control state actions had been made by representatives of the states. Consequently, the justices realized that they would need something more concrete than the natural law as the basis for their decisions if they voided state legislative or executive actions. The original Constitution, however, offered little basis for assuming control of state activities through a natural law formula.

The Bill of Rights could have provided a number of specific provisions for controlling the activities of state governments. The history of the Bill of Rights, however, clearly showed that the authors of the amendments intended that they only apply to the federal government. Anti-federalists had objected to the new Constitution because the document contained no specific guarantees that the new national government would not infringe on certain individual rights. The Federalists, on the other hand, had argued that no such enumeration was necessary because no power delegated to the natural government in the body of the Constitution would enable it to legitimately eliminate individual liberties. Indeed, the Federalists argued that listing protected rights would be dangerous because a government may interpret the enumeration of specific protected rights as an implied exclusion of those rights not

so listed because of drafting or timing limitations. The Anti-federalists, however, sought and gained assurances that the federal government, by amendment to the Constitution, would guarantee certain individual liberties. This resulted in the first Congress drafting the Bill of Rights. The ratification process for the ten amendments went swiftly and they were ratified in 1791. The history of the Bill of Rights revealed the difficulty the Supreme Court would have had in suggesting that the amendments were intended as a check on the powers of state governments. Indeed, the Court soon held that the Bill of Rights only limited the acts of the federal government. In *Barron v. Mayor and City Council of Baltimore* [6] the Court confronted the question of whether or not the fifth amendment prohibition on taking private property for a public use without just compensation applied to state governments. Chief Justice Marshall answered that none of the first ten amendments could apply to the state governments because the history of the Bill of Rights supported their application only to the activities of the newly formed central government.[7] Thus, limitations on state governments would have to exist either in natural law or in the specific portions of the text of the Constitution.

The text of the Constitution contains some specific checks on the powers of state government. Article 1, section 10 of the Constitution limits the ability of state governments to take certain specific actions absolutely or to take other actions without the consent of Congress.[8] The prohibitions against bills of

---

6.　32 U.S. (7 Pet.) 243 (1833). For references to historical materials concerning the ratification process and the call for a Bill of Rights, see Chapter 3, section I, and Chapter 4, section I.

7.　Id. at 249.

8.　"No State shall enter into any Treaty, Alliance, or Confederation; grant Letters of Marque and Reprisal; coin Money; emit Bills of Credit; make any thing but gold and silver coin a Tender in Payment of Debts; pass any Bill of Attainder, ex post facto Law, or Law impairing the Obligation of Contracts, or grant any Title of Nobility.

"No State shall, without the Consent of the Congress, lay any Imposts or Duties on Imports or Ex-

ports, except what may be absolutely necessary for executing its inspection Laws: and the net Produce of all Duties and Imposts, laid by any State on Imports or Exports, shall be for the Use of the Treasury of the United States; and all such Laws shall be subject to the Revision and Controul of the Congress.

"No State shall, without the Consent of Congress, lay any Duty of Tonnage, keep Troops, or Ships of War in time of Peace, enter into any Agreement or Compact with another State, or with a foreign Power, or engage in War, unless actually invaded, or in such imminent Danger as will not admit of delay."

U.S. Const. art. I, § 10.

attainder [9] or *ex post facto* laws [10] eliminated the ability of state governments to imprison people by legislative act, but these prohibitions had little to do with general police power legislation. Only a few of the Constitution's provisions served as a limit on the general types of police power legislation that would infringe individual liberties or vested property rights. Indeed, only the provision prohibiting the states from "impairing the obligation of contracts" [11] offered any hope for controlling legislation that eliminated vested property rights.

The Court used the contract clause in its attempt to gain some control over the substance of general police power legislation during the years prior to the Civil War. In 1810 Chief Justice Marshall wrote the opinion in *Fletcher v. Peck.*[12] In this decision the Chief Justice, with the approval of a unanimous Court, found that a state legislature could not rescind grants of land to original purchasers. So long as the original purchasers transferred the land to innocent third parties, the contract clause protected the original grant even though the original purchaser had bribed the members of the legislature to acquire the property initially. *Fletcher* was one of the most important decisions in the history of the Court notwithstanding the contract clause issue. The Court had just survived many threats to its existence ranging from the wrath expressed by President Jefferson following the *Marbury* decision to the attempted impeachment of Justice Chase for partisan activities.[13] Having survived these challenges to its authority, the Marshall Court embarked on a main effort to control state legislation through the contract clause. Moreover, *Fletcher* was a rather adventuresome interpretation of the contract clause because the Court had to find that the clause applied to

contracts made by the state as well as to state invalidation of private contracts. Furthermore, the Court was required to hold that grants of property rights by the state could be construed as contracts. Nevertheless, once he laid the groundwork for these positions in *Fletcher*, Marshall quickly enlarged upon these findings so that they could become a basis for the control of state legislation.

In the famous case of *Dartmouth College v. Woodword*[14] the Court confronted the question of whether a state legislature could control a college established by grant of the British Crown to publicly appointed trustees. Chief Justice Marshall found that the corporate charter was a contract within the meaning of the contract clause and that the state could not alter the charter materially without violating the prohibition of Article I. *Dartmouth College* could have established a basis for controlling many forms of state legislation. The decision logically implied that all businesses or corporations chartered by the state had a right to use their property free of government regulation, because the limitation of the rights of the chartered business would violate the contract of the state. Indeed, Marshall apparently favored this reasoning because it would have fully protected vested property rights. The other justices, however, were unwilling to extend the *Dartmouth* opinion this far. For example, in 1827, the Supreme Court upheld state bankruptcy laws that provided for the discharge of debts and held that the contract clause did not control prospective state interference with free use of property.[15]

The development of both natural law and the contract clause as protection for the individual against the actions of government was centered on the freedom to use property without government restriction. Professor

---

9.   Id.

10.   Id.

11.   Id.

12.   10 U.S. (6 Cranch) 87 (1810).

13.   See R. McCloskey, The American Supreme Court 44–53 (1960).

14.   17 U.S. (4 Wheat.) 518 (1819).

15.   Ogden v. Sanders, 25 U.S. (12 Wheat.) 213 (1827); For an examination of this and other contract clause issues, see section VI, A of this Chapter.

Corwin, in his classic works on the nature of liberty in the American system, has called this "the doctrine of vested rights."[16] He stated that the general theme of the concept of vested rights "was that the effect of legislation on existing property rights was a primary test of its validity; for if these were essentially impaired then some clear constitutional justification must be found for the legislation or it must succumb to judicial condemnation."[17] But at the same time that the judiciary was accepting the "doctrine of vested rights", another legal concept was developing which would oppose it. Political and judicial thought prior to the Civil War had begun to recognize the inherent need of governments to protect the safety and welfare of their citizens from the unrestrained liberty of some individuals.[18] This came to be known as the "police power" concept. This does not relate to any specialized power of government. Instead, the "police power" encompasses the inherent right of state and local governments to enact legislation protecting the health, safety, morals or general welfare of the people within their jurisdiction.

In 1837 the Court recognized that state and local governments had an inherent police power to protect the health, safety, welfare or morals of their people and that the reasonable exercise of the police power did not violate the contract clause. In *Charles River Bridge v. Warren Bridge Co.*[19] the owners of a state-chartered toll bridge contended that the legislature could not authorize any competing bridges. The owners argued that any authorization of competing bridges would diminish the worth of their chartered monopoly. The Court held that, although it would construe the charter as a contract that bound the state, it would interpret the contract narrowly in favor of the state. The justices here recognized the need of the legislature to act to provide for the welfare of its citizens. Consequently, the Court held that, whenever possible, it would interpret public grants and business charters so as to allow reasonable police power regulation. Thus, the contract clause was severely limited as a tool for controlling the substance of the state legislation. The clause would not become an important consideration again, because after the Civil War new means would exist to control the states through the Civil War Amendments.[20]

Other than the provisions of Article I, the Court had few bases for controlling state legislation prior to the Civil War. Any legislation of state or local governments that conflicted with federal legislation would be invalidated under the supremacy clause.[21] Pre-Civil War federal legislation, however, was limited in scope; consequently, the Court had little opportunity to find that state legislation was void because of a direct conflict with federal law or preempted by related, though not directly conflicting, federal acts. The commerce clause provided the Court a method to control state legislation and, thus, to protect private property rights prior to the Civil War. The Court held that the commerce clause prohibited state legislation that would interfere unreasonably with the free flow of commerce between the states.[22] A broad interpretation of the clause was necessary not only to increase the scope of powers of the federal government but also to allow the federal judges to protect to some extent vested rights by controlling some state commercial legislation.

A review of judicial control of the substance of legislation would be incomplete without some discussion of the philosophy of

---

16. E. Corwin, Liberty Against Government 72 (1948).

17. Id.

18. Id. at 88.

19. 36 U.S. (11 Pet.) 420 (1837).

20. U.S. Const. amend. XIII, XIV, XV. The growth of judicial review following the Civil War is discussed in the next section of this Chapter.

21. "This Constitution, and the Laws of the United States which shall be made in Pursuance thereof . . . shall be the Supreme Law of the Land." U.S. Const. art. VI.

22. The development of the commerce clause is examined in Chapter 9.

substantive due process.[23] Substantive due process began to develop before the Civil War. Both the English concept of due process of law and the early American legal theorist's idea of due process focused on the procedural feature of the concept. With the rise of natural rights philosophy, however, some theorists intimated that due process also should have a substantive content. Under this theory, if a legislature passed any law which restricted vested rights or violated natural law, it exceeded all bounds of the social compact in restricting the freedom of some individuals. Therefore, some authorities reasoned that the legislature had denied due process of law to those individuals whose rights or liberties were limited by such legislation because the legislature had denied those deprived persons the guarantees of the basic social compact. Indeed, in several of the contract clause cases, the Marshall Court indicated that state laws that interfered with the free use of property by a chartered corporation violated not only the contract clause but also an inherent right of individuals to be free of legislation which interfered with vested property rights. The theory gained additional credence during this period because a number of state judiciaries held that laws that violated either natural law or vested rights philosophy were invalid under the due process clauses of state constitutions. The most famous federal and state pre-Civil War cases that indicated a judicial acceptance of substantive due process were rendered in 1856 and 1857.

The clearest use of substantive due process in the states occurred in the New York Court of Appeals decision in *Wynehamer v. People.*[24] It held that a prohibition statute violated the state due process clause to the extent that it applied to liquor owned prior to the passage of the statute. Because the measure affected the vested rights of owners in their property (in this case the alcoholic beverages intended for further sale), the court held that the law's enactment was be-

yond any power given to the legislative body under the state's social compact with its citizens.

The federal decision invalidating a law as totally beyond the legislative power came in the case of *Dred Scott v. Sandford.*[25] Dred Scott had been taken as a slave into the state of Illinois and the northern part of the Louisiana Purchase territory. Not only had Illinois forbidden slavery, but the territory into which Scott's "owner" had taken him had been declared a free territory by the Missouri Compromise. Dred Scott sued his present owner and argued that, having been taken into free areas, he had been made a free man. In a decision which almost ended the concept of judicial supremacy, the Court ruled against Dred Scott. The eight separate opinions filed in the case make the basis of the holding and the exact principle of the case unclear. Three reasons, however, do appear for the ruling. First, black slaves were not citizens of the United States. Second, the Supreme Court must respect the Missouri law declaring Scott a slave notwithstanding his previous entry into "free" area. Third, and most important for the growth of the concept of due process, the Missouri Compromise exceeded Congress' power. On this last rationale Chief Justice Taney suggests that the original Constitution had not given Congress any power to interfere with an "owner's" vested rights in his slaves. Thus, the Missouri Compromise was invalid because it deprived the owners of their rights without due process. The decision, at a minimum, shows a pre-war willingness both to adopt substantive due process and the natural law philosophy of Justice Chase. However, Northern leaders saw the *Dred Scott* decision as a judicial attempt to protect the system of slavery and the reaction to the decision was violent. In light of this reaction, it is not surprising that the Court after the war sought to control state and federal legislation under specific provisions of the Constitution rather than the due pro-

---

23. For a detailed study of this concept and its growth prior to the Civil War, see E. Corwin, Liberty Against Government 58–115 (1948).

24. 13 N.Y. 378 (1856).

25. 60 U.S. (19 How.) 393 (1857).

cess clauses. However, the concept of substantive due process, while slow to develop, would dominate constitutional adjudication during the next phase of the country's history.[26]

II. THE GROWTH OF THE CONCEPT—1865 TO 1900

The end of the Civil War prompted a great flurry of Congressional activity. Much of the legislation that Congress passed in the years immediately following the Civil War was designed to punish the southern states for their attempt to secede from the Union. Congress, however, did pass some measures intended to improve the plight of blacks in the South. Although the thirteenth amendment forbidding involuntary servitude was ratified in 1865, the former slaves were unable to enjoy their new freedom. The southern states enacted "Black Codes" and other repressive measures to restrict the ability of blacks to enjoy and exercise their rights. To counteract these repressive measures Congress passed the Civil Rights Act of 1866.[1] The Act made all people born in the country citizens of the United States and gave to such citizens the same rights and "equal benefits of all laws and proceedings for the security of person and property, as is enjoyed by white citizens . . . ."[2]

As Congress was enacting the Civil Rights Act of 1866, it recognized the need to remove doubts about the constitutional ability of Congress to pass such legislation. Therefore, a week after Congress passed the Civil

Rights Act a congressional committee submitted an early version of the fourteenth amendment for Congress' approval.[3] Finally, after several revisions Congress approved the present version of the fourteenth amendment and sent it to the states for ratification.[4] The ratification process for the fourteenth amendment was completed in 1868.

Unlike the Congress during the Civil War and the Reconstruction years, the Supreme Court at this time largely was inactive, exercising its power of judicial review infrequently, perhaps because of it reluctance to entangle itself in the passions and emotions that the War had aroused in the nation. Although the Court reviewed the Constitutionality of federal and state legislation only on a few occasions, it did void several state and federal measures that violated the provisions of the Constitution.[5]

On those occasions that the Court invalidated state and federal legislation, it used the specific language of the Constitution to strike the measures rather than concepts of natural law or fundamental rights. The Court relied on the Constitution's proscription of *ex post facto* laws and bills of attainder to void state legislation in *Cummings v. Missouri*[6] and *Ex parte Garland*.[7] In *United States v. DeWitt*[8] the Court struck federal legislation because it believed the commerce clause had not granted Congress the power to pass the legislation at issue. In short, the Court had abandoned the concept of natural law that had been referred to

---

26. Professor Corwin concludes:

"In less than twenty years from the time of its rendition the crucial ruling in 'Wynehamer' was far on the way to being assimilated into the accepted constitutional law of the country. The 'due process' clause, which had been intended originally to consecrate a mode of procedure, had become a constitutional test of ever increasing reach of the substantive content of legislation. Thus was the doctrine of vested rights brought within the constitutional fold, although without dominating it. For confronting it was the still-expanding concept of the police power."

E. Corwin, Liberty Against Government at 114–15 (1948).

1. 14 Stat. 27 (1866); Cong. Globe, 39th Cong., 1st Sess. 1809, 1861 (1866).

2. 14 Stat. 27, § 1 (1866).

3. Fairman, Does the Fourteenth Amendment Incorporate the Bill of Rights?, 2 Stan.L.Rev. 5, 41 (1949).

4. Cong. Globe, 39th Cong., 1st Sess. 2545, 3042, 3149 (1866). For further references to the history of the Civil War Amendments, see Chapter 16, section II, C.

5. B. F. Wright, The Growth of American Constitutional Law at 80–82 (1942) [hereinafter cited as Wright].

6. 71 U.S. (4 Wall.) 277 (1867).

7. 71 U.S. (4 Wall.) 333 (1861).

8. 76 U.S. (9 Wall.) 41 (1870).

in some earlier decisions. Instead, the Court followed the advice of Justice Iredell to use the specific language and specific prohibitions of the Constitution to check the actions of the state and federal governments.

The Supreme Court's reluctance to give an expansive reading to the Constitution was exemplified dramatically in its first major attempt to interpret and apply the provisions of the new fourteenth amendment. The language of section one of the amendment was broad and sweeping. The amendment prevented any state from making and enforcing any measure that "shall abridge the privileges or immunities of citizens of the United States . . ."[9] Moreover, the amendment adopted the due process language of the fifth amendment and made that language applicable to the states.[10] Finally, the amendment mandated that no state shall "deny to any person within its jurisdiction the equal protection of the laws."[11] Although the amendment's language was capable of a broad and expansive reading, the intent of the Congress that approved the amendment was at best vague and ambiguous. Consequently, the Court was free to exercise discretion when it interpreted the language of the fourteenth amendment. At first the Court opted for a restrictive reading of the amendment's provisions.

The *Slaughter-House Cases*[12] concerned a Louisiana statute that prohibited livestock yards and slaughterhouses within New Orleans and the immediate area surrounding the city. The same statute, however, had an exception to its proscription which allowed the Crescent City Company to operate a slaughterhouse in a specified area of New Orleans. Butchers and others adversely affected brought an action to have the measure declared void, but the Louisiana state courts sustained the statute. The butchers appealed to the Supreme Court. The butch-

ers contended that the Louisiana law violated both the thirteenth and fourteenth amendments. Specifically, under the fourteenth amendment the butchers argued that the statute transgressed not only the amendment's privileges and immunities clause, but also the amendment's due process and equal protection clauses. The Court, however, rejected not only the thirteenth amendment argument, but also all three fourteenth amendment contentions.[13] The Court reasoned that the sole purpose behind the thirteenth amendment was to abolish slavery, and, therefore, the amendment had no application to this case. The Court's reasons for rejecting the fourteenth amendment contentions, however, were more complex.

The majority opinion by Justice Miller focused on the first sentence of the fourteenth amendment, which declared that "[A]ll persons born . . . in the United States . . . are citizens of the United States and of the state wherein they reside."[14] The majority read this language to mean that two types of citizenship existed: state citizenship and national citizenship.[15] The second sentence of the amendment, therefore, only prohibited states from making and enforcing laws that infringed on the privileges and immunities of national citizenship. The Court listed some of the rights that it considered to be the privileges and immunities of United States citizenship. These rights included: the privilege to come to the seat of government to assert a claim; the right of free access to the country's seaports; the right to travel to the government's sub-treasuries, land offices, and courts; the right to assemble peaceably and petition for redress of grievances; the privilege of the writ of habeas corpus; the right to use the nation's navigable water; rights secured for citizens by national treaties; and the rights secured by the thirteenth and fifteenth amendments and the other provisions of the

---

9. U.S. Const. amend. XIV, § 1.

10. ". . . nor shall any State deprive any person of life, liberty, or property, without due process of law . . . ." Id.

11. Id.

12. 83 U.S. (16 Wall.) 36 (1873).

13. Id. at 65–81.

14. U.S. Const. amend. XIV, § 1.

15. 83 U.S. (16 Wall.) at 73–74.

fourteenth amendment.[16] The Louisiana statute that granted the legislatively created monopoly to the Crescent City Co. did not infringe on any of the privileges and immunities of the United States Citizenship. Thus, the Court held that the butchers had no cause of action under the privileges and immunities clause of the fourteenth amendment.

The Court easily disposed of the butchers' contentions under the fourteenth amendment's due process and equal protection clauses. The Court decided that the due process provision only guaranteed that states would enact laws according to the dictates of procedural due process. Thus, the law did not deprive the butchers of their property or their rights without due process of law. In short, the due process clause of the fourteenth amendment did not guarantee the substantive fairness of laws passed by state legislatures. Moreover, the Court rejected the butchers' equal protection argument because it believed that the drafters of the fourteenth amendment only intended to protect blacks from discriminatory actions by a state.[17]

Justice Field and Justice Bradley strongly dissented.[18] Justice Field contended that the majority's reading of the fourteenth amendment's privileges and immunities clause rendered that clause useless. The Constitution already protected the privilege and immunities that the majority listed. Justice Field believed that the fourteenth amendment protected those privileges and immunities *"which of right belong to the citizens of all free governments."* [19] Among these privileges was the right to pursue lawful employment. The Supreme Court never did accept Justice Field's view of the fourteenth amendment's privileges and immunities

clause, and the majority's interpretation in the *Slaughter-House Cases* is still the accepted reading of that provision, rendering the clause inoperative as a check on state laws.[20]

Nevertheless, both dissenting justices did express views about the proper scope of the fourteenth amendment that later Supreme Courts did accept. Both Justice Field and Justice Bradley, joined by Chief Justice Chase and Justice Swayne, argued that the fourteenth amendment did guarantee equal protection of the laws to all persons in all the states.[21] They believed that the drafters of the fourteenth amendment did not intend to limit the application of the equal protection clause to black citizens. Moreover, these justices believed that the fourteenth amendment protected the natural and inalienable rights of all citizens. In their view, the amendment prevented states from enacting arbitrary laws that limited these natural rights.[22] Their opinions echoed somewhat the beliefs of Justice Chase on the philosophical limitations on governmental power.[23] A majority of the immediate post-Civil War Supreme Court, however, was not willing to read into the fourteenth amendment any substantive due process guarantee. Therefore, for the time being at least, the Court refused to accept the views of Bradley and Field. The economic and political realities of the late nineteenth century United States, however, soon would move the Court to accept the legal theories of the dissenting justices.

The great industrial revolution the country experienced during the latter half of the nineteenth century had a profound influence on the growth of judicial review. The rapid growth of transportation and communication during this period led many states to at-

---

16. Id. at 79–80.

17. Id. at 80–81.

18. Id. at 83 (Field, J., dissenting, joined by Chase, C.J. & Swayne & Bradley, JJ.); id. at 111 (Bradley, J., dissenting); see also id. at 124 (Swayne, J., dissenting).

19. Id. at 98.

20. Only one decision struck a state law on the basis of the privileges or immunities clause, Colgate v.

Harvey, 296 U.S. 404 (1935) and that decision was quickly overruled, Madden v. Kentucky, 309 U.S. 83 (1940).

21. 83 U.S. (16 Wall.) at 105–11 (Field, J., dissenting, joined by Chase, C.J. & Swayne & Bradley, JJ.).

22. Id. at 106–11; 118–19.

23. See section one of this chapter for a review of the Chase "natural law" philosophy.

tempt to regulate these industries.[24] As the states attempted to control industry, representatives of the regulated businesses would seek to have the state regulatory schemes declared unconstitutional. Initially, the Supreme Court's reaction to these attempts to seek judicial invalidation of the state regulatory measures was restrained. The Court willingly recognized that the states had a legitimate authority under their police powers to control business activity within their borders. The Court, therefore, would void a state regulatory measure usually only if the law violated a specific prohibition contained in the Constitution or if the law interfered with interstate commerce. Indeed, in the period between 1874 and 1898, only in sixty-five cases did the Court hold a state law unconstitutional.[25] On most of those occasions when the Court did invalidate a state law, it did so because it believed the law infringed on Congress' power under the commerce clause.[26]

At the same time that the legal representatives of large businesses were pressing the Court to take a bold and affirmative stance to protect rapidly growing industries from government regulations, contemporary legal thought began actively to advocate a substantive interpretation of the due process clauses. Thomas M. Cooley in his influential treatise *Constitutional Limitations* strongly supported substantive due process concepts.[27] Many judges relied on Cooley's book as an authoritative analysis of the state and federal constitutions. Moreover, Justice Field continued to argue in his dissents for an interpretation of the due process clause that would protect the freedom of contract. Such an interpretation of that clause would void many of the state regulatory laws and would accord well with the *laissez-faire* view of economic development that prevailed during this period of Ameri-

can history. Although the Court continued to defer to legislative judgments when it reviewed the constitutionality of state and federal laws, it began to suggest that certain limits existed that would control the legislative power.

The Court in *Munn v. Illinois* [28] gave an indication that the due process clause contained some implied and inherent restrictions on the police power of the states. Illinois had enacted laws regulating the rates of grain elevators. The grain elevator operators argued that the Illinois statutes violated not only the commerce clause but also the due process clause of the fourteenth amendment. The Court rejected the commerce clause contention because the statutes regulated businesses exclusively within the boundaries of the state. The Court also rejected the due process argument. The Court noted that a state could exercise its police power to control the use of property when it is necessary for the public good. The regulation of private property in this case was particularly appropriate because the operation of grain elevators was "affected with a public interest." [29] The Court even refused to evaluate the reasonableness of the established rates because the state legislature had the implied authority to establish maximum rates. The Court, however, qualified its approval of a state's use of its police power when it stated that "[u]ndoubtedly, in mere private contracts, relating to matters in which the public has no interest, what is reasonable must be judicially ascertained . . . this is because the legislature has no control over such a contract." [30]

The Court continued through 1886 to follow a policy of noninterference with legislative judgments. Occasionally, however, the Court would warn that the legislatures must recognize a limit to their law-making power. Although the Court sustained the state reg-

---

24. Wright, supra note 5, at 87.

25. Id. at 87–88.

26. Id.

27. See R. G. McCloskey, The American Supreme Court 131 (1960).

28. 94 U.S. 113 (1877).

29. Id. at 130.

30. Id. at 134.

ulation of railroad rates in the *Railroad Commission Cases*,[31] it explicitly recognized a limit to the state's regulatory power. The Court observed that a state cannot set rates so low as to "require a railroad corporation to carry persons or property without reward."[32] Moreover, the Court reasoned that a state cannot use regulatory measures as a pretense for what "amounts to a taking of private property for public use without just compensation, or without due process of law."[33]

Finally, the Court explicitly stated in *Mugler v. Kansas*[34] that it would use substantive due process to determine the constitutionality of governmental regulatory measures. In *Mugler* the Court sustained a statute that prohibited the sale of alcoholic beverages. The Court recognized that the legislature could exercise its police powers once it determined what laws were needed to protect the public health, morals, and safety. At the same time, however, the *Mugler* Court stated that limits existed beyond which the legislature could not go. Moreover, the courts had the responsibility to determine whether the legislature had exceeded these limits. The *Mugler* Court decided that the judiciary must look to the substance of the laws to see if the legislature had surpassed its authority.[35]

The *Mugler* decision gave notice that the Court would begin evaluating the relationship of a law to its purported purposes. A statute required a substantial relation to the protection of the public health, morals, or safety before the Court would sustain the measure as a valid exercise of the state's police power.

In the year before the Court decided *Mugler*, it held, without discussion, that corporations were included under the term "persons" as that word was used in the fourteenth amendment.[36] Therefore, any protection of fundamental or natural rights that the fourteenth amendment offered was afforded to incorporated business entities as well as to people. The Court, thus, had laid the framework for using the fourteenth amendment as a broad shield to protect industry from governmental regulation.[37]

In *Allgeyer v. Louisiana*,[38] the Supreme Court used the substantive due process framework already created to invalidate a state statute. This decision concerned a Louisiana statute which prohibited anyone from giving effect to marine insurance on any Louisiana property if the insurance company that issued the policy had not complied in all respects with Louisiana law. The state had convicted Allgeyer for violating the statute when he mailed a letter advising a New York insurance company about the shipment of some insured goods. The New York insurer was not registered to do business in Louisiana. The Supreme Court reversed the conviction and held that the statute violated the fourteenth amendment because it deprived the defendant of his liberty without due process of law.

The *Allgeyer* Court reasoned that the state of Louisiana had no jurisdiction over contracts made outside of the state with a foreign corporation. Although the Court primarily relied on this jurisdictional reasoning to void the law, it went on and extensively discussed the liberty of contract and the fourteenth amendment's protection of liberty interests. The *Allgeyer* Court reasoned that the "liberty" that the fourteenth amendment protected was a more extensive liberty than merely the right of a person to be free of physical restraints. The fourteenth amendment's due process clause also

31. 116 U.S. 307 (1886).

32. Id. at 331.

33. Id.

34. 123 U.S. 623 (1887).

35. Id. at 661.

36. Santa Clara County v. Southern Pacific R.R. Co., 118 U.S. 394 (1886).

37. The Court first used this concept to strike a state law in Missouri Pacific Ry. v. Nebraska, 164 U.S. 403 (1896). The Court there held that a law requiring railroads to allow privately owned grain elevators on their right of way denied the railroad company property without due process of law. There was no further exposition of the due process concept in the opinion.

38. 165 U.S. 578 (1897).

guaranteed that a person would be free to enjoy "all his faculties; to be free to use them in all lawful ways . . . ."[39] to insure that a person could enjoy "all his faculties," the *Allgeyer* Court believed that the fourteenth amendment permitted a person to seek any type of employment or to pursue any type of avocation, and, to facilitate this liberty, the amendment protected the freedom of contract. The Louisiana statute deprived *Allgeyer* of his liberty to contract "which the state legislature had no right to prevent. . . ."[40]

The Supreme Court during last half of the nineteenth century had undergone a major philosophical transformation. The Court of the immediate post-Civil War years willingly deferred to the legislature's judgment on policy issues. The Court readily would recognize that the state's police powers gave the legislatures ample authority to impose regulatory schemes on the industries within their borders. The Court usually would invalidate these schemes only if they either violated a specific prohibition of the Constitution, or if they interfered with the federal government's power under the commerce clause. The Court, however, began slowly to abandon its non-interventionist philosophy. The economic, social, and intellectual thought of the late nineteenth century persuaded the Court that it must do more to protect business interests from encroaching governmental control. The idea of substantive due process became the most viable concept for the Court to adopt as a legal theory to protect industry from government regulation. By the turn of the century the Court had embraced the concept fully and was ready to use it as a rationale for striking legislation that attempted to restrain the freedom of businesses to contract.

III. SUBSTANTIVE DUE PROCESS FROM 1900 TO 1936

By the turn of the century the Supreme Court had indicated its complete acceptance of the substantive due process doctrine. The dicta of *Allgeyer v. Louisiana*[1] revealed the Court's willingness to use the substantive due process doctrine to void any economic or social legislation that the Court believed unreasonably infringed on the liberty to contract. The substantive due process test could be easily stated: the government had to employ means (legislation) which bore some reasonable relation to a legitimate end. As the doctrine had developed, it held that any law which the justices did not believe related to a legitimate end was void as government had no power to enact this limitation of liberty. Similarly, no matter how temperate the legislation might seem to others, it would be void if the justices thought it related to some end which they considered beyond the proper role of government. Freedom in the marketplace and freedom to contract were viewed as liberties which were protected by the due process clause. Thus the justices would invalidate a law if they thought it restricted economic liberty in a way that was not reasonably related to a legitimate end. But as they did not view labor regulation, price control, or other economic measures as legitimate "ends" in themselves, only a limited amount of business regulation could pass this test. Only when the Justices were convinced that the regulation actually promoted public health, safety, or some other important "public interest" would they uphold the law. While the "test" might sound mild, independent judicial review of such legislation made the constitutionality of these laws dependent on the justices' individual views. While many laws were invalidated on this basis, we will examine only a representative sample of the Court's actions during this period.

Although state legislatures were adopting a variety of methods to regulate businesses, one of the most popular regulations was setting the maximum number of hours that an employee could work in one week in a particular business. In 1898 the Supreme Court

---

39. Id. at 589.
40. Id. at 591.

1. 165 U.S. 578 (1897). See the preceding section for the development of the doctrine.

upheld a Utah statute that limited the hours men could work in mines and smelters.[2] After noting the extremely unsafe and unhealthy working conditions of mines, the Court declared Utah's passage of the regulatory measure as a reasonable exercise of the state's police powers in relation to this type of occupation. Although the law limited the liberty of contract, the opinion sustained the Utah statute because it was a valid health law.[3] The Court, however, retained the authority under the substantive due process theory to invalidate any similar measure that the Court did not believe was a legitimate health measure.

The State of New York enacted a law that limited the number of hours a baker could work to only 60 hours a week or 10 hours a day. The issue of the constitutional validity of the New York statute came before the court in the now infamous case of *Lochner v. New York*.[4] A majority of the Court held the law unconstitutional because it was an arbitrary and unnecessary interference with the liberty to contract between an employer and employee—a liberty protected by the fourteenth amendment. New York had infringed unreasonably on "the freedom of master and employee to contract with each other in relation to their employment."[5] The majority found no legitimate purpose of government in regulating labor conditions or practices where the regulation was not a true health or safety measure. The Court rejected any suggestion that the New York law was a health measure. The majority refused to accept the argument that the legislature might rationally have taken these steps to protect the health of the workers. While the *Lochner* majority stated that it would not "substitut[e] the judgment of the court for that of the legislature,"[6] it also stated, in a more frank passage, that "[w]e

do not believe in the soundness of the views which uphold this law."[7] Consequently, the provision, in the Court's view, was purely a piece of labor legislation and as such was an improper exercise of the state's police power.

Justice Holmes and Justice Harlan wrote famous dissents to the *Lochner* majority opinion.[8] Justice Holmes believed that the majority was imposing its own theory of a proper economic policy on the state of New York by invalidating this law. The Constitution, however, did not allow the Court to force a certain economic concept on the country. His remark that "[t]he 14th Amendment does not enact Mr. Herbert Spencer's Social Statics"[9] has become one of the most famous in constitutional history. On the contrary, the founding fathers created a Constitution "for people of fundamentally differing views,"[10] and the Court should not void a law simply because a legislature enacted the measure to implement an economic policy the justices do not believe proper. Justice Holmes stated that the Court should invalidate a law only when "a rational and fair man necessarily would admit that the statute proposed would infringe fundamental principles as they have been understood by the traditions of our people and our law."[11]

Justice Harlan's dissent followed a somewhat different analysis than Justice Holmes. Justice Harlan was willing to accept the New York statute as a valid health measure. He cited the evidence that supported the contention that limiting the number of hours bakers could work would protect the welfare of these workers whose health standard was below the national average.[12] Justice Harlan believed that as long as the statute arguably was a health measure the Court should sustain the law.

2. Holden v. Hardy, 169 U.S. 366 (1898).

3. Id. at 393–98.

4. 198 U.S. 45 (1905).

5. Id. at 64.

6. Id. at 56–57.

7. Id. at 61.

8. Id. at 65, 74.

9. Id. at 75.

10. Id. at 76.

11. Id.

12. Id. at 71.

The majority and dissenting opinions of *Lochner* classically reveal the problem the Supreme Court experienced between 1900 and 1937. The state legislatures and the national government were enacting an ever-increasing amount of legislation that regulated the economic and social life of Americans. Many of the Supreme Court justices believed they had an obligation to protect the free enterprise system as it was embodied in the concept of laissez faire.[13] It must be stressed that their position resulted from their independent reading of the Constitution and the historic economic freedom of action in American life rather than from some arbitrary desire to protect big business. While they would uphold some laws which they felt were needed for health or safety, they were inclined to fully protect freedom of contract and liberty in the market place. Consequently, these justices, as exemplified by the *Lochner* majority opinion, were willing to use not only the substantive due process concept, but also the commerce clause, the contract clause, and the equal protection clause to void those laws that they believed unreasonably infringed on free enterprise. At the same time, however, the Court had a tradition of judicial forbearance.[14] As the *Lochner* dissents indicated, the Court historically sustained legislation that arguably fell within the confines of constitutionality. Because this tension existed, the Court of the early twentieth century failed to follow a systematic and uniform approach to the legislation it reviewed.

Three years after *Lochner* the Court sustained state legislation that regulated the number of hours women could work. In *Muller v. Oregon*[15] then attorney Louis D. Brandeis presented the Court with the now-famous "Brandeis brief," a brief that contained massive documentation to justify the regulation of the work hours for women. Nine years after *Muller* the Court, without mentioning *Lochner*, sustained statutes that limited the work hours for men in certain industries.[16] Again, the supporters of the measure used a Brandeis brief to present the necessary documentation to justify the law. But the Court had not abandoned its use of substantive due process. The states had to be prepared to present sufficient evidence in support of legislation that controlled the hours of labor to convince the Court that the legislation was a proper exercise of the state's police power. If the states failed to justify adequately a particular labor regulation as an appropriate police power measure, the Supreme Court would invalidate the statute as violative of due process.

The Court not only relied on the due process clause as a standard to determine the constitutionality of labor or business legislation but also relied on the fourteenth amendment's equal protection clause.[17] The Court on several occasions also held state legislation that taxed certain businesses unconstitutional because the particular tax classifications denied businesses equal protection of the laws.[18] The Court's use of the equal protection clause to invalidate economic legislation that discriminated against certain industrial enterprises demonstrated the justices' view that economic freedom was as constitutionally significant as any civil liberty. The authors of the fourteenth amendment drafted the equal protection clause as a protective provision to shield blacks from laws that discriminated against them unfairly,[19] but the Court during this period found

---

13. B.F. Wright, The Growth of American Constitutional Law 109–12 (1942) [Hereinafter cited as Wright]; R.G. McCloskey, The American Supreme Court 137–39 (1960) [Hereinafter cited as McCloskey].

14. McCloskey, supra note 13, at 138–39.

15. 208 U.S. 412 (1908).

16. Bunting v. Oregon, 243 U.S. 426 (1917).

17. See, e.g., Gulf, C. & S. F. Ry. Co. v. Ellis, 165 U.S. 150 (1897) (attorney's fees provisions for certain suits against railroads denies the railroads equal protection); Louisville Gas & Elec. Co. v. Coleman, 277 U.S. 32 (1928) (mortgage recording fee and tax classifications violate equal protection); Wright, supra note 13, at 157–63.

18. See, e.g., Quaker City Cab Co. v. Pennsylvania, 277 U.S. 389 (1928); Stewart Dry Goods Co. v. Lewis, 294 U.S. 550 (1935); Wright, supra note 13, at 158–62.

19. See Chapter 16, section II, C.

discrimination in favor of certain economic groups to be similarly objectionable.

The Supreme Court did begin to use the equal protection clause to invalidate state laws that denied black citizens equal protection of the laws. In *Nixon v. Herndon* [20] the Court relied on the equal protection clause to void a Texas statute that precluded blacks from participating in the Democratic primary. Similarly, the Court held unconstitutional a subsequent Texas statute that permitted the executive committee of the Democratic party to prescribe membership requirements.[21] Because the Court found the committee was an agent of the state, the Texas law violated the equal protection guarantee when the committee excluded blacks from party membership. Although these two cases reveal the Court's awareness of the original intent behind the drafting of the equal protection clause, the Court only infrequently confronted racially discriminatory laws during the early part of the twentieth century.[22]

During the early part of the century the Court decided against the validity of state laws in many cases because these laws improperly burdened interstate commerce.[23] At the same time, however, only a relatively few cases arrived before the Court where the constitutionality of federal legislation enacted under Congress' authority under the commerce clause was an issue.[24] Between 1900 and 1910 Congress repeatedly increased the power and authority of the Interstate Commerce Commission. The Court usually sustained this legislation. In *The Minnesota Rate Cases* [25] the Court recognized Congress' authority over interstate transportation. In a subsequent railroad

regulation case the Court noted that simply because some elements of a transaction have intrastate features does not preclude congressional control over that transaction if the intrastate and interstate operations "are so related that the government of the one involves the control of the other." [26] The Court also established that when interstate and intrastate transactions are intertwined, Congress "is entitled to prescribe the final and dominant rule." [27]

In *The Lottery Case* [28] the Court held that because the federal government had the power to regulate commerce between the states, the government had the authority to prohibit certain articles from interstate commerce. The Court reasoned that the power to regulate necessarily included the power to prohibit. The Court subsequently used this reasoning to sustain the Pure Food and Drug Act and the Mann Act; [29] the Mann Act prohibited the transportation of women across state lines for immoral purposes. Although these acts were, in reality, primarily health and moral provisions, the Court willingly sustained these measures as a valid exercise of congressional supervision over interstate commerce. The Court, however, set limits to its deference to congressional judgments exercised under the commerce clause. Those limits were revealed in *Hammer v. Dagenhart*.[30]

Congress had passed a law that excluded from interstate commerce products of mines and manufacturing enterprises that employed children under a certain age. Congress clearly intended to reduce the use of child labor by enacting this law. In *Dagenhart* the Court labeled the provision as an improper exercise of Congress' author-

---

20. 273 U.S. 536 (1927).

21. Nixon v. Condon, 286 U.S. 73 (1932).

22. Wright, supra note 13, at 148–50.

23. Id. at 113.

24. Id.

25. 230 U.S. 352 (1913).

26. Houston, East & West Texas Ry. Co. v. United States, 234 U.S. 342, 351–52 (1914).

27. Id.

28. 188 U.S. 321 (1903). The docket title was Champion v. Ames.

29. Wright, supra note 13, at 121. See Hipolite Egg Co. v. United States, 220 U.S. 45 (1911) (Pure Food & Drug Act of 1906); Hoke v. United States, 227 U.S. 308 (1913) (Mann Act); Caminetti v. United States, 242 U.S. 470 (1917) (Mann Act upheld in context where there was no business transaction).

30. 247 U.S. 251 (1918).

ity under the commerce clause.[31] The Court believed that the tenth amendment had given the states the exclusive power to regulate manufacturing done within their borders. Under the statute at issue, however, Congress had attempted to regulate the production of articles before their interstate transportation had begun. Therefore, Congress, by enacting this child labor statute, had exceeded its authority under the commerce clause.[32]

Justice Holmes, as he had in *Lochner*, dissented. He failed to discern any conceptual difference between the statute at issue in *Hammer* and the statutes sustained in previous cases that had prohibited from interstate commerce certain other designated products. Justice Holmes would have deferred to Congress' judgment because to him it "did not matter whether the supposed evil precedes or follows the transportation. It is enough that in the opinion of Congress the transportation encourages the evil."[33] The Justice remained consistent with his *Lochner* dissent.

Similar to the substantive due process cases, the commerce clause cases reveal the tension between the justices' desire to protect business from increasing government control and the Court's traditional forbearance when it exercised its power of judicial review.

Often the justices' concern over governmental intervention with business expressed itself in the Court's invalidation of legislation that regulated the relationship between employer and employee.[34] The Court, however, also voided some legislation that regulated the rates certain businesses could

charge customers. The issue in many of these rate regulation cases was whether the regulated business was one "affected with a public interest."[35] In *Munn v. Illinois*[36] the Court upheld a state statute that controlled the rates grain elevator operators could charge farmers because the grain elevators were businesses "affected with a public interest," and, thus, were subject to a state's police powers. During the early part of the twentieth century the Court sustained many regulatory schemes because the regulated businesses were affected with a public interest.[37] Beginning in 1923, however, the Court began to use the negative implications of the public interest concept to void legislative regulation. The Court decided a series of cases where it held various regulatory devices violative of the fourteenth amendment because the regulated businesses were not affected with a public interest. Unless the business either resulted from a public grant or franchise, was subject traditionally to regulation, or "which though not public at their inception may be said to have risen to be such and have become subject in consequence to some government regulation,"[38] the state could not regulate the business. The Court's guidelines to determine whether a state properly could regulate a business were of little help to the states. Those businesses that fell within the first two categories always had been subject to state supervision. The third category was the critical class of businesses, and the Court retained the power to determine subjectively the parameters of that class of businesses. The Court's approach to the public interest line of cases was as unprincipled as its applica-

---

31. Id. at 271–73.

32. Id. at 276.

33. Id. at 280.

34. See, e.g. Adair v. United States, 208 U.S. 161 (1908) (Court's invalidation of federal law prohibiting anti-union "yellow dog" employment contracts as violation of due process); Coppage v. Kansas, 236 U.S. 1 (1915) (state law prohibiting anti-union activity contracts held invalid as violation of due process).

35. See, e.g., Tyson & Bro. v. Banton, 273 U.S. 418 (1927) (theater ticket sales regulation invalidated); Rib-

nik v. McBride, 277 U.S. 350 (1928) (employment agency practice and rate regulation invalid). The "public interest" issue concerned the Court majority whenever it reviewed new forms of business regulation. Wright, supra note 13, at 166.

36. 94 U.S. 113 (1877).

37. McCloskey, supra note 13, at 157.

38. Wolff Packing Co. v. Court of Industrial Relations, 262 U.S. 522, 535 (1923).

tion of the substantive due process doctrine and the commerce clause.

In *Nebbia v. New York* [39] the Court reversed the public interest line of cases. New York had established a regulatory board that had the authority to set minimum prices for the retail sale of milk. The Court sustained the legislation as a legitimate exercise of the state's police power. The petitioner contended that the milk industry was not a business affected with a public interest, and consequently, the state could not control the retail price of milk. The Court rejected the contention with the recognition that "there is no closed class or category of businesses affected with a public interest. . . ." [40] The *Nebbia* Court stated that the Court's function "is to determine in each case whether circumstances vindicate the challenged regulation as a reasonable exertion of governmental authority or condemn it as arbitrary or discriminatory." [41] The opinion contained language that suggested that the Court's use of the substantive due process doctrine to invalidate economic or welfare legislation was at an end. The Court stated that "a state is free to adopt whatever economic policy may reasonably be deemed to promote public welfare, and to enforce that policy by legislation adopted to its purpose." [42] Moreover, the *Nebbia* Court observed that the courts did not have the authority either to establish an economic policy or to overrule the legislative choice of an appropriate policy. The Court apparently had adopted Justice Holmes' *Lochner* dissent as the proper approach to economic legislation. The language of *Nebbia*, however, was deceiving because the Court continued to use the substantive due process concept to invalidate legislation.

Immediately after his election to his first term in office President Roosevelt marshalled his support in Congress and persuaded Congress to enact his New Deal legislation designed to help the nation recover from the Great Depression. [43] The issue of the constitutionality of some of this legislation came before the Supreme Court between 1934 and 1936. With a remarkable series of decisions the Court invalidated many of the New Deal acts. [44] The New Deal legislation presented to a majority of the justices of the Court the greatest threat to their concept of free enterprise that they could imagine. Therefore, the Court used a narrow interpretation of the commerce clause to declare New Deal provisions unconstitutional. [45] The Court also refused to follow *Nebbia's* formulation of the Court's proper role when reviewing economic legislation under the due process clause.

Two years after *Nebbia* the Court declared unconstitutional another New York statute that had established a minimum wage for women. In *Morehead v. New York ex rel. Tipaldo* [46] the Court used the substantive due process doctrine much as it had before *Nebbia*. The minimum wage law violated the fourteenth amendment because it impaired the liberty to contract. The *Morehead* opinion's use of substantive due process was not unique. Nevertheless, the opinion is important because of its timing. The Court decided this case shortly after it invalidated much of President Roosevelt's New Deal legislation. Hence, the *Morehead* decision announced to the states, as the Court's decision on the New Deal legislation had announced to Congress, that the Court would continue to construe strictly the powers the government had to control business.

The Court's refusal to sustain much of the New Deal-type legislation of the early 1930's precipitated a constitutional crisis. The voters re-elected Franklin Roosevelt to a second presidential term by an overwhelming margin in 1936. [47] The President interpreted his

---

39.   291 U.S. 502 (1934).

40.   Id. at 536.

41.   Id.

42.   Id. at 537.

43.   McCloskey, supra note 13, at 163.

44.   See Chapter 4, section III, C; Wright, supra note 13, at 180–82.

45.   Id. McCloskey, supra note 13, at 165–66.

46.   298 U.S. 587 (1936).

47.   Wright, supra note 13, at 200–201.

landslide margin of victory as a mandate from the people to do whatever was necessary to end the Depression. Before, however, he could implement that mandate, he had to eliminate the Supreme Court as an obstacle to his programs. Therefore, Roosevelt proposed a plan whereby the President could appoint a new justice if an incumbent justice failed to retire when he reached seventy. Roosevelt wanted the opportunity to appoint justices who would interpret the Constitution in a way that would allow the New Deal legislation to stand.

The President's plan confronted the Court with the most serious threat to its constitutional authority since the Court's inception. The President was proposing to "pack" the Court with his appointees largely because he disapproved of the Court's invalidation of his legislation. This plan threatened to destroy the concept of the Court as a neutral arbiter of constitutional issues. Congress debated the merits of the plan for almost six months. Ultimately Congress voted against the plan.[48] At this time the Court reversed its position and began to sustain much of the economic and labor legislation enacted by Congress and the states. The Court began to abandon its substantive due process review of economic and welfare legislation as well as broadening its interpretation of the federal commerce power.[49]

Before turning to the "modern era," we should mention that the Court during the first third of the twentieth century also started to apply the doctrine to the area of civil rights. Although the number of civil liberty cases the Court decided was small, the number increased as the years passed. The Supreme Court cases principally involved state statutes and the due process clause of the fourteenth amendment. In *Buchanan v. Warley*[50] the Court voided a Louisville city ordinance that precluded blacks from moving into areas where the residents were primarily white. The ordinance violated the due process clause because it was an unwarranted interference with property rights. The Court felt constrained to use the due process clause to protect property rights in the civil rights area as it had done in the business area.[51]

Six years after *Buchanan* the Court began to expand the impact of substantive due process in the area of civil liberties. Nebraska had enacted a statute that prohibited teaching in any language other than English. In *Meyer v. Nebraska*[52] the Court declared the provision unconstitutional because it improperly infringed upon liberty to make educational decisions.[53] Two years after *Meyer* the Court decided *Gitlow v. New York*.[54] Although the *Gitlow* Court sustained a conviction under the New York criminal anarchy statute, the ramification of the decision on civil liberties was profound. In *Gitlow* the Court assumed the fourteenth amendment's due process guarantee protect-

---

48. Id. at 202.

49. Id. at 203–08. See particularly West Coast Hotel Co. v. Parrish, 300 U.S. 379 (1937): "What is this freedom? The Constitution does not speak of freedom of contract. It speaks of liberty and prohibits the deprivation of liberty without due process of law. In prohibiting that deprivation the Constitution does not recognize an absolute and uncontrollable liberty . . . [R]egulation which is reasonable in relation to its subject and is adopted in the interests of the community is due process." Id. at 391. *West Coast Hotel* upheld a state minimum wage law for women and explicitly overruled Adkins v. Children's Hosp., 261 U.S. 525 (1923), which had declared that "freedom of contract is nevertheless the general rule and restraint the exception." Id. at 546. *Adkins* had struck down a state minimum wage law for women. See also United States v. Darby, 312 U.S. 100 (1941) (wage and hour laws for men and women upheld).

50. 245 U.S. 60 (1917). Professor Schmidt has presented substantial evidence to support the thesis that *Buchanan* should be understood as a judicial effort to restrict racially discriminatory legislation. Schmidt, Principle and Prejudice: The Supreme Court and Race in the Progressive Era, Part 1: The Heyday of Jim Crow, 82 Colum.L.Rev. 444 (1982). See Chapter 16, section II, D, 3.

51. McCloskey, supra note 13, at 171.

52. 262 U.S. 390 (1923).

53. The Court also held that the state could not prohibit private schools, although the state could require them to meet secular educational standards. Pierce v. Society of Sisters, 268 U.S. 510 (1925).

54. 268 U.S. 652 (1925).

ed the freedom of speech. The *Gitlow* assumption implied that the Court had abandoned its earlier position that the fourteenth amendment's due process clause did not apply to the states the guarantees of the Bill of Rights.[55]

Finally, in 1931 the Court decided two cases that held that state statutes violated the due process clause because the provisions impaired the liberty of speech and press.[56] To an uncertain extent, then, the provisions of the Bill of Rights did apply to the states. Moreover, in a series of cases the Court decided that the states could not deny an individual a right to counsel nor could the state use forced confessions in criminal prosecutions.[57] Under the theory of due process, the Court began to incorporate into the fourteenth amendment some of the liberty guarantees of the first eight amendments.

IV. SUBSTANTIVE DUE PROCESS SINCE 1937

The substantive guarantee of due process required that legislation have a rational relationship to a legitimate end of government. If a law did not have such a relationship, it would be an unconstitutional deprivation of liberty as to those persons it affected. Similarly, the equal protection clause required that governmental classifications have a rational relationship to a legitimate end of government. The impact of these doctrines resulted from the independent judicial review of the basis for laws under these tests. During the first third of the century, the Supreme Court did not give any deference to the opinion of other branches of government regarding the legitimate ends of legislation or the proper means for achieving those

ends.[1] A law would not be upheld unless a majority of the justices were of the opinion that its end was within the proper scope of activities for an American governmental entity. Additionally, these justices would not uphold a law unless they were of the opinion that the means employed to achieve even permissible ends were in fact reasonable. Many of the justices during this period were of the opinion that the government should not "arbitrarily" disrupt the free market economic system. But their rulings could not even be termed an economically consistent defense of laissez faire theories of economics. Instead, the justices upheld laws which they personally agreed would be necessary to protect important social goals even though the legislation involved some restraint on commerce,[2] while they struck down as arbitrary legislation laws they considered to tamper unnecessarily with the free market system.[3] Thus, the independent review of legislation during this period resulted in an unprincipled control of social and economic legislation.[4]

Although the Supreme Court of the pre-1937 era relied on the commerce clause and the contract clause to void some economic legislation, the due process clause of the fifth and fourteenth amendments and the equal protection clause provided the Court with the most useful and flexible concepts to promote and protect the economic scheme that the justices believed was best for the country.[5] These clauses allowed the justices to decide whether a regulatory program was reasonably related to a particular end, or whether a classification system was reasonably necessary for a certain economic objective. The justices had complete discretion to determine the permissibility of economic and

---

55. See Hurtado v. California, 110 U.S. 516 (1884).

56. Stromberg v. California, 283 U.S. 359 (1931); Near v. Minnesota, 283 U.S. 697 (1931).

57. Powell v. Alabama, 287 U.S. 45 (1932); Brown v. Mississippi, 297 U.S. 278 (1936).

1. See the preceding section for an examination of these cases.

2. See, e.g. Muller v. Oregon, 208 U.S. 412 (1908) where the proponents had to revert to the famous

"Brandeis Brief" to convince the Court of the necessity for, and the reasonableness of, the control over labor laws regarding women.

3. See Lochner v. New York, 198 U.S. 45 (1905).

4. See Wright, The Growth of American Constitutional Law 204–26 (1967) [hereinafter cited as Wright]; R. McCloskey, The American Supreme Court 182–85 (1960) [hereinafter cited as McCloskey].

5. McCloskey, supra note 4, at 182–84.

social welfare legislation. With the advent of the Great Depression, however, the economic beliefs of the majority of the justices failed to comport with the economic programs of the "New Deal." [6] The two branches of the federal government began to work at odds with each other, and one branch would sooner or later have to yield to the other.[7]

In 1934 the Court decided *Nebbia v. New York* [8] and revealed, for the first time, a willingness to shift its thinking on economic substantive due process. In *Nebbia* the Court sustained a state regulatory scheme for milk because the regulations were reasonable in light of the desired end. The Court stated that "a state is free to adopt whatever economic policy may reasonably be deemed to promote public welfare." [9] The *Nebbia* opinion signaled the Court's possible abandonment of the traditional economic substantive due process thinking. The Court disclosed a willingness to defer to the legislative judgment on what was reasonable to promote the public welfare. The *Nebbia* decision, however, was followed with a series of cases where the Court applied traditional economic substantive due process concepts to void business regulations.[10] The final determination on whether the Court actually would change its approach to economic legislation was left to subsequent events.

The court-packing controversy of 1937 precipitated the permanent change in the Court's application of the substantive due process concept. The Court's decisions of 1937 and the years immediately following revealed the justices' total disenchantment with substantive due process as a constitu-

tional theory that could protect property interests from government regulation and control. These decisions disclosed not only that the Court no longer believed that economic issues were of constitutional magnitude but also that the justices were prepared to apply new and objective constitutional standards to test the constitutionality of economic legislation.[11]

The first significant sign of the demise of the Court's use of substantive due process in testing the constitutionality of economic legislation came in *West Coast Hotel v. Parrish*.[12] In *Parrish* the Court sustained the constitutionality of the state of Washington's minimum wage law for women. The appellant, the owner of the hotel, alleged that the law violated substantive due process under the fourteenth amendment because it deprived him of the liberty of contract. The appellant's argument was reminiscent of the argument the Court accepted in *Adkins v. Children's Hospital* [13] in invalidating an identical law adopted for the District of Columbia. In *Parrish*, however, the Court rejected the substantive due process argument and labeled the *Adkins* decision "a departure from the true application of the principles governing the regulation by the State of the relation of employer and employed." [14]

The *Parrish* opinion marked the beginning of the end for judicial scrutiny of economic legislation under the concept of substantive due process. The Court had directly overruled a decision not only formulated during the zenith of the substantive due process concept but also decided firmly on substan-

---

6. This conflict arose even more sharply in terms of judicial restrictions of the federal commerce powers, see Chapter 4.

7. The "court packing" plan of President Roosevelt is also discussed in the preceding section and in Chapter 2, section II, E.

8. 291 U.S. 502 (1934).

9. Id. at 537.

10. See, Stewart Dry Goods Co. v. Lewis, 294 U.S. 550 (1935) (tax classifications invalid); Morehead v. New York ex rel. Tipaldo, 298 U.S. 587 (1936) (minimum wage law invalid). A similar approach was used under the commerce clause. Among these cases were

some of the decisions by which "the Court tore great holes in the New Deal program of recovery legislation." McCloskey, supra note 4, at 165–66; See Chapter 4 on the Commerce Power.

11. McCloskey, supra note 4, at 183–84.

12. 300 U.S. 379 (1937). See, Wilson P. Abraham Constr. Corp. v. Texas Industries, Inc., 604 F.2d 897, 904 n. 16 (5th Cir. 1979) (Thornberry, C.J., citing an earlier edition of this treatise), aff'd 451 U.S. 630 (1981).

13. 261 U.S. 525 (1923).

14. 300 U.S. at 397.

tive due process grounds.[15] The *Parrish* Court had sustained the Washington law as a legitimate exercise of the state's police power and discounted the statute's impact on the freedom of contract. Unlike the *Nebbia* opinion, the *Parrish* decision was not to prove to be an isolated departure from the doctrine of substantive due process because the Court followed *Parrish* with a series of cases that reflected the discredit that had befallen economic substantive due process.

A year after *Parrish* the Court decided *United States v. Carolene Products Co.*[16] The Congress had passed legislation that prohibited the interstate shipment of "filled" milk. The appellee contended that the legislation violated the fifth amendment's due process provision. The Court responded through Justice Stone that "where the legislative judgment is drawn in question, [the inquiry] must be restricted to the issue whether any state of facts either known or which could reasonably be assumed, affords support for [the legislation]."[17] The Court found sufficient facts in *Carolene Products* to support the finding of a rational basis for the measure. The legislative findings that filled milk was injurious to the public health revealed the congressional rationale behind the act. Justice Stone, however, emphasized that even absent these legislative findings the Court would have sustained the legislation because "the existence of facts supporting the legislative judgment is to be presumed, for regulatory legislation affecting ordinary commercial transactions is not to be pronounced unconstitutional unless . . . it is of such a character as to preclude the assumption that it rests on some rational basis. . . ."[18] Here the Justice made a classic statement of the distinction

between general regulatory legislation and governmental restrictions on fundamental constitutional values. In the now famous "footnote 4," which he added at the end of this sentence, he gave reasons for the continued independent judicial review of some governmental actions:

4. There may be narrower scope for operation of the presumption of constitutionality when legislation appears on its face to be within a specific prohibition of the Constitution, such as those of the first ten amendments, which are deemed equally specific when held to be embraced within the Fourteenth . . .

It is unnecessary to consider now whether legislation which restricts those political processes which can ordinarily be expected to bring about repeal of undesirable legislation, is to be subjected to more exacting judicial scrutiny under the general prohibitions of the Fourteenth Amendment than are most other types of legislation . . .

Nor need we enquire . . . whether prejudice against discrete and insular minorities may be a special condition, which tends seriously to curtail the operation of those political processes ordinarily to be relied upon to protect minorities, and which may call for a correspondingly more searching judicial inquiry . . .[19]

The exact dimension of the Court's deference to legislative economic judgments remained unclear after *Carolene Products*. The Court had suggested that it may consider the validity of the proffered rational basis for economic legislation. Subsequent Court decisions, however, disclosed that the judicial deference to the legislature's economic regulations was virtually complete. In *Lincoln Federal Labor Union v. Northwestern Iron & Metal Co.*[20] the Court upheld the constitutionality of a state's "right-to-work" law. After noting the Court's rejection of

---

15. Professor Wright viewed the Court's position in *Adkins* as "essentially that of the *Lochner* opinion." Wright, supra note 4, at 178.

16. 304 U.S. 144 (1938).

17. Id. at 154.

18. Id. at 152.

19. Id. at 152–53 n. 4. For criticisms and justifications for this controversial footnote 4, see, e.g., Frank-

furter, J., concurring in Kovacs v. Cooper, 336 U.S. 77, 89 (1949); Hand, Chief Justice Stone's Conception of the Judicial Function, 46 Colum.L.Rev. 696 (1946); Freund, The Supreme Court and Civil Liberties, 4 Vand.L.Rev. 533, 548 (1951); Powell, Carolene Products Revisited, 82 Colum.L.Rev. 1087 (1982); Lusky, Footnote Redux: A Carolene Products Reminiscence, 82 Colum.L.Rev. 1093 (1982).

20. 335 U.S. 525 (1949).

the "Allgeyer-Lockner-Adair-Coppage constitutional doctrine," [21] Justice Black stressed that the states have the authority to legislate against "injurious practices in their internal commercial and business affairs, so long as their laws do not run afoul of some specific federal constitutional prohibition, or of some valid federal law." [22] Six years later in *Williamson v. Lee Optical Co.*[23] the Court rejected the due process and equal protection arguments that the appellees made against the validity of an Oklahoma statute that restricted the ability of opticians to fit or duplicate eyeglasses. Not only was the Court unable to find a specific constitutional prohibition that the Oklahoma measure violated, but the Court was willing to conceive of possible reasons for the enactment that would furnish a rational basis for the law.[24] The *Williamson* opinion suggests that the Court will not only presume that a legislature had a reasonable basis for enacting a particular economic measure, but also will hypothesize reasons for the law's enactment if the legislature fails to state explicitly the reasons behind its judgment. Consequently, anyone attempting to argue for the invalidation of a legislative economic enactment may have to discredit the Court's conceived reasons for the legislature's actions as well as the arguments of those who support the measure. The Court's turnabout from the *Lochner* era became complete with the *Williamson* decision.

Justice Black's opinion in *Ferguson v. Skrupa*[25] provides an appropriate epilogue for the demise of economic substantive due process. In sustaining a Kansas law that prohibited anyone from conducting the business of debt adjusting unless incident to the practice of law, the Court through Justice Black stated: "[We] refuse to sit as a 'superlegislature to weigh the wisdom of legislation' . . . . Whether the legislature takes for its textbook Adam Smith, Herbert Spencer, Lord Keynes or some other is no concern of ours." [26] Justice Holmes's *Lochner* dissent had become the Court's standard.[27]

Another step in the Court's retreat from its position as guardian of the laissez faire concept of economics was taken when the Court decided that the equal protection clause did not guarantee that economic legislation would treat all businesses equally. In *Railway Express Agency v. New York* [28] the Court rejected a constitutional argument that a New York City ordinance violated the equal protection clause. The ordinance prevented owners of delivery vehicles from placing advertisements on the outside of their vehicles unless the advertisement was for the owner's business. The appellant contended that the municipal regulation violated the equal protection clause because the proffered rationale for the ordinance, to reduce distractions for vehicle drivers and pedestrians, did not comport with the ordinance's classification. As long as the classification scheme "has relation to the purpose for which it is made and does not contain the kind of discrimination against which the equal protection clause affords protection" [29] the Court will sustain the regulation against arguments based on equal protection analysis. Because the classification had an argu-

---

21. Id. at 535–36.

22. Id. at 536.

23. 348 U.S. 483 (1955).

24. Repeatedly throughout the opinion Justice Douglas rationalized some possible reasons for the Oklahoma statute: "[t]he legislature might conclude that to regulate [eyeglass lenses] effectively it would have to regulate [eyeglass frames]. Or it might conclude that both sellers of frames and sellers of lenses were in a business where advertising should be limited or abolished in the public interest." Id. at 490. Later the justice noted "it may be deemed important to effective regulation that the eye doctor be restricted to geo-

graphical location that reduce the temptations of commercialism."

Id. at 490.

25. 372 U.S. 726 (1963); Mid-State Food Dealers Ass'n v. City of Durand, 525 F.Supp. 387, 390 n. 18 (E.D.Mich.1981) (Newblatt, J.), citing earlier edition of this treatise.

26. Id. at 731–32 (footnotes omitted).

27. See discussion of *Lochner* in section III of this Chapter.

28. 336 U.S. 106 (1949).

29. Id. at 110.

able relation to the perceived goal of the legislation, the Court found that the ordinance violated no constitutional proscription.[30]

The post-1937 history of the Court's application of the equal protection clause to business regulation would correspond exactly to the history of its application of economic substantive due process concepts if the Court had not rendered the opinion in *Morey v. Doud*.[31] The Court had decided several cases after *Railway Express Co.* that strongly suggested that it would defer to legislative judgment on economic matters even if those who opposed a business regulation raised equal protection arguments against the measure.[32] In short, the Court had implied that it would not use the equal protection clause to void economic regulations. In *Morey v. Doud*, however, the Court invalidated an Illinois statute because it violated the appellees' right to equal protection under the law. The statute required currency exchanges to meet certain requirements before the State Auditor could issue a license that would allow the exchange to conduct its business. The law specifically exempted from its requirements those who issued United States Post Office, American Express Company, or Western Union Telegraph Company money orders. The Court recognized that the purpose behind the regulation was "to afford the public *continuing* protection"[33] in its dealing with currency exchange. Moreover, the Court understood that the present characteristics of the American Express Company made unnecessary any regulation of the sale of that company's money orders. The Court, however, was concerned that the American Express Company would retain its exemption even if its present characteristics changed. In essence, the act not only created advantages for a "closed class" of sellers but also only had "a

remote relationship" between its purpose and its classification scheme.[34] Consequently, the Illinois law violated the equal protection clause because a majority of the justices believed that this closed class lacked even a rational basis.

For almost twenty years *Morey v. Doud* stood as the only exception to the Court's consistent refusal to invalidate economic legislation because it allegedly violated the equal protection clause. Finally, in *City of New Orleans v. Dukes*[35] the Court declared that *Morey* was an erroneous decision and overruled it. The City of New Orleans had adopted an ordinance that prohibited pushcart vendors from selling their goods in the city's French Quarter. The law exempted from its prohibition those pushcart vendors who qualified under the ordinance's "grandfather" clause. Only two vendors qualified, and the respondent, who did not qualify under the "grandfather" clause, contended the ordinance violated the equal protection clause. The Court rejected the contention after noting that the ordinance was purely an economic regulation. The Court reminded the respondent that it consistently had deferred to legislative determinations as to the desirability of a particular statutory classification. Any reliance on *Morey v. Doud* as a basis to invalidate the ordinance was mistaken. The Court summarized its reaction to the equal protection argument when it stated that "the judiciary may not sit as a superlegislature to judge the wisdom or desirability of legislative policy determinations made in areas that neither affect fundamental rights nor proceed along suspect lines."[36]

The Court's retreat from its previous position of active interference with business regulatory measures was complete. The extent of this retreat was reflected not only in the way the Court drastically modified its appli-

---

30. Id.

31. 354 U.S. 457 (1957).

32. Williamson v. Lee Optical Co., 348 U.S. 483 (1955); Daniel v. Family Security Life Insurance Co., 336 U.S. 220 (1949); Kotch v. Board of River Port Pilot Comm'rs, 330 U.S. 552 (1947) (although decided before *Ry. Express Co.* it was reflective of the trend).

33. 354 U.S. at 466 (emphasis in original).

34. Id. at 467–69.

35. 427 U.S. 297, 306 (1976).

36. Id. at 303.

cation of the due process and equal protection clauses but also in the lenient manner the Court applied the contract [37] and commerce clauses.[38] The Court had removed itself completely from the business of protecting economic and business interests.

In sharp contrast to the Court's almost total abandonment of any real scrutiny of economic legislation under substantive due process or equal protection analysis is its increasingly strict examination of legislation and governmental actions that affect civil rights or liberties.[39] Since 1937 the Court has deferred to the legislative judgment on economic matters but it has continued to emphasize that substantive due process analysis was available to protect an individual's civil rights.[40] The rights the Court has recognized as fundamental and deserving of significant judicial protection are most of the guarantees of the Bill of Rights,[41] the right to fairness in the criminal process, the right to privacy (including some freedom of choice in matters of marriage, sexual relations and child bearing), the right to travel, the right to vote, the freedom of association and some aspects of fairness in the adjudication of individual claims against the government (procedural due process rights).

Today the due process and equal protection guarantees are not significant restraints on the government's ability to act in matters of economics or social welfare. While due process still protects a person's liberty in society, only those liberties or rights of "fundamental" constitutional magnitude will be actively protected by the Supreme Court. Where the government seeks to deprive persons of fundamental rights, it must prove to the Court that the law is necessary to promote a compelling or overriding interest. Where no such right is restricted, the law need only rationally relate to any legitimate end of government. As long as there is any conceivable basis for finding such a rational relationship, the law will be upheld. Only when a law is a totally arbitrary deprivation of liberty will it violate the substantive due process guarantee.[42]

The equal protection clause governs the classification of persons for benefits or burdens by the government. While the clause applies only to state and local government, the due process clause of the fifth amendment restricts the federal government's ability to classify persons in a similar manner and may be termed another equal protection guarantee.[43] If the government classifies persons as to their ability to exercise fundamental rights, it must show the classification to be necessary to a compelling or overriding governmental interest. Similarly, if a law burdens a class of persons because of the "suspect" traits of race, national origin or status as a resident alien, the justices will

---

37. The contract clause is examined in Chapter 13, section VI.

38. The Federal commerce power is examined in Chapter 4.

39. See generally Professor Wright's discussion of the beginning of this trend in Wright, supra note 4, at 227–31.

40. See United States v. Carolene Products, 304 U.S. 144, 152–53 n. 4 (1941). For a full discussion of the Court's application of the substantive due process and equal protection theory to protect fundamental rights, see the next section of this chapter.

41. On this basis all of the first eight amendments except for the second, third, and seventh amendments, and the grand jury clause of the fifth, have been applied to the states. See the next subsection for a discussion of the application of these guarantees.

42. Woods v. Holy Cross Hosp., 591 F.2d 1164, 1176 (5th Cir. 1979) (Tjoflat, J.), quoting an earlier edition of this treatise.

The development of fundamental rights analysis represents a partial return to the judicial use of the due process clause to justify independent judicial review of laws that do not restrict rights or liberties which have explicit recognition in the text of the Constitution or its amendments. For this reason the basic theoretical problem of judicial definition and protection of such rights is noted in Section V of this chapter. Because most Supreme Court rulings finding unconstitutional infringements of fundamental rights have been based on the equal protection guarantee, detailed analysis of the Court's fundamental rights decision is deferred to Chapter 16; Equal Protection.

43. See the introductory section to Chapter 16; Equal Protection.

See Arceneaux v. Treen, 671 F.2d 128, 132 n.8 (5th Cir. 1982); Seoane v. Ortho Pharmaceuticals, Inc., 660 F.2d 146, 171 (5th Cir. 1981); Verner v. Colorado, 533 F.Supp. 1109, 1117 (D.Colo.1982); Stang v. Waller, 415 So.2d 123, 124 (Fla.App.1982), all citing this section of an earlier edition of this treatise.

subject the law to independent "strict scrutiny" to determine if it promotes a compelling interest of the government. But where the law classifies persons on a non-suspect basis for the exercise of liberties which are not fundamental constitutional rights, the justices will not independently review the basis for the classification. The law will be upheld so long as the justices can conceive of a basis for terming the classification rationally related to a legitimate end of government.

We have come full circle with the concepts of substantive due process and equal protection in the area of general legislation. Originally there was little active review of such legislation, as it was realized that the federal courts should defer to the other branches of government unless laws were totally arbitrary deprivations of liberty. Slowly there emerged independent judicial control of all

governmental policies under the guise of enforcing the due process guarantee. Today, the justices have accepted the position that they are only to actively guard fundamental constitutional values and that they should allow other branches of government great latitude in dealing with issues of "economics and social welfare" which do not touch upon these values. The Supreme Court, in majority opinions, employs the rational basis test in reviewing the substance of laws and regulations challenged under the due process or equal protection guarantees when the regulation does not involve a fundamental constitutional right, suspect classification or the characteristics of citizenship, gender, or illegitimacy. When the Court examines procedural due process claims it must employ independent judicial review of the fairness of an administrative or judicial system.[44] But

---

44. See Chapter 12, section III regarding the difference between procedural due process and substantive due process or equal protection. See also Chapter 15, Procedural Due Process, infra.

The difficulty of separating procedural from substantive issues has caused some confusion (or at least lack of precision) in a few Supreme Court opinions in recent years.

In Logan v. Zimmerman Brush Co., 455 U.S. 422 (1982), the Court unanimously found that provisions of the Illinois Fair Employment Practices Act as interpreted and applied to a specific plaintiff violated procedural due process. The plaintiff in that case had filed a charge with the Illinois Employment Practices Commission alleging that he had been fired from his job unlawfully due to a physical handicap. Under the Act the Commission was required to hold a fact-finding conference within 120 days of the filing of the claim, but through inadvertence or neglect the Commission scheduled the hearing five days after the expiration of that 120 day period. The Illinois courts construed the 120-day requirement as jurisdictional and held that the Commission was permanently barred from hearing the employee's claim for redress for the alleged discriminatory practice. Justice Blackmun wrote for seven justices in finding that the state statute gave the plaintiff a constitutionally protected property interest to use the statutory procedure for possible redress of discriminating employment practices. The state court ruling denying the plaintiff that property interest without a hearing violated due process. Six justices also believed that the state statute as interpreted by the state supreme court violated equal protection. There was no ruling on the discharged worker's equal protection claim as these justices addressed the equal protection issue in two separate concurring opinions. Justices Powell and Rehnquist found that the challenged cut-off of discrimination claim in this case failed to have a "ra-

tional relationship to legitimate governmental objectives" because "it is unfair and unnatural to punish" individual claimants for the Commission's failure to meet its statutory obligations. These two justices did not wish to express any view on the nature of due process or equal protection review. Logan v. Zimmerman Brush Co., 455 U.S. 422, 441 (1982) (Powell, J., concurring, joined by Rehnquist, J.). Justice Blackmun wrote for four justices as he found that the Illinois rule denied the claimant equal protection. Justice Blackmun's separate opinion stated that the minimal equal protection guarantee requires judicial scrutiny of whether in fact the administrative or legislative classification promoted a legitimate end of government. "The State's rationale must be something more than the exercise of a strained imagination; while the connection between means and ends need not be precise, it, at the least, must have some objective basis." Logan v. Zimmerman Brush Co., 455 U.S. 422 (1982) (Blackmun, J., joined by Brennan, Marshall and O'Connor, JJ.). The Blackmun opinion would remove or, at least, diminish the strong presumption of constitutionality given regulations in the area of economics or social welfare since 1937. However, this opinion did not receive the support of a majority. Additionally, it may be that these four justices would differ about the nature of the rational basis standard in a case that did not involve an arbitrary denial of procedural fairness. The equal protection opinions in *Logan* are in fact no more than a response to the State of Illinois' claim that it was free to refuse hearing a discrimination claim before its commission and courts by terminating some claims based on the admittedly arbitrary refusal of its commission to hear those claims.

Another decision of the Supreme Court that is difficult, if not impossible, to reconcile with the established principle of judicial deference to legislative decisions concerning economic or social welfare also involved a

when the Court examines substantive due process or equal protection claims, a majority of the justices will uphold the challenged governmental act unless no reasonably conceivable set of facts could establish a rational relationship between the challenged regulation and a legitimate end of government.

In recent years a few justices have indicated a desire to review the reasonableness of some economic or social welfare legislation but the strong presumption for validity of such statutes provided by the rational basis test has not been removed.[45] Thus, a majority of justices today continue to use the rational basis test to approve laws allocating welfare benefits,[46] restricting the use of

mix of procedural and substantive issues. In Carter v. Miller, 434 U.S. 356 (1978) (per curiam), aff'g by an equally divided court, 547 F.2d 1314 (7th Cir. 1977). The Supreme Court affirmed by an equally divided vote, and without opinion, a decision of the United States Court of Appeals for the Seventh Circuit invalidating a classification concerning the holding of chauffeur's licenses. An ordinance of the City of Chicago prohibited the granting of public chauffeur's licenses, which were required to drive taxicabs, to persons who had been convicted of certain felonies prior to the time that they applied for such a license. However, persons who were convicted of identical offenses after they received a license did not automatically lose their license. Instead, the ordinance allowed a city official to determine whether such persons were to have their licenses revoked. The City defended this distinction on two grounds: (1) that the city owed greater fairness to those who already had licenses; and (2) that, when persons had a documented record as cab drivers, the city official could consider that record in evaluating whether the felony conviction should permanently disable a person from being a public chauffeur. A three-judge panel of the Court of Appeals found that this distinction was irrational, and violated even the traditional equal protection test. In a per curiam opinion, two of the judges of that court refused to consider whether the city could deny or revoke such licenses for all persons convicted of the listed felonies. The one concurring judge in the Court of Appeals was of the opinion that the city could not deny licenses to all persons convicted of listed felonies; he believed that such a law would create an "irrebuttable assumption" of inability to drive a public vehicle. The Supreme Court affirmed the Court of Appeals decision by an equally divided 4–4 vote; Justice Blackmun did not participate in the decision. There is no basis for determining whether this vote indicates a shift in the views of some justices concerning the use of due process and equal protection in the area of social welfare and economics. It may be that the four justices who voted to affirm the decision believed that the distinction between persons convicted of felonies before and after the granting of a license was truly irrational. It seems unlikely that four justices based their votes on the "irrebuttable presumption" doctrine; the trait used to classify persons (whether they have been convicted of felonies involving armed violence or sexual assault) does not seem of the type to invoke greater than traditional rational basis scrutiny. Perhaps four justices believe that the city owes persons applying for cab driver licenses some form of fair procedure to determine their fitness; that decision would rest on procedural due process grounds. A procedural due process ruling for the would-be

chauffeur's would be contrary to those statements in prior decisions that indicate that a person is only guaranteed procedural fairness after he has received a government benefit. However, there has been some indication that the government owes some degree of procedural fairness to those who are applying for important government benefits or licenses; the Supreme Court has not resolved this issue. Thus, the affirmance may only indicate that this procedural due process issue remains unresolved. See Chapter 15, sections II C 4 and II D 1.

45. See Schweiker v. Wilson, 450 U.S. 221 (1981) (upholding Social Security Act classification giving reduced Medicaid benefits to persons institutionalized in certain public mental care institutions; Justice Powell, joined by Justices Brennan, Marshall and Stevens, in dissent, would engage in a review of the reasonableness of this classification); Minnesota v. Clover Leaf Creamery Co., 449 U.S. 456 (1981) (reversing state court determination that classification of containers for the sale of milk violated the equal protection clause despite dissent by Justice Stevens that would have allowed the state court to use the fourteenth amendment equal protection clause to review the reasonableness of the classification); United States R.R. Retirement Bd. v. Fritz, 449 U.S. 166 (1980) (employing the rationality test to uphold a retirement act classification providing for double or windfall benefits to a limited class of employees; Justice Stevens, concurring, and Justices Brennan and Marshall, dissenting, indicate a willingness to use an independent test of reasonableness to determine the validity of the classification); see also, G.D. Searle & Co. v. Cohn, 455 U.S. 404 (1982) (court rules that state statute tolling statute of limitations period against out-of-state corporation which does not have an officer located in the state for service of process does not violate equal protection; Justice Stevens in dissent would have found that the statute denied equal protection to these corporations); see also, note 44 supra.

46. See e.g., Cleland v. National College of Business, 435 U.S. 213 (1978) (upholding restrictions on educational payments under "GI Bill" which denied benefits for educational courses taken at certain types of proprietary educational institutions); United States R.R. Retirement Bd. v. Fritz, 449 U.S. 166 (1980) (Upholding congressional elimination of payment of dual retirement benefits to some employees who had engaged in both railroad and non-railroad employment on any basis that is not "patently arbitrary or irrational"); Schweiker v. Wilson, 450 U.S. 221 (1981) (upholding Social Security Act classification giving reduced Medicaid benefits to persons institutionalized in certain public

property,[47] or regulating business or personal activity that does not involve a fundamental right.[48] Nevertheless, there is the possibility that those justices who have demonstrated an unwillingness to accept government assertions of a theoretical or conceivable rational basis for legislation will be joined by new Supreme Court appointees who would also require the government to

demonstrate a reasonable relationship between any governmental regulation of liberty or property and a constitutional end of government. Were that possibility to occur, the presumption of constitutionality for economic and social welfare legislation would disappear and the Court would return to the 1900–1936 approach to substantive due process and equal protection analysis.[49]

mental care institutions); Schweiker v. Hogan, 102 S.Ct. 2597 (1982) (upholding Social Security Act classifications that provide for reimbursement of state providing Medicaid benefits to "medically needy" but exempting from program repayment for benefits to "categorically needy".)

The Supreme Court has summarily reversed decisions of state courts which used the fourteenth amendment rather than the state constitution to invalidate economic or welfare regulations. In Idaho Dept. of Employment v. Smith, 434 U.S. 100 (1977) (per curiam), the United States Supreme Court summarily reversed a state court decision holding economic legislation to be a violation of the equal protection clause. In this case the Supreme Court of Idaho had held unconstitutional a statute that denied unemployment benefits to otherwise eligible persons if they attended school during the day; students attending night schools were allowed to receive benefits if they were otherwise eligible under the statute. As the law did not touch upon fundamental interests nor disadvantage a suspect classification, the Supreme Court of the United States described it as being only "in the field of social welfare and economics." The Supreme Court held that classifications designed to be predictable, convenient means for identifying those who would receive state benefits and permissible under the rational relationship test even though they were imperfect.

47. See, Hodel v. Indiana, 452 U.S. 314 (1981) (upholding the "prime farm land" provisions of the Surface Mining and Reclamation Control Act of 1977 against the claim that the restrictions on mining and certain farm land were arbitrary limitations of the use of property in select geographic areas). "Social and economic legislation like the Surface Mining Act that does not employ suspect classifications or impinge on fundamental rights must be upheld against equal protection attack when the legislative means are rationally related to a legitimate government purpose. Moreover such legislation carries with it a presumption of rationality that can only be overcome by a clear showing of arbitrariness and irrationality." 452 U.S. at 331 (citations omitted).

The Supreme Court summarily reversed a state court, which had employed the fourteenth amendment rather than a state constitution provision to invalidate a zoning law. In County Bd. v. Richards, 434 U.S. 5 (1977) (per curiam), the Supreme Court upheld a zoning ordinance that restricted individuals' ability to park their cars in given areas based on their relationship to residents of the area. Residents of certain areas were given free parking permits for themselves, persons doing business in the area, and some visitors. All other

persons were prohibited from weekday parking in these residential areas. The Supreme Court of Virginia had held that the ordinance violated the equal protection clause of the fourteenth amendment because it created arbitrary classifications that did not in fact promote the enunciated goals of the ordinance. The Supreme Court of the United States reversed the Virginia court. The Supreme Court employed the traditional rational basis test; under this test no proof was required that the classifications established under the ordinance in fact promoted legitimate purposes. The Supreme Court of the United States was careful to note that it was only reversing the Supreme Court of Virginia as to its ruling on the fourteenth amendment; the Supreme Court did not preclude review of the ordinance on independent state grounds by the Virginia court.

48. Thus the Supreme Court upheld a federal limitation on the liability of privately-owned nuclear power plants for accidents and resulting injuries at the plants. Since no fundamental rights were regulated by the statute, it was "a classic example of economic regulation" and was subject only to the minimum scrutiny rational basis test. Duke Power Co. v. Carolina Environmental Study Group, Inc., 438 U.S. 59 (1978).

The Supreme Court upheld a state law which prohibited the ownership of retail gas stations by petroleum producers and refiners and which regulated their pricing practices. Exxon Corp. v. Governor of Maryland, 437 U.S. 117 (1978). It took the Court only a single paragraph to dismiss the producers' argument that the law violated the principle of substantive due process; there was no problem in upholding these regulations under the rational relationship test. 437 U.S. at 125. The commerce clause ruling in this case is noted in Chapter 9. The Court also upheld a state law which charged out-of-state residents a substantially higher price for hunting licenses than was charged residents of the state. Baldwin v. Fish and Game Comm'n, 436 U.S. 371 (1978). In the opinion of a majority of the justices, the hunting fee did not violate either the privileges and immunities clause of Article IV or the equal protection clause because it was a non-invidious means of protecting big game animals in the state. [The privileges and immunities aspect of the case is noted in Chapter 10.] The interest of the out-of-state resident who sought to hunt animals in the state was not one that required the Court to invoke more than a rationality standard under the equal protection clause.

49. Several scholars have noted the similarity between many Burger Court decisions and the Supreme Court scrutiny of governmental acts in the 1900–1936 era. See, Nowak, Foreword: Evaluating the Work of the New Libertarian Supreme Court, 7 Hastings Con-

V.   A NOTE ON THE MEANING OF "LIBERTY", FUNDAMENTAL CONSTITUTIONAL RIGHTS, AND THE INCORPORATION OF THE BILL OF RIGHTS

A.   Introduction

Even before the Court had decided *Marbury v. Madison*,[1] the justices were debating the extent of their power to enforce natural law rights against the actions of other branches of government.[2] As previously noted, the philosophy that the justices would overturn acts of other branches only to protect specific constitutional guarantees has been the formal guideline of the Supreme Court at every stage in its history. However, as we have seen in this chapter, the Court has continually sought to enforce those natural law rights which the justices believed were essential in American society. Prior to the Civil War, the justices took few actions in regard to the federal government but they still maintained some control over state acts through the contract and commerce clauses of Article I.[3] Following the War the Court focused on the due process clauses as a guarantee of a virtually limitless range of interests against what the justices considered to be arbitrary limitations of economic liberty by the government. Finally, the Court was to forsake any ability to control general economic or social welfare legislation under the due process clause, but the justices did not indicate that they would refrain from enforcing what they believed to be fundamental constitutional values concerning individual freedom or liberty. One should reflect upon the relationship between the history of judicial review that we have examined in this chapter and two modern constitutional concepts: the incorporation of the provisions of the Bill of Rights and the judicial protection of "fundamental" constitutional rights.

B.   Incorporation of the Bill of Rights

Prior to the Civil War the Court had held that the provisions of the Bill of Rights were not applicable to the activities of state and local governments.[4] However, it was not long after the passage of the fourteenth amendment before individuals claimed that the guarantees of individual rights contained in those amendments were made applicable to the states by the fourteenth amendment. The Supreme Court rejected such contentions at first but the reasons for so doing may be found in decisions on other constitutional issues. First, the Court had given a restrictive meaning to the privileges and immunities clause of the fourteenth amendment in one of its first decisions on the meaning of that amendment.[5] This decision had the effect of eliminating the provision which was both historically and logically the one most likely to have been intended to include within its protections the guarantees of the Bill of Rights.[6] The second reason for the Supreme Court's failure to closely analyze the incorporation issue during this period is that there was simply no need to do so. Because of the Court's expansive reading of the due process clause, the justices were able to protect any form of individual freedom or natural law rights without resorting to a specific textual basis in the Constitution or the Bill of Rights. This fact is the key to understanding why the development of the so-called "incorporation" theory has come about only recently.

During the period from 1887 to 1934 the Supreme Court decided cases which restricted the activities of state and local governments on the basis of individual rights virtu-

---

stitutional Law Quarterly 263 (1980); Van Alstyne. The Recnudescence of Property Rights as the Foremost Principle of Civil Liberties: The First Decade of the Burger Court, 43 Law & Contemporary Problems 66 (1980).

1.   5 U.S. (1 Cranch) 137 (1803).

2.   Calder v. Bull, 3 U.S. (3 Dall.) 386 (1798); see section 1 of this chapter.

3.   See the first section of this Chapter.

4.   Barron v. Baltimore, 32 U.S. (7 Pet.) 243 (1833).

5.   Slaughter-House Cases, 83 U.S. (16 Wall.) 36 (1873).

6.   See, J. tenBroek, Equal Under Law at 223 (enlarged edition 1965); J. James, The Framing of the Fourteenth Amendment, at 180 (1965).

ally identical to those protected by one or more of the first eight amendments. However, in these cases the Court simply held that the state activity violated the due process clause because it arbitrarily limited the individual's interest in liberty. The Court invalidated a state law which prohibited private religious schools under the general concept of due process and with no need to resort to the religion clauses of the first amendment.[7] Similarly, the Court struck down a state law prohibiting the teaching of foreign languages in private as well as public schools without relying on either the first amendment or what today is known as the fundamental right of privacy.[8] Because of this approach, there was no clear focusing on whether specific provisions of the Bill of Rights were "incorporated" into the due process clause of the fourteenth amendment.

The Court during this period concentrated on whether specific interests deserved protection under the concept of "liberty." Some of the opinions are unclear as to whether the Court was focusing on only the fourteenth amendment or values reflected in other amendments when it made a particular decision. The most notable example of such confusion (in terms of modern incorporation theories) is the decision of the Supreme Court concerning the just compensation clause of the fifth amendment. In 1897 the Court decided that state and local governments were required to pay just compensation when they exercised their powers of eminent domain and took an individual's property for public use.[9] But the opinion of the Court, written by the elder Justice Harlan, did not state that the just compensation clause of the fifth amendment was applied to the states through the due process clause of the fourteenth amendment. Rather the decision only held that the due process clause protected individuals against

having their property taken without just compensation. It was unnecessary for the opinion to reflect upon the issue of "incorporation," for the justices felt quite secure in their ability to control all forms of state activities through the due process clause at this time.

As we near the close of the era of substantive due process, we find that the Court begins to concentrate its attention on whether specific guarantees of the Bill of Rights are made directly applicable to the states by the fourteenth amendment. These isolated decisions before 1937 seem to be the result of growing problems with the general concept of substantive due process and particular cases which were easier to analyze under the terms of one of the first ten amendments. Thus, in 1925 we find the Court assuming that the free speech clause of the first amendment was made applicable to the states by the due process clause in deciding a particular case.[10] In 1932 when the Supreme Court intervened to grant the defendants some protection in the now famous "Scottsboro Boys" case, the justices found that at least some elements of the right to counsel under the sixth amendment were made applicable to local governments by the fourteenth.[11] However, the Court did not develop any consistent approach towards the concept of incorporation until after its denouncement of substantive due process. As late as 1934, the Supreme Court could reject the claims of religious conscientious objectors to attending state colleges with mandatory military training requirements by concentrating on the meaning of liberty as including the right to entertain religious beliefs, rather than focusing on the first amendment religion clauses.[12]

Many of the subject areas of the Bill of Rights were either not considered by the Supreme Court or were of a type that a majori-

---

7. Pierce v. Society of Sisters, 268 U.S. 510 (1925).

8. Meyer v. Nebraska, 262 U.S. 390 (1923).

9. Chicago, B. & Q. R.R. Co. v. City of Chicago, 166 U.S. 226 (1897).

10. Gitlow v. New York, 268 U.S. 652 (1925).

11. Powell v. Alabama, 287 U.S. 45 (1932). The case involved charges of rape against some black youths by a white woman and the circumstances of the trial were highly prejudicial to the defendants.

12. Hamilton v. Regents, 293 U.S. 245 (1934).

ty of the justices were not prepared to enforce prior to 1937. For example, the Court did not require the exclusion of a coerced confession by a defendant in state criminal proceeding under the fourteenth amendment until 1936,[13] and the self-incrimination clause was not incorporated until 1964.[14] However, even federal defendants did not at this time receive significant protections in the criminal process. Until 1938 the sixth amendment right to counsel in federal courts meant only that a defendant would be able to have an attorney to represent him at certain points in the proceeding if he could afford to retain one.[15] While the Supreme Court did decide a few particular issues concerning criminal procedure prior to this time, there were really no generally significant decisions in this area until the 1930's. For reasons that still remain unclear, the Court simply did not receive or decide cases involving these issues during this period.[16] Since most of the Bill of Rights are concerned with protections relating to the criminal justice system, there was little need to focus on incorporation problems.

In the last section we saw how the Supreme Court abandoned the use of the substantive due process concept as an active check on general economic or social welfare legislation. However, the Court did not indicate that it would retreat from enforcing specific constitutional guarantees or fundamental constitutional values against infringement by the other branches of government. The majority of the justices at this time only indicated that there was no inherent ability to overturn acts of the other branches of the government merely because

they disagreed with the policy behind those acts. But the Court was soon to point out that it would not hesitate to return to a strict form of review for acts that touched upon fundamental constitutional values.[17] The issue now became one of identifying what rights or values were of such a nature that they should be judicially enforced against the other branches of government. This question led the Supreme Court to consider which of the specific guarantees of the Bill of Rights were such fundamental rights. And so the Court began to focus on whether each of the guarantees was made applicable to the states by the fourteenth amendment. Today we phrase the issue as whether the provisions of the Bill of Rights are "incorporated" into the meaning of the word "liberty" so as to be protected by the due process clause of the fourteenth amendment and applied to the states.

Following 1936 the Supreme Court decided that some, but not all, of the Bill of Rights guarantees were applicable to the states. A few justices, most notably Justice Black, argued that the history of the fourteenth amendment indicated that all of the Bill of Rights were to be made directly applicable to the states.[18] Other justices, most notably Justice Frankfurter, argued that the concept of "liberty" was to have an independent, judicially defined meaning which was not dependent upon the incorporation of specific guarantees of the Bill of Rights.[19] Some of the cases concerning the question of whether a specific guarantee was incorporated into the due process clause contained classic debates over both the history of the fourteenth amendment and the role of the judici-

---

13. Brown v. Mississippi, 297 U.S. 278 (1936).

14. Malloy v. Hogan, 378 U.S. 1 (1964); The earlier, contrary decisions were Twining v. New Jersey, 211 U.S. 78 (1908), and Adamson v. California, 332 U.S. 46 (1947).

15. Schaefer, Federalism and State Criminal Procedure, 70 Harv.L.Rev. 1 (1956); see Johnson v. Zerbst, 304 U.S. 458 (1938).

16. Schaefer, supra note 15, at 3–4.

17. United States v. Carolene Products Co., 304 U.S. 144, 152 n. 4 (1938); Skinner v. Oklahoma, 316 U.S. 535 (1942).

18. See, e.g., Adamson v. California, 332 U.S. 46, 68 (1947) (Black, J., dissenting, joined by Douglas, J.). While Black would have incorporated all of these rights and no others, some justices would have included those rights, plus implied fundamental rights. See id. at 124 (Murphy, J., dissenting, joined by Rutledge, J.).

19. See, e.g., Adamson v. California, 332 U.S. 46, 59 (1947) (Frankfurter, J. concurring); Pointer v. Texas, 380 U.S. 400, 408 (1965) (Harlan, J. concurring).

ary in enforcing natural law concepts of liberty.[20] Partially as a result of these judicial debates, scholars have labored over the question of whether or not the framers of the fourteenth amendment meant to incorporate the guarantees of the Bill of Rights into its provisions. The preponderance of historical evidence discovered by these scholars indicates that the drafters of the amendment did not specifically intend to apply all of those provisions to the states.[21] However, a number of scholars, most notably Jacobus tenBroek, have isolated a concern of a number of drafters that a set of natural law values reflected in some of the Bill of Rights, as well as other sources, should have been made applicable to the states by the passage of the fourteenth amendment.[22]

The Supreme Court did follow an approach based on the historical view as well as the majority's view of the Court's role in reviewing acts of other branches of government. The Court settled upon the concept of "selective incorporation" whereby a provision of the Bill of Rights is made applicable to the states if the justices are of the opinion that it was meant to protect a "fundamental" aspect of liberty. In the early cases the Court asked whether the specific amendment was so fundamental that it could be said to be "implicit in the concept of ordered liberty."[23] This test coincided with the emerging view of the Court's powers. It disclaimed any general right to review acts of other branches of government but held that it would enforce rights "so rooted in the

traditions and conscience of our people as to be as fundamental."[24] Eventually the Supreme Court altered the test for whether a specific provision should be incorporated into the due process clause. In 1968, the Court held that the determination of whether the right to jury trial guaranteed by the sixth amendment was incorporated into the fourteenth depended on whether that guarantee was "fundamental to the American scheme of justice."[25] This new test meant that the Court would be willing to enforce values which the justices saw as having a special importance in the development of individual liberty in American society, whether or not the value was one that was theoretically necessary in any system of democratic government.

Today virtually all of the Bill of Rights have been incorporated into the fourteenth amendment and made applicable to the states. Since 1934 there has been a steady process of judicial inclusion of provisions of the Bill of Rights into the fourteenth amendment. All of the provisions of the first amendment concerning freedoms of religion,[26] speech,[27] press,[28] assembly[29] and petition[30] have been held applicable to the states. The second amendment concerning the right to bear arms is not applicable to the states since it is perceived as primarily a guarantee that the federal government would not interfere with the state militia.[31] The third amendment, which prohibits the quartering of soldiers in private homes, has not been the subject of any constitutional lit-

---

20. See, e.g., Adamson v. California, 332 U.S. 46 (1947); Pointer v. Texas, 380 U.S. 400 (1965); Williams v. Florida, 399 U.S. 78 (1970). See also, Rochin v. California, 342 U.S. 165 (1950).

21. See Fairman, Does the Fourteenth Amendment Incorporate the Bill of Rights?, 2 Stan.L.Rev. 5 (1949).

22. See, J. tenBroek, Equal Law Under Law at 223 (enlarged edition 1965); See also J. James, The Framing of the Fourteenth Amendment (1965).

23. Palko v. Connecticut, 302 U.S. 319, 325 (1937).

24. Id.

25. Duncan v. Louisiana, 391 U.S. 145, 148–9 (1968).

26. Cantwell v. Connecticut, 310 U.S. 296 (1940) (free exercise clause); Everson v. Board of Education, 330 U.S. 1 (1947) (establishment clause).

27. Gitlow v. New York, 268 U.S. 652, 666 (1925); Fiske v. Kansas, 274 U.S. 380 (1927); Stromberg v. California, 283 U.S. 359 (1931).

28. Near v. Minnesota, 283 U.S. 697, 701 (1931).

29. DeJonge v. Oregon, 299 U.S. 353 (1937).

30. 299 U.S. at 364, 365; Hague v. CIO, 307 U.S. 496 (1939); Bridges v. California, 314 U.S. 252 (1941).

31. Cf. United States v. Cruikshank, 92 U.S. 542, 553 (1876); Presser v. Illinois, 116 U.S. 252, 265 (1886); State v. Vlacil, 645 P.2d 677, 681 n. 1 (Utah 1982) (Oaks, J., concurring), citing earlier edition of this treatise.

igation in the Supreme Court. The fourth amendment's regulation of searches and seizures has been held to be applicable to the police practices of state and local governments.[32] Of the guarantees of the fifth amendment, only the grand jury clause has been held not to be applicable to the states.[33] The Court has specifically incorporated both the double jeopardy and self-incrimination provisions of that amendment.[34] The principles of the fifth amendment just compensation clause are applied to the states although it is unclear whether it is incorporated into the fourteenth amendment or whether the amendment's due process clause merely has an identical meaning to that provision.[35] Each of several guarantees of the sixth amendment concerning rights in the criminal process has been held applicable to the states through the due process clause.[36] The seventh amendment right to jury trial in civil cases is not applicable to the states.[37]

The cruel and unusual punishment clause of the eighth amendment has been specifically made applicable to the states by the Supreme Court[38] and the excessive bail provision has been made applicable by implication.[39] There are no cases concerning the applicability of the "excessive fine" provision of the eighth amendment to the states. It would seem to be applicable because it is intertwined with the other two and the Supreme Court has already regulated the imposition of fines on indigents through the equal protection clause of the fourteenth amendment.[40] Finally, the ninth amendment has not been the source of specific rights or rulings although some justices would give it greater impact.[41] The tenth amendment, by its own terms, has no application to the states.

Some justices have believed that, even if the Bill of Rights were applicable to the states, there was no need to hold state laws to the same standards under those amendments.[42] However, a majority of the justices have rejected this concept and held that when a provision of the Bill of Rights is made applicable to the states, it applies to state and local acts in the same manner as it does to federal actions.[43] Thus, rulings on the meaning of any incorporated provision of

---

32. Wolf v. Colorado, 338 U.S. 25 (1949); Mapp v. Ohio, 367 U.S. 643 (1961).

33. Hurtado v. California, 110 U.S. 516 (1884).

34. Benton v. Maryland, 395 U.S. 784 (1969) (double jeopardy); Ashe v. Swenson, 397 U.S. 436 (1970) (collateral estoppel); Malloy v. Hogan, 378 U.S. 1 (1964) (self-incrimination); Griffin v. California, 380 U.S. 609 (1965) (self-incrimination).

35. Chicago, B. & Q. R.R. Co. v. City of Chicago, 166 U.S. 226 (1897); Webb's Fabulous Pharmacies, Inc. v. Beckwith, 449 U.S. 155, 159 (1980).

36. Klopfer v. North Carolina, 386 U.S. 213 (1967) (speedy trial); In re Oliver, 333 U.S. 257 (1948) (public trial); Duncan v. Louisiana, 391 U.S. 145 (1968) (jury trial); Impartial Jury—Irvin v. Dowd, 366 U.S. 717 (1961) (impartial jury); In re Oliver, 333 U.S. 257 (1948) (notice); Pointer v. Texas, 380 U.S. 400 (1965) (confrontation); Washington v. Texas, 388 U.S. 14 (1967) (compulsory process); Gideon v. Wainwright, 372 U.S. 335 (1963) (counsel).

37. Minneapolis & St. Louis R.R. Co. v. Bombolis, 241 U.S. 211 (1916).

38. Louisiana ex rel. Francis v. Resweber, 329 U.S. 459 (1947); Robinson v. California, 370 U.S. 660 (1962).

39. See, Schlib v. Kuebel, 404 U.S. 357, 365 (1971).

40. See, Tate v. Short, 401 U.S. 395 (1971).

41. Griswold v. Connecticut, 381 U.S. 479 (1965) (Goldberg, J., concurring); See, Redlick, Are There Rights Retained by the People?, 37 N.Y.U.L.Rev. 787 (1962).

42. See, e.g., Malloy v. Hogan, 378 U.S. 1, 14 (1964) (Harlan, J. dissenting); Benton v. Maryland, 395 U.S. 784, 808 n. 12 (1969) (Harlan, J., dissenting, citing opinions of Justice Stewart).

43. See e.g., Malloy v. Hogan, 378 U.S. 1 (1964); Duncan v. Louisiana, 391 U.S. 145 (1968); Baldwin v. New York, 399 U.S. 66 (1970); Williams v. Florida, 399 U.S. 78 (1970). A ruling has been made that there may be less than unanimous jury verdicts in state but not federal trials due to a unique division of votes on the Court and the failure of any position of the substantive issue to gain a majority. Eight justices believed that the sixth and fourteenth amendments required identical rules for state and federal trials, but four voted for a single standard of uniformity and four voted to allow nonunanimous verdicts in both systems. The decision therefore came down to how Justice Powell—the only current member of the Court believing in dual standards—would vote. He voted to allow nonunanimous verdicts in the state but not the federal case. Thus we still follow the principle of a single standard even though we have differing results in those cases. See, Apodaca v. Oregon, 406 U.S. 404 (1972); Johnson v. Louisiana, 406 U.S. 356 (1972).

In Ballew v. Georgia, 435 U.S. 223 (1978) the Supreme Court held that the sixth amendment right to jury trial, as applied to the states by the fourteenth amendment, requires states to use at least six persons

the Bill of Rights are of equal meaning for both federal and state laws. This concept is sometimes known as the "bag and baggage" theory for it holds that when a provision of the Bill of Rights is made applicable to the states it is applied with all of its previous federal interpretation—it comes to the states, complete with its "bag and baggage." This doctrine squares with the philosophy of selective incorporation. When the Supreme Court holds a provision of the Bill of Rights applicable to the states, it does so because the justices are of the opinion that it is a right which can be deemed "fundamental" to the American system of government. Accordingly, the justices will not tolerate either federal or state activities which impair the right.[44]

C. Fundamental Rights

Today the justices of the Supreme Court will apply strict forms of review under the due process clauses and the equal protection clause to any governmental actions which limit the exercise of "fundamental" constitutional rights. These are rights which the Court recognizes as having a value so essential to individual liberty in our society that they justify the justices reviewing the acts of other branches of government in a manner quite similar to the substantive due process approach of the pre-1937 period. Little more can be said to accurately describe the nature of a fundamental right, because fundamental rights analysis is simply no more than the modern recognition of the natural law concepts first espoused by Justice Chase in *Calder v. Bull*.[1]

Despite claims to the contrary, there has never been a period of time wherein the Court did not actively enforce values which a majority of the justices felt were essential in our society even though they had no specific textual basis in the Constitution. Indeed, some of the most noted "conservative" justices advocated the use of a natural law analysis to select and protect the forms of liberty under the due process clause. Thus, it was that Justice Black could accuse Justice Frankfurter of assuming too great an authority by adoption of a natural law approach to constitutional issues rather than making use of specific provisions of the Bill of Rights.[2] And it was the younger Justice Harlan who first advocated protecting a right of privacy which included the right of married persons to use contraceptive devices.[3] However, the use of a subjective natural law analysis under the due process and equal protection clauses did not work out well in the period between 1887 and 1937. When the Court rejected the substantive due process approach in 1937, it restricted the ability of the justices to rely upon a natural law or openly subjective basis for defining liberty and individual constitutional rights.

It was not long after 1937 that the Court indicated that the justices would still protect individual rights. In 1938 in *United States v. Carolene Products Co.*[4] the majority indicated that it might not follow the rejection of substantive due process in areas which touched upon specific constitutional guarantees or disadvantaged certain minority

in criminal trial juries. In the 1978–79 Term, the Supreme Court held that a state conviction on a non-petty offense rendered by a non-unanimous six-person jury violated the sixth amendment jury trial guarantee, Burch v. Louisiana, 441 U.S. 130 (1979). While conceding that the case was close, and the line drawn a fine one, the Court found that such a conviction poses a similar threat to the preservation of the substance of the jury trial guarantee as was presented by the five-member jury practice previously invalidated in Ballew.

44. The incorporation doctrine appears to have played a role in the judicial failure to address questions regarding the type of procedural fairness required by the due process clauses. See Nowak, Foreword: Due

Process Methodology in the Postincorporation World, 70 Journal of Criminal Law & Criminology 397 (1980); see generally, Chapter 15 section C, 1, infra.

1. 3 U.S. (3 Dall.) 386 (1798) (Opinion of Chase, J.). See section I of this chapter for a discussion of Chase's position.

2. Rochin v. California, 342 U.S. 165, 175–6 (1952) (Black, J., concurring); Adamson v. California, 332 U.S. 46, 89–90 (1947) (Black, J., concurring).

3. Poe v. Ullman, 367 U.S. 497, 541–3, 550–54 (1961) (Harlan, J., dissenting).

4. 304 U.S. 144 (1938).

groups.[5] In 1942 the Supreme Court struck down a statute authorizing sterilization of some convicts because it arbitrarily classified persons in terms of a fundamental right.[6] Thus, there was no real break in the use of a subjective test for finding individual rights and liberties following the 1937 renouncement of substantive due process as a control over economic and social welfare legislation. However, while the justices have retained this concept, they were now deprived of the natural law-substantive due process language to describe the process by which they identified and enforced these fundamental rights. This has lead to confusing opinions as the justices have attempted to give different justifications for actions that were simply a form of substantive due process.

A most notable example of this confusion is *Griswold v. Connecticut*[7] wherein the Court struck down a law which prohibited the use of contraceptives by married persons. The majority opinion by Justice Douglas found a fundamental "right to privacy" which was infringed by the law. He found this right in the "penumbras" of several guarantees of the Bill of Rights.[8] While the justice managed to identify some arguably related provisions of the Bill of Rights he gave no indication of how to search the shadows, or penumbras, of the Bill of Rights to find other fundamental guarantees. Justice Goldberg, who concurred in the opinion, found that the right of privacy should be recognized without reliance of any specific guarantees of the Bill of Rights.[9] He found that the ninth amendment gave textual recognition to the fact that there were other

values of equal importance to the specific provisions to the Bill of Rights even though they were not mentioned in the first eight amendments. While the ninth amendment did not directly create those rights, it authorized the Court to identify them and protect them against the acts of the other branches of government. He attempted to give some objective guidelines to the search for these values by stating that the Court should rely on "the traditions and conscience" of the nation in determining what values were to be so protected.[10] Only Justice Harlan was able to give a very clear basis for why he was recognizing the right to privacy as worthy of constitutional protection. As the justice had said years before, in a dissenting opinion, he was willing to protect the right to privacy based on a natural law approach.[11] Harlan stood quite ready to defend the judicial function as selecting values which had a historical and philosophical right to be called fundamental and enforcing them against even the will of the majority. He did not advocate a return to the pre-1937 period, for there were very few rights that he would define as truly fundamental; Harlan did not advocate overturning laws merely because they offended his individual sense of reasonableness.[12] Justice Black, who objected to this natural law approach to the definition of due process, dissented because he found no clear basis for this right in the text of the Bill of Rights.[13]

The concept of fundamental rights remains vague today. All that can be said with certainty is that the justices have selected a group of individual rights which do

---

5. Id. at 152 n. 4. See also footnote 19 in section IV of this Chapter.

6. Skinner v. Oklahoma, 316 U.S. 535, 541 (1942).

7. 381 U.S. 479 (1965).

8. 381 U.S. at 484.

9. 381 U.S. 479, 486 (1965) (Goldberg, J., concurring).

10. Id. at 493, quoting Snyder v. Massachusetts, 291 U.S. 97 (1934).

11. 381 U.S. 479, 499 (1965) (Harlan, J., concurring). Here he restated the views he expressed in Poe v. Ullman, 367 U.S. 497, 522 (1961) (Harlan, J., dissenting).

12. Thus Harlan objected to the use of fundamental rights analysis to increase scrutiny under the equal protection guarantee. He thought it was used to increase judicial power to overturn policy judgments on issues the Court felt were of practical importance. See, Shapiro v. Thompson, 394 U.S. 618, 660–62 (1969) (Harlan, J., dissenting).

13. Griswold v. Connecticut, 381 U.S. 479, 507 (1965) (Black, J., dissenting).

not have a specific textual basis in the Constitution or its amendments and deemed them to be "fundamental." There can be no doubt that this must be based on the majority's decision to enforce some natural law rights against the acts of organized society.

There has been continual criticism of this approach throughout the history of the Court. Indeed, even Justice Harlan, who was willing to recognize the right to privacy through such an approach, strongly criticized the Court's use of fundamental rights analysis in protecting a wide variety of individual interests.[14] Similarly, commentators continue to reflect upon the legitimacy of the use of judicial power to protect values which have no basis in the constitutional text. There continues to be a school of

scholars who decry as illegitimate any judicial protection of values that are not identified in the text of the Constitution or its amendments.[15] Other scholars seek to justify judicial protection of such values in terms of an historical or societal consensus on the nature of rights that should be placed beyond the power of the political process.[16] A third group of scholars has confronted this problem of judicial value selection by examining the relationship of judicial decision-making to the values of the political process. These "process oriented" theorists would justify a role for the Supreme Court in enforcing a specific constitutional provision, guaranteeing the openness of the political process, and protecting certain minority groups.[17]

14. See note 12 supra.

15. See, R. Berger, Government by Judiciary (1977); Bork, Neutral Principles and Some First Amendment Problems, 47 Ind.L.J. 1 (1971). See also, L. Lusky, By What Right? (1975).

An excellent analysis of the weakness of this literal or "interpretivist" position is contained in Ely, Constitutional Interpretivism: Its Allure and Impossibility, 53 Ind.L.J. 399 (1978) reprinted in J. Ely, Democracy and Distrust (1980). For a rejoinder see, Berger, Government by Judiciary: John Hart Ely's Invitation, 54 Ind.L.J. 277 (1979).

The late Professor Bickel, who was by no means an advocate of unrestrained judicial review, noted the difficulty of attempting to define the parameters of judicial review in terms of the words of the Constitution.

"There is a body of opinion—and there has been, throughout our history—which holds that the Court can well apply obvious principles, plainly acceptable to a generality of the population, because they are plainly stated in the Constitution (e.g., the right to vote shall not be denied on account of race), or because they are almost universally shared; but the Court should not manufacture principle. However, although the Constitution plainly contains a number of admonitions, it states very few plain principles; and few are universally accepted. Principles that may be thought to have wide, if not universal, acceptance may not have it tomorrow, when the freshly-coined, quite novel principle may, in turn, prove acceptable. The true distinction, therefore, relevant to the bulk of the Court's business, lies not so much between more or less acceptable principles as between principles of different orders of magnitude and complexity in the application. This distinction can be sensed, and can serve as a caution, but no one has succeeded in defining it, and hence it is not serviceable as a rule. Unable to cabin the Court's interventions by rule, we have been generally content with the exercise of authority not so cabined. We do not

confine the judges, we caution them. That, after all, is the legacy of Felix Frankfurter's career."

A. Bickel, The Supreme Court and the Idea of Progress, at 177 (1970).

16. The value-oriented scholars would have the Supreme Court promote the social good by requiring all branches of the government, including the judiciary, to comply with principles of moral and political philosophy which these scholars believe are evidenced by the history and provisions of the Constitution and societal consensus on fundamental values. Although there are differences in their methodology, Professors Perry and Tribe and Dean Wellington provide examples of how a value-oriented approach may be used to define the proper scope of judicial review. See M. Perry, The Constitution, the Courts and Human Rights: An Inquiry into the Legitimacy of Constitutional Policymaking by the Judiciary (1982); L. Tribe, American Constitutional Law (1978); Tribe, The Puzzling Persistance of Process-Based Constitutional Theories, 89 Yale L.J. 1063 (1980); Wellington, Common Law Rules and Constitutional Double Standards: Some Notes on Adjudication, 83 Yale L.J. 221 (1973). Professor Henry Monaghan has forged a most interesting theory of judicial review which combines elements of the interpretivist and process-oriented approaches as he has attacked those scholars who have advanced value-oriented theories. See Monaghan, Our Perfect Constitution, 56 N.Y.U.L.Rev. 353 (1981). An excellent overview of the problem of choosing between these approaches to judicial review and analysis of the basis for a value-oriented approach to constitutional theory is contained in two articles by Professor Thomas Grey. See Grey, Do We Have an Unwritten Constitution? 27 Stan.L.Rev. 703 (1975); Grey, Origins of the Unwritten Constitution: Fundamental Law in American Revolutionary Thought, 30 Stan.L.Rev. 843 (1978).

17. The school of scholars commonly described as "neutral principle" advocates or theorists provided the theoretical foundation for this process oriented analy-

The list of rights which the Court has found to be fundamental, and, therefore, worthy of strict judicial scrutiny is not a long one. While there might be other ways to describe or divide these rights, they can be best understood as falling into six substantive categories (in addition to the fundamental guarantees of the Bill of Rights discussed in the previous section of this Chapter). First, the freedom of association has been found to be a fundamental value which is implied by the first amendment guarantees even though it has no specific textual recognition in that amendment.[18] Second, the right to vote and to participate in the electoral process has been held to be a fundamental constitutional value which is reflected in several amendments and given recognition as a form of "liberty" under the due process clauses.[19] Third, the Court has found a fundamental right to interstate travel which has a long history of recognition as a right to personal mobility under several provisions of the Constitution.[20] Fourth, the Court has implicitly recognized a right to fairness in the criminal process as a fundamental right although its "fundamental" nature has not been the subject of a specific decision.[21] Fifth, the Supreme Court has recognized that there is a right to fairness in procedures concerning individual claims against governmental deprivations of life, liberty, or property. Again, this right is not reflected in a specific decision but is, rather, an implied recognition of the fundamental nature of the due process clause in those decisions dealing with "procedural due process" rights.[22] Sixth, there is a fundamental

---

sis. See, Wechsler, Toward Neutral Principles of Constitutional Law, 73 Harv.L.Rev. 1 (1959). Professor Bickel began as a neutral principle theorist but eventually came to advocate a role for the Supreme Court more limited than modern process oriented scholars. For a listing of Professor Bickel's publications see, Writings of Alexander M. Bickel, 84 Yale L.J. 201. A representative sample of the scholarship of Alexander Bickel see: Bickel & Wellington, Legislative Purpose and the Judicial Process: The Lincoln Mills Case, 71 Harv.L.Rev. 1 (1957); A. Bickel, The Least Dangerous Branch (1962); A. Bickel, The Supreme Court and the Idea of Progress (1969); A. Bickel, The Morality of Consent (1975). For insightful analysis of the development and usefulness of neutral principles theory see G. White, Patterns of American Legal Thought (1978); Greenawalt, The Enduring Significance of Neutral Principles, 78 Colum.L.Rev. 982 (1978).

Modern process-oriented scholars have followed in the steps of neutral principle theorists such as Bickel and Wechsler as they have argued that justices should state clearly the reasons which justify their definition of a particular constitutional principle and limit the judicial role to independent examination of only whose legislative acts which appear to violate the specific wording of a constitutional provision, restrict the openness of the political process, or discriminate against discrete and insular minorities. Professor Jesse Choper, while not arguing against a wider scope of judicial review than a process-oriented approach would justify, has provided much of the theoretical groundwork for the process-oriented school. See J. Choper, Judicial Review and the National Political Process: A Functional Reconsideration of the Role of the Supreme Court (1980). Commentary on Professor Choper's work includes: Monaghan, Book Review, 94 Harv.L. Rev. 296 (1980); Nowak, Book Review, 68 Calif.L.Rev. 1223 (1980). During the past decade the most widely read and influential advocate of a process-oriented approach to the subject of judicial review has been Pro-

fessor (now Dean) John Hart Ely. See J. Ely, Democracy and Distrust (1980). Commentary on Professor Ely's work includes: Grano, Ely's Theory of Judicial Review: Preserving the Significance of the Political Process, 42 Ohio St.L.J. 167 (1981); Nowak, Foreword, Evaluating the Work of the New Libertarian Supreme Court, 7 Hastings Constitutional Law Quarterly 263 (1980); Tushnet, Darkness of the Edge of the Town: The Contributions of John Hart Ely to Constitutional Theory, 89 Yale L.J. 1037 (1980).

18. NAACP v. Alabama ex rel. Patterson, 357 U.S. 449, 460–61 (1958); Bates v. City of Little Rock, 361 U.S. 516, 522–3 (1960).

19. Harper v. Virginia Bd. of Elections, 383 U.S. 663 (1966); Carrington v. Rash, 380 U.S. 89 (1965).

See National Western Life Insurance Co. v. Commodore Cove Improvement District, 678 F.2d 24, 26 n. 6 (5th Cir. 1982) (Rubin, J.), citing this section of an earlier edition of this treatise.

20. Shapiro v. Thompson, 394 U.S. 618 (1969).

21. See, e.g., Douglas v. California, 372 U.S. 353 (1963) (right to counsel in first appeal); Mayer v. Chicago, 404 U.S. 189 (1971) (right to transcript in misdemeanor appeals); Bounds v. Smith, 430 U.S. 817 (1977) (right to legal materials & access to courts).

22. See Chapter 15: Procedural Due Process. The Court sometimes defines the nature of constitutional protection for a fundamental right as it rules on the procedures constitutionally mandated to avoid the unjustified deprivation of such rights in individual cases. See e.g., Youngberg v. Romeo, 102 S.Ct. 2452 (1982) (persons committed to state mental care institutions are constitutionally entitled to reasonably safe conditions of confinement and the exercise of professional judgment regarding their care that is not a substantial departure from generally accepted professional standards); Santosky v. Kramer, 455 U.S. 745 (1982) (parental rights can only be terminated if state can prove

right to privacy which includes various forms of freedom of choice in matters relating to the individual's personal life. This right to privacy has been held to include rights to freedom of choice in marital decisions,[23] child bearing,[24] and child rearing.[25]

This list is not permanently exhaustive and the Court may alter it in years ahead.[26] Yet the subjective nature of the Supreme Court's decisions concerning the rights on this list should not give the reader a feeling of hopelessness in predicting the future actions of the Court. The prior rulings of the Court concerning these rights, and the long history of the judicial enforcement of natural law rights which we have seen in this chapter, give one a basis for anticipating that the Court will continue to honor these rights in the years ahead. Because most of the Supreme Court decisions invalidating governmental limitation of fundamental rights have been based on the constitutional guarantee of equal protection, rather than due process, detailed consideration of the definition of these fundamental rights is deferred to Chapter 16.

VI. PROHIBITIONS AGAINST RETROACTIVE LEGISLATION

A. The Contract Clause

1. Introduction

The framers drafted the contract clause to prevent the states from enacting debtor relief laws. Under the leadership of Chief Justice John Marshall, however, the clause received an expansive reading. During the Marshall years the Court used the provision to invalidate statutes that retrospectively impaired almost any contractual obligation of private parties. The Court never used the clause to void laws that prospectively modified contractual obligations. Nevertheless, until the late nineteenth century the contract clause was the principal provision the Court used to void legislation that infringed on private property rights. Within the last 100 years, however, the Court rarely has relied on the clause as a reason to invalidate state legislation that retroactively affected contractual rights or obligations.

The Supreme Court has used the contract clause to restrict the ability of states to modify or alter public charters and contracts as well as private contracts. If a state is to retain the ability to modify a charter or public contract, it must explicitly so provide in the charter or in the enabling legislation. Moreover, if third parties' rights have accrued under the charter or public contract, the state may be unable to alter the contract even if it has made a general reservation to modify the contract. On the other hand, the contract clause will not prevent a state from altering its own contractual obligations that involve its inherent police powers. The Court has recognized that a state cannot bargain away its police power. If, however, the state commits itself to a financial obligation, the Court will review both the reasonableness and the necessity of any legislation that impairs that obligation. If the Court finds that the state law at issue is unnecessary and unreasonable in the way it alters the state financial commitment, it may void the measure as violative of the contract clause.

---

allegations of parental unfitness by "clear and convincing evidence").

23. Boddie v. Connecticut, 401 U.S. 371 (1971); Loving v. Virginia, 388 U.S. 1, 12 (1967).

24. This actually involves several particular rights or freedoms, see: Carey v. Population Services International, 431 U.S. 678 (1977) (purchase of contraceptives); Roe v. Wade, 410 U.S. 113 (1973) (abortions); Skinner v. Oklahoma, 315 U.S. 535 (1942) (reproductive ability—sterilization).

25. See, Pierce v. Society of Sisters, 268 U.S. 510, 535 (1925) (private eduation); Meyer v. Nebraska, 262

U.S. 390, 399 (1923); see also Prince v. Massachusetts, 321 U.S. 158, 166 (1944). Today these particular decisions might be viewed as relating to certain first amendment rights, but the Court cites them as showing a fundamental right, see Carey v. Population Services International, 431 U.S. 678 (1977).

26. This difficulty is exacerbated by those cases in which the Supreme Court mixes procedural and substantive due process questions. See note 22 supra, and Chapter 12, Section III: Procedural Due Process vs. Substantive Review.

2. The Case Law

The contract clause of the Constitution prohibits the states from enacting any law that will impair "the Obligation of Contracts." [1] This prohibition prevents the states from passing any legislation that would alleviate the commitments of one party to a contract or make enforcement of the contract unreasonably difficult.[2] The primary intent behind the drafting of the clause was to prohibit states from adopting laws that would interfere with the contractual arrangements between private citizens.[3] Specifically, the drafters intended to inhibit the ability of state legislatures to enact debtor relief laws.[4] Those who attended the Constitutional Convention recognized that banks and financiers required some assurance that their credit arrangements would not be abrogated by state legislatures. The drafters also realized that the country's economic growth depended in large measure on providing a stable environment for those who had money to invest or loan.[5] Therefore, as a means to help provide a stable economic environment, the draftsmen not only reserved in Congress the power to establish uniform bankruptcy laws [6] but also adopted the contract clause to restrict the power of the states to annul or void valid credit arrangements.

Although the framers of the Constitution believed the contract clause would have limited application, John Marshall, as Chief Justice, saw the provision as a valuable weapon to protect property interests from unwarranted state regulation.[7] Three events that occurred before Marshall became Chief Justice helped color his view of the clause as a shield to protect property owners from state regulation. First, in 1795, the circuit court for the district of Pennsylvania decided *Vanhorne's Lessee v. Dorrance* [8] in which it declared unconstitutional a Pennsylvania law that altered the title of disputed land because the statute violated the contract clause. This decision provided Marshall with valuable case authority to apply the contract clause to invalidate state statutes other than debtor relief laws.[9] Second, in 1798, the Supreme Court decided *Calder v. Bull* [10] and stated that the ex post facto clause [11] only applied to criminal legislation. With the ex post facto clause unavailable as a vehicle to void state civil legislation, the contract clause became a viable alternative as a means to protect property from retrospective legislation. Finally, the great Yazoo land scandal of the late 1790's presented Marshall, as Chief Justice, a prime opportunity to expound on the contract clause once the litigation that resulted from that scandal finally reached the Supreme Court in 1810 in the case of *Fletcher v. Peck*.[12]

In 1794 the Georgia legislature by statute granted thirty-five million acres of land to speculators for a purchase price of $500,000. When, however, the public learned of the widespread fraud and bribery that influenced the legislation, it demanded repeal of

1. U.S. Const. art. I, § 10: "No State shall . . . pass any . . . Law impairing the Obligation of Contracts." This clause does not apply to the federal government. See note 2.

2. Edward S. Corwin's, The Constitution and What It Means Today 103 (Rev. ed. by H. Chase & C. Ducat 1973). See generally, B. Wright, The Contract Clause of the Constitution (1938); Hale, The Supreme Court and the Contract Clause, 57 Harv.L.Rev. 512, 621, 852 (1944) (three part article). For rules relating to federal government contracts, see section B, 1 infra.

3. B. Wright, The Growth of American Constitutional Law 41 (1967) [hereinafter cited as Wright].

4. Wright, supra note 3, at 64; see also Home Building & Loan Ass'n v. Blaisdell, 290 U.S. 398, 427–28 (1934) (Hughes, C.J., discussing historical background of clause).

5. D. Smith, The Convention and the Constitution: The Political Ideas of the Founding Fathers 16–17 (1965).

6. U.S.Const. art. 1, § 8, cl. 4.

7. C. Magrath, Law and Politics in the New Republic—Yazoo: The Case of Fletcher v. Peck, 70–71 (1966) [hereinafter cited as Magrath].

8. 2 U.S. (2 Dall.) 304 (1795).

9. Magrath, supra note 7, at 83.

10. 3 U.S. (3 Dall.) 386 (1798).

11. U.S.Const. art. I, § 10.

12. 10 U.S. (6 Cranch) 187 (1810).

the statutory grant, and the Georgia legislature rescinded the legislation a year later.[13] Peck had purchased some of the Georgia land from one of the original grantees and had resold the land to Fletcher. When Fletcher learned of the statutory repeal of the grant, he demanded rescission of the contract and his money back because of Peck's inability to convey good title. Peck, however, responded with the argument that he was a purchaser in due course and the rescinding act could not affect his title to the land.[14]

When *Fletcher v. Peck* came before the Supreme Court, Chief Justice Marshall was fully aware of the original limited intent behind the contract clause.[15] At the same time, however, he was also familiar with the position of Alexander Hamilton. Hamilton, like Marshall, was a leading Federalist, and he believed that Georgia's repeal of a land grant made for valuable consideration violated the prohibitions of the contract clause. Like Hamilton, Marshall believed the contract clause offered a valuable defense against reckless state legislatures which would interfere with established business and property interests.[16] These countervailing considerations that Marshall entertained appearently worked at odds with each other while he was writing his opinion. Although Marshall's opinion in *Fletcher v. Peck* declared the rescinding statute unconstitutional, the constitutional basis for the opinion is somewhat uncertain. Some language in the decision implies that the Georgia statute violated the contract clause because the grant was in the nature of a contract.[17] Other language in the opinion, however, reflects Marshall's uncertainty on whether he could rest the entire decision on

the clause. He states that the rescinding legislation violated not only general principles of society and government but also the concept of natural law.[18] Therefore, whether the contract clause, by itself, would prohibit legislation that impaired the obligation of a state to a private party was unclear. Although *Fletcher v. Peck* was the Supreme Court's first decision that addressed the clause, subsequent Court decisions soon removed any uncertainty of whether the provision would prevent a state from avoiding its own obligations to a contract.

After *Fletcher v. Peck* the Court decided *New Jersey v. Wilson*[19] and *Dartmouth College v. Woodward*[20] and removed any doubt that the contract clause would prohibit a state from abrogating agreements to which it was a party. In the *Wilson* case the New Jersey legislature enacted a statute that repealed a tax exemption which the colonial legislature had granted certain lands fifty years earlier. The Supreme Court invalidated the repealing measure as violative of the contract clause.[21] In *Dartmouth College* the Court applied the clause to a statute that attempted to change the provisions of a charter issued to Dartmouth College.[22] The Court, through Chief Justice Marshall, stated without reservation or qualification that the clause applied to a state's obligation in a contract, that a charter was a contract, and that the covenants in the charter were invoidable even though the holders of the charter, the college trustees, have no beneficial interest in the instrument.[23] Although *Dartmouth College* involved a charitable and educational institution, the Court readily expanded the principles announced in the opinion to corporate charters issued for business purposes. Consequently, the decision

---

13. Magrath, supra note 7, at 1–19.

14. Id. at 50–69.

15. Id. at 71.

16. Wright, supra note 3, at 42.

17. 10 U.S. (6 Cranch) at 136–37.

18. Id. at 139. On the uncertain foundation of the opinion see Wright, supra note 3, at 42–43.

19. 11 U.S. (7 Cranch) 164 (1812).

20. 17 U.S. (4 Wheat.) 518 (1819).

21. 11 U.S. (7 Cranch) at 166–68.

22. See Wright, supra note 3, at 43.

23. 17 U.S. (4 Wheat.) at 651–52; see also R. McCloskey, The American Supreme Court at 73–75 (1960) [hereinafter cited as McCloskey].

protected industrial and financial corporations from much government regulation.[24]

The Supreme Court in *Fletcher v. Peck, Wilson,* and *Dartmouth College* unquestionably had established that the contract clause would preclude states from passing legislation that would ameliorate the contractual commitments of a state to another party. Nevertheless, the original intent behind the provision was to inhibit the ability of states to enact debtor relief laws that would impair the contractual obligation of private parties. The Court ironically, however, did not apply the clause to invalidate a debtor relief law until *Sturges v. Crowinshield,*[25] decided in the same year that the Court rendered the *Dartmouth College* opinion. In *Sturges* the Court declared unconstitutional a New York insolvency law that discharged the obligations of debtors once they had surrendered their property. The principal constitutional defect of the law was its retroactive effect; the act released debtors from obligations assumed before the act's passage. The *Sturges* opinion, therefore, implied that the Court would sustain debtor relief legislation that had a prospective effect. In *Ogden v. Saunders*[26] the Court expressly stated the implication of *Sturges* and held a debtor relief law with prospective impact to be constitutional. Although Chief Justice Marshall contended that the contract clause prohibited states from enacting prospective debtor legislation, the majority of the Court disagreed because they believed the framers of the Constitution clearly intended the clause to prohibit only retrospective legislation.

Chief Justice Marshall's inability to persuade the majority of the Court to adopt his view of the contract clause in *Ogden v. Saunders* was one of the few setbacks the Chief Justice suffered in his campaign to make the clause a shield to protect established property and business interests from

unwarranted state intrusion. He had expanded the application of the provision beyond the original intent of the framers. The contract clause not only would inhibit states from impairing the obligation of contracts between private parties but also would prevent states from abrogating their own contractual commitments to private citizens. Under Marshall's leadership, the Court had declared that state grants and state charters were contracts and came under the protection of the contract clause. On the whole, the Chief Justice had succeeded in his efforts to make the clause a valuable provision to protect the "vested rights" of property holders and businessmen.

When Roger Taney succeeded John Marshall as Chief Justice,[27] some feared that the Court would retreat from the expansive application the contract clause had received during Marshall's tenure because of Taney's affiliation with the Jackson Democrats. The Taney Court apparently gave some substance to those fears with its opinion in *Charles River Bridge v. Warren Bridge.*[28]

In *Charles River Bridge* the issue involved was the interpretation of a charter that Massachusetts had issued to the Charles River Bridge Company. The charter gave the company the authority to construct and operate a toll bridge.[29] While this charter was in effect, however, the state issued a second charter to Warren that also gave him the authority to build a toll bridge, but his bridge would become a "free" bridge after three years. The Charles River Bridge Company contended that the second charter reduced the worth of its charter and thus impaired the obligation of the state to maintain the value of its charters.[30] The Court rejected this contention. The Court replied that the first charter was not expressly an exclusive grant to operate a bridge, and that it would construe grants strictly. Consequently, the second charter did not impair

24.   Wright, supra note 3, at 44.

25.   17 U.S. (4 Wheat.) 122 (1819).

26.   25 U.S. (12 Wheat.) 213 (1825).

27.   McCloskey, supra note 23, at 81–85.

28.   36 U.S. (11 Pet.) 420 (1837).

29.   Wright, supra note 3, at 63.

30.   Id.

the state's obligation under the contract. Justice Story dissented and argued that the Court had reversed its position on the sanctity of property rights.[31] Justice Story's argument, however, was untenable: the Court had not reversed its position because Chief Justice Marshall originally had formulated the rule of the strict construction of public grants in *Providence Bank v. Billings*.[32] On the contrary, the two important doctrines of the Marshall Court remained in force: a charter is a contract and an agreement to which the state is a party falls under the protection of the contract clause.[33]

The decisions the Court rendered during Chief Justice Taney's leadership adhered to the interpretations of the contract clause that the Marshall Court had formulated. In *Piqua Branch of the State Bank v. Knoop*,[34] for example, the Court again recognized that a grant that conferred a tax exemption received protection from the contract clause and the state could not revoke the exemption by subsequent legislation. In other cases, the Court invalidated state regulations of banks when those regulations conflicted with explicit provisions of previously issued bank charters.[35] Moreover, the Court unhesitatingly applied the contract clause to void debtor relief laws that had a retroactive effect.[36] In all, the Taney Supreme Court relied on the contract clause to void state legislation on eighteen different occasions.[37]

In several cases the Taney Court gave added definition and certainty to the scope of the contract clause. In *West River Bridge Co. v. Dix*,[38] for example, the Court emphasized that certain state powers were inalienable. Although the legislature in a corporate charter may promise not to exercise the power of eminent domain, the promise will fail to prevent the state from taking the property of the corporation with just compensation because the legislature never had the power to convey away the power of eminent domain. The Court repeated the principle of the *Dix* some thirty years later in *Stone v. Mississippi*[39] when it stated that the legislature cannot bargain away the public health and morals of the people. The legislature must allow the state to exercise its proper police powers. Moreover, the Supreme Court later extended the doctrine announced in *Dix* and stated that private parties who enter into a contract "may not estop the legislature from enacting laws for the public good."[40] In *Bronson v. Kinzie*[41] the Taney Court attempted to give added definition to the remedy-obligation distinction enunciated by the Marshall Court in *Sturges*. In *Sturges* the Supreme Court had conceded that although the contract clause precluded a state from adopting laws that impaired the obligation of contracts, the state may enact legislation that modifies the available remedies for the breach of a contract.[42] In *Bronson* the Court stated that the scope of allowable modifications of remedies under the clause depended on the reasonableness of those modifications and whether the modifying legislation affected substantial rights of the parties.[43] The Court's success, however, in defining the distinction between remedy and obligation is perhaps best reflected in Justice Cardozo's statement in *Worthen Co. v. Kavanaugh*.[44] Some ninety years after *Bronson*, Cardozo found that the distinction between obligation and remedy "is at times obscure." Never-

31. 36 U.S. (11 Pet.) at 583.

32. 29 U.S. (4 Pet.) 514 (1830).

33. See, Wright, supra note 3, at 64.

34. 57 U.S. (16 How.) 369 (1854).

35. See Wright, supra note 3, at 65–66.

36. See, e.g., Bronson v. Kinzie, 42 U.S. (1 How.) 311 (1843) (legislation granting redemption rights to mortgagors who had already lost land in foreclosures held invalid). This case is discussed below at notes 41, 43. See also, Wright, supra note 4, at 64–65.

37. Wright, supra note 3, at 64.

38. 47 U.S. (6 How.) 507 (1848).

39. 101 U.S. 814 (1880).

40. Manigault v. Springs, 199 U.S. 473, 480 (1905).

41. 42 U.S. (1 How.) 311 (1843).

42. 17 U.S. (4 Wheat.) 122, 200–01 (1819).

43. 42 U.S. (1 How.) at 315–17.

44. 295 U.S. 56, 60 (1935).

theless, highlighting the difference between the two concepts gave not only the Court but also state legislatures some flexibility in approving debtor relief statutes.

The Supreme Court from 1874–1898 used the clause in thirty-nine cases to invalidate state legislation.[45] At the same time, however, the Court had reached the end of the period of the expansive reading of the clause. During the latter part of the nineteenth century the provision lost its importance as the principal constitutional clause available to protect vested rights.

Several developments help explain the diminished value of the contract clause as a defense for property interests. First, the states were reserving the right to amend or alter the charters they granted. In *Dartmouth College* the Supreme Court held that a state could not change the provisions

of a charter after the charter had been issued. At the same time, however, the *Dartmouth College* decision conceded that if a state reserved the right to modify the terms of a charter either by a provision in the charter or by a general statutory scheme, a state could subsequently modify a granted charter without violating the contract clause.[46] Therefore, states took advantage of this concession by passing the appropriate legislation or including the necessary charter provision. Additionally, the rule that the Court would construe strictly the terms of any public grant prompted the states to write their grants carefully. Consequently, the states rarely would enact a statutory grant that would fail to give the state the necessary flexibility to pass legislation that may modify the previously issued public grant.[47] Finally, the Court began to rely on the doctrine of substantive due pro-

---

45. See Wright, supra note 3, at 96.

46. Dartmouth College v. Woodward, 17 U.S. (4 Wheat.) 518, 666 (1819) (Story, J. concurring opinion); see also, Home of the Friendless v. Rouse, 75 U.S. (8 Wall.) 430, 438 (1869); Pennsylvania College Cases, 80 U.S. (13 Wall.) 190, 213 (1873); Millers v. New York, 82 U.S. (15 Wall.) 478 (1873); Murray v. Charleston, 96 U.S. 432 (1878); Greenwood v. Freight Co., 105 U.S. 13 (1882); Wright, supra note 3, at 96.

The concept that once the rights of third parties had accrued those rights must be protected in the face of modification of the corporate charter has been maintained in subsequent decisions through the present. See Greenwood v. Freight Co., 105 U.S. 13 (1882). Where the charter of a streetcar company was repealed under a general statute, the Court fashioned a remedy for shareholders rights to real and personal property of the corporation, to contract rights, and to choses in action. See also Coombes v. Getz, 285 U.S. 434 (1934) in which a state constitutional provision for alteration of corporate charters was used to offset the protection for creditors offered in another constitutional section. In reversing the legislation the Court held (1) that the right to enforce the liability was part of the creditors' contracts which were protected and fully vested before the repeal and hence were protected by both the contract clause and due process, and (2) the reserved power of a state over corporations and their shareholders cannot be used to destroy the vested rights of third persons or to impair the obligations of their contracts.

47. Wright, supra note 3, at 96. The cases reinforcing the right of a state to alter or retract at will the terms of its agreement with a smaller governmental entity are legion. Some examples of cases expressing language that local governing power can be withdrawn at the will of the legislature are: Hunter v. Pittsburgh,

207 U.S. 161 (1907); Covington v. Kentucky, 173 U.S. 231 (1899); Meriwether v. Garrett, 102 U.S. 472 (1880). Clearly the wide discretionary power is not limited only to charters involving local government; a grant made by the state to protect local needs was also denied protection. City of Trenton v. New Jersey, 262 U.S. 182, 191 (1923). Grants of property are also vulnerable. A ferry franchise to a municipality was taken back in East Hartford v. Hartford Bridge Co., 51 U.S. (10 How.) 511 (1851). See also Hunter v. Pittsburgh, 207 U.S. 161 (1907). A state can decide to relocate a county seat and protests from the local government concerning money expended in reliance on the old location will not be heard. Newton v. Commissioners, 100 U.S. 548 (1887). New school districts can be forced to assume the debts of a previous school district, Michigan ex rel. Kies v. Lowrey, 199 U.S. 233 (1905); and a state can take administrative control of insolvent communities, Faitoute Iron & Steel Co. v. City of Asbury Park, 316 U.S. 502 (1942).

Individuals dealing with the state fare no better than corporate entities. Government appointments and elections are not contracts with the state subject to protection. Tenure, salaries, and duties all remain subject to modification unless the prerequisites have already accrued and the state has gained the benefits of the individual's reliance on the agreement. Dodge v. Board of Education, 302 U.S. 74 (1937); Mississippi ex rel. Robertson v. Miller, 276 U.S. 174 (1928); Fisk v. Jefferson Police Jury, 116 U.S. 131 (1885); Butler v. Pennsylvania, 51 U.S. (10 How.) 402 (1850). Shortening the statutory period of repose for a land grant has not been seen as a deprivation of an accrued right. City of El Paso v. Simmons, 379 U.S. 497 (1965). See also Thorpe v. Housing Authority of City of Durham, 393 U.S. 268, 278–9 (1969).

cess to void legislation that would infringe on property or business interests. More often than not, any state legislation that impaired the obligation of contract would not only violate the contract clause but also would violate the Court's notions of economic substantive due process. The substantive due process doctrine gave the Court more discretion and flexibility than the contract clause in passing on the constitutionality of state legislation. Hence, if the Court had a choice, it would use substantive due process analysis rather than contract clause analysis to void state legislation.[48]

During the Court's substantive due process era the contract clause faded in importance. When, however, the Great Depression came and states began to enact debtor relief legislation, the Court began to hear numerous cases where the opponents of the debtor relief measures relied on the clause to attack the constitutionality of the legislation. Earlier Supreme Courts had invalidated many of these laws if they had a retroactive effect. Nevertheless, in *Home Building & Loan Association v. Blaisdell*,[49] the Court sustained a debtor relief law despite its retrospective impact.

In 1933, Minnesota enacted a law that gave the state courts the authority to extend the redemption period after a foreclosure sale. However, before a court could approve an extension of the redemption period, it had to order the mortgagor to pay a reasonable part of the rental value of the property. The mortgagee in *Blaisdell* contended that the law violated the contract clause, but the Court rejected the contention. The Court recognized the economy emergency the country faced when Minnesota passed the Mortgage Moratorium Law of 1933.[50] Relying on the principle first announced in *West River Bridge Co. v. Dix*[51] and clarified in later cases, the Court stated that a state always retained a power to react to emergency situations and to protect the security of its people. Minnesota's adoption of this "Mortgage Moratorium" provision fell within this reserved power and, thus, did not violate the Constitution. The Court noted that the authority the mortgage law conferred was of limited duration and would not outlast the emergency it was designed to meet. These considerations underscored the reasonableness of the measure.

When the Court examined "emergency" debtor relief legislation which totally exempted major assets of debtors from creditors' claims or eliminated remedies for claims without protecting the creditors' rights, it found that such actions violated the contract clause.[52] Under *Blaisdell* the state could alter remedies for debts if the legislation reasonably related to a public purpose and protected the basic value of creditor claims; the states were not permitted to significantly impair the basis of creditors' accrued rights in order to improve the economic position of debtors.

Although the Court did void a few state enactments as violative of the contract clause after the *Blaisdell* decision, it did sustain the great majority of state laws against attacks to their constitutionality un-

---

Just as salaries and other employment obligations are not protected by the contract clause, neither are rights of recovery under a judgment. Crane v. Hahlo, 258 U.S. 142 (1922). The contract clause does not protect such "vested rights" as such, they must be referable to an agreement of some sort between the state and an individual. Louisiana ex rel. Folsom v. Mayor of New Orleans, 109 U.S. 285 (1883); Morley v. Lake Shore Ry. Co., 146 U.S. 162 (1892); Satterlee v. Matthewson, 27 U.S. (2 Pet.) 380 (1829); Charles River Bridge v. Warren Bridge, 36 U.S. (11 Pet.) 420 (1837).

48. See, e.g., Lochner v. New York, 198 U.S. 45 (1905). The concept of substantive due process is examined above, in sections I to IV of this chapter.

49. 290 U.S. 398 (1934).

50. Id. at 424–30.

51. 47 U.S. (6 How.) 507 (1848).

52. See, W. B. Worthen Co. v. Thomas, 292 U.S. 426 (1934) (law exempting money for or from insurance premiums or benefits from creditors' claims held to violate the contract clause); W. B. Worthen Co. v. Kavanaugh, 295 U.S. 56 (1935) (elimination of foreclosure remedies violates the contract clause when no money is paid to the creditor for loss of possession and the debtor can only gain by continued default); but see East New York Savings Bank v. Hahn, 326 U.S. 230 (1945) ("mortgage moratorium" legislation like that approved in *Blaisdell* upheld even though it was extended for over ten years; reasonable provision and consideration for creditor interests supported the Act).

der the contract clause. The Court's almost uniform refusal to use the clause to void legislation paralleled its abandonment of substantive due process analysis to void economic legislation. Perhaps the best example of the Court's reluctance to use the clause to invalidate state legislation is *El Paso v. Simmons.*[53] Texas had sold land under contract for a small down payment. The purchaser could forfeit his right to the property by failing to make interest payments on the land, but could reinstate his claim to the land by paying in full the overdue interest as long as rights of third parties had not intervened. The reinstatement right had no time limit to its exercise. Some thirty years after the initial sale of the land Texas amended the statute governing the reinstatement right and placed a five-year limit on its exercise.[54] Simmons contended that the amending legislation violated the contract clause. The Court, through Justice White, disagreed. Although Justice White was willing to assume that the statutory amendment impaired the state's obligation under the land contracts, he was unwilling to declare the law unconstitutional. The rights that the amending legislation impaired were rights left unprotected by the Constitution.[55] The unlimited reinstatement period had generated not only much land speculation but also much uncertainty over land titles. Justice White believed that the contract clause could not prevent the Texas legislature's ability to remedy this situation and to "restrict a party to those gains reasonably to be expected from the contract."[56] Therefore, although the law had modified a state's own contractual obligation, the Court sustained the measure as constitutional under the contract clause.

After the *El Paso* decision some commentators speculated that because of the recent history of the Court's application of the contract clause removal of the provision from the Constitution would not reduce the Constitution's effectiveness as a check on the arbitrary exercise of governmental power.[57] This speculation of the contract clause's complete demise, however, proved premature. In *United States Trust Co. v. New Jersey*[58] the Court revived the clause and declared a New Jersey statute unconstitutional because the law impaired the state's contractual obligation to the bondholders of The Port Authority of New York and New Jersey.

In 1962 the New York and New Jersey legislature decided that the Port Authority should take over and subsidize a bankrupt passenger railroad line that serviced the New York City metropolitan area. To reassure the Port Authority bondholders that the Authority would not be asked in the future to take over mass transit deficit operations beyond the Authority's financial reserves, the two states agreed to limit the number of such operations the Authority would absorb. In 1974 New Jersey repealed the legislation that implemented the limitation agreement. The bondholders sought a declaratory judgment that the repealing legislation violated the contract clause because it reduced the financial security of their bonds. The state responded that removing the limitation was necessary to permit the Port Authority to subsidize mass transportation programs for the New York City metropolitan area. The state highlighted the need for the repealing measure relating it to the energy crisis of 1973 and of the air pollution problems northern New Jersey faces. The Court acknowledged that it traditionally had required more than a mere technical impairment of a contractual obligation before it would void a measure as violative of the con-

53.   379 U.S. 497 (1965).

54.   Id. at 500–01.

55.   Id. at 509.

56.   Id. at 515.

57.   Edwin S. Corwin's The Constitution and What It Means Today 105 (Rev.ed. by H. Chase & C. Ducat, 1973).

58.   431 U.S. 1 (1977); Mid-State Food Dealers Ass'n v. City of Durand, 525 F.Supp. 387, 391 n. 20 (E.D. Mich.1981) (Newblatt, D.J.), citing earlier edition of this treatise.

tract clause. Moreover, the Court noted that it usually had deferred to the legislature judgment whenever a state had exercised its police power to impair retroactively the obligation of private contracts. In this case, however, the state was asking the Court to sustain a law that relieved the state of its own contractual obligation. Consequently, the Court believed that the customary deference to the legislative judgment was not in order, but on the contrary, that it should assess the necessity and reasonableness of the repealing legislation.[59]

In its assessment of the New Jersey enactment the Court first noted that the state had obligated itself to a financial contract and had not bargained away one of its police powers. Therefore, the 1962 financial restrictions were valid when the state had entered into the contract. The Court then noted that although mass transportation, energy conservation, and cleaning the environment are important goals, the state cannot refuse "to meet its legitimate financial obligation simply because it would prefer to spend the money to promote the public good rather than the private welfare of its creditors."[60] Because alternative means were available to promote these goals, the Court reasoned that the repealing measure was both unreasonable and unnecessary. Hence, the Court declared the New Jersey statute unconstitutional because it impaired the state's own obligation of contract without promoting an overriding police power interest.

The Supreme Court in 1978 resurrected the contract clause as a vehicle for judicial review of state economic legislation that altered private contracts in *Allied Structural*

Steel Co. v. Spannaus.[61] At issue in *Spannaus* was a Minnesota law which effectively increased the monetary obligations of companies which had a pre-existing pension plan for employees and which either terminated the plan or closed their business facility in Minnesota. The law required that employees who had worked for such a company for in excess of ten years be granted benefits upon termination or the closing of a plant regardless of the provisions of the employer's pension plan. The majority opinion by Justice Stewart reviewed the past decisions of the Court concerning the contract clause and recognized the general principle that states could enact legislation which limited contractual rights when that legislation was enacted to protect a basic societal interest and was a reasonable and narrow means of protecting that interest. The majority opinion noted that, while this principle was not a very strict limit on the powers of the states, the contract clause remained a meaningful part of the Constitution. The majority found this law a clear violation of the contract clause, because of the following factors: (1) the impairment of contract clause by the law was "substantial";[62] (2) the plaintiff company had "relied heavily, and reasonably" on actuarial calculations as to the amount of funding necessary to sustain the projected payouts from the pension fund only to incur unexpected additional obligations as a result of the law;[63] (3) the law was not necessary to remedy an "important and general social problem," but rather focused on a limited number of employers who "had in the past been sufficiently enlightened as voluntarily to agree to establish pen-

---

59. 431 U.S. at 25–26.

60. 431 U.S. at 29.

61. 438 U.S. 234 (1978).

62. 438 U.S. at 244–245. The opinion noted that a minimal burden on contractual interests would require less stringent review and could be upheld more easily. Id. See also Texaco, Inc. v. Short, 454 U.S. 516 (1982) (Statute providing for lapse of several mineral interest unused for 20 years constitutes permissible limitation of property interests and is not an unconstitutional impairment of contract rights.)

63. 438 U.S. at 246. The company had complied with all of its contractual pension fund obligations as well as all laws applicable to pension plans until this time. It was only the closing of the office that subjected the company to this law, which requires it to recalculate and pay out additional funds for the past ten years of pension plan contributions. The burden was so severe and the company's reliance so reasonable that the majority felt unable to presume the "necessity and reasonableness" of the law. Id.

sion plans"; [64] (4) the law was not a temporary measure to deal with an emergency situation [65] and (5) the law regulated a field which the state had not previously sought to regulate. [66]

Although the above factors appear to limit the *Spannaus* decision, Justices Brennan, Marshall and White argued, in dissent, that the decision effected an unprecedented expansion of the meaning of the contract clause. [67] The dissenters stated that the majority disregarded the substantial remedial purpose of the law. They would have accepted the state's purpose of protection of employees "within a few months of the 'vesting' of their rights" under a pension plan from unforeseen plant closings or unilateral termination of a plan by an employer. [68] Justice Brennan, writing for the three dissenters, also argued that the majority had misinterpreted the scope of the contract clause. The dissenters felt that the clause could only be read to reach acts of a legislature which impair or abrogate existing contract rights, and could not be read to reach acts which merely increase existing contractual obligations. So construed, the contract clause would have no application to this leg-

islation; the Brennan opinion could then uphold the law against a due process challenge because of its relationship to protecting pensions. [69]

Although *Spannaus* appears to be a limited holding hedged by a number of qualifying factors and tied closely to the facts before the Court, the dissent seems justified in viewing the case as an enlargement of the scope of the contract clause as it had been employed by the Court in recent years. The majority, however, was unwilling to follow an approach to contract clause adjudication that effectively would read the clause out of the Constitution. Thus, the majority refused to give total deference to state legislative decisions concerning the need to alter contractual obligations or to rule that the clause did not apply to alteration of contract terms that merely increased contractual obligations. Those asserted limitations on judicial review, employed by the dissent, were not expressly adopted in the prior decisions of the Court and they would leave the Court with no meaningful role in enforcing the substantive principles of the contract clause. The majority opinion by Justice Stewart only held that a state was not free to severely al-

---

64. 438 U.S. at 250. The fact that the law did not regulate other employers, who presented more serious problems in terms of failing to establish funds to provide for employee retirement, made the law so narrow that it seemed to have little relation to solving a general social problem. Also, the Supreme Court, in a previous decision during the 1977–78 Term, had held that Minnesota Act was not preempted by older Federal legislation but that it was preempted by recent Federal pension legislation that expressly provided for the preemption of such state laws. Malone v. White Motor Corp., 435 U.S. 497 (1978). Thus, the effective time period and application of the act was so limited that it applied to only a small classification of employers.

65. 438 U.S. at 250. In this way the Court distinguished this legislation for the economic relief legislation upheld in Home Building & Loan Ass'n v. Blaisdell, 290 U.S. 398 (1934). When a law is a temporary means of dealing with an emergency, it is more likely to be upheld as a reasonable exercise of the police power that does not violate the contract clause.

66. 438 U.S. at 250.

67. Allied Structural Steel Co. v. Spannaus, 438 U.S. 234, 251 (1978) (Brennan, J., dissenting, joined by Marshall & White, JJ.).

68. 438 U.S. at 253. The pension plan that had been created by the plaintiff in the case provided, inter

alia, for unilateral termination or modification of the plan by the employer, and gave no recourse to employees in the event of such actions. The plan also provided that there was to be no recourse against the employer if the employer failed to fund the plan adequately. See 438 U.S. at 237. In light of these facts and as noted by Justice Brennan, other common abuses of employee confidence by those employers who fail to inform their employees that their "pension plan" may not protect them, it seems that the majority might not have been justified in concluding that no "important or general" state interest was reasonably served by the Minnesota law. The majority, however, did realize that the question of reliance might "cut both ways," but the majority found that no showing was made in the case that any employees of plaintiff company had relied to their detriment on Allied's pension plan. 438 U.S. at 246 n. 18. Given the limited nature and application of the law and the fact that the surcharged company appeared to have acted in good faith, the majority could not conclude that the Act was a reasonable means of protecting employees from abuse of pension plans programs so as to justify the serious retroactive burden placed on the company.

69. 438 U.S. at 255–264.

ter contractual obligations or impair contractual rights unless the state could demonstrate that its legislation was a reasonable and narrow means of promoting important societal interests.

The Court followed the reasoning of *United States Trust Co.* and *Spannaus* when it upheld a state law placing a statutory ceiling on price increases which a natural gas supplier could charge a public utility under the escalator clause of a pre-existing contract. The Court held that to the extent that the law substantially impaired contract rights it was a narrowly tailored means of promoting the important state interest in protecting consumers from imbalance in market prices caused by federal deregulation.[70] Thus, the *Allied Structural Steel Co. v. Spannaus* decision represents only a refusal to abdicate the judicial role in the enforcement of the contract clause, rather than a return to the pre-1937 model of judicial protection of economic interests.

B. Other Forms of Restrictions on Retroactive Legislation

1. Due Process Limitations

A statute or law that attempts to establish the legal significance of transactions that have occurred before its enactment constitutes what is called "retroactive legislation."[1] The courts traditionally have op-

posed retroactive legislation not only because such legislation tends to create instability but also because the legislature can benefit or harm disfavored classes of citizens more easily with retrospective laws than it can with prospective laws.[2] The Constitution reflects this bias against retroactive statutes by prohibiting both the Congress and the states from enacting any ex post facto laws;[3] the contract clause of the Constitution prevents the states from passing any legislation that impairs the obligations of contracts.[4]

Besides the explicit constitutional provisions against retroactive laws the Supreme Court has also used the due process clauses of the fifth and fourteenth amendments to void certain legislation that has a retrospective impact.[5] The framers of the fifth and fourteenth amendment due process clauses, however, did not specifically design those provisions to cover retroactive legislation. Therefore, unlike the contract or ex post facto clauses, the due process clauses fail to provide the Court with any definite criteria to determine when retroactive legislation violates constitutional principles. Nevertheless, the cases where retroactive legislation is an issue fall into four main categories and the Court appears to treat each category differently.[6] The four categories of cases involving retroactive legislation under the due

---

70. Energy Reserves Group, Inc. v. Kansas Power & Light Co., 103 S.Ct. 697 (1983). The Court found that the natural gas company's contractual rights were not substantially impaired as the contracting parties recognized the fact that their activities were and would be subject to wide ranging government regulation. To the extent that the relationship was substantially impaired the law promoted an overriding interest in consumer protection. Id. at 708. "The threshold inquiry is whether the state law has, in fact, operated as a substantial impairment of a contractual relationship . . . If the state regulation constitutes a substantial impairment, the state, in justification must have a significant and legitimate public purpose . . . Once a legitimate public purpose is identified, the next inquiry is whether the adjustment of rights and responsibilities of contracting parties is based upon reasonable conditions and is of a character appropriate to the public purpose justifying the legislation's adoption." Id. at 704–705 quoting in part the *United States Trust Co.* and *Spannaus* decisions discussed previously in this section (citations, quotation marks, and brackets within quotes omitted).

1. Greenblatt, Judicial Limitations on Retroactive Civil Legislation, 51 Nw.U.L.Rev. 540, 544 (1956).

2. See, e.g., Dash v. Van Kleeck, 7 Johns. 477 (N.Y.1811); see also, Slawson, Constitutional and Legislative Considerations in Retroactive Lawmaking, 48 Calif.L.Rev. 216, 221 (1960); Hochman, The Supreme Court and the Constitutionality of Retroactive Legislation, 73 Harv.L.Rev. 692, 692–93 (1960) [hereinafter cited as Hochman].

3. U.S.Const. art. I, § 9, cl. 3; § 10, cl. 1.

4. U.S.Const. art. I, § 10. See, section VI, A of this chapter.

5. Hochman, supra note 2, at 693–94.

6. Compare the categories listed in Slawson, Constitutional and Legislative Consideration in Retroactive Lawmaking, 48 Calif.L.Rev. 216, 238 (1960), with the three-part test of Hochman, supra note 2, at 697. Hochman's test for the constitutionality of retroactive legislation lists three major considerations: (1) the nature of the public interest involved; (2) the extent to which the statute modifies the pre-enactment right; and (3) the nature of the pre-enactment right. Id.

process clause are: (1) cases that involve emergency retroactive legislation;[7] (2) cases that challenge the constitutionality of curative statutes;[8] (3) cases that involve the constitutional merits of retroactive taxing legislation;[9] and (4) cases that contest the constitutionality of retroactive general legislation.[10] Although the constitutional criteria for determining when retroactive legislation will violate due process is unsettled, an analysis of each of these issues may help in predicting when a certain piece of legislation will infringe on the right to due process of law.

If the constitutionality of retroactive emergency legislation is challenged, the Court usually will sustain the measure. A case that illustrates the judicial deference to emergency measures is *Lichter v. United States.*[11] Petitioner contested the constitutionality of the Renegotiation Act of 1942. This wartime measure allowed the War Department to renegotiate any contract it had with private citizens to prevent those citizens from realizing excessive profits from the government contract. The Act applied not only to contracts that arose after the law's enactment but it also applied to uncompleted contracts that the government entered into before the Act's passage. The petitioners challenged the retrospective impact of the measure under the fifth amendment. In sustaining the Renegotiation Act the Court emphasized the history of the Act as a part of the nation's wartime posture. The Court suggested that Congress could have appropriated private enterprise and placed it into a governmental unit for wartime production.[12] Congress, however, by enacting this law did less and preserved private enterprise. Therefore, because Congress unquestionably had the power to act substantively

in this area, the Court deferred to the legislative judgment on what was the best approach to restrain private enterprise in an emergency.

In most emergency situations the nature of the public interest involved is great.[13] In *Lichter* the Court recognized the need to prevent individuals from profiteering from wartime conditions. Consequently, if the constitutionality of emergency measures is questioned, the Court usually will sustain the legislation despite its retrospective effect. The nature of the public interest will outweigh the traditional reasons for viewing such legislation unfavorably. But the Supreme Court, will not always sustain emergency retroactive legislation. In *Louisville Joint Stock Land Bank v. Radford*[14] the Court invalidated an emergency depression measure because it substantially reduced the value of existing mortgages. Although the Court recognized the public interest of saving existing farms from mortgage foreclosure, the retrospective impact of the legislation deprived the mortgagees of the value of their mortgages without due process of law. However, two years later the Court upheld a federal statute modified in light of the *Radford* decision: the new statute gave the farmer normally a three-year stay of foreclosure rather than an absolute one; the property, though possessed by the debtor-farmer, was under the custody, supervision, and control of the court; if the debtor failed to pay the reasonable rental, or failed to comply with court orders, or it became evident that he could not reasonably rehabilitate himself financially within the three-year period, or if the emergency ceased to exist, the court could terminate the stay and order a sale.[15]

These considerations, however, allow the Court to assess the weight of each factor. Even Hochman separates out certain types of legislation for specific discussion. Id. at 703–08.

7. See Hochman, supra note 2, at 698–99.

8. Slawson, Constitutional and Legislative Considerations in Retroactive Lawmaking, 48 Calif.L.Rev. 216, 238 (1960).

9. Id.

10. See Hochman, supra note 2, at 697–700, 715–17, 724–25.

11. 334 U.S. 742 (1948).

12. Id. at 766–67.

13. Hochman, supra note 2, at 697–98.

14. 295 U.S. 555 (1935).

15. Wright v. Vinton Branch of the Mountain Trust Bank, 300 U.S. 440 (1937); cf. Home Building & Loan Ass'n v. Blaisdell, 290 U.S. 398 (1934).

The category of cases where the constitutionality of curative statutes is an issue presents another area where the Court will almost always sustain retroactive legislation. Curative statutes are those measures that will either ratify prior official conduct or make a remedial adjustment in an administrative scheme.[16] The Court confronted and sustained a curative statute in *F.H.A. v. The Darlington, Inc.*[17] Congress had authorized the Federal Housing Administration to insure mortgages on residential housing for veterans of World War II. The F.H.A. had established a policy that housing mortgaged under the F.H.A. program must be residential housing exclusively and not housing for transients. In 1954 the Congress ratified that policy by amending the Veterans Emergency Housing Act of 1946 with a provision that codified the F.H.A. policy. The appellee had constructed an apartment building under the F.H.A. program that contained some rentals for transients. When Congress adopted the 1954 amendment, the appellee sought a declaratory judgment that the amendment was unconstitutional if it applied to his building. He contended that a retrospective reading of the amendment would violate his right to due process of law. The Court rejected his argument. The Court noted that the appellee was not penalized for anything done in the past. On the contrary, the Court found that the Act had only a prospective effect. Moreover, the Court stated that "[F]ederal regulation of future action based upon rights previously acquired by the person regulated is not prohibited by the Constitution. So long as the Constitution authorizes the subsequently enacted legislation, the fact that its provisions limit or interfere wth previously acquired rights does not condemn it."[18]

Several reasons help explain the Court's willingness to sustain curative or remedial legislation. First, curative statutes often are the result of previous court decisions which overrule certain administrative conduct.[19] In these situations the legislature is only following a judicial suggestion on how to eliminate a defect in the existing statutory scheme and the curative legislation is simply correcting the statutory flaw. Second, the courts recognize a "strong public interest in the smooth functioning of the government."[20] Remedial statutes remove unintended flaws in existing legislation and help give full effect to the legislative intent behind the initial legislation.

The reasons for upholding curative legislation help explain the almost uniform rejection of the arguments against the constitutionality of the "Portal-to-Portal Pay Act of 1947." In *Anderson v. Mt. Clemens Pottery Co.*[21] the Supreme Court gave an unexpected interpretation to the Fair Labor Standards Act. The Supreme Court interpretation exposed coal mine operators to a potential liability of over five billion dollars in claims to their employees. To remove this liability the Congress passed the Portal-to-Portal Act which eliminated both the right to sue for the overtime pay claim at issue in *Anderson* and the jurisdiction of the courts to hear such claims. This retroactive measure not only cured a defect in the existing legislation that arose because of the Court's interpretation of that legislation but it also gave full effect to the original congressional intent behind the Fair Labor Standards Act.[22] The courts who heard the arguments against the constitutionality of the Portal-to-Portal Act rejected those arguments because they realized that "the authority of the legislative body to validate voluntary transactions which at the time they were entered in-

---

16. Slawson, Constitutional and Legislative Considerations in Retroactive Lawmaking, 48 Calif.L.Rev. 216, 238–39 (1960).

17. 358 U.S. 84 (1958).

18. Id. at 91, quoting from Fleming v. Rhodes, 331 U.S. 100, 107 (1947).

19. Hochman, supra note 2, at 704.

20. Id. at 705.

21. 328 U.S. 680 (1946). See also Jewell Ridge Corp. v. Local No. 6167, 325 U.S. 161 (1945); Tennessee Coal Co. v. Muscoda Local No. 123, 321 U.S. 590 (1944).

22. Greenblatt, Judicial Limitations on Retroactive Civil Legislation, 51 Nw.U.L.Rev. 540 556–57 (1956).

to were by statute invalid or illegal has been repeatedly upheld".[23]

Unlike retroactive emergency or curative legislation, the Supreme Court has not as consistently sustained retroactive taxing measures. Nevertheless, the cases involving retroactive revenue measures do reveal a reluctance to overrule the legislative judgment on retroactive taxation except in cases of gross unfairness to the taxpayer. In *Welch v. Henry* [24] the Court sustained a Wisconsin revenue measure adopted in 1935 that taxed corporate dividends received in 1933. The taxpayer contended that the retrospective nature of the tax violated his right to due process of law under the fourteenth amendment. To support his contention the taxpayer cited cases where the Court had declared unconstitutional retroactive estate and gift taxes. The Court rejected the taxpayer's due process argument. The Court distinguished those cases where it held unconstitutional retroactive gift and estate taxes. In the estate and gift tax area the Court reasoned that a taxpayer may not have made a gift or a bequest if he had known that the legislature would enact an oppressive transfer tax. The "voluntary act" of the taxpayer was based on certain expectations. On the other hand, the Court noted that it had repeatedly sustained retroactive property and income taxes because the taxpayer had not made an affirmative voluntary act in reliance on prior law.[25] He either had simply retained property or received income and, thus, had not based any voluntary act on justified expectations.

As the *Henry* case suggests, the Court traditionally has sustained retroactive income tax legislation. However, it has sometimes invalidated retroactive estate and gift taxes; if the Court is convinced that the taxpayer had reasonable notice that a certain type of property transfer would be taxed, the justices will uphold the measure despite its retroactive effect.[26] If, however, that reasonable notice is missing, the Court may declare the retroactive transfer tax unconstitutional as violative of the taxpayer's right to due process of law. Amendments to the provisions of the Internal Revenue Code relating to the taxation of income are normally to be anticipated by persons engaging in activities that might later be subject to a higher tax than existed at the time of the activity or transaction. Many amendments to the Internal Revenue Code will have a retroactive application of one year or less. The legislative process is such that changes in the Internal Revenue Code are often before the Congress or Congressional Committees for at least several months prior to their enactment. Therefore, it is quite difficult for a person whose federal income tax liability is retroactively increased to demonstrate that the retroactive application of the tax to him violates the due process clause. The taxpayer must demonstrate that it is fundamentally unfair to apply to him a totally new tax which he could not have anticipated at the time of the transaction of the taxed activity.[27]

The concepts of reasonable notice and reasonable expectations are important consider-

---

23. Seese v. Bethlehem Steel Co., 168 F.2d 58, 64 (4th Cir. 1948); see also, Thomas v. Carnegie-Illinois Steel Corp., 174 F.2d 711 (3d Cir. 1949); Battaglia v. General Motors Corp., 169 F.2d 254, 257 (2d Cir.), cert. denied 335 U.S. 887 (1948).

The Supreme Court never accepted a case where the constitutionality of the Act was challenged; all the cases deciding the constitutionality of the Act were decided either in the lower federal courts or in the state courts. See Greenblatt, Judicial Limitations on Retroactive Civil Legislation, 51 Nw.U.L.Rev. 540, 551–61 (1956); Rotunda, Congressional Power to Restrict the Jurisdiction of the Lower Federal Courts and the Problem of School Busing, 64 Georgetown L.J. 839, 853–59 (1976).

24. 305 U.S. 134 (1938).

25. Id. at 147–48. See also United States v. Darusmont, 449 U.S. 292 (1981) (per curiam) (upholding retroactive application of the 1976 amendments of the Internal Revenue Code minimum tax provisions as not violative of due process). "The Court consistently has held that the application of an income tax statute to the entire calendar year in which enactment took place does not per se violate the due process clause. . . . " Id. at 297.

26. Hochman, supra note 2, at 707–11.

27. See United States v. Darusmont, 449 U.S. 292 (1981) (per curiam) (change in the "minimum tax" provisions pertaining to the sale of property could be ret-

ations for the Court when it considers the constitutional validity of general retroactive legislation. When the Court confronts general retroactive legislation, it will make a threshold determination on whether the statute affects a "remedy" or a "right." [28] If the measure affects a remedy, the Court reasons that no one reasonably can expect a remedy to remain immune from legislative controls, and, consequently, it will sustain the retroactive legislation. The Court's decision in *Chase Securities Corp. v. Donaldson* [29] reflects this reasoning. The plaintiff brought an action against the defendant based on an alleged violation of the Minnesota Blue Sky Law. The defendant pleaded the bar of the statute of limitations and on an appeal to the Minnesota Supreme Court he prevailed on that issue. During the process of retrial and appeal, however, the Minnesota legislature removed the statute of limitations for certain classes of blue sky cases. This case fitted that category of cases and the plaintiff reasserted his blue sky cause of action. The defendant contended that the amending legislation violated his right to due process of law. On appeal to the Supreme Court the defendant presented his fourteenth amendment contention. The Court rejected the argument because it reasoned that a statute of limitations does not extinguish a right but only barred the remedy.[30] The plaintiff always had the right to seek recovery from the defendant and the legislation only removed a bar to the remedy. The statute of limitations was a legislative creation and the legislature could remove the statute to allow plaintiffs to pursue their remedy.

The distinction between a right and a remedy, at times, can become hazy. The Court may base the distinction on some type of ex-

pectational interest. In cases involving the alteration of statute of limitations the Court reasons that any reliance on a belief that the legislature will not alter a legislatively created procedural bar to a remedy is unreasonable and cannot rise to the status of a property right. Therefore, the Court will sustain legislation that modifies procedural rules because the expectational interest involved is minimal. The Court demonstrates great deference to the legislative judgment on procedural rules with retrospective effects.[31]

Some retrospective general legislation will directly affect property rights. In these cases the Court may demonstrate some reluctance to defer to the legislative judgment. In *Railroad Retirement Board v. Alton Railroad Co.* [32] Congress had adopted a law that required the railroads to establish a pension fund. The fund, however, would cover not only all currently employed workers but also those who had worked for the railroad within the year before Congress adopted the legislation. The Court (5–4) voided this legislation because of its retrospective impact. The Court stated that the measure violated the due process clause of the fifth amendment because it "is not only retroactive in that it resurrects for new burdens transactions long since past and closed; but as to some of the railroad companies it constitutes a naked appropriation of private property upon the basis of transactions with which the owners of property were never connected." [33] The Court apparently found that the railroad operators' interests in receiving the benefits of completed labor had risen to a property right protected by the fifth amendment. It must be remembered that this decision was rendered in 1935, by justices dedicated to the use of substantive

roactively applied to the transaction made within the year prior to this amendment to the Internal Revenue Code).

28. See, e.g. Campbell v. Holt, 115 U.S. 620 (1885).

29. 325 U.S. 304 (1945).

30. Id. at 314.

31. See generally, Gange Lumber Co. v. Rowley, 326 U.S. 295 (1945); Carpenter v. Wabash Ry. Co., 309

U.S. 23 (1940); Funkhouser v. Preston Co., 290 U.S. 163 (1933).

32. 295 U.S. 330 (1935) (Roberts, J., for the Court). Hughes, C.J., joined by Brandeis, Stone, and Cardozo, JJ., dissented. 295 U.S. at 374–92.

33. Id. at 350.

due process and the constitutional protection of economic interests.

Although the Court has never overruled *Alton*, the decision in *Usery v. Turner Elkhorn Mining Co.*[34] severely narrowed its precedential importance. Congress had enacted legislation that provided benefits to mine workers who had contracted "black lung" disease. Congress placed some of the financial responsibility for the legislation on the coal mine operators. The operators broadly attacked the constitutionality of the measure.[35] In particular, the operators contended that the law violated their right to due process of law because it required them to pay benefits to miners who had left mine employment before the effective date of the act. The operators argued that the Act charged them with a liability that was completely unexpected. The Court acknowledged that the operators may have been unaware of the danger of the disease. Moreover, the operators may have relied on the current state of the law that had failed to impose any liability on them. Therefore, the Court would not justify the legislation on any theory of deterrence or blameworthiness. Nevertheless, the Court believed the Act met the dictates of due process. Justice Marshall, writing for the Court, first noted that retroactive legislation is not unconstitutional simply "because it upsets otherwise settled expectations."[36] He believed that this measure was justified as a rational method to spread the costs of the mine workers' disabilities to those who have benefitted from their labor. Justice Marshall was unwilling to weigh competing interests to assess the constitutionality of the legislation. He deferred to the legislative judgment and refused "to assess the wisdom of Congress' chosen scheme."[37] The Court was satisfied "that the Act approaches the problem of cost-spreading rationally."[38]

The *Turner Elkhorn Mining* opinion suggests that the legislature generally may overcome the traditional bias against retrospective statutes as long as it rationally relates the legislation to a legitimate governmental purpose. If the legislation does have a rational relationship to a proper governmental end, the Court will uphold the retroactive law even though it may impair recognizable property rights. In one area of federal legislation, however—when Congress passes retroactive legislation that will alter the government's obligation in a contract—the Court may find this analysis inappropriate.

The Court has used a higher level of review to legislation that modifies the government's own contractual obligations than it does to federal legislation that alters or regulates private contracts. When the Court reviews legislation that modifies the government's obligation of contract, it will require more than a rational relationship between the modifying statutes and a governmental purpose before it will sustain the measure. In *Lynch v. United States*[39] the plaintiffs were beneficiaries of government insurance issued under the War Risk Insurance Act. The plaintiffs sought to recover amounts allegedly due under the insurance contract but the government resisted because Congress had repealed the law creating the insurance. The plaintiffs contended that the repealing measure violated their right to due process. The Supreme Court agreed. The Court stated that rights against the United States arising out of a valid contract receive protection from the fifth amendment. Therefore, Congress cannot annul these rights unless the action taken to void these rights "falls with the federal police power of some other paramount power."[40] When Congress attempts to alter its own obligation of contract, the Court will give force to its traditional bias

34. 428 U.S. 1 (1976).

35. The operators argued that the Act's definitions, presumptions, and limitations on rebuttable evidence as well as its retrospective effect were unconstitutional. 428 U.S. at 12.

36. Id. at 16.

37. Id. at 18–19.

38. Id. at 19.

39. 292 U.S. 571 (1934).

40. Id. at 579.

against retroactive legislation, and rely on the due process clause of the fifth amendment to test the constitutionality of the impairing legislation.

Much of the literature on retroactive legislation repeats the general proposition that the courts have a bias against such legislation.[41] If, however, the constitutionality of emergency or curative retroactive statutes is challenged, the Supreme Court usually will sustain such legislation because of the overriding public interest that prompted the enactment of the emergency or remedial measure. Moreover, the Court will uphold a retroactive revenue measure either if it is a tax on income or if it is a transfer tax and the taxpayer reasonably could expect that the legislature would retrospectively tax such a transfer of property. Finally, the Court will sustain retroactive general legislation if the law is rationally related to a governmental purpose or if the retrospective law affects a remedy and not a right. On the other hand, the Court will closely review any federal legislation that impairs the government's own obligation of contract. In this area of judicial review the Court still entertains a strong bias against retrospective legislation.

2. The Ex Post Facto Clauses

The Constitution contains two *ex post facto* clauses: one that applies to the states [1] and one that applies to the federal government.[2] The clauses prohibit Congress and state legislatures from enacting laws that have a retrospective effect.[3] In short, an *ex post facto* law is a measure that has an impact on past transactions.[4] Early in its history the Supreme Court determined that the

ex post facto clauses only prohibited the states and the federal government from passing criminal or penal measures that had a retroactive effect.[5]

The typical retrospective law that will violate either *ex post facto* clause is a statute that imposes a criminal penalty for past conduct that was lawful when performed. Moreover, a law that imposes a harsh penalty or a potentially harsher penalty for unlawful conduct than existed before the passage of the law will also violate the *ex post facto* prohibition.[6] Even a statute altering penal provisions "accorded by the grace of the legislature" violates the *ex post facto* clause if the statute is both retrospective and harsher than the law in effect at the time of the offense. For example, in *Weaver v. Graham*,[7] the Supreme Court held that a Florida law which retrospectively reduced the good time credits available to a prisoner violated the *ex post facto* clause. A mere change in the type of penalty, however, will not violate the provisions. If, for example, a state properly had imposed the death penalty on an individual, altering the form of capital punishment from death by hanging to death by electrocution would not violate the constitutional prohibition on *ex post facto* laws.[8] Moreover, the *ex post facto* clauses do not prevent the state legislatures or Congress from reducing either the harshness of a penalty or the scope of an existing penal statute.[9] Finally, a legislature can impose a penalty on a person for continuing once lawful conduct that the legislature has subsequently declared illegal.[10]

An issue that often arises when a law is challenged under an *ex post facto* clause is whether the legislature has actually imposed

---

41. See, e.g., Seeman, The Retroactive Effect of Repeal Legislation, 27 Ky.L.J. 75 (1938); Smead, The Rule Against Retroactive Legislation: A Basic Principle of Jurisprudence, 20 Minn.L.Rev. 775 (1936).

1. U.S. Const. art. I, § 10, cl. 1: "No state shall . . . pass any . . . ex post facto law."

2. U.S. Const. art. I, § 9, cl. 3: "No . . . ex post facto law shall be passed."

3. See, Ex parte Garland, 71 U.S. (4 Wall.) 333, 377 (1867).

4. Id.

5. Calder v. Bull, 3 U.S. (3 Dall.) 386, 390, 397 (1798).

6. Lindsey v. Washington, 301 U.S. 397 (1937).

7. 450 U.S. 24 (1981).

8. Malloy v. South Carolina, 237 U.S. 180 (1915).

9. Rooney v. North Dakota, 196 U.S. 319, 325 (1905).

10. Samuels v. McCurdy, 267 U.S. 188 (1925).

a penalty for past conduct.[11] The Supreme Court labeled as punitive a post-Civil War law that required attorneys to take an oath before they could practice law in federal court.[12] The attorneys had to swear that they had not participated in the rebellion against the Union. The law was punitive because the taking of the oath had no relationship to the professional duties of attorneys.[13] Hence, the Court found the law was penal in nature and applied to past conduct. The Court held that the law violated the *ex post facto* clause and was unconstitutional.[14]

On the other hand, laws that require deportation for past conduct [15] or statutes that deny future privileges to convicted offenders because of their previous criminal activities do not impose penalties for past conduct.[16] Such measures do not violate the *ex post facto* prohibitions. Finally, laws that alter rules of criminal procedure but do not affect the substantive rights of the defendant are not violative of the *ex post facto* clause even though the legislature makes the change during the process of the trial.[17] Laws, for example, that change the number of appellate judges [18] or enlarge the potential class of competent witnesses do not affect substantive rights and are constitutional.[19] Such laws do not impose an increased penalty for past conduct.[20]

The Court has recently held that a law which changed the procedures for imposition of the death penalty could be applied to a person whose crime predated the change. In *Dobbert v. Florida* [21] the defendant had been sentenced to death for murder in Florida. When the defendant committed the murder, Florida had a statute imposing the death sentence for that crime. However the state supreme court struck down the procedures for imposition of the sentence in accordance with decisions of the Supreme Court of the United States. Thereafter the state legislature passed a new statute for imposition of the penalty which met current constitutional standards. The defendant was sentenced under this statute and the Supreme Court of the United States upheld this sentence. The majority opinion reasoned that this new statute was only a change in procedure because the old statute had declared that murder was a capital offense, thus giving the defendant fair notice. Since the new statute made imposition of the penalty more difficult, the majority saw it as "ameliorative." While the *Dobbert* majority thus made the decision fit within established doctrine, it deems difficult to dispute the dissent's argument that there was no valid means of imposing the death sentence in Florida when the defendant committed the crime.[22] The majority dismissed this argument summarily, but the point seems well taken because the ability to revise an invalid punishment and apply it to persons whose identities or characteristics are already fixed and knowable by the law makers can be readily abused. The basic principle of the clauses would seem to deny a legislative power to design sentences for application to such persons. But this position was only recognized by the dissenters.

3. Bills of Attainder

Traditionally, bills of attainder were legislative acts that imposed the death penalty without the usual judicial proceedings on

---

11. See Flemming v. Nestor, 363 U.S. 603, 614–17 (1960) (deported alien's loss of Social Security benefits nonpunitive and valid).

12. Ex parte Garland, 71 U.S. (4 Wall.) 333 (1867).

13. See Cummings v. Missouri, 71 U.S. (4 Wall.) 277, 316 (1867) (companion case to Ex parte Garland).

14. Ex parte Garland, 71 U.S. (4 Wall.) 333, 381 (1867).

15. Marcello v. Bonds, 349 U.S. 302 (1955).

16. See Hawker v. New York, 170 U.S. 189, 190 (1898).

17. See Duncan v. Missouri, 152 U.S. 377 (1894).

18. Id. at 382.

19. Hopt v. Utah, 110 U.S. 574, 589 (1884).

20. Note, however, that the Congress or state legislatures cannot evade the proscription of the *ex post facto* clauses by fashioning a civil statute out of what is basically a criminal measure. See, Burgess v. Salmon, 97 U.S. 381 (1878).

21. Dobbert v. Florida, 432 U.S. 282 (1977).

22. 432 U.S. at 303, 307 (Stevens, J., dissenting, joined by Brennan and Marshall, JJ.).

persons allegedly guilty of serious crimes.[1] If the legislature imposed a lesser punishment than the death penalty, the measure was a bill of pains and penalties.[2] The Constitution contains two bills of attainder clauses, one that applies to the states[3] and one that applies to the federal government.[4] The Court has held that the provisions prohibit both bills of attainder and bills of pains and penalties.[5]

The bill of attainder provisions prohibit the state or federal legislatures from assuming judicial functions and conducting trials.[6] Consequently, the clauses proscribe any legislative act "no matter what [its] form, that apply[s] either to named individuals or to easily ascertainable members of a group in such a way as to inflict punishment on them without a judicial trial."[7] The Supreme Court has used the prohibition against bills of attainder to void a congressional measure that prevented the payment of salaries to three named federal employees because the House of Representatives believed the three were subversives.[8] Similarly, the Court invalidated a law that declared unlawful the employment of a member of the Communist Party in a labor union.[9] The Court reasoned that the law impermissibly designated a class of persons: members of the Communist Party. The Court, however, refused to declare unconstitutional a municipal ordinance that required municipal employees to take an oath that they were never members of the Communist Party or any similar organization that advocated the violent overthrow of the government.[10] The Court believed that the ordinance only established eligibility standards for employment.[11] Additionally, the Court sustained a state law that prevented convicted felons from holding a position with longshoremen unions.[12] The Court observed that the prohibition was based on a judicial determination of culpability. The law did not create any further implications of the convicted felon's guilt. Therefore, the state legislature had imposed a penalty on an ascertainable class only after a court had established guilt. Hence, the law did not violate the prohibitions against bills of attainder.

The Supreme Court sustained the Presidential Recordings and Materials Preservation Act,[13] which had been challenged by former President Nixon on the ground that it constituted a bill of attainder because it provided for governmental custody of only his presidential papers. In *Nixon v. Administrator of General Services*,[14] the Court ruled that the statute was not a bill of attainder within the historical meaning of that term because the law did not inflict punishment and was nonpunitive. The Act merely set the policy that historical materials should be preserved. Furthermore, the Act did not become a bill of attainder merely because it applied only to President Nixon, who was named in the Act. The Court held that the appellant constituted a legitimate class of one because the papers of all other past Presidents were already safely housed in libraries. The bill of attainder clause was not intended to be a variant of the equal protection clause; Congress constitutionally can

1. See generally, J. Story, Commentaries on the Constitution of the United States, § 1338 (1833); Note, The Bounds of Legislative Specification: A Suggested Approach to the Bill of Attainder Clause, 72 Yale L.J. 330 (1962).

2. J. Story, supra note 1.

3. U.S. Const. art. I, § 10, cl. 1: "No State shall . . . pass any Bill of Attainder."

4. U.S. Const. art. I, § 9, cl. 3: "No Bill of Attainder . . . shall be passed."

5. Cummings v. Missouri, 71 U.S. (4 Wall.) 277, 323 (1867).

6. Since the primary cases involve the freedoms of speech and association, these cases are dealt with in Chapter 18, Freedom of Speech, Section XII on Loyalty and Security requirements.

7. United States v. Lovett, 328 U.S. 303, 315 (1946).

8. Id.

9. United States v. Brown, 381 U.S. 437 (1965).

10. Garner v. Board of Public Works of Los Angeles, 341 U.S. 716 (1951).

11. Id. at 722–23.

12. De Veau v. Braisted, 363 U.S. 144 (1960).

13. 44 U.S.C.A. § 2107.

14. 433 U.S. 425 (1977).

legislate to burden some classes of individuals.

VII. THE TAKING OF PROPERTY INTERESTS: EMINENT DOMAIN

A. Introduction

One of the powers of sovereign governments is the ability upon payment of adequate compensation, to take privately owned property.[1] This ability is called the power of eminent domain. Both the federal government and the individual state governments possess the power of eminent domain. Scholars and judges generally classify eminent domain as an incidental power and a means of fulfilling other governmental responsibilities. The term "police power" is often used to define the panoply of governmental power. Throughout the rest of this text and in terms of the general principles of constitutional law, the term "police power" is used to designate the inherent power of government to take acts to promote the public health, safety, welfare or morals.[2] But in the area of eminent domain cases and analysis, "police power" is used more narrowly to designate only the power of government to regulate the use of land and property without the payment of compensation. Authorities in the law of eminent domain view that power as distinct from such powers as the general police power and the power to tax.[3]

This section will trace the historical development of the constitutional law of eminent domain. It will also describe the case law currently governing the scope of the power of the state and federal governments to affect property interests without incurring any liability to compensate property owners. No single formula exists, however, to explain what one leading commentator has called the "crazy-quilt pattern of Supreme Court doctrine"[4] governing the use of eminent domain. This section, therefore, will discuss the broad issues that arise in the context of suits involving governmental acts affecting the use and possession of private property.

In analyzing the constitutional issues concerning the law of eminent domain, it is important to grasp the theoretical and historical underpinnings of the power. The next section, therefore, examines the nature of the power of eminent domain and the historical basis for the power and its limitations. That section also examines the sources of the power of eminent domain in the state and federal systems. Following that, we will discuss what scholars describe as the "taking" issue and the tests used by courts to determine whether a private property owner must be compensated for governmental interferences with his property interests. The following section examines the "public use" limitation upon the exercise of eminent domain. We will conclude with brief notes on: (1) the rules used to determine what compensation is owing to a land owner whose property is "taken" by the exercise of eminent domain; and (2) the types of interests that can be appropriated by the government through the exercise of its eminent domain power.

B. Limitations on the Exercise of Eminent Domain

The term "eminent domain" is said to have originated with Grotius, the seven-

---

1. J. Thayer, 1 Cases on Constitutional Law 952–53 (1895).

2. Thus it is the "police power" which allows government to restrict individual freedom unless specifically forbidden by the Constitution. See E. Corwin, Liberty Against Government at 88, 173 (1948). It is an inherent power which the state governments possess but the federal government has such a power only in relation to federal property, such as the District of Columbia. As to the rest of the country, the federal government is one of enumerated powers with no express

"police power". See Chapter 3, National Powers. This power was also early conceived to be the basis for allowing state regulation of Commerce. See, F. Frankfurter, The Commerce Clause Under Marshall, Taney and Waite at 27 (1937).

3. P. Nichols, The Power of Eminent Domain §§ 9–16 (1909).

4. Dunham, Griggs v. Allegheny County in Perspective: Thirty Years of Supreme Court Expropriation Law, 1962 Sup.Ct.Rev. 63, 63.

teenth century legal scholar.[1] Grotius believed that the state possessed the power to take or destroy property for the benefit of the social unit,[2] but he believed that when the state so acted, it was obligated to compensate the injured property owner for his losses.[3] Blackstone, too, believed that society had no general power to take the private property of landowners, except on the payment of a reasonable price.[4] The just compensation clause of the fifth amendment to the Constitution was built upon this concept of a moral obligation to pay for governmental interference with private property.

The natural law philosophy that so greatly affected the development of American political and legal thought [5] also had an impact on the law of eminent domain. Early state court cases held that limitations on eminent domain existed independently of written constitutions.[6] The eminent domain clause of the fifth amendment, therefore, was not seen as creating a new legal restriction on the exercise of the power but rather as recognizing the existence of a principle of natural justice.[7] In the first half of the nineteenth century state courts applied this theory of natural law to protect private property interests from state appropriations.[8]

No provision for the power of eminent domain appears in the federal constitution.[9]

The Supreme Court, however, has said that the power of eminent domain is an incident of federal sovereignty [10] and an "offspring of political necessity." [11] The Court has also noted that the fifth amendment's limitation on taking private property is a tacit recognition that the power to take private property exists.[12]

Because the federal government is a government of enumerated powers, it must be determined, when examining a specific federal use of the eminent domain power, whether the federal government possesses the constitutional power to take property for the proposed use. As the power of eminent domain is an incidental power, it may be employed only when it is necessary and proper to the effectuation of one of the federal government's enumerated powers.[13] In general terms, therefore, the power of eminent domain may only be exercised by the federal government as a means of exercising one of its implied or enumerated powers.[14] Even if the exercise of eminent domain relates to an enumerated power, the fifth amendment also requires that private property be taken by the federal government only for a public use.[15]

The individual state governments, as political sovereigns, also possess the power of eminent domain. State constitutions now almost universally require that landowners be

---

1. See, J. Thayer, 1 Cases on Constitutional Law 945 (1895).

2. See Grotius, De Jure Belli et Pacis lib. III. C. 20 VII 1 (1625), cited in J. Thayer, 1 Cases on Constitutional Law (1895).

3. E. Freund, The Police Power 540 (1904).

4. Blackstone, 1 Blackstone's Commentaries 139 (Chitty Ed. 1829), cited in E. Freund, The Police Power 540 (1904).

5. See E. Corwin, Liberty Against Government (1948).

6. See Stoebuck, A General Theory of Eminent Domain, 47 Wash.L.Rev. 553, 555 (1972).

7. See Grant, The "Higher Law" Background of the Law of Eminent Domain, 6 Wisc.L.Rev. 67 (1931).

8. See, e.g. Gardner v. Village of Newburgh, 2 Johns. Ch. 162 (N.Y.1816).

9. Comment, State and Federal Power of Eminent Domain, 4 Geo.Wash.L.Rev. 130, 131 (1935).

10. United States v. Gettysburg Electric Ry. Co., 160 U.S. 668, 681 (1896).

11. Bauman v. Ross, 167 U.S. 548, 574 (1897).

12. United States v. Carmack, 329 U.S. 230, 241 (1946).

13. P. Nichols, The Power of Eminent Domain 23 (1909); see Comment, The Public Use Limitation on Eminent Domain: An Advance Requiem, 58 Yale L.J. 599, 609–10 (1949).

14. Note, however, that the federal government possesses the full range of legislative powers over the District of Columbia, not merely those powers that the Constitution expressly confers. Shoemaker v. United States, 147 U.S. 282, 298–300 (1893). See also the discussion of Berman v. Parker, 348 U.S. 26 (1954) in section D below.

15. The public use limitation is examined in a later sub-section, See Section III, D of this Chapter.

compensated when their property is taken by the state for a public use.[16] Only two of the original state constitutions adopted between 1776 and 1780, however, required that compensation be paid by the state when private property was taken for a public use.[17] Nevertheless, state courts applied doctrines of natural justice to require that such takings be made only for public uses [18] and only upon the payment of just compensation.[19]

Unlike the federal government, the state governments are not, for purposes of the federal Constitution, creatures of limited or enumerated powers. When examining a state exercise of eminent domain, therefore, it is not necessary to determine whether the exercise of the power is necessary and incidental to the exercise of an express power. This exercise of the power will be valid so long as it does not violate any provision of the Constitution or its amendments.

The Supreme Court, prior to the Civil War, held that the fifth amendment as part of the Bill of Rights did not apply to limit state interferences with private property.[20] In 1868 the fourteenth amendment was made part of the federal Constitution; its due process clause specifically protects property rights.[21] The fourteenth amendment, however, does not expressly require either that state "takings" of private property be for a public use or that the property owner receive just compensation for the loss. In *Davidson v. New Orleans* [22] the Supreme Court stated that "it is not possible to hold that a party has, without due process of law, been deprived of his

property, when, . . . he has, by the laws of the State, a fair trial in a court of justice, according to the modes of proceeding applicable to such a case." [23] The Court in *Davidson* also noted that the just compensation clause of the fifth amendment was omitted from the fourteenth amendment.[24] At this early stage, therefore, it appears as though the justices contemplated the due process clause as merely requiring that the state act with procedural fairness, with no requirement that state takings of private property be for a public use and only on payment of just compensation.

If indeed this was the Court's early view, it was short-lived. In two 1896 cases,[25] the Supreme Court held that the due process clause did require that land taken by the state be used for a public purpose. Finally, in 1897, in *Chicago, Burlington & Quincy R. R. Co. v. City of Chicago*,[26] the Court, in an opinion by the elder Justice Harlan, held that following prescribed procedure did not mean that requirements of due process were met, for the clause regulated the "substance" as well as the form of such a taking.[27] The Court held that due process required both that the property be taken for a public use and that the owner of the property be compensated by the state for his loss.

Although some cases and commentators have viewed these Supreme Court decisions as incorporating the compensation clause into the fourteenth amendment, this view does not appear strictly correct. Rather the Court appears to have found independent

---

16. Provisions limiting the exercise of the power of eminent domain appear in some form in every state constitution except that of North Carolina. The New Hampshire constitution states no requirement that the state provide compensation when it engages in a taking. P. Nichols, The Law of Eminent Domain (Rev. 3d ed. J. Schmar, ed.) (1976) § 1.3 at 79.

17. Grant, The "Higher Law" Background of the Law of Eminent Domain, 6 Wisc.L.Rev. 67, 69–70 (1931).

18. Lenhoff, Development of the Concept of Eminent Domain, 42 Colum.L.Rev. 596, 596–601 (1942).

19. Id.

20. See Barron v. Baltimore, 32 U.S. (7 Pet.) 243, 250–51 (1833); West River Bridge Co. v. Dix, 47 U.S. (6 How.) 507, 532 (1848).

21. "(N)or shall any State deprive any person of life, liberty, or property without due process of law; . . .." U.S. Const. Amend. XIV, § 1.

22. 96 U.S. 97 (1877).

23. Id. at 105.

24. Id.

25. Fallbrook Irrigation District v. Bradley, 164 U.S. 112 (1896); Missouri Pac. Ry. Co. v. Nebraska, 164 U.S. 403 (1896).

26. 166 U.S. 226 (1897).

27. Id. at 234–35.

public use and just compensation requirements inherent in the definition of due process. That the Court would find these limitations to exist in the concept of due process is easily understood when viewed in the light of the substantive due process doctrine prevalent at this time.[28] Today, the Supreme Court itself cites the *Chicago, Burlington & Quincy R. R. Co. v. City of Chicago* decision as incorporating the compensation clause into the fourteenth amendment.[29]

C. The "Taking" Issue

1. Introduction

The fifth amendment provides that private property may not be "taken" by the federal government without just compensation. The central issue in many eminent domain cases is whether the governmental interference amounts to a "taking". Although the concept of a taking may originally have contemplated only physical appropriation,[1] it is plain today that non-acquisitive governmental action may amount to a taking in a constitutional sense.[2] A "taking", therefore, may be found when governmental activity results in significant physical damage to property that impairs its use.[3] Although the state possesses the power to regulate property without payment of compensation, if the regulation goes too far, a taking may also be found.

It should be easy to see why so much confusion surrounds the case law relating to the doctrine of eminent domain. A "taking" may result from non-acquisitive regulation, or a regulation may be held not to constitute a compensable taking because there was no actual appropriation. Damage to property caused as an incidental result of government activity may be a "taking." Or such damage might be held to be non-compensable even though the private property is totally destroyed. To a great extent, therefore, no general rule exists to describe what constitutes a compensable taking. Eminent domain cases tend to be decided on an ad hoc basis and are often decided a certain way because of the balance of equities involved. Yet the following cases illustrate factors found significant by courts in determining whether compensation is due the affected landowner.

The seminal, though conflicting, views of the elder Justice Harlan and Justice Holmes, constitute the essence of Supreme Court theory on the exercise of eminent domain. Justice Harlan viewed literally the "taking" requirement and believed compensation was not due unless the state appropriated private property for its own use. Justice Holmes believed in requiring the government to compensate those on whose use of property the government imposed significant restriction.

In Harlan's view, taking differed qualitatively from regulation and, therefore, mere use regulation never necessitated compensation by the state. In 1887, in *Mugler v. Kansas*,[4] the Supreme Court followed Harlan's view in determining that a state statute prohibiting the manufacture of liquor did not amount to a taking of the property of a beer manufacturer. In 1880 the

---

28. See E. Freund, The Police Power 541 (1904); See also Chapter 13, Substantive Process, Section V, A Note on the Meaning of Liberty. Gordon v. City of Warren, 579 F.2d 386, 390 n. 2 (6th Cir. 1978) (Lively, J., citing an earlier edition of this work).

29. Webb's Fabulous Pharmacies, Inc. v. Beckwith, 449 U.S. 155, 159 (1980) citing Chicago, Burlington & Quincy R. R. Co. v. City of Chicago, 166 U.S. 226 (1897). In *Webb's Fabulous Pharmacies*, the Supreme Court held that a Florida county's taking of the interest earned on an interpleader fund while such fund was temporarily held by the county court, in addition to a fee for the county's services for holding such fund, constituted a taking violative of the fifth and fourteenth amendments.

1. F. Bosselman, D. Callies, J. Banta, The Taking Issue 51 (1973).

2. See e.g. Pennsylvania Coal Co. v. Mahon, 260 U.S. 393 (1922); United States v. Causby, 328 U.S. 256 (1946), both discussed later in this section. Lenoir v. Porters Creek Watershed District, 586 F.2d 1081, 1093 (6th Cir. 1978) (Engle, J., quoting an earlier edition of this work).

3. Pumpelly v. Green Bay Co., 80 U.S. (13 Wall.) 166, 179–80 (1871).

4. 123 U.S. 623 (1887).

Kansas constitution was amended to prohibit the manufacture or sale of intoxicating liquors in Kansas for all but certain limited purposes. To give effect to the amendment, the Kansas legislature, in 1881, passed a statute banning the manufacture of intoxicating liquor. Mugler, who had been engaged in the manufacture of beer in Kansas for several years prior to 1880, continued in this practice after the passage of this prohibitory legislation without the required permit. The opinion of the Court, written by Harlan, observed that, if the statute was enforced against Mugler, the value of the machinery and buildings constituting his brewery would be greatly depreciated.[5] But the opinion also found that the State possessed the power to regulate the sale of alcohol under its power to protect the health, morals and safety of its people.[6] Moreover, the Court held that the prohibitory legislation did not impair any constitutional liberty or property of alcohol manufacturers.[7] The Court, therefore, rejected Mugler's argument that the regulation was a taking of property without just compensation and that the regulation deprived him of property without due process of law. Justice Harlan stated that the regulation of the sale of alcohol in no sense involved the exercise of eminent domain.

> [A] prohibition simply upon the use of property for purposes that are declared, by valid legislation, to be injurious to the health, morals, or safety of the community, cannot in any sense, be deemed a taking or an appropriation of property for the public benefit.[8]

The Court held, therefore, that the prohibitory regulation did not constitute a taking because no property had actually physically been appropriated by the state. Although *Mugler* has never been overruled by the Supreme Court, and is, in fact, still precedent, the Court has judiciously ignored the broad language of *Mugler* in cases where non-acquisitive governmental action has been found to be a taking.

The leading exponent of a broader test of a compensable taking was Justice Holmes. Holmes, seeking a test of fairness, found the appropriation test applied by Harlan in *Mugler* inadequate.[9] Unlike Justice Harlan, Holmes viewed the distinction between taking and regulation as one of degree. In the view of Justice Holmes, if regulation reached a certain extreme, it became a "taking", though no property was actually taken in a literal sense.

In *Pennsylvania Coal v. Mahon Co.,*[10] a state statute prohibited the mining of coal in such a way as to cause the subsidence of certain types of improved property. The issue before the Court was whether, through the exercise of its police power, the state could destroy the coal company's mining rights without compensation. The Supreme Court, per Justice Holmes, held that the rights of the coal company could not, consistent with due process, be so limited without payment of compensation. Although the opinion noted that values incident to property could be reduced by non-compensable use regulation, he stated that, "when [regulation] reaches a certain magnitude, in most if not in all cases, there must be an exercise of eminent domain and compensation to sustain the act."[11] Under this view, the police power and eminent domain exist in a continuum. Once regulation went so far, there was a "taking" and compensation had to be made to the injured land owner. Here the Court found the extent of the regulation so great as to constitute a taking. "To make it commercially impracticable to mine certain coal has nearly the same effect for constitutional purposes as appropriating or destroying it."[12]

---

5. Id. at 656–57.

6. Id. at 661–62.

7. Id. at 668–69.

8. Id. at 668–69.

9. Sax, Takings and the Police Power, 74 Yale L.J. 36, 41 (1964).

10. 260 U.S. 393 (1922).

11. Id. at 413.

12. Id. at 414.

Rather than develop a single framework to define a taking, the Supreme Court, much to the consternation of commentators, has retained to some extent both the theories of Holmes and Harlan.[13] In its decisions on property use regulations and the extent of permissible government impairment of the value of private property interests the Court has issued rulings which follow no clear theoretical guidelines. The Supreme Court's decisions in "taking" issues may properly be viewed as a "crazy quilt pattern" of rulings.[14]

2. Property Use Regulations

In *Euclid v. Ambler Realty Co.*,[15] the Supreme Court dealt for the first time with the constitutionality of a comprehensive land use regulatory ordinance. In 1927 the Village Council of Euclid adopted a comprehensive zoning ordinance. The statute restricted the location of trades, industries, apartment houses, two-family houses, single-family houses and other land uses. The plan also regulated aspects of property use such as the size of lots and the size and heights of buildings.

The zoning ordinance was attacked on the ground that it deprived the property owner of liberty and property without due process of law, and that the use classifications deprived him of equal protection of law. The issue, as framed by the Court, was whether the owner was unconstitutionally deprived of property "by attempted regulations under the guise of the police power, which are unreasonable and confiscatory?"[16] The Court premised its holding by stating that, if valid, the ordinance, like all similar regulatory laws, would have to find its justification in the police power.[17] The Court concluded that the statute was a valid police power regulation because there was a sufficient public interest in the segregation of incompatible land uses to justify the diminution of property values. The Court since *Euclid* has deferred to the zoning power against due process and equal protection challenges[18] with a few exceptions in the early cases.

In two cases, considered shortly after *Euclid*, the Supreme Court held land use regulation invalid as a violation of the due process clause of the fourteenth amendment. In *Washington ex rel. Seattle Title & Trust Co. v. Roberge*,[19] the Court struck down an ordinance that allowed for the issuance of use variances upon the two-thirds consent of surrounding landowners. The Court found the variance provision to be a due process violation because the surrounding landowners would be free to withhold consent for arbitrary and capricious reasons.[20] However, there is no due process violation when exemptions from zoning requirements are granted only by a general referendum.[21]

In *Nectow v. City of Cambridge*,[22] the Supreme Court faced squarely the issue of the authority of local governments to regulate land use without payment of compensation. The Court found some outer limit to the power and struck down a Cambridge zoning ordinance on the ground that it deprived the plaintiff landowner of property without due process of law. The Court held that a zoning restriction "cannot be imposed if it does not bear a substantial relation to the public

---

13. See Sax, Takings and the Police Power, 74 Yale L.J. 36, 37 (1964).

14. Dunham, Griggs v. Allegheny County in Perspective: Thirty Years of Supreme Court Expropriation Law, 1962 Sup.Ct.Rev. 63, 63.

15. 272 U.S. 365 (1926).

16. Id. at 386.

17. Id. at 387.

18. The Court will allow the city to zone an area for "traditional" families, Village of Belle Terre v. Boraas, 416 U.S. 1 (1974). Zoning must not intrude upon the functioning of traditional families, see Moore v. City of East Cleveland, 431 U.S. 494 (1977) (city cannot require family to subdivide and exclude blood relatives). Yet the Court has upheld the separate zoning of "adult" theatres. Young v. American Mini-Theatres, 427 U.S. 50 (1976).

19. 278 U.S. 116 (1928).

20. Id. at 121–22.

21. Eastlake v. Forest City Enterprises, Inc., 426 U.S. 668 (1976).

22. 277 U.S. 183 (1928).

health, safety, morals or general welfare." [23] The Court, after reviewing the factual circumstances, found that regulation of the plaintiff's land was not necessary in order to promote the general welfare of the city's inhabitants. Under this very narrow view of the operation of a comprehensive zoning plan, the Court struck down the ordinance. The Court in *Nectow* did not dispute the legitimate nature of the zoning power; it only found that an individual landowner was denied due process when his land was arbitrarily classified.

After these early zoning cases the Supreme Court withdrew from the area for an extended period and allowed the state courts to develop rules governing the permissible scope of zoning regulation. In 1962, however, in *Goldblatt v. Town of Hempstead*,[24] the Court reexamined the constitutionality of zoning regulation and described an expansive power of local government to regulate land use. In *Goldblatt*, the landowner held a thirty-eight acre tract within the town of Hempstead. The land was used as a sand and gravel quarry and had been continuously so used since 1927. The town, having grown around the quarry, attempted through a series of ordinances to restrict the quarry's operation. In 1958, the town amended its zoning ordinance to prohibit any excavation below the water-line, which effectively prohibited continuance of the use to which the property had been devoted.[25]

Emphasizing that there was a presumption that the statute was constitutional, the Court upheld the ordinance, finding "no indication that the prohibitory effect of the [ordinance was] sufficient to render it an unconstitutional taking . . . ." [26] The Court, quoting *Lawton v. Steel*,[27] stated a two-part test to determine whether the statute was valid. First it must appear that "the interests of the public . . . require such interference; and, second, that the means are reasonably necessary for the accomplishment of the purpose, and not unduly oppressive upon individuals." [28] After evaluating the nature of the menace caused by the quarry, the availability of less drastic steps, and the loss suffered by the landowner, the Court found the statute constitutional.

Only the most unusual and totally arbitrary zoning ordinance will require the granting of compensation to a property owner. So long as the zoning ordinance reasonably advances some arguable "police power" interest and does not literally transfer an existing property interest of the owner to the government or other parties, the zoning of property should not require compensation. Although the justices may "balance" public and private interests in these cases, it is assumed that the public interest will prevail unless the regulation enriches the government or public by regulation which terminate or eliminate the primary economic value of a property interest.[29]

---

23. Id. at 188.

24. 369 U.S. 590 (1962).

25. Id. at 592.

26. Id. at 594.

27. 152 U.S. 133, 137 (1894).

28. Goldblatt v. Town of Hempstead, 369 U.S. 590, 595 (1962).

29. See generally Michelman, Property, Utility, and Fairness: Comments on the Ethical Foundation of "Just Compensation" Law, 80 Harv.L.Rev. 1165 (1967).

The state may define ownership interests in real or personal property so that they terminate or lapse without paying compensation, at least when the termination is based upon the action of the owner. See, Texaco, Inc. v. Short, 454 U.S. 516, 102 S.Ct. 781 (1982) (state statute may deem as abandoned and lapsed several mineral interests upon failure of owner to use interest for 20 years or to file claim preventing lapse).

The Court has upheld regulations promulgated by the Secretary of the Interior pursuant to the Eagle Protection Act and Migratory Bird Treaty Act which prohibited commercial transaction in parts of birds protected by the Acts, regardless of whether the birds were killed before the Acts were effective. Andrus v. Allard, 444 U.S. 51 (1979).

Regulations of property use, even those limiting expression or speech, will be found to be permissible police power regulations, for which no compensation is due, so long as the regulations might permit some public interest, even an aesthetic interest. However, laws restricting speech activity may violate the first amendment. See, Metromedia, Inc. v. San Diego, 453 U.S. 490 (1981) (ordinance prohibiting certain noncommer-

Although the Court has not found zoning ordinances to constitute a taking in recent years, opinions of the Court indicate that the justices perceive a legitimate judicial role in determining whether or not a zoning regulation is so unreasonable that it constitutes a taking. In *Agins v. Tiburon*,[30] the opinion of Mr. Justice Powell, for a unanimous Court, stated that the determination of whether property has been taken by a zoning ordinance requires a judicial weighing of private and public interest. *Agins* involved an "open space" zoning ordinance which required the owners of a five acre tract of land to build no more than five single-family residences on their property. Prior to the zoning the property owners might have been able to have subdivided their land into smaller parcels and allowed for the development of more single-family dwellings. However, the Supreme Court found that the government's interest in "assuring careful and orderly development of residential property with provision for open space areas" outweighed the property owner's interest in avoiding any diminution in the market value of their land. The Court engaged in a balancing of the public and private interest and concluded that: "it cannot be said that the impact of general land use regulations has denied the appellants the 'justice and fairness' guaranteed by the fifth and fourteenth amendments."[31]

In *Penn Central Transportation Co. v. New York*,[32] the Supreme Court held that the New York City Landmarks Preservation Law might be employed, consistently with due process, to limit building rights in the vicinity of the historic Grand Central Station. The Court ruled that the limitation imposed by New York's Landmarks Preservation Commission did not constitute a "taking" or otherwise require exercise of the eminent domain power. Under the New York law,

the Landmark Preservation Commission was empowered to designate property as a "landmark," and "landmark site," or a "historic district;" such designation was then approved by higher administrative authority in light of New York's overall zoning plan, and was ultimately subject to judicial review. Designation carried with it certain restrictions on the use of designated property, among which were that the owner must keep the property in "good repair," and that alterations of the external appearance of the property were subject to prior approval by the commission. Denial of approval was subject to judicial review. New York law also provided, however, for certain benefits to owners of property designated by the commission. Chief among these was the right of the owner to transfer unused development rights from restricted property to nearby property which had not been restricted by the commission. The effect of this allowance was to permit owners of both non-historic property and property designated as historic to exceed existing zoning regulations on the development of their non-historic property to the extent that development had been curtailed by the Landmark Law on their nearby historic property. This allowance was intended to mitigate much of the economic deprivation which would inevitably result from development restrictions on historic property. In *Penn Central*, the Landmark Preservation Commission had denied Penn Central permission to build a multi-story office building above Grand Central Station. The Commission concluded that "to balance a 55-story office tower above a flamboyant Beaux-Arts facade seems nothing more than an aesthetic joke . . . ."[33] Rather than refrain from the endeavor and transfer its unused building rights to its other adjacent property, however, Penn Central sought review of the commission's decision.

cial signs or billboards but allowing certain onsite commercial advertising violates first amendment).

30. 447 U.S. 255 (1980).

31. Id. at 262. See also Hodel v. Indiana, 452 U.S. 314 (1981) (finding that "prime farmland" provisions of Surface Mining and Reclamation Control Act did not,

on their face, deprive the property owner of economically beneficial use of his property without just compensation, even though the regulation restricted the amount, type, and profitability of mining operations).

32. 438 U.S. 104 (1978).

33. Id. at 117–118.

The Supreme Court in *Penn Central* ruled that there had been no "taking" of property. A majority of the justice found the regulations a reasonable means of promoting important general welfare interests in environmental control and historic preservation. The majority opinion found the existence of an allowance for transfer of development rights supportive of its determination of the law's reasonableness, but did not indicate that, absent such allowance, the restrictions imposed on Penn Central's property would have amounted to a "taking" for which compensation would be required.[34] The Court did, however, specifically note that the allowance of transfer rights mitigated the loss to owners of historic property, and was thus a factor both in the finding that the law itself was a reasonable exercise of the police powers and in the finding that the magnitude of Penn Central's loss did not rise to the level of a "taking."[35]

Today the Court will allow governmental entities to regulate either real or personal property for the public good without the requirement of compensation so long as the action is not an unreasonable infringement of the rights of the private property owner. The government, however, is not free to transfer property rights from one group of owners to another or to take and use private property for the public good unless the action is justified by emergency conditions or unless compensation is paid. A permanent physical occupation of private property by the government or a government regulation which allows someone other than the property owner to have permanent physical occupation of a definable part of a piece of proper-

ty should constitute a taking.[36] The government must pay compensation for such a taking of traditional property rights. However, in some cases, such as those which follow in this section, it may be difficult to determine when a transfer of property rights has taken place.

In *Kaiser Aetna v. United States*,[37] the Court held that the application of the federal navigational servitude to a lagoon on the island of Oahu constituted a taking for which compensation was required. Historically, the pond in question was considered to be private property. It was leased, along with the surrounding land, to a resort and private housing developer. The developer converted the pond into a marina, and dug channels connecting it with a bay which allowed ships to travel from the lagoon into the bay and the ocean. The federal government claimed that the connection of the waterway to the bay made it a "navigable water" of the United States and therefore subject to regulation by the Corps of Engineers and open to public use. The Supreme Court found that the lagoon was a navigable waterway and subject to regulation by the United States government and the Corps of Engineers acting under the commerce power. However, the government could not require the owners and lessees of the marina to allow the public free access without invoking the eminent domain power and paying them compensation. The Court held that although the government could have refused to allow connection of the lagoon to the bay or regulated use of the lagoon in any arguably reasonable manner, it could not simply convert private prop-

---

34. Id. at 137. The "adequate compensation" issue, as well as the taking issue, had been the focus of modern analysis of prospects for "transferable development right" (TDR) programs. [See Section VII E of this chapter] The dissenting justices would have held that the restrictions on property use constituted a "taking" because those restrictions destroyed valuable property rights. The dissenting justices would not have reached the question of whether TDR's constituted adequate compensation; they would have remanded the case to the New York Court of Appeals for an initial determining of this issue. Id. at 151 (Rehnquist, J., dissenting, joined by Burger, C.J., & Stevens, J.).

35. Penn Central Transp. Co. v. New York, 438 U.S. 104, 115–116, 139 (1978).

36. Loretto v. Teleprompter Manhattan CATV Corp., 102 S.Ct. 3164 (1982) (city ordinance requiring landlord building owner to allow installation of cable television receiver on apartment building and denying landlord the ability to demand payment in excess of $1 constitutes a compensable taking because the ordinance allowed for "permanent physical occupation" of a small part of the building).

37. 444 U.S. 164 (1979).

erty into public property without paying just compensation.[38]

The state's removal of a property owner's right to exclude others under certain circumstances does not necessarily constitute a "taking" in the constitutional sense. In order to determine whether or not such a limitation of property rights constitutes a taking, a court must consider the character of the government's action in terms of the degree to which it promotes legitimate social goals, diminishes the value of the private property owner's economic interest, and interferes with reasonable expectations regarding the use of the property. In *PruneYard Shopping Center v. Robins*,[39] the United States Supreme Court upheld a decision of the California Supreme Court ruling that the California constitution prohibited the owners of private shopping centers from excluding persons who wish to engage in nondisruptive speech and petitioning activities. Although the state had thus eliminated part of the shopping center owner's right to exclude other persons, the owners did not suffer a taking in the constitutional sense because they could not demonstrate that an unchecked right to exclude others was a basic part of the economic value of the shopping center. The state court ruling was seen as a reasonable government regulation of the use of property normally open to members of the public and not a taking of property.[40]

3. *Emergency Actions*

A number of Supreme Court decisions have dealt with the conflicting rights and duties of the government and private landowners during times of emergency. Authorities have long stated that in time of extreme emergency, the government, if the need arises, may take or even destroy private property.[41] As a general rule, the Supreme Court has been reluctant, during the time of emergency, to find that the government need compensate the injured property owner.

Military actions in time of war are often found to be noncompensable emergency measures. In *United States v. Caltex, Inc.*[42] the Supreme Court found that the Army had not "taken" property which had been destroyed to prevent its capture by enemy forces. The Army, in late 1941, destroyed the claimant's oil facilities in Manila as Japanese troops were entering the city. After the war the owner of the facilities demanded compensation for all the property destroyed by the Army. The government agreed to pay for all the petroleum products used or destroyed but refused to pay for the destroyed terminal facilities. The Court, upholding the army's refusal, held that the destruction of private property during battle is a cost that must be borne by individual owners.[43]

Similarly, regulation to help the public purpose in solving an emergency will be upheld as noncompensable measures. Thus, in *United States v. Central Eureka Mining Co.*,[44] another case arising from government

---

38. Id. at 177–181.

In Vaughn v. Vermillion Corp., 444 U.S. 206 (1979), the Court held that privately-owned canals connected with public waterways were not automatically open to general public use under the federal navigational servitude. Unless the government could show that the private canals had destroyed or diverted a pre-existing natural waterway, it would have to pay compensation to the canal owners whose private property was converted to a public waterway.

39. 447 U.S. 74 (1980).

40. The Court in *PruneYard Shopping Center* distinguished Kaiser Aetna v. United States, 444 U.S. 164 (1979), noted above, on the basis that the taking of the

right of exclusivity from property held for private use in *Kaiser* went too far in interfering with "reasonable investment backed expectations," whereas the shopping center regulation was in the nature of a reasonable regulation of commercial functions. PruneYard Shopping Center v. Robins, 447 U.S. 74, 83–85 (1980).

41. See, e.g., Comment, Land Use Regulation and the Concept of Takings in Nineteenth Century America, 40 U.Chi.L.Rev. 854, 860–61 (1973).

42. 344 U.S. 149 (1952).

43. Id. at 154–56.

44. 357 U.S. 155 (1958).

action during World War II, the Supreme Court refused to find that a War Production Board order requiring nonessential gold mines to cease operation amounted to a taking of the mines. The Court observed that the government had in no way taken physical possession of the affected mines,[45] and that the order was a reasonable means, of conserving equipment needed to promote the war effort. "War, particularly in modern times," stated the Court, "demands the strict regulation of nearly all resources. It makes demands which otherwise would be insufferable."[46]

The Court reaffirmed these principles in *National Board of Young Men's Christian Associations v. United States.*[47] Here the Court denied compensation to a private landowner where looters in the Panama Canal Zone destroyed its building because American troops had taken shelter there. The Court, concluding that the presence of the troops in the area had been for the landowner's benefit, found that "fairness and justice" did not require that the loss be compensated by the government and shifted to the public.[48] The Marines had not planned to take over the building but only sought its temporary use in an emergency; therefore there was no compensable taking.

The type of emergency situation that may enable the state to destroy property, without payment of compensation, is not limited to wartime conflict. *Miller v. Schoene* [49] involved the destruction by the State of Virginia of a large number of ornamental red cedar trees. The trees were infected with cedar rust, a disease that is highly dangerous to apple trees. The only effective means of controlling the disease is to destroy all infected red cedars growing within two miles of any apple orchards. The Supreme Court held that the trees could be destroyed by the state without incurring any constitutional duty to compensate the injured landowner. The Court observed that apple production was an important agricultural activity in Virginia while the ornamental cedar trees had only minimal importance. The Supreme Court concluded that "[w]hen forced to such a choice, the state does not exceed its constitutional powers by deciding upon the destruction of one class of property in order to save another, which, in the judgment of the legislature, is of greater value to the public."[50] Like the zoning-property use decisions, this case comports with modern substantive due process analysis by allowing the government to determine how to deal with societal problems without strict judicial review.

In *Dames & Moore v. Regan,*[51] the Supreme Court upheld the validity of executive agreements suspending claims of United States citizens against the government of Iran in exchange for a return of our citizens who were being held hostage by that country.[52] In so doing the majority opinion by Justice Rehnquist found that the Presidential order nullifying attachments on Iranian assets and allowing a transfer of those assets out of the country did not constitute a compensable taking of property because the President had statutory authority to prevent or condition the allowance of such attachments so that those bringing claims against Iran did not have a property interest in the attachment.[53] As a part of the agreement with Iran the President suspended claims of United States citizens pending in United

45. Id. at 165–66.

46. Id. at 168.

47. 395 U.S. 85 (1969).

48. Id. at 89–92.

49. 276 U.S. 272 (1928).

50. Id. at 279.

51. 453 U.S. 654 (1981).

52. The separation of powers aspects of this case are examined in Chapter 6.

53. 453 U.S. at 674 n. 6, Justice Powell was the only justice who would have found that nullification of the attachments constituted a taking of property. He believed that the attachment entitling a creditor to resort to specific property for the satisfaction for a claim was a compensable property interest which could not be made less so through the executive order making the attachments conditional. 453 U.S. at 690 (Powell, J., concurring and dissenting in part).

States courts and required their submission to a "claims tribunal." The Supreme Court refused to consider whether this suspension of claims constituted a compensable taking of property because all parties admitted that the issue was not ripe for review.[54] However, the Court found that persons whose claims were suspended by the Presidential order could bring an action in the Court of Claims to determine whether the suspension of their claim had resulted in an unconstitutional taking of property by executive action.[55]

4. Impairment of Use

The taking issue can arise even when the government has neither destroyed nor regulated the use of private property. Where, as a result of some governmental activity, a landowner's use and enjoyment of his property is impaired, there may be a "taking" for which compensation is due.

The Supreme Court has held that the Constitution does not require the literal appropriation of property before there is a "taking". In *Pumpelly v. Green Bay Co.*,[56] the Supreme Court of the United States was required to interpret the "taking" clause of a state constitution and it found that a serious interruption in the use of property might be the equivalent of a taking, so that the flooding of land by a government dam would be a "taking".[57] In *Bedford v. United States*,[58] however, the Court appeared to step back from the broad statements of *Pumpelly*. In this case the Court found noncompensable the backup of flood waters which was a consequential effect of government action. The

opinion found that a distinction between damaging and taking must be observed for purposes of determining whether a constitutional requirement of compensation exists. The Court distinguished *Pumpelly* on the ground that the landowner in that case was directly injured by the dam project. In this case the government had only fortified the banks of a river to prevent flooding at a point distant from the plaintiff's land; the plaintiff was not directly injured by this act.

In this area the Court's rulings have an *ad hoc* quality as individual decisions are based on the degree of loss to the individual and the reasonableness of the government's actions in relation to the private property. For example, in *Peabody v. United States*,[59] the Court faced the issue of whether the placement of a gun battery in the vicinity of the claimant's resort hotel amounted to a fifth amendment taking. The resort owners argued that the proximate location of the battery to the hotel property for practice purposes greatly impaired the land's recreational value. The Supreme Court found no taking, but, in *dicta*, stated that if the government had installed the battery with the intent to practice at will over the hotel property, "with the intent of depriving the owner of its profitable use," such action would constitute an appropriation of property and would require compensation.[60] Six years later in *Portsmouth Harbor Land & Hotel Co. v. United States*,[61] the hotel owners again sought recovery as a result of additional firings of the battery. The Court rejected this second claim refusing to infer an intent on the part of the government to cre-

---

54. Dames & Moore v. Regan, 453 U.S. 654, 689, (1981). Justice Stevens indicated, without taking a clear position, that he believed that requiring persons to bring their claims before an international tribunal would not constitute a taking of property. Id. at 690, (Stevens, J., concurring). Justice Powell took the position that parties whose claims were not fully adjudicated or fully paid by actions before the claims tribunal were entitled to compensation from the federal government because their property had been taken in order to advance the nation's foreign policy goals. 453 U.S. at 690–1, (Powell, J., concurring and dissenting in part).

55. 453 U.S. at 689–90. The Court was careful to note that, in finding that the President had power to

settle claims against Iran it was not indicating that individual claimants did not have a "possible taking claim against the United States." Id. at 688, n. 14.

56. 80 U.S. (13 Wall.) 166 (1871).

57. Id. at 179–80.

58. 192 U.S. 217 (1904).

59. 231 U.S. 530 (1913).

60. Id. at 538.

61. 250 U.S. 1 (1919).

ate a servitude across the hotel's property. Three years later the same parties again sought recovery urging that the cumulative effect of subsequent firings had resulted in a taking.[62] The Court, per Justice Holmes, reversed the trial court's dismissal of the action, and, adopting the theory of *Peabody*, ordered evidence be heard to determine whether the continued firings were sufficient to prove an intent to create a servitude over the hotel property.

In *United States v. Causby*,[63] the Supreme Court applied the rationale of the *Portsmouth Hotel* cases in determining whether frequent and regular flights of government planes over the plaintiffs' land had created an easement for the benefit of the government. The plaintiffs in this case owned a small chicken farm near an airport used by army and navy planes. The glide path of one of the airport runways passed directly over the property at a height of only 83 feet. The use of the runway greatly disturbed the occupants of the farm and also eventually forced the plaintiffs to give up their chicken business. The Supreme Court found that the frequent low altitude flights of government planes over the farm created an easement in the plaintiffs' land.[64] The Court held that the landowner was entitled to as much of the air space over his property as he had been reasonably using in connection with his land, and found that the government's use of this airspace resulted in the imposition of a servitude on the chicken farm.

5. Summary

The taking issue presents a most difficult conceptual problem. Damaging private property may be a taking, but in certain instances even total destruction does not require compensation. Physical occupation of private property normally will require compensation but the government was allowed to restrict a shopping center owner's ability to exclude persons without the payment of compensation. Regulation generally may be done without compensation; yet a regulation may be so restrictive as to warrant a finding that a taking has occurred. The term "taking," therefore, is best viewed not as a literal description of the governmental action. Thus, Professor Michelman, in his outstanding analysis of the philosophy and principles of adjudication in this area described the term "taking" as "constitutional law's expression for any sort of publicly inflicted private injury for which the Constitution requires judgment of compensation."[65] In connection with this analysis, Professor Michelman has described four factors, any one of which is normally determinative in evaluating whether compensation is constitutionally due:

(1) Whether or not the public, government or one of its agents have physically used or occupied something belonging to the claimant.

(2) The size of the harm sustained by the claimant or the degree to which his affected property has been devalued.

(3) Whether the claimant's loss is or is not outweighed by the public's commitant gain.

(4) Whether the claimant has sustained any loss apart from restriction of his liberty to conduct some activity considered harmful to other people.[66]

While these four factors will not definitively answer the question of whether a court will

---

62. Portsmouth Harbor Land and Hotel Co. v. United States, 260 U.S. 327 (1922).

63. 328 U.S. 256 (1946).

64. Id. at 265. The Court later held that the establishment of a county owned airport next to residential property could constitute a taking if the flight and operation of the airport made the property unusable for residential purposes. Griggs v. Allegheny County, 369 U.S. 84 (1962).

65. Michelman, Property, Utility, and Fairness: Commentaries on the Ethical Foundations of "Just Compensation" Law, 80 Harv.L.Rev. 1165, 1165 (1967).

66. Id. at 1184.

When the government takes physical possession of money or property which otherwise would accrue to the benefit of a private person, the private person's claim for just compensation is established unless the government can demonstrate that its action in fact constituted only a regulation of the property use, or payment of an amount lawfully owed to the government.

find compensation due, in a specific case, they do set the parameters for argument.

D. The "Public Use" Limitation

The government is not entirely free to take a person's property whenever it is willing to compensate him. The individual may not wish to part with his property, and under both the fifth and fourteenth amendments property may not be taken by the government, even upon payment of just compensation, unless the property is taken for a public use. Like the requirement that a landowner be compensated when his property is taken by the state, the "public use" limitation also has its roots in natural as well as constitutional law.[1] The early interpretation of this public use test was broadly viewed as properly exercisable for "the public good, the public necessity or the public utility".[2]

The broad interpretation of the public use limitation was abandoned in the later half of the nineteenth century, however, in order that the courts might better control the exercise of eminent domain by private enterprises to whom the power had been delegated.[3] The state courts developed, therefore, the "use by the public" test for determining when a public use existed. Under the "use by the public" test the public had to have a right to use or enjoy the property taken. Early in the twentieth century, however, the Supreme Court repudiated the narrow "use by the public" test[4] and returned to the broad public benefit test for determining when a use was public.

The leading modern case defining the scope of the public use limitation is the unanimous 1954 Supreme Court decision in *Berman v. Parker*.[5] This case involved the constitutionality of the 1945 District of Columbia Redevelopment Act. Under section 2 of that Act, Congress declared it the policy of the United States to eliminate all substandard housing in Washington, D.C. because such areas were "injurious to the public health, safety, morals, and welfare." The Act also created the District of Columbia Redevelopment Land Agency and granted that agency the power to assemble real property for the redevelopment of blighted areas of the city through the exercise of eminent domain. After assembling the necessary real estate, Congress authorized the Agency to lease or sell portions of the land to private parties upon an agreement that the purchasers would carry out the redevelopment plan.

The appellant in *Berman* held property within the redevelopment area upon which a department store was located. The appellants argued that their property could not constitutionally be taken for the project, first, because the property was commercial and not residential or slum housing, and second, because, by condemning the property for sale to a private agency for redevelopment, the land was being redeveloped for a private and not a public use as required by the fifth amendment. The Supreme Court,

---

See, e.g., Webb's Fabulous Pharmacies, Inc. v. Beckwith, 449 U.S. 155 (1980) (A taking occurred when a county took the interest earned on funds deposited with the clerk of the county court in an interpleader action. Since a state statute authorized a separate clerk's fee for services rendered, the taking of the interest could not be justified as payment of an obligation to the government.)

The fifth amendment limits the ability of the federal government to take property belonging to state or local governments without just compensation, even though the tenth amendment does not prohibit such federal acts. However, no person or entity may sue the United States without its permission. Legislation imposing a twelve year statute of limitations on suits challenging the taking of property by the federal government could be applied to bar state government suits against the United States. Block v. North Dakota ex rel.

Board of University and School Lands, 103 S.Ct. 1811 (1983).

1. Lenhoff, Development of the Concept of Eminent Domain, 42 Colum.L.Rev. 596, 598–99 (1942).

2. Comment, The Public Use Doctrine: "Advance Requiem" Revisited, 1959 Law and the Social Order 689, 689.

3. Comment, The Public Use Limitation on Eminent Domain: An Advance Requiem, 58 Yale L.J. 599, 602–603 (1949).

4. See Mt. Vernon—Woodberry Cotton Duck Co. v. Alabama Interstate Power Co., 240 U.S. 30 (1916). See also Sachman, The Right to Condemn, 29 Albany L.Rev. 177, 183 (1965).

5. 348 U.S. 26 (1954).

in an opinion by Justice Douglas, disagreed and upheld the use of the eminent domain power.

The opinion noted that Congress has a "police power" as to the city of Washington, D. C., which is equivalent to the police power of the individual states, to legislate as necessary for the health, safety and welfare of its residents. Congress was exercising this "police power" in *Berman*.[6] This use of the term "police power" by Justice Douglas did not indicate that the government could take property without compensation but only that the federal government is not of limited, enumerated powers when it legislates concerning the District of Columbia. The significance of the *Berman* opinion is that it confirms that the public use limitation of the fifth and fourteenth amendment is as expansive as a due process police power test.[7] The Court reaffirmed the rule that once the legislature has declared a condemnation to be for a public use, the role of the courts is an extremely narrow one.[8] The Court approved the concept of area redevelopment by holding that property which, standing by itself, was innocuous could be taken as part of the overall plan.[9] As for the power of the legislature to condemn areas for the purpose of renovation, the Court stated that "[i]t is within the power of the legislature to determine that the community should be beautiful as well as healthy, spacious as well as clean, well-balanced as well as carefully patrolled."[10]

After *Berman*, the public use limitation is easily met whenever eminent domain is exercised by either the state or federal government as a means of realizing any object within its authority. For the state governments, and for the federal government when acting within federal territory, this means that eminent domain may be exercised whenever the purpose of the action is for the benefit of the health, safety and welfare of its citizens. For the actions of federal government concerning land within the states, this public use limitation is met whenever the object of the exercise bears any reasonable relationship to one of its implied or enumerated powers.

E. A Note on the Amount of Compensation and Compensable Property Interests

The fifth and fourteenth amendments, as discussed above, require that a person receive "just compensation" for property that has been taken by the state or federal government. The Supreme Court has said that the constitutional guarantee of just compensation is not a limitation on the power of eminent domain, but only a condition of its exercise.[1] In determining what is "just compensation" the courts have developed various standards of valuation.[2]

The most basic principle for determining the amount due an individual whose property has been taken is contained in the often-quoted statement by Justice Holmes that the test is "what has the owner lost, not what has the taker gained".[3] Thus determination of what the injured property owner has lost fixes the amount for which the state is liable. Here the courts normally look to the market value of the property that has been

---

6. Id. at 31.

7. Costonis, Fair Compensation and the Accommodation Power: Antidotes for the Taking Impasse in Land Use Controversies, 75 Colum.L.Rev. 1021, 1036 (1975).

8. Berman v. Parker, 348 U.S. 26, 32 (1954). See also, Rindge Co. v. County of Los Angeles, 262 U.S. 700, 709 (1923); Old Dominion Land Co. v. United States, 269 U.S. 55, 66 (1925); and United States ex rel. Tennessee Valley Authority v. Welch, 327 U.S. 546, 551–52 (1946).

9. Berman v. Parker, 348 U.S. 26, 35 (1954).

10. Id. at 33.

1. Long Island Water Supply Co. v. Brooklyn, 166 U.S. 685, 689 (1897). See E. Freund, The Police Power 541 (1904) where the author concludes that the compensation requirement has always been an element of the exercise of eminent domain in civilized societies.

2. For an analysis of the compensation and valuation issue see, L. Orgel, Valuation Under the Law of Eminent Domain (2d ed. 1953).

3. Boston Chamber of Commerce v. City of Boston, 217 U.S. 189, 195 (1910).

taken.[4] Moreover, in determining the market value of the land, the court will normally look to the value of the property as if land were applied to its "highest and best" use. The highest and best use of a piece of property is determined by the value of the property in light of its present and potential uses if those uses can be anticipated with reasonable certainty.[5]

The market value test is not, however, a definitive test. In *United States v. Fuller*,[6] the Supreme Court stated that the overall standard is governed by basic equitable principles of fairness. In *Fuller*, the Court held that the government as a condemnor was not required to pay for elements of the property's market value that the government had created by granting the landowner a revocable permit to graze his animals on adjoining Federal lands.[7]

Related to determining the amount of compensation are issues concerning the interests that qualify as property for which

any compensation is due. The power of eminent domain enables the government to take "property" for public uses and only requires compensation for such. When the federal government acts as the condemnor, or taker, of the property the issue of what may be taken and what must be paid for is a matter of federal law.[8] The Supreme Court, for example, has held that an Indian group had an insufficient interest in unrecognized Indian land to require that compensation be paid for divestiture of that interest.[9] The Court has held, however, that a lease interest is property and that an injured lessee had a property right requiring compensation.[10] In sum, the power of eminent domain extends to tangibles and intangibles, including choses in action, contracts and charters.[11] As with the basic determination of value, this "test" combines traditional property law interests and equitable principles of fairness.

One of the most significant eminent domain issues to have arisen for several de-

---

4. Note, Valuation of Conrail Under the Fifth Amendment, 90 Harv.L.Rev. 596, 598 (1977).

5. Super-Power Co. v. Summers, 352 Ill. 610, 618, 186 N.E. 476, 479 (1933).

6. 409 U.S. 488 (1973).

7. See also, United States ex rel. Tennessee Valley Authority v. Powelson, 319 U.S. 266 (1943), where the Supreme Court held that in condemning land the federal government need not take into consideration in valuing the property the loss of business opportunity dependent on the owner's privilege to use the state's power of eminent domain.

In United States v. Bodcaw Co., 440 U.S. 202 (1979) (per curiam) the Court unanimously held that appraisal fees incurred by the owner of land in connection with a condemnation proceeding were not constitutionally compensable interests in connection with the taking of land by the federal government. While a particular legislative body might grant such costs to property owners as a part of condemnation proceedings, the government was not required by the Constitution to reimburse these costs. The Court also held that such expenses were not to be repaid under applicable federal acts.

In keeping with the requirement that condemned land be paid for at market value, absent unusual circumstances, the Court, in United States v. 564.54 Acres of Land, 441 U.S. 506 (1979), found that a private non-profit organization whose recreational camp was condemned by the government, in order that the government build the government facility, was not entitled to the replacement cost for the camp. In this case the replacement cost would have been higher than the mar-

ket value because the reestablishment of the camp was subject to new regulations which had not applied to the first facility. The Court found that this case did not present a unique situation where there was no ascertainable market value for the property or where the use of market value would create manifest injustice to the owner. It is arguable that when one governmental entity condemns the land of an inferior entity, and the inferior entity is required to continue to perform the function which it had been performing on the land, that the lower governmental entity is entitled to replacement costs rather than market value. However, the Supreme Court was unanimous in the opinion that to the extent that such an exemption from the market value principle may exist for taking from governmental units, it should not apply to taking from non-profit corporations.

8. United States ex rel. Tennessee Valley Authority v. Powelson, 319 U.S. 266 (1943). See also, annot. 1 A.L.R. Fed. 479 (1969).

9. Tee-Hit-Ton Indians v. United States, 348 U.S. 272 (1955).

10. A. W. Duckett & Co. v. United States, 266 U.S. 149 (1924). See also Armstrong v. United States, 364 U.S. 40 (1960) (materialmen's liens held to be a compensable interest).

11. City of Cincinnati v. Louisville & Nashville R.R. Co., 223 U.S. 390, 400 (1912). The Court in City of Cincinnati also held that the constitutional limitation on any state law impairing the obligation of contracts was not intended to limit the exercise of eminent domain. Id.

cades focuses on the compensation concept. In an effort to protect historical landmarks from destruction, a system termed "transferable development rights" has been developed. Under such a system, the owners of designated landmarks are given "rights" to exceed building height restrictions in their building zones as compensation for the decreased value of the building because of regulations which prohibit the modification of the landmark. Whether the system takes property or provides adequate compensation remains open to dispute.[12]

---

12. The adequate compensation issue remains undecided. The Supreme Court upheld the use of the landmark preservation—transferable development rights (TDR) system to limit the alteration of the Grand Central Station in New York on the basis that this land use "regulation" did not constitute a "taking." Penn Central Transp. v. New York, 438 U.S. 104 (1978). The justices, in *Penn Central*, did not examine the question of whether TDR's constituted adequate compensation for a taking (the decision is examined in Section VII, C, 2 of this Chapter).

The primary intellectual proponent of the transferable development rights concept has been Professor John Costonis. He has been challenged as to the worth of transferable development rights by Professor Curtis Berger. Compare Costonis, Fair Compensation and the Accommodation Power: Antidotes for the Taking Impasse in Land Use Controversies, 75 Colum.L. Rev. 1021 (1975), with Berger, The Accommodation Power in Land Use Controversies: A Reply to Professor Costonis, 76 Colum.L.Rev. 799 (1976). See generally, J. Costonis, Space Adrift (1974); Costonis, The Disparity Issue: A Context for the Grand Central Terminal Decision, 91 Harv.L.Rev. 402 (1977).

CHAPTER FOURTEEN

STATE ACTION

I. INTRODUCTION*

A. Central Theory

Most of the protections for individual rights and liberties contained in the Constitution and its amendments apply only to the actions of governmental entities. The safeguards against deprivations of individual rights which are contained in the text of the Constitution specifically apply only to the activities of either the state or federal governments. Similarly, the Bill of Rights by its terms and necessary implications has been viewed only to limit the freedom of the government when dealing with individuals. Finally, the amendments to the Constitution which protect individual liberties specifically address themselves to actions taken by the United States or a state. Only the thirteenth amendment, which abolishes the institution of slavery, is also directed to control-

ling the actions of private individuals. Thus whenever a suit is brought against private individuals on the basis that they have taken actions which have violated the civil or political rights of another, there is a question as to how the actions of the private individuals could be limited by these constitutional provisions. There must be a determination of whether defendant's actions constitute governmental or "state" action of a type regulated by the appropriate constitutional provision.

In most forms of constitutional litigation there is no state action issue involved in the case. When a legislature, executive officer, or a court takes some official action against an individual, that action is subjected to review under the Constitution, for the official act of any governmental agency is direct governmental action and therefore subject to the restraints of the Constitution. The so

* This Chapter is taken in substantial part from an article co-authored by one of the authors of this text. See Glennon and Nowak, A Functional Analysis of the Fourteenth Amendment "State Action" Requirement, 1976 Sup.Ct.Rev. 221. We express our thanks to Professor Robert J. Glennon, Jr., and to the editor of the Supreme Court Review, Professor Philip Kurland, for allowing us to make use of the article.

called "state action" issue arises only when the person or entity alleged to have violated the Constitution is not acting on behalf of the government. In such a case the person alleged to have violated the constitutional provision will argue that he is incapable of violating the Constitution because he is not part of the government, giving rise to the state action issue.

It should be noted that actions of any governmental entity give rise to state action for the purposes of constitutional limitations. Any subdivision of a state, be it an administrative agency or an independent political subdivision, such as a city, represents government or state authority to a sufficient degree to invoke constitutional restrictions on its actions. Additionally it should be noted that the phrase "state action" is a misnomer as the issue arises in an identical manner when the federal government or its agents are involved in a case. If a person or agency is alleged to have violated some constitutional provision or civil rights statute directed at the federal government there will be an issue in the case as to whether the defendant has sufficient "federal government action" to be subjected to those limitations. However, all problems relating to the existence of government action—local, state or federal—which would subject an individual to constitutional restrictions come under the heading of "state action."

All of the cases involving a state action issue have an essentially similar fact pattern. In these cases one individual citizen (the "aggrieved party") feels that his freedoms or rights have been violated by the actions of another (the "alleged wrongdoer"). The aggrieved party, or some governmental agency acting on his behalf, claims that a violation of the Constitution has taken place by the other party's actions. In a very real sense the issue is simply which party's rights are of the greater constitutional significance. This question is answered by determining whether the challenged party's activities involve sufficient governmental action so that they are subjected to the values and limitations reflected in the Constitution and its amendments. If the Court finds sufficient connections to the government it will declare that the aggrieved party's rights must prevail. In such a situation the aggrieved party has a constitutionally protected freedom of action which cannot be disregarded by the alleged wrongdoer. However, the Court may find that the alleged wrongdoer does not have sufficient contacts with the government to justify subjecting him to constitutional limitations. In that situation the alleged wrongdoer's rights will prevail and the aggrieved party will receive no relief from the federal courts. Here the activity is free from constitutional limitation and it will be allowed to continue until such time as it is made illegal under appropriate state or federal statutes.

While all state action cases arise in similar fact situations they are brought on two distinct legal bases. The first type of suit is based solely on the provisions of the Constitution or a specific amendment. In such a case the challenged party is alleged to have sufficient state action so that his activities directly violate the Constitution by limiting the rights of the aggrieved party. The second type of case is based upon a specific statute passed by the Congress pursuant to its powers to protect the principles of an amendment to the Constitution. In the second type of case there are two issues: (1) whether the seemingly private party comes within the terms of the statute and (2) whether Congress has the power to restrict the activities of private individuals in order to safeguard civil liberties.[1] The most important state action issues are involved in cases where the challenged activity is alleged to violate an amendment to the Constitution or a general civil rights statute. In these cases the Court is presented with the question of how it is to determine when a

---

1. Examination of this issue is included in a Chapter on congressional power to enforce these amendments. See Chapter 17, infra.

private individual is to be subjected to constitutional limitations. The Court's resolution of this problem will be the focus of this Chapter. But before commencing upon that inquiry let us briefly examine the decisions that gave rise to both facets of the state action issue.

B. Origins of the Problem

The issues concerning the applicability of constitutional restrictions and congressional legislation to private conduct did not rise until after the enactment of the Civil War amendments. At the time of the proposal and ratification of the thirteenth and fourteenth amendments the Congress passed a wide ranging series of civil rights statutes designed to protect blacks against the actions of both state officials and private persons. In several cases between 1875 and 1882 the Supreme Court indicated that Congress was not empowered to regulate the conduct of private persons simply because that conduct might disadvantage blacks or other persons. In the two most important cases of the period the Court held that federal criminal indictments under the Civil Rights Acts for participation in the lynchings of blacks were unconstitutional as applied to persons who had no connection to state governments and who were not interfering with uniquely federal rights such as the petitioning of Congress.[2] However the issue was not fully examined until 1883 in the *Civil Rights Cases*.[3]

The decision of the Supreme Court captioned the *Civil Rights Cases* concerned four criminal indictments and one civil action under Section 1 of the Civil Rights Act of 1875.[4] That act established criminal and civil penalties against anyone who interfered with the "full and equal enjoyment" of public facilities and conveyances by persons because of their race. The five cases were brought against individuals and railroads who had excluded black persons from railroads, hotels and theaters because of their race. The Court reversed the indictments and the civil penalty, as a majority of the justices found that these actions were immune from congressional legislation and the restrictions of the fourteenth amendment because they did not involve state action. Additionally, the Court held that the congressional acts could not be justified by the thirteenth amendment, as the justices did not believe them to be related to abolition of slavery in the United States.

As to the fourteenth amendment issue the Court's opinion was predicated upon the premise that the power of Congress to enforce the amendment comprehended no legislation which did not deal with actions that constituted a violation of section 1 of the amendment. The majority therefore examined what actions might constitute a violation of the guarantees of due process and equal protection under Section 1. The opinion found that the amendment was only meant to guarantee the existence of certain rights in law. So long as neither the state government nor its agencies established the deprivation of rights nor authorized others to impair such rights the justices could see no state violation of due process or equal protection of law.[5] In the view of these justices the aggrieved person's rights remained in full force because, in theory, the state had not taken them away. The mere fact that private persons refused to allow black persons into public accommodations or public conveyances did not mean that the state had withdrawn the right of blacks to engage in such activities.[6] These actions by a private person or a corporation amounted to merely a private wrong which had no relationship to a deprivation of rights such as was prohibited by the fourteenth amendment.

Because the majority of justices saw the harm to black persons as merely a conflict

---

2. United States v. Cruikshank, 92 U.S. 542 (1876); United States v. Harris, 106 U.S. 629 (1883). See also, United States v. Reese, 92 U.S. 214 (1876).

3. Civil Rights Cases, 109 U.S. 3 (1883).

4. Civil Rights Act of 1875, 18 Stat. 335, chap. 114.

5. 109 U.S. at 11.

6. 109 U.S. at 17, 18.

between private persons, they refused to allow the Congress to regulate these activities. The Court indicated that Congress' powers under section 5 of the fourteenth amendment could not extend beyond an enforcement of the basic provisions of Section 1 of the amendment.[7] The opinion of the Court in the *Civil Rights Cases* reflects two concerns as to congressional power. First, as the amendment was directed only to the states, direct congressional regulation of private activities would be an unwarranted expansion of the federal power over individuals. Second, if Congress had a power to protect all rights against private deprivations it would allow the federal assumption of the functions of the state in a way which would violate principles inherent in the tenth amendment.

It is interesting to note that a majority of the Court used the tenth amendment to interpret both the applicability of the fourteenth amendment and the grant of power given to Congress by that amendment.[8] This decision came at the time that justices were also beginning to restrict the scope of federal power under the commerce clause by using the tenth amendment to protect intrastate activities from federal regulation.[9] Additionally, it was during this period that the concept of substantive due process was gaining adherents on the Court.[10] The *Civil Rights Cases* can be seen then as another reflection of these justices' antipathy towards government regulation of individual activities regardless of the basis of the legislation. However, it should be noted that the Supreme Court recognized that Congress properly regulated the activities of private individuals when such regulation was based on a specific federal power such as those contained in section 8 of Article 1 of the Constitution.[11] Thus, the justices laid the basis for recognition of congressional powers to pro-

tect uniquely federal rights against interference by private persons which would be recognized by the Court in the next century.[12]

The opinion in the *Civil Rights Cases* also reviewed the permissibility of these civil rights acts as an enforcement of the thirteenth amendment.[13] This question did not involve a state action issue, for that amendment abolishes slavery and involuntary servitude in the United States regardless of whether those conditions are imposed by a government entity or private persons. However, for a law to be a valid enforcement mechanism for this amendment it would have to relate to the abolition of the incidents of slavery. The majority opinion stated that Congress had the right under this amendment to "enact all necessary and proper laws for the obliteration and prevention of slavery with all its badges and incidents."[14] However, a majority of the justices believed that they should independently determine whether the legislation in fact was related to the "badges and incidents" of slavery. Here the majority simply disagreed with the Congress. The Court refused to grant any real deference to the congressional acts as that would allow the federal regulation of all private discriminations or wrongs against blacks. The Court took the position that Congress could only eliminate legal distinctions based upon slavery and that, once those distinctions had been eliminated, any further discrimination had to be dealt with under the fourteenth amendment.

Justice Harlan dissented in these cases.[15] In his opinion the thirteenth amendment eliminated not only the institution of slavery but the continuing distinctions based on race which resulted from the slavery experience. He found that Congress could enforce the rights of the blacks in relation to public ac-

7. 109 U.S. at 14, 15.

8. 109 U.S. at 15.

9. See Chapter 4 section III.

10. See Chapter 13, sections II, III.

11. The Civil Rights Cases, 109 U.S. 3, 18 (1883).

12. See Griffin v. Breckenridge, 403 U.S. 88 (1971); for an examination of the Congressional Power to enforce these amendments see Chapter 17.

13. 109 U.S. at 20.

14. 109 U.S. at 21.

15. 109 U.S. at 26 (Harlan, J., dissenting).

commodations, facilities and public conveyances since discriminations in those "public" or "quasi-public" functions was a continuing badge of servitude.[16] Additionally, he found that the fourteenth amendment authorized Congress to grant full protection to blacks against discriminations by private persons. He noted that the first sentence of the fourteenth amendment created a national citizenship which could be protected by congressional legislation. Thus, he found that protection from race discrimination was a basic civil right and part of citizenship in the United States which could be protected by Congress.[17]

There were three distinct holdings in the *Civil Rights Cases*. First, that the guarantees of civil liberties contained in the fourteenth amendment applied only to governmental or "state" actions. Second, that the Congress was only empowered by the fourteenth amendment to regulate the activities which the Court independently would find to be a violation of section 1 of the amendment. Third, that the Court would independently review congressional legislation under the thirteenth amendment to insure that it was designed to eliminate clear vestiges of slavery. These three holdings have had varying degrees of acceptance by later justices and the Court. The final holding relating to the thirteenth amendment has clearly been overruled, for the Court will no longer strictly review legislation based on the thirteenth amendment.[18] As to the second holding relating to the power to regulate private activities the position of the current Court is something less than clear. Today, Congress may regulate private activities which infringe uniquely federal rights.[19] However it is not clear as to whether Congress may regulate private persons because their activities

would constitute a denial of due process or equal protection if done by the state. While many of the justices in recent cases have indicated that congressional action should be subject to no state action requirement the issue has not been conclusively settled.[20] Finally, the first holding of the Court—that judges should not independently find violations of the amendment absent state action—remains the position of the Supreme Court today. It is that issue which will concern us throughout most of this chapter. We will examine the bases on which the Court will find state action in the activities of a seemingly private person or entity.

The Court did not modify its strict position concerning state action until the 1940's, when the justices began to find violations of the fourteenth amendment even though the complained of activities were not formally linked to any action by state officials. From these early cases to the present the Court has developed a series of theories by which it may be established that a private person is sufficiently tied to the activities of government so that his actions might violate certain constitutional provisions. It should be remembered that in each of these cases a private person (whom we may term the aggrieved party) claims that he has been deprived of some constitutionally guaranteed right by the activities of another seemingly private person (whom we may term the alleged wrongdoer). The Court must then determine whether the alleged wrongdoer has sufficient connection to the state to subject his or her activities to constitutional restrictions. If the Court determines that sufficient state action exists, it will order a remedy for the aggrieved party and the ending of the practice of the alleged wrongdoer. If the Court finds that the alleged wrongdoer

---

16. 109 U.S. at 37–44 (Harlan, J., dissenting).

17. 109 U.S. 46–47 (Harlan, J., dissenting).

18. Jones v. Alfred H. Mayer Co., 392 U.S. 409 (1968); Runyon v. McCrary, 427 U.S. 160 (1976). For an examination of Congressional power under the thirteenth amendment, see Chapter 17.

19. United States v. Classic, 313 U.S. 299 (1941); See Chapter 17.

20. In United States v. Guest, 383 U.S. 745 (1966), six justices indicated that Congress could regulate private actions, but they did not do so in a single majority opinion, id. at 762 (Clark, J., concurring); id. at 784 (Brennan, J., concurring in part); for more on this issue, see Chapter 17.

is not involved with state action, it will afford no remedy to the aggrieved party, who must continue to suffer whatever discrimination he has complained of. The remainder of this Chapter will deal with the basis upon which the Court may find state action in the activities of the alleged wrongdoer.

II. THE PUBLIC FUNCTION CONCEPT

It is now clear that constitutional limitations on state activities restrict the manner in which government functions are conducted. If private persons are engaged in the exercise of government functions their activities are subject to similar constitutional restrictions. The state cannot free itself from the limitations of the Constitution in the operation of its governmental functions merely by delegating certain functions to otherwise private individuals. If private actors assume the role of the state by engaging in these governmental functions then they subject themselves to the same limitations on their freedom of action as would be imposed upon the state itself. The functions of government which are subjected to these restraints are termed "public functions." But, while this theory is easily justified, it is very difficult to determine what activities should be deemed public functions and subjected to constitutional limitations.

The fact that a private person engages in an activity which could be performed by a state government will not in itself subject him to such limitations, for state governments could engage virtually in any activity. It is only those activities or functions which are traditionally associated with sovereign governments, and which are operated almost exclusively by governmental entities, which will be deemed public functions. Thus, the operation of election systems, the governance of cities and towns, and, perhaps, the operation of seemingly public facilities such as parks will be deemed public functions regulated by the Constitution. However, the mere operation of businesses which could be operated by a government will not be construed as a public function as that would involve a determination based on the practical importance of the activity rather than its relation to the function of the state. Thus, the operation of a public utility such as a power company is not a public function.[1] As the Court has given us only the most general guidelines to these determinations, it is important to review the major decisions of the Court in this area.

The concept of public function appears to have originated in a series of decisions relating to the applicability of the fourteenth and fifteenth amendments to primary elections in Texas which were segregated by race.[2] As early as 1927 the Supreme Court held that the Texas state laws which excluded blacks from democratic primaries violated the fourteenth amendment.[3] A few years later the Court held that granting political party committees the authority to determine who voted in the primary was similarly unconstitutional as these committees constituted the agents of the state.[4] However, in 1935 in the case of *Grovey v. Townsend*[5] the Court held that a state political party convention which discriminated on the basis of race was not constitutionally invalid because there was no state action connected to it. However, this decision was overruled nine years later in *Smith v. Allwright.*[6]

In *Smith* the Supreme Court held that the white primary system which had been established by a state political party convention in Texas violated the fifteenth amendment. The basis for applying the fifteenth amendment to the primary system was that the election system and the fixing of qualifica-

---

1. Jackson v. Metropolitan Edison Co., 419 U.S. 345 (1974).

2. It should be remembered that Justice Harlan raised similar considerations in his examination of the rights protected by the thirteenth amendment; The Civil Rights Cases, 109 U.S. 3, 37–44 (1883) (Harlan, J., dissenting).

3. Nixon v. Herndon, 273 U.S. 536 (1927).

4. Nixon v. Condon, 286 U.S. 73 (1932).

5. 295 U.S. 45 (1935).

6. 321 U.S. 649 (1944).

tions for voters was a public function which was subjected to constitutional limitations regardless of who actually conducted the election. This decision had been foreshadowed in *United States v. Classic*.[7] The *Classic* Court had upheld congressional regulation of primary elections on the basis that the electoral system was a unitary process which was entirely subject to the regulatory powers of congress. In *Smith* the justices found that the running of elections was an essential state function, that the primary system was an integral part of the election process and that the delegation of this authority over the election system to the political party made it an agent of the state.

It should be noted that following this decision state political parties attempted to retain their racially restrictive practices but that these efforts met with little success. In *Terry v. Adams*[8] the Court reviewed a practice of the "Jay Bird Democratic Association" which was composed of supposedly voluntary clubs of white democrats in Texas. These clubs held their own private elections of nominees who then ran in the democratic primaries in Texas—usually unopposed. In this case the Supreme Court held that these pre-primary elections were subject to the restrictions of the fifteenth amendment even though there had been a "complete absence" of formal state connection to any of the activities of the political clubs. There was no majority opinion in this case but the justices seemed to agree that the relationship between the club practices and electoral system constituted the delegation of a public function to this group so as to subject it to the fifteenth amendment.[9] Justice Frankfurter noted that while the state had taken no positive action it had abdicated its respon-

sibility of insuring a racially neutral election system and that this abdication was the basis for subjecting the club to the restrictions of the fifteenth amendment.[10]

Perhaps the strongest use of the public function doctrine came in the case of *Marsh v. Alabama*.[11] This case involved a "company town" which was a privately owned area encompassing both residential and commercial districts. The Gulf Shipbuilding Corporation owned and governed this area but it had no formal ties to any state agency or authority. Agents of the corporation had ordered a Jehovah Witness to leave the privately owned business district and to refrain from distributing religious leaflets within the boundaries of the company town. If the order were valid it would have subjected the leafleter to conviction under state trespass laws for her refusal to leave the area or stop distributing literature. Unquestionably this town would have violated the first amendment if it were an agency of the state attempting to suppress the distribution of the literature. Thus, the only issue in the case was the applicability of the first and fourteenth amendments to the conduct of the corporation that owned the town. A majority of the justices, in an opinion by Justice Black, held that the company town was subjected to the limitations of the first and fourteenth amendments and that the individual had a right to distribute her leaflets within the town.

The Court relied on the fact that the state allowed private ownership of land and property to a degree which allowed this corporation to replace all of the functions and activities which would normally belong to a city. Because the privately owned business area served as the equivalent of a community

---

7. 313 U.S. 299 (1941).

8. 345 U.S. 461 (1953).

9. 345 U.S. at 469 (Black, J.); 345 U.S. at 484 (Clark, J., concurring). See generally, Chambers and Rotunda, Reform of the Presidential Nominating Conventions, 56 Va.L.Rev. 179, 194–96 (1970).

10. 345 U.S. at 477 (Frankfurter J., concurring). See Pollak, Racial Discrimination and Judicial Integrity: A Reply to Professor Wechsler, 108 U.Pa.L.Rev. 1,

23 (1959): "[O]nly a state can conduct elections—especially so where the state is one in which, under the Constitution, a republican form of government is perpetually guaranteed." See also Rotunda, Constitutional and Statutory Restrictions on Political Parties in the Wake of Cousins v. Wigoda, 53 Texas L.Rev. 935, 952–957 (1975).

11. 326 U.S. 501 (1946).

shopping district in a normal city the first amendment applied in full force to the activities which took place there. Perhaps the most revealing part of the opinion was the statement that, in the determining of the existence of a public function, the Court would "balance the constitutional rights of the owners of property against those of the people to enjoy freedom of press and religion." [12]

The public function concept appeared to include a wide range of activities when the Court decided *Evans v. Newton.*[13] This case involved the exclusion of members of racial minorities from a park in Macon, Georgia. The park had been established in 1911 by testamentary trust in the will of Senator Bacon which required that the park be used only for white persons. The city had originally been the trustee and operator of the segregated park until the decision in *Brown v. Board of Education.*[14] The city then resigned as trustee and requested the appointment of private persons to take its place. The Supreme Court of the United States held that the park could not be operated with the racial restriction even if the new trustees would have no connection to the city government. The decision of the Court seemed to center on the entanglement between the city government and the operation of the park. Indeed, this entanglement was a strong factor, for the city continued to offer certain maintenance assistance to the park even after the substitution of the private trustees. However, the opinion indicated that the park could not be operated on a racially restricted basis even if the city managed to sever all of its ties to the operation of the facilities. The majority opinion by Justice Douglas implied that the operation of the park was an essential municipal function which could not be delegated to private persons so as to avoid the restrictions of the fourteenth amendment.[15]

It should be noted that following this decision the trust was terminated by the local state courts and the land reverted to the heirs of Senator Bacon. This reversion to the heirs—for uses other than a racially restrictive park—was upheld by the Supreme Court in *Evans v. Abney.*[16] A majority of the Court found that the application of property law which ended the trust and returned the land to the heirs did not violate the Constitution as it was not premised on any continuation of racial restrictions. This holding strengthens the theory that the operation of the public park on a racially restrictive basis violated the fourteenth amendment because it constituted a public function. Once the land was being used for something other than a park it could be returned to the heirs. But as the public function concept has been narrowed in recent years, the case cannot at this time be taken to have established public amusement areas as public functions.

The most interesting developments under the public function concept occurred in relation to privately owned shopping centers. In a series of three cases between 1968 and 1976 the Supreme Court wrestled with the problem of whether there was a right to go into the open areas of privately owned shopping centers to distribute information concerning public issues. In the final analysis the Court held that there were no first amendment rights in these areas because the privately owed shopping centers did not constitute a public function and there was no state action which violated the Constitution. However, this result came about only after two totally conflicting decisions. In *Amalgamated Food Employees Union v. Logan Valley Plaza*[17] a majority of the justices held that striking laborers had a right to enter a private shopping area to picket a store with which they were having a labor dispute. The majority found that the shopping center was the functional equivalent of

12. 326 U.S. at 509.

13. 382 U.S. 296 (1966).

14. Brown v. Board of Education, 349 U.S. 294 (1955).

15. Evans v. Newton, 382 U.S. at 301–2.

16. Evans v. Abney, 396 U.S. 435 (1970).

17. Amalgamated Food Employees Union v. Logan Valley Plaza, 391 U.S. 308 (1968).

the company town involved in the *Marsh* case [18] so that no further contact between the state and the shopping center owners was necessary to establish the applicability of the first amendment. Only a few years later the Court was confronted with a case involving antiwar demonstrators who wished to enter a private shopping center mall to distribute leaflets to patrons of the center. Here the Court found that there was no first amendment right to engage in speech on privately owned property where that speech did not relate to the activities of the store owners on the property.[19] The majority opinion by Justice Powell attempted to distinguish the *Amalgamated Food Employees* case on the basis that the labor picketing had involved speech which was directly related to activities on the shopping center. However, the opinion was not clear as to why a difference in the content of the speech changed the determination of whether there was sufficient state action to invoke the protections of the first amendment. This uncertainty was clarified in *Hudgens v. National Labor Relations Board* [20] when the Court simply held that the first amendment did not apply to privately owned shopping centers and overruled the *Amalgamated Food Employees* decision. The final position of the Court was that the operation of a shopping center which was not part of a privately owned town did not involve the assumption of a public function by private persons. So long as the state did not aid, command or encourage the suppression of free speech the first amendment would not be violated by the actions of the shopping center owners.

The majority held that the right to private property encompassed the right to exclude others in this manner. Only when the property was used as a city did it lose its private character. Thus, there would have to be some additional state involvement to establish state action.[21]

The Supreme Court restricted scope of public function analysis in *Jackson v. Metropolitan Edison Co.*[22] This case concerned the activity of a privately owned electric utility and the applicability of the due process clause to its termination of services for individual customers. In this case a woman had her electrical service terminated without a final hearing to determine the status of her account with the company. She asserted that the utility company was required to give her notice and a hearing in the same manner as would a governmental agency which would terminate state benefits to her. The Court found no state action involved in the operation of this utility even though it was given virtually a monopoly status and licensed by the state.[23] The opinion found that there were insufficient contacts between the utility and the state to justify restricting its activities by constitutional limitation. As to the public function claim, the majority held that the fact that a state could have operated its own utilities did not make the activity of providing electric service a public function. Nor was the fact that these types of businesses might have a peculiar "public interest" enough to establish that the state was under an obligation to restrict them in conformity with constitutional guarantees.

---

18. Marsh v. Alabama, 326 U.S. 501 (1946).

19. Lloyd Corp. v. Tanner, 407 U.S. 551 (1972).

20. Hudgens v. NLRB, 424 U.S. 507 (1976).

21. In PruneYard Shopping Center v. Robins, 447 U.S. 74 (1980), the Supreme Court held that its ruling in the *Hudgens* case did not preclude a state from granting protection to speech and associational activities at privately owned shopping centers. In *PruneYard Shopping Center* the United States Supreme Court affirmed a decision of the California Supreme Court holding that the California state constitution prohibited the use of trespass laws by shopping center owners to exclude peaceful distribution of literature and petitions on the mall area of a shopping

center. The United States Supreme Court found that the state ruling did not constitute a taking of property from the shopping center owner; the state was free to expand its protection of civil liberties under its own constitution.

22. Jackson v. Metropolitan Edison Co., 419 U.S. 345 (1974).

23. The Supreme Court later held that utility companies that are operated by government agencies are required to provide their customers with fair notice and billing review procedures prior to termination of service if state law provides for such termination only "for cause." Memphis Light, Gas, and Water Division v. Craft, 436 U.S. 1 (1978).

The majority opinion in *Jackson* indicated that only those activities which were traditionally reserved to state authority or commonly associated with state sovereignty would be considered public functions. Thus, it would appear that few public functions will be found beyond those most essential services which are provided by governments and which have no direct counterpart in the private sector. The electoral system and the operation of towns will constitute such functions while traditional business activities such as the operation of utilities or other regulated industries will not. A majority of the current justices appear to believe that no private sector agency should be subjected to constitutional limitation of its autonomy unless it performs a delegated governmental function, or is taking actions under the direction of state authorities.[24]

A majority of the justices continued to employ restrictive definition of public functions as they approved a state law that allowed warehousemen to sell the property of their debtors. In *Flagg Brothers, Inc. v. Brooks*[25] the Supreme Court held that there was no state action in the sale of a debtor's goods by a warehouseman who had the goods in his possession and who had a lien on the goods for unpaid storage charges.[26] This was true even though a state law, patterned after the Uniform Commercial Code, authorized such sales under certain circumstances. The majority opinion refused to examine whether the procedure specified in the law, or the actions of the warehousemen, violated the due process clause, because this "private" activity of the warehousemen was not subject to the restraints of the fourteenth amendment. The majority opinion, by Justice Rehnquist, held that dispute resolution between debtors and creditors was not a public function so as to subject the debt collection practices of the creditor-warehouseman to constitutional constraints. Justice Rehnquist found that the two activities that the Court clearly has held to be public functions—operating towns and running elections—were undertaken by governmental entities to the exclusion of private actors.[27] The majority believed that the fact that an activity was traditionally within the province of government did not make it a public function; such functions exist only when there is a history of exclusive government activity of the type at issue. This use of the exclusivity concept is consistent with recent state action decisions. However, the opinion left the concept of state action more unclear than ever. The majority opinion stated that the decision in *Flagg Brothers* did not affect prior rulings concerning the existence of state action in programs providing incidental aid to segregated schools.[28] Justice Rehnquist noted that activities such as "education, fire and police protection, and tax collection" might constitute public functions, although his opinion did not resolve

---

24. The Court refused to impose due process limitations on the ability of a private school to discharge teachers or a private nursing home to discharge patients. In Rendell-Baker v. Kohn, 102 S.Ct. 2764 (1982) the Court found that a private school whose primary business was teaching students with educational or behavioral problems, and which received most of its funding from state sources, did not exercise state action when it discharged members of its staff. In Blum v. Yaretsky, 102 S.Ct. 2777 (1982) the Court held that a nursing home did not exercise state action when it discharged or transferred patients, even though the home and the patients received state funds.

25. 436 U.S. 149 (1978).

26. The charges resulted from the city marshall's arrangement for placement of Ms. Brooks household furnishings into the possession of a moving and storage company, Flagg Bros., following the eviction of

Ms. Brooks and her family from her apartment in Mount Vernon, N. Y., 436 U.S. at 153. After a series of disputes between Ms. Brooks and Flagg Bros. concerning the amount of the moving and storage bill, Flagg Bros. threatened to sell her property pursuant to the New York Uniform Commercial Code § 7–210.

An almost identical situation involved a dispute between Ms. Jones and Flagg Bros. concerning the charges from storing her goods following her eviction from another Mount Vernon apartment. Ms. Jones paid her bill under threat of a sale. Id. at 154 n. 2, n. 3.

27. Flagg Bros., Inc. v. Brooks, 436 U.S. 149, 159, 160 (1978) [the portion of the opinion holding that there was no state encouragement of the sale is noted in Section III of this Chapter.]

28. 436 U.S. at 163.

these issues.[29] Indeed, the majority refused to rule that private control of debtor-creditor disputes could never constitute a public function or state action. "This is not to say that dispute resolution between creditors and debtors involves a category of human affairs that is never subject to constitutional constraints. We merely address the public function doctrine as respondents would apply it in this case."[30] Thus, the opinion leaves lower courts without a clear basis for distinguishing those activities which cannot be deemed public functions because they have not been considered to be the exclusive domain of government from those activities that might be held to involve state action even absent positive acts of the state involving it in the disputed activity.

So long as the Supreme Court continues to employ a formal test for determining the presence of state action in a private person's activity, the opinions on public function concepts will never be more precise than Justice Rehnquist's majority opinion in *Flagg Brothers*. In an incisive dissent, Justice Stevens noted the inconsistency of the majority defining public functions in terms of a formal test for exclusivity while simultaneously admitting that some nonexclusive activities might be restrained by the Constitution.[31] Justice Stevens went to the heart of the issue when he stated his belief that the power to order a resolution of debtor-creditor conflicts was precisely the type of power that involved the values of the due process clause.[32] He noted the danger of using a formal test for state action and that the majority's test logically should allow states to "recognize" the ability of a physically stronger disputant to take the property of

the weaker person.[33] Justice Stevens noted that the line between public and private actions was not a clear one; he would have based the state action on the relevance of the constitutional value to the "private" activity.[34]

The majority opinion in *Flagg Brothers* asserted that: "Unlike the parade of horribles suggested by our Brother Stevens in dissent, this case does not involve state authorization of private breach of the peace."[35] But, surely, this does not answer the Stevens dissent. A state statute that "recognized" a right of the strong to take the property of the weak would not "encourage" their activity anymore than the warehouseman statute encouraged sales without specific procedural protections. The real difference between permitting the warehouseman's lien sale and legitimizing the forceful taking of property by physically strong creditors, or their employees, lies in the differing potential for creditor abuse of each practice and the differing value of the debtor's interest in avoiding lien sales or avoiding loss of his property to stronger persons. But the majority's continued rejection of any "balancing" test in this area leaves them with no understandable basis for their distinctions between specific types of "private" and "state" actions.[36]

The difficulty of predicting the outcome of state action cases while the Supreme Court clings to its formal method of state action analysis is demonstrated by *Lugar v. Edmonson Oil Company*.[37] In *Lugar* the Supreme Court ruled that a debtor could challenge, as a violation of due process, the state procedure by which a creditor secured a pretrial writ of attachment against his property

---

29. 436 U.S. at 163–164.

30. 436 U.S. at 162, n. 12.

31. Flagg Bros., Inc. v. Brooks, 436 U.S. 149, 173 n. 10 (1978) (Stevens, J., dissenting, joined by White & Marshall, JJ.) (Justice Brennan did not participate in the decision).

32. 436 U.S. at 174–179 (Stevens, J., dissenting).

33. 436 U.S. at 170 (Stevens, J., dissenting).

34. 436 U.S. at 178 (Stevens, J., dissenting). As to the lack of a basis for formal distinctions between pub-

lic and private activity, Justice Stevens cited, inter alia, the article upon which Section V of this Chapter is based. 436 U.S. at 178 n. 16.

35. Flagg Bros., Inc. v. Brooks, 436 U.S. 149, 160 n. 9 (1978).

36. For an alternative to formal tests for state action, Section V of this Chapter.

37. 102 S.Ct. 2744 (1982).

based upon the creditor's ex parte petition. The involvement of the state judicial system in the issuance of the writ, and the involvement of the county sheriff in the execution of the writ, distinguished the *Lugar* case from the *Flagg Brothers* creditor "self help" decision. Thus the debtor in *Lugar* could challenge the debt collection system whereas the debtor in *Flagg Brothers* could not.[38]

III. STATE COMMANDMENT OR ENCOURAGEMENT OF PRIVATE ACTIVITIES

In other than the public function cases, the determination of state action is based on the relationship between government and the activities of the alleged wrongdoer. There is no formal test for the amount of contacts with government which will subject a private person's activities to the restrictions of the Constitution. The one constant factor in the cases is the justices' unwillingness to commit to any such test. The Court has stressed continually that it must determine on a case by case basis whether there is state action present by "sifting facts and weighing circumstances." [1] However, it is possible to isolate certain factors which have caused the Court to make a determination of state action in a particular activity.

One category of cases are those where the aggrieved party claims that the wrongdoer has been commanded or encouraged by government to engage in the activity which has harmed the aggrieved party. In these cases the Court determines whether there is a sufficient nexus between the wrongdoer and the government by assessing the degree to which the government has commanded, encouraged or otherwise directed the complained of activity. Obviously the forms of state commandment or encouragement vary depending on the type of governmental entity which is alleged to have brought about

the complained of activity. We will now examine the cases as they relate to encouragement of otherwise private activity by the legislative, executive and judicial branches of government. Finally, we will note the effect of local customs in establishing and encouraging a practice.

Cases in which alleged wrongful activity is said to have a connection to state legislation present the widest scope of factual situations. In later sections we will examine variations of these problems based upon the legislative granting of funds or special privileges to persons or entities which are alleged to have violated constitutional provisions. Our concern for the moment rests with legislation which commands or encourages a specific result which is alleged to violate the Constitution. When state legislation commands a certain activity, or officially recognizes its legitimacy, there is no question but that state action is present whenever someone follows the guidelines of the statute. In such a situation the challenged activity must be taken to exist because the state legislature has commanded its occurrence and continuation. For example, if a state legislature commands that restaurants serve food on a racially segregated basis it is clear that the action of restaurant owners who discriminate between their patrons on the basis of race will constitute state action.[2] Similarly state legislation may encourage an activity so as to give rise to state action in the activities of private persons. For example, state action will be found in a restaurant's racially restrictive practices where state legislation requires that restaurants serving members of minority races have separate toilet facilities for those persons.[3] The restaurant owner who refuses to serve members of a racial minority is restricted by constitutional provision because that decision must be held to be the

---

38. The distinction between *Lugar* and *Flagg* rests on the Court's recognition of state action when private parties act in concert with government officials. See Section III of this Chapter.

1. Burton v. Wilmington Parking Authority, 365 U.S. 715, 722 (1961).

2. Peterson v. City of Greenville, 373 U.S. 244 (1963).

3. Robinson v. Florida, 378 U.S. 153 (1964).

result of the state legislation. To hold otherwise would allow the state to have helped establish or continue a practice without any effective remedy.

The state may also command or encourage the continuation of the alleged wrongdoing through its executive officers or agencies. Again the reason for this rule is that the alleged wrongdoing appears to be connected to activities of the state in such a way that it can be said to be the denial of rights by the state itself. How much encouragement or positive action by executive officials is necessary to invoke constitutional restrictions is, to say the least, unclear. It would appear that any significant encouragement of alleged wrongdoers to impair important rights of the aggrieved parties will be sufficient. Even though the complained of practice may not have resulted from the encouragement, the actions of the private wrongdoer will be subjected to constitutional limitations. For example, in *Lombard v. Louisiana* [4] the Supreme Court reversed the trespass convictions of sit-in demonstrators because the city officials, prior to the demonstration, had condemned sit-ins and stated that the city was prepared to enforce the law. These statements were taken to be official encouragement of store owners to use the state trespass laws in a discriminatory manner. However, it was not at all clear in this case whether the store owners had refused to serve the demonstrators or called the police because of the actions of the officials.

Even very strong encouragement by state officials might not result in a finding of state action where the challenged activities of private persons were themselves worthy of some constitutional deference. For example, assume that a mayor and sheriff encouraged the citizens of their town who were of a majority race to refuse to invite members of a racial minority to dinner. It would seem highly unlikely that the Supreme Court would find sufficient state action in members of the majority race refusing to invite minorities to their private dinner parties. The importance of private property and associational rights here would seem to require that no state action be found unless the racially discriminatory dinner invitations were solely the product of the official encouragement.

Even the judiciary may imbue the actions of private individuals with state action. When judges command private persons to take specific actions which would violate the Constitution if done by the State, state action will be present in the resulting harm to constitutionally recognized rights. The classic example of such a situation appeared in *Shelley v. Kraemer.* [5] In this case a white property owner attempted to sell his property to a member of a racial minority. This land was subject to a covenant which forbade sales to racial minorities; those persons with an interest in the restrictive covenant sued to restrain the current owner from violating the covenant by selling to a black. The Supreme Court held that any court order which would enjoin the sale and enforce the covenant would violate the fourteenth amendment; the state court order would be a judicial command to the current owner—who is willing to sell to an equally willing buyer—to make a racial distinction in the sale of property. Such a command, interfering with a willing seller and a willing buyer, violates the amendment. [6]

4. Lombard v. Louisiana, 373 U.S. 267 (1963).

5. 334 U.S. 1 (1948). Cf. Gandolfo v. Hartman, 49 F. 181 (S.D.Cal.1892). See generally, VanAlstyne, Mr. Justice Black, Constitutional Review, and the Talisman of State Action, 1965 Duke L.J. 219, 241–45.

6. See, Pollak, Racial Discrimination and Judicial Integrity: A Reply to Professor Wechsler, 108 U.Pa.L. Rev. 1, 13 (1959):

"The line sought to be drawn is that beyond which the state assists a private person in seeing to it that others behave in a fashion which the state could not itself have ordained. . . .

"[Thus] an employer may freely contract with a union to maintain a lily-white shop, but that the provision is one which fails whenever the employer's self-interest so dictates: the union cannot coerce compliance through an injunction or an award for damages."

In a later case the Court also held that a white property owner who sold land to a member of a minority race could not be subjected to monetary damages for the breach of a racially restrictive covenant.[7] While this damage suit would not involve a formal judicial order to discriminate on the basis of race it would be a state imposed penalty for refusal to discriminate. Such a state penalty is the functional equivalent of a command or encouragement to refuse to sell property to members of minority races. The judicial encouragement of racial discrimination is the state action which violates the fourteenth amendment.

The *Shelley* decision should not be taken as holding that any judicial decree which disadvantages members of a racial minority violates the fourteenth amendment. A court can uphold trespass convictions which are based on a private party's decision to refuse to open their home or other private property to members of a racial minority. If a home owner refuses to allow persons into his home because of their race he is allowed to have that decision enforced by law enforcement officials and use of the trespass laws. In such a situation neither executive nor judicial action has prompted or required his decision to refuse to allow minority members onto his private property. As exclusivity is an attribute of private property, the owner may use the trespass laws to enforce his decision so long as he has no other connection to state action.

A court may enforce racially neutral principles of property law even though a contrary ruling would be helpful to some members of a minority race. In *Evans v. Abney*[8] the Court allowed land to revert to the heirs of Senator Bacon who had made a bequest of the land for the establishment of a public park that would be closed to members of racial minorities. While the city and the trustees were not allowed to conduct a racially restricted admissions policy for the park, the reverter of land to the heirs of the testator did not involve any continuing discrimination against black persons. Thus the application of the rules relating to failure of trust purpose and the reversion of land to a testator's heirs could be followed in this case. Note that this would not be true of a condition (or reverter clause) which would divest a property owner of the title to his property if he attempted to sell it to black persons. Such a clause would be the equivalent of monetary damages for failure to follow a restrictive covenant. When *Evans v. Newton*[9] and *Evans v. Abney* are read together it can be seen that the Court merely invalidated trusts for racially restrictive purposes which involved the activities of government or public functions.[10] Where grantors or testators attempt to establish such trusts in the future those provisions will be invalid *ab initio*. For already existing trusts of this type, such as the Macon Georgia park, the Court will declare an end to the discriminatory practices. The reverter in such a case will shift the use without penalizing those who would use land for racially neutral practices and without encouraging racial discrimination in the future.

Some justices have taken the position that customs which had become so strong as to have the force of law might establish state action. For example, in a town with a

7.   Barrows v. Jackson, 346 U.S. 249 (1953).

8.   396 U.S. 435 (1970).

9.   382 U.S. 296 (1966).

10.   The Court has not passed on the validity of operating private trusts for allegedly unconstitutional purposes apart from those in which there was a finding of government involvement or a public function. In Pennsylvania v. Board of Trustees, 353 U.S. 230 (1957) (per curiam) the Court found state involvement for a private trust to run a school for orphans on a racially restricted basis. Yet the Court refused to reconsider the legality of the school after both a finding by the

state courts that private trustees could continue the school and a decision by a federal court that the substitution of trustees and continued operation of the school involved unconstitutional state action. In Re Girard College Trusteeship, 391 Pa. 434, 138 A.2d 844 (1958), appeal dismissed and cert. denied 357 U.S. 570 (1958) (per curiam); Pennsylvania v. Brown, 392 F.2d 120 (3d Cir. 1968), cert. denied 391 U.S. 921 (1968). This problem is unlikely to rise again due to the Court's ruling on the scope of statutes passed pursuant to the thirteenth amendment, see section IV, C of this Chapter concerning government subsidies and Chapter 17, concerning the scope of congressional power.

strong custom of refusing to serve Blacks in public facilities, a shop owner's refusal to serve Blacks might be found to be the equivalent of state action violating the fourteenth amendment. However, a majority of the justices have never held that custom alone would be sufficient to turn private activities into state action. The Supreme Court avoided a decision on this issue in *Bell v. Maryland* [11] where a business owner refused to serve members of a minority race and had those persons prosecuted for trespass when they refused to leave his establishment. The Court as a whole avoided ruling on the merits by vacating the conviction and remanding the conviction for reconsideration in light of a new state law. An opinion by Justice Douglas, representing the views of three justices, would have prohibited the discrimination by the restaurant owner because of the local custom of refusing to serve Blacks. Justice Douglas indicated that he would not take such a position if the trespass conviction had related to the use of a private person's home,[12] but where property was used for a semi-public function Justice Douglas would subject the property owner's decisions to the restrictions of the fourteenth amendment. Justice Black, also representing two other justices, dissented and took a position opposite to Douglas.[13] He noted that any restriction of the property owners scope of decision making would go beyond all previous state action rulings. Justice Black indicated that private property rights should not be subjected to constitutional limitations absent some further connection to the government or its basic public functions.

A majority of the Court eventually followed Justice Black's position and refused to find that a private individual's or group's de-cision to exclude members of a racial minority constitutes state action violating the fourteenth amendment merely because it coincides with local custom. In *Moose Lodge Number 107 v. Irvis*[14] the Supreme Court held that there was insufficient state action connected with a private social club to review the club's racially restrictive policies. Because there was no official aid or encouragement of the club's decision to restrict its membership, it would not be subjected to constitutional restraint. It should be noted here that both the majority and dissenting opinions in *Moose Lodge* focused on whether any real harm was done to members of a minority race by the existence of the segregated club. It is possible that the real difference between those who would or would not subject the lodge to constitutional restraint relates to their view of whether or not any harm was done to members of the minority race by its policies. But the decision appears to rest on a quantitative view of the existence of state action in the club's decisions. Absent some entanglement with the government, the Court will not find state action on the basis of a club's historic practices or the customs which might have given rise to those practices.

The existence of a state law which recognizes the legitimacy of an action taken by an otherwise private person will not give rise to "state action" being present in the private activity. To imbue an activity with state action there must be some non-neutral involvement of the state with the activity.[15] Thus, the Supreme Court has held that a law which allowed a warehouseman to sell property of another against which he had a lien did not involve state action in the sale.[16] This was consistent with the Court's earlier decision that government approval of a pri-

---

11. 378 U.S. 226 (1964).

12. 378 U.S. at 253 (Douglas, J.)

13. 378 U.S. at 318 (Black, J., dissenting).

14. 407 U.S. 163 (1972). See also Section IV, infra.

15. In Martinez v. California, 444 U.S. 277 (1980), the Court held that a state parole board was not liable under federal civil rights acts for the death of a young girl killed by a parolee, five months after his release

because there was not state action connected to the death. This decision should not be understood as ruling that the decision of the parole board was not state action, but only that a parole board's failure to accurately assess the rehabilitation of prison inmates does not deprive other persons of any constitutionally protected interest, even if the parolee injures or kills those persons.

16. Flagg Bros., Inc. v. Brooks, 436 U.S. 149 (1978).

vately owned utility company's rate policies and collection practices did not establish state action in the termination of customer services without a prior hearing by the utility.[17] These situations should be distinguished from those involving the de facto authorization of activities by public officers. When a public officer takes acts relating to his office those actions should be considered to be "state action" even if they exceed the scope of the officer's authority under the law of that jurisdiction. Thus, the Court has held that law enforcement officers who beat a prisoner to death did so under "color of law." [18]

Those who conspire with a government official to take action that deprives others of federal constitutional rights do so "under color of law" and are subject to a federal lawsuit even though the official is immune from civil liability.[19] Similarly, when a private business hires an off duty police officer to act as a security guard, there is state action connected to his actions taken on behalf of the private business to the extent that he appears to the public to be exercising the authority of a police officer.[20] These cases on de facto authorization of public officials' actions should be unaffected by the decisions regarding state "recognition" of otherwise private actions. Were it not for state action, the public official would not have the opportunity to abuse his authority, nor would he be able to represent to the public that his actions were authorized by the government.

This fact distinguishes the de facto cases from the state recognition of many private "self-help" actions; the majority believes that self help remedies would exist to some extent even if the state never recognized or authorized those actions.[21]

The distinction between recognition of private action and governmental authorization of activities by public officers was demonstrated in two recent cases. In *Polk County v. Dodson*,[22] the Court held that a public defender does not act under color of state law when performing a lawyer's traditional functions as counsel to a defendant in a criminal proceeding. The public defender is serving an essentially private function, adversarial to and independent of the state.[23] She is not amenable to administrative direction in performing her duties for her client but is required to exercise her own independent judgment on behalf of the client.[24] However, the Court noted that a public defender making hiring and firing decisions on behalf of the state may be a state actor.[25]

The Supreme Court found that a private party was involved with state action in *Lugar v. Edmundson Oil Co., Inc.*[26] In *Lugar* an oil company sued an alleged debtor in Virginia state court and, pursuant to state law, obtained a prejudgment writ of attachment of some of the debtor's property. The prejudgment writ was executed by the county sheriff. In a 5 to 4 decision the Court held that the involvement of state officials in the prejudgment attachment process

---

17. Jackson v. Metropolitan Edison Co., 419 U.S. 345 (1974). The Court later held that similar customer service termination practices of government operated utility companies violated the due process clause. Memphis Light, Gas, and Water Division v. Craft, 436 U.S. 1 (1978).

18. Screws v. United States, 325 U.S. 91 (1945) (interpreting and applying Congressional Act passed in pursuance of section 5 of the fourteenth amendment that used the phrase "under color of any law".)

19. See Dennis v. Sparks, 449 U.S. 24 (1980) (those conspiring with a state judge to issue an illegal order were acting under color of law even though the judge was immune from liability.)

20. Griffin v. Maryland, 378 U.S. 130 (1964).

21. Thus, the majority opinion in *Flagg Brothers*, which upheld the warehouseman's sale, indicated that

the de facto authorization cases were correct but it did so by finding that Griffin v. Maryland (referred to in note 20, supra) was based on the finding that the police officer security guard "purported to exercise the authority of a deputy sheriff." Flagg Bros., Inc. v. Brooks, 436 U.S. 149, 163 n. 14 (1978), quoting Griffin v. Maryland, 378 U.S. 130, 135 (1964).

22. 454 U.S. 312 (1981).

23. 454 U.S. at 318.

24. 454 U.S. at 320.

25. 454 U.S. at 324 citing Branti v. Finkel, 445 U.S. 507 (1980) (which held that the discharge of assistant public defenders was subject to first amendment limitations).

26. 102 S.Ct. 2744 (1982).

provided a state action basis for the debtor's claim that he had been deprived of property without due process.[27] The Court set forth a two part test to determine if deprivation of a federal right may be fairly attributed to the state. "First, the deprivation must be caused by the exercise of some right or privilege created by the state, or by a rule of conduct imposed by the state, or by a person for whom the state is responsible . . . Second, the party charged with the deprivation must be a person who may fairly be said to be a state actor [either] because he is a state official, or because he has acted together with or has obtained significant aid from state officials, or because his conduct is otherwise chargeable to the state."[28] This two part was satisfied in *Lugar*. While the oil company's private misuse of a state statute could not be attributed to the state, the procedural scheme created by the statute was a product of state action. Second, the ex parte application of the oil company resulting in attachment of the property by the sheriff made the oil company a joint participant with state officials in the seizure of the property. The second factor differentiates *Lugar* from *Flagg Brothers, Inc. v. Brooks*, according to a majority of the justices. The debtor in *Lugar* was allowed to challenge the constitutionality of the state system of issuing prejudgment attachments because it involved judicial and executive officers of the state. The debtor could not challenge the decision of the creditor to employ the state statutory procedure as that was a decision of a private sector entity

which was not commanded or encouraged by the government.[29]

IV. MUTUAL CONTACTS—LICENSING, SYMBIOTIC RELATIONSHIPS, SUBSIDIES, AND OTHER ENTANGLEMENTS

The remaining cases concerning the existence of state action relate to the number or type of contacts between government and the challenged practices or the alleged wrongdoer. Most decisions ordinarily included in this category actually focus on the granting of direct aid to the alleged wrongdoer, the government encouragement or ordering of the specific activities, or the delegation of public functions.

In a few cases the Court has found state action in an alleged wrongful practice simply on the basis of the entanglement between the government and private practice, but no specific test has emerged from these cases.[1] The decisions merely hold that, on the facts presented by the individual case, the private wrongdoer should be subjected to constitutional restraints because of his relationship to government. It might be said that where there are sufficient contacts between a private individual and the government, then that the private individual takes on at least the appearance if not the actual authority of the state. Where the actions provide some tangible aid to both the alleged wrongdoer and the government, the two have come to be in a type of "symbiotic relationship." In such a situation the state and private individual have in effect become joint venturers

---

27. The Court held that if the challenged conduct constitutes state action, that conduct is also action "under color of state law" and will support a suit under 42 U.S.C.A. § 1983, although all conduct satisfying the "under color of law" requirement may not meet the fourteenth amendment requirement of state action. 102 S.Ct. at 2753.

"The ultimate issue in determining whether a person is subject to suit under § 1983 is the same question posed in cases arising under the Fourteenth Amendment: is the alleged infringement of federal rights fairly attributable to the state?" Rendell-Baker v. Kohn, 102 S.Ct. 2764, 2770 (1982) citing Lugar v. Edmundson Oil, 102 S.Ct. 2744, 2754 (1982).

28. 102 S.Ct. at 2754.

29. 102 S.Ct. at 2757.

1. Several of these cases were examined in Section III under the heading "State Commandment or Encouragement of Private Activities." Because the Supreme Court refuses to categorize its state action decisions, or even identify specific state action tests, there is necessary overlap between the sections of this chapter. Thus, cases involving actions undertaken by private persons acting in concert with government employees were examined in Section III but those cases could have been labeled "mutual contacts" cases and included in this section. The reader is encouraged to consider each decision examined in this section against the backdrop of all theories of state action examined in this Chapter.

even though they do not have any formalized agreements. Here the alleged wrongdoer's beneficial ties to the state justify subjecting his activities to constitutional limitations.

Cases involving determinations of state action based on the relationship between the private actor and government have fallen into three general categories. First, cases where the private actor is subjected to extensive regulation by the government. Second, cases involving a wide range of physical and economic contacts between the actor and government. Third, cases where the government has provided some sort of direct aid or subsidy to the private actor.

A. Licensing and Regulation

The fact that an otherwise private actor is regulated or licensed by a government agency will not make all of the actions of that person or business equivalent to actions of the government itself. The degree of entanglement between the government and a regulated industry is not an irrelevant fact. It may be easier to find state action in the business practices of a regulated entity than it would be of one with no formal contacts to the government. Indeed it appeared for some time that the Court might subject some businesses to constitutional restraints merely because they received an important license from the state or because their business activities were extensively regulated.

Such a position was not without some merit, for government licensing or regulation may give the appearance of an approval of the challenged action. However, the Supreme Court has refused to subject licensed entities or individuals to constitutional restraints merely because some of their activities or policies are regulated by the government. However, if the government regulation had directly approved the challenged practice of the alleged wrongdoer there is state action intertwined with that practice. This principle involves no more than the application of the "government encouragement" basis for finding state action discussed in the preceding section. When government commands, encourages, or actively approves a practice, that practice is subject to constitutional limitation. Where the government has not specifically approved the alleged wrongful activity the degree of regulation of the actor is only one factor to consider when assessing the presence of state action in the challenged activity.[2]

There are four cases which are of special significance to the state regulation or licensing theory for finding state action. *Public Utilities Commission v. Pollak*[3] involved a challenge to transit company's practice of broadcasting radio programs in its buses and street cars. The company was licensed to operate the buses in Washington, D.C., and, in the course of reviewing its activities, the Supreme Court seemed to find that the

---

2. In decisions rendered in the 1981–82 term, the Supreme Court continued to employ this method of analysis and refused to impose constitutional limitations on the autonomy of private sector actors when the justices found no specific government encouragement of the activity challenged as violating an individual's constitutional rights.

In Blum v. Yaretsky, 102 S.Ct. 2777 (1982) the Supreme Court rejected the argument that regulations imposing a range of penalties on nursing homes that fail to discharge or transfer patients whose continued stay is medically inappropriate dictate the decisions to discharge or transfer patients. Physicians make the decisions as to if a patient's care is medically necessary and those decisions ultimately turn on medical judgments made by private parties according to professional standards that are not established by the State. Adjustment in Medicaid benefit levels by the State in response to the discharge or transfer of a patient does

not constitute approval or enforcement of that decision. For these reasons the Court refused to find state action in the discharge or transfer of patients; its decision left these nursing home patients without any due process right to a hearing concerning their discharge.

In Rendell-Baker v. Kohn, 102 S.Ct. 2764 (1982). The Court held that although the state extensively regulated a private school for maladjusted students, the school's decisions to discharge several teachers were not compelled or even influenced by state regulations. The government regulation of the school's educational practices and funding of students attending the school were held to be unrelated to the private school's employment practices. Thus, the Court refused to find that the school's teachers had any due process right to a fair process regarding their discharge.

3. 343 U.S. 451 (1952).

government's regulation of the company made it subject to constitutional restraints. However, the decision was unclear, as the Court held that the activity was compatible with the Constitution even if it constituted governmental action. The majority opinion may have only assumed *arguendo*, the presence of state action in the practices of a regulated industry.[4] Twenty years passed before the Court again specifically considered whether state regulations or licensing gave rise to the state action.

In *Moose Lodge Number 107 v. Irvis*[5] the Court held that the activities of a private club were not subjected to constitutional restraint merely because it was given a liquor license by the city government. Although the granting of the license subjected the club to extensive regulation there was, the Court said, no involvement of the city with the club's racially discriminatory policies. Additionally, the action of granting the license to the racially discriminatory club did not appear to burden anyone's ability to receive alcoholic beverages, although the total number of liquor licenses that could be granted was fixed by law. The majority opinion found no state action which encouraged the racially restrictive practices of the club or caused any detriment to members of minority races.

The Supreme Court next concluded that the T.V. and radio stations were not subjected to the restraints of the first amendment because of their licensing and regulation by the federal government. In *Columbia Broadcasting System v. Democratic National Committee*[6] antiwar groups challenged an individual station's refusals to accept editorial advertising as violative of the first amendment. There was no majority opinion concerning the presence of government action in the activities of radio and television stations, as several of the justices believed that the refusal to accept editorial advertising was permissible even if it represented government action. However, three of the justices indicated that there was no government action connected to the refusal, since the federal regulation of stations did not encourage or approve the challenged practice.[7] But the issue was left unclear as only two justices found government action connected to these refusals which would violate the first amendment.[8] The remaining justices could assume the presence of some government action as they felt that allowing individual stations this editorial freedom did not violate the first amendment.[9]

The Supreme Court finally held that extensive regulation of a business would not in itself subject all of its activities to constitutional restraint. In *Jackson v. Metropolitan Edison Co.*[10] the majority held that the actions of a public utility did not involve sufficient state action to subject it to constitutional restraint on the basis of its monopoly status and government regulation. In this case an electric company terminated service to a customer without having a final hearing to determine the status of the account or the customer's willingness to pay new charges. The Court did not decide whether the customer would have been entitled to a hearing had the utility been a part of the governmental structure. Instead, a majority of the justices held that the termination of service by the utility would not be subject to constitutional review as it did not constitute state action. The majority found that the government licensing and regulation of the utility neither commanded, encouraged, nor sanctioned the termination practices of the company.[11] Even assuming the grant of a monopoly status to the utility company, the state had not been connected to the chal-

---

4. This point was emphasized in Jackson v. Metropolitan Edison Co., 419 U.S. 345, 356 n. 16 (1974).

5. 407 U.S. 163 (1972).

6. C.B.S. v. Democratic Nat. Committee, 412 U.S. 94 (1973).

7. 412 U.S. at 114–121, (Burger, C.J., joined by Stewart and Rehnquist, JJ.).

8. 412 U.S. at 172–181, (Brennan, J., dissenting, joined by Marshall, J.).

9. 412 U.S. at 147 (White, J., concurring); 412 U.S. at 148 (Blackmun, J., concurring, joined by Powell, J.).

10. 419 U.S. 345 (1974).

11. 419 U.S. at 356–59.

lenged practice. While the regulation and licensing disclosed certain continuing relationships between the company and the government, those relationships had nothing to do with the challenged activity in the view of the majority. Nor could the government and the utility be seen as joint venturers so that the utility could be subjected to constitutional restraint because of its "symbiotic relationship" to the government. Finally, the majority found that the provision of utility services did not constitute a "public function" as this did not relate to a sovereign function even though the state could operate a utility company.

B. Multiple Contacts—Symbiotic Relationships

In many situations an alleged wrongdoer appears to have a variety of physical and economic contacts to the government even though it is not an agent of the government or part of a regulated industry. These multiple or joint contacts may so intertwine the private actor and the government that the private actor will be treated as a government agent. Of course, if the private actor was the agent or business partner of the government it would be subjected to constitutional restraints. However, even though there is no partnership these contacts may give the appearance of government action. Where the private actor and government can be said to be in a "symbiotic relationship", the private actor will be subject to constitutional restraints. This category is, in reality, a "catch all" which may have little, if any, substantive meaning. All that can be said with certainty is that some otherwise private actors have been found to have sufficient state action to subject them to constitutional restraints even though no single fac-

tor indicated that the government was responsible for their activities. In these cases a majority of the justices simply found sufficient connections to hold the actor constitutionally accountable by "sifting the facts and weighing the circumstances." [12] Thus it may be said that when a private individual becomes so entangled with government policies that his actions appear to have the authorization of the state, it is likely that a majority of the justices on the Supreme Court will find state action in his activities. During the past decade three cases have focused on these types of generalized relationships to establish state action.

In *Evans v. Newton* [13] the Supreme Court determined that the continued existence of a racially segregated park devised by Senator Bacon to the town of Macon, Georgia violated the fourteenth amendment. This park had been given to the city on the basis that it would serve only white persons and city trustees in fact had operated the park in a segregated manner. Once it was apparent that the public park would have to be integrated, the city moved to have the public trustees replaced by private persons. However, even after the attempt to substitute private trustees, the city appeared to provide some services for the maintenance of the park's facilities. The Supreme Court held that the park was so imbued with state action that even the private trustees could not run the park on a segregated basis. This decision was based on a number of factors such as the appearance of government approval of the restricted practices, the past and present aid given to the running of the park, and the public nature of land used as a park within a city. Since the city and the park had been so intertwined, the operation of the park could not be considered truly pri-

---

12. Burton v. Wilmington Parking Authority, 365 U.S. 715, 722 (1961).

The decisions examined in each section of this Chapter should not be viewed in isolation. Thus the "symbiotic relationship" cases must be compared to the "government subsidies" decisions examined in the next subsection of this Chapter. The Supreme Court rejected the argument that a symbiotic relationship existed between a private school and the state in Rendell-

Baker v. Kohn, 102 S.Ct. 2764 (1982). Although the school derived its income primarily from public sources and was extensively regulated by public authorities, the Court viewed the school's fiscal relationship with the state as ". . . not different from that of many contractors performing services for the government." 102 S.Ct. at 2772.

13. 382 U.S. 296 (1966).

vate or beyond the reach of the Constitution. It should be noted that following this decision the Georgia courts held that the land reverted to the heirs of Senator Bacon as the trust failed when the racially restrictive conditions could not be fulfilled; this action was affirmed by the Supreme Court.[14] The Supreme Court allowed the land to revert because there would be no continuing contact between the government and the future use of the property so long as its use as a public park was terminated and the government did not encourage its use in a segregated manner.

The classic "joint contact—symbiotic relationship" case is *Burton v. Wilmington Parking Authority*.[15] In this decision the Court held that a privately owned restaurant which leased space in a government parking facility could not refuse service to members of racial minorities. While the restaurant did not receive any direct aid from the government it benefited from its location within the government facility. While there was no command or encouragement of its racially restrictive practices by the government, its location and status as a lessee of the government gave the appearance of government authorization of the practices. While the government and restaurant could not be termed joint venturers, they were in a "symbiotic relationship". The restaurant benefited from its location in the government facility and patronage by government workers. And to the extent the restaurant made improvements to the realty, it enjoyed the parking authority's tax exemption. The government benefited from convenience for its employees as well as the rental monies received. Although there was no single factor which indicated the presence of state action in the challenged practices, a majority of the justices felt that the totality of the circumstances showed sufficient contacts to the government to subject the restaurant's activities to constitutional restraint. When

the activities of the government and the private actor became so intertwined for their mutual benefit, the private party has no basis for complaint when his decisions are subjected to constitutional limitations in the same manner as those of the government.

The Supreme Court's decision in *Reitman v. Mulkey*[16] was the last of its generalized findings of state action. This case involved an amendment to the constitution of the state of California which repealed open housing legislation and prevented the passage of similar legislation. A majority of the justices on the Supreme Court of the United States held that this state amendment would constitute state action connected to racially discriminatory housing and land transactions so as to violate the fourteenth amendment. In traditional state action terms it would seem that the amendment was invalid because it encouraged racial bias in land transactions. However the refusal to outlaw private discrimination on the basis of race in real estate activities cannot be taken as the encouragement of such activity. Such a position would mean that the state could never repeal legislation that protected rights which have a constitutional basis. Indeed, the majority noted that it only engaged in such an assumption because the Supreme Court of California had held that in fact the amendment would cause increased discriminatory practices. A stronger rationale for *Reitman* was provided by Professor Charles Black who took the position that the same judgment could be reached without having to assume a hypothetical encouragement of racially restrictive land transactions resulting from the state amendment.[17] He noted that the ultimate effect of California's constitutional provision was to establish a legal impediment to minority access to legislative remedies for their problems in the real estate market. Thus the amendment could be considered the direct activity of a state to create a "super-majority" requirement for

---

14. Evans v. Abney, 396 U.S. 435 (1970), aff'g 224 Ga. 826, 165 S.E.2d 160 (1968). See Section III, supra, for a discussion of this issue.

15. 365 U.S. 715 (1961).

16. 387 U.S. 369 (1967).

17. Black, "State Action", Equal Protection, and California's Proposition 14, 81 Harv.L.Rev. 69 (1967).

the passage of laws which would assist racial minorities. Before a city or the state could enact open housing legislation, the state constitution would have to be amended. So viewed the state amendment would directly violate the fourteenth amendment because it restricted access to legislative remedies based on the race of those seeking legislative action.[18]

C. Government Subsidies or Aid

The final set of joint contact cases involves public funding or other direct aid to persons who are alleged to violate the Constitution. In these cases the government is giving direct aid to a person whose activities would be held to violate the Constitution if they were engaged in by the government itself. Two separate questions arise in such cases. First, does the granting of aid to a private party subject that person's activities to constitutional review? Second, even if the private activities are not subject to constitutional limitation may the government continue to grant the private wrongdoer a subsidy? For example, assume that an otherwise private school which discriminated on the basis of race receives a $5,000 yearly grant from the state. If a black student sues to gain admission to the school does the financial support by the state establish his

right to entry under the fourteenth amendment? If the court finds that there is insufficient state action present in the school's activities to subject it to constitutional restraint, may the state continue to give that school cash subsidies? It should be noted that there is nothing that requires that these two questions be answered in the same manner because the second question involves a government program rather than a limitation on the actions of private persons.

When the government provides some direct subsidy to an entity which impairs fundamental constitutional rights there can be no question but that the government aid program violates the Constitution. Regardless of whether the private party has a right to act free of constitutional restraints, it is clear that the government has no authority to provide specialized benefits to those who effectively burden the exercise of constitutional rights. For example, the Supreme Court held that private clubs such as the Moose Lodge had a right to exist as racially restrictive voluntary associations.[19] However, both before and after that decision, lower federal courts held that such clubs could not receive *specialized* tax exemptions which were the equivalent of a cash subsidy.[20] These clubs still can benefit from *generalized* government services such as police and

---

18. See also, Washington v. Seattle School District No. 1, 102 S.Ct. 3187 (1982) and Crawford v. Board of Education of the City of Los Angeles, 102 S.Ct. 3211 (1982). In *Seattle School District No. 1*, the Supreme Court found unconstitutional a state statute, adopted through voter initiative, which effectively permitted mandatory assignment or transfer of students by local school boards for any reason except for the purpose of desegregating schools. A five member majority held that the statute violated the equal protection clause because it used the racial nature of an issue to determine the governmental decisionmaking structure. Student assignment was left in the power of local school boards except when assignment related to desegregation. Assignment of students for desegregation purposes was removed from the power of local boards, and placed at the state level, thus imposing substantial and unique burdens on racial minorities seeking elimination of school segregation. *Seattle School District No. 1* was distinguished in *Crawford*, in which an eight member majority upheld a state constitutional amendment providing that state courts could not order mandatory assignment or transportation of students unless a federal court would do so to remedy a violation of the equal

protection clause of the fourteenth amendment. Stressing that the amendment did not embody a racial classification, the majority opinion held that the equal protection clause is not violated by the mere repeal of race-related legislation that was never required by the federal constitution. The state constitution did not allocate governmental or judicial power on the basis of a discriminatory principle, nor did it interfere with the school districts' obligation under state law to take steps to desegregate and their freedom to adopt reassignment and busing plans to effectuate desegregation. For a further examination of these cases see Chapter 16, Section III E 1 c(6).

19. Moose Lodge Number 107 v. Irvis, 407 U.S. 163 (1972).

20. See Pitts v. Department of Revenue, 333 F.Supp. 662 (E.D.Wis.1971) (three-judge district court); McGlotten v. Connally, 338 F.Supp. 448 (D.D.C.1972) (three-judge district court, opinion by Judge Bazelon); Falkenstein v. Department of Revenue, 350 F.Supp. 887 (D.Or.1972) (three-judge district court), appeal dismissed 409 U.S. 1099 (1973). Both decisions in *Falkenstein* came after the *Moose Lodge* decision.

fire protection or general tax exemptions. Regardless of their racially discriminatory acts they have a right to exist in the same manner as any other person or association. However, they are not able to receive any specialized benefits as that would be the equivalent of government support for their racially restrictive practices.

The central question in determining the permissibility of state subsidies to those whose actions impair constitutionally recognized rights is whether the aid amounts to something more than generalized services. There is no quantitative test by which this can be determined and it is clear that qualitative factors must be taken into account. When the aid is provided to only a limited group, rather than all members of the public, it can be viewed as equivalent of a direct subsidy to the alleged wrongdoer and the challenged practices. If the aid constitutes a subsidy to the wrongdoer then it will have to be terminated, for the government cannot aid a practice which would be in violation of the Constitution if undertaken directly by the government. In assessing the quantity of aid and whether it provides support for the challenged activity it is clear that the Court will consider both the worth of the subsidized activity and the harm to constitutionally recognized rights. Thus, in *Norwood v. Harrison*[21] the Supreme Court invalidated the granting of books to students who attended racially discriminatory schools under a state law which provided free books to all students. This was true even though the Court had previously upheld the granting of text books to children who attended religious schools under an identical statute.[22] While the form of state aid to each set of schools was identical, the Court found that the practice constituted an unconstitutional subsidy only insofar as it aided the racially restricted schools. While the sectarian schools represented the constitutionally recognized values of both free association and the free exercise of religion, the segregated schools represented no significant interest which could be accorded affirmative constitutional protection so as to sanction a disregard of the value of racial equality.[23] Similarly, the Supreme Court has held that a city could not grant exclusive use of public facilities to racially segregated groups even on a temporary basis because that would constitute a subsidy to the racially discriminatory practices.[24] The Court did note that members of racially discriminatory groups might be allowed to use the public facilities along with others as this would constitute the provision of generalized public services rather than a subsidy to them.

This analysis brings us to the question of whether state aid to a private individual will subject that individual's actions to constitutional limitations. For example, if the state grants a yearly subsidy to a social club which discriminates on the basis of race, will that require the group to end its racially biased membership policies? The Supreme Court has never examined this question directly, although its opinions indicate that financial aid which is not given as a direct subsidy to the challenged practice will not subject the private practice to constitutional restraint. For example, in *Jackson v. Metropolitan Edison Co.*[25] the public utility company certainly received some financial benefit from its licensing as the only electric company for the area. However, because this aid was not connected to the company's termination practices, those practices were not subjected to constitutional review. Similarly, the tax exempt status of the Moose Lodge and the granting of a liquor license to it might have resulted in some financial assistance to the club. But, because those forms of aid were not connected to its racially restricted practices, it was not subjected to constitutional review. However both of

---

21. 413 U.S. 455 (1973).

22. Board of Education v. Allen, 392 U.S. 236 (1968).

23. Norwood v. Harrison, 413 U.S. at 467.

24. Gilmore v. City of Montgomery, 417 U.S. 556 (1974).

25. 419 U.S. 345 (1974).

those cases made clear that if the government had authorized the challenged practices, either through direct approval of them or granting subsidies for their continuance, then those practices would be subjected to constitutional restraint.

The distinction between authorization of challenged practices through the grant of subsidies for their continuance and government aid which is not a direct subsidy to the challenged practices provided the basis for three recent Supreme Court decisions. In *Polk County v. Dodson*,[26] the Court held that a public defender's employment relationship with the state is insufficient to establish that she acts under color of state law when performing a lawyer's traditional functions as counsel to a defendant in a criminal proceeding. The public defender is not subject to administrative direction in performing her duties in the same sense as other state employees; she must exercise independent judgment on behalf of her client. The relationship of the public defender to her client was the same as that of any privately retained counsel and was unchanged by the state's employment of her.[27] Similarly, in *Rendell-Baker v. Kohn*,[28] where the discharge of certain employees of a privately owned school was alleged to be state action, the Court held that the relationship between a private school and its teachers is not changed because the state pays the tuition of most students. "The school . . . is not fundamentally different from many private corporations whose business depends primarily on contracts to build roads, bridges, dams, ships, or submarines for the government. Acts of such private contractors do not become acts of the government by reason of their significant or even total engagement in performing public contracts."[29] Because the school's employment practices were not influenced by state regulation, or the government funding programs, the discharge of the teachers did not involve state action. In other words, the current justices do not believe that constitutional principles limit the autonomy of private persons or corporations due to the receipt of government funds. Further involvement between the private actor and government must be shown before these justices will employ the Constitution to limit the decisions or actions of private entities. Thus, in *Blum v. Yaretsky*[30] the Court found that due process principles did not restrict a nursing home's freedom to discharge or transfer patients even though the home and patients received substantial government funding.[31]

It should be noted that it is possible that the most difficult state action issues concerning the granting of subsidies will not be resolved by the Supreme Court for two reasons. First, the most significant forms of aid to such institutions could be prohibited even though the actions of the private entities might not be subject to review.[32] This prohibition would have the effect of causing many of these private actors to change their

26. 102 S.Ct. 445 (1981).

27. Indeed the State was required "to respect the professional independence of the public defender whom it engages." 102 S.Ct. at 451 (footnote omitted).

28. 102 S.Ct. 2764 (1982).

29. 102 S.Ct. at 2771. The school whose employment practices were challenged in this case specialized in dealing with students who had educational or behavioral problems; public funds received for treating such students accounted for over 90% of the school's funding.

30. 102 S.Ct. 2777 (1982).

31. These patients suffered a diminution in medicaid benefits following discharge or transfer from the private nursing home. The majority opinion indicated that the justices might have imposed due process restrictions on the discharge or transfer procedures if they had found that legislation commanded or influenced the discharge or transfer decisions. However, the majority found that the reduction in benefits was merely the incidental result of the decision of a private entity; the state's decision to lower patient benefits after discharge from the home was not contested in the case. Blum v. Yaretsky, 102 S.Ct. 2777, 2786–88 (1982).

32. The ability of the Internal Revenue Service to deny tax exempt status to private schools that discriminate by race in their admission and treatment of students was before the Supreme Court at the time when this edition of the treatise was going to press. See, Goldsboro Christian Schools, Inc. v. United States, and Bob Jones University v. United States, 644 F.2d 879 (4th Cir. 1981) (listing of unpublished opinion), cert. granted 454 U.S. 892 (1981).

practices so that they might continue to receive specialized government subsidies. Second, the Supreme Court's interpretation of Section 1981 of the Civil Rights Act [33] makes it illegal for private schools and many other private businesses to discriminate between their students or customers on the basis of race.[34] As the most significant problems are connected to racially discriminatory practices of private groups, this statutory interpretation may eliminate the need to address these state action issues. Section 1981 might force all "public" groups to refrain from discrimination on the basis of race and the Court may not have to confront the more difficult fourteenth amendment state action problems.

D. The School Desegregation and "Interdistrict" Relief Cases [35]

To date, the Supreme Court has found that only *de jure* segregation in public schools violates the fourteenth amendment.[36] While this is not often thought of as a state action determination, the *de facto-de jure* distinction presents a state action decision in pristine form. The Court has held that certain acts of commission by public officials are an indispensible prerequisite to finding that patterns of segregated attendance constitute a prohibited racial classification. The Court has simply made a decision that there is no state action connected to the racial separation which justifies a judicial change of the school attendance patterns absent positive acts of segregation by the government. Individual justices have stated that there is

a duty for the state to provide integrated schools and that even *de facto* segregation violates the Constitution.[37] But a majority of the Court has so far refused to find that "one race" schools violate the Constitution where that condition did not result from some act of government connected to the educational system.[38] Thus, segregation in city schools which is not traceable to "state action" is not remediable under the fourteenth amendment.

The use of a state action analysis in desegregation cases is most striking in those involving what is termed "interdistrict" relief. Although such a "multi-district" or "interdistrict" plan may be necessary to end the segregation of a central district or city, the Supreme Court will only allow such a remedy when the acts of governmental entities in every area subject to the court order have caused the segregated conditions.

In *Milliken v. Bradley* [39] the justices determined that interdistrict relief in the form of student reassignment and busing could not include students from school districts which were not found to have engaged in *de jure* segregation. The holding in *Milliken* was that in the absence of positive acts designed to cause racial segregation a school district is immune from interference by federal courts in the name of desegregation.[40] Of course the state is always involved in segregated school districts, as the drawing of school district lines is subject to the power of the state government,[41] but this involvement is true of every type of *de facto* segregation, for it would always be within a

33. 42 U.S.C.A. § 1981.

34. Runyon v. McCrary, 427 U.S. 160 (1976). For an examination of the Congressional power to enforce the Civil War amendments see Chapter 17.

35. This section, with minor modifications is taken from Glennon and Nowak, A Functional Analysis of the Fourteenth Amendment "State Action" Requirement, 1976 Supreme Court Review 221.

36. See, Pasadena Bd. of Education v. Spangler, 427 U.S. 424 (1976); Milliken v. Bradley, 418 U.S. 717 (1974); Keyes v. School District No. 1, 413 U.S. 189 (1973); see generally, Goodman, De Facto School Segregation: A Constitutional and Empirical Analysis, 60 Calif.L.Rev. 275 (1972).

37. See Keyes v. School District No. 1, 413 U.S. 189, 214 (1973) (Opinion of Douglas, J.), Id. at 217 (Powell, J., concurring and dissenting); see also, Milliken v. Bradley, 418 U.S. 717, 793 (1974) (Marshall, J., dissenting).

38. See cases cited in the two previous notes; most of the litigation concerning this subject has remained in the lower courts, see D. Bell, Race, Racism and American Law, Chapter 9(D), pp. 530–572 (1973), and cases cited therein.

39. 418 U.S. 717 (1974).

40. 418 U.S. at 718–20.

41. 418 U.S. at 793–807 (Marshall, J., dissenting).

state's prerogative to dismantle school districts within its boundaries and restructure them so as to create a truly integrated school system. Yet the Court has been reluctant to embrace such sweeping power, in part because the justices have been unwilling to limit the property and association rights of suburban residents unless their city governments were guilty of some active form of discrimination.

The Court will allow wide remedies to remedy segregation in a district where some government action has caused that condition. For example in *Keyes v. School District No. 1;* [42] the court-ordered, city-wide desegregation was based on the school officials' intentional segregation of one area. The Supreme Court upheld this order even though it placed a burden on residents in those areas previously unaffected by the school official's actions. As all of the areas were part of a single district they could be made to bear the responsibility of those officials who acted for the district.

This view of the school desegregation cases was reinforced by the Court's reasoning in another "interdistrict" relief case. In *Hills v. Gautreaux* [43] the justices had to decide whether a federal court could order the Department of Housing and Urban Development (HUD) to locate public housing in the metropolitan area around Chicago, Illinois. In previous years the Chicago Housing Authority (CHA) had effectuated racial segregation in Chicago through its low-income housing site selection and tenant assignment practices. In federal court suits against CHA and HUD it was determined that HUD had violated the due process clause of the fifth amendment and the Civil Rights Act of 1964 by supporting the CHA practices. However, the district court refused to order HUD to do more than establish a city-wide

desegregation plan. The Court of Appeals for the Seventh Circuit, in an opinion by Justice Tom Clark, held that a metropolitan plan was required to remedy effectively the racially-discriminatory, public-housing system within the city.[44] His opinion found that in *Milliken* the Supreme Court had balanced the competing interests and had concluded that for equitable reasons the federal courts should not abridge political subdivisions in school desegregation suits. Clark reasoned that there was no equitable barrier to an interdistrict remedy since the interest of suburban residents in living in an area without public housing was less important than the interest in the educational experience of their children.

The Supreme Court affirmed the Court of Appeals decision while rejecting its reasoning. In an opinion by Mr. Justice Stewart, the majority stated that *Milliken* imposed a basic limitation on the equity power of federal courts based on the concept that court-ordered remedies must be "commensurate with the constitutional violation to be repaired." [45] Of course, this argument in substance (if not form) does no more than reaffirm the *de facto-de jure* distinction as a state action problem. Thus, Stewart found that an interdistrict remedy could be ordered in this case since HUD had authority to act throughout the metropolitan area. The Justice neglected to mention that, since HUD would be involved in all housing suits, in substance, the Seventh Circuit was correct in finding *Milliken* inapplicable to such cases.

Perhaps realizing that the Supreme Court's formulation was a purely formal change in Justice Clark's reasoning, Justice Stewart characterized the decision on how far a court could go in ordering HUD to disregard local and suburban government as a

---

42. 413 U.S. 189 (1973).

43. 425 U.S. 284 (1976).

44. Gautreaux v. Chicago Housing Authority, 503 F.2d 930, 936–939 (7th Cir. 1974), aff'd sub nom. Hills v. Gautreaux, 425 U.S. 284 (1976).

45. 425 U.S. at 294. This principle has been applied to single district cases as well; student transfer orders must be tailored to remedy the de jure segregation without undue burdens on students in the district. Dayton Bd. of Education v. Brinkman, 433 U.S. 406 (1977).

"more substantial question." [46] Actually, it was the only question. Despite the federal action—commensurate remedy rhetoric, the case came down to a question of how great a burden can be placed on a community which has not been directly implicated in a constitutional violation. The Court decided that HUD could operate under its statutory authority to place low income housing in suburban areas as long as the actual program did not undercut "the role of those governments in the federal housing assistance scheme." [47] A court order could place public housing in the suburbs as long as it did not violate the legitimate local interests in land use and city planning. The Court could claim a formal distinction between *Milliken* and *Gautreaux*, in that the former case required more direct action on local government units. However it appears that the Court realized that in housing actions the rights of suburban property owners can be adequately protected without totally eliminating interdistrict remedies for violations of the rights of minority citizens in a large city. In school desegregation cases the interests of the suburban children and their parents will outweigh the need to fully integrate city schools. [48]

V. A POSSIBLE "BALANCING AP-PROACH" TO STATE ACTION ISSUES [1]

The problem of defining "state action" has continued to haunt constitutional adjudication and legal literature. While few commentators doubt that the Bill of Rights and the fourteenth amendment apply only to those acts which are somehow connected to governmental or "state" action, there are no generally accepted formulae for determining when a sufficient amount of government action is present in a practice, thus justifying

subjecting the practice to constitutional restraints. [2] Although several tests for finding state action have emerged from Supreme Court decisions, [3] none is adequate to predict whether state action will be found in a new case. The lack of predictability stems from the Court's repeated insistence that state action depends in each case on "sifting the facts and weighing the circumstances."

While the determination of state action depends on a case-by-case analysis, the Court's development of tests has led to the widespread belief that state action is a unitary concept. Under this unitary concept the only issue is whether sufficient state contacts do, or do not, exist. If the Court finds a sufficient quantum of state connections to a particular activity, then that activity is subject in theory to the strictures of the fourteenth amendment, even though performed by a private party. Under this traditional theory of state action both the value of the challenged practice and the nature of the complainant's asserted rights are irrelevant.

When a case involves a challenge to a practice which is not an official governmental action, the ultimate issue is whether the Constitution proscribes the challenged practice. It is at least possible that the state action issue merely provides a convenient way of answering this ultimate question. Under traditional theory a holding that no state action is present is a separate ruling from a decision on the constitutionality of the challenged practice, but the consequence of such a ruling is the continuation of the challenged practice. In other words, such a ruling produces a decision that the private activity is consistent with the principles of the fourteenth amendment. Despite traditional doctrine, it can readily be seen that a ruling on the presence of state action is a decision on

---

46. 425 U.S. at 300.

47. 425 U.S. at 303.

48. For an examination of permissible judicial remedies for racially segregated school systems and state limitations on state remedies for de facto segregation in school systems, see Chapter 16, section III E 1 c(6).

1. This section, with some modification, is taken from Glennon and Nowak, A Functional Analysis of

the Fourteenth Amendment "State Action" Requirement, 1976 Sup.Ct.Rev. 221.

2. Fitzgerald v. Mountain Laurel Racing, Inc., 607 F.2d 589, 605 (3d Cir. 1979) (Adams, C.J., dissenting), cert. denied 446 U.S. 956 (1980), citing an earlier edition of this treatise.

3. These are examined in sections II–IV of this Chapter.

the merits of the underlying constitutional claim. A judicial decision focusing on the existence of state action may only be the Court's chosen manner of expressing the determination of whether the challenged nongovernmental act is compatible with the substantive guarantees of the amendment. This realization does not end the state action concept; instead it leads to a clearer understanding of the concept as a part of the basic guarantee of the fourteenth amendment. The amendment does not require the judiciary to determine whether a state has "acted", but whether a state has "deprived" someone of a guaranteed right.

It should be clear that a state may be connected to the asserted deprivation by its tolerance of the challenged practice as well as by its positive acts. To illustrate, assuming that a right to do something is protected by "due process", how may a state "deprive any person" of that right? Obviously it could do so in three formally different but substantively similar ways. First, it could act to end the right by simply outlawing activities involving exercises of that right. Second, it could create or explicitly approve activities by some nongovernmental entities which would limit or eliminate the right. Third, observing that, absent laws to the contrary, a practice of some nongovernmental persons will exist in a form which limits or eliminates the right, the state could do nothing. Despite traditional theory it seems hard to contend that the state has done less "depriving" of the right in the third alternative. The state has acted to set a priority between the two conflicting private rights if the challenged practice is lawful within the state. If the challenged practice limits the existence of the right and the practice is lawful, then the state has at some point chosen to define the ability to engage in the practice as the superior right. This result is true regardless of whether the state has explicitly authorized the challenged practice or simply allowed it to exist. The only difference is that in the last alternative the state has legitimated the practice through its common law rather than by specific statutory enactment.

When nongovernmental acts are challenged under the fourteenth amendment the complainant is claiming that the state has deprived him of some right by granting a legal preference to the challenged practice. In each case the exercise of the asserted right must in fact be limited by the existence of the practice; and the practice must be lawful or there would have been no need for challenging the practice under the amendment.

What must be determined is whether the deprivation or denial of the asserted right violates the amendment. The determination must be made as to whether the amendment guarantees individuals the ability to exercise that right free of the limitation arising from the existence of the challenged practice, since the right and the practice cannot coexist. If the right is guaranteed by the amendment the state is not permitted to maintain a legal system which legitimates or tolerates the challenged practice. The amendment's granting of the right directly to individuals would place the state under a duty to protect its existence, and its failure to do so would constitute a deprivation of the right by an "act" of omission. In this situation the amendment remedies the state's failure to protect the right by making the challenged practice unconstitutional, thus insuring the existence of a legal system which prefers the right above the challenged practice.

The state action cases involve a conflict between individual rights, and the Court must determine whether the Constitution dictates a preference for one right above the other. To resolve this conflict it would seem that the Court must balance the relative merits of permitting the challenged practice to continue against the limitation which it imposes on the asserted right. If the value of the right clearly outweighs the value of the challenged practice, the amendment proscribes the practice and the state has deprived plaintiff of a right guaranteed by the amendment by failing to protect the right from the impact of the challenged practice. If the importance of the right is not clearly greater than that of the challenged practice, the effect of the practice on the right does not violate the amendment.[4] The impact of the practice on the asserted right is in accordance with the amendment, not because state action is missing, but because it is permissible for the state to prefer the challenged practice rather than the asserted right.

The Supreme Court's decisions on state action reflect how the judicial balancing of rights functions to sort out those private activities whose collision with other rights makes them constitutionally infirm. While the balancing has nothing to do with finding a minimum quantum of state activity, the process of sorting out proscribed activities has occurred under the guise of a formulistic search for an undefined minimum amount of state acts. In practice, when the challenged practice deserved state protection the

Court has ruled that state action is lacking, declaring in effect that the practice is compatible with the fourteenth amendment. When the harm to protected rights outweighed the value of the challenged practice, the Court has found sufficient state action, which made easy a final ruling of unconstitutionality. The fact that, with only one minor exception, the Court always found a constitutional violation after a finding of state action offers strong support for this theory.[5]

While there were some early suggestions that a balancing process was central to state action decisions, these suggestions were made primarily in terms of finding private, racially-discriminatory actions unconstitutional.[6] This concept of balancing was never expanded to account for all state action decisions and the traditional, unitary concept has gone essentially unchallenged.[7] A renewed focus on the balancing of rights approach to these problems may greatly clarify the state action issue in the years ahead.[8]

---

4. The requirement is phrased so that the asserted right should clearly outweigh the challenged practice, since the judiciary in close cases should respect the preference set by the legislature.

5. The only major state action decision of the Court where state action was found and the challenged practice was upheld was Public Utilities Comm'n v. Pollak, 343 U.S. 451 (1952).

6. For an excellent exposition of a balancing test for state action issues relating to racial discrimination, see Black, "State Action," Equal Protection and California's Proposition 14, 81 Harv.L.Rev. 69 (1967). For a use of a balancing test which focuses on the need for the exercise of "national power," including congressional action, see VanAlstyne & Karst, State Action, 14 Stan.L.Rev. 3 (1961) and VanAlstyne, Mr. Justice Black, Constitutional Review, and the Talisman of State Action, 1965 Duke L.J. 219. For early suggestions of a general balancing test but with a primary focus on questions concerning racial discrimination, see Henkin, Shelley v. Kraemer: Notes for a Revised Opinion, 110 U.Pa.L.Rev. 473 (1962); Horowitz, The Misleading Search for "State Action" under the Fourteenth Amendment, 30 So.Calif.L.Rev. 208 (1957); Karst & Horowitz, Reitman v. Mulkey: A Telophase of Substantive Equal Protection, 1967, Supreme Court Review, 39. Judge Friendly proposed a balancing test as

a limited alternative to open ended state action rulings. See H. Friendly, The Dartmouth College Case and the Public-Private Penumbra 17–19, 30–31 (1960). For provocative questions speculating on the utility of a balancing approach, see G. Gunther, Cases and Materials on Constitutional Law 916–19 (9th ed. 1975).

7. Three articles have employed the unitary concept quite correctly in traditional terms, but with little indication of the possibility of using a principled balancing test in this area. See Quinn, State Action: A Pathology and a Proposed Cure, 64 Calif.L.Rev. 146 (1976); Note, State Action: Theories for Applying Constitutional Restrictions to Private Activity, 74 Colum.L.Rev. 656 (1974); Note, The Supreme Court, 1974 Term, 89 Harv.L.Rev. 49, 139–51 (1975). See also Hendy, Property Rights and First Amendment Rights: Balance and Conflict, 62 A.B.A.J. 76 (1976). For a defense of a quantitative test and an attack on the use of a balancing test to determine state action, see Winter, Poverty, Economic Equality, and the Equal Protection Clause, 1972 Supreme Court Review 41, 44–52.

8. The Supreme Court continued to reject value oriented tests, and followed a formalistic approach as it held that warehouseman's sales did not involve state action even though they were authorized by state statute. Flagg Bros., Inc. v. Brooks, 436 U.S. 149 (1978).

CHAPTER FIFTEEN

PROCEDURAL DUE PROCESS—THE REQUIREMENT OF FAIR ADJUDICATIVE PROCEDURES

I. INTRODUCTION

Both the fifth and fourteenth amendments prohibit governmental actions which would deprive "any person of life, liberty or property without due process of law." [1] But due process has several quite distinct meanings. [2] As we have seen in Chapter Thirteen, due process restricts the ways in which legislatures may limit individual freedom. This

---

1. "[N]or shall any person . . . be deprived of life, liberty or property, without due process of law; U.S.Const. Amend. V.

"[N]or shall any State deprive any person of life, liberty, or property without due process of law;" U.S. Const. Amend. XIV.

2. See generally, Ratner, The Function of the Due Process Clause, 116 U.Pa.L.Rev. 1048 (1968); Kadish, Methodology and Criteria in Due Process Adjudication—A Survey and Criticism, 66 Yale L.J. 319 (1957); Shattuck, The True Meaning of the Term "Liberty" in Those Clauses in the Federal and State Constitutions

"substantive" due process may protect certain fundamental rights or void arbitrary limitations of individual freedom of action. Part of the substantive impact of the due process clause of the fourteenth amendment is the "incorporation" of certain guarantees in the Bill of Rights. Thus state legislatures cannot pass legislation which denies freedom of speech, for to do so would violate due process in that the liberty it protects includes the freedom of speech guaranteed by the first amendment.

The due process clauses also have a procedural aspect in that they guarantee that each person shall be accorded a certain "process" if they are deprived of life, liberty or property. Where the power of the government is to be used against an individual, there is a right to a fair procedure to determine the basis for, and legality of, such action. But there is no general requirement that the government institute a procedure prior to taking acts which are unfavorable to some individuals. It is only when someone's "life, liberty or property" is to be impaired that the government owes him some type of process for the consideration of his interests. Today these concepts are being defined so as to exclude a variety of personal interests from their scope and protection even though earlier cases had recognized the phrase as virtually all encompassing.[3]

If life, liberty or property is at stake, the individual has a right to a fair procedure. The question then focuses on the nature of the "process" that is "due." In all instances the state must adhere to previously declared rules for adjudicating the claim or at least not deviate from them in a manner which is unfair to the individual against whom the action is to be taken. The government always has the obligation of providing a neutral decisionmaker—one who is not inherently biased against the individual or who has personal interest in the outcome. In instances where the person is to be deprived of his physical liberty for a substantial period of time, a trial is required. The criminal trial process must include all the safeguards of the Bill of Rights [4] as well as being a fair adjudicatory process. Where the individual is to be penalized for some infraction of civil law through a judicial action, there is also the requirement that the trial process be a fair one although the seventh amendment's guarantee of a jury trial applies only to federal actions.[5] In a number of other circumstances the government may impair someone's "life, liberty or property" without a trial-type process. These situations involve the regulation of certain specific activities or the denial of some governmental benefits. There are some very specific rulings on the types of procedures that are necessary for the taking of physical property by creditors, but other required "processes" are decided in terms of what procedures are both necessary and affordable for proper resolution of certain types of claims.

In the first major section of the chapter we will examine what interests the Supreme Court has held to come within the scope of the terms "life," "liberty" or "property", for no process is required for government actions which do not deprive an individual of one of these three interests.

Which Protect "Life, Liberty and Property," 4 Harv.L. Rev. 365 (1891).

3. VanAlstyne, Cracks In "The New Property": Adjudicative Due Process in the Administrative State, 62 Cornell L.Rev. 445, 489 (1977); Note, Statutory Entitlement and the Concept of Property, 86 Yale L.J. 695 (1977). See generally, Smolla, The Re-emergence of the Right-Privilege Distinction in Constitutional Law: The Price of Protesting Too Much, 35 Stanford L.Rev. 69 (1982); Simon, Liberty and Property in the Supreme Court: A Defense of Roth and Perry, 71 Calif.L.Rev. 146 (1983) (Professors Smolla and Simon argue that Burger Court decisions in this area properly attempt to define the judicial role in reviewing administrative

processes by examining the types of interests that should be protected under the due process clauses).

4. Of the provisions of the Bill of Rights which relate to the investigation and adjudication of criminal charges, only the grand jury clause of the fifth amendment is not applicable to the states. Hurtado v. California, 110 U.S. 516 (1884). For an overview of the "incorporation" concept see Chapter 12, section I, B, and Chapter 13, section V.

5. The seventh amendment has been held not applicable to the states. Minneapolis & St. Louis R.R. Co. v. Bombolis, 241 U.S. 211 (1916).

In the second major section we will examine the types of procedures which are due an individual when the government takes an action which deprives him of one of these interests.

II. DEPRIVATIONS OF "LIFE, LIBERTY OR PROPERTY" FOR WHICH SOME PROCESS IS DUE

A. In General

The due process clauses apply only if a government action will constitute the impairment of some individual's life, liberty or property. Where government actions adversely affect an individual but do not constitute a denial of that individual's life, liberty or property, the government does not have to give the person any hearing or process whatsoever. One might assume (incorrectly as it turns out) that the phrase "life, liberty or property" was to include all aspects of an individual's life in society,[1] but the Supreme Court has given the phrase a more restrictive meaning. Since 1972, the Court has continually held that the government need not give someone a procedure to determine the fairness of how it has treated that individual unless its actions fall within distinct rulings as to the meaning of "life," "liberty" and "property." [2]

Earlier in the century there was a distinction in constitutional law between "rights" and "privileges." The government could not deny someone a "right" except for specific reasons which complied with constitutional standards. However an individual could be denied a "privilege" by the government for any reason and with no constitutional restrictions. For example, when a policeman lost his job for engaging in political activities, the Supreme Court of Massachusetts upheld the dismissal. As Justice Oliver Wendell Holmes noted: "The petitioner may have a constitutional right to talk politics, but he has no constitutional right to be a policeman." [3] This rationale was followed by the Supreme Court of the United States in cases which upheld denials of occupational licenses for virtually any reason [4] and the placing of restrictions on who could attend state universities.[5] As such things were mere "privileges" to which no one was entitled as of right, the state had virtually unlimited discretion in its methods of disbursing such benefits. But this view was at least formally ended as the justices began to realize that, unless the government were required to accord fair treatment of individual interests that could not be termed "rights," there would be almost no check on the power of government to limit individual freedom in society.

---

1. Such a view would be pursued in a "literalist" position that the three terms are generic descriptions for all individual interests. For example, it is not uncommon for persons to refer to all matter as "animal, vegetable or mineral" with no intent to exclude fish, fruits or alloys. Yet there are impressive arguments for the position that the terms "life, liberty or property" refer to a limited group of interests and that "a textual exegesis" of the clauses should confine judicial decisions. See Monaghan, Of "Liberty" and "Property," 62 Cornell L.Rev. 405, 415 (1977). The Court's distinction between constitutionally protected and unprotected may be defended on the basis that some element of a "right-privilege" distinction has been used by the Court throughout this country to define the judicial role in reviewing administrative process established by the legislature. See Smolla, The Re-emergence of the Right-Privilege Distinction in Constitutional Law: The Price of Protesting Too Much, 35 Stanford L.Rev. 69 (1982); Simon, Liberty and Property in the Supreme Court: A Defense of Roth and Perry, 71 Calif.L.Rev. 146 (1983).

2. The first clear use of this approach in the last decade is Board of Regents v. Roth, 408 U.S. 564 (1972). It is difficult to find such a definitional focus prior to that decision. Van Alstyne, Cracks in "the New Property": Adjudicative Due Process in the Administrative State, 62 Cornell L.Rev. 445, 489 (1977). See United States Labor Party v. Oremus, 619 F.2d 683, 689 (7th Cir. 1980) (Wood, C.J., citing an earlier edition of this treatise). For commentary on the proper scope of federal court rulings defining these protected interests, see Glennon, Constitutional Liberty and Property: Federal Common Law and Section 1983, 51 So.Calif.L.Rev. 355 (1978).

3. McAuliffe v. Mayor of New Bedford, 155 Mass. 216, 220, 29 N.E. 517 (1892) (per Holmes).

4. Barsky v. Board of Regents, 347 U.S. 442, 451 (1954).

5. Hamilton v. Regents of University of California, 293 U.S. 245 (1934).

The first significant development which eroded the right-privilege distinction was the concept of "unconstitutional conditions." [6] This doctrine recognizes that a state may not do indirectly what it is forbidden from doing directly. Thus, even "privileges" may not be denied for reasons which violate constitutional guarantees. The state cannot make the gaining or keeping of government benefits conditional upon the recipient's agreement to forgo the exercise of constitutional rights. For example, a provision that government-subsidized housing would go only to those who agreed not to speak out against the foreign policy of the federal government would be an "unconstitutional condition"; although there may be no right to housing, the government cannot "buy up" first amendment freedoms which it could not restrain directly.[7]

The right-privilege distinction was also undermined by substantive due process and equal protection cases which placed limits on the government's ability to arbitrarily restrict freedoms that were not explicit constitutional rights. The rationale for the distinction was laid to rest by Professor William Van Alstyne [8] who showed the "distinction" to be mere tautology—it meant that only rights had to be recognized by the state but rights were what the state had chosen to recognize. This "epigram" solved every problem by allowing the Court total freedom to choose a few rights to defend from some government actions. Clearly there needed to be a more logical rationale

for the definition and protection of individual rights and freedom of action.

A basis for a new approach to these problems was offered by Charles Reich in his articles on "The New Property".[9] He noted that highly organized societies in which large numbers of persons were dependent on government "largess" or "privileges" resulted in the suppression of individual liberty. This result could be avoided by recognizing the individual's interest in government benefits as a "right" which could be protectable by procedural and substantive safeguards against arbitrary government action. Professor Reich believed that persons should be recognized as having a right to the forms of government benefits which they received, so as to attach constitutional safeguards to their allocation and termination. Reich used the term "entitlements" to designate these benefits as enforceable rights rather than mere privileges or gratitudes which could be denied or withheld as the government chose.[10]

For a short time it appeared as if the Supreme Court was going to truly end the right-privilege distinction and hold the government to certain standards of fairness in allocating public benefits. The Court never created any substantive rights to government subsistence payments, nor did the justices ever require any general equality of treatment for poor persons, but in decisions on procedural due process, the Supreme Court seemed ready to require fair treatment of a wide variety of individual claims or interests. The Court required the gov-

---

6. For the development of this concept see O'Neil, Unconstitutional Conditions: Welfare Benefits With Strings Attached, 54 Calif.L.Rev. 443 (1966); Note, Unconstitutional Conditions, 73 Harv.L.Rev. 1595 (1960); Hale, Unconstitutional Conditions and Constitutional Rights, 35 Colum.L.Rev. 321 (1935).

7. Professor Peter Westen has noted how the Supreme Court, and analysts of constitutional issues, can mask a decision on the constitutionality of a government practice in "unconstitutional condition" terminology. It is critical that judges focus on the constitutional values arguably impaired by a "condition" rather than the mere identification of "conditions." Professor Westen is unquestionably correct as he points out "constitutional condition arguments are conceptually *indis-*

tinguishable from ordinary constitutional problems." Westen, Incredible Dilemmas: Conditioning One Constitutional Right on the Forfeiture of Another, 66 Iowa L.Rev. 741, 751 (1981).

8. Van Alstyne, The Demise of the Right-Privilege Distinction in Constitutional Law, 81 Harv.L.Rev. 1439 (1968).

9. Reich, The New Property, 73 Yale L.J. 733 (1964); Reich, Individual Rights and Social Welfare: The Emerging Legal Issues, 74 Yale L.J. 1245 (1965). It may be of interest to the reader to note Charles Reich's later, somewhat related, work: C. Reich, The Greening of America (1970).

10. Reich, supra note 9, 74 Yale at 1256.

ernment to grant persons a hearing before terminating such interests as welfare payments [11] or driver's licenses.[12] Thus, it appeared that the due process clause would insure fairness of treatment for all aspects of individual liberty and dispensation of government benefits even though it would not be a check on substantive policy decisions concerning wealth allocations. But this was not to be.

Since 1972 a majority of the justices have chosen to take quite literally, and restrictively, the concept that due process applies only to "life, liberty or property." In recent years the decisions have narrowly construed these terms so that the government may take some actions adversely affecting people without having to give them any procedure to insure a fair treatment of their interests. Thus, as we shall see, the Court has allowed the government to injure someone's reputation or terminate his employment without a hearing since a majority of the justices did not find "liberty" or "property" present in the facts of those individual cases. The majority has also allowed the states to define the scope of government benefits to which any individual is "entitled," so that the state can insure that it has not created a property interest in government benefits which would require due process for their termination. To a significant degree this trend has resurrected the discredited "right-privilege" distinction. While the Court has forsaken those terms, it now requires due process only for certain interests defined as life, liberty or property. The distinction is now between life, recognized liberty interests and property "entitlements" as opposed to unprotected interests or "mere expectations." [13]

There follows a brief summary of the Supreme Court's current position on what constitutes life, liberty and property. Remember that unless a government action deprives an individual of one of those interests, the Court will not require any "process" or hearing be given the individual who is adversely affected by the action.

When no life, liberty or property interest is at stake, a state is free to deny privileges to individuals without any hearing and, therefore, on a totally arbitrary basis.[14] Thus, the Supreme Court summarily held, in a per curiam opinion, that out-of-state lawyers seeking to represent defendants in a state criminal proceeding were not entitled to any hearing as to whether or not they should be allowed to appear *pro hac vice*. In *Leis v. Flynt*,[15] the Court held that a lawyer has neither a liberty nor property interest in being admitted on a case-by-case basis to practice in a state in which he or she is not licensed and that there should be no inquiry into whether or not a state trial judge had been totally arbitrary in refusing to admit the attorneys to practice.[16]

---

11. Goldberg v. Kelly, 397 U.S. 254 (1970). This decision quoted from Charles Reich's article id. at 262 n. 8 quoting 74 Yale at 1255. The Court used the term "statutory entitlement" in the text but in n. 8 it quoted Reich and stated "It may be realistic today to regard welfare entitlements as more like 'property' than a 'gratuity.'" Id.

12. Bell v. Burson, 402 U.S. 535 (1971).

13. Professors Smolla and Simon have defended the use of a right-privilege distinction to define the role of the judiciary in reviewing the fairness of an administrative process. See Smolla, The Re-emergence of the Right-Privilege Distinction in Constitutional Law: The Price of Protesting Too Much, 35 Stanford L.Rev. 69 (1982); Simon, Liberty and Property in the Supreme Court: A Defense of Roth and Perry, 71 Calif.L.Rev. 146 (1983).

14. One must be careful not to confuse the concepts of substantive and procedural due process. The differences in the concepts, and the potential for confusion, was recently demonstrated in New Motor Vehicle Bd. of California v. Orrin W. Fox Co., 439 U.S. 96 (1978), upholding a law delaying the creation of certain automobile dealerships. The majority opinion correctly found that a general regulation of where and when dealerships could be established presented a substantive, rather than procedural, issue. See Chapter 12, Section III, "Procedural Due Process vs. Substantive Review."

15. 439 U.S. 438 (1979).

16. The dissent pointed out that the exclusion seemed to be totally arbitrary for there was no hearing in the state court on the issue of whether the attorneys should be allowed to appear, the trial judge issued a one-sentence opinion denying the appearance, and the trial judge did not refer to facts justifying his conclusion that he should not even hear the attorneys. Indeed, the case involved a celebrated Ohio state court prosecution of publishers accused of selling obscene magazines, and, the dissent noted, the lawyers who

B. Life

While the Supreme Court has never attempted to define the term "life", it has come very close to doing so in its decisions concerning the prohibition of voluntary abortions. In *Roe v. Wade*[1] the Court held that the term "person" in the fourteenth amendment does not apply to an unborn fetus. This conclusion was based on the majority's view of the use of the word "person" in various places in the Constitution; "in nearly all these instances the use of the word is such that it has application only postnatally."[2] When combined with the history of abortion practices prior to the adoption of the fourteenth amendment, this argument lead the Court to conclude that a fetus was not a constitutionally recognized person. Thus a fetus has no constitutional rights prior to birth, although a state may, if it chooses, restrict abortion practices to protect the fetus following its reaching a stage of "viability."[3]

The Supreme Court has not dealt with the issue of when a person's life ends following a live birth. Given the ability of medical doctors to sustain a person's life for extended periods following what otherwise would be a fatal occurrence of illness or injury,[4] the procedural due process issue would arise if the government were to authorize the removal of life support systems where the patient has not made such a request. Where the patient wishes to have the life support system removed but the state refuses to allow the doctor to do so, there will be an issue concerning the right to freedom of choice or "personal privacy" somewhat related to the right involved in the abortion case.[5] Where the refusal of medical treatment is based on the patient's religious beliefs, there are also issues concerning the first amendment guarantee of free exercise of religion.[6] The Court has allowed a person convicted of murder to accept the state-imposed death penalty and waive some forms of appellate review but the implications of this action are not at all clear.[7]

There are many serious legal as well as moral issues concerning when, if ever, the state should be allowed to take someone's life. The Supreme Court has held that the government may impose the death penalty on persons for certain crimes without violating either the due process clauses or the eighth amendment prohibition of cruel and unusual punishment.[8] To comport with the

---

were not admitted were specialists in the defense of obscenity cases, one of whom had received awards for meritorious practice by the Bar of New York, and the other who had been schooled in Ohio and had practiced as a legal intern there prior to his graduation and entry into the Bar of New York. Leis v. Flynt, 439 U.S. 438, 445 (1979) (Stevens, J. dissenting, joined by Brennan and Marshall, JJ.).

1. 410 U.S. 113 (1973).

2. 410 U.S. at 157.

3. For an analysis of the issues concerning restrictions on abortions, see Section VII, D of Chapter 16 on the Right to Privacy.

4. See generally Wassmer, Between Life and Death: Ethical and Moral Issues Involved in Recent Medical Advances, 13 Vill.L.Rev. 759 (1968).

5. See Chapter 16, Section VII E 3; The "Right to Die". See generally Cantor, A Patient's Decision to Decline Life Saving Medical Treatment: Bodily Integrity Versus the Preservation of Life, 26 Rutg.L.Rev. 228 (1973); Louisell, Euthanasia and Biathanasi: On Dying and Killing, 22 Cath.U.L.Rev. 723 (1973); Kamisar, Some Non-Religious Views Against Proposed "Mercy-Killing" Legislation, 42 Minn.L.Rev. 969 (1958). As to the problems concerned in determination of death and

transplantation cases, see Louisell, The Procurement of Organs for Transplantation, 64 Nw.U.L.Rev. 607 (1970) and materials cited therein.

6. See Chapter 19 on Freedom of Religion.

7. Gilmore v. Utah, 429 U.S. 1012, (1976) (order denying stay of execution accompanied by statements of reasons by individual justices).

8. In 1976 the Court upheld three statutes which allowed for the discretionary imposition of the death penalty where there are objective standards and rules to control the discretion of those charged with imposing the penalty, Profitt v. Florida, 428 U.S. 242 (1976); Jurek v. Texas, 428 U.S. 262 (1976); Gregg v. Georgia, 428 U.S. 153 (1976). The Court struck down statutes which had mandatory death sentences for certain crimes. Woodsen v. North Carolina, 428 U.S. 280 (1976); Roberts v. Louisiana, 428 U.S. 325 (1976). These cases were not decided with a majority opinion. Justices Brennan and Marshall voted to strike down the death penalty under the eighth amendment prohibition against cruel and unusual punishment. Chief Justice Burger and Justices White, Blackmun and Rehnquist voted to uphold the use of the death penalty in all five cases. Justices Stewart, Powell and Stevens voted to allow the discretionary systems in the first three

due process guarantee, statutory systems must allow for imposition of the death penalty only for the most serious criminal offenses [9] and only where there is a fair system for sorting out those convicted criminals who shall die from those who will only be imprisoned.[10] Additionally, the exact procedures for selection of these persons must be such that they are not slanted "in favor" of the death penalty by devices such as exclusion of jurors who might not impose the penalty [11] or the way in which information regarding the propriety of imposing the death penalty is presented.[12]

While "criminal procedure" is not within the scope of this text we must note the relationship between these decisions and other areas of procedural due process. In recent years the Supreme Court has increasingly

recognized the ability of individual states to determine the scope of rights or liberties of people in their jurisdiction. So long as the government does not violate one of a few express or implied "fundamental rights" the Court will not protect the interests of individuals against the state. Here the Court has refused to prohibit the use of the death penalty as a majority of the justices found no textual basis for such a restriction. Additionally, the Court has required that the states follow only a minimal set of guidelines to establish a fair process and has left them very free to choose the manner of selecting those convicted defendants who shall be killed.[13] As Professor Charles Black has pointed out, the amount of discretionary features of the criminal justice system when combined with elements of pure chance

cases but to invalidate the mandatory systems. It was these three swing votes that accounted for the differing results.

9. See, Coker v. Georgia, 433 U.S. 584, (1977) (death penalty may not be imposed for rape conviction because penalty is grossly disproportionate punishment for an offense that does not involve loss of life); Enmund v. Florida, 102 S.Ct. 3368 (1982) (death penalty may not be imposed on a defendant convicted of felony murder if the defendant did not himself kill or intend that lethal force be used in the crime).

If the state charges a specific crime as the basis for the death penalty and fails to prove that charge at trial or the penalty hearing, a court cannot impose a death penalty on the individual when it believes that the state proved the existence of another basis for the penalty which was not charged and upon which the defendant was not tried. Presnell v. Georgia, 439 U.S. 14 (1978).

10. See note 8 supra. The Court has invalidated a statute which imposed a mandatory death sentence for those who are found guilty of the murder of a police officer. Roberts v. Louisiana, 431 U.S. 633 (1977). In Godfrey v. Georgia, 446 U.S. 420 (1980), the Supreme Court, without a majority opinion, held that the Georgia Supreme Court's broad construction of that state's death penalty statute violated the eighth and fourteenth amendments. The Georgia court had affirmed a defendant's being subjected to the death penalty under a statute and jury instruction which allowed for the imposition of a death penalty for those murders that were "outrageously or wantonly vile, horrible, or inhuman." The United States Supreme Court found that nothing in the statute or the jury instructions imposed any limitation on possible arbitrary and capricious imposition of the death penalty. See Hicks v. Oklahoma, 447 U.S. 343 (1980) (defendant has right to have sentencing jury properly instructed regarding the jury's discretionary power); Beck v. Alabama, 447 U.S. 625 (1980) (defendant may not be sentenced to death if jury was not permitted to consider lesser included noncapi-

tal offense). But cf. Zant v. Stephens, 103 S.Ct. ___ (1983) (death penalty despite flaw in jury instructions). See also, Bullington v. Missouri, 451 U.S. 430 (1981) (once a defendant has been convicted and received a noncapital punishment, he cannot be sentenced to death following a retrial without violating the double jeopardy clause).

11. Witherspoon v. Illinois, 391 U.S. 510 (1968). See also Adams v. Texas, 448 U.S. 38 (1980) (the *Witherspoon* principle, limiting the state's power to exclude jurors based on their view of the death penalty, applies to a bifurcated procedure used to separately determine the guilt of a defendant and the propriety of imposing a death sentence).

12. See, e.g., Gardner v. Florida, 430 U.S. 349 (1977) (death sentence cannot be based on material in presentence report that was not disclosed to the defendant); Lockett v. Ohio, 438 U.S. 586 (1978) (Plurality opinion by Burger, C.J., finding state system for imposing death sentences invalid insofar as it precluded consideration by the sentencing jury or judge of factors which the defendant wished to claim should be considered as mitigating circumstances); Bell v. Ohio, 438 U.S. 637 (1978) (applying *Lockett*); Green v. Georgia, 442 U.S. 95 (1979) (sentence must be invalidated where court excludes relevant evidence from sentencing hearing); Eddings v. Oklahoma, 455 U.S. 104 (1982) (death sentence for 16-year old defendant held invalid for failure to consider all mitigating factors).

Statements made by an accused in a state-ordered competency examination prior to trial cannot be later used against the defendant at the sentencing phase of a trial for a capital offense unless the state has established procedural guarantees before and during the examination to insure that the accused's fifth and sixth amendment rights are not violated. See Estelle v. Smith, 451 U.S. 454 (1981).

13. Black, Due Process for Death: Jurek v. Texas and Companion Cases, 26 Cath.U.L.Rev. 1 (1976).

make it impossible to determine whether any system for imposing the death penalty is minimally fair or evenhanded.[14] But the current Court has not approached issues concerning the fairness of a procedural system through any comprehensive theory of value in individual liberty.[15] Instead a majority of the justices have looked to whether an individual was being deprived of a specific interest in life, liberty or property by a process with what they might view as unreasonably few procedural safeguards for these interests. This majority of the justices is satisfied that their guidelines for fairness in selection of defendants for the death penalty is all that can be reasonably required of a state. Their position that there is no specific basis for recognizing a wider interest in life thus correlates with the current approach to the due process issues which are examined in this chapter.

C. Liberty—Generally

1. Introduction

One cannot ascribe a specific meaning to the term "liberty" for it may encompass any form of freedom of action or choice which is accorded constitutional recognition by the Court.[1] Indeed, it is the concept of liberty which is the primary limitation on the action of the states as regards individual rights. Liberty under the fourteenth amendment includes those provisions of the Bill of Rights which the Court deems to be "incorporated" into the due process clause as well as "fundamental rights" which are derived either

from the concept of liberty or other constitutional values.[2] These constitute substantive prohibitions of government actions which would violate those rights. The concept of liberty in the due process clauses is also the basis for the "substantive due process" requirement that legislation must relate to a legitimate end of government.[3] In their procedural aspect the due process clauses require that no individual be singled out for a deprivation of a constitutional liberty without a fair "process." One can focus on the procedural issue by asking what types of individual freedom of action (liberty) cannot be limited by the government except with a fair procedure to determine the basis for, and legality of, the limitation.

There are two distinct ways in which a person may be deprived of liberty. First, the government might deprive the person of his freedom of action by physically restraining him. Second, the government might limit someone's freedom of choice and action by making it impossible or illegal for that person to engage in certain types of activity. This last category can also be subdivided into two parts. The government might deny a person the ability to exercise a right with special constitutional protection (such as the right to free speech or the right to privacy); this restraint would constitute a clear deprivation of liberty. There are also cases where the government forecloses a form of freedom of action to an individual which does not have special constitutional status (such as the freedom to engage in a particular business activity). Thus we may

---

14. Id. C. Black, Capital Punishment: The Inevitability of Caprice and Mistake (1974).

15. The lack of a true value theory in administrative due process decisions is examined in Mashaw, The Supreme Court's Due Process Calculus for Administrative Adjudication in Mathews v. Eldridge: Three Factors in Search of a Theory of Value, 44 U.Chi.L.Rev. 28 (1976). The Court's failure to examine the fundamental due process values in criminal procedure decisions is examined in Nowak, Foreword: Due Process Methodology in the Postincorporation World, 70 Journal of Criminal Law & Criminology 397 (1980). The relationship between judicial value judgments and proffered proof of the deterrent effect of the death penalty is examined in Zeisel, The Deterrent Effect of the Death Penalty: Facts v. Faiths, 1976 Sup.Ct.Rev. 317.

1. See generally Monaghan, Of "Liberty" and "Property," 62 Cornell L.Rev. 405, 411–16 (1977); Ratner, The Function of the Due Process Clause, 116 U.Pa.L.Rev. 1048 (1968); Kadish, Methodology and Criteria in Due Process Adjudication—A Survey and Criticism, 66 Yale L.J. 319 (1957).

2. For an outline of the content of these guarantees, see Chapter 12, and Chapter 13, Section V.

3. The substantive due process restriction is examined in Chapter 13. The distinctions between substantive and procedural rulings are examined in Chapter 12, Section III.

subdivide "liberty" into three headings involving governmental restraints on (1) physical freedom, (2) the exercise of fundamental constitutional rights and (3) other forms of freedom of choice or action.

2. Physical Liberty

The essential guarantee of the due process clauses is that the government may not imprison or otherwise physically restrain a person except in accordance with fair procedures. The first due process clause is a part of the fifth amendment, which is primarily concerned with procedures used to convict someone of crime. But the due process guarantee has long been understood to go beyond the criminal justice system; it governs all government deprivations of liberty. Indeed the protection of physical liberty is the oldest and most widely recognized part of the guarantee.[4]

The initial requirement of due process is that there be some fair procedure for determining whether an individual has lawfully been taken into custody by the government.

While an individual may be arrested without prior judicial approval, such an arrest must be based on probable cause for the police to believe that the person has committed a crime.[5] If the arrest was in fact made without a warrant, the law enforcement authorities must make prompt application to a magistrate for a neutral determination that the arrest was made upon probable cause.[6] Custody of the person even then cannot continue except in conformity with the eighth amendment's prohibition of excessive bail.[7] The entire process leading towards the trial of a criminal charge must be undertaken in a timely manner in order to comply with the due process and speedy trial guarantees of the Bill of Rights.[8] The adjudicative process itself is governed by the specific guarantees of the Bill of Rights and an independent concept of fundamental fairness which is imposed by the due process clause. The reasonable doubt standard is derived from the due process clauses themselves and is the historical barrier to arbitrary deprivation of freedom in the criminal justice system.[9] The

---

4. See, Hough, Due Process of Law—To-Day, 32 Harv.L.Rev. 218 (1918); Shattuck, The True Meaning of the Term "Liberty" in Those Clauses In the Federal and State Constitutions which Protect "Life, Liberty or Property," 4 Harv.L.Rev. 365 (1891). Williams, "Liberty" in the Due Process Clause of the Fifth and Fourteenth Amendments, 53 Colo.L.Rev. 117 (1981). The concept can be traced back to chapter twenty-nine of the Magna Carta. See generally, E. Corwin, The "Higher Law" Background of American Constitutional Law 30–33 (1928).

5. This requirement is part of the fourth amendment regulation of searches and seizures; it is incorporated into the term liberty and applied to the states through the due process clause of the fourteenth amendment. Mapp v. Ohio, 367 U.S. 643 (1961). Interstate extradition proceedings are governed by Article IV, § 2 of the Constitution. When a demanding state seeks extradition of a fugitive from another (asylum) state, the governor of the asylum state is charged under Article IV, § 2 with returning the fugitive to the demanding state. Congress has implemented this provision in 18 U.S.C.A. § 3182 and many states have adopted the Uniform Criminal Extradition Act. Extradition proceedings are summary in nature; the order of the governor granting extradition is prima facie evidence that there is a constitutional and statutory basis for the extradition. In Michigan v. Doran, 439 U.S. 282 (1978), the Supreme Court held that, once the governor of the asylum state grants extradition based on the demanding state's judicial determination that probable

cause exists for the arrest of the defendant-fugitive, the judiciary of the asylum state may not make any further inquiry into the issue of probable cause. See also Pacileo v. Walker, 449 U.S. 86 (1980) (per curiam) (courts of an "asylum" or "sending" state do not have authority to inquire into the prison conditions of a state demanding extradition. Once the governor of the asylum state issues a warrant for the arrest and rendition of the fugitive, challenges to the demanding state's penal system can only be raised in the courts of the demanding state).

6. Gerstein v. Pugh, 420 U.S. 103 (1975).

7. Stack v. Boyle, 342 U.S. 1 (1951); for a discussion of the scope of pretrial "detention", see Blunt v. United States, 322 A.2d 579 (App.D.C.1974).

8. Klopfer v. North Carolina, 386 U.S. 213 (1967).

9. In the Matter of Winship, 397 U.S. 358 (1970). Jackson v. Virginia, 443 U.S. 307 (1979).

The Supreme Court held in Taylor v. Kentucky, 436 U.S. 478 (1978) that the due process standard of proof beyond a reasonable doubt requires, under most circumstances, that a jury in a criminal trial be instructed on the "presumption of innocence" and on their duty to make a decision based solely on the evidence presented at trial. Even though the presumption of innocence may only be a part of the beyond a reasonable doubt standard, this requirement is not satisfied by only instructing the jury in terms of the proof beyond a reasonable doubt standard. However, in the following

standard requires the government to prove, within a fair procedural framework, that a person is unquestionably guilty of the crime for which he is to be incarcerated. The standard also prohibits the use of any procedure which would shift to the accused the burden of proving their innocence as to any basic element of the criminal charge.[10]

The due process guarantee also applies to restraints on physical liberty which are imposed in noncriminal settings. While the required procedures may differ depending on the type of action, the government can never impose substantial physical restraints on an individual without establishing a procedure to determine the factual basis and legality of such actions. Thus a child may not be made a ward of the state and subjected to state custody unless the child first receives a fair procedure including a notice of any charges against him and the assistance of counsel.[11] Indeed, when juvenile proceedings are based on charges of alleged criminal activity, those charges must be proven beyond a reasonable doubt.[12]

A significant number of people are also deprived of their freedom of action by being involuntarily committed to state institutions for mental treatment. While the Court has not clearly defined the procedures required, it is clear that an adult cannot be committed for a treatment of "mental illness" unless there has been a fair procedure to determine that the person is dangerous to himself or others.[13] In *Addington v. Texas*[14] the Supreme Court determined that an adult cannot be involuntarily committed to a psychiatric institution on a burden of proof that requires the state merely to show by a preponderance of the evidence that the person is dangerous to himself or another. Although the Court did not require a "beyond a reasonable doubt" standard, it held that trial courts must at least employ a "clear and convincing" evidence standard. Chief Justice Burger, writing for a unanimous Court, found that the societal and constitutional values placed on freedom from physical interment required adoption of a standard beyond the mere preponderance

---

term the Supreme Court ruled that Taylor had not established a rule requiring the presumption of innocence instruction in every case. The majority in Kentucky v. Whorton, 441 U.S. 786 (1979) found that the presence or absence of such an instruction was but one factor to be considered in determining whether a particular defendant received a constitutionally fair trial.

10. If the government formally shifts the burden of proof to the defendant regarding an essential element of the defense, it will violate due process, although the state may be able to require the defendant to bear the burden of proof regarding some affirmative defenses which are the equivalent of pleas of confession and avoidance. Compare Mullaney v. Wilbur, 421 U.S. 684 (1975), with Patterson v. New York, 432 U.S. 197 (1977).

If the state seeks to use a mandatory presumption, that presumption will violate due process unless the existence of the proved fact must lead a factfinder to conclude beyond a reasonable doubt that the presumed fact actually existed. Thus an instruction in a homicide prosecution that "the law presumes that every person intends the ordinary consequences of his voluntary acts" violated due process because a reasonable jury could have regarded this as a conclusive presumption. Such a presumption was unconstitutional because it relieved the state of its burden of proving the defendant guilty beyond a reasonable doubt. See Sandstrom v. Montana, 442 U.S. 510 (1979). However, when the state seeks to use a permissive presumption, which might be better termed an inference, the presumption

is to be judged only in terms of the specific case, not in terms of its general worth of proving the presumed fact under all possible circumstances. A permissive presumption instruction merely informs the jury that they may, but need not, infer a fact or conclusion from the existence of a proven fact. So long as the jury would be acting in a reasonable manner by using the presumption and the presumed fact to find guilt beyond reasonable doubt under the facts of the specific case, there will be no violation of due process. See, e.g., County Court v. Allen, 442 U.S. 140 (1979).

11. In re Gault, 387 U.S. 1 (1967); note that the child need not be granted trial by jury or a public trial, McKeiver v. Pennsylvania, 403 U.S. 528 (1971).

12. In the Matter of Winship, 397 U.S. 358 (1970).

13. O'Connor v. Donaldson, 422 U.S. 563 (1975). See also State ex rel. Doe v. Madonna, 295 N.W.2d 356, 363 n.9 (Minn.1980) (Kelly, J., quoting an earlier edition of this work). There must be some comparable safeguards between civil and criminal procedures for commitment. Jackson v. Indiana, 406 U.S. 715 (1972); Humphrey v. Cady, 405 U.S. 504 (1972). There are many unresolved issues regarding the types of due process safeguards that should be required in commitment proceedings. See generally, F. Miller, R. Dawson, G. Dix & R. Parnas, The Mental Health Process (1976).

14. 441 U.S. 418 (1979). This opinion was unanimous but Justice Powell did not participate in the decision.

standard. However, the nature of commitment proceedings, which are non-punitive and concerned with issues upon which there is virtually never factual certainty, did not require states to adopt a "beyond a reasonable doubt" or "unequivocal proof" standard.

The Supreme Court has not required states to provide similar due process safeguards for children who are committed to a mental health care facility by their parent or guardian. In *Parham v. J.R.*[15] the Court found that the voluntary commitment of a child to a state-operated mental health care institution by the child's parents, but over the child's objection, or by the state, if the child was a ward of the state, deprived the child of a liberty interest but that this deprivation did not require a pre-commitment adversarial hearing. The Supreme Court ruled that such a child was only entitled to have a "neutral fact finder" (such as a state-employed social worker or psychologist) determine if statutory criteria for commitment were met in the individual child's case.[16] The Court did not determine whether the commitment of a child to a private institution by his or her parents constituted state action that deprived the child of a constitutionally protected liberty interest.[17]

In a decision which involved both substantive and procedural due process analysis the Supreme Court found that an involuntarily committed person had a substantive right to reasonably safe conditions of confinement and freedom from unnecessary bodily restraint.[18] However, the Court found that those rights would be sufficiently safeguarded if courts merely determine that "professional judgment was in fact exercised" in determining the degree of restraint imposed on the individual and that the judgment was not "a substantial departure from accepted professional judgment." The Court has avoided ruling on whether involuntarily committed persons have a constitutionally protected right to minimally adequate rehabilitative treatment.[19]

Once a person has been incarcerated following a fair procedure that does not completely terminate his or her right to liberty. Persons convicted of a crime may be placed on probation in lieu of being imprisoned or paroled from prison prior to the end of their maximum sentence. If the state seeks to revoke the probation or parole and place the convicted defendant in prison, it must give him a new hearing.[20] While this hearing need not have the safeguards of a criminal trial it must constitute a fair procedure for determining the basis for the revocation of parole or probation. The Court has held that taking away early release credit from a

15. 442 U.S. 584 (1979). See also Secretary of Public Welfare of Pennsylvania v. Institutionalized Juveniles, 442 U.S. 640 (1979).

16. The procedural requirement of screening by a neutral fact finding is examined in Section III C 1 of this chapter.

17. The dissenting justices in the 1979 cases would have found state action in a parent using a private hospital and they seem to have assumed that the other justices would have applied due process principles to safeguard the minor's interest in this "private" commitment situation even though the justices in the majority might define those principles differently than the dissent. Secretary of Public Welfare of Pennsylvania v. Institutionalized Juveniles, 442 U.S. 640, 650 (1979) (Brennan, J., dissenting joined by Marshall and Stevens, JJ.). The position of the dissent on this state action deprivation issue seems most reasonable because the state by statute creates, or at least validates, the parental power to commit the child to an institution and loss of liberty. However, the majority avoided this issue. Id. at 642, n.1. It should be noted that the Supreme Court has in one case held that a

state statute only recognizing the ability of private persons to help themselves does not create state action in the acts of those private persons. See Flagg Bros., Inc. v. Brooks, 436 U.S. 149 (1978) (finding no state action in a warehouseman sale conducted without active state assistance but pursuant to a state statute; the case is noted in Chapter 14.

18. Youngberg v. Romeo, 102 S.Ct. 2452 (1982).

19. Compare Youngberg v. Romeo, 102 S.Ct. 2452 (1982) (Blackmun, J., joined by Brennan & O'Connor, JJ., noting the unresolved a difficult nature of this substantive claim) with 102 S.Ct. at 2465 (Burger, C.J., concurring in the judgment asserting that there is no substantive right to training or rehabilitation). In Mills v. Rogers, 102 S.Ct. 2442 (1982) the Court avoided reviewing a claim that mental patients have a constitutionally protected right to refuse "antipsychotic drugs."

20. Morrissey v. Brewer, 408 U.S. 471 (1972) (parole); Gagnon v. Scarpelli, 411 U.S. 778 (1973) (probation).

prisoner requires a fair procedure,[21] but it has also held that prisoners could be deprived of benefits by being transferred to a different corrections facility without a hearing.[22]

In *Vitek v. Jones*,[23] the Supreme Court clarified its rulings concerning the treatment of prisoners when it held that an involuntary transfer of a prisoner to a mental hospital implicated a protected liberty interest and that due process was not satisfied by the mere certification of the need for such treatment by a state-designated physician or psychologist. The Court found the existence of a liberty interest in this case on two separate grounds. First, the state statutes at issue in this case gave rise to a legitimate expectation on the part of the prisoner that he would only be kept in normal prison facilities and not be transferred to a mental hospital for psychiatric treatment without an accurate determination of his need for that treatment. Secondly, the involuntary commitment to a mental hospital, unlike a transfer between normal correctional facilities, in-

volved the loss of a liberty interest because it involved not only a greater degree of confinement but also the imposition of mandatory treatment and a realistic possibility of stigmatizing consequences for the defendant in the future. Because the transfer threatened a deprivation of the prisoner's protected liberty interest, he was entitled to "appropriate procedural safeguards against error."[24]

A convicted inmate of a penal institution does not have a constitutionally cognizable liberty or property interest in the possibility of receiving parole release before expiration of his prison sentence, but state law might create a specific entitlement to release under certain circumstances which would require some minimal procedures to ensure fair decision-making by a parole board. The majority opinion, by Chief Justice Burger, in *Greenholtz v. Inmates of the Nebraska Penal and Correctional Complex*[25] found that the possibility of parole release under a generalized parole system constituted no more than the state holding out a possibility

---

21. Wolff v. McDonnell, 418 U.S. 539 (1974).

22. When a person has been convicted of a crime, he has received the best process which our society can afford to justify his liberty loss. A later transfer of the prisoner to differing conditions of confinement does not require a new process unless the new conditions may be said to be outside of the normal range of (or substantive constitutional limits on) the conditions of confinement. Thus, a prisoner who is transferred to a facility for mental treatment is entitled to a hearing, Vitek v. Jones, 445 U.S. 480 (1980). However, when a prisoner is placed in administrative segregation or transferred to a different penal facility, even one in another state, no new process is required because the transfer does not implicate a liberty interest which was not adequately protected by the original criminal process and conviction. Montanye v. Haymes, 427 U.S. 236 (1976) (transfer to different prison facility); Meachum v. Fano, 427 U.S. 215 (1976) (transfer to maximum security prison); Howe v. Smith, 452 U.S. 473 (1981) (state prisoner transferred to federal penal facility); Hewitt v. Helms, 103 S.Ct. 864 (1983) (prisoner placed in administrative segregation); Olim v. Wakinekona, 103 S.Ct. 1741 (1983) (state prisoner transferred from prison in Hawaii to maximum security prison in California). If a state by statute or administrative action declares prisoners to be entitled to a hearing prior to a transfer into administrative segregation or to another penal facility, the state has given those prisoners an interest which is protected by due process. Hewitt v. Helms, 103 S.Ct. 864 (1983). Cf. Hughes v. Rowe, 449 U.S. 5 (1980) (per curiam). When

the state has given a prisoner an interest in receiving fair treatment in the decision to transfer him to administrative segregation or to another facility, that interest is adequately protected by an informal, nonadversarial proceeding to review the basis for the transfer. Hewitt v. Helms, 103 S.Ct. 864, 872–74 (1983).

It is important to note that these decisions do not hold that "liberty," like "property", is to be defined only by reference to legislative or administrative actions rather than constitutional values. Rather, they hold that a prisoner's liberty has been taken with due process by our criminal justice system. Even after incarceration, a person may not be subjected to a form of punishment—such as beating or transference to a facility for psychiatric care—not normally expected in our penal system without due process. However, the prisoner has no interest protected by due process in the place or type of confinement so long as it comports with substantive standards of due process and the prohibition of cruel and unusual punishment. A state by statute or administrative regulation may commit itself to giving prisoners a fair proceeding to review their transfer. Such legislative or administrative action restores to the prisoner a measure of the liberty properly taken from him by his criminal conviction.

23. 445 U.S. 480 (1980).

24. 445 U.S. at 495. The Court's rulings on the precise procedures to be afforded are noted in Section III, C, 1 of this chapter.

25. 442 U.S. 1 (1979).

or hope of early release—"a hope which is not protected by due process."[26] Thus the majority distinguished its earlier application of due process principles to parole and probation revocations because those determinations involved termination, upon a finding of specific facts, of a state-granted, presently enjoyed, conditional liberty interest.

The State of Nebraska, whose parole system was challenged in *Greenholtz*, required by statute that the state parole board release an inmate eligible for parole unless the board found that parole should be denied for one of several specific statutory reasons. The Supreme Court found that this particular statute created a liberty interest entitled to "some measure of constitutional protection." But the majority opinion noted that this statute was unique and each state parole statute would have to be examined, on a case-by-case basis, to determine if it created similar entitlements. The majority found that the liberty interest created by the Nebraska statute was not entitled to specific guarantees such as those required for the adversarial fact determination hearing for parole or probation revocation. Because the initial parole release decision was both a subjective and predictive one relating to prisoner rehabilitation, few procedural safeguards would be required.

The majority did not determine what particular procedural rights were necessary to protect this interest; the majority opinion merely found that the Nebraska Parole Board procedures were constitutionally sufficient. The parole board conducted an initial screening of all those persons eligible for parole, which involved an informal hearing for each prisoner without the taking of evidence. If the board believed a prisoner

was a likely candidate for parole, it then gave him a second hearing where the prisoner could present evidence on his behalf, and be represented by counsel, but which was a non-adversary hearing, without a right to hear adverse testimony. The board gave a written statement of its reason for denying parole to those who had the second hearing; a tape recording of the second hearing was preserved although there was no transcript of those proceedings. The majority found these procedures sufficient to minimize risk of error in this subjective process, which was based on but a few objective points and the evaluation of the prisoner's character by members of the board. Thus, the Supreme Court found that the lower federal courts should not have ordered a formal hearing for every inmate nor a statement of evidence relied upon by the board.

Mr. Justice Powell, who was of the opinion that all persons eligible for parole had a constitutionally protected liberty interest at stake in the proceedings, would have required more than a one-day notice of the scheduled hearing to the prisoner so that the prisoner could prepare himself for the hearing.[27] However, the majority found no significant claim of prejudice to the prisoner resulting from the late notice procedure.[28]

Based upon the rationale of the *Greenholtz* decision, The Supreme Court ruled in *Connecticut Bd. of Pardons v. Dumschat*[29] that a prisoner serving a life sentence had no right to procedural fairness in the review of his request for commutation of his life sentence. Chief Justice Burger wrote for the majority in *Dumschat*, as he had in *Greenholtz*. The Chief Justice found that, absent a state-created entitlement to fair treatment in the review of his sentence, the

---

26. 442 U.S. at 11.

27. Justice Powell found the other aspects of the Nebraska hearing system to be a fair, sufficient process to protect the inmates' interests. 442 U.S. at 18–22, (Powell, J., concurring in part and dissenting in part).

28. Justices Marshall, Brennan and Stevens, in dissent, would have found that all those eligible for parole have a constitutionally protected liberty interest at stake in the proceeding. The dissenters would have re-

quired earlier notice to each prisoner regarding the time of his hearing, notice of the factors that the Board might consider regarding his parole, and a statement of the evidence relied upon by the Board, rather than a general statement of reasons, whenever the Board denied parole. Greenholtz v. Inmates of the Nebraska Penal and Correctional Complex, 442 U.S. 1, 22 (1979) (Marshall, J., concurring and dissenting, joined by Brennan & Stevens, JJ.)

29. 452 U.S. 458 (1981).

due process clause imposed no procedural safeguards against arbitrary treatment of the defendant's request for commutation. The Court refused to find that the prisoner had a constitutionally cognizable interest at stake in the review of his sentence even though the review board commuted most of the life sentences which came before it. Correctly analyzed, the ruling in this case is no more than a finding that the prisoner's liberty had been properly taken from him through the criminal trial-and-appeal process. The Court found that the prisoner had no right to a statement of reasons for the denial of his request because it amounted to nothing more than "an appeal for clemency." [30] However, some may mistakenly view the case as propounding the principle that "liberty as well as property" is a creation of state law, a position which has no basis in prior substantive or procedural due process rulings of the Supreme Court.[31]

In closing it must be noted that any significant, even though temporary, physical restraint or punishment of a person constitutes a deprivation of liberty which requires some procedural safeguard. In *Ingraham v. Wright* [32] the Supreme Court upheld the use of corporal punishment for children by state school teachers so long as the state had some procedure to later determine the propriety of such actions and impose liability for any excessive use of force. But in so do-

ing the majority opinion fully accepted the position that physical restraint constitutes a deprivation of liberty for which some process is due unless it would be of an extremely brief and *de minimis* nature.[33]

3. *Fundamental Constitutional Rights*

Liberty includes the freedom of choice to engage in certain activities. When those activities have specific constitutional recognition, the liberty to engage in them is protected by the due process guarantee. In one sense it may be said that all activities or liberty have constitutional recognition as none is singled out for special limitations. But the government has broad powers to curtail individual freedom of action to promote the legitimate ends of society except where there is some specific constitutional limitation on its powers. Since 1937 and the rejection of the old substantive due process, the Court will actively protect only "fundamental" constitutional rights.[34] These rights are those with textual recognition in the Constitution, or its amendments, or values found to be implied because they are "fundamental" to freedom in American society, as reflected by history and the interpretation of the Supreme Court. The Court recognized the concept of fundamental rights when it incorporated most of the guarantees of the Bill of Rights into the due process clause of the fourteenth amendment and applied them

---

30. 452 U.S. at 465. Similarly, in Jago v. Van Curen, 454 U.S. 14 (1981) the Court held that a parole board could rescind its decision to grant a prisoner parole without a hearing upon learning of the falsity of statements made to the board by the prisoner.

31. See note 22, supra. Justice Brennan's concurring opinion might be taken by some persons to indicate that the state law could determine when a person had a protectable liberty interest under the Constitution, although it is doubtful that the justice meant to imply agreement with such a rule. Connecticut Bd. of Pardons v. Dumschat, 452 U.S. 458, 467 (1981) (Brennan, J., concurring). Justice White's concurring opinion noted clearly that liberty interests entitled to constitutional protection were not solely definable by state law even though due process might not guarantee the prisoner any administrative safeguards for denial of his request for release or sentence reduction. Id. at 467 (White, J., concurring). Justice Stevens, in an opinion joined by Justice Marshall, found that the prisoner had a liberty interest that survived conviction for a

criminal offense and which could not be left solely to definition by the state in keeping with the guarantees of due process. While the due process clause might not provide many safeguards for such an interest, the dissenting justices could see no reason why the state should not be required to give a statement of reasons for denial of the prisoner's request in order to provide a minimum degree of fairness in these proceedings. 452 U.S. at 468 (Stevens, J., joined by Marshall, J., dissenting). These justices had also dissented in the *Greenholtz* decision. See note 28, supra.

32. 430 U.S. 651 (1977).

33. 430 U.S. 674.

34. See Section IV of Chapter 13 on Substantive Due Process Since 1937. For a criticism of the expansion of the term "liberty" to protect values without textual recognition, combined with an acceptance of the Court's position, see Monaghan, supra note 1, at 411–16.

to the states.[35] The most significant implied "fundamental" rights are the right to freedom of association, the right to interstate travel; the right to privacy (including some freedom of choice in marital, family, and sexual matters), and the right to vote.[36]

In their procedural aspects the due process clauses require that the government not restrict a specific individual's freedom to exercise a fundamental constitutional right without a process to determine the basis for the restriction. Thus, if a filmmaker is to be subjected to a licensing system to determine whether his film is obscene, the government must establish a prompt and fair procedure to determine its obscenity or allow him to show the film.[37] Whenever the government seeks to restrain speech, there must be a prompt procedure to determine whether the speech may be limited in conformity with first amendment principles.[38]

When it appears that the government is going to punish someone for engaging in a constitutionally protected activity, a hearing is required. The Supreme Court has stated that if a government employee is to be dismissed because of his speech or writing, there must be a hearing to determine the

factual basis and permissibility of the dismissal. Since the employee could not be dismissed as a punishment for activities protected by the first amendment, a hearing is required to aid in the determination of whether the activity which is the basis for the dismissal falls outside of this protection. "Even though he could have been discharged for no reason whatever, and had no constitutional right to a hearing prior to the decision not to rehire him, . . . he may nonetheless establish a claim to reinstatement if the decision not to rehire him was made by reason of his exercise of constitutionally protected freedoms." [39]

These procedural safeguards apply whenever the government seeks to burden an individual in the exercise of fundamental constitutional rights. The right to privacy includes a right to freedom of choice in marital and family decisions. Thus, when a state seeks to take a child away from its parents, the parents must be given a hearing to determine their fitness to retain the child. Because of the fundamental nature of the interest in family autonomy, the state must prove its allegation of parental unfitness by at least "clear and convincing" evidence.[40]

---

35. For a listing of the decisions on "incorporation", see Chapter 12 and Chapter 13, Section V.

36. For a note regarding the role of fundamental rights analysis today, see Chapter 13, Section V.

37. Freedman v. Maryland, 380 U.S. 51 (1965).

38. Blount v. Rizzi, 400 U.S. 410 (1971); Southeastern Promotions Ltd. v. Conrad, 420 U.S. 546 (1975); See, Monaghan, First Amendment "Due Process," 83 Harv.L.Rev. 518 (1970).

39. Mt. Healthy City Bd. of Education v. Doyle, 429 U.S. 274, 283–4 (1977), citing Board of Regents v. Roth, 408 U.S. 569 (1972) and Perry v. Sindermann, 408 U.S. 593 (1972). This substantive first amendment restriction on the agency's powers exists unless the agency can prove that the employee would have been discharged regardless of his exercising his first amendment rights. See Mt. Healthy City Bd. of Education v. Doyle, 429 U.S. 274 (1977). In Givhan v. Western Line Consolidated School District, 439 U.S. 410 (1979) the Court unanimously held that the teacher could not be discharged for privately communicating her grievances about working conditions, or opinions concerning employment or public issues, to her employer. This decision extended the protection of Pickering v. Board of Education, 391 U.S. 563 (1968) to the private conversations of public employees. The opinion reaffirmed the

principle established in *Mt. Healthy* that when an employee has shown that constitutionally protected conduct played a role in the government's decision not to retain him in his job, the employer is required to and entitled to demonstrate "by a preponderance of the evidence that it would have reached the same decision as to [the employee's] reemployment even in the absence of the protected conduct." 439 U.S. at 416, quoting Mt. Healthy City Bd. of Education v. Doyle, 429 U.S. 274, 287 (1977). The degree of burden placed on the government agency to demonstrate that the discharge decision was not a punishment of constitutionally protected speech may vary with the nature of the employee's expression. See, Connick v. Myers, 103 S.Ct. 1684 (1983).

40. Santosky v. Kramer, 102 S.Ct. 1388 (1982). An indigent parent is not entitled to the services of state-paid counsel in such cases. Lassiter v. Department of Social Services, 452 U.S. 18 (1981). The procedures required by these cases are examined further in Section III B of this Chapter.

The Court has on several occasions granted review to cases involving substantive due process and equal protection questions concerning a state's ability to define the basis upon which parents are deemed unfit and their parental rights terminated. However, at the con-

This principle is valid even if the state seeks to take away an illegitimate child from its father. Due process requires that the child and parent be granted a hearing and the equal protection guarantee prohibits discrimination against illegitimates.[41] The state also must make some process fairly available for persons to control the exercise of their freedom of choice in marital matters. Thus the state could not refuse to grant a divorce to those persons who were unable to pay court filing fees.[42] The due process clause requires the state to allow freedom of choice in marital matters and the equal protection clause prohibits an allocation of the freedom only to those who can pay for it.

Similarly the equal protection clause forbids imposing appellate fees or transcript costs on those persons convicted of crimes who cannot pay for those procedures as this relates to the protection of a fundamental constitutional right.[43] However, fees for a judicial process need not be waived for indigents when the process is not clearly necessary to the protection of a "fundamental" constitutional right.[44]

The Supreme Court has held that, in establishing loss of citizenship, the federal government must prove that an individual intended to surrender his or her United States citizenship, not just that he or she voluntarily acted in a manner declared by Congress to be sufficient to demonstrate a basis for expatriation.[45] However, the Court found that Congress could prescribe that the standard of proof in expatriation proceedings be a preponderance of the evidence because "expatriation proceedings are civil in nature and do not threaten a loss of liberty."[46] Although inartfully phrased, this decision holds only that expatriation proceedings do not involve incarceration of the defendant and, therefore, do not require a greater standard of proof. This decision does not mean that loss of citizenship is unprotected by constitutional procedural requirements under either the citizenship

clusion of the 1981–82 Term, the Court had avoided ruling on these issues. See Moore v. Sims, 442 U.S. 415 (1979) (ruling that lower federal court should have abstained from ruling on this issue); Doe v. Delaware, 450 U.S. 382 (1981) (Brennan, White & Stevens dissenting) (dismissing appeal "for want of a properly presented federal question). The Court has also left unclear whether the relationship between a foster child and foster parents will receive due process protection. See Smith v. Organization of Foster Families for Equality and Reform, 431 U.S. 816 (1977) (upholding system for removing children from foster homes but assuming *arguendo* that the foster parent-child interest was protected by due process, a point disputed in a concurring opinion by Justices Stewart and Rehnquist and Chief Justice Burger).

41. Stanley v. Illinois, 405 U.S. 645 (1972). For an examination of the relationship between these two guarantees in protecting the father's interest, see, Nowak, Realigning the Standards of Review Under the Equal Protection Guarantee, 62 Geo.L.J. 1071 (1974). Due process also provides some procedural protection to a man charged in a paternity action with being the parent of an illegitimate child. See Little v. Streater, 452 U.S. 1 (1981) (indigent has a right to state-paid blood test in paternity action initiated by, or at the order of, a government agency). See Section III B of this chapter.

42. Boddie v. Connecticut, 401 U.S. 371 (1971). See also Zablocki v. Redhail, 434 U.S. 374 (1978) (invalidating as a violation of equal protection a state prohibition of marriage by persons who had not met financial obli-

gation to pay alimony or child support arising from an earlier marriage and divorce).

43. Griffin v. Illinois, 351 U.S. 12 (1956). However, counsel need not be provided for indigents after their first appeal as of right. Ross v. Moffit, 417 U.S. 600 (1974); see this chapter on the right of access to courts, Section IV. In Scott v. Illinois, 440 U.S. 367 (1979) the Supreme Court limited the right of indigent criminal defendants to appointed counsel at trial to those cases where the defendant in fact received a punishment of imprisonment. The Court had held that indigents had a right to appointed counsel at least when they were imprisoned for conviction on the charged offense in Argersinger v. Hamlin, 407 U.S. 25 (1972). The *Scott* majority refused to extend this right to those indigent defendants who were charged with serious offenses but who in fact received only a monetary fine rather than a sentence of imprisonment. However, if an indigent defendant is not given appointed counsel during a misdemeanor trial, his conviction cannot then serve as the basis for converting a subsequent misdemeanor into a felony under a state "enhanced penalty" statute. Baldasar v. Illinois, 446 U.S. 222 (1980).

44. United States v. Kras, 409 U.S. 434 (1973) (No right to waiver of fees for voluntary bankruptcy); Ortwein v. Schwab, 410 U.S. 656 (1973) (No right to appellate review of welfare termination.) See Section IV of this chapter for a comment on these cases.

45. Vance v. Terrazas, 444 U.S. 252 (1980).

46. 444 U.S. at 266.

clause of the fourteenth amendment or the due process clause of the fifth amendment.

4. Other Rights or "Liberties"

While the Court has not defined the exact scope of the liberties which are protected by the due process clauses, it is clear that they go beyond mere physical restraint or fundamental constitutional rights. The clauses also guarantee that each individual will have some degree of freedom of choice and action in all important personal matters. The Court has stated that the term "denotes not merely freedom from bodily restraint but also the right of the individual to contract, to engage in any of the common occupations of life, to acquire useful knowledge, to marry, establish a home and bring up children, to worship God according to the dictates of his own conscience and generally to enjoy those privileges long recognized . . . as essential to the orderly pursuit of happiness by free men." [47] However, the Court was also careful to note that not all areas of human activity could be described as "liberty" for constitutional terms and that individuals in some situations could be adversely affected by government without any substantive or procedural guarantees.[48] It would appear that whenever the government takes an action which is designed to deprive an individual, or a limited group of individuals, of the freedom to engage in some significant area of human activity, some procedure to determine the factual basis and legality for such action being taken is required by the due process clause.[49] The primary issues have

arisen in terms of restrictions on employment, the granting or withholding of important occupational licenses, and injury to the reputation of an individual.

If the government terminates an individual's ability to engage in a profession, it must grant that individual a procedure to determine his fitness to be a member of the profession.[50] Thus if an agency with governmental authority seeks to revoke the professional status or license of a doctor or lawyer, it must accord that individual a fair hearing. If the individual has been denied a license to engage in a profession, it is not clear whether he is entitled to a hearing if the denial is based on any factual matter which might be contested or clarified at a hearing. Some decisions concerning the right to "property" indicate that no hearing may be due unless the person has already received a license which the government is seeking to revoke.[51] If this is true, the individual who has been denied an initial license would have to bring a judicial action to have the basis for the denial reviewed. But a loss of liberty should be involved where government actions foreclose a wide range of employment or professional opportunities. If the government denial of a license precludes one from gaining employment in both the public and private sectors, the individual should be granted a hearing to determine the basis of the government action.[52]

If someone seeks temporary admission to practice as a licensed professional in a state, state agencies are under no obligation to grant that person a hearing prior to denying

47. Board of Regents v. Roth, 408 U.S. 564, 572 (1972), quoting Meyer v. Nebraska, 262 U.S. 390 (1923).

48. 408 U.S. at 569–70, 575.

49. See generally Monaghan, Of "Liberty" and "Property," 62 Cornell L.Rev. 405 (1977).

50. In re Ruffalo, 390 U.S. 544 (1968); Dent v. West Virginia, 129 U.S. 114, 123 (1889); cf. Withrow v. Larkin, 421 U.S. 35 (1975). Statutes defining the terms for retaining a professional license often use specific criteria for license suspension so that they may give an individual licensee a property interest or "entitlement" in the license. Thus, the New York licensing system for horse trainers created a property interest in licensed trainers that was protected by the due process

clause. Barry v. Barchi, 443 U.S. 55 (1979). The cases noted more fully in Section III C 3 of this chapter.

51. Board of Regents v. Roth, 408 U.S. 564, 576 (1972); Comment, Entitlement, Enjoyment and Due Process of Law, 1974 Duke L.J. 89, 101–2.

52. On this point, note the concurring opinion of Justice Powell in Weinberger v. Hynson, Westcott & Dunning, 412 U.S. 609, 638 (1973) (Powell, J. concurring). For a related decision on the ability of a city to deny chauffeur's (taxi) licenses to a class of persons, see Carter v. Miller, 434 U.S. 356 (1978) (per curiam), aff'g by an equally divided Court, 547 F.2d 1314 (7th Cir. 1977), which is examined in Chapter 13, Section IV.

him or her the opportunity to practice temporarily in the state, if state law has not created an "entitlement" to practice temporarily in the state. Thus, when a state court judge refused to allow attorneys, licensed only in other states, to appear *pro hac vice* in state court proceedings, there was no deprivation of property because there was no entitlement to engage in temporary practice under state law. The Supreme Court also found that the denial involved no deprivation of liberty because the attorneys' reputation and ability to practice law in other states, in which they were licensed, were not seriously damaged by the refusal.[53]

When the government acts as an employer there are special issues regarding the existence of liberty and property rights in employment. If the individual employee has not been granted a term of continued employment absent removal for just cause he will have no property right or entitlement to continued employment in that position.[54] Indeed, dismissal from a specific position does not amount to a loss of "liberty" as the Court has held that having one form of government employment foreclosed does not constitute a deprivation of freedom which is encompassed by that term.[55] However, if in dismissing the employee, the government also forecloses the individual's possible employment in a wide range of activities in both the public and private sectors, this will constitute a deprivation of liberty sufficient to require that the individual be granted a fair hearing. For example, if the government discharges a person from a position for announced reasons of incompetence or other traits which would tend to foreclose future employment opportunities, the individual will be entitled to a hearing to contest the basis for the charges and to clear his reputation in terms of the dismissal process.[56] Additionally, if the termination appears to be based upon grounds which would violate the Constitution, the individual is entitled to a hearing to determine whether he is being dismissed for constitutionally improper reasons. When the employee can make a prima facie showing that he is being dismissed for exercising his right to freedom of speech as protected by the first amendment, he will be entitled to a hearing to determine the basis for his termination.[57]

Whenever the government takes control of an important area of human activity, it must grant a hearing to those who are denied the right to engage in the activity. Because the government has taken control of who may drive automobiles on its highways, when it revokes someone's driver's license, that person is entitled to a hearing to determine the basis for the revocation.[58] However, when the revocation is based on prior judicial determinations of violations of traffic laws, no hearing will be required if there are no further factual issues to contest.[59] In that situation the person has already received the opportunity for full judicial hearings. Similarly, if the government revokes someone's license to engage in a commercial enterprise, it must grant him a hearing to determine any factual issues which relate to the basis for the revocation of the license.[60]

Even where the government has not established a licensing system to regulate an

---

53. Leis v. Flynt, 439 U.S. 438 (1979).

54. Board of Regents v. Roth, 408 U.S. 564 (1972).

55. Board of Regents v. Roth, 408 U.S. 564 (1972); cf. Cafeteria & Restaurant Workers Local 473 v. McElroy, 367 U.S. 36 (1961).

56. This position has been recently reaffirmed by the Court although it did not find a basis for a hearing in the individual case, see Codd v. Velger, 429 U.S. 624 (1977) (per curiam). Deuter v. South Dakota Highway Patrol, 330 N.W.2d 533 (S.D.1983) (citing an earlier edition of this treatise).

57. See the preceding subsection on the exercise of fundamental constitutional rights.

58. Bell v. Burson, 402 U.S. 535 (1971).

A driver may have his or her driver's license suspended for failure to take a drunk driving test under certain circumstances; see Mackey v. Montrym, 443 U.S. 1 (1979) (noted in Section III C 3 of this chapter). Admitting into evidence a defendant's refusal to take a blood-alcohol test violates neither due process nor the fifth amendment privilege against self-incrimination. South Dakota v. Neville, 103 S.Ct. 916 (1983).

59. Dixon v. Love, 431 U.S. 105 (1977).

60. Weinberger v. Hynson, Westcott & Dunning, 412 U.S. 609, 638 (1973) (Powell, J. concurring); cf. Dent v. West Va., 129 U.S. 114, 123 (1889).

activity, if it revokes someone's privilege to engage in an important area of activity it will be required to grant the individual a hearing. Thus, if the government singles out a person as a "drunkard" and eliminates his ability to purchase alcoholic beverages, it will owe him a hearing to determine whether his liberty should be thus curtailed.[61] The government also must give a hearing to resident aliens who are to be deported as the ability to remain physically within the country is protected by the concept of liberty in the fourteenth amendment.[62]

Onc of the most disputed aspects of liberty in recent years is the degree to which the due process clauses protect the interest of an individual in his reputation. The Supreme Court has held that government actions which injure a person's reputation within the community do not constitute a per se deprivation of property or liberty so as to require that the person be granted a hearing prior to the government action. In Paul v. Davis [63] a sheriff had distributed to merchants listings of "active shoplifters." The plaintiff argued that listing him on the sheet violated due process as there was no hearing to determine whether in fact he had engaged in such activities and this resulted in an injury to his reputation.[64] The Supreme Court held that this did not constitute a violation of due process. The majority opinion held that mere injury to reputation alone was not a deprivation of "liberty".[65] However, the majority opinion noted that the individual would have the right to sue the government officials who libeled him, in

a state court, as a matter of state tort law. The ruling that mere injury to reputation does not constitute a deprivation of liberty thus means only that the injured person must be satisfied with a tort remedy which follows the defamatory action. If the State had no tort action for libel against such officials, it would raise a much more serious question as to whether the State was depriving someone of liberty or property by allowing the government to damage his name with no hope of rectifying the harm done. One of the justices has indicated that he believes this "later process" is a better rationale for the opinion.[66] However, Paul seems to find that there is simply no impairment of liberty or property from an injury to one's reputation, although leaving this important individual interest outside of the Constitution is a severe departure from earlier due process theory.[67]

If a government official distributes false information about a person, there will be a deprivation of liberty if the act results in the person's freedom of choice or action being seriously curtailed. Thus if the damage to the person's reputation is so great that it will limit the individual's associational opportunities within a community or foreclose a wide range of employment to the individual, the act will constitute a deprivation of liberty. Thus, in Goss v. Lopez [68] the Court held that disciplinary actions against school students which resulted in their suspension from school would constitute a deprivation of liberty if the charges and actions were such as to damage the student's association-

---

61. Wisconsin v. Constantineau, 400 U.S. 433 (1971).

62. Ng Fung Ho v. White, 259 U.S. 276, 281 (1922). The Supreme Court has held, as a matter of statutory interpretation, that 8 U.S.C.A. § 1105a(a)(5) requires that persons who claim to be U.S. citizens, and who seek review of a deportation order, be given a de novo judicial review of the order whenever there is any "genuine issue of material fact" regarding the nationality claim. Agosto v. Immigration and Naturalization Service, 436 U.S. 748 (1978). A citizen of the United States or a permanent resident alien who makes a trip abroad is denied a constitutionally protected interest when the government seeks to prohibit him from returning to this country. Landon v. Plasencia, 103 S.Ct. 321 (1982); see Chapter 16, Section III, A and Chapter 20.

63. 424 U.S. 693 (1976).

64. The plaintiff had been arrested for shoplifting prior to the distribution of the circular but he had not yet gone to trial. His case was dismissed without a ruling as to his guilt or innocence.

65. 404 U.S. at 708–10.

66. Ingraham v. Wright, 430 U.S. 651 (1977) (Stevens, J., dissenting).

67. Monaghan, Of "Liberty" and "Property," 62 Cornell L.Rev. 405, 532–34 (1977).

68. 419 U.S. 565 (1975).

al relationships with fellow students and their future educational or employment opportunities.[69] Similarly, when one is dismissed from government employment, the person is entitled to a hearing if the method of termination or the publication of information regarding termination will foreclose a wide range of employment opportunities to that person.[70] However, to date the Court has held only that the person is entitled to a hearing where the distribution of defamatory information causes a curtailment of liberty and the information is alleged to be false.[71] Today a government employee has a right to contest the truth of information which the government will release concerning him if it will seriously limit his associational or employment opportunities. The Court has not as of yet held that there is any right to a hearing to contest whether truthful information may be acted upon by the government in such a way as to injure one's associational or employment interests.[72]

It would seem clear that liberty in its most general sense includes the ability of individuals to engage in freedom of action within a society and free choice as regards their personal lives. Of course, not every limitation of individual freedom constitutes a violation of "liberty" in a constitutional sense or requires that the government grant the individual a hearing. When the government acts so as to regulate an area of human activity for all persons, the law will be tested

under the substantive restrictions of the due process clause and the specific protections of the Constitution. But unless some specific fundamental constitutional right is involved the government will be able to regulate most areas of human activity. So long as the government does not classify persons in such a way as to violate the equal protection clause, it may also regulate certain classifications of persons. But the government's ability to regulate or eliminate an area of activity for a general class does not mean that it should be able to single out individuals for special limitations of freedom of action without granting them some process to determine the basis for such an action. One may sometimes see statements that the scope of individual liberty is to be defined by state law, but such a position seems clearly erroneous.[73] For example, while the state need not let anyone purchase alcohol, it cannot single out a specific individual for denial of the right to purchase alcohol without giving that individual a hearing to determine whether such an action is proper. This does not amount to a restriction on the substantive powers of the state to regulate activities within its jurisdiction, but only a recognition that when the state acts against a specific individual, it must do so in a procedurally fair manner. However, the Court has not accepted the concept of a general right to freedom from arbitrary adjudicative procedures.[74]

---

69. The Court has held that a medical student need not be given a hearing for an academic dismissal following notice and review of poor clinical work. In reaching this result, the Court assumed arguendo that the student had been deprived of "liberty." See Board of Curators v. Horowitz, 435 U.S. 78 (1978) (noted in Section III, C, 3 of this chapter).

See also Carey v. Pihus, 435 U.S. 247 (1978) wherein the Court held that a student was entitled to only nominal damages for a violation of his or her rights under *Goss.*

70. This is the implicit holding of Codd v. Velger, 429 U.S. 624 (1977) (per curiam); the Court held the individual was not entitled to a hearing as he did not claim the distributed information was false. The position seemed to be accepted that if the employee alleged that false information had injured him seriously, he

would be entitled to a hearing. 429 U.S. at 638 n. 11. (Stevens, J. dissenting).

71. Id.

72. Justice Stevens had advanced the position that the employee should have the right to contest whether the information justifies dismissal even if it is true. Codd v. Velger, 429 U.S. 624, 631 (1977) (Stevens, J., dissenting).

73. See note 22, supra.

74. This concept of freedom from arbitrary action against individuals as a part of liberty has been advanced by Professor William Van Alstyne and contrasted with the Supreme Court's decisions in Van Alstyne, Cracks in "The New Property": Adjudicative Due Process in the Administrative State, 62 Cornell L.Rev. 445, 487 (1977).

D. Property

1. Introduction

In one sense all property is a creature of the state as each government is free to define or limit property rights. However, the ability of either the state or federal governments to limit rights in property is subject to constitutional limitations. There are substantive limitations such as the first amendment, the equal protection guarantee and the concept of substantive due process which limit the ways in which government can define even the most general property rights. For example, the state government could not define or enforce rights in real property as contingent on the provision that the property not be turned over to a member of a racial minority, for this "definition" would violate the equal protection clause.[1] But within the few substantive guarantees of the Constitution, the government is free to define property rights as it chooses. There is still a procedural requirement that the government not deprive a person of any property unless it affords him "due process."

There are two basic questions concerning the procedural protection for property. First, when is the government depriving someone of property? Second, what constitutes "property"? The first question really is a state action issue: the due process clauses only protect against governmental, rather than private, deprivations of property. This state action issue is examined more fully in a separate chapter.[2] One should note here that, whenever the government enforces private claims to property of one person against another, it has acted to deprive someone of his property.[3] Thus the alleged debtor must be afforded some fair procedure to determine whether his property should be taken and transferred to the other party. If the government were actually taking the individual's property for public use, the person would also be entitled to just compensation for his property.[4]

The most difficult issues relate to the definition of property. Certainly all of the traditional forms of real and personal property fall within this definition, but a problem arises as to those governmental distributions which do not fit this classical concept of property ownership. Any recipient of government benefits or "largess" may be said to have no property right in the benefit because they have no traditionally recognized ownership interest therein. Under the old right-privilege distinction it would be easy to classify the interest of a recipient of welfare payments or a student's interest in receiving public education as an unprotected privilege. Since the government had no duty to create systems of welfare payments or education, its granting or withholding of such "privileges" was not restrained by constitutional guarantees during the era of this distinction. As we have already noted, the right-privilege distinction has come to an end as both courts and commentators have realized that individuals should not be subjected to the unfettered discretion of government to withhold even "privileges."[5] Such a rule would leave many individuals at the mercy of a bureaucratic system and threaten the liberties

---

For a challenge to Professor Van Alstyne's position, see Smolla, The Reemergence of the Right-Privilege Distinction in Constitutional Law: The Price of Protesting Too Much, 35 Stanford L.Rev. 69 (1982); Simon, Liberty and Property in the Supreme Court: A Defense of Roth and Perry, 71 Calif.L.Rev. 146 (1983).

1. Shelley v. Kramer, 334 U.S. 1 (1948); Barrows v. Jackson, 346 U.S. 249 (1953).

2. See Chapter 14 on State Action.

3. Sniadach v. Family Finance Corp., 395 U.S. 337 (1969).

4. See Chapter 13, Section VII concerning eminent domain powers and issues.

5. Compare Van Alstyne, The Demise of the Right-Privilege Distinction in Constitutional Law, 81 Harv.L. Rev. 1439 (1968) and Van Alstyne, Cracks in "The New Property": Adjudicative Due Process in the Administrative State, 62 Cornell L.Rev. 445 (1977), with Monaghan, Of "Liberty" and "Property", 62 Cornell L.Rev. 405 (1977); Smolla, The Reemergence of the Right-Privilege Distinction in Constitutional Law: The Price of Protesting Too Much, 35 Stanford L.Rev. 69 (1982); Simon, Liberty and Property in the Supreme Court: A Defense of Roth and Perry, 71 Calif.L.Rev. 146 (1983).

protected by the Bill of Rights.[6] When the government acts to dispense benefits, it must conform to the restrictions of the Constitution, which means that it may not deprive someone of an interest to which they are otherwise entitled without a procedure to determine the basis for the deprivation.

The definition of property since the 1972 decision in *Board of Regents v. Roth*[7] has centered on the concept of "entitlement." The Court will recognize interests in government benefits as constitutional "property" if the person can be deemed to be "entitled" to them. Thus, the applicable federal, state or local law which governs the dispensation of the benefit must define the interest in such a way that the individual should continue to receive it under the terms of the law. This concept also seems to include a requirement that the person already has received the benefit or at least had a previously recognized claim of entitlement.[8]

A person has an entitlement-property interest in employment with the government if he has already received the position and applicable law guarantees him continued employment.[9] However, if the person has not yet been hired, he has no property right which requires a hearing on the refusal to initially employ him.[10] Similarly, if one occupies a position that applicable law defines as terminable for any reason, that person can be discharged without the requirement of fair procedures.[11]

The concept of entitlement is meant to eliminate the requirement of hearings for those interests that are totally unlike traditional property. Unfortunately this analysis comes very close to the old right-privilege distinction, for states are allowed to define those interests that they will be required to protect under the due process clause. The requirement of present enjoyment also recognizes that the Constitution does not require a hearing for disappointed wishes or expectations but only for property entitlement. But this result leaves a person who must apply for even a highly defined system of general public benefits without procedural safeguards against totally arbitrary actions by government administrators. Again we see the spectre of the right-privilege distinction, for the requirement of present enjoyment places virtually no procedural check on the government's initial decision to distribute benefits. However, it should be noted that the Supreme Court has not yet been confronted with a state which refuses to give any explanation or procedure to a person who is denied an initial allocation of a very important government benefit. For example, if a town refused to accept a particular child into its primary educational system, even though the child appeared to qualify under applicable law, it is difficult to believe that the concept of present enjoyment or entitlement would eliminate the requirement of a fair procedure to determine the basis for this action. It is possible that in such a case

---

6. See the introductory section to this chapter and materials cited therein, especially Reich, The New Property, 73 Yale L.J. 733 (1964); Reich, Individual Rights and Social Welfare: The Emerging Legal Issues, 74 Yale L.J. 11245 (1965).

7. 408 U.S. 564 (1972).

8. This "present enjoyment" concept is implied by some statements of the Court but it has not been the focus of a decision. Board of Regents v. Roth, 408 U.S. 564, 576 (1972); Comment, Entitlement, Enjoyment and Due Process of Law, 1974 Duke L.J. 89, 101–02.

The lack of an immediate right to possess property will not foreclose all due process rights. Thus, the Supreme Court has held that under certain circumstances, claims (which accrued prior to the final determination of their claim) on a fund that had been deposited with a court clerk. See Webb's

Fabulous Pharmacies, Inc. v. Beckwith, 449 U.S. 155 (1980).

The Supreme Court has refused to review a case in which the Ninth Circuit Court of Appeals held that an applicant for a state's welfare benefits was entitled to procedural safeguards. Peer v. Griffeth, 445 U.S. 970 (1980) (Rehnquist, J., dissenting to denial of certiorari).

9. Perry v. Sindermann, 408 U.S. 593 (1972). In *Perry* the applicable law was found to be administrative actions and a common law of tenure; see the subsection on employment which follows in this chapter.

10. It should be noted that the present enjoyment concept is not clearly established and may be inapplicable to decisions that also concern "liberty"; see note 8 supra and Section II, C.

11. Bishop v. Wood, 426 U.S. 341 (1976).

the Court would find that the definition of eligibility constituted a previous entitlement even though there was no actual receipt of the benefit prior to the request for a hearing. However, the concept of present enjoyment is undefined at this time.

Obviously, the distinction between "entitlements" and "expectancies" offers little guidance to those who need to solve problems relating to the meaning of property under the due process clauses. All that can be said with certainty is that the Supreme Court currently focuses on local law to determine if the person can be said to have a fair claim to a continuation of the government benefit.[12] If they have an entitlement to the benefit, they must receive a fair procedure to determine the basis for the government withdrawal of the benefit. If they have no claim of entitlement under applicable law there need be no process at all. There have been three particular problems in this area: (1) transfer of property in debt actions; (2) termination of government benefits; (3) government employment. In addition, an individual's interest in his or her reputation is reconsidered as a property interest.

2. Debt Actions

Whenever property is taken from someone with the assistance of government officers, there is a deprivation of property. Thus, when the defendant in a lawsuit is ordered to pay money to a plaintiff, the defendant has been deprived of property. In such a situation, however, there is no denial of due process because the defendant received a fair process—the opportunity for a full trial.

A significant due process issue arises where the property in the possession of the alleged debtor is to be taken prior to trial. If, prior to trial the government grants the plaintiff-creditor a writ of replevin, or otherwise assists in the transfer of property to the creditor, there is a deprivation of the debtor's property, requiring that the government establish a fair procedure to determine whether the creditor should receive the use of property and to insure that the debtor's interest in the property will be safeguarded pending the outcome of the litigation.[13] Even though the property of the defendant is only "frozen" prior to trial to insure that asset will be available to any later judgments, there is a deprivation of property.[14] Although the property itself has not been transferred, the debtor-defendant is deprived of its use. Such garnishments or attachments of debtor assets thus require a fair procedure to protect the interests of the debtor-defendant. The procedures required to safeguard these interests are examined in section III of this chapter.

It should be noted that many states have provisions in their commercial codes which legitimate private repossession of goods from debtors by creditors. While the private repossession constitutes a taking of a debtor's property, only "state action" is regulated by the due process clauses. A state's formal recognition of the "self-help" remedy has not been deemed sufficient to subject the self-help remedy to the restraints of the due process clause.[15]

---

12. It is possible for a governmental unit through its statutes to create an entitlement to government services, including the courts. In Logan v. Zimmerman Brush Co., 455 U.S. 422 (1982) the Court held that an employee who alleged he had been discharged from employment because of his physical handicap had a state-created entitlement to use the state's administrative and judicial processes for examination of his claim. The state fair employment practices statute was found to give the individual state citizen a property right to use the state's adjudicatory procedures.

The Supreme Court has found that customers of a municipal utility company had a property interest in continued service from the utility. Memphis Light,

Gas, and Water Division v. Craft, 436 U.S. 1 (1978). Because state law recognized a public utility's right to terminate service only "for cause," the Court found that customers who disputed their bills had a legitimate claim of entitlement which was protected by the due process clause.

13. North Georgia Finishing v. Di-Chem, 419 U.S. 601 (1975).

14. Sniadach v. Family Finance Corp., 395 U.S. 337 (1969).

15. The Supreme Court upheld a state law, based on a provision of the Uniform Commercial Code, that allowed a warehouseman to sell the goods of another

3. Government Benefits

This category includes all forms of benefits which the government dispenses to individuals. These benefits may be paid in cash (such as social security payments or farm subsidies) or distributed in kind (such as housing in publicly-owned facilities) or given in a hybrid form (such as food stamps, which constitute a subsidy for particular items). It should be remembered that even the most basic governmental services such as police protection or public primary education are forms of public welfare benefits.

As the government is not under a duty to provide these benefits, they are sometimes referred to as government "largess." But when the government distributes these benefits, it must do so in accordance with constitutional limitations. Thus, it cannot deny benefits to someone because he or she is a member of a racial minority for that would violate the equal protection guarantee.[16] Similarly, persons cannot be denied benefits because they engage in speech or associational activities which are protected by the first amendment.[17] The Constitution may also restrain the government from making payments to some persons, such as religious societies[18] or groups that discriminate against others on the basis of race.[19] Where no fundamental constitutional principles are involved, the government has great latitude in its ability to select those to whom it will grant benefits.

Once the government has established a system of benefits, the due process clauses impose some requirement of fairness in the treatment of individual recipients of these goods or services. As Charles Reich has noted, the absence of recognition of individual "rights" in these benefits leaves the government with the power to undermine individual dignity and liberty through its dispensation of "privileges" to those dependent upon them.[20] Yet the Supreme Court has not required the government to establish fair procedures for the initial allocation of benefits. Although the Court has not resolved this issue, under the "entitlement" principle it would appear that a person has no property interest in a benefit unless he has previously been granted it by the government.[21]

A person receiving welfare payments, public housing, or public education will clearly lose an important interest if the government terminates his benefits. Yet the Supreme Court has refused to hold that prior receipt of benefits in itself gives one a right to a fair process to determine whether termination is proper. If the person's interest in the continuation of the benefit is categorized as a "mere expectancy", there is no loss of property which merits the protection of the due process clause. It is only when the person has a "claim of entitlement" that the interest rises to the level of constitutional property.[22] Entitlement is determined by looking to applicable state or federal law regarding the disposition of the particular ben-

that were in his possession and against which he had a warehouseman's lien for storage charges. The majority opinion held that the law "allowing" the warehouseman-creditor to sell the goods did not give rise to "state action" in the sale. While the majority's rationale for the decision logically would free all self-help remedies from constitutional restraints, the majority opinion specifically noted that "this is not to say that dispute resolution between creditors and debtors involves a category of human affairs that is never subject to constitutional constraints." Flagg Bros., Inc. v. Brooks, 436 U.S. 149, 162 n. 12 (1978). Thus, the extent to which states may legitimize or recognize self-help remedies remains unclear. See generally Uniform Commercial Code § 9–503; Clark & Landers, Sniadach, Fuentes and Beyond: The Creditor Meets the Constitution, 59 Va.L.Rev. 355 (1973).

16. See Section II of Chapter 16 concerning racial classifications.

17. See subsection II, C of this chapter on deprivations of liberty.

18. See Chapter 19 on Freedom of Religion.

19. See Chapter 14 on State Action, subsection IV, C concerning state subsidies.

20. Reich, The New Property, 73 Yale L.J. 733 (1964); Reich, Individual Rights and Social Welfare: The Emerging Legal Issues, 74 Yale L.J. 1245 (1965).

21. See the discussion of this issue and citations in subsection II, D, 1 supra.

22. Board of Regents v. Roth, 408 U.S. 564 (1972).

efit. If the applicable law establishes criteria for continued receipt of the benefit which the individual appears to meet, he will have a claim of entitlement to continued benefits.[23] However, if applicable law creates no claim to future payments, the person has only an "expectancy" of continued benefits.[24] Under this theory a state may be allowed to eliminate the need for hearings to determine the basis for termination of benefits by establishing a system which clearly indicates that there is no right to continuation of benefits or fairness in their termination.

Because nursing home residents could establish no government-created entitlement to continued residence at a particular nursing home, the Supreme Court, in *O'Bannon v. Town Court Nursing Center*,[25] held that those residents had no right to a hearing before a government agency revoked the home's certification to receive payments from the Medicare and Medicaid programs. Decertification of a particular nursing home did not terminate a recipient's medical assistance but merely required him to find a different institution which would accept him and which was certified as qualified for the receipt of Medicare or Medicaid funds. While the residents of a particular nursing home might feel that they would be better treated at the former institution or that it would be difficult for them to find comparable care, they had no government-created entitlement to continued benefits at a particular nursing home that had been decertified. Only the owners of the nursing home had a right to be heard in the administrative process leading to the decertification.

The Supreme Court has found that state statutes granting an individual citizen welfare benefits create a sufficient entitlement in the continued receipt of public aid or housing payments to require a hearing to determine the basis for termination of these benefits.[26] Similarly, the Court has held that when a state establishes a school system it must grant students a hearing regarding the fairness of dismissing or suspending them from the system.[27] Government licenses are also a form of property insofar as they constitute an entitlement to engage in a valuable activity. Thus the government must have a fair procedure to determine whether driver's licenses [28] or occupational licenses [29] should be revoked. In all of these cases the government had established criteria for the receipt and continuation of the benefit which the individuals appeared to meet. As the individual had present enjoyment of the benefit and a claim of entitlement to its continuation under state law, he had a property interest which was protected by the due process clause.

In theory the government might be able to "reverse" the result of these cases by enacting a law which declares that individuals may have benefits (such as welfare payments, public schooling or occupational licenses) terminated for any reason by the government without any "process." However, such laws might well be susceptible to attack under the substantive due process and equal protection guarantees as totally arbitrary and invidious uses of governmental power. As to benefits, such as education or occupational licenses, there would be an issue as to whether the government was in fact under a substantive duty to grant these items as "rights." Additionally, some terminations of benefits might also involve deprivations of liberty which would independently require a fair termination procedure. At the current time it is difficult to predict how these issues would be resolved as the entitlement theory does not match the concept of property to either traditional property

---

23. Goldberg v. Kelly, 397 U.S. 254 (1970) (welfare payments); Goss v. Lopez, 419 U.S. 565 (1975) (school attendance).

24. Bishop v. Wood, 426 U.S. 341 (1976) (government employment).

25. 447 U.S. 773 (1980).

26. Goldberg v. Kelly, 397 U.S. 254 (1970).

27. Goss v. Lopez, 419 U.S. 565 (1976).

28. Bell v. Burson, 402 U.S. 535 (1971).

29. In re Ruffalo, 390 U.S. 544 (1968); see Section II, C, 4 on "liberty."

"rights" or the importance of the interests to the individual.[30]

4. Government Employment

One form of government benefit to which the Supreme Court has strictly applied the entitlement theory is public employment.

If a person is hired for a government position which is clearly terminable at the will of his superiors, the employee does not have a property interest in the position which mandates a fair procedure for determining the basis for his termination. If the government gives the employee assurances of continual employment or dismissal for only specified reasons, then there must be a fair procedure to protect the employee's interests when the government seeks to discharge him from the position. This entitlement also may come from statutory law, formal contract terms, or the actions of a supervisory person with authority to establish terms of employment.

The dichotomy between a "claim of entitlement" to employment and a mere subjective expectancy of employment was brought out in the companion cases of *Board of Regents v. Roth*[31] and *Perry v. Sindermann*.[32] In *Roth* a teacher who was refused employment had only a one year contract and applicable state law left the retention of such persons in the total discretion of university officials. The majority opinion held that there was no claim of entitlement under local law and no deprivation of property which required a fair termination hearing. This case was the first use of the entitlement con-

cept to hold that some important individual interests could be excluded from the concept of "life, liberty or property." [33] The college teacher in *Sindermann* had a similar lack of express rights under his contract, but in this case the college officials had previously indicated that he had a claim to reemployment under a "de facto" tenure program. The Court held that this gave him a sufficient claim of entitlement to require a hearing prior to the final decision not to renew his contract.

In *Arnett v. Kennedy* [34] the Court upheld the dismissal of a nonprobationary employee by the federal government without a pretermination hearing. Although there was no majority opinion at least six Justices appeared to agree that the employee had an interest which could not be terminated without due process. The action of the Court seemed to be based on a majority view that pretermination review procedures and a post termination hearing constituted a sufficient procedure to safeguard this interest.[35] But in *Bishop v. Wood* [36] the Court went further and held that the state could define the terms of what appeared to be permanent employment so as to eliminate the need for procedural safeguards for termination. Here an employee was terminated without any hearing under a law which appeared to deem him a "permanent employee" who could be dismissed only for failure to perform his work in a competent manner. The majority opinion deferred to the district court analysis of state law that the employee held his position at "the will and pleasure" of city officials.[37] The majority then held that the

---

30. See generally, Simon, Liberty and Property in the Supreme Court: A Defense of Roth and Perry, 71 Calif.L.Rev. 146 (1983); Smolla, The Reemergence of the Right-Privilege Distinction in Constitutional Law: The Price of Protesting Too Much, 35 Stanford L.Rev. 69 (1982–83); Van Alstyne, Cracks in "The New Property": Adjudicative Due Process in the Administrative State, 62 Cornell L.Rev. 445 (1977); Note, Statutory Entitlement and the Concept of Property, 86 Yale L.J. 695 (1977).

31. 408 U.S. 564 (1972).

32. 408 U.S. 593 (1972).

33. Van Alstyne, note 30 supra, at 489; Note, supra note 30, at 698 n. 19.

34. 416 U.S. 134 (1974).

35. 416 U.S. 134, 171 (White, J., concurring).

36. 426 U.S. 341 (1976).

37. 426 U.S. at 345. The opinion of the district court on the meaning of North Carolina law was based on one opinion of the North Carolina Supreme Court which was not directly on point. The district judge had been affirmed by an equally divided vote of the Court of Appeals for the Fourth Circuit. Bishop v. Wood, 377 F.Supp. 501 (W.D.N.C.1973), aff'd 498 F.2d 1341 (4th Cir. 1974).

state was free to define the terms of employment so as to preclude claims of entitlement and procedural safeguards.

As Professor Robert Rabin has noted, the Court has created a dichotomy between a class of "entitled" employees who receive full procedural safeguards and those who have no protection against arbitrary dismissal.[38] Rabin argues that a basic procedure, involving primarily a statement of the reasons for dismissals, should be required to protect the rights of all public employees. However, the Supreme Court has not shown any inclination toward granting government employees any constitutionally guaranteed minimum of due process rights where applicable law gives them no claim to continued employment.

It should be noted in closing that even those employees who lack any entitlement to continued employment cannot be discharged for reasons which in themselves violate the Constitution. Thus nontenured teachers cannot be fired because they have engaged in speech which is protected by the first amendment.[39] However, a hearing will be required to determine the basis for the discharge of a nontenured teacher only where the individual can make a prima facie claim that he is being discharged for reasons which violated specific constitutional guarantees. Where the dismissal is based in part on the exercise of first amendment rights, the dismissal will be upheld if the government can prove that the employee would

have been discharged in any event for reasons unrelated to these activities.[40]

5. Reputation Reconsidered As A Property Right

When the government acts so as to injure an individual's reputation, it will deprive that individual of his liberty if the damage is so severe as to significantly limit his associational or employment opportunities.[41] Only in those instances will the government be required to accord the individual some procedure to determine the basis and legality of its actions. In *Paul v. Davis*[42] the Supreme Court held that injury to one's reputation does not in itself constitute a deprivation of liberty or property. In *Paul* a sheriff had distributed to local merchants a leaflet of "active shoplifters" which included the name and photograph of the plaintiff Davis. Davis had been arrested for shoplifting but his case later was dismissed without resolving the issue of his guilt. Davis brought an action in federal court against the sheriff for depriving him of liberty and property by failing to grant him a hearing before taking actions which injured his reputation. The Supreme Court held that Davis had not established a constitutionally cognizable loss of liberty or property, absent some further injury to his liberty. This conclusion seems to have very little historical or analytical basis, as Anglo-American law has long placed a value on the individual's right to one's

---

38. Rabin, Job Security and Due Process: Monitoring Administrative Discretion Through A Reasons Requirement, 44 U.Chi.L.Rev. 60 (1976).

39. Board of Regents v. Roth, 408 U.S. 564, 575 n. 14 (1972), See subsection C of this chapter concerning deprivations of liberty.

40. Mt. Healthy City School District Bd. of Education v. Doyle, 429 U.S. 274 (1977). The degree of burden placed on the government agency to demonstrate that the discharge decision was not a punishment of constitutionally protected speech may vary with the nature of the employee's expression. See, Connick v. Myers, 103 S.Ct. 1684 (1983).

41. See subsection II, C, 3 on "liberty" supra. In Givhan v. Western Line Consolidated School District, 439 U.S. 410 (1979) the Court unanimously held that the teacher could not be discharged for privately com-

municating her grievances about working conditions, or opinions concerning employment or public issues, to her employer. This decision extended the protection of Pickering v. Board of Education, 391 U.S. 563 (1968) to the private conversations of public employees. The opinion reaffirmed the principle established in *Mt. Healthy* that when an employee has shown that constitutionally protected conduct played a role in the government's decision not to retain him in his job, the employer is required and entitled to demonstrate "by a preponderance of the evidence that it would have reached the same decision as to [the employee's] reemployment even in the absence of the protected conduct." 439 U.S. at 416, quoting Mt. Healthy City Bd. of Education v. Doyle, 429 U.S. 274, 287 (1977).

42. 424 U.S. 693 (1976).

good reputation.[43] But it is important to note that the plaintiff here could have brought a defamation suit against the sheriff in state court. There was a procedure, a tort suit, available to remedy the deprivation of the individual's interest in his reputation, although the procedure followed, rather than preceded, the governmental act. Since that time, one justice has indicated that it is the finding of a sufficient, though delayed, process to protect the reputation interest that justified denial of federal relief to the plaintiff in *Paul*.[44] Thus it may come to pass that the majority of the justices will find a property interest in an individual's reputation but hold that the establishment of fair procedures for suits against responsible officials constitutes due process of law.

E. Irrebuttable Presumptions—The "Non" Liberty or Property Due Process Requirement

In a few cases the Supreme Court has held that the government could not establish an "irrebuttable presumption" which classified people for a burden or benefit without determining the individual merit of their claims. These presumptions were said to violate due process because they deprived someone of a governmental benefit without any fair process. Thus the Court struck

down a college tuition system which did not allow individuals a fair chance to prove they were residents of a state.[1] Similarly, the Court struck down employment restrictions on pregnant teachers when the system made no individualized determination of their ability to continue working during their pregnancy.[2] Indeed, the Supreme Court engaged in one of its rare invalidations of a welfare payment qualification when it struck down a food stamp act provision which disqualified a large class of households without individualized determination as to their need.[3]

It now seems readily apparent that these cases actually rest on an equal protection rationale, for the objectionable portion of each law was the way in which it classified individuals.[4] It was the arbitrary classification by previous residency for tuition, by pregnancy for employment, or by income tax status for food stamps that was the impermissible basis of these laws. In none of the cases would a "process" have saved the law because the procedure would only have determined whether an individual fitted into one of these arbitrary classifications.[5] The justices themselves realized this[6] and later upheld classifications which were not invidious against charges that they constituted irrebuttable presumptions.[7] For example, a state may ban all advertising on trucks

---

43. Monaghan, Of "Liberty" And "Property", 62 Cornell L.Rev. 405, 423–34 (1977).

44. Ingraham v. Wright, 430 U.S. 651, 700 (1977) (Stevens, J., dissenting). Stevens, J. did not participate in the *Paul* decision.

1. Vlandis v. Kline, 412 U.S. 441 (1973).

2. Cleveland Bd. of Education v. La Fleur, 414 U.S. 632 (1974), see also Turner v. Department of Employment, 423 U.S. 44 (1975) holding that women could not be excluded from unemployment compensation because they were pregnant without an individualized determination of their ability to work.

3. United States Dept. of Agriculture v. Murry, 413 U.S. 508 (1973).

4. For academic commentary to this effect see Bezanson, Some Thoughts on the Emerging Irrebuttable Presumption Doctrine, 7 Ind.L.Rev. 644 (1974); Nowak, Realigning the Standards of Review Under the Equal Protection Guarantee—Prohibited, Neutral and Permissible Classifications, 62 Geo.L.J. 1071, 1104–09 (1974); Note, Irrebuttable Presumptions as an Alternative to Strict Scrutiny: From Rodriquez to La Fleur, 62

Geo.L.J. 1173 (1974); Note, The Irrebuttable Presumption Doctrine in the Supreme Court, 87 Harv.L.Rev. 1534 (1974). Trafelet v. Thompson, 594 F.2d 623, 630 (7th Cir. 1978) (Tone, J., citing an earlier edition of this treatise).

5. See Guilliams v. Commissioner of Revenue, 299 N.W.2d 138, 144 (Minn.1980) (Simonett, J., citing an earlier edition of this treatise.)

6. Some justices attempted to make this point when concurring in the irrebuttable presumption decisions. See, e.g., Vlandis v. Kline, 412 U.S. 441, 457–8 (1973) (White, J., concurring); Cleveland Bd. of Education v. La Fleur, 414 U.S. 632, 651 (1974) (Powell, J., concurring).

7. See, e.g., Mourning v. Family Publications Service, 411 U.S. 356 (1973) (upholding classification in Truth in Lending Act); Marshall v. United States, 414 U.S. 417 (1974) (upholding sentencing classification in Narcotic Rehabilitation Act); Weinberger v. Salfi, 422 U.S. 749 (1975) (upholding eligibility classifications of surviving spouses and stepchildren under Social Security Act based on the duration of their relationship to a

which does not advertise the business interests of the truck owner. The classification between "owned" and "rented" advertising is sufficiently related to legitimate governmental concerns to pass review under the equal protection guarantee.[8] No hearing under the due process clause would be necessary unless a trucker who is fined for "rented" advertising claims his advertisement represented his own interests. To strike the law as an irrebuttable presumption against those who rented advertising space would be a resurrection of the now discredited theory of substantive due process as a check on economic or general welfare legislation.

While "irrebuttable presumption" analysis is not strictly a form of procedural due process it does highlight significant due process concerns. When the government dispenses benefits or burdens it should have some fair procedure for sorting out individual claims. This approach seems to support Professor Van Alstyne's call for recognition of a right to "freedom from arbitrary adjudicative procedures."[9] However, the Court since 1972 has found that a guarantee of procedural due process is only applicable where the government is held to deprive someone of "life, liberty, or property".[10]

By masking substantive decisions in procedural language, the Supreme Court, in the irrebuttable presumption cases, confused due process and equal protection analysis. Irrebuttable presumption analysis allowed the Court to overturn legislative decisions without having to justify the use of judicial power as would an open use of substantive due process or equal protection analysis. The use of irrebuttable presumption language was a conceptually confused, if not dishonest, method of justifying independent judicial review of legislative classifications. The declining use of irrebuttable presumption analysis may evidence increasing willingness of justices to address directly the judicial role in reviewing legislatively created classifications.[11]

III. WHAT PROCESS IS DUE? THE PROCEDURES REQUIRED BY THE DUE PROCESS CLAUSE

A. Introduction

When a person is deprived of life, liberty or property, there must be some process granted him in order to ensure that the action taken complies with the due process clauses. However, "process" is not a term with a clear definition and the nature of the procedure required to comply with the due process clause depends on many factors concerning the individual deprivation. Indeed the study of the required procedures has be-

deceased wage earner); Usery v. Turner Elkhorn Mining Co., 428 U.S. 1 (1976) (upholding classifications in Federal Coal Mine Health and Safety Act). See also, Brown v. Sibley, 650 F.2d 760, 765 (5th Cir. 1981) (Ingraham, J., citing an earlier edition of this treatise); Bryan v. Kitamura, 529 F.Supp. 394, 400 n. 26 (D.Hawaii 1982) (Pence, D.J., citing an earlier edition of this treatise.

The Court recently avoided ruling on the continued vitality of irrebuttable presumption analysis. Lower federal courts had found a state policy denying in-state tuition status at the state university to resident nonimmigrant alien students violated due process, equal protection, and irrebuttable presumption principles. The Supreme Court in Toll v. Moreno, 102 S.Ct. 2977 (1982) found that the state policy conflicted with federal law and violated the supremacy clause and did not rule on the due process or equal protection claims. The Court twice had earlier avoided ruling on the merits of this case. See Elkins v. Moreno, 435 U.S. 647 (1978) (remanding case for clarification of domicile status of aliens under state law); Toll v. Moreno, 441 U.S. 458

(1979) (remanding case for re-evaluation following clarification of University of Maryland tuition policy).

8. Railway Express Agency v. New York, 336 U.S. 106 (1949).

9. Van Alstyne, Cracks in "The New Property": Adjudicative Due Process in the Administrative State, 62 Cornell L.Rev. 445, 487 (1977).

10. Perhaps the most amazing feature of this distinction is that Justice Stewart was the author of the majority opinion in Board of Regents v. Roth, 408 U.S. 564 (1972) which was the first case to make such a distinction, and also the champion of the irrebuttable presumption analysis. See, Cleveland Bd. of Education v. La Fleur, 414 U.S. 632, 657 (1974) (Rehnquist, J., dissenting) ("My Brother Stewart thereby enlists the Court in another quixotic engagement in his apparently unending war on irrebuttable presumptions.").

11. See Chapter 13, Section IV, Substantive Due Process Since 1937, and Chapter 16, Section I, C, An Introduction to Standards of Review Under the Equal Protection Guarantee.

come splintered into several independent subject areas. Those who are interested in a detailed analysis of the procedures which are necessary to comply with due process in more specific terms are advised to consult one of the major reference works in the area of administrative law,[1] civil procedure[2] or criminal procedure.[3] In this section we will outline the constitutional framework within which the Supreme Court must determine specific cases concerning the adequacy of procedures granted an individual prior to depriving him of life, liberty or property. Our discussion will be divided into three major parts: first, a brief statement of the general principles which the Court follows in determining the adequacy of any procedure; second, a look at the most significant decisions in terms of procedures required in three areas: deprivations of physical liberty, debtor-creditor relationships and termination of government benefits; and third, a note on access to judicial process.

B. General Principles

The Supreme Court has tended to view its decisions on necessary procedures under the due process clause in an essentially utilitarian fashion. The Court has demonstrated a consistent belief that the adversary process is best designed to safeguard individual rights against arbitrary action by the government. The justices determine the scope of trial type procedures required for any particular deprivation by balancing the

worth of the procedure to the individual against its cost to the society as a whole. Professor Jerry Mashaw has exposed major flaws in the current approach of the justices to these issues. Mashaw argues that the Court should concern itself with safeguards other than adversary procedures because individual rights are often better protected by careful analysis of decision making systems rather than new adversarial procedures.[4] He also has demonstrated why the Court's decisions in this area should follow an independent theory of due process values rather than the current utilitarian approach. The utilitarian balancing process often seems to degrade the nature of the rights and, in any event, seems one for which the judicial branch of government is not apparently well suited. Nevertheless, the Supreme Court continues to view the procedures required in terms of which additional adversary procedures should be engrafted on an administrative system and it makes this determination by a balancing process.[5]

Before examining the balancing test in operation, one should note the different elements of the adversary process which may be required as part of the "due process" which must be afforded to an individual when the government deprives him of life, liberty or property.[6] The essential elements are: (1) adequate notice of the charges or basis for government action; (2) a neutral decision-maker; (3) an opportunity to make an oral presentation to the decision-maker;

1. See e.g., K. Davis, Administrative Law Treatise, Chapters 10, 12, 13, 14 (1979–80 2d ed.); E. Gellhorn, Administrative Law and Process in a Nutshell (1981); B. Schwartz, Administrative Law (1976).

2. J. Moore, Moore's Federal Practice (2d ed.) (multi-volume treatise with some differences in dates and coauthors); C. Wright, Federal Practice and Procedure (multi-volume treatise with some differences in dates and coauthors).

3. See, e.g., J. Israel & W. LaFave, Criminal Procedure—Constitutional Limitations in a Nutshell (3d ed. 1980); Y. Kamisar, W. LaFave & J. Israel, Modern Criminal Procedure: Cases—Comments—Questions (1980) (with supplement); C. Whitebread, Criminal Procedure (1980).

4. Mashaw, The Management Side of Due Process: Some Theoretical and Litigation Notes on the Assur-

ance of Accuracy, Fairness, and Timeliness in the Adjudication of Social Welfare Claims, 59 Cornell L.Rev. 772 (1974). For an insightful analysis of the adjudicative process and alternatives thereto, see Eisenberg, Participation, Responsiveness and the Consultative Process: An Essay for Lon Fuller, 92 Harv.L.Rev. 410 (1978).

5. Mashaw, The Supreme Court's Due Process Calculus for Administrative Adjudication in Mathews v. Eldridge: Three Factors in Search of a Theory of Value, 44 U.Chi.L.Rev. 28 (1976).

6. For a similar division of the procedural safeguards and a more complete discussion of each, see K. Davis supra note 1.

(4) an opportunity to present evidence or witnesses to the decision-maker; (5) a chance to confront and cross-examine witnesses or evidence to be used against the individual; (6) the right to have an attorney present the individual's case to the decision-maker; (7) a decision based on the record with a statement of reasons for the decision. Additionally there are six other procedural safeguards which tend to appear only in connection with criminal trials or formal judicial process of some type. Those are: (1) the right to compulsory process of witnesses; (2) a right to pre-trial discovery of evidence; (3) a public hearing; (4) a transcript of the proceedings; (5) a jury trial; (6) a burden of proof on the government greater than a preponderance of the evidence standard. There will also be a question concerning the burden of proof which either the individual or the government must bear. Additionally there will be a question of the individual's right to appeal from an adverse decision by the initial decision-maker. To date the Supreme Court has never found a right to appeal as inherent in the right to due process of law.[7]

The first decision which a court has to make on the due process issue is whether any hearing-type procedure is required. There had been some indication that the Supreme Court might require some type of procedure to formalize decisions involving deprivations of life, liberty or property even though there were no factual issues to resolve. But the Court finally decided that there is no requirement of a procedure to determine the basis for an action which affects an individual where there are no factual issues in dispute. Thus the Court has held that a discharged government employee has no right to a procedure when he does not challenge the truthfulness of the facts upon which his discharge was based.[8] Similarly, the Court has held that there was no right to a hearing to determine whether property previously taken for delinquent taxes could be sold when there was no challenge to the original seizure of the property by the government.[9] Cases also arise where the government makes a decision based upon facts which already have been determined through some adequate procedural system such as a trial. In these situations the individual will have no further right to a hearing if the disputed issues have already been resolved by adequate process. Thus the Court has held that there is no right to a hearing or other procedure in connection with a suspension or revocation of a person's automobile driver's license where the revocation is based on violations of traffic laws which were previously established through the judicial process.[10]

It is most common for the government to affect the life, liberty or property interest of a great number of people through its legislative functions. When the legislature passes a law which affects a general class of persons, those persons have all received procedural due process—the legislative process. The challenges to such laws must be based on their substantive compatibility with constitutional guarantees. Similarly, an administrative agency may make decisions that are of a legislative or general rulemaking character. When an agency promulgates generalized rules there is no constitutional right to a hearing for a specific individual. However when the agency makes rules that might be termed adjudicative in that they affect a very defined group of interests, then persons representing those interests should be granted some fair procedure to safeguard their life, liberty or property. The line between rulemaking and adjudication is not at all clear and it may be that the Court will move towards requiring some type of hearing for those who are affected in any constitutionally cognizable way by even general-

---

7. However, the Court has held that there must be equality of treatment of persons where fundamental rights are involved and has created some rights of access to court; see Section II, B, 1 on procedures for incarceration and Section IV on access to courts.

8. Codd v. Velger, 429 U.S. 624 (1977) (per curiam).

9. Pearson v. Dodd, 429 U.S. 396 (1977).

10. Dixon v. Love, 431 U.S. 105 (1977).

ized agency rules. However, to date the Supreme Court has not required procedural safeguards of systemic fairness in this rulemaking or quasi-adjudicative process beyond those established in the Administrative Procedure Act.[11]

When the government is required to establish some procedure concerning individual deprivations of life, liberty or property, the scope of permissible procedures is sometimes limited by specific constitutional guarantees. This limitation applies to the criminal trial process, which is specifically regulated by the Bill of Rights.[12] The civil trial process is also regulated by special constitutional guarantees such as due process restrictions on court jurisdiction[13] and certain restraints on the enforcement of judgments arising from the full faith and credit clause.[14] Additionally the federal government is required to have jury trials for civil cases under the seventh amendment.[15] Yet Congress may establish new forms of public rights and actions that may be adjudicated by agencies without jury trials.[16] In this section we are only concerned with the requirements of due process as a general guarantee of fair procedure.

The essential guarantee of the due process clause is that of fairness. The procedure must be fundamentally fair to the individual in the resolution of the factual and

---

11. Absent clear constitutional violations, the Administrative Procedure Act, 5 U.S.C.A. § 551 et seq. establishes the maximum procedural requirements for federal agency rulemaking. Reviewing courts may grant additional procedural rights regarding the rulemaking function of these agencies only if congressional authorization for such judicial review exists. In Vermont Yankee Nuclear Power Corp. v. National Resources Defense Council, Inc., 435 U.S. 519 (1978), the Court unanimously (Justices Blackmun and Powell not participating) overturned a decision by the Court of Appeals for the District of Columbia that restricted the licensing of nuclear reactors by the Atomic Energy Commission. The Supreme Court opinion stated:

"This is not to say necessarily that there are no circumstances which would ever justify a court in overturning agency action because of a failure to employ procedures beyond those required by statute. But such circumstances, if they exist, are extremely rare."

435 U.S. at 524.

The procedures used by agencies in rulemaking are left to the discretion of those agencies, within the bounds set by Congress. The Court did say that when rulemaking became "quasi-judicial," and adversely affected a clearly defined group of persons, additional procedures might be required "to afford the aggrieved individuals due process." 435 U.S. at 542. The opinion also left undecided the extent to which the judiciary might correct administrative acts when an agency disregards its own settled rules. Id. After noting that those two issues were not settled, the Court stated: "But this much is absolutely clear. Absent constitutional constraints or extremely compelling circumstances, 'the administrative agencies should be free to fashion their own rules of procedure' . . . " 435 U.S. at 543, quoting from F.C.C. v. Schreiber, 381 U.S. 279, 290 (1965), and F.C.C. v. Pottsville Broadcasting Co., 309 U.S. 134, 143 (1940). See also, Strycker's Bay Neighborhood Council, Inc. v. Karlen, 444 U.S. 223 (1980) (when a federal agency takes an action subject to the National Environmental Protection Act's procedural requirements, the only role for lower federal courts is to ensure that the agency has considered environmental consequences; those courts cannot reverse the discretionary decisions of the executive agency). See generally, K. Davis, supra note 1; Leventhal, Book Review, 44 U.Chi.L.Rev. 260 (1977).

12. For references, see notes 1 and 3 supra and Sections II, C, 2 and III, C, 1 of this Chapter.

13. See, e.g., Kulko v. Superior Court, 436 U.S. 84 (1978); Shaffer v. Heitner, 433 U.S. 186 (1977); Hanson v. Denckla, 357 U.S. 235 (1958). On these issues see generally, J. Moore, supra note 2; C. Wright, supra note 2; A. Ehrenzweig & D. Louisell, Jurisdiction in a Nutshell (3rd ed. 1974); D. Currie, Federal Jurisdiction in a Nutshell (1976).

14. Id., see generally American Law Institute, Restatement of the Law Second, Conflict of Law; E. Scoles & P. Hay, Conflict of Laws (1982); D. Siegel, Conflicts in a Nutshell (1982).

15. This provision is not applicable to the states. Minneapolis & St. Louis R.R. Co. v. Bombolis, 241 U.S. 211 (1916).

16. Atlas Roofing Co. Inc. v. Occupational Safety & Health Review Committee, 430 U.S. 442 (1977). The Supreme Court also has held that the federal common law of collateral estoppel is not dependent upon mutuality of the parties in earlier proceedings and that this use of collateral estoppel does not violate the seventh amendment. Thus, a defendant who lost a factual issue in an earlier equitable proceeding can be collaterally estopped from relitigating the same issue before a jury in a later damage action instituted by a plaintiff who was not a party to the earlier equitable proceeding. This use of collateral estoppel removes an issue, often the major element of a damage case, from jury determination, but it does not violate the seventh amendment because collateral estoppel between equitable and legal proceedings was recognized prior to 1791. The erosion of the mutuality requirement did not constitute a significant furtherance of the invasion of the province of the civil jury beyond the historic use of the doctrine. Parklane Hosiery Co., Inc. v. Shore, 439 U.S. 322 (1979).

legal basis for government actions which deprive him of life, liberty or property. While different situations may entail different types of procedures, there is always the general requirement that the government process be fair and impartial. Therefore, there must be some type of neutral and detached decision-maker, be it a judge, hearing officer or agency. The Court has continually held that "a fair trial in a fair tribunal is a basic requirement of due process."[17] This requirement applies to agencies and government hearing officers as well as judges.[18] The Supreme Court has strictly enforced this right and held that decision makers are constitutionally unacceptable where they have a personal monetary interest in the outcome of the adjudication or where they are professional competitors of the individual.[19] The rule against biased decision makers also serves to disqualify a judge in cases where that bias was solely the result of abuse or criticism from the parties appearing before him.[20] However the Court has held that a single hearing officer or agency may be given a combination of investigative and adjudicative functions. Thus the hearing officer could be charged with investigating and compiling facts in a case and making decisions based on those facts.[21] The fact that a government agency receives part of its funding from monetary penalties that it helps to assess does not necessarily make the agency a constitutionally unacceptable decision-maker. When no government official connected to the decision-making process personally profits from the decision, anyone challenging the process as inherently unfair would have to establish that the amount of agency funding traceable to the imposition of the civil penalty actually created an impermissible risk of bias in the decision-making process.[22]

One must also remember that the democratic process itself may be biased against an individual because a majority of the electorate may be biased, yet the system will still be upheld as "fair" within the meaning of due process. Thus the Court has upheld a requirement that zoning changes be subject to popular referendum, for that does no more than allow the general electorate to de-

17. In re Murchison, 349 U.S. 133, 136 (1965).

18. Withrow v. Larkin, 421 U.S. 35, 46 (1975); Gibson v. Berryhill, 411 U.S. 564, 579 (1973). In Holloway v. Arkansas, 435 U.S. 475 (1978), the Supreme Court held that, when a defense attorney requests the appointment of separate counsel for multiple defendants based on his representations regarding conflict of interest, the trial court must take adequate steps to ascertain whether the conflict of interest requires separate counsel. Failure to do so, the Court held, violated the defendant's right to counsel.

A posttrial hearing following a criminal conviction is sufficient to determine if conduct of a juror impaired his ability to render an impartial verdict. Smith v. Phillips, 455 U.S. 209 (1982).

19. Gibson v. Berryhill, 411 U.S. 564, 579 (1973); Ward v. Village of Monroeville, 409 U.S. 57 (1972); Tumey v. Ohio, 273 U.S. 510 (1927); Cf. Commonwealth Coatings Corp. v. Continental Casualty Co., 393 U.S. 145 (1968). In Friedman v. Rogers, 440 U.S. 1, 17–20 (1979) the Supreme Court noted that a person has a right to a fair and impartial hearing board in professional disciplinary proceedings even though he has no right to be regulated as a professional by a board sympathetic to his philosophy of commercial practice. However the Court refused to consider whether a disciplinary board for optometrists which, as a matter of state law, was required to have members from a specific professional association could judge fairly complaints against non-members of the association, because there was no specific disciplinary proceeding or a concrete controversy concerning this issue before the Court. In this case the Supreme Court also upheld the regulation of commercial practices of optometrists by a board composed of members of a specific professional organization; the composition of the board did not justify meaningful judicial review of the regulations for conduct of a professional practice.

See also, People ex rel. Judicial Inquiry Bd. v. Hartel, 72 Ill.2d 225, 235, 20 Ill.Dec. 592, 380 N.E.2d 801, 806 (1978) (Underwood, J., citing an earlier edition of this treatise).

20. Taylor v. Hayes, 418 U.S. 488, 501–503 (1974); Mayberry v. Penn., 400 U.S. 455 (1971); Pickering v. Board of Education, 391 U.S. 562, 568–69, n. 2 (1968); Cf. Ungar v. Sarafite, 376 U.S. 575, 584 (1964).

21. Withrow v. Larkin, 421 U.S. 35 (1975); Schweiker v. McClure, 455 U.S. 188 (1982); see generally Rotunda, The Combination of Functions in Administrative Actions, 40 Ford.L.Rev. 101 (1971).

22. Marshall v. Jerrico, Inc., 446 U.S. 238 (1980) (civil penalty provisions of Fair Labor Standards Act permissible even though the agency received partial reimbursement of its enforcement and administration expenses from the fines collected because there was no risk of personal bias by the agency decision-maker, who acted primarily as an investigator and prosecutor rather than an adjudicator).

termine whether they wish to alter their laws.[23] Yet even this procedure cannot be used to disguise a system which subjects one to a determination of his rights by a group composed of his professional or commercial competitors. Thus the Supreme Court has held that the zoning of a tract of real property cannot be left to the discretionary voting of neighboring property owners with interests adverse to the individual property owner.[24]

In addition to the guarantee of an impartial decision-maker, due process requires the government to give notice to individuals of government actions which would deprive those individuals of a constitutionally protected life, liberty, or property interest. When individual interests are adversely affected by legislative action, there is no notice issue, as publication of a statute is normally considered to put all individuals on notice of a change in the law of a jurisdiction.[25] When a government agency or a court (even in a case where no government agency is a party) considers terminating or impairing an individual's constitutionally cognizable life, liberty, or property interest,

notice must be given to the individual whose interest is at stake in the proceeding. The form of the notice and the procedure for delivery or posting of the notice must be reasonably designed to insure that the interested parties in fact will learn of the proposed adjudicative action.[26] "An elementary and fundamental requirement of due process in any proceeding which is to be accorded finality is notice reasonably calculated, under all the circumstances, to appraise interested parties of the pendency of the action and afford them an opportunity to present their objections."[27]

If there is a deprivation of life, liberty or property which is based on disputed facts or issues, then the individual whose interests are affected must be granted a fair procedure before a fair decision-maker. However this principle does not mean that the individual has the right to a hearing before the action is taken or even to any personal hearing at any time. What is required is a procedure, not necessarily a hearing. In many of the cases where the Court has found that there is a deprivation of life, liberty or property it has required that the affected individ-

---

23. Eastlake v. Forest City Enterprises, Inc., 426 U.S. 668 (1976).

24. Washington ex rel. Seattle Trust Co. v. Roberge, 278 U.S. 116 (1928); Eubank v. Richmond, 226 U.S. 137 (1912). Dukesherer Farms Inc. v. Ball, 405 Mich. 1, 37 n.1, 273 N.W.2d 877, 893 n.1 (1979) (Levin, J., concurring, citing an earlier edition of this treatise).

The Supreme Court has found that a state statute which gave to the governing bodies of schools and churches the power to prevent the issuance of liquor licenses for the dispensation of alcoholic beverages within 500 feet of a church or school violated the establishment clause of the first amendment, Larkin v. Grendel's Den, Inc., 103 S.Ct. 505 (1982). The Court in this case wished to emphasize that the government may not delegate governmental power to a private entity in order to achieve a sectarian or religious purpose. The Court, had the justices not been so desirous of making this point under the first amendment establishment clause, could have invalidated the statute as denying due process to the property owners whose zoning was subject to the total control of adjacent property owners who had economic interests adverse to theirs.

25. Texaco, Inc. v. Short, 454 U.S. 516 (1982) (owners of mineral interests which lapsed under statute terminating undeveloped mineral interests were not entitled to notice beyond publication of the statute of the actions that they could have taken during two-year

statutory grace period to avoid extinguishment of their interest).

26. See, e.g., Greene v. Lindsey, 456 U.S. 444 (1982) (posting notice of eviction action on door of apartment in public housing unit insufficient to meet due process standard); Memphis Light, Gas and Water Division v. Craft, 436 U.S. 1, 14 (1978) (notice of possible termination of utility service by government operated utility did not meet due process standard for informing individual of opportunity to present objections to termination).

The state must give notice by personal service or mail to both the owner and mortgagee of property before conducting a sale of the property for nonpayment of taxes, or a condemnation proceeding, when the name of the owner or mortgagee is known to, or easily ascertainable by, the government. Notice by publication or posting is not sufficient under these circumstances. Mennonite Board of Missions v. Adams, 103 S.Ct. ___ (1983); Schroeder v. New York, 371 U.S. 208 (1962); Walker v. Hutchinson, 352 U.S. 112 (1956).

27. Mullane v. Central Hanover Bank & Trust Co., 339 U.S. 306, 314 (1950) (notice by newspaper publication of judicial action to settle accounts of trust fund was constitutionally sufficient notice for beneficiaries whose whereabouts could not be determined but violated due process because it was insufficient notice for known beneficiaries with ascertainable residence).

ual be granted a personal hearing prior to the government action.[28] However, in some cases the Court has held that hearings which take place after the government action will be sufficient process to comply with the guarantee.[29] And in a few cases the Court has held that due process was satisfied by a procedural safeguard which did not involve any personal hearing for the affected individual.[30] The Court uses a balancing test to determine which procedures will be required. In *Mathews v. Eldridge* the Court has stated that it will consider three factors in making this determination:

First, the private interest that will be affected by the official action; second, the risk of an erroneous deprivation of such interest through the procedures used, and the probable value, if any, of additional or substitute procedural safeguards; and finally, the Government's interest, including the function involved and the fiscal and administrative burdens that the additional or substitute procedural requisites would entail.[31]

All courts must now employ the *Mathews v. Eldridge* balancing test to determine the type of procedures that are required by due process when a governmental action would deprive an individual of a constitutionally protected liberty or property interest. On the side of the individual, a court must assess two factors: (1) the importance of the individual liberty or property interest at stake; (2) the extent to which the requested procedure may reduce the possibility of erroneous decision-making. On the other side of the "balance," the court must assess the governmental interest in avoiding the increased administrative and fiscal burdens which result from increased procedural requirements.

While this test may suit the purposes of the Supreme Court, one cannot accurately predict how any specific case will be decided by using this test for two reasons. First, because it is a "balancing test", it is impossible to predict the results unless one knows the personal value systems of those doing the balancing. Second, as Professor Mashaw has demonstrated, this type of "intuitive functionalism" disregards a systematic pursuit of due process values.[32] Thus we can only advise individuals to reflect on these general principles and to examine the Supreme Court decisions on specific issues when attempting to predict how the current justices will decide a new issue.

A court may need to employ the *Mathews v. Eldridge* balancing test in three areas of procedural due process rulings. First, a court should use the test to determine if an individual is entitled to a hearing prior to (rather than after) a governmental action which would deprive him of a liberty or property interest. The government should be able to act to advance important public interests even though it deprives someone of property or liberty without a prior hearing, so long as adequate post-deprivation process provides the individual with a safeguard against arbitrary governmental actions.[33]

---

28. See, e.g., Snidach v. Family Finance Corp., 395 U.S. 337 (1969); Bell v. Burson, 402 U.S. 535 (1971); Goldberg v. Kelly, 397 U.S. 254 (1970) (terminating basic welfare benefits); Cf. Morrissey v. Brewer, 408 U.S. 471 (1972) (preliminary hearing at place of arrest for parole violation).

29. See, e.g., North Georgia Finishing v. Di-Chem, 419 U.S. 601 (1975) (attachment or replevin); Arnett v. Kennedy, 416 U.S. 134 (1974) (termination of government employment); Mathews v. Eldridge, 424 U.S. 319 (1976) (termination of Social Security disability payments). Mackey v. Montrym, 443 U.S. 1 (1979) (post-suspension hearing sufficient for suspending a person's driver's license for refusal to take a drunk driving test); Barry v. Barchi, 443 U.S. 55 (1979) (post-suspension hearing for race horse trainer sufficient where suspension is based on detection of illegal drugs in the horse immediately after the race).

30. Ingraham v. Wright, 430 U.S. 651 (1977) (possibility of tort suit sufficient to protect liberty interest of child who is subjected to physical punishment in school). Parratt v. Taylor, 451 U.S. 527 (1981) (prisoner's loss of property due to negligence of prison officials does not violate due process when state court remedy exists). Cf. Paul v. Davis, 424 U.S. 693 (1976) (holding that there is no property or liberty interest deprived by injury to one's reputation.) At least one justice is of the opinion that *Paul* should have been based on the principle that the state tort remedy was sufficient but required process. Ingraham v. Wright, 430 U.S. 651, 700 (1977) (Stevens, J., dissenting.)

31. Mathews v. Eldridge, 424 U.S. 319, 335 (1976).

32. Mashaw, supra note 5.

33. See notes 29, 30 supra. See, e.g., Calero-Toledo v. Pearson Yacht Leasing Co., 416 U.S. 663 (1974) (gov-

The existence of a state court remedy may be sufficient process to protect individuals from improper deprivations of some liberty or property interests by state employees.[34] Second, whether the court decides that a pre-deprivation or post-deprivation hearing is required, it should employ the balancing test to determine the precise procedures to be employed at the hearing. These balancing test rulings may cover the procedural spectrum from requiring only informal hearings [35] to requiring a full adversarial process.[36] Third, if the court requires a formal

adversarial process, it may use the balancing test to determine the standard of proof that the government must meet in order to justify the deprivation of the individual liberty or property interest in the individual case.[37]

The difficulty of predicting how the Supreme Court will employ the *Mathews* balancing test is demonstrated by its rulings in parental rights cases. The importance of the parent-child relationship, in theory and fact, is such that the court will strictly scrutinize the fairness of procedures used to establish or terminate that relationship.[38]　A

---

ernment seizure of ship used to transport contraband permissible without prior hearing).

In Hodel v. Virginia Surface Mining and Reclamation Ass'n, 452 U.S. 264 (1981) the Supreme Court upheld provisions of the Federal Surface Mining Control and Reclamation Act which allow the Secretary of the Interior to order partial or total cessation of a surface mining operation when federal inspectors report that operation of the mine violates provisions of the Act or creates an immediate danger to the health or safety of the public. Even though "due process ordinarily requires an opportunity for 'some kind of hearing' prior to the deprivation of a significant property interest . . . some administrative action may be justified in emergency situations." 452 U.S. at 299.

34. See notes 29, 30, 33 supra.

Post-deprivation process may be sufficient to remedy a deprivation of property interests that results from the unauthorized or negligent actions of government employees. The state cannot create a pre-deprivation administrative process to prevent such takings of property. A state law allowing a judicial remedy for such taking may preclude the finding of a violation of due process. See Parratt v. Taylor, 451 U.S. 527 (1981) (prisoner's loss of property due to negligence of prison officials does not violate due process due to existence of state court remedy for property loss).

For a most insightful analysis of this post-deprivation hearing issue, see Smolla, The Displacement of Federal Due Process Claims by State Tort Remedies: Parratt v. Taylor and Logan v. Zimmerman Brush Co., 1982 U.Ill.L.Rev. 831.

35. For example, the Supreme Court employed the Mathews v. Eldridge, 424 U.S. 319 (1976), balancing test to determine the procedural safeguards due to termination of utility services. In Memphis Light, Gas and Water Division v. Craft, 436 U.S. 1 (1978), the Court found that the utility customer's interest in continued service and the "not insubstantial" risk of computer errors and erroneous service terminations outweighed the efficiency interests of the government utility. The Court tried to fashion a process that would not unduly lessen the efficiency, or significantly increase costs of the utility service. The majority opinion held that customers had to be provided with: (1) a pre-termination notice that advised them of the pro-

posed termination and the availability of a procedure to consider complaints regarding erroneous billing, and (2) the opportunity for an "informal" pre-termination hearing before an employee who could review disputed bills and rectify errors.

36. Compare Goldberg v. Kelly, 397 U.S. 254 (1970) (formal procedure required to terminate subsistence welfare benefits), with Mathews v. Eldridge, 424 U.S. 319 (1976) (adversarial process not required prior to termination of disability benefit).

37. Compare Addington v. Texas, 441 U.S. 418 (1979) ("clear and convincing" evidence standard must be met when government seeks to commit adult to psychiatric care facility), with Parham v. J.R., 442 U.S. 584 (1979) (no formal adversarial process required to safeguard child who is committed to psychiatric care facility by parent or guardian).

38. The justices unanimously employed the Mathews v. Eldridge balancing test in Little v. Streater, 452 U.S. 1 (1981) in finding that a state's refusal to pay the cost of a blood grouping test for an indigent defendant in a paternity action violated due process. The case was nominally a paternity action brought by the mother of an illegitimate child against the alleged father. However, Chief Justice Burger, in an opinion for a unanimous Court, found that the action should be treated as one brought by the government because state law compelled the woman to disclose the name of the "putative father under oath and to institute an action to establish the paternity" of the child because the child was a recipient of public aid. Indeed, the Court found that this proceeding had "quasi-criminal overtones." In this paternity proceeding the indigent defendant had requested that the state provide him with the funds or other means for a blood test of him and the child; the test was clearly effective evidence as it could exclude the possibility of paternity in many circumstances. The Court found that when an indigent was required to face the state as an adversary in a paternity proceeding, the state's refusal to provide him with the means to obtain blood test evidence denied him a fair opportunity to be heard.

The Court carefully limited its holding in *Little*, noting that "in these specific circumstances" there was a denial of due process due to the state's failure to provide blood grouping tests for the indigent putative fa-

parent has a constitutionally protected interest in the relationship with his or her child so that the state must accord the parent a hearing before terminating that relationship.[39] However, because foster parents have a lesser interest in this relationship than do natural or adoptive parents, a less formal procedure may be used in removing children from foster homes.[40] The interest of the natural or adoptive parent is so great that the state must demonstrate by "clear and convincing evidence"—not merely a preponderance of the evidence—that statutory criteria for termination of parental rights have been met in an individual case.[41] However, the interest of the parent is not so great, in the view of a majority of the justices, to require the state to appoint an attorney for an indigent parent when the state institutes court proceedings to take a child from the parent.[42]

We will now examine three major decisional areas: loss of physical liberty, enforcement of debtor-creditor relationships, and termination of government benefits.

C. A Summary of the Major Decisional Areas

1. Loss of Physical Liberty

Before an individual is subjected to punishment upon a criminal charge, he must receive a full trial in conformity with many constitutional safeguards or waive those rights. The primary restrictions on the criminal process are the result of the application of the principles of the Bill of Rights. The guarantees of the fourth, fifth, sixth, and eighth amendments restrict the ways in which the government may investigate as well as prosecute someone for a criminal charge.[1] All of these safeguards apply to

---

ther. It seems unlikely that the Court would find that, in a truly private paternity proceeding in which the state had no involvement, the state would have to provide for the financing of blood tests for indigent male defendants. The opinion noted that the Court was only ruling on the due process claim of a defendant who faces the state as an adversary and that its ruling made it unnecessary to consider the equal protection claim of the putative father in this case.

39. Stanley v. Illinois, 405 U.S. 645 (1972); Santosky v. Kramer, 455 U.S. 745 (1982).

40. In Smith v. Organization of Foster Families for Equality and Reform, 431 U.S. 816 (1977), the Court unanimously upheld a state procedure for removal of children from foster homes upon ten-days notice. There was a hearing at the request of the foster family equivalent to the more exacting requirements of past cases. The Court overturned the district court's ruling that the procedure should be automatic and include formal consultation of the child under the balancing test. Additionally, the Court upheld the use of more summary procedures where the child was with the foster family less than eighteen months. While the justices were unanimous, it would have been difficult to predict with any assurance that: (1) the justices could not agree on whether the foster parent-foster child relationship was a cognizable "liberty" interest, (2) that the district court was wrong in its particular objections to the procedures, (3) that relationships of less than eighteen months required fewer procedural safeguards.

41. Santosky v. Kramer, 455 U.S. 745 (1982).

42. In Lassiter v. Department of Social Services, 452 U.S. 18 (1981), the Court refused to require the appointment of counsel for a woman who had her parental rights terminated by court action. The Court first found that its previous decisions under the sixth and

fourteenth amendments established "the presumption that an indigent litigant has a right to appointed counsel only when, if he loses, he may be deprived of his physical liberty." The majority opinion by Justice Stewart stated that the three elements of the balancing test would have to be weighed and then the Court would "set their net weight on the scales against the presumption" against the appointment of counsel. The majority concluded that counsel would not be appointed in every parental termination proceeding because, despite the importance of the interest of the parent at stake in the proceeding, the state had "an urgent interest" in determining the best interest of the child. The appointment of counsel, according to the majority, would not necessarily add to either the fairness of the proceedings or a correct determination as to whether the interest of the child would be advanced by a termination of an individual's parental rights. The majority opinion indicated that trial court judges would have to make a case-by-case determination of whether the failure to appoint counsel for an indigent defendant in a child custody or parental status case would make the proceedings so fundamentally unfair as to violate due process.

1. For general reference, see J. Israel & W. LaFave, Criminal Procedure—Constitutional Limitations In A Nutshell (3d ed. 1980); Y. Kamisar, W. LaFave & J. Israel, Modern Criminal Procedure: Cases—Comments, Questions (5th ed. 1980, with supp.); C. Whitebread, Criminal Procedure (1980).

When a legislature establishes a penalty for the violation of a legislative or administrative regulation a court may have to determine whether the penalty is a civil or criminal one. Only if a court determines that the penalty is a criminal one will the person or corporation charged with violation of the regulation be entitled

the criminal process of state and local governments except for the grand jury requirement of the fifth amendment.[2] These specific guarantees include almost all of the procedural safeguards that were mentioned in our general discussion. Specifically, the amendments require: (1) respect for individual rights to privacy and freedom from self-incrimination in the investigative process; (2) that the person not twice be placed in jeopardy for the same offense; (3) prompt processing of the charges; (4) that the trial of the charges be public; (5) that the charges be tried before an impartial jury; (6) fair notice of the charges and a chance to prepare a defense; (7) the right to confront and cross-examine witnesses; (8) compulsory process to obtain favorable witnesses and evidence; (9) the assistance of counsel; (10) that excessive bail not be used to keep the individual in custody prior to the termination of the prosecution; (11) that the punishment not be excessive or cruel. Additionally, due process requires that all procedures be fundamentally fair. The process must always conform to the twin guarantees of an impartial determination of guilt or innocence [3] and respect for the dignity of the individual.[4] Perhaps the most important safeguard which is implied by the due process clause in criminal trials is the requirement that no one be found guilty of a criminal offense unless the charge has been proven by the government beyond a reasonable doubt.[5] Upon

---

to the protections of the Bill of Rights guarantees concerning a criminal prosecution. There is no precise standard which the Supreme Court employs to separate civil from criminal sanctions; the justices will look at many factors surrounding the legislative act including whether the sanction involves an affirmative disability or restraint, the history of the legislation, whether the behavior to which it applies is also a crime, and the possible ends promoted by the penalty. See United States v. Ward, 448 U.S. 242 (1980); Kennedy v. Mendoza-Martinez, 372 U.S. 144 (1963).

2. The grand jury clause has been held not to apply to the States. Hurtado v. California, 110 U.S. 516 (1884). See Chapter 13, Section V B regarding the applicability of Bill of Rights provisions to state proceedings.

3. Mullaney v. Wilbur, 421 U.S. 684 (1975) (reasonable doubt requirement); Tumey v. Ohio, 273 U.S. 510 (1927) (requirement of disinterested judge). It is well established that a conviction cannot be upheld upon a charge that was never made at trial. Thus if the state charges a defendant with a specific crime, and the case is tried on that charge, a reviewing court may not uphold the conviction on the theory that a different crime was proved at trial if the state failed to prove the defendant guilty of the crime charged. Dunn v. United States, 439 U.S. 1045 (1979). This principle applies equally to the penalty determination phase of the criminal process. Thus, a defendant cannot be sentenced to death when the government fails to prove the basis for the death penalty which it charges, and upon which the penalty hearing is based, even if it produced evidence sufficient to prove a different basis for the death penalty. See, Presnell v. Georgia, 439 U.S. 14 (1978).

See also, Chandler v. Florida, 449 U.S. 560 (1981) (a court may allow for radio, television, and still photographic coverage of the criminal trial over defendant's objection if trial process and coverage is regulated so as to avoid adverse impact on the fairness of the trial).

4. The due process clause has traditionally been used to regulate objectionable police methods on this basis without having to find a violation of more specific guarantees. See, e.g., Rochin v. California, 342 U.S. 165 (1952) (evidence gained from "stomach pumping" of the defendant held inadmissible); Turner v. Pennsylvania, 338 U.S. 62 (1949) (exclusion of coerced confession even if it met a "trustworthiness" test).

In recent years the Supreme Court has failed to analyze these components of the due process, fundamental fairness principles in its criminal procedure decisions. For an analysis of this trend see, Nowak, Foreword: Due Process Methodology in the Postincorporation World, 70 Journal of Criminal Law & Criminology 397 (1980).

While plea bargaining, as such, is not covered in this treatise because it is a particular problem of the criminal adjudicative system, one plea bargaining case is worthy of noting in relation to the meaning of due process. In Bordenkircher v. Hayes, 434 U.S. 357 (1978) the Supreme Court held that the due process clause was not violated when a state prosecutor carried out a threat, made during plea negotiations, to indict the defendant as a "habitual criminal" unless the defendant pled guilty to a charge of forgery. The defendant was subjected to a life sentence following indictment and conviction as a habitual criminal. Because the defendant had committed the acts that justified punishment under the habitual criminal statute, the Supreme Court found that the prosecutor's honest statement of intention to prosecute the defendant on the greater offense was a legitimate part of the bargaining process.

See also Corbitt v. New Jersey, 439 U.S. 212 (1978), upholding a homicide sentencing system under which a defendant found guilty of first degree murder by a jury must be sentenced to life imprisonment, while a defendant pleading no contest to a murder charge might be given either life imprisonment or the lesser term of imprisonment specified for second degree murder.

5. Mullaney v. Wilbur, 421 U.S. 684 (1975).

In determining whether a defendant in a state criminal proceeding was denied due process by being convicted upon evidence that failed to satisfy the beyond a reasonable doubt standard a federal court, in a habeas

conviction, the defendant has a constitutionally protected expectation that he will only be deprived of his liberty to the extent allowed by statute and as determined by a sentencing agency, be it a judge or jury, properly exercising its discretion within the term set by the legislature.[6]

The individual may forego these procedural protections by waiving his right to any specific safeguard. While the Supreme Court has always stated that waivers of rights must be "knowing and intelligent" to be binding upon the individual, there is no single standard for determining when the waiver of a right will be sufficient.[7] The Court has adopted differing standards for determining the adequacy of an asserted waiver depending on the specific right involved in the case. The Court has required the government to specifically warn defendants who are in custody of their rights under the fifth and sixth amendments prior to any asserted waiver of those rights by the individual.[8] Indeed, the Court has held that any questioning of a defendant outside of the presence of his counsel will be held an automatic violation of the sixth amendment absent not only a warning but a most explicit waiver of that right.[9] On the other side of the scale, the Supreme Court has held that individuals may consent to searches of their persons or premises although they have not been advised of their rights by the investigative agencies or officers.[10]

When a defendant seeks pretrial suppression of statements or evidence which the government will seek to use against him at trial, his interest in the suppression hearing is of a lesser magnitude than his interest in the trial itself according to the Supreme Court. Therefore, the procedures used at a suppression hearing may be less elaborate than accorded a defendant at his trial. In *United States v. Raddatz*,[11] the Supreme Court used the *Mathews v. Eldridge*[12] balancing test in finding that the Federal Magistrates Act adequately protected a defendant's due process rights in a suppression hearing; the federal district judge was not required to personally rehear testimony submitted to a federal magistrate when the judge made a "de novo" determination of the admissibility of evidence.

Once the criminal trial is over and the defendant has been found guilty, there is no inherent right to appeal. But, while the Court has stated that there is no right to an appellate process,[13] the justices have never been

corpus proceeding, must determine for itself whether there was sufficient evidence adduced at trial to justify a rational trier of the facts finding guilt beyond a reasonable doubt. Jackson v. Virginia, 443 U.S. 307, 324 (1979). This rule has been given retroactive effect. See Pilon v. Bordenkircher, 444 U.S. 1 (1979); see also Blake v. Thompson, 444 U.S. 806 (1979) (mem.).

See also the decisions concerning the use of procedural devices to meet or shift the burden of proof in a criminal trial which are noted in Section II C 2 of this chapter.

See also Lakeside v. Oregon, 435 U.S. 333 (1978) in which the Supreme Court held that the fifth and fourteenth amendments were not violated by a jury instruction in a criminal case, given over the defendant's objection, that cautioned the jury not to draw any adverse inference from the defendant's decision not to testify in his own behalf.

6. Hicks v. Oklahoma, 447 U.S. 343 (1980) (improper instruction of a jury regarding the scope of its sentencing powers results in invalidation of the sentence imposed on a defendant even though the jury could have fixed the same sentence term under proper instructions).

7. As to the problems created by these different positions, see Dix, Waiver in Criminal Procedure: A Brief for A More Careful Analysis, 55 Texas L.Rev. 193 (1977).

8. Miranda v. Arizona, 384 U.S. 436 (1966); the requirement does not apply to noncustodial interviews, Beckwith v. United States, 425 U.S. 341 (1976) (home interview by I.R.S. agents).

9. Brewer v. Williams, 430 U.S. 387 (1977). See also United States v. Henry, 447 U.S. 264 (1980) (defendant's incriminating statements made to paid informant confined in a prison cellblock with the defendant held inadmissible as being elicited from a defendant in violation of his sixth amendment right to counsel).

10. Schneckloth v. Bustamonte, 412 U.S. 218 (1973).

11. 447 U.S. 667 (1980).

12. 424 U.S. 319 (1976).

13. See, e.g., Ross v. Moffit, 417 U.S. 600, 611 (1974).

When the government establishes an appellate system it may give the prosecution as well as the defendant the right to appeal under certain circumstances. See United States v. DiFrancesco, 449 U.S. 117 (1980) (upholding provision of Organized Crime Control Act allowing the government the right under certain specified conditions to appeal a sentence imposed upon a convicted defendant).

confronted with the situation where a state would not grant some review of decisions which resulted in conviction of criminal charges. Were such a case to arise, it is at least possible that the Court might hold that there is a right to the review of some portions of the original decision-making process wherein might lie serious errors of law or fact. The federal system of habeas corpus relief also serves some of the functions of an appellate system, at least as to jurisdictional or constitutional defects in the criminal trial.

When a state does set up an appellate system it must design that system to produce a fair review of the original trials of all persons. It may not establish a system which explicitly, or by its impact, affords fair appellate process only to those who can afford to pay for that process. Thus the state is required to waive filing fees and transcript reproduction costs for the appeals of indigent defendants.[14] Similarly, the state must provide defendants with the assistance of counsel for their first appeal as of right in order to insure that all classes of defendants receive a fair review of their trials.[15] However the state need not provide counsel for indigent defendants who seek to attack their convictions in later discretionary appeals or collateral attacks,[16] because a majority of the justices are of the opinion that the assistance of counsel at trial and on the first appeal of right insures an equality of treatment as to fundamental issues of law and fact. Apparently it is also the belief of a majority of the justices that later appeals or collateral attack are not so significantly related to fairness as to require that indigent defendants be accorded completely equal access to them. The Court has held that the right of access to the system of judicial review includes a right of persons to have legal research materials.[17] Nor can the prison authorities preclude prisoners from assisting

one another with the preparation of papers for judicial review of their convictions[18] or the filing of civil rights actions[19] if the state does not provide them with professional legal assistance. These rulings of right of access to currently established procedures may imply some duty of the state to establish systems of judicial review of criminal cases despite the language to the contrary in some decisions.

Following a criminal trial and conviction on a criminal charge, a person may be placed on conditional release from a penitentiary. The system known as probation allows one to forego serving his sentence of imprisonment so long as he meets certain conditions relating to his conduct. A person sentenced to serve a term of imprisonment may be allowed to leave prison prior to the expiration of his maximum term under a system of parole which also conditions continued release on certain standards of behavior. When the state seeks to revoke someone's continued right to parole or probation and place him in prison, it is depriving him of "liberty" within the terms of the due process clauses.[20] However, this fact does not require the government to prove that the conditions of parole or probation have been violated in the same way that it had to prove the initial charge. The procedures for revoking probation or parole must include: (1) notice of the claimed violation of parole or probation conditions; (2) disclosure of evidence to the defendant; (3) a personal hearing for the defendant; (4) the opportunity to present evidence on behalf of the defendant; (5) the right to confront and cross-examine witnesses against the defendant unless there is specific good cause for avoiding such a confrontation; (6) a written statement by the adjudicator as to the evidence relied on and the reason for revoking the parole or probation status. All of this must take place be-

14.   Mayer v. Chicago, 404 U.S. 189 (1971).

15.   Douglas v. California, 372 U.S. 353 (1963).

16.   Ross v. Moffit, 417 U.S. 600 (1974).

17.   Bounds v. Smith, 430 U.S. 817 (1977).

18.   Johnson v. Avery, 393 U.S. 483 (1969).

19.   Wolff v. McDonnell, 418 U.S. 539 (1974).

20.   Morrissey v. Brewer, 408 U.S. 471 (1972) (parole); Gagnon v. Scarpelli, 411 U.S. 778 (1973) (probation).

fore a neutral hearing examiner or board. However, the previously convicted defendant does not have an absolute right to counsel at either the probation or parole revocation hearing. Instead, the Court has held that the decision as to whether counsel must be allowed at the proceedings must be made on a case by case basis. There will be a need for counsel wherever the charges concerning the parole or probation violation are such that they could not adequately be defended against by the defendant alone.[21]

An individual does not lose all of his constitutional rights by being imprisoned for commission of a crime.[22] Specifically, if there are further significant deprivations of life, liberty, or property following imprisonment, the prisoner is entitled to a fair procedure to determine the basis for the deprivations. Because of the limited nature of a prisoner's constitutional rights, it is very difficult to determine when there is a constitutionally cognizable interest in life, liberty or property being denied a prisoner.[23] In *Wolff*

v. McDonnell[24] the Court held that where a state establishes a system of "good time credits" which reduce a defendant's time until possible parole, the state must accord the defendant a fair procedure prior to eliminating his good time credits. This hearing would not be an extensive one and would require only written notice of the violation, an opportunity for the convict to present evidence in his behalf and a written statement as to why the disciplinary action is being taken.[25] However these procedural requirements will not apply to all prison disciplinary actions. The majority opinion in *Wolff* indicated that a prisoner would be entitled to a hearing whenever disciplinary actions were so serious as to cause a significant change in the individual's circumstances, such as the imposition of a punishment of solitary confinement.[26] However the Court has held that prisoners could be transferred to "administrative segregation" or to prisons with less favorable conditions without any procedure.[27] These decisions might be taken to in-

---

21. Gagnon v. Scarpelli, 411 U.S. 778, 790 (1973).

22. For general references on prisoner's rights, see S. Krantz, Law of Corrections & Prisoners Rights (1973); S. Rubin, Law of Criminal Correction (2 ed. 1973); R. Singer & W. Statsky, Rights of the Imprisoned (1974). Secret v. Brierton, 584 F.2d 823, 829–830 (7th Cir. 1978) (Pell, J., citing an earlier edition of this treatise).

23. The Supreme Court has held that a prisoner's interest in a fair process to review his eligibility for parole is not protected by due process unless the state has by statute entitled him to a fair parole granting process. See Greenholtz v. Inmates of the Nebraska Penal and Correctional Complex, 442 U.S. 1 (1979) which is discussed in Section II C of this chapter.

24. 418 U.S. 539 (1974).

25. 418 U.S. at 563–72.

26. 418 U.S. at 571–2 n. 19.

27. When a person has been convicted of a crime, he has received the best process which our society can afford to justify his liberty loss. A later transfer of the prisoner to differing conditions of confinement does not require a new process unless the new conditions may be said to be outside of the normal range of (or substantive constitutional limits on) the conditions of confinement. Thus, a prisoner who is transferred to a facility for mental treatment is entitled to a hearing, Vitek v. Jones, 445 U.S. 480 (1980). However, when a prisoner is placed in administrative segregation or transferred to a different penal facility, even one in another state, no new process is required because the

transfer does not implicate a liberty interest which was not adequately protected by the original criminal process and conviction. Montanye v. Haymes, 427 U.S. 236 (1976) (transfer to different prison facility); Meachum v. Fano, 427 U.S. 215 (1976) (transfer to maximum security prison); Howe v. Smith, 452 U.S. 473 (1981) (state prisoner transferred to federal penal facility); Hewitt v. Helms, 103 S.Ct. 864 (1983) (prisoner placed in administrative segregation); Olim v. Wakinekona, 103 S.Ct. 1741 (1983) (state prisoner transferred from prison in Hawaii to maximum security prison in California). If a state by statute or administrative action declares prisoners to be entitled to a hearing prior to a transfer into administrative segregation or to another penal facility, the state has given those prisoners an interest which is protected by due process. Hewitt v. Helms, 103 S.Ct. 864 (1983). Cf. Hughes v. Rowe, 449 U.S. 5 (1980) (per curiam). When the state has given a prisoner an interest in receiving fair treatment in the decision to transfer him to administrative segregation or to another facility, that interest is adequately protected by an informal, nonadversarial proceeding to review the basis for the transfer. Hewitt v. Helms, 103 S.Ct. 864, 872–74 (1983).

It is important to note that these decisions do not hold that "liberty," like "property", is to be defined only by reference to legislative or administrative actions rather than constitutional values. Rather, they hold that a prisoner's liberty has been taken with due process by our criminal justice system. Even after incarceration, a person may not be subjected to a form of punishment—such as beating or transference to a facil-

dicate that the degree of liberty which a prisoner enjoyed might be dependent solely upon state law but this position seems to conflict with established notions of the meaning of liberty.[28] In any event, it appears that the Supreme Court will only require a minimally fair procedure for the imposition of very severe and very formal disciplinary actions within a prison. Of course, in an emergency situation greater latitude would clearly be allowed to prison authorities to impose order and safe conditions in a prison without engaging in any formalized procedures.[29]

The Court has held that the mere possibility of receiving parole is not a liberty interest protected by the due process clauses and that even a state created entitlement of prisoners to receive parole under specific circumstances requires no more than informal hearings at which a parole board can receive a presentation by the prisoner.[30]

In *Vitek v. Jones*,[31] the Supreme Court held that an involuntary transfer of a prisoner to a mental hospital implicated a protected liberty interest and that due process was not satisfied by the mere certification of the need for such treatment by a state-designated physician or psychologist. The Court found that the transfer constituted a deprivation of liberty both because state statutes at issue in the case gave rise to a legitimate expectation on the part of the prisoner that he would only be kept in normal prison facilities and because this transfer involved a significantly greater degree of confinement,

the imposition of mandatory treatment, and a realistic possibility of stigmatizing consequences for the defendant. The majority opinion by Justice White recognized that the state's interest in treating mentally ill patients was quite strong, but found that it was outweighed by the prisoner's interest in not being arbitrarily classified as mentally ill and subjected to treatment. Five justices agreed that due process required: (1) notice to the prisoner of the intended transfer and of his rights to contest that transfer; (2) time for the prisoner to prepare his arguments; (3) a hearing where the prisoner has the opportunity to be heard in person, to present evidence and witnesses, and to cross examine state witnesses, except where good cause exists for limiting confrontation; (4) an independent decision-maker; (5) a written statement by the decision-maker detailing the evidence and rationale underlying a decision to transfer. Four of the justices in the majority also believed that the prisoner was entitled to appointed counsel if he was indigent. Although earlier prison discipline and probation cases had not created a general right to appointed counsel, these justices reasoned that the prisoner identified for possible transfer to a mental institution is more likely to need assistance in understanding and exercising his rights.[32] Justice Powell, the fifth vote for the majority in this case, believed that the inmate should have "qualified and independent assistance" at the hearing but that it need not necessarily be provided by a licensed attorney.[33] The four

---

ity for psychiatric care—not normally expected in our penal system without due process. However, the prisoner has no interest protected by due process in the place or type of confinement so long as it comports with substantive standards of due process and the prohibition of cruel and unusual punishment. A state by statute or administrative regulation may commit itself to giving prisoners a fair proceeding to review their transfer. Such legislative or administrative action restores to the prisoner a measure of the liberty properly taken from him by his criminal conviction.

28. Id. The concept of liberty has historically been a federal issue, see subsection II, C, supra; Meachum v. Fano, 427 U.S. 215, 230 (1976) (Stevens, J., dissenting).

29. Prison authorities may even have the right to very temporarily segregate prisoners by race in order to stop an outbreak of disorder based on racial tension. See Lee v. Washington, 390 U.S. 333, 334 (1968) (Black, J., concurring).

30. Greenholtz v. Inmates of the Nebraska Penal and Correctional Complex, 442 U.S. 1 (1979). This decision is examined in Section II C of this chapter.

31. 445 U.S. 480 (1980).

32. Id. at 497 (Opinion of White, J., joined by Brennan, Marshall & Stevens, JJ.).

33. 445 U.S. at 498–500 (Powell, J., concurring).

remaining justices dissented on jurisdictional grounds.[34]

When the state seeks to impose physical restraints of significant duration on a person it must afford him fair procedure to determine the basis and legality of such a deprivation of liberty, even when the nature of the state's action may be considered civil rather than criminal. When the state seeks to take custody of juveniles, it must accord the child a fair procedure.[35] This includes: (1) adequate notice of the charges; (2) a right to counsel; (3) the appointment of counsel for indigents; (4) the right to confrontation and cross-examination of witnesses and (5) the privilege against self-incrimination. Additionally, when the action is based upon a charge which would constitute a crime if committed by an adult, the state must prove its case beyond a reasonable doubt.[36] However, the state does not have to grant the juvenile either a jury trial or a public hearing.[37]

When the state seeks to commit someone for mental care on an involuntary basis, it must establish a fair procedure for determining that the individual is dangerous to himself or others due to a mental problem.[38] The Supreme Court has not yet settled many issues concerning the number of procedural safeguards which must be accorded a person whom the state seeks to commit for mental care.[39] However, the Court has held that the state must grant equivalent procedural safeguards to individuals whom it seeks to commit in civil proceedings and who have been found mentally incompetent in connection with criminal trials.[40]

In *Addington v. Texas*[41] the Supreme Court determined that an adult cannot be involuntarily committed to a psychiatric institution on a burden of proof that requires the state merely to show by a preponderance of the evidence that the person is dangerous to himself or another. Although the Court did not require a "beyond a reasonable doubt" standard, it held that trial courts must at least employ a "clear and convincing" evidence standard. Chief Justice Burger, writing for a unanimous Court, found that the societal, constitutional value placed on freedom from physical interment required adoption of a standard beyond the mere preponderance standard. However, the nature of commitment proceedings, which are nonpunitive and concerned with issues upon which there is virtually never factual certainty, did not require states to adopt a "beyond a reasonable doubt" or "unequivocal proof" standard.

The Supreme Court has held that minors who were admitted to state mental care institutions at the request of their parents, or by the order of governmental child care authorities if the minor was a ward of the state, were entitled to a fair review of their condition at the time of their admission, but not to an adjudicative or adversarial hearing. In *Parham v. J. R.*[42] a majority of the justices held that such children, who were "voluntarily" committed by their parents or the state guardian, were entitled only to an admission screening procedure or inquiry by a "neutral fact finder" to determine if the statutory criteria for commitment to the mental health unit were met in the individual child's case. The inquiry may be conducted by a staff physician so long as the doctor is free to independently evaluate the child and refuse to commit the child if commitment is not justified. This inquiry must include a

---

34. Vitek v. Jones, 445 U.S. 480, 500 (1980) (Stewart, J., dissenting joined by Burger, C. J., & Rehnquist, J.), id. at 501 (Blackmun, J., dissenting).

35. In re Gault, 387 U.S. 1 (1967).

36. In the Matter of Winship, 397 U.S. 358 (1970).

37. McKeiver v. Pennsylvania, 403 U.S. 528 (1971).

38. O'Conner v. Donaldson, 422 U.S. 563 (1975).

39. See F. Miller, R. Dawson, G. Dix & R. Parnas, The Mental Health Process, Chapters 6 & 8 (1976).

40. Humphrey v. Cady, 405 U.S. 504 (1972); Jackson v. Indiana, 406 U.S. 715 (1972); McNeil v. Director,

407 U.S. 245 (1972). However, a defendant acquitted of a criminal charge on the basis of an insanity defense may be committed to a psychiatric facility on that basis, even though the defense was established by a "preponderance of the evidence" rather than by "clear and convincing" evidence. Jones v. United States, 103 S.Ct. ___ (1983).

41. 441 U.S. 418 (1979). This opinion was unanimous but Mr. Justice Powell did not participate in the decision.

42. 442 U.S. 584 (1979).

careful probing of the child's background as well as a personal interview with the child. The majority opinion employed the *Mathews v. Eldridge* [43] balancing test in determining that no quasi-formal hearing was required. The child has an important liberty interest at stake, but the state is free to recognize the interest of parental authority so long as it creates some procedural safeguard against completely arbitrary or erroneous commitments.

The justices were unanimous in rejecting the assertion that the state should be required to have an adjudicative or adversarial hearing for the juvenile prior to the commitment to the mental institution. [44] The state had legitimate interests in recognizing parental authority, in providing health care for children by allocating more resources to treatment rather than administrative hearings, and removing procedural barriers that might deter parents acting in good faith from seeking care for children who needed treatment. All of the justices recognized that a requirement of an adversarial hearing prior to the initial commitment would have been arguably applicable to any hospitalization or health care decision made by a parent over a child's objection.

Justices Brennan, Marshall and Stevens dissented concerning the ability of the state to commit wards of the state to such facilities. [45] Although, as the dissent pointed out, the state in this situation did not have an interest in deferring to parental authority, and there was no individual guardian of the child's interest, a majority of the justices refused to distinguish the interests of these wards of the state from the interests of children committed by their parents or individu-

al guardians. The majority found no evidence that the decisions of state agencies to have children committed to mental health units were more likely to be arbitrary or erroneous than decisions made by parents. [46]

Justices Brennan, Marshall, and Stevens also dissented from the majority's analysis of the process due a child once the child had been admitted to a state mental health care facility. Once the child was admitted to the facility, the dissent argued, there was no harmonious family unit for the state to defer to, and the child should be protected by an adjudicative hearing on the issue of whether the child should remain in the custody of the state at the mental health facility. [47] This is a strong argument as the child is clearly deprived of a significant constitutional freedom so long as he is kept in custody against his will. However, the majority refused to determine what type of post-admission procedures would be required to safeguard the child's interest and held only that "the child's continuing need for commitment must be reviewed periodically by a similarly independent procedure." [48] In a companion decision, *Secretary of Public Welfare of Pennsylvania v. Institutionalized Juveniles*, [49] the Court, by the same 6–3 vote, upheld a state statute which allowed for "voluntary" commitment of juveniles to such facilities by parents or guardians after examination by mental health professionals and which required review of the continuing need for commitment of the child every 30 days by hospital staff, but did not provide for any adjudicative hearings. While the Court found that the admission procedure was sufficient to meet due process standards, the majority was careful to note that

---

43. 424 U.S. 319 (1976).

44. Three justices dissented to the rulings that gave no pre-admission hearing to wards of the state and only informal review procedures to juveniles after they had been hospitalized, but these justices concurred in the ruling that children were entitled only to a neutral inquiry, and not an adjudicative hearing, prior to their commitment by their parents. Parham v. J. R., 442 U.S. 584, 625 (1979) (Brennan, J., joined by Marshall and Stevens, JJ., concurring in part and dissenting in part).

45. Id.

46. 442 U.S. at 618. The majority left open the issue of whether these wards were entitled to more formal post-admission review procedures. Id.

47. 442 U.S. at 633–37 (Brennan, Marshall & Stevens, JJ., concurring and dissenting).

48. Parham v. J. R., 442 U.S. 584, 605 (1979) (footnote omitted).

49. 442 U.S. 640 (1979).

it was not deciding what standards states had to meet for the periodic review of committed children.[50]

It should be noted that the Court did not decide what, if any, procedures were required to safeguard the interest of a child committed by his parents to a mental health care institution that was not operated by the state.[51] The majority noted that, so long as the hospital was a government institution, the individual child could bring a suit to determine if the standards and procedures had been properly applied to the child in his individual case.[52]

Whenever the government seeks to restrain someone physically, it is depriving him of a constitutionally significant liberty interest so long as the restraint is more than momentary. Where the physical restraint is of a very brief duration, lesser procedures may be required to determine the legitimacy of the action. Thus when an individual is arrested by a police officer without an arrest warrant, the state must seek validation of the arrest from a judicial officer within a relatively short period of time.[53] This procedure will amount to no more than an ex parte determination of the officer's probable cause to arrest the defendant. While this procedure is very limited in its scope, it only authorizes the temporary detention of the defendant, who still has the safeguards of the speedy trial and excessive bail provisions

to restrict the state's power to subject him to indefinite pre-trial incarceration. Similarly, the Supreme Court has held that a public school student is deprived of liberty when he is subjected to physical punishment by school authorities.[54] However the majority held that this liberty interest was adequately safeguarded by the creation of a cause of action in tort against teachers who exceeded their authority in imposing physical punishments on the child.[55]

2. Enforcement of Debtor-Creditor Relationships

When a creditor uses government-enforced procedures to take the property of his alleged debtor, the debtor-defendant is deprived of a constitutionally significant interest in property. This deprivation exists whether the government transfers the property from the debtor to the creditor or merely prevents the debtor from using the property until the termination of the judicial proceeding instituted by the creditor. Of course, once the creditor has established his claim through a trial, the debtor has been accorded due process of law and the state may aid the creditor to enforce his judgment. However, the creditor may wish to have the property kept from the alleged debtor's use prior to trial in order to insure a recovery. When the government assists the creditor prior to trial, it must establish certain proce-

50.   442 U.S. at 650 n. 9.

51.   The dissenting justices in the 1979 cases would have found state action in a parent using a private hospital and they seem to have assumed that the other justices would have applied due process principles to safeguard the minor's interest in this "private" commitment situation even though the justices in the majority might define those principles differently than the dissent. Secretary of Public Welfare v. Institutionalized Juveniles, 442 U.S. 640, 642 (1979) (Brennan, J., dissenting joined by Marshall and Stevens, JJ.). The position of the dissent on this state action-deprivation issue seems most reasonable because the state by statute creates, or at least validates, the parental power to commit the child to an institution and loss of liberty. However, the majority avoided this issue. Id. at 642 n. 1. It should be noted that the Supreme Court has in one case found that a state statute which only recognized the ability of private persons to help themselves did not create state action in the acts of those private

persons. See Flagg Brothers, Inc. v. Brooks, 436 U.S. 149 (1978) (finding no state action in a warehouseman sale conducted without active state assistance but pursuant to a state statute).

52.   Parham v. J. R., 442 U.S. 584 (1979); Secretary of Public Welfare v. Institutionalized Juveniles, 442 U.S. 640, 650 n. 9 (1979).

53.   Gerstein v. Pugh, 420 U.S. 103 (1975). When a person is arrested by police officers acting pursuant to a facially valid arrest warrant, or a proper determination of probable cause to believe that the person has committed a crime, the person has not been unconstitutionally deprived of liberty, or a fourth amendment right, even if the police have made a mistake and the person is in fact innocent. See, Baker v. McCollan, 443 U.S. 137 (1979).

54.   Ingraham v. Wright, 430 U.S. 651, 672 (1977).

55.   430 U.S. at 682.

dures to safeguard the interests of the alleged debtor.

The government cannot garnish the wages of an alleged debtor without granting that individual the right to a hearing to determine whether there is a legitimate basis for keeping a portion of his wages from him. In *Sniadach v. Family Finance Corp.*[1] the Supreme Court held that garnishing a portion of a wage earner's salary to safeguard the interest of an alleged creditor was impermissible absent either a prior hearing for the debtor or an extraordinary emergency situation which justified foregoing the hearing. The majority opinion did not explain what type of emergency situation might justify garnishing someone's wages without a hearing but, presumably, it would have to be one which would render the interest of the creditor virtually worthless before a hearing could be held. While the Court has made many conflicting statements about due process in the years since *Sniadach*, it has not withdrawn the strict requirement of a hearing prior to wage garnishments.[2]

A creditor may seek to have assets other than wages of an alleged debtor seized by the government to insure that there will be a source for recovery of later judgments against the debtor. Where the creditor has a specific interest in the property, he may seek return and use of the property prior to trial. These pre-judgment remedies against debtors include procedures such as replevin, attachment of assets and garnishment of property other than wages. For a time it appeared that the Supreme Court would always require a hearing prior to an attachment of the debtor's property; subsequently it appeared that the Court would allow credi-

tors to regain such property with almost no procedural safeguards. In *Fuentes v. Shevin*[3] the Court by a vote of four to three, indicated that there would be a requirement of a prior hearing in pre-judgment attachments or replevin just as there was for wage garnishments. Only two years later the Court held, by a vote of five to four, that a state trial judge could order sequestration of personal property on the application of a creditor with very few safeguards, in *Mitchell v. W. T. Grant Co.*[4] Indeed, in *Mitchell* the dissenting justices thought that *Fuentes* had been implicitly overruled.[5] But such was not the case and *Fuentes* was given renewed, if somewhat restricted, life in *North Georgia Finishing v. Di-Chem.*[6] Here the Court, by a six to three vote, invalidated a statute which allowed the creditor to garnish property of an alleged debtor with certain procedural safeguards but without a hearing prior to the garnishment or attachment of the debtor's assets. In so doing, the majority set four requirements for pre-judgment replevin, attachment or garnishment statutes which did not provide a prior hearing for the debtor. If the state gave the debtor a hearing prior to the attachment, it would have met the procedural due process requirement of even the strict *Sniadach* standard. Without such a prior hearing, the statute must have the following four features: (1) the creditor must post a bond to safeguard the interest of the debtor; (2) the creditor or someone with personal knowledge of the facts must file an affidavit which sets out a prima facie claim for prejudgment attachment of the property; (3) a neutral magistrate must determine that the affidavit is sufficient before issuing the writ of attachment or replevin;

---

1.   395 U.S. 337 (1969).

2.   In Mathews v. Eldridge, 424 U.S. 319, 333–4 (1976) the majority opinion by Justice Powell might be read as indicating that *Sniadach* did not impose such a clear requirement. Such a position would be clearly in error as the majority opinion in *Sniadach* stated: "absent notice and a prior hearing . . . this prejudgment garnishment procedure violates the fundamental principles of due process." Sniadach v. Family Finance Corp., 395 U.S. 337, 342 (1969). One would hope that if the prior hearing requirement for wage garnishments

is to be changed, the justices will find a more principled way of doing this than simply misreading the *Sniadach* opinion. However the *Mathews* opinion may only have meant to indicate that *Sniadach* left the scope of the hearing unclear.

3.   407 U.S. 67 (1972).

4.   416 U.S. 600 (1974).

5.   416 U.S. at 631 (Stewart, J., dissenting).

6.   419 U.S. 601 (1975).

(4) there must be a provision for a reasonably prompt post-attachment hearing for the debtor.

There are two exceptions to the general procedural due process requirements in commercial cases: waiver and emergency. It would seem that one can waive his rights to procedural due process in a commercial setting, but the proper basis for finding a waiver is not at all clear. The Supreme Court has considered only one instance of a contractual waiver of due process rights in the commercial setting. In *Overmyer v. Frick* [7] the Court upheld a waiver of process clause which had been negotiated in a contract between two independent businesses. However, the Court did not indicate that it would be willing to uphold such waivers of process when it was unclear if the parties had truly bargained over the provision. Thus the validity of form contract provisions by which one party waives his rights to notice or process remains an open question.[8] If the Court were to apply the "knowing and intelligent" waiver standard of the criminal cases, it would be virtually impossible to uphold such provisions where the parties were of clearly unequal bargaining strength or where there was no real attempt to inform the debtor of the meaning of the provision.

These requirements as to due process in the taking of property may also be modified by extraordinary or emergency conditions. Most states have provisions for pre-judgment sequestration or attachment of the assets of an alleged debtor where a creditor can make a prima facie claim that the assets are liable to be hidden or destroyed before the claim can be resolved by the trial process. These provisions would seem to be permissible so long as they are reasonably tailored to dealing with emergency situations rather than merely providing a form for creditors to avoid the pre-trial hearing process. This theory was carried to its furthest extreme in *Calero-Toledo v. Pearson Yacht Leasing Co.* [9] when the Court upheld the government seizure of a ship used to transport contraband without a prior notice or hearing. The seizure was upheld because the majority saw it as serving a significant governmental interest in asserting jurisdiction over a moveable item of property against which it could legitimately conduct forfeiture proceedings. The Court held that this was an "extraordinary situation in which postponement of notice and hearing until after seizure did not deny due process."[10]

In conclusion, it must be noted that these cases examined in this subsection concerned debt enforcement procedures that involved at least the formal use of courts or government personnel. In *Flagg Brothers, Inc. v. Brooks*,[11] the Supreme Court found that there was no "state action" connected with a sale of an alleged debtor's goods by a warehouseman when the sale did not involve use of a government agency. It remains to be seen whether the court will allow states to enact laws that give creditors in a wide variety of circumstances the right to take the property of persons whom they allege to be their debtors. The Court did not specify the extent to which a state may authorize creditor "self-help" remedies.[12] The majority opinion in *Flagg Brothers* refused to determine whether there might ever be constitutional restraints on the "private" resolution of creditor-debtor conflicts.[13] One can only hope that the majority will place some limits on the mere "recognition" of self-help remedies and, thereby, prevent a state from freeing a wide variety of creditor-debtor conflict resolution procedures from constitutional values and restraints. As noted by Mr. Jus-

---

7.   405 U.S. 174 (1972).

8.   405 U.S. at 188; Swarb v. Lennox, 405 U.S. 191 (1972).

9.   416 U.S. 663 (1974).

10.   416 U.S. at 680; see also id. at 680 n. 15, indicating that the Court was not assessing the sufficiency of the postseizure notice procedures.

11.   436 U.S. 149 (1978).

12.   For an analysis of "self-help" remedies see Clark & Landers, Sniadach, Fuentes and Beyond: The Creditor Meets the Constitution, 59 Va.L.Rev. 355 (1973).

13.   Flagg Bros., Inc. v. Brooks, 436 U.S. 149, 162 n. 12, (1978).

tice Stevens in his dissent in *Flagg Brothers*: "[T]he state power to order binding, nonconsensual resolution of a conflict between a debtor and a creditor is exactly the sort of power with which the Due Process Clause is concerned."[14] However, at the present time the Court will find sufficient "state action" in a creditor remedy only when the creditor employs the help of the judicial or executive branches of government to seize or attach the property of the alleged debtor.[15]

3. Deprivations of Government Benefits

In the sections on liberty and property we saw a variety of situations in which the termination of government benefits could be deemed a cognizable interest under the due process clauses. In these situations there is no uniformity as to the nature of the procedures required to give someone "due process." Instead the justices will merely apply the general principles described in subsection B of this section. The justices use a balancing test to determine whether the individual interest merits a specific procedure in view of its cost to the government and society in general. Not surprisingly, this balancing process has yielded varying rules whereby some deprivations of government benefits can only be accomplished with very detailed hearings while others can be summarily terminated. A sampling of the major decisions in this area should give one a feeling for the way in which the current justices are striking the balance.[1]

The interest which requires the greatest procedural protection in the view of the Supreme Court is that of subsistence payments to indigent individuals. In *Goldberg v. Kelly*[2] the Court required a trial-type hearing before basic welfare benefits could be terminated. This case involved the termination of basic subsistence benefits and the Court found that the interest in those benefits was such that it could be likened to a property right.[3] While the majority opinion stated that a "quasi-judicial trial" would not be required,[4] it went on to hold that a pre-termination hearing must be granted, including such procedures that one could accurately describe it as a quasi-judicial trial. The Court required that the welfare beneficiary be granted a hearing which included: (1) adequate notice; (2) an opportunity for oral argument to the adjudicator; (3) a chance to present evidence in his behalf; (4) an opportunity to confront any witnesses who are adverse to his claim; (5) an opportunity to cross-examine those witnesses; (6) disclosure of all evidence against him; (7) a right to have an attorney present his case; (8) a decision based solely on the evidence produced at the hearing; (9) that the decision-maker state the reasons for his determination and the evidence he relied on and (10) that the decision-maker in fact be unbiased and impartial. The only basic administrative procedural requirements that the Court left out were the right to a complete record or comprehensive opinion, the assignment of counsel, and a formal finding of fact or opinion.[5] The guaranteed procedures come very

---

14. 436 U.S. at 176 (Stevens, J., dissenting, joined by White and Marshall, JJ.). Justice Brennan did not participate in the decision.

15. In Lugar v. Edmondson Oil Co., 102 S.Ct. 2745 (1982) the Supreme Court ruled that a debtor stated cause of action for deprivation of property under color of law by alleging that private creditor used state procedures to perfect an attachment of the debtor's property which involved court issuance of writ of attachment that was executed by county sheriff. The debtor was challenging "state action" insofar as he claimed that the state statute and involvement of state officers in the attachment process deprived him of property without adequate procedural safeguards.

1. For further examination and critique of these decisions, see K. Davis, Administrative Law Treatise,

Chapters 10, 12, 13, 14 (1979–80 2d ed.); Mashaw, The Supreme Court's Due Process Calculus for Administrative Adjudication in Mathews v. Eldridge: Three Factors in Search of a Theory of Value, 44 U.Chi.L.Rev. 28 (1976); Mashaw, The Management Side of Due Process: Some Theoretical and Litigation Notes in the Assurance of Accuracy, Fairness and Timeliness in the Adjudication of Social Welfare Claims, 59 Corn.L.Rev. 772 (1974).

2. 397 U.S. 254 (1970).

3. 397 U.S. at 262 n. 8, quoting Reich, Individual Rights and Social Welfare: The Emerging Legal Issues, 74 Yale L.J. 1245, 1255 (1965).

4. 397 U.S. at 266.

5. K. Davis, supra note 1 at 244.

close to an administrative trial and indicate the Court's belief that the full adversary process is necessary to protect an interest of this importance.

Lying in the middle range of interests, in terms of the procedural safeguards which they require, are terminations of important licenses or liberties. Two of the most important cases in this area involve the suspension of driving privileges and the suspension of students from school. In *Bell v. Burson* [6] the Court invalidated a statute which suspended the licenses of drivers involved in automobile accidents unless they furnished security to satisfy a judgment or gave proof of financial responsibility. The Court found that due process required a prior hearing to determine the probability of a judgment against an individual that would require proof of his financial responsibility. While the Court did not delineate all of the rights which would be involved in such a procedure, the opinion indicated that the procedures would be somewhat less than the administrative trial required in *Goldberg*. The Court later held that suspension of an individual's driver's license based on the number of times he has been convicted of traffic law violations does not require a hearing as there is no disputed issue of fact. [7]

In *Mackey v. Montrym* [8] the Court, by a 5-4 vote, upheld a state statute requiring the 90-day suspension of a person's driver's license for failure to take a chemical test or breath analysis test for usage of alcohol while driving a vehicle but allowing for prompt post-suspension administrative hearings. Those administrative hearings would determine three issues: (1) whether the po-

lice officer who requested the driver to take the test had reasonable grounds to believe that the driver was under the influence of intoxicating liquor; (2) whether the person was in fact arrested by the officer; (3) whether the person in fact refused to take the test. Applying the *Mathews v. Eldridge* [9] balancing test, the majority found that the individual's interest in a pre-suspension hearing to minimize the risk of erroneous deprivation of the driver's license for a 90-day period was outweighed by the governmental interest in protecting the safety of the populace through strict drunk driving penalties and prompt procedures for removing the drunk drivers from the highways. [10]

Also in the middle range of interests for due process protection are the interests of students who are suspended from public schools. In *Goss v. Lopez* [11] the Court held that high school students who were suspended for up to ten days were entitled to procedural protections against unfair or illegal suspensions. The applicable state law established an entitlement to attend school so as to create a constitutional property interest. The suspension also was found to impinge upon the "liberty" of the students as it might limit their employment or associational opportunities. But the process that was required to safeguard these interests was less complex than the *Goldberg* administrative trial procedures. The majority opinion indicated that the procedure would require that the student be given some oral or written notice of the charges and an opportunity to explain his position to the school authorities. [12] The Court also noted that in situations that called for immediate action to es-

---

6. 402 U.S. 535 (1971).

7. Dixon v. Love, 431 U.S. 105 (1977).

8. 443 U.S. 1 (1979).

9. 424 U.S. 319 (1976).

10. The dissenting justices believed that these state interests could be served by a prompt hearing on the issue of whether the driver had been intoxicated; this pretermination hearing could, in the view of the dissent, insure a fair determination of the ultimate issue while allowing for prompt removal of driving privileges from persons who had in fact used a vehicle while intoxicated. Mackey v. Montrym, 443 U.S. 1, 19 (1979)

(Stewart, J., dissenting, joined by Brennan, Marshall, and Stevens, JJ.). The admission into evidence of a defendant's refusal to take a blood-alcohol test does not violate either due process or the fifth amendment privilege against self-incrimination. South Dakota v. Neville, 103 S.Ct. 916 (1983).

11. 419 U.S. 565 (1975).

12. The opinion also noted that more severe deprivation such as longer suspensions might require more safeguards, 419 U.S. 565, 583. In Carey v. Piphus, 435 U.S. 247 (1978) the Supreme Court held that elementary and secondary school students who had been sus-

tablish discipline or order within a school, the school authorities could act prior to taking any procedures to safeguard the student interest.[13] Later the Court was to hold that school authorities were free to impose physical discipline on children so long as there was some state law limitation of the authority to impose such punishments and the possibility of later judicial actions against teachers who exceeded their authority.[14]

The Supreme Court dealt with a number of procedural due process issues regarding the dismissal of students from institutions of higher education in *Board of Curators v. Horowitz*.[15] In this decision the Court upheld the dismissal of a student from a medical school, without a formal hearing, based on low evaluations of her clinical work. As a medical student, the plaintiff had been required to achieve satisfactory evaluations from faculty member doctors regarding her clinical performance in a variety of hospital departments. After a faculty doctor expressed dissatisfaction with her performance in the pediatrics department, a faculty-student council recommended that she be advanced to her second and final year on probationary status. She continued to receive unsatisfactory evaluations of her clinical performance and was notified of this fact by the Dean. Thereafter, the council recommended that she not be allowed to graduate and that she be dropped from school unless her performance greatly improved. The plaintiff was allowed to "appeal" from this recommendation by taking a set of oral and practical exams, which were reviewed by seven practicing physicians. Only two of those physicians thought that she should be allowed to graduate on schedule. Following further low evaluations of her clinical work, the council recommended that she not be al-

lowed to re-enroll in the School of Medicine. This recommendation was approved by the Dean and a university provost after review of her academic record. All nine justices agreed that there had been no deprivation of procedural due process rights in this case.

Because the plaintiff was given a fair procedure, if not a hearing, the Court found it unnecessary to decide whether this student had been denied a "liberty" or "property" interest. The majority opinion by Mr. Justice Rehnquist noted that it would be difficult to determine whether the student had been deprived of a significant liberty interest because it was not clear whether this action would significantly restrict her ability to pursue a medical education at another institution. Assuming arguendo the existence of a liberty or property interest, the majority opinion found that the student had no right to a formal hearing at which she might challenge the basis for her dismissal. The opinion distinguished *Goss v. Lopez* on the ground that it involved a disciplinary procedure. An informal hearing was necessary to allow a student to present his or her side of a disciplinary issue so as to diminish the possibility of wrongful suspensions. Although the severity of the deprivation might be greater in the academic dismissal situation, under the *Mathews v. Eldridge* balancing test fewer safeguards were required because there was less chance of wrongful dismissal. All that was required was notice to the student and some form of fair procedure for evaluation and review of the student's academic record. The student in this case had received more than a minimally fair review of the facts upon which her dismissal was based. The majority opinion noted that the school had followed all of the rules that it had previously established for such cases.

pended from school without procedural due process were entitled to only nominal damages, absent proof of actual damages due to the constitutional deprivation. It should be noted that the Supreme Court, in Carey v. Piphus, did not have to determine whether the plaintiffs had asserted valid due process claims because the defendant school board failed to contest this issue. It was not clear whether the students adequately alleged that they wanted to contest some fact at the informal

hearing which might have affected the decision regarding their suspensions. Thus, it is at least possible that some of the students were not deprived of procedural due process.

13. 419 U.S. at 582–3.

14. Ingraham v. Wright, 430 U.S. 651 (1977).

15. 435 U.S. 78 (1978).

The opinion stated that the failure to follow previously established rules would result in invalidation of a federal administrative action as a matter of federal administrative law,[16] but the opinion indicated that this was not a constitutional principle binding upon the states.[17] However, failure of an institution to follow its own established procedural rules might weigh in the determination of whether or not an individual had been treated in such an arbitrary manner as to constitute a violation of due process. The majority opinion also found that there was no violation of substantive due process in this case, even assuming that the judiciary could legitimately review standards for academic dismissals. So long as the announced basis for reviewing academic performance is arguably reasonable, the courts have no function in reviewing the substantive basis for dismissals under the due process clause unless those dismissals were shown to be clearly arbitrary or invidious.[18]

One of the interests which has received less procedural protection is the right to a continuation of disability or welfare payments under the Social Security Act. In *Mathews v. Eldridge* [19] the Court held that such benefits could be terminated under a system which accorded the individual no right to a hearing until after the termination of his benefits. Here the Court found that there were sufficient procedural safeguards other than a hearing to lessen the chances of improper terminations. A majority believed that the termination would be based on medical decisions concerning which written evidence would have been considered by the agency prior to the termination decision. The Court also felt that the interest in disability payments was not as significant as that in subsistence payments.[20] Finally the majority simply held that the benefits to the government and society in general from foregoing these administrative burdens outweighed the interests of the individual recipient of disability payments. While Professor Mashaw has shown that this type of utilitarian balancing process seems improper due to its focus on technique and disregard of due process of values,[21] a majority of the justices seem committed to the *Mathews* balancing approach.

The Court has also been fairly restrictive in its view of what procedures are necessary to safeguard the interest of government employees who are discharged from their positions. As we have already noted, the Court will not find a significant property interest in government employment unless applicable law creates an entitlement or property right to the position. Nor will the Court find the deprivation of a liberty interest by the dismissal unless there is an injury to reputation

16. 435 U.S. at 92 n. 8. See Service v. Dulles, 354 U.S. 363 (1957); United States ex rel. Accardi v. Shaughnessy, 347 U.S. 260 (1954).

17. 435 U.S. at 92 n. 8.

18. Three dissenting justices would have remanded the case to the lower court for further examination of the substantive due process ruling. 435 U.S. at 97 (Marshall, J., concurring and dissenting); Id. at 108 (Blackmun & Brennan, JJ., concurring and dissenting).

19. 424 U.S. 319 (1976).

20. The Social Security Act authorizes the Department of Health, Education and Welfare to seek recoupment of overpayments to beneficiaries but it allows the individual beneficiaries to apply for reconsideration of whether an overpayment occurred over a waiver of the recoupment. In Califano v. Yamanski, 442 U.S. 682, (1979) the Supreme Court found that the recipient beneficiary need not be given a hearing concerning a request for reconsideration of whether an overpayment occurred but that the recipient was entitled to a "pre-recoupment hearing" when the recipient sought a waiv-

er because, under the statute and regulations, the department would have to make a determination of whether the recipient was a person who had received the overpayment "without fault" and from whom recoupment would defeat the purpose of the act by depriving the recipient of current income needed for living expenses. Written review of the payment records was a sufficiently fair process for determining whether overpayments occurred and therefore did not violate due process. The statute itself however required a pre-recoupment hearing for those seeking a waiver. The Court did not hold that due process would require such a hearing but its opinion indicated that this determination was one that could not be fairly made without some type of personal hearing.

See also Richardson v. Perales, 402 U.S. 389 (1972) (written reports of physicians who examined the claimants were sufficient to support denials of disability benefits).

21. Mashaw, supra note 1.

so serious as to limit one's future associational or employment opportunities. But when such interests are involved, there must be fair procedures to determine the basis for the dismissal of the public employee. However in *Arnett v. Kennedy* [22] the Court upheld the discharge of such an employee without a prior hearing where there were other procedures to review the decision to dismiss the employee. There was no majority opinion in this case, but there appeared to be a "working majority" which held that there must be a procedure to make a pretermination review of the initial decision to dismiss the employee by an impartial decision-maker and a post-termination hearing which would take place before the employee was permanently deprived of the interest in the job. [23]

There also seems to be an emerging concept that in some instances due process is fulfilled by a "post-deprivation" hearing or suit. This type of hearing would be in accordance with the utilitarian balancing test and might in fact result in a wider role for due process. It may be that the Court will be less fearful of recognizing a wide variety of interests as life, liberty or property if such recognition does not require universal government hearings prior to affecting those interests.

As predicted in the first edition of this treatise [24], the Supreme Court in recent years is finding that an increasing number of liberty or property interests are adequately protected by procedures which take place after the governmental termination of that liberty or property interest. In these cases the Court rules that the insignificant nature of the individual liberty or property interest at stake, or the magnitude of the government's need to take action without administrative delay, justifies a government action temporarily depriving a person of a liberty in property interest until a "post-deprivation" hearing can be held. In a few cases the Court has ruled that the government need not initiate post-deprivation process because the individual's interest is adequately protected by state law which allows the individual to bring a state court action against the government agency or employees who allegedly wrongfully deprived him of a liberty or property interest. [25]

When the deprivation of life, liberty, or property is a severe one, and the risk of erroneous governmental action is substantial, the Supreme Court is not likely to find that post-deprivation judicial remedies constitute sufficient process, absent emergency justification for the governmental action. Thus, a majority of the justices found that government utility companies were required to establish a process for hearing customer billing disputes prior to termination of utility services. Both pre-deprivation and post-deprivation judicial remedies were rejected by the Court as insufficient to protect the individual's interest in avoiding wrongful termination of utility service. [26]

When the government acts to protect the public interest for harmful acts of individuals it may temporarily limit those arguably harmful actions. Based upon this rationale, the Court has upheld temporary suspension of surface mining operation pending a review of allegations that the mine operator

---

22. 416 U.S. 134 (1974).

23. 416 U.S. at 171 (White, J., concurring). Professor Robert Rabin has argued that the most significant safeguard would be a reasoned explanation for the dismissal and that reduction in the number of other procedures required might lead the Court to recognize greater interests in public employment. Rabin, Job Security and Due Process: Monitoring Administrative Discretion Through A Reasons Requirement, 44 U.Chi. L.Rev. 60 (1976); see subsection II, D of this chapter concerning rights to public employment.

24. J. Nowak, R. Rotunda & J. Young, Constitutional Law 511 (1st ed. 1978).

25. The most significant decisions of this type are noted in the following paragraphs. See notes 31, 32 infra and accompanying text. For an insightful analysis of this trend and issues left unresolved by these decisions, see Smolla, The Displacement of Federal Due Process Claims by State Tort Remedies: Parratt v. Taylor and Logan v. Zimmerman Brush Co., 1982 Ill. L.Rev. 831 (1982).

26. Memphis Light, Gas and Water Division v. Craft, 436 U.S. 1 (1978).

was violating environmental regulations.[27] Similarly, the Court has upheld a statutory system imposing a temporary suspension of a person's license to drive an automobile when that person refused to take a drunk driving test.[28] A majority of the justices also found that a state did not have to give a pre-suspension hearing to a race horse trainer before suspending his license temporarily when one of his horses was found to have been drugged prior to a race, but that the state had to give the suspended trainer a prompt post-suspension hearing to verify the drug charge and to determine if the trainer was at fault.[29]

When the Court finds both that the nature of the individual liberty or property at stake is minor and that the governmental interest in acting without unnecessary administrative delay is significant, it is likely to find a post-deprivation process sufficient to protect the asserted liberty in property interest. These lesser interests may be adequately safeguarded by state law giving the individual the right to bring a state court action against the government agency which deprived him of the interest. Such a system allows for judicial determination of whether the government acted lawfully or whether the individual has a right to a remedy for wrongful deprivation of his liberty or property interest.[30] Thus the Court found that a child who is subjected to physical punishment by a teacher in a state school was subjected to a loss of liberty, but that this liberty interest was adequately protected by state law allowing the child to seek a judicial remedy for excessive, unjustified infliction of physical harm by the teacher.[31]

The Supreme Court adopted the post-deprivation hearing approach in deciding that

unintentional deprivations of property by government employees did not violate the due process clause under certain circumstances. *Parratt v. Taylor*[32] involved a claim brought under 42 U.S.C.A. § 1983[33] by a prisoner who alleged that prison officials negligently lost hobby materials delivered to the prison for him. The hobby materials were valued at $23.50 and the state allowed tort actions for redress of property deprivations by government officials. The defendant was able to bring a civil rights claim because § 1983 imposed no dollar limitation nor a formal requirement that the defendant pursue his remedy in state court. The majority opinion, by Justice Rehnquist, found that the negligent loss of the prisoner's hobby kit amounted to a deprivation of property by persons acting "under color of state law." However, the majority found that the prisoner could not maintain an action under § 1983 because the property deprivation was not one which occurred without "due process of law." The provision of a tort remedy by the state provided a sufficient means for redress of property deprivations so as to satisfy the requirement of due process. Because these were unintentional and unauthorized actions of state employees, the state government could not have had a system for pre-deprivation hearings to protect the individual's property interest. Thus, a finding that post-deprivation tort remedies were not sufficient protection for the individual's property interest would have made a constitutional violation out of every property injury caused any individual by any government employee. The Court concluded: "We do not think that the drafters of the Fourteenth Amendment intended the amendment to play such a role

---

27. Hodel v. Virginia Surface Mining and Reclamation Ass'n, Inc., 452 U.S. 264 (1981).

28. Mackey v. Montrym, 443 U.S. 1 (1979).

29. Barry v. Barchi, 443 U.S. 55 (1979).

30. See Smolla, supra note 25.

31. Ingraham v. Wright, 430 U.S. 651 (1977).

32. 451 U.S. 527 (1981).

33. 42 U.S.C.A. § 1983 provides:

"Every person who, under color of any statute, ordinance, regulation, custom, or usage of any State or Territory, subjects, or causes to be subjected, any citizen of the United States or other person within the jurisdiction thereof to the deprivation of any rights, privileges, or immunities secured by the Constitution and laws, shall be liable to the party injured in an action at law, suit in equity, or other proper proceeding for redress."

in our society."[34] The defendant had not been able to show that the procedures for compensation of property loss established by the state were in any way inadequate or that it was at all practicable for the government to provide a pre-deprivation hearing. The Court found that "[a]lthough the state remedies may not provide the respondent with all the relief which may have been available if he could have proceeded under § 1983 . . . [t]he remedies provided could have fully compensated the respondent for the property loss he suffered, and we hold that they are sufficient to satisfy the requirements of due process."[35] The Court seems firmly committed to finding that the state's granting of a post-deprivation hearing or the possibility for a state court action to redress property or liberty deprivations of a minor nature which are the result of the unintentional and unauthorized actions of state agents constitutes due process. However, it is not clear whether the justices will find that such remedies are sufficient to justify the state's limitation or deprivation of substantial property or liberty rights without a pre-deprivation hearing.[36]

IV. THE RIGHT TO JUDICIAL PROCESS—ACCESS TO THE COURTS

In the cases concerning "procedural due process" which we have examined, the issue

has been whether the government must afford a hearing to a person whom it is about to deprive of life, liberty, or property. In these situations the government is either operating one of its own administrative systems or instituting judicial process against an individual. However, in some instances a person will want access to the judicial process whether or not he is about to be deprived of a constitutionally cognizable interest in life, liberty or property. This desire normally presents no problem, for individuals are free to file their suits and make use of the judicial process within the generally applicable rules of civil procedure. If state law allows persons to bring suit in state court to redress alleged grievances against public or private agencies, it cannot arbitrarily deny an individual the ability to use those judicial procedures. The arbitrary refusal to allow individuals to use the established state court process would seem to be invalid under even the most minimal due process or equal protection standards.[1]

A significant issue in terms of a right of access to courts arises when some individuals cannot pay the fees required by the government for the use of the courts.[2] The Supreme Court has not held that there is any right to judicial process for an individual who seeks to use that process to his benefit. However, the state may not withhold this

34. Parratt v. Taylor, 451 U.S. 527 (1981).

35. Id.

36. Justice Rehnquist's opinion in *Parratt*, as a technical matter, was written for seven members of the Court. However, there were five other opinions filed in the case. Justice Stewart concurred in the opinion while noting that he doubted that there was a deprivation of property for fourteenth amendment purposes presented by these facts and that the post-deprivation process was "all that the Fourteenth Amendment requires in this context." Parratt v. Taylor, 451 U.S. 527, 544 (1981) (Stewart, J., concurring). Justice Blackmun joined the opinion of the Court but indicated that he understood that the provision of post-deprivation remedies would only constitute due process where there was a negligent deprivation of property interest and that it could not cure the unconstitutionality of an intentional deprivation of property; Justice White indicated agreement with Justice Blackmun's "reservations" about the majority opinion. 451 U.S. at 545, (Blackmun, J., concurring); Id. at 545 (White, J., concurring). Justice Powell would have found that the

negligent deprivation of property interest did not constitute a deprivation of property under color of law for the purposes of the Civil Rights Act or the fourteenth amendment; he did not make clear his position on the extent to which he would find that deprivations of property interest need only be protected with post-deprivation hearings. 451 U.S. at 546 (Powell, J., concurring in the result). Justice Marshall agreed that "an adequate post-deprivation cause of action for damages under state law" could preclude a finding of a due process violation for the negligent deprivation of property but believed that a prisoner did not have a meaningful opportunity to exercise the option of redressing his deprivation through a tort action. 451 U.S. at 554 (Marshall, J., concurring in part and dissenting in part).

1. Logan v. Zimmerman Brush Co., 455 U.S. 422 (1982). This case involved some confusion of substantive and procedural issues; it is examined in Chapter 13, Section IV, footnote 44.

2. See generally Michelman, The Supreme Court and Litigation Access Fees: The Right to Protect One's Rights—Part I, 1973 Duke L.J. 1153.

process when to do so would constitute the deprivation of a fundamental constitutional right. The government is also restrained by the equal protection guarantee in its granting of access to the judicial process. Filing fees are merely a way of allocating the judicial process to a certain class of plaintiffs— those who are willing and able to pay. The government may not impose filing fees which prohibit access to the courts by indigents when that would impair a fundamental constitutional right of the indigent or when the fees are so arbitrary that they invidiously exclude poor persons from the judicial process.

An example of filing fees which restrict a fundamental constitutional right are those imposed before married persons may receive a divorce. In *Boddie v. Connecticut*[3] the Supreme Court held that the filing fee requirement for divorce actions could not be applied to indigents who sought a divorce. The application of fees to indigent persons would effectively preclude them from exercising their constitutionally guaranteed right of freedom of choice in marital decisions. Similarly, when the government attempts to impose prior restraints on the freedom of speech, it must not only grant access to the courts to challenge these restraints but it must also institute judicial proceedings against the would-be speakers so as to insure that there will be judicial review for the censorship system.[4] These procedures are necessary to insure that problems of access

to judicial review do not result in suppression of protected ideas.[5]

The Court has held that there is a right of access to courts for the purpose of reviewing individual claims in the criminal justice system. Through a series of decisions the Court has recognized that fairness in the criminal justice system is a fundamental right. Thus the state may not impose filing fees for appellate procedures on indigent defendants as that would deny them equal protection of the law.[6] Similarly, the indigent defendant must be provided with transcripts for appeal, or a suitable alternative, for denial of a transcript would effectively preclude their access to the appellate process.[7] The government is also required to provide counsel for indigent defendants in their first appeal as they would be denied equal protection of the law by a system which provided meaningful review only for those who could afford to retain an attorney.[8]

The Court has recently held that indigents do not have a right to state appointed counsel for discretionary review or collateral attack proceeding.[9] A majority of the justices believed that the grant of counsel through the first appeal of right provided the defendant with sufficient opportunity for meaningful review of his conviction. However, this holding does not allow the government to deny the indigent access to the courts for these proceedings. If the government does not provide counsel for the defendant, it cannot prohibit prisoners from assisting each

3. 401 U.S. 371 (1971). Woods v. Holy Cross Hosp., 591 F.2d 1164, 1173 n. 16 (5th Cir. 1979) (Tjoflat, J., citing an earlier edition of this treatise).

4. Freedman v. Maryland, 380 U.S. 51 (1965); Blount v. Rizzi, 400 U.S. 410 (1971); Southeastern Promotion Ltd. v. Conrad, 420 U.S. 546 (1975).

5. Monaghan, First Amendment "Due Process," 83 Harv.L.Rev. 518 (1970).

6. Burns v. Ohio, 360 U.S. 252 (1954); Smith v. Bennett, 365 U.S. 708 (1961).

7. Griffin v. Illinois, 351 U.S. 12 (1956); Long v. District Court, 385 U.S. 192 (1966); Mayer v. Chicago, 404 U.S. 189 (1971).

8. Douglas v. California, 372 U.S. 353 (1963). In Scott v. Illinois, 440 U.S. 367 (1979) the Supreme Court limited the right of indigent criminal defendants to ap-

pointed counsel at trial to those cases wherein the defendant in fact received a punishment of imprisonment. The Court had held that indigents had a right to appointed counsel at least when they were imprisoned for conviction on the charged offense in Argersinger v. Hamlin, 407 U.S. 25 (1972). The *Scott* majority refused to extend this right to those indigent defendants who were charged with serious offenses but who in fact received only a monetary fine rather than a sentence of imprisonment. However, if an indigent defendant is not given appointed counsel during a misdemeanor trial, his conviction cannot then serve as the basis for converting a subsequent misdemeanor into a felony under a state "enhanced penalty" statute. Baldasar v. Illinois, 446 U.S. 222 (1980).

9. Ross v. Moffitt, 417 U.S. 600 (1974).

other in the preparation of petitions for discretionary review procedures.[10] Indeed the Court has found that there is a right of access to the courts for the submission of civil rights actions following imprisonment.[11] In 1977 the Court explicitly recognized that defendants retained this "right of access" following their conviction and imprisonment when the justices required the states to furnish prisoners with adequate legal research materials.[12]

Where access to the judicial process is not essential to the exercise of fundamental constitutional rights the state will be free to allocate access to the judicial machinery on any system or classification which is not totally arbitrary. Thus, filing fee requirement for such actions may be enforced so as to bar indigents from using the judicial process unless the fees are totally arbitrary. In *United States v. Kras* [13] the Supreme Court held that access to the bankruptcy courts could be denied those who were unable to pay the $50 filing fee for voluntary bankruptcy. Unlike divorce, bankruptcy is not the only method available for a debtor to adjust his legal relationship with his creditors. The debtor can settle his debts out of court. The Court justified its holding that, in effect, some people could be found too poor to go bankrupt by ruling that a congressional desire to make the bankruptcy system somewhat self supporting was a permissible justification for the fee. Because the bankruptcy process was not essential to the exercise of any fundamental constitutional right, Congress was free to allocate access to the system on such a basis without violating either the due process or equal protection guarantees. Similarly, the Court has upheld a system which imposed $25 filing fees for appellate court review of welfare eligibility

determinations, thereby effectively precluding indigent welfare recipients from receiving judicial review of the termination of their benefits.[14] While individuals whose welfare benefits were terminated were entitled to due process, that included only a fair initial hearing. As there is no fundamental constitutional right to welfare payments, the state could impose such filing fees on all persons.

Filing fees for causes of actions which are not essential to the exercise of fundamental rights will still be invalidated if it can be shown that they are totally irrational and can serve no purpose other than to deter suits by poor persons. Thus, in *Lindsey v. Normet* [15] the Court invalidated a requirement that tenants who wish to appeal from summary eviction proceedings post appeal bonds in twice the amount that would be required to safeguard the interests of the landlord. This double bond requirement clearly served no purpose other than to deter appeals by low income tenants and it was stricken on this basis by the Court.[16] However, the Court also held that the state was free to create a summary system for eviction of tenants after non-payment of rent and preclude defenses based on landlord breaches of duty to these tenants.[17] The summary action in such a situation was held to comply with both the due process and equal protection clauses because the Court found no fundamental constitutional liberties involved in such cases. The Supreme Court has continually allowed states to create laws which rationally further governmental purposes even though they burden poor persons so long as they do not allocate the exercise of fundamental constitutional rights on the basis of wealth.[18]

10. Johnson v. Avery, 393 U.S. 483 (1969).

11. Wolff v. McDonnell, 418 U.S. 539, 577–80 (1974).

12. Bounds v. Smith, 430 U.S. 817 (1977).

13. 409 U.S. 434 (1973).

14. Ortwein v. Schwab, 410 U.S. 656 (1973) (per curiam).

15. 405 U.S. 56 (1972).

16. 405 U.S. at 74–79.

17. 405 U.S. at 64–69.

18. See Chapter 16, Sections VI & XII. For a comparison of these cases and the Supreme Court's treatment of wealth classifications generally, see Nowak, Realigning the Standards of Review Under the Equal Protection Guarantee, 62 Georgetown L.J. 1071 (1974).

CHAPTER SIXTEEN

EQUAL PROTECTION

I. INTRODUCTION TO EQUAL PROTECTION

A. Introduction—Application to State and Federal Acts

The fourteenth amendment commands that no person shall be denied equal protection of the law by any state. This clause introduced a new concept into constitutional analysis by requiring that individuals be treated in a manner similar to others as an independent constitutional guarantee. There are similar concepts in the privileges and immunities clause of Article IV, and the commerce clause requirement that states not discriminate against interstate transactions, but these relate only to state treatment of certain specific matters. The equal protection guarantee, however, governs all governmental actions which classify individuals for different benefits or burdens under the law.

In recent years the equal protection guarantee has become the single most important concept in the Constitution for the protection of individual rights. As we have seen, substantive due process analysis was disclaimed after 1937 and the justices today are not willing to restrict the legislative ability to deal with a subject under that analysis. And the privileges or immunities clause of the fourteenth amendment has never been a meaningful vehicle for the judicial review of state actions,[1] although it may have been intended to be a primary safeguard of natural law rights by the drafters of the amend-

ment.[2] Instead, the Court has increasingly focused upon the concept of equal protection to guarantee that all individuals are accorded fair treatment in the exercise of fundamental rights or the elimination of distinctions based on impermissible criteria. It was not long ago that Justice Holmes could categorize the concept of equal protection as "the last resort of constitutional arguments."[3] However the Court now recognizes that in some circumstances the review of legislative classifications is a permissible part of the judicial function, particularly since it entails only the requirement that the government either forego an action or include within it all persons of a similar position.[4]

The equal protection guarantee applies to both the state and federal governments although the restrictions have two totally distinct bases. The equal protection clause of the fourteenth amendment by its own terms applies only to state and local governments.[5] There is no equal protection clause that governs the actions of the federal government, and the Court has not attempted to make the clause itself applicable to federal acts. However, if the federal government classifies individuals in a way which would violate the equal protection clause, it will be held to contravene the due process clause of the fifth amendment. As we shall see in the following sections, the standards for validity under the due process and equal protection clauses are identical.[6]

The difference in the method of analysis under the due process and equal protection

---

1. The meaning of the clause was restricted to protecting very limited "national" rights in The Slaughter-House Cases, 83 U.S. (16 Wall.) 36 (1873). In one case the Court did find that a state statute violated this clause but it reversed the decision within a few years. See, Colgate v. Harvey, 296 U.S. 404 (1935), overruled in Madden v. Kentucky, 309 U.S. 83 (1940). See King v. Schweiker, 647 F.2d 541, 546 (5th Cir. 1981) (Geuin, J., citing an earlier edition of this treatise).

2. See J. tenBroek, Equal Under Law at 223 (Enlarged Edition 1965); cf. James, The Framing of the Fourteenth Amendment at 180 (1965).

3. Buck v. Bell, 274 U.S. 200, 208 (1927).

4. See, Tussman and tenBroek, The Equal Protection of the Laws, 37 Calif.L.Rev. 341, 344 (1949).

5. "No State shall . . .; nor deny to any person within its jurisdiction the equal protection of the laws." U.S.Const. amend. XIV, § 1.

6. See, e.g., Bolling v. Sharpe, 347 U.S. 497 (1954); Weinberger v. Wiesenfeld, 420 U.S. 636, 638 n. 2 (1975); Schlesinger v. Ballard, 419 U.S. 498, 500 n. 3 (1975), see generally, Karst, The Fifth Amendment's Guarantee of Equal Protection, 55 N.C.L.Rev. 540 (1977).

There is dicta indicating that the Court will subject federal laws which burden aliens as a class to a more lenient standard of review because of unique federal interests in this area. See, e.g., Nyquist v. Mauclet, 432 U.S. 1, 7 n. 8 (1977). The case is discussed in Section III, of this Chapter.

guarantees relates only to whether or not the governmental act classifies persons. Whenever fundamental rights are limited the laws will have to promote an overriding or compelling interest of government in order to be valid under either clause. When the governmental action relates only to matters of economics or general social welfare, the law need only rationally relate to a legitimate governmental purpose. If the law does not classify individuals, it will be subjected to the due process guarantee under these standards. However, if the means the law employs to achieve its end is the classification of persons for differing benefits or burdens, it will be tested under the equal protection guarantee. If the classification does not meet the appropriate standard of review then the legislation has failed to have a sufficient relationship to the required governmental purpose. A law which violates this concept also denies the individuals classified due process of law because the means employed by the government do not relate to a compelling or legitimate end of government. Thus, federal classifications in the area of fundamental rights or suspect classifications which do not promote a compelling governmental interest violate the due process clause.[7] Similarly, a federal law in the area of economics or social welfare which classifies persons will be upheld under the equal protection guarantee of the due process clause so long as it rationally relates to a legitimate governmental purpose.[8] Federal laws are therefore tested under the same standards as state laws and we will refer to both tests under the term "equal protection guarantee." It must be remembered, however, that classifications established by federal law are reviewed under the implied equal protection guarantee of the fifth amendment due process clause.

In the following two sections we will briefly introduce the basic concepts of classification and standards for judicial review that emanate from the equal protection guarantee. For those seeking a more extensive introduction to the equal protection concept we strongly recommend the article "The Equal Protection of the Laws" by Joseph Tussman and Jacobus tenBroek.[9] Although written in 1949, that article contains not only a description of equal protection analysis but also the basis of virtually all forms of standards of review issues which are only now beginning to emerge in the cases. In the next section, we will describe the basic equal protection concept in relation to the ways in which government may classify people. We will then give a brief outline of the ways in which the Court has reviewed these classifications. The history of the provision is dealt with in a summary fashion, together with a description of the historical background of the Civil War Amendments in a later section of the text dealing with the constitutionality of classifications based on race or national origin.

B. Government Classifications and the Concept of Equal Protection

The equal protection clause guarantees that similar individuals will be dealt with in a similar manner by the government. It does not reject the government's ability to classify persons or "draw lines" in the creation and application of laws, but it does guarantee that those classifications will not be based upon impermissible criteria or arbitrarily used to burden a group of individuals. If the government classification relates to a proper governmental purpose, then the classification will be upheld. Such a classification does not violate the guarantee when it distinguishes persons as "dissimilar" upon some permissible basis in order to advance

---

7. See, e.g., Bolling v. Sharpe, 347 U.S. 497 (1954) (segregated schools in District of Columbia).

8. See, e.g., United States v. Kras, 409 U.S. 434 (1973) (bankruptcy fees and access to courts).

See, King v. Schweiker, 647 F.2d 541, 546 (5th Cir. 1981) (Gewin, C. J., citing an earlier edition of this trea-

tise); Silva v. Vowell, 621 F.2d 640, 647 (5th Cir. 1980), rehearing denied 625 F.2d 1016, certiorari denied 449 U.S. 1125, (Tate, C. J., citing an earlier edition of this treatise), cert. denied 449 U.S. 1125 (1981).

9. Tussman and tenBroek, The Equal Protection of the Laws, 37 Calif.L.Rev. 341 (1949).

the legitimate interests of society. Those who are treated less favorably by the legislation are not denied equal protection of the law because they are not similarly situated to those who receive the benefit of the legislative classification.

It should be noted that the equal protection guarantee has nothing to do with the determination of whether a specific individual is properly placed within a classification. Equal protection tests whether the classification is properly drawn. It is the guarantee of procedural due process that determines what process is necessary to find that an individual falls within or outside of a specific classification.[1] Equal protection deals with legislative line drawing; procedural due process deals with the adjudication of individual claims.

However, it is incorrect to say that the equal protection has nothing to do with the application of a law. Some legislative acts will have, by their own terms, a classification which is to be tested under the equal protection guarantee. The Court will then determine whether the law is valid "on its face." In some instances this judicial review will involve a further inquiry into the nature of the legislative classification and its purpose and effect. For example, a zoning ordinance may be found to constitute a racial classification if, but only if, it can be proven that the purpose and effect of the ordinance is the exclusion of members of a racial minority from a residential area.[2] In other situations a law may have no impermissible classification by its own terms but it may be applied in such a way as to create a classification. Then the Court will test the law "in its application" to determine whether the classification established by administrative actions is permissible. For example, a law which eliminated the use of wooden buildings for hand laundries was found to constitute a racial classification in its administration when all Chinese persons owning such laundries were forced to give up their businesses while all non-oriental persons who had similar laundries were granted exemptions from the prohibition.[3] Again, it should be noted that in these cases equal protection is used to determine whether the classification established by the administrative acts is permissible and not whether a given individual falls within the terms of the classification.[4]

Equal protection is the guarantee that similar people will be dealt with in a similar manner and that people of different circumstances will not be treated as if they were the same.[5] In reviewing any classification it must be determined whether or not the persons classified by the law for different treatment are in fact "dissimilar." The question relates to the bases upon which the government can distinguish between individuals in society. There is no requirement that government follow natural classifications and it may subdivide persons as it deems proper for the advancement of legitimate governmental purposes. Conversely, classifications are not tested by whether or not the individuals are truly different in some absolute sense from those who receive different treatment. For example, it is undeniably true that men and women are biologically different. However that difference does not mean that gender-based classifications will be generally upheld, for most often there is no difference between men and women in terms of the promotion of a legitimate governmental end. Thus, sex cannot be the ba-

1. See Chapter 15, Procedural Due Process.

2. Arlington Heights v. Metropolitan Housing Development Corp., 429 U.S. 252 (1977).

3. Yick Wo v. Hopkins, 118 U.S. 356 (1886).

4. The problems of "proving" classification are examined later in this introduction see Section I, D of this chapter.

5. Tussman and tenBroek, The Equal Protection of the Laws, 37 Calif.L.Rev. 341 (1949).

See United States of America v. Horton, 601 F.2d 319 (7th Cir. 1979) (Pell J., quoting an earlier edition of this treatise); United States v. Horton, 601 F.2d 319, 324 (7th Cir. 1979) (Pell, C. J., quoting an earlier edition of this treatise) cert. denied 444 U.S. 937 (1979); Levine v. New Jersey Department of Institutions and Agencies, 84 N.J. 234, 256, 418 A.2d 229, 240–41 (1980) (Handler, J., quoting an earlier edition of this treatise).

sis for determining whether an individual is able to be the executor of an estate [6] or mature enough to drink alcoholic beverages.[7]

Usually one must look to the end or purpose of the legislation in order to determine whether persons are similarly situated in terms of that governmental system.[8] The judiciary need not always review the permissibility of the legislative purpose, but it must decide what is the end of the legislation to be tested. Once a court has found an end of government which does not in itself violate the Constitution, it can analyze the way in which the government has classified persons in terms of that end. Classifications can relate to government "ends" in any one of five ways,[9] any one of which may be determined to be constitutional or unconstitutional depending on the nature of the legislation in the specific case. First, the classification could be perfect in that it treats all similar persons in a similar manner. Second, the classification could be totally imperfect in that it selects exactly the wrong class for a burden or a benefit while excluding the class of persons who do relate to the legitimate purpose of the statute. Third, the classification can be under-inclusive in that it includes a small number of persons who fit the purpose of the statute but excludes some who are similarly situated. Fourth, the classification can be over-inclusive in that it treats in a similar manner not only those persons whose characteristics similarly relate to the purpose of the law but also some additional persons who do not share the legitimately distinguishing characteristic. Fifth, there can be a mixed relation of over and under-inclusions. Some examples should help to clarify this breakdown of classifications.

The perfect classification involves the legislative use of a classifying trait which exactly fits the purpose of law and treats all similar people in a similar manner. On the other hand, a perfectly bad classification benefits a classification of persons who have no relationship to the legitimate purpose of the statute. Neither such relationship is likely to exist, for perfect line drawing, be it good or bad, is a rarity and we may best analyze classifications in terms of the difficult burden of trying to prove such a relationship. For example, let us assume that a state government passes a law which allows men but not women to be bartenders. We will assume that the permissible purposes of the law are to have efficient bartenders and to avoid disturbances of the peace in establishments serving alcohol. The legislative classification would be perfect if it could be proven that all men would be good bartenders who would maintain discipline and that women bartender always caused inefficient service or disturbances of the peace. The classification would be perfectly bad if it could be shown that all women made excellent bartenders but that male bartenders always caused inefficiency or disturbances of the peace.

An under-inclusive classification contains all similarly situated people but excludes some people who are similar to them in terms of the purpose of the law.[10] To return to our bartender example, the law could be construed as an under-inclusive burden if it were found that no women would be good bartenders and that only some men would be good bartenders. In this situation all the women are similarly situated but a similar group of men is excluded from the imposition of the burden. The same law might be deemed an under-inclusive benefit if it could be shown that some women would not make good bartenders but that all men and some women would provide efficient and peaceful service. In this situation the law is under-inclusive because it fails to extend the benefit of a bartenders license to women who are

---

6. Reed v. Reed, 404 U.S. 71 (1971).

7. Craig v. Boren, 429 U.S. 190 (1976).

8. Tussman and tenBroek, supra note 5 at 367.

9. For further analysis of these possible relationships see Tussman and tenBroek, supra note 5.

10. Barnhorst v. Missouri State High School Activities Ass'n, 504 F.Supp. 449, 459 (W.D.Mo.1980) (Clark, D.J., quoting an earlier edition of this treatise).

similar in their abilities as bartenders to the men who receive the license.

A law may be said to be over-inclusive when the legislative classification includes all persons who are similarly situated in terms of the law plus an additional group of persons. In our bartender example the law could be construed as an over-inclusive burden if it could be proven that all men and some women made good bartenders but that a sub-group of women could not be efficient bartenders or gave rise to disturbances of the peace. The law would be over-inclusive because it burdened not only the group of women who would be bad bartenders but also those who would provide efficient service and avoid disturbances of the peace. Note that the same law might be construed as an over-inclusive benefit if it was shown that only a small group of men could give efficient bartender service and maintain the peace in these establishments. Were that the case, the law would be over-inclusive as a benefit measure because it gave the benefit of a bartenders license to not only qualified men but to all men.

Many classifications can be said to be a mix of both over and under-inclusions. The ease with which we could change labels by viewing the statute as one dispensing benefits or burdens in our bartenders example should highlight the fact that many classifications can have this mixed quality. Thus in our bartenders example it would be easiest to construe the statute as being both under and over-inclusive, because some women and some men make good bartenders while some women and some men cannot give efficient service or control discipline within the establishments. In other words, we cannot identify the class of persons who will promote the end of the statute by the characteristic of gender. Thus, it can be said that men and

women are similarly situated in terms of their abilities to be bartenders.[11]

It is important to analyze classifications in terms of their relationship to the legitimate purposes of the statute. This analysis will be the basis for determining whether the classification has a sufficient relationship to a proper governmental purpose so as to withstand a challenge under the equal protection guarantee. However, the labeling of a classification as over-inclusive or under-inclusive will not establish its compatibility with the equal protection clause. It is sometimes said that under-inclusive burdens are not reviewed as strictly by the Court because those burdened by the classification are properly identified as deserving the burden or regulation[12] and that the legislature may seek to solve social problems "one step at a time."[13] As the foregoing examples should demonstrate, almost any classification can be alternatively analyzed as over or under-inclusive depending on one's view of the statutory system and the facts developed in the course of a challenge to the statute. Very few classifications will be either a perfect promotion of an articulated governmental purpose or a clearly irrational mismatch of classifications with ends. The key factor in reviewing classifications is the degree of correlation between the means and the ends that is required by the judiciary and the extent to which the judiciary will analyze the permissible purposes of the legislation. If under-inclusive classifications are usually upheld it is because they tend to appear in general as "economic" or "social welfare" regulations where the Court does not require the legislature to demonstrate a very close relationship between its classifications and the purposes of the statute. It was on this basis that the Supreme Court upheld a law which excluded some women from being bartenders in a case very close

11. But the Court in fact upheld a law which denied bartenders licenses to all women except the wives or daughters of male owners of bars. Goesaert v. Cleary, 335 U.S. 464 (1948); For an analysis of the varying degree of strictness with which the Court has reviewed sex-based classifications, see Section V of this Chapter.

12. See, Developments in the Law Equal Protection, 82 Harv.L.Rev. 1065, 1084–6 (1969).

13. Williamson v. Lee Optical, 348 U.S. 483, 489 (1955).

to our example.[14] Thus a key factor becomes the standard under which the justices will review the permissibility of the government ends and the degree of relationship between the classification and these ends.

C. An Introduction to Standards of Review Under the Equal Protection Guarantee

As should be clear from the example in the previous subsection, the degree to which a classification can be said to meet the equal protection guarantee depends on the purpose which one attributes to the legislative act and the determination of whether there is a sufficient degree of relationship between the asserted governmental end and the classification. It is rare that a classification can be so artfully drawn that it can be said to promote perfectly any but the most peculiar or narrowly defined ends. Thus the ultimate conclusion as to whether a classification meets the equal protection guarantee in large measure depends upon the degree of independent review exercised by the judiciary over the legislative line-drawing in the establishment of the classification. To the extent that the Court defers to the legislature's choice of goals or determination of whether the classification relates to those goals, the justices have in fact taken the position that it is the function of the legislature rather than the judiciary to make the equal protection determination as to the particular law. To the extent that the justices independently determine whether the law has a purpose which conforms to the Constitution and whether the classification in fact relates to that purpose, the justices are taking the position that the Court is able to assess these issues in a manner superior to, or at least different from, the determination of the legislature. Thus, the Court must decide whether it will engage in any realistic scrutiny of legislative classifications, and

thereby assume the power to override democratic process, or whether, by deferring to that process, it will limit the concept of a unique judicial function. As Professors Tussman and tenBroek have stated the problem:

> The United States Supreme Court attempts to meet these difficulties by maintaining that it is not its function, as it reviews legislation, to substitute its views about what is desirable for that of the legislature. It thus bows in the direction of the functional separation theory. But at the same time the Court speaks of judicial self-restraint as the answer to the undemocratic aspects of the check and balance system. Kept apart from each other, the essential incompatibility of these two attitudes often escapes notice. For self-restraint is no virtue if the Court has a unique function to perform. If, on the other hand, the self-restraint is justified, the belief in a unique judicial function is untenable. These difficulties plague the Court at every stage in the process of applying the equal protection clause.[1]

The Court's institutional decision as to the degree of unique judicial function and the amount of deference that should be paid to legislative policy decisions in equal protection issues has mirrored that made in terms of substantive due process. As we have seen in an earlier Chapter, the Court from 1887 to 1937 used equal protection as well as due process to invalidate those forms of social welfare or economic legislation with which the justices were in fundamental disagreement.[2] The justices did not defer to legislative decisions but instead independently determined what ends the government might pursue in conformity with their view of the role of government in a free economy.

When the Court renounced the theory of substantive due process, it also rejected the claim to an institutional ability to determine the reasonableness of classifications when reviewing laws under the equal protection guarantee.[3] However, as we noted in the chapter concerning substantive due process,

---

14. Goesaert v. Cleary, 335 U.S. 464 (1948); see note 11 supra and accompanying text.

1. Tussman and tenBroek, The Equal Protection of the Laws, 37 Calif.L.Rev. 341, 366 (1949).

2. See Chapter 13, Substantive Due Process, Section III.

3. See Chapter 13, Substantive Due Process, Section IV, 1937 to Present.

the Court did not at this time reject its function of protecting what the justices believed were fundamental constitutional values.[4] Thus, in the post 1937 period we have had a dichotomy between the judicial review of classifications employed in economic and general social welfare regulation and review of classifications which touch upon fundamental constitutional values or use a criterion for classification which itself violates a fundamental constitutional value. Classifications of the first type will be upheld so long as they arguably relate to a legitimate function of government. Classifications of the second type, however, will be subjected to "strict scrutiny" by the Court and upheld only if they are necessary to promote an extremely important or "compelling" end of government. These are the same tests, or standards of review, that have been employed by the Court in resolving substantive due process issues after 1937. When the judiciary examines the constitutionality of a governmental classification these methods of analysis are referred to as equal protection "standards of review." It is possible to rationalize all equal protection decisions as judicial determinations of whether the government has fairly classified persons and argue that there is only one equal protection standard of review. However, such an argument fails to recognize that the Supreme Court justices perform quite different functions when they: (1) virtually prohibit governmental use of some classifications, (such as racial classifications); (2) independently examine the reasonableness and legitimacy of some classifications (such as gender classifications); and (3) presume that the use of some classifications is within the constitutional prerogative of the legislature (such as classifications relating to economic or social welfare matters). Although the justices have agreed in majority opinions to only two

standards of review of general applicability, there appears to be at least three standards of review that may be employed in equal protection decisions.[5]

The first standard of review is the rational relationship test which we saw developed for use in both equal protection and substantive due process issues in the post 1937 decisions of the Court. The Court will not grant any significant review of legislative decisions to classify persons in terms of general economic legislation. In this area the judges have determined that they have no unique function to perform; they have no institutional capability to assess the scope of legitimate governmental ends in these areas or the reasonableness of classifications that is in any way superior to that of the legislature. Thus, if a classification is of this type the Court will ask only whether it is conceivable that the classification bears a rational relationship to an end of government which is not prohibited by the Constitution. So long as it is arguable that the other branch of government had such a basis for creating the classification the Court will not invalidate the law.

The second type of review under the equal protection guarantee is generally referred to as "strict scrutiny". This test means that the justices will not defer to the decision of the other branches of government but will instead independently determine the degree of relationship which the classification bears to a constitutionally compelling end.[6] This test is identical to that employed in the post 1937 decisions on fundamental rights under the due process concept. The Court will not accept every permissible government purpose as sufficient to support a classification under this test, but will instead require the government to show that it is pursuing a "compelling" or "overriding" end—one whose value is so great that it justifies the

4. See Chapter 13, Substantive Due Process, Section IV, 1937 to Present, and Section V, A Note on the Meaning of Liberty, Fundamental Values and the Incorporation of the Bill of Rights.

5. Ktsanes v. Underwood, 467 F.Supp. 1002, 1007 (N.D.Ill.1979) (Pell, J., citing an earlier edition of this treatise).

6. Horton v. Califano, 472 F.Supp. 339, 343 (W.D. Va.1979) (Williams, D.J., citing an earlier edition of this treatise).

limitation of fundamental constitutional values. Even if the government can demonstrate such an end, the Court will not uphold the classification unless the justices have independently reached the conclusion that the classification is necessary to promote that compelling interest. If the justices are of the opinion that the classification need not be employed to achieve such an end, the law will be held to violate the equal protection guarantee.

Under the due process guarantee the Court will employ this level of strict scrutiny only in reviewing legislation which limits fundamental constitutional rights. However the Court will use this standard of review under the equal protection guarantee in two categories of civil liberties cases: first, when the government act classifies people in terms of their ability to exercise a fundamental right; second, when the governmental classification distinguishes between persons, in terms of any right, upon some "suspect" basis. The reason for the difference in treatment of these two types of cases stems from Justice Stone's reference to the existence of an important judicial function in protecting certain fundamental constitutional rights and "discrete and insular minorities."[7]

Because equal protection problems involve classifications rather than the limitations of rights for all persons, the Court is sometimes called upon to exercise strict scrutiny of legislation because of the classifying traits employed by the legislature rather than the nature of the right touched upon by the legislative act. However, the Supreme Court will not strictly scrutinize all legislative classifications of persons for that would merely return to the pre-1937 general review of economic and social welfare legislation.[8] The Court will only employ the strict scrutiny standard to review the legitimacy of classifications when they are based upon a trait which itself seems to contravene established constitutional principles so that any use of the classification may be deemed "suspect".[9] Due to the justices' views of the history and purpose of the fourteenth amendment, laws that classify persons on the basis of either their status as a member of a racial minority or on the basis of their national origin will be deemed suspect and subject to this strict standard of review.[10] The Court has also held that laws which classify persons in terms of alienage, by treating resident aliens less favorably than citizens, will be deemed suspect and subject to this test. However the test does not seem to be enforced quite as strictly in terms of the review of these classifications.[11]

At the close of the 1960's it was still possible to do a detailed analysis of all Supreme Court equal protection decisions in terms of a "two-tiered" model involving recognition of only the two previously described standards of review.[12] However, in the past doz-

---

7. United States v. Carolene Product Co., 304 U.S. 144, 152 n. 4 (1938):

"4. There may be narrower scope for operation of the presumption of constitutionality when legislation appears on its face to be within a specific prohibition of the Constitution, such as those of the first ten amendments, which are deemed equally specific when held to be embraced within the Fourteenth . . .

It is unnecessary to consider now whether legislation which restricts those political processes which can ordinarily be expected to bring about repeal of undesirable legislation, is to be subjected to more exacting judicial scrutiny under the general prohibitions of the Fourteenth Amendment than are most other types of legislation . . .

Nor need we enquire . . . whether prejudice against discrete and insular minorities may be a special condition, which tends seriously to curtail the op-

eration of those political processes ordinarily to be relied upon to protect minorities, and which may call for a correspondingly more searching judicial inquiry . . . ."

8. See Three Rivers Cablevision, Inc. v. City of Pittsburgh, 502 F.Supp. 1118, 1133 (W.D.Pa.1980) (Diamond, D.J., citing an earlier edition of this treatise).

9. The phrase originated in Korematsu v. United States, 323 U.S. 214, 216 (1944); see, Brest, Forword: In Defense of the Antidiscrimination Principle, 90 Harv.L.Rev. 1, 7 n. 35 (1976).

10. See, this chapter, Section II, Classification Based on Race or National Origin.

11. See this chapter, Section III, Classifications Based on Alienage.

12. See Developments in the Law—Equal Protection, 82 Harv.L.Rev. 1065 (1969).

en years there have appeared a number of cases in which the Court has given very little deference to legislative judgments when reviewing legislation classifications but in which the Court has not employed either the traditional rational basis or compelling interest standard.[13] This form of independent but not technically "strict scrutiny" review has appeared in a variety of modern cases. The only category of cases in which a majority of the justices have clearly adopted a standard of review falling between the two traditional is the category of cases involving gender-based classifications. A majority of the justices will uphold a gender classification only when the government can demonstrate that the classification it has employed is "substantially related" to an "important governmental objective."[14] The standard of review in these cases eliminates the strong presumption of constitutionality that exists under the rational basis standard of review but it allows the government to employ a gender-based classification so long as it is a reasonable means of achieving substantial government ends and not merely the arbitrary classifying of people by sexual stereotypes.[15]

In some instances the justices appear to be employing a standard of review close to the intermediate "substantial relationship to an important interest" standard adopted in the gender cases without formal adoption of that standard of review. When examining governmental classification of persons for burdens or benefits based upon whether they were technically "legitimate" at birth the Court has invoked a rational basis standard but it has invalidated illegitimacy classifications which appear to a majority of justices to be arbitrary.[16] At times the Court has described the standard employed in these cases as "not toothless";[17] at times it has said that the classification must be "substantially related to a legitimate state interest."[18] The fact that the justices have upheld the use of an illegitimacy classification when the government could demonstrate that its use of the classification was reasonably related to achieving an identifiable social end indicates that this test is far less strict than the compelling interest test even though it involves independent judicial review of the legislative action.[19] Conversely to the approach taken in the illegitimacy cases, the Supreme Court at times has described classifications based upon United States citizenship as "suspect" but has failed to employ the compelling interest test in many alienage cases.[20] In both the illegitimacy and alienage cases the Supreme Court appears to be using an intermediate or middle level standard of review but it has failed to identify the test used in those cases.

The Supreme Court in recent years appears to have altered the standard of review for laws regulating the exercise of fundamental constitutional rights. In many cases the Court still maintains that it will employ the compelling interest test when the government allocates the ability to exercise fundamental rights differently among various classifications of persons. The identification of a right as "fundamental" is a substantive

---

13. See generally, Alabama State Federation of Teachers v. James, 656 F.2d 193, 195 (5th Cir. 1981); Torres v. Portillos, ___ Colo. ___, 638 P.2d 274, 276 (1981); Lujan v. Colorado State Bd. of Educ., ___ Colo. ___, 649 P.2d 1005, 1015 n.9 (1982), citing an earlier edition of this treatise. In a landmark article Professor Gunther identified this trend virtually at its inception. Gunther, Foreword: In Search of Evolving Doctrine on a Changing Court: A Model for a Newer Equal Protection, 86 Harv.L.Rev. 1 (1972).

14. Craig v. Boren, 429 U.S. 190, 197 (1976).

15. See Section V of this chapter concerning gender classifications.

16. See Section IV of this chapter concerning illegitimacy classifications.

17. Mathews v. Lucas, 427 U.S. 495, 510 (1976).

18. Mills v. Habluetzel, 102 S.Ct. 1549, 1554 (1982).

19. See, e.g., Lalli v. Lalli, 439 U.S. 259 (1978) (upholding law prohibiting inheritance from deceased father by illegitimate child who failed to receive judicial order of paternity during father's lifetime).

20. See Section III of this chapter concerning alienage classification. The problem of deterring the proper standard of review for alienage classification was highlighted by the Court's ruling that a state violated the equal protection clause by denying free public education to the children of "illegal aliens." Plyler v. Doe, 457 U.S. 202 (1982).

decision unrelated to equal protection or technical standards of review.[21] However, the Court in the 1960's and early 1970's had indicated that laws making differentiations between persons exercising fundamental rights would be subject to strict judicial scrutiny and would not be upheld unless the government could demonstrate that it was necessary for it to use the classification in order to promote a compelling interest.[22] Although some majority opinions continue to invoke strict scrutiny—compelling interest language in fundamental rights cases, it has been more common in the late 1970's and early 1980's for the Court to review the legitimacy of such laws without stating a clear standard of review.[23] For example, the Court has found the right to vote to be fundamental but has in some cases upheld regulations of voting rights or the rights of candidates without requiring that the government formally demonstrate a compelling interest.[24] In those cases the justices seem to exercise independent judicial review in order to insure that the regulation of the voting process reasonably promotes important ends (such as the governmental interest in running efficient and honest elections) and does not unreasonably restrict the voting rights of any class of individuals. This would appear to involve a middle level standard of review which neither prohibits all regulation of the right to vote nor presumes that the government is free to limit voting rights as it would be under the traditional rational basis standard of review. Similarly, the Supreme Court sometimes invokes the compelling interest test when it examines laws that restrict the ability of some persons to migrate from one state to another but in other cases it has upheld laws imposing some burden on the right to interstate travel without requiring that the government demonstrate that such laws were necessary to promote a compelling interest.[25]

It would be helpful to lower courts, lawyers, and students of constitutional law if the Supreme Court would formally adopt three or more standards of review. The first standard would be the traditional rational basis test which the Court would in-

---

21. This decision involves a judicial determination that the text or structure of the Constitution evidences the existence of a value that should be taken from the control of the political branches of government. The decision is one that can be best characterized as a substantive due process decision because it involves judicial protection of a substantive value and a limitation in the substance of laws or regulations which restrict that value or right. Most fundamental rights cases involve equal protection rulings because the cases involve review of laws which classify persons and impose differing restrictions on the ability of those classifications of person to exercise a fundamental right. See Chapter 13, Substantive Due Process, Sections IV and V; M. Perry, the Constitution, the Courts, and Human Rights, Chapter 4 (1982). See generally, Westen, the Empty Idea of Equality, 95 Harv.L.Rev. 537 (1982); Burton, Comment on "Empty Ideas": Logical Positivist Analysis of Equality and Rules, 91 Yale L.J. (1982); Westen, On "Confusing Ideas": Reply, 91 Yale L.J. 1153 (1982); Chemerinsky, In Defense of Equality: A Reply to Professor Westen, 81 Mich.L.Rev. 575 (1983); D'Amato, Comment: Is Equality a Totally Empty Idea, 81 Mich.L.Rev. 600 (1983); Westen, The Meaning of Equality in Law, Science, Math and Morals: A Reply, 81 Mich.L.Rev. 604 (1983).

22. See, e.g., Loving v. Virginia, 388 U.S. 1 (1967) (marriage); Kramer v. Union Free School District, 395 U.S. 621 (1969) (voting); Shapiro v. Thompson, 394 U.S. 618 (1969) (interstate travel); Dunn v. Blumstein, 405 U.S. 330 (1972) (travel and voting).

23. See, e.g., Zablocki v. Redhail, 434 U.S. 374 (1978) (restrictions of marriage—examined in Section VII of this chapter); Zobel v. Williams, 457 U.S. 55 (1982) (right to travel—examined in Section X of this Chapter).

24. The voting and candidates' rights cases are examined in Section VIII of this chapter. See, e.g., Ball v. James, 451 U.S. 355 (1981) (limitation on voting for election of limited purpose governmental unit upheld); Clements v. Fashing, 102 S.Ct. 2836 (1982) (limitation on candidacy for a governmental office of persons who hold a different public office upheld).

25. See, e.g., Sosna v. Iowa, 419 U.S. 393 (1975) (one year residency requirement for divorce upheld). Compare, Dunn v. Blumstein, 405 U.S. 330 (1972) (one year residency requirement for voting invalidated) with Marston v. Lewis, 410 U.S. 679 (1973) (per curiam), Burns v. Fortson, 410 U.S. 686 (1973) (per curiam) (50 day residency requirement for voting upheld). The difficulty of identifying the proper standard of review to be used in right to travel cases was discussed in several opinions in Zobel v. Williams, 457 U.S. 55 (1982) in which the Court invalidated a distribution of state oil revenues to citizens based upon the length of each citizen's residence in the state. See Section X of this chapter for an examination of the right to travel decisions.

voke when it found no reason to independently examine the permissibility of a legislative classification. This test gives a strong presumption of constitutionality to governmental acts and involves no truly independent judicial review. The second test would be the traditional strict scrutiny or compelling interest test by which the Court has virtually forbidden the use of classifications involving race or national origin. The third standard of review would have some ad hoc quality to it for it would describe a test by which the justices would independently examine some classifications (perhaps those touching upon some fundamental rights or involving alienage, gender or illegitimacy classifications) but which were not totally prohibited from legislative use. It may be that the Court would define this middle level standard of review as a balancing test.[26] Alternatively, this test might be described—as it was in the gender classification cases—as requiring the government to demonstrate that the classification at issue

bears a substantial relationship to an important governmental interest.[27]

The Supreme Court's failure to openly adopt a middle level standard of review with applicability to a defined set of legal issues poses two dangers for constitutional decision-making in the future. First, it is possible that the Court will weaken the traditional "strict scrutiny" or "compelling interest" test by invoking that language in cases in which the justices do not mean to restrict greatly the power of a legislature to employ a classification. Thereafter, those cases might be used as precedents for weakening the very strong strict scrutiny test which has posed a virtually impenetrable barrier to legislatures desiring to use racial classifications which would burden members of minority races or ethnic groups. The second, and perhaps more realistic, danger is that the failure to define a middle level of review will result in indiscriminate exercise of independent judicial review of all legislative classifications under the guise of a rational basis test. This would result in the Supreme

---

26. Justice Marshall has long advocated use of a balancing test in equal protection cases. See, e.g., Dandridge v. Williams, 397 U.S. 471, 591–22 (1970) (Marshall, J., dissenting); Massachusetts Board of Retirement v. Murgia, 427 U.S. 307, 318–21 (1976) (Marshall, J., dissenting). For analysis of the possibility for developing a principled used of a balancing approach to equal protection decisions, see, Simson, A Method of Analyzing Discriminatory Effects Under the Equal Protection Clause, 29 Stan.L.Rev. 663 (1977); Barrett, Judicial Supervision of Legislative Classifications—A More Modest Role for Equal Protection? 1976 B.Y.U. L.Rev. 89; Lowey, A Different and More Viable Theory of Equal Protection, 57 N.C.L.Rev. 1 (1978).

27. See Notes 14 and 15 supra. Some scholars have advocated use of a middle level standard of review under which judges would independently examine the relationship of the classification to the asserted governmental interest or demand a governmental demonstration of the legitimacy of the end to be promoted by the classification. See Gunther, supra note 13; Nowak, Realigning the Standards of Review Under the Equal Protection Guarantee—Prohibited, Neutral and Permissive Classifications, 62 Georgetown L.J. 1071 (1974). Other scholars have suggested that the Court focus its decisions on the value—such as political equality—which is at stake in an equal protection case rather than employ a standard which would involve independent judicial review of all governmental classifications. Compare, Wilkinson, The Supreme Court, the Equal Protection Clause and the Three Faces of Constitutional Equality, 62 Va.L.Rev. 94 (1975), with Perry,

Modern Equal Protection: A Conceptualization and Appraisal, 79 Colum.L.Rev. 1023 (1979) (reprinted in M. Perry, supra note 21). For an analysis of the difficulty of applying the various "tests" to a governmental action regulating important areas of human activity that have not been declared to be fundamental rights, see Spece, A Purposive Analysis of Constitutional Standards of Judicial Review and a Practical Assessment of the Constitutionality of Regulating Recombatant DNA Research, 51 So.Cal.L.Rev. 1281 (1978). Professor (now Dean) John Hart Ely has published a scholarly monograph examining the role of the Supreme Court in a political process based upon democratic ideals. He would circumscribe judicial power by limiting the justices to independent review of only those laws which seem to transgress express constitutional limitations, operate to disadvantage certain minority groups, or impede the democratic process itself. J. Ely, Democracy and Distrust (1980). Professor Ely's work has given rise to reconsideration of, and renewed debate concerning, the role of judicial review in our society. Commentary on Professor Ely's work includes: Grano, Ely's Theory of Judicial Review: Preserving the Significance of the Political Process, 42 Ohio St.L.J. 167 (1981); Nowak, Foreword: Evaluating the Work of the New Libertarian Supreme Court, 7 Hastings Con.L.Q. 263 (1980); Tribe, The Puzzling Persistence of Process-Based Constitutional Theories, 89 Yale L.J. 1063 (1980); Tushnet, Darkness on the Edge of Town: The Contributions of John Hart Ely to Constitutional Theory, 89 Yale L.J. 1037 (1980).

Court returning to the unrestrained form of judicial review employed from the late 1800's through 1936 under the due process and equal protection labels.[28]

The Supreme Court today in majority opinions employs the rational basis test when reviewing a governmental classification under equal protection guarantee when that classification does not involve a fundamental constitutional right, suspect classification, or the characteristics of alienage, sex or legitimacy. A majority of the justices today will uphold governmental classifications under this standard unless no reasonably conceiva-

ble set of facts could establish a rational relationship between the classification and an arguably legitimate end of government. In recent years some justices have indicated a desire to review the reasonableness of virtually all legislative classifications in a realistic manner but they have been unable to remove the strong presumption of validity for classifications in the economic and social welfare area.[29] Thus, a majority of the justices today continue to use the traditional rational basis test to approve classifications related to welfare benefits,[30] property use,[31] or business or personal activity that does not

28. See Chapter 13, Substantive Due Process, Sections III & IV.

29. See Schweiker v. Wilson, 450 U.S. 221 (1981) (upholding Social Security Act classification giving reduced Medicaid benefits to persons institutionalized in certain public mental care institutions; Justice Powell, joined by Justices Brennan, Marshall and Stevens, in dissent, would engage in a review of the reasonableness of this classification); Minnesota v. Clover Leaf Creamery Co., 449 U.S. 456 (1981) (reversing state court determination that classification of containers for the sale of milk violated the equal protection clause despite dissent by Justice Stevens that would have allowed the state court to use the fourteenth amendment equal protection clause to review the reasonableness of the classification); United States R.R. Retirement Bd. v. Fritz, 449 U.S. 166 (1980) (employing the rationality test to uphold a retirement act classification providing for double or windfall benefits to a limited class of employees; Justice Stevens, concurring, and Justices Brennan and Marshall, dissenting, indicate a willingness to use an independent test of reasonableness to determine the validity of the classification). See also, G.D. Searle & Co. v. Cohn, 455 U.S. 404 (1982) (Supreme Court rules that state statute tolling statute of limitations period against out-of-state corporation which does not have an officer located in the state for service of process does not violate equal protection; Justice Stevens in dissent would have found that the statute denied equal protection to these corporations). See also, note 33 infra.

An excellent example of the confusion caused by the failure to identify the proper standard of review for overly generalized classifications is New York City Transit Authority v. Beazer, 440 U.S. 568 (1979). In this case the Supreme Court upheld a rule of the New York Transit Authority that excluded from employment all users of drugs, including those who were receiving methadone under a physician's supervision. After concluding that there was no issue presented for decision under the Federal Rehabilitation Act and no apparent violation of other federal statutes, the Court examined the equal protection challenge in a most unusual manner. The majority opinion, by Justice Stevens, indicated both that the law was a reasonable means of identifying candidates for employment and

that the law need not be precisely tailored for this purpose because the Court should defer to the state's decision concerning the type of persons who were suitable for employment by the Transit Authority. The opinion never explained what standard of review was used to review the classification and it avoided any consideration of whether the rule would be valid, or even reviewed more strictly, if it were used to exclude those who had completed methadone treatment for earlier drug use and who were applying for positions that did not involve the safety of passengers of the Transit Authority. Thus, the result of the case is consistent with the multi-tiered formulation, but the opinion may evidence a desire of some justices to engage in some meaningful review of laws burdening "disfavored" groups.

30. See, e.g., Cleland v. National College of Business, 435 U.S. 213 (1978) (upholding restrictions on educational payments under "GI Bill" which denied benefits for educational courses taken at certain types of proprietary educational institutions); United States R.R. Retirement Bd. v. Fritz, 449 U.S. 166 (1980) (upholding congressional elimination of payment of dual retirement benefits to some employees who had engaged in both railroad and non-railroad employment on any basis that is not "patently arbitrary or irrational"); Schweiker v. Wilson, 450 U.S. 221 (1981) (upholding Social Security Act classification giving reduced Medicaid benefits to persons institutionalized in certain public mental care institutions; Schweiker v. Hogan, 102 S.Ct. 2597 (1982) (upholding Social Security Act classifications that provide for reimbursement of state providing Medicaid benefits to "medically needy" but exempting from program repayment for benefits to "categorically needy".)

The Supreme Court has summarily reversed decisions of state courts which used the fourteenth amendment, rather than the state constitution, to invalidate economic or welfare regulations. In Idaho Dept. of Employment v. Smith, 434 U.S. 100 (1977) (per curiam), the United States Supreme Court summarily reversed a state court decision holding economic legislation to be a violation of the equal protection clause. In this case the Supreme Court of Idaho had held unconstitutional

31. See note 31 on page 597.

involve a fundamental right.[32] But there is the possibility that the confusion over the nature of standards of review under the equal protection guarantee will contribute to a return to the pre-1937 approach to equal

protection with justices invoking rational basis language while independently scrutinizing the reasonableness of government classifications.[33] There is the possibility that the justices who have demonstrated an unwill-

a statute that denied unemployment benefits to otherwise eligible persons if they attended school during the day; students attending night schools were allowed to receive benefits if they were otherwise eligible under the statute. As the law did not touch upon fundamental interests or disadvantage a suspect classification, the Supreme Court of the United States described it as being only "in the field of social welfare and economics." The Supreme Court held that classifications designed to be predictable, convenient means for identifying those who would receive state benefits and permissible under the rational relationship test even though they were imperfect.

31. See, Hodel v. Indiana, 452 U.S. 314 (1981) (upholding the "prime farm land" provisions of the Surface Mining and Reclamation Control Act of 1977 against the claim that the restrictions on mining and certain farm land were arbitrary limitations of the use of property in select geographic areas). "Social and economic legislation like the Surface Mining Act that does not employ suspect classifications or impinge on fundamental rights must be upheld against equal protection attack when the legislative means are rationally related to a legitimate government purpose. Moreover, such legislation carries with it a presumption of rationality that can only be overcome by a clear showing of arbitrariness and irrationality." Id. at 331 (citations omitted).

The Supreme Court summarily reversed a state court which had employed the fourteenth amendment rather than a state constitution provision to invalidate a zoning law. In County Board v. Richards, 434 U.S. 5 (1977) (per curiam), the Supreme Court upheld a zoning ordinance that restricted individuals' ability to park their cars in given areas based on their relationship to residents of the area. Residents of certain areas were given free parking permits for themselves, persons doing business in the area, and some visitors. All other persons were prohibited from weekday parking in these residential areas. The Supreme Court of Virginia had held that the ordinance violated the equal protection clause of the fourteenth amendment because it created arbitrary classifications that did not in fact promote the enunciated goals of the ordinance. The Supreme Court of the United States reversed the Virginia court. The Supreme Court employed the traditional rational basis test; under this test no proof was required that the classifications established under the ordinance in fact promoted legitimate purposes. The Supreme Court of the United States was careful to note that it was only reversing the Supreme Court of Virginia as to its ruling on the fourteenth amendment; the Supreme Court did not preclude review of the ordinance on independent state grounds by the Virginia court.

32. The Supreme Court upheld a state law which prohibited the ownership of retail gas stations by petroleum producers and refiners and which regulated their pricing practices in Exxon Corp. v. Governor of Maryland, 437 U.S. 117 (1978). It took the Court only

a single paragraph to dismiss the producers' argument that the law violated the principle of substantive due process; there was no problem in upholding these regulations under the rational relationship test. 437 U.S. at 125. The commerce clause ruling in this case is noted in Chapter 9.

The Court also upheld a state law which charged out-of-state residents a substantially higher price for hunting licenses than was charged residents of the state. Baldwin v. Fish and Game Comm'n, 436 U.S. 371 (1978). In the opinion of a majority of the justices, the hunting fee did not violate either the privileges and immunities clause of Article IV or the equal protection clause because it was a non-invidious means of protecting big game animals in the state. [The privileges and immunities aspect of the case is noted in Chapter 10.] The interest of the out-of-state resident who sought to hunt animals in the state was not one that required the Court to invoke more than a rationality standard under the equal protection clause.

33. The confusion of procedural due process and equal protection issues in some cases has also contributed to the difficulty of identifying the proper standard of judicial review to be employed in equal protection decisions. When reviewing the permissibility of the procedures by which the government identifies a person for the granting or withholding of entitlements, the justices must independently review the fairness of those procedures. However, when reviewing the legislative or regulatory classifications, the Court should grant a presumption of constitutionality to those classifications that do not touch upon a fundamental right nor employ racial, ethnic, citizenship, gender or legitimacy characteristics. See Chapter 12, Section III regarding the difference between procedural due process and substantive due process or equal protection. See also Chapter 15, Procedural Due Process.

The difficulty of separating procedural from substantive issues caused particular confusion in Logan v. Zimmerman Brush Co., 455 U.S. 422 (1982). In that case the justices unanimously found that provisions of the Illinois Fair Employment Practices Act as interpreted and applied to a specific plaintiff violated procedural due process. The plaintiff in that case had filed a charge with the Illinois Employment Practices Commission alleging that he had been fired from his job unlawfully due to a physical handicap. Under the Act, the Commission was required to hold a fact-finding conference within 120 days of the filing of the claim, but through inadvertence or neglect the Commission scheduled the hearing five days after the expiration of that 120-day period. The Illinois courts construed the 120-day requirement as jurisdictional and held that the Commission was permanently barred from hearing the employee's claim for redress for the alleged discriminatory practice. Justice Blackmun wrote for seven justices in finding that the state statute gave the plaintiff a constitutionally protected property interest to use the statutory procedure for possible redress of discriminat-

ingness to accept government assertions of a theoretical or conceivable rational basis for legislation will be joined by new Supreme Court appointees who would also require the government to demonstrate a reasonable relationship between any classification and a significant end of government. Were that possibility to occur, the presumption of constitutionality for economic and social welfare legislation and classifications would disappear. If the Court, in majority opinions, would clearly define a middle level standard of review, it would be forced to justify the use of that standard in particular cases and there would be less danger that all equal protection decisions in the years ahead will be ad hoc evaluations of the reasonableness of legislative classifications.

It must be remembered that today the Court does employ the traditional rational basis test when the classification to be tested does not involve a fundamental right, and does not employ the characteristics of race, national origin, citizenship, sex or legitimacy of birth to define the benefited or burdened class. The justices will not review the reasonableness of laws tested under the rationality test. Even though the classification may seem unreasonable or unfair, a majority of the justices will not strike the law so long as it is conceivable that the classification might promote a legitimate governmental interest. The Courts' decisions on mandatory retirement laws for government employees demonstrate the strong presumption of constitutionally afforded a classification in the area of economics or social welfare. Such laws require all employees of a governmental unit to retire at a statutorily fixed age. These laws may result in many otherwise qualified people losing their employment and may not in fact promote efficiency in government. However, such laws have been upheld under the rational basis standard. There is no fundamental right to government employment. Classifications based on age are not treated as suspect or even deserving of the middle level standard of review used in gender discrimination cases.[34]

ing employment practices. The state court ruling denying the plaintiff that property interest without a hearing violated due process. Six justices also believed that the state statute as interpreted by the state supreme court violated equal protection. There was no ruling on the discharged worker's equal protection claim as these justices addressed the equal protection issue in two separate concurring opinions. Justices Powell and Rehnquist found that the challenged cut-off of discrimination claim in this case failed to have a "rational relationship to legitimate governmental objectives" because "it is unfair and unnatural to punish" individual claimants for the Commission's failure to meet its statutory obligations. These two justices did not wish to express any view on the nature of due process or equal protection review. Logan v. Zimmerman Brush Co., 455 U.S. 422, 444 (1982) (Powell, J., concurring, joined by Rehnquist, J.). Justice Blackmun wrote for four justices; he found that the Illinois rule denied the claimant equal protection. Justice Blackmun's separate opinion stated that the minimal equal protection guarantee requires judicial scrutiny of whether in fact the administrative or legislative classification promoted a legitimate end of government. "The State's rationale must be something more than the exercise of a strained imagination; while the connection between means and ends need not be precise, it, at the least, must have some objective basis." Logan v. Zimmerman Brush Co., 455 U.S. 422, 442 (1982) (Blackmun, J., joined by Brennan, Marshall and O'Connor, JJ.). The Blackmun opinion would remove or, at least, diminish the strong presumption of constitutionality given regu-

lations in the area of economics or social welfare since 1937. However, this opinion did not receive the support of a majority. Additionally, it may be that these four justices would differ about the nature of the rational basis standard in a case that did not involve an arbitrary denial of procedural fairness. The equal protection opinions in *Logan* are in fact no more than a response to the State's claim that it was free to deny some persons access to its courts by terminating their claims based on the admittedly arbitrary refusal of its commission to hear those claims.

34. The Court has avoided addressing the issue of the standard of review that should be employed when reviewing laws which deny equal access to business establishments to persons below a specified age. See, Mesquite v. Aladdin's Castle, Inc., 455 U.S. 283 (1982) (Court avoids ruling on law prohibiting persons under the age of 17 from operating electronic amusement devices unless accompanied by adult because state court may rule law invalid under state constitution). Nevertheless, it is difficult to believe that the Court will subject such laws to meaningful judicial review and thereby make a serious constitutional issue of statutes restricting the age of persons entering amusement businesses be they electronic arcades or pool halls. Of course, when a state allocates a fundamental right on the basis of age that law may be subjected to meaningful judicial review. See, e.g., Carey v. Population Services International, 431 U.S. 678 (1977) (invalidating law prohibiting sale of contraceptives to persons under age of 16). Compare Bellotti v. Baird, 443 U.S. 622

Thus, the Court used the deferential rational basis test in upholding these classifications.

In *Vance v. Bradley* [35] the Supreme Court, with only one dissent, upheld a requirement that participants in the foreign service retirement system [36] retire from their government positions at age 60. The plaintiff employees had alleged that the distinction between the mandatory retirement at age 60 for their job classifications and the general federal requirement of retirement at age 70 for the federal Civil Service Retirement System personnel violated the equal protection component of the fifth amendment. The Court, in an opinion by Mr. Justice White, found that the retirement classification should be tested by general equal protection principles,[37] but that it did not violate the equal protection guarantee. Although the parties agreed that the law should be tested under the traditional rational basis standard, Justice White's opinion stressed that the federal judiciary is not to review seriously those classifications that do not involve fundamental rights or suspect classifications:

The Constitution presumes that, absent some reason to infer antipathy, even improvident decisions will eventually be rectified by the democractic process and that judicial intervention is generally unwarranted no matter how unwisely we may think a political branch has acted. Thus, we will not overturn such a statute unless the varying treatment of different groups or persons is so unrelated to the achievement of any combination of legitimate purposes that we can only conclude that the legislature's actions were irrational.[38]

The majority then applied the rational basis test, which had been employed in *Massachusetts Board of Retirement v. Murgia* [39] to uphold a mandatory retirement of state police officers at age 50, to the retirement classification. Although it appeared that the plaintiffs had abandoned their claim that the classification between those over and under age 60 was irrational, and only pressed the claim of discrimination between foreign service employees and civil service employees, the majority opinion made it clear that the rational relationship test was the only form of review justified for reviewing any aspect of this mandatory retirement program.[40]

(1979) (invalidating law severely restricting ability of minor female to have an abortion) with H. L. v. Matheson, 450 US. 398 (1981) (upholding law requiring doctor to notify parents of unemancipated minor female before performing an abortion).

While the Court may not give significant protection to non-suspect classifications, it must be remembered that Congress may protect such groups through legislation. Age classifications are not suspect and, to date, they have not been subjected to any meaningful form of judicial review. However, Congress has made it unlawful for many employees to discriminate in employment practices or benefits for most employees between the ages of 40 and 70 because of their age. Age Discrimination in Employment Act of 1967, 29 U.S.C.A. § 621 et seq. as amended by the Age Discrimination in Employment Act Amendments of 1978, Pub.L.No. 95–256 (April 6, 1978).

35. 440 U.S. 93 (1979).

36. This retirement system and requirement applied to career foreign service officers, foreign service information and certain other career staff in the International Communications Agency.

37. 440 U.S. at 94 n. 1. This point corresponds with the well established principle that the equal protection guarantee of the due process clause of the fifth amendment mirrors that of equal protection clause of the fourteenth amendment.

38. 440 U.S. at 97 (footnote omitted).

39. 427 U.S. 307 (1976).

40. The majority opinion repeatedly stressed that, while there were facts that supported the government's claims, it was not the responsibility of the government to justify the classification and that the lower courts had erred when they refused to accept a hypothetical rational basis for sustaining the Retirement Act and instead engaged in some realistic review of the classification. There was no reason to assume that Congress was rewarding "youth *qua* youth"; it was at least arguable that a significant percentage of people over age 60 might not perform their duties as foreign service officers as ably as those who were younger. It was the responsibility of those challenging the legislative classification to "convince the court that the legislative facts on which the classification is apparently based could not reasonably be conceived to be true by the governmental decisionmaker. Vance v. Bradley, 440 U.S. 93, 101, 111 (1979).

Justice Marshall, the only dissenter, argued that the Court should consider the age distinction, as well as the retirement system distinction, as a basis for engaging in some meaningful form of review of the classifications. Vance v. Bradley, 440 U.S. 93, 113 (1979) (Marshall, J., dissenting). While other members of the Court have at times joined Justice Marshall in seeking to use an intermediate form of review where it is re-

D. Establishing and Testing Classifications of a Law: "On Its Face", in Its "Application", or in Its "Purpose and Effect"—The Problem of Statistics

As can be seen from the foregoing introductory sections, in order to subject a law to any form of review under the equal protection guarantee, one must be able to demonstrate that the law classifies persons in some manner. And even this first step will not be of much help to a person challenging the law for, as we have seen, a classification in the area of "economics or social welfare" will not be subjected to a very meaningful form of judicial review. Thus, one challenging the law will need to show either that it classifies persons in terms of their ability to exercise a fundamental right or establishes a classification on the basis of race, national origin, alienage, illegitimacy or gender. In the course of litigation questions may often arise as to whether such a classification exists at all; if it does not the law will not be subjected to strict scrutiny. This issue may often involve difficult problems of proof and intricate statistical demonstrations. The details of those litigation problems are beyond the scope of this treatise [1] but we do wish to introduce the basic concepts of how a court determines the existence of a classification.

A classification within a law can be established in one of three ways. First, the law may establish the classification "on its face." This means that the law by its own terms classifies persons for different treatment. In such a case there is no problem of proof and the court can proceed to test the validity of the classification by the appropriate standard. Second, the law may be tested in its "application." In these cases the law either shows no classification on its face or else indicates a classification which seems to be legitimate, but those challenging the legislation claim that the governmental officials who administer the law are applying it with different degrees of severity to different groups of persons who are described by some suspect trait. Here the challengers must establish that there is an administrative classification used to implement the law which merits some increased standard of review. Finally, the law may contain no classification, or a neutral classification, and be applied evenhandedly. Nevertheless the law may be challenged as in reality constituting a device designed to impose different burdens on different classes of persons. If this claim can be proven the law will be reviewed as if it established such a classification on its face. However, because all laws are susceptible to having their impact analyzed in a variety of ways, it will be most difficult to establish this claim for the purpose of seeking strict judicial review of a legislative act.

The approach which the Court has taken on these issues over the years has not changed abruptly but many of its recent results may seem inconsistent with earlier decisions. One of the reasons for this apparent inconsistency is that the Supreme Court also reviews classifications under statutes which allow for easier proof as to the existence of discriminatory classifications than would be acceptable if the Court were only enforcing the equal protection guarantee. With this in mind, let us examine briefly the problems involved in establishing classifications based on the application or effect of a law.

Any law may be applied in a manner that creates a classification. For example, let us

---

quired by the constitutionally significant nature of the rights effected or personal "status" basis of a classification, no other justice was willing to engage in such wide ranging review of statutory employment criteria. Justice Marshall was also the only dissenter when the Court upheld the 50 year old retirement provision for a state police force. Massachusetts Bd. of Retirement v. Murgia, 427 U.S. 307, 317 (1976). Justice Stevens did not participate in the Massachusetts decision but he joined the majority in *Vance.*

1. For an analysis of many of these problems see, A. Larson, Employment Discrimination (multi-volume 1975); H. Edwards, R. Clark & C. Craver, Labor Relations in the Public Sector (2 ed. 1979); A. Smith, C. Craver & L. Clark, Employment Discrimination Law (2 ed. 1982); C. Sullivan, M. Zimmer & R. Richards, Federal Statutory Law of Employment Discrimination (1980); M. Player, Federal Law of Employment Discrimination in a Nutshell (2 ed. 1981); A. Ruzicho, Civil Rights Litigation (1976).

assume that it could be proven that a local police force only enforces an anti-littering ordinance against members of a minority race. This evidence would establish that the law as applied involved a racial classification so that enforcement of the law could be enjoined, at least until such a time as the authorities could show that there would be no further discriminatory application. The first and leading case in this area is *Yick Wo v. Hopkins* [2] where the Court held unconstitutional the enforcement of a San Francisco ordinance banning the operation of hand laundries in wooden buildings. It was demonstrated in that case that the vast majority of such laundries were owned and operated by Chinese residents of the city, but the Court did not rest its ruling on the direct impact of the statute. It was also demonstrated that all non-oriental launderers who had applied for an exemption from the statute had received one, while no Chinese applicant had been granted an exemption. This discriminatory application of the law constituted a racial classification which had to be invalidated.

The decisions of the Supreme Court make it easier to prove that a government impermissibly classifies persons in the administration of neutral laws than to prove that a seemingly neutral law has an impermissible discriminatory effect. The reason is a relatively simple one: the administrative discretionary selection process deserves less deference than rule-making for society's benefit, whether that rule-making is done by a legislative body or administrative agency. What is being tested in the application cases is the administrative selection of persons for a burden or benefit. The problem of proof in showing that the actions have been taken with a discriminatory purpose is far less than proving the intent of a legislative body. For example, the Supreme Court has held that the fact that a criterion for government employment, such as a written objective test, has a greater degree of impact on one race than another does not in itself constitute purposeful discrimination.[3] However, in that case the Court noted that there was no challenge to the individual selection of police officers for government employment.[4] To the extent that those officials who hired police officers were allowed to use subjective criterion, statistical proof as to the result of how they exercised their hiring discretion would be extremely relevant; such proof might establish a prima facie case that they were in fact employing racial criteria which were not expressed in the statute. Similarly, when the Court upheld a zoning ordinance against the challenge that its effect was racially disproportionate, the opinion note that an opposite result would be reached if there were proof that the city had granted exemptions from the zoning restrictions on a racially discriminatory basis.[5]

Throughout its decisions in cases concerning the existence of classifications, the Court has held that statistical proof is usually relevant but rarely determinative. The problem to be confronted is whether the decision maker is employing some form of suspect criterion and thereby establishing a classification within the law or in its application. Where the statistical proof is overwhelming, it may be sufficient to establish a prima facie case. Proof by statistics is especially useful when one is challenging an individual selection or application process; there the criterion is subjective and unknowable to all those except the officials charged with the enforcement or application of the law. It is less difficult to inquire into their motivation for there is no need to pay them the deference that the judiciary should afford either an independent branch of government or an administrative agency when it is acting in a rule making capacity. However, to the extent that the Court finds some independent societal value in the discretionary system it will be more hesitant to employ statistical

---

2. 118 U.S. 356 (1886).

3. Washington v. Davis, 426 U.S. 229 (1976).

4. 426 U.S. at 235.

5. Arlington Heights v. Metropolitan Housing Development Corp., 429 U.S. 252, 267 (1977).

proof to establish a prima facie case of discrimination. This factor is demonstrated quite clearly by the jury selection cases. The Court has long held that it is unconstitutional to exclude members of racial minorities, or to allow only for their disproportionately low representation, on either grand juries or petit juries in criminal cases.[6] Following this ruling, states have enacted a variety of measures for selecting jurors which have been challenged and overturned by the Court as constituting racial classifications. In these cases the Court has continually allowed statistics to establish a prima facie case of discrimination whenever there was a statistically significant underrepresentation of minority members on juries or the panels from which juries were selected.[7] It is clearly established that no individual has a right to have their particular grand jury or petit jury reflect the racial composition of the community,[8] but it is equally clear that there must be an equal opportunity for such persons to serve on juries. The reason for the Court's use of statistics in these cases is that the challenged procedures have included some form of subjective selection process by judicial or executive officials. Procedures using juror selectors or allowing officials to select jurors from lists which made them consciously aware of the individual's race were stricken when the statistics showed racially disproportionate results.[9] So too, the use and review of questionnaires or other qualifications for jury service has been overturned when the statistics indicated that the selectors were using their discretion in a racially discriminatory manner.[10] However, when the selection process did not involve any subjective elements but only the random selection of persons from tax lists the Court did not overturn the law because of its statistical impact.[11] In that situation there was no subjective discretion to test and the challenge constituted one to the terms of the law in its necessary effect rather than its application. Similarly, a jury selection procedure will not be stricken "on its face" because it grants officials some discretion, for the law is valid unless there is a prima facie statistical demonstration that it is being applied in a discriminatory manner.[12]

It is also clear that when there is some independent, legitimate reason for committing discretionary functions to a government officer then the burden of proving discrimination by statistical impact will be much

6. Strauder v. West Virginia, 100 U.S. 303 (1880); Norris v. Alabama, 294 U.S. 587 (1935); Avery v. Georgia, 345 U.S. 559 (1953).

7. For an analysis of the problems of statistical proof see, Finkelstein, The Application of Statistical Decision Theory to the Jury Discrimination Cases, 80 Harv.L.Rev. 338 (1966).

8. See, Akins v. Texas, 325 U.S. 398 (1945).

9. Whitus v. Georgia, 385 U.S. 545 (1967).

10. See, e.g., Casteneda v. Partida, 430 U.S. 482 (1977); Alexander v. Louisiana, 405 U.S. 625 (1972); Cassell v. Texas, 339 U.S. 282 (1950); Hill v. Texas, 316 U.S. 400 (1942); cf. Eubanks v. Louisiana, 356 U.S. 584 (1958).

11. Brown v. Allen, 344 U.S. 443 (1953).

12. Carter v. Jury Comm'n, 396 U.S. 320 (1970). This case did not represent a change in position as the Court struck down a system in the same day where statistical proof of discriminatory selection was not rebutted. Turner v. Fouche, 396 U.S. 346 (1970).

In Duren v. Missouri, 439 U.S. 357, 368 n. 26 (1979), the Supreme Court, in a majority opinion by Justice White, indicated that statistical proof of the underrepresentation of a distinctive community group on juri-

ry venires is sufficient to establish a prima facie violation of a defendant's sixth amendment right to a jury drawn from a fair cross section of the community, whereas statistical proof challenging exclusionary practices in the selection of jury venires on equal protection grounds was only one form of evidence concerning the ultimate question of discriminatory purpose. In Duren the Court invalidated a statutory exemption for any or all women, upon their request, because it violated the sixth amendment.

The Court has held that claims of racial discrimination in the selection of members of a state grand jury were cognizable in a federal habeas corpus action and that a defendant could bring that action to have his indictment quashed and conviction set aside even though there was no racial discrimination in the selection of his petit jury and his guilt had been established beyond a reasonable doubt at trial. Rose v. Mitchell, 443 U.S. 545 (1979). However, in Rose the Court rejected the defendants' claim because they failed to demonstrate the substantial underrepresentation of members of minority races on the grand juries, or in the position of grand jury foreman. Because the defendants failed to make out a prima facie demonstration, the burden did not shift to the state to justify its grand jury member or foreman selection process.

greater. In these cases there exists a separate reason to defer exercise of the discretion. In *Swain v. Alabama*[13] the Court upheld the use of peremptory challenges to strike persons from petit jury service in criminal cases. This procedure was upheld even though there was statistical evidence to show that black persons were excluded by the prosecution more often than white persons. However the Court was clearly subjecting this challenge to stricter proof than the other jury selection cases, because it noted that the record did not indicate that the prosecutor would systematically strike all blacks regardless of trial considerations.[14] The reason for the need to have an overwhelming statistical case, or other proof of purposeful discrimination, in this challenge may relate to the Court's belief that the practice of peremptory challenge helps to insure truly fair trials and this practice therefore ought not to be overturned by a judicial decision without clear and convincing proof.

Similarly, in *Mayor of Philadelphia v. Educational Equality League*[15] the Court upheld a mayor's practices in selecting persons for a nominating panel for the school board despite the fact that statistical analysis indicated that blacks were continually underrepresented on this panel. It found that the "simplistic percentage comparisons" used by the lower court did not have any "real meaning" in this case.[16] A chief executive officer's ability to choose persons for administrative positions of importance is a function that the Court felt should be deferred to by the judiciary. Thus it would not restrict the mayor's power absent clear proof of discrimination beyond statistical impact.[17]

The most difficult problem regarding classifications is proving that a properly enacted law or agency regulation which is neutral on its face, and in its application, nevertheless constitutes a purposeful device to classify persons on a suspect criterion. In these cases the Court is confronted by decision-making entities to whom it feels it owes some deference. The problems of proof are initially greater than in the cases of proving discriminatory application because of the general principle against inquiring into the "motives" of proper rule-making or legislative authorities. In only rare cases would the direct testimony of members of the agency or legislative body be admitted, due both to problems of separation of powers and the announced principle against searching inquiries into legislative motives.[18] The most extensive problems concerning an agency have occurred in connection with school desegregation cases but even there the Court has required objective proof that school board policies were designed to create a segregated school system.[19]

It is not easy to establish the proper role of the Court in this area. In these cases the Court is not merely determining whether the law has differing impact upon different racial groups. Nor is the test solely one of legislative "motive" in the sense of looking into the subjective intent of individual legislators. That would not only raise severe problems of separation of powers in specific cases, it would also overturn many acts which might have come out of a non-discriminatory democratic process merely because some of the people voting for the acts were prejudiced. On the other hand, the Court

---

13. 380 U.S. 202 (1965).

14. 380 U.S. at 223–6.

15. 415 U.S. 605 (1974).

16. 415 U.S. at 620.

17. This attitude was also evidenced in Carter v. Jury Comm'n, 396 U.S. 320 (1970) where the Court indicated it would not strike the mere grant of discretion to the executive absent such proof.

18. The Court has taken the position that only the most extreme circumstances might allow for the use of such testimony although it recognized this as a possi-

bility. See, Arlington Heights v. Metropolitan Housing Development Corp., 429 U.S. 252, 268 n. 18, 270 n. 20 (1977); Citizens to Preserve Overton Park v. Volpe, 401 U.S. 402, 420 (1971); See also Mayor of Philadelphia v. Educational Equality League, 415 U.S. 605, 618–9 (1974); The origin of this position has been traced by the Court to Fletcher v. Peck, 10 U.S. (6 Cranch) 87, 130–31 (1810).

19. These cases are examined in Chapter 16, Equal Protection, Section II, E, 1, b, (1), Institutions Subject to the Desegregation Principle: The De Jure-De Facto Distinction.

cannot allow all laws to stand unchallenged when they may constitute devices used by another branch of government to subvert the equal protection guarantee. Thus, the Supreme Court is faced with a most difficult problem in these cases, and there has been brilliant scholarship advocating that the Court take both very active and very passive roles in this area. Professor Paul Brest has advocated that the Court search all sources to determine if some illicit motive played a significant role in the decision-making process and, if so, to construe the law in terms of the classifications established by impact.[20] Conversely, Professor John Hart Ely has advocated that the Court should employ a "random choice" model and defer to the legislative rule-making power whenever there can be advanced a neutral, rational justification for the law.[21] Under the Brest formulation, substantial proof of discriminatory factors entering the decision-making process triggers a demand for extraordinary justification by the state. This theory focuses on the judicial power to enforce the equal protection guarantee. Under Ely's model, strict suspect classification analysis is reserved for the laws which discriminate on their face or for which there is no neutral justification. This theory avoids denying the democratic process the choices it might have arrived at through a totally non-prejudiced system.

The Court has attempted to take a middle road between these two positions.[22] It gives significant deference to other branches of government while searching all sources outside of inquiries into particular legislator's motives to determine if a law constitutes a purposeful device for discriminatory treatment. Three sources may be used to establish such a conclusion: (1) the different practical or statistical impact upon differing classifications of persons; (2) the general history concerning the problems which the legislative or administrative rule seeks to solve; (3) the history of the passage or enactment of the legislation or agency rule.[23]

For some time it had been thought that statistics alone would prove the existence of such classifications, but this belief was built upon the theory used in cases under specific civil rights statutes. The Court has determined that some statutes allow for easier proof of discriminatory classifications when applicable.[24] When enforcing the general equal protection guarantee, the Court will not allow legislative or administrative rules to be overturned on the basis of statistics alone unless the statistical proof is so great that it establishes a clear and convincing case that the legislation had to be adopted for a discriminatory purpose—thus somewhat conforming to the Ely model. However the Court will allow for other proof of discrimination and when it is convinced that the background of the legislative decision or its particular history shows discriminatory purpose, it will strike down the law. Here the Court has said that it will only require the showing of the entry of discriminatory considerations as a motive for the action—not necessarily the sole or dominant motive of

---

20. Brest, Palmer v. Thompson: An Approach to the Problem of Unconstitutional Legislative Motive, 1971 Sup.Ct.Rev. 95.

See also Ely, The Centrality And Limits Of Motivation Analysis, 15 San Diego L.Rev. 1155 (1978). Professor (later Dean) Ely, in this article, explains his position that the judiciary should employ the strict scrutiny-compelling interest test to guard against the misuse of suspect classifications. However, Professor Ely continues to hold the belief that courts should not find that facially neutral laws constitute racial classifications based solely on the statistical impact of the classification in most cases. See generally, J. Ely, Democracy and Distrust, Chapter 6 (1980).

21. Ely, Legislative and Administrative Motivation in Constitutional Law, 79 Yale L.J. 1205 (1970).

22. It should be noted that a student commentator has suggested a different approach in connection with school board cases that closely parallels this general approach. See, Note, Reading the Mind of the School Board: Segregative Intent And the De Facto/De Jure Distinction, 86 Yale L.J. 317 (1976).

23. Arlington Heights v. Metropolitan Housing Development Corp., 429 U.S. 252, 266–68 (1977).

24. See, e.g. Griggs v. Duke Power Co., 401 U.S. 424 (1971); Dothard v. Rawlinson, 433 U.S. 321 (1977).

the decision-making body—thus somewhat conforming to the Brest model.[25]

The way in which the Court looks at proof of discriminatory purpose in legislation may be demonstrated by decisions concerning literacy tests for voting. The Court struck down the use of a literacy test where it exempted all persons who had qualified to vote at an earlier time. The reason for this ruling was that the "grandfather clause" related to a period when blacks were excluded from voting within the state so that it had the effect of imposing the test upon all blacks but on only a small fraction of white voters.[26] Following this case, the state enacted a registration requirement which also gave preferential treatment to those previously registered and the Court invalidated this requirement as well.[27] When viewed against the background of racial discrimination within the state, the Court could easily reach the conclusion that these requirements constituted a racial classification. However, the Court later upheld a literacy test after the state supreme court had independently stricken down the "grandfather clause" so that the law would be applied equally to persons of all races.[28] The Court held that there was no basis on the record for finding that the law would be applied in a discriminatory manner. The fact that members of one racial group might be disproportionally affected by the law was not enough to overturn the otherwise valid decision to require some demonstrated ability, in terms of literacy, in order to exercise the franchise.

A similar contrast exists between the rulings of the Court concerning the creation of electoral subdivisions. The Court in *Gomillion v. Lightfoot*[29] held that the alteration of a town's boundaries constituted a racial classification. However, in this case the town had altered its structure in a very detailed and peculiar manner that created a shape with 25 sides and resulted in the virtually total separation of black and white voters. Here there was little need for proof of a background of racial discrimination in political matters in the area because the statistical proof was so overwhelming that it would have been difficult to imagine that the subdivision was made for any purpose other than racial discrimination. But the Court has refused to overturn legislative districting which complies with the one-person, one-vote principle because the particular districting plan has a disproportionate effect on racial minorities.[30] Where the statistical proof is supplemented with other evidence of discrimination on the part of those engaged in the districting, the Court will overturn a plan that otherwise complies with the one-person, one-vote principle unless the state can demonstrate that the plan in fact was not created for a discriminatory purpose.[31]

Even an at-large voting system may be held to violate equal protection if it is created or maintained to dilute the voting power of racial minorities. Statistical proof of an electoral system's adverse impact on the voting power of minority citizens will be relevant but not determinative in such a case. The plaintiff attacking the at-large system must prove that it was created or maintained for a racially discriminatory purpose. Thus, in *Mobile v. Bolden*[32] the Supreme Court refused to invalidate a city commission system whereby all three members of the city's governing body were elected at-large. Although no black person had ever been elected to the city commission, there was no proof that the electoral system was

---

25. Arlington Heights v. Metropolitan Housing Development Corp., 429 U.S. 252, 266 n. 12 (1977) citing Brest, supra note 20.

26. Guinn v. United States, 238 U.S. 347 (1915).

27. Lane v. Wilson, 307 U.S. 268 (1939).

28. Lassiter v. Northampton County Bd. of Elections, 360 U.S. 45 (1959).

29. 364 U.S. 339 (1960).

30. Whitcomb v. Chavis, 403 U.S. 124 (1971).

31. White v. Regester, 412 U.S. 755 (1973). Note that the attempt to assure minimally fair representation of minorities without the intent to disenfranchise another group will not violate the fourteenth amendment or Voting Right Act, see, United Jewish Organizations of Williamsburgh, Inc. v. Carey, 430 U.S. 144 (1977).

32. 446 U.S. 55 (1980).

maintained for a racially discriminatory purpose. Conversely, in *Rogers v. Lodge*,[33] the Supreme Court approved federal district court and court of appeals rulings invalidating an at-large election system for a rural county's board of commissioners. The Supreme Court found that the lower courts had correctly determined that the electoral system could only be invalidated upon a showing of discriminatory purpose. Although black persons were a majority of the population, the at-large system examined in *Rogers* had prevented black representation on the county board. The statistical evidence in *Rogers* was supported by other facts showing that elected officials in the county had been insensitive to the needs of the black community and had maintained the at-large voting system for the purpose of minimizing the voting strength of black persons.

The Supreme Court has also tried to walk a middle ground in two cases dealing with the termination of municipal services.[34] In *Griffin v. Prince Edward County School Board*[35] the Court found that the closing of local schools constituted a racially discriminatory act which justified a judicial order to reopen those schools. In this case the governmental decision followed a desegregation order and there was evidence that the local government then offered aid to private schools which discriminated on the basis of race. However, the Court in *Palmer v. Thompson*[36] allowed a city to close its public pools after a judicial desegregation order. The city maintained that the pools could no longer be operated safely or economically and the Court found no independent proof of

discriminatory purpose on the part of the city authorities. It was true in this case that the closing of the pools would have a greater impact on blacks than whites for there were private pools which served only whites, but there was no proof that the city aided the establishment or maintenance of those pools.

The Court has continued to follow this middle ground by finding that statistical proof alone will not be sufficient to establish that an otherwise neutral law constitutes a racial classification unless the statistical proof is overwhelming or there is some other evidence of discriminatory purpose. Thus the Court has upheld a referendum procedure for allowing low income housing into an area [37] but overturned a referendum system which was required to authorize the implementation of open housing or desegregation ordinances.[38] Similarly, the Court refused to find that the provision of a lower percentage funding to a welfare program for Aid to Families with Dependent Children as compared to those programs for the Aged, Blind or Disabled constituted racial discrimination merely because the differing statistical impacts upon racial groups.[39]

The Court was also confronted with classification problems by employment cases under Title VII of the Civil Rights Act.[40] In those cases it found that statistical proof that employment criterion excluded a disproportionately high percentage of racial minority members constituted a prima facie case of racial discrimination. In the leading case

---

33. 102 S.Ct. 3272 (1982). See generally, Hartman, Racial Vote Dilution and Separation of Powers: An Exploration of the Conflict Between Judicial "Intent" and the Legislative "Results" Standards, 50 Geo.Wash.L. Rev. 689 (1982).

34. This issue is also considered in Chapter 16, Equal Protection Section II, E, Implementation of the Desegregation Decisions.

35. 377 U.S. 218 (1964).

36. 403 U.S. 217 (1971).

37. James v. Valtierra, 402 U.S. 137 (1971) (statistical proof not sufficient).

See, Bell, The Referendum: Democracy's Barrier to Racial Equality, 54 U.Wash.L.Rev. 1 (1978).

38. Hunter v. Erickson, 393 U.S. 385 (1969). Here the Court considered the discriminatory impact so clear that it constituted a racial classification "in its face." See also Reitman v. Mulkey, 387 U.S. 369 (1967). The Court has employed similar analysis in examining the constitutionality of voter approved amendments to stale laws which restrict the transferring or "busing" of students. See Section II E 1c(6) of this chapter.

39. Jefferson v. Hackney, 406 U.S. 535 (1972).

40. 42 U.S.C.A. § 2000e–2(a).

of *Griggs v. Duke Power Co.*[41] the Court held that a violation of the Act could be established for the requirements of a high school diploma and intelligence tests simply because they had a disproportionate impact on racial minority job applicants. As the Court continued to enforce this rule, hopes were raised that it would find violations of the equal protection guarantee upon a similar statistical basis.[42] However, such hopeful predictions overlooked the fact that in Title VII cases the Court is enforcing a decision of the federal legislature to totally eliminate racial discrimination in public and private employment to which the statute applies. Thus there was no need for a policy of deference to employment decisions or criteria under the terms of such statutes.

When the Supreme Court returned to issues under the equal protection guarantee, however, it continued to hold that statistical proof of differing impact upon racial groups would not be sufficient to establish a racial classification absent some other proof that the law was adopted for a racially discriminatory purpose. Thus, in *Washington v. Davis*[43] the Court found that the District of Columbia did not violate the equal protection guarantee by employing a form of intelligence test for prospective police officers. The Court noted that there was no accusation that those selecting the officers had used their discretion to eliminate members of racial minorities but only that the otherwise neutral test had a disproportionate impact on blacks. In conformity with its earlier constitutional decisions, the Court found that this evidence was insufficient to establish a prima facie case of racial discrimination. If the challengers to the test could es-

tablish some other proof of racially discriminatory purpose either from the general background of employment conditions or the history of the process which resulted in the establishment of the test, then they might prevail, but not otherwise.[44]

The next year, the Court upheld a suburban zoning plan which eliminated multi-family housing and the decision of city authorities not to grant an exemption from that zoning plan for a multi-family project which would have dramatically increased the percentage of minority residents in the city.[45] The Court noted that there was no proof that the city had granted exemptions from the zoning plan on a discriminatory basis; the ultimate question was whether the adoption and enforcement of the zoning plan constituted a purposeful device to exclude black persons.[46] While the statistical proof was significant, many types of zoning plans have been adopted for totally race neutral reasons which might also have such a disproportionate impact. Since there was no proof in this case that the law had been adopted for a discriminatory purpose, either from the history of the town or the process which resulted in the plan, the city's actions were upheld.

In *Personnel Administrator of Massachusetts v. Feeney*[47] the Supreme Court, by a vote of 7 to 2, upheld a state statute granting a strict, lifetime preference for state civil service employment to veterans of American military service. There was no doubt that the preference had a severe disparate impact upon women; of the one quarter of the Massachusetts population who were veterans over 98% were male. The lower court had found that the Massachusetts preference was not established, either at its incep-

---

41. 401 U.S. 424 (1971).

42. See, e.g., Albemarle Paper Co. v. Moody, 422 U.S. 405 (1975).

43. 426 U.S. 229 (1976).

44. The Court found the record also indicated a sufficient relationship between the test and employment qualification that it would be upheld under statutory standards as well. 426 U.S. at 250–52.

45. Arlington Heights v. Metropolitan Housing Development Corp., 429 U.S. 252 (1977).

46. 429 U.S. at 265.

Following the remand of the decision in *Arlington Heights*, the Court of Appeals found that the racially disparate impact might show a violation of the Fair Housing Act, 42 U.S.C.A. § 3601 et seq.; the Supreme Court declined to review this decision. Metropolitan Housing Development Corp. v. Village of Arlington Heights, 558 F.2d 1283 (7th Cir. 1977), cert. denied 434 U.S. 1025 (1978).

47. 442 U.S. 256 (1979).

tion in 1896 or in later amendments, as a means for preferring males generally; yet the lower court and the plaintiffs had claimed that the absolute preference was so serious a burden on women that legislators must have appreciated that they were disfavoring women as a class.

The Supreme Court, in an opinion by Justice Stewart, noted that the degree of burden placed upon a class was not relevant to determining the nature of the classification or whether the legislature had engaged in invidious gender classification; the legislature was not free to impose even minor invidious discriminations against women but it need not forego valid non-discriminatory laws because of the impact of those laws.[48] The majority recognized that the legislation was non-neutral, in the sense that it preferred the class of veterans over the class of non-veterans, but the purpose of the law demonstrably was to prefer veterans over non-veterans; there was no proof that the laws were ever enacted for the purpose of preferring men over women. Mere appreciation by the legislature of the fact that the veterans preference would have adverse consequences for women as a class did not make the legislative act purposefully discriminatory. To establish that a law neutral on its face is in fact one based on a specific classification meriting increased judicial scrutiny, those challenging the law must demonstrate "that the decision-maker, in this case a state legislature, selected or reaffirmed a particular course of action at least in part 'because of', not merely 'in spite of' its adverse effects upon an identifiable group." [49] It was clear to the majority that the history of the

veterans preference legislation in Massachusetts showed that the preference was enacted to reward and aid all veterans, male or female, and not to purposely prefer men over women in government employment. Thus the legislation was a non-invidious, neutral classification that was upheld against an equal protection challenge.

These cases did not indicate that the Court was stepping back from its historic position concerning the ways in which subjective decisions were tested when laws were challenged as establishing classifications in their application. In the same term that the Court upheld the Arlington Heights zoning plan, it struck down a system for juror selection on the basis of statistical proof showing a vastly disproportionate impact on members of racial minorities from a subjective selection process.[50] The Court found a prima facie case that the discretion of the jury selectors had been used in a discriminatory manner and this evidence would prove a racial classification absent contrary proof by the state.

Similarly, the Court has not diminished the protection accorded individuals by the civil rights legislation in its recent rulings. In the same term in which the Supreme Court refused to invalidate an at-large electoral system under the fourteenth or fifteenth amendment because of a plaintiff's failure to prove discriminatory purpose,[51] the Court ruled that Congress by statute could bar changes in local electoral systems that had the effect of diluting the voting power of racial minorities without a showing of discriminatory purpose.[52] The Court upheld

---

48. 442 U.S. at 279.

49. 442 U.S. at 281 (footnote omitted). In the accompanying footnote to this statement the majority indicated that the consequences of a law might be relevant to proving discriminatory purpose though the statistical impact in itself would not establish the classification or purpose. 442 U.S. at 279 n. 25.

In McCarty v. McCarty, 453 U.S. 210 (1981) the Supreme Court held that federal law prohibited state courts from dividing military retirement pay pursuant to state community property law upon dissolution of a marriage in which one of the spouses was a member of the U.S. armed forces. Although the case involved no

gender discrimination issue, the ruling will make it more difficult for the divorced spouses of military personnel to receive adequate financial support. The class most affected by the ruling, of course, is composed of women who are the ex-wives of male armed forces personnel and who have not made dollar contribution to a retirement system during the period of their marriage.

50. Castaneda v. Partida, 430 U.S. 482 (1977).

51. Mobile v. Bolden, 446 U.S. 55 (1980). See notes 32, 33, supra.

52. Rome v. United States, 446 U.S. 156 (1980).

the use of seniority systems which might have had the effect of continuing discrimination which occurred before the Civil Rights Act because it found these to be authorized under the terms of the Act unless they were clearly proven to have been adopted for the specific purpose of establishing racially discriminatory benefit systems.[53] However, the Court strictly enforced the basic anti-discrimination portions of Title VII when it found that statistical proof alone constituted a sufficient basis for finding a prima facie case that a city school system had discrimi-

nated on the basis of race in the hiring of teachers.[54] Similarly, the Court struck down, as violation of the Act, height and weight qualifications for prison guards; it found them to constitute sex discrimination because of their effect.[55] These rulings will always be open to criticism because they are by their nature *ad hoc*; they must be made on the basis of individual records and evidence before the Court.[56]

When the Supreme Court examines a claim that a defendant has violated a federal

---

53. International Brotherhood of Teamsters v. United States, 431 U.S. 324 (1977).

A bona fide seniority system will be upheld under Title VII even though it serves to disadvantage minority workers so long as the differences are not the result of an intent to discriminate by race. 42 U.S.C.A. § 2000e–2(h). This exemption has been applied to a collective bargaining agreement which required workers to be employed for 45 weeks before they were classified as permanent employees and then were entitled to greater employment benefits. California Brewers Ass'n v. Bryant, 444 U.S. 598 (1980).

54. Hazelwood School District v. United States, 433 U.S. 299 (1977).

In National Education Ass'n v. South Carolina, 434 U.S. 1026 (1978), the Supreme Court summarily affirmed a lower court decision that the state's use of the National Teachers Examination in hiring teachers and classifying them for differing pay levels did not violate either the fourteenth amendment or Title VII. Mr. Justice White, joined by Mr. Justice Brennan, dissented on the basis that the discriminatory impact of the test on black applicants required that the test be validated by proof of its relation to job performance. 434 U.S. at 1027.

In Board of Education v. Harris, 444 U.S. 130 (1979) the Court found that a school district could be declared ineligible for federal funds to which it would otherwise be entitled under the 1972 Emergency School Aid Act (20 U.S.C.A. §§ 3191–3207) on the basis of racially disproportionate faculty assignments; and a prima facie case of discriminatory impact may be made on the basis of a proper statistical study.

55. Dothard v. Rawlinson, 433 U.S. 321 (1977).

See generally, Sirota, Sex Discrimination: Title VII and The Bona Fide Occupational Qualification, 55 Texas L.Rev. 1025 (1977).

56. The Supreme Court in New York City Transit Authority v. Beazer, 440 U.S. 568 (1979) determined that the exclusion of drug users, including those receiving methadone treatment for the curing of heroine addiction, from employment by the New York City Transit Authority violated neither Title VII nor the equal protection clause. Unfortunately, the opinion was confusing to the point of obscurity regarding the proper use of statistical proof.

When considering the Title VII claim, the majority opinion by Justice Stevens refused to indicate whether the statistical evidence showing that 81% of the transit authority employees investigated or suspected of rules violations were either black or hispanic, and that 63% of the persons in public methadone maintenance programs were black or hispanic, demonstrated a prima facie case of racial discrimination under Title VII. The opinion described the statistical proof as "weak" because it was not based on the total number of employees who were using methadone, the proof did not examine the racial composition of all persons in public and private methadone programs, and it did not describe the racial composition of the class of persons otherwise qualified for employment who were using methadone under a physician's supervision. This portion of the opinion constitutes an unusually strict examination of statistical proof of discriminatory effects and subdivision of the relevant labor market. However the plaintiffs, and the lower courts, had described the plaintiff class as those who were capable of fulfilling the job requirement of the Transit Authority but for their use of methadone; this fact may have caused the Court to engage in a detailed analysis of the relationship between adverse impact on the plaintiff class and the establishment of a claim of racial discrimination.

The majority opinion also stated that even if this weak showing was sufficient to establish a prima facie case, it failed to demonstrate a violation of Title VII because the Transit Authority had demonstrated that its rule was "job related." 440 U.S. at 587 n. 31. The majority opinion accepted the demonstration of relatedness between the rule and safety and efficiency for all Transit Authority positions when that demonstration could be made only for some classes of Transit Authority employees. The requirement clearly was "job related" for train operators and electrical workers, but it hardly seems relevant to the positions of secretary or janitor. Since this point was made strongly by the dissent, it seems difficult to believe that the majority could have failed to appreciate that it was employing the job related test in a very imprecise manner. See 440 U.S. at 596–603 (White, J., dissenting joined by Brennan and Marshall, JJ.).

It appears that, the majority opinion attempted to go no further than to find that on the specific facts before the Court the Transit Authority rules should be upheld.

civil rights statute because of the allegedly racially or sexually discriminatory impact of the defendant's actions, the Court confronts the discriminatory effect versus discriminatory purpose issue. However, in statutory cases the issue is resolved by examining the purpose of the statute at issue and the intention of Congress in passing the statute. Thus the Court has found that an employer's use of hiring or promotion tests that have an adverse impact on women or racial minorities is presumptively invalid under Title VII of the Civil Rights Acts passed in 1964,[57] but that statutes passed in 1866 to prevent racial

discrimination against black persons in property or contract opportunities are only violated by actions undertaken with a discriminatory purpose.[58] Congress can outlaw those practices which have a discriminatory impact on women or minorities but the Court will follow the discriminatory purpose analysis in the absence of such statutory action.

The Court's treatment of statistics as a form of proof which is of great worth in the Civil Rights Act cases, somewhat less in the discriminatory application cases, and very little in the "effect" cases is certainly open to criticism from those who desire a single

Thus the majority opinion seemed to issue simultaneous rulings that the plaintiffs had failed to show that the drug user-methadone prohibition was racially discriminatory and that there was a sufficient claim of job relatedness in any event. However, we must await future decisions of the Supreme Court to determine whether this opinion will have any impact on the use of statistical proof in other Title VII cases.

57. For a complete analysis of the use of statistical proof in Title VII employment cases, see Shoben, Differential Pass-Fail Rates in Employment Testing: Statistical Proof Under Title VII, 91 Harv.L.Rev. 793 (1978); Shoben, Probing the Discriminatory Effects of Employee Selection Procedures with Disparate Impact Analysis Under Title VII, 56 Texas L.Rev. 1 (1977).

In Connecticut v. Teal, 102 S.Ct. 2525 (1982), the Supreme Court held that an employer's use of employment tests or standards which had a disparate impact on members of racial minorities established a prima facie case of a Title VII violation. The employer could not rebut that case merely by showing that the final or "bottom line" result of his hiring or promotional system demonstrate a fair racial balance.

Once a prima facie showing of racial discrimination in an employer's hiring practices has been made by a plaintiff, the burden shifts to the employer to demonstrate that there is a legitimate business purpose for the practices which resulted in the alleged discrimination. This rule applies regardless of whether the prima facie showing is based on statistical proof or an inference of racial discrimination that might arise from an employer's rejection of qualified minority applicants. If the employer can demonstrate that the practices are justified by business necessity, or if he can rebut the plaintiff's prima facie case, the employer will prevail unless the plaintiff can demonstrate that the employer has used the practice or job qualification in question as a mere pretext to achieve discriminatory ends. Furnco Constr. Corp. v. Waters, 438 U.S. 567 (1978). In demonstrating that the employment practice was undertaken for legitimate reasons and without intent to further discriminatory ends, the employer may introduce statistical evidence that the employer's workforce contains a percentage of minority workers of the group against which discrimination is alleged which is equal to or greater than the percentage of such workers in the relevant labor pool. Although such evidence is not conclusive on the issue, the Court

has held that it might be considered in reaching a determination as to whether racial discrimination has in fact occurred. Id. When an employer presents evidence to rebut a prima facie case under Title VII the trial court must decide the ultimate issue of discrimination rather than merely assessing the plaintiff's prima facie case. United States Postal Serv. Bd. of Governors v. Aikens, 103 S.Ct. 1478 (1983).

In Board of Trustees of Keene State College v. Sweeney, 439 U.S. 24 (1978) (per curiam), the Supreme Court held that the employer could rebut the prima facie showing of discrimination by articulating some legitimate nondiscriminatory reason for rejecting the applicant. Justice Stevens, joined by Justices Brennan, Stewart, and Marshall in dissent, noted that *Furnco* appeared to rest a more substantial burden on the defendant to rebut the prima facie case. The dissenters objected to the Court vacating and remanding a decision to the Court of Appeals when the circuit judges had attempted to fairly apply a basic decisional rule. 439 U.S. at 26–29 (Stevens, J., dissenting).

In Los Angeles Dept. of Water v. Manhart, 435 U.S. 702 (1978), the Supreme Court held that Title VII prohibited the collection of larger pension contributions from female employees than from male employees. Although statistically valid mortality tables showed that women live longer than men, Title VII prohibits giving different treatment to any individual because of his or her sex. See also, Arizona Governing Committee for Tax Deferred Annuity and Deferred Compensation Plans v. Norris, 103 S.Ct. ____ (1983) (employer and insurance company practice of paying lower monthly annuity retirement benefits to women than men on the basis of projected longer life span of women as a class violates Title VII).

58. General Building Contractors Ass'n, Inc. v. Pennsylvania, 102 S.Ct. 3141 (1982) (proof of discriminatory intent is required to establish a violation of 42 U.S.C.A. § 1981, enacted in 1866 and based on Congress' thirteenth amendment power, which guarantees to all persons the same contract rights as those "enjoyed by white citizens"). See also, Memphis v. Greene, 451 U.S. 100 (1981) (closing of street passing through white neighborhood and going into neighborhood with a predominantly black population does not violate 42 U.S.C.A. § 1982 granting all citizens those property rights "enjoyed by white citizens").

standard for testing the impact of all rules that might have differing effects on racial or sexual classifications of persons. Yet the Court's approach is not new; it is clear that the Court opinions in recent years have not dramatically changed from those that went before and that the Court continues to attempt to walk the middle ground between the Brest and Ely models.

II. CLASSIFICATIONS BASED ON RACE OR NATIONAL ORIGIN

A. Introduction

Today the equal protection clause of the fourteenth amendment mandates that no governmental entity shall burden persons, or deny a benefit to them, because they are members of a racial minority. After many years of indifference to the use of racial classifications, the Supreme Court has in the last forty years enforced the constitutional principle of racial equality. Of course, there was no such principle prior to the Civil War when slavery existed with constitutional and Supreme Court sanction. Following the War the thirteenth, fourteenth and fifteenth amendments were passed as part of an effort to grant by constitutional decree equal rights to black persons. Although it appeared at the outset as though the Supreme Court might strongly enforce the equal protection guarantee, the Court endorsed racial segregation of public facilities and functions, other than overt discrimination in jury selection, by accepting the concept of "separate but equal."

Following 1930 the Court began to evidence a growing distaste for having to place a constitutional imprimatur on racial discrimination. In the mid 1940's, the Court upheld the wartime restrictions on Japanese residents but indicated that classifications based on race or national origin would not be consistent with constitutional principles absent the most important justification. Finally the Supreme Court began to enforce the concept of equal protection by forbidding the establishment of separate educational facilities for blacks. Thereafter the

Court was to strike down every form of government action that discriminated against members of a minority race or segregated public facilities by race.

Classifications based on race or national origin have been held to be "suspect," that is, the justices will use "strict scrutiny" to determine whether the law is invidious. The use of these classifications will be invalid unless they are necessary to promote a "compelling" or "overriding" interest of government. Burdening someone because of his national origin or status as a member of a racial minority runs counter to the most fundamental concept of equal protection. To legitimate such a classification the end of the governmental action would have to outweigh the basic values of the amendment. For this reason no such classification has been upheld since 1945 when the Supreme Court accepted the argument that the classification at issue would burden racial minorities. However, the Court has not held that all government acts must be race-neutral (or "color-blind") and we do not yet know whether the government may use racial classifications to grant special benefits to members of minority races except where the classification is used to remedy proven discrimination.

We stress the term "governmental action" for the equal protection guarantee extends to all governmental acts. The fourteenth amendment applies to any state, including all subdivisions or local governments within a state. The due process clause of the fifth amendment imposes a similar equal protection guarantee upon the federal government. The Court has held that any classification which would violate the equal protection clause when done by the federal government is an arbitrary and invidious use of power which constitutes an independent violation of the due process clause of the fifth amendment.

The actions of persons with no connection to any governmental entity are not subject to either the fifth or fourteenth amendments. A discussion of the relationships to government that subject someone to constitutional constraint is contained in Chapter 14, State Action.

What follows is a development of these principles and a study of their application. While the section on classification is complete in itself, the following section, on the problems of implementing integration, provides additional insight into the principles of racial equality. The section on affirmative action and benign classifications examines the arguments relating to a most important but unresolved undecided issue.

B. Racial Discrimination Prior to the Civil War[1]

Prior to the Civil War there was no constitutional safeguard against depriving persons of rights or privileges because of their race, the inevitable position of a system which legitimized slavery.

There was some sentiment in colonial America for total abolition of slavery. During the period under which the states followed the Articles of Confederation slavery was prohibited in the territories by the Northwest Ordinance.[2] At the constitutional convention the various sectional groups approached the problem of slavery as an economic and political one. The northern delegates were not ready to risk their economic and political unification with the south over the slavery issue. The southern representa-

tives sought some assurances that the new federal government would not take steps to abolish slavery in their states. Eventually the convention agreed that the federal government should not be able to limit the importation of slaves for a period of time and that southern slaveholders should have full recognition of their right to hold slaves. Thus Article I forbade Congress to restrict the slave trade prior to 1808[3] and Article V prohibited amendments which would remove this restriction.[4] The rights of slaveholders were recognized in the fugitive slave clause of Article IV.[5]

No branch of the new federal government moved to curtail slavery within the states following the formation of the union. The second Congress passed the "fugitive slave act" which established the slaveowners' rights to the return of slaves who escaped into free states.[6] The Supreme Court of the United States upheld and enforced the act as a proper implementation of the slave clause of Article IV.[7] The Court struck down state laws that punished those who "kidnapped" fugitive slaves in free states as conflicting with the federal policy[8] and upheld state laws that punished those who harbored fugitive slaves.[9]

The Supreme Court also proved unhelpful to former slaves who asserted that they had become free. The Court generally ruled in favor of the slaveholders who asserted that the individuals making the claim had not

---

1. For a more complete treatment of this period see D. Bell, Race, Racism and American Law (2d ed. 1980) and materials cited therein.

2. The Northwest Ordinance of July 13, 1787, Journals of the Continental Congress Vol. IV, pp. 752–54 reprinted in H. Commanger, 1 Documents of American History 128 (5th ed. 1949).

3. The provision allowed for taxation but not prohibition. U.S. Const. art. I, § 9, cl. 1:

"The Migration or Importation of Such Persons as any of the States now existing shall think proper to admit, shall not be prohibited by the Congress prior to the Year One thousand eight hundred and eight, but a Tax or duty may be imposed on such Importation, not exceeding ten dollars for each Person."

4. U.S. Const. art. V:

". . . Provided that no Amendment which may be made prior to the Year One thousand eight hun-

dred and eight shall in any Manner affect the first and fourth clauses in the Ninth Section of the first Article."

5. U.S. Const. art. IV, § 2, cl. 3:

"No Person held to Service or Labour in one State, under the Laws thereof, escaping into another, shall, in Consequence of any Law or Regulation therein, be discharged from such Service or Labour, but shall be delivered up on Claim of the Party to whom such Service or Labour may be due."

6. Act of Feb. 12, 1793, 1 Stat. 302.

7. Jones v. Van Zandt, 46 U.S. (5 How.) 215 (1847); Ableman v. Booth, 62 U.S. (21 How.) 506 (1859).

8. Prigg v. Pennsylvania, 41 U.S. (16 Pet.) 539 (1842).

9. Moore v. Illinois, 55 U.S. (14 How.) 13, 17 (1853).

been freed according to the laws of the appropriate jurisdiction.[10] Individuals seeking to establish that they had been freed from slavery were dependent upon local courts to enforce their rights.

In the north, states systematically began eliminating slavery within their jurisdictions.[11] If a slave became subject to the jurisdiction of a free state for a sufficient period of time, he would become free according to the laws of that state. Until approximately 1830 most state courts applied a rule of "reasonableness" to determine whether a slave had remained in a free state long enough to become free.[12] Northern states would not declare slaves free if they were brought into free territory for only a short time, while southern states would honor the free status of slaves emancipated this way.[13] As the rivalry between the free and slave states intensified, the rule of reasonableness and judicial cooperation came to an end.[14] Northern states would declare a slave free even though that person had been in the state only a short time, while southern states would refuse to honor the free status of former slaves who returned to slave states. The abolitionist movement and the southern defense of slavery simply could not be reconciled by local legal systems, and the need for some sort of federal action intensified.

The federal government moved to limit the slave trade after the constitutional prohibition in Article I expired.[15] The restriction on the importation of slaves was enforced by the Supreme Court in an attempt to greatly restrict the slave trade.[16] However, the Court was unwilling to move to strike down the slave trading practices. Justice Johnson, as a Circuit Justice, struck down a state law regulating and enslaving free blacks incident to slave trade regulation as invalid under the commerce clause,[17] but the Court as a whole only pronounced dicta against the immorality of slavery while refusing to limit slavery beyond the statutory trade restrictions.[18] However, it is interesting to note that the Supreme Court recognized that foreign black Africans were free persons who had, and retained, individual rights if they were brought into this country in violation of the congressional restriction of slave trade.[19]

Some protection was given to those blacks unlawfully brought into the country, but free blacks were not given rights against racial discrimination. The Supreme Court had no conception of a right of free blacks to equal protection of the laws. In the southern states not only was there unequal treatment of blacks, but white abolitionists who traveled into slave territory were unlikely to receive the protection of the southern legal

10. See, e.g., Queen v. Hepburn, 11 U.S. (7 Cranch) 290 (1813); Scott v. Negro Ben, 10 U.S. (6 Cranch) 3 (1810); but see, McCutchen v. Marshall, 33 U.S. (8 Pet.) 220 (1834); see generally, Roper, In Quest of Judicial Objectivity: The Marshall Court and the Legitimation of Slavery, 21 Stan.L.Rev. 532 (1969).

11. L. Litwack, North of Slavery 3–20 (1961) D. Bell, supra note 1.

12. Note, American Slavery and the Conflict of Laws, 71 Colum.L.Rev. 74 (1971).

13. During this period at least some southern courts also enforced the prohibition of slavery contained in the Northwest Ordinance, supra note 2, by declaring free those who had become subject to the jurisdiction of the territory. Merry v. Chexnaider, 8 Martin (N.S.) 699, 5 La.Ann. part 3 at 224, (La.1830); Forsyth v. Nash, 4 Martin (O.S.) 385, 1 La.Ann. part 4 at 117 (La.1816).

14. Note, American Slavery and the Conflict of Laws, 71 Colum.L.Rev. 74, 92–8 (1971).

15. 2 Stat. 426 (1807) (Act of March 2, 1807, to be effective on January 1, 1808); 3 Stat. 450 (1818); 3 Stat. 600 (1820).

16. See, e.g., The Josefa Segunda, 18 U.S. (5 Wheat.) 338 (1820).

17. Elkison v. Deliesseline, 8 Fed.Cas. 493 (No. 4366) (C.C.S.C.1823). (Johnson sitting as Circuit Justice).

18. The Antelope, 23 U.S. (10 Wheat.) 66 (1825) (dicta that slave trade had to be authorized by statute as it was contrary to national law); see Roper, In Quest of Judicial Objectivity: The Marshall Court and the Legitimation of Slavery, 21 Stan.L.Rev. 532 (1969).

19. The Amistad Case, 40 U.S. (15 Pet.) 518 (1841). The Court here set free a group of black Africans who had revolted against their captain on a Spanish schooner and landed in the United States. The Court recognized these persons as kidnapped free persons. The case was argued for the Africans by former president John Quincy Adams, who was a part of the abolitionist effort.

authorities.[20] The North provided no more meaningful protection for free blacks against unequal distribution of rights based on a race.[21] Indeed it was the Supreme Court of Massachusetts that created the concept of "separate but equal" when it upheld a separate school system for black students.[22] In some states only blacks could be slaves.[23] In others, all blacks were presumed to be slaves.[24]

The move to abolish slavery steadily gained momentum following the turn of the century. The American Anti-Slavery Society was founded in 1833 and thereafter the abolitionist movement became a more potent political force. As the abolitionists had little hope of limiting or ending slavery by local legislation in the south, they turned to the national government to advance this cause. A battle ensued in Congress over not only congressional power to limit slavery but also over the whole scope of federal power under the Constitution. At first the abolitionists sought only an end to slavery in federally held areas such as the District of Columbia. Eventually they sought the total abolition of slavery by Congressional act. These pressures were resisted by southern representatives whose position changed from arguing the tacit recognition of slavery in the Constitution to asserting the right of individual states to refuse to follow or "nullify" federal laws.[25] In 1820 Congress had found a temporary solution in the Missouri Compromise.[26] This compromise did not change the balance of power or the slavery system within the country, but it avoided battles over the admission of new states by dividing

them into "free" and "slave" states. Following 1820 the political struggle had intensified and the constitutionality of congressional action affecting slavery was in doubt. Arguments over slavery, congressional power, nullification and possible secession were inexorably linked. Indeed it can be fairly said that, by the time the Supreme Court spoke on these issues, the country was in the midst of a constitutional as well as a political crisis.

In 1857, in its only attempt to constitutionally resolve the slavery conflict, the Court displayed an amazing lack of moral or political wisdom. At issue in *Dred Scott v. Sandford*[27] was the effect of state and federal laws granting freedom and citizenship to former slaves. Scott had been taken as a slave by his owner into Illinois, a free state, and an area of the Louisiana Purchase territory which had been made a free territory under the Missouri Compromise. Upon returning to Missouri, Scott sued his owner in federal court to establish his freedom. The Supreme Court could have avoided the most difficult issues by finding that the federal court was bound to follow Missouri law, under which Scott was still considered a slave or even that proper diversity jurisdiction was not present.[28] Perhaps due to the fact that at least one dissenting Justice intended to defend the Missouri Compromise and the Congressional power to free slaves, a six member majority of the Court went far beyond the basic issues in resolving Scott's claim.[29] There were eight separate opinions which covered over 200 pages of the U. S. Reports, but it is the majority opinion by

20. For a recounting of the history of attacks on the abolitionists and their response see, J. tenBroek, Equal Under Law 35–40 (1965).

21. D. Bell, supra note 1; L. Litwack, North of Slavery (1961); L. Greene, The Negro in Colonial New England (1942). Some "free" states actually prohibited the immigration of black persons into the states. See, e.g., Nelson v. People, 33 Ill. 390 (1864).

22. Roberts v. City of Boston, 59 Mass. (5 Cush.) 198 (1850).

23. Gaines v. Ann, 17 Tex. 211 (1856). Contra, State v. Van Waggoner, 6 N.J.Law (1 Halst.) 374 (1797); See also Scott v. Ralib, 88 Va. 721, 14 S.E. 178 (1892).

24. Forsyth v. Nash, 4 Martin (O.S.) 385, 1 La.Ann. part 4 at 117 (La.1816).

25. An excellent history of the times in terms of conflicting political theories is J. tenBroek, Equal Under Law (1965) (first published as "The Antislavery Origins of the Fourteenth Amendment").

26. 3 Stat. 545–48 (1820).

27. 60 U.S. (19 How.) 393 (1857).

28. Such a course had been followed six years earlier in Strader v. Graham, 51 U.S. (10 How.) 82 (1850).

29. It may well have resulted from a combination of the possible dissent and the majority's belief in its own ability to save the country from a major social conflict.

Chief Justice Taney which was, and is, the center of controversy. The opinion by Taney found that neither black slaves nor their descendants could be considered citizens of the United States or persons who received any individual rights under the Constitution. This conclusion was based on the majority's historical and legal perception of blacks as persons of an inherently inferior position in society. In the view of the majority, no state could alter the status of slaves or their descendants by granting them citizenship. The majority opinion went even beyond these assertions to hold that Congress could not grant citizenship to these persons. The Missouri Compromise was held unconstitutional; the majority found that Congress was without power to grant citizenship to slaves or their descendants, based on the majority's view that the original Constitution and Bill of Rights by implication precluded any possibility of constitutional protection for black slaves or their descendants. The opinion implied that any congressional action to emancipate slaves would violate the substantive due process protections for a

slaveholder and his interest in his "property."

Taney's majority opinion in *Dred Scott* may well have been based on an honest and fairly objective view of the attitudes of some of the founders of the country, but the majority could not be excused from using its interpretative powers to reach out and protect the morally reprehensible practice of slavery from reform through the democratic process. The opinion was greeted with unmitigated wrath from every segment of the United States except the slave holding states, causing the Court to lose both its moral authority and political base until after the Civil War when it slowly began to reassert its power and align itself with national economic interests.[30]

Prior to the Civil War the Court showed no interest as an institution in limiting slavery or racial discrimination. It would take the Civil War Amendments to establish some basis for black citizenship and constitutional rights for members of racial minorities. It should be noted in closing, however, that both the Court and country have tried to excise the *Dred Scott* decision from our legal

R. McCloskey, The American Supreme Court 92–95 (1960).

30. The late Professor McCloskey summarized the aftermath, R. McCloskey, The American Supreme Court 95–97:

"The tempest of malediction that burst over the judges seems to have stunned them; far from extinguishing the slavery controversy, they had fanned its flames and had, moreover, deeply endangered the security of the judicial arm of government. No such vilification as this had been heard even in the wrathful days following the Alien and Sedition Acts . . .

"The extent of that tragedy is revealed by the peculiar transvaluation of values that took place in connection with the case of Ableman v. Booth in 1859. Ableman, a Milwaukee editor, had assisted a fugitive slave to escape from federal custody, and was therefore arrested for violation of the national Fugitive Slave Law. The Wisconsin Supreme Court ordered him released on a writ of habeas corpus, and the order was obeyed. However, the national government then appealed to the Supreme Court of the United States, which held that the state courts had no business to interfere with the conduct of federal law and that the Fugitive Slave Law was constitutional.

"Now the first point was of course the very keystone of the Supreme Court's jurisdictional arch;

this was the principle for which Marshall has fought so shrewdly and effectively. If the national government and its judicial arm can operate only by the leave of the several states, the nation is not a nation and the Supreme Court is not a supreme court. Yet the decision was violently attacked, the state was urged to resist, the cry that the Court had no power thus to overrule a state was heard, not only in Wisconsin, but throughout the North.

"This was the doctrine of nullification, familiar since the Virginia and Kentucky resolutions of 1798–99, re-energized by the mordant genius of Calhoun in 1832, and now becoming an article of faith below the Mason-Dixon line. That it should be invoked by a northern state as a challenge to the Court is a measure of the witless inconsistency of some Northern opinion but is also a measure of judicial bankruptcy. The Court's effective existence depended on acceptance of the principle of national authority, and there was no hope that this principle would be entertained in the South one minute after an anti-slavery opinion was rendered. The judicial constituency had always been drawn from those who had a stake in nationalism, and in 1859 that meant the North. But the monumental indiscretion of *Dred Scott* had forfeited Northern allegiance. For the first time in its history, the Court seemed almost friendless (for the fair-weather friendship of the South provided very cold comfort)."

heritage. As Professor Bell has summarized:

> The understandable desire on the part of the legal profession to finally erase what Chief Justice Charles Evans Hughes called the Court's "self-inflicted wound" has resulted in the Dred Scott case's being the most frequently overturned decision in history. The final demise of Dred Scott has been attributed to the following: (1) the Civil War—"The law of the case was lost in the maelstrom which engulfed North and South," A. Blaustein and C. Ferguson, Desegregation and the Law 85 (1957); (2) the Thirteenth Amendment, according to The Civil Rights Cases, 109 U.S. 3 . . . (1883); (3) the Fourteenth Amendment, by H. Horowitz and K. Karst, Law, Lawyers and Social Change 102 (1969); (4) all three Civil War Amendments, by former Chief Justice Earl Warren: E. Warren, A Republic If You Can Keep It, 46 (1972); (5) Brown v. Board of Education, . . . (1954), . . . by Judge John Minor Wisdom in United States v. Jefferson County Board of Education, 372 F.2d 836, 873 (5th Cir. 1966), and (6) Jones v. Mayer Co., . . . (1968) . . . by Larsen, The New Law of Race Relations, 1969 Wis.L.Rev. 470, 486.[31]

C. The Civil War Amendments and Racial Discrimination—An Introductory Note

1. The Text of the Amendments

The Civil War was to change the basic features of the Constitution just as it altered the country's political and social structure. Three amendments to the Constitution were proposed after the war and were ratified by 1870. These three amendments—the thirteenth, fourteenth, and fifteenth—are often referred to as the Civil War Amendments because they are the direct outgrowth of the war and its political aftermath. As the amendments are closely tied to the earlier abolitionist movement and the post war struggle concerning the rights of freed blacks, we shall briefly review these amendments prior to continuing our discussion of racial classifications.

The thirteenth amendment, proposed by Congress and ratified by the states in 1865, consists of two sections.[1] The first section prohibits "slavery" and "involuntary servitude" throughout the United States or its territories. This prohibition applies to all persons subject to the jurisdiction of the United States and is not dependent on the existence of government action. It proscribes such practices even where they are imposed by individuals with no connection to any governmental entity. The only exception is that made by section one for the punishment of properly convicted criminals. Section two of the amendment grants Congress the power to make laws to enforce the amendment.

The fourteenth amendment, proposed by Congress in 1866 and ratified in 1868, has five sections dealing with separate issues.[2]

---

31. D. Bell, Race, Racism and American Laws at 21–22 (1st ed. 1973); See generally D. Bell, supra note 1.

1. U.S.Const. amend. XIII:

"Section 1. Neither slavery nor involuntary servitude, except as a punishment for crime whereof the party shall have been duly convicted, shall exist within the United States, or any place subject to their jurisdiction.

"Section 2. Congress shall have power to enforce this article by appropriate legislation."

2. U.S.Const. amend. XIV:

"Section 1. All persons born or naturalized in the United States, and subject to the jurisdiction thereof, are citizens of the United States and of the State wherein they reside. No State shall make or enforce any law which shall abridge the privileges or immunities of citizens of the United States; nor shall any State deprive any person of life, liberty, or property, without due process of law; nor deny to any person within its jurisdiction the equal protection of the laws.

"Section 2. Representatives shall be apportioned among the several States according to their respective numbers, counting the whole number of persons in each State, excluding Indians not taxed. But when the right to vote at any election for the choice of electors for President and Vice President of the United States, Representatives in Congress, the Executive and Judicial officers of a State, or the members of the Legislature thereof, is denied to any of the male inhabitants of such State, being twenty-one years of age, and citizens of the United States, or in any way abridged, except for participation in rebellion, or other crime, the basis of representation therein shall be reduced in the proportion which the number of such male citizens shall bear to the whole

Section one is the provision that has been the source of most "civil rights" rulings by the Supreme Court. This section consists of two sentences containing a total of four clauses. Sentence one grants citizenship to everyone "born or naturalized in the United States, and subject to the jurisdiction thereof . . . ." The three clauses of sentence two grant important individual rights, but they secure these rights only against interference by the states. Thus sentence two appears to be inapplicable to the actions of private persons or the federal government. The first clause of sentence two prohibits the states from abridging "the privileges or immunities of citizens of the United States." The second clause mirrors the language of the fifth amendment due process clause and prohibits the states from depriving anyone of "life, liberty or property, without due process of law." The last clause of section one contains the only equal protection clause in the Constitution, and it prohibits the states from depriving anyone of "the equal protection of the laws."

Section 2 of the fourteenth amendment altered the regulation of the electoral franchise in two ways. First, blacks were counted as full citizens for purposes of representation in the Congress by replacing the provisions of Article I Section 2 which counted only three-fifths of "all other persons" (meaning slaves—a term the Constitution's drafters avoided). Second, representation in the federal Congress would be

reduced for those states which denied any adult male citizen the right to vote except for "participation in rebellion, or other crime. . . ." In these ways the drafters of the Amendment hoped to encourage the states to grant universal male suffrage without direct federal action.

Sections three and four of the fourteenth amendment relate to political problems of the period. Section three bars from federal office, except by vote of Congress, any previous government office holder who participated in a rebellion or gave aid to the enemies of the United States. Section four insulates the government debt, including the Union war debt, from legal attack. It also insures that the federal government would never pay any of the Confederate debt.

Section five of the fourteenth amendment gives Congress the power to enforce the amendment.

The fifteenth amendment,[3] proposed by Congress in 1869 and ratified in 1870, enfranchised blacks by prohibiting both the state and federal governments from denying anyone the right to vote "on account of race, color, or previous condition of servitude." Section two of the amendment grants enforcement powers to Congress.

2. A Capsule History

As we saw in the previous section, slavery and racial discrimination were given constitutional protection prior to the Civil War.

---

number of male citizens twenty-one years of age in such State.

"Section 3. No person shall be a Senator or Representative in Congress, or elector of President and Vice President, or hold any office, civil or military, under the United States, or under any State, who having previously taken an oath, as a member of Congress, or as an officer of the United States, or as a member of any State legislature, or as an executive or judicial officer of any State, to support the Constitution of the United States, shall have engaged in insurrection or rebellion against the same, or given aid or comfort to the enemies thereof. But Congress may by a vote of two-thirds of each House, remove such disability.

"Section 4. The validity of the public debt of the United States, authorized by law, including debts incurred for payment of pensions and bounties for ser-

vices in suppressing insurrection or rebellion, shall not be questioned. But neither the United States nor any State shall assume or pay any debt or obligation incurred in aid of insurrection or rebellion against the United States, or any claim for the loss or emancipation of any slave; but all such debts, obligations and claims shall be held illegal and void.

"Section 5. The Congress shall have power to enforce, by appropriate legislation, the provisions of this article."

3. U.S.Const. amend. XV:

"Section 1. The right of citizens of the United States to vote shall not be denied or abridged by the United States or by any State on account of race, color, or previous condition of servitude.

"Section 2. The Congress shall have power to enforce this article by appropriate legislation."

Although there were many economic or political influences that took part in causing the war, the Northern Abolitionists and their goals of abolishing slavery and providing for the freed blacks were of critical importance in the shaping of postwar history. While the three amendments were not part of a preconceived legislative "package" or plan, they represent the natural progression of the abolitionist goals as these goals were represented in Congress by the "Radical Republicans." Each of the amendments can be traced in part to particular political considerations, but most of the leading Republican members of Congress were confirmed abolitionists. The desire to secure freedom and safety, if not social equality, for freed black persons was shared by a large part of the population, at least in the North. During this period, there were times in which the people of the northern states seemed to want all reconstruction issues to end and the southern states to be "readmitted" to the Union. Indeed, the continued discrimination against black persons in the northern states gives one cause to doubt the popular strength of the abolitionist movement after the war. Yet the continued mistreatment of freed blacks in the South resulted in renewed Northern dedication to the abolitionists' goals. Thus, following a period of seemingly lessening Northern interest, we find the fifteenth amendment being ratified in 1870 and the major civil rights act being passed in 1871.

Emancipation from slavery for black persons began with the Civil War. Congress ended slavery in the territories [4] and authorized the emancipation of slaves who served with the Union armed forces. [5] President Lincoln, in his famous Emancipation Proclamation, declared slaves held in Confederate territory to be free. [6] However, total abolishment of slavery awaited the end of the War; it was accomplished by the ratification

of the thirteenth amendment in 1865. The congressional debates on the amendment answer very few questions, for there was very little opposition or debate. With no southern representation in Congress, there were no defenders of the slavery system. It seems clear that the drafters intended to enhance federal power and actions were taken at the expense of older concepts of federalism and state sovereignty. A small segment of Congress objected to the amendment on the grounds that it would give vast power to Congress and replace the states as the prime entity for dealing with personal rights. [7] Such objections were for naught as Congress saw the need to revise older conceptions of federalism in order to guarantee human liberty. Yet the degree of liberty protected by the amendment is not clear. With a fair amount of certainty one can say that the framers wanted to do more than abolish the traditional slavery system. All forms of involuntary servitude were to be eliminated whether they were applied to blacks or whites and regardless of the formal legal categorization of the system. Unfortunately, the framers were not at all clear about the extent to which the amendment would prohibit legal discriminations that were the result of the slavery experience.

The uncertainty over the meaning of the thirteenth amendment in large measure gave rise to the need for the fourteenth amendment. Shortly after the passage of the thirteenth amendment new civil rights legislation was introduced in Congress. This bill sought to protect both blacks and whites from deprivation of their civil liberties. The bill was aimed at the southern states, where both before and after the War abolitionists had encountered violent opposition to their attempts to organize programs for black persons. The Civil Rights Act was critically important; the rights declared in

4.   12 Stat. 432 (1862).

5.   12 Stat. 597–600 (1862). Congress also amended the Articles of War to prohibit members of the Union forces from returning any fugitive slave. 12 Stat. 359 (1862).

6.   Presidential Proclamation of January 1, 1863, 12 Stat. 1268 (1863).

7.   J. tenBroek, Equal Under Law at 159–173 (1965).

section one of the Act were virtually identical to those eventually embodied in the fourteenth amendment. But even after the thirteenth amendment some members of Congress opposed the bill as beyond federal power.[8] Radical Republicans in those debates expressed their belief that the federal government should protect all those civil rights that had been disregarded by the slavery system. They saw section two of the amendment as authorizing Congress to guarantee the civil rights of every individual because the amendment eliminated the remnants of pre-war discrimination and slavery. Although virtually all the Republicans lauded the goal of federal action to promote and protect civil rights, some Republicans doubted that the thirteenth amendment gave Congress such a power. This feeling of uncertainty about the basis for such federal action gave impetus to the movement for another, clearer amendment to the Constitution. But, at the same time, Congress was solidified enough in its view of federal power to pass a sweeping Civil Rights Act and to repass it over the veto of President Johnson.[9] They also passed, over Johnson's veto,[10] the second Freedman's Bureau bill to protect those deprived of civil rights in the south.

The history of the fourteenth amendment is complicated if often told. We will only sketch its outline here.[11]

The Thirty-Ninth Congress began with an abolitionist movement to secure full civil rights for all persons and a "hard-core" Republican movement to postpone returning any power to the Democrats.[12] Congress faced a President who wanted the nation reunited on terms at least partially acceptable to all the major pre-war elements of political society. It was President Johnson's desire to reunite the nation without unduly punishing the southern states that led to his impeachment and trial in Congress.

The first proposals in the thirty-ninth Congress for a new amendment were very general. John Bingham, a representative who was to play a major role in the drafting of the amendment, first proposed an amendment simply giving Congress the power to declare and to enforce civil rights.[13] This proposal and all others were referred to by a special joint committee of the Congress created to draft a proposed amendment.[14] Because this committee was dominated by Rad-

---

8. Id. at 174–197.

9. 14 Stat. 27 (1866). The votes overriding President Johnson's veto appear in Congressional Globe, 39th Cong., 1st Sess. (1866) at 1809 (Senate), 1861 (House).

10. 14 Stat. 173 (1866). The override of President Johnson's veto appears in Congressional Globe, 39th Cong. 1st Sess. (1866) at 3842. There was an earlier bill to continue the Freedman Bureau which passed the Congress and was also vetoed by President Johnson. The attempt to override his veto at that time failed in the Senate. Id. at 943.

11. For good summaries and analyses of the history of the fourteenth amendment, see H. Flack, The Adoption of the Fourteenth Amendment (1908); J. James, The Framing of the Fourteenth Amendment (1956); Kendrick, The Journal of the Joint Committee of Fifteen on Reconstruction, in Columbia Univ. Studies in History, Economics and Public Law (vol. 62, 1914); J. tenBroek, Equal Under Law (1965). The history of the amendment is also summarized in relation to three more particular legal inquiries in: Fairman, Does the Fourteenth Amendment Incorporate the Bill of Rights?, 2 Stan.L.Rev. 5 (1949); Bickel, The Original Understanding and the Segregation Decision, 69 Harv. L.Rev. 1 (1955); Nowak, The Scope of Congressional

Power to Create Causes of Action Against State Governments and the History of the Eleventh and Fourteenth Amendments, 75 Colum.L.Rev. 1413 (1975); Dimond, Strict Construction and Judicial Review of Racial Discrimination Under the Equal Protection Clause: Meeting Raoul Berger on Interpretivist Grounds, 80 Mich.L.Rev. 462 (1982).

12. An especially good treatment of the political consideration is to be found in James, supra note 11.

13. Congressional Globe, 39th Cong., 1st Sess. (1866) at 813. The Proposal read:

"The Congress shall have power to make all laws which shall be necessary and proper to secure to the citizens of each state all privileges and immunities of citizens in the several states [Art. 4, Sec. 2]; and to all persons in the several states equal protection in the rights of life, liberty and property [5th amendment]."

14. The Journal of that Committee is contained in Kendrick, supra note 11. For a brief time some thought that there was a "conspiracy" to create an amendment that could later be used to protect "big business", but this thesis has been completely disproved. See Graham, The "Conspiracy" Theory of the Fourteenth Amendment, 47 Yale L.J. 371 (1938).

ical Republicans and abolitionists, one can only assume that these original drafters attempted to create civil liberties of wide scope and to grant Congress virtually unchecked power to expand and to protect those rights.[15] Nevertheless, they had to deal with more conservative elements in their own party as well as with Democrats who wished to limit federal power in the hope of regaining strength with the renewed representation for southern states. Additionally, there was growing public sentiment in the North for a speedy resolution of these issues and a normalization of relations between all states. This meant the drafters had to settle for a proposal that could secure a consensus for ratification within a fairly short period of time. Tailoring the proposal to gain a wide base for support thus became a necessity for the drafters.[16] Sections three and four of the amendment, for example, were obviously designed to aid passage of the amendment by capitalizing on specific regional concerns.

The final product of Congress, which is now the fourteenth amendment, is difficult to interpret historically because of these competing influences. At least one goal of the Republican-Abolitionist movement, that of universal black suffrage, was not pursued directly. The grant to blacks of the right to vote would have helped to secure their equality before the law as well as to dilute Democratic voting majorities in the South. However, the drafters did not believe that they could get a direct grant of suffrage through the ratification process.[17] This be-

lief did not mean that they did nothing on the issue. The second section of the amendment was intended to punish states that refused to grant suffrage to black males. Additionally, section one declared the right to equality before the law, and section five created a congressional power to enforce the amendment. Did this enforcement power mean that the equal protection clause itself might be the basis for enforcing the voting rights of black citizens, at least if it was done by Congressional action? The answer may never be known, for the passage of time has obscured the meaning of vague statements and competing influences.[18]

The history of the amendment yields virtually no clear-cut answers to modern issues concerning civil rights. On a few issues one may find easy answers in quotations from individual representatives, but these must be tempered by the realities of a time long past. For example, there are many statements by key drafters of the amendment, including Representative Bingham, to the effect that the amendment would apply the "Bill of Rights" to the states. However, it is also clear that Bingham, in conformity with abolitionist theory, was referring to a morally dictated set of rights rather than the specific guarantees of the first ten amendments.[19] Even when the intent of the drafters seems clear, one must remember that part of the debates focused on the expected immediate impact of the amendment rather than the principles which were to govern future generations. For example, one can find many statements that indicated that the drafters

15. On the influence of these persons see tenBroek, supra note 11.

16. The Republicans were under a great deal of political pressure to adopt a workable plan for guaranteeing the civil rights of freedmen. Sentiment in the North was quickly turning against "racial" proposals and delay in "readmitting" the Southern states. The radical Republicans clearly appreciated the danger of adopting proposals which went beyond the moderate feeling of the general populace and were willing to settle for more limited guarantees of civil rights so that they would not be defeated in the upcoming elections. Cong. Globe, 39th Cong., 1st Sess. (1866), at 2332 (Rep. Dixon), 2459 (Rep. Stevens), 2506 (Rep. Eldridge); Bickel, The Original Understanding and the Segregation Decisions, 69 Harv.L.Rev. 1, 61–62 (1955). It must

be remembered that the final ratification was accomplished by a narrow margin. James, supra note 11, at 192.

17. James, supra note 11, at 55–66.

18. While Justice Harlan thought that the history showed that the amendment should not apply to equal protection issues in voting, Reynolds v. Sims, 377 U.S. 533, 589 (1964) (Harlan, J., dissenting), Professor William Van Alstyne has shown how the history of the amendment may support such rulings, Van Alstyne, The Fourteenth Amendment, The Right to Vote, and the Understanding of the Thirty-Ninth Congress, 1965 Sup.Ct.Rev. 33.

19. tenBroek, supra note 11, at 231–2; Fairman, supra note 11.

did not believe the amendment would require the integration of schools. But these representatives lived in a world in which there was no uniform system of public education and in which the Supreme Court had attempted to uphold slavery against congressional limitation. That they did not anticipate the fourteenth amendment giving rise to an integrated system of public education under the guidance of the Supreme Court is not surprising. This belief does not mean that they intended to create a constitutional principle other than full equality and integration of the races.[20]

Although they do not provide answers to specific issues, the congressional debates on the fourteenth amendment indicate four general goals of the drafters. First, the amendment was to guarantee to all persons a set of civil liberties that could be judicially enforced against any state action. While it is unclear which parts of the Bill of Rights were included in the amendment the drafters followed abolitionist theory by attempting to guarantee a set of civil liberties that they believed no government could disregard.[21] Second, the drafters intended to promote the legal status and rights of black persons. The degree to which they would have required full integration or "colorblind" principles is unknown. Their central concern throughout the debates was securing some rights for freed blacks which state governments (or a future Democratic Congress) could not disregard.[22] The declaration of citizenship in section one and the provision on voting in section two were clearly designed as specific protections for black persons. Third, the Congress was to be given extremely wide powers to enforce the amendment. Again, there is no specific delineation of this power in the debates, but the drafters indicated a belief that Congress could expand and enforce civil rights through this power.[23] Fourth, the amendment was intended to alter the system of "federalism" and to centralize power over civil rights matters in the federal government. Opponents of the amendment continually stressed that it would allow a federal take over of legal relationships between persons and usurp the power of the states. All the participants in the debates, for example, understood that the amendment would authorize the Civil Rights Bill and future legislation of a similar type.[24] With the theoretical battle lines clearly drawn, the Congress

---

20. Bickel, The Original Understanding and the Segregation Decisions, 69 Harv.L.Rev. 1 (1955).

For an excellent defense, rooted in the history of the fourteenth amendment, of a meaningful judicial role in eliminating racial segregation and discrimination see, Dimond, Strict Construction and Judicial Review of Racial Discrimination Under the Equal Protection Clause: Meeting Raoul Berger on Interpretivist Grounds, 80 Mich.L.Rev. 462 (1982).

21. This goal seems universally agreed upon by legal historians; see sources in notes 11, 16, and 18 supra.

22. The most crass political considerations revolved around eliminating the power of Democrats by enacting strong measures to protect blacks. Such measures meant both continued power over southern states and increase in the strength of the Republican majority. See generally, James, supra note 11. Yet it should not be forgotten that the key drafters of the amendment were dedicated abolitionists who also acted from a moralist desire to help blacks, see generally, tenBroek, supra note 11.

23. For an analysis of this power see Chapter 17. A more complete discussion of the history relative to Congressional power under section 5 is contained in Nowak, supra note 11. Part of the "evidence" of a broad power was the failure of most members of Congress to discuss section 5 during the debates while going over in detail all other sections. See, e.g., Congressional Globe, 39th Cong., 1st Sess. (1866) at 2469 (Rep. Kelley) 2502, 2512 (Rep. Raymond). The failure to discuss the section seems to stem from a widely held belief that it was an open ended grant of power to enforce the other sections. Representative Miller summarized:

"The fifth section gives to Congress the power to enforce the provisions of this article by appropriate legislation. This clause is requisite to enforce the foregoing sections, or such of them as may be adopted, and is too plain to admit of argument; and in fact is not, as I am aware, contested by any gentlemen in this House."

Id. at 2510–11.

24. It is clear that opponents of the amendment task understood this aspect of the amendment and made it a specific point of debate. See the comments of those who were in opposition to the amendment because it "constitutionalized" the Civil Rights Bill, e.g., Cong. Globe, 39th Cong. 1st Sess. (1866) at 2461 (Rep. Flinck), 2506 (Rep. Eldridge), 2538 (Rep. Rogers). See also, id. at 2512–13 (exchange between Reps. Raymond and Wilson).

and the country rejected the "states' rights" position.[25] Regardless of any strong theoretical basis for respecting state autonomy in a federal system, the concept of state sovereignty had no place in American political life during the period when the fourteenth amendment was drafted and ratified.[26]

Ratification of the fourteenth amendment, perhaps because of its four general goals, was not easily gained. The amendment was forced on unwilling southern states and some northern states had "controversial" ratifications.[27] As soon as he had enough formal ratifications to accept the amendment, Secretary of State Seward proclaimed it adopted. And in a most unusual action, Congress passed a resolution accepting the amendment as ratified, perhaps to forestall or prevent legal attacks on its ratification.[28] Later decisions of the Supreme Court indicated that the legal objections to the ratification would be left to the decision of the political branches of government.[29] The Court thus removed any lingering theoretical doubts as to the legality of the ratification.

A most interesting fact about this period is that interest in securing the rights of blacks increased after the passage of the fourteenth amendment. That amendment and the earlier civil rights legislation clearly failed to bring about any meaningful protection for blacks. The rights of blacks in the south clearly were not being respected by white citizens or local governments. Reports of the atrocities committed against blacks stirred congressional and popular sentiment for new measures. The abolitionist influence in Congress became strong enough to mount a campaign for what was thought to be the ultimate goal—guaranteed electoral suffrage for black men. Abolitionists hoped that the franchise would guarantee blacks sufficient political power to insure that all of their rights would be respected. But there was fear of black suffrage both in the north and south by those who saw it diluting their political power. The amendment was passed after a difficult political struggle, and ratification was hard to gain. With most of the southern states fully represented in Congress, both passage and ratification seemed for a time to be impossible. However, ratification of the amendment was made a condition of "readmittance" for those southern states who had not had their representation restored, a procedure neces-

25. Public debate also focused on the fact that all branches of the federal government would be given increased power over individual rights to the detriment of state autonomy. See, e.g., The New York Herald, Oct. 25, 1866 at 6, col. 4; N.Y. Times, Oct. 25, 1866, at 4, col. 3. For a summary of newspaper articles endorsing the concept of a federal power to protect certain "natural law" rights, see Fairman, supra note 11 at 68–81. Perhaps the most widely debated public attack on the amendment was made by Secretary of the Interior Browning who wrote a lengthy "letter" containing a detailed attack on the proposed amendment and arranged to have it published by the newspapers. This letter apparently had been approved by President Johnson and was widely commented upon as the official administration argument against the amendment. In arguing against the first section of the amendment he focused this attack on the power given each branch of the federal government and the ways in which it would lead to an end of any true independence for the states. "Letter of Secretary Browning to Col. Benessen and Major Sullivan of Quincy, Illinois," printed in The Cincinnati Commercial, Oct. 26, 1866, at 2, Cols. 4–6. Major excerpts of the letter appear in Nowak, supra note 11, at 1457, 1462.

26. For an analysis of this rejection of older concepts of federalism in regard to specific issue see Nowak, The Scope of Congressional Power to Create Causes of Action against State Governments and the History of the Eleventh and Fourteenth Amendments, 75 Colum.L.Rev. 1413 (1975).

27. The provisional governments of southern states which refused to ratify were replaced with one that did ratify the Amendment. In Oregon the ratification passed narrowly and a later Democratic controlled Oregon legislature claimed the ratification was illegal. See, J. James, The Framing of the Fourteenth Amendment, at 192–3 (1965).

28. Seward "proclaimed" the Amendment twice, 15 Stat. 706 (July 20, 1868), 15 Stat. 708 (July 28, 1868). In between each house of Congress passed an acceptance resolution, Congressional Globe, 40th Cong., 1st Sess. at 4266 (Senate) 4295–96 (House) (1868).

29. Coleman v. Miller, 307 U.S. 433 (1939); Corwin & Ramsey, The Constitutional Law of Constitutional Amendment, 26 N.D. Lawyer 187 (1951); as to the amendment process generally see Chapter 2, Section IV, E, 2, b.

sary to ratification since a number of "union" states rejected the amendment.[30]

Although the fifteenth amendment did not in fact secure equal political rights for blacks, it accomplished two goals of importance for the future. First, at a later, more tranquil time the Supreme Court had a basis, more specific than the fourteenth amendment, for invalidating voting systems which discriminated against black citizens.[31] Second, the grant of power to Congress would one day be used to dramatically increase the political power of members of racial minorities.[32] Sadly, the changes did not take place until the next century; political equality in any meaningful form has been a recent development.

In closing this section we should note that the Congress realized that the passage of the amendments alone would not secure equality for blacks or stop the atrocities committed against them. As news of lynchings and other violent acts against blacks reached Washington, northern congressmen sought legislation to stop these practices. This resulted in the Civil Rights Act of 1871 which was known at the time as the "Ku Klux Klan Act."[33] The Act was designed to civilly and criminally punish those who acted to deprive others of their civil rights. The total Act granted sweeping presidential powers to use the armed forces to enforce its provisions and even to suspend the right to habeas corpus when necessary to restore order to areas dominated by violent organizations. Although these provisions were the focus of most of the debate in Congress, the most important section was to be the civil penalty provision. Now usually referred to as simply "section 1983",[34] it provides the cause of action and general basis for federal courts to protect individual civil rights.[35]

We now turn back to a legal history of the constitutional decisions concerning racial discrimination. These sections deal with the impact of the fourteenth amendment equal protection clause and the fifth amendment due process clause. The thirteenth and fifteenth amendment have been the subject of only limited rulings and their primary impact has been in connection with federal legislation. They will be examined in connection with the congressional power to enforce the Civil War Amendments.[36]

D. Classifications Based on Race or National Origin Following the Civil War

1. Introduction

The problem of racial classification is most easily analyzed as an equal protection issue. The fourteenth amendment prohibits states from denying any person the "equal protection of the laws."[1] Whenever any governmental entity classifies persons by their race for dispensation of benefits or burdens it probably has violated the equal protection clause, which requires that similar persons be dealt with in a similar manner.[2] Therefore, it must be determined when, if ever, the government may rule that a person is "dissimilar" from others for the purpose of a law because of that person's race. The Supreme Court has considered race and national origin classifications together for they

---

30. See D. Bell, Race, Racism and American Law at 119–127 (1st ed. 1973) and sources cited therein, see generally D. Bell, supra note 1.

31. See Smith v. Allwright, 321 U.S. 649 (1944); Terry v. Adams, 345 U.S. 461 (1953).

32. South Carolina v. Katzenbach, 383 U.S. 301 (1965) (upholding Voting Rights Act of 1965). For an examination of Congressional power see Chapter 17.

33. Act of April 20; 17 Stat. 13 (1871).

34. 42 U.S.C.A. § 1983 (From Act April 20, c. 22, § 1, 17 Stat. 13 (1871): "Every person who, under color of any statute, ordinance, regulation, custom, or usage, of any State or Territory, subjects, or causes to be sub-

jected, any citizen of the United States or other person within the jurisdiction thereof to the deprivation of any rights, privileges or immunities secured by the Constitution and laws, shall be liable to the party injured in an action at law, suit in equity, or other proper proceeding for redress."

35. For an analysis of the statute as it relates to grant of federal jurisdiction over state governments see Nowak, supra note 26, at 1464–68.

36. See Chapter 17.

1. U.S.Const. amend. XIV.

2. For an overview of basic equal protection-classification analysis see Section I, B of Chapter 16.

both involve the government's treatment of persons on the basis of their ethnic ancestry rather than individual actions. Classifications based on alienage—the status of not being a citizen—relate to the personal attributes of citizenship rather than ancestry alone and they are dealt with in a separate section.[3]

Today classifications based on race or national origin are "suspect;" courts will make an independent inquiry to determine whether they should be stricken as "invidious" discrimination.[4] Such classifications are permissible only if they are necessary to promote a compelling or overriding interest of government. This conclusion requires a judicial finding that the use of the classification is so important as to outweigh the central purpose of the amendment. But this present position of the Court was not easily arrived at: the Court went through a long period of allowing the use of racial classifications, especially for segregating public facilities. The sections which immediately follow deal with the development of standards for the permissibility of explicit classifications based on race or national origin which are used by any branch of the government, including both state and federal governments. Although the federal government is not subject to the fourteenth amendment, the due process clause of the fifth amendment has been interpreted to encompass an equal protection guarantee.[5]

The thirteenth amendment has not served as a significant prohibition of racial discrimination absent congressional action. The amendment prohibits "slavery" or "involuntary servitude" throughout the United States or any territory under its jurisdiction. The Supreme Court acknowledged shortly after the ratification of the amendment that it prohibited systems of peonage as well as the type of slavery that existed prior to the Civil War.[6] However, only a few years later the Court found that racial discrimination by private persons did not violate the amendment because it did not involve imposition of the incidents of slavery upon those against whom the discriminatory actions were taken nor did it involve a slavery or peonage system.[7] By ruling that "mere discriminations on account of race or color were not regarded as badges of slavery,"[8] the Court restricted the application of section one of the thirteenth amendment to a prohibition of peonage or slavery. However, in the next century the Supreme Court would rule that Congress has the power under section two of the amendment to outlaw by statute almost any form of racial discrimination even though section one of the amendment did not in itself outlaw such discrimination.[9]

The Court has enforced the thirteenth amendment's prohibition of slavery or peonage.[10] A state may force individuals to perform duties traditionally demanded of citizens by government such as military service, jury duty, or work during imprisonment.[11] Similarly, the state may enforce labor con-

---

3. See Section III of Chapter 16.

4. For an overview of classification analysis see Section I of Chapter 16.

5. Bolling v. Sharpe, 347 U.S. 497 (1954); Weinberger v. Wiesenfeld, 420 U.S. 636, 638 n. 2 (1975); Schlesinger v. Ballard, 419 U.S. 498, 500 n. 3 (1975).

6. Slaughter-House Cases, 83 U.S. (16 Wall.) 36 (1873).

7. Civil Rights Cases, 109 U.S. 3, 20–25 (1883).

8. Id. at 25.

9. Jones v. Alfred H. Mayer Co., 392 U.S. 409 (1968); Runyon v. McCrary, 427 U.S. 160 (1976). The power of Congress to expand the scope of the thirteenth amendment is examined in Chapter 17, Section III.

10. For a most thorough and insightful analysis of the Court's peonage decisions at a pivotal historical period in the development of legal protection for racial minorities see Schmidt, Principle and Prejudice: The Supreme Court and Race in the Progressive Era, Part 2: The Peonage Cases, 82 Columbia L.Rev. 646 (1982).

11. See Butler v. Perry, 240 U.S. 328 (1916), in which the Supreme Court stated:

"[The Thirteenth Amendment] certainly was not intended to interdict enforcement of those duties which individuals owe to the State, such as services to the army, militia, on the jury, etc." 240 U.S. at 333.

In *Butler* the Court upheld a state statute requiring able-bodied males between 21 and 45 years of age to work on public roads for a certain time. A State "has

tracts [12] but it may not compel a person to work for another to repay a debt or place a person into forced labor or prison for failure to pay a debt.[13]

In a previous section of this chapter we dealt with the problem of determining when a law which appears neutral on its face might be found in fact to be a racial classification due to its necessary statistical impact.[14] In a separate chapter we examine the problem of determining when the actions of seemingly private persons may be found to have sufficient "state action" to subject them to constitutional limitations such as the equal protection guarantee.[15]

2. The First Cases—Institutional Uncertainty

Shortly after the ratification of the fourteenth amendment, the Court decided *Strauder v. West Virginia*.[16] In this case, the justices invalidated a state statute excluding blacks from juries because it violated the equal protection clause. A West Virginia statute provided that only white male citizens were eligible to serve on juries and the Court had to consider whether the defendant, a black citizen, had the right to trial by a jury selected without discrimination against persons of his race or color. As the Court specifically noted, the question was not whether he had the right to have persons of his own race serve on the jury but, rather, whether the law might exclude all blacks solely because of their race or color. With two dissents the Court held this to be a violation of the amendment which justified the removal of the case to federal court.[17] In reaching this result, the majority opinion examined the conditions which had led to the passage of the fourteenth amendment. The opinion described the fourteenth amendment as one of a series of constitutional provisions with a common purpose, namely, securing to blacks "all the civil rights that the superior race may enjoy." Federal protection was necessary because it was recognized that the states might attempt to perpetuate the distinctions between the races. In the opinion of the majority, blacks as a race were unprepared or unable to take an equal place in post Civil War society. Thus they were in need of federal protection and, accordingly, the fourteenth amendment was adopted.[18]

The opinion next discussed the meaning and the effect of the amendment. The

---

inherent power to require every able-bodied man within its jurisdiction to labor for a reasonable time on public roads near his residence without direct compensation." 240 U.S. at 330. The military draft laws in effect requiring labor by soldiers and conscientious objectors have also been upheld. Arver v. United States, 245 U.S. 366, 390 (1918).

12. See International Union v. Wisconsin Employment Relations Bd., 336 U.S. 245 (1949) (injunctions issued in labor disputes preventing interference with business activity do not violate the thirteenth amendment). See also Robertson v. Baldwin, 165 U.S. 275, (1897) (labor contract of seamen enforced). The *Robertson* case may be of little precedential value as it is based on nineteenth century social and legal views of the unique obligation of sailors to their employer. 165 U.S. at 282–3.

13. "The state may impose involuntary servitude as a punishment for crime, but it may not compel one man to labor for another in payment of a debt, by punishing him as a criminal if he does not perform the service or pay the debt." Bailey v. Alabama, 219 U.S. 219, 244 (1911). Similarly, the state may not "indirectly" reach this result "by creating a statutory presumption which upon proof of no other fact [than failure or refusal to serve without paying his debt] exposes him to conviction and punishment." Id. at 244.

N.R. & Y. Const.Law 2nd Ed. HB—15

See also, United States v. Reynolds, 235 U.S. 133 (1914) (holding invalid a state law system allowing a "surety" to collect his debt for payment of a debtor's fine in the form of court approved labor); Taylor v. Georgia, 315 U.S. 25 (1942) (holding invalid a statute which in effect established a presumption that a defendant committed a criminal fraud by non-payment of a debt); Pollock v. Williams, 322 U.S. 4 (1944) (same). For an excellent historical analysis of these decisions see Schmidt, supra note 10.

A few lower courts enforced the thirteenth amendment prohibition even before these Supreme Court decisions. See Peonage Cases, 123 F. 671 (M.D.Ala.1903). The federal "Anti-Peonage Act" was enacted in 1864 and is codified in 42 U.S.C.A. § 1994.

14. See Section I, D of Chapter 16.

15. See Chapter 14 on State Action.

16. 100 U.S. 303 (1879).

17. Justices Clifford and Field dissented without opinion. Congressional power to enforce the amendment is discussed in Chapter 17. The jurisdictional basis for "removal" of state cases to a federal court is examined in Chapter 2.

18. 100 U.S. at 306.

Court found that laws must be the same for all persons, black or white, and prohibited discrimination against blacks because of their color. The prohibitory language of the amendment contained a necessary implication of a right for blacks—the right to be exempt from unfriendly legislation, to be exempt from legal discriminations, "implying inferiority in civil society, lessening the security of their enjoyment of the rights which others enjoy," and "which are a step toward reducing them to the condition of a subject race." [19] The majority found the exclusion from juries to be a proscribed discrimination because it expressly denied blacks the right to serve as jurors because of their color. However, the Court would not strike down a conviction where a black defendant had been tried before an all white jury if blacks were not excluded from jury service. [20]

The next major decision involved statutes proscribing interracial marriages or providing stricter punishment for fornication or adultery when the partners were of different races. Such statutes had become numerous in this country [21] in *Pace v. Alabama*, [22] the Court upheld an Alabama statute which provided for more severe penalties for adultery and fornication if the couple were composed of a white and a black than if the two members were of the same race. If both partners were of the same race, the punishment for the first such offense was a fine of not less than $100 and a possible sentence of not more than six months imprisonment. On the other hand, the penalty for adultery, fornication, or marriage where one partner was white and other black was a sentence of not less than two years imprisonment. The statute was upheld because, in the unanimous view of the justices, it applied to both races equally. If both partners were of the same race, whether white or black, one penalty was imposed. If the partners were of different races, the same sentence applied to both. Any discrimination was not between races but between offenses. While the marriage portion of the statute was not relevant to the *Pace* case, the Court there seemed to approve that provision. The Court did not directly rule on interracial marriage prohibitions until 1967, when it invalidated all such laws. [23] Until that time *Pace* stood as authority for such laws, although *Pace* and its reasoning had been explicitly overruled earlier in *McLaughlin v. Florida*. [24]

In 1883, the Court struck down certain federal civil rights legislation as beyond the power granted Congress by the Civil War Amendments. In the *Civil Rights Cases* [25] the Court held that Congress could not impose sanctions against private persons for interfering with the civil liberties of others. In the opinion of a majority of the justices, the thirteenth amendment prohibited only the direct badges or incidents of slavery and could not be used to remedy private discrimination. The fourteenth amendment, in their opinion, could only be violated by "state action" and not by the acts of private individuals. The majority limited congressional power to remedy that which the Justices felt would violate the amendments and thus struck down the legislation. Justice Harlan dissented because he saw these amendments as granting a full panoply of civil liberties to blacks and empowering Congress to fully

19.   100 U.S. at 307–08.

20.   Virginia v. Rives, 100 U.S. 313 (1879).

21.   D. Bell, Race, Racism and American Law, chapter 2 (2 ed. 1980); Applebaum, Miscegenation Statutes: A Constitutional and Social Problem, 53 Georgetown L.J. 49 (1964).

22.   106 U.S. 583 (1882).

23.   Loving v. Virginia, 388 U.S. 1 (1967).

24.   379 U.S. 184, 189–90 (1964). The Court, however, did not reach the question of the constitutionality of laws against interracial marriage. 379 U.S. at 195. See text at notes 96 & 97 infra.

It is interesting, if sad, to note that the Supreme Court refused to adjudicate and denied certiorari to a miscegenation case shortly after its decision in Brown v. Board of Education (discussed infra). Jackson v. State, 37 Ala.App. 519, 72 So.2d 114, cert. denied sub nom.; Jackson v. Alabama, 348 U.S. 888 (1954). See also, Naim v. Naim, 350 U.S. 891 (1955), and Naim v. Naim, 350 U.S. 985 (1956) (denial of appeal from Supreme Court of Virginia, affirming annulment of marriage as violating Virginia's miscegenation statute), discussed in H. Hart & H. Wechsler, The Federal Courts and the Federal System 660–62 (2d ed. 1973).

25.   109 U.S. 3 (1883).

protect their rights.[26] The decision is discussed in greater detail in the section on state action,[27] but it should be noted here as evidencing the tendency of the Court during this period to refrain from fully protecting the rights of black citizens.

In 1886 the Supreme Court again announced a prohibition of explicit racial discrimination. In *Yick Wo v. Hopkins*,[28] the Court held that an ordinance could not be enforced where its application was designed to burden one race. A San Francisco ordinance prohibited the operation of laundries in wooden buildings without the consent of a board of supervisors. The defendant and all other Chinese persons had been denied permission to operate such laundries, while all non-Chinese persons operating laundries in wooden buildings were given permission to do so. This application of the law was found to constitute explicit racial discrimination which violated the fourteenth amendment.[29] The Court found that these facts established "an administration directed so exclusively against a particular class of persons as to warrant and require the conclusion, that, whatever may have been the intent of the ordinances as adopted, they are applied * * * with a mind so unequal and oppressive as to amount to a practical denial by the State of [equal protection]."[30] No reason for the discrimination could be shown other than hostility against the Chinese. Therefore, the ordinance could not be enforced.

3. 1896–1954: The "Separate but Equal" Doctrine and Its Limitation

During the period from 1896 to 1954 there existed a concept known as "separate but equal." Under this "principle," persons of minority races could be given separate services or treatment so long as it was equal to that provided for whites. Of course this amounted to no more than the Court giving racial discrimination a constitutional imprimatur. Although the concept has been totally rejected since 1954, these rulings are still important. It is only against the background of these decisions that one can understand the basis for recent decisions and the degree to which the Supreme Court as an institution has helped, or failed to help, establish the rights of racial minorities.

The separate but equal concept made its first appearance in a pre-Civil War decision of the Massachusetts Supreme Court. In *Roberts v. City of Boston*,[31] suit was brought on behalf of a black child who was denied admission to the elementary school nearest her home because it was an all-white school. The applicable statutes did not mention race or color restrictions, providing simply that each child was to attend the school nearest to his or her residence unless special provisions were made. Nevertheless, the Massachusetts court held that she could be required to attend a school established for blacks although it was further from her home because it was in all other respects "equal". That court noted that there was no tradition of local schools in Boston and that a child's education would not be hurt by having to travel across Boston to go to school. It was more than a century before this position was rejected.[32]

The Supreme Court of the United States skirted the separate but equal issue until 1896 [33] when the Court adopted the doctrine

---

26. 109 U.S. 3, 26 (1883) (Harlan, J., dissenting).

27. See Chapter 14, Section I.

28. 118 U.S. 356 (1886).

29. The problems of proving racially biased application of laws or racially disproportionate impact is discussed in Section I, D of Chapter 16.

30. 118 U.S. at 373.

31. 59 Mass. (5 Cush.) 198 (1850).

32. The same arguments accepted by the Massachusetts court were rejected in Brown v. Board of Education, 347 U.S. 483 (1954). It is ironic that one of the greatest public controversies in recent years over the implementation of *Brown* is whether a federal court should be allowed to alter student attendance in Boston schools to remedy racial segregation.

33. Questions of "separate but equal" accommodations had risen in earlier cases in other contexts. Congress agreed to allow a railroad to pass through the District of Columbia, but required that "no person shall be excluded from the cars on account of color." The Court, construing this statute in Railroad Co. v. Brown, 84 U.S. (16 Wall.) 445 (1873), ruled that it meant that blacks must be permitted to travel on the

in *Plessy v. Ferguson*.[34] A Louisiana statute required that all railway companies provide "equal but separate accommodations" for black and white passengers, imposing criminal penalties for violations by railway officials. Plessy, who alleged his ancestry was seven-eighths Caucasian and one-eighth African, attempted to use the coach for whites. The Louisiana Supreme Court denied his request for a writ of prohibition against the judge who was to try him for a violation of the statute. The Supreme Court of the United States affirmed the denial of the writ and held that the statute was not violative of fourteenth amendment.

The majority in *Plessy* summarily dismissed any thirteenth amendment claim. The opinion simply held that the amendment was meant to insure only the basic legal equality of blacks as was necessary to the abolition of involuntary servitude. The majority at this time refused to add any judicial restrictions on classification by race under that amendment.

The fourteenth amendment's equal protection clause did not present much more of a barrier to such practices. The majority of the justices fully adopted the separate but equal doctrine: "The object of the amendment was undoubtedly to enforce the absolute equality of the two races before the law, but in the nature of things, it could not have been intended to abolish distinctions based upon color, or to enforce social, as distinguished from political equality, or a commingling of the two races upon terms unsatisfactory to either."[35] Laws requiring racial

separation, according to the Court, did not necessarily imply the inferiority of either race and had been recognized to be within the police power of a state. The Court then referred to the custom of separate schools and the Massachusetts decision in *Roberts*.

The Court went on to define the nature of the power to afford black persons separate but equal treatment. The majority held that persons could be legally classified and treated in such a manner because of their race when the classifying law was a reasonable exercise of the police power. This meant that such laws must be reasonable, good faith attempts to promote the public good and not be designed to oppress a particular class.

The question in any particular case, according to the *Plessy* majority, was whether the statute was reasonable. The Court recognized the great discretion in the legislature. In determining reasonableness, the legislature might look to established usages, customs, and traditions of the people and act with a view to the promotion of their comfort and the preservation of public peace and good order. Under the reasonableness standard, the majority refused to say that a statutory authorization or requirement of separate accommodations was unreasonable or obnoxious to the fourteenth amendment. The majority found both that the enforced separation of the races did not mark the black race with a badge of inferiority and that social prejudice could not be overcome by law. The opinion stated that "if the two races are to meet upon terms of social equal-

---

same cars with whites; the requirement was not satisfied by the provision of separate cars for blacks, even upon a showing that the cars were equal to the cars provided whites and the cars sometimes were used exclusively for whites.

The constitutionality of statutes requiring separate but equal accommodations had also risen in two cases prior to *Plessy*, but in a very different context—the provisions were challenged by the railroads as being a burden on interstate commerce. In Hall v. DeCuir, 95 U.S. 485 (1877) the Court invalidated the statutory requirement, stating that although the requirement was applicable only within the state, the train would be required to carry extra cars and therefore would be affected outside the state as well, and thus create a di-

rect burden on interstate commerce. In Louisville, New Orleans, and Texas Ry. Co. v. Mississippi, 133 U.S. 587 (1890), the Court upheld a similar statute finding it was applicable only to intrastate commerce and therefore imposed no direct burden upon interstate commerce.

34. 163 U.S. 537 (1896). For an excellent in depth examination of the philosophy of Justice Brown, who wrote the opinion, and the social theories which might have given rise to this opinion, see, Glennon, Justice Henry Billings Brown: Values in Tension, 44 U.Colo.L. Rev. 553 (1973).

35. 163 U.S. at 543–44.

ity, it must be the result of natural affinitives, a mutual appreciation of each other's methods and a voluntary consent of individuals." [36]

Only Justice Harlan dissented in *Plessy*. [37] He viewed the Civil War Amendments as together removing "the race line from our governmental systems." [38] In the opinion of the Justice, the Constitution was now "colorblind" [39] so that government could not use a person's color to determine his rights. It should be noted that Justice Harlan was speaking to a system that he saw as designed to protect "a dominant race—a superior class of citizens", [40] while imposing a "badge of servitude" [41] on others. Thus it is not certain how the Justice would have enforced his color-blind principle in a case involving affirmative government action to aid members of minority races. [42] However, the Justice was an accurate prophet when he viewed the *Plessy* separate but equal doctrine as one which "will, in time prove to be quite as pernicious as the decision made by this tribunal in the Dred Scott Case." [43]

Although the separate but equal doctrine in *Plessy* applied only to accommodations on public conveyances, it was used to uphold widespread segregation in public schools and other state institutions and statutory requirements of segregation in privately-owned business. The Court did not fully reconsider the validity of the separate but equal doctrine again until 1954. Prior to that time, the Supreme Court decided a number of issues within the framework of that doctrine, many of them in the context of education.

In *Cumming v. Board of Education* [44] the Court did not seriously attempt to enforce the "equal" requirement of the separate but equal doctrine. In this case, a local school board was allowed to close down the black high school for "purely economic reasons" and convert the school to a primary school for a larger number of black children. The Court, per Justice Harlan, considered only the question whether the white high school should be closed until equal provisions were made for blacks. The Court decided that such an action would only deprive whites of education without providing anything for blacks, and therefore, upheld the action.

The Court continued to uphold statutes requiring segregation of blacks by private enterprises. Thus, in *Berea College v. Kentucky*, [45] the Supreme Court upheld a fine imposed by Kentucky upon a private college because white and black students were taught together. The act under which the school had been incorporated reserved to the legislature the right to repeal any charter or alter it in any way which did not substantially impair the object of the grant. In the opinion of the Court, the requirement that members of different races be taught at different times or in different places did not impair the object of educating those attending the college and, accordingly, was valid. In *McCabe v. Atchison, T. & S. F. Ry. Co.* [46] the Court upheld a statute that required "separate but equal accommodations" on trains. However, the opinion indicated that a company which provided a dining car for whites also had to provide a dining car for blacks even if there was not a sufficient volume of black traffic to support the cost of a separate dining room.

The justices were willing to strike segregation laws when they could not accept the separation as incident to a valid police power

---

36. 163 U.S. at 551.

37. Plessy v. Ferguson, 163 U.S. 537, 552 (Harlan, J. dissenting). Justice Brewer did not participate in the decision.

38. 163 U.S. at 555.

39. 163 U.S. at 559.

40. 163 U.S. at 560.

41. 163 U.S. at 562.

42. The "affirmative action" issue is discussed in Section II, F of this chapter.

43. 163 U.S. at 559 (Harlan, J. dissenting).

44. 175 U.S. 528 (1899).

45. 211 U.S. 45 (1908).

46. 235 U.S. 151 (1914).

end. Accordingly, the Court in *Buchanan v. Warley* [47] unanimously struck down a law entitled "An ordinance to prevent conflict and ill-feeling between the white and colored races in the city of Louisville, and to preserve the public peace and promote the general welfare, by making reasonable provisions, requiring, as far as practicable, the use of separate blocks, for residences, and places of assembly by white and colored people respectively." The ordinance prohibited a black from moving into a neighborhood which was predominantly white at the time the ordinance was passed and vice versa. The ordinance was held invalid under the due process clause of the fourteenth amendment because it arbitrarily eliminated the right to acquire, use, and dispose of property. The Court distinguished this case from *Plessy* and *Berea* because in those cases blacks were not deprived of transportation or education; they were merely required to conform to "reasonable rules" concerning the separation of races. In this case, however, the statute effectively deprived persons of the right to acquire land in a neighborhood predominated by members of the other race or to dispose of their property to a member of the race which was not predominant. It always has appeared to the authors of this treatise that *Buchanan* can only be explained by the desire of Supreme Court justices during this era to protect property rights, given that fact that these justices did not otherwise strive to promote the goals of racial equality or desegregation. However, as Professor Benno Schmidt's masterful study of the Court's decisions during this era concluded, decisions such as *Buchanan* provided the foundation for the equal protection decisions which came later in this century. [48]

In *Gong Lum v. Rice* [49] the separate but equal doctrine was also implicitly accepted in the context of public education. Suit was brought on behalf of an American citizen child of Chinese ancestry who was denied admission to a school established for whites in Mississippi. The Court found the only issue to be whether a Chinese child was denied equal protection when she was classified as "colored" and, therefore, only entitled to attend the school for nonwhites. The Court referred to other state and federal cases upholding segregation and then stated that although the cases referred only to whites and blacks, "we cannot think that the question is any different, or that any different result can be reached, assuming the cases cited to be rightly decided, where the issue is as between white pupils and the pupils of the yellow race." [50] Therefore, the Court unanimously found there was no violation of the fourteenth amendment.

Following 1930, there was a series of cases in which the Court, without re-examining the separate but equal doctrine, found that the black plaintiffs were entitled to relief because they had not in fact been offered "equal" educational opportunities. In the first of these cases, *Missouri ex rel. Gaines v. Canada,* [51] an admittedly qualified black applicant to the state law school was denied entrance solely because of his color. Because there was no law school for blacks in Missouri, the state sought to fulfill its obligation to provide blacks an education that was "substantially equal" to the education provided whites by paying plaintiff's tuition at a comparable out-of-state school that did admit blacks. The Court, however, found that this procedure did not satisfy the state's duty—the question was not whether the legal education a black could receive at the out-of-state school was equal to the legal

---

47. 245 U.S. 60 (1917).

48. Schmidt, Principle and Prejudice: The Supreme Court and Race in the Progressive Era, Part 1: the Hayday of Jim Crow, 82 Columbia L.Rev. 444 (1982); Schmidt, Principle and Prejudice: The Supreme Court and Race in the Progressive Era, Part 2: The Peonage Cases, 82 Columbia L.Rev. 646 (1982); Schmidt, Principle and Prejudice: The Supreme Court and Race in the

Progressive Era, Part 3: Black Disfranchisement from the KKK to the Grandfather Clause, 82 Columbia L.Rev. 835 (1982).

49. 275 U.S. 78 (1927).

50. 275 U.S. at 87.

51. 305 U.S. 337 (1938).

education received at the Missouri school, but what opportunities Missouri provided for whites, but not blacks, solely on the basis of color.

In subsequent cases, the Court began to examine intangible as well as tangible factors in determining if the educational opportunities offered to blacks were equal. In *Sweatt v. Painter*, [52] the petitioner again was a black who was seeking admission to a law school and who was turned down solely on the basis of race. The trial court recognized that this situation was a denial of equal protection, but instead of ordering the school to admit petitioner, it continued the case to allow the state to supply substantially equal facilities. A school for blacks was established while petitioner's appeal was pending and as a result the case was remanded. The trial court found the new school for blacks was "substantially equivalent", and petitioner, therefore, was not entitled to be admitted to the law school for whites. This decision was reversed by the Supreme Court. The Court expressly reserved the question of the validity of the separate but equal doctrine, holding that the newly established law school was not substantially equal. The white law school had a better faculty, a better offering of courses, a better library, and a wider range of activities than the law school established for blacks. Furthermore, the white school possessed those qualities which are immeasurable but make a superior law school, e.g., reputation of the faculty, position and influence of alumni.

In *McLaurin v. Oklahoma State Regents for Higher Education*, [53] decided the same day, a different facet of the question was presented—whether a state after admitting a black graduate student to its university might afford him different treatment because of his race. McLaurin had been admitted to a previously all-white school after a court ruling at an earlier stage of the litigation. However, he was admitted upon a

specially segregated basis. He was required to sit at a desk in a classroom anteroom behind a railing with a sign "for colored's only", to sit at a designated desk on the mezzanine floor of the library and to eat at a different time and at a specified table in the cafeteria. During the course of litigation, the requirements were changed so that he was allowed a seat in the classroom but in a special row for black students, was assigned a desk on the main floor of the library, and was allowed to eat at the same time as the white students but still at a specified table. The Court held that such state-approved restrictions based on race produced inequality in educational opportunities that violated even the separate but equal test. The restrictions impaired and inhibited "his ability to study, to engage in discussions, and exchange views with other students, and in general, to learn his profession." [54] As in *Sweatt*, the Court relied on intangible factors in making its determination that blacks were not being offered equal educational opportunities. The Court agreed that McLaurin might still have been set apart in the absence of state-approved restrictions but held that to be immaterial. There was a vast difference—a constitutional difference—between a state-imposed prohibition of the intellectual commingling of students and the voluntary refusal of individuals to commingle socially.

4. The Modern Position on Racial Restrictions

a. The World War II Japanese "Restriction" Cases—A turning Point for "Suspect Classifications"

Out of a fear of espionage by Japanese persons in the United States or an invasion by Japanese military, severe restrictions were placed on the rights of persons of Japanese ancestry during World War II. In our Western states Japanese persons, whether aliens or citizens, were subject to detention

52. 339 U.S. 629 (1950).

53. 339 U.S. 637 (1950).

54. 339 U.S. at 641.

in guarded camps whether or not they were as individuals at all likely to engage in disloyal acts. These actions were taken with the unanimous concurrence of the various branches of government. As a security measure, President Roosevelt issued an executive order authorizing military commanders to exclude persons from vast areas.[55] Congress then made it a federal crime to violate military orders made pursuant to this authority.[56] Beginning in March 1942 an appropriate army general issued a series of such orders for "Military Area No. 1"—the Pacific coast states. These included a curfew which kept Japanese persons in their residences all night and required the movement of Japanese persons from certain areas to inland "relocation centers". In a series of three cases in 1943 and 1944, the Supreme Court upheld the curfew and the temporary relocation and temporary detention practices, while invalidating the indefinite detention of admittedly loyal persons as beyond the scope of the executive order.

It is obvious that the result in these cases does not represent a favorable "turning point" in the treatment of persons by their race or national origin. However, in the course of these opinions a majority of the justices indicated that such restrictions were contrary to the basic purpose of the Civil War Amendments and constitutionally disfavored even when employed by the federal government. Only the majority's belief in the need of the executive to have a wide scope of powers during wartime resulted in the actions being upheld. When combined with the position of the dissenters, the opinion indicated that the justices were ready to revise the constitutional doctrines concerning the permissibility of racial restrictions. This change in judicial perspective could be seen in the stricter application of the last separate but equal cases that we have examined. Indeed, these cases stand today as the last decisions upholding classifications burdening minority races and the only such cases which have not been at least implicitly overruled.[57]

Two of the opinions are of little importance beyond the impact of the result reached in the individual cases. In *Hirubayashi v. United States* [58] the Court upheld the 8 p.m. to 6 a.m. curfew requirement as within the discretion granted the executive to wage war. In *Ex parte Endo* [59] the Court held that President Roosevelt's executive order did not authorize the continued detention of Japanese persons following an initial evacuation and determination of their loyalty. This opinion did indicate that the justices would have stricken such an order as being beyond any reasonable exercise of war powers, but the decision was based on the president's order.

The decision in the third case, *Korematsu v. United States*, [60] was the start of a revolution in constitutional analysis of equal protection issues. In this case the Court upheld, by a 6 to 3 vote, the temporary exclusion and detention of persons of Japanese ancestry. The opinion gave great deference to the combined war powers of the president and Congress as these detentions far exceeded anything necessary to protect the country.[61] The dissenting justices would not

---

55. Executive Order 9066; 7 Fed.Reg. 1407 (Feb. 19, 1942).

56. Public Law 77–503; 56 Stat. 173 (Act of March 21, 1942).

57. This has led at least one author to conclude that classifications burdening minority races should actually be termed "prohibited" in order to clarify equal protection theory. Nowak, Realigning the Standards of Review Under the Equal Protection Guarantee—Prohibited, Neutral and Permissive Classifications, 62 Geo. L.J. 1071 (1974).

The Court has summarily approved the keeping of government records which included racial information

kept to further race-neutral goals. See Hamm v. Virginia State Bd. of Elections, 230 F.Supp. 156 (E.D.Va. 1964) aff'd per curiam sub nom. Tancil v. Woolls, 379 U.S. 19 (1964) (invalidating the keeping of separate lists of voters and taxpayers by race but permitting the state to require that the race of a husband and wife be identified in a divorce decree).

58. 320 U.S. 81 (1943).

59. 323 U.S. 283 (1944).

60. 323 U.S. 214 (1944).

61. For an examination of the War Power see Chapter 6, Section III.

have tolerated any but the most necessary restrictions to promote the war effort. Indeed, the three dissenting opinions remain as classic statements against the false security which results from using war powers to burden minorities.[62] The majority opinion agreed with the dissent as to the general unconstitutionality of imposing burdens on a person because of his race but these justices felt that the needs of the nation, as perceived at the start of the war, justified these measures.

The majority opinion by Justice Black established the basis for a new constitutional standard of review of race classifications:

> It should be noted, to begin with, that all legal restrictions which curtail the civil rights of a single racial group are immediately suspect. That is not to say that all such restrictions are unconstitutional. It is to say that courts must subject them to the most rigid scrutiny. Pressing public necessity may sometimes justify the existence of such restrictions; racial antagonism never can.[63]

This opinion thus established three points for future analysis of classifications based on race or national origin. First, these classifications were "suspect" which meant, at a minimum, that they were likely to be based on an impermissible purpose. Second, these classifications were to be subject to independent judicial review—"rigid scrutiny."[64] Third, the classification would be invalid if based on racial antagonism and upheld only if they were based on "public necessity."[65]

From this opinion came the concepts of "strict judicial scrutiny" and the requirement that some restrictions on liberty must be necessary to promote "compelling" or "overriding" interests.[66]

b. *The Rejection of Separate but Equal and Establishment of Racial Equality as a Constitutional Principle*

The final period of Court rulings concerning racial discrimination can be rather confusing unless one has some appreciation of the current position of the Court. As we have seen, by the late 1940's the justices had deemed classification based on race or national origin to be suspect and subject to strict review under the equal protection guarantee. In the early 1950's the Court ended the concept of separate but equal, although this doctrine was not finally eradicated until a series of summary rulings had stricken down every manner of state enforced segregation. During this period the Court also held that the due process clause of the fifth amendment would be violated whenever the federal government used invidious classifications. Thus, the federal government was subjected to an equal protection guarantee even though the equal protection clause of the fourteenth amendment could only apply to the states.[67] In the 1960's the Court at last began to enforce the concept of racial equality by striking down government actions which burdened mem-

62. 323 U.S. at 225–33 (Roberts, J., dissenting); 323 U.S. at 233–42 (Murphy, J., dissenting); 323 U.S. at 242–8 (Jackson, J., dissenting).

63. Korematsu v. United States, 323 U.S. 214, 216 (1944).

64. There continues to be some debate over Justice Black's personal intentions when he used the word "suspect." See, Brest, Foreword: In Defense of the Antidiscrimination Principle, 90 Harv.L.Rev. 1, 7 n. 35 (1976).

While Justice Black may have meant to advance only an initial theory of independent judicial review, the continual invalidation of statutes under this standard has led Professor Gunther to aptly describe it as "strict in theory and fatal in fact." Gunther, Foreward: In Search of Evolving Doctrine on a Changing Court: A Model for a Newer Equal Protection, 86 Harv.L.Rev. 1, 8 (1972).

65. In fact no such "necessities" have been found, see note 57 supra. It may be possible for government agencies to use a racial classification in dealing with an emergency situation when separation of persons by race is demonstrably necessary to promote an end which the government is obligated to pursue—such as the protection of the lives of those persons in its custody. Thus, Justice Black was of the opinion that prison authorities could separate persons by race in order to stop an outbreak of disorder based on racial conflict in the prison. Lee v. Washington, 390 U.S. 333, 334 (1968) (Black, J., concurring).

66. For an overview of the different standards of review see Section V of Chapter 12, and Section I, C of this Chapter.

67. For a description of the relationship between the two clauses see Section I, A of Chapter 16.

bers of minority races in addition to those which required segregation of public facilities. By the end of the 1960's it was clear that the Court had finally accepted what seemed to be the correct original position: that the government could not classify persons by race to impose a burden on, or deny benefits to, members of minority races. Today we await word from the Court on the final classification question in this area— whether the government may have "affirmative action" programs which classify persons by race in order to grant some remedial preferences to members of minority races.[68]

It should be noted that the Supreme Court during this period dealt with racial issues which are analyzed in other sections of this text. First, while legal segregation was declared invalid in the 1950's, the problem of remedying official segregation, especially in schools, remains. This issue is the focus of the next section.[69] Second, during the 1960's the Supreme Court protected those persons publicly protesting racial discrimination by enforcing their first amendment rights in a variety of settings. These cases are primarily examined in the section on "public forums" in our Chapter on The Freedom of Speech.[70] Third, the Court has had to settle a variety of issues concerning seemingly private racial discrimination which might have some connection to government action. These problems are dealt with in our Chapter on State Action.[71] Fourth, the Court has resolved some specific issues concerning the thirteenth and fifteenth amendments. Since virtually all of these cases had to do with the application of federal laws prohibiting racial discrimination, they are dealt with in our section on congressional power to enforce the Civil War Amendments.[72] These cases are extremely important for the broad interpretation given these statutes has resulted in the statutory prohi-

bition of many forms of overt private racial discrimination.[73]

With this overview in mind, we can now turn to the period from 1954 to the present to examine the basic racial-equal protection issue: When may the government classify persons for different treatment because of their race or national origins. Not surprisingly, the cases begin with the first school desegregation decision.

In 1954, the Court in *Brown v. Board of Education* [74], for the first time since *Plessy*, fully examined the validity of the separate but equal doctrine. The Court did not expressly overrule *Plessy*, but held simply that the separate but equal doctrine had no place in education. *Brown* involved four consolidated cases focusing on the permissibility of local governments conducting school systems which segregated students by race. In each case blacks sought admission to public schools on a nonsegregated basis and in each the state court based its decision upon the separate but equal doctrine. The plaintiffs challenged the validity of the doctrine, arguing that segregated schools were not "equal" and could not be "equal."

The case was briefed and argued at two successive terms of Court. The reargument before the Supreme Court centered largely around the circumstances surrounding the adoption of the fourteenth amendment and the intentions of its framers. Because it was a constitutional amendment rather than a statute that the Court was interpreting, the search for the intent of the framers had two facets: whether the drafters contemplated that the amendment would immediately abolish segregation in public schools and, if not, whether the amendment was to embody a principle that would allow Congress or the judiciary to abolish segregation in the future.[75] The Court in *Brown* found

---

68. The arguments for and against such programs are discussed in Section II, F of this Chapter.

69. See Section II, E of this Chapter.

70. See Chapter 18.

71. See Chapter 14.

72. See Chapter 17.

73. See the discussion of these matters in Chapter 14 on State Action, Sections I, IV.

74. 347 U.S. 483 (1954).

75. Bickel, The Original Understanding and the Segregation Decision, 69 Harv.L.Rev. 1, 59 (1955).

that the legislative history was inconclusive at best.[76] The conflicting statements of the drafters gave little guidance as to the anticipated effect of the principles of equality on future generations. Indications that they did not expect segregation to end seemed to relate to their predictions of what in fact would happen in society and were clouded by the limited nature of public school systems. Thus the Court could honestly deem history inconclusive and interpret the principles of the amendment as they should apply to modern society.[77]

The Court in *Brown* next traced the development of the separate but equal doctrine. Cases decided shortly after the adoption of the amendment construed it as a prohibition of all state-imposed discrimination against blacks. In 1896, the separate but equal doctrine appeared in the Court in the field of transportation. American courts have since that time labored with the doctrine. As we have seen, the Court had grown increasingly uneasy about the doctrine. Because recent cases had found inequality in challenged practices, there had been no necessity to reexamine the doctrine in order to grant the requested relief.

Here the question was directly presented. The record showed that the schools were equalized or being equalized with respect to the buildings, curricula, qualifications and salaries of teachers, and other tangibles. The decision, therefore, could not turn on measurable inequalities; it was necessary to look to the effects of segregation itself. Having previously determined history to be inconclusive, the Court gave no more thought to the past but instead looked only to the present. The opinion noted that the Court could not "turn the clock back to 1868 when the amendment was adopted, or even

to 1896 when *Plessy v. Ferguson* was written."[78] It stated the question presented as: "Does segregation of children in public schools solely on the basis of race, even though the physical facilities and other 'tangible' factors may be equal, deprive the children of the minority group of equal educational opportunities?"[79] The justices unanimously found that it did and, in so doing, sounded the death knell for legally enforced segregation.

The Court, however, did not explicitly overrule *Plessy* or hold the separate but equal doctrine unconstitutional. Instead, it limited its holding to the conclusion "that in the field of public education the doctrine of 'separate but equal' has no place."[80] The opinion referred to the earlier recognition in *Sweatt* and *McLaurin* that intangibles played a considerable role in the value educational opportunities offered. Although all tangibles such as faculty, books, or buildings were "equal", a difference in "intangibles" such as separation would render a school unequal. To separate black children "from others of similar age and qualifications solely because of their race generates a feeling of inferiority as to their status in the community that may affect their hearts and minds in a way unlikely ever to be undone."[81] The Court stated that this finding was "amply supported by modern authority" and in a footnote cited findings of sociologists, anthropologists, psychologists, and psychiatrists who had done work in race relations.[82] The reliance on social science data and limited approach of the opinion were later subject to criticism.[83] The Court, however, evidently sought to reduce public hostility by presenting only a limited ruling supported by some factual evidence. The

---

76. 347 U.S. at 489.

77. Bickel, supra note 75 at 59–65.

78. Brown v. Board of Education, 347 U.S. 483, 492 (1954).

79. 347 U.S. at 493.

80. 247 U.S. at 495.

81. 347 U.S. at 494 (the Court here is quoting from lower court rulings).

82. 347 U.S. at 494 n. 11.

83. Compare, Wechsler, Toward Neutral Principles of Constitutional Law, 73 Harv.L.Rev. 1 (1959), with, Pollak, Racial Discrimination and Judicial Integrity: A Reply to Professor Wechsler, 108 U.Pa.L.Rev. 1 (1959) and Black, the Lawfulness of the Segregation Decisions, 69 Yale L.J. 421 (1960).

rulings which followed *Brown* made clear what we take for granted today—no governmental entity may segregate or burden people because of their race or national origin.

On the same day, the Court invalidated segregation of public schools in the District of Columbia in *Bolling v. Sharpe*.[84] Because the equal protection clause of the fourteenth amendment, upon which the decision in *Brown* was based, is inapplicable to the federal government, the precise legal question differed from that of *Brown*. The issue was whether racial segregation violated the due process clause of the fifth amendment. Although "liberty" had not been defined with precision, it included educational opportunities. Because no sufficient governmental objective could be shown which required segregation of schools, such segregation imposed upon blacks a burden that constituted a deprivation of their liberty. Racial segregation constituted an impermissible means of accomplishing even legitimate government goals. Thus the practice violated the due process clause. In view of *Brown*, it was unthinkable that the Constitution would impose a lesser burden on the federal government. Today it is accepted that the due process clause imposes an equal protection guarantee on the federal government.[85]

Although *Brown* technically invalidated the separate but equal doctrine only as applied to education, a series of Court decisions soon came down which indicated the in-

validity of that doctrine in other areas as well: public beaches and bathhouses,[86] municipal golf courses,[87] buses,[88] parks,[89] public parks and golf courses,[90] athletic contests,[91] airport restaurants,[92] courtroom seating,[93] and municipal auditoriums.[94] These decisions were short, per curiam opinions which often only cited *Brown*. Thus, through *Brown* and these subsequent cases the entire separate but equal doctrine was invalidated, requiring that classifications be subject to "strict scrutiny" and prohibited.

In 1964 the Court also rejected the limited view of equal protection which had allowed the use of racial classifications to determine whether certain activity was criminal so long as the same sanctions were given members of each race.[95] In *McLaughlin v. Florida*[96] a statute prohibiting a white person and black person from living together or occupying the same room at night was found violative of the equal protection clause because such behavior between persons of the same race was not proscribed. The Court in *McLaughlin* stated that, while statutory classifications normally would be upheld if they were not totally arbitrary, when the classification was drawn on the basis of race the legislature was without its normally wide discretion. The statute would be upheld only if the state were able to show an overriding purpose requiring proscription of the specified conduct when engaged in by members of different races but not when engaged in by persons of the same race. Be-

84. 347 U.S. 497 (1954).

85. Weinberger v. Wiesenfeld, 420 U.S. 636, 638 n. 2 (1975); Schlesinger v. Ballard, 419 U.S. 498, 500 n. 3 (1975).

86. Mayor of Baltimore v. Dawson, 350 U.S. 877 (1955).

87. Holmes v. City of Atlanta, 350 U.S. 879 (1955).

88. Gayle v. Browder, 352 U.S. 903 (1956).

89. Muir v. Louisville Park Theatrical Ass'n, 347 U.S. 971 (1954).

90. New Orleans Park Development Ass'n v. Detiege, 358 U.S. 54 (1958).

91. State Athletic Comm'n v. Dorsey, 359 U.S. 533 (1959).

92. Turner v. City of Memphis, 369 U.S. 350 (1962).

93. Johnson v. Virginia, 373 U.S. 61 (1963).

94. Schiro v. Bynum, 375 U.S. 395 (1964).

95. During this period the Supreme Court unaccountably refused to consider the appeal of one accused of violating a miscegenation statute, although this refusal was arguably based on the procedural posture of the decision below. Naim v. Naim, 197 Va. 80, 87 S.E.2d 749, vacated 350 U.S. 891 (1955), on remand 197 Va. 734, 90 S.E.2d 849, appeal dismissed 350 U.S. 985 (1956). As to the propriety of the procedural ruling, compare Weschler, Toward Neutral Principles of Constitutional Law, 73 Harv.L.Rev. 1, 34 (1959), with Pollak, The Supreme Court and the States: Reflections on Boynton v. Virginia, 49 Calif.L.Rev. 15, 45 n. 79 (1961).

96. 379 U.S. 184 (1964).

cause no such purpose could be shown, the statute was invalid.

It should be noted that Justices Douglas and Stewart concurred in the Court's opinion but objected to the implication that it might be possible for a state to show an overriding purpose which would validate such a statute.[97] In the view of these justices, any statute which made the color of the actor the test for whether his conduct was criminal was an invidious discrimination and per se unconstitutional.

It was not until 1967 that the Supreme Court held antimiscegenation statutes, which existed in many states, unconstitutional.[98] In *Loving v. Virginia*[99] the Court ruled that an antimiscegenation statute violated both the equal protection and due process clauses. The Court rejected the notion that the mere "equal application" of a statute containing a racial classification was enough to remove the classification from the fourteenth amendment's proscription of racial classifications. While some weight was to be given statements made at the time of passage of the amendment about miscegenation, historical sources were inconclusive and insufficient to resolve the problem. The purpose of the fourteenth amendment was clearly to remove invidious racial classifications. There was no question that the Vir-

ginia statute, by proscribing behavior if the couple were of different races which was accepted if they were of the same race, was based on an invidious racial classification and therefore invalid. The fact that it "burdened" members of both races was irrelevant as it used a person's race to determine his right to marry another. The statute also had an obvious stigmatizing effect on blacks, implying they were inferior and must be kept separate. Additionally, this statute suffered from the vice of arbitrarily limiting the freedom to marry.[100]

Since the early 1960's the Court has consistently invalidated explicit governmental discrimination against minorities. Even before this period, the Supreme Court in a number of decisions reaffirmed its holding in *Strauder* that blacks may not be excluded from jury service.[101] In *Carter v. Jury Commission of Greene County*,[102] the Court found that black citizens who were qualified to be jurors, as well as black defendants tried by juries from which blacks had been excluded, had standing to challenge the exclusion. The Court will find a violation of these rights where statistics on jury service in a jurisdiction give rise to an inference of racial discrimination, unless the evidence of racial imbalance is clearly rebutted by the government.[103]

---

97. 379 U.S. at 198 (Stewart and Douglas, JJ., concurring).

98. For the history and application of such laws, see D. Bell, Race, Racism and American Law, Chapter 2 (2 ed. 1980). At the time of this decision such statutes were found in fifteen states: Alabama, Alaska, Arkansas, Florida, Georgia, Kentucky, Louisiana, Mississippi, Missouri, North Carolina, Oklahoma, South Carolina, Tennessee, Texas, and West Virginia. They had been outlawed within 15 years in 14 other states: Arizona, California, Colorado, Idaho, Indiana, Maryland, Montana, Nebraska, Nevada, North Dakota, Oregon, South Dakota, Utah, and Wyoming. Loving v. Virginia, 388 U.S. 1, 6 n. 5 (1967).

99. 388 U.S. 1 (1967).

100. Because the right to marry was a protected right and the statute interfered with the exercise of that right, the due process clause was violated. See the discussion of right to privacy in Chapter 16, Section VIII.

101. Virginia v. Rives, 100 U.S. 313 (1874); Neal v. Delaware, 103 U.S. 370 (1880); Bush v. Kentucky, 107

U.S. 110 (1882); Gibson v. Mississippi, 162 U.S. 565 (1896).

102. 396 U.S. 320 (1970). The Court, however, denied relief on the particular facts.

103. Castaneda v. Partida, 430 U.S. 482 (1977). On proving the discrimination in such case, see Section I, D of this chapter.

The Court has held that claims of racial discrimination in the selection of members of a state grand jury were cognizable in a federal habeas corpus action and that a defendant could bring that action to have his indictment quashed and conviction set aside even though there was no racial discrimination in the selection of his petit jury and his guilt had been established beyond a reasonable doubt at trial. Rose v. Mitchell, 443 U.S. 545 (1979). However, in *Rose* the Court rejected the defendants' claim because they failed to demonstrate the substantial underrepresentation of members of minority races on the grand juries, or in the position of grand jury foreman. Because the defendants failed to make a prima facie demonstration, the burden did not

In matters relating to the integration of public facilities and services, the Court has come to the position that no continued racial discrimination will be constitutionally tolerated.[104] This rule has the effect of prohibiting most forms of official racial discrimination. Additionally, the application of federal civil rights statutes to persons who refuse to contract with others because of their race [105] also evidences the modern Supreme Court's position that racial discrimination is incompatible with essential constitutional values.

The constitutional prohibition against burdening members of racial minorities in election systems has also been the focus of a series of Supreme Court decisions. Where a governmental unit discriminates by race in the granting of voting rights it will violate the fifteenth amendment as well as the equal protection guarantee.[106] Going beyond such obvious discrimination, the Court has also prohibited attempts to use the electoral system to discriminate against racial minorities. For example, the Court struck down a system whereby the race of each candidate for elective office was noted on the ballot, as this requirement was certain to support and facilitate, if not induce, racial prejudice.[107]

Similarly, requiring racial minorities to take their problems to public referenda rather than to the normal legislative process will also violate equal protection. In *Reitman v. Mulkey* [108] the Court struck down a California Constitutional provision which would have prohibited open housing statutes because it would have encouraged racial discrimination and prevented minorities from seeking the help of the legislature to remedy their specific problems. A state may not place "in the way of the racial minority's attaining its political goal any barriers which, within the state's political system taken as a whole, are especially difficult of surmounting, by comparison with those barriers that normally stand in the way of those who wish to use political processes to get what they want."[109] In *Hunter v. Erickson,* [110] after the enactment of a fair housing ordinance, the voters amended the city charter to provide that no ordinance dealing with racial, religious, or ancestral discrimination in housing could be implemented without the approval of a majority of the voters. The Court held the provision invalid, finding it was a violation of the equal protection guarantee. It contained "an explicitly racial classification" by disadvantaging persons who would benefit from the prohibition of racial, religious, or ancestral discrimination, *i.e.,* minority groups. Similarly, the Supreme Court has invalidated a state law, enacted through a voter initiative, which effectively prohibited local school boards from transferring students to achieve racial integration but allowed the school boards the ability to transfer students between schools for many other reasons.[111] Relying on *Hunter,* the Court ruled that this restriction of school board powers was an invalid allocation of governmental power and benefits based on racial criteria.[112]

---

shift to the state to justify its grand jury member or foreman selection process.

104. The tolerance of racial discrimination while government proceeded to integrate schools "with all deliberate speed" has ended. Alexander v. Holmes County Bd. of Education, 396 U.S. 19 (1969).

105. See, e.g., Runyon v. McCrary, 727 U.S. 160 (1977); Jones v. Alfred H. Mayer Co., 392 U.S. 409 (1968). These statutes and cases are discussed in Chapter 17.

106. This rule applies even if the state attempts to freeze out minority participation by having "private" elections which exclude members of minority races. For a discussion of these "White Primary" cases, see Chapter 14, State Action, Section II.

107. Anderson v. Martin, 375 U.S. 399 (1964).

108. 387 U.S. 369 (1967). This case is analyzed in Chapter 14 on State Action.

109. Black, Foreword, "State Action", Equal Protection, and California's Proposition 14, 81 Harv.L.Rev. 69, 82 (1967).

110. 393 U.S. 385 (1969).

111. Washington v. Seattle School District, 102 S.Ct. 3187 (1982).

112. Id. The Court upheld, however, an amendment to a state constitution which prohibited state courts from transferring or busing students to different schools unless such an order was necessary to remedy a violation of federal law. Crawford v. Los Angeles Bd. of Education, 102 S.Ct. 3211 (1982). These cases are contrasted in Section II, E, 1, c, (6) of this Chapter.

Just as governmental units cannot lock minorities out of the political process, they may not seek to dilute the voting power of members of racial minorities. There is no constitutional violation if such persons are underrepresented statistically in the governing bodies because their candidates fail to attract the support of a majority of voters.[113] But if the electoral districts are "gerrymandered" to dilute the voting power of racial minorities, the districting system is invalid even if it otherwise represents perfect compliance with "one person-one vote" principles.[114] However, racial considerations may be used to protect the voting strength of minorities. In *United Jewish Organizations v. Carey* [115] the Court upheld a state legislative districting plan which was designed to protect the representation of minorities, but which caused a decrease in the voting strength of other ethnic groups. However, the plan showed an overall fairness to all races and two of the justices concurred only because they saw no evidence that the plan had the purpose or effect of burdening the right to vote of white persons.[116] While the case settles very little beyond its precise facts, it raises important questions concerning statistical information and affirmative action.

Although racial considerations may not be used to burden members of minority races, the government appears to have some right to know the racial impact of its actions. Thus, it would appear that the government can compile racial information so long as it

is not used to burden anyone because of his race.[117] At least it is clear that some compilation of racial statistics will be required when issues of racial discrimination in public services are litigated. Although statistics on racial impact do not decide substantive issues regarding discrimination, the information is relevant to determine government purposes.[118]

Finally, we have an open question as to the permissibility of racial classifications which burden members of a majority race in order to benefit members of a minority. Should these "affirmative action" programs be subjected to the compelling interest test and stricken? This issue is the subject of a later section. Before addressing that issue we will examine the implementation of the desegregation rulings.

E. Implementation of the Desegregation Decisions

1. Desegregation of the Schools

a. The Rise and Fall of "All Deliberate Speed"

In 1954 the Court decided *Brown v. Board of Education (Brown I)* [1] which held that segregated school systems violated the equal protection guarantee. But that decision postponed any ruling as to the relief to be granted in the cases. The Court heard new arguments concerning the proper scope of its decree in the next term. In *Brown v.*

---

113. Whitcomb v. Chavis, 403 U.S. 124 (1971).

114. White v. Regester, 412 U.S. 755 (1973). Compare, Mobile v. Bolden, 446 U.S. 55 (1980) (at-large voting system for county board is not invalid merely because racial minorities are not represented on board), with, Rogers v. Lodge, 102 S.Ct. 3272 (1982) (at-large voting system violates equal protection when maintained for the purpose of diluting racial minority voting power). See Section I, D of this Chapter.

115. 430 U.S. 144 (1977).

116. 430 U.S. 144, 179 (1977) (Stewart & Powell, JJ., concurring).

117. The Court has summarily approved the keeping of government records which included racial information kept to further race-neutral goals. See Hamm v. Virginia State Bd. of Elections, 230 F.Supp. 156

(E.D.Va.1964) aff'd per curiam sub nom. Tancil v. Woolls, 379 U.S. 19 (1964) (invalidating the keeping of separate lists of voters and taxpayers by race but permitting the state to require that the race of a husband and wife be identified in a divorce decree).

118. The use of statistics to prove discrimination is examined in Section I, D of Chapter 16.

1. 347 U.S. 483 (1954); Bolling v. Sharpe, 347 U.S. 497 (1954) (Federal segregation of public schools is denial of due process). The Court in these decisions fashioned no immediate relief, setting the question of relief for reargument. An invitation to submit briefs to aid in the formulation of decrees was extended to the Attorney General of the United States and the attorney generals of all states which by law required or permitted segregation. 347 U.S. at 495–496.

Board of Education (Brown II) [2] the Supreme Court addressed the question of the manner in which relief should be accorded black students who previously had been found to have been denied equal protection of the laws due to the segregation of public schools. Generally when a court finds there has been a constitutional violation, it will order an immediate end to the unconstitutional practice. In *Brown II*, however, because of the complexities the Court anticipated would occur nationwide in the transition to a system of public education freed of racial discrimination, the Court required only that school authorities dismantle segregated school systems with "all deliberate speed." [3] A "prompt and reasonable start toward full compliance" [4] was required. Once such a start had been made, school authorities might be permitted additional time to comply if "necessary in the public interest" and "consistent with good faith compliance at the earliest practicable date." [5]

2. 349 U.S. 294 (1955).

3. 349 U.S. at 301. Cf. Virginia v. West Virginia, 222 U.S. 17, 19–20 (1911) (Holmes, J.): "A question like the present should be disposed of without undue delay. But a State cannot be expected to move with the celerity of a private business man; it is enough if it proceeds, in the language of the English Chancery, with all deliberate speed". Cf. also, The Hound of Heaven, 1 The Works of Francis Thompson 107 (1913): "But with unhurrying chase,/and unperturbed pace,/Deliberate speed, majestic instancy . . . ."

See also, Radio Station WOW, Inc. v. Johnson, 326 U.S. 120, 134 (1945) (using all deliberate speed language in an FCC case).

4. 349 U.S. at 300.

5. Id.

6. Id. at 299.

7. Id. at 300.

8. Virginia enacted a new rule aimed at civil rights attorneys which would have disbarred those who represented organizations with "no pecuniary interest" in litigation. The statute was stricken on first amendment grounds in NAACP v. Button, 371 U.S. 415 (1963). The issues are examined in depth in Bell, Serving Two Masters: Integration Ideals and Client Interests in School Desegregation Litigation, 85 Yale L.J. 470, 493–505 (1976).

The problems of resistance and implementation are examined in two leading texts. D. Bell, Race, Racism and American Law Chapter 7 (2 ed. 1980); N. Dorsen, P. Bender, B. Neuborne & S. Law, Political and Civil

This decision was in part predicated on faith in state and lower federal courts, which, because of their proximity to local conditions, were best suited to perform the duty of insuring good faith implementation of the decision. [6] The lower courts, like the school authorities, were given no specific guidelines. They were to be guided by equitable principles, which traditionally had been characterized by practical flexibility and facility for balancing public and private needs. [7] Unfortunately, local courts were not able to measure up to this task.

The decision was met with massive resistance in the states with official segregation. Their tactics included inaction, defiance by political leaders, and vigorous defensive action in the legislatures, including attempts to punish civil rights attorneys. [8] The resistance was typified by the occurrences in Little Rock, Arkansas, in 1957 which resulted in an important Court decision regarding these tactics. School authorities developed a plan for desegregation, but the legislature

Rights in the United States, Vol. II, Chapter XXVIII (4th ed. 1979). Some examples follow:

In Arkansas and Mississippi a state sovereignty commission was formed to protect the sovereignty of the state from encroachment by the federal government. Miss. Acts 1956, ch. 365, p. 520, 1 Race Rel.L.Rep. 592 (1956); Ark. Acts 1957, No. 83, p. 271, 2 Race Rel.L. Rep. 491 (1957). Other southern states simply relied upon interposition, the argument that a state may, in the exercise of its sovereignty, reject any mandate of the federal government deemed to be unconstitutional or beyond the scope of its delegated powers. Ala. Acts 1956, Spec.Sess., Act No. 42, p. 70, 1 Race Rel.L.Rep. 437 (1956); Fla. Acts 1956, Spec.Sess. SC.R. No. 17–XX, 1 Race Rel.L.Rep. 948 (1956); Fla. Acts 1957, H.C.R. No. 174, p. 1217, 2 Race Rel.L.Rep. 707 (1957); Ga. Acts 1956, H.R. 185, 1 Race Rel.L.Rep. (1956); Miss. Acts 1956, ch. 466, p. 741, 1 Race Rel.L.Rep. 440 (1956); Va. Acts 1956, S.J.R. 3, p. 1213, 1 Race Rel.L. Rep. 445 (1956).

Legislatures also passed legislation relieving school children from compulsory attendance at racially segregated schools. The formation of pupil assignment boards was also common. Children were supposedly no longer automatically sent to a particular school on the basis of race, they were instead placed by the board. However, typically all black children were assigned to one school and all white children to another.

For a further discussion of tactics adopted by states in an attempt to avoid desegregation, see Section II, E, I, c, below on the permissibility of certain state acts in relation to integration.

engaged in a program to perpetuate racial segregation.[9] When the governor sent state troops to prevent blacks from entering the previously white high school he was enjoined from further interference by a federal court.[10] To enforce the constitutional ruling, federal troops were sent to allow the blacks to attend the schools. School authorities requested postponement of their desegregation plan because they believed that the extreme public hostility caused by the actions of the governor and the legislature made it impossible to maintain a sound education program with the black students in attendance.

In *Cooper v. Aaron*,[11] the Supreme Court of the United States denied the city any additional time to comply with the ruling. The opinion was headed by the names of all nine justices of the Court to emphasize the strength of the ruling that was to "unanimously reaffirm" the holding in *Brown*. The Court accepted without reservation the assertions that the school board had acted in good faith and that the educational process

of all students would suffer if the prevailing conditions of the previous year continued but stated that the rights of black children were not to be sacrificed to violence and disorder engendered by the actions of state officials. *Brown* could not be nullified either "openly and directly by state legislators or state executive or judicial officers" or "indirectly by them through evasive schemes for segregation whether attempted 'ingeniously or ingenuously.'"[12]

Many school districts persisted in the use of dilatory practices to avoid complete desegregation.[13] As time passed and no appreciable progress toward integration was made, the Court manifested its impatience.[14] In 1963, the Court noted that "the context in which we must interpret and apply this language to plans for desegregation has been significantly altered."[15] The following year in *Griffin v. Prince Edward County Board of Education*,[16] the Court stated "the time for mere deliberate speed had run out;"[17] black children who had been denied admission to public schools on the basis of race

9. An amendment to the state constitution was passed, commanding the General Assembly to oppose "in every constitutional manner the un-constitutional desegregation decisions of May 17, 1954 and May 31, 1955 of the United States Supreme Court." Ark.Const. amend. 44. Pursuant to the amendment, the General Assembly enacted a pupil assignment law, Ark.Stats. §§ 80–1519 to 80–1524, a law relieving school children from compulsory attendance at racially mixed schools, Ark.Stats. § 8–1525, and a law enacting a State Sovereignty Commission, Ark.Stats. §§ 6–801 to 6–824.

10. Aaron v. Cooper, 156 F.Supp. 220 (E.D.Ark. 1957), affirmed sub nom. Faubus v. United States, 254 F.2d 797 (8th Cir. 1958).

11. 358 U.S. 1 (1958).

12. 358 U.S. at 17. The Supreme Court found that its earlier rulings on desegregation were "the supreme law of the land" and bound all state officials. 358 U.S. at 18. Professor Daniel Farber has published an excellent analysis of the relevance of *Cooper* and the Court's position on the supremacy of its decisions to the concept of "law" in "constitutional law". Farber presents a most insightful defense of the Court's position and the need to regard Supreme Court decisions as binding law. See, Farber, The Supreme Court and the Rule of Law: Cooper v. Aaron Revisited, 1982 U.Ill.L. Rev. 387.

13. The Court, for eight years after *Brown*, refused to review cases questioning the validity of pupil placement regulations or the appropriateness of applying

the doctrine of exhaustion of administrative remedies to frustrate suits challenging segregated school systems. D. Bell, Race, Racism and American Law 458 (1973); Covington v. Edwards, 264 F.2d 780 (4th Cir. 1959), cert. denied 361 U.S. 840 (1959); Carson v. Warlick, 238 F.2d 724 (4th Cir. 1956), cert. denied 353 U.S. 910 (1956); Hood v. Board of Trustees, 232 F.2d 626 (4th Cir. 1956), cert. denied 352 U.S. 870 (1956), Shuttlesworth v. Birmingham Bd. of Education, 162 F.Supp. 372 (N.D.Ala.1958), aff'd 358 U.S. 101 (1958).

14. In 1963, the Court ruled that the doctrine requiring exhaustion of administrative remedies before relief could be sought in a federal court was not applicable in school desegregation cases. McNeese v. Board of Education, 373 U.S. 668 (1963).

In the same term the Court invalidated a transfer policy which allowed students assigned to a school where their race was in the minority to transfer to a school where their race was in the majority because the policy's inevitable effect was the perpetuation of school segregation. Goss v. Board of Education, 373 U.S. 683 (1963).

15. Goss v. Board of Education, 373 U.S. 683, 689 (1963).

16. 377 U.S. 218 (1964). The case is discussed more fully in the subsection on state acts relating to integration, Section II, E, I, c.

17. 377 U.S. at 234.

were entitled to quick and effective relief. In 1968, in *Green v. County School Board*,[18] the Court restated the need for prompt adoption and effectuation of a plan that would actually disestablish a dual system. *Brown II* had recognized that the dismantling of a segregated school system was complex and would thus require time, but school boards were nevertheless charged with the affirmative duty to take the necessary steps to eliminate racial discrimination. The Court stated further that "[t]he burden on a school board today is to come forward with a plan that promises realistically to work, and promises realistically to work now." [19]

By 1969, the Supreme Court was no longer willing to tolerate delay. Reviewing a Fifth Circuit decision granting more time for the desegregation of a public school system, the Court ruled "the Court of Appeals should have denied all motions for additional time because continued operation of segregated schools under a standard of allowing 'all deliberate speed' for desegregation is no longer constitutionally permissible. Under explicit holdings of this Court the obligation of every school district is to terminate dual systems at once and to operate now and hereafter only unitary schools." [20] Acknowledging the Court's holding, the Fifth Circuit nevertheless permitted a semester delay in the implementation of a court order to desegregate because the order was issued in the middle of the school year. The Supreme Court summarily reversed in a per curiam opinion.[21] Two concurring justices thought that the time between a finding of noncompliance and the effective date of the remedy, including any judicial review, should not exceed eight weeks.[22] Four other justices thought that even that delay would be too long.[23]

Once there has been a showing of deliberate segregation of schools, school authorities must develop a plan which will provide immediate relief. State legislatures and governors will not be allowed to hinder the implementation of desegregation plans.[24] The courts are empowered to act if school authorities fail to discharge their duties or if state officials thwart desegregation.

However, despite these rulings, many black children are still denied their right to equal educational opportunities. School boards rarely take action to desegregate schools except under the threat of a court order.[25] Courts can order desegregation only if there has been a showing of purposeful segregation.[26] Another problem is that orders for the integration of city schools often lead to "white flight" from a city, which leads to increasingly black public schools, which in turn reduces the likelihood of political support for education—which leaves

18. 391 U.S. 430 (1968).

19. 391 U.S. at 438–39.

20. Alexander v. Holmes County Bd. of Education, 396 U.S. 19, 20 (1969) (per curiam).

21. Singleton v. Jackson Municipal Separate School District, 419 F.2d 1211, 1216 (5th Cir.) (per curiam), rev'd sub nom. Carter v. Western Feliciana Parish School Bd., 396 U.S. 290 (1970) (per curiam).

22. 396 U.S. at 291–93 (Harlan & White, JJ., concurring).

23. 396 U.S. at 293 (opinion of Black, Douglas, Brennan, & Marshall, JJ.); cf. Dowell v. Board of Education, 396 U.S. 269, 271 (1969) (desegregation should not be stayed pending appeal). See, Rotunda, Congressional Power to Restrict the Jurisdiction of the Lower Federal Courts and the Problem of School Busing, 64 Georgetown L.J. 839, 864–66 (1976).

24. North Carolina State Bd. of Education v. Swann, 402 U.S. 43, 46 (1971) (unanimous Court invalidated state statute banning involuntary bussing); Cooper v. Aaron, 358 U.S. 1 (1958).

25. For further analysis of the Supreme Court's desegregation rulings see Wilkinson, The Supreme Court and Southern School Desegregation, 1955–70: A History and Analysis, 64 Va.L.Rev. 485 (1978). Jones, Strategies for completing the Job of School Integration, 19 How.L.J. 82 (1975). For a detailed attack on the school desegregation rulings, see L. Graglia, Disaster By Decree (1976).

26. See Keyes v. School District No. 1, 413 U.S. 189 (1973) discussed infra this section.

Professor Robert Allen Sedler has made a powerful argument that the Supreme Court should find that the fundamental values inherent in the concept of equal protection give rise to a right of children to attend a racially integrated school. See Sedler, The Constitution and School Desegregation: An Inquiry Into the Nature of the Substantive Right, 68 Ky.L.J. 879 (1979).

black children disadvantaged, as before.[27] Professor Bell has noted that the economic and political realities of urban America may mean that earnest implementation of the desegregation principle can actually hurt the educational opportunities afforded black children.[28] This result may be corrected by litigation designed to protect or upgrade educational quality,[29] but given the increasingly restrained judicial attitudes towards educational issues, success in litigation may be very difficult to accomplish.[30]

All desegregation suits proceed through three stages. First, it must be shown that the school system is subject to *Brown* because it has engaged in purposeful or de jure segregation. Second, the school system or state is given the opportunity to devise a plan for ending the segregation system and creating an integrated one. Finally, if the state will not devise a plan, the court must issue orders to integrate the school system. The remainder of this section will discuss the schools subject to the integration principle, the permissibility of certain state acts in relation to integration and, finally, the scope of federal court power to act if the state or city refuses to fully correct its segregated school system.

b. Institutions Subject to the Desegregation Principle

(1) The De Jure-De Facto Distinction

Neither *Brown I* nor later decisions of the Supreme Court require all public schools to be racially integrated. Rather, the decisions require that public schools not be racially segregated. School systems which have not been segregated by law need not take steps to integrate their school system even though their individual schools have racially unbalanced student populations. However, if a school district has operated a racially segregated system, it must entirely eradicate that practice by integrating its schools. These historical differences are the core of the de jure-de facto distinction. De jure ("by law") segregation is racial separation which is the product of some purposeful act by government authorities. De facto ("by the facts") segregation occurs because of housing and migration patterns and is unconnected to any purposeful governmental action to racially segregate schools. If a school system involves de jure segregation, it violates the equal protection guarantee; the courts will intervene if necessary to remedy this situation. But if a school district has become unintentionally (de facto) segregated, there is no constitutional violation and the courts will not intervene. In the South where it was easy to show schools had been segregated by law, desegregation orders were issued and compliance slowly followed. In the North and West, however, where there were no express statutory provisions authorizing segregation of schools, blacks faced the difficult task of showing purposeful discrimination in school assignments even where segregation resulted from discriminatory housing practices or gerrymandering of school districts. As a result, in 1970 in the South only 39.4% of black students attended predominantly minority schools, while in northern and western states the figure was 57.6%.[31]

Today a central issue in school desegregation suits is whether the school system constitutes de jure rather than de facto segregation. Mere statistics showing an imbalance between the racial make-up of in-

---

27. Abramowitz and Jackson, Desegregation: Where Do We Go From Here?, 19 How.L.J. 92, 93 (1975).

28. Bell, Serving Two Masters: Integration Ideals and Client Interests In School Desegregation Litigation, 85 Yale L.J. 470 (1976).

29. "Correspondence", 86 Yale L.J. 378–384 (1976) (letter of Nathaniel Jones, general counsel for N.A. A.C.P. Special Contribution Fund Concerning Professor Bell's article; reply by Professor Bell.)

30. On this issue see, e.g., the next section on de jure segregation and San Antonio Independent School District v. Rodriquez, 411 U.S. 1 (1973). The Court has held that federal courts could order remedial and compensatory education programs as part of a school desegregation decree. Milliken v. Bradley, (Milliken II), 433 U.S. 267 (1977); see Section II, E, 1, d.

31. J. Barron and C. Dienes, Constitutional Law: Principles and Policy 622 (1st ed. 1975).

dividual schools will not in itself be sufficient, for such an imbalance could have arisen unintentionally from housing and migration patterns. The Supreme Court has held that de jure segregation is only present when there has been "segregative purpose or intent" and government action to maintain segregated schools.[32] Unfortunately the Court has not clarified the way in which "purposeful" segregation may be proven. Some clarity is added by the Court's opinions on the use of statistics to prove the existence of racial classifications by the disproportionate impact of other types of laws. In those cases the Court has indicated that only in the most rare case will statistical proof be so overwhelming as to prove discrimination from the evenhanded application of a seemingly race-neutral law.[33] Instead, some additional proof of discrimination is needed.[34]

There are three possible ways to prove a discriminatory purpose, although the Supreme Court has yet to clearly choose one of them. First, the Court could require proof of the subjective motive to discriminate on the part of individual legislators or school board members. This alternative seems unlikely as the Court has in other areas continued to adhere to the position that "motivation" of legislators is irrelevant.[35] However, the purpose versus motivation distinction makes little sense in school board inquiries because there is less reason to respect the decision making process as one of a primary branch of government. But this theory would mean that educational policies would

stand or fall on the subjective intent of those who adopted it rather than on the educational worth of the policy itself. A second approach to the problem would be to view school districts as having purposeful segregation whenever the school board practices can objectively be said to have encouraged or maintained segregation in the system. This alternative has the advantage of avoiding vague inquiries into the motives of school board members, but it is a most imprecise tool to determine purpose. If it were applied strictly it could end the de jure-de facto distinction because a wide variety of practices might be found (using statistical hindsight) to have maintained racial segregation even though the policies appeared to be race-neutral to those who adopted them. In any event, it focuses the inquiry on statistics to the exclusion of all else, a result which recent cases on statistical proof attempt to avoid.[36]

A third approach to determine purpose has recently been advocated by a law review commentator [37] and some lower courts.[38] This approach is a hybrid of the two other methods. The third position would allow objective criteria of school board policies to establish a prima facie case of purposeful segregation; this case could be disproved by the school board showing that the policies were adopted for race-neutral educational reasons. Accurately labeled an "institutional intent" test,[39] it exposes the basis for the adoption of school board policies. When objective criteria show that the policies en-

---

32. Keyes v. School District No. 1, 413 U.S. 189, 208 (1973).

33. See Section I, D of Chapter 16 on proving the existence of classifications.

34. Id. For the pronouncement of the general rule, see Washington v. Davis, 426 U.S. 229 (1976).

35. For an examination of this problem, see Section I, D of Chapter 16. For discussion and critique of the distinctions, see Brest, Palmer v. Thompson: An Approach to the Problem of Unconstitutional Legislative Motive, 1971 Sup.Ct.Rev. 95; Ely, Legislative and Administrative Motivation in Constitutional Law, 79 Yale L.J. 1205 (1970).

36. Arlington Heights v. Metropolitan Housing Development Corp., 429 U.S. 252 (1977); Washington v. Davis, 426 U.S. 229 (1976).

37. Note, Reading the Mind of the School Board: Segregative Intent And the De Facto/De Jure Distinction, 86 Yale L.J. 317 (1976).

38. Oliver v. Michigan State Bd. of Education, 508 F.2d 178 (6th Cir. 1974), cert. denied 421 U.S. 963 (1975); see also United States v. School District of Omaha, 521 F.2d 530 (8th Cir. 1975), cert. denied 423 U.S. 946 (1975); Amos v. Board of School Directors, 408 F.Supp. 765 (E.D.Wis.1976).

39. See Note, Reading the Mind of the School Board: Segregative Intent and the De Facto/De Jure Distinction, 86 Yale L.J. 317 (1976). The author describes in the Note how he would employ the test to determine institutional intent. Of course, courts might adopt a different manner of applying the test while still agreeing with the basic concept.

couraged or maintained segregation, a presumption of unconstitutional segregation acts is permissible. If the governmental entity (normally the school board) that adopted the school policy can show that it was the most efficient way for achieving race-neutral educational goals, the presumption is rebutted. If the school board cannot do this, it is fair to conclude that the policies were adopted for segregative (as opposed to irrational or otherwise unknown) purposes. A similar approach to discovering racial discrimination in the calling of jurors has worked well and been approved by the Supreme Court in that context.[40] Thus, it seems that this approach is the one most likely to be adopted by the Court. But as the issue remains unsettled; we will discuss the most important decisions of the Court on this issue before turning to our next subject.

In 1973 in *Keyes v. School District No. 1*,[41] the Supreme Court for the first time considered a charge of racially discriminatory behavior against a school system in a large metropolitan area outside the South. The Denver school district had never operated under a constitutional or statutory provision that explicitly required or permitted racial segregation in the public schools. However, there was proof that at least some of the schools had been used to isolate blacks and Hispanic-Americans. The Court adopted the de jure-de facto analysis and held that there was a constitutional violation to the extent there was "segregative purpose or intent" in school board actions.

The Court first discussed the method of defining a "segregated school." Because the Court found Hispanic-Americans and blacks suffer identical discrimination in treatment when compared to whites, schools with a combined predominance of blacks and Hispanic-Americans may be considered "segregated" schools.[42] The majority opinion

then went on to find that government designed segregation as to a substantial portion of the school system could not be viewed in isolation from the rest of the district. If plaintiffs prove that school authorities have carried out a systematic program of segregation affecting a substantial portion of the students, schools, teachers, and facilities within the school system, it is logical to assume there is a predicate for a finding of the existence of a dual school system.[43] Normally, racially discriminatory actions will have an impact beyond the particular schools. However, it is possible that the school board might be able to show that the segregated portion did not directly affect the other schools.

The Court noted that even if the board were able to prove this contention, the finding of intentional segregation on the part of the school board in one portion of the school system is highly relevant to the question of the board's intent with respect to other segregated schools in the system. A "finding of intentionally segregative school board actions in a meaningful portion of a school system, as in this case, creates a presumption that other segregated schooling within the system is not adventitious."[44] Such a finding establishes a prima facie case of unlawful segregation and shifts the burden to school authorities to prove that other segregated schools are not also the result of deliberate racial discrimination. In discharging this burden, the school board must do more than simply offer some allegedly logical, racially neutral explanation for their actions. They must produce proof sufficient to support a finding that segregative intent was not among the motivating factors for their actions. If segregative intent has been shown, the board can rebut the prima facie case only by showing that past discriminatory acts did not create or contribute to the

40. See, e.g., Castaneda v. Partida, 430 U.S. 482 (1977).

41. 413 U.S. 189 (1973). For a detailed analysis criticizing this case, see L. Graglia, Diaster by Decree: The Supreme Court Decisions on Race and Schools, 160–202 (1976).

42. 413 U.S. at 198.

43. 413 U.S. at 201.

44. 413 U.S. at 208.

current segregated condition of the schools.[45]

Justices Powell and Douglas each filed separate opinions, stating that the de jure-de facto distinction is no longer viable. Justice Douglas would have required a remedy for de facto segregation in recognition of the fact that many state policies contribute to neighborhood segregation.[46] Justice Powell argued that the Courts could not resolve problems of subjective intent to determine the existence of constitutionally impermissible segregation. He proposed a new standard: "where segregated public schools exist within a school district to a substantial degree, there is a prima facie case that the duly constituted public authorities [are] sufficiently responsible to warrant imposing upon them a nationally applicable burden to demonstrate they nevertheless are operating a genuinely integrated system."[47] But, unlike Douglas, he moved to an objective criterion to determine responsibility rather than suggest the elimination of all segregation.[48]

The de jure-de facto distinction was strengthened when the Court held that suburbs with de facto segregation could not be ordered to integrate with a neighboring system involving de jure segregation. In *Milliken v. Bradley*[49] the question, as phrased by the Court, was "whether a federal court may impose a multidistrict, areawide remedy to a single-district de jure segregation problem absent any finding that the other included school districts have failed to operate unitary school systems within their district, absent any claim or finding that the boundary lines of any affected school district were established with the purpose of fostering racial segregation in public schools, absent any finding that the included districts committed acts which effected segregation within the other districts, and absent a meaningful op-

portunity for the included neighborhood school districts to present evidence or be heard on the propriety of a multidistrict remedy or on the question of constitutional violation by those neighboring districts."[50] As indicated by the manner in which the opinion stated the question, the answer of the majority was no.

In the *Milliken* case, the Detroit public schools were found to be unlawfully segregated. The federal district court found that the plans proposed for the desegregation of Detroit would only make the Detroit system even more clearly a one race system, with the suburban schools becoming the white school system. The district court, therefore, adopted a metropolitan plan, in which fifty-three Detroit suburbs were included in the "desegregation area." The Supreme Court of the United States, however, found it impermissible for the lower court to decree inter-district relief simply to produce area-wide integrated schools.

According to the majority opinion, school district lines are not sacrosanct, but local autonomy in education is of great importance. In determining the validity of a court decree requiring cross-district or inter-district consolidation in order to remedy segregation found in one district, the Court stated that the controlling principle is that the scope of the remedy must be determined by the extent and the nature of the constitutional violation. "Before the boundaries of separate and autonomous school districts may be set aside by consolidating the separate units for remedial purposes or by imposing a cross-district remedy, it must first be shown that there has been a constitutional violation within one district that produces a significant segregative effect in another district."[51] Thus, inter-district relief would be appropriate where it is shown either that the

45. 413 U.S. at 211.

46. Keyes v. School District No. 1, 413 U.S. 189, 214–17 (1973) (opinion of Douglas, J.).

47. 413 U.S. at 224 (Powell, J., concurring and dissenting).

48. Justice Powell has reemphasized his view that court-ordered remedial measures to establish integra-

tion in a school system should not exceed the degree to which there was objective proof of segregation. Austin Independent School District v. United States, 429 U.S. 990, 991–95 (1976) (Powell, J., concurring).

49. 418 U.S. 717 (1974).

50. 418 U.S. at 721–2.

51. 418 U.S. at 744–5.

racially discriminatory acts of one district affected an adjacent district or where district lines have been drawn according to race. To order such relief absent such a showing would be impermissible.

Four of the justices dissented.[52] Although their opinions differed in part, they all believed that once there has been a finding of state-imposed segregation, it becomes the duty of the state to remove all traces of racial segregation. Here, black students were denied the only effective relief because of administrative inconvenience and undue regard for school district lines. They would have held that the constitutional rights of black students were too fundamental to be abridged on such grounds. The school district decision remains undisturbed, but the Court has approved inter-district housing remedies for racial segregation in public housing under limited circumstances.[53]

In *Pasadena City Board of Education v. Spangler*[54] the Supreme Court invalidated the district court's requirement as a part of a desegregation plan that the composition of the student body of particular schools fit a certain ratio every year. Because the system involved de jure segregation the initial use of a statistical goal for racial integration was proper, but once a racially neutral school system had been established the lower court exceeded its authority in requiring annual readjustment to racial balance. Later changes in racial mixture were not caused

by segregative acts of school or state authorities and, therefore, the new racial imbalance constituted only de facto segregation. This decision evidences some movement by the justices of the Supreme Court to make the de facto-de jure distinction more important but more objective. Similarly, the Court has summarily remanded a lower court decision on segregation for lower court consideration of whether there was sufficient evidence of purposeful school segregation.[55] In remanding the case, several justices indicated their view that remedies designed to promote school integration could not exceed the scope of purposeful segregation that had been established at trial.[56] Such an approach would make the finding of de jure discrimination more important than ever before.

In recent years the justices appear to be attempting to employ an "institutional intent" approach for identifying de jure racial segregation while tailoring the scope of judicial remedies to correction of the identified segregation. The institutional intent test, described above,[57] allows for the objective identification of purposely discriminatory acts by school boards in order to identify de jure segregation in the absence of explicit racial classifications in city or state laws. However, this test does not justify the imposition of integration orders upon school districts that have a racial imbalance in their schools due only to de facto segregation. While statistical proof of racial disparity in

52. Milliken v. Bradley, 418 U.S. 717, 757 (1974) (Douglas, J., dissenting); id. at 762 (White, J., dissenting); id. at 781 (Marshall J., dissenting). Justice Brennan joined in the dissent of Justices White and Marshall.

53. Hills v. Gautreaux, 425 U.S. 284 (1976). This case is discussed at the end of this section on implementation of the desegregation principle and in Chapter 14 on State Action, Section IV, D.

54. 423 U.S. 1335 (1976).

Following the remand of this case, the district judge entered an order deleting the provision of his earlier order that had required annual readjustment of attendance zones to prohibit schools with a majority of minority race students. The district judge also prohibited the school board from making further changes in the method of student assignment. Members of the school board then sought to have a writ of mandamus issue to

the district court as they believed that statements made by the judge would continue to pose a continuing no "school with a majority of minority students" requirement on the school district. Justice Rehnquist, sitting as a Circuit Justice, denied their application for a stay order. Justice Rehnquist believed that the district court order in fact eliminated the "no majority" continual reassignment provision. Vetterli v. United States District Court, 435 U.S. 1304 (1978) (Rehnquist, Circuit Justice).

55. Austin Independent School District v. United States, 429 U.S. 990 (1977), vacating and remanding United States v. Texas Education Agency, 532 F.2d 380 (5th Cir. 1976).

56. 429 U.S. at 990 (Opinion of Powell, J., joined by Burger, C. J., and Rehnquist, J.).

57. See notes 35–40 supra, and accompanying text.

schools will not in itself establish unconstitutional segregation, proof that a school board has been aware of serious racial imbalance in its schools and that it has knowingly adopted policies that have been designed to maintain or exacerbate the racial imbalance will give rise to an inference of purposeful discrimination on the part of the school board.

> Proof of purposeful and effective maintenance of a body of separate black schools in a substantial part of the system itself is prima facie proof of a dual school system and supports a finding to this effect absent sufficient contrary proof by the [school] Board . . . .[58]

The school board's recognition of the foreseeable effects of its actions on the racial imbalance in the schools is one element of proof of purposeful discrimination, and the establishment of purposeful discrimination as to one area of school board activity or one part of the school system will give rise to an inference of system wide discrimination. However, these inferences only shift the burden to the state or local government to demonstrate that the school board policies were intended to promote important educational objectives and did not constitute purposeful discrimination.

In two highly publicized but relatively simple cases, the Court upheld lower court findings that two cities in Ohio had engaged in purposeful discrimination in their school districts and that their refusal to remedy past discrimination was a violation of the constitutional obligation to dismantle de jure segregated school systems and to avoid any action that would impede the disestablishment of such an unconstitutional system. By a vote of 7 to 2, the Court upheld a District Court and Court of Appeals finding that the schools in Columbus, Ohio had been purposely discriminating against black students and

intentionally maintaining a dual school system through the early 1950's and that, after the Supreme Court's initial rulings that such systems violated the fourteenth amendment, the Columbus school board had not only failed to dismantle its dual school system but also had intentionally adopted policies such as the establishment of optional attendance zones and boundary changes that maintained and increased the system wide segregation.[59]

By a 5 to 4 vote the Court also found that the Court of Appeals for the Sixth Circuit had been correct in ordering system wide desegregation plans for the school district of Dayton, Ohio.[60] There was little doubt that Dayton had maintained a dual school system through the early 1950's, and both the District Court and Court of Appeals had found that the Dayton school board had violated the fourteenth amendment in the past. There was a closer division of the justices in this case, however, because there was less proof that the school board's actions had been designed to maintain a dual school system throughout the school district. The District Court had found that the constitutional violation was limited to a few schools within the district, but the Court of Appeals had found that the school board had not effectively rebutted the inference of area wide discrimination that arose once there was proof of purposeful discrimination as to some schools in the district. A majority of the justices of the Supreme Court agreed with the Court of Appeals because, "given intentionally segregated schools in 1954", the school board had an obligation to dismantle the dual system and to refrain from taking "any action that would impede the process of disestablishing the dual system." Because "the board has never seriously contended that it fulfilled its affirmative duty

---

58. Columbus Bd. of Education v. Penick, 443 U.S. 449, 458 (1979).

59. Columbus Bd. of Education v. Penick, 443 U.S. 449 (1979). Justice White wrote a majority opinion in this case, joined by Justices Brennan, Marshall, Blackmun, and Stevens. Justice Stewart filed an opinion concurring in the judgment as to this case but dissenting as to the judgment in the Dayton, Ohio case (see

footnote 60 infra), joined by the Chief Justice. Justices Powell and Rehnquist dissented, for they felt that the Court's use of inferences to shift burdens of proof to the school board had the effect of justifying remedies for de facto segregation.

60. Dayton Bd. of Education v. Brinkman, 443 U.S. 526 (1979).

or heavy burden of explaining its failure to do so," the majority of the justices found that the Court of Appeals was justified in finding that the board had purposely maintained a dual school system throughout the district. The fact that the original decisions resulting in the segregated system may have occurred over 20 years ago did not relieve the board from its duty of undoing the segregative effect, which it simply exacerbated by its continual refusal, in over a quarter of a century, to integrate its previously segregated school system.

(2) The Desegregation Principle and Private Schools

Private schools which segregate on the basis of race do not violate the Constitution unless they have sufficient contacts with the state or the federal government to allow description of their acts as "state action," because the equal protection clause of the fourteenth amendment applies only to the states and the due process clause of the fifth amendment applies only to the federal government. Thus, private segregated schools present a classic "state action" issue and under traditional analysis, they are not subject to constitutional restraint absent further contacts with the government.[61] However, the government may not give any aid to these schools because that would constitute government support for and facilitation of racial segregation. Therefore, these schools could be put to an election between receiving assistance from the government and maintaining the segregative practices.

Although these schools do not violate the Constitution, they are illegal under federal civil rights statutes insofar as they refuse to contract with persons on the basis of the person's race. The major issue now is whether the government must permit the existence of (and perhaps offer neutral educational benefits to) religious schools that segregate because of the principles of their religion. The few decisions of the Supreme Court concerning private school segregation sharpen these issues.

The Supreme Court has invalidated all attempts to aid segregative schools that exceed generalized governmental services such as police and fire protection. In several cases the Court affirmed lower court decisions which enjoined states from making tuition grants to students attending segregated schools.[62] In *Norwood v. Harrison*[63] the Court held that a state could not lend textbooks to students at such schools even though the program was identical to one under which the Court had allowed textbooks to go to students of religious schools.[64] The Court held that state aid to racially discriminatory schools was not permissible even where the aid and the discrimination were not tied together. The state could give limited assistance to children at parochial schools because of the constitutionally recognized value in the free exercise of religion. However, there is no constitutionally significant value or support for racial discrimination.

The Supreme Court clarified the state aid issue when it held that racially discriminatory schools could not be allowed to reserve public recreational facilities for temporary exclusive use. In *Gilmore v. Montgom-*

---

61. See Chapter 14 on State Action. It might have been argued that education was a public function and, therefore, that all accredited schools embodied state action. However the cases in this area leave little doubt that the Court would not accept such an argument. See Section II of Chapter 14.

62. Norwood v. Harrison, 413 U.S. 455, 463 n. 6 (1973). The Court lists the following decisions in its note 6: Brown v. South Carolina Bd. of Education, 296 F.Supp. 199 (D.S.C.), aff'd per curiam, 393 U.S. 222 (1968); Poindexter v. Louisiana Finance Assistance Comm'n, 275 F.Supp. 833 (E.D.La.1967), aff'd per curiam 389 U.S. 571 (1968). See Wallace v. United

States, 389 U.S. 215 (1967), aff'g Lee v. Macon County Bd. of Education, 267 F.Supp. 458, 475 (M.D.Ala.1967). Mississippi's tuition grant programs were invalidated in Coffey v. State Educational Finance Comm'n, S.D. Miss., C.A. No. 2906, decided Sept. 2, 1970 (unreported). The latter case involved a statute which provided for tuition loans rather than tuition grants. See Green v. Connally, 330 F.Supp. 1150 (D.D.C.1971), aff'd sub nom. Coit v. Green, 404 U.S. 997 (1971).

63. 413 U.S. 455 (1973).

64. Board of Education v. Allen, 392 U.S. 236 (1968).

ery [65] the Court found that this connection constituted aid to the racially discriminatory entity. A majority of the justices did not decide whether the nonexclusive use of public recreational facilities by such groups was also prohibited. [66] If the use amounted to an informal use of the facilities with other persons on a desegregated basis, it might be viewed as no more than a generalized service such as police and fire protection. Yet there was no decision on this point, and four justices indicated that they would not allow any use of public facilities that was part of the segregated school program or that otherwise aided the school. [67]

Another form of aid to segregated schools comes from tax exemptions. Lower federal courts had invalidated any exemptions which could be viewed as specific aid (such as tax exempt status) rather than as a generalized grant to all persons (such as depreciation deductions). [68] Such a decision would seem to cast doubt on state property tax exclusions for such groups. [69] Although property tax exemptions for churches have been upheld, under the rationale of *Norwood*, this aid should be classified as specific aid which may be granted to insure religious freedom but not to allow racially segregative practices. The Internal Revenue Service agreed with this position and ruled that racially discriminatory entities would not receive tax exempt status. [70] This ruling is valid, even though it is applied to deny tax exempt status to a religiously affiliated college which discriminates racially because, while the government may aid religious schools in certain limited ways, it need not offer any aid to them. On the other hand, the government is prohibited from aiding segregation. Thus, the refusal to extend aid to religious schools which discriminate by race constitutes the neutral enforcement of a secular constitutional value rather than the burden of some religion because of its beliefs. [71]

The existence of racially discriminatory schools may now be coming to an end since the Supreme Court has upheld the application of civil right statutes prohibiting racial discrimination to them. In 1976, in *Runyon v. McCrary*, [72] it held that a private school that excluded children because of their race violated 42 U.S.C.A. § 1981, the Civil Rights Act. This statute declares that all persons shall have the same right to contract as white persons. The statute was passed pursuant to congressional power granted by the thirteenth amendment and was to be applied to the actions of private persons or groups. The Court dismissed challenges to the validity of applying the statute to private schools, as past cases had established beyond peradventure that the Civil War Amendments did not recognize any associational-privacy right to segregate in public dealings or contracts. The Court did not decide whether a school which did not offer its services to all whites but only to an "invited" group would come under the terms of the statute. Additionally, there is a question as to the application of the statute to religious schools that segregated because of principles of their religion.

65. 417 U.S. 556 (1974).

66. 417 U.S. at 570.

67. 417 U.S. at 576 (Marshall, J., concurring); id. at 577 (Brennan, J., concurring); id. at 581 (White and Douglas J.J., concurring).

68. McGlotten v. Connally, 338 F.Supp. 448 (D.C. 1972) (three judge court per Bazelon, C.J.); Green v. Connally, 330 F.Supp. 1150 (D.D.C.1971) (three judge court per Leventhal, J.), aff'd sub nom. Coit v. Green, 404 U.S. 997 (1971).

69. See Pitts v. Department of Revenue, 333 F.Supp. 662 (E.D.Wis.1971) (three judge court); Falkenstein v. Department of Revenue, 350 F.Supp.

887 (D.Or.1972) (three judge court), appeal dismissed 409 U.S. 1099 (1973).

70. Rev.Rul. 71–447; 1971–2 Cum.Bull. 230.

71. Bob Jones University v. United States, 103 S.Ct. 2017 (1983). Earlier litigation concerning this issue was dismissed because it was brought in a manner which violated the tax injunction statutes. Bob Jones University v. Simon, 416 U.S. 725 (1974). See Chapter 19 on Freedom of Religion; Simon, The Tax-Exempt Status of Racially Discriminatory Religious Schools, 36 Tax L.Rev. 477 (1981).

72. 427 U.S. 160 (1976).

This question is more serious than the tax exemption issue for it would end the existence of these schools by government rule. The Court reserved this question for the future [73] and a prediction at this time would be speculative. It may be that the religion clauses of the first amendment requires the government to tolerate the existence of such schools while the equal protection clause of the fourteenth amendment requires the government to refrain from giving them any aid. Yet if these schools have any significant impact on the desegregation of other schools, it may be that the Civil War amendments will authorize the total prohibition of these racially discriminatory practices.

(3) Colleges and Universities

The deliberate speed concept was never applicable to state universities. The desegregation of higher education had begun prior to *Brown* in a series of Court decisions in which findings that educational facilities and opportunities afforded blacks were not equal resulted in the mandate of immediate admission of black students to previously white universities and law schools on a nonsegregated basis.[74] Following *Brown II*, some efforts were made to use the deliberate speed formula to slow down integration.[75] The Supreme Court rejected all such attempts, stating that qualified blacks seeking to enter colleges, graduate or professional schools were entitled to prompt relief.[76] In regard to private colleges and universities, the statutory prohibition of discriminatory admission practices by private schools, discussed in the previous section, will apply. The problem regarding religiously affiliated colleges will remain.

c. State School Programs Relating to Desegregation

As discussed briefly above, in connection with massive resistance, school authorities and state legislatures often adopted measures in an attempt to evade compliance with the principle of *Brown*. When faced with desegregation orders, some authorities reacted by closing public schools and giving financial support to private schools; others attempted to form new school districts. In other cases, school authorities superficially indicated compliance with the desegregation mandate but adopted desegregation plans which did not effectively integrate schools. These included freedom-of-choice plans or grade-a-year plans. In recent years, state legislatures have attempted to evade *Brown* through the passage of "antibusing" statutes. The Supreme Court has invalidated all of the above methods when used in an attempt to perpetuate segregated school systems.

(1) Grade-A-Year Plans

The grade-a-year plan, under which one school grade was desegregated per year, was a method commonly used in the desegregation of Southern schools. However, after the Supreme Court held that the time for mere deliberate speed had run out,[77] the Court invalidated a grade-a-year plan because the plan was too slow. In *Rogers v. Paul*[78] the Court was confronted with a school board which adopted such a plan, beginning with the first grade in 1957. Thus, in 1966 the 10th, 11th, and 12th grades remained segregated by law. The Court in a per curiam decision reversed the lower court's denial of the request by black high school students for immediate integration. The Court again noted that delays were no longer tolerable. Clearly such tactics could

---

73. 427 U.S. 160, 167 n. 6.

74. Sweatt v. Painter, 339 U.S. 629 (1950); McLaurin v. Oklahoma State Regents, 339 U.S. 637 (1950).

75. E.g., Board of Supervisors of Louisiana State University v. Tureaud, 225 F.2d 434 (5th Cir. 1956), cert. denied 351 U.S. 924.

76. Florida ex rel. Hawkins v. Board of Control, 350 U.S. 413 (1956) (per curiam).

77. Griffin v. County School Board of Prince Edward County, 377 U.S. 218 (1964).

78. Rogers v. Paul, 382 U.S. 198 (1965).

not be used to evade a constitutional mandate any longer.

(2) Freedom-of-Choice Plans

Some school authorities in districts with official segregation adopted free transfer or freedom-of-choice plans which gave the student some voice in deciding which school he would attend. In 1963, the Court invalidated a transfer policy that allowed students assigned to a school where their race was in the minority to transfer to a school where their race was in the majority because its inevitable effect was the perpetuation of school segregation.[79]

Five years later, in *Green v. County School Board*[80] the question before the Court was whether the school board's adoption of a freedom-of-choice plan that permitted a student to choose his own public school constituted adequate compliance with the board's responsibilities, as stated in *Brown*, "to achieve a system of determining admission to the public schools on a nonracial basis."[81] The Supreme Court invalidated the plan. Pursuant to state statute, a segregated school system had been established and had been perpetuated by the formation of a board to assign children to segregated schools. After being enrolled in a school, a child could request reassignment, but as of 1964, no pupil ever applied for admission to a school maintained for the other race. In 1965, following the initiation of this suit, the school board adopted the freedom-of-choice plan in order to desegregate the schools and remain eligible for federal financial aid. Under the plan, first and eighth graders were to choose a school. Pupils in other grades could annually choose a school, but if they did not, they simply remained assigned to the school they were attending. The Court stated that "in the context of the state-imposed segregated pattern of long standing, the fact that in 1965 the Board opened the

doors of the former 'white' school to Negro children and of the 'Negro' school to white children merely begins, not ends, our inquiry whether the Board has taken steps adequate to abolish its dual, segregated system."[82] The Court then examined the plan to see whether it realistically could be expected to provide immediate relief. Here, no white had enrolled at any black school, and 85% of the black students continued to attend all-black schools. The Board, therefore, was required to present an effective desegregation plan.

The Court in *Green* did not hold that the freedom-of-choice plan could not be adopted, but, rather, that in desegregating a school system such a plan might be of use under some circumstances. However, if there were reasonable alternatives available which would provide for speedier, more effective desegregation of schools, a freedom-of-choice plan was clearly unacceptable.

As indicated by *Green*, freedom-of-choice plans seldom achieved the desegregation required by *Brown*. Whites did not choose to attend black schools, and blacks were often discouraged from electing white schools because they feared retaliation or exertion of undue pressure by school officials; other times they were simply deterred by poverty. Where they did elect white schools, they were often targets of violence.[83] In *Raney v. Board of Education*,[84] a companion case to *Green*, the Court found that a freedom-of-choice plan was inadequate when blacks seeking admission to the white school were denied entrance because of overcrowding. In a third case, the Court struck down a free transfer plan that had not significantly affected the racial composition of segregated schools. The duty of school authorities who have run a de jure segregated system is to integrate the system, not to maintain the status quo created by prior official segregation.[85]

---

79. Goss v. Board of Education, 373 U.S. 683 (1963).

80. 391 U.S. 430 (1968).

81. 391 U.S. at 431–32.

82. 391 U.S. at 437.

83. 391 U.S. at 440, n. 5.

84. 301 U.S. 443 (1968).

85. Monroe v. Board of Comm'rs, 391 U.S. 450 (1968).

(3) Closing Public Schools

Another tactic employed to avoid desegregation of schools was to close public schools and to give financial support to private segregated schools. For example, when the Prince Edward County School Board was ordered in 1959 to take "immediate steps" beginning in September toward desegregation, the public schools simply did not open in the fall; instead private schools were established for whites. Most of the financial support of these private schools was in the form of indirect state and county tuition grants available for all students who attended private nonsectarian schools or in the form of private contributions prompted by the creation of a property tax exemption. In *Griffin v. County School Board of Prince Edward County*, [86] the Court affirmed that the closing of the Prince Edward County public schools was a denial of equal protection to black students. This decision is correct as the record clearly indicated that the state and county financially supported the private discriminatory schools; all other Virginia counties maintained public schools; and the only purpose for closing the public schools was to avoid desegregation. Because of the need for immediate relief, the Court upheld the district court's order that the payment of local tuition grants, the allowance of tax exemptions, and the processing of applications for state grants be suspended as long as the public schools remained closed. The Supreme Court also indicated that the district court could order appropriate local authorities to reopen and to financially support the public schools.[87]

(4) Creation of New School Districts

School authorities sometimes redesigned or established new school districts surprisingly soon after being ordered to desegregate a de jure segregated district. In 1972, in *Wright v. City Council of Emporia* [88] and *United States v. Scotland Neck City Board of Education*,[89] the Court forbade the creation by local authorities of new school districts which would adversely affect the effectiveness of an earlier desegregation order.

In *Wright*, a five to four majority upheld an injunction prohibiting subdivision of a school district based on the impact of such an action. The City of Emporia, Virginia and the county had entered a contractual agreement by which the county would continue to provide public schooling to Emporia residents along with others, with Emporia sharing the costs. The lower court found de jure segregation; therefore, Emporia and the county were ordered to have a desegregated school system. Two weeks after the desegregation decree was entered, Emporia began its plans to operate its own unitary school system. Because Emporia had long been part of the de jure segregated county school system and had decided to withdraw only after the issuance of the desegregation decree, a showing of an independent constitutional violation did not have to be made.[90] The proposal for the new school system was to be judged by the standard stated in freedom-of-choice plan decisions; it would be found invalid if it hindered rather than furthered school desegregation. The finding of the district court that the establishment of the new school system would deprive blacks living in the county of their right to desegregated public schooling was supported by adequate evidence, including *inter alia* the resulting racial disparity between the city and county schools, the timing of Emporia's action, and the superior quality of the previously white schools located in the city compared to the outlying black schools. Thus, Emporia could not now create a new district, claim that it involved only de facto segregation, and avoid the desegregation ruling.

---

86. 377 U.S. 218 (1967).
87. 377 U.S. at 233–4.
88. 407 U.S. 451 (1972).

89. 407 U.S. 484 (1972).
90. 407 U.S. at 459.

The four dissenting justices [91] agreed with the principles stated by the majority but disagreed with the findings of fact. Chief Justice Burger summarized their position when he stated that the city should have a right to terminate its own system unless there were a clearer showing that it would frustrate the dismantling of the dual school system.[92]

In *Scotland Neck* the Supreme Court unanimously upheld the District Court's decision to enjoin the carving out of a new school district from a larger district which had been ordered to desegregate. The majority here simply relied upon the holding in *Wright*. The four justices dissenting in *Wright* filed a concurring opinion to explain why they distinguished *Wright* and *Scotland Neck*.[93] Here, the operation of a separate school system would preclude meaningful desegregation. Additionally, Emporia had been accepting its responsibility as an independent governmental entity to provide independent education whereas this change was clearly motivated by desire to avoid desegregation.

(5) Legislative Modifications of Federal Desegregation Remedies

The transferring of students to achieve integration of schools has met with public disapproval. But if legislatures respond to public pressure with "antibusing" statutes, the courts must respond by striking them down. In *North Carolina State Board of Education v. Swann* [94] the Supreme Court affirmed the lower court decision striking a North Carolina statute that forbade the school assignment of any student on the basis of race or for the purpose of creating a racial balance in the schools and forbade the use of busing for such purpose. Under the fourteenth amendment and the supremacy clause of Article VI, the States may not interfere with federal remedies for constitutional violations.[95]

There have been a variety of proposals before the Congress to restrict the authority of federal courts to remedy racial segregation in public school systems. Congress did pass legislation providing for the stay of busing orders pending appeal [96] and setting forth a priority of remedies which indicated that the transportation of students should be used only as a last resort.[97] But these statutes did not limit the authority of federal courts to issue orders calling for the redistricting of schools or transportation of students in order to correct de jure segregation.[98] As of December, 1982, the Congress had not approved legislative proposals to restrict federal court authority to remedy a racially segregated school system which had been judicially determined to be in violation of the fourteenth amendment.[99]

(6) Modification of State Remedies

In two states, voters expressed their dissatisfaction with the busing of students pursuant to state law by enacting legislation limiting remedies available for desegregating schools. However, because of the different methods employed to limit the

---

91. Justices Burger, Blackmun, Powell, and Rehnquist dissented. 407 U.S. at 471.

92. 407 U.S. at 471–72 (Burger, C.J., dissenting).

93. 407 U.S. at 491 (Burger, C.J., concurring).

94. 402 U.S. 43 (1971).

95. Cf. New York v. Cathedral Academy, 434 U.S. 125, 130 (1977), wherein the majority opinion stated that a state legislature may not "effectively modify a federal court's injunction whenever a balancing of constitutional equities might conceivably have justified the court's granting similar relief in the first place." (This decision is also noted in Chapter 19: Freedom of Religion.)

96. Education Amendments Act of 1972, Pub.L. No. 92–318 § 803, 82 Stat. 235. See generally, Hearings on

Proposed Amendments to the Constitution and Legislation Relating to Transportation and Assignment of Public School Pupils, Before Subcommittee No. 5 of the House Committee on the Judiciary, 92d Cong., 2d Sess. (1972).

97. Education Amendments Act of 1974, Pub.L. 93–380, 88 Stat. 484.

98. Such was the position of Justice Powell. See Drummond v. Acree, 409 U.S. 1228 (1972) (opinion of Justice Powell as Circuit Justice) denying stay in Acree v. County Bd. of Education, 458 F.2d 486 (5th Cir. 1972), cert. denied 409 U.S. 1006.

99. For an examination of this issue see Chapter 2, Section III.

transfer of students to achieve integration, only one state's action was upheld. In Washington, voters adopted, through a statewide initiative, a state which effectively permitted assignment and transfer of students for all purposes except for the purpose of integration of schools.[100] The Supreme Court in *Washington v. Seattle School District No. 1*[101] held that the statute was a violation of the equal protection clause of the fourteenth amendment because it did not allocate governmental power on the basis of any general principle, but instead ". . . uses the racial nature of an issue to define the governmental decision-making structure, and thus imposes substantial and unique burdens on racial minorities."[102] Rejecting the state's argument that the legislation has no racial overtones, the Court saw the statute as removing the authority to address a racial problem, and that problem only, from the local school board and placing it in the hands of the state legislature. This restructuring of governmental power places special, impermissible burdens on minority interests, because those seeking integration of Washington schools must now seek relief from the statewide electorate or the state legislature, a new and remote level of government.

In California, voters adopted a state constitutional amendment providing that state courts cannot order mandatory student assignment or transportation unless a federal court would do so to remedy a violation of the equal protection clause of the fourteenth amendment. In *Crawford v. Board of Education*,[103] the Supreme Court upheld the amendment, rejecting the argument that the mere repeal of race related legislation embodies a presumptively invalid racial classification. The Court refused to see the amendment as allocating governmental or judicial

power on the basis of a discriminatory principle. Having gone beyond the requirements of the fourteenth amendment, California was free to return to the standard of the federal Constitution. The Court saw the amendment as removing simply one means of achieving integrated schools because under California law, the local school districts still retain the obligation to alleviate segregation regardless of cause and they remain free to adopt busing plans to effectuate desegregation.

Justice Powell, writing the majority opinion in *Crawford* and a dissenting opinion in *Seattle*, viewed the two decisions as incompatible.[104] Crucial distinctions, however, underlie the two holdings. The Washington statute embodied an explicit racial classification in that it reallocated decision-making authority in such a way as to make it more difficult for minority groups than other community members to obtain legislation in their interest. By singling out minorities for particularly disadvantageous treatment within the political process, the statute did more than the California constitutional amendment, which merely repealed the right to invoke a state judicial busing remedy heretofore available. Though the California amendment, like the Washington statute, may make it more difficult to achieve school integration, it does not do so by altering the political process in such a way as to burden minority interests.[105] Also underlying the *Crawford* holding is a concern over limiting a state's authority to deal with racial problems. To hold that the mere repeal of race related legislation is unconstitutional would imply that such legislation could never be repealed and discourage the states from experimenting with legislation designed to im-

---

100. The statute allowed busing for racial purposes in one circumstance: it did not "prevent any court of competent jurisdiction from adjudicating constitutional issues relating to the public schools." Wash.Rev. Code § 28A.26.060 (1981). Washington v. Seattle School District No. 1, 102 S.Ct. 3187, 3191 (1982).

101. 102 S.Ct. 3187 (1982).

102. 102 S.Ct. at 3195.

103. 102 S.Ct. 3211 (1982).

104. Washington v. Seattle School District No. 1, 102 S.Ct. 3187, 3204 (1982) (Powell, J., dissenting, joined by Burger, C.J., Rehnquist and O'Connor JJ.).

105. See the concurring opinion of Justice Blackmun, joined by Justice Brennan, in Crawford v. Board of Education, 102 S.Ct. at 3222–23.

prove race relations.[106] Further, the people of the state, as the final authority over their state constitution, have the right to determine the nature of the judicially enforceable desegregation obligation under their constitution.[107] To define that obligation in terms of the principles of the fourteenth amendment does not violate that amendment.

d. Federal Court Remedial Powers

When, in the years following *Brown*, little progress was made toward the desegregation of schools, the Supreme Court stated the need for immediate relief but said little about what form this relief should take. The result was confusion. The problems encountered by judges of the lower federal courts made clear their need for guidance from the Supreme Court as to the scope of federal court powers to dismantle de jure segregated school systems. Therefore, in 1971, in *Swann v. Charlotte-Mecklenburg Board of Education*[108] the Court discussed in more precise terms the scope of the duty of school authorities and district courts to fashion an end to racially segregated school systems.

A federal court is not empowered to take any action or to require the school authorities to take any action until there has been a showing of de jure segregation. The Court has preserved the de jure-de facto distinction. Only if there is a showing of purposeful discrimination in a substantial portion of a school district is there a presumption of intentional discrimination in the rest of the district. The presumption can be rebutted only by showing that no such intent existed.[109]

Even when the Court finds there has been purposeful discrimination, school authorities will be given the opportunity to submit a plan for desegregation. Only when the school authorities are found to be engaged in de jure segregation and also fail to submit an adequate desegregation plan does the district court have the authority to order specific steps to desegregate the schools. The Court in *Swann* first discussed the responsibilities of school authorities in regard to nonstudent remedies. The existing policy and practices with regard to faculty, staff, transportation, extracurricular activities, and facilities are among the most important indicia of a segregated school system. If it is possible to identify a school as a white school or a black school by the racial composition of the faculty and staff, the quality of the school buildings or equipment, or the organization of sport activities, a prima facie case of an equal protection violation is established.[110]

When there has been a violation of equal protection the first duty of school authorities is to eliminate all invidious racial discriminations. The action should be immediate with respect to transportation, supporting personnel, extracurricular activities, maintenance of buildings and distribution of equipment.[111] Faculty assignment and the construction of new schools offer easy, flexible ways to achieve integration. The Court, therefore, upheld the district court's use of a fixed ratio in making faculty assignments to achieve an initial degree of desegregation and correction of the de jure segregation. Because the location of school buildings may determine the racial composition of individual schools, particular care must be given by school authorities and courts to prevent the use of future school construction and abandonment to perpetuate or re-establish the dual system.[112]

The Court then turned its attention to the question of remedies for the de jure racial

106. See 102 S.Ct. at 3219.

107. The right of each state to determine what its constitution means, as long as it meets the minimum guarantees of the federal Constitution, is the basis of each state's power to expand its constitutional protection of individual rights beyond those established by the federal Constitution. See Section III, B of Chapter I.

108. 402 U.S. 1 (1971).

109. Keyes v. School District No. 1, 413 U.S. 189 (1973). See generally, L. Graglia, Disaster by Decree (1976) for a thorough criticism of this case and similar decisions.

110. Swann v. Charlotte-Mecklenburg Bd. of Education, 402 U.S. 1, 18 (1971).

111. Id.

112. 402 U.S. at 20–21.

segregation of students. Where such practices have existed they must be terminated and a nondiscriminatory school system must be established. Here the school authorities are given an opportunity to correct the system by presenting an effective plan for desegregation. As already discussed, grade-a-year plans, freedom-of-choice plans, or other preferred "remedies" that do not truly reverse the segregation are inadequate. In such situations, the district court is forced to use student remedies.

The Court in *Swann* discussed the extent to which attendance zones may be remedially altered by district courts. The redesign of school districts and attendance zones has been one of the tools most frequently used by both school planners and courts to eliminate dual systems. As an interim measure such zoning, including the creation of attendance zones neither compact nor contiguous, is within the remedial powers of a court.[113] If all things are equal, students should be assigned to the school closest their homes. But all things are not equal in a deliberately segregated school system; the students formerly segregated must be mixed to desegregate the system. Although the remedy may be administratively awkward or burdensome for some students, some reasonable amount of inconvenience or burden cannot be avoided in the transition from segregation to integration. In determining the validity of a particular attendance plan the lower court should make its decision in light of the objective sought and its knowledge of local conditions. Reasonable decrees will meet with the approval of the Supreme Court.

The Court also discussed busing, which has been an important tool for the desegregation of schools. If, as in *Swann*, the assignment of students to the schools nearest their homes would not effectively dismantle the segregated school system, the court may order the assignment of some students to schools at a distance which requires the pro-

vision of some transportation for students. Because of the infinite variety of local problems and conditions, the Supreme Court did not set rigid guidelines in *Swann*. It simply stated that neither the time nor the distance involved should be so great as to risk the health of the children or to significantly impinge on the educational process.[114] The age of the children is probably the primary factor for the courts to consider in determining the limits on travel time.[115] Very young children are not to be assigned to schools far from their homes. Older children such as those in high school can ride buses to school with little impact on their education.

Amazingly, there is little else to the "busing" problem. Where a school district has engaged in de jure segregation and has refused to submit an effective plan to end segregation, the district court must fashion for them a remedial decree to end segregation. The district judge's only other option would be to violate his oath to support the Constitution by simply allowing a school district to refuse to comply with the requirements of the fourteenth amendment. The district court may decree that some students be assigned to schools other than those closest to their home in order to desegregate the student bodies of the schools. If the reassignment is beyond normal walking distance for a child, the court may order the school district to provide transportation for the students. Often this reassignment seems to be linked in public debate to some concept of "statistical ratios" being imposed by judges. However, as discussed in a previous section, statistical imbalance alone will not establish de jure segregation. The extent to which children are reassigned to eliminate segregation does involve the use of statistics as explained in *Swann*.

The Court has upheld the use of an initial statistical ratio for faculty assignment. The Supreme Court also found that the limited use of mathematical ratios in student assignment was valid, especially if the school

---

113. 402 U.S. at 27–28.

114. 402 U.S. at 30–31.

115. Id.

board fails to submit an effective plan. But there is no requirement that every school reflect the racial composition of the school system as a whole.[116] Indeed, the Court ruled in *Swann* that there was no absolute requirement that every one-race school be eliminated. Schools whose students are all, or virtually all, of the same race would require close scrutiny, but their existence alone is not a sufficient indication of a segregated system.[117] Because the goal is to end de jure segregation, school and judicial authorities would necessarily be concerned with the elimination of such schools. The strict use of ratios is not permissible. Courts cannot require schools to maintain a certain ratio but, instead, must tailor their decrees to provide a reasonable remedy. In a later case, the Supreme Court held that the district court could not require an annual adjustment in the student ratios in the absence of a showing that the shift in racial balance was the result of purposeful discrimination.[118]

The final, and most important, limit on federal court remedial powers arose in *Milliken v. Bradley*.[119] A majority in that case prohibited district courts from fashioning remedies that included more than one school district absent any finding that the other included school districts have failed to operate unitary, integrated school systems or that the boundary lines of the affected school districts were established with the purpose of fostering racial segregation.

The Supreme Court followed these previously agreed upon principles in two unanimous decisions on school desegregation orders. In *Milliken v. Bradley (Milliken II)*,[120] the Court held that a federal district court could order the State of Michigan to pay a share of the cost of compensatory and remedial educational programs. These programs were found necessary to correct the effects of past de jure discrimination in the establishment and maintenance of the Detroit school system for which the State had some responsibility. The order violated neither the tenth nor eleventh amendments since the order required prospective compliance with the requirements of the fourteenth amendment.

In the second case, the Court remanded for reconsideration and clarification, a case wherein a district judge had ordered a wide ranging student transfer plan for a seemingly minor occurrence of segregation in a school district. In *Dayton Bd. of Education v. Brinkman*,[121] the Court unanimously held that, if the evidence in the record supported a finding of segregation throughout the school system, the judge might be able to order system-wide busing if it did not impair educational interests. If the segregation in fact occurred only in a part of the system, the remedy must be limited to that area.

Following the remand of the *Dayton* case, the district court found that there was a violation of the Constitution as to only a limited number of schools in the district, but the court of appeals reversed and found that the proof of purposeful discrimination as to a selected group of schools gave rise to an inference of area wide discrimination and that the school board had failed to meet its burden of showing that it had not engaged in area wide discrimination. The Supreme Court upheld the court of appeals and found clear proof that the Dayton school board had intentionally discriminated against black students and operated segregated schools in 1954, that the board had never taken any action to dismantle its dual school system, and that the board had simply refused to attempt to integrate the school system which had been admittedly segregated in the

---

116. Swann v. Charlotte-Mecklenburg Bd. of Education, 402 U.S. 1, 24–5 (1971).

117. Id.

118. Pasadena City Bd. of Education v. Spangler, 427 U.S. 1335 (1976).

119. 418 U.S. 717 (1974), discussed in text at n. 49, supra.

120. 433 U.S. 267 (1977).

121. 433 U.S. 406 (1977).

past.[122] The clear establishment of a continuing violation as to a few schools gave rise to an inference of area wide discrimination, and the school board was unable to demonstrate that the inference was unjustified; it did not show that its policies had been clearly designed to achieve important educational goals rather than to maintain the segregated school system.[123]

2. Desegregation of Other Facilities

Although the Supreme Court delayed implementation of public school desegregation, it did order an immediate end to state-imposed racial segregation in other public facilities. In the decade following *Brown I*, primarily in a series of per curiam decisions, the Court invalidated the segregation of: public beaches and bathhouses,[124] golf courses,[125] buses,[126] parks,[127] athletic contests,[128] public restaurants,[129] auditoriums,[130] and courtroom seating.[131] The lower courts followed suit[132] so that where racial segregation was found in contexts other than public education, immediate relief was ordered so long as state action was found. However, many of the public facilities that excluded or segregated blacks were privately owned and, therefore, not subject to the restrictions of the equal protection clause.

Further desegregation of public facilities was required after the enactment of the Civil Rights Act of 1964, which prohibits racial discrimination in "establishments affecting interstate commerce or supported in their activities by State action as places of public accommodation, lodgings, facilities principally engaged in selling food for consumption on the premises, gasoline stations [and] places of exhibition or entertainments."[133] The act was upheld by the Court as an exercise of congressional power to regulate interstate commerce.[134] Similarly, the Court has upheld and applied statutes passed pursuant to the Congressional power under the thirteenth amendment to eliminate racial discrimination in property sales and business contracts.[135] Of course, there have been tremendous problems in enforcing these statutes.[136]

---

122. Dayton Bd. of Education v. Brinkman, 443 U.S. 526 (1979).

123. The Supreme Court has avoided ruling on the details of desegregation plans adopted by lower federal courts since the 1979 Ohio cases. See, e.g., Delaware State Bd. of Education v. Alexis I. duPont School District, 447 U.S. 916 (1980) (Rehnquist, Stewart, and Powell, JJ., dissenting to denial of certiorari). The Supreme Court declined to review a case where a district court order to remedy school segregation involved student reassignment beyond the boundaries of an individual city. However, in this case the lower courts had found evidence of purposeful segregation in the establishment of attendance zones within a system that included a variety of municipalities. Cleveland Bd. of Education v. Reed, 445 U.S. 935 (1980) (Rehnquist, J., joined by Burger, C.J., and Powell, J., dissenting to denial of certiorari). During the 1979–80 Term, the Court refused to review a decision of the United States Court of Appeals which remanded a case to the district court to provide for more extensive pupil reassignment, busing, and statistically better racial balance in public schools than the district judge had originally required. See Estes v. Metropolitan Branches of Dallas NAACP, 444 U.S. 437 (1980) (dismissing writs of certiorari as improvidently granted) (Powell, Stewart, and Rehnquist, JJ., dissenting).

124. Mayor of Baltimore v. Dawson, 350 U.S. 877 (1955) (per curiam).

125. Holmes v. City of Atlanta, 350 U.S. 879 (1955) (per curiam). Orleans Park Development Ass'n v. Detiege, 358 U.S. 54 (per curiam) (1958).

126. Gayle v. Browder, 352 U.S. 903 (1956) (per curiam).

127. Muir v. Louisville Park Theatrical Ass'n, 347 U.S. 971 (1954) (per curiam); New Orleans Park Development Ass'n v. Detiege, 358 U.S. 54 (1958) (per curiam).

128. State Athletics Comm'r v. Dorsey, 359 U.S. 533 (per curiam) (1959).

129. Turner v. City of Memphis, 369 U.S. 350 (1962).

130. Schiro v. Bynum, 375 U.S. 395 (1964) (per curiam).

131. Johnson v. Virginia, 373 U.S. 61 (1963).

132. D. Bell, Race, Racism and American Law, 208–15 (1st ed. 1973); see also Chapter 3 of the second edition of D. Bell, Race, Racism and American Law (2d ed. 1980).

133. 42 U.S.C.A. § 2000a(b).

134. Heart of Atlanta Motel, Inc. v. United States, 379 U.S. 241 (1964); Katzenbach v. McClung, 379 U.S. 294 (1964).

135. Runyon v. McCrary, 727 U.S. 160 (1976); Jones v. Alfred H. Mayer Co., 392 U.S. 409 (1968).

136. For an examination of these enforcement issues, see D. Bell, Race, Racism and American Law, supra note 132; N. Dorsen, P. Bender, B. Neuborne & S.

The closing of public facilities and the re-opening of privately-owned facilities in their stead has also occurred in other contexts besides schools as in the *Griffin v. Prince Edward County Board of Education* case discussed above. In *Palmer v. Thompson* [137] the Court faced the issue of the constitutionality of shutting down city pools allegedly in response to a court decree that pools could not be racially segregated. The Court affirmed the lower court's decision that closing the pools did not violate the equal protection clause. The city was under no affirmative duty to operate any swimming pools. Although one pool previously leased from the YMCA by the city apparently was being run by that organization for whites only and another pool previously owned by the city was owned and operated by a predominantly black college, there was no evidence to show the city was directly or indirectly involved in the funding or operation of either pool. The majority would not examine the motivation of the legislators. [138] The dissenting justices disagreed with the assertion that it was impermissible to find invidious purpose on the evidence in the case. The closing came only after a desegregation order and the dissent believed the ruling came dangerously close to allowing a town to evade the mandate of the fourteenth amendment. [139]

Interdistrict relief problems have also arisen apart from school integration. In *Hills v. Gautreaux* [140] the question before the Court was the appropriateness of interdistrict relief in the context of public housing. The Court distinguished this case from *Milliken v. Bradley* [141] and held that district court

should have considered the possibility of ordering a metropolitan area remedy.

In 1969 summary judgment was entered against the Chicago Housing Authority (CHA) on the basis of uncontradicted evidence showing that it had selected public housing sites and had made tenant assignments on the basis of race. CHA was accordingly directed to locate its new family public housing in predominantly white neighborhoods. Summary judgment was also entered against the U.S. Department of Housing and Urban Development (HUD) for its violation of the fifth amendment and Civil Rights Act of 1964 by assisting the CHA discriminatory actions. In formulating a remedy, the district court rejected a plan for metropolitan relief, finding that there had been no proof of separate racially discriminatory acts in the suburbs of Chicago into which the public housing might be placed. [142] The United States Court of Appeals for the Seventh Circuit reversed and remanded the case for the adoption of a "comprehensive area plan." [143]

The Supreme Court rejected HUD's contentions that *Milliken* barred the adoption of a metropolitan area plan and found that the district court had the authority to order remedial action by HUD outside the city limits. HUD, unlike the suburban school districts in *Milliken,* had been found to have violated the Constitution, thereby providing the necessary predicate for the entry of a remedial order against HUD. [144] Following the finding of a Constitutional violation, the district court has broad authority to provide for an effective remedy. Nothing in *Milliken* suggested the federal courts lack the au-

---

Law, Political & Civil Rights in the United States Vol. II (4th ed. 1979); J. Greenberg, Judicial Process and Social Change 1–327 (1977).

137. 403 U.S. 217 (1971).

138. On the problem of establishing classifications which do not openly appear in government acts and the question of legislative purpose see Chapter 16, Section I, D.

139. 403 U.S. at 231 (Douglas, J., dissenting); id. at 240 (White, J., dissenting); id. at 271 (Marshall J., dissenting). Justice Brennan joined in the dissent of Justices White and Marshall.

140. 425 U.S. 284 (1976).

141. 418 U.S. 717 (1974). The distinction between the cases is also considered in Chapter 14, Section IV, D on State Action.

142. Gautreaux v. Romney, 363 F.Supp. 690 (N.D. Ill.1973).

143. Gautreaux v. Chicago Housing Authority, 503 F.2d 930 (1974) (opinion per Clark, J.).

144. Hills v. Gautreaux, 425 U.S. 284, 297–300 (1976).

thority to order parties guilty of unconstitutional behavior to undertake remedial efforts beyond the boundaries of the city where the violation occurred. Rather, they lacked the authority to interfere with the operations of governmental units that had not been implicated in any wrongdoing.

The Court then turned to the contention that the order would impermissibly interfere with local governments and suburban housing authorities by requiring HUD to "ignore the safeguards of local autonomy and local political processes." [145] The Court found that no such interference would result from the remedy in this situation. In contrast to the *Milliken* desegregation order, a metropolitan relief order would not consolidate or restructure local political units; the decree would have the same effect as a discretionary decision by HUD to offer alternatives to the segregated Chicago public housing system created by CHA and HUD. The case was therefore remanded to the district court for further consideration of the appropriateness of metropolitan area relief in the specific case.

F. "Benign" Racial Classifications—Affirmative Action Programs

1. Introduction

As Justice Brennan has stated, "[f]ew constitutional questions in recent years have stirred as much debate" [1] as the question of "benign" discrimination—the use of racial classifications to benefit rather than burden particular racial or ethnic minorities. We have seen in this Chapter that the Supreme Court has held that racial classifications which discriminate against minorities are inherently "suspect" and will be subject to "strict scrutiny" and upheld only if necessary to promote a "compelling" state interest. [2] However, it is unclear whether the same

standard of review should be applied to government action which discriminates in favor of racial or ethnic minorities. Is strict scrutiny required under the equal protection clause only where legislation discriminates against a "discrete and insular" minority so that reasonable affirmative action programs are permissible? Alternatively, is the test designed to enforce a constitutional principle of race neutrality so that affirmative action programs violate a "color-blind" principle of the fourteenth amendment? Before turning to the limited Supreme Court rulings in this area, which resolve few affirmative action issues, we should briefly note the parameters of the affirmative action problem.

The debate on "affirmative action" has focused on three practices: using quotas in making public housing assignments to insure the housing is integrated; giving minority members preferential treatment in hiring and promotions to atone for past discriminatory actions; and adopting preferential admission programs for minority students at universities and professional schools. The goals of racial equality and integration have never been the subject of serious constitutional challenge; the objections have been directed at the means used: racial preferences and quotas. [3] The controversy over the constitutionality of such programs stems largely from the apparent conflict between two equal protection goals: the removal of any remaining barriers to full racial equality and the requirement of governmental treatment of individuals on the basis of their personal merit rather than their race. [4]

In judging the constitutionality of affirmative action programs, a distinction must be drawn between two basic forms of affirmative action. A quota may be set reserving a specific number of places for minority members and a specific number for nonminority

---

145. 425 U.S. at 300.

1. DeFunis v. Odegaard, 416 U.S. 312, 350 (1974) (Brennan, J., dissenting).

2. For a discussion of the judicial treatment given to racial classifications see Sections II, A to II, E of this chapter.

3. See Lavinsky, DeFunis v. Odegaard: The Non-Decision With A Message, 75 Columbia L.Rev. 520 (1975).

4. See Greenawalt, Judicial Scrutiny of "Benign" Racial Preference in Law School Admissions, 75 Columbia L.Rev. 559 (1975).

members. Alternatively, separate standards may be set giving preferential treatment to minority members without the use of a quota. The quota programs are difficult, if not impossible, to defend. When the government distributes benefits under a strict quota system, it totally disregards individual circumstances and also burdens members of minority races.[5] For example, if a government housing project consists of 100 units to be assigned 50% to white families and 50% to black families, the fifty-first black family to apply will be denied housing because of its race even if there are housing units available. This system disregards both the need for benefits and the availability of government benefits. That the program burdens both white and black should be irrelevant given past decisions of the Supreme Court.[6] One lower federal court upheld such a system on the basis that the quotas prevented "white flight" and maintained integrated public housing.[7] Yet a majority member's dislike of living near a large number of minority persons hardly seems to be a sufficient reason for refusing to extend benefits to the "excess" black person. Indeed, this use of the quota system stands integration on its head; it becomes a tool for limiting the rights of minorities by accepting the bias of members of the majority race.[8]

When a program gives members of minority races clearly preferential treatment, such as guaranteeing them a minimum (but not fixed) share of benefits, the problem becomes more complex. Here the goals of racial equality for the minority and integration both seem to be effectively promoted by the affirmative action program. The issue is whether the use of a racial classification is prohibited because the Constitution prohibits limiting the opportunities of anyone on the basis of his race. The decisions of the Supreme Court to date do not resolve the question of whether the government may use such racial classifications to dispense benefits.

The Supreme Court has consistently invalidated racial classifications, but it has never held that racial classifications are unconstitutional per se.[9] The Court seems to have approved at least the keeping of some statistical information by race as that may further race-neutral purposes.[10] But this holding could be seen as the Court's approval of truly neutral actions. The Supreme Court has ruled that the use of racial classifications by school authorities to implement the desegregation of an intentionally segregated school system is not only constitutionally permissible but, in fact, may be mandated by court order.[11] Similarly, in the field of employment giving preference to qualified minority

---

5. Developments in the Law-Equal Protection, 82 Harv.L.Rev. 1065, 1117 (1969).

6. Loving v. Virginia, 388 U.S. 1 (1967) (striking miscegenation statute though state argued it limited the marital rights of both black and white persons).

7. Otero v. New York City Housing Authority, 484 F.2d 1122 (2d Cir. 1973).

8. In this way the case seems at odds with the Supreme Court's decision in Cooper v. Aaron, 358 U.S. 1 (1958) where it held that violent reaction of white persons could not justify a delay in integrating schools. Indeed, Plessy v. Ferguson, 163 U.S. 537 (1896) was based in part on the belief that white persons would react violently if they had to ride a train with blacks and that the state could grant "separate but equal" facilities to blacks to avoid this. Since the overruling of Plessy, one is surprised to find a federal court raising "white flight" to a constitutional consideration. See also, United States v. Scotland Neck City Bd. of Education, 407 U.S. 484, 491 (1972) (fear of white flight "cannot . . . be accepted as a reason for achieving

anything less than complete uprooting of the dual public school system.").

For an analysis of this issue see Smolla, Integration Maintenance: The Unconstitutionality of Benign Programs That Discourage Black Entry to Prevent White Flight, 1981 Duke L.J. 891.

9. See Henkin, DeFunis: An Introduction, 75 Columbia Law Review 483, 485–86 (1975).

10. The Court has summarily approved the keeping of government records which included racial information kept to further race-neutral goals. See Hamm v. Virginia State Bd. of Elections, 230 F.Supp. 156 (E.D. Va.1964) aff'd per curiam sub nom. Tancil v. Woolls, 379 U.S. 19 (1964) (invalidating the keeping of separate lists of voters and taxpayers by race but permitting the state to require that the race of a husband and wife be identified in a divorce decree).

11. See Swann v. Charlotte-Mecklenburg Bd. of Education, 402 U.S. 1 (1971); O'Neil, Racial Preference and Higher Education: The Larger Context, 60 Va.L. Rev. 917, 928 (1974).

employees to remedy past discriminatory practices has been judicially approved. While the Court has not upheld using minimum quotas for hiring new employees where past discrimination is found, it has upheld other remedial practices under the civil rights acts.[12]

A difficult question arises where there has been no finding of de jure segregation and such remedial measures are undertaken voluntarily.[13] The Supreme Court has suggested that a school board does have the authority to use racial classifications to produce a mixed student body which reflects society.[14] Voluntary measures to end de facto school segregation in elementary and high schools by use of racial classifications and integration programs have been upheld consistently by both federal and state courts.[15] These situations may be differentiated from preferential admissions to professional schools because all students are provided with a public education and no one has a right to

attend segregated schools. However, some students may suffer because they are no longer able to attend the best schools, but schools should be relatively equal within a school district unless the authorities have engaged in other discriminatory acts. The difference in degree should not determine the resolution of the constitutional issue.[16] It has been argued that it would be anomalous to require remedial measures where there has been a showing of explicit government discrimination but not to permit such measures to be voluntarily undertaken where there had been de facto segregation.[17]

Unfortunately these remedial action cases do not necessarily resolve the affirmative action issue.[18] The question is whether the strict scrutiny-compelling interest test should be employed to determine the permissibility of these racial classifications. If this test is used, one should expect that most affirmative action programs will be held invalid, for the Court would be adopting a race

---

12. In United Steel Workers of America v. Weber, 443 U.S. 193 (1979), the Court held that Title VII of the Civil Rights Acts did not prohibit the voluntary use of affirmative action programs by private employers.

Franks v. Bowman Transp. Co., 424 U.S. 747 (1976) (retroactive seniority may be given to those discriminated against in previous hiring practices). The Court has held that the civil rights acts relating to employment and contracts protect white persons as well as minorities. McDonald v. Santa Fe Trail Transp. Co., 427 U.S. 273 (1976).

13. See note 14, infra; Developments in the Law—Equal Protection, 82 Harv.Law Rev. 1065, 1104 (1969).

14. The Court stated in Swann v. Charlotte-Mecklenburg Bd. of Education, 402 U.S. 1, 16 (1971):

"School authorities are traditionally charged with broad power to formulate and implement educational policy and might well conclude, for example, that in order to prepare students to live in a pluralistic society each school should have a prescribed ratio of Negro to white students reflecting the proportion for the district as a whole. To do this as an educational policy is within the broad discretionary power of the school authorities; absent a finding of a constitutional violation, however, that would not be within the authority of a federal court."

15. When state agencies or courts engage in the transferring or busing of students to achieve a racially balanced school system which is not mandated by the fourteenth amendment, state law may be amended to end that action if, but only if, the state does so without employing a racial classification. Compare, Washington v. Seattle School District, 102 S.Ct. 3187 (1982),

with, Crawford v. Los Angeles Bd. of Education, 102 S.Ct. 3211 (1982). These cases are examined in Section II E, 1, c, (6) of this Chapter. Developments, supra note 13 at 1108. See Offermann v. Nitkowski, 378 F.2d 22 (2d Cir. 1967); Tometz v. Board of Education, 39 Ill.2d 593, 237 N.E.2d 498 (1968); School Comm'n v. Board of Education, 352 Mass. 693, 227 N.E.2d 729 (1967), appeal dismissed 389 U.S. 572 (1968); Booker v. Board of Education, 45 N.J. 161, 212 A.2d 281 (1965).

16. Ely, Reverse Racial Discrimination, 41 U.Chi.L. Rev. 723, 724 (1974); J. Ely, Democracy and Distrust 61–2, 170–72 (1980).

17. O'Neil, Racial Preference and Higher Education: The Larger Context, 60 Va.L.Rev. 925, 930 (1974).

18. For further examination of these issues see "DeFunis" Symposium, 75 Columbia Law Review 483 (1975); Sandalow, Racial Preferences in Higher Education: Political Responsibility and the Judicial Role, 42 U.Chi.L.Rev. 653 (1975); O'Neil, Preferential Admissions: Equalizing the Access of Minority Groups to Higher Education, 80 Yale L.J. 699 (1971); Developments, supra note 13; Note, Ameliorative Racial Classifications Under the Equal Protection Clause, 1973 Duke L.J. 1126; Redish, Preferential Law School Admissions and the Equal Protection Clause: An Analysis of the Competing Arguments, 22 U.C.L.A.L.Rev. 343 (1974); Ely, supra note 16; Posner, The DeFunis Case and the Constitutionality of Preferential Treatment of Racial Minorities, 1974 Sup.Ct.Rev. 1; Smolla, supra note 8; Choper, The Constitutionality of Affirmative Action: Views From the Supreme Court, 70 Ky.L.J. 1 (1981). See note 35 infra.

neutral standard for government action apart from specific remedies for past discrimination. If the Court finds that there is only an absolute prohibition of racial classifications used to burden a minority, some of the affirmative action programs would be upheld. A valid program would have to be one which is reasonable in terms of promoting racial equality and integration. Totally arbitrary programs resulting in burdening some minority members or members of the majority without reasonably advancing racial equality and integration would be invalid under equal protection analysis. The Court could declare that all racial classifications are "suspect" but that these classifications are used to advance "compelling interests." This approach would amount to no more than placing affirmative action classifications under a separate reasonableness test while adding further to the confusion over the meaning of the term "compelling interest." [19] Alternatively, the Court could declare the correction of the effects past societal racial discrimination to be a sufficiently important end to support any reasonable program. This would place affirmative action programs under the same standard of review as gender classifications.[20] The question remains: what approach should or will the Supreme Court take?

It may seem ironic that a measure enacted to protect a minority from adverse treatment could be used to bar programs designed to remedy past discrimination.[21] While the equal protection clause undoubtedly protects majorities as well as minorities, the traditional rationale for strict scrutiny may not be applicable.[22] One reason race classifications traditionally have been regarded as "suspect" is that their historic use was to discriminate against discrete and insular groups which were politically subordinate and subject to public prejudice and discriminations. Such measures were often motivated by hostility toward a particular group; their effect was to stigmatize members of the group.[23] However, when a majority burdens itself to give preferential treatment to minorities, neither of these factors is present; the motive is to remedy past discrimination and whites are not stigmatized by such programs. It is argued, however, that the quantum of proof required to uphold racial classifications must not depend upon "subjective evaluations as to whether a particular discriminatory act merits such adjectives as 'invidious' or 'stigmatizing'." [24] It may be that all racial classifications "stigmatize" by government action declaring a person's race to be more important than his individual actions or merit.

Race classifications have also been considered "suspect" because race is generally an irrelevant characteristic but, when the purpose is to remedy the effects of past racial discrimination, race may be relevant.[25] If a black is preferentially awarded a job or entrance to a university and a non-black is thereby denied it, both the award and the denial may seem to be based on an irrelevant characteristic. However, race is not the reason for the preferential treatment. Preference is given to blacks not because they are black, it is argued, but because they are more likely to have been victimized by discrimination. It is disputed whether there is a sufficiently high correlation between the relevant characteristics and membership in a minority group to justify the governmental use of racial classifications. It is argued that such classifications are both overinclusive and underinclusive because minority members are eligible for preferential treat-

19. Nowak, Realigning the Standards of Review Under the Equal Protection Guarantee, Prohibited, Neutral and Permissive Classifications, 62 Georgetown L.J. 1071, 1093 n. 111 (1974).

20. The standard is derived from Craig v. Boren, 429 U.S. 190 (1976). See generally Section I, C of this chapter "An Introduction to Standards of Review Under the Equal Protection Guarantee" and Section V "Classifications Based on Gender."

21. Note, Ameliorative Racial Classification, supra note 18, at 1149; Redish, supra note 18, at 358.

22. Henkin, supra note 9, at 488–489; Developments, supra note 13, at 1107.

23. Redish, supra note 18, at 362; Developments, supra note 13, at 1107.

24. Lavinsky, supra note 3, at 526.

25. Developments, supra note 13, at 1108.

ment even if they personally have managed to escape effects of racial discrimination and nonminority members who may have been subject to equally onerous burdens are excluded.[26]

The Supreme Court has approved the use of compensatory or benign classifications in several cases that did not involve racial classifications. The Court has upheld an affirmative action classification for members of Indian tribes, but this decision was based on the unique relationship of Indians to the federal government.[27] The Court has also upheld some financial aid benefits for women but required equal benefits for men where the program was not reasonably related to compensation for previous discrimination against women.[28] The Court has upheld shaping voting districts to insure that minorities were represented by elected officials but the districting did not serve as an "invidious" denial of the right to vote to white persons.[29] All were left with equal votes; the state merely took cognisance of the fact that, where minority voters are splintered, those persons could easily be left without a voice in the government.

As of December, 1982, the Supreme Court had not resolved the affirmative action issue. In a few narrow rulings, the Court has upheld or stricken such programs without addressing the basic constitutional issue of the standard of review that should be employed to determine the compatibility of a benign racial classification with the equal protection guarantee.[30] The Court has been unable to produce an opinion on this issue which has the support of a majority of the justices. A majority of the justices have rejected the "color-blind" argument and would uphold some affirmative action programs. However, there is little agreement among the justices as to the standards to be used in such cases or the types of programs which might be upheld. Currently, two justices would prohibit all racial classifications including benign ones,[31] one justice would subject these classifications to a compelling interest test which could be met by the government in some instances,[32] and three justices would require that the government demonstrate that the benign racial classification is substantially related to the important interest of correcting the effects of racial discrimination.[33] Three justices have taken

26. Nichel, Preferential Policies in Hiring and Admissions, a Jurisprudential Approach, 75 Colum.L.Rev. 534 (1975).

27. Morton v. Mancari, 417 U.S. 535 (1974) (preferential hiring of members of federally recognized American Indian Tribes for Bureau of Indian Affairs positions). For a note on the special constitutional status of American Indian Tribes see Chapter 4, The Federal Commerce Power, Section I, B the Power to Regulate Commerce with Foreign Nations and Indian Tribes.

For an excellent analysis of equal protection issues involving American Indian classifications see, Johnson & Crystal, Indians and Equal Protection, 54 U.Wash.L. Rev. 587 (1979).

28. Compare Califano v. Webster, 430 U.S. 313 (1977) (Social Security benefits increase valid); Kahn v. Shevin, 416 U.S. 351 (1974) (tax benefit for widows valid); with, Califano v. Goldfarb, 430 U.S. 199 (1977) (requiring only males to prove dependency on deceased wage earner for social security benefits invalid); see Section V of this chapter.

29. United Jewish Organizations v. Carey, 430 U.S. 144 (1977).

30. Regents of the University of California v. Bakke, 438 U.S. 265 (1978) (medical school affirmative action program found to violate federal statute); United Steel Workers of America v. Weber, 443 U.S. 193

(1979) (Title VII of Civil Rights Acts does not prohibit private employees from voluntarily using an affirmative action employment program); Fullilove v. Klutznick, 448 U.S. 448 (1980) (federal public works statute setting aside contract funds for businesses owned by members of minority races upheld).

31. See Fullilove v. Klutznick, 448 U.S. 448, 523 (1980) (Stewart, and Rehnquist, JJ., dissenting). Justice Stewart has since retired from the court.

Justice Stevens appears to be unwilling to uphold any racial classification although he has not been clear in explaining his position in this issue. See, Fullilove v. Klutznick, 448 U.S. 448, 532 (1980) (Stevens, J., dissenting).

32. See, Regents of the University of California v. Bakke, 438 U.S. 265 (1978) (judgment of Court announced in an opinion by Justice Powell but without a majority opinion); Fullilove v. Klutznick, 448 U.S. 448, 502 (1980) (Powell, J., concurring).

33. See, Fullilove v. Klutznick, 448 U.S. 448, 517 (1980) (Marshall, J., joined by Brennan and Blackmun, JJ., concurring in the judgment); Regents of the University of California v. Bakke, 438 U.S. 265, 324 (1978) (Brennan, Marshall, White and Blackmun, JJ., concurring in part and dissenting in part). Justice White's position on this issue is not clear, see note 34, infra.

no clear position on this issue.[34]   Thus, in the next section we examine the Court's decisions, and the opinions of individual justices, in this area so that the reader may assess the difficulty of resolving affirmative action issues.

2. Supreme Court Decisions

a. *Overview*

The Supreme Court has not defined the constitutional standards to be applied in reviewing benign racial classifications.[35] The Supreme Court dealt with the question of the legality of racial preferences in higher education admission programs in *Regents of the University of California v. Bakke.*[36] However, the decision turned on the applicability and meaning of Title VI of the Civil Rights Act,[37] which prohibits racial discrimination in federally funded programs. Although five justices voted to recognize the

validity of some race-conscious government programs, the case did not resolve the issue of whether "benign" racial classifications or "affirmative action" programs in higher education, or any other government program, comply with the equal protection guarantee. While a five member majority voted to invalidate the specific program that was before the Court in *Bakke*, there was no majority opinion regarding the basis for that invalidation. One or more justices voted for one of three different bases for these rulings. Thus, one must examine the posture of the case as it was presented to the Supreme Court and the votes of the individual justices in order to understand the decision.

The Court also determined that Title VII of the Civil Rights Acts, which literally forbids race discrimination in private employment, did not prohibit an employer from adopting a voluntary affirmative action program. By a 5 to 2 vote, in *United Steel*

---

34. Chief Justice Burger voted to uphold a federal program giving preferential treatment to businesses owned by members of minority race in the awarding of public contracts but he did not define in his opinion the proper standard of review to be applied to affirmative action programs. See, Fullilove v. Klutznick, 448 U.S. 448 (1980) (Burger, C.J., announcing the judgment of the Court in an opinion joined by White and Powell, JJ.).

Justice White's position is unclear as he joined Chief Justice Burger's opinion in *Fullilove,* supra, and Justice Brennan's opinion in *Bakke,* supra note 33.

At the time when this edition of the treatise was going to press, Justice O'Connor had not yet voted in a racial affirmative action case.

35. See notes 30–34, supra, and accompanying text.

The Court several times has avoided these issues after taking jurisdiction of cases which presented affirmative action problems. See, e.g., DeFunis v. Odegaard, 416 U.S. 312 (1974), dismissing as moot a case wherein an unsuccessful white applicant to a state law school challenged the school's granting preferential admissions for members of minority races. After oral argument the Court dismissed the case as moot because the white student had attended the school for a time under court order and, thereafter, the school had agreed to let him complete his legal education there even if he lost his case before the Supreme Court. See also Minnick v. California Dept. of Corrections, 452 U.S. 105 (1981) (dismissing case for lack of "Final judgment").

The holding the case moot has been much debated. See Pollak, DeFunis Non Est Disputandum, 75 Columbia Law Review 495 (1975) (arguing Court correctly found case moot); O'Neil, after DeFunis: Filling the

Constitutional Vacuum, 27 U. of Fla.L.R. 315 (1975) (arguing Court correctly deferred decision until better case was presented); Baldwin, DeFunis v. Odegaard, The Supreme Court and Preferential Law School Admissions: Discretion Is Sometimes Not the Better Part of Valor, 27 U.Fla.L.R. 343 (1975) (arguing the need for express constitutional sanction is so great decision should not have been delayed). It should be noted (in the Court's defense) that Mr. DeFunis in fact did graduate from this law school following the mootness determination. See Chapter II, Section IV, B, 3, infra.

There are too many articles on the subject of affirmative action in general and *Bakke* in particular to list all of the well written articles here. An entry into the literature may be found, however, by examination of the following scholarly considerations of this topic: Symposium, 67 Calif.L.Rev. 1–255 (1979): Symposium, 14 Harv.C.R.—C.L.L.Rev. 1–327 (1979); Symposium, 26 Wayne L.Rev. 1201–1411 (1980); Van Alstyne, Rites of Passage: Race, the Supreme Court, and the Constitution, 46 U.Chicago L.Rev. 775 (1979); see notes 3, 4, 8, 9, 11, 15, 16, 17, 18, 21 & 26, supra.

36. 438 U.S. 265 (1978).

37. 42 U.S.C.A. § 2000d et seq. The statute is referred to as "Title VI" because that was the designation of the relevant provisions in the Civil Rights Act of 1964. 78 Stat. 252, Pub.L. 88–352, Title VI, § 601 et seq. (July 2, 1964). This statute governs the operation of "any program or activity receiving Federal financial assistance" and prohibits racial discrimination in such programs. Thus, the judgment of the Court on the Title VI issue applies to any such program, the application of the statute is not limited to programs involving "state action."

Workers of America v. Weber[38] the Court interpreted Title VII to permit such programs, voluntarily adopted by employers or bargained for by employers and unions, because the Congress which adopted the statute was demonstrably concerned with discrimination against members of minority races, there was no evidence that Congress would have prohibited these programs, and the statute only stated that it did not "require" such programs, thus leaving open the possibility of voluntary programs. But the majority opinion in *Weber* was careful to note that the case did not involve a challenge to an affirmative action program undertaken with state action so that there was no need to consider the constitutionality of such programs. In *Weber* the Court held only that Title VII did not prohibit employers or unions from seeking to remedy racial imbalances in traditionally segregated job categories.

In *Fullilove v. Klutznick*[39] a fragmented Supreme Court upheld a federal statute which required 10% of federal public works project funds be expended on bids from businesses owned by members of certain minority racial or ethnic groups. The *Fullilove* decision helped to clarify the position of some justices on affirmative action issues while leaving a new set of questions regarding the constitutionality of affirmative action programs. The *Bakke* decision remains singular in the depth of analysis of constitutional issues relating to affirmative action programs. For this reason, we will examine the

opinions of the justices in *Bakke* in detail and then summarize the additional insights into these issues provided by the opinions of various justices in the *Fullilove* case.

b. *Regents of the University v. Bakke*[40]

Allan Bakke had been denied admission to the Medical School of the University of California at Davis [hereinafter referred to as Davis] in both 1973 and 1974 because the admissions committee did not believe that his qualifications justified admitting him under the general admissions program, even though his academic qualifications were substantially equivalent to those of other students being admitted under the program at that time. However, during each of those years Davis operated a special admissions program to consider the applications of candidates who asked to be considered as "economically and/or educationally disadvantaged," or as members of a "minority group." Under the Davis program, membership in certain racial or ethnic minorities—Black, Mexican-American (Chicano), Asian, or American Indian—qualified one for consideration under the special admissions program. Bakke was not a member of the specified racial minority groups and, therefore, was not eligible for consideration for admission under the special admissions program. Since a certain number of places in the class were reserved for these minority or disadvantaged students, Bakke contended that the refusal to admit him was the result of the special admissions program.[41]

---

38. 443 U.S. 193 (1979). This case was decided by a 5 to 2 vote. The majority opinion in *Weber* was written by Justice Brennan. Justice Blackmun concurred in both the opinion and result, but he added a separate statement as well. Justices Powell and Stevens did not participate in the decision. Only the Chief Justice and Justice Rehnquist dissented in *Weber*. It is interesting to note that Justice Stewart voted with Justice Brennan in *Weber* and with Justice Stevens in *Bakke*, thus reflecting his own judgment as to the proper statutory interpretation of Title VI (in *Bakke*) and Title VII (in *Weber*). The Supreme Court also has ruled that Title VII does not require an employer to engage in affirmative action for female or minority job applicants or employees. Texas Department of Community Affairs v. Burdine, 450 U.S. 248 (1981). The Court in *Burdine* held that Title VII does not require an employer to hire

a female or minority job applicant or promote a female or minority employee whenever their qualifications are equal to those of white male applicants or employees.

39. 448 U.S. 448 (1980).

40. 438 U.S. 265 (1978).

41. Bakke applied late in 1973, and would perhaps have gained admission in that year had it not been for this fact. See 438 U.S. at 276–277 (Opinion of Powell, J.). In 1974 Bakke applied early. In that year he also possessed academic credentials above the average of persons admitted in 1974 to the medical school at Davis under the regular admissions program. See id. at n. 7. There is some suggestion in the opinion of Justice Powell that Bakke was perhaps denied admission in 1974 because he had previously criticised Davis's affirmative action program. See 438 U.S. at 278–279 (Opinion

Bakke brought suit in state court alleging that the Davis special admissions program caused him injury by effectively excluding him from the freshman medical classes during 1973 and 1974 and that the Davis program violated the constitution of the state of California, Title VI of the Federal Civil Rights Act of 1964, and the equal protection clause of the fourteenth amendment to the United States Constitution. The state trial court found that the Davis program violated all three provisions, but held that Bakke was not entitled to a judgment in his favor because he could not demonstrate that he would have been admitted to Medical School if the special admissions program had not been in operation.

The Supreme Court of California reversed the holding of the state trial court; it ruled that the trial court erred by requiring Bakke to demonstrate that he would have been admitted but for the special admissions pro-

gram.[42] The Davis Medical School did not challenge this ruling of the California Supreme Court and, therefore, there was no issue concerning Bakke's ability to demonstrate that he was injured by the special admissions program in the case as it was presented to the Supreme Court of the United States.[43]

The Supreme Court of California avoided ruling on either the state constitutional issue or the applicability of Title VI of the Civil Rights Act to the Davis program. That court held that the Davis admissions program violated the equal protection clause of the fourteenth amendment because that amendment, in the view of a majority of the state court justices, meant that the government could not take cognizance of race in dispensing governmental benefits. The state supreme court therefore ordered the admission of Mr. Bakke to the Medical School.[44]

of Powell, J.). The extent to which this submerged first amendment issue may have influenced the opinion of Justice Powell remains unclear. In 1973 Davis allowed special consideration to these "economically and/or culturally disadvantaged," while in 1974 the special program was altered to consider only "minority groups." It appears however, that even in 1973 whites were effectively denied consideration under the special program. See id. (Opinion of Powell, J.).

42. Regents of University of California v. Bakke, 18 Cal.3d 34, 132 Cal.Rptr. 680, 553 P.2d 1152 (1976).

43. This point was noted by Justice Powell, 438 U.S. at 280 n. 13, and by Justice Stevens, 438 U.S. at 410: Justice Powell indicated that Bakke had standing due to his exclusion from consideration for the special admissions program. Id. at n. 14.

Several amicus briefs had argued that the suit should be dismissed as collusive because Mr. Bakke had received information and counseling from an assistant dean at the Medical School who was not very favorably disposed toward the special admissions program. This person was no longer at the University at the time of the decision, and neither the Medical School nor the University had been involved with Mr. Bakke's case in a manner that could be deemed collusive. 438 U.S. at 278 n. 8 (Opinion of Powell, J.).

44. Some of the justices of the United States Supreme Court disagreed as to the scope of the California Supreme Court decision and the precise question upon which they were compelled to rule. Justice Powell maintained that the California decision invalidated the Davis program because it took account of race and asserted that the California court had held that all educational admissions programs had to operate on a colorblind basis. 438 U.S. at 1318 (Opinion of Powell, J.).

Justice Powell was correct in his characterization of the California opinion. See Regents of the University of California v. Bakke, 18 Cal.3d 34, 54–56, 132 Cal. Rptr. 680, 683, 694, 533 P.2d 1152, 1155, 1166 (1976). Justice Powell believed both that the Davis program was illegal and that Davis and other institutions could employ some race conscious programs.

Therefore Justice Powell had to vote to reverse the part of the judgment of the California Supreme Court that prohibited race conscious programs even though he voted to affirm the order of the California court that required Davis to accept Mr. Bakke and to refrain from using its present special admissions program. Justice Stevens speaking for the other four members of the United States Supreme Court who voted to affirm the California Supreme Court, stated that the California court had ordered only the admission of Mr. Bakke to the Davis Medical School and that there was no outstanding order prohibiting race conscious programs on a constitutional basis. 438 U.S. at 409–410 (opinion of Stevens, J., joined by Burger, C. J., & Rehnquist & Stewart, JJ.). Because Justice Stevens was correct in noting that the judgment of the California Court which was affirmed by the United States Supreme Court, technically applied only to Mr. Bakke and his exclusion from the Davis program, and because Justice Stevens believed that federal statutes precluded any race conscious admission program in an institution receiving federal funds, he could vote to affirm the judgment of the California Supreme Court without reaching the constitutional issue. Thus, the disagreement between Justices Powell and Stevens regarding the scope of the California decision was highly technical and related to their views of the proper resolution of the federal issue; this issue amounted to little more than a procedural skirmish between the justices. The

The justices of the Supreme Court of the United States affirmed the decision of the California Supreme Court; however, they came as close to being evenly divided as they could with all nine justices voting on the legality of the Davis program. Four of the justices—Chief Justice Burger and Justices Stewart, Rehnquist, and Stevens—concluded that the Davis program violated Title VI of the Federal Civil Rights Act.[45] They found that the application of Title VI to the admissions program made it unnecessary to reach any constitutional issue. Four justices—Justices Brennan, White, Marshall and Blackmun—were of the opinion that Title VI was meant to bar only such racial discrimination as was prohibited by the fourteenth amendment and that the Davis program did not violate either the equal protection clause or Title VI.[46] Thus, the ruling of the case turned on the vote of Justice Powell, even though his analysis of the issues was not supported by a majority of justices. Justice Powell found that the equal protection clause and, therefore, Title VI, required invalidation of the Davis program. But Justice Powell was of the opinion that neither provision would require the invalidation of all race conscious affirmative action programs. He therefore voted with the group of four justices who ruled only on the Title VI issue to the extent of finding the Davis program a violation of Title VI and ordering Davis to accept Mr. Bakke into medical school. However, Justice Powell voted to reverse the California decision insofar as it required state governmental units to avoid all consideration of race in affirmative action programs. Only two portions of Justice Powell's opinion were joined by four other

justices: the statement of facts and the paragraph in which he stated that not all racial classifications were invalidated by the fourteenth amendment.[47] Nevertheless, he cast the fifth vote that resulted in the affirmance of the order that required Davis to accept Mr. Bakke while allowing it and other educational institutions to make some use of race conscious admissions criteria.

Thus, the Bakke decision means that an admissions program of an institution receiving federal funds which uses clear, strict racial preferences, such as that of the Davis Medical School, will be held to violate Title VI of the Civil Rights Act because five justices would find it to be a Title VI violation, although for differing reasons. A program of admissions to institutions of higher education that allows admissions officers to consider race as an affirmative factor without using clear racial preferences will be held to violate neither the equal protection clause nor Title VI because a different alignment of five justices would vote to uphold such programs. In Bakke, five justices, with no majority opinion, did vote for the proposition that Title VI bars only such racial discrimination as would violate the equal protection clause if it involved state action.

Bakke leaves many important issues regarding racial preferences unsettled. There was no ruling on the constitutionality of any affirmative action program other than those relating to admission to higher education. The Court did not determine whether other federal civil rights acts can or do mandate or restrict the use of such benign classifications; the statutory ruling involved only Title VI.[48]

---

reader may understand this point more fully after consideration of the substantive positions of the justices. The four justices who voted to reverse the California Supreme Court in total did not have to enter this procedural debate as they simply would have reversed the decision of the California Supreme Court regardless of how its judgment might be described.

45.　438 U.S. at 421 (Stevens, Rehnquist, Stewart, JJ., & Burger, C. J., concurring in the judgment in part and dissenting in part).

46.　438 U.S. at 325 (Brennan, Marshall, Blackmun & White, JJ., concurring in the judgment in part and dissenting in part).

47.　438 U.S. at 271–284, 320 (Opinion of Powell, J.).

48.　Indeed, the Court did not decide whether Title VI creates a private cause of action that would allow persons, other than Mr. Bakke, to bring suit for either monetary or injunctive relief from educational institutions that employ programs similar to that used at the Davis Medical School. Four members of the Court—Justices Powell, Brennan, Marshall and Blackmun—appeared to assume a private cause of action under Title

The Supreme Court ruled only that the Davis program violated Title VI. It did not hold that the Davis program violated the equal protection clause. It is important to note that the Court also did not establish the constitutional standards to be employed in reviewing benign or affirmative action race classifications. Four of the five justices who reached the constitutional issue would have used an intermediate standard of review for affirmative action classifications.[49] Justice Powell was the only justice reaching the constitutional issue who would have subjected all race conscious affirmative action programs to strict judicial scrutiny and the most exacting test of constitutionality.[50] Four justices ruled only that Congress could and did require that recipients of federal funds dispense the benefits of programs employing those funds on a purely "colorblind" basis.[51]

Justice Powell, in a portion of his opinion that was not joined by any other justice, analyzed Title VI of the Civil Rights Act before turning to the constitutional issues. Justice Powell turned to the language of the section of Title VI that might bar the Davis program, characterizing it as "majestic in its sweep."[52] Section 601 of the Civil Rights Act reads as follows:

> No person in the United States shall, on the ground of race, color, or national origin, be excluded from participation in, be denied benefits of, or be subjected to discrimination under any program or activity receiving Federal financial assistance.[53]

Justice Powell noted that this statute was subject to varying interpretations because of the lack of precision in the words used by Congress. He rejected the views expressed in the plurality opinion of Justice Stevens and found that Title VI prohibited only those activities that, if they involved state action, would violate the equal protection clause of the fourteenth amendment. This conclusion, although not Justice Powell's opinion, was joined by four other justices—Justices Brennan, White, Marshall and Blackmun[54]—so

---

VI in order to find Title VI protection equivalent to that of the fourteenth amendment, and ultimately to address the constitutional issue. See 438 U.S. 284 (Opinion of Powell, J.); Id. at 328 (Opinion of Brennan, Marshall, White & Blackmun, JJ. concurring in part and dissenting in part). Four members of the Court apparently found the existence of such a private cause of action under Title VI. See 328 U.S. at 420 (Stevens, J., joined by Burger, C. J., & Rehnquist & Stewart, JJ., concurring in the judgment in part and dissenting in part). In a separate opinion Justice White expressly found no private cause of action under Title VI. See 438 U.S. at 379–380 (Separate opinion of White, J.).

In Cannon v. University of Chicago, 441 U.S. 677 (1979) the Supreme Court held that an implied cause of action existed under Title IX, which would allow a woman allegedly discriminated against by sex in the admission process of a medical school receiving federal funds to seek a remedy against the school in federal court. The Court reasoned in part that Title IX, which forbids discrimination on the basis of sex by educational programs that are federally funded, was patterned on Title VI and that Congress was aware when it passed Title IX that several federal courts had found an implied private cause of action under Title VI. Although the Court in Cannon technically did not resolve the question of whether there would be a similar implied cause of action under Title VI, the majority opinion strongly indicates that a majority of the justices agree that Title VI, as well as Title IX, gives rise to an individual cause of action. Justices White, Blackmun, and Powell dissented in Cannon.

49. 438 U.S. 355–362 (Brennan, Marshall, White & Blackmun, JJ., concurring in part and dissenting in part).

50. 438 U.S. 287–305 (Powell, J.). The position of Justice White on the applicable standard of review is not entirely clear. On the one hand, the Justice joined that portion of Justice Powell's opinion which calls for exacting strict scrutiny. See Id. at 387 n. 7 (Separate opinion of White, J.). On the other hand, Justice White specifically stated that he joined the views of the Brennan, Marshall, White and Blackmun opinion on "the equal protection issue." Id. at 387 (Separate opinion of White, J.). It would appear that Justice White believes that any affirmative action program that is truly benign and meets the Brennan tests will also satisfy the proper strict scrutiny standard.

51. In Fullilove v. Klutznick, 448 U.S. 448 (1980) Justices Stewart, Rehnquist and Stevens took strict positions against the use of racial classifications for affirmative action purposes, while Chief Justice Burger refused to commit to a specific standard for the review of such programs. There is still no majority position regarding the appropriate standard of review for the benign use of racial classifications for affirmative action programs. The *Fullilove* case is examined following the examination of the opinions of individual justices in *Bakke*.

52. Regents of the University of California v. Bakke, 438 U.S. 283–284 (Powell, J.).

53. 42 U.S.C.A. § 2000d; see footnote 37 supra.

54. 438 U.S. at 328–55 (Brennan, J. joined by White, Marshall & Blackmun, JJ.).

that Title VI now will prohibit only those programs that would not survive scrutiny under the fourteenth amendment if they involved state action.

Justice Powell found that all racial classifications are inherently suspect and subject to the strictest judical scrutiny. As to the test employed to review such classifications, the Justice was not entirely clear, but he did note that strict scrutiny was an "inexact term".[55] At several points in his opinion Justice Powell endorsed the traditional view that such classifications must be necessary to promote a "compelling" interest, although he also refers to the test as one under which the means employed must be precisely tailored to promote a "substantial" interest.[56] This linguistic disparity should be of no consequence, as the Justice made it clear that the test, however labeled, would require the Court to subject all racial and ethnic distinctions or classifications to "the most exacting judicial examination."[57] Taken as a whole, Justice Powell's opinion indicates that he would subject all racial classifications, whether "stigmatizing" or "benign," to a form of strict scrutiny test that would be almost impossible to meet absent a showing that the classification was necessary to promote an interest of overriding magnitude.

Justice Powell also found that there was no difference between setting racial quotas and establishing "goals" of minority representation; in so doing the Justice was taking the position that he would subject any use of racial criteria to the most strict equal protection test.[58] Justice Powell argued that application of the strictest equal protection test to racial and ethnic classifications was required by the "constitutional and demographic history" of the country. He concluded that it was "far too late to argue that the guarantee of equal protection to all persons permits the recognition of special wards entitled to a degree of protection greater than that accorded others."[59]

In reaching the conclusion that all racial and ethnic classifications should be subjected to the most exacting scrutiny, Justice Powell distinguished three groups of prior Supreme Court decisions. First, he found that the school desegregation cases were not relevant to the affirmative action decision because they involved only remedies designed to redress specific constitutional violations.[60] Second, the employment discrimination cases decided under Title VII of the Civil Rights Acts were not relevant because the affirmative action remedies were ordered in such cases only after a judicial or administrative finding of discrimination against a racial minority in a particular business or industry.[61] Third, the Justice found that the use of less than the most strict

---

55. 438 U.S. at 287–288 (Powell, J.).

56. Compare 438 U.S. at 314 with 438 U.S. at 265, 320 (Powell, J.).

57. 438 U.S. at 291 (Powell, J.).

58. 438 U.S. 287–299. It was in Part III–A of his opinion that Justice Powell concluded that the "quota"—"goal" distinction was irrelevant and that all such racial classification were subject to the strict scrutiny test. Justice White stated that he joined Part III–A of the Powell opinion, even though he also joined in all of Justice Brennan's opinion. 438 U.S. at 387, n. 7 (Separate Opinion of White, J.); Justice White did not join in any of Justice Powell's explanation of the standard or Powell's analysis of the statutory or equal protection issues. No other justice joined Part III–A of the Powell opinion.

59. 438 U.S. at 295 (Powell, J.).

60. 438 U.S. at 300–01 (Powell, J.).

61. 438 U.S. at 301. Justice Powell's comments indicate that he will be favorably disposed toward approving most, if not all, types of race conscious remedies for employment discrimination that are ordered by an executive agency or federal legislation relating to problems of identifiable race discrimination which Congress seeks to remedy by using its powers under section 2 of the thirteenth amendment or section 5 of the fourteenth amendment. 438 U.S. at 302, n. 41 (Powell, J.).

Justice Powell also stated that no other decision of the Supreme Court regarding any civil rights legislation mandated the approval of racial classification under less than a strict scrutiny standard. He found that Lau v. Nichols, 414 U.S. 563 (1974), which on the basis of Title VI, had required a city to provide remedial English instruction for students of oriental ancestry, was based both on the Court's deference to an agency decision that prior practices had had the effect of subjecting individuals to discrimination on the basis of their national origin, and the Court's recognition that the program did not result in denial of benefits to members of any other racial or ethnic group. Similarly, Justice

standard in gender-based classification cases was irrelevant to the race affirmative action question.[62] The special societal and constitutional history of race discrimination in America made racial classification qualitatively different. Additionally the greater judicial ability to deal with gender-based classifications, which involve only two possible groups, justified the greater allowance of their use for remedial purposes by government units.

Justice Powell applied his strict scrutiny-compelling interest test to the Davis program and found it wanting. In order to test the Davis program he examined each of the asserted purposes of the state and school. First, the school could not assert as a legitimate purpose the attainment of a minimum specified percentage of a particular racial or ethnic group in the class; in Justice Powell's view, that purpose would be "facially invalid."[63] Second, the Justice recognized that the state had a legitimate interest in eliminating the effects of "identified discrimination," but he found that this end would only support programs that were judicially, legislatively, or administratively found to be necessary to remedy violations of the constitution or statutes which had been passed to promote constitutional purposes.[64] Because the University could not claim any ability, or any state granted authority, to make find-

ings of particular discrimination in its or other educational programs, the Davis special admissions program could not be held to further the governmental interest in ending the effect of prior acts of racial discrimination. Third, the Justice found that the program was not a reasonably necessary way of improving health care for communities that currently did not receive adequate medical services. Even assuming that in some situations an interest in health care might be compelling, the Justice found that there was no proof that the Davis program would in fact substantially increase the number of doctors or the quality of health care available to economically deprived citizens.[65] Fourth, Justice Powell found that the attainment of a "diverse student body" would be a compelling interest under some circumstances; it was on this basis that he would approve some of the race-conscious admissions programs that had been employed by universities other than Davis.

Justice Powell found that the attainment of a diverse student body related to "academic freedom," which in turn was related to the guarantees of the first amendment.[66] Because this interest embodied a value of independent constitutional importance, it would be considered compelling by the Justice under some circumstances. In graduate and professional schools, as well as under-

Powell found that United Jewish Organizations v. Carey, 430 U.S. 144 (1977), in which the Court had approved the use of race-conscious criteria in creating voting districts, was irrelevant because it was based on an administrative finding that the measures were necessary to improve the ability of previously disadvantaged racial groups to participate in the voting process, and because the creation of such districts did not deny any person their right to vote in any meaningful matter.

62. 438 U.S. at 302–303 (Powell, J.). Justice Powell also found that the cases regarding congressional treatment of American Indians were inapposite because of the unique relationship between the government and Indian tribes. Id. at 304 n. 42 [on the unique nature of American Indian classification see Chapter 4, Section I, B.]

63. 438 U.S. at 307 (Powell, J.).

64. 438 U.S. at 307–10 (Powell, J.). Justice Powell indicates in his footnote 44 that the statistically demonstrated "disparate impact" of an employment practice

or job qualification is not sufficient in itself to establish a violation of Title VII of the Civil Rights Acts. Proof of such disparate impact does establish a prima facie case of such discrimination and it will suffice as the basis for a finding of a Title VII violation if the employer whose employment practice is challenged cannot show that the practice is not discriminatory but, instead, is justified by business necessity or relationship to job performance. Carefully read, Justice Powell's footnote only indicates that courts do not order remedies for Title VII violation until all evidence in a case is considered and the court concludes that the challenged practice in fact violates Title VII.

Justice Powell also noted that the University had been unable to demonstrate that the special admissions program was necessary to evaluate minority applicants due to some inherent cultural bias in grading or testing procedures. 438 U.S. at 306 n. 43.

65. 438 U.S. 311 (Powell, J.).

66. Id. at 311–314 (Powell, J.).

graduate colleges, a faculty could attempt to insure that students and teachers would be exposed to a wide variety of diverse social and political interests. The use of racial or ethnic classifications, whether described as "goals," quotas or something else, did not further this goal, however, because it set aside places in the class for persons solely on this basis, without regard to whether the acceptance or rejection of specific individuals on the basis of their race was promoting true diversity within the university. "The diversity that furthers a compelling state interest encompasses a far broader array of qualifications and characteristics of which racial or ethnic origin is but a single though important element."[67] Thus the Justice found that strict racial "track" programs for admission, no matter how many special groups they might include, did not further a compelling interest. Instead, if a university wished to assert this "compelling interest" to justify its admissions program, it would have to establish an admissions procedure that would consider all facets of an applicant's background when that applicant was considered for admission on the basis of particular personal characteristics, or for the attainment of diversity in the student body. In attaining this diversity the educational institution, in Justice Powell's opinion, may consider or give positive weight to virtually any personal characteristic of the applicant. "An otherwise qualified medical student with a particular background—whether it be ethnic, geographic, *culturally advantaged or disadvantaged*—may bring to a professional school of medicine experiences, outlooks and ideas that enrich the training of its student body and better equip its graduates to render with understanding their vital service to humanity."[68]

Justice Powell did not limit consideration of these personal factors only to granting a "plus" because an individual was a member of a racial or disadvantaged minority rather than an educationally advantaged member of a racial majority. Indeed, his statement regarding "cultural advantage or disadvantage," and his statement that "the weight attributed to a particular quality may vary from year to year depending upon the 'mix' both of the student body and the applicants for the incoming class,"[69] make it appear that Justice Powell would allow a university to give a "plus" to economically advantaged white students over minorities once it had a sufficient "mix" of minority members. While it seems hard to believe that the Justice meant to approve of systems that subtly disadvantaged a minority member because of his or her race, the opinion provides little basis for limiting this use of the "diversity" goal. Justice Powell noted that others had claimed that such discretionary programs could be a subtle means of employing a racial preference. The Justice found that there would be no "facial infirmity" in such programs and that the Court, in his opinion, would not allow such an admissions program

---

67. 438 U.S. at 315 (Powell, J.).

68. 438 U.S. at 314 (Powell, J.) (emphasis added).

In order to explain the type of program which he found constitutional, Justice Powell described the Harvard College admissions program as it had been described to the Court in the brief of several *amici curiae*. In the Harvard program the grades and test scores as well as the personal background of each individual was evaluated by a committee. In such a program the applicant's race or ethnic background would be considered, as would the person's age, achievements in nonscholastic areas, economic background, and other characteristics. In this way the admissions committee would attempt to achieve a "mix" of a wide variety of people within the student body. Justice Powell found that such a procedure would be permissible even though it was race conscious and even though some candidates of equal ability would lose out on the "last"

places in the class to persons who had received a "plus" because of their racial or ethnic background. However, the Justice found that this type of race consciousness in admissions procedures was permissible because the candidate who had been denied admission had not been denied a benefit solely on the basis of race; he had been considered for all of the places in the class and the decision was simply that "his combined qualifications, which may have included similar nonobjective factors, did not outweigh those of the other applicant."

Columbia University, Harvard University, Stanford University and the University of Pennsylvania filed a brief with the Court as Amici Curiae. 438 U.S. 316, 321 (Opinion of Powell, J., and Appendix to his Opinion).

69. 438 U.S. at 318 (Powell, J.).

to be challenged on the basis of its disparate impact on persons of similar races because "good faith would be presumed" in the absence of a showing of a discriminatory purpose.

Justice Powell concluded that affirmative action programs would be constitutional if they followed the race consciousness approach without the use of predetermined racial classifications preferences, quotas, or goals. For this reason he voted with Justice Brennan and the other justices who would have upheld the Davis program in total, but he did so only to the extent of reversing the California Supreme Court ruling that race could never be considered in educational admissions programs. The only portion of Justice Powell's opinion concerning the constitutionality of racial classifications that received five votes was the following paragraph:

In enjoining petitioner from ever considering the race of any applicant, however, the courts

70. Id. at 320 (Powell, J.).

71. Regents of The University of California v. Bakke, 438 U.S. at 324 (1978) (Brennan, Marshall, White & Blackmun, JJ., concurring in the judgment in part and dissenting in part); 438 U.S. at 379 (Separate Opinion of White, J.); id. at 387 (Separate Opinion of Marshall, J.); id. at 402 (Separate Opinion of Blackmun, J.).

Justice White, in his separate opinion, examined only whether Title VI implicitly created a private right of action.

Justice Marshall's separate opinion emphasized the history of racial discrimination both in the nation at large and in the decisions of the Supreme Court. He noted the pervasive historic discrimination against Blacks by both society at large and the government; for him the continuing impact of this discrimination justified affirmative action programs. He noted that the primary motivation for passing the fourteenth amendment was to protect the recently freed slaves, and that this goal had not been met. The discriminatory treatment of Blacks throughout our history was different in kind from that towards any other group. Although Justice Marshall's concurrence in the Brennan opinion indicates that he believes that the history of discrimination against Blacks justifies affirmative action programs that would benefit many racial minorities who have been the victims of discrimination, his analysis of the special concern that the fourteenth amendment shows for Blacks indicates that he might approve an affirmative action program designed to help only Blacks. Neither Justice Marshall nor Justice Brennan discussed the point explicitly. 438 U.S. at 387–402 (Separate Opinion of Marshall, J.).

below failed to recognize that the State has a substantial interest that legitimately may be served by a properly devised admissions program involving the competitive consideration of race and ethnic origin. For this reason, so much of the California court's judgment as enjoins petitioner from any consideration of the race of any applicant must be reversed.[70]

Justices Brennan, White, Marshall and Blackmun voted to uphold the Davis program under both Title VI and the equal protection clause. They joined Justice Powell to form a majority in holding that some affirmative action programs are both constitutional and legal under Title VI, but they differed from Justice Powell in that they would have found that the Davis program, or ones employing similar racial goals or preferences, met the relevant constitutional and statutory standards. These four justices joined in an opinion written by Justice Brennan, although each of the other three justices added additional comments in separate concurring opinions.[71]

Justice Blackmun added several important points in his separate opinion concerning the justification for the use of the judicial power to approve affirmative action programs and the lack of similar justification for judicial disapproval of affirmative action programs. In his opinion affirmative action programs such as the Davis special admissions program were a reasonable means of redressing the effects of racial discrimination. He expressed regret that the country had not achieved a degree of equality sufficient to render the effects of racial discrimination only "an ugly feature of history that is instructive but that is behind us." He believed that, while the "Harvard program" might be preferable to the Davis program for policy reasons, the Constitution did not prohibit universities from using explicit racial criteria in their admissions programs. He noted that the Davis program might only be "barely" constitutional but that, because it met Justice Brennan's two-pronged test, it should be upheld. Justice Blackmun pointed out the irony of a ruling that would not allow universities to give explicit preferences to members of racial minorities when those institutions had a history of freely granting preferences based on "geography, athletic ability, anticipated financial largess, alumni pressure, and other factors of that kind." Justice Blackmun believed that it was quite reasonable for state agencies to use benign racial classifications in affirmative action programs because the goal of eliminating the effects of racial discrimination could not reasonably be advanced in a racially neutral manner. "In order to get beyond racism, we must first take account of race. . . . We cannot—we dare not—let the Equal Protection Clause perpetuate racial supremacy." The Justice concluded his opinion by citing Chief Jus-

Justice Brennan noted that he and the three justices who joined in his opinion agreed with Justice Powell only to the extent of finding that neither the fourteenth amendment nor Title VI prohibited the use of race in an affirmative action setting; Justice Brennan's opinion would establish criteria for legality and constitutionality quite different from those set forth by Justice Powell. Justice Brennan recognized that racial classifications advancing interests of racial minorities might disadvantage white persons because of their race. But the Brennan plurality believed that there was no justification for judicial protection of members of the white majority with a test so strict that it would bar virtually all such remedial programs.[72] These persons did not constitute a minority whose interests were likely to be disregarded by the political process because of the history of their unequal treatment or their failure to have a voice in the political process. However, Justice Brennan went on to explain that classifications which burden white persons incident to such programs should not be tested under the "very loose rational basis standard of review that is the very least that is always applied" when reviewing equal protection claims. The Justice instead found for two reasons that classifications which burden white persons incident to remedial programs should be subjected to a standard of review similar to that employed in the gender and illegitimacy cases. First, such classifications might often be used to "stereotype and stigmatize" a small, powerless segment of individuals. Second, these racial classifications, like gender and illegitimacy classifica-

tions, were based on "immutable characteristics which its possessors are powerless to escape or set aside."

The key paragraph, setting forth the "tests" the Brennan plurality will apply a racial affirmative action case, reads as follows:

> In sum, because of the significant risk that racial classifications established for ostensibly benign purposes can be misused, causing effects not unlike those created by invidious classifications, it is inappropriate to inquire only whether there is any conceivable basis that might sustain such a classification. Instead, to justify such a classification an important and articulated purpose for its use must be shown. In addition, any statute must be stricken that stigmatizes any group or that singles out those least well represented in the political process to bear the brunt of a benign program. Thus our review under the Fourteenth Amendment should be strict—not "strict in theory and fatal in fact", because it is stigma that causes fatality—but strict and searching nonetheless.[73]

Justice Brennan, it appears, would describe laws that burden members of racial minorities because of their racial status would as ones that "stigmatize" that group and are not truly benign. Such laws must be subjected to the strict scrutiny—compelling interest test that Professor Gunther had described as "fatal in fact."[74] However, when a government program could be described as "benign" to racial minorities, it would be subjected to a form of intermediate standard of review that allows for independent judicial evaluation of both the substantiality of the articulated purposes of the program and the reasonableness of the means

tice Marshall's statement, justifying the Court's use of wide interpretative powers, that "we must never forget, that it is a *constitution* that we are expounding." Justice Blackmun believed that the Court has the institutional responsibility to avoid interpreting the fourteenth amendment and the concept of equal protection in a manner that would inhibit the attainment of true racial equality. 438 U.S. 402–408 (separate opinion of Blackmun, J.) quoting McCulloch v. Maryland, 17 U.S. (4 Wheat.) 316, 407 (1819) (Opinion by Marshall, C.J.).

72. 438 U.S. at 361–362 (quoting from Gunther, The Supreme Court 1971 Term-Foreword: In Search of

Evolving Doctrine on a Changing Court: A Model for a Newer Equal Protection, 86 Harv.L.Rev. 1, 8 (1972)).

73. 438 U.S. at 361–362 quoting Gunther, Foreword: In Search of Evolving Doctrine on a Changing Court: A Model for a Newer Equal Protection, 86 Harv.L.Rev. 1, 8 (1972). Justice Brennan cites to Professor Gunther's article concerning equal protection standards of review wherein he refers to the strict scrutiny standard "strict in theory and fatal in fact."

74. Id.

employed to promote that purpose.[75] In the quoted paragraph Justice Brennan was explaining the test that these four justices would employ to determine whether a challenged program constituted a truly "benign" racial classification which only incidentally burdened members of the majority race. Such classifications would have to meet this test; a test that the Justice described as "two-pronged" later in his opinion.[76] To be a valid benign racial classification program, in the view of these four justices, a program must: (1) be justified by an articulated purpose of demonstrably sufficient importance to justify burdening members of the racial majority, and (2) be precisely and narrowly related to that purpose to avoid stigmatizing any racial group or singling out powerless persons to bear the burden of the program.

In reviewing the constitutionality of the Davis special admissions program, Justice Brennan first examined whether Davis had demonstrated an articulated purpose for the program that was of sufficient importance to justify the racial classification. Justice Brennan found that the attempt to remedy past societal discrimination was sufficient to justify the use of race conscious admissions programs, at least when there was a reason-

able basis for concluding that minority underrepresentation in such programs would be both substantial and related to past racial discrimination.[77]

After finding Davis' remedial purpose to be sufficient to meet the first part of the two part test, Justice Brennan's plurality opinion then went on to determine whether the program met "the second prong of our test—whether the Davis program stigmatizes any discrete group or individual and whether race is reasonably used in light of the program's objective." [78] The four justices who joined this opinion found that the Davis program met this test and, therefore, that it comported with the equal protection guarantee. The Brennan opinion found that the program did not stigmatize members of the racial majority because Bakke, or others in his situation, were not "in any sense stamped as inferior by their rejection." [79] Justice Brennan also found that the Davis program was a sufficiently narrow and reasonable means of rectifying the under-representation of minorities, even though it employed an explicit racial classification that operated to exclude members of the majority from consideration for some places in the medical school class.[80]

75. See Section I, C of this chapter regarding equal protection "standards of review."

76. 438 U.S. at 373–74.

77. 438 U.S. at 362.

Justice Brennan stated:

"[O]ur prior cases unequivocally show that a state government may adopt race-conscious programs if the purpose of such programs is to remove the disparate racial impact its actions might otherwise have and if there is reason to believe that the disparate impact is itself the product of past discrimination, whether its own or that of society at large."

Id. at 369.

78. Id. at 373–374.

79. Id. at 375. Justice Brennan's opinion thus distinguished Davis' benign racial classification from those racial classifications which burdened minorities and which had been invalidated in prior decisions of the Court.

80. If the Davis program had not been a truly benign and reasonable means of promoting its objectives, the Brennan plurality would have held it unconstitutional because it would not have been a narrow means of remedying past discrimination without stigmatizing

or burdening some other group of persons by race or political powerlessness. According to the four-member plurality, the Davis program was truly benign and reasonable because it did not place a ceiling on the number of minority applicants admitted to medical school (the general admissions program did not exclude or limit the consideration of minority students); it did not stigmatize members of the group that were excluded from consideration; it did not arbitrarily advance unqualified persons (all students would have to meet the same academic requirements once admitted); and it did not place a burden on a politically powerless minority. In the opinion of these four justices the Davis program was reasonable because, in fact, there was no other practical means to achieve the end of remedying the effect of racial discrimination in medical school admissions and the medical profession. The Brennan opinion stated that the school did not have to use only "objective" factors to identify "disadvantaged" persons for special admissions because that would not be a more reasonable means of achieving the goal of ameliorating the effects of past racial discrimination in society. 438 U.S. at 376–377.

The Brennan opinion also noted that the Davis program "does not simply equate minority status with disadvantage." However, while Davis evaluated the

Justice Stevens wrote an opinion joined by Chief Justice Burger and Justices Stewart and Rehnquist.[81] These four justices found it unnecessary to address the constitutional issue in *Bakke* because both Davis' special admissions program and, therefore, the exclusion of Mr. Bakke from medical school violated Title VI.[82]

Justice Stevens concluded that Section 601 of the Civil Rights Act of 1964 required complete racial neutrality, or "colorblindness," by all administrators of programs accepting federal funds. He found that the "plain language of the statute" required this result absent clear legislative history indicating an intent to give the words a meaning other than their normal ordinary reading.[83] Justice Stevens read the legislative history of Title VI as affirmatively supporting a literal reading of the statute, which appears to require "colorblind" programs. He based this conclusion on several statements of proponents of the statute who had assured their colleagues in Congress that no person of any race would be disadvantaged because of their race in any Federally funded program if this statute were enacted. Having found that Title VI required programs involving federal funds to be totally race-neutral, Justice Stevens stated that it was not necessary to decide "the congruence—or lack of congruence" between the statute and the fourteenth amendment because Congress could go beyond the basic prohibitions of the amendment and establish a principle of total race neutrality even if no such principle was

embodied in the equal protection clause.[84] Finally, these justices stated that the Court should hold that Title VI created a cause of action so that private persons could seek a judicial remedy for injuries caused them by violation of the Act, although they did not approve the allowance of private suits to terminate federal funding of such programs.[85] Justice Stevens carefully drafted this plurality opinion to indicate that these four justices joined Justice Powell's conclusion that Davis' program violated Title VI, but none of his reasoning. Thus, five justices voted to require the Davis medical school to admit Bakke, but there is no majority opinion as to why he should be admitted.

The result of the division of the justices in *Bakke* is that even though five members of the Supreme Court of the United States have ruled that some affirmative action programs are constitutional and legal under Title VI, only those programs in federally funded colleges that meet the Powell criteria will be upheld. As to those types of race-conscious programs, Justice Powell will vote with Justices Brennan, White, Marshall and Blackmun to uphold the program. Justice Powell will vote to strike down any program that employs explicit, rigid, racial classifications or preferences; if Title VI applies to such programs he will form a majority with Chief Justice Burger, and Justices Rehnquist, Stevens, and O'Connor (assuming that she will vote for a "strict" application of Title VI as did Justice Stewart) to invalidate

background and credentials of minority applicants it did not make any determination of whether each applicant had been disadvantaged due to his or her race. Justice Brennan found that the Constitution did not require Davis to determine that the specific persons admitted had been "victimized by discrimination." 438 U.S. at 377.

81. 438 U.S. 408–421 (Stevens, Stewart, Rehnquist, JJ., & Burger, C.J.), concurring in part and dissenting in part).

82. 438 U.S. at 411. Justice Stevens first noted that the case was an individual's suit, not a class action, and found the distinction significant because the trial court's order and the California Supreme Court's reversal thereof could be read narrowly. Justice Stevens argued that the California Supreme Court had only ordered the individual plaintiff admitted to medical

school, and not ordered all state agencies or all schools to stop considering race when processing applications for educational or other benefits. These justices believed that Title VI itself precluded any race-conscious admissions program; therefore, for this plurality, the Title VI ground for affirming the California Supreme Court's decision obviated any need to reach the constitutional issues. "It is . . . perfectly clear that the question whether race can ever be used as a factor in an admissions decision is not an issue in this case, and that discussion of that issue is inappropriate."

83. 438 U.S. at 412–3. The statute appears in the text accompanying note 53 supra.

84. 438 U.S. at 414, 417–418.

85. 438 U.S. at 418–419.

such programs under Title VI of the Civil Rights Acts.

c.   The Fullilove Decision and Federal Affirmative Action Programs

In *Fullilove v. Klutznick* [86] the Supreme Court upheld the constitutionality of the minority business enterprise provision of the Public Works Employment Act.[87] This provision required 10% of the amount of every federal public works project grant be expended for work done by minority business enterprises. The statute defines such businesses as ones in which a majority of the equity interest is owned by "citizens of the United States who are Negroes, Spanish-speaking, Orientals, Indians, Eskimos, [or] Aleuts." [88]

While the federal program was upheld in this case, and all nine of the justices voted on the constitutionality of this affirmative action program, no single theory concerning the constitutionality of affirmative action programs commanded the votes of more than three justices. The Court seemed to split evenly between three different methods of analysis. First, Chief Justice Burger, in an opinion joined by Justices White and Powell, found the Act to be a permissible use of the federal power to eliminate or redress discrimination in federal contract practices without ever specifying a test for the constitutionality of such programs. Although the Chief Justice refused to employ a specific test in his opinion, Justice Powell, while concurring in the Chief Justice's opinion, found that the federal program could be upheld under a compelling interest test. Second, Justice Marshall, in an opinion joined by Justices Brennan and Blackmun, advocated the use of a test which would require remedial racial classifications to be substantially related to an important governmental objective. Finally, Justices Stewart, Rehnquist, and Stevens dissented and opposed the use of racial classifications for the granting of government benefits, although Justice Stevens was unwilling to vote for an absolute prohibition of classifications based upon race.

Several factors indicate that the *Fullilove* case will not serve as a guide for future constitutional decisions concerning affirmative action. First, the case concerned a unique federal program that could be rationalized as a congressionally created remedy for past discrimination in public works projects against minority-owned enterprises. Second, the fact that Justice White joined the opinion of the Chief Justice rather than that of Justice Marshall seems to have reduced from four to three the number of justices who are committed to the use of an intermediate standard of review for affirmative action programs. Third, Justice Stewart's retirement from the Court lessens the number of justices who have committed to a position that would find most if not all affirmative action programs invalid. Finally, while three justices appeared willing to uphold most affirmative action programs

---

86.   448 U.S. 448 (1980).

87.   Public Works Employment Act of 1977, Pub.L. 95–28, 91 Stat. 116. The statute amended the Local Public Works Capital Development and Investment Act of 1976, Pub.L. 94–369, 90 Stat. 999. The statute states in relevant part:

"Except to the extent that the Secretary determines otherwise, no grant shall be made under this Act for any local public works project unless the applicant gives satisfactory assurance to the Secretary [of Commerce] that at least 10 per centum of the amount of each grant shall be expended for minority business enterprises. For purposes of this paragraph, the term 'minority business enterprise' means a business at least 50 per centum of which is owned by minority group members or, in case of a publicly owned business, at least 51 per centum of the stock

of which is owned by minority group members. For the purposes of the preceding sentence minority group members are citizens of the United States who are Negroes, Spanish-speaking, Orientals, Indians, Eskimos, and Aleuts."

88.   The Economic Development Administration (EDA), a part of the commerce department charged with administration of the public works grant program, issued guidelines which set standards for determining when a business enterprise qualified as a minority business enterprise. As a part of these regulations the EDA defined the six minorities that were to receive a preference in terms of the geographic or ethnic origin of an individual. Relevant portions of the guidelines are quoted in the Appendix to the opinion of Chief Justice Burger, Fullilove v. Klutznick, 448 U.S. 448, 492 (1980) (Appendix to opinion of Burger, C.J.).

and three would have invalidated almost all such programs, the three justices whose votes will decide the outcome of future affirmative action cases were less than clear on the standards which they will employ in those cases.

Chief Justice Burger took a curious path in coming to the conclusion that the public works set-aside program was valid.[89] The Chief Justice decided that the analysis must proceed "in two steps."[90] First, he would inquire "whether the *objectives* of this legislation are within the power of Congress" and, if so, "whether the limited use of racial and ethnic criteria, in the context presented, is a constitutionally permissible *means* for achieving the congressional objectives."[91] This approach deviates from traditional equal protection analysis under any standard of review as the Chief Justice totally fails to tell us whether his assessment of the "objectives" of the legislation is only to determine whether they are legitimate and not prohibited by the Constitution or whether the ends will be independently evaluated by the Court to determine if they are sufficiently important or compelling to justify the use of a racial classification. Similarly, no standard is set forth for determining the relationship between the means employed and promotion of the congressional goals. The Chief Justice had little problem in determining that the goals of the congressional action were within the federal power. The Chief Justice's conclusion that public works projects could be funded by the federal government under the commerce and spending powers was hardly a startling decision.

The Chief Justice also focused on the power of Congress under section 5 of the fourteenth amendment "to regulate procurement practices of state and local grantees of federal funds." The Chief Justice's opinion was unclear on this issue. At some points in the opinion he seemed to conclude that Congress has the power under the fourteenth amendment to take affirmative steps to aid members of racial or ethnic minorities to achieve social or economic equality. At other points he appeared only willing to rule that Congress could, and had, determined that minority owned businesses had been subject to unconstitutional and illegal discrimination in federal procurement programs in the past and that affirmative steps needed to be taken to remedy such prior discrimination. If the Chief Justice was indicating agreement with the first position one might expect him to vote to uphold a wide variety of affirmative action programs, at least if they were enacted by the Congress. If he was only indicating that the federal government could move to correct its own past discriminatory practices his opinion was indeed a narrow one.

When the Chief Justice looked at the means which Congress used to accomplish "these plainly constitutional objectives" he, in a single paragraph, indicated that the Court must pay significant deference to the congressional choice of means to promote its goals but that there had to be "careful judicial evaluation" to ensure racial or ethnic criteria were not used in an unconstitutional manner.[92] At this point in his opinion Chief Justice Burger described the congressional action as "remedial," perhaps to indicate that the goal Congress was pursuing was the undoing of the effect of past racial discrimination in federal public works projects. The Chief Justice specifically rejected "the contention that in the remedial context the Congress must act in a wholly 'colorblind' fashion."[93] This is the most significant passage in the Chief Justice's opinion because, for the first time, we are assured that there are not five justices who would vote to strike out virtually all benign racial classifications. However, the statement is of limited importance because the Chief Justice justified the congressional use of race in this

---

89. Fullilove v. Klutznick, 448 U.S. 448 (1980) (Burger, C.J., announcing judgment of the Court in an opinion joined by White and Powell, JJ.).

90. 448 U.S. at 473.

91. Id. (emphasis in original).

92. 448 U.S. at 478–82.

93. 448 U.S. at 482–84.

manner by likening the Act to a decree by a court which formulated a remedy for proven unconstitutional racial discrimination. The Chief Justice did indicate that Congress was to have a reasonable degree of latitude to frame its remedial statute so that a minor amount of over-inclusiveness or under-inclusiveness in the granting of the benefit should not make it invalid. Yet the Chief Justice was not willing to endorse a congressional power to use racial classifications whenever Congress wished to remedy the effects of past discrimination. Instead, the Chief Justice noted that the program before the Court was reasonably tailored to promote a remedial objective.[94] Those who sought to take advantage of the minority preference by the creation of "front entities" could be identified and eliminated from participation by administrative agencies. Waivers could be granted to public works grantees who could show that their best efforts could not produce 10% minority firm participation; the 10% target was not a rigid quota but a means of assuring fair treatment of minority business enterprises. The program, therefore, was not a strict racial quota or preference, in the view of the Chief Justice. In conclusion the Chief Justice stated that "[t]his opinion does not adopt, either expressly or implicitly, the formulas of analysis articulated in such cases as *University of California Regents v. Bakke.*"[95] The Chief Justice found that the program at issue in *Fullilove* would survive either of the tests used by Justices Powell and Brennan in the *Bakke* decision.

Justice Powell joined in the opinion of Chief Justice Burger but "would place greater emphasis than the Chief Justice on the need to articulate judicial standards of review in conventional terms."[96] In other words, Justice Powell realized that Chief Justice Burger's opinion told us how impor-

tant the Chief Justice thought it was for Congress to remedy past discrimination but totally failed to put that statement into the framework of equal protection analysis. Justice Powell applied the compelling interest test as he had done in *Bakke.*[97] While racial preference could never constitute a compelling state interest, the remedying of identified discrimination by a government body competent to make a finding of discrimination could be a compelling interest. Justice Powell found that Congress had the authority under the commerce power as well as the Civil War Amendments to identify and remedy the continuing effects of racially discriminatory practices.[98] Congress thus survived the "ends" test and Justice Powell required only that the means employed by Congress be "reasonable remedies to advance the compelling state interest in repairing the effects of discrimination."[99] Justice Powell placed special emphasis on the enforcement clauses of the thirteenth and fourteenth amendments; he would give Congress some latitude in the employment of a race conscious remedy for discrimination, although he would review state affirmative action programs more strictly. Even as to congressional action the Justice required a showing that the program was reasonable and did not shift the burden for the remedy of racial discrimination to innocent third parties in an unreasonable manner.

Justice Marshall built upon the opinion of Justice Brennan in *Bakke* as he advocated the use of an intermediate standard of review, between the deferential rationality test and the insurmountable strict scrutiny standard.[100] Justice Marshall, and Justices Brennan and Blackmun, endorsed the use of a strict scrutiny standard for determining the validity of laws which burden members of racial or ethnic minorities because they stigmatize members of the minority in a way

---

94. 448 U.S. at 486.

95. 448 U.S. at 490.

96. Fullilove v. Klutznick, 448 U.S. 448, 494 (1980) (Powell, J., concurring).

97. Regents of the University of California v. Bakke, 438 U.S. 265 (1978) (Powell, J.).

98. Fullilove v. Klutznick, 448 U.S. 448, 502 (1980) (Powell, J., concurring).

99. 448 U.S. at 510.

100. Fullilove v. Klutznick, 448 U.S. 448, 517 (1980) (Marshall, J., joined by Brennan and Blackmun, JJ., concurring in the judgment).

that is contrary to the fundamental principles of equal protection. Even laws that are defended as benign racial classifications should be examined with more than the deferential rational basis standard of review for they may be easily misused either to mask discrimination against a racial minority or to burden another politically powerless segment of society. For these reasons the Justices found that "the proper inquiry is whether racial classifications designed to further remedial purposes serve important governmental objectives and are substantially related to achievement of those objectives." [101] Under this standard the validity of the public works law was "not even a close one." The purpose of remedying the effects of past racial discrimination against minority-owned businesses was clearly an important one and the program was a reasonable method of insuring an end to the harshest effects of past discrimination in this area.

Justices Stewart and Rehnquist took the position that the guarantee of equal protection inherent in the due process clause of the fifth amendment and the equal protection clause of the fourteenth amendment prohibited any governmental entity from using race as the basis for allocating benefits or burdens. [102] "Under our Constitution, any official action that treats a person differently on account of his race or ethnic origin is inherently suspect and presumptively invalid." [103] These justices found that the history of the fourteenth amendment, and the philisophic premises of past Supreme Court decisions invalidating racial classifications, precluded the use of racial criteria to assign benefits or burdens in our society. The most fundamental value of an equal protection guarantee was undercut by such laws; the framers of the fourteenth amendment had seen the effects of governmental definitions of race and ethnicity. The Act before the Court in *Fullilove* involved the categorization of persons by race with accompanying regulations establishing the criteria for inclusion of persons into racial groupings. This division of society along racial lines was antithetical to the equal protection guarantee in the view of Justices Stewart and Rehnquist. However, they would approve the limited use of racial classifications by a court formulating a specific remedy for a proven violation of a law prohibiting racial discrimination. Judicial formulation of such remedies does not involve the division of society along racial lines.

Justice Stevens was unwilling to join Justices Stewart and Rehnquist but he took a position against racial classifications nearly as strict. [104] Justice Stevens found that "[r]acial characteristics may serve to define a group of persons who have suffered a special wrong and who, therefore, are entitled to special reparations." [105] He might allow narrowly tailored laws to give reparations to specific groups against whom the government has committed a demonstrable wrong in the past, such as American Indians or some segment of Black citizens. However Justice Stevens would not allow Congress to use racial criteria to remedy the effects of societal discrimination against members of racial minorities. There was insufficient proof for the Justice that any specific minority business enterprise in the past was denied access to public contracts and that the federal progam was a means of remedying such specific acts of discrimination rather than the granting of a general preference by race. Justice Stevens requires such an exact matching of remedial programs to demonstrations of specific instances of past discrimination that it is difficult to envision what types of programs for the benefit of

---

101. 448 U.S. at 518.

102. Fullilove v. Klutznick, 448 U.S. 448, 523 (1980) (Stewart, J., joined by Rehnquist, J., dissenting).

103. Id.

104. Fullilove v. Klutznick, 448 U.S. 448, 532 (1980) (Stevens, J. dissenting).

105. Id. at 537.

racial minorities could survive his searching form of judicial review.[106]

III. CLASSIFICATIONS BASED ON ALIENAGE

A. General Status of Aliens: Citizenship, Immigration, Deportation, Naturalization, and Expatriation [1]

Many types of laws or executive actions may distinguish between citizens of the United States and noncitizens. Such actions raise the question of the constitutionality of classifications based on "alienage", the status of being a noncitizen. Aliens do not receive the protection of constitutional guarantees that by their terms apply only to "citizens." [2] However, aliens are protected by those provisions which refer to "persons." [3] Thus, they receive the protection of the Bill of Rights, including the fifth amendment due process clause, and the fourteenth amendment due process and equal protection clauses.[4]

Questions concerning discrimination based on alienage, analyzed in Section B below, or on immigration status, considered in Section C below, must be separated from those concerning immigration, deportation, naturalization or expatriation, considered briefly in this subsection and more thoroughly in Chapter 20.

Citizenship is defined and conferred by section one of the fourteenth amendment which states: "All persons born or naturalized in the United States, and subject to the jurisdiction thereof, are citizens of the United States and of the State wherein they reside." [5]

The Congressional ability to set standards for naturalization of aliens has never been significantly limited by the Court. But the fourteenth amendment grant of citizenship contains no provision for termination of citizenship. Thus problems have arisen as to expatriation—the termination of a person's citizenship. Voluntary expatriation is permissible so that a person may renounce his citizenship.[6] The Court, however, has strick-

---

106. The strictness of his approach may best be captured in the following statements indicating his belief that the program was not a narrowly tailored means for redressing past discrimination.

"Even if we assume that each of the six racial subclasses [receiving a preference from the statutes] has suffered its own special injury at some time in our history, surely it does not necessarily follow that each of those subclasses suffered harm of identical magnitude. Although 'the Negro was dragged to this country in chains to be sold in slavery,' *Bakke* opinion of Marshall, J., [citation omitted], the 'Spanish-speaking' subclass came voluntarily, frequently without invitation, and the Indians, the Eskimos and the Aleuts had an opportunity to exploit America's resources before most American citizens arrived. There is no reason to assume, and nothing in the legislative history suggests, much less demonstrates, that each of these subclasses is equally entitled to reparations from the United States Government." 448 U.S. at 537 (Stevens, J., dissenting).

This passage by Justice Stevens ended with the following inexplicable footnote: "8. Ironically, the Aleuts appear to have been ruthlessly exploited at some point in their history by Russian fur traders. See The New Columbia Encyclopedia, p. 59." Id. at 538, n. 8 (Stevens, J., dissenting).

1. For a discussion of alien rights concerning naturalization see Chapter 20. For treatment of other matters concerning international relations see Chapter 6. For a more in depth treatment of constitutional issues

in foreign affairs, see L. Henkin, Foreign Affairs and the Constitution (1972).

2. E.g., aliens are not entitled to protection under Section 1 of the Fourteenth Amendment, which provides that "No State shall make or enforce any law which shall abridge the privileges or immunities of citizens of the United States." Furthermore, the validity of citizenship as a prerequisite of voting is impliedly recognized by the constitutional guarantees of the Fifteenth and Nineteenth Amendments that the right of citizens to vote would not be denied or abridged on the basis of race or sex and by Supreme Court opinions. E.g. Sugarman v. Dougall, 413 U.S. 634, 649 (1973). The Constitution expressly makes citizenship a requirement to hold the office of representative, senator, or president. Article II Section 2 makes citizenship for seven years a requirement for representative. Article II Section 3 requires senators to have been citizens nine years. Article II Section 1 requires that the President be a natural born citizen (or a citizen when the Constitution was adopted).

3. Yick Wo v. Hopkins, 118 U.S. 356 (1886).

4. Wong Wing v. United States, 163 U.S. 228, 238 (1896) (due process clause of fifth amendment applicable to aliens); Yick Wo v. Hopkins, 118 U.S. 356 (1886) (equal protection).

5. U.S. Const. amend. 14, § 1.

6. "By the Act of July 27, 1868 [15 Stat.L. 223, chap. 249] Congress declared that 'the right of expatriation is a natural and inherent right of all people.' Ex-

en several congressional attempts to provide for involuntary termination of citizenship. Thus, the Court has held that persons could not be deprived of their citizenship because of refusal to serve in the armed forces or for voting in a foreign election.[7] However there may still be a question as to whether Congress might by statute require a person to elect to reject his citizenship for an act totally opposed to that status, such as service in the armed forces of a nation at war with the United States. While the Court has taken the position that Congress was without power to deprive a person of citizenship since the fourteenth amendment was meant to be an irrevocable grant of citizenship to certain persons,[8] it might be argued that at some point a person's actions might constitute voluntary expatriation.[9]

In *Vance v. Terrazas*,[10] the Court held that an individual cannot be deprived of his United States citizenship unless the government demonstrates not only that he voluntarily took an action which Congress has deemed to be expatriating, but also that he intended to renounce his citizenship when he took that action. The government, however, need only prove the elements of voluntariness and specific intent by a preponderance of the evidence. A five member majority of the Court also upheld the statutory presumption that any person who committed an

act of expatriation listed by Congress did so voluntarily. However, this presumption was upheld only insofar as it could be used to demonstrate the voluntariness of the action; it could not be used to establish intent to relinquish citizenship. In this case, a young man born with dual citizenship in the United States and Mexico had applied for a certificate of Mexican nationality. In so doing, he had sworn allegiance to that government and had stated that he was renouncing citizenship in all other governments, including the United States. The Court found that the declaration of allegiance to the Mexican government did not in itself establish a basis for expatriation despite a statute to that effect.[11] The young man, however, would be deprived of his United States citizenship if the Secretary of State could demonstrate that the oath was taken voluntarily and with an actual intent to relinquish citizenship. The Secretary would be helped in meeting this burden by the statutory presumption of voluntariness, but there would have to be some other basis for showing intent.

A person who has not been born in this country may become a naturalized citizen if he or she complies with the conditions for naturalization set by Congress.[12] Following naturalization in this country the naturalized citizen is not subject to involuntary expatriation to any greater extent than a natural

patriation is the voluntary renunciation or abandonment of nationality and allegiance." Perkins v. Elg, 307 U.S. 325, 334 (1939). The Act has since been repealed and the right of expatriation is covered by 8 U.S.C.A. §§ 1482, 1483. See also Kennedy v. Mendoza-Martinez, 372 U.S. 144, 159 n. 11 (1963) where Court states there is no disagreement that citizenship may be voluntarily relinquished either expressly or by conduct.

7. Kennedy v. Mendoza-Martinez, 372 U.S. 144 (1963) (Expatriation of one who departed from or remained outside the United States in time of War or during a period of national emergency for the purpose of evading military service found unconstitutional); Trop v. Dulles, 356 U.S. 86 (1958) (Expatriation for desertion of military services during war held unconstitutional as applied to native born citizen); Afroyim v. Rusk, 387 U.S. 253 (1967) (Expatriation of citizen for voting in foreign election found unconstitutional, overruling Perez v. Brownell, 356 U.S. 44 (1958)).

8. Afroyim v. Rusk, 387 U.S. 253 (1967).

9. See, e.g. Chief Justice Warren's dissent in Perez v. Brownell, 356 U.S. at 68–69 (1958), with which the

Afroyim majority declared its agreement. *Afroyim* overruled *Perez*.

10. 444 U.S. 252 (1980).

11. 8 U.S.C.A. § 1481(a)(2).

12. The Constitution vests Congress with the power "to establish an Uniform Rule of Naturalization." Art. I, § 8, cl. 4. The Supreme Court has given Congress great latitude in selecting the appropriate conditions. United States v. Macintosh, 283 U.S. 605, 615 (1931); Congress has provided by statute that the right to become a citizen may not be denied on the basis of race, sex, or marital status. § 311, 66 Stat. 239 (1952), 8 U.S.C.A. § 1422. The right will be denied where, for example, a person is or has been a member of an organization advocating the violent overthrow of the government. § 313(a) and (c), 66 Stat. 240 (1952), 8 U.S.C.A. § 1424(a) and (c). "Good moral character" is also a prerequisite, § 316(a)(3), 66 Stat. 242, 8 U.S.C.A. § 1427(a)(3).

born citizen with an exception; if the person engages in fraud or misrepresentation in the naturalization process later discovery of the fraud will annul the grant of citizenship.[13] Congress may also attach reasonable conditions to the original grant of citizenship under which the person might later be divested of citizenship, if the person is naturalized outside of the United States. Thus, in *Rogers v. Bellei* [14] the Court upheld the requirement for children born abroad with only one parent of United States citizenship that they later spend 5 continuous years in the United States between the ages of 14 and 28 in order to retain United States citizenship. Since these persons were not born in the United States or finally naturalized there, they were not granted citizenship by the fourteenth amendment. Congress could grant the conditional citizenship just as it could have refused to make any grant of citizenship until they fulfilled the residence requirement.[15]

Congress also has a virtually unrestricted power to set the terms for alien immigration [16] and this power may be delegated in part to the executive.[17] The immigration acts have set conditions and quotas for entry into this country.[18] Whether the alien seeks entry for a temporary visit or to establish residence he has no right to entry and Congress may exclude any alien or noncitizen group as it pleases. For many years, Congress set quotas for immigration based on nationality [19] and, despite the racial-national origin classification, the law was never seriously questioned.[20] The executive branch also has been given the authority to exclude individual aliens whom are either unqualified for immigration or who may present some moral or social danger.[21] Not only are these general powers subject to no significant limitation, the individuals who are refused entry do not have a right to a hearing to determine the basis for their exclusion.[22] Indeed the Supreme Court once upheld the refusal to

---

13. § 340(a), 66 Stat. 260 (1952), 8 U.S.C.A. § 1451(a). Proof of fraud or misrepresentation may be proved and result in loss of citizenship at any time regardless of how long ago person became a citizen. Costello v. United States, 365 U.S. 265 (1961) (27 years); Polites v. United States, 364 U.S. 426 (1960) (10 years); Knauer v. United States, 328 U.S. 654 (1946) (6 years). Affiliation with an organization which advocates violent over throw of the government within five years after becoming a citizen is prima facie evidence of fraud. § 340, 66 Stat. 261 (1952), 8 U.S.C.A. § 1451(c). Schneider v. Rusk, 377 U.S. 163 (1964). (Court struck provision that naturalized citizen lost his citizenship if he resided continuously for three years in the country of which he was formerly a national or in which he was born.)

In Fedorenko v. United States, 449 U.S. 490 (1981), the Supreme Court upheld the deportation of a person who was proven to have given false and incomplete information on his visa application and, therefore, to have "illegally procured" his naturalization. The person had failed to disclose facts concerning his service as a concentration camp guard which made him ineligible for a visa; the federal courts had no "equitable discretion" to refrain from entering a judgment of denaturalization.

14. 401 U.S. 815 (1971).

15. Justices Black, Brennan, Douglas, and Marshall dissented. But see Schneider v. Rusk, 377 U.S. 163 (1969).

16. Congress does not derive its power to regulate immigration from a specific constitutional grant. It is simply regarded as a power inherent to a sovereignty. See Chinese Exclusion Case, 130 U.S. 581 (1889). For a

further discussion of Congressional authority and foreign affairs, see L. Henkin, Foreign Affairs and the Constitution (1972).

17. U. S. ex rel. Knauff v. Shaughnessy, 338 U.S. 537, 543 (1950).

18. Aliens presently excludable are listed in 8 U.S. C.A. § 1182. The method of allocation of immigration is found in 8 U.S.C.A. § 1153.

19. The first Congressional act limiting immigration on the basis of race or nationality was the Chinese Exclusion Act of 1882, Act of May 6, 1882, 22 Stat. 58, which remained in effect until 1943. In 1924 Congress set up the national origin quota system, Act of May 26, 1924, 43 Stat. 153, which remained in effect until 1965. Act of October 3, 1965, P.L. 89–236, 79 Stat. 911. 8 U.S.C.A. § 1152(a) now prohibits the use of race, national origin, sex, place of birth, or place of residence to determine the eligibility of an alien to immigrate.

20. See Ozawa v. United States, 260 U.S. 178 (1922); United States v. Bhagat Singh Thind, 261 U.S. 204 (1923); Toyoto v. United States, 268 U.S. 402 (1925); Morrison v. California, 291 U.S. 82 (1934). The Court refused to review the only case in which the constitutional issue was raised and rejected, Kharaiti Ram Samras v. United States, 125 F.2d 879 (9th Cir. 1942), cert. denied 317 U.S. 634 (1942).

21. 8 U.S.C.A. §§ 1103, 1104.

22. For aliens who have never been naturalized nor acquired residence in the United States, the decision of an executive or administrative officer, acting within the powers conferred by Congress is due process. United States v. Ju Toy, 198 U.S. 253, 263 (1905). See,

grant a hearing to an alien who sought re-entry to the country after an absence even though no other country would accept this person.[23] This decision should now be considered constitutionally infirm even though it has never been overruled, but it demonstrates the historic refusal of the Court to review immigration decisions.

The congressional power to regulate immigration and naturalization includes the power to regulate the behavior of aliens who are in this country.[24] Pursuant to statute, aliens may be deported for a variety of activities deemed harmful to this country.[25] These conditions will be upheld as within the power of Congress because the Court defers to the legislature in such matters. But the resident alien will have a right to a hearing prior to the deportation.[26] The hearing will determine whether the person is an alien or a citizen, and, if he is an alien, whether the conditions for continuing residence have been violated. While the procedural aspects of the due process clause requires this hearing to establish the basis for the deportation, an alien who has violated the statutes or conditions of entry has no right to continued residence in this country.

The Court recently has extended the protection of the fourteenth amendment equal protection clause to illegally resident aliens but, in so doing, it did not impliedly limit the power of the federal government to exclude or deport such persons.[27] Thus, when we examine the rights of an alien in this country we are really looking primarily at the rights of lawful resident aliens apart from questions of immigration, deportation or nat-

Hart & Wechsler, The Federal Courts and the Federal System 352–53 (2d ed. 1973) (the "Dialogue").

Either a citizen of the United States or a permanent resident alien who makes a trip abroad is denied a constitutionally protected interest when the government seeks to exclude him from returning to the country. It would appear that the citizen who wishes to return to the country always has a claim that he has lost liberty in such a situation. The alien who was lawfully resident in the United States before his trip abroad has a claim that he had a statutory entitlement to residence which was denied him by the government when it prevented him from reentering the country. If the resident alien's absence from the country was extended he may lose his entitlement. When the absence was brief he should be entitled to some type of a due process hearing, in the nature of a deportation hearing, to determine the reasonableness of prohibiting him from reentering the country. The cases finding that an alien seeking initial admission to the United States has no constitutional rights regarding his application do not bar the granting of a hearing to either the citizen or lawfully resident alien who has been temporarily absent from the country and wishes to return. See, Landon v. Plasencia, 103 S.Ct. 321 (1982).

23. Shaughnessy v. United States ex rel. Mezei, 345 U.S. 206 (1953), see note 22, supra.

24. See the dissenting opinion of Justice Rehnquist in Hampton v. Mow Sun Wong, 426 U.S. 88 (1976).

25. 8 U.S.C.A. § 1251. Reasons for deportation include non-compliance with eligibility requirements for entrance, a conviction of a crime of moral turpitude within five years after entry, and membership in proscribed organizations. The latter provision was upheld as to aliens who had become members of the communist party before the law was established. See Harisiades v. Shaughnessy, 342 U.S. 580 (1952) (interpreting and upholding predecessor section, 54 Stat. 670, 8 U.S.C.A. § 137).

26. 8 U.S.C.A. § 1252(b). A person arrested and held for deportation who claims to be a citizen is entitled to his day in court. Ng Fung Ho v. White, 259 U.S. 276, 281 (1922).

The Supreme Court has held, as a matter of statutory interpretation, that 8 U.S.C.A. § 1105a(a)(5) requires that persons who claim to be U. S. citizens, and who seek review of a deportation order, be given a de novo judicial review of the order whenever there is any "genuine issue of material fact" regarding the nationality claim. Agosto v. Immigration and Naturalization Service, 436 U.S. 748 (1978). A person who is deported is entitled not only to a fundamentally fair hearing but a procedure which follows the dictates of federal statues. However, the question of whether the Immigration and Naturalization Service has properly followed statutory requirements is one of statutory interpretation rather than an analysis of due process principles. See Immigration and Naturalization Service v. Miranda, 103 S.Ct. 281 (1982).

Under federal statutes the Attorney General or his delegates may suspend for reasons of "extreme hardship" the deportation of an otherwise deportable alien who has resided in the United States for seven years and is of "good moral character." The statute does not grant a deportable alien a right to a hearing as to whether the Attorney General should use his authority to suspend the deportation; federal courts are not to substitute a judicial determination of extreme hardship for that made by the Attorney General or his delegates. Immigration and Naturalization Service v. Wang, 450 U.S. 139 (1981) (per curiam).

See also note 22, supra.

27. Plyler v. Doe, 457 U.S. 202 (1982). This case is examined in subsection C of this section of Chapter 16.

See also notes 22, 26, supra.

uralization. The ability of the government to treat resident aliens differently from citizens depends on the degree to which alienage is relevant to legitimate goals of government programs. It is this problem of classification and discrimination which is the subject of the next subsection.

B. The Classification Problem

1. Overview

Aliens are persons, so they receive the protection of the due process clauses and the equal protection clause.[28] It should be noted that, while the equal protection clause does not apply to the federal government, the fifth amendment's due process clause guarantees equal protection in the application of federal law.[29] State classifications which treat aliens differently on the basis of that status are reviewed under the equal protection clause of the fourteenth amendment while federal acts are subject to the due process clause of the fifth amendment.

The equal protection guarantee requires that the government treat similar persons in a similar manner. When testing a classification based upon alienage the issue is whether the status of being a United States citizen differentiates persons in terms of a proper governmental purpose. If not, it should be invalidated as an arbitrary refusal to accord equal treatment to lawfully resident persons who are not citizens. The Supreme Court has refused to enunciate a single test to be used when determining the compatibility of alienage classifications with the equal protection guarantee of the fourteenth amendment equal protection clause or the fifth amendment due process clause.

All of the Court's decisions since 1970 on this issue would appear to be consistent if the Court were using an intermediate standard of review—between the traditional rational basis test and the strict compelling interest test—which required the government to demonstrate that a citizenship classification bore a reasonable and substantial relationship to an important government interest.[30] Since state and local governments have no interest in foreign affairs, their use of alienage classifications would have to be reasonably justified by a significant local interest. Thus, state laws prohibiting aliens from voting or holding important government positions could be upheld as related to the important local interest in the self-governance process. However, state citizenship restrictions on eligibility for welfare payments or the practice of a profession would not in most instances be reasonable ways of promoting an important local interest because the lawfully resident noncitizen is not be distinguishable for the citizen in terms of local economic interests. Federal laws employing citizenship classifications would almost always be upheld under a substantial relationship to an important interest standard. The federal interest in international affairs, as well as the federal power over immigration and naturalization, should justify the use of alienage classifications. So long as a federal alienage classification was not a totally arbitrary means of disfavoring lawfully resident aliens, the classification would be upheld. Such rulings would assure the federal government freedom to pursue national goals without simultaneously granting the government a virtually unchecked power to make use of arbitrary and invidious classifications burdening noncitizens. Unfortunately, the Court has chosen not to analyze all alienage classifications in terms of a single standard of review. Instead, the Court has divided alienage cases into three categories.

First, when state of local laws classify persons on the basis of United States citizenship for the purpose of distributing economic benefits, or limiting the opportunity to engage in private sector economic activity, the law will be subjected to strict judicial scruti-

---

28. See note 4, supra.

29. Bolling v. Sharpe, 347 U.S. 497 (1954). See Sections I, A & C of this Chapter.

30. See Section I, C of this Chapter, An Introduction to Standards of Review Under the Equal Protection Guarantee.

ny. In this situation, the Court recognizes that classifications based on alienage should be deemed "suspect" and upheld only if necessary to promote a compelling or overriding interest.[31] Until recently, the Court upheld alienage classifications whenever the justices believed that the state had a "special public interest" in granting privileges only to citizens. Now that the Court has subjected these economic citizenship classifications to strict scrutiny, the state must demonstrate a compelling purpose for treating aliens in a less favorable manner than citizens. This test will be quite difficult for the state to meet because in almost all instances the lawfully resident noncitizen is subject to federal and state taxation just as is the resident citizen. The lawfully resident alien is not reasonably distinguishable from the citizen in terms of legitimate, nondiscriminatory economic goals of the state.

Second, an alienage classification created by state or local law which relates to allocating power or positions in the political process will be upheld under the traditional rational basis test. The state clearly has a legitimate interest in reserving positions in the self-governance process for United States citizens. The state need not allow noncitizens the right to vote or hold elective office. Indeed, it appears that the state need not allow the noncitizen to hold an important governmental position of any type.[32] The trait of being an United States citizen does define a class of persons, in the view of the Court, who have a special affiliation to both the federal and state governments and, therefore, who may be given a priority for employment in governmental positions. A political, as opposed to economic, alienage classification will be upheld so long as it is rationally related to the state interest in preserving the governmental process for citizens. Even in the political area, a state may not be totally arbitrary in its use of the alienage classification.[33] If the alienage classification does not relate to this self-governance interest, the state classification will be tested under the strict scrutiny standard. It must be remembered that states may not pursue foreign policy objectives; state classifications must relate to a legitimate local interest. Additionally, states will not be allowed to intrude into the foreign relations interests of the United States and any state law regulating aliens which might interfere with federal policy in this area will be held void under the supremacy clause or preempted by federal law.[34]

Third, alienage classifications created by federal law will be subjected to only the rational basis standard of review. Although, the Court has not been clear in identifying the proper standard of review to be employed in these cases, it would appear that the federal government may use a citizenship classification so long as it is arguably related to a federal interest.[35] Although some judicial opinions read as if every federal alienage classification will be upheld, a federal alienage classification should be invalid if it is an arbitrary and invidious classification designed only to burden a disfavored group of persons. Most, if not all, federal alienage classifications would be upheld under any standard of review other

---

31. See, e.g., Graham v. Richardson, 403 U.S. 365 (1971); In re Griffiths, 413 U.S. 717 (1973). These cases are examined in the next subsection of this section of Chapter 16.

32. See, e.g., Ambach v. Norwick, 441 U.S. 68 (1979); Cabell v. Chavez-Salido, 454 U.S. 432 (1982). These cases are examined in the next subsection of this section of Chapter 16.

33. See, Sugarman v. Dougall, 413 U.S. 634 (1973) (total exclusion of noncitizens from state civil service position held invalid).

34. See, e.g., Toll v. Moreno, 102 S.Ct. 2977 (1982) (state university regulated denying "in-state" tuition status to nonimmigrant aliens with federal visa for employees of international organizations violated supremacy clause of Article VI by interfering with federal policy; Hines v. Davidowitz, 312 U.S. 52 (1941) (state law regarding registration of aliens is preempted by federal law). State power in this area may be expanded when the state assists in the fulfillment of federal policy. See DeCanas v. Bica, 424 U.S. 351 (1976).

35. See, Mathews v. Diaz, 426 U.S. 67 (1976). The federal, as well as state, cases are examined in the next subsection of this Section of Chapter 16.

than the strictest form of the compelling interest test. The proper differentiation between federal and state laws in this area is not in terms of the standard of review to be employed, but in the nature of the governmental interest which justifies the classification. The federal government has an important interest in foreign affairs and foreign relations. The federal government should be allowed to classify persons by their citizenship when that classification is arguably related to foreign policy interests. Such interests include the manner in which our citizens might be treated in other countries, bargaining power with other governments, national security, or simply the image which the nation wishes to present to the world. However, if the federal government does not appear to be pursuing such ends, it should not be allowed the freedom to engage in invidious classification of aliens and such a federal action should be invalidated as a totally arbitrary imposition of burdens on a group of persons whom the federal government has allowed to remain in this country.

2. Supreme Court Decisions Before 1970

In *Yick Wo v. Hopkins* [36] the Supreme Court found that aliens are "persons" so as to enjoy the protection of the equal protection clause. The case involved a challenge to the licensing system for laundries in San Francisco. It was found that the system had been used to deny licenses to resident Chinese aliens. The application of the law violated the Fourteenth Amendment as the distinction was based on "no reason . . . except hostility to the race and nationality to which petitioners belong." [37] But the Court

was not clear as to what other "reasons" might support an alienage classification. [38]

In the period from the *Yick Wo* decision until 1948, aliens were not accorded very significant constitutional protection. Aliens could be treated differently than citizens when the alienage status made them dissimilar for some legitimate reason. Had the Supreme Court been willing to strictly review legislation to determine if alienage was in fact being used as an arbitrary classification aliens might have received equal protection of the law. But the Court allowed aliens to be treated in a less favorable manner whenever the alienage classification related to a "special public interest". The special public interest doctrine permitted alienage classifications except where the state had no interest of any significance other than a mere hostility toward aliens. [39] If no public interest could be shown in the classification, it would be a violation of the equal protection clause. [40] The restriction on aliens fell into three main categories: use of natural resources, ownership of land, and employment.

During this period the Court recognized a "special public interest" in the preservation of natural resources, both animal and mineral. Aliens could be forbidden from taking possession of these resources for their benefit as the state had a significant legitimate interest in reserving use of these resources for its citizens. Thus aliens were prohibited from various activities relating to natural resources including the killing of wild game [41] or the planting and taking of shellfish. [42] These results were compatible with the Court's general deference to the state interest in natural resources during this period.

---

36. 118 U.S. 356 (1886).

37. 118 U.S. at 374.

38. The reader must remember that insofar as a classification is deemed to be based on the "race" or "national origin" of the persons classified, rather than their citizenship, it will be deemed "suspect" on subject to strict judicial scrutiny under the compelling interest test. See Section II of this Chapter.

39. The Court at the time upheld licensing statutes which prohibited issuance to aliens, thereby closing them out of many occupations. E.g., Ohio ex rel. Clarke v. Deckebach, 274 U.S. 392 (1927).

40. In Truax v. Raich, 239 U.S. 33 (1915), the Court struck a statute requiring Arizona employers with more than five employees to hire eighty per cent qualified voters or native-born citizens. The provision was invalid because it was directed to private persons and did not pertain in any way to the protection of the public domain. Where statutes requiring that citizens be hired were limited to "public works," they were upheld. Heim v. McCall, 239 U.S. 175 (1915); Crane v. New York, 239 U.S. 195 (1915).

41. Patsone v. Pennsylvania, 232 U.S. 138 (1914).

42. McCready v. Virginia, 94 U.S. 391 (1876).

At this time the Court also allowed the states to reserve the use of natural resources for its own citizens to the detriment of citizens of other states as well as aliens.[43]

Laws prohibiting the ownership of land by aliens were also upheld by the Supreme Court. The state interest in regulating the use of its territory was considered a "special public interest." The Court found that aliens were distinguishable as to land ownership and use for reasons other than hostility to race. The Court took this position in *Terrace v. Thompson* [44] and rejected the argument that such laws were based on hostility to persons of certain races or nationality. This was a very significant holding since persons from Oriental nations were not then eligible for citizenship under federal statutes; upholding these classifications allowed the western states to prohibit Chinese and Japanese persons from owning and using land in any significant manner. Thus when the Court upheld a California statute prohibiting the use of land by "ineligible" aliens it, in effect, sanctioned a racial classification.[45] As there was a special public interest in prohibiting the ownership of lands by ineligible aliens the Court also allowed the states to prohibit the indirect control of lands by aliens. Similarly, laws prohibiting food crop contracts with aliens [46] or the transfer to aliens of shares of a land owning corporation were also upheld.[47] The Court upheld statutes under which land would escheat to the state if the owner attempted to convey it to an alien.[48]

Finally, in 1948, the Supreme Court indicated that statutes restricting land ownership by aliens might be invalid. In *Oyama v. California* [49] the Court struck down a

state presumption that land transfers to citizens which were paid for by an ineligible alien were an illegal attempt to transfer property to that alien. Here the state sought to take land which was conveyed to the citizen son of an ineligible alien because the alien father paid the consideration. The Supreme Court held that the presumption and escheat of the property denied the citizen son equal protection of laws but the opinion also cast doubt on the validity of land laws based on alienage.

In 1948, the Court eroded the "special interest" theory in *Takahashi v. Fish & Game Commission*.[50] Takahashi was a resident Japanese alien who was ineligible for citizenship under federal law, which excluded certain national and racial groups from naturalization. He had held a fishing license in California for over 25 years prior to World War II. Following the evacuation of all Japanese from the area, California amended the statute which had previously authorized the issuance of commercial fishing licenses to all qualified persons. The statute prohibited issuance to any "person ineligible for citizenship." Takahashi, on his return, was unable to get a license solely because of his ineligibility for citizenship and, therefore, he was no longer able to make his living by fishing in the ocean.

The Supreme Court of California upheld the statute on the basis of the state's proprietary interest in the fish.[51] The question presented was whether California could constitutionally "use this federally created racial ineligibility for citizenship as a basis for barring Takahashi from earning his living as a commercial fisherman in the ocean waters off the coast of California." [52]

---

43. Id.

44. 263 U.S. 197 (1923).

45. Porterfield v. Webb, 263 U.S. 225 (1923). The statute in question was similar to that found in *Terrace* except that instead of the total exclusion of aliens, only "ineligible" aliens were unable to own land. The Court in *Terrace* had rejected the argument that because pursuant to the congressional act only free whites and Africans could become citizens, the Act invidiously discriminated against Orientals; any naturalization classification made by Congress was presumed

to be reasonable. In *Porterfield*, the Court simply relied upon *Terrace*.

46. Webb v. O'Brien, 263 U.S. 313 (1923).

47. Frick v. Webb, 263 U.S. 326 (1923).

48. See Cockrill v. California, 268 U.S. 258 (1925).

49. 332 U.S. 633 (1948).

50. 334 U.S. 410 (1948).

51. 30 Cal.2d 719, 185 P.2d 805 (1963).

52. 334 U.S. at 412.

The United States Supreme Court found it could not. The fact that the United States regulated immigration and naturalization on the basis of racial classifications did not mean the state could adopt such classifications to prevent an alien from earning a living in the same manner as citizens. The states do not have the broad power the federal government has to regulate the admission and naturalization of aliens; they may not add or subtract from the conditions imposed by Congress. State laws which impose discriminatory burdens on the entrance or residence of aliens are therefore invalid. The Court found it unnecessary to resolve whether the motivation for the statute was a desire to conserve fish or to discriminate against the Japanese, simply analyzing the statute in terms of the former. The power of the state to apply its laws exclusively to its alien inhabitants, particularly certain racial groups, is limited by the Fourteenth Amendment. The Court was unable to find that the "special public interest" on which California relied provided support for the state ban on Takahashi's commercial fishing. The Court stated "to whatever extent the fish in the three-mile belt off California may be 'capable of ownership' by California, we think that 'ownership' is inadequate to justify California in excluding any or all aliens who are lawful residents of the state from making a living by fishing in the ocean off its shore while permitting all others to do so." [53]

3. Supreme Court Decisions After 1970

It was not until very recently that the Court again ruled on the validity of state classifications based on alienage under the equal protection clause. In *Graham v. Richardson* [54] the Court held that the equal protection clause prevented a state from conditioning welfare benefits either upon the possession of United States citizenship or residence in this country for a specified numer of years. The opinion noted that prior decisions had equated classifications based on alienage with those based on race or national origin and declared that such classifications are inherently suspect and subject to close judicial scrutiny. The classification would only be valid if it was necessary to promote a compelling state interest.

The state sought to justify the restrictions on the basis of a "special public interest" in favoring its own citizens over aliens in the distribution of limited resources such as welfare benefits. The Court noted that it had previously upheld statutes upon such grounds, but that the decision in *Takahashi* had cast doubt on the continuing validity of the special public-interest doctrine in all contexts. The Court stated further: "whatever may be the contemporary vitality of the special public-interest doctrine in other contexts after *Takahashi*, we conclude that a state's desire to preserve limited welfare benefits for its own citizens is inadequate to justify Pennsylvania's making noncitizens ineligible for public assistance, and Arizona's restricting benefits to citizens and long time resident aliens." [55]

The special public interest doctrine had been heavily grounded in the notion that whatever is a privilege, rather than a right, may be dependent upon citizenship; this distinction between rights and privileges no longer exists. Absent the special public-interest doctrine, there was no compelling reason for the classification. The Court had held in *Shapiro v. Thompson* [56] that fiscal integrity was not a "compelling interest" and the same conclusion was true here. Although, unlike *Shapiro*, no fundamental right was invoked in this case, the use of a suspect classification required application of the compelling interest test. The justifica-

---

53. 334 U.S. at 421.

54. 403 U.S. 365 (1971).

55. 403 U.S. at 374.

56. 394 U.S. 618 (1969). The Court invalidated a state residency requirement which had to be met by

persons wishing to receive welfare benefits. The preservation of fiscal integrity was not a sufficient justification to inhibit the exercise of the right of interstate travel.

tion of limiting expenses was especially inappropriate where the class discriminated against was aliens who also pay taxes and may have lived and worked in the state for many years.

The Court in *Graham* also held the statute invalid because it interfered with the exclusive exercise of the federal government's control of aliens. Congress has broad powers to determine who may enter and reside in this country and Congress has not barred any aliens who become indigent after entry into the country. Thus the opinion found that "state laws that restrict the eligibility of aliens for welfare benefits merely because of their alienage conflict with these overriding national policies in an area constitutionally entrusted to Federal Government." [57]

The Court went further in requiring only narrow uses of alienage classifications in *In re Griffiths*.[58] In this case, the Court invalidated a state court requirement of citizenship for admission to the bar. The majority opinion stated that, because alienage is a suspect classification, the classification must promote a substantial state interest. The opinion equated the term "substantial," "overriding" and "compelling" in describing the type of state end that would justify such a classification. The state asserted that a person's citizenship affected his or her ability to fulfill the responsibilities of an attorney, but the state could not prove the truth of this assertion. The Court found it did not denigrate lawyers' high responsibilities to observe that their duties hardly involve matters of high state policy or acts of such unique responsibility so as to entrust them only to citizens. The possibility that some resident aliens are unsuited to the practice of law cannot be a justification for a wholesale ban. Since the state could not demonstrate that the classification was a narrow means of promoting a compelling or "substantial" end, the rule was invalid.

While the Court has been quite strict in recent years in prohibiting the use of alienage classifications in the economic area, it has allowed the states much wider latitude to use alienage classifications which are related to the self-governance process. When the government claims that an alienage classification serves political goals, the Court must determine whether the classification is so overinclusive or underinclusive that the claim should not be believed. When the state uses such a classification to exclude noncitizens from holding government employment, the Court should ask whether the positions from which the noncitizens are excluded relate to the self-governance process.

In *Sugarman v. Dougall*,[59] the Supreme Court invalidated a law making citizenship a requirement for any position in the competitive class of a state civil service system. The competitive class included all positions for which it was practicable to determine merit by a competitive exam and reach various positions in nearly the full range of governmental services. The state asserted that its goal was to employ only persons with undivided loyalty, but this prohibition was applicable to many positions whose function had no relationship to the loyalty, or citizenship, of the individual excluded. Since the Court exercises some form of realistic judicial scrutiny in determining whether an alienage classification is related to legitimate political ends, this classification could not withstand analysis. The state showed no need to require citizenship for all government positions other than simple economic preference for its citizens. The state also could not justify the statute on the grounds that it desired long-time employees; it offered no proof that aliens were a poorer risk in this regard than were citizens of another state within the Union. The sweeping prohibition on the employment of aliens in the public sector appeared so broad as not to be reasonably tailored to promote a legitimate interest in reserving the political process for

57. 403 U.S. at 378.

58. 413 U.S. 717 (1973).

59. 413 U.S. 634 (1973).

members of the political community. It appeared only to grant an arbitrary economic preference to residents of the state who were also United States citizens. The Court noted that its holding was a narrow one: it did *not* hold that "on the basis of individualized determination, an alien may not be refused, or discharged from, public employment, even on the basis of noncitizenship, if the refusal to hire, or the discharge rests on legitimate state interests that relate to qualifications for a particular position or to the characteristics of the employee."[60] Nor did the Court hold that a state may not, in an appropriately defined class of positions, require citizenship as a valid qualification for employment. In later cases, the Court upheld laws which reserved positions in state governmental agencies for citizens.

In *Foley v. Connelie*,[61] the Supreme Court upheld, by a 6–3 vote, a state law which excluded aliens from appointment as members of the state police force. The majority opinion by Chief Justice Burger stated that the earlier cases "generally reflect a close scrutiny" of alienage classifications, at least when they are used by state governments, but that the Supreme Court "never suggested that such legislation is inherently invalid, nor . . . held that all limitations on aliens are suspect."[62] Of course, this statement is incorrect to the extent that it would deny that alienage classifications have been held to be "suspect." The statement is correct to the extent that prior cases make it clear that alienage classifications are not to be reviewed as strictly as the suspect classifications of race or national origin. The majority opinion notes that the Court has recognized that obtaining the status of a citizen is a significant act because many rights relating to self-government may be properly reserved to citizens. In this way the Chief Justice is able to harmonize the substance of prior cases even though prior opinions use inconsistent language. Prior cases have rec-

ognized that reasonable alienage classification may be employed to pursue substantial state interests, such as that of self-governance, although prior "strict scrutiny" language has clouded these rulings. The majority in *Foley* believed that the great discretion granted police officers made individual officers important components of the system of government. Thus, the majority concluded that these positions could be reserved for those who have a right to participate in the governance process.

In his concurrence, Justice Blackmun, the author of the majority opinions in *Graham v. Richardson* and *Nyquist v. Mauclet*, found that the law could be upheld even though alienage classifications had been deemed to be inherently "suspect" and subject to close scrutiny.[63] Justice Blackmun found that, when a state is pursuing goals related to self governance, the use of citizenship classifications need only be shown to have some rational relationship to the interest in preserving the political community.

Justice Marshall, in a dissent joined by Justices Brennan and Stevens, was of the opinion that a compelling interest test should be used to review alienage classifications, but that the statute had to be invalidated so long as any form of review above the most minimal was employed. Justice Marshall stated that officers below a policy making level in the police department were involved in the application of public policy rather than the formulation of policies relating to self-governance. Thus, there was no permissible basis upon which to exclude all aliens because these classifications did not promote any interest relating to self-governance.[64] The dissenting opinion of Justice Stevens, joined by Justice Brennan, found that there was no group characteristic of aliens that would serve as a permissible classifying trait for their total exclusion from

---

60.   413 U.S. at 646–7.

61.   435 U.S. 291 (1978).

62.   435 U.S. at 294.

63.   435 U.S. at 300–301 (Blackmun, J., concurring).

64.   Foley v. Connelie, 435 U.S. 291, 303 n. 1 (1978) (Marshall, J., dissenting).

employment in the state police department.[65] Justice Stevens stated that in a representative democracy neither the police nor the military has broad policy making responsibilities, and, therefore, that the qualifying traits would have to be job related. Justice Stevens pointed out that the Court in *Elrod v. Burns* [66] had held that most public employees were protected from patronage discharges because such dismissals would punish them for their political beliefs. Thus, the refusal to allow aliens to hold non-policy making positions could not be treated as a permissible means of dispensing rewards for voting or participation in the political system.[67]

In recent years, the Supreme Court sought, perhaps unsuccessfully, to add some framework to its alienage decisions of the 1970's. By a 5 to 4 vote, in *Ambach v. Norwick*,[68] the Court upheld a state law prohibiting the employment as a teacher, in any publicly operated grade school or high school, of any person who was not a citizen of the United States unless that person had manifested an intention to apply for citizenship or was not yet eligible for citizenship. The majority opinion by Mr. Justice Powell admitted that the decisions of the Supreme Court regarding alienage classifications "have not formed an unwavering line over the years." The Justice noted the history of the public interest doctrine and its rejection in recent years, and he attempted to avoid any resurrection of that doctrine even though the majority was upholding an alienage classification.

Justice Powell's majority opinion cited with approval the earlier cases of the 1970's finding alienage classifications to be "inherently suspect" and rejecting the general public interest doctrine. However, the majority opinion went on to find that a state alienage classification would be judged by a rational basis test when the classification related to a state function that was "bound up with the operation of the State as a governmental entity." [69] The Court had long recognized that only citizens had a right to participate in the voting and self-governance processes; the majority noted that the Constitution itself reserved the right to direct participation in the governance process to citizens and made citizenship a meaningful distinction. The majority would apply a rational basis standard if the state could assert the promotion of a "governmental function" as the basis for the classification.

Thus, there were two issues to be considered: first, whether public school teachers were a part of a governmental function; second, whether the classification rationally related to that function. The majority found that the role of teachers in publicly funded and operated grade schools and high schools constituted a significant governmental function. Teachers in these schools were employed, in part, to prepare young persons for participation in the governance process as citizens. Public school teachers were also to foster and preserve many societal values, including those relating to self-governance. The majority found that standardization of teaching materials would not fulfil this important role because teachers served as a "role model" of persons involved in the American democratic system. Having found that teachers were a part of a government function the majority upheld the alienage classification as rationally related to the promotion of a self-governance, or governmental, function. For the majority this distinguished the teacher and police officer cases from the earlier cases finding that aliens

---

65. 435 U.S. at 308 (Stevens, J., dissenting).

66. 427 U.S. 347 (1976).

67. Justice Stevens also noted that there should be some similarity between the non-policy making class of jobs that were protected from patronage firing by the *Elrod* decision and that classification of jobs from which aliens could not be excluded. He noted it would be impermissible to dismiss a citizen state police officer

on the basis of his political affiliation because under *Elrod* this would not be considered a high policy making position. Nevertheless, after *Foley*, aliens could be excluded from being employed in the same positions on the rationale that the jobs were high ranking, policy making positions.

68. 441 U.S. 68 (1979).

69. 441 U.S. at 73, 74.

could not be excluded from becoming licensed attorneys or engineers. The attorney and engineer positions were not positions of government employment and the exclusions of aliens from those professions, therefore, was not related to a governmental function.[70] The majority noted that the state had not attempted to bar aliens from positions as teachers in public institutions of higher education or from any teaching positions in private schools.[71] It would be most difficult to uphold the bar of aliens as teachers in private schools, if they met educational requirements, because those schools do not perform the same government function as do publicly operated schools.

Justice Blackmun, author of the early alienage decisions of the 1970's, wrote a dissenting opinion that was joined by Justices Brennan, Marshall, and Stevens.[72] The dissent examined the classification in a more traditional manner; it employed a realistic standard of review to determine whether the alienage characteristic was a demonstrably reasonable way of determining that the burdened class was not similar to the benefited class. The dissent found nothing in the role of high school teachers that involved them in the creation or execution of significant public policy. There was nothing in the characteristic of being a lawfully resident alien that made one less able to be a grade school or high school teacher of most basic subjects. Justice Blackmun pointed out that the New York statutory scheme itself failed to promote any significant purposes for three reasons: (1) it contained an exception for persons ineligible to be United States citizens; (2) its exclusion was not related to whether the failure to apply for citizenship related to the individual fitness to teach; (3) the scheme would prefer a less qualified candidate as teacher over a better candidate if the poorer teacher were a United States citizen and the better candidate a resident alien.

Indeed, it appeared that the classification was merely one of a general list of positions that were denied to aliens by the State of New York after World War I.

Although the dissenters may have been correct in finding the restriction unreasonable; a majority of the justices rejected the dissenter's claim that it was "logically impossible" to differentiate this case from those striking the exclusion of aliens from practice as attorneys or engineers. The majority opinion found that the dissenters "missed the point" by failing to ask first if the public employment position were a part of a governmental (in the sense of self-governance) function.[73] An affirmative answer to that question, for the majority, allows the state to use any classification that will pass a rational basis test. It now appears that state governments cannot employ alienage classifications in a burdensome manner in their police power regulations or their granting of social welfare benefits but they will receive greater latitude in excluding aliens from public employment as well as from direct participation in the governance process. While the states will not be allowed to have a blanket exclusion of aliens from public employment, they will be able to exclude aliens from positions that are part of a governmental function.

The Court's last pronouncement on the ability of states to exclude aliens from public employment involved a state statute that provided that a person must be a citizen of the United States to be a peace officer or to occupy any government position at the state or local level which is declared by state law to have the powers of a peace officer. In *Cabell v. Chavez-Salido*,[74] the Supreme Court held that the California statutory requirement that peace officers be citizens was not unconstitutional and that it could be applied to exclude lawfully resident aliens from holding positions as deputy state pro-

---

70. 441 U.S. at 76 n. 6.

71. 441 U.S. at 70 n. 1, 3.

72. Ambach v. Norwick, 441 U.S. 68, 81 (1979) (Blackmun, J., dissenting, joined by Brennan, Marshall,

and Stevens, JJ.). Justice Blackmun wrote the majority opinions in *Graham* and *Sugarman*.

73. Ambach v. Norwick, 441 U.S. 68, 76 n. 6 (1979).

74. 454 U.S. 432 (1982).

bation officers. After reviewing the decisions noted previously in this section, the majority opinion by Justice White stated, "while not retreating from the position that restrictions on lawfully resident aliens that primarily affect economic interest are subject to heightened judicial scrutiny . . . we have concluded that strict scrutiny is out of place when the restriction primarily serves a political function." [75] The majority found that aliens could be excluded from the governmental process because this was not the arbitrary imposition of burdens on a disfavored class but "a necessary consequence of the community's process of political self-definition." [76] When the state excluded persons from exercising political power or holding government offices its action was not initially subject to strict judicial scrutiny. "[A] claim that a particular restriction on legally resident aliens serves political and noneconomic goals is to be evaluated in a two-step process. First, the specificity of the classification will be examined: a classification that is substantially over or under-inclusive tends to undercut the governmental claim that the classification serves political ends . . . Second, even if the classification is sufficiently tailored, it may be applied in the particular case only to 'persons holding state elective or important non-elective executive, legislative, and judicial positions,' those officers who 'participate directly in the formulation, operation, or review of broad public policy' and hence 'perform functions that go to the heart of representative government.'" [77] The Court found that the exclusion of citizens from the position of deputy probation officer met these tests. The general law enforcement character of all peace officers, including probation officers, resulted in the Court finding that the exclusion was "sufficiently tailored" to the legitimate political purpose of limiting the exercise of important governmental powers to members of the political community.

Justice Blackmun, author of the early 1970's decisions which had appeared to extend the protection of the compelling interest test to alienage classifications, dissented in *Cabell*. He and three other justices believed that the exclusion of aliens from the position of deputy probation officer could not withstand any realistic form of judicial review.[78] It was their belief that the exclusion "stemmed solely from state parochialism and hostility towards foreigners." [79] Nevertheless, a majority of the justices refused to subject the classification to rigorous judicial scrutiny once they believed that it was tailored to serve legitimate political ends.

The Supreme Court has employed a lenient standard of review when examining federal laws which employ citizenship classifications. The Court has not clarified the standard of review to be employed when examining federal alienage classifications but it seems apparent that most, if not all, such classifications will be upheld under any but the strictest form of judicial review. Because of the important nature of the federal interest in foreign affairs and foreign relations, as well as the federal power to regulate immigration and naturalization, the Court will defer to the Congress and uphold alienage classifications so long as they are not clearly an arbitrary and invidious imposition of burdens upon a politically powerless group.

In *Mathews v. Diaz* [80] the Court held Congress could condition an alien's eligibility for participation in a federal medical insurance program on continuous residence in the United States for a five-year period. The Court found that Congress had no duty to give all aliens the full benefits of citizens. The opinion noted that illegal or temporary

---

75.   454 U.S. at 437–39.

76.   454 U.S. at 439–41.

77.   Cabell v. Chavez-Salido, 454 U.S. 432, 439–41 (1982) in part quoting Sugarman v. Dougall, 413 U.S. 634 (1973).

78.   Cabell v. Chavez-Salido, 454 U.S. 432, 447–49 (1982) (Blackmun, J., dissenting, joined by Brennan, Marshall & Stevens, JJ.).

79.   454 U.S. at 461–63.

80.   426 U.S. 67 (1976).

resident aliens could present no substantial claims. The question was whether Congress could impose a durational residency requirement in order to define who was eligible for the benefits. As some line had to be drawn, the opinion held it reasonable for Congress to make an alien's eligibility for benefits depend on the "character and the duration of his residence." The determination of precisely where to fix the line for eligibility was for Congress, as any cutoff would produce some apparently arbitrary consequences for those falling slightly short of the requirement.

While the *Diaz* case makes it clear that the federal government may use alienage classifications to a greater degree than classifications based on the other suspect criteria of race or national origin, this decision is not inconsistent with recent alienage cases. Classifications based on race, national origin or alienage are "suspect", for they are highly likely to be used to arbitrarily disadvantage these groups. The history of the civil war amendments and post-war racial discrimination justify a judicially imposed prohibition against using race and national origin to disfavor these minorities. However, aliens bear a relationship to this country which is in fact different from that of citizens. They have yet to establish a permanent commitment to this country and they retain the obligations and benefits of citizenship in another nation. Another nation continues to have a legitimate interest in their treatment by this government. These factors may distinguish them, for some government programs, for nonarbitrary (nonprejudiced) reasons from citizens. These differences, however, relate only to national citizenship. The states have no interest in regulating aliens and their legitimate local interests do not relate to national citizenship. Thus, the states will rarely be able to show that they need to distinguish between

aliens and citizens to promote substantial state interests.[81] States may restrict the employment of those who are not lawful residents of the United States.[82]

Only the federal government may conduct foreign relations activities; therefore it alone has a need to distinguish between citizens and aliens. Since the treatment of aliens is intertwined with our relations with foreign nations, distinguishing aliens and citizens does not demonstrate prejudice against aliens or an arbitrary treatment of them. Thus the federal government has a "substantial" or "compelling" interest in the conduct of foreign relations and it may make reasonable use of alienage classifications to promote those ends.[83]

Because the national treatment of aliens is interwoven with foreign policy the Supreme Court will grant Congress some deference in its use of alienage classifications even though they are suspect. Where, as in *Mathews*, the classification appears to relate to national policy and is not based on a prejudice against aliens the Court will uphold the classification. However, even the federal government cannot make free use of alienage classifications which do not relate to foreign policy. Thus, in *Hampton v. Mow Sun Wong*[84] the Court held unconstitutional a regulation of the United States Civil Service Commission barring resident aliens from employment in the competitive federal civil service. The majority struck down the regulation because it was unclear whether the classification was to promote foreign policy or only employment efficiency. If the purpose were to promote foreign policy, it might well be valid, although the majority did not decide this issue. The majority also did not invalidate the regulation as an unconstitutional delegation of authority from Congress, reserving the question of congressional power to authorize the classification. Instead, the majority opinion for the Court

---

81. Thus, Puerto Rico could not restrict the practice of engineering by aliens. Examining Bd. of Engineers, Architects & Surveyors v. Flores de Otero, 426 U.S. 572 (1976).

82. DeCanas v. Bica, 424 U.S. 351 (1976).

83. For a further discussion of constitutional issues in foreign affairs, see generally, L. Henkin, Foreign Affairs and the Constitution (1972).

84. 426 U.S. 88 (1976).

only held that the regulation appeared to exceed the actual grant of authority from Congress to the Commission. The Congress could have given the agency some role in pursuing foreign policy through employment regulation but it did not appear to have done so in the past. Thus, the agency might be exceeding its powers by making such a decision. If Congress in fact had not granted it such a power, the regulation would have to be judged merely in terms of employment efficiency and it would be invalid under *Sugarman*. After *Hampton*, the Congress could establish the employment restriction on its own and the Supreme Court would assume that it was to promote foreign policy, since the Court would assume that the Congress was basing the law on its full power in the area. If Congress actually delegated the authority to the Commission to make such restrictions based on foreign policy considerations, the Court would review the regulation as an act of Congress. While the Court reserved the question, the regulation would not be stricken if it appeared to be related to national policy other than the arbitrary treatment or exploitation of aliens. But where the Civil Service Commission did not appear to consider foreign policy or even to be empowered to pursue such policy, the statute was invalidated.

The Supreme Court attempted to clarify the constitutional status of resident aliens in *Nyquist v. Mauclet.*[85] In this case the Court invalidated a state law which granted aid for higher education to citizens and resident aliens who were or would be applying for citizenship. By a 6 to 3 vote the Court found no compelling state interest in encouraging citizenship or limiting general programs to those who determine its policy.

The most important point of the decision is not the result of the case, which is in complete conformity with earlier rulings, but a statement in the majority opinion, written by Justice Blackmun, that "classifications by a state that are based on alienage are inherently suspect and subject to close judicial scrutiny."[86] In an accompanying footnote to this statement the Justice states that the Court used "relaxed scrutiny" in upholding the federal welfare requirements in *Diaz* because "Congress, as an aspect of its broad power over immigration and naturalization, enjoys rights to distinguish among aliens that are not shared by the states."[87]

The decision in *Nyquist v. Mauclet* has the distinction of leaving this area even more unclear than it was before that decision. The use of two totally different tests (strict scrutiny-compelling interest v. great deference-rational basis) for federal and state laws under the equal protection guarantee seems both analytically and historically unsound.[88] Not only is this contrary to the long development of uniform standards of review, it would allow the federal government to engage in the arbitrary and discriminatory treatment of aliens. It seems unlikely that such a result was intended to be

---

85. 432 U.S. 1 (1977).

86. 432 U.S. 7 at n. 8.

87. 432 U.S. at 7, n. 8:

"In Mathews v. Diaz, 426 U.S. 67 (1976), the Court applied relaxed scrutiny in upholding the validity of a federal statute that conditioned an alien's eligibility for participation in a federal medical insurance program on the satisfaction of a durational residency requirement, but imposed no similar burden on citizens. The appellants can draw no solace from the case, however, because the Court was at pains to emphasize that Congress, as an aspect of its broad power over immigration and naturalization, enjoys rights to distinguish among aliens that are not shared by the States. Id., at 84–87. See Hampton v. Mow Sun Wong, 426 U.S. 88, 100–101 (1976); De Canas v. Bica, 424 U.S. 351, 358 n. 6 (1976).

"It is perhaps worthy of note that the Medicare program under consideration in Diaz granted a permanent resident alien eligibility when he had resided in the United States for five years. Five years' residence is also the generally required period under federal law before an alien may seek to be naturalized. 8 U.S.C. § 1427(a). Yet, ironically, this is precisely the point at which, in New York, a resident must petition for naturalization or, irrespective of declared intent, lose his eligibility for higher education assistance."

88. The development of congruence of standards is examined in Karst, The Fifth Amendment's Guarantee of Equal Protection, 55 N.C.L.Rev. 541 (1977).

achieved with what appears to be the most casual dictum in a footnote. The footnote does not mention any of the cases stating the principle of congruence of standards of review under the equal protection guarantees. Nor does it note that the Congressional power to create general classifications for non-sensitive employment was not deferred to in *Hampton* as the Court expressly reserved the question in that case. Thus it may be that the dictum here was only intended to establish that there was a clear basis for a realistic review of state law in this case regardless of what the ultimate conclusions might be on the review of federal alienage classifications. To the extent this is true, it leaves untouched our earlier analysis.

As we have seen, the Court employs different standards of review for different types of alienage cases. When a state or local government distributes economic benefits on the basis of United States citizenship, the classification will be deemed "suspect" and subject to heightened judicial scrutiny and some form of the compelling interest test. When the State seeks to allocate political power, including the opportunity to hold important government positions, it will be able to do so whenever a majority of the justices believe that the law is reasonably tailored to further a legitimate political end. When the federal government employs an alienage classification, the Court will invoke only the rational basis test and defer to Congressional judgment over the dispensation of either economic benefits or political rights on the basis of citizenship. The cases could be made consistent by recognition of an intermediate standard of review for alienage cases but the split among the justices concerning the proper judicial role in reviewing alienage classifications may mean that this area will remain one of great theoretical confusion.

C. Classifications Burdening "Illegal Aliens"

As noted in the introductory subsection, Congress has virtually plenary power to define the class of persons who may lawfully reside in this country. The Supreme Court has never exercised meaningful judicial review over the exclusion or deportation of noncitizens from this country. However, the Court has long held that all persons within the country are protected by the due process guarantee; any person within the jurisdiction of the United States is entitled to a fair process to determine whether he may be deported from, or prohibited from returning to, the United States for violation of a federal statute or regulation.[89] The Court has not yet imposed any substantive restrictions on the ability of Congress to define the class of persons who may lawfully reside in the country or the ability of Congress to disfavor unlawfully resident persons in the distribution of federal benefits.

During the 1981–82 Term, however, the justices, by a 5 to 4 vote, for the first time extended the scope of the equal protection clause of the fourteenth amendment to give limited protection to unlawfully resident aliens from state or local laws which arbitrarily denied them benefits or imposed burdens upon them. In so doing, the Court employed a middle level standard of review by which it required the state to demonstrate that a classification burdening the children of illegal aliens in fact furthered a substantial goal of the state. The Court indicated that states might be given greater leeway in burdening unlawfully resident aliens when they were acting pursuant to authority given them by the federal government or promoting an articulable federal policy. Indeed, the Court did not prohibit states from taking all actions which give preferential treatment to citizens and lawfully resident aliens in the dispensation of governmental benefits. Because of the limited nature of the Court's ruling it is difficult to predict at this time the nature of the equal protection

89. See subsection A of this Section of Chapter 16.

guarantee which will limit the ability of state and local governments to differentiate between lawfully and unlawfully resident aliens.

In *Plyler v. Doe*,[90] the Court held that a Texas statute which withheld from local school districts any state funds for the education of children who were not "legally admitted" into the United States, and which authorized local school districts to deny enrollment in their schools to children who were not "legally admitted" to the United States, violated the equal protection clause of the fourteenth amendment. The State of Texas had argued that the equal protection clause was not applicable to this law and that it only protected those persons lawfully within the state. The majority opinion by Justice Brennan totally rejected that argument. There was nothing in the history of the fourteenth amendment or its language which indicated that the scope of the equal protection clause was meant to be narrower than that of due process. The fourteenth amendment reads in relevant part: "No state shall . . . deny to any person within its jurisdiction the equal protection of the laws." Justice Brennan found no reason not to apply the equal protection clause literally; the majority ruled that laws which gave unequal treatment to unlawfully resident aliens were subject to some form of judicial review under the terms of the equal protection clause.

The majority opinion by Justice Brennan focused on the precise problem before the Court and did not make a sweeping ruling on the nature of rights that must be granted to illegal aliens. Brennan noted that the state had made powerful arguments that it should be allowed to withhold its benefits from those persons whose very presence in the state was the result of their own unlawful conduct. However, in this case, the state was denying its benefits to the children who had been brought into the country illegally.

"Even if the state found it expedient to control the conduct of adults by acting against their children, legislation directing the onus of a parent's misconduct against his children does not comport with fundamental conceptions of justice."[91] The Court refused to recognize illegal aliens as a suspect class, which would have required that laws burdening this class of persons be subject to strict judicial scrutiny.[92] The majority opinion also refused to find that all laws burdening illegal aliens should be subject to a meaningful form of judicial review, such as were laws that employed gender or illegitimacy classifications, because the status of being an undocumented alien was not "an absolutely immutable characteristic since it is the product of conscious, indeed unlawful, action."[93] The fact that the Texas law at issue was directed against the children of those persons who entered the country illegally required, in the majority's view, some realistic examination of whether it was arbitrary to penalize these children for the actions of their parents.

In examining the permissibility of excluding the illegally resident children from public education, the Court noted that education is not a right specifically granted by the Constitution, nor a right which in the past has been found by the Supreme Court to be a fundamental constitutional right.[94] Thus, there was no basis for subjecting the law to strict scrutiny and requiring a compelling state interest to justify the exclusion of these children. However, the importance of education to a person's ability to function in society, and the fact that denial of all educational benefits to these children would result in their being deprived of any opportunity to advance their personal or economic interests on the basis of individual merit, led the majority to the conclusion that the Court should not simply defer to the state decision to deny an education to these children. The federal government might exclude or deport these

90. 457 U.S. 202 (1982).

91. 457 U.S. at 218–220.

92. 457 U.S. at 219 n. 19.

93. 457 U.S. at 218–222.

94. 457 U.S. at 220–222.

children, but the state was not entitled to a strong presumption of constitutionality for a law which would impose "a lifetime hardship on a discreet class of children not accountable for their disabling status." [95] For this reason, the Court found that laws which disfavored the children of undocumented aliens should be subjected to some form of realistic judicial review and "the discrimination contained in § 21.031 [the statute at issue] can hardly be considered rational unless it furthers some substantial goal of the state." [96]

In examining the state law under this realistic but less than strict form of judicial scrutiny, Justice Brennan's majority opinion initially noted that the state action was not taken pursuant to a federal mandate. The state's authority might be expanded when it was pursuing a clearly articulated federal policy and assisting Congress with the pursuit of important federal interests.[97] However, the majority found no indication that Congress had intended to allow aliens to remain within the country illegally and have the children of these aliens be subjected to arbitrary burdens. The majority then noted that the state might in some circumstances have an interest in employing a classification which disfavored illegal aliens when that classification would limit serious economic effects of sudden shifts in population. But the state could not demonstrate that its denial of services to the children of illegal aliens was a reasonable disincentive to illegal entry into the state as the dominant incentive for illegal immigration appeared to be the availability of employment rather than free education. Nor could the state demonstrate that the exclusion of the children of illegal aliens would improve the quality of public education because the legality of the residency of a child was not related to the cost which that child imposed upon the state by

going to school. A child who is not fluent in English imposed the same burden on a public school system regardless of whether he was lawfully or unlawfully resident within the state. Indeed, the state could not demonstrate that the children of unlawfully resident aliens were less likely than other children to remain within the boundaries of the state because the state did not structure its education system based on the assurance that any child, whether or not he or she was a citizen, would employ his eduction for the good of the state by remaining within the state.

Chief Justice Burger in a dissent joined by Justices White, Rehnquist and O'Connor, found no reason to engage in realistic judicial review of laws which burdened illegal aliens generally or their children in particular. "Once it is conceded—as the court does—that illegal aliens are not a suspect class, and that education is not a fundamental right, our inquiry should focus on and be limited to whether the legislative classification at issue bears a rational relationship to a legitimate purpose." [98] After noting that the burden on the children was not insubstantial, Chief Justice Burger indicated that denying them education "is not a choice I would make were I a legislator." [99] Nevertheless, the Chief Justice found no reason to give any protection from the arbitrary denial of benefits and imposition of burdens on these children. In the view of the dissent it was not unconstitutional to deny any opportunity for an education to these children because it was not irrational for a state to conclude that it did not have the responsibility to provide benefits for persons whose presence in the country was illegal.

The closeness of the vote in *Plyler* and the narrowness of the ruling, striking down only a law which denied an education to the chil-

---

95. Plyler v. Doe, 457 U.S. 202, 222–224 (1982).

96. Id., 457 U.S. at 222–224.

97. 102 S.Ct. at 2399. The opinion made reference to De Canas v. Bica, 424 U.S. 351 (1976) wherein the Court had upheld state legislation requiring employers to hire lawfully resident persons in part because it reflected a similar federal policy.

98. Plyler v. Doe, 457 U.S. 202, 247–249 (1982) (Burger, C.J., dissenting, joined by White, Rehnquist & O'Connor, JJ.).

99. 457 U.S. at 250–252 (Burger, C.J., dissenting).

dren of illegal aliens, make it difficult to predict the nature of the equal protection guarantee that will be defined in future cases involving the rights of illegal aliens.[100]

IV. CLASSIFICATIONS BASED ON ILLEGITIMACY

A. Introduction

An illegitimate child is one whose parents were not lawfully married to each other at the time of his birth.[1] Some statutes have accorded more favorable treatment to legitimate children than to illegitimate children, particularly when dispensing benefits following the death or disability of one of the children's parents. Although legitimacy classifications have not been held to be among those classifications that are deemed "suspect", they do receive a meaningful review under the equal protection guarantee. The compelling interest test has not been applied to these classifications, but the justices will independently review the basis of these clas-

sifications to determine if they reasonably advance a legitimate government purpose. The Court has stated that because sensitive personal rights are involved, the judicial scrutiny of classifications based on this form of personal status will be subject to a greater scrutiny than general economic or social welfare legislation.[2] The Court has stated that "imposing disabilities on the illegitmate child is contrary to the basic concept of our system that legal burdens should bear some relationship to individual responsibility or wrongdoing.[3]

Classifications that distinguish illegitimate from legitimate children may be upheld if the Court finds that they advance permissible government purposes and are not burdens placed on the illegitimate child because of his status. Neither state nor federal laws may use these classifications to punish the parent's behavior for giving birth to an illegitimate child. Nor can illegitimate children be burdened on the theory that unfavorable treatment of them will encourage legitimate

---

100. Indeed three of the justices who joined the Brennan majority opinion found it necessary to add concurring opinions. Justice Marshall noted that he remained committed to the view that laws denying educational benefits to a class of persons should be subjected to some realistic form of judicial review even though such laws might not be subjected to the traditional strict scrutiny or compelling interest test. Plyler v. Doe, 457 U.S. 202, 230–232 (1982) (Marshall, J., concurring). Justices Blackmun and Powell had voted in San Antonio School District v. Rodriguez, 411 U.S. 1 (1973), to employ only the traditional rational basis test in cases in which a state classified persons for the dispensation of educational benefits along lines that were not suspect. Justices Blackmun and Powell concurred in *Plyler* because they thought that realistic review of the Texas law was necessitated by the fact that it did not merely allocate different amounts of educational benefits to different classes of persons but in fact excluded a class of children from any opportunity to receive public education. The decision of the state to subject a class of children to a type of permanent disadvantage in society through the denial of any opportunity for state funded education had to be subject to meaningful judicial review. Plyler v. Doe, 457 U.S. 202, 230–232 (1982) (Blackmun, J., concurring); 457 U.S. at 235–237 (Powell, J., concurring).

The Supreme Court, by an eight to one vote, upheld a state statute which permitted a school district to deny tuition free education to a child who lived apart from his parent or lawful guardian if the child's presence in the school district was "for the primary purpose" of attending school in the district. Martinez v.

Bynum, 103 S.Ct. 1838 (1983). "A bona fide residence requirement, appropriately defined and uniformly applied, furthers the substantial state interest in assuring that services provided for its residents are enjoyed only by residents." Id. at 1842. The majority opinion found that this residence requirement did not violate the equal protection clause because it was not based on a suspect classification and it did not limit the exercise of a fundamental right. The Court noted that public education was not such a right. Id. at 1842–43 n.7. *Martinez* held that the statute at issue was a bona fide residence requirement because it provided free education for all children who resided in the school district with the intent to remain in the district indefinitely. The Court did not pass upon the residency claim of the child in this case, a United States citizen whose parents were non-resident aliens living in Mexico. See Id. at 1845 (Brennan, J., concurring). Only Justice Marshall would have invalidated the residency requirement on its face. Id. at 1845–54 (Marshall, J., dissenting).

1. For a complete examination of the status of illegitimacy and related legal issues, see, H. Krause, Illegitimacy: Law and Social Policy (1971); H. Krause, Family Law—Cases and Material, Chapter 7 (1976); H. Krause, Family Law in a Nutshell, Chapter 12 (1977); Krause, Equal Protection for the Illegitimate, 65 Mich. L.Rev. 477 (1967). For an examination of illegitimacy issues in relation to child support, see H. Krause, Child Support in America: The Legal Perspective (1981).

2. See Levy v. Louisiana, 391 U.S. 68 (1968).

3. Weber v. Aetna Casualty & Surety Co., 406 U.S. 164, 175 (1972).

family relationships.[4] Legitimacy classifications created for impermissible reasons constitute the arbitrary burdening of the child or his parents rather than mere regulation of activities that the state has a right to proscribe.

The state may not disadvantage illegitimate children in the dispensation of government benefits, or of property rights from their parents, merely because the problem of proving parentage may be difficult.[5] Statutes must include procedures to resolve questions of parentage; difficulties of proof may not be used as a barrier to the rights of illegitimate children. But the government need not give all children an equal presumption of a support or dependency relationship to their parents if that classification is not based on the status of illegitimacy. Governmental benefit systems designed to give support to those children dependent upon a parent who is deceased or disabled may presume dependency for legitimate children and certain classes of illegitimates who have a relationship to the parent that indicates a support obligation from the parent to the child. This classification will be valid even though it excludes from the presumption some classes of illegitimate children. However, to survive scrutiny under the reasonable basis test, the classification must be narrowly drawn to identify those with a likelihood of dependency upon the parent, and it must grant a presumption of dependency to illegitimate children whose personal circumstances indicate that they have been acknowledged or supported by the parent.

Furthermore, these laws should also permit other illegitimate children to prove their actual entitlement to benefits because of their continuing relationship to the parent, even though they do not have a presumption of dependency.[6]

Because the decisions on illegitimacy have been made under a "middle level" scrutiny test for validity of classifications, they have a certain ad hoc quality. The Court's rulings on the permissibility of a classification depends in part on the justices' view of the purpose of the classification and whether it is used to invidiously burden illegitimate children. Analysis of the Court's position on illegitimacy is further clouded by three cases, decided in the 1978–79 term, which involved combined illegitimacy and gender classifications.[7] All of the cases were divided by 5-4 votes and there was a majority opinion in only one case.[8] In that case the Court applied an intermediate level of scrutiny for gender classifications that requires such classifications to bear "a substantial relationship to an important state interest." The Court did not adopt any specific test for illegitimacy classifications, although a majority of the justices appear to be employing some form of realistic scrutiny, or middle level test, for such classifications. The most recent Supreme Court case involving an illegitimacy classification required that classification to be substantially related to a legitimate state interest.[9]

It is helpful to note the range of results in the illegitimacy decisions before going on to examine them individually. Statutes grant-

---

4. Trimble v. Gordon, 430 U.S. 762 (1977). See also Mills v. Habluetzel, 456 U.S. 91, 99–101, n. 8 (1982). But cf. Parham v. Hughes, 441 U.S. 347, 353 (1979).

5. Gomez v. Perez, 409 U.S. 535 (1973). The problems in this area may be lessened with the drafting of the proposed Uniform Parentage Act, see H. Krause, Family Law Cases, supra note 1; H. Krause, Family Law in a Nutshell, Chapter 14 (1977). See also H. Krause, Child Support in America; The Legal Perspective (1981).

6. Mathews v. Lucas, 427 U.S. 495 (1976).

7. Lalli v. Lalli, 439 U.S. 259 (1978); Parham v. Hughes, 441 U.S. 347 (1979); Caban v. Mohammed, 441 U.S. 380 (1979). Although the opinions in these cases discussed the constitutionality of gender classifications

more than illegitimacy classifications, we shall examine these cases together in this section because the decisions also illuminate the Court's position on the constitutional worth of asserted state interests in illegitimate children, the status of those children, and the permissible distinctions between maternal and paternal relationships to illegitimate children.

8. Caban v. Mohammed, 441 U.S. 380 (1979); see also Orr v. Orr, 440 U.S. 268 (1979) invalidating a state law allowing only for alimony payments from husbands to wives upon the dissolution of marriages. For a further examination of this case, see Section V, Chapter 16.

9. Pickett v. Brown, 103 S.Ct. 2199 (1983) (see notes 71–74, infra).

ing causes of action for wrongful death cannot deny a right of recovery to either illegitimate children or to their mothers.[10] The Court has held that such actions should be unrelated to the fact of illegitimacy and should depend upon the continuing relationship between the child and the mother. However, fathers of illegitimates may be prohibited from suing for the wrongful death of an illegitimate child unless the father has legitimated or formally acknowledged the child during the child's lifetime.[11] Neither the Social Security System[12] nor state worker's compensation provisions may deny benefits to all illegitimate children.[13] Such laws must be based upon the relationship between the child and the parent and cannot arbitrarily exclude all illegitimates because of the status of their birth. If a state grants legitimate children a right of support from either their mothers or their fathers, it must grant similar support rights to illegitimates who can prove their parentage.[14] The fact that it will be difficult for the state to create systems for proving parentage will not excuse it from its obligation of treating illegitimates in a fair manner.[15] For a time the Court held that illegitimate children could be treated less favorably than legitimate children in the property distribution from the estate of a male parent who died without a will.[16] The Court then adopted the position that illegitimate children cannot be arbitrarily excluded from inheriting from either their mother or their father, even though allowing inheritance rights to il-

legitimates will raise problems of proof of parentage.[17] More recently, however, the Court upheld a state law that excluded illegitimates from inheriting from their father unless they had been found, in a judicial proceeding, to be the children of the decedent father during his lifetime.[18] The Court also upheld a federal immigration law allowing Congress to subject illegitimate children of American fathers to immigration quotas.[19] That decision is based on the Court's historic deference to Congress in setting the terms for immigration and naturalization.[20]

The Court has looked with disfavor upon laws based on an arbitrary view of the worthiness of the parents of illegitimate children or family units containing illegitimate children to receive governmental benefits or equal treatment of laws relating to family matters. Households cannot be disqualified from receiving benefits because they contain illegitimate children.[21] However, the Court held that a Social Security Act provision which restricted surviving parent benefits to persons who have been lawfully married to a deceased wage earner prior to the wage earner's death did not discriminate against illegitimates.[22] States may not presume that the father of an illegitimate child is unfit to take custody of the child but must allow fathers some opportunity to retain custody following the death of the child's mother.[23] Similarly, the Court overturned a statute that required the consent of the mother but not the father of illegitimate children prior to their adoption, at least insofar as the stat-

---

10. Levy v. Louisiana, 391 U.S. 68 (1968); Glona v. American Guarantee & Liability Insurance Co., 391 U.S. 73 (1968).

11. Parham v. Hughes, 441 U.S. 347 (1979).

12. Jimenez v. Weinberger, 417 U.S. 628 (1974).

13. Weber v. Aetna Casualty & Surety Co., 406 U.S. 164 (1972).

14. Gomez v. Perez, 409 U.S. 535 (1973). See also Mills v. Habluetzel, 456 U.S. 91 (1982).

15. Trimble v. Gordon, 430 U.S. 762 (1977).

16. Labine v. Vincent, 401 U.S. 532 (1971).

17. Trimble v. Gordon, 430 U.S. 762 (1977).

18. Lalli v. Lalli, 439 U.S. 259 (1978).

19. Fiallo v. Bell, 430 U.S. 787 (1977).

20. See Kleindeinst v. Mandel, 408 U.S. 753 (1972) (attorney general's discretion on the entry of aliens not limited by the First Amendment); Mathews v. Diaz, 426 U.S. 67 (1976) (different standard of review applied to laws governing aliens; Congress may make rules for aliens that would be unacceptable if applied to citizens); cf. Hampton v. Mow Sun Wong, 426 U.S. 88 (1976) (Civil Service Commission could not bar aliens from employment unless Congress empowers it to do so).

21. New Jersey Welfare Rights Organization v. Cahill, 411 U.S. 619 (1973).

22. Califano v. Boles, 443 U.S. 282 (1979).

23. Stanley v. Illinois, 405 U.S. 645 (1972).

ute excluded the known or ascertainable fathers of older children.[24]

B. Wrongful Death Actions

In a series of decisions since 1968 the Court has employed a standard of review that must be implied from its rulings. In that year the Court, in *Levy v. Louisiana*,[25] overturned a state statute denying recovery to an illegitimate child for the wrongful death of his mother. The majority opinion first noted that illegitimate children were persons entitled to the full protection of the equal protection guarantee. The general rule that states could not invidiously discriminate against a particular class of people was of special importance because the classifications involved intimate family relationships and basic civil rights. The Court indicated that it would be sensitive to misuse of these classifications because they touched upon such relationships and were burdens based on religious or philosophical views of the worth of illegitimates or their parents. In this case, the Louisiana wrongful death statute denied to a child the right to sue for the death of his parent merely because he had been born out of wedlock. The right to sue was not based upon past support by the parent or continuing relationships with the parent but solely upon the fact of legitimacy. The United States Supreme Court held that the legitimacy of one's birth had no relationship, rational or otherwise, to the wrong inflicted upon the mother, which is the basis for wrongful death suits. The opinion stated that "it is invidious to discriminate against [illegitimate children] when no action, conduct, or demeanor of theirs is possibly relevant to the harm that was done the mother."[26]

In a companion case, *Glona v. American Guarantee & Liability Insurance Co.*,[27]

the Court refused to allow the state of Louisiana to deny an illegitimate child's mother the right to bring suit for the child's death. Employing an analysis similar to *Levy*, the Court held that the state had no rational basis to believe that denying recovery to mothers of illegitimates would tend to reduce illegitimate births. The disability had no causal relationship to the earlier actions or to any continuing wrongdoing by the mother. The opinion acknowledged that false claims of motherhood might arise following the death of children but held that these problems would not excuse the state's invidious classification. Justices Harlan, Black, and Stewart dissented in *Levy* and *Glona*.[28] The dissent noted that wrongful death was a statutory rather than common law cause of action and argued that the legislatures could draw almost any line for the allocation of this benefit.

In *Parham v. Hughes*,[29] the Supreme Court upheld a Georgia statute which allowed the father of an illegitimate child to sue for the wrongful death of that child only if the mother of the child was deceased and the father had legitimated the child before the child's death. While the justices examined this law in terms of sex discrimination rather than as an illegitimacy classification, none of the five justices in the majority talked about the generalized gender discrimination in the Georgia statutes which prohibited any father from suing for the wrongful death of the child if the mother was alive. For a majority of the justices, the case focused solely on the requirement that the father legitimate the child before its death to be entitled to sue.

Justice Stewart wrote a plurality opinion for four members of the Court.[30] He treated the law, in part, as one which did not classify either by an illegitimacy or gender trait

24. Caban v. Mohammed, 441 U.S. 380 (1979).

25. 391 U.S. 68 (1968).

26. 391 U.S. at 72.

27. 391 U.S. 73 (1968).

28. 391 U.S. 73, 76 (1968) (dissent applying to both *Levy* and *Glona*).

29. 441 U.S. 347 (1979).

30. The Stewart opinion was joined by the Chief Justice and Justices Rehnquist and Stevens. It is interesting to note that Justices Blackmun and Stevens switched sides between *Parham* and Lalli v. Lalli, 439 U.S. 259 (1978) (discussed in Section C, supra). Apparently, Justice Stevens found the *Lalli* distinction arbi-

and, in part, as one that survived whatever the appropriate test might be for such classifications. The plurality opinion noted that state laws are generally entitled to a strong presumption of validity and would be stricken only if they "bear no rational relationship to a permissible state objective." But the opinion stated that not all such classifications or statutes were "entitled to the same presumption of validity;" that presumption would be undermined by the use of suspect classifications or "other immutable human attributes."[31] The plurality opinion then found that the classification was not an invidious one based on illegitimacy or gender, which would require increased scrutiny, but the opinion also seemed to employ a realistic standard for reviewing whether or not the classification was permissible. The plurality endorsed the *Weber v. Aetna Casualty & Surety Co.*[32] position that classifications based on illegitimacy at birth appeared contrary to a principle requiring that burdensome classifications bear some relationship to individual responsibility, but the opinion also stated that fathers of illegitimates who had not legitimized their children were "responsible for fostering an illegitimate child and for failing to change its status."[33]

The plurality also found that the law was not one invidiously based on gender. Although the opinion recognized that a state was not free to make overbroad generalizations involving sex classifications, it stated that "in cases where men and women are not similarly situated, however, and a statutory classification is realistically based upon the differences in their situations, this Court has upheld its validity."[34] Justice Stewart then found that the fathers and mothers of illegitimate children were not similarly situated; only the father had to, or could, legiti-

mate a child under Georgia statutes. Because the mothers of illegitimates were readily identifiable, and more directly responsible for the care of a child immediately following its birth, it was reasonable to establish separate standards for when fathers might be entitled to recover for the death of the illegitimate child.

Having found that the classification was not invidiously based on illegitimacy or gender, the plurality readily accepted the assertion that the goals of the statute were promoted by the classification. Only the mothers of illegitimate children had a right to sue for the wrongful death of the child. A majority of the justices appear to believe that the distinction between mothers and fathers of illegitimates is demonstrably related to the important state goals of encouraging the legitimization of illegitimate children and guarding against spurious claims relating to paternity.

In a concurring opinion, Justice Powell mirrored much of the analysis used by the plurality but did so with a clearer statement of the appropriate standard of review for gender-based classifications.[35] He applied the intermediate standard of review adopted in *Craig v. Boren*[36] for reviewing gender classifications. Those classifications must "serve important governmental objectives and must be substantially related to the achievement of those objectives." But Justice Powell found that this statute was a realistic and reasonable way of achieving the state interest in avoiding problems of proof of paternity after the death of the child as well as encouraging the legitimization of illegitimate children.

Justice White, writing for four justices in dissent, also employed the *Craig v. Boren* standard.[37] The dissenters found

---

trary and the *Parham* one reasonable, while Justice Blackmun would defer to the state interest in regulating intestate succession but realistically review the *Parham* distinction. However, neither justice explained his position in these decisions.

31. 441 U.S. at 351.

32. 406 U.S. 164 (1972).

33. 441 U.S. at 353.

34. 441 U.S. at 354.

35. Parham v. Hughes, 441 U.S. 347, 359 (1979) (Powell, J., concurring).

36. 429 U.S. 190 (1977).

37. Parham v. Hughes, 441 U.S. 347, 361 (1979) (White, J., dissenting, joined by Brennan, Marshall, and Blackmun, JJ.).

that the statute reflected only one facet of a generalized assumption about the difference in the relationships between fathers and mothers and their children: the statute denied recovery to any father so long as the mother of the child was alive.

Justice White found no important state interest that was advanced by the distinction between the fathers and mothers of illegitimate children for three reasons. First, the end of promoting family unity or establishing standards of morality through the placing of burdens on illegitimates or their parents at the time of death was irrational, and rejected in previous decisions. Second, the goal of avoiding problems of proof in paternity cases could be met by more narrow and less burdensome means than a total bar on suits by fathers of illegitimates. The state was free, in the view of the dissent, to require specific forms of proof of paternity in order to meet these problems. Third, the assertion that in all cases fathers who failed to legitimate their children suffered no real loss upon the death of the child was totally unreasonable; the state could set standards for reducing or denying recovery to parents who in fact had little or no interest in the lives of their children while they were alive. There was no basis or need for the generalized assumption that no father of an illegitimate ever had a relationship with his child equal to that of a mother.

C. Government Benefits, Inheritance and Support Rights

The Supreme Court, in *Labine v. Vincent*,[38] had upheld a law which allowed illegitimate children to receive equal treatment in the intestate distribution of their father's estate only if they had been formally acknowledged by the father during his life. The majority apparently based the entire decision upon deference to the states' right to regulate property distributions after the death of a citizen. However, the opinion is almost indecipherable. It applies the equal protection analysis only in a footnote[39] and spends the entire text on a discussion of why these laws should be beyond the reach of the equal protection guarantee, a position with no support in any case prior to or following this one. The opinion may have turned on the fact that the state-created barrier to inheritance was not insurmountable; the illegitimate child could have been acknowledged by his parent or left property in a valid will.[40] The four dissenting justices argued that it was not rational to disfavor children in intestate distributions; it was an arbitrary burden based on status and an attempt to punish them because of the illegitimacy of their birth.[41]

This case existed for six years as the one case in which the Court had upheld a burden based solely on a social view of the status of illegitimates. In the years after *Labine* the composition of the Court changed, and the majority returned to an equal protection analysis. In *Weber v. Aetna Casualty & Surety Co.*,[42] the Court invalidated a Louisiana workman's compensation law that granted full recovery for injury to parents by legitimate and acknowledged illegitimate children but limited benefits to unacknowledged illegitimates. The Court held that when unacknowledged children had been dependent upon the injured parent, there was no basis for denying them full benefits. The majority opinion distinguished *Labine* as being based on a deference to the states' power over property distribution. However, its discussion of illegitimacy classifications thoroughly undercut the result in *Labine*. The majority opinion by Mr. Justice Powell explained that these classifications touched upon fundamental personal interests and that they appeared to run contrary to basic concepts of fairness. The opinion stated that the Court would exercise a "stricter scrutiny" over these classifications. It did not hold them to be suspect classifications

---

38. 401 U.S. 532 (1971).

39. 401 U.S. at 536, n. 6.

40. 401 U.S. at 538.

41. 401 U.S. 532, 541.

42. 406 U.S. 164 (1972).

subject to the most exacting tests.[43] Instead, the opinion held that in these situations "the essential inquiry [is] however, inevitably, a dual one: What legitimate state interest does the classification promote? What fundamental personal rights might the classification endanger?"[44] Here the law did not rationally promote legitimate state concerns because the state could not use later punishment of these persons to discourage illicit relationships in the future nor did this constitute a scheme to distinguish between those children dependent upon a wage earner and those not dependent. The personal rights involved were extremely sensitive because they involved family relationships and punishments of children who were not responsible for their status at birth.

In *Gomez v. Perez*,[45] the Court held that Texas could not deny illegitimate children the right to financial support from their natural fathers when this right was given to legitimate children. Without explaining the standard which it employed, the opinion held that the legislature could not permissibly decide to give parental support only to legitimate children. The opinion admitted that enforcement of support rights for illegitimates would be more difficult because of the problems of resolving complex factual questions of paternity. The Court decided, however, that the state could not justify on the ground of difficulty of birth the creation of "an impenetrable barrier that works to shield otherwise invidious discrimination."[46]

In response to *Gomez*, Texas enacted a statute establishing procedures to be followed in a paternity suit to identify the natural father of an illegitimate child for pur-poses of obtaining support. The state required that the suit be brought before the child was one-year old, or it was barred. In *Mills v. Habluetzel* [47] the Supreme Court held that the one-year period denied illegitimate children equal protection of law. Equal protection, the Court held, requires first that the period for obtaining support must be of sufficient duration to present "a reasonable opportunity for those with an interest in such children to assert claims on their behalf," and, second, that "any time limitation placed on that opportunity must be substantially related to the state's interest in avoiding the litigation of stale or fraudulent claims."[48] Problems of proving paternity may justify greater restrictions on support suits by illegitimate children than on those by legitimate children,[49] but the support opportunity provided to illegitimate children "must be more than illusory."[50]

In the next several years following *Gomez*, the Supreme Court invalidated several other laws burdening illegitimates. In *New Jersey Welfare Rights Organization v. Cahill*,[51] the Court invalidated a program providing welfare to low-income family units consisting of married couples with either natural or adopted children. The opinion held that the states could not deny benefits to family units simply because they contained illegitimate children. The effect of the statute was to punish illegitimate children by denying benefits to them and their families. The Court concluded that there was not an acceptable justification for distinguishing between legitimates and illegitimates when the purpose of the benefits should be to support needy persons rather

---

43.   406 U.S. at 172.

44.   405 U.S. at 173.

45.   409 U.S. 535 (1973).

46.   409 U.S. at 538.

47.   456 U.S. 91 (1982).

48.   456 U.S. at 99–101.

49.   456 U.S. at 95–99. Texas allows legitimate children to sue their natural father for support at any time until the age of eighteen. 456 U.S. at 99–101.

50.   456 U.S. at 95–97. For a complete examination of child support and illegitimacy issues, see H. Krause,

Child Support in America: The Legal Perspective (1981); see note 74, infra.

51.   411 U.S. 619 (1973). See also Davis v. Richardson, 342 F.Supp. 588 (1972), affirmed 409 U.S. 1069; Griffin v. Richardson, 346 F.Supp. 1226 (1972), affirmed 409 U.S. 1069. These cases, which were affirmed by the Supreme Court, held a provision of the Social Security Act unconstitutional because it tended to disfavor illegitimates by allowing them to receive benefits only if favored classes did not qualify for full benefits. Both lower courts applied the strict scrutiny—compelling state interest test in reviewing the statute.

than single out a class of children as unworthy because of their status at birth. Similarly, *Jimenez v. Weinberger*,[52] the Court invalidated a provision of the federal Social Security Act barring recovery by illegitimate children born after the onset of the worker's disability. These children were not distinguishable in terms of the purpose of the law, which was aimed at supporting disabled workers or their dependents. The law violated the equal protection component of the fifth amendment due process clause. There was no legitimate governmental interest, compelling or otherwise, which was related to dispensing support benefits on the basis of a child's status at birth. The Court found it unnecessary to determine whether illegitimacy classifications were suspect. It found the laws constitutionally invalid under the equal protection guarantees using a lesser test.[53]

In 1976 the Supreme Court held that the Social Security Act could condition the eligibility for survivor's benefits of certain illegitimate children upon a showing that the deceased wage earner was both the child's parent and was supporting the child at the time of his death. In *Mathews v. Lucas*,[54] the Court examined under the fifth amendment equal protection guarantee the permissibility of a law which granted a presumption of dependency to legitimate children and illegitimates who were entitled to inherit from the decedent under state law. Other illegitimate children were allowed to establish their dependency upon the deceased wage earner and to collect survivor's benefits, but they had to produce evidence of their dependency. The Court upheld the law because it found that the reduction in administrative problems and expense in avoiding a

proof of dependency requirement for all children could support this classification. The classification was not strictly a division between legitimate and illegitimate children because those illegitimate children whose circumstances indicated that the children were dependent on the wage earner were treated in a manner similar to legitimate children. Illegitimate children were entitled to a presumption of dependency if they could inherit personal property from the parent under state law, if their parents had ever gone through a purported marriage ceremony or had acknowledged the children, if they had been decreed by a court to be the wage earner's children, or if the wage earner had ever been ordered by a court to support the children. Thus, only a small group of illegitimate children were not entitled to a presumption of dependency upon the death of their parents. Furthermore, the remaining children were allowed to prove their dependency, in which case they would be qualified for benefits. The law was upheld because it was not an attempt to burden illegitimate children but only a narrow way of easing administrative problems for the establishment of dependency.[55]

Lucas did not indicate a change in the Court's analysis of illegitimacy classifications as was shown by the decision in *Trimble v. Gordon*.[56] *Trimble* involved a challenge to an Illinois statute which allowed illegitimate children to inherit by intestate succession from the estates of their mothers but not their fathers. The state supreme court had sustained the law on the authority of *Labine;* the United States Supreme Court held the law unconstitutional. The majority opinion by Justice Powell held that the Illinois act was not a reasonable way of pro-

52. 417 U.S. 628 (1974).

53. 417 U.S. at 631–31.

54. 427 U.S. 495 (1976).

55. See also United States v. Clark, 445 U.S. 23 (1980) holding that Civil Service Retirement Act provision 5 U.S.C.A. § 8341 (which automatically grants survivors' benefits to the legitimate children of a federal service employee, but allows "recognized natural" children to qualify only if they lived with the employee in a

family relationship), requires payment of benefits to an employee's illegitimate child who had once lived with him, but who no longer lived with the employee at the time of his death. The Court construed the statute to avoid the constitutional question of whether a narrower grant of benefits to illegitimate children is an impermissible illegitimacy classification.

56. 430 U.S. 762 (1977).

moting any legitimate governmental purpose. Nothing but conjecture suggested that such burdens upon illegitimates would promote legitimate family relationships or influence the actions of unmarried persons. Nor could the theory that intestate succession laws were "statutory wills" support the law because the possibility that many citizens would disfavor their illegitimate children upon death could not justify a total barrier to inheritance by illegitimates. Nor could the fact the father might leave these children property by will save the law; it still constituted a differentiation between children based solely upon their legitimacy.[57] The Court did not overrule *Labine* and indicated that, if in nothing else, the Louisiana statute was different because it had created different subclasses of illegitimates with different rights.

In *Lalli v. Lalli*,[58] the Supreme Court distinguished *Trimble* and upheld a requirement that in order for an illegitimate child to qualify as an heir of his or her father, and share in the intestate estate of the father, the child had to receive "an order of filiation declaring paternity" from a court of "competent jurisdiction" during the father's life. The proceeding, in which the illegitimate child received a judicial declaration of paternity of the alleged father prior to the death of the father, could have been initiated by the child, the child's mother, or the father during his lifetime. The plurality opinion by Justice Powell used a realistic form of review that might be described as a middle level equal protection test, even though the Justice did not state the test with particularity. The plurality opinion noted that classifications based on illegitimacy were not subject to strict scrutiny but that "they nevertheless are invalid under the Fourteenth Amendment if they are not related to a permissible state interest." The plurality also referred to the state interests in the case as "important" and "articulated." It appears that a majority of the justices favor some form of realistic scrutiny of whether the use of an illegitimacy classification relates to a significant, in the sense of articulated and not impermissible, state interest. However, the precise nature of the test is unclear since four of the seven justices who employed realistic scrutiny dissented in this case.

The Powell plurality distinguished New York's requirement of a judicial finding of paternity from the Illinois statute in *Trimble v. Gordon* which had excluded an illegitimate child from the father's estate unless the child was legitimated through the intermarriage of the natural parents and the father's acknowledgement of paternity. The requirement of intermarriage was an arbitrary and unreasonable means of attempting to encourage legitimate family relationships by burdening illegitimate children. The plurality found that the New York paternity order requirement was demonstrably related to the state interest in the orderly disposition of property and the accurate determination of paternity suits. While evidence regarding the actual purpose of the legislature was unclear, the law did not appear to be designed to penalize illegitimates as a class; there was some legislative history indicating that the law had been designed to treat illegitimate children in an equitable manner while insuring efficient and accurate proceedings for the establishment of paternity.[59] The plurality recognized that there might be other legitimate ways of providing for inheritance by illegitimates that would promote the state's interest, but the plurality did not require the legislature to achieve its ends through the means least burden-

---

57.   430 U.S. at 775.

58.   439 U.S. 259 (1978). Justice Powell announced the judgment in an opinion joined only by the Chief Justice and Justice Stewart. Justices Rehnquist and Blackmun concurred in the judgment but would have employed a significantly less strict standard to test the classification than did the Powell plurality. They would defer totally to the state interest in determining

the system of devolution of property from its citizens who die without a will and overturn Trimble v. Gordon. 439 U.S. at 276 (Rehnquist, J., concurring), 439 U.S. at 276, 277 (Blackmun, J., concurring).

59.   Lalli v. Lalli, 439 U.S. 259, 268–272 (1978). The plurality noted and relied upon the work of a state commission that had examined the need for revision of the state intestacy laws regarding illegitimates.

some on illegitimates as a class. The justices in the plurality believed that a requirement only of acknowledgement during the father's life would not provide the same degree of proof and certainty for the determination of heirs and avoidance of spurious paternity claims as would the New York judicial order requirement. Thus, in the view of the plurality, the requirement was "substantially related to the important state interest the statute is intended to promote." [60] In *Lalli* the Court did not consider whether the New York statutes established impermissible gender discrimination by allowing illegitimates to be heirs of their mothers without a declaration of maternity while requiring a judicial declaration of paternity for them to be intestate heirs of their natural fathers.

Justice Brennan, in a dissent joined by Justices White, Marshall and Stevens, employed a degree of scrutiny or equal protection test greater than the rational basis test but less than the strict scrutiny-compelling interest standards.[61] Although the dissent did not specify the precise test that should be used to review the legitimacy classifications, it examined the importance of the ends asserted by the state and the relationship between those ends and the classification. Justice Brennan found that the state goals of avoiding spurious paternity claims and the efficient identification of heirs could be achieved substantially by the "less drastic means" of requiring illegitimates to prove their paternity by a higher standard of proof following the death of the father or by accepting some forms of acknowledgement in lieu of a judicial declaration of paternity.

D. Adoption Problems

The Court has recognized that the fathers of illegitimates are entitled to some constitutional protection of their relationship to the child even though they have not married the mother of the child. In *Stanley v. Illinois*,[62]

the Court invalidated a statute which denied the father of illegitimate children a hearing prior to their adoption by another person. In this case the father had lived with the mother and the illegitimate children until the mother's death. At that time, the state sought to remove the children from the custody of the father without making an individual determination of the fitness of the father to retain custody. The Court held that the state denied the father his due process right to a determination of his fitness and a continuation of his relationship with the children. Just as there is no reason to arbitrarily burden the illegitimate child in his relationship to his parents, there is no basis for presuming that such fathers are unfit to retain custody of their children.

In *Caban v. Mohammed*,[63] the Supreme Court invalidated a New York law which required the consent of the mother of an illegitimate child prior to its adoption but which did not give equal consent rights to the father of the child. The majority found that the law constituted an impermissible form of gender-based discrimination between the parents of illegitimate children, although the majority did not reach the question of whether such discrimination would be allowed when the father of the child was not readily ascertainable or during the period when the child was in its infancy.

Under the New York statutes, a legitimate child could not be adopted over the objection of either its mother or father unless the parent had abandoned the child or otherwise been judicially determined to be incompetent to care for the child. The mothers of illegitimate children were treated like the parents of legitimates; the natural father of an illegitimate child had only the right to protest adoption proceedings involving his child. If the natural father exercised his right to object, then the trial court would determine whether the would-be adoptive parents were qualified to care for the child,

60. 439 U.S. at 275, 276.

61. Lalli v. Lalli, 439 U.S. 259, 277–278 (1978) (Brennan, J., dissenting, joined by White, Marshall, & Stevens, JJ.).

62. 405 U.S. 645 (1972).

63. 441 U.S. 380 (1979).

whereas the mother's objection would block the adoption under any circumstances.

The majority opinion adopted the intermediate standard of review which requires that gender-based classifications bear a "substantial relation to some important state interest." [64] Employing this test, the majority rejected the two bases which the state asserted for the classification. First, the majority found that maternal and paternal relationships to illegitimates were not so inherently different as to justify the conclusion that all mothers of illegitimates had a more significant interest in the well-being of the child than did any father. Second, while recognizing the importance of the interest in promoting the adoption and legitimization of these children, the majority found that the means used to promote adoption were unreasonable because there was no demonstration that fathers were more likely than mothers to object to adoptions for reasons that did not involve the well being of the children. Nor was there proof that the difficulty in locating fathers would interfere with the adoption of children beyond the infancy stage. The majority did not consider whether a

statute could be drafted that would grant adoption consent rights to only the mothers of illegitimates when the father could not be easily ascertained or when the child was to be adopted during the "infancy stage." The majority merely held that the "undifferentiated distinction between unwed mothers and unwed fathers, applicable in all circumstances where adoption of a child of theirs is at issue, does not bear a substantial relationship to the State's asserted interest." [65] Although the Court has not settled the rights of fathers of illegitimate children to gain initial custody of the children, *Caban, Stanley, Quilloin v. Walcott,* [66] and summary decisions of the Court indicate that fathers of illegitimate children should be given notice and a hearing before the child can be adopted by another person, at least where the natural father can be located and identified without unreasonably complicated or expensive administrative systems. [67]

The dissenting justices in *Caban* did not employ a significantly different standard of review than the majority, but they reached an opposite conclusion on the ultimate issue in the case due to their assessment of the

64. 441 U.S. at 388.

65. 441 U.S. at 394 (footnote omitted).

66. 434 U.S. 246 (1978). The Supreme Court unanimously rejected the claim of the natural father of an illegitimate child who sought to veto the adoption of that child by the husband of the natural mother. The opinion by Mr. Justice Marshall recognized that parent-child relationships received significant protection under the due process and the equal protection clauses. However, there was no violation of the natural father's procedural due process rights since his petition to stop the adoption and formally acknowledge the child was rejected only after a full hearing and a determination that the adoption would be in the "best interest of the child." Thus, there was no violation of the *Stanley* requirement that the father be afforded some form of fair procedure. The Court found that even if the "best interest of the child" standard might be challengeable in other situations, it was a permissible basis for determining whether to allow a child to be adopted over the objections of a parent (such as the natural father in this case) who had never sought actual nor legal custody of his child prior to the time when the child was to be adopted. The statutes reviewed in *Quilloin* granted fathers of legitimate children an absolute veto power over adoptions of those children. The father of a legitimate child retained this right until he specifically surrendered his rights in the child, abandoned the child, or had his rights terminated by a court for cause. The Supreme Court found no violation of equal protec-

tion in denying a similar veto power to fathers who had never sought custody of, nor taken significant responsibility for, the child in question. The fact that married fathers of legitimate children, at least for some period of time, had legal custody and responsibility for those children was a permissible basis to distinguish their rights from those of persons such as the unmarried father in this case.

67. Rothstein v. Lutheran Social Services, 405 U.S. 1051 (1972), summarily vacating 47 Wis.2d 420, 178 N.W.2d 56 (1972); Vanderlaan v. Vanderlaan, summarily vacating 126 Ill.App.2d 410, 262 N.E.2d 717 (1970). On June 23, 1983, in Lehr v. Robertson, 103 S.Ct. ___ (1983), the Supreme Court held that the state was not required by due process or equal protection to provide notice and a hearing to the putative father of a two year old illegitimate child when the father had never sought to establish a substantial relationship with, or accept responsibility for, the child. In *Lehr* the state allowed a man who claimed to be the father of an illegitimate child to file a statement to that effect in the "putative father registry"; that registration would guarantee that the man received notice of future adoption proceedings. Due process did not require a more extensive system to identify or notify fathers who had never claimed responsibility for the child; equal protection did not require that such fathers be granted rights equal to those who had established a substantial custodial, legal, or financial relationship with the child.

importance of facilitating adoptions.[68] Given the state interest in promoting adoptions and relationship of the mother to the child, the dissenting justices believed it was permissible to give a veto/consent right to the mother alone. Although Justices Stewart and Stevens were writing in dissent, they did note several important points that are critical to an understanding of the majority opinion. First, it is not at all clear whether this decision will have a retroactive effect; given the reasonableness of reliance on the previous adoption processes, it would seem unconscionable to call into question untold numbers of completed adoptions. Second, the problem of questioning mothers of newborns to ascertain the male parentage of newborns may constitute a basis for distinguishing between mothers and fathers when the adoption concerns an infant, a point not reached by the majority. Third, not even the dissenters would appear to endorse a principle that would distinguish between the legal status of mothers and fathers of legitimate children. Indeed, there is no indication that any of the justices would allow for termination of parental rights in relationship to a legitimate child absent a finding of unfitness on the part of the parent.

E. Immigration

In *Fiallo v. Bell*,[69] the Supreme Court held that the federal government could grant special preferences in immigration which excluded the illegitimate children of foreign national fathers seeking their admission. Under these laws legitimate children of either male or female parents, or the illegitimate children of a foreign national mother seeking admission to this country, were not subject to certain immigration quotas. However these quotas applied to the illegitimate children of fathers seeking admission to this country. The Court was not in this case indicating that illegitimacy classifications were subject to only traditional standards of review, or that the fifth amendment included a lesser equal protection guarantee. Rather, the federal government has a strong interest in setting standards for immigration and naturalization which the Court has always respected. This decision comports with decisions deferring to the legislative power over immigration and naturalization.[70]

F. Conclusion

Prior to the illegitimacy-gender cases decided in the 1978–79 Term, the Supreme Court had quite consistently invalidated laws which discriminated against illegitimate children or their parents. Illegitimacy classifications which were allowed to stand were narrowly drawn and did not stand as impenetrable barriers to obtaining benefits, or they related to an overriding governmental interest such as immigration. The illegitimacy-gender cases, however, allowed legislatures to erect some classifications which could deprive an illegitimate child, or his or her father, of benefits due to failure to comply with legal requirements even where there was a continuing relationship between the parent and child. Perhaps these decisions can be made consistent with prior cases upon the assumption that the Supreme Court will guard against the arbitrary use of gender or illegitimacy classifications, while attempting to allow legislatures to deal with significant social problems through the use of such classifications when they are not based on stereotypes. Yet the decisions are difficult to analyze because of the alignments of different justices that brought about the particular result in each case.

What emerges as clear from the Court's decisions is that classifications based on illegitimacy will be reviewed in some meaningful way. The precise nature of the test is unclear, but a majority of the justices require some demonstration that the classification is not an arbitrary burden on illegitimates or their parents due to moral

---

68. Caban v. Mohammed, 441 U.S. 380, 395 (1979) (Stewart, J., dissenting). 441 U.S. at 401 (Stevens, J., dissenting, joined by Burger, C.J., and Rehnquist, J.)

69. 430 U.S. 787 (1977).

70. See n. 15 supra and Chapter 16, Section III, and Chapter 20.

approbation or stereotypes. Results in particular cases, however, may be difficult to predict because they will depend on the different justices views of the purpose and effect of the classifications. Gender classifications must bear a substantial relationship to important state interests, but the Court may sustain some gender classifications concerning relationships of mothers and fathers to illegitimate children because some justices believe that the difference in proving paternity and maternity justifies the distinction.

The most recent illegitimacy decisions of the Supreme Court, in some ways seems to return to the principles of the early illegitimacy decisions. Under the state statute at issue in *Mills v. Habluetzel*,[71] the failure of an illegitimate child (with his guardian) to file a paternity suit within the first year of the child's life resulted in the illegitimate being forever barred from the right to sue his natural father for support. In that case, the Court required that restrictions relating to illegitimacy must be substantially related to a legitimate state interest.[72] The Court rejected the state assertion that legitimacy classifications promoted the continuation of the institutions of family and marriage; the Court repeated that imposing disabilities on the illegitimate child is contrary to the basic principle of our law that burdens should bear some relationship to individual responsibility or wrongdoing.[73] It should be noted, however, that the unanimous judgment of the Court was made in the context of a strict and substantial restriction on the rights of illegitimates to obtain parental support. Restrictions of lesser magnitude on the rights of an illegitimate child to seek support from his or her natural father may result in a di-

vided Court upholding or striking a particular illegitimacy classification based on the justices' differing views of the purpose and effect of the restriction.[74]

V. CLASSIFICATIONS BASED ON GENDER

A. Introduction

Men and women were not originally considered to stand as equals before the law. The married woman in particular was subject to severe legal disabilities at common law.[1] The passage of the fourteenth amendment, had no immediate effect upon the use of sex-based classifications. States continued to pass, and courts continued to uphold, legislation which reflected traditional beliefs of sex-defined roles and provided distinct treatment for men and women, notably in regard to employment opportunities and jury duty.

The earliest challenge to unequal treatment of women arose under the privileges and immunities clause of the fourteenth amendment. These challenges were unsuccessful chiefly because of the narrow construction given to this phrase by the Supreme Court. The clause was construed to encompass only those privileges or immunities which resulted from national, as opposed to state, citizenship.[2] Similarly, the Court originally gave the equal protection clause a very narrow interpretation which indicated that it would not provide any support for equal rights for women. Discussing the scope of the clause, the Court, in 1872, stated that it very much doubted "whether any action of a state not directly

---

71. 456 U.S. 91 (1982).

72. 456 U.S. at 97–99.

73. 456 U.S. at 99–101 n. 8.

74. In Pickett v. Brown, 103 S.Ct. ___ (1983), Justice Brennan wrote for a unanimous Court in holding invalid a state law which required a support or paternity action to be filed against the father of an illegitimate child before the child was two years old. The law did not provide a reasonable opportunity for illegitimate children to bring support claims. Citing the *Mills* "substantially related to a legitimate interest" test the Court's opinion found that the two-year limitation,

which provided exceptions only for acknowledged children or children likely to become "a public charge", was not substantially related to preventing the litigation of stale or fraudulent claims. See also Mills v. Habluetzel, 456 U.S. 91, 101 (O'Connor, J., concurring); id. at 105 (Powell, J., concurring).

1. The married woman would for example lack the legal capacity to contract or convey property. She could also not be held criminally responsible for an act done at her husband's direction.

2. Slaughter-House Cases, 83 U.S. (16 Wall.) 36 (1872).

by way of discrimination against the [N]egro as a class, or on account of their race, will ever be held to come within the purview of this provision." [3]   Although the clause was soon found to apply to other arbitrary classifications besides race, prior to 1971 sex-based classifications were treated exactly as were general economic regulations.   When the Court was taking an active role in the evaluation of economic regulation under substantive due process, it took a correspondingly active role in the evaluation of statutes which treated women differently from men. The Court generally upheld these statutes because it agreed with the legislatures that it was necessary to give women special treatment; however, where the Court found special treatment was not needed, it struck the legislation.   Following the repudiation of substantive due process,[4] the Court treated all "economic and social welfare" legislation—including all sex-based classifications—with great judicial deference.   The Court engaged in independent judicial review only when a fundamental right or suspect class was involved.

In 1971, in *Reed v. Reed*,[5] the Supreme Court broke from this tradition and engaged in the independent judicial review of a statute which discriminated between persons on the basis of sex, without declaring sex to be a suspect classification.   It soon became clear that the Court would no longer treat sex-based classifications with the judicial deference given economic regulations; however, it became equally clear that such classifications are not subject to the "strict scrutiny" given to truly suspect classifications such as those based upon race.   For a five year period, the Court struggled with the appropriate standard of review to be applied in

gender-based discriminations.   In 1976, in *Craig v. Boren*,[6] a majority of the justices defined an intermediate level of review for the examination of sex-based classifications. "To withstand constitutional challenge, classifications by gender must serve important governmental objectives and must be substantially related to achievement of those objectives." [7]   This "substantial relationship to an important interest" standard has been applied by a majority of the justices in the gender discrimination cases following *Craig*.

One must evaluate the decisions of the United States Supreme Court based on the results of its cases rather than an enunciation of a standard of review.   In the cases since *Craig*, the justices have often been divided on the meaning of the *Craig* standard and the degree of freedom that will be allowed the government to employ sex-based classifications.   The Court has invalidated statutory provisions which entitled women workers to less benefits for their family than their male counterparts.[8]   Preferential treatment for women has been upheld where it is compensatory for past discrimination against women as a class,[9] but not when it unreasonably denied benefits to men.[10] Age-sex deferentials have been invalidated both in the context of entitlement to support payments [11] and the sale of alcoholic beverages.[12]   But the Court has upheld sex-based classifications when a majority of the justices believed that the classification reasonably advanced a state interest which the majority found to be significant.   Thus, the Court has upheld differentiations between the rights of mothers and fathers of illegitimate children to bring a wrongful death action following the death of the child,[13] a statutory rape law that punished only adult men

---

3.   Slaughter-House Cases, 83 U.S. at 81.

4.   See Chapter 13, Section IV.

5.   404 U.S. 71 (1971).

6.   429 U.S. 190 (1976).

7.   429 U.S. at 197.

8.   Frontiero v. Richardson, 411 U.S. 677 (1973); Weinberger v. Wiesenfeld, 420 U.S. 636 (1975); Wengler v. Druggists Mutual Insurance Co., 446 U.S. 142 (1980).

9.   Kahn v. Shevin, 416 U.S. 351 (1974); Califano v. Webster, 430 U.S. 313 (1977).

10.   Califano v. Goldfarb, 430 U.S. 199 (1977); Wengler v. Druggists Mutual Insurance Co., 446 U.S. 142 (1980).

11.   Stanton v. Stanton, 421 U.S. 7 (1975).

12.   Craig v. Boren, 429 U.S. 190 (1976).

13.   Parham v. Hughes, 441 U.S. 347 (1979).

who had sexual intercourse with a child of the opposite sex,[14] and the exemption of women from military draft registration.[15] The exclusion of insurance payments for costs related to pregnancy from employee benefits has been found not to constitute a classification by gender and upheld by a majority of the justices,[16] even though overly restrictive maternity leave regulations and ineligibility for unemployment benefits based upon pregnancy status were found to be violative of due process.[17] While the Court has invalidated a state law that prohibited men from attending a state operated nursing school, it is not clear that a majority would find "separate but equal" male only and female only state-funded schools to violate the equal protection guarantee. These rulings lead one to believe that the Court's decisions in this area are ad hoc decisions dependent on whether the justices believe that a law is based on a sexual stereotype or was intended to promote a significant governmental interest. Perhaps it is inevitable that Court decisions will have an ad hoc quality to them whenever judges employ an intermediate standard of review that requires them to examine the asserted governmental interests and the relationship of the law to those interests. It is important to remember, however, that the Court continues to formally employ the substantial relationship to an important state interest standard when reviewing governmental classifications that are based on sex.

B. Cases Prior to REED v. REED

Bradwell v. Illinois,[18] in 1873, was the first case in which the constitutionality of different treatment for men and women was challenged. Relying upon the privileges and immunities clause of the fourteenth amendment, Bradwell challenged the refusal of the Illinois Supreme Court to grant her a license to practice law solely because she was a woman. The applicable statute required only that a person desiring a license obtain a certificate of good moral character from a local court. Bradwell, in compliance with the statute, submitted such a certificate with her application for a license but, in an oral opinion, was denied the license because as a married woman she "would be bound neither by her express contracts nor by those implied contracts which it is the policy of the law to create between attorney and client."[19] After announcement of the decision, Bradwell filed an argument maintaining her right, as a married woman, to practice law. The Court in response issued a written opinion in which it denied her a license on the basis of her gender.[20]

On appeal to the Supreme Court, Bradwell maintained that she was entitled to a license to practice because the fourteenth amendment "opens to every citizen of the United States, male or female, black or white, married or single, the honorable professions as well as the simple enjoyments of life."[21] The Supreme Court rejected this argument, affirming the state court decision with but one dissent.[22] Earlier that term the Court had held that the privileges and immunities clause protected only those privileges and immunities which were the result of United States citizenship.[23] Admission to practice in state courts was, if anything, dependent upon state citizenship and, therefore not within the scope of the amendment.[24]

---

14. Michael M. v. Superior Court, 450 U.S. 464 (1981).

15. Rostker v. Goldberg, 453 U.S. 57 (1981).

16. Geduldig v. Aiello, 417 U.S. 484 (1974).

17. Cleveland Bd. of Education v. LaFleur, 414 U.S. 632 (1974); Turner v. Department of Employment, 423 U.S. 44 (1975).

18. 83 U.S. (16 Wall.) 130 (1873).

19. 83 U.S. at 131 (1873).

20. 83 U.S. at 131 (1873).

21. 83 U.S. at 137 (1873), argument of Mr. Matthew Hall Carpenter for the plaintiff-in-error.

22. Chief Justice Chase, the lone dissenter, filed no opinion.

23. Slaughter-House Cases, 83 U.S. (16 Wall.) 36 (1872).

24. The privileges and immunities clause of Article IV § 2 was inapplicable because Bradwell was an Illinois citizen.

The concurring justices upheld the different treatment of women because it was mandated by "the law of the creator." Job opportunities for women were necessarily more limited than for men; women were not suited for occupations with highly special qualifications and responsibilities. The "paramount destiny and mission of womanhood are to fulfill the noble and benign offices of wife and mother." The views quoted here were representative of the attitudes women met when they attempted to challenge sex-based classifications.[25]

Because of the restrictive constitutional construction given the privileges and immunities clause and the determination that neither admission to the bar nor voting were privileges arising from federal citizenship, the Court in two cases following *Bradwell* upheld the denial of these rights to women.[26] However, these decisions are without contemporary effect. Subsequent Supreme Court decisions have forbidden arbitrary denial of admission to state bars [27] and the passage of the nineteenth amendment in 1920 extended to women the right to vote.

Prior to 1937, the Court took an active role in the review of economic regulation.[28] During this period a majority of the justices engaged in an independent review of the reasonableness and legitimacy of sex-based classifications just as they did for other forms of legislation. As a result of independent judicial review, the Court held in *Lochner v. New York* [29] that a state law setting maximum hours for bakers was invalid because it was not a legitimate exercise of police power and, in the Court's view, an unnecessary regulation which interfered with an individual's liberty to contract. However, three years later in *Muller v. Oregon*,[30] the Court upheld a statute prohibiting the employment of women "in any mechanical establishment, or factory, or laundry for more than ten hours a day." The Court rejected the argument of the defendant, a male laundry operator charged with violating the statute, that *Lochner* was controlling. That position incorrectly "assume[d] that the difference between the sexes [did] not justify a different rule respecting a restriction of the hours of labor." [31]

After stating the right to contract was not absolute but subject to reasonable restrictions, the majority opinion engaged in an extended discussion of the differences between men and women which justified the special legislation. That a woman's physical structure and her performance of maternal functions rendered her less capable of prolonged toil was a widespread belief as well as a proposition supported by medical testimony.[32] "[A]nd as healthy mothers are essential to vigorous offspring, the physical well-being of a woman becomes an object of public interest and care in order to preserve the strength and vigor of the race." [33]

Although the Court continued to uphold similar legislation prescribing maximum hours for women,[34] it did not uphold all laws designed to give women separate treatment. The justices determined for themselves

---

25. Although the method of communication between the Creator and the judge was never disclosed, "divine ordinance" was a dominant theme in justifying sex classifications. R. Ginsburg, Constitutional Aspects of Sex-Based Discrimination (1974).

26. In re Lockwood, 154 U.S. 116 (1894) (Woman admitted to bars of Supreme Court and District of Columbia could be denied admission to state bar of Virginia); Minor v. Happersett, 88 U.S. (21 Wall.) 162 (1874) (Statute limiting right to vote to men).

27. In re Griffiths, 413 U.S. 717 (1973) (aliens). The issue has not arisen in recent years in regard to women.

28. For a discussion of the Court's role prior to 1937, see Chapter 13, Section III.

29. 198 U.S. 45 (1905).

30. 208 U.S. 412 (1908).

31. 208 U.S. at 419 (1908).

32. In a footnote the Court referred to the brief of those who sought to uphold the law (now known as the "Brandeis brief" but which was primarily the work of Josephine Goldmark) which contained citations to state and foreign laws restricting hours of labor and extracts of over 90 reports of detrimental effects of long working hours upon women. 208 U.S. at 419 n. 1.

33. 208 U.S. at 421 (1908).

34. Bosley v. McLaughlin, 236 U.S. 385 (1915); Miller v. Wilson, 236 U.S. 373 (1915); Hawley v. Walker, 232 U.S. 718 (1914); Riley v. Massachusetts, 232 U.S. 671 (1914).

whether such treatment was a reasonable means of promoting legitimate state goals. Where the Court was in disagreement with the legislature, the statute was invalid. In *Adkins v. Children's Hospital* [35] the Court found the setting of minimum wages for women was a violation of due process, because it restricted the liberty to contract and there was no showing of a need for women to be treated differently in that regard. Due to the change in the contractual, political, and civil status of women, the differences between men and women, with the exception of physical differences, had come almost to "the vanishing point." "[W]hile the physical differences must be recognized in appropriate cases, and legislation fixing hours or conditions of work may properly take them into account, we cannot accept the doctrine that women of mature age, sui juris, require or may be subjected to restrictions upon their liberty of contract which could not lawfully be imposed in the case of men under similar circumstances." [36] However, in 1937, the Court, giving great deference to the legislative judgment, upheld a minimum wage standard for women and reversed *Adkins*. [37] Four years later the Court upheld federal maximum hours and minimum wage requirements for both men and women. [38]

As the decisions concerning minimum wage legislation indicate, the Supreme Court in 1937 retreated from its active role and began to treat economic regulations with great deference. [39] The Court employed independent judicial review only where a statutory provision affected a "fundamental right" or contained a classification by a "suspect class" such as race, a category which did not and still does not include sex. Classifications based on sex therefore were treated with the same deference given economic legislation and were upheld if they rationally related to a legitimate goal of the legislature.

A classic example of post-1937 judicial deference to the use of sex-based classifications is *Goesaert v. Cleary*. [40] In this case the Court upheld a Michigan statute which provided that no female would be licensed as a bartender unless she was the wife or daughter of the male owner of a licensed liquor establishment. The statute was challenged as being violative of equal protection because it discriminated between the wives and daughters of owners and the wives and daughters of non-owners. The majority began with the proposition that Michigan could bar all women. The issue of total exclusion was not addressed by the dissent and even the plaintiff centered her argument on the exception for wives and daughters of male owners rather than on the general exclusion. [41]

The question addressed by the majority, therefore, was whether, in view of the general prohibition of women bartenders the state could make an exception in favor of the wives and daughters of bar owners. The majority opinion found that bartending by women might "in the allowable legislative judgment" create the need for preventive measures against moral and social problems. The majority would defer to the legislative belief that for a defined class of women other factors reduced these problems so that different treatment could be accorded them. As long as the belief in the distinction was "entertainable"—not totally irrational—the classification did not violate the equal protection clause. The Court did not question whether this rationale was supportable in fact.

35.   261 U.S. 525 (1923).

36.   261 U.S. at 553 (1923). *Adkins* was reaffirmed in Morehead v. New York ex rel. Tipaldo, 298 U.S. 587 (1936). See Chapter 13, Section III.

37.   West Coast Hotel Co. v. Parish, 300 U.S. 379 (1937).

38.   United States v. Darby, 312 U.S. 100 (1941).

39.   For a discussion of the Court's retreat and its post-1937 treatment of economic legislation, see Chapter 13, Sections IV, V.

40.   335 U.S. 464 (1948).

41.   R. Ginsburg, Constitutional Aspects of Sex-Based Discrimination 24 (1974).

When freed of the need to defer to legislative or executive judgments, the Court showed some awareness of the claim to sexual equality. In *United States v. Dege* [42] the Court rejected the argument that a husband and wife were incapable of conspiracy. Such an immunity would require one of two assumptions: either that responsibility of both for joint participation in crime would cause marital disharmony or that the wife must be presumed to act under the coercive influence of her husband and, therefore, could never be a willing participant. "The former assumption is unnourished by sense; the latter implies a view of American womanhood offensive to the ethos of our society." [43] The latter would also require the disregard of the "vast change in the status of women—the extension of her rights and correlative duties." [44]

A year later, in *Hoyt v. Florida* [45] the Court upheld statutory provisions which made males eligible for jury duty unless they requested an exemption but granted females an exemption unless they waived it and registered their desire to be placed on the jury list. The Court declined the invitation to consider the continuing validity of earlier dictum to the effect that a state may constitutionally confine jury duty to males. [46] This case presented the narrower issue of the validity of the exemption of women. The relevant inquiry was whether the exemption itself was based upon a reasonable classification. [47] The Court found that "despite the enlightened emancipation of women from the restrictions and protections of bygone years, and their entry into many parts of community life formerly considered to be reserved to men, woman is still regarded as the center of the home and family life." [48] The Court could not say that "it is constitutionally impermissible for a state, acting in pursuit of its general welfare, to conclude that a woman should be relieved from the civic duty of jury service unless she herself determines that such service is consistent with her own special responsibilities." [49] The state might have exempted only those women with family responsibilities, but it was not irrational for a state to decide on a broad exemption, if it found such an exemption more administratively feasible.

C.   Definition of a Standard: From REED v. REED to CRAIG v. BOREN

It must be remembered that prior to 1971 the Supreme Court had always reviewed sex-based classifications under the equal protection clause in the same manner that it reviewed purely economic classifications. In 1971, in *Reed v. Reed* [50] the Supreme Court for the first time offered realistic protection against sex discrimination under the equal protection guarantee. *Reed* involved a challenge to an Idaho statute which established a scheme for the selection of the administrator of an intestate estate. Under the statute eligible persons were grouped into eleven categories by their relationship to the decedent and the categories were ranked in an order which was to be determinative if it was necessary to select between two competing applicants. The challenged portion of the statute provided that if it was necessary to select between two competing applicants in the same category the male was to be preferred over the female. As construed by the Idaho Supreme Court, the statutory preference for males was mandatory and was to be given effect without regard to individual qualifications.

The Supreme Court of the United States unanimously held that the arbitrary preference for males could not withstand constitutional attack. The opinion did not find sex classifications to be "suspect" and there was

42.   364 U.S. 51 (1960).

43.   364 U.S. at 53 (1960).

44.   364 U.S. at 54 (1960).

45.   368 U.S. 57 (1961).

46.   Strauder v. West Virginia, 100 U.S. 303 (1880).

47.   Chief Justice Warren and Justices Douglas and Black concurred, finding that the statute did not discriminate on the basis of sex. 368 U.S. at 69.

48.   368 U.S. at 61–62.

49.   368 U.S. at 62.

50.   404 U.S. 71 (1971).

no direct challenge to a legislature's power to classify persons by gender. But the opinion impliedly challenged the power to provide different treatment of persons on the basis of their sex when that was unrelated to the legitimate objective of a statute. "A classification must be reasonable, not arbitrary and must rest upon some ground of difference having a fair and substantial relation to that object of the legislation, so that all persons similarly circumstanced shall be treated alike." [51]

The question thus presented in *Reed* was whether the difference in the sex of the administrator had a rational relationship to some permissible objective of the statute. While the objective of reducing the workload by eliminating one class of contests is not without some legitimacy, the crucial question is whether the preference of males advances that objective in a manner consistent with the command of the equal protection clause. The Court's conclusion was that it did not. "To give a mandatory preference to members of either sex over members of the other, merely to accomplish the elimination of hearings on the merits, is to make the very kind of arbitrary legislative choice forbidden by the Equal Protection Clause of the Fourteenth Amendment; and whatever may be said as to the positive values of avoiding intrafamily controversy, the choice in this context may not lawfully be mandated solely on the basis of sex." [52]

As can be seen, the test was not the traditional rational relation test applied by the Court in *Goesaert* and *Hoyt*. Under the rationality test used in those cases, the statute could have been found to be related to a permissible purpose similar to the administrative convenience purpose of the statute in *Hoyt*. It would have been easier and less costly for the probate courts to choose ad-

ministrators if one class of claimants (women) were eliminated. The Court, however, found that the manner by which the objective was to be accomplished was arbitrary. Clearly the statute was not designed to pick the most competent administrators unless it was based on a theory that women were not as capable as men to administer the estate; the Court's refusal to defer to the use of such an assumption allowed it to find the classification arbitrary. The Court determined that the state's interest in judicial efficiency was less important than the interest of women in equal treatment with respect to the purpose of choosing qualified administrators of decedents' estates. [53]

In the five years following *Reed*, the Court considered a variety of sex-based classifications without agreement among the justices on the appropriate standard of review. A majority of the justices were committed to independently reviewing the reasonableness of these classifications but could not agree on a standard of review between the traditionally weak rational basis test and the almost insurmountable "strict scrutiny" or "compelling interest" test. Cases decided during this five-year period are instructive both in terms of giving one a basis for predicting the outcome of future cases and for help in understanding that different justices may be employing quite differing tests for the legitimacy of gender classifications even though they assert in their opinions to be applying a test agreed upon by a majority of the justices.

In the term following *Reed* the Court in *Frontiero v. Richardson* [54] faced a question concerning the rights of a female member of the uniformed services to claim her spouse as a "dependent" for the purposes of obtaining increased quarters allowances and medical and dental benefits. A serviceman

---

51. 404 U.S. at 76, quoting Royster Guano Co. v. Virginia, 253 U.S. 412, 415 (1920).

52. 404 U.S. at 76–77.

53. Note, Legislative Purpose, Rationality, and Equal Protection, 82 Yale L.J. 123, 150–51 (1972). For a discussion of tests being used by the Court in these cases see Gunther, In Search of Evolving Doctrine on a

Changing Court: A Model for a Newer Equal Protection, 86 Harv.L.Rev. 1 (1972); Nowak, Realigning the Standards of Review Under the Equal Protection Guarantee—Prohibited, Neutral, and Permissive Classifications, 62 Georgetown L.J. 1071 (1974).

54. 411 U.S. 677 (1973).

could automatically claim his wife as a dependent without regard to whether she was in fact dependent upon him; a servicewoman was required to show her husband was in fact dependent upon her for over half of his support. The question before the Court was whether this difference in treatment constituted a violation of the due process clause of the fifth amendment.[55] With one dissent,[56] the Court found it was.

Justice Brennan, in a plurality opinion, stated that sex was a suspect class, finding implicit support in the unanimous decision in *Reed*. Brennan reached this decision after examining the history and nature of discrimination against women. However, this view of sex as a suspect class never gained the support of a majority of justices voting in a single case. Furthermore, later opinions show that although Justices Douglas and White joined in the Brennan opinion even they did not actually mean that sex was a suspect class in the same way as racial classifications. The concurring justices found that such a declaration was unnecessary to reach a decision in this case and that the Court should await the outcome of the proposed Equal Rights Amendment before ruling on the suspect class issue.

After concluding sex was a suspect class, Justice Brennan engaged in a discussion of the rationale behind the statutory provision. The only justification offered by the government for the differential treatment was administrative convenience. Congress might have found it easier to conclusively presume wives were dependent, but require proof that a servicewoman's husband was in fact dependent. However, no concrete evidence was introduced which showed that the government did in fact save money. The government's explanation failed to convince the Court that there were sufficient grounds up-

on which to base the classification. As in *Reed*, the legislative judgment was no longer treated with great judicial deference; the Justices asked for proof that the classification actually achieved legitimate legislative goals.

In *Kahn v. Shevin* [57] a widower brought suit claiming denial of equal protection of the laws because a Florida statute allowed widows a $500 property tax exemption but provided no analogous exemption for widowers. The Court believed that the financial difficulties confronting a surviving wife exceed those facing a husband. Whether due to overt discrimination or the socialization process of a male dominated culture, she was more likely to be subject to an inhospitable job market. The difference in treatment therefore bore a sufficient relation to the legislative objective as required by *Reed*.

Justices Brennan and Marshall dissented because the governmental purpose could be served equally well by a more narrowly drafted statute. Consistent with their statement in *Frontiero* that sex was a suspect class, these justices found that gender-based classifications could not stand merely because they promoted legitimate governmental interests. The exemption, in their opinion was plainly overinclusive and should have been limited to widows needing financial assistance.

In *Schlesinger v. Ballard* [58] a male Naval line officer who after nine years of active service was passed over for promotion and consequently discharged, as required by statute, unsuccessfully claimed his discharge constituted unconstitutional discrimination because women were not discharged for lack of promotion until they had been in the Navy for thirteen years. The Court distinguished the provision from those in *Reed* and *Frontiero* in two respects. First, the

---

55. While the fifth amendment contains no equal protection clause as the fourteenth amendment does, it has been recognized that a classification may be so arbitrary as to be a denial of due process. E.g., Bolling v. Sharpe, 347 U.S. 497 (1954).

The Court has held that gender discrimination by the federal government or its agents gives rise to a cause

of action under the due process clause of the fifth amendment. See Davis v. Passman, 442 U.S. 228 (1979).

56. Rehnquist, J., dissented.

57. 416 U.S. 351 (1974).

58. 419 U.S. 498 (1975).

differential treatment involved here was not based on an overbroad generalization as in those cases, but rather on the fact that promotion opportunities for male and female line officers differed (due to the exclusion of women from all combat and most sea duty) which might have led Congress to rationally believe that women line officers had less opportunity for promotion. Secondly, the purpose of the classification is a flow of promotion commensurate with the Navy's current needs, not mere administrative convenience.

The dissenting justices found nothing in the legislative history to support the majority's suggestion that different treatment might have been provided to compensate women for "disadvantages visited upon them by the Navy." Futhermore, they found "quite troublesome the notion that a gender-based difference in treatment can be justified by another, broader, gender-based difference in treatment imposed directly and currently by the Navy itself." [59] The need for a correct flow of promotions could not be used to justify the distinct treatment given male and female line officers. The issue should be not whether the discharge policy promoted a legitimate or compelling state interest, but whether the differences in treatment accorded men and women could be justified.

In 1975, in *Taylor v. Louisiana* [60] the Court rejected *Hoyt* by holding that the practice of automatically exempting a woman from jury duty unless she waived her exemption violated a defendant's sixth amendment right. The exemption operated to virtually exclude women from jury venires and thus denied a criminal defendant his sixth amendment right to have a jury drawn from a fair cross-section of society. It was no longer tenable to suggest that jury duty would be a hardship for all women or that women could not be spared from their other duties.[61]

In *Weinberger v. Wiesenfeld* [62] the Supreme Court struck statutory provisions which conferred payments based on the earnings of a deceased husband and father upon his widow and minor children but which conferred payments based on the earnings of a deceased wife and mother only upon her minor children. While the statute could clearly have been regarded as discrimination against widowers who received no benefits, the basis of the Court's decision was the discriminatory effect upon women workers who received less protection for their survivors. The Court found the distinction between men and women was indistinguishable from the distinction invalidated in *Frontiero* because both rested upon the

59. 419 U.S. at 511 n. 1 (1975) (dissenting opinion).

60. 419 U.S. 522 (1975).

61. In Duren v. Missouri, 439 U.S. 357 (1979), the Court held that a statute granting all women an exemption from jury duty upon their request also violated a defendant's sixth amendment right to a jury drawn from a fair cross section of the community. The exclusion of any or all women upon request could not be justified by a desire to allow some persons to stay home to meet their family responsibilities; the exception was both under and over inclusive in terms of that end. But the majority opinion, by Justice White, indicated that a precisely drawn exemption for persons that was based on individual hardship, incapacity, or other important reasons, including the fulfillment of family responsibilities, would survive the requirement that the state demonstrate that the exemption classification serve a significant state interest.

After *Duren* the Supreme Court vacated and remanded for reconsideration decisions in which other defendants had been tried by juries subject to similar exclusions. The Court did not indicate that those decisions would have to be reversed, as such errors

may be subject to the harmless error rule. The Supreme Court has held that the *Duren* decision is retroactive to the extent that, in any case in which a jury was sworn after the decision in Taylor v. Louisiana it was error to impanel a jury chosen by a system that effectively excluded potential women jurors. However, if the defendant's jury was sworn after that date and the defendant failed to raise his objection to the jury in a timely manner, the defendant's petition for habeas corpus will be dismissed unless he can show good cause for having failed to properly raise the claim in state courts. Thus, the rule may only have significant retroactive impact on those cases that were or are on direct appeal after the *Duren* decision. See Lee v. Missouri, 439 U.S. 461 (1979); Harlin v. Missouri, 439 U.S. 459 (1979).

62. 420 U.S. 636 (1975).

The Supreme Court later upheld the restriction of "mothers insurance benefits", extended to fathers in *Wiesenfeld*, to those mothers or fathers of a deceased wage earner's child who had been married to the deceased wage earner prior to his or her death. Califano v. Boles, 443 U.S. 282 (1979).

assumption that the earnings of male workers were vital to a family while those of female workers were not.

Justice Rehnquist concurred for he found the statute did not even pass the rational relationship test as the restriction of benefits to mothers did not rationally serve any valid legislative purpose. He found it irrational "to distinguish between mothers and fathers when the sole question [was] whether a child of a deceased contributing worker should have the opportunity to receive the full time attention for the only parent remaining to it.[63]

In *Stanton v. Stanton* [64] the Court for the first time addressed age-sex differentials. In *Stanton* the statute in question provided that females reached majority at 18 and males at 21. As a result, the appellee had discontinued support payments ordered by the divorce decree for his daughter when she reached 18. The state court upheld the statute despite the equal protection challenge, finding that the classification had a reasonable basis in the belief that males were to provide the primary support of a home and, therefore, should receive an education. The Supreme Court reversed, relying on *Reed*. The differences between genders did not warrant the statutory distinction in the appellee's obligation to support them. The place of women was no longer solely the home; an education was equally important for females. The Court found that "under any test—compelling state interest, or rational basis, or something in between—the different ages for reaching majority in the context of child support could not survive an equal protection attack.[65]

The Supreme Court also invalidated an Oklahoma law which permitted the sale of 3.2% beer for off-premises consumption to women at age eighteen but required males to be twenty-one in *Craig v. Boren*. [66] The Court began with the statment that previous cases had established the principle that to

withstand constitutional challenge, classifications by gender must serve important governmental objectives and must be substantially related to the achievement of those objectives. A majority of the justices now had agreed upon a specific definition for the intermediate level of review applied in gender discrimination cases. Indeed, the Court's agreement on a standard of review was much more important than the holding in *Craig*. Under almost any form of realistic judicial review, the classification examined in *Craig* could not withstand analysis. The Court accepted traffic safety as the goal of the legislation, but found the statistical evidence could not support a conclusion that the classification reasonably served to achieve that objective. The relationship between traffic safety and the gender classification was too tenuous. While it might be true that more teenage males were involved in car accidents than females, and that more teenage males were arrested for driving while intoxicated than were teenage females, there was no evidence that would substantiate the claim that a person's gender made him or her more or less likely to become a drunken driver. The classification was based upon a stereotype perception of teenage males and females. It was not substantially related to the important state interest in traffic safety.

D. Recent Decisions Under the Intermediate Standard of Review

After 1976, a majority of the justices in each case involving gender discrimination have asserted that they are applying the substantial relationship to a important interest test. However, the meaning of this test is less than clear. As would be true of any intermediate standard of review, the test is one which neither prohibits the use of all gender classifications nor one which requires the justices to defer to legislative decisions. Thus, each justice may independently evaluate the importance of the

63. 420 U.S. 655.

64. 421 U.S. 7 (1975).

65. 421 U.S. at 17.

66. 429 U.S. 190 (1976).

interest which the government asserts to justify the gender classification and the reasonableness of the relationship between the gender classification and that interest. The Court's decisions appear to be *ad hoc* judgments based upon justices' perceptions of the gender classification at issue in each case. The major emphasis of the post-*Craig* cases has been the elimination of governmental classifications that arbitrarily burden one gender in terms of economic rights. Such laws are almost always viewed as based upon little more than sexual stereotypes. When the government employs a gender classification which does not allocate economic rights, the Court has a difficult time analyzing the constitutionality of that gender classification.

Not all laws which allocate economic rights on the basis of gender will be invalid. Those laws which appear to the justices to be a reasonable means of compensating women as a class for past economic discrimination will be upheld. Thus, the Court was unanimous in upholding a now superceded provision of the Social Security Act which allowed women to compute their benefits with a more favorable formula relating the past earnings than could be used by men at retirement.[67] Giving women some preference on a scale for retirement benefits which was keyed to earnings was reasonable because it compensated for the fact that discrimination in the employment market might have kept an undefinable class of women from achieving their highest potential in terms of earnings and contributions to the Social Security System. Conversely, the Court will strike down laws giving preference to women in the economic area if the justices believe that those laws are not reasonable means of com-

pensating for past discrimination against women as a class. Thus, the Court struck down a provision of the Social Security System that required male, but not female, spouses of deceased wage earners to prove actual dependency in order to receive survivor's benefits.[68]

In *Orr v. Orr*,[69] the Supreme Court employed the substantial relationship to an important governmental interest standard as it struck down a state law which provided that the state courts could grant alimony payments only from husbands to wives and never from wives to husbands. The majority opinion, by Mr. Justice Brennan, rejected the permissibility of any goal of the state related to insuring that the husband was allocated primary responsibility for the family; the Court has consistently rejected any state interest in keeping men in a role of primary responsibility in the family. The majority opinion did note that there were two possible objectives for such laws that might be considered sufficiently important to support a gender based classification: providing help for needy spouses and compensating women for past economic discrimination. However, the majority found that the law was impermissible because the classification did not substantially promote either important governmental interest. Indeed, the majority opinion noted that the Court did not have to engage in an analysis that would require the justices to determine if this gender based classification was a "sufficiently accurate proxy" for need or for compensating women as a class for past societal discrimination because the Alabama system in fact could not promote either purpose. Alabama, like virtually all other states, required an individualized court hearing at which the parties' fi-

---

67. Califano v. Webster, 430 U.S. 313 (1977). The Court also upheld a provision of the Act that provided greater secondary benefits for a woman married to a retired wage earner than for divorced spouse of wage earner. Mathews v. de Castro, 429 U.S. 181 (1976). The Supreme Court summarily affirmed a district court decision upholding a provision of the Railroad Retirement Act that allowed women to retire at age 60 while men could not retire, with equivalent benefits, until age 65. The lower court found that Title VII did not repeal this provision and that the system was justified

by historic discrimination against women in this field. Lewis v. Cowen, 443 F.Supp. 544 (E.D.Pa.1977) (three judge court), aff'd 435 U.S. 948 (1978).

68. Califano v. Goldfarb, 430 U.S. 199 (1977).

69. 440 U.S. 268 (1979). The relevance of this decision to an analysis of laws giving preferential treatment to women is examined in Kanowitz, "Benign" Sex Discrimination: Its Troubles and Their Cure, 31 Hastings L.J. 1379 (1980).

nancial circumstances were examined before the court entered an alimony order. Because the state required individualized hearings there was no demonstrable need to use the gender based classification as a proxy for need or as compensation for past discrimination. It would cost the state nothing to determine, at that hearing, whether the woman was financially secure and the husband in need of financial support. As there was no state goal that could not be achieved by applying a sex neutral rule at the hearing, the statutory classification was invalid.

The Court also employed the substantial relationship-important interest test in *Califano v. Westcott* [70] to invalidate a gender based classification used to allocate benefits to families with dependent children. The Social Security Act system of aid to families with dependent children provided benefits to families with children deprived of parental financial support because of the unemployment of the father only; no benefits were paid when support was lost due to the unemployment of the child's mother. Although the government claimed that there was no "gender bias" in the statute because it always affected a family unit with a male and a female parent and one or more children, the justices unanimously found that the law discriminated against mothers who in fact were the primary economic providers for their families. The classification was invalid under the equal protection component of the fifth amendment because it did not substantially advance the government interests in identifying children in need of support or reducing the unemployed fathers' incentive to desert his family, which had been encouraged by earlier federal aid programs. In *Westcott* the Court concluded that the program should be extended to all families where a parent was unemployed. Although

the decision as to extension of benefits or termination of the program is a non-constitutional one, as invalidating the statute also would eliminate the unconstitutional classification, a majority of the justices concluded that the congressional objective of providing for needy children and families would be best effectuated by extension of benefits in this case. [71]

The middle level standard of review should allow the Court to analyze clearly the validity of gender-based discrimination. For example, in *Wengler v. Druggists Mut. Ins. Co.* [72] the Court held, by an 8 to 1 vote, that a state worker's compensation law which provided death benefits (upon the work-related death of a spouse) to a widower only if he was mentally or physically incapacitated or could prove actual dependence on his wife's earnings, but automatically granted such benefits to a widow, was unconstitutional. The Court found that the statute discriminated against both men and women. The Court has consistently used a middle level standard of review in cases where discrimination is said to exist against working women because lesser benefits are granted to their spouses or dependents than are granted to the spouses or dependents of their male counterparts. Justice Stevens, in a concurring opinion, thought that the statute only discriminated against men, but he believed that the statute should still be subjected to the middle level standard of review. [73] The majority opinion stated that, "[h]owever the discrimination is described in this case, our precedents require that gender-based discriminations must serve important governmental objectives and that the discriminatory means employed must be substantially related to the achievement of those objectives." [74] Providing benefits for needy spouses of deceased workers was

70.   443 U.S. 76 (1979).

71.   Four justices concurred in the finding that the classification was unconstitutional but dissented as to the extension of benefits ruling; they would have invalidated the unemployed parent aid provisions on the basis that Congress had never intended to pay benefits based on the unemployment of the child's mother. Califano v. Westcott, 443 U.S. 76, 93 (1979). (Powell,

J., concurring and dissenting, joined by Burger, C.J., and Stewart and Rehnquist, JJ.). Of course, Congress has the choice of continuing the program on a gender neutral basis or terminating this aid program.

72.   446 U.S. 142 (1980).

73.   446 U.S. at 152–155, (Stevens, J., concurring).

74.   446 U.S. at 148–150.

deemed to be an important government objective, but that objective could have been achieved in a non-discriminatory manner by giving benefits only to widows and widowers who could demonstrate need. The state made only a generalized claim of administrative convenience for employing the classification, asserting that it might result in the savings of dollars that could then be used to pay benefits. The Court stated that "[i]t may be that there are levels of administrative convenience that will justify discriminations that are subject to heightened scrutiny under the equal protection clause, but the requisite showing has not been made here by the mere claim that it would be inconvenient to individualize determinations about widows as well as widowers." [75]

It seems difficult to believe that a showing of administrative convenience will ever be found sufficient to support a gender-based discrimination because the state could always be charged with finding some way to determine need as regards beneficiaries and challenged worker's compensation systems and doing so in a manner that would not seriously deplete the resources available for paying benefits under those systems. In *Wengler* the Supreme Court remanded the case to the state supreme court for a determination as to whether the classification should be made equal by granting benefits to all widows and widowers automatically or by requiring proof of dependency or need from all widows and widowers following the work-related death of their spouses.

Laws which allocate property or economic rights on the basis of gender should be invalidated under the intermediate level of review. In *Kirchberg v. Feenstra,*[76] the Supreme Court invalidated a Louisiana statute which gave a husband, as "head and master" of the family, the unilateral right to dispose of property jointly owned with his wife without her consent. Because neither the state nor the husband who was a party to the case could identify any important state interest which was in fact promoted by such a law, this granting of special rights to men violated the equal protection clause. Louisiana statutes allowed a wife to take steps to protect her property interest and avoid some of the discriminatory impact of the statute, but this fact could not save the gender-based classification because the degree of burden placed upon women is irrelevant when the gender-based classification fails to serve any important governmental objective.

The Court has had a great deal of difficulty in analyzing the constitutionality of a gender classification when the classification at issue did not allocate property or economic rights. While the Court in these cases also applies the substantial relationship to an important interest test, the outcomes of the cases vary with the judicial assessment of the asserted governmental interests. In two cases that involved combined gender and illegitimacy classifications [77] the Court applied this standard in differentiating between the rights and duties of fathers and mothers of illegitimate children.[78] The justices, by a 5 to 4 vote, invalidated a state law which granted a veto power over the adoption of such children to all mothers but no fathers because the state failed to show that such discrimination was necessary to achieve important interests in the facilitation of adoptions of illegitimates.[79] By a 5 to 4 vote, but without a majority opinion, the Court approved the denial of a right to sue for the wrongful death of an illegitimate to a father, but not a mother, if the father had failed to acknowledge the child during its life; the interest in determining paternity before the death of the child, as well as encouraging the legitimization of these children, supported such a distinction.[80] In a related illegitimacy case the Court upheld the exclusion of illegitimates from the intestate

75.　446 U.S. at 152–54.

76.　450 U.S. 455 (1981).

77.　These cases are examined in detail in Section IV of this Chapter.

78.　Caban v. Mohammed, 441 U.S. 380 (1979); Parham v. Hughes, 441 U.S. 347 (1979).

79.　Caban v. Mohammed, 441 U.S. 380 (1979).

80.　Parham v. Hughes, 441 U.S. 347 (1979).

estates of their decedent fathers if they failed to get a judicial order of paternity before the death of the father; the difference in the difficulty of proving paternity, as opposed to maternity, justified the state's desire to have such suits settled before the death of the father.[81] These decisions seem to reflect the opinions of a majority of the justices concerning the importance of state interests in illegitimate children more than they reflect a majority view of the proper degree of scrutiny for gender based classifications.

In *Michael M. v. Superior Court*,[82] the Supreme Court, without a majority opinion, upheld California's "statutory rape" law which defined as unlawful sexual intercourse "an act of sexual intercourse accomplished with a female not the wife of a perpetrator, where the female is under the age of 18 years." Although the statute provided only for the punishment of males who engaged in sexual intercourse with minor females and not for females who engaged in sexual activity with minor males, the Court did not overturn the statute. Justice Rehnquist, writing for four members of the Court, found that the state had an important interest in preventing illegitimate pregnancies and that the gender-based classification was sufficiently related to that end "[b]ecause virtually all of the significant harmful and inescapably identifiable consequences of teenage pregnancy fall on the young female."[83] Justice Stewart also noted that there was a variety of statutes in California which made unlawful various types of sexual activity with both males and females below specified ages; the statutory rape law was merely the imposition of an additional sanction which promoted the state's interest in avoiding illegitimate teenage pregnancies and the unique harm caused by

them to young females.[84] Justice Blackmun, concurring in the judgment, made it clear that he would apply the substantial relationship-important state interest test in this case even though he found that the law was valid because it substantially promoted the interest in the avoidance of illegitimate teenage pregnancies.[85] Justice Brennan, in a dissent joined by Justices White and Marshall, believed that the Court had either not applied or misapplied the substantial relationship-important interest standard because it was not clear that young women needed greater protection from the criminal law than did young men so that the law appeared to be one based only on "sexual stereotypes."[86] Justice Stevens dissented because he found the law not only unreasonable but irrational in its total failure to provide for punishment of females who engage in sexual intercourse with young men, particularly when the age of the persons engaged in the sexual intercourse might be quite close or identical.[87]

The Supreme Court upheld the constitutionality of the military selective service act, which exempted women from the draft registration process, in *Rostker v. Goldberg*.[88] The majority opinion, by Justice Rehnquist, stated that the Court should accord Congress great deference when reviewing laws having to do with the establishment or regulation of the military, but went on to find that the gender-based classification would survive scrutiny under the substantial relationship-important interest test. The majority found "the government's interest in raising and supporting armies" was an important governmental interest under the *Craig v. Boren*[89] standard.[90] Congress had not legislated on the basis of stereotypes of the roles of the genders but had given detailed consideration to both the constitutionality and wisdom of a registration system

---

81. Lalli v. Lalli, 439 U.S. 259 (1978).

82. 450 U.S. 464 (1981).

83. 450 U.S. at 476 (Rehnquist, J., joined by Burger, C.J., and Stewart and Powell, JJ.).

84. 450 U.S. at 476–77 (Stewart, J., concurring).

85. 450 U.S. 464 at 482 (Blackmun, J., concurring in the judgment).

86. Michael M. v. Superior Court, 450 U.S. 464, 488 (1981) (Brennan, J., joined by White and Marshall, JJ., dissenting).

87. 450 U.S. at 496 (Stevens, J., dissenting).

88. 453 U.S. 57 (1981).

89. 429 U.S. 190 (1976).

90. 453 U.S. at 70.

which would include both men and women and a registration system for males only. The majority opinion found that Congress was acting within its authority to raise and support armies in its decision that only men would be eligible for combat roles and that the draft registration should be used to prepare for an enlistment of combat troops. Congress could conclude that although there might be a need for women in noncombat roles during the mobilization, such a need could be met through volunteers or means other than the draft process. Men and women, because of the combat restrictions on women, are not similarly situated for purposes of a draft or registration for a draft.[91] For this reason the congressional decision to authorize only the registration of men did not violate the equal protection component of the fifth amendment due process clause. The majority found that "the exemption of women from registration is not only sufficiently but closely related to Congress' purpose in authorizing registration."[92]

The uncertain meaning of the intermediate standard of review employed in gender discrimination cases was demonstrated in *Mississippi University for Women v. Hogan*.[93] Mr. Hogan was a registered nurse in Mississippi who did not hold a baccalaureate degree in nursing. He applied for admission to the Mississippi University for Women [MUW] School of Nursing, which offered a four-year baccalaureate program in nursing and a graduate program. Although Mr. Hogan was otherwise qualified for admission, he was denied admission to the school of nursing solely because of his sex. Mississippi statutes, which included the charter of the university, limited the enrollment at Mississippi University for Women to women. The exclusion of males from the state nursing

school was invalidated by only a 5 to 4 vote. Indeed, the majority opinion left open the question of whether the Mississippi University for Women could deny admission to men because of their sex to schools within the university other than the school of nursing.

Justice O'Connor wrote for the majority *Mississippi University for Women*. The majority opinion, like those since 1976, stated that the classification would only be upheld if it served important governmental objectives and if the classification was substantially related to the achievement of those objectives.[94] "That this statute discriminates against males rather than against females does not exempt it from scrutiny or reduce the standard of review."[95] Mississippi justified the single sex admissions policy on the basis that it compensated for discrimination against women. However, the fact that women were not under-represented in the field of nursing undercut the reasonableness of the state's argument. Indeed, "rather than compensate for discriminatory barriers faced by women, MUW's policy of excluding males from admission to the school of nursing tends to perpetuate the stereotyped view of nursing as an exclusively woman's job."[96] The majority was unwilling to take a position against the dispensation of educational benefits by gender. Justice O'Connor's opinion, in a footnote, stated: "we decline to address the question of whether MUW's admissions policy, as applied to males seeking admission to schools other than the school of nursing, violates the fourteenth amendment."[97] It might be that one or more justices in the five member majority would view the limiting of admissions to other schools in the university, or other types of state supported schools, to one gender as being a permissible means of compen-

---

91. 453 U.S. at 77.

92. Id. Three justices dissented because they believed the government failed to show that there was a need to draft only combat troops, or that there was a need to draft men for noncombatant as well as combat positions, while exempting females from any need to register for or be subject to a draft for noncombatant military positions. 453 U.S. at 83, (White, J., joined by

Brennan, J., dissenting); Id. at 86, (Marshall, J., joined by Brennan, J., dissenting).

93. 102 S.Ct. 3331 (1982).

94. 102 S.Ct. at 3336.

95. Id.

96. 102 S.Ct. at 3339.

97. 102 S.Ct. at 3335 n. 7.

sating for past discrimination against persons of one gender or to achieve some other asserted governmental interest in the education process. Four justices dissented *Mississippi University for Women.* They believed that the fact that the state offered some coeducational nursing programs at other state schools justified limiting this nursing program or that the entire university to a single gender.[98] The dissent is based on these justices' belief that the equal protection guarantee does not justify judicial interference with traditionally accepted distinctions in the educational area. These justices need only one more vote in order to uphold the concept of "separate but equal" provision of educational benefits and services based upon gender.

The adoption of the substantial relationship to an important governmental interest standard by a majority of the justices has settled, at least formally, the issue of the proper definition of a middle level standard of review for gender classifications. However, that standard of review is such that it allows justices to base their votes upon individual perceptions of the reasonableness of a gender classification and the governmental interest asserted in each case. Were our country to adopt a constitutional amendment prohibiting gender discrimination by governmental agencies, the Court would have to employ some form of strict scrutiny or compelling interest test under that amendment which would limit the ability of individual judges to argue for the legitimacy of gender classifications based upon their personal perceptions of the reasonableness of allocating rights by gender.[99] Absent the adoption of such an amendment, the Court will continue to apply the middle level standard of review and it will be difficult to predict the degree of protection that will be given to persons against the arbitrary assignment of rights and benefits in society on the basis of gender. For instance, the Court has yet to decide whether general physical differences between the genders may constitute a basis for classifications which afford separate

---

98. Chief Justice Burger, dissented separately in his words: "to emphasize that the Court's holding today is limited to the context of a professional nursing school . . . it suggests that a state might well be justified in maintaining, for example, the option of an all-women's business school or liberal arts program." Mississippi University for Women v. Hogan, 102 S.Ct. 3331, 3341 (1982) (Burger, C.J., dissenting). Justice Blackmun, in dissent, stated: "I hope that we do not lose all values that some think are worthwhile (and are not based on differences of race or religion) and regulate ourselves to needless conformity." 102 S.Ct. at 3342 (Blackmun, J., dissenting). Justice Powell believed that the majority's opinion would lead inevitably to prohibiting states from providing one gender schools. Justice Powell believed that so long as men had some opportunity to receive the educational benefit, even if a somewhat different form and at a different location, they were treated substantially equally and found no justification for judicial intervention based upon the fact that Mr. Hogan could have received his education at another state school. Justice Powell concluded: "this is simply not a sex discrimination case. The equal protection clause was never intended to be applied to this kind of case." 102 S.Ct. at 3342, 3348 (Powell, J., dissenting, joined by Rehnquist, J.).

99. The proposed Equal Rights Amendment, which recently failed to win ratification read as follows:

Section 1. Equality of rights under the Law shall not be denied or abridged by the United States or by any state on account of sex.

Section 2. The Congress shall have the power to enforce, by appropriate legislation, the provisions of this article.

Section 3. The amendment shall take effect two years after the date of ratification.

The possible impact of this amendment on constitutional analysis of gender classifications was noted in the first edition of this treatise. See J. Nowak, R. Rotunda & J. Young, Constitutional Law 618 (1st ed. 1978). We also noted the progress of the proposed amendment through the ratification process. See id. at App. C, and 1982 Supplement to the first edition at Appendix C.

See generally B. Babcock, A. Freedman, E. Norton & S. Ross, Sex Discrimination and the Law (1975); R. Ginsburg, Constitutional Aspects of Sex-Based Discrimination (1974); H. Kay, Cases and Materials in Sex-Based Discrimination (1981); Brown, Emerson, Falk and Freedman, the Equal Rights Amendment: A Constitutional Basis for Equal Rights for Women, 80 Yale L.J. 871 (1971); Equal Rights for Women: A Symposium on the Proposed Constitutional Amendment, 6 Harv.Civ.Rts.—Civ.Lib.L.Rev. 125 (1971); Ginsburg, Sexual Equality Under the Fourteenth and Equal Rights Amendments, 1979 Wash.U.L.Q. 161; Van Alstyne, The Proposed Twenty-Seventh Amendment: A Brief, Supportive Comment, 1979 Wash.U.L.Q. 189.

governmental treatment to men and women without consideration of their individual abilities, such as the establishment of "separate but equal" schools or interscholastic athletic teams.[100] Additionally, it must be remembered that the review of gender-based classifications may still be complicated by issues concerning whether a law, neutral on its face, constitutes gender discrimination.[101]

E. Pregnancy Classifications and Irrebuttable Presumptions

In *Cleveland Board of Education v. La-Fleur*[102] the Supreme Court ruled that mandatory maternity leaves for teachers violated due process. Under the Cleveland rule, a pregnant teacher had to take a maternity leave beginning five months before the expected birth of her child and could not return without a doctor's certificate of physical fitness or until the semester which began after her child had reached the age of three months. A Virginia rule, which was challenged in a companion case, required a woman to leave four months before the expected birth, but guaranteed her re-employment the first day of the school year after she had received a doctor's certificate of physical fitness and could assure the school that child care would not interfere with her teaching.

The mandatory maternity leave provisions involved in these cases placed a heavy burden on a woman's exercise of her freedom of personal choice in matters of marriage and family life, a fundamental right. The question was whether there was a state interest sufficient to justify the rules. The firm cut-off dates were claimed to be necessary to maintain the continuity of classroom instruc-

tion. The Court recognized this purpose was a significant and legitimite educational goal, but found that the arbitrary cut-off date bore no rational relationship to the promotion of that goal as long as the school received substantial advance notice. Requiring women to leave at a later date would serve the same purpose while imposing a lesser burden. Furthermore, because pregnancies fell at different times of the school year, the cut-off date often hindered rather than promoted continuity as in the present case where the teachers were required to leave shortly before the end of the term. Nor could the arbitrary cut-off date be justified by the necessity of keeping physically unfit teachers out of the classroom. The Court found that this reason was a legitimate purpose and it would assume arguendo that some pregnant teachers became unfit to teach during the latter stages of pregnancy. However, this rationale could not justify the "irrebuttable" presumption that every pregnant teacher reaching the fifth or sixth month of pregnancy was physically incapable of teaching. Finding that the firm cut-off dates were invalid, the Court turned to the evaluation of the provisions regarding the return to teaching. The Court noted there was no serious challenge made to the medical requirement of an individual determination of the teacher's health or to the requirement of waiting for a new term following birth before resumption of teaching duties. However, the Court could find no reasonable justification for requiring that the woman's child be older than three months before she could return. The age of the child was entirely unrelated to the continuity of education and the medical certificate served to protect the school interest.

---

100. See Mississippi University for Women v. Hogan, 102 S.Ct. 3331 (1982) [examined previously in this section]. See also, Vorchheimer v. School District of Philadelphia, 430 U.S. 703 (1977) affirming by an equally divided court, 532 F.2d 880 (3d Cir. 1976) (establishment of two single sex schools with voluntary attendance upheld); O'Connor v. Board of Education, 449 U.S. 1301 (Stevens, as Circuit Justice, refusing to vacate lower court order which allowed a public school to refuse to allow a junior high school girl to try out for the interscholastic boys basketball team. At the end of

this opinion Stevens indicates that he believes that gender based classifications can be justified in giving separate treatment to boys and girls in contact sports).

101. This issue was examined as the Court upheld a state employment preference for veterans. See Personnel Administrator of Massachusetts v. Feeney, 442 U.S. 256 (1979) [this case is examined in Section I, D of this Chapter].

102. 414 U.S. 632 (1974).

Thus, this requirement was also a violation of due process.

Relying on *LaFleur*, the Court in a per curiam decision invalidated a statutory provision which declared a pregnant woman ineligible for employment benefits from twelve weeks before the expected birth until six weeks after birth.[103] The presumption of incapacity and unavailability for employment was found to be virtually identical to the presumption invalidated in *LaFleur*. In both these cases, the provisions were invalidated not because they were a denial of equal protection but because they constituted "irrebuttable presumptions." The relationship between this due process rationale and equal protection is examined in Chapter 15.

In *Geduldig v. Aiello*[104] the Court rejected the claim that a California disability insurance system which covered all disabilities of a prescribed duration[105] with the sole exception of disabilities resulting from normal pregnancy resulted in an invidious discrimination under the equal protection clause. The program might rightfully exclude some risks and the exclusion of pregnancy served a legitimate interest in keeping costs low. The majority rejected the contention that this exclusion was a sex-based classification, stating there was no evidence that the selection of risks which were covered harmed any definable group. There were no risks from which men were protected that women were not and vice versa.

Justices Brennan, Marshall, and Douglas dissented. The program paid for disabilities regardless of whether they were costly, voluntary, as with cosmetic surgery, unique to one sex such as prostatectomies or hemophilia, or statistically more likely to occur to one race, such as sickle-cell anemia, or the result of a preexisting condition. Despite this otherwise broad coverage, the program denied compensation for disabilities suffered in connection with "normal pregnancy", disabilities unique to women. Women suffering such disabilities had equivalent medical and economic needs as persons suffering from disabilities covered by the program. The dissent therefore would have found that the sex-based discrimination violated the equal protection clause.

A suit attacking a similar provision under Title VII[106] was equally unsuccessful.[107] Relying on *Geduldig* the Court stated that the exclusion of pregnancy from a disability benefits plan providing general coverage was not a gender-based distinction. A prima facie case of discrimination could admittedly have been established by showing that the effect of the "facially neutral" plan was discriminatory against a protected class, but the Court found no attempt had been made to show this effect in this case. In a later decision the Court found that Title VII did prohibit the use of pregnancy classifications or regulations that imposed a substantial burden on women employees.[108] Congress has amended Title VII so that discriminatory

---

103. Turner v. Department of Employment, 423 U.S. 44 (1975) (per curiam).

104. 417 U.S. 484 (1974).

105. Statute excluded coverage for disabilities lasting less than 8 days or greater than 26 weeks. There was also an exception mentioned for drug addicts, sexual psycopaths and dipsomania—these exclusions however were not strictly adhered to.

106. Suit was brought under § 703(a) "It shall be an unlawful employment practice for an employer (1) . . . or otherwise to discriminate against any individual with respect to his compensation, terms, conditions, or privileges of employment, because of such individual's race, color, religion, sex, or national origin" 42 U.S.C.A. § 2000e–z.

107. General Electric Co. v. Gilbert, 429 U.S. 125 (1976).

108. The next year the Court held that an employer's practice of taking away accumulated seniority from women who had to take mandatory pregnancy leave constituted a form of sex discrimination prohibited by Title VII. Nashville Gas Co. v. Satty, 434 U.S. 136 (1977). In that case the Supreme Court found that the substantial burden imposed on women by this practice rendered it a form of sex discrimination. This was true even though the same statistical impact analysis would not establish as a form of sex discrimination the employer's failure to grant insurance or sick leave pay benefits to pregnant employees. The Court did remand the case for a determination of whether the particular employer's sick pay policy was a mere pretext for invidious sex discrimination barred by Title VII. See also, Newport News Shipbuilding and Dry Dock Co. v. EEOC, 103 S.Ct. ___ (1983) (discrimination re-

treatment of employees on the basis of pregnancy is now prohibited by statute.[109]

VI. CLASSIFICATIONS BASED ON WEALTH

The constitutional protection for classifications burdening poor persons, sometimes called wealth classifications, can be described as nothing more than the protection given to any other classification of persons or business entities which are described by criterion which the Court does not regard to be suspect. The Court will uphold legislative actions which burden poor persons as a class under the equal protection or due process guarantee if the actions have any rational relationship to a legitimate end of government. So long as these laws do not involve the allocation of fundamental rights, the Court will consider them to be regulations concerning economic and social welfare policy. As such, these laws have no relationship to values with constitutional recognition so as to merit active judicial review under the strict scrutiny-compelling interest standard. It is apparently the view of the majority of the justices that there is nothing in the judicial function which makes them institutionally capable of deciding economic policy as to the allocation of income and wealth through the review of legislative classifications. However, the justices will actively review those classifications which burden the exercise of fundamental rights even when such classifications are based upon wealth.

The Supreme Court has consistently held that the government is not permitted to restrict the ability to engage in fundamental constitutional rights on the basis of individual wealth.[1] However, the Court has held that the state need not subsidize the financing of abortions for women who lack the economic resources to obtain an abortion during the first two trimesters of their pregnancy. This distinction is based upon the Court's view that the right to privacy concerning abortions involves only the absence of express governmental limitations on the abortion decision and that the failure to subsidize these practices constitutes no more than a policy choice not to give increased wealth or welfare benefits to a class of people who are not described by any suspect trait.[2]

In a series of decisions in the 1960's concerning rights to fair treatment in the criminal process,[3] voting rights,[4] and ability to engage in interstate travel[5] opinions of the Supreme Court had indicated that classifications which burden the poor were to be reviewed under an increased standard of review as suspect classifications. However, the Court had not yet squarely faced a law which burdened a class of persons who lacked financial resources for the allocation of benefits which had no other constitutional recognition. In *Dandridge v. Williams*[6] the Court reviewed a statute which set a formula for the provision of aid to families with dependent children that in effect did not offer any benefits for children born to families over a certain size. Since the Court has never recognized the interest of an individual in government subsistence benefits as a fundamental constitutional interest, there was no fundamental right present in this case. The majority opinion then upheld the

garding pregnancy benefits for employee spouses violates Title VII).

109. Pub.L. 95–555, 92 Stat. 2076 (1978) [adds Section 701(k) to Title VII proscribing as sex discrimination discriminatory treatment based on pregnancy or childbirth].

1. See, e.g., Douglas v. California, 372 U.S. 353 (1963) (counsel in first appeal for criminal conviction); Harper v. Virginia Bd. of Election, 383 U.S. 663 (1966) (invalidation of tax as prerequisite to voting in state elections); Boddie v. Connecticut, 401 U.S. 371 (1971) (filing fees for divorce cannot bar indigent).

2. See Maher v. Roe, 432 U.S. 464 (1977); Poelker v. Doe, 432 U.S. 519 (1977); Beal v. Doe, 432 U.S. 438 (1977); Harris v. McRae, 448 U.S. 297 (1980); Williams v. Zbaraz, 448 U.S. 358 (1980).

3. See, e.g., Douglas v. California, 372 U.S. 353 (1963).

4. Harper v. Virginia Bd. of Elections, 383 U.S. 663 (1966).

5. Shapiro v. Thompson, 394 U.S. 618 (1969).

6. 397 U.S. 471 (1970).

law under a rational relationship test, finding an arguable basis for relating the classification to the state interest in economy and the provision of certain families. This result was reached over the strong dissent of Justice Marshall who argued that classifications which burden poor persons in the ability to obtain the basic necessities for functioning in society should be judged by some meaningful standard of review even if they were not subjected to the compelling interest test.[7] However, the majority found no basis for distinguishing this law from any other economic regulation since all such measures to some extent involved the reallocation of resources or wealth. Thus, the majority found that these regulations constituted "economic and social welfare" legislation which merited only the traditional standard of review.[8]

This position has been consistently followed by the Court; it has held that there was no basis for using any form of strict scrutiny, or increased standard of review, to test legislation which burden classifications of poor persons in the receipt of other forms of welfare benefits,[9] public housing,[10] or access to the judicial process when no fundamental right is involved.[11] The Court again explicitly confronted the contention that some forms of wealth classifications should be held to be suspect in *San Antonio Independent School District v. Rodriquez.*[12] In that case the Court upheld the constitutionality of a property tax system which financed primary and secondary education in a school district in such a way as to create

subsidiary districts with large differences in the amount of money spent on the education of individual children. The Court found nothing in the allocation of educational opportunities based on the wealth of the district in which a child resided which furnished a constitutionally cognizable basis for close judicial supervision of legislative policies in this area. In so doing the opinion noted that in no case had the Court ever engaged in an active standard of review solely because the law burdened poor persons in the allocation of benefits which could not be deemed to be fundamental constitutional rights.[13]

The Court has held that governmental entities may not take actions which limit the capabilities of a class of persons to engage in the exercise of fundamental constitutional rights because of their lack of economic resources. In this area the Court has a separate basis for engaging in the active review of the actions of other branches of government: these laws burden interests which the Court has found to be of such a value as to merit special protection against arbitrary limitations. The state may be free to allocate economic benefits on any economic policy it chooses but the fact that these rights are of fundamental constitutional magnitude means that they cannot be given only to those who can afford to pay for them.[14] Thus the Court has held that indigents must be granted equal access to all the aspects of the criminal process which are basic to the fair determination of their guilt or innocence.[15] However, once the state has fulfilled this duty by granting them the oppor-

7. 397 U.S. 508 (Marshall, J., dissenting).

8. 397 U.S. at 485.

9. See, e.g., Schweiker v. Wilson, 450 U.S. 221 (1981); Jefferson v. Hackney, 406 U.S. 535 (1972). But cf., United States Dept. of Agriculture v. Moreno, 413 U.S. 528 (1973) (unrelated household members exclusion of food stamp act held to violate rationality test); United States Dept. of Agriculture v. Murry, 413 U.S. 508 (1973) (food stamp act exclusion of households based on previous status of individual member invalidated as an irrebuttable presumption).

10. James v. Valtierra, 402 U.S. 137 (1971), see also Lindsey v. Normet, 405 U.S. 56 (1972); Arlington Heights v. Metro. Housing Development Corp., 429 U.S. 252 (1977).

11. United States v. Kras, 409 U.S. 434 (1973) (bankruptcy fee); Ortwein v. Schwab, 410 U.S. 656 (1973) (filing fee to appeal from decision to terminate welfare benefits).

12. 411 U.S. 1 (1973).

13. 411 U.S. at 28. The Court has held that a state may not arbitrarily deny all access to education to a class of children. See, Plyler v. Doe, 457 U.S. 202 (1982) (invalidating statute denying education to children of illegal aliens).

14. The reader should examine the sections in this Chapter on each "fundamental right" for a more detailed examination of these cases.

15. See, e.g., Smith v. Bennett, 365 U.S. 708 (1961) (filing fees may not bar collateral attack); Douglas v.

tunity for a fair trial and access to the initial appellate process, there is no requirement that the state go further and level all economic distinctions by continuing to provide counsel for the individual throughout successive appeals or collateral attacks.[16]

In a decision concerning the right to vote the Court has held that any form of voter taxes is an impermissible way to limit access to the ballot.[17] The right of an individual to stand for elective office is also part of that fundamental right. The state may impose filing fees on candidates who can afford to pay them, for this is a reasonable means of determining which candidates are seriously interested in running for office, but the same filing fees cannot be applied to a person without the funds to pay them; otherwise the right to run for elective office would be allocated on the basis of individual financial resources.[18] Similarly the state cannot establish residency requirements for government benefits when that would penalize the right to interstate travel for poor persons.[19] And where access to the courts is necessary to protect one of these fundamental rights the process may not bar litigants because of their inability to pay filing fees.[20]

It should be noted that the issue in fundamental rights cases is whether the individual statute constitutes a limitation of the fundamental right that violates the Constitution and not whether it is fair or unfair to poor persons. The law may be invalidated as a violation of the fundamental constitutional right even though it seeks to level wealth distinctions in the exercise of the right rather than to create them. Thus in *Buckley v. Valeo* [21] the Court invalidated limits on campaign spending by candidates for public office as an unconstitutional burden on the right to freedom of speech. While the legislation was in part designed to equalize the ability to run for office between persons of differing wealth status, the majority found no interest of a sufficiently compelling magnitude to justify the limitation on the first amendment right to free speech.

The Court has ruled that states need not subsidize abortions during the first two trimesters of pregnancy for women who are unable to pay for those abortions. The majority opinions in these cases construed a woman's right to an abortion, as protected by the constitutionally fundamental value of privacy, to entail only a freedom from direct government restraints on her ability to choose to have an abortion.[22] Thus, the majority considered the legislature's policy to encourage childbirth by providing benefits

California, 372 U.S. 353 (1963) (counsel in first appeal); Mayer v. Chicago, 404 U.S. 189 (1971) (transcript fees).

16. Ross v. Moffit, 417 U.S. 600 (1974).

In Scott v. Illinois, 440 U.S. 367 (1979) the Supreme Court limited the right of indigent criminal defendants to appointed counsel at trial to those cases wherein the defendant in fact received a punishment of imprisonment. The Court had held that indigents had a right to appointed counsel at least when they were imprisoned for conviction on the charged offense in Argersinger v. Hamlin, 407 U.S. 25 (1972). The *Scott* majority refused to extend this right to those indigent defendants who were charged with serious offenses but who in fact received only a monetary fine rather than a sentence of imprisonment. However, if an indigent defendant is not given appointed counsel during a misdemeanor trial, his conviction cannot then serve as the basis for converting a subsequent misdemeanor into a felony under a state "enhanced penalty" statute. Baldasar v. Illinois, 446 U.S. 222 (1980).

17. Harper v. Virginia Bd. of Elections, 383 U.S. 663 (1966) (State and local fees). Poll taxes for federal elections are proscribed by the Twenty-Fourth Amendment. U.S. Const. amend. XXIV.

18. Lubin v. Panish, 415 U.S. 709 (1974); Bullock v. Carter, 405 U.S. 134 (1972).

19. Shapiro v. Thompson, 394 U.S. 618 (1969); Memorial Hosp. v. Maricopa County, 415 U.S. 250 (1974).

20. Boddie v. Connecticut, 401 U.S. 371 (1971) (divorce); Smith v. Bennett, 365 U.S. 708 (1961) (collateral attack on criminal conviction).

21. 424 U.S. 1 (1976).

22. Harris v. McRae, 448 U.S. 297 (1980) (limitation on payments for abortions under Social Security-Medicaid program upheld); Williams v. Zbaraz, 448 U.S. 358 (1980) (Federal statutes do not require payment for abortions. See also, Maher v. Roe, 432 U.S. 464 (1977) (payments for nontherapeutic abortions may be denied poor women); Beal v. Doe, 432 U.S. 438 (1977) (Social Security Act does not require such payments); Poelker v. Doe, 432 U.S. 519 (1977) (City hospital may provide free child birth assistance without providing corresponding services for nontherapeutic abortions).

These decisions are examined in Section VII, The Right to Privacy.

for childbirth procedures and other maternity requirements, but not for abortions, as a permissible social welfare measure. To the majority this limitation amounted to nothing more than the refusal to offer to increase the income position of persons who wished to enjoy a benefit available in the private sector which they could not afford given the other allocations of their resources. This classification did not burden the fundamental right and did not merit any increased standard of review. The majority opinion noted that wealth classification have never been granted the protection of a standard of review above the rationality test.[23]

The dissenting opinions in these cases pointed out that this decision did not seem to correlate with the many instances in which the Court had invalidated state burdens on the exercise of fundamental rights by poor persons.[24] The differences between the majority and the dissent are truly irreconcilable for these Justices have totally different views of the Court's role in insuring free exercise of fundamental rights by persons of extremely limited economic resources. The view of the dissent is that the state is not only required to respect the exercise of fundamental rights but also to facilitate their exercise within its existing wealth and income reallocation systems. The majority views the duty of the state only in terms of

an inability to create barriers to the exercise of those rights. In those instances where the state controls the means necessary to the exercise of the right, or to their protection through litigation, the majority will engage in some redistribution of economic benefits by allowing indigent persons free access to those governmental "benefits." However, it is the view of the majority that the state is not required to equalize the ability to exercise fundamental rights in the private sector for persons of differing wealth classifications. To this extent the case may be seen as consistent with the decision refusing to engage in a meaningful review of welfare programs. Any denial of a welfare benefit to class of poor persons can be said to make them less able to exercise a variety of fundamental rights in society by decreasing their total resources.[25]

VII.　THE RIGHT TO PRIVACY

A.　Introduction

Today the "right to privacy" has varied meanings. In the common law of torts the right encompasses a freedom from intrusion by others into privately owned areas as well as freedom from disclosures of information about an individual's private life.[1] The phrase also has several meanings in terms of constitutional analysis. The oldest consti-

---

23. See, Maher v. Roe, 432 U.S. 464, 471 (1977); Harris v. McRae, 448 U.S. 297, 323 (1980).

For an excellent analysis of this position see, Perry, Why The Supreme Court was Plainly Wrong in The Hyde Amendment Case, 32 Stanford L.Rev. 1113 (1980).

24. See, Harris v. McRae, 448 U.S. 297, 329 (1980) (Brennan, J., dissenting, joined by Marshall & Blackmun, JJ.); id. at 337 (Marshall, J., dissenting); id. at 348 (Blackmun, J., dissenting). See also, id. at 349 (Stevens, J., dissenting). See generally, Perry, supra note 23.

25. For an examination of the trends in the Supreme Court rulings concerning issues involving poor persons and wealth reallocation programs see Nowak, Foreword: Evaluating the Work of the New Libertarian Supreme Court, 7 Hastings Constitutional Law Quarterly 263 (1980). For commentary on wealth classifications see Michelman, On Protecting The Poor Through the Fourteenth Amendment, 83 Harv.L.Rev. 7 (1969) (arguing that the Court should guarantee a minimum allocation of basic interests); Nowak, Realigning

the Standards of Review Under the Equal Protection Guarantee—Prohibited, Neutral and Permissive Classifications, 62 Georgetown L.J. 1071 (1974) (criticizing the failure of the Court to analyze these classifications in terms of a meaningful standard of review); Wilkinson, The Supreme Court, The Equal Protection Clause and the Three Faces of Constitutional Equality, 61 Va. L.Rev. 945 (1975) (supporting the Court protecting fundamental rights but not economic equality); Winter, Poverty, Economic Equality and the Equal Protection Clause, 1972 Sup.Ct.Rev. 41 (using economic analyses to argue that the Court has gone too far in attempting to level economic distinctions). For sources and materials on a great many legal issues concerning proverty, see B. Brundo, Poverty, Inequality and the Law: Cases—Commentary—Analyses (1976); A. La France, M. Schroeder, R. Bennett & W. Boyd, Law of the Poor (1973).

1. For an original analysis of this concept, see Warren & Brandeis, The Right to Privacy, 4 Harv.L.Rev. 193 (1890).

tutional right to privacy is that protected by the fourth amendment's restriction on governmental searches and seizures. The first amendment has been held to protect some rights to privacy in speech or association.[2] The Court has also confronted the tort right to privacy in determining when suit may be brought against a person whose speech has invaded the privacy of another.[3]

But in terms of due process and equal protection the "right to privacy" has come to mean a right to engage in certain highly personal activities. More specifically, it currently relates to certain rights of freedom of choice in marital, sexual, and reproductive matters. Even this definition may be too broad, for the Court still has not recognized any general right to engage in sexual activities that are done in private. Instead, the justices have acknowledged the existence of a "right" and defined it by very specific application to laws relating to reproduction, contraception, abortion, and marriage.[4]

This general constitutional right to privacy may have had its inception in an article written in 1890 by Samuel Warren and Louis D. Brandeis.[5] The article attacked intrusions by newspapers into the private affairs of individuals and advocated the protection of the "inviolate personality" of each person. In contemporary terms Warren and Brandeis were advocating protection, under the law of torts, for dissemination or use of facts relating to an individual's private life. They did not consider the problem of government intrusion into the "inviolate personality" of each individual, but they did help to establish recognition in American legal thought that each person had a cognizable legal interest in a private life, both physical and emotional. Later, as a Justice of the Supreme Court, Brandeis would advocate a wide reading of the fourth amendment in order to insure that government did not intrude into the "privacy of the individual." While the Justice did not foresee the issue of government restrictions or decision making in private matters, he laid the basis for the modern right when he recognized a right to protection of one's private life from government intrusion or "the right to be alone—the most comprehensive of rights and the right most valued by civilized man."[6]

During the first part of this century the Supreme Court held that the liberty protected by the due process clause included the freedom to make decisions which did not adversely affect legitimate state interests. In *Meyer v. Nebraska*[7] the Court invalidated a statute which prohibited all grade schools from teaching subjects in any language other than English. In *Pierce v. Society of Sisters*[8] a statute which required students to attend public rather than private schools was found repugnant to the due process clause of the fourteenth amendment. In each case the majority found that the law restricted individual freedom without any relation to a valid public interest. Freedom of choice regarding an individual's personal life was recognized as constitutionally protected. These decisions may only have reflected the attitude of the Court towards government regulation during the apex of "substantive due process."[9] While these decisions might today be grounded on the first amendment, their existence is important to the growth of the right to privacy. If nothing else, they show a historical recognition of a right to private decision making regarding family matters as inherent in the concept of liberty.

---

2. For a discussion of the First Amendment, see Chapter 18, Sections XII, XIII.

3. E.g., Gertz v. Robert Welch, Inc., 418 U.S. 323 (1974); Cox Broadcasting Corp. v. Cohn, 420 U.S. 469 (1975). See also Chapter 18, Section X.

4. For this reason we have divided this section into subsections dealing with specific privacy issues.

5. Warren & Brandeis, The Right of Privacy, 4 Harv.L.Rev. 193 (1890).

6. See his dissenting opinion in Olmstead v. United States, 277 U.S. 438, 478 (1928).

7. 262 U.S. 390 (1923).

8. 268 U.S. 510 (1925).

9. For a discussion of "substantive due process" and government regulation, see Chapter 13.

B. Sterilization and Contraception

The development of the contemporary concept of a constitutionally protected "right of privacy" in sexual matters can be traced to the Supreme Court's decision in *Skinner v. Oklahoma*.[10] On the basis of the equal protection clause, the Court held unconstitutional a statute which authorized the sterilization of persons previously convicted and sentenced to imprisonment two or more times of crimes "amounting of felonies of moral turpitude" in the state. Under the statute persons convicted of "offenses arising out of the violation of the prohibitory laws, revenue acts, embezzlement, or political offenses" were excepted from sterilization. A person was subjected to sterilization only if their crimes were classified (perhaps arbitrarily) as ones involving moral turpitude. Under this system grand larceny was deemed to be such a crime while embezzlement was not. Thus a person convicted three times of larceny could be subjected to sterilization while the embezzler was free from the risk of sterilization no matter how often he committed the crime or how large a sum of money he appropriated. The Court did not "stop to point out all the inequities of the Act," but instead rested the decision upon the artificiality of the distinction drawn between larceny and embezzlement, crimes of intrinsically the same nature. Despite the broad police powers of the state, this classification violated the equal protection clause because it could not withstand the scrutiny to which the fundamental nature of the right involved demanded it be subjected. The Court noted that the Act dealt with "one of the basic civil rights of man. . . . Marriage and procreation [were] fundamental to the very existence and survival of the race".[11] In the Court's view this required strict scrutiny of the classification for "[w]hen the law [laid] an unequal hand on those who [had] committed intrinsically the same quality of offense and sterilize[d] one and not the other, it [made] as invidious a discrimination as if it had selected a particular race or nationality for oppressive treatment."[12] In this way the Court went beyond traditional rational relationship standard of review. This rationale was to have two important ramifications. First, it established the basis for "fundamental rights" analysis under the due process and equal protection guarantees by finding that some rights deserved special judicial protection from the majoritarian process. Second, while the opinion never mentioned a "right of privacy" relating to sexual matters, it established interests in marriage or procreation as ones of special constitutional significance.

It should be noted that the Supreme Court has not ruled that involuntary sterilization is *per se* unconstitutional. *Skinner* was an equal protection ruling in which the Court held that classifications of persons who were sterilized would be subjected to strict scrutiny. This holding therefore does not establish a constitutional prohibition of all such statutes. Previously, in *Buck v. Bell*,[13] the Court had upheld a sterilization statute, in an opinion by Justice Holmes, stating that the legislature was the branch of government most suited to defining the necessity of these procedures. However, this decision came prior to the use of the fundamental rights—strict scrutiny analysis. Because the statute would interfere with the fundamental right of privacy (the freedom of choice regarding the individual's ability to reproduce) it could only be justified by a compelling governmental interest. Some lower courts have allowed states to order sterilization of mentally retarded persons

10. 316 U.S. 535 (1942).

11. 316 U.S. at 541.

12. 316 U.S. at 541.

13. 274 U.S. 200 (1927).

See also Stump v. Sparkman, 435 U.S. 349 (1978), wherein the Supreme Court held that state judges were immune from suits under the Civil Rights Acts for acts done in their official capacity. The case involved the unjustified granting of an order to sterilize a fifteen year old female.

both in criminal and civil proceedings.[14] But it is doubtful that the Supreme Court would follow *Buck v. Bell* today. If the justices find no compelling interest to justify the prohibition of abortions, any state interest in sterilization should be held insufficient to impair this fundamental right.

The right to privacy was given its first exposition by Justice Harlan in his dissent in *Poe v. Ullman.*[15] The majority did not reach the merits and held that the challenges to Connecticut statutes prohibiting the use of contraceptive devices, and the giving of medical advice on the use of such devices, did not present a justiciable controversy as there was no apparent intent by state officials to enforce these statutes. Justice Harlan dissented on this issue; he saw the statute and its possible enforcement as imposing a burden on the plaintiffs. More importantly, he reached the merits of their claims and found that application of the statute to married persons would violate the due process clause because the regulation invaded marital "privacy." In his opinion, the statute intruded upon "the most intimate details of the marital relation" and prosecution under the statutes would require disclosure of those relationships.

In *Griswold v. Connecticut,*[16] the Court held the same Connecticut statutes invalid because they restricted the right of married persons to use contraceptive devices. The appellants in this case, a doctor and executive of the Planned Parenthood League, were convicted for giving information and medical advice to married persons concerning means of preventing conception. The majority opinion by Justice Douglas found that the statute impermissibly limited the right of privacy of married persons. The law violated the due process clause because

it deprived these married persons of the liberty protected by this fundamental right. There was some confusion caused by Douglas' attempt to find a specific textual basis for a "right of privacy" that would include the right of married persons to use contraceptives, but it should be realized that this confusion was not the sole fault of the Douglas opinion. The Court continued to formally reject the substantive due process decisions of the first part of the century.[17] Thus, Douglas was forced to repudiate *Lochner v. New York*[18] and state that the Supreme Court "did not sit as a super-legislature."[19] Yet he had to justify the decision of the Court to invalidate this law on the basis that it infringed the general area of liberty. It was too close—in terms of decisional, if not calendar, time—to the period of substantive due process to admit that the Supreme Court had to protect some individual rights against government intrusion in much the same manner as the Court had done in *Lochner*. The difference was, of course, in the nature of the right to be protected and the role of the Court as the proper entity to define and protect the right. But at this time Douglas had to create a more specific right and relate it to the text of the Constitution in order to formally differentiate this decision from earlier uses of substantive due process.

In order to justify the decision as one mandated by specific constitutional principles, the majority opinion created a new "right to privacy." Justice Douglas found that the "penumbras" and "emanations" of several guarantees of the Bill of Rights established this right to privacy. The right of parents to send their children to parochial schools[20] and the freedom of private schools from excessive restrictions[21] evidenced special values in the liberty to make personal

---

14. See, e.g., In re Cavitt, 182 Neb. 712, 157 N.W.2d 171, appeal dismissed sub nom. Cavitt v. Nebraska, 396 U.S. 996 (1968); the relevant cases are collected in annot., 53 A.L.R.3d 960; annot., 74 A.L.R.3d 1210; annot., 74 A.L.R.3d 1224.

15. 367 U.S. 497, 522 (1961) (Harlan, J., dissenting).

16. 381 U.S. 479 (1965).

17. For discussion of substantive due process, see Chapter 13.

18. 198 U.S. 45 (1905). For a discussion of this case see Chapter 13, Section III.

19. 381 U.S. at 482.

20. Pierce v. Society of Sisters, 268 U.S. 510 (1925).

21. Meyer v. Nebraska, 262 U.S. 390 (1923).

decisions free of governmental restrictions. Indeed, the entire freedom of association was implied from the express guarantees of the first amendment. This amendment included a right to privacy, as the government could force disclosure of association or speech only in the most limited circumstances. The fourth and fifth amendments also reflected sources for individual privacy and freedom from government demands for information. Thus the opinion found that a right to privacy existed within the bases for these express rights.

It is fair to say that the right of privacy was created in *Griswold* as no specific, Court-defined right to engage in private acts had existed before this decision. But the opinion was nonetheless correct in finding that the values of privacy, including freedom from government intrusion with private thoughts, association, and liberty, had long been part of American legal philosophy. These values indeed had been the basis for the arguments of Brandeis and the earlier opinions cited by Justice Douglas. The Douglas opinion turned these historical values into a specific guarantee to help justify the Court's enforcing the values against a legislative decision. The Connecticut legislature banned the use of contraceptives by married persons, which contravened the established values of privacy in three ways: (1) it regulated a personal marital relationship without an identifiable, legitimate reason; (2) it gave government the right to inquire into these private marital relationships; (3) prosecution under the statutes would often require husbands and wives to testify to the intimate details of their relationship.

Separate concurring opinions brought foward reasons for judicial protection of these privacy values against legislative or executive actions. Justice Goldberg took the position that it was the function of the Court to defend certain fundamental rights

under the due process clause even though these rights were not expressed in the first eight amendments. Goldberg was of the opinion that the ninth amendment evidenced the historic belief that certain fundamental rights could not be restricted by the government even though it did not create specific rights. The Court should look to the "tradition and [collective] conscience of our people" [22] to determine if a right was fundamental and one which should be judicially protected from infringement by other branches of government. There was no doubt that "marital privacy" was such a right because there were clear historic values in freedom of choice in marital relationships. As Justice Goldberg noted, if a law required husband and wives to be sterilized after having two children, any justice would have held it unconstitutional absent the most compelling justification regardless of the "implied" nature of the guarantee.

Justice Harlan concurred in the decision, also finding that the due process clause protected fundamental liberties which were not expressed in the Bill of Rights. Just as in his dissent in *Poe v. Ullman*, [23] the Justice found that marital privacy was a basic part of the liberty "protected by the fourteenth amendment." In Harlan's opinion it was the role of the justices to decide when legislation violated "basic values 'implicit in the concept of ordered liberty.' " [24] Justice White's concurrence followed through on this due process theory; he found no legitimate end of government which could support this law. The state claimed that the statute was to deter illicit sexual relationships but there was no likelihood that a ban on contraceptives for married persons would promote that end. Thus the statute restricted a fundamental constitutional value arbitrarily.

Justices Black and Stewart dissented in *Griswold*. They could find no basis for judicial protection of a right to privacy and they were committed to the view that the justices

---

22. 381 U.S. at 493 (Goldberg, J., concurring).

23. 367 U.S. 497, 539–55 (1961) (Harlan, J., dissenting).

24. 381 U.S. at 500, quoting Palko v. Connecticut, 302 U.S. 319, 325 (1937).

should not follow in the steps of the substantive due process decisions by enforcing values which had no textual basis in the constitution. It is interesting to note that by the time of the decision on abortion regulations in 1973, Justice Stewart had come to accept this decision as a permissible use of substantive due process theories.

The Court has restricted the ability of states to punish the use of contraceptives by adults. In *Griswold* the Court held that the use of contraceptives by married persons could not be prohibited. Seven years later, in *Eisenstadt v. Baird* [25] the Court invalidated a statute which prohibited distribution of contraceptives to unmarried persons because a majority found that this separate treatment of unmarried persons violated the equal protection clause. In *Eisenstadt* the Court did not explicitly rely on the fundamental rights-strict scrutiny analysis. Instead, the majority opinion simply found no legitimate way to distinguish between use of contraceptives by married or unmarried persons. While the majority opinion, by Justice Brennan, proported to apply only the traditional equal protection standard of review, the majority clearly employed some form of independent judicial scrutiny. One conceivable purpose of the statute was the prevention of premarital, as opposed to extramarital sex. The opinion conceded that the state, consistent with the equal protection clause, could treat differently the problems of premarital and extramarital sexual relations. The majority found, however, that prevention of premarital sexual relations was not in fact the purpose of the statute because to accept that interest it would have had to impute to the legislature an intent to punish premarital relations by forced pregnancy and birth of an unwanted child—a conclusion the majority was unwilling to reach. Nor could it be demonstrated that the statute significantly furthered that end. The same statute permitted distribution of contraceptives to unmarried persons for pre-

vention of disease, an exception which diminished considerably the statute's potential effectiveness. The state also asserted its interest in regulating medically harmful substances as a basis for the legislation, but this interest could not support the classification for several reasons. First, the Court concluded that the statute was not in fact a health measure, because it was contained in a chapter of the Massachusetts laws dealing with "Crimes Against Chastity, Morality, Decency and Good Order" and was cast only in terms of morals. Second, the statute was underinclusive because it could not be shown that the health needs of unmarried persons were greater than those of married persons. Finally, the statute was overbroad in restricting distribution of all contraceptives, while only some could be demonstrated to be dangerous.

Following *Griswold* and *Eisenstadt* it was clear that states may not eliminate the use of contraceptives by adults; however, the states should be able to restrict the manufacturers and sale of contraceptive devices to insure that the products meet health and safety standards. For such restrictions the state will have to show that the regulations in fact promote health or safety. Mere assertion of police power ends will not justify limitation of the right to privacy.

In *Carey v. Population Services International*,[26] the Court invalidated a law which allowed only pharmacists to sell non-medical contraceptive devices to persons over 16 years of age and prohibited the sale of such items to those under 16. As to the general restriction, there was a majority opinion that the burden on an adult's freedom of choice could only be justified by a compelling interest and that distribution only through pharmacists did not advance such an end. The Court struck the restriction on children without a majority opinion. Writing for four members of the Court, Justice Brennan implied that even young persons have some rights to freedom of choice in these mat-

25. 405 U.S. 438 (1972).

26. 431 U.S. 678 (1977).

ters.[27] The other three justices voting to strike the law wanted to avoid any implication of a right of minors to engage in sexual activity. They would allow prohibition of sexual activity, including use of the contraceptives by minors. But, as there has never been any evidence that denial of contraceptives to young persons deterred them from such activities, for the state to require them to assume greater risks of pregnancy and disease if they violated the law was therefore so arbitrary as to violate due process.[28] Thus when these three are combined with the two dissenting Justices, there appears to be a majority that would allow statutes strictly regulating the sexual activity of minors.

C. Marriage as a Part of the Right to Privacy

The right to freedom of choice in marriage and family relationships lies at the heart of the right to privacy. The early due process cases regarding the education and rearing of children showed special concern for the values of free choice in such matters. Justice Harlan first described the modern "right to privacy" in terms of the historic values of privacy and freedom of choice in marriage relationships.[29] On this basis, the right to freedom of choice in marriage relationships is itself a fundamental right. Thus, laws which restrict individual choice regarding marriage or divorce will be subjected to "strict scrutiny" under the due process or equal protection clauses. A law which generally limits freedom of choice in marriage for all persons will be invalid under the due process test unless the state can show an overriding or compelling interest in the re-

striction. Similarly, a law which restricts or inhibits the right of class of persons to marry will be invalid under the equal protection guarantee unless the state can show that the classification in fact promotes a compelling interest.

A case of special significance in establishing marriage as a fundamental right is *Loving v. Virginia*.[30] In this case the Court held unconstitutional a statute prohibiting interracial marriage.[31] The statute was found violative of equal protection because it rested solely upon distinctions drawn according to race. It was a denial of due process, for it deprived each individual of significant freedom of choosing whom to marry. Since marriage is a fundamental right, the state could not restrict the right to marry for less than compelling reasons.

In *Boddie v. Connecticut*[32] the Supreme Court held invalid a statute making the payment of Court costs a prerequisite to obtaining access to state courts, as applied to persons seeking a divorce who were unable to pay such costs. Appellants were welfare recipients who had been unable to bring a divorce action in a state court solely because of their inability to pay the court fees. Because courts were usually not the sole means available for resolving private disputes, the Supreme Court had seldom been asked to view the access to courts in a civil context as an element of due process. Here, however, divorce was available only through the judicial machinery of the state. The state's refusal to admit these appellants to its courts, the sole means for obtaining a divorce, was the equivalent of denying them the freedom of choice regarding the dissolution of their marriage. Because the State

---

27. 431 U.S. at 694–95 (opinion of Brennan, J., joined by Stewart, Marshall, & Blackmun, JJ.).

28. The three concurrences actually rested on the dual basis: (1) that the prohibition of distribution violated fundamental rights when applied to interfere with family relations in that it included young married females and distribution from a parent to a child; (2) the ban constituted a totally arbitrary infliction of risk and harm upon children who would violate the laws against sexual relationships in any event. 431 U.S. at 702 (White, J., concurring); id. at 703 (Powell, J. con-

curring); id. at 712 (Stevens, J., concurring). Only Chief Justice Burger and Justice Rehnquist dissented from the ruling on the invalidity of the law.

29. See his dissenting opinion in Poe v. Ullman, 367 U.S. 497, 522 (1961) (Harlan, J., dissenting).

30. 388 U.S. 1 (1967).

31. The statute provided that if a white and nonwhite were to marry, each would be subject to imprisonment for one to five years.

32. 401 U.S. 371 (1971).

could show no overriding state interest, this barrier to freedom of choice in marriage was a denial of due process. The Court's decision was predicated upon the fundamental nature of the right to marry or dissolve that relationship, as well as the monopoly held by the states over the means of dissolution. Indeed, the Court pointed out that its holding was extremely narrow; one could not be denied access to the sole means to adjust a fundamental human relation because of inability to pay court costs. The importance of this observation became clear in later years when the Court refused to order that persons be granted access to courts for such nonfundamental claims as welfare rights[33] or bankruptcy discharges.[34]

Although governmental regulation of the ability to enter or withdraw from a marriage is subject to close judicial scrutiny, the government may employ marital status classifications in welfare systems. In *Califano v. Jobst* [35] the justices had little problem in upholding the provisions of the Social Security Act which terminated the benefits of a disabled person, who received benefits as a disabled dependent child of a deceased wage earner covered by the Act, when that person married someone who was not receiving Social Security benefits. An exemption from the "marriage termination rule" for those disabled children who married other persons entitled to benefits under the Social Security Act was held not to be so under-inclusive as to violate the equal protection guarantee embodied in the due process clause of the fifth amendment. The opinion by Mr. Justice Stevens for a unanimous court found the traditional rational relationship test applicable because the law could not be characterized as one based on "stereotyped generalization about a traditionally disadvantaged group, or as an attempt to interfere with the individual's freedom to make a decision as important as marriage." [36] It was not irrational for Congress to terminate secondary benefits for the disabled children of deceased social security wage earners when those children were married, even if termination created financial hardship for these persons. Congress sought to alleviate the hardship on some persons dependent upon deceased wage earners and social security benefits by exempting those whose spouse was also entitled to benefits under the Social Security Act. The legislative exemption was not irrationally under-inclusive; Congress was entitled to deal with these economic problems and hardships one at a time. The result in *Califano v. Jobst* is easily justified because the law placed little burden on the right to marry and it was a reasonable means of identifying a group of financially needy persons for special economic benefits.

In *Zablocki v. Redhail* [37] the justices experienced little difficulty in striking a law which restricted the ability of economically poor persons to marry. Yet the justices had considerable difficulty in deciding why the law violated the equal protection clause. The Wisconsin statute in question prohibited any Wisconsin resident from marrying without court permission if that person had minor issue who were not in his custody and whom he was required to support according to a court order or judgment. A state court could grant such persons permission to marry only if they submitted proof of compliance with the support obligation and demonstrated that the children covered by the court order were not likely to become "public charges." Justice Marshall wrote a majority opinion for five members of the Court which was somewhat unclear as to the nature of the right to marriage and the standard of review used in the decision. Justice Marshall described the right to marry as one of "fundamental importance" and a "part of the fundamental right to privacy implicit in the fourteenth amendment's due process clause." Thus, the majority opinion seems to continue to recognize marriage as a fun-

---

33. Ortwein v. Schwab, 410 U.S. 656 (1973).

34. United States v. Kras, 409 U.S. 434 (1973).

35. 434 U.S. 47 (1977).

36. 434 U.S. at 54 (footnotes omitted).

37. 434 U.S. 374 (1978).

damental right although the language used is weaker than that of previous majority opinions. Justice Marshall also stated that all regulations of the incidents of marriage need not be subjected to "rigorous scrutiny." The majority opinion referred to the *Califano v. Jobst* decision, and observed that "reasonable regulations that do not significantly interfere with decisions to enter into the marital relationship may be legitimately imposed." [38] The opinion did not specify the types of regulations that need not to be tested by "rigorous scrutiny." The opinion by Justice Marshall found that the permission to marry statute was invalid, even assuming that the state had a substantial interest in its announced goals of counselling applicants for such marriages and protecting the welfare of the children. The statute neither afforded any significant counselling to persons who might be entering marriages that would injure their economic status nor did it reasonably protect the financial status of children from earlier marriages. The statute prevented a person's marriage but it did not insure support for the children from that person's prior marriage.

The majority opinion left the exact nature of the standard of review employed in this case unclear, but that has been true in many of the "fundamental rights" cases. [39] The concurring opinion of Justice Stevens helped to clarify this point by noting that the classification based on marital status in *Califano v. Jobst* simply was not as significant a burden on the right to marriage as was the law reviewed in this case. Justice Stevens indicated that the fact the ability to marry was limited by a law precluded reviewing that law under the most minimal rational relationship test even though such a law need not be subjected to a "level of scrutiny so

strict that a holding of unconstitutionality is virtually foreordained." [40] Indeed, the majority opinion by Justice Marshall stated that "when a statutory classification significantly interferes with the exercise of a fundamental right, it cannot be upheld unless it is supported by sufficiently important state interests and is closely tailored to effectuate only those interests." [41] These statements indicate that the Court used a standard of review that approximates one or more of the "middle level standard of review" that have been previously advocated by Justice Marshall and several legal scholars. [42]

Justice Powell concurred in the judgment although he felt the majority opinion swept too broadly by indicating that there might be strict scrutiny of a variety of traditional marriage regulations. He stated that the Court had never required "the most exacting judicial scrutiny" for all laws touching upon the marriage relationship; he noted that laws prohibiting marriages that would involve incest, bigamy, and homosexuality had been assumed to be within the constitutional scope of state powers. [43] Justice Powell based his decision on the fact that the state had been unable to establish any reasonable basis for foreclosing marriage to citizens who were willing but unable to make payments to meet their previous child support obligations; this was not a reasonable manner of providing for the support of those children.

Justice Stewart would have abandoned the equal protection rationale as he did not feel that this law created any testable classification. He viewed the decision as one based on the concept of substantive due process. Justice Stewart found that marriage was not a constitutional right but only a "privilege" that was protected to some extent by the

---

38.   434 U.S. at 386.

39.   See Section I, C of this chapter for an analysis of "standards of review" issues. Chief Justice Burger concurred in the opinion on the understanding that this ruling would not require the Court to impose some form of "strict scrutiny" when reviewing classifications such as those in *Jobst*. 434 U.S. at 391 (Burger, C.J., concurring).

40.   434 U.S. at 406–407 n. 10 (Stevens, J., concurring).

41.   434 U.S. at 388.

42.   See Section I, C of this Chapter.

43.   Zablocki v. Redhail, 434 U.S. 374 (1978) (Powell, J., concurring).

concept of liberty in the due process clauses. For him, this explains why a state may legitimately create regulations of the marriage relationship so long as the justices agree that the regulations are reasonable means of promoting important concerns of the state. Justice Stewart voted to strike this law because it contained no exception for those who were truly indigent and could not afford to pay their child support obligations. Like Justice Powell, he found that the law was not a reasonable means of furthering important state interests. But Justice Stewart found no purpose in using equal protection language when "the doctrine is no more than substantive due process by another name." Justice Stewart believed that recognition of the use of substantive due process demonstrates why the Supreme Court should be hesitant to reject the decisions of the democratic process concerning important social questions.[44]

Only Justice Rehnquist would have upheld the law in *Zablocki*. In rejecting substantive due process and equal protection strict scrutiny, apart from racial classification cases, the Justice consistently has taken the position that the Court should only determine whether laws which do not touch upon explicit constitutional guarantees bear some rational relationship to legitimate governmental interest. Under the traditional test, of course, the law would have to be upheld; the law was an arguably, though not demonstrably, rational means of preventing an increase in the number of children for whom the state would bear financial responsibility. However, Justice Rehnquist recognized the possibility that the law could not be applied to persons who were truly indigent; under those circumstances the prohibition of marriage might not be even arguably a rational way of enforcing support obligations. He did not have to reach this question for, in his opinion, the litigant did not have standing to raise this issue. It is interesting to note that at the start of Justice Rehnquist's dissent he explicitly rejected the use in this case of either "the strictest judicial scrutiny" or any "intermediate standard of review."[45]

D. Abortion

1. An Introductory Note

Why an interpretive note before an analysis of the cases? Because even the reader who is about to consider the abortion decisions for the first time is likely to have some previously formed conclusions about how to approach and evaluate these cases. As all are aware, in 1973 the Supreme Court declared that statutes prohibiting abortion unconstitutionally infringed upon a pregnant woman's right to privacy. The abortion decisions have been subjected to both telling criticism and great praise. But regardless of one's view of the ultimate rulings in these cases, it must be appreciated that this use of the right to privacy was developed without great difficulty from the earlier opinions. Because the right had been given a separate existence similar to an express guarantee in cases such as *Griswold* the justices had little need to explain why they were enforcing this right against the will of the majority. And the Court's previous use of the term "privacy" to cover a variety of values in personal, associational, family and sexual matters reduced the need for the justices to clearly explain how freedom to abort a fetus came within the constitutional guarantee. The earlier cases had established the value in privacy as a constitutional right, albeit a vague one, which was now interpreted and applied by the justices. This change in the law was similar to the development of the concept of substantive due process in the last part of the nineteenth century.[46] In both instances the Court initially protected a few activities in the name of a new implied constitutional value. In both instances the early establishment of the right was later relied on as if the libertarian guarantee were

---

44. 434 U.S. at 395 (Stewart, J., concurring).

45. 434 U.S. at 407 (Rehnquist, J., dissenting).

46. For an in-depth treatment of substantive due process, see Chapter 13.

an express provision of the constitution. In both instances the Court was then able to interpret the value that it had earlier found implied so as to protect a freedom of action from restrictions by the legislature. But these similarities do not show which, if either, set of decisions was proper or improper.

Virtually all of the justices who have sat on the Court have realized that they must protect values which are only implied by the text of the Constitution or its amendments.[47] Chief Justice Marshall realized this when he established the Constitution as "law" and the Court as the interpreter of this law which was to meet changing circumstances.[48] Even the justices who have advocated restraint in overturning the acts of the legislature at times voted to overturn legislation because it conflicted with protection values not clearly expressed in the Constitution. But such an argument is not to say that any decision of the Court is proper simply because a majority of the justices agree that it is a correct interpretation of the Constitution. Instead it is to suggest that the one should not dwell on whether the Court has injected values into the Constitution which lack a clear textual or historical basis, for this "injection" is part of the Supreme Court's historical function. The question to consider is whether these cases represent values that should be given judicial protection against the majoritarian process. In terms of the abortion cases, rather than considering whether the Court has taken on a new function here, a more fruitful area for consideration lies in whether the justices should have refrained from using their traditional powers because there was no interest which merited judicial protection against the majoritarian process. Some scholars have been unable to identify any value which the justices are able to define or protect better than the democratic process and so they have criticized the use of the "substantive due process" power in these cases.[49] Others have seen the woman's freedom of choice as a value which is most properly protected by a nonmajoritarian entity which can impartially define decision making roles.[50] But the reader should remember that none of the learned critics or defenders of these cases is focusing on whether the Court, as an institution, should have the power to make these rulings. While some scholars claim that the Court should be "interpretive" and protect only values with clear textual support, they do not seek to limit the Court's function to applying only the few literal checks on legislation which appear in the Constitution.[51] As the late Professor Bickel stated in a relevant inquiry into the functions of the Supreme Court:

> There is a body of opinion—and there has been, throughout our history—which holds that the Court can well apply obvious principles, plainly acceptable to a generality of the population, because they are plainly stated in the Constitution (e.g., the right to vote shall not be denied

---

47. See Chapter 13, Section V, A Note on the Meaning of Liberty.

48. Marbury v. Madison, 5 U.S. 137 (1 Cranch) 137 (1803). For a discussion of this case, see Chapter 1. McCulloch v. Maryland, 17 U.S. (4 Wheat.) 316 (1819). For a discussion of this case, see Chapter 3.

49. See Ely, The Wages of Crying Wolf: A Comment on Roe v. Wade, 82 Yale L.J. 920 (1973).

Professor Ely has published a scholarly monograph examining the role of the Supreme Court in a political process based upon democratic ideals. He would circumscribe judicial power by limiting the justices to review of only those laws which seem to transgress express constitutional limitations, operate to disadvantage certain minority groups, or impede the democratic process itself. J. Ely, Democracy and Distrust (1980). Professor Ely's work has given rise to reconsideration of, and renewed debate concerning, the role of judicial review in our society. Commentary on Professor Ely's work includes: Grano, Ely's Theory of Judicial Review: Preserving the Significance of the Political Process, 42 Ohio St.L.J. 167 (1981); Nowak, Foreward: Evaluating the Work of the New Libertarian Supreme Court, 7 Hastings Con.L.Q. 263 (1980); Tribe, The Puzzling Persistence of Process-Based Constitutional Theories, 89 Yale L.J. 1063 (1980); Tushnet, Darkness on the Edge of Town: The Contributions of John Hart Ely to Constitutional Theory, 89 Yale L.J. 1037 (1980).

50. See Tribe, Toward a Model of Roles in the Due Process of Life and Law, 87 Harv.L.Rev. 1 (1973).

51. See T. Grey, Do We Have an Unwritten Constitution?, 27 Stan.L.Rev. 703 (1975). Grey, Origins of the Unwritten Constitution: Fundamental Law in American Revolutionary Thought, 30 Stan.L.Rev. 843 (1978).

on account of race), or because they are almost universally shared; but the Court should not manufacture principle. However, although the Constitution plainly contains a number of admonitions, it states very few plain principles; and few are universally accepted. Principles that may be thought to have wide, if not universal, acceptance may not have it tomorrow, when the freshly-coined, quite novel principle may, in turn, prove acceptable. The true distinction, therefore, relevant to the bulk of the Court's business, lies not so much between more and less acceptable principles as between principles of different orders of magnitude and complexity in the application. This distinction can be sensed, and can serve as a caution, but no one has succeeded in defining it, and hence it is not serviceable as a rule. Unable to cabin the Court's interventions by rule, we have been generally content with the exercise of authority not so cabined. We do not confine the judges, we caution them. That, after all, is the legacy of Felix Frankfurter's career.[52]

2. The Cases

a. Roe v. Wade

In *Roe v. Wade*[53] the Supreme Court overturned a Texas statute which proscribed procuring or attempting the abortion of a human fetus except when necessary to save the life of the mother. The Court held that the statute violated the due process clause of the fourteenth amendment as an unjustified deprivation of liberty in that it unnecessarily infringed on a woman's right to privacy. The majority opinion, by Justice Blackmun, noted the broad range of decisions involving the right to privacy. With virtually no further explanation of the privacy value the opinion found that the right of privacy, regardless of exactly what constitutional provision it was ascribed to, "is broad enough to encompass a woman's decision whether or not to terminate her pregnancy."[54] As this was now a part of the liberty protected by the fourteenth amendment, the

right could not be restricted without due process of law.

Normally the legislature may regulate activities so long as the legislation has some rational relationship to a legitimate state interest. However, where the legislature restricts the exercise of fundamental constitutional rights it will only be upheld if it is necessary to promote a compelling state interest. In this case the Court found that the right to an abortion was not absolute and so it could be limited in some circumstances. But the majority found the right to privacy which included the woman's right to an abortion was "fundamental." Thus, the Court held that limitations on the woman's right to have an abortion would only be upheld where they furthered a "compelling state interest."

There were two state interests which the Court found might support some limitations on the right to an abortion—the interest in the health of the mother and in the life of the fetus. The only interest which might have supported a total ban on abortion was the protection of the fetus as a human life. But the majority found no basis, apart from certain philosophies or religions, for calling the fetus a person. While this argument did not establish the invalidity of the Act, the refusal of the Court to recognize this interest required the states to demonstrate some independent interest in the life of the mother or the fetus. There would be a "compelling interest" in the mother's life where restriction on the right was needed to protect her life or safety. There would be a "compelling interest" in the fetus when the state could show a viable life which it had an interest to protect.

Through approximately the first third of a pregnancy, abortion performed under a doctor's care was as safe, if not safer, for a woman's health as was completion of the pregnancy. Thus the opinion held there could be no significant restriction on the right of the

---

52. A. Bickel, The Supreme Court and the Idea of Progress 177 (1970).

53. 410 U.S. 113 (1973).

54. 410 U.S. at 153.

woman to have an abortion during the first trimester of the pregnancy. The woman was free to have an abortion during this time subect only to her ability to find a licensed physician who would perform the operation. The state could require a few minimal medical safeguards during this period such as requiring that the abortionist be a licensed medical doctor.

The risk to the pregnant woman's health increased after the first trimester. Thus the Court found a "compelling interest" in establishing further medical regulations on abortions performed after that stage of the pregnancy. Later decisions made it clear that the reasonableness of these restrictions would be subjected to independent judicial review and that only of those truly necessary to protect the health of the woman during a second trimester abortion would be upheld.[55]

With respect to the state's interest in the existence of the fetus the majority found that the state had a "compelling interest" when the fetus became viable—normally considered to be the beginning of the third trimester (end of the sixth month) of the pregnancy. At this point the fetus could have "meaningful life" outside the mother and the state could demonstrate an important interest in its existence apart from moral philosophy concerning the beginning of life. The Court held that after the time of viability the legislature could prohibit abortions except where necessary to protect the life or health of the mother. It should be noted that all of the opinions have assumed that an exception would be made to such a proscription to secure the mother's life or prevent serious injury to her health.

The separate opinions of individual justices foreshadowed the debate over the legitimacy of these decisions. In concurring opinions, Justice Stewart accepted this ruling as a permissible use of the substantive due process theory and Justice Douglas elaborated on the concept of unwritten fundamental values recognized by the ninth and fourteenth amendments. There were only two dissents but they touched on the points that would lead to later criticism of the decisions. Justice White explained that there was no basis for finding that the judiciary should make decisions concerning the competing values of the mother and the potential life of the fetus. He saw the decision as the "exercise of raw judicial power" rather than the protection of clear constitutional values. Justice Rehnquist noted the similarity in the use of substantive due process between these decisions and the formally repudiated position of the Court in *Lochner v. New York*.[56]

b. Regulations of Abortion Procedures

After *Roe v. Wade*, all governmental regulations of a woman's ability to obtain an abortion are formally subject to strict judicial scrutiny and the compelling interest test.[57] The *Roe* majority opinion stated that

---

55.　See note 57, infra.

56.　198 U.S. 45 (1905).

57.　On June 15, 1983, the Supreme Court ruled on the constitutionality of several government regulations of abortion procedures. Those rulings did not alter the theories outlined in this section or the problems noted therein, although the rulings clarified several technical issues. Six justices remain committed to the principle that a woman has a fundamental constitutional right to choose to have an abortion free of interference by the state with her decision or the professional judgment of her attending physician. These justices require that government regulations of abortion comply with the principles set forth in *Roe*; regulations of pre-viability abortions must be reasonably related to the "compel-ling" interest in protecting the health of the woman. Akron v. Akron Center for Reproductive Health, Inc., 103 S.Ct. ___ (1983) (majority opinion by Powell, J., joined by Burger, C.J., and Brennan, Marshall, Blackmun, and Stevens, JJ.). Three justices would uphold any government regulation of abortions which is not totally arbitrary; they call into question the legitimacy of judicial control of abortion regulations. Id. at ___ (O'Connor, J., dissenting, joined by White and Rehnquist, JJ.). Because the six justices who exercise strict judicial scrutiny when reviewing abortion regulations sometimes split over the constitutionality of specific regulations, some cases may turn on the fact that two or more of those six justices will join with Justices O'Connor, Rehnquist, and White to uphold a specific regulation. See notes 71, 103, infra.

it was to be read in conjunction with *Doe v. Bolton*,[58] where the justices examined procedural requirements of abortion statutes. In *Doe* the Court invalidated a number of procedural restrictions on the woman's ability to secure an abortion. These provisions were invalid as they unnecessarily restricted the woman's right to privacy and, therefore, violated due process. One requirement was that the abortion be performed in a hospital accredited by a special committee although no such requirement was imposed for non-abortion surgery. The Court held the requirement could not withstand constitutional scrutiny; the State could not show that this distinction was based on differences reasonably related to the purpose of the Act. The State failed to show why the abortion should have to be performed in a licensed hospital rather than some other appropriately licensed institution. The statute also required the approval of two other physicians, despite the fact the performing physician had already been required to exercise his "best clinical judgment" in determining that an abortion was necessary. This requirement was also stricken, for if the physician is licensed and recognized as competent, the required acquiescence has no rational connection with the patient's needs. For almost identical reasons, the Court struck the requirement that the physician's decision to abort be approved by a committee of at least three hospital staff members.

Other medical and procedural restrictions in the woman's right to receive an abortion were considered in *Planned Parenthood v. Danforth*.[59] The statute in *Planned Parenthood* was challenged on the basis of its definition of viability and its prohibition of the use of saline amniocentesis as a means of abortion after the first twelve weeks. The statute defined viability as "that stage of fetal development when the

life of the unborn child may be continued indefinitely outside the womb by natural or artificial life support systems." [60] The Court upheld this definition, finding it consistent with *Roe v. Wade.* Viability is basically a medical term, and as such it need not be defined as occurring at a specific point in the gestation period, but may be left to the judgment of the attending physician.

The ban on saline amniocentesis was stricken because it could not be shown, as required by *Roe*, to be a restriction reasonably related to the preservation and protection of maternal health, though it was related to fetal health. The state general assembly had stated in its statute that the saline amniocentesis type of abortion "for the purpose of killing the fetus and artificially inducing labor is deleterious to maternal health and is hereby prohibited after the first twelve weeks of pregnancy." But saline amniocentesis was the method most commonly used nationwide after the first twelve weeks of pregnancy and was safer than most other methods used to terminate a pregnancy, none of which were banned, and in fact saline amniocentesis was safer than childbirth. Therefore, the majority found that the state law forced women who wished to exercise their right to terminate a pregnancy to use methods more dangerous to maternal health. The law could not withstand the strict judicial scrutiny mandated by *Roe*. [61]

Prior to the 1978–79 Term the Supreme Court's rulings, if not its opinions, in the area of abortion rights at least had the virtue of clarity. But in 1979 the Court decided an abortion case in which it may have expanded the scope of a woman's right to an abortion but which left the scope of state powers concerning abortion regulations undefined and confused. In *Colautti v. Franklin*,[62] the Court held void for vague-

---

58. 410 U.S. 179 (1973).

59. 428 U.S. 52 (1976).

60. 428 U.S. at 63.

61. The Court in *Danforth* upheld a requirement that each woman sign a written consent to an abortion

and that the hospital keep records of abortions performed because these requirements reasonably promoted health interests. 428 U.S. at 65–67, 79–81. See also note 71, infra.

62. 439 U.S. 379 (1979).

ness a Pennsylvania abortion regulation which required a doctor to make a determination of viability prior to performing an abortion. If the doctor determined that the fetus was "viable", or if there was "sufficient reason to believe that the fetus may be viable," the doctor was required to "exercise that degree of professional skill, care and diligence to preserve the life and health of the fetus which such person would be required to exercise in order to preserve the life and health of a fetus intended to be born." The statute required that the doctor aborting such a fetus use the abortion technique which "would provide the best opportunity for the fetus to be aborted alive so long as a different technique would not be necessary in order to preserve the life or health of the mother." [63] The statute also stated that a doctor who failed to make the viability determination, or to exercise a required degree of care, would be subject to the same criminal or civil liability as would apply if the fetus had been intended to be born alive.

The majority opinion, by Justice Blackmun, found that this statute was unconstitutionally vague in two distinct aspects: first, the requirement that the doctor determine if there was sufficient reason to believe the fetus may be viable was vague and, second, the standard of care that the doctor must use, including the guidelines for choosing between a technique to save the fetus and one to protect the health of the mother, also was unconstitutionally vague. Unfortunately, the majority opinion itself was less than a model of clarity and it is difficult, if not impossible, to decide what, if any, principles are established by this opinion.

Before examining the particularities of the Pennsylvania Act the majority discussed the earlier decisions in the abortion area in order to provide "essential background" and, in so doing, seems to have established a significant new principle in this area. The majority opinion by Justice Blackmun focused on the language in *Roe v. Wade* that discussed the difficulty of predicting an exact point for viability and which referred to the 24–28 week period as a likely time for viability. The opinion then indicated that the Court had upheld the statutory prohibitions of abortions of viable fetuses in *Doe v. Bolton* and *Planned Parenthood of Central Missouri v. Danforth* because each statute left the determination of viability to the judgment of the physician attending the pregnant woman. Justice Blackmun's opinion concluded that these cases meant that the woman's attending physician have unlimited discretion to determine when viability was attained; the opinion excluded any possibility of a legislative or judicial definition of viability based on objective factors.

"Viability is reached when, in the judgment of the attending physician on the particular facts of the case before him, there is a reasonable likelihood of the fetus' sustained survival outside the womb, with or without artificial support. Because this point may differ with each pregnancy, neither the legislature nor the courts may proclaim one of the elements entering into the ascertainment of viability—be it weeks of gestation or fetal weight or any other single factor—as the determinant of when the

---

63. The relevant portions of the statute, as reprinted in 439 U.S. at 380 n. 1 are as follows:

1. Section 5 reads in pertinent part:

"(a) Every person who performs or induces an abortion shall prior thereto have made a determination based on his experience, judgment or professional competence that the fetus is not viable, and if the determination is that the fetus is viable or if there is sufficient reason to believe that the fetus may be viable, shall exercise that degree of professional skill, care and diligence to preserve the life and health of the fetus which such person would be required to exercise in order to preserve the life and health of any fetus intended to be born and not aborted and the abortion technique employed shall be that which would provide the best opportunity for the fetus to be aborted alive so long as a different technique

would not be necessary in order to preserve the life or health of the mother.

"(d) Any person who fails to make the determination provided for in subsection (a) of this section, or who fails to exercise the degree of professional skill, care and diligence or to provide the abortion technique as provided for in subsection (a) of this section . . . shall be subject to such civil or criminal liability as would pertain to him had the fetus been a child who was intended to be born and not aborted."

The Pennsylvania Abortion Control Act also contained a number of other provisions that presented a variety of issues resolved in the lower court and which were not before the Supreme Court. These issues and the history of the lower court proceeding are referred to at 439 U.S. at 383–388.

State has a compelling interest in the life or health of the fetus. Viability is the critical point. And we have recognized no attempt to stretch the point of viability one way or the other." [64]

This portion of the opinion would appear to work a dramatic change in the constitutional principles regarding abortion; it indicates that a state can do no more than write a general statute prohibiting abortions after viability and hope that physicians will not be willing to perform an abortion of a viable fetus. Although the Court left open the question of how the state might establish criteria for prosecution of physicians who act in "bad faith," [65] its discussion of the Pennsylvania statute showed that it will be difficult for a legislature to establish criteria to prove the intent of such doctors.

The majority began its analysis of the vagueness issue by noting that due process required that criminal statutes give fair notice of what conduct is forbidden and that this principle was particularly important where the vagueness of the statute might inhibit the exercise of important constitutional rights. As a woman's right to abortion, like the rights to speech and association, is one to which the Court has afforded significant constitutional protection, the principles of vagueness and adequate notice had to be applied with particularity to this statute. The majority found that the requirement that a physician performing an abortion make a judgment that the fetus is viable or if there is "sufficient reason to believe that the fetus may be viable" was unconstitutionally vague for three reasons. First, it was unclear whether the statute imposed a subjective or a "mixed subjective and objective standard." That is, it was unclear whether the physician was to make the determination based only on his best judgment or on the objective facts that other physicians might think of particular relevance to a viability determination. Second, the phrase "may be viable" might refer either to viability (the point at which abortions could be prohibited) or to a "grey" area immediately prior to the viability of the fetus. This uncertainty might inhibit physicians from performing abortions when they did not believe that the fetus was viable but where there were indications that it "may be" viable. Third, the vagueness regarding the standards was exacerbated by the fact that the statute did not punish only those physicians who knowingly or intentionally aborted a viable fetus; the majority opinion described this failure as "the absence of a scienter requirement." The Pennsylvania homicide statute, which was made applicable to physicians by Section 5d of the Abortion Act, required a mental state of "intentionally, knowingly recklessly, or negligently" taking a human life. Justice Blackmun noted this fact and stated that it was "different from a requirement that the physician be culpable or blameworthy." [66] The majority appears to indicate that a statute with a required mental element of only recklessness or negligence would always be invalid; but the majority stated that, "we need not now decide whether, under a properly drafted statute, a finding of bad faith or some other type of scienter would be required before a physician could be held criminally responsible for an erroneous determination of viability." [67]

---

64. 439 U.S. at 388, 389.

65. 439 U.S. at 396. The Pennsylvania Abortion Control Act itself prohibited all abortions after the term of viability and punished as second degree murder the killing of a child born alive after an attempted abortion. Neither of these provisions was challenged before the Supreme Court.

In Anders v. Floyd, 440 U.S. 445 (1979) the Court, in a brief per curiam opinion, vacated a ruling of a district court that enjoined prosecution of a doctor for an abortion of a 25 week old fetus. The district court had held that the doctor could not be punished for criminal abortion or murder. The Supreme Court indicated the district court might have based its ruling on an erroneous concept of viability, "which refers to potential, rather than actual, survival of the fetus outside the womb." The Court only remanded the case for reconsideration in light of Colautti.

When a state establishes a valid regulation of abortion procedures, it may provide an exception to the procedures based upon medical necessity. The state may write its statutes so that the concept of medical necessity is an affirmative defense for doctors prosecuted under the statute; it need not initially plead or prove a lack of necessity in such prosecutions. See Simopoulous v. Virginia, 103 S.Ct. ___ (1983).

66. 439 U.S. at 395, n. 12.

67. 439 U.S. at 396.

The Court also determined that the standard of care provision was unconstitutionally vague, although the majority did not reach the question of whether or not it would be overbroad if it also applied to abortions prior to the time of viability.[68] The Court examined the testimony taken at the lower court that indicated that many physicians appeared to be unclear as to the types of abortion techniques that were required by the act and when a physician could use a procedure that was slightly more safe for a woman even though it increased the likelihood of destroying a fetus that might be viable. Not only was the standard of care requirement unclear, it might inhibit abortions by making them more expensive or by imposing serious burdens on the physical well being of the woman because of its effect on the physician's choice of abortion techniques. The majority refused to reach the question of whether the state could ever impose regulations on the precise type of abortion technique in order to protect a fetus; the opinion stated, "we hold only that where conflicting duties of this magnitude are involved, the State, at the least, must proceed with greater precision before it may subject a physician to possible criminal sanctions."[69]

Little can be gained, in the terms of definite rules, from this opinion. It would appear that the state may not define the point of viability other than by stating that a fetus is viable when it has the potential to live outside of the mother's womb in the judgment of the attending physician. Perhaps a state might be able to define more clearly what abortion techniques might be used af-

ter the time of viability, as determined by the attending physician. However, given the Court's prior invalidation of a ban of saline abortions in *Planned Parenthood* and the analysis used in *Colautti*, it would seem virtually impossible for a state to eliminate any form of abortion that was safe for the woman prior to the time of viability.

The ability of a woman to have an abortion seems to have been increased by the decision. The dissent by Justice White[70] noted in that a requirement that physicians know that the fetus is viable when they abort it, in order to make their actions criminal, will mean that it is practically impossible to convict a physician in a marginal case. There may be many instances when most doctors would have determined that the fetus was viable but where a particular physician will assert that he believed that the fetus was not viable when he performed the abortion. Whether states will be able to effectively enforce a prohibition of abortions of viable fetuses is not at all clear; the majority refused to indicate what type of statute might be used to punish the abortion of a viable fetus or what factors might be used to prove bad faith on the part of the attending physician.

Because "strict" judicial scrutiny of abortion regulations involves ad hoc decisionmaking, the determination of whether any specific regulation of abortion procedures is constitutional will depend on whether a majority of the justices believe that the regulation is reasonably designed to protect the health of women or only intended to deter abortions.[71]

---

68. 439 U.S. at 397, n. 17.

69. 439 U.S. at 400, 401. The Court has also invalidated as unconstitutionally vague a criminal statute requiring physicians after performing an abortion to dispose of the fetal remains in a "humane and sanitary manner." Akron v. Akron Center for Reproductive Health, Inc., 103 S.Ct. ___ (1983).

70. Colautti v. Franklin, 439 U.S. 380, 402 (1979) (White, J., dissenting). This dissent was joined by Chief Justice Burger and Justice Rehnquist.

71. See note 57, supra, and note 103, infra. Compare Akron v. Akron Center for Reproductive Health, Inc., 103 S.Ct. ___ (1983) (statute requiring abortions after first trimester reviewed by six justices on the basis of current standards of the medical profession and held invalid because it was not reasonably designed to

protect health of the woman) with Simopoulous v. Virginia, 103 S.Ct. ___ (1983) (requirement that second trimester abortions be performed in a "hospital" upheld where "hospital" included "outpatient clinics" meeting criteria designed to protect health of women patients).

Statutes requiring women to wait 24 hours after giving their consent to an abortion before receiving the abortion and statutes requiring attending physicians to inform each woman patient considering abortion of the details of fetal development, abortion techniques, emotional complications that may accompany abortion, and availability of abortion alternatives have been invalidated when a majority of justices have found that the consent requirement was not designed to protect the patient (as are standard medical consent procedures) or that the consent requirement intrudes upon the discre-

c. Spouse or Parent Consent Requirements

The Supreme Court has examined several types of statutes which required a woman to obtain the consent of her spouse or parents prior to having an abortion. The Court has not hesitated to strike down spouse consent requirements. However, the justices have not precisely defined in a majority opinion the legitimate degree of parental control over a minor female's ability to obtain an abortion.

In *Planned Parenthood v. Danforth* [72] the Supreme Court examined both a spouse and parent consent requirement. The abortion statute in question required the written consent of the spouse or parents of a minor unless the life of the mother was in danger.

The Court found that the state could not require the consent of the spouse during the first twelve weeks. The state could not delegate powers it was prohibited from exercising. Although it was manifest that the decision to terminate a pregnancy should be the decision of both husband and wife, it was equally clear that where they disagreed, one must prevail. Since "it [was] the woman who physically [bore] the child and who [was] the more directly and immediately affected by the pregnancy, as between the two, the balance weigh[ed] in her favor." [73] The Court held that the state had no legitimate interest in granting any pre-birth parental rights to a father if that limited the woman's freedom.

The requirement of parental consent was also stricken because of the inability of the state to grant the power of an absolute veto over the woman's decision. The state did have broader authority to regulate where a

juvenile was concerned, [74] but "[a]ny independent interest the parents [might] have in the termination of the minor daughter's pregnancy [was] no more weighty than the right of privacy of the competent minor mature enough to have become pregnant." [75]

The question of parental consent requirements has not been finally settled as a majority of the justices have not agreed to the proper scope of parental control. In *Bellotti v. Baird* [76] the statute in question also contained a provision requiring parental consent if a minor wished to secure an abortion. If the parents refused, the necessary consent could be obtained by order of a judge. The Court abstained from deciding the constitutionality of the statute because there were two possible interpretations of the statute. It was possible that the statute might be construed to grant the right of parental veto which, if exercised, gave the minor the burden of proving the necessity of the abortion, thus requiring a choice between the privacy rights of the woman and the state-created right of the parents. On the other hand, the statute could be construed as a "statute that prefer[red] parental consultation and consent but permit[ted] a mature minor capable of giving informed consent to obtain without undue burden an order permitting the abortion without parental consultation . . . where there [was] a showing that the abortion would be in her best interests, [77] an interpretation, which the Court found, would be quite different from a statute creating a parental veto. Accordingly, the Court abstained.

When the *Bellotti v. Baird* [78] litigation returned to the Supreme Court [79] the Court invalidated the Massachusetts parental con-

---

tion of a physician to deal with his patient or is unreasonable in requiring physicians rather than other hospital staff to provide information to the woman abortion patient. Akron v. Akron Center for Reproductive Health, Inc., 103 S.Ct. ___ (1983).

A majority of the justices, although not in a majority opinion, recently voted to uphold government regulations reasonably designed to protect the life of a viable fetus or the health of a woman patient. Planned Parenthood Association v. Ashcroft, 103 S.Ct. ___ (1983) (upholding requirement that separate physician be present at post-viability abortion to care for viable fetus and upholding statutory requirement that a pa-

thology report be completed and filed after every abortion).

72. 428 U.S. 52 (1976).

73. 428 U.S. at 71.

74. 428 U.S. at 72, 74–75.

75. 428 U.S. at 75.

76. 428 U.S. 132 (1976).

77. 428 U.S. 132, 145 (1976).

78. 428 U.S. 132 (1976).

79. Following the Supreme Court decision in *Bellotti I* the federal district court certified questions to the

sent for abortion statute but, in so doing, found that state could restrict the ability of female children to obtain an abortion. In *Bellotti v. Baird* [80] (*Bellotti II*) a plurality opinion, written by Justice Powell and joined by three other justices, found that the constitutional rights of minors were not always coextensive with those of adults and that this right to an abortion could be subject to some reasonable limitations. Justice White dissented, as he had in earlier invalidations of parental consent requirements,[81] because he would uphold strict parental consent requirements. White's position indicates that there may be a majority of justices voting to uphold parental consent laws whenever those laws meet the test of the Powell plurality. Four other justices simply found the Massachusetts requirement invalid and refused to indicate if they would vote to uphold any parental notice or consent requirements.[82]

The Powell opinion stated that there were three reasons for finding that some constitutional rights of children were not to be equated with those of adults: "the peculiar vulnerability of children; their inability to make critical decisions in an informed, mature manner; and the importance of the parental role in child rearing." [83]

Based upon these principles the justices of the Powell plurality found that the ability of

a truly "immature" minor female to have an abortion could be restricted to those situations where the immature child received consent for the abortion from one or both parents or when a fair administrative agency or court found that the abortion would be in the best interest of the child. These justices voted to invalidate the Massachusetts law because that statute, as interpreted by the state courts, did not allow for the prompt judicial authorization of an abortion for an immature minor where the abortion was in the best interest of the minor even though she failed to receive parental consent. The statute also failed to make any provision for determining whether a minor was mature enough to make the abortion decision without being subjected to parental or judicial control.

Specifically, the Powell plurality set forth the following rules for a statute which would seek to restrict the ability of a minor female to obtain an abortion. First, the state law must create a prompt procedure for making the determination of whether the child may have an abortion so that the law does not effectively cut off the right to an abortion through delay. Second, the minor must have an opportunity to go directly to a court, or perhaps an administrative tribunal,[84] to show that she is mature enough to make the decision to have an abortion without the necessity of either parental consent

Supreme Judicial Court of Massachusetts pursuant to a state procedure whereby the Supreme Judicial Court will answer questions concerning the meaning of state laws that are at issue in federal litigation. The Massachusetts Supreme Court authoritatively construed the statute and the federal district court then invalidated the statute based upon its understanding of the principles established by the earlier abortion decisions of the Supreme Court of the United States. The history of the litigation is set out at the beginning of the *Bellotti II* opinion.

80. 443 U.S. 622 (1979). The plurality opinion of Justice Powell was joined by Chief Justice Burger, and Justices Stewart and Rehnquist. Justice Rehnquist indicated in a separate opinion that he would be willing to reconsider the entire question of a minor's right to an abortion but that he would join the opinion of Justice Powell rather than the dissent of Justice White because he believed that, until a majority of the justices were willing to reconsider their basic abortion rights decisions, the states and lower court judges needed

guidance from less fragmented holdings of the Supreme Court.

81. Justice White has consistently dissented to the Court's rulings concerning the rights of adult or minor women to receive abortions. He had voted to uphold a generalized parental consent requirement in Planned Parenthood of Missouri v. Danforth, 428 U.S. 52, 94 (1976) (White, J., dissenting).

82. Bellotti v. Baird (Bellotti II), 443 U.S. 622, 652 (1979) (Stevens, J., concurring in the judgment, joined by Brennan, Marshall, and Blackmun, JJ.).

83. 443 U.S. at 633.

84. In a footnote the Powell plurality opinion indicated that these states might be able to establish nonjudicial hearing agencies for determining whether the child was mature or whether the abortion should be allowed in the best interest of the child even though she was immature and had failed to receive parental consent. 443 U.S. at 643 n. 22.

or judicial control.[85] Third, if the state court finds that the child is not mature it can refuse the child the ability to seek an abortion only if two factors are present: (1) the child fails to obtain the consent of one or both parents as required by state law,[86] and (2) that court finds that the abortion is not in the best interest of the child. Thus, if the statutory provision allows the child to receive an abortion with the consent of one or both parents if she is immature and, in the alternative, offers a prompt fair determination of whether the child is mature enough to make the decision by herself or whether, even if she is immature, an abortion would be permitted when in her best interest, the statute might be upheld by a majority of the justices. Although not subscribed to by a majority of the justices, Justice Powell's opinion provides constitutional guidelines for the drafting of parental consent laws.

The Supreme Court once again faced the issue of defining the scope of a minor female's right to an abortion when it upheld a Utah statute which required a physician to give notice to the parents of a minor female whenever possible before performing an abortion on the minor.[87] In *H.L. v. Matheson*,[88] the appellant, a fifteen year old, sought to terminate her pregnancy without the consent or knowledge of her parents with whom she lived. Although the appellant's attending physician and social worker agreed that the abortion was in her best medical interest, her physician refused to perform the abortion without first notifying her parents in accordance with the terms of the Utah statute. The Supreme Court in an opinion by Chief Justice Burger tracked the reasoning of Justice Powell's plurality opinion in *Bellotti II* concerning the special constitutional status of minors and concluded that the Utah statute furthered "significant state interest[s]" that justified the incidental burden it placed on the minor's ability to secure an abortion. Chief Justice Burger reasoned that the Utah statute "furthers a constitutionally permissible end by encouraging an unmarried pregnant minor to seek the help and advise of her parents in making the very important decision whether or not to bear a child."[89] The majority opinion seemed to attach equal constitutional significance to the state's interest in promoting the relationship between the parent and child which, the Chief Justice noted, historically has been granted constitutional recognition.[90]

The minor female appellant, Ann Matheson, had attempted to have the statute judicially invalidated on the basis that it was overbroad in requiring notice to the parents of all minor females seeking an abortion, even the parents of a minor female who was independent of her family. The majority opinion framed the issue in the case narrowly and avoided the appellant's overbreadth attack on the statute. The Chief Justice found that neither the appellant nor any member of the class[91] alleged any basis for

---

85. The Powell plurality opinion indicated that the state would be able to identify some reasonable criteria for determining maturity including the use of some objective factors "such as age limits, marital status, or membership in the armed forces . . . " 443 U.S. at 643 n. 23.

86. The Powell plurality opinion held that the state was free to require the consent of both parents, rather than merely requiring the consent of one parent, at least when both parents were living together with the child so that identification of the parents would not unduly delay the proceeding. However the Powell plurality stated, in a footnote, that if the child did receive the support of even a single one of the child's parents that the mutual decision by the child and one of her parents "should be given great, if not dispositive weight." 443 U.S. at 649 n. 29.

87. The relevant portion of the Utah statute, as reprinted in H.L. v. Matheson, 450 U.S. 398, 400 (1981) is as follows:

§ 76–7–304, enacted in 1974, provides:

"To enable a physician to exercise his best medical judgment [in considering a possible abortion], he shall: (2) *Notify, if possible, the parents or guardian of the woman upon whom the abortion is to be performed, if she is a minor* or the husband of the woman, if she is married." (emphasis supplied by the Court.)

88. 450 U.S. 396 (1981).

89. 450 U.S. at 409 (citing the concurring opinion in Bellotti II).

90. Id.

91. The appellant sought to represent a class of unmarried, minor pregnant women who wished to have

finding that they were sufficiently mature to make an independent decision regarding an abortion or that they had become emancipated from their family in any way. Thus, the Court analyzed the constitutionality of the statute only in terms of its application to an unemancipated minor female such as the appellant, a fifteen year old unmarried minor who was dependent upon and residing with her parents. The appellant had failed to demonstrate her independence or maturity or that the relationship with her parents would be detrimentally effected by the giving of such notice. The majority opinion found that the appellant lacked standing to challenge the statute because of its possible overbroad application to mature or emancipated minor females.[92]

The Chief Justice's opinion for the Court found that the notice requirement did not burden the unemancipated minor's right to privacy in any constitutionally significant degree. The Chief Justice distinguished the statute at issue in *Bellotti II* from the Utah statute on the basis that the statute at issue in *Bellotti II*, as construed by the state court, established an absolute parental veto power over the minor's decision to terminate her pregnancy. That statute had been stricken because it had not allowed a minor female who was capable of making an informed and rational decision concerning the pregnancy to have an abortion. The statute at issue in *Matheson*, however, did not es-

tablish a parental veto; it required only the giving of notice to the parents. In the Court's view, the Utah statute "does not violate the constitutional rights of an immature, dependent minor." [93] Rather, the Utah statute as "applied to immature and dependent minors" furthers two important state interests: (1) the general protection of the family relationship, which includes incidental protection of the interests of adolescents; and (2) providing an opportunity for parents to furnish medical and other important information to the physician prior to the performing of an abortion. The Court determined that the minor's right to an abortion was sufficiently guaranteed by the state; the statute promoted significant state interests with only an indirect burden, if any, on the freedom of choice of the minor. The Court refused to consider whether the state had a sufficient interest in requiring the giving of notice to the parents of an emancipated minor that would outweigh the incidental burden on that person's ability to seek an abortion.

Justice Stevens concurred in the judgment of the Court but disagreed with the narrowness of the majority's ruling.[94] According to Justice Stevens, the issue presented the Court was whether the Utah statute was constitutional as applied to all members of the asserted class of unmarried minor women wishing to terminate their pregnancies.[95] Stevens analyzed the Utah

---

an abortion but who were prohibited from doing so without notice to and the effective consent of their parents. The United States District Court had held that the Utah notice provision would be unconstitutional if it were applicable to emancipated minors. 450 U.S. at 405 citing L.R. v. Hansen (D.Utah) (1980) (unpublished opinion).

According to the dissent, the narrowness of the majority opinion meant merely that a more "carefully drafted" complaint, specifically asserting a minor's emancipation or maturity and that it was in her best interest not to have her parents notified prior to the abortion, would provide another plaintiff with standing to challenge the statute on the basis of overbreadth. 450 U.S. at 425 (Marshall, J., joined by Brennan and Blackmun, JJ., dissenting).

92. Chief Justice Burger's majority opinion supported a strict application of standing rules in this case because the United States District Court had decided

that the statute did not apply to emancipated minors, although that court was of the opinion that the statute would be unconstitutional if it were applicable to such women. The United States Supreme Court found no reason to believe that the statute would not be properly construed only to apply to unemancipated and immature minors. "Since there was no appeal from that ruling, it is controlling on the State. We cannot assume that the statute, when challenged in a proper case, will not be construed also to exempt demonstrably mature minors." H.L. v. Matheson, 450 U.S. at 405 (1981) (footnote omitted).

93. 450 U.S. at 409 (citing Bellotti II).

94. H.L. v. Matheson, 450 U.S. 398, 420 (1981) (Stevens, J., concurring in the judgment).

95. 450 U.S. at 420 (Stevens, J., concurring). Stevens had also written a separate opinion in *Bellotti II*, concurring only in the judgment. In *Bellotti II*, how-

statute in terms of the two prior decisions concerning parental notice. Stevens found that neither *Bellotti v. Baird* [96] nor *Planned Parenthood of Central Missouri v. Danforth* [97] controlled the *Matheson* decision because a statute "which does no more than require notice to the parents, without affording them or any other third party an absolute veto" in fact does not deprive a minor of her ability to secure an abortion. [98] The fact that a state statute may have a practical impact on a minor's ability to exercise her right would not render the statute unconstitutional according to Stevens. While the majority refused to make a determination as to the nature of the state's interest in requiring a notice to all the parents of unemancipated minors, Justice Stevens found that the state's interests "protecting a young pregnant woman from the consequences of an incorrect abortion decision is sufficient to justify the parental-notice requirement." [99]

Justice Marshall, in his dissent, noted that the Court's ruling was narrow in its refusal to consider the constitutionality of applying the statute to emancipated or otherwise mature minor females who sought an abortion. [100] However, the dissent found that the notice requirement for any or all females constituted a significant burden on the right of the minor female to exercise a fundamental constitutional right and that there was no sufficient state reason for the notice requirement. According to the dissent, if the family unit were truly harmonious the state had no need to require by law the notification of the parents. If members of a particular unit would attempt to interfere with the minor's ability to have an abortion or delay the possibility for her to have an abortion until af-

ter the first trimester of pregnancy, the minor might face significantly greater health risks when she finally secured an abortion or would have to forsake her constitutionally guaranteed freedom of choice.

Concurring, Justice Powell, joined by Justice Stewart, sought a middle course between the positions taken by the Stevens concurring opinion and the dissent. [101] Justice Powell, after noting that the Court left open the question of whether the statute would burden the rights of a mature minor or a minor whose best interest would not be served by parental notification stated that "I continue to entertain the views on this question stated in my opinion in *Bellotti II*." [102] Justice Powell continues to find that the state could subject a minor female's ability to have an abortion to the control of her parents only so long as it provides some procedure for freeing a mature minor or minor whose best interest would be served by self-determination regarding an abortion decision from the general requirement of notice to or approval of her parents.

The Court has avoided ruling on the constitutionality of requiring notification of the parents of an "emancipated" minor before providing the minor with an abortion and it has voided state attempts to give parents a veto power over a minor's abortion decisions, regardless of the maturity of the minor female. However, in accordance with the principles set forth in the Powell plurality opinion in *Bellotti II*, the government may require an unemancipated minor female to receive either parental consent for her abortion or to receive judicial approval of her decision to have an abortion. [103]

---

ever, Stevens took the narrower position; he found the Massachusetts statute at issue invalid but refused to indicate whether he would invalidate all parental notice or consent requirements.

96. 443 U.S. 622 (1979).

97. 428 U.S. 52 (1976).

98. H.L. v. Matheson, 450 U.S. at 420 (1981) (Stevens, J., concurring).

99. 450 U.S. at 425 (Stevens, J., concurring).

100. H.L. v. Matheson, 450 U.S. 398, 425 (1981) (Marshall, J., joined by Brennan and Blackmun, JJ., dissenting).

101. H.L. v. Matheson, 450 U.S. 398, 413 (1981) (Powell, J., joined by Stewart, J., concurring).

102. 450 U.S. at 413 (Powell, J., concurring).

103. On June 15, 1983, the Supreme Court, by a 5 to 4 vote, upheld a state law requiring a minor, pregnant female to receive the consent of her parent for her abortion or, in the alternative, to obtain the consent of a juvenile court judge. Planned Parenthood Associa-

d. *Public Funding of Abortions*

The Supreme Court's rulings on abortion have proven to be more libertarian than liberal.[104] The Court defines a woman's right to an abortion in terms of her freedom to make a decision free of government restraints. Indeed, a majority of the justices refuse to accept government attempts to demonstrate a societal interest in preservation of the fetus that would limit this freedom of choice by the woman. Yet the Court has found that indigent women have no claim of right to public funding for abortions. The woman's right includes only her own decision to attempt to secure an abortion in the private sector; the Court will not issue a ruling here which might have wealth reallocation effects even though it will leave many women without a realistic chance to secure the abortion which they have a fundamental right to choose.

In 1977 the Court had upheld the refusal of federal and local governmental entities to fund abortions that were not necessary to preserve the health of a pregnant woman. In *Maher v. Roe*,[105] the Court held that

neither the state nor federal governments were required to subsidize non-therapeutic abortions. Indeed, the Court upheld a variety of systems granting payments for maternity and childbirth costs but not abortions.[106] The majority saw these programs as merely the encouragement of childbirth rather than the penalizing of those who sought abortion but could not afford to pay for them. The three dissenting justices viewed this case as a retreat from the recognition of the right as truly fundamental.[107] But the majority was convinced that the right to privacy did not include a right to government benefits for the procurement of an abortion.

Three years later, in *Harris v. McRae*,[108] the Court upheld the federal government's exclusion from federal medical benefits programs of funding for abortion for indigent women even when a woman's attending physician had determined that an abortion was necessary to safeguard her health. The Court found that the "Hyde Amendment" not only eliminated federal funding for almost all abortions,[109] but also freed the

---

tion v. Ashcroft, 103 S.Ct. ___ (1983). There was no majority opinion regarding this issue. The consent requirement was upheld because it met the standards set out in the Powell plurality opinion referred to earlier in the text. See notes 83–86, supra. In *Ashcroft*, Justice Powell wrote only for himself and Chief Justice Burger in finding that the consent requirement at issue was valid only because it did not give parents a veto power over the minor's right and it allowed judges to withhold judicial consent for "good cause" only after a determination that the minor female was not mature enough to make the abortion decision independently. Planned Parenthood Association v. Ashcroft, 103 S.Ct. ___ (1983) (Powell, J., joined by Burger, C.J., in part V of opinion announcing judgment of Court). Justices O'Connor, White, and Rehnquist also voted to uphold the parental consent requirement but indicated that they would vote to give greater control to parents over the decisions of immature females to have an abortion. See, id. at ___ (O'Connor, J., concurring in part and dissenting in part, joined by White and Rehnquist, JJ.); Akron v. Akron Center for Reproductive Health, Inc., 103 S.Ct. ___ (1983) (O'Connor, White, and Rehnquist, JJ., dissenting).

Justices Blackmun, Brennan, Marshall, and Stevens adhere to the position that a pregnant, minor female's decision to have an abortion should not be subjected to an effectively absolute veto power of parents and judges. Planned Parenthood Association v. Ashcroft, 103 S.Ct. ___ (1983) (Blackmun, J., concurring in part and dissenting in part, joined by Brennan, Marshall, and Stevens, JJ.). Whenever an abortion statute grants control over a minor female's abortion decision to par-

ents and judges in violation of the rules set forth by Justice Powell, he and Burger will join with Justices Blackmun, Brennan, Marshall, and Stevens to invalidate the consent statute. See Akron v. Akron Center for Reproductive Health, Inc., 103 S.Ct. ___ (1983).

104. See Nowak, Forward: Evaluating the Work of the New Libertarian Supreme Court, 7 Hastings Constitutional Law Quarterly 263 (1980); note 118, infra.

105. 432 U.S. 464 (1977).

106. Id.; Beal v. Doe, 432 U.S. 438 (1977) (Social Security Act does not require abortion payments); Poelker v. Doe, 432 U.S. 519 (1977) (city hospital may provide childbirth procedures and refuse abortions).

107. Maher v. Roe, 432 U.S. 464, 482 (1977) (Brennan, Marshall & Blackmun, JJ., dissenting).

108. 448 U.S. 297 (1980).

109. There were three versions of the Hyde Amendment. As originally passed for the 1977 Fiscal Year, the amendment prohibited federal funding for abortions except where "the life of the mother would be in danger if the fetus were carried to term." For the majority of the 1978 and all of the 1979 Fiscal Year, the amendment additionally provided for funds in cases where "such medical procedures [are] necessary for the victims of rape or incest when such rape or incest has been reported promptly to a law enforcement agency or public health service" and in "instances where severe and long-lasting physical health damage to the mother would result if the pregnancy were carried to term when so determined by two physicians." For the 1980 Fiscal Year, Congress amended the previous version of the Hyde Amendment to exclude federal fund-

states of any duty to fund abortions that were not funded by the federal Medicaid program.[110] The majority opinion, written by Justice Stewart, found that the Court's previous decisions in the area of abortion established only a fundamental right of a woman to be able to choose to have an abortion without direct government interference. The government could not attempt to limit a woman's right to an abortion with an artificial definition of the time at which a fetus became viable, or medical regulations which were designed to inhibit a woman's access to abortion services, because such laws interfered with a fundamental right of the woman and were not supported by a compelling government interest. Justice Stewart reasoned that the Hyde Amendment "places no governmental obstacle in the path of a woman who chooses to terminate her pregnancy, but rather, by means of unequal subsidization of abortion and other medical services, encourages alternative activity deemed in the public interest."[111] The fact that a woman could not exercise her fundamental right to secure an abortion in the private sector was of no concern to the justices, for her inability to exercise her freedom of choice was the result of her own lack of resources rather than government action. The government was not required to reallocate resources so as to enable persons to exercise their rights, according to the majority.[112]

Having thus dispensed of the claim that failure to provide a woman with resources for exercising her right to choose to have an abortion violated the fundamental right of privacy, the Court had little problem in dismissing the indigent women's equal protection claim. Because the failure to provide

funds for such women did not deprive them of a fundamental right, the law was not to be tested by the compelling interest test. Rather, the majority found that it need only determine whether the Hyde Amendment "bears a rational relationship to [the government's] legitimate interest in protecting the potential life of the fetus."[113] The Court had no problem in upholding the statute against the equal protection attack under the deferential rational basis standard. Unless a law allocates the ability to exercise a fundamental right by economic status, the Court refuses to scrutinize rigorously the validity of wealth classifications.[114]

The Court quickly dispensed with the claim that the Hyde Amendment violated the religion clauses of the first amendment. The fact that the Hyde Amendment coincided with the doctrines of certain religious sects did not provide a basis for its invalidation because the amendment could be seen as having a secular purpose in encouraging childbirth. To use the establishment clause to prohibit laws which have an ethical basis in some religion would be to deprive the government of an ability to act in many areas traditionally recognized as being within the police power of the state.[115] No plaintiff attacking the validity of the Hyde Amendment in these cases had standing to claim that the law violated the free exercise clause of the first amendment as, not unexpectedly, none were able to demonstrate that they must procure an abortion under compulsion of their religious beliefs.[116]

Four justices dissented from these rulings denying indigent women funding for therapeutic abortions.[117] Justice Stewart, a mem-

---

ing for the last described category of abortions. Harris v. McRae, 448 U.S. 297 (1980).

110. In Williams v. Zbaraz, 448 U.S. 358 (1980), decided the same day as *McRae*, the Court relied on its ruling in *McRae* that state governments were not required to fund abortions not covered by the federal Medicaid plan and that the refusal of the state to fund such abortions did not violate the due process or equal protection clauses of the fourteenth amendment. The Court in *Williams* relied entirely on the *McRae* opinion to establish the constitutionality of the state refusal to fund medically necessary abortions.

111. Harris v. McRae, 448 U.S. 297, 314 (1980).

112. 448 U.S. at 316–320.

113. 448 U.S. at 324.

114. The Court's refusal to find wealth classifications to be deserving of meaningful judicial reveiw is examined in Section VI of this chapter.

115. Harris v. McRae, 448 U.S. 297, 320 (1980).

116. 448 U.S. at 320.

117. Justices Brennan, Marshall, and Blackmun focused their dissents on the Hyde Amendment's effective interference with an indigent pregnant woman's freedom of choice to have an abortion, which they found to be a fundamental constitutional right. Justice Stevens would have employed a reasonableness standard to find that there was no basis for exclusion from a government "pool of benefits" of individuals who had a medical need for an abortion. Harris v. McRae, 448 U.S. 297, 329 (1980) (Brennan, J., joined by

ber of the five person majority and author of the *Harris* opinion, has resigned from the Court since the date of these rulings. However, it seems unlikely that the Court in the near future will find that the government must provide resources for the funding of an abortion for this seems to be contrary to the libertarian political philosophy which currently holds sway on the Supreme Court.[118] Were the Court to find that the government must use reasonable classifications in its allocation of "welfare" benefits in order to avoid effectively denying a woman her fundamental right to an abortion, it would be only a short philosophic step away from justifying judicial review of the reasonableness of welfare classifications and a wide variety of laws which have a disparate impact on economically disadvantaged persons.

E. Emerging Issues Regarding the Right to Privacy

1. Right to Engage in Sexual Acts

In a highly publicized ruling several years ago, the Supreme Court refused to review a sodomy conviction of an adult person who had engaged in a private, consensual homosexual act with another adult;[1] this ruling was consistent with decisions of the Court in previous years.[2] Despite the growing

amount of litigation concerning the ability of individuals to engage in sexual acts prohibited by state or local legislation, the Supreme Court has given no indication that a significant number of the justices consider this issue to be a serious constitutional question.[3] As noted elsewhere in the text, the Court has never indicated that there is any constitutionally guaranteed right to live a particular "lifestyle."[4]

Although it has been argued that a right of adults to engage in voluntary sexual acts in private should be considered a part of the right to privacy,[5] the previously decided cases do not seem to support such a result. The cases which come closest to supporting the theory are the contraception cases. *Griswold v. Connecticut*,[6] however, was grounded on the "right to privacy" that existed in the relationship between partners in a traditional marriage. In *Eisenstadt v. Baird*,[7] the Court ruled that it was a violation of equal protection to punish unmarried persons for purchasing items that would prevent disease or pregnancy because there was no clear proof that a ban of such purchases in fact would deter persons from committing illegal sexual acts. The *Eisenstadt* opinion did describe the right to privacy as a right to be "free from unwarranted governmental intrusion into matters so fundamentally affecting a person as the deci-

---

Marshall and Blackmun, JJ., dissenting); Id. at 337 (Marshall, J., dissenting); Id. at 348 (Blackmun, J., dissenting); Id. at 349 (Stevens, J., dissenting).

118. For an examination of the political and judicial philosophy evidenced by the "Burger Court" as compared to the "Warren Court" see Nowak, Foreword: Evaluating the Work of the New Libertarian Supreme Court, 7 Hastings Constitutional Law Quarterly 263 (1980). Excellent examinations of the Court's recent abortion rulings appear in: Perry, Why the Supreme Court was Plainly Wrong in the Hyde Amendment Case: A Brief Comment on Harris v. McRae, 32 Stanford Law Review 1113 (1980); Bennett, Abortion and Judicial Review: Of Burdens and Benefits, Hard Cases and Some Bad Law, 75 Northwestern University Law Review 978 (1981).

1. Enslin v. Bean, 436 U.S. 912 (1978).

2. Two years earlier the Court had summarily affirmed a similar conviction. See Doe v. Commonwealth's Attorney, 425 U.S. 901 (1976), aff'g mem., 403 F.Supp. 1199 (E.D.Va.1975) (three judge court) (upholding such a statute as not vague or violative of the right

to privacy). See also Wainwright v. Stone, 414 U.S. 21 (1973) (upholding the use of a sodomy statute to punish voluntary sexual conduct as it was not vague when viewed in terms of state court rulings).

3. For example, only Justices Brennan and Marshall voted to grant certiorari in *Enslin*. See Enslin v. Bean, 436 U.S. 912 (1978).

4. The concept of "lifestyle" might include freedom to live, dress, or act in a manner that is inconsistent with any number of state laws ranging from mandatory education requirements to single family zoning regulations. See subsections A & B of this section of Chapter 16 and Chapter 16, Section XII C. For a thorough analysis of "lifestyle" issues, see Wilkinson & White, Constitutional Protection for Personal Lifestyles, 62 Cornell L.Rev. 563 (1977).

5. See Richards, Unnatural Acts and the Constitutional Right to Privacy: A Moral Theory, 45 Fordham L.Rev. 1281 (1977).

6. 381 U.S. 479 (1965).

7. 405 U.S. 438 (1972).

sion whether to bear or beget a child." [8] This language might be taken to mean that unmarried individuals have a right to make similar decisions concerning whether to engage in private sexual acts, but the two issues were separated in *Carey v. Population Services International.* [9] In *Carey*, the Court based its decision that minors could not be prohibited from purchasing contraceptives solely on the ground that the prohibition was not a rational way of deterring children from engaging in illegal sexual activities. At the same time, however, there seemed to be a clear majority of justices who would allow punishment of minors who use contraceptives for their intended purpose. [10]

Other right to privacy cases offer even less support for this theory of sexual freedom than do the contraception cases. Most of the cases relate either to unique intrafamily decision-making problems, or to the ability of persons to engage in traditionally recognized forms of marriage. One justice recently has noted that the restriction of marriage to heterosexual unions between unrelated adults had never been thought to present a significant constitutional problem. [11] Similarly, the decisions of the Supreme Court relating to sterilization or abortion do not logically necessitate the finding of a further right to commit otherwise illegal sexual acts with another; those decisions are based on the ability of an individual to make certain decisions deemed "fundamen-

tal." To a majority of the justices it does not appear unreasonable to find that an individual's freedom to have an abortion, or to become permanently sterilized, involve significantly more fundamental rights than the ability to engage in legally proscribed sexual practices.

It may be that the right to privacy should encompass some right to be free of government regulation of one's personal lifestyle. However, it is difficult to distinguish such "lifestyle" interests from individual interests which are often infringed by modern "economic and social welfare" legislation. The failure to make such a distinction could lead the Court back into the morass of pre-1937 substantive due process rulings. There is a strong argument that the right to privacy should include, at minimum, a ban on criminal sanctions against adults who engage in voluntary acts that do not demonstrably harm anyone else. [12] Such a right would be based on the philosophy which underlies the recognition of any true right to privacy: that society may not limit individual freedom unless it does so to prevent an individual from harming others. [13] A future set of justices might well find that the previous right to privacy decisions support inclusion of such a right within the concept of "liberty" protected by due process. At present, however, the cases do not necessitate such a conclusion. [14] Thus, the Supreme Court recently denied certiorari to a case in which a government employed librarian and

---

8. Eisenstadt v. Baird, 405 U.S. 438, 453 (1972).

9. 431 U.S. 678 (1977).

10. See subsection B of this section of Chapter 16.

11. See Zablocki v. Redhail, 434 U.S. 374, 398 (1978) (Powell, J., concurring). In noting that marriage was not a right but only a "privilege" and that the Court should be hesitant to overturn societal decisions in this area, Justice Stewart indicated that he would not subject traditional marriage restrictions to strict scrutiny. Id. at 391–396 (Stewart, J., concurring in the judgment). See subsection C of this section of Chapter 16.

12. One might find support for this position in Stanley v. Georgia, 394 U.S. 557 (1969) which allowed a person to possess pornographic material in the home. But the Court has refused to find in *Stanley* a right to secure such material, or to view pornographic materials "in private" outside the home. One (now retired) Jus-

tice has recently noted that *Stanley* had not created a generalized right to privacy but instead was based on an interpretation of the first amendment. Whalen v. Roe, 429 U.S. 589, 609 (1977) (Stewart, J., concurring).

13. See J. S. Mill, On Liberty.

14. It would be quite difficult to justify the judicial imposition of this philosophy on society when the societal judgment seems at best divided concerning the asserted right. See generally, A. Bickel, The Morality of Consent 25–30 (1975). Former Justice Stewart has noted that the right to privacy decisions are a form of substantive due process adjudication, and that the Court should be hesitant to employ this doctrine to overturn societal decisions concerning morality and social welfare. Compare, Roe v. Wade, 410 U.S. 113, 167 (1973) (Stewart, J., concurring) with Zablocki v. Redhail, 434 U.S. 374, 391 (1978) (Stewart, J., concurring).

the custodian at the library were discharged from their employment because they lived together and had a child out of wedlock.[15] Similarly, the Court refused to review a state supreme court's decision taking away custody of children from a divorced mother based upon a presumption that her cohabitation with an unmarried adult male adversely affected the well being of her children.[16]

In connection with this issue it should be noted that the Supreme Court refused to review a ruling of the Court of Appeals for the Eighth Circuit that prohibited a state university from refusing to recognize, or grant access to campus facilities to, an organization whose goals were to provide information concerning homosexuality and to secure recognition of rights for homosexuals.[17] The ruling of the lower court, however, was based on the first amendment freedoms of speech and association, and not on a right to engage in homosexual acts.[18]

2. Accumulation and Distribution of Data Concerning Individual Citizens

The Supreme Court has not yet held that the right to privacy limits governmental powers relating to the collection of data concerning private individuals. In *Whalen v. Roe*,[19] the Court unanimously upheld a New York law that required physicians and pharmacists to forward to state authorities copies of prescriptions for medicines containing certain narcotics. The majority opinion by Justice Stevens held that the statute was valid even if the right to privacy places some

restriction on the ability of government to collect data concerning individual citizens. The New York law was found to be related to the legitimate goal of controlling illegal drug distribution and reasonable in its limitations on the use and distribution of the collected data. The mere possibility that the data would be used improperly did not void the law. Justice Stevens noted, however, that government data collection did threaten individual privacy, and, for that reason, that the right to collect such data normally would be limited by a duty to avoid unwarranted disclosure of the information collected. The majority opinion stated that this duty "arguably has its roots in the Constitution," but did not rule on this issue. In a concurring opinion, Justice Brennan stated his belief that governmental data collection practices that were not carefully limited as to the use of information concerning private persons would deprive those persons of a constitutionally protected privacy interest.[20] In a separate concurring opinion, Justice Stewart noted that the majority had not adopted Justice Brennan's views. Justice Stewart was of the opinion that the Constitution, apart from the fourth amendment, did not create a general right to privacy that would restrict governmental activities of this nature.[21]

The Supreme Court has confronted the question of the propriety of government collection of data only in terms of the fourth amendment right to be free from unreasonable searches and seizures, and the fifth amendment prohibition against compelling

---

15. Hollenbaugh v. Carnegie Free Library, 436 F.Supp. 1328 (W.D.Pa.1977) 578 F.2d 1374 (3rd Cir. 1978) cert. denied 439 U.S. 1052 (1978) (Justice Marshall dissented to the denial and wrote a dissenting opinion. Justice Brennan noted that he would grant certiorari). The lower court had found that the exclusion should be judged only under the minimum rationality test under the equal protection clause; the court of appeals issued no opinion and affirmed on the basis of the district court opinion. Justice Marshall, in dissent, objected to the Supreme Court's continued refusal to openly deal with issues regarding choice of lifestyle and the degree of scrutiny which such actions merited under the equal protection clause.

16. Jarrett v. Jarrett, 78 Ill.2d 337, 400 N.E.2d 421 (1979), cert. denied 449 U.S. 927 (1980). Justice Bren-

nan filed an opinion dissenting to the denial of certiorari which was joined by Justice Marshall. Justice Blackmun voted to set the case for oral argument and dissented without opinion.

17. See Gay Lib v. University of Missouri, 558 F.2d 848 (8th Cir. 1977) cert. denied sub. nom. Ratchford v. Gay Lib, 434 U.S. 1080 (1978).

18. See Healy v. James, 408 U.S. 169 (1972).

19. 429 U.S. 589 (1977).

20. Whalen v. Roe, 429 U.S. 589, 606–607 (1977) (Brennan, J., concurring).

21. 429 U.S. at 607–609 (Stewart, J., concurring).

persons to incriminate themselves.[22] Indeed, in its determination of this application and meaning of the fourth and fifth amendments, the Court has failed to acknowledge the possibility of other "privacy" limitations on governmental data collection practices. The Supreme Court has held that neither amendment was violated by a federal law requiring banks to obtain and record information concerning their customers and their customer's financial transactions.[23] Thereafter, in *United States v. Miller*,[24] the Court held that the government could subpoena bank records of specific persons in an investigation of criminal activity. The majority opinion in *Miller* found that individuals had no expectation of privacy in the records, checks, or deposit slips which were kept by their bank. Unless the Court would begin to recognize some general right of privacy limitation on government data collection, *Miller* would allow the government to engage in the wholesale collection and examination of data concerning the financial transactions of persons not connected to criminal activity.[25]

22. In several cases the Court has noted the existence of issues relating to a possible right of privacy regarding personal data without ruling on these issues.

Using an analysis similar to that employed in *Whalen*, the Supreme Court upheld a state statutory requirement that records of all abortions be maintained by doctors and hospitals involved in these abortions. Planned Parenthood of Central Missouri v. Danforth, 428 U.S. 52 (1976). Because the regulation could relate to legitimate concerns regarding regulation of health care services, and because there was no demonstration that the data would be misused by the government, the Court upheld the general requirement without ruling on what, if any, right of privacy limitations might be placed on data collection practices.

In Nixon v. Administrator of General Services, 433 U.S. 425 (1977), the Court upheld the Presidential Recordings and Materials Act and the requirement that former President Nixon leave certain papers and tapes in control of the government. Because of the overriding interest of the nation in these records, the Court upheld the Act, even assuming that Mr. Nixon had a constitutionally protected privacy interest as to some portion of these items.

In cases dealing with the ability of Congress to inquire into, and disclose, the political beliefs of private individuals, the Supreme Court has indicated that congressional investigations cannot have as their sole purpose the disclosure of such information. However, this limitation is based on an analysis of the congressional investigatory power and the first amendment; the principle has not seriously restricted the ability of Congress to investigate the actions of private individuals or to disclose its findings concerning private individuals. See Chapter 8, Sections I, D & E.

The Court did give protection to individual privacy interests when it held that a company cannot be compelled by the National Labor Relations Board to disclose to a union results of psychological tests on individual employees without the employees' consent. As a matter of federal labor law, the Court held that a union assertion of need for data regarding the employees did not justify this inquiry. The employees' right to confidentiality outweighed the burden on the union. Detroit Edison Co. v. NLRB, 440 U.S. 301 (1979).

The Freedom of Information Act (5 U.S.C.A. § 552) and the Trade Secrets Act (18 U.S.C.A. § 1905) both govern the control of data regarding private individuals that is in the possession of the federal government. The Court has held that neither act grants an implied private right of action to enjoin disclosure by a government agency, but under § 10 of the Administrative Procedure Act (5 U.S.C.A. § 702) there is judicial review of an agency's decision to release information to ensure that agency disclosure is authorized by law. Chrysler Corp. v. Brown, 441 U.S. 281 (1979).

23. California Bankers Association v. Shultz, 416 U.S. 21 (1974). This decision upheld the general record keeping requirements because the majority saw that as reasonable regulation of financial institutions and related to the preservation of information that might be used for legitimate governmental purposes. The Court upheld the regulations, which required banks to report information concerning individual accounts, against a fourth amendment challenge; the Court avoided ruling on whether the first amendment implied right of association, or related privacy interests, placed any limits on these regulations, because a majority of the justices did not find the question ripe for review at this time. In a later decision, the Supreme Court upheld the Internal Revenue Service's use of a warrant to examine all the records of a bank to determine which of its customers had given it $40,000 in cash that was in a deteriorated condition, indicating it had been in storage for a long time. As the facts of the particular case showed a basis for concluding that these records might disclose further proof of tax evasion, the Court upheld the "John Doe" warrant and examination of the bank's records regarding many of its customers. Bisceglia v. United States, 420 U.S. 141 (1975).

24. 425 U.S. 435 (1976).

25. Similarly, the Court has held that telephone companies could be directed to assist federal law enforcement officials in the installation of pen register devices on telephone lines, so long as the federal authorities had secured a search warrant authorizing the installation of such devices. United States v. New York Telephone Co., 434 U.S. 159 (1977). And in 1979 the Supreme Court held that the fourth amendment did not restrict the use of pen register devices, which record the telephone numbers dialed from a particular telephone, at telephone company offices because the person using the telephone does not have a "legitimate expectation of privacy" in the dialed phone numbers. Smith v. Maryland, 442 U.S. 735 (1979).

The Court has also held that a search of newspaper offices, pursuant to warrant, for photographic evidence of the identity of demonstrators who had severely beaten police officers was not unconstitutional. In *Zurcher v. Stanford Daily*,[26] a majority of the Court found that a search pursuant to a valid warrant is constitutionally sound even when the owner or possessor of the premises searched is not suspected of any crime. The Court then went on to hold that the first and fourth amendments permit searches of press offices pursuant to warrant and do not require use of the less intrusive subpoena *duces tecum* where practicable. The Court reasoned that the reasonableness, specificity, and probable cause requirements of the warrant procedure provided sufficient protection to first amendment interests, and noted that, where such requirements were properly applied, there would be no occasion for police to "rummage at large in newspaper files."[27] *Zurcher* makes plain the fact that, in the context of a criminal investigation, privacy interests endangered by government actions will be tested and protected almost exclusively under the fourth amendment. The majority opinion, however, did emphasize that where "the materials sought to be seized may be protected by the first amendment, the requirements of the fourth amendment must be applied with scrupulous exactitude."[28] In dissent, Mr. Justice Stewart, with whom Mr. Justice Marshall joined, observed that the majority holding would allow police to "ransack the files of a newspaper," and would ultimately result in a chilling of confidential sources and a suppression of news.[29] But this dissent did not challenge the general ability of government agents to search for evidence of a crime in the possession of innocent persons.

Only Justice Stevens noted the relationship between the *Zurcher* decision and the danger posed to the privacy interests of private, non-media persons. He would have required the police to use the subpoena procedure in order to limit the number and scope of searches of persons not suspected of committing a crime.[30] For many years it was held that the fourth amendment allowed searches only for instrumentalities or fruits of a crime, or other contraband items. In *Warden v. Hayden*[31] the Court ruled that a search for evidence of a crime based upon probable cause and, in most instances, a procedurally proper warrant would comply with the fourth amendment. This opened two new privacy issues: (1) whether government agents could search for a defendant's records or other written evidence of his criminal activity, and (2) whether searches for "mere evidence" of a crime believed to be possessed by persons not suspected of criminal activity required special justification. In *Andresen v. Maryland*[32] the Court resolved the first issue by finding that the police could search for records of criminal activity even though the records were "testimonial" in nature. In *Zurcher* the Court resolved the second issue by finding that third person searches were allowed upon a basic

When the Court is confronted with invasions of privacy that involve traditional searches it often finds a textual basis in the fourth amendment for protecting privacy interests. See, e.g., Brown v. Texas, 443 U.S. 47 (1979) (state cannot authorize police officers to stop individuals without cause and demand identification); Ybarra v. Illinois, 444 U.S. 85 (1979) (search warrant for a specific premises does not justify the search of a person present at the scene who is neither suspected of a crime nor believed to be armed or dangerous); Payton v. New York, 445 U.S. 573 (1980) (police are required, absent exigent circumstances, to have an arrest or search warrant when entering a private home to make an arrest).

26. 436 U.S. 547, 98 S.Ct. 1970 (1978).

27. 436 U.S. at 566.

28. 436 U.S. at 564. Justice Powell, in a concurring opinion, noted that, as the Court's opinion makes clear, newspapers might receive added protection because magistrates considering warrants for searches of press facilities "can and should take cognizance of the independent values protected by the First Amendment." 436 U.S. at 570 (Powell, J., concurring).

29. Zurcher v. Stanford Daily, 436 U.S. 547, 571–574 (1978) (Stewart & Marshall, JJ., dissenting.)

30. Zurcher v. Stanford Daily, 436 U.S. 547, 582–583 (1978) (Stevens, J., dissenting).

31. 387 U.S. 294 (1967).

32. 427 U.S. 463 (1976).

finding of probable cause to believe that the person possessed evidence of a crime, even though he had not been involved in the criminal activity. Whether these decisions foreclose the use of a more generalized right to privacy analysis to limit probable cause searches by the police remains unclear.[33]

Today, the justices of the Supreme Court appear to be willing to limit governmental activity relating to the collection and distribution of data only when that activity impairs first amendment rights [34] or constitutional restrictions on the criminal justice process. Yet the concept of a "right to privacy" should impose some requirement of reasonableness on government officials who engage in such activity.

In considering the extent to which the right to privacy may limit the government collection and use of data concerning private individuals, it is important to remember that the Supreme Court has held that the press could not be prohibited, consistently with the first amendment, from reporting information which was lawfully obtained from public records.[35] Nor can persons who are not participants in confidential judicial proceeding be subject to criminal sanctions for publishing accurate reports of such proceedings.[36] As individuals can not be punished for reporting information lawfully obtained from government records, the government might be under some duty to exclude public access to records concerning private individuals. The extent to which the government will be able to keep such records secret depends upon what, if any, right of access to government records is granted to members of the press or public under the first amendment.[37]

33. The Supreme Court in recent years seems to have narrowed the fourth amendment definition of the right of privacy protected from governmental intrusion as it has been increasingly strict in allowing defendants in criminal cases to challenge searches and seizures only when they can demonstrate that their own fourth amendment rights were violated. An illegal search or seizure only violates the rights of those persons who have a legitimate expectation of privacy with respect to the place searched or item seized. Strict enforcement of this "standing" principle comes close to requiring persons to have a legally cognizable property interest before they can complain of improper police activities and gathering of evidence to be used against them. See, e.g., United States v. Payner, 447 U.S. 727 (1980) (federal courts had no inherent power to exclude evidence obtained in an illegal search of a third party's premises no matter how flagrantly illegal were the activities of the investigating officers); United States v. Salvucci, 448 U.S. 83 (1980) (rejecting the doctrine of "automatic standing" and requiring defendants to assert an interest in the possession of contraband goods before they could complain of an illegal seizure of such items); Rawlings v. Kentucky, 448 U.S. 98 (1980) (defendant may not complain of the illegal search of a companion's person or property even though that search produced evidence to be used against the defendant); Dalia v. U.S., 441 U.S. 238 (1979) (fourth amendment does not prohibit covert entry to install "bugging" equipment pursuant to a warrant authorizing the electronic surveillance but silent as to the entry).

See generally, W. LaFave, Search and Seizure: A Treatise on the Fourth Amendment (3 vol. 1979, with annual supplement).

34. Laws requiring disclosure of information regarding political candidates, political parties or campaign contributors are subject to independent judicial review to determine if they comply with the principles of the first amendment. The campaign disclosure law which requires every political party to disclose the names of members of the party or campaign contributors may not be applied to a minor political party which has demonstrated that it is subject to private or governmental hostility and that disclosures will impair the rights of the freedom of speech and association of members of the party. See, Brown v. Socialist Workers '74 Campaign Committee, 103 S.Ct. 416 (1982). See Chapter 18, Section XV.

35. Cox Broadcasting Corp. v. Cohn, 420 U.S. 469 (1975). See Chapter 18.

36. Landmark Communications, Inc. v. Virginia, 435 U.S. 829 (1978).

See also Smith v. Daily Mail Publishing Co., 443 U.S. 97 (1979) (state may not punish a newspaper's truthful publication of an alleged juvenile delinquent's name lawfully obtained by a newspaper).

37. See, Philadelphia Newspapers, Inc. v. Jerome, 434 U.S. 241 (1978) (remanding for clarification of record, and declining to rule on, a case involving an assertion of a right of reporters to attend pretrial suppression hearing); Nixon v. Warner Communications, Inc., 435 U.S. 589 (1978) (press had no right to record copies of presidential tape recording). See also Kissinger v. Reporters Committee for Freedom of the Press, 445 U.S. 136 (1980), and Forsham v. Harris, 445 U.S. 169 (1980) (strictly interpreting the Freedom of Information Act not to include items not technically within the possession and control of an agency covered by the Act, even though the agency could have acquired or once had possession of the documents which contained information concerning the individual claimant).

It should also be noted that, even if the Supreme Court were to define a right to privacy that would limit government data collection practices, it might be quite difficult for anyone to maintain a law suit that would vindicate that right. The Court has held that an injury to an individual's reputation through the release of even false data about him does not establish a constitutional violation, although this decision may be only a limitation of procedural due process principles.[38] In any event, unless an individual could show identifiable harm from government investigation or data collection practices that individual would not have standing to maintain a suit to limit such practices.[39]

3. The "Right to Die"

To date the Supreme Court has not determined whether an individual has a constitutional right to forego life saving medical treatment. As noted elsewhere in the text, a claim to such a right might be based on either the free exercise clause of the first amendment or the right to privacy inherent in the concept of liberty.[40] As the issue receives greater attention, it is important that courts and legislators clearly separate the question of whether an individual should have the right to forego medical treatment from the question of whether other persons can determine when life support or life saving techniques need not be employed to continue an individual's existence.

Professor Yale Kamisar has advanced the analysis of such problems by showing that no "right to die" issue is presented by a situation absent a clear demonstration that the patient knowingly desires to refuse medical treatment.[41] To allow a patient's doctor, family, or friends to determine whether life support systems should be employed is to give those persons a "right to kill" under Professor Kamisar's analysis. As he notes, it is virtually impossible to draw a line between active and passive euthanasia; it does no good to pretend that life is not being terminated in any case where a person could continue their existence for more than a brief period of time. When dealing with the person who cannot make or express an intelligent decision concerning this subject, there is no medical distinction between killing that person and letting him or her die. It may be that society will recognize some ability of family members or doctors to engage in "passive euthanasia" based on a societal decision that the quality of an individual's life is such that it should not be continued under certain circumstances. Nevertheless, failure to recognize this decision as one allowing persons to take the life of another will lead to poorly reasoned decisions. In *In re Quinlan*,[42] for example, the New Jersey Supreme Court granted a right to parents to terminate the life of their daughter while leaving the issue submerged in a discussion of the daughter's "right" to forego medical treatment. That court recognized that there was no significant proof that the daughter-

---

38. Paul v. Davis, 424 U.S. 693 (1976). See Chapter 15, Section II, D5.

39. Laird v. Tatum, 408 U.S. 1 (1972).

40. See Chapter 18, Section III, D, and Chapter 15, Section II, B.

The Supreme Court has held that the federal Food, Drug, and Cosmetic Act, 21 U.S.C.A. §§ 321, 355 supported the prohibition of interstate distribution of the drug "Laetrile" and that the Act could not be interpreted to contain an exemption for terminally ill cancer patients. United States v. Rutherford, 442 U.S. 544 (1979). The Court in *Rutherford* did not review the patients' claim that they had a substantive due process "privacy" right to use Laetrile because the case presented only an issue of statutory construction. However, Justice Marshall's opinion for a unanimous Court emphasized the possible dangers presented even for

terminal patients by ineffective drugs, the wide variety of products whose producers claimed "cured" cancer, and the difficulty of reviewing all such claims and products. Thus it appears unlikely that the Supreme Court will find that due process principles authorize strict judicial review of medical regulations or an exemption from reasonable regulation for terminally ill patients. Nevertheless, resolution of those issues must await future cases.

41. Y. Kamisar, A Life Not (Or No Longer) Worth Living: Are We Deciding the Issue Without Facing It? [1977 Mitchell Lecture delivered at the University of New York at Buffalo; on file at the University of Illinois College of Law and the University of Michigan Law School].

42. 70 N.J. 10, 355 A.2d 647 (1976).

patient would have rejected the treatment; the court's decision was based on a factually unsupported conclusion as to when most individuals would reject such treatment. The New Jersey court made a ruling on the quality of human life that justified medical treatment without medical support or clear legal analysis. Indeed, the daughter-patient in that case continues to live and it is unlikely that the New Jersey court would deny her the reduced medical treatment that now sustains her life.

Under Professor Kamisar's analysis the determination of whether or not persons may withdraw life support systems used for other persons should be recognized as a decision with respect to legalized euthanasia. The Professor hopes that recognition of this decision as a euthanasia decision may help to preclude courts from too readily allowing families to decide to terminate the lives of incompetent or ill family members. It should be noted that merely recognizing "living wills" whereby an individual can state in advance whether or not they want to have their life supported by "extraordinary means," should the necessity arise, will not avoid the societal problem referred to, and analyzed by, Professor Kamisar. A jurisdiction that recognizes such instruments must still determine what medical techniques it is willing to consider "extraordinary" and what circumstances will demonstrate that the person's previously expressed desire to forego treatment continued up to the time immediately prior to his or her medical disability. Absent such legislative decisions the problem of defining the nature of a life that deserves to be continued will fall to the courts.

VIII. THE RIGHT TO VOTE

A. The Electoral Franchise as a Fundamental Right

1. Introduction

The Constitution initially contained two provisions that related to the exercise of the electoral franchise. Article I, section two of the Constitution mandates that electors for members of the House of Representatives shall meet the same qualifications as "Electors for the most numerous Branch of the State Legislature."[1] Article II, section one and the twelfth and twentieth amendments, establish the procedure whereby members of the Electoral College select the President and Vice-President.[2] Article II, section one grants the states discretion in the manner of selecting the members of the Electoral College. The Supreme Court has used these provisions to support the proposition that the states, because of this inherent constitutional authority to control the electoral process, can require persons to meet certain reasonable requirements before they vote in state or national elections.[3] Later amendments to the Constitution, however, have placed restrictions on the ability of states to impose franchise requirements. The fifteenth amendment, for example, prohibits the states from impairing the franchise on the basis "of race, color, or previous condition of servitude".[4] The nineteenth amendment forbids discrimination in voting by sex. The twenty-fourth amendment prevents the states from imposing "any poll tax or other tax" on a person before that person can vote

1. "The House of Representatives shall be composed of Members chosen every second year by the People of the Several States, and the Electors in each State shall have the Qualifications requisite for Electors of the most numerous Branch of the State Legislature." U.S. Const. art. 1, § 2, cl. 1.

2. "Each State shall appoint, in such Manner as the Legislature thereof may direct, a Number of Electors, equal to the whole Number of Senators and Representatives to which the State may be entitled in the Congress; but no Senator or Representative, or Person holding an Office of Trust or Profit under the United States, shall be appointed an Elector." U.S. Const. art.

2, § 1, cl. 2. See U.S. Const. amends. XII and XX for current procedures.

3. See, e.g., Kramer v. Union School District, 395 U.S. 621, 625 (1969). The Court sustained residency and citizenship requirements in Marston v. Lewis, 410 U.S. 679 (1973); Burns v. Fortson, 410 U.S. 686 (1973). The Court discussed age requirements in Oregon v. Mitchell, 400 U.S. 112 (1970).

4. "The right of citizens of the United States to vote shall not be denied or abridged by the United States or by any State on account of race, color, or previous condition of servitude." U.S. Const. amend. XV, § 1.

for a candidate for a federal office.[5] The twenty-sixth amendment grants the right to vote to all citizens of the United States who are eighteen years of age or older.

Besides the explicit constitutional provisions that pertain to the election process, the Supreme Court has held that the fourteenth amendment restricts the power of the states to place qualifications on the exercise of the franchise in several ways. The Court has used the amendment to fashion a fundamental right to vote.[6] It has recognized that the right to vote is one of those rights that "is preservative of other basic civil and political rights."[7] Therefore, any alleged impairment of the right should be subjected to "strict scrutiny" by the Court.[8] Because the right to vote is a fundamental right, any classification defining the ability to exercise the right must meet, under a strict scrutiny review, the dictates of the equal protection guarantee before the Court can sustain the measure as constitutional.[9] Additionally because the fourteenth amendment does apply to state laws that regulate the election process, the Court has recognized that Congress has some power to legislatively override the states' authority to govern the exercise of the franchise.[10]

Although the Supreme Court has restricted the authority of the states over the electoral process, at the same time, it has acknowledged the states' right to impose some restrictions on the right to vote. The right to vote is a fundamental right and restrictions on it are subject to "strict scrutiny" but in this context "strict scrutiny" means only that judges must independently review the voting regulation or restriction. If restriction is in fact related to important or overriding state interests, the Court will sustin that regulation or restriction. For example, the Court has upheld reasonable age, citizenship, and residency requirements.[11] The determination, however, of what is a reasonable restriction or impairment on the voting right often is difficult to make. In the area of reapportionment the Court has used mathematical criteria to determine whether a state's legislative apportionment has diluted the right to vote.[12] This subject is discussed in a later section.[13] In this section we will focus on the Court's determination of constitutionality of other laws that either impair or dilute the right to vote.

It is important to remember that the Court's rulings concerning the right to vote have come in terms of equal protection. The decision to find the right to vote to be constitutionally "fundamental" and subject to a meaningful form of judicial review may best be described as a substantive due process decision because it is based on an analysis of the importance of that right and it restricts the substance of legislation regulating the exercise of the electoral franchise.[14] How-

---

5. "The right of citizens of the United States to vote in any primary or other election for President or Vice President, for electors for President or Vice President, or for Senator or Representative in Congress, shall not be denied or abridged by the United States or any State by reason of failure to pay any poll tax or other tax." U.S. Const. amend. XXIV, § 1.

6. See Reynolds v. Sims, 377 U.S. 533 (1964).

7. Id. at 562.

8. See Kramer v. Union School District, 395 U.S. 621, 626 (1969).

9. See Harper v. Virginia Bd. of Elections, 383 U.S. 663, 666 (1966).

10. See Katzenbach v. Morgan, 384 U.S. 641 (1966). See Chapter 17 for a discussion of the Congressional power to enforce the Civil War Amendments.

11. The Court has upheld 50 day residency requirements for voting in local elections. Marston v. Lewis, 410 U.S. 679 (1973); Burns v. Fortson, 410 U.S. 686

(1973). The Court has also held that only resident citizens of a municipality need be given a vote in local elections and upheld the denial of voting privileges to persons in unincorporated residential areas adjacent to a city. Holt Civic Club v. Tuscaloosa, 439 U.S. 60 (1978). The Court discussed the validity of age requirements in Oregon v. Mitchell, 400 U.S. 112 (1970); much of that discussion was made irrelevant by the twenty-sixth amendment.

12. See, e.g., Gaffney v. Cummings, 412 U.S. 735 (1973); White v. Weiser, 412 U.S. 783 (1973).

13. See Section IX, infra.

14. Professor John Hart Ely has published a scholarly monograph examining the role of the Supreme Court in a political process based upon democratic ideals. He would circumscribe judicial power by limiting the justices to review of only those laws which seem to transgress express constitutional limitations, operate to disadvantage certain minority groups, or impede the democratic process itself. J. Ely, Democracy and Dis-

ever, the Court has never held that all important governmental positions must be elective, rather than appointive, or that all restrictions on voting activities will be subject to some virtually insurmountable test such as the traditional strict scrutiny-compelling interest test. Thus, in *Rodriguez v. Popular Democratic Party*,[15] the Court upheld a statute of Puerto Rico that provided that vacancies in the Puerto Rican legislature caused by the death, resignation or removal of a legislator would be filled until the next regularly scheduled election by the political party with which the previous incumbent was affiliated. The Court noted that the seventeenth amendment permitted a vacancy in the United States Senate to be filled by appointment by the state's governor and found that "no provision of the federal constitution" mandated the procedures by which a state or Puerto Rico must follow in filling vacancies in its legislature. Similarly, the Court has rejected challenges to "supermajority" requirements that subject the decision on some public issues, such as tax increases, to a voter referendum and require that more than 50 percent of the voters approve the referendum issue.[16]

The Court has not required that all important governmental positions be filled by election or that all important public issues be settled by a majoritarian election process. However, the Supreme Court has required that judges to exercise independent judicial review when examining classifications that allocate voting rights. It is important that the judiciary not simply defer to legislative decisions in this area but, instead, insure that voting classifications promote important societal interests and are not simply attempts by persons in power to impair or dilute the right to vote of disfavored classes.

2. *Restricting the Ballot to Interested Voters*

In *Kramer v. Union Free School District*[17] the Court examined a New York state law that provided that residents of a school district either had to own or lease taxable property or had to have children enrolled in the district's schools before they could vote in school district elections. The appellant in *Kramer*, a resident of the school district, was a bachelor who neither owned or leased any property and was prevented from voting in school elections. He lived with his parents. He argued that, as a resident of the district, any decisions made by the local school board would affect him, and, consequently, he and the class he represented suffered discrimination that violated equal protection. The state, on the other hand, contended that it had an interest in limiting the election to interested persons because they would have a better understanding of the complexity of school affairs. The state argued that the classification achieved this purpose.

The Supreme Court reviewed the New York classification scheme under the strict scrutiny standard, because the law denied persons the fundamental right to vote.[18] It was willing to assume arguendo that a state constitutionally could limit the election to interested voters. Nevertheless, this particular New York method for restricting the vote was unconstitutional because it failed to achieve the purpose for which it was designed "with sufficient precision to justify denying appellant the franchise."[19] The

trust (1980). Professor Ely's work has given rise to reconsideration of, and renewed debate concerning, the role of judicial review in our society. Commentary on Professor Ely's work includes: Grano, Ely's Theory of Judicial Review: Preserving the Significance of the Political Process, 42 Ohio St.L.J. 167 (1981); Nowak, Foreword: Evaluating the Work of the New Libertarian Supreme Court, 7 Hastings Con.L.Q. 263 (1980); Tribe, The Puzzling Persistence of Process-Based Constitutional Theories, 89 Yale L.J. 1063 (1980); Tushnet, Darkness on the Edge of Town: The Contributions of

John Hart Ely to Constitutional Theory, 89 Yale L.J. 1037 (1980).

15. 457 U.S. 1 (1982).

16. Gordon v. Lance, 403 U.S. 1 (1971) (sixty percent voter approval requirement for bond issue upheld).

17. 395 U.S. 621 (1969).

18. Id. at 626–28.

19. Id. at 632.

statute was both underinclusive and overinclusive as the lines it drew excluded interested persons and included persons who only had "a remote and indirect interest in school affairs." [20] Therefore, the law violated the equal protection clause.

The Court in *Kramer* suggested that in some situations a state legitimately could limit an election to interested voters. Such a law would have to restrict the election precisely to those voters that would be primarily affected by the election. In *Salyer Land Co. v. Tulare Water District* [21] the Court encountered such a law. Certain landowners, lessees, and residents of a water storage district in California attacked the constitutionality of the voter qualification provision of the district. They contended the statute violated the equal protection clause because it allowed only landowners to vote in the water storage district elections. They argued that non-landowners had a substantial interest in the operation of the water storage district.[22] The Court, however, believed that the *Kramer* analysis was inappropriate for this case. It observed that the water storage district possessed only limited authority and did not provide general public services like schools or housing. Moreover, the district's operations affect primarily the land within the district, and not residents as residents. Therefore, because the district served a special purpose that had a disproportionate effect on landowners the state could legitimately impose a landownership restriction as a means to establish a demonstrated interest in the election.[23]

It is difficult to reconcile *Kramer* with *Tulare Water District*. But the functions of the water storage district were more specialized than those of a school board and the Court in *Hill v. Stone* [24] found this distinction would reconcile the cases.

In *Hill*, the Court examined the Texas "dual box" voting technique for bond elections. Property owners would place their ballots in one ballot box, and non-property owners in another. Before a bond issue could pass, it must receive not only a majority of the total votes cast but also a majority of the votes cast by property owners. The Court declared this scheme unconstitutional. The Court first noted that any restriction on the vote must promote a compelling state interest unless it is an age, citizenship, or residence requirement. The Court then stated that, if the election is of special interest, the state can limit the election to those who will be primarily affected. The election in *Kramer* was not a special interest election, unlike the election in *Tulare Water District* in the view of the Court. Therefore, the Court reasoned that "as long as the election in question is not one of special interest, any classification restricting the franchise on grounds other than residence, age, and citizenship cannot stand unless the district or State can demonstrate that the classification serves a compelling state interest." [25] In a previous case the Court had declared that a general obligation bond issue is of general interest.[26] Therefore, because the election scheme at issue in *Hill* failed to serve a compelling state interest, the dual box voting device violated the equal protection clause.

As a result of these decisions a state can impose a "demonstrated interest" requirement on the exercise of the franchise only for special interest elections. Although the Court has failed to define exactly the nature of a special interest election, it has stated that it will sustain a "demonstrated interest" restriction for such elections as long as a reasonable basis exists for the limitation. On the other hand, the Court will review strictly any "demonstrated interest" requirement for general interest elections.

20. Id. Accord Phoenix v. Kolodziejski, 399 U.S. 204 (1970); Cipriano v. City of Houma, 395 U.S. 701 (1969).

21. 410 U.S. 719 (1975).

22. Id. at 726.

23. Id. at 729; accord, Associated Enterprises Inc. v. Toltec District, 410 U.S. 743 (1973).

24. 421 U.S. 289 (1975).

25. Id. at 297.

26. Phoenix v. Kolodziejski, 399 U.S. 204 (1970).

Although the Court has not allowed state or local governments to limit referenda or elections for representation on governmental bodies with generalized powers to a subclass of registered voters, the Court appears to have become lenient in its determination of what governmental entities qualify as ones exercising "general governmental power" requiring an unrestricted grant of the franchise to all otherwise eligible voters in compliance with the one person, one vote rule.

In *Ball v. James* [27] the Supreme Court allowed the State of Arizona to create a system for electing directors of a water reclamation district which limited voting eligibility to land owners who were otherwise eligible to vote and which apportioned voting power according to the amount of land owned by each voter. The Arizona system was in essence a one acre, one vote system. Fractional votes were given to those persons who owned less than an acre of land within the district and no vote to tenant farmers. The majority opinion by Mr. Justice Stewart had little trouble in upholding this system under the Court's ruling in *Salyer Land Co. v. Tulare Water District* [28] but the water district in the *Salyer* case had in fact engaged in few activities other than the allocation of irrigation water. The Arizona water district whose voting system was at issue in *Ball* was not only authorized to but, in fact, did generate and sell electric power to a large portion of the state and distribute water to urban areas as well as farming areas, and issued tax exempt bonds. The majority opinion found that the district's absence of a general taxing power or other typical "governmental powers" exempted it

from the one person, one vote rule. While its control over the allocation of water, the regulation of flood control, and the sale of electricity, might have economic repercussions throughout the state or district, it was only a "limited purpose" governmental entity whose actions had a "disproportionate relationship . . . to the specific class of people whom the system makes eligible to vote." [29] The majority upheld the restriction of the right to vote because it found that everyone affected by the operations of a government entity need not be enfranchised and that "the question was whether the effect of the entity's operations on them [the persons allowed to vote] was disproportionately greater than the effect on those seeking the vote." [30] If a state government cannot convince the Court that it has created only a limited purpose governmental entity, or that one group of citizens is distinctly affected by the action of a governmental entity, it will be able to limit the vote to a group of interested voters only if a majority of the justices find that the law bears a reasonable relationship to important statutory objectives.[31]

3. Voting Taxes

The twenty-fourth amendment prohibits the states from imposing a poll tax as a prerequisite for voting in presidential and congressional elections.[32] The amendment does not apply to local or state elections.[33] Nevertheless, the Supreme Court has declared poll taxes for state and local elections unconstitutional under the fourteenth amendment.

In *Harper v. Virginia Board of Elections* [34] the Court entertained a direct chal-

---

27. 451 U.S. 355 (1981).

28. 410 U.S. 719 (1973).

29. Ball v. James, 451 U.S. 355, 369 (1981).

30. 451 U.S. at 369–71.

31. Four justices did dissent to the Court's lenient approach to defining limited versus general purpose elections. Ball v. James, 451 U.S. 355 (1981) (White, J., joined by Brennan, Marshall, and Blackmun, JJ., dissenting). With a slight change in the membership of the Court the approach to such decisions could change in the future.

See also Holt Civic Club v. City of Tuscaloosa, 439 U.S. 60 (1978) (upholding residency requirement for voting in municipal election although municipality exercises some powers over bordering, unincorporated community).

32. U.S. Const. amend. XXIV.

33. See, e.g., Harman v. Forssenius, 380 U.S. 528 (1965).

34. 383 U.S. 663 (1966).

lenge to the Virginia poll tax for state elections. Although the Court recognized that the Constitution did not grant an expressed right to vote in state elections, the opinion stated that once the state granted the franchise the state must follow the dictates of the equal protection clause. The Court reasoned that because the ability to vote has no relationship to wealth, any impairment of the voting right based on wealth would violate the fourteenth amendment. In short, "a state violates the equal protection clause of the fourteenth amendment whenever it makes affluence of the voter or payment of any fee an electoral standard." [35]

4. Literacy tests

Traditionally, the most common restriction on the franchise based on "ability" was the literacy test. The Court considered the constitutionality of literacy tests in *Lassiter v. Northampton Election Board*.[36] The appellants, black citizens from North Carolina, asked the Court to declare unconstitutional on its face a state statute that required a person to pass a literacy test before he could vote in state elections. The Court previously had held literacy tests constitutional in *Guinn v. United States*[37] and it refused to overrule *Guinn*. The *Lassiter* Court believed that the states have broad power to establish requirements that a person must meet before exercising the franchise. As long as the states do not use literacy tests to promote discrimination, the Court will refuse to declare the use of literacy tests unconstitutional.[38] The Court added that the ability to read and write has a direct relationship to the intelligent use of the voting right, and, therefore, classifications based on literacy are neutral.

Although the Court sustained the use of literacy tests, Congress later declared that the states cannot use these tests as a voting requirement. Congress began the process of outlawing literacy tests with the 1965 Voting Rights Act.[39] In a series of cases the Court sustained the Act against several challenges to its constitutionality. The Act gave the Attorney General the authority to prohibit the states from using literacy tests whenever less than half of the state's eligible voters were registered to vote.[40] The Court held that the fifteenth amendment gave Congress the power to prohibit racial discrimination in voting and it deferred to the congressional judgment on the most appropriate means to eliminate any discrimination that existed. Using the same reasoning the Court sustained an extension of the Voting Rights Act that prohibited voting literacy tests anywhere within the nation.[41]

5. Physical Access to Polling Places—Inmates of Correctional Facilities

A state's authority to restrict the franchise based on a physical ability to go to the polls was challenged in *McDonald v. Board of Election Commissioners*.[42] The appellants were inmates confined in the Cook County Jail while awaiting trial. They were qualified voters but were unable to get to the polls to vote. A state statute only allowed Illinois election officials to give absentee ballots to the physically handicapped and to those who would be outside of the county on election day. The appellant failed to qualify for absentee ballots and they contended that the state's refusal to provide them with such ballots violated their fundamental right to vote. A unanimous Court disagreed, but on narrow grounds. The Court first noted that the statute's classifications as to who could receive absentee ballots were not based on race or wealth. The burden, the Court said, speaking through

---

35.   Id. at 666.

36.   360 U.S. 45 (1959).

37.   238 U.S. 347 (1915).

38.   Louisiana v. United States, 380 U.S. 145 (1965); Alabama v. United States, 371 U.S. 37 (1962).

39.   See Katzenbach v. Morgan, 384 U.S. 641 (1966).

40.   See South Carolina v. Katzenbach, 383 U.S. 301, 317 (1966).

41.   See Oregon v. Mitchell, 400 U.S. 112, 131–34 (1970).

42.   394 U.S. 802 (1969).

Chief Justice Warren, was on securing an absentee ballot, not on voting. "It is thus not a right to vote that is at stake here but a claimed right to receive absentee ballots." [43] Moreover, the record was too sparse:

> Appellants agree that the record is barren of any indication that the State might not, for instance, possibly furnish the jails with special polling booth or facilities on election day, or provide guarded transportation to the polls themselves for certain inmates, or entertain motions for temporary reductions in bail to allow some inmates to get to the polls on their own. [44]

The statute denying the appellants absentee ballots was then judged constitutional under traditional, deferential equal protection standards and the state law was upheld.

In *Goosby v. Osser* [45] the Court emphasized that *McDonald* was concerned with a barren record and that a different record, in which it were shown that a statutory scheme absolutely prohibited otherwise confined inmates from voting, might result in a different decision. In *O'Brien v. Skinner* [46] the Court was faced with a sufficient record in a case brought by imprisoned persons who were either awaiting trial or convicted of misdemeanors. None was subject to any voting disability under state law. Chief Justice Burger, who delivered the opinion of the Court, distinguished *McDonald* as a case disposed of only on failure of proof. [47] The New York election and correctional officials refused either to issue ballots, to establish registration or voting facilities within the jail, or to transport the appellants to the polls. The decision as to who would receive

absentee ballots, as the state's election statutes were construed by its highest courts, was found to be "wholly arbitrary." [48] For example, those held in jail awaiting trial in a county other than their residence were permitted to register by mail and vote by absentee ballot, but if a person were confined for the same reason in the county of their own residence, he would be completely denied the ballot. The state cannot, the Court concluded, deny voters "any alternative means of casting their vote although they are legally qualified to vote." [49]

It is unclear how broadly one should read *O'Brien*. The basis of its decision was not that absentee ballots are constitutionally required but that if the state has this absentee procedure it cannot be "wholly arbitrary" in deciding what classes of voters may use it. But the majority's broad concluding dictum supports a view that a state cannot refuse to provide means for qualified citizens to exercise the franchise who are physically unable to get to the polls. In any event, this line of cases should be distinguished from the power of the state to deny completely the ballot (absentee or otherwise) from certain classes of voters, for example, convicted felons. [50]

6. *Residency Requirements*

The Supreme Court has recognized that the state may qualify the voting right with reasonable residency restrictions. Several Court decisions have given some insight into what the Court considers reasonable. In *Carrington v. Rash*, [51] for example, the Court declared unconstitutional a Texas statute that prevented members of the armed

---

43. Id. at 807.

44. Id. at 808, n. 6.

45. 409 U.S. 512 (1973).

46. 414 U.S. 524 (1974).

47. Id. at 529.

48. Id. at 530.

49. Id.

50. The Court, however, has sustained the states' authority to deny the vote to those convicted of felonies even though the convicted individual has completed serving his sentence. The Court found support for the prohibition in section two of the Fourteenth

Amendment. Richardson v. Ramirez, 418 U.S. 24 (1974).

The specific language reads: "But when the right to vote at any election for the choice of electors . . . is denied to any of the male inhabitants, . . . or in any way abridged, except for participation in rebellion, or other crime. . . ." The section also guarantees that equal representation shall be apportioned among the states. The states may exclude from representation only those who participated in a rebellion or other crime. U.S. Const. amend. XIV, § 2.

51. 380 U.S. 89 (1965).

services who moved to Texas from voting in state elections regardless of the length of time they had lived in Texas or their status as property-owners.[52] The Court held that the law violated the equal protection clause of the fourteenth amendment, and that Texas must develop a more precise means to determine the validity of a claim of residency than the challenged statute's classification scheme.[53]

Another residency limitation the states may use to restrict the voting right is to impose a durational residency requirement. The Congress, however, abolished residency requirements for presidential elections with the 1970 Voting Rights Act, and the Court sustained this provision of the Act.[54] Nevertheless, the Voting Rights Act allowed the states to place a durational residency restriction on the right to vote in state elections.

In *Dunn v. Blumstein*[55] the Court considered the constitutionality of Tennessee's durational residency requirement. Tennessee law provided that before a person could vote in state elections that person not only had to meet age and citizenship requirements but also had to be a resident of the state for one year and of the county for three months. Although the *Dunn* Court acknowledged that the states can require their voters to be residents, this particular durational requirement was unwarranted and violated the fourteenth amendment. Tennessee's durational residency restriction on the right to vote impaired both voting rights and the right to travel. The Court reasoned that other means were available to determine bona fide residence and that with the prevalence of mass communications, citizens who have moved into an area can learn about local affairs quickly.[56] Consequently, Tennessee's one year requirement was invalid. The test appears to be one of reasonableness. The Court has upheld a fifty-day durational

restriction.[57] A restriction of less than two months may be necessary to verify voter lists or records and prevent fraud.

The exercise of extra-territorial jurisdiction by a municipality over nonresidents who could not vote in municipal elections was approved in *Holt Civic Club v. Tuscaloosa.*[58] Holt, an unincorporated community, was within three miles of Tuscaloosa, Alabama; under relevant Alabama statutes Holt residents were subjected to the police and sanitary regulations of Tuscaloosa, a major municipal entity. Under these statutes, Tuscaloosa also had the power to license certain businesses, trades, and professions in Holt; however, license fees collected by a city from businesses in an unincorporated community could not exceed one-half the fee charged similar businesses in the city. Holt residents sought a ruling that the extension of Tuscaloosa's jurisdiction over them was unconstitutional because they were not given the opportunity to participate in elections for city officials; they sought invalidation of the extra-territorial powers of the city or, in the alternative, extension of the right to vote in municipal elections to all those subjected to the municipality's jurisdiction.

In *Holt*, the Supreme Court, in a majority opinion by Justice Rehnquist, rejected the equal protection and due process claims of the Holt residents. In so doing the majority opinion went through three analytical steps relevant to determination of similar extra-territorial jurisdiction cases. First, the majority concluded that this case involved no denial of the right to vote that was cognizable under the equal protection clause or previous rulings of the Court. The opinion noted that the previous decisions of the Court concerning the exclusion of some persons from the voting process because of residency or special interest requirements had invalidated only unreasonable durational residen-

---

52. Id. at 89–90, n. 1.

53. Id. at 75–76.

54. See Oregon v. Mitchell, 400 U.S. 112, 118–19 (1970) (opinion of Black, J.).

55. 405 U.S. 330 (1972).

56. Id. at 349–60.

57. See Marston v. Lewis, 410 U.S. 679 (1973); Burns v. Fortson, 410 U.S. 686 (1973).

58. 439 U.S. 60 (1978).

cy requirements and impermissible definitions of the special interest that could be solely represented in an election.[59] The Court found that the use of residency as a requirement for voting was permissible because the use of a governmental "impact analysis" to determine who should vote in city elections was unworkable. Municipal actions often may affect many persons living immediately outside city boundaries in a variety of ways. The Court therefore concluded that "the line heretofore marked by this Court's voting qualification decision coincides with the geographical boundary of the governmental unit at issue."[60]

The second step was to determine if there was another equal protection problem with the classification. If there were no voting rights issue involved in the analysis then the equal protection test to be applied to this economic and social welfare legislation was the traditional rational basis test. This test required only a determination of "whether any state of facts reasonably may be conceived to justify Alabama's system of police jurisdiction."[61] The majority concluded that the Alabama legislature might have conceived that the extension of city jurisdiction was a reasonable means of facilitating possible future annexation of territory to cities, helping to insure that the population outside of its cities do not go without basic municipal services, and insuring that businesses were regulated without the extraction of onerous license fees.

In the third phase of its analysis in *Holt*, the Court found no basis for a due process claim to participate in the election. The opinion noted that the Court has never declared any generalized right to vote under the due process clause, and upheld the law since the classification was not totally arbitrary. Justice Brennan, joined by Justices White and Marshall in dissent, would have found that the Alabama system violated the equal protection clause.[62] Because the residents of Holt were directly affected by Tuscaloosa's police jurisdiction and governed in a substantial manner by the officials of Tuscaloosa, the dissenters would have required the city and state to demonstrate a "compelling interest" in denying the franchise to the residents of the unincorporated area. Indeed, Justice Brennan found that the distinction between city residents and unincorporated community residents to be "irrational"; the city was not merely affecting people in the surrounding area, it was governing them as it did city residents. However, this view was rejected by the majority and it would appear that most statutes of this type will be approved if they are arguably reasonable and not in fact based on an invidious classification such as race.[63]

7. Restrictions Based on Party Affiliation

States often conduct primary elections before the final general election. The primary election will provide political parties with a means to select their candidates for the next

---

59. See the cases examined previously in this section. See also Evans v. Cornman, 398 U.S. 419 (1970) (persons living on the grounds of the National Institute of Health, a federal enclave located within Maryland's boundaries, cannot be denied the right to vote in Maryland elections; the state treats such persons as residents in its census and in determining congressional apportionment and the fiction that the enclave is not part of Maryland is rejected). *Evans* was specifically distinguished in *Holt* because the NIH inhabitants were, under a federal law, residents of Maryland.

60. 439 U.S. at 70.

61. 439 U.S. at 73.

62. 439 U.S. at 79 (Brennan, J. dissenting, joined by White & Marshall, JJ.).

63. If the voting classification or boundary was drawn on the basis of race it would be invalid, see Gomillion v. Lightfoot, 364 U.S. 339 (1960).

Justice Stevens, in a concurring opinion, appeared to use a more realistic test, approaching one of the middle level standards of review. Yet he concluded that the residents of Holt were not denied equal protection because he found that their ability to vote for county, state, and federal officials allowed them to participate in the governance process and that residents had not been subjected to clearly unreasonable burdens or cost for municipal services. However, Justice Stevens left open the possibility that he would vote against the extension of extraterritorial jurisdiction in particular cases wherein the exercise of jurisdiction, or the denial of the vote, could be demonstrated to be truly arbitrary or invidious. Holt Civic Club v. City of Tuscaloosa, 439 U.S. 76–79 (1978) (Stevens, J., concurring).

at-large election the state will conduct. To prohibit voters who belong to one political party from voting for a weak candidate in another party's primary, the states may restrict a person's ability to vote in party primary elections.[64] In *Rosario v. Rockefeller*[65] the state of New York required its voters to register with the state and to select their party thirty days before the November election; otherwise they could not vote in the next primary. The registration deadline generally occurred eight to eleven months before the primary. The primary registration statute was challenged as unconstitutional because it placed a limitation on the right to vote. The Court, however, sustained the law because it furthered the legitimate state goal of preventing party raiding.[66] The time limit the statute imposed bore a reasonable relationship to that goal because a voter probably would not register in one party when he intended to vote the other party's ticket in the November election.[67] If the relationship between the means and the end had not been so direct, the Court would have declared the law void.

The party affiliation statute challenged in *Kusper v. Pontikes*[68] was related directly to the legitimate state purpose of preventing voting raids in party primaries, but the Court declared it unconstitutional. The Court held that the law placed unnecessary restrictions on the voting right. Illinois prohibited a person from voting in the primary election of one political party if that person had voted in another party's primary election anytime within the previous twenty-three months.[69] The Court reasoned that the Illinois provision "locked-in" a voter into

a particular party affiliation and the only way a person could break free was to forego voting in primaries for almost two years.[70] The Court believed that less drastic alternatives were available to Illinois to prevent party raiding.

Justice Blackmun dissented in *Kusper*.[71] He believed Illinois' scheme had a more rational relationship to its goal than New York's. New York used a flat time limit that would affect not only "primary raiders" but also persons who simply failed to register through an oversight. Illinois, "on the other hand, affects only party switchers,"[72] because those who regularly vote in party primaries usually will belong to "the group most amenable to organized raiding."[73] Moreover, the Justice reasoned that the twenty-three month limitation in practice amounted only to a one year limitation and in this context the state legislators had drawn the classification scheme as narrowly as possible.

8. *Racial Restrictions*

Restrictions on the voting right based on racial classifications are unconstitutional. A series of cases commonly called the *White Primary Cases*,[74] clearly established that a state could not exclude a minority race from the franchise. In the first of the *White Primary Cases, Nixon v. Herndon*,[75] the Court declared unconstitutional a Texas law that expressly excluded blacks from voting in the Democratic primary. The law violated the fourteenth amendment because it impaired the right to vote on account of race or color. Later White Primary Cases declared unconstitutional other schemes that states adopted

---

64. See, Note, Developments in the Law—Elections, 88 Harv.L.Rev. 1111, 1164 (1975).

65. 410 U.S. 752 (1973).

66. Id. at 760–62.

67. Id. at 762.

68. 414 U.S. 51 (1973).

69. Id. at 57.

70. Id.

71. 414 U.S. 51, 61 (1973) (dissenting opinion, Blackmun, J.).

72. Id. at 65.

73. Id.

74. Terry v. Adams, 345 U.S. 461 (1953); Smith v. Allwright, 321 U.S. 649 (1944); Nixon v. Condon, 286 U.S. 73 (1932); Nixon v. Herndon, 273 U.S. 536 (1927). On the White Primary Cases, see Chapter 16, Section VIII, C.

75. 273 U.S. 536 (1927).

in attempts to circumvent *Nixon v. Herndon.*[76]

Not only does the Constitution prohibit the states from expressly infringing the right to vote on the basis of race, but it also prohibits the states from applying facially neutral laws to disenfranchise racial minorities. In *Gomillion v. Lightfoot*[77] an Alabama statute altered the city limits of Tuskegee. It changed the shape of the city from a square to a twenty-eight sided figure. The record also indicated that the modification of the city boundaries removed nearly 400 black voters but no white voters from the city.[78] The opinion stated that the Constitution limits the states' regulatory powers over their political subdivisions. The Court held that this affirmative legislative action deprived citizens of the vote on the basis of race and thus Alabama had violated the fifteenth amendment. The Court recognized the racial purpose of the state's action, and declared the law unconstitutional.[79]

In *Mobile v. Bolden,*[80] the Supreme Court refused to invalidate a city commission system whereby all three members of the city's governing body were elected at-large. The system was challenged by black voters who claimed that the city's refusal to elect commission members by district ensured that no black person could ever be elected to city government. In accordance with the Court's rulings concerning the proof of racial discrimination through statistical evidence, the challenge to the city's election system had to be dismissed because of the plaintiff's failure to prove that the at-large voting system was created or maintained for a "racially discriminatory purpose." Statistical proof of the racially discriminatory impact of a

voting regulation is relevant but not determinative proof in cases wherein a governmental act is challenged on the basis of the fourteenth or fifteenth amendment.[81] In *Rogers v. Lodge,*[82] the Supreme Court upheld federal district court and court of appeals rulings finding that an at-large election system for the commissioners of a rural county violated the equal protection clause. In *Rogers,* the majority opinion found that the lower courts had properly required plaintiffs to prove that the voting system was maintained for a racially discriminatory purpose and that there was sufficient evidence that that standard had been met in this case. It was not only the fact that no black person had ever been elected to the county board of commissioners in *Rogers* that supported the lower federal courts' rulings. Those courts had also found evidence that the system was maintained by persons holding political power in the county so that they could consistently disregard the interests and concerns of members of racial minorities within the county. The Supreme Court found that this issue of intent was primarily a factual matter and it would not disturb the finding of the two lower federal courts. Election regulations that have a disparate impact on minority races will not be invalidated on that basis alone; only those laws which are enacted or maintained for the purpose of diluting or impairing the votes of members of a racial minority will be held to violate the equal protection guarantee or the fifteenth amendment. However, Congress, by statute, may invalidate state or local laws which have a discriminatory impact on the voting power of minority racial groups.[83]

---

76. Terry v. Adams, 345 U.S. 461 (1953); cf. Georgia v. United States, 411 U.S. 526 (1973); Tancil v. Woolls, 379 U.S. 19 (1964).

77. 364 U.S. 339 (1960).

78. Id. at 341.

79. Id. at 342. For a detailed discussion of this case, see Chapter 16, Section I, D.

80. 446 U.S. 55 (1980).

81. See Section I, D of this Chapter regarding the use of statistical evidence to prove discrimination.

82. 102 S.Ct. 3272 (1982).

83. See generally, Chapter 17, Congressional Enforcement of Civil Rights, and Section ID of this chapter. Congress may regulate or prohibit state election regulations which have the effect of diluting the voting rights of members of racial minorities even if those regulations were not enacted for a discriminatory purpose. Rome v. United States, 446 U.S. 156 (1980).

The Supreme Court has held that a federal district court did not exceed its authority under the Voting Rights Act by conditioning the approval of a reappor-

9. Adjusting the Majority Requirement

The Court has recognized that the states legitimately may require more than a simple majority of the vote cast before the government can adopt certain programs. In *Gordon v. Lance*,[84] for example, voters challenged the constitutionality of a provision in the West Virginia Constitution that prevented political subdivisions of the state from incurring bonded indebtedness unless sixty percent of the voters approved the bond issue in a referendum. They contended that the provision violated the fourteenth amendment; the Court rejected the contention. The state constitutional scheme did not single out any discrete or insular minority. Moreover, the Court realized that although "any departure from strict majority rule gives disproportionate power to the minority,"[85] the Constitution fails to contain any requirement that a simple majority must always prevail.

The Court in *Town of Lockport v. Citizens for Community Action*[86] confronted another challenge to a state law that required more than a simple majority before a political subdivision of a state could act. A New York statute required that, before a county could adopt a new county charter, a majority of all the voters in the cities of the county must approve the charter and also a majority of all the non-city voters must approve the charter. In this particular case a majority of the city voters had approved the new charter. A majority of the non-city voters, however, had rejected the charter. Even though an overall majority of all the county voters had approved the charter, the measure was defeated. The disappointed city voters contended that this concurrent majority requirement violated the equal protection clause of the fourteenth amendment. The federal district court agreed and held that the concurrent majority requirement violated the one person-one vote principle. The Supreme Court, however, reversed. The Court decided that the one person-one vote analysis was inappropriate. That analysis is applicable for the election of representatives not for referendums.[87] A referendum is an expression of direct voter will. Consequently, the Court concluded that two considerations became important. First, the Court must consider whether a genuine difference in interests exists in the two groups of voters the statute created. Second, if a genuine difference does exist, the Court must determine whether the enhancement of the minority voting strength worked an "invidious discrimination."[88] The Court found a genuine difference in interests because the cities were more autonomous from county government than were non-city areas. Moreover, the Court failed to find that the statutory scheme invidiously discriminated against city voters. Because such referenda can shift political power from towns to the city, the state can recognize "constituencies with separate and potentially opposing interests."[89] Thus, the Court held that the New York concurrent majority requirement did not violate the equal protection clause.

B. The Right to Be a Candidate

1. Introduction

The Constitution contains no express provision that guarantees the right to become a candidate.[1] The states are free, therefore, to create restrictions on the ability to become a candidate, but the restrictions creat-

---

tionment plan for a racially divided city (whose annexations reduced its Black population from 45 to 40 percent of the city population) on elimination of a majority vote requirement for the election of two of three at-large seats on a nine-member city council. Port Arthur v. United States, 103 S.Ct. 530 (1982).

84.   403 U.S. 1 (1971), on the requirements of "one man, one vote" and super-majorities, see Chapter 16, Section IX, C, 6.

85.   403 U.S. at 6.

86.   430 U.S. 259 (1977).

87.   430 U.S. at 266.

88.   430 U.S. at 268.

89.   430 U.S. at 271.

1.   See Note, Development in the Law—Elections, 88 Harv.L.Rev. 1111, 1218 (1975) [hereinafter cited as Elections].

ed must not violate provisions of the Constitution that are of general application.[2] The states have exercised their discretion and have placed conditions on the right to candidacy. They have justified the creation of these conditions with several arguments. First, the restrictions on the right to become a candidate have helped the state to limit the size of the ballot, and thus reduce the potential for voter confusion.[3] Second, limiting the number of potential candidates will help insure that the candidate that eventually wins will have received a majority of the popular vote. Having an elected official who has received a majority of the popular vote will give citizens additional confidence in the ability of the official and faith in the democratic form of government. The state does not have an interest in minimizing the number of candidates who appear on the ballot but it has an interest in political stability.[4] Finally, restricting the right to candidacy will help avoid the potential for frivolous candidacies and thus preserve the integrity of the electoral process.[5] The Supreme Court has recognized these reasons as legitimate interests of the states and as acceptable justification for some restrictions on access to the ballot.[6]

The states have used several methods to qualify the right to become a candidate. These methods include: (1) wealth restrictions;[7] (2) residency restrictions;[8] (3) property ownership requirements;[9] (4) party affiliation[10] and demonstrated support limitations,[11] and (5) racial classifications.[12] Although the Supreme Court has recognized

the power of the states to control the electoral process in some ways, it also has held that various constitutional provisions will limit the state's power to regulate access to the ballot. Ballot access restrictions, for example, must follow the dictates of the equal protection clause.[13] Moreover, the individual rights that the Constitution protects may have more weight with the Court than the right of the states to regulate the right to candidacy. The right to vote and the right to associate are the principal individual rights that may restrict the ability of the states to control candidate access to the ballot.[14] Consequently, the Court may use several constitutional provisions to void state restrictions on the right to become a candidate. Although the Supreme Court has recognized that basic constitutional rights are intertwined in the electoral process, the Court also has noted that elections are largely political creatures and that the courts should refrain from getting too involved in basically political decisions. Restrictions on candidacy for elective office impair the right of voters to cast a ballot for the candidate of their choice, protected by the fourteenth amendment due process and equal protection clauses, and the right of persons to associate in the expression of views in a political campaign, which is protected by the first amendment. Therefore, the judiciary must independently scrutinize the basis for such legislation to insure that ballot access restrictions are a reasonable, nondiscriminatory means of promoting important state interests.[15]

2. See e.g. Storer v. Brown, 415 U.S. 724, 728 (1974); Bullock v. Carter, 405 U.S. 134, 142–43 (1972).

3. See e.g., Storer v. Brown, 415 U.S. 724, 732 (1974).

4. See Anderson v. Celebrezze, 103 S.Ct. 1564 (1983); William v. Rhodes, 393 U.S. 23, 32 (1968).

5. See American Party of Texas v. White, 415 U.S. 767, 781–85 (1974).

6. Id.

7. See Lubin v. Panish, 415 U.S. 709 (1974).

8. See, e.g., Chimento v. Stark, 353 F.Supp. 1211 (D.N.H.1973), aff'd mem. 414 U.S. 802 (1973).

9. See Turner v. Fouche, 396 U.S. 346 (1970).

10. See McCarthy v. Briscoe, 429 U.S. 1317 (1976).

11. See Williams v. Rhodes, 393 U.S. 23 (1968).

12. Anderson v. Martin, 375 U.S. 399 (1969). Cf. United Jewish Organizations v. Carey, 430 U.S. 144 (1977).

13. Bullock v. Carter, 405 U.S. 134, 141 (1974).

14. See, e.g., Williams v. Rhodes, 393 U.S. 23, 30 (1968).

15. See, Anderson v. Celebrezze, 103 S.Ct. 1564 (1983) (invalidating March deadline for filing nominating petition of independent presidential candidate for November election). The method of judicial review used by the majority in *Anderson* involved the open

The ability of persons to be a candidate for political office is certainly intertwined with the freedom of choice of voters to place persons into electoral office. Nevertheless, it would be misleading to characterize the right to be a candidate as a fundamental right which requires the Court to employ "strict scrutiny" and the "compelling interest" test to all laws restricting candidate access to the ballot. Laws which regulate candidacy for elective office certainly should be subject to independent judicial review. While the justices should not impose unduly strict limitations on states' abilities to promote legitimate goals through regulating the candidacy of persons for elective office, the justices should not simply defer to legislative judgments in this area.

The difficulty of employing a standard of review, such as a balancing test, which is less than strict, but not merely deferential is demonstrated by the Court's decision in *Clements v. Fashing*.[16] In *Clements* the Court upheld provisions of the Texas constitution that restricted a public official's ability to become a candidate for a public office other than that office which he already held. The Texas constitution prohibited certain state and county officeholders from becoming candidates for another state or federal office. These provisions were upheld by a 5 to 4 vote and without a majority opinion. Four justices who voted to uphold the law found that candidacy for elective office was not a fundamental right which subjected all candidate regulations to strict judicial scrutiny.[17] Because the law did not allocate the ability

to become a candidate based upon wealth nor impose arbitrary burdens on small political parties or independent candidates, these justices found no reason to independently review the reasonableness of the regulation. Justice Stevens, concurring in the judgment of the Court, found that requiring certain state officers to forego seeking another elective office until they fulfilled their duties, and their term of office did not impinge upon any interest protected by the federal constitution.[18] It is unfortunate that there was no majority opinion in this case and that some justices made it appear as if there should be no independent judicial review of laws regulating candidacy for elective office that do not involve wealth classifications or small political parties. The dissent in *Clements* accused the majority of abdicating the proper judicial role in the review of candidacy classification by failing to require the classification of officeholders prohibited from being candidates for another office was reasonably related to a legitimate legislative purpose.[19] However, the dissent failed to focus on the question of whether all candidacy regulations should be subjected to strict judicial review or whether the Court should only subject to strict scrutiny those classifications which appeared to disadvantage a disfavored classification of persons such as economically poor persons or independent candidates.[20]

2. *Wealth Restrictions*

Many states require potential candidates for public office to pay a filing fee before

---

use of a balancing test. The justices balanced the degree of impact of the ballot restriction on first and fourteenth amendment rights against the interests asserted by the state and the relationship between the restriction and these interests. See also, Cousins v. Wigoda, 419 U.S. 477 (1975); see generally, Rotunda, Constitutional and Statutory Restrictions on Political Parties in the Wake of Cousins v. Wigoda, 53 Tex.L. Rev. 935 (1975).

16. 102 S.Ct. 2836 (1982). Justice Rehnquist delivered an opinion which was a majority opinion as to certain jurisdictional and first amendment issues. The first amendment aspect of the case is noted in Chapter 18. Those portions of Justice Rehnquist's opinion which addressed the equal protection issue was joined

only by Chief Justice Burger and Justices Powell and O'Connor.

17. 102 S.Ct. 2843–44 (Rehnquist, J., joined by Burger, C.J., and Powell & O'Connor, JJ.)

18. Clements v. Fashing, 102 S.Ct. 2836, 2848 (1982) (Stevens, J., concurring).

19. Clements v. Fashing, 102 S.Ct. 2836, 2850 (1982) (Brennan, Jr., joined by Marshall, Blackmun & White, JJ., dissenting).

20. 102 S.Ct. at 2854. The dissent did not address this point because the dissenters believed that the classification could not survive even the minimal rationality test.

the state will place their names on the ballot. In *Bullock v. Carter* [21] the appellees challenged the constitutionality of the Texas filing fee requirement. The appellees met all the other qualifications necessary to become candidates for public office but could not afford to pay the requisite fee of $1000. These candidates, contended that the fee requirement violated the equal protection clause.

As a preliminary issue the *Bullock* Court had to determine the level of review it would use to assess the constitutionality of the Texas wealth restriction. The opinion recognized that the states had broad powers under the Constitution to establish the rules and regulations for elections.[22] Moreover, the state of Texas imposed the fee requirement on candidates and not voters, and the Constitution did not explicitly guarantee any right to candidacy. Nevertheless, the filing fee requirement did affect voters because it limited the choice on the ballot. The size of the fee at issue was "patently exclusionary" and could exclude qualified candidates from the election.[23] Consequently, the effect on qualified voters was direct and obvious; their choice of candidates became limited and the poor voter may not have a qualified representative running for office. Because the filing fee requirement affected the fundamental right to vote, the Court would use strict scrutiny to review the Texas law.[24]

In support of the filing fee requirement the state argued that the fee was necessary to limit the size of the ballot and to frustrate frivolous candidates. Furthermore, the state contended that the filing fee helped finance the election. The Court acknowledged the state's legitimate interest in protecting the integrity of the ballot, but the Court also observed that appellees were not unwilling to pay the fee but simply were unable to pay. Hence, the filing fee requirement excluded legitimate as well as frivo-

lous candidates.[25] As to Texas' financing argument the Court held that the purpose of financing the election served a rational basis for the fee requirement. However, the opinion employed a strict scrutiny level of review and the state failed to show that the fee requirement was necessary to finance the election.[26] Moreover, the force of the financing argument was diluted by the realization that candidates for statewide office paid a lower fee than candidates for local office. Hence, the *Bullock* Court held that the Texas filing fee requirement was unconstitutional because it violated the equal protection clause.

Two years after *Bullock* the Court decided *Lubin v. Panish* [27] in which candidates for local and state offices attacked the constitutionality of the California filing fee requirement. The fee equaled two per cent of the annual salary of the state office sought. The Court decided that the California filing fee violated the equal protection clause of the fourteenth amendment insofar as it was applied to indigent candidates. Again the Court recognized the legitimate needs of the state to keep the size of the ballot manageable. To achieve that end, however, the state must adopt means that will not "unreasonably burden either a minority party's or individual candidate's equally important interest in the continued availability of political opportunity." [28] The states must allow voters a reasonable choice of candidates, and an absolute filing fee requirement unconstitutionally limited that choice. The opinion reasoned that the state may require a filing fee only if a reasonable alternative to the fee exists to gain access to the ballot. The Court believed that a minimum wealth requirement does not reflect a potential candidate's popular support or the seriousness of the candidacy. Hence, the state must provide alternative means for indigent candidates to qualify for a ballot position.

---

21. 405 U.S. 134 (1972).

22. Id. at 141.

23. Id. at 143.

24. Id. at 144.

25. Id. at 146.

26. Id. at 147.

27. 415 U.S. 709 (1974).

28. Id. at 716.

3. Residency Restrictions

State election laws often require persons running for elective office to meet durational residency requirements. Lower federal courts and state courts have considered durational residency restrictions on the right to be a candidate on several occasions.[29] The Supreme Court has affirmed by memorandum several three-judge district court decisions that have decided the constitutionality of such limitations on the right to access to the ballot.[30] But memorandum affirmances are of limited precedential value,[31] and the constitutionality of durational residency requirements is still an open question.[32]

A three-judge federal district court in *Chimento v. Stark*[33] sustained the constitutionality of New Hampshire's durational residency requirement for elective office. The New Hampshire statute required gubernatorial candidates to have resided within the state for seven years before running for office. Those challenging the statute's constitutionality contended that the law violated the equal protection clause by impairing the right to travel and the right to associate. Because the *Chimento* court agreed that the statute affected these fundamental rights, it decided that it must use a strict standard of review.[34] The court, however, sustained the law. It reasoned that the durational residency requirement only delayed the opportunity to become a candidate. Therefore, the court decided that the law only imposed a minimal burden on potential candidates and voters. Moreover, the state imposed the seven year requirement only on candidates for the state's highest elective office. The

court suggested it might have reached a different result if the requirement existed for lesser public offices.[35] Finally, the court concluded that the state had a legitimate interest in creating the seven year durational requirement. The restriction helps insure not only that candidates will become familiar with local issues, but also that local voters will become familiar with the candidates. Therefore, the restriction both can promote the integrity of the election process and avoid voter confusion.

Frustrated candidates for elective office face a major constitutional obstacle whenever they challenge durational residency requirements. The Constitution itself requires candidates for federal elective office to meet certain residency standards.[36] Therefore unless the residency requirement is patently unreasonable in length for the particular elective office the courts usually have sustained such qualifications on the right to candidacy. The Supreme Court, however, has not explained what constitutes a reasonable and constitutional residency requirement.

4. Property Ownership Requirements

To date the Supreme Court has assessed the constitutionality of a property ownership restriction on the access to ballot position only in *Turner v. Fouche*,[37] where black citizens brought a class action challenging the constitutionality of Georgia's statutory restriction on school board candidates. Georgia limited school board membership to those with an interest in real property. This restriction was found to violate the equal

---

29. See, e.g., Woodward v. City of Deerfield Beach, 538 F.2d 1081 (5th Cir. 1976); Sununu v. Stark, 383 F.Supp. 1287 (D.N.H.1974); Chimento v. Stark, 353 F.Supp. 1211 (D.N.H.1973), aff'd mem. 414 U.S. 802 (1973).

30. See, e.g., Chimento v. Stark, 353 F.Supp. 1211 (D.N.H.1973), aff'd mem. 414 U.S. 802 (1973).

31. See Chapter 2, Section II, C.

32. See Comment, Durational Residence Requirements for Candidates, 40 U.Chi.L.Rev. 357 (1973); Note, Age and Durational Residency Requirements as Qualifications for Candidacy: A Violation of Equal Protection?, 1973 U.Ill.L.F. 161.

33. 353 F.Supp. 1211 (D.N.H.1973), aff'd mem. 414 U.S. 802 (1973). Accord, Sununu v. Stark, 383 F.Supp. 1287 (D.N.H.1974), aff'd mem. 420 U.S. 958 (1975) (seven years residence for state senatorial candidate).

34. 353 F.Supp. at 1214.

35. Id. at 1215–16 n. 10.

36. U.S.Const. art. I, §§ 2, 3 and art. II, § 1.

37. 396 U.S. 346 (1970); Elections, supra note 1, at 1220–21.

protection clause. The Court stated that the appellants "have a federal constitutional right to be considered for public service without the burden of invidiously discriminatory qualifications."[38] The Court reasoned that the property ownership restriction failed to serve a valid state purpose. The status of being a non-freeholder did not reflect any lack of attachment to the local community or the local schools. Hence, Georgia's classification scheme for school board candidates was unconstitutional.

5. Party Affiliation and Demonstrated Support Requirements

A party affiliation qualification requires persons who want to run for elective office to be a member of certain political parties; this requirement gives candidates who are members of major political parties certain advantages over independent candidates.[39] In *Storer v. Brown*[40] California prohibited independent candidates from running in the general election if the candidates either had voted in an immediately preceding party primary or had registered their party affiliation with a qualified party within one year of the primary. Storer challenged the constitutionality of the prohibition. He had been a registered Democrat and the state had disqualified him from running as an independent candidate. He contended that the provision violated his first amendment rights and the dictates of the fourteenth amendment.[41] The Supreme Court, however, sustained the law. The opinion held that the Constitution did not prevent California from adopting a party affiliation statute. The state, however, must adopt reasonable alternative means for independent candidates and minor political parties to get a ballot position, and the alternative means must not place too heavy

a burden on the right to vote and the right to associate.

The Court noted in *Storer* that the state has an interest in imposing some candidate qualifications to avoid voter confusion, to prevent burdening the election process, and to facilitate the election winner receiving a majority.[42] The California party affiliation restriction helped achieve these goals because it kept a loser in the party primary from running in the general election. Therefore, the state reduced the potential for political factionalism and splintered parties, and prevented the general election ballot from becoming a forum for intra-party feuds. Moreover, the state provided the necessary alternative means for ballot qualification. A party member who intended to run as an independent could disaffiliate himself from the party before the deadline and, by using the alternative methods to a primary election, gain a position on the general election ballot. Consequently, the Court found the California party affiliation provision constitutional.

Justice Powell, sitting as a Circuit Justice, summarized the Court's present position on party affiliation statutes in *McCarthy v. Briscoe.*[43] Supporters of Eugene McCarthy sought a mandatory injunction to force the state of Texas to place his name on the general election ballot as a presidential candidate. Texas required presidential candidates to be members of a major organized political party before they could gain access to the ballot. The only alternative for independent candidates was a "write-in" campaign. Justice Powell granted the injunction. He noted that the Court in *Storer v. Brown* rejected the idea that a state could force an independent candidate to join or organize a political party to gain access to the ballot. The state could require some show-

---

38. 396 U.S. at 362. The Court has summarily reversed a state court decision that upheld a requirement that appointed members of an airport commission (with some governmental powers) own property in the locality. The Supreme Court merely cited *Turner* and reversed the state decision. Chappelle v. Greater Baton Rouge Airport District, 431 U.S. 159 (1977).

39. Elections, supra note 1, at 1124–25.

40. 415 U.S. 724 (1974).

41. Id. at 727.

42. Id. at 732.

43. 429 U.S. 1317 (1976).

ing of demonstrated support but it had to provide alternative means to an independent candidate to get a position on the ballot. Therefore, Texas had to place former Senator McCarthy's name on the ballot as a candidate for President.

The states usually impose demonstrated support requirements on independent candidates or minor political parties.[44] Typically, the demonstrated support statute requires independent candidates or minor parties to submit petitions containing a certain number of signatures from qualified voters before they can receive access to the ballot. The number of signatures required is often related to the percentage of votes cast in the last general election. States will relieve a political party of the petition requirement if the party's candidates received a minimum percentage of the votes cast in the previous election. In short, these statutes require independent candidates or minor political parties to demonstrate their popular support before they gain a ballot position.

The Court has considered several challenges to the constitutionality of demonstrated support requirements. One of the first cases was *Williams v. Rhodes.*[45] Members of a minor political party contended that the Ohio demonstrated support statute strongly favored the established political parties, and thus violated the equal protection clause. Ohio required new political parties to submit petitions with signatures of qualified voters equaling in number fifteen per cent of the number of votes cast in the last gubernatorial election. Moreover, Ohio had an early filing deadline for the petition. No petition was required if the party received ten per cent of the vote in the previous gubernatorial election. The state contended that the law was constitutional because it furthered three state interests. First, the measure promoted the two party system. Second, the law would insure that

the voters would elect a candidate with a majority vote. Third, the statute helped prevent voter confusion, the standard state interest argument. The Court reviewed the requirements under the strict scrutiny standard as it burdened both the right to vote and the right to associate.[46] Consequently, the state had to justify these burdens with a compelling state interest and the Court found the proffered state interests less than compelling. Although the Ohio scheme did support the two party system, it did so by favoring two particular parties—the Democratic and Republican parties. The Court agreed that Ohio's law assured the election of majority candidates but it did so by suppressing the growth of new parties. Finally, the Court acknowledged that the statute helped avoid voter confusion, but the Court believed that the means Ohio chose to achieve this goal were not necessary to that end. Thus, it could not justify the burden on the fundamental rights to vote and associate.[47] Under this strict level of review the Court found that the Ohio law violated the equal protection clause.

A demonstrated support statute may discriminate against some voters as well as some candidates. In *Moore v. Ogilvie*[48] Illinois required independent candidates for President and Vice President to submit petitions with signatures from 25,000 qualified voters. The Illinois law, however, also required that among these signatures at least 200 signatures had to come from each of fifty different Illinois counties out of the state's 102 counties. The state argued that this additional requirement was necessary to insure that the independent candidate had statewide support. The Supreme Court found that the law discriminated against the more populous counties. Nearly 94% of Illinois voters, who lived in only forty-nine counties, could not form a new party, but 6.6% of the voters in the remaining 53 coun-

44. Note, Developments in the Law—Elections, 88 Harv.L.Rev. 1111, 1124–25 (1973).

45. 393 U.S. 23 (1968).

46. Id. at 30.

47. Id. at 33–34.

48. 394 U.S. 814 (1969).

ties could form a new party.[49] The law violated the principle of equality among voters and was an unreasonable burden on candidates.

After *Moore v. Ogilvie*, the Illinois election code required that new political parties and independent candidates obtain the signatures of 25,000 qualified voters to appear on the ballot for statewide elections; they did not have to receive a specific number of votes from specific counties, the requirement which was invalidated in *Moore*. However, the Illinois election code required that independent candidates, or candidates of new parties, for offices of political subdivisions in Illinois had to receive signatures from at least five percent of the number of people who had voted in the previous election of that particular subdivision. The distinction in the statute, as applied to City of Chicago or Cook County elections, required that these candidates receive substantially more signatures to gain access to the Chicago or Cook County ballots than would similar independent candidates for statewide office. Thus, an independent candidate would need 35,000 signatures for inclusion on the ballot in a Chicago election, while a candidate for statewide office would need only 25,000 signatures. In *Illinois State Board of Elections v. Socialist Workers Party*,[50] the Supreme Court unanimously held that this political subdivision requirement violated equal protection and that the new political

cal parties or independent candidates could not be required to obtain more signatures than the statewide requirement (25,000) for city or county elections. The majority opinion, by Justice Marshall, found the classification subject to the compelling interest test because it affected the fundamental rights of association and voting. Justice Marshall's opinion seemed to indicate that exclusion of frivolous candidates was an acceptable purpose for the legislation, although he described that goal only as a "legitimate" one. The majority held that the subdivision signature requirement was invalid because it was not the most narrow, or least restrictive, means of excluding frivolous candidates from the ballot.[51]

Not all demonstrated support states are unconstitutional. The Supreme Court sustained Georgia's demonstrated support requirement in *Jenness v. Fortson*.[52] Georgia law required candidates for elective office who ran without winning a primary election to file petitions with signatures from qualified voters equaling five per cent of the vote cast in the last general election for that office. If the candidate belonged to a political party that received more than twenty per cent of the votes in the last gubernatorial election, the state relieved the candidate of the petition requirement. The Court distinguished *Williams* by suggesting that the Ohio statute challenged in that case presented an " 'entangling web of election laws.' "[53]

---

49. Id. at 819.

50. 440 U.S. 173 (1979).

51. 440 U.S. at 188. Mr. Justice Blackmun concurred in the result but not in the use of the "compelling interest test." He believed that the law should be subject to "strict scrutiny" but that the phrases "compelling state interest" and "least drastic means" were vague and an open ended invitation to lower court judges to engage in a form of substantive due process analysis similar to that used earlier this century in the economic area. 440 U.S. at 188–189 (Blackmun, J., concurring). Justice Stevens also concurred separately in the judgment; he would have preferred to rest the decision on a due process rationale. Justice Stevens thought that there might sometime be sufficient reasons for distinguishing city and state election requirements but that the 5% requirement was excessive, given the fact that the state did not defend it as other than an historical remnant of an earlier election code.

Thus, Justice Stevens believed that this particular requirement deprived the candidates of liberty without due process. 440 U.S. at 189 (Stevens J., concurring). Justice Rehnquist concurred because he found no rational basis for the higher requirement for the city elections, but he noted that the unreasonableness of this requirement stemmed from the Supreme Court action in *Moore* and lower court invalidation of other portions of the election code. Had it not been for these judicial actions, which the Justice apparently did not agree with, the election code would have been reasonable in requiring statewide candidates to have a lesser number of signatures but requiring that set numbers of signatures be obtained in a specific number of counties around the state. 440 U.S. at 189–90 (Rehnquist, J., concurring).

52. 403 U.S. 431 (1971).

53. Id. at 437 (quoting *Williams*).

Georgia, on the other hand, not only permitted independent candidates but also did not require any unreasonable early filing deadline. Moreover, the five per cent Georgia requirement was not a "suffocating" restriction like the fifteen per cent Ohio requirement. Finally, the Court noted that, unlike Ohio, Georgia often had independent candidates running for election office. The Court thus concluded that the Georgia election scheme did not violate either the first amendment or equal protection clause.[54]

A demonstrated support statute may be unconstitutional if it limits too narrowly the pool of available voters who can sign the required petition, or if it limits too severely the time period to submit the petition. Those who challenged the California Election Code in *Storer v. Brown*[55] specifically questioned the constitutionality of the demonstrated support provisions. The provisions allowed non-qualified political parties twenty-four days to gather the necessary signatures on the support petition. Furthermore, the statute discounted any signature from a qualified voter who had voted in the primary election. The Court found that the record provided insufficient information on whether these requirements excessively burdened the ability of minor political parties to gain access to the ballot. Consequently, the Court remanded this phase of the *Storer* litigation back to the district court with an order to gather the necessary facts and make the determination on the extent of the burden. The Court indicated that if these requirements were too severe on minor political parties they would violate the equal protection clause.[56]

Demonstrated support requirements may impair the ability of minor political parties

and independent candidates to run an effective campaign in several ways. The Federal Elections Campaign Act of 1971, for example, granted an amount of federal funds to minor or new political parties that was less than that for the major parties. In *Buckley v. Valeo*[57] the Supreme Court considered constitutional challenges to these restrictions. The Court initially decided that it would review this portion of the Act under a rational relationship standard of review.[58] Although the Court realized that restrictions on access to the electoral process may limit a voter's choice, it reasoned that a denial of public financing did not directly infringe the right to vote.[59] Moreover, the restriction promoted a proper governmental purpose: prohibiting an artificial incentive for splinter parties and avoiding factionalism. Hence, the Court concluded that Congress properly may require " 'some preliminary showing of a significant modicum of support' . . . as an eligibility requirement for public funds."[60]

The *Buckley* Court also assessed a provision of the Federal Elections Campaign Act that required political committees and candidates to keep detailed records and to disclose the sources of contributions.[61] It was contended that the government's interest in such information was minimal but the danger of impairing rights of association and free expression was great. The Court rejected the arguments and indicated that an impairment of first amendment rights was only speculative. Before the Court would order minor parties or independent candidates to be exempted from this provision, it would require evidence of a reasonable probability that harassment or threats to contributors resulted from the compelled disclosures. The Court stated that if such evi-

---

54. Id. at 439–40; see Note, Developments in the Law—Elections, 88 Harv.L.Rev. 1111, 1133–42 (1975).

55. 415 U.S. 724 (1974).

56. Id. at 746; but see American Party of Texas v. White, 415 U.S. 767 (1974) where the Court sustained the Texas Election Code that had a fifty-five day time period for filing election petitions, and a restriction on the size of the pool of voters who could sign an election petition. Id. at 779–88.

57. 424 U.S. 1 (1976).

58. Id. at 85.

59. Id. at 93–97.

60. Id. at 96 (quoting from Jenness v. Fortson, 403 U.S. 431, 442 (1971)).

61. 424 U.S. at 60 (1976).

dence existed, it would review the constitutionality of the disclosure requirement with strict scrutiny.[62] Until the production of such evidence, however, the Court would sustain the provision under the reasonable relationship test because it furthered governmental interests in the deterrence of corruption and the prevention of fraud.[63]

Any restriction on the ability of potential candidates to appear on the general election ballot may implicate the first amendment associational rights and the fourteenth amendment due process and equal protection rights of voters. However, the states must impose some candidate access restrictions in order to run honest, efficient elections in which the populace may choose its government officials. As the Court has stated: "the state's important regulatory interests [in orderly, honest elections] are generally sufficient to justify reasonable, nondiscriminatory restrictions."[64] The judiciary must independently review ballot access regulations to insure that they are justified by such state interests.

In *Anderson v. Celebrezze*[65] the Court, by a 5 to 4 vote, invalidated a state statute which required an independent candidate for President to file his nominating petition in March prior to the general election. This March filing date preceded the time when major political parties, which had sufficient demonstrated support to reserve a place on the ballot, named their candidates. The state could justify some date certain cutoff for candidate filing but not one so far in advance of the general election. The majority stated that judges, in reviewing such a restriction, were to balance the degree to which the regulation impaired the first and

fourteenth rights of voters against the degree to which the regulation advanced important state interests. The Court concluded the early filing date did not sufficiently advance the interests in political stability, voter awareness, or equal treatment of candidates to justify such a significant restriction on the voter's freedom of choice and freedom of association.

6. *Racial Classifications*

Any state law that impairs a person's ability to become a candidate for elective office because of that person's race is unconstitutional. Such a law would violate the fourteenth and fifteenth amendments.[66] The Constitution prevents the states from directly dictating, casually promoting, or facilitating "a distinction in the treatment of persons solely on the basis of race."[67] Thus, a state could not designate on a ballot which candidates were black and which were white.[68] Such a designation requirement would provide an easy means of discrimination. Moreover, race has no relationship to the determination of a person's capabilities to function in public office.

7. *Judicial Involvement in the Selection of Candidates for Elective Office*

At the 1972 National Democratic Party Convention the Party's Credentials Committee prevented the Illinois delegation aligned with Mayor Richard Daley from participating in the Convention. Although the delegates loyal to Mayor Daley had been selected to attend the Convention under provisions of Illinois law, the manner of their selection violated Democratic Party rules.[69] The unseated Illinois delegates obtained an injunc-

---

62. Id. at 73–85, see note 63, infra.

63. A campaign disclosure law cannot be applied to a minor political party when that party can demonstrate reasonable probability that disclosure will result in harassment of party members or contributors. Forced disclosure in these circumstances would violate the first amendment. Brown v. Socialist Workers '74 Campaign Committee, 103 S.Ct. 416 (1982).

64. Anderson v. Celebrezze, 103 S.Ct. 1564, 1569–70 (1983) (footnote omitted).

65. 103 S.Ct. 1564 (1983).

66. Cf. Georgia v. United States, 411 U.S. 526 (1973); Gomillion v. Lightfoot, 364 U.S. 339 (1960).

67. Hamm v. Virginia State Bd. of Elections, 230 F.Supp. 156, 157 (E.D.Va.1964), aff'd sub. nom. Tancil v. Woolls, 379 U.S. 19 (1964).

68. Anderson v. Martin, 375 U.S. 399 (1964).

69. See generally Rotunda, Constitutional and Statutory Restrictions on Political Parties in the Wake of Cousins v. Wigoda, 53 Tex.L.Rev. 935, 935–37 (1973).

tion from an Illinois state court but the Convention seated a replacement delegation and refused to recognize the Daley "loyalists." Contempt proceedings were brought against the substitute delegation and were pending when the Supreme Court decided *Cousins v. Wigoda.*[70] The Court held that the contempt proceedings impaired the replacement delegates' and the Party's rights of association. The contempt proceedings also infringed on the Democratic Party's right to determine the composition of its National Convention in accordance with its own standards.[71] Consequently, the injunction was unconstitutional.

The *Wigoda* opinion reveals the Court's reluctance to involve the judiciary in intraparty disputes. The Court has indicated that the process of delegate selection and the management of political conventions are the business of private political parties and not of the government.[72] The Court has reasoned that the probability that political parties will enact and enforce arbitrary and unreasonable rules is minimal. A viable political party needs loyal party members to win elections. Moreover, the Court has realized that a political party can possess interests that particular states do not share.

The *White Primary Cases* together with *Wigoda* establish that at some point a court must act to prevent the political parties from acting unconstitutionally. A party convention—at least one held by one of the two major parties—should not discriminate on the basis of race. *Wigoda* indicates that the

Court will sustain party rules governing prenomination activities only as long as the party acts in conformity with basic constitutional principals.[73] Furthermore, a state may not attempt, as it did in *Wigoda*, an extraterritorial extension of state jurisdiction to enforce even otherwise valid laws.[74] Because political party autonomy is related to the first amendment freedoms of speech and association, the state would need a compelling interest to burden the national party before the Court will sustain its law over the party rule.[75]

C. The Right to Vote and Racial Discrimination

1. The White Primary Cases

The *White Primary Cases*[1] represented the major effort by the Court prior to the 1960's to prevent racial discrimination in voting. In this sequence of cases the Supreme Court steadily loosened the constitutional requirements of state action in order to protect the effectiveness of the voting franchise. The Supreme Court prohibited states from forbidding black participation in state primaries;[2] struck down an analogous resolution passed by a party executive committee acting pursuant to the authority of a state statute;[3] held that the failure of state officials acting under color of law to count ballots properly in a primary election was a violation of a section in the United States Code prohibiting such "state action;"[4] over-

---

70. 419 U.S. 477 (1975).

71. Id. at 489.

72. Buckley v. Valeo, 424 U.S. 1, 235, 250 (1976) (Burger, C.J., concurring in part and dissenting in part).

73. Rotunda, supra note 69, at 937.

74. Id. at 936.

75. See Democratic Party v. LaFollette, 450 U.S. 107 (1981) (state law requiring party to have "open" primary violates first amendment), examined in the next section of this chapter.

In Marchioro v. Chaney, 442 U.S. 191 (1979) the Supreme Court upheld a state statute that required each major political party to create a state central committee composed of two members from each county in the state against a claim that the statute violated the free-

dom of association. The requirement was related to the state interest in insuring a fair, orderly election process; it touched upon "internal" party affairs only because the party chose to give the committee powers and duties beyond the limited statutory power to call conventions, create a process for delegate election, and to fill vacancies on a party ticket.

1. E.g., Terry v. Adams, 345 U.S. 461 (1953); Smith v. Allwright, 321 U.S. 649 (1944); United States v. Classic, 313 U.S. 299 (1941); Nixon v. Condon, 286 U.S. 73 (1932); Nixon v. Herndon, 273 U.S. 536 (1927); Baskin v. Brown, 174 F.2d 391 (4th Cir. 1949); Rice v. Elmore, 165 F.2d 387 (4th Cir. 1947).

2. Nixon v. Herndon, 273 U.S. 536 (1927).

3. Nixon v. Condon, 286 U.S. 73 (1932).

4. United States v. Classic, 313 U.S. 299 (1941).

ruled a prior decision to find that the right to vote free of racial discrimination embodied in the fifteenth amendment applied to primaries as well as a general election;[5] and barred racial discrimination in an unofficial primary conducted by a private group.[6] An analysis of the *White Primary Cases* and their progeny suggest that the unarticulated premise and most easily understood reasoning behind the cases is that all integral steps in an election for public office are public functions and therefore state action subject to some constitutional scrutiny, particularly if a complaint is based on racial discrimination. The *White Primary Cases* thus carry the seed of an expansive reading.

The first white primary case was *Nixon v. Herndon,*[7] where a black plaintiff sued the Judges of Elections for refusing to allow him to vote in a Texas state primary for senator and representatives of Congress and for various state offices. A Texas statute provided that "in no event shall a negro be eligible to participate in a Democratic party election held in the State of Texas."[8] Justice Holmes, speaking for a unanimous Court, in a very short opinion, held that the statute violated the fourteenth amendment's equal protection clause, finding it "unnecessary to consider the fifteenth amendment."[9]

The state of Texas reacted to this case by repealing its statute and enacting another which provided that "every political party in this State through its State Executive Committee shall have the power to prescribe the qualifications of its own members and shall in its own way determine who shall be qualified to vote or otherwise participate in such political party . . . ."[10] The State Executive Committee of the Democratic Party then adopted a resolution providing that only white democrats could vote in the Democratic party. Nixon was again denied participation in the primary because of his color, and once again the Supreme Court decided in his favor in *Nixon v. Condon,*[11] a 5–4 decision. The respondents argued that it was not the state but a political party, "a voluntary" association, which denied Nixon his ballot; private associations, it was contended, have the inherent power to determine their own membership. The Court rejected this argument but appeared to decide on narrow grounds: the state delegated power to the executive committee, which then became an agency of the state for this purpose. The executive committee, by virtue of the state statute, became a repository of official power, and therefore became subject to the equal protection clause.[12]

Texas refused to give up. After the *Condon* decision the Texas Democratic Convention itself barred blacks from voting in its primaries. This time, in *Grovey v. Townsend,*[13] the Court upheld the color bar. Since no state statutes authorized any color discrimination or delegated that power to any party organ and since the party convention did have inherent power to set up the qualifications of its members, there was no state action. Less than a decade later *Grovey* was overruled in *Smith v. Allwright,*[14] with Justice Roberts complaining that such prompt reversals of direction by the Court "tends to bring adjudications of this tribunal into the same class as a restricted railroad ticket, good for this day and train only."[15] *Grovey's* speedy rejection was made possible by the leading decision in *United States v. Classic,*[16] which occurred between *Grovey* and *Allwright.*

5. Smith v. Allwright, 321 U.S. 649 (1944).

6. Terry v. Adams, 345 U.S. 461 (1953). See Chapter 14, State Action, Section II.

7. 273 U.S. 536 (1927).

8. See 273 U.S. at 540.

9. 273 U.S. at 540.

10. Quoted in Nixon v. Condon, 286 U.S. 73, 82 (1932).

11. 286 U.S. 73 (1932).

12. 286 U.S. at 85–88.

13. 295 U.S. 45 (1935).

14. 321 U.S. 649 (1944).

15. 321 U.S. at 669 (Roberts, J., dissenting).

16. 313 U.S. 299 (1941). Cf. United States v. Saylor, 322 U.S. 385 (1944). See, Bixby, The Roosevelt Court, Democratic Ideology, and Minority Rights: Another Look at United States v. Classic, 90 Yale L.J. 741 (1981).

In *Classic* a federal indictment was upheld charging various state officials, who were conducting a primary election under Louisiana law, with willfully altering and falsely counting the ballots.

> The questions for decision are whether the rights of qualified voters to vote in the Louisiana primary and to have their ballots counted is a right "secured by the Constitution" within the meaning of [certain statutes of the Criminal Code] . . .[17]

In *Classic*, the Court concluded:

> Where the state law has made the primary an integral part of the procedure of choice, or where in fact the primary effectively controls the choice, the right of the elector to have his ballot counted at the primary is likewise included in the right protected by Article 1, § 2. . . . Here . . . [t]he right to choose a representative is in fact controlled by the primary . . . the practical influence of the choice of candidates may be so great as to affect profoundly the choice at the general election, even though there is no effective legal prohibition. . . .[18]

The Court was concerned with reality, not merely the formal fact of state regulation and therefore the Court found it essential that congressional power over "elections" extend to primary elections.[19] As if to anticipate the argument that a private primary or party convention would not constitute state action, the Court noted that the Article I, § 2 command "unlike those guaranteed by the fourteenth and fifteenth amendments, is secured against the action of individuals as well as of states."[20] *Grovey* was not discussed.

Smith v. Allwright,[21] relying on the fifteenth amendment, expanded *Classic* by finding state action in a party primary election; it explicitly overruled *Grovey*.[22] In *Allwright*[23] the Court struck down a party convention resolution forbidding blacks from voting in a party primary regulated by the state. The Court reasoned that when a state delegated the power to fix voting qualifications to a party which made party membership necessary for voting in a primary, then the state had made the action of the party action of the state.[24] The constitutional "grant to the people of the opportunity for choice [without regard to race] is not to be nullified by a State casting its electoral process in a form which permits a private organization to practice racial discrimination in the election."[25]

While the *Allwright* Court emphasized the state's close regulation of political parties, such a factor should not be crucial in determining state action for purposes of the fourteenth or fifteenth amendments, since the absence of state regulation of party elections in effect produces a delegation of the state's possible authority to the party. *Terry v. Adams*[26] illustrates this point. There, a racially discriminatory primary was conducted by the Jaybird party, a private organization operating without state aid of any kind. This primary was conducted prior to the Democratic primary. The Court explained that the distinction between the private primary and the Democratic primary it preceded was merely a distinction of form, even though the Jaybird nominees entered their own names as candidates in the Demo-

---

17. 313 U.S. at 307.

18. Id. at 318–19.

19. Id. at 315–16.

20. Id. at 315. Art. I, § 2 deals with the states' power to regulate the selection of Representatives. Art. II, § 1 deals with the states' power to regulate the election of presidential electors. A comparison of the two sections indicates that if there is no state action requirement limiting the rights secured by art. I, § 2, there must be no state action requirement for art. II,

§ 1. Similarly, there appears to be no state action requirement limiting the rights secured by the seventeenth amendment (election of U.S. Senators).

21. 321 U.S. 649 (1944).

22. 321 U.S. at 666.

23. 321 U.S. 649 (1944).

24. 321 U.S. at 664–65.

25. 321 U.S. at 664.

26. 345 U.S. 461 (1953).

cratic primary.[27] While the plurality opinion noted that the Democratic primary and the general election following it had only been the "perfunctory ratifiers" of the choice made in the prior Jaybird primary, the language of Justice Black's opinion went well beyond relying on the peculiar power of the Jaybird election. The state had violated the Fifteenth Amendment by *permitting* within its borders a private device that would have been forbidden in a public election.[28]

The rulings in the *White Primary Cases* provided a needed basis for judicial intervention in the voting process to prevent racial discrimination in the allocation of power within the self-governance system. In other sections of this treatise, we have examined in greater detail the requirement that those attacking an electoral system as racially biased must prove that the system was created or maintained for a racially discriminatory purpose.[29] In this section of Chapter 16, we examine the question of whether these cases provide a basis for judicial intervention in the activities of political parties.

2. The "Public Function" Analysis of Each Stage of the Election Process

The logic of the *White Primary Cases* supports the conclusion that an election for public office is a public function and that any integral part of that function must conform to the Constitution. In fact, probably only the public function analysis adequately explains the extension of constitutional restrictions against racial discrimination to private groups such as the Jaybirds. The Court has held that constitutional restrictions and limitations apply to those who assume governmental functions. This concept should easily apply to what is in essence the holding of an election for public office. The nomination process may appear to be more a private than a governmental function because it is generally carried on by individuals in their role as private citizens. But even the process of a final election is carried on only by the individual *qua* private citizen. Conversely, as Dean Pollak has urged, "only a state can conduct elections—especially so where the state is one in which, under the Constitution, a republican form of government is perpetually guaranteed."[30]

If an election is state action, any integral part of that election is also state action. Several circuits have already explicitly adopted the public function rationale with respect to judicial review of political parties.[31] It is this rationale which most naturally explains the *White Primary Cases*. Several state courts have also accepted the principle that state action exists whenever the party performs a public electoral or nominating function.[32] The public function analysis does not even break down if the nominating vehicle is a convention rather than a primary. The Supreme Court in *Classic* adopted for constitutional purposes a definition of "election" that was "no less than the expression by qualified electors of their choice of candidates,"[33] a definition sufficient to include a primary, caucus, or convention.

27. 345 U.S. at 465–66. (Plurality opinion by Black, J., joined by Douglas & Burton, JJ.) There was no opinion by the Court.

28. 345 U.S. at 469 (Black, J., joined by Douglas & Burton, JJ.).

29. See Chapter 16, Section I, D, Section VIII, A, 8, Section VIII, B, 6. See also Chapter 14 (State Action) for an examination of the basis upon which the judiciary may find that a seemingly private entity, such as a political party, has sufficient contacts with the government to subject it to the constitutional limitations on its action.

30. Pollak, Racial Discrimination and Judicial Integrity: A Reply to Professor Wechsler, 108 U.Pa.L.Rev. 1, 23 (1959). See generally, Chapter 14, State Action.

With respect to presidential, senatorial, and congressional elections, it should be noted that the rights secured respectively by Article II, § I; Art. I, § II; and the seventeenth amendment are not limited to state action. Cf. New York v. United States, 326 U.S. 572, 582 (1946) (Concurring opinion of Frankfurter, J.).

31. Seergy v. Kings County Republican County Committee, 459 F.2d 308, 313 (2d Cir. 1972); Lynch v. Torquato, 343 F.2d 370, 373 (3d Cir. 1965) (dictum).

32. E.g., Bentman v. Seventh Ward Democratic Executive Committee, 421 Pa. 188, 203, 218 A.2d 261, 269 (1966) (right to select party nominees for public office is state action under the fourteenth amendment); Wagner v. Gray, 74 So.2d 89, 91 (Fla.1954).

33. 313 U.S. at 318.

Decisions subsequent to the *White Prima-ry Cases* have continued to define "election" broadly in order to subject to constitutional scrutiny all state action relevant to the electoral process.[34] For example, even the procedures for selecting delegates to the national nominating conventions amount to state action, as a practical matter, because, in virtually all states, selection is either regulated by state statute or explicitly delegated to the state political party.[35] It is difficult to argue persuasively for purposes of prohibiting racial discrimination that even the Democratic or Republican presidential nominating convention is not an integral part of the presidential election or that it is less an integral part than a state primary. The state's power under article II, section I to appoint presidential electors as their legislatures direct is for constitutional purposes not just a power but a nondelegable duty. The state may by statute, as in *Allwright,* authorize the state parties to set up certain procedures. Or, as in *Terry,* the state may remain silent, allowing the parties to enact their own rules and regulations. But for constitutional purposes it is the state that is acting and that must be held responsible. The duty under article II, section I should not be immune from review but should be subject to the fourteenth and fifteenth amendments and judged by their standards.[36] Similarly, the state's duties with respect to congressional elections under article I, section II and senatorial elections under the seventeenth amendment are also subject to the fourteenth amendment. The Supreme Court in *Ray v. Blair*[37] explicitly adopted the view that any integral part of the presidential election process is a nondelegable state duty, subject to constitutional limitations. In that case, a state statute had allowed the party executive committee to determine qualifications for primary candidates, and pursuant to this delegation of power the Democratic Party required a loyalty pledge from each candidate for presidential elector. While the Court upheld the loyalty pledge as a legitimate party objective, it recognized that both the state and the party were subject to possible constitutional limitations when the former so delegated power to the latter.[38]

The broad *Classic* definition of "election" provided that an election in the constitutional sense occurs, regardless of how small the universe of possible electors or candidates. The smallness of the universe is merely a possible constitutional argument for striking the whole procedure, not an argument for immunizing the scheme from constitutional scrutiny. For example, Georgia law formerly allowed the chairman of the party's state executive committee to appoint delegates to the Democratic National Convention.[39] While only one "voter" existed, the procedure still represented an election which was an integral part of the presidential electoral process. Under *Moore v. Ogilvie*[40] the procedure could have been subject to challenge

---

34. In Williams v. Rhodes, 393 U.S. 23 (1968), the Court held that the state power under the Constitution to appoint presidential electors is subject to the fourteenth amendment. A state law that makes it more difficult for third parties to be placed on the ballot violated the voters' right to effectively exercise their franchise. Id. at 30. It follows that if this right does not extend to the nominating process, the right to vote effectively will be stripped of its constitutional protection. In a subsequent fourteenth amendment case the Court again maintained that all state procedures that are an integral part of the election process must not discriminate, nor abridge the right to vote, Moore v. Ogilvie, 394 U.S. 814, 818 (1969).

35. Chambers & Rotunda, Reform of Presidential Nominating Conventions, 56 Va.L.Rev. 179, 195 (1970). Terry v. Adams, 345 U.S. 461, 469 (1953), supports the argument that even if the state withdrew from such regulation, the pre-election selection process might still be an integral part of the election. It is immaterial under *Terry* whether or not the state has given a preferred position on the ballot to the nominee of a completely private primary. 345 U.S. at 465 n. 1.

36. See, e.g., Williams v. Rhodes, 393 U.S. 23 (1966).

37. 343 U.S. 214 (1952).

38. 343 U.S. at 227, 231.

39. See Chambers & Rotunda, Reform of Presidential Nominating Conventions, 56 Va.L.Rev. 179, 185 (1970).

40. 394 U.S. 814 (1969). An Illinois statute required nominating petitions for independent candidates to demonstrate broad geographic support. The Court found the procedure to be an integral part of the electoral process and struck the requirement as discriminatory.

as discriminatory and an abridgment of the right to vote.[41] The *White Primary Cases* as supported by later case law may be read to support some federal judicial intervention to protect the constitutional "right of qualified voters . . . to cast their votes effectively." [42]

A Supreme Court decision breaking new ground may not be entirely clear until later cases interpret and better articulate the grounds of the earlier decision.[43] Later lower court and Supreme Court cases appear to have read the *White Primary* decisions broadly, making clearer their expansive, public function rationale. In *Moore v. Ogilvie*,[44] a fourteenth amendment case, the Court cited *United States v. Classic* and *Smith v. Allwright* as authority for the proposition that no procedures used by a state as an integral part of the election process may operate discriminatorily or abridge the right to vote.[45] The Supreme Court's reliance on *Classic* and *Allwright* to create a fourteenth amendment right suggests that the cases have fourteenth amendment implications. Similarly, in *Hadley v. Junior College District*,[46] a fourteenth amendment reapportionment case,[47] the Court relied in part on *Classic* for the proposition that a voter has a constitutional right not to have his vote "wrongfully denied, debased, or diluted." [48] *Classic*, an article I case, involved state election officials charged with altering and falsely counting ballots, and the dilution referred to in *Hadley* was the fourteenth amendment dilution that occurs when the one man, one vote standard is not followed. The premise behind *Classic* must, however,

also be relevant to an understanding of fourteenth amendment rights, or its citation by the Supreme Court was frivolous.[49]

3. *Judicial Control of Political Parties*

One of the major issues left unresolved by the *White Primary Cases* and other such election cases decided in their wake is the extent to which the judiciary will exercise review of political parties when the nominating process takes place by convention or caucus rather than by primary. A recent case which suggests the direction of the Supreme Court is *Cousins v. Wigoda*,[50] arising out of a 1972 credentials challenge to Mayor Daley's Illinois delegation at the Democratic National Convention. In response to the unseating of Mayor Daley and his loyalists by the convention's Credentials Committee, the Court held that the national interest in selecting candidates for national office and the party members' freedom of association overcame an admitted state interest in the interest in the integrity of its election process; thus party rules on delegate selection might legitimately disqualify delegates selected according to state law.

Arguably *Cousins* may be read to urge, if not to require, courts and legislatures to stay out of the national nominating convention process at any stage. But the Court was careful to point out that no claim was made that the party delegate selection rules violated the Constitution. If the party rules complained of involved racial discrimination such as that involved in the *White Primary*

---

41. Id. at 818.

42. Williams v. Rhodes, 393 U.S. 23, 30 (1969).

43. See generally Wright, Professor Bickel, The Scholarly Tradition, and the Supreme Court, 84 Harv.L. Rev. 769 (1971).

44. 394 U.S. 814 (1969).

45. Id. at 818.

46. 397 U.S. 50 (1970).

47. Id. at 51.

48. Id. at 52.

49. Cf. Bullock v. Carter, 405 U.S. 134 (1972); Nixon v. Herndon, 273 U.S. 536 (1927). In Ray v. Blair,

343 U.S. 214 (1952), the Court explained that the fourteenth amendment forbids a state from excluding voters from any integral part of the general election unless the exclusion "is reasonably related to a legitimate legislative objective." Id. at 226 n. 14. The legislative objective was measured in terms of a party objective. Thus, the state statute in *Blair* allowed the party to require candidates for presidential elector to take a party loyalty pledge; the Supreme Court upheld the pledge as constitutional.

50. 419 U.S. 477 (1975). Cf. Gottlieb, Rebuilding the Right of Association: The Right to Hold a Convention as a Test Case, 11 Hofstra L.Rev. 191 (1982) (objecting to legislative regulation or political parties).

Cases, Cousins does not preclude the Court from acting:

> [W]hatever the case of actions presenting claims that the Party's delegate selection procedures are not exercised *within the confines of the Constitution—and no such claims are made here*—this is a case where "the convention itself [was] the proper forum for determining intra-party disputes as to which delegates [should] be seated".[51]

Perhaps it should be noted for comparison that a decision by the Court to outlaw racial discrimination by political parties at their conventions or in their primaries would not require the prohibition of religious parties, if such might be formed, that have religious qualifications. Unlike racial discrimination, religious liberty is explicitly protected by the first amendment. A different balance of interests may allow a party to discriminate if motivated by religious grounds while that discrimination may not be justified if motivated by racial grounds.[52]

The Court followed the implications of *Cousins* in *Democratic Party v. LaFollette*.[53] Though National Democratic Party rules provided that only those willing to affiliate publicly with the Democratic Party may participate in the process of selecting delegates to the Party's National Convention, Wisconsin state law allowed anyone to vote in the state primary without requiring a public declaration of party preference. In this "open" primary, Wisconsin voters did not vote for delegates but only expressed their choice among the Democratic Party presidential candidates. Later, the Democratic Party caucuses, made up of people who had publicly stated their affiliation with the Democratic Party, selected the delegates to the National Convention. Wisconsin law then purported to bind these delegates to vote at the National Convention in accord with the results of the open presidential preference primary. Although Wisconsin's open presidential preference primary did not itself violate National Party rules, the state's mandate that the results of the primary must determine the allocation of votes cast by the state's delegates at the National Convention did violate the Democratic Party rule that the procedure by which delegates to the Convention are bound to vote must be limited to those who have publicly declared the Democratic Party preference. The majority found that any issue as to the validity of the state law was foreclosed by *Cousins.* "[T]he freedom to associate for 'the common advancement of political beliefs' necessarily presupposes the freedom to identify the people who comprise the association, and to limit the association to those people only."[54]

IX. THE REAPPORTIONMENT CASES AND THE RULE OF ONE PERSON, ONE VOTE

A. The Creation of Justiciability

The first major case to reach the Supreme Court claiming that Congressional election districts for the House of Representatives were malapportioned because they lacked compactness of territory and approximate equality of population was *Colegrove v. Green.*[1] A majority of the voting Justices dismissed the suit, but there was no majority for treating reapportionment as a political question. Justice Frankfurter in an opinion concurred in by only Justices Reed and Burton argued that "due regard for the effective working of our Government revealed this issue to be of a peculiarly political nature and therefore not meet for judicial determination."[2] He strongly urged that "Courts ought not to enter this political thicket."[3] Three justices found jurisdiction

---

51.   419 U.S. at 491 (emphasis added).

52.   In a similar manner, the Court has held that the state could give text books to students attending religious schools, Board of Education v. Allen, 392 U.S. 236 (1968), but not to those attending racially discriminatory schools, Norwood v. Harrison, 413 U.S. 455 (1973).

53.   450 U.S. 107 (1981).

54.   450 U.S. at 120 (internal citation and footnote omitted).

1.   328 U.S. 549 (1946).

2.   328 U.S. at 552.

3.   328 U.S. at 556.

and one concurred on nonjurisdictional grounds.[4]

The next major case to reach the Supreme Court was *Gomillion v. Lightfoot*.[5] Here the Court acted, but purportedly on a narrow ground, in the majority opinion for the Court, written by Justice Frankfurter. In this case black voters, who had been residents of the City of Tuskegee, complained after the Alabama legislature enacted a statute redefining the City of Tuskegee by altering its shape from a square to a strangely shaped twenty-eight-sided figure.[6] Plaintiffs relied on the equal protection guarantees of the Fourteenth Amendment and the right to vote under the Fifteenth Amendment, and claimed that the gerrymandered boundaries were created solely for the purpose of fencing out black voters from the town to deprive them of the pre-existing right to vote in the municipal election. The Court agreed that the claim was justiciable, relying only on the Fifteenth Amendment.[7] By placing the case on such grounds, Frankfurter perhaps hoped to isolate it from a more general precedent. Justice Whittaker's concurrence was analytically more satisfying; he relied on equal protection:

> It seems to me that the "right . . . to vote" that is guaranteed by the Fifteenth Amendment is but the same right to vote as is enjoyed by all others within the same . . . political division. . . .

> But . . . "fencing Negro citizens out of" Division A and into Division B is an unlawful segregation of races of citizens, in violation of the Equal Protection Clause of the Fourteenth Amendment. . . .[8]

Finally, in *Baker v. Carr*,[9] two years after *Gomillion*, the Court found reapportion-ment cases to be justiciable based on the more general equal protection clause of the Fourteenth Amendment. *Colegrove* was distinguished and the Court held that debasement of a person's vote by malapportionment is a violation of the equal protection guaranty of the Fourteenth Amendment. This claim was significantly different from those based on the nonjusticiable republican form of government clause.[10]

> The question here is the consistency of state action with the Federal Constitution. We have no question decided, or to be decided, by a political branch of government coequal with this Court. Nor do we risk embarrassment of our government abroad, or grave disturbance at home if we take issue with Tennessee as to the constitutionality of her action here challenged. Nor need the appellants, in order to succeed in this action, ask the Court to enter upon policy determinations for which judicially manageable standards are lacking.[11]

Malapportionment claims were now before the Court. But the nature of the Constitutional right had yet to be decided.

B.   The Origins of One Person, One Vote

The value of the right recognized in *Baker* was explained in *Reynolds v. Sims*,[1] which created the one person, one vote principle grounded in the Equal Protection Clause. But before that case the Supreme Court laid the groundwork in two others, *Gray v. Sanders*,[2] and *Wesberry v. Sanders*.[3] In *Gray* the Court invalidated the county unit system of nominating the Governor and other officials of Georgia. Under the Georgia law challenged in *Gray*, each candidate in the primary election who won a plurality of

---

4. Justice Rutledge assumed jurisdiction but declined to exercise it for other reasons, including the shortness of time remaining before the election. 328 U.S. at 564, 565 (Rutledge, J., concurring). Justices Black, joined by Douglas and Murphy, dissented. 328 U.S. at 566. Justice Jackson took no part in the consideration of the case. 328 U.S. at 556.

5. 364 U.S. 339 (1960).

6. 364 U.S. at 340.

7. 364 U.S. at 341–43.

8. 364 U.S. at 349.

9. 369 U.S. 186 (1962). See G. Graham, One Man, One Vote: Baker v. Carr and the American Levellers (1972), for a fascinating study of the young lawyers who made the case for reapportionment in the courts.

10. U.S.Const. art. IV, § 4.

11. 369 U.S. at 226.

1. 377 U.S. 533 (1964).

2. 372 U.S. 368 (1963).

3. 376 U.S. 1 (1964).

the popular vote in any county was entitled to all of the county's electoral "units." A majority of the county unit votes nominated the Governor and the United States Senator; the other nominees needed only a plurality of unit votes.[4] Although the units were not assigned among counties according to population, the Court suggested that apportionment of units on a one person, one vote basis could not cure the constitutional flaws of the unit system because the winner of a county won all of its unit votes. Using the entire state as the appropriate geographic unit, the Court interpreted the Constitution to require the addition of a minority candidate's votes in one county to the votes he received in the other counties.[5] Thus:

> Once the geographic unit for which a representative is to be chosen is designated, all who participate in the election are to have an equal vote—whatever their race, whatever their sex, whatever their occupation, whatever their income, and wherever their home may be in the geographic unit. This is required by the Equal Protection Clause of the Fourteenth Amendment.[6]

In *Wesberry* the Court required that congressional districts be apportioned equally, but the Court did not base its holding on the Equal Protection Clause but rather the command of Article I, section 2, that the Representatives be chosen "by the People of the several States." That clause, said Justice Black speaking for the Court, "means that as nearly as practicable one man's vote in a congressional election is to be worth as much as another's. . . . To say that a vote is worth more in one district than in another would not only run counter to our fun-

damental ideas of democratic government; it would cast aside the principle of a House of Representatives elected 'by the People'. . . . ."[7]

In *Reynolds v. Sims* the Court was faced with a challenge to the malapportionment of the Alabama state legislature. This time, relying on the equal protection clause, Chief Justice Warren formulated the broad one person, one vote rule:

> Legislators represent people, not trees or acres. . . . And, if a State should provide that the votes of citizens in one part of the State should be given two times, or five times, or 10 times the weight of votes of citizens in another part of the State, it could hardly be contended that the right to vote of those residing in the disfavored areas had not been effectively diluted . . . the Equal Protection Clause requires that the seats in both houses of a bicameral state legislature must be apportioned on a population basis.[8]

In one of the companion cases[9] the Court struck down an election apportionment scheme in which one house was malapportioned by use of an area representation system analogous to the U.S. Senate.[10] While it was contended that the state voters in every county of the State had approved of their malapportioned State Senate, the malapportionment was still flawed: "An individual's constitutionally protected right to cast an equally weighted vote cannot be denied even by a vote of a majority of a State's electorate. . . . ."[11] The majority cannot waive the rights of the minority, nor should the majority be able to waive the rights of future generations of voters.

---

4. 372 U.S. at 371–72.

5. 372 U.S. at 381 n. 12.

6. 372 U.S. at 379. *Gray* explicitly declined to address the situation in which a convention instead of a primary election nominates the candidates. 372 U.S. at 378 n. 10. See Chambers & Rotunda, Reform of Presidential Nominating Conventions, 56 Va.L.Rev. 179, 199–203 (1970).

7. 376 U.S. at 7–8 (footnote omitted).

8. 377 U.S. at 562, 568.

9. The companion cases were Lucas v. Forty-fourth General Assembly, 377 U.S. 713 (1964) (Colorado); WMCA, Inc. v. Lomenzo, 377 U.S. 633 (1964) (New York); Maryland Committee for Fair Representation v. Tawes, 377 U.S. 656 (1964) (Maryland); Davis v. Mann, 377 U.S. 678 (1964) (Virginia); Roman v. Sincock, 377 U.S. 695 (1964) (Delaware).

10. Lucas v. Forty-fourth General Assembly, 377 U.S. 713 (1964).

11. 377 U.S. at 736.

C. The Application of One Person, One Vote

1. To the Appointment of the State Governor and Other Such Officials

In *Fortson v. Morris* [1] the Supreme Court upheld the election of Georgia's Governor by the state legislature. When no candidate had received a majority of the votes cast in the state's general election, the state constitution allowed the General Assembly to elect the Governor from the two front runners.[2] The voters of each legislative district elected the state representatives who in turn elected the Governor. One major procedural defect struck down in *Gray v. Sanders* [3]—not adding a minority candidate's votes in one part of the state to the votes he receives in other parts—was approved in *Fortson* as it applied to the "delegates" who elect another person. The case indicates that the equal protection principle underlying *Gray* and other reapportionment cases should be inapplicable to voting by bodies which, like party conventions, performs a deliberative, but non-legislative function.

Gray and *Fortson* are in one sense difficult to reconcile with one another. On one level they appear directly contradictory. *Gray*, on the one hand, seems to hold that where the voters are asked or required to participate, equal protection mandates that each vote be counted equally. *Fortson*, on the other hand, upholds the selection of a state official by what had earlier been ruled to be a malapportioned legislature.[4] On another level, however, *Fortson* sanctions a representative process in the performance of a nonlegislative task, after the voters have exercised untrammeled their right to choose first-tier spokesmen. *Fortson* and *Gray* together thus appear to permit selection of an officer through indirect "election"—i.e., appointment—by a state legislature, but not by a mechanical unit system.

The *Fortson-Gray* theory developed above would permit multi-stage representative selection of delegates to the national conventions. A majority of the registered voters in a particular area—a county, for example—could constitutionally elect a delegate to a state convention, which in turn chooses the national delegates. The minority voters in the county are not disenfranchised, as they would be under a unit system, because they will be represented at higher levels by a delegate who, though committed to a differing point of view, can think, compromise and change in the deliberative process, the purpose of which is to select the "best man" for the Presidency.[5]

Pragmatic reasons may also explain *Fortson*: Georgia already had two primaries, one general election, and still failed to choose a governor. Justice Black argued that "State-wide elections cost time and money and it is not strange that Georgia's people decided to avoid repeated elections".[6]

---

1. 385 U.S. 231 (1966).

2. Ga.Const. art. V, § 1, para. IV (1945). The Court noted that this provision had been in the Georgia Constitution since 1824 and had been readopted by Georgia voters in the 1945 constitution, 385 U.S. at 233. In 1968 the voters ratified an amendment which repealed this procedure and substituted a provision which calls for a run-off election between the two candidates with the highest number of votes. Ga.Const. art. V, § 1, para. IV (1945), as amended, 1968 Ga.Laws 1562–63, ratified Nov. 5, 1968 (codified in Ga.Code Ann. § 2–2704 (1977).)

3. 372 U.S. 368 (1963).

4. The Court relied on its ruling in Toombs v. Fortson, 384 U.S. 210 (1966), aff'g per curiam 241 F.Supp. 65 (N.D.Ga.1965), that the Georgia Assembly as then constituted could function until May 1, 1968, to hold that the Assembly was not disqualified to elect the Governor. But see Fortson v. Morris, 385 U.S. 231,

245 (Fortas, J., dissenting) ("We have declined to deprive a malapportioned legislature of its de facto status as a legislature. But not until today has this Court allowed a malapportioned legislature to be the device for doing indirectly what a State may not do directly.")

5. Cf. Burke's Politics 115–16 (R. Hoffman & P. Levack eds. 1949) (Speech of Edmund Burke to the Electors of Bristol, Nov. 3, 1774). Consider also the historical reasons for the electoral college. See, e.g. The Federalist No. 68 (A. Hamilton). The concept of the national party convention as a deliberative body searching to select the "best man" appears to be fictional. The same is true of the Georgia legislature when it elected the Governor after *Fortson* was decided, for the ballots followed straight party lines.

6. 385 U.S. at 234. The speed with which *Fortson* was heard on both district and Supreme Court levels bespeaks the simple need for Georgia to have a Governor: the general election took place on November 8, a

In any event, *Fortson*, at the least, shows that the Constitution does not require that the Governor of a state be popularly elected. The state can choose to appoint members to an official position rather than elect them. If there is no popular election, the one person, one vote rule does not apply.

Thus, for example, a state or commonwealth statute may provide that if an interim vacancy in the state legislature is created, then the political party with which the previous incumbent was a member may fill that vacancy.[7] Such a statute does not restrict access to the electoral process because the interim appointment is not an election. Nor is such a statute defective because the appointment power is given to a political party rather than to an elected official: the legislature "could reasonably conclude that appointment by the previous incumbent's political party would more fairly reflect the will of the voters than appointment by the Governor or some other elected official."[8]

2. *To Local Government Elections*

In *Sailors v. Board of Education*,[1] the Supreme Court approved the choosing of county school board members by a method whereby each local school board appointed only one delegate and was allowed only one vote at the caucus convened to elect the county school board, even though the districts represented by the local school boards were of disproportionate population.[2] The Supreme Court held that the state has discretion to decide whether or not such a board shall be appointed by a representative process, or popularly elected, and that if the board is appointed, the districts its members represent need not be equal in population. The Court stated that "we see nothing in the Constitution to prevent experimentation."[3] In *Sailors* the school board was not found to exercise legislative powers but only administrative powers. This purported distinction between administrative and legislative powers was continued in a case decided a year later. In *Avery v. Midland County*[4] the Court required that county commissioners who exercised "general governmental powers over the entire geographic area served by the body"[5] and who are popularly elected be districted according to population.

Finally in *Hadley v. Junior College District*[6] the Court seemed to abandon the distinction between administrative and legislative powers and fashion a new test. The trustees in *Hadley* could levy and collect taxes, issue some bonds, hire and fire teachers, perform other activities and in general manage the junior college. While the powers were less than those in *Avery*, where the commissioners maintained the county jail, set the county tax rate, built and ran hospitals, airports, and libraries and similar duties,[7] the Court found the governmental powers general enough and of sufficient impact to justify the one person, one vote rule. But the decision appeared to find crucial another factor:

three-judge federal court gave its decisions on November 17, the Supreme Court heard arguments on December 5 and rendered its decision on December 12.

7. Rodriguez v. Popular Democratic Party, 102 S.Ct. 2194 (1982). See also Valenti v. Rockefeller, 393 U.S. 405 (1969) (per curiam), aff'g 292 F.Supp. 851 (S.D.N.Y.1968) (three judge court) (Governor may fill vacancy in U.S. Senate by appointment pending next regularly scheduled congressional election, even though the wait in that case was over 29 months; the court relied on the seventeenth amendment).

8. Rodriguez v. Popular Democratic Party, 457 U.S. 1, 11–13 (1982) (footnote omitted).

1. 387 U.S. 105 (1967).

2. In *Fortson* it was clear that the Georgia legislature was malapportioned and had been ordered to reapportion itself. Toombs v. Fortson, 241 F.Supp. 65 (N.D.Ga.), aff'd mem. 384 U.S. 210 (1966). But in *Sailors* the Board was not required to reapportion itself though it was clearly malapportioned. One district with a population of over 200,000 could send one delegate to the caucus selecting the county school board; another district, with fewer than 100 people, also had one delegate. Brief for Appellants at 4, Sailors v. Board of Education, 387 U.S. 105 (1967).

3. 387 U.S. at 111.

4. 390 U.S. 474 (1968).

5. 390 U.S. at 485.

6. 397 U.S. 50 (1970).

7. Compare 397 U.S. at 53 with 390 U.S. at 476–77.

[While] the case now before us . . . differs in certain respects from those offices considered in prior cases, it is exactly the same in one crucial factor—*these officials are elected by popular vote.* . . . If there is any way of determining the importance of choosing a particular governmental official, we think the decision of the State to select that official by popular vote is a strong enough indication that the choice is an important one.[8]

The Court then refused to distinguish for purposes of the apportionment rule between elections for "legislative" officials and those for "administrative" officials.[9] And it held that:

[A]s a general rule, whenever a state or local government decides to select persons by popular election to perform governmental functions, [equal protection] requires that each qualified voter must be given an equal opportunity to participate in that election, and when members of an elected body are chosen from separate districts, each district must be established on a basis which will insure, as far as is practicable, that equal numbers of voters can vote for proportionally equal numbers of officials. It is of course possible that there might be some case in which a State elects certain functionaries whose duties are so far removed from normal governmental activities and so disproportionately affect different groups that a popular election in compliance with [one man, one vote] might not be required.[10]

Sailors and *Fortson v. Morris* [11] were distinguished as cases where the State chose to appoint members to an official body rather than elect them.[12] But once a popular election mechanism is chosen one person, one vote must apply. If an official is appointed to a position, then one person, one vote need not apply.

However, the Court has found, in conformity with the *Hadley* principle, that some elected entities are so specialized that the one person, one vote rule need not be applied to them. In several cases the Court upheld the restriction of votes to elected members of a water storage district which gave the franchise only to local owners and weighted the votes according to the amount of property the individuals held. While not a classic districting case, these franchise restrictions did allow for differing degrees of voter participation. The activities of the water storage district fell disproportionally on the landowners as a group. The Court upheld this deviation from the one person, one vote principle because in these cases the restrictions furthered the interest of insuring that land owners controlled the limited water supply in these areas.[13]

In *Town of Lockport v. Citizens for Community Action at the Local Level, Inc.,*[14] a unanimous Court upheld a provision of New York law which provided that a new county charter could go into effect only if it is approved by a referendum election by separate majorities of the voters who live in the cities within the county and those who live in the county but outside of the cities. The Court noted that in order to determine whether a concurrent majority requirement violates the principle of one person, one vote, the Court will focus on two inquiries: first, is there a genuine difference in the relevant interests of the groups that the state electoral classification has created; second, if there is such

---

8. 397 U.S. at 54, 55 (emphasis added).

9. 397 U.S. at 55.

10. 397 U.S. at 56.

11. 385 U.S. 231 (1966).

12. 397 U.S. at 58.

13. Salyer Land Co. v. Tulare Lake Basin Water Storage District, 410 U.S. 719 (1973); Associated Enterprises, Inc. v. Toltec Watershed Improvement District, 410 U.S. 743 (1973).

Over the strong dissents of four justices the Court applied the principle of these cases in Ball v. James, 451 U.S. 355 (1981), where it upheld the constitutionali-

ty of the system for electing the directors of a large Arizona water reclamation district which limited voter eligibility to landowners and apportioned voting power according to the amount of land a voter owns. The Court concluded that the "peculiarly narrow function of this local governmental body and the special relationship of one class of citizens to that body release[d] it from the strict demands of the one-person-one-vote principle. . . . " 451 U.S. at 357.

14. 430 U.S. 259 (1977); cf. Hill v. Stone, 421 U.S. 289 (1975); Phoenix v. Kolodziejski, 399 U.S. 204 (1970); Cipriano v. City of Houma, 395 U.S. 701 (1969).

a difference, does the enhancement of minority votes nonetheless amount to invidious discrimination. The Court analyzed the purposes of the New York law; noted that in some counties the city voters outnumbered the town voters and in other counties the situation was the reverse; and recognized that a new or amended county charter will frequently operate to transfer functions from cities to county. Just as in annexation proceedings the residents of the annexing city and the area to be annexed have sufficiently different constituencies and interests, the decision to restructure county government is similar in impact and justifies the concurrent majorities requirement.

Finally, it should be remembered that the one person, one vote principle applies where the representative is elected by district and not where the area serves not as a voting district but only as a basis for residence. For example, where the residents of a city are allowed to vote to elect all the representatives but these representatives are required to live in certain areas, the one person, one vote rules do not apply to these areas. Since each person votes for all the representatives, even though each representative must live in a given area, there is no districting of voters. The areas where the representatives live need not be equal in population.[15]

3. *Mathematical Precision*

a. *In Federal Elections*

In *Wesberry v. Sanders*[1] the Supreme Court required states to draw their congressional districts so that "*as nearly as is prac-*

ticable one man's vote in a congressional election is to be worth as much as another's."[2] In subsequent litigation the Court has had occasion to explain what it meant, and the Court's explanation has shown it to be literally minded. In *Kirkpatrick v. Preisler*,[3] for example, a decision rendered when Earl Warren was Chief Justice, the Court struck down a congressional districting plan where "the most populous district was 3.13% above the mathematical ideal, and the least populous was 2.84% below."[4] The Court found no justification for even this small deviation and explicitly rejected any argument that there is any variance small enough to be considered de minimis. Moreover, it was no justification that the State attempted to avoid fragmenting political subdivisions by drawing the Congressional districts along existing county lines or other political subdivisions. In districting for the House of Representatives the State must "make a good-faith effort to achieve precise mathematical equality."[5] That same day the Court invalidated a New York plan with slightly larger variations.[6]

The Court has continued to follow this principle. Thus in *White v. Weiser*[7] the Court invalidated a reapportionment plan where the differences were even smaller than *Kirkpatrick*. In *White* the average deviation of all districts from the ideal was .745%; the largest district exceeded the ideal by 2.43% and the smallest district under the ideal by only 1.7%. The plan was rejected in favor of one where the largest district exceeded the ideal by .086% and the smallest was under the ideal by .063%.[8] Again it should be remembered that the one person,

---

15. Dallas County v. Reese, 421 U.S. 477 (1975) (per curiam).

1. 376 U.S. 1 (1964).

2. Id. at 7–8 (emphasis added).

For an argument that the fourteenth amendment and the census clause (U.S. Const. Art. I, § 2, cl. 3) grant each citizen a right to an accurate census, and for a discussion of the lower court cases on this issue, see, e.g., Note, Constitutional Implications of a Population Undercount: Making Sense of the Census Clause, 69 Georgetown L.J. 1427 (1981).

3. 394 U.S. 526 (1969).

4. 394 U.S. at 528–29 (footnote omitted).

5. 394 U.S. at 530–31.

6. Wells v. Rockefeller, 394 U.S. 542 (1969) (most populous district 6.488% above the mean; smallest district 6.608% below the mean).

7. 412 U.S. 783 (1973).

8. 412 U.S. at 786, 796–97. See also, Karcher v. Daggett, 103 S.Ct. ___ (1983) (disparity between largest district and smallest district of 0.6984%; plan invalidated).

one vote requirement in federal elections is based on Article I rather than the Equal Protection Clause of the Fourteenth Amendment.

b. In State Elections

As we have seen, the one man, one vote mandate with respect to Congressional districting is based on Article 1, § 2 of the Constitution, but the apportionment in elections for state or local offices is justified by the Equal Protection Clause of the Fourteenth Amendment. Thus the strict application of the one man, one vote standard for Congressional districting does not require a similar rule for other elections, where the Court has been more flexible. In *Abate v. Mundt*,[9] the Court allowed deviations in a County Board of Supervisors election where the most underrepresented town deviated from the ideal by 7.1% and the most overrepresented deviated 4.8%. The Court found justification on the "long tradition of overlapping functions and dual personnel in Rockland County government and on the fact that the plan before us does not contain a built-in bias tending to favor particular political interests or geographic areas." [10]

In *Mahan v. Howell* [11] the Court formally recognized that while population alone is the sole criterion to judge a congressional districting scheme, "broader latitude has been afforded the States under the Equal Protection Clause in state legislative redistricting . . . ." [12] In *Mahan* the most overrepresented district exceeded the ideal by 6.8%, the most underrepresented exceeded the ideal by 9.6%, these variations were found justified by the state policy of respecting political subdivision boundaries.

Subsequently, de minimis variations were found to require no justifications at all: in a case where the most overrepresented district exceeded the ideal by 5.8% and the most underrepresented was under by 4.1%, for a total variation of 9.9%, the Court held that 9.9% total variation does not make out a prima facie case and does not require any special justification.[13] However, deviations of up to 16.5% for state senate districts and 19.3% for state house of representative districts have been held to violate the one person, one vote principle.[14]

While the Court has not created a special test for local governmental units, it seems clear that deviations in the one person, one vote principle will be held to, at most, no higher a standard than that imposed on state governments. The Court has upheld a deviation of 11.9% for a local government unit at a time before it recognized the reasonableness test for state governments.[15]

c. Who Counts?

The Court has not created a rule which sets a fixed requirement of who must be counted to determine the equality of representation. In general the cases have required that the apportionment be made on the basis of total population even though the actual voters may be apportioned differently because of peculiar distribution of persons of certain ages or other characteristics which may properly preclude them from voting.[16] Thus, the Court has not required the states to "include aliens, transients, short-term or temporary residents, or persons denied the vote for conviction of crime, in the apportionment base by which their legislators are distributed . . . ." [17] However

---

9. 403 U.S. 182 (1971).

10. 403 U.S. at 187.

11. 410 U.S. 315 (1973).

12. 410 U.S. 322.

13. White v. Regester, 412 U.S. 755, 763 (1973); accord, Gaffney v. Cummings, 412 U.S. 735 (1973).

14. Connor v. Finch, 431 U.S. 407 (1977). Contrast Brown v. Thomson, 103 S.Ct. ___ (1983) (maximum deviation of 89% allowed under peculiar circumstances: plaintiffs asked for relief which would not really solve

the malapportionment; state plan followed a neutral principle).

15. Abate v. Mundt, 403 U.S. 182, 185 (1971) (Court notes that local government needs "considerable flexibility" to meet "changing societal" needs).

16. Burns v. Richardson, 384 U.S. 73, 91–92 (1966); see WMCA, Inc. v. Lomenzo, 377 U.S. 633 (1964) (apportionment based on United States citizenship population).

17. Burns v. Richardson, 384 U.S. 73, 92 (1966).

the state cannot reduce the voting strength of an area because it contains military personnel.[18] "The difference between exclusion of all military and military-related personnel and exclusion of those not meeting a State's residence requirements is a difference between an arbitrary and constitutionally permissible classification"[19] because the former discriminates on the basis of employment while the latter does not offer voting strength to those who validly do not have the vote.

The Court has also upheld a state plan which used registered voters as the population basis when the state has a large transient population and the use of the registered voter figure was not substantially different than a result based on state citizen population.[20]

4. *Multimember Districts*

The Court early held that the Equal Protection Clause does not require that even one house of a bicameral state legislature consist of single-member election districts.[1] But multimember districts will be invalidated if "designedly or otherwise" they operate "to minimize or cancel out the voting strength of racial or political elements of the voting population."[2] Multimember districts are not per se unconstitutional, even if a group with distinctive interests is found numerous enough to command at least one seat and represents a majority in an area sufficiently compact enough to constitute a single-member district. Otherwise it would be "difficult to reject claims of Democrats, Republicans, or members of any political organization . . . who live in what would be safe districts in a single-member district

system but who in one year or another, or year after year, are submerged in a one-sided multi-member district vote."[3] Also, the State may use such multimember districts in one part of the state and single member districts in other parts.[4]

However, in *White v. Regester*,[5] the Court upheld a judgment of a District court which invalidated two multimember districts, one found to discriminate against blacks, the other against Mexican-Americans. The Court found that plaintiffs had proven that "the political processes leading to nomination and election were not equally open to participation by the group in question—that its members had less opportunity than did other residents in the district to participate in the political processes and to elect legislators of their choice."[6] With respect to the multimember district found to discriminate against blacks, for example, the District Court had noted a past history of official racial discrimination against blacks which at times related to their right to vote and otherwise participate in the Democratic processes. Certain characteristics of state electoral system—for example, requiring a majority vote to secure nomination in a primary election—while not improper did enhance "the opportunity for racial discrimination."[7] The lower court also found that since Reconstruction days, there have been only two blacks elected to the state's lower house, and then only after being slated by "a white-dominated organization that is in effective control" of the County's slating.[8] And that organization was found not to have shown any concern for the needs of the black community. Given the trial court's findings, its ruling as

---

18. Davis v. Mann, 377 U.S. 678, 691 (1964).

19. Burns v. Richardson, 384 U.S. 73, 92 n. 21 (1966); see Hadley v. Junior College District, 397 U.S. 50, 57 n. 9 (1970).

20. Burns v. Richardson, 384 U.S. 73, 91–97 (1966).

1. Fortson v. Dorsey, 379 U.S. 433 (1965); Burns v. Richardson, 384 U.S. 73 (1966).

2. 379 U.S. at 439; 384 U.S. at 88.

3. Whitcomb v. Chavis, 403 U.S. 124, 156 (1971) (footnote omitted).

4. E.g., 403 U.S. at 127–28 (8 out of 31 senatorial districts and 25 out of 39 house districts multimember; upheld.).

5. 412 U.S. 755 (1973).

6. 412 U.S. at 766.

7. Id.

8. Id. at 766–67.

to these multimember districts was upheld in these circumstances.

However, when the district court is itself forced to fashion a reapportionment plan, "single-member districts are preferable to large multi-member districts as a general matter." [9]

In *Wise v. Lipscomb* [10] the Court affirmed the principles that multimember legislative districts are not per se unconstitutional, that federal courts should make every effort not to preempt legislative bodies from devising their own reapportionment plans, that only when the legislative body does not respond or a state election is imminent should a federal court impose a reapportionment plan, that federal courts, when imposing such a reapportionment plan, are held to "stricter standards" on review, and that one of these stricter standards is that "a court-drawn plan should prefer single member districts over multimember districts, absent persuasive justification to the contrary." [11] The real issue in *Wise* was how to determine whether the plan was court-drawn or legislatively derived.

In *Wise*, six members of the Court agreed that the plan was really legislatively enacted, and therefore there was no need to satisfy the special test applicable to a court plan creating a multimember district; however, the majority could not agree how to determine if a plan is really legislatively derived.

Two justices of the majority argued that a plan cannot be considered legislatively imposed if the political body offering it to the district court lacks the legal power to reapportion itself. These justices also found

that there was no evidence under state law that in the circumstances of this case the city council exceeded its authority. [12]

Four justices thought that the crucial factor was that the city council exercised its legislative and popular judgment, which justifies a lesser amount of judicial review. Under this theory it is irrelevant if state law does not allow the legislative body, in this case the city council, to reapportion itself. [13]

The three justices dissenting agreed that before a plan can be treated as legislatively devised, the legislative body must have the legal authority to reapportion itself but that such authority was lacking here because under state law, in the view of the dissent, the city council could only be reapportioned by popular referendum. [14]

5. *Political Gerrymandering*

Related to, but still distinct from, the racial and political issues involved in multimember districts are similar issues involved in political gerrymandering, i.e., drawing political lines to take into account various political strengths. "But compactness or attractiveness has never been held to constitute an independent federal constitutional requirement for state legislative districts." [1] In fact, such political considerations are inherent in any reapportionment scheme:

District lines are rarely neutral phenomena. They can well determine what district will be predominately Democratic or predominately Republican, or make a close race likely. Redistricting may pit incumbents against one another or make very difficult the election of the most experienced legislator. . . .

It may be suggested that those who redistrict and reapportion should work with census,

---

9. Connor v. Johnson, 402 U.S. 690, 692 (1971).

10. 437 U.S. 535 (1978).

11. Part II of Justice White's opinion, joined by Justice Stewart, articulated these principles. 437 U.S. at 539. Justice Marshall, dissenting, joined by Justices Brennan and Stevens, agreed with Part II, thus five justices agreed on these principles. 437 U.S. at 550. The concurring opinion of the four other justices did not dispute Part II of Justice White's opinion. See 437 U.S. at 549. (Powell, J., joined by Burger, C.J., and Blackmun and Rehnquist, JJ.).

12. 437 U.S. at 544–545 & n. 8, relying on and distinguishing East Carroll Parish School Board v. Marshall, 424 U.S. 636 (1976) (per curiam).

13. 437 U.S. at 547–548, relying on Burns v. Richardson, 384 U.S. 73 (1966), distinguishing *East Carroll*, supra note 12, and reading it "as turning on its peculiar facts."

14. 437 U.S. at 552.

1. Gaffney v. Cummings, 412 U.S. 735, 752 n. 18 (1973).

not political, data and achieve population equality without regard for political impact. But this politically mindless approach may produce, whether intended or not, the most grossly gerrymandered results; and, in any event, it is most unlikely that the political impact of such a plan would remain undiscovered by the time it was proposed or adopted, in which event the results would be both known and, if not changed, intended.[2]

To be distinguished from this "political fairness" issue is racial gerrymandering. To draw political boundaries to fence out racial groups is unconstitutional and the Court has acted to enforce such minority rights even before the one man, one vote rule was created.[3]

6. Departures From Strict Majority Rule

In *Gordon v. Lance* [1] the Court upheld a West Virginia law requiring a 60% vote requirement before political subdivisions of the State incurred bonded indebtedness or increased tax notes above a certain amount. The 60% vote requirement constituted no geographic discrimination unlike the typical reapportionment case. The Court also appeared not to disapprove a requirement that more than a majority vote be assembled for some issues in a state legislature or that a given issue be approved by a majority of all registered voters.[2] "[T]here is nothing in the language of the Constitution, our history, or our cases that requires that a majority always prevail on every issue." [3]

Explicitly not considered in *Gordon* was whether a provision requiring unanimity or giving a veto to a "very small group" would be constitutional, or whether it was proper to require "extraordinary majorities" to elect public officers.[4]

X. THE RIGHT TO TRAVEL

A. The Right to Travel Abroad

The right to travel abroad pits the constitutional right of travel against the broad power of the government in the international area. Just as the equal protection rights of illegitimates are significantly lessened in the context of the government's foreign affairs power over immigration,[1] so also when the right to travel is exercised in the context of international travel, governmental power frequently overcomes this right.

The three leading Supreme Court cases which introduce this area of the law are: *Kent v. Dulles,*[2] *Aptheker v. Secretary of State,*[3] and *Zemel v. Rusk.*[4]

Kent v. Dulles, as Justice Douglas, writing for the Court specifically noted, did "not reach the question of constitutionality." [5] Its importance stems from its broad dictum. Passports had been denied to two applicants because of their communist background. Douglas first discussed the history of passports in this country. Except for certain intervals in our history, particularly in wartime, for "most of our history a passport was not a condition to entry or exit." [6] It was a document addressed to foreign powers, requesting that the bearer be allowed to pass safely and freely as an American citizen; [7] and it established citizenship to enable the bearer to reenter the United States.[8]

---

2. Id. at 753.

3. Gomillion v. Lightfoot, 364 U.S. 339 (1960). Cf. United Jewish Organizations of Williamsburgh, Inc. v. Carey, 430 U.S. 144 (1977) (racial reapportionment decision under section 5 of Voting Rights Act, 42 U.S.C.A. § 1973c).

1. 403 U.S. 1 (1971).

2. 403 U.S. at 7.

3. 403 U.S. at 6.

4. 303 U.S. at 8 n. 6. Cf. Town of Lockport v. Citizens for Community Action, 430 U.S. 259 (1977) (concurrent majority requirements upheld for local government units under special circumstances).

1. Compare Fiallo v. Bell, 430 U.S. 787 (1977), with Trimble v. Gordon, 430 U.S. 762 (1977).

2. 357 U.S. 116 (1958).

3. 378 U.S. 500 (1964).

4. 381 U.S. 1 (1965).

5. Kent v. Dulles, 357 U.S. 116, 129 (1958).

6. Id. at 123.

7. Urtetiqui v. D'Arcy, 34 U.S. (9 Pet.) 692, 699 (1885).

8. Browder v. United States, 312 U.S. 335, 339 (1941).

Douglas next noted that it has often been said that the issuance of passports is a discretionary act, but the justice was unwilling to accept this earlier dictum. He argued: "The right to travel is part of the 'liberty' of which the citizen cannot be deprived without due process of law under the Fifth Amendment." [9] Moreover, while the dictum of discretion as to the issuance of passports is broad, in fact the power over issuance has been exercised quite narrowly. Thus, the Court hesitated to impute to Congress, "when in 1952 it made a passport necessary for foreign travel and left its issuance to the discretion of the Secretary of State, a purpose to give him unbridled discretion to grant or withhold a passport from a citizen for any substantive reason he may choose." [10] The Court did not decide that the reasons relied on by the Secretary of State could not be enacted by Congress nor did it decide that such broad delegation could not occur; it simply said that such broad delegation had not occurred. But within this context the dictum supporting the right to travel abroad seemed quite broad.

In *Aptheker* the Court appeared to follow the broad language of *Kent*, but again its decision rested on narrower grounds. In this case several ranking officials of the Communist Party of the United States had their passports revoked. This time there was no question of whether Congress had delegated such power to the Secretary of State; it had. Section 6 of the Subversive Activities Control Act of 1950 provided that it was unlawful for any member of a Communist organization which was registered or under a final order to register, to use, apply for, renew a passport if the applicant had knowledge or notice that the organization is registered or that an order to register was final. Justice Goldberg's opinion for the Court quoted with approval the language in

Kent as to the right to travel abroad. [11] But Goldberg's opinion actually decided the case on another ground. Given the importance of the right to travel, the degree of the legislative abridgement must be restricted to the least drastic means of achieving the same purpose. [12] In this case, Section 6 was overbroad on its face. The section applied whether or not the member actually knew or believed he was associated with what was deemed to be a communist-action or communist-front organization. The section also included both knowing and unknowing members. For these and similar reasons the section was held unconstitutional on its face. But the Court did not hold that Congress could not enact a more narrowly drawn statute.

Finally, in *Zemel v. Rusk* [13] the Court was faced with an explicit, narrow Congressional prohibition of travel to Cuba. This prohibition was upheld, with Chief Justice Warren writing the opinion of the Court. The opinion found, first, that Congress had authorized the Secretary of State to refuse to validate American passports for travel to Cuba—where the United States had broken diplomatic and consular relations—and second, that the exercise of that authority is constitutional. The Court admitted that the legislative history of the basic passport act does not affirmatively indicate an intention to authorize area restrictions on travel abroad, but "its language is surely broad enough to authorize area restrictions . . . " [14] This reading of Congressional delegation illustrates an approach not displayed in *Kent v. Dulles*. [15] *Kent* was distinguished first, because the history of administrative practice in *Kent* was different than that shown in *Zemel*, and second, because the issue involved in *Kent* was whether a citizen could be denied a passport because of his political beliefs or associations, while in *Zemel* the Secretary of State refused to vali-

9.   357 U.S. at 125.

10. Id. at 128.

11. 378 U.S. at 505–06.

12. Id. at 508.

13. 381 U.S. 1 (1965).

14. Id. at 8.

15. 357 U.S. 116 (1958).

date the passport "not because of any characteristic peculiar to appellant, but rather because of foreign policy considerations affecting all citizens." [16]

The constitutionality of the Secretary's decision was then upheld basically by relying on the foreign policy context of the case. "That the restriction which is challenged in this case is supported by the weightiest considerations of national security is perhaps best pointed up by recalling that the Cuban missile crisis of October 1962 preceded filing of appellant's complaint by less than two months." [17] The majority again cited with approval the *Kent* dictum that the right of travel is a part of the liberty of which a citizen cannot be deprived without due process, but it pointedly noted that the fact "a liberty cannot be inhibited without due process of law does not mean it can under no circumstances be inhibited." [18] In this case, the inhibition was proper.[19]

Following these three cases the Court was asked to rule on the constitutionality of congressional restrictions on the payment of certain Social Security benefits; these restrictions limited payments to those who, in certain circumstances, exercised their right to engage in international travel. In *Califano v. Aznavorian* [20] a unanimous Supreme Court upheld a provision of the Social Security Act which provided that benefits would not be paid to a recipient residing outside of the United States for 30 days until that person once again had been a resident of this country for 30 days.

The Court first found that the constitutionality of welfare legislation should be upheld if a *rational basis* existed for the classification; scrutiny of the law would be intensified only if the classification related to a fundamental right or employed a suspect classification. The right to travel *abroad*, however, is not judged by the same standards applied to laws which directly burden the right of *interstate* travel by use of durational residence requirements.[21] Moreover, this law had a lesser impact on international travel than those examined in *Kent*, *Aptheker*, or *Zemel* because here the statutory provision did not limit the availability of passports nor burden the exercise of first amendment rights. "It merely withdraws a governmental benefit during and shortly after an extended absence from the country. Unless the limitation imposed by Congress is wholly irrational, it is constitutional in spite of its incidental effect on international travel." [22]

The next major case was *Haig v. Agee*,[23] where the Court, relying on *Zemel v. Rusk*,[24] upheld the powers of the Secretary of State to revoke the passport of one Philip Agee, an American residing abroad, on the grounds that his activities caused or were likely to cause serious damage to American national security or foreign policy. In *Agee*, however, unlike *Zemel* the Court did not rely

---

16. 381 U.S. at 13.

17. 381 U.S. at 16.

18. Id. at 14 (footnote omitted).

As to the test to govern federal burdens on travel between the states of the United States and the District of Columbia on the one hand, and Puerto Rico on the other, see Harris v. Rosario, 446 U.S. 651 (1980), holding that Congress may treat Puerto Rico differently so long as there is a rational basis for its actions. In that case Congress could provide less federal welfare benefits to Puerto Rican residents, who do not pay U.S. income taxes. See also, Califano v. Gautier Torres, 435 U.S. 1 (1978) (per curiam) (unique status of Puerto Rico justified federal limitations on payment of supplemental social security).

19. Justices Black, Douglas, and Goldberg all dissented. 381 U.S. at 20 (Black, J.); at 23 (Douglas J., joined by Goldberg, J.); at 27 (Goldberg, J.).

20. 439 U.S. 170 (1978).

21. Cf. Section X, B, infra.

22. 439 U.S. at 177. Justices Marshall and Brennan concurred in the result but objected to the "wholly irrational" test if that standard implied a lesser standard of review than the traditional rational basis test. 439 U.S. at 178. Congress may pass separate legislation for territories and may treat a territory, such as Puerto Rico, differently than the states in terms of federal assistance. This disparate treatment will be upheld "so long as there is a rational basis for its [the Congress'] actions." Harris v. Rosario, 446 U.S. 651 (1980) (per curiam) (upholding lower level of federal reimbursement to Aid to Families with Dependent Children program in Puerto Rico).

23. 453 U.S. 280 (1981).

24. 381 U.S. 1 (1965).

on prior administrative *practice* but rather on administrative *policy*.

Agee was a former employee of the Central Intelligence Agency who had been trained in clandestine operations. In 1974 he publicly announced his intention to expose CIA officers and agents. To carry out his program he would travel to a given country and consult with people within the local diplomatic service he knew based on his prior CIA experience. "He recruit[ed] collaborators and train[ed] them in clandestine techniques designed to expose the 'cover' of CIA employees and sources." [25]

In 1979 the Secretary of State revoked Agee's passport, pursuant to Departmental regulations and based on a determination that his activities "are causing or are likely to cause serious damage to the national security of the United States." [26] Agee sued claiming that Congress had not authorized the regulation and that it was unconstitutional. He moved for summary judgment and for "purposes of that motion, Agee conceded the Government's factual averments and its claim that his activities were causing or were likely to cause serious damage to the national security or foreign policy of the United States." [27]

The Court first concluded that although the Passport Act of 1926 "does not in so many words confer upon the Secretary a power to revoke a passport," [28] the fact that there was no evidence that Congress intended to repudiate the prior administrative construction led the Court to find that Congress, in 1926, adopted the previous assertions of executive power. An "unbroken line of Executive Orders, regulations, in-

structions to consular officials, and notices to passport holders" [29] evidenced the prior interpretation.

Agee responded that in order for the Executive to establish implicit congressional approval it must show "longstanding and consistent *enforcement* of the claimed power: that is, by showing that many passports were revoked on national security and foreign policy grounds." [30] The Court rejected that argument. "[I]f there were no occasions—or few—to call the Secretary's authority into play, the absence of frequent instances of enforcement is wholly irrelevant." [31] It is enough that the Executive's announcement of policy was " 'sufficiently substantial and consistent' to compel the conclusion that Congress has approved it." [32]

Justice Blackmun, in his concurrence, correctly recognized that the majority opinion, although purporting to rely upon *Zemel v. Rusk* [33] and *Kent v. Dulles,* [34] was actually cutting back on their reasoning because those cases required not merely the announcement of administrative *policy* but also substantial and consistent administrative *practice* in order to establish that Congress had implicitly approved the administrative interpretation.[35] Justice Brennan, joined by Justice Marshall, agreed with that analysis, but supported the original reasoning of *Zemel* and *Kent* and therefore dissented in a forceful opinion.[36]

The majority also rejected the other grounds which Agee raised. Relying on *Califano v. Aznavorian* [37] the Court majority found no violation of the freedom to travel abroad because the restriction on travel

---

25. 453 U.S. at 284. See also, 453 U.S. at 283 & n. 2. See generally, P. Agee & L. Wolf, eds., Dirty Work: The CIA in Western Europe (1978).

26. 453 U.S. at 286.

27. 453 U.S. at 287 (footnotes omitted).

28. 453 U.S. at 290.

29. 453 U.S. at 298.

30. 453 U.S. at 301–02 (emphasis in original). Agee relied on Kent v. Dulles, 357 U.S. 116, 127–28 (1958).

31. 453 U.S. at 302. The Court contended that *Kent* was "not contrary" to its ruling in *Agee*. Id. at

303. However, the Court of Appeals had ruled that *Kent* required a ruling in Agee's favor. 629 F.2d 80, 87 (D.C.Cir.1980).

32. 453 U.S. at 306.

33. 381 U.S. 1 (1965).

34. 357 U.S. 116 (1958).

35. 453 U.S. at 310 (Blackmun, J., concurring).

36. 453 U.S. at 310–21 (Brennan, J., joined by Marshall, J., dissenting).

37. 439 U.S. 170 (1978).

served a reasonable, indeed compelling, governmental interest: protecting the security of the nation.[38]

The Court then quickly turned to and rejected without any substantial discussion Agee's other constitutional arguments that the passport violated his free speech and constituted a taking of his liberty interests without procedural due process.[39] Agee responded by securing a new passport from Grenada; he announced that he would continue his activities against the CIA.[40]

This case probable signals an increased judicial deference to the Executive Branch in matters of foreign affairs.[41]

B. The Right to Interstate Travel

The right to travel between and among the states has been recognized as a fundamental constitutional right. Any governmental act which restricts the right to interstate migration should be subject to independent judicial review to determine whether it serves a sufficiently important governmental interest to offset the impairment of the right to travel. A law regulating the right to change residency should be tested under the due process guarantee if it is a general limitation on the ability of all persons to travel and under the equal protection guarantee if it is a denial of the right to travel on only a limited class of persons. It is often said that regulations restricting the right to travel are subject to strict judicial scrutiny and will be upheld only if the government can demonstrate that the regulation serves an overriding governmental interest. However, such statements may be misleading in describing the type of judicial limita-

tion placed upon the government's ability to create laws which may have some effect on interstate mobility. The Court has identified a federal interest, and a fundamental right, regarding the ability of persons to change their residency from one state to another. A law which restricts that aspect of the right to travel will be subject to close judicial scrutiny and should not be upheld unless the law serves an important governmental interest. Of special importance in this area are laws which establish residency requirements for certain governmental benefits. The state may be free to limit welfare benefits to those who are lawfully resident within the state but it should not be allowed to impose durational residency requirements for government benefits which effectively make it impossible, or at least very difficult, for a class of persons to migrate into the state. Similarly, states should not be able to differentiate between "old" and "new" citizens in the dispensation of governmental services. If the right to interstate mobility means anything, it should mean that a state should not be able to use the length of a person's residency as an arbitrary means of defining that person to be "different" and not deserving of equal treatment with other persons in the state. Not all laws which restrict interstate mobility need be subject to close judicial scrutiny. In some instances those laws serve important state interests and have little or no effect on the ability of persons to migrate into the state. The state should be able to control the dispensation of governmental benefits so long as it does not unreasonably interfere with the ability of persons to change their residency.[1]

38. 453 U.S. at 308.

39. 453 U.S. at 308–09.

40. Newsweek, Aug. 10, 1981, at 15 ("Philip Agee's Grenadian Passport").

41. See generally, Farber, National Security, The Right to Travel, and the Court, 1981 S.Ct.Rev. 263. Cf. Nowak and Rotunda, A Comment on the Creation and Resolution of a "Non-Problem": Dames & Moore v. Regan, the Foreign Affairs Power, and the Role of the Court, 29 U.C.L.A. L.Rev. 1129 (1982) for a discussion of judicial deference in the foreign affairs area.

1. Compare Shapiro v. Thompson, 394 U.S. 618 (1969) (durational residency requirement for subsistence welfare benefits held invalid as a restriction on the fundamental right to travel) with Sosna v. Iowa, 419 U.S. 393 (1975) (one-year residency requirement for divorce upheld as not interfering with the right to relocate from one state to another). Compare Jones v. Helms, 452 U.S. 412 (1981) (upholding statute making abandonment of child by a parent a felony if the parent leaves the state after abandonment) with Zobel v. Williams, 457 U.S. 55 (1982) (invalidating state distribution of state money to citizens in varying amounts based

The right to travel has been recognized in one form or another throughout the history of the Republic. The Articles of Confederation explicitly recognized the right of the people of each state to "have free ingress and regress to and from any other State".[2] This provision was not included in the text of the Constitution or the proposed Bill of Rights and the reason for its exclusion is not clear. It has been suggested that it was believed to be so basic a right that it need not be expressed in the text.[3] Another possibility is that the framers of the original Constitution believed that the guarantee was subsumed in the other protections given the citizens of each state by the privileges and immunities clause of Article IV and by the granting of the national commercial power to Congress.[4] This explanation has a textual basis in that these provisions of the Constitution are similar to those which were joined with the mobility provision in the Articles of Confederation;[5] the concept of interstate travel may have been considered to be a subset of these other rights. Prior to the Civil War the Court did not directly consider the scope of the right to travel between the states.[6] The Court in 1837 did approve a law which required the registration of passengers entering a state and in so doing indicated that the individual states had some inherent power to limit the terms upon which people entered the state.[7] However, the case did not involve a direct burden or prohibition and the language was limited only a few years later in *The Passenger Cases*[8] when the justices invalidated state legislation that imposed a tax upon alien passengers arriving from foreign ports.

Following the Civil War the Supreme Court held that there was an inherent right to individual travel between the states. In *Crandall v. Nevada*,[9] the Court held unconstitutional a statute which imposed a tax on railroads for every passenger carried out of the state. The majority opinion held the matter to be an unconstitutional interference with the inherent right of a citizen to travel. When the Court limited the scope of the privileges or immunities clause of the fourteenth amendment in *The Slaughter-House Cases* the opinion still recognized that one of the attributes of national citizenship was the freedom to travel through individual states.[10]

The Court did not expand this concept in terms of an independent national right for some years, although it would occasionally mention the right as one pertaining to national citizenship. The laws relating to travel which were reviewed by the Supreme Court during this period related to the entrance of interstate commerce into a state. However, during this period the Court did uphold a two year residence requirement to

---

upon the length of each citizen's residence). The Court's rulings in right to travel cases are discussed in this section. The reader should also consider how these cases fit into the Court's general approach to "standards of review" under the equal protection and due process guarantees. See Section I, C of this Chapter.

2. Articles of Confederation, art. IV (1778) (reprinted, e.g., in Chapter 21, of the Lawyer's Edition of J. Nowak, R. Rotunda, & J. Young, Constitutional Law (West Hornbook Series, 2d Ed. 1983).

3. United States v. Guest, 383 U.S. 745, 758 (1966) (majority opinion by Stewart, J.); Z. Chafee, Three Human Rights 185 (1956).

4. The basis for the right to personal mobility is examined in connection with the Commerce Clause restrictions on the states and the Interstate Privileges and Immunities Clause in Chapter 9, Section IV.

5. The Articles of Confederation, art. IV in part read:

"[T]he free inhabitants of each of these States, paupers, vagabonds and fugitives from justice excepted, shall be entitled to all privileges and immunities of free citizens in the several States; and the people of each State shall have free ingress and regress to and from any other State, and shall enjoy therein all the privileges of trade and commerce, subject to the same duties, impositions and restrictions as the inhabitants thereof respectively . . . "

6. There were statements in commerce clause cases indicating that some right existed, see notes 7 and 8 infra; see also Corfield v. Corgell, 6 Fed.Cas. 546, 552 (No. 3230) (C.C.E.D.Pa.1823).

7. Mayor and City of New York v. Miln, 36 U.S. (11 Pet.) 102 (1837).

8. 48 U.S. (7 How.) 283 (1849).

9. 73 U.S. (6 Wall.) 35 (1867).

10. The Slaughter-House Cases, 83 U.S. (16 Wall.) 36, 79 (1873).

become an insurance broker within a state.[11] This comported with the Court's view that the insurance industry was a matter for local regulation and that laws which burdened the entry of new insurance businesses into the state did not violate the commerce clause.[12]

The Court's next opportunity to confront the issue of a personal right to travel came in *Edwards v. California.*[13] In an effort to keep out indigents fleeing the economic depression in other parts of the country, the State of California passed the statute which penalized the bringing into the state of any non-resident person by anyone knowing the individual to be "an indigent person." The majority opinion held that this statute violated the commerce clause. Even accepting the state's argument that the migration of poor persons had brought grave problems of health and finance to the state, the majority opinion found that the state's attempt to lock out the transportation of persons across its borders was a classic trade barrier which fell within the prohibition of the commerce clause.[14] Four of the justices, in concurring opinions, would have held that the statute violated the Constitution because the right to interstate travel was one of the privileges or immunities protected by the fourteenth amendment.[15] Justice Jackson's opinion in that case has become not only the best exposition of the inherent right to travel but also a classic statement regarding the fact that fundamental constitutional rights should not be allocated by wealth. He stated:

> That choice of residence was subject to local approval is contrary to the inescapable implication of the westward movement of our civilization . . . We should say now, and in no uncertain terms, that a man's mere property

status, without more, cannot be used by a state to test, qualify, or limit his rights as a citizen of the United States. "Indigence" itself is neither a source of rights nor a basis for denying them . . . If I doubted whether his federal citizenship alone were enough to open the gates of California to Duncan, my doubt would disappear on consideration of the obligations of such citizenship . . . Rich or penniless, Duncan's citizenship under the Constitution pledges his strength to the defense of California as a part of the United States, and his right to migrate to any part of the land he must defend is something she must respect under the same instrument. Unless this Court is willing to say that citizenship of the United States means at least this much to the citizen, then our heritage of constitutional privileges and immunities is only a promise to the ear to be broken to the hope, a teasing illusion like a munificent bequest in a pauper's will.[16]

The Court next examined the right to interstate travel in connection with the review of a federal statute designed to protect that right. In *United States v. Guest*[17] the Supreme Court upheld the application of the criminal conspiracy provision of the Civil Rights Acts to private individuals who attempted to deprive black persons of the right to enjoy public facilities connected with interstate travel. The majority opinion did not state that Congress could prohibit the actions of private persons that interfere with any rights that might be protected by the fourteenth amendment although a majority appeared to accept this position.[18] Justice Stewart had the clear support of more than a majority of the Justices when he held that the right to interstate travel was a fundamental incident of federal citizenship which the Congress was free to protect to its fullest extent. Justice Stewart noted the history of the right which dated back to the Arti-

11. LaTourette v. McMaster, 248 U.S. 465 (1919).

12. Paul v. Virginia, 75 U.S. (8 Wall.) 168 (1868).

13. 314 U.S. 160 (1941).

14. 314 U.S. at 173–74.

15. 314 U.S. 160, 177 (Douglas, J., concurring, joined by Black and Murphy, JJ.); id. at 181 (Jackson, J., concurring).

16. Edwards v. California, 314 U.S. 160, 183–86 (1941) (Jackson, J., concurring).

17. 383 U.S. 745 (1966).

18. 383 U.S. at 762 (Clark, J., concurring, joined by Black and Fortas, JJ.). Id. at 782 & n. 6 (Brennan J., concurring, joined by Warren, C.J., and Douglas, J.). Justice Harlan found it "to say the least, extraordinary" that some of the justices would "cursorily pronounc[e] themselves" on "far-reaching constitutional questions . . . ." 383 U.S. at 762 n. 1 (Harlan, J., concurring in part and dissenting in part).

cles of Confederation and had continual, if implicit, recognition in the cases of the Court throughout history.[19] This ruling set the stage for full recognition of the right a few years later when the Court was confronted by state actions which inhibited the right to travel.

The landmark decision concerning the right to travel and the permissible scope of the burdens on that right which result from residency requirements came in *Shapiro v. Thompson*.[20] In this case the justices reviewed the permissibility of two state statutes and a District of Columbia statute which denied welfare benefits to persons who had not resided within the jurisdiction for at least one year. The Court found that the state statutes violated the equal protection clause of the fourteenth amendment and District act violated the equal protection guarantee of the due process clause of the fifth amendment. The basis for this equal protection ruling was that a residency requirement has the effect of deterring the entry of indigent persons into these jurisdictions, thereby limiting their rights to engage in interstate travel. The majority opinion held that, because the right limited was a fundamental constitutional right, the classification had to be invalidated unless it was "shown to be necessary to promote a *compelling* governmental interest." [21] The state's argument that it was attempting to deter indigents who entered the state solely to obtain larger benefits would not be permissible as the states had no right to exclude poor persons from their borders.[22] And the majority found that it was impermissible for the state to try to distinguish between old and new residents when that burdened fundamental rights. While the state might have some requirement that the persons be residents at the time they applied, they could not create subclasses of cit-

izens based on the duration of time that persons had been residents of the state. There was also no proof that the system significantly promoted the budgeting process of the state and the Court found that administrative efficiency was not such a compelling interest as to support the limitation of a fundamental right.

The primary dissent in *Shapiro* was that of Justice Harlan who attacked not only the Court's strict protection of the right to travel but the entire fundamental rights branch of equal protection analysis.[23] He found no basis for elevating the right to travel to a status under which the Court could review governmental policy in so strict a manner and he believed that protecting rights in this way because of their importance to daily life allowed the Court to sit as a super legislature.

The *Shapiro* analysis has been followed in a series of cases dealing with durational residence requirements. These statutes require not only that persons declare themselves to be residents of the state but that they maintain that residency status for a set duration of time prior to being eligible to receive some benefit or exercise some right. The right involved need not be a fundamental right in order to require the strict scrutiny analysis, for a durational residency requirement burdens the right to travel which is itself a fundamental right. Thus, any classification which burdens the right will be subject to strict judicial scrutiny to determine its legitimacy. In many of these cases the Court has invoked the language of the "compelling interest" test to indicate that these laws must meet a high standard before the justices will uphold them. However, in other cases the Court has issued rulings both upholding and striking residency requirements which indicate that the Court

---

19. 383 U.S. at 758.

20. 394 U.S. 618 (1969).

21. 394 U.S. at 634 (emphasis in original).

22. The Court later summarily affirmed the invalidation on a similar basis of a statute which was intended to bar only those persons who came into a state for

the sole purpose of obtaining welfare benefits. Gaddis v. Wyman, 304 F.Supp. 717 (N.D.N.Y.1969), affirmed sub nom. Wyman v. Bowens, 397 U.S. 49 (1970).

23. Shapiro v. Thompson, 394 U.S. 618, 655 (1969) (Harlan, J., dissenting). Justice Black and Chief Justice Warren also dissented.

may only be employing some form of true "reasonableness" test or an ad hoc balancing test when deciding whether these laws serve legitimate governmental purposes which justify a limitation of the right to travel.

The Supreme Court has never held that a state or local government is prohibited from requiring persons to be residents of that location in order to receive government benefits. The state may restrict some welfare benefits to *bona fide* residents.[24] The *Shapiro* rationale only requires close judicial scrutiny of durational residency requirements, a distinction between new and old residents. Each jurisdiction has a right to

limit voting to residents of that jurisdiction,[25] and the Court has held that residence within a specific area can be a requirement for public employment.[26] The Court has never foreclosed the possibility that some residence requirement for securing benefits may violate the right to travel, but neither has it indicated that a resident would be entitled to keep any form of state dispensed benefit upon leaving the state.[27]

The Supreme Court has dealt with the right to travel in terms of restrictions on voting eligibility in several cases. In these cases it has stricken the residency requirement whenever it was a period beyond that which was truly reasonable or necessary to

---

24. The Supreme Court has upheld a state statute which permitted a school district to deny tuition free education to a child who lived apart from his parent or lawful guardian if the child's presence in the school district was "for the primary purpose" of attending school in the district. Martinez v. Bynum, 103 S.Ct. 1838 (1983). "A bona fide residence requirement, appropriately defined and uniformly applied, furthers the substantial state interest in assuring that services provided for its residents are enjoyed only by residents." Id. at 1842. The majority opinion found that this residence requirement did not violate the equal protection clause because it was not based on a suspect classification and it did not limit the exercise of a fundamental right. The Court noted that public education was not such a right. Id. at 1842–43 n.7 *Martinez* held that the statute at issue was a bona fide residence requirement because it provided free education for all children who resided in the school district with the intent to remain in the district indefinitely. The Court did not pass upon the residency claim of the child in this case, a United States citizen whose parents were non-resident aliens living in Mexico. See Id. at 1845 (Brennan, J., concurring). Only Justice Marshall would have invalidated the residency requirement on its face. Id. at 1845 (Marshall, J., dissenting).

The Supreme Court has found that some types of preferential treatment for state residents violate neither the commerce clause nor the interstate privileges and immunities clause. See e.g., Reeves, Inc. v. Stake, 447 U.S. 429 (1980) (state may limit sales from state owned cement plant to instate residents); Baldwin v. Fish and Game Commission of Montana, 436 U.S. 371 (1978) (upholding disparity between fees for recreational hunting for resident and nonresident hunters). These cases, however, did not involve "right to travel" claims.

25. See Rosario v. Rockefeller, 410 U.S. 752 (1973).

26. McCarthy v. Philadelphia Civil Service Comm'n, 424 U.S. 645 (1976).

27. The Court noted that this problem might arise in the future but that it did not have to resolve the issue at this time. In Califano v. Torres, 435 U.S. 1

(1978) (per curiam), the Supreme Court, in a brief per curiam opinion, held that neither the right to travel, nor the equal protection guarantee of the fifth amendment due process clause prohibited the limitation of Social Security Act supplemental security income payments to aged, blind, or disabled persons who are residents of the United States, which was defined by statutes as the fifty states and the District of Columbia. The Court held that the exclusion of Puerto Rico residents from the program did not create a significant equal protection problem because of the unique status of Puerto Rico. (435 U.S. 3 n. 4.) The majority opinion noted that the ability to engage in international travel could be regulated in a reasonable manner by the federal government even though the right of interstate travel is virtually unqualified (435 U.S. at 4 n. 6). The majority held that, even if there were an extensive constitutional right to travel between Puerto Rico and any of the fifty states, the denial of benefits to those leaving the fifty states did not constitute a restriction on the right to travel. These persons were not being denied any benefit given to long term residents of Puerto Rico; they were only required to give up a benefit that belonged to a resident of the state they left. The opinion noted that conditioning of benefits on residency within a state was presumptively permissible, and that none of the cases under the right to travel had allowed a person to continue to invoke the law of the state from which he came to secure benefits from either it or the jurisdiction of his new residence. The Court did not exclude the possibility that such cases might arise; the majority only ruled that the claim to the payment of monetary benefits from the prior jurisdiction in this case did not constitute an infringement of the right to travel.

See also Harris v. Rosario, 446 U.S. 651 (1980), reh. denied 448 U.S. 912 (per curiam). (Congress may treat Puerto Rico differently so long as there is a rational basis for its actions; it is proper for Congress to provide less welfare benefits to Puerto Rican residents, who do not pay U.S. taxes; also increased benefits would disrupt the Puerto Rican economy and greatly burden the treasury).

protect the electoral process from fraudulent practices or administrative breakdowns. In *Dunn v. Blumstein* [28] the Court struck down a state law which required a voter to be a resident of the state for one year and the county for 3 months before he could vote. The Court found that this law had to be reviewed under the compelling interest test for it touched upon the right to travel as well as the right to vote. Since there was no dispute that the person was a resident, the state could not deny the individual the vote simply because he had not been present within the state for this duration of time. The opinion found that there was no sufficient connection between a person's ability to intelligently exercise the electoral franchise and the time spent within the state. The small chance of greater familiarity with local issues could not justify this burdening the right to travel. States could limit the right to vote to residents, and take reasonable measures to protect the integrity of their system, but they could not allocate fundamental rights in this manner. In later cases the Court, in per curiam decisions, upheld statutes which required voters to be resident in a jurisdiction for close to two months prior to the time of an election. Registration requirements up to fifty days were upheld upon the basis that the state needed a reasonable period of time in which to finalize its voter registration list before an election in order to prevent fraud and allow for efficient administration of the system.[29]

The Court in *Rosario v. Rockefeller* [30] upheld a statute which required voters to enroll in the party of their choice thirty days before a general election as a prerequisite to voting in the following primary. This requirement has the effect of requiring persons to register almost a year before the primary, thus requiring their presence and residency in the state at that time. Although this had the effect of a durational residency requirement which served as a limitation on both the right to vote and the right to travel, the law was upheld. The majority opinion found that the state interest in avoiding inter-party rating in primary elections was sufficient to uphold this classification. But in *Kusper v. Pontikes* [31] the Court struck down a state statute which prohibited a person from voting in a primary election of a particular party if he had voted in the primary of another party within the preceding twenty-three months. While this was not strictly a durational residency requirement the Court in striking the classification indicated that a requirement of registration twenty-three months before a primary simply was not legitimate means of protecting state interests in the election.

On this basis, it can be expected that any residency requirement for primary elections which exceeds a year would be found to be an illegitimate manner of protecting the party system and that any requirement of residency or registration for more than two months prior to a general election would be found to be an impermissible way of protecting the integrity of the balloting on election day. However, the Court has not decided whether candidates may be subjected to a durational residency requirement that exceeds that of voters, although the basis for such laws appears to be undercut by the Court's conclusion in *Dunn* that residency could not be equated with knowledge of electoral issues. But the extent to which the Court will move to allow states to prohibit "carpetbagger" candidates remains to be seen.[32]

That the right to travel will be protected even when no other fundamental right is involved became clear when the Court decided *Memorial Hospital v. Maricopa County.* [33] In this case an Arizona statute required one year residence in a county as a condition to receiving non-emergency hospitalization or

---

28. 405 U.S. 330 (1972).

29. Marston v. Lewis, 410 U.S. 679 (1973); Burns v. Fortson, 410 U.S. 686 (1973).

30. 410 U.S. 752 (1973).

31. 414 U.S. 51 (1973).

32. See Note, Durational Residency Requirements for Candidates, 40 U.Chi.L.Rev. 357 (1973).

33. 415 U.S. 250 (1974).

medical care at public expense. The Court found that this classification impinged upon interstate travel and, in so doing, found that it was irrelevant that classification also burdened travel by persons within their own state. This fact could not protect the discrimination against the interstate traveller anymore than discrimination against some in-state businesses could justify discrimination against interstate commerce.[34] The Court has never found medical care to be a fundamental right just as it has never found that any form of necessary welfare assistance payment or general government benefit constitutes such a right. But the majority found it was required to use the compelling interest test to protect the right to interstate travel in this setting. With an analysis quite similar to that employed in *Shapiro* the opinion found that the denial of medical services to indigents from others states constituted a severe penalty on their right to engage in interstate travel. The majority opinion found that the denial of this "basic necessity of life" to be such a severe burden on the right to travel that it could not be justified by the state's interest in administrative efficiency or general pursuit of economic policies. The opinion noted that the Court's review of residency requirements for all government benefits might not be scrutinized with such a strict analysis, but that where the state burdened the right to travel by denial of benefits which were essential to the daily life of the new indigent in the state, the Court would require that the state meet his "heavy burden of justification."[35]

As indicated in the *Memorial Hospital* opinion, the Court may not be ready to apply the strict scrutiny analysis of *Shapiro* to every durational residency requirement. Where the requirement relates to activities which are not directly related to the exercise of other rights or the individual's ability to function in a meaningful manner as a new resident of the state, these laws may be upheld on a test which comes close to the rational basis standard. It should be noted that Justice Douglas indicated that he shared the doubts about the usefulness of the strict scrutiny analysis of residency requirements because it offered little basis for deciding complex questions of the allocation of state resources and wealth. However, the Justice concurred in *Memorial Hospital* because the line drawn on medical aid was so arbitrary, and the importance of the interest so great, that the requirement could only be described as "invidious discrimination against the poor."[36] Thus, there are significant questions as to whether the Court will require that there be only very short durational residency requirements for other governmental benefits.

The Supreme Court has not yet prohibited states from charging lower tuition at state universities for persons who have been residents for some significant period. In *Vlandis v. Kline*[37] the Court invalidated a Connecticut statute which permanently barred a non-resident student from becoming an in-state resident for the purposes of lower tuition rates in the state university system of higher education. The opinion characterized the statute as creating a permanent and "irrebuttable presumption" of nonresidency. However, the only issue in the case was the statutory definition of residency rather than the legitimacy of any durational residency requirement. Under the statute an unmarried student was classified as a non-resident if his address for any part of one year prior to his application for admission had been outside of the state of Connecticut. However a married student would be classified as a resident so long as he had an in-state address at the time of his application. These classifications were permanent and the student could do nothing to change

---

34. As to the invalidity of local burdens on interstate commerce, see Dean Milk Co. v. City of Madison, 340 U.S. 349 (1951).

35. Memorial Hosp. v. Maricopa County, 415 U.S. 250, 263 (1974).

36. 415 U.S. at 270, 273 (Douglas, J., concurring).

37. 412 U.S. 441 (1973).

his residency status throughout his career at the university. The Supreme Court found that the classification was an irrebuttable presumption against those who might be able to prove residency at some later time. However, the Court did cite with approval its decision in *Starns v. Malkerson* [38] which summarily affirmed a decision upholding Minnesota's requirement that students be residents of the state for one year prior to qualifying for lower tuition. One may conclude that there will be a reasonableness test for durational residency requirements in the area of education which will be similar to the test which the Court has used in the primary election cases.

The Supreme Court, in *Martinez v. Bynum*,[39] upheld a state statute which permitted a school district to deny tuition-free education to a child who lived apart from his parent or lawful guardian if the child's presence in the school district was "for the primary purpose" of attending school in the district. Justice Powell wrote for eight justices when he stated: "A bona fide residence requirement, appropriately defined and uniformly applied, furthers the substantial state interest in assuring that services provided for its residents are enjoyed only by residents." The majority opinion by Justice Powell found that this residence requirement did not violate the equal protection clause because it was not based on a suspect classification and it did not limit the exercise of a fundamental right, because public education was not such a right.[40] The statute at issue in *Martinez* was held to be a bona fide residence requirement because it provided free education for all children who resided in the school district with the intent to remain in the district indefinitely. The Court did not pass upon the residency claim of the child in this case, a United States citizen whose parents were non-resident aliens living in Mexico.[41]

The Supreme Court has indicated that some burdens on the right to travel will be upheld so long as the Court finds them not to be arbitrary in fact. In *Sosna v. Iowa* [42] the Court upheld a one year residency requirement for parties seeking a divorce from state courts. The Court found that there was no due process violation here because there was no deprivation of access to the state courts but only a delay before they could be used by the parties. This delay was justified by the state's interest in ensuring that it had a real interest in those who sought to use its courts to alter fundamental family relationships and by a desire to insulate state divorce decrees from successful collateral attacks. The opinion distinguished *Shapiro, Dunn,* and *Memorial Hospital* on the basis that this classification did not prevent the woman who sought the divorce from receiving support or functioning as a citizen of the state during this period.

The dissent accused the majority of making a significant departure from *Shapiro* and its progeny.[43] However several factors demonstrate the compatibility between *Sosna* and the earlier decisions. The residency requirement here related to an interest which, while it was of great importance to the individual, was not such that it would usually deter travel. Additionally, the delay was for one year—a length similar to that which the Court had upheld as a residency requirement for such interests as voting in primary elections and receiving lower college tuition. Finally, the opinion in *Sosna* was careful to note that the law was justified by ends which were of greater significance than administrative efficiency or mere dollar savings.[44]

---

38. 401 U.S. 985 (1971), affirming 326 F.Supp. 234 (D.Minn.1970), cited in 412 U.S. at 452–53 n. 9.

39. 103 S.Ct. ___ (1983).

40. 103 S.Ct. at 1842–43 n.7.

41. Martinez v. Bynum, 103 S.Ct. 1838, 1845 (1983) (Brennan, J., concurring). Only Justice Marshall voted

to invalidate the statute on its face. Id. at 1845 (Marshall, J., dissenting).

42. 419 U.S. 393 (1975).

43. 419 U.S. 393, 418 (1975) (Marshall, J., dissenting).

44. 419 U.S. at 406.

The Supreme Court in recent years has endorsed strict judicial review of those state laws which serve as impediments to interstate relocation but it has not been ready to endorse strict judicial supervision of all laws that might serve as some type of barrier to interstate travel. Strict judicial scrutiny of state laws which serve as an impediment to immigration into a state is necessary to avoid states giving preferential treatment to in-state residents in the dispensation of state resources and erecting barriers to immigration from less wealthy states. Strict judicial review of laws regulating or restricting a person's right to cross state lines may be less important to preserving our national cohesion as a single social and economic unit. An example of judicial review of a right to travel claim on somewhat less than the strictest standard of judicial review is *Jones v. Helms* [45] in which the Supreme Court upheld a Georgia statute making willful abandonment of a child by a parent a misdemeanor if the parent remained in the state and a felony if the parent left the state after the abandonment. The majority opinion, by Mr. Justice Stevens, found that the statute did not violate the equal protection clause because a parent who abandoned his child had "qualified his right to travel interstate before he sought to exercise that right." [46] The restriction on the interstate travel of such persons promoted the state interest in ascertaining the guilt of persons who abandoned their child and facilitating remedies which the state might otherwise lawfully seek against the parents who had abandoned their child. The Court found that, "although a simple penalty for leaving a State is simply impermissible," the restriction of travel on the part of those who had engaged in otherwise punishable conduct was permissible. [47]

Having found that the fundamental right to interstate travel was not restricted by the Georgia statute, the Court had no trouble in finding that placing a burden on parents who left the state following an abandonment of their child did not violate equal protection but was a nondiscriminatory law applying to all parents residing in Georgia. [48]

In *Zobel v. Williams* [49] the Court was confronted with a case wherein the decision on the merits was easy but the rationalization of the Court's role in reviewing travel restrictions was quite difficult for the justices. By an 8 to 1 vote, the Court invalidated a statute which distributed state money to residents based upon the length of their residency in the state. The Court did not in this case attempt to define the appropriate standard of review for state laws which impose economic barriers to interstate migration. In *Zobel*, the Court examined an Alaska statute which distributed money from a state fund which had been enriched by the state's share of oil exploration revenues. Under the state statutes, each citizen of the age of 18 years or more received one "dividend unit" for each year of residency after 1959, which was the first year of Alaska's statehood. The statute fixed the value of each unit at $50 so that a one-year resident would receive $50 while a resident of Alaska since 1959 would receive $1,050. The Court had little trouble invalidating this program; only Justice Rehnquist believed that the Court should defer to the legislative judgment to prefer old residents over new residents in this case.

The *Zobel* majority opinion, by Chief Justice Burger, asserted that the Court would not in this case define the appropriate standard of review for right to travel cases. The Chief Justice correctly noted that "if the

45. 452 U.S. 412 (1981).

46. 452 U.S. at 419.

47. 452 U.S. at 422.

48. 452 U.S. at 423–26. Justice White's concurring opinion was much clearer in terms of his equal protection analysis of the fundamental rights problem than was the majority opinion by Justice Stevens. Justice White employed the compelling interest test analysis

used in Shapiro v. Thompson, 394 U.S. 618 (1969) but concluded that the state's interests were significant enough to justify the burden on the right to travel of parents who had abandoned their child in the state. Jones v. Helms, 452 U.S. 412, 426 (1981) (White, J., concurring), on remand 660 F.2d 120.

49. 457 U.S. 55 (1982).

statutory scheme could not pass even the minimal proposed by the state [the rationality standard], we need not decide whether any enhanced scrutiny is called for." [50] The majority then found that the law could not withstand even the minimal "rational relationship to a legitimate state interest" test. The state had argued that the law served three purposes. First, the state claimed that the law created a financial incentive for individuals to establish and maintain their residence in Alaska. But the Court found that the law as did not rationally promote that interest because the statute gave benefits retroactively rather than awarding benefits to those who remained in the state after the passage of the act. Second, the state claimed that the law related to the prudent management of its oil revenue fund. However, the Court found that the law did not rationally promote that end by retroactively granting greater dividends to those who resided in Alaska during the 21 years prior to the enactment of the statute.

Finally, the state claimed that the apportionment of benefits by length of residency was done in recognition of "contributions of various kinds, both tangible and intangible, which residents have made during their years of residency." [51] The law certainly furthered this end. Indeed, the end was defined in terms of the discrimination between new and old residents which the state wished to maintain. The Court found that the state's goal of awarding citizens for past contributions to the state standing on its own was "not a legitimate state purpose . . . the equal protection clause prohibits such an apportionment of state services." [52] While claiming not to establish any important principles regarding the judicial review of laws that burden the right to travel, Chief

Justice Burger's offers an insight into the judicial role in this area. The Chief Justice noted that "right to travel analysis refers to little more than a particular application of equal protection analysis." [53] The justices must independently examine state laws which seriously restrict the ability of persons to migrate from one state to another or laws which make distinctions between new and long-term residents. As was pointed out in Justice Brennan's concurring opinion, the Court has long recognized that the structure of the federal union requires justices to actively review laws which burden the right to interstate migration; the basic concept of equality between citizens requires that the state not define citizens as deserving of more or less favorable treatment merely because of the length of their residence in the state. [54]

In the future the Court may invoke "strict scrutiny" or "compelling interest" language when it examines laws which impose direct barriers on the right of persons to migrate into the state or which allocate governmental benefits on the basis of the length of a person's residence in the state. However, state laws which limit the ability to move from state to state may be upheld when those laws are not serious impairments of the right to interstate migration. Laws which have a significant impact on interstate migration may be upheld if they serve reasonable state interests unrelated to deterring migration and do not arbitrarily award benefits to longtime state residents. Additionally, states may be able to limit the dispensation of benefits to those who are *bona fide* residents. It may even be possible for states to "rebate" a specific portion of residents' taxes for past years, although it may be difficult for states to do this after *Zobel*. [55]

50. 457 U.S. 60–62.

51. 457 U.S. 60–62.

52. 457 U.S. 62–64, in part quoting Shapiro v. Thompson, 394 U.S. 618, 632–33 (1969).

53. 457 U.S. at 60 n. 6.

54. Zobel v. Williams, 102 S.Ct. 2309, 2315 (1982) (Brennan, J., dissenting, joined by Marshall, Blackmun & Powell, JJ.).

55. The majority opinion by Chief Justice Burger in Zobel v. Williams, 457 U.S. 55, 64 n. 13 (1982) found that Starns v. Malkerson, 419 U.S. 393 (1975), referred to in the previous paragraphs, could not be read as contradicting the Court's position in Zobel that the state could not dispense benefits based solely upon a person's length of residency in the state. The Chief Justice, in that footnote, noted that *Starns* was only a "summary affirmance" and that the one-year residency

The basic guarantee of equal protection is that government will treat similar persons in a similar manner and the structure of our federal system requires judges to keep states from arbitrarily defining persons as "dissimilar" based solely on the date upon which they entered into the state.

XI. THE GUARANTEES OF THE BILL OF RIGHTS AS FUNDAMENTAL RIGHTS FOR EQUAL PROTECTION ANALYSIS

A. Introduction

The Court has applied most of the provisions of the Bill of Rights to the states because it found them to be fundamental to the American system of government and inherent in the concept of liberty under the due process clause.[1] These rights also are to be considered as fundamental rights for the purposes of equal protection analysis. However, laws which classify persons in terms of their abilities to exercise rights which have specific recognition in the first eight amendments do not generally arise as equal protection issues. In these instances the denial of the right to one class of persons is likely to be held a violation of the specific guarantee without any need to resort to equal protection analysis. Thus, if the state or federal government were to deny to a specific class of persons the right to bail upon certain criminal charges, the classification should be analyzed to determine the compatibility of the law with the substantive guarantees of the eighth amendment prohibition of excessive bail, although it could just as easily be analyzed as an equal protection issue. There are two areas of rights which deserve some specific mention because they have been the subject of particular interest in terms of the government's ability to establish laws which burden particular classes of persons in the exercise of these rights. The areas involve the exercise of rights protected by the first amendment and the concept of fairness in the criminal justice system, which is derived from the various restraints placed upon the criminal process by the Bill of Rights.

B. First Amendment Guarantees

Each of the guarantees of the first amendment has been held to be a fundamental right and made applicable to the states through the due process clause of the fourteenth amendment. Thus whenever a state

---

requirement for in-state tuition status examined in *Starns* was reviewed as a "test of bona fide residence, not a return on prior contributions to the state." The Chief Justice may have meant to indicate that the state could limit education benefits to those persons who were in-state residents but that the state could not make distinctions in the education benefits it gave to persons based upon their length of residency within the state. The tuition law must be reasonably related to determining that a person was a *bona fide* resident.

Justice O'Connor, in a concurring opinion joined by no other justice, found Alaska's distribution scheme invalid under privileges and immunities clause of Article IV. Zobel v. Williams, 457 U.S. 55, 71–73, (1982) (O'Connor, J., concurring). Justice O'Connor focused on the privileges and immunities clause as a means for justifying independent judicial review of laws which make distinctions between persons on the basis of the length of their residence in a state. She was quite correct in noting that in order to justify a state citizenship or length of citizenship classification under Article IV, the state should be required to show both that the noncitizen or new resident will "constitute a particular source of the evil at which the statute is aimed" and that there is a "substantial relationship" between that evil and the classification employed by the state. Jus-

tice O'Connor's analysis is helpful in that it explains why the Court might allow the state to rebate some specific portion of each person's taxes. If the state wished to rebate 10 percent of each person's actual tax payments to the state over the past 21 years, rather than merely awarding a set amount of dollars to all persons based upon their length of residency, it might justify that rebate as a reasonable return of contributions to the state treasury. Regardless of whether one employs Justice O'Connor's Article IV analysis or Chief Justice Burger's equal protection analysis, the Court, in such a "rebate" case, would have to confront the basic question of whether the law is a reasonable way of distinguishing persons in the dispensation of government benefits. Perhaps Justice O'Connor's Article IV analysis would help limit the scope of judicial review in the right to travel area. However, her opinion has come after so many previous "right to travel" opinions that it would seem to add little but confusion to the Court's attempt to define the judicial role in this area.

1. See Chapter 13, Substantive Due Process, Section V, A Note on the Meaning of "Liberty," Fundamental Constitutional Rights and the Incorporation of the Bill of Rights.

burdens the freedom of religion,[2] speech,[3] press,[4] assembly,[5] or petition [6] the law must be analyzed under the strict scrutiny required by the first amendment as well as the general guarantees of the due process and equal protection provisions. The right of freedom of association is not mentioned in the first amendment but is implied by its provisions and analyzed in the same manner as those specific guarantees.[7] Whenever a state law impermissibly burdens the exercise of one of these rights there is actually a violation of the due process guarantee. Since the provisions are made applicable to the states by the due process clause, state laws which burden these rights constitute a denial of liberty as protected by that clause. Because the interpretation of the substantive guarantees of the first amendment are the same regardless of whether the provisions are being applied to state or federal actions, there is little need to discuss substantive due process guarantees in these cases. This same analysis applies in equal protection cases.

It is generally unnecessary to analyze laws which burden the exercise of first amendment rights by a class of persons under the equal protection guarantee, because the substantive guarantees of the amendment serve as the strongest protection against the limitation of these rights. Laws which classify persons in their exercise of these rights will have to meet strict tests for constitutionality without need to resort to

the equal protection clause. Should the laws survive substantive review under the specific guarantees they are also likely to be upheld under an equal protection analysis, for they have already been found to represent the promotion of government values which override the individual interest in exercising the specific right. For example, a law which requires public employees to refrain from partisan political activities creates a classification in terms of first amendment rights. But the Court has decided that this restriction promotes an overriding governmental interest and is valid under the first amendment. Therefore it is a permissible classification in terms of the equal protection guarantee.[8] Similarly if a law favors or burdens a religious group it will undergo strict scrutiny under the establishment and free exercise clauses of the first amendment, so that we do not tend to see such laws analyzed as equal protection issues.[9]

Although the analysis of first amendment classification under the equal protection guarantee is not common, it is important to remember that it is always permissible to review such laws under the guarantee. The first amendment rights have been held to be fundamental and, therefore, the classifications in terms of the ability to exercise those rights are subject to strict judicial scrutiny. For example in *Police Department of Chicago v. Mosley* [10] the Court invalidated a statute which prohibited pickets and demonstrations within 150 feet of local schools dur-

---

2. Cantwell v. Connecticut, 310 U.S. 296 (1940) (free exercise clause); Everson v. Board of Education, 330 U.S. 1 (1947) (establishment clause).

3. Gitlow v. New York, 268 U.S. 652, 666 (1925); Fiske v. Kansas, 274 U.S. 380 (1927); Stromberg v. California, 283 U.S. 359 (1931).

4. Near v. Minnesota, 283 U.S. 697, 701 (1931).

5. DeJonge v. Oregon, 299 U.S. 353 (1937).

6. DeJonge v. Oregon, 299 U.S. 353 at 364, 365 (1937); Hague v. CIO, 307 U.S. 496 (1939); Bridges v. California, 314 U.S. 252 (1941).

7. NAACP v. Alabama ex rel. Patterson, 357 U.S. 449, 460–61 (1958); Bates v. City of Little Rock, 361 U.S. 516, 522–3 (1960).

8. Broadrick v. Oklahoma, 413 U.S. 601, 607 n. 5 (1973).

See also California Medical Ass'n v. Federal Election Comm'n, 453 U.S. 182 (1981) (holding that limitations on contributions to multicandidate political committees which differed from the limitation placed on union and corporate contributions do not violate either the first amendment or the equal protection component of the fifth amendment).

9. See, e.g., McGowan v. Maryland, 366 U.S. 420 (1961) (Sunday closing law upheld against both claims); Sherbert v. Verner, 374 U.S. 398 (1963) (law refusing unemployment benefits to those who will not work on Saturday violates free exercise clause; no need to examine equal protection).

10. 408 U.S. 92 (1972).

ing school hours, but which exempted "peaceful picketing" caused by a labor dispute within the school. The Court found that the classification regarding permissible picketing was a violation of the equal protection guarantee for there was no overriding state interest to support a distinction between labor pickets and other forms of speech. While local governments might create laws to protect schools from disruption that were compatible with both the first and fourteenth amendments they could not classify the ability to speak in a manner that was not supported by overriding interest. In this case the Court specifically found that where statutory classifications affected conduct within the protection of first amendment rights, it would be inappropriate to review them under traditional rational basis standards of the equal protection guarantee.[11] It should be noted that this form of analysis may offer some benefits in decisions where the Court feels that the classification in terms of the fundamental right is not permissible but, for some reason, is unwilling to interpret the substantive guarantee of the first amendment in terms of the state activity involved in the case.

C. Rights to Fairness in the Criminal Justice System

There is no single decision of the Court in which a majority of the justices specifically recognize a "fundamental right" to fair treatment in the criminal justice system for purposes of equal protection analysis. However, the Court has established this right through a series of related decisions. Most of the guarantees of the Bill of Rights concern fairness in the investigation and adjudication of criminal charges against individuals. All of these provisions except for the grand jury clause of the fifth amendment[12] have been found to be fundamental and made applicable to the states through the due process clause of the fourteenth amendment.[13] The Court has also found that the concept of due process itself requires the establishment of procedures which will result in the fair treatment of individuals when the state seeks to prosecute them on criminal charges.[14] In cases dealing with required filing fees or other practices which hamper the review of criminal convictions, the Supreme Court has established a right of access to courts to vindicate claims of mistreatment of individuals within the criminal justice system.[15] Taken together these cases recognize fairness in the criminal justice system as a fundamental right of each individual.

When a state takes actions which treat an individual unfairly in terms of the adjudication of his individual case, those actions may be reviewed under the due process guarantee as well as under specific amendments.[16] When the government takes actions that burden the rights of a classification of persons in terms of their treatment in a criminal justice system it is proper to review

---

11. 408 U.S. at 98–99, 102.

In Carey v. Brown, 447 U.S. 455 (1980), the Supreme Court invalidated a state statute which prohibited the picketing of residences or dwellings but exempted from its prohibition the peaceful picketing of a residence which was also a place of employment involved in a labor dispute. The statute was found to violate the equal protection clause because it discriminated among picketers on the basis of the subject matter of their speech. As was true in *Mosley*, the Court chose to rest its decision on an equal protection rather than first amendment rationale.

12. Hurtado v. California, 110 U.S. 516 (1884).

13. See Chapter 13, Substantive Due Process, Section V, A Note on the Meaning of "Liberty," Fundamental Constitutional Rights and the Incorporation of the Bill of Rights.

14. In re Winship, 397 U.S. 358 (1970) (beyond a reasonable doubt standard—juvenile cases); Bounds v. Smith, 430 U.S. 817 (1977) (prison law libraries).

In recent years the Supreme Court formally has stated no disagreement with this principle but its decisions have evidenced a failure to consider whether a defendant has been treated in a fundamentally unfair manner in the procedures leading to his conviction. See Chapter 15, Procedural Due Process, Section III, C, 1; Nowak, Foreword: Due Process Methodology in the Post-incorporation World, 70 Journal of Criminal Law & Criminology 397 (1979).

15. See, e.g., Burns v. Ohio, 360 U.S. 252 (1959) (appellate filing fees); Bounds v. Smith, 430 U.S. 817 (1977) (prison libraries necessary for access).

16. Rochin v. California, 342 U.S. 165 (1952); Mullaney v. Wilbur, 421 U.S. 684 (1975).

these laws under the strict scrutiny standard for equal protection. However, it is often unnecessary to resort to equal protection analysis because the legitimacy of the law may be determined by the substantive interpretation of a specific guarantee of the Bill of Rights. For example, if a state refuses to provide the assistance of counsel to indigent defendants at any "critical stage" of the proceedings prior to appeal it will have violated the sixth amendment guarantee of a right to counsel.[17] In these cases it is unnecessary to rely on an equal protection analysis since the sixth amendment itself requires equal opportunities for indigents. However, following conviction at trial the right to counsel has been analyzed under an equal protection analysis.[18] The Court has held that counsel need only be provided in the first appeal.[19] It was not until 1956 that the Court used equal protection analysis to require the government to provide a guaranteed minimum form of fairness to all defendants, regardless of whether the claim related to a right with specific recognition in the first eight amendments. In *Griffin v. Illinois*[20] the Supreme Court held that the state had to provide a defendant with a stenographic transcript of criminal trial proceedings where that was necessary to his appeal. The state could not provide these transcripts to only a small class of defendants or those who offered to pay for them; the Court found that all defendants were entitled to some form of "equal justice." Although the state might not be required to provide an appellate system, once it did so, it was required to grant access to the system in ways de-

signed to ensure fair treatment of individuals. This principle has been continually upheld by the Court. In the years since *Griffin* it has ruled that indigents must be provided with transcripts, or their functional equivalent, for appeal and post conviction proceedings.

The type of charge involved in the case does not alter the indigent's right to equal treatment as the Court has held that the state must waive transcript fees required for appeal even in cases which do not involve incarceration of the defendant. In *Mayer v. Chicago*[21] a unanimous Court held that the state must provide transcripts in all cases. The state's fiscal and other interests could not be promoted by eliminating access to basic review procedures for indigent defendants. The Court stated, "*Griffin* does not represent a balance between the need of the accused and the interest of society; its principle is a flat prohibition against pricing indigent defendants out of as effective an appeal as would be available to others able to pay their own way."[22]

The Court has recognized through a series of decisions that part of the right to fair treatment in the criminal justice system is a right of access to review procedures. The state may not impose burdens on the indigent's right to access to courts unless it can demonstrate some truly compelling interest in the limitation. The Court has held that defendants may not be required to pay filing fees in order to have access to appellate courts[23] or even as a requirement for post conviction proceedings following appeals.[24]

17. Gideon v. Wainwright, 372 U.S. 335 (1963); Coleman v. Alabama, 399 U.S. 1 (1970) (right to counsel at preliminary hearing—plurality opinion).

In Scott v. Illinois, 440 U.S. 367 (1979) the Supreme Court limited the right of indigent criminal defendants to appointed counsel at trial to those cases wherein the defendant in fact received a punishment of imprisonment. The Court had held that indigents had a right to appointed counsel at least when they were imprisoned for conviction on the charged offense in Argersinger v. Hamlin, 407 U.S. 25 (1972). The *Scott* majority refused to extend this right to those indigent defendants who were charged with serious offenses but who in fact received only a monetary fine rather than a sentence of imprisonment. However, if an indigent de-

fendant is not given appointed counsel during a misdemeanor trial, his conviction cannot then serve as the basis for converting a subsequent misdemeanor into a felony under a state "enhanced penalty" statute. Baldasar v. Illinois, 446 U.S. 222 (1980).

18. Douglas v. California, 372 U.S. 353 (1963).

19. Ross v. Moffitt, 417 U.S. 600 (1974).

20. 351 U.S. 12 (1956).

21. 404 U.S. 189 (1971).

22. 404 U.S. at 196–97.

23. Burns v. Ohio, 360 U.S. 252 (1959).

24. Smith v. Bennett, 365 U.S. 708 (1961).

Even after the defendant's right to counsel has expired, states may not take other actions to limit his access to the court. Thus the Court has held that where counsel is not provided to defendants for collateral attack proceedings, the state cannot prohibit prisoners from assisting each other with the preparation of papers seeking further review of their criminal convictions.[25] The Supreme Court has also extended this principle to include a right of access to the courts to contest deprivations of rights while in prison. Thus it held that the states could not prohibit inmates from providing assistance to each other in the filing of civil rights actions while they were in prison.[26] This right of access to courts includes a right to the materials that are necessary to prepare and file documents seeking review of criminal convictions or civil rights actions. Recently, the Court required the states to provide prisoners with adequate legal research materials for these purposes.[27]

The Court has not guaranteed that all defendants will be able to present their defense or prosecute their appeals with equal resources, for it is incapable of leveling the economic ability of some defendants to pay for superior legal or investigative services that may be of some assistance to them. However the Court has sought to guarantee a basic level of fair treatment as a fundamental constitutional right.[28] This distinction between insuring required fair treatment and leveling economic distinctions is the basis for the Court's rulings concerning the scope of counsel following a criminal conviction. In *Douglas v. California*[29] the

Court held that a state could not dismiss the appeals of indigent criminal defendants with a separate system which did not include representation by counsel for the defendant. While the state might not be required to establish an appellate system, it could not grant appellate review on the basis of the wealth of the individual defendants. Thus it was required to provide counsel for indigent defendants in their first appeal as of right in order to grant them a meaningful form of judicial review. A decade later, however, the Supreme Court held that this principle did not require states to provide attorneys for indigent defendants in discretionary appeals or collateral attack proceedings following their first appeal as of right. In *Ross v. Moffitt*,[30] the Court held that these proceedings were not so essential to a fair determination of the individual criminal defendant's claims regarding his trial that they required the assistance of counsel. Furnishing the individual defendant with counsel and transcripts during his first appeal as of right sufficiently enabled him to receive fair treatment in the process of applying for discretionary appeals or collateral review of his conviction.

The Supreme Court has not yet considered whether the right to fairness in the criminal process requires states to provide indigent defendants with access to other forms of assistance, or aid to present a defense or to prosecute an appeal.[31] The issue is most likely to arise in terms of whether an indigent defendant's inability to retain an expert witness such as a psychiatrist or scientific analyst violates the equal protection guaran-

---

25. Johnson v. Avery, 393 U.S. 483 (1969).

26. Wolff v. McDonnell, 418 U.S. 539 (1974).

27. Bounds v. Smith, 430 U.S. 817 (1977).

28. United States v. Chavez, 627 F.2d 953, 958 (9th Cir. 1980) (Kilkenny, C.J., quoting an earlier edition of this treatise) cert. denied 450 U.S. 924 (1981).

29. 372 U.S. 353 (1963).

30. 417 U.S. 600 (1974).

In Scott v. Illinois, 440 U.S. 367 (1979) the Supreme Court limited the right of indigent criminal defendants to appointed counsel at trial to those cases wherein the defendant in fact received a punishment of imprison-

ment. The Court had held that indigents had a right to appointed counsel at least when they were imprisoned for conviction on the charged offense in Argersinger v. Hamlin, 407 U.S. 25 (1972). The *Scott* majority refused to extend this right to those indigent defendants who were charged with serious offenses but who in fact received only a monetary fine rather than a sentence of imprisonment.

31. For a collection of materials regarding these issues, see Y. Kamisar, W. LaFave & J. Israel, Modern Criminal Procedure Cases—Comments—Questions, Chapter 3, § 4 (5th ed. 1980).

tee, although the issue may also arise in terms of investigative services which would be related to the effective presentation of a defense in a particular case. The issue has not arisen in a manner which has received extensive judicial review, because many jurisdictions already provide for some form of investigative services or expert assistance, either through a public defender's office or direct payment for services in a limited group of cases. In addition to the unresolved equal protection issues there are also questions as to whether the sixth amendment right to compulsory process of witnesses might include some right to state assistance to secure expert testimony to aid in the presentation of a defense. If analysis in this area follows that used in the right to counsel decisions, one could expect the Court to find a right, under either the sixth amendment or the equal protection guarantee, to those forms of assistance which are necessary to a fair presentation of a particular defense but not to every form of assistance that a person of greater resources might secure in the private sector.

The right to equality in the criminal justice system also includes the right to fair treatment in sentencing. Most sentencing decisions are dealt with through the use of standards governing the discretion of the trial court and a determination of whether an individual sentence violates the cruel and unusual punishment clause of the eighth amendment.[32] The equal protection issue arises where indigent defendants are incarcerated because they cannot pay a fine. The Court has used equal protection analysis rather than the eighth amendment prohibition of excessive fines to determine the constitutionality of these procedures.[33] The

Court has held that the inability to pay a fine could not be used as a basis for extending the prison term of a defendant beyond the maximum period fixed by statute or imposing any incarceration on the individual when there was only a system of fines for punishment of those who were able to pay them.[34]

It must be emphasized in closing that the rights in the criminal justice system relate either to specific guarantees or to fairness in the system of investigating and adjudicating individual claims. The Court has not held that the government is required to grant any permanent form of economic benefits to persons in the criminal process because they are without funds to pay for them. Thus, the Court has upheld statutory provisions that require convicted indigent defendants to repay the state for the services of counsel that was provided them at trial or on appeal,[35] but those statutes which subjected these persons to arbitrary classifications in the enforcement of debts will be held to violate equal protection.[36]

XII. INTERESTS WHICH DO NOT CONSTITUTE FUNDAMENTAL RIGHTS

A. Introduction

In this Chapter we have outlined those rights which the Supreme Court has held to be fundamental for purposes of reviewing classifications under the equal protection guarantee. When combined with the sections on the incorporation of the Bill of Rights,[1] we have a complete listing of all interests which the Supreme Court has found to be fundamental constitutional rights. While laws limiting these rights will be subjected to strict review under the due process

---

32. See Solem v. Helm, 103 S.Ct. ___ (1983) (life sentence without possibility of parole for repeated minor offenses held invalid).

33. Revocation of a defendant's probation for failure to pay a fine absent a determination that the defendant was responsible for the failure and that alternative forms of punishment are inadequate will violate the principle of fundamental fairness protected by the due process and equal protection clauses. Bearden v. Georgia, 103 S.Ct. 2064 (1983).

34. Williams v. Illinois, 399 U.S. 235 (1970) (exceeding maximum sentence invalid); Tate v. Short, 401 U.S. 395 (1971) (incarceration in lieu of fine invalid).

35. Fuller v. Oregon, 417 U.S. 40 (1974).

36. Rinaldi v. Yeager, 384 U.S. 305 (1966); James v. Strange, 407 U.S. 128 (1972).

1. Chapter 13, Section V, A Note on the Meaning of Liberty, Fundamental Constitutional Rights and the "Incorporation" of the Bill of Rights.

and equal protection guarantees, laws limiting other rights will be subjected only to the rationality test because the Court finds them to be matters of "economics or social welfare." Under the due process guarantee of fair adjudicative procedures,[2] the Court has granted some protection against the termination of individual interests which do not qualify as fundamental constitutional rights. Yet such procedural rights have not increased the substantive protection of those interests. It would be fruitless to try to list all of the interests that the Court has held not to be fundamental, for it is composed of the entire universe of individual interests other than those which we have detailed in previously mentioned sections.[3] However, it is worth noting four particular interests that have been the subject of great debate as to their constitutional significance. The Court has refused to declare these to be of fundamental constitutional value. Even as to these interests we will list only the most recent, or major, decisions of the Court since the findings of "non-fundamentality" are part of every case in which the Court has considered a law burdening these interests. The four interests are: (1) governmental subsistence payments or welfare; (2) housing; (3) education; and (4) government employment.

When considering these rights one should also reflect upon the Supreme Court's refusal to find that classifications based on wealth are "suspect" or otherwise deserving of significant protection under the equal protection guarantee.[4] The rights which have been the subject of the most debate concerning whether they should be accorded fundamental constitutional recognition are those which relate to the allocation of resources to provide basic subsistence benefits. The argument that these rights should be recognized as fundamental involves the concept that individuals are entitled to a minimum quantum of the items or benefits necessary to be a productive member of society and to enjoy other rights. This concept relates in large measure to the philosophy expounded by John Rawls in *A Theory of Justice*,[5] and brilliantly transformed into equal protection arguments by Professor Frank Michelman.[6] Professor Michelman has argued that the rights for the poor should be thought of not as requiring equal protection but as a constitutionally guaranteed "minimum protection." Under this theory of the equal protection guarantee the Court would have to decide upon the basic quantum of these items which was necessary for an individual to be a functioning member of modern American society who might enjoy a significant degree of liberty and the ability to exercise other fundamental rights. However, any such determination, no matter how strong the philosophy behind it, clearly does involve the reallocation of wealth through the means of judicial decisions.

Decisions which distribute benefits by striking wealth classifications may be attacked on an economic basis, in that these decisions may decrease the total "efficiency" or "product" of society and, thereby, injure all of society despite the original good motives of those making the reallocation of wealth. This argument against the Rawls-Michelman position was most ably expounded by Professor (now Judge) Ralph Winter, who took the position that the Court is institutionally incapable of making wealth reallo-

---

2. Chapter 15, Procedural Due Process.

3. Thus in Section VIII of this Chapter, on the Right to Privacy, we noted that the Court had not created a right to engage in consensual conduct or to live a particular "life style." For an in-depth analysis of these issues, see Wilkinson & White, Constitutional Protection for Personal Lifestyles, 62 Cornell L.Rev. 563 (1977).

4. See Chapter 16, Section VI, Classifications Based on Wealth.

For an examination of the trends in the Supreme Court rulings on issues involving poor persons and wealth reallocation programs see Nowak, Foreword: Evaluating the Work of the New Libertarian Supreme Court, 7 Hastings Constitutional Law Quarterly 263 (1980).

5. J. Rawls, A Theory of Justice (1971).

6. Michelman, On Protecting the Poor Through the Fourteenth Amendment, 83 Harv.L.Rev. 7 (1969).

cation decisions.[7] Thus, he argued the Court should withdraw from reviewing legislative decisions on the allocation of basic benefits since there is no clear textual basis for such a judicial role. Indeed, he uses economic analysis to demonstrate that the justices cannot be sure whether they are helping or hurting any specific class of individuals in making such economic impact decisions. Professor Winter's position may also be supported by a libertarian philosophy which advocates great freedom of individual action and a correspondingly limited role for government. Robert Nozick has advanced this type of political philosophy as a jurisprudential answer to the theory of Rawls.[8]

As we have noted in our discussion of wealth classifications, the Court has taken a middle road between these two positions. The justices have held that fundamental rights may not be allocated by an individual's ability to pay for them; where no fundamental rights are involved the Court will not engage in active review of wealth classifications. Let us now briefly consider the major decisions of the Supreme Court by which it has refused to hold that basic economic benefits should be the subject of active judicial review.

B. Subsistence or Welfare Payments

There is no opinion of the Supreme Court in which a majority of justices have held that there is any right to receive subsistence payments or welfare benefits of any kind. Instead the justices have considered such programs as general economic and social welfare measures which are to be reviewed under the basic rationality standard of the due process and equal protection guaran-

tees.[9] These laws will be subjected to strict scrutiny if they dispense the benefits upon suspect criterion or exclude classes of persons upon a status which deserves active protection by the judiciary.[10] Similarly, these laws will be subject to the strict scrutiny test if the welfare system has limitations which burden other fundamental constitutional values such as the right to travel.[11] Where the state has declared that someone is "entitled" to receive these benefits, the individual has a right to a hearing, in accordance with the procedural due process guarantee, prior to their termination.[12] But even in the area of procedural due process the Court has left the states free to determine the basis upon which they will grant these benefits and the definition of those persons who are entitled to receive or retain them.[13]

The most vivid example of this type of analysis is contained in *Dandridge v. Williams*.[14] In this case the Court upheld a state law for the administration of Aid to Families with Dependent Children (AFDC) which in effect put an upper limit on the number of children for which any family could receive subsistence payments. The majority opinion by Justice Stewart not only upheld the law but found that it was one concerning only "economics and social welfare".[15] Thus, the majority subjected the classification and allocation of benefits to only the rational relationship-invidious discrimination test. The Court stated that although the classification "involved the most basic needs of impoverished human beings . . . we can find no basis for applying a different constitutional standard." [16] This case also gave rise to the first exposition of a theoretical basis for a middle level stan-

---

7. Winter, Poverty, Economic Equality and the Equal Protection Clause, 1972 Sup.Ct.Rev. 41.

8. R. Nozick, Anarchy, State and Utopia (1974).

9. See Section I C of this Chapter for a more detailed examination of this "standards of review" problem and a more complete listing of cases in which the Court has refused to employ strict judicial scrutiny to review welfare statutes.

10. See, e.g., Graham v. Richardson, 403 U.S. 365 (1971) (aliens); see also New Jersey Welfare Rights Organization v. Cahill, 411 U.S. 619 (1973) (illegitimates).

11. Shapiro v. Thompson, 394 U.S. 618 (1969).

12. Goldberg v. Kelly, 397 U.S. 254 (1970).

13. This includes some ability to define the scope of even procedural guarantees, see Mathews v. Eldridge, 424 U.S. 319 (1976); see also Bishop v. Wood, 426 U.S. 341 (1976). For an examination of these issues see Chapter 15, Procedural Due Process.

14. 397 U.S. 471 (1970).

15. 397 U.S. at 485.

16. Id.

dard of review between the strict scrutiny-compelling interest test and the minimal protection-rationality test. In a dissenting opinion, which was joined by Justice Brennan, Justice Marshall took the position that the "mere rationality test," while well suited for testing economic and business regulations, should : ot be applied to the interests of the poor in basic subsistence. While these interests might not qualify as ones which deserved a form of strict review under which almost any legislative classification would be invalid, they did merit some meaningful form of judicial review. To Justice Marshall it made no sense to have equal protection or due process standards be an all or nothing dichotomy.[17] Instead, the Court should realize that there was a wide range of interests which required an independent determination of whether people were being treated in a nonarbitrary manner in terms of permissible governmental goals and the importance of the interested individual freedom in society. Although the Court has never adopted such an approach to welfare classifications Justice Marshall's views have given rise to a variety of academic justifications for a third standard of review under the equal protection guarantee.[18]

Following *Dandridge* the Court continued to uphold classifications relating to welfare benefits under the rationality test. Thus the Court has upheld classifications for the payment of different forms of welfare which left families with dependent children in a

much worse position, in terms of the percentage of their need that was met, than to other forms of welfare.[19] The Court's use of the rationality test to review welfare classifications has not been limited to those systems dispensing only cash subsistence payments. The Court has also upheld classifications relating to public housing,[20] and public education[21] under this standard because it found no basis to strictly review any welfare distribution system which does not allocate fundamental constitutional rights or employ suspect criteria.[22]

It should be noted, however, that in two cases the Court did invalidate provisions of the Food Stamp Act under what seemed to be a more meaningful standard of review than the basic rationality test. In *United States Department of Agriculture v. Moreno*[23] the Court invalidated a section of the Food Stamp Act which made any household comprised of unrelated individuals ineligible to receive food stamps. Writing for six members of the Court, Justice Brennan indicated that the traditional rationality test was being employed,[24] although both the concurring and dissenting Justices could not agree to this position.[25] The majority opinion found that the disqualification of these households could further no legitimate governmental interests and that it seemed only to be the arbitrary and invidious exclusion of household units for which there was some public animosity. In a companion decision, *United States Department of Agriculture*

---

17. Dandridge v. Williams, 397 U.S. 471, 517–22 (1970) (Marshall, J., dissenting).

18. See, e.g., Gunther, In Search of Evolving Doctrine on a Changing Court: A Model for a Newer Equal Protection, 86 Harv.L.Rev. 1 (1972); Nowak, Realizing the Standards of Review Under the Equal Protection Guarantee—Prohibited, Neutral and Permissive Classifications, 62 Georgetown L.J. 1071 (1974). See Chapter 16, Section I, C.

19. Jefferson v. Hackney, 406 U.S. 535 (1972).

20. James v. Valtierra, 402 U.S. 137 (1971).

21. San Antonio Independent School District v. Rodriguez, 411 U.S. 1 (1973).

22. The Supreme Court recently reaffirmed the principle that classifications relating to welfare benefits are to be upheld under the rational basis test so

long as they conceivably might relate to a legitimate governmental purpose, when the justices unanimously upheld a federal law denying social security benefits to recipients who left the United States for 30 days. Califano v. Aznavorian, 439 U.S. 170 (1978). See also United States R.R. Retirement Bd. v. Fritz, 449 U.S. 166 (1980) (Congress may eliminate payment of dual retirement benefits to some employees who had engaged in both railroad and non-railroad employment on any basis that is not "patently arbitrary or irrational"). For a more complete listing of recent decisions on this issue see Section I, C of this Chapter.

23. 413 U.S. 528 (1973).

24. Id. at 533.

25. 413 U.S. at 542–3 (Douglas, J., concurring); Id. at 546–7 (Rehnquist, J., dissenting).

v. Murry [26] the Court invalidated a section of the act which disqualified any household that included a member who was over 18 years of age and who had been claimed as a tax dependent by a nonmember of the household in the previous year. The majority opinion invalidated this classification as an "irrebuttable presumption" due to the failure to make an individualized determination of need. However, Justice Marshall, in a concurring opinion, seems correct in noting that the due process and equal protection guarantees seem to merge in this situation. [27] Unfortunately the Court did not in either instance explain why it was employing an increased standard of review, if indeed the justices even appreciated that they were going beyond the rationality test. It may be that the justices were less hesitant to strike a classification which separated very similar groups of claimants. It is also possible that a few justices felt that this was so arbitrary that the classification violated the rationality test and that these justices, when combined with the votes of justices who would use an increased standard to review all classifications within welfare systems, formed a majority. In any event, these two decisions stand out as atypical findings that a law fails to meet the rationality test.

Although a particular classification defining eligibility for welfare payments may have significant impact on a group composed primarily of women or illegitimates, that fact alone will not render the classification gender-based or illegitimacy-based for purposes of equal protection analysis. [28] Thus, the Court has upheld laws which required a spouse or a stepchild to have established their relationship to a deceased wage earner several months prior to the wage earner's death as a qualification for Social Security

Act death benefits [29] and which gave greater benefits to a married, as opposed to divorced, spouse of a retired wage earner. [30]

The Supreme Court also upheld the Social Security Act restriction which makes "mother's insurance benefits" available to widows and divorced wives of a deceased wage earner if that spouse supports the children of the wage earner; the provision denied benefits to the mother of the wage earner's children if she was never married to the wage earner. [31] The provision was no longer gender based because the Supreme Court previously had invalidated the mother-father distinction in this program. [32] It was not a law discriminating on the basis of legitimacy or illegitimacy because the benefits were for the surviving parent and the qualification was a reasonable means of identifying surviving parents who were dependent upon a deceased wage earner at the time of the wage earner's death. [33] Because the law did not employ a suspect classification or discriminate between claimants based upon the immutable characteristics of gender or illegitimacy it was to be upheld under the rational basis test.

C. Housing

The Supreme Court has never found that there is any right to government assistance to secure adequate housing or other forms of shelter. Indeed, the Court has not subjected governmental actions which might burden persons' abilities to find adequate private housing to any standard of review above the rationality test of the due process and equal protection guarantees. Of course, if these laws involve the use of suspect classifications or burden fundamental rights they will be subjected to the strict scrutiny standard of review. This dichotomy has

---

26. 413 U.S. 508 (1973).

27. Id. at 517–19 (Marshall, J., concurring).

28. See Section I, D of this Chapter.

29. Weinberger v. Salfi, 422 U.S. 749 (1975).

30. Matthews v. DeCastro, 429 U.S. 181 (1976).

31. Califano v. Boles, 443 U.S. 282 (1979).

32. Weinberger v. Weisenfeld, 420 U.S. 636 (1975).

33. Four justices would have found that the primary purpose of the Social Security Act program in question related to providing support for children of the deceased wage earners through the surviving parent; these justices would have invalidated the program as being impermissible based on a distinction between legitimate and illegitimate children. Califano v. Boles, 443 U.S. 282 (1979) (Marshall, J., dissenting joined by Brennan, White, and Blackmun, JJ.)

been brought out in a series of decisions by the Court.

The Court has held that a city charter which required a referendum to implement a fair housing ordinance was invalid because the Court found it to effectively constitute a classification designed to exclude members of minority races from the locality.[34] However, when there was no proof that a referendum system was used to exclude minority members, the Court upheld a state constitutional provision that prohibited the development of low rent public housing projects unless approved by a vote of the residents of the locality in which the housing unit was to be placed.[35] Although this voter approval clearly imposed a significant barrier to the establishment and dispensation of public housing, it did not constitute the limitation of a fundamental constitutional right such as would require a meaningful form of review in the opinion of the majority. Similarly, the justices have held that statistical disparities between racial representation in a locality will not prove that its exclusion of multi-family housing units constitutes a racial classification, absent proof that the zoning system is designed to purposely exclude racial minorities.[36] Thus, the Court has indicated that there is no right to the development of either multi-family or low income housing which justifies overturning a municipality's decision to exclude these uses from its zoning plan.

A similar refusal to recognize a right to housing in the private sector was evidenced in the Court's decision that states were free to enact summary eviction statutes which gave landlords a right to repossession of premises while excluding defenses based on the landlord's failure to meet his obligations under a building code.[37] The Supreme Court has also held that municipalities may zone residential areas for traditional families (those composed of persons related by blood or marriage) since this restriction did not burden any fundamental interest.[38] But the Court struck down a zoning plan that would have required families to exclude collateral relatives living with them since this restriction touched upon important interests in the family relationship.[39]

D. Education

The Supreme Court has not held that publicly financed primary or secondary education is a fundamental right. It has avoided the ultimate issue, but it has refused to impose upon the states the requirement that they provide equal access to high quality forms of education.[1] However, the Court has held that once educational rights are granted a student, they cannot be terminated without procedural due process safeguards,[2] although these safeguards will not protect the individual student against certain actions, such as physical punishment, within the school system.[3] Under the guarantees of due process and freedom of religion the Court has recognized that individuals have the right to withdraw their children from the public school system and send them to private schools.[4] These private schools may be made to meet certain educational standards, but the state may not control all facets of their curriculum.[5]

The most important decision of the Court concerning a "right" to education is *San Antonio Independent School District v. Rodriguez*.[6] In this case the Supreme

---

34. Hunter v. Erickson, 393 U.S. 385 (1969); see also Reitman v. Mulkey, 387 U.S. 369 (1967).

35. James v. Valtierra, 402 U.S. 137 (1971).

36. Arlington Heights v. Metropolitan Housing Development Corp., 429 U.S. 252 (1977).

37. Lindsey v. Normet, 405 U.S. 56 (1972).

38. Village of Belle Terre v. Boraas, 416 U.S. 1 (1974).

39. Moore v. City of East Cleveland, 431 U.S. 494 (1977).

1. San Antonio Independent School District v. Rodriguez, 411 U.S. 1 (1973).

2. Goss v. Lopez, 419 U.S. 565 (1975).

3. Ingraham v. Wright, 430 U.S. 651 (1977).

4. Pierce v. Society of Sisters, 268 U.S. 510 (1925); see also, Wisconsin v. Yoder, 406 U.S. 205 (1972).

5. Meyer v. Nebraska, 262 U.S. 390 (1923).

6. 411 U.S. 1 (1973).

Court, by a 5 to 4 vote, upheld the use of local property taxes to finance primary and secondary education, although the system allowed areas within a single school district to have great disparities in the amount of money spent per student on educational programs and resources. The majority opinion, by Justice Powell, applied the standard of minimal scrutiny; it found it arguably reasonable for the legislature to use local property taxation to advance goals of local control over schools. The Court accepted these interests at face value and never inquired whether the system in fact bore a rational relationship to a state interest of a quality sufficient to justify the lower standard of education for children in the least wealthy districts. The majority opinion never found it necessary to inquire as to whether the state's legitimate goals would still be met if an equal amount of money was expended on the education of each child in the state. The Court found that no suspect classification was involved since there was no correlation in this case between district wealth and race.

It had been argued that the relationship between education and fundamental freedoms of speech and voting should establish education as a fundamental right, but the opinion found no authority to guarantee the citizenry the most effective participation in the public process. The majority opinion did not exclude the possibility that some level of educational opportunity might be a fundamental right but it stated that—

[e]ven if it were conceded that some identifiable quantum of education is a constitutionally protected prerequisite to the meaningful exercise of either right we have no indication that the [low taxation] system fails to provide each child with an opportunity to acquire the basic minimal skills.[7]

Thus, there appears to be no fundamental right to receive publicly funded education above the possibility of some amount so minimal that it could be provided by a very small, and unequal, expenditure of public funds.

Because education has not been deemed to be a "fundamental right," most laws which regulates access to education or allocate differing amounts of educational benefits to different classes of persons will not be subject to strict judicial scrutiny. However, if a state singles out a class of children and denies them all educational opportunity, that classification should be subject to some form of independent judicial review. The basis upon which the class is defined need not be suspect because the singling out of an identified class of children for complete denial of this important governmental benefit would seem to be arbitrary on its face. For example, if a state denied all state funded education to left-handed children or red-haired children, one would assume that the law would be subject to some meaningful form of judicial review and that the justices would not simply presume that the legislature was acting within its constitutional authority by refusing to grant any educational benefits to these children. Thus, the Court invalidated a state statute which denied public education to the children of illegally resident aliens, even though the Court refused to find that education was a fundamental right or that illegal aliens constituted a class of persons who merited close judicial scrutiny of laws which disadvantaged them.[8]

Because education is not a fundamental right, the Supreme Court has allowed states to restrict the provision of tuition-free education to children who are bona fide resi-

---

7. 411 U.S. at 36–7.

8. Plyler v. Doe, 457 U.S. 202 (1982). This case is analyzed in Section III of this Chapter.

Congress may extend educational rights by statute, particularly where local educational programs are funded with federal money. However, the question of whether congressional regulations relating to educational programs funded by federal money require state and local agencies to provide special educational ser-

vices to some or all children is a question to be determined on the basis of congressional intent rather than constitutional principles. See, Board of Education v. Rowley, 102 S.Ct. 3034 (1982) ("education for all handicapped children act" did not require state to provide individualized programs for all deaf children, at least when the particular child was able to receive educational benefits without specialized care).

dents of the state or local school district.[9] Of course, a state may not deny educational benefits or even limit educational opportunities to persons because of constitutionally suspect criteria. Laws that allocate educational benefits on the basis of race, national origin or United States citizenship should be subject to strict judicial scrutiny.[10] The Court has not yet prohibited states from offering "separate but equal" educational opportunities to males and females on the basis of their gender. However, any law allocating educational benefits on the basis of gender should be held invalid unless the state can demonstrate that the classification is substantially related to an important state interest.[11]

While the Court has not authorized judicial intervention in school regulations generally, the judiciary should protect students in the exercise of their fundamental rights even though they seek to exercise those rights in an educational setting. Thus, the Court has required that school systems respect student's rights to speak and present ideas in a manner compatible with the orderly operation of the school.[12]

While the Court has not granted strict review over the substantive limitations on access to public education it has applied the procedural due process requirements to the denial of educational benefits. In *Goss v. Lopez*[13] the Court held that fair procedures had to be established for determining the basis of the suspension of students from public school systems. Since state law appeared to allow students to continue with their education, absent dismissal for cause, they had a property right or "entitlement" to continued access to the educational system. When the suspension or termination of their educational benefits may affect their employment or associational opportunities in the future, they may also be deprived of a constitutionally significant interest in liberty by such a suspension. However, the Court has refused to extend the rationale of *Goss* to protect the student's interests against the arbitrary imposition of disciplinary actions which do not involve the termination or suspension of the educational benefits. Thus, in *Ingraham v. Wright*[14] the Court refused to impose any meaningful federal limitations on the imposition of corporal punishment on students in public school systems. The ma-

9. The Supreme Court, by an eight to one vote, upheld a state statute which permitted a school district to deny tuition free education to a child who lived apart from his parent or lawful guardian if the child's presence in the school district was "for the primary purpose" of attending school in the district. Martinez v. Bynum, 103 S.Ct. 1838 (1983). "A bona fide residence requirement, appropriately defined and uniformly applied, furthers the substantial state interest in assuring that services provided for its residents are enjoyed only by residents." Id. at 1842. The majority opinion found that this residence requirement did not violate the equal protection clause because it was not based on a suspect classification and it did not limit the exercise of a fundamental right. The Court noted that public education was not such a right. Id. at 1842–43 n.7. *Martinez* held that the statute at issue was a bona fide residence requirement because it provided free education for all children who resided in the school district with the intent to remain in the district indefinitely. The Court did not pass upon the residency claim of the child in this case, a United States citizen whose parents were non-resident aliens living in Mexico. See Id. at 1845 (Brennan, J., concurring). Only Justice Marshall would have invalidated the residency requirement on its face. Id. at 1845 (Marshall, J., dissenting).

10. See Section II of this Chapter concerning classifications based upon race and Section III of this chap-

ter regarding alienage classifications. In order to demonstrate that a school system is allocating benefits on a constitutionally and permissible criteria such as race or national origin, the person attacking the system must show that the law on its face allocates educational benefits on that basis or that the law which has a disadvantageous impact on a racial or ethnic minority was enacted or maintained for a racially discriminatory purpose, see Section I, D of this Chapter.

11. See, Mississippi University for Women v. Hogan, 102 S.Ct. 3331 (1982) (invalidating state exclusion of men from state operated nursing schools under the substantial relationship test but refusing to address the question of whether states can provide separate but equal educational benefits for persons based upon their gender). The decision is examined in Section IV of this chapter.

12. See, Tinker v. Des Moines Independent Community School District, 393 U.S. 503 (1969).

13. 419 U.S. 565 (1975). Even this limited recognition of a right in education has been challenged as unjustified interference with an important state function. Wilkinson, Goss v. Lopez: The Supreme Court as School Superintendent, 1975 Sup.Ct.Rev. 25.

14. 430 U.S. 651 (1977).

jority held that the eighth amendment prohibition of cruel and unusual punishment did not apply outside of the criminal setting. As the dissent pointed out, this reading of history makes the safeguard apply only to areas in which punishments are least likely to offend the principles of society.[15] The majority opinion did recognize that the taking of physical discipline against the student did constitute a deprivation of his or her liberty[16] but it found that the possibility of later tort suits against the teachers was a sufficient process to safeguard this interest under the due process clause.

E. Government Employment

It should be noted that, so long as the government does not employ suspect criteria or burden fundamental rights, the Court defers to legislative and executive judgments concerning the terms of public employment in the same way it treats other forms of economic and social welfare legislation. Thus, the Court has upheld mandatory retirement from government service at age 50 since classifications by age are not "suspect" or of special constitutional significance.[17]

In *Vance v. Bradley*[18] the Supreme Court, with only one dissent, upheld a requirement that participants in the foreign service retirement system[19] retire from their government positions at age 60. The plaintiff employees had alleged that the distinction between the mandatory retirement at age 60 for their job classifications and the general federal requirement of retirement at age 70 for the federal Civil Service Retirement System personnel violated the equal protection component of the fifth amendment. The Court, in an opinion by Mr. Justice White, found that the retirement classification should be tested by general equal protection principles,[20] but that it did not violate the equal protection guarantee. Although the parties agreed that the law should be tested under the traditional rational basis standard, Justice White's opinion stressed that the federal judiciary is not to review seriously those classifications that do not involve fundamental rights or suspect classifications.

The Constitution presumes that, absent some reason to infer antipathy, even improvident decisions will eventually be rectified by the democratic process and that judicial intervention is generally unwarranted no matter how unwisely we may think a political branch has acted. Thus, we will not overturn such a statute unless the varying treatment of different groups or persons is so unrelated to the achievement of any combination of legitimate purposes that we can only conclude that the legislature's actions were irrational.[21]

---

15. 430 U.S. 692 (White, J., dissenting).

16. 430 U.S. at 674.

17. Massachusetts Board of Retirement v. Murgia, 427 U.S. 307 (1976). It should be noticed that the mandatory retirement policy did not constitute an invalid "irrebuttable presumption" of inability to fasten in a position. See Chapter 15, Procedural Due Process, Section II, E, Irrebuttable Presumptions. See Trafelet v. Thompson, 594 F.2d 623, 626 (7th Cir. 1978) (Tone, J., citing an earlier edition of this treatise).

Congress in the Age Discrimination in Employment Act of 1967, 29 U.S.C.A. § 621 et seq. as amended by the Age Discrimination in Employment Act Amendments of 1978, Pub.L. No. 95–256 (April 6, 1978), has made it unlawful for covered employers to discriminate against or discharge individuals between the ages of 40 and 70 due to their ages. The Court has held that the prior Act, by its own terms, does not apply to a retirement plan established prior to its enactment that requires employees to retire before age 65 if the plan was established prior to passage of the Act so long as the plan was instituted in good faith and was not used to evade the act. United Air Lines, Inc. v. McMann, 434 U.S. 192 (1977). The Act, as amended, sets new effective dates for its coverage. The Supreme Court has held that in a private action for damages brought under the 1967 Act a jury trial would be available when requested by one of the parties. Lorillard v. Pons, 434 U.S. 575 (1978). The Act, as amended, now provides for jury trials regardless of whether damages or equitable relief is sought.

18. 440 U.S. 93 (1979).

19. This retirement system and requirement applied to career foreign service officers, foreign service information officers and certain other career staff in the International Communications Agency.

20. 440 U.S. at 94 n. 1. This point corresponds with the well established principle that the equal protection guarantee of the due process clause of the fifth amendment mirrors that of equal protection clause of the fourteenth amendment. See Section IC of this chapter.

21. 440 U.S. at 97 (footnote omitted).

The majority then applied the rational basis test, which had been employed in *Massachusetts Board of Retirement v. Murgia*[22] to uphold a mandatory retirement of state police officers at age 50, to the retirement classification. Although it appeared that the plaintiffs had abandoned their claim that the classification between those over and under age 60 was irrational, and only pressed the claim of discrimination between foreign service employees and civil service employees, the majority opinion made it clear that the rational relationship test was the only form of review justified for reviewing any aspect of this mandatory retirement program.[23]

The United States, in *Vance*, argued that it had legitimate goals in recruiting foreign service personnel and assuring their physical and mental competence and that the retirement requirement at age 60 furthered these ends by: (1) assuring potential recruits, and younger members of the service, that there would be predictable openings at the highest level of foreign service, and (2) removing those who were less likely to be able to face the difficult task of foreign service officers, which included regular overseas duty. The majority opinion repeatedly stressed that, while there were facts that supported the government's claims, it was not the responsibility of the government to justify the classification and that the lower courts had

erred when they refused to accept a hypothetical rational basis for sustaining the Retirement Act and instead engaged in some realistic review of the classification. There was no reason to assume that Congress was rewarding "youth *qua* youth";[24] it was at least arguable that a significant percentage of people over age 60 might not perform their duties as foreign service officers as ably as those who were younger. It was the responsibility of those challenging the legislative classification to "convince the court that the legislative facts on which the classification is apparently based could not reasonably be conceived to be true by the governmental decisionmaker."[25]

Government employees may be ordered to take certain actions which could not be imposed on the public generally, such as regulation of their appearance[26] or requirement of residency within a specific area,[27] when these regulations are reasonably related to the efficient operation of the governmental unit or the pursuance of other legitimate purposes. Indeed, an employee's right to engage in political activities may be limited as a means of establishing fairness in government agencies.[28]

A government employee who will have a liberty or property interest deprived by termination of his or her employment does not

22. 427 U.S. 307 (1976) [see note 20 supra].

23. Justice Marshall, the only dissenter, argued that the court should consider the age distinction, as well as the retirement system distinction, as a basis for engaging in some meaningful form of review of the classifications. Vance v. Bradley, 440 U.S. 93, 113 (1979) (Marshall, J., dissenting). While other members of the court have at times joined Justice Marshall in seeking to use an intermediate form of review where it is required by the constitutionally significant nature of the rights effected or personal "status" basis of a classification, no other justice was willing to engage in such a wide range review of statutory employment criteria. Justice Marshall was also the only dissenter when the Court upheld the 50 year old retirement provision for a state police force. Massachusetts Bd. of Retirement v. Murgia, 427 U.S. 307, 317 (1976). Justice Stevens did not participate in the Massachusetts decision but he joined the majority in *Vance*.

24. Vance v. Bradley, 440 U.S. 101 (1979).

25. 440 U.S. at 111. The Supreme Court has refused to review a state law imposing a mandatory re-

tirement age for elected state court judges which was challenged as an age classification violative of equal protection and a restriction on the ability of voters to elect the person of their choice violative of the fundamental right to vote. Trafelet v. Thompson, 444 U.S. 906 (1979) (White, J., dissenting to denial of certiorari).

26. Kelley v. Johnson, 425 U.S. 238 (1976) (hair length requirement).

27. McCarthy v. Philadelphia Civil Service Comm'n, 424 U.S. 645 (1976).

28. Civil Service Comm'n v. National Ass'n of Letter Carriers, 413 U.S. 548 (1973); Broadrick v. Oklahoma, 413 U.S. 601 (1973); however, those who are employed at less than high level policy making position may not be discharged under a patronage system because of their political affiliation. Elrod v. Burns, 427 U.S. 347 (1976). For a discussion of other restrictions on government employment in terms of the rights of speech and association see Chapter 18, Section XII.

receive any added substantive protection against the loss of his or her job. An employee entitled to a government position has only a procedural right to a fair process for determining whether he or she violated the substantive conditions of their employment.[29] Thus, in *Harrah Independent School District v. Martin*,[30] the Supreme Court unanimously rejected the substantive due process and equal protection claims of a tenured school teacher who was dismissed under the "willful neglect of duty" clause in her contract for failure to follow a school board regulation that teachers with only bachelor's degrees obtain five semester hours of college credit every three years. Since the teacher had been given a hearing on her reasons for refusal to comply with the regulation, there was no procedural issue in this case. The Supreme Court unanimously reversed the Court of Appeals, which had overturned the boards actions as "arbitrary and capricious." Even if the underlying regulation was arbitrary, that fact would not convert the issue into a procedural one so as to justify significant judicial review of the action. In a per curiam opinion, the Supreme Court held that school board rules, like legislative actions, are entitled to

a strong presumption of validity; the Court noted that there was no possible claim of a connection between the rule and the restriction of a fundamental constitutional interest, such as the right to privacy, which might cause the Court to employ a stricter form of review under the principle of substantive due process. The board could argue rationally that non-renewal of teacher contracts was a reasonable means of promoting its policy of continuing education for certain classes of teachers. Thus, the rule could not be described as totally arbitrary and lacking a rational basis. The substantive due process claim, in the opinion of the Court, was "wholly untenable." The Supreme Court also employed the minimal scrutiny-rational basis test when it examined and rejected the teacher's claim that the rule violated the equal protection clause, because the teacher was unable to demonstrate that the classification related to a suspect class or to the deprivation of a fundamental constitutional right. Because the rule requiring additional college education might arguably relate to teacher quality and because the firing of teachers might be rationally related to that end, the equal protection claim had to be rejected.

---

29. See Chapter 15, Procedural Due Process, Section II D.4.

30. 440 U.S. 194 (1979) (per curiam).

CHAPTER SEVENTEEN

CONGRESSIONAL ENFORCEMENT OF CIVIL RIGHTS

I. INTRODUCTION

Following the Civil War, Congress enacted a series of civil rights statutes to counter the Southern Black Codes which were being passed to take away from the blacks the rights thought to be associated with the thirteeth amendment outlawing slavery and its badges.[1] One of these acts, passed over President Andrew Johnson's veto, was the Civil Rights Act of 1866, grounded on the thirteenth amendment, giving citizens, inter alia, the same right "as is enjoyed by white citizens" to give evidence in court, sue and be sued, to make and enforce contracts, and to buy, sell, inherit, and lease property.[2]

Whether the thirteenth amendment offered sufficient constitutional power to justify Congressional inroads on matters which had normally been entrusted to the states led to the adoption of the fourteenth amendment, the last section of which gave Congress explicit power to "enforce by appropriate legislation the provisions of this article."[3] Several years later the fifteenth amendment was also enacted. The Civil Rights Act of 1866 was then reenacted,[4] along with other civil rights legislation in 1870,[5] and in the subsequent years further protective laws were enacted.[6] We shall not focus on the various interpretations of the civil rights statutes except to the extent they

1. See generally Maslow & Robison, Civil Rights Legislation and the Fight for Equality, 1862–1952, 20 U.Chi.L.Rev. 363 (1953), Gressman, The Unhappy History of Civil Rights Legislation, 50 Mich.L.Rev. 1323 (1952); R. Carr, Federal Protection of Civil Rights: Quest for a Sword (1947).

2. Civil Rights Act of 1866, 14 Stat. 27 (April 9, 1866). See Gressman, The Unhappy History of Civil Rights Legislation, 50 Mich.L.Rev. 1323, 1328 (1952).

3. Some lower courts found the 1866 Act to be unconstitutional. E.g., People v. Brady, 40 Cal. 198 (1870). Contra, In re Turner, Fed.Cas. No. 14,247 (C.C. Md.1867); People v. Washington, 36 Cal. 658 (1869).

4. 16 Stat. 114 (May 31, 1870). See Slaughter-House Cases, 83 U.S. (16 Wall.) 36, 96–97 (1873) (Field, J., dissenting).

5. E.g., § 6 of the Civil Rights Act of 1870, 16 Stat. 190 (May 31, 1870), now codified at 42 U.S.C.A. § 241. See generally United States v. Williams, 341 U.S. 70, 73–82 (1951). (Opinion of Frankfurter, J.) See also id. at 83–84 (Appendix to Opinion of Frankfurter, J.).

6. E.g. the Ku Klux Klan Act, 17 Stat. 13 (April 20, 1871), now codified in 42 U.S.C.A. §§ 1983, 1985(3). See also the Civil Rights Act of 1875, 18 Stat. 335 (Mar. 1, 1875). See Civil Rights Cases, 109 U.S. 3 (1883). The main civil rights statutes of the Reconstruction legislation are now codified in 42 U.S.C.A. §§ 1981

significantly illuminate congressional power under the thirteenth and fourteenth amendments. First we shall discuss congress' power under section 5 of the fourteenth amendment; then we shall turn to the scope of congress' power under the thirteenth amendment; finally we will turn to the fifteenth amendment.

II. CONGRESSIONAL POWER UNDER SECTION 5 OF THE FOURTEENTH AMENDMENT

A. The Historical Background and the Developing Case Law

There was much evidence that the congressional framers of the Civil War Amendments "meant them to serve as a basis for a positive, comprehensive federal program—a program defining fundamental civil rights protected by federal machinery against both state and private encroachment."[1] The hearings on the fourteenth amendment:

> [R]evealed that most of the abuses still being suffered by the Negro were at the hands of individual white persons rather than state governments or those acting under color of state law. Such private invasions of civil liberties were testified to by the vast majority of the 125 witnesses appearing before the committee. These hearings further demonstrated that the Negro was not alone in his tribulations; white persons who had supported the Union cause or who were bold enough to advocate civil rights for the Negro were also the victims of terrorism in the South. These factors were thus clearly in the minds of the committee members

when they drafted the all-important first section of the Fourteenth Amendment. The demonstrated fact that violations of civil rights were primarily the product of individual rather than state action made it unreasonable for the committee to limit the scope of the amendment to state action.[2]

Yet the early case law under section 5 was not conducive to such a broad reading. In the *Civil Rights Cases*,[3] Justice Bradley speaking for the Court read much of the power out of section 5:

> [T]he last section of the [Fourteenth] Amendment invests Congress with power to enforce it by appropriate legislation. To enforce what? . . . It does not invest Congress with power to legislate upon subjects which are within the domain of state legislation; but to provide modes of relief against state legislation, or state action . . . . It does not authorize Congress to create a code of municipal law for the regulation of private rights; but to provide modes of redress against the operation of state laws, and the action of state officers . . . . [C]ivil rights, such as are guaranteed by the Constitution against state aggression, cannot be impaired by the wrongful acts of individuals, unsupported by state authority in the shape of laws, customs, or judicial or executive proceedings.[4]

Because of such decisions, when nearly a century later Congress enacted the Civil Rights Act of 1964 providing, inter alia, for injunctive relief against discrimination in places of public accommodation,[5] it did so on the basis of the Congress' interstate commerce power, not on the basis of section 5 of

---

(Equal Rights Under the Law); 1982 (Property Rights of Citizens); 1983 (Civil Action for Deprivation of Rights); 1985(3) (Depriving Persons of Rights or Privileges); 18 U.S.C.A. §§ 241 (Conspiracy Against Rights of Citizens); 242 (Deprivation of Rights Under Color of Law); and 28 U.S.C.A. § 1443 (Jurisdiction of Civil Rights Cases).

Some of these statutes require that the defendant act "under color of law." E.g., 18 U.S.C.A. § 242; 42 U.S.C.A. § 1983. Others maybe read to reach private conduct, without any "color of law" requirement. E.g., 18 U.S.C.A. § 241, 42 U.S.C.A. §§ 1981, 1982, 1985(3).

"Under color of law" has been said to mean under pretense of law, Screws v. United States, 325 U.S. 91 (1945); defendant need not be a state official; he need only be "a willful participant in joint activity with the

state or its agents." United States v. Price, 383 U.S. 787 (1966).

On the Civil Rights Statutes, see generally, C. Abernathy, Civil Rights: Cases and Materials (1980); T. Eisenberg, Civil Rights Legislation: Cases and Materials (1981); S. Nahmod, Civil Rights & Civil Liberties Litigation: A Guide to § 1983 (1979).

1. R. Carr, Federal Protection of Civil Rights: Quest for a Sword 36 (1947).

2. Gressman, The Unhappy History of Civil Rights Legislation, 50 Mich.L.Rev. 1323, 1329–30 (1952).

3. 109 U.S. 3 (1883).

4. 109 U.S. 3, 11, 17 (1883).

5. Now codified as 42 U.S.C.A. §§ 2000a–2000a–6.

the fourteenth amendment.[6] Yet the more modern suggestions of lower courts supported a much broader reading of section 5. Thus, in 1956, only one year after *Brown v. Board of Education* (*Brown II*)[7] the Eighth Circuit held that a school district could sue to prevent private individuals from interfering with its duty to desegregate.[8]

In 1966, the Supreme Court decision of *United States v. Guest*[9] recognized a wide power in Congress to enforce this amendment. An indictment was brought under a law passed in 1870 outlawing, inter alia, two or more persons going "in disguise on the highway, or on the premises of another, with intent to prevent or hinder his free exercise or enjoyment of any right or privilege so secured . . . ."[10] The fourth count of the indictment in *Guest* is of particular interest for our purposes. It charged the defendants, private individuals, with conspiring to intimidate some black citizens to prevent them from exercising the right to use the facilities of interstate commerce within the State of Georgia. The Court held that the indictment should not have been dismissed as to this paragraph because a conspiracy against the constitutional right to use the facilities of interstate commerce, whether or not motivated by racial discrimination [is] a proper object of the federal law."[11]

The Court specifically disavowed any intent to consider "the question of what kinds of other and broader legislation Congress might constitutionally enact under § 5 of the fourteenth amendment . . . ."[12] Separate opinions did reach that question. Justice Clark, concurring, and joined by Black and Fortas, argued that "the specific language of section 5 empowers the Congress to enact laws punishing all conspiracies— with or without state action—that interfere with fourteenth amendment rights."[13] Justice Brennan concurring and dissenting in part, and joined by Warren and Douglas, contended that under section 5 Congress could reach private discrimination and that Congress in fact had exercised that power in the statute construed by the Court.[14]

Six members of the Court were now on record as approving Congressional legislation that reached private discriminatory actions, though that conclusion was not expressed as a holding. Indeed the Court has never adopted this position in a majority opinion. But at least the way was now clear for a definite test of Congressional power under section 5. The test came very soon.

In *Katzenbach v. Morgan*,[15] the Supreme Court upheld the constitutionality of section 4(e) of the Voting Rights Act of 1965. That section provided that no person who has completed the sixth grade in a Puerto Rican school in which the predominant classroom language was not English may be denied the right to vote in any election because of his or her inability to read or write English. The statute *pro tanto* prohibited enforcement of the laws of New York requiring an ability to read and write English as a condition of voting.[16] The question in *Morgan*, as stated by the Court, was whether the Congress could prohibit enforcement of the state law by legislating under section 5 of the fourteenth amendment, regardless of whether the Court would find that the equal protection clause itself nullified New York's literacy requirement.[17]

---

6. See 42 U.S.C.A. § 2000a–1(b); Hearings before the Senate Commerce Committee on S. 1732, 88th Cong., 1st Sess., Parts 1 & 2 (1963). The Supreme Court affirmed the constitutionality of the law on the basis of the commerce clause. Heart of Atlanta Motel v. United States, 379 U.S. 241 (1964); Katzenbach v. McClung, 379 U.S. 294 (1964).

7. 349 U.S. 294 (1955).

8. Brewer v. Hoxie School District No. 46, 238 F.2d 91 (8th Cir. 1956).

9. 383 U.S. 745 (1966).

10. Now codified in 42 U.S.C.A. § 241.

11. 383 U.S. 745, at 780 (1966).

12. 383 U.S. 745, at 755 (1966).

13. 383 U.S. 745, at 762 (1966) (Clark, J., concurring).

14. 383 U.S. 745, at 777 (1966) (Brennan, J., concurring and dissenting in part).

15. 384 U.S. 641 (1966).

16. 384 U.S. 641, 643–44.

17. Id. at 649. In Lassiter v. Northampton Election Bd. the Court refused to strike down state literacy requirements for voting as a violation of the equal pro-

The Court utilized a two-part analysis to uphold the federal statute. The Court first construed section 5 as granting Congress "by a specific provision applicable to the fourteenth amendment, the same broad powers expressed in the necessary and proper clause." [18] Under this interpretation, the Court held it within the power of Congress to determine that the Puerto Rican minority needed the vote to gain nondiscriminatory treatment in public services and that this need warranted federal intrusion upon the states.[19] The Court reached the same result in the second part of its analysis. Since it perceived a basis, upon which Congress might reasonably predicate its judgment that the New York literacy requirement was invidiously discriminatory, the Court was willing to uphold the legislation.

Congress, in the statute upheld in *Katzenbach*, explicitly relied on section 5, but years later the Court made it clear that when Congress legislates under section 5, it need not do so explicitly. The Court must determine what is the intent of Congress, but Congress need not "recite the words 'section 5' or 'Fourteenth Amendment' or 'equal protection' . . . ." [20]

If the Court in *Morgan* had limited its rationale to the first conclusion, that Congress may extend the vote to a class of persons injured by discriminatory allocation of government services by a state, *Morgan* would offer no support for arguments that legislation could restrict the reach of the equal protection guarantee. A court still would retain authority to determine whether discrimination exists and whether the legislative remedy is reasonably related to the proper goal. By suggesting that Congress can legislate to address specific violations of the equal protection clause, however, the Court in *Morgan* may have conferred on Congress the power to define the reach of equal protection.[21] Justice Harlan specifically attacked this portion of the majority's opinion as allowing Congress to define constitutional rights "so as in effect to dilute [the] equal protection and due process decisions of this Court.[22]

Justice Harlan's fears may prove accurate. That various justices of the Supreme Court have explicitly acknowledged and relied on *Morgan* as the reason to respect congressional accommodations of conflicting rights and powers gives additional support to Harlan's concerns.[23]

In an influential discussion of congressional power under section 5, Professor Archibald Cox concluded that Congress does have broad power to determine what constitutes a violation of equal protection. Cox observed that section 5 makes it irrelevant whether the relief for violations of the fourteenth amendment granted under a legislative enactment is greater or lesser than the courts

---

tection clause in the absence of any showing of discriminatory use of the test. 360 U.S. 45, 53–54 (1959). The *Morgan* court acknowledged *Lassiter* and refused to disturb its earlier ruling. See 384 U.S. at 649–50.

18. 384 U.S. at 650.

19. Id. at 652–53. See generally Hawkins v. Town of Shaw, 437 F.2d 1286 (5th Cir. 1971); Fessler & Haar, Beyond the Wrong Side of the Tracks: Municipal Services in the Interstices of Procedure, 6 Harv.Civ. Rights-Civ.L.Rev. 441 (1971).

20. EEOC v. Wyoming, 103 S.Ct. 1054, 1064 n.18 (1983). Cf. Katzenbach v. Morgan, 384 U.S. 641, 643 n.1 (1966), quoting § 4(e).

21. See id. at 653; Burt, Miranda and Title II: A Morganatic Marriage, 1969 Sup.Ct.Rev. 81, 133. According to Burt, "*Morgan* allows a restrained Court, intent perhaps on undoing the work of its active predecessors, [to] permit a graceful and selective retreat limited to those areas where the political branch gives an explicit and contrary judgment." Id.

22. 384 U.S. at 668 (Harlan, J., dissenting). See also, Note, Toward Limits on Congressional Enforcement Power Under the Civil War Amendments, 34 Stanford L.Rev. 453 (1982).

23. See Trafficante v. Metropolitan Life Insurance Co., 409 U.S. 205, 212 (1972) (White, with Blackmun & Powell, JJ., concurring) (white tenants given standing under section 8(10)(a) of Civil Rights Act of 1968 despite doubts of case or controversy under article III of Constitution); Welsh v. United States, 398 U.S. 333, 371 (1970) (White, J., with Burger, C. J., & Stewart, J., dissenting) (argument for respecting congressional judgment accommodating right to free exercise of religion with statute for raising armies). See also, Fullilove v. Klutznick, 448 U.S. 448, 476–78 (1980) (Opinion of Burger, C. J., joined by White & Powell, JJ.) (relying on § 5 of fourteenth amendment to justify Congressional decision to set aside 10% of funds for federal work projects for minority group members). On *Fullilove*, see Section II, D, infra and Chapter 16, Section II, F, supra.

would order.[24] Cox concluded that the *Morgan* rationale requires judicial deference to congressional judgments to limit rights as well as to decisions to extend them.[25]

Reliance on *Morgan* to support, e.g., the position that Congress has the power to restrict court-ordered remedies rests on three questionable predicates: that congressional power to override state law under the fourteenth amendment is as broad as an expansive reading of *Morgan* would suggest; that *Morgan* authorizes Congress to override not only state actions, but also federal court constructions of the fourteenth amendment that are too restrictive; and that section 5 permits Congress to interpret the equal protection clause not only more broadly than the federal courts, but also more narrowly. Congress can rely on a broad reading of *Morgan* to dilute rights under section 5 of the fourteenth amendment only if each of these premises is correct.

B. The Proper Reach of MORGAN

The broad language in *Morgan*, purporting to give Congress power to define equal protection, was unnecessary to the decision of the case. The Court's language appears to be an alternative holding rather than dictum, but subsequent decisions show that the Court has retreated from the more far-reaching implications of *Morgan*.

In *Oregon v. Mitchell* [26] the Court faced challenges to the constitutionality of provisions of the Voting Rights Act Amendments of 1970 [27] which lowered the minimum voting age in state and federal elections from 21 to 18, barred the use of literacy tests under certain circumstances, and forbade state imposition of residency requirements for presidential and vice-presidential elections. If

the *Morgan* holding granted Congress carte blanche to enact legislation to remedy what Congress regards as denials of equal protection, the Court would have upheld the federal statute on that basis. Instead, the Court, in five separate opinions, struck down the section of the Act that extended the franchise to 18 year-olds in state and local elections.[28]

Four justices,—Douglas, Brennan, White, and Marshall—maintained that Congress had the power under section 5 to determine equal protection requirements as applied to the voting rights of 18 to 21 year-olds in state and federal elections. Justice Brennan argued that since Congress had sufficient evidence to conclude that exclusion of such citizens from the franchise was unnecessary to promote any legitimate state interest, it could properly extend the franchise, regardless of the Court's view of the matter.[29] None of the other justices of the fragmented Court saw Congress' role as that extensive. Justice Stewart, joined by Chief Justice Burger and Justice Blackmun, found that Congress could not usurp the role of the courts by determining the boundaries of the equal protection clause.[30] Rather than reading *Morgan* as granting Congress power to define the reach of the equal protection clause, Justice Stewart reasoned that the Court in *Morgan* only accepted an undoubtedly correct congressional conclusion that a state statute denying a racial group the right to vote amounts to invidious discrimination under the equal protection clause.[31] Justice Harlan agreed that Congress could not define the reach of equal protection; he reasoned that constitutional interpretation by the Congress conflicts with the procedures for amending the constitution, particularly because legislative determinations normally

---

24. Cox, The Role of Congress in Constitutional Determinations, 40 U.Cinn.L.Rev. 199, 259 (1971). See also Cox, Constitutional Adjudication and the Promotion of Human Rights, 80 Harv.L.Rev. 91 (1966).

25. Id. at 259–60.

26. 400 U.S. 112 (1970).

27. Pub.L. No. 91–285, 84 Stat. 314, amending 42 U.S.C.A. § 1973.

28. 400 U.S. 112, 118, 124–31.

29. Id. at 240, 280–81 (Brennan, J., with White & Marshall, JJ., concurring and dissenting); Id. at 135, 141–42 (Douglas, J., concurring and dissenting).

30. Id. at 296 (Stewart J., with Burger, C. J., & Blackmun, J., concurring and dissenting).

31. Id. at 295–96.

are accorded deferential judicial review.[32] Justices Black and Douglas disagreed on the validity of the Voting Rights Act Amendments of 1970 because of their differing conceptions of the reach of the equal protection clause, but each assumed that the legal question was for the courts, not Congress, to decide.[33]

The opinions of the seven justices who concurred in *Mitchell* indicate that section 5 does not confer unlimited power on Congress to determine the meaning of equal protection. Although the fragmented Court does not provide a precise guide to the proper limitations, a majority did reject the contention that section 5 authorizes Congress to define the substantive boundaries of the equal protection clause by invalidating state legislation.[34]

Whatever the reach of section 5 as a vehicle for augmenting the power of Congress to regulate matters otherwise left to the states, it does not provide in itself authority for Congress to interfere with the execution or enforcement of federal court judgments or to overturn federal judicial determinations of the requirements of the fourteenth amendment. The question turns on the history of the amendment and its perceived purpose as an enduring principle to govern the country.

C. Application of Section 5 to Federal Court Determinations

The framers of section 5 considered it a tool to enable "Congress, in case the States shall enact laws in conflict with the principles of the amendment, to correct that legis-

lation by a formal congressional enactment".[35] Senator Trumbull of Illinois viewed section 5 as the means of "destroy[ing] all these discriminations in civil rights [by the states] against the black man . . . ."[36] Other participants in the debates added that the purpose of the proposed section was to give Congress a means to enforce the fourteenth amendment[37] to see that it "was carried out in good faith, and for [no] other [purpose] . . . ."[38]

Strong evidence supports the view of section 5 as a plenary power. An original draft of section 1 of the fourteenth amendment provided that "Congress shall have power to make all laws . . . to secure . . . to all persons . . . equal protection . . . ,"[39] but the framers of the Amendment in rejecting that formulation desired to secure the stated guarantees against a future unsympathetic Congress as well as the courts.[40] The history will always be unclear, for the drafters had no reason to anticipate a time when the Court might be more liberal in granting and enforcing fourteenth amendment rights than the Congress. We must remember that Congress at this time was dominated by the Radical Republicans, who viewed themselves as the principal protectors of the recently freed slaves. The only Supreme Court that the members of Congress knew was a Court which had not applied the Bill of Rights to the states; had not assisted in giving the protection of the law to the abolitionists in the South prior to the War; had enforced the fugitive slave laws; and had invalidated congressional legislation limiting the expansion of slavery into new territories. There was simply no rea-

---

32. Id. at 205 (Harlan, J., concurring and dissenting).

33. Id. at 117–35 (Black, J., announcing judgments of the Court); Id. at 135–52 (Douglas J., separate opinion).

34. See Cox, The Supreme Court 1965 Term—Foreword: Constitutional Adjudication and the Promotion of Human Rights, 80 Harv.L.Rev. 91, 106–07 (1966). See generally Engdahl, Constitutionality of the Voting Age Statute, 39 Geo.Wash.L.Rev. 1 (1970). Cox does not appear to have been persuaded that the *Mitchell* case should be read to constrict the broad language of *Morgan*.

35. Cong. Globe, 39th Cong., 1st Sess. 2768 (1866) (remarks of Senator Howard, who reported the amendment to the Senate from the Joint Committee on Reconstruction).

36. Id. at 322 (debate on Freedman's Bureau bill).

37. See Cong. Globe, 39th Cong., 1st Sess. 41 (1865) (remarks of Senator Wilson).

38. See id. at 43 (remarks of Senator Trumbull).

39. Cong. Globe, 39th Cong., 1st Sess. 1033–34 (1866).

40. See Burt, Miranda and Title II: A Morganatic Marriage, 1969 Sup.Ct.Rev. 81, 92–93.

son for the framers to anticipate a Court which would liberally recognize individual rights more expansively than the Congress, and therefore there is no evidence that they considered this issue. But some limit on the congressional restriction of judicial power did exist, in the first section of the fourteenth amendment, for that section established blacks as citizens, overturning *Dred Scott* and protecting these newly acquired citizenship rights of the blacks against a future Congress.

Thus we must turn to judicial interpretations of the scope of the section 5 power. The early cases arising under section 5 focused initially on the new relationship between Congress and the states and later on the role of the courts in determining violations of equal protection. In 1879 the Supreme Court in *Ex parte Virginia* [41] described the new federalism:

> The prohibitions of the Fourteenth Amendment are directed to the States, and they are to a degree restrictions of State power. It is these which Congress is empowered to enforce, and to enforce against State action, ... Such enforcement is not invasion of State sovereignty . . . . [T]he constitutional amendment was ordained for a purpose. [42]

In 1976 the Supreme Court reaffirmed and cited the *Virginia* Court's view that "the fourteenth amendment was 'intended to be what [it] really [is], a limitation of the power of the State and [an] enlargement of the power of Congress.' " The tenth amendment does not limit section 5. [43] Other, earlier decisions suggest that section 5 empowers Congress to enforce the guarantees of

the amendment only when Congress and the courts agree that the states have abridged them. [44] Indeed, the Court twice rejected the judgment of Congress expressed in federal legislation that actions of a state government violated the fourteenth amendment. [45]

Although *Morgan* and *Mitchell* may permit Congress to find a state law invalid even if a court would not, neither the legislative history of section 5 nor the subsequent case law authorizes Congress to invalidate federal court action enforcing the fourteenth amendment. *Morgan* allows congressional intrusion into state sovereignty where necessary to secure fourteenth amendment guarantees. *Morgan* does not relax such other limitations on congressional power as those inherent in the fifth amendment. [46]

D. Section 5 Power to Narrow Federal Judicial Interpretations of Equal Protection

Although the Court in *Morgan* found broad congressional power under section 5 to determine that state practice interferes with fourteenth amendment rights, it also examined the federal statute for consistency with constitutional requirements. [47] The Court's analysis confirms that federal courts will scrutinize congressional action under section 5 to assure that it meets the equal protection requirements embodied in the fifth amendment. [48] If the legislation includes a suspect classification or affects a fundamental right, then under traditional equal protection analysis only a compelling

---

41. 100 U.S. 339 (1879).

42. Id. at 346–47.

43. Fitzpatrick v. Bitzer, 427 U.S. 445, 454 (1976). Thus it is quite clear that Congress' powers under section 5 are not limited by the tenth amendment even though the tenth amendment does place some limits on Congress' exercise of the commerce power. EEOC v. Wyoming, 103 S.Ct. 1054, 1064 n.18 (1983).

44. See Virginia v. Rives, 100 U.S. 313, 317–19 (1879) (under section 5 mode of enforcement of prohibition against discriminatory state action left to discretion of Congress; one means of enforcement is removal from state to federal court); Strauder v. West Virginia, 100 U.S. 303, 307–09 (1879) (same).

45. See Civil Rights Cases, 109 U.S. 3, 18–19 (1883) (law preventing private citizens from depriving individuals of equal protection); United States v. Harris, 106 U.S. 629, 639 (1882) (same).

46. See Cohen, Congressional Power to Interpret Due Process and Equal Protection, 28 Stan.L.Rev. 603, 614 (1975).

47. See Katzenbach v. Morgan, 384 U.S. 641, 656 (1966).

48. See Bolling v. Sharpe, 347 U.S. 497, 499–500 (1954) (racial discrimination so unjustifiable as to be also a denial of due process; racial segregation in District of Columbia schools such a denial under Fifth Amendment).

state interest will support its constitutionality.[49]

The Voting Rights Act of 1965 at issue in *Morgan*, the 1970 Amendments to that Act reviewed in *Mitchell*, and the reconstruction laws involved in earlier cases were attempts by Congress to expand the power of the federal government over the states and to extend protection to a group whose rights had been denied in violation of the fourteenth amendment. The statutes in these cases were upheld on the rational relationship test. If Congress were to limit federal courts' power to extend to racial minorities constitutionally protected rights, such statutes would place special burdens on those minorities seeking to implement their constitutional rights and would dilute their equal protection rights. A court must strictly scrutinize such a legislative scheme and uphold it only if supported by a compelling state interest.[50] The decision in *Morgan*, upholding the requirement of a more liberal voting eligibility standard than the judicially defined constitu-

tional requirement, does not support the argument that Congress may restrict a court's power to interpret the requirements of the fourteenth amendment or may limit the available remedies for violations of those rights.[51]

A caveat to the Court's opinion in *Morgan* emphasizes the distinction between the power to expand and the power to restrict the reach of equal protection:

> Section 5 does not grant Congress power to exercise discretion in the other direction and to enact "statutes so as in effect to dilute equal protection and due process decisions of this Court." We emphasize that Congress' power under section 5 is limited to adopting measures to enforce the guarantees of the Amendment; section 5 grants Congress no power to restrict, abrogate, or dilute these guarantees. Thus, for example, an enactment authorizing the States to establish racially segregated systems of education would not be—as required by section 5—a measure "to enforce" the Equal Protection Clause since that clause of its own force prohibits such state laws.[52]

---

49. See e.g. San Antonio Independent School District v. Rodriguez, 411 U.S. 1, 17 (1973); Developments in the Law—Equal Protection, 82 Harv.L.Rev. 1065, 1087–132 (1969). The right to an unrestricted exercise of the franchise is fundamental, requiring a compelling state interest to justify any restrictions. Harper v. Virginia Bd. of Elections, 383 U.S. 663, 670 (1966). In *Morgan*, however, Congress did not restrict the franchise, but extended it.

50. Cf. Hunter v. Erickson, 393 U.S. 385 (1969). In *Hunter* the Court held that a provision in a city charter prohibiting the city council from implementing any ordinance dealing with racial, religious, or ancestral discrimination in housing without the approval of the majority of the city's voters was unconstitutional. The Court found that although the statute did not discriminate on its face, its effect was to place a burden on the minority. Id. at 391. The Court asserted that a state may not make it more difficult to enact legislation for one group than for another. Id. at 392–93. See also Reitman v. Mulkey, 387 U.S. 369, 380–81 (1967); Black, The Supreme Court 1966 Term—Foreword: "State Action," Equal Protection and California's Proposition, 14, 81 Harv.L.Rev. 69, 82 (1967). A congressional attempt to make it more difficult for the members of one group to enforce their constitutional rights to, e.g. integrated public education, should be subject to this same equal protection strict scrutiny.

51. See Shapiro v. Thompson, 394 U.S. 618, 641 (1969) (rejecting argument that congressional approval of one year residence requirement for welfare recipients authorizes states to impose such requirements); accord, Graham v. Richardson, 403 U.S. 365, 382 (1971).

But cf. Welsh v. United States, 398 U.S. 333, 368 (1970) (White, J., with Burger, C. J. & Stewart, J., dissenting) (argument for respecting congressional judgment accommodating right to free exercise of religion with statute for raising army).

Neither may Congress use its power to limit standing so as to affect substantive constitutional rights if it could not do so directly. The courts have often asserted that if a dispute is otherwise justiciable, the question whether a litigant is a proper party to request adjudication of an issue is within the power of Congress to determine. E.g., Sierra Club v. Morton, 405 U.S. 727, 731–32 (1972). Yet, such statements should not control where a restriction on standing may affect a constitutional right. Rather, they should be limited to cases where Congress has created and expanded standing by statute.

The Court has indicated that Article III also limits the power to restrict or grant standing. See Association of Data Processing Service Organizations, Inc. v. Camp, 397 U.S. 150, 154 (1970). "Apart from Article III jurisdictional questions, . . . Congress can, of course, resolve the question [of standing] one way or another, *save as the requirements of Article III dictate otherwise.*" Id. (emphasis added). Presumably due process creates another limitation. See Switchmen's Union v. National Mediation Bd., 320 U.S. 297, 301 (1943).

52. 384 U.S. at 651–52 n. 10. See also Oregon v. Mitchell, 400 U.S. 112, 128–29 (1970) (opinion of Black, J.).

Although the Court may not have articulated precisely why the power to enforce does not include the power to dilute, it did recognize that section 5 power to dilute would conflict with a primary purpose of the equal protection clause, to protect citizens' rights under the fourteenth amendment against a hostile Congress.[53] The command of the equal protection guarantee of section 1 should control the section 5 power: neither the states nor the Congress should have the power to violate the equal protection clause, as defined by the courts, if the guarantee is to be meaningful.[54]

Reading section 5 as authorizing only extensions of fourteenth amendment guarantees accords with both *Morgan* and the general scheme of the Constitution. Professor Archibald Cox has admitted:

> There is no *a priori* reason for linking power to expand constitutional safeguards with power to dilute them. One can assert without logical fallacy that, since the chief function of the Supreme Court is to protect human rights, it should never defer to any legislative determination which restricts those rights without making its own investigation and characterization of the interest affected, even though it welcomes any legislative determination that extends human rights and is subject to challenge only as an unconstitutional extension of federal power at the expense of the States.[55]

Morgan provides strong support that section 5 of the fourteenth amendment does give Congress broad power to ban state laws authorizing discriminatory acts. But as many commentators contend,[56] and as the Court itself recognized in *Mississippi University for Women v. Hogan*,[57] this power should not be considered a power to dilute.

Less clear is the power of Congress to use section 5 of the fourteenth amendment to justify federal statutes which distribute benefits or burdens on the basis of race for the purpose of affirmative action. In *Fullilove v. Klutznick*[58] a fragmented Court rejected a challenge on its face to the minority business enterprise (MBE) section of a federal public works act which required that, unless there was an administrative waiver, at least 10% of the federal funds granted for local public works projects must be used by the state or local grantees to purchase services or supplies from businesses owned and controlled by minority group members, defined by statute as American citizens who are "Negroes, Spanish-speaking, Orientals, Indians, Eskimos, and Aleuts."

The plurality opinion of Chief Justice Burger, joined by Justices White and Powell, specifically relied on Congress' power under section 5 of the fourteenth amendment.

---

53. See 384 U.S. at 651–52 n. 10.

54. Bolling v. Sharpe, 347 U.S. 497, 499 (1954).

55. Cox, The Role of Congress in Constitutional Determination, 40 U.Cinn.L.Rev. 199, 253 (1971).

56. The literature in this area is vast; some of the articles include:

Emerson, The Power of Congress to Change Constitutional Decisions of the Supreme Court: The Human Life Bill, 77 Nw.U.L.Rev. 129 (1982); Estreicher, Congressional Power and Constitutional Rights: Reflections on Proposed "Human Life" Legislation, 68 Va.L.Rev. 333 (1982); Choper, Congressional Power to Expand Judicial Definitions of the Substantive Terms of the Civil War Amendments, 67 Minn.L.Rev. 299 (1982); Note, Congressional Power to Enforce Due Process Rights, 80 Colum.L.Rev. 1265 (1980); Cohen, Congressional Power to Interpret Due Process and Equal Protection, 27 Stan.L.Rev. 603 (1975); Gordon, The Nature and Uses of Congressional Power Under Section Five of the Fourteenth Amendment to Overcome Decisions of the Supreme Court, 72 Nw.U.L.Rev. 656 (1977); Buchanan, Katzenbach v. Morgan and Congressional Enforcement Power Under the Fourteenth

Amendment: A Study in Conceptual Confusion, 17 Hous.L.Rev. 69 (1979); Burt, Miranda and Title II: A Morganatic Marriage, 1969 Sup.Ct.Rev. 81; Rotunda, Congressional Power to Restrict the Jurisdiction of the Lower Federal Courts and the Problem of School Busing, 64 Georgetown L.J. 839, 858–67 (1976).

57. 102 S.Ct. 3331 (1982), where the Court quoted footnote 10 of Katzenbach v. Morgan, 384 U.S. 641, 651 n. 10 (1966) and added: "Although we give deference to congressional decisions and classifications, neither Congress nor a State can validate a law that denies the rights guaranteed by the Fourteenth Amendment." In *Hogan* the Court held that the state, under the fourteenth amendment, could not have a female-only nursing school; no congressional statute could excuse the state from such gender discrimination. See also, e.g., Califano v. Goldfarb, 430 U.S. 199, 210 (1977). Cf. Williams v. Rhodes, 393 U.S. 23, 29 (1968) (the powers granted by the Constitution to Congress or the states "are always subject to the limitation that they may not be exercised in a way that violated other specific provisions of the Constitution.").

58. 448 U.S. 448 (1980).

These justices were satisfied that Congress, although it made no factual findings, had before it abundant historical evidence "from which it could conclude that traditional procurement practices, when applied to minority businesses, could perpetuate the effects of prior discrimination."[59] This opinion explicitly did not adopt any of the formulas advanced in *Bakke*.[60]

The Burger plurality was narrowly drafted, and found it "significant that the administrative scheme provides for waiver and exemption."[61] In rejecting a facial attack on the statute, the Chief Justice noted the law provides for administrative scrutiny to remove from the program non-bona-fide, spurious minority front entities. A waiver procedure was also available to avoid dealing with an MBE attempting to exploit the program by charging an unreasonable price, that is a price not justified by the present effects of past discrimination. "That the use of racial and ethnic criteria is premised on assumptions rebuttable in the administrative process gives reasonable assurance that application of the MBE program will be limited to accomplishing the remedial objectives contemplated by Congress and that misapplications of the racial and ethnic criteria can be remedied . . . . The MBE provision may be viewed as a pilot project, appropriately limited in extent and duration, and subject to reassessment and reevaluation by the Congress prior to any extension or reenactment."[62] This plurality opinion did conclude, however, that under section 5

"congressional authority extends beyond the prohibition of purposeful discrimination to encompass state action that has discriminatory impact perpetuating the effects of past discrimination."[63]

Given that this opinion was written narrowly and did not command a majority, it is difficult to determine to what extent section 5 may be used to justify affirmative action programs enacted by Congress.

Also difficult to determine is the extent to which section 5 may be used to reach private conduct. While *Morgan* and its progeny confirm Congressional power to override state *laws* which interfere with fourteenth amendment rights, there has not yet been a Supreme Court case precisely holding that Congress, by statute, may reach purely private actions, though some lower courts have so held.[64] The main cases dealing with Congressional power to enforce civil rights against purely private acts have, on the Supreme Court level, been justified by a thirteenth amendment analysis. It is to those cases that we now turn.

III. CONGRESSIONAL POWER UNDER SECTION 2 OF THE THIRTEENTH AMENDMENT

The thirteenth amendment is fairly unique in two respects. First, it contains an absolute bar to the existence of slavery or involuntary servitude; there is no requirement of "state action." Thus it is applicable to individuals as well as states. "By its own un-

---

59. 448 U.S. at 481.

60. 448 U.S. at 491, citing University of California Regents v. Bakke, 438 U.S. 265 (1978). See Chapter 16, Section II, F, supra.

61. 448 U.S. at 485.

62. 448 U.S. at 487.

Justice Powell's separate concurrence did apply the analysis he had advocated in *Bakke*, though he too also relied on Congress' power under section 5. 448 U.S. at 500. Justice Marshall concurring, joined by Justices Brennan and Blackmun, relied on the Marshall analysis earlier promulgated in *Bakke* and therefore did not find it necessary to rely on section 5. The other three justices dissented, objecting strongly to the use of racial criteria for the purposes of distributing government benefits. Two of these justices, Rehnquist and

Stewart, believed that the Constitution absolutely prohibited the use of racial criteria, and the third, Stevens, objected because the statute was not narrowly tailored, was not adequately preceded by a consideration of less drastic alternatives, and was not adequately explained by a statement of legislative purpose.

63. 448 U.S. at 477.

64. E.g., Westberry v. Gilman Paper Co., 507 F.2d 206 (5th Cir. 1975) (42 U.S.C.A. § 1985(3) applicable to private discriminatory acts; here private persons allegedly conspired to kill plaintiff in violation of 14th amendment equal protection and due process guarantees); but see, Bellamy v. Mason's Stores, Inc., 508 F.2d 504 (4th Cir. 1974) (while 42 U.S.C.A. § 1985(3) does not apply to private acts, perhaps Congress could enact such a statute).

aided force and effect it abolished slavery, and established universal freedom." [1] Secondly, like the fourteenth and fifteenth amendments, it contains an enforcement clause, enabling Congress to pass all necessary legislation.

The Supreme Court was first required to comprehensively examine the scope of the thirteenth amendment in the *Civil Rights Cases* [2] in 1883. Five cases were joined, all arising originally from criminal prosecutions against private citizens who denied blacks the privileges and accommodations of hotels or theatres. The question before the Court was the constitutionality of the Civil Rights Act of 1875, which provided that all persons were entitled to equal access to inns, public conveyances and places of amusement regardless of race and that any person denying another such access was subject to suit. It was contended that the Thirteenth Amendment constituted a basis for the statute.

The Court found that the amendment abolished slavery and that the prohibition against subjecting another to slavery or involuntary servitude was directed to individual citizens, as well as the states. The Court also found that "the power vested in Congress to enforce the article by appropriate legislation, clothes Congress with power to pass all laws necessary and proper for abolishing all badges and incidents of slavery in the United States. . . ." [3] The question then became whether "the denial to any person of admission to the accommodations and privileges of an inn, a public conveyance, or a theatre [subjected] that person to any form of servitude or [tended] to fasten upon him any badge of slavery." [4] The Court found it did not and that therefore Congress

was without authority under the thirteenth amendment to have enacted a statute with this effect. The purpose of the amendment was to vindicate "those fundamental rights which appertain to the essence of citizenship" [5] not to adjust "social rights." [6] The Court said it would be carrying the slavery concept too far if it were applied to denying blacks access to inns or theatres. "Mere discriminations on account of race or color were not regarded as badges of slavery." [7] The Court found the Civil Rights statute invalid under the thirteenth amendment as not involving the badges of slavery and not valid under the fourteenth amendment as not involving state action. [8] However, the Court did carefully distinguish Congress' enforcement powers under the thirteenth and fourteenth amendments:

> Under the thirteenth amendment, the legislation, so far as necessary or proper to eradicate all forms and incidents of slavery and involuntary servitude, may be direct and primary, operating upon the acts of individuals, whether sanctioned by State legislation or not; under the fourteenth as we have already shown, it must necessarily be, and can only be, corrective in its character, addressed to counteract and afford relief against state regulations or proceedings. [9]

Justice Harlan dissented vigorously. He did not believe the Court should place a limitation on the Congress' power to define and prohibit badges of slavery. He stated further that discrimination on the basis of race could constitute a badge of slavery, that the rights involved here were also fundamental rights. No class of people should be in practical subjection to another class. [10] For the most part, after the *Civil Rights* decision the thirteenth amendment lay dormant for nearly a century after its passage. [11]

---

1. The Civil Rights Cases, 109 U.S. 3, 20 (1883).

2. 109 U.S. 3 (1883).

3. 109 U.S. at 20.

4. 109 U.S. at 21.

5. 109 U.S. at 22.

6. 109 U.S. at 23.

7. 109 U.S. at 25.

8. 109 U.S. at 24.

9. 109 U.S. at 23.

10. 109 U.S. at 27–62.

11. An important case during this period is Butler v. Perry, 240 U.S. 328 (1916). The Supreme Court there stated:

> "[The Thirteenth Amendment] certainly was not intended to interdict enforcement of those duties which individuals owe to the State, such as services to the army, militia, on the jury, etc."

The Supreme Court finally gave the anti-slavery amendment new force in *Jones v. Alfred H. Mayer Co.*[12] The controversy in *Jones* arose when defendants, a subdivision developer, builder, and realtor, refused as a matter of policy to sell housing or land to blacks. No state action was involved because all facilities such as sewer, garbage collection and sidewalks were provided by the defendant developers. And no federal aid was involved which might have subjected the defendants to executive orders or federal statutes prohibiting discrimination in publicly financed projects. The principal issue was, then, one of private discrimination in refusing to sell housing.[13] The controversy involved the right of citizens to buy and lease housing without regard to their race, and to solve the problem the Court resurrected a provision of the 1866 Civil Rights Act as a basis for its decision.[14]

Notwithstanding some arguable ambiguities,[15] the Court read the legislative history of Section 1982, along with its language and judicial history,[16] as proof that the act was intended to apply to private as well as public acts of discrimination. The Court reasoned that legislation *rationally* connected with eradicating slavery is valid under the thirteenth amendment and that private discrimination could constitute such a badge or incident of slavery.[17] It then concluded that Section 1982, construed as reaching private discrimination in the sale of property, was a valid enactment under the thirteenth amendment.[18] Thus, the primary basis upon which the decision rested became the thirteenth amendment. What had been described as "an unserviceable antique"[19] now became

240 U.S. at 333.

In *Butler* the court upheld a state statute requiring able-bodied males between 21 and 45 years of age to work on public roads for a certain time. A State "has inherent power to require every able-bodied man within its jurisdiction to labor for a reasonable time on public roads near his residence without direct compensation." 240 U.S. at 330. The military draft laws in effect forcing labor out of soldiers and conscientious objectors has also been upheld. Arver v. United States, 245 U.S. 366, 390 (1918). Injunctions in labor disputes also do not involve involuntary servitude. International Union v. Wisconsin Employment Relations Bd., 336 U.S. 245 (1949). Cf. Robertson v. Baldwin, 165 U.S. 275, 282 (1897) (labor contracts of seamen enforced).

However, the state may not engage a person in forced labor in order to liquidate a civil debt or obligation. Peonage Cases, 123 F. 671 (M.D.Ala.1903). "The state may impose involuntary servitude as a punishment for crime, but it may not compel one man to labor for another in payment of a debt, by punishing him as a criminal if he does not perform the service or pay the debt." Bailey v. Alabama, 219 U.S. 219, 244 (1911). Similarly, the state may not "indirectly" reach this result "by creating a statutory presumption which upon proof of no other fact [than failure or refusal to serve without paying his debt] exposes him to conviction and punishment." Id. at 244. Other statutes also conducive to peonage have been invalidated under the Thirteenth Amendment. United States v. Reynolds, 235 U.S. 133 (1914); Taylor v. Georgia, 315 U.S. 25 (1942); Pollock v. Williams, 322 U.S. 4 (1944). See generally, 42 U.S.C.A. § 1994 (The Anti-Peonage Act).

See generally, Schmidt, Principle and Prejudice: The Supreme Court and Race in the Progressive Era, Part 2: The Peonage Cases, 82 Colum.L.Rev. 646 (1982).

12. 392 U.S. 409 (1968).

13. A second issue involved the Paddock Country Club, which was joined in the suit. The Club was a corporation controlled by the developer which provided recreational facilities to residents of Mayer's subdivision. The *Jones* decision was not clear as to whether the Club must admit the plaintiffs. Compare the discussion below of Sullivan v. Little Hunting Park, Inc., 396 U.S. 299 (1969).

14. Ch. 31, § 1, 14 Stat. 27 (1866), codified at 42 U.S.C.A. § 1982 (1964).

15. Section 1982, guaranteeing to all citizens "the same right, in every State and Territory, as is enjoyed by white citizens thereof to inherit, purchase, lease, sell, hold and convey real and personal property", had been interpreted to have an enforcement provision (now codified as 18 U.S.C.A. § 242 (1964) which applied to only acts committed under color of state law. See Civil Rights Cases, 109 U.S. 3, 16–17 (1883). The state action requirement, though an arguable limitation on the substance of § 1982, was neither clearly applicable nor clearly inapplicable to the provision.

16. See Section IV of Justice Stewart's opinion, 392 U.S. at 422 (legislative history); Section III, 392 U.S. at 420 (plain meaning); Section II, 392 U.S. at 417 (judicial history).

17. 392 U.S. at 437–44. See also id. at 440–41: "Nor can we say that the determination Congress has made is an irrational one."

18. The majority in the *Civil Rights Cases*, 109 U.S. 3 (1883) was able to avoid the question of the constitutionality of § 1982 by noting that it was limited in its scope by the enforcement provision, now 18 U.S.C.A. § 242 (1964), which applies only to state action. 109 U.S. at 16–17.

19. Note, The "New" Thirteenth Amendment: A Preliminary Analysis, 82 Harvard Law Review 1294 (1969).

the basis for a broad Congressional protection of civil rights without a "state action" limitation. The enabling clause of the amendment was, the Court held, a grant of power to Congress not only to outlaw forced labor but also to identify "badges of slavery" and pass legislation " 'necessary and proper' " to eliminate them.[20] If Congress could not act to insure minorities at least the "freedom to buy whatever a white man can buy, the right to live wherever a white man can live," the thirteenth amendment promise of freedom would be a "mere paper guarantee."[21]

The Court also found it necessary to make several incidental holdings in order to reach this conclusion. Section 1982 was deemed to provide an equitable remedy despite the fact that it is declaratory in nature.[22] The Court also overruled *Hodges v. United States*,[23] a case which had denied that the thirteenth amendment affected individual rights, unconnected with the institution of slavery.[24]

The principles enunciated in *Jones* were extended by lower federal courts to the sale of used homes,[25] and the leasing of housing and apartments.[26] In *Sullivan v. Little Hunting Park, Inc.*,[27] the Supreme Court extended *Jones* to hold that discrimination in certain community facilities in connection with the rental of property entitles the injured party to a private right of action for damages under section 1982.

Petitioner Sullivan was a white member of Little Hunting Park, Inc., a corporation organized for the benefit of residents in a subdivision of Fairfax County, Virginia. Membership entitled a resident and his family to use various recreational facilities. The share in the corporation designating membership could be assigned by the shareholder to the lessee of his residence, subject to approval by the board of directors. Sullivan attempted such an assignment to his black lessee, T. R. Freeman, but Freeman was refused admittance to the nonstock corporation and was denied use of its facilities.[28] In addition, the defendant corporation expelled Sullivan after he began a campaign to convince the board to reverse its decision.

Petitioners brought action for monetary and injunctive relief under the Civil Rights Act of 1866.[29] In reversing the trial court's judgment[30] the Supreme Court held that the corporation could not refuse to approve an assignment on the basis of the lessee's race. *Sullivan* has extended the reach of § 1982 beyond the interpretation in *Jones* by holding that distinctions between real and personal property in characterizing the membership share were immaterial, as § 1982 covers both types of property.[31] The Supreme Court rejected the Virginia trial court's finding the Little Hunting Park was a private social club.

> There was no plan or purpose of exclusiveness. It is open to every white person within the geographic area, there being no selective element other than race.[32]

The Supreme Court further expanded the range of federal civil remedies available to

---

20. 392 U.S. at 439–40.

21. 392 U.S. at 443.

22. 392 U.S. at 414, n. 13.

23. 203 U.S. 1 (1906).

24. 392 U.S. at 441–43, n. 78.

25. Contract Buyers League v. F. & F. Investment, 300 F.Supp. 210 (N.D.Ill.1969).

26. Vaughn v. Ting Su, 1 Race Rel.L.Survey 45 (N.D.Cal. July 19, 1968); Bush v. Kaim, 297 F.Supp. 151 (N.D.Ohio 1969); Pina v. Homsi, 1 Race Rel. L.Survey 183 (D.Mass. July 10, 1969).

27. 396 U.S. 299 (1969).

28. After Sullivan's assignment of the membership share to the lessee, the board of directors for the corporation refused to approve petitioner Freeman's membership. Sullivan had third party standing to maintain this action. "[T]he white owner is at times 'the only effective adversary' . . . ." 396 U.S. at 237, citing Barrows v. Jackson, 346 U.S. 249, 259 (1953).

29. Ch. 31, § 1, 94 Stat. 27 (1866), now U.S.C.A. § 1982 (1964), which reads as follows:

"All citizens of the United States shall have the same right in every State and Territory, as is enjoyed by white citizens thereof to inherit, purchase, lease, sell, hold and convey real and personal property."

30. The trial court had upheld the board's action and the Supreme Court of Appeals of Virginia refused to review the decision.

31. 396 U.S. 229 at 236 (1969).

32. 396 U.S. 229 at 236 (1969).

victims of private racial discrimination when it determined in *Griffin v. Breckenridge* [33] that actions for damages under 42 U.S.C.A. § 1985(3) [34] did not have to allege the presence of state action. *Griffin* was based on events which occurred in the summer of 1966, when the civil rights movement was at its peak and racial tensions were high, particularly in the South. Plaintiffs, four black residents of Mississippi, were passengers in a car being driven on a public highway in Mississippi by a black resident of Tennessee. Two local white residents, mistaking the driver of the car for a civil rights worker, blocked the car on the highway, forced the occupants to get out, and then severely beat them with clubs.

The four black passengers, sustaining severe physical injuries and emotional damage, brought suit under § 1985(3) seeking damages for the alleged racially motivated assault and conspiracy to interfere with the right of a citizen to travel. The district court dismissed the complaint for failure to state a cause of action because there was no allegation that the defendants were acting under color of state law. The Court of Appeals for the Fifth Circuit affirmed, relying on an earlier case which held that § 1985(3) applied only to conspiracies involving state action.[35] The Supreme Court reversed and remanded for trial on the merits holding that actions can be brought under § 1985(3) against private conspiracies which interfere with the right of interstate travel.

The Court thus eliminated the "color of law" requirement which it had read into § 1985(3) earlier,[36] at least for plaintiffs alleging racial motivation. The *Griffin* Court looked at the equal protection language of § 1985(3) and found "nothing inherent in the phrase that requires the action working the deprivation to come from the State." [37] The Court interpreted the terms "equal protection" and "equal privileges", at least as applied to private action in § 1985(3), to mean the "equal enjoyment of legal rights" free from all interference.[38] Writing for a unanimous Court, Justice Stewart stated that, as applied to the complaint in *Griffin*, § 1985(3) is constitutional under the enforcement clause of the thirteenth amendment. The Court did not reach the fourteenth amendment question. Alternatively, the Court held, by a vote of 8 to 1, that the statute as applied was constitutional as an exercise of congressional power to protect the fundamental right of interstate travel.[39]

The statute's requirement of a purpose to deprive of equal rights makes the only limit to § 1985(3) liability the need to show some "racial, or perhaps otherwise class-based, invidiously discriminatory animus behind the conspirators' action." [40] This statute is not a general federal tort law. However, the Court explicitly stated that proof of specific intent was not necessary to establish a cause of action under the statute.[41] In contrast with *Griffin*, the first part of § 1985(2), which prohibits intimidation of witnesses in federal court, requires no allegation of class

---

33. 403 U.S. 88 (1971).

34. 42 U.S.C.A. § 1985(3) provides in part:

"If two or more persons . . . conspire or go in disguise on the highway . . . for the purpose of depriving, either directly or indirectly, any person or class of persons of the equal protection of the laws, or of equal privileges and immunities under the laws; . . . whereby another is injured in his person or property, or deprived of having and exercising any right or privilege of a citizen of the United States, the party so injured or deprived may have an action for the recovery of damages . . ."

35. See Collins v. Hardyman, 341 U.S. 651 (1951).

36. Collins v. Hardyman, 341 U.S. 651 (1951). *Collins* was not a constitutional decision, only one of statutory interpretation.

37. 403 U.S. at 97.

38. 403 U.S. at 102–103.

39. Justice Harlan declined to rely on the right to interstate travel as a constitutional basis for the statute as applied. 403 U.S. at 107. His vote was not necessary to the opinion of the Court which all the other justices joined in its entirety.

40. 403 U.S. at 102. Cf. General Building Contractors Ass'n, Inc. v. Pennsylvania, 102 S.Ct. 3141 (1982) holding that proof of racially discriminatory intent is necessary to make out a violation of 42 U.S.C.A. § 1981.

41. 403 U.S. at 102 n. 10. This test differs from 18 U.S.C.A. § 241, the criminal analogue to § 1985(3), which requires proof of specific intent to deprive the victims of the conspiracy of a constitutional right.

based animus because of its plain language, its legislative history, the federal government's unquestioned and inherent authority to protect the processes of its own courts, and the absence of any need to limit this section in order to avoid creating any general federal law of torts.[42]

Prior to *Griffin*, federal civil remedies against purely private conduct protected only racially motivated denials of a few specific rights.[43] Although 42 U.S.C.A. § 1983 protects civil rights in general, it requires action under color of law. *Griffin* established § 1985(3) as a major federal remedy giving broad protection against private racial discrimination.

While § 1982 prohibits racial discrimination in property, § 1981 regulates the making and enforcing of contracts and other rights.[44] The question of whether federal law prohibits denial of admission by private schools to qualified applicants solely because of their race (a contract right) came before the Supreme Court in *Runyan v. McCrary*.[45] Respondents Michael C. McCrary and Colin M. Gonzales, two black children, brought suit through their parents alleging that they had been denied entrance to the petitioner schools because of their race in violation of 42 U.S.C.A. § 1981.

Bobbe's Private School in Arlington, Virginia, and Fairfax-Brewster School, Inc., of Fairfax County, Virginia, were privately owned schools which regularly and widely advertised for applicants, but neither school

had ever accepted a black applicant. In response to a mailed brochure addressed "resident" and an advertisement in the "Yellow Pages" of the telephone directory, Mr. & Mrs. Gonzales inquired into the Fairfax-Brewster School and, after a visit, they submitted an application on behalf of their son Colin. The school refused his admission for the stated reason that the school was not integrated. Mr. Gonzales then telephoned the Bobbe's School, from which the family had also received a mailed brochure addressed to "occupant". Once again, Colin was refused admission on the ground that he was not white. In August, 1972, Mrs. McCrary phoned the same school in response to an advertisement in the telephone book. She, too, was told the school was not integrated when she inquired about nursery school facilities for her son. Suit was brought against the schools under § 1981 [46] seeking declaratory and injunctive relief and damages. The lower courts found for the children and petitioners appealed.

The Court held that Section 1981 prohibits private, commercially operated, non-sectarian schools from denying admission to prospective students because of their race because § 1981 prohibits racial discrimination in the making and enforcement of private contracts. The private schools had violated the respondent's contractual rights by not offering services on an equal basis to white and nonwhite students.

---

42. Kush v. Rutledge, 103 S.Ct. 1483 (1983) (Stevens, J., for a unanimous Court). The Court said that a similar result would be reached with respect to 42 U.S.C.A. § 1985(1) (federal officers); the first part of § 1985(2) (federal judicial proceedings); and the second part of § 1985(3) (federal elections). In contrast, the second part of § 1985(2) (conspiracies to obstruct justice in state courts) and the first part of § 1985(3) (conspiracy to go in disguise on the highway) are not institutionally linked to federal interests and do require that the conspirators' actions be motivated by intent to deprive victims of equal protection.

43. See, e.g., 42 U.S.C.A. § 1982 (the right to purchase or rent property); 42 U.S.C.A. § 2000a–3.

44. 42 U.S.C.A. § 1981 provides:

"All persons within the jurisdiction of the United States shall have the same right in every State and Territory to make and enforce contracts, to sue, be parties, give evidence, and to the full and equal benefit of all laws and proceedings for the security of persons and property as is enjoyed by white citizens, and shall be subject to like punishment, pains, penalties, taxes, licenses, and exactions of every kind, and to no other."

45. 427 U.S. 160 (1976).

46. Suit was also brought under Title II of the Civil Rights Act of 1964, 42 U.S.C.A. § 2000a et seq., but the Title II claim was withdrawn before trial.

Section 1982 had earlier been held to reach purely private acts of racial discrimination in *Jones v. Alfred H. Mayer Co.*,[47] and

[j]ust as in *Jones* a Negro's [§ 1982] right to purchase property on equal terms with whites was violated when a private person refused to sell to the prospective purchaser solely because he was a Negro, so also a Negro's [§ 1981] right to "make and enforce contracts" is violated if a private offeror refuses to extend to a Negro, solely because he is a Negro, the same opportunity to enter into contracts as he extends to white offerees.[48]

The schools had advertised and offered their services to the members of the general public in what was clearly an offering of a contractual relationship. The schools were to have performed educational services for the plaintiffs and in return would receive payments for the instructions. The findings of facts in the lower court showed that the parents of Michael McCrary and Colin Gonzales had tried to enter into contractual relationships with these schools and had been refused solely because they were black. This racial exclusion the Supreme Court found to amount to a "classic violation" of § 1981.[49]

The Court carefully limited its decision to the question of private discrimination in contracts. Unlike the facts in *Moose Lodge No. 107 v. Irvis*,[50] the Court in *Runyan* did not have before it any question of the right of a private social organization to limit membership on the basis of race. The *Moose Lodge* decision had held that the grant of a state liquor license to a private club which refused to serve blacks, and the continuing regulation of the liquor served in the club by the state liquor control board, did not constitute sufficient state action to invoke the equal protection clause of the fourteenth amendment. Although the Court allowed private discrimination in *Moose Lodge* and barred it in *Runyan*, the distinction between the cases did not rely on the fact that the first involved liquor and the second education, nor in the fact that *Moose Lodge* did not purport to resolve the section 1981 issue. Both involved private contracts, but the key to distinguishing these cases lies in the nature of the facility itself.

Runyan involved educational facilities which were open to any white who could pay the set fees. The only applicants refused were those who were black. *Moose Lodge*, on the other hand, was not open to the general public. One could become a member only by invitation and thus some whites as well as all blacks were denied membership. Although plaintiff in *Moose Lodge* did not attempt to rely on § 1981, the key between the cases lies in the public nature of these schools. The schools avidly solicited applications from all parents in the area and then denied contracts only to blacks. *Moose Lodge* did not solicit applications from the general public and therefore presents a stronger case for an exception. One would expect that section 1981 would not apply to truly private matters such as marriage contracts or other similar contracts where parties discriminate not merely because of race. Such contracts are not solicited from the general public. The Court also specifically left open the question of whether section 1981 would apply to a school which discriminated on the basis of race for religious reasons. Unlike pure racial discrimination, which has no constitutional protection, religiously based discrimination may possibly find some protection in the first amendment.

Section 1981 was also found to provide blacks with a federal remedy against racial discrimination in private employment contracts through the ruling of the Supreme Court in *Johnson v. Railway Express Agency, Inc.*[51] One year after *Johnson*, the Court ruled that the same remedy is available to any victim of racial discrimination in employment, white as well as black. This issue was brought before the Court in *McDonald v. Santa Fe Trail Transportation Co.*[52] when two white employees, discharged

47.   392 U.S. 409, 441–43 (1968).

48.   427 U.S. 160, 170–71 (footnote omitted).

49.   427 U.S. 160 (1976).

50.   407 U.S. 163 (1971).

51.   421 U.S. 454 (1975).

52.   427 U.S. 273 (1976).

for misappropriating cargo from one of the company's shipments, challenged their dismissal as racially discriminatory because a black accused of the same theft remained on the job. Relying on the language and legislative history of the act,[53] the Court held that whites were not prohibited from using this remedy despite possible contrary interpretations based on the description in the law of the protected rights as those "enjoyed by white citizens."[54] This phrase, in the Court's view, merely "emphasiz[ed] 'the racial character of rights being protected'" and did not preclude use of the section by non-blacks.

One of the most important issues in this area of civil rights litigation involves the question of the inferences to be drawn from undisputed evidence. This problem is well illustrated by *Memphis v. Greene*,[55] where the Court upheld a city's closing of one end of a street traversing a white residential community. The street led to a neighborhood with a predominantly black population. The closing forced residents of the adjoining black neighborhood to use alternative routes for certain trips within the city. The majority found that legitimate, nonracial reasons existed to justify the street closing and that the impact on the black citizens and neighborhood could not be characterized as a badge or incident of slavery violative of either the thirteenth amendment or 42 U.S. C.A. § 1982: "[T]he inconvenience of the drivers is a function of where they live and where they regularly drive—not a function of their race . . . ."[56] And "it does not involve any impairment to the kind of property interests that we have identified as being within the reach of § 1982."[57]

In *Greene* the majority[58] did not reach the issue of whether a violation of § 1982 could be established without proof of purposeful discrimination. But the Court did reach that

---

53. Section 1981, now codified under 42 U.S.C.A., was derived from the Civil Rights Act of 1866.

54. Section 1981 gives "[a]ll persons . . . the same right . . . to make and enforce contracts . . . as is enjoyed by white citizens." 42 U.S.C.A. § 1981. But cf. United Steelworkers v. Weber, 443 U.S. 193 (1979) (as a matter of statutory construction, Title VII and *McDonald* do not apply to affirmative action plans voluntarily adopted by private parties to eliminate traditional patterns of racial segregation).

55. 451 U.S. 100 (1981).

56. 451 U.S. at 128.

"[T]he inconvenience of the drivers is a function of where they live and where they regularly drive—not a function of their race; the hazards and the inconvenience that the closing is intended to minimize are a function of the number of vehicles involved, not the race of their drivers or of the local residents. Almost any traffic regulation—whether it be a temporary detour during construction, a speed limit, a one-way street, or a no parking sign—may have a differential impact on residents of adjacent or nearby neighborhoods. Because urban neighborhoods are so frequently characterized by a common ethnic or racial heritage, a regulation's adverse impact on a particular neighborhood will often have a disparate effect on an identifiable ethnic or racial group. To regard an inevitable consequence of that kind as a form of stigma so severe as to violate the Thirteenth Amendment would trivialize the great purpose of that charter of freedom. Proper respect for the dignity of the residents of any neighborhood requires that they accept the same burdens as well as the same benefits of citizenship regardless of their racial

or ethnic origin. This case does not disclose a violation of any of the enabling legislation enacted by Congress pursuant to § 2 of the Thirteenth Amendment. To decide the narrow constitutional question presented to this record we need not speculate about the sort of impact on a racial group that might be prohibited by the Amendment itself. We merely hold that the impact of the closing of West Drive on nonresidents of Hein Park is a routine burden of citizenship; it does not reflect a violation of the Thirteenth Amendment." 451 U.S. at 128–29.

57. 451 U.S. at 124.

58. Justice White, concurring in the judgment, objected to the majority acting as a fact-finder and "rehash[ing]" the evidence. 451 U.S. at 130. Without reaching the thirteenth amendment he would have held that a violation of section 1982 requires some showing of racial animus or an intent to discriminate on the basis of race; and that since the district court had found no discriminatory purpose—a finding not disturbed by the circuit court—the circuit court was in error in finding a violation of section 1982. 451 U.S. at 129–35.

Only Marshall, joined by Brennan and Blackmun, JJ., dissented. They believed that "a more careful review and a 'more detailed study' of the record" that the majority ignored "the plain and powerful symbolic message of the inconvenience," 451 U.S. at 138, created by the road closing. The dissent believed that the record, "combined with a dab of common sense," paints a picture of a group of white citizens acting "to keep Negro citizens from traveling through their urban 'utopia'" and the city has placed its seal of approval on the scheme." 451 U.S. at 155.

issue—at least as to § 1981—in *General Building Contractors Association, Inc. v. Pennsylvania.*[59] The Court there held that to make out a violation of § 1981 it is not enough to prove disproportionate impact; there must be proof of a racially discriminatory intent, and, absent such proof, liability in the form of a detailed and burdensome injunction[60] cannot be imposed or vicariously on employers and trade associations.

In *General Building* the employers and trade associations, pursuant to collective bargaining agreements, used union hiring halls to select workers. The unions had intentionally discriminated on the basis of race, but the contractors and trade associations had not; nor was there evidence that they were aware of the union's discrimination. The Court therefore held that the employers and trade associations did not violate § 1981; nor were they liable under a theory of *respondeat superior* or similar theory: the union is not the fiduciary and agent of the employer, which has no right to control the union.

The requirement of purposeful discrimination necessary to make out a violation of § 1981 should also exist with respect to § 1982, which the Court specifically noted was a companion statute with similar origins and scope.[61]

IV. CONGRESSIONAL ENFORCEMENT OF THE FIFTEENTH AMENDMENT

With the enactment of the fifteenth amendment in 1870, the Reconstruction Congress was not content to rely on its self-executing section 1, but passed implementing legislation pursuant to section 2. The Enforcement Act of 1870[1] made it a criminal offense for either public officials or private persons to obstruct the right to vote. The next year Congress tightened that law by careful federal supervision of registration through the certification of election returns.[2] But "[a]s the years passed and fervor for racial equality waned, enforcement of the laws became spotty and ineffective, and most of their provisions were repealed in 1894."[3]

Portions of the country responded by vigorous efforts to disenfranchise the blacks through the use of grandfather clauses, procedural hurdles, primary elections open to whites only, improper challenges, racial gerrymandering, and discriminatory application of voting tests, all struck down in a long series of Supreme Court opinions.[4] In 1965, Congress again entered the battle in a major way with a new weapon, the Voting Rights Act of 1965.[5]

The leading recent case interpreting Congress' power under section 2 of the fifteenth amendment to enforce its guarantees to citizens of the United States that the right to vote may not be denied on account of race, color, or previous condition of servitude is *South Carolina v. Katzenbach.*[6] In this case the Court upheld certain challenged portions of the Voting Rights Act of 1965. South Carolina brought this original case in the Supreme Court pursuant to Article III, section 2, granting original jurisdiction between a state and a citizen of another state. All states were invited to submit amicus briefs and a majority did so, some support-

---

59. 102 S.Ct. 3141 (1982).

60. 102 S.Ct. at 3154–55. The Court did note: "This is not to say that defendants in the position of petitioners might not, upon a showing, be retained in the lawsuit and even subjected to such minor and ancillary provisions of an injunctive order as the District Court might find necessary to grant complete relief to respondents from the discrimination they suffered at the hands of the Union." 102 S.Ct. at 3154.

Cf. Hacker & Rotunda, The Reliance of Counsel Defense in Securities Cases: Damage Actions vs. Injunctive Actions, 1 Corp.L.Rev. 159, 161–62 (1978) (discussing relevance of good faith in decision to grant injunctive relief).

61. 102 S.Ct. at 3146. Marshall J., joined by Brennan, J., filed a dissenting opinion; O'Connor J., joined by Blackmun, J., filed a concurring opinion.

1. 16 Stat. 170 (1870).

2. 16 Stat. 433 (1871).

3. South Carolina v. Katzenbach, 383 U.S. 301, 310 (1966), footnote omitted, citing the repealing legislation, 28 Stat. 36 (1874).

4. See, 383 U.S. at 310–12 and cases cited therein.

5. 79 Stat. 437, 42 U.S.C.A. § 1973.

6. 383 U.S. 301 (1966).

ing South Carolina and others supporting the Attorney General.[7] The Court upheld the attacked sections of the Act and refused to enjoin their operation.

Chief Justice Warren, writing the opinion for the Court, first noted that Congress, prior to passage of the Voting Rights Act, "explored with great care the problem of racial discrimination in voting."[8] This Congressional investigation showed, first, that certain parts of the country had long sought by various means to defy the command of the fifteenth amendment, and that, second, more federal legislative remedies were therefore in order. For example, in spite of previous court actions and earlier federal legislation,[9] the registration of voting age blacks in Mississippi rose from only 4.9% to 6.4% between 1954 and 1964.[10]

One of the sections attacked was the Act's coverage formula. This formula provides coverage as to any state, county, parish, or similar political subdivision, that the Attorney General has determined that on November 1, 1964, maintained a "test or device" to qualify voting rights and, that the Director of the Census has determined that less than 50% of its voting age residents were registered on November 1, 1964, or voted in that year's presidential election. The term "test or device" is defined as any requirement that the registrant be able to read or interpret any matter, or demonstrate any educational achievement or knowledge of any particular subject, or possess good moral character, or prove his voting qualifications by the voucher of registered voters or

others. The findings of the Attorney General or the Census Director under these sections are not reviewable in any court. Such statutory coverage is terminated if the area persuades a court to grant it a declaratory judgment that tests and devices have not been used within the last five years to abridge the vote on racial grounds. This declaratory judgment must be obtained from a three judge court of the District Court for the District of Columbia with a direct appeal to the Supreme Court.

As long as the statutory coverage is effective, the state or political subdivision is barred from enforcing its tests or devices. Also, before the state or political subdivision may change its election qualifications or procedures, it must submit its changes to the Attorney General for approval or obtain a declaratory judgment from a three-judge court of the District Court for the District of Columbia, with direct appeal to the Supreme Court.

If the Attorney General certifies certain facts to the Civil Service Commission, it must appoint voting examiners. The Attorney General's certification is either that he has received meritorious written complaints alleging racial discrimination in voting from at least twenty residents or that the appointment of the examiners is otherwise necessary to implement the guarantees of the fifteenth amendment. These certifications are also not reviewable in any court. These examiners test the voting qualifications of applicants; any applicant meeting the nonsus-

---

7. 383 U.S. at 307 & n. 2.

8. 383 U.S. at 308.

9. Previous legislative remedies included the Civil Rights Act of 1957, 71 Stat. 634, which authorized the Attorney General to sue to enjoin public and private racial interference with the right to vote; amendments to the Civil Rights Act of 1960, 74 Stat. 86, which allowed states to be joined as defendants, gave the Attorney General access to local voting records, and authorized courts to register voters in areas of systematic voting discriminations; and the Civil Rights Act of 1964, title I, 78 Stat. 241, 42 U.S.C.A. § 1971, which expedited voting cases heard by three-judge courts, and outlawed various tactics used to disenfranchise blacks. See 383 U.S. at 313.

The 1965 Voting Rights Act was extended by the Voting Rights Amendments of 1970, Pub.L. No. 91–285, 84 Stat. 314. That Act, among other things, forbade literacy tests in all elections, throughout the country, for a five year period. This provision was upheld in Oregon v. Mitchell, 400 U.S. 112 (1970), by a unanimous Court. The Voting Rights Act was extended for seven years in 1975, Pub.L. No. 94–73, 89 Stat. 400. Congress also expanded its coverage in this extension to include language minorities. See Briscoe v. Bell, 432 U.S. 404 (1977).

10. 383 U.S. at 313.

pended portions of state law is to be promptly placed on the list of eligible voters.

After reviewing these and other portions of the Act, the Court turned to the various challenges. The argument that the Act violated the due process rights of the states by employing an invalid presumption was quickly disposed of: the word "person" in the due process clause of the fifth amendment does not include the states of the Union.[11] The objection that the statutory bar to judicial review of administrative findings constituted an unconstitutional bill of attainder and violated the separation of powers by adjudicating guilt through legislation was similarly disposed of for these principles apply only to protect individual persons and private groups, not the state. Nor does a state have standing to invoke these provisions on behalf of its citizens.[12]

The Supreme Court next rejected the argument that only the judiciary may strike down state statutes and procedures. Section 2 of the fifteenth amendment contemplates a role for Congress.[13] "As against the reserved powers of the States, Congress may use any rational means to effectuate the constitutional prohibitions of racial discrimination in voting."[14] To determine if this Congressional legislation is valid, the basic test is to apply Chief Justice Marshall's test for the validity of legislation under the necessary and proper clause.

Let the end be legitimate, let it be within the scope of the constitution, and all means which are appropriate, which are plainly adapted to that end, and which are not prohibited, but consist with the letter and spirit of the constitution, are constitutional.[15]

Thus, Congress under section 2 may do more than to forbid violations of the fifteenth amendment in general terms.[16]

It was a legitimate response for Congress to prescribe voting discrimination remedies without going into prior adjudication given the ample evidence showing that case-by-case litigation was inadequate to combat the persistent discrimination.[17] It was no flaw in the statute that the remedies were confined to certain locations because Congress had learned that the problem was localized and in these areas immediate action seemed necessary. "The doctrine of the equality of States, invoked by South Carolina, does not bar this approach, for that doctrine applies only to the terms upon which States are admitted to the Union and not to the remedies for local evils which have subsequently appeared."[18]

The coverage formula Congress devised to determine the applicability of the Act was proper because it was "rational in both theory and practice."[19] The rules relating to statutory presumptions in criminal cases does not bind Congress when it is prescribing civil remedies against other organs of government pursuant to section 2 of the fifteenth amendment.[20]

It was also proper for Congress to limit litigation under challenged provisions of the Act to a single court in the District of Columbia. And, when this litigation does occur, the burden of proof of nondiscrimination which the state must shoulder is bearable, particularly since the relevant facts are peculiarly within the knowledge of the states and political subdivisions involved. The bar to judicial review of certain findings is not invalid because these findings consist of objective statistical determinations and

---

11. Id. at 323.

12. Id. at 324.

13. Id. at 325–26.

14. Id. at 324. See also, Briscoe v. Bell, 432 U.S. 404 (1977) (no judicial review of determination of coverage); cf. Morris v. Gressette, 432 U.S. 491 (1977).

15. 383 U.S. at 326, quoting McCulloch v. Maryland, 17 U.S. (4 Wheat.) 316, 421 (1819). See also Id. at 327, quoting Ex parte Virginia, 100 U.S. 339, 345–46 (1879)

and citing James Everard's Breweries v. Day, 265 U.S. 545, 558–59 (1924).

16. 383 U.S. at 327.

17. Id. at 328.

18. Id. at 328–29, citing Coyle v. Smith, 221 U.S. 559 (1911) and cases cited therein.

19. 383 U.S. at 330.

20. Id. at 330.

routine analysis of state statutes. Moreover, the state can always go to the district court to seek termination of its statutory coverage provided that it has not been guilty of voting discrimination in recent years.[21]

The provisions of the Act suspending literacy tests and devices for a period of five years from the last occurrence of substantial voting discrimination were a proper Congressional response under section 2 of the fifteenth amendment.[22] The provisions of the Act suspending new voting regulations pending scrutiny by federal authorities to determine whether their use would violate the fifteenth amendment may be "an uncommon exercise of congressional power"[23] but the exceptional circumstances justify it.[24]

The Court also concluded that the District Court's opinions issued under the Act are not advisory since the state seeking to change its voting laws has a concrete controversy with the federal government. The appointment of federal examiners and the expeditious challenge procedure of those whom the examiners list as qualified to vote were also an appropriate response to the problem. Thus, the majority upheld all of the provisions of the Voting Rights Act challenged in that case.

Justice Black concurred and dissented in part. First, he objected to the part of the Act providing that in no way may a state covered by the Act amend its constitution or laws relating to voting without first trying to persuade the Attorney General or a federal district court that the changes do not have the purpose or effect of denying citizens the right to vote on the basis of color. This provision was unconstitutional, he thought, because it required the district court to issue an advisory opinion.[25] Secondly, if the dispute can be brought in a court, the appropriate court, given the dignity of a state and the fact that it is a party to the litigation, is the Supreme Court. If the Voting Rights Act, by seeking to limit litigation to the District Court for the District of Columbia, is an attempt to limit the constitutionally created original jurisdiction of the Supreme Court, then that section, Black argued, was also unconstitutional.[26] The provision giving federal officials the power to veto state laws, Justice Black thought, violated the obligation of the United States to guarantee to every state a republican form of government.[27]

> Certainly if all the provisions of our Constitution which limit the power of the Federal Government and reserve other power to the States are to mean anything, they mean at least that the States have power to pass laws and amend their constitutions without first sending their officials hundreds of miles away to beg federal authorities to approve them.[28]

---

21. 383 U.S. at 331–33. See n. 26, infra.

22. Id. at 334.

23. Id.

24. Id. at 335.

25. Id. at 357 (Black, J., dissenting).

26. 383 U.S. at 357 n. 1 (Black, J., dissenting).

There seems to be no support for the suggestion that § 14(b) would be interpreted to limit what Justice Black referred to as "the constitutionally created original jurisdiction of this Court . . . ." Id. The majority, after all, accepted South Carolina's bill of complaint filed in the Supreme Court. "Original jurisdiction," held the Court, "is founded on the presence of a controversy between a State and a citizen of another State under Art. III, § 2, of the Constitution." 383 U.S. at 307.

See also, Hathorn v. Lovorn, 457 U.S. 255, 265–270 (1982), holding that state courts have the power and duty to decide whether § 5 of the Voting Rights Act applied to a change in election procedures; to hold otherwise would require state courts to ignore the Voting

Rights Act and enter a decree violating federal law. Section 14(b) of the Voting Rights Act, the Court explained, governs only declaratory judgments approving proposed changes in voting procedures. It does not prevent a state court from deciding a federal question collaterally. See generally, Note, Exclusive Jurisdiction of the Federal Courts in Private Civil Actions, 70 Harv.L.Rev. 509 (1957); cf. Cooper, State Law of Patent Exploitation, 56 Minn.L.Rev. 313 (1972).

27. 383 U.S. at 359 (Black, J., dissenting).

28. Id. footnote omitted, noting that this "requirement that States come to Washington to have their laws judged is reminiscent of the deeply resented practices used by the English crown in dealing with the American colonies . . . ." Id. at 359 n. 2.

The Court has interpreted the preclearance requirement vigorously. See McDaniel v. Sanchez, 452 U.S. 130 (1981) (the preclearance requirement of § 5 of Voting Rights Act of 1965 applies to a reapportionment plan submitted to a federal district court by the legislative body of a covered jurisdiction even though that plan was submitted in response to a judicial determina-

Cases since *South Carolina v. Katzenbach* [29] have illustrated the effectiveness of the new Voting Rights Act. In *Allen v. State Board of Elections* [30] the Court held that private litigants have standing to invoke the jurisdiction of the district court to assure that their political subdivision complies with the requirement of section 5 of the Act that no person shall be denied the right to vote for failure to comply with an unapproved new enactment subject to section 5.[31] The Court stated also that "Congress intended to reach any state enactment which altered the election law of a covered State in even a minor way." [32] In *Georgia v. United States* [33] the Court squarely held that reapportionment plans come within section 5 of the Voting Rights Act. In *Beer v. United States* [34] the Court held that the Voting Rights Act does not permit implementation of a reapportionment plan which "would lead to a retrogression in the position of racial minorities with respect to their effective exercise of the electoral franchise." [35]

In *United Jewish Organizations of Williamsburgh, Inc. v. Carey* [36] a fragmented Court approved the use of racial criteria by the State of New York in its attempt to comply with section 5 of the Voting Rights Act and secure the approval of the Attorney General. While there was no opinion of the Court, a majority found that—in the circumstances of that case—use of such racial criteria did not violate either the fourteenth or fifteenth amendments. These changes, which did not change the number of districts with nonwhite majorities but did change the size of the nonwhite majorities in most of those districts, created more substantial nonwhite majorities in two assembly districts and two senate districts. To create substantial nonwhite majorities in these districts, the changes split an Hasidic Jewish Community between two senate and two assembly districts.[37]

In *United States v. Board of Commissioners,*[38] the Court applied section 5 of the

---

tion that the existing apportionment of its electoral districts is unconstitutional; therefore it is error for the district court to act on a county's proposed plan before it had been submitted for preclearance to the Attorney General or to the District of Columbia district court).

29. 383 U.S. 301 (1966).

30. 393 U.S. 544 (1969).

31. 393 U.S. at 557. These private litigants, the Court also held in interpreting the statute, may bring their suit in any federal district court and, unlike the state, are not limited to the District Court for the District of Columbia. Id. at 560. But the dispute must still be heard by a three judge court. Id. at 563.

32. Id. at 566. The Court held that the Voting Rights provisions did apply to the enactments at issue in this case. Id. at 569. The Court left "to another case" any consideration of possible conflict between "our interpretation of the statute and the principles involved in the reapportionment cases." Id. See also, Perkins v. Matthews, 400 U.S. 379 (1971); Holt v. City of Richmond, 406 U.S. 903 (1972).

33. 411 U.S. 526 (1973). White, Powell, and Rehnquist, JJ., dissented. 411 U.S. at 542.

34. 425 U.S. 130 (1976).

35. 425 U.S. at 141. See also, City of Richmond v. United States, 422 U.S. 358 (1975); City of Lockhart v. United States, 103 S.Ct. 998 (1983).

36. 430 U.S. 144 (1977).

37. Notwithstanding this benign racial gerrymandering, "four of the five 'safe' (65%+) nonwhite districts established by the 1974 plan have since elected

white representatives." Burger, C.J., dissenting, 430 U.S. at 185.

Cf. Gomillion v. Lightfoot, 364 U.S. 339 (1960), where the Court invalidated racial gerrymandering. In that case, however, the power of Congress under section 2 of the fifteenth amendment was not involved. Also, in *Gomillion* there was a fencing out of the black population from the political process and their voting strength was invidiously minimized; in the New York plan, in contrast, "there was no fencing out of the white population from participation in the political process of the county, and the plan did not minimize or unfairly cancel out white voting strength." 430 U.S. at 165 (opinion of White, J.).

38. 435 U.S. 110 (1978). Justice Powell concurred in part and in the judgment; he also indicated that his reservation to the constitutionality of the Act as to its selective coverage and intrusive preclearance procedure had not abated. 435 U.S. at 139 & n.*. Justice Stevens, joined by the Chief Justice and Justice Rehnquist dissented.

In Gaston County v. United States, 395 U.S. 285 (1969), the Court upheld the finding of a three judge lower court that the County had not met its burden of proving that its use of literacy tests, in the context of its historic maintenance of segregated and unequal schools, did not discriminatorily deprive blacks of the franchise.

See also, Dougherty County Bd. of Education v. White, 439 U.S. 32, 44–46 (1978). In that case the majority also held that in a state covered by the Voting Rights Act of 1965, a county school board's rule requir-

Voting Rights Act of 1965 to a municipality plan to employ an at-large method of electing city councilmen. The opinion held that a city in Alabama (a state covered by section 5) must obtain the Attorney General's preclearance even though the city has never conducted voter registration. Section 5 is not limited only to counties and to the political units which conduct registration, but applies to all entities exercising control over the electoral processes within the covered states or subdivisions. The majority also held that the Attorney General's failure to object to the holding of a referendum election which adopted a voting charge did not constitute federal approval of the change because, among other things, the proposal had not been properly submitted to him.

In *City of Rome v. United States* [39] the Court also upheld the constitutionality of broad federal power under section 5 of the Voting Rights Act of 1965. In that case the

Attorney General had declined to approve certain city annexations and other electoral changes after concluding that in a city such as Rome, Georgia, where whites were in the majority and there was racial bloc voting, the city had not met its burden of showing that the disapproved changes would not dilute the black vote. The disapproved changes were not made for any discriminatory *purpose* but did have a discriminatory *effect*. The Attorney General's refusal to clear the practice was proper, the Court ruled, since the statute required that the electoral change must have neither the purpose nor effect of abridging the right to vote on the basis of color.[40] This interpretation, the Court held, was constitutional even if section 1 of the fifteenth amendment prohibits only purposeful discrimination because Congress has broad power under section 2 of that amendment.[41]

ing its employees to take unpaid leaves of absence had sufficient potential for discrimination to require federal preclearance. Cf. Blanding v. DuBose, 454 U.S. 393 (1982) (per curiam).

39. 446 U.S. 156 (1980).

40. The majority also held the political units of a state may not independently bring a bailout action under section 4(a) of the Act. Only a state can bring a declaratory judgment proving that no prohibited "test or device" had been used in the past 17 years.

41. On the same day that it decided *City of Rome* a fragmented Court could not agree as to whether section 1 of the fifteenth amendment only applied to purposeful discrimination. See City of Mobile v. Bolden, 446 U.S. 55 (1980). In Rogers v. Lodge, 102 S.Ct. 3272 (1982), the Court, per White, J., applied *Mobile v. Bolden*, and, in a 6 to 3 opinion, upheld the district court finding that the at-large electoral system in Burke County, Georgia was being maintained for the purpose of diluting the voting strength of the black population. A dissent by Stevens, J. acknowledged

that there could be no doubt that an amendment to the Voting Rights Act (which would require Burke County and other covered jurisdictions to abandon specific types of at-large voting schemes that perpetuate the effects of past discrimination) would be constitutional. 102 S.Ct. at 3283.

See also, City of Port Arthur v. United States, 103 S.Ct. 530 (1982) upholding a District of Columbia district court ruling that the electoral plan for the Port Arthur, Texas, City Council could not be approved under § 5 of the Voting Rights Act because it insufficiently neutralized the adverse impact on black voting strength caused by the expansion of the city's borders, and it was appropriate for the district court to rule that it would approve the plan if it were modified to eliminate a majority vote requirement as to the two at-large, non-mayoral candidates and to permit the election to these two seats to be made by plurality vote. Cf. City of Richmond v. United States, 422 U.S. 358 (1975); City of Peterburg v. United States, 354 F.Supp. 1021 (D.D.C.1972), aff'd 410 U.S. 962 (1973).

CHAPTER EIGHTEEN

FREEDOM OF SPEECH

I. INTRODUCTION

In this Chapter we focus on the free speech clause of the first amendment. First we begin with an historical summary and philosophical background of some of the important English and American experiences with laws restricting speech, primarily political speech. Then we shall turn to some of the techniques used or attitudes expressed by the Court in reviewing a statute affecting speech. Here we will identify the primary techniques used by the Court to balance speech interests against the interests of the state in laws alleged to infringe on free speech. The Court often engages in a close analysis of the statute under attack to determine if it is overly broad or too vague; that is, though a narrowly drawn statute could validly restrict certain activity, the fatal flaw in the particular statute may be that it is drafted so that it may be read to restrict valid speech interests. Additionally, the judges will independently determine if the statute alleged to restrict speech can achieve its legitimate goals by less restrictive means.

In the last part of this Chapter, and by far the bulk of it, we consider in the main how the Court has dealt with specific types or categories of speech in concrete situations: subversive speech; obscene speech; the speech of the broadcast media and of the traditional print media; libelous speech;

speech affecting associational rights; "fighting words" and speech before hostile audiences; symbolic speech; restrictions on speech that affect the gathering and reporting of news in the context of fair trials and investigative reporting; and speech associated with rights of assembly and petition.

One must bear in mind that these categories are not exhaustive, and they are certainly not airtight. But they are useful in that the Court oftentimes develops different tests for the permissible scope of restrictions on the various types of speech. This difference in treatment is really to be expected because to the extent there is ever a balancing of interests, the relevant interests of one type of speech, e.g., subversive speech, may vary from those of another, e.g., obscene speech. Moreover, the techniques of reviewing alleged restrictions on speech (overbreadth, vagueness, and so on) may be applied differently to each category, either consciously or unconsciously.

II.   HISTORICAL BACKGROUND

A.   Introduction

Freedom of speech has been recognized as one of the preeminent rights of Western democratic theory, the touchstone of individual liberty.[1] Justice Cardozo characterized it as ". . . the matrix, the indispensible condition of nearly every other form of freedom." [2] The consequences of an application of this theory, however, has often provoked bitter public controversy. As Justice Holmes has observed, ". . . it is . . . not free thought for those who agree with us, but freedom for the thought that we hate," [3] which gives the theory its most en-

during value. One can readily appreciate the wisdom of Professor Thomas Emerson's emphasis on the importance as well as the difficulty of arriving at an understanding of the system of freedom of expression as envisioned by the language of the First Amendment.

> [T]he theory of freedom of expression is a sophisticated and even complex one. It does not come naturally to the ordinary citizen but needs to be learned. It must be restated and reiterated not only for each generation, but for each new situation.[4]

Consequently, it is necessary to examine the historical and philosophical context out of which the concept of free speech emerged.

B.   The English Background

The intransigence of the developing nation-states toward the idea that speech, regardless of its content, is entitled to a public forum, was a natural outgrowth of the authoritarian nature of those societies following the Middle Ages. Political authority derived its legitimacy from religious authority, where truth was determined by divine revelation. Controversies were, therefore, to be resolved by God through his infallible human agents in the government and churches. Dissent from this authority meant not only to be wrong, but to be damned. Dissent was no more tolerable when governments became responsive to political, rather than spiritual needs. It was essential, if divine authority were removed, that the popular opinion of the government be preserved in order that the obligations which the government required of the people, primarily taxes and military conscription, were to be efficiently obtained.[5]

---

1.   Dunagin v. City of Oxford, 489 F.Supp. 763, 769 (N.D.Miss.1980) (Keady, D.J., quoting an earlier edition of this work).

2.   Palko v. Connecticut, 302 U.S. 319, 327 (1937).

3.   United States v. Schwimmer, 279 U.S. 644, 654–55 (1929) (dissenting opinion).

4.   T. Emerson, Toward A General Theory of the First Amendment, 72 Yale L.J. 877, 894 (1963). For an excellent introduction to, and analysis of, the free speech clause, see Van Alstyne, A Graphic Review of the Free Speech Clause, 70 Calif.L.Rev. 107 (1982).

The article was "[w]ritten principally for students" and aims "to determine what is at stake among contending interpretations, and to see why great importance tends to be attached to such matters." Id. at 107.

5.   Thus, Lord Holt in Rex v. Tuchin, Holt 424 (1704) reasoned:

> "If men should not be called to account for possessing the people with an ill opinion of the government, no government can subsist; for it is very necessary for every government, that the people should have a good opinion of it. And nothing can be worse

In England, the situation was exacerbated by the schism between the English and Roman Catholic Church as well as the protracted struggle for supremacy between the King and Parliament. Thus, in the three centuries prior to the Declaration of Independence, the battle for the hearts and minds of the English people required the suppression of ideas antagonistic to the controlling power. The two primary methods by which this suppression was effectuated were the doctrine of seditious libel and the licensing and regulation of the press.[6]

1. Seditious Libel

The publication of statements critical of the sovereign or his agents was considered seditious libel. The theory of the action, as developed in the Court of the Star Chamber and utilized in subsequent common law courts, was that the King, as the originator of justice, was above popular criticism. Publication of opinions which were censurious of the government constituted, therefore, a criminal assault. Truth was not a defense, for "the greater the truth, the greater the libel" against the government.[7] There was no need to prove intent to incite insurrection for if one intended to publish criticism, he acted unlawfully merely by finding "fault with his masters and betters."[8] Prosecution was vigorous; then there was the passage of Fox's Libel Act[9] in 1792, which turned the issue of guilt to the jury, who could bring in a general verdict of guilty or not guilty. No longer could the judge direct the jury to find the defendant guilty merely on proof of the publication. After Fox's Libel Act, seditious prosecutions in England "went on with shameful severity" but the new Act was still a "safeguard."[10] But the Act was silent as to whether truth should be allowed as a defense.

2. Prior Restraints

In addition to punishment following the publication of an article, English authors, until 1694, had to contend with an elaborate system of licensing. All writing that was to be published had to be licensed prior to publication; without the license, there could be no lawful publication. "The struggle for the freedom of the press was primarily directed against the power of the licensor."[11] The history of this censorship is concisely summarized by Justice Story, in his Commentaries on the Constitution:

> The art of printing soon after its introduction, we are told, was looked upon, as well in England as in other countries, as merely a matter of state, and subject to the coercion of the crown. It was, therefore, regulated in England by the King's proclamations, prohibitions, charters of privilege, and licenses, and finally by the decrees of the Court of Star-Chamber, which limited the number of printers and of presses which each should employ, and prohibited new publications, unless previously approved by proper licensers. On the demolition of this odious jurisdiction, in 1641, the Long Parliament of Charles the First, after their rupture with that prince, assumed the same powers which the Star-Chamber exercised with respect to licensing books; and during the

to any government, than to endeavor to produce animosities as to the management of it. This has always been looked upon as a crime, and no government can be safe unless it be punished."

Quoted in Z. Chafee, Free Speech In the United States 180 (1941).

6. See generally, C. D. Bowen, The Lion and the Throne: The Life and Times of Sir Edward Coke: 1552–1634 (1956); B. Schwartz, The Roots of Freedom: A Constitutional History of England (1967).

A third, but less used, method of suppression was that of conviction for constructive treason. See 1 H. Taylor, The Origin and Growth of the English Constitution 511 (1898); 3 id. 250–51 (1911); C. D. Bowen, supra note 6, at 200–203.

7. W. Prosser, Handbook of the Law of Torts 796–97 (4th ed. 1971); II J. S. Stephen, A History of the Criminal Law of England 381 (London 1883); L. Levy, Judgments: Essays on American Constitutional History 119 (1972); Z. Chafee, Free Speech in the United States 500 (1941).

8. Z. Chafee, Free Speech in the United States 19 (1941).

9. 32 Geo. 3, c. 60 (1792). See generally, II J. S. Stephen, A History of the Criminal Law of England 340–49 (1882).

10. Z. Chafee, Free Speech in the United States 23, 35 (1941).

11. Lovell v. Griffin, 303 U.S. 444, 451 (1938).

Commonwealth (such is human frailty and the love of power even in republics!) they issued their ordinances for that purpose, founded principally upon a Star-Chamber decree in 1637. After the restoration of Charles the Second, a statute on the same subject was passed, copied, with some few alterations, from the parliamentary ordinances. The act expired in 1679, and was revived and continued for a few years after the revolution of 1688. Many attempts were made by the government to keep it in force; but it was so strongly resisted by Parliament that it expired in 1694, and has never since been revived.[12]

C. Colonial Background

Although the initial emigration to the New World is credited to the repressive religious policies prevalent in Europe, the colonies exhibited no tendencies to liberalize free communication within their own communities. "Colonial America was an open society dotted with closed enclaves, and one could generally settle with his co-believers in safety and comfort and exercise the right of oppression."[13]

The decline in the use of censorship in England no doubt contributed to its relative absence in pre-Revolutionary America. However, the doctrine of seditious libel was in full force on both sides of the Atlantic. Although the last prosecution for seditious libel in the colonies, that of New York printer John Peter Zenger, occurred in 1735, the

threat of prosecution in the ensuing years did not cease.[14]

The trial of Zenger was the first cause célèbre in the name of free speech in America. Zenger had published articles critical of the policies of New York's Governor Cosby, for which the royal governor instituted suit, over the reluctance of the colonial legislature. The defense, organized and argued by a prominent attorney, Andrew Hamilton, centered on the assertion that truth should be a proper defense to the crime. Hamilton recognized that truth, if determined by the jury, would exculpate his client since the intrusion of the King into colonial affairs was already deeply resented. This position was not the broad libertarian theory of freedom of the press which was being advanced, but merely the right of the press to publish articles in accord with that ephemeral concept known as "popular opinion." The Court rejected Hamilton's argument, but he prevailed by persuading the jury to ignore the law and return a general verdict of acquittal.[15]

At the same time, the popularly elected legislatures were imposing rather draconian punishments, through summary contempt procedures upon printers who criticized their policies.[16] Liberty to speak critically of the government was cherished in the abstract, but manipulated in practice to suit the politics of the time.

---

12. 2 J. Story, Commentaries on the Constitution of the United States, § 1882 (5th ed. 1891) (footnote omitted).

13. J. Roche, American Liberty: An Examination of the "Tradition" of Freedom, in Shadow and Substance: Essays on the Theory and Structure of Politics 11 (1964), as quoted in L. Levy, Judgments: Essays in American Constitutional History 121 & n. 37 (1972).

14. Z. Chafee, Free Speech in the United States 21 (1941). See, also the thorough historical discussion in Rabban, The First Amendment in Its Forgotten Years, 90 Yale L.J. 514 (1981).

For a discussion of state court protections of free speech based on state constitutions, see generally, Developments in the Law—The Interpretation of State Constitutional Rights, 95 Harv.L.Rev. 1193, 1398–1428 (1982).

15. Several accounts of the Zenger trial have been published. A bibliography is available in L. Rutherford, John Peter Zenger: His Press, His Trial, and a

Bibliography of Zenger Imprints 249–53 (1904). Zenger's counsel argued to the jury: "Men who injure and oppress the people under their administration and provoke them to cry out and complain should not also be allowed to make that very complaint the foundation for new oppressions and prosecutions." Trial of John Peter Zenger, 17 Howell's State Tr. 675, 721–22 (1735). See also, L. Levy, ed., Liberty of the Press from Zenger to Jefferson (1966); F. Latham, The Trial of John Peter Zenger, August, 1735 (1970). In England, it was not until 1843 that there was a defense of truth, if publication was for the public benefit. See Lord Campbell's Act, 6 & 7 Vict. (1843), c. 96; T. Plucknett, A Concise History of the Common Law 444 (2d ed. 1936).

16. Leonard Levy provides detailed accounts of the willingness of the colonial legislatures to honor free speech in accord with their political views, but dishonor it when the criticism was directed at them, in his book, Judgments: Essays on American Constitutional History 125–34 (1972).

Although issues of free speech were by and large subsumed in the general debate over the revolution, the common law view at the time the Constitution was drafted is generally conceded to be that expressed by Blackstone in his Commentaries, first published in 1765. At that time, it will be remembered, the practice of censorship had withered away, but the law of seditious libel was still viable.[17]

> The liberty of the press is indeed essential to the nature of a free state; but this consists in laying no *previous* restraint upon publications, and not in freedom from censure for criminal matter when published. Every freeman has an undoubted right to lay what sentiments he pleases before the public; to forbid this, is to destroy the freedom of the press; but if he publishes what is improper, mischievous, or illegal, he must take the consequences of his own temerity . . . . [T]hus, the will of individuals is still left free; the abuse only of that free-will is the object of legal punishment. Neither is any restraint hereby laid upon freedom of thought or enquiry: liberty of private sentiment is still left; the disseminating, or making public, of bad sentiments, destructive of the ends of society, is the crime which society corrects.[18]

D. Enactment of the First Amendment

The framers of the Constitution felt no need to include in the original document a provision expressly upholding a general theory of freedom of speech, undoubtedly holding to the belief that the government they envisioned, limited to the enumerated powers, could not constitutionally enact a law in derogation of the principle of free speech. Popular pressure, however, demanded a more articulate expression of the guarantees of individual rights from governmental interference, which culminated in the adoption of the Bill of Rights in 1791. The first amendment states:

> Congress shall make no law respecting an establishment of religion, or prohibiting the free exercise thereof; or abridging the freedom of speech, or of the press; or the right of the people peaceably to assemble, and to petition the Government for a redress of grievances.

Little can be drawn from the debates within the House concerning the meaning of the first amendment,[19] nor are there any records of debates in the Senate[20] or the states[21] on its ratification. Perhaps the members were following Madison's dictum that they should avoid discussing with particularity "abstract propositions, of which judgment may not be convinced . . . . If we confine ourselves to an enumeration of simple, acknowledged principles, the ratification will meet with but little difficulty."[22] Interpretation of this language has not proved as simple as Madison expected, however. A question of the intent of the Framers has been continually raised when considering the meaning of the first amendment, although its significance is more historical than legal following the expansion of the constitutional guarantee in recent years.

Professor Zachariah Chafee contends that the limited, legalistic view of free speech expounded by Blackstone was supplemented in the New World by a tangible popular meaning; the right of unrestricted discussion of public affairs. Thus, the amendment was intended to serve the dual purpose of eliminating all vestiges of censorship in America and destroying the viability of the doctrine of seditious libel. As the practice of censorship was abandoned well before the drafting of the first amendment, Chafee contends that it could not have been intended solely as a prohibition against a non-existent practice. Further support is derived from the Zenger

---

17. There were 70 prosecutions and 50 convictions for seditious libel by the English authorities from 1760 to 1776. 2 T. S. May, Constitutional History of England 9n (2d ed. 1912).

18. Commentaries on the Laws of England, Book IV pp. * 151–152 (T. Cooley ed., Chicago: 2d ed., rev. ed. 1872) (emphasis in original).

19. Constitution of the United States: Analysis & Interpretation, 92d Cong., 2d Sess., Senate Document 92–82 (1973), at p. 936.

20. Id.

21. Id.

22. 1 Annals of Congress, 738 (August 15, 1789).

trial, which is, in the Chafee view, not only a repudiation of the legitimacy of seditious libel in the colonies but an expression of the colonists' cherished belief in the principle of free speech.[23]

Leonard Levy, however, maintains that a careful historical study of this period will show that a notion that a broad libertarian approach to freedom of speech was a cherished principle is merely a "sentimental hallucination." There was nothing in the tradition of the colonists to influence them to overthrow seditious libel, and their activities would indicate that free speech in the revolutionary period was accorded only to those who propounded favorable opinions of the struggle for independence.[24]

Whatever the view of the Framers at the time of the drafting of the amendment, a broader interpretation of that language was ensured by the controversy surrounding the Alien and Sedition Acts of 1798.[25] Under the Alien Act, the President could order to leave the country all aliens "as he shall judge dangerous to the peace and safety of the United States. . . ."[26] It was never formally invoked, and expired after two years, but its existence did result in some aliens leaving the country or going into hiding.[27]

The Sedition Act prohibited "publishing any false, scandalous and malicious writing or writings against the government of the United States, or either house of Congress . . . or the President . . . with intent to defame . . . or to bring them . . .

into contempt or disrepute . . . ."[28] Truth was a defense and the jury had a right to determine the law and facts under the direction of the court. In this respect the Act was actually a fairly liberal one for its time. England did not establish a defense of truth until 1843,[29] though a general verdict of the jury was allowed in the 1790's.[30] Yet the Sedition Act was employed by President Adams' Federalist administration against members of Jefferson's Democratic-Republican party for their criticism of his administration. Despite the subsequent retaliation in kind by the Republicans upon Jefferson's election,[31] their attack upon the politically motivated prosecutions and the resulting restriction upon free expression provided the foundation for the modern theory of the first amendment.

Although these Acts were never required to withstand judicial scrutiny under the first amendment, the Alien and Sedition Acts remain the epitome of an unconstitutional abridgement of free speech. Justice Brennan later wrote that it was the Sedition Act "which first crystallized a national awareness of the central meaning of the First Amendment."[32] He added:

Although the Sedition Act was never tested in this Court, the attack upon its validity has carried the day in the court of history. Fines levied in its prosecution were repaid by Act of Congress on the ground that it was unconstitutional. . . . Calhoun, reporting to the Senate on February 4, 1836, assumed that its invalidity was a matter "which no one now doubts." . . . Jefferson, as President,

---

23. Z. Chafee, Free Speech in the United States (1941) at 19–21.

24. L. Levy, Legacy of Suppression: Freedom of Speech and Press in Early American History, ch. 2 (1960). Also published in 1963 as Freedom of Speech and Press in Early American History.

25. J. Smith, Freedom's Fetters—The Alien and Sedition Laws and American Civil Liberties (1956); L. Levy, Legacy of Suppression: Freedom of Speech and Press in Early American History, ch. 6 (1960).

26. 1 Stat. at Large 570 (June 25, 1798).

27. 1 Emerson, Haber, & Dorsen's Political and Civil Rights in the United States 21 (4th ed., Law School ed. 1976). Hereinafter all citations are to the law school edition of this book, not the lawyer's edition.

28. 1 Stat. at Large 596 (July 14, 1798).

29. 6 & 7 Vic. c. 96 (1843) (Lord Campbell's Act); II J. F. Stephen, A History of the Criminal Law of England 383 (London, 1883).

30. Fox's Libel Act, 32 Geo. 3, c. 60 (1792).

31. L. Levy, Jefferson & Civil Liberties—The Darker Side 58–59 (1963). Levy reports an incident in which Jefferson, in a letter to the Governor of Pennsylvania, noted that the Federalists having failed to destroy the press by their gag law, now appeared to be doing so by encouraging its licentiousness, and that a few well-placed prosecutions might be necessary to restore the integrity of the press.

32. New York Times v. Sullivan, 376 U.S. 254, 273 (1964).

pardoned those who had been convicted and sentenced under the Act . . . . The invalidity of the Act has also been assumed by Justices of this Court . . . . These views reflect a broad consensus that the Act, because of the restraint it imposed upon criticism of government and public officials, was inconsistent with the First Amendment.[33]

E. The Value of Speech and the Function of the First Amendment

Reliance solely on the intent of the founders for an appraisal of the scope of first amendment protections is inadequate for several reasons. First, as we have seen, the tools available to calibrate such intent are imprecise and capable of divergent interpretations. Second, and more importantly, such reliance imposes a narrow view upon the role of the Constitution by ignoring the dynamic nature of its provisions.[34] Justice Holmes, for example, thought that the main purpose of the free speech guarantee of the first amendment "is 'to prevent all such *previous restraints* upon publications as had been practiced by other governments', and they do not prevent the subsequent punishment of such as may be deemed contrary to the public welfare."[35] Yet he also admitted: "There is no constitutional right to have all general propositions of law once adopted remain unchanged."[36] Thus, it is appropriate to briefly note the underlying values of free speech in order to ascertain the proper degree of judicial solicitude to be afforded such a concept.

First, it should be recognized, as Professor Meiklejohn has observed, that the first amendment does not forbid the abridging of speech, but abridging the *freedom of speech.*[37] "The First Amendment is not the guardian of unregulated talkativeness."[38]

Therefore, the values perceived in a system of free expression will be determinative of whether there exists an inhibition upon that freedom.

The initial justification for a system of free speech has long been held to be its value in preventing human error through ignorance. One of the most eloquent defenses of free speech is derived from John Milton's battle with the English censorship laws. In his tract, Areopagitica, Milton said:

[T]hough all the winds of doctrine were let loose to play upon the earth, so truth be in the field, we do injuriously, by licensing and prohibiting, to misdoubt her strength. Let her and falsehood grapple; whoever knew truth put to the worse in a free and open encounter?[39]

John Stuart Mill expanded Milton's arguments two centuries later in his 1859 essay, *On Liberty,* by his recognition of the public good which results from the free exchange of ideas.

First, if any opinion is compelled to silence, that opinion for aught we can certainly know, be true. To deny this is to assume our own infallibility. Secondly, though this silenced opinion be in error, it may, and very commonly does, contain a portion of the truth; and since the generally prevailing opinion on any subject is rarely or never the whole truth, it is only by the collision of adverse opinions that the remainder of the truth had any chance being supplied. Thirdly, even if the received opinion be not only true but the whole truth; unless it is suffered to be, and actually is, vigorously and earnestly contested, it will, by most of those who receive it, be held in the manner of a prejudice, with little comprehension of feeling of its rational grounds. And not only this, but fourthly, the meaning of the doctrine itself will be in danger of being lost or enfeebled. . . .[40]

---

33. 376 U.S. 254, 276 (1964) (footnote omitted).

34. See, e.g., P. Brest, Process of Constitutional Decisionmaking, ch. 2 (1975).

35. Patterson v. Colorado, 205 U.S. 454, 462 (1907) (emphasis in original).

36. 205 U.S. 454, 461 (1907).

37. A. Meiklejohn, Free Speech and Its Relation to Self Government (1948) p. 19.

38. Id. at 26.

39. Areopagitica, A Speech for the Liberty of Unlicensed Printing to the Parliament of England (1644). Milton was not as assured of the strength of truth as it appeared, however, for he disavowed any legitimacy for popery, open superstition, impiety, or evil. Id.

40. J. S. Mill, On Liberty, (1859), Ch. II.

These statements are strongly supportive of Justice Holmes' "marketplace of ideas" theory of free speech.[41] This theory is built upon the premise that the first amendment prohibits government suppression of ideas because the truth of any idea can only be determined in the "marketplace" of competing ideas. There are, of course, other justifications.

It has been urged that an important function of free speech is to enhance the potential of individual contribution to the social welfare, thus enlarging the prospects for individual self-fulfillment.[42] Another function, a corollary of the first, is that the health of a society of self-government is nurtured by the contributions of individuals to its functioning.[43] In addition, once we allow the government any power to restrict the freedom of speech, we may have taken a path which is a "slippery slope." Particularly so since a central value of the free press, speech, and assembly lies in "checking" the abuse of power by public officials.[44] Line-drawing in such an abstract area is always difficult and especially so when a government's natural inclination is moving the line towards more suppression of criticism and unpopular ideas. Thus, even if one could distinguish between illegitimate and legitimate speech, it may still be necessary to protect all speech in order to afford real protection for legitimate speech.[45]

III. SOME BASIC TESTS AND ATTITUDES

A. Balancing vs. Absolutism

1. A Preferred Position for Free Speech?

In *United States v. Carolene Products Co.*,[1] the Court upheld the power of Congress to regulate "filled milk" as it endorsed the post-1937 concept of judicial deference to acts of other branches of government in their regulation of economic activities. In the course of the now famous footnote 4 of the opinion, Chief Justice Stone indicated that certain other rights might properly receive more active judicial protection against the democratic process:

> There may be narrower scope for operation of the presumption of constitutionality when legislation appears on its face to be within a specific prohibition of the Constitution, such as those of the first ten amendments, which are deemed equally specific when held to be embraced within the Fourteenth. . . .

> It is unnecessary to consider now whether legislation which restricts those political processes which can ordinarily be expected to bring about repeal of undesirable legislation, is to be subjected to more exacting judicial scrutiny under the general prohibitions of the Fourteenth Amendment than are most other types of legislation. . . .[2]

A few years later this view was made more explicit when the Court asserted: "Freedom

---

41. Abrams v. United States, 250 U.S. 616, 630 (dissenting opinion).

42. See Redish, The Value of Free Speech, 130 U.Penn.L.Rev. 591, 593 (1982), emphasizing the value of "individual self-realization." For comment on this thesis, see Baker, Realizing Self-Realization: Corporate Political Expenditures and Redish's *The Value of Free Speech*, 130 U.Penn.L.Rev. 646 (1982), and the reply: Redish, Self-Realization, Democracy, and Freedom of Expression: A Reply to Professor Baker, 130 U.Penn.L.Rev. 678 (1982).

Professor Chevigny has argued that a right to free expression may also be derived from and rooted in, the nature of language itself; the necessity of a dialogue in order to understand words at all means that society should allow the dialogue to proceed. Chevigny, Philosophy of Language and Free Expression, 55 N.Y.U.L.Rev. 157 (1980). In reply see, Martin, On a New Argument for Freedom of Speech, 57 N.Y.U.L.Rev. 906 (1982), and Chevigny, A Dialogic

Right of Free Expression: A Reply to Michael Martin, 57 N.Y.U.L.Rev. 920 (1982).

43. See T. Emerson, The System of Freedom of Expression (1970) for an elaboration and integration of these theses in a more complete form.

44. Blasi, The Checking Value in First Amendment Theory, 1977 A.B. Foundation Res.J. 521. For a careful analysis of the greater immunity from government regulation of expression than most other forms of human conduct, see Wellington, On Freedom of Expression, 88 Yale L.J. 1105 (1979).

45. On the other hand, it has been argued that protection should only be afforded to explicitly political speech, and not to scientific, literary or obscene speech. See, Bork, Neutral Principles and Some First Amendment Problems, 47 Ind.L.J. 1 (1971).

1. 304 U.S. 144 (1938).

2. 304 U.S. at 152–53 n. 4 (1938).

of press, freedom of speech, freedom of religion are in a preferred position." [3] It should be recognized that the position advanced by footnote 4 is not merely an assertion; it does have a strong rationale. Unlike economic legislation, which is only a product of the political process, and therefore may to some extent be subject to an inner political check, speech is part of the legislative process itself; restriction of speech alters the democratic process and undercuts the basis for deferring to the legislation which emerges. Additionally, the restraint of speech may often be seen as a short range aid to societal programs by insulating the current government from criticism caused by debate. This natural tendency conflicts with the first amendment value of open debate. Thus the judiciary may need to be more active to protect this value against the will of a temporary majority.

Justice Frankfurter strongly criticized the use of the "preferred position" terminology, because of his belief its use might imply ". . . that any law touching communication is infected with presumptive invalidity . . . it radiates a constitutional doctrine without avowing it." [4] Such criticism may be regarded as a warning against unwarranted extension of judicial principle rather than an attack upon established judicial dogma, for in that same opinion, Justice Frankfurter wrote most eloquently of the rationale and meaning of the "preferred position of freedom of speech."

[S]ociological conclusions are conditioned by time and circumstance. Because of this awareness Mr. Justice Holmes seldom felt justified in opposing his own opinion to economic views which the legislature embodied in law. But since he also realized that the progress of civilization is to a considerable extent the displacement of error which once held sway as official truth by beliefs which in turn have yielded to other beliefs, for him the right to search for truth was of a different order than some transient economic dogma. And without freedom of expression, thought becomes checked and atrophied. Therefore, in considering what interests are so fundamental as to be enshrined in the Due Process Clause, those liberties of the individual which history has attested as the indispensable conditions of an open as against a closed society come to this Court with a momentum for respect lacking when appeal is made to liberties which derive merely from shifting economic arrangements. Accordingly, Mr. Justice Holmes was far more ready to find legislative invasion where free inquiry was involved than in the debatable area of economics. [5]

Since Frankfurter's sharp attack on the language of "preferred position," the words have been avoided but the substance remains. The preferential treatment of the first amendment is exemplified by the variety of judicial tools utilized by the Court in its review of challenged legislation. As we shall see, the Court has used the clear and present danger test, applied a narrowed presumption of constitutionality, strictly construed statutes to avoid limiting first amendment freedoms, restricted prior restraint and subsequent punishment, relaxed general requirements of standing to sue and generally set higher standards of procedural due process in order to give vitality to those freedoms over ordinary governmental functions. [6]

2. Is Free Speech an Absolute?

The first amendment appears to speak in absolutist terms: "Congress shall make no

---

3. Murdock v. Pennsylvania, 319 U.S. 105, 115 (1943). See also, Herndon v. Lowry, 301 U.S. 242, 258 (1937); Thornhill v. Alabama, 310 U.S. 88, 95 (1939); Schneider v. State, 308 U.S. 147, 161 (1939); Bridges v. California, 314 U.S. 252, 262–63 (1941); Prince v. Massachusetts, 321 U.S. 158, 164 (1943); Follett v. McCormick, 321 U.S. 573, 575 (1943); Marsh v. Alabama, 326 U.S. 501, 509 (1945); Saia v. New York, 334 U.S. 558, 562 (1947); West Virginia State Bd. of Education v. Barnette, 319 U.S. 624, 639 (1943); Thomas v. Collins, 323 U.S. 516, 530 (1945). The attempt to recognize

First Amendment freedoms as being in a "preferred position" was first made by Chief Justice Stone in his dissent in Jones v. Opelika, 316 U.S. 584, 600, 608 (1942).

4. Kovacs v. Cooper, 336 U.S. 77, 90 (1949) (concurring opinion).

5. 336 U.S. 77, 95 (1949) (concurring opinion).

6. McKay, The Preference for Freedom, 34 N.Y. U.L.Rev. 1182, 1184 (1959).

law . . . abridging the freedom of speech . . ." The strict language is emphasized by a comparison with the fourth amendment's prohibition against "*unreasonable* searches and seizures." If free speech is an absolute right it is certainly in a preferred position vis-a-vis the majority of rights in the Constitution, which like the fourth amendment, are not expressed in absolute terms. An absolute right, by definition, is not subject to balancing. Considerable controversy has arisen over the appropriate degree of judicial responsibility in appraising and preserving the rights of free speech. In approaching the significant problem of interpreting the meaning of "free speech", an initial problem must be to determine the strength of first amendment rights in relation to the other individual rights and whether, in light of that, it is appropriate for the judiciary to balance free speech with legitimate governmental objectives. The problem is virtually unique to free speech and its corollaries, freedom of the press and the right to petition the Government for a redress of grievance. Even the freedom of religion is on a slightly different plane, for the first amendment may be read to require some balancing of interests—laws must neither establish a religion nor prohibit its free exercise.

The absolutist view of free speech has been championed and most closely associated with Justices Black and Douglas,[7] but it has never persuaded a majority of the Court. As Black himself has summarized his views in *Konigsberg v. State Bar of California:*[8]

The recognition [that a State] has subjected "speech and association to the deterrence of

subsequent disclosure" is, under the First Amendment, sufficient in itself to render the action of the State unconstitutional unless one subscribes to the doctrine that permits constitutionally protected rights to be "balanced" away whenever a majority of this Court thinks that a State might have interest sufficient to justify abridgement of those freedoms . . . I do not subscribe to that doctrine for I believe that the First Amendment's unequivocal command that there shall be no abridgement of the rights of free speech and assembly shows that the men who drafted our Bill of Rights did all the "balancing" that was to be done in this field . . . . [T]he very object of adopting the First Amendment . . . was to put the freedoms protected there completely out of the area of any congressional control that may be attempted through the exercise of precisely those powers that are now being used to "balance" the Bill of Rights out of existence . . . . I fear that the creation of "tests" by which speech is left unprotected under certain circumstances is a standing invitation to abridge it . . . . [T]he Court's "absolute" statement that there are no "absolutes" under the First Amendment must be an exaggeration of its own views.[9]

Justice Harlan has often been associated with the "balancing view." In *Konigsberg*, where Black wrote his defense of the absolutist position, Harlan wrote for the Court, and presented his justification for judicial balancing.

[W]e reject the view that freedom of speech and association . . . as protected by the First and Fourteenth Amendments, are "absolutes," not only in the undoubted sense that where the constitutional protection exists it must prevail, but also in the sense that the scope of that protection must be gathered solely from a literal reading of the First Amend-

---

7. Konigsberg v. State Bar of California, 366 U.S. 36, 56 (1961) (dissenting opinion); Braden v. United States, 365 U.S. 431, 441 (1961) (dissenting); Barenblatt v. United States, 360 U.S. 109, 140–44 (1959) (dissenting); Wilkinson v. United States, 365 U.S. 399, 422 (1961) (dissenting); Uphaus v. Wyman, 364 U.S. 388, 392 (1960) (dissenting); American Communications Ass'n v. Douds, 339 U.S. 382, 443 (1950); Communist Party v. SACB, 367 U.S. 1, 137 (1961) (dissenting); Beauharnais v. Illinois, 343 U.S. 250, 367 (1952) (dissenting); New York Times Co. v. Sullivan, 376 U.S. 254, 293 (1964) (concurring); New York Times Co. v. United States, 403 U.S. 713, 714 (concurring); Roth v.

United States, 354 U.S. 476, 508 (1957) (dissenting); Brandenburg v. Ohio, 395 U.S. 444, 450 (1969) (concurring). See generally, R. Rotunda, ed., Six Justices on Civil Rights, at 11 (Frank, "Hugo L. Black: Free Speech and the Declaration of Independence"), and at 107 (Countryman, "Justice Douglas and Freedom of Expression") (Oceana Publications, Inc. 1983).

8. 366 U.S. 36 (1961).

9. Konigsberg v. State Bar of California, 366 U.S. 36, 60–61, 63, 68 (1961) (Black, J., dissenting, joined by Douglas, J., and Chief Justice Warren) (footnote omitted).

ment. Throughout its history this Court has consistently recognized at least two ways in which constitutionally protected freedom of speech is narrower than an unlimited license to talk. On the one hand, certain forms of speech, or speech in certain contexts, has been considered outside the scope of constitutional protection . . . . On the other hand, general regulatory statutes, not intended to control the content of speech but incidentally limiting its unfettered exercise, have not been regarded as the type of law the First or Fourteenth Amendment forbade Congress or the States to pass, when they have been found justified by subordinating valid governmental interests, a pre-requisite to constitutionality which has necessarily involved a weighing of the governmental interest involved. . . .[10]

Stylistically, Harlan's balancing approach is not inconsistent with the language of the first amendment. It is not "speech" which is absolutely protected from restriction but only "free speech." How does the Court decide what speech should be free? Must it balance?

Harlan never advocated an *ad hoc* balancing. The result of his balancing was a rule of law with precedential effect. Moreover Harlan's balancing view should not be regarded as necessarily more subservient to state authority than Black's approach. Thus in *Street v. New York,*[11] a flag burning case, Harlan wrote the majority opinion sustaining the First Amendment challenge on the facts of that case, while Black dissented. Black believed the prosecution permissible because it did not rest on spoken words; the "talking that was done took place 'as an integral part of conduct' ".[12] Similarly, Black did not believe that the right of free speech granted "a constitutional right to engage in the conduct of picketing or patrolling,

whether on publicly owned streets or on privately owned property." [13]

Black's view may be criticized because, contrary to his assertion, he may be using the balancing test to decide what is speech and what is only expressive conduct. His balancing is more covert and intuitive than Harlan's frank balancing of interests.[14] On the other hand, Harlan's balancing may appear to invite if not justify legislative attempts to encroach on the guarantees of free speech.

Professor Alexander Meiklejohn has modified Justice Black's absolute test in his theory that the first amendment is designed to provide unequivocal protection to speech related to self-government while relegating speech that falls outside of this protective zone to the due process safeguards of the fifth and fourteenth amendments.[15] While it would appear that this analysis offers some middle ground between the "absolutists" and the "balancers" as well as giving some weight to the absolute, unequivocal language of the amendment, there is little support for such an interpretation in the history surrounding the amendment, nor does it appear to command much weight with the Court.[16] Moreover, it replaces the question of the scope of protection with the equally perplexing question of the relation of a particular type of speech to "self-government", a phrase which is by no means self-defining.

B. The Overbreadth Doctrine

Two closely related doctrines particularly important in dealing with free speech issues are the prohibitions against the overbreadth and vagueness of a statute. Because of the importance of the free speech guarantee,

---

10. 366 U.S. 36, 49–51 (1961) (footnote omitted).

11. 394 U.S. 576 (1969).

12. 394 U.S. 576, 610 (1969) (Black, J. dissenting). Black emphasized: "I would not balance away the First Amendment mandate that speech not be abridged in any fashion whatsoever . . . [But it] is immaterial to me that words are spoken in connection with the burning [of an American flag.]" Id.

13. Cox v. Louisiana, 379 U.S. 559, 578 (1965) (Black, J. dissenting).

14. See Mendelson, The First Amendment and the Judicial Process: A Reply to Mr. Frantz, 17 Vand.L. Rev. 479, 482 (1964).

15. Meiklejohn, Free Speech and Its Relation to Self Government (1948); What Does the First Amendment Mean? 20 U. of Chi.L.Rev. 461 (1953); Political Freedom (1960). For criticism, see Chafee, Book Review, 62 Harv.L.Rev. 891 (1949).

16. Chafee, Book Review, 62 Harv.L.Rev. 891, 894 (1949).

even when the state does have the power to regulate an area, it "must be so exercised as not, in attaining a permissible end, unduly to infringe the protected freedom." [1] In this section we consider the overbreadth doctrine and in the next section we turn to the vagueness doctrine.

An overbroad statute is one that is designed to burden or punish activities which are not constitutionally protected, but the statute includes within its scope activities which are protected by the first amendment. In a case of a statute which is overbroad on its face, the speaker's actions or speech may not be protected by the first amendment and thus the act could have been prohibited under a carefully drawn statute. Nevertheless the Court will strike the overbroad statute because it might apply to others, not before the Court, who may engage in protected activity which the statute appears to outlaw. [2] As Justice Brennan explained for the Court in *NAACP v. Button:* [3]

> [T]he instant decree may be invalid if it prohibits privileged exercises of First Amendment rights *whether or not* the record discloses that the petitioner has engaged in privileged conduct. For in appraising a statute's inhibitory effect upon such rights, this Court has not hesitated to take into account possible applications of the statute in other factual contexts besides that at bar. [4]

On the other hand, in non first amendment areas, "one to whom application of a statute is constitutional will not be heard to attack the statute on the ground that impliedly it

might also be taken as applying to other persons or other situations in which its application might be unconstitutional." [5] Two cases illustrate the power of the overbreadth doctrine as a first amendment test; to those cases we now turn.

Karl Kunz, a Baptist Minister, was convicted of violating an ordinance which prohibited holding a religious meeting on streets without a permit. The conviction was affirmed by the New York Court of Appeals, [6] and reversed by the Supreme Court, in *Kunz v. New York.* [7] Under the city ordinance those desiring to conduct religious worship meetings on the street had to first obtain a permit from the city police commissioner. Kunz received a one year permit in 1946 which was revoked in November 1946 on the basis of evidence that the appellant had "ridiculed and denounced other religious beliefs in his meeting." [8] No mention was made in the ordinance of grounds for revoking or refusing permits. Kunz reapplied for a permit in 1947 and 1948; his application was rejected in both years. In 1948 he was arrested and convicted for speaking without a permit. [9]

Writing for the Court, Chief Justice Vinson stated, "We are here concerned only with the propriety of the action of the police commissioner in refusing to issue that permit." [10] An administrative official, the police commissioner, was empowered under the ordinance to deny a permit application for conduct he determined, in his discretion, to be condemned by the ordinance. Ordinances

1. Cantwell v. Connecticut, 310 U.S. 296, 304 (1940).

See also, International Union of Police Associations, Local 189 v. Barrett, 524 F.Supp. 760, 765 (N.D.Ga. 1981) (overbreadth and vagueness are two separate concepts that often go hand in hand), citing an earlier edition of this treatise.

2. People v. Holder, 103 Ill.App.3d 353, 356, 59 Ill. Dec. 142, 145, 431 N.E.2d 427, 430 (2d Dist. 1982) (Hopf, J.), quoting this portion of an earlier edition of this treatise.

3. 371 U.S. 415 (1963).

4. 371 U.S. 415, 432 (1963) (emphasis added). See also NAACP v. Alabama, 377 U.S. 288, 307 (1964); Keyishian v. Board of Regents, 385 U.S. 589, 609 (1967) (statutes which "seek to bar employment both for association which legitimately may be proscribed and for

association which may not be proscribed consistently with First Amendment rights" are struck down and not construed narrowly).

5. United States v. Raines, 362 U.S. 17, 21 (1960). See also Yazoo & M. V. R. v. Jackson Vinegar Co., 226 U.S. 217, 219–20 (1912). An excellent example of a conviction for unprotected activity which was nevertheless reversed because the statute affected the first amendment and was overbroad is Kunz v. New York, 340 U.S. 290 (1951).

6. 300 N.Y. 273 (1949).

7. 340 U.S. 290 (1951).

8. 340 U.S. at 292.

9. Id. at 293.

10. Id.

giving discretionary power to administrative officials over a citizen's right to speak about religion on the city streets was held to be an invalid prior restraint on a first amendment right.[11] Vinson indicated the decision was in no way an opinion delineating which punitive remedies authorities may implement, but, "New York can not vest restraining control over the right to speak on religious subjects in an administrative official when there are *no appropriate standards* to guide his action."[12]

In a lengthy dissent Justice Jackson stated that Kunz's speech fell into the inflammatory, insulting or "fighting words" category which traditionally has not been considered to be constitutionally protected.[13] The Court, he urged, should recognize some speech as being outside the first amendment privilege and set up a standard to determine what types of speech should be unprotected.[14] The majority's analysis however never reached this issue. While a narrowly drawn statute, with appropriate standards, might validly have been used to deny Kunz's permit, the overbroad statute must fail under the first amendment standards. Jackson's argument that one must consider the statute only as applied, while acceptable in a non first amendment context, was not acceptable when dealing with a statute affecting free speech.[15]

Another, more recent, example of the application of the overbreadth doctrine is *Lewis v. City of New Orleans*,[16] where the appellant had been convicted for violating a city ordinance making it unlawful "to curse or revile or to use obscene or opprobrious language toward or with reference" to a police officer performing his duties.[17] The Louisiana Supreme Court sustained the ap-

pellant's conviction and the Supreme Court reversed.[18]

The Court held that the ordinance as construed by the Louisiana Supreme Court was overbroad and consequently invalid as a violation of the first and fourteenth amendments.[19] Justice Brennan, writing for the Court, indicated the ordinance had gone beyond the bounds of *Chaplinsky v. New Hampshire*[20] and *Gooding v. Wilson*[21] where "fighting words," "which 'by their very utterance inflict injury or tend to incite an immediate breach of the peace,'" were held to be without constitutional protection.[22] The ordinance proscribed the use of "opprobrious language" a term not limited to words which could be categorized as "fighting words."[23] Earlier, the Louisiana Supreme Court had contended the ordinance's wording was narrow and specific and not in need of refinement.[24] The Louisiana Supreme Court had emphasized that there would be a damaging effect on the stature of police in the performance of their jobs if it was permissible to address curses and obscenities to officers on duty.[25] Nothing in the Louisiana Supreme Court opinion, noted Brennan, limited the ordinance in accordance with the *Chaplinsky* and *Gooding* decisions.[26]

Brennan, for the majority, concluded that it was immaterial that the appellant's words might have been constitutionally unprotected under a properly drawn statute or ordinance. The ordinance effectively punished all vulgar and offensive speech even though some of this speech may have been protected by the first amendment. Since the ordinance as construed by the Louisiana Supreme Court was "susceptible of application to protected speech, the section is constitu-

---

11. Id.

12. Id. at 295 (emphasis added).

13. Id. at 298 (Jackson, J., dissenting).

14. Id. at 299 (Jackson, J., dissenting).

15. Id. at 304–305 (Jackson, J., dissenting).

16. 415 U.S. 130 (1974).

17. Id. at 132.

18. 415 U.S. at 130.

19. Id. at 131–132.

20. 315 U.S. 568, 572 (1942).

21. 405 U.S. 518, 522 (1972).

22. 415 U.S. at 133.

23. Id.

24. 263 La. 809, 269 So.2d 450 (1972).

25. 415 U.S. at 132.

26. Id. at 133.

tionally overbroad and . . . facially invalid." [27]

In a separate concurring opinion Justice Powell stated the Louisiana Supreme Court had construed the ordinance as a *per se* rule punishing all obscene language directed at city police.[28] Powell agreed that the ordinance was overbroad and expressed concern that such a regulation:

> confers on police a virtually unrestrained power to arrest and charge persons with a violation. . . . The opportunity for abuse, especially where a statute has received a virtually open-ended interpretation, is self-evident.[29]

Justices Blackmun, Rehnquist and Chief Justice Burger joined in dissent. Blackmun writing for the dissenters stated the overbreadth and vagueness doctrines had been indiscriminately invoked by the Court without regard to the nature of the speech in question. The Court, he criticized, was not just applying constitutional limitations but was invalidating statutes because they might at a future time restrict protected speech.[30] Blackmun quoted Justice Jackson's dissenting opinion in *Saia v. New York:* [31]

> [T]he issue before us is whether what has been done has deprived this appellant of a constitutional right. It is the law *as applied* that we review, not the abstract academic questions which it might raise in some more doubtful case.[32]

The appellant's speech had plainly been "fighting words," and should be within the reach of the ordinance, Blackmun concluded.[33]

It is difficult to determine how creative a challenging party must be in conceiving of situations where the language of a statute might be applied to protected speech which is not before the Court. It has been sug-

gested that in all first amendment overbreadth cases, a statute should fall only if it is "substantially overbroad and not readily reconstructed to avoid privileged activity. . . . [because if it] is not substantially overbroad [it] is unlikely to have a drastic inhibitory impact." [34] The Supreme Court in *Broadrick v. Oklahoma,*[35] has noted that the overbreadth doctrine is "strong medicine," [36] and consequently has attempted to place some limits on it. By a 5 to 4 vote, the Court ruled that substantial overbreadth may be a requirement to invoke the doctrine, particularly when the speech is joined with conduct:

> [The function of the overbreadth doctrine is] a limited one at the outset, [and] attenuates as the otherwise unprotected behavior that it forbids the State to sanction moves from "pure speech" toward conduct and that conduct— even if expressive—falls within the scope of otherwise valid criminal laws that reflect legitimate state interests in maintaining comprehensive controls over harmful, constitutionally unprotected conduct. . . . To put the matter another way, particularly where conduct and not merely speech is involved, we believe that the overbreadth of a statute must not only be real, but substantial as well, judged in relation to the statute's plainly legitimate sweep.[37]

Such a test is hardly a mechanical one and, perhaps, is most important in showing an attitude of hesitancy to employ the doctrine. Elsewhere in *Broadrick,* the Court offered a more specific test when it stated that it would invalidate statutes for overbreadth "only when the flaw is a substantial concern in the context of the statute as a whole." [38]

A lengthy consideration of the case law suggests that three types of overbreadth statutes may be distinguished for purposes of the overbreadth doctrine: censorial laws, inhibitory laws, and remedial laws. The

---

27.   Id. at 134.

28.   Id. at 134–135.

29.   Id. at 135–136.

30.   Id. at 137.

31.   334 U.S. 558 (1948).

32.   334 U.S. 558, 571 (1948) (emphasis added).

33.   415 U.S. at 141.

34.   Note, The First Amendment Overbreadth Doctrine, 83 Harv.L.Rev. 844, 918 (1970).

35.   413 U.S. 601 (1973).

36.   413 U.S. 601, 613.

37.   413 U.S. 601, 615.

38.   413 U.S. 601, 616 n. 14. See also Village of Schaumburg v. Citizens for a Better Environment, 444 U.S. 620, 636–38 (1980).

first type, censorial laws (such as criminal syndicalism laws), seek to burden the advocacy of matters of public concern.[39] The Court is less tolerant of overbreadth statutes in this area than it is of inhibitory laws, "which impinge on expressive and associational conduct but whose impact tends to be neutral as to viewpoints sought to be advocated. . . . "[40], such as libel laws. The Court is less tolerant of overbreadth in this area of inhibitory laws than it is of remedial laws, those "which hamper first amendment activities for the purpose of promoting values which are within the concern of the amendment."[41] Such remedial laws include, for example, the fairness doctrine of the broadcast media,[42] as well as laws regulating lobbying, campaign contributions, and union elections.[43] The law upheld in *Broadrick* fits under this analysis for it was a remedial law: it regulated partisan political activity of state employees.[44]

Within this framework, it is not entirely clear to what extent the overbreadth doctrine applies to so-called commercial speech.[45] In *Ohralik v. Ohio State Bar*,[46] the Supreme Court upheld the Ohio state bar's discipline of an attorney for in-person solicitation under the circumstances of that case. In the course of the opinion the majority opinion stated that such in-person solicitation was commercial speech and such speech "is not as likely to be deterred as noncommercial speech, and therefore does not require the added protection afforded by the overbreadth doctrine".[47] But the majority immediately went on to say that "[e]ven if the commercial speaker could mount an overbreadth attack. . . . " then the requirements of *Broadrick v. Oklahoma*[48] must be met. In the case companion to *Ohralik, In re Primus*,[49] the Court did in fact apply the overbreadth doctrine,[50] however there the majority did not find the attorney solicitation to be "commercial" speech. Thus, if speech is deemed to be commercial speech, then the overbreadth analysis is at this point probably inapplicable. "Because of the special character of commercial speech and the relative novelty of First Amendment protection for such speech, we act with caution in confronting First Amendment challenges to economic legislation that serves legitimate regulatory interests."[51]

C. The Void-for-Vagueness Doctrine

Closely related to the overbreadth doctrine is the void for vagueness doctrine. The problem of vagueness in statutes regulating speech activities is based on the same rationale as the overbreadth doctrine and the Supreme Court often speaks of them together.[1] There are several objections to vague statutes that affect first amendment rights. Because the first amendment needs breathing space, the governmental regulation that is tolerated must be drawn with "narrow

---

39. E.g., Brandenburg v. Ohio, 395 U.S. 444 (1969) (per curiam); Herndon v. Lowry, 301 U.S. 242 (1937); DeJonge v. Oregon, 299 U.S. 353 (1937).

40. Note, The First Amendment Overbreadth Doctrine, 83 Harv.L.Rev. 844, 918 (1970).

41. Id.

42. See Red Lion Broadcasting Co. v. FCC, 395 U.S. 367 (1969).

43. Note, The First Amendment Overbreadth Doctrine, 83 Harv.L.Rev. 844, 920 (1970).

44. Broadrick v. Oklahoma, 413 U.S. 603, n. 1 (1973).

45. See Chapter 18, Section IX, infra.

46. 436 U.S. 447 (1978).

47. 436 U.S. at 462–63.

48. 413 U.S. 601, 615 (1973).

49. 436 U.S. 412 (1978).

50. 436 U.S. at 433, 438–39.

51. Friedman v. Rogers, 440 U.S. 1, 11 n. 9 (1979). The Court also noted: "Our decisions dealing with more traditional first amendment problems do not extend automatically to this as yet uncharted area." Id. at 11 n. 9. In deferring to commercial regulation, however, the Court should recognize that when this regulation takes the form of restrictions on truthful speech, the first amendment interests should be considered compelling. Cf. Rotunda, The First Amendment Now Protects Commercial Speech, 10 The Center Magazine: A Publication of the Center for the Study of Democratic Institutions 32, 33 (May/June 1977).

1. E.g., Dombrowski v. Pfister, 380 U.S. 479, 486 (1965); Keyishian v. Board of Regents, 385 U.S. 589, 609 (1967); NAACP v. Button, 371 U.S. 415, 433 (1963). Commentators also often consider them indistinguishable. E.g., Note, The Void-for-Vagueness Doctrine in the Supreme Court, 109 U.Pa.L.Rev. 67, 110–13 (1960).

specificity." [2] Such narrow, clear statutes are more likely to reflect the considered judgment of the legislature that certain speech activities must be regulated.[3] Moreover there is a special danger of tolerating in the first amendment area "the existence of a penal statute susceptible of sweeping and improper application. . . . These freedoms are delicate and vulnerable, as well as supremely precious in our society. The threat of sanctions may deter their exercise almost as potently as the actual application of sanctions." [4] As a result the doctrine consists of a strict prohibition of statutes which burden speech in terms that are so vague as either to allow including protected speech in the prohibition or leaving an individual without clear guidance as to the nature of speech for which he can be punished.[5]

One case illustrating the use of the vagueness doctrine is *Smith v. Goguen*,[6] where appellee had been convicted of violating a state flag-misuse statute for sewing a small United States flag to the seat of his pants.[7] Under the statute an individual who "publicly mutilates, tramples upon, defaces or treats contemptuously the flag of the United States . . . " was subject to criminal liability.[8] The Supreme Court held the statutory language was void for vagueness under the fourteenth amendment due process clause.[9] Justice Powell, writing the opinion

for the Court, explained that the void for vagueness doctrine:

> incorporates the notions of fair notice or warning. . . . [I]t requires legislatures to set reasonably clear guidelines for law enforcement officials and triers of fact in order to prevent "arbitrary and discriminatory enforcement." Where a statute's literal scope, unaided by a narrowing state court interpretation, is capable of reaching expression sheltered by the First Amendment, the doctrine demands a greater degree of specificity than in other contexts.[10]

The flag-misuse state was vague because no clear distinction had been made between what type of treatment of the flag was or was not criminal.[11] In addition to the statute's failure to provide any warning or notice, the standard of "contemptuous treatment of the flag" was found to be so ambiguous that police, judges and juries were able to determine what actions were contemptuous on the basis of their personal preferences.[12] This lack of ascertainable standards for defining "treats contemptuously" violated the due process clause.[13]

Powell concluded there was no reason to give police and courts such broad discretion as to what constitutes flag contempt. Flag etiquette changes from generation to generation, he noted, making it necessary for the legislature to specify what behavior has been outlawed.[14]

---

2. NAACP v. Button, 371 U.S. 415, 433 (1963), citing Cantwell v. Connecticut, 310 U.S. 296, 311 (1940). See generally, Schauer, Fear, Risk and the First Amendment: Unraveling the "Chilling Effect," 58 Boston U.L.Rev. 685 (1978).

3. But Cf. NAACP v. Button, 371 U.S. 415, 432–33 (1963): "The objectionable quality of vagueness and overbreadth does not depend upon absence of fair notice to a criminally accused or upon unchanneled delegation of legislative powers. . . ."

4. NAACP v. Button, 371 U.S. 415, 433 (1963) (footnote omitted).

5. State v. Princess Cinema of Wisconsin, Inc., 96 Wis.2d 646, 292 N.W.2d 807, 813 (1980) (Day, J., citing an earlier edition of this work).

6. 415 U.S. 566 (1974). See also, Erznoznik v. City of Jacksonville, 422 U.S. 205 (1975); Hynes v. Mayor and Council of Oradell, 425 U.S. 610 (1976).

7. 415 U.S. at 568–70.

8. 415 U.S. at 568–69.

9. 415 U.S. at 572.

10. 415 U.S. at 572–73 (footnotes omitted).

11. 415 U.S. at 574.

12. 415 U.S. at 575.

13. 415 U.S. at 578.

14. 415 U.S. at 581–82.

See also, e.g., City of Mesquite v. Alladin's Castle, Inc., 455 U.S. 283, 291, (1982) (city ordinance directing police chief to consider whether applicant for license to operate coin-operated amusement establishment has any "connections with criminal elements" is not unconstitutionally vague because the applicant's possible connection with criminal elements is merely a subject that the ordinance directs the Police Chief to investigate before he makes his recommendation to the City Manager; the test—"connections with criminal elements"—is not used as the standard by the City Man-

D. The Least Restrictive Means Test

Even if the legislative purpose is a legitimate one of substantial governmental interest, "that purpose cannot be pursued by means that broadly stifle fundamental personal liberties when the end can be more narrowly achieved. The breadth of legislative abridgement must be viewed in the light of less drastic means for achieving the same basic purpose."[1] The least restrictive means test has also been applied in non-speech areas, such as state regulation affecting interstate commerce,[2] but it is particularly important to the free speech area.

Shelton v. Tucker[3] is an important case illustrating the doctrine of least restrictive means. In *Shelton* each Arkansas teacher was required by statute to file an annual affidavit listing all organizations to which he belonged or contributed in the last five years. Petitioner Shelton and others refused to file an affidavit and his teaching contract was not renewed. The trial showed that he was not a member of the Communist Party or any organization advocating the overthrow by force of the Government, but he was a member of the NAACP. The trial court found the information requested in the affidavit relevant.

The Supreme Court readily agreed that the state had an interest in investigating the competence and fitness of its teachers[4] but the Arkansas statute went well beyond its legitimate purposes. The information filed under the statute was not kept confidential, allowing public exposure and risks of offending superiors by belonging to an unpopular group. Moreover the state disclosure requirement was "completely unlimited."[5] The teacher was required to list any associational tie—social, professional, religious, avocational—and his financial support, even though many such relationships had no possible bearing on the teacher's occupational fitness. The "unlimited and indiscriminate sweep of the statute" went "far beyond what might be justified in the exercise of the State's legitimate inquiry into the fitness and competence of its teachers"[6] and thus it was struck down.[7]

IV. "CLEAR AND PRESENT DANGER" AND THE ADVOCACY OF VIOLENCE OR OTHER ILLEGAL CONDUCT

A. Introduction

First amendment guarantees prohibiting Congress from passing laws abridging speech, press, or peaceful assembly have never been treated as absolute by the Supreme Court. In spite of the possibility of reading the first amendment literally, the Court has preferred the view that in certain situations an individual's rights to freely express his or her beliefs must be subordinated to other interests of society.[1] Yet a will-

---

ager for approval or disapproval of the application: "The Federal Constitution does not preclude a city from giving vague or ambiguous directions to officials who are authorized to make investigations and recommendations."); Village of Hoffman Estates v. Flipside, Hoffman Estates, Inc., 456 U.S. 489 (1982) (Court rejected pre-enforcement challenge, on its face, to city ordinance requiring a business to obtain a license if it sells any items "designed or marketed for use with illegal drugs;" the Court rejected challenges based on vagueness, overbreadth, and free speech).

Contrast Kolender v. Lawson, 103 S.Ct. 1855 (1983) (Court, distinguishing *Flipside*, invalidated, on grounds of vagueness, state statute requiring "credible and reliable" identification of persons found to loiter or wander on the streets; the statute gave too much discretion to the police and thus allowed the police to interfere with freedom of movement).

1. Shelton v. Tucker, 364 U.S. 479, 488 (1960) (footnotes omitted). See also Schneider v. State, 308 U.S. 147, 161, 165 (1939); American Communications Ass'n v. Douds, 339 U.S. 382 (1950); Louisiana ex rel. Gremillion v. NAACP, 366 U.S. 293 (1961); NAACP v. Alabama, 377 U.S. 288, 307–08 (1963); Talley v. California, 362 U.S. 60 (1960).

2. See, e.g., Dean Milk Co. v. Madison, 340 U.S. 349 (1951).

3. 364 U.S. 479 (1960).

4. 364 U.S. 479, 485 (1960).

5. 364 U.S. 479, 488 (1960).

6. 364 U.S. 479, 490 (1960).

7. Another example of a recent case employing the least restrictive means test is Virginia State Bd. of Pharmacy v. Virginia Citizens Council, Inc., 425 U.S. 748 (1976).

1. Whitney v. United States, 274 U.S. 357, 375–376 (1927) (Brandeis, J., concurring).

ingness to balance first amendment rights against other interests has not diminished the importance of the first amendment, for the prevailing view is that the Constitution has placed the burden of reconciling the conflicting interests of the individual and society on the Court.[2] One of the standards the Supreme Court first developed to justify abridgement of freedom of expression for the benefit of society is the "clear and present danger" test.

There are three phases in the development of the "clear and present danger" doctrine. The test originated in a number of opinions and dissents written by Justice Holmes and Justice Brandeis dealing primarily with the Espionage and Sedition Acts of World War I. In the second phase, when the Cold War was at its height, a later generation of Supreme Court Justices and federal judges, including Chief Justice Vinson and Judge Learned Hand, applied the "clear and present danger" doctrine in a manner restricting first amendment freedoms more severely than Holmes and Brandeis contemplated. This restrictive approach influenced the Court to develop a "balancing test" for protecting freedom of expression.[3] Finally, in the 1960's the Supreme Court has attempted to breathe new life into the doctrine and, as we shall see, has formulated a more strict test, but with strong historical origins in the original clear and present danger standard. This most recent test is more protective of free speech.

B. The Holmes-Brandeis "Clear and Present Danger" Test

1. The Origins and Development

From the time the first amendment was ratified until just prior to World War I the Supreme Court had little exposure to freedom of expression issues. Except for the passage of the 1798 Alien and Sedition Acts [4] Congress followed the First Amendment directive that "Congress shall make no law" restricting free speech, assembly or press, but Congressional adherence to the literal meaning of the amendment was abandoned when the United States involvement in World War I met with vocal resistance. Congress in response to the domestic political unrest passed the Espionage Act of 1917 [5] and the Sedition Act of 1918.[6] This legislation provided the Supreme Court with the opportunity to develop standards for approaching first amendment questions at a time when the climate was not conducive to an expansive reading of the free speech guarantee.

In 1919, the year that first saw the Palmer raids,[7] the Supreme Court handed down two important decisions involving free speech issues, *Schenck v. United States* [8] and *Abrams v. United States.*[9] In these decisions the Court first discussed "clear and present danger" theory. In *Schenck* the appellants' conviction for conspiracy to violate the Espionage Act of 1917 was affirmed. Appellants had mailed leaflets to men eligible for military service asserting that the

2. Emerson, Toward a General Theory of the First Amendment, 72 Yale L.J. 877, 905 (1963).

3. For discussions of the balancing test, see generally, Dennis v. United States, 341 U.S. 494, 517 (1951) (J. Frankfurter concurring); Emerson, Toward a General Theory of the First Amendment, 72 Yale L.J. 877, at 912–14 (1963).

4. Alien Act of June 25, 1798, ch. 58, 1 Stat. 570. Sedition Act of July 14, 1798, ch. 74, 1 Stat. 596.

5. Espionage Act of June 15, 1917, ch. 30, 40 Stat. 217.

6. Sedition Act of May 16, 1918, ch. 75, 40 Stat. 553.

7. See, e.g., A. Kelly & W. Harbison, The American Constitution: Its Origins and Development 690 (1970):

"In 1919 a great Red scare began, inspired by Communist successes in Russia and central Europe. This fear was aggravated by the activities of a few bomb-throwing anarchists and of the Industrial Workers of the World. . . . In January 1919, Attorney-General A. Mitchell Palmer launched a gigantic two-year Red hunt, highlighted by mass arrests without benefit of habeas corpus, by hasty prosecutions, and by mass deportation of Communists and other radicals."

8. 249 U.S. 47 (1919).

9. 250 U.S. 616 (1919).

draft violated the thirteenth amendment.[10] These leaflets, the government argued, were prohibited by provisions in the Espionage Act forbidding obstruction of military recruiting.

Justice Holmes, writing for the Court, upheld the convictions and the restraint on freedom of expression as necessary to prevent grave and immediate threats to national security. Ordinarily, Holmes, believed, the leaflets would have been constitutionally protected but:

> [T]he character of every act depends upon the circumstances in which it is done. . . . The most stringent protection of free speech would not protect a man in falsely shouting fire in a theater and causing a panic. It does not even protect a man from an injunction against uttering words that may have all the effect of force. . . . The question in every case is whether the words used are used in such circumstances and are of such a nature as to create a clear and present danger that they will bring about the substantive evils that Congress has a right to prevent. It is a question of proximity and degree.[11]

Holmes concluded that first amendment protection could not be extended during war-

time to protect speech hindering the war effort.[12]

In a dissenting opinion in *Abrams v. United States*,[13] Holmes further explained his "clear and present danger" test. The appellants were convicted of conspiracy to violate the Espionage Acts amendments which prohibited speech encouraging resistance to the war effort and curtailment of production "with intent to cripple or hinder the United States in the prosecution of the war." [14] They had distributed pamphlets criticizing the United States' involvement in the effort to crush Russia's new Communist Government.

The majority in *Abrams* was unimpressed with Holmes' clear and present danger test as outlined in *Schenck*, and affirmed without being much concerned at all with the free speech interests involved.[15] Because of the "bad tendency" of the defendants' speech, the majority affirmed, even though the defendants' sentences were twenty years.[16] Under the majority's use of the bad tendency test, speech could be prohibited if it was of a type that would tend to bring about harmful results.

---

10. 249 U.S. at 49–51.

11. Id. at 52. See generally, Bogen, The Free Speech Metamorphasis of Mr. Justice Holmes, 11 Hofstra L.Rev. 97 (1982). Cf. Ragan, Justice Oliver Wendell Holmes, Jr., Zechariah Chafee, Jr., and the Clear and Present Danger Test for Free Speech: The First Year, 1919, 58 J.Am.Hist. 24 (1971).

12. One week after writing the *Schenck* opinion Holmes wrote two other opinions for the Court affirming convictions in similar cases. In Frohwerk v. United States, 249 U.S. 204 (1919) he stated that: "[T]he First Amendment while prohibiting legislation against free speech as such cannot have been, and obviously was not, intended to give immunity for every possible use of language. . . . Whatever might be thought of the other counts on the evidence, if it were before us, we have decided in Schenck v. United States, that a person may be convicted of a conspiracy to obstruct recruiting by words of persuasion." 249 U.S. at 206.

In Debs v. United States, 249 U.S. 211 (1919) Holmes affirmed the conviction of Eugene Debs, a prominent Socialist of the time, for allegedly encouraging listeners to obstruct the recruiting service. Holmes in this case spoke more in common law speech terms which were adopted later by the Court (but not by Holmes) in the *Abrams* and *Gitlow* cases discussed below. Holmes said in the *Debs* case:

"We should add that the jury were most carefully instructed that they could not find the defendant guilty for advocacy of any of his opinions unless the words used had as *their natural tendency and reasonably probable effect* to obstruct the recruiting service, &c., and unless the defendant had the specific intent to do so in his mind."

249 U.S. at 216 (emphasis added).

13. 250 U.S. 616, 624 (1919).

14. Espionage Act of June 15, 1917, ch. 30, 40 Stat. 217, as amended May 16, 1918, 40 Stat. 553.

15. The United States at this time was at war with Germany, not Russia. The actual statute involved forbade conspiracies to interfere with production with the intent to hinder the prosecution of the war. The theory of the trial court and the Supreme Court majority was that to reduce arms production for the Russian fight might aid Germany (with whom the United States was at war) because the United States would have less total arms. The Court did not require any specific intent by defendants. 250 U.S. at 621: "Men must be held to have intended, and to be accountable for, the effects which their acts were likely to produce." The free speech defense was very briefly dismissed as "sufficiently discussed and is definitely negatived in *Schenck* . . ." and other cases. 250 U.S. at 619.

16. 250 U.S. at 629.

Holmes criticized the Court's decision to uphold the conviction arguing that it was ridiculous to assume these pamphlets would actually hinder the government's war efforts in Germany, with which the United States was at war; as a matter of statutory construction Holmes would have reversed the convictions. But he also quickly moved to consider the constitutional issues. Holmes contended that the government could only restrict freedom of expression when there was "present danger of immediate evil or an intent to bring it about . . . Congress certainly cannot forbid all effort to change the mind of the country." [17] Laws regulating free speech, Holmes conceded, would be an effective way for the government to stifle opposition, but he maintained hope that people would realize that:

> the ultimate good desired is better reached by free trade in ideas—that the best test of truth is the power of thought to get itself accepted in the competition of the market. . . . That . . . is the theory of our Constitution.[18]

Holmes warned against overzealous repression of unpopular ideas:

> [W]e should be eternally vigilant against attempts to check the expression of opinions that we loathe and believe to be fraught with death, unless they so imminently threaten immediate interference with the lawful and pressing purposes of the law that an immediate check is required to save the country.[19]

Holmes concluded that the appellants had been unjustly convicted for exercising their first amendment rights.

Six years later the Court continued to use the bad tendency test and remained reluctant to apply the clear and present danger doctrine in the manner Justice Holmes intended. The appellants in *Gitlow v. New York* [20] were convicted of violating New York's "criminal anarchy statute" which prohibited advocating violent overthrow of the government. They had printed and circulated a radical manifesto encouraging political strikes. There was no evidence that the manifesto had any effect on the individuals who received copies.

The majority of the Court upheld the conviction and the statute, finding the "clear and present danger test" inapplicable. The Court reasoned that only when a statute prohibits particular acts without including any restrictions on language should the "clear and present danger" standard be employed to determine if the particular speech should be constitutionally protected. In such a case the government must prove the defendants' language brought about the statutorily prohibited result.[21] But in *Gitlow*, the Court noted that the legislature had already determined what utterances would violate the statute. The government's decision that certain words are likely to cause the substantive evil "is not open for consideration." [22] The government must then show only that there is a reasonable basis for the statute. It is irrelevant that the particular words do or do not create a "clear and present danger." [23]

Holmes and Brandeis dissented. Holmes wrote that if the "clear and present danger"

Disquieting echoes of the majority's bad tendency test are found in Haig v. Agee, 453 U.S. 280 (1981). There the majority upheld the power of the Secretary of State to revoke the passport of Agee, a former CIA agent engaged in a policy of exposing clandestine CIA agents abroad. In rejecting Agee's first amendment claims the majority said: "Agee's disclosures, among other things, have the declared purpose of obstructing intelligence operations and the recruiting of intelligence personnel. They are clearly not protected by the Constitution." 453 U.S. at 308–09. Note the similarities with Abrams v. United States, 250 U.S. 616, 620–21 (1919): "The purpose of this [published article] was to persuade the persons to whom it was addressed to turn a deaf ear to patriotic appeals in behalf of the Govern-

ment of the United States, and to cease to render it assistance in the prosecution of the war."

17. 250 U.S. at 628.

18. Id. at 630.

19. Id. at 630.

20. 268 U.S. 652 (1925).

21. Id. at 670–71.

22. Id. at 670.

23. Id. at 671. Accord, Bork, Neutral Principles and Some First Amendment Problems, 47 Ind.L.J. 1, 23 (1971).

test was properly applied it would be obvious there was no real danger that the appellants' pamphlets would instigate political revolution. If the manifesto presented an immediate threat to the stability of the government then there would be a need for suppression.[24] But in the absence of immediate danger, Holmes concluded, the appellants were entitled to exercise their first amendment rights.

Two years later, in 1927, the "clear and present danger" test made its appearance once again, but this time at least it was in a concurrence. In *Whitney v. California*,[25] the Court affirmed the conviction of Mrs. Whitney for violating the California Criminal Syndicalism Act by assisting in the organization of the Communist Labor Party of California. The statute defined criminal syndicalism as any doctrine "advocating teaching or aiding and abetting . . . crime, sabotage . . . or unlawful acts of force and violence" to effect political or economic change.[26]

Whitney contended that she had argued at the organizing convention for political reform through the democratic process. The majority of the convention, however, supported change through violence and terrorism. She maintained that she had not assisted the Communist Party with knowledge of its illegal purpose; her conviction was based on her presence at the convention and consequently she alleged deprivation of liberty without due process.[27] The Court held the jury had resolved adversely to her the question of fact regarding her participation at the convention, that the united action of the Communist Party threatened the welfare of the state, and Mrs. Whitney was a part of that organization.[28] The conviction was affirmed.

The concurring opinion by Justice Brandeis was joined in by Justice Holmes. But while the opinion was labelled a "concurrence" it read like a dissent. Brandeis specifically objected to any notion, first presented in *Gitlow*, that the enactment of a statute foreclosed the application of the clear and present danger test by the Court. "[T]he enactment of the statute cannot alone establish the facts which are essential to its validity." [29]

He then proceeded to justify the clear and present danger test. In language perhaps a little more restrained than Holmes had used, he argued that the "state is, *ordinarily*, denied the power to prohibit dissemination of social, economic and political doctrine which a vast majority of its citizens believe to be false and fraught with evil consequence." [30] The framers "valued liberty both as an end and as a means. They believed liberty to be the secret of happiness and courage to be the secret of liberty." [31] Brandeis also argued that public order was secured by free speech. "[R]epression breeds hate; . . . hate menaces stable government; . . . the path of safety lies in the opportunity to discuss freely supposed grievances and proposed remedies . . . ." [32] Parts of Brandeis' concurrence appeared to place strong emphasis on the need to show incitement:

> "But even advocacy of [law] violation however reprehensible morally, is not a justification for denying free speech where the advocacy falls short of incitement and there is nothing to indicate that the advocacy would be immediately acted on. . . . [N]o danger flowing from speech can be deemed clear and present, unless the incidence of the evil apprehended is so imminent that it may befall before there is opportunity for full discussion." [33]

---

24. 268 U.S. at 673.

25. 274 U.S. 357 (1927).

26. Id. at 359–360.

27. Id. at 363–67.

28. Id. at 367–72.

29. 274 U.S. at 374 (Brandeis, J., concurring). See generally, R. Rotunda, ed., Six Justices on Civil Rights 161–71 (Nathanson, "The Philosophy of Mr. Justice Brandeis and Civil Liberties Today") (Oceana Publications, Inc. 1983).

30. Id. (emphasis added).

31. Id. at 375.

32. Id.

33. Id. at 376–77.

Only when speech causes unthinking, immediate action is the protection of the first amendment withdrawn.

Brandeis then concluded that in situations where the rights of free speech and assembly were infringed the defendant may contest this suppression alleging that no "clear and present danger" actually existed. Mrs. Whitney should have argued her conviction was void because no "clear and present danger" of a serious evil resulted from the convention activities. Instead Whitney had challenged her conviction on the basis of denial of due process; therefore, Brandeis was unable to pass on the "clear and present danger" issue.[34] Brandeis' concurrence was a dissent in all but name, upholding the conviction only on this narrow procedural ground. But calling the opinion a concurrence perhaps lent a little more authority to the doctrine which Holmes and Brandeis were unsuccessfully urging.

While the Supreme Court, in a few cases during this period, did reverse convictions of speech advocacy, it did not do so under the clear and present danger rationale.[35] Finally, the Holmes doctrine of "clear and present danger was relied on in a majority opinion in *Herndon v. Lowry*,[36] a 5 to 4 decision. The Court reversed a conviction for violating a statute prohibiting attempts to incite insurrection, in effect rejecting the *Gitlow* test.

The Court held that a state could not restrict words which had a "tendency" to be dangerous. Power to abridge individual rights to freely express themselves "even of utterances of a defined character must find its justification in a reasonable apprehension of danger to organized government." [37]

Almost immediately after using the doctrine the Court began to expand its application. For a few years, the "clear and present danger" test was employed in a number of cases, not involving sedition, challenging the constitutionality of governmental suppression of free expression.[38] Perhaps the most important of these cases—and the type of speech to which the "clear and present danger" language is applied to this day—involved a series of contempt-of-court decisions. It is to that issue we now turn. Outside of these contempt of court cases the Court has developed different tests to determine when governmental restraints may be placed on different types of speech.[39]

2. *Present Application in the Contempt of Court Cases*

Originally, in contempt of court cases, the Court had held that any spoken or printed criticism of courts obstructed the administration of justice and therefore was not con-

---

34. Id. at 379.

35. In Fiske v. Kansas, 274 U.S. 380 (1927), decided immediately after the *Whitney* decision, the Court—in a decision written not by Justice Holmes but by Justice Sanford—reversed a conviction of a member of the Industrial Workers of the World under the Kansas Criminal Syndicalism Act. The test of *Whitney* was applied; the State simply did not meet it:

"The result is that the Syndicalism Act has been applied in this case to sustain the conviction of the defendant, without any charge or evidence that the organization in which he secured members advocated any crime, violence or other unlawful acts or methods as a means of effecting industrial or political changes or revolution." 274 U.S. at 387.

The simple reference in the I.W.W.'s Constitution to a class struggle was insufficient.

Several years later, in Stromberg v. California, 283 U.S. 359 (1931), the Court, in an opinion by Chief Justice Hughes, reversed, on vagueness grounds, a convic-

tion under California's statute forbidding the display of the red flag for various reasons, including display "as a sign, symbol and emblem of opposition to organized government . . . ." Id. at 361.

36. 301 U.S. 242 (1937). Cf. DeJonge v. Oregon, 299 U.S. 353 (1937) (peaceable assembly for lawful discussion cannot be made a crime; the Court talked of the need to show incitement; id. at 359–65).

37. 301 U.S. at 258.

38. Thornhill v. Alabama, 310 U.S. 88 (1940) (peaceful picketing); Cantwell v. Connecticut, 310 U.S. 296, 308 (power of state to punish clear and present danger of riot) (1940); West Virginia State Bd. of Education v. Barnette, 319 U.S. 624 (1941) (flag salutes); Terminiello v. Chicago, 337 U.S. 1, 4–5 (1949) (breach of the peace).

39. For a modern defense of the clear and present danger standard, see Redish, Advocacy of Unlawful Conduct and the First Amendment: In Defense of Clear and Present Danger, 70 Calif.L.Rev. 1159 (1982).

stitutionally protected.[1] In *Bridges v. California*,[2] however, a contempt case, Justice Black writing for the majority applied the "clear and present danger" test stating "the substantive evil must be extremely serious and the degree of imminence extremely high before utterances can be punished."[3] The petitioners' statements criticizing pending court proceedings were not likely, Black reasoned, to bring about a "substantive evil" requiring abridgement of free expression.[4]

The Court struck down another contempt conviction in *Pennekamp v. Florida*[5] holding that the danger to be avoided, interference with the administration of justice, was not a clear and immediate enough danger to justify suppressing public comment. The Court also set aside a contempt citation for publishing inaccurate articles criticizing procedures in a trial, in *Craig v. Harney*,[6] where it held:

> The vehemence of the language used is not alone the measure of the power to punish for contempt. The fires which it kindles must constitute an imminent, and not merely a likely, threat to the administration of justice. The danger must not be remote or even probable; it must immediately imperil.[7]

Later in *Nebraska Press Association v. Stuart*[8] the Court used the language of "clear and present danger" and reversed a court order restraining reporters from publishing allegedly prejudicial pretrial material.

The application of the test to contempt of court cases perhaps indicated that the Court intended to employ the "clear and present danger" standard as a general test for determining the constitutionality of restrictions on speech.[9] However, outside of the contempt of court cases, different tests had to be developed to evaluate the competing interests where the governmental restraints are placed on different types of speech, such as obscenity or defamation. Even in cases involving the advocacy of violence, breach of the peace, or criminal syndicalism, the "clear and present danger" test was to undergo revision, though the historical debt to Holmes and Brandeis is unmistakable.

C. Revision of the "Clear and Present Danger" Test

In the early 1950's the Supreme Court decided to reexamine the validity of the Holmes-Brandeis "clear and present danger" doctrine. With the advent of the cold war and the McCarthy paranoia, freedom of expression, especially speech or actions criticizing the government or threatening national security, was severely restricted. The tone of the times was reflected in the Court's opinions, as it managed to avoid direct confrontation with the other branches of government over these issues.

Petitioners in *Dennis v. United States*[1] were convicted of violating the Smith Act by

---

1. Toledo Newspaper Co. v. United States, 247 U.S. 402 (1918). This history is reflected in Canon 20 ("Newspaper Discussion of Pending Litigation"), American Bar Association, Canons of Professional Ethics (1908, amended), and also in D.R. 7–107 ("Trial Publicity"), American Bar Association, Model Code of Professional Responsibility (1970, as amended). See also, id., D.R. 1–102(A)(5) (a lawyer shall not "engage in conduct that is prejudicial to the administration of justice").

These broad restrictions have come under constitutional attack. See, e.g., Chicago Council of Lawyers v. Bauer, 522 F.2d 242 (7th Cir. 1975), cert. denied sub nom. Cunningham v. Chicago Council of Lawyers, 427 U.S. 912 (1976); Hirschkop v. Snead, 594 F.2d 356 (4th Cir. 1979) (per curiam). See generally, T. Morgan & R. Rotunda, Professional Responsibility: Problems and Materials 310–18 (2d ed. 1981).

2. 314 U.S. 252 (1941).

3. Id. at 263.

4. Id. at 270, 278.

5. 328 U.S. 331, 350 (1946).

6. 331 U.S. 367 (1947).

7. Id. at 376.

8. 427 U.S. 539, 562–63 (1976), citing United States v. Dennis, 183 F.2d 201, 212 (2d Cir. 1950) (L. Hand, J.), aff'd 341 U.S. 494 (1951). Cf. 427 U.S. at 569 (1976).

See Landmark Communications, Inc. v. Virginia, 435 U.S. 829, 844 (1978), noting that older cases have shown that out of court comments concerning pending cases or grand jury investigations do not constitute a clear and present danger to the administration of justice and cannot be punished by contempt.

9. See Strong, Fifty Years of "Clear and Present Danger": From Schenck to Brandenburg—And Beyond, 1969 Sup.Ct.Rev. 41, 52.

1. 341 U.S. 494 (1951).

conspiring to organize the Communist Party of the United States. The party's goal allegedly was to overthrow the existing government by force and violence. There was no majority opinion in this case. Chief Justice Vinson, writing for himself and three other justices, indicated Congress possessed the power to promulgate laws restricting speech. The issue the Court had to decide, thought Vinson, was whether the means Congress employed in suppressing free expression conflicted with first amendment guarantees. He believed the questions would most effectively be resolved by applying the "clear and present danger" test.[2] But that test, as he construed it, meant much less than the original Holmes-Brandeis theory. It contained two steps. First, the Government had to show a substantial interest in limiting the speech. Congress, the Court held, did have a substantial interest here in preventing violent overthrow of the government. Second, the words or actions restricted in the legislation must be shown to constitute a "clear and present danger." Vinson's theory of "clear and present danger" was decidedly different from that of Holmes and Brandeis:

> [T]he words cannot mean that before the Government may act, it must wait until the *putsch* is about to be executed. . . . If Government is aware that a group aiming at its overthrow is attempting to indoctrinate its members . . . action by the Government is required. . . . Certainly an attempt to overthrow the Government by force, even though doomed from the outset because of inadequate numbers or power of the revolutionists, is a sufficient evil for Congress to prevent.[3]

Speech which advocates more extreme dangers, such as overthrow of the Government, may be prohibited even though the danger is more remote. Vinson contended it was no longer realistic to assert that probability of success should be the basis of determining whether the danger is clear and present. The Court adopted the lower court's interpretation of the rule, quoting Chief Judge Learned Hand:

> In each case [courts] must ask whether the gravity of the "evil," discounted by its improbability, justifies such invasion of free speech as is necessary to avoid danger.[4]

In other words, the greater the gravity of the act advocated, the less clear and present danger needed to justify governmental intrusion. So rephrased, the clear and present danger test became a disguised balancing test which weighed the seriousness of the danger against competing interest in free speech. Petitioners' conspiracy to advocate revolution, even though it was merely in a preparatory stage, was held to create "clear and present" danger.

> It is the existence of conspiracy which creates the danger. . . . If the ingredients of the reaction are present, we cannot bind the Government to wait until the catalyst is added.[5]

As one commentator has noted, the Vinson-Hand reformulation of clear and present danger meant that in practice "any radical political doctrine would receive little or no protection, since it would always appear as a threat to the nation and thus as the most serious of all possible evils. This is simply the remote bad tendency test dressed in modern style."[6] Under traditional criminal conspiracy law the Government could always prosecute a criminal agreement coupled with some overt act. Such an indictment, which places on the Government the burden of proving the elements of a traditional conspiracy, does not require that the "putsch is about to be executed" nor raise substantial free speech problems.[7] But the strategy of

---

2. Id. at 501–505.

3. Id. at 509.

4. Id. at 510, citing 183 F.2d 201, 212 (2d Cir. 1950).

5. Id. at 511.

6. Shapiro, Freedom of Speech: The Supreme Court and Judicial Review 65 (1966). The author also notes that the *Dennis* test is even less hospitable to free

speech than the bad tendency test since it "considers the gravity of the evil discounted by *its* improbability— not the improbability that the speech in question will bring the evil about, but that it will occur from any cause." Id. (emphasis in original).

7. Nathanson, The Communist Trial and the Clear-and-Present-Danger Test, 63 Harv.L.Rev. 1167, 1172–1173 (1950).

the Government approved by the *Dennis* Court was in effect to replace the burden of showing conspiracy with the much lighter burden of showing tendencies and probabilities.

Justice Frankfurter concurred in the affirmance but criticized the clear and present danger test as too inflexible:

> The demands of free speech in a democratic society as well as the interest in national security are better served by candid and informal weighing of the competing interests, within the confines of the judicial process.[8]

He would have not affirmed the convictions in the *Gitlow* case because the circumstances then did not justify serious concern, but he thought that the conspiracy the Government faced in 1951 justified the legislative judgment that saw a substantial threat to national order and security. He advocated acceptance of a "balancing" test to determine the constitutionality of speech restrictions as a replacement for the now vague clear and present danger theory.

In *Yates v. United States*[9] the Supreme Court strove to retreat from the broad doctrine of the *Dennis* decision. Yates and other Communist party officials were convicted for conspiring to "advocate and teach the necessity of overthrowing the federal government by violence" and organizing the Communist party to carry out this revolution in violation of the Smith Act.[10] The Supreme Court held that the trial court had incorrectly interpreted the *Dennis* precedent.

In the Court's opinion, Justice Harlan indicated the District Court had "apparently thought that *Dennis* obliterated the traditional dividing line between advocacy of abstract doctrine and advocacy of action."[11]

Relying on the *Dennis* decision, the trial court had refused to instruct the jury that the statute prohibited advocacy actually inciting violent revolution and actions but not a mere abstract doctrine of forcible overthrow.[12] It was apparent from legislative history that Congress intended the Smith Act to be "aimed at the advocacy and teaching of concrete action for forcible overthrow of the Government, and not at principles divorced from action," the Supreme Court ruled.[13]

The essence of the *Dennis* holding, Harlan stated, was that teaching and preparing a group for immediate or future violent action are not constitutionally protected, if it is reasonable to believe based upon the circumstances, size, and commitment of the group that the action or revolution will occur:

> *Dennis* was . . . not concerned with a conspiracy to engage at some future time in seditious advocacy, but rather with a conspiracy to advocate presently the taking of forcible action in the future. It was action not advocacy, that was to be postponed until "circumstances" would "permit."[14]

Harlan concluded the petitioners' statements advocated a philosophy and did not incite action. Without evidence of any actual action or possibility of action the Court would not affirm the convictions.[15]

But the *Yates* decision did not spell the end to Communist membership prosecutions. In *Scales v. United States*[16] the Court affirmed the petitioners' conviction for violating the membership clause of the Smith Act.[17] The trial court found the petitioners were active members of the Communist Party who were aware of the illegality of their

---

8. 341 U.S. at 524–25 (Frankfurter, J., concurring).

9. 354 U.S. 298 (1957).

10. 18 U.S.C.A. §§ 371, 2385.

11. 354 U.S. at 315–318.

12. Id. at 312–313.

13. Id. at 319–320.

14. Id. at 324.

15. *Yates* reversed the conviction of five defendants and remanded for retrial as to the remaining nine; the

charges against these nine were dismissed at the request of the Government, which found that it could not meet the tougher evidentiary requirements set out in *Yates.* Mollan, Smith Act Prosecutions: The Effect of the Dennis and Yates Decisions, 26 U.Pitt.L.Rev. 705, 732 (1965).

16. 367 U.S. 203 (1961).

17. 18 U.S.C.A. § 2385.

teachings and advocated violent revolution and overthrow of the government "as speedily as circumstances would permit." Justice Harlan, again writing the Court's opinion, upheld the lower court's findings, indicating its interpretation of the membership clause did not impute "guilt to an individual merely on the basis of his associations and sympathies." [18] This holding limited both the freedom of speech and of association. The freedom of association is implied from the express guarantees of the first amendment and is subject to the same standards as freedom of speech. Harlan emphasized that the Court's narrowing construction of the membership clause supported the constitutionality of the membership clause of the Smith Act:

> [T]he statute [as interpreted] is found to reach only "active" members having also a guilty knowledge and intent, and which therefore prevents a conviction on what otherwise might be regarded as merely an expression of sympathy with the alleged criminal enterprise, unaccompanied by any significant action in its support or any commitment to undertake such action.[19]

Though the record in *Scales* did not show advocacy of immediate violence, it did show present advocacy of future action for violent overthrow, which satisfied the limited requirements of *Dennis* and *Yates:*

> *Dennis* and *Yates* have definitely laid at rest any doubt that present advocacy of *future* action for violent overthrow satisfies statutory and constitutional requirements equally with advocacy of *immediate* action to that end. . . . [T]his record cannot be considered deficient because it contains no evidence of advocacy for immediate overthrow.[20]

Appellant's advocacy of violent revolution was intended to be a guide for future revolutionary action and consequently violated the Smith Act. If the record did not evidence support for at least advocacy of future action, the Court would dismiss the prosecution for Communist Party membership.[21] Justice Douglas dissented to this whole theory, arguing that "the essence of the crime . . . is merely belief," and the conviction was a "sharp break with traditional concepts of First Amendment rights." [22]

After the *Dennis* and *Yates* decisions the "clear and present danger" doctrine was rejected to a great extent by the Court.[23] The doctrine as defined by Holmes proved no longer to be a viable method for restricting governmental invasion of free expression. To many people the cold war threat of a communist takeover was a very real possibility. The requirement that the danger resulting from speech or action must be imminent before first amendment protection was denied was unsettling to those living in fear of communism,[24] and as a result the "balancing test" replaced the "clear and present danger" doctrine. The case law was ripe for the third phase of the clear and present danger test, for while the Holmes-Brandeis test was discarded, it had not been forgotten.

D. Current Status of the "Clear and Present Danger" Doctrine

The Holmes and Brandeis "clear and present danger" theory was refined during the late 1960's as the Court focused on protecting the unpopular advocacy of ideas. This modification of the Holmes-Brandeis theory was particularly apparent in three cases decided by the Court in the late 1960's: *Bond v. Floyd,*[1] *Watts v. United States,*[2] and *Brandenburg v. Ohio.*[3]

---

18. 367 U.S. at 220.

19. 367 U.S. at 228.

20. Id. at 251 (emphasis in original).

21. E.g. Noto v. United States, 367 U.S. 290 (1961) (conviction reversed).

22. 367 U.S. at 262–65.

23. Cf. Brennan, The Supreme Court and the Meiklejohn Interpretation of the First Amendment, 79 Harv.L.Rev. 1, 8 (1965).

24. Emerson, Toward a General Theory of the First Amendment, 72 Yale L.J. 877, 911 (1963).

1. 385 U.S. 116 (1966). See generally, J. Barron and C. Dienes, Handbook of Free Speech and Free Press 11–31 (1979).

2. 394 U.S. 705 (1969) (per curiam).

3. 395 U.S. 444 (1969) (per curiam).

Members of the Georgia House, in *Bond v. Floyd*,[4] challenged the right of a duly elected representative, Julian Bond, to be seated. Bond had publicly expressed his support of a statement issued by the Student Nonviolent Coordinating Committee (SNCC) criticizing the United States' involvement in Viet Nam and the operation of the draft laws.[5] The Georgia legislature conducted a special hearing to determine if Bond could in good faith take the mandatory oath to support the Constitution. At the hearing Bond argued he was willing and able to take his oath of office. He testified that though he supported individuals who burned their draft cards he had not burned his own or counseled anyone to burn their card.[6] The Georgia House voted not to administer the oath or seat Bond.

The Supreme Court held that the action of the Georgia House violated Bond's right of free expression.[7] Although the oath of office was constitutionally valid, Chief Justice Warren wrote, this requirement did not empower the majority of the representatives to challenge a duly elected legislator's sincerity in swearing allegiance to the Constitution. Such authority could be used to stifle dissents of legislators who disagreed with majority views.[8] Convicting Bond under the Selective Service Act for counseling or aiding persons to evade or refuse registration, Warren believed would have been unconstitutional. Bond's statements could not be interpreted "as a call to unlawful refusal to be drafted."[9] He actually appeared to have been advocating legal alternatives to the draft, not inciting people to violate the law. The Court, citing *Yates v. United States*,[10] concluded that Bond could not have been convicted for these statements consistently with the First Amendment.[11]

Traces of a "clear and present danger" analysis are also evident in *Watts v. United States*.[12] In a per curiam opinion the Supreme Court reversed the appellant's conviction for violating a statute prohibiting persons from "knowingly and willfully . . . threat[ening] to take the life of or to inflict bodily harm upon the President." Watts, during a public rally in Washington, D.C., stated he would not report for his scheduled draft physical, continuing:

> If they ever make me carry a rifle the first man I want to get in my sights is L.B.J. They are not going to make me kill my black brothers.[13]

On its face the statute was held constitutional: the nation certainly has a valid interest in protecting the President.

A statute criminalizing certain forms of pure speech must, however, "be interpreted with the commands of the First Amendment clearly in mind. What is a threat must be distinguished from what is . . . protected speech."[14] Watts' statement was held to be a "political hyperbole" and not a true threat. The Court maintained the nation was committed to unrestrained expression and debate, including criticism of the government and public officials.

> The language of the political arena . . . is often vituperative, abusive and inexact. [The petitioner's] . . . only offense here was "a kind of very crude offensive method of stating a political opposition to the President."[15]

Considering in context the conditional nature of the remarks and the fact the listeners had laughed at the statement, the words could only be interpreted as an expression of political belief. Had the circumstances of the speech amounted to incitement of violence, the Court's decision might have been different.

---

4. 385 U.S. 116 (1966).

5. Id. at 118–21.

6. Id. at 123–124. The constitutionality of federal laws punishing draft card burning was subsequently upheld by the Supreme Court. United States v. O'Brien, 391 U.S. 367 (1968).

7. 385 U.S. at 137.

8. Id. at 132.

9. Id. at 133.

10. 354 U.S. 298 (1957).

11. 385 U.S. at 134.

12. 394 U.S. 705 (1969) (per curiam).

13. Id. at 706.

14. Id. at 707.

15. Id. at 708.

The influence of the "clear and present danger" doctrine is obvious in both of these cases. The pivotal determination in *Bond* [16] was the fact that the appellant was merely expressing his grievances with the government, not inciting unlawful action. This distinction appeared to be based on the identical distinction made by Brandeis in his concurrence in *Whitney v. California*. [17] The petitioner's conviction in *Watts* [18] was reversed when the Court concluded the statement did not clearly present an imminent threat to the President.

Finally in the *Brandenburg v. Ohio*, [19] a per curiam opinion, the Warren Court seemed to follow the reasoning of "clear and present danger" as Holmes and Brandeis had originally interpreted the test, but with differences in phrasing and emphasis to assure that its protections would not be diluted. The Court in *Brandenburg* overruled the *Whitney* [20] decision, but without ever explicitly referring to the "clear and present danger" standard. However it completely supported and added new vigor to the reasoning of the Brandeis concurrence in *Whitney*, and eliminated the open-ended use of the test that prevailed in the "bad tendency" and "balancing" years.

The *Brandenburg* Court's per curiam opinion reversed the conviction of a Ku Klux Klan leader for violating Ohio's Criminal Syndicalism statute. The appellant had been charged with advocating political reform through violence and for assembling with a group formed to teach criminal syndicalism. A man identified as the appellant arranged for a television news crew to attend a Klan rally. During the news film made at the rally, Klan members, allegedly including Brandenburg, discussed the group's plan to march on Congress. [21]

The Court acknowledged a similar criminal syndicalism statute had been upheld in *Whitney*, but it recognized that later decisions discredited *Whitney*, and held advocacy of violence protected by the First Amendment as long as the advocacy did not incite people to *imminent* action. The Court then formulated the test for speech which advocates unlawful conduct: "[The state may not] forbid or proscribe advocacy of the use of force or of law violation except where such advocacy is directed to inciting or producing imminent lawless action and is likely to incite or produce such action." [22] Mere teaching of abstract doctrines, the Court noted, was not like leading a group in a violent action. Moreover, the statute must be narrowly drawn, and if it failed to distinguish between advocacy of a theory and advocacy of action, it abridged first amendment freedoms. [23]

Criminal syndicalism as defined in the Ohio statute could not meet the *Brandenburg* test. The statute forbade teaching of violent political revolution with the intent of spreading such doctrine or assembling with a group advocating this doctrine. At the appellant's trial no attempt was made to distinguish between incitement and advocacy. The statute consequently was held to be an abridgement of the First and Fourteenth Amendments. Any law punishing mere advocacy of Ku Klux Klan doctrine and assembly of Klan members to advocate their beliefs was unconstitutional. [24]

Justice Douglas concurred separately entering the caveat that there was no place for the "clear and present danger" test in any cases involving First Amendment rights. He was distrustful of the test, which he believed could be easily manipulated, as it was in *Dennis*, to deny constitutional protection

16. 385 U.S. 116 (1966).

17. 274 U.S. 357, 372–80 (1927) (Brandeis, J., concurring).

18. 394 U.S. 705 (1969) (per curiam).

19. 395 U.S. 444 (1969) (per curiam).

20. 274 U.S. 357 (1927).

21. 395 U.S. at 446.

22. 395 U.S. at 447 (footnote omitted).

23. Id. at 447–49.

24. Id. at 448–449.

to any speech critical of existing government.[25]

Brandenburg's new formulation appeared to offer broad new protection for strong advocacy. Its major focus is on the inciting language of the speaker, that is, on the objective words, in addition to the need to show not only that the speech is directed to produce immediate lawless action but that in fact the situation makes this purpose likely to be successful.[26]

Hess v. Indiana,[27] a post-Warren Court decision, indicates that the Court is serious and literal in its application of the test proposed in *Brandenburg.* Hess had been arrested and convicted for disorderly conduct when he shouted "we'll take the fucking street later (or again)" during an antiwar demonstration. Two witnesses testified Hess did not appear to exhort demonstrators to go into the street just cleared by the police, that he was facing the crowd, and that his tone of voice was not louder than any of the other demonstrators, although it was loud.[28] The Indiana Supreme Court upheld the trial court's finding that the remarks were intended to incite further riotous behavior and were likely to produce such a result, but the United States Supreme Court reversed, and in a per curiam opinion the Court stated:

> At best . . . the statement could be as counsel for present moderation; at worst it amounted to nothing more than advocacy of illegal action at some indefinite future time. This is not sufficient to permit the state to punish Hess' speech. Under our decisions, "the Constitutional guarantees of free speech and free press do not permit a state to forbid or proscribe advocacy of the use of force or of

law violation except where such advocacy is directed to inciting or producing *imminent* lawless action and is likely to incite or produce such action."[29]

The Court concluded that since Hess' speech was "not directed to any person or group of persons" Hess had not advocated action which would produce imminent disorder. His statements, therefore, did not violate the disorderly conduct statutes.[30]

Justice Rehnquist, joined by Chief Justice Burger and Justice Blackmun, strongly dissented. The dissent objected to the per curiam opinion's "somewhat antiseptic description of this massing" of people and preferred to rely on the decision of the trial court which was free to reject some testimony and accept other testimony. The majority, Justice Rehnquist claimed, was merely interpreting the evidence differently and thus exceeding the proper scope of review.[31]

The new *Brandenburg* test—a test more vigorously phrased and strictly applied than the older clear and present danger test—now probably appears to be the proper formula for determining when speech which advocates criminal conduct may constitutionally be punished. With its emphasis on incitement, imminent lawless action, and the objective words of the speaker, it should provide a strong measure of first amendment protection.

But the Court has yet to face the most troublesome question under this test. Should the Court confront a situation where a speaker advocates violence through the use of a speech which does not literally advocate action, such as Marc Antony's funeral oration for Caesar,[32] the majority might

---

25. Id. at 450–452. (Douglas, J., concurring). Justice Black also concurred separately, and similarly objected to the clear and present danger test as construed in *Dennis.* Id. at 449–450.

26. Gunther, Learned Hand and the Origins of Modern First Amendment Doctrine: Some Fragments of History, 27 Stan.L.Rev. 719 (1975).

27. 414 U.S. 105 (1973).

28. Id. at 106–107.

29. Id. at 108 (emphasis in original), citing Brandenburg v. Ohio, 395 U.S. 444, 447 (1969).

30. Id. at 108–109.

31. Id. at 109–112.

32. For example, the *Brandenburg* test would even appear to protect Marc Antony's funeral oration in Shakespeare's *Julius Caesar*, Act III, scene ii.

In National Broadcasting Co., Inc. v. Niemi, 434 U.S. 1354 (1978) (Rehnquist, Circuit Justice), the respondent sought damages from a television network and publisher for injuries allegedly inflicted upon her by persons acting under the stimulus of observing a scene of brutality broadcast in a television drama. The petitioners

be urged to look for proximity to violence rather than to the literal words of incitement.[33] However, only time will tell whether the Court will apply the test in a strict manner or whether it will be subject to the same periods of vague interpretation as was the old "clear and present danger" test.

V. PRIOR RESTRAINT OF POLITICAL SPEECH

A. The Distinction Between Prior Restraint and Subsequent Punishment of Speech

Since the expiration of the English licensing system in 1695 under which nothing could be published without prior approval of the church or state authorities,[1] prior restraint has been considered a more drastic infringement on free speech than subsequent punishment. Thomas M. Cooley's Treatise on Constitutional Limitations summarized the old law:

The constitutional liberty of speech and of the press, as we understand it, implies a right to freely utter and publish whatever the citizen may please, and to be protected against any responsibility for so doing, [but after he has done so he is not protected] so far as such publications, from their blasphemy, obscenity, or scandalous character, may be a public offense, or as by their falsehood and malice they may injuriously affect the standing, reputation, or pecuniary interests of individuals.[2]

Cooley's view of prior restraint reflected the prevailing view at the time of the first amendment's adoption. Blackstone's Commentaries was the harbinger of Cooley's restatement of the law:

The liberty of the press is indeed essential to the nature of a free state; but this consists in laying no *previous* restraints upon publications, and not in freedom from censure for criminal matter when published. . . . To subject the press to the restrictive power of a licenser, as was formerly done, both before and since the revolution, is to subject all freedom of sentiment to the prejudices of one man, and to make him the arbitrary and infallible judge of all controverted points in learning, religion and government. But to punish (as the law does at present) any dangerous or offensive writings, which, when published, shall on a fair and impartial trial be adjudged of a pernicious tendency, is necessary for the preservation of peace and good order, of government and religion, the only solid foundations of civil liberty.[3]

While it is no longer true that the first amendment means only freedom from prior restraint of speech, prior restraint is still considered to be more serious than subsequent punishment. As the modern Supreme Court has repeatedly recognized, "liberty of the press . . . has meant, principally al-

---

sought a stay of the state court order remanding for a trial. While Circuit Justice Rehnquist denied the stay for procedural reasons, he noted that the trial judge had rendered judgment for petitioners because he found that the film "did not advocate or encourage violent and depraved acts and thus did not constitute an incitement." 434 U.S. at 1356. The *Brandenburg* test would appear to be applicable to determine the free speech defense to plaintiff's tort claim.

33. Cf. NAACP v. Claiborne Hardware Co., 102 S.Ct. 3409, 3434 (1982):

"The emotionally charged rhetoric of Charles Evers' speeches did not transcend the bounds of protected speech set forth in *Brandenburg*. The lengthy addresses generally contained an impassioned plea for black citizens to unify, to support and respect each other, and to realize the political and economic power available to them. In the course of those pleas, strong language was used. *If that language had been followed by acts of violence, a substantial question would be presented whether Evers could be held liable for the consequences of that unlawful conduct.* In this case, however—with the

possible exception of the Cox incident—the acts of violence identified in 1966 occurred weeks or months after the April 1, 1966 speech; the chancellor made no finding of any violence after the challenged 1969 speech. Strong and effective extemporaneous rhetoric cannot be nicely channeled in purely dulcet phrases. An advocate must be free to stimulate his audience with spontaneous and emotional appeals for unity and action in a common cause. When such appeals do not incite lawless action, they must be regarded as protected speech." (emphasis added).

1. Near v. Minnesota, 283 U.S. 697, 713–14 (1931).

2. 2 T. Cooley, A Treatise on the Constitutional Limitations which Rest Upon the Legislative Power of the States of the American Union 886 (8th Ed. by W. Carrington, 1927) (footnote omitted).

3. 4 W. Blackstone, Commentaries on the Laws of England * 151–52 (2d ed. rev. 1872). T. Cooley was the editor. See generally L. Levy, Legacy of Suppression: Freedom of Speech and Press in Early American History (1960). Also published in 1963 as Freedom of Speech and Press in Early American History.

though not exclusively, immunity from previous restraints or censorship." [4]

In modern times prior restraint has generally taken the form of court injunctions rather than a system of licensing by a Board of Censors. The only major exception is the case of allegedly obscene speech, where, in practice, often there may be censorship by board review prior to court action. The courts have generally tolerated more prior restraint in situations involving allegedly obscene materials, but even in such cases restraint is still suspect. Another section of this chapter discusses prior restraint of allegedly obscene speech.[5] Here we are primarily concerned with the prior restraint of other types of speech, which often but not necessarily occur in a political context.[6]

If a given utterance may be punished, is there any real difference if one is enjoined from making the speech or whether one is punished after having made the speech? In addition to historical distinctions discussed in the beginning of this Chapter, the "marketplace" theory of speech supports the distinction between prior restraint and subsequent punishment. While subsequent punishment may deter some speakers, at least the ideas or speech at issue can be placed before the public. Prior restraint limits public debate and knowledge more severely. Additionally, some of the procedural aspects of enjoining speech make subsequent punishment a less serious alternative.

If the subsequent punishment is criminal, the state is encouraged to use the procedural device of a prior restraint. Procedurally it is easier to initiate a civil injunction action than to start a criminal prosecution. An application for a temporary restraining order is filed in cases where immediate and expeditious relief is needed. Once the court grants a temporary restraining order it sets a hearing, for the earliest possible date, to determine if a preliminary injunction should be issued.[7] In contrast to the rapid disposition of injunctive actions, a criminal prosecution must proceed through indictment or information,[8] arraignment,[9] pleadings, pretrial motions,[10] and jury selection if there is a possibility of imprisonment of six months or more,[11] before the accused is even brought to trial.

The hearing on an application for an injunction, an historically equitable action, is before a judge sitting without a jury.[12] If the injunctive order is violated there is generally no right to a jury at the contempt proceedings [13] except in some cases of criminal contempt.[14] The standard of proof in injunc-

---

4. Near v. Minnesota, 283 U.S. 697, 716 (1931). See also, New York Times v. United States, 403 U.S. 713, 714 (1971); Organization for a Better Austin v. Keefe, 402 U.S. 415, 419 (1971); Bantam Books v. Sullivan, 372 U.S. 58, 70 (1963).

For a well-developed and contrary view, see Mayton, Toward a Theory of First Amendment Process: Injunctions of Speech, Subsequent Punishment, and the Costs of the Prior Restraint Doctrine, 67 Cornell L.Rev. 245 (1982), concluding: "Because injunctions are necessarily the product of a judicial process, they should be preferred to subsequent punishment." Id. at 281. See also, Hunter, Toward a Better Understanding of the Prior Restraint Doctrine: A Reply to Professor Mayton, 67 Cornell L.Rev. 283 (1982).

5. See Chapter 18, § XVII, F, 3.

6. E.g., Southeastern Promotions, Ltd. v. Conrad, 420 U.S. 546 (1975) (denial by city of the use of a municipal theater for showing the musical "Hair"); Blount v. Rizzi, 400 U.S. 410 (1971) (postal stop orders); Freedman v. Maryland, 380 U.S. 51 (1965) (movies allegedly obscene).

7. See Fed.R.Civ.P. 65; see also United States v. United Mine Workers, 330 U.S. 258 (1947); Houghton

v. Meyer, 208 U.S. 149 (1908); Moore, Federal Practice and Procedure, § 65.07.

8. Fed.R.Crim.P. 7. Cf. Nebraska Press Ass'n v. Stuart, 427 U.S. 539, 559 (1976).

9. Fed.R.Crim.P. 10.

10. Fed.R.Crim.P. 11.

11. Baldwin v. New York, 399 U.S. 66, 69 (1970).

12. See Ross v. Bernhard, 396 U.S. 531 (1970); Beacon Theatres, Inc. v. Westover, 359 U.S. 500 (1950); Dairy Queen, Inc. v. Wood, 369 U.S. 469 (1962).

13. Shillitani v. United States, 384 U.S. 364, 365 (1966).

14. See Gompers v. Buck's Stove & Range Co., 221 U.S. 418, 449 (1911); 18 U.S.C.A. § 402.

If the length of the sentence is in the judge's discretion rather than fixed by statute, the Sixth Amendment requires a jury trial in criminal contempt cases if the sentence imposed is in fact more than six months. In contrast, in ordinary criminal cases defendant has a right to a jury trial if the sentence that *could* be imposed is in excess of six months. Codispoti v. Pennsylvania, 418 U.S. 506 (1974); Muniz v. Hoffman, 422

tive actions, as in most equitable proceedings, is not the strict criminal requirement of "beyond a reasonable doubt" [15] but the more lenient "clear and convincing proof" standard.[16] Unlike an injunctive case, in criminal prosecutions the government generally has no right of appeal,[17] a limitation imposed by the double jeopardy provision of the Fifth Amendment.[18] Since injunctive cases are civil proceedings, the Government's right to appeal in civil cases is limited only by the nonconstitutional principle of res judicata.[19]

The injunctive remedy with its speedier procedural framework is thus more subject to abuse and to indiscriminate application, whereas criminal prosecution entails a more thorough self-selection process resulting in fewer applications and successes. The over-all chilling effect on speech is consequently less with criminal prosecution. Also, even if a temporary restraining order is ultimately found to have been improperly granted, the Government may have in fact achieved its end by restraining speech at a crucial time.[20] Although the speech may be subsequently allowed, its impact may then be negligible because of the time elapsed.

It has been argued that the courts have treated violations of prior restraint orders as a more serious offense than deliberate refusals to abide by a statute. A significant illustration of this principle is found in a comparison of two Supreme Court cases. In one,

the High Court reversed the conviction of civil rights demonstrators who had been convicted of violating an ordinance found to be unconstitutionally vague. The ordinance forbade issuance of a license for a protest march if "the public welfare, peace, safety, health, decency, good order, morals or convenience" require that it be refused.[21] Justice Stewart writing for the Court said that "a person faced with such an unconstitutional licensing law may ignore it and engage with impunity in the exercise of the right of free expression for which the law purports to require a license." [22]

The Court earlier had upheld the conviction of marchers who violated that same statute *after* the statute had been copied into an ex parte injunction. While the statute could have been violated with impunity, violation of the state court's ex parte injunction was another matter:

> The breadth and vagueness of the injunction itself would also unquestionably be subject to substantial constitutional question. But the way to raise that question was to apply to the Alabama courts to have the injunction modified or dissolved.[23]

In short, while one is free to violate an unconstitutional statute restricting free speech, one is not free to violate the same words when written as a court injunction.

This rule reflects the fact that courts are more adamant in punishing contempts of their orders than in punishing violations of

---

U.S. 454, 476 (1975). As for fines, in criminal contempt cases there is no fixed line that determines when the Constitution requires a jury trial. Thus in Muniz v. Hoffman, 422 U.S. 454 (1975) the Court held that the Constitution did not require a jury trial, given the facts of that case, when the fine for criminal contempt was $10,000. If the case had involved an ordinary crime a jury would be required if the fine could exceed $500. 18 U.S.C.A. § 1(3). Subsequently a lower court, in the exercise of its supervisory power, limited fines for criminal contempt to $500. Douglass v. First Nat. Realty Corp., 543 F.2d 894 (D.C.Cir. 1976). See generally, Y. Kamisar, W. LaFave, & J. Israel, Modern Criminal Procedure 1318–20 (5th ed. 1980).

15. In re Winship, 397 U.S. 358, 361 (1970).

16. McCormick, Evidence, § 340 at 796 (2d ed., E. Cleary, ed. 1972); see, e.g., Fisher v. Miceli, 291 S.W.2d 845, 848 (1956); Hyder v. Newcomb, 236 Ark. 231, 365 S.W.2d 271, 274 (1963).

17. Ashe v. Swenson, 397 U.S. 436, 445 (1970); Benton v. Maryland, 395 U.S. 784, 793–795 (1969).

18. United States v. Ball, 163 U.S. 662, 668–670 (1896).

19. Cf. 28 U.S.C.A. § 1292.

20. Cf. Walker v. City of Birmingham, 388 U.S. 307, 336 (Douglas, J., dissenting):

> "For if a person must pursue his judicial remedy [of lifting an injunction] before he may speak, parade, or assemble, the occasion when protest is desired or needed will have become history and any later speech, parade, or assembly will be fruitless or pointless."

21. Shuttlesworth v. Birmingham, 394 U.S. 147, 150–151 (1969).

22. Id. at 151.

23. Walker v. Birmingham, 388 U.S. 307, 317 (1967).

criminal statutes. Because the defendant has violated a specific order of the judge, Chief Justice Warren had argued in dissent that Courts may interpret a contempt action as an attack on the courts themselves or as a violation of the respect that judges feel is due them; however, this self-interest of the court is not present in criminal cases, where there is no personal stake in enforcement of the criminal statute.[24] Because the judge may object more to the violation of his own order than to the violation of a state's statute, he may correspondingly be more severe in enforcing prior restraints relative to subsequent punishments. The Court majority appears to have focused on the principle that the individual before the courts in a case where the judge is issuing the prior restraint has access to receive a neutral determination of the issue. If there were no reasonable review procedures available there might be a different conclusion. But so long as there is outstanding a judicial order, the legal process cannot tolerate an individual's choice to disregard a court order and then claim a right to attack that order collaterally.

In the case of prior restraint of controversial political speech touching on national security or similar interests, new problems emerge. In such cases the government may argue that an injunction should issue because publication will cause substantial damage to the United States. In ruling on the application, the Court is really asked to predict the future; that is, will publication in fact cause this vague but substantial damage? Courts are ill-equipped for such a

task. If the Court says no damage will occur and allows publication, there are two possible consequences. The damage may actually occur (or some damage may occur and appear to have been linked with earlier publication) and the Court consequently will share the blame for the damage to the United States' security. If, alternatively, the asserted damage does not occur, the judiciary has still engaged in a risky expenditure of its esteem without noticeable advantage.

On the other hand, if the Court does not allow publication, the public will probably never know if the Court was wrong, since the allegedly damaging papers may never be published or, if they are printed, may be seized prior to distribution. The public then is never able to judge for itself the importance of the suppressed speech.[25] The Court will never lose esteem or share blame in such cases, and there will be little or no damage to its reputation from nonpublication. Prior restraint, with its emphasis on predicting an unknowable future, encourages courts to overpredict the potential damage from publication. The dangers of underprediction and the lack of burdens attached to overprediction furnish an important incentive to the Courts, which makes prior restraint a more serious and more effective weapon against free speech.

It should also be noted that any governmental order which restricts or prohibits speech prior to its publication constitutes a prior restraint. Such orders may include

---

24. Cf. Walker v. Birmingham, 388 U.S. 307 (1967) where the Court held that even though a state injunction forbidding a demonstration was unconstitutional, the subjects of it could be prosecuted for violating it rather than appealing it and seeking reversal. Chief Justice Warren in dissent noted:

> "It has never been thought that violation of a statute indicated such a disrespect for the legislature that the violator always must be punished even if the statute was unconstitutional. . . . Indeed it shows no disrespect for law to violate a statute on the ground that it is unconstitutional and then to submit one's case to the courts with the willingness to accept the penalty if the statute is held to be valid. . . . [But an ex parte] injunction [is] such potent

magic that it transformed the command of an unconstitutional statute into an impregnable barrier, challengeable only in what likely would have been protracted legal proceedings and entirely superior in the meantime even to the United States Constitution."

388 U.S. 307, 327, 330 (1967).

25. Cf. United States v. Marchetti, 466 F.2d 1309 (4th Cir. 1972), cert. denied 409 U.S. 1063 (prior restraint of former CIA employee's publication discussing CIA activities; at time of employment the employee contractually agreed to submit such writings to the CIA for approval). But cf. Snepp v. United States, 444 U.S. 507, 509 n. 4 (1980) (per curiam) (distinguishing *Marchetti*).

censorship of movies,[26] denial of mail privileges,[27] refusal of access to a public forum [28] and judicial protective or "gag" orders against the press in criminal cases.[29]

For these historical, procedural, and substantive reasons prior restraint—particularly in the context of political speech attacking governmental policies—has long been suspect. Just as the common law forbade equity from enjoining a crime [30] the overeffectiveness of prior restraint and its strong potential for abuse has made it much more chilling on the exercise of first amendment rights, than subsequent punishments.[31]

B. From NEAR to the Pentagon Papers and Beyond

The doctrine of prior restraint was used to dismiss injunctions against the press in two leading cases. *Near v. Minnesota* [1] firmly embedded the doctrine in modern jurisprudence, and *New York Times Co. v. United States* [2] applied the principles of *Near* to the special problem of national security. *Near v. Minnesota* involved a state statute which permitted enjoining as a nuisance any "malicious, scandalous and defamatory newspaper, magazine or other periodical." [3] Defendant published "The Saturday Press" and had printed articles with strong antisemitic overtones critical of local officials. The trial court issued a permanent injunction against

defendant, which was affirmed by the highest state court.

The Supreme Court reversed the conviction on the grounds that it was an infringement of the liberty of the press as guaranteed in the first and fourteenth amendments. In reaching this conclusion, the Court enumerated the gravity of the statute's consequences: (1) In order to obtain an injunction under the statute, one did not need to prove the falsity of the charges made in the publication, as in libel law. The statute only permitted the defense that "truth was published with good motives and for justifiable ends." [4] (2) The statute was directed to publications critical of private citizens and public officers. (3) The object of the statute was not ordinary punishment but suppression. (4) The statute operated not only to suppress the publication but also to effectively place the publisher under censorship.[5]

The Court summarized the working of the statute:

> The operation and effect of the statute in substance is that public authorities may bring the owner or publisher of a newspaper or periodical before a judge upon a charge of conducting a business of publishing scandalous and defamatory matter—in particular that the matter consists of charges against public officers of official dereliction—and unless the owner or publisher is able and disposed to bring competent evidence to satisfy the judge that the

---

26. Freedman v. Maryland, 380 U.S. 51 (1965). For the procedural requirements of prior restraint, see Section XVII, F, 3 of this chapter.

27. Blount v. Rizzi, 400 U.S. 410 (1971).

28. Southeastern Promotions, Ltd. v. Conrad, 420 U.S. 546 (1975).

29. Nebraska Press Ass'n v. Stuart, 427 U.S. 539 (1976); see Section VIII, C of this chapter.

30. Miliken v. Stone, 16 F.2d 981, 983 (2d Cir. 1927), cert. denied 274 U.S. 748; In re Debs, 158 U.S. 564, 593–94 (1894).

31. Contra, Mayton, Towards a Theory of First Amendment Process: Injunctions of Speech, Subsequent Punishment, and the Costs of the Prior Restraint Doctrine, 67 Cornell L.Rev. 245 (1982); but compare Hunter, Toward a Better Understanding of the Prior Restraint Doctrine: A Reply to Professor Mayton, 67 Cornell L.Rev. 283 (1982).

1. 283 U.S. 697 (1931).

2. 403 U.S. 713 (1971). Organization for a Better Austin v. Keefe, 402 U.S. 415 (1971) was another prior restraint case. Chief Justice Burger, for the Court, reversed a prior restraint on the OBA which, to encourage integrated housing, had peacefully distributed leaflets objecting to block busting and panic peddling. The leaflets specifically criticized Keefe, a real estate broker.

3. 283 U.S. 697, 701–02.

See generally, Symposium: Near v. Minnesota, 50th Anniversary, 66 Minn.L.Rev. 1 (1981): Gillmor, Prologue, 66 Minn.L.Rev. 1 (1981); Toward a Theory of Prior Restraint: The Central Linkage, 66 Minn.L.Rev. 11 (1981); Murphy, Near v. Minnesota in the Context of Historical Developments, 66 Minn.L.Rev. 95 (1981); Knoll, National Security: The Ultimate Threat to the First Amendment, 66 Minn.L.Rev. 161 (1981); Linde, Courts and Censorship, 66 Minn.L.Rev. 171 (1981).

4. 283 U.S. at 702.

5. Id. at 710–12.

charges are true and are published with good motives and for justifiable ends, his newspaper or periodical is suppressed and further publication is made punishable as a contempt. This is the essence of censorship.[6]

According to the Court, a statute which functioned in this way was inconsistent with the historical conception of the freedom of the press guarantee.[7]

In order to reach this conclusion the Court made a major initial presumption: that the chief purpose of the freedom of the press guarantee was to prevent prior restraints on publication.[8] Thus, there could be very few exceptions to the principle of immunity from previous restraint. The Court listed only three "exceptional cases" which *might* justify previous restraint:[9] (1) if it were necessary so that "a government might prevent actual obstruction to its recruiting service or the publication of the sailing dates of transports or the number and location of troops;"[10] (2) the requirements of decency could justify prior restraint on obscene publications; (3) if it were necessary to avoid "incitements to acts of violence and the overthrow by force of orderly government."[11] Because none of these exceptions was applicable to the statute so far as it authorized the proceedings of this action, prior restraint was not constitutionally justified in *Near*.

Forty years later, in 1971, the doctrine of prior restraint of political speech again received special attention in *New York Times*

Co. v. United States (The Pentagon Papers Case)[12] when the Court dismissed temporary restraining orders and stays against the *New York Times* and the *Washington Post* and refused to enjoin the newspapers from publishing a classified study on United States policy-making in Viet Nam. The fragmented Court, which decided the case in nine separate opinions by a 6 to 3 majority, agreed on only two general themes—any system of prior restraint of expression bears a heavy presumption against its constitutional validity, and the Government carries a "heavy burden" to justify enforcing any system of prior restraint.[13]

The opinions in this case can be grouped in three categories: Justices Black and Douglas, maintained that there can never be prior restraint on the press; Justices Brennan, White, Stewart and Marshall, maintained that there could be prior restraint on the press in some circumstances but not in this case; and Justices Burger, Harlan, and Blackmun, maintained that the prior restraint was appropriate in this case.

Justices Black and Douglas argued that no system of prior restraint was ever justified. A holding that the publication of news may sometimes be enjoined, according to Justice Black, would "make a shambles of the First Amendment," and the operation of the injunctions was a "flagrant, indefensible, and continuing violation of the First Amend-

---

6. Id. at 713.

7. Id.

8. Id.

9. Id. at 716.

10. Id.
The majority relied on this dictum in upholding the power of the Secretary of State to revoke the passport of a former CIA agent who was seeking to expose CIA agents abroad. Haig v. Agee, 453 U.S. 280 (1981). The passport revocation, the majority reasoned, did not violate Agee's first amendment rights because it only inhibited Agee's *"action"*, not his "speech." 453 U.S. at 309 (emphasis in original). Just as the hypothetical disclosures in *Near* obstruct the government's recruiting services, Agee's disclosures "have the declared purpose of obstructing intelligence operations and the recruiting of intelligence personnel." 53 U.S. at 308–09.

Brennan, J., in dissent, found *Near* to be an irrelevant and unconvincing precedent and commented that under the majority's speech-action rationale, "a 40 year prison sentence imposed upon a person who criticized the Government's food stamp policy would represent only an 'inhibition of action.' After all, the individual would remain free to criticize the United States Government, albeit from a jail cell." 453 U.S. at 320–21 n. 10.

11. 283 U.S. at 716.

12. 403 U.S. 713. The Court therefore reversed the Second Circuit and affirmed the D.C. Circuit. The Court also lifted its own stay. 403 U.S. 943 (1971). The D.C. Circuit had refused to enjoin but still restrained the *Post* pending Supreme Court review.

See J. Barron and C. Dienes, Handbook of Free Speech and Free Press 42–57 (1979).

13. 403 U.S. at 714.

ment." [14] Black characterized the very purpose of the press as exposing the secrets of government and informing the people; "paramount among the responsibilities of a free press is the duty to prevent any part of the government from deceiving the people and sending them off to distant lands to die of foreign fevers and foreign shot and shell." [15] Rather than be enjoined or condemned for publishing the Pentagon Papers, these newspapers should be "commended for serving the purpose that the Founding Fathers saw so clearly. . . . The Press was to serve the governed, not the governors." [16]

Justice Douglas deplored governmental restraint on the press and also interpreted the dominant purpose of the First Amendment to be "to prohibit the widespread practice of governmental suppression of embarrassing information." [17] Although Douglas left unanswered the question whether the war power of Congress might change the doctrine of prior restraint, as the doctrine exists now, even serious impact from disclosures of publication cannot justify prior restraint on the press.

Justice Brennan did leave open the possibility of some constitutional prior restraints, but his test was so strict that none might pass any realistic review. Brennan first pointed out the impropriety of granting injunctive relief in the instant case. The basis of the Government's argument was that publication might damage the national interest but, according to Brennan, "the First Amendment tolerates absolutely no prior judicial restraints of the press predicated upon surmise or conjecture that untoward consequences may result." [18] Brennan did find one situation which would justify an exception to the first amendment ban on prior restraint, cases which may arise when the nation is at war. However, Brennan invoked a high standard for imposition of prior restraint even then. The Government must allege and prove that the publication of information must "inevitably, directly, and immediately" cause the happening of an event such as nuclear holocaust. [19] Thus, although Brennan conceptually allowed the possibility of prior restraint, his test is so strict as to be virtually a prohibition.

Justice Stewart argued that prior restraint imposed by the Executive could be justified in order to maintain internal security, because the Executive has a constitutional obligation to preserve the confidentiality required to effectively perform its duties related to national defense and foreign affairs. [20] However, the Executive must show that disclosure of information will result in "direct, immediate, and irreparable damage to our Nation or its people," and the Government did not meet this test for all the documents involved in the instant case. [21]

Even though he was convinced disclosure of the material would do substantial damage to the public interest, Justice White concurred in the Court's judgment also because the Government did not satisfy the "very heavy burden" it must meet to justify prior restraint. [22] White implied that Congressional authorization for prior restraint might lessen this "very heavy burden" and emphasized that the Government could still proceed against the newspapers for criminal publication.

Justice Marshall based his concurrence on the absence of Congressional authorization for prior restraint in this situation. He argued that it would be against the separation of powers concept for the Court, through use of the contempt power, to restrain actions Congress has chosen not to prohibit. [23] Although the power of the Executive could constitutionally justify prior restraint, Congress had clearly refused to give the president the power he sought to exercise here

14. Id. at 715.

15. Id. at 717.

16. Id.

17. Id. at 723–24.

18. Id. at 725–26 (footnote omitted).

19. Id. at 726–27.

20. Id. at 729–30.

21. Id. at 730.

22. Id. at 731.

23. Id. at 742.

by enjoining publication of these materials. Marshall dismissed the injunction because "[w]hen Congress specifically declines to make conduct unlawful it is not for this Court to redecide those issues—to overrule Congress." [24]

The remaining three justices dissented and found that the injunction was proper in the instant case. Chief Justice Burger did not speak directly to the merits of the case, arguing instead that undue haste in the proceedings removed any possibility of orderly litigation of the proceedings and meant that the justices "literally do not know what we are acting on." [25] He would have upheld the injunction to allow the Court enough time for an orderly hearing on the merits. However, Burger criticized the New York Times as being largely responsible for the "frenetic haste" of the proceedings and his sympathies were apparent in that he "agreed generally" with Harlan's dissent. [26] Harlan did uphold use of the injunction on the merits, albeit "within the severe limitations imposed by the time constraints." [27]

Unlike Justice Marshall, Harlan used the constitutional separation of powers to justify prior restraint of the Pentagon Papers. Harlan argued that the Executive has "constitutional primacy in the field of foreign affairs" and that the judiciary has only two narrow areas of inquiry over Executive decisions in foreign policy. [28] The Judiciary can (1) insure that the area of dispute actually lies within the scope of the president's foreign relations power; and (2) insure that the decision that disclosure of the subject matter would irreparably impair the national security be made by the head of the executive department concerned, such as the Secretary of State or the Secretary of Defense. But it is not within the power of the Court to redetermine the probable impact of disclosure on national security once this decision has been made by the Executive. [29]

Justice Blackmun added that there was need for developing proper standards between the "broad right of the press to print and . . . the very narrow right of the Government to prevent." [30] Representing the opposite extreme from Black's praise for the action of the New York Times, Blackmun included a strong attack on the newspapers and concurring justices who comprised the majority of the Court:

> [I]f, with the Court's action today, these newspapers proceed to publish the critical documents and there results therefrom "the death of soldiers, the destruction of alliances, the greatly increased difficulty of negotiation with our enemies, the inability of our diplomats to negotiate," to which list I might add the factors of prolongation of the war and of further delay in the freeing of United States prisoners, then the Nation's people will know where the responsibility for these sad consequences rests. [31]

The Government lost its injunctive suit and the newspaper proceeded to finish publishing the excerpts of the Pentagon Papers which they had secured by an unauthorized leak from a former government employee, Daniel Ellsberg. The Government never prosecuted any of the newspapers—an option not foreclosed by the Pentagon Papers case [32] but it did prosecute Daniel Ellsberg.

---

24. Id. at 745–46.

25. Id. at 751.

26. Id. at 751–52.

27. Id. at 755.

28. Id. at 756.

29. Id. at 757.

30. Id. at 761.

31. Id. at 763.

32. Cf. Landmark Communications, Inc. v. Virginia, 435 U.S. 829 (1978). The holding in *Landmark*—protecting third party publication of confidential judicial disciplinary proceedings—may not be applicable to a situation like the Pentagon Papers case, where a newspaper might be subject to subsequent punishment for publishing allegedly top secret national security data since the interests of the state in protecting such information is much greater. However, a major issue in such a case would still be whether or not such data was properly classified as top secret, since a "legislature appropriately inquires into and may declare the reasons impelling legislative action but the judicial function commands analysis of whether the specific conduct falls within the reach of the statute. . . ." 435 U.S. at 844.

See also, Smith v. Daily Mail Publishing Co., 443 U.S. 97, 104 (1979) (if a newspaper lawfully obtains truthful

The trial judge directed a verdict of acquittal for Ellsberg because of various prosecution improprieties.

Following the Pentagon Papers Case, the Court decided *Snepp v. United States*.[33] *Snepp* was only a brief per curiam opinion, but significantly it held that a former agent of the Central Intelligence Agency breached his fiduciary obligation and his employment contract when he failed to submit for prepublication review a book concerning the CIA, even though the Government conceded, for the purposes of the case, that the book divulged no classified information. Therefore, the Court put into constructive trust for the Government all the profits from Snepp's book.

The majority explained that the proper procedure that Snepp should have followed, in light of his explicit employment agreement to submit all material to the CIA, for prepublication review, would be to submit the material so that the Agency could determine if it contained harmful disclosures. If Snepp and the CIA failed to agree on this issue, the Agency would have the burden to seek an injunction against publication.[34] Without any further discussion the Court appeared to approve of what amounts to prior restraint in those special cases where former CIA employees have been in a position of trust and have agreed to sign employment contracts accepting prepublication review of information dealing with the CIA.

The dissent objected: "the Court seems unaware of the fact that its drastic new rem-edy [of a constructive trust for failure to abide by prepublication clearance] has been fashioned to enforce a species of prior restraint on a citizen's right to criticize his government." [35]

VI. THE OTHER SIDE OF THE COIN FROM PRIOR RESTRAINT OF THE PRESS: ACCESS TO AND BY THE PRESS

A. A Right of Access to the Press

1. The Fairness Doctrine and the Regulation of the Broadcast Media

Due to the unique nature of electronic media and the present state of the art, there is no comparable right of everyone to broadcast on radio and television what one could speak, write, or publish elsewhere.[1] Frequencies presently available to broadcast are finite, and when some are given the privilege to use them, others must be denied. No particular licensee has a first amendment right to broadcast and his existing privilege may be qualified through regulation. In general it may be said that the award of a broadcast license may be subjected to reasonable regulation with goals other than the suppression of ideas. Such regulation is permissible because it is the right of the listeners and viewers which is paramount, not the rights of the broadcasters.

information about a matter of public significance "then state officials may not constitutionally punish publication of the information, absent a need to further a state interest of the highest order.")

33. 444 U.S. 507 (1980) (per curiam). When Saigon fell on April 30, 1975, Frank W. Snepp III, a senior analyst for the C.I.A., was one of the last Americans evacuated by helicopter from the roof of the American embassy. He was awarded the C.I.A.'s Medal of Merit when he returned to the United States, but he quit the Agency and wrote *Decent Interval* (1977), which was his version of the final days, and which criticized, inter alia, the C.I.A.'s evacuation planning. See R. Rotunda, Modern Constitutional Law: Cases and Notes 783 (1981). See generally, Medow, The First Amendment and the Secrecy State: Snepp v. United States, 130

U.Penn.L.Rev. 775 (1982). See also, Section XII, B, 3, infra.

34. 444 U.S. at 515, n. 8.

35. 444 U.S. at 527 (footnote omitted) (Stevens, J., dissenting, joined by Brennan and Marshall, JJ.).

1. While the Supreme Court has often commented on the monopoly nature of broadcasting, e.g., National Broadcasting Co. v. United States, 319 U.S. 190, 226 (1943); Red Lion Broadcasting Co. v. FCC, 395 U.S. 367, 376–77 (1969), this premise has been attacked. See, e.g., R. Posner, Economic Analysis of Law § 22.3 at 312–13 (1972); Fowler and Brenner, A Marketplace Approach to Broadcast Regulation, 60 Tex.L.Rev. 207 (1982). Powe, "Or of the [Broadcast] Press, 55 Tex.L.Rev. 39, 55–62 (1976).

In *National Broadcasting Co., Inc. v. United States* [2] the Supreme Court first recognized that, since no one has a first amendment right to a radio license or to monopolize a radio frequency, to deny a station a license on the grounds of public interest is not a denial of free speech. In this action challenging the FCC's regulations of multiple station "chain" broadcasting as an unconstitutional restraint on free speech, the opinion of the Court made much of the fact that broadcasting is a limited media and that an absolute first amendment right of access is not feasible in such circumstances.

Writing for the Court, Justice Frankfurter emphasized that regulation was essential to develop the full potential of radio [3] and that the overriding interest to be served must be "the interest *of the listening public* in 'the larger and more effective use of radio'." [4] To further the public interest in use of this limited resource, government must allocate use of the airways:

> Freedom of utterance is abridged to many who wish to use the limited facilities of radio. Unlike other modes of expression, radio inherently is not available to all. That is its unique characteristic and that is why, unlike other modes of expression, it is subject to governmental regulation. [5]

The extent of the right of the government to control the electronic media was not made clear by *NBC*, but it was brought into sharp focus by *Red Lion Broadcasting Co. v. Federal Communication Commission*, [6] which challenged the right of the FCC to require broadcasters to follow a "fairness doctrine." The fairness doctrine required broadcasters to allow reply time to the public in cases involving personal attacks or political editori-

als. The case was the first time that the Supreme Court ruled on a challenge made to the FCC's fairness doctrine on constitutional grounds.

In *Red Lion*, the petitioner operated a radio station under FCC license. During a broadcast on the station the Reverend Billy James Hargis verbally attacked author Fred J. Cook. [7] Cook demanded free reply time and, upon the station's refusal, filed a formal letter of complaint with the Federal Communications Commission. The Commission deemed the incident a "personal attack" and, citing its *Times-Mirror Broadcasting Co.* doctrine [8] as requiring a station to offer free reply time in such a situation, ordered the station to grant Cook the time requested. Upon appeal by the station, the D.C. Circuit Court of Appeals affirmed [9] and the Supreme Court granted certiorari.

After the *Red Lion* litigation had commenced, the FCC issued its Personal Attack Rules, which codified the *Times-Mirror* doctrine and the Commission's ad hoc ruling in *Red Lion* for all personal attacks. [10] The Radio-Television News Directors Association (RTNDA) immediately sought review of the rule-making proceeding in the Court of Appeals for the Seventh Circuit, where the rules were declared unconstitutional abridgments of free speech. [11] The Supreme Court granted certiorari for consideration of the issues together with *Red Lion*. [12]

The broadcasters challenged the fairness doctrine and its specific manifestations in the personal attack and political editorial rules on conventional first amendment grounds as abridging freedom of speech and press. Their argument was based on the

2. 319 U.S. 190 (1943).

3. 319 U.S. at 217–27.

4. 319 U.S. at 216 (emphasis added).

5. 319 U.S. at 226.

6. 395 U.S. 367 (1969). See Van Alstyne, The Möbius Strip of the First Amendment: Perspectives on Red Lion, 29 So.Car.L.Rev. 539 (1978).

7. During part of a "Christian Crusade" broadcast series, Hargis discussed Cook's book, Goldwater—Extremist on the Right. Hargis claimed that Cook had been fired from a newspaper for leveling false charges

at a city official and had subsequently worked for "one of the most scurrilous publications of the left (The Nation)." 395 U.S. at 371–372, n. 2.

8. 24 P & F Radio Reg. 404 (1962).

9. Red Lion Broadcasting Co. v. FCC, 381 F.2d 908 (D.C.Cir. 1967).

10. 47 C.F.R. §§ 73.123, 73.300, 73.598, 73.679 (1969).

11. RTNDA v. United States, 400 F.2d 1002 (7th Cir. 1968).

12. 393 U.S. 1014 (1969).

contention that the first amendment protected their desire to use their allotted frequency continuously to broadcast whatever they choose, and to exclude whomever they choose from using that frequency; if no man could be prevented from publishing or saying what he thinks, or from refusing in his speech to give equal weight to the views of his opponents, then broadcasters must have a similar first amendment right it was argued.

The Supreme Court unanimously rejected this contention of a right to free speech for broadcasters identical to published or spoken speech.[13] It emphasized that "differences in the characteristics of news media justify differences in the First Amendment standards applied to them,"[14] and stressed that a limited media could not support an absolute right of free speech:

> Where there are substantially more individuals who want to broadcast than there are frequencies to allocate, it is idle to posit an unabridgeable First Amendment right to broadcast comparable to the right of every individual to speak, write, or publish.[15]

The Court reasoned that the fiduciary nature of the relationship between the licensee and the general public put those who hold a license in no more favored position than those to whom licenses are refused. Where the public interest requires, the government could demand that a licensee fulfill his obligation "to present those views and voices which are representative of his community and which would otherwise, by necessity, be barred from the airwaves."[16] Because of this fiduciary role, the rights of the broadcasters must be subordinate to the right of

viewers and listeners to suitable access to ideas and information.

It is important to note that while the *Red Lion* case only upheld a Federal Communication Commission rule, parts of the Court's opinion appeared to go much farther and were written as if the fairness doctrine is constitutionally required:

> It is the right of the public to receive suitable access to social, political, esthetic, moral, and other ideas and experiences which is crucial here. That right may not constitutionally be abridged either by Congress or by the [Federal Communication Commission].[17]

Yet other portions were more narrow:

> [W]e do hold that the Congress and the Commission do not violate the First Amendment when they require a radio or television station to give reply time to answer personal attacks and political editorials.[18]

While the fairness doctrine regulations do not constitute a prior restraint in the classic sense,[19] they do place a recognizable burden upon broadcaster programming discretion. The *Red Lion* Court, however, spent little time discussing the competing considerations involved in placing this additional burden upon the broadcast industry. The broadcasters' claims that they would be forced into self-censorship and would substantially curtail coverage of controversial issues under a right-to-reply rule was summarily dismissed as "at best speculative."[20] The Court did admit that if the rules should result in such a reduction of coverage, then "there will be time enough to reconsider the constitutional implications".[21] While as a practical matter, it should be hard to measure a drop in the amount of free speech

---

13. Justice Douglas was not present at oral argument and therefore abstained from taking part in the decision.

14. 395 U.S. at 386–87, citing Joseph Burstyn, Inc. v. Wilson, 343 U.S. 495, 503 (1952).

15. 395 U.S. at 388.

16. 395 U.S. at 389.

17. 395 U.S. at 390.

18. 395 U.S. at 396.

19. See, e.g., Near v. Minnesota, 283 U.S. 697 (1931).

20. 395 U.S. at 393.

21. 395 U.S. at 393. Assuming that the broadcaster does indeed have a monopoly, the fairness doctrine as an economic matter might not at all increase the publication of ideas. "On the contrary, it penalizes [the broadcaster] for presenting controversial ideas by requiring him to present all sides of a controversy. The element of penalty lies in the fact that the doctrine comes into play only when the broadcaster's welfare would be maximized by his not presenting all sides." R. Posner, Economic Analysis of Law § 22.3 at 313 (1972).

caused by the fairness doctrine, the Court's acknowledgement of a reconsideration of the fairness rule in such circumstances suggests that, in spite of the Court's earlier strong language, the fairness doctrine is not constitutionally required.[22]

Notwithstanding the Court's suggestion, the generally broad language of *Red Lion* led some commentators to argue that there is a constitutional right of individual access to the airwaves beyond the scope of the fairness doctrine. This right was perceived both in the decision's qualifications on the broadcaster's first amendment rights and in the FCC's power to compel presentation of individual responses to personal attacks and political editorials.[23] Only a slight extension of the *Red Lion* holding would recognize a right of access to electronic media by individuals wishing to make minority views on issues of public importance known. The Democratic National Committee (DNC) and an anti-war group called the Business Executive's Movement for Vietnam Peace (BEM) tried to establish the existence of such a constitutional right in *Columbia Broadcasting System v. Democratic National Committee*.[24]

The issue presented in *CBS* was whether "responsible" groups have a constitutional right under the first amendment to purchase air time for the presentation of ads and programs in order to make known their views about controversial issues of public importance. The two groups claiming such a right, DNC and BEM, were challenging separate decisions of the FCC. In the case of BEM, the FCC had held that a radio station acted within its authority in refusing to air BEM's spot advertisement opposed to the Vietnam conflict; in the case of DNC, the FCC had held that as a general matter the DNC did not have a right to purchase time to air its views on controversial public issues.[25]

The Supreme Court held that there is no such right of access under the Constitution. Though the Court divided on several issues, six Justices agreed that the first amendment would not require the sale of time to responsible groups even if state action was involved.[26] The Court of Appeals below had held that "a flat ban on paid public issue announcements is in violation of the First Amendment, at least when other sorts of paid announcements are accepted."[27]

The opinion of the Supreme Court emphasized that a balancing of the first amendment interests involved must be carried out within the framework of the regulatory scheme already imposed by Congress on the broadcast media. It noted that Congress had formerly dealt with and firmly rejected the argument "that the broadcast facilities

---

22. See, FCC v. WNCN Listeners Guild, 450 U.S. 582 (1981), in which the Court held that neither federal statutes nor the U.S. Constitution require the Commission to review past or anticipated changes in a station's entertainment programming when it rules on an application for renewal or transfer of a radio broadcast license. The Commission may rely on market forces to promote diversity and serve the public interest in entertainment programming. Although *Red Lion* acknowledged that a debate of public issues promotes the public interest it "did not imply that the First Amendment grants individual listeners the right to have the Commission review the abandonment of their favorite entertainment programs." 450 U.S. at 604.

23. See, e.g., Note, Freedom of Expression—Violation of First Amendment for Radio and Television Stations to Deny Completely Broadcasting Time to Editorial Advertisers When Time Is Sold to Commercial Advertisers, 85 Harvard L.Rev. 689 (1972); Marks, Broadcasting and Censorship: First Amendment Theory After Red Lion, 38 Geo.Wash.L.Rev. 974 (1970); But see, Jaffe, The Editorial Responsibility of the Broad-

caster: Reflections on Fairness and Access, 85 Harv.L. Rev. 768 (1972). See generally, Barron, Access to the Press—A New First Amendment Right, 80 Harv.L. Rev. 1641 (1967); Barron, An Emerging First Amendment Right of Access to the Media?, 37 G.W.L.Rev. 487 (1969); J. Barron, Freedom of the Press for Whom? (1973); Lange, The Role of the Access Doctrine in the Regulation of the Mass Media, 52 N.Car.L.Rev. 1 (1973).

24. 412 U.S. 94 (1973).

25. Business Executive's Movement for Vietnam Peace, 25 F.C.C.2d 242 (1970); Democratic National Committee, 25 F.C.C.2d 216 (1970).

26. The majority opinion consisted of Parts I, II, and IV of Chief Justice Burger's opinion, which Justices Rehnquist, White, Blackmun, and Powell joined. The latter three emphasized in their concurring opinion, 412 U.S. at 146-48, that the state action question had not been decided. For an analysis of the state action issues, see Chapter 14.

27. BEM v. FCC, 450 F.2d 642 (D.C.Cir. 1971).

should be open on a nonselective basis to all persons wishing to talk about public issues."[28] Although a Congressional decision or viewpoint cannot be deemed decisive in an issue of constitutional interpretation, the Court was persuaded that the rationale behind this legislative decision was based on sound principles. The *CBS* decision made it clear that any right of access to the electronic media is very limited and that in balancing the competing interests involved "[o]nly when the interests of the public are found to outweigh the private journalistic interests of the broadcasters will government power be asserted within the framework of the [Federal Communications] Act."[29]

The Court concluded that an unlimited right of access would not best serve the public interest. The views of the affluent could still prevail because they could purchase more time to air their views. Valuable broadcast time might be wasted by groups concerned with trivialities. The Court was reluctant to allow full access by individuals who had no responsibilities or accountability to act in the public interest; complete access rights might exchange "public trustee" broadcasting for "a system of self-appointed editorial commentators."[30] The fairness doctrine was not thought to be applicable to editorial advertisements and the BEM and DNC's argument on this basis was inappropriate.[31]

In a later case the Court held that the Communications Act not only does not mandate any claimed right of access,[32] but neither that Act nor the Constitution authorizes or permits the FCC to require broadcasters to extend a range of public access. The majority relied on the fact that section 3(h) of the Act stipulates that broadcasters shall not be treated as common carriers; and it distinguished the fairness doctrine because that rule contemplates a wide range of licensee discretion and does not mandate access to anyone.

The Court in *CBS* was strongly split on the question of whether state action was involved but the decision is of little precedential value on this issue. Justice Burger, joined by Justices Stewart and Rehnquist, emphasized that the government was not a "partner" nor in a "symbiotic relationship" with the licensee;[33] they saw no governmental action involved here which would invoke the proscriptions of the first amendment. Justices White, Blackmun and Powell on the other hand emphasized in their concurring opinions that the case had been decided on other grounds and that the state action issue had not been reached.[34] Justice Douglas, in his concurrence, argued that "the activities of licensees of the government operating in the public domain are governmental actions, so far as constitutional duties and responsibilities are concerned,"[35] but admitted that this view "has not been accepted."[36] Justice Brennan, joined by Justice Marshall, dissented and argued that there was governmental action and that it was improper to rely on the fairness doctrine as the sole means of presenting controversial ideas; rather citizens should be permitted some opportunity to speak directly for themselves.[37]

---

28. 412 U.S. at 105.

29. 412 U.S. at 110.

30. 412 U.S. at 125.

31. 412 U.S. at 124–26. The Court did not clearly discuss this issue, although some lower courts had already developed a theory that commercial advertising is subject to the fairness doctrine. See, e.g., Friends of Earth v. FCC, 449 F.2d 1164 (D.C.Cir. 1971); Retail Store Employees Union v. F.C.C., 436 F.2d 248 (D.C.Cir. 1970).

32. FCC v. Midwest Video Corp., 440 U.S. 689, 705 n. 14 (1979). The Court reserved the question whether it would be constitutional for Congress to give the FCC the power to treat broadcasters as common carriers.

Cf. FCC v. WNCN Listeners Guild, 450 U.S. 582, 603–04 (1981) (FCC may rely on market forces to promote diversity in radio entertainment formats).

33. 412 U.S. at 119.

34. 412 U.S. at 146–148.

35. 412 U.S. at 150.

36. 412 U.S. at 150. Because of this admission, Douglas argued that, since broadcasters are like newspapers, these should be treated no differently. Id. Stewart said that Douglas' views "closely approach" his own. 412 U.S. at 132.

37. 412 U.S. at 180, 189–90 (Brennan, J., dissenting).

In *FCC v. National Citizens Committee for Broadcasting*,[38] the Court held that the FCC, consistent with first amendment, may enact a rule prospectively barring the common ownership of a radio or television station and a daily newspaper located in the same community, and retroactively requiring divestiture of such co-located newspaper-broadcast combinations in the "most egregious" cases. Such regulations further both antitrust and first amendment goals and do not violate the first amendment rights of newspapers because—given the physical limitations of the broadcast spectrum—there is no unabridgeable first amendment right to broadcast comparable to the right of persons to speak, write, or publish.

The Court acknowledged that the government may not restrict the speech of some in order to enhance the relative voice of others, but noted that this general rule does not apply to the broadcasting media which poses unique problems justifying special regulations. These FCC regulations are not content related, nor do they unfairly single out newspaper owners, since owners of radio stations, television stations, and newspapers are, by the new rule, treated alike in their ability to acquire licenses for co-located broadcast stations.

Later, in *C.B.S., Inc. v. F.C.C.*[39] the Court upheld, as consistent with the first amendment, the power granted to the F.C.C. under 47 U.S.C.A. § 312(a)(7). This law gives legally qualified candidates for federal elective office an affirmative, promptly enforceable right of reasonable access, to purchase broadcast time without reference to whether an opponent has secured time. Violation of this section authorizes the F.C.C. to revoke a broadcaster's license. The Court empha-

sized that it was not approving any *"general right of access to the media."* [40] But section 312(a)(7) is constitutional and properly balances the first amendment rights of the public, the broadcasters, and the candidates because it "creates a *limited* right to 'reasonable' access that pertains only to legally qualified federal candidates and may be invoked by them only for the purpose of advancing their candidacies once a campaign has commenced." [41]

Note that in *C.B.S., Inc. v. Democratic National Committee* [42] the Court refused to create a right of access. In *C.B.S., Inc. v. F.C.C.*, on the other hand, the Court upheld the constitutionality of a carefully drawn statute providing for limited access. In both cases the Court was deferring to the judgment of Congress and the F.C.C. in their regulation of the broadcast media. Given the complexity of this area it is not unusual that the Court relies so heavily on congressional judgment and administrative expertise.[43]

Constitutional issues in the area of electronic media such as radio and television have presented unique problems to the courts and will continue to do so. While *Red Lion* emphasized that the monopoly nature which arises from inherent technological restraints on these media probably requires, or at least permits, implementation of a fairness doctrine to best serve the public interest, later case law has made clear, however, that restriction on access deemed to be reasonable are not prohibited by the Constitution.[44]

The first amendment rights of free speech in a broadcasting context raise questions not only of access but also of censorship. In

---

38. 436 U.S. 775 (1978).

39. 453 U.S. 367 (1981).

40. 453 U.S. at 396 (emphasis in original).

41. 453 U.S. at 396 (emphasis in original).

42. 412 U.S. 94 (1973).

43. Cf. Radio Corp. of America v. United States, 341 U.S. 412, 420 (1951): "[C]ourts should not overrule

an administrative decision merely because they disagree with its wisdom."

44. See generally, Bollinger, Freedom of the Press and Public Access: Toward a Theory of Partial Regulation of the Mass Media, 75 Mich.L.Rev. 1 (1976). Cf. Kreiss, Deregulation of Cable Television and the Problem of Access Under the First Amendment, 54 So.Calif. L.Rev. 1001 (1981).

FCC v. Pacifica Foundation [45] a sharply divided Court upheld the power of the FCC to regulate "adult speech" over the radio air waves, at least in some limited circumstances. The Court held that the FCC does have statutory and constitutional power to regulate a radio broadcast that is "indecent" but not "obscene" in the constitutional sense [46] and also does not constitute "fighting words" in the constitutional sense.[47]

In the particular case a radio station broadcast for nearly 12 minutes a record of a George Carlin humorous monologue. This broadcast occurred in the early afternoon when children were likely to be in the audience. During this monologue Carlin repeatedly used various words [48] referring to sexual and excretory activities and organs, and mocked middle class attitudes toward them. The FCC, after having received a complaint from a man who had heard the broadcast with his son on the car radio, issued a "Declaratory Order" against Pacifica. While the FCC did not impose formal sanctions it did add the complaint to the station's license file and noted that if subsequent complaints were received the FCC would then decide whether to utilize any of the sanctions it has, ranging from issuing a cease and desist order or imposing a fine, to revoking the station's license.

First, the justices considered the statutory authority of the FCC to take such actions.

One statutory provision forbids the FCC from engaging in "censorship;" [49] another prohibits "obscene, indecent, or profane" broadcasts.[50] Five members of the Court held that the censorship language only prohibits the Commission from engaging in prior censorship. While the Commission cannot excise material in advance, it can review the content of completed broadcasts in fulfilling its regulatory duties.[51] Second, the majority held that the second statutory provision prohibits not only constitutionally "obscene" language but also "indecent" language, defined as "nonconformance with accepted standards of morality."[52]

Next the Court had to decide if the statute as construed by the majority was constitutional. Five members agreed that broadcasting receives "the most limited" free speech protections of all forms of communication because it is "a uniquely pervasive presence in the lives of all Americans" and "is uniquely accessible to children, even those too young to read." [53] But they could not agree any further on the constitutional rationale for their holding.

In one opinion Justice Stevens, joined by Chief Justice Burger and Justice Rehnquist, thought that "indecency is largely a function of context . . . " and that "a broadcast of patently offensive words dealing with sex and excretion may be regulated because of its content." [54]

45. 438 U.S. 726 (1978). See Krattenmaker and Esterow, Censoring Indecent Cable Programs: The New Morality Meets the New Media, 51 Ford.L.Rev. 606 (1983); Krattenmaker and Powe, Televised Violence: First Amendment Principles and Social Science Theory, 64 Va.L.Rev. 1123 (1978).

46. For an analysis of obscenity, see Section XVII, infra. The present definition of obscenity is found at Section XVII, E, infra.

47. For an analysis of the "fighting words" doctrine, see Section XI, infra.

48. The seven words "that you can't say" were: "shit, piss, fuck, cunt, cocksucker, motherfucker, and tits." Later Carlin added "three more words . . . you could never say on television, and they were fart, turd and twat . . . ." 438 U.S. at 751, 755 (appendix).

The entire monologue is reprinted in an appendix to the opinion.

49. 47 U.S.C.A. § 326.

50. 18 U.S.C.A. § 1464.

51. 438 U.S. at 735. This five person majority also said: "Respect for that [congressional] intent requires that the censorship language be read as inapplicable to the prohibition on broadcasting obscene, indecent, or profane language." 438 U.S. at 738. This language, however, would appear to allow even prior censorship of indecent language. Since the rationale of the opinion does not support this broad language, the majority should not be considered to have embraced it.

52. 438 U.S. at 439–40 (footnote omitted).

53. 438 U.S. at 749.

54. 438 U.S. at 743. (Separate Opinion of Stevens, J., joined by Burger, C. J., and Rehnquist, J.). Another important case in which Justice Stevens has propounded his viewpoint (also not accepted by a majority of the Court) that there can be valid regulations on speech

Justice Powell, joined by Justice Black-mun, wrote a separate opinion. They specif-ically rejected Justice Stevens' view that the Court is "free generally to decide on the ba-sis of its content which speech protected by the First Amendment is most valuable . . . . The result turns instead on the unique characteristics of the broadcast me-dia, combined with society's right to protect its children from speech generally agreed to be inappropriate for their years, and with the interest of unwilling adults in not being assaulted by such offensive speech in their homes."[55]

Justices Stewart and White dissented only on statutory grounds and did not read the constitutional issues.[56] Justice Brennan, joined by Justice Marshall, did reach the con-stitutional issues and strongly dissented. They argued that when an individual turns to a radio station or any transmission broad-cast to the public at large, there is no funda-mental privacy interest implicated. The lis-tener has, by tuning in, decided to take part in an on-going public discussion. Neither, they believed, is the FCC regulation justified by the need to protect children. While par-ents have the right to make certain decisions for their children, it is the parents and not the Government who are to make these deci-sions: "As surprising as it may be to individ-ual members of the Court, some parents may actually find Mr. Carlin's unabashed at-titude towards the seven 'dirty words' healthy, and deem it desirable to expose

their children to the manner in which Mr. Carlin defuses the taboo surrounding the words."[57] Justice Brennan accused the ma-jority of attempting "to unstitch the warp and woof of First Amendment law . . . ."; and he added, the majority's "fragile sensibilities" were the result of "an acute ethnocentric myopia."[58]

The five member majority emphasized that the decision was very narrow, not in-volving a two-way radio conversation, an Elizabethan comedy, a closed-circuit trans-mission, or an occasional expletive. The time of day and the content of the program in which the language is used may also be relevant, as well as the type and amount of punishment imposed.[59] Yet the three mem-ber plurality's willingness to allow govern-ment regulation of content, so long as the regulation appears to these justices to pro-mote reasonable ends—in this case, the end of prohibiting "nonconformance" with ac-cepted standards of morality—is a disquiet-ing and a significant departure from tradi-tional first amendment theory, which normally subjects any type of content regu-lation to very careful and principled judicial review.

In other types of speech, not involving broadcasting, the Court has been much more protective of the first amendment. Thus, the Supreme Court has allowed prohibition of speech which incites illegal conduct within

based on the *content* of the communication in his sepa-rate opinion in Young v. American Mini Theatres, 427 U.S. 50, 52 (1976), noted infra, Section XVII, F, 4.

55. 438 U.S. at 761–762 (Powell, J., joined by Black-mun, J., concurring).

56. The four in dissent argued that "indecent" means no more than "obscene" in the constitutional sense. A related federal statute, the dissent noted, forbade the mailing of every "obscene, . . . inde-cent, . . . or vile article," and the Court had previ-ously construed that language as only referring to ob-scenity in the constitutional sense. Since Carlin's monologue was conceded to be not obscene, the dissent argued that the FCC had no statutory grounds to regu-late it. See 438 U.S. at 779–780 (Stewart, J., dissent-ing, joined by Brennan, White, & Marshall, JJ.).

57. 438 U.S. at 770.

58. 438 U.S. at 775. Justice Brennan feared that the majority's various rationales could justify banning from FCC regulated media the Nixon tapes and impor-tant literary works, including the Bible, all of which uses one or more of the indecent words of the Carlin monologue. See 438 U.S. at 770–771, & n. 5 (footnote 5 of Justice Brennan's dissent quotes several passages from the Bible using several of Carlin's indecent words).

The majority thought such examples to be distin-guishable: "Even a prime time recitation of Chaucer's Miller's Tale would not be likely to command the atten-tion of many children who are both old enough to un-derstand and young enough to be adversely affected by passages such as, 'And prively he caughte hir by the queynte.' G. Chaucer, The Miller's Tale, 1. 3276 (c. 1386)." 438 U.S. at 750, n. 29.

59. 438 U.S. at 750.

the meaning of *Brandenburg v. Ohio* [60] because when a speaker uses speech to cause unthinking, immediate lawless action and is likely to produce such action, one cannot rely on more speech in the marketplace of ideas to correct the errors of the original speech, and the state has signficant interests in and no other means of preventing the resulting lawless conduct.[61] When the Court allowed the prohibition of obscenity, it found, inter alia, that such speech when taken as a whole, lacked any serious literary, artistic, political, or scientific value.[62] It did not judge some types of obscene speech to be more worthy of protection than other types, nor find that obscenity in an Elizabethan comedy is permissible but obscenity in a modern comedy is not. Rather it attempted to fashion a principled means of distinguishing a certain type of speech. But Justice Stevens would prohibit the use of a word in the Carlin monologue though he would allow the same word to be used in a reading of Chaucer's Miller's Tale,[63] or an Elizabethan comedy,[64] apparently because he feels the latter types of speech are more valuable than the Carlin satire. Similarly, he would allow the same words to be used if he thought the monologue to have political content.[65]

The four member dissent, as well as Justices Powell and Blackmun in their concurring opinion, specifically disavoided a theory that the degree of protection of speech varies with the ad hoc view of five members of the Court as to its social value, but the latter two justices did agree that the FCC action was constitutional. With this decision, then,

one is left in doubt as to the strictness with which the Court will review content regulation—at least as regards the electronic media—in the future. It appears that the permissibility of such regulation may depend on the personal notions of at least five justices concerning the worth of the regulated speech. As Justice Stevens concluded in a portion of his opinion joined by four justices:

> We simply hold that when the Commission finds that a pig has entered the parlor [instead of the barnyard], the exercise of its regulatory power does not depend on proof that the pig is obscene.[66]

2. The Fairness Doctrine and the Regulation of Traditional Print Media

Traditional media, particularly newspapers, have come under pressure from those advocating a first amendment right of access to make their views on public issues known, similar to the restrictions placed on the electronic media.[1] In general, it is argued that the right of free speech guaranteed by the Constitution is meaningless if the speakers are not also given access to the media necessary to present these views to the general public[2] because of the monopolistic nature of modern newspapers.

The Supreme Court however has strongly rejected the notion that a government guaranteed right of access or a fairness doctrine can apply to the press. In *Miami Herald Publishing Co., Inc. v. Tornillo*,[3] a unanimous Court struck down, as violative of the first amendment, a Florida statute that required newspapers to give free reply space to political candidates whom they had at-

60. 395 U.S. 444 (1969) (per curiam).

61. 395 U.S. 44 (1969) (per curiam). See Section IV, D, supra.

62. See Section XVII, E, supra. Note also that the zoning of adult movies allowed in Young v. American Mini Theatres, 427 U.S. 50 (1976), see n. 54, supra, involved valid goals other than the regulation of speech, 427 U.S. at 71 n. 34 (Stevens, J.) & 427 U.S. at 80 (Powell, J.). See also 438 U.S. at 774 (Brennan, J., dissenting).

63. See note 58, supra.

64. See text at note 58, supra.

65. 438 U.S. at 746.

66. 438 U.S. at 750–51.

1. Cf. Red Lion Broadcasting Co. v. FCC, 395 U.S. 367 (1969) (fairness doctrine upheld); CBS, Inc. v. Democratic National Committee, 412 U.S. 94 (1973) (no right of access to broadcast media is constitutionally required for groups seeking to place editorial advertisements).

2. E.g., Barron, Access to the Press—A New First Amendment Right, 80 Harv.L.Rev. 1641 (1967); Cf. T. Emerson, The System of Freedom of Expression 671 (1970).

3. 418 U.S. 241 (1974).

tacked in their columns. The Court based its holding on the premise that a statute which told a newspaper what it must print in fact was exacting a penalty on the basis of the content of the newspaper; this, the Court felt, was unconstitutional censorship.[4]

Although not subject to the same finite limitations of the broadcast media which were deemed so important in the electronic media cases [5] the opinion of the Court recognizes that newspapers are also subject to space limitations which must be considered in balancing the public interest in access against the rights of the publishers.[6] But such physical limitations were not seen to be the primary concern in denying reply space in newspapers, an issue which in fact was only briefly discussed.[7] Even if a compulsory law did not create economic problems or cause the newspaper to have to forego printing something else to give space to a reply, the reply law's great evil was that it intruded on the rights and functions of the newspaper and its editors and reporters:

> It has yet to be demonstrated how governmental regulation of this crucial process can be exercised consistent with First Amendment guarantees of a free press as they have evolved to this time.[8]

Miami Herald firmly established that the right of newspaper editors to choose what they wish to print or not to print cannot be abridged to allow the public access to the newspaper media. The "virtually insurmountable barrier" [9] which freedom of the press erects between governmental regulation and the print media stands firm.

An important distinction between the fairness doctrine as applied to electronic media and the fairness doctrine which cannot be applied to the print media is that the former enjoys a legal monopoly, which justifies FCC regulations requiring "fairness." [10] There is no legal monopoly of newspapers. While some local towns may be served by only one paper, yet other print media—nationwide newspapers such as the New York Times, weekly newsmagazines, or so-called underground newspapers—are not legally barred from these same "channels." If someone is not satisfied that the local newspaper is printing his views he may publish his pamphlets, posters, or leaflets—all without securing a Government license and opening up his channels of communication to others of opposing views. Moreover if a newspaper is sufficiently insensitive to the needs of its readers, the economic system will develop competitors who are.[11]

Finally, if we assume that the problem of lack of access is as serious as those arguing for government regulation of the print me-

---

4. In discussing precedent, the Court noted that "[T]he clear implication has been that any such a compulsion to publish that which 'reason' tells them [newspaper publishers] should not be published is unconstitutional." And it went on to say "The Florida statute exacts a penalty on the basis of the content of a newspaper." 418 U.S. at 256.

5. See, e.g., National Broadcasting Co. v. United States, 319 U.S. 190 (1943); Red Lion Broadcasting Co. v. FCC, 395 U.S. 367 (1969); Columbia Broadcasting System v. Democratic National Committee, 412 U.S. 94 (1973).

6. "It is correct, as appellee contends, that a newspaper is not subject to the finite technological limitations of time that confront a broadcaster but it is not correct to say, that, as an economic reality, a newspaper can proceed to infinite expansion of column space to accommodate the replies that a government agency determines or a statute commands the readers should have available." 418 U.S. at 256–57. (footnote omitted).

7. 418 U.S. at 256–57.

8. 418 U.S. at 258. Accord, 2 Z. Chafee, Government and Mass Communications 709–10 (1947) ("If officials can tell newspapers what to put into their editorial pages, . . . [the next] step [is] to tell them what to leave out.").

9. 418 U.S. at 259 (White, J., concurring opinion). However, the right of the press to make the editorial judgment to print or not print does not protect the press from appropriate libel actions and, in such libel actions, the press has no immunity from a libel plaintiff inquiring about the editorial process. Herbert v. Lando, 441 U.S. 153, 166–69 (1979).

10. Red Lion Broadcasting Co. v. FCC, 395 U.S. 367 (1969).

11. Cf. R. Posner, Economic Analysis of Law § 22.3 at 314 (1972).

dia assert, the solution of access overestimates its effectiveness:

> To say that the media have great decision-making powers without defined legal responsibilities or any formal duties of public accountability is both to overestimate their power and to put forth a meaningless formula for reform. How shall we make the *New York Times* "accountable" for its anti-Vietnam policy? Require it to print letters to the editor in support of the war? If the situation is as grave as stated, the remedy is fantastically inadequate. But the situation is not that grave. The *New York Times*, the *Chicago Tribune*, NBC, ABC, and CBS play a role in policy formation, but clearly they were not alone responsible, for example, for Johnson's decision not to run for re-election, Nixon's refusal to withdraw the troops from Vietnam, the rejection of the two billion dollar New York bond issue, the defeat of Carswell and Haynsworth, or the Supreme Court's segregation, reappointment and prayer decisions. The implication that the people of this country—except the proponents of the theory—are mere unthinking automatons manipulated by the media, without interests, conflicts, or prejudices is an assumption which I find quite maddening. The development of constitutional doctrine should not be based on such hysterical overestimation of media power and underestimation of the good sense of the American public.[12]

In the same term with *Miami Herald* the Court considered another access case, this time not involving the private press but rather the use of billboard space on a city-owned public transportation system. In *Lehman v. City of Shaker Heights*,[13] a divided Court

held, 5–4,[14] that a city which operates a public rapid transit system does not violate the first or fourteenth amendments by selling commercial advertising space for cigarette companies, banks, liquor companies, churches, and public service groups on its vehicles while refusing to accept any political advertising on behalf of candidates for public office or public issue advertising.[15]

The essential problem in *Lehman* was not a pure right to access, but rather a right of equal access. Plaintiffs argued that by making the advertising space available for some uses, the city had created a public forum and could not now censor the content of speech in that forum by banning political advertisements. The majority of the Court firmly rejected the contention that card space on a city transit system is to be deemed a public forum for a variety of reasons, to minimize chances of abuse, the appearance of favoritism, and the risk of imposing upon a captive audience.[16] Justice Douglas' concurring opinion emphasized the distinctions between this claimed forum and the situations which had previously given rise to the concept of a "public forum."

> But a streetcar or bus is plainly not a park or sidewalk or other meeting place for discussion, any more than is a highway. It is only a way to get to work or back home. The fact that it is owned and operated by the city does not without more make it a forum. . . .

> And if we are to turn a bus or streetcar into either a newspaper or a park, we take great liberties with people who because of necessity

---

12. Jaffe, The Editorial Responsibility of the Broadcaster: Reflections on Fairness and Access, 85 Harv.L. Rev. 768, 786–87 (1972). See also, Abrams, Book Review, 86 Yale L.J. 361, 363–64 (1976). But see, B. Schmidt, Freedom of the Press vs. Public Access 13, 227–29 (1976).

13. 418 U.S. 298 (1974).

14. Justice Blackmun's opinion was joined in by three other Justices; Justice Douglas, the fifth vote, wrote his own concurrence, relying heavily on the idea that the audience of a bus is captive. 418 U.S. 298, 305–308.

15. 418 U.S. 298, 300–301. See also, United States Postal Service v. Council of Greenburgh Civic Associations, 453 U.S.114 (1981) (18 U.S.C.A. § 1725, prohibiting the deposit of unstamped, "mailable matter" in a letter box approved by the U.S. Postal Service is consti-

tutional; mail boxes are not public forums, and section 1725 does not regulate on the basis of content).

16. 418 U.S. at 304. "These are reasonable legislative objectives advanced by the city in a proprietary capacity. In these circumstances, there is no First or Fourteenth Amendment violation." 418 U.S. at 304.

Contrast Metromedia, Inc. v. City of San Diego, 453 U.S. 490 (1981). There a fragmented Court invalidated laws restricting the display of billboards. The zoning laws, inter alia, drew a distinction between on-site commercial advertising (allowed) and on-site noncommercial advertising (not allowed). The Court found this distinction unconstitutional. In this case, however, the city could not advance adequate justification for the distinction; moreover it was not acting in a proprietary capacity.

become commuters and at the same time captive viewers or listeners.[17]

The Court noted that the city, like a newspaper or the electronic media, could exercise its discretion concerning the types of advertising it accepted,[18] although because of the state action involved, policies governing access by advertisers must not be "arbitrary, capricious, or invidious."[19]

The four dissenters[20] were seemingly not as concerned with the rights of the commuter because they felt that a public forum had been created:

> [T]he city created a forum for the dissemination of information and expression of ideas when it accepted and displayed commercial and public service advertisements on its rapid transit vehicles.[21]

Having once created a public forum, the dissent argued, the city could not discriminate on the basis of message content between types of advertising,[22] and the fact that entire classes of advertising were banned, rather than particular ads, did not make the city's choice any less censorship.[23]

Although later cases have extended the public forum concept to go beyond parks and streets, to include a public auditorium,[24] the Court in *Lehman* refused to expand the doctrine to include public transportation facilities. "If a bus is a forum it is more akin to a newspaper than to a park," and newspapers cannot be forced to include items "which outsiders may desire but which the owner abhors."[25]

B. A Right of Access by the Press: Speech in a Restricted Environment

In the companion cases of *Pell v. Procunier*[1] and *Saxbe v. Washington Post Co.*,[2] the Supreme Court rejected claims by prisoners and the press that the first amendment guaranteed a right of access to the newspapers to interview individual prisoners; California and federal prison regulations which prohibited face-to-face interviews between prisoners and members of the news media were upheld.[3]

The constitutional right of inmates to seek individual interviews with members of the press was not explored in *Saxbe* because inmates were not a party to the litigation.[4] In *Pell v. Procunier*,[5] however, the Court ex-

17. 418 U.S. at 306–07 (concurring opinion). See also 418 U.S. at 304 (Blackmun, J.) Cf., Hague v. CIO, 307 U.S. 496, 515–516 (1939), where Justice Roberts argued parks and streets are public forums whose use "may be regulated in the interest of all . . . but it must not, in the guise of regulation, be abridged or denied". While a majority of the Court at this time did not join in this view, the Court has now adopted it. E.g., Schneider v. State, 308 U.S. 147, 163 (1939); Kunz v. New York, 340 U.S. 290, 293 (1951). See Section XIII of this chapter.

18. 418 U.S. at 303. Cf. Public Utilities Comm'n v. Pollak, 343 U.S. 451 (1952).

19. 418 U.S. at 303.

20. Brennan, J., filed a lengthy dissenting opinion, in which Stewart, Marshall, and Powell, JJ., joined. 418 U.S. at 308–22.

21. 418 U.S. at 310 (Brennan, J., dissenting opinion).

22. 418 U.S. at 310 (Brennan, J., dissenting opinion).

23. 418 U.S. at 316 (Brennan, J., dissenting opinion).

24. See, e.g., Southeastern Promotions Ltd. v. Conrad, 420 U.S. 546 (1975). Here the Court evidenced willingness to apply public forum analysis whenever use of a public facility is denied those who wish to exercise their free speech rights; held: a municipal auditorium is a public forum. See also, Note, Constitutional Law—Southeastern Promotions, Ltd. v. Conrad: A

Contemporary Concept of the Public Forum, 54 N. Carolina L.Rev. 439 (1976).

25. 418 U.S. 298, 306 (Douglas, J., concurring); Miami Herald Publishing Co. v. Tornillo, 418 U.S. 241 (1974).

1. 417 U.S. 817 (1974).

2. 417 U.S. 843 (1974).

3. *Pell* challenged regulation section 415.071 of the California Department of Corrections Manual (Aug. 23, 1971) which reads as follows: "Press and other media interviews with specific individual inmates will not be permitted." 417 U.S. at 819. In *Saxbe*, the Washington Post and one of its reporters challenged Policy Statement 1220 1A para. 4b(6) of the Federal Bureau of Prisons (February 11, 1972), which reads as follows:

> "Press representatives will not be permitted to interview individual inmates. This rule shall apply even where the inmate requests or seeks an interview. However, conversation may be permitted with inmates whose identity is not to be made public, if it is limited to the discussion of institutional facilities, programs and activities." 417 U.S. at 844 at n. 1.

4. Only the newspaper involved, the Washington Post, and one of its reporters brought suit against the Attorney General to challenge the regulation.

5. 417 U.S. 817 (1974).

plored this aspect of the first amendment in light of the prisoners' unique position in society. Justice Stewart, writing for the majority,[6] began by noting that while an absolute ban on interviews applied to the public at large would clearly involve a freedom of speech issue, the right to hold a press conference does not necessarily survive incarceration. Starting from the proposition that "[l]awful incarceration brings about the necessary withdrawal or limitation of many privileges and rights, a retraction justified by the considerations underlying our penal system",[7] the Court proceeded to balance the rights of inmates against the state's legitimate interests in security and rehabilitation of prisoners.[8]

Great emphasis was placed on the fact that the prisoners had alternative means of communication with the press, including uncensored mailing privileges and a visitation policy allowing face-to-face conversation with family, attorneys, the clergy and long-standing friends. Determining that these alternative channels were sufficient to ensure that reasonable and effective means of communication with the outside remain open to the prisoner, the Court refused to find that a restriction of one manner of communication

was sufficient to violate a prisoner's first amendment rights.[9]

While the Court admitted "we would find the availability of such alternatives unimpressive if they were submitted as justification for governmental restriction of personal communication among members of the general public,"[10] it went on to recognize that prisoners are in a closer relationship with their wardens than the average person is with the state and "[s]o long as reasonable and effective means of communication remain open and no discrimination in terms of content is involved, we believe that in drawing such lines, 'prison officials must be accorded latitude'."[11]

Both *Pell* and *Saxbe* considered the issue of whether this limitation on press interviews violates freedom of the press as guaranteed by the Constitution. The press contended that, irrespective of any first amendment rights of the prisoners, members of the press have a constitutional right of access to interview any willing inmate. This right, they claimed, could only be abridged if the prison authorities made an individualized determination that interviewing a particular inmate would constitute a clear and present danger to prison security or another substantial interest of the prison

---

6. Justice Powell concurred in the majority opinion but dissented on the issue of the press' right. 417 U.S. at 835–36 (1974). Justice Douglas, joined by Justices Brennan and Marshall, dissented on both U.S. 319, 321 (1972). Cf. Jones v. North Carolina Prisoners' Labor Union, Inc., 433 U.S. 119 (1977).

7. 417 U.S. at 822, quoting Price v. Johnson, 334 U.S. 266, 285 (1948). See also, Cruz v. Beto, 405 U.S. 319, 321 (1972). Cf. Jones v. North Carolina Prisoners' Labor Union, Inc., 433 U.S. 119 (1977).

The principle that a convicted prisoner does not possess the full range of freedoms of an unincarcerated person "applies equally" to lawfully incarcerated pretrial detainees, although the detainers have not yet been convicted beyond a reasonable doubt. Bell v. Wolfish, 441 U.S. 520, 545–547, 553 (1979).

8. 417 U.S. at 822–24. It is interesting to note that at the time that these regulations were adopted, prison officials were very concerned that press attention to individual inmates was fostering a "big wheel" syndrome and causing certain prisoners to gain prestige and undue influence over the other inmates. The California regulation had been enacted two days after one of these "big wheels" had engineered an escape attempt

which resulted in the deaths of three staff members and two inmates.

9. 417 U.S. at 824–28. It should be noted that some forms of prisoner communication are protected, but based on the right of the nonprisoner correspondent, not on the rights of prisoners. Procunier v. Martinez, 416 U.S. 396, 412–13 (1974). Thus, prison officials cannot censor mail from prisoners "simply to eliminate unflattering or unwelcome opinions or factually inaccurate statements." 396 U.S. at 413. Cf. Procunier v. Navarette, 434 U.S. 555, 563–66 (1978).

Consistent with the first amendment, prison authorities may prohibit the receipt, by prisoners, of hardcover books unless they are mailed directly from publishers, book stores, or book clubs. That restriction is a limited one and a "rational response by prison officials to an obvious security problem" because hardback books are especially serviceable for smuggling contraband, and it is difficult and time consuming to search them effectively. Bell v. Wolfish, 441 U.S. 520, 548–51 (1979).

10. 417 U.S. at 825.

11. 417 U.S. at 826, citing Cruz v. Beto, 405 U.S. at 321.

system. The press did not claim a violation or restriction of their right to publish, only of their right to gather news.

The Court rejected this argument in both cases, stating in *Pell* that: "[N]ewsmen have no constitutional right of access to prisons or their inmates beyond that afforded the general public." [12] While agreeing that a journalist is free to seek out sources of information, the Court pointed out that this was a far cry from saying that the Constitution places upon the State "the affirmative duty to make available to journalists sources of information not available to members of the public generally." [13]

The majority of the Court found *Saxbe* to be "constitutionally indistinguishable" from *Pell* on these issues.[14] In *Saxbe*, the Court pointed out that the record revealed that the press had actually been given more access to the prisoners than the general public had,[15] noting that newsmen could tour, take pictures, and even conduct on-the-spot interviews with inmates they ran into. Justice Powell, dissenting in *Saxbe*,[16] felt that testimony had shown that personal interviews are crucial to effective reporting in a prison context and rejected the idea of alternative means of communication as adequate.[17]

Pell and *Saxbe* may not have much precedential value outside the restricted environment of a prison, for they do not apply usual first amendment standards. However, the cases do firmly reject a right of access by the press greater than that of the general public, a holding which appears to go beyond prison cases, although *Pell* acknowledged that "news gathering is not without its First Amendment protections." [18]

A few years later, in another prison case, *Houchins v. KQED, Inc.*[19] the Supreme Court, in a four to three vote, with two justices not participating, reversed a lower court injunction ordering prison officials to grant access to the press to certain prison facilities; however, the fragmented court produced no majority opinion. Chief Justice Burger, joined by Justices White and Rehnquist, found that there is no first or fourteenth amendment right of access to government information or sources of information within the government's control. Further, the press has no greater right of access than that of the public generally.

Justice Stewart concurred in the judgment, but on much narrower grounds. He agreed the press has no right of access "superior to that of the public generally," but that the concept of equal access must be flexibly applied "to accommodate the practical distinctions between the press and the general public." [20] In the context of this case, he believed that flexibility could require reasonable use of camera and sound equipment to members of the press in the

---

12. 417 U.S. at 834.

13. 417 U.S. at 834.

14. 417 U.S. at 850.

15. 417 U.S. at 849.

16. Powell was joined by Brennan and Marshall, 417 U.S. at 850. Douglas dissented from both *Pell* and *Saxbe* in the same opinion, 417 U.S. at 836.

17. 417 U.S. at 853–54.

18. 417 U.S. at 833, quoting Branzburg v. Hayes, 408 U.S. 665, 707 (1972).

See also, Burger, C. J., concurring in First Nat. Bank v. Bellotti, 435 U.S. 765, 795, 798 (1978), where the Chief Justice noted that the "Court has not yet resolved whether the Press Clause confers upon the 'institutional press' any freedom from government restraint not enjoyed by all others"; however, after a careful and powerful analysis he concluded that there is no difference in rights guaranteed by the speech vs. press clauses.

See generally, Halle, The News-Gathering/Publication Dichotomy and Government Expression, 1982 Duke L.J. 1.

19. 438 U.S. 1 (1978).

See also Gannett Co., Inc. v. DePasquale, 443 U.S. 368, 391–93 (1979) (assuming that members of the press and public have a constitutional right of access to pretrial hearings, this alleged right was given appropriate deference by the state trial court when it closed a pretrial hearing; the press did not object immediately to defendant's closure motion and any denial of access was not absolute but only temporary because a transcript of the suppression hearing was made available after the dangers of pretrial prejudice dissipated).

20. 438 U.S. at 16 (Stewart, J., concurring). Contra, Burger, C. J., concurring in, First Nat. Bank v. Bellotti, 435 U.S. 765, 795 (1978).

areas open to both press and public, because the fact that "the First Amendment speaks separately of freedom of speech and of the press is no constitutional accident, but an acknowledgement of the critical role played by the press in American society." [21] Because the lower court injunction was overbroad and had granted the press greater access to prison areas than the public generally, he agreed with the reversal, but would not prohibit more carefully tailored relief on remand.

Justice Stevens, joined by Justices Brennan and Powell, dissented. They distinguished *Pell* and *Saxbe* [22] as limited to the case where there already was substantial press and public access to the prison. The dissent would grant a right of public and press access to prisons, while allowing the prison officials only a right to regulate reasonably the time and manner of that access. The dissent agreed that the press has "no greater right of access to information than that possessed by the public at large" but would not have reversed the lower court injunction granting a greater access to the press since the public generally had not requested separate relief and it was proper for the lower court to fashion relief to the needs of the litigant before it.

Since there was no majority opinion and two justices—Marshall and Blackmun—did not participate, the *Houchins* decision probably will not end litigation over public access to prisons in cases where there is only limited access to parts of the jail. [23] However, the seven justices did agree that there the press has no greater right of access to prisons than the public generally.

The Supreme Court has invalidated a state employment commission's order requiring a school board to prohibit teachers who are not union representatives from speaking at open meetings at which public participation is permitted, even if the speech is addressed to the subject of pending collective bargaining negotiations, [24] thus giving the press and the public a similar right of access to such speech.

However, the state's power to restrict the use which the press makes of its access in a *nonprison* setting was approved in the facts of *Zacchini v. Scripps-Howard Broadcasting Co.* [25] There the Court held the right of a state to grant a "right of publicity" to an individual, such as a performer (a person with a name having commercial value) by protecting the proprietary interest in his act, in part to encourage such entertainment. The freedom of speech protections do not immunize the news media from a damage action by the performer when it broadcasts the performer's entire act (in this case a 15 second act) for which he normally gets paid. "The Constitution no more prevents a state from requiring respondent to compensate petitioner for broadcasting his act on television than it would privilege respondent to film and broadcast a copyrighted dramatic work without liability to the copyright owner." [26]

The press has no constitutional right to access to evidence given at trials greater than that of the general public. In *Nixon v. Warner Communications, Inc.,* [27] the Court held that neither the first amendment guarantee of free speech and press nor the sixth amendment guarantee of a public trial gives the press the right to copy evidence given at trial. News organizations sought to copy several Watergate tapes that had been introduced at the trial of several defendants, but

---

21.   438 U.S. at 17 (Stewart, J., concurring).

22.   Pell v. Procunier, 417 U.S. 817 (1974); Saxbe v. Washington Post Co., 417 U.S. 843 (1974).

23.   Cf. Philadelphia Newspapers, Inc. v. Jerome, 434 U.S. 241 (1978) (per curiam) (raising issue of press and public access to pretrial suppression hearings; state court judgment vacated to clarify the record).

24.   City of Madison v. Wisconsin Employment Relations Comm'n, 429 U.S. 167 (1976).

25.   433 U.S. 562 (1977).

26.   433 U.S. at 575. The Court specifically distinguished Time, Inc. v. Hill, 385 U.S. 374 (1964), as a false light privacy case not involving an appropriation of a name or likeness for purposes of trade. For a further discussion of *Hill*, see this chapter, Section X, B. For further discussion of the *Zacchini* case, see Section X, E of this Chapter.

27.   435 U.S. 589 (1978).

the Court held that the opportunity to listen to the tapes at trial and to receive transcripts of them had satisfied both constitutional guarantees. The Court held that within the courtroom, the press enjoys no greater rights than does the public, but that the press is free, within broad limits, to report what its representatives have seen at the proceeding.[28]

VII. OTHER REGULATION OF THE PRESS—ANTITRUST, LABOR RELATIONS, AND TAXATION

The Court has clearly established that the first amendment does not bestow antitrust immunity on newspapers, broadcasters, and other news media even though enforcement of the antitrust laws might cause a newspaper to go bankrupt.[1] The principle underlying the Court's position was described by Justice Black in *Associated Press v. United States*.[2]

> Freedom to publish means freedom for all and not for some. Freedom to publish is guaranteed by the Constitution, but freedom to combine to keep others from publishing is not. Freedom of the press from governmental interference under the First Amendment does not sanction repression of that freedom by private interests [through conspiracies in restraint of trade]. The First Amendment affords not the slightest support for the contention that a combination to restrain trade in news and views has any constitutional immunity.[3]

The test in such cases should be that the applicable antitrust laws should be even-handed, nondiscriminatory and neutral on their face and in effect. A state antitrust law that was written only to apply to the dissemination of news would raise more substantial first amendment issues.[4]

On a similar theory, the Court held that the first amendment does not bar nondiscriminatory application of the National Labor Relations Act to the news media in *Associated Press v. NLRB*.[5] The law in question did not affect the impartial distribution of news.[6]

The Government may not impose flat taxes which serve to burden a privilege guaranteed by the Bill of Rights.[7] Thus, in *Follett v. McCormick*,[8] the Court struck down a flat license tax as applied to one who earns his livelihood as an evangelist or preacher. Those who preach, "like other citizens, may be subject to general taxation [but that] does not mean that they can be required to pay a tax for the exercise of that which the First Amendment has made a high constitutional privilege."[9]

The Court has also invalidated discriminatory taxes on the dissemination of news. The leading case is *Grosjean v. American Press Co.*[10] where the Court struck down a

---

28. 435 U.S. at 608–609. The Court also held that the common law right of access to judicial records does not authorize release of the tapes, in light of the Presidential Recordings Act. Justices Marshall and Stevens dissented, each writing a separate opinion, and Justice White dissented in part, joined by Justice Brennan.

1. Citizen Publishing Co. v. United States, 394 U.S. 131 (1969). See also Lorain Journal Co. v. United States, 342 U.S. 143 (1951); United States v. Radio Corp. of America, 358 U.S. 334 (1959).

2. 326 U.S. 1 (1945).

3. Id. at 20 (footnote omitted).

4. Cf. Grosjean v. American Press Co., 297 U.S. 233, 250–51 (1936).

5. 301 U.S. 103 (1937).

6. Associated Press v. NLRB, 301 U.S. at 132 (1937). See also Oklahoma Press Publishing Co. v. Walling, 327 U.S. 186 (1946) (Wage and hour laws).

7. Murdock v. Pennsylvania, 319 U.S. 105, 113 (1943).

8. 321 U.S. 573 (1944).

As to the constitutionality of a license tax in a non-religious context, see Corona Daily Independent v. City of Corona, 115 Cal.App.2d 382, 252 P.2d 56, cert. denied 346 U.S. 833 (1953). Justice Douglas, joined by Justice Black, dissented from the denial of certiorari. He summarized the case as follows:

> "Petitioners publish a newspaper in Corona, California. The city has by ordinance imposed a license tax for the privilege of engaging in any business in the city, including the business of publishing a newspaper. Petitioners refused to pay the license fee, and the California courts have held that they may be compelled to do so." (346 U.S. at 833).

Justice Douglas argued that such a license tax violates the First Amendment because "No government can exact a price for the exercise of a privilege which the Constitution guarantees." 346 U.S. at 834.

9. 321 U.S. at 578.

10. 297 U.S. 233 (1936).

state tax (which was in addition to other taxes of general applicability) on 2% of the gross receipts of advertising in those newspapers with circulation of more than 20,000 copies per week. The Court explained:

> It is not intended by anything we have said to suggest that the owners of newspapers are immune from any of the ordinary forms of taxation for support of the government. But this is not an ordinary form of tax . . . It is bad because, in the light of its history and of its present setting, it is seen to be a deliberate and calculated device *in the guise of a tax* to limit the circulation of information to which the public is entitled in virtue of the constitutional guaranties. . . .
>
> The form in which the tax is imposed is in itself suspicious. It is not measured or limited by the volume of advertisements. It is measured alone by the extent of the circulation of the publication in which the advertisements are carried, with the plain purpose of penalizing the publishers and curtailing the circulation of a selected group of newspapers.[11]

Though the state may apply general business taxes without violating the first amendment, even though some of these business activities relate to free speech,[12] it may not enact laws, in the guise of a tax, designed to limit the circulation of newspapers.

In *Minneapolis Star and Tribune Co. v. Minnesota Comm'r of Revenue*[13] the Court interpreted *Grosjean* as dependent on the legislature having improper censorial goals or motive.[14] However, even without such improper goals a tax may be invalid. In Minnesota periodic publications were exempt from the state's general sales and use taxes. But Minnesota had a special "use" tax on the cost of paper and ink products consumed in the production of periodic publications after the first $100,000 worth of ink and paper consumed in a calendar year.

The Court invalidated this tax, which singled out the press for special tax burdens. The state's interest in revenue "cannot justify the special treatment of the press" because the state could "raise the revenue by taxing businesses generally . . . ."[15] The Court emphasized this point by noting that a nondiscriminatory sales tax, which also taxed the sale of newspapers would be constitutional.[16] Finally, the Court found the Minnesota use tax improper because it targeted a small group within the press, those who would exceed the $100,000 exemption. Singling out only the larger publishers had a strong potential for abuse.[17]

VIII. THE PRESS AND THE CRIMINAL JUSTICE SYSTEM

A. Introduction

It has been said that the press and the government are natural adversaries. An appreciation of the conflicting functions with which each is endowed will aid in an understanding of their adversarial roles in the area of criminal justice. The Supreme Court has observed:

> A responsible press has always been regarded as the handmaiden of effective judicial administration, especially in the criminal field. Its function in this regard is documented by an impressive record of service over several centuries. The press does not simply publish information about trials but guards against the miscarriage of justice by subjecting the police, prosecutors, and judicial processes to extensive public scrutiny and criticism.[1]

It is not surprising that this relationship is accompanied by a certain degree of rancor as well as suspicion that each is attempting to stunt the effectiveness of the other by intruding unnecessarily into the other's respective sphere of responsibility. The

---

11. 297 U.S. 233, 250–51 (emphasis added).

12. Cf. Cammarano v. United States, 358 U.S. 498 (1959) (Government may forbid as a business deduction, money spent on lobbying activities).

13. 103 S.Ct. 1365 (1983).

14. 103 S.Ct. at 1369.

15. 103 S.Ct. at 1372 (footnote omitted).

16. 103 S.Ct. at 1373 n.9. The Court rejected a rule which would allow the state to single out the press for

a different method of taxation so long as the effective tax burden was no greater, because differential treatment threatens the press and "courts as institutions are poorly equipped to evaluate with precision the relative burdens of various methods of taxation." 103 S.Ct. at 1374 (footnote omitted).

17. 103 S.Ct. at 1375.

1. Sheppard v. Maxwell, 384 U.S. 333, 350 (1966).

courts have been charged with the duty of maintaining this dynamic tension without diminishing the independence of either. The central question which confronts the judiciary in this area is whether there exists any order of pre-eminence among the conflicting rights and duties with constitutional recognition? This question has been assessed in two contexts concerning the press and the criminal justice system. First, does the first amendment provide for the protection of confidential sources when such information is relevant to a criminal investigation or prosecution? Second, does there exist any power in the government to restrain the publication of information which may jeopardize a defendant's rights to a fair trial?

B. The Protection of Confidential Sources

In *Branzburg v. Hayes*,[2] the Supreme Court, by a 5 to 4 majority, rejected a reporter's claim that, as the flow of information available to the press would be impeded if newsmen were compelled to release the names of confidential sources for use in a government investigation, the first amendment must be held to embrace a privilege to constitutionally refuse to divulge such information in order to protect the reporter's channels to the community. Though the issue before the Court and the *Branzburg* decision itself has far-reaching implications, Justice White in speaking for the majority phrased the question and his holding narrowly: "The issue in these cases is whether requiring newsmen to appear and testify before state or federal grand juries abridges the freedom of speech and press guaranteed by the First Amendment. We hold that it does not."[3] Left undecided was the scope of a newsman's privilege, if any, in testimony before administrative hearings, legislative hearings, and in civil suits.

The issue of the existence of such a constitutional privilege was initially raised in 1958 before the Second Circuit in *Garland v. Torre*,[4] but had generally been rejected by the lower courts. *Branzburg* was the first time the Supreme Court had granted certiorari to review the issue. Although the Court noted that some protection of news sources was necessary unless the information-gathering process was to be totally eviscerated, petitioners had not established that such a result would occur unless greater protection than that traditionally afforded the press was made available.

> Only where news sources themselves are implicated in crime or possess information relevant to the grand jury's task need they or the reporter be concerned about grand jury subpoenas. Nothing before us indicates that a large number or percentage of *all* confidential news sources falls into either category and would in any way be deterred by our holding that the Constitution does not, as it never has, exempt the newsman from performing the citizen's normal duty of appearing and furnishing information relevant to the grand jury's task.[5]

Even if it were assumed that the flow of news would be greatly diminished by sources who were not subject to a grand jury subpoena, the public interest in the investigation and prosecution of crimes outweighs that public interest in the availability of sources for future use, the Court concluded.

Moreover, the opinion emphasized that the difficulties of administering such a privilege would be enormous. It would eventually be necessary to categorize the various individuals and organizations participating in the distribution of information to determine those qualified to exercise the privilege. This would be a most "questionable procedure in light of the traditional doctrine that liberty of the press is the right of the lonely pam-

---

2. 408 U.S. 665 (1972). See generally, V. Blasi, Press Subpoenas: An Empirical and Legal Analysis (1972).

3. 408 U.S. at 667.

4. 259 F.2d 545 (2d Cir. 1958), cert. denied 358 U.S. 910. Prior to *Garland*, newsmen had attempted, gen-

erally unsuccessfully to establish a common law privilege in the federal courts, see e.g., Brewster v. Boston Herald-Traveler Corp., 20 F.R.D. 416 (D.Mass.1957).

5. Branzburg v. Hayes, 408 U.S. 665, 691 (1972) (emphasis in original).

phleteer . . . as much as of the large metropolitan publisher . . . ." [6] In addition, as the privilege claimed was only conditional, each assertion would require a judicial determination that it was properly invoked; i.e., there existed alternative methods to obtain this information, that it was not relevant to the subject of the investigation, or that such information is not intrinsic to a successful prosecution.[7]

In spite of these arguments the Court did leave open an avenue of redress for newsmen who feel they are being harassed by government officials.

> [G]rand jury investigations if instituted or conducted other than in good faith, would pose wholly different issues for resolution under the First Amendment. Official harassment of the press undertaken not for purposes of law enforcement but to disrupt a reporter's relationship with his news sources would have no justification. Grand juries are subject to judicial control and subpoenas to motions to quash.[8]

Justice Powell, who cast the crucial fifth vote, strikes a somewhat problematical note for future litigation relying upon *Branzburg.* Believing that the "state and federal authorities are not free to 'annex' the news media as 'an investigative arm of government,'" he indicated in his concurrence a broader test than mere "good faith" for assessing the need to disclose confidential sources. In his view:

> [I]f the newsman is called upon to give information bearing only a remote and tenuous relationship to the subject of the investigation, or if he has some other reason to believe that his testimony implicates confidential source relationships without a legitimate need of law enforcement, he will have access to the Court on

a motion to quash and an appropriate protective order may be entered.[9]

The ambiguity surrounding "a legitimate need of law enforcement" arguably suggests an approach not too dissimilar to that rejected in the majority opinion due to inherent administrative difficulties.[10] Indeed, Justice Stewart's dissent interpreted this ambiguity as offering "some hope of a more flexible view in the future." [11] Nevertheless, clarification has not been forthcoming despite the numerous appeals from contempt citations against newsmen in the wake of *Branzburg.*[12]

Despite intensive lobbying efforts, there has not yet been any federal bill enacted which would provide a statutory privilege for newsmen.[13] However, several states have enacted "state shield" laws which vary in the range of protection, depending upon the statute and the interpretation it has received from the state court.[14] Of course, under the supremacy clause of the Constitution such state shield laws could not apply to limit the power of federal courts exercising jurisdiction over federal questions.

State shield laws may vary greatly in how they are applied in state cases to prevent a state court from subpoenaing information from a newsreporter when such information may be helpful to a criminal defendant. For example, the New Jersey Supreme Court has declared that its seemingly strong shield law must yield to sixth amendment rights and the state constitutional provisions relating to the rights of criminal defendants. The state court said: "[W]hen faced with the shield law, [the criminal defendant] invokes the rather elementary but entirely sound proposition that where the Constitu-

---

6. Id. at 704.

7. Id. at 705. Petitioner did not assert an absolute privilege, but one where information could be compelled only upon a showing of exhaustion of alternative sources and under strict guidelines as to relevance, see 408 U.S. at 630.

8. Id. at 707–708 (footnote omitted).

9. Id. at 710.

10. See Note, The Supreme Court, 1971 Term, 86 Harv.L.Rev. 1, 144 (1972).

11. Branzburg v. Hayes, 408 U.S. 665, 725 (1972).

12. Citation of cases in which the Supreme Court has denied certiorari may be found at e.g., 1, Dorsen, Bender, and Newborne, Emerson, Haber, and Dorsen's Political and Civil Rights in the United States, p. 309, n. 1 (4th ed. Law School 1976).

13. Id. at 311.

14. Id. at 314.

tion and statute collide, the latter must yield. Subject to what is said below, we find this argument unassailable." [15] The state court held that the press would have a right to a preliminary determination (before being required to submit materials to the trial judge for *in camera* inspection) that there was a reasonable likelihood that the information sought was material and relevant, that it could not be secured from any less intrusive source, and that the defendant had a legitimate need to see and use it.

The U.S. Supreme Court denied certiorari in this case,[16] but two justices suggested their views on the merits when they both earlier refused to stay an order of the New Jersey Superior Court holding the reporter, Myron Farber, and the New York Times Co. in civil contempt. Justice White, sitting as a circuit justice, noted that even if four or more justices of the full Court would hold that a reporter's obligation to comply with a subpoena is subject to some special showing of materiality not applicable to ordinary third party witnesses, the Court would not likely accept review "at this time." "The order at issue directs submission of the documents and other materials for only an *in camera* inspection; it anticipates a full hearing on all issues of federal and state law; and it is based on the trial court's evident views that the documents sought are sufficiently material to warrant at least *in camera* inspection." [17]

Justice Marshall also denied a stay because he did not believe it likely that four justices would vote to grant certiorari, but he explicitly differed with Justice White as to the merits of the constitutional issue involved because even a judge's *in camera* inspection might burden the ability of the news media to gather information.[18] The is-

sue thus remains unresolved, though several state courts have shown hostility to state shield laws both on federal and state constitutional law grounds.[19]

Branzburg v. Hayes [20] specifically had recognized that Congress has the freedom to fashion a statutory reporter's privilege "as narrow or broad as deemed necessary. . . . " ; moreover, the state legislatures are also free "within First Amendment limits, to fashion" their own shield laws, and state courts could construe their state constitutions "so as to recognize a newsman's privilege, either qualified or absolute." [21]

One should also note that many statutory or judge-made laws create a host of privileges that serve to deprive the accused or the prosecutor of relevant evidence. The attorney-client privilege, the doctor-patient privilege, the husband-wife privilege—all serve certain important social policies and none of them has been found to violate the accused's rights. To illustrate, if a client confesses to a particular crime to his attorney, the attorney may not (without the client's consent) breach the wall of secrecy, even to offer the evidence in order to help acquit an innocent man wrongfully accused of that same crime. If that "shield" law is constitutional, may one logically treat the reporter-source privilege any differently?

Assertion of such a privilege in civil cases has met with a qualified success, the lower courts distinguishing *Branzburg* on the grounds that a civil action does not present as significant a countervailing interest as a criminal prosecution, particularly where the plaintiffs seeking access to a reporter's notes are not parties to a pending criminal action, but merely prospective witnesses. Thus, in one district court case where the privilege has been sustained, the standard

---

15. In re Farber, 78 N.J. 259, 394 A.2d 330, cert. denied 439 U.S. 997 (1978).

16. Id.

17. New York Times Co. (and Myron Farber) v. Jascalevich, 439 U.S. 1317, 1322, 1323 (1978) (White, Circuit Justice).

18. New York Times Co. (and Myron Farber) v. Jascalevich, 439 U.S. 1331, 1334 (1978) (Marshall, Circuit

Justice). See also, New York Times Co. v. New Jersey, 439 U.S. 886 (1978) (Marshall, J., dissenting).

19. See generally, e.g., Goodale, Courts Begin Limiting Scope of Various State Shield Laws, 1 Nat'l Law Jrl. 28 (Dec. 11, 1978).

20. 408 U.S. 665 (1972).

21. 408 U.S. 706 (1972).

required the party seeking discovery to exhaust alternative sources and to show that the information requested is central to the party's claim.[22] Such a claim may well be present in libel suits brought by public officials and figures against the media, since the plaintiff needs to establish "malice" or *New York Times* scienter in publishing the defamatory information in order to be successful.[23] If the story is purportedly based on the information obtained from a confidential source, scienter can be proven by a showing that the source is non-existent.[24]

In *Zurcher v. The Stanford Daily*,[25] the Supreme Court refused to create any special protections for newspapers that might be searched by government authorities pursuant to a search warrant which had been based on probable cause to look for evidence of a crime in the newspaper office. The majority opinion quickly dismissed arguments based on the need to protect confidential sources:

> Nor are we convinced, anymore than we were in *Branzburg v. Hayes*, 408 U.S. 665 (1972), that confidential sources will disappear and that the press will suppress news because of fears of warranted searches. Whatever incremental effect there may be in this regard if search warrants, as well as subpoenas, are permissible in proper circumstances, it does not make a constitutional difference in our judgment.[26]

Thus there are no special privileges for the press to refrain from responding to either subpoenas or search warrants for evidence of a crime.

In *Zurcher* the police had probable cause to believe that the files of the student newspaper at Stanford University would contain photographs of persons who had assaulted police officers during a sit-in demonstration. On this basis they secured a search warrant to search for and seize such photographs in the newspaper office. Though locked drawers and rooms were not opened, the police did have an opportunity to read the newspaper's notes and correspondence, and the police did search the newspaper's photographic laboratories, filing cabinets, desks and waste paper baskets. No materials were removed from the newspaper offices. The newspaper later sued in federal court seeking, among other things, a declaratory judgment that the search violated the first and fourth amendments, as applied to the states through the fourteenth amendment. The district granted the declaratory judgment but the Supreme Court reversed.

First, the majority rejected any argument that the fourth amendment establishes different requirements for search warrants that are issued to search for material in possession of one not suspected of a crime, such as the student newspaper which only was thought to have evidence of a crime committed by others. The Supreme Court held that the fourth amendment is not a barrier to search for property on which there is probable cause to believe that the fruits, instrumentalities, or evidence of a crime is located, whether or not the owner or possessor of the premises covered by the warrant is reasonably suspected of involvement in the crime being investigated.

Secondly, the majority rejected any rule based on the first amendment that would require the use of subpoenas, rather than the more intrusive search procedure, when the premises to be searched are a newspaper's offices. The Supreme Court, however, did emphasize that where "the materials sought to be seized may be protected by the First Amendment, the requirements of the Fourth Amendment must be applied with 'scrupulous exactitude.'"[27] Thus in prior cases the Court has invalidated a search warrant authorizing a search of a private home for all

---

22. Democratic Nat. Committee v. McCord, 356 F.Supp. 1394 (D.D.C.1973).

23. New York Times Co. v. Sullivan, 376 U.S. 254 (1964). See Chapter 18, section X.

24. See, e.g., Carey v. Hume, 492 F.2d 631 (D.C.Cir. 1974).

25. 436 U.S. 547 (1978).

26. 436 U.S. at 566.

27. 436 U.S. at 564, citing Stanford v. Texas, 379 U.S. 476, 485 (1965).

books, records, and other materials relating to the Communist Party. The warrant in that context was the functional equivalent of a general warrant, which was prohibited by the fourth amendment.[28] Similarly, before a warrant may be issued for the seizure of allegedly obscene material, there must be an opportunity for the judicial officer to " 'focus searchingly on the question of obscenity;' ".[29] Because of first amendment concerns, the police officer is not allowed to rely on merely his own judgment of what is obscene either in securing the warrant or seizing material without a warrant incident to an arrest.[30]

The majority in *Zurcher* did not believe that its ruling would result in a rash of incidents of police rummaging through newspaper files. First, there have been only a few instances since 1971 that search warrants have been issued to apply to newspaper premises,[31] and search warrants themselves—which are only issued by the judiciary upon proof of probable cause—are more difficult to obtain than subpoenas.[32] In addition, the local prosecutor would not likely choose the more difficult procedure unless he or she had a special reason. The prosecutor may wish to utilize the warrant procedure because of fear that the evidence might be destroyed if the less intrusive subpoena method were used. In *Zurcher*, the student newspaper had an announced policy of destroying photographs that could aid in the prosecution of protestors.[33] Finally, while a

subpoena is less intrusive, it is also much less satisfactory for prosecutorial purpose than a search warrant because the fifth amendment privilege against self incrimination is not available to one resisting a search warrant.[34] Thus, there are practical reasons supporting the majority's holding and past practices do not suggest that the warrant powers applied to newspaper premises will be abused. Nevertheless, Congress responded to *Zurcher* by enacting the Privacy Protection Act;[35] this law applies to state as well as federal law enforcement personnel. It limits their power to secure evidence from the news media by search warrant, and requires in many circumstances that they prefer a subpoena.

C. Judicial Protective Orders and the Press

The compatibility of a commitment to an "uninhibited, robust, and wide-open" discussion of public issues in a free press [36] with a commitment to a criminal process in which the "conclusions to be reached in a case will be induced only by evidence and argument in open court" [37] has been a subject of long standing debate.[38] The problem becomes more acute with the growth of national news coverage and the electronic media. The prominent issue within this area is the extent to which a trial judge may insulate his courtroom procedures from the intrusion of outside prejudice caused by publicity sur-

---

28. Id.

29. 436 U.S. at 565, citing Marcus v. Search Warrant, 367 U.S. 717, 732 (1961); A Quantity of Books v. Kansas, 378 U.S. 205, 210 (1964); Lee Art Theatre, Inc. v. Virginia, 392 U.S. 636, 637 (1968); Roaden v. Kentucky, 413 U.S. 496, 502 (1973); and Heller v. New York, 413 U.S. 483, 489 (1973).

30. The Court, however, has upheld the use of a search warrant to search a law office for business records of criminal activity. Andresen v. Maryland, 427 U.S. 463 (1976).

31. 436 U.S. at 566. The problem raised by *Zurcher* would not have arisen prior to 1967 when the Supreme Court finally rejected the "mere evidence" rule and thus allowed search warrants for mere evidence of a crime. Warden v. Hayden, 387 U.S. 294 (1967). After that case, the focus of a special reporter's privilege was on the question of subpoenas, the is-

sue dealt with in Branzburg v. Hayes, 408 U.S. 665 (1972).

32. 436 U.S. at 562–63.

33. 436 U.S. at 568 n. 1 (Powell, J., concurring).

34. Maness v. Meyers, 419 U.S. 449 (1975). Both Justice Stevens' dissent in *Zurcher*, and Justice Stewart's dissent (joined by Justice Marshall) did not answer this point.

35. Pub.L. 96–440, 94 Stat. 1879 (1980), codified at 42 U.S.C.A. §§ 2000aa–2000aa–12.

36. New York Times Co. v. Sullivan, 376 U.S. 254 (1964).

37. Patterson v. Colorado, 205 U.S. 454 (1907).

38. See Chief Justice Burger's discussion of the history of this conflict in Nebraska Press Ass'n v. Stuart, 427 U.S. 539, 547–51 (1976).

rounding the case. In this area the rights of the press often conflict with the rights of the accused. The Supreme Court offered a qualified response to this question when it invalidated a Nebraska district court "gag order" which prohibited the press from the publication of certain implicative evidence pertaining to a murder suspect until the jury selection process was completed.[39]

Earlier the danger to the sixth amendment guarantee of a fair trial posed by inflammatory publicity had become apparent following a series of cases in which the Court reversed state convictions upon a finding that pre-trial publicity had so infected the trial atmosphere to amount to a denial of due process. The first reversal of a state conviction due to prejudicial pre-trial publicity occurred in 1961 [40] in *Irvin v. Dowd*.[41] In that case, ninety percent of the venire and eight of the twelve members of the petit jury admitted that they had formed opinions based on the publicity surrounding the murder, and this result was obtained *after* a change of venue to an adjoining county. The unanimous opinion of the Court, by Justice Clark, stated:

> To hold that the mere existence of any preconceived notion as to the guilt or innocence of an accused, without more, is sufficient to rebut the presumption of a prospective juror's impartiality would be to establish an impossible standard. It is sufficient if the juror can lay aside his impression or opinion and render a verdict based on the evidence presented in court . . . With his life at stake, it is not requiring too much that petitioner be tried in an atmosphere undisturbed by so huge a wave of public passion and by a jury other than one in which two-thirds of the members admit, before hearing any testimony, to possessing a belief in his guilt.[42]

Although concurring in the judgment of the Court, Justice Frankfurter portended the future by acerbically noting the omission of any discussion of the responsibilities of the press in protecting the fair trial guarantee:

> The Court has not yet decided that, while convictions must be reversed and miscarriages of justice result because the minds of jurors or potential jurors were poisoned, the poisoner is constitutionally protected in plying his trade.[43]

Nevertheless, the Court continued to avoid this issue as the appeals mounted following *Irvin*. In *Rideau v. Louisiana*,[44] the Court found that a denial of a request for change in venue offended due process based upon a local television broadcast of a film of the defendant confessing to the crimes in response to leading questions by the sheriff. The opinion indicates that the Court's reaction may be attributable to the coercive and pervasive nature of the television medium and the apparent complicity of the state in the broadcast.[45] This view of the case is buttressed by the result in *Estes v. Texas*,[46] in which the presence of television cameras recording the trial proceedings for rebroadcast over the defendant's objections was found to be so inherently intrusive that a violation of due process was inevitable. As the majority opinion of Justice Clark observed,

> It is true that in most cases involving claims of due process deprivations we require a showing of identifiable prejudice to the accused. Nevertheless, at times a procedure employed by the state involves such a probability that prejudice will result that it is deemed inherently lacking in due process.[47]

The incremental value of television reporting over traditional print reporting in serving the press function of providing the public with information on the operation of the criminal justice system was thought to be

---

39. Nebraska Press Ass'n v. Stuart, 427 U.S. 539 (1976).

40. Federal convictions had previously been overturned in the exercise of the federal supervisory power, see Marshall v. United States, 360 U.S. 310 (1959).

41. 366 U.S. 717 (1961).

42. Id. at 723, 728.

43. Id. at 730.

44. 373 U.S. 723 (1963). Clark and Harlan, JJ., dissented.

45. Justice Clark's dissent found this conduct reprehensible, but argued that, as state officials, they violated no constitutional mandate and remedies were properly left to the states. 373 U.S. at 727–33.

46. 381 U.S. 532 (1965). Justices Black, Brennan, Stewart and White dissented.

47. Id. at 542–43.

negligible and could justifiably be sacrificed in light of the impact television cameras had upon the judicial process. However Justice Harlan's concurring opinion left open the possibility that future experimentation with the television might produce admirable results.[48]

Nearly two decades later the Supreme Court retreated from the broad implications of Justice Clark's opinion in *Estes* and instead followed the direction of Justice Harlan's *Estes'* concurring opinion.[49] The Court, in *Chandler v. Florida*,[50] held that there is no per se constitutional prohibition against Florida providing for radio, television, and still photographic coverage of a criminal trial for public broadcast, notwithstanding the objection of the accused.

In *Chandler*, Chief Justice Burger speaking for the Court, first concluded that *Estes* did not establish a per se rule. The Court then noted that many of the negative factors relating to television coverage that existed in 1962, when Estes was tried—"cumbersome equipment, cables, distracting lighting, numerous camera technicians—are less substantial factors today than they were at that time."[51] In addition, the Florida program avoided many of the most egregious problems that had concerned the justices in *Estes*. Under the program the Florida courts are admonished to protect certain witnesses, e.g., children, victims of sex crimes, some informants, the very timid, from the tensions of being televised. If the accused objects to broadcast coverage, the trial judge may define the steps necessary to eliminate the risks of prejudice to the accused.[52] The Florida guidelines also provided for other safeguards such as the use of only one television camera in a fixed position, only one technician, no artificial lighting, no changing of film, videotape and lenses while court is in session, and no filming of the jury.[53]

The Court concluded that due process did not require any per se prohibition against broadcasting of criminal trials. Since the defendants did not demonstrate with "specificity that the presence of cameras impaired the ability of jurors to decide the case on only the evidence before them or that the trial was affected adversely by the impact on any of the participants of the presence of cameras and the prospect of broadcast," the convictions were affirmed.[54]

In addition to problems related to the general topic discussed above and often called "cameras in the courts," the Supreme Court has had to lay guidelines governing judicial power to restrict prejudicial pretrial publicity. *Sheppard v. Maxwell*,[55] the appeal from the celebrated Dr. Sam Sheppard murder trial, found the Court again concerning itself with the manner in which conduct of the press offended defendant's due process rights to a fair trial. Holding that the trial judge had failed to properly protect the defendant, jurors, and witnesses from the firestorm of publicity, much of which was erroneous and prejudicial, the conviction was reversed. The Court found that there were more than adequate procedures at the judge's disposal to prevent a murder trial from being converted into a "carnival." In particular, the Court emphasized stricter control over the activities of the press within the courtroom and provision for the insulation of witnesses.[56] Moreover, when it is apparent that the crime has already attracted massive publicity, the trial judge must take pre-trial steps to remove the prejudice inherent in such publicity from the trial itself.[57]

Initially, the Court said, the judge has the duty of intensive voir dire examination of

---

48. Justice Harlan limited the majority holding to merely stating that no requirement existed that television be allowed in a courtroom over the defendant's objections, particularly on a case of great notoriety, 381 U.S. at 587.

49. 381 U.S. at 587.

50. 449 U.S. 560 (1981).

51. 449 U.S. at 575.

52. 449 U.S. at 577.

53. 449 U.S. at 565.

54. 449 U.S. at 582.

55. 384 U.S. 333 (1965).

56. Id. at 358.

57. Id. at 358–59.

prospective jurors to assure himself that excessive pre-trial publicity has not clouded the juror's presumed impartiality. Once a jury is selected, sequestration will protect its members from being subjected to the opinions and possible intimidations of an aroused community. Should the judge determine that such procedures have already been rendered inadequate by press accounts of the crime and its investigation, the alternatives of a continuance or a change of venue should be considered.

The opinion in *Sheppard* also stressed the responsibilities of the parties to the case, i.e. defense and prosecution counsel, police officers, and witnesses, not to release information to the press. Should they evidence an inclination to abdicate this responsibility, the judge should re-impose it by court order.

> Had the judge, the other officers of the court, and the police placed the interest of justice first, the news media would have soon learned to be content with the task of reporting the case as it unfolded in the courtroom—not pieced together from extrajudicial statements.[58]

And in a highly significant passage, the Court concluded,

> From the cases coming here we note that unfair and prejudicial news comment on pending trials has become increasingly prevalent . . . [T]here is nothing that proscribes the press from reporting events that transpire in the courtroom . . . But we must remember that reversals are but palliatives; the cure lies in those remedial measures that will prevent the prejudice at its inception. The courts must

take such steps by rule and regulation that will protect their processes from prejudicial outside interferences.[59]

Within those words lay the genesis of future controversy. Faced with increasing claims of prejudice following *Sheppard*,[60] trial courts began increasing utilization of protective orders to prevent the publication of inflammatory material, at least until a jury was impaneled. The dilemma confronting the courts and law enforcement officials was a real one, since the most heinous crimes attracted the greatest publicity, some of which was irresponsible, and were thus the most prone to be prejudicially affected by that publicity.[61] Protective orders provided a method of controlling this possibility. However it was neither the least restrictive nor the most efficacious method of resolving the dilemma, as early recognized by Justice Powell, speaking in his capacity as Circuit Judge for the Fifth Circuit, in *Times-Picayune Publishing Corp. v. Schulingkamp*.[62] He stayed a protective order promulgated by a criminal court judge in New Orleans which banned the publication of information on a murder trial until a jury had been selected, because there had been no showing of an imminent threat to a fair trial or that the alternative measures outlined in *Sheppard* would be insufficient to protect the accused's rights.[63]

The full Court did not get an opportunity to hear arguments on this basic issue until two years later, in another case, *Nebraska Press Association v. Stuart*,[64] an appeal by

---

58. Id. at 362.

59. Id. at 362–65.

60. E.g., Doggett v. Yeager, 472 F.2d 229 (3d Cir. 1973).

61. See Report of the President's Commission on the Assassination of President Kennedy, 94–99 (Assoc. Press ed. 1964) for the publicity of the Lee Harvey Oswald case.

62. 419 U.S. 1301 (1974).

63. While attention has focused on the extent of a court's power to issue restraining orders in criminal cases, the first amendment implications of such orders in civil cases is also not to be forgotten. In Gulf Oil Co. v. Bernard, 452 U.S. 89 (1981), for example, the Court, speaking through Justice Powell, restricted the

scope of a federal district court's authority to limit communications from named plaintiffs and their counsel to prospective class members during the pendency of class action. Although the Court based its ruling on its interpretation of the Federal Rules of Civil Procedure, particularly Rule 23, it acknowledged the first amendment interests and ruled that any order limiting communications between parties and potential class members should be based on a clear record and specific findings that reflect a weighing of the need for a limitation and the potential interference with the right of the parties.

64. 427 U.S. 539 (1976). See Marcus, The Media in the Courtroom, Attending, Reporting, Televising Criminal Cases, 57 Ind.L.J. 235 (1982), arguing for less judicial deference to the media.

members of the state press association challenging a restraining order prohibiting them
from publishing confessions by an accused
in a murder trial (except those made directly
to members of the press) as well as other
facts "strongly implicative" of the accused.[65]
In this posture, the case is removed from the
due process cases previously discussed by
its direct challenge, by the press, to the validity of such an order in light of the hostility of the first amendment toward prior restraints.[66] The Court unanimously held the
order invalid, but there were five separate
opinions.

The opinion of the Court, written by Chief
Justice Burger, was subscribed to by four
other members.[67]

The Chief Justice, after narrating the history of those cases invalidating prior restraints, characterized them as follows:

> Prior restraints on speech are the most serious
> and least tolerable infringement on First
> Amendment rights . . . A prior restraint
> . . . has an immediate and irreversible sanc-
> tion. If it can be said that a threat of criminal
> or civil sanctions after publication "chills"
> speech, prior restraint "freezes" it at least for
> the time.[68]

By contrast, deprivations of due process did
not inevitably result from unregulated publicity surrounding notorious crimes. Rather,
it was only in a rare circumstance that publicity could be regarded as fatally infecting
the judicial process.[69]

This view does not indicate that the rights
of an accused awaiting trial are always subordinated to those of the press as embodied
in the first amendment. While the barriers
to the validity of prior restraints remain
high, they are not insuperable, as the Chief
Justice took pains to point out.

> If the authors of these guarantees, fully aware
> of the potential conflicts between them, were

unwilling or unable to resolve the issue by as-
signing to one priority over the other, it is not
for us to rewrite the Constitution by undertaking what they declined to do.[70]

However, despite the fact that pretrial
press coverage posed a severe danger to the
neutrality of the trial, the trial court in *Nebraska Press* had not made a showing that
the entire panoply of procedures outlined in
Sheppard would be insufficient to forestall
this occurrence; for example, continuance,
change of venue, intensive voir dire examination, sequestration of the jurors, instruction on the duty of each juror to decide the
issues on the evidence, and restraining orders on the parties involved and their attorneys in discussing issues with the press. In
the absence of such a showing, the imposition of a protective order could never overcome the heavy presumption against constitutionality which inevitably attaches to prior
restraints.

Further, there existed no assurance that
such an order would even have served to
eliminate the offending danger. Jurisdictional difficulties exist, as the editors of
some of the publications might well lie beyond the reach of the *in personam* jurisdiction of the court while their publications are
distributed throughout the country or district from which the jurors are drawn.
Moreover, the speculative nature of a protective order created problems in drafting since
it appeared to prohibit the publication of material which would not possess a prejudicial
effect while not encompassing seemingly innocent information which would later develop into very damaging evidence.

Finally, the Court emphasized that that
portion of the order which prohibited the
publication of information obtained in open
court could under no circumstances prevail.
As was said in *Sheppard*, "there is nothing
which proscribes the press from reporting

65. 427 U.S. at 541.

66. See Near v. Minnesota, 283 U.S. 197 (1931);
New York Times v. United States, 403 U.S. 713 (1971).

67. Justices White, Blackmun, Powell, and Rehnquist joined in the majority opinion. Justice Brennan
(with Justices Stewart and Marshall joining) and Jus-

tices White, Powell, and Stevens all wrote separate
concurring opinions.

68. Nebraska Press Ass'n v. Stuart, 427 U.S. 539,
559 (1976).

69. Id. at 560–61.

70. Id. at 561.

events that transpire in the courtroom".[71] The judge may in his discretion, if the relevant statutes allow, and subject to constitutional limitations discussed below, close the courtroom during portions of the proceedings, but if that alternative is bypassed, it cannot be effectuated retroactively by a protective order. If the information is lawfully obtained from an open hearing in court, its republication by the press cannot be restrained.[72]

Justice Brennan in his separate opinion argued that the only instance in which the presumption against prior restraints is rebuttable is in crises affecting national security. In all other situations, the protections of the first amendment must remain preeminent. The defendant's rights to a fair trial must rest upon those procedures which had traditionally been within the province of the trial judge.[73] However, five of the justices felt that it was unnecessary to formulate such a broad rule on the basis of the facts. Because the state courts had made no finding as to the efficacy of these alternative procedures, it still remains possible to argue that in a given set of circumstances a fair trial will be impossible to obtain without a limitation upon the information the press can publish.[74] Such a position might possibly be acceptable to a majority of the justices but only as a last resort.

Perhaps the most important practical result of the *Nebraska Press Association* case may be the increase of restraining orders upon the parties under the trial court's control: the attorneys, the police, and witnesses. Such "silence orders" have been upheld in lower courts, even in the absence of any showing of imminent peril to an unprejudiced trial, although the issue has yet to appear before the Supreme Court.[75] Such orders will perhaps prove more effective than in the past due to the holding in *Branzburg v. Hayes*[76] that supports the power of the courts to compel reporters to reveal the source of their information.

To cope with problems of pretrial publicity, courts at times have sought to close portions of the proceedings to the public, because at least in those cases where the press lawfully obtains information the court cannot then prohibit the press from publishing it.[77] In *Gannett Co., Inc. v. DePasquale*,[78] the Supreme Court upheld this practice under the narrow circumstances of that case. The Court held, by a five to four vote, that neither the public nor the press has an inde-

---

71. Sheppard v. Maxwell, 384 U.S. 333 (1966); cf. Cox Broadcasting Corp. v. Cohn, 420 U.S. 469 (1975).

72. Cf. Cox Broadcasting Corp. v. Cohn, 420 U.S. 469 (1975); Virginia State Bd. of Pharmacy v. Virginia Citizens Consumer Council, Inc., 425 U.S. 748 (1976). See also, Oklahoma Publishing Co. v. District Court, 430 U.S. 308 (1977) (per curiam).

In Landmark Communications, Inc. v. Virginia, 435 U.S. 829 (1978) the Court held that a state cannot punish a newspaper or other third party who is neither an employee nor participant of a judicial disciplinary commission for publishing truthful information about a confidential investigation in progress. The Court noted that such publication lies "near the core" of the First Amendment and that criminally punishing was not justified by the interests advanced by the state, the Supreme Court found the state's justifications insufficient, noting that New York Times v. Sullivan, 376 U.S. 254, 272–73 (1964), had "firmly established" that injury to official reputation was insufficient reason "for repressing speech that would otherwise be free." There was no support for the claim that without criminal sanctions against nonparticipants the objectives of the statutory scheme would be seriously undermined, since the advantages of confidentiality may still be served without such sanctions.

See also Smith v. Daily Mail Publishing Co., 443 U.S. 97 (1979) (state may not punish a newspaper's truthful publication of an alleged juvenile delinquent's name lawfully obtained by a newspaper).

73. 427 U.S. at 572–613, Justices Stewart and Marshall joining.

74. See United States v. Abbott Laboratories, 369 F.Supp. 1396 (E.D.N.C. 1973) an unusual case, in which the court dismissed the indictment for introduction of adulterated drugs into interstate commerce on the grounds that alternative procedures were insufficient to ensure a fair trial. This case is most difficult to justify, for its logical conclusion is that if a crime is heinous enough—perhaps even was committed on television—the resulting publicity (created by the crime itself) should be enough to prevent a trial.

75. E.g., United States v. Tijerina, 412 F.2d 661 (10th Cir.), cert. denied 396 U.S. 990 (1969). But see, Chicago Council of Lawyers v. Bauer, 522 F.2d 242 (7th Cir. 1975), cert. denied sub nom., Cunningham v. Chicago Council of Lawyers, 427 U.S. 912 (1976).

76. 408 U.S. 665 (1972).

77. See n. 54, supra.

78. 443 U.S. 368 (1979).

pendent constitutional right to insist upon access to a *pretrial* suppression hearing, *if* the accused, the prosecutor, and the trial judge all agree that the proceeding should be closed in order to assure a fair trial.

The majority first noted that to safeguard the due process rights of the accused a trial judge may take "protective measures [to minimize the effects of prejudicial pretrial publicity] even when they are not strictly and inescapably necessary."[79] Publicity as to pretrial suppression hearings is particularly unfair because the purpose of such hearings is to screen out unreliable or illegally obtained evidence and insure that the prospective jury does not learn of such evidence. After the trial has begun and the jury chosen, on the other hand, the trial court has a variety of other means to keep information from the jury.

Second, the majority emphasized that the sixth amendment guarantee of a public trial is a right personal to the accused.[80] Although the majority conceded that "there is a strong societal interest in public trials" it held that interest does not involve a constitutional right on the part of the public.[81] Yet the *Gannett* Court would not grant defendant a right to insist on a closed hearing since the five member majority emphasized that the waiver of the defendant was joined with the consent of the prosecutor and the approval of the court. To these participants is delegated the duty to protect the public interest.[82] Also, the majority phrased the issue narrowly: "whether the Constitution *requires* that a pretrial proceeding such as this one be opened to the public even though

the participants in the litigation agree that it should be closed to protect the defendant's right to a fair trial."[83] The majority answered this question in the negative, but also stated that a court's failure to close a pretrial hearing does not necessarily require reversal of a subsequent conviction.[84] Thus it would appear that the defendant does not have an absolute right to close a hearing over the objection of the judge and prosecutor.

There were other suggestions in *Gannett* that the opinion should be read narrowly. The majority emphasized that any denial of public access was only temporary, since once the danger of prejudice had dissipated the court made available a transcript of the suppression hearing.[85] The majority also discussed the dangers of pretrial publicity in this particular case.

In addition, the decision was a five to four opinion, so a shift of even one vote would change the result. Three of the five member majority wrote separate concurrences. Chief Justice Burger emphasized that what was involved in their case was "not a *trial;* it is a *pre*trial hearing."[86] Justice Powell concurring, stated that he would have held that the press, as an agent of the public, does have a first amendment right to be present at the pretrial suppression hearing but that on balance this nonabsolute right was adequately respected in the present case.[87] Only Justice Rehnquist, concurring, argued that if the parties agreed to a closed proceeding, the trial court need not advance any reason whatsoever for declining to open a

---

79. 443 U.S. at 377–78 (1979).

80. 443 U.S. at 380, quoting Blackmun, J., dissenting in Faretta v. California, 422 U.S. 806, 846 (1975): "[T]he specific guarantees of the Sixth Amendment are personal to the accused." Justice Blackmun, joined by Brennan, White, and Marshall, JJ., dissented in *Gannett* on all issues except in the majority's holding that the case was not moot. Justice Blackmun thought it "clear" from the prior cases that "the fact that the Sixth Amendment casts the right to a public trial in terms of the right of the accused is not sufficient to permit the inference that the accused may compel a private proceeding simply by waiving the right." 443 U.S. at 417. On the facts of this case Justice Black-

mun concluded that there was an insufficient showing to establish "the strict and inescapable necessity that supports a suppression order." 443 U.S. at 447.

81. 443 U.S. at 382.

82. 443 U.S. at 384, & n. 12.

83. 443 U.S. at 384 (emphasis in original) (footnote omitted).

84. 443 U.S. at 379 n. 6.

85. 443 U.S. at 392.

86. 443 U.S. at 394 (Burger, C. J., concurring) (emphasis in original).

87. 443 U.S. at 403.

pretrial hearing "or trial" to the public.[88] The four member dissent would have held that pretrial hearings could be closed only upon a showing of "strict and inescapable necessity. . . . "[89]

A narrow interpretation of *Gannett* limited to pretrial hearings is supported by the decision shortly thereafter in *Richmond Newspapers, Inc. v. Virginia*.[90] The fragmented Court, with only Justice Rehnquist dissenting (and Justice Powell not participating), rejected the asserted power of a state trial judge to close a criminal trial. The state judge had relied on a state statute granting broad discretion in such matters.

Chief Justice Burger, joined by Justices White and Stevens, concluded that the first and fourteenth amendments give the public the right of access to criminal trials. There is a "presumption of openness,"[91] and that "[a]bsent an overriding interest articulated in findings, the trial of a criminal case must be open to the public."[92]

Justice Brennan, joined by Justice Marshall, concurred in the judgment, though they did not appear to disagree with any of the substance of Chief Justice Burger's opinion. They also noted that mere agreement of the trial judge and parties cannot constitutionally close a trial to the public in light of the first amendment guarantees. And, since the state statute in this case authorized the trial judge and parties to engage in trial closures with unfettered discretion, "[w]hat countervailing interest might be sufficiently compelling to reverse this presumption of openness need not concern us now . . . . "[93]

Justice Stewart, concurring in the judgment, also relied on a first amendment right of access. Justice Blackmun, also concur-

ring in the judgment, relied principally on the sixth amendment, but also acknowledged the secondary role of the first amendment as a source of this right to access.

In *Globe Newspapers Co. v. Superior Court*[94] the Court produced a majority opinion, elaborated on the meaning of *Richmond Newspapers*, and invalidated a state statute, unique to Massachusetts, which *required* trial judges to exclude the press and general public from the courtroom during the testimony of the victim in cases involving certain specified sexual offenses. Although the Court invalidated the mandatory state law (which required no particularized determinations in individual cases), it left open the possibility that under appropriate circumstances and in individual cases the trial court could exclude the press and public during the testimony of minor victims of sex crimes.

Justice Brennan, for the Court, explained that under *Richmond Newspapers* the first amendment, as applied to the states, grants to the press and general public "a right of access to *criminal trials*"[95] under the first amendment because historically such trials have been open and such openness aids in the functioning of the judicial process and the government of the whole.[96] Thus states may deny access only if denial serves "a compelling governmental interest, and is narrowly tailored to serve that interest."[97]

The statute was said to serve two basic state interests: first, protecting minor victims of sex crimes from further trauma and embarrassment and, second, encouraging victims to come forward and testify truthfully. Though this first interest was compelling, it did "not justify a *mandatory*-closure rule, for it is clear that the circumstances of the particular case may affect the signifi-

88. 443 U.S. at 404.

89. 443 U.S. at 447–48 (Blackmun, J. dissenting and concurring, joined by Brennan, White, and Marshall, JJ.).

90. 448 U.S. 555 (1980).

91. 448 U.S. at 576. As Justice Stevens noted in a concurring opinion, this case is the first ever to find constitutional protection for a right of access, a right to acquire newsworthy information. 448 U.S. at 583.

92. 448 U.S. at 587 (footnote omitted).

93. 448 U.S. at 600 (footnote omitted).

94. 102 S.Ct. 2613 (1982).

95. 102 S.Ct. at 2619 (emphasis in original).

96. 102 S.Ct. at 2619–20.

97. 102 S.Ct. at 2620.

cance of the interest." [98] The judge should consider the minor victim's wishes regarding disclosure, as well as the victim's age and maturity, the interests of relatives, the nature of the crime, and so on. In the present case the defendant objected to closure, the state made no motion for closure, and the victims may have been willing to testify without closure.

The second interest—to encourage witnesses to come forward—was speculative, and, given the nature of the statute, illogical: the statute did not deny the press access to the transcript or other possible sources that could provide an account of the testimony; the press could still publish the victim's identity and the substance of the testimony. Finally, the state's interest is not compelling. The asserted state interest would justify too many types of closure because "minor victims of sex crimes are [not] the *only* crime victims who, because of publicity attendant to criminal trials, are reluctant to come forward." [99]

IX. REGULATION OF COMMERCIAL SPEECH

A. Introduction

Commercial speech, for purposes of our discussion, may be understood as speech of any form that advertises a product or service for profit or for business purpose. This definition is not precise, nor consistently applied by the courts. Neither is it self-evident why this category of speech should be treated differently from other types of speech. Flawed as this definition is, it is at least helpful in understanding the earlier cases.

Commercial speech, such as advertising, has always been subject to substantial governmental regulation. If all commercial speech, even truthful advertising, is excluded from the coverage of the First Amendment, the extent and nature of such regulation will create no free speech problems. And until recently it has commonly been assumed that such is the case. Under the most recent case law this category of speech may well have been abandoned, for, as we shall see, commercial speech appears now to be vested with full First Amendment protection. The state can issue reasonable time, place, or manner regulations of such speech, and it also appears that the state has a broader power to regulate misleading commercial speech than its power to regulate misleading or libelous speech of public officials or public figures.

B. Origins of the Commercial Speech Doctrine

In *Valentine v. Chrestensen*,[1] an entrepreneur in New York City distributed a leaflet containing on one side an advertisement for a commercial exhibition of a former Navy submarine and on the other side a message protesting the City's denial of wharfage facilities for the exhibition. The entrepreneur was convicted of violating a sanitary code provision forbidding the distribution of advertising matter in the streets.

The Supreme Court upheld the conviction unanimously. Three years earlier, the Court had struck down several municipal ordinances applied to severely restrict the distribution of political or religious handbills in

---

98. 102 S.Ct. at 2621.

99. 102 S.Ct. at 2622 (emphasis in original).

O'Connor, J., concurred in the judgment and emphasized her view that neither *Richmond Newspapers* nor this case carried implications outside of criminal trials. Burger, C. J., joined by Rehnquist, J., dissented and objected to the paradox that the Court decision "denies the victim the kind of protection routinely given to juveniles who commit crimes." 102 S.Ct. at 2627.

Stevens, J., dissented because he believed that the case was moot, since, as presently construed, it had

never been applied in a live controversy: the trial court had interpreted the statute to require closure of the entire trial; after the defendant had been acquitted the Massachusetts Supreme Judicial Court interpreted the statute to require closure only of the portions of the trial when the minor sex victim testified. All the Justices except for Stevens thought that the issue was "capable of repetition, yet evading review."

1. 316 U.S. 52 (1942). See generally, Rotunda, The Commercial Speech Doctrine in the Supreme Court, 1976 U.Ill.L.Forum 1080.

the streets or in house-to-house canvassing.[2] The Court had stated that "the public convenience in respect of cleanliness of the streets does not justify an exertion of the police power which invades the free communication of information and opinion secured by the Constitution."[3] But the Court had carefully noted that it did not hold "that commercial soliciting and canvassing may not be subjected to such regulation as the ordinance requires."[4] In *Chrestensen*, the Court took this proviso and expanded it into what has become known as the "commercial speech" doctrine:

> This court has unequivocally held that the streets are proper places for the exercise of the freedom of communicating information and disseminating opinion and that, though the states and municipalities may appropriately regulate the privilege in the public interest, they may not unduly burden or proscribe its employment in these public thoroughfares. We are equally clear that the Constitution imposes *no such restraint on government as respects purely commercial advertising.*[5]

This pronouncement, as we shall see, was long read to completely exclude so-called "commercial speech" from any protection of the First Amendment.[6]

In distributing his leaflet, the entrepreneur in *Chrestensen* was, in the Court's view, attempting to "pursue a gainful occupation in the streets,"[7] and his right to do so was purely a matter for "legislative judgment."[8] By implication this judgment need not have been justified by an overriding or compelling state interest, or balanced against any inherent right to employ advertising as a business technique. The Court

reasoned that if speech is "purely commercial," it is subject to regulation to the same extent and for the same reasons as other forms of commercial activity. As commentators have argued, the *Chrestensen* Court, "without citing precedent, historical evidence, or policy considerations, . . . effectively read commercial speech out of the first amendment."[9] Commercial speech, under this ruling, is not subject to less First Amendment protection; rather it is subject to no first amendment protection.

As to the political protest message the entrepreneur had placed on the back of his advertising leaflet, the Court said it was "enough" that the message had admittedly been designed "with the intent, and for the purpose, of evading the prohibition of the ordinance."[10] Thus, although the Court declined to "indulge nice appraisals based upon subtle distinctions,"[11] it did point to the primary purpose of the protest message. The Court might have issued a narrower ruling, by simply approving the regulation as a reasonable one under the circumstances. Instead it fashioned a more general approach for future cases: when the primary purpose of the speech is "commercial," it falls within a category of speech that is not within the protection of the First Amendment.

Apparently it was the "speech-on-the-handbill" which was considered "commercial" and thus not within the First Amendment. It is not clear that even the *Chrestensen* Court would have allowed the entrepreneur to be enjoined from merely telling someone about his submarine. If the *Chrestensen* Court would indeed have made

---

2. Schneider v. State (Town of Irvington), 308 U.S. 147 (1939); see also Lovell v. City of Griffin, 303 U.S. 444 (1938). In both cases the ordinances were held unconstitutional, apparently for reasons of overbreadth.

3. Schneider v. State (Town of Irvington), 308 U.S. 147, 163 (1939).

4. Id. at 165.

5. 316 U.S. at 54 (emphasis added).

6. This broad holding of *Chrestensen* has occasionally been attacked in several strong dissents in the high court. E.g., Lehman v. City of Shaker Heights, 418 U.S. 298, 314–15 (1974) (Brennan, J., dissenting); Pittsburgh Press Co. v. Pittsburgh Commission on

Human Relations, 413 U.S. 376, 398 (1973) (Douglas, J., dissenting), and 413 U.S. at 401 & n. 6 (Stewart J., dissenting); Dun & Bradstreet, Inc. v. Grove, 404 U.S. 898, 904–06 (1971) (Douglas, J., dissenting from denial of certiorari).

7. Valentine v. Chrestensen, 316 U.S. 52, 54 (1942).

8. Id.

9. Redish, The First Amendment in the Marketplace: Commercial Speech and the Values of Free Expression, 39 Geo.Wash.L.Rev. 429, 450 (1971).

10. 316 U.S. at 55.

11. Id.

a distinction between the "speech" vs. the "speech-on-the-handbill" then the difficulty of defining "commercial" speech with any precision is emphasized.

C. Subsequent Development of the Commercial Speech Doctrine

The significant reach of *Chrestensen* and its primary purpose test was clarified in *Murdock v. Pennsylvania*[12] and *Breard v. City of Alexandria*.[13] In *Murdock*, the Court overturned the convictions of several Jehovah's Witnesses who had violated an ordinance by selling religious books without paying a license tax. The Court stated flatly that a "state may not impose a charge for the enjoyment of a right guaranteed by the Federal Constitution" and equated the power to impose the license tax with "the power of censorship which this Court has repeatedly struck down."[14] The Court stressed that the fact that the books had been sold did not automatically bring the books within the Commercial Speech doctrine nor diminish the petitioners' First Amendment privileges; the sales had been "merely *incidental* and collateral" to a principal purpose of disseminating religious beliefs.[15] It might be added that the petitioners had not attempted to profit from the sales, and indeed there is some suggestion in the Court's opinion that this fact influenced the Court nearly as much as the petitioners' religious motives.[16] At one point the Court stated in dictum that the "constitutional rights of those spreading their religious beliefs through the spoken and printed word are not to be gauged by standards governing retailers or wholesalers of books."[17] In its holding, however, *Murdock* is authority for the more limited principle that the exercise of an established First

Amendment right cannot be circumscribed merely because it contains an incidental commercial aspect. Apparently, however, if the profit in the sales had been the primary purpose of the speech, *Chrestensen* would have applied.[18]

This view is supported by *Breard*, where the Court faced the profit motive squarely in upholding an ordinance prohibiting unsolicited door-to-door magazine subscription sales. Earlier, in *Martin v. City of Struthers*,[19] the Court, pointing to the freedoms of speech and religion, had voided a similar ordinance applied to prevent Jehovah's Witnesses from distributing free religious tracts door-to-door. The Court in *Breard* agreed that "the fact that periodicals are sold does not put them beyond" the First Amendment, but it reasoned that in *Martin* "no element of the commercial" had entered into the distribution, and here, the "selling . . . brings into the transaction a commercial feature."[20] The Court found that the appellant's sales pitch was not itself protected speech: "Only the press or oral advocates of ideas could urge this point. It was not open to the solicitors for gadgets or brushes."[21] The Court did not hold, of course, that the First Amendment does not extend to any speech possessing a commercial feature,[22] but the *profit motive* underlying magazine sales was sufficient in *Breard* to deprive those sales of at least some First Amendment protection.

However, the Court reached this result not by a subjective, factual inquiry into motive but by "balancing . . . the conveniences between some householders' desire for privacy and the publisher's right to distribute publications in the precise way that those soliciting for him think brings the best

---

12. 319 U.S. 105 (1943).

13. 341 U.S. 622 (1951).

14. 319 U.S. at 113.

15. Id. at 112 (emphasis added).

16. The Court noted that the Witnesses' "main object . . . was to preach and publicize the doctrines of their order". 319 U.S. at 112.

17. 319 U.S. at 111.

18. Although *Murdock* did limit somewhat the reach of the *Chrestensen* doctrine it left unclear how a court should determine the "primary purpose" of a communication.

19. 319 U.S. 141 (1943).

20. Breard v. City of Alexandria, 341 U.S. 622, 642–43 (1951).

21. 341 U.S. at 641.

22. 341 U.S. at 642.

results." [23] At first glance, the Court's reliance on this balancing process would appear to have been a rather severe departure from the categorizing approach in *Chrestensen*. In *Chrestensen* once speech fell into the category of commercial speech, it became mere commercial activity, held to be a matter for legislative judgment; suddenly in *Breard* it was a "right" to be balanced against that of privacy. But the two cases are not really inconsistent. In *Breard* the Court did not directly hold that door-to-door magazine subscription solicitation is "purely commercial" in the sense contemplated by *Chrestensen*. While the Court did not dwell on the extent to which effective competition is necessary to a free press, a factor discussed at length in the dissent,[24] it was undoubtedly aware that if subscription solicitation were deemed purely commercial, logically the state arguably could ban all such solicitation without regard to the inevitable effects of such a ban on the content of magazines. Viewed conversely, *Breard* might be interpreted to stand for the concept that the First Amendment does not automatically extend to profit-making aspects of otherwise protected activity. As such *Breard* is consistent with the line of decisions upholding the neutral application of the antitrust, labor, and tax laws to newspapers and other communications media.[25]

D. What Is "Commercial" Speech?

For many years, the extent to which *Chrestensen* and its progeny have been controlling beyond their own facts was unclear. If speech is labeled "commercial", it loses, under this line of cases, all First Amendment protection. But when is speech commercial? Shortly after *Breard* was decided,

for example, the Court, in rejecting the argument that motion pictures are unprotected because they are made and exhibited for profit, stated that the fact that "books, newspapers, and magazines are published and sold for profit does not prevent them from being a form of expression whose liberty is safeguarded by the First Amendment. We fail to see why operation for profit should have any different effect in the case of motion pictures." [26] Later, in *New York Times v. Sullivan*,[27] the Court declined to apply *Chrestensen* to sustain a libel action against a newspaper which had published an allegedly offensive paid political advertisement. The advertisement in *New York Times*, said the Court,

> was not a "commercial" advertisement in the sense in which the word was used in *Chrestensen*. It communicated information, expressed opinion, recited grievances, protested claimed abuses, and sought financial support on behalf of a movement whose existence and objectives are matters of the highest public interest and concern.[28]

If nothing else, *New York Times* suggests in this context that the primary purpose test for determining commercial speech, to the extent it had been adopted in the past, was laid to rest. The newspaper's commercial motives in publishing the advertisement were irrelevant; it was the advertisement's content that swayed the Court to apply First Amendment protection.

The "purely commercial advertising" which appeared to have been carved out from protected speech in the case law following *Chrestensen* and *New York Times* was—to say the least—confused. While financial motive is not enough to make speech "commercial," [29] where product sales are the so-called "primary purpose" of the speech,

---

23. 341 U.S. at 644.

24. 341 U.S. at 646–48.

25. Citizen Publishing Co. v. United States, 394 U.S. 131 (1969) (antitrust); Associated Press v. NLRB, 301 U.S. 103 (1937) (labor laws); Oklahoma Press Publishing Co. v. Walling, 327 U.S. 186 (1946) (wage and hour laws). Cf. Cammarano v. United States, 358 U.S. 498 (1959) (business deduction on federal income tax of sums spent for lobbying activities disallowed).

26. Joseph Burstyn, Inc. v. Wilson, 343 U.S. 495, 501–502 (1952) (footnote omitted).

27. 376 U.S. 254 (1964).

28. 376 U.S. 254, at 266 (1974).

29. See, e.g., New York Times v. Sullivan, 376 U.S. 254 (1964) (protection of publication of public political advertisement is not diminished by the fact that newspaper was paid to carry the ad); Cammarano v. United States, 358 U.S. 498, 514 (1959) ("The profit motive

inclusion of political comment or other material which itself could be protected will not suffice to pull the speech within the ambit of the Amendment.[30] This primary purpose test apparently looks, not to the form, but to the function of the publication. Under this test, a book or other expression which itself could fall within the guarantee of free speech can be the subject of otherwise prohibited regulation if either the book is promoted by advertising, in which case the advertising may be regulated,[31] or the book itself is used to advertise or promote the sale of another product.[32] Second, statements which might be considered non-commercial if made by persons not materially interested in the affected trade apparently can take on a different character when made by one involved in trade.[33]

E. Rationales for the Commercial Speech Doctrine

The validity of *Chrestensen's* Commercial Speech doctrine has been subject to much dispute, a dispute which is encouraged by the uncertain and confusing tests to determine the types of speech which are commercial. In 1959, Mr. Justice Douglas stated that the "ruling [in *Chrestensen*] was casual, almost offhand. And it has not survived reflection." [34] But the view was expressed in a concurring opinion and not embraced by the full Court. Other justices have on occasion agreed with Justice Douglas,[35] and commentators have also criticized the doctrine as inflexible and insensitive to the informational value of commercial advertising; [36] *Breard* has similarly been attacked as demonstrative of "the Court's general lack of enthusiasm for the commercial element in first amendment questions." [37]

One obvious logical problem in distinguishing commercial speech from political expression is the simple fact that inherent in every speech labeled as "commercial" is at least some noncommercial message: the expression of ideas and values such as materialism or capitalism. There is no such thing as "pure" commercial speech.[38] Certainly the first amendment makes no obvious dis-

should make no difference."); Thornhill v. Alabama, 310 U.S. 88, 102 (1940) (purely informational union picketing is protected); Grosjean v. American Press Co., 297 U.S. 233 (1936) (newspaper successfully challenges discriminatory tax on its publication). Indeed, even selling is not itself enough to make speech unprotected where the sale activity is "merely incidental and collateral." Murdock v. Pennsylvania, 319 U.S. 105, 112 (1943) (holding unconstitutional a tax on the sale of religious material where the "main object [was] to preach and publicize the doctrines."); see also Jamison v. Texas, 318 U.S. 413 (1943); Cantwell v. Connecticut, 310 U.S. 296 (1940); Harman v. City of Haverhill, 120 F.2d 87 (1st Cir. 1941) cert. denied 314 U.S. 641.

30. Valentine v. Chrestensen, 316 U.S. 52, 55 (1942) (advertising handbill not protected where political statement was included "with the intent, and for the purpose, of evading the prohibition" on commercial handbills).

31. See Bantam Books, Inc. v. F.T.C., 275 F.2d 680 (2d Cir. 1960), cert. denied 364 U.S. 819 (F.T.C. regulation of book labeling upheld without discussion of First Amendment); Witkower Press, Inc., 57 F.T.C. 145 (1960); cf., M.B. Waterman & Co., 46 F.T.C. 133 (1949) (deceptive advertising of religious objects).

32. Compare United States v. 8 Cartons, Etc., 103 F.Supp. 626, 628 (W.D.N.Y.1951) ("The seizure relates not to books offered for bona fide sale but to copies of the book claimed to be offending against the Act by being associated with the article . . . in a distribution plan in such a way as to misbrand the product.")

and United States v. Articles of Drug, 32 F.R.D. 32, 35 (S.D.Ill.1963), with Koch v. F.T.C., 206 F.2d 311, 317–18 (6th Cir. 1953).

33. Compare, Scientific Manufacturing Co. v. F.T.C., 124 F.2d 640, 644 (3d Cir. 1941), with Perma-Maid Co. v. F.T.C., 121 F.2d 282 (6th Cir. 1941).

34. Cammarano v. United States, 358 U.S. 498, 514 (1959) (Douglas, J., concurring).

35. Lehman v. City of Shaker Heights, 418 U.S. 298, 314–15 (1974) (Brennan, J., dissenting); Pittsburgh Press Co. v. Pittsburgh Comm'n on Human Relations, 413 U.S. 376, 401 & n. 6 (Stewart, J., dissenting).

36. See Note, Deceptive Advertising, 80 Harv.L. Rev. 1005, 1029–34 (1967); see also Redish, The First Amendment in the Marketplace: Commercial Speech and the Value of Free Expression, 39 Geo.Wash.L.Rev. 429, 432–38 (1971); Rotunda, The Commercial Speech Doctrine in the Supreme Court, 1976 U.Ill.L.Forum 1080.

37. Redish, The First Amendment in the Marketplace: Commercial Speech and the Value of Free Expression, 39 Geo.Wash.L.Rev. 429, at 454 (1971).

38. E.g., Black, He Cannot Choose But Hear: The Plight of the Captive Auditor, 53 Colum.L.Rev. 960 (1953):

"One Article of Faith in this [advertising] Gospel emerges as a matter of soundest induction, commerical by commercial: Prices were never so reasonable, products never so fine . . . . We know another

tinction between commercial and non-commercial speech, and the difficulty of the Court over the years in defining commercial speech at least suggests that the distinction does not really exist.

In an attempt to rationalize the doctrine, some have argued that since "state and federal governments enjoy wide powers of regulation" over "the economic welfare of business enterprises", therefore the "possibly desirable objectives furthered by advertising would not seem to require its protection by the first amendment. . . ."[39] That argument, however, appears to assume the point in dispute: how wide should the government's power over advertising be? And when the form of the regulation over business is not a direct economic matter (such as taxes, subsidies, minimum wages), but direct control over speech, should there be some role for the Court in reviewing the reasonableness of the restrictions on speech?

Unlike straightforward economic regulation, speech is preservative of other rights. While regulatory legislation affecting ordinary commercial transactions is usually presumed constitutionally valid, regulation restricting or forbidding speech restricts the public process of debate and exchange of ideas which can ordinarily be expected to bring about repeal of undesirable legislation.[40] The regulation of speech, including commercial speech, inhibits public debate and evaluation of proposed regulatory measures.

Others still justify the doctrine on the grounds that only minimal protection of commercial advertising is necessary because there is little risk that its regulation will exist "for political purposes or even that its regulation will hamper the workings of democracy."[41] But this empirical assertion certainly cannot be assumed. Moreover, as a constitutional matter, the Court implicitly has rejected this justification by its refusal to construe the antitrust laws to prohibit anticompetitive activities which are sheltered by the first amendment.[42]

If a political candidate is selling himself, the first amendment applies; yet if he sells peanuts, the commercial speech doctrine asserts that there is *no* first amendment protection. Rationalizing these results is more than a little difficult. Certainly this commercial speech doctrine cannot be based on a realistic belief that the dangers of falsehood are less likely when the speech is political. One commentator has asserted that the "government is more likely to be impartial in censoring speech influencing commercial decisions than in regulating speech affecting its own policies and composition."[43] This assertion is not supported by any authority and it is difficult to believe that it could be. Commercial regulation usually is enacted to benefit one economic group (businessmen, a certain class of businessmen, consumers, a certain class of consumers) and impose a burden on other classes. The government merely responds to these pressures. Why we would always expect the result of these

Article well, for it is the easily tallied integral sum of all advertising, and its deepest philosophic wellspring: material possessions produce happiness . . . . The adman has every right to preach his Gospel." (53 Colum.L.Rev. at 968).

See also, R. Posner, Economic Analysis of Law § 22.4 at 316 (1973).

39. Note, Freedom of Expression in a Commercial Context, 78 Harv.L.Rev. 1191, 1195 (1965).

40. United States v. Carolene Products, Co., 304 U.S. 144, 152–153 n. 4 (1938) (Stone, J.); cf. Wright, Professor Bickel, the Scholarly Tradition, and the Supreme Court, 84 Harv.L.Rev. 769, 787–89 (1971).

41. Cooper, The Tax Treatment of Business Grassroots Lobbying: Defining and Attaining the Public Policy Objectives, 68 Colum.L.Rev. 801, 832 (1968).

42. In two related cases, Eastern R.R. Presidents Conference v. Noerr Motor Freight, Inc., 365 U.S. 127 (1961) and United Mine Workers of America v. Pennington, 381 U.S. 657 (1965), the Court held, on First Amendment grounds, that the Sherman and Clayton Acts do not extend to exercises of the right to petition the government in either a legislative or administrative setting, despite anticompetitive effects. Compare, Nat. Society of Professional Engineers v. United States, 435 U.S. 679 (1978).

See generally, Fische, Antitrust Liability for Attempts to Influence Government Action: The Basis and Limits of the *Noerr-Pennington* Doctrine, 45 U.Chi.L. Rev. 80 (1977).

43. Note, Freedom of Expression in a Commercial Context, 78 Harv.L.Rev. 1191, 1195 (1965).

conflicting pressures to be impartial is a mystery.

Perhaps because neither the states nor the federal government have until recently had much interest in prohibiting truthful advertising, the older cases concerned either control of false or misleading speech or regulations, like those in *Valentine* and *Breard*, or those affecting the time and manner of the communication.[44] But now government is asserting broader prohibiting regulations on speech affected by a commercial interest, and some of the most recent cases have illustrated some of the possible dangers of the commercial speech doctrine. It is to those cases we now turn.

F. The Modern Commercial Speech Doctrine

In *Capital Broadcasting Co. v. Mitchell*,[1] the commercial speech doctrine was given its most far-reaching interpretation by a three-judge district court, which the Supreme Court affirmed without opinion. This decision upheld a flat statutory ban on the advertising of cigarettes over any medium of electronic communications subject to F.C.C. jurisdiction. The district court reasoned that "advertising is less vigorously protected than other forms of speech" and, thus, that "Congress has the power to prohibit the advertising of cigarettes in any media" as an exercise of its power to regulate commerce. The district court's analysis belies any effort to limit its approval of Congressional regulation either to cigarettes (on the theory that they are uniquely hazardous) or to electronic media (which are necessarily subject to regulation).

The dissent argued, to no avail, that since cigarette advertising has been held to express a position on a matter of public controversy,[2] it is not merely commercial speech but comes "within the core protection of the First Amendment." The dissent did not expressly dispute the proposition that commercial speech may be regulated by Congress, but it did implicitly reject the primary purpose test in favor of a content-analysis test, though it may be read to implicitly reject the commercial speech doctrine. The Supreme Court affirmed the majority position of the district court without opinion.

Capital Broadcasting is a troublesome case. If Congress may forbid truthful advertising urging the purchase of a legal, validly offered item, it is hard to see a way to establish a principled limitation in its power to restrict advertisements for anything it chooses to consider "harmful." May Congress prohibit the advertising of movies which are not obscene,[3] or of political pamphlets which do not constitute advocacy directed "to inciting or producing imminent lawless action and [are] likely to incite or produce such actions?"[4] These were serious questions following *Capital Broadcasting*.

In a series of three decisions—*Pittsburgh Press Co. v. Pittsburgh Commission on Human Rights*,[5] *Bigelow v. Virginia*,[6] and *Virginia State Board of Pharmacy v. Virginia Citizens Council, Inc.*[7]—the Supreme Court recognized these problems and rejected the commercial speech doctrine. In *Pittsburgh Press*, a newspaper had been charged with violating an ordinance prohibiting sex-designated help-wanted advertisements except where the employer or advertiser would be free to make hiring decisions

---

44. One important exception may be Williamson v. Lee Optical Co., 348 U.S. 483, 489–90 (1955), where the Court upheld a state law prohibiting solicitations for the sale of optical appliances. However, the First Amendment issues were not discussed; the Court relied on the state's asserted special interest in the underlying health related conduct.

1. 333 F.Supp. 582 (D.D.C.1971), aff'd without opinion sub nom. Capital Broadcasting Co. v. Acting Attorney General Kleindienst, 405 U.S. 1000 (1972).

2. Banzhaf v. F.C.C., 405 F.2d 1082 (D.C.Cir. 1968), cert. denied 396 U.S. 842 (1969).

3. See Miller v. California, 413 U.S. 15 (1973).

4. Brandenburg v. Ohio, 395 U.S. 444, 447 (1969) (footnote omitted) (per curiam).

5. 413 U.S. 376 (1973).

6. 421 U.S. 809 (1975).

7. 425 U.S. 748 (1976).

on the basis of sex. The newspaper argued that the advertisements involved the exercise of editorial judgment, as to where to place the advertisement, rather than its commercial context. Therefore the advertisements, it was argued, were sufficiently noncommercial to fall within the ambit of the first amendment. The Supreme Court disagreed.

The Court conceded that the newspaper does make a judgment as to whether or not to allow the advertiser to select the column in which the want-ad should be placed. And, also, the newspaper's profit motive alone could not be determinative because then all aspects of the newspaper business—"from selection of news stories to choice of editorial position"—would come under the commercial speech doctrine. But relying heavily on *New York Times*, the Court found that the advertisements constituted "in practical effect an integrated commercial statement" [8] devoid of any truly editorial expression on matters of public interest or social policy. "The advertisements are thus classic examples of commercial speech" of the sort left unprotected in *Chrestensen*.[9] Once again, the Court appeared to examine the content rather than the primary purpose underlying the advertisements in reaching its decision. Yet this factual conclusion in *Pittsburgh Press* illustrates that a determination of commercial speech is a fruitless task: what if the want-ad had been placed to protest the laws relating to sex discrimination? Chief

Justice Burger in dissent attempted to point out the problem of having judges make page by page determinations of what parts of a newspaper were commercial speech.[10]

If *Pittsburgh Press* had stopped here in its analysis, it would have merely given further support to a broad reading of the *Capital Broadcasting* case. But significantly, the Court noted the argument that "the exchange of information is as important in the commercial realm as in any other," [11] a view which is a common basis for criticism of the rationale in *Chrestensen*. And, the Court did not reject that argument, but said, in response to the urging of the newspaper that the justices abrogate the distinction between commercial and other speech:

> Whatever the merits of this contention may be in other contexts, it is unpersuasive in this case. Discrimination in employment is not only commercial activity, it is *illegal* commercial activity under the Ordinance. We have no doubt that a newspaper constitutionally could be forbidden to publish a want ad proposing a sale of narcotics or soliciting prostitutes. Nor would the result be different if the nature of the transaction were indicated by placement under columns captioned "Narcotics for Sale" and "Prostitutes Wanted" rather than stated within the four corners of the advertisement.[12]

Even more importantly, after emphasizing the illegal nature of this activity, the opinion cited in a footnote the dissent in Capital Broadcasting.[13] The Court, while not yet rejecting *Chrestensen*, relied on a much narrower and more concrete test: if an activity

---

8. 413 U.S. at 388.

9. 413 U.S. at 385.

10. 413 U.S. at 393 (Burger, C.J., dissenting).

11. 413 U.S. at 388.

12. 413 U.S. at 388 (emphasis in original) (footnote omitted).

See also, Village of Hoffman Estates v. Flipside, Hoffman Estates, Inc., 455 U.S. 489 (1982). In that case a city ordinance required a business to obtain a license if it sells any items "designed or marketed for use with illegal drugs." The Court, in rejecting a preenforcement challenge on its face to the ordinance on the grounds of vagueness and overbreadth, turned to the free speech claims. The ordinance did not infringe noncommercial speech interests of drug paraphernalia stores, or "head shops" ("head" is slang for frequent user of drugs), even though the city guidelines treated

the proximity of drug related literature to paraphernalia as evidence that the paraphernalia was marketed for use with illegal drugs: the ordinance did not prohibit the sale of the literature itself but "simply regulates the commercial marketing of items that the labels reveal may be used for an illicit purpose." As far as commercial speech is concerned, the ordinance's restriction on the manner of marketing does not significantly limit the store's communication of information with the exception of "commercial activity promoting or encouraging illegal drug use. If that activity is 'speech,' then it is speech proposing an illegal transaction, which a government may regulate or ban entirely." 455 U.S. at 496.

13. 413 U.S. 376, 388 n. 12, citing Wright J., dissenting, in Capital Broadcasting Co. v. Mitchell, 333 F.Supp. 582, 593 n. 42 (D.D.C.1971).

is illegal, the state may prohibit the advertising or touting of that activity. Its reasoning to support this test follows a traditional balance of interests:

> Any First Amendment interest which might be served by advertising an ordinary commercial proposal and which might arguably outweigh the governmental interest supporting the regulation is altogether absent when the commercial activity itself is illegal and the restriction on advertising is incidental to a valid limitation on economic activity.[14]

In *Bigelow v. Virginia*[15] the Court began to establish a corollary principle: If an activity is legal, the state cannot prohibit advertising it. In *Bigelow* a newspaper publisher had been convicted of violating a state statute outlawing advertisements that "encourage or prompt the procuring of abortion."[16] The advertisement in question had been placed by a profit-making organization in New York which had offered to arrange for legal abortions in New York. The Court stated that

> Viewed in its entirety, the advertisement conveyed information of potential interest and value to a diverse audience—not only to readers possibly in need of the services offered, but also to those with a general curiosity about, or genuine interest in, the subject matter or the law of another State and its development, and to readers seeking reform in Virginia. [Also], the activity advertised pertained to constitutional interests . . . . Thus, in this case, appellant's First Amendment interests coincid-

ed with the constitutional interests of the general public.[17]

With this, however, the Court did not rule that the advertisement was sufficiently editorial or noncommercial in nature to fall outside the ambit of *Chrestensen*. For the opinion in *Bigelow* proceeded with a reinterpretation of *Chrestensen*:

> the holding [in *Chrestensen*] is distinctly a limited one: the ordinance was upheld as a reasonable regulation of the manner in which commercial advertising could be distributed. The fact that it had the effect of banning a particular handbill does not mean that *Chrestensen* is authority for the proposition that all statutes regulating commercial advertising are immune from constitutional challenge.[18]

This view of *Chrestensen* was a new one, to say the least. As Justice Rehnquist argued in his dissent, *Chrestensen* had been considered authority for the proposition that the First Amendment cannot be used to attack a statute regulating commercial advertising, assuming, as Mr. Justice Rehnquist did, that the "[w]hatever slight factual content the advertisement may contain and whatever expression of opinion may be laboriously drawn from it does not alter its predominantly commercial content."[19] Thus the Court in *Bigelow*, by reducing *Chrestensen* to an exercise in a generalized balancing process, might well have interpreted the commercial speech doctrine out of existence.

One might have argued that, in spite of language of *Bigelow*, its facts allow a very

---

14. 413 U.S. at 389. See also, National Society of Professional Engineers v. United States, 435 U.S. 679, 697–698 & nn. 26–27 (1978). In that case the Court held that the Professional Society's canon of ethics prohibiting competitive bidding violates section 1 of the Sherman Act. Hence, the district court could enjoin the Society from adopting any official opinion, policy statement, or guideline stating or implying that competitive pricing is unethical, even though the Society can seek to influence governmental action. "While the resulting order may curtail the exercise of liberties that the Society might otherwise enjoy, that is a necessary and, in cases such as this, unavoidable consequence of the violation. Just as an injunction against price fixing abridges the freedom of businessmen to talk to one another about prices, so too the injunction in this case must restrict the Society's range of expression on the ethics of competitive bidding." 435 U.S. at 697 (footnote omitted).

On the relationship between professional ethics, the antitrust laws, and free speech, see, e.g., Morgan, The Evolving Concept of Professional Responsibility, 90 Harv.L.Rev. 702 (1977); Rotunda, The Word "Profession" Is Only a Label—And Not a Very Useful One, 4 Learning and the Law 16 (No. 2, Summer, 1977); Rotunda, The First Amendment Now Protects Commercial Speech, 10 The Center Magazine: A Publication of the Center for the Study of Democratic Institutions 33 (May/June 1977).

15. 421 U.S. 809 (1975).

16. 421 U.S. at 812–813.

17. 421 U.S. at 822.

18. 421 U.S. at 819–20.

19. 421 U.S. at 831–32 (Rehnquist, J., dissenting).

narrow interpretation: the state may not prohibit one from advertising an activity which is a constitutional right. In this case, the right is that very special right created in *Roe v. Wade*,[20] the right to obtain an abortion, particularly during the first trimester. Under *Pittsburgh Press*, the state may prohibit advertisements of *illegal* commercial activity; under *Bigelow*, the state may not prohibit advertisements of activity which enjoys special constitutional protection. However, a later decision, *Virginia State Board of Pharmacy v. Virginia Citizens Consumer Council, Inc.*[21] indicates that a narrow view of *Bigelow* is inappropriate and that commercial speech is now within the protection of the First Amendment.

In *Virginia State Board of Pharmacy*, a consumer group claimed that the first amendment prohibited a statute making illegal the advertisement of prescription drug prices as unprofessional conduct. The statute was defended on the grounds that it was a permissible regulation of commercial speech that had the effect of maintaining professional standards of pharmacy. Justice Blackmun, writing for the majority, phrased the issue simply:

> Our pharmacist does not wish to editorialize on any subject, cultural, philosophical, or political. He does not wish to report any particularly newsworthy fact, or to make generalized observations even about commercial matters. The "idea" he wishes to communicate is simply this: "I will sell you the X prescription drug at the Y price." Our question, then, is whether this communication is wholly outside the protection of the First Amendment.[22]

The Court held that the consuming public had a protected first amendment interest in the free flow of truthful information concerning lawful activity.[23]

At the same time, the *Virginia State Board of Pharmacy* opinion reaffirmed the states' authority to issue regulations of the time, place, and manner of speech, if such restrictions are justified without reference to the content of the speech, serve a significant governmental interest and leave open other channels of communication.[24] Also untruthful speech, "commercial or otherwise, has never been protected for its own sake."[25] Thus the state may continue to regulate so as to prohibit false or even misleading speech.

In disposing of the claim that the advertising prohibition protected professional standards, the Court rejected the rationale that banning advertising was justified by the alleged salutary results—more small pharmacies, less demand for potentially dangerous drug consumption, and high public esteem for the pharmaceutical profession. Conceding the desirability of those results, the Court rejected the advertising ban as a paternalistic means of securing them. In essence, the state was taking away the consumer's ability to choose among economic decisions (where to shop, what prescription to request, and so on) by depriving him of the information needed to make these decisions intelligently. Such pre-emption of individual decision-making is deemed by the Court to be objectionable in a free-market economy. But the Court did not use neo-

---

20. 410 U.S. 113 (1973).

21. 425 U.S. 748 (1976). See generally, Rotunda, The First Amendment Now Protects Commercial Speech, 10 The Center Magazine: A Publication of the Center for the Study of Democratic Institutions, 32–33 (May/June 1977).

22. 425 U.S. at 761. To emphasize the lack of any nice distinction between commercial and noncommercial speech, the Court noted that "[o]ur pharmacist, for example, could cast himself as a commentator on store-to-store disparities in drug prices, giving his own and those of a competitor as proof. We see little point in requiring him to do so, and little difference if he does not." 425 U.S. at 764–65.

23. 425 U.S. at 773.

24. Id. at 771.

25. Id. Justice Stewart, in his concurrence, elaborates on this issue. Unlike libel actions, where the First Amendment offers some protection in appropriate cases even for false factual assertions, New York Times Co. v. Sullivan, 376 U.S. 254 (1964), the commercial advertiser generally is not under the deadline pressures of the press, generally knows the product or service he seeks to sell and is in a position to verify the accuracy of his factual assertions, and consequently there is little danger that state regulation of false or misleading price or product advertising will chill nondeceptive commercial expression. 425 U.S. at 777–78 (Stewart, J., concurring).

classical, laissez-faire economic thinking to restrict the government's ability to regulate industry, only to show that it could not accomplish these ends by suppression of first amendment freedoms. It clearly allowed Virginia to subject its pharmacists to "close regulation", to adopt other professional standards or to "subsidize them or protect them from competition in other ways." [26] What the state cannot do is to completely suppress dissemination of concededly truthful information about entirely lawful activity.

The advertising prohibition in this case was really being used to implement hidden policy decisions that were better left to be decided by free and open debate. For example, the statute allegedly protected the small, high service pharmacy by keeping the consumer uninformed as to the cost he pays for such services. The Court suggested the desired results of the statute may yet be attained in a non-paternalistic fashion by *encouraging* dissemination of information, rather than restricting it. Presumably, if there is value to individual service from pharmacists, a fully informed consumer (or a sufficient number of them) will choose to bear the cost of such service. Alternatively, the government may choose to subsidize low-volume, high-service pharmacies by free individual choice, through tax advantages, or outright subsidies, and this decision itself may be the subject of public debate. Similarly, if it is socially desirable to discourage the indiscriminate consumption of drugs, warnings of the hazards of consumption may prevent abuses; if not, an informed public may choose to discourage consumption by taxing or prohibiting certain drugs.

After *Virginia State Board of Pharmacy* the state may reach the same policy goals as it chose to reach before, but it may not use the means of prohibiting the dissemination

of truthful information about lawful activity. The purpose of this holding is not merely to tidy-up the interpretation of the first amendment; rather it is to encourage more rational majority decision-making and a more open weighing of the advantages and disadvantages of policy alternatives by preventing the use of the "commercial speech" concept to deny entirely first amendment protection to an important area of speech.

Two additional aspects of the decision should be noted. First, the decision by implication raises anew the question of the constitutionality of restrictions on the advertising of cigarettes in the electronic media. Despite Justice Blackmun's offhand dismissal of the point as having been based on the "special problem of the electronic broadcast media" not present in this case,[27] we have already seen that the *Capital Broadcasting* decision was not based upon any special aspects of the broadcast media; rather it was squarely based on a view of the commercial speech doctrine promulgated in *Chrestensen*, that so-called commercial speech is completely outside the protections of the first amendment. Justice Rehnquist's conclusion in his dissent that television cigarette ads may no longer be completely prohibited is probably correct. The state, of course, may tax cigarettes to discourage their use and the federal government may place a nationwide tax on cigarettes, or prohibit their production and sale entirely. To prevent misleading advertisements the FCC may require warnings to be placed in the commercials, as well as requiring anticigarette ads under the fairness doctrine. But unless Congress outlaws cigarettes, it cannot prohibit "concededly truthful information"—e.g., brand X cigarettes offer less tar and nicotine than any other cigarette—about "entirely lawful activity"—the smoking of cigarettes. Any other conclusion would allow Virginia to pro-

---

26. Id. at 770. Cf. Parker v. Brown, 317 U.S. 341 (1943).

27. 425 U.S. at 773. See Lamar Outdoor Advertising, Inc. v. Mississippi State Tax Comm'n, 701 F.2d 314 (5th Cir. 1983), petition for rehearing en banc granted, March 11, 1983 (citing an earlier edition of this trea-

tise). The *Lamar* fifth circuit panel, in an opinion by Judge Gee, invalidated, as a violation of free speech, certain statutes and regulations of Mississippi which effectively banned liquor advertising on billboards and in printed and electronic media originating within the state.

hibit the advertising of drug prices on radio or television. Perhaps the Court may one day fashion some special constitutional rules dealing with this problem in the still formative area of the first amendment and the broadcast media.[28] But the Court has not yet done so; certainly Justice Blackmun's brief, inaccurate reference to the *Capital Broadcasting* decision banning cigarette advertising on television hardly qualifies as a legal distinction of constitutional proportions.

Moreover, Chief Justice Burger's attempt, in his concurrence, to distinguish between advertisements by "true professionals" (doctors and lawyers) and advertisements by pseudo-professionals (pharmacists)[29] creates a distinction as unworkable as that inherent in the *Chrestensen* doctrine itself, and since rejected in *Bates v. State Bar*,[30] discussed below.

The Court has continued the principle of *Virginia Board of Pharmacy* in *Linmark Associates, Inc. v. Township of Willingboro*.[31] There the unanimous Court ruled that the First Amendment did not permit a municipality to prohibit by ordinance the posting of "For Sale" or "Sold" signs even though the town acted to stem what it perceived as the flight of white homeowners from a racially integrated community. The respondent argued that the First Amendment concerns were less because the ordinance only restricted one form of communication. The Court decided, however, that the other forms of advertising—mainly by newspapers and realtor listings—were more

costly and less effective. Second, the Court emphasized that the Township's ordinance, by its own terms, made clear that it was not concerned with the time, place, or manner of the speech but its content. It did not prohibit all lawn signs, or all lawn signs of a particular size, in order, perhaps, to promote aesthetic values or other goals unrelated to the suppression of free expression. In addition, the "respondents have not demonstrated that the place or manner of speech produces a detrimental 'secondary effect' on society. . . . Rather, Willingboro has proscribed particular types of signs based on their content because it fears their 'primary' effect—that they will cause those receiving the information to act upon it."[32]

Finally, the Court was unwilling to regard the governmental objective of assuring that Willingboro remains an integrated community as sufficient to justify the ordinance. The Court rejected this rationale on two grounds, one very narrow and one much broader. First, the Court concluded that the record before it did not support the township's fears that it was experiencing panic selling by white homeowners because of a belief the township was changing from a white to a black community.[33] More broadly, the Court found the defect in the ordinance "more basic" because if "dissemination of this information can be restricted, then every locality in the country can suppress any facts that reflect poorly on the locality, so long as a plausible claim can be made that disclosure would cause the recipi-

---

28. Compare Red Lion Broadcasting Co. v. FCC, 395 U.S. 367 (1969), with Columbia Broadcasting System v. Democratic Nat. Committee, 412 U.S. 94 (1973).

29. 425 U.S. at 774 (Burger, C.J., concurring).

30. 433 U.S. 350 (1977). It should be noted that the scope of attorney advertising when restricted by professional association rather than by the state also raises important issues of antitrust law. The Justice Department for example sued the American Bar Association claiming its advertising restrictions in the Code of Professional Responsibility violate the antitrust laws. See Bar News, A Special Report on the Justice Department Antitrust Suit Against the ABA (Summer 1976); see generally T. Morgan & R. Rotunda, Prob-

lems and Materials on Professional Responsibility 95–132 (1976), and its 1978 Supplement, ch. 4. This suit was later settled.

31. 431 U.S. 85 (1977).

32. 431 U.S. 85 at 94, citing Young v. American Mini Theatres, 427 U.S. 50, 70 n. 34 (1976).

33. The Court specifically distinguished Barrick Realty, Inc. v. City of Gary, 491 F.2d 161 (7th Cir. 1974) which upheld Gary, Indiana's prohibition of "For Sale" signs on a record which showed that whites were fleeing en masse. "We express no view as to whether *Barrick Realty* can survive *Bigelow* and *Virginia Pharmacy*." 431 U.S. 85 at 95, n. 9.

ents of the information to act 'irrationally.' " [34]

In *Carey v. Population Services International*,[35] the Court invalidated a prohibition of any advertisement or display of contraceptives, a product which was not only legal but constitutionally protected. The arguments that such a prohibition was necessary because advertisements would be offensive or embarrassing to some or would legitimize sexual activities were rejected as "classically not justifications . . . ." [36]

That same year, in *Bates v. State Bar* [37] the Court struck down state limitations on attorney advertising. The majority noted that the case did not involve person-to-person solicitation nor advertising as to the quality of legal services, but only the question of whether lawyers may constitutionally advertise the prices of routine services, such as uncontested divorces, uncontested adoptions, simple personal bankruptcies, and changes of name.[38] Such advertising is constitutionally protected. The Court left open the extent to which certain types of advertising may be misleading, though it found appellants' particular advertisement not misleading. The Court also raised the question of whether advertising claims as to the quality of services "may be so likely to be misleading as to warrant restriction . . . . And the special problems of advertising on the electronic broadcast media will [also] warrant special consideration." [39]

Later, in *In re R.M.J.*,[40] a unanimous Supreme Court, in an opinion by Justice Powell, applied *Bates* and invalidated various restrictions on lawyer advertising. The state supreme court had reprimanded R.M.J. because he had deviated from the precise listing of areas of practice included in the state's Rule 4 governing lawyer advertising; for example, his advertisement listed "real estate" instead of "property," and he listed "contracts," although Rule 4 did not list that latter term at all. Since the state did not show that R.M.J.'s listing was deceptive and because the state could show no substantial interest which its restriction on advertising promoted, the Court invalidated it. Similarly the Court invalidated a part of Rule 4 prohibiting a lawyer from identifying the jurisdictions in which he is licensed to practice law.[41] The Court also struck a prohibition against the lawyer widely mailing announcement cards to persons other than lawyers, former clients, personal friends, and relatives. These cards announced the opening of his law office.[42] The state produced no evidence justifying such a restrictive prohibition.

A year after *Bates, First National Bank v. Bellotti*,[43] held that states cannot prohibit corporations from spending money to ex-

---

34. 431 U.S. 85 at 96.

35. 431 U.S. 678 (1977).

36. 431 U.S. at 701. See also Bolger v. Youngs Drug Products Corp., 103 S.Ct. ___ (1983) (law prohibiting mailing of unsolicited advertisements for contraceptives invalid).

37. 433 U.S. 350 (1977). See generally, e.g., Andrews, Lawyer Advertising and the First Amendment, 1981 A.B.Found.Res.J. 967 (1981).

38. 433 U.S. at 366.

39. 433 U.S. at 383–84.

After this case the American Bar Association's Model Code of Professional Responsibility was amended to allow radio and television advertising subject to certain restrictions. See, e.g., D.R. 2–101(D): "If the advertisement is communicated to the public over television or radio, it shall be prerecorded, approved for broadcast by the lawyer, and a recording of the actual transmission shall be retained by the lawyer."

40. 455 U.S. 191 (1982). See Blackmar, the Missouri Supreme Court and Lawyer Advertising: *RMJ* and its Aftermath, 47 Mo.L.Rev. 621 (1982).

41. 455 U.S. at 205.

R.M.J. also emphasized in large boldface type that he was a member of the U.S. Supreme Court bar, a "relatively uninformative fact" but the record did not show that it was misleading. Rule 4 did not specifically identify this information as misleading, nor place a limitation on the type size, nor require any explanation of the significance of admission to the U.S. Supreme Court bar. 455 U.S. at 205–06.

42. 102 S.Ct. at 939. See text at nn. 65–66, infra.

43. 435 U.S. 765 (1978). See generally, Note, The Corporation and the Constitution: Economic Due Process and Corporate Speech, 90 Yale L.J. 1833 (1981); Patton and Bartlett, Corporate "Persons" and Freedom of Speech: The Political Impact of Legal Mythology, 1981 Wisc.L.Rev. 494.

press their views on referendum questions even if such issues are not directly related to their business interests.[44] The Court characterized its recent commercial speech decisions as illustrating that the first amendment prohibits government from limiting the stock of information from which the public may draw, and noted that the state's argument that it could not regulate commercial speech of corporations but could ban their political speech, would reverse the traditional constitutional values attaching to political and commercial speech.[45]

Shortly after *Bellotti,* the Court began to define the limits of state regulation of attorney solicitation of clients in two cases decided the same day, *Ohralik v. Ohio State Bar*[46] and *In re Primus.*[47] In so doing the

majority, speaking through Justice Powell, appeared to resurrect some elements of the "commercial" speech distinction that had been discredited by the earlier cases. Justice Powell said in *Ohralik* that the distinction between other types of speech and commercial speech is a "commonsense" one,[48] though later he stated in *Primus* that the line between commercial and noncommercial speech "will not always be easy to draw,"[49] an admission that suggests the distinction is not so commonsensical.

It is difficult to derive any specific principle of law from *Ohralik* and *Primus* because language in each case suggests both broad and narrow holdings.[50] The decisions in the two cases, taken together, indicate that the state may regulate lawyer solicita-

44. 435 U.S. at 783–784 & n. 20. The Court did caution that "our consideration of a corporation's right to speak on issues of general public interest implies no comparable right in the quite different context of participation in a political campaign for election to public office. Congress might well be able to demonstrate the existence of a danger of real or apparent corruption in independent expenditures by corporations to influence candidate elections." 435 U.S. at 788 n. 26.

Justice Rehnquist, dissenting, argued that corporations as creatures of the state, have only those rights granted them and those necessarily incident to their business purposes. 435 U.S. at 822–28. Justice White, joined by Justices Brennan and Marshall, also dissented.

45. In Consolidated Edison Co. of New York, Inc. v. Public Service Comm'n, 447 U.S. 530 (1980), the Court, applying a similar analysis, invalidated a state public utility commission order which prohibited a utility from inserting in monthly electric bills inserts discussing controversial issues of public policy. In this case the utility advocated nuclear power. See also, Central Hudson Gas & Elec. Corp. v. Public Serv. Comm'n, 447 U.S. 557 (1980), noted infra, text as nn. 90–93.

See Comment, Public Utility Bill Inserts, Political Speech, and the First Amendment: A Constitutionally Mandated Right to Reply, 70 Calif.L.Rev. 1221 (1982), arguing that the first amendment requires opposing groups a right to reply to billing envelope inserts which voice opinions on controversial subjects.

46. 436 U.S. 447 (1978).

47. 436 U.S. 412 (1978).

48. 436 U.S. at 455–456.

49. 436 U.S. at 438, n. 32. Justice Powell said that the line is "based in part on the motive of the speaker and the character of the expressive activity. . . . ." Id. Justice Rehnquist, dissenting, noted that to the extent this "'commonsense' distinction focuses on the content of the speech, it is at least suspect under many

of the Court's First Amendment cases . . . and to the extent it focuses upon the motive of the speaker, it is subject to manipulation by clever practitioners." 436 U.S. at 441–42.

Moreover, Justice Powell's tortured discussion of attorney's fees—in which he sought to demonstrate that there are differences in counsel fees awarded by the court and counsel fees awarded in a "traditional" manner—demonstrates that distinguishing between commercial and noncommercial speech is a fruitless endeavor. Justice Powell said, inter alia, that:

"Counsel fees [here] are awarded in the discretion of the court; awards are not drawn from the plaintiff's recovery, and are usually premised on a successful outcome; and the amounts awarded may not correspond to fees generally obtainable in private litigation." 436 U.S. at 430.

All of these characteristics, even the last one supposedly unique to the ACLU litigation, apply to many private securities lawsuits where the attorneys secure a benefit for shareholders but create no res. Similar types of fees may be generated by truth in lending cases. See, e.g., Mills v. Electric Auto-Lite Co., 396 U.S. 375, 389–97 (1970); Mirabal v. General Motors Acceptance Corp., 576 F.2d 729 (7th Cir. 1978).

50. For example, in *Ohralik*, Justice Powell for the majority summarized *Primus* as follows:

"We hold today in *Primus* that a lawyer who engaged in solicitation as a form of protected political association may not be disciplined without proof of actual wrongdoing that the State constitutionally may proscribe." 436 U.S. at 462–463 n. 20.

Yet in *Primus* itself, Justice Powell for the majority spoke more hesitantly, stating, for example, that "[w]e express no opinion whether an analysis of this case [*Primus*] would be different [if the ACLU had shared court awarded fees between the state chapter and the private attorney cooperating with the ACLU]." 436 U.S. at 430 n. 24.

tion in order to protect the public from false or deceptive commercial practices, so long as the regulations are reasonable and are not applied to speech that does not clearly present such dangers to the public.[51]

The Court recognized that the state has an interest in *Ohralik* in protecting the "unsophisticated, injured, or distressed lay person" from "those aspects of solicitation that involve fraud, undue influence, intimidation, overreaching, and other forms of 'vexatious conduct.'"[52] This rule is justified in part because of the special nature of "in-person" solicitation. In general advertising the recipient may simply turn away, but in-person solicitation may exert pressure and seek an immediate response from the prospective client, who then has less opportunity for reflection. The Bar and supervisory authorities have less opportunity to engage in counter education in such circumstances. And there is less opportunity for public scrutiny because the in-person solicitation often takes place in private, with no witness other than the lawyer and the prospective client.[53]

However, even these distinctions apparently do not justify a broad, per se rule against in-person solicitation, for the *Ohralik* majority seemed careful to limit its holding to the facts before the Court. The opinion emphasized that the issue was whether the antisolicitation rule could constitutionally be applied to the appellant,[54] and that "the appropriate focus is on appellant's conduct."[55] Justice Powell began the opinion by summarizing in detail the appellant's

outrageous in-person solicitation, and concluded by restating the factual context:

> On the basis of the undisputed facts of record, we conclude that the disciplinary rules constitutionally could be applied to appellant. He approached two young accident victims at a time when they were especially incapable of making informed judgments or of assessing and protecting their own interests. He solicited Carol McClintock in a hospital room where she lay in traction and sought out Wanda Lou Holbert on the day she came home from the hospital, knowing from his prior inquiries that she had just been released. Appellant urged his services upon the young women and used the information he had obtained from the McClintocks, and the fact of his agreement with Carol, to induce Wanda to say "O.K." in response to his solicitation. He employed a concealed tape recorded, seemingly to insure that he would have evidence of Wanda's oral assent to the representation. He emphasized that his fee would come out of the recovery, thereby tempting the young women with what sounded like a cost-free and therefore irresistible offer. He refused to withdraw when Mrs. Holbert requested him to do so only a day after the initial meeting between appellant and Wanda Lou and continued to represent himself to the insurance company as Wanda Holbert's lawyer.[56]

Justice Marshall's thoughtful concurring opinion specifically would allow "benign" commercial solicitation, that is "solicitation by advice and information that is truthful and that is presented in a noncoercive, nondeceitful and dignified manner to a potential client who is emotionally and physically capable of making a rationale decision either to accept or reject the representation with respect to a legal claim or matter that is not frivolous."[57] Nothing in the majority

---

51. The distinction between this type of regulation and unjustified prohibition of lawyer advertising is evidenced by the fact that the majority in *Ohralik* accepted reasons for regulating attorney solicitation that would not be sufficient to ban attorney advertising. Thus in *Ohralik* the Court emphasized that law is a "profession," that the transaction in question was commercial in nature, and that a strong prophylactic rule was necessary to protect the unsophisticated, even though there is no explicit proof or finding of harm. Such rationales were rejected in Bates v. State Bar, 433 U.S. 350 (1977) when they were used to prohibit attorney advertising.

52. 436 U.S. at 462 (footnote omitted). See Reich, Preventing Deception in Commercial Speech, 54 N.Y. U.L.Rev. 775 (1979).

53. 436 U.S. at 466.

54. 436 U.S. at 462–463 n. 20.

55. 436 U.S. at 463. The attorney who argued the *Ohralik* case on behalf of the state bar also believes that the case should be limited to its facts. (June 13, 1978) (Report of A.B.A. Disciplinary Workshop, in 46 U.S.L.W. 2662).

56. 436 U.S. at 467.

57. 436 U.S. at 472 n. 3 (Marshall, J., concurring).

opinion rejects Justice Marshall's conclusions.

In the companion case, *In re Primus*,[58] a lawyer whose firm was cooperating with the American Civil Liberties Union (ACLU) wrote to a woman who had been sterilized as a condition of receiving public medical assistance. The lawyer offered the ACLU's services to represent her. The state had disciplined the attorney for this action but the Supreme Court of the United States reversed that decision.

The Court distinguished *Ohralik* because of the nature of the interests involved. Solicitation for private gain under the circumstances of *Ohralik* could be proscribed without showing harm in a given case because the circumstances were likely to result in the misleading, deceptive, and overbearing conduct, but solicitation on behalf of nonprofit organizations which litigate as a form of political expression may be regulated only when actual harm is shown in the particular case.[59] The Court reviewed the record in *Primus* and found nothing indicating fraud, overreaching or other regulable behavior; consequently, it held the solicitation within the zone of political speech and association protected in *NAACP v. Button*.[60]

Under *Ohralik*, the states are free to proscribe in-person solicitation for gain in circumstances where it is likely to be fraudulent, misleading, or overreaching, but under *Primus* they may only proscribe solicitation on behalf of nonprofit political organizations if it is in fact misleading, and then regulations must be "carefully tailored" so as not to "abridge unnecessarily the associational freedom of nonprofit organizations, or their members, having characteristics like those of the NAACP or the ACLU."[61]

Justice Powell's opinion for the Court seems to emphasize two factors distinguishing *Primus* from *Ohralik*: the absence of misrepresentation and pressure tactics, and the lack of major pecuniary award. Yet a careful reading of the *Primus* opinion indicates a third, equally important factor: the form of the solicitation. In *Ohralik* the solicitation was "in-person," *face-to-face*.[62] In *Primus*, the attorney first was invited to address a gathering of women and then sent a letter to one of them offering free representation after being advised that the woman wished to sue the doctor who had sterilized her. This "act of solicitation took the form of a letter. . . . This was not *in-person* solicitation for pecuniary gain."[63]

Later the Court was more specific in recognizing that a letter is not face-to-face solicitation but is more like the advertising protected in *Bates*:

> The transmittal of this letter—as contrasted with in-person solicitation—involved no appreciable invasion of privacy; nor did it afford any significant opportunity for overreaching or coercion. Moreover, the fact that there was a written communication lessens substantially the difficulty of policing solicitation practices that do offend valid rules of professional conduct.[64]

As Justice Powell himself earlier recognized in his separate opinion in *Bates*: "No distinction can be drawn between newspapers and a rather broad spectrum of other means—for example, magazines, signs in buses and subways, posters, handbills, and mail circulations."[65] The letter in *Primus* seems

---

58.   436 U.S. 412 (1978).

59.   436 U.S. at 435. The Court noted that in *Primus* the lawyer did not attempt to "pressure" the prospective client into filing the suit. 436 U.S. at 417 n. 7. "[A]ppellant's letter cannot be characterized as a pressure tactic." 436 U.S. at 435 n. 28.

60.   371 U.S. 415 (1963).

61.   436 U.S. at 439.

62.   It does not matter whether the face-to-face solicitation was by the lawyer himself or one of his agents or "runners." 436 U.S. at 464 n.22. Accord,

D.R. 1–102(A)(2), A.B.A. Model Code of Professional Responsibility (1970, as amended).

63.   436 U.S. at 422 (emphasis added).

64.   436 U.S. at 435–436 (footnote omitted) (emphasis added).

65.   Bates v. State Bar, 433 U.S. 350, 402 n. 12 (1977). See also, Koffler v. Joint Bar Ass'n, 51 N.Y.2d 140, 432 N.Y.S.2d 872, 412 N.E.2d 927 (1980) (direct mail communications are not "in-person" solicitation within the meaning of *Ohralik* and therefore protected under *Bates)*; Kentucky Bar Ass'n v. Stuart, 568

identical to the "mail circulations" referred to in *Bates.*

In a later case a unanimous Court, in an opinion by Justice Powell, invalidated a state rule which prohibited mailing cards (which announced the opening of his office) to persons other than "lawyers, former clients, personal friends and relatives." The silent record did not justify the reason for the absolute prohibition. Even if a reason existed, the state could use less restrictive means, such as requiring that a copy of any mailings be filed with the state, if the state wished to supervise mailings. "[A]lthough the states may regulate commercial speech, the First and Fourteenth Amendments require that they do so with care and in a manner no more extensive than reasonably necessary to further substantial interests." [66] Thus, letters and other non-face-to-face solicitation may not even be "in-person" solicitation for purposes of *Ohralik,* even if the lawyer seeks pecuniary gain.

Separate treatment of face-to-face solicitation by the state can be justified by the greater public need to guard against possible deceptive or coercive advertising practices. Of course, actual misrepresentation and overreaching can always be prohibited.

As Justice Marshall's concurrence emphasized, "[w]hat is objectionable about Ohralik's behavior here is not so much that he solicited business for himself, but rather the circumstances in which he performed that solicitation and the means by which he accomplished it." [67]

The direction in which the Supreme Court is turning in the commercial speech area was somewhat clarified by the position of the majority of the justices in *Friedman v. Rogers.* [68] In this case the Court held that Texas constitutionally could prohibit the practice of optometry under a trade name, assumed name, or corporate name.

It now appears that the Court, under the leadership of Justice Powell in this area, will engage in a series of *ad hoc* decisions as to the permissible scope of regulation of commercial speech. In so doing, the majority appears to shift away from Justice Blackmun's principled position that the state may not regulate commercial speech so long as the underlying activity advertised is legal, and the speech itself is not actually misleading. While Justice Blackmun authored the most of the majority opinions in the initial round of modern commercial speech cases, [69]

S.W.2d 933 (Ky.1978) (same). Contra, Allison v. Louisiana State Bar Ass'n, 362 So.2d 489 (La.1978). See generally, T. Morgan and R. Rotunda, Problems and Materials on Professional Responsibility 204–06 (2d ed. 1981).

66. In re of R.M.J., 455 U.S. 191, 207 (1982). See also, text at nn. 40–43, supra.

67. 436 U.S. at 470 (Marshall, J., concurring).

At the end of *Primus,* Justice Powell for the majority stated in dictum:

"And a State may insist that lawyers not solicit on behalf of lay organizations that exert control over the actual conduct of any ensuing litigation."

436 U.S. at 439.

The only authority for that assertion was dictum by Justice White concurring and dissenting in NAACP v. Button, 371 U.S. 415, 447 (1963). Justice Powell's dictum—at least in its broad form—is not even supported by the American Bar Association. See A.B.A. Formal Opinion 334 (Aug. 10, 1974) (dealing with restrictions on lawyers' activities by legal services offices as they affect independence of professional judgment). Justice

Marshall specifically disassociated himself from Justice Powell's dictum and noted that it "is by no means self-evident, has never been the actual holding of this Court and is not put in issue by the facts presently before us." 436 U.S. at 447. See also 436 U.S. at 439 (Blackmun, J., concurring).

68. 440 U.S. 1 (1979).

The Court also upheld regulations in this case that required four of the six members of an optometrist regulatory board to be members of a specific professional organization. Because this regulation governed general and economic welfare matters, the Court applied only the minimum rationality test to this law. 440 U.S. at 17. The Court also refused to consider whether or not a board composed of members of a particular trade association could fairly judge disciplinary proceedings brought against a non member. 440 U.S. at 17.

69. Bates v. State Bar, 433 U.S. 350 (1977); Virginia State Bd. of Pharmacy v. Virginia Citizens Consumer Council, Inc., 425 U.S. 748 (1976); Bigelow v. Virginia, 421 U.S. 809 (1975).

more recently it has been Justice Powell who has authored the majority opinions.[70]

In upholding the ban on trade names the majority refrained from establishing rigid rules for the regulation of commercial speech, but it established some guidelines that tie together the earlier cases and help provide a framework for the future determination of the permissibility of particular regulations of commercial practices involving speech.

The majority opinion by Justice Powell differentiated "commercially motivated" speech, which appears entitled to full first amendment protection, from "commercial speech," which is subject to the *ad hoc* approach.[71] It is now clear that cases such as *New York Times v. Sullivan*[72] and *First Nat. Bank of Boston v. Bellotti*[73] did not involve "commercial speech" in the sense of speech designed to sell a product or solicit patronage for profit. Instead, as was suggested in each of those decisions, those cases involved speech concerning non-commercial issues, even though the speech might have been motivated by commercial and monetary desires of the speakers. This commercially motivated speech is not "commercial speech" and it is protected by all first amendment principles.[74]

The majority opinion indicated that commercial speech is speech connected to the selling of a product or service. Such speech has more limited first amendment protection than does non-commercial speech. Justice Powell noted that principles relating to "more traditional first amendment problems" are not to be applied automatically to commercial speech regulations in a "yet uncharted area."[75]

For example, the majority treated *Bigelow v. Virginia*[76]—which invalidated a law forbidding a profit making organization's advertisement offering to arrange for legal abortions out of state—as "more than" a commercial speech case because it "did more than simply propose a commercial transaction."[77] By way of contrast, *Virginia State Bd. of Pharmacy v. Virginia Citizens Council*[78]—invalidating a law forbidding advertisements offering prescription drugs for sale at certain prices—is, in the view of the majority, commercial speech because the advertisements simply offered to make an economic exchange for profit. Yet the law was invalidated because of "the other interests in the advertisements. . . ." For example, information about prices at competing pharmacies would enable consumers to enjoy, at a lesser cost, the "basic necessities."[79]

Once the speech is found to be commercial speech, the majority opinion found that the

---

70. Ohralik v. Ohio State Bar, 436 U.S. 447 (1978); In re Primus, 436 U.S. 412 (1978). Justice Blackmun wrote a concurring opinion in these two cases.

71. 440 U.S. at 11 n. 10.

72. 376 U.S. 254 (1964). See Section X, B, infra.

73. 435 U.S. 765 (1978). See text at nn. 40–41, supra.

74. See also, Village of Schaumburg v. Citizens for a Better Environment, 444 U.S. 620, 636 (1980): "[B]ecause charitable solicitation does more than inform private economic decisions and is not primarily concerned with providing information about the characteristics and costs of goods and services, it has not been dealt with in our cases as a variety of purely commercial speech." (footnote omitted).

75. 440 U.S. at 10 n. 9.

76. 421 U.S. 809 (1975).

77. Friedman v. Rogers, 440 U.S. 11 n. 10 quoting Bigelow v. Virginia, 421 U.S. at 822.

78. 425 U.S. 748 (1976).

The majority's efforts to distinguish commercial from noncommercial speech made no effort to explain why movies exhibited purely for profit and advertisements of such movies—"a mere solicitation of patronage. . . ." 440 U.S. at 11 n. 10 is nonetheless apparently entitled to full first amendment protection under the prior case law. See, e.g., Joseph Burstyn, Inc. v. Wilson, 343 U.S. 495, 501–02 (1952). Perhaps, under Justice Powell's theories, such advertisements are entitled to lessened first amendment protection. He has joined in cases offering lessened first amendment protection for nonobscene but "adult" movies. Young v. American Mini Theatres, Inc., 427 U.S. 50, 73 (1976) (Powell, J., concurring). Cf. FCC v. Pacifica Foundation, 438 U.S. 726, 759–763 (1978) (Powell, J., concurring) (FCC may regulate radio broadcast which is not obscene in a constitutional sense but is "indecent").

79. 440 U.S. at 8. See generally, De Vier, Justice Powell and the First Amendment's "Societal Function": A Preliminary Analysis, 68 Va.L.Rev. 177 (1982).

government could place more general restrictions on the time, place, or manner of commercial speech than on noncommercial speech and that the government would be given greater latitude in forming regulations of the content of commercial speech to avoid potentially false, deceptive, or misleading commercial practices. The government was given greater powers in controlling this type of speech for several reasons: commercial speech is more verifiable because it relates to a particular product or service; the communicative value of this speech is less likely to be inhibited or deterred by regulations due to the economic incentive to engage in alternative forms of commercial communication; effective rules to prevent false, deceptive or misleading practices may not be too precise.

Although the Court did not establish rigid categories of commercial speech, the *Friedman* majority indicated that there would be a distinction in the degree of permissible government regulation related to the types of commercial speech. For regulations of commercial speech that contain explicit product, price, or service information the state must demonstrate a clear relationship between the regulation and the avoidance of false, deceptive, or misleading practices. If it cannot do so, the state must demonstrate that the regulation of this commercial speech is a demonstrably reasonable restriction of the time, place, or physical manner of the commercial expression. However when the "commercial speech" conveys less substantive information the government has greater latitude in regulating the speech. The majority deemed such speech to have little first amendment value because it does not (in the view of the majority) clearly communicate information. In so holding, the majority stated that there was no requirement that states tolerate practices with little or no communicative content that might be

used in a deceptive or misleading manner, even though the possible deception could also be cured by less drastic means, for example, if the state were to require the publication of additional information to clarify or offset the effects of the spurious communication.[80]

Based upon this analysis Justice Powell found it easy to allow the prohibition of the use of trade names by optometrists. The opinion noted that the use of these trade names had a purpose which was "strictly business" and was "a form of commercial speech and nothing more."[81] This point differentiated the case from the commercially motivated speech cases in which the speaker desires more than simply an offer to sell goods or solicit patronage.

Justice Powell also sought to distinguish this prohibition from the earlier prohibitions on advertising service and price information that had been overturned in *Virginia Pharmacy*, and *Bates*. While both of those cases simply proposed a commercial transaction—an offer to sell prescription drugs for a price in the former case, and an offer to sell legal services for a price in the latter—those messages contained useful information, which inherently has meaning. Trade names, on the other hand, do not have any inherit meaning.

In both the *Virginia Pharmacy*[82] case, involving pharmacists, and the *Bates*[83] case, involving lawyers, the Court was not moved by the argument that these occupations were "professions," a title which was supposed to justify lessened first amendment protection. But in *Friedman* the majority, without explanation, found it important to emphasize that the Texas legislature considered optometry to be a profession.[84]

The majority did concede that trade names might acquire some meaning over a period of time, and become a valuable property right. But such a property interest in the

---

80. 440 U.S. at 12 n. 11.

81. 440 U.S. at 11 (footnote omitted).

82. Virginia State Bd. of Pharmacy v. Virginia Citizens Consumer Council, Inc., 425 U.S. 748 (1976).

83. Bates v. State Bar, 433 U.S. 350 (1977).

84. 440 U.S. at 5, n. 7.

trade name only meant that such property could not be taken without due process of law. The fact of a property interest neither enlarged nor diminished first amendment rights.[85]

Because this use of trade names, or any commercial speech practice, has the potentiality of conveying information, the majority indicated that the state had to assert some reasonable basis for the prohibition. But the majority readily accepted the state's assertion that some optometrists in the past had used trade names in a misleading manner and that this history justified the general prohibition of trade names even if the particular plaintiff in this case had never engaged in a misleading practice.

Thus it appears that the Court will not exercise active review and will use a test approaching the traditional "rational basis" test when reviewing statutes which regulate speech in circumstances where the speech is found to be commercial speech, *and* that speech does not explicitly convey product, service, or price information. Yet, the scope of the majority decision remains unclear. For example, may the state prohibit lawyers from practicing under a trade name while allowing lawyers to use the name of one or more deceased or retired partners as the firm name?[86] May the state consistently contend that trade names are inherently misleading while at the same time maintaining that a firm named after lawyers who died and left the firm years ago is not in reality a trade name?

Justice Blackmun wrote a vigorous dissent, joined by Justice Marshall.[87] Justice Blackmun noted that the use of trade names would allow for more efficient advertisement of eye glasses and therefore a lowering in the price of such items, which he described as one of the basic necessities of life. He found, as he had indicated in some of his earlier opinions, that the increase in informational transaction costs was prohibited unless the state could demonstrate an overriding reason for the speech prohibition.

Justice Blackmun, who had written the majority opinion in *Virginia Pharmacy*, readily agreed with Justice Powell that misleading speech can be regulated, but denied trade names are inherently misleading. But while Justice Powell thought that "because a trade name has no intrinsic meaning it can cause deception," the dissent countered that "[b]ecause a trade name has no intrinsic meaning, it cannot by itself be deceptive. A trade name will deceive only if it is used in a misleading context."[88] Justice Blackmun thus would have required the state to tolerate the use of trade names and only to prosecute those who in fact used them in a misleading manner.

While Justice Blackmun's approach is a principled one, the majority of the justices do not seem ready to follow Justice Blackmun's active review of all commercial speech cases, perhaps in part because of fears of returning to the discredited substantive economic due process rulings of the pre 1937 Court.[89] Instead the Court has granted only limited protection to commercial speech.

---

85. 440 U.S. at 12 n. 11.

86. Compare, Police Dept. of Chicago v. Mosley, 408 U.S. 92 (1972); see A.B.A. Code of Professional Responsibility, D.R. 2–102(B): "A lawyer in private practice shall not practice under a trade name, a name that is misleading . . . or a firm name containing names other than those of one or more of the lawyers in the firm, *except* . . . a firm may use as, or continue to include in its name, the name or names of one or more deceased or retired members of the firm or of a predecessor firm in a continuing line of succession." (emphasis added).

87. 440 U.S. at 19 (Blackmun, J., concurring and dissenting joined by Marshall, J.). Justice Blackmun joined in part III of the Court's opinion which validated the composition of the optometry board.

88. 440 U.S. at 24 (Blackmun, J., joined by Marshall, J., dissenting and concurring in part).

89. See Jackson and Jeffries, Commercial Speech: Economic Due Process and the First Amendment, 65 Va.L.Rev. 1 (1979). Farber, Commercial Speech and First Amendment Theory, 74 Nw.U.L.Rev. 372 (1979), concluding that while the informative function of speech deserves traditional first amendment protection, "commercial speech also serves a contractual function which does not directly implicate first amendment interests. Regulations aimed at this contractual function, though they relate to the meaning of the speech, should not be tested under the stricter scrunity reserved for 'content related' regulation. Most traditional consumer protection legislation is based on the contractual nature of the speech. Misrepresentation, duress, overreaching, and unconscionability are well-known

It appears that the justices will prohibit states from banning the truthful conveyance of commercial information but that they will allow the state a much greater leeway in protecting against false, deceptive or misleading practices. The lower the informational content of the regulated speech, the greater latitude the Court will give the government in drafting such regulations. Thus it appears that future rulings will of necessity have an *ad hoc* quality in determining the degree of informational content of a regulated commercial speech practice and the reasonableness of the regulation, but there will not be an absolute prohibition of regulating any speech activity that might increase information or transaction costs in the marketplace.

This analysis is supported by *Central Hudson Gas & Electric Corporation v. Public Service Commission*.[90] The Court invalidated a regulation of the state Public Service Commission which completely banned all public utility advertising which promoted the use of electricity. The Commission argued that all such promotional advertising was contrary to the national policy of conserving energy. The Court, per Justice Powell, applied a four-part analysis to the question:

> At the outset we must determine whether the expression is protected by the First Amendment. For commercial speech to come within that provision, it at least must concern lawful activity and not be misleading. Next we ask whether the asserted governmental interest is

substantial. If both inquiries yield positive answers, we must determine whether the regulation directly advances the governmental interest asserted, and whether it is not more extensive than is necessary to serve that interest.[91]

Applying this test the Court invalidated the New York regulation. Promotional advertising is lawful commercial speech;[92] the state interests in conservation are substantial; the ban on promotional advertising advances this ban; but the state's complete suppression of speech was more extensive than necessary to further energy conservation.[93] For example, some promotional advertising would cause no net increase in energy use. Also more limited restrictions might promote conservation sufficiently. The state could "require that the advertisements include information about the relative efficiency and expense of the offered service, both under current conditions and for the foreseeable future."[94]

X. LIBEL AND INVASION OF PRIVACY

A. Introduction—The Problem of Group Libel Laws

The Supreme Court upheld the constitutionality of a state criminal statute prohibiting libel of a class of citizens in *Beauharnais v. Illinois*.[1] Petitioner had distributed a leaflet calling for white unity against further "encroachment . . . by the Negro" and urging "the need to prevent the white

contract doctrines. When the state attacks these problems with modern regulatory tools, it can legitimately claim an interest quite distinct from the suppression of free expression." Id. at 407–08. See generally, Rotunda, The Commercial Speech Doctrine in the Supreme Court, 1976 U.Ill.L.Forum 1080.

90. 447 U.S. 557 (1980). See Note, Constitutional Protection of Commercial Speech, 82 Colum.L.Rev. 720 (1982).

91. 447 U.S. at 571.

92. Accord, Consolidated Edison Co. of New York, Inc. v. Public Serv. Comm'n, 447 U.S. 530 (1980). See also Bolger v. Youngs Drug Products Corp., 103 S.Ct. ___ (1983) (law prohibiting mailing of unsolicited advertisements for contraceptives invalid).

93. Cf. N.L.R.B. v. Retail Store Employees Union, Local 1001, 447 U.S. 607, 618 (1980) (Powell, J., joined by Burger, C.J., Stewart, and Rehnquist, JJ.) (Congress, consistent with first amendment, may prohibit secondary picketing calculated "to persuade the customers of the secondary employer to cease trading with him in order to force him to cease dealing with, or put pressure upon, the primary employer;" such picketing spreads labor discord by coercing neutral party to join the dispute and furthers an unlawful objective).

94. 447 U.S. at 576.

1. 343 U.S. 250 (1952). See generally, J. Barron and C. Dienes, Handbook of Free Speech and Free Press, ch. 6, "The Rise of the Public Law of Defamation," pp. 222–361 (1979).

race from becoming mongrelized by the negro [sic] . . . "[2] The Court could have reached a decision based on the narrow facts of the case, avoiding the issue of the constitutionality of the statute and holding that the particular pamphlet did not violate the terms of the Illinois group libel law.[3] Speaking for the Court, Justice Frankfurter affirmed the conviction in a broad holding that libelous, insulting, or fighting words are not within the realm of constitutionally protected speech.[4] State statutes which curtail group libel do not raise a constitutional problem, he said, unless they are a "wilful and purposeless restriction unrelated to the peace and well being of the state."[5] Frankfurter pointed out that the judiciary should not interfere with the state legislature's choice of policy, emphasizing the Court's position that state libel laws were not within a constitutionally protected category of speech.

The dissenting views in *Beauharnais* were a precursor to the future position of the Court concerning libel. Justice Douglas argued that the expansion of individual and criminal libel to include group libel constituted an invasion of free expression which should occur only in circumstances wherein the "peril of speech must be clear and present . . . raising no doubts as to the necessity of curbing speech in order to prevent disaster."[6] The balancing between private vindication of reputation and free expression should be in favor of free expression, Justice

Black argued, because of the "unequivocal First Amendment command that its defined freedoms shall not be abridged."[7] Black noted as especially restrictive the potential that under the Illinois statute one could proceed against a book publisher, newspaper, radio or television station. Any danger in public discussion was outweighed "by the danger incident to the stifling of thought and speech."[8]

As we shall see in this section, it has been the views of Justices Black and Douglas that to a great extent have prevailed in later cases. And while *Beauharnais* has never been expressly overruled, it would seem to be impossible to reach its results under the modern cases.[9]

B. NEW YORK TIMES v. SULLIVAN and Libel of a Public Official

1. The Case

Although *Beauharnais v. Illinois* has never been explicitly rejected, it is unlikely to represent present law in light of *New York Times v. Sullivan,*[10] decided in 1964. The Court there held for the first time that constitutional protections for speech and press do limit state powers to award damages in libel actions brought by public officials against critics of official conduct.

Sullivan, one of three elected commissioners of Montgomery, Alabama, brought the action against four individuals and the *New York Times*, claiming he had been libeled in

---

2. 343 U.S. 252.

3. The law proscribed "any lithograph, moving picture, play, drama, or sketch," which was libelous to a class of citizens. The Court called Beauharnais' leaflet, a "lithograph," but to avoid the broad constitutional issue it could have held that as a requirement of fair warning, the statute would be unduly vague if so construed, and thus the statute by its term did not forbid libelous pamphlets.

4. 343 U.S. at 256–57.

5. 343 U.S. at 258.

6. 343 U.S. at 285.

7. 343 U.S. at 269.

8. 343 U.S. at 275.

9. The Court of Appeals for the Seventh Circuit has held invalid local ordinances designed to prevent a

march of a Nazi organization. That court found that the *Beauharnais* rationale would not justify prohibition of a peaceful march based on its implied message of racial animosity or the racial beliefs of the marchers. Collin & National Socialist Party v. Smith, 578 F.2d 1197 (7th Cir. 1978), cert. denied 439 U.S. 916 (Blackmun, J., joined by White, J., dissented).

10. 376 U.S. 254 (1964). See Collin & Nat. Socialist Party v. Smith, 578 F.2d 1197 (7th Cir. 1978), cert. denied 439 U.S. 916. See also, Shiffrin, Defamatory Non-Media Speech and First Amendment Methodology, 25 U.C.L.A.L.Rev. 915 (1978); Arkes, Civility and the Restriction of Speech: Rediscovering the Defamation of Groups, 1974 Sup.Ct.Rev. 281; Delgado, Words that Wound: A Tort Action for Racial Insults, Epithets, and Name-Calling, 17 Har.Civ.Rts.-Civ.Lib.L.Rev. 133 (1982).

two paragraphs of a full page advertisement. Even though he was not mentioned by name in the advertisement, Sullivan recovered $500,000 damages against the *New York Times*, based on a state legal doctrine whereby criticism of the Montgomery Police Department was transmuted to criticism of him as the official in charge. The state court instructed the jury that such criticism was libel per se. Under such instruction Sullivan need only prove that the statement was false and that it referred to him.

The Supreme Court reversed in a holding broader than was strictly necessary given the facts of the case. The Court might have reversed by creating a narrower constitutionally based theory: no defamation on its face existed in the ad since Sullivan was not mentioned; alternatively, it might have held that the only amount of damages was constitutionally regulated and only actual damages would be allowed; or, it could have held that a newspaper which merely republished an advertisement drawn up by others should have some constitutional protection; it also might have created a defense that the statements alleged in the advertisement were substantially true. Instead, the majority opinion by Justice Brennan expounded a much more dramatic change in state libel law, which now must be measured against the first amendment.

The Court reasoned that a state must safeguard freedom of speech and press in its libel laws as required by the first amendment as applied to the states through the fourteenth amendment. This first amendment protection exists against the background of "profound national commitment to the principle that debate on public issues should be uninhibited, robust, and wide-open, and that it may well include vehement, caustic, and sometimes unpleasantly sharp attacks on government and public officials." [11] Neither erroneous statement nor

injury to official reputation forfeits the first amendment protection, which should provide "breathing space" for freedom of expression. The Court drew an analogy to the Sedition Act of 1798,[12] an early attempt to prohibit criticism of the government. The Court noted that state statutes punishing libel of public officials must likewise be restricted by the first amendment, for a broad libel law serving to protect public officials from criticism is closely analogous to the Sedition Laws. The Alabama statute did provide for a defense of truth, but given the importance of safeguarding the "breathing space" necessary so as not to discourage valid criticism of public officials, a "defense for erroneous statements honestly made" was essential.[13]

Given this general and basic policy, the Court laid out the standard for recovery of any alleged defamatory falsehood relating to a public official's conduct. First, the defamatory statement would have to relate to the individual plaintiff-government official;[14] no generalized criticism of government policy could be punished, for that would constitute a sedition action. The plaintiff-government official would also have the burden of proving that the statement was false. Citizens are certainly free to disclose truthful information about their officials. Finally, and most significantly, for there to be a defamation action, the plaintiff must allege and prove that the defendant had made the defamatory statements with "malice." On this point the Court said:

> The constitutional guarantees require, we think, a federal rule that prohibits a *public official* from recovering damages for a defamatory falsehood relating to his official conduct unless he proves that the statement was made with *"actual malice"* . . .[15]

The Court defined "actual malice" as "knowledge that [the defamation that was published] was false or with reckless disre-

---

11. 376 U.S. at 270.

12. 376 U.S. at 273–77. See Section II, C, of this Chapter, supra.

13. 376 U.S. at 278.

14. See also Rosenblatt v. Baer, 383 U.S. 75 (1966).

15. 376 U.S. 279–80 (emphasis added).

gard of whether it was false or not." [16] while the Court used the word "malice," it was not referring to the old, common law libel meaning of "malice" as hatefulness or ill will; [17] rather, from its definition, the Court meant "*scienter.*" [18]

2. New York Times Scienter

This scienter requirement was clearly applied in *Garrison v. Louisiana.* [19] There the Supreme Court struck down a Louisiana statute which permitted liability for true statements about public officials made with "actual malice" in the common law sense. The Court reiterated that only the knowing or reckless falsehood could be subject to civil or criminal sanction.

Four years later the Court made clear that "reckless disregard" could not be shown by proof of mere negligence; for "reckless disregard" there must be "serious doubts as to the truth of [the] publication." [20] The standard seems to be one of the knowing lie—at the time of publication defendant must have had serious doubts as to the statement's truth and have published it despite these doubts. Thus, where one defendant had relied solely on a union member's affidavit charging a public official with criminal conduct and did not verify the charges with other union members, the Court would not allow plaintiff to go to the jury with a charge of reckless falsity. [21] Similarly, the Court has not found "reckless falsity" when de-

fendant has failed to conduct an affirmative investigation, [22] or for omissions which could constitute merely an error of judgment. [23]

In subsequent cases, the Supreme Court also clarified other issues first raised in *New York Times v. Sullivan*—the burden of proof requirement and the definition of "public official."

3. Burden of Proof

According to *New York Times v. Sullivan,* plaintiff bears the burden of proving actual malice with "convincing clarity." [24] This standard is apparently somewhere between "preponderance of the evidence" and "beyond a reasonable doubt," because later the Court uses the term "clear and convincing," [25] a standard of proof which historically has required plaintiff in a civil case to bear more of a burden than a bare "preponderance."

The "clear and convincing" standard has its origins in the standards used by the chancellors finding facts in equity cases. It has now been expanded in many states to include other classes of cases such as charges of fraud. In general this standard is used "where there is thought to be special danger of deception, or where the court considers that the particular type of claim should be disfavored on policy grounds." [26]

It remains unclear whether the "clear and convincing" standard is only applied on review to determine if there was a sufficient

---

16. 376 U.S. at 280.

17. W. Prosser, Torts 771–72 (4th ed. 1971). See also, Cantrell v. Forest City Publishing Co., 419 U.S. 245, 251–52 (1974).

18. Cf. Herbert v. Lando, 441 U.S. 153, 199 (1979) (Stewart, J., dissenting): "Although I joined the Court's opinion in *New York Times,* I have come greatly to regret the use in that opinion of the phrase 'actual malice.' . . . In common understanding, malice means ill will or hostility. . . . [but *New York Times* malice] has nothing to do with hostility or ill will. . . ."

The Court also held unconstitutional the Alabama proposition that criticism of a government agency is transmuted to criticism of the official in charge, a practice which strikes at the center of constitutionally protected area of free expression by expanding the law of libel beyond the requirement of scienter.

19. 379 U.S. 64 (1964).

20. St. Amant v. Thompson, 390 U.S. 727, 730–33 (1968).

21. Id.

22. Beckley Newspaper Corp. v. Hanks, 389 U.S. 81 (1967).

23. St. Amant v. Thompson, 390 U.S. 727 (1968).

24. 376 U.S. 254 at 285–86.

25. Gertz v. Robert Welch, Inc., 418 U.S. 323, 331–32 (1974); see also Beckley Newspapers Corp. v. Hanks, 389 U.S. 81, 83 (1967) (per curiam).

26. E. Cleary, et al., McCormick's Handbook of the Law of Evidence § 340, at 798 (2d ed. 1972).

basis for the verdict or whether the jury must be instructed in these terms. To be a meaningful restriction, the jury should be so instructed.

In meeting his or her burden of proof, plaintiff may directly depose the defendants about their thought processes and state of mind. In *Herbert v. Lando*,[27] the press urged the Supreme Court to create a privilege based on the first amendment that would bar a plaintiff suing for libel to inquire into the editorial processes of those responsible for the publication. The majority refused.

Plaintiffs are not limited to proving intent by inferences from objective circumstances; they may also ask about the ultimate fact directly. "*New York Times* and its progeny made it essential to proving liability that plaintiffs focus on the conduct and state of mind of the defendant. . . . Inevitably, unless liability is to be completely foreclosed, the thoughts and editorial processes of the alleged defamer would be open to examination."[28]

The majority noted that in past cases plaintiffs had asked direct questions about the editorial processes, with no one objecting to plaintiffs treading on allegedly forbidden areas, and in other cases libel defendants have offered such evidence to show good faith.[29] Similarly, there is no privilege for collegiate conversations or exchanges with fellow editors or damaging admissions to third persons;[30] nor must plaintiff first prove a prima facie case of falsity before asking about such questions.[31]

However, there may be some first amendment protection from discovery in other cir-

cumstances. The majority specifically stated that: "There is no law that subjects the editorial process to private or official examination merely to satisfy curiosity or to serve some general end such as the public interest; and if there were, it would not survive constitutional scrutiny as the First Amendment is presently construed. No such problem exists here, however, where there is a specific claim of injury arising from a publication that is alleged to have been knowingly or recklessly false."[32]

4. Public Officials

A special reason for the constitutional restriction on libel laws is that they might deter criticism of official conduct. As we have seen, the requirement of *New York Times* scienter was limited to public officials. Sullivan himself was an elected official in Montgomery, Alabama, and some commentators speculated that the definition of "public official" would be limited to elected officials. However, the Court later extended the *New York Times* privilege by expanding the definition of "public official" to include those who were candidates for public office and to statements that did not relate to official conduct but did relate to fitness for office.[33] The Court also included non-elected persons in the expanded definition of "public official."[34]

The breadth of the concept of "public official" is illustrated in *Rosenblatt v. Baer*,[35] where the Court applied the *New York Times* privilege to the discharged supervisor of a county-owned ski resort. The Court held that in order to encourage criticism of government, the "public official" designa-

---

27. 441 U.S. 153 (1979).

28. 441 U.S. at 160.

29. 441 U.S. at 160, & n. 6, 165 & n. 15.

30. 441 U.S. at 169–171.

31. Justice Brennan, dissenting, took that position, 441 U.S. at 180, but the majority specifically rejected such a bifurcated approach. 441 U.S. at 174 n. 23.

32. 441 U.S. at 174 (footnote omitted). Justice Powell joined in the six member majority, but also wrote a concurring opinion to emphasize that the trial judge has some discretion to control discovery to protect the

parties from undue burden or expense. Justice Brennan dissented in part. Justices Stewart and Marshall each wrote separate dissenting opinions. See generally, Bezanson, Herbert v. Lando, Editorial Judgment, and Freedom of the Press: An Essay, 1978 U.Ill.L.Forum 605, for a careful analysis of the competing considerations.

33. Monitor Patriot Co. v. Roy, 401 U.S. 265 (1971).

34. Rosenblatt v. Baer, 383 U.S. 75 (1966).

35. 383 U.S. 75 (1966).

tion must apply "at the very least to those among the hierarchy of government employees who have, or appear to the public to have, substantial responsibility for or control over the conduct of governmental affairs." [36]

The *New York Times* privilege exists for criticism of any government position of such "apparent importance that the public has an independent interest in the qualifications and performance of the person who holds it." [37] Thus, while persons occupying low level technical positions might not be included in this category, any government employee with discretionary power in matters of public interest should be considered a public official.

C. Libel of Public Figures

The Supreme Court extended the *New York Times v. Sullivan* doctrine when it held that the standard of "actual malice," that is, scienter, applied to alleged defamations against people who did not fit into the definition of "public official" but who were nonetheless "public figures." In *Curtis Publishing Co. v. Butts* and *Associated Press v. Walker*, [38] Chief Justice Warren's concurring opinion noted that the distinction between government and the private sector was increasingly blurred. He therefore created a new category within the *New York Times* rule beyond that of public official. He called this category "public figure" and

defined such figures as those who are "intimately involved in the resolution of important public questions or, by reason of their fame, shape events in areas of concern to society at large." [39] Warren reasoned that the *New York Times v. Sullivan* standard should apply to these people precisely because they are not subject to the restraints of the political process—"public opinion may be the only instrument by which society can attempt to influence their conduct." [40] The broad range of those whom the Court intended to classify as "public figures" is evident in that in the *Curtis Publishing* case, Walker was a retired army general, while in *Associated Press*, Butts was athletic director of the University of Georgia. [41]

More recently, the Court has explained:

> For the most part [public figures are] those who attain this status [by assuming] roles of especial prominence in the affairs of society. Some occupy positions of such persuasive power and influence that they are deemed public figures for all purposes. More commonly, those classed as public figures have thrust themselves to the forefront of particular public controversies in order to influence the resolution of the issues involved. [42]

Thus, a research scientist who is the recipient of a government grant, the award of which a U.S. Senator attacked as wasteful in allegedly defamatory statements, is not a "public figure" even for the limited purpose of comment on his receipt of public funds. [43] The mere receipt of public funds did not con-

---

36. 383 U.S. at 85 (footnote omitted).

37. 383 U.S. at 86. See also, Hutchinson v. Proxmire, 443 U.S. 111, 119 n. 8 (1979) ("public official" cannot "be thought to include all public employees. . . . ").

38. 388 U.S. 130 (1967).

39. 388 U.S. at 164 (Warren, C.J., concurring). There was no majority opinion.

40. Id.

41. In a 9–0 decision, the Supreme Court reversed a Mississippi jury award of $500,000 compensatory and $300,000 punitive damages for the eyewitness news report which stated that Walker had personally taken command of a violent crowd's charge against federal marshalls who were enforcing a court decree ordering the University of Mississippi to enroll a Black student. According to the Court, the situation involved reporting "hot" news by a trustworthy and competent report-

er. The evidence was insufficient to support even a finding of negligence.

In a 5–4 decision, however, the Court affirmed Butts' damage award for an article in the Saturday Evening Post which accused him of conspiring to fix a football game by divulging information on Georgia plays. Four Justices held that the Post had met Harlan's negligence test of "highly unreasonable conduct" and Chief Justice Warren joined them to create a majority by holding that the Post had met the New York Times v. Sullivan standard of "reckless disregard" and that the jury had been properly instructed.

42. Gertz v. Robert Welch, Inc., 418 U.S. 323, 345 (1974).

43. Hutchinson v. Proxmire, 441 U.S. 111 (1979). See also Wolston v. Reader's Digest Ass'n, 439 U.S. 1066 (1979) (court rejects the argument that any person who engages in criminal conduct automatically be-

fer public figure status; nor could it be said in this case that the scientist-libel plaintiff assumed any role of public prominence in the broad question of public expenditures. The scientist's limited access to the media for the purpose of responding to the Senator's charges did not establish the regular and continuing access to the media that is a sign of a public figure.

D. Private Individuals

1. TIME, INC. v. HILL

Because of their general fame and notoriety both Walker and Butts could be considered public figures for all purposes. However, in *Time, Inc. v. Hill*[44] the Supreme Court faced the issue of a private individual being thrust into the limelight for the purpose of one particular event. In 1952, the Hill family had been the subject of national news coverage when three escaped convicts held them hostage in their home. The incident was fictionalized in a play, and in 1955 Life Magazine published a picture story which showed the play's cast re-enacting scenes from the play in the former Hill house. The Hills sued on the basis of a New York state privacy statute which made truth a complete defense but allowed a privacy action to "newsworthy people" or "events" in case of "[m]aterial and substantial falsification."[45] However, the Supreme Court applied the *New York Times* standard of "knowing or reckless falsity" to alleged defamations concerning false reports of matters of public interest.[46]

In determining the standard of liability for private individuals, the Court looked to whether these individuals were involved in a matter of public interest. If they were so involved, the Court held the more stringent

standard of recovery defined in *New York Times v. Sullivan* to be applicable, even in the circumstances like that of the Hills, who were thrust into the limelight by events not of their own doing.

Although the Court applied the *New York Times* standard to the Hill's privacy action, it left open the question of whether the same standard of liability should be applicable in a libel action to persons voluntarily and involuntarily thrust into the public limelight.[47] Four years later the Court offered a tentative answer to this question in *Rosenbloom v. Metromedia*,[48] a fragmented plurality decision containing 5 separate opinions. The Court held, in a decision which did not attract even a bare majority of the justices, that the *New York Times v. Sullivan* standard must apply to private citizens caught up in events of public interest—whether voluntarily or involuntarily so involved. But this concept ended as abruptly as it appeared.

2. GERTZ v. ROBERT WELCH, INC.

The *Rosenbloom* issue was still open and three years later the Court, in a 5 to 4 decision, rejected the extension of the *New York Times v. Sullivan* doctrine to publication of all matters of public interest. Instead, in *Gertz v. Robert Welch, Inc.*,[49] the Court created a third category within which the *New York Times v. Sullivan* doctrine applied: private citizens who obviously are not public officials and who are not public enough to be public figures for all purposes, may be public figures with respect to a particular controversy. Now, clarifying the issues in *Hill* and in similar cases, the Court decided that the important question was not whether the alleged defamation was a matter of public interest but whether the individual defamed

---

comes a public figure for purposes of a limited range of issues relating to his conviction).

44. 385 U.S. 374 (1967).

45. 385 U.S. at 383, 386.

46. 385 U.S. at 387–88.

47. 385 U.S. at 390–91.

48. 403 U.S. 29 (1971).

49. 418 U.S. 323 (1974). See generally, Christie, Injury to Reputation and the Constitution: Confusion Amid Conflicting Approaches, 75 Mich.L.Rev. 431 (1976); Shiffrin, Defamatory Non-Media Speech and First Amendment Methodology, 25 U.C.L.A.L.Rev. 915 (1978); Christie, Underlying Contradictions in the Supreme Court's Classification of Defamation, 1981 Duke L.J. 811.

was a private citizen for purposes of that activity. If the plaintiff were a private person, he could collect damages based on evidence in the record (actual money damages) on the basis of the defendant's neligence, although strict liability for defamatory speech would not be tolerated.[50]

Of course all such rewards have to be supported by competent evidence, "although there need be no evidence which assigns an actual dollar value to the injury."[51] Such private plaintiffs would have to prove *New York Times* "malice" by the defendant only if they sought punitive damages or damages not supported by the evidence (presumed damages).

The Court stated that a person is not to be considered a public figure for the purpose of libel actions absent clear evidence of general fame and notoriety in the community or the assumption of roles of special prominence in the affairs of society. But even though one is not a public figure for all purposes, one may be a public figure for a particular incident. The Court suggested this view by explaining that an individual's status as "public figure" can be determined by looking specifically to his participation in the *particular* controversy giving rise to the defamation;"[52] that is, he may be a public figure for some purpose but not for others. According to the Court, private individuals may be "public figures" for purposes of *New York Times* if they have "thrust themselves to the forefront of particular public controversies in order to influence the resolution of the issues involved."[53] The truly involuntary public figure is considered rare.

Under this newly defined category, Gertz was an example of a private citizen who was not public enough to be a public figure for all purposes and who was not a public figure with respect to the particular controversy giving rise to the defamation. In the facts

of that case a Chicago policeman, Richard Nuccio, shot and killed a young man, Nelson. Nuccio was ultimately convicted of murder in the second degree. Gertz filed his libel action after a 1969 article in American Opinion Magazine, a monthly outlet for the views of the John Birch Society, alleged that he had been the architect of a Communist frameup which led to Nuccio's murder conviction. Gertz, a reputable Chicago lawyer, had acted as counsel for the Nelson family in civil litigation and had attended the coroner's inquest, but Gertz did not discuss Nuccio with the press and was not involved in the criminal proceedings against Nuccio.[54] Although Gertz had been active in community affairs, according to the Court he was not a "public figure" for all purposes of libel law. In making this determination, the Court relied on the fact that Gertz seemingly did nothing to thrust himself into the public eye nor did he attempt to engage the public's attention during the period in which the controversy arose.

Since Gertz was not sufficiently public to be a public figure, nor was he "public" with respect to the particular controversy, the Court had to determine the standard of libel recovery for such private individuals. It held that the standard was a matter for the States to determine: "[S]o long as they do not impose liability without fault, the States may define for themselves the appropriate standard of liability for a publisher or broadcaster of defamatory falsehood injurious to a private individual."[55] The Court found this solution to be an equitable balance for the competing interests. "It recognizes the strength of the legitimate state interest in compensating private individuals for wrongful injury to reputation, yet shields the press and broadcast media from the rigors of strict liability for defamation."[56] The Court suggested the possibility of a difference in libel standards between the speech and

---

50. 418 U.S. at 350. See text at note 58, infra, for definition of "actual" damages.

51. Id.

52. 418 U.S. at 352 (emphasis added); see also id. at 345.

53. 418 U.S. at 345; see also id. at 352.

54. 418 U.S. at 352.

55. 418 U.S. at 347.

56. 418 U.S. at 348.

press clauses of the first amendment by specifically using such terms as "publisher," "broadcaster" and "press" in this part of its holding. However the reference was only an offhand one and in fact there may be no distinctions between freedom of speech and freedom of the press.

The Supreme Court also held that a plaintiff must prove actual damages in order to recover under a standard requiring less than knowing or reckless falsity in a libel action: "The States may not permit recovery of presumed or punitive damages, at least when liability is not based on a showing of knowledge of falsity or reckless disregard for the truth." [57] However the Court defined actual damages quite broadly to include not only out-of-pocket loss but also "impairment of reputation and standing in the community, personal humiliation, and mental anguish and suffering." [58] While the Court did leave open the possibility that a private person could recover punitive damages if knowing or reckless falsity were proven, it left unresolved the question of whether a public figure or public official could recover punitive damages at all. The Court in fact condemned the inhibiting effect of damage awards in excess of any actual injury, so it should not be surprising if it were held that any punitive damage awards for libels directed against public figures or officials impinge upon the "breathing space" required in the exercise of first amendment freedoms.

3. TIME, INC. v. FIRESTONE

Two years after its decision in *Gertz v. Robert Welch, Inc.*,[59] the Court re-emphasized the narrow applicability of the *New York Times* scienter test when one moves outside the category of "public official" into the "public figure" domain of *Gertz*. In *Time, Inc. v. Firestone*,[60] a libel action was brought after *Time Magazine* reported that plaintiff's husband divorced her "on grounds of extreme cruelty and adultery." [61] The state court had actually granted the divorce on the grounds that "neither party is domesticated, within the meaning of that term as used by the Supreme Court of Florida." [62]

The Court decided that *New York Times* scienter should not be the standard of recovery in the case; plaintiff's role in Palm Beach society did not make her a "public figure" for the purpose of the libel action, nor did plaintiff "thrust herself to the forefront of any particular public controversy in order to influence the resolution of the issues involved in it." [63] The Court said that a "public controversy" is not *any* controversy of interest to the public—it had rejected that definition of "public controversy" when it repudiated *Rosenbloom v. Metromedia* in *Gertz*.[64] Firestone had no choice but to go to Court in order to dissolve her marriage, the Court reasoned, and by this action she did not freely choose to publicize her marital problems nor did she assume "special prominence in the resolution of public questions." [65] Significantly the Court also said that Firestone's several press conferences during divorce proceedings did not convert her into a "public figure." The press conferences were not an attempt to influence the outcome of the divorce proceedings nor were they an attempt to influence the outcome of some unrelated controversy, according to the court.[66]

The Court thus limited the media's ability to make an issue a "public controversy" and then claim the *New York Times* standard of recovery in libel actions arising therefrom. Mere existence or generation of public interest is not sufficient to define someone as a

---

57. 418 U.S. at 349.

58. 418 U.S. at 350.

59. 418 U.S. 323 (1974). See Ashdown, *Gertz* and *Firestone*: A Study in Constitutional Policy-Making, 61 Minn.L.Rev. 645 (1977).

60. 424 U.S. 448 (1976).

61. 424 U.S. at 452.

62. 424 U.S. at 450–51.

63. 424 U.S. at 453.

64. 424 U.S. at 454.

65. 424 U.S. at 454–55.

66. 424 U.S. at 454–55 n. 3.

"public figure" for the purpose of libel law. *Firestone* therefore applied the *Gertz* standard.

The rationale of *Firestone* may indicate that *Time v. Hill* may no longer govern the standard for "false light" privacy suits. Such suits are based on a theory that the disclosure of private facts is made in a way that casts the individual in a false and possibly unflattering light before the public. Unless the Court were to resurrect the *Rosenbloom* plurality opinion, it may well be the case that the *Gertz* standard should apply to these cases where the plaintiff is a private person. However it is also possible that the Court will preserve *Hill* and instead rely on one element of the *Rosenbloom* public issues concept for people caught up in public issues by finding such people to be involuntary public figures. Yet the Court in *Firestone* emphasized that Mrs. Firestone had not voluntarily placed herself in the public domain. *Hill*, discussed above, involved the opening of a new play linked to an actual incident that had been a matter of public interest; the Hill family was involuntarily a part of this actual incident, and, like Mrs. Firestone, the Hills did not voluntarily place themselves in the public domain.[67]

E. Privacy Cases

In addition to the categories of public officials, public figures, and *Gertz*-public figures, we have true privacy cases: the accurate description of private facts. May the state, to protect an individual's privacy, prohibit the publication of information which is true but which admittedly relates to and infringes on private matters? This general issue was raised in *Cox Broadcasting Corp. v. Cohn*[68] but the Court decided the case on narrow grounds.

Cohn, father of a deceased rape victim, brought suit against an Atlanta, Georgia, television station after a news broadcast reported the name of his victim-daughter. The name had been obtained from judicial records open to public inspection which were maintained in connection with public prosecution.

The Supreme Court held that a state may not impose right of privacy liability for public dissemination of true information derived from official court records open to public inspection. Since the state allowed the court records to be public, it could not forbid the republication of the information by the press. The Court reasoned that the strong interest of the public to know about governmental operations and the strong interest in a free press not subject to self-censorship outweighed the individual's interest in privacy concerning information already appearing in public records. The public interest was presumedly being served, the Court continued, when the information was placed in the public domain on official court records. Privacy interests must be protected by means which avoid public documentation or other disclosure of private information, concluded the Court, not by limiting the press.

The Supreme Court confined its holding to the narrow facts of the case—information in court records lawfully available to the public which was accurately republished. Explicitly left unresolved was the constitutional question of a state policy which denies access to the public and press of certain kinds of official records which are not public information and normally cannot be lawfully obtained by the press, such as juvenile court proceedings.[69] The Court also reserved the question of whether truth must be recognized as a defense in a defamation action

---

67. See Fitzgerald v. Penthouse International, Ltd., 525 F.Supp. 585, 602 (D.Md.1981) (Miller, D.J.), citing an earlier edition of this treatise.

68. 420 U.S. 469 (1975). See generally, Warren and Brandeis, The Right to Privacy, 4 Harv.L.Rev. 193, 196 (1890). See also, Kalven, Privacy in Tort Law—Were Warren and Brandeis Wrong?, 31 Law & Contemp. Prob. 326 (1966).

See generally, J. Barron and C. Dienes, Handbook of Free Speech and Free Press, ch. 7, "The New Public Law of Privacy," pp. 363–406 (1979).

69. 420 U.S. at 496 n. 26. See Oklahoma Publishing Co. v. District Court, 430 U.S. 308 (1977) (per curiam).

brought by a truly private person (as distinguished from a public official or public figure) and noted that *Time, Inc. v. Hill*,[70] had reserved the question of whether truthful publication of private matters could ever be constitutionally proscribed.

In *Landmark Communication, Inc. v. Virginia*,[71] the Supreme Court answered one of the questions reserved in *Cox Broadcasting Corp.* when it held that the first amendment prohibits the criminal punishment of persons who are not participants to a judicial disciplinary inquiry, including newspapers, from divulging or publishing truthful information regarding confidential proceedings of the judicial inquiry board. The Court found it unnecessary to hold broadly that truthful reporting about public officials in connection with their official duties is always insulated from criminal punishment by the first amendment, nor did the Court consider any special right of access to the press or the applicability of the state confidentiality statutes to one who secures the information by illegal means and thereafter divulges it.[72]

In *Zacchini v. Scripps-Howard Broadcasting Co.*[73] the Court upheld, in a 5 to 4 decision, the power of the state to allow a damage action brought by a performer against the operator of a television broadcasting station when it telecast a videotape of the plaintiff's entire 15 second act. The majority stressed that it was the entire act that was telecast. Plaintiff was a "human cannonball" who was shot from a cannon into a net at a county fairgrounds. The videotaping was done after Zacchini had asked the freelance reporter not to do it.

Relying on Dean Prosser, the majority divided privacy into four branches. (1) *Time, Inc. v. Hill* was a "false-light" privacy case; there also are cases: (2) involving an "appropriation" of a name or likeness for the purposes of trade; or (3) publicizing "private details" about a nonnewsworthy person or event; or (4) involving a performer, a person with a name having commercial value with a claim to a "right of publicity."[74]

The plaintiff, Zacchini, fell into the fourth category of a person with a right to publicity, and the majority found that the unauthorized telecast of his entire performance (even though accompanied by favorable commentary) injured his proprietary interest. Without violating free speech guarantees, the state need not, but may, protect this interest, which the Court found analogous to the goals of the copyright and patent laws.

It is unclear, given the majority's emphasis on the telecast of the "entire" performance, whether *Zacchini* has any application to cases where the videotaping is less than the entire act. Even in Zacchini's case, Justice Powell's dissent noted that the plaintiff-Zacchini might not be able to bring himself within the Court's holding because it is unlikely that the "entire" act took only 15 seconds. It was likely to have been accompanied by some fanfare.[75] Also unclear is the measure of damages in the case. The majority said that Zacchini had to prove his damages, which apparently could be eliminated if the "respondent's newsbroadcast increased the value of petitioner's performance by stimulating the public's interest in seeing the act live."[76]

---

70. 385 U.S. 374 (1967). See 420 U.S. at 490–91. Justice Powell, concurring in *Cox*, thought that Gertz v. Robert Welch, Inc., 418 U.S. 323 (1974) "largely resolves this issue" and makes truth a complete defense. 420 U.S. at 498.

71. 435 U.S. 829 (1978).

72. 435 U.S. at 837–838. See also Smith v. Daily Mail Publishing Co., 443 U.S. 97 (1979) (state may not punish a newspaper's truthful publication of an alleged juvenile delinquent's name lawfully obtained by a newspaper).

73. 433 U.S. 562 (1977).

74. 433 U.S. at 571–72 & nn. 7 & 8. Cf. Nimmer, Does Copyright Abridge the First Amendment Guarantees of Free Speech and Press, 17 U.C.L.A.L.Rev. 1180 (1970); cf. also, Maggs, New Directions in US–USSR Copyright Relations, 68 Am.J.Internat'l L. 391 (1974). See Gordon, Right of Property in Name, Likeness, Personality and History, 55 Nw.U.L.Rev. 553 (1960) for an analysis of the early cases.

75. 433 U.S. at 579 n. 1 (Powell, J., dissenting, joined by Brennan & Marshall, JJ.).

76. 433 U.S. at 575 n. 12. See generally, Shipley, Publicity Never Dies; It Just Fades Away: The Right

XI. FIGHTING WORDS AND HOSTILE AUDIENCES

A. Introduction

Government regulation of speech has been allowed when the purpose of the statute was to proscribe "fighting words." While the definition of this phrase is best left to case analysis below, it is helpful in understanding the underlying rationale to reconsider the dichotomy between action and speech traditionally illustrated by the hypothetical situation of the individual shouting "fire" in a crowded theater. In an absolutist sense, convictions for fighting words are a regulation of speech. Yet it is the better analysis to regard fighting words as within the ambit of action rather than speech as there is no intellectual content to be conveyed to the listener, but merely a provocative, emotional message intended and likely to incite an *immediate*, violent response. Thus, the state's interest in order overshadows the minimal protection to be afforded the "slight social value as a step to truth" [1] of the speech. The theory of the regulation of "fighting words" is not contrary to the theory of the free marketplace of ideas because this speech triggers an automatic reaction, with no thinking, rather than a consideration of an idea.

B. The Doctrine Emerges

In 1942, the United States Supreme Court in *Chaplinsky v. New Hampshire* [2] unanimously upheld a statute which had previously been construed by the state court to ban "face-to-face words plainly likely to cause a breach of the peace by the addressee." [3] Chaplinsky's conviction was based on his encounter with the City Marshal of Rochester whom he described as a "God damned racketeer and a damned fascist" [4] as a policeman was leading Chaplinsky away from a public sidewalk because of fear that his distribution of religious literature was causing a public disturbance. It is important to remember that Chaplinsky was not convicted for his distribution of religious literature or the policeman's fear of a public disturbance, but for his denunciations made directly to the fire marshal. The Court argued that Chaplinsky's epithet was without communicative value, since "[a]rgument is unnecessary to demonstrate that the appellations . . . are epithets likely to provoke the average person to retaliation, and thereby cause a breach of the peace." [5] Justice Murphy stated in dictum that " 'fighting' words—those which by their very utterance inflict injury or *tend to incite* an *immediate* breach of the peace"—are not constitutionally protected because their "slight social value as a step to truth . . . is clearly outweighed by the social interest in order and morality." [6] The Court indicated that breach of the peace convictions can be upheld when there is merely a danger the listener will be incited to violence. There was no need to prove actual violence between the fire marshal and Chaplinsky. Neither was it error for the state court to refuse "to admit evidence of provocation and evidence bearing on the truth or falsity of the utterances . . . ." [7] The rationale of the Court, as noted above, was that in the balance, the state's interest outweighed the slight value of communication demonstrated by the appellant's remark. *Chaplinsky* may be read to stand for the broad proposition that breach of the peace convictions can be upheld when there is merely a danger the lis-

of Publicity and Federal Preemption, 66 Cornell L.Rev. 673 (1981).

    1. Chaplinsky v. New Hampshire, 315 U.S. 568, 572 (1942). On hostile audiences and fighting words, see generally, J. Barron and C. Dienes, Handbook of Free Speech and Free Press 63–93 (1979).

    2. Id.

    3. Id. at 573. The state statute forbade a person to address "any offensive, derisive or annoying word to

any other person who is lawfully in any street or other public place." Id. at 569.

    4. Id. at 569.

    5. Id. at 574.

    6. Id. at 572 (footnotes omitted) (emphasis added).

    7. Id. at 574.

tener will be incited to violence, for the Court in that case was presuming fighting words would produce an "uncontrollable impulse" to violence and thus their harm easily outweighed their social value.[8] The test outlined in *Chaplinsky* was whether or not men of common intelligence would understand the words as likely to cause the average addressee to fight, "words and expressions which by general consent are 'fighting words' when said without a disarming smile. . . . "[9] There was no consideration as to whether fire marshals or policemen could be (or should be) expected to resist epithets which would produce violent responses in the average citizen who has not been trained to prevent breaches of the peace.[10]

C. Subsequent Modifications

Decisions following *Chaplinsky* reflect the Court's desire to limit the broad implications of the doctrine outlined there and the recognition of the potential social value in statements that might come under the initial definition of "fighting words."

In *Terminiello v. Chicago*,[11] the Supreme Court overturned a municipal ordinance prohibiting breaches of the peace. The trial court's instruction to the jury construed the statute as prohibiting conduct which "stirs the public to anger, invites dispute, brings about a condition of unrest or creates a disturbance."[12] Terminiello's address was a denunciation of Jews and blacks. Outside of the auditorium where he spoke, a "howling" crowd gathered in protest and he denounced them as well. The majority opinion of Justice Douglas analyzed the purpose of free speech and found it contradictory to the jury instruction

[A] function of free speech . . . is to invite dispute. It may indeed best serve its high purpose when it induces a condition of unrest, creates dissatisfaction with conditions as they are, or even stirs people to anger. Speech is often provocative and challenging. It may strike at prejudices and preconceptions and have profound unsettling effects as it presses for acceptance of an idea . . . the alternative would lead to standardization of ideas either by legislatures, courts, or dominant political or community groups.[13]

The Court's invalidation of the statute as vague and overbroad allowed it to avoid the more difficult question of whether the speech was protected under the First Amendment. The strong language of the majority opinion does, however, indicate a retreat from the *Chaplinsky* "uncontrollable impulse" test by recognizing that a certain amount of provocative and challenging speech is protected.[14]

Two years after *Terminiello*, in *Feiner v. New York*,[15] the Court upheld the conviction of petitioner under a state disorderly conduct statute. *Feiner* directly raised the question of the hostile audience. Feiner's address included descriptions of President Truman as a "bum", the mayor of Syracuse as a "champagne sipping bum", the American Legion as a "Nazi Gestapo" and the need for blacks to "rise up in arms and fight for equal rights."[16] The speaker's racial statements " 'stirred up a little excitement.' Some of the onlookers made remarks to the police about their inability to handle the crowd and at least one threatened violence if the police did not act. There were others who appeared to be favoring petitioner's ar-

---

8. Rutzick, Offensive Language and the Evolution of First Amendment Protection, 9 Harv.Civ.Rts.-Civ. Lib.L.Rev. 1, 8, n. 36 (1974).

9. Chaplinsky v. New Hampshire, 315 U.S. at 573. See also id. at 572.

10. Rutzick, supra note 8, 9 Harv.Civ.Rts.-Civ.Lib.L. Rev. 1, 10.

11. 337 U.S. 1 (1949).

12. Id. at 3. Four justices dissented on the grounds that the instructions issue was not properly preserved for review.

13. Terminiello v. Chicago, 337 U.S. 1, 4 (1949).

14. Rutzick, supra note 8, 9 Harv.Civ.Rts.-Civ.Lib.L. Rev. 1, 12–13; Kaufman, The Medium, The Message, and the First Amendment, 45 N.Y.U.L.Rev. 761, 767 (1970).

15. 340 U.S. 315 (1951).

16. Id. at 330 (Douglas, J. dissenting).

guments." [17] The police asked Feiner to stop, but he refused. After their request, the officer arrested Feiner, who had been speaking for over a half hour.[18] The majority opinion of Chief Justice Vinson stressed that the arrest was not an attempt to censor the content of the speech, but an effort to protect the peace before the threatened violent reaction took place.

> It is one thing to say that the police cannot be used as an instrument for the suppression of unpopular views, and another to say that, when as here the speaker passes the bounds of argument or persuasion and undertakes incitement to riot, they are powerless to prevent a breach of the peace.[19]

Feiner's claim differed from Terminiello's in that he did not assert that the statute was unconstitutionally broad or vague, but that the police had abused their discretion and were motivated by a desire to suppress the content of his speech, an assertion which the majority found unsupported by evidence.

Justices Douglas and Black dissented vigorously, arguing that the minimal threat of violence was insufficient to justify this suppression. Moreover, both Justices emphasized that the first duty of the police is to protect the speaker's rights by dissuading those threatening violence, an attempt not evidenced in this case. By immediately acquiescing in the face of a single threat by one individual, the police had acted merely as conduits for the desires of suppression and denied the provocation value attributed to speech in Terminiello,[20] regardless of the impetus which motivated the policemen. Thus, the dissent raised the ultimate question in "fighting words" cases: whose rights are pre-eminent in a Feiner situation, the audience voluntarily listening or the speaker? [21]

The authority of Feiner has been undercut significantly in subsequent cases where the Court applied the language of Terminiello and distinguished Feiner on the factual situation, although at times it may appear to be a distinction without a difference. Edwards v. South Carolina,[22] for example, involved a civil rights demonstration on the grounds of the state legislature. Although the state officials and lower courts found that the crowd observing the demonstration was growing increasingly restive, and the demonstrators refused to leave when requested, the Court (in 1963) refused to consider the conduct of the demonstrators—the singing of religious and patriotic hymns and a "religious harangue" urging them to go to segregated lunch counters—to constitute "fighting words." Neither did the "hostile audience" doctrine apply. Although the situation in Edwards might have been potentially more dangerous than that of Feiner (a 1951 "hostile audience" case) the Court was appreciative of the ability of an expansive Feiner doctrine to serve effectively as a vehicle for the suppression of civil rights demonstrations by persons falsely claiming that their emotions were uncontrollably aroused. The discretion to halt the demonstration of those "sufficiently opposed to the views of the majority" [23] was lodged in individuals without an effective measure to determine whether the motivation was to preserve peace or suppress content of the speech. And as a factual matter the Court found the situation in Edwards a "far cry" from the hostile audience problem in Feiner.[24]

It is important to distinguish the Terminiello, Feiner, and Edwards cases from that of Chaplinsky. The latter case involved face-to-face confrontation where insults were delivered which were likely to provoke violence by the listeners. The harangues delivered in the former cases were not anger which focused on the audience—"fighting words" directed at particu-

---

17. Id. at 317.

18. Id. at 318.

19. Id. at 321.

20. Id. at 326–27 (Black, J., dissenting) and 331 (Douglas, J., dissenting).

21. One Circuit at least had held that hecklers would be arrested rather than speakers when the for-

mer arrived with preconceived intent to commit violence. Sellers v. Johnson, 163 F.2d 877 (8th Cir. 1947), cert. denied 332 U.S. 851 (1948).

22. 372 U.S. 229 (1963); see also Cox v. Louisiana, 379 U.S. 536 (1965).

23. 372 U.S. at 237.

24. Id. at 236.

lar members of the audience—nor was the audience even compelled to listen. While such speech may have offended the listeners' sensibilities, the Court has generally emphasized that regulation of speech needs more compelling justification in this context to avoid the censorship of ideas which are unpopular.

Cohen v. California,[25] decided in 1971, provides important support for this distinction and leaves the authority of *Feiner* in a very questionable state. *Cohen* was appealing his conviction for breach of the peace based on his presence in a Los Angeles courthouse wearing a jacket bearing the clearly printed words "Fuck the Draft." Stating that people in public places must be subject to some objectionable speech, the Court could not state that the expletive was totally devoid of social value. The Court, in the majority opinion of Mr. Justice Harlan, stated that

> [T]he ability of government, consonant with the Constitution, to shut off discourse solely to protect others from hearing it is . . . dependent upon a showing that substantial privacy interests are being invaded in an essentially intolerable manner.[26]

The fact that an offensive expletive was utilized does not detract from the protection afforded the speech, since, in Justice Harlan's phrase, "one man's vulgarity is another's lyric." [27] Moreover, the offensive words were not "a direct personal insult" specifically directed at the hearer; neither was the state exercising its police power (as in *Feiner*) "to prevent a speaker from intentionally provoking a given group to a hostile reaction." [28]

It remains to be considered whether, after the *Cohen* limitations, *Chaplinsky* remains a viable precedent allowing the States to proscribe these words "likely to provoke the average person to retaliation." The Court in

Cohen now appears to favor a more critical examination of the audience, the results of the speech, the length of the speech, the actual results of the speech, and the wording of the statute:

> [W]e do not think the fact that some unwilling "listeners" in a public building may have been briefly exposed to [the offensive speech] can serve to justify this breach of the peace conviction where, as here, there was no evidence that persons powerless to avoid appellant's conduct did in fact object to it, and where that portion of the statute upon which Cohen's conviction rests evinces no concern, either on its face or as construed . . . with the special plight of the captive auditor . . .[29]

D. The Present Status of the "Fighting Words" and "Hostile Audience" Doctrines

In addition to the explicit limitations on *Chaplinsky* created by the *Cohen* court, more recent cases have illustrated that the Court does not look with favor on prosecutions for "fighting words." However, to avoid a direct overruling of *Chaplinsky*, the Court in recent cases has employed the vagueness and overbreadth standards to avoid upholding convictions. Thus, in *Gooding v. Wilson*,[30] a 1972 case, the defendant addressed a policeman, "you son of a bitch I'll choke you to death." Similarly, in *Lewis v. City of New Orleans*,[31] the defendant said "you goddamn motherfucking police." Both convictions were overturned as the statutes were held vague and overbroad. Though the Court in *Gooding* noted that when the statute is narrowly drawn or construed, such convictions may be upheld under the *Chaplinsky* standard,[32] it also conducted its own examination of state case law and held that the state decisions did not limit the statute "to words that 'have a direct tendency to cause acts of violence by the person to whom individually, the remark is ad-

---

25. 403 U.S. 15 (1971).

For a different and interesting analysis of this case, and possible limits on its holding, see Farber, Civilizing Public Discourse: An Essay on Professor Bickel, Justice Harlan, and the Enduring Significance of Cohen v. California, 1980 Duke L.J. 283.

26. 403 U.S. at 21.

27. Id. at 25.

28. Id. at 20.

29. Cohen v. California, 403 U.S. 15, 22 (1971).

30. 405 U.S. 518 (1972).

31. 415 U.S. 130 (1974).

32. 405 U.S. 518, 523.

dressed.' " [33] And in *Lewis* the Court made clear that words conveying or intended to convey disgrace are not "fighting words." [34] In *Norwell v. City of Cincinnati*,[35] the Court refused to uphold the conviction of one "verbally and negatively" protesting his arrest, finding no fighting words. Also, in *Hess v. Indiana* [36] the Court held the speaker's statement during an antiwar protest that "We'll take the fucking street later" was constitutionally protected, for, as in *Cohen*, the words were not aimed at anyone in particular.

The result of these cases appears to be that the "fighting words" doctrine is still alive, but the Court will carefully scrutinize any convictions under it. Alternatively, Justice Blackmun may be correct when he complained in his dissent in *Gooding v. Wilson*,[37] that "the Court, despite its protestations to the contrary, is merely paying lip service to *Chaplinsky.*" [38] Similarly, while *Feiner* has never been overruled, the Court has distinguished it on its facts and not allowed the state to justify the prosecution of speakers for breach of the peace on the grounds that the speech invites dispute by hostile audiences.[39]

XII. FREEDOM OF ASSOCIATION AND THE PROBLEM OF LOYALTY AND SECURITY REQUIREMENTS

A. Introduction—The Freedom to Associate and Not to Associate

In *NAACP v. Alabama ex rel. Patterson*,[1] a unanimous Court, speaking through Justice Harlan, held that the state of Alabama could not compel the National Association for the Advancement of Colored People to reveal to the state's Attorney General the names and addresses of all of its Alabama members without regard to their positions and functions in the association. The NAACP made a showing that compelled disclosure of its rank and file members on past occasions exposed them to economic reprisal, loss of employment, threat of physical coercion, and general public hostility. Unlike an organization with illegal ends [2] the NAACP's nondisclosure interest was directly related to the right of the members to pursue their lawful interests privately. In reaching this conclusion, the Court announced in clearest form the right of association:

> Effective advocacy of both public and private points of view, particularly controversial ones, is undeniably enhanced by group association, as this Court has more than once recognized by remarking upon the close nexus between the freedoms of speech and assembly. . . . It is beyond debate that freedom to engage in association for the advancement of . . . the "liberty" assured by the Due Process Clause of the Fourteenth Amendment, which embraces freedom of speech. . . . Of course, it is immaterial whether the beliefs sought to be advanced by association pertain to political, economic, religious or cultural matters, and state action which may have the effect of curtailing the freedom to associate is subject to the closest scrutiny.[3]

This right of association takes many forms, many of which are considered elsewhere in this Chapter.[4] Thus, a state col-

---

33. 405 U.S. 518, 524.

34. 415 U.S. 130, 133 (1974).

35. 414 U.S. 14 (1973).

36. 414 U.S. 105 (1973).

37. 405 U.S. 518 (1972).

38. 405 U.S. at 537 (Blackmun, J., dissenting).

39. E.g., Gregory v. City of Chicago, 394 U.S. 111 (1969) (civil rights demonstration); see also, Cox v. Louisiana, 379 U.S. 536, 551 (1965) (citing *Feiner* but distinguishing it as a "far cry" from the civil rights demonstration involved in the instant case); Bachellar v. Maryland, 397 U.S. 564, 567 (1970) (antiwar demonstration); Edwards v. South Carolina, 372 U.S. 229, 236 (1963) (civil rights demonstration; a "far cry from the situation . . . " in *Feiner*).

1. 357 U.S. 449 (1958); see also Bates v. City of Little Rock, 361 U.S. 516 (1960); Louisiana ex rel. Gremillion v. NAACP, 366 U.S. 293 (1961); Brown v. Socialist Workers '74 Campaign Committee, 103 S.Ct. 416 (1982).

2. The Court so distinguished Bryant v. Zimmerman, 278 U.S. 63 (1928) where the Court upheld a New York State requirement of disclosure of the roster of membership of all unincorporated associations which required an oath as a condition to membership, as applied to the Ku Klux Klan. See 357 U.S. at 465. See Note, The First Amendment and Law Enforcement Infiltration of Political Groups, 56 So.Calif.L.Rev. 207 (1982) arguing for first amendment limits on such infiltration.

3. 357 U.S. 449, 460–61.

4. See this Chapter, Sections XV & XVI.

lege cannot deny official recognition (and the loss of privilege to distribute literature on campus and other such privileges which such denial entails) to a student organization because of its parent organization's history.[5] Under the freedom of association the Court has also struck down laws which prevented the NAACP from assisting individuals [6] and which prevented a labor union from assisting its members [7] in retaining lawyers to assert the legal rights of these individuals. Also, the freedom of association allows political parties, within certain bounds, to regulate the selection of delegates to their national conventions even when such regulations are contrary to state law.[8]

Similarly, the right of association raises some issues of whether organizations which persons are required to join—for example a union, as a requirement to work, or a state bar, as a requirement in some states to practice law—may, consistent with the freedom

of association, use the dues required of their members to advance causes not favored by all of the members.[9] In *Abood v. Detroit Board of Education*,[10] the Court held that the state may require a public worker to pay dues or a service fee equal to dues insofar as the money is used to finance expenditures by the union for the purposes of collective bargaining, contract administration, and grievance adjustment. But under the first amendment, the workers may not be compelled to contribute to political candidates, and the workers may constitutionally prevent the union's spending a part of its required fees to contribute to political candidates and to express political views unrelated to its duties as exclusive bargaining representative.

In the remainder of this section we shall examine some of the basic issues of freedom of association by focusing on the major

5. Healy v. James, 408 U.S. 169 (1972).

6. NAACP v. Button, 371 U.S. 415, 429–30 (1963).

7. Brotherhood of R.R. Trainmen v. Virginia, 377 U.S. 1 (1964); United Mine Workers v. Illinois State Bar Ass'n, 389 U.S. 217 (1967); United Transp. Union v. State Bar of Michigan, 401 U.S. 576 (1971).

See also Ohralik v. State Bar, 436 U.S. 447 (1978); In re Primus, 436 U.S. 412 (1978).

8. See, Democratic Party v. LaFollette, 450 U.S. 107 (1981). See generally, Gottlieb, Rebuilding the Right to Association: The Right to Hold a Convention as a Test Case, 11 Hofstra L.Rev. 191 (1982). See also, Anderson v. Celebrezze, 103 S.Ct. 1564 (1983), invalidating Ohio's excessive restrictions on ballot eligibility for independent presidential candidates because of the voter's freedom of choice and freedom of association.

9. International Ass'n. of Machinists v. Street, 367 U.S. 740 (1961) (statute construed to avoid association issue by holding that union dues money could only be used, under the statute, to support collective bargaining and not to support political causes); Lathrop v. Donohue, 367 U.S. 820 (1961) (integrated bar; issue of whether dues money could constitutionally be used to support causes opposed by a member not reached by the Court). In both of these cases Justices Harlan and Frankfurter would have reached the issue and allowed the compelled dues money to be spent for causes not approved by the involuntary members. Justices Douglas and Black also would have reached the issue and both would have found the use of dues money in this way unconstitutional.

In First Nat. Bank v. Bellotti, 435 U.S. 765 (1978), the Court held that states cannot prevent corporations from spending money to influence referendum questions, even if such referenda do not affect business interests. The state asserted as one interest to support the restriction on corporate speech the protection of shareholders by preventing waste of corporate resources to further views with which some shareholders disagreed. The Court noted that the statute was over-inclusive because it precluded corporations all of whose shareholders voted to allow the expenditure to engage in public debate.

The Court dismissed *Street* and *Abood* as "irrelevant," because in those cases the employees were required either by state law or union agreement to pay dues or a service fee to the union. The shareholder was free to withdraw his investment, but the union member could disassociate himself from the debate only at the cost of his job. 435 U.S. at 792–794 & n. 34.

Justices White, Brennan, and Marshall, dissenting, argued that the state interests in protecting stockholders from waste of corporate assets, in preventing corporations from dominating political debate, and in promoting economically efficient corporate decisionmaking overrode the first amendment restriction. 435 U.S. at 802–822.

The majority did not decide whether it may be possible for the state to place greater restrictions on corporate expenditures to influence candidate elections. 435 U.S. at 788 n. 26.

10. 431 U.S. 209 (1977).

cases dealing with loyalty and security requirements.

B. Public Employment Restrictions

1. Political Affiliation

The Courts have developed over the years guidelines which affect the legislature's ability to impose restrictions upon public employment. This result was given impetus by the emergence of the doctrine of unconstitutional conditions, discussed below. As a result, denial of public employment on the basis of political affiliation is in violation of the first amendment, unless the proscribed organization is one legitimately designated as "subversive", that is, dedicated to the use of illegal means to effectuate its political or social objectives, and the prospective employee is one who is aware of those objectives and intends specifically to further those objectives.[1] The development of these standards and the rationale for their implementation is left for consideration within the factual situations in which they developed.

Adler v. Board of Education,[2] the first significant venture of the Court into loyalty programs, involved an appeal from the dismissal of a teacher pursuant to a New York statute which disqualified from civil service and public school employment any person advocating, advising, or teaching governmental overthrow by force or violence.[3] Appellant's claim that his freedom of speech and association had been infringed by the statutes was not deemed persuasive because employment was not considered to be constitutionally a "right," thus removing it from the spectrum of constitutional protection. As the majority opinion phrased it,

> They [appellants] may work for the school system upon the reasonable terms laid down by the proper authorities of New York. If they do not choose to work on such terms, they are at liberty to retain their beliefs and associations and go elsewhere.[4]

Thus, the Court employed the then traditional view that public employment was a privilege rather than a right, illustrated by Justice Holmes' famous dictum, ". . . petitioner may have a constitutional right to talk politics, but he has no constitutional right to be a policeman."[5] However, the subsequent erosion of the doctrine that public employment, as a mere privilege, could be conditioned upon a surrender of constitutional rights,[6] forced a re-examination of the basic tenets of *Adler* and eventually removed *Adler's* constitutional underpinnings.

Wieman v. Updegraff,[7] decided the same term as *Adler*, demonstrated that the Court would not allow even a privilege to be withdrawn on the basis of certain broad classifications. Oklahoma required of its state employees an oath disclaiming membership in the Communist Party or

> any agency, party, organization, association or group whatever which has been officially determined . . . to be a communist front or subversive organization . . . that advocated the overthrow of the Government of the United States or of the State of Oklahoma by force or violence or other unlawful means.[8]

Reacting to the Oklahoma Supreme Court's interpretation of that language as including within the proscription persons "solely on the basis of organizational membership, regardless of their knowledge"[9]

---

1. For more detailed and interpretive analyses, T. Emerson, The System of Freedom of Expression (1970); and Note, Developments In the Law—The National Security Interest and Civil Liberties, 85 Harv.L. Rev. 1130 (1972).

2. 342 U.S. 485 (1952) (Justices Black, Douglas, & Frankfurter dissented).

3. Id. at 487–89 n. 3.

4. 342 U.S. at 492.

5. McAuliffe v. New Bedford, 155 Mass. 216, 220, 29 N.E. 517 (1892).

6. See Van Alstyne, The Demise of the Right—Privilege Distinction in Constitutional Law, 81 Harv.L.Rev. 1439 (1968); see Chapter 15, Section II, D, 4.

7. 344 U.S. 183 (1952).

8. Id. at 184–85 n. 1.

9. Id. at 190.

concerning the activities of such organizations, the Court determined that the oath offended due process.[10] The majority found that the denial of public employment for subversive association stigmatizes the individual and is unjustified when the member is innocent of the group's illegal and subversive goals:

> [U]nder the Oklahoma Act, the fact of association alone determines disloyalty and disqualification; it matters not whether association existed innocently or knowingly. To thus inhibit individual freedom of movement is to stifle the flow of democratic expression and controversy at one of its chief sources . . . Indiscriminate classification of innocent with knowing activity must fall as an assertion of arbitrary power.[11]

In subsequent years, the Supreme Court added no new substantive protections, choosing instead to deal with loyalty qualifications by the use of the vagueness and overbreadth doctrines. Thus, in *Shelton v. Tucker*,[12] the Court invalidated an Arkansas statute requiring teachers to file an affidavit listing all the organizations to which they had belonged or contributed within the past five years. The state's legitimate interest in investigating the loyalty of its teachers did not justify the "unlimited and indiscriminate sweep" of the statute when less restrictive alternatives, offering less impingement upon the teachers' freedom of association, were available.

In *Cramp v. Board of Public Instruction*,[13] the Court unanimously invalidated a Florida statute requiring employees to swear, "I have not and will not lend my aid, support, advice, counsel or influence to the Communist Party."[14] The consequences of such vague and ambiguous wording would not only inhibit legitimate activity by those whose "conscientious scruples were the

most sensitive," but would increase the likelihood of prosecution for ideas antithetical to those held by the general community. Employing a similar rationale in *Baggett v. Bullitt*,[15] the Court invalidated two Washington loyalty oath requirements. The first required the affiant to promote, by teaching and example, "respect for the flag and the institutions of the United States of America and the State of Washington" and the second, to swear that he was not a member of a "subversive organization." Once again, the language was found susceptible of an interpretation applying to a broad spectrum of behavior with which the State could not interfere. Moreover, the lack of any criminal sanction for its future violation did not prevent the oath from being stricken since this would not avoid the prohibited deterrent effect upon those who will only swear to that which they can obey.

More precisely drawn oaths were invalidated in 1966 and 1967 as the Court found that the *Wieman* standard, mere knowledge of illegal aims of the organization, was insufficient to terminate an individual's employment. *Elfbrandt v. Russell*[16] involved a challenge to an Arizona statute imposing an oath upon the prospective employee that he had not knowingly and willfully become or remained a member of an organization dedicated to the overthrow by force or violence of the government with knowledge of its illegal aims. The majority opinion found this to prohibit "knowing, but guiltless" behavior as the oath did not require the individual to have participated in or subscribed to the unlawful activities for employment to be terminated and prosecution for perjury to be instituted. The Court relied on previous decisions involving criminal prosecutions under the Smith Act[17] and held that the same standards were applicable to employment

---

10. See Garner v. Board of Public Works, 341 U.S. 716 (1951).

11. 344 U.S. at 191.

12. 364 U.S. 479 (1960) (Frankfurter, Harlan, Clark, & Whittaker, JJ., dissented).

13. 368 U.S. 278 (1961).

14. Id. at 279 n. 1, and 286–287.

15. 377 U.S. 360 (1946); see generally Israel, Elfbrandt v. Russell, The Demise of The Oath? 1966 Sup. Ct.Rev. 193.

16. 384 U.S. 11 (1966).

17. Scales v. United States, 367 U.S. 203 (1961) and Noto v. United States, 367 U.S. 290 (1961).

discrimination; "knowing membership" coupled with a specific intent to further the illegal aims of the organizations would be required since "quasi-political parties or other groups . . . may embrace both legal and illegal aims." [18]

In *Keyishian v. Board of Regents*,[19] the Court finally came full circle and invalidated the Feinberg Law which had been upheld in *Adler* fifteen years before. Noting the pertinent constitutional doctrines which had arisen in the interim, and the absence of any claim of vagueness in *Adler*, the Court determined *Adler* to be no longer controlling. Examining the complex interdependence of the various provisions of the New York law, Justice Brennan, speaking for the Court, found them unconstitutionally vague.

> The very intricacy of the plan and the uncertainty as to the scope of its proscriptions make it a highly efficient *in terrorem* mechanism. It would be a bold teacher who would not stay as far as possible from utterances or acts which might jeopardize his living by enmeshing him in this intricate machinery . . . The result must be to stifle that free play of the spirit which all teachers ought especially to cultivate and practice.[20]

Further, a provision added to the statute since the *Adler* decision stated that mere membership in a prohibited organization, as determined by the State Board of Regents, created *prima facie* evidence of disqualification for employment which could be rebutted by appellant only in one of three ways: denial of membership, denial that the organization advocated overthrow, or denial that appellant had knowledge of such advocacy. The provision was invalidated as overbroad relying on *Elfbrandt*, as the law did not allow the presumption to be rebutted by denial of specific intent to further the unlawful

aims of the organization or denial of active membership.[21]

In the same year, the Court, in *United States v. Robel*,[22] dealt with employment restrictions in federal legislation. The majority opinion of Chief Justice Warren determined that § 5(a)(1)(D) of the Subversive Activities Control Act was unconstitutionally overbroad by denying to members of designated "communist-action" groups employment in any defense facility. The Court refused to narrow the application of the statutory prohibition to bring it within constitutional standards, as had been done in *Scales*,[23] noting:

> the clarity and preciseness of the provision in question make it impossible to narrow its indiscriminately cast and overly broad scope without substantial rewriting.[24]

This statutory language made irrelevant the active or passive status of the individual's membership, his knowledge of the illegal aims of the organization or lack of it, the degree of his agreement or disagreement with those aims, and the sensitive nature of his position of employment as it affected national security. The Court held that the statute literally established guilt by association and inhibited the exercise of First Amendment rights while less restrictive means of achieving the legislative objective were at hand.

Thus, the constitutional requirements involving loyalty-security qualifications for employment by either federal or state governments parallel each other quite closely. An individual may not be punished or deprived of public employment for political association unless: (1) he is an active member of a subversive organization; (2) such membership is with knowledge of the illegal aims of the organization; and (3) the individual has a specific intent to further those illegal

---

18. Elfbrandt v. Russell, 384 U.S. at 15, quoting Scales v. United States, 367 U.S. 203, 229 (1961).

19. 385 U.S. 589 (1967).

20. Id. at 601, citing Wieman v. Updegraff, 344 U.S. 183, 195 (Frankfurter, J. concurring).

21. In light of Speiser v. Randall, 357 U.S. 513 (1958), it is doubtful that the addition of those require-

ments would save the statute since the burden remains on the affiant to establish his innocent connection with the organization.

22. 389 U.S. 258 (1967).

23. Scales v. United States, 367 U.S. 203 (1961).

24. Id. at 262, quoting Aptheker v. Secretary of State, 378 U.S. 500, 515 (1964).

ends, as opposed to the general support of the general objectives of an organization.

Robel does leave an indication, however, that the federal government's interest in national security may on occasion override individual rights of association, depending upon the sensitivity of the proffered employment. Denial of a position with a demonstrable relationship to important national security interests might be justified on a finding that the person's status is nothing more than active, knowing membership in a subversive organization, since the potential conversion of such an individual to the adoption of illegal means to achieve the organization's political objectives would not offer the government an adequate opportunity to forestall the implementation of those means.[25]

The subsequent decisions have had little impact on the prior law governing the ability of the government to discharge workers for their associational or speech activities. In *Connell v. Higginbotham*,[26] the Court in a per curiam opinion invalidated a section of a Florida loyalty oath requiring the affiant to disclaim belief in the overthrow of the federal or state government by force or violence. The statute's requirement of dismissal without notice or hearing for failure to take the oath was violative of due process since the appellant was afforded no opportunity to explain his refusal, thus potentially allowing dismissal for possible protected activity. The Court applied similar standards to access to the ballot in unanimously invalidating an Indiana oath requiring political parties to disclaim *any* advocacy of overthrow of the government by force.[27]

However in *Cole v. Richardson*,[28] an opinion of significant impact upon statutory oaths as opposed to substantive legislative

restrictions, the Court indicated a greater willingness to construe arguably overbroad or vague requirements so as to comport with constitutional guidelines. Previous decisions of the Court had established a distinction between oaths which require individuals to swear to the appropriateness of their past conduct, so-called negative oaths, and oaths which merely require the individual to swear his support in the future to the constitutional processes of government, so-called affirmative oaths.[29] Such affirmative oaths have traditionally been viewed as constitutionally permissible despite the inherent vagueness of the terms employed. The primary justification for overlooking the inability of the wording to distinguish between protected and unprotected activity which must be defended against by the affiant is the presence of such wording in the body of the Constitution for the presidential oath[30] and that for federal and state officials.[31] The purpose motivating the enactment of such oaths is looked upon as merely "to assure that those in positions of public trust were willing to commit themselves to live by the constitutional processes,"[32] and the effect is substantially equated with that of a vow of allegiance.[33]

The challenged oath in *Cole*, which Massachusetts required of its state employees, read as follows:

> I do solemnly swear (or affirm) that I will uphold and defend the Constitution of the United States . . . and the Constitution of the Commonwealth of Massachusetts and that I will oppose the overthrow of the government of the United States of America or of this Commonwealth by force, violence or by any illegal or unconstitutional method.[34]

Chief Justice Burger, writing for a four to three majority, read the first portion of the

---

25. See 389 U.S. at 266–68.

26. 403 U.S. 207 (1971).

27. Communist Party of Indiana v. Whitcomb, 414 U.S. 441 (1974).

28. 405 U.S. 676 (1972).

29. See Bond v. Floyd, 385 U.S. 116, 135 (1966); Knight v. Board of Regents, 269 F.Supp. 339 (S.D.N.Y. 1967), aff'd per curiam 390 U.S. 36 (1968).

30. Art. II, § 1, cl. 8.

31. Art. VI, cl. 3.

32. Cole v. Richardson, 405 U.S. at 684 (1976).

33. Knight v. Board of Regents, 269 F.Supp. 339, 341 (S.D.N.Y.1967), aff'd per curiam 390 U.S. 36 (1968).

34. 405 U.S. at 677–78 (footnote omitted).

oath, swearing to "uphold and defend", as a permissible "affirmative oath." This result allowed the Court to conclude that a literal reading of the second part, requiring opposition to attempted overthrow, would be inconsistent. Rather, it should be read as merely a negative restatement of the "support" oath:

> [A] commitment not to use illegal and constitutionally unprotected force to change the constitutional system. The second clause does not expand the obligation of the first; it simply makes clear the application of the first clause to a particular issue. Such repetition, whether for emphasis or cadence, seems to be the wont of authors of oaths. That the second clause may be redundant is no ground to strike it down; we are not charged with correcting grammar but with enforcing a constitution.[35]

The dissenters, Justices Douglas, Marshall, and Brennan, ignored the nebulous nature of the positive portion of the oath, but argued that the vagueness of "oppose" left the affiant in a quandary concerning when and by what method he must demonstrate his opposition. As Justice Douglas put the dilemma, the oath "requires that appellee 'oppose' that which she has an indisputable right to advocate." [36]

The *Cole* decision has not signaled any diluting of the basic proposition that one may not be excluded from public employment on the basis of political affiliation unless the proscribed organization is truly subversive. The Court emphasized this constitutional rule in *Elrod v. Burns*,[37] where it invalidated political patronage dismissals by the Democratic Sheriff of Cook County. Respondent's discharge was unrelated to membership in any subversive organization.

While individuals affiliated with subversive organizations may be denied public employment pursuant to the safeguards outlined in *Keyishian* and *Robel*, dismissal merely for membership in an opposing political party which poses no illegal threat to the democratic process falls squarely within the overarching principle of those cases; the imposition of burdens based solely upon political association is forbidden. The Court did entertain arguments alleging the existence of a significant state interest in political patronage, primarily the preservation of the two party system and promotion of interest in lower echelon elections, but such interests were unpersuasive when weighed against the restraint such practices placed upon the freedoms of belief and association.

It is important to note that, while the broad language of the plurality opinion of Justice Brennan questioned the validity of patronage practices at all levels of government, the pivotal concurrences of Justices Stewart and Blackmun narrowed the effect of the case. In their view, *Elrod* held only that the dismissal of a non-policy making, non-confidential government employee could not be constitutionally justified by the alleged benefits of political patronage.[38] Different considerations, alluded to in the majority opinion, attend those higher-echelon government employees because they are principally responsible for promulgating and implementing the goals of the party attaining office in the election.

The Court reaffirmed the *Elrod* protection against political patronage dismissals in *Branti v. Finkel*,[39] an opinion which, unlike *Elrod*, attracted a majority. The proper test, said the majority, to determine whether political affiliation is a legitimate factor to consider in government employment "is not whether the label 'policymakers' or 'confidential' fits a particular position; rather, the question is whether the hiring authority can demonstrate that party affiliation is an appropriate requirement for the effective performance of the public office involved." [40]

---

35. Cole v. Richardson, 405 U.S. at 684.

36. Id. at 689 (dissenting opinion).

37. 427 U.S 347 (1976).

38. 427 U.S. 347, 374–75 (1976).

39. 445 U.S. 507 (1980). See generally, Note, First Amendment Limitations on Patronage Employment Practices, 49 U.Chi.L.Rev. 181 (1982).

40. 445 U.S. at 521. Stewart, J., dissented because he disagreed with the standard created by the majority; he found the professional and confidential nature

Thus a state's election laws could require that there be two election judges each representing one of the two main parties, even though the job of election supervision does not involve policy making or access to confidential information. Similarly, the state could not fire a state university football coach because of his political affiliation, even though his job involves some policy making.

The majority, thus held that a state official may not terminate the employment of a public defender for purely political grounds because any policy making role he might have should not relate to partisan political interests; his confidential information based on the attorney client relationship has no relation to partisan political concerns; and to make his tenure depend on his political affiliation would not advance the effective performance of his duties.[41]

Elrod and *Branti* serve to silhouette the basic legislative goals that may serve as a constitutional basis for denial or termination of public employment. The initial focus must be on the character of the organization; unless it is one posing a threat to democratic government not only in terms of its advocacy but also its ultimate goals there is little chance that there can be found to be significant state interest in prohibiting its members *qua* members from the public payroll. Moreover, even if the organization is one which may constitutionally be guarded against, only those members who have

knowledge of its illegal goals and have a specific intent to further those goals may be precluded from public employment.[42]

As applied to oaths, it is clear that they must be clear, concise, and narrow in scope, although affirmative oaths, relating only to allegiance to constitutional processes of government, are accorded a wider range of permissibility. Negative oaths cannot require a disclaimer of past conduct or belief other than that for which the employee may be constitutionally denied employment pursuant to an investigation, i.e. the two step standard of *Elfbrandt*.

2. Exercise of the Fifth Amendment

Questions occasionally arise as to the legitimacy of sanctions applied against a public employee who has asserted the Fifth Amendment privilege against self-incrimination when questioned as to his political associations. In *Slochower v. Board of Higher Education of New York City*,[43] the Court ruled that a summary dismissal of a teacher following his refusal to answer such questions in effect indicated that the matter was taken as confessed and served as the basis for his dismissal. Without further evidence, independent of the assertion of the privilege, such a dismissal violated due process. However, the Fifth Amendment does not serve as an impenetrable barrier which will protect the identity of one's political affiliations. The Court has held that if "use

---

of employment to be determinative. Justice Stewart relied on the distinction that he had drawn in his concurrence in *Elrod* (a concurrence joined by Justice Blackmun), in which he argued that *Elrod* only ruled that the dismissal of a nonpolicy making, nonconfidential governmental employee could not be constitutionally justified by the alleged benefits of political patronage. 427 U.S. at 374–75. Powell, J., joined by Rehnquist, J., objected to the majority creating a first amendment protection in the first place.

41. Contrast Connick v. Myers, 103 S.Ct. 1684 (1983), where the Court, in a 5 to 4 decision, upheld the firing of an assistant district attorney for circulating a questionnaire regarding office policies. The questionnaire did not touch upon matters of public concern in any real sense. The employer need not tolerate action which he reasonably believed would disrupt the office, undermine his authority, and destroy close working re-

lationships. "We hold only that when a public employee speaks not as a citizen upon matters of public concern, but instead as an employee upon matters of personal interest, absent the most unusual circumstances, a federal court is not the appropriate forum in which to review the wisdom of a personnel decision taken by a public agency allegedly in reaction to the employee's behavior." 103 S.Ct. at 1690.

42. As discussed above, *Robel* offers a potential exception for individuals in highly sensitive governmental jobs who are knowing members, as they may adopt, subsequent to their employment, the illegal aims of the organization. See text at notes 24–25, supra.

43. 350 U.S. 551 (1956); see also Konigsberg v. State Bar of California, 353 U.S. 252 (1957) discussed below.

immunity"[44] is granted the employee, he can no longer assert the privilege, and may be compelled to answer.[45] However, if no immunity is offered, the employee cannot be forced to choose between forfeiture of his public employment or self-incrimination.[46] Under the narrow use immunity, his answers may be used against him in a decision to terminate his employment since use immunity only bars use of the testimony in a criminal case.[47]

3. National Security Restrictions

In recent years the Supreme Court has justified various first amendment restrictions on the activities of present or former government employees. In the leading case the litigant against whom the Court upheld restraints was a former employee of the Central Intelligence Agency. In *Snepp v. United States*,[1] a former CIA agent, Frank W. Snepp, III, published a book concerning CIA involvement in South Vietnam, without seeking or securing the Agency's prepublication approval, in violation of his employment contract promising that he would "not . . . publish . . . any information or material relating to the Agency, its activities or intelligence activities generally, either during or after the term of [his] employment . . . without specific prior approval of the Agency."[2] He also agreed not to disclose any classified material without proper authorization.

Because Snepp published his book without submitting it for prepublication review, the CIA sued for an order enjoining him to submit future writings for prepublication review, a declaration that he had breached his contract, and a constructive trust for the Government of all profits earned from the publication of the book. For purposes of this litigation the Government conceded that Snepp's book disclosed *no* classified intelligence.

The Supreme Court, in a short per curiam opinion, delivered without benefit of oral arguments or full briefing, granted all of the Government's requested relief. In a footnote the majority dismissed Snepp's first amendment claims: "[E]ven in the absence of an express agreement—the CIA could have acted to protect substantial government interests by imposing reasonable restrictions on employee activities that in other contexts might be protected by the First Amendment. The Government has a compelling interest in protecting both the secrecy of information important to our national security and the appearance of confidentiality so essential to the effective operation of our foreign intelligence service. The agreement that Snepp signed is a reasonable means for protecting this vital interest."[3]

The majority contended that because Snepp's employment involved a high degree of trust and his explicit obligation to submit

---

44. Use immunity, as defined in 18 U.S.C.A. § 6002, provides immunity from the use of the compelled testimony and evidence derived therefrom.

45. Kastigar v. United States, 406 U.S. 441 (1972).

46. Garrity v. New Jersey, 385 U.S. 493 (1967).

Lefkowitz v. Cunningham, 431 U.S. 801 (1977) (state statute which provided that if an officer of a political party subpoenaed by a grand jury or other authorized tribunal to testify concerning the conduct of his office refuses to testify or refuses to waive immunity from later prosecution from the use of his testimony, then the statute immediately terminates his party office and prohibits him from holding any other party or public office for a period of five years, held unconstitutional as a violation of the self incrimination clause of the fifth amendment as applied to the states through the fourteenth amendment).

If the employee is given "use immunity" and forced to testify that testimony cannot be used in a later crim-

inal prosecution. In New Jersey v. Portash, 440 U.S. 450 (1979) that grand jury testimony given under such immunity cannot be used even for impeachment purposes at trial. The Court found use of a balancing approach to be impermissible as testimony given under immunity is compulsory self-indiscrimination in its most "pristine" form.

47. Kastigar v. United States, 406 U.S. 441, 453 (1972). Cf. In re Schwartz, 51 Ill.2d 334, 282 N.E.2d 689 (1972).

1. 444 U.S. 507 (1980) (per curiam). See generally, Medow, The First Amendment and the Secrecy State: Snepp v. United States, 130 U.Penn.L.Rev. 775 (1982). See also Section V, B, supra.

2. 444 U.S. at 509.

3. 444 U.S. at 511, n. 3 (citations omitted).

for prepublication review all material, whether classified or not, Snepp's violation impaired the CIA's statutory functions by limiting the CIA's ability to guarantee the security of information and protect intelligence sources. What Snepp should have done, rather than flout his preclearance obligation, said the majority, was to submit the book for prepublication review. This Agency clearance would be subject to judicial review. Thus if the CIA claimed that the book contained harmful classified disclosures and Snepp disagreed, the CIA then would have the burden of seeking an injunction against publication.[4]

The strong dissent of Justice Stevens, joined by Brennan and Marshall argued that since it was stipulated that the book contained no classified nonpublic material, the interest in confidentiality that Snepp's employment agreement was designed to protect had not been affected. Moreover there was no precedent to authorize a constructive trust because his book did not use, or profit from, confidential information as the Government stipulated.[5]

C. Regulation of Labor Organizations

The Court has on several occasions dealt with federal legislation attempting to limit subversive influence in the labor hierarchy. As the decisions are quite dissimilar in both approach and result, it is difficult, if not impossible, to draw any thread of uniformity for future application. The easy answer may be simply that the difference in the membership of the Court as well as the political climate in each decision best explains the philosophical disparity. Moreover, the major cases delineating the protections afforded political association were not decided until after these opinions were handed down, leaving the implication that wholly new consider-

ations may apply to any future attempts by Congress to control subversives in the labor movement.

The first case, *American Communications Association v. Douds*,[1] decided in 1950, considered a challenge to § 9(h) the "non-Communist affidavit" provision of the Taft-Hartley Act of 1947.[2] Pursuant to that provision, any labor organization which desired the benefits of the National Labor Relations Act (N.L.R.A.) was required to have its officers file annually with the National Labor Relations Board affidavits disavowing membership in or support of the Communist Party as well as disclaiming membership, support, or belief in any organization which advocates or believes in the overthrow of the federal government by force or any illegal or unconstitutional means.[3] Legislative findings of fact supporting this statute determined that strikes called to achieve political rather than economic goals posed a severe threat to the flow of interstate commerce. The past beliefs and associations of the individuals designated by the provision would serve as a reasonable method to identify them as potential instigators of such strikes and the presence of such individuals in positions of influence in labor unions would greatly increase their potential. The Court found that there existed a reasonable relationship between the evil and the means implemented to avoid that evil, as past beliefs and associations are sufficient criterion to infer future conduct consistent with those beliefs.[4] However, further analysis was required since the means employed discouraged the lawful exercise of first amendment freedoms.

The Court rejected appellant's claim that whenever rights of free speech and association are impaired the clear and present danger test is the appropriate adjudicative stan-

---

4. 444 U.S. at 513, n. 8.

5. 444 U.S. at 516–26.

1. 339 U.S. 382 (1950).

2. Officially known as the Labor-Management Relations Act; 61 Stat. 136, 146, 29 U.S.C.A. §§ 141, 159(h). Section 159(h) was later repealed by the Labor-Manage-

ment Reporting and Disclosure Act of 1959, 73 Stat. 519, 525, 29 U.S.C.A. § 201(d).

3. 339 U.S. at 385–86.

4. American Communications Ass'n v. Douds, 339 U.S. 382, 391 (1950).

dard. In the Court's view, Congress had focused the thrust of its prohibition at preventing conduct and the subsequent effect on speech was merely incidental. The government's interest was:

> not in preventing the dissemination of Communist doctrine . . . because it is feared that unlawful action will result . . . such strikes are called by persons who, so Congress has found, have the will and power to do so *without* advocacy or persuasion that seeks acceptance in the competition of the market.[5]

As the effect upon the first amendment was minimal and the public interest in an untrammelled flow of commerce great, the Court felt that a requirement of showing imminent national peril to invoke prophylactic measures would be an absurdity.[6] Rather, the competing values of free speech and the public interest in a responsible exercise of the power vested in labor by the N.L.R.A. must be weighed and the appropriate balance struck.[7] In view of the great public interest in protecting the flow of commerce and the relative handful of individuals whose beliefs may actually be restrained by their desire for union office, as well as the fact that those individuals who were affected were not required to forego their beliefs since they could resign their position with the union with their beliefs intact, the Court found that Congress had not contravened the purposes of the first amendment.[8] Moreover, the Court construed the portions of the Act prohibiting mere belief to encompass only those union officials who held the belief in violent overthrow of the Government to be an objective, as opposed to a prophecy.[9]

Following *Douds*, there were 18 prosecutions instituted by the Government for the filing of false affidavits.[10] In only one of these cases did the appeal reach the Supreme Court, *Killian v. United States*.[11] The Court reversed petitioner's conviction on procedural grounds, but in the course of this decision it approved a broad interpretation of the requirement of "membership or affiliation" as related to the Communist Party. Emphasizing that no criminal sanctions applied to membership in or affiliation with the Communist Party under the terms of the Act, the Court rejected petitioner's claim that membership could only be determined by factual phenomena, such as a "specific formal act of joining."[12] The instruction to the jury which was approved allowed membership to be shown by state of mind; "the desire on the part of the individual to belong to the Communist Party and a recognition by that Party that it considers him as a member."[13]

In 1959, Congress repealed § 9(h) and provided, in its stead, § 504 of the Landrum-Griffin Act[14] which provided:

> No person who is or has been a member of the Communist Party . . . shall serve . . . as an officer, director, trustee, member of any executive board or similar governing body, business agent, manager, organizer, or other employee . . . of any labor organization.[15]

In *United States v. Brown*,[16] this provision was invalidated as a bill of attainder.[17] The

---

5. Id. at 396 (emphasis in original; footnote omitted).

6. Id. at 397.

7. Id. at 400.

8. Id. at 404.

9. Id. at 407; Justice Jackson, although concurring in the decision as it related to the prohibition upon members of the Communist Party, dissented as to the prohibition upon those for mere belief. Id. at 437–43; Justice Black dissented, stating that the statute should have outlawed political strikes and avoided the unnecessary impairment of First Amendment freedoms. Id. at 445; Justices Douglas, Clark, and Minton did not participate.

10. N. Dorsen, P. Bender, B. Newborne, Emerson, Haber, & Dorsen's Political and Civil Rights in the United States, 111 (4th ed. 1976), vol. I.

11. 368 U.S. 231 (1961).

12. Id. at 247.

13. Id. at 247 n. 5.

14. Officially, the Labor-Management Reporting and Disclosure Act, 73 Stat. 536, 29 U.S.C.A. § 504.

15. Id.

16. 381 U.S. 437 (1965).

17. For an extensive analysis of bills of attainder, see Note, The Bounds of Legislative Specification: A Suggested Approach to the Bill of Attainder Clause, 72 Yale L.J. 330 (1962).

Court did not deny the legislative power to prevent political strikes by rationally related means, but a blanket decree that all individuals on the membership rolls of the Communist Party was unjustifiable in that it determined guilt by legislative fiat. In language implicating the reasoning in *Douds*, Chief Justice Warren's majority opinion declared:

> The designation of Communists as those persons likely to cause political strikes . . . rests, as the Court in *Douds* explicitly recognized . . . upon an empirical investigation by Congress of the acts, characteristics, and propensities of Communist Party members. In a number of decisions, this Court has pointed out the fallacy of the suggestion that membership in the Communist Party, or any other political organization, can be regarded as an alternative, but equivalent expression for a list of undesirable characteristics.[18]

However, since § 9(h) of the Taft-Hartley Act had permitted Communists to resign their membership in the Party if they wished to remain in their position as union officials, *Douds* was not explicitly overruled. While the decision may have blurred the lines between a bill of attainder and an *ex post facto* law, the Court in *Brown* held that, since former Communists could not serve as union officials for five years after their resignation, the statute served as prohibited legislative punishment,[19] regardless of the argument that the function of the statute was preventive rather than retributive.

> It would be archaic to limit the definition of "punishment" to "retribution." Punishment serves several purposes: retributive, rehabilitative, deterrent—and preventive.[20]

The authority of *Douds* in the wake of the language quoted above is nebulous, although *Brown* has not been relied on as precedent to overturn any further restrictions banning Communists or other political groups.

Moreover, the rise of the doctrine of unconstitutional conditions in the public employment area[21] seems to conflict with the *Douds* reasoning that § 9(h) imposed no unreasonable restraint on beliefs as the official had the option of resigning his position. However, *United States v. Robel*,[22] as discussed above, leaves the implication that mere beliefs may be restrained without a specific intent to further illegal goals if the individual occupies a sensitive position, which is precisely the rationale which motivated Congress to enact the provision.[23]

Nevertheless, there is as yet no successor to § 504.[24] In the absence of federal regulation, many unions have provided for limitation of subversive influence in their constitutions or have excluded subversives without the benefit of a constitutional provision.[25] The courts have declined to interfere in such intra-union activities.[26]

D.   Restrictions on Entry into the Bar

States routinely require that applicants for membership to the bar possess certain attributes of character which are consistent with the practice of law. A significant component of this character, as a prospective member of a "profession dedicated to the peaceful and reasoned settlement of disputes between men, and between a man and his government,"[1] is loyalty to that system

18.   381 U.S. at 455.

19.   The statute must impose punishment to be voided as a bill of attainder; Cummings v. Missouri, 71 U.S. (4 Wall.) 277 (1867).

20.   381 U.S. at 458.

21.   See Section XII, B on employment restrictions.

22.   389 U.S. 258 (1967).

23.   However, see Osman v. Douds, 339 U.S. 846 (1950), where the Court evenly split on the belief provisions of § 9(h), Justice Clark not participating.

24.   Note that § 703(f), Civil Rights Act of 1964, 42 U.S.C.A. § 2000e–2(f), denies to Communist Party members and members of other subversive groups the benefits of the fair employment practices provision of that statute.

25.   See Summers, The Right to Join a Union, 47 Colum.L.Rev. 33 (1947); Paschell and Theodore, Anti-Communist Provisions in Union Constitutions, 77 Monthly Lab.Rev. 1097 (1954).

26.   N. Dorsen, P. Bender, B. Newborne, Emerson, Haber and Dorsen's Political and Civil Rights in the United States, 114 (4th ed. 1976), vol. I.

1.   Law Students Civil Rights Research Council v. Wadmond, 401 U.S. 154, 166 (1971).

of government fostered by the Constitution and a devotion to "the law in its broadest sense, including not only its substantive provision, but also its procedures for orderly change." [2] Not surprisingly, denials of admission to the bar on grounds of disloyalty have produced a spate of litigation alleging that such requirements restrict the applicant's rights of belief and association. Such cases have generally been presented in two basic contexts: the legitimacy of a denial based upon inferences of disloyalty due to specific incidents or circumstances in the applicant's past or the legitimacy of a denial due to a refusal to answer questions delving into the applicant's past political associations.[3]

Ex parte Garland,[4] the initial case dealing with loyalty oaths for attorneys, invalidated as a bill of attainder and an ex post facto law an oath that the individual had never supported or expressed sympathy for the enemies of the United States, foreign or domestic. Although *Garland* did not rest on the First Amendment, which was not applicable to the states at that time, the modern cases make it clear that the statute would be invalid under present First Amendment theory.

Political association cannot be construed as evidence of disloyalty unless the standard for criminally punishable political affiliation delineated in *Scales v. United States* [5] is satisfied.[6] The rationale is also much the same. Disabilities imposed by the legislatures upon an organization's ability to attract members cannot be justified unless the goals of such an organization encompass violent overthrow of the constitutionally established governments. Therefore, a member cannot be punished for his political affiliations unless he has knowledge of those illegal goals

and has evidenced a specific intent to aid in the implementation of those goals.

The question of whether active membership status is required to infer disloyalty as a character trait was raised in *Schware v. Board of Bar Examiners*,[7] in which the New Mexico Board of Bar Examiners disqualified the petitioner on the grounds of membership in the Communist Party fifteen years prior to his application for admission to the bar. The Court was unanimous in reversing this decision. As Mr. Justice Black noted in his majority opinion, membership in the Communist Party had not even been illegal at the time of Schware's membership. Moreover, the affirmative evidence produced by the petitioner as to his loyalty during the intervening fifteen years had demonstrated that his affiliation with the Party was sufficiently attenuated from his present life so as to remove any justification for relying on it as grounds for disloyalty.

There is no general rule to be gleaned from the cases. At the least, it may be stated that past membership in a subversive organization cannot create an irrebuttable presumption of unfitness for the bar; also the First Amendment will not protect an active, knowing member of the Communist Party with specific intent to aid in its illegal goals. The area between these extremes necessarily rests with the equities inherent in the particular fact situation.[8]

Following *Schware*, the Supreme Court was confronted with a series of cases in which there was no claim that past incidents in the applicant's life had revealed characteristics incompatible with the practice of law. Rather, the applicants had asserted a privilege in refusing to answer questions which they believed intruded unnecessarily into their first amendment freedoms.

---

2. Konigsberg v. State Bar of California, 366 U.S. 36, 52 (1961) (Konigsberg II).

3. The early cases are collected in Note, 18 A.L.R.2d 268, 283–291, 335–336 (1951).

4. 71 U.S. (4 Wall.) 333 (1867).

5. 367 U.S. 203 (1961). See Section XII, B, 1, supra.

6. T. Emerson, The System of Freedom of Expression 240–41 (1970); and Note, Developments in the Law—The National Security Interest and Civil Liberties, 85 Harv.L.Rev. 1130, 1137–38, 1172–76 (1972).

7. 353 U.S. 232 (1957).

8. See also In re Summers, 325 U.S. 561 (1945).

The first case of this posture, *Konigsberg v. State Bar of California* [9] *(Konigsberg I)*, decided the same term as *Schware*, dealt with the range of inferences which could properly be drawn from the applicant's refusal to answer questions relating to his past political affiliations. The California Bar had determined that petitioner's refusal to respond to inquiries into his membership in the Communist Party, coupled with other characteristics, required it to deny admission on the grounds that the petitioner had failed to establish his good moral character as well as his non-advocacy of illegal overthrow of the government. The Court found such a conclusion unjustified based upon the evidence presented to the bar examiners. There must exist some authentic, affirmative evidence of disloyalty to deny admission to an applicant, not a conclusion of disloyalty based upon suspicions deduced from a refusal to answer questions. The majority opinion by Justice Black noted,

> We recognize the importance of leaving States free to select their own bars, but it is equally important that the State not exercise this power in an arbitrary or discriminatory manner nor in such way as to impinge on the freedom of political expression or association . . . A lifetime of good citizenship is worth very little if it is so frail that it cannot withstand the suspicions which apparently were the basis for the Committee's action. [10]

The decision expressed no opinion as to the propriety of denying admission to the bar solely on the basis of an applicant's refusal to answer, as that issue was not presented. Four years later the same parties appeared before the Court to litigate that question. [11] On re-hearing for Konigsberg's application for admission to the bar of California, the applicant introduced further evidence of his good character and reiterated that he did not believe in or advocate violent overthrow of the government. Further he

stated that he had never knowingly been a member of any organization with such objectives. Nevertheless, he steadfastly refused to answer questions concerning possible membership in the Communist Party. Relying solely on this refusal as an obstruction to a legitimate investigation, the bar examiners again denied him certification to practice law in that State.

In *Konigsberg (II)* the majority opinion of Justice Harlan rejected the claim that the State had placed upon Konigsberg the burden of establishing his loyalty, which would contravene the holding of *Speiser v. Randall.* [12] In the view of the majority, the denial had not been based upon any inference as to Konigsberg's character, but simply on his obstruction of the investigation. Since the state had the burden of producing evidence as to disloyalty, an applicant could not be allowed to frustrate that burden by refusing to submit relevant information. This conclusion was dictated by the majority's view that, as the regulatory statute imposed only an incidental infringement upon speech, the state's interest in such regulation must be weighed against the appellant's interest in remaining silent. The balance was struck in favor of the state; the rationale for this conclusion being implicit in the Court's characterization of the competing values:

> [W]e regard the State's interest in having lawyers who are devoted to the law in its broadest sense, including not only its substantive provisions, but also its procedures for orderly change, as clearly sufficient to outweigh the minimal effect upon free association occasioned by compulsory disclosure in the circumstances here presented. [13]

Nor did the petitioner's voluntary disclosure of his general beliefs and associations moot the issue or make the question irrelevant, for the Committee is entitled to conduct its investigation in the manner it deems best suited to its purposes. Thus, although a de-

---

9. 353 U.S. 252 (1957) (Frankfurter, Harlan and Clark, JJ., dissented).

10. Id. at 273–74.

11. Konigsberg v. State Bar of California, 366 U.S. 36 (1961) (Konigsberg II).

12. 357 U.S. 513 (1958).

13. 366 U.S. at 52.

nial of admission to the bar may not be premised on arbitrary or irrelevant information, there exists no privilege to refuse to provide legitimate information and denial of the application to practice is an appropriate device to prevent such frustrations of the investigative purpose.[14]

Justice Black, in dissent, wrote one of his most celebrated attacks upon the theory of "balancing" in the first amendment area. Although he disagreed with the majority's characterization of this scheme as an "incidental" abridgement of speech,[15] the brunt of his attack was focused upon his philosophical antipathy towards balancing.

> I fear that the creation of "tests" by which speech is left unprotected under certain circumstances is a standing invitation to abridge it . . . The Court suggests that a "literal reading of the First Amendment" would be totally unreasonable because it would invalidate many widely accepted laws . . . it certainly would invalidate all laws that abridge the right of the people to discuss matters of religious or public interest, in the broadest meaning of those terms, for it is clear that a desire to protect this right was the primary purpose of the First Amendment.[16]

Balancing, in his view, is inherently dangerous and wholly lacking in judicial integrity because ". . . the application of such a test is necessarily tied to the emphasis particular judges give to competing societal values."[17] As if to illustrate this dictum, he stated that the appropriate characterization of these values would give emphasis to the social value of maintaining unimpaired freedoms of association and belief over a bar committee's curiosity concerning the applicant's possible membership in the Communist Party.

The validity of *Konigsberg II* was reemphasized and amplified by a trio of cases decided by the Court in 1971. The primary case, *Law Students Civil Rights Research*

Council, Inc. v. Wadmond,[18] involved an attack upon the manner in which New York screened its applicants for the bar. The appellants had challenged, inter alia, that the appellees' use of a questionnaire, which bifurcated inquiry between knowing membership and membership with intent to further illegal goals, unnecessarily intruded into rights of association by requiring applicants to divulge knowing membership although there could be no inference of disloyalty based on such information. The Court, however, held that it was within reasonable legislative boundaries to inquire into knowing membership as a preliminary inquiry upon which to base further investigation.

Thus, an applicant to the bar may be required to answer a question concerning only his knowing membership on pain of denial of certification. If the applicant responds affirmatively, the examiners may probe more deeply into the nature of that association to determine if it is appropriate to deny admission. Judicial review is available to remedy any abuses resulting from solely an admission of knowing membership. Moreover, the Court found that there was no constitutional infirmity in inquiring into the applicant's ability to take the oath required of attorneys without any mental reservations,[19] as such inquiry is incorporated into the federal oath for uniformed and civil service personnel.

In the two accompanying decisions also handed down in 1971, *Baird v. State Bar of Arizona*[20] and *In re Stolar*,[21] the Court reaffirmed the rationale of *Wadmond* by invalidating denials of admission to the bar based on the petitioners' refusal to answer questions which were not limited to ascertaining "knowing" membership. As the questions were overbroad and beyond the legitimate interest of the State in the affilia-

---

14. See also In re Anastapolo, 366 U.S. 82 (1961).

15. 366 U.S. at 71 (Black, J., dissenting joined by Warren, C.J., and Douglas, J.).

16. 366 U.S. at 63–64 (Black, J., dissenting).

17. Id. at 75.

18. 401 U.S. 154 (1971). (Justices Black, Douglas, Brennan and Marshall dissented).

19. See also In re Summers, 325 U.S. 561 (1945).

20. 401 U.S. 1 (1971).

21. 401 U.S. 23 (1971).

tions of its attorneys, the sanction of denial of admission to the bar was improper.

Thus, at present, the first amendment does not provide an unlimited sanctuary for a bar applicant who does not desire to disclose his political affiliations. The state has an interest in informing itself of the philosophical context of the bar, particularly since it has the burden of establishing affirmative evidence of disloyalty. Frustration of a legitimate inquiry is subject to a denial of application for membership in the bar. However, the state's interest does not extend beyond interrogation concerning knowing membership, and a question beyond that permissible spectrum may be refused without penalty.

XIII. REGULATION OF THE TIME, PLACE, AND MANNER OF SPEECH IN PUBLIC PLACES AND THE PUBLIC FORUM

A. Introduction

Justice Roberts, in his concurring opinion in *Hague v. CIO*,[1] expressed a narrow view of the Government's power to control speech that takes place on public property: "Wherever the title of streets and parks may rest, they have immemorially been held in trust for the use of the public and, time out of mind, have been used for purposes of assembly, communicating thoughts between citizens, and discussing public questions."[2] Yet other justices have inserted language in later opinions which treats public property as if it were private property for free speech purposes. Thus Justice Black, who had con-

curred with Roberts, later stated that he did not think the first and fourteenth amendments granted "a constitutional right to engage in the conduct of picketing or patrolling, whether on publicly owned streets or on privately owned property."[3] Justice Black's position, if taken literally, is an echo of Justice Holmes' view when he was a state court judge: "For the Legislature absolutely or conditionally to forbid public speaking in a highway or public park is no more an infringement of the rights of a member of the public than for the owner of a private house to forbid it in his house."[4]

One's judgments between these competing viewpoints should be a function of how one weighs the interests at stake, that is, "the right to disseminate ideas in public places as against claims of an effective power in government to keep the peace and to protect other interests of a civilized community."[5] To this balance some would add claims of a special right of access by the public to commandeer such public places so that they can become a Public Forum.[6] We shall examine some of the leading cases in this area in order to illustrate the major rules which have developed.[7]

B. Licensing Schemes Implemented by Administrators and Injunctions Issued by the Courts

Often the state seeks to exercise time, place, or manner restrictions on speech in public places by use of licensing schemes. Justice Frankfurter has warned that the administrator's "net of control must not be

---

1. 307 U.S. 496 (1939).

2. 307 U.S. 496, 515 (1939) (Roberts, J., concurring, joined by Black, J.). Note that subsequently Justice Black appeared to retreat from this narrow view. E.g., Cox v. Louisiana, 379 U.S. 559, 578 (1965) (Black, J., concurring and dissenting in part); Adderly v. Florida, 385 U.S. 39, 47–48 (1966) (Black, J.).

3. Cox v. Louisiana, 379 U.S. 559, 578 (1965) (Black, J. concurring and dissenting in part).

4. Commonwealth v. Davis, 162 Mass. 510, 511 (1895), aff'd sub nom., Davis v. Massachusetts, 167 U.S. 43 (1897).

5. Niemotko v. Maryland, 340 U.S. 268, 273–274 (1951) (Frankfurter, J., concurring).

6. See Kalven, The Concept of the Public Forum: Cox v. Louisiana, 1965 S.Ct.Rev. 1.

7. Other commentators have taken broader or narrower views of the concept of the "Public Forum." For a broad view, see vol. I of N. Dorsen, P. Bender, & B. Neuborne, Political and Civil Rights in the United States, 236–302 (4th ed. 1976) which includes within the topic of the Public Forum other questions, such as advocacy of criminal activity and picketing in private shopping centers, all considered elsewhere in this book.

cast too broadly." [8] Thus, a "licensing standard which gives an official authority to censor the content of a speech differs *toto caelo* from one limited by its terms, or by nondiscriminatory practice, to considerations of public safety and the like." [9] This rule may be illustrated by briefly reviewing some of the important cases.

In *Lovell v. Griffin*,[10] a member of the Jehovah's Witnesses [11] was prosecuted for disobeying a city ordinance which forbade the distribution of circulars, advertising matter, and similar material unless one secured a permit from the city manager. The city argued that its sanitary and litter problems made "apparent" the reasons for the ordinance.[12]

In *Lovell* the defendant was convicted for distributing religious tracts. Since she had not secured a license nor even applied for it, the city argued that in such a case she was not in the "position of having suffered from the exercise of the arbitrary and unlimited power of which she complains." [13] If she had applied and then been denied, the city argued, then she would have suffered loss of constitutional right; in other words, only then would she have standing to complain. The Supreme Court, in a unanimous opinion, was unpersuaded. The vague ordinance—

which prohibited the distribution of literature of any kind under every sort of circulation, at any time, at any place, and in any manner, without a permit from the City Manager—was held to be invalid on its face, as a prior restraint of free speech.[14] Since the ordinance was void on its face, it was not necessary for the defendant to apply for a permit under it before she could contest it.

Other decisions, when faced with similar fact situations, have followed this basic principle.[15] As the Court articulated most clearly in *Thornhill v. Alabama:* [16] "One who might have had a license for the asking may therefore call into question the whole scheme of licensing when he is prosecuted for failure to procure it." [17]

To be distinguished from the *Lovell* case and its progeny is the line of cases illustrated by *Poulos v. New Hampshire*,[18] another Jehovah's Witness case. In *Poulos* the defendant was convicted for conducting a religious service in a public park without a proper license. Unlike *Lovell*, the defendant did apply for the license. He was denied the license and did not appeal that denial in the state court system. And, one would think it equally important, his defense in the criminal charge was not that the licensing statute was so vague or overbroad as to be void on

---

8. Niemotko v. Maryland, 340 U.S. 268, 282 (1951) (concurring).

9. Id.

10. 303 U.S. 444 (1938).

11. In the approximately three decades following *Lovell*, there were more than thirty cases in the Supreme Court raising issues of the regulation of speech in the public forum. A large majority of these cases involved the Jehovah's Witnesses. Kalven, The Concept of the Public Forum: Cox v. Louisiana, 1965 S.Ct. Rev. 1 n. 2.

12. 303 U.S. at 445 (argument for appellee).

13. Id. at 446.

14. Id. at 451.

15. E.g., Thornhill v. Alabama, 310 U.S. 88 (1940); Cantwell v. Connecticut, 310 U.S. 296, 304–305 (1940); Thomas v. Collins, 323 U.S. 516 (1945); Niemotko v. Maryland, 340 U.S. 268 (1951); Kunz v. New York, 340 U.S. 290 (1951); Staub v. Baxley, 355 U.S. 313 (1958); Shuttlesworth v. Birmingham, 394 U.S. 147 (1969).

16. Thornhill v. Alabama, 310 U.S. 88 (1940).

17. 310 U.S. at 97. In *Thornhill* the Court also held, inter alia, "the dissemination of information concerning the facts of a labor dispute must be regarded as within that area of free discussion that is guaranteed by the Constitution." 310 U.S. at 102. But the modern view does not grant full first amendment protection to all forms of peaceful labor picketing. Thus, "a State, in enforcing some public policy, whether of its criminal or its civil law, and whether announced by its legislature or its courts, could constitutionally enjoin peaceful picketing aimed at preventing effectuation of that policy." International Brotherhood of Teamsters v. Vogt, Inc., 354 U.S. 284, 293 (1957). See also, e.g., Giboney v. Empire Storage & Ice Co., 336 U.S. 490 (1949) (state court injunction of peaceful labor picketing upheld where state court found purpose of violating state statute forbidding agreements in restraint of trade); Local Union No. 10, United Ass'n of Journeymen Plumbers & Steamfitters v. Graham, 345 U.S. 192 (1952) (injunction against peaceful labor picketing upheld where picketing carried on for purposes in conflict with state statute). But cf. Youngdahl v. Rainfair, Inc., 355 U.S. 131, 139–140 (1957).

18. 345 U.S. 395 (1953).

its face but rather that the City Council arbitrarily and unreasonably refused his application for a license.

The state trial court held that, on its face, the ordinance in question was constitutional, as a reasonable restriction of the time, place, and manner of speech in public places.[19] The court also found that the refusal of the City Counsel to grant the requested license was arbitrary and unreasonable, but it nonetheless upheld the criminal prosecution, and the state supreme court affirmed because, since "the ordinance was valid on its face the state court determined the [defendant's] remedy was by certiorari to review the unlawful refusal of the [city] Council to grant the license, not by holding public religious services in the park without a license, and then defending because the refusal of the license was arbitrary."[20]

The Supreme Court affirmed, with Justice Frankfurter concurring in the result and only Justices Black and Douglas dissenting. First, the Supreme Court majority found that the licensing statute, as construed by the state court to require uniform, nondiscriminatory, and consistent treatment of the granting of licenses for public meetings on public streets and parks, was constitutional on its face.[21] The Supreme Court found it provided only a ministerial role for the police.[22]

Secondly, the defendant could be convicted for holding his religious meeting without a license, even though it had wrongly been denied to him by the city. The Court recognized that:

It must be admitted that judicial correction of arbitrary refusal by administrators to perform official duties under valid laws is exulcerating and costly. But to allow applicants to proceed without the required permits to . . . hold public meetings without prior

safety arrangements or take other unauthorized action is apt to cause breaches of the peace or create public dangers. . . . Delay is unfortunate, but the expense and annoyance of litigation is a price citizens must pay for life in an orderly society where the rights of the First Amendment have a real and abiding meaning.[23]

There are some exceptions to the *Poulos* rule regarding the failure to obtain a license where the relevant licensing statute is not void on its face. The *Poulos* majority noted that a state may always, if it chooses, make an unlawful refusal a defense to a licensing statute.[24] But it also said that if the statute is valid on its face, a defense of failure to apply for a license on the ground that such application would be unavailing is not allowed.[25]

Justice Frankfurter's concurrence explained that nothing in the record even suggested that the judicial remedy in the state court that Poulos must utilize was a procedural pretense or even would effectively frustrate by delay his right to speech. Poulos did not show the unavailability of a prompt judicial remedy, particularly given the fact that Poulos was denied his license on May 4 for meetings that were not to be held until June 25 and July 2.[26] If there were no prompt judicial remedy in the state court system, *Poulos* should probably have come out differently.

Finally, we must remember that the *Poulos* Court upheld the statute as construed by the state court. This power of a state court to save the constitutionality of one of the state's statutes by narrow interpretation has some limits, for it can deprive a litigant of fair warning if a statute that appears void on its face is later upheld in the very case in which the litigant is protesting its application. Therefore, even though the state court

---

19. The state trial court relied on the reasoning and holding of an earlier U. S. Supreme Court decision upholding the constitutionality of another section of the same New Hampshire statute. Cox v. New Hampshire, 312 U.S. 569 (1941). See 345 U.S. at 399–400.

20. 345 U.S. at 400.

21. 345 U.S. at 402–403.

22. 345 U.S. at 403, 404.

23. 345 U.S. at 409.

24. 345 U.S. at 409 n. 13.

25. 345 U.S. at 410 n. 13.

26. 345 U.S. at 420 (Frankfurter, J., concurring).

may authoritatively construe a statute for its future application, when the interpretation is "a remarkable job of plastic surgery"[27] and it would have taken "extraordinary clairvoyance"[28] to anticipate the decision,[28] a conviction under the statute, when one could not know its limited construction, could not stand.

To be distinguished from the *Lovell* and *Poulos* line of cases, where the application for the license is made to an administrator, is the fact situation when the speaker is prevented from speaking, not by the denial of a license, but by a court injunction or temporary restraining order. The basic rule now appears to be that, although one may collaterally attack a licensing ordinance that is invalid on its face, under the doctrine of *Lovell v. Griffin*,[29] one may not disregard a court injunction or temporary restraining order that is equally void on its face in the hope of having the injunction overturned in a later proceeding. The proper procedure is a direct appeal and therefore the individual may be barred in a collateral proceeding from contesting the validity of the injunction, if he is prosecuted for violating it.[30]

In *Walker v. Birmingham*[31] the Court upheld the contempt of court convictions of Martin Luther King Jr. and other black ministers who participated in civil rights marches and parades in violation of an *ex parte* temporary injunction issued by a state circuit court.[32] The Supreme Court found that the state court had jurisdiction over the petitioners and over the subject matter of the controversy. Moreover the injunction was not "transparently invalid" nor did it have "only a frivolous pretense to validity."[33] The majority did not define those terms, but it should be understood that it would be the most atypical injunctive order that could probably meet this test, for the *Walker* order, as the majority admitted, was written in terms of such "breadth and vagueness" as to "unquestionably" raise a "substantial constitutional question."[34] In fact, two terms later, the Supreme Court held that marchers in the same events involved in *Walker* did not have to comply with the same Birmingham licensing ordinance, because it was invalid on its face and could not be saved even by judicial construction applied to the parties before the state court.[35] Thus, an *ex parte* court order is not "transparently invalid" simply because it "recites the words of the invalid statute."[36]

The majority was concerned that the petitioners did not even attempt to appeal within the Alabama court system the lower court's order. The proper procedure was to apply to the Alabama courts to have the injunction modified or dissolved.[37] If petitioners had done so and had been met with delay or frustration of their constitutional claims the case "would arise in quite a different constitutional posture."[38] Finally, the majority concluded:

This Court cannot hold that the petitioners were constitutionally free to ignore all the pro-

---

27. Shuttlesworth v. Birmingham, 394 U.S. 147, 153 (1969).

28. 394 U.S. 147, 156 (1969).

29. 303 U.S. 444 (1938).

30. Compare Walker v. Birmingham, 388 U.S. 307 (1967), with Shuttlesworth v. Birmingham, 394 U.S. 147 (1969).

31. 388 U.S. 307 (1967).

32. Petitioners were each sentenced to five days in jail and $50 fine. 388 U.S. at 312.

33. 388 U.S. at 315.

34. 388 U.S. at 317. The order was reprinted in 388 U.S. at 321–322.

35. Shuttlesworth v. Birmingham, 394 U.S. 147 (1969). The Court noted that: "a person faced with such an unconstitutional licensing law may ignore it,

and engage with impunity in the exercise of the right of free expression for which the law purports to require a license." 394 U.S. at 151 (footnote omitted). The Court also acknowledged that the "petitioner here was one of the petitioners in the *Walker* case. . . . " 394 U.S. at 157.

36. Walker v. Birmingham, 388 U.S. 307, 346 (1967) (Brennan, J., dissenting, joined by Warren, C. J., and Douglas and Fortas, JJ.).

37. 388 U.S. at 317.

38. 388 U.S. at 318. Cf. National Socialist Party v. Village of Skokie, 432 U.S. 43 (1977) (per curiam).

See also, National Socialist Party v. Village of Skokie, 434 U.S. 1327 (1977) (Stevens, Circuit Justice) (refusing to allow a stay of lower court injunction of march of Nazi group where there was no showing that the state supreme court would not review the decision

cedures of the law and carry their battle to the streets. One may sympathize with the petitioners' impatient commitment to their cause. But respect for judicial process is a small price to pay for the civilizing hand of law, which alone can give abiding meaning to constitutional freedom.[39]

Chief Justice Warren, Justices Douglas, Brennan, and Fortas all dissented vigorously.[40] As Chief Justice Warren argued in his dissent, the petitioners should be treated as persons who challenge the constitutionality of a statute and then defend themselves on the grounds that the statute is unconstitutional. "It has never been thought that violation of a statute indicated such a disrespect for the legislature that the violator always must be punished even if the statute was unconstitutional." [41]

Several years later the Supreme Court held unconstitutional the *ex parte* procedure in free speech cases such as *Walker*, where officials obtain an *ex parte* court order restraining the holding of meetings or rallies. An order in such cases is defective if it is issued *ex parte*, without notice to the subjects of the order, and without any effort, even an informal one, to invite or permit their participation, unless a showing is made that it is impossible to serve or to notify the opposing parties and give them an opportunity to respond.[42] In the case in which this holding was announced the petitioners obeyed the order and then appealed it rather

than disobeying it and attacking it collaterally; thus the *Walker* rule did not apply.

C. Reasonable Time, Place, and Manner Restrictions on Speech, Without Regard to Content

1. Introduction

In general it may be said that the state may place reasonable time, place, or manner restrictions on speech that takes place in the public forum, but these regulations must be implemented without regard to the content of the speech.[43] Otherwise the state can cloak restrictions on speech itself in the guise of regulations of the mode of speech or the place—the streets, the parks, public buildings—which is used for the speech. To prevent abuse of the power to exercise such reasonable regulations, and to help assure that the regulations are in fact reasonable, the Court will independently determine if the regulation is a narrow means of protecting important interests unrelated to content.

2. Regulation of Sound and Noise

Thus, in *Saia v. New York* [44] the Court, in a 5–4 decision, invalidated a city ordinance which forbade the use of sound amplification devices such as loudspeakers on trucks, except with permission of the Chief of Police. The ordinance was unconstitutional on its face because of the uncontrolled discretion of the Chief of Police. The abuses of loudspeakers can be controlled, the majority agreed, if the control is pursuant to a nar-

---

promptly); Collin & Nat. Socialist Party v. Smith, 578 F.2d 1197 (7th Cir. 1978), cert. denied 439 U.S. 916 (1978) (holding unconstitutional village ordinances designed to stop the same march by the Nazi group).

39. 388 U.S. at 321.

40. 388 U.S. at 324–349.

41. 388 U.S. at 327 (Warren, C. J., dissenting, joined by Brennan and Fortas, JJ.).

42. Carroll v. President and Comm'rs of Princess Anne, 393 U.S. 175 (1968); cf. A Quantity of Books v. Kansas, 378 U.S. 205 (1964).

43. E.g., Madison School District v. Wisconsin Employment Relations Comm'n, 429 U.S. 167, 176 (1976) ("when the board sits in public meetings to conduct public business and hear the views of citizens, it may not be required to discriminate between speakers on the basis of their employment, or the content of their

speech."); Linmark Associates, Inc. v. Township of Willingboro, 431 U.S. 85 (1977) (ordinance banning "for sale" and "sold" signs for the purpose of stemming the flight of white homeowners from racially integrated town invalidated; ordinance concerned with content of speech).

But cf. Young v. American Mini Theatres, 427 U.S. 50 (1976) (zoning of "adult" theatres upheld); FCC v. Pacifica Foundation, 438 U.S. 726 (1978) (FCC may regulate radio broadcast which is "indecent" but not "obscene"). See also, Farber, Content Regulation and the First Amendment: A Revisionist View, 68 Georgetown L.J. 727 (1980); Redish, The Content Distinction in First Amendment Analysis, 34 Stan.L.Rev. 113 (1981). See generally, Stephan, The First Amendment and Content Discrimination, 68 Va.L.Rev. 203 (1982).

44. 334 U.S. 558 (1948).

rowly-drawn statute.[45] In *Kovacs v. Cooper*[46] the Court upheld such a statute, though the fragmented Court could not agree on the reasons.[47] Justice Reed's opinion found the city ordinance of Trenton, New Jersey in *Kovacs* not overbroad nor vague. It prohibited sound trucks and similar devices from emitting "loud and raucous noises." These words were found not to be too vague. Moreover the New Jersey courts by construction had narrowed the ordinance's applicability only to vehicles containing a sound amplifier or any other instrument emitting loud and raucous noises, when operated or standing in the public streets, alleys or thoroughfares of the city.[48] Justice Reed added that just as unrestrained use of all sound amplifying devices in a city would be intolerable, "[a]bsolute prohibition within municipal limits of all sound amplification, even though reasonably regulated in place, time and volume, is undesirable and probably unconstitutional as an unreasonable interference with normal activities."[49]

Somewhat related is the class of cases in which recipients of information claim a right not to hear a message. A leading case in this area is *Public Utilities Commission v. Pollak*,[50] where the majority found no deprivation of either the first or fifth amendment because a city-regulated bus company broadcast FM music, news, and commercials to buses and streetcars, in return for money payments.[51] The Court refused to upset the ruling of the Public Utilities Commission allowing the practice.[52] *Pollak*, however, does not forbid the state from deciding to protect those who do not wish to be recipients. Thus, it is constitutional for a statute to provide that any addressee of mail may request the post office to prohibit all future mailings from any particular sender. The law was upheld because the government made no decision on the basis of the content of the speech but only allowed the addressee to act in his sole discretion.[53] Without a request by the addressee, the post office could not require the addressee to have the burden to request certain mail. Such a statute would "chill" the addressee by requiring him to request mailings which the Government determined that he not receive. Also, less drastic means of protecting recipients are available, for the law could place the burden on the un-

45. 334 U.S. at 562.

46. 336 U.S. 77 (1949).

47. Justice Reed announced the judgment of the Court, in an opinion by Vinson, C. J., and Burton, J.; Murphy, J. dissented without opinion. Frankfurter, J. concurred. Jackson, J. also concurred, but in a separate opinion. Black, J., dissented in an opinion joined by Douglas and Rutledge, JJ. Rutledge, J., also wrote a separate dissent.

48. 336 U.S. at 83 (opinion of Reed, J.).

49. 336 U.S. at 81–82 (opinion of Reed, J.). Examples of more recent loudspeaker cases include Phillips v. Township of Darby, 305 F.Supp. 763 (E.D.Pa.1969); Phillips v. Borough of Folcroft, 305 F.Supp. 766 (E.D. Pa.1969); Maldonado v. County of Monterey, 330 F.Supp. 1282 (N.D.Cal.1971). See also Grayned v. Rockford, 408 U.S. 104, 107–121 (1972) (antinoise ordinance prohibiting a person while on grounds adjacent to a building in which school is in session from making a noise or diversion that disturbs the peace and good order of the school session is not unconstitutionally vague or overbroad).

50. 343 U.S. 451 (1952). See generally, Black, He Cannot Choose But Hear: The Plight of the Captive Auditor, 53 Colum.L.Rev. 960 (1953).

51. The majority was "assuming that the action of Capital Transit in operating the radio service, together with the action of the Commission in permitting such operation, amounts to sufficient Federal Government action to make the First and Fifth Amendments applicable thereto." 343 U.S. at 462–463.

52. Justice Black issued a separate opinion dissenting insofar as the majority allowed the passengers of Capital Transit to be subjected to news, public speeches, views, or propaganda of any kind. He would only allow musical programs. Douglas also dissented in a separate opinion. And Justice Frankfurter disqualified himself for the following reasons:

"My feelings are so strongly engaged as a victim of the practice in controversy that I had better not participate in judicial judgment upon it. I am explicit as to the reasons for my non-participation in this case because I have for some time been of the view that it is desirable to state why one takes himself out of a case." (343 U.S. at 467).

53. Rowan v. Post Office Dept., 397 U.S. 728 (1970). Cf. United States v. Ramsey, 431 U.S. 606 (1977) (border searches of foreign mail upheld over fourth amendment and first amendment objections; the letters were not read and there was no "chill".)

willing addressees to request that certain types of mail not be delivered.[54]

Similarly, a city may protect householders from unwanted solicitors knocking on their doors, but the means selected must not be unreasonably harsh: thus, a city ordinance may prohibit the business practice of soliciting magazine subscriptions door-to-door without prior invitation of the homeowner.[55] The balance of interests was struck differently, however, in *Martin v. Struthers*,[56] where the Court was confronted with a far broader ordinance. There the city of Struthers enacted an ordinance which forbade any person to knock on doors, ring doorbells, or otherwise summon any residents to the door for the purpose of receiving handbills or other distributions. The Court was particularly concerned that the *Struthers* ordinance made one a criminal trespasser if he entered the property of another for an innocent purpose and without an explicit command from the owners to stay away.[57] Moreover the Court was aware that door to door distribution of circulars is "essential to the poorly financed causes of little people." [58] The defendant in *Struthers* was a Jehovah's Witness who sought to distribute to households a leaflet advertising a religious meeting. Thus:

> A city can punish those who call at a home in defiance of the previously expressed will of the occupant and, in addition, can by identification devices control the abuse of the privilege by criminals posing as canvassers. . . . [W]e conclude that the [*Struthers*] ordinance is invalid because in conflict with the freedom of speech and press.[59]

Under analogous reasoning, a city cannot forbid all leaflet distribution in order to prevent littering, fraud, or disorder, since the state can less drastically prohibit only the actual littering, fraud, or disorder.[60]

3. Where the Speech Takes Place: The Degrees of Public Forum

The substantive rules for public demonstrations and other such speech activities in the public forum are in part a function of where the speech takes place.[61] In *Police Department of Chicago v. Mosley*[62] the Court considered the constitutionality of a city ordinance that prohibited picketing on a public way within 150 feet of a grade or high school from one-half hour before the school was in session until one-half hour after the school session had been concluded. Exempted from this prohibition was peaceful labor picketing. The ordinance was invalidated. While it purported to regulate the time, place, and manner of speech activities in the public forum, it did so with regard to the content of the speech, and that content regulation was the fatal flaw in the ordinance:

> The central problem with Chicago's ordinance is that it describes permissible picketing in terms of its subject matter. Peaceful picketing on the subject of a school's labor-management dispute is permitted, but all other peaceful picketing is prohibited. The operative distinction is the message on a picket sign. But, above all else, the First Amendment means that government has no power to restrict expression because of its message, its ideas, its subject matter, or its content. . . .

> Necessarily, then, under the Equal Protection Clause, not to mention the First Amendment it-

---

54. Lamont v. Postmaster General, 381 U.S. 301 (1956).

55. Breard v. Alexandria, 341 U.S. 622 (1951). The Court specifically relied on the commercial nature of the transactions in question. One should compare this case with the modern view of the commercial speech doctrine. See Section IX of this Chapter.

56. 319 U.S. 141 (1943).

57. 319 U.S. at 148.

58. 319 U.S. at 146.

59. 319 U.S. at 148–49 (footnote omitted).

60. Schneider v. Irvington, 308 U.S. 147 (1939).

61. Cf. Niemotko v. Maryland, 340 U.S. 268, 282–283 (1951) (Frankfurter, J., concurring):

> "Where does the speaking which is regulated take place? Not only the general classifications—streets, parks, private buildings—are relevant. The location and size of a park; its customary use for the recreational, esthetic and contemplative needs of a community; the facilities, other than a park or street corner, readily available in a community for airing views, are all pertinent considerations in assessing the limitations [of] the Fourteenth Amendment. . . . "

62. 408 U.S. 92 (1972).

self, government may not grant the use of a forum to people whose views it finds acceptable, but deny use to those wishing to express less favored or more controversial views. . . . Once a forum is opened up to assembly or speaking by some groups, government may not prohibit others from assembling or speaking on the basis of what they intend to say.[63]

In *Cary v. Brown* [64] the Court invalidated an Illinois statute which prohibited all picketing of residences or dwellings except for the peaceful picketing of a place of employment involved in a labor dispute. The majority relied on the earlier analysis in *Mosley* and concluded that the residential picketing statute accorded preferential treatment to the expression of views on one particular subject and thus allowed only certain types of residential picketing based on the content of the message. The state cannot ban speech based on its content. The state's goal of protecting privacy may not be advanced in such a constitutionally impermissible manner; nor was the statute narrowly drawn to protect residential privacy in light of the fact it allowed all labor picketing regardless of how disruptive that was. The majority, however, made clear that it was not implying that the first amendment would prohibit an antiresidential picketing statute that was uniform and nondiscriminatory in its regulation.

If a statute is sufficiently narrow in scope, and applied without regard to content, it can apply to remove certain public areas from the public forum. *Adderly v. Florida* [65] illustrates this principle. In *Adderly* 32 students were convicted of a statutory crime of

"trespass with malicious and mischievous intent" on the grounds of a county jail. The students had demonstrated at the jail to protest the earlier arrests of other protesting students and to protest the state's segregated practices, including the policy of racial segregation of the jail. The local sheriff tried to persuade the students to leave and when that failed, he warned them that he would charge them with trespassing.

The Supreme Court affirmed the convictions and distinguished earlier protest cases where the convictions had been reversed.[66] Unlike one of the earlier cases, where the Court reversed the trespass convictions of demonstrators on the state capitol grounds, the *Adderly* demonstrators were on jailhouse grounds. While state capitol grounds are traditionally open to the public, jails, "built for security purposes, are not." [67] Moreover, unlike the breach-of-the-peace statutes involved in the earlier cases the trespass statute in *Adderly* was not unnecessarily vague or overbroad.[68] The majority was apparently not concerned that the state convicted the defendants under the statute which did not apply specifically to jails or even to public property but seemed to be limited to private property.[69] The majority appeared to simply treat jailhouse property as private property.[70]

Adderly stands out as one of the few cases in this period involving demonstrations on public property where the Supreme Court affirmed the conviction. Normally the Supreme Court reversed, sometimes on narrow or unusual grounds.[71]

---

63. 408 U.S. 92, 95–96. Accord Grayned v. Rockford, 408 U.S. 104, 105–107 (1972). See also, Niemotko v. Maryland, 340 U.S. 268 (1951) (Jehovah's Witnesses cannot be denied permit to use a city park for Bible talks when other religious and political groups had been allowed to use the park for similar purposes); Fowler v. Rhode Island, 345 U.S. 67 (1953) (same).

64. 447 U.S. 455 (1980). Rehnquist, J., joined by Burger, C. J., and Blackmun, J., dissented.

65. 385 U.S. 39 (1966).

66. 385 U.S. at 41–42, distinguishing Edwards v. South Carolina, 372 U.S. 229 (1963), and Cox v. Louisiana, 379 U.S. 536 (1965).

67. 385 U.S. at 41.

68. 385 U.S. at 42.

69. The Florida statute spoke of "[e]very trespass upon the property of another . . . ." 385 U.S. at 40 n. 1.

70. Justice Douglas, joined by Chief Justice Warren and Justices Brennan and Fortas. 385 U.S. at 48–56.

71. E.g., Gregory v. Chicago, 394 U.S. 111 (1969) (disorderly conduct conviction reversed; protest to press claim for desegregated schools); Edwards v. South Carolina, 372 U.S. 229 (1963) (breach of the peace conviction reversed; demonstration against racial segregation); Cox v. Louisiana, 379 U.S. 536 (1965) (breach of the peace conviction, obstructing of public passages conviction, and picketing near courthouse

Later, the Supreme Court upheld military regulations of Fort Dix, New Jersey, which banned speeches and demonstrations of a partisan political nature.[72] The Court found, inter alia, that this regulation had been rigidly and neutrally enforced and that civilians were freely permitted to visit unrestricted areas of the military reservation. The Court ruled that federal military reservations are not like municipal streets and parks because only the latter have traditionally served as a public forum; the business of a military installation is to train soldiers, not to provide a public area for debate. The Fort Dix policy of keeping official military activities wholly free of entanglement with any partisan political campaigns was reasonable. Thus, while individual soldiers could attend military political rallies, out of uniform and off-base, "the military as such is insulated from both the reality and the appearance of acting as a handmaiden for partisan political causes or candidates." [73]

The Court also upheld a regulation authorizing the Fort Dix commander to prohibit the distribution of literature that he finds consti-

tutes a clear danger to military loyalty, discipline, or morale; he was not to prohibit distribution of a publication because he does not like it or even because it unfairly criticized the governmental policy or governmental officials. The Court found no evidence the authorities had applied this regulation arbitrarily.

Similarly the Court later upheld Air Force regulations prohibiting members of the service from circulating petitions on Air Force bases unless they first secured the approval of their commanders. A commander could deny permission only if he found that distribution of the material would cause "a clear danger to the loyalty, discipline, or morale of the Air Force, or material interference with the accomplishment of a military mission." The regulations were not invalid on their face.[74]

To be distinguished is the case where a street, technically within the jurisdiction of a military fort, had in fact been treated by the military as a public thoroughfare of the city, with the military abandoning any special interest and any right to exclude civilian vehic-

---

conviction all reversed; demonstration against racial segregation), cf. the anti-racial discrimination "sit-in" cases, e.g. Peterson v. Greenville, 373 U.S. 244 (1963); Lombard v. Louisiana, 373 U.S. 267 (1963); Garner v. Louisiana, 368 U.S. 157, 184 (1961); Bell v. Maryland, 378 U.S. 226 (1969); Hamm v. City of Rock Hill, 379 U.S. 306 (1964).

72. Greer v. Spock, 424 U.S. 828 (1976).

73. 424 U.S. 828 at 839.

74. Brown v. Glines, 444 U.S. 348, & 354 n. 2 (1980).

See also United States Postal Service v. Council of Greenburgh Civic Associations, 453 U.S. 114 (1981), where the Court upheld the constitutionality of 18 U.S. C.A. § 1725 prohibiting the deposit of unstamped "mailable matter" in a letter box approved by the U. S. Postal Service, although the appellees had argued that the law violated the first amendment. The Postal Service justified the law as protecting mail revenues; facilitating the efficient and secure delivery of mail; preventing overcrowding of the mailboxes; and promoting the privacy of mail patrons. Testimony also showed that the statute aided in the investigation of mail theft by restricting access to mailboxes, thus allowing postal inspectors to assume that anyone who opens a mailbox other than a mailman or householder may be engaged in a violation of law. About 10% of the arrests made under the external theft statute resulted from surveillance operations aided by the enforcement of 18 U.S. C.A. § 1725.

The Court majority reasoned that mailboxes, unlike streets or parks, are not public forums but more like prisons, as in Adderly v. Florida, 385 U.S. 39 (1960). Nor does section 1725 regulate speech on the basis of content.

Brennan, J., concurred in the judgment, concluding that a mailbox is a public forum but that § 1725 was a reasonable time, place, and manner regulation that was content neutral and the burden on expression advanced a significant governmental interest: preventing loss of mail revenue. White, J., also concurred in the judgment, relying on the Government's interest in defraying its operating expenses: "stuffing the mailbox with unstamped materials is a burden on the system."

Marshall, J., dissenting, argued that mailboxes are public forums. Stevens, J., also dissenting, did not accept the public forum argument but concluded that the Government's justifications for § 1725 were inadequate and less restrictive alternatives would meet its interests. For example, the Government could require that if the homeowner opted to receive unstamped mail in his mailbox, an overstuffed box must be replaced with a larger one.

See also, Consolidated Edison Co. of New York, Inc. v. Public Service Comm'n, 447 U.S. 530 (1980) (Public Service Commission order banning public utilities from inserting in monthly electric bills inserts discussing controversial issues of policy constitutes invalid attempt to regulate speech based on content).

ular and foot traffic. The military authorities could not then order a person to leave the public street because he was distributing leaflets any more than a city policeman could order someone off a city street.[75]

The Supreme Court made the first major effort to classify the types of public forums involved in the previous cases in *Perry Educational Ass'n v. Perry Local Educators' Ass'n*.[76] In that case a teachers' union, the Perry Education Association (PEA), was the duly elected exclusive bargaining representative of the teachers in a certain school district. A collective bargaining agreement granted this union, and no other union, the right to access to the interschool mail system and teacher mailboxes in that school system. The rival union, the Perry Local Educators' Association (PLEA), sought similar access. In a five to four opinion the Supreme Court, in an opinion by Justice White, found that the school's denial of access to the rival union of the mailboxes and interschool mail system was no violation of free speech.

Of significance is the majority's reasoning. The Court first recognized that there were degrees of public forums. Along the spectrum, three major distinctions exist:

> In places which by long tradition or by government fiat have been devoted to assembly and debate, the rights of the state to limit expressive activity are sharply circumscribed. At one end of the spectrum are streets and parks which "have immemorially been held in trust for the use of the public, and, time out of mind, have been used for purposes of assembly, communicating thoughts between citizens, and discussing public questions." In these quintessential public forums, the government may not prohibit all communicative activity. For the state to enforce a content-based exclusion it must show that its regulation is necessary to serve a compelling state interest and that it is narrowly drawn to achieve that end. The state may also enforce regulations of the time,

place, and manner of expression which are content-neutral, are narrowly tailored to serve a significant government interest, and leave open ample alternative channels of communication.[77]

The restrictions on residential picketing on the public streets—which the Court invalidated in *Carey v. Brown*[78]—fall in this first category, where the Court is most likely to invalidate regulation.

The Court then turned to the second category:

> A second category consists of public property which the state has opened for use by the public as a place for expressive activity. The Constitution forbids a state to enforce certain exclusions from a forum generally open to the public even if it was not required to create the forum in the first place. Although a state is not required to indefinitely retain the open character of the facility, as long as it does so it is bound by the same standards as apply in a traditional public forum. Reasonable time, place and manner regulations are permissible, and a content-based prohibition must be narrowly drawn to effectuate a compelling state interest.[79]

Thus in *Widmar v. Vincent*[80] a state university made its facilities generally available for the activities of registered student groups. Having done so, it could not discriminate among those groups on the basis of content without a compelling justification. In that case the Court therefore held that the state university could not close its facilities to a registered student group desiring to use its facilities for religious worship and discussion. Since the university created the forum, it had to justify its discriminations and exclusions.

Finally the Court turned to the third category:

> Public property which is not by tradition or designation a forum for public communication is governed by different standards. We have recognized that the "First Amendment does not guarantee access to property simply be-

---

75. Flower v. United States, 407 U.S. 197, 198 (1972) (per curiam).

76. 103 S.Ct. 948 (1983).

77. 103 S.Ct. at 954–55 (internal citations omitted without indication).

78. 447 U.S. 455 (1980). See text at n. 64, supra.

79. 103 S.Ct. at 955 (internal citations omitted without indication).

80. 454 U.S. 263 (1981).

cause it is owned or controlled by the government." In addition to time, place, and manner regulations, the state *may reserve the forum for its intended purposes, communicative or otherwise, as long as the regulation on speech is reasonable* and not an effort to suppress expression merely because public officials oppose the speaker's view. As we have stated on several occasions, "the State, no less than a private owner of property, has power to preserve the property under its control for the use to which it is lawfully dedicated." [81]

A few years earlier the Supreme Court had held that a U.S. mailbox was not a public forum, and that therefore it was constitutional to prohibit the deposit of unstamped, "mailable matter" in a mailbox approved by the U.S. Postal Service.[82] Now the Court ruled that the school mail facilities also fell in this third class.

Obviously the school's internal mail system was not a traditional public forum like a street or park. All of the parties agreed that the school board could close its mail system to all but official business. Presumably the board could also simply close down the system entirely.

While the internal mail system was not open to the public generally, the PLEA argued that the school at times allowed private, nonschool groups to use the mail system. Also, prior to the certification of the PEA, the PLEA had unrestricted access. However, the fact that groups like the Cub Scouts and YMCA had access did not convert the mailboxes to a public forum. Such users had to secure permission, which would not be granted to all; the access was selec-

tive. Also, the Court reasoned, even if the permission granted to such groups created a limited public forum, the constitutional right of access would only extend to other entities of similar character.[83] When the school did decide to preclude the PLEA, it did not discriminate against the content of the speech of the PLEA: "We believe it more accurate to characterize the access policy as based on the *status* of the respective unions rather than their views. Implicit in the concept of the nonpublic forum is the right to make distinctions in access on the basis of subject matter and speaker identity."[84]

The PLEA, in short, could say what it wanted and communicate with teachers on school property, post notices on school bulletin boards, and make announcements on the public address system.[85] It simply could not use the mailboxes. The school's policies were quite reasonable in this regard, and consistent with preserving the property for the use to which it was lawfully dedicated. The school allowed the PEA to use the mailboxes, which facilitated its obligations to represent all of the teachers. In contrast, the PLEA had no official responsibility.[86] "[W]hen government property is not dedicated to open communication the government may—without further justification—restrict use to those who participate in the forum's official business." [87]

Two months later the Supreme Court applied the *Perry* analysis and invalidated a portion of a federal statute prohibiting picketing on the public sidewalks surrounding the United States Supreme Court building.[88] The public sidewalks are in the first catego-

---

81. 103 S.Ct. at 955 (emphasis added) (internal citations omitted without indication).

82. United States Postal Serv. v. Council of Greenburgh Civic Associations, 453 U.S. 114 (1981). See n. 74, supra.

83. "While the school mail facilities thus might be a forum generally open for use by the Girl Scouts, the local boys' club and other organizations that engage in activities of interest and educational relevance to students, they would not as a consequence be open to an organization such as PLEA, which is concerned with the terms and conditions of teacher employment." 103 S.Ct. at 956. See also, Greer v. Spock, 424 U.S. 828, 838 n. 10 (1976).

84. 103 S.Ct. at 965 (emphasis in original).

85. 103 S.Ct. at 952.

86. 103 S.Ct. at 958.

87. 103 S.Ct. at 959 (footnote omitted). Brennan, J., joined by Marshall, Powell, and Stevens, JJ., dissented, arguing that the exclusive access provision in the collective bargaining agreement was viewpoint discrimination and violated the first amendment.

88. United States v. Grace, 103 S.Ct. 1702 (1983). Marshall, J., and Stevens, J., each filed separate opinions concurring in part and dissenting in part. However, neither these justices nor any other objected to the majority's reliance on the *Perry* analysis.

ry under *Perry* and the Government could not present the strong justification needed to allow such a restriction on the public forum. There was no evidence, for example, that the picketing obstructed access to the Supreme Court building.

4. *Regulation to Prevent Fraud*

A state statute banning anonymous handbills was struck down as invalid on its face in *Talley v. California*,[1] where the Court recognized that throughout history some persecuted groups have been able to criticize oppressive practices either anonymously or not at all. This right to anonymity is a function of the freedom of association,[2] for identification and the subsequent fear of reprisal could well effectively chill legitimate discussions of public interest. The *Talley* Court specifically did not pass on the validity of an ordinance limited to prevent the evils of identifying those responsible for fraud, false advertising, or libel.[3]

If a city seeks to regulate to prevent fraud, its law must be carefully tailored to achieve this purpose without unduly limiting speech. In *Village of Schaumburg v. Citizens for a Better Environment*[4] the Court invalidated as overbroad a local ordinance which prohibited the solicitation of contributions by charitable organizations which do not use at least 75% of their receipts directly for "charitable purposes," which the law defined as excluding the expenses of solicitation, salaries, overhead, and other administrative expenses.

The Village justified its regulation primarily as a prevention of fraud. It argued that if an organization spends more than one quarter of its fundraising receipts on over-head, it really is engaged in a profit enterprise benefiting itself. But the Court said that this reasoning cannot hold as to those organizations "that are primarily engaged in research, advocacy, or public education and that use their own paid staff to carry out these functions as well as to solicit financial support."[5] The Village could protect its antifraud interests by more narrowly drawn regulations which would directly prohibit fraudulent misrepresentations, or require that charitable organizations inform the public how their moneys are spent. Nor did the law serve to protect privacy since it could hardly be maintained that solicitors covered by the 75 percent rule were somehow more intrusive than solicitors not within the ordinance's prohibition. Since the ordinance did not serve a "strong, subordinating interest that the Village is entitled to protect" and is a "direct and substantial limitation on protected activity" the Court invalidated it under the first and fourteenth amendments.[6]

5. *Zoning Regulations*

In recent years the Court has scrutinized with particular care state zoning laws which have the effect of restricting speech. In addition to *Carey v. Brown*[1], dealing with state restrictions on residential picketing, other cases include *Heffron v. International Society for Krishna Consciousness, Inc.*,[2] governing state "zoning" restrictions on solicitation of donations at a state fair; *Metromedia, Inc. v. City of San Diego*,[3] zoning restrictions on billboards; and *Schad v. Mount Ephraim*,[4] zoning restrictions on live entertainment.

In *Schad*[5] a zoning ordinance banned *all* live entertainment in a commercial zone.

---

1. 362 U.S. 60 (1960).

2. See, e.g., Gibson v. Florida Legislative Committee, 372 U.S. 539 (1962); Louisiana ex rel. Gremillion v. NAACP, 366 U.S. 293 (1961); NAACP v. Alabama, 357 U.S. 449 (1958); Thomas v. Collins, 323 U.S. 516 (1945). Cf. Note, The First Amendment and Law Enforcement Infiltration of Political Groups, 56 So.Calif.L.Rev. 207 (1982).

3. 362 U.S. at 64. See also Section XII of this Chapter on freedom of association.

4. 444 U.S. 620 (1980).

5. 444 U.S. at 639.

6. 444 U.S. at 639. Justice Rehnquist was the sole dissent.

1. 447 U.S. 455 (1980), discussed in text at Section XIII, C, 3, note 64, supra.

2. 452 U.S. 640 (1981).

3. 453 U.S. 490 (1981).

4. 452 U.S. 61 (1981). See also Section XVII, F, 4, infra.

5. Id.

But an adult bookstore operating in the commercial zone wished to introduce a special type of coin operated machine whereby a customer, having inserted a coin, could then watch a live nude dancer performing behind a glass panel. The Court invalidated the ordinance under the first amendment as overbroad. The Borough argued that it was a reasonable time, place and manner restriction, yet it did not "identify the municipal interests making it reasonable to exclude all commercial live entertainment but to allow a variety of other commercial uses in the Borough." [6] The Borough presented no evidence that the manner of expression—live entertainment—is basically incompatible with the normal activities allowed in the commercial zone.

Secondly, "[t]o be reasonable, time, place and manner restrictions not only must serve significant state interests but also leave open adequate alternative channels of communication." The Borough did not leave open alternative channels because it totally banned live entertainment. Unlike *Young v. American Mini Theatres, Inc.*[7] where the Court had upheld a zoning law which had dispersed but not completely banned theatres showing nonobscene "adult films," the zoning law in *Schad* completely excluded live entertainment. The Borough argued that live entertainment, including nude dancing, was available in nearby areas. This "position suggests the argument that if there were countywide zoning, it would be quite legal to allow live entertainment in only selected areas of the county and to exclude it from primarily residential communities, such as the Borough of Mount Ephraim." The Court said that this argument "may well be true" but it was of no help to Mount Ephraim.[8] There was no countywide zoning and, the record did not show that such entertainment was available in reasonably nearby areas.

Finally—and somewhat incongruously, in light of its earlier apparent emphasis that the ordinance should have left open alternative channels of speech—the Court stated: " '[O]ne is not to have the exercise of his liberty of expression in appropriate places abridged on the plea that it may be exercised in some other place.' " [9]

In *Heffron v. International Society for Krishna Consciousness, Inc.*[10] the Court held that a state may require a religious organization which desired to distribute and sell religious literature and to solicit donations at a state fair to do so only at an assigned booth within the fairgrounds. These booths were rented to anyone on a first come, first serve basis. This Minnesota state fair rule applied to all enterprises, whether nonprofit, charitable, or commercial. It also allowed anyone to engage in face to face discussions with fair visitors anywhere on the fairgrounds.

The Krishna Society argued that one of its religious rituals, called "Sankirtan," required its members to distribute and sell religious literature and solicit donations. The Court, however, upheld the rule as reasonable time, place, and manner regulation, not violative of the first and fourteenth amendments. First, the rule was not based on the content or subject matter of the speech. Second, the method of allocating rental space was nondiscriminatory and not open to arbitrary application. Third, the rule served a significant government interest because of the state's special need to maintain the orderly movement of the crowd, given the large number of exhibitors and visitors attending the fair. Unlike a city street which is "continually open, often congested, and constitutes not only a necessary conduit in the daily affairs of a locality's citizens, but also a place where people may enjoy the open air or the company of friends and neighbors in a relaxed environment," a state fair "is a temporary event attracting great

---

6.   452 U.S. at 74–75 (footnote omitted).

7.   427 U.S. 50 (1976).

8.   452 U.S. at 76.

9.   452 U.S. at 76–77 quoting Schneider v. State, 308 U.S. 147, 163 (1939).

10.   452 U.S. 640 (1981).

numbers of visitors who come to the event for a short period to see and experience the host of exhibits and attractions at the fair. The flow of the crowd and demands of safety are more pressing in the context of the fair." [11]

Finally, less restrictive alternatives, such as directly penalizing disorder, and disruption, would probably not work to meet the state's interests because any exemption applied to the Krishna Society would also have to apply to a large number of other groups. These other groups would include religious, social, political, charitable, and perhaps even commercial organizations. The Court stated that none of its previous cases suggest that the Krishna Society and the ritual of Sankirtan have any "special claim to First Amendment protection as compared to that of other religions who also distribute literature and solicit funds . . . but do not purport to ritualize the process. Nor for present purposes do religious organizations enjoy rights to communicate, distribute, and solicit on the fairgrounds superior to those of other organizations having social, political, or other ideological messages to proselytize." [12] A decision favoring the Krishna Society would also raise the question whether commercial organizations have a similar right under the first amendment,[13] a question avoided by the majority's disposition of this case.[14]

The question of the constitutionality of zoning laws restricting billboards severely fragmented the Supreme Court in *Metromedia, Inc. v. City of San Diego*,[15] a case producing five separate opinions.[16] San Die-

go, in an attempt to eliminate the hazards caused by "distracting sign displays" and to "improve the appearance of the City," enacted a comprehensive zoning ordinance prohibiting outdoor display signs, subject to several important restrictions.

These exceptions fell into two main categories. First, the law allowed "on-site signs." On-site signs are those "designating the name of the owner or occupant of the premises upon which such signs are placed, or identifying such premises; or signs advertising goods manufactured or produced or services rendered on the premises upon which such signs are placed." The second category of exemptions were really twelve specified exemptions: "government signs; signs located at public bus stops; signs manufactured, transported or stored within the city, if not used for advertising purposes; commemorative historical plaques; religious symbols; signs within shopping malls; for-sale and for-lease signs; signs on public and commercial vehicles; signs depicting time, temperature, and news; approved temporary, off-premises, subdivision directional signs; and 'temporary political campaign signs.' " [17] Companies in the outdoor advertising business sued, claiming a violation of their first amendment rights in that enforcement of the ordinance would in effect destroy their business.

The plurality opinion of Justice White first turned to the zoning law insofar as it regulated commercial speech and found that portion of the ordinance constitutional.[18] However the plurality was less tolerant of the

---

11. 452 U.S. at 651.

12. 452 U.S. at 652.

13. 452 U.S. at 653: "The question would also inevitably arise as to what extent the First Amendment also gives commercial organizations a right to move among the crowd to distribute information about or to sell their wares as respondents claim they may do."

14. Brennan, J., joined by Marshall and Stevens, JJ., concurred in part and dissented in part. 452 U.S. at 656. They would not allow the state to prohibit the distribution of literature because they did not find the crowd control justification applicable. But they would allow the state to ban the sale of literature and solicitation of funds. Blackmun, J., in a separate opinion, also

concurring in part and dissenting in part, agreed with Justice Brennan's conclusions. 452 U.S. at 663.

15. 453 U.S. 490 (1981).

16. White, J., announced the judgment of the Court and delivered an opinion joined by Stewart, Marshall, and Powell, JJ. Brennan, J., joined by Blackmun, J., concurred in the judgment. 453 U.S. at 521. Stevens, J., Burger, C. J., and Rehnquist, J., each wrote dissenting opinions. 453 U.S. at 540, 555, 569.

17. 453 U.S. at 494–95. See also, 453 U.S. at 495 n. 3.

18. Because the outdoor advertising was concerned with lawful activity and was not misleading, it was pro-

distinctions the city drew as to noncommercial advertising. Because the city allowed on-site commercial advertising it had to allow on-site *non*commercial advertising so that an occupant could display its own ideas or the ideas of others. The noncommercial billboard would not be any more distracting or nonaesthetic than a permitted, on-site commercial billboard.[19] Nor was the ordinance a time, place, or manner restriction because it completely banned on-site noncommercial billboards based on content, i.e., that their content was noncommercial. The plurality then concluded that because the ordinance reached "too far into the realm of protected speech," it was "unconstitutional on its face"; on remand the state court could decide if the unconstitutional portions of the ordinance could be severed from the constitutional parts.[20]

Justice Brennan, joined by Justice Blackmun, concurred in the judgment. However they analyzed the case quite differently; gave much less deference to the legislative judgment; and found the entire ordinance unconstitutional. They reasoned that the practical effect of the ordinance was to ban

totally all billboards and that such a ban was unconstitutional because the city had not provided "adequate justification" for its assertion that billboards actually impair traffic safety in San Diego.[21] Similarly these justices believed that the city's interests in aesthetics was not "sufficiently substantial in the commercial and industrial areas of San Diego," which might already be so blighted that the removal of billboards would have a negligible impact.[22]

The three dissenters all would have upheld the billboard ordinance in its entirety. Justice Stevens would have upheld the ordinance and uphold as constitutional a law entirely banning billboards, but he would not reach the question of whether the ordinance could ban on-site noncommercial signs. He had no trouble with "the content neutral exception" of the ordinance.[23]

Justice Rehnquist believed that the aesthetic justification for the ordinance was sufficient to sustain the law. He did not believe that judges were better qualified than local planning commissions to decide whether removal of billboards "would have more than a negligible impact on aesthetics."[24]

tected as commercial speech. But the governmental regulations in this case were valid restrictions on commercial speech, meeting the four part test of Central Hudson Gas & Electric Corp. v. Public Service Comm'n, 447 U.S. 557 (1980). That is, the two goals that the ordinance furthered were substantial: traffic safety and the city's esthetic interests. The ordinance directly advanced those interests and regulated no further than necessary. Although the law did permit on-site commercial advertising while prohibiting off-site billboards, it was permissible for the city to conclude that off-site advertising, with "periodically changing content, presents a more acute problem than does on-site advertising." 453 U.S. at 511, citing Railway Express, Inc. v. New York, 336 U.S. 106, 110 (1949).

19. 453 U.S. at 513. See also, 453 U.S. at 515: "Because some noncommercial messages may be conveyed on billboards throughout the commercial and industrial zones [e.g., commemorative plaques of recognized historical societies; signs telling time or temperature; signs erected in discharge of a governmental function; temporary political campaign signs] San Diego must similarly allow billboards conveying other noncommercial messages throughout those zones." (footnote omitted)

The Court had earlier allowed a city to ban noncommercial speech but to allow commercial speech in the use of billboard space on a city-owned public transpor-

tation system. Lehman v. City of Shaker Heights, 418 U.S. 298 (1974). In that case, however, the Court was persuaded that the commercial space available on city buses, etc., was not a public forum. The city could limit noncommercial speech in order to limit chances of abuse, the appearance of favoritism, and the risk of imposing on a captive audience. 218 U.S. at 304. See section VI, A, 2, supra.

20. 453 U.S. at 521 & n. 26.

21. 453 U.S. at 528. These justices analogized the case to Schad v. Borough of Mt. Ephraim, 452 U.S. 61, 72 (1981).

22. 453 U.S. at 530–31. At one point Brennan suggested that "San Diego could demonstrate its interest in creating an aesthetically pleasing environment is genuine and substantial" by "showing a comprehensive commitment to making its physical environment in commercial and industrial areas more attractive and by allowing only narrowly tailored exceptions if any. . . ." 453 U.S. at 532 (footnotes omitted). Yet at another point Brennan suggested that San Diego might never meet this burden: "I express no view on whether San Diego or other large urban areas will be able to meet the burden." 453 U.S. at 534 (footnote omitted).

23. 453 U.S. at 542.

24. 453 U.S. at 570.

Chief Justice Burger also wrote a very strong dissent. He rejected the view of the plurality which apparently gave the city a choice of banning all signs (a choice that the plurality might not allow if actually faced with deciding that issue) or permitting all noncommercial signs without any restriction. "This is the long arm and voracious appetite of federal power—this time judicial power—with a vengeance, reaching and absorbing traditional concepts of local authority." [25] The distinctions and exceptions in the City's ordinance—"the presence of which is the plurality's sole ground for invalidating the ordinance—are few in number, are narrowly tailored to peculiar public needs, and do not remotely endanger freedom of speech." The ordinance "has not preferred any viewpoint and, aside from these limited exceptions, has not allowed some subjects while forbidding others. [I]n no instance is the exempted topic controversial . . . ." And the distinctions that the City made are reasonable. For example, "on-site signs, by identifying the premises (even if in the process of advertising), [could] actually promote traffic safety [because prohibiting] them would require motorists to pay more attention to street numbers and less to traffic." [26]

The Court's decisions raise more questions than the case settles. It is likely that if a city enacts a law that restricts billboards on-

ly to the extent that they convey commercial speech, a majority of the Court (composed of the White plurality and the three dissenters) would uphold the ordinance. If litigants attacked the constitutionality of the federal Highway Beautification Act of 1965,[27] it is unclear how the Court would respond. The three dissenters would no doubt uphold this law, but the other six justices specifically refused to reach this question though the White plurality, at least, hinted that the federal law might be distinguishable.[28]

XIV. SYMBOLIC SPEECH

A. Introduction

The notion that speech may be nonverbal had been recognized by the Supreme Court as far back as 1931.[1] In *Stromberg v. California*,[2] the Court provided first amendment protection to certain forms of symbolic expression. A state statute which prohibited the displaying of a red flag "as a sign, symbol or emblem of opposition to organized government" was found to be unconstitutional on first amendment grounds because it was so vague as to allow punishment for the fair use of "the opportunity for free political discussion." [3]

Twelve years later, in *West Virginia State Board of Education v. Barnette*,[4] another form of symbolic speech was given

---

25. 453 U.S. at 556. He added: "The Court today unleashes a novel principle, unnecessary and, indeed, alien to First Amendment doctrine announced in our earlier cases." 453 U.S. at 569.

26. 453 U.S. at 564–65 & n. 6.

27. 23 U.S.C.A. § 131. That law also regulates billboards and permits on-site commercial billboards in certain circumstances where it forbids billboards carrying noncommercial messages.

28. 453 U.S. at 515 n. 20: "[U]nlike the San Diego ordinance, which prohibits billboards conveying noncommercial messages throughout the city, the federal law does not contain a total prohibition of such billboards in areas adjacent to the Interstate and primary highway systems." (White, J.) See also 453 U.S. at 534 n. 11: "I express no opinion on the constitutionality of the Highway Beautification Act . . . ." (Brennan, J.).

1. Stromberg v. California, 283 U.S. 359 (1931). See generally, J. Barron and C. Dienes, Handbook of Free Speech and Free Press 189–219 (1979).

2. 283 U.S. 359 (1931).

3. 283 U.S. at 369. On the importance of symbolic speech, see, e.g., F. Haiman, Speech and Law in a Free Society 6 (U.Chi.Press 1981): "Symbolic behavior is one of the most fundamental ways in which human beings express and fulfill themselves. Its exercise thus lies at the core of a free society." See, Rotunda, The "Liberal" Label: Roosevelt's Capture of a Symbol, 17 Public Policy 377 (Harv.U.Press 1968): "Symbols and labels . . . can substitute for political action; they reflect people's innermost thoughts and ideas; and they even determine the way people think." (footnote omitted); B. Whorf, Language, Thought, and Reality 251 (Carroll, ed. 1956): "Natural man, whether simpleton or scientist, knows no more of the linguistic forces that bear upon him than the savage knows of gravitational forces."

4. 319 U.S. 624 (1943). The remedy in this case was to allow the Jehovah Witness children to refuse to salute the flag. This remedy itself indicates that the case is a free-speech case and not an establishment of

first amendment protection: Public school children could not be compelled to salute the flag in violation of their religious beliefs. The Court recognized the expressive nature of certain actions in this decision:

> "[N]o official . . . can prescribe what shall be orthodox in politics, nationalism, religion or other matters of opinion or force citizens to confess by word or *act* their faith therein." [5]

The Court has not retreated from the position that certain actions may be entitled to first amendment protection. Thus, in *Brown v. Louisiana*,[6] a 1966 decision which involved a peaceful sit-in at a segregated public library, the opinion of Justice Fortas (there was no opinion of the Court), reemphasized that first amendment rights "are not confined to verbal expression [but] embrace appropriate types of action which certainly include the right in a peaceable and orderly manner to protest . . . unconstitutional segregation of public facilities." [7]

B. Fashioning a Test for First Amendment Protection for Symbolic Speech and the Role of Improper Legislative and Administrative Motivation

Although the Court has long accepted the premise that certain "expressive" acts are entitled to first amendment protection, presumably not all activity with an expressive component will be afforded first amendment protection; and these early cases did not create a test for defining what kinds of actions, in what circumstances, fall within the speech orbit of the first amendment. The Court finally began to set boundaries for the extent of first amendment protection afforded to

symbolic speech in 1968, in *United States v. O'Brien*.[8] O'Brien burnt his selective service registration certificate on the steps of the South Boston Courthouse and was convicted in federal court for violating sec. 462(b) of the Universal Military Training and Service Act of 1948. As amended by Congress in 1965, sec. 462(b) made it an offense for any person who "forges, alters, knowingly destroys, knowingly mutilates. . . ." [9] or changes such certificate in any manner.

O'Brien argued that the 1965 Amendment was unconstitutional as applied to him because it restricted his freedom of expression. The Court rejected this contention: "We cannot accept the view that an apparently limitless variety of conduct can be labeled 'speech' whenever the person engaging in the conduct intends thereby to express an idea." [10] The Court likewise rejected the contention that an action with a clearly noncommunicative aspect is outside any first amendment consideration. Rather, the Court presumed that O'Brien's action had a "communicative element . . . sufficient to bring into play the First Amendment." [11] However, this presumption does not mean that the conduct automatically receives full first amendment protection. The government may prohibit such conduct in certain circumstances: "[W]hen 'speech' and 'non-speech' elements are combined in the same course of conduct, a sufficiently important governmental interest in regulating the non-speech element can justify incidental limitations on First Amendment freedoms." [12]

The Court set out a four-part test for determining when a government interest suffi-

---

religion case, for if it were the latter, the remedy should have been to enjoin all flag salutes. Cf. Engel v. Vitale, 370 U.S. 421 (1962) and, School District of Abington Township v. Schempp, 374 U.S. 203 (1963) (Establishment of Religion clause bars school prayer whether or not the laws establishing prayer operate directly to coerce nonobserving individuals).

5. 319 U.S. at 642 (emphasis added).

6. 383 U.S. 131 (1966).

7. 383 U.S. at 142 (footnote omitted).

8. 391 U.S. 367 (1968). See generally Ely, Flag Desecration: A Case Study in the Roles of Categorization and Balancing in First Amendment Analysis, 88 Harv.L.Rev. 1482 (1975).

9. 391 U.S. at 370 (emphasis eliminated).

10. 391 U.S. at 376.

11. Id.

12. Id.

ciently justifies the regulation of expressive conduct:

> [A] government regulation is sufficiently justified [1] if it is within the constitutional power of the Government; [2] if it furthers an important or substantial governmental interest; [3] if the governmental interest is unrelated to the suppression of free expression; and [4] if the incidental restriction on alleged First Amendment freedoms is no greater than is essential to the furtherance of that interest.[13]

The 1965 Amendment of the Universal Military Training and Service Act met the requirements of the above test, according to the Court, and "consequently . . . O'Brien can be constitutionally convicted for violating it."[14]

The 1965 Amendment met the requirements of the first part of the test because it is within the constitutional power of the Government "to raise and support armies and to make all laws necessary to that end . . . ."[15] According to the Court, part two of the test was fulfilled because the Selective Service certificate served a number of purposes in addition to initial notification. These purposes include quick determination of those registrants delinquent in Selective Service obligations; facilitation of quick induction in time of national crisis; facilitation of communication between registrants and local boards; reminders of notification of changes in status; deterrence for deceptive use of certificates. These important governmental interests met the requirements of part three of the test because they were unrelated to the suppression of free expression; the Court noted a distinction between the case at bar and one where "the commu-

nication allegedly integral to the conduct is itself thought to be harmful."[16] For example, the 1965 Amendment did not bar only *contemptuous* destruction, or only bar *public* destruction; if the act had been written in the former terms, it would have indicated that its purpose was to punish the publication of certain opinions, in violation of part three of the *O'Brien* test. Finally, the Court concluded that the 1965 Amendment was sufficiently limited to insure the smooth functioning of the Selective Service System towards the purposes enumerated, meeting the requirements of part four of the *O'Brien* test.

The Court, under "settled principles,"[17] refused to examine subjective legislative motive in deciding a statute's constitutionality. Thus, after *O'Brien* it seemed that so long as a statute on its face serves one "important governmental interest," unrelated to the regulation or suppression of speech, with only incidental restrictions on free speech no greater than necessary, there is an opportunity for the legislature to regulate symbolic speech without further review by the Court. The Court claimed that O'Brien was convicted because "he willfully frustrated this governmental interest. For this noncommunicative impact of his conduct, and for nothing else, he was convicted."[18]

One year after *United States v. O'Brien,*[19] the Court decided a case involving a similar form of expressive conduct, the wearing of black armbands to show objection to the Vietnam War.[20] In *Tinker v. Des Moines School District,*[21] petitioners were high school and junior high school students

---

13. 391 U.S. at 377.

14. Id.

15. Id.

16. 391 U.S. at 382.

17. 391 U.S. at 383. But see the discussion of Board of Education, Island Trees Union Free School District No. 26 v. Pico, 102 S.Ct. 2799 (1982), discussed at n. 58 et seq., infra.

18. 391 U.S. at 382.

Some commentators criticized the *O'Brien* Court for not disposing of O'Brien's action in terms of a more

traditional first amendment balancing of speech and nonspeech interests. They claimed that the Court should have discussed the constitutional impact of the *speech* element of O'Brien's action rather than the nonspeech regulatory aspects of the statute. See Alfange, Free Speech and Symbolic Conduct: The Draft-Card Burning Case, 1968 Sup.Ct.Rev. 1.

19. 391 U.S. 367 (1968).

20. See generally, Note, Symbolic Conduct, 68 Colum.L.Rev. 1091 (1968).

21. 393 U.S. 503 (1969).

who had been suspended and sent home for refusing to remove the armbands pursuant to a school policy adopted two days earlier in anticipation of the protest. Petitioners were denied injunctive relief from the federal courts on the grounds that school authorities acted reasonably in order to prevent disturbance, but the Supreme Court upheld petitioners' right to wear the armbands by characterizing the act as one "closely akin" to "pure speech." [22]

The Court characterized the wearing of armbands in the circumstances of *Tinker v. Des Moines School District* [23] as an action which involved "direct, primary First Amendment rights," [24] and the participants were entitled to comprehensive protection under the first amendment. Although the wearing of armbands was symbolic speech, the school regulation which forbade the action clearly failed the third part of the *O'Brien* test: the regulation was *not* unrelated to the suppression of free expression.

Unlike the statute in *O'Brien*, which banned all draft card burning, the school authorities did not ban all political symbols—students were even allowed to wear the Iron Cross, and some did. "Instead, a particular symbol—black armbands worn to exhibit opposition to this Nation's involvement in Vietnam—was singled out for prohibition." [25] This governmental interest is definitely related to the suppression of free expression. Indeed, it is not clear that the prohibition of all political symbols would be upheld. So long as these symbols were not physically used to disrupt order in the schools the prohibition would relate to the regulation of ideas rather than conduct.

Having failed the *O'Brien* test, the regulation must be analyzed within general first amendment principles. Thus, according to the Court, the problem in *Tinker* was really one of balancing the students' exercise of

first amendment rights against the conflicting rules of school authorities. To resolve this conflict, the Court adopted and quoted the standard used by the Fifth Circuit in *Burnside v. Byars:* [26] such conduct cannot be prohibited unless it " 'materially and substantially interfere[s] with the requirements of appropriate discipline in the operation of the school.' " [27] According to the Court, there was no such showing in the instant case. Petitioners' action was a "silent, passive expression of opinion" and there was "no indication that the work of the schools or any class was disrupted." [28]

The Court made two further points in concluding that the facts of the instant case did not meet the requirements of *Burnside* for prohibiting expression in schools. First, the school officials' ban of the armbands was not based on disruptive effect on school work or impingement on other students' rights. Rather, the purpose of the prohibition was to avoid legitimate controversy: the ban on armbands did "not concern aggressive, disruptive action or even group demonstrations . . . [but only] silent, passive expression of opinion . . . ." [29] The "undifferentiated fear" stemming from this silent expression of political opinion was not enough "to overcome the right to freedom of expression." [30]

Second, the Court emphasized that the prohibition of one particular opinion was not constitutionally permissible. The regulation failed the *O'Brien* test for symbolic speech and failed the *Burnside* test for prohibiting expression in schools. The wearing of armbands in the instant case was thus permitted under the strong first amendment protections for speech:

[I]n our system, undifferentiated fear or apprehension of disturbance is not enough to overcome the right to freedom of expression . . . Any word spoken, in class, in the lunch-

---

22. 393 U.S. at 505. See also id. at 508.

23. 393 U.S. 503 (1969).

24. 393 U.S. at 508.

25. 393 U.S. at 510–11.

26. 363 F.2d 744, 749 (5th Cir. 1966).

27. 393 U.S. 503, 509 (1969).

28. 393 U.S. at 508.

29. Id.

30. Id.

room, or on the campus that deviates from the views of another person may start an argument or cause a disturbance. But our Constitution says we must take this risk . . . and our history says that it is this sort of hazardous freedom—this kind of openness—that is the basis of our national strength and of the independence and vigor of Americans who grow up and live in this relatively permissive, often disputatious society.[31]

Tinker raised, but does not decide, the issue of whether the protections for symbolic speech encompass other school regulations, such as hair or shirt length or style or types of clothing.[32] The lower courts have split on such issues.[33]

Another area in which the Supreme Court has been called upon to elaborate the test it set out in *O'Brien* is in litigation surrounding flag desecration statutes. The first case was *Street v. New York*.[34] In response to the slaying of a civil rights leader, Street burned his personally-owned flag on a street corner in New York while "talking out loud" to a group of approximately thirty people.[35] The arresting officer testified that he heard Street say, *inter alia*, " 'We don't need no damn flag.' "[36] Street was convicted under a statute making it a misdemeanor "publicly [to] mutilate, deface, defile or defy, trample upon, or cast contempt upon either by *words* or *act* [any flag of the United States] . . . .' "[37]

The Court overturned Street's conviction in a narrow holding which avoided the issue of the constitutionality of a statute prohibiting flag desecration by action. The case was decided in terms of the first amendment protection afforded verbal expression. On the basis of the record, it was possible that Street's words alone or his words and actions together were the basis of his conviction. According to the Court, a conviction based on Street's words—totally or in part—would be unconstitutional.

The Court did not prohibit outright on first amendment grounds the desecration of the flag by words. Rather, there were four possible governmental interests which could justify Street's conviction for defiling the flag by words, none of which existed in this case, so Street's conviction had to be overturned. The Court first rejected the argument that there was a government interest in preventing incitement, because Street's words "did not urge anyone to do anything unlawful"—they amounted only to "excited public advocacy of [an] idea."[38] The Court next rejected the possibility that Street's remarks were "fighting words," sufficient to provoke violent retaliation.[39] Nor could Street be punished for his words because they might shock passersby because "[i]t is firmly settled that under our Constitution the public expression of ideas may not be prohibited merely because the ideas are themselves offensive to some of their hearers."[40] Finally, the Court rejected the governmental interest in demanding that every citizen show certain respect for the national symbol, citing Justice Jackson's opinion in *Board of Education v. Barnette*[41] that it is " '. . . the right to differ as to things that touch the heart of the existing order.' "[42] This right to "differ" includes the right to make publicly defiant or contemptuous statements about the flag.[43]

---

31. 393 U.S. at 508–09.

32. Id. at 507–08.

33. See generally, Casenote, 84 Harv.L.Rev. 1702 (1971); see also, Rider v. Board of Education, 414 U.S. 1088 (1974) (Douglas, J., joined by Marshall, J., dissenting from denial of certiorari.) Cf. Kelley v. Johnson, 425 U.S. 238 (1976) (county regulation of police hair length upheld based on fact that policeman is not an ordinary citizen).

See also, J. Barron and C. Dienes, Handbook of Free Speech and Free Press 212–19 (1979).

34. 394 U.S. 576 (1969).

35. 394 U.S. at 578.

36. 394 U.S. at 579.

37. 394 U.S. at 578 (emphasis added).

38. 394 U.S. at 591.

39. 394 U.S. at 592.

40. Id.

41. 319 U.S. 624 (1943).

42. 394 U.S. 576, 593.

43. Id.

It is interesting that the *Street* Court focused not on the first amendment protection for expressive action discussed in *Barnette*, but rather on general first amendment protection for speech. While citing *Barnette*, one of the early cases in symbolic speech, the *Street* Court would not consider two of Street's contentions: that the statute "is vague and imprecise because it does not clearly define the conduct which it forbids;" and that publicly destroying or damaging an American flag as a means of protest is constitutionally protected expression.[44]

The Court held that an individual's alteration of a flag under specific circumstances was protected by the first amendment in *Spence v. Washington*.[45] Appellant had affixed to both surfaces of a personally-owned flag peace symbols made from black masking tape and had displayed the flag upside down in the window of his apartment. He was convicted under the state's "improper use" statute which prohibited placing a figure, design or mark on a United States flag or exposing any such flag to view.[46] In a narrow holding, the Court overturned appellant's conviction because he had engaged in a form of constitutionally protected first amendment activity. The Court enumerated several facts important in its decision: the flag was privately owned; the flag was displayed on private property; there was no evidence of any risk of breach of the peace. Absent the specific circumstances of this case, the general applicability of this decision could thus be extremely limited.

Another fact important to the Court was that the state had conceded that appellant had engaged in a form of communication. The framework set out in *United States v. O'Brien*[47] for determining when a governmental interest sufficiently justifies expressive conduct was thereby applicable, according to the Court. However, the Court

considered not only the nature of appellant's activity (as in *O'Brien*), but also "the factual context and environment in which it was undertaken."[48] The context was important because it helped define the communicative component of the symbol:

> [A]ppellant's activity was roughly simultaneous with . . . the Cambodian incursion and the Kent State tragedy. . . . A flag bearing a peace symbol and displayed upside down by a student today might be interpreted as nothing more than bizarre behavior, but it would have been difficult for the great majority of citizens to miss the drift of appellant's point at the time that he made it.[49]

With this reasoning the Court departed from several assumptions in *O'Brien*, where it had refused to consider appellant's *motivation* to communicate and the clearly communicative nature of the draft card burning. The Court openly discussed both these considerations in *Spence v. Washington*.[50] A subtle shift seems to have occurred from the speech/conduct distinction relied upon in *O'Brien* to a more general balancing of first amendment interests against other governmental interests.

This shift becomes more apparent when the *Spence* Court went on to apply an analysis similar to the one employed in *Street v. New York*.[51] Only now the *Street* framework of governmental interests was balanced against expressive *activity* rather than against words. The Court concluded that none of the four possible governmental interests was compelling enough to uphold Spence's challenged conviction, according to the facts of the case. However, the Court did leave open the possibility that there could be a legitimate state interest in preserving the flag as an "unalloyed symbol of our country."[52] The Court concluded that even if there were a legitimate governmental interest here, it would be unconstitution-

---

44. 394 U.S. at 580–81.

45. 418 U.S. 405 (1974) (per curiam).

46. 418 U.S. at 407.

47. 391 U.S. 367 (1968).

48. 418 U.S. 405, 410.

49. Id.

50. 418 U.S. 405, 410–11 (1974).

51. 394 U.S. 576 (1969).

52. 418 U.S. 405, 412–14.

al as applied to Spence's activity. The Court did not conclude, on the other hand, that there was no government interest in preserving the flag as a national symbol strong enough to outweigh first amendment considerations. This state interest yet to be found may fulfill the requirements of the first two parts of the four-part test of *O'Brien*.

Another case involving flag desecration was *Smith v. Goguen*,[53] where the defendant wore a small flag sewn to the seat of his trousers and was convicted under a Massachusetts flag misuse statute which made it a crime if one "publicly . . . treats contemptuously" the United States flag.[54] Justice Powell, for the Court, avoided an analysis based on symbolic speech and instead overturned defendant's conviction on the basis that the statute was "void for vagueness." [55] According to Justice Powell, the statute failed to give fair notice by not providing clear guidelines as to what treatment of the flag was criminal. Although the Court did not rely on the *O'Brien* test, the "treats contemptuously" language would appear to fall within the prohibition of part three: the governmental interest is, as expressed in the statute in *Goguen*, related to the suppression of free expression. However, given the apparent recognition by the Supreme Court of the state interest in somehow protecting the flag as a symbol of the Nation, the failure of such statutes under the *O'Brien* test may not be fatal to their constitutionality.

In *Wooley v. Maynard*,[56] the Court applied settled symbolic speech principles and held that a motorist has a free speech right

not to be prosecuted for obscuring on his own license plates the state's motto, "Live Free or Die." The individual (who was a Jehovah's Witness) claimed political, moral, and religious objections to the views expressed by the motto. The Court held that the state cannot force an individual to be an instrument of an ideological point of view with which he disagrees. The state's claimed interests of facilitating identification of passenger vehicles and promoting state pride and an appreciation of history and individualism were insufficient to justify the restriction on free speech.

Though *Wooley* raised no difficult problem of the motivation of the legislative or administrative decision-maker, and the judicial use of that motivation in order to invalidate state action restricting speech, the Court certainly did return to that issue and elaborate on the uses of motivation and the implications of *Tinker v. Des Moines School District* [57] in the case of *Board of Education, Island Trees Union Free School District No. 26 v. Pico*.[58] The Court was asked to decide what were the first amendment restrictions on a decision of a local school board to remove certain books from high school and junior high school libraries. The books were not obscene in a constitutional sense but the board had concluded that the books were "anti-American, anti-Christian, anti-Semitic, and just plain filthy." [59] The Court could produce no majority opinion and returned the case to the lower courts for a trial on the merits, in order to determine the motivation of the school board.

53.   415 U.S. 566 (1974).

54.   Id. at 568.

55.   Id. at 582.

56.   430 U.S. 705 (1977).

57.   393 U.S. 503 (1969). See text at nn. 21–33, supra.

58.   102 S.Ct. 2799 (1982).

59.   102 S.Ct. at 2803. See the lower court decision at 474 F.Supp. 387, 390 (E.D.N.Y.1979).

The Board, after objections were raised by a parents group, decided (contrary to the recommendations of a Book Review Committee which it had appointed) that

the book, *Black Boy*, by Richard Wright, should be made available in the high school library subject to parental approval and that nine other books should be removed from elementary and secondary libraries and from use in the curriculum. These books were: *Slaughter House Five*, by Kurt Vonnegut, Jr.; *The Naked Ape*, by Desmond Morris; *Down These Mean Streets*, by Piri Thomas; *Best Short Stories of Negro Writers*, edited by Langston Hughes; *Go Ask Alice*, of anonymous authorship; *A Hero Ain't Nothin' But a Sandwich*, by Alice Childress; *Soul on Ice*, by Eldridge Cleaver; *A Reader for Writers*, edited by Jerome Archer; and *The Fixer*, by Bernard Malamud.

Justice Brennan, in an opinion joined by Justices Marshall and Stevens, and in part by Justice Blackmun, emphasized that the Court was dealing with a case that did not involve any textbooks or required reading; nor did the case involve judicial intrusion on the Board's discretion to prescribe curricula. "[T]he only books at issue are *library* books, books that by their nature are optional rather than required reading." [60] And even as to these books, Brennan noted, the decision of the Court was narrow would not affect the discretion of the local school board to decide which books to add. "Rather, the only action challenged in this case is the *removal* from school libraries of books originally placed there by the school authorities, or without objection from them." [61] Thus, since this case is concerned with the suppression of ideas, "our holding today affects only the discretion to *remove* books." [62] Brennan then focused heavily on the subjective motivations of the decision-makers.

Students have a "right to receive ideas." [63] Although first amendment rights must be interpreted in light of the special characteristics of the school environment, under *Tinker* the school library, said Brennan, is a special locus of first amendment freedoms. Thus—

Petitioners rightly possess significant discretion to determine the content of their school libraries. But that discretion may not be exercised in a narrowly partisan or political manner. If a Democratic school board, motivated by party affiliation, ordered the removal of all books written by or in favor of Republicans, few would doubt that the order violated the constitutional rights of the students denied access to those books. . . . Our Constitution does not permit the official suppression of *ideas.* Thus whether petitioners' removal of books from their school libraries denied respondents their First Amendment rights depends upon the motivation behind petitioners' actions. If petitioners *intended* by their removal deci-

sion to deny respondents access to ideas with which petitioners disagreed, and if this intent was the decisive factor in petitioners' decision, then petitioners have exercised their discretion in violation of the Constitution. . . . On the other hand, respondents implicitly concede that an unconstitutional motivation would *not* be demonstrated if it were shown that petitioners had decided to remove the books at issue because those books were pervasively vulgar. And again, respondents concede that if it were demonstrated that the removal decision was based solely upon the "educational suitability" of the books in question, then their removal would be "perfectly permissible." In other words, in respondents' view such motivations, if decisive of petitioners' actions, would not carry the danger of an official suppression of ideas, and thus would not violate respondents' First Amendment rights. In brief, we hold that local school boards may not remove books from school library shelves simply because they dislike the ideas contained in those books and seek by their removal to "prescribe what shall be orthodox in politics, nationalism, religion, or other matters of opinion." Such purposes stand inescapably condemned by our precedents.[64]

Justice Blackmun concurred in part and in the judgment; he emphasized that school officials may not remove books "for the *purpose* of restricting access to the political ideas or social perspectives discussed in them, when that action is motivated simply by the officials' disapproval of the ideas involved." [65] For example, "removing a learned treatise criticizing American foreign policy from an elementary school library because the students would not understand it is an action unrelated to the *purpose* of suppressing ideas. In my view, however, removing the same treatise because it is 'anti-American' raises a far more difficult issue." [66] Justice Blackmun also was dubious that the distinction between removing and failing to acquire a book was analytically sound, but he did recognize that there was a

60. 102 S.Ct. at 2805 (emphasis in original).

61. 102 S.Ct. at 2807 (emphasis in original).

62. 102 S.Ct. at 2810 (emphasis in original).

63. 102 S.Ct. at 2808, citing, inter alia, Martin v. Struthers, 319 U.S. 141, 143 (1943); Stanley v. Georgia,

394 U.S. 557, 564 (1969); Kleindienst v. Mandel, 408 U.S. 753, 762–63 (1972).

64. 102 S.Ct. at 2810 (emphasis in original).

65. 102 S.Ct. at 2814 (emphasis in original).

66. 102 S.Ct. at 2815 (emphasis in original).

practical and evidentiary distinction because removal of a book (more than a mere failure to acquire) it suggests an impermissible motive. Many justifications, including finite resources, could explain why a book was not purchased, but it is more difficult to explain why it would be removed from a library not filled to capacity.[67]

Justice White, concurring in the judgment, abstained from issuing what he called a "dissertation" on the Constitutional issues involved until after a full trial as to why the Board removed the books.[68]

Chief Justice Burger, joined by Powell, Rehnquist, and O'Connor, dissented. They reasoned that the Board placed no restraints of any kind on the students. They could read the books, available from public libraries, bookstores, or elsewhere; they could discuss the books in class.[69] But the school library need not be the conduit; there is no "'right' to have the government provide continuing access to certain books," to be made "a slavish courier of the materials of third parties."[70] The plurality's test allowing the books to be withdrawn if "educationally unsuitable" is standardless, argued the dissent. Why also must a book be "pervasively vulgar" before it is offensive; would not "random" vulgarity be enough to make the book inappropriate?[71] The Burger dissent also found no justification in the plurality's distinction between "school libraries or school classrooms, between *removing* unwanted books and *acquiring* books." Books do not have any constitutional tenure, argued the dissent.[72]

Justice Rehnquist's dissent, joined by Burger, and Powell, stated that it could agree

with the plurality that a Democratic school board could not order the removal of all books written by Republicans, but "would save for another day" such extreme examples because the books here were removed because of their vulgarity and profanity.[73] Moreover, if Justice Brennan "truly has found a 'right to receive ideas,'" his "distinction between acquisition and removal makes little sense."[74]

XV. REGULATION OF THE ELECTORAL PROCESS BY RESTRICTIONS ON CAMPAIGN FINANCING AND BY LIMITATIONS OF POLITICAL ACTIVITY OF GOVERNMENT EMPLOYEES

A. Introduction

There can be little question now that political expression lies at the core of first amendment values.[1] Nonetheless, political expression is subject to government regulation provided the state can show a substantial interest in such regulation. The transcendent legislative objective in this field is the elimination of corruption as well as the appearance of corruption in order that public participation in the electoral process is not dampened by cynicism or alienation. As a result, reasonable legislative proscriptions upon political activity by government employees have been consistently upheld,[2] as well as regulation of the conduct of, and contributions to, political campaigns deemed to serve this purpose.[3]

On the other hand, as the Supreme Court noted without dissent in *Brown v. Hartlage* [4] a state may not punish a political candidate because he made a campaign state-

---

67. 102 S.Ct. at 2814 n. 1.

68. 102 S.Ct. at 2816.

69. 102 S.Ct. at 2818.

70. 102 S.Ct. at 2819.

71. 102 S.Ct. at 2820.

72. 102 S.Ct. at 2821 & n. 8 (emphasis in original).

73. 102 S.Ct. at 2829.

74. 102 S.Ct. at 2830. O'Connor and Powell, JJ., each also wrote dissenting opinions. 102 S.Ct. at 2822 (Powell, J.), id. at 2835 (O'Connor, J.).

1. Buckley v. Valeo, 424 U.S. 1 (1976) (per curiam); Williams v. Rhodes, 393 U.S. 23 (1968); Cf. United States v. O'Brien, 391 U.S. 367 (1968).

2. United Public Workers v. Mitchell, 330 U.S. 75 (1947); United States Civil Service Commission v. National Ass'n of Letter Carriers, 413 U.S. 548 (1973); Broadrick v. Oklahoma, 413 U.S. 601 (1973); Keyishian v. Board of Regents, 385 U.S. 589, 605–06 (1967); Pickering v. Board of Education, 391 U.S. 563 (1968).

3. Buckley v. Valeo, 424 U.S. 1 (1976) (per curiam).

4. 456 U.S. 45 (1982). In this case, the Kentucky Corrupt Practices Act prohibited a candidate from

ment that he intended, if elected, to serve at a salary less than that "fixed by law." The state claimed that such statements violated a statute prohibiting candidates from offering material benefits to voters in consideration for their votes, but the Court held that the statute could not constitutionally be applied in such circumstances; the promise hardly fitted into the category of a private, politically corrupt arrangement. The state can prohibit bribes, but not such open promises to voters generally.

B. Regulation of Campaign Financing

1. Introduction

Due to the disclosures concerning the scandals in financing surrounding recent elections as well as concern for the possible effects upon democratic government of the spiraling costs of election campaigns, Congress enacted the Federal Election Campaign Act of 1971 and added more stringent amendments with the Federal Election Campaign Act Amendments of 1974.[5] These

statutes involved the federal government in the regulation of much of the day-to-day operation of political campaigns for federal office. There are four primary regulations: (1) regulating the amounts contributed to or expended by the candidate or his campaign committee; (2) forbidding "dirty tricks" by creating penalties for the "fraudulent misrepresentation of campaign authority"; (3) requiring public disclosure of contributions to and expenditures by a candidate, his campaign committee or individual expenditures on behalf of a candidate; (4) providing for public financing of all phases of presidential elections.

The Supreme Court heard a comprehensive challenge to this statute in *Buckley v. Valeo*[6], in which significant first amendment issues were raised relating to central provisions of the Act. Distinguishing between the speech interest inherent in campaign contributions and campaign expenditures, the Court, per curiam, upheld the limitations imposed on contributions, but invalidated those related to expenditures. The

---

making an expenditure, loan, or promise as to action to be taken when elected, in consideration for a vote or support of any person. Carl Brown, a candidate for the office of County Commissioner, promised the voters in a press conference that if elected he would lower his salary $3,000 per year. Because the salary had been "fixed by law" the Kentucky Court of Appeals held that the Corrupt Practices Act prohibited Brown's promise. Since Brown had been elected the state court declared the election void and found that free speech guarantees were inapplicable. After the press conference Brown retracted his pledge when he discovered that it might be illegal. Instead he promised to seek corrective legislation. The Kentucky appellate court found that the retraction was irrelevant.

The U. S. Supreme Court readily agreed that the state could prohibit bribes or agreements to buy votes. While there might be some borderline cases between such corrupt arrangements and normal, open, candidate promises (e.g., to lower taxes, to provide some group with public services), this case lies far from the border. Brown's promise, even though if it could not legally be kept, was not a private, politically corrupt arrangement. Brown's "generalized" commitment "scarcely contemplated a particularized acceptance;" it "was conditioned not on any particular vote or votes, but entirely on the *majority's* vote." 456 U.S. at 58 (emphasis in original). A "candidate's promise to confer some ultimate benefit on the voter, *qua* taxpayer, citizen, or member of the general public, does not lie beyond the pale of the First Amendment protection." 456 U.S. at 58–59. Nor does the state's fear that vot-

ers might make an ill-advised choice provide any compelling justification for such a limitation on speech.

Finally, even the state's interest in protecting voters from falsehoods did not offer any compelling justification for the law. Under the state law the candidate's liability for error is absolute: "His election victory must be voided even if the offending statement was made in good faith and was quickly repudiated. The chilling effect of such absolute accountability for factual misstatements in the course of political debate is incompatible with the atmosphere of free discussion contemplated by the First Amendment in the context of political campaigns. Although the state interest in protecting the political process from distortions caused by untrue and inaccurate speech is somewhat different from the state interest in protecting individuals from defamatory falsehoods, the principles underlying the First Amendment remain paramount. . . . In a political campaign, a candidate's factual blunder is unlikely to escape the notice of, and correction by, the erring candidate's political opponent. The preferred First Amendment remedy [is] 'more speech, not enforced silence' . . . ." 456 U.S. at 61. The state, in short, offered no compelling justification for its restriction on free speech.

5. Federal Election Campaign Act of 1971, Pub.L. No. 92–225, 86 Stat. 3, as amended by Federal Election Campaign Act Amendments of 1974, Pub.L. No. 93–443, 88 Stat. 1263.

6. 424 U.S. 1 (1976) (per curiam).

disclosure and reporting requirements were sustained as necessary for the enforcement of the Act.[7]

Initially, it is important to note the underlying rationale for the result in *Buckley*. Employing Justice White's observation, the Court has granted constitutional recognition to the maxim "money talks," [8] for the opinion rests on the foundation that campaign contributions and expenditures are speech or are so intrinsically related to speech that any regulation of such funding must be constrained by the prohibitions of the first amendment.[9]

2. *Campaign Contributions and Expenditures*

The primary importance of the *Buckley* decision lies in the Court's distinction between campaign contributions and expenditures.[10] The Court found that the speech interests in campaign contributions are marginal, as they convey only an undifferentiated expression of support rather than the specific values which motivate that support.[11] Such a tangential relationship to first amendment values cannot be successfully balanced against the primary purpose and effect of the limitation on those contributions—a reduction in the probability of corruption and the concomitant reduction in the appearance of corruption. As the limitations imposed on contributions do not have a substantial effect on the ability of a candidate to obtain funding requiring only that a broader base of contributors be drawn upon rather than lessening the total funds used, such contribution limitations were within the power of the legislature to control.[12] However, the Court ruled that expenditures, as

directly related to the expression of political views, are on a higher plane of constitutional values; thus justifications for such legislative intrusion into protected speech require a more exacting scrutiny.

> A restriction on the amount of money a person or group can spend on political communication during a campaign necessarily reduces the quantity of expression by restricting the number of issues discussed, the depth of their exploration, and the size of the audience reached. This is because virtually every means of communicating in today's mass society requires the expenditure of money.[13]

The effectiveness of such limitations to reduce corruption diminishes as the value of the communication increases. Since there exists little relationship between the campaign expenditures in bulk and the corruptive influence upon the electoral process, particularly in light of the limitations on the amount an individual may contribute, the Court held that the amount of money an individual can spend to advocate either his own candidacy or that of another is a matter within his own discretion.

Nor could such limitations be saved by the ancillary justification of limiting the escalating costs of political campaigns, thus increasing the possibilities for those candidates less able to attract massive amounts of capital. Such a justification necessarily implies that the regulation must impinge upon the operation of the political marketplace by restricting the effectiveness of a candidate's most salable commodity, his appeal to the voters, to the benefit of those whose attraction is less. The Court found nothing "invidious, improper, or unhealthy" [14] in allowing the possibility of a political campaign

---

7. In holdings unrelated to first amendment considerations, the Court invalidated the provisions of the Act creating a Federal Election Commission appointed by the Congress; public financing of campaigns was upheld as a legitimate exercise of the taxing and spending power.

8. 424 U.S. at 262 (1976) (White, J. concurring in part and dissenting in part).

9. Id. at 18–23 (per curiam). Cf. United States v. O'Brien, 391 U.S. 367 (1968); Tinker v. Des Moines School District, 393 U.S. 503 (1969); West Virginia

State Bd. of Education v. Barnette, 319 U.S. 624 (1943); Stromberg v. California, 283 U.S. 359 (1931).

10. Congress had defined contributions to include not only funds given directly to the campaign, but also money spent in support of a candidate which was within the candidate's control and coordination.

11. 424 U.S. at 19, 20.

12. 424 U.S. at 21–22.

13. 424 U.S. at 19 (footnote omitted).

14. 424 U.S. at 44.

turning on the ability of a candidate to attract a broad base of financial support, since the contributors' limitations eliminated the possibility that *quid pro quos* would be offered for large contributions, thus allowing one individual to gain an inordinate amount of influence among the supporters on the basis of financial support.

In *First National Bank v. Bellotti*,[15] the Court, in a five to four decision, found unconstitutional a Massachusetts law which prohibited corporate expenditures for the purpose of influencing the vote on any referendum submitted to the voters other than one materially affecting the property, business, or assets of the corporation. The statute was applied to corporations which had sought to spend money to publicize their view in opposition to a proposed progressive income tax on corporations.

The majority first rejected the argument that corporate speech is protected only when it pertains directly to the corporation's business interests. Then the Court considered the question of whether the state statute, which restricted corporate speech, could "survive the exacting scrutiny necessitated by a state-imposed restriction on freedom of expression." [16] Measured by this test, the state did not show a compelling, subordinating interest. There was no showing that corporate participation would exert an undue influence on the outcome of a referendum. More importantly, "the fact that advocacy may persuade the electorate is hardly a reason to suppress it." [17] Finally, the purpose of allegedly protecting corporate shareholders was contradicted by the over-and under-inclusiveness of the statute. Thus, the statute did not prohibit the use of corporate

funds for lobbying nor allow the prohibited expenditures if all the shareholders would unanimously authorize the spending.

The dissent noted that the majority holding calls into question federal law barring corporate contributions to political campaigns.[18] However the Court distinguished corporate contributions to referenda from corporate contributions to political candidates on the grounds that the latter raises more clearly problems of corruption through the creation of political debt which the government has an important interest in protecting. The majority also emphasized that laws prohibiting corporate gifts to candidates were not before the Court, and that "Congress might well be able to demonstrate the existence of a danger of real or apparent corruption in independent expenditures by corporations to influence candidate elections." [19] The issue of the constitutionality of the complete prohibition of corporate contributions to political candidates (as opposed to limiting the amount of such expenditures as discussed in the *Buckley* case [20]) appears open after the *Bellotti* decision.

In *California Medical Association v. Federal Election Commission*,[21] a fragmented Court rejected new challenges to the Federal Election Campaign Act of 1971. The California Medical Association (CMA), an unincorporated association of doctors, formed a political committee, the California Medical Political Action Committee (CALPAC), which was registered with the Federal Election Commission. The Federal Election Commission charged CMA with making contributions in excess of $5000 to CALPAC and also charged CALPAC with knowingly accepting such contributions in violation of

---

15. 435 U.S. 765 (1978). See generally, Lowenstein, Campaign Spending and Ballot Propositions: Recent Experience, Public Choice Theory and the First Amendment, 29 U.C.L.A.L.Rev. 505 (1982), for a thorough empirical study. See also, Wright, Money and the Pollution of Politics: Is the First Amendment an Obstacle to Political Equality, 82 Colum.L.Rev. 609 (1982) (attacking both *Buckley* and *Bellotti*); Note, Regulation of Campaign Contributions: Maintaining the Integrity of the Political Process Through an Appearance of Fairness, 56 So.Calif.L.Rev. 669 (1983), discussing limitations on contributions to local officials responsible for

single issues, e.g., land use decisions affecting land developers.

16. 435 U.S. at 786.

17. 435 U.S. at 790.

18. 435 U.S. at 811 (White, J., dissenting, joined by Brennan and Marshall JJ.). Justice Rehnquist filed a separate dissent.

19. 435 U.S. at 788 n. 20.

20. Buckley v. Valeo, 424 U.S. 1 (1976) (per curiam).

21. 453 U.S. 182 (1981).

the Act, which prohibits individuals and unincorporated associations from contributing more than $5000 per year to any multicandidate political committee such as CALPAC. The Act similarly prohibits political committees such as CALPAC from knowingly accepting contributions in excess of this limit.

The Court formed a majority on this issue, and ruled that although a corporation or labor union's contributions to a segregated political fund are unlimited under the Act, the limitation on the unincorporated association's contributions did not violate the equal protection aspects of the fifth amendment. "Appellants' claim of unfair treatment ignores the plain fact that the statute as a whole imposes far *fewer* restrictions on individuals and unincorporated associations than it does on corporations and unions."[22] For example, individuals and unincorporated associations may contribute to candidates, and their committees, and to all other political committees while corporations and unions are absolutely barred from making any such contributions. The different restrictions "reflect a judgment by Congress that these entities have differing structures and purposes, and that they therefore may require different forms of regulations in order to protect the integrity of the electoral process."[23]

Nor did the law violate the first amendment. Marshall's plurality opinion on this issue, joined by Brennan, White, and Stevens, found, first, that the statute did not limit the amount that CMA or its members may independently spend to advocate political views. Rather the law only limits the amount that CMA may contribute to CAL-

PAC. The analysis in *Buckley v. Valeo*[24] allows this limitation:

> If the First Amendment rights of a contributor are not infringed by limitations on the amount he may contribute to a campaign organization which advocates the views and candidacy of a particular candidate, the rights of a contributor are similarly not impaired by limits on the amount he may give to a multicandidate political committee, such as CALPAC, which advocates the views and candidacies of a number of candidates.[25]

Justice Blackmun, concurred in part and in the judgment. As to the first amendment claim, he rejected the contribution-expenditure distinction that gives less protection to contributions; he nonetheless concluded that the contribution limit to multicandidate political committees was valid in order to prevent evasion of the Act's contribution limitations upheld in *Buckley*. He analogized it to the $25,000 limitations on total annual contributions upheld in *Buckley*.[26]

3. *Disclosure and Reporting Requirements*

The statutes challenged in *Buckley*,[27] also required the campaign committees to disclose a list of their contributors as well as requiring individual contributors to report contributions to a candidate or expenditures in support of a candidate.[28] In the only previous case challenging the disclosure of campaign finances, decided in 1934, the Court upheld the requirement over claims that such a disclosure impaired the individuals' right of association.[29] Following that decision, the Court recognized that compelled disclosure of membership lists may constitute a restraint upon the associational rights

---

22. 453 U.S. at 200 (emphasis in original).

23. 453 U.S. at 201.

24. 424 U.S. 1 (1976) (per curiam).

25. 453 U.S. at 197 (footnote omitted). See also the unanimous opinion in Federal Election Comm'n v. National Right to Work Committee, 103 S.Ct. 552 (1982), per Rehnquist, J., holding that a provision of the Federal Election Campaign Act of 1971, 2 U.S.C.A. § 441b(b) (4)(C), is constitutional and does not violate any first amendment association rights because of the important interests which Congress has sought to protect. The section provided that a nonstock corporation cannot so-

licit contributions from persons other than its "members" when the nonstock corporation uses these funds for certain designated political federal election purposes.

26. 453 U.S. at 203. Stewart, J., joined by Burger, C. J., and Powell and Rehnquist, JJ., dissented on jurisdictional grounds.

27. Buckley v. Valeo, 424 U.S. 1 (1976) (per curiam).

28. 2 U.S.C.A. § 431 et seq.

29. Burroughs and Cannon v. United States, 290 U.S. 534 (1934).

of the members, as there may often exist an interest in maintaining the privacy of such associations.[30] In *NAACP v. Alabama*,[31] the Court had denied the State the right to compel the disclosure of the NAACP's members for the purpose of ferreting out subversives within the association. Such an interest was only tenuously related to the request and was overborne by the fears of the members that they would be subject to harassment and intimidation if their associational ties were made public, regardless of the presence of any subversive connection.

The appellant in *Buckley* relied on this case as precedent to argue that such disclosure in campaign financing would violate those interests in private political associations. *NAACP v. Alabama*[32] was distinguished because, unlike that case, the countervailing interests of the state, to be served by such disclosure—providing information in order to allow the voter a more informed judgment as to the candidates future performance in office; deterring corruption by providing notice that contributions and expenditures would be exposed; and establishing machinery for the enforcement of the Act—were directly related to the purposes in requiring the disclosure.[33] Moreover, the Court emphasized that there had been no showing in *Buckley* that potential contributors were deterred by fear of humiliation or public ridicule if their identities were linked to a particular candidate.[34] Although such fears were not unreasonable when related to

the funding of minority parties, there also existed no evidence that legitimate associational activity would necessarily be dampened in all minority parties by disclosure. Therefore, only if a party could show a reasonable probability that compelled disclosure of the list of its contributors—or the recipients of campaign disbursements—would subject those contributors or recipients to threats, harassment, or reprisals from either government officials or private parties, an exemption from the disclosure provisions for that organization may be granted.[35] The creation of a blanket exemption, for all minority parties, irrespective of the inherent administrative difficulties, was simply not shown to be necessary to protect the individual member's rights of association.

C. Regulation of Political Activity of Government Employees

The Court has on several occasions held that a governmental interest in fair and effective operation of the federal government justified regulation of partisan political activities of government employees.[36] The statute in question in both cases was § 9(a) of the Hatch Act[37] which forbids government employees from taking "an active part in political management or political campaigns. All such persons shall retain the right to vote as they may choose and to express their opinions on all political subjects."

30. E.g., United States v. Rumely, 345 U.S. 41 (1953); NAACP v. Alabama, 357 U.S. 449 (1958); Bates v. Little Rock, 361 U.S. 516 (1960); Talley v. California, 362 U.S. 60 (1960); Louisiana ex rel. Gremillion v. NAACP, 366 U.S. 293 (1961); Gibson v. Florida Legislative Investigation Committee, 372 U.S. 539 (1963); DeGregory v. Attorney General of New Hampshire, 383 U.S. 825 (1966).

31. 357 U.S. 449 (1958); see also Talley v. California, 362 U.S. 60 (1960).

32. 357 U.S. 449 (1958).

33. 424 U.S. at 66, 67.

34. 424 U.S. at 72–73.

35. 424 U.S. at 74. *Buckley* actually referred only to "a party's contributors' names . . . " but in a later case the Court made clear that the *Buckley* dictum sets forth the correct test to determine when the first

amendment protects minor parties from compelled disclosure and that test applies not only to contributors but also to the recipients of campaign disbursements. Brown v. Socialist Workers '74 Campaign Committee, 103 S.Ct. 416 (1982) (holding that an Ohio statute was unconstitutional as applied to the Socialist Workers Party, given the evidence of threats, harassment, and reprisals).

36. United Public Workers v. Mitchell, 330 U.S. 75 (1947) and United States Civil Service Comm'n v. National Ass'n of Letter Carriers, 413 U.S. 548 (1973); see also Broadrick v. Oklahoma, 413 U.S. 601 (1973) applying the same principles to a state restriction on political activities of public employees.

37. 5 U.S.C.A. § 7324. See United States Civil Service Comm'n v. National Ass'n of Letter Carriers, 413 U.S. 548, 560–61 (1973).

In *United States Civil Service Commission v. National Association of Letter Carriers*,[38] the Court reaffirmed its 26 year old holding in *United Public Workers v. Mitchell*[39] that such restrictions upon public employment were valid, since they served an overriding state interest which only restricts certain methods of political expression, and does not deny governmental employees the right to hold political views or express those views outside the context of a political campaign.

The Court has recognized that the government's interest in regulating the speech and conduct of its employees differs from its interest in such regulation of general citizens for two reasons.[40] First, government employees by virtue of their position exert a great deal of influence as the growth of government increasingly affects the daily life of private citizens. To allow that employee to reap political dividends by virtue of his employment demeans the government and induces disrespect for its functionaries.[41] Second, political participation by public employees may threaten the effective operation of government. It is essential that employees implement the will of Congress, unswayed by the directives of a political party.[42] The prohibitions on political activity also serve the related concern of insuring that government employees are not required to engage in partisan political support in order to retain their positions, not only so that governmental employees avoid engaging in "political justice" but also that they "appear to the public to be avoiding it. . . ."[43] As the interest of the employee in the right to political association is not dampened, but only his right to participate in political campaigns, the overwhelming governmental interest must prevail.

Thus, in *Letter Carriers* the Court held that federal employees can be prevented from engaging in "plainly identifiable acts of political management and political campaigning"[44] such as holding a party office, working at the polls, acting as a party paymaster for other party workers, organizing a political party or club, actively participating in fund-raising activities for a partisan candidate, becoming a partisan candidate or campaigning for an elective political office, initiating or circulating a partisan nominating petition, soliciting votes for a partisan candidate for political office, or serving as a delegate to a political party convention.[45]

Such governmental interests are not boundless however. Rather, the regulations must be narrowly drawn to serve the objectives of effective government without intruding unnecessarily into the private associations and beliefs of its employees. As the Court noted in *Pickering v. Board of Education*,[46]

The problem in any case is to arrive at a balance between the interests of the [employee], as a citizen, in commenting upon matters of public concern and the interest of the [government], as an employer in promoting the effi-

---

38. 413 U.S. 548 (1973).

39. 330 U.S. 75 (1947).

40. See Pickering v. Board of Education, 391 U.S. 563 (1968).

41. 413 U.S. at 565.

42. Id.

43. Id. at 566.

44. Id. at 567.

45. Id. at 554–67.

See also, Clements v. Fashing, 102 S.Ct. 2836 (1982). The Court found not first amendment defect in two provisions of the Texas Constitution. The first, § 19, insofar as it was before the Court, prohibited state judges from being eligible to serve in the Texas legislature until the judge had completed his term of judicial office. The second, § 65, provided that holders of certain state and county officers, if they become candidates for any other state or federal office, automatically resigned their positions unless the unexpired portion of their current terms were less than one year. Neither provision violated the first amendment (nor also the equal protection clause). First, state interests justified the *de minimis* interference with one's interest in candidacy. Second, " § 19 and § 65 are in reality no different than the provisions we upheld in" *Letter Carriers* and similar cases. "Appellees are *elected* state officeholders who contest restrictions on partisan political activity. Section 19 and § 65 represent a far more limited restriction on political activity than this Court has upheld with regard to civil *servants*." 102 S.Ct. at 2848 (emphasis in original).

46. 391 U.S. 563 (1968).

ciency of the public services it performs through its employees.[47]

Thus the Board of Education was prohibited from firing a teacher who wrote and published in a newspaper a letter criticizing the Board's budgetary policies and public information methods.[48] As to those charges by the teacher which were substantially correct, they were also matters of "public concern" and presented no issues of faculty discipline or harmony; hence they did not justify dismissal. The charges which were false were also concerned with issues of public concern and similarly were not shown to have interfered with the teacher's job or with the school's general operation. In the absence of the scienter required in *New York Times v. Sullivan*[49] of a knowing or reckless falsehood, the Board could not fire the teacher from his public employment.

Similarly, in *Elrod v. Burns*,[50] the Court struck down a system of political patronage in determining eligibility for government employment. Such a program delved into beliefs and associations of the employees without a significant countervailing interest. And *Givhan v. Western Line Consolidated School District*[51] made clear that the first amendment protection of public employees is not limited by any requirement that the speech must be public. The Court explained that no first amendment freedom "is lost to the public employee who arranges to communicate privately with his employee rather than to spread his views before the public." [52]

Thus, while *Letter Carriers* indicates that certain modes of actively expressing partisan political belief may be banned in the interest of preserving a non-partisan government work force, *Pickering* and *Burns* establish that political beliefs themselves and their reasonable expression are not subject to the dictates of the government employer. This principle was reaffirmed in *Madison School District v. Wisconsin Employment Relations Committee*,[53] where the Court held that the state employment commission could not bar a public school board from allowing a teacher to address it at a public meeting; the teacher addressed the board on pending labor negotiations and the employment commission had sought to bar this speech because the teacher was not a union representative and in fact was not even a union member. However the meeting was public, and public participation was generally permitted.

Although the state cannot punish a public employee because of his associations or because he speaks freely, the state has no obligation to listen, to recognize the association, and bargain with it. Thus, a state agency can refuse to consider or act upon grievances when filed by the union rather than by the employee directly.[54]

---

47. 391 U.S. 563, 568 (1968).

48. See also, Givhan v. Western Line Consolidated School District, 439 U.S. 410 (1979) where the Court unanimously held that the teacher could not be discharged for privately communicating her grievances about working conditions, or opinion concerning employment or public issues, to her employer. The opinion reaffirmed the principle established in *Mt. Healthy* that when an employee has shown that constitutionally protected conduct played a role in the government's decision not to retain him or her in their job that the employer is required and entitled to demonstrate "by a preponderance of the evidence that it would have reached the same decision as to [the employee's] reemployment even in the absence of the protected conduct." 439 U.S. at 416, quoting Mt. Healthy City Bd. of Education v. Doyle, 429 U.S. 274, 287 (1977).

In *Givhan* the statements were a matter of public concern: the school's district's allegedly racially discriminatory policies were the subject of the conversa-

tion. Contrast Connick v. Myers, 103 S.Ct. 1684 (1983) where the Court, in a 5 to 4 decision, upheld the firing of an assistant district attorney for circulating a questionnaire regarding office policies; the questionnaire did not touch upon matters of public concern. A federal court is not the appropriate forum to review the wisdom of such personnel decisions. The employer need not tolerate action which he reasonably believes would disrupt the office, undermine his authority, and destroy close working relationships.

49. 376 U.S. 254 (1964).

50. 427 U.S. 347 (1976). Accord, Branti v. Finkel, 445 U.S. 507 (1980).

51. 439 U.S. 410 (1979).

52. 439 U.S. at 415.

53 429 U.S. 167 (1976).

54. Smith v. Arkansas State Highway Employees, Local 1315, 441 U.S. 463 (1979) (per curiam). Accord,

XVI.　ASSEMBLY AND PETITION

When King John signed the Magna Carta in 1215, he established a base to which our modern right of petition for redress of grievances can, to some extent, be traced. The right to petition the Crown for redress of grievances originally given to both houses of the English Parliament, and to Commons in particular, was gradually taken over by the House of Commons. As Commons became more important, petitions for redress grievances began to be directed to it, instead of the Crown. The right to petition the House of Commons, as an extension of the original Magna Carta provision was later guaranteed to every commoner.[1]

The last clause of the first amendment provides: "Congress shall make no law . . . abridging . . . the right of the people peaceably to assemble and to petition the Government for a redress of grievances." The first clear test under this clause took place in 1836. The United States House of Representatives, having found itself inundated with abolitionist petitions, adopted in 1836 a gag rule that limited acceptance of those petitions. The rule had the effect of tabling, without discussion, petitions concerned with slavery or the abolition of slavery received by the House of Representatives. John Quincy Adams of Massachusetts, who had opposed adoption of the gag rule as a direct violation of the Constitution of the United States, was even more strongly opposed to the strengthening of that rule in 1840, to prohibit the receipt of any petition on the subject of slavery. The former President was finally successful in obtaining repeal of the rule in 1844, when the strength of antislavery views in the North intensified.[2]

It was not until 1876 that the first major United States Supreme Court interpretation of the rights of assembly and petition took place in *United States v. Cruikshank*.[3] The majority opinion by Chief Justice Waite narrowly interpreted the right of assembly as an attribute of national citizenship.[4] That is, the Court held that in order to claim the protection of the first amendment, it must have been asserted that a peaceful assembly existed in order to petition the *national* government for redress of a grievance connected with the powers and duties of the national government. It must be alleged that this right had been violated or in some way restricted.[5] Since the defendants in *Cruikshank* had been indicted only in general language of having prevented an assembly for a lawful purpose, the Supreme Court found the indictment insufficient, since the case was only within the domain of the states.[6]

It was not until *Hague v. C.I.O.*,[7] that protection against state abridgment of the rights of assembly and petition was recognized when the Supreme Court found the first amendment rights applicable to the states through the fourteenth amendment. A majority of the Court used two different lines of reasoning in striking down a Jersey City, New Jersey ordinance. Justice Roberts, with Chief Justice Hughes and Justice Black concurring, found protection for the right of assembly as a privilege and immunity of a United States citizen, within the meaning of the fourteenth amendment.[8] The opinion of Justice Stone, with Justice Reed concurring, while agreeing that the ordinance was in violation of the fourteenth amendment, found protection for the right of assembly in the due process clause.[9] The due process viewpoint has prevailed and it is

---

Babbitt v. United Farm Workers Nat. Union, 442 U.S. 289 (1979).

1.　C. Stephenson & F. Marcham, Sources of English Constitutional History 125 (2d ed. 1972). See Sherrard v. Hull, __ Md.App. __, 456 A.2d 59, 64 (1983), citing an earlier edition of this treatise.

2.　A. H. Kelly & W. H. Harbison, The American Constitution: Its Origins and Development, 357–58 (4th ed. 1970).

3.　United States v. Cruikshank, 92 U.S. 542 (1876).

4.　Id. at 552.

5.　Id. at 553.

6.　Id. at 552.

7.　Hague v. C.I.O., 307 U.S. 496 (1939).

8.　Id. at 512.

9.　Id. at 525.

into that broad clause that the Supreme Court has breathed an expansive interpretation of civil rights.[10]

In *Schneider v. Smith,*[11] the Supreme Court reaffirmed the importance and central meaning of the rights to peacefully assemble and petition. In striking down regulations dealing with "the reading habits, political philosophy, beliefs, and attitudes on social and economic issues of prospective seamen" on United States Merchant vessels,[12] the Court, through Justice Douglas, explained:

> The purpose of the Constitution and Bill of Rights, unlike more recent models promoting a welfare state, was to take government off the backs of the people. The First Amendment's ban against Congress "abridging" freedom of speech, the right peaceably to assemble and to petition, and the "associational freedom" . . . that goes with those rights create a preserve where the views of the individual are made inviolate. This is the philosophy of Jefferson, that "the opinions of men are not the object of civil government, nor under its jurisdiction . . . ."[13]

Later cases indicate that it is not significant whether one is engaged in speech, association, assembly, or petition. All four rights are now considered to be elements of a broad right to freedom of expression.[14] Nonetheless, some specific cases particularly related to assembly and petition are worthy of mention.

The first amendment allows a peaceful gathering of persons for almost any lawful purpose.[15] The Supreme Court had early recognized that it could not be made a crime to participate in a peaceful assembly.[16] Thus, participation in a Communist Party political meeting cannot be a crime unless violence is advocated,[17] and under the broad category of civil rights, assembly for marches, demonstrations, and picketing have been protected as lawful assemblages.[18] Labor organizing meetings have also been found lawful exercises of the first amendment right of assembly.[19]

Implicit in the right of assembly is the right of association which is implied from the expressly listed rights concerning free expression in the first amendment. Association is more than the right to attend a meeting: "it includes the right to express one's attitudes or philosophies by membership in a group, or affiliation with it or by other lawful means."[20] The Supreme Court in *Bates v. Little Rock,*[21] recognized that a corollary of this right is the right of an association to conceal from the state the names of the individual members if it is likely that a deprivation of the personal liberty of the individuals would result which was not balanced by the state demonstrating a "controlling justification" for the information.[22]

The right to petition the government for redress of grievances has been before the

---

10. E.g., DeJonge v. Oregon, 299 U.S. 353, 364 (1937); Thomas v. Collins, 323 U.S. 516, 532 (1945); Douglas v. Jeannette, 319 U.S. 157, 162 (1942); Shelton v. Tucker, 364 U.S. 479, 493 (1960).

11. Schneider v. Smith, 390 U.S. 17 (1968).

12. Id. at 24.

13. Id. at 25 (footnote omitted).

14. E.g., DeJonge v. Oregon, 299 U.S. 353, 364 (1937); Thomas v. Collins, 323 U.S. 516 (1945); Schneider v. Smith, 390 U.S. 17 (1968); United Mine Workers v. Illinois State Bar Ass'n, 389 U.S. 217 (1967).

15. Griswold v. Connecticut, 381 U.S. 479, 482 (1965). But cf. Jones v. North Carolina Prisoners' Labor Union, Inc., 433 U.S. 119 (1977) where the Court upheld prison regulations which made more difficult the organizing efforts of a prisoners' union. The restrictive environment of a penal institution was emphasized. While the prison authorities had forbade union solicitation, the union itself was allowed.

16. DeJonge v. Oregon, 299 U.S. 353 (1937).

17. Id. at 363–65.

18. Hague v. CIO, 307 U.S. 496 (1939).

19. Thomas v. Collins, 323 U.S. 516 (1945).

20. Griswold v. Connecticut, 381 U.S. 479, 483 (1965); see also Bates v. Little Rock, 361 U.S. 516, 523 (1960), and Chapter 13, Section V.

21. 361 U.S. 516 (1960); see also, NAACP v. Alabama, 357 U.S. 449 (1958); Shelton v. Tucker, 364 U.S. 479 (1960).

22. 361 U.S. 516, 527 (1960).

See also, Brown v. Socialist Workers '74 Campaign Committee, 103 S.Ct. 416 (1982), holding that certain disclosure requirements of the Ohio Expense Reporting Law cannot constitutionally be applied to the Socialist Workers Party, a minor political party which historically both government officials and private parties have harassed. The Court applied the test of Buckley v.

Supreme Court in civil suits against state and federal governmental units. One group of these cases involve the efforts of several different groups and associations to refer their members to lawyers after having first advised their members of their legal rights.[23] The Court upheld that practice based in part on the first amendment right of every person to petition for redress of grievances. In many situations, litigation is the only practical method open to a minority for redress of their grievances.[24] As to the union workers, the Court recognized a similar broad justification. The Court has found that a "common thread" of cases in this area is that "collective activity undertaken to obtain meaningful access to the courts is a fundamental right within the protection of the First Amendment." [25]

The Court has also held that the right is not limited solely to religious or political causes, but is applicable to any field of human endeavor including business or other economic activity.[26] Thus in the context of labor unions, a state statute cannot require labor union organizers to register with a state official before urging workers to join a union, for such a statute imposes a prior restraint on free speech and free assembly.[27] Similarly, business interests may combine and lobby to influence the legislative, executive, or judicial branches of government or the administrative agencies without violating the antitrust laws,[28] for such activities are protected by the right of petition.[29] The right to petition for redress of grievances has been found as a defense to criminal actions brought for violation of various assembly laws.[30] As long as the assembly to petition for redress of grievances is peaceful, and no violence is advocated, it may not be restricted.[31]

Even if violence is advocated, the first amendment rights require that the state may not impose tort liability for business losses caused by violence or the threat of violence, if such conduct occurs in the context of constitutionally protected activity, unless there is "precision of regulation." [32] Thus in *NAACP v. Claiborne Hardware Co.*,[33] the Court, without a single dissent, overturned a Mississippi state court judgment of over one

Valeo, 424 U.S. 1, 74 (1976) (per curiam), that the state cannot compel such disclosures from minor parties which can demonstrate a "reasonable probability" that such disclosures will subject those identified to "threats, harassment, or reprisals."

23. United Transp. Union v. State Bar of Michigan, 401 U.S. 576 (1971); United Mine Workers v. Illinois State Bar Ass'n, 389 U.S. 217 (1967); Brotherhood of Ry. Trainmen v. Virginia, 377 U.S. 1 (1964); NAACP v. Button, 371 U.S. 415 (1963). See also Ohralik v. State Bar, 436 U.S. 447 (1978); In re Primus, 436 U.S. 412 (1978).

24. NAACP v. Button, 371 U.S. at 429–30.

25. United Transp. Union v. State Bar of Michigan, 401 U.S. at 585.

26. Thomas v. Collins, 323 U.S. 516 (1945).

27. 323 U.S. at 532.

28. Eastern R.R. President's Conference v. Noerr Motor Freight, 365 U.S. 127 (1961); United Mine Workers v. Pennington, 381 U.S. 657 (1965); California Motor Transport v. Trucking Unlimited, 404 U.S. 508 (1972).

See generally, Fische, Antitrust Liability for Attempts to Influence Government Action: The Basis and Limits of the *Noerr-Pennington* Doctrine, 45 U.Chi.L. Rev. 80 (1977). See also, Kennedy, Political Boycotts, the Sherman Act, and the First Amendment: An Accommodation of Competing Interests, 55 So.Calif.L.

Rev. 983 (1982) (arguing that political boycotts can be regulated by the Sherman Act without violating the first amendment).

29. California Motor Transport v. Trucking Unlimited, 404 U.S. 508 (1972).

Cf. Citizens Against Rent Control/Coalition for Fair Housing v. Berkeley, 454 U.S. 290, 294 (1981): "[T]he practice of persons sharing common views banding together to achieve a common end is deeply embedded in the American political process. The 18th-century Committees of Correspondence and the phamphleteers were early examples of this phenomena and the Federalist Papers were perhaps the most significant and lasting example."

30. DeJonge v. Oregon, 299 U.S. 353 (1937); Thomas v. Collins, 323 U.S. 516 (1945); Edwards v. South Carolina, 372 U.S. 229 (1963); Bridges v. California, 314 U.S. 252 (1941).

31. DeJonge v. Oregon, 299 U.S. 353, 364 (1937); Thomas v. Collins, 323 U.S. 516, 532 (1945); Douglas v. Jeannette, 319 U.S. 157, 162 (1942); Shelton v. Tucker, 364 U.S. 479, 493 (1960); Edwards v. South Carolina, 372 U.S. 229 (1963).

32. NAACP v. Button, 371 U.S. 415, 438 (1963).

33. NAACP v. Claiborne Hardware Co., 102 S.Ct. 3409 (1982). Rehnquist, J., concurred in the result, without opinion. Marshall, J., took no part in the consideration or decision of the case.

and one quarter million dollars against the NAACP and certain individuals for business losses suffered by several white merchants because of an economic boycott against them. On October 31, 1969, after black citizens in Clairborne County failed to achieve their demands met for racial equality and integration several hundred blacks at a local NAACP meeting voted to boycott white merchants. Although some boycott supporters engaged in acts of violence, most of the practices used to encourage support for the boycott were peaceful, orderly, and protected by the first amendment. All of the marches were carefully controlled.

The Court first held that the state could constitutionally impose liability for "the consequences of violent conduct [but] it may not award compensation for the consequences of nonviolent, protected activity. Only those losses proximately caused by unlawful conduct may be recovered."[34] Nor can a member of a group be liable simply because another member of the same group proximately caused damage by violence:

> Civil liability may not be imposed merely because an individual belonged to a group, some members of which committed acts of violence. For liability to be imposed by reason of association alone, it is necessary to establish that the group itself possessed unlawful goals and that the individual held a specific intent to further those illegal goals.[35]

Thus mere association cannot make one liable, but those persons who actually engaged in violence or other illegal activity can be held liable for the injuries that they caused.[36]

The Court then turned to the NAACP and ruled that the lower court findings were also not adequate to support the judgment against it. "To impose liability without a finding that the NAACP authorized—either actually or apparently—or ratified unlawful conduct would impermissible burden the rights of political association that are protected by the First Amendment."[37]

Protection for the actions of groups or individuals is not unlimited under the first amendment rights of assembly and petition. In several instances, courts have justified limitations on those rights. The initial broad limitation on these rights is that they must be enjoyed in a law abiding manner.[38] Courts have stated that the rights may not be used as a shield to violate valid statutes,[39] nor may they be used as the means or pretext for achieving substantive evil.[40] Thus the antitrust laws may be applied to groups that conspire to bar competitors from meaningful access to the agencies and the courts.[41] Similarly, a conspiracy with a licensing authority to eliminate a competitor may be prosecuted under the antitrust laws.[42] And of course criminal conspiracy laws deserve no first amendment protection if the conspiracy is to achieve a criminal end in the immediate future rather than merely a combination to advocate ideas (even violent ideas) to promote future change.[43] In general, when the rights of assembly and petition are limited, the state must demonstrate a compelling interest in an area in which it can otherwise lawfully regulate.[44]

34. 102 S.Ct. at 3429.

35. 102 S.Ct. at 3430 (footnote omitted).

36. 102 S.Ct. at 3433.

37. 102 S.Ct. at 3435. See also, Douglas, J., dissenting from a dismissal of a writ of certiorai, in NAACP v. Overstreet, 384 U.S. 118 (1966). Douglas, J., in his opinion, was joined by Warren, C. J., and Brennan & Fortas, JJ.

38. Cox v. Louisiana, 379 U.S. 559 (1965).

39. California Motor Transport v. Trucking Unlimited, 404 U.S. 508 (1972).

40. NAACP v. Button, 371 U.S. 415, 438 (1963).

41. California Motor Transport v. Trucking Unlimited, 404 U.S. 508, 512 (1972).

42. Walker Process Equipment v. Food Machinery & Chemical Corp., 382 U.S. 172, 175–77 (1965).

43. Brandenburg v. Ohio, 395 U.S. 444 (1969), discussed in this Chapter, Section IV, D. See also, NAACP v. Claiborne Hardware Co., 102 S.Ct. 3409, 3434 (1982).

44. Williams v. Rhodes, 393 U.S. 23, 31 (1968); American Party of Texas v. White, 415 U.S. 767 (1974).

XVII. OBSCENITY

A. Introduction

Edmund Wilson was, without question, one of the most influential literary critics of the twentieth century. A conservative and exacting man, he was to F. Scott Fitzgerald "my artistic conscience," [1] an admission that in all honesty might well have been made by many of the American novelists of the 1920's and 1930's whose work, taken together, is now an indelible part of the American self-image.

Wilson was also a novelist himself. In 1946, at the peak of his reputation, he published his second novel, *Memoirs of Hecate County*, in which he related two rather spiritless passages describing sexual intercourse. Upon complaint of the New York Society for the Suppression of Vice, the novel's publisher, Doubleday & Co., was charged under a state criminal obscenity statute. Despite the testimony of Columbia University Professor Lionel Trilling, who said that the allegedly-obscene passages were inextricably related to the novel's literary merit, a three-judge trial panel found Doubleday guilty. This verdict was upheld by the Appellate Division and the New York Court of Appeals,[2] and the United States Supreme Court, in one of the first major obsenity cases to reach it, affirmed without opinion in a four-to-four vote.[3]

The Court's affirmation came down in 1948. A year later, in Philadelphia, several booksellers were charged with violating a Pennsylvania criminal statute that outlawed the sale of "any obscene, lewd, lascivious, filthy, indecent or disgusting book . . . ." [4] Among the books to which the Commonwealth applied these adjectives were James T. Farrell's *Studs Lonigan* trilogy, William Faulkner's *Sanctuary* and *The Wild Palms*, and Erskine Caldwell's *God's Little Acre*, books which are now familiar items on a college English major's required-reading list. In this case, however, the prosecution failed. In his trial opinion, Judge Curtis Bok granted the "several general dicta by the Supreme Court to the effect that obscenity is indictable just because it is obscenity," [5] but he reasoned that constitutionally, conviction under a criminal obscenity statute requires a "causal connection" [6] beyond a reasonable doubt between the allegedly-obscene activity—here, the sale of the books—and actual or imminent criminal behavior in individuals exposed to the activity. On this basis, Judge Bok found the booksellers not guilty.

Among the "several general dicta" to which Judge Bok referred was Justice Murphy's statement in *Chaplinsky v. New Hampshire* [7] that the "lewd and obscene" are among "certain well-defined and narrowly limited classes of speech, the prevention and punishment of which have never been thought to raise any Constitutional problem." [8] The dicta continued after Judge Bok's decision. In *Beauharnais v. Illinois*,[9] decided in 1952, Justice Frankfurter equated

---

1. F. S. Fitzgerald, Pasting It Together, in The Fitzgerald Reader 415 (A. Mizener ed. 1963).

2. People v. Doubleday & Co., 272 App.Div. 799, 71 N.Y.S.2d 736 (1947), aff'd 297 N.Y. 687, 77 N.E.2d 6.

3. Doubleday & Co. v. New York, 335 U.S. 848 (1948) (Justice Frankfurter not participating). For a more detailed discussion of the *Doubleday* case, see M. Konvitz, Fundamental Liberties of a Free People 159 (1957). A few years later the Court did strike down a New York statute banning motion pictures on the ground that they were "sacrilegious." The Court held that motion pictures are not precluded from First Amendment protection even though they are sold for profit. The statute was then struck down as too vague. Joseph Burstyn, Inc. v. Wilson, 343 U.S. 495 (1952). This case thus does have important implications for obscenity legislation, although the Court did

not specifically decide it on such grounds. See also, Kingsley International Pictures Corp. v. Regents of New York, 360 U.S. 684 (1959) (denial of license to show the film "Lady Chatterley's Lover" is reversed; decision not on obscenity grounds).

4. As cited in M. Konvitz, Fundamental Liberties of a Free People 160 (1957).

5. Commonwealth v. Gordon, 66 Pa.D. & C. 101, 146 (1949), aff'd sub nom. Commonwealth v. Feigenbaum, 166 Pa.Super. 120, 70 A.2d 389 (1950) (per curiam), discussed in M. Konvitz, supra note 4 at 160.

6. 66 Pa.D. & C. 101 at 156.

7. 315 U.S. 568 (1942).

8. Id. at 571–72.

9. 343 U.S. 250 (1952).

obscenity with group libel as being beyond "the area of constitutionally protected speech." [10] Frankfurter did not elaborate his point; neither, for that matter, had Murphy, whose inclusion of obscenity with libel and "fighting words" in a single, undifferentiated constitutional classification seemed offhand, almost peremptory. To Justice Murphy, the "lewd and obscene" were among the utterances about which "[i]t has been well observed that [they] are no essential part of any exposition of ideas, and are of such slight social value as a step to truth that any benefit that may be derived from them is clearly outweighed by the social interest in order and morality." [11]

In making this statement, Justice Murphy cited and paraphrased the work of Professor Zechariah Chafee, Jr. [12] It is to Chafee, then, that we must turn for a fuller explication of the legal principle emerging at that time which argued that "obscenity is indictable just because it is obscenity." To Chafee, "profanity and indecent talk and pictures" were inheretly void of "any exposition of ideas, ... The harm is done as soon as they are communicated, or is liable to follow almost immediatley in the form of retaliatory violence. The only sound explanation of the punishment of obscenity and profanity is that the words are criminal, not because of the ideas they communicate, but like acts because of their immediate consequences to the five senses." [13] As Professor Konvitz pointed out, Chafee's treatment of obscenity as verbal "acts" comported with legal analogy drawn by Justices Murphy and Frankfurther between obscenity, libel, and "fighting words," and further justified the Court's reluctance to confer first amendment protection. [14]

On the other hand, two years before he discussed obscenity in the *Chaplinsky* case,

Justice Murphy himself delivered the Court's opinion in *Thornhill v. Alabama*, [15] a case dealing with labor picketing in a rural company town. In *Thornhill*, Justice Murphy did not deny that picketing is an "act" in any meaningful sense of the word. But he stated that picketing and similar activities "may enlighten the public on the nature and causes of a labor dispute," and that "[t]he safeguarding of these means is essential to the securing of an informed and educated public opinion with respect to a matter which is of public concern." [16] In *Thornhill*, then Justice Murphy allowed that a verbal "act" may, under certain circumstances, be deemed "speech" within the meaning of the first amendment.

So Justice Murphy created a definitional dilemma for the Court. This dilemma was obvious in the prosecutions involving Edmund Wilson, James T. Farrell, and William Faulkner. If Faulkner, whose work brought him a Nobel Prize, played an "essential part" in the "exposition of ideas," if his Snopes trilogy, for example, may be taken as "a step to truth," then under the dictum in *Chaplinsky*, Faulkner's work could not have been obscene to Justice Murphy. But according to Professor Chafee, upon whom Justice Murphy so heavily relied, the more enticing passages in some of Faulkner's novels were by definition unrelated to the useful exposition of ideas, and were thus as a matter of law of "such slight social value" as to be beyond the protection of the first amendment. Yet Faulkner surely addressed himself to matters "of social concern"; while under *Chaplinsky* his use of obscenity constituted a verbal "act," under *Thornhill* it surely constituted a literary device, "essential to the securing of an informed and educated public opinion . . . ." under the first amendment. It may be easy to draw a distinction between labor picketing and 50-

---

10. Id. at 266.

11. Chaplinsky v. New Hampshire, 315 U.S. 568, 572 (1942).

12. Z. Chafee, Free Speech in the United States (1941).

13. Id. at 150.

14. M. Konvitz, Fundamental Liberties of a Free People 158 (1957).

15. 310 U.S. 88 (1940).

16. Id. at 104.

cent peep shows, but can the distinction be drawn where the "obscenity" at issue takes the form of a paragraph in *Sanctuary?*

In 1946, Justice Douglas noted in passing in *Hannegan v. Esquire, Inc.,*[17] that:

[u]nder our system of government there is an accommodation for the widest varieties of tastes and ideas. What is good literature, what has educational value, what is refined public information, what is good art, varies with individuals as it does from one generation to another. There doubtless would be a contrariety of views concerning Cervantes' *Don Quixote,* Shakespeare's *Venus and Adonis,* or Zola's *Nana.* But a requirement that literature or art conform to some norm prescribed by an official smacks of an ideology foreign to our system.[18]

Nonetheless, when Judge Bok observed in 1949 that to the Supreme Court, "obscenity is indictable just because it is obscenity," he was alluding to an accurate contemporary legal principle. He was also alluding to the core problem of this area of first amendment law: What is obscenity?

B. Obscenity: The ROTH Case

The dicta on obscenity in *Chaplinsky v. New Hampshire*[1] and *Beauharnais v. Illinois*[2] raised the obvious question of how the Court would treat the issue when it rendered its first decision on the subject. That decision, *Roth v. United States,*[3] was handed down in 1957, and at its core it is still the law of obscenity under the Constitution. In *Roth,* two state criminal statutes were invoked against the publication and sale of obscene matter. After stating in a footnote that "No issue is presented [here] concerning the obscenity of the material involved,"[4] Justice Brennan, writing for the Court, stated that: "The dispositve question is whether obscenity is utterance within the area of pro-

tected speech and press."[5] On the basis of a series of earlier cases in which obscenity had been discussed in dictum, including *Chaplinsky* and *Beauharnais,* it had always been "assumed" that obscenity was not protected by the first amendment.[6] The Court thereupon discussed several historical elements underlying the phrasing of the first amendment, and concluded that "All ideas having even the slightest redeeming social importance—unorthodox ideas, controversial ideas, even ideas hateful to the prevailing climate of opinion—have the full protection of the guaranties [of the first amendment], unless excludable because they encroach upon the limited area of more important interests. But implicit in the history of the first amendment is the rejection of obscenity as utterly without redeeming social importance."[7] Then, after quoting the *Chaplinsky* dictum at some length, the Court converted its traditional assumption into a rule of law, and held that "obscenity is not within the area of constitutionally protected speech or press."[8]

At this point the Court attempted to dispose of two lingering issues. First, it rejected the contention that there is a burden on the state to prove that a given piece of obscene material must be related to antisocial conduct. The Court adopted Justice Frankfurter's comment in *Beauharnais* and held that if obscenity is without constitutional protection, it may be proscribed by statute without further justification.[9] Second, the Court drew a distinction between sex and obsenity. "Obscene material," said the Court, "is material which deals with sex in a manner appealing to prurient interest," while the mere portrayal of sex in art, literature, scientific works, and similar forums "is not itself sufficient reason to deny material the constitutional protection of freedom of

---

17. 327 U.S. 146 (1946).

18. Id. at 157–58.

1. 315 U.S. 568, 571–72 (1942).

2. 343 U.S. 250, 266 (1952).

3. 354 U.S. 476 (1957). *Roth* was consolidated with Alberts v. California, and all references herein to *Roth* shall include *Alberts.*

4. Id. at 481 note 8.

5. Id. at 481 (footnote omitted).

6. Id.

7. Id. at 484.

8. Id. at 485.

9. Id. at 486-87.

speech and press." [10]   In fleshing out this distinction, the Court adopted the standard of whether "to the average person, applying contemporary community standards, the dominant theme of the material taken as a whole appeals to prurient interest." [11]   The Court closed its opinion with the observation that in accordance with *United States v. Petrillo*,[12] a statute outlawing obscenity will not violate due process by a mere lack of precision.   Except in marginal cases, the Court suggested that the language of such a statute will be sufficient if it gives "adequate warning of the conduct proscribed" and enables the law to be administered fairly.[13]

Thus when reduced to a formula, *Roth* provided that material may be deemed obscene, and therefore wholly without constitutional protection, if it (a) appeals to a prurient interest in sex, (b) has no serious literary, artistic, political, or scientific merit, and (c) is on the whole offensive to the average person under contemporary community standards.

There are two elements in *Roth* that deserve special attention.   First, there is the problem with the word "prurient."   This single word was quite clearly the touchstone of Justice Brennan's analysis of the case.   Its application spelled the difference between sex and obscenity, between applicable community standards and mere community prejudice, between material that is sanctioned by the Constitution and material that may be subject to criminal penalty.   To the Court, prurient material was that which has "a tendency to excite lustful thoughts." [14] This definition deserved some further explication, and the Court provided it with excerpts from Webster's Second New Interna-

tional Dictionary, i.e., that "prurient" is ". . . [i]tching; longing; uneasy with desire or longing; of persons, having itching, morbid, or lascivious longings; of desire, curiosity, or propensity, lewd. . . . " [15]

It is obviously possible that material can be prurient and political; that it can be possessed of a tendency to excite lustful thoughts and contain profound social commentary; or that it can create in an individual morbid and lascivious desires and constitute poetry of the highest order.   It was with this in mind, perhaps, that Chief Justice Warren stated in concurrence that the "conduct of the defendant is the central issue, not the obscenity of a book or picture.   The nature of the materials is, of course, relevant as an attribute of the defendant's conduct, but the materials are thus placed in context from which they draw color and character.   A wholly different result might be reached in a different setting." [16]

In a separate opinion, Justice Harlan, concurring and dissenting, carried Chief Justice Warren's observation further and objected to the very concept of reducing a constitutional question to a "distinct, recognizable and classifiable . . . poison ivy" under the term "prurient." [17]   To Justice Harlan, obscenity was by its nature an abstraction; and under the Constitution it presents a problem that "cannot be solved in such a generalized fashion." [18]   Justice Harlan preferred a case-by-case approach in which a reviewing court could take into account the fact that "[e]very communication has an individuality and 'value' of its own": [19]

The suppression of a particular writing or other tangible form of expression is, therefore, an *individual* matter, and in the nature of things every such suppression raises an individual

---

10.   Id. at 487.

11.   Id. at 489.   The Court explicitly rejected the leading English case holding that obscenity is to be judged merely by the effect of an isolated passage upon particularly susceptible persons.   Regina v. Hicklin, [1868] L.R. 3 Q.B. 360.

12.   332 U.S. 1, 7–8 (1947), cited in *Roth* at 491.

13.   *Roth* at 491.

14.   Id. at 487 n. 20.

15.   Id.

16.   Id. at 495 (concurring opinion).

17.   Id. at 497 (concurring in the result in *Alberts*—the state case—and dissenting in *Roth*—the federal case).

18.   Id.

19.   Id.

constitutional problem, in which a reviewing court must determine for *itself* whether the attacked expression is suppressable within constitutional standards. Since those standards do not readily lend themselves to generalized definitions, the constitutional problem in the last analysis becomes one of particularized judgments which appellate courts must make for themselves.[20]

The second element in *Roth* to which one might pay special attention is the now-famous dissent of Justices Douglas and Black. This short dissent, which is often cited as evidence of its authors' "absolutist" approach to speech and press issues under the first amendment, should be read in its entirety. It contains a direct challenge to Justice Harlan's view that "in the last analysis [obscenity] becomes one of particularized judgments which appellate courts must make for themselves." Justice Harlan assumed these judgments would be made under the applicable constitutional standard; but to Justices Douglas and Black the appropriate standard should not in any event give "the censor free range over a vast domain. To allow the State to step in and punish mere speech or publication that the judge or jury thinks has an *undesirable* impact on thoughts but that is not shown to be a part of unlawful action is drastically to curtail the First Amendment. . . ."[21]

They concluded that obscenity, under any definition in any environment, is a form of expression, and as such "can be suppressed if, and to the extent that, it is so closely brigaded with illegal action as to be an inseparable part of it. . . . As a people, we cannot afford to relax that standard."[22] Thus Justices Douglas and Black adopted Judge Curtis Bok's appoach in *Commonwealth v. Gordon*,[23] and argued that there must be a causal connection between the allegedly-obscene expression—which at all times must, for analytical purposes, be deemed to be within the protection of the first amendment—and illegal conduct, which, under long-established principle, could be sufficient to render the expression unlawful.

C. The Implications of ROTH

There is a small curiosity in the *Roth* opinion that, in some respects, symbolizes the nature and import of the opinion as a whole. As we have noted, Justice Brennan placed this prefatory footnote at the beginning of his majority opinion: "No issue is presented [here] concerning the obscenity of the material involved."[1] Apparently, the purpose of this footnote was to clarify the Court's limited task on review, which was to determine the facial validity of two state criminal obscenity statutes rather than the validity of those statutes in light of the circumstances under which they were invoked. This disclaimer points to a broad technical problem in the case. Because the Court dealt only with the facial validity of two typically-comprehensive anti-obscenity statutes, the Court was able to treat obscenity as an abstract proposition and to formulate a definitional standard for obscenity in terms of abstract Constitutional principle. While in a limited technical sense, there was nothing "advisory" about *Roth*, and while the *Roth* test was not dictum, the opinion came perilously close to a loose theoretical exercise in Constitutional law. Unburdened by the factual circumstances that triggered the case in the first place, the Court in *Roth* rendered a decision that was framed in terms that would not easily address themselves to the plethora of varying factual circumstances that would burden the Court in obscenity cases in the years to come.

Shortly after *Roth* was handed down, Dean William B. Lockhart and Professor Robert C. McClure of the University of Minnesota Law School wrote two often noted

---

20. Id. (emphasis in original).

21. Id. at 509 (dissenting opinion) (emphasis in original).

22. Id. at 514 (dissenting opinion).

23. 66 Pa.D. & C. 101 (1949), aff'd sub nom. Commonwealth v. Feigenbaum, 166 Pa.Super. 120, 70 A.2d 389 (1950).

1. 354 U.S. 476, 481 n. 8.

law review articles [2] which have "greatly influenced" the "struggle for a fair and realistic definition of obscenity in the wake of *Roth* . . . ." [3] In these articles Lockhart and McClure proposed two alternative approaches to an understanding of *Roth*. First, they suggested that the case settled only two aspects of the obscenity question: [4] (1) that the material in question must be considered as a whole, and cannot be condemned on the basis of isolated passages; and (2) that the material, taken as a whole, must be examined in light of the average person whose attitudes reflect a common community standard, not in terms of the material's impact on the exceptional individual who is particularly susceptible to the material's prurient aspects. [5] Second, Lockhart and McClure argued that the attention paid by the Court in *Roth* to the possibly redeeming social importance of allegedly-obscene material indicated an implied acceptance of a concept they termed "variable obscenity." Under this concept the pivotal word "prurient" can be understood only in a relative sense; its meaning and application would vary according to the tastes and sophistication of the audience at which the material is directed. [6]

An example of the application of the "variable obscenity" approach might be litigation over the obscenity of some of the later drawings of Aubrey Beardsley, the late-nineteenth century English illustrator and art editor of the somewhat infamous *Yellow Book*. To an average audience, Beardsley's elaborate, neo-Baroque renditions of homosexual and lesbian sexual activity would perforce be prurient, and thus obscene; but to an audience of art historians or aficionados of Victorian social psychology, the drawings, while doubtless titillating, would carry a so-cial importance that would override a prosecutor's objections to their sexual content.

It was this sort of situation, perhaps, that Chief Justice Warren had in mind when he stated in his concurrence in *Roth* that the central issue in obscenity is the conduct of the defendant himself, and thus the "context from which [the materials] draw color and character." This situation certainly lends support to Justice Harlan's objections to a rigid, undifferentiating approach to obscenity under the term "prurient." In any event the Court did move in the direction of "variable obscenity" in *Ginzburg v. United States* [7] and *Ginsberg v. New York*, [8] which are discussed below.

The value of Lockhart and McClure's scholarship, however, must be balanced against the inherently insoluble enigma of *Roth* that renders virtually any theoretical attempt to "explain" the case into an exercise in apologetics. The enigma was perhaps best described by Justice Stewart in his short concurring opinion in *Jacobellis v. Ohio*, [9] one of a series of cases in which the Court applied *Roth* to an allegedly obscene motion picture. Justice Stewart's concurrence, in its entirety, with only citations omitted, is as follows:

It is possible to read the Court's opinion in Roth v. United States and Alberts v. California . . . in a variety of ways. In saying this, I imply no criticism of the Court, which in those cases was faced with the task of trying to define what may be indefinable. I have reached the conclusion, which I think is confirmed at least by negative implication in the Court's decisions since *Roth* and *Alberts*, that under the First and Fourteenth Amendments criminal laws in this area are constitutionally limited to hard-core pornography. I shall not today attempt further to define the kinds of material I

---

2. Censorship of Obscenity: The Developing Constitutional Standards, 45 Minn.L.Rev. 5 (1960); Obscenity Censorship: The Core Constitutional Issue—What is Obscene?, 7 Utah L.Rev. 289 (1961).

3. J. Barron & C. Dienes, Constitutional Law: Principles and Policy 905 (1975).

4. W. Lockhart & R. McClure, Censorship of Obscenity: The Developing Constitutional Standards, 45 Minn.L.Rev. 5, 53 (1960).

5. Id.

6. Id. at 68–70.

7. 383 U.S. 463 (1966).

8. 390 U.S. 629 (1968).

9. 378 U.S. 184 (1964).

understand to be embraced within that short-hand description; and perhaps I could never succeed in intelligibly doing so. But I know it when I see it, and the motion picture involved in this case is not that.[10]

Perhaps, when all else is said, that is the best that any judge can do; he cannot define obscenity, but he can admit that "I know it when I see it."

It is worth noting that Edmund Wilson, whose novel *Memoirs of Hecate County* was the subject of the Court's first decision of record on obscenity, somewhat accidentally stumbled into an "art" movie house in Utica, New York in the summer of 1968. He found himself watching a movie consisting largely of an actress manipulating her genitals, which, he said, "close up and magnified, had the thoroughly repellant appearance of the pieces of raw meat in a butcher's shop." [11] The great critic concluded with little explanation that "I do not think that such films should be allowed." [12] Perhaps he thought that the subject did not deserve detailed discussion, that his judgment required no justification. He, too, knew it when he saw it; and for him that was the beginning and the end of the matter.

D. The Development of the Case Law under Roth

Two years after *Roth* the Court held that the state could not eliminate the need to prove *scienter* in an obscenity prosecution, in a case where it reversed the conviction of a bookseller under a statute which dispensed with any requirement of knowledge of the contents of the books on the part of the seller.[1]

Then, in *Jacobellis v. Ohio*, the Court held, *inter alia*, "that, in 'obscenity' cases as in all others involving rights derived from

the First Amendment guarantees of free expression, this Court cannot avoid making an independent constitutional judgment on the facts of the case as to whether the material involved is constitutionally protected." [2] In short, a trial court's findings as to the obscenity of the material at issue is not binding on review—if the appellate court takes the case, it will have to watch the movie or read the book itself.

Thus, the import of *Roth* would unfold as the Supreme Court was forced to reconsider the implications of the *Roth* test in terms of the problems of specific areas. As one might expect, the applications of *Roth* eventually subverted some of the major analytical elements of the opinion itself as well as revealing the failure of the Supreme Court to agree on any real tests to apply in practice to allegedly obscene material.

Two examples illustrating this problem may be found in the decisions of the Court's 1966 term. First, a fragmented Supreme Court used the "social value" test to overturn a conviction under the Massachusetts obscenity statute that held the book *Fanny Hill* to be obscene, in *A Book Named "John Cleland's Memoirs of a Woman of Pleasure" v. Attorney General of Massachusetts*.[3] Justice Brennan announced the judgment of the Court reversing the state court's finding of obscenity, but Brennan's opinion was only joined by Chief Justice Warren and Justice Fortas.

Brennan argued that each of the three elements of the *Roth* test must be applied independently,[4] and thus that material cannot be adjudged obscene if it passes muster under any of them. Justice Brennan reasoned that *Fanny Hill*, which has long been a classic of ribald literature, could not properly be deemed to be *"utterly* without redeeming

---

10. Id. at 197 (concurring opinion) (citations omitted).

11. E. Wilson, Upstate: Records and Recollections of Northern New York 311 (1971).

12. Id.

1. Smith v. California, 361 U.S. 147 (1959). See generally, Kalven, The Metaphysics of the Law of Ob-

scenity, 1960 Sup.Ct.Rev. 1; Magrath, The Obscenity Cases: Grapes of Roth, 1966 Sup.Ct.Rev. 7; Henkin, Morals and the Constitution: The Sin of Obscenity, 63 Colum.L.Rev. 391 (1963).

2. 378 U.S. 184, 190 (1964) (footnote omitted).

3. 383 U.S. 413 (1966).

4. Id. at 419.

social value," [5] and thus is sheltered by the First Amendment. By applying the elements of the *Roth* test independently, Justice Brennan stepped away from the strict definitional approach employed in *Roth*. *Fanny Hill* may or may not have appealed to prurient interests under any definition or under any set of community standards, but this was now irrelevant; the book contained at least a modicum of literary value, and that was enough to save it from suppression by the Attorney General of Massachusetts. Suddenly "pruriency" was no longer the pivotal element of obscenity under the first amendment.

Justice Stewart concurred in the reversal for a different reason: he felt that the material was not hard core pornography. Justice Black in his separate concurrence emphasized that the Court's opinions in this area agreed only on results and not on reasons, offering no useful tests or guidance for lower courts or laymen. Justice Douglas, composing the sixth vote, concurred because he believed that the first amendment forbade censorship of any expression not intertwined with illegal conduct. And the three remaining Justices (Clark, Harlan, and White) dissented, each writing separate opinions.

Far more important, however, was Justice Brennan's opinion for the Court in *Ginzburg v. United States*.[6] In *Ginzburg*, the Court was faced with three professionally produced publications devoted to sex, including EROS, which the Court described as "a hard-cover magazine of expensive format." [7] The Court found the publications to be obscene because they represented "commercial exploitation of erotica solely for the sake of their prurient appeal." In reaching this conclusion, the Court stated that the "leer of the sensualist" had "permeate[d]" the man-

ner in which the publications had been distributed and advertised: [8] mailing privileges had been sought from Intercourse and Blue Ball, Pennsylvania, and Middlesex, New Jersey; and the advertising circulars describing the publications "stressed the sexual candor of the respective publications, and openly boasted that the publishers would take full advantage of what they regarded as an unrestricted license allowed by law in the expression of sex and sexual matters." [9] The Court reasoned that the "brazenness" [10] of the defendant's marketing tactics unveiled his intent in distributing the materials, and that this intent was the heart of the matter: "Where the purveyor's sole emphasis is on the sexually provocative aspects of his publications, that fact may be decisive in the determination of obscenity." [11]

In the *Memoirs* case, Justice Brennan emphasized that "the social value of the book can neither be weighed against nor cancelled by its prurient appeal or patent offensiveness." [12] But in *Ginzburg*, the Court, per Justice Brennan, did not even address the question of the social value of the three publications—its decision rested solely on the defendant's intent, his pandering. Thus an intent to appeal "solely" to prurient interests *can* outweigh the social value of the materials in question while the prurient appeal of the materials, of itself, cannot.

In a series of obscenity decisions the rationales of the individual members became more, rather than less, divergent. There was never majority agreement concerning the "contemporary community standards" aspect of the *Memoirs* plurality, with some justices favoring a national community standard; [13] others favoring a national standard for federal prosecutions; [14] still others favor-

---

5.   Id. (emphasis in original).

6.   383 U.S. 463 (1966).

7.   Id. at 466.

8.   Id. at 468.   Later pandering cases include Splawn v. California, 431 U.S. 595 (1977), and Hamling v. United States, 418 U.S. 87, 130 (1974).

9.   383 U.S. at 468.

10.   Id. at 470.

11.   Id.

12.   383 U.S. 413, 419 (1966).

13.   Jacobellis v. Ohio, 378 U.S. 184, 192–195 (1964) (Brennan, J., joined by Goldberg, J.).

14.   Manual Enterprises v. Day, 370 U.S. 478, 488 (1962) (Harlan, J., joined by Stewart, J.).

ing local community or flexibility for state standards.[15] As to the "prurient interest" aspect, some justices held that if the material was designed for and primarily disseminated to a clearly defined deviant sexual group rather than the public at large, the prurient-appeal requirement is satisfied by looking to that group and not to the "average" or "normal" person referred to in *Roth*.[16] Other cases emphasized the element of "pandering" in close cases [17] or defined obscenity in terms of the juvenile audience.[18] And various justices also had differing views of the tests used to determine the "social value" aspect of the *Memoirs* test.[19] As Justice Brennan later openly acknowledged:

> In the face of this divergence of opinion the Court began the practice in *Redrup v. New York*, 386 U.S. 767 (1967) of *per curiam* reversals of convictions for the dissemination of materials that at least five members of the Court, applying their separate tests, deemed not to be obscene. This approach capped the attempt in *Roth* to separate all forms of sexual oriented expression into two categories—the one subject to full governmental suppression and the other beyond the reach of governmental regulation to the same extent as any other protected form of speech or press.[20]

No fewer than 31 cases had followed this *Redrup* approach.[21]

E.   The MILLER Decision

Finally, in *Miller v. California*,[22] the Court decided to abandon the *Memoirs* approach entirely, and for the first time since

Roth a majority of the justices agreed to the proper test for obscenity:

> While *Roth* presumed "obscenity" to be "utterly without redeeming social importance," *Memoirs* [the *Fanny Hill* case] required that to prove obscenity it must be affirmatively established that the material is "*utterly* without redeeming social value." Thus, even as they repeated the words of *Roth*, the *Memoirs* plurality produced a drastically altered test that called on the prosecution to prove a negative, *i.e.*, that the material was "*utterly* without redeeming social value"—a burden virtually impossible to discharge under our criminal standards of proof. Such considerations caused Mr. Justice Harlan to wonder if the "*utterly* without redeeming social value" test had any meaning at all.[23]

The *Miller* Court might well have been correct in pointing to the difficulties the *Memoirs* approach imposed on the practicalities of meeting the burden of proof where the state is asked, in effect, to prove a negative. But in *Memoirs* the Brennan plurality emphasized the adjective "utterly" in order to give the word an independent significance, not to give it an overriding meaning as suggested in *Miller*.

In any event, in rejecting the *Memoirs* approach, the Court in *Miller* had to return to the problems that the *Memoirs* plurality had tried to resolve. The Court in *Miller* carefully noted that "in the area of freedom of speech and press the courts must always remain sensitive to any infringement on genuinely serious literary, artistic, political, or scientific expression. This is an area in

---

15. Jacobellis v. Ohio, 378 U.S. 184, 200–201 (1964) (Warren, C. J., joined by Clark, J. dissenting) (local community standards); Hoyt v. Minnesota, 399 U.S. 524 (1970) (Blackmun, J., joined by Burger, C. J., and Harlan J., dissenting) (flexibility of state standards).

16. Mishkin v. New York, 383 U.S. 502, 508 (1966) (Brennan, J., for the Court, with Douglas, Black, and Stewart, JJ., dissenting, and Harlan, J., concurring).

17. Ginzburg v. United States, 383 U.S. 463 (1966) (Brennan, J., for the Court, with Black, Douglas, Stewart, and Harlan, JJ., each dissenting separately).

18. Ginsberg v. New York, 390 U.S. 629 (1968) (Brennan, J., for the Court, with Stewart, J., concurring in the result; Fortas, J., dissenting; and Harlan, J., concurring).

19. E.g., A Book Named "John Cleland's Memoirs of a Woman of Pleasure" v. Attorney General of Massachusetts, 383 U.S. 413, 445 (1966) (Clark, J., dissenting) (consider "social importance" together with evidence that the material in question "appeals to prurient interest and is patently offensive"); Id. at 462 (social importance not an independent test of obscenity but "relevant only to determin[e] the predominant prurient interest of the material . . . ").

20. Paris Adult Theatre I v. Slaton, 413 U.S. 49, 82–83 (1973) (Brennan, J., dissenting) (footnote omitted).

21. Id. at 82 n. 8.

22. 413 U.S. 15 (1973).

23. Id. at 21–22. (emphasis in original).

which there are few eternal verities." [24]   On this basis the Court stated that "State statutes designed to regulate obscene materials must be carefully limited"; [25] and thus the Court held that "we now confine the permissible scope of [state] regulation [of obscenity] to works which depict or describe sexual conduct."   The actual test for obscenity set forth in *Miller* is as follows:

> The basic guidelines for the trier of fact must be: (a) whether "the average person, applying contemporary community standards" would find that the work, taken as a whole, appeals to the prurient interest, (b) whether the work depicts or describes, in a patently offensive way, sexual conduct specifically defined by the applicable state law, and (c) whether the work, taken as a whole, lacks serious literary, artistic, political, or scientific value. [26]

The third element of the *Miller* test— "whether the work, taken as a whole, lacks serious literary, artistic, political, or scientific value"—appears on its face considerably more restrictive than the "utterly without redeeming social value" test in *Roth* given independent significance in *Memoirs* through the emphasis on the word "utterly." The shift from "utterly" to "serious" indicates that juries may be given greater leeway under this standard.   In addition, the Court eliminated the concept of "social value" and replaced it with "literary, artistic, political, or scientific value"—a distinction without a difference, perhaps, unless one believes that material can contain "social" value without being literary, artistic, political, or scientific.   However, to the extent that the Court requires judicial supervision of these issues and the directing of verdicts when the evidence shows the speech to be "serious" or nonpornographic in nature, there may be little practical difference. [27]

With respect to the second part of the *Miller* test, the Court offered "a few plain examples of what a state statute could define for regulation under part (b) of the standard announced in this opinion . . . ." [28]

These examples were:

> (a) Patently offensive representations or descriptions of ultimate sexual acts, normal or perverted, actual or simulated.

> (b) Patently offensive representations or descriptions of masturbation, excretory functions, and lewd exhibition of the genitals. [29]

The Court explicitly acknowledged that under *Miller*, "no one [may] be subject to prosecution for the sale or exposure of obscene materials unless these materials depict or describe patently offensive 'hard core' sexual conduct specifically defined by the regulating state law, as written or construed." [30] This portion of the test might have served as a basis for improving the ability of individuals to engage in publishing or film-making by offering them clear notice of what is prohibited by statute.   But the Court has allowed state courts to save their statutes by construction and in so doing expand the Court's list of examples.   Thus sadomasochistic materials may be constitutionally prohibited even though not listed in *Miller*: the *Miller* specifics "were offered merely as 'examples' . . . , they 'were not intended to be exhaustive.' " [31]

The most controversial aspect of the *Miller* decision, however, may be the first part of its test with its rejection of the national-standards test.   The national standards concept had never been adopted by a majority of the Court. [32]   It was only the most restrictive concept that could get a working majority of five justices to suppress an item as obscene.   Now a majority finally agreed on the national standards test—and they rejected it.

---

24. Id. at 22–23.

25. Id. at 23–24.

26. Id. at 24.

27. See Jenkins v. Georgia, 418 U.S. 153 (1974).

28. 413 U.S. at 25.

29. Id.

30. Id. at 27.

31. Ward v. Illinois, 431 U.S. 767, 773 (1977), quoting Hamling v. United States, 418 U.S. 87, 114 (1974). Cf. Mishkin v. New York, 383 U.S. 502 (1966).

32. See Jacobellis v. Ohio, 378 U.S. 184 (1964) (no opinion of the Court).

In *Miller*, the Court decided to give the "community standards" aspect of the *Roth* test a more literal meaning, and it held that trial courts may draw upon actual community standards in determining whether the material at issue is factually obscene. As *Miller* explicitly stated: "In resolving the inevitable sensitive questions of fact and law, we must continue to rely on the jury system, accompanied by the safeguards that judges, rules of evidence, presumption of innocence, and other protective features provide . . . ." [33]

Curiously, in *Miller* the Court reiterated the notion that had provided the basis for the plurality *Jacobellis* national-standards test in the first place, that "fundamental First Amendment limitations on the powers of the States do not vary from community to community." [34] Thus the Constitutional source for the *Miller* "community standards" test is difficult to locate. Any implication in *Miller* of a broader role for the jury, as we shall see in the next section below, has not proven correct. It may be that the Court only meant that the trier of fact should not be required to guess at some hypothetical "median" standard.

Justice Brennan, in a dissent in another case filed the same day as *Miller*, expressed deep concern with the vagueness of the obscenity tests as developed from *Roth* to *Miller*. He felt that the differences between *Miller* and his plurality opinion in *Memoirs* "are, for the most part, academic," [35] but he nonetheless felt compelled to reject it as well as his earlier *Roth* opinion. [36] After considering and rejecting a wide variety of tests for the validity of obscenity legislation he offered his own brightline approach:

> In short, while I cannot say that the interests of the State—apart from the question of juveniles and unconsenting adults—are trivial

or nonexistent, I am compelled to conclude that these interests cannot justify the substantial damage to constitutional rights and to this Nation's judicial machinery that inevitably results from state efforts to bar the distribution even of unprotected material to consenting adults. . . . I would hold, therefore, that at least in the absence of distribution to juveniles or obtrusive exposure to unconsenting adults, . . . the First and Fourteenth Amendments prohibit the State and Federal Governments from attempting wholly to suppress sexually oriented materials on the basis of their allegedly 'obscene' contents. Nothing in this approach precludes those governments from taking action to serve what may be strong and legitimate interests through regulation of the manner of distribution of sexually oriented material. [37]

Justice Brennan's position has not persuaded his colleagues, who have followed *Miller*. But then a majority has always held that some speech known as "hard core" pornography can be banned. Indeed for fifteen years Justice Brennan had espoused this view.

F. Special Considerations in Light of the MILLER Case

1. *Private Possession*

In *Stanley v. Georgia*,[1] the Court, relying on the first and fourteenth amendments, held that "mere private possession of obscene matter" [2] is not a crime. *Stanley*, however, must be read quite narrowly. The crucial fifth vote in *Stanley* was Justice Harlan's; thus, in spite of the broad language of the opinion, the *Stanley* Court's own summary of its decision emphasized that while "the States retain broad power to regulate obscenity; that power simply does not extend to mere possession by the individual in the privacy of his own home." [3] The Court itself had previously emphasized, in

---

33. 413 U.S. at 26.

34. Id. at 30.

35. Paris Adult Theatre I v. Slaton, 413 U.S. 49, 95 (1973) (Brennan, J., dissenting) (footnote omitted).

36. Id. at 98.

37. Id. at 112–13.

1. 394 U.S. 557 (1969).

2. Id. at 568.

3. 394 U.S. at 568.

other contexts, the privacy of the home [4] and Justice Harlan in particular had been concerned with the sanctity of the home,[5] although he repeatedly has emphasized the broad power of the state over obscenity outside of the home.[6]

While the Court has refused to expand *Stanley* it has also not explained why a seller of obscenity may not raise the third-party right of persons to keep the obscenity in the home. In other contexts the Supreme Court has allowed such derivative rights.[7] Thus under *Stanley* one may enjoy obscene material in one's own home, but the state may prohibit an individual from transporting the material for private use,[8] and may also prohibit the individual from receiving the materials through the mails,[9] or from importing them from foreign countries [10] or regulate obscene materials even if those using them voluntarily sought them out.[11] Though the private possession of obscene materials in the home is protected activity, virtually any process that leads to such possession may be declared illegal.

2. *Protection of Minors*

In *Ginsburg v. New York*,[12] the Court adopted the "variable obscenity" approach suggested by Professors Lockhart and McClure and held that a statute defining obscenity in terms of an appeal to the prurient interest of minors was constitutional. As such, *Ginsburg* represents a departure from a pure or neutral concept of "pruriency" as explicated in *Roth*; it is also a departure from the "average man" standard. In light of the Court's revision of the *Roth* test in *Miller*, however, *Ginsburg* may be theoretically reconcilable within the "community standards" test currently in operation.

Such statutes for the protection of children must be narrowly drawn in two respects. First, the statute must not be overbroad; the state cannot prevent the general public from reading or having access to materials on the grounds that it would be objectionable if read or seen by children. Thus in *Butler v. Michigan* [13] the Court reversed a conviction under a statute which made it an offense to make available to the general public materials found to have a potentially deleterious influence on minors. The state argued that by "quarantining the general reading public against books not too rugged for grown men and women in order to shield juvenile innocence, it is exercising its power to promote the general welfare." [14] The unanimous Court answered: "Surely, this is to burn the house to roast the pig." [15] Second, the statute must not be vague. The problem of vagueness is "not rendered less objectionable because the regulation is one of classification rather than direct suppression . . . . Nor is it an answer to an argument that a particular regulation of expression is vague to say that it was adopted for the salutary purpose of protecting children." [16]

---

4. E.g., Griswold v. Connecticut, 381 U.S. 479 (1965).

5. E.g., Griswold v. Connecticut, 381 U.S. 479, 499 (1965) (concurring opinion); Poe v. Ullman, 367 U.S. 497, 550 (1961) (dissenting opinion).

6. E.g., Smith v. California, 361 U.S. 147, 169 (1959) (concurring opinion).

7. Griswold v. Connecticut, 381 U.S. 479 (1965); Carey v. Population Services International, 431 U.S. 678 (1977) (third party standing and right to distribute contraceptives).

8. United States v. Orita, 413 U.S. 139 (1973).

9. United States v. Reidel, 402 U.S. 351 (1971).

10. United States v. 12 200 Ft. Reels of Film, 413 U.S. 123 (1973); see also United States v. 37 Photographs, 402 U.S. 363 (1971).

11. Paris Adult Theatre I v. Slaton, 413 U.S. 49 (1973).

12. 390 U.S. 629 (1968). See generally, e.g., Krislov, From Ginzburg to Ginsberg: The Unhurried Children's Hour in Obscenity Litigation, 1968 Sup.Ct.Rev. 153; F. Schauer, The Law of Obscenity 77–95 (1976).

13. 352 U.S. 380 (1957). Cf. FCC v. Pacifica Foundation, 438 U.S. 726 (1978) (FCC has power to regulate radio broadcast which is "indecent" but not "obscene" because in part, of the presence of children in the early afternoon audience).

14. Id. at 383.

15. Id.

16. Interstate Circuit, Inc. v. Dallas, 390 U.S. 676, 688–89 (1968) (footnote omitted); see also, Erznoznik v. Jacksonville, 422 U.S. 205 (1975) (ordinance prohibiting drive-in movie theatre from showing nudity invalid on

A law which met both of these requirements and was designed to prevent the abuse of children was a state statute which the Court upheld, without a dissent, in *New York v. Ferber*.[17] New York statutes made it a crime for a person knowingly to promote sexual performances by children under the age of 16 by distributing material which depicts such performances [18] even though the materials themselves were not necessarily "obscene" in a constitutional sense.[19]

The Court articulated five basic premises. First, the state's interests in protecting the physical and psychological well being of minors was compelling. Second, prohibiting the distribution of films and photos depicting such activities was closely related to this compelling governmental interest in two ways: the permanent record of the child's activity and its circulation exacerbates the harm to the minor, and also the distribution encourages the sexual exploitation of the children and the production of the material. Third, the advertising and selling of the material encourages the evil by supplying an economic motive. Fourth, the value of allowing live performances and photographic reproduction of children engaged in lewd sexual conduct in *de minimis*. And, fifth, the classification of child pornography as outside of first amendment protection is consistent with earlier precedent and justified by the need to protect the welfare of the children.

The Court cautioned that there were limits to the extent to which child pornography is unprotected speech. The conduct prohibited must be adequately defined and described. And, the circumstances of this case require that the crime "be limited to works that *visually* depict conduct by children below a specified age." [20]

The Court then explained how the test of *Miller* [21] must be modified when dealing with child pornography:

> The *Miller* formulation is adjusted in the following respects: A trier of fact need not find

---

its face; the broad nudity ban exceeds the permissible restraints on obscenity and thus applies to protected speech; assuming that the law is aimed at youths, it is still not sufficiently limited—the law would seek to bar even a baby's buttocks from being shown on the drive-in movie screen).

17. 102 S.Ct. 3348 (1982). Blackmun, J. concurred in the result without opinion. O'Connor, J., filed a concurring opinion. Brennan, J., joined by Marshall, J., filed an opinion and concurred in the judgment. Stevens, J., wrote a separate opinion also concurring in the judgment. White, J., wrote the opinion of the Court.

18. The Supreme Court described the New York statutory framework:

In 1977, the New York legislature enacted Article 263 of its Penal Law. Section 263.05 criminalizes as a class C felony the use of a child in a sexual performance:

"A person is guilty of the use of a child in a sexual performance if knowing the character and content thereof he employs, authorizes or induces a child less than sixteen years of age to engage in a sexual performance or being a parent, legal guardian or custodian of such child, he consents to the participation by such child in a sexual performance."

A "sexual performance is defined as 'any performance or part thereof which includes sexual conduct

by a child less than sixteen years of age,' " § 263.1. "Sexual conduct" is in turn defined in § 263.3:

"'Sexual conduct' means actual or simulated sexual intercourse, deviate sexual intercourse, sexual bestiality, masturbation, sado-masochistic abuse, or lewd exhibition of the genitals."

A performance is defined as "any play, motion picture, photograph or dance" or "any other visual presentation exhibited before an audience." § 263.4.

At issue in this case is § 263.15, defining a class D felony:

"A person is guilty of promoting a sexual performance by a child when, knowing the character and content thereof, he produces, directs or promotes any performance which includes sexual conduct by a child less than sixteen years of age."

To "promote" is also defined:

"'Promote' means to procure, manufacture, issue, sell, give, provide, lend, mail, deliver, transfer, transmute, publish, distribute, circulate, disseminate, present, exhibit or advertise, or to offer or agree to do the same."

A companion provision bans only the knowing dissemination of obscene material. § 263.10.

102 S.Ct. at 3351–52 (footnote omitted).

19. The films in this case primarily depicted young boys masturbating. 102 S.Ct. at 3352.

20. 102 S.Ct. at 3358 (emphasis in original) (footnote omitted).

21. Miller v. California, 413 U.S. 15 (1973).

that the material appeals to the prurient interest of the average person; it is not required that sexual conduct portrayed be done so in a patently offensive manner; and the material at issue need not be considered as a whole. We note that the distribution of descriptions or other depictions of sexual conduct, not otherwise obscene, which do not involve live performance or photographic or other visual reproduction of live performances, retains First Amendment protection. As with obscenity laws, criminal responsibility may not be imposed without some element of scienter on the part of the defendant.[22]

The Court then rejected the argument that the New York statute was overbroad within the meaning of *Broadrick v. Oklahoma*.[23] Since the facts of *Ferber* involved conduct plus speech, the Court held that *Broadrick* required substantial overbreadth.[24] Under this test, section 263.15 [25] was not substantially overbroad. True, the statute might be applied to pictures in medical textbooks or National Geographic pictorials, but "we seriously doubt, and it has not been suggested, that the *arguably impermissible applications* of the statute amount to more than a tiny fraction of the materials within the statute's reach." [26]

Justice O'Connor, in her separate concurring opinion, argued that it may well be the case that it would be constitutional to ban clinical pictures in medical textbooks.[27] In contrast, Justice Brennan's opinion, concurring in the judgment, concluded that application of the New York statute to depictions of children when those depictions have serious literary, artistic, scientific, or medical value would violate free speech.[28] Justice Stevens

would have avoided the overbreadth analysis in this case because, for him, the question of whether a specific act of communication is protected as free speech involves a consideration not only of content but context.[29]

3. *Prior Restraint*

The Court has often stated that "Any system of prior restraints of expression comes to this Court bearing a heavy presumption against its constitutional validity." [1] Obscenity, however, is one of a few areas of the law in which prior restraint has been upheld.

There are, however, certain fifth and fourteenth amendments safeguards that the Court has imposed on the procedures employed in the prior restraint of allegedly-obscene materials. In *Freedman v. Maryland*,[2] the Court held that a local censorship board authorized to revoke a book or motion-picture distributor's license for the sale or display of obscene materials, or otherwise authorized to engage in the prior restraint of allegedly-obscene materials, (1) must afford the accused party a prompt hearing; (2) has the burden of showing that the material is, in fact, obscene; (3) must defer to a judicial proceeding for the imposition of a valid final restraint on the material; and (4) must either refrain from making a finding of obscenity or, as a requirement of law under the board's enabling statute or clear judicial mandate, take action on its own behalf in a court of law to seek an affirmation of its initial finding of obscenity. In the court proceeding the distributor or retailer may con-

---

22. 102 S.Ct. at 3358.

23. 413 U.S. 601 (1973). See Section III, B, supra.

24. 102 S.Ct. at 3362.

25. See n. 18, supra.

26. 102 S.Ct. at 3363 (emphasis added).

27. 102 S.Ct. at 3364 (O'Connor, J., concurring).

28. 102 S.Ct. at 3365 (Brennan, J., joined by Marshall, J., concurring in the judgment).

29. 102 S.Ct. at 3366 (Stevens, J., concurring in the judgment).

1. Bantam Books, Inc. v. Sullivan, 372 U.S. 58, 70 (1963).

2. 380 U.S. 51 (1965); see also, e.g., Carroll v. President and Comm'rs of Princess Anne, 393 U.S. 175 (1969). It is unlikely that the *Freedman* rule of prior restraints would apply if the allegedly obscene material were not films but only books.

In an injunctive proceeding, which is civil, there is no federal constitutional requirement that proof be beyond a reasonable doubt, Cooper v. Mitchell Bros.' Santa Ana Theatre, 454 U.S. 90 (1981) (per curiam). Nor is there a federal constitutional requirement of a jury. Alexander v. Virginia, 413 U.S. 836 (1973) (per curiam).

test the issue of obscenity even though the book or film has been found to be obscene in other cases to which he was not a party.[3] Even if a judge rather than an administrative tribunal initially enters the prior restraint, the procedural safeguards of *Freedman* must be followed, in order to mitigate the unconstitutional consequences if the restraint were erroneously entered.[4]

It should be noted, however, that where the censorship board or other state body confiscates a single piece of allegedly obscene material (while others are available for exhibition) for the purpose of preserving it as evidence, the board need not provide a hearing so long as the confiscation is made pursuant to a warrant issued upon a showing of probable cause. Even here, though, a prompt judicial hearing is required to determine whether the material is obscene. If a showing is made to the trial court that other copies of the film are not available for exhibition, the trial court should permit the seized film to be copied so that the exhibition can be continued until the obscenity issue is resolved in an adversary hearing. Otherwise the film must be returned.[5]

Before a search warrant may be issued for the seizure of allegedly obscene material, there must be an opportunity for a neutral and detached judicial officer to focus searchingly on the question of obscenity. That neutrality and detachment do not exist when the Town Justice signed an open-ended warrant and then joined the law enforcement officials in conducting a search of the book store lasting nearly six hours and examining and seizing numerous films and magazines. The judicial officer in effect conducted a prohibited generalized search and seizure and became "a member, if not,

the leader of the search party which was essentially a police operation." [6]

4. Zoning Laws and Public Exhibition of "Adult" Non-obscene Material

In *Paris Adult Theatre v. Slaton*,[1] decided by the Court on the same day as *Miller*, the Court further restricted *Stanley v. Georgia*[2] in holding that the state may prohibit public exhibitions or displays of obscenity even if access to the exhibitions is limited to consenting adults. The Court carried *Paris Adult Theatre* a step further in *Young v. American Mini Theatres, Inc.*,[3] in which it held that an appropriately definite zoning ordinance prohibiting the location of an "adult movie theatre" within 1000 feet of any two other "regulated uses," including 10 different kinds of establishments in addition to adult theatres, is constitutionally permissible *even* if the theatre is not displaying obscene material. While the ordinance in question characterized an adult theatre as one presenting certain specified "sexual activities" or "anatomical areas," the Court reasoned that the ordinance did not constitute an exercise in prior restraint, but rather a valid use of the city's zoning power to regulate the location of commercial establishments. The Court specifically held that this zoning power overrides the first amendment element in the display of the material at any locality the distributor chooses. However the Court placed great emphasis on the continual availability of these movies and the fact that the restrictions were unrelated to the suppression of ideas.

It was true that a concentration of these theatres brought certain physical changes to the neighborhoods where they were located. These changes were due not only to the ad-

---

3. McKinney v. Alabama, 424 U.S. 669 (1976) (in rem proceeding not bar to litigation of the obscenity issue of the material as to a distributor not party to the in rem proceeding).

4. Vance v. Universal Amusement Co., Inc., 445 U.S. 308 (1980) (per curiam).

5. Heller v. New York, 413 U.S. 483 (1973).

6. Lo-Ji Sales, Inc. v. New York, 442 U.S. 319, 325–27 (1979), distinguishing Heller v. New York, 413 U.S. 483 (1973).

1. 413 U.S. 49 (1975).

2. 394 U.S. 557 (1969).

3. 427 U.S. 50 (1976). See also, Bellanca v. New York State Liquor Authority, 54 N.Y.2d 228, 241, 445 N.Y.S.2d 87, 93, 429 N.E.2d 765, 771 (1981) (Gabrielli, J., dissenting), citing an earlier edition of this treatise.

vertisements and posters associated with the theatres but also to the size and type of crowd they attracted. The zoning of a reasonable amount of space between such theatres avoided the concentration of this physical effect on a neighborhood. Nevertheless the regulation describes the theatres in terms of the content of their films. Whether this doctrine will be expanded to other types of speech will have to await future cases, though the language of Justice Stevens' plurality opinion in *American Mini Theatres* appears to allow the doctrine to be confined:

> [E]ven though we recognize that the First Amendment will not tolerate the total suppression of erotic materials that have some arguably artistic value, it is manifest that society's interest in protecting this type of expression is of a wholly different, and lesser, magnitude than the interest in untrammeled political debate. . . . But few of us would march our sons and daughters off to war to preserve the citizen's right to see "Specified Sexual Activities" exhibited in the theaters of our choice. Even though the First Amendment protects communication in this area from total suppression, we hold that the State may legitimately use the content of these materials as the basis for placing them in a different classification from other motion pictures.

> . . .

> Since what is ultimately at stake is nothing more than a limitation on the place where adult films may be exhibited, even though the determination of whether a particular film fits that characterization turns on the nature of its content, we conclude that the city's interest in the present and future character of its neighborhoods adequately supports its classification of motion pictures.[4]

Thus the Court held that *non*-obscene motion pictures involving the display of sexual activities are entitled to a lesser degree of protection under the first amendment than other forms of protected expression, at least in the context of the otherwise valid purposes of a zoning ordinance. In so doing, the Court made it clear that the artistic value of a non-obscene display of sexual activity is of less value to society than political expression, and implied that a zoning ordinance based upon the latter would not pass constitutional muster. The implications of this distinction has stirred up a great deal of controversy, for the Court in this case allowed time, place or manner restrictions on speech based on the content of the speech.[5]

In *Schad v. Borough of Mount Ephraim*[6] the Court distinguished *American Mini Theatres*[7] and invalidated a zoning ordinance that, as construed by the state courts, forbade *all* "live entertainment," including nonobscene nude dancing, in a commercial zone. "[N]o property in the Borough may be principally used for the commercial production of plays, concerts, musicals, dance, or any other form of live entertainment."[8] An adult book store, operating in a commercial zone in the Borough of Mount Ephraim, introduced a coin operated device: a customer, after inserting a coin, would be able to watch a live dancer, usually nude, perform behind a glass panel; the store was therefore found guilty of violating the ordinance.

Justice White, for the Court, reasoned, first, that nude dancing is entitled to some first amendment protection.[9] The Court also allowed the appellants to raise an overbreadth challenge to the ordinance.[10] The

---

4. 427 U.S. at 70–72 (footnote omitted) (opinion of Stevens, J., joined by Burger, C. J., and White & Rehnquist, JJ.).

5. See Section XIII, C of this Chapter.

See also, e.g., FCC v. Pacifica Foundation, 438 U.S. 726 (1978) (FCC has power—in order to protect children—to regulate radio broadcast which is "indecent" but not "obscene"). Note that Justice Stevens' separate opinion, joined by Chief Justice Burger and Justice Rehnquist, specifically relied on a power to regulate speech based on its content, but the other two members of the majority rejected this analysis.

6. 452 U.S. 61 (1981).

7. Young v. American Mini Theatres, Inc., 427 U.S. 50 (1976).

8. 452 U.S. at 66 (footnote omitted).

9. 452 U.S. at 66, citing Doran v. Salem Inn, Inc., 422 U.S. 922 (1975), and Southeastern Promotions, Ltd. v. Conrad, 420 U.S. 546 (1975).

10. 452 U.S. at 66; see Section III, B of this Chapter, supra, for a discussion of the Overbreadth Doctrine.

ordinance on its face did not even seek to justify the exclusion of such a broad category of protected expression—all live entertainment.

Before the Supreme Court, counsel for Mount Ephraim presented some justifications, but none of these were persuasive and none had been articulated by the state courts. the Borough argued that it could allow a broad range of commercial uses but nonetheless exclude live entertainment because that use led to special problems such as increased need for parking, trash pick-up, police protection, and medical facilities. However the Borough presented no evidence to support this assertion, and the Court did not find it "self-evident that a theatre, for example, would create greater parking problems than would a restaurant." [11] Assuming that live entertainment would create special problems not associated with other commercial uses, the Borough had not narrowly tailored a zoning law to address any unique problems. The Borough's claim that its zoning restriction was an attempt to create a commercial area catering only to the residents' "immediate needs" also did not survive scrutiny. The Borough introduced no evidence to support this assertion and the face of the ordinance contradicted it, for the ordinance permitted car showrooms, hardware stores, offices, etc.

Nor did the *American Mini Theatres* analysis support the constitutionality of the ordinance, for the restriction in *American Mini Theatres* did not ban all adult theatres or even affect the number of adult movie theatres in the city; "it merely dispersed them." [12] And in *American Mini Theatres*

the city had presented evidence that a concentration of adult theatres led to a deterioration of surrounding neighborhoods. Finally, the Court could not accept the ordinance as a reasonable "time, place, and manner" restriction. The Borough presented no evidence that the manner of expression—live entertainment—is basically incompatible with the normal activity in a commercial zone. Thus the Court invalidated the ordinance with only two justices dissenting. [13]

5. Obscenity and the Twenty-First Amendment

Related to the state's power to use the zoning laws to restrict "adult" speech which is not constitutionally obscene is the state's power, under the twenty-first amendment, to regulate "adult" speech in establishments licensed by the state to serve liquor. As the Court stated in *New York State Liquor Authority v. Bellanca*: [1]

> Pursuant to its power to regulate the sale of liquor within its boundaries, [the New York Legislature] has banned topless dancing in establishments granted a license to serve liquor. The State's power to ban the sale of alcoholic beverages entirely includes the lesser power to ban the sale of liquor on premises where topless dancing occurs. [2]

The legislature judged that "mixing alcohol and nude dancing" causes disturbances which the state sought to avoid by a reasonable restriction on places which sell liquor for consumption on the premises. The Court would respect this judgment, to which the twenty-first amendment gave an "added presumption." [3] In contrast, a statute prohibiting nude entertainment in places that serve no alcohol but only food or nonal-

---

11. 452 U.S. at 74 (footnote omitted).

12. 452 U.S. at 71. Later in the opinion the Court rejected Mount Ephraim's argument that residents could view nude dancing in nearby areas outside of the limits of the Borough. Since there was no countywide zoning, the Borough could not argue that the county wished to exclude live entertainment only from residential areas within the county. Further, no evidence supported the assertion that nearby areas offered nude dancing as a form of entertainment. Finally, one " 'is not to have the exercise of his liberty of expression in appropriate places abridged on the plea that it may be

exercised in some other place.' " 452 U.S. at 76–77, quoting Schneider v. State, 308 U.S. 147, 163 (1939).

13. Burger, C. J., joined by Rehnquist, J., dissented. 452 U.S. at 85.

1. 452 U.S. 714 (1981) (per curiam). Accord, California v. LaRue, 409 U.S. 109 (1972).

2. 452 U.S. at 717.

3. 452 U.S. at 718, quoting California v. LaRue, 409 U.S. 109, 118. Only Stevens, J., dissented. Marshall J., concurred in the judgment but filed no written opinion. Brennan, J., dissented from the summary disposi-

coholic beverages, violates the first amendment. Nudity alone is not obscene in the constitutional sense, and since such a law applies to establishments which do not serve liquor, it is overbroad.[4]

The twenty-first amendment has long been used to grant the states extensive authority over liquor, and to some extent immunize state regulation from commerce clause challenge.[5] However, the twenty-first amendment has never been read to immunize state regulation over liquor from the civil liberties guarantees of the Constitution.[6] Thus, *Bellanca* should be read narrowly: it does *not* stand for the proposition that the first and fourteenth amendments are inapplicable to the states when they regulate liquor. Rather the twenty-first amendment only allows the states greater freedom to regulate "adult" speech in connection with its power to regulate the sale of liquor within its boundaries. This state regulatory power appears to be similar to its zoning power to restrict "adult," nonobscene speech.

6. *Non-pictorial Obscenity*

On the same day that *Miller v. California*[1] was decided, the Court ruled in *Kaplan v. California*[2] that books alone, containing only words and no pictures, may be obscene.[3] The Court recognized that books "have a different and preferred place in our hierarchy of values . . . ."[4] But they nonetheless may be found to be obscene.

7. *Use of Experts*

Once the allegedly obscene material is actually placed into evidence the state need not present expert testimony that the material is obscene, lacks serious artistic value, or any other ancillary evidence of obscenity.[5] The defense, however, is free to introduce appropriate expert testimony.[6]

---

tion of the case and would have set it for oral argument.

On remand the New York State Court of Appeals held that the state statute violated the free speech provisions of the state constitution, because the twenty-first amendment does not confer a power on the states that is superior to, or free from, state constitutional restraints. 54 N.Y.2d 228, 445 N.Y.Supp.2d 87, 429 N.E.2d 765 (1981). See also, 54 N.Y.2d at 241, 445 N.Y.Supp.2d at 93, 429 N.E.2d at 771, citing treatise (Gabrielli, J., dissenting).

4. Chase v. Davelaar, 645 F.2d 735 (9th Cir. 1981); Morris v. Municipal Court for San Jose-Milpitas Judicial District of Santa Clara County, 32 Cal.3d 553, 186 Cal.Rptr. 494, 652 P.2d 51 (1982).

5. See, e.g., State Bd. of Equalization v. Young's Market Co., 299 U.S. 59 (1936) (California may impose $500 fee for privilege of importing into that state beer from a sister state even though such a fee would have violated the commerce clause prior to the twenty-first amendment).

6. See, e.g., Craig v. Boren, 429 U.S. 190 (1976), where the Court invalidated a state statute prohibiting the sale of 3.2% beer to males under 21 and females under 18; the discrimination based on gender violated the equal protection guarantees of the fourteenth amendment:

"Once passing beyond consideration of the Commerce Clause, the relevance of the Twenty-First Amendment to other constitutional provisions becomes increasingly doubtful. . . . [T]he Court has never recognized sufficient 'strength' in [that] Amendment to defeat an otherwise established claim

of invidious discrimination in violation of the Equal Protection Clause." 429 U.S. at 206–207.

See also, Moose Lodge No. 107 v. Irvis, 407 U.S. 163, 178–79 (1972). Cf. California Retail Liquor Dealers Ass'n v. Midcal Aluminum, Inc., 445 U.S. 97 (1980) (state wine pricing statute violates Sherman Act, notwithstanding twenty-first amendment); Department of Revenue v. James B. Beam Distilling Co., 377 U.S. 341 (1964) (state tax on Scotch violates export-import clause, notwithstanding twenty-first amendment); R. Rotunda, Modern Constitutional Law: Cases and Notes 147–48 (1981).

1. 413 U.S. 15 (1973).

2. 413 U.S. 115, 116 (1973).

3. Only once since *Roth*, in Mishkin v. New York, 383 U.S. 502 (1966), did the high Court hold books to be obscene, and in that case most if not all of the books were illustrated. 383 U.S. at 505. See also Kaplan v. California, 413 U.S. 115, 118 n. 3 (1973).

4. 413 U.S. at 119.

5. 413 U.S. at 121; Paris Adult Theatre I v. Slaton, 413 U.S. 49, 56 (1973).

There might be a case where the allegedly obscene material is directed at such a bizarre deviant group that the experience of the jurors would be inadequate to judge if the material appeals to the particular prurient interest. In such a case, the government may have to use expert testimony. Pinkus v. United States, 436 U.S. 293, 303 (1978).

6. 413 U.S. at 121; Smith v. California, 361 U.S. 147, 164–65 (1959) (Frankfurter, J., concurring).

8. National vs. Local Standards

In *Miller v. California*[1] the Court held, *inter alia*, that obscenity is to be determined by applying contemporary community standards, not national standards. In that case, the trial court instructed the jury to consider state community standards. The following year the Court extended that holding to apply to a federal prosecution:

> Since this case was tried in the Southern District of California, and presumably jurors from throughout that judicial district were available to serve on the panel which tried petitioners, it would be the standards of that "community" upon which the jurors would draw. But this is not to say that a district court would not be at liberty to admit evidence of standards existing in some place outside of this particular district, if it felt such evidence would assist the jurors in the resolution of the issues which they were to decide.[2]

The Court has since made clear that *Miller* did not mandate use of a statewide standard; the trial court may use a national standard and it may instruct the jury to apply "community standards" without instructing it what community was specified.[3] It is unclear if such holdings mean that a trial court may instruct the jury to apply national standards even if it could be shown that national standards apply a stricter definition of obscenity than local standards.

In *Smith v. United States*[4] the Court placed some limits on the power of the state to attempt to define legislatively the contemporary community standard of appeal to prurient interest or patent offensiveness. First, in state obscenity proceedings:

> [The state could, if it wished] impose a geographic limit on the determination of community standards by defining the area from which

the jury could be selected in an obscenity case, or by legislating with respect to the instructions that must be given to the jurors in such cases. . . . [However] the question of the community standard to apply, when appeal to prurient interest and patent offensiveness are considered, is not one that can be defined legislatively.[5]

As to federal obscenity proceedings, no state law can regulate distribution of obscene materials and define contemporary standards. Thus, in a federal prosecution for wholly intrastate mailings of allegedly obscene material it is irrelevant that the state in which the mailings took place did not regulate at all obscenity aimed at adults. A state's laissez-faire attitude towards obscenity cannot nullify federal efforts to regulate it. In federal obscenity prosecutions federal jury instructions as to community standards will be given.[6]

In *Pinkus v. United States*,[7] the Court clarified several requirements concerning jury instructions in federal obscenity prosecutions which were governed by the standards of *Roth v. United States*.[8] While *Pinkus* was decided under the *Roth* test of obscenity, the instructions approved of as to who in the community still should be law under *Miller*[9] since—as to that issue—*Miller* only rejected the national standards test in favor of a smaller geographic area: the actual local community.

The Court overturned Pinkus' conviction for mailing obscene materials based on its statutory interpretation that children had been improperly included in determining community standards. "[C]hildren are not to be included . . . as part of the 'community' as that term relates to the 'obscene materials' proscribed by 18 U.S.C.A.

---

1. 413 U.S. 15 (1973).

2. Hamling v. United States, 418 U.S. 87, 105–06 (1974).

3. Jenkins v. Georgia, 418 U.S. 153 (1974).

4. 431 U.S. 291 (1977).

5. 431 U.S. 291 at 303 (dictum).

6. 431 U.S. 291 at 304.

Note that the standards of Miller v. California, 413 U.S. 15 (1973) are not applied retroactively to the ex-

tent that they burden criminal defendants but they are applied retroactively to the extent they benefit criminal defendants. Marks v. United States, 430 U.S. 188 (1977).

7. 436 U.S. 293 (1978).

8. 354 U.S. 476 (1957).

9. 413 U.S. 15 (1973).

§ 1461." [10] The Court went on to state that under the Constitution, it was permissible to include "particularly sensitive persons" when considering community standards, since the "community includes all adults who comprise it." The jury may not be instructed to focus on the most susceptible and sensitive members of the community, but the jury need not exclude such people from the community as a whole for purposes of judging the material's obscenity. [11] Finally, the Constitution allows an instruction on prurient appeal to deviant sexual groups as part of the instruction concerning the appeal of the materials to the average person when the evidence supports such a charge.

9. Role of the Jury After MILLER

While *Miller v. California* [12] talked of the necessity of relying on the jury system and suggested that it might thus have a lesser role for appellate courts in reviewing obscenity convictions, such a rule of law has not come to pass. In *Jenkins v. Georgia* [13] the Court held that even though "questions of appeal to the 'prurient interest' or of patent offensiveness are 'essentially questions of fact'; it would be a serious misreading of *Miller* to conclude that juries have unbridled discretion in determining what is 'patently offensive.'" [14] The appellate courts can conduct an "independent review" of the constitutional claims where necessary. [15] In *Jenkins* itself the Court concluded that "Our own viewing of the film satisfies us that . . . ." it is not obscene. [16] Justice Brennan, concurring in the result and joined by Justices Stevens and Marshall thought that *Miller* and *Jenkins* brought the Court back to the case-by-case approach. [17]

The Court has also held that in civil cases there is no federal constitutional mandate requiring the states to use a jury. [18]

10. Burden of Proof

If the government brings a *criminal* prosecution in an obscenity case, then it must prove its charges "beyond a reasonable doubt" because this burden of proof requirement is an element of due process binding on both the state and federal governments. [1] But an obscenity case may be a *civil* proceeding as well, such as a proceeding to abate a public nuisance. In such instances, there is no federal constitutional requirement of proof beyond a reasonable doubt. [2]

---

10. 436 U.S. at 297. Since the Court specifically referred to the federal statute it appears that the decision is based on an interpretation of that statute. Whether the states, as a matter of constitutional law, must follow this ruling, remains unclear.

11. 436 U.S. at 299–300.

12. 413 U.S. 15 (1973).

13. 418 U.S. 153 (1974).

14. Id. at 160.

15. Id.

16. Id. at 161.

17. Id. at 162–165. See, Note, An Empirical Inquiry Into the Effects of Miller v. California on the Control of Obscenity, 52 N.Y.U.L.Rev. 819 (1977) (arguing that *Miller* has had little effect on the day-to-day regulation of obscenity).

18. Melancon v. McKeithen, 345 F.Supp. 1025, 1035–45, 1048 (E.D.La.1972), aff'd sub nom. Mayes v. Ellis, 409 U.S. 943 (1972); Alexander v. Virginia, 413 U.S. 836 (1973) (per curiam). Brennan, J., joined by Marshall, J., dissented for the reasons stated in his separate opinion, concurring in part, in McKinney v. Alabama, 424 U.S. 669, 687–89 (1976).

1. In re Winship, 397 U.S. 358, 364 (1970).

2. Cooper v. Mitchell Bros.' Santa Ana Theatre, 454 U.S. 90 (1981) (per curiam). The Court noted that in some civil areas of great importance it has required the "clear and convincing" standard of proof in civil cases, rather than the "preponderance of the evidence" test normally used. 454 U.S. at 93. See, e.g., Addington v. Texas, 441 U.S. 418, 431 (1979) (clear and convincing standard in civil commitment); Rosenbloom v. Metromedia, 403 U.S. 29, 52 (1971) (clear and convincing standard in libel cases) (opinion of Brennan, J.); Woodby v. INS, 385 U.S. 276, 285–86 (1966) (deportation); Chaunt v. United States, 364 U.S. 350, 353 (1960) (deportation); Schneiderman v. United States, 320 U.S. 118, 159 (1963) (denaturalization). But see Vance v. Terrazas, 444 U.S. 252 (1980) (constitutional for Congress to establish preponderance of evidence standard in expatriation cases).

The Court in *Cooper* did not decide whether or not the clear and convincing standard was necessary, but rather remanded the case. Brennan, J. joined by Marshall, J., filed a dissenting opinion arguing for the standard of beyond a reasonable doubt, based on Brennan's separate opinion in McKinney v. Alabama, 424 U.S. 669, 683–87 (1976). Stevens, J., also filed a dissenting opinion.

CHAPTER NINETEEN

FREEDOM OF RELIGION

I. INTRODUCTION

A. The Natural Antagonism Between the Two Clauses

There are two clauses of the first amendment which deal with the subject of religion.[1] The amendment mandates that "Congress shall make no law respecting an establishment of religion, or prohibiting the free exercise thereof . . . ." The first clause is referred to as the establishment clause; the second is the free exercise clause. The Supreme Court has held that both of these clauses are made applicable to the states by the due process clause of the fourteenth amendment.[2]

There is a natural antagonism between a command not to establish religion and a command not to inhibit its practice. This tension between the clauses often leaves the Court with having to choose between competing values in religion cases. The general guide here is the concept of "neutrality." The opposing values require that the government act to achieve only secular goals and that it achieve them in a religiously neutral manner. Unfortunately, situations arise where government may have no choice but to incidentally help or hinder religious groups or practices.

Professor Philip Kurland has advanced the theory that government can only remain neutral by prohibiting the use of religion as a standard for government action.[3] So long as a law avoids "classification in terms of religion either to confer a benefit or to impose a burden"[4] he would find it in conformity with both clauses. This position has much to recommend it, for insistence on avoiding incidental aid to religion is likely to inhibit its free exercise. Similarly, requiring a great degree of government accommodation of religious practices might result in impermissible aid to religion. However, despite the great theoretical appeal of the Kurland position the Court has never adopted such a theory. Instead the Court has reviewed the claims under the different clauses on independent bases and has developed separate tests for determining whether a law violates either clause.[5] While "neutrality" is still a central principle of both clauses, we have no single standard for determining what is a religiously neutral act. Instead, we must examine the neutrality or permissibility of a law in terms of the challenge to it.

B. The Appeal to History

There is a seemingly irresistible impulse to appeal to history when analyzing issues under the religion clauses. This tendency is unfortunate because there is no clear history as to the meaning of the clauses. It is of course true that many of the colonists fled religious persecution, but in this country the experience differed widely throughout the colonies. It is common to refer to the Virginia experience when arguing for a complete separation of religious matters from

---

1. It should also be noted that art. VI, cl. 3, of the constitution provides that "no religious Test shall ever be required as a Qualification to any Office of Public Trust under the United States."

2. The free exercise clause was first held applicable to the states in Cantwell v. Connecticut, 310 U.S. 296 (1940). The establishment clause was held applicable to the states in Everson v. Board of Education, 330 U.S. 1 (1947).

3. P. Kurland, Religion and Law 112 (1962).

4. Id.

5. See Choper, The Religion Clauses of the First Amendment: Reconciling the Conflict, 41 U. Pittsburgh L.Rev. 673 (1980), in which Professor Choper proposes that the conflict can be resolved by only applying the establishment clause to forbid government action undertaken for a religious purpose and likely to result in coercing, compromising or influencing religious beliefs.

secular government. In Virginia, Jefferson and Madison led a continuing battle for total religious freedom and an end of government aid to religion. Their position was most clearly stated by Madison in his "Memorial and Remonstrance" against an assessment bill to aid religion.[6] The first amendment was a product of Madison and the Virginia influence in the first Congress. However, this is not the only history that is relevant to these issues. The clauses were ratified as a part of the Bill of Rights, and the intention of those in the ratifying states should be as important as that of the Virginia representatives. Moreover, as the first amendment was only a limitation on the actions of the federal government,[7] one could read this history as an affirmance of state sovereignty over this subject.

In other states close ties existed between church and state, with a number of states having established churches until well after the time of the revolution.[8] For these states the amendment insured that the federal government could not interfere with their state preferences for certain religions. It also would forbid the federal government from benefiting one religion over another. The close ties between religion and state governments indicate that many states would not have opposed federal government aid to all religions on an equal basis. Indeed, Justice Story was certain that the federal government was barred only from punishing or benefiting specific religions.[9] He thought the amendment allowed for aid to all religions on an equal basis. However, beyond

this little can be said with any certainty. Even after the established churches had ended in the states, aid to religious entities continued. For example, religious teachers often made use of public schools, and the tax exempt status of churches was guaranteed in many states.[10] Since assessing history to determine the exact meaning of the religious freedom that was to be guaranteed by the first amendment will not produce clear answers to current issues, we must plunge ahead and study the development of the separate doctrines in the case law. Here we will find that the Court has both found and created certain "historic" principles which are suited to protecting religious freedom—past and present. As almost all of the important Supreme Court decisions in this area have come after 1940, we have only the modern Court's view of history and the justices' current tests to guide us.[11]

II. THE ESTABLISHMENT CLAUSE

A. Introduction

The establishment clause applies to both the federal and local governments. It is a prohibition of government sponsorship of religion which requires that government neither aid nor formally establish a religion. While at its inception the clause might not have been intended to prohibit governmental aid to all religions, the accepted view today is that it also prohibits a preference for religion over non-religion. However, the government simply cannot avoid aiding religion in some manner unless it actively opposes

---

6. This Madison "Remonstrance" was reprinted in Walz v. Tax Comm'n, 397 U.S. 664, 719–27 (1970) (Douglas, J., dissenting, app. II).

7. In Barron v. City of Baltimore, 32 U.S. (7 Pet.) 243 (1833) the Court, per Chief Justice Marshall, held that the Bill of Rights was not applicable to the activities of state or local governments. See note 2, supra, as to the application of these guarantees to the states by the fourteenth amendment.

8. For an excellent presentation of early history of church-state relationship and theories, see C. Antieau, A. Downey, & E. Roberts, Freedom From Federal Establishment (1964).

9. J. Story, Commentaries on the Constitution of the United States 627-34 (5th Ed. 1891).

10. For some examples of this see, Choper, The Establishment Clause and Aid to Parochial Schools, 56 California L.Rev. 260, 263 (1969); C. Antieau, P. Carroll, & T. Burke, Religion under the State Constitutions (1965).

11. The Supreme Court did decide several important cases under the free exercise clause between 1878 and 1940. These are discussed in section III B of this chapter. State courts were confronted with problems of religious freedom at an earlier time, e.g., Donahoe v. Richards, 38 Me. 379 (1854) (schoolchildren can be forced to participate in religious exercises).

religion—something that it is forbidden to do by the free exercise clause. For example, the granting of police or fire protection to churches clearly aids the practice of religion, but the withholding of such services would single out religious activities for a special burden. Thus it is clear that some test is required to determine when such incidental aid is permissible and when it is prohibited.

When a law is challenged under the establishment clause it must pass a three part test. First, it must have a secular purpose. Second, it must have a primary secular effect. Third, it must not involve the government in an excessive entanglement with religion. When the potentiality for excessive entanglement must be determined another three part test is employed. The degree of entanglement is estimated by evaluating: (1) the character and purpose of the religious institution to be benefited, (2) the nature of the aid, and (3) the resulting relationship between the government and religious authorities. Additionally (although this may be considered a part of the entanglement test) the law must not create an excessive degree of political division along religious lines.

An outline of the history of the establishment clause tests may give the reader some added perspective. There were only two significant decisions under the establishment clause prior to 1947. In that year, the Court

held the clause applicable to the states, while approving the reimbursement of bus fees for all students, including those attending parochial schools. It did so without a clear standard, as a majority simply found that no prohibited form of aid was involved in that program. In the cases dealing with prayers and Bible reading in the public schools the Court enunciated a "secular purpose and primary effect" test. This two part test was the sole standard for a time and was used in reviewing the permissibility of loaning textbooks to parochial school students. In 1970, the Court upheld property tax exemptions for churches while using for the first time the present purpose-effect-entanglement test.

To withstand analysis under the establishment clause a government act must have not only a secular purpose and a primary effect which neither advances nor inhibits religion, it also must avoid creating the type of entanglement between government and religion which might lead to an erosion of the principle of government neutrality in religious decisionmaking.[12] The government may take action for secular purposes which aid all persons in a religiously neutral manner even though there is some incidental aid to religious organizations.[13] Additionally, the Supreme Court in limited circumstances has allowed the government to recognize the historic role of religion in American society.[14]

---

12. In Larkin v. Grendel's Den, Inc., 103 S.Ct. 505 (1982), the Court found that a zoning law violated the first amendment establishment clause by granting to all churches or schools a veto power over the issuance of liquor license for any premises within a 500 foot radius of the church or the school. The Court applied the three-part test under the establishment clause. Although the law might have had a secular purpose, (the promotion of a quiet atmosphere around certain cultural and educational centers) that purpose could not alone sustain the statute's constitutionality. The zoning statute was clearly susceptible being used to promote religious rather than secular ends. The churches had a power under the statute which was subject to no clear secular standards; that power could be used to promote primarily religious goals. Even if one assumed that the statute had both a secular purpose and primary effect, the law clearly failed the excessive entanglement test. A law which vested governmental authority in churches, "enmeshes churches in the exercise of substantial governmental powers contrary to

our consistent interpretation of the establishment clause." 103 S.Ct. at 512. The excessive entanglement branch of the establishment clause test was meant to avoid the danger to both secular government and religious autonomy that accompanies a sharing of power and entanglement of administrative agencies.

13. See Section II B of this Chapter regarding aid to religious institutions.

14. See Walz v. Tax Commission, 397 U.S. 664 (1970) (exemption from state tax for property and income of religious organization upheld on basis of separate tax treatment of such property by federal and state governments since the American Revolution). On July 5, 1983, the Supreme Court ruled that a state legislature could employ a chaplain and open each legislative day with a prayer. Chief Justice Burger, writing for the majority, upheld these practices on the basis of history of legislative prayer, which dated back to the same Congress which drafted the first amendment. Marsh v. Chambers, 103 S.Ct. ___ (1983).

B. Aid to Religious Institutions

1. Primary and Secondary Schools

There is very little state aid that may go to religious primary and secondary schools without violating the establishment clause. As the Supreme Court has held that these schools are permeated by religious teaching, any significant aid will have a high potentiality for having the effect of aiding religion. The only way to avoid such an effect would be the imposition of so many procedural checks that the program would result in the excessive entanglement between government and religious entities. Additionally, these programs have a history of causing serious political divisions.[1] For these reasons the Court has been quite strict in applying the purpose-effect-entanglement test to these programs. Because the first amendment principles which govern this area are the product of a series of Supreme Court decisions on very specific types of aid to religiously affiliated schools, we must review those decisions to understand these first amendment principles.[2]

In *Everson v. Board of Education*[3] the Court, by a 5 to 4 vote, upheld a program which in effect paid the transportation costs of parochial school students. Pursuant to a state statute, a local school board established a program which reimbursed the parents of students at public and non-profit private schools for the amounts they spent for bus transportation.[4] The only private non-profit school in the district was a Catholic school. A majority of the justices upheld this program even though they took the position that no aid could be given to a religion in accordance with the establishment clause. The majority was of the view that the provi-

sion of free bus transportation to all school children on an equal basis constituted only a general service to benefit and safeguard children rather than an aid to religion. The opinion noted that basic governmental services, such as fire and police protection, could be extended to religious institutions along with the rest of the public without aiding religion. As the majority saw the general provision of free transportation to be akin to such a service, the program was approved. This position was taken over several vigorous dissents[5] and at a later time one member of the majority in *Everson* indicated that he felt the case was wrongly decided.[6] However, *Everson* remains the law today and the Court has shown no inclination to reverse its position on basic bus fare reimbursement programs, even though, as discussed at the end of this section, the state cannot pay for parochial school "field trips." If a similar aid program were limited to public and parochial school students by statute, the Court would come to a different conclusion. Such a statute would have the effect of preferring religious school students over students at other nonprofit schools and this preference should be held to violate the establishment clause.

By the time that the Court was next confronted with a program of aid to parochial school students, it was employing the "purpose and effect" test to resolve establishment clause claims.[7] Under this test the purpose of a state program must be secular in nature. Additionally, the program may not have a primary effect of either advancing or inhibiting religion or religious practices to withstand review under this test.

In *Board of Education v. Allen*[8] the Court upheld a program of providing text-

---

1. See Section II, B, 4, infra, for further analysis of the "excessive entanglement" principle.

2. Related decisions concerning governmental acts that arguably advance religious goals in a public school system are examined in Section II, C, infra.

3. 330 U.S. 1 (1947).

4. There is no serious problem presented by the exclusion of students at private profit making or proprietary schools. To date the legislature is free to classify on the basis of wealth or financial characteristics so long as the classification is not irrational or clearly invidious. Cf., San Antonio Independent School District

v. Rodriguez, 411 U.S. 1, 28 (1973). See Chapter 16, Section VI.

5. The dissent of Justice Rutledge is worth noting for it contains a history of many of the circumstances that led to the drafting of the amendment. 330 U.S. 1, 33–43 (1947) (Rutledge, J., dissenting).

6. Engel v. Vitale, 370 U.S. 421, 443–44, 601 (1962) (Douglas, J., concurring).

7. This test was developed in the "school prayer" cases, see Section II, C, 3, infra.

8. 392 U.S. 236 (1968).

books to parochial school students under the purpose and effect test. The New York textbook law under review required school boards to loan textbooks to students in all public or private schools. This resulted in books being given to parochial school students for their studies in the religious schools. However, only books for secular studies could be loaned to students and the books had to be either ones used in public schools or approved by the school board as being secular in nature. The opinion found no religious purpose in this law as it accepted the position that the program was designed to aid the secular education of students. This secular purpose—the improvement of the educational opportunities for all children—has sufficed in every case relating to aid for religious schools.[9]

The *Allen* majority also found that the program did not have a primary effect of advancing religion. At this time a majority of the justices refused to assume that the religious schools—including Catholic primary and secondary schools—were so permeated by religion that even classes in secular subjects advanced religion. Thus the majority could find that the books were used only for the secular teaching component of such schools. The local board's insuring that only secular books were loaned, and the absence of proof that secular classes were used to advance religion, were the mainstays of the majority position.[10] But *Allen* marks the outermost reaches of permissible aid to parochial school students. Like *Everson*, it remains the law solely on the basis of *stare*

decisis,[11] since the Court has become increasingly strict in the scope of aid that may be afforded to such schools. Additionally, it must be noted that even these programs would be invalid if they aided schools that discriminated on the basis of race.[12]

In *Walz v. Tax Commission*[13] the Court expanded the establishment clause tests while upholding another form of aid to religious entities. In this case the Court upheld the granting of exemptions from property taxes to churches as a part of a general exception for a wide variety of nonprofit institutions.[14] Presumably this validates the granting of tax exemptions to religious schools so long as the exemption is granted to all nonprofit schools. The majority opinion by Chief Justice Burger required that the program withstand a three-part test to avoid invalidation under the establishment clause. The program would be invalid unless it: (1) had a secular purpose, (2) had no primary effect of advancing or inhibiting religion, and (3) avoided causing an "excessive entanglement" between government and religion.[15] The general tax exemption was found to have a secular purpose and provide only incidental aid to religion. The majority opinion also found that the taxation of church property would cause at least as much administrative entanglement between government and religious authorities as did the exemption. The Court was clearly persuaded by the long history of such exemptions: more than 200 years of a virtually uniform practice in the states without any further "establishment" effects.[16]

---

9. The only cases which center on a finding of religious purpose are Epperson v. Arkansas, 393 U.S. 97 (1968) which is discussed in Section II, C, 4 infra, and Stone v. Graham, 449 U.S. 39 (1980), which is examined in Section II, C, 3 infra.

10. Board of Education v. Allen, 392 U.S. 236, 245–48 (1968).

11. See notes 29–31 of this section, infra, and accompanying text.

12. As to the validity of programs which aid such schools, see Section II, B, 3, b of this Chapter. As the second edition of this treatise was going to press the issue was before the Supreme Court. Goldsboro Christian Schools Inc. v. United States and Bob Jones University v. United States, 644 F.2d 879 (4th Cir. 1981), cert. granted, 454 U.S. 892 (1981). On May 24, 1983, in

Bob Jones University v. United States, 103 S.Ct. 2017 (1983) the Court, with only one dissent, upheld the authority of the Internal Revenue Service to deny tax exempt status to private schools which practice racial discrimination in their admissions standards due to their religious doctrine.

13. 397 U.S. 664 (1970).

14. It should be noted that the opinion did not approve granting exemptions for church property where no similar exemption existed for other social service or nonprofit activities. Such a preferential exemption would almost certainly constitute a prohibited direct aid to certain religious entities.

15. 397 U.S. at 664.

16. 397 U.S. at 676–80.

The Court invalidated two state attempts to subsidize the costs of parochial school education in *Lemon v. Kurtzman*.[17] Rhode Island provided a fifteen percent salary supplement to teachers of secular subjects in private schools where the per-pupil expenditure was below that of the public schools. In the second program, Pennsylvania authorized the reimbursement of nonpublic schools for a fraction of teacher salaries and instructional materials in secular subjects. Under both state systems, Catholic schools were the main beneficiaries of the programs.[18] Once again, the Court accepted the legislatures' position that they were pursuing the secular end of promoting the nonreligious education of young children. The Court did not come to an exact ruling on whether the programs had a primary effect of advancing religion.[19] However, the Court's discussion of the need for avoiding administrative entanglement indicated that such programs could have a prohibited effect. As the majority assumed that religious elementary and secondary schools were likely to advance religion even in their secular subjects, it would seem that these subsidies would constitute direct aid to religion.

Instead of basing the ruling on the effect of these programs, the opinion in *Lemon* struck down these statutes because it found that they fostered an excessive entanglement between church and state. Chief Justice Burger, writing for the majority, held that, in assessing the degree of entanglement, three factors were to be considered: (1) the character and purpose of the institution benefited; (2) the nature of the aid; (3) the resulting relationship between government and religious authorities.[20] In applying this three part test the majority opinion first found that Catholic elementary and secondary schools were an integral part of the religious program of that church. The religious atmosphere and control of this type of school showed that religious teaching might be advanced, even inadvertently, in secular courses. Second, the aid here was a subsidy for teacher salaries. The Court noted that, unlike textbooks, teachers could not be checked in advance to insure that they would not teach religion. Though the teachers could in good faith promise to remain neutral, they might inadvertently advance religion in the classroom. Finally, the majority found that in order to insure that religious activities or teaching were not aided by the program, the state would have to place a great number of restrictions on the schools and engage in a monitoring program which would be little short of ongoing surveillance. Thus, the character of the school and the aid required complex ongoing relationships between secular and religious authorities. This three part analysis showed that the program would result in an excessive entanglement violative of the establishment clause.

The Chief Justice also stressed the fact that these types of programs were politically divisive. The provision of significant ongoing aid to parochial elementary and secondary schools injected an explosive political issue which caused division along religious lines. These programs virtually guarantee that there will be yearly public debate and political conflict between religious factions. The majority opinion stated that this division was to be eliminated by the establishment

---

17. 403 U.S. 602 (1971). At this time the Court also decided Tilton v. Richardson, 403 U.S. 672 (1971) involving aid to religious colleges. This subject is examined in the next section of this chapter.

18. While the majority has noted this fact it is difficult to see its relevance. It might be used in an attempt to show a religious "purpose" but the Court has never looked into the motives of the legislature in such a manner. The religious effect of administrative entanglements might be quantitatively (but not qualitatively) greater if a large number of parochial schools were aided. This would not relate to the number or

names of the religions involved. The justices may feel that Catholic primary schools are uniquely permeated with religion, but that raises questions as to the basis for such a judicial ruling and why other parochial schools are treated in the same manner by the Court. Finally, the justices might feel that Catholic schools generate greater political division. One might question both the propriety and usefulness of such judicial assumptions.

19. 403 U.S. at 613–14.

20. 403 U.S. at 615.

clause [21]. However, the opinion was not clear as to whether this was merely the reason for strict application of the purpose-effect-entanglement test, a branch of the entanglement test, or a fourth test. Thus, we can only say that where the majority views an aid program as causing an undue amount of political division along religious lines the program is likely to be invalidated.

In 1973 the Court decided several cases involving aid to religious schools.[22] The Court held invalid a law granting all private schools a payment for services mandated by state law in *Levitt v. Committee for Public Education*.[23] The lump sum per pupil payment was to cover the cost of keeping certain records, preparation of various reports to the state, and the testing of students on required subjects. The largest amount was for required tests, some of which were prepared by the private school teachers and some by the state. A majority of the justices easily concluded that these grants constituted a prohibited form of aid to religion. Given the nature of religious primary and secondary schools these unrestricted lump sum grants might go to advance the sectarian activities as well as the secular functions of these schools. The fact that these services were required by the state could not furnish a way to avoid the prohibition against subsidizing religious activities.

The Court examined the constitutionality of tuition reimbursement and tax credit programs in *Committee for Public Education*

v. *Nyquist* [24] and *Sloan v. Lemon*.[25] In these cases New York and Pennsylvania had attempted to reimburse the parents of students attending nonpublic schools for a portion of the tuition which they paid to those schools. Once again, the greatest number of these schools were Catholic schools, and both programs were invalidated by the Court. The *Nyquist* case gave rise to the more significant opinion as New York had attempted to insure the secular effect of its program by making the payments and granting the tax credits directly to the parents, limiting the amounts to no more than one-half of the tuition paid, and excluding high income families.[26]

The Court invalidated both programs as it found that the programs had the effect of advancing religion. The state had to insure that these funds did not advance religion and the majority was unwilling to accept statistical guarantees that only the secular function could benefit from this aid.[27] In *Nyquist* and *Sloan*, the Court invalidated statutory grants, tax credits, and tax deductions that reimbursed only private school students for educational costs. A statute which granted tax deductions to all students or parents based upon actual expenditures for attending public or private schools would appear to have a religiously neutral purpose and effect. Such a statute might not require an excessive entanglement between government and religion in order to limit deductions to secular expenses.[28]

---

21. 403 U.S. at 622.

22. In Hunt v. McNair, 413 U.S. 734 (1973) the Court examined a program of aid to religious colleges. This subject is examined in the next section in this chapter.

23. 413 U.S. 472 (1973).

24. 413 U.S. 756 (1973).

25. 413 U.S. 825 (1973).

26. The law provided for payments to parents with an annual taxable income of under $15,000 and tax credits to those with an adjusted gross income of under $25,000. In no event could the payment exceed the lesser of the statutory limits (set between $50 and $100) or 50 percent of the tuition actually paid. Law of 1972, Ch. 414, §§ 1–5 [1972] N.Y. Laws 1669. The law, complete with tax tables, is reprinted at 413 U.S. at 761–67.

27. 413 U.S. at 787–89 (1973).

28. On June 28, 1983, the Supreme Court upheld a state statute allowing taxpayers to deduct, when computing their income tax liability, the cost of "tuition, textbooks, and transportation" expenses incurred to send their children to either a public or private school. Because the deduction was available to all students or parents, not just those who attended private or religious schools, five justices found that the law had both a nonreligious purpose and effect. Because only neutral, incidental aid was given to students attending religious schools, the majority ruled that the government involvement in audits of deductions to insure proper tax computations, and disallowance of deductions for textbooks used to teach religious doctrines, did not constitute an excessive entanglement between government and religion. Mueller v. Allen, 103 S.Ct. ___ (1983). The dissenters believed that there was no meaningful

In *Meek v. Pittenger*[29] the Court invalidated several new forms of aid to nonpublic schools. Following the rejection of its earlier program, Pennsylvania had adopted three new forms of aid for students at nonpublic schools: (1) a textbook-loan program similar to the one approved in *Allen;* (2) the loaning to nonpublic schools of instructional materials of a secular nature; (3) the provision of auxiliary guidance, testing, remedial and therapeutic services by public school employees who would provide services at the private schools. The Court upheld the textbook program but invalidated the other two forms of aid. The textbook program was upheld on the basis of the *Allen* decision. But, due to the view of parochial schools taken in later cases and the new entanglement test, some justices would even have reconsidered the validity of such programs.[30] However, it appears that *Allen* will not be reexamined and that these textbook programs will be upheld on the basis of *stare decisis.*

The loaning of instructional materials, such as recording equipment, laboratory materials or maps was held invalid because it had the impermissible effect of aiding religion. Although the majority accepted the lower court characterization of these materials as so secular that they were "self-policing,"[31] the opinion found an impermissible degree of aid to religion in this program. The granting of materials to the schools aided their operation and made the entire religious enterprise a more viable institution. As the function of parochial primary and secondary schools was inherently religious, this constituted impermissible aid to religion in the majority's view. This "aid-to-the-enterprise" theory is the culmination of the view of parochial schools taken in earlier cases and it eliminates most forms of aid which might help these schools.

The provision of auxiliary services was also invalidated in *Meek.* The state sought to avoid a religious effect by using its own employees to provide assistance in developing purely secular educational skills. In this way the state hoped to also avoid the necessity for a surveillance of the teachers and programs which might constitute an excessive entanglement. Justice Stewart, writing for the majority, found the use of state employees insufficient to guarantee a purely secular program. In the majority's view there remained the possibility that even a public school employee might advance religious ends in such a situation. Consequently, the Court held that it is impossible to avoid all possible religious effect, even in secular programs for remedial students, without supervision of the programs on a scale that would result in a prohibited form of entanglement. Once again the majority was of the view that the politically divisive nature of these programs required their invalidation under the establishment clause. However, it remains unclear whether this is a separate test, a part of the entanglement test, or merely the majority's policy reason for the strict application of other tests.

In *Meek* the majority did indicate that certain diagnostic health or speech services might be compatible with the establishment clause. Thus, if a state uses its own employees to go into public schools to make diagnosis of illness or educational disabilities and, perhaps, offer some basic treatment the program may withstand constitutional challenge. As to the diagnosis of speech or other education related skills, it was questionable whether state employees could do more than come into the nonpublic school to make a basic evaluation and diagnosis of students. Treatment which would constitute remedial educational training seemed difficult, if not impossible, to uphold after *Meek.* Thus it

---

distinction between *Mueller* and *Nyquist.* Id. at ___ (Marshall, Brennan, Blackmun, & Stevens, JJ., dissenting).

29. 421 U.S. 349 (1975).

30. 421 U.S. at 378–9 (Brennan, J., concurring in part, dissenting in part).

31. Meek v. Pittenger, 421 U.S. 349, 365 (1975) quoting Meek v. Pittenger, 374 F.Supp. 639, 660 (E.D. Pa.1974).

was not surprising that the Court later held that these remedial services could only be given to parochial students at a site away from the parochial school.[32]

It should be noticed that there may be emerging issues relating to federal aid for remedial instruction under Title I of the Federal Elementary and Secondary Education Act of 1965.[33] This act makes money available for a variety of services for private school students, especially for the educationally disadvantaged. In *Wheeler v. Barrera*[34] the Court held that the requirement of giving equal services to both public and private school students did not necessarily violate the Constitution. As there was no specific program before the Court in this case, the Court held only that state education authorities were not barred from attempting to provide comparable services for all students. However, it noted that on the premises instruction for private school students was not required by the Act and that all programs were restricted by state constitutional provisions limiting the scope of aid to religious schools. The case did not approve of any specific program and indicated that only very limited programs were likely to be found valid.

In recent decisions the justices have been sharply divided over the meaning of the three part establishment clause test and the permissible scope of governmental aid to parochial school students. In a complicated statutory program, Ohio attempted to aid private schools, which were primarily Catholic schools. This program consisted of six types of aid for all nonpublic elementary and secondary schools: (1) a textbook program like the ones approved before; (2) the provision of funds to distribute and score standardized educational tests; (3) diagnostic services with state personnel testing the individual children for specified health and educational problems; (4) therapeutic services

for health and educational disabilities provided by state personnel at sites outside of the parochial school; (5) loans to students of instructional materials and equipment; (6) funds for commercial transportation or the use of state school buses for field trips.

The rulings on these provisions were consistent with earlier cases, and basic tests remained the same, but the Court showed itself hopelessly fragmented in *Wolman v. Walter*.[35] The Court continues to have a majority that formally supports the three part test, though fewer justices may actually wish to employ the test in this school aid area. The *Wolman* opinion by Justice Blackmun was a majority opinion in part and a plurality opinion in part. The opinion applied the standard three part test in a straight forward manner and the results are best understood in the terms of this opinion. The textbook program (# 1) was upheld by a vote of 6 to 3 on the basis of *Allen*. The testing and scoring provision (# 2), by a 6 to 3 vote, was upheld because, unlike *Levitt*, these were standard educational tests prepared by state employees and designed to insure that private school students are in fact being properly educated. The diagnostic services (# 3) were upheld by a vote of 8 to 1, as there was an important secular goal in caring for children and no possible religious effect. The therapeutic services (# 4) were upheld by a vote of 7 to 2, as the removal of the services from the school eliminated the danger of religious permeation of the program. The instructional materials program (# 5) was held invalid, by a 6 to 3 vote, on precisely the same basis as was the similar program in *Meek*. The provision of transportation aid was held invalid, by a 5 to 4 vote, on an aid to the religious enterprise concept quite similar to *Meek* rationale.

The reason for the differing votes in *Wolman* was that the justices were evenly split between three positions. Chief Justice Bur-

---

32. Wolman v. Walter, 433 U.S. 229 (1977); see notes 34 & 35, and accompanying text.

33. Title I of the Elementary and Secondary Education Act of 1965, as amended, 20 U.S.C.A. § 241a et seq.

34. 417 U.S. 402 (1974), judgment modified 422 U.S. 1004 (1975).

35. 433 U.S. 229 (1977).

ger and Justices White and Rehnquist would allow the state to help the education of all children so long as there is no clear aid to religion. Justices Stewart, Blackmun and Powell believed that an independent application of the three part test will allow the state to promote secular education without impermissibly fostering religion. Justices Brennan, Marshall and Stevens are committed to the position that the first amendment was designed to prohibit any aid to religion, although only Justice Brennan could follow this position when voting on the diagnostic services.

In *Committee for Public Education and Religious Liberty v. Regan*,[36] the Supreme Court upheld, by a 5 to 4 vote, a state statute which reimbursed nonpublic schools for expenses incurred in administering and scoring standardized educational achievement tests; recording and reporting data concerning student attendance; and compiling and reporting statistical information about the students, staff, and facilities of each institution. Writing for the majority, Justice White found that the program had a secular purpose, that its principal or primary effect neither advanced nor inhibited religion, and that it did not foster an excessive government entanglement with religion. The promotion of quality nonreligious education of students in private schools was once again found sufficient to pass the first prong of the three part test. The Court found that the program did not have a religious effect because, unlike the state law stricken in *Levitt v. Committee for Public Education*,[37] this program involved repayment for administrative costs connected to specific state-required functions and, therefore, had virtually no potential for aiding the propagation of religious beliefs. The Court already had approved the use of state standardized educational achievement tests in private schools in

Wolman v. Walter. It also found here that direct cash reimbursement to nonpublic schools for administering and grading the examinations did not promote sectarian beliefs because the content of the tests was controlled by public authorities and the grading of the objective and essay questions did not provide any realistic opportunity to advance religious beliefs. The other administrative and record-keeping expenses reimbursed by the state involved the collection and reporting of attendance records and information concerning the personnel, facilities, and curriculum of each school. The majority found that state payment of such costs creates no appreciable risk of aiding the religious function of the school even though the reimbursement might free other funds within the school's budget for unspecified purposes. Finally, the majority concluded that there was no excessive entanglement fostered by this program even though the program required the schools to maintain separate accounts for the reimbursable expenses and to submit the accounts for audits by public authorities. Since the services were "discrete and clearly identifiable" the Court held that the review process did not pose a danger to either government neutrality or religious freedom. In this case Justices Stewart and Powell, who had often voted to apply the three part test very strictly in order to invalidate state programs aiding religious schools, joined with Chief Justice Burger and Justices White and Rehnquist.

Although the justices may feel bound by the principle of *stare decisis* to follow the previously described technical distinctions between permissible and impermissible forms of aid to religiously affiliated schools and their students, there now appears to be a majority of justices who will vote to uphold religiously neutral forms of general aid to public and private students.[38]

---

36. 444 U.S. 646 (1980).

37. 413 U.S. 472 (1973).

38. In 1983, Justice O'Connor, who replaced retired Justice Stewart, joined with the Chief Justice and Jus-

tices Powell, Rehnquist, and White to uphold a state income tax deduction for tuition paid to private, religiously affiliated schools. See note 28, supra.

2. Aid to Colleges and Universities

Although aid to nonpublic institutions of higher education has been the subject of only a few Supreme Court decisions, it is clear that government programs aiding these schools must be tested under the same tests that have been employed in the primary school cases. The aid must have a secular purpose, its primary effect cannot advance or inhibit religion, and it must avoid creating an excessive entanglement between government and religion. In determining whether excessive entanglement exists, three factors are examined: (1) the character of the institutions benefited; (2) the nature of the aid provided; (3) the resulting relationship between government and church authorities. Additionally, the program must not be of a type which will cause political division along religious lines. Once again, the Court will accept the legislative purpose of the aid programs as secular in nature. The announced intention of the legislature to assist the secular portion of all students' education has never been challenged by the Court in any school aid case.

These programs also have been held not to have a primary effect of aiding religion where there was at least some formal guarantee by the college authorities that the funds would not be used for religious instruction or other sectarian activities. The Court has refused to assume that religious colleges are so permeated with religion that their secular functions cannot be separated from their religious mission. Thus, a program which is tied to only secular instruction will not have an effect of advancing religion. However, if the institution to be aided is sectarian to the extent that the advancing of religious beliefs permeated its entire program then this analysis could not apply. Such an institution would be similar to the parochial elementary and secondary schools which the majority of justices have deemed to have a primary function of propagating religious doctrine. In such a situation the secular teaching function could not be sufficiently separated from the religious mission of the school. Thus any significant aid to the school would have the prohibited effect of advancing religion.

In conclusion, there is a two part test to determine whether a specific aid program for religiously affiliated colleges and universities has a "primary effect" of advancing religion. To avoid such an effect: (1) the institution's secular function must not be permeated with a religious atmosphere, and (2) there must be assurances by the college and the government authority that the aid will not be used for religious teaching or other religious activities.

It is also relatively easy for these programs to pass the three factor test for determining the presence of excessive entanglement. First, since the institutions are not "permeated" with religion, there is little need for extensive controls to insure against advancing religion. Second, the aid is usually granted for a specific secular purpose. If so, it is likely to be only a one-time grant which is easily monitored. However, the Court has upheld annual general grants to colleges where the college and government authorities would give assurances of their use for secular purposes. Third, the administrative contacts between government and religious authorities can easily be kept to a minimum in such programs. As the nature of the institution and aid do not have a high potential for advancing religion, the state need not engage in a program of constant surveillance. As long as the Court is of the impression that the program invokes little more contact between the religious authorities and the state than the normal accreditation procedures, no excessive administrative entanglement will be found. Finally, these programs have not been found to be politically divisive by the Court. The one-time grants for specific purposes rarely stir emotion concerning government subsidies to religion. Even annual grant programs are not the subject of debate along religious lines. The largely secular atmosphere of these institutions, and the public evaluation of higher education, helps to keep debate on such subjects focused on educational and fiscal policy rather than religion. Additionally, the high percentage of nonsectarian private colleges prevents these programs from becoming religious issues.

Government aid to religiously affiliated institutions of higher education has been the subject of three Supreme Court decisions. In *Tilton v. Richardson* [39] the Court, by a 5 to 4 vote, upheld the federal Higher Education Facilities Act. Under this act federal grants were made for the construction of college facilities for other than religious activities or religious instruction. In accordance with the analysis outlined above, the program was found to be permissible under the purpose-effect-entanglement test. First, the purpose of the program was to aid secular education. Second, the court found that aid to these religious colleges did not have a primary religious effect. Their dedication to secular educational goals, the policy of academic freedom and the nature of higher education were such that these colleges were not found to be permeated with religion; the program did not have the effect of advancing religion so long as the government was given assurances that the buildings were not to be used for a sectarian purpose. Third, no excessive entanglement was created by these programs. This conclusion followed from three factors: (1) the institution was not permeated with religion, (2) the aid was a one-time grant for specific building, and (3) the resulting contact between church and state could be kept to a minimum. Finally, the majority found that this program was not likely to result in political division.

It should be noted that one section of the federal law was held invalid in *Tilton*. Under the act the government gave up any ability to demand a return of funds after twenty years even if the buildings then were used for religious purposes. But a majority of the justices concluded that the limitation of the government's enforcement powers after twenty years would be the equivalent of an unrestricted gift to the college after that

time. Since this delayed grant could have the effect of advancing religion, the Court held that both the assurance of secular use and the government power to demand return of money used for religious purposes must continue so long as the facility was of any value. [40]

In *Hunt v. McNair* [41] the Court upheld a state program of issuing revenue bonds for the benefit of private colleges, including religiously affiliated schools. An "Educational Facilities Authority" issued bonds to finance construction of facilities which did not involve sectarian uses and the schools repaid these bonds from their own revenues. Although the state incurred no financial obligation under the program, the state authority issued the bonds, financed the construction with the bond revenues and leased the facilities to the institution. The use of the state bonding system allowed these schools to sell bonds at a reduced interest rate; this saved the schools significant interest payments. The Authority also was authorized to establish regulations and conduct inspections to insure secular use of the buildings which were conveyed to it. This program easily withstood review under the three part purpose-effect-entanglement test. The Court found no impermissible effect in this case. There would be a primary effect of advancing religion if either (1) the institution was so religious in character that its function was subsumed in the religious mission, or (2) the funded activity was religious in nature. Under this program the institutions aided were not subsumed in their religious mission and only secular facilities were financed by the bonds. The Court also found the act permissible under the excessive entanglement test. The three factor entanglement analysis required this result: (1) the institution was not permeated with religion, (2) the aid was not of a general character, and (3) the state authority would not be involved in detailed relationship with the college. While it was possible that the state

---

39. 403 U.S. 672 (1971). Justice White, who does not believe that the excessive entanglement test is required to protect establishment clause values, also voted to uphold the program. Thus the 5 to 4 ruling does not constitute a true application of the three-part test.

For a similar voting alignment in another case see notes 43, 45 to this section, infra.

40. 403 U.S. at 682–84.

41. 413 U.S. 734 (1973).

authority might be involved in such a relationship if it had to help a program which was becoming financially insolvent, no such case was before the Court.[42]

Finally, in *Roemer v. Board of Public Works*,[43] the justices approved an annual grant program which benefited religious colleges. Maryland established a program of annual grants which provided for each full time student (excluding those enrolled in seminary or theological programs) a grant of 15% of the per-pupil amount that the state spent in the public college system. Originally this program was subject to virtually no restrictions on the use of the grant money. However, Maryland had amended the act to provide that the Maryland Council of Higher Education screen the institution application to insure that the institution was not pervasively religious and that the institution had given adequate assurance that the funds would be used for a secular purpose. The Court by a 5 to 4 vote upheld this amended program.[44]

Justice Blackmun, in *Roemer*, wrote an opinion joined by Chief Justice Burger and Justice Powell which found that the amended program passed the three part purpose-effect-entanglement test. Justices White and Rehnquist agreed that the program had a secular purpose and effect, but they did not apply an entanglement test as they believe that no such test is mandated by the establishment clause.[45] The plurality opinion of Justice Blackmun accepted the purpose of the act as secular. He found that it did not have a primary effect of aiding religion as it neither aided an institution subsumed in religion nor in a specific religious activity. As these institutions were not "pervasively sectarian," the requirement of assurance of secular use and review by the Council on Higher Education was sufficient guarantee to avoid an effect of advancing religion.

The plurality found that using the three factor assessment did not result in a finding of excessive entanglement. First, the character of the institution was not pervasively sectarian so as to require constant surveillance of the aid. Second, the nature of a specific program was not before the Court and so the justices could only consider the character of an annual grant program in the last part of the test. Third, the resulting relationship was not materially distinguishable from earlier cases. While the aid consisted of annual grants, the justices were of the opinion that this would not involve significantly greater contact between the state and the colleges than did normal accreditation procedures. Finally, Justice Blackmun noted what may be the key factor that has caused the Court to uphold these programs—the absence of political division resulting from the enactment of such aid programs. Debate on aid to institutions of higher education, Justice Blackmun found, does not involve lobbying by churches and intense divisions among religious sects. Instead, those programs tend to be evaluated on their educational and fiscal merits. A majority of the justices have not been disposed to overturn such programs without a very clear showing of an impermissible purpose, effect or excessive administrative entanglement.[46]

---

42. For this reason the majority specifically refused to consider the degree to which the state could become involved in such a situation. 413 U.S. at 748–49.

43. 426 U.S. 736 (1976) (plurality opinion by Blackmun, J.).

44. The invalidity of the first program was in effect conceded by the state and the Court did not consider it. The status of the payments under programs which are later held invalid is considered in the next section of this chapter.

45. Roemer v. Board of Public Works, 426 U.S. 736, 767 (1976) (White, J., concurring).

46. During the 1977–1978 Term, the Supreme Court summarily affirmed two cases that upheld state programs which provided scholarships, tuition assistance, and financial aid to college students, including some students attending religiously affiliated schools. Smith v. Board of Governors, 434 U.S. 803 (1977), affirming 429 F.Supp. 871 (W.D.N.C.1977) (three-judge court); Americans United for Separation of Church and State v. Blanton, 434 U.S. 803 (1977), affirming 433 F.Supp. 97 (M.D.Tenn.1977) (three-judge court). Justices Brennan, Marshall, and Stevens voted to review each case.

3. Other Issues in Aid to Religious Institutions

a. Payments Under Programs Later Held Invalid

Even though a program of aid to religious schools has been held invalid under the establishment clause, payments may have been made to schools under the law prior to its invalidation. The question then arises as to whether the recipient institutions should be ordered to return the funds. This is precisely the situation that was present in *Lemon v. Kurtzman (Lemon II).*[47] Prior to the Supreme Court's decision in *Lemon I*[48] Pennsylvania had made substantial payments to parochial schools under the challenged act. The Court held that two factors were relevant in determining whether to grant a retroactive remedy: (1) the reasonableness and degree of reliance by the institution on the payments, and (2) the necessity of refunds to protect the constitutional right involved. Here the Court held that reimbursement was not required as reliance had been reasonable. Additionally, the return of funds would not be necessary to guard against impermissibly aiding religion as the money had been spent on secular purposes under the supervision of secular authorities.[49]

In *New York v. Cathedral Academy,*[50] the Court invalidated a state statute that would have granted reimbursement to private schools for state mandated record keeping and testing services under a program that previously had been held to violate the first and fourteenth amendments. A federal district court had found the original state act regarding payments for record keeping and testing to be unconstitutional; this had been

upheld by the Supreme Court.[51] The district court had enjoined the distribution of funds for this program including distribution of funds for the last half of the 1971–72 school year. In June 1972, the state legislature attempted to limit the impact of the district court injunction by passing a new state statute granting reimbursement for expenses incurred prior to July, 1972, by schools that had attempted to follow the previous record keeping and testing requirements. In *Cathedral Academy*, the Supreme Court held that this reimbursement act was invalid, and distinguished it from the situation in *Lemon II*. In *Lemon I* the state program violated the first amendment because it created an excessive entanglement between government and religion. The lower court's refusal to grant retroactive injunctive relief in that case was justified because allowing payments for the prior period did not do any further damage to constitutional values; those payments involved no further entanglement between government and religion, and the payments did not serve a religious purpose. In *Cathedral Academy*, the district court had enjoined all payments in the original action; the Supreme Court indicated that it could not allow state legislators to modify the impact of such injunctions. However, the opinion recognized that the primary issue was whether the new act itself violated the religion clauses of the first amendment, as applied to the states by the fourteenth amendment. The Court found that the reimbursement statute failed the three part establishment test on two bases: (1) the reimbursement payments would have a religious effect because the grant program itself had been a prohibited form of aid to religion; (2) the procedures required by the

47. Lemon v. Kurtzman, 411 U.S. 192 (1973).

48. Lemon v. Kurtzman, 403 U.S. 602 (1971). In this case the Court invalidated a Pennsylvania program involving payments to religious primary schools. The case is discussed in Section II, B, 2 of this Chapter.

49. This reasoning was reaffirmed in Roemer v. Board of Public Works, 426 U.S. 736, 745 n. 11, 767 n. 23 (1976) (plurality opinion by Blackmun, J.). Here the Court did not have to consider the constitutionality of payments made under a superceded statute which was

admittedly unconstitutional. However, the opinion indicated that the earlier payments to religious colleges under the invalid program need not be returned to the state as the state's actions were reasonable. It was also noted that the separation of church and state would not be promoted by making the state a judgment creditor of these religious institutions.

50. 434 U.S. 125 (1977).

51. Levitt v. Committee for Public Education, 413 U.S. 472 (1973).

Act to insure the secular nature of the reimbursement payments would involve an excessive entanglement between state and religious authorities. Thus, there could be no reimbursement payments under the statute even though some religious schools might have relied on the original statute, prior to the first federal court action, when they incurred these expenses. The differences in the original trial court actions in *Lemon I* and *Levitt*,[52] as well as the nature of the aid programs, resulted in the different holdings in *Lemon II* and in *Cathedral Academy*.

b. Aid to Schools That Discriminate on the Basis of Race

Although a program of state aid to a private school may not violate the establishment clause, it cannot aid a school that discriminates on the basis of race. In *Norwood v. Harrison*[53] the Supreme Court held that textbooks could not be loaned to students of a school which discriminated on the basis of race. Such a textbook program may aid religious schools as they represent a value in the free exercise of religion which offsets any slight aid to religion. However, there is no countervailing constitutional value which could justify state aid to a racially discriminatory system. Thus, the aid to these students would violate the equal protection clause of the fourteenth amendment.

A related issue is the question of whether Congress can prohibit a private school from discriminating on the basis of race because it is affiliated with a religion which requires segregation as a tenet of the religious belief.[54] It may well be that the free exercise clause requires only that such religious-segregated schools be accommodated in that their existence is not made illegal. Indeed, it is not clear whether the mere existence of such schools is prohibited by the thirteenth amendment or legislation passed pursuant to it.[55] The Civil War Amendments might be found to establish racial equality as a preeminent goal which overrides the interests of religiously affiliated schools.

At a minimum, the thirteenth and fourteenth amendments represent values that should prevent the government from actively aiding these schools. Because those schools represent values opposed to constitutional rights of racial minorities, only accommodation of their existence and the provision of such general governmental services as police and fire protection might be required. In *Bob Jones University v. United States*,[56] the Court upheld the authority of the Internal Revenue Service to deny tax exempt status to private schools which practice racially discriminatory admissions standards on the basis of their religious doctrine. The Court noted that the denial "of tax benefits will inevitably have a substantial impact

52. See note 51, supra.

53. 413 U.S. 455 (1973).

54. The Court might have confronted this problem in Bob Jones University v. Simon, 416 U.S. 725 (1974). In that case a private university sought to enjoin the Internal Revenue Service for denying it tax exempt status because it discriminated by race in its admissions. The school argued that the religion it represented required racial segregation and that to deny it favorable tax treatment on this basis would violate the free exercise clause. However, the Court did not reach this issue since it held that the suit was barred by the tax "anti-injunction" statutes. Also, in Runyon v. McCrary, 427 U.S. 160 (1976), the Court explicitly excluded from its decision—holding 42 U.S.C.A. § 1981 to forbid private racial discrimination in private schools—the case where the racial discrimination is required by religious doctrine. 427 U.S. at 167 n. 6.

The Supreme Court declined to review a decision that might have resolved the issue of whether a religious

school could exclude racial minorities. Brown v. Dade Christian Schools, Inc., 556 F.2d 310 (5th Cir. 1977) (en banc), cert. denied 434 U.S. 1063 (1978). However, the lower court had found that the school in question was secular and that the school could not base a claim on the religious principles of some of its students. The application of 42 U.S.C.A. § 1981 to this school presented little problem once the lower court determined that the exclusion policy was based on social policy rather than religious belief.

55. The Supreme Court has held that legislation passed pursuant to the thirteenth amendment prohibits the racial discrimination by private schools. Runyon v. McCrary, 427 U.S. 160 (1976), this case is discussed in Chapter 17, Section III. The Court specifically left open the case where a school discriminated by race due to religious beliefs, 427 U.S. at 167 n. 6.

56. 103 S.Ct. 2017 (1983), decided on May 24, 1983, as the second edition of this treatise was going to press.

on the operation of private religious schools, but will not prevent those schools from observing their religious tenets." Moreover, "the Government has a fundamental, overriding interest in eradicating racial discrimination in education" and this interest "substantially outweighs whatever burden denial of tax benefits places on petitioners' exercise of their religious beliefs."

c. State Constitutional Restrictions

A number of states have constitutional provisions that specifically restrict aid to religious institutions.[57] In such states even such forms of aid as bus fees, textbooks, and tax exemptions might be denied to religious institutions by the state constitution. As the Supreme Court of the United States has only indicated that such forms of aid are permissible if the state desires to furnish them, there is no violation of the first amendment if a state refuses to aid religious schools. If a state went so far as to deny basic governmental services such as police and fire protection to religious institutions, there would be a significant issue as to whether the denial of services so inhibited the practice of religion as to amount to a violation of the free exercise clause. However, no state has done this.

d. Government Payments of Money "Owned" by Private Individuals

The government may pay the tuition of students at religious schools if the tuition payment is made with money owned or earned by the students. In *Quick Bear v. Leupp*[58] the Supreme Court upheld a federal government payment to religious organizations on Indian reservations since the money used was owned by the Indian tribes and only held in trust by the federal government. A similar analysis might support the use of tuition payments for veterans of the armed services to religious colleges, or the government loaning money at reduced interest rates to all students regardless of whether they attend religiously affiliated schools. However, no Supreme Court decision has addressed the permissibility of these programs.

e. Financial Aid to Religiously Affiliated Institutions Other Than Schools

If the government is granting financial aid to a religiously affiliated institution of any type, the program must be tested under the establishment clause in the same manner as are programs which aid schools. Thus, the program must have a secular purpose, no primary effect which either advances or inhibits religion and no excessive entanglement between government and religious authority. Again, excessive entanglement will be looked at in terms of: (1) the character of the institution, (2) the type of aid, and (3) the resulting administrative relationships. Additionally, the potential of the program for causing political division along religious lines will be an important factor in determining its validity.

The key to analysis of any such program is the determination of the degree of the independent secular function in the institution to be aided. If the institution is pervasively religious, it will be practically impossible to aid the institution without either having the impermissible effect of aiding religion or else having to establish so many procedural safeguards that an excessive entanglement results. However, if the institution has a clearly independent secular function the state should be able to design a program which aids only the secular activities. This type of institution can then be aided with a minimum of administrative entanglement, as the lesser potential for aiding the religious function requires fewer safeguards.

During the last century the Supreme Court upheld grants to church affiliated hospitals in *Bradfield v. Roberts*,[59] recently cited with approval by the Court.[60] As reli-

---

57. For a review of such provisions see, C. Antieau, P. Carroll & T. Burke, Religion Under the State Constitutions (1965).

58. 210 U.S. 50 (1908).

59. 175 U.S. 291 (1899).

60. Roemer v. Board of Public Works, 426 U.S. 736, 746 (1976) (plurality opinion by Blackmun, J.).

gious hospitals seem to have an independent secular function, the analysis should be the same as that for religious colleges—the state need only avoid aiding pervasively religious institutions or clearly religious activities. So long as the hospital aided is not so "pervasively sectarian" as to subsume its role as a hospital in its religious mission, its secular medical function may receive state aid.

4. A Comment on the Emergence and Impact of the Excessive Entanglement Test [1]

Prior to the Supreme Court decisions of the 1970's, it appeared that the states would be able to give financial assistance to children who chose to receive their educations away from the public school system. As the Court had refused to assume that there was no independent secular function in parochial schools, the "purpose and effect" test did not bar general aid to students in all private schools. But one leading scholar, Professor Paul Freund, thought that the incidental aid to religion which resulted from government transportation payments or textbook programs violated the first amendment principles of government neutrality and separation between church and state.[2] However another leading scholar in this area, Professor Jesse Choper, attempted to keep the Court from a more restrictive approach by

demonstrating how the government might aid only the secular function of religiously affiliated schools.[3]

Economic and statistical analysis shows that it is possible to construct a tuition tax credit or voucher system, which reimburses families for part of the expense of sending their children to private schools, without aiding religion.[4] So long as the amounts would be less than the amount expended for the secular courses in these schools, no funds inure to the benefit of religious education. It would be true that more families might be able to to "opt out" of the public school system and send their children to parochial schools if such a refund or voucher program existed. But this would not be the result of any government encouragement or aid to religion. Instead these programs merely offer families a choice of receiving their educational benefits "in kind" at the local public school or "in cash" if the chose to send their children to an alternative school system.

The most important effect of a general aid program to students attending alternative systems of education is that such a program provides a more meaningful equality of educational opportunity for children from low-income families. The provision of subsidized education only through a government operated school system imposes very severe hardships on children from low-income fami-

---

1. This comment was taken with very few changes from Nowak, The Supreme Court, the Religion Clauses and the Naturalization of Education, 70 Nw.U.L.Rev. 883 (1976). On June 29, 1983, the Supreme Court upheld a state statute that allowed taxpayers to deduct, in computing their income tax liability, expenses incurred in providing tuition, textbooks, or transportation for children attending either public or private schools. In this 5 to 4 decision the majority used a conception of government neutrality close to that advocated in this comment; the dissent claimed that this approach disregarded previous Supreme Court rulings. Mueller v. Allen, 103 S.Ct. ___ (1983).

2. Freund, Public Aid to Parochial Schools, 82 Harv.L.Rev. 1680 (1969).

3. Choper, The Establishment Clause and Aid to Parochial Schools, 56 Calif.L.Rev. 260 (1968). This article contains a comprehensive analysis of the history and effect of programs of aid to religious schools.

4. For an economic analysis of these programs and the rulings of the Supreme Court, see Nowak, The Su-

preme Court, the Religion Clauses and the Nationalization of Education, 70 Nw.U.L.Rev. 883 (1976). The voucher system and economic analysis which follow were first suggested in A. Smith, The Wealth of Nations 736–38 (Mod.Lib. ed. 1937). The concept was fully developed and the analysis refined by Professor Friedman. M. Friedman, Capitalism & Freedom 85–107 (1962). The problems of zero tuition and higher education which were explored by Professor Alchian also relate directly to the analysis of the voucher program. Alchian, The Economic and Social Impact of Free Tuition, in H. Manne, The Economics of Legal Relationships 598–613 (1975). Those who have not been exposed previously to economic analysis might wish to consult the following introductory works: A. Alchian & W. Allen, University Economics—Elements of Inquiry 1–27, 487–528 (3d. ed 1972); R. Posner, Economic Analysis of Law 110, 252–65 (1973); L. Reynolds, Microeconomics—Analysis & Policy 3–22, 346–65 (1973); P. Samuelson, Economics 1–17, 58–100, 801–22 (9th ed. 1973).

lies who seek a superior education. If the local public school system seems insufficient for developing the intellectual abilities of their children, higher income parents may move to a place where the public school system is superior or simply withdraw their child from the public system and provide the child with a privately financed education. Neither of these options is available to low-income families. The low-income parents may be equally desirous of improving the education of their children, especially if they perceive that their children have exceptional intellectual abilities or that the local public schools fail to provide even a minimally adequate education. Indeed these parents might well be willing to do without many other "basic necessities" in order to provide their children with a superior education. However, because subsidized education is provided only in kind, they can only change the quality of their child's education with a massive dollar supplement which is beyond their means. If the state would give them the dollar equivalent of the per-pupil cost of the local public school, they could supplement this figure with some of their own resources and use the increased amount to send their child to another school. However, where the subsidized education is provided only in kind, the parents would have to be able to move to a substantially richer neighborhood or to bear the entire cost of private education themselves in order to improve the educational opportunities of their children. These options, of course, will be beyond the means of such families.

The administrative regulation of religious activities would pose great danger to the values of government neutrality in religious matters. First, programs which call for a high degree of administrative contact and regulation might leave the impression that those groups which survive regulation are governmentally approved. Such regulation also endangers the freedom of religious societies by requiring them to be responsive to government administrators in order to maintain the flow of benefits. Additionally, this type of involvement may undermine the neutrality of the government itself. A high degree of regulation will require some formal administration to insure that the day-to-day regulations are followed and that reporting requirements are met. However, in the long run, administrators and those who are being regulated frequently develop a mutuality of interest. It is in the interest of the public administrators to please those who are regulated in order to maintain their position and increase the power of their agency. Similarly, it is in the interest of the regulated entities to accommodate, if not control, those who regulate them so that they will receive favorable rulings in areas where the administrators exercise some discretion. This mutuality of interest can lead to the "capture" of administrative agencies by those whom they are supposed to regulate and make it difficult to determine whether such agencies are acting on behalf of the public or the regulated entity.[5] There is no reason to believe that the regulation of religious activities would follow a different pattern.[6]

5. K. Davis, Administrative Law Treatise § 1.03 (1958); T. Morgan, Economic Regulation of Business—Cases and Materials 21–23 (1976); Posner, Theories of Economic Regulation, 5 Bell J. of Econ. & Mgt. Science 335 (1974); Stigler, The Theory of Economic Regulation, 2 Bell J. of Econ. & Mgt. Science 3 (1970). See also, L. Kohlmeier, The Regulators—Watchdog Agencies and the Public Interest 69–82 (1969).

6. In Larkin v. Grendel's Den, Inc., 103 S.Ct. 505 (1982), the Court found that a zoning law violated the first amendment establishment clause by granting to all churches or schools a veto power over the issuance of liquor license for any premises within a 500 foot radius of the church or the school. The Court applied the three-part test under the establishment clause. Although the law might have had a secular purpose, (the promotion of a quiet atmosphere around certain cultur-

al and educational centers) that purpose could not alone sustain the statute's constitutionality. The zoning statute was clearly susceptible being used to promote religious rather than secular ends. The churches had a power under the statute which was subject to no clear secular standards; that power could be used to promote primarily religious goals. Even if one assumed that the statute had both a secular purpose and primary effect, the law clearly failed the excessive entanglement test. A law which vested governmental authority in churches "enmeshes churches in the exercise of substantial governmental powers contrary to our consistent interpretation of the establishment clause." 103 S.Ct. at 512. The excessive entanglement branch of the establishment clause test was meant to avoid the danger to both secular government

Thus, Chief Justice Burger was quite correct in concluding that the first amendment forbids any program of government aid which would require substantial reporting and regulation [7] since it is the first step to agency regulation of religious societies. However, so long as the aid program does not involve a substantial probability that the benefits could be used directly for sectarian functions, there is no need for a reporting and regulation system which would lead to administrative entanglement. For example, vouchers which are computed by a formula which gives statistical assurance that no aid will be provided to sectarian activities should not require further regulation of this type.[8] Similarly, the provision of truly neutral educational materials which are not readily adaptable for religious education requires no further regulation to insure that they are not used for the religious orientation of students.[9]

Economic and statistical analysis proves that no danger to the values of the religion clauses results from school aid programs which have statistical assurances against aid to religious teaching. Programs such as those described by Professor Choper cannot aid the religious function of parochial schools because the dollar supplement is less than their cost for the teaching of secular subjects. No principle of voluntarism is endangered by such a program as no tax dollars go to the funding of religious activities. There is no danger to government neutrality since the programs merely allow low-income families to exercise freedom of choice in educational matters. Such programs offer no incentive or encouragement for parents to send their children to parochial schools, so long as they could receive at least as great a financial benefit by sending their children to

the public schools. Finally, the principle of mutual abstention is preserved by providing only services or dollar amounts which are not likely to aid religious activities and which avoid administrative entanglement.

As we saw in the previous sections of this chapter, the Court in the 1970's rejected the use of statistical guarantees to prove that an educational assistance program did not aid religion. Instead, the majority held that any significant aid to children attending religious elementary or secondary schools would be presumed to aid the religious function of those schools. This impermissible effect could only be avoided if administrative systems were designed to prevent any aid to religious teaching. Of course, if a state used such a system, it would give rise to an excessive entanglement between government and religion which would violate the first amendment. To insist that any form of aid, no matter how neutral, continually be reported on to insure its neutrality but then to invalidate the program because of the reporting requirement seems circular. This result is justified, in the view of a majority of the Court, by the political divisiveness principle and the first amendment prohibition of government aid to religion.

The origin of the excessive entanglement-political divisiveness test merits attention. The concept was introduced by Justice Harlan in his concurring opinions in *Board of Education v. Allen* [10] and *Walz v. Tax Commission.* [11] However, he only meant to use the concept to indicate that the Court should be careful not to encourage such political fragmentation. His conclusions as to the validity of the textbook program and the tax exemption show that he did not intend to use the concept as a strict test of constitu-

---

and religious autonomy that accompanies a sharing of power and entanglement of administrative agencies.

7. The administrative entanglement test was added in Walz v. Tax Comm'n, 397 U.S. 664 (1970).

8. Choper, The Establishment Clause and Aid to Parochial Schools, 56 Calif.L.Rev. 260, 287–90 (1968).

9. Even the new majority of the Court has admitted that a variety of instructional materials may be "self-

policing" in this sense. Meek v. Pittenger, 421 U.S. 349, 365 (1975).

10. 392 U.S. 236, 249 (1968) (Harlan, J., concurring).

11. 397 U.S. 664, 694 (1970) (Harlan, J., concurring); the concept of entanglement was also used by the majority in *Walz* without defining the principle. Id. at 670, 674–5.

tional validity.[12] Similarly, in the *Lemon* and *Tilton* decisions, it appeared that the Chief Justice was only using this concept to reinforce the conclusions of the Court. He found that the programs of aid to religious primary, secondary and college level schools all had a secular purpose. However, the challenged forms of aid to primary and secondary schools were found to be extremely susceptible to use for religiously oriented activities, which meant that the government would have to engage in a prohibitive form of day-to-day regulation to insure that no aid was given to religious functions. At the college level, the greatly decreased likelihood that the forms of aid could or would be used for sectarian activities meant that the government could rely on milder forms of reporting and regulation to insure secular use of funds. Thus the real distinction between the two programs was not in the politically divisive nature of each program, but that one form of aid invited excessive administration while the other did not.[13] The Chief Justice merely reinforced the Court's conclusions by noting that there was political division over the primary school aid programs, but not the college grant programs.[14]

The test, however, took on a life of its own in *Nyquist*. Here a form of completely neutral aid—a tuition-voucher plan—was stricken in part because of the belief that any significant aid to students in sectarian schools caused political division.[15] This principle was invoked again in *Meek* to justify the prohibition of furnishing auxiliary educational aids and services to students, a form of aid with little potential for use in sectarian functions.[16] Indeed, three of the justices were so committed to this concept that they favored invoking it to strike down the *Allen* textbook program.[17] They were correct in noting that no significant aid to parochial schools is permissible under the political divisiveness test. There was no principled way to distinguish the textbook program under the test [18] since any form of aid which would enable children to go to parochial schools will carry with it the seeds for debate cast in religious terms about its merits.

If the political divisiveness test is in fact being used by the majority to ban religious conflict, the attempt would appear to be futile at best. The prohibition of aid to parochial schools cannot end sectarian debate over educational programs and budgets—it can only shift its focus. By prohibiting even neutral aid to parochial schools, the Court has seriously disadvantaged them in competing with the governmentally operated school system. Instead of religious groups proposing legislation which would benefit the students who would attend their schools, they will be forced to oppose aid to public schools so as to benefit their schools indirectly. Insofar as the proponents of religious education can reduce the amounts spent on public schools, they will decrease the economic incentive for parents to send their children to such schools. Opposition to public school bond referendums by religious groups will occur in the future unless those groups are content to watch increasing student transfers to the better financed systems. It seems unlikely that this will reduce political division.

The shifted focus of the political conflict may well increase political division along religious lines. If inner city school performance continues to decrease, one would expect increased pressure on government to

12. Thus, although Justice Harlan cited the Freund article, Public Aid to Parochial Schools, 82 Harv.L.Rev. 1680 (1969), in his *Walz* concurrence, 397 U.S. at 695, he showed no inclination to reconsider his position in *Allen* because of this concept. Id.

13. Compare Lemon v. Kurtzman, 403 U.S. 602, 618–22 (1970), with Tilton v. Richardson, 403 U.S. 672, 685–88 (1971) (Burger, C.J., plurality opinion).

14. Lemon v. Kurtzman, 403 U.S. 602, 622–25 (1971); Tilton v. Richardson, 403 U.S. 672, 689 (1971) (Burger, C.J., plurality opinion).

15. Committee for Public Education v. Nyquist, 413 U.S. 756, 795–97 (1973).

16. Meek v. Pittenger, 421 U.S. 349, 365 n. 15, 372 (1975).

17. Id. at 374–78 (Brennan, J.). This opinion was joined by Justices Douglas and Marshall.

18. Id. at 377–78 (Brennan, J.).

aid private schools so that the residents of the city have an alternative to the public school system.[19] However, it will be in the interest of those who favor religiously oriented education to oppose such aid if it is not provided on an equal basis to parochial schools. Those who favor parochial schools will perceive that aid to nonreligious private schools directly threatens their existence by offering an alternative to the public school system which the state has placed in an economically preferred position to their schools. This would leave religious schools at a dual disadvantage in the market place. Public schools would have the benefit of the highest governmental subsidy, while private nonreligious schools would have a lower subsidy but greater responsiveness to parents and teachers. Those who favor the continued existence of parochial schools would find it beneficial to oppose aid to both the public schools and nonreligious private schools. Thus, new forms of political division along religious lines may result from the Court's ban on aid to parochial schools. If the Court were to approve religiously neutral forms of government aid to both public and private school students, it would aid the quality of education without endangering the first amendment values or creating political divisions along religious lines.

C. Religion and the Public Schools

1. Introduction

Questions concerning the introduction of religion into the governmentally operated school system may arise in several ways.

The issue was considered by the Court prior to 1980 in cases which involved the release of public school students for religious instruction, the use of prayers or Bible readings in the classroom and the legislative banning of certain biological theories. All of these cases were decided prior to the emergence of the excessive entanglement test; indeed, the released time cases arose before the clear emergence of the purpose-and-effect test. Since 1980 the Court has used the three-part purpose-effect-entanglement test when examining these issues.[1]

2. Released or Shared Time

The Supreme Court has twice considered public school programs involving the exemption of public school students from class so that they could receive religious instruction. The Court has held that the students could not be given religious instruction on the public school premises as such a program has the direct effect of aiding the establishment of religious beliefs. However, the state may release students from school so that they may attend religious instruction away from the public school. This early release of students is viewed as only an accommodation of individual religious preferences rather than an aid to the religions.

In *Illinois ex rel. McCollum v. Board of Education* [2] the Court held invalid a system whereby religious teachers came into the public school to give instruction to students. The program allowed members of any religious organization to instruct those students who had requested the instruction. Stu-

---

19. In fact, this is exactly what has happened in major urban areas. The majority of parochial schools exist in the most populous states and serve urban areas. U. S. Department of Health, Education & Welfare, Digest of Education Statistics 39–41 (1973). In those low-income areas the quality of education can be expected to decline in the presence of increasing problems of financing and overcrowding. See, President's Panel on Nonpublic Education and the Public Good (1972). The eight most populous states face even greater problems in the years ahead if parochial schools close and the government operated systems are forced to serve additional students who otherwise would have attended these schools. See Swartz, The Estimated Marginal Costs of Absorbing All Nonpublic

Students into the Public School System, in President's Commission on School Finance, Economics of Nonpublic Schools, 301, 347 (1972). For further analysis of the restrictive effect of the current public school system on lower income groups and economic mobility, see Clark, Alternative Public School Systems, in Equal Educational Opportunity (Harv.Educ.Rev. ed. 1969). See generally, J. Coons, W. Clune & S. Sugarman, Private Wealth and Public Education (1970).

1. Stone v. Graham, 449 U.S. 39 (1980), see Section II C3 infra; Widmar v. Vincent, 454 U.S. 263 (1981), see Section II, C, 5, infra.

2. 333 U.S. 203 (1948).

dents who did not request instruction remained in the school, as the programs took place during a time when the compulsory attendance laws required all students below the age of 17 to be in school. The Court found a direct aid to religion as government facilities were being used for the propagation of religious beliefs. While no formal test was employed, the opinion noted that this policy removed any "wall" between church and state as it had the government giving direct help to the advancing of religion. It was irrelevant that all religions might be helped by the program as the first amendment was held to forbid the advancing of religious beliefs over non-religious ones as well as the advancement of a particular sect.

Only four years later, in *Zorach v. Clausen*,[3] the Court upheld a program where students were released from public schools so that they could receive religious instruction at other locations. Although all children were required to be either in school or at religious classes during this period, a majority of the justices found that the program did not constitute government aid to religion. As no government funds or other support went to the advancing of religious ends, this was considered to be only the accommodation of the desires of individual students and their families to be free of the public school system so that they could receive their religious education. Moreover, there was no religious doctrine taught on public property, in the public schools. The key concept here is the neutral principle of "accommodation." If there had been proof that the program coerced students into attending religious classes, the state support of those programs would violate both the free exercise and the establishment clauses.[4] However, there was no such proof in this case and, on this basis,

the majority found the program to be a mere accommodation of the desires of individual students to exercise rights whose values are reflected in the free exercise clause.

3. Prayers or Bible Reading

The use of officially authorized prayers or Bible readings for motivational purpose constitutes a direct violation of the establishment clause. Even though a practice may not be coercive, active support of a particular belief raises the danger of eventual establishment of state approved religious views. Although a given prayer or practice may not favor any one sect, the principle of neutrality in religious matters is violated by any program which places tacit government approval on "religious" views or practices. Under the basic purpose-and-effect test these programs must be found to violate the first amendment. The purpose of the program might be a neutral or secular one of state accommodation of student desires. However, the effect of any such practice is to give government aid and support to the advancing of religious beliefs. Thus the programs were held invalid even prior to the use of the additional entanglement test.

It should be noted that not all religious references have been banned from the public schools. Religion and religious literature, including the Bible, may be studied in a purely academic manner. So long as the study does not amount to prayer or the advancement of religious beliefs, a teacher may discuss such materials in the secular course of study.[5] Finally, religious references in official ceremonies, including some school exercises, will be allowed as a part of our secularized traditions and not an advancement of religion similar to state approved prayer.[6]

3. 343 U.S. 306 (1952).

4. 343 U.S. at 311.

5. School District v. Schempp, 374 U.S. 203, 225 (1963).

6. Engel v. Vitale, 370 U.S. 421, 435 n. 21 (1962). On July 5, 1983, the Court upheld a state legislature's

employment of a chaplain and use of an opening prayer. These practices were upheld on the basis of the history of legislative prayer, which dated back to the Congress which drafted the first amendment. The ruling does not modify the principles regarding religious activity in public schools. Marsh v. Chambers, 103 S.Ct. ___ (1983).

In *Engel v. Vitale*[7] the Supreme Court held that the use of a "nondenominational prayer" written by government authorities violated the establishment clause. The decision was easily reached as the government writing of a prayer was sponsorship of religious views similar to the official establishment of religion, which many of the framers of the first amendment had fled from and feared. Moreover, like the program in *Illinois ex rel. McCollum v. Board of Education*, discussed above, the religious exercise was performed on school property.

In a second case, *School District v. Schempp*,[8] the Court examined school programs of voluntary Bible reading or the use of the "Lord's Prayer." Unlike *Engel*, it was not part of the job of any public official to compose a prayer. Yet this difference did not save the program from Constitutional attack. In *Schempp* the Court used the purpose and effect test to review the programs under the establishment clause. Although the program was voluntary and did not favor any sect, the effect was to aid the advancement of religion; it constitutes a generalized religious ceremony. Thus, it violated the concepts of separation and neutrality between government and religion and there was but one dissent to the invalidation of these practices.[9]

An important part of the *Schempp* decision was the majority's answer to the argument that elimination of voluntary prayers would amount to government sponsorship of an anti-religious position. The Court found that neutrality in religious matters did not constitute the implied teaching of a "religion of secularism."[10] This viewpoint is important to the decisions involving aid to religious schools for it rejects the argument that providing publicly funded education only in secular schools inhibits the free exercise of religion by those who want their children trained in a religious manner. So long as the state does not legally prohibit private, religious schools, its offering of public education in this manner is not a violation of the religion clauses.[11]

In *Stone v. Graham*,[12] the Supreme Court held that a Kentucky statute requiring the posting of the Ten Commandments on the wall of each public classroom in the state violated the establishment clause. Any use of prayers or Bible passages in school must be reviewed under the three part test for compatibility with the establishment clause. First, the statute must have a secular legislative purpose. Second, its primary effect must neither advance nor inhibit religion. Third, the statute must not create an excessive entanglement between government and religion.[13] Any use of prayers or religious literature for inspirational purpose would violate the purpose and effect tests for validity. The Supreme Court's opinion stated that the preeminent purpose of the Kentucky statute was "plainly religious in nature" and had no secular legislative purpose, even though the legislation included a statement of avowed secular purpose.[14] The fact that the Bible verses were to be posted rather than read aloud and the fact that they were to be financed by voluntary private contributions had no bearing on the validity of the statute because it had a plainly religious purpose and "it is no defense to urge that the religious practices here may be relative-

---

7. 370 U.S. 421 (1962).

8. 374 U.S. 203 (1963).

9. Justice Stewart was the sole dissenter. 374 U.S. at 308. It is interesting to note that while these decisions were the subject of intense public debate, there was virtual unanimity among the justices on these issues.

10. 374 U.S. at 225–26.

11. The Court's rulings on aid to parochial schools and the refusals to recognize a state interest in enabling students to attend those schools are the subject of Section II, B, 1 of this Chapter.

12. 449 U.S. 39 (1980).

13. 449 U.S. at 40, citing Lemon v. Kurtzman, 403 U.S. 602, 612–13 (1971).

14. The Kentucky legislation required the following notation in small print at the bottom of each posted copy of the Ten Commandments: "The secular application of the Ten Commandments is clearly seen in its adoption as the fundamental legal code of Western Civilization and the Common Law of the United States." K.R.S. 158.178 (1980). Stone v. Graham, 449 U.S. 39, 40 n. 1 (1980).

ly minor encroachments on the first amendment." [15]

4. Modification of the Curriculum for Religious Purposes

The Supreme Court has ruled that a state may not eliminate the teaching of certain ideas related to normal classroom subjects because they conflict with religious beliefs. In *Epperson v. Arkansas* [16] the Court reviewed a statute which made it unlawful for teachers in state schools to teach a theory of human biological evolution. The Court held that the statute violated the establishment clause because it had a religious purpose—thus failing the secular purpose test. It was an impermissible breach of the principle of government neutrality for the state to eliminate a particular piece of information from a course merely because it conflicted with religious beliefs.

It should be noted that this case does not, by itself, eliminate the ability of the state to adjust or eliminate the subjects that are taught in its school system. Justice Black, in a concurring opinion, noted that a state should be able to eliminate any given subject matter from its school system without raising a first amendment issue. [17] This principle would seem to be true, for if the state is under no obligation to teach a specific subject there should be nothing wrong with eliminating a given course. However, there are two bases for making an exception to this deference to state educational authority. First, where the state has eliminated only one element from a course of study for religious reasons it has attempted to help the religious point of view by eliminating ideas which would challenge that view. Second, where the state can offer no secular educational reason for altering the curriculum there is no reason to defer to the state's educational policy. It was this unusual case of an open attempt to aid certain religious views that was presented to the Court in *Epperson*. This official attempt to aid a specific religious view openly breached the principle of neutrality, which is the core of the Religion Clauses.

5. Equal Access to School Facilities

In *Widmar v. Vincent* [18] the Supreme Court invalidated a state university regulation which denied access to school facilities to religious student organizations as a violation of the freedom of speech. [19] In so doing the Court provided some insight into the related problem of defining the scope of university involvement with religious organizations.

In 1977 the University of Missouri at Kansas City began to enforce a policy prohibiting the use of university buildings or grounds "for purposes of religious worship or religious teaching." University officials informed a registered student religious group that the University was discontinuing what had been a four-year practice of permitting the group to conduct its meetings in university facilities. The majority opinion in *Widmar* by Justice Powell found that once it had opened its facilities for use by student groups the university had created a public forum. It was then required to justify any content-based exclusions under the applicable standard of review and the regulation would be upheld only if it was necessary to serve a compelling state interest and if it was narrowly drawn to achieve that end.

Justice Powell's opinion stated that the university's interest in maintaining a strict separation of church and state, as mandated by the establishment clauses of the federal and Missouri constitutions was compelling. However, Justice Powell, applying the three pronged purpose-effect-entanglement test, did not agree that a policy allowing equal access to university facilities to religious groups would violate the establishment

---

15. 449 U.S. at 42, citing School District v. Schempp, 374 U.S. 203 (1963).

16. 393 U.S. 97 (1968).

17. 393 U.S. at 113–14 (Black, J., concurring).

18. 454 U.S. 263 (1981).

19. See Chapter 18, Section XIII for analysis of this and other "public forum" problems.

clause. He found that the first and last parts of the test—purpose and entanglement were clearly met: a policy fostering an open university forum for all registered student groups has a secular purpose. Opening facilities to all students would not involve excessive entanglement between government and religion. In addition, the Court was satisfied that the "primary effect" of allowing student religious groups to share the limited public forum, open to all forms of discourse, was not to benefit religion. Any religious benefits would be merely incidental for two reasons. First, the creation of a limited public forum at the university, and allowing religious groups access to that forum, does not confer state approval on any religious sect or practice. Second, the forum was available to a broad class of non-religious, as well as religious, groups. In the absence of concrete evidence that campus religious groups would dominate the open forum, the Court was unwilling to find that the benefits to religion were to any degree greater than the general benefits such as police and fire protection which were clearly compatible with the establishment clause.

Justice Powell also held that, despite the fact that the Missouri constitution required stricter separation of church and state than the federal Constitution, the State's interest in achieving complete separation of church and state was limited by the free exercise and free speech clauses of the first amendment and was not sufficiently compelling to justify the content-based discrimination against these students' speech activities.

It should be noted that in *Widmar* the Court ruled only that a state university could not engage in content-based discrimination against religious speech. If the university had not created the "public forum" it would not have been required to furnish facilities for use by religious groups. Thus, the case may be of little relevance to determining if high school student religious organizations must be allowed access to high school facilities, where there may be no "public forum."

III. THE FREE EXERCISE CLAUSE

A. Introduction

The first amendment provides that Congress shall make no law "prohibiting the free exercise" of religion.[1] This clause, which has since been applied to the states, provides protection for the practice of any religion. It absolutely prohibits the proscription of any religious belief by the government. Additionally, it requires that the government make some accommodation for the practice of religious beliefs when it pursues ends which incidentally burden religious practices. However, the accommodation required by this clause is not great. Burdens on the practice of religion will be tolerated whenever they are incident to a regulation of secular activities and the state interest is of a magnitude that overrides the claims for a religious exemption.

The prohibition of any religious belief by the government could never withstand analysis under the religion clauses. These clauses have proscribed all government judgments concerning the propriety or truthfulness of religious doctrine. Correspondingly, government may not confer any benefits or impose any burden on individuals because of their religious beliefs. A law which would deny government employment to people who held certain religious beliefs would violate the free exercise clause because of its burden on those persons and the establishment clause because it preferred other religions. The text of the Constitution contains a specific provision which prohibits any religious tests for a position in the federal government[2] and the religion clauses also prohibit such tests. In *Torcaso v. Wat-*

---

1. "Congress shall make no law respecting an establishment of religion or prohibiting the free exercise thereof . . . ." U.S. Const.Amend. I. The free exercise clause was first held applicable to the states in Cantwell v. Connecticut, 310 U.S. 296 (1940).

2. "[N]o religious Test shall ever be required as a Qualification to any Office or Public Trust under the United States." U.S. Const. art. VI.

kins [3] the Supreme Court unanimously invalidated a state requirement that a person take an oath which required a belief in God in order to qualify for public employment. As the justices found that aid could not be given to religion over "non-religion" and that non-religious beliefs could not be burdened, the law violated both of the religion clauses.

A government regulation may also burden the practice of a religion because it inhibits or prohibits the taking of actions important to the practice of that religion. Such burdens may be "direct" in the sense that an activity essential to the religious practice is prohibited, or "indirect" in that the regulation makes the practice of religion more difficult. An example of a direct burden would be the legal prohibition of polygamy which was considered an essential part of the practice of the Mormon religion at one time. An indirect burden would be the requirement that shops close on Sunday which has the effect of imposing additional economic costs on Sabbatarians whose religion also requires them to refrain from work on Saturdays. Although earlier cases implied that indirect burdens were at least presumptively permissible, today it is clear that both direct and indirect burdens must be reviewed under the same standards. Any substantial burden on free exercise is reviewed by the Court under a test which balances the burden on religion against the state's interest in the regulation.

In presenting these issues it is the burden of the party who is challenging the law, or claiming a religious exemption from a regulation, to show that the law does burden the practice of their religion. While there is no formal test for a *de minimis* burden, there must be a substantial burden—that is, one which would inhibit the practice of the religion and in effect be a coercion to forego the practice.[4] In earlier cases the Court mentioned the need to show that the state regulation amounted to "coercion." Today any regulation which substantially impairs the practice of a religion will be sufficiently "coercive" to merit further review under the balancing test. Once it is shown that the law burdens the practice of a religious belief the state must show that it has an overriding or compelling secular reason for refusing to grant an exemption from the regulation. In balancing the interests the court must first determine the degree of burden on the religious practice. Then, in assessing the state's interest, the court will have to determine the importance of the secular interest and the extent to which that interest would be impaired by an exemption for the religious practice. If the state interest is truly compelling, there will be no requirement that the state diminish the effectiveness of its regulation by granting the exemption. However, if the state could achieve its goal as well by a means which would not burden the religious practice, it will be required to adopt the alternative means. If the state's interest is of a lesser magnitude it will be required to grant the exemption and accept a less effective means of fulfilling its goal.

B. The Early Decisions

The claims of religious minorities received little serious attention from the Supreme Court through the first part of this century. In *Reynolds v. United States* [5] the Supreme Court upheld the application of a federal law prohibiting polygamy to a Mormon whose religion required him to engage in that practice.[6] The majority opinion indicated that Congress was free to prohibit any action regardless of its religious implications so long as it did not formally prohibit a belief.[7]

---

3. 367 U.S. 488 (1961).

4. Walsh v. Louisiana High School Athletic Ass'n, 616 F.2d 152, 158 (5th Cir. 1980) (Clark, C. J., citing an earlier edition of this treatise), cert. denied 449 U.S. 1124 (1981).

5. 98 U.S. 145 (1879).

6. Actually the church required polygamy by male members only "when circumstances would admit," but it was conceded that Mr. Reynolds' second marriage was sanctioned by the church as being within the requirement. 98 U.S. at 161.

7. The majority opinion by Chief Justice Waite stated: "Congress was deprived of all legislative power

Thus construed, the clause would give no protection against the proscription of actions deemed central to a religion unless the legislature formally outlawed the belief itself. The cases for some years implicitly supported this view, as the Court upheld other laws which burdened the practice of the Mormon religion by imposing various penalties on polygamy.[8] Similarly the Court also upheld a government system of compulsory vaccinations as applied to those who objected to vaccinations on a religious basis.[9] It should be noted that while this action-belief distinction has been eliminated, the holdings in these cases have gone unchallenged.

Prior to the application of the religion clauses to the states the Supreme Court decided two cases under the due process clause of the fourteenth amendment which have significant free exercise implications. In *Hamilton v. Regents of the University of California*,[10] the Court held that requiring male students at a state university to take courses in military training was not a denial of liberty which violated due process. This decision is highly suspect in light of the Court's recent decision in the conscientious objector cases and the demise of the "right-privilege" distinction,[11] but it serves to emphasize the absence of significant judicial protection for religious minorities during this period. The second major due process case in this area was *Pierce v. Society of Sisters*.[12] In this case the Court struck down a statute which required that children attend only public schools as an undue re-striction on the freedom of both parents and students. Today *Pierce* stands for the right of children to attend private (including religious) schools so long as they meet basic educational standards. In this regard it should be noted that the state apparently cannot control the subjects taught in those schools beyond its assurance that children are given competent instruction in specified secular subjects and that they are in a safe and healthy environment; further restrictions on the educational process would have to be necessary to promote important secular interests.[13]

During the 1940's and 1950's, the Supreme Court invalidated a number of laws which restricted religious practices primarily on the basis that they interfered with the free speech protection of the first amendment. The most important of these cases was *Cantwell v. Connecticut*,[14] wherein the Court struck down the conviction of several Jehovah's Witnesses for soliciting funds without a license because they were engaged in the distribution of religious materials. It was in this decision that the Court held the free exercise clause applicable to the states. However, the majority noted that while the freedom to believe was absolute, the freedom to act was not. A general regulation of solicitation which left no room for official discretion and did not unduly obstruct religious practices would have been permissible. But, as this statute allowed a licensing officer discretion to determine whether the solicitation was for a religious

---

over mere opinion, but was left free to reach actions which were in violation of social duties or subversive of good order." 98 U.S. at 164.

8. Davis v. Beason, 133 U.S. 333 (1890); Church of Latter Day Saints v. United States, 136 U.S. 1 (1890), see also State v. Barlow, 107 Utah 292, 153 P.2d 647 (1944), appeal dismissed 324 U.S. 829 (1945) (state bigamy law upheld); In re State in Interest of Black, 3 Utah 2d 315, 283 P.2d 887 (1955), appeal dismissed 350 U.S. 923 (1955) (Parents might lose custody of children for teaching polygamy).

9. Jacobson v. Massachusetts, 197 U.S. 11 (1905); Zucht v. King, 260 U.S. 174 (1922).

10. 293 U.S. 245 (1934).

11. The conscientious objector cases are discussed in Section III, D, 1 of this Chapter. At an earlier time the Court protected only those interests which could be termed "rights" to which one was entitled rather than a "privilege" which was a benefit (such as a college education) which the government need not provide. This distinction has been eliminated and the Constitution now protects all interests. For a discussion of the procedural protection of "privileges" under the due process clause see Chapter 15.

12. 268 U.S. 510 (1925).

13. Even prior to the *Pierce* decision the Court held that a state violated the due process clause when it prohibited the teaching of any language other than English in private (and parochial) schools. Meyer v. Nebraska, 262 U.S. 390 (1923).

14. 310 U.S. 296 (1940).

cause it was invalid. This would allow the officer to determine who would be allowed to engage in solicitation based on his view of that religious content of their message. Such a statute would violate both the freedoms of speech and religion.

Cantwell was followed by a number of decisions which overturned statutes regulating the dissemination of religious views because they interfered with both the freedom of speech and religion. In each case, however, it appeared that the free speech claim was central to the decision. In a series of decisions the Court struck down licensing systems for demonstrations or meetings which gave government officials discretion to deny licenses on the basis of the content of the speech, while upholding ones which had permit requirements based on nondiscriminatory "time, place or manner" factors.[15] In these cases the fact that religious meetings were suppressed under discretionary statutes indicated a violation of free exercise rights, but the statutes were invalid in total because they conflicted with the free speech clause. Similarly, the Court invalidated laws prohibiting the distribution of handbills on city streets or in residential neighborhoods as applied to those who sought to distribute religious literature.[16] In a decision which focused on religious freedom, the Court held that a license tax on all persons soliciting orders for goods could not be applied to a Jehovah's Witness who went door to door distributing religious literature and asking for contributions.[17]

It must be remembered that *Cantwell* and the other solicitation and licensing cases were decided on the basis of freedom of speech principles. Laws that impose time, place, or manner limitations on literature distribution or funds solicitation can be validly applied to activities conducted by members of religious sects if the laws are compatible with the freedom of speech.[18]

One of the most interesting problems concerned the requiring of school children to take part in a flag salute ceremony. The Court overruled a decision rendered only three years earlier and held that students could not be compelled to salute the flag against their beliefs.[19] Once again basing the decision on the right of free speech, a majority of the justices found that the requirement invaded the sphere of free intellect and belief that was the core of these first amendment principles. It must be remembered that in these cases it was the limitation of freedoms essentially protected by the free speech clause which made the requirements unconstitutional. Although the Jehovah Witnesses brought these cases because of their religious objections to the honoring of "idols," the infringement of religious beliefs was not crucial to the decision. Anyone opposed to saluting the flag had to be excused from the requirement without re-

---

15. See, e.g., Schneider v. Town of Irvington, 308 U.S. 147 (1939); Largent v. Texas, 318 U.S. 418 (1943) (discretionary sales license system invalid); Kunz v. New York, 340 U.S. 290 (1951) (discretionary public meeting licensing system invalid); Cox v. New Hampshire, 312 U.S. 569 (1941) (non-discretionary parade licensing system upheld); Poulos v. New Hampshire, 345 U.S. 395 (1953) (non-discretionary system upheld).

16. Jamison v. Texas, 318 U.S. 413 (1943); see also Martin v. Struthers, 319 U.S. 141 (1943).

17. Murdock v. Pennsylvania, 319 U.S. 105, 117 (1943), overruling Jones v. Opelika, 316 U.S. 584 (1942); see, also, Jones v. Opelika, 319 U.S. 103 (1943) (per curiam), vacating Jones v. Opelika, 316 U.S. 584 (1942); Follett v. Town of McCormick, 321 U.S. 573 (1944).

18. In Heffron v. International Society for Krishna Consciousness, Inc., 452 U.S. 640 (1981), the Court upheld a state fair rule whereby a non-discretionary licensing system forced all persons to confine distribu-

tion or sales of literature and solicitation activities to a fixed location. The rule was upheld on its face and as applied to members of a religious sect. The majority opinion stated:

> "None of our cases suggest that the inclusion of peripatetic solicitation as part of a church ritual entitles church members to solicitation rights in a public forum superior to those of members of other religious groups that raise money but do not purport to ritualize the process. Nor for present purposes do religious organizations enjoy rights to communicate, distribute, and solicit on the fairgrounds superior to those of other organizations having social, political, or other ideological messages to proselytize."

Id. at 652.

19. West Virginia State Bd. of Education v. Barnette, 319 U.S. 624 (1943), overruling Minersville School District v. Gobitis, 310 U.S. 586 (1940).

gard to whether their refusal was based on religious or non-religious grounds.

Despite these seemingly liberal free speech-free exercise decisions, the Supreme Court did not give significant independent protection to the free exercise of religion against police power regulations during this period. Thus, in *Prince v. Massachusetts*,[20] the Court upheld the application of a law prohibiting the selling of merchandise in public places by minors to a nine year old child who was distributing religious literature with her guardian. The majority found that the state's interest in the health and well being of young people was a significant secular end which justified the incidental burden on religion.

As of 1960, no case in the Supreme Court had resulted in the overturning of police power regulations solely on the basis that they had a coercive effect on the free exercise of religion. If the end pursued was a significant secular goal, the Court would uphold incidental restrictions on religiously motivated activity. Only when the law proscribed beliefs or interfered with free speech as well as the exercise of religion would the Court overturn the law. After 1960, the belief-action distinction would be replaced by tests that would place meaningful limits on the government's ability to regulate actions essential to the exercise of religion. Yet the distinction is still of some importance for there is still an absolute prohibition of governmental proscription of beliefs. Incident to this prohibition, the Court has precluded the government from inquiring into the truth of religious teaching or resolving ecclesiastical disputes on the basis of religious doctrine.[21]

C. The Modern Cases

Since 1961, the Supreme Court has established new standards for determining the va-

lidity of state regulation which places incidental burdens on religion. The Court has also reaffirmed the absolute prohibition against government interference with beliefs. In *Torcaso v. Watkins*[1] the Court invalidated a state constitutional provision which required a declaration of a belief in God as a prerequisite to taking public office. The majority noted that the Constitution itself prohibits the use of religious tests for office,[2] and that the first amendment prohibits the promotion of religious beliefs. Thus, the state may not impose any burden on someone due to his religious beliefs or the lack thereof. However, the current position of the Court on the permissibility of regulating religiously motivated activity developed slowly across this period. The Court's position can only be understood by reviewing the three significant decisions on this issue.

In *Braunfeld v. Brown*[3] the Court considered the constitutionality of applying Sunday closing laws to Orthodox Jews whose beliefs required them to observe another day as the Sabbath. A majority of the justices held that the economic burden placed on a Sabbatarian did not violate the free exercise clause, although no opinion gathered a majority vote. The Sabbatarians' claim for an exemption was based on the fact that their religious beliefs required them to abstain from commercial activity on Saturday. Thus the statutory prohibition of shopping or selling on Sunday placed an added economic burden on them because of their religious practices. Chief Justice Warren, writing for four members of the Court, found that this law placed a severe burden on Sabbatarian retailers. But the Chief Justice held that, since the burden was the indirect effect of a law with a secular purpose, it would violate the free exercise clause only if there were alternative ways of achieving the state's interest.[4] He then employed a test of validity which essentially was a two-part bal-

---

20. 321 U.S. 158 (1944).

21. Both of these problems are reviewed in the last section of this chapter.

1. 367 U.S. 488 (1961).

2. "[No] religious Test shall ever be required as a Qualification to any Office of public Trust under the United States." U.S. Const. art. VI.

3. 366 U.S. 599 (1961).

4. 366 U.S. at 606–07.

ancing test. First, the plaintiff had to show that there was some real burden placed on the exercise of his religion by the regulation. Second, this burden would be upheld only if the state was pursuing an overriding secular goal by the means which imposed the least burden on religious practices. The plurality opinion by Chief Justice Warren found that the state had an overriding secular interest in setting aside a single day for "rest, recreation and tranquility." Although some states exempted Sabbatarians from the closing laws, the opinion found that an exemption for those whose beliefs required them to close on another day might undermine the state's goal. Additionally, the Chief Justice noted that the state could choose to avoid a system whereby it would have to examine the good faith of those who claimed religious exemption in order to make effective its laws.[5]

Justice Frankfurter, in a concurring opinion joined by Justice Harlan, was most open in using a balancing test to determine whether the state could pursue its secular end in a manner which burdened the practice of certain religions. He noted that the interest of the state in the preservation of the "traditional institution" of a day of rest and repose was to be balanced against the economic disadvantage to the retailer who had to close an extra day per week.[6] He found the economic disadvantage to be of a lesser importance and one that would exist if there were no Sunday closing laws at all as the Sabbatarian would still lose a day of sales. Thus he found that the secular state interest could incidentally burden the practice of these religions.

The dissenting justices were more concerned with the added economic burden to Sabbatarian sellers as the statute would literally drive those persons out of business because of their religious beliefs.[7] In their

view, the additional commercial activity which would result in the exemption for such persons would not destroy the state's interest in the traditional day of rest. Indeed most states granted such exemptions. To the extent that a state sought a more perfectly non-commercial day its interest was overridden by the individual freedom to practice their religion guaranteed by the free exercise clause, in the view of these justices. It should be stressed that this is still a minority position. Although the free exercise clause standards have been applied with increasing rigor by the Court, there has been no indication that the *Braunfeld* decision will be overturned.

The second major decision of this era was *Sherbert v. Verner*.[8] In this case a majority of the justices held that state unemployment benefits could not be denied to a Seventh Day Adventist because she refused to work on Saturday due to her religious beliefs. Justice Brennan, writing for a seven member majority, stated that for the denial of benefits to withstand scrutiny under the free exercise clause "it must be either because her disqualification as a beneficiary represents no infringement by the state of her constitutional right of free exercise, or because any incidental burden on the free exercise of appellant's religion may be justified by a compelling state interest in the regulation. . . . "[9] Thus the majority continued to employ a two-part balancing test. First, plaintiff had to show a substantial burden on the exercise of her religion from the law under review. Second, such a burden would only be valid if the Court found it necessary to a "compelling state interest" which outweighed the degree of impairment of free exercise rights. This test implies that the degree of burden on religious activity is to be balanced against the importance of the state interest and the degree to which it would be impaired by an ac-

---

5. 366 U.S. at 609.

6. 366 U.S. at 521–22 (Frankfurter, J., concurring).

7. Braunfeld v. Brown, 366 U.S. 599, 610–11 (1961) (Brennan, J. dissenting); 366 U.S. at 616 (Stewart, J., dissenting).

8. 374 U.S. 398 (1963).

9. 374 U.S. at 403.

commodation for the religious practice. Relevant to such an inquiry is the importance of the state's interest [is it a "compelling" one?] and the degree to which there are alternative means to achieve it which do not burden religious practices [least restrictive means are required].

In *Sherbert* the majority found that the denial of unemployment benefits was invalid under this two part test. First, there was a significant coercive effect on the practice of religion as the Sabbatarian was forced to make a choice between receiving state benefits or following her beliefs. Second, no compelling or overriding interest in the regulation was shown by the state. The state claimed only that this restriction avoided fraudulent claims, but this contention had not been raised in the state courts and was not sustained by the record.[10] Additionally, even if this were assumed *arguendo* to be a compelling interest there had been no demonstration that alternative means of avoiding fraud were not available. In conclusion, there was no demonstration by the state that the denial of benefits was necessary to promote a compelling interest and, therefore, the state was required to exempt such workers from its requirement that they be available for work on Saturdays. It is interesting that the majority opinion noted that the case was not one where "an employee's religious connections made her a nonproductive member of society."[11] This language indicates that the state would not have to give benefits to those who were permanently unemployable because of their religious beliefs since that would interfere with the state's goal of providing benefits to those involuntarily unemployed but available for work. While the state might have to accommodate certain religious practices which it had no real need to burden, it would not be required to abandon the goal of its program in order to accommodate everyone who might be unemployed for religious reasons.

In *Wisconsin v. Yoder*[12] the Court held Wisconsin could not require members of the Amish Church to send their children to public school after the eighth grade. The majority opinion by Chief Justice Burger employed the two part balancing test. First, a significant burden on the free exercise of religion would have to be shown. Second, this burden would be balanced against the importance of the state's interest and the degree to which it would be impaired by a religious exemption.

In finding that there was a significant burden on the free exercise of religion, the Court had to determine whether the parents' refusal to send their children to school was based on religious beliefs. As the Court noted, a claim based on a personal or philosophical rejection of secular values would not be protected by the free exercise clause. Thus, if the Amish refused to send their children to school merely to preserve a "traditional way of life", their claim would be denied. However, the Court found that the Amish lifestyle, educational practices and refusal to submit their children to further secular education were religious. Central to this determination were the following facts: (1) this was a shared belief by an organized group rather than a personal preference, (2) the belief related to certain theocratic principles and interpretation of religious literature, (3) the system of beliefs pervaded and regulated their daily lives, (4) the system of belief and lifestyle resulting therefrom had been in existence for a substantial period of time.[13] It is not clear as to which, if any, of those factors determines the presence of a "religion" or a "religious belief." Indeed, the question of how one determines a religious practice cannot be answered as this is the only case in which the Supreme Court

10. 374 U.S. at 407.

11. 374 U.S. at 410.

12. 406 U.S. 205 (1972). The Court was unanimous as to the result in this case, but three justices filed separate opinions. 406 U.S. at 237 (Stewart and Brennan, J.J., concurring), 406 U.S. at 241 (Douglas, J., concurring). Two Justices (Powell & Rehnquist) did not participate.

13. 406 U.S. at 215–17.

has addressed the issue of defining religion apart from a statutory determination.[14] A narrow definition of religion, perhaps recognizing only very structured religions, should be employed in establishment clause cases as no real danger is posed to religious freedom by government aid to unusual or nonstructured groups even if they could arguably be deemed religious. It would seem that the Court should be more lenient in defining "religious" or "religion" in cases under the free exercise clause. These claims seek only to protect private individual liberty rather than to overturn governmental social welfare programs.[15] Yet, under the free exercise clause one cannot allow individuals to grant themselves a "religious exemption" from laws which displease them. As Chief Justice Burger stated for the majority, "although a determination of what is a 'religious' belief or practice entitled to constitutional protection may present a most delicate question, the very concept of ordered liberty precludes allowing every person to make his own standards on matters of conduct in which society as a whole has important interests."[16]

Because the Amish had shown their refusal to send children to school after the eighth grade was religiously based, the Court determined the permissibility of applying the compulsory education laws to them under the two part balancing test. However, this time the Court did not use the "compelling interest" language, thus suggesting the use of a more open balancing test.[17] The compulsory attendance laws could be applied to the Amish if "the State does not deny the free exercise of religious belief by its requirement, or that there is a state interest of sufficient magnitude to override the interest claiming protection under the Free Exercise Clause."[18]

The first part of the test—the demonstration of a burden on the exercise of religion—was met by the Amish. The education of their children in the public schools beyond the eighth grade was in conflict with their religious principles and threatened the entire religious training of their children. As there was a burden on the exercise of religion incident to a state regulation of general activity, the Court had to balance the interests of the state against those of the Amish. Here the state would have to show both that it was promoting an interest which was superior to these free exercise rights and that this goal would be unduly impaired by granting an exemption to the Amish. The state asserted that the attendance of these children at school between the ages of 14 and 16 was necessary to their development as citizens and members of society. However, the Court found that these goals would not be impaired by an exemption for the Amish. The first eight years of formal education and the home training of young people by the Amish parents made the children both able citizens and productive members of society. The state also argues that its interest in the children's health and well being justified an absolute rule to grant secondary education to all children. The Court recognized that this interest would overcome a claim for religious freedom where the practice was detrimental to the health, training or well

---

14. It appears that the Supreme Court may require courts to avoid ruling on this issue whenever an individual has any nonfrivolous claim that his belief is religious. See notes 23–29, infra, and accompanying text. The Court has interpreted the conscientious objector provision of the military conscription laws so as to avoid a definition which would prefer certain theocratic religions. These cases are discussed in Section III, D, 1 of this Chapter.

For a scholarly examination of this problem focusing the particular anguish caused persons who are forced to forsake certain types of beliefs see Choper, Defining "Religion" in the First Amendment, 1982 U.Ill.L.Rev. 579 (1982).

15. Freund, Public Aid to Parochial Schools, 82 Harv.L.Rev. 1680, 1686–87 n. 14 (1969); see also, Galanter, Religious Freedoms in the United States: A Turning Point?, 1966 Wis.L.Rev. 217, 266–67.

16. Wisconsin v. Yoder, 406 U.S. 205, 215–16 (1972).

17. While the word "compelling" appears at several points in the majority opinion, it was not used as part of the statement of the test to be employed in reviewing claims under the free exercise clause.

18. 406 U.S. at 214.

being of a child.[19]   But since the record showed that the Amish children were well cared for and well trained in their community, the state's goals would not be impaired by an exemption for the Amish children.   It should be noted that the majority did not find it necessary to discuss the interest of Amish children who wished to attend school after the eighth grade against the wishes of their parents.   Absent an actual case involving such a parent-child conflict, the Court refused to decide if the state's interest in the child would allow the government to require a parent to send a child to school at the child's request over the religious objections of the parent.[20]

In the 1961–72 period the Court developed a two part balancing test to determine when police power regulations may be applied to restrict religiously based activity.   First, the persons claiming an exception from the regulation must show that it burdens the practice of their religion.   This requirement expands on an earlier concept of state "coercion" but it requires only that the regulation has a coercive tendency in that it substantially burdens a religious practice.   Second, the restriction on the free exercise of religion will be balanced against the importance of the state interest in the regulation. Even if the state interest appears to be of a greater magnitude, the regulation will be invalid unless it burdens religion no more than is necessary to promote the overriding secular interest.   This "least restrictive means" test is merely another way of saying that an important state interest will not justify the limitation of the free exercise of religion unless an exemption for religiously motivated activity would unduly interfere with the achievement of that state interest.[21]   The Supreme Court has continued to apply this two part balancing test in recent cases.[22]

In *Thomas v. Review Board*[23] the Supreme Court was required to determine the validity of an individual's claim that he was acting on the basis of a religious belief when a state asserted that the motivation for his action was nonreligious.   Mr. Thomas, a Jehovah's Witness, quit his job when his employer transferred him from a metal foundry to a factory department that produced parts for military tanks and gave him no opportunity to transfer to another job.   Thomas testified that he believed his religion prohibited him from working on war materials although he had been advised by at least one fellow employee who was a friend and a Jehovah's Witness that such work did not violate the principles of the religion.   Thomas was denied unemployment compensation because state law precluded the granting of benefits to a person who voluntarily terminated his employment for reasons other than "good cause [arising] in connection with [his] work."   The unemployment compensation hearing officer and state review board found that Thomas had left his job for reli-

---

19.   406 U.S. at 229–30.   In this way the Court distinguished the earlier cases relating to child labor or the protection of their health.   See Jacobson v. Massachusetts, 197 U.S. 11 (1925) (vaccinations required); Prince v. Massachusetts, 321 U.S. 158 (1944) (child labor law upheld as applied to child distributing religious materials).

20.   Justice Douglas would have reached this point and was of the opinion that the child's decision should be honored under these circumstances.   Wisconsin v. Yoder, 406 U.S. 205, 241 (1972) (Douglas, J. dissenting in part).   However, the other Justices were of the opinion that the issue was not present in these cases.   406 U.S. at 236–37 (Stewart, J., concurring).

21.   Moody v. Cronin, 484 F.Supp. 270, 273–74 (C.D. Ill.1979) (Ackerman, D.J., quoting an earlier edition of this treatise).

22.   The Court has examined free exercise claims in several military draft cases, as well as in the cases not-

ed in the following paragraphs.   The draft cases are examined in the next section of this chapter.

A case that should be noted at this point is *Johnson v. Robison*, 415 U.S. 361 (1974), as it involves a basic application of the rules described above.   The Court upheld the granting of educational benefits to veterans who served active duty but denied them to conscientious objectors who performed alternate service.   In finding that there was no violation of the free exercise clause, the majority first noted that there was little, if any, real burden on religious practices which resulted from these programs.   Second, the government interest in the raising and supporting of armies was of a "kind and weight" sufficient to overcome the alleged burden on the free exercise right of those who did not receive the educational benefits.   Thus, the program survived scrutiny under the balancing test.

23.   450 U.S. 707 (1981).

gious reasons but that he did not qualify for benefits under the statute. The state supreme court found that the denial of benefits for voluntary termination of employment did not violate the free exercise clause for three reasons: (1) Thomas's belief was more a "personal philosophical choice" than a religious belief; (2) the burden on Thomas's religious belief was only "indirect"; and (3) the granting of benefits only to persons who voluntarily left employment for religious reasons would violate the establishment clause. The United States Supreme Court had little difficulty finding that the denial of benefits to Thomas violated the free exercise clause; only Justice Rehnquist would have upheld the state supreme court and denied the claim.[24]

The majority opinion in *Thomas*, like many of the key opinions in the free exercise and establishment clause field, was written by Chief Justice Burger. The Chief Justice avoided ruling on what type of beliefs were "religious" although the majority opinion indicated that judges had to accept an individual's assertion that his belief or motivation for his actions was religious so long as the person asserts the claim in good faith and so long as the belief could arguably be termed religious.

"Courts should not undertake to dissect religious beliefs because the believer admits that he is 'struggling' with his position or because his beliefs are not articulated with the clarity and precision that a more sophisticated person might employ . . . one can, of course, imagine an asserted claim so bizarre, so clearly nonreligious in motivation, as not to be entitled to protection under the Free Exercise Clause; but that is not the case here, and the guarantee of free exercise is not limited to beliefs which are shared by all members of a religious sect. . . . Courts are not arbiters of scriptural interpretation.

The narrow function of a reviewing court in this context is to determine whether there was an appropriate finding that petitioner terminated his work because of an honest conviction that such work was forbidden by his religion . . . . . On this record, it is clear that Thomas terminated his employment for religious reasons." [25]

Once Thomas' reasons were found to be religious the case was easily disposed of under the first amendment. Conditioning a significant benefit upon conduct prohibited by a religious belief places a substantial burden on the individual regardless of whether the burden can be labeled direct or indirect.[26] The state's asserted interests in denying benefits to those leaving employment for religious reasons were the avoidance of large scale unemployment and the avoidance of employer inquiries into religious beliefs. However, the state was unable to prove that granting benefits to such persons would lead to either widespread unemployment or detailed questioning of beliefs by employers. Thus, the Court held that "[n]either of the interests advanced is sufficiently compelling to justify the burden upon Thomas' religious liberty." [27] On the basis of *Sherbert v. Verner* the majority opinion by Chief Justice Burger found that the granting of an exception to the conditions for unemployment compensation based upon religious objectives did not promote the establishment of religion but only moved the government to a position of neutrality toward religious beliefs.[28]

In *United States v. Lee*,[29] the Court denied an Amish employer of Amish workmen an exemption from compulsory participation in the social security system. The majority opinion, again written by Chief Justice Burger, first held that the employer could not claim the statutory exemption allowed self-employed individuals who had religious ob-

---

24. 450 U.S. at 720 (Rehnquist, J., dissenting). Justice Blackmun joined parts of the majority opinion by Chief Justice Burger and concurred in the result but not the Court's opinion holding that the granting of benefits to religious persons under these circumstances did not constitute an aid to religion. 450 U.S. at 720 (Blackmun, J., concurring).

25. 450 U.S. at 713–716. See note 14, supra.

26. 450 U.S. at 717–18.

27. 450 U.S. at 719.

28. Thomas v. Review Bd., 450 U.S. 707, 719 (1981).

29. 455 U.S. 252 (1982).

jections to payment of the tax. The Chief Justice went on to apply the balancing test. First, the opinion asked whether the payment of social security taxes by an Amish employer or the receipt of benefits by Amish employees from the system interfered with the free exercise of their religious beliefs. In accord with *Thomas v. Review Board*, the majority refused to decide the correct interpretation of any religious belief because such a decision was neither a judicial function nor within judicial competence. The Chief Justice accepted Lee's claim that both payment of taxes and receipt of benefits were forbidden by the Amish faith. Therefore, because compulsory participation in the social security system violated Lee's and his employee's beliefs, such compulsion constituted a burden on their free exercise rights.

In the second part of the test, the Chief Justice asked if this burden on the free exercise of religion was justified by an overriding governmental interest and, if so, whether the religious belief could be accommodated without unduly interfering with the achievement of that interest. The Chief Justice found that the governmental interest in the social security system was compelling. This was a nationwide system of comprehensive insurance providing a variety of benefits and contributed to by both employers and employees. The government viewed compulsory payments as necessary for the vitality of the system because voluntary participation would undermine its soundness and would be difficult to administer.

The Court did not examine whether alternative means were available to achieve this compelling interest which would not burden the Amish beliefs. The Chief Justice stated that this complex taxing system was organized in such a way that it would be difficult to accommodate exceptions which might arise from a large spectrum of religious beliefs, except to the extent such accommodation had already been made by the existence of the self-employment exemption. The category exempted by statute was narrow (self-employed members of a religious group which made sufficient provision for its dependent members) and readily identifiable. The Court seemed to be concerned, as Justice Stevens recognized in his concurrence,[30] that granting the exemption in this case, although actually not difficult to administer, would result in numerous other claims far more difficult to process. Thus, the government's interest in an efficient social security system justified forcing Lee to comply with the law in violation of his faith.

D. Recurrent Free Exercise Problems

1. Exemptions From Military Service

The Supreme Court has never held that the religion clauses require the government to grant an exemption from military service to persons who object to such service on a religious basis. However, it is at least arguable that such an exemption should be required if the interests of those who object to military service were balanced against the government's need for universal conscription in the same manner as interests are balanced under the modern free exercise clause cases.[1] While there are early decisions which state that the war powers of the government should not be required to yield for the accommodation of individual beliefs,[2] strong considerations weigh in favor of requiring such an exemption under modern free exercise clause analysis.[3] The individual interest in adhering to religious beliefs

---

30. 455 U.S. at 262–64 (1982) (Stevens, J., concurring).

1. In assessing the need for a religious exemption from state regulation, the court employs a two part balancing test. First, the claimant must show that the regulation substantially burdens the practice of his religion. Second, the government interest in the regulation is weighed against the burden on free exercise

rights. For a more complete discussion of the modern cases see Section III, C of this Chapter.

2. See, The Selective Service Draft Law Cases, 245 U.S. 366, 389–90 (1918); United States v. MacIntosh, 283 U.S. 605 (1931); Dickinson v. United States, 346 U.S. 389 (1953).

3. For an excellent discussion of this and other issues raised by conscientious objectors, see Greenawalt,

which prohibit the use of violence would seem strong and the burden imposed on those beliefs by universal conscription is severe. Additionally, the government's interest in raising armies might be adequately met without the conscription of these persons. The possible lack of suitability for armed combat on the part of these persons and the social problems created by the forced conscription of religious objectors also indicates that no important government interest would in reality be furthered by the drafting of these persons into the armed services. Yet the government interest in defense, especially in time of war, has been historically deferred to by the Supreme Court.[4] Thus, the Court could find that it was not the proper branch of government to weigh these individual interests against the national interest in defense. Indeed, the Court in 1971 approved the government's refusal to exempt those who objected only to particular wars and indicated that even today no exemption might be required.[5] In short, there are good arguments on both sides of this issue. Absent congressional authorization for universal conscription and a case concerning the need for a religious exemption, the question will remain unresolved.

Despite the lack of certainty regarding the need for any religious exemption, the history of statutory exemptions and their interpretation gives us insights into this clash between religious beliefs and the military powers. While no exemption need be granted, if the government grants an exemption to any persons who object to war on a religious basis it must do so in a way which violates neither religion clause. Any exception must be so broad in nature that it does not benefit particular religions and thereby violate the establishment clause.[6] Thus, any exemption

must have a secular purpose, a secular effect and avoid giving rise to an excessive entanglement between government and religion. Establishment clause considerations favor broad exemption from military service for conscientious objectors as narrow definitions are likely to favor a given religion or, at a minimum, common religious beliefs which are theistic (God-centered). In refusing anyone an exemption under a statute, the government must not violate the free exercise clause. This will require the government to grant the exemption to all whose conscription into military service would not aid the defense effort because their beliefs make them similarly unsuited for service. The government remains free to draft those whose objections to war could be differentiated on a secular basis from those it exempted from service.

The Supreme Court decisions regarding conscientious objectors have followed this analysis. The Court has deferred to the interest in defense and refused to declare a first amendment right to avoid military service. However, the Court has read the statutory exemption from service to apply to all persons who are opposed to war in any form on the basis of beliefs which are the functional equivalent of a theistic religious belief.[7] Thus, any persons who objected to all wars on the basis of sincerely held personal principles which occupied a place in their lives similar to religion would receive an exemption. Problems under the religion clauses were avoided by interpreting the exemption so that all those who objected to participation in any war received an exemption. The only ones who failed to qualify for an exemption were those whose objections were not sincere or whose objections were based "solely upon considerations of policy, pragmatism or expediency."[8]

All or Nothing at All; The Defeat of Selective Conscientious Objection, 1971 Supreme Court Rev. 31.

4. See, e.g., United States v. O'Brien, 391 U.S. 367 (1968 prohibition of destroying draft cards upheld); Korematsu v. United States, 323 U.S. 214 (1944) (domestic detention of Japanese persons in World War II upheld).

5. Gillette v. United States, 401 U.S. 437, 461 n. 23 (1971).

6. Welsh v. United States, 398 U.S. 333, 356 (1970) (Harlan, J., concurring).

7. United States v. Seeger, 380 U.S. 163 (1965).

8. Welsh v. United States, 398 U.S. 333, 342–43 (1970) (Plurality opinion by Black, J.), the scope of

The history of military conscription and statutory exemptions has avoided clear constitutional rulings beyond these guidelines. Prior to the Civil War, the conscription of men into the armed service was a matter regulated to state law. During this time it was customary to allow a person to avoid service by the payment of a fee. Near the middle of the nineteenth century, some states began to allow those who opposed service on a religious basis to do alternative noncombatant work in lieu of joining the army.[9] By 1864, after the federal government had taken over the administration of the armed services, the first federal statute considering conscientious objectors was passed, providing for alternate service in military hospitals. The Selective Service Law of 1917 provided an exemption from compulsory combatant service to anyone belonging to a "well-recognized" religious sect or organization whose creed forbade members to participate in war in any form and whose religious convictions were against war or participation in it. This provision was upheld by the Supreme Court but it must be remembered that the Court did not actively protect religious values during this period.[10] The Selective Training and Service Act of 1940 broadened the classification by exempting those who by "religious training and belief" were opposed to participation in war in any form. Eight years later, in the Selective Service Act of 1948, the exemption section was narrowed with the addition of a clarification of "religious training and belief" as "belief in relation to a Supreme Being" and not "essentially political, sociological, or philosophical views or a merely personal moral code." [11]

The "Supreme Being Clause" of the 1948 Act was interpreted by the Selective Service System, and the Department of Justice, as excluding those whose objections to service were not based on theistic beliefs. But in *United States v. Seeger*[12] the Supreme Court interpreted the statute as granting an exemption to all those whose nontheistic beliefs occupied in their lives the place of a religion. The Military Service Act of 1967 reflected the *Seeger* decision and deleted the reference to the "Supreme Being." The exemption clause is not phrased thusly:

> [Nothing] contained in this Act shall be construed to require any person to be subject to combatant training and service in the land or naval forces of the United States who, by reason of religious training and belief, is conscientiously opposed to participation in war in any form. As used in this subsection, the term religious training and belief does not include essentially political, sociological, or philosophical views, or a merely personal code.[13]

In 1970 the Court interpreted this language to include all those whose sincere beliefs required them to refuse to participate in any war for other than purely pragmatic reasons.[14] It should be noted that Justice Harlan concurred in this result because he was of the opinion that the statute's restriction to only religious beliefs violated the establishment clause.[15] But there was no ruling on this issue as the new statutory interpretation avoided the question.

Gillette v. United States[16] was a case where the Court was required to address the compatibility of the statutory exemption with the religion clauses. The current statutory exemption is clearly granted only to those who oppose participation in any war and denied to those who object only to some wars. This was challenged by those whose

---

court authority to inquire into the sincerity of religious beliefs is examined in Section IV B of this chapter.

9. E. N. Wright, Conscientious Objectors in the Civil War (1931).

10. The Selective Service Draft Law Cases, 245 U.S. 366, 389–90 (1918). For a discussion of the Court's position on religious issues during this period see Section III B of this chapter.

11. 50 U.S.C.A. § 301.

12. 380 U.S. 163 (1965).

13. P.L. No. 90–40, June 30, 1967, 81 Stat. 100, 50 U.S.C.A. § 451 et seq.

14. Welsh v. United States, 398 U.S. 333 (1970) (Plurality opinion by Black, J.).

15. 398 U.S. at 344 (Harlan, J., concurring).

16. 401 U.S. 437 (1971).

formal religion or religious philosophy required them to refrain only from participation in "unjust" wars. A majority of the justices found that the narrow definition of the statute was compatible with both religion clauses. The Court held that the granting of exemption only to those whose beliefs opposed all war did not violate the establishment clause. The majority found that the limitation was based on secular reasons relating to the persons involved rather than adherence to accepted beliefs. The Court found a secular purpose in defining the exemption so as to exclude in the most fair way those persons not readily available or suitable for service due to their beliefs. The effect of the statute was not religious as it served only to insure a fair process by avoiding a definition which would complicate the determination of those with such claims. The definition did not have the effect of aiding religion as it did not encourage any belief. Finally, the narrow definition avoided further entanglement between government and religion as there was less need to examine the sincerity and character of individual beliefs.

The claimants in *Gillette* also argued that failure to grant an exemption to those who opposed only unjust wars on a religious basis violated the free exercise clause. The majority opinion found that the burden on these persons was justified by substantial government interests in defense and the power to raise armies. It was clear that the Court reached this result by granting great deference to these governmental interests and without any real weighing of the individual interests. With these important national interests at issue, the Court simply refused to review the legislative determination of who should serve in the armed forces as the justices did not view the law as a penalty against any belief or religion.[17]

Finally, the treatment of those who had done alternative service as conscientious objectors did raise one further issue. The per-

sons who were granted this exemption but required to do alternative service did not receive the same benefits as those who served in normal military operations. In *Johnson v. Robison*,[18] the Court found that this differing treatment did not violate the first amendment. Since the majority found both a secular distinction between the types of service and a minimal burden on the practice of religion resulting from that distinction, the justices had little trouble in ruling that the secular governmental interest was sufficient to overrule the conscientious objector's claim for further benefits.

2. *Health and Medical Regulations*

It has been the time honored position of American courts that the government interest in health and medical treatment of the populace will override individual religious objections to such regulation. These brief notes describe the main issues that have arisen in this area and the historic responses of the courts to these issues. However, it should be noted that all of these issues were resolved prior to the development of the modern balancing test under the free exercise clause. It is always possible that the Supreme Court would reverse its position on these questions and the reader should evaluate these issues under the modern approach. But, despite the possibility of contrary rulings in the future, it must be remembered that the following notes do reflect the current position of the Court.

a. *Vaccinations*

The Supreme Court very early in this century held that an individual could be required to receive a vaccination against disease.[1] Although the submission to such a program might violate the individual's religious beliefs, this is a direct method of effectuating the secular interest in public health. While the chance of epidemics may have been small, the courts have continually

---

17. 401 U.S. at 461–62.

18. 415 U.S. 361 (1974).

1. Jacobson v. Massachusetts, 197 U.S. 11 (1905).

upheld vaccination requirements as a precondition to a child's attendance at public school.[2]

b. Treatment of Children

American courts have upheld the right of the state to protect the health and safety of minor children over the religiously based objections of the child or their parent. Thus, courts have appointed guardians to consent to necessary medical treatment (such as blood transfusions) for children even though the treatment violates the child's or parent's religion.[3] Similarly appropriate action may be taken against parents for the neglect of the health or safety of their children regardless of whether the parent acted on the basis of religious principles.[4]

c. Blood Transfusions and the "Right to Die"

Current developments in medicine have permitted the continuation of a person's life for extended periods of time after it is apparent that the person will never recover from some eventually terminal illness or injury. This has raised serious questions as to whether an individual can be required to undergo such treatment or whether that person has a "right to die." This problem, in terms of modern life support techniques, has not yet been finally resolved by the state or federal courts. It should be noted, however, that there is no issue under the religion clauses unless the individual's desire to forego medical treatment and die a "natural" death is based on religious beliefs.[5] If the individual's preference is not religious in nature there is only a conflict between personal choice relating to health and state medical regulations. Such a conflict would be resolved under the due process clauses.[6] When the objection to medical treatment is based on religious principles, however, a serious free exercise clause problem is presented. While the modern life support issue has not been resolved, courts have been confronted with cases in which a person has refused medical treatment (usually a blood transfusion) on the basis of religious beliefs. Where the person who needed treatment was a minor [7] or mentally incompetent,[8] the courts have ordered the treatment, but where the person is a mentally competent adult, there is a split among the cases as to whether the life saving treatment may be ordered. Those courts who view the state as having an identifiable interest in the life of each person will order the treatment as this state interest will outweigh the individual's right to freedom of conscience.[9] Some courts have taken the position that the state has no interest in protecting a person's life against his own wishes. These courts have approached the problem in a manner similar to that of John Stuart Mill, whose philosophy mandated the primacy of an individual decision to die unless a contrary state decision could be justified by a very narrow and

---

2. See, e.g., Wright v. DeWitt School District, 238 Ark. 906, 385 S.W.2d 644 (1965); Vonnegut v. Baun, 206 Ind. 172, 188 N.E. 677 (1934); McCartney v. Austin, 57 Misc.2d 525, 293 N.Y.S.2d 188 (N.Y.Sup.Ct. 1968).

3. See, e.g., In re Sampson, 29 N.Y.2d 900, 278 N.E.2d 918, 328 N.Y.S.2d 686 (1972); People ex rel. Wallace v. Labrenz, 411 Ill. 618, 104 N.E.2d 769 (1952); Jehovah's Witnesses v. King County Hosp., 278 F.Supp. 488 (W.D.Wash.1967), affirmed 309 U.S. 598 (1968). In a few cases a court has refused to order medical treatment which was beneficial but not related to the preservation of the child's life. See, In re Green, 448 Pa. 338, 292 A.2d 387 (1972).

4. See State v. Perricone, 371 U.S. 890 (1962).

5. In Wisconsin v. Yoder, 406 U.S. 205 (1972) the Court made it clear that exemption from regulations on the basis of the free exercise clause required a show-

ing that the regulation interfered with religious beliefs and practices. This decision is noted in Section III, C of this Chapter.

6. The issues in such a case are essentially the same as that presented in the abortion cases—whether a law controlling the treatment of a person's body deprives them of liberty in violation of the due process clauses. For a discussion of the abortion decisions and the right to privacy basis for a "right to die" see Chapter 16, Section VII.

7. See notes 3 and 4 of this section, supra.

8. See, e.g., Application of the President and Director of Georgetown College, 331 F.2d 1000 (D.C.Cir. 1964); Winters v. Miller, 404 U.S. 985 (1969).

9. See, e.g., Kennedy Memorial Hosp. v. Heston, 58 N.J. 576, 279 A.2d 670 (1971); United States v. George, 239 F.Supp. 752 (D.Conn.1965).

important social interest.[10] Such an approach has led these courts to take the position that life saving procedures cannot be ordered for a competent adult who refuses treatment on a religious basis.[11] Yet it should be noted that even judges who are philosophically disposed to such a view may in fact order treatment when the patient indicates that they want to live but that they simply will not sign the required consent forms.[12] As the Supreme Court has not resolved this issue, no final opinion can be given regarding the propriety of such orders. However, in considering this issue it should be remembered that the balancing test will yield either result—depending on whether the court would or would not accept the legitimacy of the state interest in individual life.

d. Drugs

Prior to the emergence of the modern balancing test it was assumed that laws prohibiting the use of certain drugs could be applied to those who wished to use the drugs as a part of their religion. As the state has a clear secular interest in the regulation or prohibition of such drugs, the courts saw no free exercise interest which required an exemption for any religious use. Following the development of a balancing test, a new approach to these problems is called for even though the same results might be reached. First, the plaintiff would have to show that the inability to use the drug seriously burdened the practice of his religion. Second, the state interest in the regulation of the drug and the impact of an exemption from religious use would have to be assessed. Where it is clear that the drug was dangerous, the state's interest would be of a magnitude that should not permit even religious use of the drug. If for no other rea-

son, the danger of accidental distribution of a dangerous drug to persons outside of the religious sect claiming the exemption should constitute a compelling interest. However, it is possible that some proscribed drugs are not so dangerous that a narrow exemption for religious use would impair state interest in safety or health.

How a court decides this issue will depend on the judges' view of the deference that should be paid to legislative determinations regarding health, especially in drug regulation. A court which believes that even these laws should be subject to independent judicial scrutiny might order an exemption for those whose religion requires the use of a drug which poses little societal danger. Thus, in *People v. Woody* [13] the Supreme Court of California created an exemption from laws prohibiting the use of peyote for members of an American Indian religion which required its use. As there was little evidence that either these persons would be seriously hurt or that this would lead to a wider distribution of the drug, the state's interest did not require application of the law to this group. Other courts might well defer to the legislature on the issue of the dangerousness of drug use, and find that the state had a compelling interest in drug regulations. Indeed, this is the historic position of American courts. Most courts can be expected to refuse to independently consider the necessity for religious exemption from drug regulation.[14]

While the Supreme Court has not resolved this issue of whether these exemptions should be judicially ordered, there appears to be agreement as to two related issues concerning such exemptions. First, exemptions will not be granted to any person or group who cannot demonstrate that their belief is sincere and that they are not merely

---

10. J. S. Mill, On Liberty 9–10 (Crofts Classics ed.).

11. See In re Estate of Brooks, 32 Ill.2d 361, 205 N.E.2d 435 (1965); see also the opinion of Judge (now Chief Justice) Burger in Application of the President and Directors of Georgetown College, 331 F.2d 1010, 1015 (D.C.Cir. 1964) (Petition for rehearing en banc— Burger, J., dissenting).

12. Application of the President and Directors of Georgetown College, 331 F.2d 1000, 1010 (D.C.Cir. 1964) (Wright, J.).

13. 61 Cal.2d 716, 394 P.2d 813 (1964).

14. See, e.g., Lewellyn v. State, 489 P.2d 511 (Okl. 1971); Leary v. United States, 383 F.2d 851, 861 (5th Cir. 1967), rev'd on other grounds 395 U.S. 6 (1969); State v. Big Sheep, 75 Mont. 219, 243 P. 1067 (1926).

attempting to subvert the drug laws.[15]　Second, if an exemption is granted by legislation it must not be so narrow as to prefer one religion above others.[16]

IV.　OTHER ESTABLISHMENT–FREE EXERCISE PROBLEMS

A.　Sunday Closing Laws

In four companion decisions the Supreme Court upheld "Sunday closing laws" over objections based on the establishment clause, the free exercise clause, and the due process and equal protection clauses.[1]　These laws prohibited most forms of commercial activity on Sundays.　Several forms of retail commercial activities were allowed to operate on Sunday but these classifications were easily upheld.　Absent consideration under the religion clauses, the goal of providing a uniform day of rest must be held to be a legitimate government goal for the purposes of the due process and equal protection clauses.　To rule otherwise would involve a return to the position that it is not a lawful end of government to regulate the hours and conditions of labor.　The issue under the equal protection clause was whether the exemptions were reasonable in view of the legislative goal.　As this involved purely economic legislation the classification had to be upheld as long as it was arguable that it related to the legitimate state end.[2]

The question of whether these laws violated the establishment clause received the most comprehensive analysis in *McGowan v. Maryland*.[3]　Writing for the majority, Chief Justice Warren found that the present "purpose and effect" of these laws was not religious, even though the laws originally had a religious character.　Crucial to the majority

determination of this question was the history of these laws.　Despite their religious origin, such laws had existed in Virginia following the passage of the act for religious freedom that embodied the views of Jefferson and Madison.　The existence of such legislation in virtually every one of the original states, including Virginia, detracted from the view that the amendment was necessarily incompatible with all Sunday closing laws.

If those laws had retained their religious character the majority would nevertheless have found them invalid as an attempt to advance religion, but the history of these laws showed that they had become non-religious over the years.　Sunday closing laws now appeared in some form in every state and these laws had the support of labor and trade associations as measures for the health and welfare of commercial workers.　Modern statutory programs appeared to be designed to insure a uniform day of rest and non-commercial activity.　Undoubtedly this made attendance at religious services easier for workers of majority Christian sects.　However, given the secular purpose of the law, this was seen only as an effect which happened to coincide with certain religious beliefs and not a real aid to those religions.　To hold otherwise would be to require the state to pursue its goal of establishing a uniform day of rest by choosing a day when the least number of people might use the time to attend religious services.　In the Court's view such a result would be hostile to the public welfare without promoting the separation of church and state.

While a majority of the justices had little trouble in upholding these laws against a general establishment clause challenge,[4] a much more difficult problem was presented

---

15.　United States v. Kuch, 288 F.Supp. 439 (D.D.C. 1968); In re Grady, 61 Cal.2d 887, 394 P.2d 728 (1964). The general problem of testing religious sincerity is discussed in Section IV B of this chapter.

16.　Kennedy v. Bureau of Narcotics and Dangerous Drugs, 459 F.2d 415 (9th Cir. 1972), cert. denied 409 U.S. 1115 (1973); see also Dalli v. Board of Education, 358 Mass. 753, 267 N.E.2d 219 (1971) (exemptions from vaccination requirement must not prefer some religions).

1.　McGowan v. Maryland, 366 U.S. 420 (1961); Two Guys from Harrison—Allentown, Inc. v. McGinley, 366

U.S. 582 (1961); Braunfeld v. Brown, 366 U.S. 599 (1961); Gallagher v. Crown Kosher Market, 366 U.S. 617 (1961).

2.　McGowan v. Maryland, 366 U.S. 420, 425–28 (1961).

3.　Id.

4.　Justice Douglas was the only one who would have held that the laws were invalid under the establishment clause, 366 U.S. at 561 (Douglas, J., dissenting).

by the application of these laws to Sabbatarians. But, as we have seen, the Court held that the state's interest in promoting a uniform day of rest justified the incidental economic burden on these people.[5]

B. Inquiries Into Religious "Frauds"

A question may arise in some cases as to whether an individual is seeking to perpetrate a fraud on others through the false representation of religious beliefs. It is clear that the religion clauses forbid an inquiry by any branch of government, including the courts, into the truth or falsity of asserted religious beliefs. However, it is not clear when an inquiry may be made as to whether an individual is sincerely advocating a religious doctrine (regardless of the truth or falsity of that doctrine) or falsely professing such a belief for fraudulent purposes.

In *United States v. Ballard* [6] the defendants were charged with using the mail to obtain money by fraud. The two defendants, Edna and Donald Ballard, claimed that they had been made divine messengers by "Saint Germain" who was Gary Ballard when he (Gary Ballard) was alive. They represented themselves as the divine messengers and teachers of the "I am" movement with powers to heal many diseases, including some classified medically as incurable. The indictment charged that they "well knew" that these representations were false and that they made the representations to fraudulently collect donations from their followers for themselves. The district court had submitted the jury the question of whether the defendants in good faith believed the representations. The trial judge, however, did not submit to the jury any issue as to the truth or falsity of the representations. The Court of Appeals reversed the defendants convictions on the basis that it was necessary to prove that the representations were in fact false. The Supreme Court in turn reversed the Court of Appeals decision.

In an opinion by Justice Douglas, a majority of the justices held that the guarantees against the establishment of any creed and the assurance of the free exercise of any religion constituted a prohibition of inquiries into the truth or falsity of an asserted religious belief. To hold otherwise would allow a trial for heresy. The majority noted that any religion could be made the subject of such a trial, but that we are free to believe what we cannot prove. The "falsity" may rest only in the views of more common faiths rather than in any absolute definition of true religion. But while holding that a court could never inquire into the falsity of a religious belief, the Supreme Court did not rule on whether a court could inquire into whether the defendant honestly held the belief. This issue was never ruled on by the Court, for when the case was returned to it a majority of the justices reversed the indictment because of the exclusion of women from the jury.[7]

Justice Jackson dissented from the remanding of the case to the circuit court as he found that any inquiry into religious "fraud" was prohibited by the first amendment.[8] He argued that to allow inquiry into a defendant's good faith in asserting a belief was not materially different from a testing of the belief itself. Unless one proves that the asserted religion is not worthy of belief it is not likely that anyone will be convinced of a defendant's bad faith. Additionally, the possibility that government might begin testing when "preachers" lack true belief is in itself dangerous to religious freedom. The Justice noted that a purely secular fraud such as using, for private purposes, money solicited for building a church could be prosecuted since the prosecution would not involve the testing of beliefs. But to find that a would-be religious leader was getting money for his general support through fraud because he did not really believe what he preached could endanger, or

5. The claims under the free exercise clause are examined in Section III, C of this Chapter.

6. 322 U.S. 78 (1944).

7. Ballard v. United States, 329 U.S. 187 (1946).

8. United States v. Ballard, 322 U.S. 78, 92 (1944) (Jackson, J., dissenting).

"chill", every religious teacher of any faith. That people may give their money or, more importantly, their minds and hopes to religions of dubious merit preached by persons with questionable faith is the price we pay for religious freedom.

It is not at all clear whether a majority of the justices would accept the Jackson position that the sincerity of one asserting a religious belief may not be put in issue in a prosecution for fraud. However, two points must be noted in relation to both the *Ballard* opinion and Justice Jackson's dissent. First, the inability to inquire into religious beliefs does not prevent the outlawing of actions based on those beliefs. Thus, the issue of whether the government may ban the taking of money for curing cancer by any means other than accepted medical procedure has no relation to an inquiry into religious beliefs. If the government prohibits the act regardless of whether it is done on a religious basis there is no inquiry into the merit of any religious belief. The only issue is whether the prohibition of this activity violates the free exercise rights of those who believe in faith healing.[9] Second, even if the Court were to adopt the Jackson view, the sincerity of one who requested a religious exemption from some general regulation might still be tested by government agencies or the courts. Justice Jackson only took the position that the government could not prosecute a person for his failure to truly believe in some religious principle. He did not examine the question of whether anyone who seeks a benefit from government because of his religious beliefs must be taken at his word. For example, if a person claims the right to be exempted from work on Saturday because he is a Sabbatarian, may the unemployment compensation agency inquire as to whether he honestly holds the belief? This

question was not answered in *Sherbert v. Verner* [10] wherein Sabbatarians were exempted from the six-day work requirement as the issue had not been raised in the case. However, in the draft exemption cases the Court assumed that the sincerity of one seeking a conscientious objection exemption could be tested both by the draft boards and the courts.[11] There would seem to be merit in allowing these tests of sincerity when the person seeks to use his religious beliefs in this manner. In this situation the law allows for a special treatment of some individuals in order to accommodate their religious beliefs. This promotion of the values of the free exercise clause is only applicable where the person in fact does want to practice a religion. There is little or no danger of persecuting unorthodox beliefs here as the individual has requested the exemption. Thus, it is possible that the Court might adopt the Jackson view and prohibit inquiries into the sincerity of one asserting a religious belief where the action is one relating to misrepresentation of religious teaching to others, while requiring those seeking a religious exemption from secular regulatory statutes to demonstrate their sincerity in the asserted religious belief.[12] Of course, in neither case could the agency or the court inquire into the truth or falsity of the belief itself—that is clearly barred by the decision in *Ballard*.

C. State Involvement in Ecclesiastical Disputes

When there is a dispute bewteen factions of a religious organization, one or more of the parties may seek resolution of the dispute by a state court. Of course, the government cannot declare which party is correct in matters of religion, for that would violate the principles of both religion clauses. A judicial declaration of such mat-

---

9. This is a basic issue in all claims raised under the free exercise clause, see Section III of this Chapter.

10. 374 U.S. 398 (1963). The majority opinion noted that it was not necessary to decide this issue. 374 U.S. at 407–08.

11. These cases are examined in Section III, D, 1 of this Chapter.

12. This position has received support from some legal scholars. See Giannella, Religious Liberty, Nonestablishment and Doctrinal Development—Part I: The Religious Liberty Guarantee, 80 Harv.L.Rev. 1381, 1417–18 (1967); Greenawalt, All or Nothing At All: The Defeat of Selective Conscientious Objection, 1971 Sup.Ct.Rev. 31, 57 n. 92.

ters would simultaneously establish one religious view as correct for the organization while inhibiting the free exercise of the opposing belief. Yet when the opposing groups both claim the church property the state will have to make some judgment as to who is entitled to possession. This must be done under carefully circumscribed rules which guarantee the avoidance of civil court rulings on matters of religious belief.

Where the disputed property is subject to some express condition in a deed, a court can rule on the occurrence of the condition if that does not involve a ruling on religious matters. Thus, if a building is deeded to a church for so long as it is used as a place of religious worship the court could order the return of the property if it were used as a retail sales establishment. But if the condition was that the general church could keep the property so long as it was true to its doctrine, that condition could not be enforced. Any ruling requiring the return of such property would involve a state ruling on religious beliefs.

Most disputes center around property which is not subject to such a specific condition. In these situations two or more groups present themselves to a court and claim the right to possess and control church property. The permissible basis for court rulings in these situations varies with the type of church involved in the dispute. Where the church group is an independent congregation, not subject to a general or higher church authority, the will of a majority of the members must control the decision. As this is a self-governing unit, the only secular basis for a ruling between competing groups is based on the preferences of a majority of the members. There might be a separate secular way to determine ownership if the deed or incorporation documents specified some other form of resolving disputes which did not require the court to review religious doctrine. As it is highly un-

likely that such a neutral, secular rule for dispute resolution could be found, it is only safe to assume that the majority rule principle must prevail in these cases.

Most commonly, disputes arise between a local congregation and a general church with which it has been affiliated in the past. Where the dispute involves a hierarchical church, or organized body of churches of a similar faith and subject to a common ecclesiastical authority, different principles apply. Here there are only two questions for state court resolution: (1) whether this is a hierarchical church, (2) whether the local group in the past affiliated itself and its property with the hierarchical church. If either of these questions were answered in the negative, the local group would be an independent congregation. However, when these questions are answered affirmatively the courts must defer to the hierarchical authority. The rulings of the highest ecclesiastical authority must be enforced by the civil courts. Only in the case of clear fraud by persons in that authority could the court question the judgment of ecclesiastical authority—and even this possible exception is subject to dispute. The highest ecclesiastical authority—an assembly in some religions or a clerical superior in others—is the final arbiter of the church doctrine and authority. As the few decisions in this area deal with widely varying fact situations, it is important to review the individual rulings of the Supreme Court.

Watson v. Jones,[13] the first case involving internal ecclesiastical dissension,[14] was decided on common law principles rather than a constitutional basis. With jurisdiction based on diversity of citizenship, the federal courts were required to determine which of two contesting groups would be deemed to lawfully control the property of the Walnut Street Presbyterian Church of Louisville. In this case the local elders and trustees had been decreed by a state court to control the

---

13. 80 U.S. (13 Wall.) 679 (1872).

14. There was an earlier decision concerning property held by religious organizations but it did not ex-

amine the issues discussed in this section. Terrett v. Taylor, 13 U.S. (9 Cranch) 43 (1815).

church property, even though they had been replaced by the edict of the highest council of the "Presbyterian Church in the United States of America." The Supreme Court held that in this situation the state courts were required to follow the edicts of the highest ecclesiastical tribunal. Although the first amendment had not yet been made applicable to the States, the decision is now recognized as reflecting the values of the religion clauses. The majority found three general rules applicable to civil court resolution of internal ecclesiastical disputes. First, if property is given to a congregation with an express condition in the terms of the grant that it shall be used only to support a specific purpose, the civil courts could order a return of the property if the property is no longer used for that purpose. Second, where property has been given to the general use of an independent religious group the property must be used as determined by a majority of the society or by another manner that the group has previously established for this purpose. Third, where property has been acquired by a society or group which constitutes a part of a general religious organization, the established tribunals of that organization must be deferred to by civil courts. The right to church property insofar as it is dependent on questions of religious doctrine or ecclesiastical law must be settled by the highest tribunal or authority of the religious organization.

Since the time of the *Watson* decision the ability of a civil court to resolve questions of "departure from purpose" has been limited in light of the principles of the first amendment. However, the principles of deference to a congregational polity or hierarchical authority has been strengthened by later decisions. Two other decisions relating to church disputes were rendered by the Supreme Court prior to the application of the first amendment to the States. In *Bouldin v. Alexander* [15] the Court held that a civil court could declare who was entitled to con-

trol the property of an independent congregational church. In this case a minority of the congregation had met and expelled the majority of the members and the trustees in whom the title to the church property was formally vested. The Court found that civil courts must follow the will of the majority of this congregational Church to decide the question of legal title. While it is not clear that this decision was based on first amendment principles, it is the only case in which the Supreme Court has been presented with a dispute over the property of a clearly independent local congregation and it follows the principle stated in *Watson*.

In *Gonzalez v. Roman Catholic Archbishop of Manila*,[16] the Court refused to allow a civil court to determine the qualification of a chaplain of the Roman Catholic Church. A testatrix had given funds to the Church to establish a "chaplaincy" to which her nearest male relative was to be appointed whenever possible. One of her descendants sought the post, and the income from the fund, but was refused appointment by the church authorities due to his failure to qualify under ecclesiastical law. The Supreme Court held that a civil court could not award the fund or the position to the heir as it could not disturb the judgment of the church authorities. As the chaplaincy was a part of a hierarchical church, the rulings on ecclesiastical matters by the church organization could not be reviewed. However, the Court noted that this conclusion was true in the absence of "fraud, collusion or arbitrariness." [17] In later years this statement has been regarded as dicta and there is no general ability of courts to review church decisions to determine if they are arbitrary.

Following the application of the religion clauses to the States, the Supreme Court was confronted with legislative and judicial attempts to grant sole control of the property held by the Russian Orthodox Church to American members of that Church. But in both instances the Court refused to allow

---

15.   82 U.S. (15 Wall.) 131 (1872).

16.   280 U.S. 1 (1929).

17.   280 U.S. at 16.

the government to interfere with the authority of the hierarchical church even though the highest authority of that church resided in a country hostile to the interests of the United States. New York passed legislation which would have placed control of the church property of the Russian Orthodox Church in an autonomous part of that church in New York. This was challenged by an archbishop of the church who had been appointed by the ecclesiastical authority of the central church in Moscow. The Russian Orthodox Church was admittedly a hierarchical church to which the American groups had been joined in the past. However, formal title was in a corporation with officers who were citizens of the United States. At issue was whether the American churches could renounce their affiliation to the central church and retain the church property. In *Kedroff v. St. Nicholas Cathedral* [18] the Supreme Court invalidated the New York legislation which would have given control to the American controlled sect. In the majority's view, this legislation violated the principles of the free exercise clause by interfering with the control and decisions of the ecclesiastical authority. A hierarchical church is one which is "organized as a body with other churches having a similar faith and doctrine with a common ruling convocation or ecclesiastical head." [19] If state law allowed one group to take control of the property of such a church against the will of the formal ecclesiastical authority, the state would be determining the status of one faction as the "true" church. As a contrary ruling would prevent the free operation of the hierarchical church, the state must accept the decisions of the highest formal authority in the church when it resolves such disputes. This is true even in the absence of legislation, for civil courts have no more

power to review the decisions of a church than does the legislature.[20]

It is now clear that civil courts may not make any inquiry into the correctness of decision concerning religious doctrine. In *Presbyterian Church v. Mary Elizabeth Blue Hull Memorial Presbyterian Church* [21] the state courts were confronted with a withdrawal of two local churches from the general Presbyterian Church. The state courts applied a rule of law which granted a trust of church property to a general church on the sole condition that it adhere to the faith and doctrine which existed when the local churches affiliated with it. The Supreme Court of the United States ruled that no inquiry could be made into whether the general church had deviated from its doctrine. This was unquestionably a decision that belonged to the hierarchical church authority, as only that authority could decide the true faith of the church. Thus, the local churches could not retain their property as they had subjected themselves and their property to church control and there was no basis for granting them the property without an inquiry into religious matters.

It should be noted that the state courts can resolve these conflicting claims for property so long as they do not rule on religious matters. These decisions might occur in several ways. For example, a donor might grant property to a church with the provision that the property will revert to the donor on the happening of a specific condition. This condition could be enforced so long as the happening of the event could be determined without a court ruling on religious doctrine. Similarly, state law could establish a purely secular or non-religious basis for finding title in a local church unless title had been formally granted to the general

---

18. 344 U.S. 94 (1952).

19. 344 U.S. at 110.

20. After this decision, the New York courts held that the American controlled faction of the Russian Church was entitled to the property even though the statute had been held invalid. In Kreshik v. St. Nicholas Cathedral, 363 U.S. 190 (1960) the Supreme

Court overruled the decision of the New York court. The Supreme Court held that civil courts had to defer to the ecclesiastical authorities and that there could be no judicial review of those decisions—regardless of whether the review was based on statute or "common law."

21. 393 U.S. at 440 (1969).

church. This law would be proper as long as the question of whether control over the property had been given to the general church could be determined without a judicial inquiry into religious doctrine. Thus, even though a local group belonged to a hierarchical church, they could withdraw from the church and retain their property when the state property law, and the deeds for the property, made it clear that the property had never been given over to the control of the general church.[22]

It must be remembered that civil courts can never question a church's rulings on matters of religious doctrine or even authority. When a church is truly local or congregational the will of a majority controls the decision. Once it is found that a group has submitted itself and its property to the control of a hierarchical church, the rulings of the highest formal authority in that church must be accepted by the civil courts. There is the possibility that the Supreme Court may allow a further inquiry into whether the general church has replaced local authority over the property for reasons of "fraud or collusiveness." However, if such an inquiry can be made at all the civil court could only prevent a clear theft of local church property for the personal benefit of members of the hierarchical organization. The Court has made it clear that the hierarchical authority cannot have its decisions overturned because they are "arbitrary" or contrary to the church's own rules. In a case concerning this issue, a hierarchical church replaced one of its higher clerics and granted control of the church property to a new officer seemingly in violation of its own rules of procedure. But in *Serbian Eastern Orthodox Church v. Milivojevich*,[23] the Court ruled that any review of the jurisdiction of the general church authorities or whether they acted in conformity with the church

laws would result in undue interference with the freedom of religion. Any review of such principles would require a state judgment on the meaning and applicability of religious rules and doctrine. This review can only be avoided by accepting the judgment of the highest formal authority of the hierarchical organization. Therefore, state courts must refrain from ruling contrary to such authorities unless their decision is clearly based on principles which have no reference to religious doctrines or rulings.

The justices were closely divided by the application of these principles to the resolution of a complex dispute between some members of a local religious group and the church with which they had been affiliated. In *Jones v. Wolf*[24] the Court examined a dispute between members of the Vineville Presbyterian Church of Macon, Georgia and between some members of that local church group and the Augusta-Macon Presbytery of the Presbyterian Church in the United States. Approximately 40 years earlier a local group in Macon, Georgia had founded a congregation and property had been acquired in the name of the trustees of the Vineville Presbyterian Church. When it was organized the Vineville Church group became a member church of the Presbyterian Church in the United States (PCUS). PCUS has a higher hierarchical form of government, as contrasted with a congregational form, but the local church property was never formally deeded over to the general church or subjected to the control of the general church according to any identifiable document.

In 1973 a congregational meeting of the local Vineville Church, at which a quorum of its members were present, voted to separate from PCUS and to unite with another Presbyterian denomination, the Presbyterian Church in America (PCA). A minority of

---

22. Such a situation was presented in Maryland & Virginia Eldership of the Churches of God v. Church of God, 396 U.S. 367 (1970). A discussion of the secular basis for ruling on such conditions is contained in the concurring opinion of Justice Brennan. 396 U.S. at 368.

23. 426 U.S. 696 (1976).

24. 443 U.S. 595 (1979). The majority opinion in this case was written by Justice Blackmun and joined by Justices Brennan, Marshall, Rehnquist and Stevens.

the local church wished to stay with PCUS and in response to the schism in the local congregation PCUS appointed a commission to resolve the dispute and found that the minority faction was the "true congregation" of the Vineville Church. There then ensued a dispute brought to state court over whether the PCUS and the local minority controlled title to the property or whether the majority which had disaffiliated itself from PCUS, controlled title.

By a 5 to 4 vote the Supreme Court found that the Georgia courts could apply "neutral principles" of property law to determine that title remained in the local congregation and was to be controlled by a majority vote of that congregation. The majority opinion appears to be consistent with earlier Court decisions. The majority held only that state courts may examine the language of real and personal property deeds, the terms of church charters or state statutes relating to the control of property, and documents affiliating the local group with the general church and the constitution of the general church in order to determine technically if the local group had become a member of an hierarchical church and subjected its property to control of that church. The majority opinion noted that the "neutral principles approach" was to rely only on "objective, well established concepts of trust and property law" and that any examination of the instruments of ownership that were religious documents must be examined in a strictly secular manner to determine whether those documents technically place property ownership in the local group or the general church. The majority refused to adopt a rule of compulsory deference to the higher church authority in all instances because it felt that the neutral principles approach would involve less entanglement with religious doctrine by requiring judges to abstain from a determination as to what authority is the highest in a church organization and simply to examine the documents in a secular manner to determine where title to the property had been formally placed.

Applying this rule to the specific case before it, the majority found that the Georgia courts could have found that the deeds, contracts of conveyance and trust, and church charters left title to the property in the local church. However, the Georgia courts had not explained how they had determined that the local church was represented by the majority rather than the minority. In determining which group would control the use of property by the local congregation the state was still required to adopt rules that did not involve an examination of religious doctrine. The state could adopt a presumptive rule of majority representation, which could be changed by a showing that the local church group had chosen another means for property control through contract or deed terms. In fact the state could adopt any method of overcoming the majoritarian presumption so long as the civil courts did not entangle themselves in religious controversy or impair free exercise rights. However, it was unclear whether the Georgia courts had applied a truly neutral rule of majority ownership or a neutral examination of property and contract terms to determine if majority rule was to control under the terms of the property contracts and deeds of the Vineville Church. Thus, the Supreme Court remanded the case to the Georgia courts to determine if Georgia had a rule requiring deference to a majority of the local congregation or whether state law provided that the identity of the controlling local group was to be determined on the basis of religious principles. The latter position would require a granting of automatic deference to the general church (PCUS) because otherwise the civil court would be involved in questions of religious doctrine rather than the following of neutral principles of contract and property law.

The dissenting justices would have required automatic deference to the general church councils (PCUS) because they believed that only such deference could avoid impermissible entanglement between the state and religious authorities.[25] Whenever a local group affiliates technically with a hierarchical church the dissent would subject the local group to the control of the higher church authorities with no recourse to civil courts. These justices felt that it would be impossible to apply the Court's neutral principles approach without examining religious documents and effectively making decisions on questions of religious doctrine.

If the majority in *Jones* is correct and the state courts can be kept to a purely secular examination of documents relating to formal control of property then its neutral principles approach does not deviate from the analysis employed in earlier Supreme Court decisions. But if ruling on these property disputes involves government agents or judges in examining religious charters in a manner that calls for some evaluation of religious principles or doctrine, the neutral principles approach will lead to what should be deemed an unconstitutional entanglement between government and religion.

D. Congressional Action to End Religious Discrimination in Private Employment

Title VII of the Civil Rights Act of 1964 [26] prohibits employers covered by the Act from discriminating against persons because of their religion. This statute has a great impact on the employment market as it applies to most forms of private, as well as governmental, employment and the activities of labor unions.[27] The Act itself is fairly straightforward in its approach to this problem. It prohibits an employer from discriminating in the hiring, payment or treatment of employees on the basis of their religion.[28] Similarly, the statute makes it unlawful for a labor organization to exclude or burden a worker on the basis of their religion.[29] In 1972, the Act was amended to include a definition of religion which also defines an employer's duties in this area. The Act now reads:

> The term "religion" includes all aspects of religious observance and practice, as well as belief, unless an employer demonstrates that he is unable to reasonably accommodate to an employee's or prospective employee's religious observance or practice without undue hardship on the conduct of the employer's business.[30]

This amendment to the Act confirmed some of the previous rulings of the Equal Employment Opportunity Commission (EEOC), which is the agency empowered to promulgate regulation to implement Title VII.[31] Employers now are required not only to refrain from discriminating against persons

---

25. Jones v. Wolf, 443 U.S. 595, 610 (1979) (Powell, J., dissenting, joined by Burger, C. J., and Stewart and White, JJ.).

26. 42 U.S.C.A. § 2000e et seq. (Civil Rights Act of 1964, Pub.L. No. 88–352, title VII, § 701 et seq., 78 Stat. 253).

27. Employers with over 15 employees, most forms of government employment and most labor unions are covered by the Act. For the exact coverage see 42 U.S.C.A. § 2000e & 2000e–1 (as amended).

28. 42 U.S.C.A. § 2000e–2(a) provides in part:

"It shall be an unlawful employment practice for an employer—(1) to fail or refuse to hire or to discharge any individual or otherwise to discriminate against any individual with respect to his compensation, terms, conditions, or privileges of employment, because of such individual's race, color, religion, sex, or national origin; . . ."

29. 42 U.S.C.A. § 2000e–2(c) provides:

"It shall be an unlawful employment practice of a labor organization—(1) to exclude or to expel from its membership, or otherwise to discriminate against, any individual because of his race, color, religion,

sex, or national origin; (2) to limit, segregate, or classify its membership or applicants for membership, or to classify or fail or refuse to refer for employment any individual, in any way which would deprive or tend to deprive any individual of employment opportunities, or would limit such employment opportunities or otherwise adversely affect his status as an employee or as an applicant for employment, because of such individual's race, color, religion, sex, or national origin; or (3) to cause or attempt to cause an employer to discriminate against an individual in violation of this section."

30. Act of March 24, 1972, Pub.L. No. 92–261, § 2, 86 Stat. 103, codified at 42 U.S.C.A. § 2000e, amending 42 U.S.C.A. § 2000e (1970).

31. At first the EEOC interpreted the statute as only prohibiting discriminatory practices and allowing the application of a uniform work week even though it burdened some religions. 29 C.F.R. § 1605.1(a)(3), 31 Fed. Reg. 8370 (1966). In 1967 the EEOC required reasonable accommodation such as granting Sabbatarians exemptions from Saturday work requirements. 29 C.F.R. § 1605.1(b), 32 Fed.Reg. 10298 (1967).

because of their religion but also to accommodate a wide variety of religious practices.[32]

Whether this statute as it has been applied by the EEOC and lower courts, would withstand attack under the first amendment remains an open question. Twice the Justices of the Supreme Court have split 4 to 4 in cases which presented this issue.[33] In its third attempt at resolving the issue the Court interpreted the statute in a manner that avoided a constitutional ruling. In *Trans World Airlines v. Hardison*,[34] the Court held that the statute did not require the employer to alter Saturday work schedules in violation of a seniority system established by collective bargaining. By a vote of 7 to 2 the Court held that requiring the employer to bear more than *de minimis* costs was not required by the act. Thus the Court recognized that further congressional action of this type raises most serious issues under the religion clauses.

E. Prohibiting "Ministers" From Holding Public Office

Early in the country's history, several states by statute or constitutional provision, had prohibited members of religious orders or ministers from holding public office. By the turn of this century it was generally recognized that these laws conflict with the free exercise and establishment clauses, and although the Court had not held them to be *per se* invalid, these laws were repealed or annulled in almost every state that had adopted them. Tennessee had, by statute, barred "ministers of the gospel, or priest[s]

of any denomination whatever," from serving as delegates to the state's constitutional convention; this statute mirrored a provision of the state constitution barring such persons from membership in the state legislature. The Supreme Court unanimously found that the statute was unconstitutional in *McDaniel v. Paty*.[35] There was no majority opinion in *McDaniel*, however, because the justices could not agree on exactly why the statute was unconstitutional. The Court had previously held, in *Torcaso v. Watkins*,[36] that the states could not require persons to take a religious oath before accepting public employment or office. This holding was based on the principle that no individual can be punished for his religious beliefs. The relevance of *Torcaso* to the Tennessee disqualification laws divided the Court.

Chief Justice Burger wrote an opinion, joined by Justices Powell, Rehnquist and Stevens, which concluded that the disqualification statute violated the free exercise clause. The opinion by the Chief Justice found that the law was not one that infringed the "freedom to believe," and, therefore, was not automatically invalid under *Torcaso*.[37] The Chief Justice noted that the history of such disqualification clauses in the original states indicated that such laws had been aimed merely at restricting acts of religious groups that would have further entangled the states with religion. The Tennessee law, however, regulated actions that related to the individual's religion, and, therefore, it was to be tested by the free exercise clause balancing test. Under this

---

32. By far the most common issue is the exemption of employees from work on their Sabbath. However, there may be claims for exemption from religious services at business meetings, Young v. Southwestern Savings & Loan Ass'n, 509 F.2d 140 (5th Cir. 1975), or exemption from dress or hair style regulations, EEOC Dec. No. 71–2620, 1973 C.C.H. EEOC Dec. 4500 (June 25, 1971).

33. In each of these cases one justice did not participate in the decision or the remaining eight Justices were evenly divided. In such instances the lower court ruling is affirmed, normally without opinion. Dewey v. Reynolds Metals, 402 U.S. 689 (1971), affirming Dewey v. Reynolds Metals, 429 F.2d 324 (6th Cir. 1970);

Parker Seal Co. v. Cummins, 429 U.S. 65 (1976), affirming Cummins v. Parker Seal Co., 516 F.2d 544 (6th Cir. 1975).

34. 432 U.S. 63 (1977).

35. 435 U.S. 618 (1978) (Justice Blackmun did not participate in the decision). A history of the use and repeal of disqualification statutes appears in the plurality opinion written by the Chief Justice. Id. at 622–625 (Burger, C. J.).

36. 367 U.S. 488 (1961).

37. McDaniel v. Paty, 435 U.S. 618 (1978) (Burger, C. J., plurality opinion).

test, the State's failure to demonstrate that participation by clergy in the political process would bring about further "establishment" problems indicated that this law in fact did not promote a strong state interest. Thus, the law was invalid because it burdened religious practices without advancing overriding state interests. The Chief Justice found no reason to examine whether the state's asserted interest in furthering separation of church and state under other circumstances, might constitute a permissible legislative goal.

Justice Brennan, joined by Justice Marshall, found that the statute violated both the free exercise and establishment clauses of the first amendment, which applied to the states through the fourteenth amendment. Unlike the Chief Justice, Justice Brennan found that this law disadvantaged the person because of his religious belief. So construed, the law was a *per se* violation of the free exercise clause; there was no reason to employ the balancing test in such a case. The Justice noted that requiring a minister to forego either his ministry or public office constituted a sufficient burden to invoke the free exercise prohibition against burdening religious beliefs.[38] Justice Brennan also found that the law violated the establishment clause. He agreed that a purpose of the establishment clause was to eliminate religious divisiveness, but believed that the state could not pursue that goal through the use of religious classifications. Justice Brennan noted that this law might fail the secular purpose test, as it was at least possible that it was based on the religious beliefs of a dominant sect within the jurisdiction; but he found it unnecessary to resolve this issue.[39] The statute was invalid in Justice Brennan's view because it failed the primary secular effect test. He believed that a primary effect of this statute was the inhibition

of the practice of religion. Justice Stewart concurred in the judgment because he believed, as did Justice Brennan, that the law constituted a restriction on religious beliefs. In his opinion, such restrictions were prohibited by *Torcaso*.[40]

Justice White was the only justice who did not believe that the disqualification law was invalid under the free exercise clause; he did not believe that the law, in any meaningful way, compelled a person to abandon the ministry. However, the Justice found that it was a significant limitation on the right to seek elective office; many ministers would be deterred from running for office by the law, even though they would not feel compelled to abandon their ministries. For this reason, he found the law to be unconstitutional as a violation of the equal protection clause of the fourteenth amendment. In support of his position, Justice White noted that the Court had held that the right to vote and the right to be a candidate were of sufficient constitutional magnitude to require the states "to provide substantial justification for any requirement that prevents a class of citizens" from exercising these rights. He found that, while the state's interest in separating church and state might be legitimate, "close scrutiny reveals that the challenged law is not 'reasonably necessary to the accomplishment of . . .' that objective."[41]

F. Regulation of the Conditions of Labor in Parochial Schools

In *National Labor Relations Bd. v. Catholic Bishop of Chicago*[42] the Supreme Court, by a 5 to 4 vote, held that the National Labor Relations Board (N.L.R.B.) was not authorized by the National Labor Relations Act to regulate the unionization of lay faculty members at schools affiliated with

38. 435 U.S. at 632 (Brennan, J., concurring in the judgment).

39. 435 U.S. at 636 n. 9 (Brennan, J., concurring in the judgment).

40. 435 U.S. 642–643 (Stewart, J., concurring in the judgment).

41. 435 U.S. at 645 (White, J., concurring in the judgment), quoting from Bullock v. Carter, 405 U.S. 134 (1972).

42. 440 U.S. 490 (1979).

the Roman Catholic Church. In so doing, the majority opinion by Chief Justice Burger indicated that it was unlikely that the Court would allow secular authorities to engage in detailed regulation of the conditions of labor or the employer-employee relationship at church affiliated schools. The N.L.R.B. had asserted jurisdiction to resolve questions regarding elections for union representation and union representatives at Catholic schools in Chicago and Indiana.[43] The majority stated that it would have to determine if this extension of jurisdiction gave rise to "serious constitutional questions" and, if so, whether those questions could be avoided by construing the statute to avoid jurisdiction.[44] The Chief Justice noted that the Court had stressed in past decisions the important role of a teacher in a church affiliated school. Indeed, this fact has formed the basis for the invalidation of some state laws that would have allowed for government subsidies to parochial schools to offset the cost of teachers for subjects that were not sectarian in nature.[45] The N.L.R.B. claimed that its jurisdiction would only require it to resolve factual issues in disputes between union groups and the church employer and that it could avoid religious issues when ruling on teacher disputes. But the majority opinion found that a significant risk of greater and unconstitutional entanglement between the government agency and church authority would be created if the Board were to regulate this important component of religious education. The Court noted that the resolution of many disputes concerning "terms and conditions of employment" might involve inquiries into the good faith of positions asserted on a religious basis by administrators of these school systems. Indeed, the majority added an appendix to its opinion which was an excerpt of an inquiry by the Board's hearing officer regarding prayers at Catholic schools that involved the questioning of a member of the Catholic clergy concerning the nature of Catholic liturgy and its use at such schools. The Chief Justice, for the majority, noted that this type of involvement between secular and religious authorities presented significant dangers to the values protected by the first amendment.[46]

The majority opinion then went on to examine whether there was a clear congressional authorization of N.L.R.B. jurisdiction over parochial schools, so as to require the Court to face the issue of whether the asserted jurisdiction violated the first amendment. The majority found the statutes might have been interpreted to allow for such jurisdiction and the necessary conflict with church operated schools, but that Congress had not clearly demonstrated an intent to bring teachers at such schools within the jurisdiction of the N.L.R.B. Therefore, the congressional act would be construed so as to avoid the constitutional question. The dissenting justices found that the history of the National Labor Relations Act demonstrated a clear intent to allow the Board to assert jurisdiction over all non-profit institutions that affected commerce, including private schools affiliated with religious organizations.[47] But the dissent did not express a view on the ultimate constitutional issue be-

43. The Chicago parochial schools involved in the case were related to the training of young men for the Roman Catholic priesthood; the Indiana schools were more traditional high schools. This distinction, however, played no part in the decision. Both sets of schools were certified by their respective states as meeting the basic requirements for private educational institutions.

44. 440 U.S. at 501. See also St. Martin Evangelical Lutheran Church v. South Dakota, 451 U.S. 772 (1981) in which the Supreme Court construed the Federal Unemployment Tax Act (FUTA) and the Unemployment Compensation Amendments of 1976 so that non-profit church-related schools were not subject to FUTA's unemployment tax on school personnel. The Court thus avoided ruling on first amendment, objec-

tions to the tax and related regulations, raised by the church.

45. 440 U.S. at 501–2.

46. Chief Justice Burger has provided the leadership in defining the concept of excessive entanglement so as to protect both the autonomy of religious organizations and to avoid providing aid to religious entities. See Section II, B, 4 of this Chapter for a critique of the history and usefulness of the excessive entanglement concept.

47. National Labor Relations Bd. v. Catholic Bishop of Chicago, 440 U.S. 490, 508 (1979) (Brennan, J., dissenting, joined by White, Marshall & Blackmun, JJ.).

cause the majority opinion had avoided the issue.[48]

G. Direct Regulation of Religious Organizations

In *Larson v. Valente*,[49] the Court held that a section of the Minnesota Charitable Solicitation Act, which imposed registration and reporting requirements upon only those religious organizations which solicit more than 50% of their funds from non-members, discriminated against those organizations in violation of the establishment clause of the first amendment. The Unification Church, a religious organization heavily involved in fund-raising activities aimed at non-members, sought a declaration that statute denied its members free exercise of their religion and that it favored some religious organizations over others, contrary to the establishment clause.

Before addressing the establishment clause issue, the Supreme Court, in an opinion by Justice Brennan noted that the Unification Church was a religious organization within the meaning of the statutory section in question. The State of Minnesota had attempted to force the Church to comply with a rule which applied only to religious organizations and could not now claim that the Church was a religion. The Court then went on to hold that the denominational preference inherent in the "fifty percent" classification, the statute must be invalidated unless it was justified by a compelling government interest, and unless it was "closely fitted" to further that interest.

"The clearest command of the establishment clause is that one religious denomination cannot be officially preferred over another."[50] Justice Brennan acknowledged Minnesota's significant interest in protecting its citizens from abusive practices in the solicitation of funds for religious organizations. However, the majority found that the fifty percent classification was not tailored to advance this purpose. There was no factual support for the state's claim that members can and will effectively control an organization if they contribute more than half of its solicited income or that religious organizations are any less able to regulate themselves than other charitable organizations. The Court also found it more plausible that the need for public disclosure rose in proportion to the absolute amount, as opposed to the percentage, of non-member contributions.

Although he deemed it "unnecessary" because the classification was invalid under the compelling interest test that must be applied to denominational classifications, Justice Brennan also applied the three-pronged purpose-effect-entanglement test. Brennan found that the law violated all three parts of the test. This type of law created a danger of "politicizing religion," because it imposed selective legislative burdens and advantages on particular denominations. This risk was made startlingly clear by this law's legislative history, which indicated that the legislature's intention was to include certain religious groups within the regulatory requirements and to exclude others.[51]

---

48. See D. Laycock, Towards a General Theory of the Religion Clauses: The Case of Church Labor Relations and the Right to Church Autonomy, 81 Col.L.Rev. 1373 (1981), for the view that a constitutional right to church autonomy exists based on the free exercise clause, so that any regulation of churches must be justified by a compelling governmental interest.

49. 456 U.S. 228 (1982).

50. 456 U.S. at 244–45.

51. See also Larkin v. Grendel's Den, Inc., 103 S.Ct. 505 (1982) (zoning law violates establishment clause by granting to churches or schools a veto power over the issuance of liquor licenses for any premises within a 500-foot radius of the church or school) (the case is noted in section II of this Chapter).

CHAPTER TWENTY

NATIONALIZATION AND CITIZENSHIP

I. INTRODUCTION

In Section III of Chapter 16 on Equal Protection we considered the constitutionality of laws that classify on the basis of alienage. In this chapter we will analyze other constitutional guarantees relating to alienage; congressional power over admission, immigration and naturalization; voluntary and involuntary expatriation or repudiation of citizenship; and deportation. In considering the cases that follow, it is important to remember that Congress enjoys "broad power over immigration and naturalization . . . ." [1]

II. ADMISSION, IMMIGRATION, AND ACQUISITION OF CITIZENSHIP

A. Admission

In a long line of cases the Supreme Court has stated that the power of Congress over the admission of aliens to this country is absolute. This principle is illustrated in *The Chinese Exclusion Case* [1] where the Supreme Court upheld the application of a federal statute which prohibited Chinese nationals from entering the United States to persons who had departed before that statute's enactment with a certificate issued under an earlier act granting them permission to return. The later act was attacked as a violation of existing treaties between the United States and China and in violation of rights vested in Chinese laborers by the previous acts. As to the conflict of the later statute with the earlier treaty, Justice Field, speaking for a unanimous Court, held that the "last expression of the sovereign must control." [2] Turning to congressional power to exclude aliens, the Court emphasized Congress' absolute power:

> [These Chinese laborers who seek to return to the United States] are not citizens of the Unit-

---

1. Fiallo v. Bell, 430 U.S. 787, 792 (1977); see also Galvan v. Press, 347 U.S. 522, 530–32 (1954). In Nyquist v. Mauclet, 432 U.S. 1, 7 n. 8 (1977), the Court said that because of this broad power it would apply "relaxed scrutiny" in judicial review of such statutes. *Nyquist* is considered in Chapter 1, Section II, B, 2.

1. 130 U.S. 581 (1889). The case is also titled Chae Chan Ping v. United States.

2. 130 U.S. at 600.

ed States; they are aliens. That the government of the United States, through the action of the legislative department, can exclude aliens from its territory is a proposition which we do not think open to controversy. Jurisdiction over its own territory to that extent is an incident of every independent nation.[3]

The power of the government to exclude foreigners from the country whenever, in its judgment, the public interest requires such exclusion, has been asserted in repeated instances, and never denied by the executive or legislative departments.[4]

Congress, in "broad terms," may also authorize the executive to exercise this power.[5]

Notwithstanding this broad power, Congress enacted no laws regulating immigration for about a century, though in 1798 it did pass the short-lived and ill-fated Alien Act[6] as part of its Alien and Sedition Laws.[7] In 1875, it enacted a statute barring convicts and prostitutes; there followed a series of other acts,[8] and in 1924 it enacted a national origins quota system that was not repealed until 1965.[9]

The broad power to exclude aliens has not been weakened by more recent Supreme Court decisions, though several justices have dissented from this position. In *Kleindienst v. Mandel*[10] the Supreme Court upheld a decision of the Attorney General refusing to grant a temporary nonimmigrant visa to an alien scholar and a self-proclaimed "revolutionary Marxist" who also claimed not to be a member of the Communist Party. He had entered the country twice before to accept invitations to speak and at those times the Attorney General had exercised his statutory discretion, under the Immigration and Nationality Act of 1952,[11] to admit him temporarily despite the fact he was ineligible under section 212(a)(28) as an alien who is, or at any time has been, inter alia, advocating economic doctrines of world communism or writing or publishing the economic doctrines of world communism. But this time the Attorney General denied his application for a temporary visa.

The Court, after quoting many of the earlier cases that said the legislative power of Congress to exclude aliens or prescribe the conditions for their entry is plenary, declined to reach the issue of whether the first amendment rights of the listeners in this country (who are citizens) should prevail when the Attorney General advanced no reason for his denial of a waiver.[12] The Attorney General had in fact written the alien's counsel that the reason he (Mandel) was denied a waiver was that Mandel had engaged in previous abuses by violating the terms of his earlier waivers. But Mandel apparently was not made aware of the conditions attached to his previous waivers,[13] and the

3. Id. at 603.

4. Id. at 606–607. See also, e.g., The Japanese Immigrant Case (Yamataya v. Fisher), 189 U.S. 86 (1903); Oceanic Steam Navigation Co. v. Stranahan, 214 U.S. 320, 339 (1909). Bugajewitz v. Adams, 228 U.S. 585 (1913); Hines v. Davidowitz, 312 U.S. 52 (1941).

But note: "It is well established that if an alien is a lawful permanent resident of the United States *and remains physically present there*, he is a person within the protection of the Fifth Amendment. He may not be deprived of his life, liberty or property without due process of law." Kwong Hai Chew v. Colding, 344 U.S. 590, 596 (1953) (emphasis added) (footnote omitted). Cf. Section IV of this Chapter, infra.

5. United States ex rel. Kanuff v. Shaughnessy, 338 U.S. 537, 543 (1950); Shaughnessy v. United States ex rel. Mezei, 345 U.S. 206 (1953).

6. Act of June 25, 1798, 1 Stat. 570.

7. See Chapter 18 on Free Speech, Section II, C.

8. 18 Stat. 477 (1875); see Kleindienst v. Mandel, 408 U.S. 753, 761 (1972). The Constitution of the Unit-

ed States: Analysis and Interpretation, 92d Cong. 2d Sess. Document 92–82 (1973), at 295–96. See, e.g., id. at 295, n. 4, citing 22 Stat. 214 (1882) (exclusion of idiots, lunatics, convicts, and persons likely to become public charges); 26 Stat. 1084 (1891) (exclusion of persons suffering from certain diseases, those convicted of crimes involving moral turpitude, paupers, and polygamists); 32 Stat. 1213 (1903) (exclusion of epileptics, insane persons, professional beggars, and anarchists); 34 Stat. 898 (1907) (exclusion of feeble minded, children unaccompanied by parents, tuberculosis sufferers, women entering for prostitution and other immoral purposes).

9. Act of May 26, 1924, § 11, 43 Stat. 153, 159; Act of Oct. 3, 1965, § 2, 79 Stat. 911 (repealing legislation).

10. 408 U.S. 753 (1972).

11. 66 Stat. 182, 8 U.S.C.A. § 1101 et seq.

12. 408 U.S. at 766–69.

13. Id. at 758 n. 5, 759.

Government chose not to rely on this letter to counsel, either at the district court or at the Supreme Court.[14] Nonetheless, the Court held:

> The fact remains, however, that the official empowered to make the decision stated that he denied a waiver because he concluded that previous abuse by Mandel made it inappropriate to grant a waiver again. With this, we think the Attorney General validly exercised the plenary power that Congress delegated to the Executive. . . . We hold that when the Executive exercises this power negatively on the basis of a facially legitimate and bona fide reason, the courts will look neither behind the exercise of that discretion, nor test it by balancing its justification against the First Amendment interests of those who seek personal communication with the applicant.[15]

The Court distinguished *Lamont v. Postmaster General*[16] where the Court had held that a statute permitting the Government to hold "communist political propaganda" arriving in the mails from abroad unless the addressee affirmatively requested in writing that it be delivered to him placed an unjustifiable burden on the addressee's first amendment rights, since that case did not involve the Government's plenary power over admission of aliens.[17]

Even more recently, the Supreme Court upheld other sections of the Immigration and Nationality Act which had the effect of excluding the relationship between an illegitimate child and his natural father—but not his natural mother—from the special preference immigration status given to a "child" or "parent" of a United States citizen or lawful permanent resident.[18] The Court again reviewed the relevant line of cases and said it was "no more inclined to reconsider this line of cases today than we were five years

ago. . . ."[19] Justices Marshall, Brennan, and White dissented on constitutional grounds. That same day the Supreme Court did strike a state law which allowed illegitimate children to inherit by intestate succession only from their mothers while legitimates were allowed in such cases to inherit from both parents.[20] The federal law which discriminated against certain types of illegitimates, unlike the state law, was apparently saved from unconstitutionality by its reliance on Congress' plenary power over the admission of aliens.

B. Immigration and Acquisition of Citizenship

One method of acquiring United States citizenship is to be born in the United States. One born in the United States and subject to the jurisdiction thereof is a citizen of the United States by virtue of the first sentence of the first section of the fourteenth amendment. "Subject to the jurisdiction thereof" means that the person is not born of parents who are employed in a diplomatic or official capacity of a foreign government. For example, in *United States v. Wong Kim Ark*,[1] the Supreme Court held that a child born in the United States of parents of Chinese descent, who at the time of his birth, were subjects of the Emperor of China, but had a permanent domicil and residence in the United States and were there carrying on business but were not employed in any diplomatic or official capacity under the Emperor of China became at the time of his birth a citizen of the United States by virtue of the first clause of the fourteenth amendment. Thus, even the child of illegal immigrants is a United States citizen if he or she is born in the United States, even though the illegal

14. Id. at 769.

15. Id. at 769–70.

16. 381 U.S. 301 (1965).

17. Justice Douglas dissented on statutory grounds, 408 U.S. at 770–74. Justice Marshall, joined by Justice Brennan, dissented on constitutional grounds. 408 U.S. at 774–85.

18. Fiallo v. Bell, 430 U.S. 787 (1977).

19. 430 U.S. 787, at 793 n. 4 (1977).

20. Trimble v. Gordon, 430 U.S. 762 (1977).

1. 169 U.S. 649 (1898).

immigrants are not, and never become, United States citizens.

The other means of obtaining citizenship is through naturalization.

Article I, Section 8, Clause 4, gives Congress the power to "establish an uniform Rule of Naturalization. . . . " Like the power of admission, this power seems to be virtually unchecked by the due process clause of the fifth amendment and other constitutional restrictions, though once naturalization is conferred, due process and other restrictions limit Congress' power to involuntarily expatriate a citizen, as discussed in the next subsection. As the Supreme Court stated in *United States v. Macintosh:* [2]

> Naturalization is a privilege, to be given, qualified or withheld as Congress may determine, and which the alien may claim as of right only upon compliance with the terms which Congress imposes.[3]

Throughout the years Congress has by statute imposed various qualifications, such as those based on race and beliefs. In 1790 only a "free white person" was eligible for naturalization pursuant to an act of the First Congress.[4] It was not until after the Civil War that those of "African" birth or descent were eligible to be naturalized.[5] In 1882, Congress excluded Orientals.[6] Belief in doctrines such as anarchy or belief in or advocacy of the overthrow by force or violence of the Government of the United States made one ineligible as of 1903.[7]

In the next subsection we consider the main Supreme Court cases dealing with the involuntary expatriation of naturalized citizens. In this section it is important to note that Congress' power over naturalization differs when the person who is naturalized becomes so while in this country. The first sentence of the first clause of the fourteenth amendment provides: "All persons born or naturalized in the United States and subject to the jurisdiction thereof, are citizens of the United States and of the State wherein they reside." The purpose of this sentence was "to make citizenship of Negroes permanent and secure" and not subject to loss by any statutory change,[8] but this sentence of the fourteenth amendment "has not touched the acquisition of citizenship by being born abroad of American parents; and has left that subject to be regulated, as it had always been, by Congress, in the exercise of the power conferred by the Constitution to establish an uniform rule of naturalization." [9] Thus, as to persons naturalized in the United States, Congress may only establish conditions precedent to naturalization.[10] But if the person has been naturalized abroad—as is one who has the benefit of a federal statute granting United States citizenship by virtue of having been born abroad to parents, one of whom is an American citizen—Congress may also impose conditions subsequent. In *Rogers v. Bellei,*[11] also discussed in the subsection below, the majority noted:

> The central fact, in our weighing of the plaintiff's claim to continuing and therefore current United States citizenship, is that he was born abroad. He was not born in the United States. He was not naturalized in the United States. And he has not been subject to the jurisdiction of the United States. All this being so, it seems indisputable that the first sentence of the Fourteenth Amendment has no application . . . . He simply is not a Fourteenth-Amendment-first-sentence citizen.[12]

---

2. 283 U.S. 605 (1931).

3. Id. at 615.

4. Act of Mar. 26, 1790, 1 Stat. 103 (1790).

5. Act of July 14, 1870, § 7, 16 Stat. 254, 256 (1870).

6. Act of May 6, 1882, § 1, 22 Stat. 58 (1882). See Toyota v. United States, 268 U.S. 402 (1925); Kharaiti Ram Samras v. United States, 125 F.2d 879 (9th Cir. 1942), cert. denied 317 U.S. 634.

7. Act of March 3, 1903, 32 Stat. 1213 (1903). The constitutionality of this act was upheld in United States

ex rel. Turner v. Williams, 194 U.S. 279 (1904). Aliens now excludable are listed in 8 U.S.C.A. § 1182.

8. Afroyim v. Rusk, 387 U.S. 253, 263, 268 (1967); H. Flack, Adoption of the Fourteenth Amendment 88–94 (1908).

9. United States v. Wong Kim Ark, 169 U.S. 649, 688 (1898).

10. Schneider v. Rusk, 377 U.S. 163 (1964).

11. 401 U.S. 815 (1971).

12. Id. at 827.

The restriction on Congress' power to take away citizenship conferred by the use of conditions subsequent over such persons is not governed by the specific guarantees of the first sentence of the fourteenth amendment but rather by the more generalized restrictions of the due process clause and other constitutional safeguards. It is to this power of involuntary expatriation we now turn.

III. VOLUNTARY AND INVOLUNTARY EXPATRIATION

A. Voluntary Expatriation

Early in our history Justice Story for the Court argued that the "general doctrine is, that no persons can, by any act of their own, without the consent of the government, put off their allegiance, and become aliens." [1] But now it is agreed that an American citizen may voluntarily relinquish, repudiate, or renounce his or her citizenship.[2] "Voluntary" in this sense is used literally: a free giving up of a known right.

Sometimes it is not clear whether a U.S. citizen had earlier relinquished his or her citizenship voluntarily. The leading case on the constitutional power of Congress to prescribe rules of evidence and burdens of proof on this question is *Vance v. Terrazas*,[3] where the Court construed and ruled on the constitutionality of various sections of the Immigration and Nationality Act. One section of that Act provides: "a person who is a national of the United States . . . shall lose his nationality by . . . taking an oath or making an affirmation or other formal declaration of allegiance to a foreign

state . . . ." [4] The party claiming such loss of U.S. citizenship must "establish such claim by a preponderance of the evidence," and the voluntary nature of the expatriating conduct is rebuttably presumed.[5] In *Vance* the United States claimed that Laurence Terrazas, a dual United States and Mexican citizen by birth, had lost his American citizenship at age 22 when in his application for a certificate of Mexican nationality—swore allegiance to Mexico and "expressly renounced" his "submission, obedience, and loyalty to any foreign government, especially to that of the United States of America. . . ." [6]

The Court first held that the mere taking of an oath of allegiance to a foreign power or other expatriating acts as defined by Congress do not per se amount to a loss of citizenship. Congress may not simply specify those acts which cause a renunciation of citizenship. The Government therefore must prove not only the voluntary commission of an expatriating act specified in the statute but also the citizen's specific intent to renounce U.S. citizenship. "In the last analysis, expatriation depends on the will of the citizen rather than on the will of Congress and the assessment of his conduct." [7]

However, it is constitutional for Congress to provide, by statute, evidentiary rules to govern what the Government must prove, pursuant to Congress' traditional powers to establish rules of evidence and standards of proof in federal courts. In *Vance* the Court held that the particular evidentiary standards which Congress had prescribed to determine expatriation violated neither the due process nor citizenship clauses of the four-

---

1. Shanks v. Dupont, 28 U.S. (3 Pet.) 242, 246 (1830); Inglis v. Trustees of Sailor's Snug Harbour, 28 U.S. (3 Pet.) 99 (1830); cf. Talbot v. Janson, 3 U.S. (3 Dall.) 133, 153–54 (1795) (opinion of Paterson, J.); id. at 161–66 (opinion of Iredell, J.); See also 4 Annals of Cong. 1005, 1027–1030 (1794) (view of some Congressmen also accepting this doctrine of perpetual allegiance); 7 Annals of Cong. 349 et seq. (1797) (same); 31 Annals of Cong. 495 (1817) (introduction of bill to allow for voluntary repudiation of citizenship).

2. Perkins v. Elg, 307 U.S. 325, 334 (1939); Kennedy v. Mendoza-Martinez, 372 U.S. 144, 159 n. 11

(1963); Perez v. Brownell, 356 U.S. 44, 66 (1958) (Warren, C. J., dissenting). See also 8 U.S.C.A. §§ 1482, 1483.

3. 444 U.S. 252 (1980).

4. 8 U.S.C.A. § 1481(a)(2).

5. 8 U.S.C.A. § 1481(c).

6. 444 U.S. at 256–58.

7. 444 U.S. at 262, relying on Afroyim v. Rusk, 387 U.S. 253 (1967). Accord, 42 Op.Atty.Gen. 397 (1969).

teenth amendment. The statute in question provided that the party claiming voluntary expatriation must prove one of the expatriating acts by a preponderance of the evidence. If proved, it is presumed to have been committed voluntarily, but this presumption of voluntariness could be rebutted, also by a preponderance of the evidence. In addition the party claiming expatriation must also prove, also by a preponderance of the evidence (and without the benefit of any presumption), that the act had been performed with the specific intent to relinquish American citizenship.[8] Although this statutory rule of evidence rule reversed a previous Supreme Court decision,[9] the previous case had not been based on the Constitution.

B. Involuntary Expatriation of One Born or Naturalized in the United States

More difficult is the question of involuntary expatriation; that is, does Congress have the power to take away someone's citizenship by providing that the doing of a certain act forfeits citizenship or implies its repudiation? A brief history of the case law is necessary to answer this question and illuminate the various distinctions.

In *Perez v. Brownell*[10] a 5–4 majority of the Supreme Court upheld the constitutionality of a federal statute which deprived the plaintiff, a national of the United States by birth, of his American citizenship for voting in a Mexican political election. Justice Frankfurter for the bare majority reviewed the earlier case law and concluded that the statute was within Congress' foreign affairs

power. The statute was upheld because there was a "rational nexus" between the withdrawal of citizenship and the regulation of foreign affairs.[11] In a footnote Frankfurter dismissed in one sentence the argument that the fourteenth amendment restricted Congressional power.[12] He declined to decide whether it was constitutional for Congress to strip away citizenship of a person who remains outside of the United States to avoid military service.[13] Chief Justice Warren and Justices Black and Douglas dissented on broad constitutional grounds,[14] and Justice Whittaker also dissented, though on narrower constitutional grounds, for he agreed with the "major premise" of the majority.[15]

The same day that the Court decided *Perez* it decided *Trop v. Dulles*.[16] A fragmented Court, with no majority opinion, found unconstitutional on various grounds a federal statute providing that a citizen loses "his nationality" if he deserts the United States military or naval forces in time of war provided that he is convicted for that offense by court martial and as a result "is dismissed or dishonorably discharged from the service." Chief Justice Warren, again joined by Justices Black and Douglas, and also Justice Whittaker adhered to their views in their *Perez* dissents and in addition found that the statute in question violated the eighth amendment because it was penal and "cruel and unusual."[17] Justice Black, joined by Douglas, also wrote a separate opinion arguing that even if citizenship could be involuntarily divested, the authority to do so could

8. But see, Woodby v. INS, 385 U.S. 276, 285–86 (1966) (clear and convincing standard in deportation proceedings); Schneiderman v. United States, 320 U.S. 118, 159 (1943) (clear and convincing standard in denaturalization proceedings).

9. The statutory rule of evidence upheld in *Vance* reversed a previous Supreme Court decision, Nishikawa v. Dulles, 356 U.S. 129 (1958) (requiring Government to prove voluntary expatriating act by clear and convincing evidence, without any benefit of a presumption), but that previous case had not been based on the Constitution.

In *Vance* Marshall, J. and Stevens, J., each concurring in part, and Brennan, J., joined in part by Stewart, J., dissenting, believed that a citizen should not lose his

citizenship unless there was clear and convincing evidence that he so intended.

10. 356 U.S. 44 (1958).

11. Id. at 58.

12. Id. at 58 n. 3.

13. Id. at 62.

14. Id. at 62 (Warren, C. J., dissenting, joined by Black and Douglas, JJ.); Id. at 79 (Douglas, J., dissenting, joined by Black, J.).

15. Id. at 84 (Memorandum of Whittaker, J.).

16. 356 U.S. 86 (1958).

17. Id. at 87–104.

not be placed in the hands of the military.[18] And Justice Brennan also concurred, though still agreeing with the majority he had joined in *Perez*.[19] Justices Frankfurter, Burton, Clark, and Harlan all dissented.[20]

Five years later a majority of the Court answered the question reserved in *Perez* and held that Congress could not constitutionally strip someone of his citizenship because he remained outside the jurisdiction of the United States in time of war or national emergency to avoid military service.[21] Justice Goldberg was now on the Court and he wrote the opinion for the 5 to 4 majority. *Perez* was distinguished, and Justice Brennan who joined the majority, stated in a concurring opinion that the "instant cases do not require me to resolve some felt doubts of the correctness of *Perez*, which I joined."[22] A year later, in a short opinion, Justice Douglas for the majoirty struck a federal statute which sought to divest citizenship from a German born woman who came to this country as a child and acquired derivative American citizenship on the grounds that a naturalized citizen (with certain exceptions not applicable here) loses her citizenship by continuous residence for three years in the country of origin.[23] Justice Douglas noted, in an understatement, that the "[v]iews of the Justices have varied when it comes to the problem of expatriation."[24]

Finally, in 1967 a 5 to 4 majority of the Supreme Court in *Afroyim v. Rusk*[25] explicitly overruled the already eroded doctrine of *Perez*. Justice Black now wrote for the ma-

jority. He upheld the citizenship claims of a naturalized American of Polish birth who, nearly a quarter of a century after naturalization, went to Israel and voted in an Israeli legislative election in 1951.

First he argued Congress has no general power, express or implied, to strip people of their citizenship without their assent. The power to take away citizenship cannot be sustained as an implied attribute of sovereignty possessed by all nations: "Other nations are governed by their own constitutions, if any, and we can draw no support from theirs."[26]

Then, unlike the other majority opinions in the previous cases, Justice Black specifically relied on the first sentence of the first section of the fourteenth amendment: "All persons born or naturalized in the United States . . . are citizens of the United States . . . ."

Black explained that this sentence granted permanence and security of citizenship in order to protect the freed black slaves. Just a few years before the ratification of the fourteenth amendment, the *Dred Scott v. Sanford*[27] case had denied any power of Congress to grant citizenship to blacks. The Civil Rights Act of 1866[28] had attempted to confer citizenship on all persons born or naturalized in the United States, but the Senate sponsors of the soon to be enacted fourteenth amendment were afraid that this statutory right might later be taken away by another Congress. "[I]t was to provide an insuperable obstacle against every governmental effort to strip Negroes of their new-

---

18. Id. at 104–05.

19. Id. at 105–14.

20. Id. at 114–28.

21. Kennedy v. Mendoza-Martinez, 372 U.S. 144 (1963).

22. 372 U.S. at 187 (Brennan, J., concurring).

23. Schneider v. Rusk, 377 U.S. 163 (1964).

24. Id. at 166.

25. 387 U.S. 253 (1967), overruling Perez v. Brownell, 356 U.S. 44 (1958).

26. Id. at 257. Justice Black also relied on some frequently quoted dictum by Chief Justice Marshall in

Osborn v. Bank of United States, 22 U.S. (9 Wheat.) 738, 827 (1824):

"[The naturalized citizen] becomes a member of the society, possessing all the rights of a native citizen, and standing, in the view of the constitution, on the footing of a native. The constitution does not authorize Congress to enlarge or abridge those rights. The simple power of the national Legislature, is to prescribe a uniform rule of naturalization, and the exercise of this power exhausts it, so far as respects the individual."

See 387 U.S. at 261.

27. 60 U.S. (19 How.) 393 (1857).

28. 14 Stat. 27.

ly acquired citizenship that the first clause was added to the Fourteenth Amendment." [29] This purpose "would be frustrated by holding that the Government can rob a citizen of his citizenship without his consent by simply proceeding to act under an implied general power to regulate foreign affairs or some other power generally granted." [30]

The general state of the law now appears to be as follows. If a person is born in the United States and subject to the jurisdiction thereof, he or she is a citizen by virtue of the first sentence of the first section of the fourteenth amendment. Such citizenship cannot be taken away. If a person is naturalized in the United States and subject to the jurisdiction thereof, the same clause confers the same rights. However, Congress may confer preconditions to achieving such naturalization. Once those preconditions are filled, the recipient is within the protection of the fourteenth amendment and the full force of the *Afroyim* rule applies, although, as Justice Black specifically noted in *Afroyim*, "naturalization unlawfully procured can be set aside." [31] Thus, if the person engages in fraud or misrepresentation in the naturalization process, later discovery will annul the grant.[32]

The only exception to this irrevocable grant of citizenship to one born or properly naturalized in the United States and subject to the jurisdiction thereof is one suggested by some justices in the older cases, arguing that Congress, by statute, may require a person to reject one's citizenship for an act totally opposed to that status, such as service in the armed forces of a nation at war with the United States.[33] However, this position was definitely rejected in *Vance v.*

Terrazas [34] where the Court stated that the fourteenth amendment constitutional definition of citizenship "cannot coexist with a congressional power to specify acts that work a renunciation of citizenship even absent an intent to renounce. In the last analysis, expatriation depends on the will of the citizen rather than on the will of Congress and its assessment of his conduct." [35]

C. Involuntary Expatriation of One Born and Naturalized Outside of the United States

Thus far we have only considered the involuntary expatriation of one born or naturalized in the United States. The case of one born outside of the United States and naturalized outside of the United States is subject to different considerations. The leading case in this area is *Rogers v. Bellei.*[36] Bellei was born abroad to parents, one of whom was an American citizen. By statute he, therefore, acquired United States citizenship. But the statute also imposed a condition subsequent: One who so acquires United States citizenship loses it unless he resides in this country continuously for five years between the ages of 14 and 28. A 5 to 4 majority upheld the constitutionality of this statute on the grounds that Congress has the power to impose the condition of subsequent residence in this country on one who does not come within the fourteenth amendment's definition of citizens as those "born or naturalized in the United States . . . ." These conditions subsequent are only subject to the general requirements of due process and other such restrictions. To determine, in a *Bellei* type of problem whether the condition subsequent causing

---

29. 387 U.S. at 262–63 (footnote omitted).

30. 387 U.S. at 263.

31. Id. at 267 n. 23. Cf. Luria v. United States, 231 U.S. 9 (1913).

32. 8 U.S.C.A. § 1451(a); e.g., Costello v. United States, 365 U.S. 265 (1961). See also, Fedorenko v. United States, 449 U.S. 490 (after the Government proves that a naturalized citizen has procured citizenship illegally or by wilful misrepresentation, the federal courts lack equitable discretion to refrain from entering a judgment of naturalization).

33. See, e.g., Warren, C. J., dissenting (joined by Black and Douglas, JJ.), in Perez v. Brownell, 356 U.S. 44, 68 (1958): "Any action by which he manifests allegiance to a foreign state may be so inconsistent with the retention of citizenship as to result in loss of that status." (footnote omitted).

34. 444 U.S. 252 (1980), on remand 494 F.Supp. 1017.

35. 444 U.S. at 262.

36. 401 U.S. 815 (1971).

the involuntary expatriation is valid, one must use the *Perez* [37] line of cases concerning due process which, it would appear, are still good law as to a *Bellei* issue.

IV. DEPORTATION

Congress has the power to regulate the behavior of aliens in this country.[1] To enforce these restrictions, Congress may deport aliens for a wide variety of activities Congress deems harmful.[2] In interpreting the constitutional restraints on this substantive power, the Court has exercised very little review. So long "as aliens fail to obtain and maintain citizenship by naturalization, they remain subject to the plenary power of Congress to expel them under the sovereign right to determine what noncitizens shall be permitted to remain within our borders."[3]

However, procedural guarantees do exist for the alien to be deported, in sharp contrast to the absence of similar procedures for the alien seeking admission.[4] The resident alien has a right to procedural due process, including a hearing prior to deportation;[5] at this hearing it is determined if he is an alien and if the conditions for continuing residence have been met. However, the congressional delegation of discretion to the Attorney General to detain aliens without

bail pending deportation hearings does not constitute an unlawful delegation nor violate the due process clause because the statute contains definite legislative standards; moreover, according to the Court, there is no denial of due process in the detention of alien communists without bail in such cases where there is reasonable cause to believe that their release on bail would endanger the safety and welfare of the United States.[6] Finally, the distinction between the rights of deportees versus the rights of aliens seeking admission should not be overdrawn, for the deportees' substantive rights and rights of judicial review are narrow, and the Immigration and Naturalization Service's discretion not to seek deportation is narrowly exercised even in cases of extreme hardship.[7]

Under the statutory scheme, which has been upheld as constitutional, if a permanent resident alien leaves this country's borders for an "innocent, casual, and brief excursion," then the government—if it desires to determine his or her admissibility and deny him or her entry back into the United States, must proceed by way of a deportation hearing rather than an exclusion hearing.[8] The deportation hearing is the usual way that the government must use to proceed against an alien already physically within this coun-

---

37. See Section III, B, supra.

1. See, e.g., Justice Rehnquist dissenting in Hampton v. Mow Sun Wong, 426 U.S. 88, 117 (1977).

2. 8 U.S.C.A. § 1251.

3. Carlson v. Landon, 342 U.S. 524, 534 (1952) (footnote omitted). See also Ludecke v. Watkins, 335 U.S. 160 (1948) (Congressional power to deport enemy alien after cessation of actual hostilities); Harisiades v. Shaughnessy, 342 U.S. 580 (1952) (Congressional power to deport a legally resident alien because of membership in the Communist Party, which membership terminated before the enactment of the Alien Registration Act of 1940. See also Galvan v. Press, 347 U.S. 522 (1954); Rowoldt v. Perfetto, 355 U.S. 115 (1957); Berenyi v. District Director, 385 U.S. 630 (1967).

4. See Section II, A of this Chapter.

5. See 8 U.S.C.A. § 1252(b); Ng Fung Ho v. White, 259 U.S. 276, 281 (1922) (Habeas corpus proceeding; Court holds that Ng Fung Ho entitled to trial de novo and an independent judicial judgment on the issue of citizenship); see also Kwong Hai Chew v. Colding, 344 U.S. 590 (1953); Wong Yang Sung v. McGrath, 339 U.S. 33, 48–51 (1950); Heikkila v. Barber, 345 U.S. 229

(1953); See generally, H. Hart & H. Wechsler's, The Federal Courts and the Federal System 351–354 nn. 40–44 (2d ed. 1973).

The Supreme Court has held, as a matter of statutory interpretation, that 8 U.S.C.A. § 1105a(a)(5) requires that persons who claim to be U.S. citizens, and who seek review of a deportation order, be given a de novo judicial review of the order whenever there is any "genuine issue of material fact" regarding the nationality claim. Agosto v. INS, 436 U.S. 748 (1978).

6. Carlson v. Landon, 342 U.S. 524 (1952). For a discussion of the extent to which an administrator may combine in himself the functions of a prosecutor and judge in the context of deportation cases, see Rotunda, The Combination of Functions in Administrative Actions: An Examination of European Alternatives, 40 Ford.L.Rev. 101, 102–103 (1971).

7. See, e.g., Dunn v. INS, 419 U.S. 919 (1974) (Stewart, J., joined by Douglas, J., dissenting from denial of certiorari); Bufalino v. Holland, 277 F.2d 270 (3d Cir.), cert. denied 364 U.S. 863 (1960).

8. Rosenberg v. Fleuti, 374 U.S. 449, 462 (1963).

try. The exclusion hearing is, in contrast, the usual method of proceeding against an alien who is physically outside of the United States and seeking entry.[9] The distinction, as noted above, is not only in name, for a deportation hearing carries with it important procedural and substantive rights that do not exist for exclusion hearings.[10]

If the permanent resident alien's purpose for leaving the United States is in order to "accomplish some object which is itself contrary to some policy reflected in our immigration laws, it would appear that the interruption of residence thereby occurring would properly be regarded as meaning-ful,"[11] requiring the alien to submit to an exclusion hearing. Therefore when a permanent resident alien sought to return to this country after a brief visit to Mexico, and the government charged that the purpose of her trip had been to smuggle aliens for gain, then her departure was "meaningfully interruptive" of her residence here, and under the statute, she was subject to an exclusion hearing.[12] Even though a *resident* alien returning from a brief trip out of United States has a right to due process, it is not the same due process rights to which a *continuously present* resident alien is entitled.[13]

9. Landon v. Plasencia, 103 S.Ct. 321, 325 (1982).

10. See text at nn. 4–7, supra. See generally, Maldonado-Sandoval v. INS, 518 F.2d 278, 280 n. 3 (9th Cir. 1975); Landon v. Plasencia, 103 S.Ct. 321, 325–26 (1982).

11. Rosenberg v. Fleuti, 374 U.S. 449, 462 (1963).

12. Landon v. Plasencia, 103 S.Ct. 321, 328 (1982).

13. Compare Kwong Hai Chew v. United States, 344 U.S. 590, 596 (1953), with Landon v. Plasencia, 103 S.Ct. 321, 328 (1982).

*

APPENDICES

APPENDIX A

THE JUSTICES OF THE SUPREME COURT *

Prepared by JOHN J. COUND

Professor of Law, University of Minnesota

The data which follow, summarizing the prior public careers of the many individuals who have served upon the Supreme Court of the United States, are not presented with any notion that they did presage or now explain their judicial performance or constitutional philosophy. The experience which the justices have at any one time brought to bear upon the issues before the Court, however, seem worthy of interest, and may serve as a consideration in assessing charges that the Court has in particular cases rendered "ivory tower" decisions, unaware or heedless of "the realities."

Two conclusions are manifest. First, the diversity of distinguished experience which the bench of the Court has at all times reflected, always among its members and frequently in a single justice, is startling. William Howard Taft is unique, but surely few Americans have lived lives of diversified public service so rich as John Jay, Levi Woodbury, Lucius Q. C. Lamar, Charles Evans Hughes and Fred M. Vinson. Second, a broad background in public service has not assured prominence upon the Court, nor has its absence precluded it. Gabriel Duvall, with prior executive, legislative and judicial experience, was forgotten in the first edition of the *Dictionary of American Biography.* Samuel F. Miller and Joseph P. Bradley, with no prior public offices, surely stand among the front rank of the justices. (The interested student will find stimulation in Frankfurter, *The Supreme Court in the Mirror of Justice,* 105 U.Pa.L.Rev. 781 (1957), which treats particularly of the relevance of prior judicial office).

---

* Adapted, with permission, from W. Lockhart, Y. Kamisar, and J. Choper, Constitutional Law: Cases—Comments—Questions, appendix A (4th ed. 1975), with the addition of information relating to the more recent apointments and retirements.

The accompanying Table of Justices has been planned so that the composition of the Court at any time can be readily ascertained.

1789 1790 1791 1793 1795 1796 1798 1799 1801 1804 1806 1807 1811 1823 1826 1829 1830 1835 1836 1837 1841 1845 1846 1851 1853 1858 1862 1863 1864 1865 1867 1870 1872 1874 1877 1880 1881 1882 1888 1889

Jay — Rutledge, J. — Johnson, T. — Paterson — Rutledge, J. — Ellsworth — Marshall, J. — Taney — Chase, Salmon — Waite — Fuller

Cushing — Livingston — Thompson — Story — Nelson — Woodbury — Curtis — Clifford — Hunt — Blatchford — Gray

Wilson — Washington — Baldwin — Grier — Strong — Woods — Lamar, L.

Blair — Chase, Samuel — Duval — Barbour — Daniel — Miller

Iredell — Moore — Johnson, W. — Wayne — Bradley

Todd — Trimble — McLean — Swayne — Matthews — Brewer

Catron — McKinley — Campbell — Davis — Field — Harlan

* Catron died in 1865, Wayne in 1867; their positions were abolished by Congress to prevent their being filled by President Johnson; a new position was created in 1869, which traditionally has been regarded as a re-creation of Wayne's seat.

Years (top and bottom axis): 1890, 1892, 1893, 1894, 1895, 1898, 1902, 1903, 1906, 1909, 1910, 1912, 1914, 1916, 1921, 1922, 1923, 1925, 1930, 1932, 1937, 1938, 1939, 1940, 1941, 1943, 1945, 1946, 1949, 1953, 1955, 1956, 1957, 1958, 1962, 1965, 1966, 1967, 1968, 1969, 1970, 1972, 1975, 1976, 1977, 1978, 1979, 1980, 1981, 1982, 1983

[C7563]

Justices (by seat line):

McKenna — Stone — ** Jackson, R. — Harlan — Rehnquist

Pitney — Sanford — Roberts — Burton — Stewart — O'Connor

Hughes — Clarke — Sutherland — Reed — Whittaker — White, B.

Shiras — Day — Butler — Murphy — Clark — Marshall, T.

Brown — Moody — Lamar, J. — Brandeis — Douglas — Stevens

Jackson, H. — Peckham — Lurton — McReynolds — Byrnes — Rutledge — Minton — Brennan

Holmes — Cardozo — Frankfurter — Goldberg — Fortas — Blackmun

White, E. — ** Van Devanter — Black — Powell

White, E. — Taft — Hughes — Stone — Vinson — Warren — Burger

** Fuller died in 1910, and White was named Chief Justice. Hughes resigned in 1941, and Stone was named Chief Justice.

In the data, the first dates in parentheses are those of birth and death; these are followed by the name of the appointing President, and the dates of service on the Court. The state in which the justice was residing when appointed and his political affiliation at that time are then given. In detailing prior careers, I have followed chronological order, with two exceptions: I have listed first that a justice was a signer of the Declaration of Independence or the Federal Constitution, and I have indicated state legislative experience only once for each justice. I have not distinguished between different bodies in the state legislature, and I have omitted service in the Continental Congresses. Private practice, except where deemed especially significant, and law teaching have been omitted, except where the justice was primarily engaged therein upon his or her appointment. (Blackmun, Burger, Douglas, Fortas, Holmes, Hughes, L. Q. C. Lamar, Lurton, McReynolds, Murphy, Roberts, W. Rutledge, Stevens, Stone and Van Devanter, in addition to Taft and Frankfurter, had all taught before going on the Court; Story, Strong and Wilson taught while on the Court or after leaving it). The activity in which a justice was engaged upon appointment has been italicized. Figures in parentheses indicate years of service in the position. In only a few cases, a justice's extra-Court or post-Court activity has been indicated, or some other note made. An asterisk designates the Chief Justices.

For detailed information on the individuals who have served as members of the Supreme Court, see L. Friedman & F. Israel, eds., *The Justices of the United States Supreme Court 1789–1969: Their Lives and Major Opinions* (Chelsea House, 1969), and the bibliographical references collected therein.

(This material has been compiled from a great number of sources, but special acknowledgment must be made to the *Dictionary of American Biography* (Charles Scribner's Sons), the A. N. Marquis Company works, and Ewing, *The Judges of the Supreme Court, 1789–1937* (University of Minnesota Press, 1938).)

BALDWIN, HENRY (1780–1844; Jackson, 1830–1844). Pa. Dem.—U.S., House of Representatives (5). *Private practice.*

BARBOUR, PHILIP P. (1783–1841; Jackson, 1836–1841). Va. Dem.— Va., Legislature (2). U.S., House of Representatives (14). Va., Judge, General Court (2); President, State Constitutional Convention, 1829–30. *U.S., Judge, District Court (5).*

BLACK, HUGO L. (1886–1971; F. D. Roosevelt, 1937–1971). Ala. Dem.—Captain, Field Artillery, World War I. Ala., Judge, Police Court (1); County Solicitor (2). *U.S., Senate (10).*

BLACKMUN, HARRY A. (1908– ——; Nixon, 1970– ——). Minn. Rep.— Resident Counsel, Mayo Clinic, (10). *U.S., Judge, Court of Appeals (11).*

BLAIR, JOHN (1732–1800; Washington, 1789–1796). Va. Fed.—Signer, U.S. Constitution, 1787. Va., Legislature (9); Judge and Chief Justice, General Court (2), *Court of Appeals (9).* His opinion in *Commonwealth v. Caton,* 4 Call 5, 20 (Va.1782), is one of the earliest expressions of the doctrine of judicial review.

BLATCHFORD, SAMUEL (1820–1893; Arthur, 1882–1893). N.Y. Rep.—U.S., Judge, District Court (5); *Circuit Court (10).*

BRADLEY, JOSEPH P. (1803–1892; Grant, 1870–1892). N.J. Rep.—Actuary. *Private practice.*

BRANDEIS, LOUIS D. (1856–1941; Wilson, 1916–1939). Mass. Dem.— *Private practice.* Counsel, variously for the government, for industry, and "for the people", in numerous administrative and judicial proceedings, both state and federal.

BRENNAN, WILLIAM J. (1906– ——; Eisenhower, 1956– ——). N.J. Dem.—U.S. Army, World War II. N.J., Judge, Superior Court (1); Appellate Division (2); *Supreme Court (4).*

BREWER, DAVID J. (1837–1910; B. Harrison, 1889–1910). Kans. Rep.—Kans., Judge, County Criminal and Probate Court (1), District Court (4); County Attorney (1); Judge, Supreme Court (14), *U.S., Judge, Circuit Court (5).*

BROWN, HENRY B. (1836–1913; B. Harrison, 1890–1906). Mich. Rep.—U.S., Assistant U.S. Attorney (5). Mich., Judge, Circuit Court (1). *U.S., Judge, District Court (15).*

＊ BURGER, WARREN E. (1907– ——; Nixon, 1969– ——). Va. Rep.—U.S., Assistant Attorney General, Civil Division (3), *Judge, Court of Appeals (13).*

BURTON, HAROLD H. (1888–1964; Truman, 1945–1958). Ohio Rep.—Capt., U.S.A., World War I. Ohio, Legislature (2). Mayor, Cleveland, O. (5). *U.S., Senate (4).*

BUTLER, PIERCE (1866–1939; Harding, 1922–1939). Minn. Dem.—Minn., County Attorney (4). *Private practice.*

BYRNES, JAMES F. (1879–1972; F. D. Roosevelt, 1941–1942). S.C. Dem.—S.C., Solicitor, Circuit Court (2). U.S., House of Representatives (14); *Senate (12).* Resigned from the Court to become U.S. Director of Economic Stabilization.

CAMPBELL, JOHN A. (1811–1889; Pierce, 1853–1861). Ala. Dem.—*Private practice.* After his resignation, he became Assistant Secretary of War, C.S.A.

CARDOZO, BENJAMIN N. (1870–1938; Hoover, 1932–1938). N.Y. Dem.—N.Y., Judge, Supreme Court (6 weeks); Associate Judge and *Chief Judge, Court of Appeals (18).*

CATRON, JOHN (1778–1865; Van Buren, 1837–1865). Tenn. Dem.—Tenn., Judge and Chief Justice, Supreme Court of Errors and Appeals (10). *Private practice.*

＊ CHASE, SALMON P. (1808–1873; Lincoln, 1864–1873). Ohio Rep.—U.S., Senate (6). Ohio, Governor (4). *U.S., Secretary of the Treasury (3).*

CHASE, SAMUEL (1741–1811; Washington, 1796–1811). Md. Fed.—Signer, U.S., Declaration of Independence, 1776. Md., Legislature (20); Chief Judge, Court of Oyer and Terminer (2), *General Court (5).* Impeached and acquitted, 1804–05.

CLARK, TOM C. (1899–1977; Truman, 1949–1967). Tex. Dem.—U.S. Army, World War I. Tex., Civil District Attorney (5). U.S., Assistant Attorney General (2), *Attorney General (4).*

CLARKE, JOHN H. (1857–1945; Wilson, 1916–1922). Ohio Dem.—*U.S., Judge, District Court (2).*

CLIFFORD, NATHAN (1803–1881; Buchanan, 1858–1881). Me. Dem.—Me., Legislature (4); Attorney General (4). U.S., House of Representatives (4); Attorney General (2); Minister Plenipotentiary to Mexico, 1848. *Private practice.*

CURTIS, BENJAMIN R. (1809–1874; Fillmore, 1851–1857). Mass. Whig.—Mass., Legislature (1). *Private practice.*

CUSHING, WILLIAM (1732–1810; Washington, 1789–1810). Mass. Fed.—Mass., Judge, Superior Court (3); Justice and *Chief Justice, Supreme Judicial Court (14).*

DANIEL, PETER V. (1784–1860; Van Buren, 1841–1860). Va. Dem.—Va., Legislature (3); Member, Privy Council (23). *U.S., Judge, District Court (5).*

DAVIS, DAVID (1815–1886; Lincoln, 1862–1877). Ill. Rep.—Ill., Legislature (2); *Judge, Circuit Court (14).* His resignation to become U.S. Senator upset the agreed-upon composition of the Hayes-Tilden Electoral Commission.

DAY, WILLIAM R. (1849–1923; T. Roosevelt, 1903–1922). Ohio Rep.—Ohio, Judge, Court of Common Pleas (4). U.S., Assistant Secretary of State (1), Secretary of State ($\frac{1}{2}$); Chairman, U.S. Peace Commissioners, 1898; *Judge, Circuit Court of Appeals (4).*

DOUGLAS, WILLIAM O. (1898–1980; F. D. Roosevelt, 1939–1975). Conn. Dem.—Pvt., U.S. Army, World War I. *U.S., Chairman, Securities and Exchange Commission (3).* His was the longest tenure in the history of the Court.

DUVAL(L), GABRIEL (1752–1844; Madison, 1811–1935). Md. Rep.—Declined to serve as delegate, U.S. Constitutional Convention, 1787. Md., State Council (3). U.S., House of Representatives (2). Md., Judge, General Court (6). *U.S., Comptroller of the Treasury (9).*

* ELLSWORTH, OLIVER (1745–1807; Washington, 1796–1800). Conn. Fed.—Delegate, U.S. Constitutional Convention, 1787. Conn., Legislature (2); Member, Governor's Council (4); Judge, Superior Court (5). *U.S., Senate (7).*

FIELD, STEPHEN J. (1816–1899; Lincoln, 1863–1897). Calif. Dem.—Calif., Justice, and *Chief Justice, Supreme Court (6).*

FORTAS, ABE (1910–1982; L. B. Johnson, 1965–1969). Tenn. Dem.—U.S. Government attorney and consultant (A.A.A., S.E.C., P.W.A., Dep't of Interior (9); Undersecretary of Interior (4). *Private practice in Washington, D.C.* Nominated as Chief Justice; nomination withdrawn, 1968. Resigned.

FRANKFURTER, FELIX (1882–1965; F. D. Roosevelt, 1939–1962). Mass. Independent.—U.S., Assistant U.S. Attorney (4); Law Officer, War Department, Bureau of Insular Affairs (3); Assistant to Secretary of War (1). *Professor of Law (25).*

* FULLER, MELVILLE W. (1833–1910; Cleveland, 1888–1910). Ill. Dem.—Ill., Legislature (2). *Private practice.*

GOLDBERG, ARTHUR J. (1908– ——; Kennedy, 1962–1965). Ill. Dem.—Major, U.S.A., World War II. General Counsel, USW–AFL–CIO (13). *U.S., Secretary of Labor (1).* Resigned to become Ambassador to U.N.

GRAY, HORACE (1828–1902; Arthur, 1881–1902). Mass. Rep.—*Mass., Associate Justice and Chief Justice, Supreme Judicial Court (18).*

GRIER, ROBERT O. (1794–1870; Polk, 1846–1870). Pa. Dem.—*Pa., Presiding Judge, District Court (13).*

HARLAN, JOHN M. (1833–1911; Hayes, 1877–1911). Ky. Rep.—Ky., Judge, County Court (1). Col., Union Army, 1861–63. Ky., Attorney General (4). U.S., Member, President's Louisiana Commission, 1877. *Private practice.* Grandfather of:

HARLAN, JOHN M. (1899–1971; Eisenhower, 1955–1971). N.Y. Rep.—Col., U.S.A.A.F., World War II. N.Y. Chief Counsel, State Crime Commission (2). *U.S., Judge, Court of Appeals (1).*

HOLMES, OLIVER W., JR. (1841–1935; T. Roosevelt, 1902–1932). Mass. Rep.—Lt. Col., Mass. Volunteers, Civil War. *Mass., Associate Justice, and Chief Justice, Supreme Judicial Court (20).*

* HUGHES, CHARLES E. (1862–1948; Taft, 1910–1916, and Hoover, 1930–1941). N.Y. Rep.—N.Y., Counsel, legislative committees investigating gas and insurance industries, 1905–06. U.S., Special Assistant to Attorney General for Coal Investigation, 1906. *N.Y., Governor (3).* [Between appointments to the Supreme Court: Presidential Nominee, Republican Party, 1916. U.S., Secretary of State (4). *Member, Permanent Court of Arbitration, The Hague (4). Judge, Permanent Court of International Justice (2).*] Chief Justice on second appointment.

HUNT, WARD (1810–1886; Grant, 1872–1882). N.Y. Rep.—N.Y., Legislature (2). Mayor of Utica, N.Y. (1). N.Y Associate Judge, and Chief Judge, Court of Appeals (4); *Commissioner of Appeals (4).* He did not sit from 1879 to his retirement in 1882.

IREDELL, JAMES (1750–1799; Washington, 1790–1799). N.C. Fed.— Comptroller of Customs (6), Collector of Port (2), Edenton, N.C., N.C., Judge, Superior Court ($\frac{1}{2}$); Attorney General (2); Member, Council of State, 1787; *Reviser of Statutes (3).*

JACKSON, HOWELL E. (1832–1895; B. Harrison, 1893–1895). Tenn. Dem.—Tenn., Judge, Court of Arbitration (4); Legislature (1). U.S. Senate (5); *Judge, Circuit Court of Appeals (7).*

JACKSON, ROBERT H. (1892–1954; F. D. Roosevelt, 1941–1954). N.Y. Dem.—U. S., General Counsel, Bureau of Internal Revenue (2); Assistant Attorney General (2); Solicitor General (2); *Attorney General (1).*

* JAY, JOHN (1745–1829; Washington, 1789–1795). N.Y. Fed.—N.Y., Chief Justice, Supreme Court (2). U.S., Envoy to Spain (2); Commissioner, Treaty of Paris, 1782–83; Secretary for Foreign Affairs (6). Co-author, The Federalist.

JOHNSON, THOMAS (1732–1819; Washington, 1791–1793). Md. Fed.—Md., Brigadier-General, Militia (1); Legislature (5); Governor (2); *Chief Judge, General Court (1).*

JOHNSON, WILLIAM (1771–1834; Jefferson, 1804–1834). S.C. Rep.— S.C., Legislature (4); *Judge, Court of Common Pleas (6).*

LAMAR, JOSEPH R. (1857–1916; Taft, 1910–1916). Ga. Dem.—Ga., Legislature (3); Commissioner to Codify Laws (3); Associate Justice, Supreme Court (4). *Private practice.*

LAMAR, LUCIUS Q. C. (1825–1893; Cleveland, 1888–1893). Miss. Dem.—Ga., Legislature (2). U.S., House of Representatives (4). Draftsman, Mississippi Ordinance of Secession, 1861. C.S.A., Lt. Col. (1); Commissioner to Russia (1); Judge-Advocate, III Corps, Army of No. Va. (1). U.S., House of Representatives (4); Senate (8); *Secretary of the Interior (3).*

LIVINGSTON, (HENRY) BROCKHOLST (1757–1823; Jefferson, 1806–1823). N.Y. Rep.—Lt. Col., Continental Army. *N.Y., Judge, Supreme Court (4).*

LURTON, HORACE H. (1844–1914; Taft, 1909–1914). Tenn. Dem.— Sgt. Major, C.S.A. Tenn., Chancellor (3); Associate Justice and Chief Justice, Supreme Court (7). *U.S., Judge, Circuit Court of Appeals (16).*

McKENNA, JOSEPH (1843–1926; McKinley, 1898–1925). Calif. Rep.— Calif., District Attorney (2); Legislature (2). U.S., House of Representatives (7); *Judge, Circuit Court of Appeals (5); Attorney General (1).*

McKINLEY, JOHN (1780–1852; Van Buren, 1837–1852). Ala. Dem.— Ala., Legislature (4). U.S., Senate (5); House of Representatives (2); *re-elected to Senate,* but appointed to Court before taking seat.

McLEAN, JOHN (1785–1861; Jackson, 1829–1861). Ohio Dem.—U.S., House of Representatives (4). Ohio, Judge, Supreme Court (6). U.S., Commissioner, General Land Office (1); *Postmaster-General (6)*.

McREYNOLDS, JAMES C. (1862–1946; Wilson, 1914–1941). Tenn. Dem.—U. S., Assistant Attorney General (4); *Attorney General (1)*.

*MARSHALL, JOHN (1755–1835; J. Adams, 1801–1835). Va. Fed.— Va., Legislature (7); U.S., Envoy to France (1); House of Representatives (1); *Secretary of State (1)*.

MARSHALL, THURGOOD (1908– ——; L. B. Johnson, 1967– ——). N.Y. Dem.—Counsel, Legal Defense and Educational Fund, NAACP (21). U.S., Judge, Court of Appeals (4); *Solicitor General (2)*.

MATTHEWS, STANLEY (1824–1889; Garfield, 1881–1889). Ohio Rep.—Ohio, Judge, Court of Common Pleas (2); Legislature (3). U.S., District Attorney (3). Col., Ohio Volunteers. Ohio, Judge, Superior Court (2). Counsel before Hayes-Tilden Electoral Commission, 1877. U.S., Senate (2). *Private practice.* His first appointment to the Court by Hayes in 1881 was not acted upon by the Senate.

MILLER, SAMUEL F. (1816–1890; Lincoln, 1862–1890). Iowa Rep.— Physician. *Private practice.*

MINTON, SHERMAN (1890–1965; Truman, 1949–1956). Ind. Dem.— Capt., Inf., World War I. U.S., Senate (6); *Judge, Court of Appeals (8)*.

MOODY, WILLIAM H. (1853–1917; T. Roosevelt, 1906–1910). Mass. Rep.—U.S., District Attorney (5); House of Representatives (7); Secretary of the Navy (2); *Attorney General (2)*.

MOORE, ALFRED (1755–1810; J. Adams, 1799–1804). N.C. Fed.—N.C., Col. of Militia; Legislature (2); Attorney General (9). U.S. Commissioner, Treaty with Cherokee Nation (1); *N.C., Judge, Superior Court (1)*.

MURPHY, FRANK (1893–1949; F. D. Roosevelt, 1940–1949). Mich. Dem.—Capt., Inf., World War I. U.S., Assistant U.S. Attorney (1). Mich., Judge, Recorder's Court (7). Mayor, Detroit, Mich. (3). U.S., Governor-General, and High Commissioner, P.I. (3). Mich., Governor (2). *U.S., Attorney General (1)*.

NELSON, SAMUEL (1792–1873; Tyler, 1845–1872). N.Y. Dem.—N.Y., Judge, Circuit Court (8); Associate Justice, and *Chief Justice, Supreme Court (14)*.

O'CONNOR, SANDRA DAY (1930– ——; Reagan, 1981– ——). Ariz.— Rep. Private practice & Assistant Ariz. State Atty. Gen.; Ariz. State Senate (5); Judge, Superior Court (trial court) Maricopa County, Ariz. (5); *Judge, Ariz. Appellate Court (2)*.

PATERSON, WILLIAM (1745–1806; Washington, 1793–1806). N.J. Fed.—Signer, U.S. Constitution, 1787. N.J., Legislature (2); Attorney General (7). U.S., Senate (1). *N.J., Governor (3)*. Reviser of English Pre-Revolutionary Statutes in Force in N.J.

PECKHAM, RUFUS W. (1838–1909; Cleveland, 1895–1909). N.Y. Dem.—N.Y., District Attorney (1); Justice, Supreme Court (3); *Associate Judge, Court of Appeals (9)*.

PITNEY, MAHLON (1858–1924; Taft, 1912–1922). N.J. Rep.—U.S., House of Representatives (4). N.J., Legislature (2); Associate Justice, Supreme Court (7); Chancellor (4).

POWELL, LEWIS F. (1907– ——; Nixon, 1972– ——). Va. Dem.—Col., U.S.A.A.F., World War II. *Private practice.*

REED, STANLEY F. (1884–1980; F. D. Roosevelt, 1938–1957). Ky. Dem.—Ky., Legislature (4). 1st Lt., U.S.A., World War I. U.S., General Counsel, Federal Farm Board (3); General Counsel, Reconstruction Finance Corporation (3); *Solicitor General (3).*

REHNQUIST, WILLIAM H. (1924– ——; Nixon, 1972– ——). Ariz. Rep.—U.S.A.F., World War II. Law Clerk, Justice Jackson, 1952–53. *U.S., Assistant Attorney General (3).*

ROBERTS, OWEN J. (1875–1955; Hoover, 1930–1945). Pa. Rep.—Pa., Assistant District Attorney (3). U.S., Special Deputy Attorney General in Espionage Act Cases, World War I; Special Prosecutor, Oil Cases, 1924. *Private practice.*

* RUTLEDGE, JOHN (1739–1800; Washington, 1789–1791, and Washington, 1795). S.C. Fed.—Signer, U.S. Constitution, 1787. S.C., Legislature (18); Attorney General (1); President and Governor (6); *Chancellor (7).* [Between appointments to the Supreme Court: *S.C., Chief Justice, Court of Common Pleas and Sessions (4).*] He did not sit under his first appointment; he sat with a recess appointment as Chief Justice, but his regular appointment was rejected by the Senate.

RUTLEDGE, WILEY B. (1894–1949; F. D. Roosevelt, 1943–1949). Iowa Dem.—Mo., then Iowa, Member, National Conference of Commissioners on Uniform State Laws (10). *U.S., Judge, Court of Appeals (4).*

SANFORD, EDWARD T. (1865–1930; Harding, 1923–1930). Tenn. Rep.—U.S., Assistant Attorney General (1); *Judge, District Court (15).*

SHIRAS, GEORGE (1832–1924; B. Harrison, 1892–1903). Pa. Rep. *Private practice.*

STEWART, POTTER (1915– ——; Eisenhower, 1958–1981). Ohio Rep.—Lt., U.S.N.R., World War II. *U.S., Judge, Court of Appeals (4).*

STEVENS, JOHN PAUL (1920– ——; Ford, 1975– ——). Ill. Rep.—U.S. Navy, 1942–1945. Law Clerk, Justice Wiley Rutledge, 1947–1948. Associate Counsel, House Judiciary Committee's Subcommittee on Study of Monopoly Power, 1951–52; member of Attorney General's National Committee to Study Antitrust Laws, 1953–1955; Counsel to special commission to investigate allegations of misconduct on Illinois Supreme Court, 1969. *U.S. Court of Appeals (5).*

* STONE, HARLAN F. (1872–1946; Coolidge, later F. D. Roosevelt, 1925–1946). N.Y. Rep.—*U.S., Attorney General (1).* Chief Justice, 1941–1946.

STORY, JOSEPH (1779–1845; Madison, 1811–1845). Mass. Rep.—Mass., Legislature (5). U.S., House of Representatives (2). *Private practice.*

STRONG, WILLIAM (1808–1895; Grant, 1870–1880). Pa. Rep.—U.S., House of Representatives (4). Pa., Justice, Supreme Court (11). *Private practice.*

SUTHERLAND, GEORGE (1862–1942; Harding, 1922–1938). Utah Rep.—Utah, Legislature (4). U.S., House of Representatives (2); Senate (12). *Private practice.*

SWAYNE, NOAH H. (1804–1884; Lincoln, 1862–1881). Ohio Rep.—Ohio, County Attorney (4); Legislature (2). U.S., District Attorney (9). *Private practice.*

* TAFT, WILLIAM H. (1857–1930; Harding, 1921–1930). Conn. Rep.—U.S., Collector of Internal Revenue (1). Ohio Judge, Superior Court (3). U.S., Solicitor General (2); Judge, Circuit Court of Appeals (8); Governor-General, P.I. (3); Secretary of War (4); President (4). *Professor of Law.*

* TANEY, ROGER B. (1777–1864; Jackson, 1836–1864). Md. Dem.—Md., Legislature (7); Attorney General (2). U.S., Attorney General (2), Secretary of the Treasury ($^3/_4$; rejected by the Senate). *Private practice.*

THOMPSON, SMITH (1768–1843; Monroe, 1823–1843). N.Y. Rep.—N.Y., Legislature (2); Associate Justice, and Chief Justice, Supreme Court (16). *U.S., Secretary of the Navy (4).*

TODD, THOMAS (1765–1826; Jefferson, 1807–1826). Ky. Rep.—*Ky.*, Judge, and *Chief Justice, Court of Appeals (6).*

TRIMBLE, ROBERT (1777–1828; J. Q. Adams, 1826–1828). Ky. Rep.—Ky., Legislature (2). Judge, Court of Appeals (2). U.S., District Attorney (4); *Judge, District Court (9).*

VAN DEVANTER, WILLIS (1859–1941; Taft, 1910–1937). Wyo. Rep.—Wyo., Legislature (2); Chief Justice, Supreme Court (1). U.S., Assistant Attorney General (Interior Department) (6); Judge, Circuit Court of Appeals (7).

* VINSON, FRED M. (1890–1953; Truman, 1946–1953). Ky. Dem.—Ky., Commonwealth Attorney (3). U.S., House of Representatives (14); Judge, Court of Appeals (5); Director, Office of Economic Stabilization (2); Federal Loan Administrator (1 mo.); Director, Office of War Mobilization and Reconversion (3 mo.); *Secretary of the Treasury (1).*

* WAITE, MORRISON R. (1816–1888; Grant, 1874–1888). Ohio Rep.—Ohio, Legislature (2). Counsel for United States, U.S.–Gr. Brit. Arbitration ("Alabama" Claims), 1871–72. *Private practice.*

* WARREN, EARL (1891–1974; Eisenhower, 1953–1969). Calif. Rep.—1st Lt., Inf., World War I. Deputy City Attorney (1); Deputy District Attorney (5); District Attorney (14); Attorney General (4); *Governor (10).*

WASHINGTON, BUSHROD (1762–1829; J. Adams, 1798–1829). Pa. Fed.—Va., Legislature (1). *Private practice.*

WAYNE, JAMES M. (1790–1867; Jackson, 1835–1867). Ga. Dem.—Ga., Officer, Hussars, War of 1812; Legislature (2). Mayor of Savannah, Ga. (2). Ga., Judge, Superior Court (5). *U.S., House of Representatives (6).*

WHITE, BYRON R. (1917– —; Kennedy, 1962– —). Colo. Dem.—U.S. N.R., World War II. Law Clerk, Chief Justice Vinson, 1946–47. *U.S., Deputy Attorney General (1).*

* WHITE, EDWARD D. (1845–1921; Cleveland, later Taft, 1894–1921). La. Dem.—La., Legislature (4); Justice, Supreme Court (2). *U.S., Senate (3).* Chief Justice, 1910–1921.

WHITTAKER, CHARLES E. (1901–1973; Eisenhower, 1957–1962). Mo. Rep.—U.S., Judge, District Court (2); *Court of Appeals (1).*

WILSON, JAMES (1724–1798; Washington, 1789–1798). Pa. Fed.—Signer, U.S. Declaration of Independence, 1776, and U.S. Constitution, 1787. Although he was strongly interested in western-land development companies for several years prior to his appointment, his primary activity in the period immediately preceding his appointment was in obtaining ratification of the Federal and Pennsylvania Constitutions.

WOODBURY, LEVI (1789–1851; Polk, 1845–1851). N.H. Dem.—N.H., Associate Justice, Superior Court (6); Governor (2); Legislature (1). U.S., Senate (6); Secretary of the Navy (3); Secretary of the Treasury (7); *Senate (4).*

WOODS, WILLIAM B. (1824–1887; Hayes, 1880–1887). Ga. Rep.—Mayor, Newark, O. (1). Ohio, Legislature (4). Brevet Major General, U.S. Vol., Civil War. Ala., Chancellor (1). *U.S., Judge, Circuit Court (11).*

APPENDIX B

PROPOSED AMENDMENTS NOT RATIFIED BY THE STATES *

During the course of our history, in addition to the 26 amendments which have been ratified by the required three-fourths of the States, six other amendments have been submitted to the States but have not been ratified by them.

Beginning with the proposed Eighteenth Amendment, Congress has customarily included a provision requiring ratification within seven years from the time of the submission to the States. The Supreme Court in *Coleman v. Miller*, 307 U.S. 433 (1939), declared that the question of the reasonableness of the time within which a sufficient number of States must act is a political question to be determined by the Congress. See generally Chapter 2, Section IV, E, 3, b, supra.

In 1789, at the time of the submission of the Bill of Rights, twelve proposed amendments were submitted to the States. Of these, Articles III–XII were ratified and became the first ten amendments to the Constitution. Proposed Articles I and II were not ratified. The following is the text of those articles:

ARTICLE I. After the first enumeration required by the first article of the Constitution, there shall be one Representative for every thirty thousand, until the number shall amount to one hundred, after which the proportion shall be so regulated by Congress, that there shall be not less than one hundred Representatives, nor less than one Representative for every forty thousand persons, until the number of Representatives shall amount to two hundred; after which the proportion shall be so regulated by Congress, that there shall not be less than two hundred Representatives, nor more than one Representative for every fifty thousand persons.

ARTICLE II. No law varying the compensation for the services of the Senators and Representatives shall take effect, until an election of Representatives shall have intervened.

Thereafter, in the 2d session of the 11th Congress, the Congress proposed the following amendment to the Constitution relating to acceptance by citizens of the United States of titles of nobility from any foreign government.

The proposed amendment which was not ratified by three-fourths of the States reads as follows:

Resolved by the Senate and House of Representatives of the United States of America in Congress assembled (two-thirds of both Houses concurring), That the following section be submitted to the legislatures of the several states, which, when ratified by the legislatures of three fourths of the states, shall be valid and binding, as a part of the constitution of the United States.

If any citizen of the United States shall accept, claim, receive or retain any title of nobility or honour, or shall, without the consent of Congress, accept and retain any present, pension, office or emolument of any kind whatever, from any emperor, king, prince or foreign power, such person

* Adapted from, The Constitution of the United States of America: Analysis and Interpretation, Senate Document No. 92–82, 92d Cong., 2d Sess., 51–52 (1973).

shall cease to be a citizen of the United States, and shall be incapable of holding any office of trust or profit under them, or either of them.

During the second session of the 36th Congress on March 2, 1861, the following proposed amendment to the Constitution relating to slavery was signed by the President. It is interesting to note in this connection that this is the only proposed amendment to the Constitution ever signed by the President. The President's signature is considered unnecessary because of the constitutional provision that upon the concurrence of two-thirds of both Houses of Congress the proposal shall be submitted to the States and shall be ratified by three-fourths of the States.

Resolved by the Senate and House of Representatives of the United States of American in Congress assembled, That the following article be proposed to the Legislatures of the several States as an amendment to the Constitution of the United States, which, when ratified by three-fourths of said Legislatures, shall be valid, to all intents and purposes, as part of the said Constitution, viz:

"ARTICLE THIRTEEN

"No amendment shall be made to the Constitution which will authorize or give to Congress the power to abolish or interfere, within any State, with the domestic institutions thereof, including that of persons held to labor or service by the laws of said State."

In more recent times a proposed amendment which has not been ratified by three-fourths of the States is the proposed child-labor amendment, which was submitted to the States during the 1st session of the 68th Congress in June 1924, as follows:

JOINT RESOLUTION PROPOSING AN AMENDMENT TO THE CONSTITUTION OF THE UNITED STATES

Resolved by the Senate and House of Representatives of the United States of America in Congress assembled (two-thirds of each House concurring therein), That the following article is proposed as an amendment to the Constitution of the United States, which when ratified by the legislatures of three-fourths of the several States, shall be valid to all intents and purposes as a part of the Constitution:

ARTICLE —

SECTION 1. The Congress shall have power to limit, regulate, and prohibit the labor of persons under 18 years of age.

SECTION 2. The power of several States is unimpaired by this article except that the operation of State laws shall be suspended to the extent necessary to give effect to legislation enacted by the Congress.

On March 22, 1972, Congress submitted to the States for ratification the proposed Equal Rights Amendment. The resolution accompanying this proposed amendment states that "[t]his article shall be valid to all intents and purposes as part of the Constitution of the United States when ratified by the legislatures of three-fourths of the several States within seven years from the date of its submission by the Congress." When it appeared that a sufficient number of the States would not ratify within the required period of time, Congress extended the period for ratification until June 30, 1982. H.J.Res.

638, 92 Stat. 3799 (1978). However, no new States ratified, and the proposed amendment therefore died. It would have provided:

ARTICLE —

SECTION 1. Equality of rights under the law shall not be denied or abridged by the United States or by any State on account of sex.

SECTION 2. The Congress shall have the power to enforce, by appropriate legislation, the provisions of this article.

SECTION 3. This amendment shall take effect two years after the date of ratification.

The House of Representatives on March 2, 1978, and the Senate on March 6, 1978, passed a proposed amendment to provide for representation of the District of Columbia in Congress. It was then sent to the States for ratification. The proposed amendment provides:

ARTICLE —

SECTION 1. For purposes of representation in the Congress, election of the President and Vice President, and article V of this Constitution, the District constituting the seat of government of the United States shall be treated as though it were a State.

SECTION 2. The exercise of the rights and powers conferred under this article shall be by the people of the District constituting the seat of government, and as shall be provided by Congress.

SECTION 3. The twenty-third article of amendment to the Constitution of the United States is hereby repealed.

SECTION 4. This article shall be inoperative, unless it shall have been ratified as an amendment to the Constitution by the legislatures of three-fourths of the several States within seven years from the date of its submission.

APPENDIX C

THE CONSTITUTION OF THE UNITED STATES *

1787 [1]

---

* Adapted, with permission, from United States Code Annotated, Constitution of the United States, Annotated (West Publishing Co. 1968).

1. In May, 1785, a committee of Congress made a report recommending an alteration in the Articles of Confederation, but no action was taken on it, and it was left to the State Legislatures to proceed in the matter. In January, 1786, the Legislature of Virginia passed a resolution providing for the appointment of five commissioners, who, or any three of them, should meet such commissioners as might be appointed in the other States of the Union, at a time and place to be agreed upon, to take into consideration the trade of the United States; to consider how far a uniform system in their commercial regulations may be necessary to their common interest and their permanent harmony; and to report to the several States such an act, relative to this great object, as, when ratified by them, will enable the United States in Congress effectually to provide for the same. The Virginia commissioners, after some correspondence, fixed the first Monday in September as the time, and the city of Annapolis as the place for the meeting, but only four other States were represented, viz.: Delaware, New York, New Jersey, and Pennsylvania; the commissioners appointed by Massachusetts, New Hampshire, North Carolina, and Rhode Island failed to attend. Under the circumstances of so partial a representation, the commissioners present agreed upon a report, (drawn by Mr. Hamilton, of New York,) expressing their unanimous conviction that it might essentially tend to advance the interests of the Union if the States by which they were respectively delegated would concur, and use their endeavors to procure the concurrence of the other States, in the appointment of commissioners to meet at Philadelphia on the second Monday of May following, to take into consideration the situation of the United States; to devise such further provisions as should appear to them necessary to render the Constitution of the Federal Government adequate to the exigencies of the Union; and to report such an act for that purpose to the United States in Congress assembled as, when agreed to by them, and afterwards confirmed by the Legislatures of every State, would effectually provide for the same.

Congress, on the 21st of February, 1787, adopted a resolution in favor of a convention, and the Legislatures of those States which had not already done so (with the exception of Rhode Island) promptly appointed delegates. On the 25th of May, seven States having convened, George Washington, of Virginia, was unanimously elected President, and the consideration of the proposed constitution was commenced. On the 17th of September, 1787, the Constitution as engrossed and agreed upon was signed by all the members present, except Mr. Gerry, of Massachusetts, and Messrs. Mason and Randolph, of Virginia. The president of the convention transmitted it to Congress, with a resolution stating how the proposed Federal Government should be put in operation, and an explanatory letter. Congress, on the 28th of September, 1787, directed the Constitution so framed, with the resolutions and letter concerning the same, to "be transmitted to the several Legislatures in order to be submitted to a convention of delegates chosen in each State by the people thereof, in conformity to the resolves of the convention."

On the 4th of March, 1789, the day which had been fixed for commencing the operations of Government under the new Constitution, it had been ratified by the conventions chosen in each State to consider it, as follows: Delaware, December 7, 1787; Pennsylvania, December 12, 1787; New Jersey, December 18, 1787; Georgia, January 2, 1788; Connecticut, January 9, 1788; Massachusetts, February 6, 1788; Maryland, April 28, 1788; South Carolina, May 23, 1788; New Hampshire, June 21, 1788; Virginia, June 26, 1788; and New York, July 26, 1788.

PREAMBLE

———

We the People of the United States, in Order to form a more perfect Union, establish Justice, insure domestic Tranquility, provide for the common defence, promote the general Welfare, and secure the Blessings of Liberty to ourselves and our Posterity, do ordain and establish this Constitution for the United States of America.

Article I

Section 1. All legislative Powers herein granted shall be vested in a Congress of the United States, which shall consist of a Senate and House of Representatives.

Section 2. [1] The House of Representatives shall be composed of Members chosen every second Year by the People of the several States, and the Electors in each State shall have the Qualifications requisite for Electors of the most numerous Branch of the State Legislature.

[2] No Person shall be a Representative who shall not have attained to the Age of twenty five Years, and been seven Years a Citizen of the United States, and who shall not, when elected, be an Inhabitant of that State in which he shall be chosen.

[3] [Representatives and direct Taxes shall be apportioned among the several States which may be included within this Union, according to their respective Numbers, which shall be determined by adding to the whole Number of free Persons, including those bound to Service for a Term of Years, and excluding Indians not taxed, three fifths of all other Persons.] The actual Enumeration shall be made within three Years after the first Meeting of the Congress of the United States, and within every subsequent Term of ten Years, in such Manner as they shall by Law direct. The Number of Representatives shall not exceed one for every thirty Thousand, but each State shall have at Least one Representative; and until such enumeration shall be made, the State of New Hampshire shall be entitled to chuse three, Massachusetts eight, Rhode Island and Providence Plantations one, Connecticut five, New York six, New Jersey four, Pennsylvania eight, Delaware one, Maryland six, Virginia ten, North Carolina five, South Carolina five, and Georgia three.

> **The clause of this paragraph inclosed in brackets was amended, as to the mode of apportionment of representatives among the several states, by the Fourteenth Amendment, § 2, and as to taxes on incomes without apportionment, by the Sixteenth Amendment.**

[4] When vacancies happen in the Representation from any State, the Executive Authority thereof shall issue Writs of Election to fill such Vacancies.

[5] The House of Representatives shall chuse their Speaker and other Officers; and shall have the sole Power of Impeachment.

The President informed Congress, on the 28th of January, 1790, that North Carolina had ratified the Constitution November 21, 1789; and he informed Congress on the 1st of June, 1790, that Rhode Island had ratified the Constitution May 29, 1790. Vermont, in convention, ratified the Constitution January 10, 1791, and was on March 4, 1791, by an act of Congress approved February 18, 1791, "received and admitted into this Union as a new and entire member of the United States."

Section 3. [1] [The Senate of the United States shall be composed of two Senators from each State, chosen by the Legislature thereof, for six Years; and each Senator shall have one Vote.]

This paragraph and the clause of following paragraph inclosed brackets were superseded by the Seventeenth Amendment.

[2] Immediately after they shall be assembled in Consequence of the first Election, they shall be divided as equally as may be into three Classes. The Seats of the Senators of the first Class shall be vacated at the Expiration of the Second Year, of the second Class at the Expiration of the fourth Year, and of the third Class at the Expiration of the sixth Year, so that one third may be chosen every second Year; [and if Vacancies happen by Resignation, or otherwise, during the Recess of the Legislature of any State, the Executive thereof may make temporary Appointments until the next Meeting of the Legislature, which shall then fill such Vacancies.]

See note to preceding paragraph of this section.

[3] No Person shall be a Senator who shall not have attained to the Age of thirty Years, and been nine Years a Citizen of the United States, and who shall not, when elected, be an Inhabitant of that State for which he shall be chosen.

[4] The Vice President of the United States shall be President of the Senate, but shall have no Vote, unless they be equally divided.

[5] The Senate shall chuse their other Officers, and also a President pro tempore, in the Absence of the Vice President, or when he shall exercise the Office of President of the United States.

[6] The Senate shall have the sole Power to try all Impeachments. When sitting for that Purpose, they shall be on Oath or Affirmation. When the President of the United States is tried, the Chief Justice shall preside: And no Person shall be convicted without the Concurrence of two thirds of the Members present.

[7] Judgment in Cases of Impeachment shall not extend further than to removal from Office, and disqualification to hold and enjoy any Office of Honor, Trust, or Profit under the United States: but the Party convicted shall nevertheless be liable and subject to Indictment, Trial, Judgment, and Punishment, according to Law.

Section 4. [1] The Times, Places and Manner of holding Elections for Senators and Representatives, shall be prescribed in each State by the Legislature thereof; but the Congress may at any time by Law make or alter such Regulations, except as to the Places of chusing Senators.

[2] The Congress shall assemble at least once in every Year, and such Meeting shall be on the first Monday in December, unless they shall by Law appoint a different Day.

Section 5. [1] Each House shall be the Judge of the Elections, Returns, and Qualifications of its own Members, and a Majority of each shall constitute a Quorum to do Business; but a smaller Number may adjourn from day to day, and may be authorized to compel the Attendance of absent Members, in such Manner, and under such Penalties as each House may provide.

[2] Each House may determine the Rules of its Proceedings, punish its Members for disorderly Behavior, and, with the Concurrence of two thirds, expel a Member.

[3] Each House shall keep a Journal of its Proceedings, and from time to time publish the same, excepting such Parts as may in their Judgment require

Secrecy; and the Yeas and Nays of the Members of either House on any question shall, at the Desire of one fifth of those Present, be entered on the Journal.

[4] Neither House, during the Session of Congress, shall, without the Consent of the other, adjourn for more than three days, nor to any other Place than that in which the two Houses shall be sitting.

Section 6. [1] The Senators and Representatives shall receive a Compensation for their Services, to be ascertained by Law, and paid out of the Treasury of the United States. They shall in all Cases, except Treason, Felony and Breach of the Peace, be privileged from Arrest during their Attendance at the Session of their respective Houses, and in going to and returning from the same; and for any Speech or Debate in either House, they shall not be questioned in any other Place.

[2] No Senator or Representative shall, during the Time for which he was elected, be appointed to any civil Office under the Authority of the United States, which shall have been created, or the Emoluments whereof shall have been increased during such time; and no Person holding any Office under the United States, shall be a Member of either House during his Continuance in Office.

Section 7. [1] All Bills for raising Revenue shall originate in the House of Representatives; but the Senate may propose or concur with Amendments as on other Bills.

[2] Every Bill which shall have passed the House of Representatives and the Senate, shall, before it become a Law, be presented to the President of the United States; If he approve he shall sign it, but if not he shall return it, with his Objections to the House in which it shall have originated, who shall enter the Objections at large on their Journal, and proceed to reconsider it. If after such Reconsideration two thirds of that House shall agree to pass the Bill, it shall be sent together with the Objections, to the other House, by which it shall likewise be reconsidered, and if approved by two thirds of that House, it shall become a Law. But in all such Cases the Votes of both Houses shall be determined by yeas and Nays, and the Names of the Persons voting for and against the Bill shall be entered on the Journal of each House respectively. If any Bill shall not be returned by the President within ten Days (Sundays excepted) after it shall have been presented to him, the Same shall be a Law, in like Manner as if he had signed it, unless the Congress by their Adjournment prevent its Return in which Case it shall not be a Law.

[3] Every Order, Resolution, or Vote, to Which the Concurrence of the Senate and House of Representatives may be necessary (except on a question of Adjournment) shall be presented to the President of the United States; and before the Same shall take Effect, shall be approved by him, or being disapproved by him, shall be repassed by two thirds of the Senate and House of Representatives, according to the Rules and Limitations prescribed in the Case of a Bill.

Section 8. [1] The Congress shall have Power To lay and collect Taxes, Duties, Imposts and Excises, to pay the Debts and provide for the common Defence and general Welfare of the United States; but all Duties, Imposts and Excises shall be uniform throughout the United States;

[2] To borrow money on the credit of the United States;

[3] To regulate Commerce with foreign Nations, and among the several States, and with the Indian Tribes;

[4]   To establish an uniform Rule of Naturalization, and uniform Laws on the subject of Bankruptcies throughout the United States;

[5]   To coin Money, regulate the Value thereof, and of foreign Coin, and fix the Standard of Weights and Measures;

[6]   To provide for the Punishment of counterfeiting the Securities and current Coin of the United States;

[7]   To Establish Post Offices and Post Roads;

[8]   To promote the Progress of Science and useful Arts, by securing for limited Times to Authors and Inventors the exclusive Right to their respective Writings and Discoveries;

[9]   To constitute Tribunals inferior to the supreme Court;

[10]   To define and punish Piracies and Felonies committed on the high Seas, and Offenses against the Law of Nations;

[11]   To declare War, grant Letters of Marque and Reprisal, and make Rules concerning Captures on Land and Water;

[12]   To raise and support Armies, but no Appropriation of Money to that Use shall be for a longer Term than two Years;

[13]   To provide and maintain a Navy;

[14]   To make Rules for the Government and Regulation of the land and naval Forces;

[15]   To provide for calling forth the Militia to execute the Laws of the Union, suppress Insurrections and repel Invasions;

[16]   To provide for organizing, arming, and disciplining, the Militia, and for governing such Part of them as may be employed in the Service of the United States, reserving to the States respectively, the Appointment of the Officers, and the Authority of training the Militia according to the discipline prescribed by Congress;

[17]   To exercise exclusive Legislation in all Cases whatsoever, over such District (not exceeding ten Miles square) as may, by Cession of particular States, and the Acceptance of Congress, become the Seat of the Government of the United States, and to exercise like Authority over all Places purchased by the Consent of the Legislature of the State in which the Same shall be, for the Erection of Forts, Magazines, Arsenals, dock-Yards, and other needful Buildings;—And

[18]   To make all Laws which shall be necessary and proper for carrying into Execution the foregoing Powers, and all other Powers vested by this Constitution in the Government of the United States, or in any Department or Officer thereof.

Section 9.   [1]   The Migration or Importation of Such Persons as any of the States now existing shall think proper to admit, shall not be prohibited by the Congress prior to the Year one thousand eight hundred and eight, but a Tax or duty may be imposed on such Importation, not exceeding ten dollars for each Person.

[2]   The privilege of the Writ of Habeas Corpus shall not be suspended, unless when in Cases of Rebellion or Invasion the public Safety may require it.

[3]   No Bill of Attainder or ex post facto Law shall be passed.

[4]   No Capitation, or other direct, Tax shall be laid, unless in Proportion to the Census or Enumeration herein before directed to be taken.

[5]   No Tax or Duty shall be laid on Articles exported from any State.

[6]   No Preference shall be given by any Regulation of Commerce or Revenue to the Ports of one State over those of another: nor shall Vessels bound to, or from, one State be obliged to enter, clear, or pay Duties in another.

[7]   No money shall be drawn from the Treasury, but in Consequence of Appropriations made by Law; and a regular Statement and Account of the Receipts and Expenditures of all public Money shall be published from time to time.

[8]   No Title of Nobility shall be granted by the United States: And no Person holding any Office of Profit or Trust under them, shall, without the Consent of the Congress, accept of any present, Emolument, Office, or Title, of any kind whatever, from any King, Prince, or foreign State.

Section 10. [1]   No State shall enter into any Treaty, Alliance, or Confederation; grant Letters of Marque and Reprisal; coin Money; emit Bills of Credit; make any Thing but gold and silver Coin a Tender in Payment of Debts; pass any Bill of Attainder, ex post facto Law, or Law impairing the Obligation of Contracts, or grant any Title of Nobility.

[2]   No State shall, without the Consent of the Congress, lay any Imposts or Duties on Imports or Exports, except what may be absolutely necessary for executing it's inspection Laws: and the net Produce of all Duties and Imposts, laid by any State on Imports or Exports, shall be for the Use of the Treasury of the United States; and all such Laws shall be subject to the Revision and Controul of the Congress.

[3]   No State shall, without the Consent of Congress, lay any Duty of Tonnage, keep Troops, or Ships of War in time of Peace, enter into any Agreement or Compact with another State, or with a foreign Power, or engage in War, unless actually invaded, or in such imminent Danger as will not admit of delay.

Article II

Section 1. [1]   The executive Power shall be vested in a President of the United States of America. He shall hold his Office during the Term of four Years, and, together with the Vice President, chosen for the same Term, be elected, as follows:

[2]   Each State shall appoint, in such Manner as the Legislature thereof may direct, a Number of Electors, equal to the whole Number of Senators and Representatives to which the State may be entitled in the Congress; but no Senator or Representative, or Person holding an Office of Trust or Profit under the United States, shall be appointed an Elector.

[3]   [The Electors shall meet in their respective States, and vote by Ballot for two Persons, of whom one at least shall not be an Inhabitant of the same State with themselves. And they shall make a List of all the Persons voted for, and of the Number of Votes for each; which List they shall sign and certify, and transmit sealed to the Seat of the Government of the United States, directed to the President of the Senate. The President of the Senate shall, in the Presence of the Senate and House of Representatives, open all the Certificates, and the Votes shall then be counted. The Person having the greatest Number of Votes shall be the President, if such Number be a Majority of the whole Number of Electors appointed; and if there be more than one who have such Majority, and have an equal Number of Votes, then the House of Representatives shall immediately chuse by Ballot one of them for President; and if no Person have a Majority, then from the five highest on the List

the said House shall in like Manner chuse the President. But in chusing the President, the Votes shall be taken by States the Representation from each State having one Vote; A quorum for this Purpose shall consist of a Member or Members from two thirds of the States, and a Majority of all the States shall be necessary to a Choice. In every Case, after the Choice of the President, the Person having the greater Number of Votes of the Electors shall be the Vice President. But if there should remain two or more who have equal Votes, the Senate shall chuse from them by Ballot the Vice President.]

This paragraph, inclosed in brackets, was superseded by the Twelfth Amendment, post.

[4]   The Congress may determine the Time of chusing the Electors, and the Day on which they shall give their Votes; which Day shall be the same throughout the United States.

[5]   No person except a natural born Citizen, or a Citizen of the United States, at the time of the Adoption of this Constitution, shall be eligible to the Office of President; neither shall any Person be eligible to that Office who shall not have attained to the Age of thirty five Years, and been fourteen Years a Resident within the United States.

[6]   In case of the removal of the President from Office, or of his Death, Resignation or Inability to discharge the Powers and Duties of the said Office, the Same shall devolve on the Vice President, and the Congress may by Law provide for the Case of Removal, Death, Resignation or Inability, both of the President and Vice President, declaring what Officer shall then act as President, and such Officer shall act accordingly, until the Disability be removed, or a President shall be elected.

[7]   The President shall, at stated Times, receive for his Services, a Compensation, which shall neither be increased nor diminished during the Period for which he shall have been elected, and he shall not receive within that Period any other Emolument from the United States, or any of them.

[8]   Before he enter on the Execution of his Office, he shall take the following Oath or Affirmation: "I do solemnly swear (or affirm) that I will faithfully execute the Office of President of the United States, and will to the best of my Ability, preserve, protect and defend the Constitution of the United States."

Section 2.   [1]   The President shall be Commander in Chief of the Army and Navy of the United States, and of the militia of the several States, when called into the actual Service of the United States; he may require the Opinion, in writing, of the principal Officer in each of the Executive Departments, upon any Subject relating to the Duties of their respective Offices, and he shall have Power to grant Reprieves and Pardons for Offenses against the United States, except in Cases of Impeachment.

[2]   He shall have Power, by and with the Advice and Consent of the Senate to make Treaties, provided two thirds of the Senators present concur; and he shall nominate, and by and with the Advice and Consent of the Senate, shall appoint Ambassadors, other public Ministers and Consuls, Judges of the supreme Court, and all other Officers of the United States, whose Appointments are not herein otherwise provided for, and which shall be established by Law; but the Congress may by Law vest the Appointment of such inferior Officers, as they think proper, in the President alone, in the Courts of Law, or in the Heads of Departments.

[3] The President shall have Power to fill up all Vacancies that may happen during the Recess of the Senate, by granting Commissions which shall expire at the End of their next Session.

Section 3. He shall from time to time give to the Congress Information of the State of the Union, and recommend to their Consideration such Measures as he shall judge necessary and expedient; he may, on extraordinary Occasions, convene both Houses, or either of them, and in Case of Disagreement between them, with Respect to the Time of Adjournment, he may adjourn them to such Time as he shall think proper; he shall receive Ambassadors and other public Ministers; he shall take Care that the Laws be faithfully executed, and shall Commission all the Officers of the United States.

Section 4. The President, Vice President and all civil Officers of the United States, shall be removed from Office on Impeachment for, and Conviction of, Treason, Bribery, or other high Crimes and Misdemeanors.

Article III

Section 1. The judicial Power of the United States, shall be vested in one supreme Court, and in such inferior Courts as the Congress may from time to time ordain and establish. The Judges, both of the supreme and inferior Courts, shall hold their Offices during good Behaviour, and shall, at stated Times, receive for their Services a Compensation, which shall not be diminished during their Continuance in Office.

Section 2. [1] The judicial Power shall extend to all Cases, in Law and Equity, arising under this Constitution, the Laws of the United States, and Treaties made, or which shall be made, under their Authority;—to all Cases affecting Ambassadors, other public Ministers and Consuls;—to all Cases of admiralty and maritime Jurisdiction;—to Controversies to which the United States shall be a Party;—to Controversies between two or more States;—between a State and Citizens of another State;—between Citizens of different States;—between Citizens of the same State claiming Lands under the Grants of different States, and between a State, or the Citizens thereof, and foreign States, Citizens or Subjects.

[2] In all Cases affecting Ambassadors, other public Ministers and Consuls, and those in which a State shall be a Party, the supreme Court shall have original Jurisdiction. In all the other Cases before mentioned, the supreme Court shall have appellate Jurisdiction, both as to Law and Fact, with such Exceptions, and under such Regulations as the Congress shall make.

[3] The trial of all Crimes, except in Cases of Impeachment, shall be by Jury; and such Trial shall be held in the State where the said Crimes shall have been committed; but when not committed within any State, the Trial shall be at such Place or Places as the Congress may by Law have directed.

Section 3. [1] Treason against the United States, shall consist only in levying War against them, or, in adhering to their Enemies, giving them Aid and Comfort. No Person shall be convicted of Treason unless on the Testimony of two Witnesses to the same overt Act, or on Confession in open Court.

[2] The Congress shall have Power to declare the Punishment of Treason, but no Attainder of Treason shall work Corruption of Blood, or Forfeiture except during the Life of the Person attainted.

Article IV

Section 1. Full Faith and Credit shall be given in each State to the public Acts, Records, and judicial Proceedings of every other State. And the Congress may by general Laws prescribe the Manner in which such Acts, Records and Proceedings shall be proved, and the Effect thereof.

Section 2. [1] The Citizens of each State shall be entitled to all Privileges and Immunities of Citizens in the several States.

[2] A Person charged in any State with Treason, Felony, or other Crime, who shall flee from Justice, and be found in another State, shall on demand of the executive Authority of the State from which he fled, be delivered up, to be removed to the State having Jurisdiction of the Crime.

[3] No Person held to Service or Labour in one State, under the Laws thereof, escaping into another, shall, in Consequence of any Law or Regulation therein, be discharged from such Service or Labour, but shall be delivered up on Claim of the Party to whom such Service or Labour may be due.

Section 3. [1] New States may be admitted by the Congress into this Union; but no new State shall be formed or erected within the Jurisdiction of any other State; nor any State be formed by the Junction of two or more States, or Parts of States, without the Consent of the Legislatures of the States concerned as well as of the Congress.

[2] The Congress shall have Power to dispose of and make all needful Rules and Regulations respecting the Territory or other Property belonging to the United States; and nothing in this Constitution shall be so construed as to Prejudice any Claims of the United States, or of any particular State.

Section 4. The United States shall guarantee to every State in this Union a Republican Form of Government, and shall protect each of them against Invasion; and on Application of the Legislature, or of the Executive (when the Legislature cannot be convened) against domestic Violence.

Article V

The Congress, whenever two thirds of both Houses shall deem it necessary, shall propose Amendments to this Constitution, or, on the Application of the Legislatures of two thirds of the several States, shall call a Convention for proposing Amendments, which, in either Case, shall be valid to all Intents and Purposes, as part of this Constitution, when ratified by the Legislatures of three fourths of the several States, or by Conventions in three fourths thereof, as the one or the other Mode of Ratification may be proposed by the Congress; Provided that no Amendment which may be made prior to the Year One thousand eight hundred and eight shall in any Manner affect the first and fourth Clauses in the Ninth Section of the first Article; and that no State, without its Consent, shall be deprived of its equal Suffrage in the Senate.

Article VI

[1] All Debts contracted and Engagements entered into, before the Adoption of this Constitution shall be as valid against the United States under this Constitution, as under the Confederation.

[2] This Constitution, and the Laws of the United States which shall be made in Pursuance thereof; and all Treaties made, or which shall be made, under the Authority of the United States, shall be the supreme Law of the Land; and the Judges in every State shall be bound thereby, any Thing in the Constitution or Laws of any State to the Contrary notwithstanding.

[3] The Senators and Representatives before mentioned, and the Members of the several State Legislatures, and all executive and judicial Officers, both of the United States and of the several States, shall be bound by Oath or Affirmation, to support this Constitution; but no religious Test shall ever be required as a Qualification to any Office or public Trust under the United States.

Article VII

The Ratification of the Conventions of nine States shall be sufficient for the Establishment of this Constitution between the States so ratifying the Same.

DONE in Convention by the Unanimous Consent of the States present the Seventeenth Day of September in the Year of Our Lord one thousand seven hundred and Eighty seven and of the Independence of the United States of America the Twelfth. IN WITNESS whereof We have hereunto subscribed our Names,

Go. WASHINGTON—*Presidt. and deputy from Virginia*

New Hampshire

JOHN LANGDON   NICHOLAS GILMAN

Massachusetts

NATHANIEL GORHAM   RUFUS KING

Connecticut

WM. SAML. JOHNSON   ROGER SHERMAN

New York

ALEXANDER HAMILTON

New Jersey

WIL: LIVINGSTON   WM. PATERSON
DAVID BREARLEY   JONA: DAYTON

Pennsylvania

B. FRANKLIN   THOS. FITZSIMONS
THOMAS MIFFLIN   JARED INGERSOLL
ROBT. MORRIS   JAMES WILSON
GEO. CLYMER   GOUV MORRIS

Delaware

GEO: READ   RICHARD BASSETT
GUNNING BEDFORD jun   JACO: BROOM
JOHN DICKINSON

Maryland

JAMES MCHENRY   DANL. CARROLL
DAN OF ST THOS. JENIFER

Virginia

JOHN BLAIR   JAMES MADISON, JR.

North Carolina

WM. BLOUNT   HU WILLIAMSON
RICHD. DOBBS SPAIGHT

South Carolina

J. RUTLEDGE   CHARLES PINCKNEY
CHARLES COTESWORTH PINCKNEY   PIERCE BUTLER

Georgia

WILLIAM FEW   ABR BALDWIN

Attest   WILLIAM JACKSON
                                              Secretary

ARTICLES IN ADDITION TO, AND AMENDMENT OF, THE CONSTITUTION OF THE UNITED STATES OF AMERICA, PROPOSED BY CONGRESS, AND RATIFIED BY THE LEGISLATURES OF THE SEVERAL STATES PURSUANT TO THE FIFTH ARTICLE OF THE ORIGINAL CONSTITUTION.[1]

AMENDMENT [I] [1791] [2]

Congress shall make no law respecting an establishment of religion, or prohibiting the free exercise thereof; or abridging the freedom of speech, or of the press; or the right of the people peaceably to assemble, and to petition the Government for a redress of grievances.

AMENDMENT [II] [1791]

A well regulated Militia, being necessary to the security of a free State, the right of the people to keep and bear Arms, shall not be infringed.

1. All of the Amendments except the 13th, 14th, 15th, and 16th, were not specifically assigned a number in the resolution proposing the Amendment. Brackets enclose the number for such Amendments. The 13th, 14th, 15th, and 16th Amendments were ratified by number and thus no brackets enclose such Amendment numbers. See, The Constitution of the United States of America: Analysis and Interpretation, Senate Document No. 92–82, 92d Cong., 2d Sess., at 25 n. 2 (1973).

2. The first ten amendments to the Constitution of the United States were proposed to the legislatures of the several States by the First Congress, on the 25th of September 1789. They were ratified by the following States, and the notifications of ratification by the governors thereof were successively communicated by the President to Congress: New Jersey, November 20, 1789; Maryland, December 19, 1789; North Carolina, December 22, 1789; South Carolina, January 19, 1790; New Hampshire, January 25, 1790; Delaware, January 28, 1790; Pennsylvania, March 10, 1790; New York, March 27, 1790; Rhode Island, June 15, 1790; Vermont, November 3, 1791, and Virginia, December 15, 1791. The legislatures of Connecticut, Georgia, and Massachusetts ratified them on April 19, 1939, March 24, 1939, and March 2, 1939, respectively.

Note: other amendments have also been ratified by states after the amendment has been announced as ratified; these other, after-the-fact ratifications are not usually noted in this appendix.

Amendment [III] [1791]

No Soldier shall, in time of peace be quartered in any house, without the consent of the Owner, nor in time of war, but in a manner to be prescribed by law.

Amendment [IV] [1791]

The right of the people to be secure in their persons, houses, papers, and effects, against unreasonable searches and seizures, shall not be violated, and no Warrants shall issue, but upon probable cause, supported by Oath or affirmation, and particularly describing the place to be searched, and the persons or things to be seized.

Amendment [V] [1791]

No person shall be held to answer for a capital, or otherwise infamous crime, unless on a presentment or indictment of a Grand Jury, except in cases arising in the land or naval forces, or in the Militia, when in actual service in time of War or public danger; nor shall any person be subject for the same offence to be twice put in jeopardy of life or limb; nor shall be compelled in any criminal case to be a witness against himself, nor be deprived of life, liberty, or property, without due process of law; nor shall private property be taken for public use, without just compensation.

Amendment [VI] [1791]

In all criminal prosecutions, the accused shall enjoy the right to a speedy and public trial, by an impartial jury of the State and district wherein the crime shall have been committed, which district shall have been previously ascertained by law, and to be informed of the nature and cause of the accusation; to be confronted with the witnesses against him; to have compulsory process for obtaining witnesses in his favor, and to have the Assistance of Counsel for his defence.

Amendment [VII] [1791]

In Suits at common law, where the value in controversy shall exceed twenty dollars, the right of trial by jury shall be preserved, and no fact tried by jury, shall be otherwise re-examined in any Court of the United States, than according to the rules of the common law.

Amendment [VIII] [1791]

Excessive bail shall not be required, nor excessive fines imposed, nor cruel and unusual punishments inflicted.

Amendment [IX] [1791]

The enumeration in the Constitution, of certain rights, shall not be construed to deny or disparage others retained by the people.

Amendment [X] [1791]

The powers not delegated to the United States by the Constitution, nor prohibited by it to the States, are reserved to the States respectively, or to the people.

AMENDMENT [XI] [1798]

The Judicial power of the United States shall not be construed to extend to any suit in law or equity, commenced or prosecuted against one of the United States by Citizens of another State, or by Citizens or Subjects of any Foreign State.

Historical Note

This amendment was proposed to the legislatures of the several States by the Third Congress, on the 5th September, 1794, and was declared in a message from the President to Congress, dated the 8th of January, 1798, to have been ratified by the legislatures of three-fourths of the States.

AMENDMENT [XII] [1804]

The Electors shall meet in their respective states and vote by ballot for President and Vice-President, one of whom, at least, shall not be an inhabitant of the same state with themselves; they shall name in their ballots the person voted for as President, and in distinct ballots the person voted for as Vice-President, and they shall make distinct lists of all persons voted for as President, and of all persons voted for as Vice-President, and of the number of votes for each, which lists they shall sign and certify, and transmit sealed to the seat of the government of the United States, directed to the President of the Senate;—The President of the Senate shall, in the presence of the Senate and House of Representatives, open all the certificates and the votes shall then be counted;—The person having the greatest number of votes for President, shall be the President, if such number be a majority of the whole number of Electors appointed; and if no person have such majority, then from the persons having the highest numbers not exceeding three on the list of those voted for as President, the House of Representatives shall choose immediately, by ballot, the President. But in choosing the President, the votes shall be taken by states, the representation from each state having one vote; a quorum for this purpose shall consist of a member or members from two-thirds of the states, and a majority of all the states shall be necessary to a choice. And if the House of Representatives shall not choose a President whenever the right of choice shall devolve upon them before the fourth day of March next following, then the Vice-President shall act as President, as in the case of the death or other constitutional disability of the President.—The person having the greatest number of votes as Vice-President, shall be the Vice-President, if such number be a majority of the whole number of Electors appointed, and if no person have a majority, then from the two highest numbers on the list, the Senate shall choose the Vice-President; a quorum for the purpose shall consist of two-thirds of the whole number of Senators, and a majority of the whole number shall be necessary to a choice. But no person constitutionally ineligible to the office of President shall be eligible to that of Vice-President of the United States.

Historical Note

This amendment was proposed to the legislatures of the several States by the Eighth Congress, on the 12th of December, 1803, in lieu of the original third paragraph of the first section of the second article, and was declared in a proclamation of the Secretary of State, dated the 25th of September, 1804, to have been ratified by the legislatures of three-fourths of the States.

Amendment XIII [1865]

Section 1. Neither slavery nor involuntary servitude, except as a punishment for crime whereof the party shall have been duly convicted, shall exist within the United States, or any place subject to their jurisdiction.

Section 2. Congress shall have power to enforce this article by appropriate legislation.

Historical Note

This amendment was proposed to the legislatures of the several States by the Thirty-eighth Congress, on the 1st of February, 1865, and was declared, in a proclamation of the Secretary of State, dated the 18th of December, 1865, to have been ratified by the legislatures of twenty-seven of the thirty-six States, viz: Illinois, Rhode Island, Michigan, Maryland, New York, West Virginia, Maine, Kansas, Massachusetts, Pennsylvania, Virginia, Ohio, Missouri, Nevada, Indiana, Louisiana, Minnesota, Wisconsin, Vermont, Tennessee, Arkansas, Connecticut, New Hampshire, South Carolina, Alabama, North Carolina, and Georgia.

Amendment XIV [1868]

Section 1. All persons born or naturalized in the United States, and subject to the jurisdiction thereof, are citizens of the United States and of the State wherein they reside. No State shall make or enforce any law which shall abridge the privileges or immunities of citizens of the United States; nor shall any State deprive any person of life, liberty, or property, without due process of law; nor deny to any person within its jurisdiction the equal protection of the laws.

Section 2. Representatives shall be apportioned among the several States according to their respective numbers, counting the whole number of persons in each State, excluding Indians not taxed. But when the right to vote at any election for the choice of electors for President and Vice President of the United States, Representatives in Congress, the Executive and Judicial officers of a State, or the members of the Legislature thereof, is denied to any of the male inhabitants of such State, being twenty-one years of age, and citizens of the United States, or in any way abridged, except for participation in rebellion, or other crime, the basis of representation therein shall be reduced in the proportion which the number of such male citizens shall bear to the whole number of male citizens twenty-one years of age in such State.

Section 3. No person shall be a Senator or Representative in Congress, or elector of President and Vice President, or hold any office, civil or military, under the United States, or under any State, who having previously taken an oath, as a member of Congress, or as an officer of the United States, or as a member of any State legislature, or as an executive or judicial officer of any State, to support the Constitution of the United States, shall have engaged in insurrection or rebellion against the same, or given aid or comfort to the enemies thereof. But Congress may by a vote of two-thirds of each House, remove such disability.

Section 4. The validity of the public debt of the United States, authorized by law, including debts incurred for payment of pensions and bounties for services in suppressing insurrection or rebellion, shall not be questioned. But neither the United States nor any State shall assume or pay any debt or obligation incurred in aid of insurrection or rebellion against the United States, or any claim for the loss or emancipation of any slave; but all such debts, obligations and claims shall be held illegal and void.

Section 5. The Congress shall have power to enforce, by appropriate legislation, the provisions of this article.

Historical Note

This amendment was proposed to the legislatures of the several States by the Thirty-ninth Congress, on the 16th of June, 1866. On the 21st of July, 1868, Congress adopted and transmitted to the Department of State a concurrent resolution, declaring that "the legislatures of the States of Connecticut, Tennessee, New Jersey, Oregon, Vermont, New York, Ohio, Illinois, West Virginia, Kansas, Maine, Nevada, Missouri, Indiana, Minnesota, New Hampshire, Massachusetts, Nebraska, Iowa, Arkansas, Florida, North Carolina, Alabama, South Carolina, and Louisiana, being three-fourths and more of the several States of the Union, have ratified the fourteenth article of amendment to the Constitution of the United States, duly proposed by two-thirds of each House of the Thirty-ninth Congress: Therefore, Resolved, That said fourteenth article is hereby declared to be a part of the Constitution of the United States, and it shall be duly promulgated as such by the Secretary of State." The Secretary of State accordingly issued a proclamation, dated the 28th of July, 1868, declaring that the proposed fourteenth amendment had been ratified, in the manner hereafter mentioned by the legislatures of thirty of the thirty-six States, viz: Connecticut, June 30, 1866; New Hampshire, July 7, 1866; Tennessee, July 19, 1866; New Jersey, September 11, 1866, (and the legislature of the same State passed a resolution in April, 1868, to withdraw its consent to it;) Oregon, September 19, 1866; Vermont, November 9, 1866; Georgia rejected it November 13, 1866, and ratified it July 21, 1868; North Carolina rejected it December 4, 1866, and ratified it July 4, 1868; South Carolina rejected it December 20, 1866, and ratified it July 9, 1868; New York ratified it January 10, 1867; Ohio ratified it January 11, 1867, (and the legislature of the same State passed a resolution in January, 1868, to withdraw its consent to it;) Illinois ratified it January 15, 1867; West Virginia, January 16, 1867; Kansas, January 18, 1867; Maine, January 19, 1867; Nevada, January 22, 1867; Missouri, January 26, 1867; Indiana, January 29, 1867; Minnesota, February 1, 1867; Rhode Island, February 7, 1867; Wisconsin, February 13, 1867; Pennsylvania, February 13, 1867; Michigan, February 15, 1867; Massachusetts, March 20, 1867; Nebraska, June 15, 1867; Iowa, April 3, 1868; Arkansas, April 6, 1868; Florida, June 9, 1868; Louisiana, July 9, 1868; and Alabama, July 13, 1868. Georgia again ratified the amendment February 2, 1870. Texas rejected it November 1, 1866, and ratified it February 18, 1870. Virginia rejected it January 19, 1867, and ratified October 8, 1869. The amendment was rejected by Kentucky January 10, 1867; by Delaware February 8, 1867; by Maryland March 23, 1867.

AMENDMENT XV [1870]

Section 1. The right of citizens of the United States to vote shall not be denied or abridged by the United States or by any State on account of race, color, or previous condition of servitude.

Section 2. The Congress shall have power to enforce this article by appropriate legislation.

Historical Note

This amendment was proposed to the legislatures of the several States by the Fortieth Congress, on the 27th of February, 1869, and was declared, in a proclamation of the Secretary of State, dated March 30, 1870, to have been ratified by the legislatures of twenty-nine of the thirty-seven States. The dates of these ratifications (arranged in the order of their reception at the Department of State) were: from North Carolina March 5, 1869; West Virginia, March 3, 1869; Massachusetts, March 9–12, 1869;

Wisconsin, March 9, 1869; Maine, March 12, 1869; Louisiana, March 5, 1869; Michigan, March 8, 1869; South Carolina, March 16, 1869; Pennsylvania, March 26, 1869; Arkansas, March 30, 1869; Connecticut, May 19, 1869; Florida, June 15, 1869; Illinois, March 5, 1869; Indiana, May 13–14, 1869; New York, March 17–April 14, 1869, (and the legislature of the same State passed a resolution January 5, 1870, to withdraw its consent to it;) New Hampshire, July 7, 1869; Nevada, March 1, 1869; Vermont, October 21, 1869; Virginia, October 8, 1869; Missouri, January 10, 1870; Mississippi, January 15–17, 1870; Ohio, January 27, 1870; Iowa, February 3, 1870; Kansas, January 18–19, 1870; Minnesota, February 19, 1870; Rhode Island, January 18, 1870; Nebraska, February 17, 1870; Texas, February 18, 1870. The State of Georgia also ratified the amendment February 2, 1870.

Amendment XVI [1913]

The Congress shall have power to lay and collect taxes on incomes, from whatever source derived, without apportionment among the several States, and without regard to any census or enumeration.

Historical Note

This Amendment was proposed to the legislatures of the several States by the Sixty-First Congress, on the 31st of July, 1909, and was declared, in a proclamation by the Secretary of State, dated the 25th of February, 1913, to have been ratified by the legislatures of the states of Alabama, Kentucky, South Carolina, Illinois, Mississippi, Oklahoma, Maryland, Georgia, Texas, Ohio, Idaho, Oregon, Washington, California, Montana, Indiana, Nevada, North Carolina, Nebraska, Kansas, Colorado, North Dakota, Michigan, Iowa, Missouri, Maine, Tennessee, Arkansas, Wisconsin, New York, South Dakota, Arizona, Minnesota, Louisiana, Delaware, and Wyoming, in all, thirty-six. The legislatures of New Jersey and New Mexico also passed resolutions ratifying the said proposed amendment.

Amendment [XVII] [1913]

[1] The Senate of the United States shall be composed of two Senators from each State, elected by the people thereof, for six years; and each Senator shall have one vote. The electors in each State shall have the qualifications requisite for electors of the most numerous branch of the State legislatures.

[2] When vacancies happen in the representation of any State in the Senate, the executive authority of such State shall issue writs of election to fill such vacancies: *Provided,* That the legislature of any State may empower the executive thereof to make temporary appointments until the people fill the vacancies by election as the legislature may direct.

[3] This amendment shall not be so construed as to affect the election or term of any Senator chosen before it becomes valid as part of the Constitution.

Historical Note

This amendment was proposed to the legislatures of the several states by the Sixty-Second Congress, on the 16th of May, 1912, in lieu of the original first paragraph of section 3 of article I, and in lieu of so much of paragraph 2 of the same section as related to the filling of vacancies, and was declared, in a proclamation by the Secretary of State, dated the 31st of May, 1913, to have been ratified by the legislatures of the states of Massachusetts, Arizona, Minnesota, New York, Kansas, Oregon, North Carolina, California, Michigan, Idaho, West Virginia, Nebraska, Iowa, Montana, Texas, Washington, Wyoming, Colorado, Illinois, North Dakota, Nevada, Vermont, Maine, New Hampshire, Oklahoma, Ohio, South Dakota, Indiana, Missouri, New Mexico, New Jersey, Tennessee, Arkansas, Connecticut, Pennsylvania, and Wisconsin, said states constituting three-fourths of the whole number of states.

AMENDMENT [XVIII] [1919]

Section 1. After one year from the ratification of this article the manufacture, sale, or transportation of intoxicating liquors within, the importation thereof into, or the exportation thereof from the United States and all territory subject to the jurisdiction thereof for beverage purposes is hereby prohibited.

Section 2. The Congress and the several States shall have concurrent power to enforce this article by appropriate legislation.

Section 3. This article shall be inoperative unless it shall have been ratified as an amendment to the Constitution by the legislatures of the several States, as provided in the Constitution, within seven years from the date of the submission hereof to the States by the Congress.

Historical Note

This amendment was proposed to the legislatures of the several states by the Sixty-Fifth Congress, on the 19th day of December, 1917, and was declared, in a proclamation by the Acting Secretary of State, dated on the 29th day of January, 1919, to have been ratified by the legislatures of the states of Alabama, Arizona, California, Colorado, Delaware, Florida, Georgia, Idaho, Illinois, Indiana, Kansas, Kentucky, Louisiana, Maine, Maryland, Massachusetts, Michigan, Minnesota, Mississippi, Montana, Nebraska, New Hampshire, North Carolina, North Dakota, Ohio, Oklahoma, Oregon, South Dakota, South Carolina, Texas, Utah, Virginia, Washington, West Virginia, Wisconsin, and Wyoming.

AMENDMENT [XIX] [1920]

[1] The right of citizens of the United States to vote shall not be denied or abridged by the United States or by any State on account of sex.

[2] Congress shall have power to enforce this article by appropriate legislation.

Historical Note

This amendment was proposed to the legislatures of the several states by the Sixty-Sixth Congress, on the 5th day of June, 1919, and was declared, in a proclamation by the Secretary of State, dated on the 26th day of August, 1920, to have been ratified by the legislatures of the states of Arizona, Arkansas, California, Colorado, Idaho, Illinois, Indiana, Iowa, Kansas, Kentucky, Maine, Massachusetts, Michigan, Minnesota, Missouri, Montana, Nebraska, Nevada, New Hampshire, New Jersey, New Mexico, North Dakota, New York, Ohio, Oklahoma, Oregon, Pennsylvania, Rhode Island, South Dakota, Tennessee, Texas, Utah, Washington, West Virginia, Wisconsin and Wyoming.

AMENDMENT [XX] [1933]

Section 1. The terms of the President and Vice President shall end at noon on the 20th day of January, and the terms of Senators and Representatives at noon on the 3d day of January, of the years in which such terms would have ended if this article had not been ratified; and the terms of their successors shall then begin.

Section 2. The Congress shall assemble at least once in every year, and such meeting shall begin at noon on the 3d day of January, unless they shall by law appoint a different day.

Section 3. If, at the time fixed for the beginning of the term of the President, the President elect shall have died, the Vice President elect shall become President. If the President shall not have been chosen before the time fixed for the beginning of his term, or if the President elect shall have failed to qualify, then the Vice President elect shall act as President until a President shall have qualified; and the Congress may by law provide for the case wherein neither a President elect nor a Vice President elect shall have qualified, declaring who shall then act as President, or the manner in which one who is to act shall be selected, and such person shall act accordingly until a President or Vice President shall have qualified.

Section 4. The Congress may by law provide for the case of the death of any of the persons from whom the House of Representatives may choose a President whenever the right of choice shall have devolved upon them, and for the case of the death of any of the persons from whom the Senate may choose a Vice President whenever the right of choice shall have devolved upon them.

Section 5. Sections 1 and 2 shall take effect on the 15th day of October following the ratification of this article.

Section 6. This article shall be inoperative unless it shall have been ratified as an amendment to the Constitution by the legislatures of three-fourths of the several States within seven years from the date of its submission.

Historical Note

This amendment was proposed to the legislatures of the several states by the Seventy-Second Congress, on March 3, 1932, and was declared, in a proclamation by the Secretary of State, dated Feb. 6, 1933, to have been ratified by the legislatures of the states of Alabama, Arizona, Arkansas, California, Colorado, Connecticut, Delaware, Georgia, Idaho, Illinois, Indiana, Kansas, Kentucky, Louisiana, Maine, Massachusetts, Michigan, Minnesota, Mississippi, Missouri, Montana, Nebraska, New Jersey, New York, North Carolina, North Dakota, Ohio, Oklahoma, Pennsylvania, Rhode Island, South Carolina, South Dakota, Texas, Utah, Virginia, Washington, West Virginia, Wisconsin, and Wyoming.

AMENDMENT [XXI] [1933]

Section 1. The eighteenth article of amendment to the Constitution of the United States is hereby repealed.

Section 2. The transportation or importation into any State, Territory, or possession of the United States for delivery or use therein of intoxicating liquors, in violation of the laws thereof, is hereby prohibited.

Section 3. This article shall be inoperative unless it shall have been ratified as an amendment to the Constitution by conventions in the several States, as provided in the Constitution, within seven years from the date of the submission hereof to the States by the Congress.

Historical Note

This amendment was proposed to the several states by the Seventy-Second Congress, on Feb. 20, 1933, and was declared, in a proclamation by the Secretary of State, dated Dec. 5, 1933, to have been ratified by conventions in the States of Arizona, Alabama, Arkansas, California, Colorado, Connecticut, Delaware, Florida, Idaho, Illinois, Indiana, Iowa, Kentucky, Maryland, Massachusetts, Michigan, Minnesota, Missouri, Nevada, New Hampshire, New Jersey, New Mexico, New York, Ohio, Oregon, Pennsylvania, Rhode Island, Tennessee, Texas, Utah, Vermont, Virginia, Washington, West Virginia, Wisconsin and Wyoming.

AMENDMENT [XXII] [1951]

Section 1.   No person shall be elected to the office of the President more than twice, and no person who has held the office of President, or acted as President, for more than two years of a term to which some other person was elected President shall be elected to the office of President more than once. But this Article shall not apply to any person holding the office of President when this Article was proposed by the Congress, and shall not prevent any person who may be holding the office of President, or acting as President, during the term within which this Article becomes operative from holding the office of President or acting as President during the remainder of such term.

Section 2.   This article shall be inoperative unless it shall have been ratified as an amendment to the Constitution by the legislatures of three-fourths of the several States within seven years from the date of its submission to the States by the Congress.

Historical Note

Proposal and Ratification.   This amendment was proposed to the legislatures of the several States by the Eightieth Congress on Mar. 24, 1947 by House Joint Res. No. 27, and was declared by the Administrator of General Services on Mar. 1, 1951, to have been ratified.   The legislatures ratified this Amendment on the following dates: Maine, Mar. 31, 1947; Michigan, Mar. 31, 1947; Iowa, Apr. 1, 1947; Kansas, Apr. 1, 1947; New Hampshire, Apr. 1, 1947; Delaware, Apr. 2, 1947; Illinois, Apr. 3, 1947; Oregon, Apr. 3, 1947; Colorado, Apr. 12, 1947; California, Apr. 15, 1947; New Jersey, Apr. 15, 1947; Vermont, Apr. 15, 1947; Ohio, Apr. 16, 1947; Wisconsin, Apr. 16, 1947; Pennsylvania, Apr. 29, 1947; Connecticut, May 21, 1947; Missouri, May 22, 1947; Nebraska, May 23, 1947; Virginia, Jan. 28, 1948; Mississippi, Feb. 12, 1948; New York, Mar. 9, 1948; South Dakota, Jan. 21, 1949; North Dakota, Feb. 25, 1949; Louisiana, May 17, 1950; Montana, Jan. 25, 1951; Indiana, Jan. 29, 1951; Idaho, Jan. 30, 1951; New Mexico, Feb. 12, 1951; Wyoming, Feb. 12, 1951; Arkansas, Feb. 15, 1951; Georgia, Feb. 17, 1951; Tennessee, Feb. 20, 1951; Texas, Feb. 22, 1951; Utah, Feb. 26, 1951; Nevada, Feb. 26, 1951; Minnesota, Feb. 27, 1951, and North Carolina, Feb. 28, 1951.

Subsequent to the proclamation, Amendment XXII was ratified by South Carolina on Mar. 13, 1951; Maryland, Mar. 14, 1951; Florida Apr. 16, 1951, and Alabama, May 4, 1951.

Certification of Validity.   Publication of the certifying statement of the Administrator of General Services that the Amendment had become valid was made on Mar. 1, 1951, F.R.Doc. 51-2940, 16 F.R. 2019.

AMENDMENT [XXIII] [1961]

Section 1.   The District constituting the seat of Government of the United States shall appoint in such manner as the Congress may direct:

A number of electors of President and Vice President equal to the whole number of Senators and Representatives in Congress to which the District would be entitled if it were a State, but in no event more than the least populous state; they shall be in addition to those appointed by the states, but they shall be considered, for the purposes of the election of President and Vice President, to be electors appointed by a state; and they shall meet in the District and perform such duties as provided by the twelfth article of amendment.

Section 2. The Congress shall have power to enforce this article by appropriate legislation.

Historical Note

Proposal and Ratification. This amendment was proposed by the Eighty-sixth Congress on June 16, 1960 and was declared by the Administrator of General Services on Apr. 3, 1961, to have been ratified.

The amendment was ratified by the following States: Hawaii, June 23, 1960; Massachusetts, Aug. 22, 1960; New Jersey, Dec. 19, 1960; New York, Jan. 17, 1961; California, Jan. 19, 1961; Oregon, Jan. 27, 1961; Maryland, Jan. 30, 1961; Idaho, Jan. 31, 1961; Maine, Jan. 31, 1961; Minnesota, Jan. 31, 1961; New Mexico, Feb. 1, 1961; Nevada, Feb. 2, 1961; Montana, Feb. 6, 1961; Colorado, Feb. 8, 1961; Washington, Feb. 9, 1961; West Virginia, Feb. 9, 1961; Alaska, Feb. 10, 1961; Wyoming, Feb. 13, 1961; South Dakota, Feb. 14, 1961; Delaware, Feb. 20, 1961; Utah, Feb. 21, 1961; Wisconsin, Feb. 21, 1961; Pennsylvania, Feb. 28, 1961; Indiana, Mar. 3, 1961; North Dakota, Mar. 3, 1961; Tennessee, Mar. 6, 1961; Michigan, Mar. 8, 1961; Connecticut, Mar. 9, 1961; Arizona, Mar. 10, 1961; Illinois, Mar. 14, 1961; Nebraska, Mar. 15, 1961; Vermont, Mar. 15, 1961; Iowa, Mar. 16, 1961; Missouri, Mar. 20, 1961; Oklahoma, Mar. 21, 1961; Rhode Island, Mar. 22, 1961; Kansas, Mar. 29, 1961; Ohio, Mar. 29, 1961, and New Hampshire, Mar. 30, 1961.

Certification of Validity. Publication of the certifying statement of the Administrator of General Services that the Amendment had become valid was made on Apr. 3, 1961, F.R.Doc. 61–3017, 26 F.R. 2808.

Amendment [XXIV] [1964]

Section 1. The right of citizens of the United States to vote in any primary or other election for President or Vice President, for electors for President or Vice President, or for Senator or Representative in Congress, shall not be denied or abridged by the United States or any State by reason of failure to pay any poll tax or other tax.

Section 2. The Congress shall have power to enforce this article by appropriate legislation.

Historical Note

Proposal and Ratification. This amendment was proposed by the Eighty-seventh Congress by Senate Joint Resolution No. 29, which was approved by the Senate on Mar. 27, 1962, and by the House of Representatives on Aug. 27, 1962. It was declared by the Administrator of General Services on Feb. 4, 1964, to have been ratified.

This amendment was ratified by the following States: Illinois, Nov. 14, 1962; New Jersey, Dec. 3, 1962; Oregon, Jan. 25, 1963; Montana, Jan. 28, 1963; West Virginia, Feb. 1, 1963; New York, Feb. 4, 1963; Maryland, Feb. 6, 1963; California, Feb. 7, 1963; Alaska, Feb. 11, 1963; Rhode Island, Feb. 14, 1963; Indiana, Feb. 19, 1963; Utah, Feb. 20, 1963; Michigan, Feb. 20, 1963; Colorado, Feb. 21, 1963; Ohio, Feb.

27, 1963; Minnesota, Feb. 27, 1963; New Mexico, Mar. 5, 1963; Hawaii, Mar. 6, 1963; North Dakota, Mar. 7, 1963; Idaho, Mar. 8, 1963; Washington, Mar. 14, 1963; Vermont, Mar. 15, 1963; Nevada, Mar. 19, 1963; Connecticut, Mar. 20, 1963; Tennessee, Mar. 21, 1963; Pennsylvania, Mar. 25, 1963; Wisconsin, Mar. 26, 1963; Kansas, Mar. 28, 1963; Massachusetts, Mar. 28, 1963; Nebraska, Apr. 4, 1963; Florida, Apr. 18, 1963; Iowa, Apr. 24, 1963; Delaware, May 1, 1963; Missouri, May 13, 1963; New Hampshire, June 12, 1963; Kentucky, June 27, 1963; Maine, Jan. 16, 1964; South Dakota, Jan. 23, 1964.

Certification of Validity. Publication of the certifying statement of the Administrator of General Services that the Amendment had become valid was made on Feb. 5, 1964, F.R.Doc. 64–1229, 29 F.R. 1715. President Johnson and the Administrator signed this certificate on Feb. 4, 1964.

AMENDMENT [XXV] [1967]

Section 1. In case of the removal of the President from office or of his death or resignation, the Vice President shall become President.

Section 2. Whenever there is a vacancy in the office of the Vice President, the President shall nominate a Vice President who shall take office upon confirmation by a majority vote of both Houses of Congress.

Section 3. Whenever the President transmits to the President pro tempore of the Senate and the Speaker of the House of Representatives his written declaration that he is unable to discharge the powers and duties of his office, and until he transmits to them a written declaration to the contrary, such powers and duties shall be discharged by the Vice President as Acting President.

Section 4. Whenever the Vice President and a majority of either the principal officers of the executive departments or of such other body as Congress may by law provide, transmit to the President pro tempore of the Senate and the Speaker of the House of Representatives their written declaration that the President is unable to discharge the powers and duties of his office, the Vice President shall immediately assume the powers and duties of the office as Acting President.

Thereafter, when the President transmits to the President pro tempore of the Senate and the Speaker of the House of Representatives his written declaration that no inability exists, he shall resume the powers and duties of his office unless the Vice President and a majority of either the principal officers of the executive department or of such other body as Congress may by law provide, transmit within four days to the President pro tempore of the Senate and the Speaker of the House of Representatives their written declaration and the President is unable to discharge the powers and duties of his office. Thereupon Congress shall decide the issue, assembling within forty-eight hours for that purpose if not in session. If the Congress, within twenty-one days after receipt of the latter written declaration, or, if Congress is not in session, within twenty-one days after Congress is required to assemble, determines by two-thirds vote of both Houses that the President is unable to discharge the powers and duties of his office, the Vice President shall continue to discharge the same as Acting President; otherwise, the President shall resume the powers and duties of his office.

Historical Note

Proposal and Ratification. This amendment was proposed by the Eighty-ninth Congress by Senate Joint Resolution No. 1, which was approved by the Senate on

Feb. 19, 1965, and by the House of Representatives, in amended form, on Apr. 13, 1965. The House of Representatives agreed to a Conference Report on June 30, 1965, and the Senate agreed to the Conference Report on July 6, 1965. It was declared by the Administrator of General Services, on Feb. 23, 1967, to have been ratified.

This amendment was ratified by the following States: Nebraska, July 12, 1965; Wisconsin, July 13, 1965; Oklahoma, July 16, 1965; Massachusetts, Aug. 9, 1965; Pennsylvania, Aug. 18, 1965; Kentucky, Sept. 15, 1965; Arizona, Sept. 22, 1965; Michigan, Oct. 5, 1965; Indiana, Oct. 20, 1965; California, Oct. 21, 1965; Arkansas, Nov. 4, 1965; New Jersey, Nov. 29, 1965; Delaware, Dec. 7, 1965; Utah, Jan. 17, 1966; West Virginia, Jan. 20, 1966; Maine, Jan. 24, 1966; Rhode Island, Jan. 28, 1966; Colorado, Feb. 3, 1966; New Mexico, Feb. 3, 1966; Kansas, Feb. 8, 1966; Vermont, Feb. 10, 1966; Alaska, Feb. 18, 1966; Idaho, Mar. 2, 1966; Hawaii, Mar. 3, 1966; Virginia, Mar. 8, 1966; Mississippi, Mar. 10, 1966; New York, Mar. 14, 1966; Maryland, Mar. 23, 1966; Missouri, Mar. 30, 1966; New Hampshire, June 13, 1966; Louisiana, July 5, 1966; Tennessee, Jan. 12, 1967; Wyoming, Jan. 25, 1967; Washington, Jan. 26, 1967; Iowa, Jan. 26, 1967; Oregon, Feb. 2, 1967; Minnesota, Feb. 10, 1967; Nevada, Feb. 10, 1967; Connecticut, Feb. 14, 1967; Montana, Feb. 15, 1967; South Dakota, Mar. 6, 1967; Ohio, Mar. 7, 1967; Alabama, Mar. 14, 1967; North Carolina, Mar. 22, 1967; Illinois, Mar. 22, 1967; Texas, Apr. 25, 1967; Florida, May 25, 1967.

Certification of Validity. Publication of the certifying statement of the Administrator of General Services that the Amendment had become valid was made on Feb. 25, 1967, F.R.Doc. 67–2208, 32 F.R. 3287, and signed on July 23, 1967.

AMENDMENT [XXVI] [1971]

Section 1. The right of citizens of the United States, who are eighteen years of age or older, to vote shall not be denied or abridged by the United States or by any State on account of age.

Section 2. The Congress shall have power to enforce this article by appropriate legislation.

Historical Note

Proposal and Ratification. This amendment was proposed by the Ninety-second Congress by Senate Joint Resolution No. 7, which was approved by the Senate on Mar. 10, 1971, and by the House of Representatives on Mar. 23, 1971. It was declared by the Administrator of General Services on July 5, 1971, to have been ratified.

This amendment was ratified by the following States: Connecticut, Mar. 23, 1971; Delaware, Mar. 23, 1971; Minnesota, Mar. 23, 1971; Tennessee, Mar. 23, 1971; Washington, Mar. 23, 1971; Hawaii, Mar. 24, 1971; Massachusetts, Mar. 24, 1971; Idaho, Mar. 30, 1971; Montana, Mar. 31, 1971; Arkansas, Apr. 1, 1971; Iowa, Apr. 1, 1971; Nebraska, Apr. 2, 1971; Kansas, Apr. 7, 1971; Michigan, Apr. 7, 1971; Indiana, Apr. 8, 1971; Maine, Apr. 9, 1971; Vermont, Apr. 16, 1971; California, Apr. 19, 1971; South Carolina, Apr. 28, 1971; West Virginia, Apr. 28, 1971; Pennsylvania, May 3, 1971; New Jersey, May 4, 1971; Texas, May 5, 1971; Maryland, May 6, 1971; New Hampshire, May 13, 1971; Arizona, May 17, 1971; Colorado, May 24, 1971; Louisiana, May 27, 1971; Rhode Island, May 27, 1971; New York, June 2, 1971; Oregon, June 5, 1971; Missouri, June 14, 1971; Wisconsin, June 18, 1971; Illinois, June 29, 1971; Alabama, June 30, 1971; Ohio, June 30, 1971; North Carolina, July 1, 1971; Oklahoma, July 1, 1971.

Certification of Validity. Publication of the certifying statement of the Administrator of General Services that the Amendment had become valid was made on July 7, 1971, F.R.Doc. 71–9691, 36 F.R. 12725, and signed on July 5, 1971.

*

TABLE OF CASES

References are to Pages

I

N

O

T

INDEX

†